# Concise Chronology of World Events
## (to c.1000AD)

| MIDDLE AND NEAR EAST | ASIA AND THE FAR EAST | AUSTRALASIA AND THE PACIFIC | |
|---|---|---|---|
| | c.50 000 BC Modern humans arrive in Asia | c.40 ... humans in | 125 000 BC – 5000 BC |
| 10 000 BC Agriculture begins | 18 000 BC First rock reliefs ca... | | |
| c.7500 BC–6500 BC Settlement of Çatal Hüyük in Anatolia inhabited | | | |
| c.3760 BC Bronze in use | 3500 BC Copper in us... ...ailand | 4000 BC Colonization of the Pacific islands | 5000 BC – 1000 BC |
| 3200 BC Sumerians invent cuneiform writing | | | |
| 3000 BC Wheeled vehicles in use | | | |
| c.2100 BC Abraham leaves Ur | c.2300–1750 BC Indus Valley civilization | 2000 BC First settlers arrive in New Guinea | |
| 1950 BC End of Empire of Ur | 1766–1122 BC Chinese Shang Dynasty | | |
| 1595 BC Hittites conquer Babylon | c.1500 BC Aryans in India | 1300 BC First settlers arrive in Fiji, Tonga and Samoa | |
| c.1100–612 BC Assyrian Empire; Assyrians conquer Babylon (1116) and Israel (721) | 1122–256 BC Chinese Zhou Dynasty | | |
| | 800 BC Development of India's caste system | | 1000 BC – AD100 |
| 550 BC Foundation of Persian Achaemenid Empire by Cyrus II, the Great | 563–483 BC Life of Buddha | | |
| 525 BC Persia conquers Egypt | 551–479 BC Life of Confucius | | |
| c.499 BC Persian Empire at its height | | | |
| 344 BC Alexander the Great invades Persia | 321–185 BC N Indian Mauryan Empire | | |
| 312–64 BC Seleucid Empire | 273–232 BC Buddhism introduced into India by Mauryan ruler Ashoka | | |
| | 221 BC Construction of Great Wall of China begins | | |
| | 206 BC – AD220 Chinese Han dynasties | | |
| 5 BC – AD30 Life of Jesus Christ | 202 BC – AD50 Buddhism introduced into China | | |
| 70 Destruction of Jerusalem by Romans | | c.100 First settlers arrive in Hawaiian islands | |
| 224–651 Sassanian Dynasty rules in Persia | 220–589 Civil War in China | | AD100 – AD1000 |
| | 250 Yamato dominates Japan | | |
| 330 Constantinople becomes capital of Roman Empire | 266–317 Chinese Jin Dynasty | c.300 First settlers arrive in Tahiti | |
| | 320–535 N Indian Gupta Dynasty | | |
| | 582 Chinese Sui Dynasty reunites the country | c.400 Polynesians reach Easter Island | |
| | 594 Buddhism becomes Japan's official religion | | |
| 632 Death of Muhammad; Islamic Empire begins to expand | 618–907 Chinese Tang Dynasty | | |
| 642 Arabs conquer Persia and overthrow Sassanian Empire | | 650 All Polynesian islands are now colonized except New Zealand | |
| 661–750 Umayyad Dynasty | | | |
| 756 Islamic Empire stars to break up in separate countries | | | |
| 762 Foundation of Baghdad | | | |
| 962–1186 Ghaznevid Dynasty | 918–1392 Koryo Dynasty in Korea | | |

# CHAMBERS

## DICTIONARY OF
# WORLD
# HISTORY

# CHAMBERS

# DICTIONARY OF WORLD HISTORY

*Consultant Editor*
Bruce P Lenman

*Editor*
Hilary Marsden

**CHAMBERS**

CHAMBERS
An imprint of Chambers Harrap Publishers Ltd
7 Hopetoun Crescent,
Edinburgh,
EH7 4AY

This edition first published by Chambers Harrap Publishers Ltd 2005

© Chambers Harrap Publishers Ltd 2005

Second edition published in 2000
First edition published in 1993

A CIP catalogue record for this book is available from the British Library.

ISBN 0550 10094 6

Designed and typeset by Chambers Harrap Publishers Ltd, Edinburgh
Printed in Great Britain by Bath Press Ltd

# Contents

# Preface

This is the third edition of a work of reference that was welcomed as a comprehensive single-volume survey of the political, military, diplomatic and social history of the past 1,000 years when the first edition appeared in 1993, and has remained in demand since. In this new edition Chambers has sought to retain and strengthen the features that make the dictionary an accessible and valued source of information for users, and at the same time to add to the coverage events and people of historical significance that have come to the fore in the five years since the second edition was published in 2000.

One innovation of the second edition that enhanced the dictionary's usefulness was the use of panels to handle broader topics than could easily be accommodated within the shorter and more detailed entries. More of these panels have been included in the current edition. They cover aspects of social and cultural history that, as well as being intrinsically important, were significant in shaping the mental worlds within which political, military and diplomatic decisions were taken, establishing what was thinkable and what was not in different historical eras. They also provide information on the period before the year 1000, especially where this is essential for an understanding of subsequent developments. New panels in this edition cover topics such as the environment and the globalization of trade that have assumed a greater importance in national and, particularly, international politics in recent years. We hope that these, along with relevant new individual entries, will maintain this work's tradition of responding to readers' reactions and changing needs.

The cartographic content of the second edition was much appreciated; for this new edition, all the maps have been redrawn and new maps added. The presentation of the text has been redesigned also, enabling more information to fit into a single volume while remaining easily accessible.

The core of the book remains the individual entries. These draw on a wide range of sources and expertise, ranging from the substantial body of experts who have compressed their knowledge within compact entries, to the reference publishing resources of Chambers. This edition contains a significant proportion of new entries in response to major events of the past five years; the subjects cover a wide range, though the impact on international politics of the events of September 11, 2001, and increasing concern about the impact of globalization and environmental issues, are major themes. Also, the existing entries have been surveyed and, where necessary, modified. Sometimes modification has been purely for the sake of clarity in a work that is meant to be easy to use, but where entries reflected outdated and obsolete scholarship, they have been rewritten.

Although physically the book has been kept at a manageable size, this edition is a different and matured version that benefits from the cumulative efforts and experience of earlier editions.

Bruce P Lenman

# Using the Dictionary

The Chambers Dictionary of World History aims to be both comprehensive (within the scope defined in the Preface) and as accessible and easy to use as possible.

It is arranged in a straightforward A–Z format, with each entry placed according to what has been judged to be the most familiar form. Where there is any potential for confusion, either in the order of the elements in a headword (eg **ALLIANCE, HOLY ► HOLY ALLIANCE**) or in terminology (eg **WAR OF INDEPENDENCE ► AMERICAN REVOLUTION**), a cross-reference is provided.

Some foreign words and names present special difficulties insofar as they may be transliterated in a variety of ways. In such instances, the most commonly used forms have been chosen, and cross-references have been given from other less widely found or up-to-date forms of words and names. As far as Chinese names are concerned, most entries are listed alphabetically under the Pinyin transliteration, with a cross-reference given from the corresponding Wade-Giles transliteration; exceptions to this rule are specific Chinese names which are traditionally expressed in the Wade-Giles system and which would therefore be unfamiliar to most readers if given in the Pinyin form (eg Chiang Kai-shek, Sun Yat-sen) and Taiwanese names (since the Wade-Giles system is always used to transliterate these). Each of these entries is listed under its Wade-Giles transliteration (although, in the case of People's Republic of China names, a cross-reference is still provided from the Pinyin form).

Highlighted in bold type, either in the body of an entry or following the arrow symbol (►) at the end of an entry, are other biographical or topic entries found in the dictionary which provide additional information. The arrow symbol is also used to direct the reader to relevant panels, tables or maps.

The panel entries included in this edition cover a wide range of subjects. Alongside each panel is a highlighted icon representing one of five subject areas:

War & Warfare

Science & Technology

Art & Literature

Transport & Travel

Culture & Society

# Contributors

*Consultant Editor*
Bruce P Lenman
Emeritus Professor of Modern History,
University of St Andrews

Honorary Professor of History,
University of Dundee

*Editor*
Hilary Marsden

*Compilers*
Nancy Bailey
Catherine Gaunt
Michael Munro

*Managing Editor*
Camilla Rockwood

*Publishing Manager*
Patrick White

*Prepress Controller*
David Reid

*Prepress Manager*
Sharon McTeir

*Contributors to Previous Edition*
The Editors wish to acknowledge the contributions made by
the following to the previous edition of the dictionary:
Trevor Anderson, Steve Curtis, Sian Hayton, Jim Horsford,
Min Lee, Melanie Parry, David Reid and John Widdows.

# *Panels*

# Maps

# Tables

**Abahai** (1592–1643)
Manchu (Jurchen) leader. He was the eighth son of
**NURHACI**, whom he succeeded as dominant leader
of the Manchu tribes in 1626. He enhanced his power
by gradually reducing the influence of other senior
princes, or banner chiefs, thereby transforming a collective leadership into unitary rule. Under Abahai, the
Manchus extended their control over Korea and
Mongolia and conducted raids into north China.
With the assistance of captured Chinese officials
and scholars, Abahai created the structures of a bureaucratic state modelled on that of China. In 1636, at
his capital in Mukden, Abahai proclaimed himself
Emperor of the **QING DYNASTY**, and by the time of his
death the Manchus were poised to launch a full-scale
invasion of China. ➤ **BANNER SYSTEM**

**Abalkin, Leonid Ivanovich** (1930– )
Soviet economist. He has been Director of the Institute of Economics of the Russian Academy of
Sciences (formerly the USSR Academy of Sciences)
since 1986 and was a member of the Supreme Soviet
of the USSR, with special responsibility for economic
affairs. His published works centre on the theoretical
problems of political economy under socialism.
Under Mikhail **GORBACHEV** he was one of the
major advocates of rapid economic reform, and in
1998 became a member of the Economic Crisis
Group.

**'Abbas I** (1813–54)
Khedive of Egypt (1848/54). A grandson of the great
**MUHAMMAD 'ALI**, he took an active part in his grandfather's Syrian war, but later did much to undo the
progress made under him, for example by blocking
the construction of the Suez Canal.

**'Abbas I, the Great** (1571–1629)
Safavid Shah of Persia (1588/1629). After his accession, he set about establishing a counterweight to
the Turkmen tribal chiefs who under his father, Muhammad Khudabanda, had constituted the principal
political and military powers in the state, and whose
propensity for feuding was a major cause of instability. This was achieved by the creation of a standing
army drawn especially from Caucasian prisoners
and immigrants and financed by an increase in the
extent of the crown lands. From 1598 he was able to
recover Azerbaijan and parts of Armenia from the Ottomans, and Khurasan from the Uzbeks. He transferred his capital from Qazvin to Isfahan, which he
developed with a major programme of public works,
and established diplomatic and economic relations
with Western Europe.

**'Abbas II** (1874–1943)
Khedive of Egypt (1892/1914). He succeeded his
father, **TEWFIK PASHA**, and attempted to rule independently of British influence. At the outbreak of **WORLD
WAR I** in 1914 he sided with Turkey and was deposed
when the British made Egypt a protectorate.

**Abbas, Ferhat** (1899–1985)
Algerian nationalist leader. He founded a Muslim
Students' Association in 1924, before becoming a
chemist. He served as a volunteer in the French army
in 1939, but after France's defeat he produced in 1942
a 'Manifesto of the Algerian People'. In 1955 he joined
the *Front de Libération Nationale* (**FLN**), the main Algerian resistance organization, and worked with **BEN
BELLA** in Cairo, before founding in 1958 a 'Provisional Government of the Algerian Republic' in Tunis.
After independence in 1962, he was appointed President of the National Constituent Assembly but he fell
out of favour and was exiled. He was rehabilitated
shortly before his death. ➤ **ALGERIAN WAR OF INDE-
PENDENCE**

**Abbas Hilmi Pasha** ➤ **'ABBAS II**

**'Abbasid Dynasty**
A dynasty of caliphs, which replaced that of the
Umayyads in 749, establishing itself in Baghdad until
its sack by the **MONGOLS** in 1258. Early 'Abbasid
power reached its peak under Harun al-Rashid
(786/809). The 'Abbasids traced their descent from
the family of the Prophet Muhammad's uncle, 'Abbas,
and were thus able to claim legitimacy in the eyes of
the pious. ➤ *See table*

**'Abbas Pasha** ➤ **'ABBAS I**

**Abboud, Ibrahim** (1900–83)
Sudanese soldier. Commander-in-Chief of the Sudanese Army from the attainment of independence
(1956), he was the leader of the military regime in
the Sudan which obtained power when Abdullah
Khalil surrendered the reins of government to the
army in 1958. Abboud's regime was unable either politically or economically to maintain effective rule
over the country, and was overthrown in 1964. Abboud himself resigned and retired into private life.

**Abd al-Hadi, Awni** (1889–1970)
Palestinian politician. He was involved in Arab na-
tionalist activity directed against the Turks prior to
**WORLD WAR I**, and helped to organize the first Arab
Congress in Paris in 1913. A member of King Abdul-
lah of Transjordan's staff after the so-called 'libera-
tion' of **PALESTINE** in the latter years of the war,
Abd al-Hadi subsequently became involved in the

## 'ABBASID DYNASTY

| Regnal Dates | Name | Regnal Dates | Name | Regnal Dates | Name |
|---|---|---|---|---|---|
| *Caliphs in Iraq and Baghdad* | | 946/74 | al-Muti' | 1362/77 | al-Mutawakkil I |
| 749/54 | al-Saffah | 974/91 | al-Ta'i' | | (1st reign) |
| 754/75 | al-Mansur | 991/1031 | al-Qadir | 1377 | al-Mu'tasim (1st reign) |
| 775/85 | al-Mahdi | 1031/75 | al-Qa'im | 1377/83 | al-Mutawakkil I |
| 785/6 | al-Hadi | 1075/94 | al-Muqtadi | | (2nd reign) |
| 786/809 | Harun al-Rashid | 1094/1118 | al-Mustazhir | 1383/5 | al-Wathiq II |
| 809/13 | al-Amin | 1118/35 | al-Mustarshid | 1385/9 | al-Mu'tasim (2nd reign) |
| 813/33 | al-Ma'mun | 1135/6 | al-Rashid | 1389/1406 | al-Mutawakkil I |
| 833/42 | al-Mu'tasim | 1136/60 | al-Muqtafi | | (3rd reign) |
| 842/7 | al-Wathiq | 1160/70 | al-Mustanjid | 1406/14 | al-Musta'in |
| 847/61 | al-Mutawakkil | 1170/80 | al-Mustadi' | 1414/41 | al-Mu'tadid II |
| 861/2 | al-Muntasir | 1180/1225 | al-Nasir | 1441/51 | al-Mustakfi II |
| 862/6 | al-Musta'in | 1225/6 | al-Zahir | 1451/5 | al-Qa'im |
| 866/9 | al-Mu'tazz | 1226/42 | al-Mustansir | 1455/79 | al-Mustanjid |
| 869/70 | al-Muhtadi | 1242/58 | al-Musta'sim | 1479/97 | al-Mutawakkil II |
| 870/92 | al-Mu'tamid | | | 1497/1508 | al-Mustamsik |
| 892/902 | al-Mu'tadid | *Caliphs in Cairo* | | | (1st reign) |
| 902/8 | al-Muktafi | 1261 | al-Mustansir | 1508/16 | al-Mutawakkil III |
| 908/32 | al-Muqtadir | 1261/1302 | al-Hakim I | | (1st reign) |
| 932/4 | al-Qahir | 1302/40 | al-Mustakfi I | 1516/17 | al-Mustamsik |
| 934/40 | al-Radi | 1340/1 | al-Wathiq I | | (2nd reign) |
| 940/4 | al-Muttaqi | 1341/52 | al-Hakim II | 1517 | al-Mutawakkil III |
| 944/6 | al-Mustakfi | 1352/62 | al-Mu'tadid I | | (2nd reign) |

pan-Arab movement, was a member of the Arab Higher Committee in 1936 and was also behind the Arab 'Rebellion' of the same year. Exiled by the British from 1937 until 1941, he was subsequently involved in the formation of the **LEAGUE OF ARAB STATES** in 1945. He was Jordanian Ambassador to Britain (1951–5) and, despite holding government posts in Jordan, spent the later years of his life in Egypt. ► **ALEXANDRIA PROTOCOL**

### Abd al-Krim, Muhammad (1882–1963)
Berber chief. Born at Ajdir, Morocco, he led revolts in 1921 and 1924 against Spain and France, but surrendered before their combined forces in 1926. He was exiled to the island of Réunion, and later amnestied (1947). He then went to Egypt, where he formed the North African Liberation Committee. He died in Cairo.

### Abd al-Qadir (1807–83)
Algerian military and religious leader. After the French conquest of Algiers, the Arab tribes of Orán elected him as their Amir. He waged a long struggle against the French (1832–47), defeating them at Makta (1835). Eventually crushed by overpowering force, he took refuge in Morocco and began a crusade against the enemies of Islam. He finally surrendered in 1847 and was sent to France. He later lived in Bursa and in Damascus, where he died.

### Abd al-Rahman (c.1840–1901)
Amir of Afghanistan. The grandson of **DOST MUHAMMAD**, he was driven into exile in Russia in 1869. He was brought back and proclaimed Amir with British support in 1880. Abd al-Rahman consolidated his power and arranged for the withdrawal of British troops, leaving Britain in control of foreign affairs, and in 1893 subscribed to the Durand Line as the India–Afghanistan border.

### Abd el Kader ► ABD AL-QADIR

### Abduh, Muhammad (1849–1905)
Egyptian reformer. A prime mover behind the reform movement in late 19c Egypt, after graduating from the Azhar he became convinced of the need for educational reorganization and a reappraisal of Islam's position in the modern world. Exiled after the suppression of the **'URABI REVOLT**, he went eventually to Paris, where he renewed his acquaintanceship with Jamal al-Din al-**AFGHANI**. Permitted to return to Cairo, by 1889 he had been appointed to the highest (clerical) post, that of state Mufti, which he held until his death. His activities were dominated by a strong Egyptian patriotism and he was thus opposed to control of Egypt being vested in despots, whether European or Oriental. He was, however, first and foremost a theologian, and the maintenance of the true religion of Islam, shorn of falsifying abuses, was his prime motivation.

### Abd ul-Aziz (1830–76)
Ottoman Sultan (1861/76). He succeeded his brother, **ABD UL-MAJID I**, and continued his brother's liberal and westernizing reforms. He promulgated the first Ottoman civil code, and visited Western Europe (1871). Thereafter, he became more autocratic and, after revolts in Bosnia, Herzegovina and Bulgaria, was forced to abdicate. He was found dead five days later.

### Abd ul-Hamid II (1842–1918)
Ottoman Sultan (1876/1909). Known as the 'Great Assassin', he was the second son of Sultan **ABD UL-MAJID I** and successor to his brother, Murad V. He promulgated the first Ottoman constitution in 1876, but his reign was notable for his cruel suppression of revolts in the Balkans, which led to wars with Russia (1877–8), and especially for the appalling Armenian massacres of 1894–6. He suspended the constitution in 1878 and ruled autocratically. Revolts in Crete in 1896–7 led to war with Greece. Later a

reform movement by the revolutionary **YOUNG TURKS** forced him to restore the constitution and summon a parliament in 1908, but he was deposed and exiled in 1909.

**Abdullah, Sheikh Muhammad** (1905–82)
Kashmiri politician. Known as the 'Lion of Kashmir', he was a leading figure in the struggle for India's independence and the fight for the rights of Kashmir. He participated actively in the Muslim struggle to overthrow the Hindu maharajah and substitute constitutional government, for which he was imprisoned several times. He was the founder of the Kashmir Muslim (later, National) Conference, and then the Quit Kashmir movement in 1946, when he was again detained. A year later he was released by the emergency administration, and in 1948 he was appointed Prime Minister of Kashmir. However, for his championing of the cause of an independent Kashmir, and his subsequent treasonable refusal to pledge his loyalty to India, he was again imprisoned for most of the period 1953–68. He contested the 1972 elections at the head of his Plebiscite Front, but lost to the Congress Party. As Chief Minister of Jammu and Kashmir from 1975 until his death, he was instrumental in persuading the Indian Prime Minister, Indira **GANDHI**, to grant Kashmir a degree of autonomy, making him a central figure in the fight for Kashmiri national rights.

**Abdullah ibn Husayn** (1882–1951)
King of Jordan (1946/51). Born in Mecca, he was the second son of **HUSAYN IBN 'ALI**, and the grandfather of King **HUSSEIN**. He was made the ruler of the British-mandated territory of Transjordan in 1921, and became the first King of Jordan when the mandate ended in 1946. He was assassinated in Jerusalem.

**Abd ul-Majid I** (1823–61)
Ottoman Sultan (1839/61). He succeeded his father, **MAHMUD II**, and continued the reforms of the previous reign, reorganizing the court system and education, and granting various rights to citizens, including Christians. In 1850 he chivalrously refused to give up the Hungarian political refugee Lajos **KOSSUTH** to the Habsburgs. In 1854 he secured an alliance with Britain and France to resist Russian demands, thus precipitating the **CRIMEAN WAR** (1854–6). Thereafter, however, the **OTTOMAN EMPIRE** was increasingly weakened by financial difficulties and internal nationalist problems. ► **HABSBURG DYNASTY**

**Abdul Rahman, Tunku Putra** (1903–90)
Malaysian politician. The son of the Sultan of Kedah, he trained as a lawyer and joined the Civil Service in Kedah in 1931, becoming a public prosecutor in 1949. In 1952 he was nominated to the Executive and Legislative Councils of the Federation of Malaya, becoming Chief Minister in 1955 and Prime Minister, on independence, in 1957. He negotiated the formation of the Federation of Malaysia, to embrace Sabah, Sarawak and Singapore (1961–2) and remained Prime Minister of that enlarged entity when it came into being in 1963. After the outbreak of violent Malay-Chinese riots in Kuala Lumpur (May 1969), he withdrew from active politics. In his later years, he became an outspoken newspaper columnist.

**Abercromby, Sir Ralph** (1734–1801)
British general. He studied law at Edinburgh and Leipzig, then joined the Dragoons in 1756 and fought in the **SEVEN YEARS' WAR**. He became an MP in 1774, later serving in Holland and the West Indies, capturing Trinidad (1797). In 1800 he commanded the expedition to the Mediterranean, and effected a successful landing at Aboukir Bay, but was mortally wounded in the ensuing battle against the French. ► **NAPOLEONIC WARS**

**Aberdeen, George Hamilton Gordon, 4th Earl** (1784–1860)
British politician. He succeeded to his earldom in 1801, and became a Scottish representative peer (1806), Ambassador to Vienna (1813–14) and Foreign Secretary (1828–30 and 1841–6). From 1852 to 1855 he headed a coalition ministry, which for some time was extremely popular. However, vacillating policy and mismanagement during the **CRIMEAN WAR** led to his resignation.

**Abernathy, Ralph** (1926–90)
US **CIVIL RIGHTS** leader. A Baptist minister, he became chief aide to Martin Luther **KING**, and helped organize the boycott of buses by the black community in Montgomery in 1955. He assumed the presidency of the **SCLC** (Southern Christian Leadership Conference) after King was assassinated in 1968 and continued in that post until his resignation in 1977. ► **CIVIL RIGHTS MOVEMENT, MONTGOMERY BUS BOYCOTT, PARKS, ROSA LEE**

**Abgrenzung**
A German term meaning 'delimitation'. Following the success of Federal (West) Germany's **OSTPOLITIK** in the early 1970s, the East German authorities feared that increased personal contact between East and West Germans might undermine the GDR's legitimacy. They therefore stressed the differences between 'socialist' and 'capitalist' Germany, which were deemed more significant than a common German nationhood.

**Abiola, Moshood Kastumawo** (1937–98)
Nigerian politician. In 1979 he was elected to parliament as a member of the National Party. As a member of the Social Democratic Party he successfully contested the 1993 presidential elections but was arrested and charged with treason following a military coup. He spent the rest of his life in prison and died shortly before his scheduled release.

**ABM Treaty (Anti-Ballistic Missile Treaty)** (1972)
A treaty between the USA and USSR restricting the construction of defensive missile systems to protect against nuclear ballistic weapons attack. The treaty was signed at the same time as the first **SALT** agreement limiting the nuclear weapons arsenals built up during the **COLD WAR**. The USSR claimed the USA was in breach of the treaty when it began to develop a space-based weapons defence system (**SDI**) and this caused a short hiatus in the **START** talks. President George W **BUSH** advocated an enhanced system (**NMD**) and, feeling that the ABM Treaty hindered NMD development, he abrogated the treaty with effect from Jun 2002.

**abolitionism**
A 19c movement to end **SLAVERY** in the US South, it

was distinguished from earlier anti-slavery movements by its uncompromising attitude. It crystallized around the American Anti-Slavery Society, founded in 1833, and made slavery an issue that could not be ignored. Blacks as well as whites, and women as well as men, actively participated in the movement. ► **DOUGLASS, FREDERICK**; **GARRISON, WILLIAM LLOYD**; **HOWE, JULIA WARD**

## Aboriginals
The native inhabitants of Australia, who reached the country some 40,000 years ago. By 1788 there were c.600 territorially defined groups, with a population of 300,000–1 million. Numbers fell dramatically thereafter, partly through conflict with Europeans, but mainly through epidemics of European diseases such as smallpox, and by 1933 the population was only c.66,000. As white settlement progressed, the Aboriginals lost control of the land and their daily lives. Government actions and those of Christian missionaries, whilst well-intentioned, attempted to 'civilize' the Aboriginals in the European image. The alternative to assimilation was segregation: in the 1830s the government of Van Diemen's Land (Tasmania) attempted to clear the island, removing the Aboriginals to Flinders Island. Elsewhere, most Aboriginals were confined to government or mission reserves, which offered little protection against the demands for land from pastoral and, later, mining interests, or from the government's own policies such as **CLOSER SETTLEMENT**. Social Darwinist theories that the Aboriginals, as an inferior race, were doomed to extinction, made the Aboriginal question appear temporary. Defying European theory, the Aboriginal population rose from the nadir of the 1930s to reach 145,000 in 1981. Aboriginal confidence also grew: a day of mourning was planned to mark the 150th anniversary of the European invasion in 1838 and Aboriginal stockmen went on strike for better wages, with the Arbitration Commission awarding them equal pay in 1965. In 1967 a referendum gave the federal government powers to legislate for Aboriginals, making aid available. Aboriginal Land Trusts, to which remaining reserves were transferred, were set up in most states from the mid-1960s, but the European doctrine of *terra nullius*, reaffirmed by the courts, left the Aboriginals with little or no claim to the land in law. Aboriginal activism, however, kept the issue alive. The **WHITLAM** government set up the Aboriginal Land Fund and the Aboriginal Land Rights (Northern Territory) Act (1976) to enable land transfers. In 1981, land for Aboriginal use amounted to some nine per cent of the total land area, but much of this was in the desert centre. Since then, the momentum has slowed, with growing opposition from commercial interests and economic difficulties reducing the scope for positive government action. Although Aboriginals have gradually been appointed in the Department of Aboriginal Affairs, they remain the most deprived section of the population. Aboriginal activism, however, kept the issue of *terra nullius* alive, and the doctrine was overturned by a High Court ruling in 1992; thus, the Aboriginals are now, at least in principle, legally entitled to their ancestral lands.

## aboriginal subsistence whaling
Certain aboriginal groups (in Greenland, Alaska, parts of Siberia, Dominica, Grenada and St Lucia) maintain a whaling tradition that is important culturally and for subsistence. Despite the moratorium on commercial whaling, the **INTERNATIONAL WHALING COMMISSION** (IWC) allows limited aboriginal subsistence whaling because it is much less intensive and so has a lower impact on whale populations.

## Aboukir Bay, Battle of (Aug 1798)
A naval battle during the War of the Second Coalition, in which the British Admiral **NELSON** destroyed the French fleet under Brueys off the coast of Egypt; the engagement is also known as the Battle of the Nile. This victory forced **NAPOLEON I** to abandon his Egyptian campaign, aimed at threatening British territory in India, and return to France.

## Aboukir Bay, Battle of (July 1799)
The last French victory of the Egyptian campaign, in which **NAPOLEON I**'s Army of Egypt captured Aboukir citadel, north-east of Alexandria, defeating an Ottoman Turkish force over twice its size, led by Mustafa Pasha.

## Absalon (1128–1201)
Danish prelate and statesman. The foster-brother of **VALDEMAR I, THE GREAT** whom he helped to the throne in 1157, he was appointed Bishop of Roskilde in 1158 and elected Archbishop of Lund in 1177. As Chief Minister to Valdemar, he led an army against the Wends in 1169 and extended Danish territories in the Baltic by capturing Rügen. In 1169 he built a fortress at Havn which became the nucleus of Copenhagen. As Chief Minister to Knud VI, he led an expedition in 1184 that captured Mecklenburg and Pomerania. As Archbishop of Lund, he was largely responsible for the systematization of Danish ecclesiastical law.

## absolutism
The prevalent type of government in 17–18c continental Europe, characterized by the concentration of all state power in the hands of the ruler and best exemplified by France under **LOUIS XIV**. The establishment of absolute rule involved the suspension of the estates' tax-voting rights and the streamlining of all intermediate authorities between subject and state. This required, and thus caused, the creation of a standing army and an efficient bureaucracy. State and monarch were conceived of as one and regarded as above the law. The notion of the '**DIVINE RIGHT OF KINGS**' provided the justification for this claim to undivided sovereignty, which found its visible expression in a magnificent court. In many countries the arbitrariness of monarchical power was later tempered by concepts of responsibility to God and the common good, and used to implement a variety of reforms. ► **ENLIGHTENED DESPOTS**

## Abu Nidal, originally Sabri Khalil al-Banna (1937–2002)
Palestinian terrorist. Having joined Yasser **ARAFAT**'s al-**FATAH** guerrilla group in the late 1950s, he grew impatient with its relatively 'moderate' stance and established his own group, the 'Revolutionary Council of Fatah' (often simply called the 'Abu Nidal Group'), in 1973. Sentenced to death for his extremism by the 'mainstream' **PLO** the following year, Abu Nidal went on to head a group which gained notoriety for its

brutal activities. The group targeted Arabs viewed as traitors to the Palestinian cause, and its attacks included the killing of 'moderate' PLO member Issam Sartawi in 1983 and that of the Israeli-appointed Mayor of Nablus in 1986. It also killed passengers at Rome and Vienna airports. Bowing to pressure from Arab states and the PLO, in 1988 Abu Nidal reportedly agreed to abide by the latter's ban on **TERRORISM**. However, the assets of the Abu Nidal Group, along with 11 other organizations, were frozen by President **CLINTON** in 1995 for undermining the Middle East peace process. He was living in Baghdad at the time of his death in Aug 2002 from gunshot wounds that the Iraqi government said were self-inflicted.

## Abyssinia, Conquest of (1935)

The bellicose venture by **MUSSOLINI** aimed at winning popular support at home, an increase in Italian prestige and strategic gains to pressurize the British in the Eastern Mediterranean. The invasion began in Oct 1935, against the advice of **VICTOR EMMANUEL III** and most of his generals. Victory was achieved by General **BADOGLIO** in May 1936 and the King was declared Emperor. However, the campaign was not a success: Italy had to commit over 650,000 men to subduing an ill-equipped and badly organized army and won the profound enmity of the British government. Limited economic sanctions were also imposed by the **LEAGUE OF NATIONS**. ➤ **AUTARCHIA**; **DE BONO, EMILIO**

## Acadia

Part of France's American empire; what is today Prince Edward Island, Nova Scotia, New Brunswick and the mainland coast from the Gulf of St Lawrence to Maine. The first settlement was established at Port Royal in 1605 by the sieur de Monts, and the area was exchanged between France and England until the Peace of **UTRECHT** (1713) handed most of Acadia to Britain. In 1755, 10,000 Acadians were evicted from the territory for resolving to pursue a policy of neutrality in the conflicts between France and Britain. The last French stronghold, **LOUISBOURG**, fell in 1758. ➤ **NEW FRANCE**

## Aceh

A major state at the northern extremity of the island of Sumatra, renowned for the fierceness of its Islamic tradition and for its trading prowess. As Dutch rule advanced from Java though the outer islands of the Indonesian archipelago in the second half of the 19c, the Acehnese put up the most stubborn resistance. The Dutch occupied the capital of the sultanate in the early 1870s but then found themselves drawn into a protracted resistance struggle. The colonial power launched ceaseless attacks from 1896 and subdued the sultanate by 1902. Since Indonesian independence (1945) there has been fighting between armed separatists in Aceh and government troops. This was suspended in December 2004 after the Indian Ocean tsunami, of which Aceh bore the brunt.

## Acheampong, Ignatius Katu (1931–79)

Ghanaian soldier and politician. He taught in commercial colleges before joining the army in 1953. Trained in the UK and USA, he served with the **UN** in the Congo and, following the 1966 military overthrow of **NKRUMAH**, was Chairman of the Western Region's administration for the National Liberation Council. Acting head of the 1st Brigade when he led the coup overthrowing Kofi **BUSIA** (13 Jan 1972), he became Chairman of the National Redemption Council and then Chairman of the Supreme Military Council and head of state (1972–8), until he was deposed and later executed.

## Acheson, Dean Gooderham (1893–1971)

US lawyer and politician. Educated at Yale and Harvard, he was Under-Secretary (1945–7) and then Secretary of State (1949–53) in the Truman administration. He developed US policy for the **CONTAINMENT** of **COMMUNISM**, helped to formulate the **MARSHALL PLAN** (1947–8) and participated in the establishment of **NATO** (1949).

## Achille Lauro Hijacking (7–9 Oct 1985)

The Italian cruise liner *Achille Lauro* was hijacked by four members of the Tunis-based faction of the Palestine Liberation Front (PLF), part of the **PLO** (Palestine Liberation Organization), when sailing between Alexandria and Port Said. The hijackers demanded the release of 50 Palestinians being held in Israel and threatened to kill the ship's 180 passengers if their demands were not met. However, after negotiations with Egyptian and Italian intermediaries and PLO officials, the terrorists surrendered. Despite the hijackers' claims that no one had been harmed, after their surrender it transpired that a US Jewish passenger, Leon Klinghoffer, had been shot dead and thrown overboard. The hijackers and an alleged Syrian accomplice were tried on charges of illegal possession of arms and explosives in Genoa the following month; all were convicted and sentenced to between four and nine years' imprisonment.

## Achimota College

A college founded in the Gold Coast by the Governor Sir Gordon Guggisberg in 1924 with the intention of developing an educated African élite capable of taking over a large proportion of the administrative tasks in the colony. By 1938 it was offering degree courses to a small number of students.

## Achin War ➤ ATJEH WAR

## Acker, Achille Henry van (1898–1975)

Belgian politician. A socialist, he began his career in trade unions after **WORLD WAR I** and was MP for his home town of Bruges (1927–74). He was appointed Cabinet Minister for Labour and Social Affairs in 1944, and thereafter became Prime Minister on four occasions. He is remembered for his role in the education debate, in the controversy leading to King **LEOPOLD III**'s abdication, and in social legislation. After 1958 he took less controversial political roles, first as a minister of state, and then as chairman of the House of Representatives until 1974. ➤ **BELGIAN SOCIALIST PARTY**

## ACLU ➤ AMERICAN CIVIL LIBERTIES UNION

## Adalbert (c.1000–72)

German prelate. Born of a noble Saxon family, in 1043 he was appointed Archbishop of Bremen and Hamburg. As papal legate to the north (1053), he extended his spiritual sway over Scandinavia and carried Christianity to the Slavonic Wends. In 1063 he became tutor to the young **HENRY IV** (of the Germans) and ruled over the whole kingdom for three years until he was deposed by enemy princes in 1066. He never regained his earlier authority and even lost Bremen, from which he was banished for three years.

**Adams, Charles Francis** (1807–86)
US diplomat. The son of John Quincy **ADAMS**, he studied at Harvard, was admitted to the Bar (1828), and became a representative from Massachusetts (1858–61). As Minister to Britain (1861–8), he strove to maintain British neutrality during the **AMERICAN CIVIL WAR**.

**Adams, Gerry**, properly **Gerard Adams** (1948–)
Northern Ireland militant nationalist politician. He emerged as a republican leader in the late 1960s through the civil rights movement and was briefly interned in 1972 before being released to take part in peace talks in London. He was interned again (1973–7, 1978), then became Vice President of **SINN FÉIN** in 1978 and President in 1983. A radical, he advocated a 'bullet and ballot box' strategy of electoral politics and paramilitarism, but he did not take his seat in the UK parliament when elected MP for West Belfast in 1983. He announced the **IRA** ceasefire in 1994, and took Sinn Féin into the multiparty talks resulting in the **GOOD FRIDAY AGREEMENT**. He committed Sinn Féin in public to 'all aspects' of the Agreement, enabling the start of power-sharing in a devolved Northern Ireland government, but the **STORMONTGATE** scandal and the Northern Bank raid in 2004 raised doubts about the sincerity of this commitment and underlined the speciousness of his insistence that Sinn Féin and the IRA are distinct organizations.

**Adams, Sir Grantley Herbert** (1898–1971)
Barbadian politician. After studying classics at Oxford, he was called to the English Bar in 1924 and returned to the West Indies to practise. He was a prominent figure in Caribbean politics and became Premier of Barbados (1954–8) before being elected the first Prime Minister of the short-lived Federation of the **WEST INDIES** (1958–62), which would have united seven former British colonies into a single state.

**Adams, John** (1735–1826)
US politician and 2nd President. Educated at Harvard, and admitted to the Bar in 1758, he emerged as a leader of US resistance to Britain's imposition of the **STAMP ACT** (1765), and led the debate that resulted in the **DECLARATION OF INDEPENDENCE**. He served in **CONGRESS** until 1777, after which he had an extensive diplomatic career in Europe. He took part in negotiating a peace treaty with Great Britain, and then served as Minister to Great Britain (1785–8). He became the first US Vice-President, under George **WASHINGTON** (1789), an office he found frustrating. Both were re-elected in 1792, and in 1796 Adams was elected President with Thomas **JEFFERSON** as Vice-President. Adams's presidency was marked by factionalism within his cabinet and his party, especially over the issue of war with France. Adams opposed a war, which made him an unpopular President, and he was defeated by Jefferson on seeking re-election in 1800. He retired to his home at Quincy, where he died. ▬ **FEDERALIST PARTY**

**Adams, John Quincy** (1767–1848)
US politician and 6th President. The son of John **ADAMS**, he studied at Harvard, and was admitted to the Bar in 1790. He had an extensive and brilliant diplomatic career between 1794 and 1817, except when he served in the US **SENATE** (1803–8). As Secretary of State under James **MONROE**, he negotiated with Spain the treaty for the acquisition of Florida, and played an important part in the formulation of the **MONROE DOCTRINE**. As President (1825–9), he failed to establish a strong base of public and political support and was therefore frustrated by executive and congressional factionalism. After his defeat by Andrew **JACKSON** in 1828, he was elected to the **HOUSE OF REPRESENTATIVES**, where through the 1830s and 1840s he became a strong opponent of the extension of **SLAVERY**.

**Adams, Samuel** (1722–1803)
American revolutionary political leader. Educated at Harvard, he became Lieutenant-Governor (1789–94) and Governor (1794–7) of Massachusetts. He was a strong supporter of revolution against Britain, and helped to plan the **BOSTON TEA PARTY**. Adams was a member of the **CONTINENTAL CONGRESS** (1774–81) and one of the signatories of the **DECLARATION OF INDEPENDENCE**. ▬ **AMERICAN REVOLUTION**

**Adams, Will(iam)** (1564–1620)
English sailor. He was pilot of a Dutch ship stranded off Japan in 1600, and was kept by **TOKUGAWA IEYASU**, the first **SHOGUN**, as an adviser on such areas as shipbuilding, navigation, gunnery, foreign relations and trade. He built the first European type of ocean-going vessel in Japan. The first Englishman to enter the service of a Japanese ruler, he lived at **EDO** (now Tokyo), where he was given an estate by Ieyasu. He is buried at Pilot Hill, Yokosuka, and is commemorated by monuments at Ito and Tokyo. ▬ **TOKUGAWA SHOGUNATE**

**Addams, Jane** (1860–1935)
US social reformer. She founded the first US settlement house, Hull House in Chicago, dedicated to settlement work among the immigrant poor, where she made her home. Addams worked to secure social justice by sponsoring legislation relating to housing, factory inspection, female suffrage and the cause of pacifism. She also campaigned for the abolition of **CHILD LABOUR** and the recognition of labour unions. Many of these reforms were adopted by the Progressive Party as part of its platform in 1912; Addams seconded Theodore **ROOSEVELT**'s nomination for President and was an active campaigner on his behalf. In 1931 she shared the **NOBEL PEACE PRIZE**, awarded in recognition of her efforts to end hostilities in **WORLD WAR I**.

**Addington, Henry** ▬ SIDMOUTH, HENRY ADDINGTON, 1ST VISCOUNT

**Addison, Joseph** (1672–1719)
English essayist and poet. In 1708–11 he was Secretary to the Lord-Lieutenant of Ireland, where he formed a warm friendship with Jonathan Swift. He became an MP, and contributed largely to the *Tatler*. In 1711 the *Spectator*, 274 numbers of which were his work, was founded. He was satirized by Alexander Pope in the famous character of Atticus (*An Epistle to*

*Dr Arbuthnot*). Addison was made a commissioner for trade and the colonies, and in 1717 was appointed Secretary of State, but a year later resigned his post on health grounds.

## Addled Parliament
In Britain, the name given to the brief parliament of Apr–June 1614 which saw disputes over money between **JAMES VI AND I** and the House of **COMMONS**. The Commons attempted to coerce the King into giving up prerogative revenue from 'impositions' on goods entering and leaving the country. The King dismissed the parliament, which passed no legislation.

## Adelfi
Secret society inspired and organized by the Tuscan revolutionary Filippo **BUONARROTI**, which pursued radical and patriotic goals from the 1790s until the Restoration era. ➤ **CARBONARI**

## Adenauer, Konrad (1876–1967)
German politician. He studied at Freiburg, Munich and **BONN**, before practising law in Cologne, where he became Lord Mayor (1917). He was President of the Prussian State Council (1920–33). In 1933 the Nazis dismissed him from all his offices, and imprisoned him in 1934, and again in 1944. In 1945, under Allied occupation, he helped to found the Christian Democratic Union (**CDU**) and served briefly again as Lord Mayor of Cologne. As the first Chancellor of the Federal Republic of Germany (1949–63), he established closer links with the French, and aimed to rebuild West Germany on a basis of partnership with other West European nations through **NATO** and the **EEC**. Although relations were restored with the USSR, relations with other countries in Eastern Europe remained frigid.

## ADGB (*Allgemeiner Deutscher Gewerkschaftsbund,*'General German Trade Union Federation')
The predominant, socialist-inclined German trade union organization in the **WEIMAR REPUBLIC**. Founded in 1919, the ADGB strove to unite all employees in a single federation and to gain recognition from the employers as the legitimate representative of German labour. Initial successes were undermined by a vigorous employers' counter-offensive, but the ADGB remained a significant organization with a membership of around 4 to 5 million. On 2 May 1933 it was banned by the National Socialist government. ➤ **NAZI PARTY**

## Adolf Frederick (1710–71)
King of Sweden (1751/71). The first king of the House of Holstein-Gottorp, he was the son of Christian Augustus, Prince-Bishop of Lübeck, and was descended on his mother's side from King **CHARLES XI** of Sweden. A favourite of Empress **ELIZABETH PETROVNA** of Russia, he was imposed by her on the Swedes as successor-designate to the childless King Frederick I in 1743 as a condition for ending a war in which Sweden had been humiliatingly defeated. The following year he married **LOVISA ULRIKA**, the sister of King **FREDERICK II, THE GREAT** of Prussia, by whom he was dominated. His powers as king were severely limited by the constitution of the 'AGE OF LIBERTY', but in 1768 his brief abdication forced the calling of an election to the Diet, which returned the Hat Party to power.

## Adolf of Nassau (1250–98)
King of Germany (1292/8). Relatively powerless himself, Adolf was unanimously elected King in 1292 as a means of refuting Habsburg claims to a hereditary right to the monarchy, represented by Albert of Austria. Adolf attempted to build up a power base in Meissen and Thuringia and had military successes there in 1294–5, but his ambitions alarmed the **ELECTORS** and he was deposed in 1298 by a coalition of Bohemia, Austria and Mainz. He fell in battle against Albert of Austria (**ALBERT I**) and was buried in the cathedral in Speyer in 1309. ➤ **GÖLLHEIM, BATTLE OF; HABSBURG DYNASTY**

## Adowa, Battle of (1 Mar 1896)
A battle between Ethiopian forces, under Emperor **MENELIK**, and Italian forces, in which the latter were decisively defeated. In the 1880s Italy had become involved in the Scramble for Africa, taking Eritrea (1884) and the Indian Ocean coast of Somalia (1890). The Italian defeat at Adowa was the worst reverse suffered by Europeans in the Partition of **AFRICA**, ensuring Ethiopian independence for another 40 years. It was also probably the biggest factor in bringing down the second **CRISPI** ministry. **MUSSOLINI**'s invasion of 1935 was a conscious act of revenge.

## Adrian IV, originally Nicholas Breakspear (c.1100–1159)
English pope (1154/9). The only Englishman to hold the office, he became first a lay brother in the monastery of St Rufus, near Avignon, and in 1137 was elected its Abbot. His zeal for strict discipline led to an attempt to defame his character, and he had to appear before **EUGENIUS III** at Rome. Here he not only cleared himself, but acquired the esteem of the pope, who appointed him Cardinal Bishop of Albano in 1146. As pope, he is said to have granted the Lordship of **IRELAND** to **HENRY II** of England.

## Adrian VI, originally Adrian Dedel (1459–1523)
Dutch pope (1522/3). After studying with the Brethren of the Common Life and in Leuven (Louvain), he was made Professor of Theology (1491) and was appointed tutor in 1507 to the 7-year-old Charles (later Charles I of Spain and Emperor **CHARLES V**), who in 1516, commencing rule in Spain, made Adrian Inquisitor-General of Aragon and effective co-regent with Ximenes, the choice of the dying **FERDINAND II, THE CATHOLIC**. On Ximenes's death, Charles worked closely with Adrian and made him regent in his absence from 1520, but in 1522 on the death of **LEO X**, Adrian was almost unanimously elected pope. He tried to attack the sale of indulgences which had prompted Martin **LUTHER**'s first revolt, but was blocked by interested officials. He called openly for widespread reform of the curia at the Diet of Nuremberg, but also demanded Luther's punishment for heresy. He allied with the Emperor, England and Venice against France, thus failing to unite Christendom against the Turks, who captured Rhodes. He died before his attempted reforms could be effective, and was the last non-Italian pope before **JOHN PAUL II** in 1978.

## Adrianople, Treaty of (1829)
The treaty ending the Russo-Turkish War of 1828–9 which began when, partly as a diversion from

domestic unrest, **NICHOLAS I** of Russia renewed his predecessors' policy of southwards expansion by moving his forces across the River Danube in 1828. It marked an important stage in the advance of both Serbia and Greece towards independent statehood. Russian troops also crossed the Balkan Mountains for the first time; and, although under the treaty Russia gave up all its conquests, it gave notice that it was now a military power to be reckoned with in the Near East and the Mediterranean. ▶ **RUSSO-TURKISH WARS**

### Adullamites
A nickname coined by the radical British Liberal MP John **BRIGHT** to describe those in his party who opposed **GLADSTONE's** parliamentary reform bill in 1866. Bright's reference was to the 'Cave Adullam' in the First Book of Samuel which housed 'everyone that was in distress ... and everyone that was discontented'. The Adullamite leaders, Robert Lowe and Lord Elcho, succeeded in bringing down the Liberal government (1866). ▶ **RADICALISM**

### Aerssen, Cornelis van (1546–1627)
Founder of an important Dutch political family of the 16–17c. He became Pensionary of Brussels in 1580, and then Secretary to the States General in 1584, a post he held until 1623. He was closely involved in the negotiations leading to the **TWELVE YEARS' TRUCE**. His son François (1572–1641) became Lord of Sommelsdijk in 1612 and was a diplomat and adviser to **OLDENBARNEVELDT**, but later transferred his allegiance to Prince **MAURICE**, and exerted a major influence on the foreign policy of the Dutch Republic. François' son Cornelis (1600–62), a military leader, was thought to be the richest man in Holland of his day. Several other members of the family achieved prominence in the public life of the republic.

### Aethelred the Unready ▶ ETHELRED THE UNREADY

### affirmative action
The name given to US policies requiring businesses and other institutions to enact employment practices concerning minorities, ranging from the employment and promotion of ethnic minorities and women, to the setting of employment quotas. Such policies were established in the early 1970s to counteract discrimination in the past, but have been challenged in recent times as 'reverse discrimination'. ▶ **BAKKE CASE**

### Afghani, Jamal al-Din al- (1838/9–97)
Muslim reformer and political agitator. Born at Asadabad near Kabul, his life's work was directed towards fomenting agitation for his country's liberation from European exploitation, the independent internal development of Muslim countries along liberal lines, and towards his overriding vision of a union of all Islamic states under a single caliph ('Pan-Islam'). He visited India, Egypt and Turkey, where he fell foul of the authorities and returned to Cairo. In what was to become a familiar pattern, after an initially good reception, he annoyed both the British and the Azharis by his inflammatory behaviour and was deported to India. Noted particularly for his later opposition to the Persian tobacco concession, which became a *cause célèbre*, he became a thor-

oughly embarrassing figure to the authorities in the countries he had visited. In 1892 he was, however, invited to retire to Turkey, where he spent the last five years of his life. His activities were primarily directed towards the goal of universal Pan-Islam. He sought to achieve this by means of inflammatory articles, appearing notably in two major publications, *Al-Urwa al-Wuthqa* (in collaboration with Muhammad **ABDUH**), and the bilingual Arabic–English monthly, *Diya' al-Khafiqin*, which contained many attacks on the Shah of Persia and his government.

**AFGHANISTAN** official name **Islamic State of Afghanistan**

A landlocked, mountainous republic in south central Asia, bounded to the north by Turkmenistan, Uzbekistan and Tajikistan; to the east and south by Pakistan; to the west by Iran; and in the extreme north-east by China and India. The nation first formed in 1747 under **AHMAD SHAH DURRANI**. In the 19c and early 20c Britain saw Afghanistan as a bridge between India and the Middle East, but failed to gain control during the **AFGHAN WARS**. The feudal monarchy survived until after **WORLD WAR II**, when the constitution became more liberal under several Soviet-influenced five-year economic plans. In 1973 the king was deposed and a republic was formed. A new constitution was adopted in 1977, but a coup in 1978 installed a new government under the communist leader Nur Muhammad Taraki; a further coup in 1979 brought to power Hafizullah Amin. This led to invasion by Soviet forces, fiercely resisted by the **MUJAHIDIN**, with US backing. In 1989 the Soviet troops finally withdrew, and in 1992 Mujahidin groups forced the resignation of the communist government of Muhammad **NAJIBULLAH** and proclaimed the Islamic State of Afghanistan. Fighting between factions continued until the rise in 1994 of the **TALIBAN**, who sought to replace the factionalism with Islamic law. Within two years the Taliban had taken Kabul, executed Najibullah, and the civil war had resulted in 25,000 to 45,000 Afghan deaths. In 1998 they controlled almost 90 per cent of the country. The Taliban allowed **AL-QAEDA** to base terrorist training camps in Afghanistan, and its refusal to hand over Osama bin Laden and other al-Qaeda leaders after the **SEPTEMBER 11 ATTACKS** led to the regime's overthrow in 2001 by a US-led international coalition, supported by the Afghani Northern Alliance (**AFGHAN WAR**). Following approval of a new constitution, Hamid Karzai was elected President in Oct 2004. Although allied forces remain in Afghanistan, the government does not control the whole of the country because of factionalism and Taliban-inspired violence.

### Afghan War (Oct–Dec 2001)
The first conflict in the war on **TERROR**, the objectives

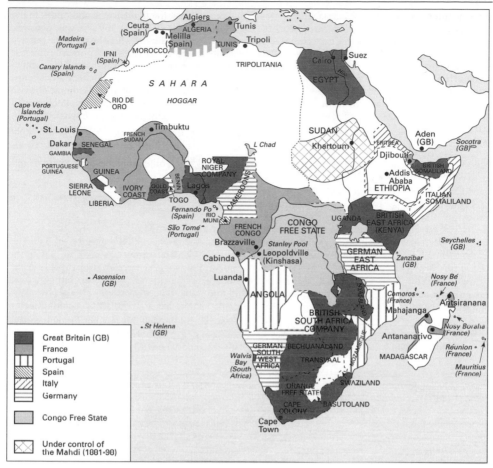

**Great Britain (GB)**
**France**
**Portugal**
**Spain**
**Italy**
**Germany**

**Congo Free State**

**Under control of**
**the Mahdi (1881-98)**

**Africa, 1895**

of Operation Enduring Freedom were to eliminate terrorist training camps in Afghanistan and to capture Osama bin Laden and other **AL-QAEDA** leaders. A coalition of 38 countries, in an uneasy alliance with the Northern Alliance (United Front), internal opponents of the **TALIBAN** regime, supported a US-led invasion. The conflict began on 7 Oct and by 13 Nov the major cities had fallen and the Taliban had been ousted. No al-Qaeda leaders of significance were captured. Suspected Taliban and al-Qaeda supporters were detained, many at Camp X-ray in the US base at Guantanamo Bay, Cuba, without charge or access to legal assistance for some years despite international representations to the US government over the terms of their detention and the USA's intention to try them before military tribunals.

**Afghan Wars** (1838–42, 1878–80 and 1919)
A series of wars between Britain and Afghanistan, prompted by the British desire to extend control in the region to prevent the advance of Russian influence towards India. The treaties which followed the third Afghan War (1919) reinforced the country's independent political status.

**Aflaq, Michel** (1910–89)
Syrian politician. A schoolteacher and then journalist in Damascus, he was, with Salah al-Din **BITAR**, the founder of the **BA'ATH PARTY**. The ideology behind the

party was essentially socialist, with an emphasis on Arab unity. It was also anti-Zionist and instrumental in the foundation with Gamal Abd al-**NASSER** of the **UNITED ARAB REPUBLIC** (1958–61). Ousted from Syria in 1966, his own political influence declined, but even today (hostile) Arab presses are inclined to refer to the Ba'ath Party as being 'Aflaqi'.

**AFL–CIO (American Federation of Labor and Congress of Industrial Organizations)**
A federation of labour unions in the USA, Canada, Mexico, Panama and US dependencies, formed in 1955 from the merger of the AFL (mainly craft unions, founded in 1886) with the CIO (mainly industrial workers' unions, founded in 1935). Its aims include educational campaigns on behalf of the labour movement, the settlement of disputes among affiliates, and political support for beneficial legislation. ➤ **LEWIS, JOHN L**; **UNITED AUTOMOBILE WORKERS**

**Afonso I, Henriques** (c.1110–1185)
King of Portugal (1139/85). He was only two years old at the death of his father, Henry of Burgundy, first Count of Portugal. Wresting power from his mother in 1128, he fought the **MOORS**, defeating them at Ourique (1139), and proclaimed himself King. He took Lisbon (1147), and later all Galicia, Estremadura and Elvas.

## afrancesados

The term applied to those 'Frenchified' Spanish politicians and intellectuals who during the War of Independence (1793–1814) supported Joseph **BONAPARTE** and the programme of reforms introduced by the French administration. They were opposed by the 'patriot' reformers who supported Ferdinand VII. When the French troops withdrew from Spain, some 10,000 *afrancesados* were driven into exile by a decree of 1814.

## Africa, Partition of

The division of the continent of Africa into colonial territories, which occurred in the last three decades of the 19c. Europeans had traded with Africa for several centuries, using a series of coastal settlements. Portuguese efforts to penetrate the interior in the 16–17c had largely failed, and only the Dutch at the Cape had been able to establish a dynamic permanent settlement. In the course of the 19c, efforts to abolish the slave trade, missionary endeavours, and optimistic views of African riches helped to encourage colonial ambitions. The countries involved in the Partition included Britain, France, Germany, Portugal and Italy, as well as the Boers in the south, and (in his private capacity) King **LEOPOLD II** of the Belgians. When the French and the Italians completed

the Partition of North Africa in the years before **WORLD WAR I**, only Liberia and Ethiopia remained independent. At the end of the two World Wars, a repartitioning occurred with the confiscation of German and Italian territories. Most of the countries created by the Partition achieved independence in or after the 1960s, and the **ORGANIZATION OF AFRICAN UNITY** pledged itself to the maintenance of the existing boundaries.

## African Development Bank

Established in 1963, the same year as the **ORGANIZATION OF AFRICAN UNITY**, and based in Abidjan, Côte d'Ivoire, it began operations in 1966. Its funds come from both individual countries and multilateral sources and loans are made, at preferential rates, for development schemes.

## African Lakes Company

A company founded in 1878, originally called the Livingstonia Central Africa Company, to assist the Scottish Presbyterian missionaries in Nyasaland, now Malawi. Its founders, the two brothers Fred and John Moir, placed steamers on Lake Nyasa and became embroiled in campaigns against Muslim rivals. The under-capitalized company was poorly managed and it was bought out by Cecil **RHODES** who, in 1893, turned it into the African Lakes

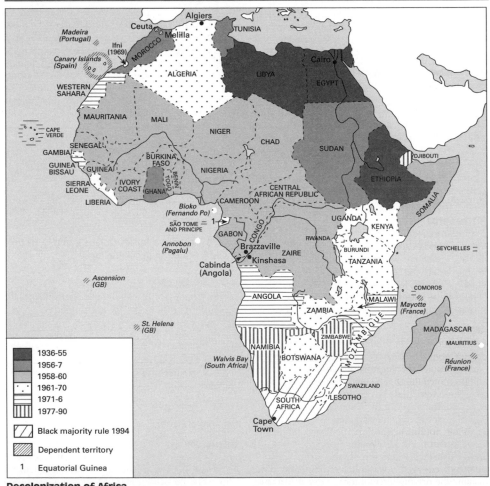

**Decolonization of Africa**

Trading Corporation. It remained a leading trading and retailing company throughout the period of colonial rule in central Africa.

### African National Congress ► ANC

### African National Council

A Zimbabwean political organization founded in 1972 on the roots of ZAPU to express to the Pierce Commission black opposition to a proposed constitutional arrangement agreed between Ian SMITH and British Prime Minister Sir Alec Douglas-Home. Its leader was Bishop Abel MUZOREWA, who developed it into a political party. Its success in the late 1970s depended upon the continued banning of its forerunners, and its strength rapidly reduced after independence in 1980. ► HOME OF THE HIRSEL, BARON

### African Union (AU)

An organization established in 2002 by the 53 members of the ORGANIZATION OF AFRICAN UNITY (OAU) as a successor body to it. While the OAU functioned within the framework of individual nation states, the African Union is modelled on the EU, and plans to maintain a range of institutions, including an assembly of heads of state and of government, a secretariat, and a peace and security council. It intends to set up an African Court of Justice and a range of financial institutions to support development, and supports a Pan African Parliament, based in South Africa. It aims to achieve further development and the economic integration of the continent, but it is a body whose rhetoric is at odds with the realities of African life.

### Afrifa, Akwasi Amankwaa (1936–79)

Ghanaian soldier and politician. Educated at Adisadel College, he joined the colonial army in 1956, trained at Sandhurst and twice served with the UN in the Congo. He was one of the group that overthrew NKRUMAH in 1966 and became a member, later chairman, of the National Liberation Council. He handed power over to civilians in 1969, but, when the military intervened again in 1972, he was for a while detained. When civilian rule returned, he was tried and executed for corrupt practices.

### Afrika Corps

A German expeditionary force of two divisions under the command of ROMMEL, sent to North Africa (Mar 1941) to reinforce Italian troops there. It had been given special desert training in Germany, and proved highly effective in desert warfare between 1941 and 1943. ► NORTH AFRICAN CAMPAIGN; WORLD WAR II

### Afrikaner Bond

A society founded in 1880 as part of the political and cultural revival of the Boers or AFRIKANERS in South Africa. It coined the slogan 'Afrika voor de Afrikaners' and promoted the Dutch language and strict Calvinism. There were branches in the Cape, Orange Free State and Transvaal. At the Cape the Bond was prepared to form a political alliance with English-speaking South Africans, particularly supporting Cecil RHODES, but elsewhere it became virulently anti-British. In 1918 a new body, the Afrikaner BROEDERBOND, emerged. It was much more secretive and became the driving force of more radical Afrikaner nationalism in the 20c.

### Afrikaners

An early 18c term to describe those Europeans who had been born in the Dutch colony at the Cape and were therefore 'Africans', also known as Boers (in Dutch, 'farmers'). They emerged as a separate people derived from an admixture of Dutch, German, French and non-white. During the 18c they penetrated the interior of the Cape as pastoral farmers. After 1835, groups left Cape Colony and established independent republics in the interior, which later coalesced into the Orange Free State and the South African Republic. After the Boer War (1899–1902) the British hoped to encourage emigration to South Africa, transforming the Afrikaners into a minority. Such large-scale emigration failed to materialize. Even before the Union of South Africa in 1910, the Afrikaners had become the dominant force in white South African politics, and maintained their ascendancy until the dismantling of APARTHEID under F W DE KLERK and the elections of 1994 which brought the ANC to power. ► BOER WARS; GREAT TREK; SMUTS, JAN

### Agadir

A port on the Atlantic coast of Morocco which was visited in July 1911 by the German gunboat *Panther*, supposedly to protect German interests in Morocco threatened by the French, whom Kiderlen-Wächter had accused of acting contrary to the agreements reached at the 1906 Conference of ALGECIRAS. It was the British government, however, who were the more alarmed by the presence of the *Panther* in a port relatively close to Gibraltar. They suspected the Germans of seeking to establish a naval presence in Agadir, thereby posing a threat to British trade routes. The 'Second Moroccan Crisis' came close to precipitating hostilities. These were, however, averted.

### Aga Khan

The title of the hereditary head of the Nizari Isma'ilian sect of Muslims, notably Aga Khan III (1877–1957) (in full, Aga Sultan Sir Mohammed Shah, born at Karachi), who succeeded to the title in 1885. He worked for the British cause in both World Wars, and in 1937 was President of the LEAGUE OF NATIONS. He owned several Derby winners. He died at Versoix, Switzerland, and was succeeded as 49th Imam by his grandson, Karim (1936– ), the son of Aly Khan. ► WORLD WAR I; WORLD WAR II

### Aganbegyan, Abel Gazevich (1932– )

Soviet economist. Part-Armenian, part-Hungarian, he was born in Tbilisi in Georgia, studied economics in Moscow and made his name in the Institute of Industrial Production in Novosibirsk, eventually as Director (1967–85). He met Mikhail GORBACHEV through ZASLAVSKAYA and was initially one of the main contributors to his reform programme. An early influence on Gorbachev's PERESTROIKA, although he transferred to Moscow he fell into the background in the late 1980s, subsequently becoming Rector of the Academy of National Economy.

### Agenda 21

Agenda 21 was endorsed by the EARTH SUMMIT in 1992 but is not binding on participants. It provides a framework for sustainable development, avoiding waste and inefficient consumption, and creating a

# Agriculture

*Culture & Society*

### Origins
After the last Ice Age ended, c.10,000 BC, a favourable climate and a good supply of food resulted in an expansion of the human population; a more certain source of food than the hunter-gatherer mode of living could provide was required. In the Near East from 8000 BC and a little later in the Far East and Mesoamerica, wild grains were collected for food, and began to be grown in areas around settlements. By 7000 BC the cultivation of wheat and barley had moved into Greece. Animals were domesticated for their milk, meat and hides: goats and sheep from 7000 BC, pigs in Turkey at the same time, and cattle in the Aegean c.6000 BC. In Mesoamerica maize was cultivated, and in Peru the llama and alpaca were used as draught animals before 5000 BC. In north China millet was cultivated from 5000 BC, and in the south, around the Yangzi delta, rice was grown from 4000 BC. The cultivation of rice had spread to Japan and Persia by the 1c AD. In tropical Africa yams, sorghum and finger millet were grown c.4000 BC, cotton in the Indus Valley c.5500 BC, flax for linen in ancient Egypt (found as shrouds), and manioc in the Amazon basin c.1500 BC.

### Crops and animals
At first, plants occurring naturally in each region were the ones grown. Cereals were important from the beginning, producing the most food value from the land and capable of being stored. As the population of each country grew, means were sought to increase crop yields. As well as cereals, other foods are known to have been grown from the beginnings of agriculture: squash in Mexico, olives and grape vines (for wine) in the Near East and Europe, and fruits indigenous to each area.

With the 16c voyages of discovery, exotic foods were taken from their places of origin and introduced to Europe, most significantly potatoes (originating in Peru) to the north, and maize (originating in Mesoamerica) to the south. Later, in the era of colonization, tea, coffee and cocoa plants were introduced to new areas, and rubber, sugarcane, coconuts and bananas were farmed on plantations.

Pigs were farmed all over Asia and Europe, goats and sheep in the Near and Middle East, sheep and cattle all over Europe, and reindeer in Scandinavia; every part of the animal was used. Poultry were kept for their eggs, flesh and feathers; cattle, especially oxen, could be used for transport as well. The horse had been domesticated on the Asian steppes at an early stage, and its introduction to farms by those who could afford one was a great benefit in many tasks.

In the 19c when new areas opened up for raising livestock in North America, Australia and New Zealand, cross-breeding created breeds of cattle and sheep that could meet the challenges of unfamiliar conditions.

### Methods and tools
Stone adzes and sickles were the first tools. A digging stick helped prepare the ground for planting (a tool still in use in Mesoamerica, India and parts of the Pacific in the 20c), or a branch might serve as a rudimentary plough. Ploughs were improved in shape, and with the coming of the Iron Age acquired a metal share. The use of animals to pull the ploughs meant that earth could be penetrated more deeply, and the wheeled plough in use in Europe from about the 5c enabled heavier soils to be turned. The all-steel plough was invented by blacksmith John Deere in the USA in 1830, and the advent of the internal-combustion engine provided ploughing capabilities unimagined in medieval times.

An early innovation that was essential to agriculture in many parts of the world was irrigation, used in the Nile Valley as early as 5000 BC (the *shadoof*, a bucket on a weighted pole is still in use there and elsewhere), in China in 2200 BC (now the greatest irrigator in the world, because of rice production), in Peru, and in North America by **Native Americans** in Arizona.

Until the 20c much of southern Europe followed the farming practices followed by the Romans. Holdings were mostly small, and used to grow cereals, vines, olives and fruits. Worked by mattocks, hoes and a wooden plough with an iron share (ploughed three times a year) on a two-field system, where one of the two was left fallow each year, they were

---

sustainable balance between consumption, population and use of the Earth's resources. Chapter 28 of Agenda 21 emphasizes the importance of local authorities in sustainable development, and recommended that by 1996 every local authority should have developed a local Agenda 21 for its community. Progress on implementation was assessed in 1997. A follow-up, Local Action 21, was launched at the World Summit on Sustainable Development in 2002.

### Age of Greatness (Sweden)
The period in the 17c when Sweden acquired and maintained the status of a great European power. It is usually taken to begin with the accession of **GUSTAV II ADOLF** in 1611 and to end with the Peace of Nystadt in 1721 at the end of the **GREAT NORTHERN WAR**. During this time Sweden won Livonia in the southeastern Baltic, western Pomerania, the city of Wismar and the bishoprics of Bremen and Verden in northern Germany, as well as the provinces of Halland, Skåne and Blekinge from Denmark, and Bohuslän, Jämtland and Härjedalen from Norway. Under a series of ca-

pable kings and ministers, Sweden's government and military machine became among the most efficient in Europe.

### Age of Liberty (Sweden)
The period between the death of **CHARLES XII** in 1718 and the coup d'état of **GUSTAV III** in 1772, when Sweden was governed under a constitution (finalized in 1720) which granted political power to the Diet dominated by the Estate of Nobles. It saw the rise of political parties, divided on foreign, economic and social policy, beginning with the pro-French Hat Party in the later 1730s, which dominated the scene until ousted in 1765 by the Cap Party, which then developed a social policy that aimed to reduce noble privileges. The intensity of the struggle between these two groups was ended by Gustav III, who restored a degree of monarchical power.

### Agincourt, Battle of (1415)
A battle between France and England during the **HUNDRED YEARS' WAR**. **HENRY V** of England was

fertilized with the contents of the compost pit (human and animal waste, kitchen waste and weeds). Crops were harvested with a sickle, threshed by being trodden by animals, and winnowed in the wind. Sheep, goats, pigs, cattle and fowl were kept, pasture animals being moved seasonally.

Northern Europe followed different methods from about AD 800. The land around villages was divided into long strips (of about one acre), each man working several (separated) strips. From the 10c to the 13c the acreage of agricultural land was increased by the clearing of forests and draining of marshes. The events of the 14c – famine, floods and plague – saw a change in the social order as labour became scarce and the peasants revolted against their lot.

From the beginning of the 18c changes began in England – later referred to as the Agricultural Revolution – that would be followed eventually in other parts of Europe. Common lands were enclosed for the pasture of sheep for their wool, and arable lands were consolidated and fenced to form coherent farms. The serfs had been permitted to remit service to their feudal lords in cash rather than service, so that they could devote all their time to their own farms; **feudalism** was abolished by statute in 1660. However, this change did not occur in some other parts of Europe until after the **French Revolution**, and not in Russia until the **Russian Revolution**. In England there was incentive to improve farms' output, and in the 18c the Norfolk four-course (root crops, barley, clover and wheat) crop rotation, an idea borrowed from the Netherlands by Lord **Townsend**, revolutionized land management in Britain and spread to other parts of Europe. As well as improving the land by the inclusion of clover, the root crops in the rotation (usually turnips) provided winter fodder for the animals so that they did not have to be slaughtered in the autumn. The animals also provided more manure to put on the fields. The rate of enclosures increased – six million acres being enclosed between 1700 and 1845 – and some peasant farmers were turned out of their homes. Veterinary schools were established to train people to care for the improved livestock, and a more intensive form of farming began. New machinery such as Jethro Tull's seed drill led to greater productivity, an aim much encouraged by governments. Although farm workers opposed mechanization it continued apace, particularly after the internal-combustion engine prompted the invention of tractors and combine harvesters. In the USA in particular, the lack of available labour encouraged the development of mechanical devices, which grew ever larger in the 20c as farms turned into big businesses.

### Changes in the 20c

Understanding the chemical requirements of plants came in the 19c. Following that, a fertilizer industry emerged that could supply these nutrients to farmers in concentrated form, so that they did not have to rely on animal manures. Alongside fertilizers, the chemical industry was able to supply herbicides to combat weeds, and insecticides and fungicides to fight pests and diseases. With the development of insecticides such as DDT and organophosphates in the middle of the century, farmers thought that they had reached a golden age. But all too soon it became apparent that insects, fungi and bacteria could develop resistance to sprays, and the harm done to the environment was a side-effect difficult to quantify.

Scientific plant breeding led to increased yields, and genetic engineering promised 'better' animals and crops for the farmers' purposes. The '**Green Revolution**' of the 1960s saw increased crop yields in many developing countries, but again there were problems with the need for increased irrigation, fertilizers and pesticides placing a strain on the local growers. Despite this, in industrialized societies farms grew bigger and even more mechanized, greatly increasing output and efficiency.

### Social and economic implications

When groups of hunter-gatherers became farmers as well, they settled in one place. This paved the way for permanent settlements, cities and complex civilizations. More goods were collected than had been possible in the old nomadic life, sometimes there was a surplus. They also desired goods they could not make or grow themselves, so trade began.

Very desirable crops, such as the spices of the East, inspired voyages of exploration. The growth of large cities meant many people needed to be fed by products farmed elsewhere. Civilizations rose on the success of their agriculture, but also failed when it failed; one of the problems of long-term irrigation is the increasing salinity of the soil, and the

---

forced to fight near Hesdin (Pas-de-Calais) by the French who, ignoring the lessons of the Battles of **CRÉCY** and **POITIERS** (1356), pitched cavalry against dismounted men-at-arms and archers. Though heavily outnumbered, the English won another overwhelming victory, and returned in 1417 to begin the systematic conquest of **NORMANDY**.

### Agitprop

An abbreviation for the Department of Agitation and Propaganda, established in 1920 as a section of the Central Committee Secretariat of the Soviet Communist Party. Its role was to ensure the compatibility of activities within society with Communist Party ideology. The term later came to be widely used in an artistic or literary context for works which adopted an ideological stance. ► **COMMUNISM**

### Agnew, Spiro Theodore (1918–96)

US politician. The son of a Greek immigrant, after service in **WORLD WAR II** he studied law at the University of Maryland. In 1966 he was elected Governor of

Maryland on a liberal platform, supporting anti-discrimination and anti-poverty legislation, but by 1968, he had become considerably more conservative. As a compromise figure acceptable to many in the **REPUBLICAN PARTY**, he became Richard **NIXON**'s running mate in the 1968 election, and took office as Vice-President in 1969. He resigned in 1973 after charges of corruption during his years in Maryland politics were brought against him.

### Agrarian Party (Sweden) ► CENTRE PARTY (SWEDEN)

### Agrarian Reform Law (1950)

One of the first measures implemented by the Chinese People's Republic established in 1949. It aimed to complete the process, begun in the late 1940s in areas under communist control, to redistribute land amongst landless and poor peasants. In contrast to previous measures, however, agrarian reform in 1950 was to be relatively moderate, in line with the prevailing view that there was to be a gradual

Mesopotamian civilization fell victim to that.

The introduction of new crops such as potatoes and maize from America to Europe created new cheap food for the poor; in Ireland by 1846 (when potato blight led to famine and starvation for many) the population had grown to almost four times the size it had been at the time of the potato's introduction. Agricultural enterprises in the colonies meant a change in the way of life for the people who provided the work force, and riches for many of the companies who handled the import of products to the developed world. Coffee, believed to have been grown first in Arabia around the 6c, was first imported into Europe in 1517, and by the 18c plantations were being developed in Latin America. Tea was adopted by the English after its introduction in 1657 (it had been drunk in China from before 1000 BC) and plantations made throughout the British Empire. So too with cocoa, after the introduction of chocolate to Europe by explorers returning from Mexico. Tobacco, sugarcane and cotton in the West Indies and USA gave impetus to the slave trade. These products could not be grown in Europe; even those that could were in short supply in the big cities that developed in the **Industrial Revolution**. The demand for wheat stimulated the economies of eastern Europe, Canada and the USA.

The dependence of city-dwellers on others to produce their food led at the end of the 20c to fears and concerns about its safety, and to the desirability of certain farming practices over others. Some people reacted against the intensive farming that had kept the price of some products, such as chicken and pork, very low, either by refusing to eat meat, or by turning to 'organic' produce grown or raised without the use of pesticides or chemical fertilizers. Concerns about pollution from fertilizers in the water table and pesticides in the food chain increased each decade after the 1960s. The scandals of salmonella poisoning, BSE and dioxin contamination point to the importance of agriculture to everyone and the difficulty of imposing effective controls in an age when ease of transport means products are dispersed quickly and widely from the point of production. Nor could the pace of scientific change in agriculture be expected to slacken. On the contrary, research into genetically modified (GM) crops such as soy beans and maize has led to widespread cultivation of such crops in North America; so far, GM crops have been grown in the UK only in farm-scale trials, to test the effects on the environment, and it is not expected that commercial cultivation in the UK will begin until at least 2008. Advances have been made in selective breeding and in animal husbandry; for example, chickens can be reared to attain full size in a lifetime of only 50 days. The great supermarket chains in advanced countries, with their search for low-cost bulk producers, more or less mandated an endless search for cost efficiency through innovation in agriculture.

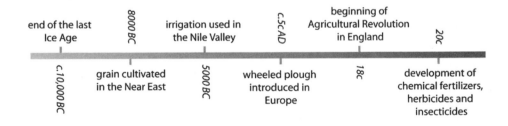

transition towards socialism and collectivization. Although the land and property of landlords (who made up about four per cent of the population and owned 30 per cent of the cultivated land) were to be confiscated and redistributed, dispossessed landlords could still be given a share. Moreover, land worked by rich peasants was protected and they could even rent land to tenant farmers, providing it did not exceed the amount of land they cultivated themselves. Nevertheless, agrarian reform, completed in 1952, produced a large class of individual peasant owner-cultivators. Socially and politically, the influence of the landlord class was eliminated; many landlords were subject to denunciation and even execution by communist-organized peasant associations.

**agregado**

A term used in Brazil (literally, 'a dependant') with various connotations, all of which denote the dependence of the *agregado* on the patronage of a powerful proprietor. The agregado was a rural labourer, depen-

dent on the favour of a landowner for access to a subsistence plot and hut, in exchange for labour services specified by customary law. Such agreements were always verbal, and could generally be revoked by the landowner. Agregados were often tied by fictitious rental agreements, which obliged them to vote for the candidate chosen by the landowner. They were seen variously as the property of the landowner or as his personal militia.

**Agriculture** ► *See panel*

**Aguinaldo, Emilio** (1870–1964)
Filipino revolutionary. He was a central figure in the rising against Spain (1896–8), and against the USA (1899–1901). After capture by the Americans in 1901, he took the oath of allegiance to the USA, the new colonial power.

**Aguirre, José Antonio** (1904–60)
Basque politician. Born into a middle-class, Carlist family, he became leader of the conservative Basque Nationalist Party (**PNV**), the main Basque party of the

1930s. He was elected as the first President (or *Lendakari*) of the Basque country (or *Euzkadi*) after the Republic passed the Autonomy Statute in Oct 1936. After the fall of Bilbao in June 1937, Aguirre took the government into exile in France. Following the outbreak of **WORLD WAR II**, he was denied passage to England, and so undertook an extraordinary journey via Nazi Germany (complete with artificial moustache and glasses), Sweden and Brazil to Uruguay. After the war, he headed the government in exile in France. ➤ **BASQUE AUTONOMY STATUTES**

## Aguiyi-Ironsi, Johnson (1925–66)
Nigerian soldier and politician. He joined the colonial army in 1942 and was trained in the UK before commanding the Nigerian contingent in the **UN** involvement in the Congo (Zaire). Appointed Commander-in-Chief in 1965, he assumed power following the officers' coup of Jan 1966, but was killed in the counter-coup, led by **GOWON** (July 1966).

## Ahidjo, Ahmadou (1924–89)
Cameroonian politician. Educated at the École Supérieure d'Administration, Yaoundé, he was a radio operator in the post office before entering politics in 1947, being elected to the Territorial Assembly. He represented Cameroon in the Assembly of French Union 1953–7. From 1957 to 1960 he held senior positions in the Territorial Assembly of Cameroon. In 1960, when most of the British Cameroons was amalgamated with the French Cameroons, he became President and was re-elected to that post in 1972, 1975 and 1980. He resigned in 1982 and went into voluntary exile in France. His one-party state, although severe on the rival, but outlawed, *Union des Populations Camerounaises* (UPC), was relatively successful economically and less repressive than many West African states.

## Ahmad al-Mansur (1549–1603)
Sultan of Maghrib (Morocco) (1578/1603). He brought peace and prosperity to the country, instituting administrative reforms and developing trade, especially in sugar and saltpetre.

## Ahmad Gran (c.1506–1543)
Sultan of Adal in Somalia. He declared a **JIHAD** or holy war against Christian Ethiopia in the 1530s and, with assistance from the Ottomans, he was able to maintain control of the empire until his defeat in battle by Emperor **GALAWDEWOS** in 1543.

## Ahmad Khan, Sir Sayyid (1817–98)
Indian lawyer and educator. One of the most important and influential Indian Muslims of the 19c, he was an employee of the British **EAST INDIA COMPANY** and later a judge, who embraced European civilization and many aspects of British rule and worked to further the Muslim cause in India within the British system. An opponent of Muslim participation in the **INDIAN NATIONAL CONGRESS**, following the **INDIAN UPRISING** of 1857–8, Khan wrote a widely read book and a pamphlet demonstrating that Muslims were neither primarily responsible nor generally involved in the rebellion. He held progressive views on the issue of the social position of women, which brought him into conflict with orthodox Islamic leaders, but his greatest legacy was his establishment of the Mo-

hammedan Anglo-Oriental College (now Aligarh Muslim University) in 1875 and the development of the Muslim Educational Conference, which eventually spread across India.

## Ahmad of Rai Bareilly, Sayyid (1786–1831)
Muslim Indian leader hostile to British rule. Sayyid Ahmad of Rai Bareilly came from the circle of Islamic thinkers whose spiritual forebears had tried to convince the Afghan Shah Ahmad to wage a **JIHAD** against all non-Muslim powers in India. Sayyid Ahmad led an Islamic revival in the early 19c, seeking to rid Indian Islam of all Hindu practices, to end popular belief in the intercessionary power of Sufi saints, and to establish an exemplary Muslim society in India. In order to wage jihad upon the Sikhs, Sayyid Ahmad and his followers eventually moved into the North-West Frontier, where he was killed in 1831.

## Ahmad Shah Durrani (1722–73)
Central Asian warlord. He was the founder of the short-lived Durrani empire in Afghanistan and northern India. A commander of the Afghan ruler **NADIR SHAH**'s bodyguard, Ahmad Shah founded his own regime in Kandahar after Nadir's death in 1747. By 1761, through decisive victory at the Battle of **PANIPAT**, he had established supremacy over the Marathas and much of north-western India. After severely weakening the Mughal power base, however, Ahmad Shah and his successors were unable to exploit fully his opportunity and it was left to European powers, most notably Britain, to fill the vacuum.

## Ahmadu ibn Hammadu (c.1775–1844)
West African Islamic leader. Influenced by the example of **USMAN DAN FODIO** in northern Nigeria, he led a **JIHAD** or holy war in the western Sudan. It started about 1818 and made Ahmadu master of a state of some 50,000 sq mi/130,000 sq km, including within its borders the important centres of Jenne and Timbuktu. In 1862 it was conquered by another leader of a jihad, al-Hajj **UMAR IBN TAL**.

## Ahmad 'Urabi ➤ 'URABI PASHA

## Ahmed I (1590–1617)
Ottoman Sultan (1603/17). He was the son of **MEHMED III**, whom he succeeded. The most notable feature of his reign was the losing war he waged against Persia (1602–12).

## Ahmed II (1642–95)
Ottoman Sultan (1691/5). He was the son of Ibrahim, whom he succeeded. The disastrous Ottoman defeat at **SLANKAMEN** (1691) at the hands of the Habsburgs lost him Hungary. ➤ **HABSBURG DYNASTY**

## Ahmed III (1673–1736)
Ottoman Sultan (1703/30). He was the son of **MEHMED IV**. He sheltered **CHARLES XII** of Sweden after the Battle of **POLTAVA** (1709), thus falling foul of **PETER I, THE GREAT**, with whom he waged a successful war which was terminated by the Peace of the Pruth (1711). He successfully fought the Venetians (1715), but soon after was defeated by the Austrians, losing territories around the Danube. He was deposed by the **JANISSARIES** (1730) and died in prison.

# *Aircraft*

*Transport & Travel*

A dream machine throughout most of history, the aircraft, in both its lighter-than-air and heavier-than-air forms, became a practical and widely useful reality only in the 20c. Like many other technological achievements, in the course of that century it rapidly attained a degree of sophistication and a prevalence that would perhaps have been surprising to the early pioneers.

### Beginnings
Early attempts at flight were thwarted by the inherent unsuitability of the human body for travel through the air. Those like the monk Eilmer of Malmesbury, who attached an apparatus of struts and cloth, or feathers, to their bodies, or wrapped themselves in voluminous cloaks, and launched themselves from high places (in Eilmer's case the tower of Malmesbury Abbey), were lucky if their 'wings' enabled them to survive the fall. Nor were machines in which the lifting power was provided by human muscular effort alone, such as the helicopter-like rotor device sketched by Leonardo da Vinci (1452–1519), a realistic way forward. However, there were devices in existence during the **Middle Ages** which did contribute to the development of the technology necessary for flight. The kite, flown in China and other parts of Asia from ancient times, was observed by Marco **Polo**, who reported that the Chinese were able to build kites of sufficient size and strength to be able to lift a man into the air. The windmill, likewise, pointed the way to the airscrew that would 'bite' the air and enable an aircraft to be propelled through it.

### Lighter-than-air craft
From the 18c onwards, attempts to get human beings off the ground and into the air were guided by modern science. The observation of the rising and lifting properties of hot air, and the isolation of a lighter-than-air gas, hydrogen, led to the first balloon ascents in 1783. The Montgolfier brothers, Joseph Michel and Jacques Étienne, who were paper manufacturers from Annonay in France, sent up an uncrewed hot air balloon in 1782 and organized the first crewed flight the next year; the balloon travelled over 7mi/11km and rose to 3,000ft/914m. In Dec 1783, Jacques Alexandre César Charles made an ascent in a hydrogen-filled balloon. Jean Pierre Blanchard, the inventor of the parachute, made the first balloon crossing of the English Channel with John Jeffries in 1785. Thereafter, balloon flights continued achieving greater heights and distances. First used for aerial reconnaissance in warfare by French revolutionary forces in 1794, they were also called into service in the **American Civil War** and the **Franco-Prussian War**. Nevertheless, the flight of a free balloon remained dependent on the wind for speed and direction. In 1852 the French inventor Henri Giffard achieved the first powered and controlled flight in a cigar-shaped semi-rigid airship fitted with a propeller and rudder, and driven by a 3-horsepower steam engine. Giffard's airship was still only operable and controllable in relatively calm weather. Larger and more powerful airships were developed in the latter part of the 19c, but it was the invention and development of the internal-combustion engine that enabled airships to develop further. Count Ferdinand von Zeppelin completed his first rigid airship powered by internal-combustion engines in 1900. In 1910 a zeppelin began the first regular passenger airship service, and zeppelins made long-range bombing attacks on Britain during **World War I**.

After World War I there was considerable interest in airship development, especially with the prospect of helium becoming available in large enough quantities to fill the gas-bags of the bigger ships. (Helium gas, first isolated in 1895, has 92 per cent of the lifting power of hydrogen and, crucially, is, unlike hydrogen, non-flammable.) A British airship completed a transatlantic crossing in 1919, the US Navy introduced the first helium-filled zeppelin-type ship, *Shenandoah*, in 1923, and for a time lighter-than-air craft appeared to offer competition to their faster and more manoeuvrable heavier-than-air counterparts in the field of commercial air transport. But the *Shenandoah* was wrecked in 1925, and other losses, especially the crash of the British *R101* in 1930 and the destruction by fire of the German *Hindenburg* in 1937, recorded on film, hastened the abandonment of commercial airship development. The US Navy used helium-filled blimps for convoy escort duties and anti-submarine patrols during **World War II**, and finally discontinued airship use in 1961.

The use of airships to replace or supplement aeroplanes in various roles has again been mooted in recent times, but the idea has not as yet been pursued on a large scale. Balloons continue to be used for sport and for scientific research into the atmosphere. The first successful round-the-world flight in a balloon was completed in Mar 1999.

### Heavier-than-air craft
The principle governing the behaviour of fluids in motion, formulated by the Swiss physicist Daniel Bernouilli in 1738 and known by his name, provided a foundation for the work of the man generally known as the father of aerodynamics and fixed-wing aviation, the British baronet and engineer Sir George Cayley (1773–1857). Cayley designed, constructed and flew model and full-size gliders, and in 1853, the year following Giffard's airship flight in France, Cayley's coachman reluctantly made what is generally reckoned to be the first glider flight in history. Various designs for powered heavier-than-air flying machines were published or patented around the middle of the 19c, such as William Samuel Henson's *aerial steam carriage* which in outline bears a striking resemblance to a modern monoplane, although it never flew. A

**Aidid, Muhammad Farrah** (1934–96)
Somali soldier and politician. Born in Italian Somaliland, he served in the colonial police force and transferred to the Somali army following the country's independence in 1960. During the war with Ethiopia over the possession of Ogaden province, he was promoted general by President Siad **BARRE**. In the early 1970s he lost that support and was imprisoned. Freed following Barre's overthrow, he was appointed ambassador to India. In 1993 he was elected leader of the Hebr Gader clan during a civil war which ruined Somalia and led to intervention by **UN** forces. He died of gunshot wounds in 1996 and his son assumed control of the country.

**Ain Jalut, Battle of** ► AYN JALUT, BATTLE OF

steam-powered machine designed and built by the US inventor Samuel Pierpont Langley successfully flew in 1896, but was never able to fly with a human being on board. The use of an internal-combustion engine as a power source, together with refinements in the design of the body of the craft and its control surfaces, enabled the brothers Wilbur and Orville Wright to make the first successful crewed, powered and controlled flight at Kitty Hawk, North Carolina, on 17 Dec 1903. The distance flown by Orville Wright in the first ever flight, 120ft/37m, was, it has been noted, less than the length or wingspan of a large modern jet. For a few years the Wright brothers remained the only men in the world building successful flying machines. From 1906 others began to catch up. The first cross-Channel flight was made in 1909 by Louis Blériot in a monoplane of his own design. Before the outbreak of World War I the first mail had been carried by air (1911) and the first commercial passenger service had been introduced in Florida.

Aircraft development was accelerated by World War I. Planes became faster, more manoeuvrable and more reliable, and were used not only for observation and bombing but engaged in combat with each other. Control of the air as a factor affecting military strategy, however, only became important in World War II, during which aircraft design and production took a further leap forward.

Commercial aviation developed fairly slowly between the wars, though aircraft flew longer and longer distances. The first transatlantic flights were made in 1919 and the first round-the-world flight in 1924. It was after World War II that commercial aviation became really big business, especially after the introduction of jet airliners during the 1950s.

### Jet propulsion
The basic principle of jet propulsion had been known since at least the 3c BC. The first potentially workable design for a jet plane was produced in France in 1865 and the first flight in a jet-propelled plane was made in 1910 by the Romanian-born engineer Henri Coanda in an aircraft of his own design. Coanda's pioneering work was initially neglected in favour of propeller-driven planes, though by the 1930s progress towards a modern jet engine was well advanced. The British engineer Sir Frank Whittle (1907–96) is credited with designing the prototype gas turbine jet engine. By the time a plane first flew with a Whittle engine in Britain in 1941, however, German and Italian jet-powered aircraft had already flown. Jet fighters were used by the **Luftwaffe** in the latter stages of World War II, but on a limited scale. The first large-scale air battles to be fought by jet aircraft took place during the **Korean War**.

The jet engine gradually began to overhaul the propeller as the main means of aircraft propulsion after World War II. A rocket-powered experimental plane, the American Bell X-1, was the first to deliberately fly above the speed of sound in 1947. The world's first commercial jet airliner, the British De Havilland Comet, entered service in 1952, but was withdrawn two years later after two disastrous crashes. The entry into regular service of the Boeing 707 in 1958 ushered in the age of the modern passenger jet. The joint development by Britain and France of the world's first supersonic jet airliner, Concorde, during the 1960s, was a technical but not a commercial success. Though jet aircraft now dominate both military and commercial aviation, and are in use all over the world, their enormously high development and production costs mean that the number of countries able to maintain a viable front-rank aviation industry has shrunk to very few.

### The helicopter
Foreshadowed in one of Leonardo da Vinci's most famous technical sketches, the helicopter was developed more or less simultaneously in Europe and the USA in the first quarter of the 20c. The first flight in a helicopter is usually credited to an American, Henry Berliner, while the first truly successful helicopter is said to be a twin-rotored machine designed by the German engineer Heinrich Focke that flew in 1936. In 1939, the Russian-born naturalized American Igor Sikorsky flew the first successful single-rotor helicopter. During and after World War II, Sikorsky machines set new distance records and were largely responsible for shaping the helicopter's present role in both civilian and military life. ▶ **Air Force**

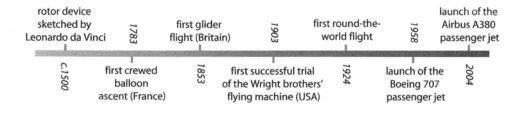

---

**Aircraft** ▶ See panel

**Air Force** ▶ See panel

### Akali Movement and Akali Dal
Primary Sikh political organization in Punjab. The original Akalis were 17c Sikh zealots who became censors for the community. During the Independence movement, the Akalis cooperated with Congress but tended to promote Sikh communal concerns. They were especially concerned with the control of Sikh shrines. Following Muslim agitation for the creation of Pakistan, the Akalis agitated for an independent Sikh state within the Punjab, but settled for a greater language-based autonomy in 1966. Still active in the Sikh independence cause, the Akali Dal split into several factions in 2003.

# *Air Force*

War & Warfare

War first took to the air in the late 19c when hot-air balloons began to be used in Europe for observing the movements of enemy forces and, later, to help direct the fire of artillery. A British Army Balloon School was set up at Woolwich in 1878 to train soldiers in this sphere. Balloons were very limited in manoeuvrability and were soon superseded by dirigible airships, with the Germans in particular making great progress with their zeppelin airships. Powered aircraft developed rapidly in the years following the first successful flight by the Wright brothers in 1903, and it was in France that the potential military value of aeroplanes was first recognized. By the time **World War I** broke out in 1914, aeroplanes were available that could fly at speeds up to 75mph/120kph and stay in the air for over two hours.

In 1914 the British established two air forces: one, the Royal Flying Corps, was to be a part of the army, and the other, the Royal Naval Air Service, was a wing of the navy. At first military aircraft fulfilled the role that balloons had performed in reconnaissance and artillery-spotting, but their potential as offensive weapons was quickly realized. They began to carry bombs, at first crude examples dropped by hand by the pilot or observer, later specially designed weapons with release mechanisms. As true anti-aircraft weapons had not yet emerged, troops on the ground were extremely vulnerable to bomb attacks or to strafing with machine guns, and it was largely to counter the bombers that the first fighter planes were brought into service.

As all major combatants in the Great War developed both bombers and fighters, the number of machines increased and aerial battle became a new sphere of warfare, particularly above the Western Front. Pilots emerged who had particular ability in this form of combat, downing several of their foes and becoming known as 'aces', such as the German Max Immelmann (1890–1916). Larger formations of fighters were built up, flying together for mutual protection, and these became known as 'circuses'. The most famous of these was Richthofen's Circus, commanded by the German ace Baron Manfred von Richthofen (1892–1918), known as the 'Red Baron' due to the distinctive colour of his Fokker triplane; he was credited with 80 victories before he himself was shot down.

The Germans used zeppelin airships as bombers and created great alarm when they carried out bombing raids on the south of England. Although this caused more terror than actual damage, it was a foreshadowing of the mass bombing to come a generation later. Between the wars the development of aeroplanes continued apace while airships became seen as dangerous, particularly after terrible accidents like the destruction of the British *R101* in 1930 and the German *Hindenburg* in 1937, and were largely sidelined into use as static anti-aircraft defences. The **Spanish Civil War** was used, especially by the fascist powers, as a proving ground for new military aircraft designs, both bombers and fighters, most strikingly in the terror bombing of the village of Guernica by the German **Luftwaffe.**

Air power was a vital component of the German **Blitzkrieg** which was demonstrated to the world in the Nazi invasion of Poland in 1939. German bombers pounded the enemy forces, disrupting communications and causing chaos, and dive-bombers were used to great effect, especially the Stuka, which was fitted with a siren to increase the terrifying noise of its dive. German fighters attacked the Polish air force and succeeded in destroying most of its aircraft on the ground. The dropping of assault troops by parachute was another new use of air power that the German military pioneered, particularly in their airborne conquest of Crete in 1941.

It was in the skies over Britain that the first major aerial battle was fought, the Battle of **Britain** (Aug–Oct 1940). As a prelude to a projected invasion, the Luftwaffe mounted a strategic bombing campaign as part of their effort to gain mastery of the air over the English Channel and the south of England. Although outnumbered, the Royal Air Force had the advantage of radar and a centralized early warning system, allowing air defences to be marshalled to meet individual

---

**Akbar I, the Great**, originally **Jalal ud-Din Muhammad Akbar** (1542–1605)
Mughal Emperor of India (1556/1605). He succeeded his father, **HUMAYUN**, in 1556, and took over the administration from his regent in 1560. Within a few years, he had gained control of the whole of India north of the Vindhya Mountains. He constructed roads, established a uniform system of weights and measures, and adjusted taxation. He was unusually tolerant towards non-Muslims, and greatly encouraged literature and the arts. ► **MUGHAL EMPIRE**

**Akhromeyev, Sergei Fedorovich** (1923–91)
Soviet commander in **WORLD WAR II**. He joined the **RED ARMY** in 1940 and was in command of a tank battalion by 1945. He then rose steadily to be First Deputy Chief of the General Staff by 1979 and Marshal by 1981. Opposed to escalating military expenditure, he was called in to replace **OGARKOV** as Chief of the General Staff in 1984 and aided Mikhail **GORBACHEV** in his post-1985 arms control talks. He tried, but failed, to accommodate fully to the Gorbachev era, and resigned in 1988 in disgust at Gorbachev's unilateral troop cuts. He committed suicide in the aftermath of the attempted coup in 1991, in apparent dismay at **PERESTROIKA**'s results. ► **AUGUST COUP**

**Akihito** (1933– )
Emperor of Japan (1989/ ). The eldest son of Emperor **HIROHITO**, he was born and educated in Tokyo, where he studied politics and economics. Invested as Crown Prince in 1952, he became the first Crown Prince to marry a commoner, Michiko Shoda, in 1959.

**Akkerman, Convention of** (1826)
The Russians imposed terms upon the Ottoman Sultan **MAHMUD II** whereby Russia was acknowledged as the protector of Serbia and the Danubian Principalities. The internal organization of the Principalities was also to be modified: new statutes were to be drawn up for the administration of each province and the *hospodars* (governors) were to be elected by the boyar divans for seven years subject to Russian and Ottoman approval. The terms of the Convention, which were met in the course of the **GREEK WAR OF INDEPENDENCE**, built upon the Treaty of **BUCHAREST** (1813) and confirmed Russian influence over the emergent Balkan nations. ► **HOSPODAR; MOLDAVIA**

raids. Using their Hurricanes and Spitfires, British and Allied airmen destroyed such large numbers of enemy bombers and their fighter escorts that the German invasion was never mounted.

The Luftwaffe switched to mass bombing of British cities, which came to be known as the **blitz**, causing great destruction and loss of life not only in London but in population centres such as Belfast, Coventry and Clydebank. The same tactics were later used against Germany by the RAF by night, and the USAAF by day, in raids deploying up to 1,000 bombers.

In the Pacific, the Japanese air force began the war with the USA by striking at the US naval base at **Pearl Harbor**. Japan had made great strides in the building of aircraft-carriers, ships especially built to act as floating airstrips, and it was able to launch over 400 bombers and fighter-bombers from six carriers in this attack. Aircraft-carriers dominated the great sea battles of the **Pacific War**, such as the Battle of the Coral Sea (May 1942) which was almost entirely fought by carrier-based fighters, bombers, and torpedo-bombers attacking enemy ships and aircraft, while the great US and Japanese fleets never so much as sighted each other.

This pattern was repeated at the Battle of **Midway** (June 1942), and US aircraft-carriers played a pivotal role in the reconquest of the Pacific Islands. It was air power that finally brought the war to a close with the dropping of atomic bombs on the Japanese cities of **Hiroshima** and **Nagasaki**.

**Nuclear weapons** were increasingly deployed by air forces after **World War II**, with both long-range strategic bombers and intercontinental ballistic missiles able to threaten the very heartland of the enemy with terrible destructive power. Air forces played vital roles in subsequent conflicts, the skies over Korea seeing the first dogfights by jet fighters. In South-East Asia the Americans carried out mass strategic bombing in Vietnam and Cambodia, and made great use of helicopters in ground attack roles as gunships and as troop carriers. The dominance of air power in modern warfare was further shown by the Allies' decisive use of bombing against Iraq in the **Gulf War** of 1991, and by **NATO**'s exclusive use of air strikes to arrest the **ethnic cleansing** of Albanians in **Kosovo** in 1999. But the experience of the **Iraq War** (2003) suggested that while precision weapons had made air power dominant on formal battlefields and an effective means of coercion against vulnerable governments, it was a blunt tool against insurgency, especially resistance in the form of urban guerrilla warfare. ► **Aircraft**; **Army**; **Navy**; **Warfare**

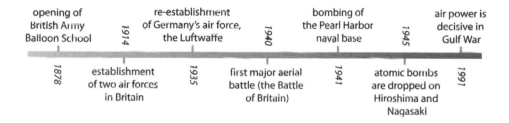

| opening of British Army Balloon School | 1914 | re-establishment of Germany's air force, the Luftwaffe | 1940 | bombing of the Pearl Harbor naval base | 1945 | air power is decisive in Gulf War |
|---|---|---|---|---|---|---|
| 1878 | establishment of two air forces in Britain | 1935 | first major aerial battle (the Battle of Britain) | 1941 | atomic bombs are dropped on Hiroshima and Nagasaki | 1991 |

**Akritas, Digenis** ► GRIVAS, GEORGEIOS

**Aksakov, Ivan Sergeevich** (1823–86)
Russian lyric poet and publicist. Born in Nadeshdino, he was the son of Sergei Aksakov. He was the founder and editor of various Slavophil and Pan-Slavic periodicals, and a supporter of the liberation of **SLAVS** in the Balkans.

**Akwamu**
A state founded c.1600 by the Abrade people, an Akan group in the Gold Coast in the immediate hinterland of Accra. It commanded trade routes and eventually built up its power along almost the entire length of the Gold Coast to Dahomey. It collapsed in 1730 when conquered by Akim, its neighbour to the west.

**Ala al-Din Khalji** (1296/1316)
Second ruler of the Khalji Dynasty in Delhi. After murdering his uncle and seizing power in 1296, Ala al-Din embarked on a programme of southward expansion made possible by the recession of the Mongol threat to the north. In a series of brutal military expeditions he subdued the Gujarat and the Rajput

princes, spreading his rule and Islam deep into south India. During his reign, Delhi enjoyed a prosperity sustained by the spoils of war, and was transformed by the Sultan's grandiose building campaign.

**Alabama Claims** (1869–72)
A diplomatic dispute in which the USA held Britain accountable for damage inflicted to the Union during the **AMERICAN CIVIL WAR** by Confederate naval vessels (the *Alabama*, *Florida* and *Shenandoah*) built in Britain. The dispute was resolved in 1872 when an international tribunal (Italy, Switzerland and Brazil), ruled that Britain should pay an indemnity to the USA of US$15.5 million. ► **WASHINGTON, TREATY OF**

**Alamán, Lucas** (1792–1853)
Mexican politician and historian. The intellectual father of Mexican conservatism, his views were shaped by the wrecking of Guanajuato (his birthplace) in **HIDALGO (Y COSTILLA)**'s revolt in 1810, and his training as a mining engineer. Repelled by the aftermath of the Riego Revolt in Spain (1820), he argued that monarchical rule would provide stability for an independent Mexico. After independence

(1821), he negotiated with the Vatican and France to set up a Mexican royal house. Minister of State under **ITURBIDE**, and Foreign Minister and Minister of State for Anastasio **BUSTAMANTE** and **SANTA ANNA**, he was a friend of the Church and writer of the monumental, and still readable, *Historia de México.*

### Alamo, The

A fortified mission in San Antonio, Texas, held in 1836 during the Texas War of Independence against Mexico. In a heroic act of resistance, some 180 Texans defended the Alamo for 12 days against several thousand Mexicans, until the last survivors were overwhelmed. ► **MEXICAN WAR**

### Alanbrooke, Alan Francis Brooke, 1st Viscount (1883–1963)

British field marshal and leading strategist of **WORLD WAR II**. He joined the Royal Field Artillery in 1902, and fought in **WORLD WAR I**. He commanded the 2nd Corps of the **BRITISH EXPEDITIONARY FORCE** in France (1940), and later was Commander-in-Chief Home Forces. Chief of the Imperial General Staff 1941–6, he was Winston **CHURCHILL**'s principal strategic adviser at the conferences with **ROOSEVELT** and **STALIN**. He was created baron (1945) and viscount (1946).

### Alaska, Sale of (1867)

Tsarist Russian interests in Alaska were sold to the USA for US$7 million, a price which seemed so high at the time that the Tsarist government had to spend a large sum of money influencing both members of **CONGRESS** and influential newspapers. Russian efforts to establish a position on both sides of the North Pacific had begun more than a century before. However, defeat in the **CRIMEAN WAR** and the acquisition of the Amur Basin from China by the Treaty of **BEIJING** (1860) made **ALEXANDER II** decide to concentrate on the north-west Pacific. Once the **AMERICAN CIVIL WAR** was over, Secretary of State William **SEWARD** was quick to realize the long-term strategic and economic value of Alaska both for the continental USA and for its expansion into the Pacific.

### Ala-ud-Din Khilji ► ALA AL-DIN KHALJI

### Alaunghpaya (1714–60)

Founder of the Konbaung Dynasty in Burma (the country's last royal line). He came to prominence during the final collapse of the restored Toungoo Dynasty at the beginning of the 1750s. A local official, he rapidly brought under his authority, by skilful organization, the great force of his personality and also by military might, the many competing elements jostling for power in the vacuum left by the disintegration of the old state. With the fall of Pegu to Alaunghpaya's forces in May 1757, internal consolidation was complete. He then turned his attention to the Tai states to the east, but in an unsuccessful attack on the Thai capital of **AYUDHYA** (May 1760), he was fatally wounded, dying on the retreat.

### Alava, Don Miguel Ricardo de (1771–1843)

Spanish soldier and politician. He served under **WELLINGTON** in the **PENINSULAR WAR** (from 1811) and was Ambassador to the Netherlands for King **FERDINAND VII**. However, as President of the **CORTES** in 1822, he aided in the deposition of the monarch. He fled when the French reinstated Ferdinand in

1823, but later served Queen **MARÍA CRISTINA** as Ambassador to London and Paris. Having refused to take the oath to the Constitution of 1837, he went into exile in France, where he died.

### Alawi

An alternative name for Nusayri **SHIITES**, who currently hold power in Syria. The Syrian leader Hafez al-**ASAD** was an Alawi (Alawite).

### Alba, Fernando Álvarez de Toledo, 3rd Duke of (1507–82)

Spanish general and political figure. He served with distinction in Germany under Emperor **CHARLES V** against the Protestant princes, notably at the siege of Metz (1552). Under **PHILIP II** of Spain his three most important commands were in the **ITALIAN WARS** against the forces of Pope **PAUL IV**, in the army of Flanders, and in the conquest of Portugal (1580). He also served in several diplomatic roles. He is primarily associated with the Flanders campaigns, when he was sent (1567) to deal with the Dutch Revolt and, as Regent, adopted a hardline policy through the Council of **BLOOD**, the body he set up to try rebels and heretics. His harsh policies, including his prosecution of ferocious military campaigns against the rebels and the introduction of new centralized taxes, aggravated rather than calmed the revolt, which he was unable to subdue militarily; his actions signalled the start of the **EIGHTY YEARS' WAR** in 1568. Recalled in 1573, he was pulled out of retirement to lead the successful occupation of Portugal in 1580.

---

**ALBANIA**   official name **Republic of Albania**

A mountainous republic in the western part of the Balkan Peninsula, bounded to the west by the Adriatic Sea; to the north by Montenegro and Serbia; to the north-east by Macedonia; and to the south-east by Greece. The history of the Albanians dates back to the 2c AD, when Ptolemy referred to a tribe, the Albanoi, in the region of modern Albania. The Albanian **GHEGS** and **TOSKS** speak two forms of an Indo-European language now considered a dialect of Illyrian, the Albanians being recognized as descendants of the ancient Illyrians but with Slav, Greek, Vlach and Turkish blood. In the **MIDDLE AGES** they were included within the empires of Byzantium, **SAMUEL** (of Macedonia) and **STEPHEN I NEMANJA** of **SERBIA**, but from the 12c an independent Albanian enclave developed around Krujë. Their decentralized tribal way of life was little changed under Ottoman rule (1503–1913) and was only destroyed with the establishment of the communist regime (1945). After local uprisings against Ottoman officials, the Albanian national movement formally began with the League of **PRIZREN** (1878–81). The first general uprising resulted in independence in 1912, and in 1913 the first independent Albanian state was established. Its boundaries excluded many Albanians, many of whom still live in the Serbian province of **KOSOVO**. Albania's independence was short-lived at first, as Italian forces occupied the country from 1914 until 1920; however, it became a republic in 1925, and a monarchy, under King **ZOG I**, in 1928. During **WORLD WAR II** Albania was occupied by Germany and Italy, and it again became a republic in 1946. After a dispute with the USSR in 1961, it withdrew from the **WARSAW PACT** in 1968 but maintained close links with communist China until 1978. The Socialist People's Republic was instituted in 1976. The country gradually began to move towards democratic reform and westernization in the late 1980s, and the first free elections were held in 1991. The communists retained power in 1991 but were defeated the following year by the Democratic Party. In the early 1990s the economy declined and severe food shortages led to violent rioting. There was further rioting in early 1997 when many Albanians lost their life savings in the collapse of investment schemes. In 2003 Albania began talks with the **EU** about membership. ► **BALLI KOMBËTAR**; **LNC**; **LONDON, TREATIES OF**

### Albanian League ► PRIZREN, LEAGUE OF

### Albany Congress (1754)
A meeting in Albany, New York, of representatives from seven British colonies in North America at which Benjamin **FRANKLIN** proposed his 'plan of union' to unite the separate American British colonies. The Albany Plan of Union was rejected by the Colonial governments and the Crown. However, the plan served as a model for the joint action of the mainland colonies in the **AMERICAN REVOLUTION**.

### Albany Regency
A group of Democrats organized (c.1817) by Martin **VAN BUREN** to run New York while he served in the US **SENATE** in Washington. Situated in Albany, New York, which he had established as his power base, the Regency was one of the first effective political machines using the **SPOILS SYSTEM** to fill public office, and influenced the future development of US political parties.

### Alberdi, Juan Bautista (1810–84)
Argentine political thinker. A **CREOLE** of Basque inheritance, he studied law in Buenos Aires. Persecuted by Juan Manuel de **ROSAS**, he was exiled to Montevideo in 1839, travelled in Europe and returned to Valparaíso in Chile for 10 years. Author of a treatise which profoundly influenced the Constituent Congress of Santa Fé, which drew up the constitution of 1853, he is regarded as its intellectual godfather. He argued that a democratic future for Argentina could only be guaranteed by the attainment of economic and educational equality. To achieve this, European immigration should be encouraged and the economy opened up to foreign investment by a strong federal government. He coined the phrase 'To govern is to populate' which had an enduring, if equivocal, impact on modern Argentina. Appointed Minister to

France and England in 1854 by General Justo José de **URQUIZA**, Alberdi spent most of the remainder of his life in Europe.

### Albero (c.1080–1152)
Archbishop of Trier. The son of a noble family, he held many high offices in the Church, culminating in his election as Archbishop of Trier in 1131. A supporter of the papacy against Emperor **HENRY V**, he was made papal legate in Germany in 1137. The following year he was instrumental in having the papal candidate, **CONRAD III**, elected to the German throne, bypassing **LOTHAIR III**'s designated successor, Henry the Proud, and strengthening his own political and territorial position. As a church reformer he had close links with Pope **EUGENIUS III** and **BERNARD OF CLAIRVAUX**.

### Alberoni, Giulio (1664–1752)
Spanish-Italian cardinal and statesman. After a diplomatic career in France and Spain, he gained the favour of **PHILIP V** of Spain, and arranged his marriage to Elizabeth Farnese (1714), daughter of the Duke of Parma. He used his influence to develop the resources of Spain, remodel the army and fleet, increase foreign trade, and extend Spanish power in Italy. His aggressive European foreign policy finally lost him Philip's support. He was banished, fled to Rome (1721), and through papal influence resumed his career in the Church. ► **FARNESE FAMILY**

### Albert (1819–61)
Prince Consort of Queen **VICTORIA** of Great Britain. The youngest son of the Duke of **SAXE-COBURG-GOTHA**, he married his cousin, an infatuated Queen Victoria, in 1840. He became her chief adviser, first as Consort (1842), then as Prince Consort (1857). Ministerial distrust and public misgivings combined to obstruct his interference in politics, but he developed a congenial sphere of self-expression by encouraging the arts and social and industrial reforms. It was largely on his initiative that the **GREAT EXHIBITION** of 1851 took place.

### Albert I (c.1255–1308)
King of Germany (1298/1308). The son of **RUDOLF I** of Habsburg, he was elected King of Germany in opposition to the deposed **ADOLF OF NASSAU**, whom he then defeated and killed in battle at **GÖLLHEIM** (1298). He proceeded energetically to restore the power of the monarchy and reduce that of the electoral princes, but was murdered while crossing the River Reuss by his disaffected nephew, John. ► **HABSBURG DYNASTY**

### Albert I (1875–1934)
King of the Belgians (1909/34). The younger son of Philip, Count of Flanders, he succeeded his uncle, **LEOPOLD II**. At the outbreak of **WORLD WAR I** he refused a German demand for the free passage of their troops, and after a heroic resistance led the Belgian army in retreat to Flanders. He commanded the Belgian and French army in the final offensive on the Belgian coast in 1918, and re-entered Brussels in triumph on 22 Nov. After the war he took an active part in the industrial reconstruction of the country; the Albert Canal, linking Liège with Antwerp, is named after him. He was killed in a climbing accident in the Ardennes, and was succeeded by his son, **LEOPOLD III**.

**Albert V** (1528–79)
Duke of Bavaria. Educated at the Jesuit College at Ingolstadt, he was a strong Roman Catholic, and established the pattern of Wittelsbach **ABSOLUTISM** in Bavaria based upon the suppression of Protestantism and the centralization of ducal authority.

**Albert of Hohenzollern** (1490–1568)
Last Grand Master of the **TEUTONIC KNIGHTS** (1510/23). The younger son of the Margrave of Ansbach, he failed to shake off Polish overlordship but, embracing the **REFORMATION**, was able to convert the Order's lands into a hereditary duchy. In 1525, he became the first secular Duke of Prussia, a title which subsequently passed to the Brandenburg line of the House of Hohenzollern. ► **HOHENZOLLERN DYNASTY**

**Albert the Bear** (1100–70)
First Count of Brandenburg. The only son of Otto of Ballenstädt, he succeeded his father in 1123. Thwarted in his ambitions to become Duke of Saxony by King **LOTHAIR III** in 1127 and then, after becoming Duke in 1138, by the **WELFS**, to whom he lost the title irrevocably in 1142, he expanded his territory instead to the east.He gained control of the North Mark, Pomerania and Brandenburg, and settled and Christianized the area with the help of settlers from the Rhineland and Saxony. He is regarded as the founder of the state of Brandenburg and the first to begin German colonization east of the River Elbe.

**Albigenses** or **Albigensians**
Followers of a form of Christianity which in the 11c and 12c especially had its main strength in the town of Albi, south-western France. It was derived from 3c followers of the Persian religious teacher Mani, whose ideas gradually spread along trade routes to Europe, especially Italy and France. Also known as Cathars or Bogomils, they believed life on earth to be a struggle between good (spirit) and evil (matter). In extreme cases, they were rigidly ascetic, with marriage, food and procreation all condemned. They believed in the transmigration of souls. Condemned by Rome and the **INQUISITION**, they were devastated in the early 13c crusade against them, which also broke down the distinctive civilization of Provence, France.

**Albright, Madeleine Korbel** (1937–)
US diplomat. Born in Czechoslovakia, she was educated at Wellesley College and Columbia University. She was a staff member of the National Security Council during the administration of President **CARTER**, and has been a senior adviser to prominent Democrats. She was the USA's permanent representative to the **UN** (1993–6), the first US ambassador to the UN to have been born outside the USA, and was Secretary of State in President **CLINTON**'s cabinet from 1997 to 2001.

**Albuquerque, Afonso de, the Great** (1453–1515)
Portuguese Viceroy of the Indies. He landed on the Malabar coast of India in 1502, and conquered Goa, Ceylon, the Sundra Islands, Malacca and (in 1515) the island of Hormuz in the Persian Gulf. He gained a reputation for wisdom and justice, but through his enemies at court he was replaced in office, and died soon afterwards at sea near Goa.

**alcabala**
A traditional Spanish sales tax, also imposed in Spanish America (in Mexico from 1575 and in Peru from 1591). Generally ten per cent in **CASTILE** and six per cent in Spanish America, its collection was often farmed out to local traders and continued to be the major source of revenue for local governments in the first decades after independence. Its abolition, in the late 19c, marked the emergence of effective national governments under rulers such as Mexico's Porfirio **DÍAZ** and the development of the railroads. Equivalent taxes (*registros*) continued to be levied in Brazil until the **VARGAS** governments of the 1930s.

**Alcalá Zamora, Niceto** (1877–1949)
Spanish politician. A lawyer and landowner from Andalusia, he was Liberal Minister of Development in 1917 and Minister of War in 1922. In opposing the dictatorship of **PRIMO DE RIVERA**, he joined the Republican cause and, with the establishment of the Republic, headed both the provisional government and the Constituent **CORTES**'s first administration. He resigned in Oct 1931 over the new constitution's anticlerical clauses, but accepted the presidency in Dec of the same year. A florid orator, he proved a highly conscientious if conservative and interventionist President, finally being removed in Apr 1936 after a decisive vote of the Cortes (238–5) against him. He died in exile in Buenos Aires.

**Alcántara, Order of**
One of the military orders founded in **CASTILE** during the **RECONQUEST** of Spain. It was founded in 1156, with a green cross as its symbol, and came to possess extensive estates (*encomiendas*), numbering 38 in 1616. Members were in theory subject to semimonastic discipline. From 1523, the crown of Spain became, with papal permission, head of the order. ► **ENCOMIENDA**

**Alcazarquivir, Battle of** (4 Aug 1578)
The battle fought by the young King **SEBASTIAN** of Portugal at the head of the flower of Portuguese nobility and troops, whom he led into a disastrous adventure in Morocco, where they were annihilated by superior Muslim forces. Some 7,000 of the Portuguese troops were killed, and 8,000 were taken prisoner. King Sebastian's body was never clearly identified, leading to later claims by impostors; the throne was left without an heir, as a consequence of which **PHILIP II** of Spain was able to claim the succession in 1580.

**Alcock Convention** (1869)
A proposed treaty agreed upon by the British ambassador to China, Sir Rutherford Alcock, and Chinese officials in Beijing. Reflecting the British government's view that undue pressure to extract greater trade concessions should not be exerted on the Chinese government, the proposed treaty allowed the Chinese government to increase import duties on opium and export duties on silk, as well as to open a consulate in the British colony of Hong Kong. However, due to protests from British merchant interests eager for a considerable expansion of commercial opportunities in China, the treaty was not ratified by the British government.

**Alessandri Palma, Arturo** (1868–1950)
Chilean politician. He became a member of the Chamber of Deputies (1897–1915), Senator (1915–18 and 1944–50) and Minister of the Interior (1918–20). Elected President on a reform platform in 1920, he was ousted, but was soon recalled by the armed forces (1924–5). In 1932–8 he served a second, more conservative, term.

**Alexander** (1893–1920)
King of Greece (1917/20). The second son of **CONSTANTINE I** and Queen Sophia, he became King in June 1917 after his father, under pressure from Eleuthérios **VENIZÉLOS** and the Allies to enter **WORLD WAR I**, was obliged to abdicate. Greece then entered the war on the side of the Allies and Venizélos returned as Prime Minister. Alexander's death in Oct 1920, after being bitten by a pet monkey, precipitated a constitutional crisis which led to the election defeat of Venizélos and the triumphant return of his father as king.

**Alexander I** (c.1077–1124)
King of Scots (1107/24). He ruled north of the Forth–Clyde line while his younger brother David (later **DAVID I**) controlled southern Scotland in his name. The second of the three sons of **MALCOLM III, CANMORE** and Queen (later St) Margaret to become king, he succeeded his brother, Edgar. He founded an Augustinian monastery at Scone, and maintained friendly relations with England by marrying Sybilla, an illegitimate daughter of **HENRY I**, and fighting alongside Henry in Wales (1114). ➤ **MARGARET, ST**

**Alexander I** (1777–1825)
Emperor of Russia (1801/25). The grandson of **CATHERINE II, THE GREAT**, the early years of his reign were marked by the promise of liberal constitutional reforms and the pursuit of a vigorous foreign policy. In 1805 Russia joined the coalition against Napoleon, but after a series of military defeats was forced to conclude the Treaty of Tilsit (1807) with France. When Napoleon broke the Treaty by invading Russia in 1812, Alexander pursued the French back to Paris. At the Congress of **VIENNA** (1814–15) he laid claim to Poland. During the last years of his reign his increased political reactionism and religious mysticism resulted in the founding of the **HOLY ALLIANCE**. His mysterious death at Taganrog caused a succession crisis which led to the attempted revolutionary coup of the **DECEMBRISTS**. ➤ **NAPOLEON I; ROMANOV DYNASTY; TILSIT, TREATIES OF**

**Alexander II** (1198–1249)
King of Scots (1214/49). The son and successor of **WILLIAM I, THE LION**, he supported the English barons against King **JOHN**, later concluding a peace treaty with **HENRY III** (1217) and marrying Henry's eldest sister, Joan (1221). In 1239 he married Marie, the daughter of Enguerrand de Coucy. His reign represents an important landmark in the making of the Scottish kingdom. He renounced his hereditary claims to Northumberland, Cumberland and Westmorland by the Treaty of York (1237), and concentrated on the vigorous assertion of royal authority in the north and west. He died of a fever on Kerrera, near Oban, while leading an expedition to wrest the Western Isles from Norwegian control. ➤ **BARONS' WARS**

**Alexander II** (1818–81)
Emperor of Russia (1855/81). The son of **NICHOLAS I**, the main achievement of his reign was the emancipation of the serfs (1861), followed by local government judicial and military reforms. During his reign, the Russian Empire was widely extended in central Asia and the Far East. He defeated Turkey in the war of 1877–8. The latter part of his reign was marked by the struggle with populist terrorists. One of their organizations, the People's Will, finally succeeded in assassinating him by bombing his coach in St Petersburg. ➤ **ROMANOV DYNASTY; RUSSIAN SERFS, EMANCIPATION OF THE**

**Alexander II**, originally **Anselm of Lucca** (d.1075)
Italian pope (1061/73). Bishop of Lucca from 1057, he undertook reforms and campaigned against immorality and corruption in the Church. He was a founder of the Patarine Party, which opposed the marriage of priests. On his election in 1061 as the choice of Hildebrand (the future Pope **GREGORY VII**), the German court elected Honorius (II) as anti-pope (1061/72).

**Alexander III** (1241–86)
King of Scots (1249/86). The son of **ALEXANDER II** of Scotland, in 1251 he married Margaret, eldest daughter of **HENRY III** of England. Soon after he had come of age, he defended the kingdom against the Norwegians, who were routed at Largs (1263). By the Treaty of Perth (1266), Scotland gained the Hebrides and the Isle of Man. In the later part of his reign, the kingdom enjoyed a period of peace and prosperity. He was killed in a riding accident.

**Alexander III** (1845–94)
Emperor of Russia (1881/94). The son of **ALEXANDER II**, his reign was marked by policies of extreme political reactionism, Great Russian chauvinism, religious bigotry and attempts to reverse some of his father's liberal reforms. On the other hand, the Russian economy made some progress and the foundations were laid for the industrial boom of the late 1890s. ➤ **ROMANOV DYNASTY**

**Alexander III**, originally **Rolando Bandinelli** (c.1105–1181)
Italian pope (1159–81). He taught law at Bologna, and became adviser to Pope **ADRIAN IV**. As pope, he was engaged in a struggle with the Emperor **FREDERICK I, BARBAROSSA** who supported anti-popes against him. The Emperor was finally defeated at the Battle of **LEGNANO** (1176) and peace was concluded by the Treaty of Venice (1177). The other notable conflict of Church and State in which he was involved was that between **HENRY II** of England and Thomas à **BECKET**. He also called the third Lateran Council (1179). ➤ **LATERAN COUNCILS**

**Alexander VI**, originally **Rodrigo Borgia** (1431–1503)
Spanish pope (1492/1503). He was made a cardinal (1455) by his uncle, Calixtus III, and became pope on the death of Innocent VIII as a result of flagrant bribery. Father to Cesare and Lucrezia **BORGIA**, and two other illegitimate children, he endeavoured to break the power of the Italian princes, and to gain their possessions for his own family. Under his pontificate, he apportioned the New World between Spain and Portugal, and despite introducing the

censorship of books, he was a generous patron of the arts. ► BORGIA

**Alexander VII**, originally **Fabio Chigi** (1599–1667) Italian pope (1655/67). As nuncio, he had protested against the Peace of WESTPHALIA (1648), which ended the THIRTY YEARS' WAR. His election was said to have been clinched by belief in his opposition to nepotism, to which he later succumbed. He supported the Jesuits against the Jansenists and forbade the translation of the Roman missal into French. He was also responsible for the construction of the colonnade in the piazza at St Peter's, Rome.

**Alexander VIII**, originally **Pietro Vito Ottoboni** (1610–91) Italian pope (1689/91). On his death-bed he issued the Bull *Inter multiplices*, based on ideas already developed by INNOCENT XI, which reaffirmed the papal condemnation of the Gallican Articles published by the French Synod summoned by LOUIS XIV in 1682. Despite this, it was during Alexander's pontificate that the bases were established for the reconciliation which took place between France and the papacy under INNOCENT XII.

**Alexander I Karageorgević** (1888–1934) King of the Kingdom of Serbs, Croats and Slovenes (1921/9) and King of Yugoslavia (1929/34). The second son of PETER I KARAGEORGEVIĆ of Serbia, he was Commander-in-Chief of the Serbian Army during WORLD WAR I while acting as Prince-Regent of Serbia (1914/21). A Serbian nationalist, he aimed to create a centralized state governed from Belgrade and roused the resistance of non-Serb national groups in the kingdom. In 1929, after the collapse of the constitutional system hastened by the murder of the Croatian leader Stjepan RADIĆ, he imposed a royal dictatorship, dissolving the assembly, abolishing the political parties and imprisoning many of their leaders. Supported by the LITTLE ENTENTE and France, in 1934 he was assassinated while on a state visit to Marseilles by a Macedonian terrorist linked to the Italian-backed Croatian USTAŠA. ► KOROŠEC, ANTON; MAČEK, VLADKO; PAVELIĆ, ANTE; PRIBIĆEVIĆ, SVETOZAR; TRUMBIĆ, ANTE; VMRO

**Alexander Karageorgević** (1806–85) Prince of Serbia (1842/58). The son of KARAGEORGE, he lived in exile until he was chosen as the new Prince of Serbia after the regency of Michael OBRENOVIĆ collapsed (1842). The Constitutionalist Party hoped to control the new prince through a constitution and to establish a civil code and a centralized, bureaucratic state system. In 1844 Ilija GARAŠANIN presented the weak and inexperienced Alexander with a programme for government, the NACERTANIJE, but relations between the prince and the Constitutionalists swiftly deteriorated. He further lost support through his conciliatory policy towards Austria which led him to remain neutral during the Serbian revolt in Hungary (1848) and during the CRIMEAN WAR (1854–6). On St Andrew's Day 1858, the assembly deposed Alexander and called for the return of the old absolutist prince Miloš OBRENOVIĆ.

**Alexander Nevsky** (c.1220–1263) Russian Grand Prince, hero and saint. He received his surname from his victory over the Swedes on the River NEVA (1240). He later defeated the TEUTONIC KNIGHTS (1242) and the Lithuanians (1245), and also helped maintain Novgorod's *de facto* independence from the Mongol Empire. He died at Gorodets, and was canonized by the Russian Church in 1547. ► GOLDEN HORDE

**Alexander of Tunis, Harold Rupert Leofric George Alexander, 1st Earl** (1891–1969) British field marshal. In WORLD WAR I he commanded a brigade on the Western Front, and in 1940 was the last officer out of Dunkirk. He served in Burma (now Myanmar), and in 1942–3 was Commander-in-Chief, Middle East, his NORTH AFRICAN CAMPAIGN being one of the most complete victories in military history. Appointed field marshal on the capture of Rome in June 1944, he became Supreme Allied Commander, Mediterranean Theatre, for the rest of the war. He later became Governor-General of Canada (1946–52) and Minister of Defence (1952–4), and was created viscount (1946) and earl (1952). ► WORLD WAR II

**Alexander, Sir William** ► STIRLING, WILLIAM ALEXANDER, 1ST EARL OF

**Alexandra Feodorovna** (1872–1918) Empress of Russia. A princess of Hesse-Darmstadt, and granddaughter of Queen VICTORIA, she became Empress upon her marriage to NICHOLAS II in 1894. Alexandra came under the influence of RASPUTIN, and meddled disastrously in politics, being eventually imprisoned and shot by Bolshevik revolutionaries, along with her husband and children, at Ekaterinburg. ► BOLSHEVIKS; FEBRUARY REVOLUTION (Russia)

**Alexandria Protocol** (1944) This agreement was the outcome of a conference of Arab states convened in Alexandria by the Egyptian Prime Minister Mustafa al-NAHHAS. His aim was to determine the form that future Arab unity should take. Al-Nahhas, backed on this issue by King FAROUK, wished to obtain agreement to the formation of a 'League of Arab States' consisting of the sovereign states in the Arab world, and this was embodied in the Alexandria Protocol. ► ARAB LEAGUE

**Alexei**, originally **Sergei Vladimirovich Simansky** (1877–1970) Russian Orthodox ecclesiastic. He accommodated to the Soviet regime to save Orthodoxy. First elected to a bishopric in 1913, he was made Metropolitan of Leningrad in 1933 and, despite one spell of exile, he was able to survive to earn a reputation for his courage during the Siege of LENINGRAD. He was then elected Patriarch of Moscow and All Russia in 1944, in succession to Patriarch SERGEI, and generally supported Soviet attitudes to the world at large in order to protect his Christian flock at home, in which he was certainly not unsuccessful.

**Alexeiev, Mikhail Vasilevich** (1857–1918) Russian soldier. He fought in the RUSSO-JAPANESE WAR (1904–5) and was promoted general. In WORLD WAR I he was appointed Chief of the Imperial General Staff in 1915, and directed the retreat from Warsaw after the crushing German victory. After the RUSSIAN

**REVOLUTION** in 1917 he organized the volunteer army against the **BOLSHEVIKS**.

**Alexei Mikhailovich** (1629–76)
Romanov Tsar of Russia (1645/76). He succeeded his father, **MICHAEL ROMANOV** and, although personally pious and abstemious, presided over a court notorious for its splendour and excess. Abroad, he waged war against Poland (1654–67), regaining Smolensk and Kiev, while at home his attempts to place the Orthodox Church under secular authority brought him into conflict with Patriarch **NIKON**. In 1670–1 he suppressed a great peasant revolt; and his new code of laws (1649) legitimized peasant serfdom in Russia. By his second wife he was the father of **PETER I, THE GREAT**. ► **ROMANOV DYNASTY**

**Alexei Petrovich** (1690–1718)
Heir to the Russian throne. Having opposed the reforms and wars of his father, **PETER I, THE GREAT**, he was excluded from the succession when Peter's second wife, Catherine, provided him with another male heir. Alexei fled to Vienna, where he was sheltered by the Holy Roman Emperor **CHARLES VI**, and Naples. Having been induced to return to Russia by Peter, who was fearful of the possibility of foreign support for his son, Alexei found himself condemned to death on a charge of treason. He was later pardoned, only to die in prison under torture a few days later. Alexei's son subsequently became Tsar as **PETER II**.
► **CATHERINE I**

**Alexius I Comnenus** (1048–1118)
Byzantine Emperor (1081/1118). The founder of the Comnenian Dynasty, he strengthened the weakened Byzantine state, and defeated the attacking Turks and Normans. He was able to use the warriors of the First **CRUSADE** to Palestine (1095–9) to recover lands in Asia Minor, but relations with them were complicated by the setting up of the Latin States in Antioch, Edessa, Jerusalem and Tripoli.

**Alfonsín (Foulkes), Raúl** (1927– )
Argentine politician. Educated at military and law schools, he joined the Radical Union Party (UCR) in 1945. He later served in local government (1951–62), but was imprisoned by the **PERÓN** government for his political activities in 1953. During two brief periods of civilian rule, between 1963 and 1976, he was a member of the Chamber of Deputies, at other times practising as a lawyer. When constitutional government returned in 1983, he was elected President. He ensured that several leading military figures were brought to trial for human rights abuses, and in 1986 was joint winner of the **COUNCIL OF EUROPE**'s human rights prize. His conduct of economic policy remained equivocal: an initial success, the *Plao Austral*, failed to dampen inflation, and he proved unable to open up the economy to international investment. The failure of economic policy under the UCR resulted in the election in 1989 of Carlos **MENEM**, of the Peronist Party, as President. Alfonsín resigned as leader of the UCR in 1995 and was elected to the Senate in 2001.

**Alfonso V, the Magnanimous** (1394–1458)
King of **ARAGON** (1416/58). He took the Catalan–Aragonese empire to its peak of expansion. After his succession, Alfonso largely neglected his peninsular dominions and devoted himself to campaigns against the Mediterranean islands of Corsica and Sardinia. He was concerned, above all, with the capture of the Kingdom of Naples, which he secured in 1442.

**Alfonso X, the Wise** or **the Astronomer** (1221–84)
King of Leon and Castile (1252/84). He succeeded his father, **FERDINAND III**, in 1252. His victories over the **MOORS** enabled him to unite Murcia with Castile, but an insurrection headed by one of his sons in 1282 seriously undermined his power. He was the founder of a Castilian national literature, and fostered work on Spanish history and the Bible, as well as compiling a code of laws and a planetary table.

**Alfonso XII** (1857–85)
King of Spain (1874/85). After a period of Republican rule following the overthrow of his mother, **ISABELLA II**, by the army in 1868, he was formally proclaimed King in 1874. In 1876 he suppressed the last opposition of the Carlists (supporters of the Spanish pretender, Don Carlos (1788–1855) and his successors). Alfonso summoned the **CORTES** to provide a new constitution and, under the influence of his Prime Minister, **CÁNOVAS DEL CASTILLO**, a parliamentary system based on rigged elections was introduced to protect the interests of the predominantly landed oligarchy. The last years of his reign were beset by difficulties, including several military revolts, a devastating cholera epidemic, and continuing unrest in Cuba. In 1879 he married María Cristina, daughter of Archduke Charles Ferdinand of Austria, and was succeeded by his posthumously born son, **ALFONSO XIII** Alfonso XII's reign was distinguished more by hope than accomplishment, its major achievement being the stabilization of the dynasty.

**Alfonso XIII** (1886–1941)
King of Spain (1886/1931). A member of the Spanish House of Bourbon, he was the posthumous son of **ALFONSO XII**. Until 1902, his mother, María Cristina of Austria, acted as regent on his behalf. At 16 he assumed his majority, thereafter frequently attempting to influence politics, and showing marked sympathy for the Spanish army. In 1923 he allowed General Miguel **PRIMO DE RIVERA** to destroy the parliamentary system and establish a dictatorship: the dictator's fall in 1930 left Alfonso discredited and, in 1931, after sweeping Republican gains in local elections, he left Spain, never to return. In 1941, shortly before his death in Rome, he 'abdicated' in favour of his third son, Don Juan.

**Algeciras, Conference of** (1906)
This conference was called to defuse the differences between France and Germany which derived from the First Moroccan Crisis. The conference resulted in the acceptance by Germany, outmanoeuvred diplomatically by the French and particularly by the British, of the Act of Algeciras. The Germans had hoped both to curb the growth of French influence in Morocco and to harm the developing cordiality in relations between France and Britain. They were, however, constrained under the Act to accept provisions whereby, with due respect to the authority of the Sultan of Morocco, France and Spain were authorized to 'police' Morocco under the supervision of a Swiss Inspector-General.

**ALGERIA** official name **Democratic and Popular Republic of Algeria**

A North African republic, bounded to the west by Morocco; to the south-west by **WESTERN SAHARA**, Mauritania and Mali; to the south-east by Niger; to the east by Libya; to the north-east by Tunisia; and to the north by the Mediterranean Sea. The indigenous peoples of Algeria (**BERBERS**) have been driven back from the coast by many invaders, including the Phoenicians, Romans (Algeria became a province of the Roman Empire), Vandals, Arabs, Turks and French. Islam and Arabic were introduced by the Arabs in the 8–11c, and Islam (Sunni Muslim) is now the chief religion. The Turks invaded in the 16c, and the 19c French colonial campaign resulted in control by 1902. The **FLN** (*Front de Libération Nationale*) engaged in guerrilla war with French forces in 1954–62, and Algeria gained independence in 1962. The first President of the republic, Ahmed **BEN BELLA**, was replaced after a coup led by Houari **BOUMÉDIENNE** in 1965, who governed by decree until 1976, when elections were held and a new constitution declared him President. He was succeeded in 1979 by **CHADLI BENJEDID**. In 1992 a state of emergency was declared as a result of clashes between government forces and the Islamic Salvation Front, and for the rest of the 1990s Algeria was wracked by a bloody civil war between its secular government and Islamic fundamentalist insurgents in which an estimated 100,000 people died. The level of violence fell after 1999, when the newly elected President Abdelaziz **BOUTEFLIKA** instituted a policy of reconciliation with the Islamists.

**Algerian War of Independence** (1954–62)
Growing resentment against French colonial rule in Algeria, fuelled by Arab nationalism (which had been gathering strength since **WORLD WAR II**) and ignited by the **FLN** (*Front de Libération Nationale*), first expressed itself on the night of 1 Nov 1954, when Algerian nationalists attacked French military and civilian targets. By 1956, guerrilla warfare was widespread in rural areas; by the late 1950s, between 60,000 and 100,000 nationalists, with Tunisian support, were actively involved in the fight for independence. The 400,000–500,000-strong French army under General Jacques Massu, responded, but its harsh methods led to widespread criticism and public opinion in France began to turn. In May 1958 there was a revolt in Algiers by French officers under Massu, who suspected that the **MENDÈS-FRANCE** government might enter negotiations with the FLN. This came close to triggering civil war in France, and brought about the fall of the government. This led to the inauguration of the Fifth Republic of General de **GAULLE** (1 June 1958) who, later that year, promised self-determination to Algeria. Despite subsequent attempts by right-wing French colonists, the army general Raoul **SALAN** and the **OAS** (*Organisation de l'Armée Secrète*) to prevent the attainment of Algerian independence, peace talks began at Evian-les-Bains in France (Mar 1962), and a ceasefire was agreed. Algeria was declared independent on 3 July 1962, with Ahmed **BEN BELLA** as Premier of the new Algerian government. ►— **EVIAN AGREEMENTS**; **REPUBLIC, FIFTH** (France)

**Algiers Agreement** (1975)
This agreement, negotiated between the government of the Shah of Iran and Saddam **HUSSEIN** of Iraq, granted a considerable area of border territory north of the **SHATT AL-ARAB** waterway to Iran, coupled with the recognition of the waterway itself as constituting the border between the two states (as opposed to the low-water mark on the Iranian side), in return for a cessation of military assistance by Iran to the **KURDS** in the north of Iraq. The abrogation of this agreement by Saddam Hussein may be regarded as effectively provoking the 1980–8 **IRAN–IRAQ WAR**.

**Algonquin**
A small group of Native North Americans speaking Algonquian languages and living along the Ottawa River in Canada. They were allied with the French during the **FRENCH AND INDIAN WAR**, and most were killed by the Iroquois. The few remaining Algonquin live near Quebec and Ontario.

**Ali, Maulana Muhammad** (1878–1931) and **Ali, Maulana Shaukat** (1873–1938)
Muslim Indian political activists and leaders of the **KHILAFAT MOVEMENT**. Muhammad Ali was closely associated with the states of Rampur and Baroda, and in the internal politics of Aligarh College prior to **WORLD WAR I**. In 1911 he founded *Comrade*, an English-language weekly paper espousing Pan-Islamic views. Shortly thereafter he moved the paper to the new seat of government, Delhi, and also bought an Urdu paper, *Hamdard*, which he used to set forth his political views. Shaukat Ali was also prominent in Aligarh College politics and in 1913 organized *Anjuman-i-Khuddam-i-Kaaba* to provide Indian support of Muslim causes in the Middle East. The continued activities of this movement after the outbreak of World War I resulted in the detention of both brothers between 1915 and 1919. On their release, they joined the Khilafat Conference, of which Muhammad soon became the leader. Because of M K **GANDHI**'s support of the Khilafat Movement, the brothers allied with the **INDIAN NATIONAL CONGRESS** and Muhammad convinced the Khilafat Conference to adopt M K Gandhi's **SATYAGRAHA** strategy. As a result of a Khilafat Conference resolution calling upon Muslims to refuse to serve in the Indian army, the brothers were again arrested in 1921. In 1923, Muhammad Ali was elected President of the Congress. Mustafa Kemal **ATATÜRK**'s 1924 abolition of the Caliphate undermined the Khilafat movement, which continued on with dwindling support and influence. During the late 1920s both brothers broke with Congress over the issue of safeguards for Muslims in an autonomous India. Following this, they concentrated on

affairs solely concerning the Muslim community, although they remained highly influential national political leaders.

**Ali, (Chaudri) Muhammad** (1905–80)
Pakistani politician. He was educated at Punjab University and, in 1947, on the partition of India, became the first Secretary-General of the Pakistani government. In 1951 he became Finance Minister, and in 1955 Prime Minister. He resigned a year later because of lack of support from members of his own party, the **MUSLIM LEAGUE**.

**Alia, Ramiz** (1925–)
Albanian communist leader. Born of poor Muslim peasants, during **WORLD WAR II** he fought in the Army of National Liberation, attaining in 1945 the rank of Lieutenant Colonel and receiving a Yugoslav military decoration. In 1949 he became a member of the Central Committee of the Albanian Workers' Party, was Minister for Education and Culture (1955–8), and member of the Agitation and Propaganda Department (1958). He was made an alternate member of the Politburo in 1966, becoming a full member and Secretary of the People's Assembly in 1982. As Chairman of the Presidium of the People's Assembly, in 1982 he became nominal head of state. On the death of Enver **HOXHA** (1985), he took over as First Secretary of the Albanian Workers Party Central Committee, thus becoming the national leader. He resigned as head of state in 1992 and shortly afterwards was placed under house arrest and later sentenced to nine years' imprisonment for abuse of power and violation of citizens' rights.

**'Ali Bey** (1728–73)
Caucasian slave. In 1763 he rose to be chief of the **MAMLUKS** in Egypt. After being proclaimed Sultan (1768), he made himself independent of Turkey, and conquered Syria and part of Arabia. He died soon after being defeated by an army raised by one of his sons-in-law.

**Alien and Sedition Acts** (1798)
Four US laws passed by a Federalist-controlled **CONGRESS** intended to restrain the political opposition at a time of crisis in US relations with the warring powers of Europe. The Alien Acts delayed citizenship and gave the President great power over foreigners, while the Sedition Act authorized fining and imprisonment for public criticism of the government. ▶ **KENTUCKY AND VIRGINIA RESOLUTIONS**

**Aliev, Geidar Alievich** (1923–2003)
Azerbaijani secret police officer and politician. He moved into politics and survived from Leonid **BREZHNEV**'s to Mikhail **GORBACHEV**'s time. His move to the Central Committee came in 1971 and to the Supreme Soviet in 1974. Yuri **ANDROPOV** made him a full member of the **POLITBURO** in 1982 as someone from a non-Russian republic, and in this respect he was useful to Gorbachev too. The latter, however, pushed him out in 1987 for his lack of enthusiasm for reform, and on account of allegations of corruption. In 1993 he returned to the political spotlight when he became President of Azerbaijan, serving until 2003, when he withdrew from the presidential race due to health problems; he endorsed the candidacy of his son, Ilham, who was elected president. ▶ **PERESTROIKA**

**Alinagar, Treaty of** (7 Feb 1757)
The treaty concluded by **CLIVE OF PLASSEY** following his recapture of Calcutta from the Nawab of Bengal, **SIRAJ UD-DAULA**. Under its terms, Calcutta was returned to the British **EAST INDIA COMPANY**, its privileges were renewed and the rights to fortify the town and mint money were secured. This absolutely secured a bridgehead from which to increase the Company's power in Bengal.

**Ali Pasha** (1744–1822)
Rumeliot notable (*ayan*). A semi-independent feudal lord in south Albania, he became Pasha of Trikala in 1787 and was known as 'the Lion of Janina' after the region of Greece which he took in 1788. In 1803 he became *beglerbeg* (governor) of **RUMELIA**. He received at his court Lord Byron and other European travellers and developed contacts with Britain and with revolutionary France and the **FILIKI ETAIRIA**, which worked for independence from the Ottoman Porte. Anticipating Russian support, in 1819 he declared his independence from the Porte but after the long siege of Janina he surrendered to the Sultan **MAHMUD II**, and was put to death in 1822. ▶ **GREEK WAR OF INDEPENDENCE**; **OTTOMAN EMPIRE**; **PORTE, THE SUBLIME**

**Ali Salim Rubay** (1934–78)
Yemeni politician. He was the President of the People's Democratic Republic of Yemen during the period of left-wing socialist rule there and was overthrown and executed in 1978.

**Alivardi Khan** (1678–1756)
Ruler of Bengal, Bihar and Orissa. He was an officer in the Mughal bureaucracy who rose steadily to become Deputy Governor of Bihar under the Nawab of Bengal, Shuja-ad-Din. Following Shuja's death, his successor was overthrown by Alivardi. His reign was largely spent suppressing rebellions and unsuccessfully defending Bengal against the Maratha invasion. A strong ruler, Alivardi was independent of Delhi, but never secure in his position due to the method of its attainment.

**Aliyah**
The name given to the Jewish migrations from Europe to Palestine, which started in 1882, and laid the foundations of the modern state of Israel. The ideals of the second Aliyah (1904–14) were redemption of the soil, and personal labour as a means of salvation. It pioneered the cooperative settlement which was to develop into the modern kibbutz. The third Aliyah was associated with a search for a National Home, while the fourth (1925) reflected Jewish persecution in Eastern Europe, mainly Poland. The fifth Aliyah (1932) represented flight from early Nazi persecution. ▶ **ZIONISM**

**Al-Kasr al-Kabir, Battle of** ▶ ALCAZARQUIVIR, BATTLE OF

**Allan, Sir Hugh** (1810–82)
Canadian entrepreneur. He emigrated to Montreal in 1826, became partner in an ocean-going shipping line and by 1859 was one of the wealthiest men in the province. His relationship with Conservative

politicians enabled him to win back the contract to deepen the St Lawrence in 1854. In 1862 the British Secretary for War accused him of charging excessive fares, and causing the death of many immigrants. He was also charged with bribery in the **PACIFIC SCANDAL** of 1872–3 which brought down the Conservative government. In return for donating campaign funds to the party, he had hoped to receive the charter for building the Canadian Pacific Railway.

### Allawi, Iyad (1945– )
Iraqi neurologist and politician. Born into a prominent Shia family, he studied medicine in Baghdad and London. By 1975 he had become disenchanted with and left the **BA'ATH PARTY**. His links to exiled or dissident security and military personnel led to the creation in 1990 of the Iraqi National Accord (INA). Despite the failure of the INA's attempted coup against President Saddam **HUSSEIN** in 1996, Allawi was able to remain in touch with government officials. He was the source, through a third party, of British intelligence claims in 2002 that Iraq could deploy weapons of mass destruction (**WMD**s) within 45 minutes, precipitating the **IRAQ WAR** (2003). He returned to Iraq after the allied occupation in 2003, and became interim Prime Minister in Jun 2004 until elections in Jan 2005.

### Allen, Ethan (1738–89)
American soldier, revolutionary leader and writer. Allen distinguished himself early in the Revolutionary War when he led Vermont's **GREEN MOUNTAIN BOYS** in the capture of **FORT TICONDEROGA** from the British (10 May 1775). He then assisted in an effort to capture Montreal, but was himself captured. He returned to Vermont and continued to campaign for its independence. ► **AMERICAN REVOLUTION**

### Allenby, Edmund Henry Hynman, 1st Viscount (1861–1936)
British field marshal. As Commander of the 3rd Army during the Battle of Arras (1917), he came close to breaching the German line. He then took command of the Egyptian Expeditionary Force, and conducted a masterly campaign against the Turks in Palestine and Syria, capturing Jerusalem (1917), Damascus and Aleppo (1918), and securing an armistice. He was made a viscount in 1919. ► **WORLD WAR I**

### Allende (Gossens), Salvador (1908–73)
Chilean politician. A medical doctor who helped found the Chilean Socialist Party (1933), he was a member of the Chamber of Deputies (1937–9), Minister of Health (1939–41) and Senator (1945–70). Unsuccessfully standing for the presidency in 1952, 1958 and 1964, he was finally elected in 1970 as leader of the left-wing **UNIDAD POPULAR** ('Popular Unity') coalition, which promised a 'transition to socialism'. Undermined by US policy under Richard **NIXON** and Henry **KISSINGER**, he was overthrown in 1973 by the army under General Augusto **PINOCHET** and gunned down in the presidential palace in Santiago.

### Alliance, Holy ► HOLY ALLIANCE

### Alliance, Triple ► TRIPLE ALLIANCE

### Alliance for Progress
A ten-year programme (1961–71) of modernization and reform for 22 countries in Latin America, sponsored by the US government in reaction to the advent of Fidel **CASTRO**'s Cuba and **KUBITSCHEK (DE OLIVEIRA)**'s abortive 'Operation Pan-American' initiative. However, it fell foul of the Kennedy administration's **COLD WAR** impulse and its partiality for orthodox economic policies, and few of its aims were achieved. ► **KENNEDY, JOHN F**

### Alliance of Free Democrats
A Hungarian political party founded in 1988; it was the most immediately successful of the new non-communist parties in Hungary after the Democratic Forum. Events in 1989 intensified public interest in reform and many new groupings emerged. The Alliance showed greater concern for marketization and, in coalition with the Democratic Forum following the 1990 elections, it moved policy in this direction. After the 1994 elections, in which the Hungarian Socialist Party (HSP) won 54 per cent of the vote and the Free Democrats 18 per cent, it joined with the HSP in a coalition government.It lost ground in the 1998 and 2002 general elections but remains in coalition with the ruling HSP.

### Allied Intervention in Russia (1918–22)
The term refers to the intervention of foreign troops in Russian affairs following the Bolshevik **OCTOBER REVOLUTION** (1917). France, Britain, Japan and the USA were initially concerned to stiffen resistance to Germany by landing contingents in the north and the south of Russia and in eastern Siberia. Before these could become effective, **LENIN** had concluded the separate Treaty of **BREST-LITOVSK** (Mar 1918), and they were drawn instead into the **RUSSIAN CIVIL WAR** on the side of his opponents. This did nothing to help defeat Germany and soured Western–Soviet relations for years to come. Most of the troops had been withdrawn by 1920, but it was Oct 1922 before the Japanese left Vladivostok. ► **BOLSHEVIKS**

### All-India Muslim League ► MUSLIM LEAGUE

### Allon, Yigal (1918–80)
Israeli military commander and politician. After Israeli independence in 1948, he attended university in Jerusalem and Oxford. Under the British Mandate, Allon was prominent in the **HAGANAH** and Palmach, involved both in the allied occupation of Syria and Lebanon and in military activities against the British administration in **PALESTINE**. Having played a vital role in the War of Independence, Allon turned to academia and politics during the 1950s and 1960s. He became Deputy Prime Minister in 1968, having helped to shape Israeli strategy in the **SIX-DAY WAR**, and became Foreign Minister in 1974.

### Almagro, Diego de (c.1475–1538)
Spanish conquistador and collaborator of Francisco **PIZARRO**. He briefly invaded Chile in 1536. Bitter rivalry then developed between Almagro and Pizarro, who defeated him in a desperate engagement near Cuzco. Shortly thereafter, Almagro was executed.

### Almansa, Battle of (25 Apr 1707)
A crucial episode in the War of the **SPANISH SUCCESSION** in the Iberian Peninsula. The Franco-Spanish army of some 25,000 men under the Duke of **BERWICK** was faced by the Allied forces, mainly Portuguese and English, numbering some 15,000 and

commanded by the Earl of Galway and the Portuguese general Das Minas, near the town of Almansa (Valencia). Berwick won a decisive victory which, despite subsequent minor reverses, permanently assured the Bourbon cause in Spain.

**Almanzor** ► MANSUR, AL-

**Almeida-Garrett, João Baptista da Silva Leitão** (1799–1854)
Portuguese writer and politician. Brought up in the Azores, he graduated in law from the University of Coimbra in 1820. He was exiled after the 1820 revolt because of his liberalism, but returned to support PEDRO I, becoming Minister of the Interior. He was also a pioneer of the romantic movement and of modern Portuguese drama.

**Almohads**
The Muslim dynasty which began to displace the Almoravid rulers of North Africa from c.1100. They invaded the Iberian Peninsula in 1160, establishing their control over the Muslim kingdoms there. In Andalusia and North Africa, their rule lasted until c.1200. ► ALMORAVIDS

**Almoravids**
The Muslim dynasty which dominated North Africa from c.1055 to c.1147. They invaded Spain during the same period and controlled the Muslim kingdoms there from 1091 to 1146. They were noted for their severe religious principles. ► ALMOHADS

**Alp Arslan** (1029–72)
Seljuk Sultan (1063/72). He succeeded his uncle, TUGHRUL BEG. A skilful and courageous commander, he devoted his energies to extending the frontiers of the Seljuk Empire, entrusting the central administration to his capable vizier, Nizam al-Mulk. He restored good relations with the 'Abbasid Caliph and, in his role as protector of the caliphate, was about to launch a major offensive against its rivals, the Fatimids, when he was recalled to meet a Byzantine offensive in Armenia. At Manzikert (1071) he defeated a numerically superior army and captured the Emperor Romanus IV, opening up the interior of Anatolia to penetration by the nomadic Turkmen tribes. Killed in a struggle with a prisoner while on campaign in Persia, he was succeeded by his son, Malik Shah. ► 'ABBASID DYNASTY; FATIMID DYNASTY

**Alpujarras, Revolts of** (1499–1501 and 1568–70)
The Alpujarra Mountains in the formerly Muslim kingdom of Granada were the setting for several revolts after the kingdom was captured by Christian Spain in 1492. The Islamic faith had been guaranteed in the terms of surrender, but social exploitation and religious persecution fuelled rebellions in 1499 and 1500. These led to the government of Queen ISABELLA I, THE CATHOLIC decreeing (12 Feb 1502) that all MUDEJARS of CASTILE must choose either conversion or exile. Continued pressures provoked another great revolt in 1568–70, which was put down in 1570 by Don JOHN OF AUSTRIA. Thousands of MORISCOS were slaughtered, and some 80,000 were forcibly expelled to other parts of Spain; the population of Granada was reduced by a third.

**al-Qaeda**
The term describes a loose collection of groups and individuals associated by sympathetic goals, which range from the expulsion of non-Muslims from Islamic countries to the overthrow of non-Islamic regimes in order to establish a pan-Islamic caliphate, and was coined by Western intelligence agencies after the 1998 bombings of the US embassies in Africa. Most closely associated with the grouping are Osama bin Laden, Ayaman al-Zawahiri, founder of Islamic Jihad, and Khalid Sheikh Mohammed, believed to have masterminded the SEPTEMBER 11 ATTACKS in 2001. The attack on the USS *Cole* in Yemen (2000), the Bali bombing (2002) and the Madrid train bombings (2004) were claimed by al-Qaeda, but it is unclear how solid the organization actually is, and some analysts argue for a more realistic assessment of its capabilities, spread, and influence. ► AFGHAN WAR; TALIBAN; TERROR, WAR ON

**Alsace**
The region of north-east France, comprising the departments of Bas-Rhin and Haut-Rhin, occupying part of the Upper Rhine Plain on the frontier with Germany. A traditional scene of Franco-German conflict, it was historically part of Lorraine before becoming part of the German Empire. The Peace of WESTPHALIA (1648) and Treaty of RIJSWIJK (1697) ceded most of Alsace to France, but it was reannexed by Germany in 1871. Alsace was subsequently returned to France in 1919 and temporarily regained by Germany in WORLD WAR II. Predominantly Germanic in language and culture, various autonomist movements have, since 1871, sought a special cultural or political status in Germany/France respectively.

**Altan Khan** (1507–82)
Leader of the Tumet MONGOLS (a branch of the KHALKAS who inhabited eastern Mongolia). He asserted control over the Western Mongols, or Oirat, and captured the former imperial Mongol capital at Karakorum. Altan Khan was responsible for the revival of Tibetan Buddhism (or Lamaism), whose influence in Mongolia had waned from the 14c onwards. In particular he patronized the Yellow Sect of Lamaism, personally conferring on the sect's leader, Sonam Gyatso, the title of DALAI LAMA. Altan Khan's settlement at Köke Qota became the first permanent Mongol city of modern times. After his death, the influence of the Tumet Mongols waned and all the Khalka Mongols came under the sway of the QING DYNASTY in the 17c.

**Alternate Attendance System** (*Sankin-kotai*)
An arrangement in 17–19c Japan whereby the TOKUGAWA SHOGUNATE was able to ensure its control over the feudal lords, or DAIMYO. Each *daimyo* was required to spend six months of the year in the Tokugawa capital of EDO (present-day Tokyo). Such a prolonged stay, along with the need to maintain a large household, was a continual drain on the daimyo's financial resources. When the daimyo returned to his own domain, his family had to remain in Edo as virtual hostages. With the weakening of the shogunate from the 1850s, such controls lapsed in 1862.

**Althing**
The Icelandic parliament. The original *Althing* was established in 930 at Thingvellir, near the modern capital of Reykjavik. It met for two weeks in the summer of

each year and was attended by the leaders of Icelandic society and their followers. Its legislative assembly of 48 chieftains, presided over by a 'lawspeaker' elected every three years, considered changes in the law code. It survived the loss of Iceland's independence in 1262/4, but by the end of the 18c had become purely a court of law, and in 1800 was abolished. It was, however, revived as a consultative body by the Danish crown in 1843, and in 1874 was granted legislative powers. From 1983 it has had 63 members, divided after election into an upper and (smaller) lower chamber.

## Alumbrados (Illuminists)

The name applied to groups of religious mystics active in **CASTILE** in the 16c. The first groups appeared between 1510 and 1520 in the area between Toledo and Valladolid and were patronized by elements of the higher aristocracy. Their members were mostly of Jewish descent (**CONVERSOS**), with women (*beatas*) playing a prominent role. From 1525 they were persecuted by the **INQUISITION**, but without any of them suffering grave penalties. A later group, also subsequently persecuted by the Inquisition, appeared in Llerena in 1570. Illuminism was regarded with suspicion largely because it appeared at a period when Protestant heresy was spreading outside Spain.

## Alva, Fernando Álvarez de Toledo, 3rd Duke of ►

ALBA, FERNANDO ÁLVAREZ DE TOLEDO, 3RD DUKE OF

## Alvarado, Pedro de (c.1485–1541)

Spanish conquistador. The companion of Hernán **CORTÉS** during the conquest of Mexico (1519–21), he became Governor of **TENOCHTITLÁN**, where the harshness of his rule incited an Aztec revolt which drove the Spaniards out. In the following year Tenochtitlán was recaptured and razed, and Mexico City built in its place. From 1523 to 1527 he was sent by Cortés on an expedition to Guatemala, which also conquered parts of El Salvador. He returned to Spain, and in 1529 was appointed Governor of Guatemala. He embarked on an expedition to conquer Quito (Ecuador) in 1534, but was bought off by Francisco **PIZARRO**.

## Álvarez (Mendizábal), Juan (1790–1853)

Spanish politician. He was Liberal Minister of Finance in 1835 and Prime Minister in 1835–6. Álvarez initiated one of the most important programmes of **DISENTAILMENT** in Spanish history in an endeavour to reduce the government's debts and create an independent peasantry.

## Amadeus VIII, the Peaceful (1383–1451)

Anti-pope, as Felix V (1439/49). Count and Duke (from 1416) of Savoy, he became ruler of Piedmont in 1419. In 1434 he retired to the monastery of Ripaille beside Lake Geneva, but in 1439 was elected pope as Felix V (an anti-pope, in opposition to **EUGENIUS IV**). He resigned in 1449.

## Amal

A Lebanese Shiite movement established by the Imam Musa Sadr in the early 1970s. After Sadr's disappearance in 1978 during a trip to Libya, Nabih **BERRI** assumed the leadership of the organization. With the end of the civil war, Amal transformed itself from a military force into a political party and holds

several parliamentary seats. ► **SHIITES**

## Amanullah Khan (1892–1960)

Amir and King of Afghanistan (1919/29). He established Afghan independence (1922) after a war with Britain. His push for internal reforms provoked opposition, and led to his abdication. He spent the rest of his life in exile, and died in Zurich, Switzerland.

## amban

Civil officials (usually Manchu or Chinese) appointed by the authorities of the **QING DYNASTY** from the 18c onwards to supervise administration in Tibet and Mongolia, with the support of armed garrisons. With the abolition of the Tibetan monarchy in 1750, the *amban* ('imperial resident') assumed a more extensive supervision of the Tibetan government, while in Mongolia the amban was also responsible for regulating the increasing numbers of Chinese traders and merchants entering the region.

## Ambedkar, Bhimrao Ranji (1893–1956)

Indian politician. A champion of the depressed castes, he was born in a Ratnagiri village, Bombay. Educated in Bombay, New York and London, he became a London barrister, later a member of the Bombay Legislative Assembly and leader of 60 million untouchables. Appointed Minister of Law in 1947, he took a leading part in framing the Indian Constitution. With thousands of his followers, he publicly embraced the Buddhist faith not long before his death, in New Delhi. ► **INDIA, PARTITION OF**

## Amboise, Georges d' (1460–1510)

French prelate and statesman. A cardinal, he became Prime Minister under **LOUIS XII** in 1498. In an attempt to secure his election as pope, he encouraged a schism between the French Church and Rome. An able minister, in 1505 he effected the Treaty of Blois which brought about an alliance between France and Spain.

## Amboyna or Ambon, Massacre of (1623)

The execution by the Dutch authorities of 10 Englishmen, 10 Japanese and a Portuguese on the island of Ambon in the Dutch East Indies. The Governor of Ambon, Herman van Speult, ordered the arrests after learning of an alleged plot by the English (who were permitted to reside in the Dutch fort at Victoria on Ambon) to overthrow the Dutch authorities with the help of some Japanese soldiers in Dutch service. The prisoners were tortured, confessed, and were executed; this was subsequently used as a symbol for Dutch brutality and barbarism, especially during the **ANGLO-DUTCH WARS** of the 17c.

## Amelioration

The term used to denote the various improvements in slave conditions urged on the British West Indies between 1807 and 1831. The abolition of the slave trade led to the abolitionists seeking to attack **SLAVERY** itself, and in 1815 parliament secured the compulsory registration of slaves in Crown Colonies. Pressure from the abolitionists and the self-interest of some sections of the West India lobby produced the Amelioration Proposals of Lord Bathurst (1823). The instructions of the Colonial Secretary included the abolition of the flogging of women, punishment record books, religious instruction for slaves and the acceptance of slave testimony in law. They were widely resisted by the plantocracy and only produced unfulfilled slave expectations which led to revolts in Demerara (1823) and Jamaica (1831–2).

### Amendola, Giovanni (1882–1926)

Italian journalist, politician and philosopher. He was elected to parliament in 1919 and was made Under-Secretary for Finances in the **NITTI** government (1920) and Minister for Colonies under **FACTA** (1922). He vehemently opposed the fascist seizure of power and led the **AVENTINE SECESSION**. Attacked several times by fascist thugs, he fled to France after a particularly savage beating, dying shortly afterwards of his injuries. ► **FASCISM**

### Amer, Abd al-Hakim (d.1967)

Egyptian politician. He was one of the nine officers who, meeting in the aftermath of the disastrous 1948 war, formed the original constituent committee of the **FREE OFFICERS** Movement in 1949. In 1950 Gamal Abd al-**NASSER** was elected chairman of this committee and, when he became Prime Minister in 1954, it was Amer (by this time a general) who took over the War Ministry. In 1967, following the **SIX-DAY WAR**, Amer (now a field marshal), disillusioned by what he saw as Nasser's betrayal of the army, allegedly took part in a conspiracy against him. Arrested for his supposed part in this plot, Amer was arrested and subjected to a campaign of vilification by the press. He committed suicide while in custody.

### America, Hispanic

This term, used to define the region of the Western hemisphere from the Rio Grande 7,000mi/11,300km to Cape Horn, emerged as late 19c scholars attempted to coin a word which would encapsulate the Iberian heritage of the region. It was convenient in that it emphasized European and non-Anglo-Saxon roots, in contrast to those of the rapidly emerging 'Colossus of the North', the USA. It reiterated the importance of Roman law and Catholicism, tracing its roots back to the Roman Empire. Inherently élitist, the term implicitly excludes those many and varied peoples of the region whose heritage is either Indian or African. Nevertheless, its prevalence indicates the extent of the difficulties embraced when the history of this vast region is summarized.

### America First Committee

Political organization (1940–1) opposing US involvement on behalf of the Allies in **WORLD WAR II**. The committee attracted support from many conservatives fearing costly military commitment as well as from pro-Nazi sympathizers, and the renowned aviator Charles **LINDBERGH** was a chief spokesman. It campaigned unsuccessfully against the **LEND–LEASE AGREEMENT** and the repeal of the **NEUTRALITY ACTS**, but its propaganda was undoubtedly effective in the early years of the war. After the Japanese attack on **PEARL HARBOR** (7 Dec 1941), however, the committee ended its activities, urging its members to support the war effort.

### American Civil Liberties Union (ACLU)

US legal defence association founded to protect the constitutional rights of free speech, privacy and equal protection under the law. The ACLU board selects areas where **CIVIL RIGHTS** and liberties are under threat and provides legal assistance and expenses for litigants in its test cases. In its early days the ACLU provided the defence counsel in the **SACCO AND VANZETTI AFFAIR** and the Scopes Monkey Trial. During **WORLD WAR II** it protested against the internment of the Nisei and in the post-war years acted on behalf of many harassed by McCarthyism and subjected to blacklisting. Throughout its existence it has been associated with unpopular political causes and has won cases concerning academic freedom, labour/business relations and civil rights. ► **DARROW, CLARENCE; MCCARTHY, JOSEPH**

### American Civil War (1861–5)

A conflict between Northern states (the Union) and Southern states that had seceded (the Confederacy). The causes of the war included disagreement over **SLAVERY** (which by then existed only in the South) and conflict over how much control the federal government should exert over the states (**STATES' RIGHTS**). The election in 1860 of Abraham **LINCOLN**, who was hostile to slavery and opposed its extension to new territories (although he did not believe at first that he could interfere with it where it already existed) precipitated the conflict. South Carolina seceded almost at once from the Union, followed within a short time by 10 other states. These 11 states formed the **CONFEDERATE STATES OF AMERICA** early in 1861. War broke out on 12 Apr 1861, when Southern forces opened fire on **FORT SUMTER**, South Carolina, and took possession of the fort. Most of the Civil War battles were fought in the South, and the Confederacy won some early victories, particularly at **BULL RUN** and **FREDERICKSBURG** and in the **PENINSULAR CAMPAIGN**. But **ANTIETAM** (1862) was a victory for the North. Shortly after Antietam, President Lincoln signed the **EMANCIPATION PROCLAMATION** freeing all slaves in the Confederacy. This further reduced the available manpower in the South and as the war continued, the Union, with its far greater manpower and industrial resources, gradually began to prevail. The Battle of **VICKSBURG** in 1863 was a major victory, and the Battle of **GETTYSBURG**, followed by Lincoln's **GETTYSBURG ADDRESS**, marked a turning point in the war. By 1864, Union forces captured Atlanta and completed a march of destruction through Georgia to the sea. The war ended on 9 Apr 1865, when Confederate General Robert E **LEE** surrendered to Ulysses S **GRANT** at **APPOMATTOX COURT HOUSE**. At enormous cost of life, the war had succeeded in keeping the Union together and in bringing an end to slavery in the USA. ► *See map*

### American Colonization Society

A US group founded in 1816 whose goal was to resettle freed slaves in Africa. By 1860, 11,000 former slaves had been transported to Liberia. The society was attacked by abolitionists but supported by some slaveholders anxious to keep freed blacks separate from slaves. It was dissolved in 1912. ► **ABOLITIONISM**

### American Federation of Labor ► AFL–CIO

### American Indians ► NATIVE AMERICANS

### American Legion

In the USA, an association for former members of the armed forces (veterans) of **WORLD WAR I** and **WORLD**

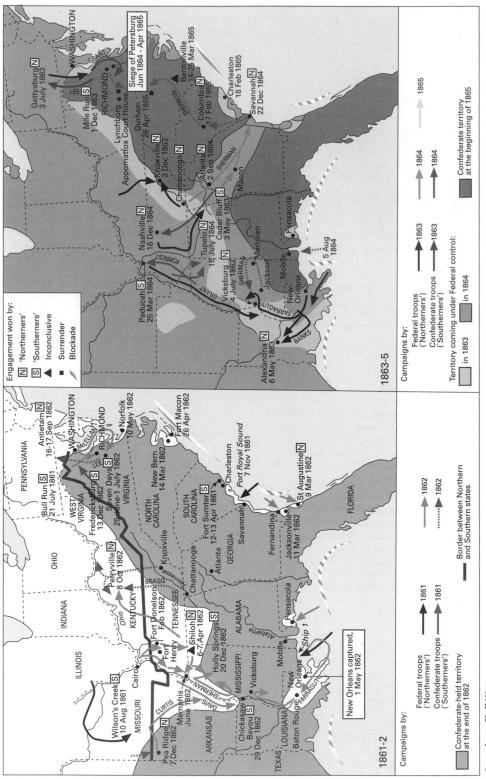

**American Civil War**

**1863-5**

Engagement won by:
- N 'Northerners'
- S 'Southerners'
- ▲ Inconclusive
- ■ Surrender
- Blockade

Campaigns by:

Federal troops ('Northerners')
- → 1863
- → 1864
- → 1865

Confederate troops ('Southerners')
- → 1863
- → 1864

Territory coming under Federal control:
- in 1863
- in 1864

Confederate territory at the beginning of 1865

**1861-2**

Campaigns by:

Federal troops ('Northerners')
- → 1861
- → 1862

Confederate troops ('Southerners')
- → 1861
- → 1862

Border between Northern and Southern states

Confederate-held territory at the end of 1862

American victory
at Saratoga
17 Oct 1777

Rochambeau
1781

Washington
1776

Valley Forge

Washington and the French
1781

Lafayette
1781

Cornwallis
1781

Cornwallis
1780

Charleston

Savannah

Montreal

Burgoyne
1777

Lexington  Boston

Newport

New York

Philadelphia      Howe
1776

Rochambeau
1781

de Grasse
1781

Franco-American
victory at Yorktown
19 Oct 1781

Cornwallis
1779

L. Huron

L. Erie

→ Americans

-▶ British

▪▪▪▪▶ French

The 13 rebel colonies
(1776)

✕ Battle

**American Revolution**

WAR II, the KOREAN WAR and the VIETNAM WAR. It is
the largest such organization in the world. Incorporated in 1919, its aims are to rehabilitate veterans, promote child welfare, ensure a strong national defence,
and encourage patriotism.

### American Revolution (1775–83)

The war that established the 13 American colonies as
independent from Britain, often called the American
War of Independence. In the years 1763 to 1775
relations between the North American colonies and
Britain became increasingly strained as Britain began
taking measures to tighten control over the colonies.
Colonial resistance was especially high over the issue
of whether the British parliament had the right to tax
the colonies without their representation. Anti-
British sentiment was more organized in the major
port towns, with considerable support coming from
the elected assemblies. The tension during this period
was reflected in the STAMP ACT crisis (1765–6), resistance to the TOWNSHEND ACTS (1767–70), the BOS-
TON MASSACRE (1770), the burning of the customs
cruiser *Gaspée* (1772) and the BOSTON TEA PARTY
(1773). The British parliament's passage of the INTOL-
ERABLE ACTS (1774) to punish Massachusetts for the
Tea Party led to the calling of the First CONTINENTAL
CONGRESS (1774). In Apr 1775 fighting broke out be-
tween British troops and the colonial militia known
as the MINUTEMEN at the Battles of LEXINGTON AND
CONCORD in Massachusetts. Other military engage-
ments followed, including the colonial capture of
FORT TICONDEROGA (May 1775), the Battle of BUN-
KER HILL and the unsuccessful colonial expedition in
Quebec, Canada. In June 1775 the Second Continental
Congress elected George WASHINGTON to command

the Continental Army and in July adopted the DEC-
LARATION OF INDEPENDENCE. Following the British
evacuation of Boston in May 1776, the main theatre
shifted to New York, New Jersey and Pennsylvania.
Washington's troops suffered a number of defeats in
the New York area, including the Battle of Long Island
(Aug 1776), but his surprise attacks at Trenton (25
Dec 1776) and Princeton (Jan 1777), New Jersey,
though small victories, did much to reinvigorate the
colonial cause. In the Battle of BRANDYWINE (Sep
1777) in Pennsylvania, however, Washington's troops
were once again defeated. In June 1777 British troops
had begun to move down from Canada and at
first seemed assured of victory, but shrewd
American manoeuvring resulted in defeat of the
British and the surrender of Burgoyne following the
Battle of Saratoga in upstate New York. This American
triumph convinced the French to enter the war
officially, bringing to the colonists badly needed
material support, troops, monetary credit and a
fleet. During the winter of 1778 Washington's troops
suffered great hardship while wintering in VALLEY
FORGE. By the spring the colonial forces had
regathered their strength and Washington's men
made a good showing at the Battle of Monmouth
(June). Later that year fighting shifted southward,
when Sir Henry Clinton commanded an invasion of
South Carolina. Clinton's successor, Lord CORNWAL-
LIS, led the army gradually north until Washington
and the French Admiral de Grasse trapped him on
the Yorktown Peninsula in Virginia, where he surrendered in 1781. The defeat resulted in the fall of the
British Prime Minister, Lord North, who had prosecuted the war, and ended British will for further fighting. After almost two years of negotiating, the Treaty
of Paris was signed in Sep 1783, recognizing the independence of the USA. The revolution had an impact
felt far beyond the battlefield. Although support had
not been universal – many loyalists fled at the war's
end and became the core of English-speaking Canada – the various coalitions uniting entrepreneurs,
professionals, planters, farmers and urban working
people had given form to the most advanced political
hopes of their time. The newly created republic was
an institution that political thinkers of the day had
doubted was capable of governing a large area or of
even surviving at all. The new country, founded by a
democratic movement and based on an ideology of
'equal rights' opened the way for the long-term decline of monarchy in the rest of the world. ➤ CAM-
DEN, BATTLE OF; CHARLESTON, BATTLES OF;
COMMITTEES OF CORRESPONDENCE; CONSTITU-
TIONAL CONVENTION; COWPENS, BATTLE OF; GAS-
PÉE; GREEN MOUNTAIN BOYS; SONS OF LIBERTY;
SUGAR ACT; THIRTEEN COLONIES; YORKTOWN CAM-
PAIGN

### American System

An economic programme designed by US politician
Henry CLAY in the 1820s which developed into the
backbone of Whig economic policy. It aimed to stimulate national economic development by imposing
protective tariffs, by creating a national bank which
would stabilize currency and regulate business
conducted between states (which in turn would
lessen the dependence on other countries), and by
giving federal subsidies for internal improvements,

particularly transportation projects.

**American War of Independence** ► AMERICAN RE-
VOLUTION

**Amhara**
A Semitic-speaking people of the Ethiopian central
highlands who, with the Tigray, dominate the country.
They are descended from the original Semitic conquerors from southern Arabia. The Christian empire
of Ethiopia was ruled by Amhara dynasties
(1260–1974) which, by intermarriage and cultural
assimilation, incorporated people from almost every
ethnic group of the empire. Amharic is the official
language of Ethiopia.

**Amherst, Jeffrey Amherst, 1st Baron** (1717–97)
British general. He successfully commanded an expedition against the French fortress at LOUISBOURG
(Nova Scotia) in 1758. After the fall of QUEBEC the
following year, he completed the conquest of Canada
by taking Montreal in 1760. He became a peer in 1776,
and served as Commander-in-Chief of the British
Army.

**Amiens, Treaty of** (1802)
A treaty between Britain and France, marking the end
of the first stage of the wars with revolutionary
France. Most of the conquests made by either power
since 1793 were agreed to be returned. The peace held
for only a brief period; war broke out afresh in 1803
and continued until 1815. ► NAPOLEONIC WARS

**Amin (Dada), Idi** (c.1925–2003)
Ugandan soldier and President. He joined the King's
African Rifles in 1946, fought with the British Army in
the Kenyan MAU MAU uprising and was heavyweight
boxing champion of Uganda. He benefited from the
rapid Africanization of the army after Uganda's independence in 1961 and became major-general in
1968. He seized power from President OBOTE in
Jan 1971, dissolved parliament and was proclaimed
President. During his presidency, there was widespread violence in Uganda, a mass expulsion of British Asians and the massacre of opponents, especially
from the Langi and Acholi peoples. Deposed by exiled Ugandans with the help of the Tanzanian army
in 1979, he fled to Libya and thence to Saudi Arabia
(1980–8). After a brief sojourn in Zaire (now Democratic Republic of Congo), he returned to Saudi Arabia, where he remained until his death.

**Amitabha**
A Buddhist deity, or bodhisattva, worshipped by the
Pure Land Sect, a branch of Mahayana Buddhism that
teaches salvation through faith rather than good
deeds. The worship of Amitabha originated in India
during the 2c and was introduced to China from the
5c and to Japan from the 7c, where he was known as
Amida. The worship of Amitabha became a feature of
popular Buddhist sects in imperial China, which at
times of economic crisis and government suppression often resorted to open rebellion against the state.

**Amnesty International**
A British-based pressure group, founded in London
in 1961, that campaigns for the release of any person
detained for their political or religious beliefs or who
has been unjustly imprisoned for any other reason.

**Amritsar Massacre** (13 Apr 1919)
On 10 Apr 1919 riots broke out in Amritsar in the
Punjab in the course of an agitation for Indian self-
rule. A gathering assembled three days later at Jallianwalla Bagh, a public park, on the festive occasion of
Baisakhi. While they were being addressed, General
Dyer, the local British commander, marched in. With
barely a warning to the assembly and leaving no adequate means for the crowd to disperse, he ordered his
troops to fire on the unarmed crowd, which included
women and children, killing 379 Indians and wounding nearly 1,200. A government commission of inquiry severely censured Dyer and he had to resign
his commission. Back in England, however, the
House of LORDS passed a motion approving of his actions and Dyer was widely acclaimed as 'the man who
saved India' (the *Morning Post* launched a fund for
him, raising £26,000 towards his retirement). The
long-term effect of the massacre was the reverse of
what Dyer had intended: many Indians were driven
into supporting the INDIAN NATIONAL CONGRESS,
and M K GANDHI himself became convinced of the
impossibility of just rule under the British and the necessity for Indian independence.

**Amselfeld, Battle of** ► KOSOVO, BATTLE OF

**Anabaptists (Rebaptizers)**
The collective name given to various groups of believers on the radical wing of the 16c Reformation
committed to the baptism of believing adults only.
They emphasized adherence to the word of scripture
and strict Church discipline as ranking higher than
the law of the state, which made them liable to much
harassment and persecution. Infant baptism was first
challenged by the 'Zwickau Prophets' who visited
Wittenberg in 1521, and their protests were carried
further by Thomas MÜNTZER, whose religious reforming zeal soon escalated into advocacy of social
revolution. After his execution in 1525 Switzerland,
Moravia and Holland emerged as the main centres of
Anabaptist activity and, most spectacularly, Münster,
where a short-lived 'Kingdom of the Saints' was established (1533–5), the antics of which did much to
discredit the movement. Redoubled persecution by
both Roman Catholics and Protestants followed, and
Anabaptism was all but stamped out. Some of its
more pacifically minded followers were able to re-
group under the name of Mennonites, while modern-
day Baptists can be considered a more distant
offshoot.

**anarchism**
A generic term for political ideas and movements that
reject the state and other forms of authority and coercion, in favour of a society based exclusively upon
voluntary cooperation between individuals. To anarchists the state, whether democratic or not, is always
seen as a means of supporting a ruling class or élite,
and as an encumbrance to social relations. However,
they differ in their view of the nature of their future
society, their proposals ranging from a communist
society based on mutual aid to one based on essentially self-interested voluntary exchange. They reject
involvement in political institutions, and support
civil disobedience action against the state, and on occasions political violence. Anarchist movements
were most prevalent in Europe in the second half of

the 19c and early 20c, but virtually died out apart from fringe groups after the SPANISH CIVIL WAR.

**Anastasia**, in full **Grand Duchess Anastasia Nikolaievna Romanova** (1901–19)
Daughter of Tsar NICHOLAS II. She is thought to have died when the royal family was executed by the BOLSHEVIKS in Ekaterinburg (19 July 1918). Several women claimed to be Anastasia, notably Anna Anderson, from the Black Forest (d.1984). Conflicting opinions by members of the Romanov family and others failed to establish the truth, and her claim was finally rejected by a Hamburg court in May 1961. The mystery has been the theme of books, plays and films, and has not been resolved by further evidence produced following the collapse of the USSR. ► ROMANOV DYNASTY; RUSSIAN REVOLUTION

**ANC (African National Congress)**
The most important of the South African nationalist organizations opposed to white minority rule. It began in 1912 as the South African Native National Congress and, under the influence of M K GANDHI, organized passive resistance to white power. Led by members of a growing black middle class, it steadily extended its support both into the urban black community and also into some liberal white quarters. Its central policy document, the FREEDOM CHARTER, was issued in 1956 and is social democratic, believing in non-racialism rather than the racial exclusivity of its rival PAN-AFRICANIST CONGRESS. When the party was declared an unlawful organization (Apr 1960), it began a campaign of industrial and economic sabotage through its military wing (UMKHONTO WE SIZWE), but essentially followed a two-track policy of direct action within South Africa and diplomacy abroad. It was generally recognized as the dominant voice of black protest, by the NATIONAL PARTY inside South Africa as well as the international community, and was unbanned in Feb 1990. It suspended its armed struggle in Aug 1990 and its leaders, notably Nelson MANDELA, Walter SISULU and Cyril RAMAPHOSA, negotiated with the government under President F W DE KLERK for a transition to a democratic South Africa. The new constitution gave the vote to all South African adults, and in 1994 the ANC won the country's first all-race elections and Mandela became President. In Dec 1997 Thabo MBEKI succeeded Mandela as ANC leader, and became President of South Africa following the ANC's landslide victory in the 1999 elections. The party retained power in 2004 with an increased majority.

**ancien régime**
The social and political system of France existing from the late 16c to the outbreak of the FRENCH REVOLUTION (1789). The term denotes a hierarchical, corporative society, bound closely to the dynastic state, and is associated particularly with mechanisms upholding traditional orders and privileges. ► PARLEMENT

**Anckarström, Johan Jakob** (1762–92)
Swedish army officer and assassin of King GUSTAV III of Sweden. He served as the instrument of a ring of nobles opposed to the King's autocracy and, in 1792, mortally wounded Gustav during a masked ball in the Royal Opera House in Stockholm. He was soon seized and executed.

**Andean Community** ► CAN

**Andean Group**, also called **Andean Pact**, official name **Acuerdo de Cartagena**
A South American organization formed in 1969 by the Cartagena Agreement to stimulate industrial development and economic cooperation among members. The group originally consisted of Bolivia, Colombia, Ecuador, Peru (suspended 1992–3) and Chile (left 1977); Venezuela joined in 1973. In addition to its main aim of economic integration, the organization was concerned with monetary exchange, tourism and social affairs. In 1987 member countries signed the Quito Protocol to modify some of the more ambitious industrial projects and to lessen the strict controls which had been placed on foreign investors. In 1997 it changed its name to the Andean Community (CAN). ► MERCOSUR

**Anders, Władysław** (1892–1970)
Polish general. He was Commander-in-Chief of the Polish forces in the Middle East and Italy in WORLD WAR II. After the war, deprived of his nationality by the Polish communist government (1946), he became Inspector-General of the Polish forces in exile, and a leading figure in the 140,000-strong Free Polish community in Britain. He died in London.

**ANDORRA** also called the **Valleys of Andorra**, official name **Principality of Andorra**

A small, mountainous, semi-independent, neutral state on the southern slopes of the central Pyrenees between France and Spain. One of the oldest states in Europe, it has been under the joint protection of France and Spain since 1278, and became an independent parliamentary democracy in 1993.

**Andrada e Silva, José Bonifácio de** (1763–1838)
Brazilian politician and geologist. After holding academic posts in Portugal, he returned to Brazil in 1819 to take part in the independence movement that overturned the Portuguese regency of Prince Pedro in 1820–2. He was adviser and First Minister to Pedro in 1822, forming his first administration under the new empire of Brazil. Authoritarian by instinct, he closed newspapers and advocated a strong executive, but argued for the gradual end of the African slave trade as a means of eradicating SLAVERY from the empire. Deported once PEDRO I had dissolved the constituent assembly, he returned in 1829. After Pedro's abdication in Apr 1831, he served as tutor to the young PEDRO II.

## Andrada Family

Arguably one of the most impressive political dynasties of Latin America, founded by three brothers, José Bonifácio de **ANDRADA E SILVA**, Antônio Carlos de Andrada e Silva and Martim Francisco Ribeiro de Andrada. All educated at Coimbra University, Portugal, they played major roles in the making of the Brazilian empire between 1815 and 1826, either as First Minister to **PEDRO I**, or as protagonists of constitutional reform. All headed powerful regional factions, and were known for taking fearless, if highly controversial, stances on constitutional issues as well as **SLAVERY** and the abolition of the slave trade. Their descendants often achieved powerful positions as councillors to **PEDRO II**, and as senators or deputies, generally for São Paulo and Minas Gerais; they were often lawyers and drawn from families holding landed property in the most prosperous regions of those provinces. The more conservative, Minas, branch of the family played a leading role in support of Getúlio **VARGAS**'s 1930 'revolution' as Governor of Minas and during his subsequent vice-presidency. José Bonifácio de Andrada e Silva served as President of the Chamber under the Costa e Silva government in 1967–9.

## Andrássy, Gyula, Count (1823–90)

Hungarian politician. A supporter of Lajos **KOSSUTH**, he was prominent in the struggle for independence (1848–9), after which he remained in exile until 1858. When the Dual Monarchy came into being, he was made Prime Minister of Hungary (1867–71). ► **AUSTRIA-HUNGARY, DUAL MONARCHY OF**

## Andrássy, Gyula, Count (1860–1929)

Hungarian politician. The son of Count Gyula **ANDRÁSSY** (1823–90), he became Minister of the Interior in 1900, and Foreign Minister in 1918. In 1921 he attempted to restore the monarchy, and was imprisoned, but after his release became leader of the royalist opposition.

## Andreev, Andrei Andreevich (1895–1971)

Russian government minister and long-serving apparatchik. He joined the Communist Party in 1914 and was active in the Petrograd metal workers union in the period 1917–19. He was a member of the Central Committee by 1935 and a secretary by 1938. In 1946 he moved on to be Deputy Chairman of the Ministerial Council and, as such, had special responsibility for improving agriculture. Pressure did little to increase yields, though, and in the early 1950s Nikita **KHRUSHCHEV** took on the job and began enlarging collectives instead. However, this did very little good either, and agriculture became institutionalized as the major economic problem.

## Andreotti, Giulio (1919– )

Italian Christian Democrat politician. Born in Rome and educated at the University of Rome, he was elected to the first post-war Constituent Assembly in 1945 and to parliament in 1947. He was appointed Minister of the Interior in 1954 and served as Minister of Finance (1955–8), Minister of the Treasury (1958) and Minister of Defence (1959–66). He was first appointed Prime Minister in 1972 and served two further terms (1976–9, 1989–92).

## Andropov, Yuri (1914–84)

Soviet politician. The son of a railwayman, he became head of the **KGB** (1967–82), and in 1973 was made a member of the **POLITBURO**. On the death of Leonid **BREZHNEV** (1982), he became General-Secretary of the Soviet Communist Party, consolidating his power (June 1983) with the presidency. He fell ill later that year, and died soon after, in Moscow. ► **COMMUNISM**

## Andrusovo, Treaty of (1667)

The treaty ending the Russo-Polish War which began when Tsar **ALEXEI MIKHAILOVICH** agreed (1654) to give military assistance to the Ukrainian Cossack rebel Bohdan Khmelnitsky. The River Dnieper became the new frontier, except that Kiev on the right bank went to Russia. While the Ukrainians were fortunate to escape from the Poles, they were subsequently to consider that they had gone from the frying pan into the fire.

## Angevins

The name conventionally given to the English monarchs from 1154 to 1216: **HENRY II** and his sons, **RICHARD I** and **JOHN**. It derives from the lordship of the medieval county (and later, duchy) of Anjou in western France via Henry, son of Geoffrey Plantagenet, Count of Anjou. Henry created a wider 'Angevin Empire' comprising also Normandy, Maine and Aquitaine. The Angevin line continued as Plantagenets after the death of John, although John is usually considered the last Angevin king because it was during his reign that Anjou was lost to the French. ► **PLANTAGENET DYNASTY**

## Angkor ► SOUTH-EAST ASIA PRE-1000AD

## Angkor Thom

The ancient capital of the **KHMER EMPIRE**, 150mi/240km north-west of Phnom Penh, Cambodia. The moated and walled city was built on a square plan, extending over 40 sq mi/100 sq km, and completed in the 12c. Abandoned in the 15c, it was rediscovered in 1861. Angkor Wat is the largest of the temples surrounding the site – linked, richly sculpted sanctuaries on a massive platform, the work of Suryavarman III (1112–52).

## Anglesey, Henry William Paget, 1st Marquis of (1768–1854)

British field marshal, who commanded the British cavalry at the Battle of **WATERLOO** (1815), where he lost a leg. He sat in parliament at various times between 1790 and 1810, succeeding his father as Earl of Uxbridge in 1812. He served in the army with distinction in Flanders (1794), Holland (1799) and the **PENINSULAR WAR** (1808–14), and was made Marquis of Anglesey for his services at Waterloo. He was Lord Lieutenant of Ireland (1828–9 and 1830–3), where he supported Catholic emancipation, and Master-General of the Ordnance (1846–52).

## Anglo-Burmese Wars (1824–6, 1852–3 and 1885)

Three wars which secured British control of Burma (now Myanmar): the first (1824–6) brought control of Arakan and Tehnasserim; the second (1852–3) led to the occupation of Pegu; the third (1885) saw the occupation of Upper Burma, and in 1886 all Burma was proclaimed a province of British India.

**Anglo-Dutch Wars** (1652–4, 1665–7, 1672–4 and 1780–4)
Four naval wars fought between the Dutch Republic and England caused mainly by commercial and colonial rivalry between the two great sea powers. The first three, in the second half of the 17c, did not result in the supremacy of either nation; the fourth (1780–4), shortly before the French Revolutionary period, was heavily lost by the Dutch, and signalled the end of their claims to commercial domination. The wars were the occasion of great naval heroics on both sides, for instance in the persons of Robert **BLAKE**, Maarten and Cornelis **TROMP**, and Michiel de **RUYTER**. ► **FRENCH REVOLUTION**

**Anglo-Egyptian Treaty** (1936)
In 1922 the British government had issued a declaration which recognized Egypt as an 'independent sovereign state', but retained for Britain control of the Suez Canal, the right to keep troops in the Canal Zone and the **CONDOMINIUM** in the Sudan. The 1936 treaty gave more of the substance of independence to Egypt. British residents in Egypt lost their legal and financial privileges, the British occupation was formally ended and Egypt gained control of her armed forces for the first time since 1882. In wartime, the British had the right to reoccupy the country, a right they exercised in 1939.

**Anglo-Iraqi Treaty** (1930)
This treaty prepared the way for ending Britain's mandate in Iraq. The two countries formed a 25-year alliance in which they agreed to consult each other where they had common interests in foreign policy. Britain would retain the use of some air bases in Iraq and would train the Iraqi army. In 1932 Iraq became independent and joined the **LEAGUE OF NATIONS**.

**Anglo-Irish Agreement** (1985)
A joint agreement allowing the Irish Republic to contribute to policy in Northern Ireland for the first time since 1922, signed (15 Nov 1985) by the British and Irish Prime Ministers, Margaret **THATCHER** and Garrett **FITZGERALD**. It established an intergovernmental conference to discuss political, security and legal matters affecting Northern Ireland; early meetings focused on border cooperation. Both governments pledged not to change the status of Northern Ireland without the consent of the majority. The agreement was opposed by the Irish Republic's opposition party, **FIANNA FÁIL**; in Northern Ireland, Unionist leaders withdrew cooperation with ministers and boycotted official bodies.

**Anglo-Japanese Alliance** (1902)
The first modern alliance between a Western and Asian power, which lasted until 1921. It reflected the anxiety both countries felt at increasing Russian encroachment in **MANCHURIA**. The alliance took account of each country's interests in China, as well as Japan's interests in Korea, and provided for joint action in the event that either of the signatories was involved in war with more than one power in East Asia. Each signatory would remain neutral if the other fought only one power. The alliance was renewed twice (1905 and 1911), extending its scope to the protection of Britain's interests in India and recognizing Japan's annexation of Korea in 1910. Although the al-

liance brought benefits to both countries, the irrelevance of Russia as a threat in East Asia after 1918 and persistent US hostility led to its replacement in 1921 at the **WASHINGTON CONFERENCE** by a much looser consultative Four-Power Pact (USA, Britain, France and Japan).

**Anglo-Maori Wars** ► **MAORI WARS**

**Anglo-Russian Entente** (1907)
A crucial settling of differences between Russia and Britain which in the event almost amounted to an alliance. The Russian and British empires had been rivals in the Near, Middle and Far East for at least a century. However, they were gradually brought together by mutual distrust of an aggressive Germany and mutual interest in friendship with a worried France, with which Russia had had an alliance since 1894 and Britain an entente since 1904. Neither was prepared to sink their differences so far as to conclude a treaty. However, agreeing their respective spheres of influence, particularly in Persia, enabled them to operate as a diplomatic bloc that went to war in 1914.

**Anglo-Tibetan Agreement** (1904)
The agreement reached in Lhasa between Tibetan officials and a British expeditionary force (under Sir Francis Younghusband) fearful of potential Russian influence. Tibet recognized British overlordship of Sikkim and agreed to open relations with India. Trade marts were also to be opened in Gyantse and Gartok (western Tibet), where British officials and troops could be stationed. This agreement was virtually repudiated by the British government when it signed a convention with China in 1906 reaffirming China's position in Tibet and promising not to interfere in Tibetan affairs, in return for China's guarantee to keep Tibet free from encroachment by a third power.

---

**ANGOLA**  official name **Republic of Angola**, formerly (until 1992) **People's Republic of Angola**

A republic in south-west Africa, bounded to the south by Namibia; to the east by Zambia; and to the north by the Democratic Republic of Congo; the separate province of Cabinda to the north is bounded by the Congo in the north and the Democratic Republic of Congo in the south. The area became a Portuguese colony after exploration in 1483; an estimated 3 million slaves were sent to Brazil during the next 300 years. Boundaries were formally defined during the Congress of BERLIN in 1884–5. Angola became an Overseas Province of Portugal in 1951 and gained independence in 1975. Shortly afterwards, civil war broke out between the Marxist MPLA (Popular Movement for the Liberation of Angola) government and two factions: UNITA (National Union for the Total Independence of Angola), and the FNLA (National Front for the Liberation of Angola), both of which received arms from the USA in 1975–6. In 1976 Cuban combat troops arrived to support the MPLA. South African forces occupied an area along the Angola–Namibia frontier in 1975–6, and were active again in support of UNITA in 1981–4. Meanwhile, Angola backed the Namibian independence movement SWAPO (South West Africa Peoples' Organization), which launched attacks on Namibia from Angolan territory in the 1970s. Eventually an international agreement signed in Geneva in 1988 linked arrangements for the independence of Namibia with the withdrawal of Cuban troops and the cessation of South African support for UNITA. In 1991 a peace agreement between UNITA and the Angolan government was followed by multiparty elections but subsequently fighting resumed and continued – despite another peace agreement (1994–8) and UNITA's proposed inclusion in a government of national unity (1997) – until 2002, when a ceasefire was called after the death of the UNITA leader Jonah SAVIMBI and UNITA demobilized.

### Angry Brigade
A left-wing group with anarchist sympathies, active in Britain in the 1960s and early 1970s, which took sporadic violent action against representatives of the establishment in the name of the working class. Its leaders were tried and imprisoned for a bomb attack on the home of Robert Carr, Secretary of State for Employment, in 1971. ➤ ANARCHISM

### Anhalt
A principality of the HOLY ROMAN EMPIRE, originally a part of the Duchy of Saxony, then ruled by Brandenburg. Prince George III introduced Lutheranism in 1526. Anhalt was devastated in the THIRTY YEARS' WAR as a result of the activities of the Prince, Christian I, in siding against the Empire. The principality straddles the River Elbe between Magdeburg and Wittenberg.

### Ankara, Battle of (21 July 1402)
This represented a devastating defeat for the Ottomans at the hands of TIMUR. Throughout the 14c, the Ottomans had gradually increased their hold over Anatolia and in the second half of the century they had established a European capital at Edirne (Adrianople). Their defeat by Timur lost them Anatolia at a stroke. It was as well for the Ottomans that they had invaded Europe as their sultanate was able to hold on in the Balkans with its capital at Edirne until, after Timur's departure, they were able in the 15c to re-establish themselves in their former territories. ➤ EDIRNE, CAPTURE OF; OTTOMAN EMPIRE

### Anna Comnena (1083–1148)
Byzantine Princess. The daughter of Emperor ALEXIUS I COMNENUS, she tried in vain to secure the imperial crown, and failed in her attempt to overthrow or poison her brother (1118). Disappointed and ashamed, she withdrew from the court, and sought solace in literature. On the death of her husband (1137), she wrote a life of her father, the *Alexiad*, which contains an account of the First CRUSADE. ➤ COMNENUS FAMILY

### Anna Ivanovna (1693–1740)
Empress of Russia (1730/40). She was the younger daughter of Ivan V and the niece of PETER I, THE GREAT. In 1710 she married the Duke of Courland, who died the following year. After the early death of PETER II, she was elected to the throne by the Supreme Council in 1730, with conditions that severely limited her authority. She trumped the council by abolishing it and ruled as an autocrat with her German favourite, Ernst Johann BIRON, who assumed the title of Duke of Courland and became the real power behind the throne. Together they established a reign of terror, in which 20,000 people are said to have been banished to Siberia.

### Annam
A French protectorate, occupying the central part of Vietnam. The name was originally a Tang Chinese term for Vietnam (literally, 'the pacified south'), but was then revived by the French. The French protectorate was established in 1883, following the final French assault on the Vietnamese court. In 1887 Annam was brought together with the French colony of COCHIN-CHINA and the Cambodia and Tonkin protectorates to form the *Union Indochinoise*. Economic conditions in parts of Annam were notably harsh. This was an important element in the fierceness of the local opposition to French rule, as demonstrated in the uprisings in Nghe-An and Ha-Tinh at the beginning of the 1930s. The imperial capital of Vietnam, Hue, was situated in Annam. ➤ NGHE-AN/HA-TINH UPRISINGS

### Annan, Kofi Atta (1938– )
Ghanaian diplomat. Educated in Ghana, the USA and Switzerland, he began his career at the UN with the WORLD HEALTH ORGANIZATION (1962–71). After various posts in administration, budget and personnel, he became UN Special Envoy to former Yugoslavia (1995–6) and succeeded BOUTROS-GHALI as Secretary-General of the UN in 1997, the first incumbent to attain the post by promotion through UN ranks; he was re-appointed for a second term in 2002. In 2001 he was the joint winner (with the UN) of the NOBEL PEACE PRIZE.

### Anna Pavlovna (1795–1865)
Queen of the Netherlands. She was Tsar ALEXANDER I's sister, and married the Dutch Crown Prince, the future King WILLIAM II, in 1816. They ascended the throne in 1840 on the abdication of William's father, William I. William himself died in 1849 and was succeeded by their son, WILLIAM III. An indefatigable charity organizer, she is remembered as a stickler for ceremony, and brought international sophistication to the Dutch court.

### Anne (1665–1714)
Queen of Great Britain and Ireland (1702/14). The second daughter of JAMES VII AND II, she was the last Stuart sovereign. In 1672 her father became a

Catholic, but she was brought up in the Church of England. In 1683 she married Prince George of Denmark (1653–1708); Sarah Jennings (1660–1744), the wife of Lord Churchill (afterwards 1st Duke of **MARLBOROUGH**), was appointed a lady of her bedchamber. Lady Churchill speedily acquired supreme influence over her, which she exerted in favour of her husband. During her father's reign, Anne lived in retirement, taking no part in politics, but later was drawn into intrigues for his restoration, or to secure the succession for his son. She was herself childless when she succeeded to the throne in 1702. She bore 17 children, but only William, Duke of Gloucester, survived infancy. The influence of Marlborough and his wife was powerfully felt in all public affairs during the greater part of her reign, which was marked by pronounced party political conflict between **WHIGS** and **TORIES**, the Union of England and Scotland (1707), and the long struggle against **LOUIS XIV** of France known as the War of the **SPANISH SUCCESSION**. Towards the end of her reign she quarrelled with the Marlboroughs and **GODOLPHIN**, her Lord Treasurer. Anne found a new favourite in Abigail Masham, and under her influence appointed a Tory government (1710), but quarrels between the new ministers prevented her securing the succession for her brother. ► **STUART, HOUSE OF**; **UNION, ACTS OF**

### Anne of Austria (1601–66)
Queen of France. The eldest daughter of **PHILIP III** of Spain, she married **LOUIS XIII** of France in 1615. Their first son was born in 1638; he succeeded to the throne on his father's death in 1643, as **LOUIS XIV**, with Anne as regent. She wielded power with her lover, Cardinal Jules **MAZARIN**, as Prime Minister. They steered France through the difficult period of the **FRONDE** and, although Louis came of age in 1651, they continued to rule the country jointly until Mazarin's death (1661), when Anne retired to the convent of Val de Grâce and Louis XIV became absolute monarch.

### Anne of Brittany (1477–1514)
Duchess of Brittany (1488/1514). She married **CHARLES VIII** (1491), then **LOUIS XII** of France (1499), and devoted herself to preserving the autonomy of Brittany, her hereditary dominion.

### Anne of Cleves (1515–57)
Lutheran princess. She became the fourth queen of **HENRY VIII** of England in Jan 1540, as part of Thomas **CROMWELL**'s strategy of developing an alliance with German Protestant rulers. The marriage was declared null and void on grounds of non-consummation six months afterwards. On agreeing to the divorce, Anne was given a large income, and she remained in England until her death.

### Anne of Denmark (1574–1619)
Wife (from 1589) of James VI of Scotland, later James I of England. Much of her time was spent in planning extravagant court entertainments, and she became a patron of the masque and other art forms. ► **JAMES VI AND I**

### Annexation Manifesto (1849)
A Canadian proposal (produced chiefly by Montreal **TORIES**, A T **GALT** among them, and some **ROUGES**), which argued that annexation to the USA was preferable to the proposed union of the colonies. Since the ending of colonial preference, Canadian trading problems had become very severe, and with the repeal of the **NAVIGATION ACTS** it looked as if the colonies were being abandoned. Annexation would raise farm prices, lower import costs, and make US capital available for industrial development. The reaction to the proposal was disappointing for the signatories: not only were the French thoroughly opposed, but the USA showed little interest.

### Anno, St (c.1010–1075)
Archbishop of Cologne. Elected Archbishop of Cologne in 1056, after Emperor **HENRY III**'s death he led the opposition to the Regent, the Empress Agnes; he seized the young King, **HENRY IV**, and took control of the Empire (1062). From 1063 onwards he was forced to share government with **ADALBERT** of Bremen and increasingly lost the favour of Henry IV, although he continued to support him, even when the King sided with the people of Cologne in their revolt against the Archbishop in 1074. Anno contributed greatly to the power of the Church and created a centre for reform in the Rhineland. He was canonized in 1183.

### Ansbach-Bayreuth
A principality of the **HOLY ROMAN EMPIRE** in Franconia which became Lutheran under Margrave George (d. 1543). Margrave Christian Ernst (d.1712) settled Huguenots in Erlangen, where a university was founded in 1743. It was annexed to Bavaria in 1810.

### Anschluss
The concept of union between Austria and Germany, expressly forbidden by the Treaties of **VERSAILLES** and **ST GERMAIN** (1919), but with widespread support, especially in Austria, after the collapse of the Habsburg Empire. A proposed customs union (1931) was vetoed by France and Czechoslovakia. **HITLER** pursued the idea once in power, and in 1938, after the forced resignation of the Austrian Chancellor von **SCHUSCHNIGG**, the Germans occupied Austria. The union of Austria and Germany was formally proclaimed on 13 Mar 1938. ► **HABSBURG DYNASTY**

### Anson, George Anson, Baron (1697–1762)
English naval commander. Born in Shugborough Park, Staffordshire, he joined the navy in 1712, and was made a captain in 1724. In 1739, on the outbreak of the War of **JENKINS' EAR**, he received the command of a Pacific squadron of six vessels, and sailed from England in 1740. With one ship and fewer than 200 men, but with £500,000 of Spanish treasure, he returned to Spithead in 1744, having circumnavigated the globe. He defeated the French off Cape Finisterre (1747), capturing £300,000. As First Lord of the Admiralty from 1751 he played a key role in Britain's unprecedented successes in the **SEVEN YEARS' WAR**. In 1761 he was appointed Admiral of the Fleet.

### Antall, József (1932–93)
Hungarian historian and reforming politician. After working as an academic in Budapest, he came to politics in 1956 when he led one of the revolutionary committees. Active in the Smallholders Party, he was arrested in 1957 and banned from practising his profession until 1963. He did not enter politics again until the late 1980s, when he became President of

the Democratic Forum in 1989. He entered parliament in 1990 and was chosen Prime Minister later the same year, with the difficult task of presiding over a coalition government.

### Anthony, Susan Brownell (1820–1906)
US reformer and champion of **WOMEN'S RIGHTS**. After teaching and pursuing temperance work, she was instrumental in the passage of the Women's Property Rights Act (1860). From 1869 she was a leader of the National Woman Suffrage Association, becoming President of the US branch in 1892. ► **NATIONAL AMERICAN WOMAN SUFFRAGE ASSOCIATION**

### Anthracite Strike (1902)
A strike by the **UNITED MINE WORKERS OF AMERICA** in the anthracite coalfields of the USA in which the union demanded recognition, an increase in wages and shorter hours. The coalfield operators refused to arbitrate and violence broke out. President Theodore **ROOSEVELT**, facing the prospect of cold homes, hospitals and schools in the early winter, considered the conflict to be of national economic importance. Threatening to use the army to operate the mines, he won an agreement to mediate and secured a wage increase for the miners. The strike is noteworthy because it marked the first time that the federal government had intervened in a labour dispute of this kind.

### Anti-Comintern Pact
An agreement between Germany and Japan, concluded in 1936, which outlined both countries' hostility to international **COMMUNISM**. The pact was also signed by Italy in 1937. In addition to being specifically aimed against Soviet Russia, it also recognized Japanese rule in Manchuria. ► **COMINTERN**

### Anti-Confucian Campaign (1973–4)
An ideological campaign launched by the Chinese Communist Party on the eve of its Tenth Congress (Aug 1973). It was apparently the inspiration of **MAO ZEDONG**'s radical supporters who used the campaign, ostensibly to condemn the persistence of traditional ideas, as a veiled attack on the policies of Premier **ZHOU ENLAI**. Just as Confucius and his followers attempted to restore feudal society and practices, so Zhou was seen as trying to roll back **CULTURAL REVOLUTION** innovations (in such areas as education) and rehabilitate purged party officials. After the Congress, however, the campaign was specifically linked to a denunciation of **LIN BIAO**, Mao's former deputy, who was identified with the excesses of the Cultural Revolution, suggesting that the campaign had been taken over by Zhou and his more moderate allies.

### Anti-Corn Law League
An association formed in Manchester in Sep 1838, largely under the patronage of businessmen and industrialists, to repeal the British **CORN LAWS**, which imposed protective tariffs on the import of foreign corn. League propaganda aided the growing movement for free trade in early 19c Britain, and the league was an influential political pressure group with many supporters in parliament. The Corn Laws were repealed by Robert **PEEL** (1846). ► **BRIGHT, JOHN**

### Antietam, Battle of (16–17 Sep 1862)
A battle of the **AMERICAN CIVIL WAR** (also known as the Battle of Sharpsburg), fought in Maryland. In military terms the North won a technical victory, but both McClellan's and Robert E **LEE**'s troops suffered huge casualties. The Union cause gained enough credibility to allow President **LINCOLN** to issue his preliminary **EMANCIPATION PROCLAMATION**. ► **CONFEDERATE STATES OF AMERICA**

## ANTIGUA AND BARBUDA

An independent group of three tropical islands in the Leeward group of the Lesser Antilles in the eastern Caribbean Sea: Antigua, Barbuda and the uninhabited Redonda. Antigua was discovered by **COLUMBUS** in 1493. It was colonized by the English in 1632 and ceded to England in 1667. Barbuda was colonized from Antigua in 1661. Administered as part of the Leeward Islands Federation from 1871 until 1956, it became an associated state of the UK in 1967. Full independence of Antigua and Barbuda was achieved in 1981. The head of state remains the British monarch, represented by the Governor-General. The Prime Minister on independence was Vere Cornwall **BIRD** of the Antigua Labour Party, who held power until he was succeeded by his son, Lester Bird, in 1994. The islands' prosperity is founded on financial services; allegations of corruption and money laundering, with political connivance, have been made.

### Anti-Masonic Party (1830–6)
US political party. Dedicated to driving Freemasons out of public life, it arose from the highly publicized disappearance (1826) of the author of a book revealing Masonic secrets. It was the first 'third party' in the USA, nominating a presidential candidate in 1832 at the first national party convention. ► **FREEMASONRY**

### Antioch, Capture of (June 1098)
After the successes of the First **CRUSADE** over the Turks at Dorylaeum and Heraclea, the main body of the Crusader army split up and moved on Antioch (which had been lost to the Turks in 1085). The city was taken after a seven-month siege, Bohemond having achieved this success by obtaining a betrayal from one of its citizens. The Crusaders repelled an attempt to recapture the city by the Seljuk Atabeg of

Mosul, Kitbugha, and the gateway to northern Syria was in Crusader hands.

### Anti-Party Plot (1957)

The name given by Nikita **KHRUSHCHEV** to the attempt made by senior opponents to oust him from his position as First Secretary of the Communist Party. Ever since **STALIN**'s death he had been strengthening his position and, in the process, introducing changes to existing policies. He had therefore incurred the hostility of hardliners and opponents of reform such as **MALENKOV, MOLOTOV, KAGANOVICH** and **SHEPILOV**, who succeeded in defeating his decentralization proposals at a meeting of the Party Presidium. However, Khrushchev managed with great skill to convene a meeting of the Central Committee, where he commanded a majority, and had the Presidium vote overturned and the plotters expelled. In a similar situation in 1964, he was unable to repeat his success since many of his reforms had proved useless.

### anti-pope

In the Roman Catholic Church, a claimant to the office of **POPE** in opposition to one regularly and canonically appointed. Anti-popes featured prominently in the period of **GREAT SCHISM** in the Western Church (1378–1417). They included Clement VII and Benedict XIII (in Avignon, France), and Alexander V and **JOHN XXIII** (in Pisa, Italy).

### Anti-Revolutionary Party (Anti-Revolutionaire Partij, ARP)

Dutch political party founded in 1878 by Abraham **KUYPER** on principles of Calvinist opposition to the **ENLIGHTENMENT** and the **FRENCH REVOLUTION** (hence 'anti-revolutionary'). Since the 1840s there had been a loose grouping of Dutch MPs calling themselves 'Anti Revolutionaries', led by **GROEN VAN PRINSTERER**, but in 1878 under Kuyper it became the first true political party in the Netherlands, with a published manifesto and a quasi-democratic structure. Its programme was for limited social and political reform, together with a Calvinist approach to all things including politics: thus, it was an early Christian–Democrat party. From 1888 the ARP regularly took part in Dutch government coalitions, usually with the Catholics. Kuyper's successor, **COLIJN**, led the country during the 1930s, and in 1973 the ARP joined the other Dutch confessional political parties in the **CHRISTIAN DEMOCRATIC APPEAL**. As a result of this merger, the ARP ceased to exist in Sep 1980.

### Anti-Saloon League

US organization. Established in 1893, its aim was to end the use of alcohol by state and local anti-alcohol laws, and by amending the **US CONSTITUTION**. The League remained in existence during and after the **PROHIBITION** period, and became part of the National Temperance League in 1950.

### Anti-Spiritual Pollution Campaign (1983)

Ideological campaign promoted by the Chinese Communist Party and initially encouraged by **DENG XIAOPING**. At a time of economic reform, which aimed to dismantle state controls, and increasing contacts with the West, 'spiritual pollution' referred to pernicious Western influences in the realm of political thought and culture that were seen to encourage excessive individualism and hedonism. Intellectuals were criticized for their espousal of humanism and the notion that alienation could exist in a socialist society, while Western trends in dress and music were condemned as decadent.

### Anti-Trust Acts

US legislation passed to control the development of monopoly capitalism. The Sherman Act (1890) forbade all combinations 'in restraint of trade'. Ambiguities in wording led to its use against labour unions instead of corporations, or *trusts*. The Clayton Act (1914) was intended to clear up the ambiguities and make enforcement easier.

### Antonescu, Ion (1882–1946)

Romanian general and politician. He was military attaché in Rome and London, and served as Minister of War from 1934 to 1938. Right-wing and nationalistic, while out of office he maintained links with the **IRON GUARD**. In 1940 he established a dictatorship with the trappings of fascism, taking the title *conducător* ('leader') and assuring **HITLER** of his support. In Jan 1941, to maintain the internal stability essential for German interests, he crushed an uprising of the Iron Guard with the Romanian army backed by German forces. He was executed as a war criminal. ► **CODREANU, CORNELIU ZELEA**; **MICHAEL** (of Romania)

### Antraigues, Emanuel Delaunay, Count of (1755–1812)

French politician. His *Mémoires sur les États-généraux* (1788) was one of the first sparks of the **FRENCH REVOLUTION**, but in 1789, when he was chosen a Deputy, he defended the hereditary privileges and the kingly veto, and ranked himself against the union of the three estates. After 1790 he was employed in diplomacy at St Petersburg, Vienna and Dresden. In England he acquired great influence with George **CANNING**. He was murdered, with his wife, near London, by an Italian servant.

### Antwerp, Sack of (Nov 1576)

Also known as the Spanish Fury, the Sack occurred during the **EIGHTY YEARS' WAR** when the prosperous trading port was plundered by mutinous Spanish troops who had not been paid in campaigns against the northern Dutch provinces. The sack lasted several days and cost 7,000 citizens their lives, together with huge amounts of booty.

### Anuradhapura

A city in northern Sri Lanka, which was the centre of the island's Buddhist kingdoms from 4c BC to 12c AD. The centre of government then shifted to **POLONNARUWA**, partly as a result of hostile invasions from South Indian kingdoms. In the late 19c the city became the focus of archaeological attention and in the 20c many of its monuments were restored by Buddhist revivalists.

### ANZAC (Australia and New Zealand Army Corps)

A unit in which troops from both countries fought during **WORLD WAR I** in the Middle East and on the Western Front. Anzac Day (25 Apr) commemorates the Gallipoli landing in 1915. ► **GALLIPOLI CAMPAIGN**

### Anzio Landing (22–23 Jan 1944)

Landing by 50,000 US and British troops during

WORLD WAR II at a small port 60 miles behind the German defences of the so-called Gustav Line. Although the Germans were taken by surprise, they were able to confine the Allied troops and prevent them from using Anzio as a bridgehead. In late May the forces at Anzio eventually made contact with the advancing troops of General Alexander who had overrun the Gustav Line.

## ANZUS (1951)
An acronym for the treaty concluded between Australia, New Zealand, and the United States for mutual security in the Pacific against armed attack. The treaty encompasses not only the metropolitan territories of the three, but also island territories under their jurisdiction, their armed forces, and their aircraft and shipping. New Zealand participation lapsed in 1985 following that country's refusal to admit US nuclear-powered warships to its waters.

## Apache
Native North Americans of the Athapascan linguistic group, who originally migrated from Canada, settling in the south-western USA. During the 19c their fierce warriors dominated the region, leading raids against both Native American and white settlements. They proved formidable opponents of the US Army when from 1861, led by COCHISE and GERONIMO, they fought against federal troops in the Apache Wars. Following their defeat in 1886, they were assigned to reservations in Arizona and New Mexico. Their present population is c.90,000. ► INDIAN WARS; NATIVE AMERICANS

## apartheid (Afrikaans, 'apartness')
The policy of separate racial development in the Republic of South Africa, supported traditionally by the Nationalist Party, and more recently by other right-wing parties. The ideology has several roots: Boer concepts of racial, cultural and religious separation arising out of their sense of national uniqueness; British liberal notions of indirect rule; the need to preserve African traditional life while promoting gradualism in their Christianization and westernization; and the concern for job protection, promoted by white workers to maintain their status in the face of a large and cheaper black proletariat. Under the policy, different races were given different rights. In practice, the system was one of white supremacy, blacks having no representation in the central state parliament. Many of the provisions of apartheid regarding labour, land segregation (reserves, Homelands, Bantustans), municipal segregation, social and educational separation, and a virtually exclusive white franchise, were in place before the Nationalist victory of 1948, but after that date it was erected into a complete political, social and economic system, down to the provisions of 'petty apartheid' relating to transport, beaches, lavatories, park benches, etc. Its principal architect, Hendrik VERWOERD, was assassinated in 1966. Some of its provisions began to be dismantled in the mid-1980s, for example the abolition of the 'pass laws' in 1986 and the modification of the Group Areas Act, and in 1991 President F W DE KLERK bowed under international pressure and internal unrest to repeal all remaining apartheid legislation. In Dec that year the Convention for a Democratic South Africa was created to draft a new constitution, which

enfranchised blacks and other racial groups, and in 1994 the first multiracial elections were won by Nelson MANDELA and the ANC. ► AFRIKANERS; BLACK CONSCIOUSNESS MOVEMENT; INDIRECT RULE; SHARPEVILLE

## Apartheid Laws
A body of legislation in South Africa passed by the Nationalist government after its victory in 1948. APARTHEID was based on a combination of ideas derived both from the Boers' sense of separateness and from the British colonial practice of indirect rule (ruling through chiefs on reserves). Earlier laws such as the Natives Land Act of 1913 and the Natives (Urban Areas) Act of 1923 created a foundation for the more extreme form of separation promoted by the Nationalists. The laws included the Prohibition of Mixed Marriages Act and the Population Registration Act (both 1949), the Immorality Act and the Group Areas Act (1950), the Prevention of Illegal Squatting Act (1951), the Bantu Authorities Act and the Bantu Education Act (1953). The intention of these Acts was to separate white and black living areas, educational provision and social intercourse. Jobs were also reserved according to race, but the apartheid system was ultimately destroyed because it failed to match economic realities. Most of these laws were repealed in 1990–1 after F W DE KLERK, who had become President of South Africa in 1989, announced the abandonment of the apartheid programme. In 1993 a new constitution gave the vote to all South African adults, and in 1994 the first multiracial elections were won by the ANC.

Apis ► DIMITRIJEVIĆ, DRAGUTIN

## APO (Ausser-Parlamentarische Opposition, 'Extra-parliamentary Opposition')
After the formation of an SPD–CDU coalition in Federal Germany in 1966, there was no effective opposition in the BUNDESTAG. Radical, student-dominated, groups therefore took their opposition to the political system into the streets, declaring the Federal Republic to be a parliamentary dictatorship. The formation of an SPD–FDP coalition in 1969 (leaving the CDU/CSU as a credible opposition) defused much of the criticism, but the BAADER–MEINHOF GROUP had roots in the APO.

## Apollo–Soyuz Project
A landmark joint space mission conducted by the USA and USSR in July 1975, following an agreement signed by President Richard NIXON and Premier Alexei KOSYGIN in May 1972. A project of the period of US–Soviet DÉTENTE, Apollo–Soyuz also demonstrated the capability for joint operations between the major space powers and, as such, the potential for on-orbit emergency rescue missions. The rendezvous (17 July 1975) lasted nearly two days. The crews (T Stafford, V Brand, D Slayton and A Leonov, V Kubasov) conducted a series of joint experiments. A special adaptor docking module was constructed for the mission. ► SPACE EXPLORATION

## apparat
The aggregate of full-time officials of the COMMUNIST PARTY OF THE SOVIET UNION (apparatchiki). Originally drawn from professional revolutionaries, and based on LENIN's doctrine of democratic centralism,

the role of the *apparat* is to execute the decisions of the party leadership in a disciplined, bureaucratic manner with little scope for discussion or discretion. The term *apparatchik* is used to refer to a functionary.

**appeasement**
A foreign policy based on conciliation of the grievances of rival states by negotiation and concession to avoid war. The term is most often applied to the unsuccessful British and French attempts before WORLD WAR II to satisfy HITLER's demands over German grievances arising out of the Treaty of VERSAILLES. As a result, Hitler remilitarized the RHINELAND, secured ANSCHLUSS with AUSTRIA, and gained the SUDETENLAND from Czechoslovakia. ► CHAMBERLAIN, NEVILLE

**Appomattox Court House**
The site in Virginia, USA, of the surrender (9 Apr 1865) of the Confederate Army under Robert E LEE to Union forces under Ulysses S GRANT. Although a few Confederates remained under arms, the surrender marked the effective end of the AMERICAN CIVIL WAR.

**Apponyi, Albert Georg, Count** (1846–1933)
Hungarian politician. He entered the Hungarian Diet in 1872, and showing himself to be a brilliant orator, soon became leader of the moderate opposition which became the National Party in 1891. In 1899 he and his supporters went over to the Liberal Government party, and from 1901 to 1903 he was President of the Diet. From 1906 to 1910 he was Minister of Culture and, a devout Roman Catholic, gave asylum to the expelled French Jesuits. He introduced free public education. In 1920 he led the Hungarian peace delegation, protested bitterly against the terms imposed under the Treaty of TRIANON and resigned. He frequently represented his country at the LEAGUE OF NATIONS.

**Apprenticeship System** (1834–8)
The technique introduced into the British West Indies after emancipation in order to preserve the labour force of the plantation economy. Fearful of the expected social upheaval and economic consequences of the immediate freedom of some 750,000 slaves, the British government totally freed only children under six years in 1834. Field slaves remained apprenticed to their masters for another six years and domestic slaves for four years, and were bound to give 40 hours of unpaid work weekly. Stipendiary magistrates were appointed to oversee apprenticeship, which worked well only in colonies without large tracts of crown land. Antigua ignored apprenticeship, while slaves in Guyana and Jamaica left to found 'free villages'. In all the British West Indies the system was ended in 1838.

**Apraxin, Fyodor Matveevich, Count** (1671–1728)
Russian naval commander, known as the 'Father of the Russian Navy'. In the service of PETER I, THE GREAT from 1682, he was appointed admiral in 1707 and built up the navy into a powerful fighting force. In the GREAT NORTHERN WAR (1700–21) he fought off the Swedes at St Petersburg (1708), captured Viborg, Åbo and Helsinki, and routed the Swedish fleet in 1713, thus taking control of the Baltic. Later he commanded successful engagements against Turkey and Persia.

**Apraxin, Stephen Fyodorovich, Count** (1702–58)
Russian soldier. The nephew of Count Fyodor APRAXIN, he served in the war against the Turks (1736–9), and at the outbreak of the SEVEN YEARS' WAR (1756–63) was appointed marshal. He commanded the Russian forces invading East Prussia in 1757, and defeated the Prussians at the Battle of Gross-Jägersdorf, but fell from favour and died in prison. ► RUSSO-TURKISH WARS

**April Movement** (1853)
Popular Protestant protest in the Netherlands against the re-establishment of the Roman Catholic episcopal hierarchy. On 4 Mar 1853 Pope PIUS IX set up five new bishoprics (Breda, Haarlem, 's-Hertogenbosch, Roermond, and the Archbishopric of Utrecht) in the Netherlands, which had not had a proper hierarchy since the REFORMATION (the country had been a 'mission area', under the *Propaganda Fide* in Rome). Petitions were raised, demonstrations took place, Catholic employees were dismissed, Catholics were molested on the streets, and the liberal government of the day was forced to resign. Thereafter the row subsided, and the new bishops took over their sees.

**April Theses**
A programme of revolutionary action announced by LENIN in Apr 1917 shortly after the FEBRUARY REVOLUTION and his return to Russia. In it he advocated the transformation of the Russian 'bourgeois-democratic' revolution into a 'proletarian-socialist' revolution under the slogan of 'All power to the Soviets'. ► BOLSHEVIKS; JULY DAYS; OCTOBER REVOLUTION; RUSSIAN REVOLUTION

**Aquino, Benigno**, nicknamed **Ninoy** (1932–83)
Filipino politician. Born into a political family, he rose rapidly through provincial politics to become a senator at the age of 35. He was the principal opposition leader during the period of martial law declared by President Ferdinand MARCOS in 1972. It is generally accepted that if martial law had not been declared then, and the 1973 presidential election thereby abandoned, Aquino would have succeeded Marcos as President. However, Aquino was arrested and sentenced to death on charges of murder and subversion (Nov 1977). In 1980, suffering from a heart condition, he was allowed to leave for the USA for surgery (and exile). On his return to the Philippines (21 Aug 1983), he was assassinated at Manila airport; this, it was widely believed, on the orders of the established regime. His death unleashed mass demonstrations against the Marcos order, which were to lead, in Feb 1986, to the collapse of the Marcos presidency and the succession of Benigno's widow, Cory AQUINO.

**Aquino, Cory (Maria Corazón)** (1933–)
Filipino politician. In 1956 she married Benigno AQUINO, and after his imprisonment in 1972 by President MARCOS kept him in touch with the outside world. She lived in exile with Benigno in the USA until 1983, when he returned to the Philippines and was assassinated at Manila airport. She took up her husband's cause, and with widespread support claimed victory in the 1986 presidential elections, accusing President Marcos of ballot-rigging. The non-violent 'people's power' movement which

followed brought the overthrow of Marcos and Aquino's installation as President. Her presidency was, however, much troubled by internal opposition; in 1989 the sixth, and most serious, attempted coup against her was resisted with assistance from the USA. In 1992 she did not run for the presidency, but supported the successful bid of General Fidel Ramos.

## Arab Cooperation Council (ACC)

The ACC was founded by Egypt in 1989 in cooperation with Iraq, Jordan and Yemen when Saddam **HUSSEIN** appeared to have been excluded from the Gulf Cooperation Council (GCC). Its establishment had as its formal aim economic cooperation between the member states, but the underlying objective was to establish a consultative assembly whereby the more extravagant policies of Iraq might be subjected to at least some form of control. The ACC ceased to function as an effective body when Saddam Hussein annexed Kuwait (Aug 1990).

## Arabi Revolt ► 'URABI REVOLT

## Arab–Israeli Wars

Four wars (1948, 1956, 1967 and 1973) fought between Israel and the Arab states over the existence of the state of Israel and the rights of the Palestinians. The June 1967 war is known by supporters of Israel as the '**SIX-DAY WAR**' and by others as 'The June War.' The 1973 war is called the '**YOM KIPPUR WAR**' by Israelis, the 'Ramadan War' by Arabs, and the 'October War' by others. ► **ZIONISM**

## Arab Legion (1921)

Established in the state of Transjordan in 1921, initially as a police force, command of the force passed in 1939 to Major John Bagot **GLUBB** (later known as Glubb Pasha), under whose training it developed into a military force of the highest discipline and quality. Making a considerable contribution to the **WORLD WAR II** effort in the Middle East, the legion was also instrumental in the 1948 struggle with Israel in retaining East Jerusalem and the **WEST BANK** for the Arabs. This provided the basis of additional territory, which enabled King **ABDULLAH** to proclaim his Hashemite Kingdom of Jordan, consisting of the former Transjordan and the territories won by the legion. Glubb Pasha (now Colonel Sir John Glubb), resigned in 1956, at which time the legion became part of the regular Jordanian army.

## Arab Revolt (1916)

The result of British negotiations with Sharif **HUSAYN IBN 'ALI** of Mecca, in part at least encouraged by the **HUSAYN–MCMAHON CORRESPONDENCE**, the revolt was led by the Sharif's son, Faysal. Attached to the Arab forces during the revolt was T E **LAWRENCE** ('Lawrence of Arabia'). Amongst the achievements of the revolt was the destruction of the **HIJAZ RAILWAY** between Ma'an and Medina, and the capture of Aqaba. Essentially a revolt against Turkish occupation, the Arabs were also under the impression that a greater Arab nation had been promised them by the British. The revolt cleared the way for British troops under **ALLENBY** to advance northwards into Syria, where the capture of Damascus effectively brought Turkish hegemony to a close. Unsurprisingly, the Arabs felt aggrieved, if not betrayed, by the provisions of the subsequent **BALFOUR DECLARATION** (providing for a national home for the Jews in **PALESTINE**) and by the provisions for British and French 'spheres of influence', initially negotiated by Sykes and Picot and confirmed after **WORLD WAR I** by the **LEAGUE OF NATIONS**. ► **FAYSAL I**; **SYKES–PICOT AGREEMENT**

## Arabs

A diverse group of people, united by their use of Arabic as a first language, who live primarily in southwest Iran, Iraq, Syria, the Arabian Peninsula, the Maghrib region of North Africa, Egypt and Mauritania. They are mostly Caucasoid, but with Negroid and Mongoloid admixture in certain areas. A great unifying force is Islam, the religion of 95 per cent of all Arabs. The majority live in cities and towns; five per cent are pastoral nomads living in deserts.

## Arab Socialism

This was the ideology of President Gamal Abd al-**NASSER** of Egypt. He denounced Western parliamentary democracy as 'a shameful farce' because the masses were still exploited. 'Democracy', he wrote, 'means that the government should not be the monopoly of feudalism and exploiting capitalism but should be for the welfare of the whole nation.' Nasser put his ideas into practice by nationalizing nearly all large-scale businesses and landholdings in 1961 and by forming the Arab Socialist Union, with 'basic units' in villages, factories and workshops. There were elected councils at local levels, rising to the National Executive, headed by Nasser himself. In all elected bodies, half the seats were reserved for farmers and workers, so that for the first time all Egyptians could participate in running the country.

## Arab States, League of

An association of Arab states, founded (Mar 1945) with the aim of encouraging Arab unity. The League's headquarters was established in Egypt, moved to Tunis after the signing of Egypt's peace treaty with Israel in 1979, and returned to Cairo in 1990 after Egypt's suspension was lifted. It has 22 member states including **PALESTINE**, and has observer status at the **UN**.

## Arafat, Yasser or Yasir, originally Mohammed Abed Ar'ouf Arafat (1929–2004)

Palestinian resistance leader, born in Cairo of Palestinian parents. He led the Palestinian Students' Union at Cairo University, and co-founded the **FATAH** resistance group in 1956, which gained control of the Palestinian Liberation Organization (**PLO**) in 1964. Acknowledged (though not universally popular) as the PLO leader, he skilfully managed the uneasy juxtaposition of militancy and diplomacy, and gradually gained world acceptance of the PLO. In 1983, however, his policies lost majority PLO support, and he was forced to leave Lebanon with his remaining followers, establishing new headquarters in Tunis. The **INTIFADA** ('uprising') in the **WEST BANK** in 1988 paved the way for his dramatic recognition of Israel and renunciation of **TERRORISM** in Dec 1988. In Sep 1993 he signed, with the Prime Minister of Israel, Yitzhak **RABIN**, the first of the **OSLO ACCORDS** granting a a measure of self-government to Palestinians in the **GAZA STRIP** and parts of the **WEST BANK**. In 1994 he became President of the Palestinian National Authority. Implementation of the Accords and initiatives

# Archaeology

Culture & Society

Archaeology as a systematic, scientific pursuit, as opposed to the discovery and collection of antiquities, is largely a product of the 19c, and its beginnings can be traced to excavations made in the Middle East.

## Mesopotamia
This region was the cradle of several warring or successive civilizations, notably the Sumerians, Akkadians, Assyrians and Babylonians. In the 1840s the Englishman Sir Austen Henry Layard (1817–94) carried out excavations on a mound that was reputed to be the site of ancient Nineveh. Work on the translation of Assyrian–Babylonian cuneiform script by such scholars as Sir Henry Rawlinson (1810–95) assisted greatly in the identification of his finds. Layard discovered remains of the palaces of the Assyrian kings Shalmaneser III (858/824 BC) and Ashurbanipal (7c BC), including huge statues of winged bulls and sculptured lions. He went on to find the palace of Sennacherib (d.681 BC) before transferring his attention to the site of Nimrud in 1845. Here he excavated the remains of the Assyrian city of Calah, rebuilt by Ashurnasirpal in 879 BC, and discovered the Black Obelisk of Shalmaneser III. Layard also excavated at the Sumerian city of Ur, discovering the Temple of the Moon God, although most of the discoveries here were made later by Sir Leonard Woolley (1880–1960) in the 1920s and 1930s. The important Sumerian city of Lagash was excavated in the 1870s by Ernest de Sarzec (1832–1901), who found sculptures and relics of Sumerian kings, as well as of Gudea (c.2150–c.2050 BC), the city's seventh governor.

Much of the impetus for this sort of work, especially that carried out by archaeologists from the UK and USA, was rooted in the contemporary controversy over the validity of Old Testament narratives.

## Egypt
The French were the pioneers in Egyptian archaeology because of the team of savants who accompanied the Napoleonic invasion of Egypt. Their discovery in 1799 of the Rosetta Stone, inscribed with parallel texts in hieroglyphics, demotic Egyptian characters, and Greek, allowed hieroglyphics to be translated. In 1851 Auguste Mariette (1821–81) discovered the Serapeum at Saqqarah, in which were interred the mummified remains of the holy Apis bulls. He also excavated temples at Giza, Abydos, Dendara and Edfu, and exposed the columns of Karnak. Gaston Maspéro (1846–1916) worked on sites at Luxor and Giza and made the vitally important discovery in 1886 of many royal mummies, including that of Ramesses II at Deir el-Bahari, which had been removed from their tombs and hidden to protect them from grave robbers. The British Egyptologist Flinders Petrie (1853–1942) excavated at Faiyum, Tanis and Tel-el-Amarna, as well as discovering (1884–5) the 'lost' Greek city of Naukratis. Arguably his most important finds were at Nagada (1904–5), where he discovered traces of hitherto unknown pre-dynastic cultures, and Thebes (1896), where he found a stele of King Meneptah (1213/1204 BC) that mentioned Israel by name. Undoubtedly the best-known discovery in Egyptian archaeology is that of the tomb of Tutankhamun in 1922 by the British archaeologist Howard Carter (1873–1939) and his patron Lord Carnarvon. Unlike so many previous finds, this tomb was unplundered and was found to contain an amazing hoard of treasures, including the pharaoh's gold funerary mask.

## Greece
By the late 19c, ancient Greece was re-invented, especially in Germany and the UK, as a more appropriate classical ancestor for a liberal bourgeois society than imperial Rome. The Earl of Elgin collected marbles from the Parthenon and eventually sold them to the British government, but this was a variation on the old practice of importing classical sculpture from Italy. The field of archaeology at this time was led by Heinrich Schliemann (1822–90), who may not unfairly be described as an enthusiastic amateur. Having made a fortune in commerce, Schliemann was free to indulge his dream of finding the actual sites mentioned by his beloved Homer. In 1870 he excavated at a site in Turkey (Hissarlik) where he believed Troy to have stood. He discovered the remains of nine cities superimposed one upon the ruins of another, and claimed to have found the treasure of the Trojan King Priam. While he was wrong in this attribution, it is accepted that he had indeed found where the Trojan War took place. At Mycenae (1876), Schliemann excavated several shaft graves, in a number of which the dead were richly adorned with gold. The splendour of one golden death mask

such as the **ROADMAP PEACE PLAN** stalled over issues such as Jewish settlements on the West Bank and the future of Jerusalem. The second *intifada*, his inability to rein in radicals, his corrupt regime and his stubborn clinging to power discredited him, and became obstacles to peace. He remained at his compound at Ramallah until his final illness, dying in Paris in Nov 2004. Although he had done much to achieve nationhood for the Palestinians, his death was felt to improve the prospects of reaching a successful peace settlement, especially after the election of a moderate, Mahmoud Abbas, as his successor in Jan 2005.

**Arago, Dominique François Jean** (1786–1853)
French scientist and politician. At 17 he entered the Polytechnic, in 1804 became Secretary to the Observatory, and in 1830 its Chief Director. He took a prominent part in the **JULY REVOLUTION** (1830), and as a member of the Chamber of Deputies voted with the extreme Left. In 1848 he was a member of the provisional government, but refused to take the oath of allegiance to **NAPOLEON III** after the events of 1851–2. His achievements were mainly in the fields of astronomy, magnetism and optics.

**Aragon, House of**
The ruling house of one of Spain's component kingdoms, founded in 1035 by Ramiro I, the illegitimate son of Sancho the Great of Navarre. It was united by marriage with the ruling house of Barcelona in 1131. Fernando II of Aragon (**FERDINAND II, THE CATHOLIC**) married Isabella of Castile in 1469, and the crowns of Aragon and **CASTILE** were finally united in 1479. ► **ISABELLA I, THE CATHOLIC**

**Aragon, Kingdom of**
The kingdom, with its capital in Saragossa, began to

prompted him to claim to have looked upon the face of Agamemnon. While he was once again presumptuous in his boast, his discoveries here and at Tiryns created the basis of our knowledge of the Mycenaean civilization that dominated Greece c.1400–c.1100 BC. The Bronze Age Minoan civilization, based on Crete c.3000–c.1100 BC, was discovered through the work of Sir Arthur Evans (1851–1941). Evans excavated the chief Minoan city of Knossos from 1900 onwards, discovering a magnificent palace lavishly decorated with colourful frescoes and containing numerous clay tablets inscribed with what was later decided to be Mycenaean Greek. Further palaces were later excavated on the island, for example at Phaistos and Malia. Elsewhere in Greece important excavations were made at Delos, Olympia, Eleusis, Corinth and Delphi, and great works of ancient Greek sculpture were found, including the Aphrodite of Melos (better known by its French name of Venus de Milo) in 1820 and the Winged Victory of Samothrace (on that island) in 1863.

### Other world regions

Archaeological work in East Africa, particularly the area around the Olduvai Gorge in northern Tanzania, yielded many important fossil finds in the 20c that expanded knowledge of early humankind. The British anthropologist and archaeologist Louis Leakey (1903–72) led expeditions that discovered remains of various human-like apes. In 1959 his wife Mary (1913–96) found a skull estimated to be over 1.75 million years old. This was first classified as *Zinjanthropus*, but later renamed *Australopithecus boisei*. The following year Louis Leakey labelled a 1.8 million-year-old skull as *Homo habilis*, because he believed the species capable of using tools. It was Mary Leakey again, in 1974, who discovered fossils of the earliest known human species, belonging to a female *Australopithecus afarensis* (known as 'Lucy'), estimated to be over 3.6 million years old. The Leakeys' work was carried on by their son Richard (1944– ) who found human fossil remains over 2 million years old. In North America, where controversy over the date and origin of human settlement in the Americas has been a source of both interest and funds for excavation, remains were found in the 20c of a Pleistocene culture, named Folsom Man after a nearby town in New Mexico. These early humans used leaf-shaped flint projectile points and seem to have lived mainly by hunting bison.

One of the most striking archaeological finds of the later 20c was excavated in China in 1974. This was the burial mound of the Emperor Shi Huangdi (d.210 BC) of the Qin Dynasty in the northern Shanxi province. Archaeologists gradually revealed an army of over 6,000 life-size terracotta warriors made with great individual detail, some of which were exhibited around the world. As in Egypt and Greece from the 19c, archaeology here was immediately enlisted in the service of tourism.

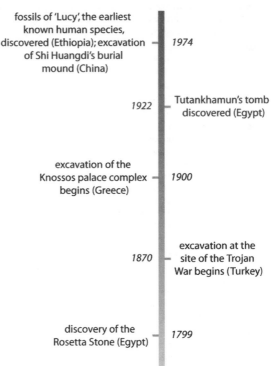

fossils of 'Lucy', the earliest known human species, discovered (Ethiopia); excavation of Shi Huangdi's burial mound (China) — 1974

1922 — Tutankhamun's tomb discovered (Egypt)

excavation of the Knossos palace complex begins (Greece) — 1900

1870 — excavation at the site of the Trojan War begins (Turkey)

discovery of the Rosetta Stone (Egypt) — 1799

---

emerge in the 11c. It came to form part of the confederation of the 'Crown of Aragon', which took shape from the 12c, when Aragon and Catalonia came under one ruler. Subsequent territorial extensions took in Valencia and much of the western Mediterranean. The Aragonese empire reached its height in the 13c.

### Arai Hakuseki (1657–1725)

Japanese Confucian scholar and official. He came from a SAMURAI family and in 1694 was appointed personal tutor to the future sixth Tokugawa SHOGUN, later becoming his adviser. Arai vainly attempted to transform the shogunate from a military-style government to a Confucian monarchy replete with the appropriate rituals and ceremony. He also wrote extensively on early Japanese myths and history, military affairs, and geography. ➤ TOKUGAWA SHOGUNATE

### Arakcheev, Alexei Andreevich, Count (1769–1834)

Russian landowner, officer and imperial minister. Commandant of St Petersburg for a time under PAUL I, he became Minister of War under ALEXANDER I in 1807 and then a state councillor in 1810. He did much to improve the efficiency of the army, but he also acted as a conservative counterweight to the reformist Count SPERANSKY. Then, and also for a time under NICHOLAS I, he was responsible for the notorious military colonies which organized ex-soldiers and their families in agricultural settlements run along military lines. Typical of the best and the worst of Tsarist rule, he acquired a reputation for brutality excessive even for the administration of his time.

### Araki Sadao (1877–1966)

Japanese soldier and politician. An ultra-nationalist, he was a leader of the right-wing IMPERIAL WAY

# *Architecture*

*Art & Literature*

Traditionally, the term architecture has tended to be associated with those buildings considered to represent great works of art, like the Parthenon or the Taj Mahal. However, the practice of architecture in the 19–20c increasingly involved a greater number of varied skills, including technical and functional considerations as well as aesthetic ones.

From the earliest times, buildings to honour the gods, to shelter worshippers, or to house rulers after their deaths tended to combine grandeur and ornamentation. Buildings to house rulers and their attendants in life often incorporated aspects of defence as well. These splendid edifices were often decorated with sculpture and painting, sometimes to an extent that it is hard to differentiate sculpture from architecture.

### Egyptian
The impressive buildings to have survived are the pyramids, funerary monuments and temples to honour the pharaohs. Their proportions are vast: the Great Pyramid (c.2600 BC) of Khufu at Giza is approximately 482ft/146m high, covering 13 acres/5.3 hectares at the base. The pyramids were designed to house the necessities of the king's journey to the afterlife, in such a way as to be safe from future tomb robbers. The temples were built with bare outside walls, monolithic columns on the inside, and were approached down an avenue lined with sculptures, such as sphinxes, statues of the king and obelisks near the entrance.

### Minoan
Excavations in Crete have revealed a number of palace complexes. The one at Knossos (c.500 BC) was built around a central courtyard (165ft × 100ft/50m × 30m), with extensive corridors and suites of rooms, including deep storerooms, a theatre and state rooms. Like Egyptian buildings they are on a monumental scale. Unlike the later Mycenaean buildings they were not fortified, suggesting that there was no fear of attack in a country whose navy ruled the Mediterranean.

### Mesopotamian
The monumental temple building of the Sumerians dates from at least as early as 3000 BC. Their temples were built of mud brick, often raised on platforms, and faced with copper sheathing or wooden pillars. These temples developed into ziggurats – stepped towers rising above walled temple enclosures. In the later period grand royal palaces were built, a dominant feature of which was a large outer courtyard with a raised audience chamber. Babylon, the capital of the Babylonian Empire, was defended by a double wall and a ditch, and the wall could be entered by one of eight gates. The eighth, the Ishtar Gate, more than 40ft/12m high, was decorated with glazed tiles and reliefs of dragons and young bulls. The stone and brick-paved Processional Way passed through it. At the centre of the city was the temple of Marduk, with its ziggurat (identified with the Tower of Babel).

### Greek
The main material used in the ancient Greek buildings that have survived (mostly temples) is stone. This was used in the way that clay and wood had been used, so post and lintel construction was still the mainstay, although in the massive Temple of Zeus in Sicily (c.600 BC) the half-columns are engaged against a solid wall, to spread the load. Columns were placed on the outside of buildings, the styles following the Doric, Ionic or Corinthian order. The summit of Greek architecture was achieved in the buildings on the Acropolis in Athens: the Doric Parthenon, the temple to Athena with its Ionic sculptural frieze, and the contrasting Ionic Erechtheum.

### Roman
Roman engineering skills developed some new construction methods. Materials for large buildings were *tuff* (a volcanic stone), travertine (a limestone used for facing) and concrete. Marble was much sought after for interior decoration. The Romans developed concrete, leading to an increase in arch construction, the use of the barrel vault, and finally the dome. These features made possible their extensive aqueducts and bridges, some of which survive (eg the aqueduct at Segovia, and the bridge across the Tagus, Alcántara, both in Spain). Concrete also enabled the construction of round buildings, a favourite form for temples. Grand public buildings, religious and secular, became the goal, exemplified by the baths and

---

FACTION of the army. He was Minister for War (1931–3) and for Education (1938–40). After WORLD WAR II he was convicted as a war criminal and sentenced to life imprisonment, but was released in 1965.

### Arana Goiri, Sabino de (1865–1903)
Basque nationalist. From a well-to-do Carlist family, he created much of the language and symbolism of Basque nationalism. Not only did he revive the Basque language by publishing grammars, textbooks, histories, newspapers and magazines, but he also created the word *Euzkadi* for the Basque ethnic nation, designed the first Basque flag (the *ikurrina*), founded the first Basque cultural club, and coined many of its key political slogans. He founded the Basque Nationalist Party (PNV) in 1895. He was also the first Basque nationalist to win public office. ►
CARLISM

### Aranda, Pedro Pablo Abarca y Bolea, Count of (1718–99)
Spanish statesman and general. He was made Ambassador to Poland in 1760, but in 1766 was recalled to Madrid and made Prime Minister in the wake of the ESQUILACHE riots of that year. He engineered, in 1767, the expulsion from Spain of the Jesuits, who were blamed for the risings, but in 1773 fell from power and was sent to France as ambassador. Returning in 1787, he became Prime Minister again in 1792, but antagonized Manuel de GODOY, and died in Aragon in enforced retirement.

### Arapaho
A Native American people of the northern Great Plains, members of the Algonquian linguistic group. Although they inhabited permanent settlements in the eastern woodlands in the 17c, they gradually

palaces of Nero, the Trajan Forum in Rome, and the Pantheon (AD 120–4), a rotunda 141ft/43m in diameter, through which light is admitted via one central hole in the dome. Public buildings for pleasure were practically designed as well as impressively large: the Colosseum amphitheatre (AD 62–72), a concrete shell faced on the outside with travertine and inside with marble, had 80 entrances to speed the arrival and departure of some 50,000 spectators.

### Islamic
The main thrust of monumental building was at first mosques, then palaces. The style of the mosque was dictated by the need for a large internal space to accommodate worshippers. A mosque at Damascus was built on the remains of a Roman temple and the towers were used as minarets. A minaret to call the faithful to prayer became standard; inside rich decorations of marble and mosaic were used, and were always geometric since the representation of the human figure is forbidden in Islamic religious art. Construction was with mud or stone bricks, and roofs were supported on walls or slender pillars. The arch was a recurrent feature, used to special effect in the Great Mosque at Córdoba, where the building is heightened by two rows of horseshoe arches, the alternating stone and brick providing the distinctive decoration. Domes symbolizing the heavens were used on minarets, the most famous being the Dome of the Rock in Jerusalem (AD 691). Later palace architecture became the focus of Islamic architecture, as exemplified in the Alhambra Palace (1238–1358) in Granada, Spain, with its elegant courts, where waters flow to refresh and delight, and its interior walls richly decorated with calligraphy.

### Indian
The Mughal emperors revived Islamic style in India in the 16–17c, and also drew influence from Persian buildings. Mosques, the fort at Agra and the tomb of Akbar were surpassed by **Shah Jahan**'s mausoleum for his wife, and its surrounding complex, the Taj Mahal (1632–49). White marble was used for the double-domed construction, in a park-like setting. Other religions generated their own styles. The early Buddhist stupas (dome-like mounds) evolved into temples and are found across South-East Asia. Jain and Hindu styles exhibit ornateness and pyramidal roofs. The temples usually have grand gates and ceremonial halls.

### Asian
In China the Buddhist stupas evolved into pagodas. There, and in Japan, the temples were made of wood, with gardens to aid contemplation. In Indonesia the stupas are organized in a complex architectural form on eight terraces, the first five square, the top three round, and crowned with a stupa. This design probably influenced the **Angkor Thom** and Angkor Wat temples in Cambodia.

### Pre-Columbian America
The surviving architecture of the Americas shows many factors common to the various civilizations. The main form of construction was post and lintel. Ceremonial buildings, temples, palaces, pyramids and tombs were constructed from rubble and mud brick, and faced with stone. Most pyramids were used as bases for temples, although burials have been discovered in some. The Aztec complex in Teotihuacán featured a geometric style that made impressive use of sun and shadow; the interiors were decorated with murals. The Pyramid of the Sun in Teotihuacán, and the Pyramid of Quetzalcoatl at Cholula, are larger than any Egyptian pyramid. The Maya building style was similar, with the addition of the false arch; the Maya also made extensive use of sculptured decoration. The Inca of Peru created a style sympathetic to the grandeur of the setting of their buildings in the Andes, employing undecorated stonemasonry.

### Europe and the West
After the fall of the Roman Empire, the dominant architectural style to emerge was the Romanesque. The most frequent display of this massive solidity with its rounded arches was in churches and cathedrals, such as Durham Cathedral, England. The Gothic style that followed was a result of the development of the ribbed vault to support the roof, and flying buttresses that allowed the walls to be thinner, with large windows inserted. The arches became pointed and the whole effect less grand. The cathedrals of northern France exhibit the development of Gothic styles; the bar tracery in the windows that was to become typical of all later Gothic churches was used first in Reims Cathedral.

In Italy the architects of the **Renaissance** turned to classical styles for inspiration, and developed a fascination with the dome. This period saw the building of Florence Cathedral and the beginning of St Peter's in Rome. In Roman Catholic countries the grandeur of the High Renaissance building style was embellished in the 17c and early 18c by the Baroque,

adopted a nomadic lifestyle and moved westwards until, around 1830, they split into northern and southern groups. The latter lived along the Arkansas River and became associated with the **CHEYENNE**, whom they fought alongside in the Battle of **LITTLE BIGHORN**. By the Treaty of Medicine Lodge (1867) the northern group was assigned to a reservation in Wyoming with the Shoshone (where by the early 21c they numbered c.6,500), and the southern group was assigned to a reservation in Oklahoma with the Cheyenne, where by the early 21c the Arapaho and Cheyenne together numbered c.7,400. ► **INDIAN WARS**; **NATIVE AMERICANS**

### Araucanians
A South American Indian group of central Chile. Two divisions, the Picunche, who were first encountered by the Spanish in the 1530s, and the Huilliche, were assimilated into Spanish society in the 17c. The Mapuche, however, resisted assimilation for over three centuries, and the word **GUERRILLA** was coined to describe their hit-and-run tactics, or small wars. They were finally defeated by the Chilean army in the 1880s and were settled on reservations, which were abolished in the 1980s. They now live on private former reservations and in towns and cities in Chile and Argentina, and number c.200,000.

### Arawaks
The original inhabitants of the Bahamas (Lucayos) and the Greater Antilles (Tainos) who practised a subsistence agriculture based on seafood, game, maize and cassava using Neolithic technology. They lived mainly in coastal settlements of large villages with *caneyes* (family houses) and *bohios* (chiefs' houses), and had a hierarchical politico-religious

an elaborate celebration of religious fervour in art and architecture. This was also the style chosen by **Louis XIV** for the Versailles complex, bringing together architecture, painting, sculpture and landscape gardening to proclaim his royal magnificence. A further development of this in France was the Rococo style, a lighter, more playful version of the rich and complex Baroque. It spread through Europe, but mainly into Roman Catholic countries. A reaction against the elaboration of Rococo and a new concern with the ancient world led to the spread of Neoclassicism at the end of the 18c and into the 19c. The style is exemplified by the Pantheon in Paris, by Edinburgh's New Town and by the White House in Washington, DC. Alongside this simplicity ran the Gothic Revival associated with the Romantic movement. Romanticism extolled the individual: Antoni Gaudí (1852–1926) was commissioned to build the Sagrada Familia in Barcelona, and although unfinished at his death, he made it an expression of his own interpretation of curving, sinuous Art Nouveau forms. Other examples of Art Nouveau can be seen in the Paris Métro entrances by Hector Guimard (1867–1942) and the work of Charles Rennie Mackintosh (1868–1928) in the UK.

In Chicago, Louis Sullivan (1856–1924) and other architects began to work with new construction techniques that used steel frameworks. The invention of the elevator made practical the construction of skyscrapers, and often these had a classical or beaux-art decoration. But the next generation of architects, including Frank Lloyd Wright (1867–1959), who had trained in Sullivan's office, promoted buildings with clean lines and cubic shapes, free of ornamentation. Wright used smooth expanses of cantilevered concrete and glass walls to mingle interior and exterior in his design for Fallingwater in Pennsylvania. The other great exponents of the Modern Movement are Walter Gropius (1883–1969, founder of the Bauhaus), Ludwig Mies van der Rohe (1886–1969, director of the Bauhaus in 1930–3) and Le Corbusier (1887–1965). Le Corbusier stressed the importance of modern materials and conceived the design of a 'carpet' of low buildings and open spaces in which high-rise buildings form a pattern. His town planning designs had worldwide influence.

The Modern style was challenged in the 1950s by a rougher style known as brutalism, characterized by chunky forms and exposed concrete. Brutalism was succeeded in the 1970s by the High Tech style, in which the constructive and technological aspects of a building are placed prominently on the exterior (eg the Pompidou Centre, Paris, 1971–2, and Lloyds of London, 1979–85, both by architect Richard Rogers (1933– )). The end of the 20c saw an unprecedented internationalization of the architecture of prestigious buildings, allied to a more successful, varied and imaginative integration of technological developments and new materials than had been achieved in the building boom of the 1960s, many of whose structures were being demolished after only a 40-year life. Something like the infinite range of styles available in the high Victorian era, though on a vastly more sophisticated material basis, seemed to be emerging as the norm. ► **Painting**; **Sculpture**

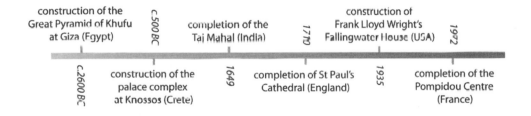

structure based on a hereditary ruler, the *cacique*, who possessed a ceremonial stool (*duho*). A priestly caste controlled worship of gods of place and nature (*zemis*), and ceremonies which led to *coyaba* (heaven). Notable Arawak caciques included Hautey (Cuba), and Guarionex and Anacaona (Hispaniola). They were exterminated as a people by the Spanish after 1519. The words maize, tobacco, potato, hammock, canoe and hurricane all derive from the Arawak language.

**Arbatov, Georgi Arkadevich** (1923–)
Soviet journalist, academic, party official and adviser to Mikhail **GORBACHEV**. A Russian born in the Ukraine, he graduated in international relations, was a contributor to serious periodicals and got his first academic posting in 1962. His first Communist Party appointment came in 1964 and his major break-

through was in 1967, becoming Director of the Institute for American Studies. This made him chief Soviet interpreter of US policies, a role that acquired a new importance with Gorbachev's rise to power. He clearly influenced the Gorbachev–**REAGAN** link that ended the **COLD WAR**. In the late 1980s, however, the need for his talents declined.

**Arbenz (Guzmán), Jácobo** (1913–71)
Guatemalan soldier and politician. He joined the Revolutionary Action Party and was one of the group who overthrew the dictator Jorge Ubico Castañeda in 1944. In 1949 he was appointed Minister of War in Juan José **ARÉVALO**'s government, and in 1951 he succeeded Arévalo as President of Guatemala, supported by the army and by various left-wing parties. He introduced wide-ranging agrarian reforms, including the increase of taxes on large landowners

and the attempted expropriation of foreign holdings, both of which affected the huge US-based UNITED FRUIT COMPANY. Before long Arbenz's administration was branded communist and EISENHOWER ordered the CIA to muster troops in neighbouring countries. The Guatemalan army heard exaggerated stories of the size of the US force and refused to fight for Arbenz, who in 1954 was forced to resign to give way to a military junta led by Colonel Carlos Castillo Armas.

## arbitristas

The name given to the writers who put forward proposals (*arbitrios*) to solve the problems of CASTILE in the late 16c and early 17c. The majority of them were concerned with questions of economy, inflation, taxation and population decline; but some were also concerned with questions of imperial power. Among the best known of them were Martín González de Cellorigo, Sancho de Moncada and Pedro Fernández de Navarrete.

## Arbroath, Declaration of (6 Apr 1320)

A response by Scottish barons, with the support of the Church, to a demand from Pope JOHN XXII that the Scots make peace with England. The pope did not recognize Robert BRUCE as King of Scotland. Almost certainly written by Bruce's Chancellor, Bernard de Linton, also Abbot of Arbroath, the declaration asserted the separate nationhood of Scotland and the integrity of its 'uninterrupted succession of 113 Kings, all of our own native and royal stock'. The declaration, a skilful and effective piece of anti-English propaganda, declared that the signatories would never 'consent to subject our selves to the dominion of the English' and urged the pope to take note of the wrong and calamities to the Church and State which had been wrought by the English incursions. Unsurprisingly, it became a key document for supporters of a separate Scottish nation.

## Archaeology ▶ *See panel*

## Architecture ▶ *See panel*

## Arcot

Small town and principality in India near Madras, capital of the Carnatic under the MUGHAL EMPIRE. Arcot is principally known for the daring diversionary tactic of CLIVE OF PLASSEY, embarking on his first command in 1751. By capturing the town and defending it against a much larger force of French and Carnatic troops, Clive forced the Nawab and the French to move troops from Trichinopoly, ending the stalemate which had pervaded the war. Ultimately, Clive's victory at Arcot resulted in British control of the Madras region.

## Arditi

Volunteer commandos set up in Italy by General DÍAZ towards the end of WORLD WAR I. Many joined the FASCIST PARTY after the war, feeling betrayed by the peace settlements. It was in imitation of their uniform that the fascists adopted black shirts. ▶ MUTILATED VICTORY

## Aref, Abd al-Salam (1921–66)

Iraqi politician. He took over as Ba'ath socialist President of Iraq from Abd al-Krim QASSIM in 1963. Amongst his achievements were improved relations with Gamal Abd al-NASSER's Egypt and the nationalization of the oil industry. Under Ba'athist ideological influences, he moved further towards the establishment of Iraq as a secular state, but his rule ended suddenly with his death in a helicopter crash. He was succeeded by his brother, Abd al-Rahman Aref, until he was toppled in the Ba'ath coup of July 1968 and replaced as President by Hasan al-BAKR, who ruled in concert with the Ba'ath leader, Saddam HUSSEIN.

## Arens, Moshe (1925– )

Israeli politician, born in Lithuania. Educated at Massachusetts and California Institutes of Technology, he lectured in aeronautical engineering at the Israel Institute of Technology, Haifa, and was Deputy Director of Israel Aircraft Industries before entering the Knesset in 1973. He served as Ambassador to the USA (1982–3), Minister of Defence (1983–4) and then as a Minister without portfolio until 1987, when he was appointed Foreign Minister (1987–90). He then returned to his former role of Minister of Defence (1990–2). In 1999 he briefly filled this role again in the government of Binyamin NETANYAHU which fell later that year. ▶ LIKUD

## Arévalo (Bermejo), Juan José (1904–90)

Guatemalan politician. He came to power as President of Guatemala in 1945 following the coup that had ousted the military dictator, Jorge Ubico Castañeda, the previous year. During his administration (1945–51), Arévalo encouraged the labour movement and instituted far-reaching social reforms, including the introduction of a social security system and major health and education programmes. Externally he pursued a nationalistic foreign policy, and revisited the old dispute over British-owned Belize. In 1951 he was succeeded by Jácobo ARBENZ.

## Argenson, René Louis, Marquis of (1694–1757)

French politician, the son of the Marquis of Argenson (1652–1721) who created the secret police and established the LETTRES DE CACHET. He became councillor to the PARLEMENT of Paris in 1716, and Foreign Minister (1744–7). He fell a victim in 1747 to the machinations of Madame de POMPADOUR, as ten years later did his brother, Marc Pierre, Count of Argenson (1696–1764), who became War Minister in 1743.

## ARGENTINA official name Argentine Republic

A republic in south-eastern South America, bounded to the east by the southern Atlantic Ocean; to the west by Chile; to the north by Bolivia and Paraguay; and to the north-east by Brazil and Uruguay. The majority of the population is of European origin and the remainder is of mestizo or South American Indian origin. Argentina was settled in the 16c by the Spanish. It declared its independence in 1816, and the United Provinces of the Río de la Plata were established. A federal constitution was agreed in 1853. Following a war with Paraguay in 1865–70, Argentina acquired the GRAN CHACO plain. A 1943 coup introduced military rule, before Juan PÉRON became President in 1946. His overthrow in 1955 was followed by long periods of military rule broken by brief spells of civilian rule. After an attempt to gain control of the Falkland Islands in 1982 resulted in defeat in the FALKLANDS WAR with the UK, civilian rule was re-established in 1983, when Raúl ALFONSÍN became President; he was

succeed by Carlos **MENEM** in 1989. Economic collapse in 2001 saw a return to political instability.

### Argentine–Brazilian War (1825–8)
A war fought to decide the possession of the Banda Oriental, territory to the east of the River Uruguay, whose separate status was confirmed by the adoption of a constitution in 1830. The vicissitudes of the war provoked profound political change in both major combatants, contributing to the fall of both Bernardino Rividavia and the *unitarios* in Buenos Aires and **PEDRO I** in Rio de Janeiro. ► **ARTIGAS, JOSÉ GERVASIO**; **ROSAS, JUAN MANUEL DE**

### Argyll, Archibald Campbell, 5th Earl of (1530–73)
Scottish nobleman. The son of the 4th Earl, he was a Protestant follower of **MARY, QUEEN OF SCOTS**. He succeeded to the earldom in 1558 and was involved in the assassination of her husband, Lord **DARNLEY** (1567). He later supported King **JAMES VI AND I** and became Lord High Chancellor of Scotland in 1572.

### Arias Navarro, Carlos (1908–88)
Spanish politician. Notorious as the 'Butcher of Malaga' for being state prosecutor there during the Nationalists' savage repression during the **SPANISH CIVIL WAR**, from 1957 to 1965 he was the Director-General of Security and from 1965 to 1973 the Mayor of Madrid. Named Minister of the Interior (June 1973), he became Prime Minister after the assassination of **CARRERO BLANCO** in Dec 1973. Following **FRANCO**'s death, he was confirmed as the first Prime Minister of the monarchy. He resigned in July 1976, having proven too hardline to effect the transition to democracy.

### Arias Sánchez, Oscar (1940– )
Costa Rican politician. He was educated in the UK, then returned to Costa Rica, where he started a law practice. He entered politics, joining the left-wing National Liberation Party (PLN) and eventually becoming its Secretary-General. Elected President of Costa Rica in 1986, on a neutralist platform, Arias Sánchez was the major author of a Central American peace agreement aimed at securing peace in the region, particularly in Nicaragua, and he was awarded the **NOBEL PEACE PRIZE** in 1987. Although enormously popular in Costa Rica, he was barred by the constitution from seeking re-election once his term of office ended in 1990, but in 2004 he announced his intention to run for the presidency again in 2006.

# *Armour*

*War & Warfare*

Armour is essentially any sturdy covering worn by warriors to protect them against injury in combat, and was developed in many cultures around the world in response to improvements in weaponry.

Warriors who fought on foot with spear or sword were able to use a shield, whether made of metal, wood or wickerwork, to ward off blows. Fighters who had to have both arms free, such as archers or charioteers, required a different form of protection. The first recorded type of armour was mail, small pieces of metal attached to a cloth garment, as in the metal-studded capes worn by the ancient Sumerians.

Ancient Egyptian warriors of the New Kingdom (c.1567–c.1085 BC) protected themselves against arrows with flexible coats of mail made with metal scales. Both the cavalry and infantry of the Assyrian Empire (at its height in 7–6c BC) were heavily armoured with mail.

It was in ancient Greece that the first solid-metal plate armour began to be used. A hoplite or armoured spearman went into battle in a full panoply of bronze helmet (covering the whole head, with openings at the eyes and nose), breastplate (often moulded in the shape of a naked male chest), shield and greaves (metal coverings for the shins). This type of protection was well-suited to the fairly static pitched battles of the time, based on powerful thrusting movements of the heavy infantry phalanx, but as **warfare** became more mobile, particularly with greater use of cavalry, a lighter form of protection was needed.

The Romans used the Greek style of breastplate increasingly only as a parade armour for generals. They developed chain mail (suits of interlinked metal rings) and their legionaries wore flexible coats made up of individual metal plates (*lamellae*). They improved on the Greek helmet by adding movable coverings for the cheeks.

The soldiers of the **Byzantine Empire**, both cavalry and infantry, wore steel helmets and long shirts of mail that reached to their thighs. In addition, cavalrymen were also equipped with steel shoes and gauntlets, and their horses wore breastplates in battle.

The chain mail shirt, or *byrnie*, was also developed in Western Europe, particularly among the **Franks** and Teutons, and came to replace the Roman-style breastplate. By the **Middle Ages**, improved metalworking techniques allowed the long mail tunic to be made more supple, less heavy, and more closely fitted to the body. Many fighters wore mail over a leather or quilted cloth coat called a *gambeson*, and a cloth surcoat over the mail itself. Further reinforcements were added to this in the form of plate metal coverings at vulnerable points such as elbows, knees and shins. By the time of the Crusades, the mounted knight wore a mail shirt down to his knees, chain armour on his hands and legs, a mail coif over his neck and head, and a flat-topped iron helmet, called a *pot-helm*, which protected the whole head and had slits

## Arielism

The moral credo of the Uruguayan philosopher and essayist José Enrique Rodó (1872–1917) which was set out in his highly influential work *Ariel* (1900, Eng trans 1922). At the heart of Arielism is a warning (given in the essay by the teacher Prospero) to young South Americans to shun materialism, as epitomized by North American, particularly US, society. Instead they are instructed that their idealism will create a better democracy and that they must draw on their own spiritual, intellectual and moral resources to progress through life.

## Arlington, Henry Bennet, 1st Earl of (1618–85)

English statesman. A member of the **CABAL** ministry under **CHARLES II**, and Secretary of State (1662–74), he was created Earl of Arlington in 1672. In 1674 he was impeached for embezzlement, and although cleared, resigned and became Lord Chamberlain. He negotiated the Triple Alliance against France (1668), and helped to develop the English party system.

## Armada, Spanish

A fleet of 130 Spanish ships, commanded by Medina Sidonia, carrying 20,000 soldiers and 8,500 sailors, sent by **PHILIP II** of Spain to invade England in 1588. The invasion was in retaliation for English support of Protestant rebels in the Netherlands, the execution of **MARY, QUEEN OF SCOTS** (1587), and raids on Spanish shipping, such as **DRAKE**'s at Cadiz (1587); Philip's aim was to gain control of the English Channel. The fleet, hampered by orders to rendezvous with Spanish forces in the Netherlands, was routed by English attacks off Gravelines (28–29 July 1588); 44 ships were lost in battles and during the flight home around

Scotland and Ireland. Although a victory for the English, counter-armadas were unsuccessful, and the war lasted until 1604. ► **ELIZABETH I**

## Armand, Inessa (1875–1920)

Russian politician. One of the most active women **BOLSHEVIKS**, she was a champion of Soviet women's causes. Born in Paris where her French father lived, she was brought up in Russia by a rich family after her parents died. Her intellectual interests and travels brought her into contact with **LENIN** and she joined his party in 1905. She was twice exiled, but she returned to Russia in 1917, and in 1919 became the founding head of *zhenotdel*, the women's section of the Communist Party. She set to, organizing branches everywhere, but died shortly thereafter of overwork and cholera. Zhenotdel, however, continued at least until 1930.

## ARMENIA official name **Republic of Armenia**

A mountainous republic in southern Transcaucasia, bounded to the north by Georgia; to the east and south-west by Azerbaijan; to the south-east by Iran; and to the north-west by Turkey. The Armenians are a Christian nation of Indo-European origin, speaking a language of that family with some Caucasian features. Their history goes back to the Roman period and includes years of relative independence; their highly developed ancient culture, particularly in fine art, architecture and sculpture, reached its zenith in the 14c. They are highly nationalistic, and their resentment of foreign domination during the 19c provoked their Russian and Turkish rulers. Those who were not retained under Turkish control were taken

through which the wearer could see and breathe. Armed with shield and lance, and mounted on heavy warhorses (*destriers*) which also carried some metal or padded protection, a charging force of such heavily armoured men could deliver an awesomely powerful shock to an opposing force. Not surprisingly, the cavalry charge was the most common and decisive battle tactic of the time.

As new powerful crossbows came into increasing use, it was discovered that chain mail was not proof against their bolts, and by the 13c many cavalrymen were wearing a *cuirass*, a plate metal covering for the torso that protected both the breast and back. The following century saw the development of full plate armour for mounted warriors, ending with the typical man-at-arms fighting while covered from head to toe in metal. While this afforded the wearer the ultimate in protection, apart from vulnerable spots like the armpit, it also greatly hampered the fighter's ease of movement. The making of armour became a highly skilled trade and some places, such as Milan and Nuremberg, became centres of excellence. Wealthy men were able to commission ever more elaborate and ostentatious suits of armour that were never destined to be worn in battle but were kept for ceremonial occasions or displayed in their homes.

The development and increasing use of portable firearms on the battlefield signalled the end of the widespread use of armour for the foot-soldier. None but the thickest of plate armour could withstand the strike of a bullet, and heavily laden infantrymen were no match for the highly mobile arquebusiers.

Most armour became ornamental, but many cavalrymen continued to wear cuirasses and helmets as protection against sword cuts. A notable example of this was the cavalry regiment commanded by Oliver **Cromwell** in the **English Civil Wars** (1642–8), whose use of back- and breastplates earned them the nickname of 'Ironsides'. Heavy cavalry such as the Napoleonic cuirassiers persisted with this form of armour well into the 19c, and cuirasses are worn to this day by cavalrymen on parades or performing ceremonial duties.

In other parts of the world different forms of armour were worn, using a wide range of materials, including animal bones, wood, wickerwork, quilted or studded textiles, and woven fibres. Chinese warriors often wore flexible coats of armoured plates similar to Roman designs. The mounted, highly mobile Mongol warriors of **Genghis Khan** wore light armour made of lacquered leather plate. The Japanese **samurai** typically wore a metal helmet and a layered, skirted garment of leather strengthened with iron. Such armour was often highly decorated, and the finest forms could be inlaid with silver and gold.

Although the 20c saw the eclipse of cavalry in modern warfare, perhaps surprisingly, armour experienced something of a revival. In **World War I** steel helmets to protect soldiers against shells were introduced by all the major armies, and the armoured vehicle, the tank, began to play a part on the battlefield. Other modern developments based on the introduction of new resistant materials include the flak jacket, worn by soldiers against shrapnel and bullets, the bullet-proof vest, and the types of helmets, shields and padded riot gear worn by many police forces. ▶ **Army**; **Warfare**

over by the Russians in 1828. During **World War I**, the Turks deported two-thirds of Armenians (1.75 million) to Syria and Palestine; 600,000 were either killed or died of starvation during the journey; later, many settled in Europe, the USA and the USSR. Galvanized by earlier Turkish massacres and encouraged by **Lenin**, Armenia declared its independence in 1918; however, it lost it again on Lenin's orders in 1920 for allegedly consorting with Soviet enemies. Armenia was proclaimed a Soviet Socialist Republic in 1920, and became a constituent republic of the USSR in 1936. At this time Soviet Armenia laid claim to Turkish Armenia. In 1988 there was a severe earthquake which harmed the economy, and further damage was done from 1991 by the escalation of a longstanding dispute with neighbouring **Azerbaijan** over Nagorno-Karabakh, a mountainous autonomous region ruled by Azerbaijan since 1923 despite having a mainly Armenian population. With the disintegration of the USSR, Armenia declared its independence in 1991 and became a member of the **CIS** (Commonwealth of Independent States). The follow-

ing year a state of emergency was declared as a result of the worsening economic situation, and the dispute with Azerbaijan escalated into full-scale war. A cease-fire agreement was reached in 1994 and Nagorno-Karabakh declared itself independent in 1996, but the conflict remained unresolved and the economy continued to suffer.

### Armenian Massacres (19–20c)
These killings resulted from the persecution of Armenians in the **Ottoman Empire** by Sultan **Abd ul-Hamid II** in 1894–6 and by the Young Turk government in 1915. By the late 1880s there were, in the Ottoman Empire, two and a half million Armenians who, encouraged by Russia, sought autonomy. When they refused to pay vastly increased taxes in 1894, Turkish troops killed thousands and burnt their villages. Two years later, Armenians seized the Ottoman Bank in Istanbul to draw European attention to their plight: this sparked off riots in which over 50,000 Armenians were killed. In **World War I** the secret recruitment of Turkish Armenians to fight on the side of Russia led the Turkish government to deport the Armenian population to Syria and Palestine, during which over half a million died of starvation or were killed.

### Armfelt, Gustaf Mauritz (1757–1814)
Swedish soldier and politician. Born in Finland, he was a favourite of King **Gustav III** towards the end of his reign. He fought in Gustav's war against Russia (1788–90) and helped to negotiate the Peace of Värälä. Armfelt was a member of the regency council during the minority of **Gustav IV Adolf** and was Swedish ambassador in Vienna in 1802–4. He

# Army

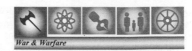

*War & Warfare*

Organized armies have been in existence since earliest recorded times. In Mesopotamia in the third millennium BC contending armies of such peoples as the Sumerians, Babylonians and Akkadians were essentially similar in composition. The basic tactic of these forces involved forming a phalanx, or tight formation, of spear-carrying infantry. Archers softened up the enemy, and war chariots were used in pursuit. Archers became more important with the introduction of the composite bow. This was made of different materials, essentially wood, horn, sinew and glue, bonded together to give greater strength and tension than a bow made purely of wood. This was the principal weapon of the armies of ancient Egypt. Egyptian pharaohs could call on a professional corps of royal guards, supplemented with militia supplied by local governors. In addition, later pharaohs such as Ramesses II (c.1290/c.1224 BC) also employed foreign mercenaries.

The armies of the Assyrians were the first to make great use of cavalry, whose mounted spearmen would charge the enemy head-on while mounted archers attacked on the wings. The cavalry would be supported by chariots and infantry consisting of spearmen, archers and slingmen. The Assyrians maintained a regular army and all males were required to perform a spell of military service. Numbers were bolstered by conquered peoples being compelled into service.

In ancient Greece armies were based on heavy infantry, with the spear as the principal weapon. Hoplites, heavy infantrymen armed with an eight-foot thrusting spear, shield, sword, helmet, breastplate and greaves were deployed in phalanxes, which decided battles by making thrusting advances against enemy formations. The militarized state of Sparta saw this type of warfare brought to its height, with the entire Spartan male population constituting a standing army, and boys being trained in fighting techniques from an early age under harsh discipline.

The phalanx was still central to the Macedonian army of Alexander III, the Great (356–323 BC), which was the most well-organized, trained, and equipped military force yet seen. The royal bodyguard of professional cavalry and infantry was supplemented by local militia as well as soldiers from allied or conquered peoples such as Cretan archers, Thessalian heavy cavalry and Thracian lancers. Alexander deployed his phalanxes to engage and hold the enemy while the decisive strokes were delivered by his cavalry.

The armies of ancient Rome developed from a citizen levy to a largely professional body maintained not by the state but by generals, to whom the soldiers thus owed their loyalty. The Roman legions that conquered an empire were organized around heavy infantry, armed with shields, javelins and short stabbing swords, supported by lighter infantry and cavalry usually supplied by allied peoples.

In the early **Middle Ages** lighter infantry and cavalry were more common, but in the Frankish army of Charlemagne (742–814) heavy, armoured cavalry became more important. The feudal system became the basis for military organization, binding fighting men to military service as payment for being granted land by an overlord, and creating more homogeneous, disciplined forces bound by mutual obligation. Feudal cavalry formed the striking force of armies

---

commanded the Swedish army against **NAPOLEON I** in Pomerania. After the deposition of Gustav IV Adolf in 1809, Armfelt was exiled by his successor, **CHARLES XIII**, and entered Russian service. He became Governor-General of Finland, now a grand duchy under the Russian tsar.

**Armour** ► *See panel*

**Army** ► *See panel*

### Army, (British) Indian (1748–1947)

British-controlled and officered military force in India in which the rank and file were recruited from the native populace, although some purely European regiments existed until 1860. The Indian Army served abroad as well as in India, and was a mainstay of the Pax Britannica. It was originally formed from guards used to protect properties of the British **EAST INDIA COMPANY** and Indian soldiers known as sepoys. In 1748 the growing French presence in Madras and continuing bad relations between France and Britain caused the Company to organize a permanent military force in India. Until 1759, when the size and organization of units were standardized, the armies of the Bengal, Bombay and Madras presidencies developed entirely independently, and expanded at different rates. By 1796, when two-battalion native infantry regiments were instituted, Bengal had twelve, Madras eleven and Bombay six. Bengal and Madras also had cavalry regiments, although these were less strictly regulated and sometimes amounted to élite private units raised and commanded by enthusiastic Com-

pany officials. The growth of the military reflected the Company's increased territorial acquisitions and responsibility for what had been Mughal administration. For all its size, the Indian Army in the first half of the 19c was inefficient and amateur; defects became apparent especially amongst the exclusively European officer cadre. Following the mutiny of the Bengal Army and the **INDIAN UPRISING** of 1857–8, the East India Company was dissolved and the Indian Army became the property of the Crown. By 1861 European regiments had been transferred to the British Army. The main functions of the Army between 1858 and 1914 were guarding the North-West Frontier and maintenance of order, although it was designed to be used in emergencies between Suez and Hong Kong. In 1895, the armies of the three presidencies were amalgamated into one British Indian Army. In 1903 Lord **KITCHENER** administratively combined the Staff and Troops, and renamed the force the Indian Army. Because of their performance during **WORLD WAR I** and the changing political climate, Indians became eligible for the King's Commission in 1917. In 1922 the Army was again reorganized and 'Indianization' of the officer corps was accelerated. By 1924 there were eight wholly Indian units and in 1934 an Indian military academy for the training of officers was opened at Dehra Dun. In **WORLD WAR II** units of the Indian Army were employed throughout the world in the Allied cause, although the bulk of the force fought in Burma (now Myanmar) and remained in India to maintain order. With Indian independence

in early medieval Europe until the development of such infantry weapons as the longbow and the pike allowed them to be effectively countered on the field, leading to the need for combinatons of weapons and paid contract service by specialists in the late medieval period.

The increasing refinement and spread of firearms brought about radical changes in the composition of armies. Arquebusiers (soldiers armed with handguns) were increasingly employed and the infantryman armed with a firearm became the most important component of any military formation, retaining its primacy until the 20c.

In the 17c armies became larger, more professional and more permanent, in what has been described as the 'Military Revolution'. Not only did states need to garrison their frontiers, but the increasing mobility and technical skill of military forces meant that they also had to be ready to maintain an army at all times of the year, not just in the 'campaigning season', even if armies usually went into winter quarters in the worst weather. These standing armies were costly to maintain but this in turn stimulated industry and agriculture at home.

All over Europe the lesser nobility increasingly adopted a military career and made up most of the officer corps. Increased professionalism was shown in the emphasis placed on drill in such armies as that of **Gustav II Adolf**. Discipline became ever more important and the introduction of uniforms helped forge unity and *esprit de corps*.

The **French Revolution** saw a huge leap in the size of armies based on the ability of the French Republic to mobilize manpower and resources on an unprecedented scale because of its ideological claims on its citizens. The core of the army remained the non-commissioned and junior officers of the old royal army, but class restrictions on access to commissions were lifted, promotion was purely on merit, and mass conscription filled the ranks. When **Napoleon I**, an artillery officer in the royal army, came to power he retained these innovations and expanded the army into a body that dominated Europe. He also built on the advanced **artillery** traditions of the pre-revolutionary French army, accelerating the emerging dominance of artillery on the battlefield in the 19c and early 20c.

The **Industrial Revolution** provided armies with new and more efficient weapons, like breech-loading rifles, as well as larger populations from which to recruit, and the growth of **railways** allowed even greater mobility, as was seen in their use during the **American Civil War**.

An arms race between conscripted mass forces took place in Europe in the later 19c until the outbreak of **World War I**, which left most armies with essentially similar armaments in rifles and artillery. Uniforms became increasingly standardized, such as the British khaki and the German field grey, while specialist units proliferated, such as engineers, signallers and medical units.

The regular British Army that entered World War I was greatly expanded by the thousands of volunteers whose patriotic fervour drove them to join up. However, as the unparalleled attrition of the Western Front claimed so many lives, mass conscription had to be introduced, even in Britain, and this took place again in **World War II**. This experience of total war and the involvement of the majority of the population in the armed forces was not typical of the later 20c, however, with the established trend being towards ever smaller standing armies, made up of regular professional soldiers viewing the army as a career, trained in specialist roles (not the least being peace-keeping duties rather than combat) and equipped with technologically advanced weaponry.

in 1947, the British Indian Army ceased to exist, its resources having been divided equally between India and Pakistan ► **BRITISH INDIA**; **SEPOY**

**Arnhem, Battle of** (Sep 1944)
Major conflict in occupied Dutch territory towards the end of **WORLD WAR II**, in which the German forces thwarted Allied attempts to break through. Operation 'Market Garden' was designed by Field Marshal **MONT-GOMERY**, and involved the largest airlift operation of the war, parachuting 10,000 troops on 17 Sep 1944 into the Dutch rivers area, to take key bridges over the Rhine, Maas and Waal. Allied forces advanced to Nijmegen, but at Arnhem met the 9th and 10th German Panzer divisions, which successfully resisted attack and eventually forced an Allied withdrawal on 25 Sep to behind the Rhine River.

**Arnim, Hans Georg von** (1581–1641)
German soldier and diplomat. Born in Brandenburg, he joined the Swedish army and served in the war with Russia (1613–17). However, after falling out with **GUSTAV II ADOLF**, he transferred to Poland to fight Sweden in 1621. Although a Protestant, he next entered the service of the emperor in 1626 and soon rose to be the right hand of **WALLENSTEIN**. However, when, in 1629, the edict of restitution was passed, Arnim resigned; he devoted himself to the formation of a third force in the raging conflict, decidedly Protestant but ready for compromise and with a view to maintaining the unity of the Reich against all foreign interventions. He took command of the Saxon army

and advocated an alliance with Sweden (1631), but stayed in close contact with Wallenstein all the same. The latter's fall destroyed what slim chances of success there were for his scheme. Lacking full support from his master, the Elector of Saxony, and distrusted by both the emperor and Sweden, Arnim retired in 1635.

**Arnold, Benedict** (1741–1801)
US general and turncoat. In the **AMERICAN REVOLUTION** he joined the colonial forces, and for his gallantry at the siege of Quebec (1775) was made a brigadier-general. He also fought with distinction at the Battles of Ridgefield and **SARATOGA**, and in 1778 was placed in command of Philadelphia. His resentment at being passed over for promotion, followed by his marriage to a woman of loyalist sympathies, led him to conspire with John André to deliver West Point to the British. When the plan was detected and André was captured, Arnold fled behind British lines, and was given a command in the royal army. After the war he lived in obscurity in London, where he died.

**Arnold of Brescia** (c.1100–55)
Italian churchman and politician. Born at Brescia, he was possibly educated in France under Abelard. He adopted the monastic life, but his preaching against the wealth and power of the Church led to his banishment from Italy (1139). He returned to Rome in 1145 and became involved in an insurrection against the papal government, which continued for some ten years. When this movement failed, he fled, but was

# Artillery

War & Warfare

The earliest form of artillery was the catapult, essentially a device for hurling a projectile at an enemy. The ancient Greeks used catapults that worked by tightening ropes, made usually of horsehair, building up sufficient tension in a single wooden arm to propel the projectile on release. The *onager* was an example of this, and was capable of throwing stones of enormous size. The Greeks also used a type of machine similar to a crossbow to fire large arrows. The Romans further developed these weapons, along with the *ballista*, a catapult in which the missile was propelled from between two uprights.

At this stage artillery was cumbersome and static and was mostly used in siege warfare, to batter enemy defences. Alexander III, the Great (356–323 BC) was the first commander to make use of artillery in the field, and catapults were carried on pack animals throughout his campaigns.

The next significant development was 'Greek fire', a petroleum-based compound that was thrown in earthenware vessels or launched from tubes, and used primarily in naval conflicts. It originated with the Byzantines in the 7c, and was in use against the Arab fleet that attacked Constantinople in 673. Although its precise ingredients remain a mystery, it was clearly a highly effective means of setting fire to the enemy and its vessels.

With the invention of gunpowder in China over 1,000 years ago, there emerged a new and highly effective artillery propellant, and by the end of the Tang Dynasty the Chinese were using gunpowder bombs in their catapults. In Europe, gunpowder was introduced in the 14c, and the first cannon were produced shortly afterwards. The English forces at the Battle of **Crécy** used six prototype cannon, although a number of these exploded before firing and probably killed more English gunners than enemy forces. More substantial bronze guns were cast, but these were difficult to manoeuvre and lacked accuracy. Their tendency to explode before firing was also a continuing problem, one notable casualty being the Scots King **James II** who was killed at the siege of Roxburgh in 1460.

As improved methods of casting resulted in stronger barrels, guns became more common in **warfare**, especially at sieges. The first strikingly decisive use of siege cannon was in 1415 when the artillery of **Henry V** destroyed the walls of Harfleur. It was widely appreciated that old methods of making fortifications impregnable were no longer valid. The French made great advances in siege artillery and it played a major part in their expulsion of the English during the **Hundred Years' War**. Their artillery commander Jean Bureau carried out dozens of successful sieges, and by the 1450s could bring as many as 250 guns into the field.

During the **Hussite War**, John **Ziska**, a commander in the forces rebelling against Emperor **Sigismund**, made the first important use of more mobile field artillery. He mounted his guns on wagons drawn by bullocks or horses and was able to bring them into use against enemy cavalry and infantry, as well as against fortifications.

By the late 15c proper, horse-drawn gun carriages were being used, which were able to keep up with an army on the march. Another contemporary improvement was the use of *trunnions*, a pair of horizontal projections on a cannon barrel, one on each side, that allowed easier and more precise elevation and depression of the gun. However, truly mobile and rapid-firing field guns did not appear until the 17c.

Engineers constructing fortifications had tried to keep pace with the more powerful siege weapons, building low, thick walls sunk in a complex of defensive ditches and studded with projecting bastions which allowed the enfilade of gunfire along the walls. First developed in Italy in the 15c, this *trace italienne* style spread all over Western Europe and into the Spanish Caribbean by the 16c. This in turn led to the increase in the size and power of siege guns brought against them. Accuracy was improved through better casting, gunpowder was refined to give more power, and longer barrels (up to 18ft/6m) giving greater range were brought in. Mortars – short-barrelled guns designed to lob missiles a short distance up and over defences – were introduced, and cheaper iron began to be used in place of bronze. Even so, the essential design of the muzzle-loading gun remained unchanged.

European artillery expertise was being adopted elsewhere during this period. In 1453 the Turkish Sultan, Mohammed II, used siege guns to pound breaches in the great walls of Constantinople in a long-lasting bombardment, making it only a matter of time before the city succumbed to his infantry.

Further advances in lighter, more mobile guns continued, and the Swedish King, **Gustav II Adolf**, exploited these to the full in his campaigns during the **Thirty Years' War**. His artillerymen made great use of weapons light enough to be drawn by a single horse, firing grapeshot and canister-shot against massed formations of enemy forces.

---

captured by the forces of Emperor **FREDERICK I, BAR-BAROSSA**, brought to Rome, condemned for heresy, and hanged.

### Arras, Union of (6 Jan 1579)

During the **EIGHTY YEARS' WAR** the southern Netherlands principalities of Artois, Hainaut and Douai formed the union with the intention of returning to the Catholic rule of **PHILIP II** of Spain. Later the same month, on 23 Jan, the other Netherlands provinces formed the Union of **UTRECHT** in opposition. Together with other French-speaking southern provinces in the Netherlands, the members of the Union of Arras signed a treaty (17 May 1579) which contributed to the final separation of the southern from the northern Netherlands, and therefore to the

eventual independence of the Dutch Republic.

### Arriaga, Manoel José de (1840–1917)

Portuguese politician. He took part in the revolution of 1910 which overthrew King **MANUEL II**, and was the first elected President of the Republic (1911–15).

### Arrow Cross (1938–45)

Hungarian right-wing fascist-type party. Like similar parties in other East European countries, it emerged from a combination of nationalist dissatisfaction, anti-**COMMUNISM** and anti-Semitism that was rooted in the failure of successive Hungarian governments to reverse the defeat marked by the Treaty of **TRIANON** in 1920 or to overcome the 1929 depression. These feelings were strengthened by the successes of

In the 18c the Duke of **Marlborough** carried on Gustav's integration of artillery with the infantry and cavalry arms, taking great care in siting his batteries. It was this period that saw the development of the prolonged artillery duel as the opening act in a pitched battle, with gunners exchanging cannonballs at long distance before switching to case-shot (canisters full of musket balls) to deal with attackers at shorter range.

**Napoleon I**, himself an artillery officer, introduced new gunnery tactics. Helped by the latest industrial techniques, he was able to deploy more guns than ever before, and he used massed artillery to punch holes in enemy formations before launching his infantry attacks.

Breech-loading weapons were increasingly introduced after 1815, although this entailed initial sacrifices to increased weight and decreased mobility. Through time, and the experience of 19c conflicts such as the **American Civil War**, where smooth-bore cannon were used at short range but where long-range rifled artillery came to dominate sieges, these problems were dealt with, and the turn of the century saw most armies equipped with the types of gun that remained the standard design through both the World Wars. These included light field weapons, long-range heavy guns, howitzers (squat-barrelled guns designed to fire at a steep angle), and, reintroduced for trench warfare, the mortar.

The world had never seen such concentrated shelling as that which took place in **World War I**. The tactic was simple: to pound the enemy's trenches and barbed wire so heavy that the infantry would merely have to advance and take possession of ground. However, as in the past, techniques of building defences improved, and soon defenders were able to sit out a bombardment in immensely strong dugouts before emerging to mow down the enemy infantry. New types of shell were developed, including high-explosive, smoke and gas, and massive railway-mounted long-range guns ('Big Berthas') appeared. Artillery tactics became very sophisticated, and it was artillery, rather than the tank, which won the war for the Allies in 1918.

**World War II** saw many a battle between artillery and tanks, and some guns became specialized for anti-tank use, firing armour-piercing rounds. Rocket-launchers were also developed, as well as the German V1 and V2 missiles. Developments in the late 20c include chemical and nuclear shells, as well as 'smart' rounds guided to the target by laser or homing devices. These 'smart' projectiles, along with sophisticated fire control, ensured that field artillery was more economical than ever before.

### Naval artillery in the 20c
The enormous discrepancy between rounds fired and hits, which was particularly marked in naval warfare in the late 19c and 20c, became a thing of the past with the advent of new technology. So did heavy naval guns. The wooden ships and ironclads of the 18c and 19c had mounted as many as 110 smooth-bore guns which were fired in broadsides at short range. With the evolution of the armoured 'Dreadnought' big-gun battleships of the early 20c, warships mounted increasingly large guns in turrets. The British Navy's standard heavy gun was eventually a 15-inch piece, but the problem of firing accurate salvoes was huge until radar control came in at the end of World War II. By the end of the 20c, naval heavy guns had been rendered obsolete by various missiles and carrier-borne **aircraft**. ► **Fortification**

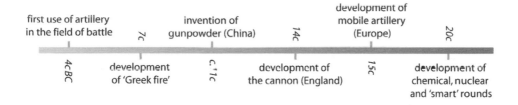

MUSSOLINI and HITLER, and leaders were found in malcontents such as SZALASI, a former officer who became Prime Minister in 1944.

### Arrow War (Second Opium War) (1856–60)
A conflict between Britain and China, which began when the Hong Kong-registered ship *Arrow*, flying the British flag, was boarded at Canton (Guangzhou) by the Chinese, who arrested most of the crew for piracy. British warships and troops then attacked Canton and were initially repulsed, but a combined British and French force took it the following year, and proceeded north, threatening Beijing. The Treaty of TIANJIN (Tientsin) that concluded hostilities opened additional TREATY PORTS to foreign trade, legalized the opium traffic, and facilitated Christian missionary activity. ► OPIUM WARS

### Arsenije III Črnojević, also known as Arsen III (1633–1706)
Serbian Patriarch of Peć. During the Vienna War (1684–99) he met General Piccolomini at Prizren in southern KOSOVO and arranged for c.20,000 Serbs and Albanians from Ottoman territory to enter the service of Emperor LEOPOLD I. In 1690 he led 70,000–80,000 Serbs into southern Hungary and established a religious and cultural centre for the Serbs at Sremski Karlovci in the VOJVODINA. During the 19c the descendants of these migrants, known as the *prečani* ('across-the-river') Serbs, were to play an important role in the Serbian national revival.

**Artevelde, Jacob van** (c.1290–1345)
Flemish statesman. A burgess of Ghent, he led his town in a revolt against the pro-French policies of Count **LOUIS OF NEVERS**. Thus he sided with England at the beginning of the **HUNDRED YEARS' WAR**. He concluded a treaty with **EDWARD III** (1340), and was effectively Governor of Flanders, but when he proposed that the Black Prince should be elected Count of Flanders, he was killed in a popular insurrection.

**Artevelde, Philip van** (1340–82)
Flemish leader. He was taken to England when his father, Jacob van **ARTEVELDE**, was murdered in 1345. He returned in 1360, and in 1382 led the people of Ghent in their uprising against Count Louis II of Flanders. Against all odds Van Artevelde won the Battle of Beverhoutsveld (May 1382), but lost to Count Louis and his French allies at the Battle of Westrozebeke (Nov 1382), where he perished.

**Arthur** (1187–1203)
Claimant to the English throne. He was the posthumous son of Geoffrey (**HENRY II**'s fourth son) by Constance, Duchess of Brittany. On the death of **RICHARD I** (1199), Arthur claimed the English crown; and the French King, **PHILIP II**, for a while supported his bid for the throne. However, King **JOHN** had him captured and murdered.

**Arthur, Chester Alan** (1830–86)
US politician and 21st President. He qualified in law, and then became leader of the **REPUBLICAN PARTY** in New York State. He was Vice-President when James A **GARFIELD** became President (1881), and succeeded him on his death, holding the presidency from 1881 until 1885. During his administration he supported civil service and vetoed a Chinese exclusion bill.

**Articles of Confederation**
The constitution of the USA from 1781 to 1788. Prepared by the **CONTINENTAL CONGRESS**, it established a single-house **CONGRESS**, with one vote for each state and with no executive, courts, or independent revenue. Its weaknesses led to its replacement by the present **US CONSTITUTION** in 1788.

**Artigas, José Gervasio** (1774–1850)
Spanish American soldier and revolutionary hero of Uruguay. A **GAUCHO** in his youth, and then army officer in Spanish service, he sided with Buenos Aires against Spain in 1811, and fought Buenos Aires in 1813–14, and the Portuguese between 1817 and 1820. Unable to hold the littoral, Artigas fled to **FRANCIA**'s Paraguay (1820), where he lived in exile until his death. Uruguay finally became independent on 27 Aug 1828. ► **SPANISH-AMERICAN WARS OF INDEPENDENCE**

**Artillery** ► *See panel*

**Artyukhina, Alexandra Vasilevna** (1889–1969)
Soviet politician. An early champion of Soviet **WOMEN'S RIGHTS**, she failed in the face of traditional male chauvinism. A textile worker, she was active in the union movement in the pre-revolutionary period and was arrested several times. She held various government jobs after the **RUSSIAN REVOLUTION**, but in 1927 she was appointed head of *zhenotdel*, the women's section of the **COMMUNIST PARTY OF THE SOVIET UNION**. In this she did much good work until

it was shut down in 1930. Thereafter, her jobs were more honorific than real, but at least she survived **STALIN**.

**Arunachalam, Ponnambalam** (1853–1924)
Ceylonese civil servant and politician. He was the first **TAMIL** to gain a place in the Ceylonese Civil Service through open competition, eventually rising to be Registrar-General of Ceylon. He later entered politics and ardently championed the cause of the Ceylon National Congress. He eventually left the Ceylonese National Congress owing to his disillusionment at the lack of Tamil representation in the Legislative Council provided for by the 1924 constitution.

**Arundel, Thomas** (1353–1414)
English prelate and statesman, third son of Robert Fitzalan, Earl of Arundel. He became Archdeacon of Taunton and Bishop of Ely (1373), then Archbishop of York (1388), and finally of Canterbury (1396). He supported the nobles opposed to **RICHARD II**, who banished him (1397), but he returned to help seat Henry of Lancaster on the throne (1399). He was a vigorous opponent of the **LOLLARDS**.

**Arusha Declaration** (29 Jan 1967)
Although strictly only Part IV, the Arusha Declaration usually refers to all of an important document, written under President Julius **NYERERE**'s direction and accepted by **TANGANYIKA AFRICAN NATIONAL UNION** (TANU)'s National Executive Committee in Arusha on 29 Jan 1967. It set out the assumptions underlying Tanzania's version of African socialism, emphasizing the dignity and equality of people, the primacy of rural production, self-reliance, the importance of hard work and the role of the party. Later documents ('Education for Self-Reliance', 'Socialism and Rural Development' and 'After the Arusha Declaration') developed Nyerere's ideas of creating a uniquely African and egalitarian socialism in Africa, but it proved economically disastrous although, for the most part, politically popular.

**Arya Samaj**
A dogmatic and militant Hindu sect (literally, 'Society of Nobles') founded c.1875 by Dyananda Sarasawati (1824–83). The latter demanded a return to the purity of the *Rig Veda* and its principles, as opposed to the accretions and corruptions that subsequently entered Hinduism. Many militant nationalists in the north-west of India, such as Lala **LAJPAT RAI**, belonged to this sect.

**Asad, Hafez al-** (1928–2000)
Syrian general and politician. He was Minister of Defence and Commander of the Air Force (1966–70), instigated a coup in 1970 and became Prime Minister and then President (1971–2000). He belonged to the minority **ALAWI** sect of Islam. After the 1973 Arab–Israeli War, he negotiated a partial withdrawal of Israeli troops from Syria. In 1976 he sent Syrian troops into Lebanon, and did so again in early 1987. By 1989 he had imposed Syrian control over the greater part of Lebanon. He enjoyed Soviet support, and was one of the few Arab leaders to support Iran in its war with Iraq. Following his sending of Syrian forces to join the **UN** coalition against Iraq in the **GULF WAR**, Syria's relations with Western nations improved. He was a

supporter of the Palestinian radicals against **ARAFAT**'s mainstream **PLO** (Palestine Liberation Organization) and in 1995 entered negotiations with Israel as part of the US-brokered Middle East peace process. He was succeeded as President by his son, Bashar al-Asad.
➤ **IRAN–IRAQ WAR**

**Asaf ud-Daula** (1775/97)
Nawab of Awadh (Oudh) during the governor-generalship of Warren **HASTINGS**. During his reign, Awadh was a Mughal buffer against the rising power of the British in Bengal. While Hastings was Governor of Bengal, his administrative council imposed the Treaty of Faizabad, also known as the Second Treaty of Benares (1775), on Asaf, increasing the subsidy he paid for the British military presence in Awadh, and ceding the sovereignty of Benares, Jaunpur and Ghazipur to the British **EAST INDIA COMPANY**. With the Treaty of Chunar (1781), Hastings attempted to interfere with the administration of Awadh. Hastings' part in the resumption of *jagirs* (government revenues from land) and removal of the treasures of Awadh formed a large part of the charges brought against him at his subsequent **IMPEACHMENT**.

**Asante** ➤ **ASHANTI**

**Asanuma Inejiro** (1898–1960)
Japanese politician. Initially he was a member of the **JAPAN COMMUNIST PARTY** and in 1924 was imprisoned for participating in anti-government demonstrations. In 1936 he was elected to the Diet as a member of the Social Masses Party (*Shakai Taishuto*), one of many pre-**WORLD WAR II** socialist parties. After 1945 he helped found the **JAPAN SOCIALIST PARTY**, becoming its Secretary-General. He acquired notoriety in 1959 on a visit to Beijing when he declared that US imperialism was the common enemy of China and Japan. In 1960 he was assassinated by a right-wing fanatic while attending a televised political rally.

**ASEAN** ➤ **ASSOCIATION OF SOUTH-EAST ASIAN NATIONS**

**Asen Dynasty**
The dynasty which ruled Bulgaria from 1187 to 1257. John (Ivan) Asen I (1187/96) with his brother Peter led the rebellion that freed Bulgaria from Byzantine suzerainty (c.1185). John then founded the second Bulgarian Empire and established his throne at Trnovo. John II (1190–1241) ruled from 1218 until his death. He renewed the Bulgarian patriarchate (1235), thereby securing the independence of the Bulgarian Church. ➤ **BULGARIAN EXARCHATE**

**Ashanti**
A Kwa-speaking Akan people of southern Ghana and adjacent areas of Togo and Côte d'Ivoire. They form a confederacy of chiefdoms, founded by the ruler Osei Tutu in the late 17c; the paramount chief was established at Kumasi, and the Golden Stool was the symbol of Ashanti unity. The independent Ashanti state was at the height of its powers in the early 19c, and became a major threat to British trade on the coast until defeated (1873) by a force under Sir Garnet **WOLSELEY**. The state was annexed by the British in 1902 after a further campaign in which the Golden Stool was seized and removed to London. Traditional culture and religion still flourish, with rich ceremonial and internationally famous art.

**Ashdown, 'Paddy' (Jeremy John Durham), Baron Ashdown of Norton-sub-Hamdon** (1941– )
British politician. After a career in the Royal Marines (1959–71) and the diplomatic service (1971–6) he entered politics, becoming Liberal MP for Yeovil (1983). He was Liberal spokesman on trade and industry (1983–6) and succeeded David Steel as leader of the Liberal Democrats (1988). In 1997 he led his party to its most successful general election result since 1929, winning 46 seats, and announced his resignation as party leader in Jan 1999. He was succeeded by Charles Kennedy, and in 2001 was made a life peer. In May 2002 the European Parliament appointed him as its High Representative in Bosnia and Herzegovina, responsible for administering the civilian aspects of the Dayton Peace Accord. ➤ **LIBERAL PARTY** (UK); **STEEL OF AIKWOOD, DAVID, BARON**

**Ashida Hitoshi** (1887–1959)
Japanese politician. Formerly a Finance Ministry bureaucrat, he was first elected to the Diet in 1932. In the first post-**WORLD WAR II** cabinet (Oct 1945) he was Minister of Health and Welfare. In 1947 he helped to organize the Democratic Party (*Nihon Minshuto*), one of the two principal conservative parties at the time. In June 1947 he joined a coalition cabinet headed by the socialist **KATAYAMA TETSU** and became Prime Minister when the coalition collapsed (Mar 1948). Ashida was a vigorous advocate of Japanese rearmament. In Oct 1948 he was forced to resign following alleged involvement in the Showa Denko scandal.

**Ashikaga Shogunate** (1338–1573)
In Japan, the second shogunal government, located in the vicinity of the imperial capital of Kyoto. The Ashikaga family, from central Honshu, was an offshoot of the **MINAMOTO FAMILY**, founders of the first shogunate. There were altogether 15 Ashikaga shoguns. Under the third **SHOGUN**, Yoshimitsu (1368/94), the imperial schism, originally caused by **DAIGO II**'s exile and establishment of a rival imperial court south of Kyoto, was ended when the two rival branches of the imperial family were united in 1392. During the 15c, however, increasingly powerful military governments undermined its control, leading to

### ASHIKAGA SHOGUNATE

| Regnal Dates | Name |
|---|---|
| 1338/58 | Ashikaga Takauji |
| 1358/67 | Ashikaga Yoshiakira |
| 1368/94 | Ashikaga Yoshimitsu |
| 1394/1423 | Ashikaga Yoshimochi |
| 1423/5 | Ashikaga Yoshikazu |
| 1429/41 | Ashikaga Yoshinori |
| 1442/3 | Ashikaga Yoshikatsu |
| 1449/73 | Ashikaga Yoshimasa |
| 1473/89 | Ashikaga Yoshihisa |
| 1490/3 | Ashikaga Yoshitane (1st reign) |
| 1494/1508 | Ashikaga Yoshizumi |
| 1508/21 | Ashikaga Yoshitane (2nd reign) |
| 1521/46 | Ashikaga Yoshiharu |
| 1546/65 | Ashikaga Yoshiteru |
| 1568 | Ashikaga Yoshihide |
| 1568/73 | Ashikaga Yoshiaki |

a series of bloody wars, with the result that the last Ashikaga shoguns became virtual puppets of their leading vassals.

**Ashikaga Takauji** (1305–58)
Japanese warrior leader. He was the founder of the second shogunal government, the ASHIKAGA (or Muromachi) SHOGUNATE. Originally sent by the previous KAMAKURA SHOGUNATE to quell forces loyal to Emperor DAIGO II, who had been exiled (1324) for attempting to assert direct imperial rule, Takauji turned against his former masters and allowed Daigo II to return. Yet in 1336 he himself forced the exile of Daigo II and installed a rival claimant on the throne, who conferred on Takauji the title of SHOGUN in 1338. For his betrayal of the Emperor, Takauji is condemned in Japanese historiography.

**Ashkenazim**
Jews of Central and East European descent, as distinguished from SEPHARDIM Jews, who are of Spanish or Portuguese descent. In the MIDDLE AGES, Europe and west Asia was divided between Christian and Islamic countries, resulting in the Ashkenazim being cut off. They developed their own customs, interpretation of the Talmud, music and language (Yiddish).

**Ashley, William Henry** (1778–1838)
US fur-trader and politician. He made money in mining, gunpowder manufacture and property speculation in the early 1800s, and in 1820 became the first Lieutenant-Governor of Missouri. In 1822 he and Andrew Henry set up the Rocky Mountain Fur Company and established a trading post at the mouth of the Yellowstone River, though Native American hostility soon drove them into the Central Rockies. They made expeditions across the mountains, travelling almost as far west as the Great Salt Lake, a route later followed by settlers journeying to Oregon. Ashley revolutionized the FUR TRADE by establishing annual meetings or temporary markets for fur-traders, which replaced the traditional trading posts and solved many difficulties the trappers had with marketing and transport. At these meetings, the first of which was held in 1825 at Green River (now in Wyoming), trappers would sell their furs to him and also buy what they needed for the year ahead. By 1827 Ashley had made a fortune and turned to politics. He was a member of the HOUSE OF REPRESENTATIVES from 1831 to 1837.

**asiento de negros**
Literally 'negro (slave) contract', this was the means whereby the Spanish crown farmed out the slave trade between Spain, Africa and the Spanish-American empire. The contractors were usually non-Spaniards: originally Genoese, from 1595 to 1640 they were Portuguese; from 1702 to 1713, French; and, from the Peace of UTRECHT in 1713 until 1750, British. ► SLAVERY

**Askiya**
The dynastic title of the rulers of SONGHAI, founded by Sunni Ali (1464/92) out of the disintegrating empire of Mali in Western Africa. The first *Askiya*, Muhammad Toure (d.1528), deposed Sunni Ali's successor c.1500 and extended the empire into Eastern Mali and the upper Volta basin. He also re-established Timbuktu as a centre of Islamic faith and

learning. He was deposed by his son in 1528 and Songhai went into decline. The empire dissolved altogether in 1591, when it was invaded by a Moroccan army, but descendants of the Songhai Askiyas continued to fight on against their Moroccan rulers well into the 17c.

**Aspromonte, Battle of** (Sep 1862)
Frustrated by the reluctance of the Italian government to seize Rome, GARIBALDI sought to take the city with a group of volunteers he had mustered in Sicily. RATTAZZI, who hitherto had not opposed Garibaldi's plans openly, feared RED SHIRTS would clash with the French garrison in Rome and sent regular troops to prevent their northward advance. The two forces met at Aspromonte, where a skirmish took place in which Garibaldi was wounded and captured. He was briefly held under arrest at La Spezia before receiving a royal amnesty.

**Asquith, H(erbert) H(enry), 1st Earl of Oxford and Asquith** (1852–1928)
British Liberal politician and Prime Minister. He was called to the Bar (1876), and became a QC (1890) and MP (1886), Home Secretary (1892–5), Chancellor of the Exchequer (1905–8) and Premier (1908–16). His regime was notable for the upholding of free trade, the introduction of old-age pensions, payment for MPs, the Parliament Act of 1911, Welsh disestablishment, suffragette troubles, the declaration of war (1914), the coalition ministry (1915) and the EASTER RISING (1916). His replacement as Premier by Lloyd George provoked lasting bitterness; in 1918 he led the Independent Liberals who rejected Lloyd George's continuing coalition with the Conservatives. He was created an earl in 1925. ► LIBERAL PARTY (UK); SUFFRAGETTES

**Assad, Hafez al-** ► ASAD, HAFEZ AL-

**Assassins**
An Isma'ili Shiite grouping. An offshoot of the FATIMID DYNASTY of Cairo, the sect was founded by an Isma'ili *da'i* ('missionary') called Hasan-i Sabbah in the late 11c in northern Persia. The name 'Assassins' is thought to have derived from their use of hashish, designed to give them the courage to carry out the attacks they believed their faith demanded as a duty. The sect's headquarters was at the virtually impregnable castle of Alamut in the Elburz Mountains in Iran, from where they achieved their ends by using murder (or assassination) as a political weapon. The sect spread also to Syria, where it was based in the Ansariyya Mountains and caused considerable problems for the Crusaders and for SALADIN. As a sect, it was finally dissolved by the MONGOLS in the mid-13c. The Nizaris, with whom the sect was linked, still exist as a sevener Shiite sect to this day, with the AGA KHAN as their leader.

**Assemblies**
A unique feature of the 'Old Representative System' which existed in the pre-19c British West Indies colonies. When the previous proprietary system of government was abolished in 1663, real legislative and financial power quickly devolved onto a forum of the unrepresentative, rich plantocracy, whose wealth made London's responsibility for the administration somewhat illusory. Aping the powers and prerogatives

of the House of **COMMONS** in England, the Assemblies resisted progressive legislation and imperial edict and countered all attempts to abolish them. So obstructive, oligarchic, self-interested and obscurantist had the Assemblies become, that when Britain took over Trinidad, Berbice-Essequibo and St Lucia after the **NAPOLEONIC WARS**, they were incorporated into the empire under **CROWN COLONY GOVERN-MENT**. Jamaica gave up its assembly after the **MORANT BAY REBELLION** (1866), but Barbados maintained an assembly until 1966.

### Assietta, Battle of (19 July 1747)
Famous Piedmontese victory in the War of **AUSTRIAN SUCCESSION** in which the troops of **CHARLES EMMAN-UEL III** halted the advance on Turin of a Franco-Spanish army.

### assignats
Originally, paper bonds issued by the Constituent Assembly in France (1789). They were later (1790) accepted as currency notes, in view of the shortage of coin, until the abolition of paper currency in 1797. ▶ **FRENCH REVOLUTION**

### Assize Court
A legal system in England and Wales, dating from the time of **HENRY II** of England, which was abolished by the Courts Act, 1971. Assize courts were presided over by High Court judges, who travelled on circuit to hear criminal and civil cases. The functions of Assize courts continue to be exercised by High Court judges sitting in Crown Courts throughout England and Wales.

### Association of German Princes
An association of 17 important German states organized by **FREDERICK II, THE GREAT** of Prussia. They agreed to uphold Imperial law and to defend one another's territory. It was designed to thwart the centralizing plans of Emperor **JOSEPH II** for the **HOLY ROMAN EMPIRE**. The association collapsed after Frederick's death (1786).

### Association of South-East Asian Nations (ASEAN)
An association formed in 1967 to promote regional stability and economic cooperation between Indonesia, Malaysia, the Philippines, Singapore and Thailand. It was later joined by Brunei (1984), Vietnam (1995), Laos (1997), Myanmar (1997) and Cambodia (1999); East Timor's post-independence attempts to join have been opposed by Indonesia and its supporters. Since 1978, when it sought by diplomatic means to end the Vietnamese occupation of Kampuchea (now Cambodia), it has become an important political force. Although it was originally strongly opposed to communist regimes in other Asian countries, its admission of communist Vietnam in 1995 showed it was becoming more flexible and comprehensive in outlook. In 1992 it took the first steps towards an ASEAN common market by creating the ASEAN Free Trade Area, and closer economic integration was initiated by a concord signed in Oct 2003.

### Astor, John Jacob (1763–1848)
German-born US millionaire. The son of a butcher, he emigrated to the USA in 1783 and eventually became the wealthiest man in America, worth more than US$20 million at his death. His first fortune was made through the Western **FUR TRADE**, the second in New York real estate. Astor used his friendship with **JEFFERSON** to advantage, in one instance gaining permission for one of his ships to sail to Canton during the 1807 embargo. Astor helped the government finance the **WAR OF 1812** by taking over and selling to the public the unsubscribed portion of a government loan. He also used his influence to ease through **CONGRESS** the Act establishing the Second Bank of the United States. His major philanthropy was the endowment of the Astor Library, now the New York Public Library.

### Astor, Nancy Witcher Langhorne Astor, Viscountess (1879–1964)
British politician. The first woman MP to sit in the House of **COMMONS** (1919–45), she succeeded her husband as MP for Plymouth in 1919, and became known for her interest in **WOMEN'S RIGHTS** and social problems, especially temperance.

### Astrid (1905–35)
Queen of the Belgians (1934/5). The daughter of Prince Charles of Sweden and Princess Ingeborg of Denmark, on 4 Nov 1926 she married **LEOPOLD III**, Crown Prince of Belgium, who succeeded to the throne on 23 Feb 1934, with Astrid as Queen. The mother of three children, Josephine-Charlotte, **BAUDOUIN I** and Albert, she was killed in a car accident near Küssnacht in Switzerland.

### Atahualpa (d.1533)
Last King of the Incas (1527/33). On his father's death (1527), he received the Kingdom of Quito, and in 1532, overwhelming his elder brother **HUÁSCAR**, seized Peru. At times over-confident of his strength, at others apprehensive of the Spaniards, his vacillations encouraged initial Spanish penetration and subsequent control. He was captured by the Spaniards, accused of plotting against **PIZARRO**, and executed.

### Atatürk, Mustapha Kemal, originally Mustafa Kemal (1881–1938)
Turkish army officer and politician. During **WORLD WAR I** he fought against the British in the **DARDANELLES** and earned the title *pasha*. He drove the Greeks from Anatolia (1919–22), raising a nationalist rebellion in protest against the post-war division of Turkey. In 1921 he established a provisional government in Ankara. The following year the Ottoman Sultanate was formally abolished, and Turkey was declared a secular republic, with Kemal as President (1923–38). The focus of a strong personality cult, he launched a programme of revolutionary social and political reform intended to transform Turkey from a feudal absolute monarchy into a modern republic. His reforms included the political emancipation of women (1934) and the introduction of the Latin alphabet to replace Arabic script, as well as increased educational opportunities and the suppression of traditional Islamic loyalties in favour of a secular Turkish nationalism. In 1934, upon the introduction of surnames into Turkey, he took the name Atatürk ('Father of the Turks'). ▶ **GRAECO-TURKISH WAR**; **LAUSANNE, TREATY OF**

### Athos, Mount
The site of a complex of 20 Orthodox monasteries on

the easternmost peninsula of Chalcidice in Greece. The first monastic community was established c.963, reaching the peak of its influence in the 15c, and later maintained good relations with the Ottoman Porte, **SELIM I, THE GRIM**, making a state visit. During the **GREEK WAR OF INDEPENDENCE** it joined the Greek insurgents but was defeated. Russian influence dominated in the period after the Treaty of **ADRIANOPLE** (1829). During the first of the **BALKAN WARS** it was occupied by Greek troops and was declared independent and neutral by the Treaties of **LONDON** (1913). In 1926 it became a theocratic republic under the suzerainty of Greece. As well as the Greek, the Russian, Bulgarian, Serbian and Romanian Orthodox Churches have communities on the mountain. ➤ **CONSTANTINOPLE, PATRIARCHATE OF**; **PORTE, THE SUBLIME**; **SAVA, ST**

**Atjeh War** (1873–1914)
Dutch colonial war fought between the Dutch East Indies (now Indonesia) and the inhabitants of Atjeh, the northernmost part of the island of Sumatra. In order to limit the activities of pirates, the Dutch sent a series of military expeditions against Atjeh which until 1900 proved unsuccessful and sometimes disastrous. The campaigns intensified as the imperialist movement meant that investment opportunities were sought in oil, mines and plantations. Under Governor-General J B van Heutsz (1851–1924) resistance was finally broken by 1912, not without reports of extreme atrocities. The Dutch then installed a full-scale civil administration in Atjeh. The war is estimated to have cost more than 100,000 lives, nearly all Indonesian.

**Atlantic, Battle of the** (1940–3)
The conflict arising out of German attacks on shipping in the Atlantic during **WORLD WAR II**. The German strategy was to cut off Britain's supplies of food and munitions by submarine action. Only at the end of 1943 were the attacks countered and the threat brought under control.

**Atlantic Charter** (Aug 1941)
A declaration of principles to govern the national policies issued by US President Franklin D **ROOSEVELT** and British Prime Minister Winston **CHURCHILL** after a secret meeting off the Newfoundland coast. Echoing Woodrow **WILSON**'s **FOURTEEN POINTS**, and the **FOUR FREEDOMS** of Roosevelt's Jan 1941 State of the Union Address, the charter called for the rights of self-determination, self-government and free speech for all peoples, promised a more equitable international economic system, and called for the abandonment of the use of force, pending the establishment of a system of general security. After the entry of the USA into the war, the charter was endorsed internationally by the inclusion of its provisions in the Declaration of the United Nations signed by the USA, the UK, the USSR and China, on 1 Jan 1942, and by 22 other states on the following day. It served as an ideological basis for Allied cooperation during the war. ➤ **WORLD WAR II**

**Attlee, Clement Richard Attlee, 1st Earl** (1883–1967)
British politician. Early converted to **SOCIALISM**, he became the first Labour Mayor of Stepney (1919–20), an MP (1922), Deputy Leader of the Op-

position (1931–5), and then Leader (1935). He was Dominions Secretary (1942–3) and Deputy Prime Minister (1942–5) in Winston **CHURCHILL**'s war cabinet. As Prime Minister (1945–51), he carried through a vigorous programme of nationalization and social welfare, including the introduction of the National Health Service (1948). His government granted independence to India (1947) and Burma (1948). He was Leader of the Opposition again (1951–5) until he resigned and accepted an earldom.

**Auchinleck, Sir Claude John Eyre** (1884–1981)
British field marshal. He joined the 62nd Punjabis in 1904, and served in Egypt and Mesopotamia. In **WORLD WAR II**, he commanded in northern Norway and India, and then moved to the Middle East (1941). He made a successful advance into Cyrenaica, but was later thrown back by **ROMMEL**. His regrouping of the 8th Army on **EL ALAMEIN** is now recognized as a successful defensive operation, but at the time he was made a scapegoat for the retreat and replaced (1942). In 1943 he returned to India, serving subsequently as Supreme Commander India and Pakistan (1947). ➤ **NORTH AFRICAN CAMPAIGN**

**audiencia**
A high court in each of the Spanish realms. First established in Santo Domingo (1511), Mexico (1535) and Lima (1544), additional *audiencias* were subsequently created in Guatemala, Guadalajara, Charcas, Quito and Panama. These courts were far more than judicial entities: they served in the Viceroy's stead, and the judges (*oidores*) stood at the apex of colonial society. Personally linked to the Council of the Indies in Madrid, the oidores brought family retinues plus lawyers and credit arrangements, which tied to them to both local and metropolitan society. Although some Spanish-born individuals (*peninsulares*) were always appointed to them, by the mid-18c the audiencias were dominated by members of Criollo (American-born) families; **CHARLES III** of Spain's reforms barely altered this trend. Additional audiencias were created in Bogotá (1739) and Buenos Aires (1776) for military and economic reasons. Their Portuguese equivalent was the *Relação*, or High Court, established in Bahia (1751) and subsequently Rio de Janeiro; judges (*desembargadores*) were recruited from among both Brazilian and Portuguese-born magistrates.

**Augsburg, League of** (1686)
The alliance against French territorial expansionism (the *réunion* policy of **LOUIS XIV**) formed by Emperor **LEOPOLD I**, Spain, Bavaria and various circles of the empire. The accession to it of England, the Netherlands and Savoy during the subsequent War of the League of Augsburg (1689–97, also known as War of the Palatinate Succession) created the so-called Grand Alliance. Following the devastation of the Palatinate (1689) and a joint English–Dutch naval victory at the Battle of La Hogue (1692), the eventual peace treaty (Treaty of **RIJSWIJK**, 1697) restored the independence of Lorraine but confirmed France's possession of Alsace.

**Augsburg, Peace of** (25 Sep 1555)
The treaty signed by Catholics and Lutherans in Germany, recognizing the legitimacy of the **AUGSBURG**

CONFESSION (1530) and the Roman Catholic faith. It marked the failure of Emperor CHARLES V's attempt to destroy Protestantism in the Empire. The treaty was negotiated by his brother, Ferdinand. It confirmed the appropriation of ecclesiastical properties by the Protestant princes and declared that each ruler should decide the religion of his state (hence the phrase: *cuius regio, eius religio*).

## Augsburg Confession
A statement of faith composed by LUTHER, MELANCHTHON and others for the Diet of Augsburg (1530), the official text being written by Melanchthon in 1531. The earliest of Protestant Confessions, it became authoritative for the Lutheran Church.

## Augsburg Interim (1548)
A formula designed at the Diet of Augsburg (30 June 1548) by CHARLES V to solve the Empire's religious divisions by devising a loosely defined Roman Catholicism acceptable to the Protestant princes. It allowed the laity to receive the Communion cup and for Protestant ministers to keep their wives. The Catholic princes signed without enthusiasm while most of the Protestant princes rejected it outright. Pope Paul refused to endorse it until Aug 1549. Most Catholic priests refused to give the wine to the laity, which they considered a Protestant innovation. The Protestant ministers considered it an attempt to reintroduce Catholicism. ► HOLY ROMAN EMPIRE

## August Coup (1991)
The conservative attempt to reverse the process of reform in the USSR, which ended in failure. Communist opponents of Mikhail GORBACHEV's policies had been able to slow down, but not to stop, the reforms. The coup's leaders included YANAEV, the Vice-President, and YAZOV, Defence Minister. The military in particular were split, and the planning left Boris YELTSIN free to act in full view of the world. The plotters achieved the very opposite of what they wanted: Yeltsin took over from Gorbachev and accelerated the reforms. Those behind the coup succeeded, however, in undermining the USSR, which was formally dissolved in Dec 1991 after 15 republics declared their independence. ► CIS

## Augustus I (1526-86)
Elector of Saxony (1553/86). The younger son of Henry, Duke of Saxony, he was raised a Lutheran and educated at Leipzig University. He became Elector upon the death of his brother, Maurice. Married (Oct 1548) to Anna, daughter of Christian III, King of Denmark, he worked hard to avoid religious disputes in the Empire and, although a Lutheran, supported the Habsburgs. He was actively involved in bringing about the Peace of AUGSBURG. He strove to unite the Lutherans and the Calvinists but after 1574 and the expulsion of the Crypto-Calvinists from Saxony he adopted a strict form of Lutheranism. He continued to hope that the Calvinists could be persuaded to accept the AUGSBURG CONFESSION. ► HABSBURG DYNASTY

## Augustus II, the Strong (1670-1733)
King of Poland (1697/1706 and 1710/33). After being elected King, he tried to recover the provinces lost to Sweden, but was defeated, and then deposed. In 1709 he returned to Poland, formed a fresh alliance with the Tsar, and recommenced a war with Sweden, which raged until the death of CHARLES XII of Sweden (1718). The Saxon court became known as the most dissolute in Europe, and poor government hastened Poland's decline. Augustus is said to have had around 300 illegitimate children; his one legitimate child became AUGUSTUS III of Poland. He died in Warsaw.

## Augustus III (1696-1763)
Elector of Saxony and King of Poland (1733/63). Unlike his father, AUGUSTUS II, he had no ambition to make his combined dominions a great power in Europe. He ruled from Dresden, not Warsaw, and made no attempt to control the Polish magnates and gentry, famed for their unpatriotic selfishness. He permitted foreign interference in Poland's internal affairs, thus preparing the ground for the partitions of Poland which followed his reign. He squandered much of the considerable wealth of the country, helped in this activity by the nobility.

## Aung San (1915-47)
Burmese nationalist. He was the dominant figure in the nationalist movement during and after the PACIFIC WAR. At the beginning of the 1940s, Aung San, working with Japanese agents, formed the anti-British Burma Independence Army, which entered Burma (now Myanmar) with the invading Japanese in Jan 1942. He rapidly became disillusioned with the Japanese, however, and, as a leading figure in the Anti-Fascist People's Freedom League (AFPFL), turned his troops against them (Mar 1945). In the immediate post-war period he became President of the AFPFL and, in 1946, was effectively Prime Minister in the Governor's Executive Council. In Jan 1947 he travelled to London to negotiate, with success, Burma's independence. On 19 July, however, he was assassinated by a political rival. His death removed the one figure who might have held together Burma's warring political interests as the country achieved independence (4 Jan 1948).

## Aung San Suu Kyi (1945- )
Burmese political leader and founder of the National League for Democracy. The daughter of Burmese nationalist hero General AUNG SAN, she studied Politics, Philosophy and Economics at Oxford University, and in 1969 worked for the UN in New York. In 1988 she returned to Burma (now Myanmar) and after appeals to the government for more open consultation on the country's future, she co-founded the National League for Democracy (NLD) and became its General Secretary. The government had established its State Law and Order Restoration Council (SLORC), introduced martial law and imprisonment without trial, and banned public meetings, forbidding Suu Kyi to hold her office. Nonetheless, she toured the country and as a result was held under house arrest by the military junta (1989–95). Despite this imprisonment of its leader, the National League for Democracy won an overwhelming victory in the elections of 1990, amounting to 80 per cent of the popular vote, although the result was ignored and many newly elected MPs were jailed. Aung San Suu Kyi has continued to call for democratic change despite further periods of house arrest (2000–2, 2003–) and imprisonment (May 2003). She was awarded the NOBEL PEACE PRIZE in 1991.

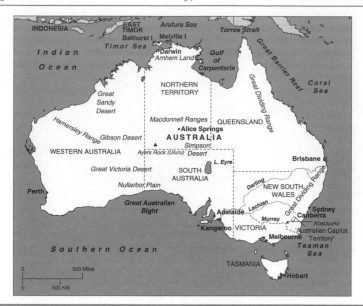

**Aurangzeb** (1618–1707)
Mughal Emperor (1658/1707). The last, and most magnificent, of the Mughal emperors of India, he took the kingly title Alamgir. The youngest son of **SHAH JAHAN**, he struggled for power with his brothers, finally putting them to death. He was a fervent Muslim, which alienated the Hindus and led to war with the Marathas and the extension of the boundaries of the Empire into the Deccan in the south. His long reign was distinguished by prosperity. However, in the long term, most of his enterprises failed, and after his death the empire began rapidly to decline. ► **MUGHAL EMPIRE**

**Auriol, Vincent** (1884–1966)
French politician. A socialist, he studied law, and was a Deputy (1914–40 and 1945–7), Minister of Finance in the **POPULAR FRONT** government (1936–7) and Minister of Justice (1937–8). He opposed the granting of power to **PÉTAIN** in 1940, and joined the French Resistance, escaping to Algeria in 1943, where he became President of the Foreign Affairs Committee of the Consultative Assembly. He represented France at the first meeting of the **UN**, was elected President of the Constituent Assembly in 1946, and was first President of the Fourth Republic (1947–53). ► **REPUBLIC, FOURTH** (France); **RESISTANCE MOVEMENT** (France)

**Aurora** (1917)
The Russian warship that went over to the **BOLSHEVIKS** in Oct 1917, and thus tipped the balance in their favour. Although ordered by the **RUSSIAN PROVISIONAL GOVERNMENT** to put to sea, it stayed in the River Neva across from the Winter Palace, fired a blank shell that frightened away many of the government's supporters and eventually fired some live shells to help overcome its defenders. Its action was, however, essentially symbolic, indicating that the authorities had lost a major source of power. ►**WINTER PALACE, STORMING OF**

**Auschwitz**
The largest Nazi **CONCENTRATION CAMP**, founded in 1941, on the outskirts of Oświecim, south-west

Poland, where 3–4 million people, mainly Jews and Poles, were murdered between 1940 and 1945. Gas chambers, watch towers and prison huts are preserved at the camp, part of which is now a museum. ► **HOLOCAUST**

**Ausgleich**
The arrangement (literally, 'compromise') made in 1867 between the Imperial government of Austria and representatives of Hungary, following the Austrian defeat by **PRUSSIA** (1866), which created the Dual Monarchy of **AUSTRIA-HUNGARY**.

**Austerlitz, Battle of** (2 Dec 1805)
The victory of **NAPOLEON I** over a combined Austrian-Russian army in Moravia. The Treaty of **PRESSBURG** (Bratislava) followed on 26 Dec, by which Austria renounced all interests in Italy, lost most of her western Alpine lands, and saw French hegemony established in western Germany.

**Austin, Stephen Fuller** (1793–1836)
US colonizer known as 'the Father of Texas' who established the first settlement of Americans in Texas in 1822, a project left incomplete by his father who had died in 1821. Austin became the leader of the colony and had influence in Mexico. However, he did not succeed in convincing Mexico, of which Texas was still a part, that Texas should have a separate state government, and was imprisoned for his efforts (1833–4). After the Texas Revolution he failed to win the presidency but served briefly as Secretary of State of the Texas Republic.

**AUSTRALIA**    official name **Commonwealth of Australia**
An independent country and the smallest continent in the world, entirely in the southern hemisphere. The **ABORIGINALS** are thought to have arrived in Australia from South-East Asia c.40,000 years ago. The first European visitors were the Dutch, who explored the Gulf of Carpentaria in 1606 and landed in 1642. Captain James **COOK** arrived in **BOTANY BAY** in 1770, and claimed the east coast for Britain. New South Wales was established as a penal colony in 1788. In

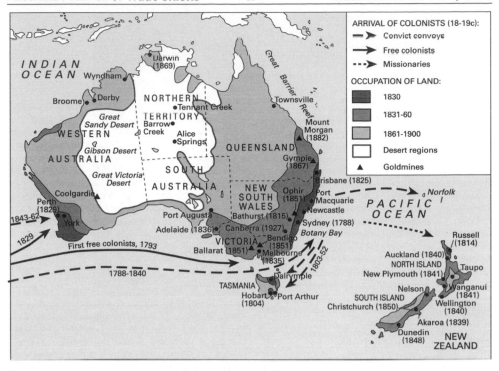

**ARRIVAL OF COLONISTS (18-19c):**
- ═══▶ Convict convoys
- ───▶ Free colonists
- ┅┅▶ Missionaries

**OCCUPATION OF LAND:**
- ▇ 1830
- ▨ 1831-60
- ░ 1861-1900
- ☐ Desert regions
- ▲ Goldmines

**British penetration of Australia and New Zealand, 18–19c**

1829, all the territory now known as Australia was constituted a dependency of Britain. It originally developed as several widely-spread colonies, relating to Britain more than to one another. Increasing numbers of settlers were attracted to Australia, especially after the introduction of Spanish Merino sheep. Gold was discovered in New South Wales and Victoria (1851) and in Western Australia (1892). **TRANSPORTATION** of convicts to eastern Australia ended in 1840, but continued until 1853 in Tasmania and 1868 in Western Australia. During this period, the colonies drafted their own constitutions and set up governments: New South Wales (1855), Tasmania and Victoria (1856), South Australia (1857), Queensland (1860) and Western Australia (1890). In 1901 a federal Commonwealth of Australia was established by agreement between the colonies, with the new city of Canberra chosen as the site for its capital. A policy of preventing immigration by non-whites stayed in force from the end of the 19c until 1974. The growing movement for independence in recent years culminated with the pledge of Paul **KEATING** in 1993 to make Australia a republic by 2001, subject to a referendum, to which Queen **ELIZABETH II** agreed. In 1996 Keating's Labor Party lost power, but the Liberal–National Party coalition led by John Howard continued the process; in Feb 1998 a constitutional convention voted in favour of adopting a republican system of government, but a referendum on the proposal in Nov 1999 rejected republican status, with 55 per cent voting against. Hardline policies on refugees and asylum seekers were adopted in 1992 and poor conditions in detention camps have led to riots and demonstrations, and international protests in 2001 after Australia forcibly diverted boats of asylum seekers to **NAURU**.

## Australian Council of Trade Unions (ACTU)

Australia's national trade union organization, formed in 1927. Its prestige has come from representing the unions' case before the Australian Conciliation and Arbitration Commission, and in helping to settle industrial disputes. By 1986, 162 unions were affiliated, with a claimed total membership of 2.6 million. The ACTU's 1983 accord with the **AUSTRALIAN LABOR PARTY** (ALP) on economic policy was in effect during the ALP's term in office from 1983 to 1996. ► **AUSTRALIAN WORKERS' UNION (AWU)**

## Australian Gold Rush

Traces of gold were first found in Australia in 1823, but the first significant find was in 1851, when Edward Hargraves publicized his find and attracted 2,000 to the site at Ophir, New South Wales. In the same year, large gold finds were made in Victoria, which accounted for 35 per cent of world gold production (1851–60). Gold was also found in Queensland (1867) and Western Australia (1893). The discovery transformed Australia: it drew thousands of immigrants (342,000 arrived from overseas, 1852–61), created a mass movement for democracy, and gave a tremendous boost to the economy. Cities, in particular Melbourne (which grew from 29,000 to 473,000 in 1851–91), symbolized the new-found prosperity. Although some miners struck it rich, most did not, and this led to pressure to open pastoral land for farming. Gold also attracted thousands of Chinese miners, who were greatly resented by the Europeans; this led to anti-Chinese laws and the beginning of the **WHITE AUSTRALIA POLICY**. ► **EUREKA**; **LAMBING FLAT RIOTS**

## Australian Labor Party (ALP)

Australia's oldest political party, founded in 1891 in

New South Wales following the defeat of the trade unions in the 1890 maritime strike. The party spread to all states by the mid-1900s and formed the world's first labour government in Queensland in 1899 for one week. It has always been a social democratic party, committed to evolutionary not revolutionary change. Despite a commitment to 'SOCIALISM', it has generally been moderate and pragmatic when in government. Three major splits in the ALP occurred: in 1916–17 over conscription, in 1931 over economic policy to combat the Depression and in 1955 over attitudes to COMMUNISM. ALP has had only some success in winning federal government (1904, 1908–9, 1910–13, 1914–16, 1929–32, 1941–9, 1972–5 and 1983–96), but has done better at state level. Its most important national figures have been Prime Ministers W M HUGHES (1915–16), James Scullin (1929–32), John CURTIN (1941–5), Ben CHIFLEY (1945–9), Gough WHITLAM (1972–5), R J L ('Bob') HAWKE (1983–91) and Paul KEATING (1991–6). When Keating was defeated in 1996, Kim Beazley took over as party leader. The party has always had fewer members than its main rival, the LIBERAL PARTY OF AUSTRALIA. ► DEMOCRATIC LABOR PARTY, AUSTRALIAN; PETROV AFFAIR

### Australian Workers' Union (AWU)
The largest Australian trade union from the early 1900s to 1970, and still one of the largest. It was formed in 1894 by the merging of the Amalgamated Shearers' Union (formed 1886) and the General Labourers' Union (formed 1890), and has traditionally recruited lesser paid workers. It has always been a conservative force in trade union and labour politics. ► AUSTRALIAN COUNCIL OF TRADE UNIONS

---

**AUSTRIA**   official name **Republic of Austria**

A mountainous republic in central Europe, bounded to the north by Germany, the Czech Republic and Slovakia; to the south by Italy and Slovenia; to the west by Switzerland and Liechtenstein; and to the east by Hungary. Austria was part of the Roman Empire until the 5c, then was occupied by Germanic tribes and in the late 8c became a frontier area of Charlemagne's empire. It became a duchy and passed to the HABSBURG family (1282), who made it the foundation of their empire; the head of the Habsburg house was almost continually the Holy Roman Emperor, making Austria the leading German state. Habsburg defeats in the 19c (notably the AUSTRO-PRUSSIAN WAR) and Hungarian nationalism led to the Dual Monarchy of AUSTRIA-HUNGARY. The assassination of Archduke Franz Ferdinand by Serbian nationalists triggered WORLD WAR I. Following the collapse of Austria-Hungary at the end of the war, those German-speaking lands of the Habsburg Empire not annexed

by other successor states constituted themselves on 12 Nov 1918 as 'German Austria', renamed Austria on the insistence of the victor powers. Between the wars the republic led an uneasy existence, with most of public opinion and most politicians seeking union with Germany. Union with HITLER's Germany, which occurred when Austria was annexed by the German Reich in Mar 1938 (ANSCHLUSS), under the name Ostmark, was more controversial. After WORLD WAR II, Austria was reconstituted as a distinct territory by the Allies and in 1955 became an independent, neutral, democratic state. Thomas Klestil succeeded Kurt WALDHEIM as President in 1992, and under Klestil Austria joined the EC in 1995. In 2000, the EU briefly imposed diplomatic sanctions on Austria because of the inclusion of extreme right-wing Freedom Party members in its coalition government.► AUSTRIAN STATE TREATY

### Austria-Hungary, Dual Monarchy of
A constitutional arrangement created by the AUSGLEICH, or 'compromise', of 1867. In Austria-Hungary the Habsburg emperors FRANCIS JOSEPH (until 1916), and CHARLES I (1916/18), ruled over the twin kingdoms of Austria (incorporating German-, Czech-, Polish-, Slovenian-, and Ruthenian-speaking regions of their empire) as well as DALMATIA and Hungary (incorporating Magyar, Romanian, Slovak, and most Croatian and Serb regions). The separate kingdoms possessed considerable autonomy over internal policy, with overall foreign and financial policy remaining in the hands of the Imperial government. The Dual Monarchy provided a temporary solution to the internal problems of the Habsburg Empire, but was ultimately destroyed by defeat in WORLD WAR I.

### Austrian State Treaty (May 1955)
The agreement between Austria and the four Allied victor powers under which Austria regained its independence as a federal republic in return for restrictions on armaments and curbs on close relations with Germany. In Oct 1955 this was supplemented by an Austrian declaration of permanent neutrality.

### Austrian Succession, War of the (1740–8)
The European conflict over the succession to the hereditary Habsburg lands of MARIA THERESA. On the death of Emperor CHARLES VI, Bavaria, Saxony and Spain, backed by France, refused to recognize the PRAGMATIC SANCTION and invaded Bohemia and Upper Austria. At this juncture, Prussia claimed and, on being rebuffed, conquered Silesia in two campaigns, the second of which ended in 1745. That year also saw the withdrawal of Bavaria from the struggle, when the son and successor of Charles Albert, holder of the Bohemian and imperial crowns, renounced all claims to them. The subsequent intervention on Austria's side of Russia led to peace negotiations and, by 1748, to the Treaty of Aachen, under the terms of which the Habsburg monarchy retained almost all her dominions with the exception of Silesia. ► HABSBURG DYNASTY

### Austro-Prussian Dualism
The period which spanned the reign of FREDERICK II, THE GREAT of Prussia. For the first time, power within the HOLY ROMAN EMPIRE was evenly divided between

PRUSSIA and Austria and they were both substantially stronger than any other Imperial state. Neither seemed inclined to strive for absolute mastery over the Empire.

### Austro-Prussian War (1866)

A war between Austria and PRUSSIA occasioned by a dispute over the Duchies of Schleswig and Holstein. It was declared on 14 June, decided by the Prussian victory at the Battle of KÖNIGGRÄTZ-SADOWA on 3 July, and ended by the Treaty of Prague on 23 Aug. Austria's defeat hastened German unification (since she had been the main advocate and defender of particularism in the GERMAN CONFEDERATION, now dissolved by Prussia), allowed Italy, Prussia's ally, to acquire Venetia, and precipitated the creation of Austria-Hungary.

### Austro-Slavism

A federalist movement among the SLAVS within the Habsburg Empire. It developed after 1848 as a reaction to German nationalism and Pan-Germanism which, in its extreme forms, denied the existence of Slav nationhood. Representatives of the Habsburg Slavs, under the leadership of the Czech František PALACKÝ, demanded the reorganization of the monarchy on a federal basis which would give full weight to the Slav nations. Having ably exploited Austro-Magyar antagonisms, the advocates of Austro-Slavism had their hopes crushed with the establishment of the Dual Monarchy. Their ideas were later taken up by the Czech national leader, Tomáš MASARYK. ►AUSTRIA-HUNGARY, DUAL MONARCHY OF

### autarchia

The Italian word ('autarchy' or 'self-sufficiency') used to describe the policy of economic self-sufficiency pursued by the fascist regime in Italy. Originally it was largely limited to a drive for greater grain production, the so-called 'battle for wheat'. However, when limited economic sanctions were imposed in response to Italy's invasion of Abyssinia in 1935, an increased effort was made to replace imports with ersatz goods. ► ABYSSINIA, CONQUEST OF; FASCISM

### authoritarianism

A form of government, or a theory advocating such government, which is the opposite of democracy, in that the consent of society to rulers and their decisions is not necessary. Voting and discussion are not usually employed, except to give the appearance of democratic legitimacy to the government, and such arrangements remain firmly under the control of the rulers. Authoritarian rulers draw their authority from what are claimed to be special qualities of a religious, nationalistic or ideological nature, which are used to justify their dispensing with constitutional restrictions. Their rule, however, relies heavily upon coercion. ► TOTALITARIANISM

### auto-da-fé (Portuguese, *auto da fé*)

Literally an 'act of faith', practised originally by the Spanish and later by the Portuguese INQUISITION, it was a public ceremony, including a procession and mass, at which prisoners were made to express repentance for sins. Very frequent in the late 15c and 16c, the ceremony was rarely held in later epochs. Burning of heretics at the stake never formed part of the *auto-da-fé*, and was carried out in a separate act afterwards.

### Autumn Harvest Uprisings (1927)

A series of attempted peasant insurrections launched by the Chinese Communist Party in the provinces of Hunan and Hubei following the collapse of the United Front (June 1927). An emergency party conference in Aug 1927 called for communist-led attacks on major cities in the hope of igniting urban revolution. MAO ZEDONG led one such uprising, but following its defeat he led the remnants of his ragtag force to the mountains of JINGGANGSHAN where he began to create a rural base area. By the end of 1927, all other insurrections had collapsed.

### Aventine Secession (June 1924)

In protest at fascist vote-rigging and the murder of MATTEOTTI, the deputies of the main Italian opposition parties staged a walk-out from parliament. Designed to register protest and deny legitimacy to MUSSOLINI's regime, the actual consequence was to hand the fascists dominance of the Italian Chamber. The measure was further undermined by the reluctance of GIOLITTI and other leading liberals to support what they felt to be a useless boycott. Those deputies who joined the walk-out were said to have 'gone to the Aventine hill'.

### Avis Dynasty

The dynasty which ruled Portugal from 1385 to 1580 and took its name from the medieval military order of Avis, founded in 1147. The first of the line was King João (John) I (1385–1433), and the last was SEBASTIAN, who died at the Battle of ALCAZARQUIVIR in 1578.

### AVNOJ (*Antifašističko Veče Narodnog Oslobodjenja Jugoslavije,* 'Anti-Fascist Council for the National Liberation of Yugoslavia')

Organized by the partisan leader TITO, the council first met at Bihać in Bosnia to establish a central government for Yugoslavia (Nov 1942). Communist-dominated, it challenged the authority of the royalist government-in-exile in London. In Nov 1943 it met at Jajce and declared itself the true representative government of Yugoslavia. Its political programme included the reorganization of the country on a federal basis and the establishment of a republic. At the end of WORLD WAR II, it had created an effective administrative structure throughout the country and became the national provisional assembly until the Nov 1945 elections. That Yugoslavia alone of the Balkan countries was under communist control at the end of the war was due to the successful organization of AVNOJ. ► DJILAS, MILOVAN; KARDELJ, EDVARD; STOJADINOVIĆ, MILAN

### Awadh, Annexation of

A semi-independent northern Indian province within the MUGHAL EMPIRE, Awadh (Oudh) was annexed in 1856 by the British EAST INDIA COMPANY. Loss of rights by hereditary land revenue receivers caused resentment, and contributed towards the 1857–8 INDIAN UPRISING.

### Awami League

East Pakistani (later Bangladeshi) political party founded initially to promote East Pakistani autonomy, and later Bangladeshi independence. The Awami League rose to political prominence in the late 1960s when, under the leadership of Sheikh MUJIBUR

**RAHMAN**, it protested against the fact that profits from jute, produced in highly populated East Pakistan, were being kept in relatively sparsely populated West Pakistan. The Awami League's second cause was for parliamentary representation by population. As the government of General **AYUB KHAN** became increasingly unstable in 1968, Sheikh Mujib and the Awami League sought to limit the powers of the central government in East Pakistan. The central government responded by imprisoning all opposition leaders. The following year Ayub Khan resigned and was replaced by General Yahya Khan, who proceeded with a policy of political militarization while preparing to restore parliamentary democracy. Although representation by population was part of Yahya Khan's plan, dissatisfaction in East Pakistan grew and popular feeling began to call for independence. In the election of 7 Dec 1970, the Awami League won 160 of 162 seats in East Pakistan. In Mar 1971 Sheikh Mujib set forth full internal autonomy as his condition for the Awami League's participation in the National Assembly. He was arrested shortly thereafter and the Awami League was outlawed. These actions on the part of the central government led directly to the bloody 1971 Pakistani civil war, which saw the emergence of the new state of Bangladesh following India's military invasion in support of the Awami League. While the League managed to retain democratic control of Bangladesh through the nation's first independent election in 1973, it was overthrown by a coup in 1975. Since then, the Awami League has remained a major political party in Bangladesh, winning power again in 1996 under Sheikh Mujib's daughter, Sheikh Hasina **WAJED**.

**AWB** (*Afrikaner Weerstandsbeweging*, 'Afrikaner Resistance Movement')
A paramilitary group founded in 1973, and led by Eugene Terre'Blanche, its aim was to preserve white control of South Africa by force. It lost much of its momentum following the dismantling of **APARTHEID** and the election of the **ANC** in 1994.

**Awolowo, Chief Obafemi** (1909–87)
Nigerian politician. Educated in Protestant schools, he was a teacher, trader, trade union organizer and journalist, before being an external student of law at London University and becoming a solicitor and advocate of the Nigerian Supreme Court. He helped found and then led the Action Group, a party based on the Yoruba of Western Nigeria, from 1951 to 1966 (when the party was banned). He was Premier of the Western Region (1954–9) and then leader of the opposition in the federal parliament from 1960 to 1962, when he was imprisoned. Released after the 1966 coup, he was Federal Commissioner for Finance and Vice-President, Federal Executive Council of Nigeria (1967–71), when he returned to private practice. But he returned to politics in 1979 as the unsuccessful presidential candidate for the Unity Party of Nigeria.

**Axel ►** ABSALON

**axis of evil**
A term used by US President George W **BUSH** in Jan 2002 in reference to North Korea, Iran and Iraq, meaning states sponsoring terrorism and having either the potential to develop or the capability of using weapons of mass destruction (**WMD**). It has

been suggested that North Korea's inclusion was an attempt to show that the war on **TERROR** is not a war on Islam. In May 2002 the USA added Cuba, Libya and Syria to the list. **► FINANCIAL ACTION TASK FORCE**

**Axis Powers**
The name given to the cooperation of Nazi Germany and fascist Italy (1936–45), first used by **MUSSOLINI**. In May 1939 the two countries signed a formal treaty, the 'Pact of Steel'. In Sep 1940, Germany, Italy and Japan signed a tripartite agreement, after which all three were referred to as Axis Powers. **► NAZI PARTY**; **WORLD WAR II**

**Ayacucho, Battle of** (9 Dec 1824)
The final major battle of the **SPANISH-AMERICAN WARS OF INDEPENDENCE**, fought in the Peruvian Andes by **BOLÍVAR** and **SUCRE** against Field Marshal José de la Serna, the last Viceroy of Peru. The revolutionary forces (comprising Venezuelans, Colombians, Argentines, Chileans and Peruvians) defeated the royalist army, and the Spanish Viceroy and his generals were taken prisoner. All Spanish forces were then withdrawn from Peru and Charcas (Bolivia), ensuring the independence of the newly emerged South American republics from Spanish rule.

**Ayans**
Muslim notables who, as landowners, enjoyed considerable political influence at local level in the **OTTOMAN EMPIRE**. Often rebellious, during the 18c their independence increased as Ottoman central authority weakened.

**Ayn Jalut, Battle of** (3 Sep 1260)
A major battle between the **MONGOLS** and the **MAMLUKS** which effectively stopped the Mongol westward advance. The armies met at Ayn Jalut near Nazareth in Palestine, where the Mongols, under Kitbugha, were trapped and suffered a crushing defeat at the hands of the Mamluks, led by Baybars. This was the Mongols' first defeat in pitched battle.

**Ayub Khan, Mohammed** (1907–74)
Pakistani soldier and politician. Educated at Aligarh Muslim University and Sandhurst, he served in **WORLD WAR II**, became first Commander-in-Chief of Pakistan's army in 1951 and field marshal in 1959. He became President of Pakistan in 1958 after a bloodless army coup, and established a stable economy and political autocracy. In Mar 1969, after widespread civil disorder and violent opposition from both right and left wings, Ayub Khan relinquished power and martial law was re-established.

**Ayudhya**
Classical Thai kingdom (1351–1767) situated in the heart of the great plain of the Chaophraya River, and the name of that kingdom's capital. Ayudhya was established (1351) by Prince U Thong as the power of the Cambodian empire of Angkor in the region began to wane. In the mid-15c, Ayudhya, securing the final collapse of Angkor and the elimination of the rival Tai state of Sukhothai, emerged as an expansive regional power. Sacked by the Burmese in 1569 and reconstructed towards the end of the 16c, Ayudhya became a major trading centre and host to many nationalities (including Europeans) in the 17c. However, in 1688,

following French intrigues at the court, an internal revolt ended the Western presence, although intra-Asian trade continued to flourish. Burmese attacks were revived from the late 1750s, and in 1767 the capital was sacked by Burmese forces. A new royal line and a new state were established at Thonburi-Bangkok in 1782.

## Ayyubid Dynasty
The Kurdish dynasty of the 12c and 13c established by **SALADIN**. His empire, based essentially on Egypt, included Yemen, Syria and enough of the Fertile Crescent to cause him at one time to be a matter of concern to the 'Abbasid Caliph al-Nasir (1180/1225). Saladin's greatest achievements were the defeat of the field army of the Latin Kingdom of Jerusalem at **HITTIN** (1187) and his subsequent capture of Jerusalem, which enabled him to negotiate a settlement with the Crusaders. By this, the latter retained control of much of the Levantine littoral, while Saladin (and his descendants) had control of the Syrian and Palestinian hinterland as well as Egypt. The failure of the Ayyubids to survive as a dynasty more than 60 years after Saladin's death was largely due to squabbling between those who considered themselves his heirs. The cession by negotiation of Jerusalem to **FREDERICK II** by the Ayyubid al-Kamil in the early 13c (which 'did not count' because Frederick was excommunicated at the time) served in some degree to emphasize the futility of the Holy Wars of the 12c and 13c. Internal disagreements in the Ayyubid House opened the way for Mamluk control of Egypt and then Palestine in the mid-13c. ➤ 'ABBASID DYNASTY; MAMLUKS

## Azad, Abu'l-Kalam (1888–1958)
Muslim Indian politician and leader of the **INDIAN NATIONAL CONGRESS**. His pan Islamic articles in his newspaper, *Al-Hilal*, resulted in detention in 1915, after release from which he became active in the **KHILAFAT MOVEMENT**. In 1923 Azad presided over a special session of the Indian National Congress, and in 1940 he was elected President – a position which he held until 1946. While President of Congress he conducted important negotiations with Sir Stafford **CRIPPS** and Field Marshal Lord **WAVELL**. He was interned throughout most of the war. Following Indian independence, Azad became India's Education Minister, a post he held until his death.

## Azaña (y Díaz), Manuel (1880–1940)
Spanish politician and intellectual. He qualified as a lawyer, served as a bureaucrat, but became eminent in the literary and political world. In 1925 he founded a political party, *Acción Republicana*. With the advent of the Second Republic (1931), he became Minister of War and then Prime Minister (1931–3) of a reforming government. An outstanding orator and thinker, he himself was closely identified with army reform and anticlericalism. In opposition from Sep 1933 to Feb 1936, he was the chief architect of the Popular Front coalition which triumphed in the general election of Feb 1936. He resumed the premiership then, and was elevated to the presidency in May 1936. He remained President during the **SPANISH CIVIL WAR** until Feb 1939, then went into exile in France, where he died. Azaña was the leading politician of the Second Republic and the greatest embodiment of its liberal, reformist vision. ➤ **REPUBLIC, SECOND** (Spain)

## Azania
The names given by ancient and medieval Greek and Arab geographers to the northern part of the East African coast. 'Azanians' were the early, pre-Bantu-speaking inhabitants of the coast. In modern times, the name Azania has been used by some nationalist groups, especially the **PAN-AFRICANIST CONGRESS**, to denote a post-**APARTHEID** South Africa.

## Azcona del Hoyo, José Simon (1927– )
Honduran politician. He trained as a civil engineer in Honduras and Mexico, and developed a particular interest in urban development and low-cost housing. As a student he became interested in politics and fought the 1963 general election as a candidate for the Liberal Party of Honduras (PLH), but his career was interrupted by a series of military coups. He served in the governments of Roberto Suazo and Walter López (1982–6), which were ostensibly civilian administrations but, in reality, were controlled by the army Commander-in-Chief, General Gustavo Álvarez. The latter was removed by junior officers in 1984, and in 1986 Azcona narrowly won the presidential election. A moderate conservative, he served as President until 1990, signing the Central American Peace Accord of 1987 despite his government's quiet acceptance of the presence in Honduras of Nicaraguan **CONTRAS** backed by the USA. He was barred by law from seeking a second term.

**AZERBAIJAN** official name **Azerbaijan Republic**

A republic in eastern Transcaucasia, bounded to the east by the Caspian Sea and to the south by Iran; Armenia splits the country in the south-west and forms the western boundary; Georgia and the Russian Federation lie to the north. The Azeris have a long history, mainly of subjection to neighbouring empires. A Turkish people converted to Islam, they came under Tsarist Russian rule in 1813. The development of the oil industry in and around Baku produced leaders who, encouraged by **LENIN**, declared independence in 1918. However, in 1920 they were reconquered on his instructions for allegedly siding with Soviet enemies, and Azerbaijan was proclaimed a Soviet Socialist Republic; it became a constituent republic of the USSR in 1936. Between Dec 1988 and Jan 1990 riots promoted by the nationalist Azerbaijan Popular Front culminated in an anti-Armenian pogrom in the capital, and Soviet troops mounted a violent assault on the city to restore order. Before emerging as an independent republic in 1991 following the disintegration of the USSR, Azerbaijan became locked in a struggle with Armenia over the autonomous region that **STALIN** had set up for the latter's co-nationals in

Nagorno-Karabakh. In 1992 this degenerated into a full-scale war in which Nagorno-Karabakh and parts of Azerbaijan were lost to Armenia. A ceasefire was announced in 1994 and Nagorno-Karabakh declared itself independent in 1996, but the conflict remained unresolved. Azerbaijan joined the CIS (Commonwealth of Independent States) in 1993.

**Azhari, Isma'il al-** (1900–69)
Sudanese politician. He was the leader of the Sudanese Unionist Party which, to the surprise and indeed disappointment of the British, was the victor of the first Sudanese parliamentary elections in 1953. Al-Azhari formed the first government in 1954. Opposed by the Mahdists, he was nonetheless able to guide the Sudan towards independence, which was achieved on 1 Jan 1956. After the deposition of Ibrahim **ABBOUD** in 1964, al-Azhari became President of the Supreme Council of the Sudan. However, a military coup in 1969 resulted in his being placed under house arrest and he died during this confinement.

**Azikiwe, Nnamdi**, known as **Zik of Africa**, originally **Benjamin Azikiwe** (1904–96)
Nigerian journalist and politician. He spent four years as a government clerk before going to the USA, where he studied at Storer College, Lincoln University and Howard University. He then taught at Lincoln, where he obtained two further degrees. He returned to Africa in 1934 and edited the *African Morning Post* in Accra before going back to Nigeria to take up the editorship of the *West African Pilot* in 1937. He was a member of the executive of the Nigerian Youth Movement (1934–41) and helped found the National Council of Nigeria and the Cameroons (NCNC), of which he was Secretary (1944–6) and President (1946–60). A member of the Nigerian Legco in 1947–51, he became Premier of the Eastern Region in 1954 after two years as Leader of the Opposition. He was appointed the first black Governor-General of Nigeria in 1960 and was President of the first Nigerian Republic in 1963–6. He was in Britain at the time of the 1966 military coup, but returned as a private citizen to Nigeria soon afterwards. He returned to politics in 1979 as leader of, and successful candidate for, the Nigerian People's Party. He was a member of the Council of State (1979–83).

**Aztecs** ► PRE-COLUMBIAN CIVILIZATIONS

## Baader–Meinhof Group

The popular name for *Rote Armee Fraktion* (RAF), after its leaders, Andreas Baader (1943–77) and Ulrike Meinhof (1934–76). A left-wing German revolutionary terrorist group, which recruited largely from the middle-class, younger generation, it carried out political bombings in Germany in the early 1970s. Baader, Meinhof and 18 other members were arrested in 1972. On a much smaller scale, RAF continued into the 1980s.

## Ba'ath Party

The political manifestation of Ba'athism, an Islamic ideology of the 1930s. Founded by Michel **AFLAQ** and Salah al-Din **BITAR**, the party's ideology faced problems in coping with combining a Marxist social analysis with an Islamic religious basis, but eventually became the ruling party in both Syria and Iraq. However, rather than fostering closer relations between the two countries, the term became divorced from its ideological bases and has in no way served to reduce the rancour which has existed between the two countries over the years. The party was banned in Iraq by the occupying forces after the overthrow of Saddam **HUSSEIN**'s regime in 2003.

## Bab al-Mandab

The straits lying between Yemen on the east and Djibouti and Ethiopia on the west. Strategically important, they lie at the southern entrance to the Red Sea and control access to Jordan's only seaport, Aqaba. The straits were of considerable importance, for example during the **IRAN–IRAQ WAR**. Since Iraq had no significant freedom of navigation in the Persian Gulf, all sea-borne material destined for Iraq had to pass through Aqaba at the head of the Red Sea, with entry to there being controlled at the Bab al-Mandab.

## Babangida, Ibrahim (1941–)

Nigerian soldier and politician. Educated at military schools in Nigeria and later in India, UK and USA, he was commissioned in 1963 and became an instructor at the Nigerian Defence Academy. During the Nigerian Civil War, he commanded an infantry battalion, then became an instructor at the Nigerian Defence Academy (1970–2) and later commander of the Armoured Corps (1975–81). Involved in the military overthrow of President **SHAGARI** in 1983, he became a member of the Supreme Military Council and Chief of Staff in 1985, and was himself the leader of the coup which overthrew **BUHARI** in 1985. He was mainly responsible for the cautious and controlled way Nigeria returned to civilian rule, imposing a two-party system and staged elections on the country. In 1993 he was replaced by General Sani Abacha following military intervention in the general elections.

## Bab-ed-Din (1819–50)

Persian religious leader. This title, meaning 'Gate of the Faith', was assumed by a merchant of Shiraz, Mirza Ali Mohammed. In 1844 he declared himself the Bab (Gateway) to the prophesied 12th Imam; later he claimed to be the Imam himself. He was imprisoned in 1847 and later executed at Tabriz. The religion he founded (Babism) was the forerunner of the Baha'i faith. ➤ **BAHA-ULLAH**

## Babeuf, François-Noël (1760–97)

French politician. During the **FRENCH REVOLUTION** (as 'Gracchus Babeuf'), he advocated a rigorous system of **COMMUNISM** (Babouvism). His conspiracy to destroy the **DIRECTORY** (1796) and establish an extreme democratic and communistic system (a 'Republic of Equals') was discovered, and he was guillotined.

## Babington, Antony (1561–86)

English Roman Catholic conspirator. He served as a page to **MARY, QUEEN OF SCOTS**, when she was a prisoner at Sheffield. In 1586, he was induced by John Ballard and others to lead a conspiracy towards **ELIZABETH I**'s murder and Mary's release (the Babington Plot). Cipher messages were intercepted by **WALSINGHAM** in which Mary warmly approved the plot, and these were later used against her. Babington fled, but was captured and executed with the others.

## Babi Yar

A huge ravine near Kiev in the Ukraine into which over 30,000 Jews were herded and massacred by Nazi German troops in 1941. It is also the title of a poem by Yevgeny **YEVTUSHENKO** (1961) and a novel by Anatoli Kuznetsov (1966) dedicated to the victims. ➤ **HOLOCAUST; NAZI PARTY**

## Babur, originally Zahir-ud-Din Muhammad (1483–1530)

First Mughal Emperor of India (1526/30). Born in Fergana, Central Asia, a small principality ruled by his father, he was a descendant of **GENGHIS KHAN** and of **TIMUR**. The nephew of Sultan Mahmud Mirza of Samarkand, he attempted unsuccessfully as a young man to establish himself as ruler there, but in 1504 turned his attention with greater success towards Afghanistan, entering Kabul in that year. A further attempt to win Samarkand in 1511 was again unsuccessful. The death of Sikandar Lodi in 1517 brought civil war to the Afghan **LODI DYNASTY** in India and Babur took advantage of this to invade India, defeating Ibrahim Lodi decisively at the Battle of **PANIPAT** in 1526 and laying the foundation for the

MUGHAL EMPIRE. The following year he defeated the Hindu Rajput Confederacy and, despite continuing resistance from the Hindus and from the Afghans, the military strength of the Mughals enabled him to consolidate his gains. A soldier of genius, he was also a cultured man with interests in architecture, music and literature. Himself a Muslim, he initiated a policy of toleration towards his non-Muslim subjects that was continued by his successors and became a hallmark of the Mughal Empire at its zenith.

### Bach, Alexander, Baron von (1813–93)
Austrian politician. A prominent supporter of the Mar 1848 revolution in Vienna, Bach became Minister of Justice in the revolutionary government of Wessenberg-Doblhof. After he resigned from office in Oct 1848 his rapid personal conversion from liberalism to neo-absolutism brought him high office in the counter-revolutionary government led by SCHWARZENBERG. Here he served as Interior Minister and achieved reforms in the system of provincial government which influence Austria to this day. ➤ REVOLUTION OF 1848

### Bacon, Francis, Viscount St Albans (1561–1626)
English philosopher and statesman. He became an MP in 1584, and was knighted by JAMES VI AND I in 1603. He was in turn Solicitor-General (1607), Attorney-General (1613), Privy Counsellor (1616), Lord Keeper (1617) and Lord Chancellor (1618). He became Lord Verulam in 1618, and was made viscount in 1621. However, complaints were made that he accepted bribes from suitors in his court, and he was publicly accused before his fellow peers, fined, imprisoned, and banished from parliament and the court. Although soon released, and later pardoned, he never returned to public office, and died deeply in debt.

### Bacon's Rebellion (1675–6)
A rising against the royal governor in the American colony of Virginia, rooted in a conflict between small frontier farmers and the indigenous peoples. The rebellion reflected the rift between the western farmers and the eastern aristocracy represented by the colonial government. When Governor William BERKELEY, perhaps protecting trading interests with the NATIVE AMERICANS, failed to respond to a Native American attack against western settlers, Nathaniel Bacon led a misguided reprisal against innocent Native Americans. In 1676 Berkeley sought to bring the farmers to trial, but the opposition escalated, resulting in the burning of JAMESTOWN. After Bacon's death, the rebellion collapsed.

### Baden, Treaty of (1714)
The treaty which ended the War of the SPANISH SUCCESSION between France and the HOLY ROMAN EMPIRE. It completed the peace process which began with the Peace of Utrecht (1713). Emperor CHARLES VI renounced his claim to the Spanish throne though he refused to recognize the French-backed claimant, PHILIP V of Spain (a Bourbon), until 1720.

### Baden-Powell, Robert Stephenson Smyth Baden-Powell, 1st Baron (1857–1941)
British general. Educated at Charterhouse, he joined the army, served in India and Afghanistan, was on the staff in Ashanti and MATABELELAND, and won fame as the defender of Mafeking in the second Boer War. He founded the Boy Scout movement (1908) and, with his sister Agnes (1858–1945), the Girl Guides (1910). ➤ BOER WARS; MAFEKING, SIEGE OF

### Badoglio, Pietro (1871–1956)
Italian general. Governor of Libya (1929–34), by 1932 he had achieved the pacification of the Sanusi tribesmen. In 1935 he replaced DE BONO at the head of the Conquest of ABYSSINIA where he conducted a campaign of extreme brutality; he became Viceroy of the new colony in May 1936. At the outbreak of WORLD WAR II he initially favoured neutrality but rapidly dropped his opposition to intervention and in June 1940 was made Commander-in-Chief. Humiliating defeats suffered by the Italian army in Greece and Albania prompted Badoglio's resignation (Dec 1940). In 1943 he was asked by VICTOR EMMANUEL III to form an anti-fascist government after the arrest of MUSSOLINI. On 25 Sep Badoglio signed an armistice with the Allies at Malta and in mid-Oct declared war on Germany. Apr 1944 saw the formation of a broad coalition government under Badoglio's leadership (including TOGLIATTI, CROCE and Carlo SFORZA), but after the liberation of Rome in June he was obliged to stand down under pressure from the Americans and politicians with better anti-fascist credentials. He was replaced by Ivanoe BONOMI.

### Bagaza, Jean-Baptiste (1946–)
Burundian politician and soldier. After attending military schools in Belgium he returned to Burundi and became assistant to the head of the armed forces, with the rank of lieutenant-colonel. In 1976 he led a coup to overthrow President Micombero and was appointed President by a Supreme Revolutionary Council. In 1984 the post of Prime Minister was abolished and Bagaza was elected head of state and government. In 1987 he was himself ousted in a coup led by Major Pierre Buyoya. During the civil war in Burundi in 1996, he was a leading supporter of the Tutsis' demands to control the country.

### Bagehot, Walter (1826–77)
British economist, journalist and political theorist. He studied mathematics at London, and spent some time as a banker in his father's firm, then became editor of the *Economist* in 1860. His *English Constitution* (1867) is still considered a standard work. His *Physics and Politics* (1872) applied the theory of evolution to politics. He advocated many constitutional reforms, including the introduction of life peers.

### Baghdad, Sack of (1258)
The sack of Baghdad carried out by the Mongol armies of Hulagu Khan, grandson of GENGHIS KHAN. The initial wrath of Genghis had been kindled by the murder of three of his diplomatic envoys by the Khwarazm-Shah, an action which made the invasion of the Khwarazm-Shah's territories inevitable. By extension, the incident led to the eventual devastation of the Muslim territories by the MONGOLS, the sack of Baghdad and the death of the last 'Abbasid Caliph of Baghdad, al-Mustasim. The latter surrendered on 10 Feb 1258 and the sack of Baghdad, beginning on 13 Feb with the concomitant pillaging, lasted for some seven days.

## Baghdad Pact
Originally a treaty between Turkey and Iraq (1955) aimed at mutual cooperation against militants of the Left. Britain, Pakistan and Iran joined later in 1955 but there was general opposition in Jordan when King **HUSSEIN** proposed becoming a signatory. The **SUEZ CRISIS** compromised Britain's position in 1956 and after the withdrawal of Iraq in 1958 (after the murder of the royal family) the pact ceased to exist as such and was supplanted by the Central Treaty Organization (**CENTO**).

## Baghdad Railway
A railway planned in 1899 by a German company to link Berlin via the Bosphorus to Baghdad and possibly to the **SHATT AL-ARAB**, thereby providing a link between Central Europe and the Persian Gulf. The British feared that this would threaten their interests in the Gulf, southern Persia, and above all India, while the Russians sought to develop Persian railways themselves. The British kept a careful watch on the progress of the line, but it was incomplete before the outbreak of **WORLD WAR I**, and by 1919 the British controlled Mesopotamia (Iraq).

## Bagot, Sir Charles (1781–1843)
British diplomat and Governor-General of Canada. On taking office in 1842, he was advised by the British Colonial Secretary to depend on the **FAMILY COMPACT**. However, he discovered that 'you cannot rule Canada without the French', and that the **DURHAM**–Sydenham programme of Anglicization was causing great resentment amongst the French-Canadians. He therefore appointed as advisers Louis H **LAFONTAINE** as well as Robert **BALDWIN**, and invariably listened to their advice. Since these two men held a majority in the Assembly, this almost amounted to ministerial government or collective responsibility, but Bagot still retained the ultimate decision-making power. In 1843 a fatal illness forced him to resign.

## Bagration, Pyotr Ivanovich, Prince (1765–1812)
Russian soldier. Descended from the royal Bagratidae of Georgia, he entered the Russian army in 1783, and, after much active service, distinguished himself by holding up **MURAT** in a rearguard action at Schöngrabern (1805). He fought too at **AUSTERLITZ** (1805), **EYLAU**, **FRIEDLAND** (1807) and the siege of Silistria (1809). He was mortally wounded at the Battle of **BORODINO**.

## THE BAHAMAS official name Commonwealth of the Bahamas

An independent archipelago of c.700 low-lying islands and over 2,000 cays, forming a chain extending c.500mi/800km south-east from the coast of Flor-

ida. The Bahamas were discovered by **COLUMBUS** in 1492, but the first permanent European settlement was not until 1647, by English and Bermudan religious refugees. The Bahamas became a British Crown Colony in 1717, and were a notorious rendezvous for buccaneers and pirates. The islands gained independence within the **COMMONWEALTH OF NATIONS** in 1973. The head of state remains the British monarch, represented by a Governor-General; the Prime Minister on independence was Sir Lynden **PINDLING**. ► **ARAWAKS**

## Baha-Ullah (1817–92)
Persian religious leader. This was the name, meaning 'Glory of God', given to Mirza Huseyn Ali, founder of the Islamic Baha'i sect. He became a follower of the Shiraz merchant Mirza Ali Mohammed (**BAB-ED-DIN**), founder of the Persian Babi sect. Persecuted and imprisoned in 1852, he was exiled to Baghdad, Constantinople and Acre. In 1863 he proclaimed himself as the prophet that Bab-ed-Din had foretold, and became the leader of the new Baha'i faith.

## Bahmani Sultanate (1347–1518)
A Muslim sultanate in the Deccan, India, founded by Ala al-Din Bahman Shah, an official of the **TUGHLAQ DYNASTY** of the **DELHI SULTANATE**, who declared his independence in that year. The early Bahmani period is mostly recalled for wars and uneasy truces with the Hindu empire of Vijayanagar, and for the brutality and intolerance of the early sultans. In sharp contrast, the later Bahmani period, beginning in the 15c, is remembered for the open-mindedness of its rulers, who practised religious tolerance towards the local majority Hindu population and promoted an air of Persian intellectual diversity similar to that of the **MUGHAL EMPIRE** at its height. The sultanate's capital was Gulbarga (Ahsanabad) until c.1425, when it was transferred to Bidar (Muhammadabad). At the peak of its power, during the period 1466–81, it ruled everything between the Penganga River in the north to Vijayanagar in the south.

## BAHRAIN official name State of Bahrain

A group of 35 islands comprising an independent sheikhdom in the Arabian Gulf, midway between the Qatar Peninsula and mainland Saudi Arabia. A causeway (16mi/25km in length) connects Bahrain to Saudi Arabia. Bahrain was a flourishing trade centre in 2000–1800BC. It was ruled by Iran from 1602 until the Iranian rulers were ousted in 1783 by the al-Khalifa family, who rule to this day. Political control of Bahrain was held by Britain from 1820 to 1971, and oil was discovered during this time, in 1932. In 1971 Bahrain gained independence and **ISA IBN SULMAN**

became ruler. He dissolved the National Assembly in 1975 as a result of disputes between Sunni and Shiite Muslims, and made moves to return to democratic rule only when civil agitation forced him to promise to do so in 1996. On his death in 1999, he was succeeded by his son Hamad bin Isa. A referendum in 2001 approved a new constitution, making Bahrain a constitutional monarchy with a partially elected parliament. The first legislative elections since 1973 were held in 2002. ▶ **GULF COOPERATION COUNCIL**

**Bailly, Jean Sylvain** (1736–93)
French astronomer and politician. From art he turned to literature, and then to astronomy, writing his great *Histoire de l'astronomie* (1775–87). As President of the National Assembly and Mayor of Paris during the **FRENCH REVOLUTION** in 1789, he conducted himself with great integrity, but lost his popularity by allowing the **NATIONAL GUARD** to fire on anti-royalist crowds. He withdrew from public affairs but was arrested and taken to Paris, where he was guillotined.

**Bairakdar, Mustafa** (1755–1808)
Turkish Grand Vizier and Pasha of Rustchuk. After the revolt of the **JANISSARIES** in 1807 by which **SELIM III** was deposed in favour of Mustafa IV, he marched his troops to Constantinople in 1808, but found Selim already dead. Bairakdar executed the murderers, deposed Mustafa, and proclaimed his brother, **MAHMUD II**, Sultan. As Grand Vizier, he endeavoured to carry out Selim's reforms and to annihilate the Janissaries who, however, rebelled and, backed by the fleet, demanded the restoration of Mustafa. Bairakdar defended himself bravely until, having strangled Mustafa, he threw the latter's head to the besiegers, and then blew himself up.

**Bakatin, Vadim Viktorovich** (1937– )
Russian politician. Educated as an engineer in Novosibirsk, he worked in the construction industry before being selected for political work in the Communist Party of the USSR. With further training in social sciences he worked his way up from First Secretary in Kirov (1985–7) and in Kemerovo (1987–8) to the Central Secretariat in Moscow. In search of new blood, Mikhail **GORBACHEV** appointed him Minister of the Interior in 1988 but dismissed him under right-wing pressure (Dec 1990) as too liberal, particularly on the nationalities question. In June 1991 he ran against Boris **YELTSIN** and others for election as President of the Russian Federation, allegedly as Gorbachev's candidate, but he came bottom of the poll. After the failure of the **AUGUST COUP** of the same year, Gorbachev appointed him head of the **KGB** with instructions to convert it to a normal police force but he left at the end of the year.

**Baker, George** ▶ **DIVINE, FATHER**

**Baker, James Addison, III** (1930– )
US public official. He was educated at Princeton and the University of Texas. He served President **FORD** as Under-Secretary of Commerce, and President **REAGAN** as White House Chief of Staff (1981–5) and Secretary of the Treasury (1985–8) before resigning to manage George H W **BUSH**'s campaign for the presidency. After winning the election, Bush made him

Secretary of State. In the final year of the Bush administration he was once again Chief of Staff, and he ran Bush's unsuccessful re-election campaign. When George W **BUSH** ran for the presidency in 2000, Baker was his legal adviser, and later served in the US administration of Iraq after the **IRAQ WAR**.

**Baker, Sir Samuel White** (1821–93)
English explorer. Born in London, in 1860 he undertook the exploration of the Nile sources. At Gondokoro (1863) he met fellow explorers who told him of a great lake, Luta Nzige. In 1864 Baker reached this inland sea into which the Nile flows and renamed it Albert Nyanza. He was knighted in 1866, joined the Prince of Wales in Egypt for the opening of the Suez Canal (1869), and was subsequently invited to command an expedition, organized by **ISMA'IL PASHA**, for the suppression of **SLAVERY** and the annnexation of the equatorial regions of the Nile Basin.

**Baker v Carr** (1962)
The US Supreme Court decision that state electoral districts must contain approximately the same voting population, bringing to an end the long-standing rural domination of state legislatures.

**Bakhtiyaris**
A nomad tribe from the south of what is now Iran. In early 20c Persia they supported the nationalist cause which had been given impetus by gaining the agreement, albeit reluctant, of the Qajar Shah Muzaffar al-Din to the formation of a national assembly. Muzaffar al-Din was succeeded by his son Muhammad Ali who was just as reluctant to have his powers circumscribed as his father had been and, after a bomb attack in an attempt to assassinate him, he called upon Russian-officered Cossack brigades to crush the nationalists in Tehran and Tabriz. Against this background, the Bakhtiyaris, under their leader Sirdari Asad, moved first against Isfahan where they put an end to the autocratic rule of the local governor, and then led a combined nationalist combat force against Tehran. The nationalists succeeded in seizing the capital and deposing the Shah. The Bakhtiyaris were thus instrumental in assisting the Persian nationalists to a triumph, albeit short-lived, as a result of great-power (in this case Russia and Britain) involvement in the politics of the country.

**Bakke case**
A landmark civil rights case challenging the constitutional basis of US **AFFIRMATIVE ACTION** programmes and their use of racial quotas and minority set-asides. The point at issue was that a white engineering graduate, Alan Bakke, who had applied to the American University of California (Davis) medical school in 1973 was not offered a place despite having higher entrance qualifications than most of the black students admitted; of the 100 available places, 16 were reserved for minorities. The US Supreme Court ruled in *Regents of the University of California v Bakke* (1978) that, although the university's actions violated the 14th Amendment and Bakke had been discriminated against and so was entitled to a place, it was nevertheless reasonable to allow race to be considered in admissions decisions. This muddled decision did little to clarify the issues while opening the door for further 'reverse discrimination' cases.

**Bakr, Hasan al-** (1914–82)
President of Iraq. He succeeded Abd al-Rahman Aref as President in 1968, following the Ba'ath coup of July 1968. A leader of the socialist **BA'ATH PARTY**, he held power with Saddam **HUSSEIN**, the Ba'ath leader. Because of his border claims against Iran, al-Bakr was involved in conflict with the **KURDS** in the north of Iraq, a problem he eventually resolved through an agreement reached in 1975. On the economic front, he developed the modernization of both agriculture and industry, the former particularly as a result of irrigation financed by oil revenues. Politically, he made an alliance with the USSR, supported the **PLO** (Palestine Liberation Organization) and was an ally of Syria and Egypt in the 1973 **YOM KIPPUR WAR**. He was succeeded by Saddam Hussein in 1979.

**Bakunin, Mikhail Alexeevich** (1814–76)
Russian anarchist. He took part in the German revolutionary movement (1848–9) and was condemned to death. Sent to Siberia in 1855, he escaped to Japan, and arrived in England in 1861. In the First International (1868), he was the opponent of Karl **MARX**; but at the Hague Congress in 1872 he was outvoted and expelled.

**Balaclava, Battle of** (25 Oct 1854)
A battle fought between British and Russian forces during the early stages of the **CRIMEAN WAR**. The Russian attack on the British base at Balaclava was unsuccessful, but the British sustained the heavier losses.
➤ **CHARGE OF THE LIGHT BRIGADE**

**Balaguer, Joaquín** (1907–2002)
Dominican Republic politician. He was Professor of Law at Santo Domingo University from 1938 and Ambassador to Colombia and Mexico in the 1940s before entering politics. He served in the dictatorial regime of Rafael **TRUJILLO**, after whose assassination in 1961 he fled to the USA in 1962, returning in 1965 to win the presidency in 1966 as leader of the Christian Social Reform Party (PRSC). He was re-elected in 1970 and 1974. The failure of the economic policies of the Dominican Revolutionary Party (PRD) brought the PRSC and Balaguer back to power in 1986, at the age of 79, retaining the presidency until 1996. In 2000 he ran for the presidency again, this time unsuccessfully.

**Balaguer (i Cirera), Victor** (1824–1901)
Catalan poet, politician and historian. A leading figure of the Catalan renaissance, he wrote a *History of Catalonia*, a *Political and Literary History of the Troubadours*, and poems in both Catalan and Spanish.

**Balbo, Cesare** (1789–1853)
Piedmontese politician and political writer. He wrote widely on political problems and Italian history, his most important work, *Delle Speranze d'Italia* ('Of the Hopes of Italy'), appearing in 1844. Echoing **GIOBERTI**, to whom it was dedicated, *Delle Speranze* called for the creation of an Italian Confederation. It also demanded the end of Austrian rule in the Kingdom of **LOMBARDY-VENETIA** and that the Habsburgs seek compensation by expansion into the Balkans. In 1847, in a growing climate of reform, Balbo accepted the invitation of **CHARLES ALBERT** to enter a moderate government and the following year fleetingly held office as Piedmont's first constitutional Prime Minister.

In his final years he supported the policies of **D'AZEGLIO** and **CAVOUR** despite reservations about their anticlericalism. ➤ **HABSBURG DYNASTY**

**Balbo, Italo** (1896–1940)
Italian politician. An early supporter of Italian intervention in **WORLD WAR I**, Balbo served from 1915 as an officer in the Alpini. From 1920 he played a key part in the fascist movement: he was one of the most energetic **RAS** and a Quadrumvir in the **MARCH ON ROME**. During 1923–4 he was commander of the **MVSN** and in 1926 became Secretary of State for Aviation. In Jan 1934 he was made Governor of Libya but was killed when his plane was accidentally brought down by Italian anti-aircraft fire in 1940. He was one of several fascist leaders who disliked **MUSSOLINI**'s move towards **HITLER** and who spoke out in defence of the Jews.

**Balboa, Vasco Núñez de** (1475–1519)
Spanish explorer. In 1511 he joined an expedition to Darién (Central America) as a stowaway. Taking advantage of an insurrection, he took command, founded a colony at Darién and extended Spanish influence into neighbouring areas. On one of these expeditions he climbed a peak and sighted the Pacific Ocean, the first European to do so, and took possession for Spain. The governorship was granted in 1514 to Pedro Arias de Ávila, for whom Balboa undertook many successful expeditions and whose daughter he married. ➤ **EXPLORATION**

**Balczerowicz, Leszek** (1947– )
Polish economist and politician. A talented economic researcher at the Central School of Planning in Warsaw, he was also a strong supporter and adviser of **SOLIDARITY**. In 1989 he was appointed Finance Minister after the **WAŁESA** revolution and achieved something of an economic miracle in stabilizing the currency and introducing the first stage of marketization. Following the 1991 elections, Wałesa judged his economic stringency too unpopular and engineered his dismissal in 1992. His achievement, nonetheless, won wide international praise.

**Baldwin I** (1172–1205)
Count of Flanders, as Baldwin IX (1194/1205), and Hainaut, as Baldwin VI (1195/1205), and Latin Emperor of Constantinople (1204/5). The youngest brother of Godfrey of Bouillon, in 1202 he joined the Fourth **CRUSADE**, and in 1204 was crowned Baldwin I of the Latin Empire in Constantinople. The Greeks, invoking the aid of the Bulgarians, rose and took Adrianople. Baldwin laid siege to the town, but was defeated in 1205 and died in captivity.

**Baldwin II** (1217–73)
Latin Emperor of Constantinople (1228/61). The nephew of **BALDWIN I**, he succeeded his brother, Robert, as fourth and last Emperor of Constantinople, the Greeks taking the city in 1261 and extinguishing the Latin Empire. Thereafter, Baldwin lived as a fugitive, having sold his rights to **CHARLES OF ANJOU**.

**Baldwin II, of Bourcq** (d.1131)
King of Jerusalem (1118/31). He was a son of Count Hugh of Rethel and succeeded his cousin, Baldwin I, as Count of Edessa (1100) and King of Jerusalem (1118).

**Baldwin III** (1129–62)
King of Jerusalem (1143/62). The grandson of **BALD-WIN II**, he succeeded his father, Fulk of Anjou, in 1143, but enjoyed sole authority only after long disputes and even civil war with his mother, Melisend. Baldwin's main achievement was the capture of Ascalon, the last Fatimid stronghold in Palestine (1153). ➤ **FATIMID DYNASTY**

**Baldwin, Robert** (1804–58)
Canadian lawyer and politician. He was the leader of the **CANADA WEST** reforming clique who formed a coalition with Louis H **LAFONTAINE** to establish a reform party, which became a precursor of the **LIBERAL PARTY**. With his father, William Baldwin, he devised the theory of **RESPONSIBLE GOVERNMENT**. This was rejected initially by the British government and governors such as Sir Francis Bond Head and Sir Charles **METCALFE**, although Sir Charles **BAGOT** accepted a level of participation by the Executive Council in government. Metcalfe's autocratic government led both Baldwin and Lafontaine to resign. In 1848 Baldwin came into power again as a partner with Lafontaine in the 'Great Ministry', during the period of transition from colonial rule to self-government.

**Baldwin of Bewdley, Stanley Baldwin, 1st Earl** (1867–1947)
British politician. He worked in his family business before becoming a Conservative MP in 1908. He was President of the Board of Trade (1921–2) and Chancellor of the Exchequer (1922–3), and then unexpectedly succeeded Bonar **LAW** as Prime Minister. His periods of office (1923–4, 1924–9 and 1935–7) included the **GENERAL STRIKE** (1926) and were interrupted by the two minority Labour governments of 1924 and 1929–31. During the **MACDONALD** coalition (1931–5), he served as Lord President of the Council. He played a leading role in arranging the abdication of **EDWARD VIII** in 1936. He resigned from politics in 1937, when he was made an earl. ➤ **CONSERVATIVE PARTY** (UK)

**Balewa, Sir Abubakar Tafawa** (1912–66)
Nigerian politician. After a career as a teacher and education officer, he entered the Nigerian Legco and was a founder-member of the Northern People's Congress. He entered the Federal Assembly in 1947 and was appointed consecutively Federal Minister of Works (1952–4), Minister of Trade (1954–7), Chief Minister (1957–9) and Prime Minister (1959–66). Essentially sympathetic to Western priorities, he was seen within Nigeria as a supporter of northern interests in the first years of independence. He was overthrown and assassinated in the 1966 coup.

**Balfour, Arthur James Balfour, 1st Earl** (1848–1930)
British politician. He entered parliament in 1874, becoming Secretary for Scotland (1886) and Chief Secretary for Ireland (1887–91), where his policy of suppression earned him the name of 'Bloody Balfour'. A Conservative, he was Prime Minister (1902–5) and First Lord of the Admiralty (1915–16). As Foreign Secretary (1916–19), he was responsible for the **BALFOUR DECLARATION** (1917), which promised Zionists a national home in **PALESTINE**. He resigned in 1922, was created an earl, but served again as Lord President (1925–9). ➤ **ZIONISM**

**Balfour Declaration** (2 Nov 1917)
A short communication from the British Foreign Secretary, A J **BALFOUR**, to Lord Rothschild, expressing the British government's disposition towards a Jewish national home in **PALESTINE**. The central portion reads: 'His Majesty's Government view with favour the establishment in Palestine of a national home for the Jewish people ... it being clearly understood that nothing shall be done which may prejudice the civil and religious rights of existing non-Jewish communities'. Britain having received the Mandate for Palestine in 1920, the vagueness of the Balfour Declaration was clarified in 1923: Jewish immigration was to be encouraged; an appropriate Jewish body formed to that end; the rights of non-Jews were to be protected; and English, Hebrew and Arabic were to be given equal status. However, the ensuing two decades showed Britain to be either unwilling or unable to deliver its promise to the Jews, especially in view of increasing Arab hostility to Jewish immigration. ➤ **HAGANAH; IRGUN; JEWISH NATIONAL FUND; ZIONISM**

**Balilla**
The umbrella term for the youth movement founded by the **FASCIST PARTY** in 1926. Its official name, the *Opera nazionale Balilla*, was altered to *Gioventù Italiana del Littorio* in 1937. The organization had many branches for boys and girls of different age groups and aimed at fascist indoctrination and the cultivation of patriotic fervour. It also provided youth clubs, sports facilities and rudimentary military training. Its success in attracting members can be largely attributed to the fascist abolition of the Catholic Boy Scouts Movement in 1928.

**Balkan Entente** (1930)
A cultural and political alliance formed between Greece, Yugoslavia, Romania and Turkey after the first Balkan Conference held in Athens. It became in effect a defensive alliance against revisionist Bulgaria, which sought to regain territory lost to Greece and Yugoslavia by the Treaty of **NEUILLY** (1919). In 1934 the member states signed a pact of mutual security and consultation, but cooperation was limited and the Entente could not counteract great-power interference in the Balkans. During the 1930s, with the establishment of authoritarian regimes in all the Balkan states, the whole region moved closer to the German and Italian camp.

**Balkan Wars** (1912–13)
A series of military campaigns fought in the Balkans. In 1912 Bulgaria, Serbia, Greece and Montenegro attacked Turkey, securing swift victories. A preliminary peace was drawn up by the Great Powers in May 1913, in which Turkey surrendered most of her European territories and the new state of Albania was created. Disputes between the Balkan allies over the spoils of war led to a second war, in which Bulgaria attacked her former allies and was defeated. As a result of the two wars, Turkish territory in Europe was reduced to an area around Adrianople and Constantinople, Albania was established, Macedonia was partitioned, Serbia and Montenegro almost doubled in size, and tension among the Great Powers in Europe was considerably increased.

**Ball, John** (d.1381)
English rebel. Born in St Albans, Hertfordshire, he was an excommunicated priest who was executed as one of the leaders in the PEASANTS' REVOLT (1381), led by Wat TYLER.

**Balli Kombëtar**
The National Front Albanian resistance movement during WORLD WAR II. Formed in Oct 1942 under Ali Klissura and Midhat Frashëri, it was nationalistic and liberal, favouring the establishment of a republic and an extensive programme of domestic reform. Relations with the communist-led resistance were vexed by the issue of KOSOVO, which since 1941 had been included within Albania by the Italians: while Balli Kombëtar wanted to retain Kosovo, the Albanian communists, under pressure from their Yugoslav masters, did not. In 1943, under Allied pressure, the two resistance groups joined to form the Committee for the Salvation of Albania, but at the end of the war many members of Balli Kombëtar fell victim to Enver HOXHA's drive to destroy all internal opposition to communist rule.

**Balliol, Edward** (c.1283–1364)
King of Scots (1332/56). He was the elder son of John BALLIOL. In 1332, accompanied by the 'disinherited barons' bent on recovering their forfeited Scottish estates, he landed with 3,400 followers at Kinghorn, Fife; and at Dupplin Moor, Perthshire, on 12 Aug, surprised and routed the Scottish army under the new Regent, the Earl of Mar. On 24 Sep he was crowned King of Scotland at Scone. Less than three months later, he was himself surprised at Annan and fled across the border on an unsaddled horse. Two further incursions into Scotland, in 1334–5, were unsuccessful and he resigned his claims to the Scottish throne to EDWARD III in 1356. He died without heirs.

**Balliol, John** (c.1250–1313)
King of Scots (1292/6). On the death of MARGARET, MAID OF NORWAY in 1290, he became a claimant to the crown of Scotland, and was supported by EDWARD I of England against Robert BRUCE, Lord of Annandale. Balliol swore fealty to Edward before and after his investiture at Scone (1292) and was forced to repudiate the Treaty of Bingham of 1290 with its guarantees of Scottish liberties. By 1295 a council of 12 of the magnates had taken control of government out of his hands and concluded an alliance with France, then at war with England; Edward invaded Scotland, took Balliol prisoner, and forced him to surrender his crown (10 July 1296). Balliol was confined for three years at Hertford and in the Tower; in 1302 he was permitted to retire to his estates in NORMANDY.

**Balmaceda, José Manuel** (1840–91)
Chilean politician. A Liberal, he was elected to Congress in 1870 and served in the cabinet of President Santa María (1881–6). His strong presidency (1886–91) provoked resistance from Congress; this led to civil war, in which the President was defeated (1891). His suicide mythologized his rule as a struggle against the dominion of foreign, principally British, interests.

**Baltimore, George Calvert, 1st Baron** ► CALVERT, GEORGE

**Baltimore and Ohio Railroad**
The first US passenger-carrying railroad. Its foundation stone was laid on 4 July 1828 by the last surviving signatory of the DECLARATION OF INDEPENDENCE. In 1830 its first section was opened, running horse-powered vehicles over the 13mi/ 21km from Baltimore to Ellicott's Mills. Later that year the railroad turned to steam after Peter Cooper's *Tom Thumb* covered the distance in one hour. By the Civil War the system had become a major element in the transportation links between the mid-west and the east coast. ► RAILWAYS

**Baltimore Incident** (1891)
A brief but serious dispute between the USA and Chile, stemming from the death of two US sailors from the cruiser *Baltimore* in a brawl in Valparaíso. A war between the two countries was averted by a Chilean apology.

**Bambuk**
A region in the valley of the middle and upper Senegal and its tributary, the Faleme, famous for its goldfields, exploited from medieval until modern times and important in trade and the rise and fall of West African kingdoms.

**Banat of Temesvár** ► TEMESVÁR, BANAT OF

**Banda, Hastings Kamuzu** (1898–1997)
Doctor and politician. He left Malawi by foot for South Africa, from where he travelled to the USA and then Britain, obtaining medical qualifications in Tennessee, and Edinburgh and Glasgow universities. He set up practice first in Liverpool and then on Tyneside before moving to London, where he became deeply involved in opposition to the CENTRAL AFRICAN FEDERATION, but, after a scandal involving his liaison with a white woman, he went to Ghana, from where he was persuaded to return to Malawi to lead the Nyasaland African National Congress there. He was jailed in 1959 but was soon released and was appointed Minister of National Resources and Local Government (1961–3), Prime Minister of Nyasaland (1963–4) and then of independent Malawi (1964–6). When the country became a republic he was its first President, and Life President from 1971. He retained many portfolios, notably Defence, throughout his period as President. He made himself Life President of the only political party, the MALAWI CONGRESS PARTY. Depending on a unique mix of populism, a functioning political party and ruthless use of his security apparatus, he survived as the dominant figure in Malawi for over 30 years. However, his popularity declined in the 1990s as demands for multiparty democracy grew and he lost his presidency in 1994 in the first all-party elections. He was later placed under house arrest and put on trial for the murder in 1983 of four politicians, but in Dec 1995 he was acquitted.

**Bandaranaike, Sirimavo Ratwatte Dias** (1916–2000)
Sri Lankan politician. The widow of S W R D BANDARANAIKE, who was assassinated in 1959, she became the first woman Prime Minister in the world when she was elected in 1960. She held office from 1960 to 1965, and again from 1970 to 1977. Her second term was especially turbulent, with the 1971 JVP

(People's Liberation Front) insurrection followed by the introduction of a new republican constitution in 1972 and a period of severe economic shortages. The UNP (United National Party) government of J R JAYAWARDENE stripped her of her CIVIL RIGHTS in 1980, forcing her to relinquish temporarily the leadership of the SLFP (Sri Lanka Freedom Party) to her son, Anura. In 1994 she was appointed Prime Minister by her daughter, Chandrika Bandaranaike KUMARATUNGA, who relinquished the post after being elected President, and served until a few months before her death.

### Bandaranaike, S(olomon) W(est) R(idgeway) D(ias) (1899–1959)
Ceylonese politician. Educated in Colombo and Oxford, he was called to the Bar in 1925. He became President of the Ceylon National Congress, and helped to found the UNP (United National Party). He was Leader of the House in Ceylon's first parliament, and Minister of Health. In 1951 he resigned from the government and organized the SLFP (Sri Lanka Freedom Party). In 1956 he was the main partner in a populist coalition which defeated the UNP in an election dominated by the issue of national language and the spirit of Buddhist revivalism. Bandaranaike's Sinhala-only proposals were opposed by representatives of the TAMIL minority and swiftly followed by outbreaks of Sinhala–Tamil violence. In 1959 he was assassinated by a Buddhist monk. ► KUMARATUNGA, CHANDRIKA BANDARANAIKE; BANDARANAIKE, SIRIMAVO

### bandeirante
A 17c Brazilian slave-raider and explorer. Parties of *bandeirantes* (literally, followers of the *bandeira* standard) sought Indian slaves from the interior from among the sedentary Jesuit-led Guaraní peoples of the Platine Basin and peoples of the Amazon to labour on the coastal plantations. Initially permitted by the colonial government, their expeditions into the interior became a means by which the Portuguese could extend their rule well beyond the formal limits established by the Treaty of Tordesillas. Their conflicts with Indian peoples took them into the gold- and diamond-bearing districts of Minas Gerais and Bahia, which had been discovered by the late 17c. Their legendary feats in securing the interior of Brazil against Spanish, French or Dutch penetration secured them the mythical role of 'pioneers' (equivalent to the Canadian Voyageurs or South African VOORTREKKERS) in Brazil's history.

### Bandiera, Attilio (1810–44) and Emilio (1819–44)
Italian revolutionaries. Sons of a Venetian admiral and lieutenants in the Habsburg navy, in 1840 they founded a nationalist secret society and planned to seize an Austrian frigate and launch a mutiny. Their plans discovered, they deserted ship in Corfu and travelled to the Kingdom of the TWO SICILIES with the intention of launching an insurrection. Captured by Neapolitan troops, they were tried and executed along with seven of their co-conspirators.

### Bandung Conference (Apr 1955)
A meeting in Bandung, Indonesia, of 29 newly independent Afro-Asian countries anxious to distance themselves from the superpower rivalry between the USA and the USSR. Representatives included ZHOU ENLAI (China), NEHRU (India), SIHANOUK (Cambodia), U NU (Burma) and Gamal Abd al-NASSER (Egypt). Communist China's participation, which signalled its emergence as an actor on the world stage, indicated Beijing's determination to pursue a foreign policy independent of that of Moscow and the desire to deal amicably with those governments (such as that of India) hitherto deemed 'lackeys' of US imperialism. Zhou Enlai expressed this new conciliatory policy with his Five Principles of Peaceful Co-Existence (first enunciated in 1954), which looked forward to peaceful relations with all countries (including the USA) on the basis of mutual respect for each other's territorial integrity, non-interference in each other's affairs and non-aggression. Thus, the conference sought to establish the non-aligned, newly emerging nations as a major force in world politics, free from the shabby self-interest and manipulative interventions practised by the established blocs. It was a major triumph, domestically and internationally, for the Indonesian President SUKARNO.

### Banerjea, Sir Surendranath (1848–1925)
Indian politician and journalist. A fervent nationalist, he founded the Calcutta Indian Association in 1876 and was editor of *The Bengali* newspaper from 1879 to 1921. Initially regarded as 'extremist' by the British, but later as a moderate, he was important in the INDIAN NATIONAL CONGRESS (of which he was President in 1902), a member of the Calcutta Corporation and twice returned to the Central Legislature. He welcomed the MONTAGU-CHELMSFORD REFORMS for the government of India, and subsequently broke with Congress over the non-cooperation question. ► NON-COOPERATION MOVEMENT

### Bánffy, Dezsö, Baron (1843–1911)
Hungarian politician. He was born into an aristocratic family in Transylvania, where the population was ethnically mixed. In 1876 he became Lord Lieutenant of the county of Szolnok-Doboka, acquiring a reputation for denying the rights of nationalities other than his fellow Magyars. In 1892 he became Speaker of the Hungarian parliament, and from 1895 to 1899 he was Prime Minister. In these capacities he was much concerned with developing the ruthless policy of enforced Magyarization as an antidote to the emerging nationalism of the subject peoples of the Hungarian half of the Austro-Hungarian Empire.

### BANGLADESH official name People's Republic of Bangladesh, formerly East Pakistan
An Asian republic lying between the foothills of the Himalayas and the Indian Ocean, bounded to the west, north-west and east by India; to the south-east by Myanmar; and to the south by the Bay of Bengal. Bangladesh formed part of the State of Bengal until Muslim East Bengal was created in 1905, separate from Hindu West Bengal. Reunited in 1911, East and West Bengal were again partitioned in 1947, with West Bengal remaining in India and East Bengal forming East Pakistan. Disparity in investment and development between East and West Pakistan (separated by over 1,000mi/1,600km), coupled with language differences, caused East Pakistan to seek autonomy. The suspension of democracy following a sweeping

electoral victory by the **AWAMI LEAGUE** in East Pakistan in 1970, the devastation of this province of Pakistan by a cyclone in the same year (it is one of the world's most densely populated areas), and the Dhaka government's ineffectual response to the disaster – which claimed 220,000 lives and countless homes and crops – triggered fighting, which developed into a full-scale civil war in 1971. Pakistan surrendered the territory only after several months, following a popular uprising and military intervention by India, which had accepted huge numbers of Bangladeshi refugees; thus the independent republic of Bangladesh was created. It joined the **COMMONWEALTH OF NATIONS** a year later. Political unrest led to the suspension of the constitution in 1975, and the assassination of the first President, **MUJIBUR RAHMAN** (Sheikh Mujib). There were further coups in 1975, when the Awami League was overthrown and disbanded, as well as in 1977 and 1982. The constitution was restored in 1986. The Awami League later regrouped and rose to become a major political force, and in 1996, led by Sheikh Hasina **WAJED**, it defeated the Bangladesh Nationalist Party of Khaleda **ZIA**, but lost the 2001 election to Khaleda Zia's coalition..

### Bani-Sadr, Abolhassan (1935– )
Iranian politician. He studied economics and sociology at the Sorbonne in Paris, having fled there in 1963 after being imprisoned in Iran for involvement in riots against the Shah's regime. He was an important figure in the **IRANIAN REVOLUTION** of 1979, a member of the Revolutionary Council, and was elected first President of the Islamic Republic of Iran in 1980. From the start, however, he was threatened by a deepening conflict with the fundamentalist Muslim clergy; he was eventually criticized by Ayatollah **KHOMEINI**, and dismissed (mid-1981). He fled to France, where he was granted political asylum. The same year, he formed the National Council of Resistance to oppose the Iranian government and was chairman until 1984.

### Bank War (1832)
An anti-national bank policy adopted by US President Andrew **JACKSON**, when he vetoed the re-charter of the Second Bank of the United States which had been passed through **CONGRESS** under the patronage of the **NATIONAL REPUBLICAN PARTY**. Like many Americans, especially in the West, Jackson believed that the bank had been responsible for the depression of the 1820s. He accused the bank of being a monopoly and representing big business, of allowing

foreigners too much influence, of showing favour to congressmen, and of having too much power over state banks. Jackson refused, against the advice of two Secretaries of the Treasury, to allow any more federal revenues to be deposited with the bank, placing them instead with favoured state banks. Flush with new deposits and without the restraints which the national Bank had placed on their activities, the state banks encouraged another speculative boom which collapsed in the panic of 1837, after Jackson had been succeeded by Martin **VAN BUREN**.

### Banna, Hasan al- (1906–49)
Islamic fundamentalist. Born at Mahmudiya, near Cairo, he was the founder in Egypt in 1928 of the Society of Muslim Brothers (better known as the **MUSLIM BROTHERHOOD** or Brethren), which preached a return to the purity of early Islam. In 1948 the Egyptian Prime Minister, Nuqrashi Pasha, was killed by a Brotherhood member, and the following year al-Banna was himself murdered, although he had condemned the assassination. His movement has had considerable influence on contemporary Islamic fundamentalism.

### Banna, Sabri Khalil al- ► ABU NIDAL

### Banner System
A system of military organization in China, created by **NURHACI** and used by the Manchu tribes. By the early 17c, the Manchus were organized into companies of 300 troops under at first four and then eight banners. By 1644, eight Chinese and eight Mongol banners had been formed, comprising an army of 170,000 men. The system survived throughout the **QING DYNASTY**.

### Bannockburn, Battle of (21 June 1314)
A battle fought near Stirling between English forces under **EDWARD II** and the Scots under Robert **BRUCE**. It resulted in a decisive victory for the Scots. The English army was largely destroyed, and many English nobles were killed or captured. The battle made Bruce a national hero, and inspired Scottish counter-attacks against northern England.

### Bantustans ► APARTHEID

### Bao Dai, originally Nguyen Vinh Thuy (1913–97)
Indo-Chinese ruler. He succeeded his father in 1925, ascending the throne in 1932. He collaborated with the Japanese during **WORLD WAR II** and, after the Japanese surrender, found very brief favour with **HO CHI MINH**. He abdicated in 1945, but returned to Saigon in 1949 (having renounced his hereditary title), as Chief of the State of Vietnam within the French Union. In 1955 he was deposed by **NGO DINH DIEM** and South Vietnam became a republic.

### Baojia (Pao-chia) System
An administrative arrangement of household control and surveillance in China dating from the **SONG DYNASTY** (960–1279). Village families were grouped into units of 100 (jia) and 1,000 (bao), presided over by local elders. Originally responsible for providing and provisioning militia conscripts, by the time of the **QING DYNASTY** (1644–1911) the baojia system simply fulfilled a police function of mutual surveillance. All households were registered and were made responsible for the actions of their members.

## Bar, Confederation of (1768)

A military alliance of Polish gentry established at Bar, Podolia, directed against the Russian-backed king, Stanisław **PONIATOWSKI**. The Confederation advocated the preservation of the privileges of the Polish aristocracy and the Roman Catholic Church. Its suppression in 1772 led to the first partition of Poland.

### BARBADOS

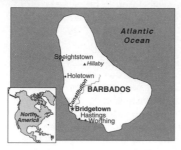

An independent state and the most easterly of the Caribbean Islands, situated in the Atlantic Ocean. It was colonized by the English in 1627 and attained self-government in 1961, becoming an independent sovereign state within the **COMMONWEALTH OF NATIONS** in 1966. ► **DEMOCRATIC LABOUR PARTY**

## Barbary Coast

The coast of North Africa from Morocco to Tripolitania (Libya), famous for piracy between the 16c and 18c. This coast and the Barbary States of Morocco, Algeria, Tunisia and Tripolitania take their name either from the pirate Barbarossa, or from the Berber people of the region.

## Barbary Wars (1801–15)

A series of intermittent armed engagements between US Navy and Marine forces and pirates who operated from the North African kingdoms of Morocco, Algeria, Tunis and Tripolitania in the early years of the 19c. The rulers of these kingdoms encouraged the pirates, and demanded tribute payments from other countries to protect their shipping from attack. At first the USA paid the tribute, but when the Pasha of Tripoli increased his demands in 1801 and the Dey of Algeria increased his demands in 1812, the USA sent naval expeditions that won quick victories; the latter expedition resulted in treaties that permanently ended pirate attacks against US shipping. The **BARBARY COAST**, an early name for the coastal, western North African region, is the source of the term 'Barbary Wars'.

## Barberini

A Tuscan family which acquired wealth by trade in the 16c, and rose to the front rank of the Roman nobility on the elevation of Maffeo to the papacy as **URBAN VIII** in 1623. Francesco (1597–1679), brother of Cardinal Taddeo, founded the Barberini Library. Antonio (1608–71) was cardinal and high chamberlain under Urban VIII. Their power and ambition aroused the jealousy of neighbouring princes and led to war (1641–4) and the defeat of papal troops by the Duke of Parma. The Barberini fled to France, but returned in 1652.

## Barbosa, Ruí (1849–1923)

Brazilian politician and lawyer. After studying law, he practised in Salvador and then in Rio de Janeiro. A Liberal, he was elected a deputy in 1878, and became prominent in 1884–5 at the peak of the anti-slavery campaign. A radical, he campaigned against the last cabinet of the monarchy, siding with the Republicans in Nov 1889. He was Finance Minister and also briefly Vice-Chief of the Provisional Government of the Republic. His controversial 14 months of power saw the introduction of financial measures which stimulated hyperinflation and massive government deficits, a legacy which meant that he never succeeded in regaining high office. As Senator for Bahia from 1891 until his death, he campaigned in favour of a more liberal regime, being exiled in 1893–4, and defeated on an 'anti-military' ticket in the presidential election of 1910. Special Ambassador to the Hague Conference in 1907, he defended the idea that all states were equal in international law.

## Barcelona, Siege of (1713–14)

The final drama of the War of the **SPANISH SUCCESSION**, when the Catalans were abandoned by their allies, the Germans and the English, and forced to defend themselves or accept unconditional surrender. After a bloody siege, the Duke of **BERWICK** at the head of the Franco-Spanish army entered the city and abolished its privileges (*fueros*) and those of all Catalonia. The date of the surrender (11 Sep) is now commemorated as the national day of Catalonia. Barcelona was the seat of a principality from the 9c, and the centre of resistance to Castilian rule during the revolution of 1640. It was besieged several times, notably by the French in 1697.

## Barclay de Tolly, Mikhail Bogdanovich, Prince (1761–1818)

Russian field marshal. He joined the Russian army in 1786, and served in Turkey, Sweden and Poland, losing an arm at the Battle of **EYLAU** (1807). He was appointed Minister of War in 1810. Defeated by Napoleon at Smolensk (1812), and replaced, he later served again as Commander-in-Chief, and took part in the invasion of France. He was made a prince in 1815, and died at Insterburg, eastern Prussia. ► **ALEXANDER I; NAPOLEON I**

## Bardi and Peruzzi

These Florentine families gave their names to two great banking companies of the 14c, commanding assets far greater than those of the later and more famous Medici bank. They advanced loans to European monarchs, most notably **EDWARD III**, who used the money to finance his campaigns in the **HUNDRED YEARS' WAR**. He reneged on his debts in 1345, which led to bankruptcy for the Bardi and Peruzzi firms and sent shock waves through the European economy.

## Bardoli

A town in Surat district, near Bombay, it was the scene of a very successful tax reduction campaign lasting from 12 Feb to 4 Aug 1928. Led by Sardar **PATEL**, using M K **GANDHI**'s **SATYAGRAHA** technique, the protest called for an impartial review of an apparently arbitrary increase in local land revenue forecast used for tax assessments. In Mar 1929 an appointed committee reported that the increase was excessive by 15.75 per cent, and the rate was lowered.

## Barebone's Parliament (4 July–12 Dec 1653)

The English 'Parliament of Saints', nominated by the

Council of Officers of the Army to succeed the **RUMP PARLIAMENT**, and named after radical member Praise-God Barebone. It instituted civil marriage and sought legal reforms but collapsed after disagreements over the abolition of tithes and lay patronage in church.

**Barère (de Vieuzac), Bertrand** (1755–1841)
French revolutionary and regicide, noted for his achievement of survival. Originally a monarchist, he went over to **ROBESPIERRE**'s camp, becoming a member of the Committee of **PUBLIC SAFETY**. He was later imprisoned (1794), but escaped into exile, not returning to Paris until 1830. ► **FRENCH REVOLUTION**

**Bar-Lev Line**
The chain of fortifications established after the **SIX-DAY WAR** on the east of the Suez Canal by Chaim Bar-Lev, Israeli Chief of Staff. This was in response to continued Egyptian attacks under Gamal Abd al-**NASSER**, despite ceasefire agreements. In the **YOM KIPPUR WAR** of 1973, however, the Bar-Lev Line was not able to withstand the initial onslaught of Egyptian forces. ► **ARAB–ISRAELI WARS**

**Barnardo, Thomas John** (1845–1905)
Irish doctor and philanthropist. Born in Dublin, he was the founder of homes for destitute children. A clerk by profession, he was converted to Christianity in 1862, and after a spell of preaching in the Dublin slums went to London (1866) to study medicine with the aim of becoming a medical missionary. Instead, he founded, while still a student, the East End Mission for destitute children in Stepney (1867) and a number of homes in Greater London, which came to be known as the 'Dr Barnardo's Homes'. The organization now flourishes under the name of Barnardos, and is the largest child care charity working in the UK.

**Barnave, Antoine Pierre Joseph Marie** (1761–93)
French revolutionary. He studied law, and became a member of the new National Assembly (1799), where he established a reputation as an orator, and helped to carry through the **CIVIL CONSTITUTION OF THE CLERGY**. He brought back the royal family from Varennes, but, after advocating more moderate courses, was guillotined. ► **FRENCH REVOLUTION**

**Barneveldt, Jan van Olden** ► **OLDENBARNEVELDT, JAN VAN**

**Barons' Wars** (1215–17 and 1263–7)
Two wars in England during the reigns of **JOHN** and **HENRY III**. The first came about after the sealing of **MAGNA CARTA**: many barons still defied John, and offered the crown to Prince Louis (later **LOUIS VIII**) of France. After John's death, the French and baronial army was routed at Lincoln (May 1217), and the war was effectively ended by the Treaty of Kingston-upon-Thames (Sep 1217). The second war broke out after the Provisions of **OXFORD** failed to achieve a settlement, and some barons led by Simon de **MONTFORT**, captured Henry III at Lewes (1264). Earl Simon was killed at Evesham (1265), and the King was restored to power by the Dictum of Kenilworth (1266).

**Barotseland** ► **LOZI STATE**

**Barras, Paul François Jean Nicolas, Count of** (1755–1829)
French revolutionary. An original member of the Jacobin Club, and a regicide, he played the chief part in the overthrow of **ROBESPIERRE**, and was given dictatorial powers by the National **CONVENTION**. In 1795, acting against a royalist uprising, he was aided by his friend Bonaparte, who fired on the rebels (the historical 'whiff of grape-shot'). Barras became one of the five members of the **DIRECTORY** (1795). Once more dictator in 1797, he guided the state almost alone, until his hedonism and corruption made him so unpopular that Bonaparte overthrew him easily (1799). After travelling abroad, he died at Paris-Chaillot. ► **FRENCH REVOLUTION**; **JACOBINS**; **NAPOLEON I**

**Barre, Muhammad Siad** (1919–95)
Somali soldier and politician. Educated locally and at an Italian military academy, he was a police officer in Somaliland, under both Italian and British trusteeship, before joining the Somali army in 1960. He led a successful coup in 1969. Using a **KGB**-trained secret service and manipulating the clan divisions of the Somalis, he was backed first by the USSR and then by the USA. When uprisings took place in 1989, his use of the air force and army to stamp out the opposition proved unavailing and he was forced to leave Mogadishu (Jan 1991), leaving behind an impoverished country divided into competing warring factions.

**Barre, Raymond** (1924– )
French conservative politician. He made his reputation as an influential neo-liberal economist at the Sorbonne and as Vice-President of the European Commission (1967–72). He was Minister of Foreign Trade under President **GISCARD D'ESTAING** and was appointed Prime Minister (1976–81) after the resignation of Jacques **CHIRAC** in 1976. Holding concurrently the Finance Ministry portfolio, he concentrated on economic affairs, gaining a reputation as a determined budget-cutter. With unemployment mounting between 1976 and 1981, he became deeply unpopular, but his term as Prime Minister was later favourably reassessed after the failure of the 1981–3 socialist administration's reflationary experiment. During the 1980s he built up a firm political base in the Lyons region, representing the centre-right Union for French Democracy (UDF). He contested the 1988 presidential election but was eliminated in the first ballot.

**Barrès, Maurice** (1862–1923)
French novelist and politician. A member of the Chamber of Deputies (1889–93), he was an apostle of nationalism, individualism, provincial patriotism and national energy. He wrote a trilogy on his own self-analysis (Le Culte du moi, 1888–91), and a nationalistic trilogy that included L'Appel au soldat (1906), and many other works, including Colette Baudoche (1909).

**Barreto, Francisco de** (1520–73)
Portuguese military commander. He attempted an ambitious conquest of the Zambezi Valley, the Mashonaland plateau and the kingdom of **MWENE MUTAPA** in 1572. In 1575 a treaty was concluded

between the Portuguese and the Mwene Mutapa ruler whereby Muslims would be expelled and the Portuguese be allowed to trade, to seek gold and conduct missionary work. The Portuguese maintained trading footholds in the interior of what is now Zimbabwe until expelled in the 1690s.

**Barrier Treaties** (1697, 1709 and 1715)
A series of agreements giving the Dutch Republic the right to garrison certain towns in the southern Netherlands as a protection against potential French encroachments. The first was signed between the Dutch and Spain in 1697, the second between the Dutch and the English in 1709, and the third between the Dutch, the English and the Austrians in 1715. In the War of the **AUSTRIAN SUCCESSION** (1740–8), the towns were overrun by the French. In 1781 Emperor **JOSEPH II** declared the treaties void and returned the garrisons to the Netherlands.

**Barrow, Errol Walton** (1920–87)
Barbadian politician. Born in Barbados, he flew with the Royal Air Force (1940–7) and then studied at London University and Lincoln's Inn. Returning to Barbados, he became active in the Barbados Labour Party (BLP) and was elected to the House of Assembly in 1951. In 1955 he left the BLP and co-founded the **DEMOCRATIC LABOUR PARTY (DLP)**, becoming its Chairman in 1958. In the elections following independence in 1961 the DLP was victorious and Barrow became the first Prime Minister. His unbroken tenure was ended in 1976 by the BLP, led by 'Tom' Adams. In 1986, a year after Adams's death, Barrow returned to power with a decisive majority but he died in the following year and was succeeded by Erskine Lloyd Sandiford.

**Barry, Marie-Jeanne Gomard de Vaubernier, Countess du** (c.1743–1793)
French noblewoman. The favourite mistress of **LOUIS XV**, her influence reigned supreme until his death (1774), when she was dismissed from court. She was tried before the Revolutionary Tribunal, and guillotined. ▶ **FRENCH REVOLUTION**

**Bart** or **Barth, Jean** (1650–1702)
French privateer. He served first in the Dutch navy, turning to French service on the outbreak of the war with Holland (1672). In 1691 he commanded a small squadron in the North Sea, where he destroyed many English vessels. In the War of the Grand Alliance (1689–97), he was taken prisoner, but escaped from Plymouth to France, where **LOUIS XIV** received him, rewarding him with command of a squadron, and later giving him noble status.

**Barthou, Jean Louis** (1862–1934)
French politician. He practised law, and was a member of parliament from 1889 until his death. From 1894 onwards he frequently held ministerial office, becoming Prime Minister in 1913, when he introduced three-year conscription. He was briefly Foreign Minister in 1917 and criticized the Treaty of **VERSAILLES** (1919) for not providing enough security for France. After **WORLD WAR I** he was again almost continually in office, as Minister of War (1921–2, 1930–1), Minister of Justice (1922–4, 1926–9) and Foreign Minister (1934). He presided over the French delegation at the Genoa Conference (1922), and was

President of the Reparations Committee. As part of his attempt to strengthen French links with the states of Eastern Europe against the threat from Germany (an 'Eastern Locarno Treaty'), he invited King Alexander I of Yugoslavia to France; he was assassinated with him by Croatian terrorists in Marseilles.

**Barton, Clara**, popular name of **Clarissa Harlowe Barton** (1821–1912)
US humanitarian and founder of the US **RED CROSS**. A schoolteacher (1836–54) and clerk in the Patent Office in Washington, DC (1854–7), during the **AMERICAN CIVIL WAR** she organized the distribution of hospital supplies and nursed the wounded, becoming known as the 'angel of the battlefield'. She worked for the International Red Cross in Europe during the **FRANCO-PRUSSIAN WAR** (1870–1). After returning to the USA she established the US branch of the Red Cross in 1881 and became its first President (1881–1904). As a result of her campaigning, in 1882 the USA signed the **GENEVA CONVENTION** for the humane treatment of the wounded and prisoners of war.

**Barton, Sir Edmund** (1849–1920)
Australian jurist and politician, the first Prime Minister of the Australian Commonwealth (1901–3). He was elected to the New South Wales legislature in 1879, becoming Speaker (1883–7) and Attorney-General (1889 and 1891–3). He was leader of the **FEDERATION** movement from 1891, headed the committee that drafted the Commonwealth Constitution Bill, and led the delegation that presented it to the British parliament in 1900. From 1903 until his death he served as a High Court judge.

**Baruch, Bernard Mannes** (1870–1965)
US financier. In 1918 he was appointed by President Woodrow **WILSON** to head the War Industries Board, with sweeping powers to establish priorities and increase production. His appointment symbolized a new alliance between a Democratic administration which had previously acted against the excesses of big business, and industry which now wished to combine patriotism with its own interests. A conservative Democrat and supporter of Alfred **SMITH**, Baruch was one of the few speculators who anticipated the **WALL STREET CRASH** and so preserved his fortune. Often critical of the more radical aspects of the **NEW DEAL**, he nevertheless frequently advised President Franklin D **ROOSEVELT**. In 1946 he presented the US plan for atomic energy control to the **UN**.

**Barzani, Mustafa al-** (1904–79)
Kurdish military leader and mullah. He commanded the Peshmerga guerrillas and negotiated a promise of autonomy for the **KURDS** in northern Iraq in 1970. However, President **BAKR**'s failure to honour his pledge led to further Iraqi–Kurdish conflict, resulting in the defeat of the Peshmerga by Saddam **HUSSEIN**, who took over the presidency in 1979.

**Basic Law** (*Grundgesetz*)
The Basic Law forms a major component within the Federal German constitutional order. In the period 1949–90, the Basic Law accepted the western Allied provision that Federal Germany have a market-oriented economy (although it did not exclude alternative options in the future) and that in political

matters ultimate sovereignty lay with the (non-functioning) Allied Control Commission. With German reunification these limitations on sovereignty lapsed. In its content the Basic Law represents a summation of previous German constitutional experience which learns from past successes and failures. It establishes the principle of constitutional democracy with ultimate sovereignty lying with the people and it defines the rights of the **BUND** and *Länder*. The Basic Law has been amended dozens of times by act of parliament and although previously regarded as a provisional creation pending eventual reunification, it has survived in slightly amended form in a reunited Germany. ► **LAND**

**Basic Treaty** (*Grundvertrag*) (8 Nov 1972)
The treaty signed between Federal (West) and East Germany under which each promised to respect the other's independence and sovereignty. East Germany claimed that the agreement finalized Germany's division, the West maintained in a note delivered to East Berlin that it did not preclude the possibility of unification in a future, more peaceful Europe. The treaty marked a key success in Willy **BRANDT**'s policy of **OSTPOLITIK**, not least because it allowed the resumption of personal contacts between East and West Germans.

**Basil II, Bulgaroctonus** (c.958–1025)
Byzantine Emperor (963 (976)/1025). The son of Romanus II, he came to the throne as sole ruler in 976. A revolt by the nobleman Bardas Sclerus was quashed with the help of the general Bardas Phocas, but a decade later both men revolted in turn with much of the army and aristocracy. Basil was saved by his alliance with **VLADIMIR I, THE GREAT**, Prince of Kiev, who married his sister Anna and converted to Christianity. In return, Vladimir sent 6,000 Russian troops who defeated the uprising (989) and became the core of the future Varangian Guard, the élite unit of the Byzantine army. Thereafter, Basil supported the peasantry at the expense of the great landowners. His 15-year war against the Bulgarians culminated in the victory in the Belasica Mountains, which earned him his surname of 'Bulgar-slayer'; thousands of prisoners were blinded and in groups of a hundred, each led by a one-eyed man, sent back to their Tsar Samuel, who died of shock (1015). Bulgaria was annexed to the empire by 1018, while the eastern frontier was extended to Lake Van in Armenia.

**Basle, Council of** (1431–49)
A controversial Council of the Church. It was intended to continue the work of the Council of Constance, against heresy and initiating reform, but fell into dispute with Pope **EUGENIUS IV** for asserting the authority of the Council over that of the Pope. When the Pope attempted to dissolve it, the Council appointed Felix V (**AMADEUS VIII, THE PEACEFUL**), the last of the anti-popes.

**Basle, Treaties of** (7 Sep 1795)
Two separate treaties were signed during the wars associated with the **FRENCH REVOLUTION**. The first was between France and Prussia (5 Apr), and accepted the French occupation of German lands west of the Rhine. In the second (22 July), Spain ceded the Dominican Republic to France. The treaty is connected with the Treaty of **RASTATT**.

**Basle, Treaty of** (22 Sep 1499)
The treaty which put an end to the so-called Swiss or Swabian War between **MAXIMILIAN I** and the Swiss Confederation. In it the Swiss obtained stewardship of the Thurgau but had to accept Austrian overlordship in Graubünden. More significantly, the treaty declared that Switzerland was not subject to the imperial court of taxes, thus hastening its separation from the **HOLY ROMAN EMPIRE**.

**Basle Convention on the Control of Trans-Boundary Movement of Hazardous Material and Disposal** (1989)
A convention monitoring the movement of hazardous (toxic, poisonous, corrosive, flammable, eco-toxic or infectious) waste across international boundaries, requiring the exporting state to give prior written notification to states involved in both import and transit. It was adopted in 1989, and came into force in 1992. The Convention's operation is hampered by the USA's failure to ratify it. It is administered by the UN Environmental Programme and the secretariat is located in Geneva, Switzerland.

**Basque Autonomy Statutes** (1936 and 1979)
One of the oldest peoples in Europe, the Basques first formed a political entity with their unification under the Kingdom of **NAVARRE** in the 10c and 11c. With the decline of Navarre, the Basque provinces became integrated into the Kingdom of **CASTILE** by the 16c. The Basques retained their feudal laws and privileges until these were steadily abolished during the 19c. The Second Republic (1931–6) created an autonomous regime through the Statute of Oct 1936, but this was rescinded at the end of the **SPANISH CIVIL WAR** by General **FRANCO**. Franco's dictatorship (1939–75) tried to suppress all aspects of Basque independence and culture. In 1979 a new Basque Autonomy Statute was passed, although it did not include Navarre, which obtained its own autonomous arrangement in 1982. The 1979 Autonomy Statute provided for the Basque country's own parliament, police force, tax authority, and control of the means vital to the survival of Basque culture, such as Basque schools and television in *Euskera* (the Basque language). The fight for outright independence is maintained by **ETA**. ► **REPUBLIC, SECOND** (Spain)

**Basque Nationalist Party** ► **PNV**

**Basques**
A people of uncertain origin living in north-west Spain and neighbouring areas in France. They are physically similar to their neighbours and are Roman Catholics, but their language, Basque, spoken by c.500,000, does not relate to any other European language and is thought to be a remnant of the languages spoken in Western Europe before the advent of the Indo-European family. Despite extensive cultural and linguistic assimilation, urbanized Basques retain a strong ethnic identity, and their main city, Bilbao, is a centre of Basque nationalism. Most Basques supported the Spanish Republic, which granted an autonomy statute in Oct 1936, during the **SPANISH CIVIL WAR**. After the fall of Bilbao (June 1937), many went into exile. Since the death of **FRANCO** (1975), the new liberal Spanish monarchy granted Basques

some local autonomy (1978–9), but the more militant continued to agitate for a separate Basque state through the terrorist organization ETA. The use of militant means to secure autonomy was first called into question when ETA announced a ceasefire in 1998, which lasted until Nov 1999.

### Bastille
A medieval fortress and prison in east Paris, the symbol of Bourbon despotism, stormed by a Parisian mob on 14 July 1789. Its destruction came to have a unique place in French revolutionary ideology as marking the end of the ANCIEN RÉGIME. The anniversary of the day is a French national holiday. ► BOURBON, HOUSE OF; FRENCH REVOLUTION

### Batavian Republic
The name given to the Dutch Republic (1795–1806), after that country had been conquered by revolutionary French forces in 1794–5. Much influence was exerted from Paris, but the Dutch retained a degree of independence, and fought out their own battles between radicals and conservatives during the revolutionary era. Between 1806 and 1810 the Kingdom of Holland was ruled by NAPOLEON I's brother, LOUIS NAPOLEON; in 1810 the Netherlands was incorporated into France until the collapse of French rule in 1813. ► FRENCH REVOLUTIONARY WARS; NAPOLEONIC WARS

### Batista (y Zaldívar), Fulgencio (1901–73)
Cuban dictator. In 1933 he organized a military coup (the 'Sergeants' Revolt'), consolidated his power, and became President (1940–4). In 1952 he overthrew President Prio Socorras, and ruled as dictator until his overthrow by Fidel CASTRO (Jan 1959), when he found refuge in the Dominican Republic.

### Batlle (y Ordóñez), José (1856–1929)
Uruguayan politician. Educated in Montevideo and Europe, he founded the newspaper El día in 1886, rallying the support of the articulate middle sectors of Montevideo. He was elected Senator (1896), then President (1903–7 and 1911–15). Nominally a Colorado (or liberal constitutionalist), he crushed the conservative Blancos (estancieros who had dominated the interior of the country). Supported by foreign immigrants and workers, he designed a political system in which power was shared between the President and a nine-member National Council. He was a notable social reformer and exponent of democratic ideals.

### Batman, John (1801–39)
Australian colonizer, the 'Founder of Victoria'. He became a grazier in Tasmania (1821) and found fame by capturing the bushranger Matthew Brady. In May 1835 he colonized the shores of Port Phillip from Tasmania. He was the main founder of Melbourne, seeing the potential of its site.

### Battenberg, Prince Alexander of (1857–93)
First Prince of Bulgaria (1879/86). The uncle of Earl MOUNTBATTEN, he was the second son of Prince Alexander of Hesse and, through his mother, a nephew of Tsar ALEXANDER II of Russia. In 1879 he was named as a suitable candidate as Prince of Bulgaria by the Great Powers which, while accepting that Russia would be Bulgaria's protector, did not want the

new principality to fall to a major ruling dynasty. A German aristocrat with military training, Prince Alexander had no sympathy with the ideas of the predominant Bulgarian Liberal Party. After the accession of his reactionary cousin ALEXANDER III as Tsar of Russia, he suspended the highly liberal Bulgarian constitution. Bulgarian–Russian relations deteriorated as the new Tsar treated Bulgaria as tantamount to a Russian province. In 1886 Prince Alexander was overpowered by pro-Russian army conspirators at Sofia and was forced to abdicate. Unable to overcome the hostility of Alexander III, he retired to Darmstadt in Austria as Count Hartenau.

### Batthyányi, Louis, Count (1806–49)
Hungarian politician. A member of the Hungarian assembly, and a leader of the independence movement, he was executed by the Austrians for his part in the Hungarian insurrection of 1849. His estates were confiscated, but were restored to his family in 1867. In 1870 his body was removed and interred anew with great solemnity.

### Baudouin I (1930–93)
King of the Belgians (1951/93). The elder son of LEOPOLD III and his first wife, Queen ASTRID, he succeeded to the throne on the abdication of his father over the controversy of the latter's conduct during WORLD WAR II. In 1960 he married the Spanish Fabiola de Mora y Aragon. He was succeeded by his brother, Albert II.

### Baudouin IX of Flanders ► BALDWIN I

### Bauer, Gustav (1870–1944)
German politician. A senior trade unionist before WORLD WAR I, Bauer became an SPD member of the REICHSTAG in 1912. In Oct 1918 he was appointed a Junior Minister of Labour and became Minister of Labour in Feb 1919. He succeeded SCHEIDEMANN as Chancellor and on 26 June 1919 headed the government that signed the Treaty of VERSAILLES under protest. He resigned as Chancellor during the KAPP PUTSCH (Mar 1920) and, after holding various further ministerial posts, eventually resigned from parliament in 1928 on becoming involved in a corruption trial.

### Bava Beccaris, Fiorenzo (1831–1924)
Italian general. His brutality in suppressing the Milan bread riots in 1898 was pivotal in both the fall of the DI RUDINI government and the decline in popularity of UMBERTO I.

### Bavaria
A south-east German region and, although much changed in size and structure in the course of time, one of the oldest existing political entities in Europe. First documented as a duchy under Frankish overlordship in the 6c, Bavaria included most of present-day Austria until 1156 and was ruled by a succession of dynasties, including the GUELFS, before the House of WITTELSBACH took over in 1180. Presiding over the country until 1918, members of this family won the German crown on two occasions (Louis IV, 1314/47 and Charles VII, 1742/5), and for centuries held the dignity of ELECTORS of the HOLY ROMAN EMPIRE. Bavaria fought in the vanguard of the COUNTERREFORMATION and was among the pioneers of

monarchical **ABSOLUTISM** in Germany. During the **FRENCH REVOLUTIONARY WARS**, she deserted the cause of the Reich by signing the Treaty of Lunéville (1803), for which Napoleon subsequently rewarded her with considerable territorial enlargement and, in 1806, elevation to the status of kingdom. One of the first German states to introduce constitutional government (1818), Bavaria tried to pursue an independent policy between Austria and Prussia during the period of the German Confederation. Having sided with Austria against Prussia in 1866 she did, however, join the newly created German Empire in 1871, and is now one of the component federal states of Germany.

### Bavarian Succession, War of the (1778–9)

A brief campaign waged by Frederick II of Prussia against Austria when, on the dying out of the Bavarian branch of the **WITTELSBACH** family, **JOSEPH II** sought to gain parts of Bavaria and thereby strengthen the Habsburg position in Germany. Military manoeuvring soon gave way to stalemate, and the Treaty of Teschen by and large reaffirmed the status quo. Austria was forced to recognize the succession of the Palatinate line of the Wittelsbachs to the Bavarian throne, but succeeded in winning the Innviertel, including the town of Braunau which was destined to become the birthplace of **HITLER**. The 'Potato War' as the whole affair is often referred to, because of the absence of any conclusive battles, further tarnished **FREDERICK II, THE GREAT**'s prestige in the last years of his reign.

### Bayard, Pierre du Terrail, Lord of (c.1473–1524)

French soldier. Known as 'the good knight without fear and without reproach', he fought for **CHARLES VIII** of France in Italy (1494–5), and for **LOUIS XII** of France in Italy and Spain. At Marignano (1515), he gained a victory for **FRANCIS I** (of France). When **CHARLES V** invaded Champagne with a large army, Bayard successfully defended Mézières. He was mortally wounded by a shot from an arquebus while defending the passage of the Sesia.

### Bayazid ► BAYEZID

### Bayezid I (c.1360–c.1403)

Ottoman Sultan (1389/1402). He succeeded his father, Murad I, who was slain in the Battle of **KOSOVO**. Within three years he had conquered Bulgaria, with parts of Serbia, Macedonia and Thessaly, and most of Asia Minor. His rapid conquests earned him the name of *Yildirim* (lightning). For 10 years he blockaded Constantinople, to rescue which King Sigismund of Hungary (later Emperor) assembled a large army, including 2,000 French nobles, and laid siege to Nicopolis, on the Danube. Bayezid hastened to meet him, and gained a decisive victory (1396). Bayezid would have entirely destroyed the Greek empire if he had not, in 1402, been completely defeated by **TIMUR** near Ankara. Bayezid himself fell into the hands of the conqueror, who treated him with great generosity (his incarceration in an iron cage being a myth), and in whose camp he died. He was succeeded by his son, Süleyman. ► ANKARA, BATTLE OF

### Bayezid II (1448–1512)

Ottoman Sultan (1481/1512). He succeeded his father, **MEHMED II**, the conqueror of Constantinople,

in 1481. His long reign was a succession of wars against Hungary, Poland, Venice, Egypt and Persia, which served on the whole to establish the Ottoman power.

### Bay of Pigs (Apr 1961)

The failed invasion of Cuba by anti-**CASTRO** Cuban exiles sponsored by the USA. The invasion force of 1,500 men landed at Bahía de Cochinos ('Bay of Pigs') on the southern coast, but failed to win local support and was rapidly overwhelmed and defeated by Cuban troops. The episode was an embarrassment to John F **KENNEDY**'s administration.

### Bazaine, Achille François (1811–88)

Marshal of France. He joined the army in 1831, serving in Algeria, Spain, the Crimea, the Italian campaign of 1859, and notably the French expedition to Mexico (1862–7). For his surrender at Metz (1870), during the **FRANCO-PRUSSIAN WAR**, he was court-martialled and imprisoned, but he later escaped and fled to Spain, where he died. ► MEXICAN WAR

### Beale, Dorothea (1831–1906)

English pioneer of women's education. In 1857 she was appointed head teacher of the Clergy Daughters' School in Westmoreland, and from 1858 to 1906 was principal of Cheltenham Ladies' College. In 1885 she founded St Hilda's College, Cheltenham, the first English training college for women teachers, and sponsored St Hilda's Hall in Oxford for women teachers in 1893.

### Beaton, David (1494–1546)

Scottish statesman and Roman Catholic prelate. He resided at the French court (1519) and was appointed Bishop of Mirepoix by **FRANCIS I** (1537). In 1525 he took his seat in the Scots parliament as Abbot of Arbroath and became Privy Seal. Elevated to cardinal (1538), and made Archbishop of St Andrews (1539), he championed French interests at the expense of English influence. A persecutor of the Scottish Protestants, he had the reformer George **WISHART** burnt at St Andrews (1546), but was murdered in revenge three months later by a group of Protestant conspirators. ► REFORMATION (Scotland)

### Beatrix, in full Beatrix Wilhelmina Armgard (1938–)

Queen of the Netherlands (1980/ ). The eldest daughter of Queen **JULIANA** and Prince **BERNHARD** zur Lippe-Biesterfeld, she acceded to the throne on the abdication of her mother. In 1966 she married West German diplomat Claus-Georg Wilhelm Otto Friedrich Gerd von Amsberg (1926–2002), causing much controversy in the Netherlands; there were hostile demonstrations at her wedding and her coronation. Their son, Prince Willem-Alexander Claus George Ferdinand, is the first male heir to the Dutch throne in over a century. There are two other sons: Johan Friso Bernhard Christiaan David and Constantijn Christof Frederik Aschwin.

### Beatty, David Beatty, 1st Earl (1871–1936)

British admiral. He served in the Sudan (1896–8), and as battleship commander took part in the China War (1900). At the outbreak of **WORLD WAR I** he steamed into Heligoland Bight and destroyed three German cruisers. He later sank the *Blücher* (Jan

1915), and took part in the Battle of JUTLAND (May 1916). He became Commander-in-Chief of the Grand Fleet in 1916 and First Sea Lord in 1919, when he was created an earl.

**Beaufort, Henry** (1377–1447)
English cardinal and political figure. He studied at Oxford and Aix-la-Chapelle, was consecrated Bishop of Lincoln (1398) and Winchester (1405), and became a cardinal in 1426. He was Lord Chancellor on three occasions (1403–5, 1413–17, 1424–6). In 1427 the pope sent him as legate into Germany, to organize a crusade against the HUSSITES; this undertaking failed and he fell from papal pleasure. During the 1430s he controlled the government of the young King HENRY VI of England. He retired from politics in 1443. ► HUSSITE WARS

**Beaufort, Margaret** (1443–1509)
Daughter of John, 1st Duke of Somerset, and great-granddaughter of JOHN OF GAUNT, Duke of Lancaster. She married Edmund Tudor, Earl of Richmond (1455), and became the mother of HENRY VII, to whom she conveyed the Lancastrian claim to the English crown. She was twice widowed before her third husband, Thomas, Lord Stanley, was instrumental in helping Henry VII assume the crown. She was a benefactress of William Caxton and of Oxford and Cambridge universities.

**Beauharnais, Alexandre Beauharnais, Viscount of** (1760–94)
French army officer. He served in the American War of Independence, and in 1789 eagerly embraced the FRENCH REVOLUTION. He was made Secretary of the National Assembly, but was guillotined (1794) for his failure to relieve Metz. In 1779 he had married JOSEPHINE, afterwards wife of NAPOLEON I, and his daughter HORTENSE in 1802 married Napoleon's brother, Louis. Beauharnais was thus the grandfather of NAPOLEON III. ► AMERICAN REVOLUTION

**Beauharnais, Eugène Rose de** (1781–1824)
French soldier. After the marriage of his mother, JOSEPHINE, to NAPOLEON I, he served with his stepfather in Italy and Egypt, and rapidly rose to the highest military rank. In 1805 he was made a prince of France, and from 1805 to 1814 was Viceroy of Italy. As Viceroy he established his court at Milan but was allowed little rein by his stepfather in running the affairs of the kingdom. In 1806 he married Augusta, daughter of Maximilian of Bavaria. In 1813–14 Beauharnais tried to resist the Austrian invasion of Italy but eventually fled to Munich where he was offered protection by his father-in-law.

**Beauregard, Pierre Gustave Toutant** (1818–93)
US Confederate general. He graduated from the US Military Academy at West Point (1838), served with distinction in the MEXICAN WAR, and was appointed by the Confederate government to the command at Charleston, where he commenced the war by the bombardment of FORT SUMTER (12 Apr 1861). He fought at BULL RUN (1861), then took command at SHILOH (1862), and later defended Charleston and Richmond. ► AMERICAN CIVIL WAR

**Bebel, Ferdinand August** (1840–1913)
German socialist. By 1871 he had become leader of the German Social Democratic movement and its chief spokesman in the REICHSTAG. He wrote much on SOCIALISM, on the PEASANTS' WAR, and on the status of women, as well as several philosophical works and an autobiography. ► SPD

**Beck, Józef** (1894–1944)
Polish colonel. He helped Marshal PIŁSUDSKI to seize control in his 1926 coup, became Deputy Foreign Minister in 1930 and was finally Foreign Minister from 1932 to 1939. Following HITLER's rise to power, he tried to maintain first an equilibrium between Nazi Germany and the USSR and then a policy of partial cooperation with Hitler to expand and defend his country. He assisted in the dismemberment of Czechoslovakia (Sep 1938) and defeated the Anglo-French bid to form an alliance with the USSR (May 1939). In Aug of the same year, he had to face the consequences when Hitler invaded a Poland that was virtually defenceless. Beck escaped abroad.

**Becket, St Thomas (à)** (1118–70)
English saint and martyr, Archbishop of Canterbury. The son of a wealthy Norman merchant, he studied canon law at Bologna and Auxerre. In 1155, he became Chancellor, the first Englishman since the NORMAN CONQUEST to hold high office. A skilled diplomat and brilliant courtly figure, he changed dramatically when created Archbishop of Canterbury (1162), resigning the chancellorship and becoming a zealous ascetic, serving the Church as vigorously as he had HENRY II. He thus came into conflict with the King's aims to keep the clergy in subordination to the state. He unwillingly consented to the Constitutions of Clarendon (1164), defining the powers of Church and State, but remained in disfavour. He fled the country after having his goods confiscated and the revenues of his sees sequestered. After two years in France, he pleaded personally to the pope and was reinstated in his see. In 1170 he was reconciled with Henry and returned to Canterbury amid great public rejoicing. New quarrels soon broke out, however, and Henry's rashly-voiced wish to be rid of 'this turbulent priest' led to Becket's murder in Canterbury Cathedral (29 Dec 1170) by four of the King's knights. He was canonized in 1173, and Henry did public penance at his tomb in 1174.

**Bedchamber Crisis**
A British political crisis which occurred in May 1839 after MELBOURNE, Prime Minister in the Whig government, offered to resign, and advised the young Queen VICTORIA to appoint PEEL and the TORIES. The Queen refused to dismiss certain ladies of the Bedchamber with Whig sympathies, whereupon Peel refused office and the Whig government continued. ► WHIGS

**Bedford, John of Lancaster, Duke of** (1389–1435)
English general and statesman. He was the third son of HENRY IV. In 1414 his brother, HENRY V, created him Duke of Bedford, and during the King's campaigns against France he was appointed Lieutenant of the Kingdom. After Henry's death (1422), he became Guardian of England and Regent of France. When CHARLES VI died, he had his nephew proclaimed King of France and England as HENRY VI. In the HUNDRED YEARS' WAR, he defeated the French in several

battles, notably at Verneuil (1424), but an army under JOAN OF ARC forced him onto the defensive (1429).

### Bedmar, Alfonso de Cueva, Marquis of (1572–1655)
Spanish conspirator. He was sent in 1607 as ambassador to Venice, and in 1618 plotted the overthrow of the republic. One of the conspirators betrayed the plot, which forms the theme of Otway's *Venice Preserved*. Bedmar was dismissed and went to Flanders, where he became President of the council. In 1622 he was made a cardinal, and finally Bishop of Oviedo.

### Bedouin
Arabic-speaking nomads of Saudi Arabia, Syria, Jordan, Iraq and other desert areas in the Middle East. They mainly herd animals in the desert during winter months and cultivate land in summer; camel herders have the highest prestige. Many have been forced to settle in one locality because of political or economic moves, such as restrictions on their grazing land or nationalization of their land. They are divided into largely independent, endogamous patrilineal tribal groups, each controlled by its sheikh and council of male elders. There are also several vassal tribes whose members work for others as artisans, blacksmiths, entertainers, etc.

### Beecher, Lyman (1775–1863)
US religious leader and temperance reformer. He was educated at Yale before being ordained a Presbyterian minister and becoming an abolitionist. He was noted for his fiery sermons which aroused opposition amongst conservative Presbyterians, and he was charged with heresy, but later acquitted. Among his 13 children were the clergyman and social reformer Henry Ward Beecher and the novelist Harriet Beecher Stowe.

### Beecroft, John (1790–1854)
British trader, explorer and consul. He was influential in promoting the conquest of Lagos in 1851. Beecroft arrived in West Africa in 1828 as a trader on the island of Fernando Po, which the British occupied as a naval base and settlement for freed slaves during the period 1827–34. He administered the island under the Spanish flag, but later he explored the Niger Delta and in 1849 was appointed Consul for the Bights of Benin and Biafra. He promoted legitimate commerce and the suppression of the slave trade.

### Beernaert, Auguste (1829–1912)
Belgian politician. He trained as a lawyer, entered politics and was appointed Minister for Public Works in 1873. He became a member of the Belgian parliament in 1874, opposing the ruling liberal governments of the day. He was appointed Minister of Agriculture, Trade, and Industry in 1884, and took over the leadership of the government in Oct of the same year. He was responsible for introducing multiple-vote universal suffrage to Belgium in 1893, and for important reforms in labour law; he was also a supporter of King LEOPOLD II's colonial policies in the Congo. He left the government in 1894, and became Chairman of the Belgian Senate for five years until 1899. His work on weapons reduction and international law earned him the NOBEL PEACE PRIZE in 1909.

### Beggars (Gueux; Geuzen)
The name given to the resistance in the Netherlands to the rule of PHILIP II of Spain in the earlier part of the EIGHTY YEARS' WAR. The name was apparently taken as a matter of inverted pride from a remark made by Count C Berlaymont (1510–78) in 1565 about the lesser nobles of the Low Countries: *Ce ne sont que les gueux* ('They're only beggars'). As well as land-based guerrilla forces (*bosgeuzen*), the Beggars took to the sea as privateers (*watergeuzen*), allied with adventurers and refugees from the Spanish campaigns in the Low Countries. The Sea-Beggars harassed the shipping and coastal positions of Spain and her allies, and on 1 Apr 1572 they took the Dutch port of Brill with the surrounding countryside, which led directly to the spread of the revolt to the northern provinces.

### Begin, Menachem Wolfovitch (1913–92)
Israeli politician. Born and educated in Brest-Litovsk, Russia (now Brest, Belarus), he studied law at Warsaw University. An active Zionist, he became head of the Polish Zionist movement in 1931. He fled to Russia in 1939, enlisted in the Free Polish Army (1941), and was sent to British-mandated PALESTINE. In 1943 he commanded the IRGUN Zvai Leumi resistance group in Israel, and in 1948 founded the Herut Freedom Movement, becoming Chairman of the Herut Party. In 1973 three parties combined to form the nationalist LIKUD Front with Begin as its leader, and in the 1977 elections he became Prime Minister at the head of a coalition government. In the late 1970s he attended peace conferences in Jerusalem (Dec 1977) and at CAMP DAVID (Sep 1978) at the invitation of President CARTER. In 1978 he and President Anwar SADAT of Egypt were jointly awarded the NOBEL PEACE PRIZE. He resigned the premiership in 1983.

### Beijing, Treaty of (1860)
The treaty which gave Tsarist Russia all the territory it wanted between the Ussuri River and the Pacific coast in order to establish a strong presence in the Far East. Russia had been expanding towards the Pacific at China's expense since the 17c. ALEXANDER II took advantage of China's weakness in the face of British and French military attacks and US diplomatic pressure to secure without war, but through the negotiating skill of Count Nikolai Pavlovich IGNATIEV, the territory on which he then built the port and naval base of Vladivostok (literally, 'Ruler of the East').

### Beiyang (Pei-yang) Army
China's first modern army dating from 1899. Under the command of YUAN SHIKAI, the Beiyang Army grew in size during the last decade of the QING DYNASTY. Many of its officers were either trained in Japan or in new military academies in China. After 1911 the Army was the basis of Yuan Shikai's power in his struggle with the GUOMINDANG. Many of Yuan's generals later went on to become influential militarists (WARLORDS) in their own right.

---

**BELARUS** official name **Republic of Belarus**, formerly known as **Belorussia**, **Byelarus** or **White Russia**

A republic in eastern Europe, bounded to the west by Poland; to the north-west by Lithuania; to the north by Latvia; to the east by Russia; and to the south by the Ukraine. The Belorussians were one of the original

Slav tribes, like the Russians themselves. They remained slightly distinct because they lived in the exposed western border area and were subject to long periods of foreign, particularly Polish, rule. Under Tsarist control from 1795, they eventually developed a national movement that declared independence in 1917. However, a feeble Belorussia had a troubled existence; it declared a Belorussian Soviet Socialist Republic in 1919 and was incorporated into the USSR in 1921. In 1945 its territory was expanded at the expense of Poland and, for Soviet political reasons, it was given separate membership of the UN. Yet its sense of national identity remained comparatively undeveloped until it achieved independence in 1991 on the disintegration of the Soviet Union. It became a founding member of the CIS (Commonwealth of Independent States) that year, and in 1997 it united with Russia as an 'integrated political and economic community'. President Alyaksandr LUKASHENKA, first elected in 1994, resisted free-market reforms, precipitating economic collapse in the late 1990s, and has become increasingly authoritarian.

### Belaúnde Terry, Fernando (1912–2002)

Peruvian politician. He was an architect before entering politics, leading the Popular Action Party (AP) in 1956. He campaigned for the presidency in 1956 and 1962, eventually winning it in 1963, but was deposed by the army in a bloodless coup in 1968. He fled to the USA where he lectured at Harvard. He returned to Peru two years later but was deported and did not re-establish himself until 1976. He won the presidency again in 1980, and was the first civilian to hand over to another constitutionally elected civilian (1985).

### Belgian Revolution ► BELGIUM

### Belgian Socialist Party (*Parti Socialiste Belge*; *Belgische Socialistische Partij*)

The principal left-wing political party in Belgium, formed in 1940 after the German invasion had caused the abolition of its predecessor, the Belgian Workers' Party (founded in 1885). The party first gained important political influence after the constitutional revision of 1893 had introduced universal male suffrage, and gave the socialists 27 MPs. After WORLD WAR I the party dropped its Marxist and revolutionary attitude, and became a regular coalition partner in Belgian governments, often leading them in the 1950s and 1960s. After years of dispute between the French-speaking and Flemish-speaking sections of the party, they formally broke apart in 1978, with their own leaders, programmes and policies. Since the mid-1950s, when the socialists had 37 per cent of the vote, their popularity has declined, but they remain a major force in Belgian politics, forming the lesser partner in a number of recent coalition

governments. Principal leaders have been Émile VANDERVELDE, Henrik de MAN, Paul H SPAAK, Achille van ACKER and Camille HUYSMANS.

---

**BELGIUM**    official name **Kingdom of Belgium**

A kingdom in north-western Europe, bounded to the north by the Netherlands; to the south by France; to the east by Germany and Luxembourg; and to the west by the North Sea. A line drawn east–west just to the south of Brussels divides the population by race and language into two approximately equal parts; north of the line the inhabitants are Flemings of Teutonic stock who speak *Flemish*, while south of the line they are French-speaking Latins known as *Walloons*. Belgium was part of the Roman Empire until the 2c AD, and after being invaded by Germanic tribes it became part of the Frankish Empire. In the early MIDDLE AGES, some semi-independent provinces and cities grew up and from 1385 were absorbed by the House of BURGUNDY. They were known as the Spanish Netherlands, and were ruled by the Habsburgs from 1477 until the Peace of UTRECHT (1713); the Spanish provinces were then transferred to Austria as the Austrian Netherlands. The country was conquered by the French in 1794 and formed part of the First French REPUBLIC and Empire until in 1815 it united with the northern (Dutch) provinces under King WILLIAM I of the Netherlands. The southern (Belgian) provinces were unhappy with the union because of William's religious, linguistic and economic policies. The Belgian Revolution began with riots in Brussels on 25 Aug 1830. A provisional government, called a National Convention, declared the independence of Belgium and drafted a new constitution (7 Feb 1831), which made Belgium a constitutional monarchy with Leopold of Saxe-Coburg as its first king (LEOPOLD I). The Great Powers recognized Belgian independence at the Conference of London (20 Jan 1831). However, William I refused to cooperate; as a result an armed standoff dragged on for most of the 1830s. Finally in Apr 1839 the Dutch government capitulated and signed a treaty which completed the independence of Belgium. During the 20c, Belgium was occupied by Germany in both World Wars, and political tension between Walloons and Flemings caused the collapse of several governments. Belgium was a founder-member of the EEC in 1958. In 1980 Wallonia and Flanders were given regional 'subgovernments', and in 1989 a new federal constitution divided Belgium into three autonomous regions: the Walloon Region (Wallonia); the Flemish Region (Flanders) and the bilingual Brussels-Capital Region. The political federalization of Belgium was completed by constitutional amendment in 1993. ► BENELUX; FLEMISH MOVEMENT

**Belgrano, Manuel** (1770–1820)
Argentine general and leader in the war for independence. He studied law and had his first military experience during Britain's unsuccessful invasion of the Viceroyalty of Río de la Plata in 1806–7. When this region gained its independence from Spain in 1810, Belgrano joined its ruling junta and attempted to protect and enlarge its territory. He later defeated pro-Spanish, royalist forces at Tucumán and Salta in north-west Argentina, only to be defeated in his northern campaign in Upper Peru (now Bolivia) in 1813. He was superseded as commander of the army in 1814 by José de **SAN MARTÍN**. His name was given to the Argentine cruiser *General Belgrano* which was sunk by the British submarine HMS *Conqueror* during the **FALKLANDS WAR**. ➤ **SPANISH-AMERICAN WARS OF INDEPENDENCE**

**BELIZE**  formerly (to 1973) **British Honduras**

An independent state in Central America, bounded to the north by Mexico; to the west and south by Guatemala; and to the east by the Caribbean Sea. There is evidence of early Maya settlement in Belize, and its coast was colonized in the 17c by shipwrecked British sailors and disbanded soldiers from Jamaica, who defended the territory against the Spanish. Created a British colony in 1862, it was administered from Jamaica until 1884. A ministerial system of government was introduced in 1961, and in 1964 full internal self-government was achieved. The country changed its name from British Honduras to Belize in 1973 and gained full independence in 1981; the People's United Party under Prime Minister George **PRICE** continued in government during the transition from self-government to independence. Guatemalan claims over Belize territory led to a British military presence, until in the early 1990s Guatemala established diplomatic relations with Belize. Belize joined the **ORGANIZATION OF AMERICAN STATES** (OAS) in 1991. Almost all of the British presence was withdrawn in 1993. The British monarch remains head of state, represented by a Governor-General. ➤ **DISTURBANCES**

**Bell, Alexander Graham** (1847–1922)
US inventor. He first worked as an assistant to his father in teaching elocution (1868–70). In 1872 he opened a school in Boston for training teachers of the deaf, and in 1873 he was appointed Professor of Vocal Physiology at Boston, where he devoted himself to the teaching of deaf-mutes and to spreading

his father's system of 'visible speech'. After experimenting with various acoustical devices, he produced the first intelligible telephonic transmission with a message to his assistant on 5 June 1875. He patented the telephone in 1876, defended the patent against Elisha Gray, and formed the Bell Telephone Company in 1877. In 1880 he established the Volta Laboratory, from where he invented the photophone (1880) and the graphophone (1887). He also founded the journal *Science* (1883).

**Bello, Sir Ahmadu** (1910–66)
Nigerian politician. Educated at Katsina College, he started his career as a teacher but became a major political figure following his appointment as Saudana of Sokoto (1938). He led the Northern People's Congress from 1951, reaching the post of Prime Minister in 1954. He was a major figure in national politics, exercising his power through the NPC from his base in the Hausa-dominated north of the country and was assassinated in the coup of Jan 1966.

**Bem, Joseph** (1794–1850)
Polish soldier. He fought against the Russians in Napoleon's army and then in the Polish insurrection of 1830–1. He commanded Hungarian forces in the unsuccessful Hungarian insurrection of 1848–9, after which he escaped into Turkey. There he became a Muslim and was appointed Governor of Aleppo, where he died of fever ten months later.

**Bemis Heights, Battle of** (7 Oct 1777)
A preliminary conflict during the Saratoga campaign, in the **AMERICAN REVOLUTION**. ➤ **SARATOGA, BATTLE OF**

**Ben Ali, Zine el Abidine** (1936– )
Tunisian politician. After studying electronics at military schools in France and the USA, he began a career in military security, rising to the position of Director-General of National Security. He became Minister of the Interior and then Prime Minister under 'President-for-life' Habib **BOURGUIBA**, who had been in power since 1956. In 1987 he forced Bourguiba to retire, assumed the presidency and immediately embarked on constitutional reforms, promising a greater degree of democracy. He retained the presidency in the elections of 1999 and 2004.

**Ben Bella, Ahmed** (1916– )
Algerian politician. A key figure in the **ALGERIAN WAR OF INDEPENDENCE** against France, he fought with the Free French in **WORLD WAR II**, and in 1949 became head of the *Organisation Spéciale* ('Special Organization'), the paramilitary wing of the Algerian nationalist *Parti du Peuple Algérien* ('Party of the Algerian People'). In 1952 he escaped from a French-Algerian prison to Cairo, where he became a key member of the **FLN** (*Front de Libération Nationale*). Captured by the French in 1956, he spent the remainder of the war in a French prison. Following independence in 1962, he became Algeria's first Prime Minister (1962–3) and President (1963–5). His deposition in 1965 was followed by 15 years of imprisonment, from which he was released in 1980. Between 1981 and 1990, he went into exile, but afterwards he returned to Algeria, promoting himself as a symbol of revolutionary spirit.

**Benbow, John** (1653–1702)
British admiral. His main engagements were in the Nine Years' War (1690, 1693 and 1694) and the War of the **SPANISH SUCCESSION**, when he came upon a superior French force in the West Indies (1702). For four days he kept up a running fight from Santa Marta, almost deserted by the rest of his squadron, until he was wounded. He was forced to return to Jamaica, where he died.

**Benckendorff, Alexander, Count** (1849–1917)
Russian diplomat. As ambassador in London (from 1903), he greatly promoted Anglo-Russian friendship and played a part in forming the Triple Entente (1907).

**Benedict VIII**, originally **Teofilatto** (d.1024)
First of the Tusculan popes (1012/24), members of the Tusculani family. He was temporarily driven from Rome by the anti-pope Gregory VI, of the Crescenti family, but was restored to the papal chair by Emperor **HENRY II**, whom he crowned in 1014. Later he defeated the **SARACENS** and the Greeks in northern Italy, and introduced clerical and monastic reforms.

**Benedict IX**, originally **Teofilatto** (d.c.1065)
Last of the Tusculan popes (1032/44, 1045 and 1047/8). The nephew of **BENEDICT VIII**, he succeeded another uncle, John XIX, in 1032, obtaining the papal throne by simony while still a youth. However, in 1036 the Romans banished him on account of his licentiousness. He was reinstalled and deposed on at least three occasions. He died in the convent of Grotta Ferrata, probably before 1065.

**Benedict XIV**, originally **Prospero Lambertini** (1675–1758)
Pope (1740/58). Perhaps the greatest of 18c pontiffs, he was a fine scholar who won praise for his moderation and reforming tendencies. In the domestic affairs of the **PAPAL STATES** he sought energetically to stimulate the economy through liberal commercial policies, the reduction of taxes and agricultural improvement. He was similarly far-sighted and realistic in the conciliatory approach he adopted towards the many monarchs of his day, who were increasingly eager to extend the realm of secular jurisdiction and to bring Church patronage under their personal control. In the face of growing interest across Europe in **ENLIGHTENMENT** ideas, he urged that restraint be exercised by those responsible for compiling the *Index* of prohibited literature. He was also anxious to avoid too open a breach with Jansenism and, in 1756, condemned those who refused last rites to clergy who opposed the Bull *Unigenitus*. However, he was not merely a doctrinal pragmatist: in the *Ex quo singulari* (1742) and the *Omnium sollicitudinum* (1744) he forcefully denounced as incompatible with the Roman Catholic faith and prohibited the various traditional practices which Jesuits had tolerated among converts in India and China. While these measures undoubtedly set back the progress of Jesuit missionary work, they were important in maintaining the theological integrity of the Church in Asia.

**Benelux**
An economic union between Belgium, the Netherlands and Luxembourg. It began as a customs union which came into existence in 1948 as the result of a convention concluded in London in 1944. Despite the difficulties of achieving economic integration and the exclusion of agriculture from the union, mutual trade between the three countries expanded. A treaty established a more ambitious economic union between the three in 1958.

**Beneš, Edvard** (1884–1948)
Czechoslovak politician. He was Professor of Sociology at Prague, then as an émigré during **WORLD WAR I** worked in Paris with **MASARYK** for Czech independence, becoming Foreign Minister of the new state (1918–35), and for a while Premier (1921–2). In 1935 he succeeded Masaryk as President, but resigned in 1938 following the **MUNICH AGREEMENT**. He then left the country, setting up a government in exile, first in France, then in Britain. Beneš returned to Czechoslovakia in 1945 and was re-elected President the following year, but resigned after the Communist takeover in 1948. ► **CZECHOSLOVAK INDEPENDENCE, DECLARATION OF**

**Benevento, Battle of** (1266)
Victory of the **GUELFS** over the **GHIBELLINES** in the papal-imperial struggle in Italy. The pope had brought **CHARLES OF ANJOU** into Italy to counterbalance the imperial power in the south. **MANFRED**, the illegitimate son of **FREDERICK II**, was killed in the battle, and the Angevin position was further consolidated by victory at the Battle of **TAGLIACOZZO** (1268), before the expulsion of the French in the **SICILIAN VESPERS** of 1282. ► **ANGEVINS**

**Bengal, Partition of** (1905)
The division of Bengal for administrative purposes, conceived and carried out by Lord **CURZON** while he was Viceroy. Because of Bengal's combination with Orissa and Bihar for administrative purposes, the provincial population was enormous and administration had become unwieldy. Largely because of this and poor communications to the east of Calcutta, East Bengal had been neglected in favour of West Bengal, Orissa and Bihar. Curzon decided to combine East Bengal with Assam, making Dhaka the capital, and to leave Calcutta as the capital of West Bengal and India. Because the partition created an East Bengal with a large Muslim majority, Hindus felt that they would be marginalized in that region. Many Bengalis believed that the partition was an attempt to destroy nationalism, which was more highly developed in Bengal than elsewhere. The public outcry was manifested in rural agitation, mass meetings, boycott of foreign goods and even **TERRORISM**. Although the partition took place, East and West Bengal were reunited in 1911, with Assam and Orissa-Bihar becoming two new administrative districts. The outrage of nationalists and Bengali Hindus over the partition was largely responsible for both Curzon's early removal from the Viceroyalty, and the transformation of the **INDIAN NATIONAL CONGRESS** from a middle-class pressure group to a popular nationwide political party.

**Bengal Presidency**
The original British **EAST INDIA COMPANY** designation for lands around Calcutta under its direct administrative control. The Bengal Presidency bordered Bihar and Orissa to the west, Sikkim and

Bhutan to the north and Assam and Burma (now Myanmar) to the east. It was from the Bengal Presidency that the Company's greatest expansion of influence and control took place in the 18c and 19c, and it was also from there that most of the old **MUGHAL EMPIRE** was informally controlled until 1858. The Bengal Presidency was the senior administrative area, and the Governor of Bengal was in fact the Governor-General of British India. The term and administrative area of the Bengal Presidency remained current even after the dissolution of the Company.

**Ben-Gurion, David** (1886–1973)
Israeli politician. Born in Poland, he emigrated to **PALESTINE** in 1906. Expelled by the Turks during **WORLD WAR I**, he recruited Jews to the British Army in North America. In Palestine in 1919 he founded a socialist party and became Secretary to the **HISTADRUT** in 1921. He led the **MAPAI PARTY** from its formation in 1930 and headed the **JEWISH AGENCY** in 1935. Ben-Gurion moulded the Mapai into the main party of the **YISHUV** during British rule and became Prime Minister after independence (1948–53), when he was responsible for Israel absorbing large numbers of refugees from Europe and Arab countries. He was Prime Minister again from 1955 to 1963. ► **JEWISH LABOUR MOVEMENT IN PALESTINE**

**BENIN** official name. **Republic of Benin**, formerly (to 1990) **The People's Republic of Benin**, and (to 1975) **Dahomey**

A republic in West Africa, bounded to the north by Niger; to the east by Nigeria; to the south by the Bight of Benin; to the west by Togo; and to the north-west by Burkina Faso. As the Kingdom of Dahomey, it was based on its capital at Abomey, and in the late 17c and early 18c extended its authority from the coast into the interior, to the west of the Yoruba states. In the 1720s the cavalry of the **OYO** Kingdom of the Yoruba devastated Dahomey, but when the Oyo Empire collapsed in the early 19c, Dahomey regained its power. It became famous for its trade in palm oil and slaves, and was influenced by the neighbouring Yoruba. The state was annexed by the French in 1883 and constituted a territory of French West Africa in 1904, but regained its independence in 1960. In 1972 it was declared a Marxist–Leninist state under the leadership of President Mathieu **KÉRÉKOU**, who renamed it Benin in 1975. The country gradually gained stability

and moved towards democratic government, abandoning Marxism–Leninism in 1989. In the first free elections (1991) Kérékou was defeated by his Prime Minister Nicéphore Soglo, but he returned to power in 1996 and was re-elected in 2001.

**Benin, Kingdom of**
A powerful kingdom in the south Nigerian rainforest, founded in the 13c, which survived until the 19c. The dynastic title of the rulers was Oba, and Benin reached its imperial apogee under Ewuare the Great (1440/73). The Portuguese turned to Benin as a source of cloth, beads and slaves in the 15–16c, and it was later involved in the slave trade. It became one of the most prosperous areas in Africa. Benin was conquered by the British in 1897, and in 1975 the name was adopted by the former French colony of Dahomey.

**Benn, Tony (Anthony Neil Wedgwood)** (1925–)
British politician and political diarist. The son of Viscount Stansgate, he became a Labour MP in 1950 but was debarred from the Commons on succeeding to his father's title. He renounced his title, and was re-elected in a by-election in 1963. He held various government posts under Harold **WILSON** and James **CALLAGHAN**, notably Minister of Technology (1966–70), Secretary for Industry (1974–5) and Secretary for Energy (1975–9). He was the main focus for the left wing challenge to the Labour leadership in the late 1970s and 1980s which ultimately failed but which persuaded some on the right to leave the party and form the **SOCIAL DEMOCRATIC PARTY**. He retired from parliament in 2001.► **FOOT, MICHAEL**; **KINNOCK, NEIL**; **LABOUR PARTY** (UK)

**Bennett, Richard Bedford, 1st Viscount** (1870–1947)
Canadian politician. Educated in Nova Scotia, he trained as a lawyer, and entered politics in 1897. He was Conservative leader from 1927, and while Prime Minister (1930–5) convened the Imperial Economic Conference in Ottawa (1932), from which emerged a system of empire trade preference. He retired to England in 1938 and was made a peer in 1941. ► **NEW DEAL** (Canada); **PRICE SPREADS COMMISSION**

**Bennington, Battle of** (16 Aug 1777)
A battle of the **AMERICAN REVOLUTION** in which a force of around 1,000 German mercenaries led by General **BURGOYNE** attempted to seize colonial military stores in Bennington, Vermont, but were defeated by General John Stark's 1,600 **GREEN MOUNTAIN BOYS**. Soon afterwards Burgoyne was forced to surrender following his defeat at the Battle of **SARATOGA**.

**Bentham, Jeremy** (1748–1832)
British writer on jurisprudence and utilitarian ethics. He was called to the Bar in 1767, though he never practised, being more interested in the theory of the law. His publications include *A Fragment on Government* (1776) and *Introduction to the Principles of Morals and Legislation* (1789), which present his theory of hedonistic utilitarianism. He held that laws should be socially useful and not merely reflect the *status quo*, and that all actions are right when they promote 'the happiness of the greatest number' (a phrase which he popularized). He travelled widely on the Continent. Supporters of his utilitarian ideas (the Benthamites) attempted to apply them to public policy (1830s and

1840s). He was also a founder of University College, London, where his skeleton, dressed in his clothes, is preserved.

**Bentinck, Hans Willem, Baron** (1649–1709)
Friend, confidant and agent of **STADHOLDER** William III (later King **WILLIAM III** of England). Bentinck was a page to William III, and in time took on vital missions for his master, such as the marriage negotiations between William and Princess Mary, daughter of **JAMES VII AND II** of Scotland and England, and the role and input of Amsterdam in the invasion of England by William's forces in 1688. When William had succeeded to the English throne, he made Bentinck the first Duke of Portland in 1689; Bentinck remained a key figure at William's court, in war, peace and diplomacy. ► **GLORIOUS REVOLUTION**

**Bentinck, Lord William Henry Cavendish** (1774–1839)
British soldier and Governor-General of India. The second son of the 3rd Duke of **PORTLAND**, in 1791 he became an army officer. Appointed Governor of Madras in 1803, he was recalled from India following a mutiny of native soldiers, and commanded troops during the **NAPOLEONIC WARS** in Spain and Sicily. A liberal Whig in his political sympathies, in 1811 he was entrusted with reorganizing Sicily where he forced a constitution on the reactionary Bourbon King, Ferdinand I. In 1814–15 he championed the cause of Italian independence and constitutional government but was unable to persuade the authorities in Britain to share his vision. On his return to Britain he was elected to parliament. He later became Governor-General of India (1828–35), where he introduced important administrative reforms.

**Benton, Thomas Hart** (1782–1858)
US politician. He was a Missouri Senator for 30 years, and a leader of the **DEMOCRATIC PARTY**, becoming known as 'Old Bullion' from his opposition to paper currency. In his later years, he adopted an anti-**SLAVERY** position which finally lost him his seat in the **SENATE**.

**Ben-Zvi, Itzhak** (1884–1963)
Israeli politician. Born in Poltava in Russia (now Ukraine), he emigrated to **PALESTINE** in 1907. He became a prominent Zionist and was a founder of the Jewish Labour Party. Ben-Zvi was elected President of Israel on the death of Chaim **WEIZMANN** in 1952. A prominent scholar and archaeologist, he wrote on the history of the Middle East. ► **ALIYAH**; **ZIONISM**

**Beran, Josef** (1888–1969)
Czech Catholic priest and archbishop. Imprisoned in **DACHAU** concentration camp in **WORLD WAR II**, he became Archbishop of Prague in 1946. Although the Roman Catholic Church was anxious to avoid too close an involvement in politics, he spoke out in favour of democracy during the communist seizure of power in Feb 1948. Within a year the Church was persecuted, and Beran and most churchmen were cut off from contact with Rome. It was 1965 before the situation eased sufficiently for him to leave for Rome, where he was appointed cardinal.

**Beran, Rudolf** (1887–1954)
Czechoslovak politician. He became Secretary-General of the powerful right-wing Agrarian Party in 1918 and its President in 1935. Torn between dislike of **HITLER** and hatred for **STALIN**, he quickly opted for a policy of appeasing Germany in the hope of securing local concessions. His behaviour in 1938 was close to treasonable as he negotiated behind President **BENEŠ**'s back. His reward was to become Prime Minister for a time after the **MUNICH AGREEMENT**, but in 1946 he was imprisoned as a collaborator. He undoubtedly undermined the Czechoslovak position in the face of Hitler.

**Berbers**
Hamito-Semitic-speaking peoples of Egypt, Algeria, Libya, Tunisia and Morocco. They were originally settled in one area, but the Bedouin Arabs who invaded North Africa in the 12c turned many of them into nomads. Most Berber tribes ultimately accepted Islam, and in the 11c formed themselves into a military federation known as the **ALMORAVIDS**, who conquered the medieval state of Ghana, Morocco, Algeria and southern Spain. In the 12c their power began to wane, and the **ALMOHADS**, a new group influenced by Sufism, by 1169 came to command the entire Maghrib to Tripoli, as well as Muslim Spain. The Almohad Empire declined in the 13c. Today, some Berbers are sedentary farmers, while others are nomadic or transhumant pastoralists. Many work as migrant labourers in southern Europe. The best-known groups include the Kabyle, Shluh and Tuareg.

**Berdyaev, Nikolai** (1874–1948)
Russian religious philosopher. Born into an aristocratic family in Kiev, he developed strong revolutionary sympathies as a student and supported the **RUSSIAN REVOLUTION** of 1917. He secured a professorship at Moscow but his unorthodox spiritual and libertarian ideals led to his dismissal in 1922. He moved to found in Berlin an Academy of the Philosophy of Religion which he later transferred to Clamart, near Paris, where he died. He described himself as a 'believing free-thinker' and his fierce commitment to freedom and individualism brought him into conflict with both ecclesiastical and political powers.

**Berezina River, Crossing of** (1812)
A typical example of **NAPOLEON I**'s mixture of skill and luck in extricating himself from complete disaster. During the retreat from Moscow, his depleted army faced crossing the Berezina River, its supplies and morale low, the bridges destroyed, and two Russian armies closing in in a pincer movement. But he deceived the enemy, found a crossing-place, built pontoons, and escaped with two-thirds of his numbers. That his losses were not greater, however, was due to Russian mistakes, and shortly afterwards he recognized defeat and hastened back to Paris.

**Berg**
A duchy of the **HOLY ROMAN EMPIRE**, it became a possession of John III, Duke of Cleves in 1511. A centre for iron and textile manufacturing in the 17c and 18c, Berg passed into Prussian hands, as the Rhine Province, after the Congress of **VIENNA** (1814–15).

**Berggrav, Eivind** (1884–1959)
Norwegian Lutheran bishop. After some years as a teacher, pastor and prison chaplain, he became Bishop of Troms and then Bishop of Oslo and Primate

of the Norwegian Church (1937–50). Following the Nazi occupation of 1940, he led the Church's opposition to the **QUISLING** government, refusing to endorse the war against Russia as a fight against atheism, and opposing Nazi attempts to monopolize the education of young people. For this he was imprisoned (1941–5). He wrote some 30 books and was a strong supporter of the ecumenical movement, becoming a President of the World Council of Churches (1950–4).

### Beria, Lavrenti Pavlovich (1899–1953)
Soviet secret police chief. After holding local positions in his native Georgia, he became Soviet Commissar for Internal Affairs in 1938. During **WORLD WAR II** he was Vice-President of the State Committee for Defence, and was active in purging **STALIN**'s opponents. After **STALIN**'s death (1953), he belonged briefly with Giorgiy **MALENKOV** and **MOLOTOV** to the collective leadership. Accused by his colleagues of conspiracy, he was shot after a mock 'treason' trial.

### Berkeley, Sir William (1606–77)
English colonial governor. He was educated at Oxford and served in the colonial office as commissioner for Canadian affairs before being appointed Governor of Virginia in 1641. He remained in this position until 1677, apart from a period lasting from the end of the **ENGLISH CIVIL WARS** until the restoration of the monarchy in 1660. Although his first period in office had been successful and peaceful, his second was marred by economic depression, crop failures, and **BACON'S REBELLION** (1675–6). When Nathaniel Bacon and an army of white settlers began attacking **NATIVE AMERICANS** in retaliation for raids on white settlements, Berkeley, who wished to foster trade with the Native Americans and had forbidden campaigns against them, declared the attacks a rebellion and mounted his own force to fight the rebels. The rebellion collapsed when Bacon died of natural causes, but not before much of Berkeley's followers' property had been plundered, **JAMESTOWN** had been burned, and several people had died. Berkeley himself died before he could answer **CHARLES II**'s call for an explanation of his actions.

### Berlin, Battle of (Apr–May 1945)
On 25 Apr 1945 advancing Soviet troops surrounded Berlin. **HITLER** had ordered the 9th and 11th Armies to relieve Berlin on 24 Apr, but they were unable to break through the Soviet lines. There followed a Soviet offensive on the city which resulted in days of bitter street fighting. On 30 Apr, Hitler committed suicide, and on 2 May the German Commander in Berlin, General Weidling, surrendered to the Soviet commander, Marshal **ZHUKOV**.

### Berlin, Congress of (1878)
An international congress following the Russian defeat of Turkey and the one-sided Treaty of **SAN STEFANO**. The chief results were: Serbia, Romania and Bulgaria had their independence from Turkey recognized but gained less territory than they were entitled to; Austria-Hungary occupied Bosnia and Herzegovina; Russia retained gains in southern Bessarabia and the Caucasus, but conceded a reduction in the size of its protégé, Bulgaria, and generally suffered a diplo-

matic defeat; and Britain occupied Cyprus. ► **OTTOMAN EMPIRE**

### Berlin, Congress of (Nov 1884–Feb 1885)
A conference summoned by the German Chancellor **BISMARCK** to consider rival claims to Africa and the internationalization of the Congo region under the aegis of the African Association of King **LEOPOLD II** of the Belgians. All the major European powers attended, together with the USA and the **OTTOMAN EMPIRE**, but there were no representatives from Africa. The General Act of the conference, signed in Feb 1885, established freedom of navigation on African rivers and free trade areas. It also effectively laid down the ground rules for the Scramble for Africa, which was speeding up even as the conference was meeting. Bismarck achieved his objective of maintaining tension between Britain and France and won electoral support in Germany by securing colonies in West, East and South-West Africa. ► **AFRICA, PARTITION OF**

### Berlin, Partition of
Founded in the 13c, Berlin became the residence of the **HOHENZOLLERN DYNASTY** and the capital of Brandenburg. Later it was the capital of **PRUSSIA**, becoming an industrial and commercial centre in the 18c. As the capital of Germany, it was partitioned during the late 1940s into East Berlin and West Berlin. In 1949, West Berlin became associated with the Federal Republic of Germany (although under Four Power control) and East Berlin became, de facto, a county of the German Democratic Republic. The two halves of the city were separated by a wall built around West Berlin in 1961 to prevent the movement of citizens from East to West. Contact between the two halves of the city was restored in Nov 1989, following the **REVOLUTION OF 1989** in East Germany, and it was made the capital of unified Germany in 1990. ► **BERLIN WALL**; **HONECKER, ERICH**; **ULBRICHT, WALTER**

### Berlin, Treaty of (1728)
The treaty by which Frederick William of Prussia accepted the **PRAGMATIC SANCTION** of **CHARLES VI** confirming the rights of Charles's daughter, **MARIA THERESA**, to succeed to the Imperial throne. Charles's machinations made him unable to deliver his part of the treaty relating to Prussia's claims to parts of Jülich and Berg. As a result, Prussia disputed Maria's right to the throne after Charles's death.

### Berlin Airlift (1948–9)
A massive airlift of essential supplies flown in to **COLD WAR** Berlin by British and US aircraft in round-the-clock missions. It was carried out in response to the action of the Soviet military authorities in Berlin, who had attempted to isolate the city from the West by severing all overland communication routes (June 1948). **STALIN** lifted the blockade in May 1949.

### Berlin–Baghdad Railway ► BAGHDAD RAILWAY

### Berlin Blockade (1948–9)
An attempt by **STALIN** to weaken US preparedness to remain in Europe indefinitely following **WORLD WAR II**, and also to secure his control over Eastern Europe by strengthening his hold on the east of Germany. Specifically, the idea was to prevent supplies getting through to the western zones of Berlin, in the hope that the Allies would withdraw. In the event, the Allies

flew in food and fuel for almost 11 months until Stalin had to back down. It was after this that the **COLD WAR** intensified, with the establishment of **NATO** and **CO-MECON** in 1949.

**Berlinguer, Enrico** (1922–84)
Italian politician. Born into a wealthy Sardinian land-owning family, from 1943 he was a member of the Italian Communist Party (PCI) and played an active role in the resistance. Secretary-General of the Federation of Young Communists (1949–56), he was elected to parliament in 1968 and became Vice-Secretary of the party in 1969; in 1972 he was made Secretary-General. In Sep 1973 he proposed the 'historic compromise' with the **CHRISTIAN DEMOCRATIC PARTY**: in return for social reforms and an increased say on policy formation, the PCI agreed to respect the Church and constitutional institutions and discourage labour militancy. Shortly afterwards, he also endorsed **NATO** and, in Dec 1977, PCI deputies voted in favour of Italy's foreign and defence policies. Under Berlinguer's influence, Italian communism flourished in the 1970s: in the 1976 elections, the PCI received 34.4 per cent of votes, rivalling the 38.7 per cent polled by the DC, and by Mar 1978 the PCI had entered the government's parliamentary majority. However, traditional DC suspicion of the Left, the openly anti-communist stance of Pope **JOHN PAUL II** (elected Oct 1978) and the anti-Soviet feeling generated by the invasion of Afghanistan undermined the coalition. So too did the more militant wing of the PCI, which never welcomed cooperation with the DC. Berlinguer was consequently forced to jettison his conciliatory position and by 1979 was once again in opposition. During the remaining years of his life, he continued to pursue his vision of '**EURO-COMMUNISM**' which rejected the rigid Stalinist doctrines of the USSR. However, support for the PCI never again reached its peak of the late 1970s.

**Berlin Wall**
A concrete wall built by the East German government in 1961 to seal off East Berlin from the part of the city occupied by the three main Western powers. Built largely to prevent mass illegal emigration to the West, which was threatening the East German economy, the wall was the scene of the shooting of many East Germans who tried to escape from the eastern sector. The wall, seen by many as a major symbol of the denial of human rights in Eastern Europe, was unexpectedly opened in Nov 1989 following revolutionary upheaval in East Germany. Following reunification, most of the wall was taken down. ► **REVOLUTION OF 1989**

**Berlusconi, Silvio** (1936– )
Italian politician and businessman. He studied law in Milan before founding a construction company that built a large residential development in the city, which he then supplied with cable television. He developed his media interests, and by 1999 was estimated to be Italy's wealthiest man, owning three television channels, a football team, the country's largest publisher and its leading daily newspaper. He entered politics in 1993, founding the broadly liberal *Forza Italia* party, which won a surprise victory in the 1994 elections. He became Prime Minister of a coalition government but came under investigation for corruption and resigned in Dec 1994 when a coalition partner withdrew. After returning to power in the 2001 elections, he retained control of his media interests, which led to charges of a conflict of interests. He was tainted by corruption scandals but avoided bribery charges by passing a law granting him immunity from prosecution while in office, although this was later annulled and he stood trial, but charges were dismissed in Dec 2004. His government was the longest in Italy's history.

**Bernadotte, Folke, Count** (1895–1948)
Swedish diplomat. He was the nephew of King **GUSTAV V** of Sweden. He acted as a mediator in **WORLD WAR I** and, as Vice-President of the Swedish **RED CROSS**, negotiated with **HIMMLER** in the spring of 1945 for the liberation of Scandinavian prisoners from German concentration camps. Appointed by the UN to try to reach a settlement of the **PALESTINE** question, he produced a plan of partition but was assassinated by the **STERN GANG** in Jerusalem.

**Bernadotte, House of**
The royal dynasty of Sweden since 1818. The House was founded by Jean Baptiste Jules Bernadotte, one of **NAPOLEON**'s marshals, who became King **CHARLES XIV JOHN**. On his death he was succeeded by his son, **OSCAR I**, only child of his marriage to Désirée Clary, sister-in-law of Napoleon's brother, Joseph **BONAPARTE**. The reigning monarchs of Denmark, Norway, Sweden and Belgium are direct descendants of the couple. Count Folke Bernadotte, nephew of King **GUSTAV V**, acted as mediator in both World Wars. ► **BERNADOTTE, COUNT FOLKE**

## HOUSE OF BERNADOTTE

| Regnal Dates | Name |
|---|---|
| 1818/44 | Charles XIV John |
| 1844/59 | Oscar I |
| 1859/72 | Charles XV |
| 1872/1907 | Oscar II |
| 1907/50 | Gustav V |
| 1950/73 | Gustav VI Adolf |
| 1973/ | Carl XVI Gustav |

**Bernadotte, Jean Baptiste Jules** ► **CHARLES XIV JOHN**

**Bernard of Clairvaux, St** (1090–1153)
French theologian and reformer. Born of a noble family, in 1113 he entered the Cistercian monastery of Cîteaux, and in 1115 became the first Abbot of Clairvaux. His studious, ascetic life and stirring eloquence made him the oracle of Christendom; he founded more than 70 monasteries, and his preaching kindled the enthusiasm of France for the Second **CRUSADE** (1146). His writings include hundreds of epistles and sermons, and several theological treatises. He died at Clairvaux, and was canonized in 1174. The monks of his reformed branch of the Cistercians are often called Bernardines.

**Bernhard Leopold** (1911–2004)
Prince of the Netherlands. The son of Prince Bernhard Casimir of Lippe and Armgard von Cramm, in 1937 he married **JULIANA**, the only daughter of **WILHELMINA**, Queen of the Netherlands. During **WORLD**

WAR II he commanded the Netherlands Forces of the Interior (1944–5). In 1976 he was involved in a bribery scandal, in which he was found to have received money for promoting the Dutch purchase of aircraft from the Lockheed Aircraft Corporation.

**Bernstein, Eduard** (1850–1932)
German socialist leader. An associate of ENGELS, he played a major part in unifying the German socialist movement in 1875. As a leading intellectual in the Social Democratic Party (SPD), he was prominent in establishing its Marxist ideology. Later he was an advocate of revisionism, an evolutionary form of MARXISM, and a member of the REICHSTAG periodically (1902–28). He was exiled for his beliefs (1888–1901), during which time he lived in London, where he influenced, and was in turn influenced by, the British Fabians and other socialists. ► FABIAN SOCIETY

**Bernstorff, Andreas Peter** (1735–97)
Danish politician. A Count of Hanoverian descent, he was Minister of Foreign Affairs (1773–80 and 1784–97) and, after the summer of 1788, he was Denmark's *de facto* Prime Minister. He was in charge of the pragmatic and cautious policy of neutrality that kept Denmark clear of the wars between the Great Powers and achieved continued Danish prosperity, while at the same time not unduly provoking British shipping and naval interests. In domestic matters, he played the role of mediator between those who demanded agricultural reforms, such as the abolition of serfdom and the introduction of freehold, and the influential landowners who saw their feudal interests threatened. On Bernstorff's death, Crown Prince Frederick (later King FREDERICK VI), took over the leading political role, resulting in a more confrontational Danish foreign policy which (Apr 1801) led to the first of two naval Battles of Copenhagen between Denmark and the UK.

**Bernstorff, Johan Heinrich, Count** (1862–1939)
German diplomat. After a varied diplomatic career, Bernstorff became German ambassador to the USA in 1908. During WORLD WAR I he sought unsuccessfully to dissuade his government from waging submarine warfare, the latter bringing the USA into the war. He then became German Ambassador to the OTTOMAN EMPIRE before serving as a member of the REICHSTAG for the liberal DDP during the Weimar era and as German delegate on the League of Nations Disarmament Commission. In 1933 he sought exile in Switzerland where he pursued his publishing interests. ► WEIMAR REPUBLIC

**Bernward** (d.1022)
Bishop of Hildesheim. After an extensive education in theology, administration and art, Bernward became tutor to OTTO III in 987. In 993 he was appointed Bishop of Hildesheim and with his brother Tammo, a Saxon count and the King's steward, he was at the centre of a Saxon faction at court. He took a less prominent role in the administration of Otto's successor, HENRY II, THE HOLY, and died as a monk in the monastery he had founded in Hildesheim. He was responsible for a period of great vitality in the arts under Otto and was canonized in 1192. ► OTTONIANS

**Berri, Nabih** (1938–)
Lebanese politician and soldier. Born in Freetown, Sierra Leone, he was the son of an expatriate Lebanese merchant. He studied law at Beirut University and practised as a lawyer for a time. In 1978 he became leader of AMAL ('Hope'), a branch of the Shiite nationalist movement founded by Iman Musa Sadr. Backed by Syria, it became the main Shiite military force in West Beirut and southern Lebanon during the country's civil wars, but in 1988 its Beirut branch was heavily defeated by the Iranian-backed HEZBOLLAH ('Party of God') and was disbanded. Berri joined the Lebanese government in 1984 as Minister of Justice, and has held the post of Speaker since 1992.

**Bersaglieri**
Piedmontese light infantry (in Italian literally 'sharpshooters') established in 1836 by General Alessandro Ferrero La Marmora (1799–1856), brother of Alfonso LA MARMORA. They fought in the CRIMEAN WAR and the campaigns of 1859–60, and were subsequently incorporated into the Italian army.

**Berthier, Alexandre** (1753–1815)
Prince of Neuchâtel and Wagram, Marshal of the First French Empire. Entering the army in 1770, he fought with LAFAYETTE in the AMERICAN REVOLUTION. In the FRENCH REVOLUTION he soon rose to be Chief of Staff in the Army of Italy (1795), and in 1798 proclaimed the republic in Rome. He became Chief of Staff to NAPOLEON I, on whose fall he had to surrender the principality of Neuchâtel, but was allowed to keep his rank as peer and marshal. Napoleon made overtures to him from Elba, but he retired to Bamberg. On 1 July 1815, at the sight of a Russian division marching towards the French frontier, he threw himself from a window.

**Berwick, James FitzJames, 1st Duke of** (1670–1734)
French and Jacobite general. He was the illegitimate son of James VII of Scotland and II of England. Educated in France as a Roman Catholic, he was created Duke of Berwick (1687), but fled from England at the GLORIOUS REVOLUTION. He fought in his father's Irish campaign (1689–91), and then in Flanders against the CAMISARDS. In 1706 he was created a Marshal of France, and in Spain established the throne of PHILIP V by the decisive victory of ALMANSA (1707) in the War of the SPANISH SUCCESSION. Appointed Commander-in-Chief of the French forces (1733), he was killed while besieging Phillippsburg. ► JACOBITES; JAMES VII AND II

**Besant, Annie** (1847–1933)
British theosophist and social reformer. Brought up in Harrow, she married the Rev Frank Besant, but was separated from him in 1873. From secularism and BRADLAUGH she passed in 1889 to Madame Blavatsky and theosophy, becoming its high priestess from 1891. In her later years she went to India, where she championed the causes of nationalism and education.

**Bessarabia**
The region between the Prut and Dniester rivers, the Black Sea and Danube delta. Settled by the SLAVS (6c), then the MONGOLS (13c), at the end of the 14c it became part of Wallachia and was named after the

ruling Wallachian Dynasty. In the 15c it passed to Moldavia and from the 16c was subject to the Ottomans until 1812 when, by the Treaty of **BUCHAREST**, together with half of Moldavia, it passed to Russia. In 1918 it declared itself independent, voted to join Romania and under the Treaty of Paris (1920) was awarded to Romania. In the **GERMAN–SOVIET PACT** (1939) the USSR was promised Bessarabia with northern **BUKOVINA** and in 1940, with part of the Ukraine, it became part of the Soviet Socialist Republic of Moldavia (now Moldova). Although occupied by the Romanian army during **WORLD WAR II**, it was returned to the USSR in 1947, after which it was an irredentist issue between the Soviet and Romanian governments. ► **MOLDAVIA AND WALLACHIA**; **ROMANIA**

**Bestuzhev-Ryumin, Alexei Petrovich, Count** (1693–1766)
Russian politician and diplomat. After foreign service in Hanover and England (1713–17), he became Russian Resident (1720) and later Ambassador (1730–40) in Denmark. In 1741 he was sentenced to death (later commuted to exile) for participation in a plot to seize the throne by the royal favourite Ernst Biron. On the accession of **ELIZABETH PETROVNA** the same year, he was pardoned, and made Chancellor in charge of foreign affairs (1744–58). At first he strengthened the alliance with England, Holland and Austria against France, Prussia and Turkey, but on the outbreak of the **SEVEN YEARS' WAR** (1756–63) was forced to ally with France. In 1758 he was banished again for complicity in the political intrigues of the future Empress **CATHERINE II, THE GREAT**, but when Catherine came to the throne (1762) he was restored to favour and granted the title of General Field Marshal. He then took no further part in political life.

**Betancourt, Rómulo** (1908–81)
Venezuelan politician and reformer. One of the founders of the *Partido Democrático Nacional* (National Democratic Party) in 1936, he held power from 1945 to 1947. On the fall of the **PÉREZ JIMÉNEZ** dictatorship (1952–8), he was elected President (1959–64) of the new Venezuelan democracy. He chose a moderate course, adopting an agrarian law in Mar 1960, and ambitious economic development plans which provided for a transition from the dictatorship.

**Bethlen, Gabriel** or **Gábor** (1580–1629)
Protestant Prince of Transylvania (1613/29). A brilliant soldier and diplomat, he opposed Emperor Ferdinand II in the **THIRTY YEARS' WAR**. In 1619 he invaded Hungary, and the following year was chosen its King; however, in 1621 he concluded peace with Ferdinand and resigned his claims, obtaining large accessions of territory. He later renewed hostilities with the Emperor (1624 and 1626), before finally withdrawing (1629).

**Bethlen, István (Stephen), Count** (1874–1947)
Hungarian politician. He was a leader of the counter-revolutionary movement after **WORLD WAR I**, and as Prime Minister from 1921 to 1931 promoted Hungary's economic reconstruction.

**Bethmann-Hollweg, Theobald von** (1856–1921)
German politician. Having qualified in law, he rose in the service of **PRUSSIA** and the German Empire, becoming Imperial Chancellor in 1909. Although not identified with the German élite's most bellicose elements, and fearing the effects of war upon German society, he nevertheless played an important part in the events which brought about general war in 1914. Anxious for a negotiated peace in 1917, he was forced from office. ► **WORLD WAR I**

**Bethune, David** ► **BEATON, DAVID**

**Bethune, Mary McLeod** (1875–1955)
US educator and administrator. She was founder and President of the National Council of Negro Women and of Bethune-Cookman College. Serving as adviser to President Franklin D **ROOSEVELT**'s **NEW DEAL** administration, she worked to expand awareness of minority issues within government agencies. She was director of the division of Negro Affairs within the National Youth Administration at a time when 40 per cent of black youths were suffering unemployment. As such she was quietly insistent that the number of blacks enrolled in the programme be increased despite the reluctance of state administrators. Black college students also benefited from the Special Negro Fund which she administered. In 1945 she was accredited by the State Department to attend the San Francisco Conference to establish the **UN**.

**Beust, Friedrich Ferdinand, Count von** (1809–86)
Saxon and Austrian politician. He was appointed Foreign Secretary (1866–71) and Imperial Chancellor (1867–71), then Ambassador in London (1871–8) and Paris (1878–82). His chief achievement was the reconciliation of Hungary to Austria (the **AUSGLEICH**, 1867).

**Bevan, Aneurin** (1897–1960)
British politician. One of 13 children, he worked in the pits on leaving school at 13, and led the Welsh miners in the 1926 **GENERAL STRIKE**. He entered parliament for the **INDEPENDENT LABOUR PARTY** in 1929, joining the **LABOUR PARTY** in 1931. He established a reputation as a brilliant, irreverent and often tempestuous orator. As Minister of Health (1945–51), he introduced the National Health Service (1948). He became Minister of Labour in 1951, but resigned in the same year over the National Health charges proposed in the Budget. From this period dated 'Bevanism', a left-wing movement to make the Labour Party more socialist and less 'reformist'. He married Jennie **LEE** in 1934, and died while still an MP. ► **SOCIALISM**

**Beveridge, William Henry Beveridge, 1st Baron** (1879–1963)
British economist, administrator and social reformer. He entered the Board of Trade (1908) and became Director of Labour Exchanges (1909–16). He was Director of the London School of Economics (1919–37) and Master of University College, Oxford (1937–45). He is best known as the author of the *Report on Social Insurance and Allied Services* (the Beveridge Report, 1942), which provided a blueprint for the creation of the Welfare State. He was knighted in 1919, became a Liberal MP (1944–6), and was made a baron in 1946. ► **LIBERAL PARTY** (UK)

**Bevin, Ernest** (1881–1951)
British politician. Orphaned by the age of seven, and self-taught, he early came under the influence of

trade unionism and the Baptists, and was for a time a lay preacher. A paid official of the dockers' union, he gained a national reputation in 1920 when he won most of his union's claims against an eminent barrister, earning the title of 'the dockers' KC'. He built up the National Transport and General Workers' Union and became its General-Secretary (1921–40). In 1940 he became a Labour MP, Minister of Labour and National Service in Winston **CHURCHILL**'s coalition government, and was Foreign Secretary in the Labour governments of 1945–51. ► **LABOUR PARTY** (UK)

## Bhadralok

A highly educated élite class distinguished by its westernizing tendencies, which flourished in late 19c and early 20c Bengal. Well represented in the **BRAHMO SAMAJ**, it played a leading role in Indian nationalist activity.

## Bharatiya Janata Party (BJP) ► JAN SANGH

## Bhattari, Krishna Prasad (1925– )

Nepalese politician. As an opponent of absolute monarchy, he was in hiding for 12 years until 1990, when, as Leader of the centrist Nepali Congress Party (NCP), he became Prime Minister in the wake of the revolution that year which ended the uncontested rule of King **BIRENDRA**. However, in May 1991, in Nepal's first multiparty elections in three decades, he offered his resignation to the King after losing his own seat in the 205-member House of Representatives to the Marxist leader of the United Communist Party, Madan Bhandari. He became Prime Minister again in May 1999 but resigned in Mar 2000 after he lost the confidence of the majority of his party and the House of Representatives.

## Bhave, Vinoba (1895–1982)

Indian social and land reformer. M K **GANDHI** took him under his care as a young scholar, an event which changed his life. Distressed in 1951 by the land hunger riots in Telengana, Hyderabad, Bhave began a walking mission throughout India to persuade landlords to give land to the peasants and thus founded the **BHOODAN** movement. A barefoot, ascetic saint, his silent revolution led to 4 million acres/1.6 million hectares of land being redistributed in four years. He was claimed to be the most notable spiritual figure in India after the death of Gandhi, whose ardent disciple he was.

## Bhindranwale, Sant Jarnail Singh (1947–84)

Indian politician and former Sikh extremist leader. Born into a poor Punjabi Jat farming family, he trained at the orthodox Damdani Taksal Sikh missionary school, becoming its head priest in 1971 and assuming the name Bhindranwale. Initially encouraged by Sanjay **GANDHI** (1946–80), the son and political adviser of Indira **GANDHI**, who sought to divide the Sikh Akali Dal movement, he campaigned violently against the heretical activities of Nirankari Sikhs during the later 1970s. His campaign broadened into a demand for a separate state of 'Khalistan' during the early 1980s, precipitating a bloody Hindu–Sikh conflict in Punjab. After taking refuge in the Golden Temple complex at Amritsar and building up an arms cache for terrorist activities, with about 500 devoted followers, he died at the hands of the Indian security forces who stormed the temple in

'Operation Blue Star'. ► **AKALI MOVEMENT**

## Bhoodan or Bhudan

Literally 'land-giving' in Hindi, Bhoodan is a late 20c agrarian Indian social movement, which encouraged the donation of land to the landless peasantry. Bhoodan was conceived in 1951 and led by Vinoba **BHAVE**. It was successful for a time in rural areas, particularly in Bihar state, but gradually lost momentum.

## Bhopal

The capital of Madhya Pradesh, central India, founded in 1723. It was the scene of a major industrial disaster in 1984, when poisonous isocyanate gas escaped from the Union Carbide factory, killing c.2,500 people and leaving 100,000 homeless.

## Bhumibol Adulyadej (1927– )

King of Thailand (1946/ ). The second son of Prince Mahidol of Songkhola and grandson of King **CHULALONGKORN**, he was educated in Bangkok and Switzerland and became monarch, as King Rama IX, after the death, in controversial circumstances, of his elder brother, King Ananda Mahidol. He married Queen Sirikit in 1950 and has one son and three daughters. As king, he has been a stabilizing influence in a country noted for its political turbulence, and was active, with popular support, in helping to overthrow the military government of Field Marshal Thanom Kittikachorn in 1973. He is a highly respected figure, viewed in some quarters as semidivine, and wields considerable political influence behind the scenes.

**BHUTAN** official name **Kingdom of Bhutan**

A small state in the eastern Himalayas, bounded to the north by China and to the south by India. British involvement dates from 1774 with the signing of a treaty of cooperation between Bhutan and the British **EAST INDIA COMPANY**; the southern part of the country was annexed by Britain in 1865. In 1910 Britain agreed not to interfere in internal affairs, transferring the supervision of Bhutan's external affairs to **BRITISH INDIA**, and in 1949 Bhutan signed a similar treaty with India. In 1990 large numbers of ethnic Nepalese moved to Nepal and India following the introduction of strict cultural laws. Bhutan has been governed since 1907 by maharajahs, now addressed as King of Bhutan. The absolute monarchy was replaced in 1969 by a form of democratic monarchy, with the King as the head of the government. The King relinquished this role in 1998 and transferred some powers to the national assembly, but political parties remain illegal.

## Bhutto, Benazir (1953– )

Pakistani politician. After an education at Oxford University, she returned to Pakistan and was placed under house arrest between 1977 and 1984 by General **ZIA UL-HAQ**, who had executed her father Zulfikar Ali **BHUTTO**, following the 1977 coup against him.

During her subsequent exile in England with her mother, she formed the Pakistan People's Party, returning to Pakistan with the lifting of martial law in 1986 and beginning her campaign for open elections. She married in 1987, and following General Zia's death the same year she was elected Prime Minister in 1988, taking Pakistan back into the Commonwealth in 1989. Increasing friction between her administration and the conservative presidency led to her government being dismissed in Aug 1990, and soon after corruption charges were made against her. Her husband was placed in custody on related alleged criminal offences. At the start of 1991, she began an international lecture tour, dismissing speculation that she was choosing self-exile in return for her husband's release. She returned to lead the opposition against her successor, Nawaz Sharif, and in 1993 was elected Prime Minister at the head of a coalition government. In 1996 her government faced renewed charges of corruption and mismanagement, and was dismissed. She was defeated in the Feb 1997 election and became leader of the opposition once more. In Apr 1999 she was relieved of her position as an MP when she and her husband, Asaf Ali Zardari (already in prison on a charge of murdering Bhutto's estranged brother), were found guilty of corruption and sentenced to five years' imprisonment and a fine of £5.3 million; soon afterwards Bhutto entered self-imposed exile in Dubai.

**Bhutto, Zulfikar Ali** (1928–79)
Pakistani politician. A graduate of the universities of California and Oxford, he began a career in law. He joined the Pakistani Cabinet in 1958 as Minister of Commerce, and became Foreign Minister in 1963. Dropped from the Cabinet, he founded the Pakistan People's Party (PPP) in 1967. After the secession of East Pakistan (now Bangladesh) in 1971, he became President (1971–3) and Prime Minister (1973–7). He introduced social and economic reforms, but opposition to his policies, especially from right-wing Islamic parties, led to the army under General ZIA UL-HAQ seizing control after the 1977 elections. Tried for corruption and murder, he was sentenced to death in 1978. In spite of worldwide appeals for clemency, the sentence was carried out in 1979.

**Biafra**
The south-eastern province of Nigeria, inhabited by the IGBO people. Under the leadership of Colonel Ojukwu, it attempted to break away from the federation, thus precipitating the civil war of 1967–70. After the war, Nigeria was reorganized into a new provincial structure in an attempt to avert continuing instability.

**Biafran War** (1967–70)
Two military coups in 1966 left Nigeria racked by ethnic divisions, and on 26 May 1967 Lt-Col Chukwenmeka OJUKWU was mandated by the IGBO consultative assembly to declare the Eastern Region of Nigeria independent as the state of Biafra. Civil war then broke out as the federal government, led by GOWON, sought to keep Nigeria one. It was not until Jan 1970 that the federal forces prevailed and, with Ojukwu's exile, peace was restored.

**Bibó, István** (1911–79)
Hungarian political writer and, briefly, revolutionary

politician. A supporter of the so-called Smallholders Party, he held middle-of-the-road views and had a difficult time practising as a writer in the early 1950s. However, in 1956, between the two Soviet interventions, he was chosen to be a member of Imre NAGY's cabinet and tried to exert a calming influence. He was subsequently condemned to death by the KÁDÁR government and was only saved by protests from the West. It was not until 1963 that he was released from prison as a sign that reform was on the way.

**Bidault, Georges** (1899–1982)
French politician. He became a professor of history, served in both World Wars, and was a member of the French Resistance. He became leader of the MRP (*Mouvement républicain populaire*), and apart from his periods as Premier (1946 and 1949–50), was Deputy Prime Minister (1950 and 1951) and Foreign Minister (1944, 1947 and 1953–4). After 1958 he opposed de GAULLE over the ALGERIAN WAR OF INDEPENDENCE, was charged with plotting against the security of the state, and went into exile (1962–8). ▸ RESISTANCE MOVEMENT (France)

**Bienville, Jean Baptiste Le Moyne, Sieur de** (1680–1747)
French explorer and colonial governor. The eighth son of Charles Le Moyne, a French colonist who had settled in Canada in 1641, he fought in 1696–7 with his brother Pierre, Sieur d'Iberville (1661–1706), in KING WILLIAM'S WAR, and later accompanied him on his expedition down the Mississippi River (1699). He was commandant of the colony of Louisiana (1701–12, 1718–23), and in 1718 founded New Orleans, which became the capital of the colony in 1722. Dismissed and recalled to France, he returned as Governor of Louisiana (1733–43) when the colony came under royal control.

**Bierut, Bolesław** (1892–1956)
Polish Communist Party functionary. In the interwar period he was in and out of prison and of Poland; then, and later, he spent formative periods in Moscow. In 1946 he was appointed Interim President, and the following year he was elected President. In 1948 he took over from GOMUŁKA as Secretary of the party, and then from 1952 to 1954 he was Prime Minister. His main claim to fame was following the Stalinist line and doing much damage to his country and colleagues in the process.

**Big-Character Poster** (*Dazibao/Ta-tzu pao*)
A form of wall-poster in China that has served as a unique means of public expression free of government or party control. Often anonymous, and handwritten, these posters have appeared on walls or billboards erected in public places. The first wall-poster to gain notoriety was the one displayed by the Philosophy Department of Beijing University on 25 May 1966, criticizing university authorities for stifling political debate. In Aug 1966 MAO ZEDONG himself wrote a wall-poster which denounced revisionism. Although the right to erect wall-posters expressing one's opinions was guaranteed in the 1975 and 1978 constitutions, such a privilege was withdrawn in 1980 following a protest movement the previous year calling for greater democracy.

**Big Sword Society** (*Dadao hui*)
A Chinese sect active in the south-western region of the province of Shandong during the 1890s. In an area of endemic economic poverty and banditry, the Big Swords were formed and led by wealthy landlords to provide protection. Like the Boxers in north-west Shandong, they practised martial arts and invulnerability rituals, as well as coming into conflict with native Christian congregations. At first tolerated by local officials, the Big Swords were finally suppressed in 1896. ➤ BOXER RISING

**Biko, Steve (Stephen)** (1947–77)
South African black activist. He studied medicine at Natal University from where he became President of the all-black South African Students Organization (1969) and Honorary President of the Black People's Convention (1972). He was the major figure in the BLACK CONSCIOUSNESS MOVEMENT, and his challenge to APARTHEID, expressed in his organization of the Black Community Programme, led to his being banned and then detained. He died in police custody as a result of beatings he received.

**Bil'ak, Vasil** (1917–)
Czechoslovak politician. He had a fairly undistinguished career in the Communist Party until 1968 when, as a Slovak, he succeeded Alexander DUBČEK as Secretary of the Central Committee of the Slovak Section. It was at this point that Dubček moved up to the secretaryship of the whole party and initiated the PRAGUE SPRING. Bil'ak was a reluctant reformer and in July and Aug of 1968 turned against Dubček, eventually welcoming the Soviet invasion. He was subsequently too unpopular to achieve high office, but he remained a member of the party presidium, resisting any change, for two decades.

**Bilingualism and Biculturalism, Royal Commission on** (1963–71)
Canadian governmental inquiry. Instituted by the Pearson administration, it was a response to the increasing separatist pressure in Quebec. Its aims were to research the origins of the crisis and to propose measures which would lead to a more equitable relationship between francophones and anglophones. Joint presidents of the commission were André Laurendeau, editor of the newspaper *Le Devoir*, and A Davidson Dunton, President of Ottawa's Carleton University. The final report revealed the extent to which French-Canadians were disadvantaged, both economically and culturally, by their origins. It recommended the adoption of both French and English as official languages throughout the federal bureaucracy and in business. Whilst the report refused to advocate separate nationhood for Quebec, it did propose the concept of a two-nation federation, and the establishment of a ministry for multiculturalism, which was enacted in 1972.

**Billaud-Varenne, Jean Nicolas** (1756–1819)
French revolutionary and supporter of the Reign of TERROR. He became Secretary, then Vice-President, of the Jacobin Club (1792), and was one of those responsible for the September Massacres (1792), in which the mob, urged on by demagogic extremists, seized and murdered innocent victims from Paris prisons. He attacked the GIRONDINS, was elected to

the Convention, and became a member of the Committee of Public Safety (1793). He supported ROBESPIERRE at first, but deserted him at the time of THERMIDOR. He was nevertheless transported to Cayenne (Guiana), where he lived until 1815. He then fled to Haiti, where he died. ➤ CONVENTION, NATIONAL; JACOBINS; PUBLIC SAFETY, COMMITTEE OF

**bill of rights**
A list of citizens' rights set out in constitutional documents. Usually accompanying the document is an elaboration of the institutional means and powers by which such rights may be enforced. The best-known example is the one adopted in 1791 as the first ten amendments to the US CONSTITUTION. The American Bill of Rights protects the liberties of private citizens in relation to the federal and state governments in such matters as freedom of speech, religion, the press and assembly, and legal procedure. It was adopted because of popular pressure during the campaign to ratify the constitution (1787–8), and its meaning has been expounded in many cases decided by the Supreme Court.

**Bill of Rights** (1689)
A Bill to enact the DECLARATION OF RIGHTS (1689), it asserted that JAMES II (of England) had abdicated, established WILLIAM III and Mary II as monarchs, forbade Roman Catholics from succeeding to the throne, and declared illegal exercise of royal power, such as the maintenance of an army in peacetime, without the consent of parliament.

**Billy the Kid** ➤ BONNEY, WILLIAM H

**Biological and Toxin Weapons Convention (BTWC)** (1975)
A convention banning the development, production and stockpiling of bacteriological (biological) and toxin weapons and on their destruction. It also bans any weapons designed to use such agents or toxins for hostile purposes. Although the Geneva Protocol (1925) banned the use in war of poison gas and bacteriological weapons, by the 1960s stronger measures to control biological weapons were thought necessary and the UN supported the drafting of the Convention, which entered into force in 1975. Scientific advances in the 1990s raised concerns about the development of dangerous viruses by unscrupulous governments and in 1991 development of legally binding verification and monitoring measures, omitted from the original Convention, began. From 1999 the Ad Hoc Group, set up in 1994, worked on a final framework for a protocol and the negotiation of key elements. Believing that such measures would impede commercial pharmaceutical research, the USA rejected the draft protocol in 2001, and subsequently called for the Group to be disbanded.

**Biological Diversity, Convention on** (1993)
A convention arising from discussions held under the UN Environment Programme, and endorsed at the EARTH SUMMIT. Its objectives are the conservation of biodiversity, the sustainable use of the Earth's resources, and the equitable sharing of genetic resources. It came into force in 1993. The Conference of the Parties (i.e. states that have ratified/acceeded to/accepted or approved the Convention) forms the governing body and the secretariat is based in

Montreal, Canada. The first protocol of the Convention, the Cartagena Protocol on Biosafety, was adopted in 2000 and came into force in 2003. It deals with the safe use of genetically modified organisms.

**Birch, John M** ➤ JOHN BIRCH SOCIETY

**Bird, Vere Cornwall** (1910–99)
Antiguan politician. In 1939 he was a founder-member of the Antigua Trades and Labour Union and then leader of the Antigua Labour Party (ALP). In the pre-independence period he was elected to the Legislative Council and became Chief Minister (1960–7) and Premier (1967–71 and 1976–81). When total independence, as Antigua and Barbuda, was achieved in 1981 he became Prime Minister; he and his party were re-elected in 1984, and again in 1989. He was succeeded as party leader in 1994 by his son Lester Bird, who took over as Prime Minister later that year.

**Birdwood, William Riddell Birdwood, 1st Baron** (1865–1951)
Australian military leader, he served in the Indian Army, became Secretary of the Indian Army Department and a member of the Viceroy's legislative council (1912). In 1914 he was put in command of the Australian and New Zealand Army contingents, and planned the landing at Gallipoli, on Anzac Cove as it was subsequently known. Upon evacuation from the peninsula, he took his troops to the Western Front, through the Battles of the Somme and Ypres in 1916 and 1917. After **WORLD WAR I** he returned to India to command the Northern Army, becoming Commander-in-Chief in 1925, and retiring in 1930.
➤ GALLIPOLI CAMPAIGN; SOMME, BATTLE OF THE

**Birendra Bir Bikram Shah Dev** (1945–2001)
King of Nepal (1972/2001). Educated at St Joseph's College, Darjeeling, Eton, and Tokyo and Harvard universities, he married Queen Aishwarya Rajya Laxmi Devi Rana in 1970, and had two sons and one daughter. Appointed Grand Master and Colonel-in-Chief of the Royal Nepalese Army in 1964, he became King on the death of his father, King Mahendra. During his reign, there was gradual progress towards political reform, but Nepal remained essentially an absolute monarchy, with political activity banned, until 1990, when Birendra was forced to concede much of his power. He was killed, along with the Queen and other members of the royal family, by Crown Prince Dipenda, who subsequently shot himself and died a few days later, when King Birendra's brother Gyanendra became king.

**Birkenhead, Frederick Edwin Smith, 1st Earl of** (1872–1930)
British politician and lawyer. A Conservative, he entered parliament in 1906, where he became known as a brilliant orator. In the Irish crisis (1914) he supported resistance to **HOME RULE**, but later helped to negotiate the Irish settlement of 1921. He became Attorney-General (1915–19) and Lord Chancellor (1919–22), and was made an earl in 1922. His conduct as Secretary of State for India (1924–8) caused much criticism, and he resigned to devote himself to a commercial career. ➤ CONSERVATIVE PARTY (UK)

**Birla, G D** (1894–1983)
Indian industrialist. He was India's biggest paper magnate, in charge of the huge Oriental Paper empire. He was also a large-scale philanthropist, contributing to the causes of scientific and medical research. Most famous for his close friendship with M K **GANDHI** and his strong support for the **INDIAN NATIONAL CONGRESS** in the 1920s, 1930s and 1940s, he was himself elected to the Indian Central Legislative Assembly in 1926. In 1944 he compiled the so-called Bombay Plan, along with two other businessmen, Thakurdas and J R D Tata, which set the pattern of state and private investment that was characteristic of India's five-year plans after independence.

**Biron, Ernst Johann** (1690–1772)
Baltic German nobleman. He assumed the name and arms of the French dukes of Biron, when, as favourite of **ANNA IVANOVNA**, he became the real ruler of Russia on her ascent to the Russian throne in 1730. He was blamed for most of the ills which befell Russia at this time, but greatly improved the country's administration. In 1737 Anna made him Duke of Courland. On the Empress's death (1740), he assumed the regency and acted with great moderation, but was arrested and banished for a time to Siberia. **PETER III** allowed him to return in 1762 and his titles were eventually restored to him.

**Biryukova, Alexandra Pavlovna** (1929– )
Soviet politician. She was trained as a textile engineer and continued until as late as 1968 with her professional job in a factory. However, she had earlier taken official jobs, and in 1968 she became Secretary of the Trade Union Presidium and in 1985 Deputy Chairman. In 1986 Mikhail **GORBACHEV** selected her for the Secretariat of the Central Committee of the Communist Party, and in 1988 appointed her Deputy Prime Minister responsible for Social Development. She was also made a candidate member of the **POLITBURO**, the first woman since **FURTSEVA** to achieve this distinction. One of the few Soviet women to reach positions of political importance, in the turmoil of 1990–1 she was, however, pushed aside.

**Bishop, Maurice** (1946–83)
Grenadian politician. He was the leader of the New Jewel Movement that overthrew the government of Eric **GAIRY** in 1979 and set up a Marxist People's Revolutionary Government. Disagreements over policy led to Bishop's overthrow and murder by his deputy, Bernard Coard, and the Commander of the Armed Forces, General Austin, in Oct 1983, and the creation of a Revolutionary Military Council (RMC). The USA and moderate Caribbean governments, shocked by the bloody coup and fearful of imagined Cuban influence, instigated military intervention to depose the RMC and arrest the coup leaders. Coard, Austin and twelve others were sentenced to death, but these sentences were commuted to life imprisonment in 1991.

**Bishops' Wars** (1639–40)
Two wars between **CHARLES I** of England and the Scottish **COVENANTERS**, caused by his unpopular policies towards the Scottish Kirk. They resulted in English defeats, and bankruptcy for Charles, who was then forced to call the Short and Long Parliaments (1640), bringing to an end his 'personal rule'

(1629–40). ► LONG PARLIAMENT; SHORT PARLIA-MENT

**Bismarck, Otto Edward Leopold von** (1815–98)
Prusso-German politician. He studied law and agriculture at Göttingen, Berlin and Greifswald. In the new Prussian parliament (1847) he became known as an ultra-royalist, resenting Austria's predominance and demanding equal rights for PRUSSIA. He was Ambassador to Russia (1859–62), and was appointed Prime Minister in 1862 with an explicit remit to thwart liberal pressure for a constitutional monarchy. During the Schleswig-Holstein question and the Seven Weeks' War between Prussia and Austria, he was a guiding figure, becoming a national hero and reconciling the liberals to Prussian monarchism. Uniting German feeling, he deliberately provoked the FRANCO-PRUSSIAN WAR (1870–1) and acted as Germany's spokesman. He was made a count in 1866, created a prince, and was the first Chancellor of the new German Empire (1871–90). After the Peace of Frankfurt (1871), his policies aimed at consolidating and protecting the young empire. His domestic policy included universal suffrage, reformed coinage, welfare legislation and the codification of the law, although he ensured that ultimate political power resided with the Emperor and aristocracy. He engaged in a lengthy conflict with the Vatican (known as the KULTURKAMPF), which proved to be a failure, and from 1878 pursued a vigorous anti-socialist policy. In 1879, to counteract Russia and France, he formed the Austro-German Treaty of Alliance, which was later joined by Italy. Called the 'Iron Chancellor', he resigned the chancellorship in 1890, out of disapproval of Emperor WILLIAM II's initially liberal policy. In the same year he was made Duke of Lauenburg, and was finally reconciled to his sovereign (1894). ► SCHLESWIG-HOLSTEIN PROBLEM

**Bitar, Salah al-Din** (1912–80)
Syrian politician. Co-founder in 1943 with Michel AFLAQ of the BA'ATH PARTY, he played a considerable part in the founding of the short-lived UNITED ARAB REPUBLIC (UAR), a union of Egypt and Syria established in 1958, from which Syria seceded in 1961. Despite a broad influence through its essentially socialist and pan-Arab ideology, the failure of the UAR dealt a considerable blow to the Ba'ath as originally conceived by Bitar and Aflaq, and paved the way for the separate development of one-party Ba'athist rule in Syria and Iraq.

**Bixio, Gerolamo**, known as **Nino** (1821–73)
Italian soldier. One of GARIBALDI's most able lieutenants and one of the few *garibaldini* to be fully accepted by the regular army, he was elected a deputy in the Italian parliament in 1861 and became a senator in 1870.

**Biya, Paul** (1933–)
Cameroonian politician. He graduated with a law degree from Paris University and entered politics under the aegis of AHIDJO. He was a junior minister in 1962, a minister of state in 1968 and Prime Minister in 1975. When Ahidjo unexpectedly retired in 1982, he became President and reconstituted the government with his own supporters. He survived a coup attempt in Apr 1984 (almost certainly instigated by Ahidjo)

and was re-elected President in 1988 with more than 98 per cent of the vote. He has held on to power in subsequent elections, winning his latest term in 2004.

**Bjelke-Petersen, Sir Joh (annes)** (1911–)
New Zealand-born Australian politician, of Danish parents. In 1913 the family moved to Kingaroy, Queensland. He entered state politics in 1947 as a Country Party (later National Party) member of the Legislative Assembly, becoming a minister in 1963. In 1968, as a result of his firm stand on law and order, he was made Police Minister, then Deputy Leader and, following the sudden death of Jack Pizzey, became Premier of Queensland. A vocal supporter of states' rights against federal intervention, he controlled a strongly right-wing government, first in coalition with the LIBERAL PARTY OF AUSTRALIA and after 1983 in his own right. He was knighted in 1982 and retired from the premiership in 1987. ► NATIONAL PARTY OF AUSTRALIA

**Björnsson, Sveinn** (1881–1952)
Icelandic diplomat and politician. Born in Copenhagen, he was the son of an Icelandic newspaper editor. He studied law in Copenhagen and was elected a member of the Icelandic parliament in 1914–16 and 1920. During WORLD WAR I he was envoy to the USA and Britain, and was ambassador to Denmark in 1920–4 and 1926–41. During the German occupation of Denmark he was elected regent of Iceland and, when Iceland declared its independence of Denmark in 1944, he was elected the new republic's first President. Re-elected in 1948, he died in office.

BJP ► JAN SANGH

**Black, Hugo Lafayette** (1886–1971)
US jurist. He practised law in his home state of Alabama and became a police court judge. In 1927 he entered the US SENATE and as a liberal leader promoted the TENNESSEE VALLEY AUTHORITY as well as legislation that would set minimum wages and impose limits on working hours. In 1937 he was appointed to the US Supreme Court, where he served until his death. Black, a libertarian, opposed undue economic regulation by the states or the federal government. Central to his philosophy was the conviction that the FOURTEENTH AMENDMENT made the Bill of Rights generally applicable to the states, and that the First Amendment's guarantees of freedoms were absolute. Late in his career he supported CIVIL RIGHTS legislation.

**Black and Tans**
Additional members of the Royal Irish Constabulary, recruited by the British government to cope with Irish nationalist unrest in 1920. The shortage of regulation uniforms led to the recruits being issued with khaki tunics and trousers, and very dark green caps, hence their name. Terrorist activities provoked severe and brutal reprisals by the Black and Tans, which caused an outcry in Britain and the USA.

**Black Churches**
In the USA from the 1720s, Christian Protestant churches that grew out of missionary activity by whites but which formed their own Afro-American congregations. Usually Baptist, but also Methodist

or Pentecostal, the churches, which often originated among black slaves, became central to black community life especially during the segregation years. They are characterized by informal and spontaneous forms of worship, including singing and dancing, the central role of preaching, a strong concern for social and political justice, and strong feelings against the oppression of minority groups and the poor. In the 1960s and 1970s they were at the forefront of the **CIVIL RIGHTS MOVEMENT**.

**Black Codes**
Laws enacted in 1865–6 by Southern state legislatures following the **AMERICAN CIVIL WAR**, which severely restricted many rights of the newly freed slaves. Varying significantly from state to state, these laws were interpreted by the North as Southern unwillingness to change its racial attitudes. The Freedman's Bureau prevented their implementation and they were later repealed.

**Black Consciousness Movement** (South Africa)
A loose movement formed by Steve **BIKO** in 1969, when he led African students out of the multiracial National Union of South African Students and founded the South African Students Organization. From this emerged the Black People's Convention in 1972, which sought to create cooperation in social and cultural fields among all non-white peoples. Banned in 1976, most of its leaders were imprisoned in 1977 and Biko himself died in police custody soon afterwards.

**Black Dragon Society** (*Kokuryukai*)
A Japanese ultra-nationalist conspiratorial organization founded in 1901 by Uchida Ryohei and Toyama Mitsuru. Strongly influenced by the concept of Pan-Asianism, the society sought to enhance Japan's influence on the Asian mainland, initially in Manchuria (and thereby eliminate Russian influence) and then throughout China. It maintained ties with a number of government officials, Diet politicians and military officers, continually pressing for an assertive foreign policy to combat Western influence in Asia, an aim that was often linked with domestic renovation. The society also carried out espionage work on the Asian mainland. As with other ultra-nationalist organizations, the Black Dragon Society was disbanded in 1945 following Japan's defeat in **WORLD WAR II**.

**Blackfoot**
Three Algonquian-speaking Native American tribes (Blackfoot, Blood and Piegan), originally from the east, who settled in Montana and in Alberta, Canada. They reached the height of their military power in the early 19c, when they occupied a vast area and earned a reputation as strong and aggressive fighters. However, many died of starvation after the bison were exterminated, or from diseases such as smallpox which took 6,000 lives in 1837; others turned to farming and raising cattle. In the early 21c, the Blackfoot population was c.32,000, with most living in Alberta, Canada, and the Blackfeet Indian Reservation in Browning, Montana. ► **NATIVE AMERICANS**

**Black Friday**
The name given to 24 Sep 1869, the day of a US financial crisis, when the price of gold dropped severely as a result of an attempt by such financiers as Jay Gould

(1836–92) and James Fisk (1834–72) to corner the gold market. Many speculators lost their fortunes in the ensuing panic.

**Black Hand**
The common name for the secret organization *Uje-dinjenje ili Smrt* ('Unification or Death'), formed by Serbian nationalist army officers in 1911. Led by Colonel Dragutin **DIMITRIJEVIĆ**, alias Apis, its objective was the political unification of all the Serbs. It lay behind the assassination by the Bosnian Serb Gavrilo **PRINCIP** of **FRANCIS FERDINAND**, Archduke of Austria, in Sarajevo (June 1914), an event which led directly to the outbreak of **WORLD WAR I**. ► **MLADA BOSNA**

**Black Hawk**, Native American name **Makataime-shekiakiak** (1767–1838)
Native American chief. He was a leader of the Sauk tribe, who, with the Fox tribe, resisted removal from their homeland when US settlers contravened a treaty and expanded westward into Illinois. During the **BLACK HAWK WAR** (1832), most of his group of warriors and their families were slaughtered by white troops under General Henry Atkinson.

**Black Hawk War** (1832)
A military conflict between the USA and Sauk and Fox peoples, which led to the completion of the policy of removing **NATIVE AMERICANS** from 'the Old North-West' to beyond the Mississippi River. ► **BLACK HAWK; INDIAN WARS**

**Black Hole of Calcutta**
A small, badly ventilated room in which surviving British defenders were imprisoned following Calcutta's capture (June 1756) by **SIRAJ UD-DAULA**, Nawab of Bengal. It was claimed that only 23 out of 146 prisoners survived. Following possibly self-serving publicity by J Z Holwell, the incident became famous in the history of British imperialism, but the circumstances are controversial, and the total number of prisoners was probably much smaller.

**Black Hundreds** (post-1905)
The name given to the right-wing terrorists opposed to the reforms conceded by **NICHOLAS II** during the Russian **REVOLUTION OF 1905**. Operating under fine-sounding names such as Union of the Russian People, Union of the Russian Land, or Russian Orthodox Committee, they were well-to-do and well-connected. Often with official connivance, they resorted to violence against individuals or groups supporting democratic reform and helped to discredit such representative institutions as were tolerated.

**Black Muslims**
A black religious movement in the USA, also known as the Nation of Islam, founded in 1930 by Wali Farad (Wallace D Fard), who proclaimed that black Americans are descended from an ancient Muslim tribe. Followers adopted Muslim names and believed Farad to be an incarnation of God. Following Farad's mysterious disappearance in 1934, Elijah **MUHAMMAD** became leader of the movement until his death in 1975. Muhammad urged his followers to avoid contact with whites, and demanded a separate state for blacks as well as reparation for past injustices. **MALCOLM X** was one of the movement's most inspiring preachers, while the boxer Muhammad Ali was one

of its most famous members. After Elijah Muhammad's son, Warith Dean (Wallace D), assumed leadership, the organization adopted orthodox Muslim beliefs. There were some, however, who continued to hold to the original tenets of the movement, including its separatist stance. Louis **FARRAKHAN** emerged as that faction's spokesman and has continued in that role.

**Black Panthers**
US militant black political party, founded by Huey P Newton and Bobby Seale in 1966, promoting the use of physical force and armed confrontation for black liberation. The party was active in the 1960s, but was split by rival groups in the 1970s and diminished in importance.

**Black Power**
The slogan used by black activists in the USA from the mid-1960s to reflect the aspiration of increased black political power. It formed part of the more radical wing of the **CIVIL RIGHTS MOVEMENT**, was against integrationist policies, and rejected non-violence. Some political results were achieved in terms of registering black voters, together with much wider attitudinal change. ► **BLACK PANTHERS**; **CONGRESS OF RACIAL EQUALITY** (CORE)

**Black Saturday** (26 Jan 1952)
After guerrilla attacks on their bases in Egypt, the British acted against suspects, including the Egyptian police. British forces surrounded police headquarters at Ismailia and called on the police to surrender; they refused and 50 were killed in the attack on their headquarters. The next day, Black Saturday, Egyptian crowds led by the **MUSLIM BROTHERHOOD** burnt down British and foreign shops and restaurants in the centre of Cairo. Egyptian troops did not intervene to bring the situation under control until evening. King **FAROUK** and the government blamed each other for the delay and there began a period of ministerial instability, as governments followed one another rapidly. This led the **FREE OFFICERS** to bring forward the coup they were planning for 1954 or 1955 to July 1952, when army units seized key points in the capital and Farouk was forced into exile.

**Black September** (Sep 1970)
This refers to the month when Fedayeen and the **PLO** (Palestine Liberation Organization) resisted an attempt by the Jordanian government to establish control over them and their guerrillas who were carrying out operations against Israel. A civil war resulted and King **HUSSEIN** was saved by the loyalty of his Bedouin regiments.

**blackshirts**
The colloquial name for members of Oswald **MOSLEY**'s British Union of Fascists (BUF), formed in Oct 1932. It derived from the colour of the uniforms worn at mass rallies and demonstrations organized by the BUF on the model of European fascist parties. After clashes and disturbances in Jewish areas of London (1936), the Public Order Act prohibited the wearing of uniforms by political groups. ► **UNION MOVEMENT**

**Black Thursday** (24 Oct 1929)
The date of the crash of the New York stockmarket that marked the onset of the **GREAT DEPRESSION**.

**Blackwell, Elizabeth** (1891–1910)
US physician and feminist. Born in Bristol, UK, she received a degree in medicine from Geneva College in New York State. Blackwell, who faced hostility throughout her education and career, was responsible for opening the field of medicine to women. She also established an infirmary for the poor of New York City. In later life she returned to England, where she died at Hastings, Sussex.

**Blaine, James Gillespie** (1830–93)
US politician. He became a member of the US **HOUSE OF REPRESENTATIVES** (1863–76), serving as Speaker from 1869 to 1875, before becoming a senator (1876–81) and Secretary of State (1881). He was the Republican candidate for President in 1884 but lost the election by a narrow margin to Grover **CLEVELAND**, a loss that might perhaps have been avoided if one of his supporters had not alienated the Roman Catholic vote in New York by assailing the Democrats as the party of 'Rum, Romanism and Rebellion'. As Secretary of State once again (1889–93), in the **HARRISON** administration, he organized the first Pan-American Conference (1889).

**Blair, Tony (Anthony Charles Lynton)** (1953– )
British Labour politician. Born in Edinburgh, he was educated at Fettes College, Edinburgh, and St John's College, Oxford. After graduating he became a barrister, specializing in trade union and employment law. He was elected to parliament as Labour MP for Sedgefield in 1983 and achieved success as opposition Home Affairs spokesman in 1992 by promoting law and order, traditionally a Conservative interest. In 1994 he succeeded John Smith as Labour leader and instituted a series of reforms to streamline and modernize his party. In 1997 Labour's landslide win in the general election made Blair Prime Minister, the third-youngest to take office after **PITT, THE YOUNGER** and Lord **LIVERPOOL**. Labour was returned to office in the 2001 general election with a slightly reduced majority, but the decision to involve the UK in the **IRAQ WAR** lost the party, and Blair in particular, public confidence, especially when the inquiry into the death of the weapons inspector Dr David Kelly revealed that the government had overstated the case for going to war.

**Blaize, Herbert Augustus** (1918–89)
Grenadian politician. After qualifying and practising as a solicitor, he entered politics and helped to found the centrist Grenada National Party (GNP), being elected to parliament in 1957. He held ministerial posts before becoming Premier in 1967. After full independence in 1974, he led the official opposition and then went into hiding (1979–83) following the left-wing coup by Maurice **BISHOP**. After the US invasion of 1983, when normal political activity resumed, he returned to lead a reconstituted New National Party (NNP) and win the 1984 general election.

**Blake, Edward** (1833–1912)
Canadian lawyer and politician. A Liberal, he became Premier of Ontario in 1871 and minister without portfolio in the **MACKENZIE** federal administration in 1873. Uncomfortable with Mackenzie's policies, he resigned in 1874, and with a fervent speech

assumed the leadership of the **CANADA FIRST** movement. He returned to government as the Minister of Justice in 1875 and succeeded in gaining the British government's acceptance of the Supreme Court Act and a reduction in the powers of the Governor-General. Leader of the Liberals (1880–7), he resigned from the party in 1891 because he could not accept its **RECIPROCITY** proposals. Long interested in the Irish question, he left Canada in 1892 and became an Irish nationalist MP in the British parliament, but eventually returned to Canada in 1906. ▶ **LIBERAL PARTY** (Canada)

**Blake, Robert** (1599–1657)
English admiral. He lived in Oxford as a quiet country gentleman until he was 40. In 1640 he was returned for Bridgwater to the **SHORT PARLIAMENT**, and later served in the **LONG PARLIAMENT** (1645–53) and the **BAREBONE'S PARLIAMENT** (1653). In 1649 he blockaded Lisbon, destroying the squadron of Prince **RUPERT**, and in 1652–3 routed the Dutch in several battles. His greatest victory was his last, at Santa Cruz, when he destroyed a Spanish treasure fleet off Tenerife. He died on the return journey to England. ▶ **ANGLO-DUTCH WARS**; **ENGLISH CIVIL WARS**

**Blamey, Sir Thomas** (1884–1951)
Australian soldier. He joined the regular army in 1906 and attended Staff College at Quetta. He saw service on the north-west frontier of India, and in **WORLD WAR I** played an important part in the evacuation of Gallipoli. He became Chief of Staff of the Australian Corps in 1918, and between 1925 and 1936 was Chief Commissioner of Police in Victoria. At the outbreak of **WORLD WAR II** he was given command of the Australian Imperial Forces in the Middle East. He had command of Commonwealth operations in Greece (1941) and served as Deputy Commander-in-Chief to **WAVELL**. On the establishment of the south-west Pacific command he became Commander-in-Chief of Allied land forces (1942) and received the Japanese surrender in 1945. In 1950 he was made a field marshal, the first Australian soldier to hold this rank. ▶ **GALLIPOLI CAMPAIGN**

**Blanc, (Jean Joseph) Louis** (1811–82)
French politician and historian. A socialist, he studied in Paris, where in 1839 he founded the *Revue du Progrès* and wrote his chief work on socialism, *L'Organisation du travail* (1839), proposing the establishment of cooperative workshops subsidized by the state. After the **FEBRUARY REVOLUTION** (1848) he became a member of the provisional government, without portfolio, acting as President of the Luxembourg Committee set up to discuss ways of improving labour conditions; it had no power and achieved nothing. Charged, unjustly, with fomenting the **JUNE DAYS** rising of Parisian workers, he fled in Aug 1848 to Belgium, moving to London in 1851. On the fall of the Second Empire, he returned to France, and was elected to the National Assembly in 1871. He opposed the **PARIS COMMUNE** (1871), but led the extreme Left in the first parliaments of the Third Republic. ▶ **EMPIRE, SECOND** (France); **REPUBLIC, THIRD** (France)

**Blanqui, (Louis) Auguste** (1805–81)
French revolutionary leader. A socialist, he studied law and medicine, demonstrated against the Bourbon regime, and organized an abortive insurrection in 1839, which led to his imprisonment until 1848. He founded the Central Republican Society, and was again imprisoned after the demonstrations of May 1848. He remained politically active during the Second Empire, and was arrested on the eve of the **PARIS COMMUNE**, of which he was nevertheless elected President (1871). A passionate extremist, whose supporters were known as Blanquists, he spent 37 years of his life in prison. ▶ **BOURBON, HOUSE OF**; **EMPIRE, SECOND** (France)

**Blasco (Ibáñez), Vicente** (1867–1928)
Spanish politician and writer. A federalist Republican leader of revolutionary leanings, he was first elected to parliament in 1898. His populist appeal laid the foundations for the PURA (Party of Republican Autonomist Union), otherwise known as the 'Blasquist' movement, which became the dominant political force in Valencia until the **SPANISH CIVIL WAR**. At the same time as the Barcelona leader Alejandro **LERROUX** (an ally), Blasco Ibáñez formed the first modern political party in Spain. Although Blasco abandoned politics for writing in 1907, his political pronouncements made a greater impact than ever. During **WORLD WAR I** he backed the Allies, most notably through his novel *The Four Horsemen of the Apocalypse*. His broadsides against the monarchy and **PRIMO DE RIVERA**'s dictatorship (1923–30) were highly effective. During the early part of the 20c he was probably the most famous living Spanish writer in the world. He died in exile in France.

**Blenheim, Battle of** (1704)
The greatest military triumph of **MARLBOROUGH** and his Imperial ally, Prince **EUGÈNE OF SAVOY**, in the War of the **SPANISH SUCCESSION**. Fought on the Danube to prevent a combined Franco-Bavarian thrust on Vienna, it marked the first major defeat of **LOUIS XIV** of France's armies, and the first major English victory on the European mainland since the Battle of **AGINCOURT**.

**Bleus**
French-Canadian moderate reform followers of Louis Hippolyte **LAFONTAINE** (the term dating from 1850 in contradistinction to the radical **ROUGES**). From 1854 they became the French-Canadian wing of the new Conservative Party. In 1862, with the introduction of the **MILITIA BILL**, the bloc split into two wings, the *Ultra-bleus*, led by Sir Hector **LANGEVIN**, who were on the extreme right, and the moderate *Bleus*, led by Adolphe **CHAPLEAU**. The party had problems when **CANADA WEST** and **CANADA EAST** were united in 1864 because the French-Canadians suffered a numerical disadvantage in the legislature. However, under the leadership of George Étienne **CARTIER**, the Bleus sought to protect the cultural rights of the French-Canadians. The support of the party was essential to the Conservative domination of federal politics during the late 19c, but with D'Alton **MCCARTHY**'s Equal Rights Association and the **MANITOBA SCHOOLS ACT** controversy, Quebec swung its vote behind the Liberals, who then won the 1896 federal election.

**Bligh, William** (1754–c.1817)
British sailor. He sailed under Captain James **COOK** in

his second world voyage (1772–4), and in 1787 was sent as commander of the *Bounty* to Tahiti. On the return voyage, the men mutinied under his harsh treatment. In Apr 1789, Bligh and 18 men were cast adrift in an open boat without charts. In June, after great hardship, he arrived at Timor, near Java, having sailed his frail craft for 3,618mi/5,822km. In 1805 he was appointed Governor of New South Wales, where his conduct led to his imprisonment for two years. He was promoted admiral in 1811.

### blitz

The colloquial name for the series of air raids on British cities by the German air force (Sep 1940–May 1941). The purpose of the raids was to weaken British resistance to a projected invasion. The cities of London and Coventry were particularly badly affected. ► BLITZKRIEG; LUFTWAFFE; WORLD WAR II

### Blitzkrieg

A term (literally, 'lightning war') coined in Sep 1939 to describe the German armed forces' use of fast-moving tanks and deep-ranging aircraft in techniques which involved bypassing resistance and aiming the focus of effort at the enemy's rear areas rather than making frontal attacks. *Blitzkrieg* tactics were used with great success by the Germans in 1939–41 to achieve rapid and conclusive victories. ► WORLD WAR II

### Bloc national (1919)

A French electoral coalition which won the 1919 elections, producing a Chamber of Deputies with a conservative majority, called the 'blue horizon' Chamber, so named after the colour of French Army uniforms. It was defeated by the CARTEL DES GAUCHES ('Left-wing Cartel') in 1924. The term 'bloc' in this context had been coined by CLEMENCEAU in 1891, in a famous phrase describing the FRENCH REVOLUTION, and first applied to the *Bloc de Défense républicaine* ('Republican Defence') at the time of the DREYFUS Affair (1899–1902).

### Bloc Populaire

Québecois nationalist political party. It was formed in 1942 by liberals who opposed Canadian participation in WORLD WAR II and the introduction of conscription, and by Catholic radicals like André Laurendeau who wished to base industrial relations on papal encyclicals and to forbid the entry of foreign capital. After winning four seats in the provincial elections of 1944, the party fragmented, with the UNION NATIONALE having benefited considerably from its extremism.

### Blood, Council of (1567–76)

A court established by the Duke of ALBA, the Spanish Habsburg military commander in the Low Countries, on PHILIP II's orders, to suppress heresy and opposition during the Revolt of the Netherlands. Also known as the Council of Troubles, it comprised seven members (three of them Spaniards). The council's proceedings were rigorous and strict, especially against Protestants, and took no account of rank or privilege. Its deliberations were widely resented, and helped intensify the EIGHTY YEARS' WAR. ► HABSBURG DYNASTY

### Blood, Thomas (c.1618–1680)

Irish adventurer. Celebrated for his activities during the ENGLISH CIVIL WARS and RESTORATION, his most famous exploit was the attempt, disguised as a clergyman, to steal the crown jewels from the Tower of London (May 1671). After nearly murdering the keeper of the jewels, he succeeded in taking the crown, while one of his associates bore away the orb. He was pursued, captured and imprisoned, but later pardoned by King CHARLES II of England.

### Blood River, Battle of (Dec 1838)

A battle in which the Boers of the trekker republic of Natalia defeated the Zulu. Andries PRETORIUS with a commando of some 500 men avenged the killing of Piet RETIEF and attacks on Boer settlements ordered by Dingane, the Zulu king, in Feb of that year. As a result, the Boers re-established themselves in Natal, although many left when the British annexed the colony in 1843. The battle has remained a central aspect of Boer mythology in relation to Africans ever since, and is the subject of annual commemorations.

### Bloody Assizes

The name given to the western circuit assizes in England in the summer of 1685, presided over by Lord Chief Justice George JEFFREYS after the defeat of the Duke of MONMOUTH at the Battle of SEDGEMOOR. About 150 of Monmouth's followers, mostly poorer farmers and clothworkers, were executed, and 800 transported to the West Indies.

### Bloody Sunday (13 Nov 1887)

The name conventionally given to clashes between police and demonstrators in Trafalgar Square, London, at a meeting called to protest against a ban on open-air meetings and to call for the release of an Irish MP who had been supporting a rent strike. Two demonstrators were killed. The meeting took place against a background of economic depression, widespread unemployment and Irish nationalist unrest.

### Bloody Sunday (9 Jan 1905)

Political opposition to Tsarist autocracy had intensified in 1904 as Russia suffered defeats in its war with Japan. In the new year, on this day, Father GAPON led a group of workers to the Winter Palace in St Petersburg to present a petition to NICHOLAS II. They were joined by a large but peaceful crowd. Troops opened fire, killing over 100 people and wounding several hundred more. This marked the beginning of the Russian REVOLUTION OF 1905 and, symbolically, made something like the FEBRUARY REVOLUTION (1917) more or less inevitable.

### Bloody Sunday (30 Jan 1972)

The name given, especially by Republicans in Northern Ireland, to events occurring during a Catholic CIVIL RIGHTS protest march in Londonderry. British troops opened fire, killing 14 demonstrators; the Army claimed that the first shots were fired at its men from the crowd. The deaths led to increased support for the IRA and to many more deaths from political violence. Indirectly, it led to the ending of the STORMONT parliament and the reimposition of direct rule by the British government over Northern Ireland. Many considered the 1972 inquiry into events (the Widgery inquiry) unsatisfactory and in 1998 the British government announced a second judicial inquiry (the Saville inquiry) to consider previously unexamined evidence. The inquiry sat from 1999 to

2004; its report was expected in summer 2005.

### Bloomer, Amelia Jenks (1818–94)
US champion of **WOMEN'S RIGHTS** and dress reform. She founded and edited the feminist paper *The Lily* (1849–55), and worked closely with Susan B **ANTHONY**. In her pursuit of dress equality she wore her own version of trousers for women which came to be called 'bloomers'.

### Blücher, Gebbard Leberecht von, Prince of Wahlstadt (1742–1819)
Prussian field marshal. He fought against the French in 1793 and 1806, and in 1813 took chief command in **SILESIA**, defeating **NAPOLEON I** at the Battle of **LEIPZIG**, and entering Paris (1814). In 1815 he assumed the general command, suffered a severe defeat at Ligny, but completed **WELLINGTON**'s victory at the Battle of **WATERLOO** by his timely appearance on the field. He was known as 'Marshal Forward', his victories being due mainly to dash and energy. ► **PRUSSIA**

### Blueshirts
The pejorative term coined by the Japanese to refer to a Chinese élite revolutionary corps set up within the **GUOMINDANG** (Nationalist Party). Founded in 1932 by close associates of **CHIANG KAI-SHEK**, it sought to root out corruption within the Guomindang, promote state-sponsored industrial development, and create a militarized and disciplined society. Admirers of European fascism, the Blueshirts also wished to see Chiang Kai-shek elevated to the position of supreme leader, around whom national unity would be forged. They made little headway amongst the entrenched interests and factions within the Guomindang, however, and were disbanded in 1938.

### bluestockings
A nickname, usually with derogatory connotations, for educated women. The term was widely used when opportunities expanded for the education of middle-class women in the late 19c, but it originated in the Blue Stocking Club at Montagu House, London, c.1750.

### Blum, Léon (1872–1950)
French politician. He trained in the law and was elected a Deputy in 1919, becoming the leader of the Parliamentary Group of Socialists, and an influential writer in the party newspaper. He was Prime Minister of the **POPULAR FRONT** governments (1936–7 and 1938). He opposed the **VICHY** regime, and was arrested and put on trial at Riom as one of those responsible for the defeat of 1940. The trial was abandoned, but he remained in prison, and was deported to Germany. He returned to France in 1944 and resumed his position as leader of the **SOCIALIST PARTY**, becoming Prime Minister of a brief caretaker government (1946–7) before retiring from active politics. ► **RIOM TRIAL**

### Blundell, Sir Michael (1907–93)
Kenyan farmer and politician, born in London. He emigrated to Kenya in 1925 to farm, and served throughout **WORLD WAR II**. He then involved himself in settler politics, being a member of Legco (1948–63) and leader of the European members in 1952–4, and then Minister of Agriculture (1955–9 and 1961–3). He broke with the dominant white group to espouse political change involving black Kenyans in national politics and was much vilified for this. However, he was an essential bridge between the white-dominated colonial years and the black majority rule of independent Kenya.

### Blunt, Anthony Frederick (1907–83)
British double agent. An art historian, he became a Fellow at Trinity College, Cambridge (1932), where he shared in the left-wing communist-respecting tendencies of the time, and first met **BURGESS, PHILBY** and **MACLEAN**. Influenced by Burgess, he acted as a 'talent-spotter', supplying to him the names of likely recruits to the Soviet communist cause, and during his war service in British Intelligence was in a position to pass on information to the Soviet government. Although his spying activities appear to have ceased after the war, he was still able to assist the defection of Burgess and Maclean in 1951 although suspected by British Intelligence. In 1964, after the defection of Philby, a confession was obtained from Blunt in return for his immunity, and he continued as Surveyor of the Queen's Pictures until 1972. His full involvement in espionage was made public only in 1979, and his knighthood (awarded 1956) was annulled.

### Blyden, Edward Wilmot (1832–1912)
West Indian writer and educational philosopher. He spent most of his life in West Africa and is generally regarded as one of the founders of the concept of **NEGRITUDE**, and the precursor of the intellectual and political nationalism of the 20c. Blyden believed in the establishment of a vast colony under British rule in West Africa as the means whereby the continent could modernize itself. Such a colony would aspire to Dominion status and be ruled by its own élite, fully educated in Western ways but also rediscovering its own essential African characteristics. At one stage he favoured Christian missionary endeavour as a means of reaching this goal, but later turned increasingly to traditional beliefs and Islam. He wrote many works on these issues and worked for the foundation of a West African University.

### Blyukher, Vasili Konstantinovich (1890–1938)
Russian soldier. A **RED ARMY** hero in the **RUSSIAN CIVIL WAR**, he ended up commanding the forces that expelled the Japanese from the Soviet Far East. In 1924–7 he was military adviser to **CHIANG KAI-SHEK**'s **GUOMINDANG**. In 1929 he was put in command of Soviet troops in the Far East and fought successfully with the Chinese that year and with the Japanese in 1938. However, he proved too successful for **STALIN**, who had him arrested, tried and executed; this, among other things, left the USSR particularly powerless against Japan.

### Boabdil, properly Abu Abdallah Muhammad (d.c.1493)
Last Moorish King of Granada (1482/92). He dethroned his father, Abu al-Hasan (1482), and while he continued to struggle for power against his father and uncle, the Christians gradually conquered the kingdom. Malaga fell in 1487, and after a two-year siege Granada itself capitulated to **FERDINAND II, THE CATHOLIC** and **ISABELLA I, THE CATHOLIC** (2 Jan 1492). Boabdil was granted a small lordship in the Alpujarras, but in 1493 sold his rights to the Spanish

crown and retired to Morocco, where he died. ► GRANADA, CONQUEST OF

## boat people

Vietnamese who fled Vietnam by boat after the communist victory in 1975, travelling to Australia, Hong Kong, Japan, and several other parts of South-East Asia. Many died on the long voyages, or were killed by pirates. Voluntary repatriation schemes gained momentum in 1989, and the first involuntary repatriation operation from Hong Kong was carried out in Dec 1989. The Comprehensive Plan of Action for Indo-Chinese refugees, launched in 1989, sought to repatriate the many thousands held in camps in South-East Asia and Hong Kong, and by its conclusion in June 1996, 100,000 Vietnamese had returned to their homeland. China's demands that the 18,000 Vietnamese held in Hong Kong should be repatriated before the Crown Colony reverted to Chinese sovereignty on 1 July 1997 led to the expulsion of all but 1,700. The term 'boat people' is also used for other refugees who escape their homelands by sea, for example the Haitians who sought asylum in the USA in 1993–4.

## Boccanegra, Simone (c.1301–1363)

Doge of Genoa. Born of an illustrious Genoese family, Boccanegra rose to power when the factional strife of Guelf and Ghibelline had plunged the city into anarchy. In the interests of order he was given the title of Perpetual Doge in 1339. The burden of taxation that he imposed provoked discontent, and he went into exile in Pisa (1344). He returned to his native city to stiffen a revolt against the VISCONTI and was again appointed Perpetual Doge in 1356. His career is the subject of Verdi's famous opera. ► GHIBELLINES; GUELFS

## Bocskai, István (1557–1606)

Prince of Transylvania (1604/6). A landowner in the region around the River Tisza, he was elected Prince of Transylvania. He made his reputation first in the long wars against the Ottoman Turks, and then in the struggle of the Hungarian nobles against Austrian Habsburg domination, culminating in the insurrection of 1604. With the Peace of Vienna in 1606, he won self-government for the Hungarian nobility and religious freedom for Protestant Transylvania. This was the foundation on which BETHLEN later built the remarkably powerful independent principality of Transylvania that made its mark on the THIRTY YEARS' WAR.

## Boers ► AFRIKANERS

## Boer Wars (1880–1 and 1899–1902)

Two wars fought by the British and the Boers for mastery of southern Africa. The British had made several attempts to re-incorporate the Boers, who had left the Cape Colony in the GREAT TREK, within a South African confederation. The first Boer War ended with the defeat of the British at MAJUBA HILL, and the signing of the Pretoria and London Conventions of 1881 and 1884. In 1896 the JAMESON RAID was a clumsy private effort to achieve the same objective. The second Boer War can be divided into three phases: (1) (Oct 1899–Jan 1900) a series of Boer successes, including the sieges of LADYSMITH, KIMBERLEY and MAFEKING, as well as victories at Stormberg, Modder River,

Magersfontein, Colenso and Modderspruit; (2) (Feb–Aug 1900) counter-offensives by Lord ROBERTS, including the raising of the sieges, the victory at Paardeberg, and the capture of Pretoria; (3) (Sep 1900–May 1902) a period of guerrilla warfare when KITCHENER attempted to prevent Boer commando raids on isolated British units and lines of communication. The Boers effectively won the peace. They maintained control of 'native affairs', won back representative government in 1907, and federated South Africa on their terms in 1910. On the other hand, British interests in South Africa were protected and, despite internal strains, the Union of South Africa entered both WORLD WAR I and WORLD WAR II on the British side. ► VEREENIGING, PEACE OF

## Bogomils

The name, meaning 'pleasing to God', given to Balkan followers of the Manichean heresy that thrived in the 10–15c, especially in Bosnia, where espousal of Bogomilism was closely tied to a desire for a national Bosnian Church free from Rome and Constantinople. The dualistic heresy – that God had two sons, Christ and Satan – first took root in Macedonia towards the end of the reign of the Bulgarian Emperor Simeon (d.927), then spread throughout the Balkans in the mid-11c, dominating intellectual life in Bulgaria and Bosnia until the 15c. It spread into Italy and thence to Lombardy and the Pyrenees, where its followers were known as the Cathars. ► ALBIGENSES

## Bogomolov, Alexei Yefremovich (born 1900)

Soviet soldier, diplomat and lecturer. He served in the RED ARMY from 1919 to 1930 and spent the period 1930–8 teaching. His career changed again in 1939 when he became a deputy, and in 1941 when he became an ambassador. He served two years in the UK, helping to get the British government accustomed to the idea of a CZECHOSLOVAK–SOVIET ALLIANCE. Later, he spent the years 1954–7 in Prague, as Czechoslovakia escaped from some of the less happy consequences of the 1943 treaty.

## Bogomolov, Oleg Timofeevich (1927– )

Soviet economist and official. He was educated at the Moscow Institute of Foreign Trade and moved, after a short spell at the Soviet Ministry of Foreign Trade, to a long spell at COMECON. He then served on the State Planning Commission and the Communist Party Central Committee, before becoming Director of the Institute of the Economics of the World Socialist System in 1969. There he was involved in attempts to improve COMECON output in Leonid BREZHNEV's time, and he became a reformist adviser to both Yuri ANDROPOV and Mikhail GORBACHEV. In 1990 he was elected to the Soviet Congress of Deputies, but his influence appeared to decline as more radical ideas came to the fore.

## bogotázo (9 Apr 1948)

A serious urban riot in Bogotá, Colombia, arising from the assassination of the popular liberal and nationalist politician Jorge Eliécer Gaitán. A turning-point in the history of modern Colombia, it resulted in hundreds of deaths and much material damage. The mob violence was inspired by both the ultra-right followers of Laureano Gómez and Gaitáns's leftists; this in turn sparked off sporadic revolts in the countryside and the spread of martial law under moderate conservative Mariano Ospina Pérez. Gómez, an admirer of **HITLER** and **FRANCO**, was elected President in 1950.

## Bohemia

An historic province of western Czechoslovakia, bounded to the east by Moravia; to the west and south by Germany and Austria; and to the north by Poland. Part of the Moravian Empire in the 9c, it was at its peak in the early Middle Ages, especially in the 14c under Charles I. Bohemia came under Habsburg rule in the early 16c and became a province of Czechoslovakia in 1918. It became part of the Czech Socialist Republic of western Czechoslovakia in 1968.

## Bohemian Museum, Foundation of the (1818)

The second most important development, after the Royal **BOHEMIAN SOCIETY**, in the Czech cultural revival. It was established under the patronage of German-speaking nobles to house important local scientific objects. However, it became a centre for Czech-speaking intellectuals and, when its German-language journal failed in 1831, the Czech-language version rapidly increased its circulation. The most famous of the Czechs who frequented it was the great historian, and subsequently politician, František **PALACKÝ**, who used the journal effectively to spread nationalist thinking.

## Bohemian Protectorate (1939–45)

The form of government **HITLER** used to control Bohemia and Moravia following the destruction of Czechoslovakia in Mar 1939. Officially, there was a Czech President, **HÁCHA**, and a ruling cabinet, but they were instruments of the German protector, particularly after the murder of **HEYDRICH** in 1942. However, while terror was used, Hitler was careful not to push the Czechs too far since their agricultural and industrial production was essential for his war effort. In the end, though, he faced resistance there as well as elsewhere in Europe.

## Bohemian Revolt (1618)

A major uprising against the Habsburgs. The revolt was led by Protestants who were unwilling to tolerate Imperial attempts to reintroduce Roman Catholicism. The revolt, one of many, can be traced to tensions which arose out of the earlier Hussite religious reforms as well as later Protestantism. By 1621 the Bohemians had been crushed and the country was subjected to strong, centralized rule by the Habsburgs. The defeat of the revolt was used as a pretext to crush Protestantism but only in those areas that rebelled. Protestants continued to enjoy their traditional rights and freedoms in other Austrian areas. ► **HABSBURG DYNASTY**

## Bohemian Society of Sciences, Foundation of the Royal (1790)

An important development in the revival of Czech culture, it was in part a product of the **ENLIGHTENMENT**. However, the nobles who founded it in Prague, German-speaking though they were, intended it as a means of resisting the centralizing pressures of the Habsburg emperors by stressing and developing their local links. The long-term effect was to contribute to the emergence of Czech nationalism.

## Boissy d'Anglas, François Antoine de (1756–1826)

French politician. A member of the **ESTATES GENERAL** (1789), he joined the successful conspiracy against **ROBESPIERRE**. He was elected Secretary of the Convention, and a member of the Committee of Public Safety, in which capacity he displayed remarkable talent. He was later called to the Senate by **NAPOLEON I** and made a peer by **LOUIS XVIII**. ► **CONVENTION, NATIONAL; PUBLIC SAFETY, COMMITTEE OF**

## Bokassa, Jean-Bédel (1921–96)

Central African soldier and politician. He was educated in mission schools before joining the French army in 1929. He rose through the ranks and, after independence, was made army Commander-in-Chief, with the rank of colonel. On 1 Jan 1966 he led the coup which overthrew President **DACKO** and steadily entrenched his own power, first making himself Life President; then in 1976, modelling himself on **NAPOLEON**, he crowned himself Emperor of the renamed Central African Empire. His rule was noted for its gratuitous violence and in Sep 1979 he was driven from the country and went into exile, first in Côte d'Ivoire and then France, being sentenced to death in absentia. However, in 1986 he returned for trial and was found guilty of murder and other crimes. He was sentenced to life imprisonment, but this was commuted to 20 years' imprisonment and he was eventually released in 1993, when, unrepentant, he applied to stand for President.

## Bokelson, Jan, also known as Jan van Leyden (d.1536)

Leader (styled King) of the radical **ANABAPTISTS**. He seized power in Münster in 1534, but was executed in 1536 with two other Anabaptist leaders after the city was captured by a combined Catholic–Protestant force in 1535. He introduced many changes into his 'New Jerusalem' (Münster), including polygamy. His views were militant and millennial.

## Boleyn, Anne (c.1504–1536)

Queen of England. She was the second wife of **HENRY VIII** and the daughter of Sir Thomas Boleyn by Elizabeth Howard. Secretly married to Henry (Jan 1533), she was soon declared his legal wife (May); but within three months his passion for her had cooled. It was not revived by the birth (Sep 1533) of a daughter (later **ELIZABETH I**), still less by that of a stillborn son (Jan 1536). She was arrested and brought to the Tower, convicted of treason on fragile evidence, and beheaded (19 May). Henry married Jane **SEYMOUR** 11 days later.

## Bolger, James Brendan (1935– )

New Zealand National Party politician. Born at Taranaki, where his family owned a large sheep and cattle farm, he became a National Party MP in 1972. His farming interests led to his appointment as Minister of Agriculture in 1977; he became Minister of Finance in 1981 and Leader of the National Party in 1986. In 1990 he was elected Prime Minister and introduced a number of free-market reforms and cuts in public spending. He was defeated in the 1996 general election and resigned as party leader in 1997.

## Bolingbroke, Henry St John, 1st Viscount (1678–1751)

English politician. After travelling in Europe, he

entered parliament (1701), becoming Secretary for War (1704), Foreign Secretary (1710), and joint leader of the Tory Party. He was made a peer in 1712. On the death of Queen **ANNE** (1714), his Jacobite sympathies forced him to flee to France, where he wrote *Reflections on Exile*. He returned for a while to England (1725–35), but unable to attain political office he went back to France (1735–42). His last years were spent in London, where his works included the influential *Idea of a Patriot King* (1749). ► **TORIES**

**Bolívar, Simón**, known as **the Liberator** (1783–1830)
A founding father of Venezuela, Colombia, Ecuador, Peru and Bolivia. Born and educated in Caracas, Venezuela, after travelling in Europe he played the most prominent part in the **SPANISH-AMERICAN WARS OF INDEPENDENCE** in northern South America. In 1819 he proclaimed and became President of the vast Republic of Colombia (modern Colombia, Venezuela and Ecuador), which was finally liberated in 1822. He then took charge of the last campaigns of independence in Peru (1824). In 1826 he returned north to face growing political dissension. He resigned office (1830), and died on his way into exile, near Santa Marta, Colombia.

---

**BOLIVIA** official name **Republic of Bolivia**

A landlocked republic in western central South America, bounded to the north and east by Brazil; to the west by Peru; to the south-west by Chile; to the south by Argentina; and to the south-east by Paraguay. Bolivia formed part of the Inca Empire in the 15c, and there is evidence of earlier civilization. It was conquered by the Spanish in the 16c, and achieved independence after the war of liberation in 1825. Much territory was lost after wars with neighbouring countries, with the **CHACO WAR** (1932–5) in particular having a devastating effect. In 1952 the *Movimiento Nacionalista Revolucionario* (National Revolutionary Movement), an alliance of mineworkers and peasants led by Víctor **PAZ ESTENSSORO**, overthrew the military dictatorship and came to power. It brought about some far-reaching social reforms during the 1950s, including universal suffrage, the nationalization of the tin mines, and the improvement in status of the South American Indians. However, Bolivia's instability continued, as evidenced by several more changes of government and military coups during the latter part of the 20c. ► **BOLÍVAR, SIMÓN; CATAVÍ MASSACRE; GUEVARA, CHE; PACIFIC, WAR OF THE; SPANISH-AMERICAN WARS OF INDEPENDENCE**

**Bollandists**
A Roman Catholic religious order of Belgian Jesuits formed to carry on the work of the hagiographer Jean

Bolland (1596–1665). Since the 17c the Bollandists have worked on and published the *Acta Sanctorum*, a set of detailed and critical biographies of the saints of the Roman Church, which has now reached well over 60 volumes but is not yet finished. Until 1778 the work was carried out in Antwerp, and after an interlude caused by the suppression of the Jesuits in 1773, was resumed in Brussels in 1837.

**Bolsheviks**
From the Russian meaning 'majority-ites', the term describes members of the hardline faction of the Marxist Russian Social Democratic Labour Party, formed by **LENIN** when he split the party at its second congress in London in 1903 and won a spurious majority; the forerunner of the modern **COMMUNIST PARTY OF THE SOVIET UNION**. In Oct 1917 the Bolsheviks led the revolution in Petrograd that established the first Soviet government. ► **APRIL THESES; CHEKA; JULY DAYS; MENSHEVIKS; OCTOBER REVOLUTION; RUSSIAN REVOLUTION**

**Bombay Presidency**
The original British **EAST INDIA COMPANY** designation for lands around Bombay under its direct administrative control. The Bombay Presidency bordered Baroda and the Rajput States to the north, the Central Provinces, the Principality of Hyderabad to the east, and Mysore to the south. The term and administrative area of the Bombay Presidency remained current even after the dissolution of the Company. ► **BRITISH INDIA**

**Bonaparte, Jérôme** (1784–1860)
Youngest brother of **NAPOLEON I**. He served in the war against Prussia, was made King and ruled Westphalia (1807–14), and fought at the Battle of **WATERLOO**. He lived for many years in exile in Florence, but in 1848 was appointed Governor of the Invalides, and in 1850 was made a French marshal by **NAPOLEON III**. His first marriage to an American, Elizabeth Patterson (1785–1879), resulted in a son, Jérôme (1805–70), who went to live in the USA.

**Bonaparte, Joseph** (1768–1844)
King of Naples (1806/8) and Spain (1808/13). The eldest brother of **NAPOLEON I**, he carried out various diplomatic duties for his brother, and was made ruler of the **TWO SICILIES** (1805) and King of Naples (1806). In 1808 he was summarily transferred to the throne of Spain, but after the defeat of the French at Vitoria (1813) he abdicated and returned to France. After the Battle of **WATERLOO** he escaped to the USA, and lived in New Jersey as a farmer, but in 1832 returned to Europe, where he died.

**Bonaparte, Napoleon** ► **NAPOLEON I; NAPOLEON III**

**Bonapartism**
The cult of Napoleon Bonaparte, inspired by the traditions of **NAPOLEON I**, the Emperor of the French (1804/14), and sustained by his heirs, notably by his nephew, Louis-Napoleon, later Emperor **NAPOLEON III** (1852/70).

**Bondfield, Margaret Grace** (1873–1953)
English Labour politician and trade unionist. Born in Somerset, she became chairman of the Trades Union Congress (TUC) in 1923, and as Minister of Labour

# Books

Art & Literature

A book has traditionally been defined as a portable collection of written or drawn material on pages. The first such object was the papyrus scroll from ancient Egypt and Greece. A length of papyrus, with writing on one side only, was fastened to a wooden roller, around which it was wound for storage. If the roll was very long (some still in existence open out to 130ft/40m) they were unwieldy, so the practice began of breaking the material up into a collection of smaller scrolls. This practice was followed by the Egyptians as well as by the Greeks and Romans (*volumen* being the Latin name for the scroll).

In India, the earliest books were produced from the 5c BC and consisted of leaves or strips of bark tied together by string. The writing material of choice came to be the palm leaf (*Corypha umbraculifera*) which was incised using an iron stylus and then covered in ink. This method prevailed until the arrival of the Islamic paper manuscript in the 13–14c.

In China, books consisted of silk, wood or bamboo strips tied together. Their production began in the 2c, and printing from wooden blocks was introduced in the 6c. In the 9c, a woodcut-printed copy of a Buddhist text, the *Diamond Sutra*, was the first book to be produced using this method. In Persia and Israel, cured animal skins (parchment and vellum) were used; these were more durable and easier to bind together in flat pages.

The Greeks invented writing tablets that consisted of wooden boards covered with a layer of wax. Writing on the wax could be erased, thereby enabling multiple use. Parchment sheets were sometimes kept between the wooden boards, and from this developed the *codex*, a collection of parchment sheets sewn together inside rigid covers. It was adopted widely in the Roman Empire, ensuring ease of use for comparison and referencing, and space-saving, since writing could be placed on both sides. Papyrus continued to be used until the 4c, but the medium of choice for the important writers of the time, churchmen, was the codex. The form was retained when paper began to be used instead of parchment, and proved a suitable model for printed books.

For the Islamic peoples in the Middle East, Arabic script became the most important means of artistic expression, and the book was its main vehicle. Calligraphy, painting, and other arts associated with book production – illumination, illustration and binding – were particularly evident in reproductions of the Quran.

In Europe until the 15c, all books were hand-copied. In ancient Rome the work was done by slaves who wrote to dictation. Due to their numbers, production could be fast. After the fall of the Empire, however, books were copied by monks in the scriptoria of monasteries, and production was slow. The text (usually in Latin) was copied, then the manuscript (if it were sufficiently important) was handed to an illustrator. The pages were then stitched together and bound between covers, which might be of wood or leather. This process made books rare and valuable items, used only by the learned.

The invention of movable type, made of baked clay and glue, in China in the 11c was followed by the introduction of movable type cast in bronze in Korea at the turn of the 15c. In Europe, the arrival of movable metal type coincided with the emergence of religious and social movements, and ensured a much wider audience for literature and a greater dissemination of knowledge. The universities founded in the 12c had been keen users of manuscript books, and were customers for the swiftly produced output of the German and Italian presses. Books printed before 1501 (about 35,000 are still in existence) are known as *incunabula*, and one of the first to be printed was Gutenberg's Bible (1456, in Latin). It was set in 'black letter', a form of type that imitated closely the manuscript style. From the time of the **Renaissance**, this style was progressively replaced in most books (though not Bibles) by Roman type, admired both for its classical associations and its elegant clarity.

Religious works were bestsellers. Their publication was encouraged by the Roman Catholic Church as an efficient means of spreading Christian teaching, but it also realized the dangers of allowing dissident opinions to be spread, and the first Index of Forbidden Books was drawn up in 1559 under Pope **Paul IV**. Governments, too, wanted to keep control over what a book might contain, and in France and England, for instance, the monarchy restricted the number of presses allowed to operate.

---

(1929–31) was the first woman to be a British Cabinet Minister.

**Bongo, El Hadj Omar**, originally **Albert-Bernard Bongo** (1935– )
Gabonese politician. Educated in Brazzaville, he joined the French civil service in 1957, becoming Head of the Ministry of Information and Tourism (1963), and then Minister of National Defence (1964–5). He was made Vice-President in 1967. When President **M'BA** died in 1967, he took over the interlocking posts of President, Prime Minister and Secretary-General of the *Parti Démocratique Gabonais*, establishing a one-party state in 1968. Converting to Islam in 1973, he has presided over the exploitation of Gabon's rich mineral resources (it has the highest per capita income of any African country) without notably diminishing inequalities. In 1998 he was re-elected for a fifth term.

**Boniface VIII**, originally **Benedetto Gaetani** (c.1235–1303)
Italian pope (1294/1303). His reign was marked by the strong assertion of papal authority, claiming supreme power in temporal affairs in the Bull *Unam Sanctam* (1302). His authority was challenged, most notably by **PHILIP IV, THE FAIR** of France, who had Boniface taken prisoner at Anagni in 1303. He died soon after and the papacy took up residence at Avignon.

**Boniface IX**, originally **Pietro Tomacelli** (c.1355–1404)
Italian pope (1389/1404). He was chosen pope in 1389 to succeed Urban VI in opposition to Clement VII, who was pope in Avignon. He was notoriously inexperienced in papal administration but acquired despotic power in Rome.

After 1500 increasing numbers of books were printed in the vernacular, with far-reaching results. It made them available to a larger readership and it began the process of standardizing language, which in its oral form varied greatly from one part of a country to another.

The growing market encouraged the development of writing for entertainment, and the 18c saw the rise of the novel. These were distributed by commercial lending libraries as well as by booksellers. National collections of books were established, such as the library of the British Museum in London (1753), which by Act of Parliament was given a copy of every book published in the UK. In the USA, the equivalent is the Library of Congress, established in 1800.

The technical advances of the **Industrial Revolution**, including steam to power the presses and the paper-mills, made books cheaper, and publishers began to put cloth-covered board covers on the books rather than leather ones. A growth in population created more potential readers, and the desirability of public literacy was recognized and fostered in the 19c by the establishment of free lending libraries.

State education in the West led to a rise in literacy and a boom in publishing in the 20c. Book production faltered during **World War I**, mainly due to a lack of paper, but after the war it developed quickly again. People wanted books to read as they travelled, and bookstalls were established on railway stations. More vigorous attempts were made by publishers to sell the books, and the first book club was established in the USA in 1926.

In Great Britain, an important landmark was the decision in the 1930s by Allen Lane of Penguin to publish a range of paperback books with good typography. The success of these led the way for the paperback revolution of the 1950s – another pause having been made for **World War II** and severe paper shortages.

In the 1950s new technology, in the form of photo-composition, brought down the cost of typesetting, and mass production for large print-runs enabled books to be sold cheaply. These cheaper books were used a great deal in developing nations in Africa and in the Indian sub-continent. In the West, at around the same time, books were sold in a greater variety of outlets. Airport bookstalls catered to millions of travellers, supermarkets stocked books along with beans, and specialist book clubs proliferated.

In the late 20c, however, the book acquired a completely new look: paperless, printless and coverless. The computer provided an obvious medium for information publishing, and the 1980s saw the use of CD-ROM technology to contain encyclopedias and dictionaries. This was a tremendous advantage for multi-volume editions – 20 volumes could be contained on two CD-ROMs and cross-references could be hyper-linked for speedy searching. Encyclopedias also went on-line, with frequent updates as necessary. In the 1990s books became available for purchase over the Internet, electronic books (e-books) could be downloaded onto a home computer or PDA (personal data/digital assistant), and hand-held portable book-readers, with books either pre loaded or loaded using storage cards, represented the cutting-edge of book publishing. This has not meant the disappearance of the traditional book, however, and both hardbacks and paperbacks remain highly popular. ► **Printing**

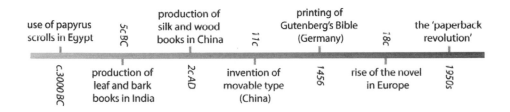

| use of papyrus scrolls in Egypt | 5c BC | production of silk and wood books in China | 11c | printing of Gutenberg's Bible (Germany) | 18c | the 'paperback revolution' |

| c.3000 BC | production of leaf and bark books in India | 2c AD | invention of movable type (China) | 1456 | rise of the novel in Europe | 1950s |

---

**Bonifacio, Andres** (1863–97)
Filipino revolutionary leader. Born in Manila in humble circumstances, he received little formal education. Bonifacio was strongly influenced by the writings of José **RIZAL** and, when the latter was sent into exile in 1892, he founded the *Katipunan*, a secret revolutionary organization. In Aug 1896 the organization was betrayed, forcing it prematurely into open rebellion. Even so, the uprising, and particularly those revolutionary forces under Emilio **AGUINALDO**, achieved considerable success against the Spanish colonial regime. In 1897, however, serious divisions appeared between Bonifacio and Aguinaldo. The former's limited educational background was held against him as the revolutionary leaders set about the task of forming an administration. These divisions threatened the revolution, and in May 1897, following a farcical trial, Bonifacio was executed, with the assent of Aguinaldo.

**Bonn**
Former capital city of West Germany (1949–90), and until Sep 1999 the seat of the administration and government (now Berlin) of Germany, in North Rhine-Westphalia. The site of an early Roman fort on the Rhine, Bonn was the seat of the **ELECTORS** of Cologne from the 13c to the 16c. In 1815, it became part of **PRUSSIA**. The city was badly bombed in **WORLD WAR II**.

**Bonner, Yelena** (1923–)
Soviet **CIVIL RIGHTS** campaigner. After the arrest of her parents in **STALIN**'s 'Great Purge' of 1937, and the subsequent execution of her father and imprisonment of her mother, Bonner was brought up in Leningrad by her grandmother. During **WORLD WAR II** she served in the army, becoming a lieutenant, but suffered serious eye injuries. After the war she married

and worked as a doctor. On separating from her husband (1965), she joined the CPSU, but became disillusioned after the Soviet invasion of Czechoslovakia (1968) and drifted into 'dissident' activities. She married Andrei **SAKHAROV** in 1971 and resigned from the CPSU a year later. During the next 14 years she and her husband led the Soviet dissident movement. Following a **KGB** crackdown, Sakharov was banished to internal exile in Gorky in 1980 and Bonner suffered a similar fate in 1984. After hunger strikes, she was given permission to travel to Italy for specialist eye treatment in 1981 and 1984. The couple were finally released from Gorky in 1986, as part of a new 'liberalization' policy under Mikhail **GORBACHEV**'s administration, and remained prominent campaigners for greater democratization.

**Bonney, William H**, also known as **Billy the Kid** (1859–81)
US outlaw. He achieved legendary notoriety for his robberies and murders in the south-west, supposedly from the age of twelve. He was captured by Sheriff Patrick F Garrett in 1880, and sentenced to hang. He escaped, but was finally tracked down by Garrett and shot.

**Bonnie and Clyde**, properly **Bonnie Parker** (1911–34) and **Clyde Barrow** (1909–34)
US criminals. Despite their popular romantic image, they and their gang were responsible for a number of murders. The pair met in 1932. When Barrow first visited Parker's house, he was arrested on seven counts of burglary and car theft. He was convicted and sentenced to two years in jail. Parker smuggled a gun to him and he escaped. Recaptured a few days later after robbing a railway office, he was sentenced to 14 years' imprisonment. He persuaded a fellow prisoner to chop off two of his toes and was subsequently released. With their gang, Parker and Barrow continued to rob and murder until they were shot dead at a police roadblock in Louisiana in May 1934.

**Bonomi, Ivanoe** (1873–1952)
Italian politician. A graduate in natural sciences and law, Bonomi took up journalism in 1898, writing for *Avanti!* and *Critica socialista*. In 1909 he was elected to parliament. Expelled from the Italian Socialist Party in 1912, he founded a reformist socialist movement. In 1916–21 he was a minister on a number of occasions, serving under **ORLANDO**, **NITTI** and **GIOLITTI**, and was briefly Premier himself (1921–2). He opposed **MUSSOLINI**'s seizure of power but left politics in 1924. From 1942, he was a leading figure in the anti-fascist struggle, replacing **BADOGLIO** as Prime Minister (June 1944) and establishing a broad, antifascist coalition government. In 1945 he was forced to resign in favour of the more radical **PARRI**; he became President of the Senate in 1948.

**Bonus Army** (June 1932)
A US protest march of some 20,000 unemployed ex-servicemen on Washington, DC, demanding Congressional passage of a bill authorizing the immediate payment of a bonus due to **WORLD WAR I** veterans. When the bill was defeated in the **SENATE**, some veterans refused to return home. At the end of July, on the orders of President Herbert **HOOVER**, General **MACARTHUR** evicted the marchers but incurred great

odium by doing so with violence and cruelty.

**Books** ► *See panel*

**Boone, Daniel** (1735–1820)
US frontiersman. He made a trail, the 'wilderness road', through the Cumberland Gap (1767) and became one of the first to explore Kentucky (1769–73). Twice captured by **NATIVE AMERICANS**, he repeatedly repelled (1775–8) native attacks on his stockade fort, now Boonesboro. Boone was a successful surveyor, trapper and landowner, ushering new settlers into Kentucky. After losing his large landholdings to debt and legal mismanagement, he moved further west into Missouri, where he died.

**Booth, John Wilkes** (1839–65)
US assassin. An actor, in 1865 he entered into a conspiracy to avenge the defeat of the Confederates and shot President Abraham **LINCOLN** at Ford's Theatre, Washington (14 Apr). He broke his leg while escaping, but managed to flee to Virginia. He was tracked down and was either shot by his pursuers or shot himself.

**bootlegging**
The manufacture, transportation or sale of an illegal product, especially alcoholic beverages during the time of **PROHIBITION** in US history. The term, which is also used of the manufacture and sale of illegally made recordings, comes from the fact that smugglers often transported liquor in their boot tops.

**Borah, William Edgar** (1865–1940)
US politician. He was elected as a Republican senator for Idaho in 1907. An advocate of disarmament and a leading isolationist, Borah was instrumental in blocking the USA's entry into the **LEAGUE OF NATIONS** in 1919.

**Borden, Sir Robert Laird** (1854–1937)
Canadian politician. He practised as a barrister, and became leader of the Conservative Party in 1901. As Conservative Prime Minister (1911–20), he led Canada through **WORLD WAR I**, the conscription crisis, and the introduction of income tax. At the Imperial War Conference of 1917, he called for greater recognition of the dominions' autonomy, a step towards the building of a commonwealth. ► **LAPOINTE, ERNEST**; **MILITARY SERVICE ACT**; **WAR MEASURES ACT**

**Borgå, Diet of** (1809) ► **PORVOO, DIET OF** (1809)

**Borghese**
A great 13c family of ambassadors and jurists of Siena, afterwards (16c) at Rome. Their members include Camillo Borghese, who ascended the papal throne in 1605 as **PAUL V**, and Prince Camillo Filippo Ludovico Borghese (1775–1832), who joined the French army, married **NAPOLEON I**'s sister Marie Pauline (1803), and became Governor-General of Piedmont. The Borghese Palace still contains one of the finest collections of paintings in Rome.

**Borgia** or **Borja**
An ancient family from Valencia in Spain. Alfonso (1378–1458) accompanied Alfonso of Aragon to Rome, and became Pope Calixtus III (1455/8). His nephew, Rodrigo, became pope as **ALEXANDER VI** (1492/1503) and sought to further the interests of his notorious children, Cesare and Lucrezia Borgia.

By contrast, a descendant of another of Alexander's sons, Francisco (1510–72), was to become General of the Jesuits. ➤ BORGIA, CESARE; BORGIA, LUCREZIA

**Borgia, Cesare** (1476–1507)
Italian soldier. He was the illegitimate son of Pope ALEXANDER VI and brother of Lucrezia BORGIA. A brilliant soldier and administrator, he succeeded his elder brother (whom he is rumoured to have murdered) as Captain-General of the armies of the Church. In two campaigns he became the master of the Romagna, Perugia, Siena, Piombino and Urbino, and planned a kingdom of Central Italy. After the death of his father (1503), his enemies rallied. He surrendered at Naples, was imprisoned and escaped (1506), only to die fighting in the service of the King of Navarre soon afterwards. His campaigns greatly impressed MACHIAVELLI, who discussed Cesare's career at length in the notorious seventh chapter of *The Prince*. ➤ BORGIA

**Borgia, Lucrezia** (1480–1519)
Illegitimate daughter of Pope ALEXANDER VI. She was three times married to further her father's political interests: first, in 1493, at the age of 12 to Giovanni Sforza, Lord of Pesaro, but this marriage was annulled by her father in 1497; second, in 1498, to Alfonso of Aragon, nephew of the King of Naples, but this marriage was ended in 1500 when Alfonso was murdered by her brother Cesare BORGIA; and third, in 1501, to Alfonso d'Este (1486–1534), son of the Duke of Este. Alfonso d'Este inherited the duchy of Ferrara, where Lucrezia established a brilliant court of artists and men of letters. ➤ BORGIA

**Boris III** (1894–1943)
King of Bulgaria (1918/43). He was the son of FERDINAND I and Maria Luisa Bourbon-Parma. After his father's abdication, he became king, the numeral III implying his succession to the great medieval Bulgarian emperors. After a series of military coups, in 1935 he established an authoritarian regime, securing the removal of Colonel Kimon Georgiev, abolishing the ZVENO-backed Military League and returning the country to civilian control. Married to the daughter of the King of Italy, and an admirer of German culture, he maintained good relations with Benito MUSSOLINI and HITLER. Although formally neutral at the outbreak of WORLD WAR II, Bulgaria through Boris's diplomacy was firmly in the Axis camp. He died suddenly, shortly after a stormy visit to Hitler, and recent research has lent credence to the rumour that he was poisoned. He was succeeded by his son, SIMEON II.

**Boris Godunov** (c.1552–1605)
Tsar of Russia (1598/1605). Of Tatar stock, he became an intimate friend of IVAN IV, THE TERRIBLE, who entrusted to Boris the care of his feeble son, Fyodor. During the reign of Tsar Fyodor (1584/98), Boris Godunov was virtual ruler of the country with the title of 'the Great Sovereign's brother-in-law', becoming Tsar himself on Fyodor's death (1598). He continued Ivan's expansionist policies, going to war against both Poland and Sweden. At home, he disposed finally of the Tatar threat but was embroiled in the last years of his reign in a civil war against a pretender claiming to be DMITRI, younger son of Ivan IV.

The pretender was murdered the year after Boris's death. Boris's reign is regarded as the beginning of the TIME OF TROUBLES.

**Borja** ➤ BORGIA

**Bormann, Martin** (1900–45)
German Nazi politician. One of HITLER's closest advisers, he became *Reichsminister* (1941) after HESS's flight to Scotland, and was with Hitler to the last. His fate was uncertain, but he is now known to have committed suicide by a poison capsule during the breakout by Hitler's staff from the Chancellory (1 May 1945). He was sentenced to death in his absence by the Nuremberg Court (1946). ➤ NUREMBERG TRIALS; WORLD WAR II

**Bornu**
A state in northern Nigeria and southern Niger lying to the west of Lake Chad. In the 15c Bornu replaced KANEM as a great trading empire linking the forest and the desert, and reached its apogee in the 16c. Its people, the Kanuri, had been Muslim since the 11c and developed a highly stratified social organization.

**Borodin, Mikhail**, originally **Mikhail Markovich Grusenberg** (1884–1951)
Russian adviser in China from 1923 to 1927, Borodin participated in the Jewish worker movement in his native Russia and met LENIN in 1904. After 1905 he lived in exile in Britain and the USA. When the United Front was formed between the GUOMINDANG and the Chinese Communist Party in 1923, Borodin, as the representative of both the COMINTERN and the Soviet Communist Party, became a personal adviser to SUN YAT-SEN. He helped transform the Guomindang into a disciplined and centrally controlled revolutionary party, as well as convincing Sun of the necessity of creating mass-based organizations. When the United Front broke down in 1927, Borodin was compelled to leave China. Made the scapegoat for the failure of STALIN's policy in China, Borodin was henceforth given only minor posts. He died in a Siberian prison camp.

**Borodino, Battle of** (7 Sep 1812)
A costly victory for NAPOLEON I's army. He inflicted 40,000 casualties on ALEXANDER I's forces, but lost 30,000 dead and wounded, a quarter of his own men. One of the Russian commanders, General BAGRATION, subsequently died of his wounds. A second, General BARCLAY DE TOLLY, showed immense courage and greatly raised his men's morale. The subsequent Russian withdrawal allowed Napoleon to briefly occupy Moscow, which was abandoned to him.

**Boscawen, Edward**, known as **Old Dreadnought** (1711–61)
English naval commander. He distinguished himself at the sieges of Porto Bello (1739) and Cartagena (1741), and in command of the *Dreadnought* in 1744 he captured the French *Médée*. He played an important part in the victory off Cape Finisterre (1747), and in command of an East Indian expedition failed to capture Pondicherry in 1748. In 1755 he intercepted the French fleet off Newfoundland, capturing two ships and 1,500 men. He was appointed Commander-in-Chief of the successful expedition against

Cape Breton (1758), and also gained victory over the French Toulon fleet in Lagos Bay (1759).

**Bosch, Johannes van den** (1780–1844)
Dutch reformer and politician. Van den Bosch took a career in the Dutch East Indian Army, rapidly reaching the rank of colonel. Returning to the Netherlands in 1815 he was put in charge of East Indies military affairs. He produced two important political essays which shaped his further career and to some extent the Dutch state as well. One was on poor relief, resulting in 1818 in the foundation of the Society for Charity, which tried to take urban paupers and compel them to be agricultural labourers in a number of 'colonies' in the east of the country. The other was his plan to make the Dutch colonies earn money for the mother country: known as the '**CULTURE SYSTEM**', it was launched in 1834, and was in time highly successful in financial terms, if not in human ones. Van den Bosch had the ear of King **WILLIAM I**; he served as Governor-General of the Dutch East Indies (1828–33), and as Minister of Colonies (1834–9).

**Bosch, Juan** (1909–2001)
Dominican Republic politician and writer. The founder of the Dominican Revolutionary Party, Bosch lived in exile in Cuba and Costa Rica during the **TRUJILLO** dictatorship. He became President in 1963 but his reformist government lasted only six months before it was overthrown by the army (Sep 1963) and he was again exiled. He was the losing candidate in every presidential election from 1966 to 1990, and although by 1990 he had moderated his **MARXISM**, his Dominican Liberation Party again lost the election of that year, despite having appeared to be the front runner.

**Bose, Subhas Chandra** (1897–1945)
Indian nationalist leader. A successful candidate for the **INDIAN CIVIL SERVICE** in 1920, he did not take up his appointment, returning instead to Calcutta to work in the **NON-COOPERATION MOVEMENT** and the **SWARAJ** Party. He also managed the Calcutta newspaper *Forward*, and became Chief Executive Officer of the Calcutta Corporation when Congress won its control in 1924. He spent the years 1925–7 under detention in Mandalay. In 1928 Bose formed an Independence League with Jawaharlal **NEHRU** in opposition to Congress's objective of dominion status. Throughout the 1930s Bose took part in the **CIVIL DISOBEDIENCE** movement, but became increasingly dissatisfied with the non-violent methods of M K **GANDHI** and increasingly radical in his beliefs. Bose felt that a disciplined mass revolutionary movement, espousing a combination of fascism and communism, was the fastest and best path toward Indian statehood. He was twice in succession President of the **INDIAN NATIONAL CONGRESS** (1938). Having resigned from the organization (1939), he formed Forward Bloc, a militant nationalist party. With the outbreak of **WORLD WAR II**, he supported the **AXIS POWERS**. Escaping from detention, he fled to Nazi Germany, then (1943) sailed to Singapore to take command of the Indian National Army (INA), a force formed of prisoners of war of the Japanese army. This force fought against the British in Burma (now Myanmar) and participated in the disastrous Japanese attempt to invade India from Burma. In Oct 1943 he

announced the formation of the Provisional Government of Free India. He was reported killed in an aircrash in Taiwan. For many years, however, his most devoted followers refused to believe that he was dead, and continued to cherish his ideas, attitudes and beliefs.

**BOSNIA AND HERZEGOVINA** official name **Republic of Bosnia and Herzegovina**

A republic in central Europe, formerly one of the six republics established in 1945 within the Socialist Federal People's Republic of Yugoslavia; bounded to the west and north by Croatia; to the south-east by Montenegro; and to the east and north-east by Serbia. In Mar 1992, under President Alija **IZETBEGOVIĆ**, it followed the republics of Slovenia and Croatia in declaring its independence from Yugoslavia. Civil war broke out between die-hard communist and nationalist elements from the Yugoslav National Army and extreme nationalist paramilitary groups, gradually and brutally engulfing the civilian population until all civil order dissolved. A three-sided civil war raged between the Muslims loyal to the government, and the Serbs and Croats who proclaimed themselves independent and began fighting for territory. By the end of 1992 the Serbs had besieged Sarajevo and were carrying out a brutal policy of **ETHNIC CLEANSING**, which **UN** peacekeeping forces attempted to stop. An alliance in 1994 between Bosnian Muslims and Bosnian Croats enabled the recapture of territory during 1995, and NATO air-strikes helped to end the Sarajevo siege. The signing of the Dayton Peace Accord in Dec 1995 brought relative, if rather tense, peace. It created a federal multiethnic Bosnian government with a rotating presidency and two separate administrations divided along ethnic and geographic lines into the Republic Srpska (Bosnian Serb) and the Bosnian Croat Federation. Civilian aspects of the Accord were overseen by the Office of the High Representative. **NATO**-led UN peacekeeping and stabilizing forces monitored the military aspects of the Accord until replaced by **EU** peacekeeping troops in Dec 2004.

**Boston Massacre** (5 Mar 1770)
The first bloodshed of the **AMERICAN REVOLUTION**. In an atmosphere of intense resentment against British troops and regulations, on 5 Mar 1770 British guards opened fire on an unruly crowd, killing five. Of the nine British soldiers tried for murder, seven, including the commander, were acquitted and two were found guilty of manslaughter.

**Boston Tea Party** (1773)
During the **AMERICAN REVOLUTION**, the climactic

event of resistance to British attempts at direct taxation, resulting in the destruction of 342 chests of dutied tea by working men disguised as **NATIVE AMERICANS**. Other ports had refused to let the tea ships enter. ► **INTOLERABLE ACTS**

**Boström, Erik Gustaf** (1842–1907)
Swedish politician. Elected to the Second Chamber of Parliament in 1876, he became leader of the protectionist wing of the Ruralist (Conservative) Party in 1888 and Prime Minister in 1891. He admired **BISMARCK** and proposed similar welfare legislation as had been introduced in Germany. He resigned in 1900, but returned to office in 1902 for three years.

**Bosworth Field, Battle of** (22 Aug 1485)
The battle that put **HENRY VII** on the English throne after victory over **RICHARD III**, who died in the conflict. Henry Tudor's forces were possibly inferior in number, but proved more loyal; they received crucial support from the Stanley family, who had feet in both camps. ► **TUDOR, HOUSE OF**

**Botany Bay**
The shallow inlet five miles south of Sydney, New South Wales, Australia (now a residential part of Sydney) where Captain James **COOK** made his first landing in 1770, naming the bay after the number of new plants discovered there. It was chosen as a penal settlement in 1787 but on his arrival Arthur **PHILLIP**, the commander of the **FIRST FLEET**, found it to be unsuitable and chose Sydney Cove instead; the name Botany Bay, however, was for many years synonymous with Australian convict settlements. ► **TRANSPORTATION**

**Botev, Khristo** (1848–76)
Bulgarian journalist, poet and revolutionary leader. A schoolteacher's son, in 1863 he went to study in Odessa, where he met members of the Russian revolutionary circle. Having returned to Bulgaria to teach, he was one of the leaders of the ill-fated Bulgarian uprising of Apr 1876 and was killed after leading a band of rebels across the Danube.

**Botha, Louis** (1862–1919)
South African politician and soldier. Born in Greytown, Natal, he was a member of the Transvaal Volksraad, and commanded the Boer forces during the war. In 1907 he became Prime Minister of the Transvaal colony, and subsequently became the first Prime Minister of the new Union of South Africa (1910–19). He suppressed De Wet's rebellion (1914), and then conquered German South West Africa (1914–15). He died at Pretoria. ► **BOER WARS**

**Botha, P(ieter) W(illem)** (1916– )
South African politician. The son of an internee in the Boer War, he was steeped in politics. His early life lacked success (he dropped out of university), but he found his métier as a party organizer. With his confidence and courage, he was a formidable operator. An advocate of **APARTHEID** before the **NATIONAL PARTY** gained power, he entered Parliament in 1948 and became Deputy Minister of the Interior (1958–61), Minister of Community Development, Public Works and Coloured Affairs (1961–6), Minister of Defence (1966–78), Prime Minister (1978–84) and State President (1984–9). Leader of the Cape section of the National Party since 1966, in 1978 he was chosen as chief leader of the Party on **VORSTER**'s resignation on the second ballot only because the Transvaal Nationalists were divided. He thus became Prime Minister. Having built up the defence forces and supported the invasion of Angola in 1975, he now sought constitutional changes, but his ideas, although too progressive for some of his Party (some members defected in 1982 to form the **CONSERVATIVE PARTY**), were too cautious to appeal to the black opposition. He suffered a stroke in 1989 and resigned later that year.

**Bothwell, James Hepburn, 4th Earl of** (c.1535–1578)
Scottish nobleman and third husband of **MARY, QUEEN OF SCOTS**. One of the greatest nobles in Scotland, he was held responsible for the abduction and murder of Mary's second husband, Lord **DARNLEY** (1567). He was made Duke of Orkney, then married Mary, but faced opposition from the nobles. He fled to Denmark after Mary's surrender to rebel forces at Carberry Hill, and was imprisoned in Dragsholm, where he died insane.

---

**BOTSWANA** official name **Republic of Botswana**, formerly (to 1966) **Bechuanaland**

A landlocked republic in southern Africa, bounded to the south by the Republic of South Africa; to the west and north by Namibia; and to the east by Zimbabwe. It was visited by missionaries in the 19c and came under British protection in 1885. The southern part became a British Crown Colony, then part of Cape Colony in 1895, while the northern part became the Bechuanaland Protectorate. In 1964 it achieved self-government, and in 1966 it gained independence and changed its name under the leadership of President Seretse **KHAMA**, who was succeeded in 1980 by Ketumile **MASIRE**. Masire was replaced by Festus Mogae in 1998. Although stable and relatively wealthy, there are high levels of **HIV/AIDS** infection, which the government has developed programmes to counter.

**Bottai, Giuseppe** (1895–1959)
Italian politician. One of the founders of the **FASCIST PARTY**, Bottai took an active part in the **MARCH ON ROME**. He was one of the **FASCIST GRAND COUNCIL** members who demanded **MUSSOLINI**'s resignation in July 1943. Sentenced to death by the Republic of **SALÒ**, and to life imprisonment by the Italian authorities after **WORLD WAR II**, he escaped and joined the French **FOREIGN LEGION**. He returned to Italy on being amnestied.

**Botzaris, Marcos** (1788–1823)
Greek patriot. In 1803 he was forced to retreat to the Ionian Islands by **ALI PASHA**. In 1820, at the head of 800 expatriated Suliotes, he gained several victories for Ali against the Sultan; in 1822 he skilfully defended Missolonghi, but was killed in an attack on the Turkish-Albanian army at Karpenisi.

**Boulanger, Georges Ernest Jean Marie** (1837–91)
French soldier and politician. Educated at Saint-Cyr, he served in Italy, China, the **FRANCO-PRUSSIAN** War (1870–1), and helped suppress the **PARIS COMMUNE** (1871). In 1886, as the protégé of **CLEMENCEAU**, he was appointed Minister of War. He introduced many reforms in soldiers' pay and living conditions and became a popular national figure with the Parisians, often appearing amongst them on horseback. When he lost office in 1887, 'Boulanger fever' only increased. He was 'exiled' by the army to a command at Clermont-Ferrand, and although deprived of his command in 1888, was immediately elected Deputy for Dordogne and Nord, and demanded a revision of the constitution. He was wounded in a duel with **FLOQUET**, the Minister-President, in the same year. 'Boulangism' became really formidable in 1889, and was supported with large sums of money by leading royalists for their own ends. Fearing a coup d'état, the government prosecuted Boulanger, who lost courage and fled the country in 1889. He was condemned *in absentia*; his schemes wholly collapsed, and he eventually shot himself on his mistress's grave in Brussels.

**Boumédienne, Houari**, originally **Mohammed Bou Kharrouba** (1925–78)
Algerian soldier and statesman. Educated at Constantine and El Azhar University in Cairo, he became a teacher. In 1954 he joined the **FLN** for whom for eight years he conducted guerrilla operations against the French, serving as Chief of Staff (1960–2) with the rank of colonel. When Algeria gained independence in 1962, he became minister of national defence. In 1965 he led a military coup against President **BEN BELLA** and established an Islamic socialist government, presiding over the Council of Revolution as effective head of state until he formally accepted election as President in 1976. In home affairs, he directed a four-year plan which increased industrial output and revolutionized agricultural production. Not long before his death, he was seeking to establish a North African socialist federation.

**Bourassa, (Joseph Napoléon) Henri** (1868–1952)
Canadian politician and journalist (as a founder and editor of *Le Devoir*). A grandson of Louis Joseph **PAPINEAU**, he was a French-Canadian nationalist who consistently opposed French-Canada's forced participation in British wars. He resigned his independent Liberal seat in the federal House of Commons when **LAURIER** sent Canadian troops to the Boer War, but since most French-Canadians felt the same way, he was returned by acclamation. Bourassa was also the focal point for French-Canadian outrage at the Naval Act of 1910, using *Le Devoir* to advocate his views and making an important contribution to the **LIBERAL PARTY** defeat in the election of 1911. He was also a vigorous opponent of Canadian involvement in **WORLD WAR I**. An advocate of European liberal Catholic thinking, he was opposed to industrial capitalism

and emerged as a social reformer in the 1920s and 1930s. ► **BOER WARS**

**Bourassa, Robert** (1933–96)
Canadian politician. Leader of the Quebec Liberal Party when it won an emphatic election victory in 1970, despite the nationalist unrest of the period. By refusing to give prominence to the constitutional and language controversies and promising to help the unemployment crisis by generating 100,000 jobs, his party won 41.8 per cent of the vote and 72 seats. During the **OCTOBER CRISIS** Bourassa was accused of being too ready to hand over power to Ottawa by those who suspected that he hoped to undermine his nationalist and left-wing opponents. Bourassa responded by reinforcing his demands for a special status for Quebec within the Confederation. He resigned as party leader when the Liberals lost the 1976 provincial elections to the Péquistes, but was re-elected in 1983 and led the party to victory in 1985. Much more popular during his second term, he attempted to pass legislation enforcing the use of French, but failed to get the **MEECH LAKE ACCORD** ratified, which again fuelled the separatist movement. He handed over the premiership and party leadership to Daniel Johnson in 1993. ► **PARTI QUÉBECOIS**

**Bourbon, Charles** (1490–1527)
French soldier. Known as 'Constable de Bourbon', he was the son of Gilbert de Bourbon, Count of Montpensier, and the only daughter of the Duke of Bourbon. For his bravery at the Battle of Marignano (1515) he was made Constable of France; but losing the favour of **FRANCIS I** of France he concluded a private alliance with Emperor **CHARLES V** and **HENRY VIII** of England. He invaded France in 1524, and was chief imperial commander at Pavia, in which Francis I was taken prisoner. He was made Duke of Milan, and commanded in northern Italy, but was killed while attacking Rome in 1527. ► **BOURBON, HOUSE OF**

**Bourbon, House of**
The French royal house descended from the Capetian St **LOUIS IX**, associated with absolutist traditions at home and the extension of French influence abroad. Succeeding the last member of the **VALOIS DYNASTY, HENRY III** (1589), Henry of Navarre (**HENRY IV**) firmly established the dynasty. Under his son (**LOUIS XIII**) and grandson (**LOUIS XIV**), the long-standing rivalry between France and the Spanish Habsburgs came to a climax. It was concluded when a descendant, Philip of Anjou, ascended to the Spanish throne (**PHILIP V**), thereby founding the Spanish House of Bourbon. Under **LOUIS XV** and **LOUIS XVI**, the prestige of the French Bourbons gradually declined; with the latter's execution (1793) the line was interrupted, to be briefly restored (1814–30). ► **CAPETIAN DYNASTY; CHARLES X** (of France); **CONDÉ, HOUSE OF; HABSBURG DYNASTY; ORLÉANS, HOUSE OF** ► *See table*

**Bourgeois, Léon Victor Auguste** (1851–1925)
French politician. A socialist, he studied law and served as Minister of Public Instruction (1890–2 and 1898), Prime Minister (1895–6) and Minister of Labour (1912–13 and 1917). A delegate to the Hague Conference (1907), he was one of the founders of the **LEAGUE OF NATIONS**, and in 1920 was awarded the

## HOUSE OF BOURBON

| Regnal Dates | Name |
|---|---|
| *France* | |
| 1589/1610 | Henry IV |
| 1610/43 | Louis XIII |
| 1643/1715 | Louis XIV |
| 1715/74 | Louis XV |
| 1774/93 | Louis XVI |
| 1793/1814 | Republican and Bonapartist regimes |
| 1814/24 | Louis XVIII |
| 1824/30 | Charles X |
| 1830/48 | Louis-Philippe (Orléans branch) |
| *Spain* | |
| 1700/24 | Philip V |
| 1724/5 | Louis I |
| 1725/46 | Philip V |
| 1746/59 | Ferdinand VI |
| 1759/88 | Charles III |
| 1788/1808 | Charles IV |
| 1808/14 | Bonapartist regime |
| 1814/33 | Ferdinand VII |
| 1833/68 | Isabella II |
| 1868/74 | First Republic |
| 1874/85 | Alfonso XII |
| 1886/1931 | Alfonso XIII |
| 1931/75 | Second Republic and Franco dictatorship |
| 1975/ | Juan Carlos I |

NOBEL PEACE PRIZE. He advocated a form of SOCIAL-ISM called *solidarisme*, which stressed the obligations of individuals as members of society.

**Bourguiba, Habib ibn Ali** (1903–2000)
Tunisian politician. He studied law in Paris and became a radical Tunisian nationalist in 1934. Over the next 20 years he served three prison sentences imposed by the French authorities. In 1956, however, the French government of MENDÈS-FRANCE in Paris recognized that, in contrast to other Arab leaders, Bourguiba was moderate in his demands and he was accepted as Tunisia's first Prime Minister, becoming President in 1957. By 1962 he had secured the withdrawal of the French from their Tunisian military bases; thereafter he was able to improve trading contacts with the former imperial power. In 1975 he was declared President for life. His authority, however, was threatened by riots instigated by Islamic fundamentalists in 1983 and 1984, and subsequently he exercised little influence on policy. In 1987 he was deposed by his prime minister, General BEN ALI, on the grounds of senility.

**Bourj al-Barajneh**
Palestinian refugee camp on the outskirts of Beirut, Lebanon. It was created following the evacuation of Palestinians from the city after Israeli attacks on Palestinians and Syrians (June 1982). The camp was the scene of a prolonged siege in 1987.

**Bouteflika, Abdelaziz** (1937–)
Algerian politician. He joined the FLN (*Front de Libération Nationale*) after leaving school and campaigned for independence from France, becoming youth, sport and tourism minister of newly independent Algeria in 1962. He was Foreign Minister from 1963 to 1979, going into exile in 1981 to avoid corruption charges made by political opponents; he re-turned in 1987 after these were dropped. In 1988 he protested against violent government attacks on demonstrators, part of the government's attempts to suppress Islamic fundamentalist groups. Although Islamist groups won the general election in 1992, the army took control of the country and unrest continued. In 1999, he stood for the presidency with army backing and was elected when the other candidates withdrew protesting that the vote was rigged. His plan for reconciliation with Islamists won support in a referendum later that year. Many Islamic rebels were released from prison and the level of violence declined. He was re-elected in 2004.

**Boutros-Ghali, Boutros** (1922–)
Egyptian politician and diplomat. Born in Cairo, he received a doctorate in international law from the University of Paris. He travelled with President Anwar SADAT to Jerusalem on the diplomatic mission that resulted in the CAMP DAVID ACCORDS (1978), and was appointed Minister of State for Foreign Affairs (1977–91). In 1992 he became Secretary-General of the UN, the first Arab and first African to do so, but he failed to be re-elected in 1996. He was succeeded by Kofi ANNAN.

**Bouvines, Battle of** (27 July 1214)
The battle near Valenciennes in northern France, at which King PHILIP II of France defeated the armies of the Holy Roman Emperor OTTO IV, the Count of Flanders, and King JOHN of England. This victory consolidated the power of the French monarchy over its vassals, led to Otto's deposition as Emperor, to the loss of NORMANDY by King John, and probably contributed to his acceptance of MAGNA CARTA (1215).

**Bowell, Sir Mackenzie** (1823–1917)
Canadian politician. In 1878, as Grand Master of the ORANGE ORDER (a position he filled with a certain tact towards the sensibilities of Roman Catholics), he was included in the cabinet of Sir John MACDONALD in order to balance the leadership of the BLEUS. In 1895 Bowell became Prime Minister, faced not only with the Depression but also with the crisis caused by the MANITOBA SCHOOLS ACT. When the province refused to restore the rights of the Catholic minority, he introduced a Remedial Bill and seven ministers resigned. They were concerned not so much with the actual issue but to remove Bowell, whose stand had alienated the Orange Order from the party, and they returned to office when he had yielded to Sir Charles TUPPER. Nevertheless, the Conservatives were defeated in the election of 1896, after which Bowell led their opposition in the Senate.

**Bowie, James ('Jim')** (1790–1836)
US adventurer. He is mainly remembered for his heroic death defending the ALAMO (1836) during the Texas Revolution. He was the inventor of the curved sheath knife named after him.

**Boxer Rising** (1898–1900)
An anti-foreign uprising in China (in Chinese, *Ye He Tuan*). Its popular name derives from the secret society to which the rebels belonged, the 'Righteous Harmonious Fists', whose members adopted boxing and ritual forms of combat in the belief that foreign weapons would thus not harm them. The movement originated in Shandong, where it destroyed churches

and expelled missionaries. It also defeated the Qing forces dispatched to suppress it. It spread across north China, invading Beijing and Tianjin. The foreign powers sent a combined force to rescue their envoys in Beijing, occupying the capital, and the rising was suppressed. By the International Protocol of 1901, the Qing court agreed to pay a massive indemnity, and a foreign garrison was established in the Legation Quarter of Beijing. ➤ **QING DYNASTY**

**Boyacá, Battle of** (7 Aug 1819)
A decisive victory for the patriot forces under Simón **BOLÍVAR** in the **SPANISH-AMERICAN WARS OF INDEPENDENCE**. It resulted in the liberation of New Granada (now Colombia) from Spanish rule and marked the beginning of the last great military campaign to destroy Spanish rule. The victory enabled Bolívar to announce the creation of **GRAN COLOMBIA** (Venezuela, New Granada and Ecuador), establish the rule of **SANTANDER**, and led to the expulsion of General Morillo's forces from the Venezuelan coastal region by 1823.

**boyars**
Members of the highest stratum of the Russian feudal aristocracy from the 10c to the early 18c. The *Boyarskaya Duma* ('Boyars' Council') was a major legislative and deliberative assembly under the early tsars. During the reign of **IVAN IV, THE TERRIBLE**, the boyars' authority was drastically curtailed, and the *Boyarskaya Duma* was finally abolished by **PETER I, THE GREAT** in 1711. ➤ **DUMA**; **FEUDALISM**

**boycott**
A general refusal to have dealings, usually in relation to trade, with a person, company or country. A trade union may boycott talks with a company as a negotiating ploy. Individuals may refuse to buy a country's goods as a gesture of political protest, for example goods from South Africa in protest against **APARTHEID**. Boycotts have also been used in international sporting events, such as by the USA and UK at the 1980 Moscow **OLYMPIC GAMES**. They are often only effective if legally enforced; for example, the ban on the import of Cuban cigars into the USA.

**Boycott, Charles Cunningham** (1832–97)
British soldier. As land agent for Lord Erne in County Mayo, he was one of the first victims in 1880 of **PARNELL**'s system of social excommunication. His name is the source of the word 'boycott' in English.

**Boyer, Jean Pierre** (1776–1850)
Haitian mulatto politician. Sent to France at an early age, in 1792 he entered the army. He distinguished himself against the British on their invasion of Haiti, and established an independent republic in the western part of the island. President Pétion, on his deathbed, recommended him as his successor (1818). After the death of Henri **CHRISTOPHE**, he united the Negro district with the mulatto in 1820. The following year he also added the eastern district, hitherto Spanish, and in 1825, for 150 million francs, obtained recognition of independence from France. He governed Haiti well for 15 years, but his partiality to the mulattos made the pure Negroes rise in 1843. Boyer fled, and died in Paris.

**Boyne, Battle of the** (12 July 1690)
A battle fought near Drogheda, County Louth, Ireland, between Protestant forces under **WILLIAM III** of Great Britain and smaller Roman Catholic forces led by **JAMES VII AND II**. William's decisive victory enabled him to capture Dublin, and marked a critical stage in the English reconquest of Ireland. It ended James's campaign to regain the English throne. The anniversary is celebrated annually by Protestant marches in Northern Ireland.

**Brabant, Duchy of**
Brabant is now the name of a province in the northern part of Belgium, and also of a province in the Netherlands (Noord-Brabant), but in the Middle Ages it was a powerful duchy covering both those areas and also the present Belgian province of Antwerp. Its nucleus was originally the County of Leuven (Louvain), whose Count Gottfried was made the first Duke in 1106. The early dukes set about increasing their power at the expense of other local magnates and then of the towns, which were rising commercial and industrial centres. The expansion of the Duchy continued throughout the 12–13c, and in 1406 the Burgundian Anton (son of **PHILIP THE BOLD**) succeeded to Brabant. The Burgundian connection was confirmed in 1430 when **PHILIP THE GOOD** inherited the Brabant Duchy. As an integral part of the Burgundian state in the Low Countries it eventually passed into Habsburg control, and at the Peace of Utrecht in 1648 the northern half was split off and went to the newly recognized Dutch Republic. The southern Duchy was dismantled under the rule of the French (1795–1813) and now the title of Duke of Brabant is given to the eldest son of the Belgian monarch. ➤ **HABSBURG DYNASTY**

**Brabant Revolution** (1789)
The name given to the revolt in the Austrian southern Netherlands (now Belgium) against the rule of the enlightened despot Emperor **JOSEPH II** of Austria, who planned a major modernization and rationalization of Church, State and legal system. The revolutionaries fell into two groups: one inspired by the ideals of the **FRENCH REVOLUTION** and led by J F Vonck (**VONCKISTS**), and the other more conservative and looking to restore the pre-Josephan *status quo*, led by H van der Noot (**STATISTS**). They had early successes, and proclaimed the independence of the 'United States of Belgium', but the Austrians regained control within a year.

**Braccio da Montone**, otherwise **Brancaccio** or **Fortebraccio** (1368–1424)
Italian mercenary captain or **CONDOTTIERE**. He commanded the troops of Queen Giovanna of Naples, and coveted the throne of Naples, but he died of his wounds in a battle before Aquila.

**bracero**
The term used to describe seasonal labour from Central and Southern Mexico working on large-scale agro-industrial enterprises in California and Texas. Often 'wetbacks' who had illegally entered the USA by crossing the Rio Grande, they did not benefit from minimum wage and employee-protection legislation in either California, Texas or New Mexico. They had often been used as 'scab' or strike-breaking labour in both states, so were not easily accepted into US trade unions. Drives to unionize them began in the

mid-1960s, thanks to the activities of leaders such as César **CHÁVEZ**; against heavy opposition from both the **AFL-CIO** and local employers, they were supported by the Republican Governor, Ronald **REAGAN**. The influx of *braceros* increased during the 1980s, in the wake of the Mexican debt crisis and the endemic civil wars of Central America.

### Bradford, William (1590–1656)

American colonist and religious leader. One of the Pilgrim Fathers, he was born near Doncaster, England. A nonconformist from boyhood, he joined a separatist group in 1606 and went with them to Holland in 1609, seeking freedom of worship. In Leiden he became a tradesman and read widely. One of the moving spirits in the Pilgrim Fathers' expedition to the New World in 1620, he sailed on the *Mayflower* and signed the Mayflower Compact. In 1621 he was elected as the second governor of Plymouth colony, taking over from John Carver. Re-elected governor 30 times between 1622 and 1656 (elections were held yearly), he guided the fledgling colony with exemplary fairness and firmness.

### Bradlaugh, Charles (1833–91)

British free-thinking social reformer. He became a busy secularist lecturer, and a pamphleteer under the name of 'Iconoclast'. In 1880 he became an MP, and claimed the right as an unbeliever to make affirmation of allegiance instead of taking the parliamentary oath; but the House refused to allow him to do either. He was re-elected on three occasions, and finally was admitted (1886). ► **BESANT, ANNIE**

### Bradshaw, Robert (1916–78)

St Kitts and Nevis politician. Bradshaw took St Kitts and Nevis to associated statehood in 1967. The founder and leader of the St Kitts and Nevis Labour Party (1940) and Federal Minister of Finance (1958–62), he briefly made the world press in 1969 when his dispute with Anguilla forced that island to declare its independence of St Kitts; this action resulted in a farcical British military intervention.

### Braganza, House of

The Portuguese royal house which originated in 1442 but succeeded to the throne only in 1640, when the rebellion against Spain put the 8th Duke, John (João), on the throne as **JOHN (JOÃO) IV**. The family ruled continuously until 1910.

### Brahmins

The highest of the four Hindu social classes. A priestly class, the Brahmins dominated Indian society for many centuries. Owing to modern economic and social changes, many of their descendants took up secular occupations. Chitpavan Brahmins figured largely amongst nationalist politicians in Western India in the late colonial period. Recently they have come under critical attack by some lower-caste movements. ► **CASTE**

### Brahmo Samaj

Literally 'Divine Society', the theistic movement founded by Ram Mohan Roy in 1828 which argued that reason should form the true basis of Hinduism. Influenced by Islam, Christianity and modern science, it sought a return to the purity of Hindu worship through an emphasis on monotheism, the rejec-

## HOUSE OF BRAGANZA

| Regnal Dates | Name |
| --- | --- |
| 1640/56 | John (João) IV |
| 1656/67 | Alfonso VI |
| 166//1/06 | Pedro II |
| 1706/50 | John (João) V |
| 1750/77 | José |
| 1777/1816 | Maria I and (until 1786) Pedro III |
| 1816/26 | John (João) VI |
| 1826 | Pedro IV (Emperor of Brazil, as Pedro I, 1822/31) |
| 1826/8 | Maria II da Gloria |
| 1828/34 | Miguel |
| 1834/53 | Maria II da Gloria |
| 1853/61 | Pedro V (Emperor of Brazil, as Pedro II, 1831/89) |
| 1861/89 | Luis I |
| 1889/1908 | Carlos I |
| 1908/10 | Manuel II |

tion of idol-worship and the reform of Hindu social practices. This, and other movements of social and religious reform, has had a profound influence on many social and political thinkers in modern India.

### Brand, Sir Jan Hendrik (1823–88)

South African politician. President of the Orange Free State from 1864 till his death, he defeated the Basutos (1865–9), and favoured friendship with Britain.

### Brandeis, Louis Dembitz (1856–1941)

US judge. He was educated in the USA and in Europe and, after graduating from Harvard Law School, he practised law in Boston. He conducted many labour arbitrations, and was frequently involved in cases challenging the power of monopolies and cartels, as well as others that dealt with the constitutionality of maximum hours and minimum wages legislation. He formulated the economic doctrine of the New Freedom adopted by Woodrow **WILSON** for his 1912 presidential campaign. Appointed to the US Supreme Court in 1916, he favoured governmental intervention to control the economy where public interest required it, but was also a strong defender of the principle of private property. Brandeis, who supported most of **ROOSEVELT**'s New Deal legislation, is remembered as one of the most perceptive and thoughtful Supreme Court judges.

### Brandenburg, Duchy of

The original core of the Kingdom of **PRUSSIA**. Effective German control was gained in 1106 by Lothair, Duke of Saxony (later German Emperor). It came under Hohenzollern control with the appointment of Frederick II as Elector by Emperor **SIGISMUND** in 1415. The **ELECTORS** Joachim and John introduced Lutheranism. Brandenburg was invaded and occupied by the Swedes in the **THIRTY YEARS' WAR**. Independence and order were restored by **FREDERICK WILLIAM, THE GREAT ELECTOR**. In 1701, Elector Frederick III (1688–1713) proclaimed himself King of Prussia, which became the new title of the region. ► **LOTHAIR III, OF SUPPLINBURG**

### Brandt, Willy, originally Karl Herbert Frahm (1913–92)

West German politician. He was an anti-Nazi who

fled in 1933 to Norway. There he changed his name, adopted Norwegian nationality and worked as a journalist until the occupation of Norway (1940) forced him to move to Sweden. In 1945 he returned to Germany, and was a member of the **BUNDESTAG** (1949–57). A pro-Western leader, he was Mayor of West Berlin (1957–66) and chairman of the Social Democratic Party (1964). In 1966 he led his party into a coalition government with the **CDU**, and in 1969 was elected Chancellor in a coalition government with the Free Democrats. Dedicated to restoring relations with Eastern Europe and especially East Germany, his success brought him the 1971 **NOBEL PEACE PRIZE**. He resigned as Chancellor in 1974, and later chaired the **BRANDT COMMISSION** on the world economy. ► **OSTPOLITIK**

**Brandt Commission**
An early attempt to address problems of global trade imbalance by proposing a major restructuring of the world economy. The Independent Commission on International Development Issues first met in 1977, chaired by Willy **BRANDT** and with members representing a broad political and regional spectrum, with the exception of the communist states. Its 1980 report, *North–South: A Program for Survival*, called for population control, **FAIR TRADE**, **THIRD WORLD DEBT** relief, better housing, education and sanitation, and increased opportunities for women but was largely ignored in the 1980s and 1990s. ► **NORTH–SOUTH DIVIDE**.

**Brandywine, Battle of** (11 Sep 1777)
A battle fought in the US **WAR OF INDEPENDENCE**, named after the Brandywine Creek near Philadelphia, Pennsylvania. British forces under William **HOWE** defeated George **WASHINGTON**'s troops, who were attempting to defend Pennsylvania.

**Brant, Joseph** (1742–1807)
**MOHAWK** chief. He fought for the British in the **FRENCH AND INDIAN WAR** and the **AMERICAN REVOLUTION**. In later years an earnest Christian, he translated St Mark's Gospel and the Book of Common Prayer into Mohawk, and in 1786 visited England, where he was received at court.

**Branting, Karl Hjalmar** (1860–1925)
Swedish politician. He was co-founder of the **SOCIAL DEMOCRATIC LABOUR PARTY** of Sweden in 1889 and was its first parliamentary representative in 1896. He became Chairman of the party in 1907 and helped to lead it away from revolutionary **MARXISM** towards a more moderate 'revisionist' programme. He was Prime Minister in 1920, 1921–3 and 1924–5. In 1921 he shared the **NOBEL PEACE PRIZE** and was Sweden's first representative at the **LEAGUE OF NATIONS** in 1922–5.

**Brătianu, Constantine** (1866–c.1948)
Romanian politician. He became the leader of the Liberal Party after the assassination of the Liberal Prime Minister Ion Duca (Dec 1933). Opposed to the dictatorship of **CHARLES II**, he operated part of the 'tolerated opposition' under Ion **ANTONESCU**. He advocated Romania's withdrawal from the war after the winning back of **BESSARABIA** and **BUKOVINA**. In 1944 he was involved in the anti-fascist coup against Antonescu and became a minister without portfolio in the new government. He refused to hold office in

the communist regime of Petru **GROZA** and was arrested and imprisoned without trial. The year of his death, in prison, is not known, but is generally held to be between 1948 and 1952.

**Brătianu, Ion** (1821–91)
Romanian politician. With his brother, Demeter (1818–92), he founded the Romanian Liberal Party. He was Premier from 1876 to 1888, while Demeter held the office for a short time in 1881. He was the father of Ion C **BRĂTIANU**.

**Brătianu, Ion Constantine** (1864–1927)
Romanian politician. A Liberal, he was the son of the great 19c minister Ion **BRĂTIANU**, and in 1916 he brought Romania into **WORLD WAR I** against the **CENTRAL POWERS**. At the **PARIS PEACE CONFERENCE** he secured maximum territorial gains for Romania. His brother, Vintila (1867–1930), was Premier from 1927 to 1928.

**Brauchitsch, Walther von** (1881–1948)
German field marshal. After studying at the War Academy, he was promoted to the rank of captain and served on the General Staff during **WORLD WAR I**. Between 1939 and 1941 he was Commander-in-Chief of the Germany Army, a period of spectacular triumphs, but was dismissed by **HITLER** following the failure of the attack on Moscow. Suffering from ill health, he was allowed to retire and played no further part in the German war effort. After the war he gave perjured evidence at the **NUREMBERG TRIALS** but died before his own case was brought to court.

**Braun, Eva** (1912–45)
German mistress of Adolf **HITLER**. Born in Munich, she was secretary to Hitler's staff photographer, became Hitler's mistress in the 1930s and married him shortly before they committed suicide together in the air-raid shelter of the Chancellory during the fall of Berlin.

**Braun, Otto** (1872–1955)
German politician. After an early career in political journalism and in municipal and Prussian state politics as a member of the **SPD**, Braun became a member of the German National (Constituent) Assembly in 1919 and a member of the **REICHSTAG** in 1920. His main role, however, was as SPD Minister-President of **PRUSSIA** from 1920 to 1932, where he carried out important welfare and civil service reforms which earned his government the hostility of the political right. The unsuccessful SPD candidate for the German presidency in 1925, he sought exile in Switzerland in 1933.

**BRAZIL**   official name **Federative Republic of Brazil**
A republic in eastern and central South America, bounded to the north by French Guiana, Suriname, Guyana and Venezuela; to the north-west by Colombia; to the west by Peru, Bolivia, and Paraguay; to the south-west by Argentina; to the south by Uruguay; and to the east by the Atlantic Ocean. It was claimed for the Portuguese after a fortuitous sighting by Pedro Cabral in 1500, and the first settlement was at Salvador da Bahía. There were 13 feudal grants, which were replaced in 1572 by a viceroyalty. The country was divided into north and south, with capitals at Salvador

and Rio de Janeiro. During the **NAPOLEONIC WARS**, the Portuguese court transferred to Brazil. Brazilian independence was declared in 1822, and a monarchy was established. In 1889 there was a coup, which was followed in 1891 by the declaration of a republic. Large numbers of European immigrants arrived in the early 20c. A revolution, headed by Getúlio **VAR-GAS**, established a dictatorship in 1930–45, but a liberal republic was restored in 1946. Another coup in 1964 led to a military-backed presidential regime, and a military junta was established in 1969. Under President Figueiredo (1979–85) the military government began a process of liberalization, allowing the return of political exiles to stand for state and federal offices, and in 1985 elections ending military rule took place. A new constitution was approved under Figueiredo's successor, José **SARNEY** (1985–9). Subsequent governments and leaders have faced a particularly difficult economic situation but plans to develop the Amazon basin have attracted controversy because they threaten the environmentally important rainforest. ► **ESTADO NOVO**; **PDS**; **PMDB**

**Brazzaville Conference** (30 Jan 1944)
French colonial governors and delegates of the French Consultative Assembly met at Brazzaville, the capital of French Equatorial Africa, in the presence of de **GAULLE**, to lay down the principles which were to govern relations between France and her colonies in the **FRENCH UNION**, created by the constitution of 1946. They envisaged assimilation and integration, rather than independence or even autonomy.

**Breda, Peace of** (31 July 1667)
The treaty which brought an end to the second of the **ANGLO-DUTCH WARS**, following hard on the heels of Michiel de **RUYTER**'s raid on Chatham Docks (June 1667). This improved the terms of the peace for the Dutch Republic: they lost their North American colonies to England (New Amsterdam became New

York, after James, Duke of York, the King's brother and a future monarch himself), but the Dutch retained Suriname in South America and the English gave up their claims to the Moluccan Islands in the East Indies. The English Navigation Acts were also relaxed to allow more Dutch trade into England. ► **CHATHAM, DUTCH DESCENT ON**

**brehon laws**
A corpus of ancient Irish customary law written down by the 8c; the name derives from Irish *breitheamh* 'judge'. Following the Anglo-Norman invasion of Ireland in the late 12c, Irish law gave much ground to English common law. It was finally abolished by statute in the early 17c.

**Breitenfeld, Battle of** (1631)
The crushing defeat inflicted upon **TILLY**, commander of the forces of the Habsburg Empire and the **CATHOLIC LEAGUE**. Tilly was overcome by the Swedes in the only major defeat he suffered in the **THIRTY YEARS' WAR**.

**Brennan, William Joseph, Jr** (1906–97)
US jurist. He was educated at the University of Pennsylvania and Harvard, and after practising law he rose in the New Jersey court system to the state Supreme Court. Named to the US Supreme Court as Associate Justice in 1956, he took an active role in the liberal decisions handed down under Chief Justice Earl **WARREN**, and worked with him in a remarkable period of judicial activism. With Chief Justice Warren E **BURGER**, Brennan upheld the rights of women, supported the Equal Rights Amendment and legalized abortion (in **ROE V WADE**, 1973). He retired from the Court in 1990.

**Breshko-Breshkovskaya, Ekaterina Konstantino-va** (1844–1934)
Russian revolutionary. The colourful and independent-minded daughter of a Polish landowner and a

Russian aristocrat, she associated with various liberal and revolutionary groups in the more open society of St Petersburg under **ALEXANDER II**. In the 1870s she worked with the **NARODNIKI** and was arrested and sent to Siberia in 1874; she was not allowed back into European Russia until 1896. In 1901 she helped to found the **SOCIALIST REVOLUTIONARY PARTY** but in 1908 she was again exiled to Siberia, from which she was able to return only in 1917. Dubbed the 'Grandmother of the Revolution', she fell out with the **BOLSHEVIKS** after their victory in Oct 1917, and died in Prague a firm anti-communist.

**Brest-Litovsk, Treaty of** (Mar 1918)
A bilateral treaty signed at Brest-Litovsk between the new Soviet state and the **CENTRAL POWERS**. Under its terms, Russia withdrew from **WORLD WAR I**, hostilities ceased on Germany's Eastern front, and the new Soviet state ceded vast areas of territory and economic resources to Germany and her newly created protectorates. **LENIN** argued against his opponents that Russia must 'sacrifice space in order to gain time'.

**Bretton Woods Conference**
An international conference held at Bretton Woods, New Hampshire, USA, in 1944, which led to the establishment of the International Monetary System, including the **INTERNATIONAL MONETARY FUND** (IMF) and the World Bank (**INTERNATIONAL BANK FOR RECONSTRUCTION AND DEVELOPMENT**). The agreement, signed by the USA, UK and 43 other nations, aimed at controlling exchange rates, which were fixed for members in terms of gold and the dollar. The system was used until 1973, when floating exchange rates were introduced.

**Brezhnev, Leonid Ilich** (1906–82)
Russian politician. Born in the Ukraine, he trained as a metallurgist and became a political commissar in the **RED ARMY** in **WORLD WAR II**. After the war, he was a party official in the Ukraine and Moldavia (now Moldova), becoming a member (1952–7) and then Chairman (1960–4) of the Presidium of the Supreme Soviet. He succeeded Nikita **KHRUSHCHEV** as General-Secretary of the **COMMUNIST PARTY OF THE SOVIET UNION** (1964–82), and gradually emerged as the most powerful figure in the USSR, the first to hold simultaneously the position of General-Secretary and President of the Supreme Soviet (1977–82). He was largely responsible for the enormous military machine and ailing economy that Mikhail **GORBACHEV** inherited. ► **BREZHNEV DOCTRINE**

**Brezhnev Doctrine**
The term applied to the policies of Leonid **BREZHNEV**, General-Secretary of the Soviet Communist Party (1964–82), which, while combining strict political control internally with peaceful coexistence and **DÉTENTE** abroad, specifically justified intervention (including military) in the internal affairs of other socialist states, as in Czechoslovakia (1968).

**Brian** (c.926–1014)
King of Ireland (1002/14). The Brian Boroimhe or Boru ('Brian of the tribute') of the annalists, in 976 he became chief of Dál Cais, and after much fighting he made himself King of Leinster (984). After further campaigns in all parts of the country, he was acknowledged as 'High King' of Ireland. This did not

mean he effectively ruled over the whole island but simply that he was the dominant king there. He was killed after defeating the **VIKINGS** at Clontarf.

**Briand, Aristide** (1862–1932)
French politician. He began his political career on the extreme Left, advocating a revolutionary general strike, but soon moved to the centre as a 'republican socialist', refusing to join the United Socialist Party (SFIO), which did not allow its members to join 'bourgeois' governments. He held ministerial office almost continuously from 1906, being a cabinet minister 25 times, and Prime Minister 11 times. Apart from his periods as Prime Minister (1909–11, 1913, 1915–17, 1921–2, 1925–6 and 1929), his most important offices were as Minister of Public Instruction and of Religion (1906–8), during which he implemented the **SEPARATION OF CHURCH AND STATE** (voted 1905), and as Foreign Minister (1925–32), when he became known as the 'apostle of peace'. He was a fervent advocate of the **LEAGUE OF NATIONS** and of Franco-German reconciliation. He shared the **NOBEL PEACE PRIZE** in 1926, concluded the **KELLOGG–BRIAND PACT** outlawing war (1928), and launched the idea of a United States of Europe (1929). ► **SOCIALIST PARTY** (France)

**Bright, John** (1811–89)
British politician and orator. A Quaker, he worked in his father's cotton mill, and took an interest in public questions. He became a leading member of the **ANTI-CORN LAW LEAGUE** (1839), and engaged in free-trade agitation. A radical-Liberal, he was MP for Durham (1843), Manchester (1847) and Birmingham (1857), and was closely associated with the Reform Act of 1867. He later held several government posts, until his retirement in 1882. ► **REFORM ACTS**

**Brisbane, Sir Thomas Makdougall** (1773–1860)
Scottish general and astronomer. He joined the army at the age of 16, served in Flanders, the West Indies, Spain and North America, and was promoted major-general in 1813. From 1821 to 1825 he was Governor of New South Wales. He improved the disorganized system of land grants, reformed the currency and improved the efficiency of several government projects. Brisbane, the capital of Queensland, is named after him.

**Brissot (de Warville), Jacques Pierre** (1754–93)
French revolutionary politician. He trained as a lawyer, but then became an author, writing on criminal law. In 1789 he was elected to the National Assembly, where he influenced all the early movements of the Revolution. He established *Le Patriote français*, the organ of the earliest republicans, and became leader of the **GIRONDINS** (or Brissotins). In the National **CONVENTION** his moderation made him suspect to **ROBESPIERRE** and the **JACOBINS**, and, with other Girondins, he was guillotined. ► **FRENCH REVOLUTION**

**Britain, Battle of** (1940)
The name given to the air war campaign of late summer 1940 in which the German **LUFTWAFFE** attempted to destroy the Royal Air Force (RAF) as a prelude to the invasion of the UK. The aerial offensive began in Aug, the German bomber aircraft and fighter escorts concentrating on wiping out the RAF both by

combat in the air and by bombing their vital airfields in the south of the country. British resistance proved stubborn, with the Spitfires and Hurricanes of RAF Fighter Command being directed by radar onto the incoming bomber streams. Badly mauled, the *Luftwaffe* switched their offensive from attacks on airfields to attacks on British cities (the '**BLITZ**'), losing their opportunity to gain true air superiority. Between 1 July and 31 Oct the *Luftwaffe* lost 2,848 aircraft to the RAF's 1,446. ► **WORLD WAR II**

### British Empire

There were in fact several British Empires: the empire of commerce and settlement in the Caribbean and North America, founded in the 17c and partly lost when the 13 colonies declared their independence in 1776; the empire in the East, founded in the 17c but developed through the extensive conquest of India (1757–1857) and the acquisition of islands, trading posts and strategic positions from Aden to Hong Kong; the empire of white settlement in Canada, Australia, New Zealand and the Cape in South Africa, each of which had been federated as 'dominions' by 1910; and the 'dependent territories' in Africa and elsewhere acquired during the 'New Imperialism' of the last few decades of the 19c. To this must be added the British 'informal empire': territories which the Empire did not rule directly, but which fell under its influence because of its industrial and commercial power. These included parts of South America, the Middle East, the Persian Gulf and China. In 1919 the Empire reached its fullest extent through the acquisition of **MANDATES** over German and Ottoman territories in Africa and the Middle East. It was this diversity which gave rise to such famous phrases as 'the empire on which the sun never sets'. By the late 19c the empire was bonded together not only by industrial strength, but by Britain's vast merchant marine and powerful navy. After **WORLD WAR I** it was apparent that Britain could not control such an extensive empire: the dominions secured effective independence in 1931; the Middle Eastern mandates were virtually lost by **WORLD WAR II**; India gained her independence in 1947, and the other Asian colonies soon followed; most of the rest of the Empire was decolonized in the 1960s. Many of the countries of the Empire remained in the British **COMMONWEALTH OF NATIONS**.

### British Expeditionary Force (BEF)

An army, first established in 1906, sent to France (Aug 1914 and Sep 1939) to support the left wing of the French armies against German attack. In **WORLD WAR II** its total strength was 394,000, of whom 224,000 were safely evacuated, mainly from Dunkirk, in May–June 1940. ► **FRENCH, JOHN; HAIG, DOUGLAS; MARNE, BATTLE OF THE; WORLD WAR I**

### British India

The term commonly used to designate the whole of India during the period of British hegemony, more properly it refers to those districts of India under direct British rule. This area may be said to have varied from the first granting of Zamindari rights over 24 parganas near Calcutta to the British **EAST INDIA COMPANY** in 1701. By 1766 the Company directly ruled the area around Madras, the Northern Circars and a sizable area of Bengal and Bihar, while the Crown had control of the city of Bombay. More properly, British India came into being in 1858 when the Company was dissolved and its lands taken over by the Crown. At its height, just before independence in 1947, British India included North-West Frontier province and the provinces of Baluchistan, Sind, Punjab, Ajmer, Merwara, Delhi, United Provinces, Bombay, Coorg, Madras, Ceylon, Central Provinces, Bihar, Orissa, Bengal and Assam; Sikkim and Bhutan were protectorates. Although not officially part of British India, there were in addition many princely states which are often viewed as part of British India. Though nominally independent vassal states of the Crown, the princely states were watched over by British residents and advisers. All control over foreign affairs and policy, and a wide variety of continent-wide matters were ceded by princely states to the government of British India, under informal terms of paramountcy by which Britain had filled the vacuum left by the **MUGHAL EMPIRE**. Although India moved gradually toward representative government between 1858 and 1947, British India was effectively governed by a viceroy or governor-general and some sort of advisory council throughout the period. Along with a small elected assembly, this was the government of India. The viceroy was responsible only to the Crown and the British government. Below the government of India was the small but effective bureaucracy of the **INDIAN CIVIL SERVICE** (**ICS**), which was focused on provincial centres, with district commissioners in rural areas. The **ICS** was supported by the local police forces under its control. The entire government was supported by the British Indian Army, which was an integral part of both government and society, especially after the **INDIAN UPRISING** (1857–8). ► **ARMY, (BRITISH) INDIAN**

### British–Iraqi Treaty (1930)

This treaty carried, amongst others, clauses providing for mutual assistance between Iraq and Britain in time of war and special rights for Britain in respect of 'essential communications' through Iraq and was, in effect, the treaty which brought to a close the British mandate in Iraq. It also granted Britain two air bases on the condition that these were not in any way to be regarded as constituting an occupation; nor were they to be seen as interfering with the principle of Iraqi sovereignty. The treaty, therefore, although ending the mandate and securing full independence for Iraq, bound Iraq to Britain in what was *de facto* a military alliance, due under the treaty to last for 25 years.

### British National Party (BNP)

An extreme right-wing political party which developed in the 1980s as an offshoot of the **NATIONAL FRONT**. It has won a small number of local council seats in England, notably in 2003.

### British North America Act (1867)

An act passed by the British parliament which sanctioned the confederation of Nova Scotia, New Brunswick, Quebec and Ontario, thus giving rise to the **DOMINION OF CANADA**. In 1982 it was renamed the Constitution Act (1867).

### British South Africa Company

A company, formed by Cecil **RHODES**, which used a series of concessions from King **LOBENGULA** and other Central African chiefs to secure a Royal Charter from the British government in 1889. Mashonaland was invaded in 1890, and by 1900 the Company ruled much of Central Africa despite considerable African resistance. In 1923–4 its territories were divided into Northern Rhodesia (Zambia, after 1964) and Southern Rhodesia (Zimbabwe, after 1980). It retained extensive mineral rights.

### British Union of Fascists ► BLACKSHIRTS

### Brizola, Leonel de Moura (1922–2004)
Brazilian politician. He became a state deputy in 1947 on a VARGAS ticket, and went on to become leader of the *Partido Trabalhista Brasileiro* (PTB, 'Brazilian Workers' Party') a decade later. As Governor of Rio Grande do Sul, his support for his brother-in-law, João GOULART, Getúlio Vargas's heir, was crucial in Aug 1961, when he enabled Goulart to assume office as President and in Mar 1964 when, as Popular Deputy for Guanabara, he urged the Left to take to the streets in defence of the President. Exiled in 1964, he advocated armed opposition to the new regime, and by the 1970s had become the standard-bearer of the exiled Social Democrats. Amnestied in 1979, he founded the *Partido Democrático Trabalhista* ('Democratic Workers' Party'), a grouping based on his personal appeal, but limited to his personal following in Rio and Rio Grande do Sul. He became Governor of Rio de Janeiro in the first direct elections in 1982 and led the successful campaign in 1985 which ended the military government. Narrowly defeated by LULA in 1989 for the left-wing candidacy for the presidency, he was elected Governor of Rio de Janeiro in 1990; he was viewed as the *éminence grise* of the nationalists.

### Broederbond
A secret Afrikaner organization founded in 1918. Membership, limited to male Afrikaners, is by invitation only and was intended to integrate potential leaders across the country first to promote Afrikaner political ambitions and then to protect them. Since the early 1980s, it has become somewhat more open as it split between its reformist (or *verligte*) and its reactionary (*verkrampte*) wings.

### Broglie, Achille Charles Léonce Victor, 3rd Duke of (1785–1870)
French politician. The grandson of Victor Broglie, and son of Prince Claude Victor (1757–94), he distinguished himself as a liberal politician and advocate of the abolition of SLAVERY. He became Foreign Secretary and Prime Minister (1835–6) under LOUIS-PHILIPPE.

### Brooke, Sir James (1803–68)
British soldier and Rajah of Sarawak. He sailed in 1838 in a schooner-yacht from London for Sarawak, on the north-west coast of Borneo, with the object of putting down piracy. Made Rajah of Sarawak (1841) for assisting the local sultan against Dayak rebel tribes, he instituted free trade, framed a new code of laws, declared the Dayak custom of head-hunting a capital crime, and vigorously set about suppressing piracy. In 1857 Brooke repelled, with native forces, a series of attacks by a large body of Chinese, who had been irritated by his efforts to prevent opium smuggling. He was succeeded as rajah in 1868 by his nephew, Sir Charles Johnson, who changed his name to Brooke. He was succeeded in turn in 1917 by his son, Sir Charles Vyner, who in 1946 ceded Sarawak to the British crown.

### Brookeborough, Basil Stanlake Brooke, 1st Viscount (1888–1973)
Irish politician. He was elected to the Northern Ireland parliament in 1929, became Minister of Agriculture (1933), Commerce (1941–5), and then Prime Minister (1943–63). A staunch supporter of union with Great Britain, he was created viscount in 1952, and retired from politics in 1968.

### Brown, George (1818–80)
Canadian politician and journalist. A supporter of RESPONSIBLE GOVERNMENT in 1848, he became a member of the Canadian legislative assembly in 1851. As editor of the *Toronto Globe* he used his considerable influence to speak for the CLEAR GRITS, pressing the case for representation-by-population ('rep by pop'), to give CANADA WEST a majority of seats in the legislature. After the Liberal-Conservatives took over government in 1854, Brown reorganized the party and won the 1857 elections by advocating the acquisition of the North West from the HUDSON'S BAY COMPANY. In 1858, in alliance with A A Dorion, the leader of the Liberals of CANADA EAST, he formed a government which survived only a few days. It was perhaps this experience which helped him to realize the inherent instability of provincial government under the system established by the Act of Union. He therefore played a major role with Alexander GALT, J A MACDONALD, and George Étienne CARTIER, in a coalition government established to devise the constitutional reforms required for confederation. This he continued to support even after resigning in Dec 1865. Brown was also an anti-SLAVERY activist, involved in the settlement of fugitive slaves during the 1850s. He was shot and killed by an employee sacked from the *Globe*. ► LIBERAL PARTY (Canada)

### Brown, Gordon (1951–)
British politician. Born in Glasgow and educated at Edinburgh University, he worked in academia and television before being elected MP for Dunfermline East in 1983. Joining the Shadow Cabinet in 1987, he became Shadow Chancellor in 1992 and then Chancellor of the Exchequer after Labour's 1997 general election victory. He reassured business and voters that Labour could manage the economy without fuelling inflation and his watchword was 'prudence', although increases in indirect taxation led to accusations that he was applying taxes by stealth. An early act as Chancellor was to give the Bank of England control over monetary policy by allowing it to set base interest rates. Although a close ally of Tony BLAIR and his chief supporter in the 1994 contest for the party leadership, relations between the two became strained in Labour's second term by policy differences and the Prime Minister's apparent failure to honour an alleged 1994 agreement to step aside in favour of Brown during his second term.

### Brown, John (1800–59)
US militant abolitionist. He supported himself with many different jobs while wandering through the

country advocating anti-**SLAVERY**. He was twice married and had 20 children. In 1859, he led a raid on the US armory at Harpers Ferry in Virginia (now West Virginia), intending to launch a slave insurrection. The raid failed, and after being convicted of treason against Virginia, he was hanged at Charlestown. The song 'John Brown's Body' commemorates the **HARPERS FERRY RAID**. ➤ **ABOLITIONISM**

**Brown v Board of Education of Topeka, Kansas** (1954)

US Supreme Court case in which Chief Justice Earl **WARREN**, speaking for a unanimous bench, declared that separate educational facilities were inherently unequal and inhumane. With this decision the court overturned **PLESSY V FERGUSON** (1896), which had supported 'separate but equal' facilities, and undermined the major principle upon which **JIM CROW LAWS** depended. Critics contended that it encroached on **STATES' RIGHTS**, and that it represented judicial legislation rather than interpretation. In 'Brown II' (1955) the Supreme Court acknowledged the problems faced by school boards in implementing the earlier decision; therefore, they ordered district courts to integrate schools 'with all deliberate speed'. ➤ **SEGREGATION**

**Broz, Josip** ➤ **TITO**

**Bruce, Blanche Kelso** (1848–98)

US politician. Born in Farmville, Virginia, he was a former slave who became a planter. He went on to become the first black American to serve a full term in the US **SENATE**.

**Bruce, Robert** (1274–1329)

King of Scots (1306/29) and hero of the **SCOTTISH WAR OF INDEPENDENCE**. As Earl of Carrick, in 1296 he swore fealty to **EDWARD I** of England, but soon joined the Scottish revolt under **WALLACE**. In 1306 he quarrelled with John Comyn, his political rival, stabbing him to death, then assembled his vassals and was crowned king at Scone. He was forced to flee to Ireland, but returned in 1307 and defeated the English at Loudoun Hill. After Edward's death (1307), the English were forced from the country and all the great castles recovered except Berwick and Stirling. This led to the Battle of **BANNOCKBURN** (1314), when the English were routed. Sporadic war with England continued until the Treaty of Northampton (1328), which recognized the independence of Scotland and Bruce's right to the throne. He was succeeded by **DAVID II**, the son of his second wife.

**Bruce of Melbourne, Stanley Melbourne Bruce, 1st Viscount** (1883–1967)

Australian politician. Bruce attended Trinity Hall, Cambridge (1902–5), and spent much time in England because of business interests. After service in **WORLD WAR I** with a British regiment, he entered Australian federal politics in 1918, representing Australia at the **LEAGUE OF NATIONS** in 1921 (and again 1932–9). He became treasurer in 1921 and Prime Minister and Minister for External Affairs (1923–9) in a coalition with **PAGE**'s Country Party. Bruce's primary concern was Australian economic development within the framework of the British Empire, to which end he encouraged immigration, overseas investment and imperial preference. Attacks on the arbitra-

tion system and the trade union movement led to the fall of his government in 1929. He led the Australian delegation at the **OTTAWA CONFERENCE** in 1932 and was High Commissioner in London (1933–45). He became Viscount Bruce of Melbourne in 1947 and was the first Chancellor of the Australian National University (1951–61). ➤ **NATIONAL PARTY OF AUSTRALIA**

**Bruges, Matins of** (18 May 1302)

The overpowering of the French garrison in the Flemish town of Bruges. The raid was carried out mainly by members of the lower classes of Bruges, who rejected the pro-French policies of the town's leaders. Thus, the incident had a democratic character; it led to a general rising of Flanders against French domination, and culminated in the Battle of the **GOLDEN SPURS** later the same year.

**Bruges, Treaty of** (15 Aug 1521)

The agreement between King **HENRY VIII** of England and the Emperor **CHARLES V** against France, despite the Anglo-French friendliness of the **FIELD OF THE CLOTH OF GOLD** the year before. The treaty meant that England was involved in long campaigns in northern Europe in support of the Emperor.

**Brühl, Heinrich, Count von** (1700–63)

Saxon courtier and diplomat. He helped his master, Elector **AUGUSTUS III**, gain the Polish crown in 1733 and was appointed Prime Minister in 1746. His aim of securing a territorial connection between Saxony and Poland at Prussia's expense aroused the unremitting hostility of **FREDERICK II, THE GREAT** and was ultimately frustrated by the outcome of the **SEVEN YEARS' WAR**. Brühl's ambitious political schemes, his generous sponsorship of baroque culture and his lavish private lifestyle drained the state's coffers and burdened the country with debt.

**Brumaire Coup** (9–10 Nov 1799)

Named after its date in the **FRENCH REPUBLICAN CALENDAR**, this was a plot, organized by **SIEYÈS**, one of the five Directors, together with **TALLEYRAND** and Cambacérès, with Napoleon Bonaparte as its military leader. Napoleon, however, bungled his part in it and had to be rescued by his brother, Lucien Bonaparte. It was intended by its organizers to produce limited constitutional changes, but ended with the overthrow of the **DIRECTORY** and the establishment of absolute power in the hands of **NAPOLEON I** as First Consul.

**Brundtland, Gro Harlem** (1939–)

Norwegian politician. She studied medicine at Oslo and Harvard, qualifying as a physician. She married (1960) a leader of the opposition Conservative Party, Arne Olav, and worked in public medicine services in Oslo until, in 1969, she joined the Labour Party and entered politics. She was appointed Environment Minister (1974–9) and then, as leader of the Labour Party group, became (1981) Prime Minister of Norway, the first woman to hold the post. She was Prime Minister two more times (1986–9, 1990–6). In 1987 she chaired the World Commission on Environment and Development which produced the report *Our Common Future*, and in 1988 she was awarded the Third World Foundation prize for leadership in environmental issues. From 1998 to 2003 she was Director-General of the World Health Organization.

**BRUNEI** official name **State of Brunei, Abode of Peace (Islamic Sultanate of Brunei)**

A state on the north-west coast of Borneo, south-eastern Asia, bounded by the South China Sea in the north-west, and on all other sides by Malaysia's Sarawak state. The Limbang River Valley in Sarawak divides the state into two sections. Formerly a powerful Muslim Sultanate, it came under British protection in 1888, achieved internal self-government in 1971, and gained independence in 1984. It is a constitutional monarchy with a Sultan (Muda Hassanal Bolkiah Mu'izzadin Waddaulah, since 1967) as head of state. In 2004 the Sultan reopened the parliament, which had been disbanded 20 years earlier.

**Brüning, Heinrich** (1885–1970)
German politician. He studied in **BONN** and at the London School of Economics, and during the **WEIMAR REPUBLIC** became (1929) leader of the predominantly Catholic *Zentrum* (**CENTRE PARTY**) and then Chancellor (1930–2). Faced with the problems of economic depression, he attempted to rule by decree, but was eventually forced out of office, to make way for the more conservative Franz von **PAPEN**. In 1934 he left Germany, spending most of the rest of his life in US universities.

**Bruno, Giordano** (1548–1600)
Italian hermetic thinker. At first a Dominican, his opinions caused him to flee to Geneva (1578). He then went to Paris (1581), where he lectured, then (1583) to London. He travelled throughout Europe until 1591, when he was arrested by the **INQUISITION** and, after an eight-year trial, burnt in Rome. His philosophy was pantheist and sympathetic to Copernicus's theory of the universe. His most famous works are *De l'infinito universo et mondi* (1584, 'On the Infinite Universe and Worlds') and *Spaccio de la bestia trionfante* (1584, 'The Expulsion of the Triumphant Beast').

**Brunswick Manifesto** (12 July 1792)
The manifesto issued by Charles William Ferdinand, Duke of Brunswick, warning the Jacobins in Revolutionary France that Paris would face heavy reprisals if any harm were to befall the French King or Queen. It marked the commencement of the Wars of the Coalition. ► **FRENCH REVOLUTION**

**Brusilov, Alexei** (1856–1926)
Russian soldier. He served in the war against Turkey (1877). In **WORLD WAR I** he led the invasion of Galicia (1914) and the Carpathians. From 1916 he distinguished himself on the eastern front, notably in command of the South Western Army Group in the only partly successful 'Brusilov Offensive' against the Austrians in 1916. He became Chief of Staff in 1917, but

the second 'Brusilov Offensive' was frustrated, many of his troops mutinied and added to the unrest that produced the Bolshevik Revolution. ► **BRUSILOV OFFENSIVES**

**Brusilov Offensives** (1916 and 1917)
Two crucial Russian actions during **WORLD WAR I**. In June 1916 General **BRUSILOV** launched a massive offensive against Austria at the request of the Western powers. He advanced into Galicia, relieved the Italians and encouraged the Romanians to enter the war. This helped eventually to destroy the Austrian Empire, but the cost in men and materials damaged Russian morale and weakened the Russian economy. The second offensive in July 1917, intended to strengthen the **RUSSIAN PROVISIONAL GOVERNMENT** that followed the **FEBRUARY REVOLUTION**, was an abysmal failure and contributed to the worsening social and political unrest that the **BOLSHEVIKS** then exploited in Oct of the same year.

**Brussels Conference, Declaration of** (1874)
An early statement of regulations covering many aspects of warfare. All the European powers were signatories, and much of the declaration was incorporated into that of the Hague Conference of 1899. ► **HAGUE PEACE CONFERENCES**

**Bryan, William Jennings** (1860–1925)
US politician. Educated at Illinois College, he entered the **HOUSE OF REPRESENTATIVES** as a Democrat in 1890 and won his party's presidential nomination in 1896 on a Populist platform. He was Democratic nominee three times, and became Secretary of State under Woodrow **WILSON**. His last public act was assisting the anti-evolutionist prosecutor in the Scopes Monkey Trial in Dayton, Tennessee. ► **DARROW, CLARENCE**; **DEMOCRATIC PARTY**; **FREE SILVER**; **POPULIST PARTY**

**Bryce, James Bryce, 1st Viscount** (1838–1922)
British politician. He entered parliament in 1880, and was made Irish Secretary (1905) and Ambassador to the USA (1907–13). As chairman of the Bryce Commission (1894–5), he recommended the establishment of a Ministry of Education. His best-known work is *The American Commonwealth* (1888).

**Bubnov, Andrei Sergeevich** (1883–1940)
Russian politician. He was a typical middle-ranking Bolshevik who suffered for the cause and was then consumed by it. Expelled from the Agricultural Institute in Moscow for political activity, he was quickly drawn into organizing and making propaganda for **LENIN** and his colleagues. He was arrested many times before 1917 and became a **POLITBURO** member in that year. Between 1918 and 1924 he was associated with **TROTSKY**, but he broke clear and was entrusted with political education in the Russian Republic in 1929. That, however, did not save him from **STALIN**'s vengeance in 1937, and he died in prison three years later.

**buccaneers**
The term used to denote legalized pirates operating in the Caribbean in the period 1650–98. The name derives from the French *boucanier* ('buyer of smoked beef'). The initial buccaneer stronghold was the island of Tortuga, off Hispaniola, but this transferred

itself to Port Royal after the English capture of Jamaica in 1655. As with the **PRIVATEERS** a century earlier, the home governments often used the buccaneers as instruments of policy, issuing them with Commissions of Reprisal entitling them to attack Spanish shipping and settlements. The most infamous buccaneers were the Frenchmen L'Olonnois, Du Casse and De Maintenon, and the Welshman Henry **MORGAN**. English buccaneering was ended by the Treaty of Madrid (1670) and French by the Treaty of **RIJSWIJK** (1697).

**Buchan, John, 1st Baron Tweedsmuir** (1875–1940)
British author and politician. During **WORLD WAR I** he served on HQ staff (1916–17), when he became Director of Information. He was MP for the Scottish Universities (1927–35), when he was made a baron, and became Governor-General of Canada until 1940. In 1937 he was made a Privy Councillor and Chancellor of Edinburgh University. Despite his busy public life, Buchan wrote over 50 books, especially fast-moving adventure stories, such as *Prester John* (1910) and *The Thirty-Nine Steps* (1915).

**Buchanan, George** (1506–82)
Scottish humanist and reformer. He was imprisoned for a satirical poem on the **FRANCISCANS**. He escaped to France (1539), and taught at Bordeaux, Paris, and Coimbra, Portugal (1549), where he was arrested as a suspected heretic. Released in 1552, he returned to Scotland in 1561, and was tutor to **MARY, QUEEN OF SCOTS**. Abandoning Mary after the death of **DARNLEY**, he became tutor to James VI, and Keeper of the Privy Seal (1570–8). His European reputation rested mainly on his skill in Latin poetry; his Latin paraphrase of the Psalms was used as a textbook until the 19c. ▸ **JAMES VI AND I**

**Buchanan, James** (1791–1868)
US politician and 15th President. Educated at Dickinson College, he was admitted to the Bar in 1812. Elected to the US **SENATE** in 1834, he became Secretary of State under President James K **POLK** (1845), an office he held during the **MEXICAN WAR**. He served as Minister to Great Britain under President Pierce (1853–6), and was elected President as a Democrat in 1856. During his administration the **SLAVERY** question came to a head and he tried to maintain a balance between pro-slavery and anti-slavery forces. He supported the establishment of Kansas as a slave state, which alienated many in the North, but his moderate position also displeased radicals in the South. He was defeated in the presidential election by Abraham **LINCOLN**, but before Lincoln's inauguration Buchanan was faced with the secession of the Southern states. Determined to avert a civil war, he rejected a military response and instead pursued a policy of compromise.

**Bucharest, Treaties of** (1812 and 1913)
Two treaties, marking important stages in the achievement of Balkan nationhood. The 1812 Russo-Turkish treaty, concluding the Serbian revolt which had begun in 1804, granted Serbia autonomy within the **OTTOMAN EMPIRE** and launched her on the path to outright independence in 1878. The treaty of Aug 1913 ended the second Balkan War between Bulgaria and Greece, Serbia and Romania, her recent allies against Turkey in the first of the **BALKAN WARS**

(1912–13). Its terms, involving Bulgaria's surrender of north Macedonia to Serbia, south Macedonia to Greece, and the south Dobrudja to Romania, finally extinguished any prospect of a 'Greater Bulgaria'.

**Buchenwald**
German **CONCENTRATION CAMP**. Established near Weimar in Aug 1937, it became a major part of the SS's economic empire during **WORLD WAR II**. Among its 239,000 internees (of whom 56,000 died) were many Soviet and Polish prisoners of war as well as German political detainees. Many major firms, as well as the SS's own Earth and Stone Co Ltd, exploited its inmates as forced labour. Liberated by the US Army in Apr 1945, Buchenwald subsequently passed under Soviet control and served as an internment camp until 1950. ▸ **HOLOCAUST**

**Buck, Edward Charles** (1838–1916)
British Indian administrator. Buck, a graduate of Clare College, Cambridge, joined the **INDIAN CIVIL SERVICE** in 1886, being immediately posted to Bengal. Having proved a great asset to the Bengal Civil Service, Buck rose through the ranks and eventually became Secretary of the government of India in 1882, a post he held until his retirement in 1897. In 1886 he represented the government of India at the Great Colonial Exhibition. In 1897, marking both his retirement and Queen **VICTORIA**'s diamond jubilee, Buck was made a Knight Commander of the Star of India.

**Buckingham, George Villiers, 1st Duke of** (1592–1628)
English statesman and court favourite. He was knighted by **JAMES VI AND I**, and raised to the peerage as Viscount Villiers (1616), Earl of Buckingham (1617), Marquis (1618), and Duke (1623). In 1623 he failed to negotiate the marriage of Prince Charles to the daughter of the Spanish King, but later arranged the marriage to Henrietta Maria of France. The abortive expedition against Cadiz (1625) exposed him to **IMPEACHMENT** by the Commons and only a dissolution rescued him. An expedition against France failed (1627), and while planning a second attack, he was assassinated at Portsmouth by John Felton, a discontented subaltern.

**Buckingham, George Villiers, 2nd Duke of** (1628–87)
English statesman. After his father's assassination, he was brought up with **CHARLES I**'s children, and went into exile after the royalist defeat in the **ENGLISH CIVIL WARS**. His estates were recovered at the **RESTORATION** and he became a member of the **CABAL** of **CHARLES II**. He was instrumental in **CLARENDON**'s downfall (1667), but lost power to **ARLINGTON** and was dismissed in 1674 for alleged Catholic sympathies.

**Buddhism** ▸ **RELIGION**

**Budenny, Simeon Mikhailovich** (1883–1973)
Russian soldier. The son of a Cossack farmer, he fought as a Cossack private in the **RUSSO-JAPANESE WAR** (1904–5) and as an NCO in **WORLD WAR I**. After the revolution he became a Bolshevik and raised a Cossack unit to fight the White forces on the Don, defeating the Whites in the battles of Tsaritsyn (1918–19). He served in the war against Poland (1920), and was made a marshal in 1935. In 1941 he

commanded the south-west sector against the German invasion, but was relieved by **TIMOSHENKO** after a disaster at Kiev. ► **BOLSHEVIKS**; **RUSSIAN REVOLUTION**

**Budi Utomo**
The first and most important of the ethnic-based organizations formed in the **DUTCH EAST INDIES** just before **WORLD WAR I**. Founded in 1908, it drew in younger members of the Dutch-educated Javanese aristocracy who, in seeking to create a modernized Javanese culture, wished to establish for themselves a greater influence in the colonial world. Moderate in tone and unable to decide whether to pursue a purely cultural programme or whether to take up political ambitions, it was soon overshadowed by overtly political indigenous movements, although it remained in existence until the mid-1930s.

**Buffalo Bill** ► **CODY, WILLIAM FREDERICK**

**Buganda**
One of the states of Uganda, occupying territory on the north-west shore of Lake Victoria. It began to expand in the 17c, and was very powerful by the 19c. It was involved in trade in ivory and other commodities with the **NYAMWEZI** in the 18c, and later became a focus of the struggle among Muslim, Catholic and Protestant parties. The British ruled Uganda through the **INDIRECT RULE** system, and the continuing existence of the kingdom caused serious strains for independent Uganda. ► **BUNYORO, KINGDOM OF**

**Buhari, Muhammadu** (1942– )
Nigerian soldier and politician. Educated locally and then at military academies in Nigeria, England and India, he was military governor of North-Eastern State (1975–6), of Bornu State (1976), and then Federal Commissioner for Petroleum Resources (1976–8) and Chairman of the Nigerian National Petroleum Corporation (1976–9). He returned to army duties (July 1976) but led the military coup which ousted Shehu **SHAGARI** (31 Dec 1983), when he became President. He was himself removed in a coup led by Ibrahim **BABANGIDA** on 27 Aug 1985 and detained, before being released in 1988. In 2003 he was an unsuccessful candidate for the presidency.

**Bukharin, Nikolai Ivanovich** (1888–1938)
Russian Marxist revolutionary and political theorist. Dubbed by **LENIN** 'the darling of the Party', he was active in the Bolshevik underground (1905–17), and after the **FEBRUARY REVOLUTION** returned to Russia, playing a leading role in the organization of the **OCTOBER REVOLUTION** in Moscow. He was a considerable theorist. As a member of the **POLITBURO** he came round to supporting Lenin's **NEW ECONOMIC POLICY**, but had an ambivalent attitude to **STALIN**'s collectivization campaign. In 1937 he was arrested in Stalin's Great Purge, expelled from the Party, tried on trumped-up charges, and shot. In 1987 he was officially rehabilitated by a board of judicial inquiry, and posthumously readmitted to the Party in 1988. ► **BOLSHEVIKS**; **BREST-LITOVSK, TREATY OF**

**Bukovina**
The region lying in the north-east of the Carpathian Mountains, which was settled by Ruthenians and Moldavians, and became part of Moldavia in the 14c.

It was ceded to Austria by the Turks (1775) and governed by a mainly Polish administration as part of Galicia, first as a duchy and then as a crown land (1786–1849). During 1848 demands were made for separation, and in 1853 it received its own diet and a separate administration. Romania, after gaining full independence (1879), sought Bukovina, occupied it during **WORLD WAR I** and received it by the Treaty of **TRIANON** (1920). The Romanian government then began to impose a Romanian cultural identity in the region. In **WORLD WAR II** Soviet troops seized northern Bukovina and in 1947 incorporated it into the Ukrainian Soviet Socialist Republic, while the southern part around Suceava remained within Romania. Populated by Ukrainians, Romanians, Germans, Jews, Poles and Hungarians, under **CEAUŞESCU** it became an irredentist issue with the USSR. ► **MOLDAVIA AND WALLACHIA**

**Bulganin, Nikolai Alexandrovich** (1895–1975)
Soviet politician. An early member of the Communist Party, he was Mayor of Moscow (1931–7), a member of the Military Council in **WORLD WAR II**, and held various defence appointments after the war. Following **STALIN**'s death he became Vice-Premier in Malenkov's government, and was Premier after Giorgiy **MALENKOV** resigned (1955–8), with Nikita **KHRUSHCHEV** wielding real power. 'B and K' travelled extensively abroad for propaganda purposes. Bulganin was dismissed in 1958, and retired into obscurity.

**BULGARIA**    official name **Republic of Bulgaria**

A republic in the east of the Balkan Peninsula, southeastern Europe, bounded to the north by Romania; to the west by Serbia and Macedonia; to the south by Greece; to the south-east by Turkey; and to the east by the Black Sea. In the 7c Bulgars crossed the Danube and gradually merged with the Slavonic population and established the Kingdom of Bulgaria, which was continually at war with the **BYZANTINE EMPIRE** until it was destroyed by the Turks in the 14c. It was under Turkish rule until 1878 but full independence was only achieved in 1908. Bulgaria was a kingdom from 1908 to 1946, after which it became a communist republic. It was aligned with Germany in the World Wars and in 1944 was occupied by the USSR. In 1990 the communist regime was ousted and in the 1990s a multiparty government introduced political and economic reforms. In 2001 the former king, **SIMEON II**, became Prime Minister following the success in the elections of his National Movement party. Bulgaria joined **NATO** in 2004 and plans to join the **EU** in 2007.

**Bulgarian Exarchate**
During the 19c, Bulgarian national sentiment first focused on founding a Bulgarian exarchate, an autonomous ecclesiastical province which would free the Bulgarians from Greek domination, although they

would still be ultimately subject to the ecumenical patriarch at Constantinople. In 1849 Sultan **ABD UL-MAJID I** allowed the Bulgarians to open a church in Constantinople, an act which for the first time recognized their existence as a separate nation. The Bulgarian Church was finally declared independent in 1872, when Antim I was appointed exarch.

### Bulge, Battle of the (1944)
The last desperate German armoured counter-offensive through the Ardennes in **WORLD WAR II** (beginning 16 Dec), to prevent the Allied invasion of Germany. It achieved early success, but ground to a halt, and the Germans were pushed into retreat by the Allies by the end of Jan 1945.

### Bull Run, Battles of (21 July 1861 and 29–30 Aug 1862)
Major victories by Confederate forces in the **AMERICAN CIVIL WAR**; also known as the Battles of Manassas. The first battle, which was the first major clash of the Civil War, pitted untrained Northern troops attempting to capture Richmond, Virginia (the Southern capital), against well-commanded Southerners. 'Stonewall' **JACKSON**'s stand caused the Northern troops to retreat, and the retreat became a rout. In the second battle, a large Northern force under John Pope was trapped by combined Confederate forces under 'Stonewall' Jackson and James Longstreet.

### Bülow, Prince Bernhard Heinrich Martin Karl von (1849–1929)
German politician. He was Foreign Secretary (1897) before becoming Chancellor, and was made a count (1899) and a prince (1905). Identified with an aggressive foreign policy in the years before **WORLD WAR I**, Bülow, as Chancellor (1900–9), was the first to govern through a parliamentary coalition, which provoked conflict with Emperor **WILLIAM II** and precipitated his dismissal.

### Bummei-kaika ('Civilization and Enlightenment')
A slogan much used by Japanese government leaders and intellectuals following the **MEIJI RESTORATION** of 1868. It was used with reference to government promotion of Western-style reforms in politics, society and the economy, with the aim of making Japan a strong and wealthy power. For a period in the 1870s and 1880s, everything Western, from constitutions to dress and eating habits, was regarded worthy of emulation. A nativist reaction set in by the end of the 1880s, when traditional values were once again championed.

### Bunau-Varilla, Philippe Jean (1859–1940)
French engineer. The chief organizer of the Panama Canal project, he was instrumental in getting the waterway routed through Panama instead of Nicaragua. He incited the Panama revolution (1903), was made Panamanian minister to the USA and negotiated the **HAY–BUNAU-VARILLA TREATY** (1903), giving the USA control of the Canal Zone. ► **CANALS**

### Bunche, Ralph Johnson (1904–71)
US diplomat. He studied at Harvard and the University of California, then taught political science at Howard University, Washington, DC (1928–50). In 1944 he assisted the Swedish Nobel Prize winner Gunnar Myrdal in the creation of *An American Dilemma*, a study on American blacks. He directed the **UN** Trusteeship department (1946–54), and became UN mediator in **PALESTINE**, where he arranged for a ceasefire. Awarded the **NOBEL PEACE PRIZE** (1950), he became a UN Under-Secretary for Special Political Affairs from 1957 to his death.

### Bund
Literally 'federation', this is the name given to the German federal level of government and its competences, as against those of the states (*Länder*) and of local government. The *Bund* shares sovereignty with the Länder. ► **BASIC LAW; LAND**

### Bund, The (1897)
The short name for the General Union of Jewish Workers in Russia and Poland. In the wave of official and popular anti-Semitism that afflicted Russia following the assassination of **ALEXANDER II** (1881), Jewish intellectuals and workers inevitably found themselves drawn into opposition activities, including Marxist groups. The Bund had its own *raison d'être*. However, in 1898 at a secret congress in Minsk, it was one of the founder-members of the Russian Social Democratic Labour Party.

### Bundesrat (1867–1918)
The upper and more powerful house of the North German (1867–70) and then German (1871–1918) parliament. Its members were appointed by the member states/princes of the German federation (**REICH**) and had extensive legislative powers as well as the power to resolve disputes between member states of the federation. Its influence declined with time as the elected, lower house of parliament (**REICHSTAG**) played a more prominent role in public affairs.

### Bundesrat (1949– )
The upper house of the current German parliament. Its members are appointed by the state (**LAND**) governments and scrutinize all federal legislation. A two-thirds majority can block legislation proposed by the lower, elected house (**BUNDESTAG**). The *Bundesrat* also serves to represent state interests at federal level. ► **BASIC LAW**

### Bundestag
The lower house of the current German parliament, elections for which are held every four years in the autumn. It is possible for the *Bundestag* to be dissolved and elections held before the end of the fixed term, as in 1972 and 1983 when the government actually lost, or contrived to lose, its majority. In addition to legislating, the Bundestag selects the Chancellor and supports his government.

### Bundeswehr (Federal German Armed Forces)
Following Federal German entry into **NATO** on 9 May 1955, the *Bundeswehr* accepted 101 volunteers on 12 Nov. This ended the period of disarmament following capitulation in May 1945. In contrast to earlier German armed forces, the Bundeswehr was unequivocally subordinated to parliament and its conscripts perceived as 'citizens in uniform'. Virtually entirely within the NATO command structure, the Bundeswehr became the largest element in NATO with 340,000 soldiers and 8,600 tanks, 104,000 airmen and 400 front-line aircraft, and 37,500 sailors. Following reunification, the Bundeswehr absorbed the

surviving elements of the East German armed forces.

**Bunge, Nikolai Khristyanovich** (1823–95)
Russian politician. Formerly Professor of Economics at Kiev University, he was Minister of Finance (1881–6). He was responsible for introducing a series of enlightened tax reforms that continued the policy of **ALEXANDER II** after the latter's assassination in 1881. Bunge also introduced labour laws, and both of these measures benefited peasants and manual workers. In 1884 he established the **PEASANTS' LAND BANK** which for a period helped peasants buy land. In addition, he began the purchasing of private railways and the building of state-owned lines as a means of promoting industrial development. He resigned rather than raise new taxes to pay for fresh foreign wars. However, despite the atmosphere of political repression, he initiated two decades of economic modernization.

**Bunker Hill, Battle of** (1775)
The first pitched battle of the **AMERICAN REVOLUTION**, technically a US defeat. The British garrison dislodged New England troops from their position overlooking occupied Boston, but very high British casualties demonstrated American fighting capacity, and forbade attempts on other American emplacements. The battle was actually fought on Breed's Hill, above Charlestown, not on nearby Bunker Hill.

**Bunyoro, Kingdom of**
One of the kingdoms of Uganda, occupying territory north of Buganda. It was formerly the most powerful of these states, originally known as Kitara, before it was colonized by the Nilotic Bito. It declined in influence when **BUGANDA** rose in the 17c.

**Buonarroti, Filippo** (1761–1837)
Italian revolutionary. One of the most colourful and radical of Italian revolutionary leaders, in the 1790s he frequented Jacobin circles in Paris and went on a number of missions to Italy, Corsica and Lyons for the revolutionary regime. After the **THERMIDOR** coup he was imprisoned twice, the second time for his involvement in **BABEUF**'s 'Conspiracy of Equals'. Freed by **NAPOLEON I**, he returned once more to conspiracy both in France and Italy, where he joined the **CARBONARI** and founded the **ADELFI**. Forced to leave Italy, he settled in Paris, mixing in revolutionary circles until the very end. ► **JACOBINS**

**Buraimi Dispute** (1952)
Buraimi, a group of oases on the borders of Abu Dhabi (now one of the United Arab Emirates) and Oman, was the subject of a territorial claim voiced by Saudi Arabia in 1949. A small armed force from Saudi Arabia occupied Buraimi in 1952, but was expelled on behalf of the rulers of Abu Dhabi and Oman by the Trucial Oman Scouts, a local force with British officers. There seems little doubt that the motivation behind the original claims and the occupation of Buraimi was the oil-bearing potential of the area recognized by the US oil concerns operating in Saudi Arabia; also that the **CIA** was involved in the organization of the attempted military seizure of the oasis.

**burakumin**
An outcaste group in Japanese society, concentrated in about 6,000 ghetto communities and numbering 1–3 million; the target of extreme discrimination with regard to employment, marriage and residential segregation. Their origins go back to the **EDO** feudal period of the 17c, when impoverished Japanese in lowly occupations were segregated. The class was officially abolished in 1871, but to no great effect: some militancy within the group since the 1920s has also had little impact.

**Bureau of Indian Affairs (BIA)**
A US government agency established in 1824 as part of the War Department and transferred in 1849 to the Department of the Interior. The BIA is in charge of the administration of Native American affairs, acting on behalf of the USA, which is the trustee of tribal lands and property. ► **NATIVE AMERICANS**

**Burgenland**
The easternmost state of the Austrian Federation. Settled by Germans in the 9c, this territory was part of Hungary until 1922 when, with the exception of its capital, Odenburg (Sopron), it passed to Austria under the terms of the Treaty of **ST GERMAIN** (1919).

**Burger, Warren Earl** (1907–95)
US jurist. Educated at the University of Minnesota, he taught and practised law in St Paul from 1931 before he became Assistant Attorney-General of the USA (1953) and US Court of Appeals judge for the District of Columbia in 1955. Appointed the 15th Chief Justice of the US Supreme Court by President Richard **NIXON** in 1969, he was conservative on criminal matters, but on social issues he proved to be more progressive than expected. He voted with the majority on **ROE V WADE** (1973), which upheld the right to abortion, and wrote the majority opinion in the 1974 decision that forced Nixon to surrender the **WATERGATE** tapes to a special prosecutor. He retired in 1986, the longest-serving chief justice of the 20c.

**Burgess, Guy Francis de Moncy** (1910–63)
British double agent. Recruited as a Soviet agent in the 1930s, he worked with the BBC (1936–9), wrote war propaganda (1939–41), and again joined the BBC (1941–4) while working for MI5. Thereafter, he was a member of the Foreign Office, and second secretary under **PHILBY** in Washington in 1950. Recalled in 1951 for 'serious misconduct', he and **MACLEAN** disappeared, re-emerging in the USSR in 1956. He died in Moscow. ► **BLUNT, ANTHONY**

**Burgh, Hubert de** (d.1243)
Justiciar of England under King **JOHN** and **HENRY III** (1215–32). He is chiefly remembered as the jailer of Prince **ARTHUR**. He was created Earl of Kent in 1227, but was imprisoned after falling from favour (1232–4), then pardoned.

**Burghers**
A term related to 'burgess', which referred to citizens of a chartered community (a burgh or borough). A burgher possessed certain civic rights and responsibilities associated with citizenship, whether by birth or through purchase of burgher status.

**Burgos, Carmen** (1879–1932)
Spanish feminist. Born in the remote province of Almeria, she married young but moved to Madrid after being abandoned by her husband. Having become a teacher, Burgos was elected to the presidency of the

International League of Iberian and Hispanoamerican Women. She was an outstanding advocate of **WOMEN'S RIGHTS**, above all through her writing. Not only did she publish a vast quantity of journalism both in Spain and Latin America (being the first Spanish female war correspondent in 1909), but also many books on women's issues under the pseudonym 'Colombine'.

**Burgos, Javier de** (1778–1849)
Spanish politician and administrative reformer. An adherent of enlightened despotism (rejecting liberalism as a political system), he was a founder of the conservative **MODERATE PARTY** in the 1830s. As a minister 1833–4, he replaced the powerful Council of Castile with a Ministry of the Interior and a Supreme Court. He also redrew the political geography of Spain into provinces.

**Burgoyne, John** (1723–92)
British general. He entered the army in 1740, and gave distinguished service in the **SEVEN YEARS' WAR** (1756–63). He then sat in parliament as a Tory, and in 1777 was sent to America, where he led an expedition from Canada, taking **FORT TICONDEROGA**, but being forced to surrender at Saratoga. He later joined the **WHIGS**, and commanded in Ireland (1782–3). ► **AMERICAN REVOLUTION; TORIES**

**Burgundy, House of**
A dynasty of French nobles, originating from the French royal family of Capet when **PHILIP THE BOLD**, the fourth son of King **JOHN II THE GOOD** of France, was made the first Duke in 1363. The family's possessions in French Burgundy were hardly more important than their holdings in the Low Countries, where the dukes began an expansion policy which continued apace throughout the 15c and early 16c. After the male line died out with the death of **CHARLES THE BOLD** in 1477, Burgundian possessions passed by marriage to the Austrian imperial house, which brought them under Habsburg control. The new leaders continued the consolidation of the Burgundian state in the Low Countries in the early 16c, which covered present-day Belgium, the Netherlands, and parts of northern France. In the 15c the court of the House of Burgundy was one of the major cultural centres of Europe, vying with France and England as the home of chivalry and art. ► **CAPETIAN DYNASTY; HABSBURG DYNASTY**

**Burgundy, Kingdom of and Duchy of**
The first Kingdom of Burgundy was a successor state of the Roman Empire in the 5c. Incorporated in the Carolingian Empire, it was divided by the Treaty of Verdun (843), and was then united with the Kingdom of Provence in the 10c. The dukes of Burgundy were some of the greatest vassals of the French monarchy, and frequently endeavoured to obtain at least *de facto* independence. They came closest to achieving this during the 15c as allies of the English during the **HUNDRED YEARS' WAR**, and under **CHARLES THE BOLD**, Duke of Burgundy (1467–77). The basis of Burgundian strength at this time was the dynastic marriages that had united Burgundy with Flanders, bringing the great wealth of the cities of the Netherlands to the dukes. However, the French monarchy retained its hold on Champagne, separating the two

parts of the ducal territory. The death of Charles the Bold in battle (1477) brought Burgundy back within the French kingdom.

**Burke, Edmund** (1729–97)
British politician and political philosopher. He began in 1750 to study law, but then took up literary work. His early writing includes his *Philosophical Inquiry into the Origin of our Ideas of the Sublime and Beautiful* (1756). He became Secretary for Ireland, and entered parliament in 1765. His main speeches and writings belong to the period when his party was opposed to Lord **NORTH**'s American policy (1770–82). His *Reflections on the French Revolution* (1790) was read all over Europe. ► **AMERICAN REVOLUTION; HASTINGS, WARREN**

**BURKINA FASO**   official name **Democratic Republic of Burkina Faso**, formerly (to 1984) **Upper Volta**

A landlocked republic in West Africa, bounded to the north and north-west by Mali; to the east by Niger; to the south east by Benin; to the south by Togo and Ghana; and to the south-west by the Côte d'Ivoire. It was part of the Mossi empire in the 18–19c before becoming a French protectorate in 1898. At first it was part of French Sudan (now **MALI**), then in 1919 it was made into Upper Volta. This was abolished in 1932, with most land incorporated into the Côte d'Ivoire. In 1947 its original borders were reconstituted, and in 1958 it gained autonomy within the French community, followed by independence as Upper Volta in 1960. It was renamed Burkina Faso in 1984. In the three decades following independence there were several military coups; the last in 1987 brought to power Blaise **COMPAORE**. Military rule ended in 1991 with multiparty elections which were won by the Popular Front and Compaoré, who was re-elected president in 1998 following an opposition boycott.

**Burlatsky, Fedor Mikhailovich** (1927– )
Soviet intellectual. Born in Kiev, he studied law and philosophy in Tashkent and Moscow, and went on to be an academic, journalist and political consultant in the 1950s and 1960s. Under a slight cloud in the 1970s, he transferred first to the Institute of State and Law, and then to the Institute of Social Sciences, where his work in political science and sociology prepared some of the ground for the 1980s. As a journalist and politician in Mikhail **GORBACHEV**'s time, he did much to propagate constitutional practices and to increase concern for Soviet human rights. He played a critical ideological role within the establishment from Nikita **KHRUSHCHEV** to Gorbachev.

**Burlingame Mission** (1868)
A Chinese official mission to the West led by the former US Minister to China, Anson Burlingame. With revision of the 1858 Treaty of Tianjin due in 1868, the Chinese government was anxious to dissuade Western governments from forcing the pace of westernization in China, and invited Burlingame to mediate on China's behalf. The mission first visited the USA, where Burlingame actually signed a treaty on his own authority with the US Secretary of State. The treaty committed the USA to a policy of non-interference in China and provided for reciprocal rights of residence, religion and travel. In London and Berlin, likewise, Burlingame extracted vague promises of restraint and moderation. While in St Petersburg, in Feb 1869, Burlingame died of pneumonia.

**Burma** ➤ MYANMAR

**Burma Campaigns** (1942–5)
The occupation of Burma (now Myanmar) in 1942 during WORLD WAR II was the result of Japanese invasion aided by the Burmese nationalist AUNG SAN, who had been persuaded by Japanese promises of independence to form the Burma Independence Army (BIA). After the capture of Rangoon, the 'BURMA ROAD', the only supply route between India and Nationalist China, was taken, and the British forces under General ALEXANDER retreated to the Indian border. From there they managed to halt the attempted Japanese invasion of Assam and northern India. In Oct 1944 British, Commonwealth, US and Chinese Nationalist forces combined to oust the Japanese from Burma and succeeded in re-opening the Burma Road. A year previously Aung San's disillusionment with the Japanese had led him to contact the Allied Commander in South-East Asia, Lord MOUNTBATTEN, to offer his support to the British, and in Mar 1945 his renamed Burma National Army joined the British side. The capture of Rangoon on 1 May 1945 by forces under William SLIM marked the final defeat of the Japanese in Burma.

**Burma Road**
A road linking the Burmese railhead at Lashio with Kunming, 700 mi/1,130 km distant in Yunnan province, China. Completed by the Chinese in 1938, it was of great strategic importance to the Allies during WORLD WAR II. ➤ BURMA CAMPAIGNS

**Burnham, (Linden) Forbes (Sampson)** (1923–85)
Guyanese politician. British-educated, Burnham represented the African element in the Guyanese population and was co-leader with JAGAN of the multiracial People's Progressive Party until 1955. In that year he split with Jagan over the latter's support for international COMMUNISM and set up a rival African-based party, the PEOPLE'S NATIONAL CONGRESS (PNC). The PNC slowly gained adherents in Jagan's troubled years after 1961, and in 1964 Burnham became Prime Minister. He negotiated an independence constitution in 1966 and in 1970 established Guyana as a 'cooperative socialist republic', remaining its President until his death.

**Burr, Aaron** (1756–1836)
US politician. Educated at Princeton and called to the Bar in 1782, he became state Attorney-General

(1789–91), then US Senator (1791–7) and Republican Vice-President (1801–5). His political career ended in 1804 when he killed his political rival Alexander HAMILTON in a duel. Thought to be conspiring to take Louisiana and establish it as an independent republic, he was tried for treason (1807) and acquitted. In 1812 he resumed his law practice in New York City, where he died.

**Bursa, Capture of** (1326)
The capture of the city by ORHAN for the Ottoman Turks, who were expanding their power in Anatolia not only at the expense of the Byzantines, but also that of other Turkish groups. Orhan's capture of Bursa took place shortly before the death of his father, OSMAN I, eponymous leader of the Osmanli (or Ottoman) Turks, whose holy city Bursa became. Bursa also became the capital of a *sanjaq* (subdivision of a province) placed initially under the control of 'Crown Prince' Murad, his father, Orhan, having succeeded to the leadership after the death of his own father.

**BURUNDI** official name **Republic of Burundi**

A small landlocked republic in central Africa, bounded to the north by Rwanda; to the east and south by Tanzania; to the south-west by Lake Tanganyika; and to the west by the Democratic Republic of the Congo. From the 16c the country was ruled by Tutsi kings who dominated a Hutu population. Today the population remains approximately 85 per cent Hutu and 14 per cent Tutsi. Germany annexed the area in 1890, and included it in German East Africa. After WORLD WAR I it became a LEAGUE OF NATIONS mandated territory, being administered by the Belgians from 1919. In 1946 it joined with Rwanda to become the UN Trust Territory of Ruanda–Urundi, but broke this union on gaining independence in 1962; it became a full republic in 1966. Civil war broke out in 1972 and there were military coups in 1976 and 1987. A multiparty constitution was adopted in 1992 which the following year saw the end of Tutsi dominance with the appointment of a Hutu head of state and a Hutu majority in the National Assembly. Soon after the election the President was killed in a coup by the Tutsi-dominated army, and his successor was killed when the plane in which he and the Rwandan President were travelling was shot down. These deaths sparked off fierce ethnic conflict which led to the loss of hundreds of thousands of lives and homes during the ensuing years. In 1996 the incumbent Hutu President was ousted by another military coup and Pierre Buyoya, a Tutsi, became head of the military junta and a multiethnic government was formed. Talks in 2001 agreed a ceasefire, which was not implemented, but rebel forces began to demobilize after further talks in 2004.

### Bush, George Herbert Walker (1924–)

US politician and 41st President. He served in the US Navy (1942–5) and after the war received a degree in economics from Yale and established an oil-drilling business in Texas. In 1966 he devoted himself to politics, and was elected to the **HOUSE OF REPRESENTATIVES**. Unsuccessful in his bid for the **SENATE** in 1970, he became US ambassador to the **UN**. During the **WATERGATE** scandal he was chairman of the Republican National Committee. Under President **FORD** he served as US envoy to China, and then became Director of the **CIA**. In 1980 he sought the Republican presidential nomination, but lost to Ronald **REAGAN**, later becoming his Vice-President. He became President in 1988, defeating the Democratic candidate, Governor Michael Dukakis of Massachusetts. As President, he focused on US foreign policy, which was changed most dramatically by the dissolution of the USSR, and he presided over the US-led UN coalition to defeat Iraq in the **GULF WAR**. In 1992 he failed to be re-elected, perhaps partly because of the perception that he had ignored US domestic issues.
► **BUSH, GEORGE WALKER**; **REPUBLICAN PARTY**

### Bush, George Walker (1946–)

US politician and 43rd President. Eldest son of President George H W **BUSH**, he received a degree in history from Yale and an MBA from Harvard Business School. In the 1970s he established an oil and gas firm in Texas, later selling it to an energy corporation. After involvement in his father's successful 1988 presidential campaign he purchased the Texas Rangers baseball franchise, serving as managing director. He was elected governor of Texas in 1994 and 1998, and in 1999 he became US President, defeating Democratic nominee Al Gore in a close and controversial election. His first term of office was characterized by increasing unilateralism in foreign affairs as his administration withdrew from the Kyoto Protocol, sought to exempt US citizens from the jurisdiction of the **INTERNATIONAL CRIMINAL COURT**, and abrogated the **ABM TREATY**. His domestic platform of 'compassionate conservatism' was all but swept away by increasing **NEOCONSERVATISM** following the **SEPTEMBER 11 ATTACKS** in 2001. He declared a 'war on **TERROR**', and in the following three years the USA and its allies fought the **AFGHAN WAR** (2001) and then the **IRAQ WAR** (2003). Bush was re-elected president in 2004, defeating Senator John Kerry by a narrow margin in a campaign dominated by issues of domestic conservatism and international security.

### Bush Doctrine

A reference to broad policies outlined by US President George W **BUSH** in a speech in Jun 2002. A response to the **SEPTEMBER 11 ATTACKS** and influenced by **NEOCONSERVATISM**, the key elements are the right of the USA to wage pre-emptive war against terrorists or 'rogue states' attempting to acquire weapons of mass destruction (**WMD**); the right of the USA to wage war unilaterally if no multilateral solution is acceptable to it; the pursuit of policies that support the current position of the USA as the sole global superpower; and the democratization of other regions and countries in the world.

### bushido

The Japanese notion of 'the way of the warrior'. The **SAMURAI** code until 1868, which taught personal loyalty to a master, death rather than capture/surrender, and stoic indifference to material goods. Like European knights, samurai rode into battle in **ARMOUR**. The bushido tradition is still seen in modern times, eg Japanese officers carried swords in **WORLD WAR II**.

### bushrangers

Australian rural outlaws who operated from 1790 to 1900. Concentrated in New South Wales, Victoria and Van Diemen's Land (Tasmania), the first bushrangers were ex-convicts (Donahoe in New South Wales, and Howe, Brady and Cash in Van Diemen's Land). The opportunities of the gold rushes led to a revival in the 1860s and 1870s. Products of a lawless frontier society, the gangs, which included Frank Gardiner, Ben **HALL** and Ned **KELLY**, relied heavily on the sympathy of the local poor settlers for whom they were symbols of resistance to a heavy-handed government. Immortalized in ballads, they became a central part of the mythology of the Australian past.

### Busia, Kofi (1913–78)

Ghanaian academic and politician. Educated in Kumasi and at Achimota College, he then obtained an external BA degree from London and a DPhil from Oxford. He was one of the first Africans to be appointed an administrative officer in the Gold Coast (Ghana). He resigned that position to become a lecturer, and later Professor of Sociology, at the University College of Ghana. Elected to Legco (1951), he became a leader of the National Liberation Movement (1954–9) in opposition to **NKRUMAH** and went into exile (1959–66), taking up the chair of sociology at Leiden University. After the 1966 coup, he returned as adviser to the National Liberation Council and then founded and led the Progress Party which won the 1969 election. He was Prime Minister (1969–72) before being overthrown in another coup, going into exile again in 1972. He held various academic posts and died in Oxford.

### Buss, Frances Mary (1827–94)

British pioneer of higher education of women. She founded the North London Collegiate School for Ladies, which became a model for the high schools of the Girls' Public Day Schools Company. She also campaigned for women to be admitted to university.

### Bustamante, Anastasio (1780–1853)

Mexican general and politician. He fought in the Spanish army against the revolutionists as early as 1808, but by 1821 supported **ITURBIDE** in the struggle for independence. He became Vice-President of the Republic under Vicente Guerrero in 1829, but entered into an alliance with **SANTA ANNA** and deposed Guerrero, becoming President of Mexico himself in 1830. Two years later he in turn was deposed by Santa Anna, but he later returned to the presidency proper in 1837–9, and nominally until 1841.

### Bustamante, Sir (William) Alexander, originally William Alexander Clarke (1884–1977)

Jamaican politician. The son of an Irish planter, he

## BYZANTINE EMPERORS

| Regnal Dates | Name | Regnal Dates | Name |
|---|---|---|---|
| 474/91 | Zeno | 1042/55 | Constantine IX |
| 475/6 | Basiliscus | 1055/6 | Theodora |
| 491/518 | Anastasius I | 1056/7 | Michael VI |
| 518/27 | Justin I | 1057/9 | Isaac I Comnenus |
| 527 (518)/65 | Justinian I, the Great | 1059/67 | Constantine X |
| 565/78 | Justin II | 1068/71 | Romanus IV |
| 578 (574)/82 | Tiberius II | 1071/8 | Michael VII |
| 582/602 | Maurice V | 1078/81 | Nicephorus III |
| 602/10 | Phocas I | 1081/1118 | Alexius I Comnenus |
| 610/41 | Heraclius | 1118/43 | John II Comnenus |
| 641 | Constantine III | 1143/80 | Manuel I Comnenus |
| 641 | Heracleon | 1180/3 | Alexius II Comnenus |
| 641/68 | Constans II | 1183/5 | Andronicus I Comnenus |
| 668/85 | Constantine IV | 1185/95 | Isaac II |
| 685/95 | Justinian II | 1195/1203 | Alexius III |
| 695/8 | Leontius | 1203/4 | Isaac II (restored) |
| 698/705 | Tiberius III | 1203/4 | Alexius IV |
| 705/11 | Justinian II (restored) | 1204 | Alexius V |
| 711/13 | Philippicus | *Latin Emperors* | |
| 713/15 | Anastasius II | 1204/5 | Baldwin I |
| 715/17 | Theodosius III | 1205/16 | Henry |
| 717/41 | Leo III | 1216/17 | Peter of Courtenay |
| 720/75 | Constantine V Copronymus | 1217/19 | Yolande |
| 775/80 | Leo IV | 1219/28 | Robert of Courtenay |
| 780/97 | Constantine VI Porphyrogenitus | 1228/61 | Baldwin II |
| 797/802 | Irene | 1231/7 | John of Brienne (co-emperor) |
| 802/11 | Nicephorus I | *Nicaean Emperors* | |
| 811 | Stauracius | 1204/22 | Theodore I Lascaris |
| 811/13 | Michael I | 1222/54 | John III |
| 813/20 | Leo V | 1254/8 | Theodore II Lascaris |
| 820/9 | Michael II | 1258/61 | John IV Lascaris |
| 829 (820)/42 | Theophilus I | 1259/61 | Michael VIII Palaeologus |
| 842/67 | Michael III | *Palaeologi* | |
| 867/886 | Basil I, the Macedonian | 1261 (1259)/82 | Michael VIII Palaeologus |
| 886/911 | Leo VI | 1282/1328 | Andronicus II |
| 912/13 | Alexander II | 1295/1320 | Michael IX (co-emperor) |
| 911/59 | Constantine VII Porphyrogenitus | 1328/41 | Andronicus III |
| 920/44 | Romanus I Lecapenus | 1341/7 | John V Palaeologus |
| 959/63 | Romanus II | 1347 (1341)/54 | John VI |
| 963 (976)/1025 | Basil II Bulgaroctonus | 1355/76 | John V (restored) |
| 963/9 | Nicephorus II Phocas | 1376/9 | Andronicus IV |
| 969/76 | John I Tzimisces | 1379/91 | John V (restored) |
| 1025 (976)/1028 | Constantine VIII | 1390 | John VII |
| 1028/50 | Zoë | 1391/1425 | Manuel II Palaeologus |
| 1028/34 | Romanus III | 1425/48 | John VIII |
| 1034/41 | Michael IV | 1448/53 | Constantine XI Palaeologus |
| 1041/2 | Michael V | | |

was adopted at the age of 15 by a Spanish seaman called Bustamante and spent an adventurous youth abroad before returning in 1932 to become a trade union leader. In 1943 he founded the JAMAICA LABOUR PARTY (JLP) as the political wing of his union and in 1962, the year Jamaica achieved independence, became its first Prime Minister. He was knighted in 1955.

**Bute, John Stuart, 3rd Earl of** (1713–92)
British politician. After early court appointments, he became a favourite of GEORGE III, who made him one of the principal Secretaries of State (1761). As Prime Minister (1762–3), his government was highly unpopular. Its principal objective was the supremacy of the royal prerogative, and he was soon forced to re-

sign. From 1768 his life was chiefly spent in the country, where he engaged in scientific study.

**Buthelezi, Chief Mangosuthu Gatsha** (1928– )
South African politician and Zulu leader. Expelled from Fort Hare University College in 1950, where he was a member of the ANC (African National Congress), he was a government interpreter in the Native Affairs Department (1951–7). Officially appointed as Chief of the Buthelezi tribe in 1957, he was also assistant to the Zulu King Cyprian (1953/68), before being elected leader of the Zulu Territorial Authority in 1970 and Chief Minister of KwaZulu in 1976, with the ANC's approval. He was sympathetic to the ANC's opposition to APARTHEID and he rejected the South African plan to turn Zululand into a 'bantustan' or

'homeland', but increasingly his readiness to work within the system and his Zulu nationalism distanced him from the radical forces of South Africa's opposition. At first refusing to participate in the 1994 election, he lifted the boycott a week before polling day when agreement was reached that the Kingdom of Zululand would be recognized in the constitution. He was Minister of Home Affairs in South Africa from 1994 to 2004. He founded, and remains President of, the INKATHA FREEDOM PARTY.

### Butler, Benjamin F(ranklin) (1818–93)
US politician, lawyer and general. He graduated from Waterville College, Maine, and was admitted to the Bar in 1840, becoming a criminal lawyer. In the AMERICAN CIVIL WAR, he and his troops took possession of New Orleans (1862), where they crushed all opposition. Elected to CONGRESS in 1866, he was prominent in the Republican efforts for the reconstruction of the Southern states and in the IMPEACHMENT of President JOHNSON. He was Governor of Massachusetts (1882–4), and unsuccessfully ran (as the candidate for the Greenback Party) for President in 1884. ➤ GREENBACK; RECONSTRUCTION

### Butler, R(ichard) A(usten) Butler, Baron (1902–82)
British politician. He became Conservative MP for Saffron Walden in 1929. After a series of junior ministerial appointments, he became Minister of Education (1941–5), introducing the forward-looking Education Act of 1944, and then Minister of Labour (1945). He became Chancellor of the Exchequer (1951), Lord Privy Seal (1955), Leader of the House of COMMONS (1955), Home Secretary (1957), First Secretary of State and Deputy Prime Minister (1962). He narrowly lost the premiership to Alec Douglas-Home in 1963, and became Foreign Secretary (1963–4). He was appointed Master of Trinity College, Cambridge (1965–78), and was made a life peer. ➤ BUTSKELLISM; CONSERVATIVE PARTY (UK); HOME OF THE HIRSEL, BARON

### Butler, Uriah 'Buzz' (1897–1977)
Grenadian-born politician and labour leader. In 1921 he emigrated to Trinidad to work in the oilfields. An industrial accident in 1929 led him towards the Moravian Baptist Church and organized labour, and in 1935 he broke with CIPRIANI's Trinidad Labour Party (TLP) and set up the British Empire and Citizens' Home Rule and Workers' Party. In 1937 his fiery oratory whipped up agitation in the oilfields, and an attempt to arrest him at Fyzabad led to rioting and several deaths at Port Fortin. Interned for sedition in WORLD WAR II, he returned to politics in 1945, but by then was a spent force.

### Butskellism
A compound of the names of British Conservative politician R A BUTLER and the Labour leader Hugh GAITSKELL, used in the 1950s and early 1960s to imply a high degree of similarity between the policies

of the two main parties. 'Mr Butskell' was first referred to in The Economist (Feb 1954).

### Buyids or Buwayhids
A twelver or imami Shiite grouping from Daylam, which lies just south of the Caspian Sea in what is now Iran. Obtaining control of much of the central Islamic lands, they achieved control of Baghdad in 945 while allowing the Sunni 'Abbasid caliph to retain his position. This gave rise to the anomalous situation of an 'Abbasid caliph's being forced to surrender secular control to twelver Shiites while himself having to be content with what was not much more under the circumstances than the relatively empty prestige of his position. Eventually declining into a group of squabbling princelings, the Buyids were ousted in the mid-11c by the Sunni Great SELJUKS (Turks who had migrated from Central Asia) who restored Sunni secular control in Baghdad. For all their differences and difficulties, however, Buyid rule saw great advances in learning and scholarship, and private patronage of scholars was encouraged.

### Byng, George, 1st Viscount Torrington (1663–1733)
English sailor. He joined the navy at 15 and gained rapid promotion as a supporter of William of Orange. Made rear-admiral in 1703, he captured Gibraltar, and was knighted for his gallant conduct at Malaga. In 1708 he defeated the French fleet of James STUART, the Old Pretender, and in 1718 destroyed the Spanish fleet off Messina. He was created viscount in 1721. ➤ WILLIAM III, OF ORANGE

### Byng, John (1704–57)
English sailor. He was the fourth son of George BYNG, 1st Viscount Torrington. He joined the navy at 14 and was rapidly promoted, becoming admiral in 1756. For his failure to relieve Minorca, blockaded by a French fleet, and for retreating to Gibraltar, he was found guilty of neglect of duty and shot at Portsmouth.

### Byng of Vimy, Julian Hedworth George Byng, 1st Viscount (1862–1935)
British general. He commanded the 9th Army Corps in the GALLIPOLI CAMPAIGN (1915), the Canadian Army Corps (1916–17), and the 3rd Army (1917–18). After WORLD WAR I he became Governor-General of Canada (1921–6) and Commissioner of the Metropolitan Police (1928–31), and was made a viscount in 1928 and a field marshal in 1932.

### Byzantine Empire
The eastern half of the Roman Empire, with its capital at Constantinople (founded AD330), formerly Byzantium. The Eastern Roman Empire survived the collapse of the Western Empire by nearly a thousand years, only falling to the Ottoman Turks in 1453, when Constantinople was taken. ➤ See table

## Cabal

An acronym taken from the initials of the five leading advisers of **CHARLES II** of England between 1667 and 1673: **C**lifford, **A**rlington, **B**uckingham, **A**shley Cooper (Shaftesbury) and **L**auderdale. The name is misleading, since these five were by no means Charles's only advisers; nor did they agree on a common policy. Arlington and Buckingham were bitter rivals. ➤ **ARLINGTON, HENRY BENNET, 1ST EARL OF**; **BUCKINGHAM, GEORGE VILLIERS, 2ND DUKE OF**; **LAUDERDALE, JOHN MAITLAND, DUKE OF**; **SHAFTESBURY, ANTHONY ASHLEY COOPER, 1ST EARL OF**

## cabildo

A Spanish (specifically Castilian) municipal council, transplanted to colonial Spanish America during the 16c. Its members were usually appointed by the colonial authorities, but membership was often bought and sold. It declined in power during the 17c, but during the later 18c re-emerged as a focus for **CREOLE** assertiveness against Spanish centralizing designs.

## Cabinet

The group of ministers in charge of the various departments of government who meet regularly for discussion with the Prime Minister. In Britain (where cabinet government originated in the 17c), although it has no constitutional status, the cabinet forms a link between the executive and legislative branches of government, as its members must be drawn from the legislature. Members are bound by the doctrine of collective responsibility, ie ministers must publicly support decisions or resign. A cabinet may also be found in non-parliamentary systems, such as the USA, where it provides the President with an additional consultative body.

## Cabot, John, originally Giovanni Caboto (c.1450–c.1500)

Italian navigator and explorer, the discoverer of mainland North America. Born in Genoa, he moved to England and settled in Bristol around 1490. In 1497 under letters patent from King **HENRY VII**, he sailed from Bristol with two ships in search of a route to Asia, accompanied by his three sons. On 24 June, after 52 days at sea, he sighted land (probably Cape Breton Island, Nova Scotia), and claimed North America for England. He is thought to have made further voyages in search of the Northwest Passage, and after setting out in 1498, died at sea.

## Cabral, Amilcar (1924–73)

Guinean nationalist leader. Educated at Lisbon University, he worked as an agronomist and agricultural engineer for the colonial authorities. He founded the PAIGC in 1956 and, after abortive constitutional discussions with the Portuguese government, initiated a revolutionary war in 1963. Noted for his commitment to politicizing the peasantry and establishing alternative institutions in liberated territories, he presided over a successful war that forced the Portuguese to concede independence. He was murdered in 1973 just as his aim was being achieved.

## Cabral, Luís de Almeida (1931–)

Guinea-Bissau nationalist leader. The brother of Amilcar **CABRAL**, he was educated in Portuguese Guinea and became a clerk and a trade union organizer. As a member of the PAIGC, he went into exile in 1960 and took part in the guerrilla struggle to win independence for Guinea-Bissau. Success made him President of the new Republic (1974–80), but he was then overthrown in a coup.

## Cabrera, Ramón (1810–77)

Spanish Carlist general and political figure. He was the leader of the Carlists in 1833–40 and 1848–9. In 1839 Don **CARLOS** created him Count of Morella in recognition of his resounding victory there the previous year against forces loyal to **ISABELLA II**. Cabrera died at Wentworth near Staines, having married a wealthy English lady.

## cacique

Originally a Caribbean Indian word meaning 'chief', the term was adapted and applied in 19c Spain to the local powerholders or bosses whose influence generally derived from their economic power, which was invariably rooted in their ownership of land. After the Restoration of 1875, the *caciques'* role as intermediaries of the state became institutionalized. They controlled political life by fixing elections so that the Liberal and Conservative parties rotated in power in a pre-arranged manner, otherwise known as the *turno pacífico* ('peaceful rotation'). The caciques thereby became the cornerstone of the **RESTORATION SYSTEM**. This fraudulent parliamentary system survived until the establishment of the dictatorship of General **PRIMO DE RIVERA** in 1923. Although the monarchist parties were disbanded by the dictatorship, the socioeconomic power of the caciques often remained intact. Consequently, under the Second Republic of 1931–6 they proved a redoubtable obstacle to the implementation of the democratic and progressive reforms envisaged by the new regime. ➤ **REPUBLIC, SECOND** (Spain)

## Cade, Jack (d.1450)

Irish leader of the insurrection of 1450 against **HENRY VI** of England. After an unsettled early career he lived in Sussex, possibly as a physician. Assuming the name of Mortimer, and the title of Captain of Kent, he marched on London with a great number of followers, and entered the city. A promise of pardon sowed dissension among the insurgents; they dispersed, and a price was set upon Cade's head. He attempted to reach the coast, but was killed near Heathfield, Sussex.

**Cadorna, Luigi** (1850–1928)
Italian general. Commander-in-Chief of the Italian Army from 1914, he held the Austrian forces successfully from the outbreak of war in Mar 1915 until the the disastrous defeat of the Battle of CAPORETTO, after which he was replaced by the more flexible DÍAZ.

**Cadoudal, Georges** (1771–1804)
French insurgent. A miller's son from Auray, Lower Brittany, from 1793 to 1800 he led the royalist CHOUANS against the republicans. He was guillotined for conspiring, with PICHEGRU, against NAPOLEON I.

**Caetano, Marcelo** (1906–80)
Portuguese politician and academic. The son of a schoolteacher, Caetano had a meteoric rise during the counter-revolution following the First Republic. He played a key judicial role in the establishment of the ESTADO NOVO. From 1944 to 1947 he was Minister of the Colonies, and from 1955 until 1958 Deputy Prime Minister. Extrovert, ambitious and less submissive than other ministers, in 1951 Caetano had attempted to replace SALAZAR as Prime Minister. Yet in 1968 he was chosen as Salazar's successor as one of the most notable figures in Estado Novo politics. From 1969 to 1971 he liberalized the country in certain respects, but there was no promise of a liberal democracy; he was simply too closely identified with the authoritarian regime to execute authentic liberalization. Enormous discontent within the army over the costly and militarily unsuccessful 13-year war waged in Portuguese Africa against independence movements led to the bloodless coup of 25 Apr 1974 which, in its turn, resulted in the revolution of 1974–5. He died in exile in Brazil. ▶ REPUBLIC, FIRST (Portugal)

**Cai Chang (Ts'ai Ch'ang)** (1900–90)
Chinese revolutionary and women's leader. The younger sister of Cai Hesen (1890–1931), friend and colleague of MAO ZEDONG, she went to France in 1919 on a work-study scheme. She returned to China in 1924 after further study in Moscow. During 1924–6 she helped organize women textile workers in Shanghai and was Head of the Women's Department in Mao Zedong's JIANGXI SOVIET from 1931 to 1934. At the Seventh National Congress of the Chinese Communist Party in 1945, Cai Chang was the sole woman elected to full membership of the Central Committee. With the establishment of the People's Republic in 1949, Cai Chang founded and led the All-China Federation of Democratic Women.

**Caillaux, Joseph** (1863–1944)
French radical politician. He was several times Finance Minister (1899–1902, 1906–9, 1911, 1913–14 and 1925), unsuccessfully advocating a progressive income tax. As Prime Minister (1911–12), he negotiated the treaty with Germany, following the AGADIR Incident, by which France was given a free hand to subjugate Morocco and to turn it into a protectorate. He was attacked for being too ready to conciliate Germany, and was arrested in 1918 on a charge of contacting the enemy. Tried by the Senate, acting as a special High Court, he was sentenced in 1920 to three years' imprisonment, and to loss of political rights. Amnestied in 1925, he resumed his political career in the influential post of President of the Finance Committee of the Senate, and as one of the leading elder statesmen of the RADICAL PARTY. In 1914 his second wife shot and killed Gaston Calmette, editor of Le Figaro, who had published letters written to her by Caillaux while he was married to his first wife; she was acquitted after a sensational trial.

**Cairo Conference** (1921)
Convened by Winston CHURCHILL, this conference had as its objective the consideration of the many problems afflicting the Middle East, particularly those thrown up by WORLD WAR I. Discussions covered such questions as defence in the area and the treatment of the Iraqi KURDS (on which no decision was reached), but perhaps the most important result (if not actual decision) of the conference was the emergence of two Hashemite rulers: the King of Iraq and the Amir of Transjordan. The latter subsequently became King of Jordan after the creation of the State of Israel and the addition to the former Transjordan of the WEST BANK and the Old City of Jerusalem.

**Cairo Conference** (1943)
A meeting held between Winston CHURCHILL and ROOSEVELT which was attended by CHIANG KAI-SHEK. Chiang was anxious that the allies continue to support the war effort in China at a time when they were considering inviting STALIN to bring the USSR into the PACIFIC WAR and whether to concentrate on capturing the Pacific Islands (from where Japan might be bombed rather than from Chinese airfields). Both developments would render the China Theatre marginal. Chiang was handicapped by both Anglo-American differences over strategy and by Roosevelt's increasing hostility to Chiang's regime, which was seen as hopelessly corrupt. The Cairo Conference was a significant turning-point in Washington's policy towards Chiang Kai-shek, hitherto considered a crucial actor in the war against Japan. Chiang did not receive the assurances he desired, while later in the same year Stalin pledged to enter the war in return for privileges in Manchuria.

**Cai Yuanpei (Ts'ai Yuan-p'ei)** (1868–1940)
Chinese educator, scholar and politician. One of the youngest candidates ever to obtain the highest degree in the classical CIVIL SERVICE EXAMINATION SYSTEM, Cai taught in various schools and colleges in his home province of Zhejiang and in Shanghai. He joined SUN YAT-SEN's anti-Manchu republican movement and in 1911 became the first Minister of Education of the new Chinese Republic, presiding over the creation of a new school system. Although he resigned in 1912, Cai continued to be active in educational affairs, helping to promote a work-study programme for Chinese students in France and assuming the chancellorship of Beijing University in 1916. He encouraged free debate and scholarship at the university, transforming it into one of the country's foremost intellectual centres. He later became a

# *Calendar*

*Culture & Society*

The calendar in general use throughout the world is the Gregorian New Style calendar, developed from the one in use in the Roman Republic.

Forms of calendar developed independently in different places, their organization being based on information provided by astronomers. In societies where astronomical skills were well developed, the calendar system was complex and worked well, usually combining a lunar and a solar calendar. In China the solar year of $365\frac{1}{4}$ days, divided into 12 lunar months of $29\frac{1}{2}$ days, was the accepted framework, with an occasional intercalation of a thirteenth month to deal with the discrepancy. The advanced astronomical abilities of the Chinese enabled them to adopt a meteorological 24-point cycle in the 3c BC, which they considered a *yin-yangli* or lunar-solar calendar, and it remained in use, despite the introduction of Hindu, Muslim and Gregorian calendars, until 1912.

The Indian classical calendar was based on the sun for purposes of astrology, but the lunar one was necessary for the sacred calendar. In the 6c AD the practice of dating years relative to the revolutions of the orbit of Jupiter was introduced, introducing a 60-year cycle. In recent times the National Calendar of India was introduced in 1957, using Gregorian dates alongside the Saka era calendar (calculated from AD 78, each year beginning on 22 Mar, or 21 Mar in a leap year). Other calendars in use include the Vikrama era calendar (calculated from 58 BC) and the Kalacuri era calendar (calculated from AD 248).

The calendars in use in the **pre-Columbian civilizations** had a common organization, and probably originated with the Olmec. The Maya had a divination calendar of 260 days, as well as a solar calendar of 365 days. The solar year was divided into 18 named months of 20 days, with 5 extra days of ill omen. The years were grouped into 52-year cycles. There were no year names but each day in the 52-year cycle was identified by a unique number. They also used a continuous count from a base date, the 'Long Count'. Their system was extremely accurate. The Aztec calendar was similar, but with less precision in date recording. Both calendars contained special days for religious celebration and sacrifice.

The Muslim calendar is calculated from the *Hegira* (the year Muhammad migrated from Mecca to Medina, and the beginning of the Muslim era) in AD 622. Still used by Muslims for religious purposes, it has 12 lunar months, with no intercalations.

The Jewish religious calendar dates in its modern form from the Babylonian Exile in the 6c BC, when the Jews adopted the Babylonian calendar. This was lunar-solar, with a lunar year of 354 days and a solar year (important to agriculture) of 365 days. By the 4c BC an accurate system of intercalation had been devised. Each month starts with the new moon, but each day begins at sunset. These features were retained in the Jewish calendar. The seven-day week was always an important feature because of the observance of the Sabbath. The year count of the Jewish era is calculated from 3761 BC, said to be the year of the creation of the world.

An attempt to move the organization of the calendar away from all religious connections was made by the French Revolutionary government with the declaration of the **French Republican Calendar**, beginning on 22 Sep 1792, the day of the proclamation of the Republic (and the autumnal equinox of that year). There were 12 30-day months, renamed to be appropriate to the season, each month divided into three periods of 10 days (*decadi*). The calendar worked well enough in France but caused problems for international communications, and **Napoleon I** replaced it with the Gregorian calendar in 1805.

The development of the calendar in the Western world incorporated the knowledge of the early civilizations. The Persian kings made the Babylonian calendar standard throughout their empire. In Egypt, the incompatibility of solar and lunar systems had been solved by using the solar calendar of 365 days (with 5 days extra at the end) for government and business, and the lunar calendar for religious affairs. The discrepancy between the two systems was solved by the intercalation of a month every 25 years. The hours were of uneven length, depending on the season, for the day began at sunrise.

The Greeks also used a dual calendar. They had one form for the civil year, and one for the agricultural; some documents were dated with both forms.

The first Roman calendar (10 months) was supposedly drawn up by Romulus. Tarquinius Priscus (617–579 BC)

---

member of the **GUOMINDANG**, but became increasingly critical of the party's suppression of free speech. He died in Hong Kong.

**Calas Affair** (1762)
A famous miscarriage of justice in Toulouse, publicized by Voltaire. A Protestant merchant, Jean Calas, whose son had committed suicide, was accused of having killed him because he wished to convert to Catholicism. He was executed in 1762, but posthumously rehabilitated in 1765 after Voltaire's campaign; the affair did much to discredit the **ANCIEN RÉGIME** in France.

**Calatrava, Order of**
One of the military orders founded in **CASTILE** during the **RECONQUEST**. It was founded in 1155, with a red cross as its symbol, and came to possess extensive

estates (*encomiendas*), numbering 51 in 1616. Members were in theory subject to semi-monastic discipline. From 1523 the crown of Spain became, with papal permission, head of the orders. ► **ENCOMIENDA**

**Calendar** ► *See panel*

**Calhoun, John Caldwell** (1782–1850)
US politician. He graduated from Yale (1804), studied law, then entered politics, becoming Secretary of War (1817), Vice-President under John Quincy **ADAMS** and **JACKSON** (1825–32), and Secretary of State under **TYLER**. He is best known for his 'nullification' theory (1828), in which he argued that states have the right to nullify laws they considered unconstitutional. He later entered the **SENATE**, where he championed the interests of the slave-holding states.

instituted the Roman republican calendar of 12 months (355 days), beginning in Mar. An intercalation was supposed to occur in Feb every second year, but the pontifices, whose duty it was to regulate the calendar, were incompetent and corrupt, and allowed the length of the year to fluctuate to suit their friends and masters. By 46 BC there was seasonal chaos and calendrical confusion. Julius Caesar enlisted the services of Sosigenes, an Alexandrian astronomer, to reform the calendar. This was achieved by two intercalations in that year, a total addition of 67 days. As a result, in the next year the day that would have marked the middle of Mar in the old Roman calendar fell instead on 1 Jan. To prevent a recurrence of the problem, Sosigenes suggested an addition of a day to the end of Feb every fourth year. This Julian calendar remained in effect until the 16c, and Julius Caesar's name was added to the list of months, replacing Quintilius. The calendar had to be corrected again by Augustus in 8 BC, as the pontifices had been intercalating every three years instead of four. His name replaced Sextilis, giving the months as they are now known. There was no division into weeks, and days were designated working days and non-working days. The days of the month were numbered in relation to the Kalendae, Nonae and Ides of each month. With the acceptance of Christianity by the Roman Empire, a seven-day week was necessary to enable observance of the Lord's Day. This was instituted by Constantine I in the 4c AD.

The Julian calendar had a shortcoming in that the value of $365\frac{1}{4}$ days placed on the solar year was too long by 11 min and 14 seconds. By 1545 the vernal equinox, used by the Church to determine the date of Easter (tied by historical events to the Passover), had moved 10 days. It took time for astronomers to work out a satisfactory method of correction, but finally Pope **Gregory XIII** issued a bull instructing that 10 days should be omitted from Oct in 1582. At the same time the rule for intercalation of leap years was formulated, dictating that only centennial years divisible by 400 should be leap years. Rules were also laid out for the calculation of the date of Easter, resolving a long controversy.

A Church calendar had been drawn up in the 6c by the theologian and astronomer Dionysius Exiguus (d.556). He had also introduced the concept of numbering years consecutively from the birth of Christ, a practice popularized by the Venerable Bede (673–735). This method of numbering accentuated the discrepancies brought about when some countries adopted the New Style (Gregorian) calendar while others retained the Old Style (Julian). In the main the New Style was adopted almost at once by European Roman Catholic countries: France, Italy, Luxembourg, Portugal, Spain, Belgium and some of the German states. Most Protestant countries did not follow suit until 100 years later. Britain adopted the New Style in 1752; by that time the difference between the two styles was 11 days. Japan adopted the New Style in 1873, Egypt in 1875, China in 1912 and Greece in 1923. The adoption of this style also meant the acceptance of 1 Jan as the beginning of the year. Although for Egyptians, Phoenicians and Persians the year had begun with the autumn equinox, and the Jews started their year in autumn, the New Year had begun at the spring equinox in the Babylonian Empire, and in Mar in Rome. 1 Jan was decreed as the start of the New Year by the Julian calendar, but the medieval West began the year on 25 Mar (the festival of the Annunciation). The worldwide use of a calendar for state and business purposes was an evident necessity. However, religious calendars remained differentiated, with traditional New Year being celebrated at different times in China, India, South-East Asia and parts of Japan.

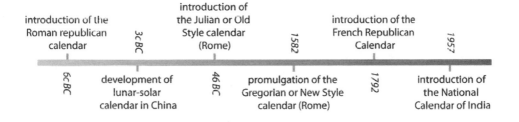

## Caliphate

The term caliph (*khalifa*), literally meaning 'successor', came to be applied to successive rulers of the Islamic state after the death of Muhammad. As an institution, it evolved slowly through the periods of the so-called Orthodox caliphs (632–61), the Umayyad Dynasty (661–750) and the **'ABBASID DYNASTY** (750–1258). Succession was always a problem in Islam as, according to the **SUNNIS**, Muhammad had made no explicit provision for a successor. The first definitive attempt to lay down qualifications for being caliph was made by al-Mawardi in his *al-Ahkam al-Sultaniyya* ('Ordinances of Government'), significantly during a period of Shiite (Buyid) control of the central Islamic lands, and is effectively a back-projection designed to bolster the position of the Sunni caliph then forced to accept Shiite secular rule,

the main qualification being that any caliph should be (however remote) a member of the Meccan tribe of Quraysh. ► **SHIITES**

**Calixtus II**, originally **Guy de Bourgogne** (d.1124) Pope (1119/24). Formerly Count of Burgundy and Archbishop of Vienne. In 1121 he overcame the anti-pope Burdinus (Gregory VIII), who was supported by the German Emperor **HENRY V**, and in 1122 concluded with Henry the Concordat of **WORMS**, which settled the **INVESTITURE CONTROVERSY**.

**Callaghan, (Leonard) James ('Jim'), Baron Callaghan of Cardiff** (1912–2005)
British politician. After a secondary education, he joined the Civil Service (1929), and in 1945 was elected Labour MP for South Cardiff. As Chancellor of the Exchequer under **WILSON** (1964–7), he intro-

duced the controversial corporation and selective employment taxes. He was Home Secretary (1967–70) and Foreign Secretary (1974–6), and became Prime Minister (1976–9) on Wilson's resignation. He resigned as Leader of the Opposition in 1980 and retired from Parliament in 1987, when he was made a life peer. ► **LABOUR PARTY** (UK)

**Calles, Plutarco Elías** (1877–1945)
Mexican politician. An ex-schoolmaster, he became Governor of Sonora (1917), and President of Mexico (1924–8). Anticlerical, he challenged the pretensions of the Church, implementing the 1917 constitution and provoking the **CRISTERO REVOLT**; he dominated the presidency until 1934, enhancing the power of the state, creating the PNR but limiting agrarian reform. Defeated by his protégé, **CÁRDENAS**, he was exiled to the USA, but was allowed to return in 1941.

**Calonne, Charles Alexandre de** (1734–1802)
French politician. In 1783 he was made Controller-General of Finance. In 1786 he advised King **LOUIS XVI** to convoke the Assembly of Notables, and distribute the burden of taxation more equally. In opening the Assembly (1787), he described the general prosperity of France, but confessed that the annual deficit of the treasury had risen to 115 million francs, and that during 1776–86 the government had borrowed 1,250 millions. The Notables demanded a statement of accounts; failing to satisfy them, he was banished to Lorraine. After this, he resided chiefly in England, until in 1802 **NAPOLEON I** permitted him to return. ► **NOTABLES, ASSEMBLIES OF THE**

**Calvert, George, 1st Baron Baltimore** (c.1580–1632)
English colonialist. He held high offices in the government, including Secretary of State (1619–25), before declaring himself a Roman Catholic in 1625 and resigning his post. That year he was created Baron Baltimore in the Irish peerage, and retired to his Irish estates. In 1627 he visited Newfoundland, where he possessed a land grant and where he had sent colonists six years before; severe winters prompted him to sail south to Virginia in 1629. His right to found a colony there was disputed, and he returned to England to obtain a fresh charter. In 1632 **CHARLES I** granted him the territory that eventually became Maryland; his goal was to create a sanctuary for practising Catholics, but he died before the colony's charter was accepted. The patent passed to his son, Cecil Calvert (1605–75), who established the Maryland colony. Leonard Calvert (1606–47), Cecil's younger brother, became Maryland's first governor (1634–47).

**Calvin, John** (1509–64)
French Protestant reformer. He studied Latin at Paris, then law at Orléans, where he developed his interest in theology. In Bourges and other centres, he began to preach the reformed doctrines, but he was forced to flee from France to escape persecution. At Basle he issued his influential *Christianae Religionis Institutio* (1536), and at Geneva was persuaded by Guillaume **FAREL** to help with the **REFORMATION**. The reformers proclaimed a Protestant Confession of Faith, under which moral severity took the place of licence. When a rebellious party, the Libertines, rose against this,

Calvin and Farel were expelled from the city (1538). Calvin withdrew to Strasbourg, where he worked on New Testament criticism, and married. In 1541 the Genevans recalled him, and he founded a theocracy which controlled almost all the city's affairs. By 1555 his authority was confirmed into an absolute supremacy. The father figure of Reformed theology, he left a double legacy to Protestantism by systematizing its doctrine and organizing its ecclesiastical discipline. His commentaries, which embrace most of the Old and New Testaments, were collected and published in 1617. ► **BASLE, COUNCIL OF**

**Calvo Sotelo, José** (1893–1936)
Spanish politician. Under the dictator **PRIMO DE RIVERA**, he was made the Director-General of Local Government, introducing the stillborn Municipal Statute in 1924. He was also a controversial Minister of Finance, attempting to overhaul the tax system (only to be thwarted by the banks) and creating state monopolies, in particular the petroleum company CAMPSA. His much-criticized monetary policies contributed to the regime's fall. He went into exile on the advent of the Second Republic in 1931, returning with the amnesty of 1934. Having founded the totalitarian National Bloc, he soon became the most powerful civilian figure on the extreme right. His assassination on 13 July 1936 triggered off the military rising that led to the **SPANISH CIVIL WAR**. ► **REPUBLIC, SECOND** (Spain)

**Camacho, Marcelino** (1918–2004)
Spanish trade union leader. He joined the Communist Party in 1934 and fought for the Republicans in the **SPANISH CIVIL WAR**. Jailed by the Nationalists, he escaped to French Morocco and then Algeria, where he earned his living as a millwright (1944–57). An amnesty in 1957 allowed him to return to Spain and during the 1960s he rose within the clandestine Workers' Commissions (**CCOO**), becoming the leading trade union leader in Spain by the early 1970s. For most of the period 1967–75 he was in jail. He was a Communist Party Deputy (1977–82) as well as being a member of the Party's Central Committee. Following the communists' dismal showing in 1982, he was one of those who pressed **CARRILLO** to resign. In 1987 he retired as Secretary-General of the CCOO, but remained its Honorary President.

**Cambacérès, Jean Jacques Régis de** (1753–1824)
French lawyer. A member of the National **CONVENTION**, he voted for the pursuit of the **GIRONDINS**, but then effaced himself during the Reign of **TERROR**, resuming a prominent role under the **DIRECTORY** and the **CONSULATE**. He became Archchancellor of the First French Empire (1804) and Duke of Parma (1808). As **NAPOLEON I**'s chief legal adviser, his civil code formed the basis of the **CODE NAPOLÉON**. ► **EMPIRE, FIRST** (France)

**Cambaluc**
The westernized term, popularized by Marco **POLO**, for *Khanbalikh* (Turkish, 'City of the Khan'), the capital **KUBLAI KHAN** built on the site of present-day Beijing. Also known as *Ta-tu* (in Chinese) and *Dadu* (in Mongol), the city was constructed between 1266 and 1272 and served as the capital of the Mongol empire. By transferring his capital from Kharakorum

(Qaraqorum) in the Mongol heartland to north China, Kublai Khan demonstrated his commitment to China, hoping thereby to gain the acceptance of Chinese élites. In order to ensure grain supplies from the south, Kublai Khan extended the Grand Canal to his new capital.

**Cambó, Francesc** (1876–1947)
Catalan politician. The leader of conservative Catalan nationalists, he was a businessman and banker, who founded with Enric **PRAT DE LA RIBA** the *Lliga Regionalista* in 1901. As a middleman for foreign companies, he became the most prominent self-made businessman of that period. His overriding political objective was to establish the Catalan bourgeoisie as the ruling class in Spain. To this end, he attempted to organize a nationwide movement for political reform, but the general strike of 1917 led him to change course. From this time on, he was closely allied to the central ruling oligarchy, joining the 'National Government' of Antonio **MAURA** in 1918 as Minister of Economic Development and remaining in government until Mar 1922. During the Second Republic he relaunched the **LLIGA** (as the *Lliga Catalana*), but his oligarchical nationalism was overshadowed throughout by the Catalan Left. He spent the **SPANISH CIVIL WAR** in Italy, thereafter living in Argentina until his death. ► **REPUBLIC, SECOND** (Spain)

**CAMBODIA** official name **Kingdom of Cambodia**, formerly (1979–89) **People's Republic of Kampuchea**, and (1976–9) **Democratic Kampuchea**, and (1970–6) **Khmer Republic**

A republic in southern Indochina, South-East Asia, bounded to the north-west by Thailand; to the north by Laos; to the east by Vietnam; and to the south and south-west by the Gulf of Thailand. Originally part of the Kingdom of Funan, it was taken over by the Khmers in the 6c. From the 15c it was in dispute with the Vietnamese and the Thais. In 1863 it was established as a French Protectorate, and it became part of **INDOCHINA** in 1887. It gained independence from France in 1953, with Prince **SIHANOUK** as Prime Minister. In 1970 Sihanouk was deposed, a right-wing government was formed, and the country was renamed the Khmer Republic. Fighting throughout the country involved troops from North and South Vietnam and the USA. In 1975 Phnom Penh surrendered to the **KHMER ROUGE**, a communist guerrilla force which opposed the government, and the following year the republic of Democratic Kampuchea was proclaimed. An attempt to reform the economy on co-operative lines and the introduction of an extreme and brutal regime by **POL POT** in 1975–8 caused the deaths of an estimated 2.5 million people. There was

further fighting in 1977–8, and Phnom Penh was captured by the Vietnamese in 1979, causing the Khmer Rouge to flee. The Vietnamese immediately established a government in Cambodia led by **HENG SAMRIN**, but fighting with the Khmer Rouge guerrillas continued. In 1983 an anti-Vietnamese government-in-exile (the Coalition Government of Democratic Kampuchea) was recognized by the **UN**. Unrest continued until 1987. A peace conference in Paris in 1988–9 between the Phnom Penh regime, the opposition coalition led by Prince Sihanouk, and the Khmer Rouge ended without agreement. In 1989 the name of Cambodia was restored and Vietnamese troops completed their withdrawal. A UN peace plan was agreed in 1991, and in 1992 a UN Transitional Authority in Cambodia was planned. The Khmer Rouge refused to comply, and UN trade sanctions were imposed in 1993. Also in 1993 a new constitution was adopted and multiparty elections took place. In the new democratic monarchy, Prince Sihanouk became king, his son Prince Norodom Ranariddh was appointed Prime Minister, and Hun Sen became second Prime Minister. The Khmer Rouge continued to launch attacks until 1996, when internal divisions caused it to weaken; Pol Pot died in Apr 1998, and the remaining Khmer Rouge surrendered in Feb 1999. Meanwhile the ruling coalition suffered divisions; in 1997 Hun Sen and his armed supporters ousted Prince Ranariddh. Following disputed elections in 1998, Hun Sen became Prime Minister; he was re-elected in 2004. In Apr 1999 Cambodia was admitted to the **ASSOCIATION OF SOUTH-EAST ASIAN NATIONS**. King Sihanouk abdicated in Oct 2004 in favour of his son, Norodom Sihamoni.

**Cambrai, League of**
An alliance, formed in 1508, as a result of Pope **JULIUS II**'s schemes to reduce the power of the Venetians and acquire their possessions in Romagna, the league included Emperor **MAXIMILIAN I, LOUIS XII** and **FERDINAND II, THE CATHOLIC**. It succeeded in the destruction of the Venetian army at the Battle of Agnadello (14 May 1509), although the Venetians subsequently recovered their territories as the victors quarrelled amongst themselves. In 1510 Julius abandoned the league to side with Venice; Ferdinand declared his neutrality, but the next year also went over to Venice. After the French victory at Ravenna (1512), even the Emperor and Swiss cantons became part of the coalition against them, and the French were driven out of Milan (May 1512). The French won a victory at Ravenna then lost at Novara in 1513 to the Swiss mercenaries who were now operating as an independent force. This was revenged by the French at Marignano amid terrible slaughter in 1515. By now it was clear that Italy was merely the theatre for the conflicts of other powers and was no longer in control of its own affairs. Pope **CLEMENT VII**, fearful of imperial dominance, dispensed Francis from his vow to keep the peace and formed the League of Cognac between the papacy, Venice, Florence and France. This was swept aside by the imperial advance and the full wrath of the unpaid imperial mercenaries was unleashed in the Sack of **ROME** in 1527, an event so shattering that in many ways it can be said to have brought the Italian **RENAISSANCE** to an end. ► **ITALIAN WARS**

**Cambrai, Treaty of** (5 Aug 1529)
A treaty concluded between **FRANCIS I** of France and Emperor **CHARLES V** in 1529, following the latter's victory at Landriano in the **ITALIAN WARS**. Francis renounced his claims in Italy and Flanders and Charles his claim to **BURGUNDY**. Although peace was short-lived, these terms were reflected in the final settlement at Cateau-Cambrésis a generation later (1559).

**Camden, Battle of** (1780)
A battle of the **AMERICAN REVOLUTION**, fought in South Carolina. After the British capture of **CHARLESTON**, Camden was the first major battle of the Southern campaign. Americans under Horatio Gates were defeated by British troops under Lord **CORNWALLIS**.

---

**CAMEROON**   official name **Republic of Cameroon**

A republic in West Africa, bounded to the south-west by Equatorial Guinea; to the south by Gabon; to the south-east by the Congo; to the east by the Central African Republic; to the north-east by Chad; and to the north-west by Nigeria. The country was first explored by the Portuguese navigator Fernando Po, and later by traders from Spain, the Netherlands and Britain. It became a German protectorate, Kamerun, in 1884, and after **WORLD WAR I** was divided into French and British Cameroon in 1919, which was confirmed by the **LEAGUE OF NATIONS** mandate in 1922. The **UN** turned **MANDATES** into trusteeships in 1946. French Cameroon acquired independence as the Republic of Cameroon in 1960, and was joined in 1961 by the southern sector of British Cameroon (the northern sector of British Cameroon voted to become part of Nigeria); the Federal Republic of Cameroon was established, with separate parliaments, in 1961. The federal system was abolished in 1972, and the country's name was changed to the United Republic of Cameroon; the word 'United' was dropped in 1984. From 1972 to 1992 it was ruled by one party, the Cameroon People's Democratic Movement, with Paul **BIYA** as President since 1982. Multi-party elections were restored in 1992. Cameroon joined the **COMMONWEALTH OF NATIONS** in 1995, the first country to do so that has never been fully under British rule at any point in its history.

**Camisards**
The last major Protestant rebellion in early modern Europe, centred on the Cévennes Mountains in northern Languedoc (1700–4). It was provoked by the revocation of the Edict of **NANTES** (1685), which

had guaranteed limited toleration, and the failure of the Treaty of **RIJSWIJK** (1697) to safeguard French Protestants. The uprising was put down with difficulty by royal troops under Marshal Villars.

**campanilismo**
The Italian word, derived from *campanile* ('bell-tower'), which is commonly used to describe the intense particularism that has always been a characteristic of Italian culture and politics.

**Campbell, Sir Colin, Baron Clyde** (1792–1863)
British field marshal. He fought in the **PENINSULAR WAR** against **NAPOLEON I**, where he was twice badly wounded, and after 30 years of duty in various garrisons, fought in China (1842) and in the second of the **SIKH WARS** (1848–9). In the **CRIMEAN WAR** he commanded the Highland Brigade in a campaign which included the renowned repulse of the Russians by the 'thin red line' at the Battle of **BALACLAVA** (1854). During the 1857–8 **INDIAN UPRISING** he commanded the forces in India, and effected the final relief of Lucknow. He was created baron in 1858. ► **LUCKNOW, SIEGE OF**

**Campbell-Bannerman, Sir Henry** (1836–1908)
British politician. He became a Liberal MP in 1868, was Chief Secretary for Ireland (1884), War Secretary (1886 and 1892–5), Liberal leader (1899), and Prime Minister (1905–8). A 'pro-Boer', he granted the ex-republics responsible government, and his popularity helped to reunite a divided **LIBERAL PARTY**. He supported the Lib–Lab pact of 1903, which played a part in the Liberal landslide of 1906. ► **BOER WARS**

**Camp David**
The US presidential retreat established as 'Shangri La' (1942) by President Franklin D **ROOSEVELT** in Catoctin Mountain Park, Maryland. Renamed in 1953 by President **EISENHOWER**, the retreat covers 200 acres/81 hectares and includes a main residence (Aspen Lodge), conference hall and office.

**Camp David Accords** (1978)
Documents signed by Anwar **SADAT**, President of Egypt, and Menachem **BEGIN**, Prime Minister of Israel, and witnessed by US President Jimmy **CARTER** at **CAMP DAVID**, Maryland, USA, in Sep 1978. Regarded by many as a triumph of US diplomacy, they were preliminary to the signing of the formal peace treaty (1979) between the two countries, which gave Egypt back the Sinai Desert, captured in the 1967 War. ► **ARAB–ISRAELI WARS**; **PLO**

**Camperdown, Battle of** (1797)
A naval battle fought between British and Dutch fleets off Texel Island, Holland. Admiral Adam Duncan (1731–1804) virtually destroyed the Dutch fleet, frustrating the attempt to disable the British North Sea squadron and thus facilitate the invasion of Britain.

**Campoamor, Clara** (1888–1972)
Spanish politician and feminist. Of working-class origin, she graduated in law in 1924, and from then onwards agitated widely on behalf of women's issues. In 1931 she was elected to the Constituent **CORTES** of the Second Republic as a deputy for the **RADICAL REPUBLICAN PARTY**. She was responsible more than anyone else for the inclusion of women's suffrage in the

Constitution of 1931. During the legislature of 1931–3 she was Vice-President of the Labour Commission and participated in the reform of the Civil Code. In addition, she represented Spain at the **LEAGUE OF NATIONS** and founded the Republican Feminine Union. In 1933–4 she was also the Director-General of Charity. During the 1930s she wrote extensively on **WOMEN'S RIGHTS** and aspirations. In 1938 she chose exile in Buenos Aires, moving in 1955 to Lausanne, where she died. She was one of the principal figures of the 20c in the struggle for women's rights in Spain. ► **REPUBLIC, SECOND** (Spain)

**Campo Formio, Treaty of** (18 Oct 1797)
A treaty between France and Austria. Negotiated and signed by **NAPOLEON I** and ratified by the **DIRECTORY**, the treaty marked the end of the first of the Wars of the Coalition and it represented the climax of the young French general's successful campaigns of 1796–7. By its terms, **FRANCIS II** of Austria recognized French possession of the Austrian Netherlands and French claims to territory on the left bank of the Rhine. The Austrian Emperor also ceded Lombardy and Mantua to the newly established **CISALPINE REPUBLIC**, receiving in compensation Venetia, Istria, **DALMATIA** and Friuli.

**Campomanes, Pedro Rodríguez, Count of** (1723–1803)
In 1762 he became *fiscal* (chief legal officer) of the Council of **CASTILE** under **CHARLES III**, King of Spain since 1759. His programme was expressed in *The Right of Mortmain* (1765), designed to limit acquisition of property by the Church, and he became identified with a liberal policy of free trade with America. Plans were interrupted by the outbreak of riots in Madrid (1766) and popular risings throughout Spain which forced the King to sack his minister **ESQUILACHE**. Under the new Chief Minister, **ARANDA**, Campomanes prepared a prosecution of the Jesuits, considered instigators of the riots; they were expelled by decree in 1767 from both Spain and America. In 1774 he encouraged the spread of Economic Societies of Friends of the Country, a group which played a key role in bringing the élite into the reform programme. In 1783 he was appointed head of the Council of Castile but was relieved of the post in 1791. An accomplished scholar, historian and practical intellectual, his writings represent the most advanced thinking of the **ENLIGHTENMENT** in Spain.

**Campos, Roberto de Oliveira** (1917–2001)
Brazilian political economist and diplomat. A Jesuit-trained economist, he served as a diplomat on the US–Brazil Economic Commission in the 1950s, and was later Director of the National Economic Development Bank (BNDE) under **KUBITSCHEK (DE OLIVEIRA)**. Associated with attempts to achieve an 'orthodox' economic policy by the nationalist press, he was the natural choice for Planning Minister under **CASTELO BRANCO**. He co-authored the 'Government Economic Action Programme, 1964–6' (PAEG), with Otávio Gouveia de Bulhões: this introduced modern fiscal and monetary policy instruments, as well as indexation and the centralization of expenditure, while encouraging 'corporate' management of the economy, drawing on the heritage of the **VARGAS** era. He espoused the trickle-down theory of economic growth and the encouragement of foreign investment.

**Campos Salles, Manuel Ferraz de** (1841–1913)
Brazilian politician. The 'Political Architect of the Republic', he was a slave-owner, **FAZENDEIRO** and lawyer in Campinas, then the centre of the coffee-growing region of Brazil. He became a Republican in the 1870s and was Minister of Justice in the Provisional Government of the Republic (1889–91), when he was responsible for the separation of Church and State and the introduction of civil marriage. He was Governor of São Paulo in 1896–8, and then became President (1898–1902). Charged with radical financial reform, designed to protect the country from foreign intervention, and pledged to a 'privatization' programme, he emasculated a nationalist Congress by agreeing a pact with incumbent governors: the President would protect them from federal intervention if they, in their turn, pledged their support for him in Congress. This system, known as the 'Politics of the Governors', led to one-party state administrations and provided the basis for political management until 1930; vestiges of it remain to this day.

**CAN** (*Comunidad Andina*, 'Andean Community')
A South American trading group comprising Bolivia, Columbia, Ecuador, Peru and Venezuela. The organization was founded in 1969 as the **ANDEAN GROUP**, changing its name to the Andean Community in 1997. CAN has attempted to achieve a high level of institutional integration, creating a commission, parliament and court of justice. By 2002 CAN regulations covered areas such as agricultural policy, control of illegal drugs and foreign policy. In 1999 negotiations began with **MERCOSUR**, the region's other main trading bloc, with the aim of creating a free-trade zone across the continent. Pacts were signed in 2004, creating the fifth-largest trading group in the world and significantly increasing the region's bargaining power with the USA in talks on the proposed free trade area of the Americas (FTAA) and **NAFTA**.

**CANADA** formerly (to 1867) **British North America**
An independent country in North America, bounded to the south by the USA; to the west by the Pacific Ocean; to the north-west by Alaska; to the north by the Arctic Ocean and Baffin Bay; to the north-east by the Davis Strait; and to the east by the Labrador Sea and the Atlantic Ocean. There is evidence of Viking settlement in c.1000. The country was visited by **CABOT** in 1497, and in 1504 St John's, Newfoundland, was established as the shore base for the English fisheries. The St Lawrence was explored for France by Cartier in 1534, and Newfoundland was claimed for England in 1583, making it England's first overseas colony. **CHAMPLAIN** founded the city of Quebec in 1608. The **HUDSON'S BAY COMPANY** was founded in 1670, and in the late 17c there was conflict between the British and the colonists of **NEW FRANCE**. Britain gained large areas from the 1713 Treaty of **UTRECHT**. After the **SEVEN YEARS' WAR**, during which **WOLFE** captured Quebec (1759), the Treaty of **PARIS** gave Britain almost all of France's possessions in North America. The province of Quebec was created in 1774, and migration of loyalists from the USA after

# *Canals*

*Transport & Travel*

The earliest man-made watercourses were almost certainly constructed for the purpose of irrigating agricultural land or of bringing water to towns and cities. In the 7c BC Sennacherib, King of Assyria, built a stone canal 50mi/80km long and 66ft/20m wide to supply drinking water to his capital, Nineveh. Similar works were carried out by the ancient Greeks and, on an even grander scale, by the ancient Romans.

Canals have also been used to drain waterlogged land. In Europe the Dutch were the masters of this craft. Besides criss-crossing their own country with dykes and drainage canals, Dutch engineers were called in to drain wetlands in other countries, notably the Fens in eastern England, which were mainly reclaimed in the 17–18c.

Despite their obvious importance as water conduits, however, the main interest in canals lies in their use as a means of communication and trade. In this respect they have a very long history.

### Early canals

Some of the great achievements of modern canal engineering were previously attempted in antiquity. The first canal across the isthmus of Suez linking the Nile delta with the Red Sea was dug around 1300 BC. For nearly 2,000 years it was periodically allowed to fall into disrepair and disuse before being re-excavated and restored. The Persian King Darius I is also said to have undertaken to link the Nile and Red Sea by canal in 510 BC, either imitating or restoring the earlier work. In a similar fashion, the Roman Emperor Nero planned to drive a canal across the isthmus of Corinth to connect the Aegean and Adriatic seas. Shafts dug by Roman engineers were reopened when the Corinth Canal was constructed in the late 19c. It eventually opened in 1893.

The longest canal in the world is also one of the oldest. The Chinese began building the Grand Canal in the 6c BC, the first and oldest section of which connects the Yangzi and Yellow rivers. In 610 AD they rebuilt and reopened this first section, and continued to extend it over the succeeding centuries until, when finally completed in the 13c, it reached Beijing – a total distance of 1,085mi/1,747km. It carried around 200,000 tons of grain north every year, using around 20,000 barges and innumerable locks. As many as 160,000 troops were deployed by the Qing emperors to guard this crucial lifeline of empire in a crisis.

Early canals for navigation were on the whole limited to fairly easy and level terrain. The Chinese had been using single-gate locks from about 500 BC. These consisted of a barrier of sluices across a waterway with a single wooden gate in the middle. When the gate was raised, the resulting 'flash' of water from behind the sluice would temporarily raise the water level below sufficiently to enable a boat to shoot through downstream or be hauled through upstream. Such locks, however, were not very efficient in water use (a great deal of water escaped downstream when the lock was opened) and were generally unsuitable for larger gradients.

The first two-gate 'pound lock' – in which the water level rises and falls within a separate chamber – was built in Holland at Vreeswijk in 1373. It still had portcullis-type gates. About a century later the first lock with 'mitre gates' of the type still in use today was built in Milan. The first pound locks in England were built on the Exeter canal in 1564–6.

### The Canal Age

In 1681 French engineers completed the Canal du Midi linking the Bay of Biscay with the Mediterranean through south-western France, and connecting the rivers Garonne and Aude. It was one of the first large canals of the modern era, a major engineering achievement involving an ascent and descent through locks to a higher plateau over which much of the canal was constructed, as well as the construction of a tunnel and three aqueducts. It showed the possibilities of the canal engineering of the time, besides giving a considerable economic stimulus to the area that it served.

Canals were also an important means of opening up a country. In the course of the 18c a large network of canals was constructed in Russia as part of the general process of modernization and westernization undertaken by a series of rulers. These waterways eventually linked St Petersburg with the Caspian Sea.

The lack of a road network and land vehicles suitable for transporting large and heavy loads was a major obstacle to trade and industry in the 18c, even in a relatively small country. By the 17–18c the Dutch had solved their internal transport problems by creating a canal network, originally designed for bulk commodities such as grain, stone and peat (the basic Dutch fuel), but soon carrying large numbers of passengers. In Britain the beginnings of the **Industrial Revolution** further stimulated the demand for a more efficient transport system, and canals were found to provide the answer. The 3rd Duke of Bridgewater employed the engineer James Brindley (1716–72) to construct a canal between Worsley and Manchester in 1759 – the Bridgewater Canal. The successful completion of this project in 1772 stimulated an enormous expansion of the canal network in Britain over the next 50 years and more. In the USA large-scale canal

---

the **AMERICAN REVOLUTION** led to the division of Quebec into Upper and Lower Canada, reunited as Canada in 1841. The **DOMINION OF CANADA** was created in 1867 by a confederation of Quebec, Ontario, Nova Scotia and New Brunswick. Rupert's Land and Northwest Territories were bought from the Hudson's Bay Company in 1869–70, and were later joined by Manitoba (1870), British Columbia (1871, after promise of a transcontinental railroad), Prince Edward Island (1873), Yukon (1898, following the **KLONDIKE GOLD RUSH**), Alberta and Saskatchewan (1905), and Newfoundland (1949). In 1982 the Canada Act gave Canada full responsibility for its constitution. There has been recurring political tension in recent decades arising from the French-Canadian separatist movement in Quebec, and from the desire for autonomy of the Native American and **INUIT** populations; a 1992 referendum approved the creation of the vast autonomous territory of Nunavut for the Inuit people, and this was implemented on 1 Apr 1999. A 1995 referendum in Quebec rejected independence by a narrow margin, and since then support for independence has fallen. Canada joined the **ORGANIZATION OF AMERICAN STATES** (OAS) in 1990. ➤

construction began somewhat later – the Erie Canal, linking the Hudson River and New York with Lake Erie, was constructed between 1817 and 1825. By that time the great age of canal expansion in Britain was nearly over. The arrival of the **railways** meant that canal traffic began to decline from about 1840, and the engineering techniques employed in canal building – the making of embankments, cuttings and tunnels to enable the canal to follow a level course – were adopted by those who engineered the first railway lines.

### The Suez and Panama canals

The Suez Canal was, as has been indicated above, an ancient idea revived. Its promoter, the French diplomat Ferdinand de Lesseps, was a cousin of **Napoleon III**'s wife, the Empress Eugénie. In 1856 he obtained a concession from **Isma'il Pasha**, the Khedive of Egypt, for the construction of a canal. Work was begun in 1859 and the canal opened 10 years later. The canal was at first operated by a private French–Egyptian company: the concession was obtained for 99 years, at the end of which time all rights were to revert to the Egyptian government. In 1875, however, the British government – which had an obvious interest in securing control of the shortest sea route to India – bought out the Egyptian interests and the canal was thereafter run as an Anglo-French concern. The right of ships of all nations to use the canal was still guaranteed. By a treaty of 1936, Britain acquired the right to maintain military forces in Egypt for the defence of the canal. This agreement remained in force until 1954, at which time British forces began a withdrawal that was completed in 1956. In that same year President **Nasser** of Egypt, angered by the Western nations' refusal to finance his project for a new Aswan Dam, abruptly nationalized the canal, provoking an attempt by British and French forces, aided by the Israelis, to seize it back. International pressure swiftly brought the war to an end, leaving the Egyptians in charge.

A political situation of similar complexity surrounds the **Panama Canal**. The possibility of a canal connecting the Atlantic and Pacific oceans across the isthmus of Panama was first mooted by Hernán **Cortés**. The project was frequently discussed, but no practical measures were taken to implement it until the end of the 19c when first de Lesseps, and then, after his company went bankrupt, the US government, attempted to obtain a concession from Colombia, to which present-day Panama then belonged. The Colombian government refused to grant the USA the strip of territory it required. Only after Panama obtained independence in 1903 was a treaty signed, enabling construction to go ahead and giving the USA a perpetual lease on the Canal Zone. The construction of the canal, and the sanitization of the surrounding area in which malaria and yellow fever were endemic, took nearly 10 years. It opened in 1914. The USA retained control of the Canal Zone until 1979 when, again under local nationalist pressure, it handed control back to Panama. Control of the canal itself reverted to Panama on 31 Dec 1999.

### The present day

Though the coming of the railways spelt the end of the operational life of many smaller canals, larger canals continued to be built and to be used throughout the 20c. The St Lawrence seaway, providing ocean-going ships access to the Great Lakes, was opened in 1959, and in 1975 the USSR opened a canal linking the Baltic and Black seas. The comparatively environmentally friendly nature of canal transportation has led to suggestions that canals should be reopened. Many smaller canals in Britain and Europe have been restored; however, their chief role is largely recreational. ► **Ships; Suez Crisis**

| | |
|---|---|
| opening of the Panama Canal | 1914 |
| 1869 | opening of the Suez Canal (Egypt) |
| development of canal networks in Russia, Holland and Britain | 18c |
| 1681 | completion of the Canal du Midi (France) |
| work begins on the Grand Canal (China) | 6c BC |
| c.1300 BC | construction of an early canal across the isthmus of Suez |

---

**CANADA, LOWER; CANADA, UPPER; CANADA EAST; CANADA WEST; LIBERAL PARTY** (Canada); **MEECH LAKE ACCORD ; NATIVE AMERICANS ; PARTI QUÉBECOIS**

### Canada, Lower (1791–1841)

The name given to Quebec by the Constitutional Act of 1791. The decision to divide Canada in two was reached with the realization that it would be impossible to establish a form of government that would satisfy both English-speaking Protestant Canadians and French-speaking Catholics. Lower Canada was dominated by French-Canadians, the Roman Catholic Church was established and the Custom of Paris accepted as its legal system. With its borders drawn up on the old seigniorial property boundaries, Montreal, despite being dominated by English merchants was also included. In Lower Canada the problems associated with colonial rule existed along with the friction caused by the fractious relationship between the two communities. This friction increased with the influx of English-speaking immigrants so that the French-Canadians were afraid for their ascendancy and the English-speaking immigrants suffered from the domination of French custom and language. In 1822 the Montreal Château Clique originated a bill

which united both provinces. They aimed to bar most Frenchmen from the vote through a high property franchise and to limit the power of the Catholic Church. The bill was dropped after PAPINEAU went to London to appeal. Although by 1831 control of the revenue had been given to the Assembly, the majority in the House was not given any official ministerial recognition. By 1834 the French only held a quarter of the public posts although they formed three-quarters of the population. The situation was aggravated by the depression of 1837, and rebellion broke out but was put down fairly quickly. With the Act of Union (1840), Lower Canada became CANADA EAST (in 1841), and was given equal representation within a united province, so the French were yet again at a disadvantage. ► CANADA, UPPER; CRAIG, SIR JAMES HENRY; DURHAM REPORT; NINETY-TWO RESO-LUTIONS

**Canada, Upper** (1791–1841)
The name given to the western region of the province of Quebec when it was made, like Lower CANADA, a separate province by the Constitutional Act of 1791. At that time it had a population of 14,000, but by 1812, with an influx of settlers mostly from the USA, it had grown to 90,000. The first governor was Sir John Graves SIMCOE, who initiated a system of distributing free land grants in return for a loyalty oath. However, the distribution of land according to social rank created an élite known as the FAMILY COMPACT. Similarly, the Anglican Church's semi-established status gave it advantages at the expense of the Methodist Church, although the latter's members outnumbered the Anglicans. These dissatisfactions led William Lyon MACKENZIE, after the failure of rebellion in Lower Canada, to call settlers to action, but his inability to organize a military uprising matched the inability of the governor, Sir Francis Bond Head, to govern. Nevertheless, it did bring the problems out into the open, and after the DURHAM REPORT, Upper Canada was made CANADA WEST in the united Province of Canada.

**Canada East** (1841–67)
The name given to Lower CANADA (Quebec) when it became a district of the united Province of Canada

established by the Act of Union in 1840 as a result of the DURHAM REPORT. After confederation in 1867, Canada East became the Province of Quebec within the DOMINION OF CANADA. ► CONFEDERATION MOVEMENT; PAPINEAU, LOUIS JOSEPH

**Canada First** (1867–76)
Canadian patriotic movement. It was founded by a number of young intellectuals who were later joined by business and professional men of Toronto disenchanted by the Treaty of WASHINGTON. Its journal, The Nation (edited by Goldwin SMITH), was noted for its political commentary, and in 1874 Edward BLAKE became the chief spokesman for the movement during his temporary defection from the LIBERAL PARTY. The CLEAR GRITS and many Liberals disliked the movement because its demand that Canada be given the authority to negotiate its own treaties seemed to imply the dissolution of the BRITISH EMPIRE. Some of its members believed in the racial supremacy of the Anglo-Saxon inheritance, thinking French-Canada corrupt and priest-ridden and therefore likely to retard Canada's progress. Many, however, like Blake, believed Canada's potential for greatness would only be realized if French-Canada's cultural inheritance was recognized, so that her leaders would be free to cooperate in federal politics.

**Canada West** (1841–67)
The name given to Upper CANADA when it became a district of the united Province of Canada established by the Act of Union in 1840 as a result of the DURHAM REPORT. After confederation in 1867, Canada West became the Province of Ontario within the DOMINION OF CANADA. ► CONFEDERATION MOVEMENT

**Canals** ► See panel

**Canaris, Wilhelm** (1887–1945)
German naval commander. He entered the Imperial German navy in 1905, and served in the Dresden at the Battles of Coronel and the Falklands in WORLD WAR I. He escaped from internment in Chile and made his way back to Germany, and served in U-boats in the Mediterranean. He retired with the rank of rear-admiral in 1934. Though disapproving of aspects of the Nazi regime, he rose under HITLER to

become admiral of the German navy and chief of the *Abwehr*, the military intelligence service of the High Command of the armed forces. Involved in the anti-Nazi resistance and associated with the 1944 bomb plot against Hitler, he was arrested, imprisoned and hanged in Apr 1945, just before the entry of the Soviet army into Berlin. ➤ **NAZI PARTY**

**Candia, War of**
The war fought between the Republic of Venice and the Turks for control of Crete. The conflict hinged on the defence of Candia, which was besieged for over 20 years before surrendering in Sep 1669. Even after the fall of Candia, the Venetians did retain a presence on the island at Grabusa, Spinalonga and Suda, but these fell to the Turks between 1691 and 1715.

**cangaço**
The golden age of the *cangaço*, the rural banditry in north-eastern Brazil, occurred between 1860 and 1930. The great droughts of 1877–9 and 1888–90, and the demise of **SLAVERY**, coincided with the decline of the region's importance in national politics and a long boom in cotton production. The result was to intensify feuding between powerful local landowners, whose ancient prerogative of *homísio* (personal protection to any individual seeking it) protected bandits. *Cangaceiros* were recruited from, and formed part of, the irregular forces which *coroneis* retained in order to preserve their local hegemonies, and their forces were enlisted by both federal and state authorities during the 1920s. Bandit leaders such as Antônio Silvino and **LAMPIÃO**, who led large and well-equipped bands in the sertão, capitalized on the notion of the 'good thief', but were liquidated by the centralized federal government after the 1930 revolution. Their defiance of authority made them popular heroes.

**Canisius, Petrus, SJ** (1521–97)
Dutch-born Jesuit reformer who was the leader of the **COUNTER-REFORMATION** in Germany. His Dutch name was Pieter Kanis, and in his function as the first Provincial of the German Jesuits he became known as the 'Second Apostle of Germany'.

**Canning, Charles John Canning, 1st Earl** (1812–62)
British politician. He entered parliament in 1836 as Conservative MP for Warwick, but next year was raised to the House of **LORDS** as Viscount Canning by his mother's death, both his elder brothers having predeceased her. In 1841 he became Under-Secretary in the Foreign Office, and in 1856 he succeeded Lord **DALHOUSIE** as Governor-General of India. The war with Persia was brought to a successful close in 1857. In the same year (10 May), the **INDIAN UPRISING** began with the outbreak at Meerut. Canning's conduct was described at the time as weak – he was nicknamed 'Clemency Canning' – but the general opinion later was that he acted with courage, moderation and judiciousness. In 1858 he became the first Viceroy of India, and in 1859 was raised to an earldom.

**Canning, George** (1770–1827)
British politician. He entered parliament for Newport, Isle of Wight (1794) as a supporter of **PITT, THE YOUNGER**. He became Under-Secretary of State (1796), Treasurer of the Navy (1804–6), and Minister for Foreign Affairs (1807). His disapproval of the Walcheren expedition led to a misunderstanding with **CASTLEREAGH**, which resulted in a duel. He became MP for Liverpool (1812), Ambassador to Lisbon (1814), President of the Board of Control (1816), and MP for Harwich (1822). Nominated Governor-General of India (1822), he was on the eve of departure when Castlereagh's suicide saw him installed as Foreign Secretary. In this post he gave a new impetus to commerce by advocating tariff reductions. He was the first to recognize the free states of Spanish America; promoted the union of Britain, France and Russia in the cause of Greece (1827); protected Portugal from Spanish invasion; contended earnestly for **CATHOLIC EMANCIPATION** (1829); and prepared the way for a repeal of the **CORN LAWS**. In 1827 he formed an administration with the aid of the **WHIGS**, but died the same year.

**Canossa** (1077)
During the conflict between the empire and the papacy known as the **INVESTITURE CONTROVERSY**, **HENRY IV** (of the Germans) had been excommunicated and his subjects thus released from their oath of allegiance to him. Henry offered unconditional submission to Pope **GREGORY VII** at Canossa, spending three days barefoot in the snow in the dress of a penitent and was freed from the ban of excommunication. This allowed him to regain the support of the majority of the German nobles. It is debatable whether his move represented a genuine change of heart or shrewd political tactics, but Canossa marks the turning point in the empire's relationship with the papacy and the end of the tradition of imperial protection and domination of the Church in Germany. ➤ **TRIBUR, PRINCES' MEETING AT**

**Cánovas del Castillo, Antonio** (1828–97)
Spanish politician and historian. A Conservative, he became a member of the **CORTES** in 1854, and was Premier in 1875–81, 1884–5, 1890–2 and 1895–7, when he was shot by an anarchist. Cánovas was the architect of the oligarchical **RESTORATION SYSTEM**, which survived until the dictatorship of General **PRIMO DE RIVERA** (1923–30).

**Cantonalist Risings** (1873)
The failure of the Spanish First Republic to establish a unitary regime led to the emergence by July 1873 of scores of independent city-states, or cantons. Inspired by the ideas of the Catalan federalist **PI I MARGALL**, the movement swept through eastern and southern Spain, embracing Barcelona, Cartagena, Granada, Malaga, Seville and Valencia. The cantonalists pursued a form of primitive communism, dividing up the large estates or common lands and adopting anticlerical measures. Under the presidency of **CASTELAR**, the cantonalists were crushed by the army under General Pavía, Cartagena holding out until Jan 1874. ➤ **REPUBLIC, FIRST** (Spain)

**Canton System**
This term refers to the trading arrangements imposed by the Qing authorities on China's south-east coast during the latter half of the 18c and early decades of the 19c. Portuguese, Spanish, Dutch and British traders had begun arriving off China's coast from the 17c onwards, but by the mid-1750s the **QING**

DYNASTY, with the aim of regulating and supervising maritime trade, had limited contact to the port of Canton (Guangzhou). Foreigners (mostly British) had to deal with a licensed group of merchants (**CO-HONG**) and could only trade at certain times of the year. While at Canton they had to reside outside the city walls and their movements were restricted. Until the British **EAST INDIA COMPANY**'s monopoly of the China trade was abolished, the system worked reasonably well; thereafter, with the increasing hostility of private British traders towards the restrictions and duties on commercial transactions, and with the Chinese government's attempts to halt the increase of illegal opium sales, the system broke down. After the first Opium War (1839–42) it was dismantled, and China was compelled to open five treaty ports in which foreigners could reside and trade freely. ➤ **OPIUM WARS**

### Canudos Campaign (1896–7)

One of the bloodiest conflicts in Brazilian history, pitting one third of the federal army and police forces from several southern states against the local populace, led by Antônio Vicente Mendes Maciel, or the 'Councillor'. An educated messianic figure, who had long preached in the drought-stricken north-eastern interior, the Councillor founded Canudos as a centre of pilgrimage, but his practice of lay preaching brought him into conflict with the Church, and the economic independence of the settlement led to violent clashes with powerful politicians. The military capabilities of the Councillor's following were such that Canudos was seen as a 'monarchist redoubt': total destruction of his forces was necessary for the consolidation of the Republic under **CAMPOS SALLES**. This was widely viewed as a titanic clash between tradition and modernity: one which precipitated the demise of Jacobin nationalism in political life.

### Canute (c.995–1035)

King of England (1016/35), Denmark (1019/35) and Norway (1028/35). The younger son of **SVEIN I HARALDSSON, FORK BEARD**, he first campaigned in England in 1013, and after his father's death (1014) successively challenged **ETHELRED THE UNREADY** and **EDMUND II, IRONSIDE** for the English throne. He defeated Edmund in 1016 at the Battle of Assandun, secured Mercia and Northumbria, and became King of all England after Edmund's death. In 1017 he married Emma of Normandy, the widow of Ethelred. He ruled England according to the accepted traditions of English kingship and maintained the peace throughout his reign. He died at Shaftesbury, Dorset. The story of his failure to make the tide recede was invented by the 12c historian Henry of Huntingdon, to demonstrate the frailty of earthly power compared to the might of God.

### Cao Dai/Hoa Hao

Two major religious movements, established in **COCHIN-CHINA** (southern Vietnam) from the final decades of French rule. The Cao Dai religion, officially founded in 1926, claimed to be heir to all the religions of the world. It preached the virtues of spiritualism, Confucian piety and vegetarianism. Hoa Hao Buddhism, founded in 1939 by a charismatic faith-healer, Huynh Phu So, was extremely puritanical. It sought to eliminate idol worship and elaborate ritual. In the late

### CAPETIAN DYNASTY

| Regnal Dates | Name |
| --- | --- |
| 987/96 | Hugh Capet |
| 996/1031 | Robert II |
| 1031/60 | Henry I |
| 1060/1108 | Philip I |
| 1108/37 | Louis VI, the Fat |
| 1137/80 | Louis VII |
| 1180/1223 | Philip II |
| 1223/6 | Louis VIII, the Lion |
| 1226/70 | Louis IX (St Louis) |
| 1270/85 | Philip III, the Bold |
| 1285/1314 | Philip IV, the Fair |
| 1314/16 | Louis X, the Quarrelsome |
| 1316 | John I |
| 1316/22 | Philip V, the Tall |
| 1322/8 | Charles IV, the Fair |

1940s the attractiveness of Cao Dai and Hoa Hao were a major obstacle to the advance of the **VIET MINH** in the rural south. The Hoa Hao was strongly hostile to the communists, to the extent that it was allied with the French against them. In 1947 the communists seized, tried and executed Huynh Phu So. The power of the sects in the politics of post-war southern Vietnam, reinforced over a number of years by French subventions, was sharply curbed by **NGO DINH DIEM** in 1955.

### Cape Coloured

A term used by the South African **APARTHEID** governments to refer to a group of people of mixed descent, arising from the unions of Europeans with slaves (from Madagascar, Mozambique, or the East) or Khoikhoi (Hottentots). They form c.9 per cent of the total population, mainly living in the towns and rural areas of the western Cape province. Culturally akin to white South Africans, most speak Afrikaans and are Christian, with a small Muslim minority (Cape Malays). They are mostly farm labourers, factory workers and artisans, with a small middle class. Rejecting the classification Cape Coloured, they referred to themselves as 'so-called Cape Coloureds'. ➤ **KHOISAN**

### Capellen tot den Poll, Joan Derk van der (1741–84)

Dutch politician. He studied in Utrecht, and joined the States (Provincial Assembly) of Overijssel in 1772, where he vigorously opposed the policies of the aristocracy and urban patricians. In 1781 he published anonymously the pamphlet *To the People of the Netherlands*, which attacked the **STADHOLDER**'s government and proposed a democratic state based on popular sovereignty. This work had a profound effect on the Dutch **PATRIOT MOVEMENT**, which spread the ideals of the **FRENCH REVOLUTION** to the Netherlands.

### Cape St Vincent, Battle of (1797)

A naval battle fought between British and Spanish fleets. Admiral Sir John Jervis (1735–1823) defeated a numerically superior Spanish force, thus preventing French plans for the assembly of a combined invasion fleet to conquer Britain. ➤ **FRENCH REVOLUTIONARY WARS**

### Capetian Dynasty

A French ruling dynasty for over 300 years

(987–1328), founded by Hugh Capet in succession to the Carolingians. Two dynamic royal descendants were **PHILIP II** of France and St **LOUIS IX**. By increasing territorial control, enforcing the right to inherit of an eldest son, and devoting themselves to administration and justice, the Capetians laid the foundations of the French nation-state. ► **BOURBON, HOUSE OF**

---

**CAPE VERDE** official name **Republic of Cape Verde**

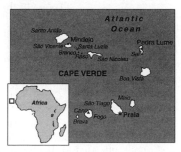

An island group in the Atlantic Ocean which lies off the west coast of Africa. It was colonized by the Portuguese in the 15c and was used as a penal colony. Administered with Portuguese Guinea until 1879, it became an overseas province of Portugal in 1951. It gained full independence in 1975 as a result of the campaign by the African Party for the Independence of Cape Verde and Guinea-Bissau (PAICV), which remained the only legal party (dropping Guinea-Bissau from its name in 1980) until multiparty elections took place in 1991. That year the new Movement for Democracy Party came to power, with Antonio Mascarenhas Monteiro as President and Carlos Veiga as Prime Minister. The PAICV returned to power in the 2001 elections.

**capitalism**
An economic system based on private, rather than state ownership, of businesses, factories, transport services and so on, with free competition and profit-making. Modern capitalism developed in 19c Western societies after the **INDUSTRIAL REVOLUTION**. According to **MARX**, capitalism depends on exploitation of the workers (or proletariat) who own nothing but their labour, which they must sell in a market controlled and owned by the capitalist class (or bourgeoisie). Non-Marxist economists define capitalism as a system in which property is privately owned and goods are sold freely in a competitive market, but without reference to exploitation. Capitalism is a highly productive economic system, although it can give rise to environmental and social (eg unemployment) problems.

**Capitalist Encirclement** (1928–53)
An excuse used by **STALIN** to justify his dictatorship. In his attitude to the outside world, Stalin moved from advocating World Revolution to accepting peaceful coexistence. However, in order to maintain his control over the Communist Party and the people, he exaggerated the hostility of surrounding states, especially Britain, Germany, Japan and the USA, by raising the spectre of a terrible capitalist encirclement.

**Capitulations**
Originally these were commercial concessions

dating back as far as Crusader and Mamluk times, such as freedom from customs duties and other forms of taxation, coupled with a civil form of diplomatic immunity so that foreign nationals were effectively under the jurisdiction of their consuls. These, as far as modern Egypt was concerned, were effectively a number of humiliating discriminatory privileges and concessions granted to certain foreign powers in Egypt, the end of which was finally negotiated in the Montreux Convention of 1937.

**Capo d'Istria, Giovanni Antonio, Count** ► **KAPODISTRIAS, IOANNIS**

**Capone, Al(phonse)** (1899–1947)
US gangster. He achieved worldwide notoriety as a racketeer during the **PROHIBITION** era in Chicago. Such was his power that no evidence sufficient to support a charge against him was forthcoming until 1931, when he was sentenced to ten years' imprisonment for tax evasion. Released on health grounds in 1939, he retired to his estate in Florida, where he died.

**Caporetto, Battle of** (24 Oct–4 Nov 1917)
The disastrous defeat for the Italian army under **CADORNA** by the Austro-German forces of General Belov. The battle broke the stalemate which had characterized the first two years of the war in Italy. The Italians lost 300,000 men and were forced back to the River Piave, where, with the assistance of French and British divisions, they managed to establish a defensive line. The defeat led to Cadorna's replacement by **DÍAZ**.

**Cap Party** (Sweden) ► **AGE OF LIBERTY**

**Caprivi, Georg Leo, Count von** (1831–99)
German soldier and politician. Entering the Prussian army in 1849, he fought in the campaigns of 1864 and 1866, and in the **FRANCO-PRUSSIAN WAR** (1870–1) was Chief of Staff to the 10th Army Corps. As head of the Admiralty (1883–8), he reorganized the navy and then was made commander of his old army corps in Hanover. On **BISMARCK**'s fall in 1890, he became Imperial Chancellor and Prussian Prime Minister. His principal measures were the army bills of 1892–3 and the commercial treaty with Russia in 1894. He was dismissed by the Emperor in 1894 for pursuing too liberal a policy. ► **PRUSSIA**

**Carabobo, Battle of** (24 June 1821)
A decisive victory by Simón **BOLÍVAR** in the **SPANISH-AMERICAN WARS OF INDEPENDENCE**, fought near Valencia, Venezuela. Bolívar and **PÁEZ**'s forces of 6,500 men defeated a smaller Spanish army, securing independence from Spanish forces demoralized by the return of General Morillo to Spain in the aftermath of the Riego revolt. However, the last royalist garrisons were not dislodged from Venezuelan soil until 1823.

**Caracciolo, Prince Francesco** (1752–99)
Neapolitan naval commander. He served with the British in the **AMERICAN REVOLUTION**, then entered the service of Ferdinand of Naples and became supreme commander of the Neapolitan navy. In Dec 1798 he fled with the King before the French from Naples to Palermo, but returned to Naples in 1798 and entered the service of the 'Parthenopean Republic'. For two months he ably directed the operations of the revolutionists, but was captured trying to escape

in peasant disguise, and was hanged.

## Carbonari

The members (literally, 'charcoal burners') of a liberal and patriotic secret society (the *Carboneria*) that emerged in southern Italy during the NAPOLEONIC WARS and which spread to other areas of Italy, particularly after the Vienna Settlement. Usually anticlerical, the society borrowed many rituals and symbols from FREEMASONRY, with which its origins are certainly connected. Although *Carbonari* were involved in a number of conspiracies and insurrections in different Italian states during the period 1817–31, they never possessed a clear programme or achieved any lasting victories. It is often hard to distinguish between the Carboneria and other similar but smaller groups such as the ADELFI, Guelfi and Federati. By the 1830s, however, most of these so-called sects had been superseded by better organized groups with more clearly defined (although by no means more realistic) liberal aims, usually seeking some degree of Italian unity and an end to Austrian hegemony in the peninsula. The Italian Carboneria was copied elsewhere in Europe, notably in Spain and France.

## Cárdenas (del Río), Lázaro (1895–1970)

Mexican general and politician. His presidency (1934–40) shaped modern Mexico. He promoted the return of the EJIDO in the south and the extension of the rancho (small property) principally in the north. His presidency also witnessed the creation of PEMEX from nationalized foreign (mainly British) companies, and the PRM (*Partido de la Revolución Mexicana*, 'Mexican Revolutionary Party'), precursor of the PRI. Left-wing in his sympathies, he introduced many social reforms and reorganized the ruling party.

## Cardigan, James Thomas Brudenell, 7th Earl of (1797–1868)

British general. He entered the army in 1824, and purchased his promotion, commanding the 15th Hussars (until 1833), and then the 11th Hussars (1836–47). He commanded a cavalry brigade in the Crimea, and led the fatal charge of the Six Hundred (the CHARGE OF THE LIGHT BRIGADE) against the Russians at the Battle of BALACLAVA (25 Oct 1854) in the CRIMEAN WAR. He then became Inspector-General of Cavalry (1855–60). The woollen jacket known as a cardigan is named after him.

## Cardozo, Benjamin (1870–1938)

US jurist. He sat on the bench of the New York Court of Appeals from 1913 to 1932, during which time the court became internationally famous. Appointed to the US Supreme Court by President Herbert HOOVER, he succeeded Oliver Wendell HOLMES, serving for six years (1932–8). Although he served for such a relatively brief time, and although many of his opinions dissented from the majority, he was remarkably influential because of his eloquence and learnedness. He was generally liberal and believed that the courts could effect social change.

## Cardwell, Edward Cardwell, 1st Viscount (1813–86)

British politician. He became a lawyer (1838) and an MP (1842). First a Peelite, then a Liberal, he served as President of the Board of Trade (1852–55), Chief Secretary for Ireland (1859–61), Chancellor of the Duchy

of Lancaster (1861–4), and Colonial Secretary (1864–6). As Secretary for War (1868–74), he carried out a major reorganization of the British Army. He was made a peer in 1874.

## Caribbean Community (CARICOM)

An association, formed in 1973, of former British colonies in the Caribbean, some of which (Barbados, Jamaica and the Leeward Islands) existed as the Caribbean Federation, with the aim of full self-government, until the establishment of the Federation of the WEST INDIES (1958–63). When Jamaica became independent in 1962, the Federation was dissolved. In 1969 certain of the remaining islands in the Windward and Leeward Islands were offered associated status within the COMMONWEALTH OF NATIONS, and in 1969 the West Indies Associated States was formed. In 1968 many of the islands agreed to the establishment of the Caribbean Free Trade Area (CARIFTA).

## Caribs

Amerindian groups of the Lesser Antilles and neighbouring South America (the Guianas and Venezuela). The island Caribs were maritime people and warriors, who slowly drove the ARAWAKS from the islands. Most were slaughtered by Spaniards or wiped out by diseases brought in by Europeans in the 16c, and the survivors mixed with Spanish conquerors and later Negro slaves. The mainland Caribs led a more peaceful existence in small autonomous settlements in the tropical forests.

## Carinthia

A federal state in southern Austria bordered by Styria, Italy and Slovenia. Part of Roman Noricum, it was settled by the Teutons, Avars and SLAVS, and in the 8c became a part of Bavaria. Briefly subject to Bohemia, it passed to RUDOLF I of Habsburg (1276) and then to the Count of Tyrol (1286), finally becoming a Habsburg crown land in 1335. Remaining a distinct district with its capital at Klagenfurt, together with Styria and CARNIOLA it formed Inner Austria. At the end of WORLD WAR I, though it remained within Austria, parts were ceded to Italy and the Kingdom of Serbs, Croats and Slovenes (later Yugoslavia). During the ANSCHLUSS it became part of the Reichsgau Kärnten (1938–45) and since 1945 has been a federal state within Austria. It is populated mainly by Germans but has a large Slovene minority.

## Carl XVI Gustav ► CHARLES XVI GUSTAV

## Carleton, Guy, 1st Baron Dorchester (1724–1808)

Acting Governor (1767–70) and Governor (1786–91) of Quebec, and Governor-in-Chief of British North America until 1798. General James WOLFE's quartermaster at the capture of QUEBEC in 1759, he realized during his first tour of duty as Governor that the 13 North American colonies were close to rebellion and that British imperial authority would require a base, which he set out to establish in Quebec. His belief that the maintenance of the seigniorial system would ensure French-Canadian loyalty was embodied in the QUEBEC ACT of 1774 which, despite protests from the increased English-speaking population, was pushed through the House of Commons against bitter opposition. Carleton refused to consider the English-speaking settlers' demands for *habeas corpus* and other aspects of English law, but in spite of resentment against this, it was they who took up arms against the US rebels when they invaded in 1775–6. Carleton's successful defence, however, was criticized for the slowness with which he pursued the rebels and he resigned. Sent out as Governor of Quebec again in 1786, he became Governor-General after the Constitutional Act of 1791. He disliked the division of Quebec into Upper and Lower CANADA, and the introduction of elected assemblies, but his advice that Montreal be retained within Lower Canada was accepted. His continued concern for the military defence of Canada was illustrated by the inflammatory speech he made to NATIVE AMERICANS just before JAY'S TREATY was signed in 1794, when he was sure that war with the USA was imminent. He resigned in 1794 and left the province in 1796.

## Carlism

A Spanish dynastic cause and political movement, officially born in 1833, but with its origins in the 1820s. Against the claim to the Spanish throne by ISABELLA II, daughter of Ferdinand VII, Carlists supported the claim of the latter's brother, Don CARLOS. In the 19c, Carlism attracted widespread popular support chiefly in conservative, Catholic districts of rural northern Spain. In 1833–40, 1846–9 and 1872–6, Carlists fought unsuccessful civil wars against Spanish liberalism. After 1876, Carlism ceased to be a vehicle for widespread anti-capitalist protest and became a narrower movement espousing ultra-rightist, 'traditionalist' principles. It took the Nationalist side in the SPANISH CIVIL WAR, providing c.100,000 volunteers. Since 1939, both during and after the FRANCO regime, the cause has suffered division and serious decline, although small Carlist groups persist.

## Carlos, Don (1545–68)

Heir to the Spanish throne. The son of PHILIP II of Spain by his first wife, Maria of Portugal, he was recognized as heir to the Spanish throne by the Cortes of CASTILE (1560). A sickly child, who later showed signs of instability, he was alienated from his father while young, and was sent to study at Alcalá de Henares. Twice (1565 and 1567) he attempted to escape from Spain, to Flanders and Germany. His hatred for his father led to his being tried for conspiracy with rebel nobles from the Spanish Netherlands. He was found guilty (although sentence of death was not formally recorded) and died shortly afterwards in prison in unclear circumstances.

## Carlos, Don (1788–1855)

Spanish pretender. He was the second son of CHARLES IV of Spain. On the accession of his niece, ISABELLA II, in 1833, he asserted his claim to the throne. This claim was reasserted by his son, Don Carlos, Count de Montemolin (1818–61), and by *his* nephew, Don Carlos (1848–1909). Carlist risings, whose principal strength lay in the Basque provinces and Navarre, occurred in 1833–40, 1846–9 and 1872–6. ► CARLISM

## Carlsson, Ingvar Costa (1934– )

Swedish politician. Educated at Lund (Sweden) and North Western (USA) universities, he was secretary in the Prime Minister's office (1958–60) before entering active party politics. He became President of the Youth League of the Social Democratic Labour Party (SAP) in 1961, and in 1964 was elected to the *Riksdag* (parliament). After holding a number of junior posts (1967–76), he became deputy to Olof Palme in 1982 and succeeded him as Prime Minister and SAP leader after Palme's assassination in 1986. He retired in 1996.

## Carmona, António (1869–1951)

Portuguese politician and soldier. Having entered the army in 1888, he was made a general in 1922 and briefly served under the First Republic as Minister of War (1923). Following the coup d'état of 28 May 1926 against the Republic, Carmona emerged as *de facto* Prime Minister (from July 1926) and as President (from Nov 1926). Although he lacked a political programme, he was able to consolidate his position by balancing the various factions within the armed forces. As military dictator for six years (1926–32), he adopted a low profile, partly because he was an uncharismatic bureaucratic officer and partly because the regime was headed by a coalition of officers. Carmona oversaw the rise of SALAZAR and the ESTADO NOVO, protecting him against opposition, especially during the major cabinet crises of 1929 and 1930. On the other hand, Salazar's success ensured Carmona's own future. Once Salazar was established as dictator, Carmona was content to act as a figurehead President. Although by 1945 he had become disillusioned with Salazar, his control over national affairs was by now negligible. He died as President, bitter at his political impotence. ► REPUBLIC, FIRST (Portugal)

## Carnegie, Andrew (1835–1919)

US industrialist and philanthropist. Born in Dunfermline, Scotland, the son of a weaver, his family emigrated to Pittsburgh in 1848. After several jobs he founded his first company, which grew into the largest iron and steel corporation in the USA. He retired in 1901, a multimillionaire, to Skibo Castle in Sutherland, Scotland, and died in Lenox, Massachusetts. His benefactions exceeded £70 million, including public libraries throughout the USA and UK, Hero Funds, the Pittsburgh Carnegie Institute, the Washington Carnegie Institution, the Hague Peace Temple, the Pan-American Union Building, and substantial gifts to Scottish and US universities.

## Carneiro Leão, Honorio Hermeto (Marquis de Paraná) (1801–56)

Brazilian politician. Born into a powerful mercantile-landowning family, he became a lawyer and then Deputy for his native Minas Gerais (1833–41). A senator and councillor of state from 1842 to 1856, he was a moderate Conservative, who led a group responsible for the charting of policies which would enable the more powerful provinces, such as Minas Gerais, to accept the centralist rule of PEDRO II. A shrewd political manager of the Chamber, he articulated the structure of the Empire, whereby central power was offset by the limited autonomy of local interests, tempered by the distribution of patronage. Master of the CONCILIAÇÃO, he was Prime Minister in 1853–6 at the head of a cabinet of 'All the Talents', drawn from the ranks of moderate Liberals and Conservatives alike, committed to a broad programme of administrative reform and railroad building.

## Carniola

A part of Roman Pannonia, it was settled by the **SLAVS** (6c), emerging as a distinct district in the 10c. Subject to various princes and bishops, it became a Habsburg crown land (1335) and, remaining a distinct district with its capital at Laibach (Ljubljana), with **CARINTHIA** and Styria formed Inner Austria. Conquered by **NAPOLEON I**, Carniola was included within the **ILLYRIAN PROVINCES** from 1809 to 1813. During the 19c it was the centre of the Slovene national awakening; in 1848, nationalists tried to form an autonomous Slovene kingdom within the Habsburg Monarchy but in 1849 Carniola was again organized as a crown land. In 1918 it became part of the Kingdom of Serbs, Croats and Slovenes (later Yugoslavia), and after 1947 was absorbed, in its entirety, within Slovenia.

## Carnot, Lazare Nicolas Marguerite (1753–1823)

French politician. Known as the 'organizer of victory' during the **FRENCH REVOLUTIONARY WARS**, he entered the army as an engineer, and in 1791 became a member of the **LEGISLATIVE ASSEMBLY** (1791–2). He survived the Reign of **TERROR**, and became one of the Directors (1795), but in 1797, suspected of royalist sympathies, he escaped to Germany. Back in Paris, he became Minister of War (1800), and helped to organize the Italian and Rhenish campaigns. He commanded at Antwerp in 1814, and during the **HUNDRED DAYS** was Minister of the Interior. ► **FRENCH REVOLUTION**

## Carnot, Marie François Sadi (1837–94)

President of the French Third Republic, grandson of Lazare **CARNOT**. He studied at the École Polytechnique, and became a civil engineer. In 1887 he was elected President and proceeded to stand firm against the Boulangist movement. Carnot was stabbed to death at Lyons by an Italian anarchist. ► **BOULANGER, GEORGES**; **REPUBLIC, THIRD** (France)

## Carol I, Carol II ► CHARLES I, CHARLES II (of Romania)

## Caroline of Brunswick, Amelia Elizabeth (1768–1821)

Wife of **GEORGE IV** of the UK, the daughter of **GEORGE III**'s sister, Augusta. She married the Prince of Wales in 1795, but the marriage was disagreeable to him, and although she bore him a daughter, the Princess Charlotte, they lived apart. When George became King (1820), she was offered an annuity to renounce the title of Queen and live abroad; when she refused, the King persuaded the government to introduce a Divorce Bill. Although this failed, she was not allowed into Westminster Abbey at the coronation (July 1821).

## Carpetbaggers

A derogatory term for US Northerners who went to the defeated South after the **AMERICAN CIVIL WAR** to aid freed blacks and take advantage of the economic opportunities offered by **RECONSTRUCTION**. The term derived from Southerners' characterization of them as opportunistic transients who carried all their worldly goods in luggage made of carpet fabric. Though many were well-intentioned, others earned their reputation of corruption and rise to political

power through exploitation of the black vote.

## Carranza, Bartolomé de (1503–76)

Spanish theologian. A Dominican, he became Professor of Theology at Valladolid, and in 1554 accompanied **PHILIP II** of Spain to England, where he was confessor to Queen **MARY I**, and where his zealous efforts to re-establish Roman Catholicism gained him the confidence of Philip and the Archbishopric of Toledo. Here, however, he was accused of heresy, and imprisoned by the **INQUISITION** in 1559. In 1567 he was removed to Rome, and confined in the castle of St Angelo. He died a few days after his release.

## Carranza, Venustiano (1859–1920)

Mexican politician. A senator under Porfirio **DÍAZ** and a supporter of **MADERO**, he emerged as the leader of Constitutionalist forces against the dictator, Victoriano **HUERTA**, in 1914. A fervent protagonist of Liberal aims, he was forced to accept the radical constitution of 1917, but limited agrarian reform to military measures, destroying **ZAPATA** and **VILLA** in the process. He was assassinated when attempting to retain the presidency.

## Carrero Blanco, Luis (1903–73)

Spanish politician and naval officer. Director of Naval Operations in 1939, he later rose to the rank of admiral (1966). In 1941 he became an under-secretary to the presidency, and for the next 32 years he was effectively **FRANCO**'s right-hand man. He became a minister in 1951, Vice-Premier in 1967 and, in 1973, the first Prime Minister other than Franco since 1939. He was the political alter ego of Franco, not only because of his absolute loyalty, but also because he shared the same ultra-reactionary outlook, hating 'communists', 'Freemasons', and 'liberals', although his visceral anti-Semitism set him apart. The key figure of the regime after Franco and the embodiment of continuity, his assassination by **ETA** (Dec 1973) was a grave blow to the regime.

## Carrier, Jean Baptiste (1756–94)

French revolutionary. In the National **CONVENTION** he voted for the death of King **LOUIS XVI**, demanded the arrest of Louis Philippe Joseph, the Duke of **ORLÉANS** (known as Philippe Égalité after renouncing his title), and assisted in the overthrow of the **GIRONDINS**. At Nantes in 1793 he massacred 16,000 prisoners, chiefly by drowning them in the Loire (the *noyades*), but also by shooting them, as in a battue. After the fall of **ROBESPIERRE** he was tried, and perished by the guillotine.

## Carrillo, Santiago (1915– )

Spanish political leader. He became Secretary-General of the Socialist Youth at only 19. Jailed for participation in the Asturian rising of Oct 1934, he was a key figure in the merger of the Socialist Youth with the communists before the **SPANISH CIVIL WAR**. He has been widely held responsible for the massacre of Nationalist prisoners at Paracuellos de Jarama in Nov 1936. Having become General-Secretary of the exiled **PCE** in 1960, he took the party from its neo-Stalinism to, in the 1970s, **EUROCOMMUNISM**. He returned to Spain in 1976. Although the PCE won 23 seats in the 1979 general election, it plummeted to a mere four in 1982. He resigned to found his own communist party, finally entering the **PSOE** in 1991. ► **STALINISM**

## Carrington, Peter Alexander Rupert Carington, 6th Baron (1919– )

British politician. A Conservative, he held several junior posts in government (1951–6), before becoming High Commissioner to Australia (1956–9). He then served as First Lord of the Admiralty (1959–63) and Leader of the House of LORDS (1963–4). He was Secretary of State for Defence (1970–4) and briefly for Energy (1974), and also Chairman of the Conservative Party organization (1972–4). Upon the Conservative return to office he was Foreign Secretary (1979–82), until he and his ministerial team resigned over the Argentine invasion of the Falkland Islands. He later became Secretary-General of NATO (1984–8), and EC mediator during the crisis in Yugoslavia (1991–2). ► CONSERVATIVE PARTY (UK)

## Carroll, Charles (1737–1832)

American Revolutionary leader. The cousin of John Carroll, the first American Catholic bishop, he was educated by Jesuits in St Omer and at the Collège de Louis le Grand, Paris. He returned to the USA in 1765 and took possession of a large family estate. As a Roman Catholic he was barred from taking part in colonial politics, but he became involved in the pamphlet wars of the mid-1770s on behalf of the colonies. He was a member of the CONTINENTAL CONGRESS (1776–8) and later became one of Maryland's first senators (1789–92.) His politics were markedly conservative, but his adherence to the Revolutionary cause represented an opportunity for full political participation and was inspirational to other American Catholics.

## Carson, Edward Henry Carson, Baron (1854–1935)

Irish politician and barrister. He became a Conservative MP (1892–1921), a QC of the Irish Bar (1880) and English Bar (1894), and in 1895 became known for his cross-examination of Oscar Wilde. He was Solicitor-General for Ireland (1892) and for England (1900–6), Attorney-General (1915), First Lord of the Admiralty (1916–17), and Lord of Appeal (1921–9). Strongly opposed to HOME RULE, he organized the Ulster Volunteers. ► CONSERVATIVE PARTY (UK)

## Carson, Kit (Christopher) (1809–68)

US frontiersman. A trapper and hunter, his knowledge of Native American habits and languages led to his becoming a guide in 1841 for John Frémont's explorations. He fought in the MEXICAN WAR, was Indian agent in New Mexico (1853), and served the Union in the AMERICAN CIVIL WAR.

## Cartel des gauches (1924)

Literally 'left-wing cartel', this term describes an electoral coalition in France of the radical, socialist and other left-wing parties which defeated the BLOC NATIONAL.

## Carter, Jimmy (James Earl) (1924– )

US politician and 39th President. Educated at the US Naval Academy, he served in the US Navy until 1953, when he took over the family peanut business and other enterprises. As Governor of Georgia (1971–5), he showed sensitivity towards the rights of blacks and women. In the aftermath of the WATERGATE crisis he won the Democratic presidential nomination in 1976, and went on to win a narrow victory over Gerald FORD. As President (1977–81), he sponsored the initiation of a protracted peace process between Egypt and Israel (1979), by means of an agreement known as the CAMP DAVID ACCORDS, and was concerned with human rights both at home and abroad. His administration ended in difficulties over the IRAN HOSTAGE CRISIS and the Soviet invasion of Afghanistan, and he was defeated by Ronald REAGAN in the 1980 election. Since then he has played a diplomatic role around the world, at first in Nicaragua and Panama, and then in a peace-brokering capacity in Ethiopia, North Korea, Haiti, and amongst the Bosnian Serbs and Muslims in the Balkans. He was awarded the NOBEL PEACE PRIZE in 2002.

## Carter Doctrine

The statement by US President Jimmy CARTER on 23 Jan 1980 that the oil reserves in the Persian Gulf were of vital interest to the USA and that any attempt by an outside nation to take the region would be met with by US military intervention. The adoption of the doctrine by President George HW BUSH resulted in the US spearheading the allied UN forces in the GULF WAR.

## Carteret, John, 1st Earl Granville (1690–1763)

English politician. He entered the House of LORDS in 1711, and became Ambassador to Sweden (1719), Secretary of State (1721), and Lord-Lieutenant of Ireland (1724–9). Chief Minister from 1742 to 1744, he was driven from power by the Pelhams (1744) because of his pro-Hanoverian policies, though from 1751 he was President of the Council under Henry PELHAM, and twice refused the premiership. ► PELHAM, THOMAS PELHAM-HOLLES, 1ST DUKE OF NEWCASTLE; WALPOLE, ROBERT

## Cartier, Sir George Étienne (1814–73)

Canadian politician. Leader of the Bleu bloc of CANADA EAST, he served with John MACDONALD in 1854 to form a Conservative ministry. Cartier believed that the French-Canadian nation would only survive if French-Canadians worked together with English-speaking Canadians. He also recognized that his people not only needed legislation to maintain their cultural identity but that their economic betterment required the development of transportation and commercial schemes. As Attorney-General for the province and solicitor for the Grand Trunk Railway he was able to advance his people's interests as well as his own. In 1858 the Macdonald Cartier administration was defeated, but reformed as the Cartier–Macdonald ministry in a mutual exchange of posts (the so-called 'double-shuffle'). This lasted until 1862, and Cartier returned to government in the great coalition of 1864 that negotiated confederation. Perhaps his greatest contribution to Canadian history was to impress the need for union upon French-Canadians, although many modern French-Canadians think of him as the first vendu. Because of his involvement with the Canadian Pacific Railway and Sir Hugh ALLAN, he was defeated in 1872, became ill and died. ► BLEUS; CONFEDERATION MOVEMENT

## Cartier, Jacques (1491–1557)

French navigator. Between 1534 and 1541 he made three voyages to North America searching for a westerly route to Asia. He discovered the St Lawrence River. ► NEW FRANCE

## Carton de Wiart, Henri, Count (1869–1951)

Belgian politician, writer and historian. A Roman Catholic, he founded the Christian-Democratic newspaper *L'Avenir Social* in 1891, and represented Brussels in the Belgian parliament. From 1911 to 1950 he was frequently a cabinet minister, holding at various times the portfolios of Justice, Home Affairs, Social Services and Public Health; in 1920–1 he was also Prime Minister.

## Cartright, Sir Richard John (1835–1912)

Canadian banker and politician. Having broken with the conservatives over the railway scandal of 1873, he became Finance Minister in Alexander **MACKENZIE**'s Liberal administration of 1873–8, when he was the most prominent advocate of free trade and alienated many transport and industrial interests by his opposition to tariffs. After the Liberals' victory in 1896 he was made Minister for Trade and Commerce in **LAUR-IER**'s cabinet. ➤ **LIBERAL PARTY** (Canada)

## Casablanca Conference (Jan 1943)

A meeting in North Africa between Franklin D **ROOSEVELT** and Winston **CHURCHILL** during **WORLD WAR II**, at which it was decided to insist on the eventual 'unconditional surrender' of Germany and Japan. Attempts to overcome friction between Roosevelt and the Free French under de **GAULLE** had only limited success. The combined Chiefs of Staff settled strategic differences over the projected invasion of Sicily and Italy.

## casa del pueblo

Spanish grass-roots political institution. Literally 'House of the People', the term describes a meeting-place and educational, social and welfare centre for political activists. Based on a Belgian socialist model, the *casa del pueblo* was introduced into Spain in 1906 by the Republican populist Alejandro **LERROUX**. The first casa del pueblo opened in Barcelona with a clinic, theatre and a consumer cooperative, which provided insurance and pension schemes as well as legal aid. It was designed to replace the traditional and more exclusive Republican casinos, thereby helping to create a truly mass party by forging a new basis for collaboration between workers and the Republicans. The casas compensated for some of the glaring deficiencies of the state's welfare provisions and became best-known as an important focus of support for the Socialist Party and its trade union movement, the **UGT**.

## Casas, Bartolomé de las (1474–1566)

Spanish priest and 'Protector of the Indians'. He sailed in the third voyage of **COLUMBUS** (1502) to Hispaniola, where he settled as an *encomendero*. Convinced of the evil of the **ENCOMIENDA**, in 1514 he gave up his Indians and began a campaign to achieve liberty for the natives with the help of the Crown. In 1517 he was appointed 'Protector of the Indians' and began a series of unsuccessful experiments to set up colonies of Indian farmers. Disappointed by his failure, he entered the Dominican Order (c.1521) and went into retirement for about 10 years, during which time he began his major writings. Thereafter he dedicated his career to the liberation of the Indians. He undertook at least one more scheme for peaceful colonization of the natives, in Guatemala (1537–50), and was the first

to suggest that black slaves be imported to substitute for Indian labour. He was influential in the Spanish court, from which in 1542 he obtained the New Laws, which decreed the end of **SLAVERY** in America. Appointed Bishop of Chiapa in Guatemala (1544), he had to resign in the face of settler protests. In Spain in 1550 he took part in a famous debate in Valladolid on the morality of conquest in America.

## Casement, Sir Roger David (1864–1916)

British consular official. He acted as Consul in various parts of Africa (1895–1904) and Brazil (1906–11), where he denounced the Congo and Putumayo rubber atrocities. Knighted in 1911, ill health caused him to retire to Ireland in 1912. An ardent Irish nationalist, he tried to obtain German help for the cause. In 1916 he was arrested on landing in Ireland from a German submarine to take part in the **EASTER RISING**, and hanged for high treason in London. Public opinion was turned against him by the circulation of his controversial 'Black Diaries', which revealed, among other things, homosexual practices.

## Casey, Richard (Gavin) Gardiner Casey, Baron (1890–1976)

Australian politician. He was elected to the House of Representatives in 1931. He became first Australian Minister to the USA in 1940, Minister of State in the Middle East (a war-cabinet rank) in 1942, and Minister for External Affairs in 1951. A life peerage was conferred on him in 1960.

## Casimir-Périer, Pierre (1777–1832)

French politician and banker. He belonged to the liberal opposition under **LOUIS XVIII** and **CHARLES X**, joining the first government of **LOUIS-PHILIPPE** after the **JULY REVOLUTION** (1830), and was Prime Minister and Minister of the Interior (1831–2). He repressed insurrections in Paris and Lyons (1832).

## Cassin, René (1887–1976)

French jurist and politician. During **WORLD WAR II** he joined General de **GAULLE** in London. He was principal legal adviser in negotiations with the British government and, in the later years of the war, held important posts in the French government in exile in London and Algiers, and subsequently in the Council of State (of which he was President, 1944–60) in liberated France. He was the principal author of the **UNIVERSAL DECLARATION OF HUMAN RIGHTS** (1948) and played a leading part in the establishment of **UNESCO**. He was a member of the European Court of Human Rights from 1959, and its President (1965–8). In 1968 he was awarded the **NOBEL PEACE PRIZE**.

## Castanos, Francisco Xavier de, Duke of Bailen (1756–1852)

Spanish soldier. During the **PENINSULAR WAR** (1808–14) he compelled 18,000 French to surrender at the Battle of Bailén (1808), but was defeated by Lannes at Tudela. Under **WELLINGTON** he took part in the Battles of Albuera, Salamanca and Vitoria (1813). In 1843 he was appointed guardian of Queen **ISABELLA II** of Spain.

## caste

A system of inequality, most prevalent in Hindu Indian society, in which status is determined by the membership of a particular lineage and associated occupational group into which a person is born. The groups are ordered according to a notion of religious purity or spirituality, thus the Brahmin or priest caste, as the most spiritual of occupations, claims highest status. Contact between castes is held to be polluting, and must be avoided. Caste was officially abolished in the constitution of independent India in 1951. However, controversy erupted in the 1980s and 1990s over the extension of 'reservations' – a policy of **POSITIVE DISCRIMINATION** in the allocation of government posts and student places in universities – intended to remove the disadvantages of, and prejudices against, the lower castes created by the caste system. ► **BRAHMINS**; **MANDAL COMMISSIONS**

## Castelar y Ripoll, Emilio (1832–99)
Spanish politician and writer. He studied at Madrid, where he was Professor of History and Philosophy (1856–65). A leader of the Republicans, he fled to Paris in 1866 but returned at the 1868 revolution, and in 1873 helped to bring about the downfall of King Amadeus I. He was made head of government in Sep 1873, crushing the **CANTONALIST RISINGS** in the provinces. He resigned in Jan 1874, and fled on **ALFONSO XII**'s accession. He returned to Spain in 1876, becoming leader of the Possibilist Republican Party, which merged with the monarchist Liberal Party upon his withdrawal from political life in 1893.

## Castelo Branco, Humberto de Alencar (1900–67)
Brazilian politician. He was educated at the Pôrto Alegre Military Academy in Rio Grande do Sul and at France's École Supérieure de Guerre, as well as the General Command course at Fort Leavenworth, USA. He went on to fight with the Brazilian army in Italy, and coordinated the anti-**GOULART** military conspiracy of 1964. Linked to other veteran officers in the Escola Superior da Guerra, founded in the 1940s in Rio de Janeiro, his foreign policy was anticommunist, and he believed that short-term arbitary technocratic measures should be taken to create the conditions for democracy. As President from 1964 to 1967, although the economy had been stabilized, the financial system reorganized and foreign debt renegotiated, his government failed to alter traditional patterns of authority and prevent the emergence of hardline factions amongst the military, which established the 'tutelary regime' that survived until 1985.

## Castiglione, Baldassare, Count (1478–1529)
Italian author and diplomat. Educated at Milan, he began a career at court, and in 1505 was sent by the Duke of Urbino as envoy to **HENRY VII** of England, who made him a knight. His chief work, *Il Cortegiano* (1528, 'The Courtier'), is a manual for courtiers. He also wrote Italian and Latin poems, and many letters illustrating political and literary history.

## Castiglione, Battle of (5 Aug 1796)
An important victory for **NAPOLEON I** over the Austrian forces commanded by General Wurmser, sent from the South Tyrol to relieve the blockade of Mantua.

## Castile, Kingdom of
The central region and component kingdom of Spain. The United County of Spain was formed in 970, and during the 11c and most of the 12c was subject to the suzerainty of Leon of Navarre. Hegemony over Leon was established in 1188, and the union of the Castilian and Leonese crowns took place in 1230. The union of crowns with the Kingdom of Aragon (1469–79), the Conquest of **GRANADA** (1492), and the annexation of Navarre (1512) created the basis of the modern Spanish state.

## Castilla (Marquesado), Ramón (1797–1867)
Peruvian general and politician. After fighting in the **SPANISH-AMERICAN WARS OF INDEPENDENCE** under José de **SAN MARTÍN** in Peru in 1820, he rose to become Chief of Staff under presidents Luís José de Orbegoso and Agustín Gamarra, and Minister of War in 1837. Following Gamarra's death in 1841 he became involved in the struggle for power, which he won in 1844. He became President of Peru the following year until replaced by José Rufino Echenique in 1851. Four years later he led the revolution that overthrew Echenique, and served as President again in 1855–62. During his presidencies, helped by the recent discovery of large guano (nitrogen-rich seabird droppings useful as fertilizer) and sodium nitrate resources, he enabled Peru to enjoy economic progress and political stability; he proclaimed a new constitution in 1860 and also built schools and railways, and abolished slavery.

## Castle of Blackburn, Barbara Anne Castle, Baroness (1910–2002)
British politician. She was Labour MP for Blackburn (1945–79) and Chairman of the Labour Party (1958–9), Minister of Overseas Development (1964–5), and a controversial Minister of Transport (1965–8), introducing a 70 mph speed limit and the 'breathalyser' test for drunken drivers. She became Secretary of State for Employment and Productivity (1968–70) and Minister of Health and Social Security (1974–8). She returned to the backbenches briefly before leaving Parliament. She represented Greater Manchester in the European Parliament from 1979 to 1989, and became Vice-Chairman of the Socialist Group in the European Parliament in 1979, a post she held until 1986. ► **LABOUR PARTY** (UK); **SOCIALISM**

## Castlereagh, Robert Stewart, Viscount (1769–1822)
British politician. The son of an Ulster proprietor, he became Whig MP for County Down in 1790, turning Tory in 1795. He was created Viscount Castlereagh in 1796, and became Irish Secretary (1797), President of the Board of Control (1802), and Minister of War (1805–6 and 1807–9). His major achievements date from 1812, when, as Foreign Secretary under Lord **LIVERPOOL**, he was at the heart of the coalition against **NAPOLEON I** (1813–14). He represented England at Chaumont and the Congress of **VIENNA** (1814–15), Paris (1815) and Aix-la-Chapelle (1818). He advocated 'Congress diplomacy' among the Great Powers, to avoid further warfare. Believing that he was being blackmailed for homosexuality, he committed suicide at Foots Cray, his home in Kent. ► **TORIES**; **WHIGS**

## Castors
Canadian political epithet. *Castor* (meaning 'beaver') was the signature on a pamphlet of 1882, entitled *Le*

*Pays, le parti et le grand homme*, which attacked Joseph Adolphe **CHAPLEAU** and J A Mousseau for becoming members of **MACDONALD**'s cabinet. The name was given to right-wing conservatives in Quebec in the following year when their newspaper adopted the beaver as its emblem. Castors were ultramontane Catholics and racialists, the counterparts of extremist British Protestants.

**Castro, Cipriano** (1858–1924)
Venezuelan general and dictator. Known as 'the Lion of the Andes', he worked as a cowboy in the mountains, became governor of the province of Táchira, and was exiled to Colombia in 1892 when the Caracas government was overthrown. Funded by his own illegal cattle trading, he amassed an army which successfully ousted the Venezuelan President, Ignacio Andrade, in 1899. Castro became 'supreme military leader' (1899–1901), then provisional President and elected President (1902–8). His administration was marked by disorder and despotism. Many political opponents were exiled or murdered, and there was trouble with foreign powers over the non-payment of debts resulting in a blockade of Venezuelan ports by British, German and Italian ships in 1902. With his health ruined by his dissolute lifestyle, he went to Paris in 1908 to seek medical help and was ousted in his absence by his Vice-President, Juan Vicente **GÓMEZ**. He spent the rest of his life in exile, plotting his return to Venezuela.

**Castro (Ruz), Fidel** (1927– )
Cuban revolutionary. He studied law in Havana and in 1953 was imprisoned after an unsuccessful rising against **BATISTA**, but released under an amnesty. He fled to the USA and Mexico, then in 1956 landed in Cuba with a small band of insurgents. Most were killed on landing, but he escaped to set up a guerrilla movement in the Sierra Madre Mountains, which grew until, by 1959, Batista was forced to flee. He became Prime Minister (1959– ), later proclaimed a 'Marxist–Leninist programme', and set about far-reaching reforms. His overthrow of US economic dominance, and the routing of the US-connived émigré invasion at the **BAY OF PIGS** (1961) was balanced by his dependence on Soviet aid. Castro became President in 1976. Although Cubans gained substantially in terms of general social provision, by the late 1980s the economic experiment had failed, and the collapse of the USSR and **COMECON** in 1990–1 isolated his regime. With Cuba having lost the commercial, military and economic support that it had enjoyed since 1960, Castro was forced to reduce public services and introduce food rationing. Cuba moved very tentatively towards a **MARKET ECONOMY**, and tourism was encouraged in order to compensate for the severe drop in sugar revenues. Following anti-government riots in 1994 he relaxed the emigration laws and thousands of Cubans left for Florida.

**Catalan Autonomy Statutes** (1932 and 1979)
Catalonia (the 'land of castles') has always been distinguished from the rest of Spain by its culture, language and geography. The dynastic union of Ferdinand of Aragon (which included Catalonia) and Isabella of Castile in 1469 allowed Catalonia to retain its laws and privileges until the end of the War of the **SPANISH SUCCESSION** in 1714. **PHILIP V** of Spain

thereupon abolished the *fueros* (medieval laws and customs) and the **GENERALITAT**, a parliament of medieval origin. During the late 19c a Catalan nationalist movement developed which eventually led to the establishment of a limited form of self-government in the shape of the Mancomunitat in 1913, only to be abolished by the dictatorship of General **PRIMO DE RIVERA** in 1923. However, the Second Republic (1931–6) provided Catalonia with an autonomy statute in Sep 1932. This restored the Generalitat, proclaimed Catalan as the official language, and gave the Catalans control over most regional issues, although the period of self-government was cut short by **FRANCO**'s victory in the **SPANISH CIVIL WAR**. In 1977 the Generalitat was revived and in 1979 Catalonia regained its autonomy with a substantial measure of home rule. ► **REPUBLIC, SECOND** (Spain)

**Catalonia**
An autonomous region of north-east Spain, comprising the provinces of Barcelona, Gerona, Lérida and Tarragona, and formerly including Roussillon and Cerdaña. Catalonia united with Aragon in 1137, and a medieval trading empire developed in the 13c and 14c. It became part of Spain following the union of the Castilian and Aragonese crowns (1469–79). There has been a strong Catalan separatist movement since the 17c, and a Catalan autonomy statute was eventually granted in Sep 1932. This was, however, abolished by **FRANCO** during the **SPANISH CIVIL WAR**. A new government was established in 1979. ► **CATALAN AUTONOMY STATUTES**

**Catalonia, Revolt of** (1640–52)
The rising that took place after decades of political tension between the Catalan authorities and the central government of **CASTILE**. It was provoked directly by the Count-Duke of **OLIVARES**, whose imperial ambitions spawned a plan for a Union of Arms, which the Catalans rejected. In 1635, when Spain went to war against France, Olivares deliberately centred the conflict on the Catalan frontier in order to stir the Catalans to defend themselves. The billeting of Castilian troops in the province provoked uprisings and the murder of the Castilian viceroy in Barcelona during the 'Corpus of Blood' in 1640. The Catalan leadership used the crisis to declare the separation of the province from Spain and its adherence to France. The experience of French rule was, if anything, worse and, after a long siege, the city of Barcelona capitulated to the Castilian army under Don **JUAN JOSÉ OF AUSTRIA** in 1652.

**Cataví Massacre** (21 Dec 1941)
An attack on striking Bolivian tin-miners and their families by Bolivian soldiers at the Cataví mining camp, in which several hundred people were killed. The incident brought about the emergence of the powerful silver miners' union, culminating in the upheaval of Dec 1943, which brought the MNR (*Movimiento Nacionalista Revolucionario*) to power, with Víctor **PAZ ESTENSSORO** as mentor. Cataví was chosen as the ceremonial site for the nationalization of Bolivia's tin mines in Oct 1952, under Estenssoro's presidency.

**Cateau-Cambrésis, Treaty of** (2–3 Apr 1559)
The treaty agreed between the French and Spanish

crowns which brought an end to the wars of **CHARLES V** in Europe. It recognized Italy as an area of Spanish influence and Franche Comté as part of the Spanish monarchy, and confirmed France in possession of Metz, Toul and Verdun. A dynastic marriage was also agreed between **PHILIP II** of Spain and Elizabeth Valois, daughter of **HENRY II** of France.

## Cathay
A name for China made famous by Marco **POLO** in the 13c. It derived from the Mongol *Khitai*, another name for the **KHITAN**, a semi-nomadic tribe that founded the Liao Dynasty (916–1125) and controlled northern China (to which this term originally referred) from its southern capital in what is now Beijing.

## Catherine I (1684–1727)
Empress of Russia (1725/7). Of lowly birth (probably Lithuanian peasant stock), she was baptized a Roman Catholic with the name of Martha. Married as a young girl to a Swedish army officer who deserted her, she subsequently became mistress to a Russian general, Boris Sheremetev, and to the Tsar's principal minister, Prince Alexander **MENSHIKOV**. In 1705 she became mistress to Tsar **PETER I, THE GREAT**, changing her name to Catherine and converting to Orthodoxy in 1708. The Tsar married her (his second wife) in 1712, following her distinguished conduct while on campaign with her husband during the wars against Sweden. In 1722 Peter passed a law allowing the tsar to nominate a successor and in 1724 chose Catherine, having her crowned Empress in that year. After his death in 1725, Prince Menshikov ensured her succession to the throne. Although she continued her husband's reforms, she had neither Peter's strong will nor his sense of purpose. She was, however, concerned to alleviate conditions for the peasantry, lowering taxation and reducing the power of local bureaucracies. She was succeeded by his grandson, **PETER II**.

## Catherine II, the Great (1729–96)
Empress of Russia (1762/96). Originally Princess Sophia Augusta of Anhalt-Zerbst, she was born at Stettin and in 1745 was married to the heir to the Russian throne (later **PETER III**). Their marriage was an unhappy one, and Catherine (now baptized into the Russian Orthodox Church under that name) spent much of her time in political intriguing and extramarital affairs. In 1762 a palace coup overthrew her unpopular husband, and she was proclaimed Empress. She carried out an energetic foreign policy and extended the Russian Empire south to the Black Sea as a result of the **RUSSO-TURKISH WARS** (1774 and 1792), while in the west she brought about the three partitions of Poland. Despite pretensions to enlightened ideas, her domestic policies achieved little for the mass of the Russian people, though great cultural advances were made among the nobility. In 1774 she suppressed the popular rebellion led by Pugachev, and later actively persecuted members of the progressive-minded nobility. Her private life was dominated by a long series of lovers, most notably **POTEMKIN**. ► **PUGACHEV, EMELYAN**; **ROMANOV DYNASTY**

## Catherine de' Medici (1519–89)
Queen of France. The daughter of Lorenzo de' Medici, she became the wife of **HENRY II** of France, and was

Regent from 1559 to 1574. During the minority of her sons, **FRANCIS II** (1559–60) and **CHARLES IX** (1560–3), she assumed political influence which she retained as Queen Mother until 1588. She tried to pursue moderation and toleration, to give unity to a state increasingly torn by religious division and aristocratic faction, but she nursed dynastic ambitions, and was drawn into political and religious intrigues, conniving in the **ST BARTHOLOMEW'S DAY MASSACRE** (1572). ► **HUGUENOTS**

## Catherine of Aragon (1485–1536)
Queen of England. The fourth daughter of **FERDINAND II, THE CATHOLIC** and **ISABELLA I, THE CATHOLIC** of Spain, she became the first wife of **HENRY VIII**. She was first married in 1501 to Arthur (1486–1502), the son of **HENRY VII**, and following his early death was betrothed to her brother-in-law, Henry, then a boy of 11. She married him in 1509, and bore him five children, of whom only the Princess Mary (later **MARY I**) survived. In 1527 Henry began a procedure for divorce, which he obtained in 1533, thereby breaking with the pope, and starting the English Reformation. Catherine then retired to lead an austere religious life until her death. ► **REFORMATION** (England)

## Catherine of Braganza (1638–1705)
Wife of **CHARLES II** of England. The daughter of King **JOHN IV** of Portugal, she was married to Charles in 1662 as part of an alliance between England and Portugal, but failed to produce an heir. She helped to convert him to Roman Catholicism just before his death, after which she returned to Portugal (1692), where she died.

## Catholic Emancipation (1829)
A reluctant religious concession granted by the British Tory government, headed by the Duke of **WELLINGTON**, following mounting agitation in Ireland led by Daniel **O'CONNELL** and the Catholic Association. Roman Catholics were permitted to become MPs, and all offices of state in Ireland, except Viceroy and Chancellor, were also opened to Catholics. ► **TORIES**

## Catholic League
The league formed during the **JÜLICH-CLEVES SUCCESSION CONFLICT** (1609–14) by the German Catholic princes, led by **MAXIMILIAN I** of Bavaria. It sided with the Emperor in the **THIRTY YEARS' WAR** and was instrumental in his victory at the Battle of the **WHITE MOUNTAIN** (1620). The league withdrew its support from Emperor Ferdinand and **WALLENSTEIN** because of the radical changes proposed by Ferdinand. The league's terms, imposed on Ferdinand with French support at Regensburg (1630), weakened the Emperor and encouraged the invasion of Pomerania by **GUSTAV II ADOLF** of Sweden. The league dissolved after the Swedes defeated the Imperial army under **TILLY** at Magdeburg (1631).

## Catholic People's Party (*Katholieke Volkspartij*, KVP)
Dutch political party, founded in 1945 as a continuation of the Roman Catholic National Party (RKSP, founded 1922). Traditionally, the Catholic Party in the Netherlands polled about a third of the votes; in the 1960s that percentage began to drop radically, due to general secularization and the departure of

various Catholic splinter groups. As a result, the KVP decided in 1973 to join the Dutch Protestant parties in an interconfessional grouping, the **CHRISTIAN DEMOCRATIC APPEAL** (CDA), and in 1980 the KVP ceased to exist as a separate party. As a centre party, the KVP was regularly in government, and it (or the CDA) has taken part in all Dutch cabinets since **WORLD WAR II**.

**Cato Street Conspiracy** (Feb 1820)
A plot formulated by Arthur Thistlewood (1770–1820) and fellow radical conspirators, to blow up the British Tory cabinet as it attended a dinner at the house of the Earl of Harrowby. The plot was infiltrated by a government agent, and the leaders were arrested and hanged. ► **RADICALISM; TORIES**

**Cats, Jacob** (1577–1660)
Dutch statesman and poet. After studying law at Leiden and Orléans, he settled at Middelburg. He rose to a position of authority in the state, and was twice ambassador in England (1627 and 1652). From then till his death, 'Father Cats' lived at his villa near the Hague, writing the autobiography printed in the 1700 edition of his *Poems*.

**Catt, Carrie Clinton Chapman** (1859–1947)
US suffragist. In 1887 she joined the Iowa Woman Suffrage Association and quickly climbed the ranks of the national movement. Succeeding Susan B **ANTHONY** as President of the **NATIONAL AMERICAN WOMAN SUFFRAGE ASSOCIATION** in 1900, her strategy of working on both state and national levels and through both political parties led to the ratification of the 19th Amendment in 1920 and secured the suffrage for women. She organized the Women's Peace Party during **WORLD WAR I**.

**Cattaneo, Carlo** (1801–69)
Italian politician and political economist. He wrote extensively during the pre-1848 period on agriculture, communications, education, finance, charity and public works. In 1835 he married an English noblewoman and was consulted during the 1830s by the British government on reform and agriculture in India and Ireland. Essentially a gradualist reformer who never preached open rebellion against Austrian rule, he nevertheless became head of the Milanese council of war during the anti-Austrian **CINQUE GIORNATE** (Mar 1848). He was, however, suspicious of the pro-Piedmontese, aristocratic faction that soon came to dominate Milan, and left for Paris. After the collapse of the **REVOLUTIONS OF 1848–9**, he spent many years in exile in Switzerland; he returned to Milan in 1859 after its annexation by the Kingdom of **SARDINIA**. He was elected Deputy in 1860 and 1867 but never attended parliament. He did, however, continue to write on politics, and in 1860 was summoned to Naples by **GARIBALDI** to serve as *prodittatore*.

**cattle trails**
Established routes along which cattle were herded from Texas to reach a railroad for despatch to eastern markets and/or a market which gave better prices. At the end of the **AMERICAN CIVIL WAR** (1861–5), cowboys rounded up herds of wild cattle roaming on the plains of Texas, branded and sold them. Two of the most-used trails were the Chisholm Trail and the Goodnight–Loving Trail. The former was blazed in 1832 by a Native American trader, Jesse Chisholm (c.1805–68); it ran originally from Fort Smith, Arkansas, to Fort Towson, in Indian Territory (later Oklahoma), and by the 1860s had been extended southwards to San Antonio, Texas, and northwards to Abilene, Kansas, where a cattle-shipping depot on the Kansas Pacific Railroad had been established by Joseph G McCoy. It handled c.1.5 million cattle between 1867 and 1871. The latter was blazed by Charles Goodnight and Oliver Loving in 1866, and went from Fort Belknap in Texas to Fort Sumner in northern New Mexico, and finally reached its destination in Denver. The importance of the trails declined in the 1880s as open-range ranching gave way to large cattle ranches fenced off with barbed wire, and many more branch lines on the railroads were built, making long cattle drives uneconomical.

**caucus**
In the USA, a group of members of a political party, or a meeting of such a group for a specific purpose, such as a meeting of local political leaders in a party in order to select convention delegates or register preferences for candidates who are running for state or national office. The term comes from the Caucus Club in Boston, Massachusetts, where the choosing of political candidates and other public matters was discussed in the early 18c. In American usage the term has been extended to denote a faction within a legislative body (eg the National Women's Political Caucus) that attempts to further its interests by influencing matters of party policy. In Britain the term was first used in 1878 by Benjamin **DISRAELI** with reference to Joseph **CHAMBERLAIN**'s reorganization of the Liberal associations, and came to be used, often disparagingly, to describe a strictly disciplined political system rather than the political meetings or people themselves.

**caudillo**
The term (literally, 'chief') often used in Spanish-speaking countries to refer to a dictator, especially (but not exclusively) in the 19c. It was much used of General **FRANCO** of Spain.

**Cavaco Silva, Anibal** (1939–)
Portuguese politician. After studying economics in Britain and the USA, he became a university teacher and then a research director in the Bank of Portugal. With the gradual re-establishment of constitutional government after 1976, he was persuaded by colleagues to enter politics and was Minister of Finance (1980–1). In 1985 he became leader of the Social Democratic Party (PSD) and Prime Minister (1985–95). He ran, unsuccessfully, for the presidency in 1996. Under his cautious, conservative leadership, Portugal joined the **EC** in 1985 and the **WESTERN EUROPEAN UNION** in 1988.

**Cavaignac, Louis Eugène** (1802–57)
French soldier. Having commanded the French army in Algeria, he became Governor-General there in 1848, but was soon recalled to Paris and became Minister of War. He quelled the formidable insurrection of the **JUNE DAYS** (1848), and ruled France thereafter as Prime Minister until the election of Louis Napoleon (**NAPOLEON III**) as President in Dec 1848. In the

coup d'état of Dec 1851, he was arrested but soon released, and though he refused to adhere to the Second Empire, he was permitted to reside in France.

## Cavalier Parliament

The name given to the British parliament of 1661–79. Until the crisis over the **POPISH PLOT**, it usually supported the King, its name deriving from royalist support during the **ENGLISH CIVIL WARS**. It passed legislation in the 1660s and early 1670s to strengthen the Church of England and to discriminate against Puritans and Nonconformists who had been dominant during the English revolution. ► **CHARLES II** (of England); **PURITANISM**

## Cavaliers

Those who fought for **CHARLES I** in the **ENGLISH CIVIL WARS**. The name was used derogatorily in 1642 by supporters of parliament to describe swaggering courtiers with long hair and swords, who reportedly welcomed the prospect of war. Similarly, the parliamentarians were labelled 'Roundheads' by Cavaliers, dating from the riotous assemblies in Westminster during **STRAFFORD**'s trial in 1641, when short-haired apprentices mobbed Charles I's supporters outside the House of **LORDS**.

## Cavell, Edith Louisa (1865–1915)

English nurse. Born in Swardeston, Norfolk, she became a nurse in 1895 and, in 1907 the first matron of the Berkendael Medical Institute in Brussels, which became a **RED CROSS** hospital during **WORLD WAR I**. In Aug 1915 she was arrested by the Germans and charged with having helped around 200 Allied soldiers to escape to the Netherlands. Tried by court martial, she did not deny the charges and was executed.

## Cavendish, Spencer Compton, 8th Duke of Devonshire (1833–1908)

British politician, known as the Marquis of Hartington. A Liberal, he entered parliament in 1857, and between 1863 and 1874 was a Lord of the Admiralty, Under-Secretary for War, War Secretary, Postmaster General, and Chief Secretary for Ireland. In 1875 he became leader of the Liberal opposition during **GLADSTONE**'s temporary abdication, later serving under him as Secretary of State for India (1880–2) and as War Secretary (1882–5). He disapproved of Irish **HOME RULE**, and, having led the break away from the **LIBERAL PARTY**, became head of the Liberal Unionists from 1886, serving in the Unionist government as Lord President of the Council (1895–1903).

## Cavendish, William, Duke of Newcastle (1592–1676)

English soldier and patron of the arts. He was created Knight of the Bath in 1610, Viscount Mansfield in 1620, and Earl (1628), Marquess (1643), and Duke (1665) of Newcastle. He gave strong support to **CHARLES I** in the **ENGLISH CIVIL WARS**, and was general of all forces north of the Trent. After the Battle of **MARSTON MOOR** (1644) he lived on the Continent, at times in great poverty, until the **RESTORATION**. A noted patron of poets and dramatists, he was himself the author of several plays, and of two works on horsemanship.

## Cavour, Camillo Benso di, Count (1810–61)

Italian politician. Abandoning his early military career, he spent most of the 1830s and 1840s concentrating on the scientific farming of his estates or travelling. His visits to England left him a deep admirer of the British liberal institutions, railways, industry and banking. In 1847 he founded a progressive journal, *Il Risorgimento*, but he played no part in the events of 1848. He entered politics in 1849, and held various ministerial posts under **D'AZEGLIO** before replacing him as Prime Minister (Nov 1852); he was to remain Premier until his death, except for a few months in 1859. Cavour's early policy was based on the economic development and modernization of the Kingdom of Sardinia-Piedmont, fostering commerce, ending restrictions on banking and improving communications. From 1855, however, he concentrated increasingly on foreign affairs, perhaps achieving his greatest success with the **PLOMBIÈRES AGREEMENT**, which laid the basis for the Piedmontese acquisition of Lombardy. In 1860 the Expedition of the **THOUSAND** to Sicily, and **GARIBALDI**'s subsequent victories in the **MEZZOGIORNO**, caused Cavour considerable anxiety: he feared that the former Mazzinian might establish a republican government in the south or attempt to capture Rome, which would jeopardize good relations with France. He consequently tried to place the south under more moderate leadership. Having failed to achieve this end, he sent Piedmontese troops through the **PAPAL STATES** (annexing Umbria and the Marche en route) to block Garibaldi's northward advance. Much to his relief, Garibaldi happily surrendered his conquests to **VICTOR EMMANUEL II**. In the last months of his life, Cavour made an abortive attempt to secure Rome through purchase and diplomacy.

## CCF (Cooperative Commonwealth Federation)

Canadian socialist political party. Founded in Calgary in 1932, its first meeting was held in Regina in 1933 by representatives of intellectual groups, organized labour, socialists and farmers. It was led by J S **WOODSWORTH**. The 'Regina Manifesto' included economic planning, central financial control and price stabilization, the extension of public ownership in communications and natural resources, the creation of a welfare state and an emergency relief programme. By 1934 the party had become the official opposition in Saskatchewan and in British Columbia, and hundreds of CCF clubs had sprung up throughout the country (except in the Maritime Provinces and Quebec). The party avoided the fate of the US **SOCIALIST PARTY** because of its strong adherence to parliamentary principles and the support it was given by both trade unionists and intellectuals, although it was damaged severely by **DUPLESSIS**'s **PADLOCK ACT**. In Ontario the CCF became the official opposition in 1943, while in the following year it was elected into government in Saskatchewan. Its challenge forced the Liberals into a far stronger emphasis on social reforms, and such federal legislation as the 1944 Families Allowances Act led to a decrease in support for CCF during the election of 1945. The continuation of this trend in **LIBERAL PARTY** policies eventually led the CCF to drop the most doctrinaire elements from its manifesto in 1956. In 1961 the party evolved into the **NEW DEMOCRATIC PARTY** with 'Tommy' **DOUGLAS**, the CCF Premier of Saskatchewan, as its leader.

**CCM** ➤ CHAMA CHA MAPINDUZI

### CCOO (Comisiones Obreras)

Spanish trade union organization (literally, 'Workers' Commissions'). Its origins lay in the spontaneous rank and file committees set up in the late 1950s in the Asturian coalfields and the Basque country to organize strike action. By the mid-1960s, it had established a parallel organization to the official syndicate, thereby becoming the first democratic broadly-based union organization in Spain since the **SPANISH CIVIL WAR**. By the late 1960s it was firmly under communist control, being severely repressed after the major demonstration of 1967 until **FRANCO**'s death in 1975. It is now one of the two main trade union forces in Spain, the other being the **UGT**.

**CDU** (*Christlich Demokratische Union*, 'Christian Democratic Union')

German political party. An ideologically heterogeneous collection of regional organizations gradually coalesced between 1947 and 1950 to form the main party of government in post-war Federal Germany. The CDU has roots in the pre-1933 **CENTRE PARTY**, but functions as a multi-denominational, 'people's' party, committed to social progress within a **SOCIAL MARKET ECONOMY**. Its membership is socially diverse, but with a definite middle-class flavour, initially more within the independent middle classes, now among salaried and professional groups. It dominated government under the leadership of Konrad **ADENAUER** (1949–63) and presided over Germany's great economic miracle (**WIRTSCHAFTS-WUNDER**), but in 1966 was forced into coalition with the **SPD** and in 1969 went into opposition. Under Helmut **KOHL** the CDU regained power in 1982 with its customary ally, the **CSU**, and with the **FDP**. This coalition oversaw the reunification of Germany during 1989 and 1990. The CDU was defeated in 1998 by the SPD, and although in 2002 it won almost as many seats as the SPD, it was kept from power by the SPD's coalition with the Greens.

### Ceauşescu, Nicolae (1918–89)

Romanian politician. Born into a peasant family, he joined the Communist Party in 1936 and was imprisoned for anti-government activities (1936–8). He became a member of the Central Committee of the Romanian Communist Party (RCP) in 1952 and of the Politburo in 1955. In 1965 he succeeded **GHEOR-GIU-DEJ** as *de facto* party leader, becoming General-Secretary of the RCP in 1965 and its first President in 1967. Under his leadership, Romania became increasingly independent of the USSR and pursued its own foreign policy, for which Ceauşescu was decorated by many Western governments. In internal affairs he extended the rigid programme of his Stalinist predecessor, instituting a strong personality cult and filling offices with his family. He manipulated Romanian nationalism and ruthlessly forced national minorities to adopt Romanian culture. His policy of 'systematization' in the countryside, uprooting traditional villages, roused an international outcry in the late 1980s. In 1989 he was deposed when elements in the army joined a popular revolt. Following a trial by military tribunal, he and his wife, Elena, who had been second only to him in political influence, were shot.

### Cecil, Robert, 1st Earl of Salisbury (c.1563–1612)

English minister, son of William **CECIL**, 1st Baron Burghley. He entered parliament in 1584. He became a Privy Councillor (1591) and was appointed **ELIZA-BETH I**'s Secretary of State (1596). His years of control in the last years of the reign helped to smooth the succession of James VI of Scotland to the English throne. James maintained him in office and he negotiated peace terms, ending the long war with Spain (1604). He was an efficient administrator and financial manager who fought a losing battle against mounting royal debts. ➤ **JAMES VI AND I**

### Cecil, Robert Arthur Talbot Gascoyne, 3rd Marquis of Salisbury (1830–1903)

British politician. He became a Conservative MP in 1853. In 1865 he was made Viscount Cranborne, and in 1868 Marquis of Salisbury. He was twice Indian Secretary (1866 and 1874), became Foreign Secretary (1878) and, on **DISRAELI**'s death (1881), Leader of the Opposition. He was Prime Minister on three occasions (1885–6, 1886–92 and 1895–1902), also serving much of the time as his own Foreign Secretary. He resigned as Foreign Secretary in 1900, but remained as head of government during the **BOER WARS** (1899–1902). He retired in 1902.

### Cecil, William, 1st Baron Burghley or Burghleigh (1520–98)

English statesman. He served under Somerset and Northumberland, was made Secretary of State (1550) and knighted (1551). During **MARY I**'s reign he conformed to Roman Catholicism. In 1558 **ELIZA-BETH I** appointed him Chief Secretary of State, and for the next 40 years he was the chief architect of the Elizabethan regime, controlling the administration, influencing her pro-Protestant foreign policy, securing the execution of **MARY, QUEEN OF SCOTS**, and preparing for the Spanish **ARMADA**. In 1571 he was created Baron Burghley, and in 1572 became Lord High Treasurer (an office he held until his death).

### CEDA (*Confederación Española de Derechas Autónomas*, 'Spanish Confederation of Autonomous Rightist Groups')

Spanish political party. The CEDA, founded in Feb 1933, was the principal non-Republican conservative force under the Second Republic. Ultimately, the proto-fascist CEDA aimed to replace the Republic by an authoritarian, corporatist state: many of its goals were assumed by **FRANCO**. The CEDA dominated the governments of 1933–5 through an alliance with the **RADICAL REPUBLICAN PARTY**, demolishing the reforms of 1931–3 and preparing the army for a rising. Its legalistic strategy for power was thwarted by the collapse of the Radicals, the President's refusal to allow the CEDA to head an administration and, finally, its failure to win the general election of Feb 1936. The party not only provided funds for the rising of July 1936, but the vast majority of its members joined the Nationalists. However, there was no place for the CEDA in Nationalist Spain, so it was dissolved in Apr 1937. ➤ **REPUBLIC, SECOND** (Spain)

## Ceka

The gang of hired thugs, often recruited from the criminal classes, employed by **MUSSOLINI** to intimidate his political opponents. Their attacks were responsible for the death of **MATTEOTTI** and for the flight from Italy of, among others, **NITTI** and **AMENDOLA**. They were also used to harass **FUORUSCITI**.

## Censorate

A Chinese government institution during imperial times with its origins in the 3c BC, which was responsible for the investigation of official conduct in central and local administration. Censors could report directly to the emperor and impeach officials for violating administrative regulations or moral standards. As the upholders of proper moral conduct in government, censors occasionally criticized emperors, although they might be treated harshly for such action. By the time of the **MING DYNASTY** and **QING DYNASTY**, the censorate had virtually become merely the emperor's tool for controlling the bureaucracy.

## CENTO (Central Treaty Organization)

A political-military alliance signed in 1955 between Iran, Turkey, Pakistan, Iraq (which withdrew in 1958) and the UK, as a defence against the USSR. The alliance effectively ended when Iran withdrew after the **IRANIAN REVOLUTION** in 1979.

## Central African Federation (1953–63)

A federal territory established by the British Government to bring together the administrations of Northern and Southern Rhodesia and Nyasaland (now Zambia, Zimbabwe and Malawi). It was designed to act as a counterweight to South Africa, which had been dominated by the Afrikaans Nationalists since the election of 1948, and to encourage investment in the region. Theoretically its society and government were to be developed on the basis of racial partnership, but in reality it became a means for the extension of white-settler power. It stimulated African nationalist resistance and an emergency was declared after disturbances broke out in Nyasaland in 1959, together with strikes and political activism in Northern Rhodesia. After the Devlin and Monckton Commission reports, the Federation was wound up, leading to the independence of Zambia and Malawi and the unilateral declaration of independence in Rhodesia.

---

**CENTRAL AFRICAN REPUBLIC**

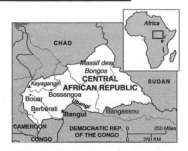

A republic in central Africa, bounded to the north by Chad; to the north-east by Sudan; to the south by Congo and the Democratic Republic of the Congo; and to the west by Cameroon. For a time part of French Equatorial Africa (known as Ubangi Shari), it became an autonomous republic within the French community in 1958 and gained independence in 1960 with David **DACKO** as President. He was deposed in 1966 by Jean-Bédel **BOKASSA**, who established a monarchy known as the Central African Empire in 1976, but was forced to flee in 1979. The country reverted to a republic with David Dacko as President until he was again ousted by a military coup in 1981, led by André-Dieudonné Kolingba. Civilian rule returned under Kolingba in 1986, and in 1992 the constitution was amended to allow for opposition parties and to reduce the powers of the President. Elections the following year brought in a coalition government and Ange-Félix Patasse as President. In 2003 François Bozize took power in a coup and suspended the constitution.

## Central American Common Market (CACM)

An economic association initiated in 1961 between Guatemala, El Salvador and Nicaragua, and (from 1962) Costa Rica and Honduras. Its early apparent success was offset by growing political crisis in the late 1970s. ► EEC (European Economic Community)

## Central American Federation (CAF)

A federation formed in 1823, following independence from Spain, by Costa Rica, Nicaragua, Honduras, El Salvador and Guatemala. Despite vigorous leadership by Francisco **MORAZÁN** of Honduras, internal tensions brought about the collapse of the federation by 1838.

## Central Committee of the Communist Party of the Soviet Union

Under Soviet party rules, this was the highest decision-making authority in the USSR, apart from the Party Congress, which elected it. However, except in rare circumstances (twice in Nikita **KHRUSHCHEV**'s time), it exercised little influence, partly because of its unwieldy size and partly because of the concentration of power in the **POLITBURO**.

## Central Intelligence Agency ► CIA

## central planning

A rigid economic system found mainly in communist countries which does not allow individual enterprise in any form. Joseph **STALIN** advocated central planning, and after coming to power in 1924 brought about the immediate collectivization of the economy: all private enterprises and capitalist markets were eliminated; private agriculture was converted into collective farming; and the direction of economic life became the responsibility of ministries and planning agencies. Largely because of too much central planning, the communist world lagged behind the West, a fact which sapped confidence in the regimes and contributed to their downfall in the period 1989–91. Since then most of the former Soviet countries have gradually developed free-market economic systems. ► **INTENSIVE DEVELOPMENT; MARKET ECONOMY**

## Central Powers

Initially, the members of the **TRIPLE ALLIANCE** (Germany, Austria-Hungary, Italy) created by **BISMARCK** in 1882. As Italy remained neutral in 1914, the term was later used to describe Germany, Austria-Hungary, their ally Turkey, and later Bulgaria, in **WORLD WAR I**.

**Centre Party** (Germany; *Zentrum*)
German political party. This interest-group party was founded in 1870–1 after the creation of the German **REICH** to defend the rights and identity of the Roman Catholic Church and the Catholic minority (33 per cent of the population) within the country. By the turn of the century, the Centre Party had long escaped the **KULTURKAMPF**, or political persecution it initially suffered under **BISMARCK**, and from 1918 onward played a key role in the creation and governance of the **WEIMAR REPUBLIC**. It contained politicians and supporters right across the social spectrum, whose politics were only accommodated with difficulty during the 20c. A staunch opponent of **HITLER** at the end of Weimar, the Centre Party then supported his enabling legislation in Mar 1933 in return for guarantees on the rights of Catholics. The Centre Party dissolved itself in July 1933.

**Centre Party** (Sweden)
The name adopted in 1958 by the Agrarian Party, which had been formed in 1921 by the union of a number of farmers' groups. It supported the Social Democrats between 1932 and the later 1950s, and indeed joined them in coalition governments in 1936–45 and 1951–7. After this, the party moved away from its former allies. It took up the environmentalist and anti-nuclear cause, and succeeded in broadening its electoral base. In 1976–82 the leader of the party, Torbjörn Fälldin, headed non-socialist coalition governments. Though essentially a non-socialist party, it has formed alliances with the socialist Social Democrats.

**Centurioni**
The members of the militia established in the **PAPAL STATES** by Cardinal Tommaso Bernetti after the liberal uprisings of the early 1830s. They were stigmatized by liberal writers as little better than bandits.

**Cerezo Arévalo, Marco Vinicio** (1942–)
Guatemalan politician. Educated at San Carlos University, Guatemala, he joined the Christian Democratic Party (PDCG), founded in 1968. From 1974 there was widespread political violence, and democratic government was virtually suspended. With the adoption of a new constitution in 1985, the PDCG won the congressional elections, and Cerezo became the first civilian President for 20 years. He remained in office until 1991, struggling to deal with a still-maleficent military, and an economy undermined by high foreign debt, and at its close his administration was widely perceived as corrupt and ineffective.

**Cerignola, Battle of** ► **ITALIAN WARS**

**Černík, Oldřich** (1921–94)
Czechoslovak politician. A man of reasonable ability, he worked his way up through the official hierarchy to become Chairman of the State Planning Commission in 1963. As such, he favoured moderate change to make the economy more efficient. However, in Jan 1968, when Alexander **DUBČEK** became General-Secretary, Černík became Prime Minister and followed a more far-reaching reform policy. In July and Aug of the same year he tried to restrain the more radical supporters of the **PRAGUE SPRING**, and after the Soviet invasion he struggled to try to retain something of its achievements. But within two years, like Dubček, he

was removed from the party and the government.

**Černý, Jan** (1874–1959)
Czechoslovak official and politician. Partly as a result of its proportional representation system, interwar Czechoslovakia had, on occasions, difficulty in finding a coalition government. In two such periods (1920–1 and 1926), President **MASARYK** employed the device of appointing a cabinet of officials. In both of these, Černý acted as Prime Minister and did an efficient job. His experience as an official in the Ministry of the Interior stood him in good stead, although it added to his unpopularity among the social democrats in particular. He subsequently served brief periods as Minister of the Interior, including just before and after the **MUNICH AGREEMENT**.

**Céspedes, Carlos Manuel de** (1819–73)
Cuban nationalist. 'The Father of the Country' came from a wealthy plantation family and studied law in Spain before returning to Cuba. There he raised a revolt against the Spanish colonial government, instigating the **TEN YEARS' WAR** in Oriente. With 200 poorly armed men, he took Santiago and freed the slaves, and in 1869 devised a constitution and was elected provisional President of the incipient republic. However, in 1873 he was deposed by the revolutionary council; he went into hiding, but was captured by the Spanish and shot.

**Cetewayo** (c.1826–1884)
King of the Zulu (1872/9). In Jan 1879 he defeated an entire British regiment at **ISANDHLWANA**, but was himself overcome by British forces under Sir Garnet **WOLSELEY** at Ulundi in July of the same year. However, so eloquently did Cetewayo present his case in London, that in Jan 1883 he was restored by the British as ruler of central Zululand. Shortly thereafter, though, he was driven out by his subjects, and died at Ekowe.

**CFE Treaty** official title **Treaty on Conventional Armed Forces in Europe** (1990)
An agreement on the reduction of conventional (ie non-nuclear) forces in Europe. Following the **HELSINKI FINAL ACT**, **CSCE** meetings sought to achieve a balance in the conventional forces of the Eastern and Western alliances, resulting in the treaty, signed by **NATO** and **WARSAW PACT** representatives in 1990. It set limits for the major weapons and equipment systems to be held by both blocs, and also specified a regime of notification and verification, on-site inspections and monitoring of destruction.

**CGT** (*Confédération générale du travail*, 'General Confederation of Labour')
French trade union organization, formed in 1895, which today claims a membership of about 2 million, mainly production and blue-collar workers. It is now closely linked to the **COMMUNIST PARTY**, but originally adopted by the Charter of Amiens (1906), a policy of avoiding all links with political parties and espousing the doctrines of revolutionary syndicalism (according to which the trade union movement should destroy capitalist society through strike action, and create a new society run by the workers' unions, as opposed to state socialism). By 1921 it had evolved to a moderate position, which led to a schism, and the founding of the CGTU (*Confédération*

*générale du travail unitaire*), which soon came to be controlled by the Communist Party. The CGT and CGTU were reunited in 1936, under the CGT banner. After being banned during **WORLD WAR II**, the CGT emerged under communist control, which led to a new schism in 1948, with the formation of the CGT *Force ouvrière*, ('Workers' Force'), close at that time to the **SOCIALIST PARTY** and consisting mainly of civil servants and clerical workers. There are several other trade union federations, of which the most important are the *Confédération française démocratique du travail* (CFDT, 'French Democratic Confederation of Labour') formed in 1964 out of the *Confédération française des travailleurs chrétiens* (CFTC, 'French Confederation of Christian Workers'), a Catholic federation originally established in 1920, which, however, also continued to exist. There is also the *Confédération générale des cadres* (CGC) founded in 1944, consisting mainly of white-collar workers. One of the largest unionized workforces, the schoolteachers, have their own *Fédération de l'éducation nationale* (FEN) independent of all the general federations. The main characteristics of French trade unionism are its fragmentation and weakness; a much smaller proportion of workers are members of any trade union than in comparable economies.

## Chaadayev, Pyotr Yakovlevich (1794–1856)
Russian writer and political critic. Particularly in periods of repression, it became the function of Russian authors overtly or covertly to discuss political issues. In 1836, during **NICHOLAS I**'s autocratic reign, Chaadayev published his *Philosophical Letters*, critical of Russia's political and cultural achievements, and specifically of the link between the State and the Orthodox Church. For a time, Nicholas declared him mad and ordered him to be examined regularly by doctors. However, his ideas were much discussed and opened what became a prolonged and heated debate between the old 'easterners' and new 'westerners'.

## Chaco War (1932–5)
A territorial struggle between Bolivia and Paraguay in the disputed Northern Chaco area. Owing to the brilliant tactics of Colonel José Félix **ESTIGARRIBIA**, Paraguay won most of the area, and a peace treaty was signed in 1938. Around 50,000 Bolivians and 35,000 Paraguayans died in the war. The outcome of the war decisively shaped the history of the decades that followed, defeat ultimately contributing to the formation of the MNR (*Movimiento Nacionalista Revolucionario*) in Bolivia, and victory to a succession of dictatorships in Paraguay, culminating in that of Alfredo **STROESSNER** in 1954.

## CHAD    official name Republic of Chad
A republic in north central Africa, bounded to the north by Libya; to the east by Sudan; to the south by Central African Republic; and to the west by Cameroon, Nigeria and Niger. It was part of French Equatorial Africa in the 19c, and became a French colony in 1920. In 1960 it gained full independence. Since 1975 the country has been politically unstable, experiencing a number of coups arising from the tension between the Muslim north, supported by Libya, and the Christian south, supported by Western states. In 1982 rebel forces supported by the West took the capital, forming a new government under Hissène

**HABRÉ**; fighting continued between Libyan-supported rebels and the new government until a ceasefire was agreed in 1987, when Libya withdrew. In 1990 Habré was deposed in another Libyan-backed coup, this time led by Idriss Déby. The country gradually underwent a process of democratization and a new constitution was approved in 1996, when Déby won the presidential election, but unrest has continued. Chad has experienced an influx of thousands of Sudanese refugees from **DARFUR** since early 2004, and its forces have clashed with Sudanese militia on the border.

## Chadli Benjedid (1929– )
Algerian politician and soldier. In 1955 he joined the guerrillas (*maquisards*) who were fighting for independence as part of the **FLN**. Under Houari **BOUMÉDIENNE**, Defence Minister in **BEN BELLA**'s government, he was military commander of Algiers, and then when Boumédienne overthrew Ben Bella in 1965 he joined the Revolutionary Council. He succeeded Boumédienne as Secretary-General of the FLN and President of Algeria in 1979. In Jan 1992 he resigned his post as President.

## chaebol
A Korean term for a conglomerate of many companies clustered around one parent company which hold shares in each other and are often run by one family; the best-known are Daewoo, Hyundai and Samsung. After the **KOREAN WAR** (1950–3) and throughout the 1960s, *chaebol* were vehicles of economic growth, usually through foreign loans and government favours, including discouragement of foreign competition. By the late 1980s, the *chaebol* dominated Korean manufacturing, trading and heavy industry but their business practices were opaque and corruption was rife. In 1997 a series of corporate failures culminated in the crashes of the South Korean stock market and currency. A $55 billion rescue package, sponsored by the **INTERNATIONAL MONETARY FUND** and the USA was linked to free market reforms.

## Chak(k)ri Dynasty
A Siamese dynasty founded in 1782 by General P'raya Chakri, who as Rama I (1782/1809) established his capital at Bangkok, and instituted a period of stability

and prosperity in Siam; also known as the 'Bangkok Dynasty'. His successors, especially Rama III (1824/ 51), Rama IV (1851/68) and Rama V (1868/1910), opened the country to foreign trade and championed modernization. The dynasty still reigns under the constitutional monarchy established after a bloodless revolution in 1932. ► CHULALONGKORN, PHRA PARAMINDR MAHA

**Chalukya** ► INDIA, PRE-ISLAMIC

## Chama cha Mapinduzi (CCM)
Sometimes referred to as the Revolutionary Party of Tanzania, this party was formed in 1977 by the merger of the TANGANYIKA AFRICAN NATIONAL UNION (TANU) and the Afro-Shirazi Party. It was the only legal party in Tanzania from 1977 to 1992, and even with the introduction of multiparty politics in 1992 it has continued to control the presidency and the National Assembly.

## Chamberlain, Sir (Joseph) Austen (1863–1937)
British politician. The eldest son of Joseph CHAMBER-LAIN, he was elected a Liberal Unionist MP in 1892, and sat as a Conservative MP until his death in 1937. He was Chancellor of the Exchequer (1903–6 and 1919–21), Secretary for India (1915–17), Unionist leader (1921–2), Foreign Secretary (1924–9), and First Lord of the Admiralty (1931). He received the 1925 NOBEL PEACE PRIZE for negotiating the LOCARNO PACT. ► CONSERVATIVE PARTY (UK)

## Chamberlain, Joseph (1836–1914)
British politician. He entered the family business at 16, and became Mayor of Birmingham (1873–5), and a Liberal MP (1876). In 1880 he became President of the Board of Trade, but in 1886 resigned over GLAD-STONE'S HOME RULE Bill, which split the LIBERAL PARTY. From 1889 he was leader of the Liberal Unionists, and in the coalition government of 1895 took office as Secretary for the Colonies. In 1903 he resigned office to be free to advocate his ideas on tariff reform, which split the Conservative and Unionist Party. In 1906 he withdrew from public life after a stroke. ► CHAMBERLAIN, AUSTEN; CHAMBERLAIN, NEVILLE; CONSERVATIVE PARTY (UK); RADICALISM

## Chamberlain, (Arthur) Neville (1869–1940)
British politician. He was the son of Joseph CHAM-BERLAIN by his second marriage. He was Mayor of Birmingham (1915–16), a Conservative MP from 1918, Chancellor of the Exchequer (1923–4 and 1931–7), and three times Minister for Health (1923, 1924–9 and 1931), where he effected notable social reforms. He played a leading part in the formation of the National Government (1931). As Prime Minister (1937–40), he advocated 'APPEASEMENT' of Italy and Germany, returning from Munich with his claim to have found 'peace in our time' (1938). Criticism of his war leadership and initial military reverses led to his resignation as Prime Minister (1940), and his appointment as Lord President of the Council. ► CON-SERVATIVE PARTY (UK); MUNICH AGREEMENT; WORLD WAR II

## Chambord, Henri Charles Dieudonné, Count of (1820–83)
French BOURBON pretender as 'Henri V', grandson of King CHARLES X of France. Born in Paris after the as-

sassination of his father, the Duke of Berry, he was taken into exile after the abdication of Charles in 1830. The National Assembly elected in 1871 had a royalist majority and his restoration to the throne seemed possible, but his refusal to accept the tricolour flag rendered this abortive.

## Chamoun, Camille (1900–87)
Lebanese politician. The curious constitutional provisions of Lebanon after its independence provided for a Muslim Prime Minister and a (Maronite) Christian President. Camille Chamoun held the presidency from 1952 until 1958. A pro-USA Maronite, his reluctance to surrender the presidency to Fuad Chehab, a Maronite more acceptable to Lebanese Muslims, led to the outbreak of civil war. His policy aimed at peaceful coexistence between Christians and Muslims, but his support for France and Britain during the SUEZ CRISIS seriously undermined the credibility of his regime. His position was only saved during the civil war by the intervention, in 1958, of US Marines (who caused a stir by coming ashore on the bathing beaches of the Lebanese coast). Although he did not seek re-election, he continued in politics and in 1980 his National Liberal Party split from the Phalangists. He survived an assassination attempt in 1987, but died later the same year.

## Champa
A state founded on the east coast of Vietnam in the 2c AD that developed along the Indian pattern of state organization and was a serious rival to Khmer and Vietnamese power in the peninsula up to the 16c.

## Champlain, Samuel de (c.1570–1635)
French navigator and Governor of NEW FRANCE. In a series of voyages he travelled to North America (1603), exploring the east coast (1604–7), and founding Quebec (1608). He was appointed commandant of New France (1612), and established alliances with several Indian nations. When Quebec fell briefly to the British, he was taken prisoner (1629–32). From 1633 he was Governor of Quebec. Lake Champlain is named after him. ► EXPLORA-TION; FUR TRADE

**Chandella** ► INDIA, PRE-ISLAMIC

## Changamire
The dynastic title of the rulers of southern Zimbabwe from 1480 until the mid-17c. In 1480 a vassal-ruler of the Changa people took advantage of the weakness of the empire of Monomotapa to declare himself an independent amir (Changa Amir). During the 17c the Changamire also conquered most of northern Zimbabwe (Mutapa) and formed a powerful barrier to the incursions of Portuguese traders eager to obtain access to the substantial gold-mining industry there.

**Chang Chih-tung** ► ZHANG ZHIDONG

**Chang Kuo-t'ao** ► ZHANG GUOTAO

**Chao Tzu-yang** ► ZHAO ZIYANG

## Chapleau, Sir (Joseph) Adolphe (1840–98)
Canadian politician. As leader of the moderate BLEUS, John MACDONALD invited him into the cabinet in 1882 to balance the inclusion of the extremist Sir Hector LANGEVIN. The Rouge leader, Honoré MER-CIER, asked him to lead the movement of protest at

the execution of **RIEL**, but since he believed the sentence was just, he refused. He resigned in 1892 to become Lieutenant-Governor of Quebec. ► **ROUGES**

**Chaptal, Jean Antoine, Count of Chantaloupe** (1756–1832)
French politician and chemist. He took a leading part in the introduction of the metric system of weights and measures. He was equally successful as a chemical manufacturer and a writer on industrial chemistry. He was Minister of the Interior from 1800 to 1804. Ennobled by **NAPOLEON I**, he served as a minister in his **HUNDRED DAYS** (1815).

**Chapultepec, Act of** (1945)
Signed in Mexico, this act established that American states should aid each other in the event of aggression from any source whatsoever. It also met the need to coordinate, by a single instrument, the various measures calling for the peaceful settlement of disputes in the Inter-American system. It was designed as a regional counterpoise to the **UN**. Its corollary was the Inter-American Treaty of Mutual Assistance (TIAR), subsequently signed in Rio de Janeiro and known as the **RIO DE JANEIRO TREATY**, and the **ORGANIZATION OF AMERICAN STATES** (OAS), drawn up in Bogotá in 1948, as well as the inter-American Treaty on Pacific Settlement (Pact of Bogotá) outlining procedures for the peaceful settlement of inter-American disputes. Subsequent amendments have strengthened the economic and social functions of the OAS.

**Charge of the Light Brigade**
An incident during the Battle of **BALACLAVA** (1854), when the Light Brigade, under the command of the Earl of **CARDIGAN**, charged the main Russian artillery. The charge involved massive loss of life. It resulted from the misunderstanding of an order given by the commanding officer, Lord **RAGLAN**, to stop guns captured by the Russians being carried away during their retreat.

**Charles (Karl Ludwig Johann)** (1771–1847)
Archduke of Austria and soldier. The third son of the Emperor **LEOPOLD II** and brother of the Emperor **FRANCIS II**, he entered the Austrian army in 1792 and became Governor-General of the Netherlands (1793). As Commander of the Austrian Army on the Rhine in 1796, he defeated Moreau and Jourdan in several battles, drove the French over the Rhine, and took Kehl. He was forced back from the Tagliamento by **NAPOLEON I** as he invaded Austria in 1797, but defeated Jourdan again at Stockach in 1799, only to be worsted by **MASSÉNA**. In 1799 he was again victorious over Jourdan. Next year ill health compelled him to accept the governor-generalship of Bohemia. Recalled after the Austrian defeat at Hohenlinden (1800) to the chief command, he checked the progress of Moreau. In 1805 he commanded against Masséna in Italy; then, after news of the crushing defeat at the Battle of **AUSTERLITZ** (1805), he made a masterly retreat to Croatia. In 1809 he won the great Battle of Aspern, but had to give best at the ferocious Battle of **WAGRAM**, leading to the Treaty of **VIENNA**. He retired thereafter and became Governor of Mainz in 1815.

**Charles I** (of Spain) ► **CHARLES V** (Holy Roman Emperor)

**Charles I** (1600–49)
King of Great Britain and Ireland (1625/49). He failed in his attempt to marry the Infanta Maria of Spain (1623), marrying instead the French princess Henrietta Maria (1609–69). This disturbed the nation, since the marriage articles permitted her the free exercise of the Roman Catholic religion. Three parliaments were summoned and dissolved in the first four years of his reign; then for 11 years (1629–40) he ruled without one, making much use of prerogative courts. He warred with France (1627–9), and in 1630 made peace with Spain, but his growing need for money led to unpopular economic policies. His attempt to Anglicize the Scottish Church brought active resistance in the **BISHOPS' WARS** (1639–40), and he then called a parliament (1640). Having alienated much of the realm, Charles entered into the first of the **ENGLISH CIVIL WARS** (1642–6), which saw the defeat of his cause at the Battle of **NASEBY**, and he surrendered to the Scots at Newark (1646). After many negotiations, during which his duplicity exasperated opponents, and a second Civil War (1646–8), he came to trial at Westminster, where his dignified refusal to plead was interpreted as a confession of guilt. He was beheaded at Whitehall (30 Jan 1649). ► **LONG PARLIAMENT**

**Charles I** (1839–1914)
King of Romania (1881/1914). He was the second son of Prince Karl Anton, head of the Roman Catholic southern branch of the Prussian ruling dynasty. Designated as a suitable candidate by the liberal Ion **BRĂTIANU**, he was made Prince of Romania in 1866 and became Romania's first king after the country received full independence from the **OTTOMAN EMPIRE**. A patriotic Prussian yet loyal to Romanian interests, active in government as a constitutional monarch and a clever politician, he became a strong and popular leader. Due to his concern for economic development, Romania was in this respect the most advanced of the Balkan states on the eve of **WORLD WAR I**.

**Charles I** (1887–1922)
Last ruler of the Austro-Hungarian monarchy (1916/18). He succeeded his grand-uncle, **FRANCIS JOSEPH**, in 1916, having become heir presumptive on the assassination at Sarajevo (1914) of his uncle, Archduke **FRANCIS FERDINAND**. In Nov 1918 he was compelled to abdicate upon the collapse of Austria-Hungary. Two attempts at restoration in Hungary (1921) failed, and he died in exile in Madeira.

**Charles II** (1630–85)
King of Great Britain and Ireland (1660/85). He was the son of King **CHARLES I**. As Prince of Wales, he sided with his father in the **ENGLISH CIVIL WARS**, and was then forced into exile. On his father's execution (1649), he assumed the title of King, and was crowned at Scone (1651). Leading poorly organized forces into England, he met disastrous defeat at the Battle of **WORCESTER** (1651). The next nine years were spent in exile until an impoverished England, in dread of a revival of military despotism, invited him back as King (1660). In 1662 he married the Portuguese Princess **CATHERINE OF BRAGANZA**. It was a childless marriage, though Charles was the father of many illegitimate children. His wars against the

Dutch (1665–7 and 1672–4) were unpopular, and the first of these led to the dismissal of his adviser Lord CLARENDON (1667), who was replaced by a group of ministers (the CABAL). He negotiated subsidies from France in the secret Treaty of DOVER (1670), by which he also promised LOUIS XIV to make England Catholic once more. He negotiated skilfully and sometimes unscrupulously between conflicting political and religious pressures, and during the EXCLUSION CRISIS (1678–81) refused to deny the succession of his Catholic brother James. For the last four years of his life, he ruled without parliament. ► ANGLO-DUTCH WARS; POPISH PLOT

**Charles II** (1661–1700)
King of Spain (1665/1700). The son of PHILIP IV of Spain, he was the last ruler of the Habsburg Dynasty in Spain. Congenital ill health made him unfit to rule, and government was conducted first by a regency under his mother, then by his half-brother, Don JUAN JOSÉ OF AUSTRIA, and finally by various noble factions. The reign was one of positive advances in many areas of economy, demography and culture, but the dominant reality was the collapse of Spanish power in Europe as a result of the aggression of LOUIS XIV of France. Peace treaties of 1684 and 1697 resulted in substantial territorial gains for France. The King's inability to produce an heir precipitated disputes over the succession, and his nomination of the French Duke of Anjou (later PHILIP V of Spain) as next king led directly to the War of the SPANISH SUCCESSION.

**Charles II** (1893–1953)
King of Romania (1930/40). Involved in a scandalous affair with Magda LUPESCU, he renounced his right of succession (1925) and went to live in Paris. In 1930 he returned to Romania as King and succeeded in concentrating political power in his own hands during the subsequent rapid changes of ministry. In 1938 he established a royal dictatorship, gaining full powers through a new constitution, organizing his own political party, the Front of National Rebirth, and adopting many of the themes of the fascist-style IRON GUARD. In 1940, after agreeing to the second VIENNA AWARD, which gave part of Transylvania to Hungary, he became so unpopular that he was obliged to abdicate in favour of his son MICHAEL.

**Charles III** (1716–88)
King of Spain (1759/88) and, as Charles IV, King of Naples and Sicily (1734/59). The younger son of PHILIP V of Spain, he conquered Naples and Sicily during the War of the POLISH SUCCESSION and, on his accession to the Spanish throne, handed them over to his son, Ferdinand I. Charles subordinated the Church to the Crown, did much to revive the economic and cultural standing of Spain in Europe, and reformed Spanish links with her colonies. He sided with France in the SEVEN YEARS' WAR, when Florida was lost to Britain. France ceded Louisiana to Spain in compensation, and Spain recovered Florida (1783) after the AMERICAN REVOLUTION.

**Charles IV** (1316–78)
Holy Roman Emperor (1346/78). He became Margrave of Moravia in 1334 and gradually assumed an increasing role in the government of the Czech lands during the frequent absences of his father, King John. On the latter's death, he became both Holy Roman Emperor and King of Bohemia. Unlike his predecessors, he tried to avoid being drawn into Italian conflicts. Instead, through shrewd diplomacy, he built up a dynastic empire based round his domains of Bohemia and Moravia, with his capital at Prague, where he founded the first university within the Empire (1348). His *Golden Bull* of 1356 became the new constitutional framework for the empire; it laid down procedure for the election of the monarch, excluded papal pretensions, and defined the rights of the seven Electors, whose domains were declared indivisible. He was the first emperor since FREDERICK I to be succeeded by his son (WENCESLAS IV).

**Charles IV** (1748–1819)
King of Spain (1788/1808). The son of CHARLES III, his government was largely in the hands of his wife, Maria Luisa (1751–1819), and her favourite, Manuel de GODOY. NELSON destroyed his fleet at the Battle of TRAFALGAR, and in 1808 he abdicated under pressure from NAPOLEON I. He spent the rest of his life in exile, and died in Rome.

**Charles IV, the Fair** (1294–1328)
King of France (1322/8) and (as Charles I) of Navarre. He renewed war with England by his invasion of Aquitaine.

**Charles V** (1500–58)
Holy Roman Emperor (1519/56). The son of PHILIP I, THE HANDSOME and JOAN THE MAD, he inherited the Habsburg lands in 1506, Spain in 1516, and was elected Holy Roman Emperor in 1519. His rivalry with FRANCIS I of France led to four wars but left him in control of the disputed territories in Italy and the Netherlands. During the REFORMATION Charles sought to defend and restore the unity of faith, and although he was forced to make concessions to the Protestants in 1532, these were revoked at the height of his power in 1546. The internally divided SCHMALKALDIC LEAGUE of Protestant princes was subsequently defeated at MÜHLBERG (1547) but the attempted reunification of the religious parties by the compromise formula of the AUGSBURG INTERIM (1548) proved unacceptable and had to be abandoned in 1555. Exhausted and frustrated, Charles abdicated in 1556, dividing the empire between his son, PHILIP II of Spain, and his brother, Ferdinand I of Austria. He retired to the monastery of San Yuste in Spain, where he died.

**Charles V, the Wise** (1337–80)
King of France (1364/80). As DAUPHIN he acted as regent during the long captivity of his father JOHN II, after the Battle of POITIERS, finally succeeding him in 1364. In a series of victories, he regained most of the territory lost to the English in the HUNDRED YEARS' WAR.

**Charles VI** (1685–1740)
Holy Roman Emperor (1711/40). As Charles III he was also a claimant to the Spanish throne. His goal was to re-establish the global empire of CHARLES V. He devised the PRAGMATIC SANCTION to ensure the succession of his daughter MARIA THERESA after the failure of the direct male Habsburg line. A son of LEOPOLD I, he attempted to seize Spain after the death of

**CHARLES II** (1700). He was initially recognized by the Netherlands, Britain and Portugal, but they abandoned him when he came to the Austrian throne. He gained lands from France in the Treaty of **RASTATT** (1714) and from the Turks in Hungary and Serbia (1716–18). He failed to secure Maria Theresa's succession, lost the War of the **POLISH SUCCESSION** (1733–8) and returned land to the Turks as a result of defeats (1736–9).

**Charles VI, the Foolish** (1368–1422)
King of France (1380/1422). He was defeated by **HENRY V** of England at the Battle of **AGINCOURT** (1415). From 1392, he suffered from fits of madness.

**Charles VII**, also known as **Albert of Wittelsbach** (1697–1745)
Elector of Bavaria (1726/45) and Holy Roman Emperor (1742/5). He opposed the Imperial claims of **FRANCIS I**, Duke of Tuscany, husband of **MARIA THERESA**, although he had originally accepted the **PRAGMATIC SANCTION** and Maria's claim to the throne. He was defeated and ousted by the Austrians but restored to his Bavarian lands by Prussia and France shortly before his death.

**Charles VII, the Victorious** (1403–61)
King of France (1422/61). At his accession, the north of the country was in English hands, with **HENRY VI** of England proclaimed King of France. However, after **JOAN OF ARC** roused the fervour of both nobles and people, the Siege of **ORLÉANS** was raised (1429), and the English gradually lost nearly all they had gained in France. Under his rule France recovered in some measure from her terrible calamities. ► **HUNDRED YEARS' WAR**

**Charles VIII** (1470 98)
King of France (1483/98). The son of **LOUIS XI**, his marriage to **ANNE OF BRITTANY** (1491) enabled him to free himself from the political domination of his sister and brother-in-law, the Beaujeus, and secure his kingdom. His Italian campaign (1494–5) initiated 60 years of French military involvement in Italy. The Kingdom of Naples was temporarily secured, but Charles was driven from Italy by the League of Venice (1495)

**Charles VIII** (of Sweden) ► **KARL KNUTSSON**

**Charles IX** (1550–74)
King of France (1560/74). The second son of **HENRY II** and **CATHERINE DE' MEDICI**, he succeeded his brother, **FRANCIS II**. His reign coincided with the Wars of **RELIGION**. He was completely subject to his mother, whose counsels drove him to authorize the slaughter of **HUGUENOTS** known as the **ST BARTHO-LOMEW'S DAY MASSACRE** (1572).

**Charles IX** (1550–1611)
King of Sweden (1604/11). He was the son of **GUSTAV I VASA** by his second wife, Margareta Leijonhuvfud. On the accession in 1592 of his Catholic nephew Sigismund, Charles led the Protestant nobility against him and secured the firm adherence of the Swedish Church to Lutheran doctrine. After Sigismund had been driven from Sweden (1598), Charles was appointed regent. He crushed Sigismund's leading supporters in Sweden in the Linköping bloodbath in 1600 and finally accepted the crown in 1604. His ac-

tion against Sigismund involved Sweden in war with Poland, to which wars with Russia and Denmark were added before the end of his reign. He alienated many nobles by his use of non-noble servants and by leaving vacant a number of the great offices of state so that his son, **GUSTAV II ADOLF**, had on his accession to promise to rule in association with the nobility.

**Charles X** (1757–1836)
Last Bourbon King of France (1824/30). The grandson of **LOUIS XV**, he received the title of Count of Artois. He lived in England during the **FRENCH REVOLUTION**, returning to France in 1814 as Lieutenant-General of the kingdom. He succeeded his brother **LOUIS XVIII**, but his repressive rule led to the **JULY REVOLUTION** (1830), and his eventual abdication and exile. ► **BOURBON, HOUSE OF**

**Charles X Gustav** (1622–60)
King of Sweden (1654/60). He was the son of John Pfalz-Zweibrücken by **GUSTAV II ADOLF**'s sister, Katarina. He served with the Swedish army in the **THIRTY YEARS' WAR**. Plans for his marriage to Queen **CHRISTINA** came to naught, but she named him her heir and on her abdication in 1654, Charles ascended the throne. In 1655 he invaded Poland and in 1657 became embroiled also in war with Denmark, which he forced to make a humiliating peace at Roskilde (1658) after a dramatic march over the frozen waters between the Danish islands. He attacked Denmark again, but died in Gothenburg before he could secure a decisive victory. In many ways his style of ruling anticipated the **ABSOLUTISM** introduced by his son and successor, **CHARLES XI**.

**Charles XI** (1655 97)
King of Sweden (1660/97). He was the son and successor of **CHARLES X GUSTAV**. After a twelve-year regency dominated by the nobility, he assumed power in 1672. Two years later he helped to staunch a Danish invasion through his leadership at the Battle of Lund, and won favourable terms at the ensuing peace treaty in 1679. In the aftermath of the war he severely punished the regents and members of the council held to be responsible for it and resumed much of the royal lands and tax revenues that had been alienated under previous monarchs (the *reduktion*). With the additional revenue this provided he reorganized the administration and armed forces, which were both placed on a much firmer financial basis. He was also no longer reliant on the Diet, and established absolute monarchy. He was married to the Danish princess Ulrika Eleonora and was succeeded by his son, **CHARLES XII**.

**Charles XII** (1682–1718)
King of Sweden (1697/1718). He was the son of **CHARLES XI** of Sweden. Three years after coming to the throne, he was attacked by an alliance of Denmark, Saxony and Russia which was attempting to deprive Sweden of its gains during the 17c. After forcing Denmark to make peace, Charles defeated the Russians at Narva (1700) and forced Augustus of Saxony to abandon the throne of Poland, on which he placed his ally, **STANISŁAW LESZCZYŃSKI**. In 1707 he turned against Russia, but was defeated by the Tsar's forces at **POLTAVA** in the Ukraine in 1709 and fled to Turkey. After a conflict with the local Turkish authorities (the

*kalabalik*) in 1713, he was taken to Constantinople as a virtual prisoner, but managed to leave Turkey the following year and reached Stralsund, Sweden's almost last remaining foothold on the southern coast of the Baltic, after a dramatic ride across central Europe. Once back in Sweden, he mobilized the country to continue the struggle against a formidable coalition. He attacked Denmark twice on Norwegian soil, but on the second of these campaigns (1718) was shot dead in the trenches before the Norwegian fortress of Frederikshald, whether by the enemy or from his own side has never been satisfactorily determined. He never married and was succeeded by his younger sister, **ULRIKA ELEONORA**.

### Charles XIII (1748–1818)

King of Sweden (1809/18) and of Norway (1814/18). The younger brother of **GUSTAV III**, he was the uncle and successor to **GUSTAV IV ADOLF**. As Duke of Södermanland, he commanded the Swedish fleet against Russia in the war of 1788–90, and after his brother's assassination in 1792 was regent until his nephew's coming-of-age in 1796. When Gustav was deposed in 1809, Charles was elected King and agreed to a new constitution which limited the monarch's powers. He had no children and in 1810 the Diet chose the French marshal Jean Baptiste Jules Bernadotte (later **CHARLES XIV JOHN**) as heir to the throne. Bernadotte in effect ruled the country until Charles's death. Charles was married to Charlotte of Oldenburg, whose diary is an important source for the history of her time. ► **BERNADOTTE, HOUSE OF**

### Charles XIV John (1763–1844)

King of Sweden (1818/44). Born Jean Baptiste Jules Bernadotte, the son of a lawyer, at Pau, France, he joined the French army in 1780, and fought his way up to become marshal in 1804. In 1799 he was Minister of War, and for his conduct at the Battle of **AUSTERLITZ** (1805) was named Prince of Pontecorvo. He fought in several Napoleonic campaigns and in 1810 was made heir to the Swedish throne by a group of Swedes who had been impressed by his conduct and wished to please Napoleon, then at the height of his power. On coming to Sweden, Bernadotte was received into the Lutheran faith and adopted the name Charles John (Karl Johan). He took control of his adopted country's foreign policy and steered it away from France. He concluded an alliance with Russia and took command of the allied forces in northern Germany in the final campaigns, forcing France's ally, Denmark, to surrender Norway to Sweden at the Treaty of Kiel (1814). His autocratic rule after his accession and his alliance with Russia caused opposition to him in the 1830s. He died in Stockholm and was succeeded by his son, **OSCAR I**. ► **BERNADOTTE, HOUSE OF**; **NAPOLEON I**

### Charles XV (1826–72)

King of Norway and Sweden (1859/72). He was the son and successor of **OSCAR I**. As Crown Prince he had been an enthusiastic supporter of the idea of the political union of the Scandinavian monarchies, but after his accession this idea died. Without consulting his ministers, he promised support to Denmark in the event of war with Germany over Schleswig-Holstein. However, when war broke out in 1864, he was unable to fulfil his promise. During his reign the old four-Estate Diet was replaced (1865–6) by a bicameral parliament, elected on a narrow franchise. A cheerful and flamboyant character, Charles was also a poet and artist. Married to Lovisa of the Netherlands, who predeceased him, he left no surviving male heir and was succeeded by his younger brother, **OSCAR II**.

### Charles XVI Gustav (1946– )

King of Sweden (1973/ ). As his father had died in an air accident in 1947, he became Crown Prince from the time of the accession of his grandfather, King **GUSTAV VI ADOLF**, in 1950. A new constitution, which reduced the king to a purely ceremonial head of state, was approved by the Swedish parliament just before his accession. In 1976 he married Silvia Sommerlath, the daughter of a West German businessman. They have two daughters, Victoria and Madeleine, and a son, Charles Philip.

### Charles, Dame (Mary) Eugenia (1919– )

Dominican politician. After qualifying in London as a barrister, she returned to the West Indies to practise in the Windward and Leeward Islands. She entered politics in 1968 and two years later became co-founder and first leader of the centrist Dominica Freedom Party (DFP). She became an MP in 1975. Two years after independence, the DFP won the 1980 general election and she became the Caribbean's first female Prime Minister, a post she held until 1995.

### Charles, Prince of Wales, in full Charles Philip Arthur George (1948– )

Eldest son of HM Queen **ELIZABETH II** and HRH Prince Philip, Duke of **EDINBURGH**, and heir apparent to the British throne. Duke of Cornwall as the eldest son of the monarch, he was given the title of Prince of Wales in 1958, and invested at Caernarvon (1969). He served in the RAF and the Royal Navy (1971–6), and in 1981 married Lady Diana Spencer, younger daughter of the 8th Earl Spencer, from whom he separated in 1992. They had two sons, Prince William and Prince Henry ('Harry'). In the 1980s he made a number of controversial statements on public issues, including architecture and educational standards. He set up the Prince's Youth Business Trust to encourage young entrepreneurs, and founded the Prince of Wales' Institute of Architecture (1992). With the news of his relationship with Camilla Parker Bowles, his divorce from Diana in 1996 and her sudden death in a car crash a year later, Charles' popularity and that of the British monarchy reached an all-time low. A more informal approach to his royal duties and the popularity of his sons helped to revive his standing, although his marriage to Camilla Parker Bowles in 2005 evoked a mixed public response.

### Charles Albert (1789–1849)

King of Sardinia-Piedmont (1831/49). Born into a junior branch of the House of **SAVOY**, Charles Albert was schooled in Paris and Geneva and made a Count of the Empire by **NAPOLEON I**. In 1821 he was made regent following the **SANTAROSA** mutiny and the abdication of the elderly **VICTOR EMMANUEL I**. Responding to popular demands he granted a liberal constitution which was promptly revoked by the new King, **CHARLES FELIX**. With the latter's accession and the collapse of the insurrection, he was exiled from the court in disgrace but was saved from disinheritance by the intervention of **METTERNICH**, who demanded in return guarantees that he would not alter the status quo. However, on ascending the throne Charles Albert embarked on a foreign policy which showed increasing readiness to resist Austrian hegemony in the Italian peninsula. Despite subsequent attempts to portray him as an Italian patriot, he was essentially reactionary and adopted very repressive measures against Mazzinian agitation in 1833–4. The surge of liberal feeling that greeted the election of **PIUS IX** and the growing strength of the moderate movement of Cesare **BALBO**, **D'AZEGLIO** and **GIOBERTI** encouraged him to appoint a more progressive ministry in Oct 1847. In Mar 1848, in the midst of a growing climate of revolution, he granted a new constitution, the **STATUTO**, and launched a somewhat half-hearted military campaign to assist the Lombard insurgents against Austrian rule. Following defeat by **RADETZKY** at **CUSTOZZA** (25 July 1848), he signed the **SALASCO ARMISTICE**. War was renewed the following year but he was once again defeated by the Austrians at the Battle of **NOVARA** (23 Mar 1849). He abdicated in favour of his son, **VICTOR EMMANUEL II**.

### Charles Emmanuel II (1634–75)
Duke of Savoy (1638/75). He was the son of Victor Amadeus I of Savoy and Christine de Bourbon (sister of **LOUIS XIII** of France). Under the regency of his mother, Savoy remained firmly within the French orbit, a policy which Charles Emmanuel did not alter when he began to govern in his own right in 1663. **LOUIS XIV** of France tended to treat him as little more than a vassal, virtually requiring him to furnish troops for his campaigns.

### Charles Emmanuel III (1701–73)
Duke of Savoy and King of Sardinia (1730/73). The second son of **VICTOR AMADEUS II**, he became heir to the throne when his brother died in 1715 and became King himself on his father's abdication. When, shortly afterwards, his father tried to return to power, Victor Emmanuel had him imprisoned in the fortress of Rivoli. Like his father, he was prepared to back either France or Austria as his interests dictated, supporting the former in the War of the **POLISH SUCCESSION** (1733–8) and the latter in the War of the **AUSTRIAN SUCCESSION** (1740–2). This policy brought territorial gains in Lombardy. He avoided involvement in the **SEVEN YEARS' WAR**, preferring instead to concentrate on domestic reform, introducing a new legal code, the *Corpus Carolinum*, in 1770.

### Charles Emmanuel IV (1751–1819)
King of Sardinia (1796/1802). The elder son of **VICTOR AMADEUS III**, he had the misfortune to come to the throne as the French armies of the **DIRECTORY** began their first great successes. He flirted with the idea of saving his dynasty through an alliance with France against Austria, but was unable to realize this scheme because of the agreement reached between **FRANCIS II** and **NAPOLEON I** at the Treaty of **CAMPO FORMIO**. In 1798 he fled to Sardinia where he abdicated in favour of his brother, **VICTOR EMMANUEL I**, in 1802. He died having entered the Church in a monastery in Rome.

### Charles Felix (1765–1831)
King of Sardinia-Piedmont (1821/31). He was the fifth son of **VICTOR AMADEUS III** and younger brother of **VICTOR EMMANUEL I**. When the latter abdicated in 1821, Charles Felix was in Modena and was horrified to discover, on his return to Turin, that the young regent, **CHARLES ALBERT**, had granted a constitution. He immediately revoked the constitution and embarked on a policy of repression, which characterized the remainder of his otherwise undistinguished reign.

### Charles Frederick of Baden (1728–1811)
Duke of Baden-Durlach (1746/1811). He was an enlightened ruler who made substantial changes in Baden (eg emancipation of the peasants). Although he opposed revolutionary France, he signed a separate truce with France and later (1806) became a Grand-Duke under Napoleon.

### Charles of Anjou (1227–85)
Angevin King of Naples and Sicily. The posthumous son of **LOUIS VIII** of France, he was invested with the crown of Naples and Sicily by Pope **URBAN IV** (1265). After defeating his Hohenstaufen rivals **MANFRED** (1266) and **CONRADIN OF SWABIA** (1268), he and his French supporters established control of the kingdom. He conquered Corfu and much of mainland Greece, and planned to capture Constantinople and re-establish the Latin Empire, but his schemes were wrecked by the revolt known as the **SICILIAN VESPERS** (1282), which allowed Manfred's son-in-law, Peter III of Aragon, to seize the entire island of Sicily. ► **ANGEVINS**; **HOHENSTAUFEN DYNASTY**

### Charles of Valois (1270–1325)
Second son of **PHILIP III** of France and Isabelle of Aragon. He was put forward as French claimant to the Kingdom of Aragon, which he was unable to conquer (1283–9). He was an unsuccessful candidate for the thrones of Constantinople (1301–7) and the **HOLY ROMAN EMPIRE** (1308), but achieved great influence during the short reigns of Philip's three sons, **LOUIS X**, **PHILIP V** and **CHARLES IV**. His only son, **PHILIP VI**, founded the **VALOIS DYNASTY**.

### Charles Robert (1288–1342)
First King of Hungary of the Angevin Dynasty (1304/42). He claimed the throne (through his mother) on the death of the last male member of the House of Árpád, Andrew III (1301), and after the defeat of rival claimants was crowned in 1308. He restored the royal authority in a struggle against the rebellious great magnates, whose lands he redistributed to the minor nobility, thus creating a new aristocracy loyal to him. The reforms that followed included the reorganization of military service and the introduction of a royal monopoly on gold and silver production. He married Elizabeth, daughter of Casimir III of Poland, and in 1337 obtained recognition of his son Louis, the future **LOUIS I, THE GREAT**, as heir also to the Polish throne.

### Charles the Bold (1433–77)
Duke of Burgundy (1467/77). Though a French vassal, he was continually at war with **LOUIS XI** of France, aiming to restore the old Kingdom of **BURGUNDY**, by conquering Lorraine, Provence, Dauphiné and Switzerland. He gained Lorraine (1475) and invaded Switzerland, but was defeated at Granson and Morat. He laid siege to Nancy, but was killed in the battle.

**Charles Theodore of Bavaria** (1724–99)
Elector of the Palatinate (1743/77) and later (1777/99) of the Palatinate and Bavaria. His control of Bavaria was recognized by his rival Charles Zweibrücken after the War of the BAVARIAN SUCCESSION (1778–9).

**Charleston, Battles of** (11 Feb–12 May 1780)
During the AMERICAN REVOLUTION, the victorious British siege of Charleston, South Carolina, which marked the beginning of the Southern phase of British strategy. At a small cost, the troops of Sir Henry Clinton (c.1738–1795) captured a 5,400-strong American garrison and a squadron of four ships.

**Charles William Ferdinand, Duke of Brunswick** (1735–1806)
A renowned military leader of the SEVEN YEARS' WAR, he began his military career as an officer to the Duke of Cumberland in 1757. A nephew of FREDERICK II, THE GREAT, he was made a Prussian field marshal. He was acclaimed as an enlightened ruler when he succeeded his father, Charles I, in 1780. He accepted command of the allied Austro-German army sent to defeat revolutionary France, having refused command of the French army shortly before.

**Charter 77** (post-1977)
An informal association of individuals devoted to the assertion of lost human rights in Czechoslovakia. The 'NORMALIZATION' following the Soviet invasion of Czechoslovakia in 1968 suppressed many CIVIL RIGHTS, including that to free expression of views. However, in 1976 the Czechoslovak government signed the international convention on human rights confirmed in the HELSINKI FINAL ACT. This gave the opposition the opportunity to protest and publish its 'charter' on 1 Jan 1977. The founders included Jiří HÁJEK (the Foreign Minister in 1968) and the writer Václav HAVEL. Charter 77 suffered much harassment, but it attracted international condemnation of the communists and eventually contributed to their downfall in 1989, when Havel became President.

**chartered companies**
A series of companies chartered to rule colonies in late Victorian times, designed to produce imperialism on the cheap. The idea for these companies was based upon the monopolistic ventures of the mercantilist period, like the EAST INDIA COMPANY of 1599 and the HUDSON'S BAY COMPANY of 1670, whose charters had been abrogated in the 19c. The British North Borneo Company was chartered in 1882 and survived until the Japanese invasion of 1941. The ROYAL NIGER COMPANY ruled in Nigeria between 1886 and 1898; the IMPERIAL BRITISH EAST AFRICA COMPANY was chartered to run British East Africa (Kenya and Uganda) from 1888 to 1893; and the BRITISH SOUTH AFRICA COMPANY received a charter to rule in Southern and Northern Rhodesia between 1889 and 1923.

**Charter Oath** (6 Apr 1868)
A broad policy statement issued in the name of the Japanese MEIJI Emperor after the overthrow of the TOKUGAWA SHOGUNATE. By calling for deliberative assemblies and public discussion of national affairs, the oath was initially designed to attract SAMURAI support for the new regime, although it was later cited

as justification for parliamentary government. The charter oath also declared that status distinctions and other backward feudal practices of the past would be eliminated, and sanctioned a policy of westernization to enhance national strength by promising to 'seek knowledge throughout the world'. The oath thus came to be seen as a manifesto anticipating the modernization programme of the new government after 1868.

**Charter of the Nobility** (1785)
The entrenchment of the privileges of the Russian nobility, intended by CATHERINE II, THE GREAT to ensure their loyalty for the future. She had already divided her empire into 50 provinces, each with approximately 10 districts. The nobles were now given the right to elect provincial and district marshals, to convene assemblies and to petition the Tsar. Their existing rights freed them from taxation and service, and they were now given fresh property rights. They had immense privileges but no obligations other than to keep down the serfs and not to question the Tsar's authority. At the same time, Catherine extended the system of serfdom and worsened the condition of the serfs. They became chattels with no privileges and few rights, forced to slave to support the Tsar and the nobles, and to fight to win the Tsar's wars: it was a political recipe for ultimate revolution.

**Chartists**
In the UK, supporters of democratic political reform, most active between 1838 and 1849. Their name derives from the 'People's Charter' presented twice to parliament (1839 and 1842) which called for universal male suffrage, voting by secret ballot, the abolition of property qualifications for MPs, payment for MPs, equal-sized constituencies and annually elected parliaments. All but the last of these were obtained but this movement, largely of working people, threatened and occasionally alarmed the authorities, who arrested and imprisoned its leaders during the main phase of the agitation. Chartism was an important cultural and educational force in working-class development. ► O'CONNOR, FEARGUS

**Chassé, David Hendrik, Baron** (1765–1849)
Dutch soldier. Nicknamed 'General Baïonette' by NAPOLEON I, he joined the French army in 1789 and fought with great distinction in Germany and Spain. As Lieutenant-General of the Dutch forces in 1815 he fought at WATERLOO against his old comrades, the French. In the struggle for Belgian independence, he held the citadel at Antwerp (1830–2), but finally surrendered to superior French and Belgian forces, with some British naval assistance.

**Chateaubriand, (François Auguste) René, Viscount of** (1768–1848)
French writer and politician. *Atala* (1801) established his literary reputation; and *Le Génie du christianisme* (1802, trans *The Genius of Christianity*, 1813) made him prominent among men of letters. He held various political and diplomatic posts after the Restoration, but was disappointed in his hope of becoming Prime Minister. In his later years, he wrote his celebrated autobiography, *Mémoires d'outre-tombe* ('Memoirs from beyond the Grave'), not published as a whole until 1902.

**Chatham, 1st Earl of** ► PITT, WILLIAM, 1ST EARL OF CHATHAM, THE ELDER

**Chatham, Dutch Descent on** (17–24 June 1667)
A Dutch naval expedition at the end of the second of the ANGLO-DUTCH WARS which had the effect of forcing the hand of the English at the negotiations for the Peace of BREDA. The Dutch Pensionary Johan de WITT sent the expedition under his brother Cornelius and Admiral Michiel de RUYTER; they sailed up the Thames and captured the fort at Sheerness. They proceeded up the Medway to the Royal Docks at Chatham, destroyed a number of ships, and carried off the English flagship the *Royal Charles*, causing panic in London. Traditionally, this event is under-reported in English history books. ► CHATHAM, DUTCH DESCENT ON

**Chatila**
Palestinian refugee camp on the outskirts of Beirut in Lebanon. It was created following the evacuation of Palestinians from the city after Israeli attacks on Palestinians and Syrians (June 1982). The camp was the scene of a massacre by Christian Phalangists (Sep 1983).

**Chattanooga Campaign** (Aug–Nov 1863)
A series of battles in Tennessee, during the AMERICAN CIVIL WAR, leading to Southern victory at Chickamauga, and Northern victories at Lookout Mountain and Missionary Ridge. It was of military importance because it placed Northern troops in a position to bisect the Confederacy on an east–west axis.

**Chatterjee, Bankim Chandra** (1838–94)
Indian author and social critic. While his primary career was as a district magistrate in Bengal, his greatest skill was as an author and philosopher. A contemporary of Rabindranath Tagore, he founded (1872) *Bangadarshan*, a Bengali newspaper that soon became a vehicle for expounding on Hindu philosophy and culture. An influential philosophical writer, Chatterjee was also a poet and a master of the historical novel, as he demonstrated in *Ananda Math*, which is set against the Sannyasi revolt in the Bengal of Warren HASTINGS. He was also a social activist, publishing *Kamalakanter Daptar* in 1885. In this novel he pleaded for a degree of social equality that was not to be found in India. Chatterjee's French rationalist bent allowed him to forge a sense of Indian nationality in his novels and at the same time point out the inequities institutionalized in Hindu society.

**Chauhans (Chahamanas) of Shakambhari** ► INDIA, PRE-ISLAMIC

**Chaumette, Pierre Gaspard** (1763–94)
French revolutionary, a shoemaker's son. At the Revolution he joined with Camille DESMOULINS, and soon gained such popularity by his extremism that he was appointed procurator of the Paris commune, the elected municipal government of the city of Paris, which played an important part in the developing extremism of the Revolution, 1792–3. His extravagances disgusted ROBESPIERRE, and he died on the scaffold. ► FRENCH REVOLUTION

**Chautauqua Movement**
A late 19c and early 20c US adult education movement, organized at Lake Chautauqua, New York,

under Methodist auspices by Lewis Miller (1829–99) and Bishop John H Vincent (1832–1920), with home reading programmes and lectures in the arts, sciences and humanities. At its peak it attracted up to 60,000 participants annually to regional centres in the USA and elsewhere.

**Chávez, César Estrada** (1927–93)
US labour leader. In 1962 he founded the National Farm Workers Association, which sought to unionize migrant workers. He used strikes, pickets and marches in the struggle to win contracts from growers, and undertook long fasts to publicize the movement. In 1968 he promoted a nationwide boycott of California grapes, which led to the table-grape growers recognition of the union in 1970. In 1972 the United Farm Workers (UFW), with Chávez as its President, became a member union of the AFL–CIO.

**Chávez (Frías), Hugo Rafael** (1954– )
Venezuelan populist politician. He came to prominence in 1992 following his involvement in a failed attempt to depose President Pérez, made unpopular by IMF-imposed austerity measures, and his great personal popularity swept him into power in the 1998 presidential election on an anti-corruption platform. By 2001 he had made fundamental changes to the government, rewriting the constitution and concentrating power in the executive. He implemented land, education and economic reforms, including an attempt to privatize the oil industry and to amalgamate the trade unions into a single government-controlled organization, but in Apr 2002 the reforms provoked a military coup supported by the now disenchanted middle and working classes. Although unsuccessful, the coup was followed by months of industrial unrest and an attempted recall vote. His 'revolutionary' policies have had little impact on the lives of ordinary citizens, and poverty and unemployment are still widespread despite the country's oil wealth.

**Chebrikov, Viktor Mikhailovich** (1923–99)
Soviet KGB operative. A Russian, he served in the army in WORLD WAR II and afterwards qualified in metallurgy in Dnepropetrovsk in the Ukraine. Having transferred to party work, he came into contact with Leonid BREZHNEV who, in 1967, appointed him to the KGB to keep an eye on Yuri ANDROPOV. He eventually switched his loyalty, and in 1982 Andropov made him chairman of the KGB. In 1985 he cast his vital vote for Mikhail GORBACHEV, who made him a full member of the POLITBURO. As he began to take fright at the implications of Gorbachev's reforms and veered towards Yegor LIGACHEV, he was carefully but firmly removed from all his posts in 1988–9.

**Chechen Wars** (1994–6 and 1999– )
Two wars between RUSSIA and CHECHNYA prompted by Chechnya's attempt to achieve independence from Russia. Although Chechnya declared itself independent in 1991 under the leadership of Dzhokar Dudyev, war did not break out until 1994, when Russian troops invaded in support of an attempt to overthrow Dudyev and met determined opposition from the Chechen army, guerrilla forces and civilians. The conflict was unpopular with the Russian public but President YELTSIN was unwilling to withdraw for fear

of encouraging other separatist groups in the Russian Federation. Following Dudyev's death in 1996, peace negotiations led to the signing of the Khasavyurt accords in Aug 1996, and Russian troops withdrew in Jan 1997. But the issue of Chechen independence was left unresolved and the uneasy peace broke down in Sep 1999 when Russian forces again invaded Chechnya. The Russians captured Grozny in Feb 2000 and in May President **PUTIN** imposed direct rule from Moscow. Violent unrest continued, accompanied by accusations of human rights violations by Russian troops, but despite this elections were held in Oct 2003 and Akhmad Kadyrov became president. He was assassinated in May 2004 and the Russian-backed Alu Alkhanov was elected president in Aug. Since the **SEPTEMBER 11 ATTACKS**, Russia has attempted to counter Western criticism of its brutal tactics by portraying Chechen fighters as part of the global terror network after attacks such as the Moscow theatre siege (2002) and the Beslan school siege (2004).

**Chechnya**
A Muslim republic in eastern Europe, formally part of **RUSSIA** but engaged in a struggle for independence. It became part of the Russian Empire in 1859 and, although briefly independent following the **OCTOBER REVOLUTION**, it was incorporated into the **USSR** as the Chechen-Ingush Autonomous Soviet Socialist Republic. After the collapse of the USSR, Chechnya attempted to assert its independence, leading to tension with Russia which culminated in the **CHECHEN WARS**. The area is strategically important to Russia because the routes from central Russia to the Black Sea and the Caspian Sea pass though it, as do oil and gas pipelines from Kazakhstan and Azerbaijan.

**Chefoo Convention** (1876)
An agreement signed by the British Minister to China, Thomas Wade, and **LI HONGZHANG**, representing the Chinese government. The previous year a British consular official, Margary, was killed in southwest China en route to meet a British expedition from Burma (now Myanmar). The agreement both provided for Chinese government compensation and an official mission of apology to Britain, as well as stipulating that four more **TREATY PORTS** were to be opened. In return, however, the Chinese government was allowed to increase taxes on opium imports and could impose the *likin* (internal transit tax) on foreign goods outside the treaty ports. These two concessions outraged British mercantile opinion, and the convention was not ratified until 1885.

**Chehab, Fuad** (1902-73)
Lebanese politician and soldier. From a Maronite Christian family who had settled initially in the Chouf Mountains of Lebanon in Ottoman times, he came to prominence when he was appointed to command the new Lebanese army in 1945. He rose to become Minister of Defence in Camille **CHAMOUN**'s government, formed in the aftermath of the **SUEZ CRISIS** in 1956. During the insurrection and disturbances following the declaration of the **UNITED ARAB REPUBLIC** of Egypt and Syria in 1958, Chehab refused to use the Lebanese army to crush the rebellion. This, coupled with the call by the rebels for the resignation of Chamoun, won Chehab the respect of the Muslim section of the community, and in July 1958 Chehab, who had by this time resigned command of the army, was elected President, to succeed Chamoun when the latter demitted office. Despite initial problems, he succeeded in restoring stability to Lebanon. His six-year term of office saw an attempt to establish a social policy aimed at improving the lot of the common people. That this was unsuccessful may be seen, to some extent, as a contributing factor to the disastrous currents which were to overwhelm Lebanon a decade later.

**Cheka**
An acronym from Russian letters che+ka, for the All-Russian Extraordinary Commission for Combating Counter-Revolution and Sabotage, established in 1917. It was in effect a political police force whose duties were to investigate and punish anti-Bolshevik activities. During the **RUSSIAN CIVIL WAR** it was responsible for executing thousands of political opponents in what came to be called the 'Red Terror'.
➤ **BOLSHEVIKS**; **COMMUNISM**

**Chelčický, Petr** (c.1390–1460)
Czech reformer and theologian. A radical follower of the **HUSSITES**, he abjured towns, commerce and violence, and founded the sect which eventually became the **MORAVIAN BRETHREN**. The Christian doctrine of his *The Net of True Faith* (1450) was later promulgated by Tolstoy.

**Chen, Eugene**, originally **Ch'en Yu-jen** (1878–1944)
Chinese lawyer and politician. Born in Trinidad he had a Catholic education and trained to be a lawyer. After the creation of the Chinese republic in 1912, Chen was appointed legal adviser to the Ministry of Communications. He became particularly close to **SUN YAT-SEN** and served as his foreign affairs adviser. Chen was identified with the left wing of the **GUOMINDANG**, which established its own government in Wuhan in early 1927 in opposition to **CHIANG KAI-SHEK**. As Foreign Minister in the Wuhan government he pursued a vigorous anti-imperialist policy, negotiating the return of the British concessions of Hankou and Jiujiang. After 1927, when the Wuhan government was dissolved, Chen was briefly associated with anti-Chiang Kai-shek separatist movements.

**Chen Boda (Ch'en Po-ta)** (1905–89)
Chinese political propagandist and interpreter of **MAO ZEDONG**'s thought. He joined the Chinese Communist Party (CCP) in 1927 and studied in Moscow until 1930. After teaching in Beijing, Chen went to the communist base at Yan'an (Yenan) in 1937. He became Mao Zedong's personal secretary and helped popularize Mao's concept of the 'Sinification of **MARXISM**' (adapting Marxism to Chinese conditions). After 1949 he continued to be influential in the party's propaganda department, becoming chief editor of the party organ, *Hongqi* ('Red Flag'), in 1958. During the **CULTURAL REVOLUTION** Chen became associated with the radicals and in 1969 reached the apogee of his influence when he was appointed to the Politburo. In the campaign against leftist excesses the following year, however, Chen was arrested and expelled from the CCP. In 1980–1 he was put on public trial along with the **GANG OF FOUR**

and sentenced to 18 years in prison, but was released later the same year. ► COMMUNIST PARTY, CHINESE

## Chen Duxiu (Ch'en Tu-hsiu) (1879–1942)

Chinese revolutionary and publicist. In 1915 Chen founded the journal *Xin Qingnian* ('New Youth'), which heralded the beginnings of a new cultural movement calling for a rejection of the Confucian tradition and the promotion of democracy and science. In 1917 he became Dean of the College of Letters at Beijing University, where he attracted a large student following. By 1920, disillusioned with the prospects of cultural change, he had become attracted to MARX-ISM and established a communist cell in Shanghai. Although Chen was in Canton when the Chinese Communist Party (CCP) was formally created in Shanghai (July 1921), he was a founder-member and was elected its first Secretary-General. With COMINTERN prodding, he led the CCP into the first United Front with the GUOMINDANG in 1923 and oversaw a considerable expansion of the party's membership. When the Guomindang turned on its erstwhile communist allies in 1927, which resulted in the near total annihilation of the party, Chen was made a scapegoat for the disaster and replaced as Secretary-General.

## Cheng Ch'eng-kung (Zheng Chenggong) ► KOXINGA

## Cheng Ho ► ZHENG HE

## Ch'en I ► CHEN YI

## Chenla ► SOUTH-EAST ASIA PRE-1000AD

## Ch'en Po-ta ► CHEN BODA

## Chen Tu-hsiu ► CHEN DUXIU

## Chen Yi (Ch'en I) (1901–72)

Chinese communist leader. He studied in France, and joined the Chinese Communist Party on his return. He supported MAO ZEDONG in the struggle with the GUOMINDANG, and the Japanese (1934). Chen Yi formed the 4th Route Army in Jiangxi (1940), commanded the East China Liberation Army (1946) and restyled the 3rd (East China) Army (1948). He prepared an amphibious operation against Taiwan, but failed to capture Jinmen (Quemoy) Island in 1949. Created Marshal of the People's Republic in 1955, he became Foreign Minister in 1958, but was dropped from the Politburo during the CULTURAL REVOLUTION in 1969.

## Chen Yong'gui (Ch'en Yung-kuei) (1915–86)

Chinese 'model' peasant and politician. During the CULTURAL REVOLUTION Chen, an illiterate peasant, was hailed as a model worker in the Dazhai Production Brigade in the north-western province of Shanxi. As leader of the brigade and supporter of Maoist policies, Chen was elected to the Central Committee in 1969 and elevated to the Politburo in 1973. After MAO ZEDONG's death in 1976, amidst a general reversal of Maoist policies, doubts were raised about Dazhai's claim as the successful embodiment of self-reliance and egalitarianism. Chen increasingly lost influence and he was dropped from the Politburo in 1981. ► MAOISM

## Chen Yün (Ch'en Yun) (1905–95)

Chinese communist leader and economic planner. Chen joined the Chinese Communist Party in 1924

and became a labour organizer in Shanghai. By 1940 he was a member of the Politburo. As Minister of Heavy Industry (1949–50) and a member of the State Planning Commission (1952–4), Chen was an important economic planner in the new communist government, helping to formulate the first Five-Year Plan. As an advocate of CENTRAL PLANNING and the need to maintain production, he clashed with MAO ZEDONG over the GREAT LEAP FORWARD campaign in 1958, which led to his official eclipse until after Mao's death. In 1978 he was reinstated as party Vice-Chairman and appointed a Vice-Premier in 1979, overseeing economic policies. He was a consistent critic of the post-Mao leadership's attempt to introduce elements of a MARKET ECONOMY, arguing for the need to maintain the dominant role of the state sector. Chen retired from party posts in 1987.

## Ch'en Yung-kuei ► CHEN YONG'GUI

## Cherasco, Peace of (1631)

The death of the last GONZAGA duke in 1627 meant that the French Prince of Nevers would inherit Mantua. The Habsburgs, fearing a French presence in northern Italy, diverted troops from the north to Mantua, and RICHELIEU countered with a French force. The Peace of Cherasco ended the war; it gave Pinerolo to France and invested Nevers with Mantua. ► HABSBURG DYNASTY

## Cherikov, V (1900–98)

Soviet marshal and typical post-RUSSIAN REVOLUTION commander. A Russian peasant, he joined the RED ARMY in 1918 and the Communist Party in 1919. He became a regimental commander in the RUSSIAN CIVIL WAR and graduated from the Frunze Military Academy in 1925. During WORLD WAR II his activities included serving as adviser to CHIANG KAI-SHEK, and then participating in the Battle of STALINGRAD (1943) and the final assault on Berlin in 1945. He was Deputy Commander (1946–53), then Commander-in-Chief of Soviet forces in Germany, and Deputy Minister of Defence (1960–5).

## Chernenko, Konstantin Ustinovich (1911–85)

Soviet politician. He joined the Communist Party in 1931, and held several local posts. An associate of Leonid BREZHNEV for many years, he became a member of the POLITBURO in 1978, and the Party's chief ideologist after the death of Mikhail SUSLOV (1982). Regarded as a conservative, Chernenko was a rival of Yuri ANDROPOV in the Party leadership contest of 1982, and became Party General-Secretary and head of state after Andropov's death in 1984. He suffered from ill health, and died soon after in Moscow, to be succeeded by Mikhail GORBACHEV.

## Chernobyl

A city in central Ukraine, situated north of Kiev, and the site of one of the world's worst nuclear accidents. In Apr 1986 the core of one of the reactors at the Chernobyl nuclear power station experienced a partial meltdown and the ensuing explosions emitted large amounts of radioactivity into the atmosphere. Traces of radioactive fallout were reported in areas of North America and Western Europe, including Scandinavia and the UK, where livestock in high-rainfall areas was contaminated for years. Over 30 people died as a direct result of the ensuing fires, and thousands more from radiation-related illnesses such as childhood leukaemia, during the following two decades. Over 135,000 were evacuated from the permanent exclusion zone set up around Chernobyl. Plans were made in the mid-1990s to encase the damaged reactor in a steel shell, to replace the 1986 'sarcophagus', which was leaking by 1996. The rest of the power station was closed in 2000. ► **THREE MILE ISLAND**

### Chernov, Viktor Mikhailovich (1876–1952)
Russian peasant politician. Although the peasants were not fully emancipated until 1905, individuals and groups participated increasingly in the opposition to **NICHOLAS II**. Chernov was originally a populist but, influenced by **MARXISM**, he helped to found the **SOCIALIST REVOLUTIONARY PARTY** in 1901, a party oscillating between **TERRORISM** and peaceful advocacy of far-reaching land reform. Half-way through the Provisional Government's life in 1917, he joined it as Minister of Agriculture and supported the peasants' seizure of all available land. This divided it in the face of the Bolshevik threat. His party gained a majority in the **RUSSIAN CONSTITUENT ASSEMBLY** elected in Nov 1917 and convened in Jan 1918 under his chairmanship. But power lay not with the peasants and their representatives, but with the **BOLSHEVIKS** and their soldiers. Within two days, **LENIN** dissolved the assembly and consigned it and Chernov to history.

### Chernyshevsky, Nikolai Gavrilovich (1828–89)
Russian writer and political activist. The well-educated son of a Saratov priest, a graduate in history from the University of St Petersburg, and a brilliant journalist, he was contributor to and editor of the critical magazine *Sovremennik* ('Contemporary') from 1855 to 1862. He abandoned the liberalism of his predecessors and developed a primitive revolutionary socialist philosophy based on his faith in the Russian peasantry. He was disappointed with **ALEXANDER II**'s rather tentative reforms and, on somewhat doubtful evidence of political subversion, he was imprisoned in 1862 and sent to Siberia in 1864. He was not allowed to return to Saratov until 1889 when he was already dying. Through his writings and his suffering he inspired a whole generation of emerging revolutionaries. ► **NIHILISM**

### Cherokee
Native North Americans formerly living in southeastern USA, now living in Oklahoma and North Carolina. They sided with the British in the **AMERICAN REVOLUTION**, and later, in 1827, established the Cherokee Nation with its own constitution and elected government. After gold was discovered on their land, they were removed by US troops and forced to move west to unsettled **INDIAN TERRITORY** in Oklahoma. Thousands died from cold, disease and starvation during their 800mi/1,300km mid-winter march that became known as the **TRAIL OF TEARS**. The survivors settled in Oklahoma with other displaced southeastern tribes. Over 700,000 Cherokee live in the USA today; most live in Oklahoma, but some who refused to leave the south-east still live in North Carolina. ► **FIVE CIVILIZED TRIBES**; **NATIVE AMERICANS**

### Cherry Blossom Society (*Sakurakai*)
The secret society formed by young Japanese army officers in 1930 under the leadership of Lieutenant-Colonel Hashimoto Kingoro of the Army General Staff. Violating the ban on army involvement in politics, the society met to discuss the renovation of the state, reflecting increasing army dissatisfaction with civilian government run by political parties. It was involved in two abortive coups in 1931, in alliance with ultra-nationalist civilians, to set up a military cabinet. The society was dissolved shortly afterwards.

### Chervenkov, Vulko (1900–80)
Bulgarian politician. He joined the Bulgarian Communist Party (BCP) in 1919 and went to the USSR where he studied at the Moscow Military Academy and Lenin International School and acted as secretary to Georgi **DIMITROV**. Returning to Bulgaria in 1944, he held a series of appointments within the BCP: Secretary for AgitProp (1949–50), Deputy Prime Minister (1949–50), General-Secretary (1950–61), Prime Minister (1950–6) and Deputy Prime Minister (1956–61). Known as Bulgaria's 'Little **STALIN**', he fell victim to Nikita **KHRUSHCHEV**'s anti-Stalinist campaign in the early 1960s. In 1962 he was expelled from the party and replaced by Todor **ZHIVKOV**, who had denounced him at the 1961 and 1962 party conferences. Later he was rehabilitated (1969) and awarded a state pension.

### Chesterfield, Philip Dormer Stanhope, 4th Earl of (1694–1773)
English politician, orator and man of letters. He studied at Cambridge, made the Grand Tour, became an MP (1715), and in 1726 succeeded his father as Earl. A bitter antagonist of **WALPOLE**, he joined the **PELHAM** ministry (1744), became Irish Lord-Lieutenant (1745), and one of the principal Secretaries of State (1746–8).

### Chetniks (*Četnici*)
Bands of royalist Serbian guerrilla fighters active in Yugoslavia during **WORLD WAR II**. Organized by Colonel Draža **MIHAILOVIĆ** and a small group of Serbian officers after the collapse of the Yugoslav army (1941), anti-communist and anti-Croat, they fought **TITO**'s communist partisans rather than the Axis occupiers and so forfeited Allied support in 1944.

### Cheyenne
Native North Americans, members of the Algonquian linguistic group, who originally lived east of the Missouri River and migrated to the Great Plains in the 17c, becoming skilled horsemen and buffalo hunters. A northern group settled along the North Platte River, while a southern contingent lived along the upper Arkansas River. Following the incursion of white prospectors and settlers on their land and attack by US troops, including a massacre at Sand Creek, Colorado, they joined the **ARAPAHO** and **SIOUX** to fight the army, taking part in the Battle of the **LITTLE BIGHORN**. Eventually defeated, their few remaining members were assigned to reservations in Oklahoma and Montana. In 1990 their population was c.11,000. ► **INDIAN WARS**; **NATIVE AMERICANS**

### Chiang Ch'ing ► **JIANG QING**

### Chiang Ching-kuo ► **JIANG JING'GUO**

**Chiang Kai-shek (Jiang Jieshi)** (1887–1975)
Chinese revolutionary leader. He was the effective head of the Nationalist Republic (1928–49), and head thereafter of the émigré Nationalist Party regime in Taiwan. Born into a merchant family in Zhejiang, he interrupted his military education in Japan to return to China and join the Nationalist revolution. In 1918 he joined the separatist revolutionary government of **SUN YAT-SEN** in Canton, where he was appointed Commandant of the new Whampoa Military Academy. After Sun's death (1925), he launched an expedition against the **WARLORDS** and the Beijing government, entering Beijing in 1928, but fixed the Nationalist capital at Nanjing (Nanking). During the ensuing decade the Nationalist Party steadily lost support to the communists. When Japan launched a campaign to conquer China (1937), Nationalist resistance was weak. Defeated by the communist forces, he was forced to retreat to Taiwan (1949), where he presided over the beginnings of Taiwan's 'economic miracle'. His son, **JIANG JING'GUO**, became Prime Minister in 1971 and President in 1978.

**Chiang Tse-min ▶ JIANG ZEMIN**

**Chibchas ▶ PRE-COLUMBIAN CIVILIZATIONS**

**Chicanos**
US citizens descended either from Mexican immigrants or from the Mexicans who once inhabited the area of the south-west USA which was taken in the **MEXICAN WAR** (1846–8). Long considered an underclass, they were encouraged during the **CIVIL RIGHTS MOVEMENT** to campaign for better treatment and by the late 20c some had secured high positions. In some parts of the USA, *chicano* (a Mexican-American man or boy) and *chicana* (a Mexican-American woman or girl) are regarded by those denoted as terms indicative of ethnic pride; in other regions, these same terms may be derogatory. ▶ **BRACERO**

**Chicherin, Grigoriy Vasilevich** (1872–1936)
Russian revolutionary, politician and diplomat. He joined the Russian Social Democratic Labour Party in 1905 and engaged in party work in Germany, France and England. At first he sided with the **MENSHEVIKS**, but after the **OCTOBER REVOLUTION** he supported the **BOLSHEVIKS** and was arrested for subversive activities in Britain. He was later exchanged for the ex-British ambassador in Russia. In 1918 he helped negotiate the Treaty of **BREST-LITOVSK**, and became People's Commissar for Foreign Affairs. During the 1920s he represented the USSR at many international conferences. In 1930, ill health and differences with **STALIN** over his conduct of foreign affairs led to his being relieved of his post, and he lived in retirement until his death.

**Chickasaw**
A Muskogean-speaking Native American tribe who originally inhabited Mississippi, south-western Kentucky and western Tennessee. They hunted, fished, farmed and battled with the **CHEROKEE** and other enemy tribes. In the 1540s they nearly stopped the advances of Spanish explorer Hernando de Sota, and in 1729 they joined forces with the **NATCHEZ** and battled the French. By the late 1830s they were forced to move westward into Oklahoma, where they became members of the **FIVE CIVILIZED TRIBES**. In 1856 they

established the Chickasaw Nation, whose prosperity declined during the **AMERICAN CIVIL WAR**. In the early 21c the Chickasaw population was c.38,000. ▶ **NATIVE AMERICANS**

**Chidzero, Bernard Thomas Gibson** (1927–2002)
Zimbabwean politician and **UN** administrator. Educated in Southern Rhodesia and Marianhill in South Africa, he went to Pius XII Catholic College in Lesotho, Ottawa University and then Nuffield Colege, Oxford, from where he graduated with a DPhil in 1960. He was successively assistant research officer at the Economic Commission for Africa in Addis Ababa (1961–3), representative of the UN Technical Assistance Board in Kenya (1963–6), Resident Representative UNDP, Kenya (1966–8), Director Commodities Division **UNCTAD** (1968–77) and Deputy President General (1977–80). Elected to the Zimbabwe Senate (1980), he was Minister of Economic Planning and Development until 1995. Although not a member of the Politburo, he was the chief architect of Zimbabwe's economic policy and the leading figure among reformists who prevailed over the radicals' wish for a more socialist and Leninist state.

**Ch'ien-lung ▶ QIANLONG**

**Chifley, (Joseph) Ben(edict)** (1885–1951)
Australian politician and Labor Prime Minister (1945–9). In early life an engine driver, he entered parliament in 1928, and became Defence Minister in 1931. Defeated in the 1931 election, he returned to parliament in 1940, becoming Treasurer in 1941, a post he combined with that of Minister for Post-War Reconstruction (1942–5), and Prime Minister on **CURTIN's** death in 1945. As Prime Minister, he expanded social services and reformed the banking system, although his attempt to nationalize the banks failed. He continued as leader of the **AUSTRALIAN LABOR PARTY** until his death.

**Childers, (Robert) Erskine** (1870–1922)
Irish nationalist and writer. He fought in the **BOER WARS** and **WORLD WAR I**, and wrote a popular spy story, *The Riddle of the Sands* (1903), and several works of non-fiction. After the establishment of the **IRISH FREE STATE**, he joined the **IRA** and was active in the **IRISH CIVIL WAR**. He was captured and executed at Dublin. His son, Erskine Childers (1905–74) was President of Ireland in 1973–4.

**child labour**
The employment of children below the minimum age specified by national or international labour laws. In Britain, although children were traditionally used in agriculture before the late 18c, the advent of the **INDUSTRIAL REVOLUTION** and their exploitation in factories and mines aroused concern for their safety in often dangerous and dirty conditions. The first law (1802) to help child labourers was ineffectual, but the **FACTORY ACTS** did limit the minimum age and working hours, and also provided for enforcement. In the USA, Jane **ADDAMS** and Frances **PERKINS** campaigned for legislation to protect children, and in 1938 the Fair Labor Standards Act (1938) brought child labour to an end. In developing countries, however, where poverty and lack of schools make a mockery of restrictive legislation, hundreds of millions of children – some as young as four – still work in

quarries, factories, fields, mines and service enterprises, and are relied upon to contribute to their meagre family incomes.

### Children's Crusade, The (1212)
The crusade began in the Rhineland and Lower Lorraine and was led by a boy called Nicholas. The children, unarmed and ranging in age from about 10 to 18, intended to travel to Jerusalem and recapture the Holy Sepulchre. When they reached Genoa they numbered around 7,000, but the Lombards refused to supply them with ships, hoped-for miracles did not happen, and they gradually dispersed. The crusade had its origins in the fanaticism of contemporary preaching against the **ALBIGENSES** and in the ideal of poverty, which suggested that the pure and innocent were the most effective servants of God.

---

**CHILE**   official name **Republic of Chile**

A republic in south-western South America, bounded to the west by the Pacific Ocean; to the east by Argentina; to the north-east by Bolivia; and to the north-west by Peru. Originally occupied by South American Indians, the arrival of the Spanish in the 16c made Chile part of the Viceroyalty of Peru. In 1810 it declared its independence from Spain, which resulted in war until the Spanish were defeated in 1818. The first President was General Bernardo O'Higgins. Border disputes with Bolivia, Peru and Argentina brought a Chilean victory in the War of the **PACIFIC** (1879–84). In the late 1920s economic unrest led to a military dictatorship until 1931. The Marxist coalition government of President **ALLENDE** was ousted in 1973 and replaced by a military junta led

by General **PINOCHET**, who banned all political activity, resulting in considerable political opposition, both at home (led by Eduardo **FREI MONTALVA**) and abroad. A constitution providing for an eventual return to democracy came into effect in 1981, and after 1988 there were limited political reforms. Free elections were held in 1989, and in 1990 the National Congress was restored and Pinochet was replaced by Christian Democrat Patricio Aylwin Azócar, who was succeeded in 1994 by Eduardo Frei Ruiz-Tagle. In 2000 the socialist Ricardo Lagos Escobar became President. ► **SPANISH-AMERICAN WARS OF INDEPENDENCE**

### Chilembwe, John (c.1871–1915)
Nyasaland religious and military leader. After receiving his education in the USA, he returned to Nyasaland (Malawi) where he established his Providence Industrial Mission, an independent African church and mission in 1906. He became increasingly discontented with white rule and petitioned for black rights in various limited areas. When his appeals were ignored, in 1915 he led a rising against the British, through which he hoped to replace white rule by divine assistance. Two Europeans were killed, but the revolt was suppressed and Chilembwe died while trying to escape. It was the first major act of black resistance in Malawi, and an inspiration to subsequent African nationalism.

### Chiltern Hundreds
In the UK, a legally fictitious office of profit under the Crown: Steward or Bailiff of Her Majesty's Chiltern Hundreds of Stoke, Desborough and Burnham. To accept this office disqualifies an MP from the House of **COMMONS**. As an MP cannot resign, application to the Chiltern Hundreds is the conventional manner of leaving the Commons.

---

**CHINA**   official name **The People's Republic of China**
A socialist state in central and eastern Asia, which also claims the island of Taiwan. The country is bounded to the north-west by Kyrgyzstan and Kazakhstan; to the north by Mongolia; to the north-east by Russia; to the east by North Korea, the Bo Hai Gulf, the Yellow Sea, and the East China Sea; to the south by the South China Sea, the Gulf of Tongking, Vietnam, Laos, Myanmar (formerly Burma), India, Bhutan and Nepal; and to the west by India, Pakistan, Afghanistan and Tajikistan. Chinese civilization is believed to date from the Xia Dynasty of c.2200–1767BC; the Shang Dynasty (c.1766–1122BC) saw the introduction of bronze, and was presided over by a chariot-riding warrior aristocracy; the western Zhou Dynasty ruled over a prosperous feudal agricultural society (c.1066–771BC); the eastern Zhou Dynasty (770–256BC) was the era of Confucius and Lao Zi (Lao-tzu); the Qin Dynasty (221–206BC) unified the warring states and provided a system of centralized control; there was expansion west during the Western and Eastern Han Dynasties (206BC–AD220). From the 4c, a series of northern dynasties was set up by invaders, with several dynasties in the south; these were gradually reunited during the Sui (581–618) and Tang (618–907) dynasties. After a period of partition into Five Dynasties (907–60) there emerged the **SONG DYNASTY** (960–1279),

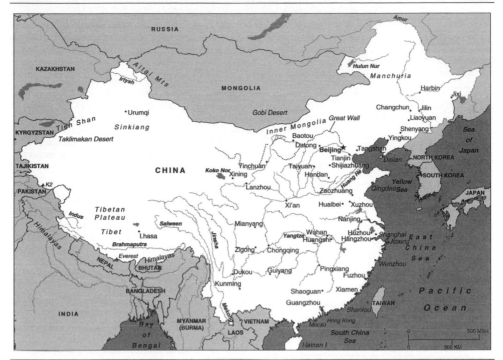

remembered for literature, philosophy and inventions (eg movable type, gunpowder); **GENGHIS KHAN** established the Mongol **YUAN DYNASTY** (1279–1368). There followed visits by Europeans, such as Marco **POLO**, in the 13–14c, and the **MING DYNASTY** (1368–1644) increased contacts with the West. It was overthrown by Manchus, who ruled until 1911, and enlarged the empire to include **MANCHURIA**, Mongolia, Tibet, Taiwan and parts of Turkestan. Opposition to foreign penetration led to the **OPIUM WARS** (1839–42, 1858–60), in which defeat compelled China to open ports to foreign trade. The **SINO-JAPANESE WAR** (1895) gave control of Taiwan and Korea to Japan. The **BOXER RISING** (1898–1900) was a massive protest against foreign influence. The Republic of China was founded by **SUN YAT-SEN** (1912) after the fall of the **QING DYNASTY**, but was followed by chaos and an era of regional **WARLORDS**. Unification came under Jiang Jieshi (**CHIANG KAI-SHEK**), who made Nanjing the capital in 1928. Conflict between Nationalists and communists led to the **LONG MARCH** (1934–5), with communists moving to north-west China under **MAO ZEDONG** (Mao Tsetung). The deeply corrupt Nationalist regime was defeated in 1950 and withdrew to Taiwan. The People's Republic of China was proclaimed in 1949, with its capital at Beijing (Peking). The first Five-Year Plan (1953–7) was a period of nationalization and collectivization; the **GREAT LEAP FORWARD** (1958–9) emphasized local authority and establishment of rural communes; the **CULTURAL REVOLUTION** was initiated by Mao Zedong in 1966; many policies were reversed after Mao's death in 1976, and there was a drive towards rapid industrialization and wider trade relations with the West. The killing of student-led pro-democracy protesters in **TIANANMEN SQUARE**, Beijing, in 1989 provoked international outrage and the introduction of economic sanctions, but these

had no effect and were relaxed after 1990. Gradual steps towards a controlled market economy continued throughout the 1990s. In 1997 China entered a new era with the death in Feb of **DENG XIAOPING**, who was succeeded as leader by **JIANG ZEMIN**, and the handover in July of former British Crown Colony Hong Kong. China was admitted to the **WORLD TRADE ORGANIZATION** in 2001 and in 2004 signed a trade agreement with ten South-East Asian countries, paving the way for a new free-trade zone. China has a population of 1,284,972,000 (2001 estimate). It is a one-party communist state governed nominally by an elected National People's Congress of 2,979 deputies and in practice by a self-perpetuating State

## DYNASTIES OF CHINA

| Dates | Name |
|---|---|
| 1766–1122 BC | Shang Dynasty |
| 1122/1066–771 BC | Western Zhou (Chou) Dynasty |
| 770–256 BC | Eastern Zhou (Chou) Dynasty |
| 403–222 BC | Warring States Period |
| 221–206 BC | Qin (Ch'in) Dynasty |
| 206 BC–AD 24 | Western ('Former') Han Dynasty |
| AD 8–23 | Interregnum (Wang Mang) |
| 25–220 | Eastern Han Dynasty |
| 220–80 | Three Kingdoms Period |
| 266–317 | Western Jin (Chin) Dynasty |
| 318–420 | Eastern Jin (Chin) Dynasty |
| 420–589 | Southern Dynasties |
| 581–618 | Sui Dynasty |
| 618–907 | Tang Dynasty |
| 907–60 | Five Dynasties and Ten Kingdoms Period |
| 960–1279 | Song (Sung) Dynasty |
| 1122–1234 | Jin (Jurchen) Dynasty |
| 1279–1368 | Yuan Dynasty |
| 1368–1644 | Ming Dynasty |
| 1644–1911 | Qing Dynasty |

# *Chinese Dynasties pre-1000* AD

*Culture & Society*

**Shang Dynasty** (1766–1122 BC)
The first Chinese dynasty for which there are historical records, although archaeological evidence suggests that the Shang monarchy emerged from an earlier Neolithic culture, the Hsia (Xia). Shang civilization stretched from the western edge of the Yellow River plain to Shandong in the east, with its core area in present-day northern Henan province (north China). There may have been several capitals although only the last one, Yin (near present-day Anyang), has been firmly identified. The inscriptions on the oracle bones excavated from the royal tombs around Anyang are the oldest known form of Chinese writing. Shang civilization, which clearly distinguished itself from non-Chinese 'barbarians' to the north, was characterized by sophisticated use of bronze, ancestor worship, large cities, a chariot-riding warrior aristocracy ruling over a dependent peasantry, and specialized craftsmen. The Shang state was overthrown by a Chinese-speaking people known as Zhou (Chou) from the west in the Wei River valley (present-day Shanxi province), who established the Zhou Dynasty.

**Zhou (Chou) Dynasty** (1122/1066–256 BC)
Accounts of the origins of the Zhou Dynasty are a mixture of history and legend. It is traditionally held to have been founded by King Wu, who overthrew the last tyrannical ruler of the Shang Dynasty, Zhouxin. Its capital was at Hao (near Xi'an) until 771 BC, and at Luoyi (near Luoyang) until its occupation by the Win in 256 BC. A form of feudal monarchy, the Zhou saw the first flowering of Chinese historical, philosophical and literary writing, most notably the **Confucian Classics**, the introduction of the doctrine of the **Mandate of Heaven**, and the establishment of many aspects of Chinese culture that have endured to the present.

**Qin (Ch'in) Dynasty** (221–206 BC)
The first dynasty to rule over a united China. Its founder, Qin Shi Huangdi, led the state of Qin (in present-day Shaanxi) to victory over the other 'warring states', and installed a regime of strict authoritarian Legalism. Its achievements include the abolition of the ancient feudal order in favour of a prefectural system, the standardization of the Chinese script, weights and measures, and the construction of roads, canals and the Great Wall of China. These achievements were made possible by a tyrannical government, which was overthrown by massive peasant uprisings.

**Han Dynasties** (206 BC–AD 220)
The name of several early Chinese dynasties, now used to distinguish those of native Chinese stock from the national minorities. The Western (or 'Former') Han (206 BC–AD 24), founded by Liu Bang, a leader of the rebellion that overthrew the Qin Dynasty, was characterized by expansion of the Chinese empire into Korea and Central Asia, incessant campaigns against the Huns, the triumph of Confucianism as state orthodoxy, and great achievements in literature and learning. Its capital was at Changan (present-day Xi'an). After an interregnum (AD 8–23), during which the reformist Wang Mang usurped the throne, the Eastern Han ruled China from Luoyang (AD 25–220). During this period Buddhism was introduced to China, and trade links developed with Europe via the Middle East.

Council of over 45 ministers, led by a Prime Minister.
➤ **CHINESE DYNASTIES PRE-1000**AD; **MONGOLS**; **MANCHU**

## China Democratic League
A political group formed in 1944 in response to **CHIANG KAI-SHEK**'s attempt to ease controls on minority party activity and thereby enhance the credibility of the **GUOMINDANG** government. Calling for constitutional guarantees and the creation of a coalition government, the league's criticism of Chiang's intransigence towards the Chinese Communist Party (CCP) and its condemnation of the renewed civil war in 1946 aroused the hostility of the authorities. Outlawed in 1947, the league was resuscitated after 1949 by the new communist regime and its leaders allowed to participate in government. In 1957, following general criticism of the CCP during the **HUNDRED FLOWERS CAMPAIGN**, the leaders of the league were accused of being rightists and were purged from official life.

## Chin Dynasty ➤ JIN (JURCHEN) DYNASTY

## Chinese Civil War (1946–9)
After Japan's **WORLD WAR II** defeat (Aug 1945), civil war broke out again in China between the communists and the **GUOMINDANG** (Nationalist) forces under **CHIANG KAI-SHEK**. A truce (14 Jan 1946), mediated by US envoy General George Marshall, broke down and US supplies to the Guomindang were stopped (July 1946). Nonetheless, the better-equipped Guomindang took the communist capital,

Yan'an, on 19 Mar 1947. The communists, meanwhile, stepped up their campaign from rural-based guerrilla warfare to full-scale battles, recapturing the city a year later. The communists' strategy of focusing on rural rather than urban areas succeeded in isolating the Guomindang and severely taxing their resources. They followed up their advantage in late 1948 and early 1949 with the so-called Battle of **HUAI-HAI**, the series of decisive engagements in the civil war, in which the Guomindang lost more than half a million men. The communists went on, in 1949, to capture Beijing and Tianjin (Jan), Nanjing (Apr), Shanghai (May) and Canton (Oct). The People's Republic of China was formally proclaimed by **MAO ZEDONG** on 1 Oct 1949; the Nationalists withdrew to Taiwan (Formosa) on 7 Dec of the same year.

## Chinese Eastern Railway (CER)
The railroad in north Manchuria, covering a distance of 1,073 mi/1,727km. In 1896 China granted Tsarist Russia the concession of building the railway as an extension of the Trans-Siberian railroad begun in 1891; Russia also obtained the right of policing the line. The 1896 agreement stipulated that the line would either be redeemed by China after 36 years for 700 million roubles or would pass to Chinese control without compensation after 80 years. Although the new Bolshevik government in 1920 promised to abolish all Tsarist Russia's privileges in China, the CER remained under Soviet control until 1935, when it was sold to Japan. In 1945 the CER

## Jin (Chin/Tsin) Dynasty (AD 266–317)

Also known as the Western Jin, this was the last native Chinese dynasty to rule over a unified China before a period of division lasting until the 6c, in which independent Chinese kingdoms confronted non-Chinese dynasties of conquest in the north. The Jin Dynasty was founded by the Sima family when it usurped power from the reigning Cao family and overthrew the Wei state. By AD 280, the Jin had completed the reunification of China, thus ending the Three Kingdoms Period, but came under increasing pressure from non-Chinese tribes in the north, who succeeded in capturing the Jin capital of Chang'an in 316. A member of the Sima family then established a separate dynasty (Eastern Jin, 318–420) in the south at Nanjing, the first of a series of independent kingdoms that engaged in constant warfare with the northern foreign dynasties.

## Sui Dynasty (581–618)

The short-lived Chinese dynasty which unified the country after three centuries of division. The founder of the dynasty, Yang Jian, came to power through a palace coup which toppled the Northern Zhou (557–81), the last of a series of 'barbarian' conquest dynasties that had held sway in north China since the 4c. Under the reign title of Sui Wendi (581/604), Yang Jian had united China by 589 and imposed centralized control, eroding entrenched aristocratic privilege. His son, Sui Yangdi (605/17), embarked on costly military adventures in Korea and Vietnam. This, together with the implementation of large-scale public works, such as the Grand Canal (built between 605 and 607) and the construction of a second capital using conscripted labour, exhausted government revenues and made the dynasty increasingly unpopular. Sui Yangdi, whose extravagance and cruelty confirmed Confucian stereotypes of the 'last bad ruler', was murdered by one of his officials in 617 amidst large-scale popular revolts.

## Tang Dynasty (618–907)

The Chinese dynasty founded by the frontier general Li Yuan (566–635), with its capital at Chang'an (present-day Xi'an). In 690 Wu Zetian, a former concubine of the second Emperor and the Empress of the third, became Emperor of China – the only woman ever to do so. In 755 the Rebellion of An Lu-shan, though crushed, left the dynasty unable to control all its provinces as before, and there resulted a period of political disunity known as the Five Dynasties and Ten Kingdoms Period. The Tang Dynasty saw the emergence of the **Civil Service Examination System** and is generally regarded as the golden age of Chinese poetry.

## Five Dynasties and Ten Kingdoms Period (907–60)

Following the collapse of the Tang Dynasty, north China was ruled by a succession of dynasties: Later Liang (907–23), Later Tang (923–36); Later Jin (936–47); Later Han (947–51); and Later Zhou (951–60). These were founded for the most part by Turkic mercenaries. Southern China came under the sway of regional warlords who established their own independent kingdoms. A period of political and social turmoil, it witnessed the further decline of aristocratic families, particularly in the north, and the emergence of new merchant and military élites. After the mid-10c, much of the area around Beijing was ceded to the Khitan nomads from the north. A general of the Later Zhou, Zhao Guangyin, succeeded in establishing his own dynasty, the **Song Dynasty**, in 960 and began the process of reuniting China.

---

came under joint Sino-Russian control as part of the price paid for Soviet entry into the war against Japan. The CER was not restored to full Chinese control until 1954.

## Chinese Labour (Canada)

The reputation of the Chinese for hard work meant they were in great demand, especially by the railway interests for the building of the British Columbian sections of the Canadian Pacific Railway. Their rate of immigration into British Columbia was such that the province attempted to restrict their entry with the introduction of a 'head tax'. This rose from C$50 in 1885 to C$100 in 1900; by 1903 it had risen to C$500, but still did not put off those seeking fortune in the 'Land of the Golden Mountains'. Anti-Chinese sentiment was pronounced among the trade unions, who feared that the labour movement would be undermined, while throughout the province there were fears that society would be destabilized. In 1902 the **LAURIER** government set up a royal commission and as a result Chinese immigration was severely restricted. In response, companies, led by the Canadian Pacific, began to bring in East Indians and Japanese in their stead. The unions became even more alarmed by the arrival of the Japanese, for they were considered more competitive and were supported by a government whom neither the Canadian nor the British governments wished to displease. With the formation of the Asiatic Exclusion League and after the violent riots of 1907, the Laurier government introduced severe restrictions on the entry of all Oriental immigrants.

## Chinese Revolution (1911)

The events relating to the overthrow of the Manchu **QING DYNASTY** and the subsequent creation of a republic in China. It broke out in Wuchang, Hubei province (central China) on 10 Oct 1911 with a mutiny in one of the new army units created by the Qing as part of its reform programme designed to strengthen the dynasty. Officers in these army units, while studying in Japan, had been influenced by the republicanism of **SUN YAT-SEN** and his followers, who attributed China's weakness to the corruption of the Qing monarchy and its subservience to the foreign powers. The anti-Qing uprising quickly spread to other central and southern provinces, where mutinous army units were joined by provincial gentry élites disillusioned with the Qing government's half-hearted attempts at constitutional reform and its failure to prevent foreign encroachment in China, particularly with regard to railway concessions. By 1 Jan 1912 delegates from 16 provinces had elected Sun Yat-sen provisional President of a Chinese republic. Aware of the weakness of his own military forces and fearful that the foreign powers might intervene to protect their economic interests, Sun offered the presidency to **YUAN SHIKAI**, commander of the Qing forces, on the condition he abide by a republican constitution. On 12 Feb 1912 the court announced the abdication of the boy-emperor **PUYI**, and Yuan Shikai became President of a

**China: the decline of the empire, 19–20c**

unified republic. The 1911 Revolution can be viewed as a nationalist revolution, but in other respects it was an ambivalent one. Spearheaded by traditional élites, who were its principal beneficiaries (rather than Sun Yat-sen's republican revolutionaries), the revolution brought no significant social change in its wake, while the new President had been an important official of the *ancien régime* who, as events were to show, had scant respect for constitutional government.

**Ch'ing Dynasty ➤ QING DYNASTY**

**Ching-Kang shan ➤ JINGGANGSHAN**

**Chioggia, War of** (1378–81)
This was the climax of the struggle between Venice and Genoa for commercial supremacy in the Mediterranean. The fact that the Genoese had reached the lagoon is commemorated in the name of the war, and, with the bell tower of St Mark's in sight, it seemed that victory would be theirs. From an apparently impossible position, the Venetians contrived an astonishing naval victory.

**Chippewa ➤ OJIBWA**

**Chirac, Jacques René** (1932– )
French politician. A Gaullist, he was first elected to the National Assembly in 1967, and gained extensive

governmental experience before being appointed Prime Minister by **GISCARD D'ESTAING**. In office from 1974 to 1976, he resigned over differences with Giscard and broke away to lead the Gaullist Party. Mayor of Paris from 1977 to 1995, he was an unsuccessful candidate in the 1981 and 1988 presidential elections, but succeeded at the third attempt in 1995. Re-elected in 2002, he alienated US opinion by opposing the **IRAQ WAR**. ➤ **GAULLE, CHARLES DE ; GAULLISTS**

**Ch'i-shan ➤ QISHAN**

**Chisholm, Caroline** (1808–77)
British-born Australian philanthropist. In 1830 she married an **EAST INDIA COMPANY** officer, Archibald Chisholm, and they moved from Madras, where she founded a school for the daughters of European soldiers, to Sydney in 1838. Concerned at the moral and physical dangers faced by poor women immigrants dumped in Sydney without resettlement facilities, she began her campaign to publicize their plight when Captain Chisholm returned to duty in 1840. She met the ships, established an employment register and a temporary Female Immigrants' Home, and sought work for the immigrants in rural areas, often accompanying groups herself. In the 1840s over 11,000 women and children passed through the network she established. Returning to England in 1846,

convinced of the positive effect women and families would have on Australian frontier society, she secured free passages for the families of emancipated convicts, and in 1849 established the Family Colonization Loan Society in London, with branches in Australia. The New South Wales government voted £10,000 to assist her work in 1852; the *Caroline Chisholm* was built for the society by a London shipbuilder. In 1854 she returned to Australia and toured the gold rush settlements, publicizing the poor conditions, but personal financial difficulties and ill health ended her philanthropic work.

**Chisholm, Shirley Anita St Hill** (1924–2005)
US politician. She was elected to the New York State Assembly in 1964, and was the first black woman to become a member of the **HOUSE OF REPRESENTATIVES** when elected as a Democrat in 1968. In the 1972 Democratic Convention she won a 10 per cent vote for the presidential nomination. ➤ **DEMOCRATIC PARTY**

**Chisholm Trail** ➤ CATTLE TRAILS

**Chissano, Joaquim Alberto** (1939–)
Mozambique politician. He graduated from high school in Maputo and went to Portugal to study medicine, where he became involved in political activity. He was a founder-member of **FRELIMO** and was in charge of its Department of Security and Defence. A close confidant of Samora **MACHEL**, he became Foreign Minister after independence in 1975, being responsible for negotiating the **NKOMATI ACCORD** with South Africa. He succeeded Machel as President in 1986 and began the process of change inside Mozambique. Faced with accusations of government corruption, he announced in 2004 that he would not to seek re-election in 2005.

**Ch'i-tan** ➤ KHITAN

**Ch'iu Chin** ➤ QIU JIN

**Ch'i-ying** ➤ QIYING

**Chłopicki, Józef** (1771–1854)
Polish soldier and patriot. He served under **NAPOLEON I**, was made a general by the Emperor **ALEXANDER I**, and took part for a time in the Polish insurrection of 1830–1. However, although declared dictator, his rather conservative attitude compelled him to give up this role and he died in exile in Krakow.

**Choctaw**
A Muskogean-speaking Native American tribe who in the 1780s inhabited western Alabama and southern Mississippi. In continuous conflict with the **CHICKASAW** from about 1720, they fought with the French against the **NATCHEZ** and Chickasaw in the Natchez War of 1730, in which they burned Natchez villages, killed around 1,000 people and sent 450 to the West Indies to be slaves. Although they had generally been allied with the French against the British and other Native American tribes, in the 18c they became allies of the British, hampering Spanish commerce during the **AMERICAN REVOLUTION**, and later helped to defeat the **CREEKS** at the Battle of Horseshoe Bend (1814). In 1831, having been forced to exchange their territory for land in Oklahoma, they became members of the **FIVE CIVILIZED TRIBES** and moved

to a reservation in Durant. They presently number c.150,000. ➤ **NATIVE AMERICANS**

**Choibalsan** (d.1952)
Mongolian revolutionary leader. Originally trained as a lamaist monk, he went to Siberia, where he made contact with Russian revolutionaries. He founded his first revolutionary organization in 1919 and joined up with Sukhe Bator in 1921 to establish the Mongolian People's Revolutionary Party. When in 1921 Soviet **RED ARMY** units entered Urga, the capital of Outer Mongolia (which had broken free of Chinese control in 1912) and sponsored the creation of a pro-Soviet government, Choibalsan became a deputy War Minister. In succeeding years he became the dominant leader of the Mongolian People's Republic (formally established in 1924) and had eliminated all his rivals by 1940. His policies were modelled on those of **STALIN**, including the cultivation of a personality cult and harsh treatment of landowners. He was also responsible for the execution of thousands of lamaist monks.

**Choiseul-Amboise, Étienne François, Duke of** (1719–85)
French politician. A minister of **LOUIS XV**, he became Duke of Choiseul and Foreign Minister in 1758. He arranged in 1756 the alliance between France and Austria against **FREDERICK II, THE GREAT**, and obtained good terms for France at the end of the **SEVEN YEARS' WAR** (1763). He improved the army and navy, and developed trade and industry. However, he was alienated from Louis by Madame du **BARRY** and he retired in 1770.

**Chola** ➤ INDIA, PRE-ISLAMIC

**Choshu**
A Japanese feudal domain (*han*) situated in southwest Honshu and founded during the **ASHIKAGA SHOGUNATE** (1338–1573). After 1603 Choshu, as one of the domains that had resisted the establishment of the **TOKUGAWA SHOGUNATE** (1603–1868), was classified as an 'outside fief' (*tozama*) and stripped of land. Middle-ranking **SAMURAI** from Choshu played an important part in the overthrow of the Tokugawa and restoration of imperial rule in 1868. In subsequent decades they occupied key posts in the national government and army.

**Chouans**
Peasant guerrilla bands from the western provinces of France, who rose against the republican government in Paris (1793), opposing attempts to enforce conscription and subdue the clergy. Their name comes from the Breton word for 'screech-owl', allegedly the nickname of their leader, Jean Cottereau. ➤ **FRENCH REVOLUTION**

**Chou En-lai** ➤ ZHOU ENLAI

**Chrétien, (Joseph Jacques) Jean** (1934–)
Canadian politician. As Chancellor in Pierre **TRUDEAU**'s administration he introduced two budgets in 1978 in an attempt to encourage industrial growth and fight inflation, but he failed in the latter since he also introduced tax cuts. In 1980 as Minister of Justice he fought against the concept of an independent Quebec, organizing the campaign leading up to the referendum. After Trudeau's resignation in 1984, the

**LIBERAL PARTY**'s tradition of alternating francophone and anglophone leaders meant that it was John Turner who took over the leadership of the party rather than Chrétien. However, following Turner's decision to step down in 1990, Chrétien was selected as party leader, and after his party's victory at the polls in 1993, he became Prime Minister. In 1995 he responded to renewed Quebec separatist sentiment by proposing to give the province greater autonomy within the Canadian Federation. He was re-elected in 1997 and 2000 but resigned as Prime Minister and party leader in 2003.

**Christelijk Historische Unie ► CHRISTIAN HISTORICAL UNION**

**Christen-Democratisch Appèl ► CHRISTIAN DEMOCRATIC APPEAL**

**Christian I** (1426–81)
King of Denmark (1448/81), Norway (1450/81) and Sweden (1457/64). The founder of the Oldenburg royal line, he was the son of Dietrich, Count of Oldenburg, and Hedvig, heiress of Schleswig and Holstein. He was elected King of Denmark in succession to Christopher III (Christopher of Bavaria). In 1450 he was accepted as King of Norway, ousting **KARL KNUTSSON** of Sweden, and in 1457 he ousted Karl from the throne of Sweden as well (although he lost the crown to Karl again in 1464). In 1460 he was elected sovereign ruler of Schleswig and Holstein. Improvident and spendthrift, he maintained a splendid court in Copenhagen, but was always chronically short of money; to provide a dowry of 60,000 guilders for the marriage of his daughter Margaret to **JAMES III** of Scotland, he mortgaged the Orkneys and Shetland for 8,000 guilders to make up the balance, a pledge that was never redeemed. In Denmark, however, he founded the University of Copenhagen in 1478. He was succeeded by his son, Hans I.

**Christian II** (1481–1559)
King of Denmark and Norway (1513/23) and Sweden (1520/3). He mounted the throne of Denmark and Norway in 1513 and, in 1515, married Elisabeth of Habsburg, sister of Emperor **CHARLES V**. In 1520 he overthrew Sten **STURE, THE YOUNGER**, the regent of Sweden, and thereafter was crowned king. But the **STOCKHOLM BLOODBATH**, his treacherous massacre of the foremost men in Sweden (8–10 Nov 1520), roused such opposition that he was driven out by **GUSTAV I VASA** in 1523, marking the end of the **KALMAR UNION** between the three kingdoms. In Denmark a popular revolt drove him for refuge to the Netherlands, and placed his uncle, **FREDERICK I**, on the throne. Assisted by Charles V, Christian landed in Norway in 1531, but at Akershus next year was totally defeated, and spent his remaining years in imprisonment.

**Christian III** (1503–59)
King of Denmark and Norway (1534/59). The elder son and successor of **FREDERICK I**, he was an ardent Lutheran, imposing the **REFORMATION** on Denmark, Norway and Iceland, and establishing the Lutheran State Church. He acceded to the throne in the midst of a civil war, the so-called 'Count's War' (1533–6) between Catholic supporters of the ex-king **CHRISTIAN II** and the Protestant son of Frederick. It ended only with the capitulation of Copenhagen (Aug 1536). Six days later, Christian arrested all the Catholic bishops who had opposed him, and confiscated Church lands. He then encouraged agriculture and trade, brought out a Danish translation of the German Bible (1550), and hugely strengthened the monarchy. He was succeeded by his son, **FREDERICK II**.

**Christian IV** (1577–1648)
King of Denmark and Norway (1588/1648). One of the best-remembered monarchs of Scandinavia, he was the son of **FREDERICK II**, whom he succeeded, ruling under regents until 1596. A man of action and heroic stature, he strengthened the Danish navy and army, and enhanced the city of Copenhagen with magnificent new buildings. He also founded the city of Kristiania (Christiania) on the site of medieval Oslo after it was burnt down in 1624. He invaded the Sweden of the young **GUSTAV II ADOLF** in 1611, but failed to capture Stockholm and made peace in 1613 with the Treaty of Knærød (Knäred). In the **THIRTY YEARS' WAR** (1618–48) he joined the Protestant Union in 1625 to help his niece, Elizabeth of Bohemia, but retired from the fray after a catastrophic defeat at Lutter am Barenberge, near Hamelin, by Count von Tilley and **WALLENSTEIN** in 1626. Denmark's power and prestige were now shattered, and the rest of Christian's reign was a story of steady decline. In 1628 he formed a defensive Baltic alliance with Gustav II Adolf against Wallenstein; but in a second war with the Sweden of Queen **CHRISTINA** in 1643–5, he lost the dominion of the Baltic he had previously gained. He was succeeded by his son, **FREDERICK III**.

**Christian VII** (1749–1808)
King of Denmark and Norway (1766/1808). The son and successor of Frederick V, from an early age he suffered from dementia praecox, aggravated by the harshness of his tutor. He married in 1766 his English cousin, Caroline Matilda, sister of King **GEORGE III** of Britain, and in 1768 made a glittering tour of Europe, accompanied by his court physician, Count Johann Friedrich **STRUENSEE**, whom he soon appointed privy councillor. Struensee became the Queen's lover and seized effective power, but in 1772 was charged with treason and executed, while the Queen was divorced and exiled to Hanover. In 1784 the king was adjudged insane, and relinquished control to his son, Crown Prince Frederick, who eventually succeeded to the throne as **FREDERICK VI**.

**Christian VIII** (1786–1848)
King of Denmark (1839/48). The son and successor of **FREDERICK VI**, as Crown Prince of Denmark he was elected King of Norway in 1814 to go with a new constitution (17 May). However, he was promptly ousted when Norway was taken by **CHARLES XIV JOHN** of Sweden. As King of Denmark he revived the ancient **ALTHING** (parliament) of Iceland as a consultative assembly (1843), and allowed freedom of trade with Iceland. Early in 1848 he signed an order abolishing monarchical **ABSOLUTISM**, which was implemented by his son and successor, **FREDERICK VII**, the following year.

**Christian IX** (1818–1906)
King of Denmark (1863/1906). A prince of Glücksburg, he succeeded the childless **FREDERICK VII**. He

was confirmed as Crown Prince of Denmark by the Protocol of London, signed by all the Great Powers in 1852 when it became clear that the old Oldenburg line would become extinct. On succeeding to the throne in 1863, he was immediately obliged to sign the 'November Constitution' of that year, incorporating Schleswig into the Danish kingdom; this led to war with **PRUSSIA** and Austria, and the loss of both Schleswig and Holstein. In 1874, on the 1,000th anniversary of the settlement of Iceland, he paid the first royal visit by a reigning monarch, and granted Iceland's first constitution, of limited autonomy under a governor. He was succeeded in 1906 by his elder son as **FREDERICK VIII**, while his younger son became King **GEORGE I** of Greece. His elder daughter, Alexandra, married the future King **EDWARD VII** of Britain, and his younger daughter, Mari Dagmar, married the future Tsar **ALEXANDER III** of Russia.

### Christian X (1870–1947)

King of Denmark (1912/47) and of Iceland (1888/1944). The son of **FREDERICK VIII**, he was revered as a symbol of resistance during the German occupation in **WORLD WAR II**. In 1915 he signed a new constitution granting the vote to women, and in 1918 signed the Act of Union with Iceland, which granted Iceland full independence in personal union with the Danish sovereign (this ended in 1944). During World War II he elected to stay on in Denmark; he would ride on horseback through the streets as a defiant reminder of his presence, until he was put under house arrest by the Germans (1943–5). He married Alexandrine, Duchess of Mecklenburg-Schwerin, and was succeeded by their son, **FREDERICK IX**.

### Christian, Fletcher (fl.18c)

British seaman. He was the ringleader in the mutiny on the *Bounty*, which sailed to Tahiti 1787–8. In 1808 his descendants were found on Pitcairn Island. ► **BLIGH, WILLIAM**

### Christian of Brunswick (1599–1626)

He was a son of the Duke of Brunswick, and a Protestant commander and mercenary during the first part of the **THIRTY YEARS' WAR**. He fought against the Spanish in the Netherlands (1521) and raised an army to support the Elector Palatine, Frederick V. He was twice defeated by **TILLY** in five years of campaigning. He was called 'mad Christian'.

### Christian Democratic Appeal (*Christen-Democratisch Appèl*, CDA)

Dutch political party, founded in 1973 as an amalgamation of the three main confessional parties: the **CATHOLIC PEOPLE'S PARTY**, the **ANTI-REVOLUTIONARY PARTY**, and the **CHRISTIAN HISTORICAL UNION**. The CDA was formed as a common defence against falling electoral support for the three member parties in the 1960s and 1970s, which was a result of general secularization. At first the CDA was a loose federation, but in 1976 it campaigned on a single electoral list, and in 1980 the member parties dissolved themselves as separate entities. The CDA, the party of Ruud **LUBBERS** (Prime Minister 1982–94), participated in all government coalitions from 1980 until 1994, when it became the opposition party to a three-way coalition of the Labour, Liberal and **DEMOCRATS 66** parties under Labour leader Wim Kok. In 2003 it re-

turned to power in coalition with Democrats 66 and the **LIBERAL PARTY** (VVD).

### Christian Democratic Party (*Partito della Democrazia Cristiana*, DC)

The largest and most powerful of Italian parties in the post-fascist era and invariably, until 1993, the chief component in the coalition governments that are the basis of modern Italian politics. Emerging in 1942 as a clandestine anti-fascist group that was Catholic but formally secular and non-confessional, it was the ideological heir of the **POPOLARI** from which its early leaders (eg **GRONCHI** and **DE GASPERI**) were drawn. Although embracing quite a wide range of views, the Christian Democratic Party was essentially one of moderate conservatives of clerical sympathies. Officially founded in 1945, it supplied the premier for every coalition government until 1993, except for 1981–2 and 1983–7, when its strength began to wane. During the wave of accusations of corruption during the 1990s, several of the DC leaders were indicted, and by the 1993 local elections its support had completely gone. It changed its name to the Italian Popular Party (*Partito Popolare Italiano*, PPI) and embarked on internal reform, but made little progress in the 1994 election and virtually disappeared. Also in 1993 the party split and a right-wing faction renamed themselves the Christian Democratic Centre. (*Centro Cristiano Democratico*, CCD).

### Christian Democratic Union (Germany) ► **CDU**

### Christian Democrats

Members of Christian Democratic political parties, most of which were formed in Western Europe after 1945, and which have since become a major political force. The Christian Democratic philosophy is based upon strong links with the Roman Catholic Church and its notions of social and economic justice. It emphasizes the traditional conservative values of the family and Church, but also more progressive, liberal values such as state intervention in the economy and significant social welfare provision. Christian Democrat parties emerged to fill the vacuum created by the general disillusionment with parties of the right and left after **WORLD WAR II**, a major exception being the UK, which has no such party. Electorally, the most successful example has been the West German Christian Democratic Union (**CDU**) which, in alliance with its Bavarian sister party, the **CSU**, polled nearly 50 per cent of the votes in 1983. ► **BUNDESTAG**

### Christian Historical Union (*Christelijk Historische Unie*, CHU)

Dutch Calvinist political party founded in 1908 as an extension of the Free **ANTI-REVOLUTIONARY PARTY** (ARP, founded 1895). At the end of the 19c, some Dutch Calvinist politicians, members of the Anti-Revolutionary Party (ARP), expressed their doubts about the democratic and religiously schismatic tendencies of the ARP leader, Abraham **KUYPER**. These more conservative and perhaps more patrician Christian Democrats eventually gathered in the CHU, led by A F de **SAVORNIN LOHMAN**. The CHU has been a regular party of government, combining with other Christian Democrat parties. In the late 1960s increasing secularization began to reduce the CHU's support, to less than 5 per cent in 1972. In

1976 it joined the **CHRISTIAN DEMOCRATIC APPEAL**, and in 1980 the CHU ceased to exist as a separate party.

**Christianity ►** RELIGION

**Christian People's Party** (*Parti Social Chrétien*, PSC; *Christelijke Volkspartij*, CVP)
Belgian Roman Catholic political party founded in 1945 as a renewal of the previous Catholic Block (founded 1936). The first modern Catholic Party in Belgium was formed in 1884 and dominated politics until 1914. Between the World Wars it underwent changes of structure and name (1921, Belgian Catholic Union), and as the largest party in the country, the PSC/CVP has participated in all Belgian coalitions since 1950, with the exception of 1954–8. In 1968 the French and Dutch-speaking wings of the party split apart over the Leuven University language affair, although they still vote together except on language-related issues. As a broad party, it has seen some friction between the representatives of employers and Catholic trade unions.

**Christian Socialism**
A range of movements aimed at combining **SOCIALISM** with Christian principles. In 19c Britain clergymen, including Charles Kingsley, voiced objections to the social consequences of competition in business and unrestricted **CAPITALISM**. Among the various organizations founded with the onset of the **INDUSTRIAL REVOLUTION** was the British Christian Social Union (1889). The movement spread to the USA where the US Society of Christian Socialists was set up, and in the early 20c the Social Gospel movement arose which turned more specifically to Christ's teachings for guidance in solving social and economic problems. One of the main aims of the early Christian Socialists was to improve the status and quality of life of workers. Christian Socialism has since spread to Scandinavia, Switzerland, France and Germany.

**Christina** (1626–89)
Queen of Sweden (1632/54). The daughter and successor of King **GUSTAV II ADOLF**, she was educated like a boy during her minority, when the affairs of the kingdom were ably managed by her father's chancellor, Count Axel **OXENSTIERNA**. After she came of age in 1644, she adopted an independent line in both domestic and foreign policy and worked to bring an end to the costly **THIRTY YEARS' WAR** in which Sweden was engaged. She patronized the arts and attracted to her court some of the best minds in Europe, including Hugo **GROTIUS**, Salamatius and Descartes, who died there in 1650. She was strongly averse to marriage and found child-bearing repugnant. She refused to marry her cousin (later **CHARLES X GUSTAV**), but instead had him proclaimed Crown Prince. Then, having secretly embraced Catholicism and impatient of the personal restraints imposed on her as a ruler, she abdicated in 1654. She left Sweden for Italy, was openly received into the Roman Catholic Church in Innsbruck and entered Rome on horseback. She spent the remainder of her life in Rome as a pensioner of the pope and a generous patron of the arts.

**Christophe, Henri** (1767–1829)
Haitian revolutionary. Born a slave on the island of Grenada, he joined the black insurgents on Haiti against the French (1790), and became one of their leaders, under **TOUSSAINT L'OUVERTURE**. He was appointed President in 1807, and despite civil war was proclaimed King, as Henri I, in the northern part of the island in 1811. He ruled with vigour, but his avarice and cruelty led to an insurrection, and his subsequent suicide.

**Christophersen, Henning** (1939–)
Danish politician. A member of the Danish parliament (**FOLKETINGET**) from 1971 to 1984, he led the Danish Liberal Party (*Venstre*) from 1978 to 1984. In 1978–9 he was Minister of Foreign Affairs and in 1982–4 was Minister of Finance and Deputy Prime Minister. He became a member of the **EC** Commission in 1984 and was a Vice-President until 1995, in charge of economic and monetary cooperation.

**Chulalongkorn, Phra Paramindr Maha**, also called **Rama V** (1853–1910)
King of Siam (1868/1910). The son of King Maha Mong Kut, he was educated largely by English teachers, acquiring Western linguistic and cultural skills, after which he went, as traditionally prescribed, to a Buddhist monastery. He succeeded his father, as a minor, in 1868 and became king in his full right in 1873. He toured India and the **DUTCH EAST INDIES**, abolished **SLAVERY**, freed his subjects from approaching him on hands and knees, built schools, hospitals, roads, railways and modernized the armed forces. He standardized the coinage, introduced posts and telegraphs, and policed, sanitized and electrified Bangkok. He sent his Crown Prince to study in Britain and visited Queen **VICTORIA** in 1897. He was forced to accept treaties with France (removing Siam's claims over Cambodia and Laos) and with Britain (removing Siamese sovereignty over the northern Malay states) as the imperial pressures bore down on his kingdom towards the end of the 19c.

**Ch'u Min-i ►** CHU MINYI

**Chu Minyi (Ch'u Min-i)** (1884–1946)
Chinese politician and educator. He studied medicine at the University of Strasbourg (1915–21) and subsequently became Vice-President of the Institut Franco-Chinois attached to Lyons University. In 1925 he joined the **GUOMINDANG** and was closely associated with **WANG JINGWEI**, leader of the party's left wing. Following their invasion of China in 1937, the Japanese sponsored a separate Chinese nationalist regime under Wang Jingwei in 1940 and Chu accepted the position of Foreign Minister in the new government. The regime gained little international support and crumbled with Japan's defeat in **WORLD WAR II**. Chu was executed in 1946 for collaborating with the Japanese.

**Chun Doo-hwan** (1931–)
South Korean soldier and politician. He trained at the Korean Military Academy and was commissioned as a second lieutenant in the South Korean army in 1955. After further training at the US Army Infantry School, in 1960 he worked with the Special Airborne Forces group and in military intelligence. After President **PARK**'s assassination (Oct 1979), he took charge of the Korean Central Intelligence Agency (KCIA) and led the investigation into Park's murder. He assumed

control of the army and the government after a coup in 1979. In 1981 he was appointed President and retired from the army to head the newly formed Democratic Justice Party (DJP). Under his rule, the country's 'economic miracle' continued, but popular opposition to the authoritarian nature of the regime mounted, eventually forcing his retirement in 1988.

**Churchill, Lord Randolph Henry Spencer** (1849–95)
British politician. He was the third son of the 7th Duke of Marlborough, and the father of Winston **CHURCHILL**. He entered parliament in 1874, and became conspicuous in 1880 as the leader of a ginger group of Conservatives known as the 'Fourth Party'. He was Secretary for India (1885–6), and for a short while Chancellor of the Exchequer and Leader of the House of **COMMONS**. His powers rapidly diminished by syphilis, he resigned after his first budget proved unacceptable, and thereafter devoted little time to politics. ► **CONSERVATIVE PARTY** (UK)

**Churchill, Sir Winston Leonard Spencer** (1874–1965)
British politician and author. The eldest son of Randolph **CHURCHILL**, he was gazetted to the 4th Hussars in 1895, and his army career included fighting at Omdurman with the 1898 Nile Expeditionary Force. During the second Boer War he acted as a London newspaper correspondent. Initially a Conservative MP (1900), he joined the Liberals in 1904, and was Colonial Under-Secretary (1905), President of the Board of Trade (1908), Home Secretary (1910), and First Lord of the Admiralty (1911). In 1915 he was made the scapegoat for the **DARDANELLES** disaster, but in 1917 became Minister of Munitions. After **WORLD WAR I** he was Secretary of State for War and Air (1919–21), and (as a 'Constitutionalist' supporter of the Conservatives) Chancellor of the Exchequer (1924–9). In 1929 he returned to the Conservative fold, but remained out of step with the leadership until **WORLD WAR II**, when he returned to the Admiralty; then, on Neville **CHAMBERLAIN**'s defeat (May 1940), he formed a coalition government, and, holding both the premiership (1940–5) and the defence portfolio, led Britain through the war against Germany and Italy with steely resolution. Defeated in the July 1945 election, he became a pugnacious Leader of the Opposition. In 1951 he became Prime Minister again, though he was less effective after a stroke (1953), which was concealed from the public. From 1955 until his resignation in 1964 he remained a venerated backbencher. He achieved a world reputation not only as a great strategist and inspiring war leader, but as a classic orator with a supreme command of English, a talented painter, and a writer with a great breadth of mind and a profound sense of history. He was knighted in 1953 and won the Nobel Prize for Literature the same year. ► **BOER WARS**; **CONSERVATIVE PARTY** (UK); **LIBERAL PARTY** (UK)

**Chu Teh** ► ZHU DE

**Chvalkovský, František** (1885–1944)
Czechoslovak politician. He was Foreign Minister in the unhappy post-Munich period. A career diplomat, he served as Ambassador to Rome, endeavouring to win strong Italian support for Czechoslovakia against

Germany. As this became impossible, he veered towards cooperation with the **AXIS POWERS**, which made him a natural choice for his post-Munich post. However, in 1939 he was bullied into accepting **HITLER**'s demands and, with President **HÁCHA**, acceding to the division and domination of Czechoslovakia in Mar. He had the dubious privilege of proving that **APPEASEMENT** backfires.

**CIA (Central Intelligence Agency)**
The official US intelligence-gathering organization responsible for external security, established under the National Security Act (1947) and reporting directly to the President. The CIA was conceived as the coordinator of foreign intelligence and counter-intelligence, but it has also engaged in domestic operations. As a result of abuses of power in both the domestic (notably in the **WATERGATE** affair) and foreign arenas, the CIA must now coordinate domestic activities with the **FBI** and report on covert activities to **CONGRESS**.

**Cialdini, Enrico, Duke of Gaeta** (1811–92)
Italian general and politician. He left Italy after his part in the abortive risings of Parma and Modena (1831), and took refuge in Paris, where he studied medicine. In 1833 he joined the liberal forces in Spain but returned to serve in the Piedmontese army in 1848–9. He remained in the service of **VICTOR EMMANUEL II** after the Battle of **NOVARA**, fighting in the Crimea, and at Palestro (1859) and Gaeta (1860). After failing as a commander in the war of 1866, he retired from the army. He subsequently pursued a successful diplomatic career: he was Ambassador to Madrid (1870–3), and to Paris (1876–81).

**Ciano, Galeazzo, Count of Cortellazzo** (1903–44)
Italian politician and diplomat. Son of an admiral, he took part in the **MARCH ON ROME** and had a successful diplomatic career from 1925 to 1930, when, after marrying **MUSSOLINI**'s daughter, he was rapidly promoted to Under-Secretary for Press and Propaganda and a seat on the **FASCIST GRAND COUNCIL**. In June 1936 he became Foreign Minister. He negotiated the Axis Agreement with Germany and supported the Italian invasion of Albania (1939) and the Balkans (1940–1), but was unenthusiastic about the invasion of France, especially after **HITLER**'s unilateral and early declaration of war. Dismissed as Foreign Minister (Feb 1943), Ciano was one of those who called for the **DUCE**'s resignation in July 1943. He fled to Germany after his father-in-law's arrest but was blamed by Hitler and **RIBBENTROP** for Mussolini's defeat and was executed.

**Cid, El** (c.1043–1099)
Spanish hero. His real name was Rodrigo (Ruy) Díaz de Vivar, but he soon became known as the *Cid* (from the Moorish *Sidi*, 'lord'); *Campeador* ('warrior') is often added. A soldier of fortune and great patriot, he was constantly fighting from 1065; his great achievement was the capture of Valencia (1094), where later he died.

**científicos**
The pejorative term (literally, 'scientists') used to describe the intellectual supporters of Mexico's President Porfirio **DÍAZ** from 1876 to 1911. *Científicos* were generally Positivists, who championed the application

# Cinema

Art & Literature

### Precursors

The human eye's ability to retain an image for a fraction of a second after the object that produced it is removed was established in 1824 by the English physician Peter Mark Roget, who later compiled the famous thesaurus. The consequent ability of the eye and brain to connect up a rapid sequence of images and produce the illusion of movement was exploited by various 19c devices, such as the zoetrope, a revolving drum with a series of drawings fixed inside it which were viewed through a slit. Still **photography** was developed by William Henry Fox Talbot and Louis-Jacques-Mandé Daguerre from 1839, and soon images could be projected onto a screen with a magic lantern. The first celluloid photographic film was produced by Eastman and Goodwin in the 1880s, and at roughly the same time Thomas Edison and his assistant William Dickson devised the Kinetoscope (patented 1891), which moved a loop of film past a magnifying viewer using a sprocket system. The Kinetoscope showed moving pictures on a film, but it was a one-person peep-show, not a device for entertaining an audience.

### Beginnings

By the 1890s the cinema was an invention whose time had come: inventors in a number of countries were advancing more or less simultaneously towards developing the first practical movie camera and projector. The credit for showing the first motion picture belongs to the German pioneer Max Skladanowsky, who in Nov 1895 exhibited pictures of, among other things, a boxing kangaroo and the Kaiser reviewing his troops. The French inventors Auguste and Louis Lumière gave their first show in Dec of the same year. Their first films were above all demonstrations of the camera's ability to record movement, a notable example being a film of a train rushing towards the spectator, which caused consternation among early audiences. Enterprising showmen rushed to capitalize on the new invention and within the next year it had been demonstrated around the world.

France made the running in the first decade of the new medium. The Lumière brothers began opening auditoria before the end of the 19c, both colour films (hand-tinted) and sound films were shown at the Paris exhibition of 1900, and by 1908 the Pathé company, founded by the brothers Charles and Émile Pathé in 1896, was distributing twice as much film in the USA as the entire US film industry. Major events had been filmed by the Lumières and other pioneers from the beginning to provide material to demonstrate their equipment. From 1908 in France and 1909 in Britain, Pathé began to produce regular newsreels of events, a practice that continued until the 1960s.

Early narrative films made in France by Georges Méliès, and in the USA by Edwin Porter, introduced basic techniques of film-making and editing, such as the fade and dissolve, and intercutting between scenes. The popularity of Porter's *The Great Train Robbery* (1903) encouraged the establishment of nickelodeons across the USA. The USA's first true movie theatre opened in 1902, and by 1908 there were 9,000 across the country. The films they showed at first consisted of one or at most two reels, and lasted roughly 10 or 20 minutes. But by 1910, three, four and five-reel films were being produced, and at the outbreak of **World War I**, having been in existence for barely 20 years, cinema was poised to take off as a major industry and art form.

### The silent era

US studios, initially located in the East, began to move west to California from 1911. In 1912 restrictions which had limited US films to two reels at most and denied screen credits to performers were lifted. Independent producers such as Cecil B de Mille and Mack Sennett set up studios in Hollywood and began to turn out films by the hundred to meet an ever-increasing popular demand. The films they produced were mainly westerns, melodramas and slapstick comedies. Charlie Chaplin made his first screen appearance in a Sennett film in 1914 and made 35 films in the first year of his cinema career. His character, the baggy-trousered tramp, was an immediate success and became immensely popular worldwide, making him the first truly international film star.

---

of practical scientific (especially social sciences') methods to the solution of national problems such as industrialization and education, arguing that 'individual absolute right is worth as much as absolute monarchy'. They were pre-eminent in the period 1876–1906, arguing that the government's duty was to assure landowners of their rights. They also believed that 'scientific-technical progress' decreed the demise of the Indian, the end to customary law which protected him, and the integration of Mexico into the international economy and European society.

### çiflik

In the **OTTOMAN EMPIRE**, a type of estate acquired by lease or as a tax farm and which, unlike a **TIMAR**, was treated by its owner as private property. Like a feudal landowner in Europe, the owner of a *çiflik* could claim labour service and between a third and a half of his tenants' produce. The çiflik system developed from the 17c in some of the best agricultural areas of the Balkans (but not in **MOLDAVIA AND WALLACHIA**)

and resulted in a shift in the balance of power between the provinces and the Ottoman Porte.

### Çiller, Tansu (1946–)

Turkish economist and politician. Born in Istanbul and educated in the USA, she worked for a time as an academic economist and was the youngest professor in Turkey before becoming responsible for government finances when the conservative True Path Party took power (1991). In 1993 she was elected head of the Party and the first woman Prime Minister of Turkey. Despite the collapse of the Turkish lira, the stock market crash, and the rise of inflation, her premiership was approved to continue following the municipal elections of 1994. In 1995 the government resigned and the ensuing general election was won by the Welfare Party, though it failed to get enough seats to govern alone. Çiller was acting Prime Minister in the coalition until 1996.

**Cinema** *See panel*

The person generally credited with making the motion picture into a serious art form is the US director D W Griffith. His epics *The Birth of a Nation* (controversial because of the way it presented Black Americans and glorified the **Ku Klux Klan**) and *Intolerance* were released in 1915 and 1916 respectively. Major contributions to the art of the cinema were made during the 1920s in Germany (especially in Expressionist films such as Robert Wiene's *The Cabinet of Dr Caligari* (1919), F W Murnau's *Nosferatu* (1922) and Fritz Lang's *Metropolis* (1926)), in the Soviet Union, where the emphasis was on celebrating and making propaganda for the new state (Sergei Eisenstein's *The Battleship Potemkin* (1925) and *Ten Days that Shook the World* (1928)), and in France with the monumental work of Abel Gance (*Napoléon*, 1927) and the early comedies of René Clair.

By the 1920s, film-making had become a major and immensely profitable industry in the USA, and US films dominated the world market. The studio system and the star system were both in place. Cinemas were built on an ever grander scale to show films featuring Mary Pickford and Douglas Fairbanks, Rudolf Valentino, Charlie Chaplin, Buster Keaton and Harold Lloyd, and the pianos that had provided an improvised sound accompaniment from the early days were often replaced by enormous cinema organs. The careers and personal lives of the stars were avidly followed by legions of fans. When the smouldering screen lover Rudolf Valentino died suddenly of peritonitis in 1926, millions of women mourned him worldwide, and the turn-out for his funeral would have done credit to a monarch or national hero.

US studios lured many of the major European film actors and directors to Hollywood, especially after the financial collapse of the **Weimar Republic** and the rise of the Nazis in Germany. The German cinema industry had been the most technically sophisticated in the world during the 1920s, and Hollywood benefited greatly from the inflow of European talent at the beginning of the sound era, continuing to do so to the present day.

### Cinema outside Europe and the USA

Cinema showings began almost simultaneously around the world. There were screenings in China, India and Japan in 1896. In countries such as these, a similar pattern was followed with local companies, often at least partly foreign-owned, gradually emerging to supplement the material provided by Europe and the USA, and to cater to local demand. Different countries developed specific types of film for their own audiences. For example, **samurai** films in Japan, tango films in Argentina, and films depicting figures from Hindu mythology in India. The development of sound technology tended initially to fragment the industry in multilingual countries such as India and China. Silent films continued to be produced in considerable numbers until 1937 in Japan, not because of linguistic diversity but because cinema had adopted the theatrical device of a narrator to voice-over the action on screen and the convention was popular with audiences.

### Talking pictures

Experimental techniques for providing a soundtrack to accompany a film had been in existence from the earliest days of cinema, and were developed further and periodically tried out in the years between then and the mid-1920s, when the Warner Brothers studio brought the silent era to an end. In 1927 it released the first motion picture with sound, *The Jazz Singer* starring Al Jolson, this used the Vitaphone process in which sound was recorded on large discs and played in synchronization with the film. The Vitaphone had distinct limitations, and by 1931 the process of recording the soundtrack on a strip at the side of the film, pioneered by the US inventor Lee de Forest in 1923, had been developed sufficiently to render the Vitaphone obsolete.

Studios, directors, actors and cinema-owners had to adapt rapidly to the demands of the new medium. Some fell by the wayside. Writing for the screen during the silent era mainly involved drawing up a scenario for the director to follow. Now screenwriters had to write dialogue and composers to provide music for the screen. The popularity of screen musicals began in the 1930s with Busby Berkeley spectaculars such as *Forty Second Street* (1933) and *Gold Diggers of 1933* (1934), and the films of Fred Astaire and Ginger Rogers.

---

### Cinque Giornate (Mar 1848)

The Italian term (literally, 'the five days') used to describe ferocious street fighting in Milan that heralded the outbreak of the anti-Austrian revolution in Lombardy. Having heard the news of the overthrow of **METTERNICH**, insurgents drove **RADETZKY** from the city, establishing a provisional government under Carlo **CATTANEO**.

### Cinque Ports

Originally, the five southern English coast ports of Dover, Hastings, Hythe, Romney and Sandwich, associated by royal authority (under **EDWARD THE CONFESSOR**) to provide ships for naval defence; Rye and Winchelsea were added later. They received royal privileges, including (from 1265) the right to send barons to parliament, and charters, the first dating from 1278; they were governed by a Lord Warden who was also Constable of Dover Castle. Their role declined with the growth of the navy under the Tudors and Stuarts, and the status was abolished in 1835. ►

### STUART, HOUSE OF; TUDOR, HOUSE OF

### Ciompi, Revolt of the (1378)

A popular rebellion in Florence during the painful adjustments which the city's economy had to make in the aftermath of the Black Death. It was led by workers who were not allowed guild membership and who were therefore disenfranchised. The merchant oligarchy was briefly overthrown in favour of popular government but returned to power in a counter-coup.

### Cipriani, Arthur 'Tattoo' (1875–1945)

Trinidadian white labour leader. Cipriani represented the working man in the Trinidad legislature in the 1920s and 1930s. Of French-Corsican origin, he served as an officer in **WORLD WAR I** and on his return set up the Trinidad Workingmen's Association (1922). Once elected to the Legislative Council, he championed the cause of the 'barefoot man' and in 1932 founded the moderate Trinidad Labour Party, which campaigned for a strong trade union

## Colour

Experiments with colour film also dated back to the early days, with colour being used occasionally for special effect in silent films. It was not until the Technicolor three-colour process was perfected in 1933 that colour films became a viable commercial proposition. Walt Disney produced the first colour animated film, *The Three Little Pigs*, in 1933, and the first colour feature, *Becky Sharp* (based on Thackeray's novel *Vanity Fair*), was released in 1935. Most films of the 1930s and 1940s continued to be made in black-and-white, including such all-time masterpieces as *Citizen Kane* (1941). But colour was used especially for big-budget spectaculars such as *Gone with the Wind* (1939). By the 1950s colour films were replacing black-and-white ones, and by the 1970s black-and-white was restricted to low-budget films or chosen for special effect.

## The post-war era

The cinema remained an enormously popular medium after **World War II**. A typical local cinema in Britain in the 1950s and 1960s showed a continuous programme consisting of a newsreel, advertisements, trailers, a B-picture (a low-budget, usually British-made, black-and-white film without big stars, running for about an hour) and a main feature. Saturday matinées for children showing cartoons, serials, and short comedies with Laurel and Hardy, or even earlier stars, were also extremely popular. The rise of **television** changed things radically, first in the USA (where estimated attendances dropped from 85 million to around 45 million by the end of the 1950s) and then in the rest of the developed world.

The artistic quality of films did not decline. Film-making enjoyed a revival in Europe, especially in Italy, France and Sweden during the late 1940s, 1950s and 1960s. Japanese films, especially those of Akira Kurosawa, won international acclaim, as did those of the Indian director Satyajit Ray. Art houses, cinemas showing foreign films, artistic films and earlier masterpieces opened (though never in very large numbers), as local mainstream cinemas closed.

Predictions of the death of the cinema proved premature. Even the advent of home videos in the 1980s failed to kill it off. Part of the US industry's response to the challenge was to produce ever bigger and more expensive spectaculars that could only be fully enjoyed on the big screen, and this strategy met with success as one blockbuster succeeded another as the highest-grossing movie of all time. Collaboration with television networks and exploitation of the market for home videos have helped to finance film projects, and the local cinema showing one film to a large auditorium was supplemented and often replaced in the 1980s and 1990s by the multi-screen complex offering a choice of screenings in auditoria of different sizes.

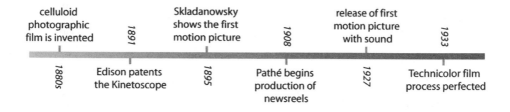

movement, racial harmony and constitutional change. His failure to effect substantial socio-political progress in part led to the **DISTURBANCES** (1935–7), and the conversion of labour to the more militant policies of Uriah **BUTLER**.

## Circles of the Empire *(Reichskreise)*

Administrative districts established (1500) by Maximilian I in the Empire. The original six (Bavaria, Swabia, Franconia, Rhineland, Westphalia, Saxony) were later (1512) joined by four more (Upper Saxony, Austria, Burgundy, Palatinate). These areas had various responsibilities associated with the Imperial administration (eg collecting tolls, taxes, customs).

## CIS (Commonwealth of Independent States)

A grouping (1991) of 12 independent states out of the 15 republics which formerly made up the Soviet Union. They are Armenia, Belarus, Kazakhstan, Kyrgyzstan, Moldova, Russia, Tajikistan, Turkmenistan, Ukraine and Uzbekistan. Azerbaijan and Georgia joined in 1993. The headquarters is in Minsk, Belarus,

and they are governed by a council made up of the presidents and prime ministers of each of the republics. The CIS members agreed in principle to co-operate in such areas as politics, economy, foreign relations, culture, education, science, trade and public health, but the policy of having unified command of each of their armed forces and of former Soviet nuclear weapons remaining in their countries has proved more problematic. In 1997 Russia and Belarus became an integrated union which was open to other CIS members, but no other country joined. ▶ **USSR**

## Cisalpine Republic

The satellite republic established by Bonaparte in Lombardy in Apr 1797. Later the same year, the territories of the smaller Cispadane Republic (Reggio, Modena, Massa and Carrara, and Ferrara and Bologna) were added, followed by the western regions of the old Venetian Republic, Mantua, the Romagna and the Valtellina. Although the republic was briefly suppressed in 1799–1800, after being overrun by

Austrian and Russian forces, it was re-established after the Battle of **MARENGO** (1800). In 1801 it was renamed the Republic of Italy. ➤ **NAPOLEON I**

### Cisař, Čestmir (1920– )

Czechoslovak communist and reformer. He worked his way up through the party apparatus to become a secretary to the Central Committee and also the Minister of Education in 1963. But, having studied in France, he proved too liberal a minister for the establishment and was appointed Ambassador to Bucharest in 1965. In 1968 he was brought back by Alexander **DUBČEK** to be Chairman of the Czech National Council and proved very popular with young people in particular. Inevitably, he was dismissed from office and from the Communist Party following the Soviet invasion: the young had to wait 20 years for their peaceful revolution.

### Cisneros, Francisco Jiménez de (1436–1517)

Castilian statesman. He entered the Franciscan Order and was appointed confessor to Queen **ISABELLA I, THE CATHOLIC** in 1492, and then Archbishop of Toledo (1495), and cardinal and Inquisitor-General (1507). He was a zealous reformer of his own Franciscan order in **CASTILE** and promoter of spiritual literature, and influenced the Queen's decision to prohibit the Muslim faith in Castile (1502). After her death he was active in military expeditions into North Africa (1507–9), resulting notably in the capture of **ORAN** (1509). Twice regent, the second time on the death of King **FERDINAND II, THE CATHOLIC**, he died on his way to greet Charles of Burgundy as the new King of Spain. His achievements for Castilian culture include the foundation of the new university at Alcalá de Henares (1508), and the publication of the famous Complutensian Polyglot Bible (1522).

### Civic Forum (1989)

The broad-based alliance of anti-communist groups in Czechoslovakia that came together to force the resignation of the communist government in Nov. This was subsequently christened the **VELVET REVOLUTION**, since the toppling of the government was achieved without serious bloodshed. The moving force had for long been **CHARTER 77** led by Václav **HAVEL**, who subsequently became President. Civic Forum became a political party and won 51 per cent of the votes in the June 1990 election but split into several rival groups in Jan 1991, agreeing to an 'umbrella' structure until the 1992 elections. The most significant group to emerge from the Civic Forum was the Civic Democratic Party, led by Václav Klaus (Prime Minister 1992–7).

### Civil Constitution of the Clergy (1790)

A decree of the National Assembly in France confiscating the property of the Roman Catholic Church, and reorganizing it on the model of the new administrative system of France. Bishops and priests were to be elected by all voters in their areas. The pope, who had not been consulted, condemned the measure in Mar 1791. The Assembly had already imposed an oath of loyalty on existing clergy. Nearly all the bishops, and about half of the parish priests, refused to take the oath, thus dividing the clergy into the constitutional clergy, those who agreed, and the refractory clergy, those who refused. This was an important fac-

tor in producing resistance to the **FRENCH REVOLUTION**. At the most extreme period of the Revolution (1793–4), attempts were made to replace Christianity with the 'Worship of Reason'; although this remained a brief aberration, the Catholic Church took a long time to recover from its persecution. It was restored to the position of an established Church by the **CONCORDAT** (1801).

### civil disobedience

A political strategy adopted by M K **GANDHI** and his followers in India in 1930, in opposition to Britain's imperial rule: launched by a march to the coast in order to break the law symbolically by making salt (on which tax was payable), it was a non-violent, mass, illegal protest, intended to discredit the authority of the state. The movement was banned, and many were arrested, including Gandhi; but a pact was reached in 1931, and Gandhi then participated in the second of the **ROUND TABLE CONFERENCES**. The strategy was later used by Martin Luther **KING** to good effect, and is a path sometimes advocated by opponents of nuclear weapons.

### Civil Guard

Founded in Spain as a militarized police force in 1844 to keep down banditry, the Civil Guard was organized like an army, led by a general and officers with military rank. Its brutal vigilance of the countryside in defence of the status quo led the ruling classes to regard it as the *Benemérita* (the 'well-deserving'), while for the lower classes its distinctive three-cornered hat, green uniforms and greatcloaks made it one of the most hated symbols of the *ancien régime*. Most of the Civil Guard sided with the Nationalists in the **SPANISH CIVIL WAR**, though it played a leading role in holding places such as Madrid and Barcelona for the Republic. Under **FRANCO** the Civil Guard's dominance of the countryside was consolidated. In 1986 the first civilian appointee was made its Director General. Today its energies are divided between controlling the traffic on the highways, patrolling the countryside, guarding foreign embassies, and combating **TERRORISM**.

### civil rights

The rights guaranteed by certain states to its citizens. Fundamental to the concept of civil rights is the premise that a government should not arbitrarily act to infringe upon these rights, and that individuals and groups, through political action, have a legitimate role in determining and influencing what constitutes them. Historically, civil rights in England have been protected by the **MAGNA CARTA**, and in the USA by the **CONSTITUTION** and **BILL OF RIGHTS**. In common usage, the term often refers to the rights of groups, particularly ethnic and racial minorities, as well as to the rights of the individual.

### Civil Rights Acts

US legislation which prohibits the states from discriminating against any citizen on the grounds of race or colour. The Act of 1866 included blacks within its definition of US citizenship. President Andrew **JOHNSON**'s veto so angered Republican moderates in **CONGRESS** that radicals were able to override the veto, and incorporated its provisions in the **FOURTEENTH AMENDMENT**. However, the Act was undermined by the Supreme Court in the Slaughterhouse Cases (1873) and US v Cruikshank (1875). The Act of 1875, passed as a memorial to Charles **SUMNER**, upheld the equal rights of blacks in the use of inns, theatres and public transport (though education was specifically excluded), but was declared unconstitutional in the **CIVIL RIGHTS** cases of 1883. By the 1950s only about a quarter of those Southern blacks who were qualified to vote could actually do so because state officials were adept at preventing them from registering. The Act of 1957 therefore established the Civil Rights Commission to examine such cases. It was backed up by a new Civil Rights Division in the Justice Department, which could seek injunctions to prevent denial of the right to vote. Even when bolstered in 1960, the Act did not prove very effective. By the Act of 1964 the Attorney-General was authorized to institute proceedings directly when voting rights were abused, and empowered to accelerate the **DESEGREGATION** of schools. Agencies which practised racial discrimination were liable to lose federal funding, and an Equal Opportunities Commission was set up to end job discrimination on the grounds of race, religion or sex. Discrimination was also prohibited in hotels and public transport. This legislation, together with the establishment of the Community Relations Service, indicated the federal government's awareness of the difficulties in dismantling the structures of white supremacy, and was more effective than any previous civil rights legislation.

## civil rights movement

A movement in the USA, especially 1954–68, aimed at securing, through legal means, the enforcement of the guarantees of racial equality contained in the Civil War Amendments to the **US CONSTITUTION**, namely, the Thirteenth, Fourteenth and Fifteenth Amendments, and by the **CIVIL RIGHTS ACTS** of the 1860s and 1870s. These guarantees were severely curtailed by later legislation. In particular, the Supreme Court rulings of 1883, which declared the Civil Rights Act of 1875 unconstitutional because **CONGRESS** had no right to trespass on the states' internal powers of economic regulation, opened the way to racial segregation. The civil rights movement began as an attack on specific forms of segregation in the South, then broadened into a massive challenge to all forms of racial discrimination. It made considerable gains, especially at the level of legal and juridical reform, culminating in the Supreme Court case of **BROWN V BOARD OF EDUCATION OF TOPEKA, KANSAS** (1954), in which Thurgood **MARSHALL** successfully argued against school segregation. The first major challenge was the **MONTGOMERY BUS BOYCOTT** of 1955, which was sparked by an incident in which a black woman, Rosa **PARKS**, refused to give up her seat to a white man. As a result of the boycott, the buses were desegregated and Martin Luther **KING** emerged as the movement's leader. King was a major force in establishing the **SCLC** (Southern Christian Leadership Conference). Forming a coalition with the **NAACP** and other organizations such as the **NATIONAL URBAN LEAGUE**, the **CONGRESS OF RACIAL EQUALITY (CORE)** and the Student Non-Violent Coordinating Committee (SNCC), he led a campaign aimed at desegregating all public facilities, including schools, restaurants, stores and transportation, by non-violent means, and at win-

ning for blacks the unrestricted right to vote and to hold public office. Major actions included the first big clash over school **DESEGREGATION** (1957), which took place in **LITTLE ROCK**, Arkansas; the efforts of the 'FREEDOM RIDERS', groups of blacks and whites who challenged segregation in interstate transport (1961); the national March on Washington (1963), in which over 200,000 blacks and whites participated; and the voter registration drive in Alabama, which culminated in the march from Selma to Montgomery (1965). As white resistance grew, many participants in the marches and demonstrations were arrested, many were beaten, and some lost their lives. But by the late 1960s most of the original goals had been achieved as a result of Court decisions, major legislation and the actions of Presidents **EISENHOWER, KENNEDY** and especially Lyndon **JOHNSON** in enforcing the law. The Civil Rights Act of 1964 barred discrimination in public accommodations and employment; the Voting Rights Act (1965) ensured blacks' right to vote in places where it had hitherto been denied; and the Civil Rights Act of 1968 prohibited discrimination in the sale or rental of housing. One result of the 1960s legislation was the increased participation of blacks in political life, even in Southern communities that were once bastions of segregation. But by the mid-1960s, different problems were arising in the black ghettos of the Northern cities when blacks began rioting to protest at their poverty, high unemployment and poor living conditions. Both King, who turned his attention northward in the last three years of his life, and more militant black leaders such as **MALCOLM X**, recognized that the struggle for equality was moving into the economic sphere. So did Jesse **JACKSON**, an associate of King's, who focused on the importance of creating jobs by investment in black businesses. But, unlike King, Malcolm X and his followers were advocating black separatism rather than integration, and the use of force to reach their goals. Significantly, widespread rioting followed King's assassination in 1968. In the decades since his death, although the economic condition of US blacks improved, the large gap between blacks and whites remained, and led to racial tensions that have yet to be resolved.

## Civil Service Examination System

A system in China for recruiting government officials based on merit rather than birth, dating from the 8c. As early as the 2c BC local officials had been called upon to 'recommend' talented candidates for official posts, but until the 8c officialdom continued to be monopolized by powerful aristocratic families. The examination system aimed to break down the hereditary principle and draw upon a larger pool from which to recruit the bureaucracy. Begun during the Tang Dynasty and systematized during the **SONG DYNASTY**, examinations were held triennially at prefectural, provincial and metropolitan levels, each one conferring a civil service degree. Initially the curriculum on which the examinations were based was a wide-ranging one, but by the 14c was limited to knowledge of the **CONFUCIAN CLASSICS**. While success at even the lowest level conferred on the candidate membership of the gentry-literati class, important official posts went to those who had passed the provincial and metropolitan level examinations.

The system became increasingly rigid and corrupt during the 19c, and was abolished in 1905, to be replaced by a network of modern schools offering a wider curriculum.

## Cixi (Tz'u Hsi) (1835–1908)
Chinese consort of the Xianfeng Emperor (1851/62). She rose to dominate China by manipulating the succession to the throne and bore the Xianfeng Emperor his only son, who succeeded at the age of five as the Tongzhi Emperor. However, Cixi (whose personal name was Yehenala) kept control even after his majority in 1873. After his death (1875), she flouted the succession laws of the Imperial clan to ensure the succession of ZAI TIAN, another minor, as the GUANG-XU (Kuang-hsu) Emperor, and continued to assert control even when the new Emperor reached maturity. In 1900 she took China into war against the combined treaty powers in support of the Boxer movement. Only after her death in Beijing was it possible to begin reforms. ▶ BOXER RISING; HUNDRED DAYS OF REFORM; QING DYNASTY

## Clam-Martinic, Jindrich, Count (1826–87)
Bohemian landowner and provincial politician. From the turn of the 18c and 19c, the landed nobility of the Czech lands, none of Czech nationality, began to associate with the emerging Czech intelligentsia and politicians as a means of asserting their provincial rights against centralist rule from Habsburg Vienna. In the 1860s and 1870s Clam-Martinic played a leading role in pursuing this policy in conjunction with František PALACKÝ and RIEGER, the leaders of the so-called Young Czech Party. But their combined tactics achieved nothing, and by the mid-1870s a purely Czech party emerged, the so-called Young Czechs, aiming for at least national autonomy with little regard for Germans, ennobled or otherwise.

## Clarendon, Constitutions of (1164)
A written declaration of rights claimed by HENRY II of England in ecclesiastical affairs, with the purpose of restoring royal control over the English Church. Promulgated at Clarendon, near Salisbury, the Constitutions (especially Clause 3, which jeopardized benefit of clergy and threatened clerical criminals with secular penalties) brought Thomas Becket and Henry II into open conflict. ▶ BECKET, ST THOMAS (À)

## Clarendon, Edward Hyde, 1st Earl of (1609–74)
English statesman and historian. He trained as a lawyer, and in 1640 became a member of the SHORT PARLIAMENT. At first he supported parliamentary claims, but in 1641 became a close adviser of CHARLES I, and headed the royalist opposition in the Commons until 1642. He was knighted in 1643, and made Chancellor of the Exchequer, became High Chancellor in 1658, and at the RESTORATION (1660) was created Baron Hyde and (1661) Earl of Clarendon. In 1660 his daughter Anne (1638–71) secretly married the King's brother, James (later JAMES VII AND II). Unpopular as a statesman, Clarendon irritated Cavaliers and Puritans alike, and in 1667 he fell victim to a conspiracy at court. Impeached for high treason, he left the country for France, where he died. ▶ ENGLISH CIVIL WARS

## Clarendon Code
A series of Acts passed by the CAVALIER PARLIAMENT (1661–79) between 1661 and 1665, which reasserted the supremacy of the Church of England over Protestant nonconformity after the collapse of the 'Puritan Revolution' in 1660. The most important were the Corporation Act (1661) and the Act of Uniformity (1662). Nonconformity was recognized as lawful, but severe restrictions were placed on the activities of Nonconformists. ▶ PURITANISM; UNIFORMITY, ACTS OF

## Clark, (Charles Joseph) Joe (1939–)
Canadian politician. At first a journalist and then Professor of Political Science, he was elected to the federal parliament in 1972, becoming leader of the Progressive Conservative Party (1976) and of the Opposition (1980–3). In 1979 he became Canada's youngest-ever Prime Minister. His minority government lost the general election the following year, and he was deposed as party leader in 1983. From 1984 to 1991 he was Secretary of State for External Affairs, and from 1993 to 1996 he was the UN representative in Cyprus. With the party facing electoral extinction, he was brought back as leader in 1998 and won a parliamentary seat in a 2000 by-election. He was credited with ensuring the party's survival before his retirement in 2003.

## Clark, George Rogers (1752–1818)
American revolutionary soldier and frontier leader. He trained as a surveyor in Kentucky, and at the start of the AMERICAN REVOLUTION persuaded the government of Virginia to make Kentucky a separate county and to authorize him to defend the frontier. In 1778 he gathered a small army of 175 men and captured the settlements of Kaskaski, Cahokia and Vincennes on the Mississippi River (in present-day Illinois), thus helping to save the Old Northwest for the colonies, before retreating to make his base at Fort Nelson (now Louisville). From 1779 until the end of the war in 1783, he was involved in battles to defend this territory from British and Native American attack. After the war in 1786, he served as Indian commissioner for a time and was involved in making a treaty with the Shawnees.

## Clark, Helen (1950– )
New Zealand politician. She was a political science lecturer before her election to the House of Representatives at the 1981 general election, representing the Labour Party. During the 1980s she served as a minister in a number of departments, including housing, conservation, health and labour, before becoming Deputy Prime Minister in 1989. After the Labour Party lost the 1990 election, she became Deputy Opposition Leader and was elected Labour Party leader in Dec 1993 after the 1993 election left the party still in opposition. She became Prime Minister in 1999 after Labour's general election victory, and continued in power after the party's success in the 2002 election. She has said that New Zealand will inevitably become a republic.

## Clark, Mark Wayne (1896–1984)
US army officer. Chosen by Dwight D EISENHOWER to plan the 1943 Allied invasion of North Africa, he became commander of the Allied armies in Italy in 1944. In 1945, after WORLD WAR II, he headed the US forces of occupation in Austria. During the KOREAN WAR he served as commander of the UN

forces, participated in the lengthy peace talks of 1952–3, and signed the armistice.

**Clark, William** (1770–1838)
US soldier, explorer and map-maker. The younger brother of George R **CLARK**, he joined the army in 1789, and was appointed joint leader with Meriwether Lewis of the successful transcontinental expedition to the Pacific coast and back (1804–6). He later became superintendent of Indian affairs in Louisiana Territory, and then Governor of Missouri Territory. ► **EXPLORATION**; **LEWIS AND CLARK EXPEDITION**

**Clarkson, Thomas** (1760–1846)
English anti-**SLAVERY** campaigner. In 1787, in association with William **WILBERFORCE** and Granville Sharp, he formed an anti-slavery society and after the passing of the British anti-slavery laws (1807) wrote *History of the Abolition of the African Slave Trade* (2 vols, 1808). He campaigned for the abolition of slavery in the colonies and saw it attained in 1833.

**classical economics** (1776–1848)
An English school of political economy, which was first outlined by Adam **SMITH** in *An Inquiry into the Nature and Causes of the Wealth of Nations* (1776) and culminated in John Stuart Mill's *Principles of Political Economy* (1848). David Ricardo's *Principles of Political Economy and Taxation* (1817) also contributed to classical economics, which remained the dominant school of economic theory until the 1870s. Its primary concern was that of economic growth, and it emphasized the need for, and consequences of, economic freedom, embracing such ideas as division of labour, free competition, the function of markets, and the international implications of a **LAISSEZ-FAIRE** economy.

**Clausewitz, Karl Philip Gottlieb von** (1780–1831)
Prussian general. He served with distinction in the Prussian and Russian armies, and ultimately became Director of the Prussian army school, and **GNEISENAU**'s Chief of Staff. His posthumously published *Vom Kriege* (1833, 'On War'), in which war was regarded as a continuation of diplomacy by other means, revolutionized military theory, and was extremely influential in Germany and beyond. ► **PRUSSIA**

**Clay, Henry** (1777–1852)
US politician. The son of a Baptist preacher, he became a lawyer (1797), entered the **HOUSE OF REPRESENTATIVES** in 1811, and was chosen its Speaker, a post he held for many years. He was one of the Congressional 'war hawks' active in bringing on the **WAR OF 1812** with Britain, and was one of the commissioners who arranged the Treaty of **GHENT** that ended it. His attempts to hold the Union together in the face of the issue of **SLAVERY** earned him the title of 'the great pacificator'. In 1824, 1832 and 1844 he was an unsuccessful National Republican and Whig candidate for the presidency.

**Clay, Lucius D(uBignon)** (1897–1978)
US army officer and director of civilian affairs in postwar Germany. He trained at West Point and was an army engineer before becoming head of the first US civil airport programme (1940–1). Soon after the USA's entrance into **WORLD WAR II** (Dec 1941), Clay directed the organization of production and supplies for the army (1942–4). In 1945 he was appointed by President Franklin D **ROOSEVELT** to the post of Deputy Military Governor in Germany under Dwight D **EISENHOWER**. Two years later he became Commander-in-Chief of the US occupation forces in Europe and military governor of the US zone in occupied Germany (1947–9), in which position, among other things, he had to satisfy the ongoing food and shelter requirements of the civilian population. In 1948–9 he oversaw the **BERLIN AIRLIFT** of vital supplies during the Soviet blockade of Berlin. After retiring from the army he entered business and politics, serving as adviser to President Eisenhower (1953–61) and as ambassador in Berlin (1961–2) on behalf of President John F **KENNEDY**.

**Clayton–Bulwer Treaty** (19 Apr 1850)
A US–British agreement on the terms for building a canal across Central America. It remained in effect until 1901, when it was superseded by the **HAYPAUNCEFOTE TREATIES**. Its major provision was to forbid either party to exercise exclusive control or to build fortifications. The parties involved were the US Secretary of State, John M Clayton, and the British Minister to Washington, Sir Henry Lytton Bulwer. The Panama Canal was not completed until 1914.

**CLC (Canadian Labour Congress)**
Canadian labour organization. It was established in 1956 with the merger of the Trades and Labor Congress (associated with the US AFL) and the Canadian Congress of Labour (similarly associated with the US CIO). Unlike the US labour movement, the CLC was ready to take direct political action, and in 1961 it united with the **CCF** (Cooperative Commonwealth Federation) to form the **NEW DEMOCRATIC PARTY**. ► **AFL–CIO**

**Clear Grits**
Canadian political party. The name given to a radical reform group in Upper **CANADA** (**CANADA WEST**/Ontario) in the 1850s. The term derived from the group's attitude of uncompromising determination. It promoted major constitutional reform, including representation by population, direct election to executive posts, and secularization of **CLERGY RESERVES**. It played an important part in Confederation and after 1867 it formed the core of the Canadian **LIBERAL PARTY**. ► **BROWN, GEORGE**

**Clemenceau, Georges Eugène Benjamin** (1841–1929)
French politician. He studied medicine and visited the USA (1865–9), where he married an American. Elected to the National Assembly (1871), he resigned his seat in protest at the actions of the government that provoked the uprising in Paris known as the **PARIS COMMUNE**. Re-elected in 1876, he became the leader of the radicals (on the extreme Left). Implication in the Panama scandal led to his defeat in the 1893 elections. He was a leader of the campaign for the rehabilitation of **DREYFUS**, which allowed his return to parliament as a Senator in 1903. Clemenceau was Prime Minister in 1906–9 and 1917–20, when his determination spurred France to make the effort to pursue victory in **WORLD WAR I**. He presided at the

PARIS PEACE CONFERENCE (1919), where he sought unsuccessfully to obtain in the Treaty of VERSAILLES a settlement that would preserve France from another German attack. Nicknamed 'the Tiger' for the ferocity of his oratorical attacks on his political opponents, he was equally renowned for his journalism, in *L'Aurore*, at the time of the Dreyfus Affair, and in his own newspaper, *L'Homme libre* (renamed *L'Homme enchainé* after a quarrel with the censor) during the war.

**Clement V**, originally **Bertrand de Got** (c.1260–1314)

French pope (1305/14). He became Archbishop of Bordeaux in 1299. As pope, he suppressed the TEMPLARS, and removed the seat of the papacy to Avignon (1309), a movement disastrous to Italy.

**Clement VII**, originally **Giulio de' Medici** (1478–1534)

Italian pope (1523/34). He allied himself with FRANCIS I of France against the Holy Roman Emperor CHARLES V, whose troops sacked Rome in 1527, and for a while became his prisoner. His indecisiveness, along with his refusal to sanction HENRY VIII's divorce from CATHERINE OF ARAGON, hastened the REFORMATION. ► ROME, SACK OF

**Clement IX**, originally **Giulio Rospigliosi** (1600–69)

Italian pope (1667/9). He was papal ambassador to Spain (1644/53) and Secretary of State to ALEXANDER VII, and sought, through the so-called Clementine Peace (Jan 1669), to prevent LOUIS XIV of France from persecuting the Jansenists. The issue of JANSENISM, however, took on a lesser significance than Louis's increasing insistence on Gallican rights to limit the authority of the papacy within France. Louis's refusal to respond to Clement's pleas that he assist the Venetians in their struggle against the Turks during the War of CANDIA further strained relations. The slight assistance the pope was able to offer was insufficient to avert Turkish victory and Clement died while mourning the Christians killed by the infidel in the final stages of the conflict.

**Clement X**, originally **Emilio Altieri** (1590–1676)

Pope (1670/6). Made a cardinal in 1669, he had previously held a number of important Church offices, including that of papal ambassador to Naples. As pope, he sought vainly to rouse Europe against the Turkish threat in the Mediterranean and in Eastern Europe. Absence of support from LOUIS XIV (caused in part by Clement's refusal to allow the French king to collect revenues from vacant sees), coupled with a general uninterest among other European princes, stymied any chance of a general crusade. However, Clement did manage to strengthen papal finances sufficiently to provide subsidies for the Poles in their struggle against the Turks.

**Clement XI**, originally **Giovanni Francesco Albani** (1649–1721)

Pope (1700/21). He was elected pope at a difficult time for the papacy, with its political role in sharp decline and its control of national Churches increasingly threatened. Although from the outset Clement hoped to avoid conflict with either of the great ruling houses of Europe, he succeeded in antagonizing first the Austrian Habsburgs, by supporting the recognition of LOUIS XIV's grandson, Philip of Anjou, as King

of Spain, and then the Bourbons, when he gave in to the demands of Joseph I of Austria to recognize his brother, Charles, as the rightful pretender to the Spanish throne. By the Treaties of UTRECHT (1713) and RASTATT (1714), Clement was forced to concede suzerainty over Naples, Sicily, Parma and Piacenza, while papal influence in France was increasingly marginalized by the growth of GALLICANISM and the rise of JANSENISM. It was against this latter that, in Sep 1713, he issued the Bull *Unigenitus*, which prompted widespread opposition among the many French clergy who supported the now outlawed heresy. ► HABSBURG DYNASTY

**Clement XIII**, originally **Carlo Rezzonico** (1693–1769)

Pope (1758/69). He held several important ecclesiastical positions before he became cardinal in 1737. As pope, he faced considerable hostility from most of Europe's more powerful Catholic princes who, at the time, were seeking to exert greater control over their own national Churches. This was especially true of the Portuguese and the Bourbon rulers of Spain, Naples and France, who were all engaged in anti-Jesuit campaigns, but it was also evident within the Habsburg Empire, which witnessed the development of Febronianism, the German equivalent of GALLICANISM. Despite Clement's attempts to defend the Jesuits, they were expelled from Portugal (1759), France and its dominions (1764), the Spanish Empire (1767) and the Kingdom of Naples and Sicily (1768). Finally in 1769 the ambassadors of the three Bourbon powers demanded that the Society of Jesus be suppressed totally; Clement refused, but within a month had a stroke and died.

**Clement XIV**, originally **Giovanni Vincenzo Antonio Ganganelli** (1705–74)

Pope (1769/74). Educated by the Jesuits, he was made a cardinal by CLEMENT XIII, who hoped he would prove a useful ally in his struggle against the rulers of Portugal, Spain, France and Naples. These had proved themselves determined to destroy the Society of Jesus, not least because it was seen as a symbol of papal interference in their domestic affairs. However, when elected pope on Clement XIII's death, he feared that open schism might emerge unless he placated the great Bourbon powers. In July 1773, therefore, he issued the *Dominus ac Redemptor* dissolving the Society; the suppression lasted until 1814.

**Clementis, Vladimír** (1902–52)

Slovak politician. He became a Czechoslovak communist MP in 1935 but criticized the Nazi–Soviet Pact in 1939 and spent WORLD WAR II in London. In 1945 he became Vice-Minister of Foreign Affairs in the first post-war government. One of the organizers of the 1948 coup, he succeeded Jan MASARYK as Foreign Minister, but was forced to resign in 1950 as a 'deviationist'. During the Stalinist purges, he was hanged along with Rudolf SLÁNSKÝ. ► GERMAN–SOVIET PACT

## Clergy Reserves

A seventh of the public land in Upper and Lower CANADA (Ontario and Quebec), set aside for the future use of Protestant clergy; established under the Constitutional Act (1791). In practice, the reserves became

# Clocks and Time Measurement

*Science & Technology*

The earliest way of measuring the passage of time was by watching the movement of the sun as it rose, passed across the sky, and sank. Humans then progressed to observing shadows cast at different periods by a fixed object, such as a stick thrust into the ground. The ancient Egyptians used a form of shadow clock in which a vertical T-shaped part cast a shadow onto a graduated horizontal piece. The most sophisticated type of shadow device is the sundial, first used around 1500 BC, in which the shadow of a stationary arm (or *gnomon*) is projected onto a circular surface which is marked off in hours and positioned at a right angle to the gnomon. The drawback with such devices is that they can only be used in sunlight, and so other methods were explored that could also indicate time in dull weather or at night, for example using flowing water. One primitive method made use of a basin with a hole in it that would sink at a known rate when placed in water, but a more sophisticated invention was the *clepsydra*, or waterclock. This worked by measuring the flow or fall of water through a narrow aperture into a vessel. Later waterclocks used a gradually-filling container in which a floating ratchet moved a hand on a dial.

Water was replaced by sand in the hour-glass, in which a quantity of fine sand fell slowly from one of two linked containers into the other at a known rate. A miniature version of this, the egg-timer, is still in use in many modern kitchens.

The rate at which something burned was another measure used, such as the Anglo-Saxon graduated candle that burned inside a horn lantern. Later, oil-burning lamps were utilized, and their rate of consumption of oil monitored as a measure of elapsed time. The mechanical clock was first invented in China in the 8c and appeared in Europe around the 14c. This worked by letting a weight fall in a controlled way, imparting motion to a wheel or system of wheels by means of an escapement, an escape wheel and anchor that converted the energy of the falling weight into a series of periodic impulses. Clocks were also developed which could strike the hours by the action of a hammer on an internal or external bell. In the next century, European clockmakers employed springs wound with a key to supply the motive force, allowing the spring to unwind in a gradual and controlled manner.

The next important advance came in the 17c with the adaptation of the pendulum: a clock weight that swings freely under the influence of gravity. The design of often highly elaborate clock cases, crafted from expensive woods and precious metals, and reflecting current trends in furniture styles, was altered to accommodate the pendulum, and the very tall longcase or grandfather clock became increasingly common. The **Industrial Revolution** saw the beginnings of the mass production of clocks, which had hitherto been expensive items made in small numbers by craftsmen. At the same time, the involvement of increasing numbers of workers in industry and the spread of regular railway services made punctuality important to larger sections of the population, thus greatly expanding the market for clocks and watches. The growing range of uses for electricity in the 19c included the supply of power for clocks, and the 19c also saw the introduction of 'standard time' and international time zones, first outlined in the 1870s by the Scots-born Canadian railway engineer Sir Sandford Fleming.

The expansion of telephone networks led to the introduction of the 'speaking clock', a pre-recorded voice continuously stating the current time to phone users dialling the service, and in 1929 the quartz crystal clock appeared, incorporating a tiny crystal of quartz which was made to vibrate by means of electricity. In turn, the piezo-electric effect of this vibration created a high-frequency electric signal which could be regulated to a frequency of one pulse per second and used as the motive force for the mechanism of the clock. These clocks were accurate to a degree that far surpassed existing mechanical or electric clocks.

---

bastions of wealth and power for the predominantly Anglican élite (the **FAMILY COMPACT**) in Upper Canada, drawing fierce criticism from Methodists and disestablishmentarians. They were secularized in 1854.

**Cleveland, (Stephen) Grover** (1837–1908)
US politician and 22nd and 24th President. The son of a Presbyterian minister, he became a lawyer, Mayor of Buffalo, and in 1883 Governor of New York. An honest and independent politician who abhorred machine politics, he was nominated for President by the Democrats in 1884 and won the election. In his first term he strongly advised a reduction in the high tariff. He was not re-elected in 1888, but regained the presidency in 1892. His second term began with an industrial depression that led to labour unrest and a split in the **DEMOCRATIC PARTY**. In foreign affairs, he took a firm stand in the boundary dispute between the UK and Venezuela, asserting the US right, under the **MONROE DOCTRINE**, to determine that boundary.
➤ **POLITICAL MACHINE**

**cliff-dwellers**
A general name for the Native American Anasazi peo-

ple and their descendants, the **PUEBLO**. The Anasazi (c.200BC–AD1500) inhabited the arid 'Four Corners' region of the south-western USA, where Arizona, New Mexico, Colorado and Utah meet. They are called cliff-dwellers because from the 10c to the 13c they built their houses along the sides and under the overhangs of cliffs. The walls and ceilings of the rooms were plastered with an adobe mixture, and the upper floors were accessed by a ladder through the ceiling on the ground floor. Several communities joined together to form a town built beneath a cliff. One of the largest examples of these remaining today is the four-storey 13c Cliff Palace in the Meso Verde National Park, which has over 200 residential rooms and 23 *kivas* or ceremonial chambers. At the end of the 13c it is thought that the Pueblo were driven by internal divisions in the communities and severe drought to build smaller communities beside better sources of water in the south. ➤ **NATIVE AMERICANS**

**Climate Change, UN Framework Convention on** (1992)
A convention dealing with the perceived threat of global warming caused by the emission of greenhouse gases, particularly carbon dioxide, and the

The next major development was the atomic clock. This is based on the phenomenon of electromagnetic waves generated during a change in the energy state of certain molecules or atoms, and the use of these waves to activate an electronic oscillator. The fact that these waves are perfectly regular and remain unaffected in frequency by outside forces means that they can be used as an extremely accurate measure of intervals of time. The first such atomic clock was invented in England in 1955, using caesium as its motivating substance. The subsequent development of even more highly accurate atomic clocks led to their adoption in setting international time standards.

## Watches

In the 15c the introduction of the spring to replace the weight in clock mechanisms allowed the manufacture of ever smaller clocks and, eventually, to the truly portable clock or watch. In Switzerland watchmaking became established as a craft by the 18c; by 1865 production at the firm of Roskopf had been taken over by mass-production techniques, and by 1880 companies such as Ingersoll, and Waterbury in the USA, were producing for a world market. Swiss watches in particular acquired an international reputation for excellence and accuracy, a reputation that persists to this day. In the late 19c watches were made that could be wound with an integral stem rather than a separate key, and at around the same time the first wristwatches were made for officers in the German navy. When they became available in the UK around 1880, they were a source of great ridicule (initially they were known as 'wristlets'), but by **World War I** they had become obligatory wear for officers. The luminous watch face was invented c.1915, and by then the wristwatch had replaced the pocket or fob watch as the most popular design. A further development was the automatic wristwatch, which did not have to be wound by hand but had a self-winding mechanism activated by the movement of the wearer's arm. Electric wristwatches became common in the late 20c, containing a replaceable battery which either powered a balance wheel or the vibration of a quartz crystal. Digital watches, showing time as digits rather than by displaying hands and a dial, became popular in the 1970s. By the late 20c, basic watch and clock technology had nearly exhausted all innovations, until multi-functional watches were introduced; some models could show not only the date and time but also the time in different parts of the world. In addition, they could function as alarm clocks, calculators or mini-computers.

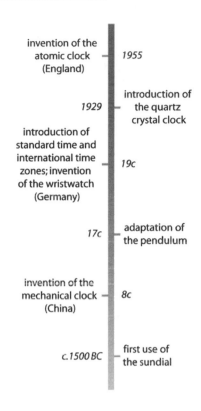

invention of the atomic clock (England) — 1955

1929 — introduction of the quartz crystal clock

introduction of standard time and international time zones; invention of the wristwatch (Germany) — 19c

17c — adaptation of the pendulum

invention of the mechanical clock (China) — 8c

c.1500 BC — first use of the sundial

---

degradation of forests and oceans, which absorb carbon dioxide. The Convention resulted from the **EARTH SUMMIT** in 1992 and came into force in 1994. It supports international cooperation to limit the causes of global warming because the threats (such as higher sea-levels and unpredictable weather patterns) are felt worldwide. It requires developed countries to reduce greenhouse gas emissions to 1990 levels, and provides technological assistance to developing countries. The Convention was strengthened by the adoption of the Kyoto Protocol in 1997.

## Clinton, Bill (William) (1946–)

US politician and 42nd President. Educated at Georgetown University and Yale Law School, and a Rhodes scholar at Oxford, he taught law at the University of Arkansas (1973–6) before being elected state Attorney-General in 1976. In 1978, at the age of 32, he was elected Governor of Arkansas, the youngest person ever to hold that office, and served for five terms (1979–81 and 1983–92). In 1992 he was elected President, campaigning on a platform of hope and change in a climate of economic recession and voter disillusionment, and ending a 12-year Republican hold on the office. During the next four years Clinton had successes in the areas of trade – both at home (he set up **NAFTA** (North American Free Trade Agreement)) and overseas (he made moves to create a trans-Pacific free-trade zone) – and foreign policy, in which US-brokered agreements were reached in the Middle East peace process (1994) and former Yugoslavia (1995), and relations with Russia improved. Despite mid-term gains by the Republicans, in 1996 Clinton became the first Democrat since Franklin D **ROOSEVELT** to win re-election. During his second term Clinton continued to be dogged by allegations of financial and sexual wrongdoing, such as the Whitewater investigation (begun in 1994 and also involving his wife Hillary), and in Dec 1998 he was impeached for allegedly seriously perverting justice whilst attempting to cover up an extra-marital affair with Monica Lewinsky by perjury, but was acquitted. Soon afterwards public attention was diverted by the Anglo-American attacks on Iraq, and then by the attacks on Serbia by US-led **NATO** forces in an attempt to stop the **ETHNIC CLEANSING** of Albanians from the Serbian province of **KOSOVO**. ▶ **CLINTON, HILLARY DIANE RODHAM**; **IMPEACHMENT**; **OSLO ACCORDS**

## Clinton, De Witt (1769–1828)

US politician. He was admitted to the Bar in 1790, sat in the New York state legislature (1798–1802) and US SENATE (1798–1802), and was three times Mayor of New York (1803–7, 1808–10, 1811–15). He was, however, defeated by James MADISON in the presidential election of 1812. He led the way in the fight to build the Erie Canal, known as 'Clinton's Ditch', which opened in 1825.

## Clinton, George (1739–1812)

American brigadier and politician. He fought with his father, Charles Clinton, and brother James Clinton, in the FRENCH AND INDIAN WAR (1755–63), including the expedition against Fort Frontenac (1758). He was a member of the New York Provincial assembly (1768–75), and in 1775 attended the second CONTINENTAL CONGRESS. In the AMERICAN REVOLUTION he was a brigadier of militia, and in 1777 was chosen first Governor of New York, a post he held for six successive terms (1777–95). In 1804 and again in 1808 he was elected Vice-President of the USA.

## Clinton, Hillary Diane Rodham (1947– )

US lawyer and politician. After graduating from Yale Law School, in 1974 she became a staff attorney for the Children's Defense Fund and also took up a position on the staff of the official inquiry into WATERGATE, then moved to a teaching post at the University of Arkansas School of Law. She married Bill CLINTON in 1975, joining the Rose Law Firm in Little Rock, Arkansas. Her law career twice brought her recognition as one of the USA's most influential lawyers (1988, 1991). She was characterized unflatteringly as a feminist and liberal by her husband's conservative opponents both during his governorship of Arkansas and during his 1992 presidential campaign. During his first term of office she was appointed head of the Task Force on National Health Care Reform and although its recommendations were rejected by Congress, her expertise on women's and children's issues and her continuing involvement in this area won her admirers. Her years as First Lady were dogged by allegations of financial impropriety (the Whitewater investigation), eventually resolved with no blame attached to her. After her husband left office and following speculation about her political future, she was elected as a Democratic senator for New York in 2000.

## Clive of Plassey, Robert Clive, Baron (1725–74)

British soldier and administrator. In 1743 he joined the British EAST INDIA COMPANY in Madras, and took part in the campaigns against the French. In 1755 he was called to avenge the so-called BLACK HOLE OF CALCUTTA, and at the Battle of PLASSEY (1757) defeated a large Indian force – much of which defected to the British side following the offer of inducements to the commanding general, Mir Jaffar, and the payment of bribes by Indian merchants to the soldiers of the Mughal Nawab (Governor) SIRAJ UD-DAULA. For three years, Clive was sole ruler in all but name of Bengal. In 1760, he returned to England, entered parliament, and was made a baron (1762). In 1765 he returned to Calcutta, effectively reformed the civil service, and re-established military discipline. His measures were seen as drastic, and he became the subject of a select committee inquiry upon his return

to England in 1767. He committed suicide in London.

## Clocks and Time Measurement ► *See panel*

## Cloots, Jean Baptiste du Val-de-Grâce, Baron de (1755–94)

French revolutionary. Born a subject of Prussia, he established himself in France in 1776. There he adopted the name Anacharsis, became one of the PHILOSOPHES and lavished his money to promote the union of all nations in one family. In the FRENCH REVOLUTION he saw the fulfilment of his dreams. He was both hated and feared by ROBESPIERRE, who involved him in HÉBERT's downfall, and he was guillotined.

## closer settlement

The name given to Australian colonial and state government laws (1894–1906) designed to settle individuals or groups of unemployed persons on small farm blocks. Based on New Zealand's example (1892), the laws provided for the repurchase of land by the government, either by arrangement or compulsorily at a fair price, and its sale in small blocks to settlers on easy terms. The principles of closer settlement and government assistance for land settlement were also applied to soldier settlement schemes after both World Wars. ► SELECTORS; SQUATTERS

## CMEA–EEC Agreement (1988)

The mutual recognition and trade agreement between COMECON, based in Moscow, and the Brussels-based EEC. Their hostility was linked with the continuance of the COLD WAR and with a specific disagreement concerning how trade should be conducted. Mikhail GORBACHEV's emergence helped calm tension and a compromise was found according to which individual CMEA members made comprehensive deals with the EEC as a whole. This further reduced tension and contributed to the dissolution of CMEA in 1990.

## CNCA (*Confederación Nacional Católico-Agraria*, 'National Catholic-Agrarian Confederation') (1917–42)

Spanish agrarian organization. Organized and funded by large landowners, the CNCA built up a large following among smallholders of north and central Spain through its propaganda and services. It claimed 500,000 members by 1919. Conservative and religious in outlook, its aim was to combat the rising power of the urban and rural working class by mobilizing middle-class support for the ruling classes. In this respect it was similar to the ACNP (National Catholic Association of Propagandists). It was an important source of support for the Right during the Second Republic, especially for the CEDA. In 1942 it was transformed into the National Union of Rural Cooperatives (UNCC), more recently the UNACO. ► REPUBLIC, SECOND (Spain)

## CND (Campaign for Nuclear Disarmament)

An organization formed in 1958 to oppose Britain's development of a nuclear weapons programme. It organized annual Aldermaston marches and briefly persuaded the Labour Party to declare a policy of unilateral disarmament in 1960, only to see it effectively reverse that decision a year later. An effective pressure group in the 1960s, its popularity and influence had already begun to decline before the signing of nuclear non-proliferation pacts in the 1980s, although supporters agreed that as part of a European movement it played a part in halting the arms race.

**CNI ▸ INDEPENDENTS** (France)

**CNT** (*Confederación Nacional de Trabajo*, 'National Confederation of Labour')
Spanish anarcho-syndicalist movement. The emergence of the CNT in 1911 provided Spanish anarcho-syndicalism with its first national framework. It was based on already existing trade unions, most of them in Catalonia, that were sympathetic to anarchism. Centred on Barcelona, Saragossa, and rural Andalucia, the CNT became the largest trade union movement in Spain during the social crisis sparked by **WORLD WAR I**. The CNT's influence in Catalonia was at its greatest from 1918 to 1923, but it met with the brutal resistance of the employers. The CNT was severely repressed under the **PRIMO DE RIVERA** dictatorship of 1923–30. Under the Second Republic, against a background of continuing if lesser repression, it spurned electoral politics (though many CNT members voted for the Left in 1931 and 1936), split over the issue of revolutionary confrontation with the Republic, and pursued a series of largely fruitless strikes and risings, most notably those of Jan and Dec 1933. However, it also extended its influence in Madrid and other areas as the voice of the marginalized sections of the working class. While the anarchist rural and industrial collectives during the **SPANISH CIVIL WAR** often proved both a social and an economic success, the failure of the anarchist militia undoubtedly undermined the Republican war effort. The CNT's revolutionary conception of the war clashed with that of most other Republican forces. Nonetheless, in Nov 1936 four anarchists joined the government – the only occasion in the history of anarchism. The communist assault on the CNT in May 1937 lost it the political initiative, and it declined thereafter. Anarchist opposition to **FRANCO** was ineffectual, its revival after his death being unimpressive.
▸ **REPUBLIC, SECOND** (Spain)

**Coastal Command**
A separate functional Command within the British Royal Air Force (1936–69). Moves to transfer it to the Royal Navy caused a political storm in 1958–9. During **WORLD WAR II**, the Command destroyed 184 German U-boats and 470,000 tonnes of enemy shipping, and played a decisive role in winning the Battle of the **ATLANTIC**.

**Cobbett, William** (1763–1835)
British journalist and reformer. The son of a farmer, he moved on impulse to London (1783), spent a year reading widely, and joined the army, serving in New Brunswick (1785–91). In 1792 he married and went to the USA, where he wrote fierce tracts against the native Democrats under the name 'Peter Porcupine'. Returning to England in 1800, he was welcomed by the **TORIES**, and started his famous *Weekly Political Register* (1802), which continued until his death, changing in 1804 from its original Toryism to an uncompromising radicalism. In 1810 he was imprisoned for two years for criticizing the flogging of militiamen by German mercenaries, and in 1817 he went again to the USA, fearing a second imprisonment. Return-

ing in 1819 he travelled widely in Britain, and finally became an MP (1832). ▸ **DEMOCRATIC PARTY**

**Cobden, Richard** (1804–65)
British economist and politician. He worked as a clerk and commercial traveller in London, then went into the calico business, settling in Manchester. In 1835 he visited the USA, and in 1836–7 the Levant, after which he published two pamphlets preaching free trade (thus earning the nickname 'the Apostle of Free Trade'), non-intervention, and speaking against 'Russophobia'. A radical-Liberal, in 1838 he helped to found the **ANTI-CORN LAW LEAGUE**, becoming its most prominent member. He became an MP in 1841. His lectures and parliamentary speeches focused opinion on the **CORN LAWS**, which were repealed in 1846.

**Cocceji, Samuel von** (1679–1755)
A famous jurist under **FREDERICK II, THE GREAT** of Prussia. In 1749–51 he wrote the *Project des Corporis Juris Fredericiani*. The *Project* formed the basis for the later Prussian Law Code of Count J H C von Carmer (1721–1801), which became (1794) Germany's first legal code.

**Cochin-China**
A French colony, occupying the southern part of Vietnam. The colony was established in 1862 when, following hostilities with the Vietnamese court, the court was forced to cede three eastern provinces to the French. Three western provinces were added in 1867. In 1887, Cochin-China was brought together with the French protectorates of **ANNAM**, Tonkin and Cambodia to form the *Union Indochinoise*. During the period of French administration, Cochin-China emerged as a major rice-exporting region. In the 1930s it became an important focus of rural unrest. In 1949, as the French sought to establish a Vietnamese alternative to **HO CHI MINH** in the north, Cochin-China became part of the Associated State of Vietnam within the French Union.

**Cochise** (c.1812–74)
Chief of the Chiricahua **APACHE**. He lived in the American south-west and was known for his bravery and military prowess. In 1861 he was wrongfully accused of stealing and abducting a rancher's child, and was arrested by the US Army. He escaped, and after hostages were taken on both sides, and eventually killed, he began a protracted guerrilla-type war against the army, together with other tribes, that lasted for ten years. In 1872, General Oliver Howard finally reached a peace settlement with Cochise by promising the Chiricahua a reservation on their native land.

**Code Napoléon**
The French civil code, introduced (though not devised) by Napoleon Bonaparte as First Consul in 1804, to fill the void left by the abolition of the legal and social customs of pre-revolutionary France. It established the principles of equality between people, liberty of person and contract, and the inviolability of private property. From 1804 the code was introduced into those areas of Europe under direct French control. The civil code of the newly united Italian state (1865) bore close affinity to it, and it was widely emulated in South America. It is still substantially

extant in France, Belgium, Luxembourg and Monaco today. ► NAPOLEON I

**Codreanu, Corneliu Zelea** (1899–1938)
Romanian political leader. From a peasant family of Ukrainian or Polish ancestry, in 1927 he organized the Legion of the Archangel Michael, the quasi-religious and nationalist organization of which the **IRON GUARD** formed the military wing. In 1938 he was tried for treason and sentenced to ten years in prison; later that year, he and a group of followers were shot, apparently while trying to escape. ► **ANTONESCU, ION**; **CHARLES II** (of Romania)

**Cody, William Frederick**, also known as **Buffalo Bill** (1846–1917)
US showman. He earned his nickname after killing nearly 5,000 buffalo in 18 months for a contract to supply workers on the Kansas Pacific Railway with meat. He served as a scout in the **SIOUX** wars, but from 1883 toured with his Wild West Show. The town of Cody in Wyoming stands on part of his former ranch.

**Coehoorn, Menno van** (1641–1704)
Dutch soldier and engineer. Coehoorn specialized in the building of fortifications. He achieved great fame through his treatises and by his practical demonstrations of his theories in the wars against France. He built the fortifications of, for example, Breda, Nijmegen, Zwolle and Bergen op Zoom. ► **FORTIFICATION**

**Coen, Jan Pieterzoon** (1587–1629)
Dutch colonial administrator. One of the founders of the Dutch East Indies, Coen joined the Dutch **EAST INDIA COMPANY** at the age of 20 as a junior merchant. In 1618 he was made Governor-General and the next year he conquered the Javanese town of Jacatra and founded in its place Batavia (now Jakarta), the capital of the Dutch East Indies. He resigned in 1623 and returned to the Netherlands, but was reappointed in 1624. He died (probably of cholera) in the capital he had founded, during its siege by a Mataram army. His achievement was crucial in setting up the colony in its early days, and in excluding English and Spanish competition in the Indonesian archipelago. He is probably best remembered for his brutal handling of the Bantanese people, which brought the Dutch a global monopoly in nutmeg and mace.

**Cohong**
The westernized form of the Chinese *gonghang* ('official firms'), which referred to a monopolistic guild of Chinese merchants licensed by the government to trade with Westerners at the port of Canton in the years 1760–1839. Each member of the Cohong was made responsible for the behaviour of Western traders, and served as intermediaries between them and local Chinese officials. Although some Cohong merchants made huge fortunes in their transactions with Westerners, the guild as a whole was always subject to arbitrary impositions by the Chinese government. The Cohong was abolished in the wake of China's defeat in the first of the **OPIUM WARS** in 1842.

**Coke, Sir Edward** (1552–1634)
English jurist. He became Speaker of the House of **COMMONS** (1593), Attorney-General (1594), Chief Justice of the Common Pleas (1606), Chief Justice of the King's Bench (1613) and Privy Councillor. He

vigorously prosecuted **ESSEX**, **RALEIGH**, and the **GUNPOWDER PLOT** conspirators, but after 1606 increasingly supported the idea of national liberties vested in parliament, against the royal prerogative. He was dismissed in 1617, and from 1620 led the popular party in parliament, serving nine months in prison. The petition of right (1628) was largely his doing. Most of his epoch-making Law Reports were published during the period 1600–15.

**Colbert, Jean Baptiste** (1619–83)
French administrator and politician. He reorganized the colonies, provided a strong fleet and introduced a code of marine law. His attempts to develop the economy through state intervention, and in the interests of state power, had some success at first, but his endeavours were undermined by court extravagance and continual warfare. His policies have been systematized by historians under the name of 'Colbertism', a term which is used in a French context as the equivalent of 'Mercantilism'. ► **LE TELLIER, MICHEL**

**Cold Harbor, Battles of** (1–3 June 1864)
A battle of the **AMERICAN CIVIL WAR**, fought in Virginia, with General Ulysses S **GRANT**'s forces suffering heavy losses (12,000 men in one day's fighting) in an ill-advised attack on General Robert E **LEE**'s secure Confederate position. The battle, however, did serve to further Grant's strategy of keeping unrelenting pressure on the South.

**Cold War**
A state of tension or hostility between states that stops short of military action or a 'hot' war. The term is most frequently used to describe the relationship between the USSR and the major Western powers, especially the USA, following **WORLD WAR II**. Tension was particularly high in the 1960s when the nuclear 'arms race' intensified. The process of **DÉTENTE**, begun in the late 1960s, led through two decades of arms reduction and control negotiations to the 'end' of the Cold War in 1990, mainly as a result of a dramatic change in the Soviet attitude under Mikhail **GORBACHEV**.

**Colenso, Battle of** (1899)
A reverse suffered by the British in the Boer War. General Sir Redvers Buller (1838–1908), fearing that his forces might be cut off in his efforts to relieve Ladysmith, changed his plans and attempted to take Colenso, an important crossing-point on the Tugela River. He was defeated by a Boer force under Louis **BOTHA**. ► **BOER WARS**

**Colfax, Schuyler** (1823–85)
US politician. Originally a newspaper editor, in 1868 he was elected Vice-President of the USA, in Ulysses S **GRANT**'s first term. Unjustly implicated in the **CRÉDIT MOBILIER SCANDAL** of 1872, he spent the rest of his life in political retirement.

**Coligny, Gaspard II de, Lord of Châtillon** (1519–72)
French Huguenot leader. He fought in the wars of **FRANCIS I** and **HENRY II** of France, and in 1552 was made Admiral of France. In 1557 he became a Protestant, and commanded the **HUGUENOTS** during the second and third Wars of **RELIGION**. **CATHERINE DE' MEDICI** made him one of the first victims in the **ST BARTHOLOMEW'S DAY MASSACRE** in Paris (1572).

**Colijn, Hendrikus** (1869–1944)
Dutch politician. His first career was in the Dutch colonial army (1892–1909), then he became a member of the Dutch parliament for the Calvinist **ANTI-REVO-LUTIONARY PARTY**, of which he was the leader from 1920. He also had business interests (as Director of the Batavian Oil Company) and was chief editor of the Calvinist daily newspaper *The Standard* from 1922. He first took cabinet office as Minister of War (1911–13) and then as Minister of Finance (1923–5). From 1925 to 1939 he was Prime Minister of no less than six cabinets, and was the figurehead of the tough deflationary Dutch government policies of the 1930s. When the Germans invaded his country in 1940 he toyed with accepting the New Order; he soon rejected this, and was interned in 1941. He died in Ilmenau in Germany.

**collaboration** (France) (1940–4)
The act of collaborating with the Germans during their occupation of France in **WORLD WAR II**. It could take various forms: economic, literary, journalistic and political. The latter applies especially to political figures who remained in Paris rather than following the French government to **VICHY**, although the distinction became blurred in 1943–4. The most extreme collaborators fought on the Eastern Front – LGF (*Légion des volontaires français contre le bolchévisme*, 'French Legion of Volunteers against Bolshevism') – or in the auxiliary police force (*Milice*) within France, which committed appalling atrocities. ► **FRENCH STATE**

**Collective Leadership** (post 1956)
In the USSR, the term used, with occasional justification, to differentiate between the leadership methods of **STALIN**, who was accused of the **CULT OF PERSON-ALITY**, and those of his successors. But as general-secretaries of the Communist Party, both Nikita **KHRUSHCHEV** and Leonid **BREZHNEV** reverted to virtual single-handed rule in the later years of their tenure. Mikhail **GORBACHEV** amended the party's rules in 1986 to include collective leadership, but had himself appointed President as well as General-Secretary in 1990.

**collective security**
The concept of maintaining security and territorial integrity by the collective actions of nation states, especially through international organizations such as the **LEAGUE OF NATIONS**, where the principle was embodied in its Covenant, and the **UN**, in its Charter. Individual member states must be prepared to accept collective decisions and implement them, if necessary, through military action. Because of the difficulty of obtaining such agreements, collective security has never been fully established.

**Collectivization** (post-1929)
The process, initiated by **STALIN** in the USSR, of forcing peasants into large communal farms where in theory they worked for one another and not for themselves or their own families. Stalin's aims were to solve the food crisis through large-scale farming, by the same means to accumulate capital and secure spare labour for industrial development, and to create a revolutionary peasantry to maintain and intensify the spirit of revolution. Despite fierce resistance

and pauses to gather breath, the main aims were achieved; casualties were, however, very high. Productivity also remained remarkably low, and agriculture became one of the weak points of the economy, leading to the collapse of Soviet socialism in the late 20c. The extension of collectivization to much of Eastern Europe after **WORLD WAR II** led to very similar results.

**Colleoni, Bartolomeo** (1400–75)
Italian soldier and **CONDOTTIERE**. He fought on both sides in the strife between Milan and Venice, where he finally settled in 1454, becoming *generalíssimo* for life. He is the subject of a famous Venetian equestrian statue by Verrochio.

**Collier, Jeremy** (1650–1726)
English bishop. He became a priest in 1677, and refused to take the oath of allegiance to **WILLIAM III** and Mary II (1689). Arrested in 1692 on suspicion of being involved in a Jacobite plot, in 1696 he was outlawed for giving absolution to two would-be assassins on the scaffold. Returning to London, he continued to preach to a congregation of those who had not taken the oath (non-jurors), and was consecrated bishop in 1713. He was also the author of a celebrated attack on the immorality of the English stage (1698). ► **JACOBITES**

**Collingwood, Cuthbert Collingwood, Baron** (1750–1810)
British admiral. He joined the navy at 11, and from 1778 his career was closely connected with that of **NELSON**. He fought at the Battles of Brest (1794), **CAPE ST VINCENT** (1797), and **TRAFALGAR** (1805), where he succeeded Nelson as commander. He was created baron after Trafalgar, died at sea, and is buried beside Nelson in St Paul's Cathedral, London.

**Collins, Michael** (1890–1922)
Irish politician and **SINN FÉIN** leader. He took part in the **EASTER RISING** and was elected an MP (1918–22). He organized the nationalist intelligence system and led ruthless attacks against British agents. With Arthur **GRIFFITH**, he was largely responsible for the negotiation of the Anglo-Irish Treaty in 1921. Commander-in-chief of the government forces in the **IRISH CIVIL WAR**, he was killed in an ambush in County Cork.

**Collor de Mello, Fernando** (1950– )
Brazilian politician. Born in the north-eastern state of Alagoas, he grew up in Rio de Janeiro. He made use of his family's extensive media holdings to lever himself into the Prefecture of Maceió (1979–82) and then become Governor of Alagoas (1986). A political conservative, he leapt to prominence as a critic of 'corruption', achieving a leading position in the race for the presidency in Nov 1989 at the head of his National Renovation Party. His ability to project the image of a young and dynamic 'messias', professing a modern social democratic approach, caught the traditional **PMDB** and radical PT off guard. Once in office (Mar 1990), he embarked on a bold programme of economic reform, before he built up a significant base within Congress. Control over Congress lay in the hands of groups that had benefited from the 1988 constitution, which protected special interests directly affected by the presidential programme. He

# *Colonization*

Culture & Society

Colonization should be distinguished both from migration and from imperialism. Migration implies a movement of large groups of people over land or over sea, often for the same motives as colonization, to find better land elsewhere or escape bad conditions at home. It does not, however, necessitate a deliberate movement from an old settlement to a new one, or the maintenance of any links between the new settlement and the old. Colonization, on the other hand, implies the existence of an established community from which people deliberately go or are sent out to establish a new settlement in other territory. That new settlement, at least initially, preserves the customs and culture of the community from which it originated and remains distinct from any local community that happens to be inhabiting the territory on which it plants itself. It also usually preserves trading and administrative links with the mother community.

Imperialism is the deliberate extension of the rule of one state over others in order to form an empire. Colonization may, and often did, form part of an imperialistic policy but is not identical with it. The British ruled India and incorporated it into their empire. It is a moot point whether they can be said to have colonized it – in the way, for example that they colonized Australia – any more than the British can be said to have colonized China by founding a colony in Hong Kong.

### Colony and colonia
The English word 'colony' comes from the Latin word *colonia*, derived from the verb *colere*: to cultivate or inhabit. A Roman colonia was both an area of territory and the community that settled on it. The territory was usually acquired by conquest, and the settlers who were awarded land in it were members of the lower social orders who contributed much of the manpower to the Roman army and whose economic aspirations could not be accommodated within Rome itself. The first *coloniae*, in the days of the early Republic, were established within Italy. Their function was partly to hold down the territory Rome had acquired from its neighbours, and partly to act as defensive buffers protecting Rome itself from attack. As the Roman army became more professionalized after the Second Punic War (218–201 BC) and it became increasingly common for men to spend many years in service abroad, the system developed whereby discharged veterans would be granted land in a self-governing colonia either in Italy or, increasingly, under the late Republic and the Empire, abroad. The German city of Cologne, for instance, gets its name from the fact that it began life as a Roman colonia. The establishment of these far-flung settlements had the same purpose as the establishment of the original ones in Italy, enabling Rome both to reward its citizens and allies, and to strengthen its hold on its territorial possessions. To the peoples amongst whom they were established, the Roman colonies brought the benefits of contact with the Roman way of life, Roman technological expertise and civilization.

### Early colonizations
Though they may have given us the word, the Romans were by no means the first colonizers. The Phoenicians established colonies along the shores of the Mediterranean from as early as 1100 BC. They lived by trade and their colonies began as trading posts – the most successful of them, Carthage, on the coast of present-day Tunisia, itself became a colonial power and waged war on Rome. The Greek city-states founded colonies. Corinth established a colony on modern-day Corfu and in 733 BC an even more important one at Syracuse in Sicily. Other Greek colonies were founded on the northern coasts of the Aegean, along the coast of the Black Sea and in Italy.

Following the fall of the Roman Empire, the most notable colonizers in northern Europe were the Viking peoples of Scandinavia. Beginning as seafaring marauders, the Vikings established bases overseas from which to conduct plundering operations; these in time became more permanent settlements. Norwegians founded Dublin; the Danes

---

resigned in Dec 1992 as his **IMPEACHMENT**, on charges of corruption, began in the Senate.

### Collot d'Herbois, Jean Marie (1751–96)
French revolutionary. Originally a provincial actor, he joined the Jacobin Club in 1791. His self-confidence, loud voice and *Almanach du Père Gérard* (1791) secured his election to the National **CONVENTION**. In 1793 he became President of the Convention and a member of the Committee of **PUBLIC SAFETY**. Sent to Lyons, he took bloody revenge by guillotine and grapeshot on the inhabitants for having once hissed him off the stage. He played a major part in the successful plot against **ROBESPIERRE** (1794), but himself was expelled from the Convention and banished to Cayenne (1795), where he died. ► **FRENCH REVOLUTION; JACOBINS**

---

**COLOMBIA** official name **Republic of Colombia**
A republic in the north-west of South America. It is bounded to the north by Panama and the Caribbean Sea; to the west by the Pacific Ocean; to the east by Venezuela; to the south-east by Brazil; and to the south by Ecuador and Peru. From the early 16c the country was conquered by the Spanish, who domi-

nated the Amerindian peoples. Governed by Spain within the Viceroyalty of Peru, it later became the Viceroyalty of New Granada. After the campaigns of Simón **BOLÍVAR**, it gained independence in 1819, and formed a union with Ecuador, Venezuela and Panama as **GRAN COLOMBIA**; the union ended with the secession of Venezuela in 1829 and Ecuador in 1830, leaving New Granada to adopt the name Colombia. Colombia suffered civil war (known as La **VIOLENCIA**)

established themselves in northern and eastern England and in northern France. Norwegians began the settlement of Iceland in 870 and towards the end of the 10c established eastern and western settlements in Greenland that survived until about 1500.

### Colonies in the New World

The conquest and colonization of the Americas began shortly after they were discovered by Europeans at the end of the 15c. The settlement of Hispaniola was begun in 1493 during **Columbus**'s second voyage. News of the conquests achieved by **Cortés** in Mexico and Francisco **Pizarro** in Peru brought a rush of emigrants from Spain, fired by the prospect of finding gold and silver in abundance. The area of Spanish rule and Spanish settlement gradually extended throughout the whole of Central America, down the western coast of South America and across the Andes to the mouth of the River Plate. Mexico City was founded in the 1520s on the site of the Aztec capital **Tenochtitlán**, which was razed by Cortés; Lima was founded by Pizarro in 1535; Asunción, the present capital of Paraguay, in the same year; and Buenos Aires, after a failed attempt in 1540, was permanently settled from Asunción in 1580.

The Portuguese, who had been granted all the territory in the New World eastward of a line of demarcation established by Pope **Alexander VI** in 1493 and amended by the Treaty of Tordesillas in the following year, were somewhat slower to settle in the territory that fell to them. In 1549 Bahia was established as the administrative capital of what was later to become Brazil, and the establishment of sugar plantations and mills led to a wave of emigration towards the end of the century.

The Spanish and Portuguese colonization of the New World was frankly exploitative. It resulted in a colonial society of a type very frequently but not universally found, where the newcomers establish themselves as a ruling class with the previous inhabitants reduced to an inferior status as small farmers, labourers or slaves.

A colonial society of a different type began to be established in the 17c along the eastern seaboard of North America. There was, to put it crudely, no loot in North America, no precious metals, and the **Native Americans** of the North did not docilely accept European domination. So although the first English settlement at **Roanoke** (1587) was established in the hope of finding gold, and although a plantation-type aristocratic colonial society later developed in the South, the **Pilgrim Fathers** and their successors in New England came with the intention of founding a conservative religious-based society, but eventually established a society which, though hierarchical, had a much less elaborate hierarchy in Church and State than the Old World, and more economic opportunity and therefore social mobility.

Something of the same process occurred later in Australia, begun as a British penal colony in 1788. By 1852, when penal transportation to New South Wales and Tasmania was finally abolished (convicts were sent to Western Australia between 1850 and 1868), over 150,000 convicts had been sent there, and a great many free settlers had also arrived. Though relations between the convicts and free settlers were often very difficult, the society that eventually shook down together was a determinedly non-hierarchical one within the Caucasian settler community. This, however, was racist as well as egalitarian: **Aboriginals** became a sub-class, and 'White Australia' was a slogan used to illustrate its exclusion of Asians.

### Colonizers and colonized

It is an understatement to say that most native populations would have preferred not to be colonized. They ran the risk not only of being reduced to an inferior status, if not enslaved, but of being decimated by diseases brought by their colonizers or conquerors – as the native populations of South and Central America, and the Australian Aboriginals were. People who set out to found and work new settlements thousands of miles away from their homelands had necessarily to be tough. They frequently endured tremendous hardships and were often only saved from disaster by being helped by the local population and learning from them how to survive in a hostile environment. Once established,

---

in the 1950s, and there has been considerable political and civil unrest since the 1980s because of left-wing insurgency, counter-attacks by right-wing paramilitaries and the activities of the drugs cartels. There is widespread illegal cocaine trafficking, which the government has been attempting to eradicate with help from the USA since 1989. A new constitution was adopted in 1991 but a state of emergency was declared in 1992 because of violence by drugs traffickers. President Álvaro URIBE was elected in 2002 on a platform of ending the insurgency and combating the drugs-trafficking. ➤ DRUGS, WAR ON; FARC

**Colombo Plan**, in full **Colombo Plan for Cooperative Economic Development in South and South-East Asia**
A plan drawn up in 1951 to assist development in the countries of South and South-East Asia. It was set up within the framework of the COMMONWEALTH OF NATIONS, although since its inception membership has extended to non-Commonwealth countries. In 1977 it was renamed the 'Colombo Plan for Cooperative Economic and Social Development in Asia and the Pacific'. It currently has 24 members and one provisional member, Mongolia.

### Colonial and Imperial Conferences

A series of conferences at which representatives of the British colonies and dominions discussed matters of common imperial concern; usually held in London. The first Colonial Conference was held in 1887, and this was followed by others in 1894, 1897, 1902 and 1907. They were particularly concerned with defence, although they also dealt with issues of trade and communications. The first Imperial Conference was held in 1911, the change of name implying a new status for the colonies, and was followed by others in 1921, 1923, 1926, 1930 and 1937, mainly concerned with constitutional changes and economic matters. After WORLD WAR II they were replaced by the Conferences of Commonwealth Prime Ministers, now the Commonwealth Heads of Government meetings. ➤ BRITISH EMPIRE; COMMONWEALTH OF NATIONS

### Colonial Development and Welfare Acts (1929, 1940, 1945, 1949 and 1950)

A series of acts designed to offer funds for the development of British colonies. They represented a departure

their main concern was to thrive, and on the whole they cared little for the rights of the natives. Both the Christian missionaries who often accompanied colonizing parties and the metropolitan governments to which they were subject usually intended that the local population should be well treated. The settlers themselves tended to write this off as pious do-gooding. The Jesuit *reducciones* in Paraguay, settlements where native converts were educated, trained and lived a variant of their traditional lifestyle under strict clerical supervision, were suppressed by the secular government in 1767. Throughout the 19c it was the official policy of the government in London and of the governors in Sydney that Australian Aboriginals should be protected. This did not prevent their land from being taken and their numbers reduced to such an extent that they only recovered to their pre-colonization levels in about 1950.

### Decolonization
The struggle for independence in the territories colonized by Europeans following the great age of exploration began with the **American Revolution** (1775–83). In the course of the early 19c all the Spanish and Portuguese possessions in South and Central America declared their independence: Chile in 1810, Mexico and Peru in 1821, and Brazil in 1822. Canada became a self-governing dominion within the British Empire in 1867, Australia in 1901, New Zealand in 1907 and South Africa in 1910. In a sense, few of these lands intended to reverse the colonization process. 'Decolonization' is a misleading term; descendants of settlers merely led them out of empires.

All these countries had largely white populations or a white ruling class. Even as they had been fighting or negotiating their way towards self-government, Britain, France, Germany and Belgium were carving out new empires for themselves in Africa. With the exception of French Algeria, however, the number of white settlers in these new territories was comparatively small, and the empires were comparatively short-lived. Following the end of **World War II** and the achievement of independence by India and Pakistan in 1947, the movement for independence in territories still under a colonial administration gathered pace. The Dutch withdrew from their possessions in South-East Asia in the late 1940s and Indonesia became independent in 1949. French rule was overthrown in **Indochina** in the mid-1950s. Ghana was the first British African territory to be granted independence under black rule in 1957. Algeria became independent of France in 1962, and during the 1960s and 1970s the rest of the subject territories in Africa, Asia and the West Indies became free. Particularly in Africa, 'decolonization' often meant the withdrawal or sharp reduction in the numbers of European settlers.

### Colonization in the late 20c
The effects of colonization for good or ill are still being felt in countries that have only recently achieved their independence and, to some extent, in those countries which once possessed a colonial empire and now no longer have one. It is a contentious point whether colonization in the traditional sense still exists. It has been suggested that a kind of reverse colonization has taken place in countries such as Britain, where considerable numbers of people from countries formerly in the British Empire, especially the West Indies, India and Pakistan, have gone to live – to some extent forming enclaves within British society, to some extent forcing it to become more pluralistic in outlook and policy to accommodate them. By the same token one might argue that the USA is being colonized by Spanish-speaking people of Latin American origin, who are challenging its English-language-based institutions and self-image perhaps in a way no previous immigrant group ever has. Alternatively, it has been argued that the great powers of the world, particularly the USA, continue to colonize large areas of the globe economically and culturally. This is, however, a classic case of muddled use of language. US domination – political, cultural and economic – is a form of imperialism, but an indirect form with no true colonization. Arguably, Zionist settlers on the **West Bank** in **Palestine** are among the last true colonists. It is perhaps safest to treat colonization in these instances as essentially a confusing metaphor whose persistence is a testament to the world-changing and often traumatic nature of the original phenomenon or experience.

from the notion that colonies should be self-supporting and a recognition that development might serve to combine colonial idealism with British economic self-interest. The 1929 Act made available £1 million. The 1940 Act was partly a response to riots in the West Indies and partly designed to encourage sympathy and loyalty during **WORLD WAR II**; £20 million was set aside, but only £3 million was spent in the first four years. The principle was extended in the post-war climate of trusteeship when £120 million was invested under the three acts introduced by Clement **ATTLEE**'s Labour government.

**Colonization** ► *See panel*

**Colonna**
Roman family, whose members included a pope (**MARTIN V**), several cardinals, generals, statesman and scholars, as well as the poet Vittoria (1492–1547), who was a close friend of Michelangelo.

**colônos**
Colonist labourers, they were introduced from Europe to Brazilian coffee plantations in the mid-19c, in order to supplant slave labourers, then declining in numbers. *Colônos* were initially allotted housing and

a given area of coffee groves, and received a cash income from sales of coffee to the **FAZENDEIRO**. By the 1880s, planters were prepared to concede fresh lands to families of Italian- and Spanish-born immigrants, many of whom cultivated and sold food crops while tending young coffee trees. Colôno settlements became crucial to the opening up of the west and south of Brazil, with distinctive patterns of landholding: they have only recently been displaced by agrobusinesses. The term is generally used to describe official settlements in the western and Amazon regions.

**Coloured** ► CAPE COLOURED

**Columbus, Christopher** (1451–1506)
Genoese explorer, and discoverer of the New World. He went to sea at the age of 14, and after being shipwrecked off Portugal, settled there in about 1470. Supported by **FERDINAND II** and **ISABELLA I**, he set sail in the *Santa María* with the aim of reaching India by sailing west from Saltes (3 Aug 1492). He reached the Bahamas (12 Oct), and then visited Cuba and Hispaniola (Haiti), where he left a small colony. He returned (15 Mar 1493), and was received with the highest honours by the court. On his second voyage

**Formation of Latin American States (19c–mid-20c)**

(1493–6) he discovered several of the Caribbean islands, though he persisted in believing he was in islands just off Japan. On his third (1488–1500) he discovered the South American mainland and seems briefly to have realized he had found a new continent. In 1500 Columbus was sent home in irons by a newly appointed royal governor after failing dismally as a colonial administrator, but the king and queen repudiated this action and restored Columbus to favour. His last great voyage (1502–4) was along the south side of the Gulf of Mexico, but by then his obsession with Asia and his general paranoia were out of hand.
➤ **EXPLORATION**

## Comanche

Shoshonean-speaking Native North American Plains people. Among the first to acquire horses from the Spanish, they migrated south into Colorado, Kansas, Oklahoma, Texas and New Mexico. They dominated the Plains and warred against both **APACHE** and white settlers. By the 1870s the Comanche were settled on reservations in Oklahoma. Today they number c.19,000. ➤ **PLAINS INDIANS**

## Combes, Émile (1835–1921)

French politician. Originally intended for the Church, after education in a seminary, he studied medicine and practised as a doctor. He was elected to the Senate (1885) and became Prime Minister (1902–4). He used the Law on Associations (1901), first presented as little more than a tidying-up of administrative regulations, but turned by strained interpretation into a measure to dissolve nearly all religious orders and confiscate their property. This opened a conflict with the papacy that led, perhaps against his own intentions, to the **SEPARATION OF CHURCH AND STATE** (1905).

### Combination Acts (1799 and 1800)
British legislation which prohibited the coming together ('combination') of workers in trade unions. The Acts were part of anti-reformist legislation passed by the Pitt government during the French wars, though combinations in many trades were already illegal. The Acts were repealed in 1824–5, and trade unions, though under severe restrictions, were legalized. ➤ **PITT, WILLIAM, THE YOUNGER**

### Combined Operations Command
A British force established in 1940 when Winston **CHURCHILL** appointed Admiral of the Fleet Lord Keyes to coordinate British commando raids against German-occupied Europe. Keyes's successor, Lord **MOUNTBATTEN** (1941–3), directed larger operations involving all three Services, and prepared for the eventual Allied invasion of France, in which Combined Operations techniques were to play a crucial role. ➤ **D-DAY**; **WORLD WAR II**

### COMECON (Council for Mutual Economic Assistance)
A body founded in 1949 by **STALIN**, dominated by the USSR, but frequently thwarted by other member states. Its purpose was ostensibly the economic integration of the Eastern bloc as a means of counteracting the economic power and political influence of the West. The ten member states were eventually the USSR, Bulgaria, Cuba, Czechoslovakia, Hungary, Poland, Romania, East Germany, Mongolia and Vietnam. With the overthrow of **COMMUNISM** in Eastern Europe in 1989–90 and the weakening of the USSR, COMECON was disbanded in 1991.

### Comenius, John Amos (1592–1670)
Czech educational reformer. He studied at Herborn and Heidelberg, and became Rector of the Moravian School in Přerov (1614–16) and minister at Fulnek, but fled to Poland in 1628 at the height of **FERDINAND II**'s oppression of Czech Protestants following his victory at the White Mountain in 1620. Settling at Leszno, he worked out a new theory of education and was chosen Bishop of the Unity of Brethren (later known as the **MORAVIAN BRETHREN**) in 1632. He visited England, the Netherlands and Sweden, and wrote and published extensively. He then settled in Holland, where he died. He tried, without success, to interest other countries in freeing the Czechs from Austrian rule, but his main contribution to history was as an influential educational innovator.

### Comines, Philippe de (c.1445–1511)
French politician and historian. In 1463 he entered the court of Burgundy, but in 1472 began to serve **LOUIS XI** of France. After Louis's death, he was imprisoned, but in 1493 was restored to favour, and accompanied **CHARLES VIII** on his Italian expedition (1494). His *Mémoires* (written 1489–98, published 1524) provide an important record of his times.

### Cominform (Communist Information Bureau)
An organization founded by **STALIN** in 1947 as a successor to the **COMINTERN**, which had been established in 1943. Its purpose was the coordination of the propaganda and politics of the communist parties of Bulgaria, Czechoslovakia, France, Hungary, Italy, Poland, Romania, the USSR and Yugoslavia. Its headquarters were moved from Belgrade to Bucharest following the break between Stalin and **TITO** which culminated in Yugoslavia's expulsion in 1948. Cominform became an instrument in the **COLD WAR**, expressing hostility towards capitalism, and was also used by Stalin as an additional means of dominating Eastern Europe. After the rapprochement between the USSR and Yugoslavia in 1956, the Cominform was dissolved.

### Comintern
An abbreviation for the Third or Communist International, founded in Moscow in Mar 1919 at the behest of the Soviet Communist Party, its purpose being to promote the expected international proletarian revolution by rallying communists and left-wing socialists. It adopted Leninist principles in its policies, rejecting reformism in favour of revolutionary action, which it encouraged against capitalist governments. It gradually became an instrument of **STALIN**'s foreign policy and was ultimately little used. It was disbanded in May 1943 when Stalin was anxious to strengthen his **WORLD WAR II** friendship with **ROOSEVELT** and Winston **CHURCHILL**. ➤ **COMINFORM**; **MARXISM–LENINISM**

### Commando
Civilian militia in the Cape, originally called out by the Dutch **EAST INDIA COMPANY** in the early 18c, but later organized by the Boers themselves and regarded as a prime symbol of their self-sufficiency in the interior of the continent. The commando was used to defend Boer settlements, but increasingly went on to the offensive, attacking **KHOISAN** and Bantu-speaking peoples as a means of expanding Boer power, landholding and herds of cattle. The word has come to mean any forces specializing in irregular actions.

### 'Commercial Union'
A Canadian movement for economic union with the USA, which became a major political issue in 1887. Confederation had failed to generate growth, probably because the number of outlets for Canadian staples had not increased, while John A **MACDONALD**'s policy of protection resulted in retaliatory tariffs in the USA. Britain, an advocate of free trade, already took half of Canada's export trade, whilst there seemed little chance that trade with other European countries or South America would expand. Canadian manufacturers, anxious to maintain their protected position, argued that 'Commercial Union' was akin to annexation, and would lead to Washington dictating fiscal policy to Ottawa. The **LIBERAL PARTY** itself was initially split, with **LAURIER** for **RECIPROCITY** rather than 'Commercial Union' and Richard **CARTWRIGHT** for free trade, and in 1888 it committed itself not to 'Commercial Union' but to 'unrestricted reciprocity'.

### Committee for the Liberation of Upper Italy
(*Comitato di Liberazione nazionale Alta Italia*, CLNAI) The organization established (Jan 1944) to coordinate the activities of anti-German and anti-fascist

partisans, often already grouped within local **COMMITTEES OF NATIONAL LIBERATION** (CLNs). Originally the CLNAI asserted its claims to power not only against the Germans and fascists but also against the Allies and the anti-fascist government in Rome. In Dec 1944, CLNAI delegates agreed to the so-called 'Protocols of Rome' by which, in exchange for a subsidy from the Allies, they promised to hand over all authority after liberation to the Allied Military Government. During the last months of **WORLD WAR II** the CLNAI burgeoned, assisted by a remarkable degree of political collaboration among the leaders of all the main anti-fascist parties. By late Apr 1945 most of the north had fallen to the CLNAI, which established its own *de facto* administration before the arrival of the Allies. Although the CLNAI laid down its weapons, it retained a strong bargaining position which its leaders used to win much greater representation in Rome, forcing the resignation of **BONOMI** and the appointment of **PARRI** as Prime Minister. The new CLNAI-dominated government carried out widespread purges against anyone associated with the former fascist regime, alienating a good deal of public opinion in the process. Blamed for the prevailing dire economic conditions and high unemployment, as well as for the anti-fascist witch-hunts, the Parri government fell from office (Dec 1945); it was replaced by the **DE GASPERI** government.

## Committee of National Liberation (Algeria)

The committee set up by Charles de **GAULLE** on 3 June 1943, through which the Algerians were promised a full voice in the running of their country. The failure to fulfil this promise was, more than any other single factor, responsible for the hardening of native Algerian resistance to the presumptions of the French in Algeria, which eventually resulted in the **ALGERIAN WAR OF INDEPENDENCE**.

## Committees of Correspondence

In the **AMERICAN REVOLUTION**, an informal network linking towns for the purpose of sharing political information. Committees, which held town meetings, began to appear in 1772. During the crisis over independence (1775–6), they assumed active power in many places.

## Committees of National Liberation (*Comitati di Liberazione nazionale*, CLNs)

The first CLN emerged in the autumn of 1943 from the 'United Freedom Front' set up by Ivanoe **BONOMI** in April of that year. Bonomi's organization was aimed at coordinating the efforts of the main anti-fascists, whether Catholic, communist or socialist. However, as the Allies advanced through Italy, autonomous CLNs were established throughout Italy to organize partisan activity; these usually had no affiliation to Bonomi's central organization. In German-occupied northern Italy especially, the CLNs often became a *de facto* government in areas where the anti-fascist resistance was victorious, and in Jan 1944 the **COMMITTEE FOR THE LIBERATION OF UPPER ITALY** was established to coordinate their efforts. ► **PARRI, FERRUCCIO**; **PARTY OF ACTION**

## Common Agricultural Policy (CAP)

The most important of the common policies of the **EC** (European Community). Its basic principles are free trade for agricultural commodities within the Community, Community preference for domestic production, control of imports from the rest of the world, and common prices and subsidization. The main objectives are increased agricultural productivity, a fair standard of living for farmers, reasonable market prices for the consumer, stability of markets, and secure food supplies. Most of these objectives have been met through the use of subsidies on certain types of farming or certain crops, which in turn have generated surpluses of most major commodities, such as the 'butter mountain' and the 'wine lake'. An important additional objective for the CAP is to contain these surpluses and limit the huge cost associated with their disposal. The CAP took up about 70 per cent of the EC budget, and showed an alarming propensity to grow, but many member governments were reluctant to undertake reform because of the wrath of the farming vote, which remains sizable in their countries. Radical reforms involving the reduction of price supports for cereals, beef and dairy produce were eventually introduced in 1992 and 1997, but the expansion of the **EU** in 2004 may further exacerbate the problems with the CAP.

## Commons, House of

The lower, and effectively the ruling, chamber of the bicameral legislature of the UK. It contains 659 members, elected by universal adult suffrage, each representing a single constituency. The Commons is elected for a maximum period of five years, though the Prime Minister may call an election at any time within that period, and the government is drawn from the party that wins the majority of seats. The ascendancy of the House of Commons over the House of **LORDS** began during the 16c, and was completed with the passage of the Parliament Acts of 1911 and 1949. The Commons is dominated by a disciplined party system, which means that governments are generally assured of a majority in the passage of legislation. In this sense the Commons serves a legitimizing rather than a legislating function.

## Commonwealth

English republican regime created by Oliver **CROMWELL**, based on the **RUMP PARLIAMENT** established in 1649, which lasted until the Instrument of Government created a **PROTECTORATE** in 1653. It failed to achieve political settlement at home, but its armies pacified Scotland and Ireland. The Navigation Acts (1650 and 1651) and the **ANGLO-DUTCH WARS** (1652–4) fostered overseas trade and colonies. ► **ENGLISH CIVIL WARS**

## Commonwealth of Independent States ► CIS

## Commonwealth of Nations

A voluntary organization of autonomous states which had been imperial possessions of Britain. Its head is Queen **ELIZABETH II**. It was formally established by the Statute of **WESTMINSTER** (1931) and meets frequently to discuss matters of mutual interest and concern. While most states, on independence, chose to become members of the Commonwealth, the Irish Republic left in 1949, South Africa left in 1961 and rejoined in 1994, Pakistan left in 1972 and rejoined in 1989, and Zimbabwe left in 2003 after having its membership suspended. A number of member countries have been suspended from the Commonwealth: Fiji (1987, readmitted 1997; suspended 2000, readmitted 2001), Nigeria (1995, readmitted 1999), Pakistan (1999, readmitted 2004), and Zimbabwe (2002).

## communalism

The term used in India to characterize the use of religion for political ends, particularly by Muslims and Hindus. Early expressions of communalism arose within the Cow Protection Societies formed by Hindus, to whom the cow is sacred; these often came into conflict with Muslims, to whom the slaughter of animals is required during some religious festivals. Conflict also arose over holy sites used by both Hindus and Muslims for worship. British intervention in such disputes often only exacerbated them: nationalists have argued that this was a conscious policy, part of the colonial tactic of 'divide and rule'. Certainly, from an early stage the British colonial government treated Hindus and Muslims (as well as tribals) as entirely separate communities, making cooperation between them very difficult to achieve. Despite this, there was a considerable degree of cooperation between Hindu and Muslim politicians in the Indian independence movement, particularly in 1915–22 when both Mohammed Ali **JINNAH** (the leader of the **MUSLIM LEAGUE**) and M K **GANDHI** (by 1917 the leader of the **INDIAN NATIONAL CONGRESS**) strove to forge a united front against the British during the Khilafat, Rowlatt and Non-Cooperation campaigns. This unity collapsed, however, in 1922 after the suspension of the **NON-COOPERATION MOVEMENT** by Gandhi. Conflict between the two communities increased markedly during the **GREAT DEPRESSION**, in the late 1930s when Congress provincial governments were formed, and during **WORLD WAR II**, when the League supported the British and the Congress was banned in the wake of the Quit India Campaign of 1942. Jinnah's demands for Muslims to have their own separate nation led ultimately to the partition of India into separate Hindu and Muslim nations (India and Pakistan) in 1947. Three wars between India and Pakistan have subsequently fuelled the conflict, and within India itself the 120 million-strong Muslim population remains the focus of fierce political dispute. A secular constitution and a secular majority amongst Indian politicians has tended to curb serious conflict, but at times of social and economic crisis the threat of 'communalism' has always re-emerged. ► **QUIT INDIA MOVEMENT**

## Commune

A sworn association of equals which developed as the distinctive political organization of European towns in the Middle Ages, first and most notably from the later 11c in northern Italy. They revived the traditions of republican Rome in the office of consul but added a corporatist dimension to civic life which reflected the new economic strength of the medieval town. The **LOMBARD LEAGUE** of Italian communes won a notable success against the feudal army of the German emperor **FREDERICK I, BARBAROSSA** at the Battle of **LEGNANO** in 1176. In the later Middle Ages in Italy and elsewhere, communal political structures proved vulnerable to family factionalism, and many succumbed to tyranny for the sake of stability and

were absorbed into larger territorial states.

## Communes, People's

The basic unit of government in the Chinese countryside, first created in 1958 as part of the **GREAT LEAP FORWARD** campaign. Originating in 1957 with the large-scale mobilization of rural labour for irrigation and water conservancy projects, the communes amalgamated previously existing collectives and combined administrative, economic and social functions. **MAO ZEDONG** hailed the communes as a symbol of China's transition to **COMMUNISM** that would boost rural productivity and enhance collective life. By the end of 1958, 740,000 collectives had been amalgamated into 26,000 communes; private plots were abolished, communal mess-halls and nurseries created, and rural industrialization promoted. Disastrous economic results and widespread peasant opposition forced the leadership after 1959 to modify the extreme forms of collectivism and devolve some of the communes' functions to the production brigade (the former collective). During the 1980s the communes were virtually dismantled as the individual peasant household became the unit of agricultural production.

## communism

A political ideology which has as its central principle the communal ownership of all property, and thereby the abolition of private property. Although examples of early social and religious groupings based upon communal sharing of property have been cited, modern communism is specifically associated with the theories of Karl **MARX**. Marx saw the emergence of a communist society as being the final stage in a historical process that was rooted in human material needs, preceded by **FEUDALISM**, **CAPITALISM** and (a transitional stage) **SOCIALISM**. Communism, according to Marx, would abolish class distinctions and end the exploitation of the masses inherent in the capitalist system. The working class, or proletariat, would be the instrument of a revolution that would overthrow the capitalist system and liberate human potential. A fully developed communist system would operate according to the principle of 'from each according to his ability, to each according to his need', and as there would be no cause for the state to regulate society, it would 'wither away'. Marx's writings provided a powerful ideological basis for communist and many socialist parties and governments, which legitimized the implementation of their policies by reference to them. The **COMMUNIST PARTY OF THE SOVIET UNION** (CPSU), first of all under **LENIN**'s leadership and then under **STALIN**'s, reinterpreted Marxist ideology as Marxism–Leninism–Stalinism, a major feature of which came to be democratic centralism. Unlike the spontaneous, decentralized organization envisaged by Marx, the CPSU was a highly centralized, monolithic and secretive organization. Under Stalin's leadership it became an instrument in the development of a totalitarian dictatorship. The CPSU provided the ideological lead for European communist parties; indeed, at the creation of the Third **INTERNATIONAL** or **COMINTERN** in 1919, it was clear that only those socialist parties which accepted the discipline, leadership and organizational structure of the Soviet Communist Party would be allowed to join. Much the same was true of the **COMINFORM**, established in 1947. Increasingly from the 1960s onwards, however, the compulsory leadership of the CPSU was questioned and challenged, partly because of the economic difficulties resulting from the rigidities of democratic centralism in industrial states, where decentralization and flexibility were required. Nonetheless, Yugoslavia was the only country to challenge Soviet dominance successfully (it was expelled from the Cominform in 1948); other countries such as Hungary (1956), Czechoslovakia (1968) and Poland (1980–1) were prevented by military force from breaking away from the Soviet model. But in 1989–90, the establishment of a non-communist government in Poland and popular uprisings elsewhere in Eastern Europe, followed by reasonably free elections, saw the almost total eclipse of communism there. The uprisings were political and economic, and one reason for their success was the changing nature of Soviet communism under Mikhail **GORBACHEV**'s reforming leadership and the growing demand in the USSR for the same kind of changes as Eastern Europe wanted. Within a year of the failed coup against Gorbachev in Aug 1991, the Soviet Communist Party was declared illegal and much of the mechanism of communist rule was dismantled. There remains the possibility of some kind of communist recovery in the USSR as well as in Eastern Europe. But faith in communism worldwide has been seriously weakened, outside exceptional cases like North Korea and Cuba. Chinese communism, which was never slavishly Soviet in its ideology and practices, has quietly abandoned its beliefs in everything except the dictatorship of the party, particularly after the death of **DENG XIAOPING** in 1997. The same is broadly true of the communist regime in Vietnam.

## Communist Party, Chinese (CCP)

Formally created in July 1921 by 14 delegates (including **MAO ZEDONG**), the party represented six communist cells established the previous year. **COMINTERN** representatives from Moscow persuaded **CHEN DUXIU**, the party's first Secretary-General, to join with the more powerful **GUOMINDANG** (Nationalist Party) in a United Front to combat imperialism and restore national unity, the long-term aim being to take over leadership 'from within'. During this period of cooperation (1923–7), the CCP increased its membership to 6,000 and gained significant influence over mass organizations. The party's urban base was destroyed after 1927 when the Guomindang turned on its erstwhile communist allies. Henceforth, Mao Zedong's strategy of protracted rural revolution, emphasizing the creation of base areas and reliance on a peasant Red Army, came to be accepted by the CCP leadership. Membership of the party again increased substantially during the war with Japan (1937–45) and reached 1.2 million by 1945. With Mao confirmed as leader at the Party's Seventh Congress (1945), the CCP emerged victorious from the civil war with the Nationalists (1946–9) and established the People's Republic in 1949. By the time of the party's Eighth Congress (1956), membership was 10.5 million. Party authority was undermined during the **CULTURAL REVOLUTION** (1966–9), but at the party's Ninth Congress (1969) the policy of rebuilding and reasserting party control was confirmed. After

Mao's death in 1976, **DENG XIAOPING** sought to rejuvenate and reform the party, but this did not prevent it gradually losing credibility amongst the population during the 1980s. Deng was committed to economic reform that embraced agriculture, industry, national defence, and science and technology, but he saw demands for a more open government and democratization as threatening a return to the populist chaos of the Cultural Revolution, and his resolute crackdown on dissenters resulted in the deaths of thousands of student demonstrators in **TIANANMEN SQUARE** in 1989. That year, **JIANG ZEMIN** became CCP General Secretary and succeeded Deng as chairman of the CCP Central Military Commission, but Deng remained paramount leader of the country until his death in Feb 1997. When Jiang retired in 2003, his successor as CCP General Secretary, Hu Jintao, sought to incorporate the burgeoning class of capitalists and entrepreneurs within the party structure.► COMMUNISM

## Communist Party, French (*Parti Communiste Français*, PCF)

Founded in 1920 when a majority of members of the **SOCIALIST PARTY** (SFIO) voted to join the Third International and to become the Communist Party, officially known until 1943 as SFIC (*Section française de l'Internationale communiste*, 'French Section of the Communist International'). The 1924 elections showed that few voters were prepared to support the new party, and by 1932 it had only 11 Deputies. It was saved by the **POPULAR FRONT**, and emerged after **WORLD WAR II** as a major political force with over a quarter of the vote and representation in a coalition cabinet (1945–7). In spite of retaining substantial electoral support (usually around 20 per cent of the vote), it never again held office until the victory of the Left in the election of 1981, when it joined in a coalition with the socialists until 1984. This apparent success coincided with a rapid fall in voting support, and this decline continues in the 21 c. ► COMMUNISM

## Communist Party of Cuba (*Partido Comunista de Cuba*, PCC)

The only political party in existence in Cuba since 1959. Originally named the Popular Socialist Party and then the United Party of the Socialist Revolution (when **CASTRO** was not yet a hard-line Marxist), it became the Communist Party of Cuba in 1965. Castro has always sought to maintain the ideological purity of the party, enunciating policy in the party newspaper *Granma* (named after the boat he landed in 1956 to start his revolution), resisting Mikhail **GORBACHEV**'s call for **PERESTROIKA** and purging the state of undesirables (no matter how high), such as General Ochao (a member of the Central Committee of the Party and a Hero of the Revolution and the Angolan War, who was executed in 1989 for drug offences). The party officially embraces the expansion of tourism as a source of income but is resistant to wider economic reform. ► COMMUNISM

## Communist Party of Finland (*Suomen Kommunistinen Puolue*, SKP)

Founded in Moscow (Aug 1918) by members of the Finnish Red Army and **SOCIAL DEMOCRATIC PARTY** who had been defeated by the Finnish Whites and their German allies in the civil war earlier in the year, its most prominent leader was Otto **KUUSINEN**. In 1919 it joined the **COMINTERN** and was declared illegal in Finland the same year. Suppressed by the Finnish authorities, it worked underground and although it failed to win the allegiance of the majority of the working class, who were loyal to the Social Democrats, it nevertheless gained significant footholds in working-class organizations through a front organization, the Socialist Workers' Party. However, its organizations in Finland were effectively smashed by anti-communist legislation introduced in 1930 under pressure from the **LAPUA MOVEMENT**. The party remained largely inactive until it was legalized in 1944, following Finland's defeat in the **CONTINUATION WAR** of 1941–4. Despite its widespread perception as a tool of Moscow, the party was able to draw on solid support among both industrial workers in the south and the small farmers of northern and eastern Finland. Through its front organization, the Finnish People's Democratic League (SKDL), the party did well in the immediate post-war period. Following electoral success in 1945, they were represented in government from 1945 to 1948, and in 1958 gained their best-ever result with 25 per cent of the vote, becoming the largest party in parliament. They were, however, kept from office for many years by the other parties' refusal to cooperate with them. From 1966 onwards the Communist Party was weakened by conflicts between Moscow loyalists and those advocating a reformist, Eurocommunist line, but it was a regular participant in government. Ultimately, the party split, with the reformist minority breaking away to form the Democratic Alternative. At the same time, the party's electoral support began a process of decline that continues still, worsened by further splits into factions. ► COMMUNISM

## Communist Party of Great Britain
Formed in 1920 through the merger of various leftist groups, it acknowledged from its inception the authority of Moscow. Its fortunes improved with Soviet intervention in **WORLD WAR II**, but it never won more than four seats in parliament and the 1956 Hungarian Uprising saw many defections. Unlike many European parties, its influence was minimal long before the collapse of the USSR (1990–1), and its subsequent history has been one of continued factionalism and declining electoral support. ► COMMUNISM

## Communist Party of Greece ► KKE

## Communist Party of India (CPI)
Founded in Dec 1926, it was an expatriate Bengali, M N Roy, who recruited and trained the first party members in the USSR. Early attempts to link up with radicals in India were frustrated by the Kanpur and Meerut conspiracy trials (1923 and 1929), but the communists, although persecuted and effectively illegal, were able to establish a network of members and supporters, infiltrating not only the **INDIAN NATIONAL CONGRESS** and trade union movements, but also setting up workers' and peasants' societies with a view to mobilizing the masses in the struggle against colonialism. Relations with the Gandhian Congress were not always easy, although members of the Congress Socialist Party and Congress leaders such as Jawaharlal **NEHRU** were sympathetic. This was due not only to disagreements over tactics, particularly the

use of violence, but also because the **COMINTERN** policy between 1929 and 1935 was to reject cooperation with bourgeois–democratic movements. Before and after these dates, however, CPI members occupied prominent positions in the Indian National Congress. Increasingly active in the late 1930s after the collapse of Gandhi's **CIVIL DISOBEDIENCE** movement, and despite the fact that officially the CPI supported the British government in the struggle against fascism during **WORLD WAR II**, local level members of the Workers' and Peasants' Parties played a prominent part in the violent Quit India agitation of 1942. In 1946 the CPI contested elections held by the British to the provincial and central assemblies and won a considerable number of votes, though a limited number of seats, as the runner-up to the Congress in most constituencies. Despite this, the CPI was not consulted by the British in the negotiations over independence, and party members organized strikes and agitation, particularly in the independent princely states, which threatened to break away from the Indian Union and set up their own autocratic regimes. Of greatest importance was the **TELENGANA DISTURBANCES** in Hyderabad. After independence, CPI members continued to contest elections and gained a number of seats in parliament. However, they were closely allied with the Congress Party (at least until 1974) and therefore generally supported the government. ► BENGAL, PARTITION OF; COMMUNALISM; COMMUNISM; GHADR PARTY AND MOVEMENT; INDIA, PARTITION OF; INDIAN NATIONAL CONGRESS; QUIT INDIA MOVEMENT

## Communist Party of India (Marxist)
The split between the USSR and China caused a split within the ranks of the Communist Party of India, the splinter group becoming the CPI (M) or CPM (where 'M' stands for 'Marxist') in 1964, a party which has since opposed the dominant political party, the **INDIAN NATIONAL CONGRESS**, in national and state elections. Its greatest success has been in Bengal, where it has been the party in power for much of the time since first forming a coalition government in 1967. The first government lasted only briefly after another faction split from the party, calling itself the CPM–L (where 'M–L' stands for 'Marxist–Leninist'), and attempted to raise a general revolt by undertaking direct action against class enemies, beginning in the district of Naxalbari, from which they derived the name 'Naxalites'. Having committed themselves, like the CPI, to the parliamentary route to socialism, violent confrontations between the CPM supporters and the CPM–L resulted, leading to intervention by the central government. After a period of Congress rule and Indira Gandhi's Emergency in 1975–7, the CPM again returned to office with a huge majority in 1977, with Jyoti Basu as Chief Minister, and it has remained there ever since, as the leading party in a Left coalition, its popularity based on its successful land reform and rural development programmes and its pragmatic, secular, social policies, which have made Bengal, despite its poverty, the only Indian state with a considerable Muslim population in recent years to have largely escaped the threat of communal violence. ► COMMUNISM; COMMUNIST PARTY OF INDIA (CPI)

**Communist Party** (Germany) ► **KPD**

**Communist Party** (Italy) ► **PCI**

**Communist Party** (Spain) ► **PCE**

**Communist Party of the Soviet Union (CPSU)**
The party that controlled political, economic and social life in the USSR from the Bolshevik Revolution in 1917 until its abolition in 1991. It was the only party with the right to put forward candidates in elections, and most of the country's important jobs were filled by selected party members. Membership comprised only c.10 per cent of the population, and the party itself was highly undemocratic, being run by the small **POLITBURO** or the slightly larger Central Committee. ► **COMMUNISM**

**Commynes, Philippe de** ► **COMINES, PHILIPPE DE**

**Comnenus Family** (1057–1461)
A family, with estates in Asia Minor, of which many members occupied the Byzantine throne from 1057 to 1185 and that of Trebizond from 1204 to 1461. David Comnenus, the last in Trebizond, was executed at Adrianople in 1462, with all his family, by **MEHMED II.** ► **ALEXIUS I COMNENUS; ANNA COMNENA; ISAAC I COMNENUS**

**COMOROS, THE** official name **Union of the Comoros** and (1978–2002) **Federal Islamic Republic of the Comoros**

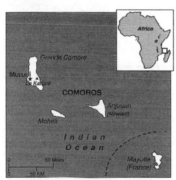

A group of three volcanic islands (Grand Comore, Anjouan and Mohéli) at the northern end of the Mozambique Channel, between Mozambique and Madagascar. Under French control from 1843 to 1912, it became a French Overseas Territory in 1947. Internal political autonomy was achieved in 1961, and unilateral independence was declared in 1975 by the Comorian President Ahmed Abdallah, who was deposed later that year. The island of Mayotte, however, decided to remain under French administration. In 1978 a group of European mercenaries staged a coup, reinstalled President Abdallah, and established the Comoros as a Federal Islamic Republic. Democracy was restored in 1984 and Abdallah ruled until 1989, but political instability continued throughout the 1980s and early 1990s. Despite promises of increased island autonomy from President Muhammad Taki Abdoulkarim, who came to power in 1996, in 1997 Anjouan and Mohéli demanded to secede from the Comoros and return to French rule. President Majiddine Ben Said Massonde agreed to grant them greater autonomy in Apr 1999 but was de-

posed a week later in a bloodless army coup. By 2002 a new constitution had been agreed that kept the three islands together as one country while granting each greater autonomy and its own leader. Leaders of each island were elected in 2002 and Azali Assoumani became president of the Union

**Compact Theory of Confederation**
Canadian constitutional theory. An interpretation of the **BRITISH NORTH AMERICA ACT** which argued that confederation meant the entrusting of certain powers to Ottawa while the provinces still retained their autonomy. As a compact, the agreement could not be altered without the acceptance of the signatories and could even be nullified if they so wished. The theory was supported in the 1880s by Quebeckers such as Honoré **MERCIER** and by English-speaking provincial leaders like Mowat in Ontario and Norquay in Manitoba. The federal power that provincial governments most wanted to remove was that of disallowing provincial legislation, because, along with a policy of economic centralization, it would result in the severe limitation of provincial rights. At the 1927 Dominion-Provincial Conference, the compact theory was proclaimed the true interpretation of confederation by both the Liberal Premier of Quebec and the Tory Premier of Ontario, and during the 1930s it was used to place the Prime Minister, Richard **BENNETT**, under political pressure. The theory actually disintegrates under examination because the original signatories comprised only three provinces.

**Compaoré, Blaise** (1940–)
Burkina Faso soldier and politician. Educated locally and in military academies in Senegal and France, including St Cyr, he joined the army in 1958, rising to command the Artillery Group (1975–6). In 1980 he was appointed Minister of Rural Development and was second in command to Thomas **SANKARA** (1983–7), when he overthrew his colleague on 15 Oct 1987 and became Chairman of the Popular Front of Burkina Faso and head of government, a position he has held since. Originally a very close friend and confrere of Sankara's, he came to reject what he felt was the overly egalitarian thrust of Sankara's policies.

**compradors**
The Chinese managers of foreign enterprises in China's **TREATY PORTS** during the 19c and early 20c. Condemned by Chinese nationalists as the tools of Western imperialism, many *compradors* in fact invested in modern Chinese-owned enterprises that successfully competed with Western-owned firms. In the late 19c some compradors were also keen advocates of political and educational reform.

**Compromise of 1850**
A major, but ultimately unsuccessful, attempt by the Congress of the USA to resolve, by legislation, the conflict between the North and the South over **SLAVERY**. Specifically involved was the expansion of slavery into new territories such as California and the South-West. Its major terms were the admission of California as a free (non-slave) state, and the passage of a strong fugitive slave law to placate the South. ►
**AMERICAN CIVIL WAR**

# *Computers*

Science & Technology

As the name suggests, the thinking behind the computer was always in terms of a machine for carrying out mechanical calculations; for relieving the human mind of some of the labour involved in simply counting. In the 1c AD the Alexandrian philosopher and mathematician Hero wrote down his idea of using a series of differentiated gearwheels to represent numbers, but there is no evidence that he gave the concept a physical form.

It was not until the 17c that the first real calculating machine appeared. This was created by the French philosopher and mathematician Blaise Pascal (1623–62). The son of a tax official, he wanted to help his father find a way of speeding up the endless addition sums that his work entailed, and in 1642 he constructed a calculating machine that could carry out simple addition and subtraction by means of cogs and wheels. This device was in essence the first computer, an achievement recognized by 20c computer scientists when they named the programming language PASCAL after him. The idea of this basic machine was further refined by the German philosopher Leibniz (1646–1716), who made a similar device that had the additional function of multiplication.

The next important advance came from the English mathematician Charles Babbage (1792–1871). In 1820 he designed a 'Difference Engine' for simple mathematical tasks that had to be carried out on a huge scale, repetitively, for the astronomical tables so essential to contemporary navigation. Babbage never actually built this device, but in the 1990s a model was constructed following his original plans and was found to work perfectly. In 1833 he designed a further device (called an 'Analytical Engine') which he intended to be programmable to execute a range of mathematical functions. In 1801–8 the French mechanic Joseph Jacquard had perfected the use of punched cards to 'programme' a mechanical loom to weave complicated designs, and Babbage used similar cards (and later perforated tape) both to feed in mathematical instructions and to record the results of calculations. Lack of money and the shortcomings of the technology of the time meant that Babbage was never able to build a fully operational model, but he had clearly demonstrated the principle of pre-programming calculations and storing results. The use of punched cards continued, and in the 1890 USA census the US inventor Herman Hollerith (1860–1929) used them to handle data.

It was in the UK, however, that the first electronic computer was invented, with, as often in history, warfare being the spur to invention. During **World War II** the British sought a way to break the codes that the Germans created on their 'Enigma' machines (one of which had been captured). To do this, scientists designed and built the computer 'Colossus'. This machine successfully carried out the function for which it had been designed, but it was too specialized to have wider applications.

The next advances came in the USA, where an electronic calculating machine was built for the Army in 1945. It was known as ENIAC (Electronic Numerical Integrator Analyzer and Computer). It could carry out several hundred multiplications per minute, but its sheer size was so great that it filled a room, and it contained thousands of valves. It was not long, however, before technological developments allowed this problem of physical bulk to be overcome.

The vital breakthrough was the invention of the transistor in the 1950s. With these components performing the functions of the much bulkier valves, it became possible to reduce the size of the internal working of computers and hence of the outer casing. Further compactness was made possible in the next decade with the development of the integrated circuit, which assembled transistors and other components on a very small unit. The microchip, invented in the 1970s, was able to contain large numbers of these integrated circuits, further scaling down the size of the machines.

It was now that the computer began to belie its name and be used for much wider applications than mathematical

---

**Compromise of Nobility** (1565)
A league of the lesser nobility of the Low Countries formed in resistance to Spanish rule at the beginning of the **EIGHTY YEARS' WAR**. In Brussels in Nov 1565 a number of the lesser aristocracy or gentry joined the compromise against the introduction of the Spanish **INQUISITION** and other forms of religious persecution; both Catholics and Calvinists were affiliated. Membership grew fast, and it provided the leadership of the revolt until there was an accord reached in late 1566 with the Spanish Regent, **MARGARET OF PARMA**, after which the compromise was dissolved.

**Compton, John George Melvin** (1926–)
St Lucian politician. He graduated from the London School of Economics and was called to the English Bar. In 1951 he established a law practice in St Lucia and three years later joined the St Lucia Labour Party (SLP), becoming its Deputy Leader. He left in 1961 to form the United Workers' Party (UWP) and, on independence in 1979, was St Lucia's first Prime Minister. He was defeated in the same year by the Labour Party but returned in 1982, and was narrowly re-elected in 1987. He retired in 1996 and was replaced as UWP leader and Prime Minister by Vaughan Lewis.

**Compton, Spencer, Earl of Wilmington** (1673–1743)
British politician. He was Paymaster-General from 1722 to 1730 and **GEORGE II** attempted to make him his First Minister on succeeding to the throne (1727), but was outmanoeuvred by **WALPOLE**. Compton remained a strong supporter of the King as Walpole's popularity waned after the outbreak of war with Spain (1739). As First Lord of the Treasury (1742–3), he was leader of the administration in name only, being overshadowed by Thomas **PELHAM**-Holles, 1st Duke of Newcastle, and **CARTERET**. ► WHIGS

**Compulsory Service Act** ► **MILITARY SERVICE ACT**

**Computers** ► *See panel*

**Comuneros, Revolt of the** (1520–1)
The name given to those who participated in the rebellion (the *Comunidades*) of the chief cities of **CASTILE** against Emperor **CHARLES V** (Charles I of Spain) in 1520–1. On Charles's arrival in Spain in 1516, the privileges awarded to his foreign entourage aggravated other complaints that the cities had against the Crown. The uprising began in Toledo, under Juan de **PADILLA**, and rapidly took in the major

calculation. Indeed, the computer was now on a course of development that would lead to its becoming almost omnipresent in modern life. Industry became increasingly 'computerized', with machines now programmable to run other machines and processes, and carry out tasks that had been done by hand in the past. Military applications were many, including the use of computers in flying aircraft, sighting weapons and targeting guided missiles. With the arrival of desktop computers, and the continuing fall in the price of the machines, the handling of data in both business and personal contexts became increasingly the main use, with the computers having such functions as record-storing, word-processing, graphic design and communications. The development of floppy discs meant that information could be stored in highly compact form as well as easily copied and circulated.

Computers moved into entertainment also, with ever more sophisticated games becoming available and increasing miniaturization allowing hand-held computer games to become a popular amusement. The sheer amount of information that could be contained on a CD-ROM allowed people to use their computers to consult multi-volume reference works at the touch of a keyboard, as well as to play music and watch videos.

Scientific research continued to make advances, particularly in the field that came to be known as 'artificial intelligence', which explored the possibility of creating computers with the ability to think in a way similar to the human brain. Another field was the use of computers to construct a simulation of the real world with which people could interact. This 'virtual reality' had both entertainment applications and more serious uses like the flight simulators on which trainee pilots could experience something like actual flight conditions without leaving the ground.

The invention of the modem (modulator–demodulator) allowed computers to interconnect via signals sent by telephone line; this opened the way for such innovations as electronic mail (email) and the late-20c creation of the Internet, the worldwide system of interconnected computer networks. Users could now communicate almost instantly all over the globe, as well as search for data, although drawbacks quickly became apparent with the development of 'spam' (unsolicited emails sent anonymously in bulk, said to constitute up to 80% of all email traffic), 'viruses' (computer programs that can damage the recipient's computer), and 'hacking' (circumvention of security measures to gain unauthorized access to confidential government or commercial information). From a simple counting device the computer has become the gateway to a world of information, and vital to the operation of modern industry, government, commerce and communications.

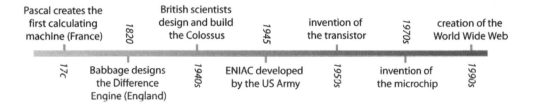

cities of central Castile, which banded themselves into a junta and sought the help of Queen **JOAN THE MAD** at Tordesillas. The nobility, however, rallied to help the royal cause, and defeated the *Comunero* forces at the Battle of **VILLALAR** (1521). Padilla and the other leading rebels were executed the following day. The popular appeal of the *Comuneros* persisted through time, and rebel movements in Spanish South America also adopted the name in the 18c.

### Comuneros, Revolt of the (1781)
One of the largest rebellions in 18c Latin America, it occurred in the Spanish viceroyalty of New Granada (now Colombia) as a protest by lower classes against new fiscal levies on tobacco and aguardiente production by the new administration under the Visitor-General, who had been appointed by **CHARLES III** to supersede previous administrations. Unlike many popular revolts, the scale of this one was substantial, involving over 20,000 armed men. Its local **CREOLE** leadership coalesced around a programme of 'capitulations', which included demands against arbitrary imprisonment, preference for local men (not Spaniards) in the distribution of patronage, and the freedom of Indians to retain their reserves as individual proprietors. Initially successful in halting the imposition of new legislation, the scale of revolt shook the viceregal administration, and the four principal leaders of the revolt were caught and executed the following year.

### concentration camp
A detention centre for political prisoners; known primarily from the camps established in Germany soon after the Nazi seizure of power, which soon came under **SS** control and were administered with extreme cruelty. The coming of war swelled the camp population with millions of Jews, Gypsies, slave workers, Soviet prisoners of war, and other 'enemies of the state' whom the SS regarded as an economic unit of resource. Following the Wannsee Conference (Jan 1942), which plotted the destruction of European Jewry, the concentration camps established in Poland, such as **AUSCHWITZ** and Treblinka, became purpose-made extermination centres in which over 6 million Jews died. ► **BUCHENWALD; DACHAU; HOLOCAUST; NAZI PARTY**

### Concessions, Scramble for (1897–8)
The term used to describe competition amongst the

foreign powers in China to secure leasehold territories from an increasingly enfeebled **QING DYNASTY**. It began in 1897 with Germany obtaining a 99-year lease on the port of Qingdao (Tsingtao) in Shandong province as 'compensation' for the murder of two German missionaries there. Russia then demanded from the Chinese government a similar lease agreement for Port Arthur, in south Manchuria. Britain obtained a lease on Weihaiwei (Shandong province) and Hong Kong's New Territories, while France acquired a lease on Guangzhou Bay in south China. At the same time, the Chinese government had to accept informal spheres of economic influence carved out by the foreign powers. Such concessions stimulated the development of Chinese nationalism.

## conciliação
The Brazilian tradition of reaching a consensus among the powerful propertied groups, rather than risk civil war. Invoked by Antônio Carlos Ribeiro de Andrada Machado é Silva in 1840, at the close of a decade of civil war, *conciliação* implied that incoming administrations would respect minor appointments made by their predecessors. This was seen as a recipe for peace in the interior and implied that the central government would mediate in local disputes, rather than allow them to threaten the political or social integrity of the empire. 'Compromise' or conciliação ministries governed the empire through the mid-19c. ➤ **ANDRADA FAMILY**

## Concordat (1516)
The agreement between King **FRANCIS I** (of France) and Pope **LEO X** that governed relations between Church and State in France until 1789. It gave the king the right to nominate bishops and abbots, and thus granted him a high degree of control over the Church.

## Concordat (1801)
The **CONCORDAT** (1516) having been broken by the **FRENCH REVOLUTION**, this new agreement between **NAPOLEON I** and Pope **PIUS VII** established a system that lasted until 1905. The government regained the right to nominate bishops, who in turn appointed parish priests; the Church did not regain its property, but the clergy were to be paid salaries by the State. The Concordat said nothing about the monastic clergy, but they came to be tolerated in practice. ➤ **SEPARATION OF CHURCH AND STATE** (France) (1905)

## Condé, House of
The junior branch of the French royal line, the House of **BOURBON**, which played a prominent role in French dynastic politics, particularly in the 16–17c. Ten generations bore the title of 'Prince of Condé', the most eminent being Louis II of Bourbon, Prince of Condé, better known as 'the Great Condé'. ➤ **CONDÉ, LOUIS I OF BOURBON, PRINCE OF**; **CONDÉ, LOUIS II OF BOURBON, PRINCE OF**

## Condé, Louis I of Bourbon, Prince of (1530–69)
French Huguenot leader. The younger brother of Antony of Bourbon, King of Navarre, he led the **HUGUE-NOTS** during the French Wars of **RELIGION**. He fought in the wars between **HENRY II** of France and Spain (1551–7), and joined the Huguenots on the accession of **FRANCIS II** (1559). He was defeated at Dreux during the first civil war (1562); and in the second war (1567–9) was defeated at Jarnac, taken prisoner, and shot. ➤ **CONDÉ, HOUSE OF**

## Condé, Louis II of Bourbon, Prince of, known as the Great Condé (1621–86)
French military leader. During the **THIRTY YEARS' WAR** he defeated the Spaniards (1643 and 1648) and Bavarians (1645–6). The court party came to terms with the **FRONDE** by his help, but his arrogance led to his imprisonment, and when he was released he joined the rebels. Defeated at the Battle of the Dunes, near Dunkirk (1658), he was then pardoned, and became one of **LOUIS XIV**'s greatest generals, defeating the Spanish in Franche-Comté (1668) and **WILLIAM III, OF ORANGE**, at Seneffe (1674). ➤ **CONDÉ, HOUSE OF**

## Condominium (Anglo-Egyptian Sudan)
After the defeat of the Mahdist forces by **KITCHENER**, the area of the Upper Nile was linked with Egypt, named the Anglo-Egyptian Sudan and controlled nominally by Britain and Egypt as a 'condominium'. In practice, though, real power lay in British hands as Britain was, at the time, in effective control of Egypt. The period of the Condominium, initially both economically and socially advantageous to the Sudan, led (through the development of an educated class) to a desire for independence. Some progress was made, and in 1948 Britain recognized the validity of these aspirations. However, the movement towards independence received a setback when, in 1951, King **FAROUK** of Egypt proclaimed himself also King of the Sudan. Farouk's subsequent fall led to Egypt's recognition, in principle, of the Sudanese right to independence, and full independence was declared in 1955.

## Condorcet, Marie Jean Antoine Nicolas de Caritat, Marquis of (1743–94)
French politician, philosopher and mathematician. He studied at Paris, and his work in mathematics became highly regarded in the 1760s. He was elected to the **LEGISLATIVE ASSEMBLY** (1791–2) and became its President, siding usually with the **GIRONDINS**. Accused and condemned by the **JACOBINS**, he was captured, and found dead in prison, at Bourg-la-Reine. In his philosophy, he proclaimed the ideal of progress, and the indefinite perfectibility of the human race. ➤ **FRENCH REVOLUTION**

## condottiere
A leader of mercenary soldiers in 14–15c Italy; from Italian *condotta* ('contract'). Hired by city-states and the papacy, they were often of foreign origin (eg the Englishman Sir John Hawkwood or Giovanni Acuto), but they also included Italian noblemen (eg the d'Este dukes of Ferrara, Gonzaga marquises of Mantua, and Sforza dukes of Milan).

## Confederacy ➤ **CONFEDERATE STATES OF AMERICA**

## Confederate States of America
The official name of the states that seceded in 1860–1, precipitating the **AMERICAN CIVIL WAR**: Virginia, North Carolina, South Carolina, Georgia, Florida, Tennessee, Alabama, Mississippi, Louisiana, Texas and Arkansas. The Confederacy's constitution was modelled on the **US CONSTITUTION**. Its only President was Jefferson **DAVIS** of Mississippi. It never

won foreign recognition, and collapsed after military defeat by the North in 1865. The other four slave states (Delaware, Maryland, Kentucky and Missouri) did not secede, and neither did the north-west counties of Virginia, which became West Virginia.

**Confederation, Articles of** ► ARTICLES OF CONFEDERATION

## Confederation Movement
Canadian political movement for unification within the British North American provinces. Prefigured at various times from the **AMERICAN REVOLUTION** onwards, consideration of the project by Earl **GREY**, the British Colonial Secretary (1846–52), set in train discussions within the maritime provinces. At the same time a growing paralysis of government was becoming evident within the Province of Canada. A T **GALT**'s entry into the **CARTIER–MACDONALD** government in 1858 was only secured on condition that it sought confederation, which was rapidly being seen as a necessity. The English-speaking business community believed it to be essential for economic growth and expansion to the west against American competition, while the threat to reciprocity demanded closer trading links between Canada and the Maritimes. The British government's commitment to Canadian defence had been called into question since the Oregon dispute, and with the onset of the **AMERICAN CIVIL WAR**, the provinces became aware that they were very vulnerable to retaliation from the Northern states because of British policies and because Confederates were ready to use Canada as a base for raids. In 1864 the 'great coalition' of Canadian reformers and conservatives under the leadership of Sir Étienne-Paschal Tache broached the idea of a general union at the Charlottetown Conference called by the Maritimes. Discussions continued at the Quebec Conference, where agreement was quickly reached. Acceptance by the provincial legislatures was much more difficult to obtain, and was achieved in Canada (where it needed all George Étienne Cartier's political acumen to persuade the French-Canadians) only after lengthy debate. In the Maritimes, Newfoundland and Prince Edward Island rejected confederation, but Samuel **TILLEY** and Charles **TUPPER** eventually secured its adoption in New Brunswick and Nova Scotia. The final resolutions were agreed at the London Conference of 1866 and embodied in the **BRITISH NORTH AMERICA ACT** of 1867. ► DOMINION OF CANADA

## Confederation of the Rhine (1806–14)
A union of all the German states except **PRUSSIA** and Austria, established by **NAPOLEON I** on the dissolution of the **HOLY ROMAN EMPIRE** in 1806. The 18 states were placed under French control to assist the French war effort, although the long-term effect was to stimulate the movement for German unification. ► **NAPOLEONIC WARS**

## Confessing Church
A Church formed in Germany by Evangelical Christians opposed to Nazism and the Nazi-supported 'German Christian Church Movement'. Its Synod of Barmen published the *Barmen Declaration* (1934), which became influential in Germany and beyond as a basis for resistance to oppressive civil authorities. It was succeeded in 1948 by the 'Evangelical Church in Germany'. ► **NAZI PARTY**

## confino
The practice of internal exile or banishment to remote provinces and islands; it was used extensively against critics of **MUSSOLINI**'s government after Nov 1926.

## conflict diamonds, also known as blood diamonds
The term describes diamonds originating in parts of Africa controlled by forces in conflict with internationally recognized governments and used to fund military action against them. The sale of rough diamonds funded civil wars in **ANGOLA**, the Democratic Republic of **CONGO**, **LIBERIA** and **SIERRA LEONE** in which c.3.7 million lives were lost. Efforts to curb the trade resulted in 2000 in a process for tracking rough diamonds and the Kimberley Process Diamond Certification Scheme, launched in 2003, took this initiative further, introducing regulatory measures such as strict import/export control and tamper-proof certificates of origin. The Kimberley Process regulations are voluntary and need member governments to enact laws to implement certification. Major diamond-trading countries such as South Africa, Canada, Israel and the USA and non-governmental organizations such as **AMNESTY INTERNATIONAL** have called for regular and impartial monitoring to ensure that the system remains credible.

## Confucian Classics
A collection of texts thought to embody the ideas of the Chinese philosopher Confucius (551–479BC) on ethics, government and ritual. Composed principally during the Zhou Dynasty and Western ('Former') Han Dynasty, these works comprised the Five Classics (Classic of Changes, Book of History, Classic of Odes, Classic of Rites and the Spring and Autumn Annals) and the Four Books (Analects of Confucius, Mencius, Book of Great Learning and Doctrine of the Mean). The former were officially canonized during the Han Dynasty, while the latter were similarly exalted during the **SONG DYNASTY**. As the official canon, these works constituted the entire curriculum of civil service examinations from the 14c onwards. ► **CHINESE DYNASTIES PRE-1000**AD; **CIVIL SERVICE EXAMINATION SYSTEM**

---

**CONGO, DEMOCRATIC REPUBLIC OF THE** formerly (1971–97) **Republic of Zaire**, and (1960–71) **Democratic Republic of the Congo**, and (1908–60) **Belgian Congo**, and (1885–1908) **Congo Free State**
A central African republic, bounded to the west by the Congo, the Angolan province of Cabinda and the Atlantic Ocean; to the south-west by Angola; to the south-east by Zambia; to the east by Tanzania, Burundi, Rwanda and Uganda; to the north-east by Sudan; and to the north and north-west by the Central African Republic. The Bantu had settled most of the country by 1000AD, and the first Europeans to visit were the Portuguese, in 1482. There were expeditions by Henry Morton **STANLEY** in 1874–7, and the country was claimed by King **LEOPOLD II** of Belgium and recognized in 1895 at the Congress of **BERLIN** as the Congo Free State. In 1908 it became a Belgian colony

and was renamed the Belgian Congo. On gaining independence in 1960 it was renamed the Democratic Republic of the Congo, and the mineral-rich **KATANGA** (later, Shaba) province claimed independence; this resulted in civil war which destroyed the new government of Patrice **LUMUMBA**. A **UN** peacekeeping force entered the country and remained until 1964. The following year President **MOBUTU SESE SEKO** seized power in a coup backed by the **CIA**. He renamed the country Zaire in 1971 and at first was credited with introducing a hitherto unknown degree of stability; however, his regime became increasingly corrupt and unpopular. Further conflict erupted in 1977–8, and there were power struggles in the early 1990s, with violent ethnic unrest in Shaba, Kivu and Kasai provinces in 1993. In addition, over 1 million refugees from the civil war in Rwanda entered Zaire in 1994. In 1996 Zaire was invaded by a rebel army led by Laurent **KABILA**, an ethnic Tutsi, who the following year succeeded in overthrowing the government and forcing Mobutu into exile. Kabila was installed as head of state but civil war with extensive foreign intervention continued, although with less intensity after a ceasefire in 1999. Kabila was assassinated in 2001 and succeeded as President by his son, Joseph. An interim government of national unity was formed in 2002 and in 2003 a new constitution provided for elections in 2005. Although most of the foreign troops involved in the civil war left the country, UN peacekeeping troops remained because of continuing clashes between rival militias.

---

**CONGO** official name **Republic of the Congo**, formerly **People's Republic of the Congo**
A west central African republic, bounded to the west by Gabon; to the north-west by Cameroon; to the north by the Central African Republic; to the east and south by the Democratic Republic of the Congo; and to the south-west by the Angolan province of Cabinda and the Atlantic Ocean. It was discovered by the Portuguese in the 14c. The French established a colonial presence there in the 19c, and from 1908 to 1958 it was part of French Equatorial Africa, known as the 'Middle Congo'. It gained independence as the Republic of Congo in 1960, and in 1968 a military coup created the first Marxist state in Africa, renaming the country the People's Republic of the Congo. **MARXISM** was renounced in 1990 and opposition parties were permitted. Elections took place in 1993 but the results were disputed and fighting between ethnic and political groups broke out. In 1997 Presi-

dent Pascal Lissouba was ousted by a military coup and replaced by former military leader and head of state (1979–92) Denis **SASSOU-NGUESSO**. Despite peace talks and settlements in 1999 and 2001, political and civil unrest continued, intensifying in 2002 after the disputed presidential election won by Sassou-Nguesso. A peace deal between the government and rebels was signed in 2003.

**Congress** (USA)
The national, or federal, legislature of the USA, consisting of two elected chambers: the **SENATE** and the **HOUSE OF REPRESENTATIVES**. The Senate contains two members from each state (irrespective of size), serving six-year terms, with a third of the terms expiring every two years. Representation in the House is for a two-year term, and is calculated on the basis of population. Congress initiates legislation, and significantly amends or rejects presidential legislative proposals. The **US CONSTITUTION** endows it with the 'power of the purse', and all revenue bills must originate in the House. For a bill to become law it must be passed in identical form by both chambers and signed by the President. A presidential veto may be overturned by a two-thirds majority in each chamber. Legislation receives detailed consideration in the powerful Congressional committees. Although the chambers are organized along party lines, party discipline is weak. The majority party leader of the House occupies the influential position of Speaker.

**Congress (I) Party** ► INDIAN NATIONAL CONGRESS

**Congress Kingdom of Poland** ► POLAND

**Congress of Racial Equality (CORE)**
US **CIVIL RIGHTS** organization founded in 1942. In the 1960s CORE sponsored sit-in demonstrations, the **FREEDOM RIDERS**' challenge to segregation on interstate public buses, and registration of black voters in the South.

**Congress Party** (India) ► INDIAN NATIONAL CONGRESS

**Conkling, Roscoe** (1829–88)
US politician. He served as a Republican for New York in the **HOUSE OF REPRESENTATIVES** (1859–63, 1865–7) and in the **SENATE** (1867–81). A loyal machine politician and an advocate of punitive measures against the South during **RECONSTRUCTION**, he contended unsuccessfully for the Republican presidential nomination in 1876. In 1880, supporting Ulysses S **GRANT** and opposing James **BLAINE**, he split the **REPUBLICAN PARTY**.

## Connubio

The Italian word (literally, 'marriage') used to describe the parliamentary alliance established by **CAVOUR** with **RATTAZZI** in 1852, ushering in a period of anticlerical legislation and paving the way for Cavour to become Prime Minister of Sardinia-Piedmont. The alliance lasted until the sweeping electoral gains of the clericals in 1857, when Cavour promptly adopted a more conservative stance.

## conquistador

Literally 'conqueror', this is the standard term for the leaders of the Spanish expeditions of the early 16c which undertook the invasion and conquest of America. The ethos of conquest pervaded Castilian society and was inherited from the long successful struggle against the Moors, permanent settlement, formal rule, a change of religion, and the division of lands among successful *conquistadores*. The expectation that conquistadores would receive labouring peoples in **ENCOMIENDA** preceded the discovery of the Americas and led to friction between the Crown, conquistadores and the Church during the early 16c.
► **CORTÉS, HERNÁN**

## Conrad II (c.990–1039)

German King (1024/39). The son of the Count of Speyer, he was crowned King in Mainz in 1024 and, after overcoming Lotharingian opposition, was crowned Emperor of the West in 1027. He restored German ascendancy over the Poles and Bohemians, and succeeded in 1032 to the Kingdom of Burgundy, but was unable to subdue rebellion in Italy in 1036–8. In 1035 he regulated the conditions of his unfree palace officials, laying the basis for the important role these **MINISTERIALES** were to play in his successors' administrations.

## Conrad III (1093–1152)

The first Hohenstaufen King of the Germans (1138/52). The son of Frederick of Swabia, he unsuccessfully contested the crown of Italy with Lothair of Saxony, and became King on his death. He was immediately involved in a quarrel with Henry the Proud, head of the **GUELFS** in Germany, the struggle being continued under Henry's son. When St **BERNARD OF CLAIRVAUX** preached a new crusade, Conrad set out for Palestine with a large army (1147). ► **CRUSADE, SECOND**; **HOHENSTAUFEN DYNASTY**

## Conrad IV (1228–54)

King of Germany and Jerusalem. The son of Emperor **FREDERICK II** and the heiress of the Kingdom of Jerusalem, Isabella of Brienne, he became Duke of Swabia in 1235 and was elected King in 1237. He ruled under the tutelage of Siegfried of Mainz (until 1241) and **HENRY RASPE** of Thuringia (until 1246). His rule in Germany was secured on the support of Swabian **MINISTERIALES** and towns. In 1251 he began the fight for his Sicilian inheritance. He landed in Apulia in 1252 and took over the government of the Norman kingdom from his half brother, Manfred, but Pope **INNOCENT III** refused to recognize his claim and excommunicated him. He died of malaria in Apulia and was succeeded by his infant son, **CONRADIN**.

## Conradin of Swabia (1252–68)

King of Jerusalem and Sicily and the last Hohenstaufen. The son of **CONRAD IV**, he was formally recognized as Duke of Swabia in 1254. His uncle, **MANFRED**, had assumed the crown of Sicily on a rumour of Conradin's death, and Pope **URBAN IV**'s hatred of the **HOHENSTAUFEN DYNASTY** led him to offer the crown of the **TWO SICILIES** to **CHARLES OF ANJOU**, who invaded Italy and slew Manfred at **BENEVENTO** (1266). Conradin, invited by the Neapolitans to assert his rights, appeared in Italy with 10,000 men, but was defeated near Tagliacozzo, taken prisoner, and executed.

## Conrad of Montferrat (d.1192)

Italian Crusader. He distinguished himself during the defence of Tyre against **SALADIN** (1187) and in 1192 he was elected King of Jerusalem as consort of the heiress Isabella, daughter of Amalric I. He was, however, murdered by the **ASSASSINS** before he could be crowned.

## Consalvi, Ercole (1757–1824)

Italian statesman and prelate. Made a cardinal and Secretary of State by **PIUS VII** (1800), he was an extremely able diplomat and administrator. In 1801 he concluded the Papal **CONCORDAT** with **NAPOLEON I**, and, at the Congress of **VIENNA** (1814–15), managed to block **METTERNICH**'s schemes to establish an Italian Confederation under Austrian presidency along the same lines as that of Germany. In domestic affairs, he was a reformer but found his policies constantly opposed by reactionary cardinals (who were known as **ZELANTI**).

## conscription

The practice of compelling young men of eligible age and fitness to serve by statute in the armed forces of a nation. To meet the huge manpower needs of **WORLD WAR I**, conscription was introduced in Great Britain in early 1916. Conscription was again in force in Britain from 1939 to 1945, continuing in peacetime as National Service, which was finally abolished in 1962. ► **DRAFT**

## Consejo Real

First created as an advisory body in 1385, as the royal council of **CASTILE** its powers and functions were specified clearly in a law of 1406 and its structure reformed in 1459, when it was laid down that eight of its twelve members must be university-trained lawyers (*letrados*). The council was further reformed in 1480, and by 1493 all its members were required to be *letrados*. The body, the supreme court of the realm, was later also known as the Council of Castile.

## Conservative Party (Sweden) ► **MODERATE UNITY PARTY**

## Conservative Party (UK)

One of the two major political parties in the UK, its full name being the Conservative and Unionist Party. It developed from the Tory Party during the 19c and pursued policies, first under **PEEL** and then **DISRAELI**, designed to broaden its appeal beyond the English landowners and supporters of the Church of England. It largely succeeded in this, having been in power either solely or as the dominant element in coalitions for approximately two-thirds of the period from Disraeli's election victory of 1874 to the end of the 20c. Its main support, however, remained English rather than British, and was generally stronger in rural than in urban areas. After 18 unbroken years in power (1979–97), it suffered a crushing defeat in the 1997 election and returned no MPs at all from either Scotland or Wales. It has since struggled to find a leader or policies that appeal to the party faithful or the wider electorate, and its position as the main parliamentary opposition party has been eroded somewhat by the Liberal Democrats. **► TORIES; WHIGS**

### Conservative Party of South Africa

A South African party formed in 1982 by reactionary (*verkrampte*) members of the **NATIONAL PARTY** who had been expelled from Parliament. It was led by Andries **TREURNICHT** and, after the 1987 general election, became the chief opposition party in the white parliament and opposed the liberalization measures of President **DE KLERK**. Once the **ANC** had been legalized in 1990, it became much less prominent in South African politics, hardly featuring at all in the results of the first multiracial elections of 1994, and by the end of the decade was effectively defunct.

### Constant (de Rebeque), (Henri) Benjamin (1767–1830)

French novelist and politician. Educated at Oxford, Erlangen, and Edinburgh, he settled in Paris (1795). As a journalist, he supported the Revolution, but was banished in 1802 for his opposition to **NAPOLEON I**. He returned in 1814, and became leader of the liberal opposition. His best-known work is the novel *Adolphe* (1816), based on his relationship with Madame de Staël. **► FRENCH REVOLUTION**

### Constantine I (1868–1923)

King of Greece (1913/17 and 1920/2). He was the son and successor of **GEORGE I**. As a military commander he was unsuccessful in the Turkish War of 1897, but led the Greeks to victory in the **BALKAN WARS** (1912–13). As the brother-in-law of Kaiser **WILLIAM II** of Germany, he insisted on Greek neutrality in **WORLD WAR I**, but was forced to retire in favour of his son, Alexander, by the rival government of Eleuthérios **VENIZÉLOS** and the Allies in 1917. In 1920 he was restored to the throne by plebiscite, but after a military revolt in 1922, abdicated again in favour of his son, **GEORGE II**.

### Constantine II (1940– )

King of Greece (1964/73). The son and successor of **PAUL I** of Greece, soon after his accession he married Princess Anne-Marie, younger daughter of **FREDERICK IX** of Denmark and sister of Queen **MARGRETHE** of Denmark. In Apr 1967 the 'Colonels' seized power in a military coup; Constantine made an abortive attempt to regain power, then fled into exile in Rome (Dec 1967). He was formally deposed in June 1973, and the monarchy was abolished by national referendum in 1974. His heir is Crown Prince Paul (1967– ). **► GREEK COLONELS**

### Constantine XI Palaeologus Dragases (1404–53)

The last Byzantine Emperor (1448/53). He was the fourth son of Manuel II and the Serbian princess Helen Dragaš. During the reign of his elder brother John VIII, he and his other brothers jointly ruled the despotate of Morea, a Byzantine apanage in the Peloponnese; on John's death (1448), Constantine succeeded to an empire consisting of little more than Constantinople and its environs, threatened by the

vast **OTTOMAN EMPIRE** which surrounded it. His proclamation of the union of the Greek Church with Rome (1452) secured only limited military assistance from the West and was repudiated by his indignant subjects. Powerless to prevent the inevitable Ottoman siege, Constantine died fighting in the final Turkish assault. **► BYZANTINE EMPIRE**

### Constantine Nikolaevich (1827–92)

Russian naval commander. A grand duke, he was the second son of Tsar **NICHOLAS I**. In the **CRIMEAN WAR** he commanded the Russian fleet, and held the British and French in check before Kronstadt. He played an important role in preparing and implementing the social and political reforms of Tsar **ALEXANDER II** after the war.

### Constantinople, Capture of (29 May 1453)

Constantinople eventually fell to the Ottoman Turks under **MEHMED II, THE CONQUEROR**. Mehmed had been provoked by the Byzantine Emperor Constantine XI, who had proposed setting up a pretender against Mehmed if the latter refused to double the financial contribution he made to Constantine for his (Constantine's) custodianship of the very prince Constantine was proposing as would-be pretender. Mehmed responded by building Rumeli Hisar, a fortress on the Constantinople side of the Bosphorus, and when envoys were sent in protest by Constantine, Mehmed had them beheaded. This was the signal for open hostilities to begin. The siege took some two months, with the Byzantines, aided only by a Genoese colony on Chios, hopelessly inadequately provided with manpower for the defence of their city. After a two-month siege, Constantinople was taken by a general frontal assault and the Emperor was killed in the mêlée.

### Constantinople, Latin Empire of

A 13c empire based at Constantinople (ancient Byzantium, modern Istanbul), the capital of the medieval (Eastern) Roman or **BYZANTINE EMPIRE**. The army of the Fourth **CRUSADE** took Constantinople (1204) and created a Latin Empire, with **BALDWIN I**, Count of Flanders as the first emperor. It succumbed in 1261 to the army of **MICHAEL VIII PALAEOLOGUS**, after a precarious existence.

### Constantinople, Latin Occupation of (1204–61)

The Fourth **CRUSADE**, originally destined for Egypt, with the Venetians supplying the ships, was tragically diverted at Venetian behest to Constantinople, because, as a result of failure to meet the cost of the ships, the Crusaders found themselves beholden to Venice virtually to the extent of being in Venetian service. It was this diversion that led to the Latins' taking Constantinople in 1204 and to the subsequent Latin occupation. Control of events appears to have been securely in the hands of Enrico **DANDOLO**, the ageing Doge of Venice, and it was he who contrived the election of Count Baldwin of Flanders as the first Latin Emperor, **BALDWIN I**. The division of imperial territory that followed was complex, but it was certainly the Venetians who gained the most. The Latin Occupation was heartily detested by the Byzantines themselves who, quite apart from their religious differences with the papacy, found the overweening arrogance of the Latins hard to stomach. It was eventually the statesmanship of **MICHAEL VIII PALAEO-LOGUS** which led to what might be seen, given the antipathy of the Byzantines towards the Latins and the constant factional differences among the Latins themselves, as the not wholly unexpected demise of the Latin 'Empire' and the restoration of the **BYZANTINE EMPIRE** as such.

## Constantinople, Patriarchate of

The highest ecclesiastical office in the Orthodox Church. Under the **OTTOMAN EMPIRE**, the ecumenical patriarch had jurisdiction over the members of the Orthodox **MILLET** and represented its interests to the Ottoman Porte. Control of the patriarchate long lay in the hands of the Greeks, who used it to dominate the cultural and religious life of the Balkans, securing the abolition of the Serb patriarchate at Peć (1766) and the Bulgarian patriarchate at Ohrid (1767). In the 19c, Bulgarian, Serb and Romanian nationalists sought to free themselves from the Greeks no less than the Turks. ► **BULGARIAN EXARCHATE**

## Constantinople, Siege of (1391–8)

In 1391 the Ottomans had conquered most of the Balkans, and from 1391 until 1398, Constantinople was in an almost continuous state of siege from the land and blockade from the sea. The only reason for its survival was the strength of its defences, which depended largely on the sea- and land-walls of the city. At this time Imperial City and Empire were almost coterminous (the principality in the Morea still held out) and, in some ways, this siege was not so much an attempt by the Ottomans to take the city, as the surrounding of Constantinople by Turks on all sides. There was little or no prospect of relief, as the Turks had reduced the surrounding area and there was nowhere whence that relief could come. This left **MANUEL II PALAEOLOGUS** (1391/1425) able to do little more than appeal for aid to Russia and the West.

## Constantinople, Siege of (1422)

A degree of relief having been afforded the beleaguered Byzantines by the devastating activities of **TIMUR**, it was not long before the Ottomans (who had lost Asia Minor after the Battle of **ANKARA** in 1402) re-established their ascendancy, having survived as a result of their foothold in the Balkans. Sultan **MURAD II** (1421/51) presided over a renewal of Ottoman aggression, and initiated (22 June) a purposeful siege of Constantinople. The strength of the Byzantine defences was again too much for the besieging Ottomans, but Murad was only deflected from his intent by having to deal with the threat to his throne posed by his younger brother Mustafa.

## Constantinople, Treaty of (1700)

The treaty ending the Russo-Turkish War that included Austria on the anti-Turkish side when it broke out in 1697. Austria made peace at **KARLOWITZ** in 1699, but **PETER I, THE GREAT** struggled on to strengthen his hold on the Black Sea. He acquired the fortress of Azov, was excused the tribute hitherto paid to the Crimean Tatars, and won the right to diplomatic representation at Constantinople. Russia now had a springboard for further encroachment on the **OTTOMAN EMPIRE**.

## Constantinople Agreements (Mar–Apr 1915)

Britain and France feared that Russia would make a separate peace with Germany unless she was offered significant territorial gains. They secretly agreed, therefore, that after **WORLD WAR I** Russia should receive Constantinople (Istanbul) and land along the Straits. This was a remarkable change in British policy particularly, as throughout the 19c Britain had opposed Russia gaining control of the Straits. After the **OCTOBER REVOLUTION**, however, the **BOLSHEVIKS** rejected all agreements made by the Tsarist government.

## Constitution Act of 1982

The statute which 'patriated' the constitution of Canada, adding a Charter of Rights and Freedoms, and a general amendment procedure. It was the result of 18 months of hectic negotiation following the 1980 Quebec referendum on independence, during which the federal government had promised a national settlement of constitutional issues. Through the summer of 1980 a series of very public discussions explored the items of a prepared agenda for a First Ministers' conference in Sep. After this broke down in acrimony, the federal government announced a unilateral approach to the British parliament, a resolution whose validity was finally accepted by the Supreme Court in Sep 1981 as allowable though objectionable. 'Constitutional convention plus constitutional law equal the total constitution of the country,' it said in a judgement that was used to support the arguments of both sides. At a final conference in Nov 1981, the so-called Kitchen Meeting paved the way for compromise, which, however, was rejected by Quebec. ► **MEECH LAKE ACCORD**

## Constitutional Convention (1787)

A gathering at Philadelphia that drafted the **US CONSTITUTION**; 12 of the original 13 states were represented (Rhode Island did not send a delegate). The term, by extension, is also used for any political meeting empowered to write a state or national constitution.

## consulado

The Spanish term used to describe the merchant guild (to which most traders belonged) established in the viceregal capitals of Mexico City (1592) and Lima (1613). Each *consulado* had the right to regulate its own custom and practice and adjudicate disputes among its members. The administrative reorganization under **CHARLES III** saw the establishment of *consulados* in Caracas, Guatemala, Buenos Aires, Havana, Cartagena, Santiago, Guadalajara and Veracruz. By the 1780s, dynasties of merchants stood at the apex of colonial society, passing the export-import business from generation to generation by the marriage of daughters to Spanish-born nephews (often from the same small towns of the peninsula), and of sons to the families of local worthies. By loans to local government and the Church, they sustained the privileges of the consulado. ► **CABILDO**

## Consulate (France) (1799–1804)

The system of government established by the constitution of the year VIII (1799). Power was placed theoretically in the hands of three consuls, but in reality was from the first monopolized by **NAPOLEON I**, who abolished the Consulate in 1804 to proclaim himself Emperor.

## Contadora Group

An alliance of Colombia, Mexico, Panama and Venezuela, whose foreign ministers met in 1983 on the Isla Contadora in the Gulf of Panama to discuss the problems of Central America. Their proposed solutions became known as the Contadora Process, and included a Central American parliament and measures to promote peace, prosperity and democratization to the region. The process failed due to lack of backing.

## containment

The action of preventing the expansion of a hostile power. It usually refers to a US policy of the 1940s and 1950s, advocated by US diplomat George F **KEN-NAN**, which aimed to prevent Soviet expansionism following **WORLD WAR II** by the formation of a circle of military pacts around the Soviet Union. President **TRUMAN** supported the policy by helping to establish **NATO** in 1949. By the 1950s the policy had been extended to include the defence of Asia against communist aggression by means of the **SOUTH-EAST ASIA TREATY ORGANIZATION**, and in the 1960s the US attempt to prevent Soviet participation in South American and African politics led to the **CUBAN MISSILE CRISIS**.

## Conté, Lansana (c.1934–)

Guinean soldier and politician. Military commander of the Boke Region, he led a bloodless coup on the death of Sékou **TOURÉ** (Mar 1984) and set up the Military Committee for National Recovery with himself as President. He relaxed the centralizing policies of Touré, continuing free-market reforms and the process of reintegrating into the Western world, and successfully encouraged many exiles to return. He has retained the presidency, largely unopposed, in subsequent elections, and survived attempted coups in 1985 and 1996.

## Continental Congress (1774–89)

In North America, the federal legislature consisting of delegates from each of the 13 colonies (the United States after 1776). The First Continental Congress met from 5 Sep to 26 Oct 1774, in response to Britain's passing the **INTOLERABLE ACTS**, and its delegates petitioned the King. When no appropriate response was received, the Second Continental Congress convened in May 1775, shortly after the Battles of **LEXINGTON AND CONCORD**, and created an army. Agreeing to seek independence in the summer of 1776, the Congress formally adopted the **DECLARATION OF INDEPENDENCE** on July 4. The Congress remained the political voice of the young country under the **ARTICLES OF CONFEDERATION** until the **US CONSTITUTION** took effect in 1789. ▶ **AMERICAN REVOLUTION; NORTHWEST ORDINANCE OF 1787**

## Continuation War (1941–4)

Known also as the Soviet–Finnish War, Finland's attack on the USSR (June 1941) in partnership with Nazi Germany was intended to reverse the outcome of the **RUSSO-FINNISH WAR** of 1939–40. After initial success, the Finnish front was stabilized until the great Russian offensive of June 1944. However, the Finnish government had decided as early as Feb 1943 that it must seek peace. With the assistance of Swedish mediation, an armistice was signed (Sep 1944) and the war was formally ended by the Treaty of **PARIS** (Feb 1947). ▶ **TANNER, VÄINÖ; WORLD WAR II**

## Contra-Remonstrants ▶ COUNTER-REMONSTRANTS

## Contras

A rebel right-wing, anti-government group in Nicaragua, consisting of the former supporters of the **SOMOZA** government and originally organized by landowners whose property had been expropriated by the **SANDINISTA NATIONAL LIBERATION FRONT**. The Contras carried out guerrilla activities against the military junta of Daniel **ORTEGA** from 1979, and during the 1980s were based in Honduras and backed by the USA (until President George H W **BUSH** came to power in 1989). The Contra war officially ended when ceasefires and disarmament were agreed in 1990, but unrest continued despite another ceasefire in 1994. ▶ **IRAN–CONTRA AFFAIR; NICARAGUAN REVOLUTION**

## Contreras, Battle of (1847)

An engagement in the **MEXICAN WAR** (1846–8) in which the Mexican army under **SANTA ANNA** was badly defeated by a smaller US force under Winfield **SCOTT**, opening the way to Mexico City and leading to the collapse of Mexican resistance.

## Convention, National (France) (1792–5)

The assembly that ruled France from 1792 to 1795. It originated with the insurrection of 10 Aug 1792, which overthrew the **LEGISLATIVE ASSEMBLY** elected in 1791 and called for new elections on a completely democratic franchise. In practice, however, very few dared to vote. The Convention proclaimed the First Republic, tried and executed King **LOUIS XVI** and allowed itself to be terrorized into authorizing the most extreme measures of the **FRENCH REVOLUTION** (1793–4) under **ROBESPIERRE** and the Committee of **PUBLIC SAFETY**. With the downfall of Robespierre at **THERMIDOR** (July 1794), the Convention recovered its authority, recalled the surviving **GIRONDINS**, established a new constitution, the **DIRECTORY** (1795), and dissolved itself. ▶ **REPUBLIC, FIRST** (France)

## Convention People's Party (CPP)

Formed in 1949 by Kwame **NKRUMAH** as a breakaway from the **UNITED GOLD COAST CONVENTION** (UGCC), the CPP appealed to a mass, especially urban, following and was instrumental in propelling Ghana to independence in 1957 and Nkrumah to the premiership. It became the only legal party in 1964 (with the slogan 'the CPP is Ghana and Ghana the CPP') and lost popular support quickly, putting up no defence for Nkrumah when he was ousted in a coup in 1966. Nevertheless, later parties were built upon CPP foundations.

## Conversos

In medieval Spain, the name given to those who had converted to Christianity from the Jewish faith; the term also applied to their descendants. Known also as New Christians to distinguish them from Old or non-Semitic Christians, they were in popular parlance vilified as **MARRANOS** (or 'pigs'). They made a major impact on public life from 1392, when anti-Jewish riots in the major Spanish towns forced most Jews to convert to Christianity. As Christians, they had right of access to public office: by the late 15c they were an influential force in many towns and could be found in the episcopate and in the royal councils. Many were suspected of still following Jewish religious practices, which helped to bring about the establishment of the Spanish INQUISITION in 1478 and the Expulsion of the JEWS in 1492. From 1480, when it commenced operations, to the 1520s, the Inquisition in Spain executed thousands of *Conversos* accused of secret judaizing. By the early 16c, judaizers were becoming a rarity and Conversos were more readily absorbed into Spanish life. Conversos made a notable contribution to cultural life through such figures as St Teresa of Ávila and the poet Luis de León.

## Cook, James (1728–79)

English navigator. He was born in Marton, Yorkshire, the son of an agricultural labourer. He joined the navy in 1755 and became master in 1759. He surveyed the area around the St Lawrence River, Quebec, and the shores of Newfoundland, then commanded the *Endeavour* for the Royal Society expedition to the Pacific to observe the transit of Venus across the Sun (1768–71). On the return, he circumnavigated New Zealand and charted the east coast of Australia. In his second voyage he sailed round Antarctica in the *Resolution* and *Adventure* (1772–5), and discovered several Pacific island groups. His third voyage (1776–9) aimed to discover a passage round the north coast of America from the Pacific, but he was forced to turn back, and on his return was killed by natives on Hawaii. He ranks with COLUMBUS as one of the two greatest European seaman-explorers of the age of sail. ► EXPLORATION

## Cook, Sir Joseph (1860–1947)

British-born Australian politician. A miner, he emigrated to Australia in 1885 and was elected to the New South Wales Assembly in 1891 as a Labor member. He left the AUSTRALIAN LABOR PARTY (1894) and joined G H REID's Liberal ministry. He entered federal politics in 1901, supporting Reid's opposition free-trade group, of which he became Deputy Leader in 1905 and Leader in 1908. By now anti-socialist, he formed a coalition government with DEAKIN in 1909, serving as Minister of Defence. He was Prime Minister (1913–14), Deputy Prime Minister in HUGHES's Nationalist government (1917), Treasurer (1920–1) and Australian High Commissioner in London (1921–7).

## Coolidge, (John) Calvin (1872–1933)

US politician and 30th President. He became a lawyer, and was Governor of Massachusetts (1919–20) when he gained national attention for his firm handling of the Boston police strike. Elected Vice-President (1921–3), on Warren G HARDING's death he became President (1923). A strong supporter of US business interests, he was triumphantly re-elected in 1924, but refused renomination in 1928. Coolidge's policies were successful while he was in office, but were partly responsible for the GREAT DEPRESSION that followed.

## Cooperative Party (UK)

A British political party which grew out of the ideas of voluntary mutual economic assistance developed in the 19c by Robert OWEN. Established in 1917, one

candidate, who joined with the parliamentary LABOUR PARTY, was elected to the House of COMMONS in 1918. Thereafter it became closely integrated with the Labour Party.

## Coornhert, Dirck Volkertzoon (1522–90)

Dutch politician, theologian, writer, poet and philosopher. One of the most important thinkers of the 16c, he was outspoken in his criticism of others and so spent most of his mature life being pursued around the Low Countries by his enemies. He became Town Clerk of Haarlem in 1562; after imprisonment in 1567 he fled to Germany where he worked for WILLIAM I, THE SILENT against Spanish rule. In 1572 he returned to Haarlem and became Secretary to the States of Holland, but regularly was obliged to flee to escape persecution. His 145 surviving publications show he was a champion of toleration and a sworn enemy of prejudice; these views brought him into conflict with both Calvinists and Catholics.

## Coote, Sir Eyre (1726–83)

Anglo-Irish soldier. He entered the British Army early and saw service in Scotland, and from 1756 to 1762 served in India. He induced Robert CLIVE to risk the Battle of PLASSEY (1757), and in 1760 he defeated Thomas, Comte de Lally (1702–66), at Wandiwash. His capture of Pondicherry in 1761 completed the downfall of the French in India. In 1777 he became Commander-in-Chief in India, and in 1781 his rout of HAIDAR ALI at Porto Novo saved the presidency again.

## Copenhagen, Battles of (1801 and 1807)

British naval operations aimed at preventing Danish neutrality from benefiting France during the NAPOLEONIC WARS. The first engagement (Apr 1801), led by Admirals Hyde Parker (1739–1807) and NELSON, resulted in Denmark's withdrawal from the Armed Neutrality. After the bombardment of Copenhagen (Sep 1807) by Admiral James Gambier (1756–1833) and Arthur Wellesley (later Duke of WELLINGTON), the Danes surrendered their fleet and stores.

## Corday (d'Armont), (Marie) Charlotte (1768–93)

French noblewoman. She sympathized with the aims of the FRENCH REVOLUTION but was horrified by the acts of the JACOBINS. Having managed to obtain an audience with the revolutionary leader Jean Paul MARAT, she stabbed him to death while he was in his bath. She was guillotined four days later.

## Cordeliers' Club

An extreme revolutionary club founded in Paris (1790) by DANTON and MARAT; also called the Society of the Friends of the Rights of Man and Citizen. Under HÉBERT's leadership its programme became increasingly radical (1792–4), contributing to the downfall of the GIRONDINS (1793). ► FRENCH REVOLUTION

## Cordobazo (May 1969)

The name given to a period of major unrest in Córdoba, Argentina, during which trade unionists and students briefly took control of the city in protest against the military dictatorship of Juan Carlos Onganía. The event indicated the potential for an alliance between left-wing PERONISM and student activists inspired by more traditional (ie European) left-wing ideologies. It also revealed the structural weaknesses of the military regime.

**Corfu, Declaration of** (20 July 1917)
During **WORLD WAR I**, in anticipation of the break-up of the Austro-Hungarian monarchy, the government of Serbia (then in exile on the island of Corfu), together with the **YUGOSLAV COMMITTEE**, agreed to work together to create a South Slav or Yugoslav state. This was to be a 'constitutional, democratic and parliamentary monarchy' under the Serbian Karageorgević Dynasty. The declaration, although it had no legal force, marked an important stage in the creation of the Kingdom of Serbs, Croats and Slovenes (later Yugoslavia).

**Corfu Incident** (Aug 1923)
When an Italian general and four members of his staff were shot while on a mission determining the Greek–Albanian frontier, **MUSSOLINI** saw it as an insult to national pride and an opportunity to test Italian strength. The Greek island of Corfu was bombarded and occupied. A Greek appeal to the **LEAGUE OF NATIONS** was successful in getting the Italians to evacuate the island, but the Greeks were also ordered to pay Italy a large indemnity. After the Corfu incident, Mussolini adopted a more conciliatory position in international relations for a number of years.

**Corn Laws**
British legislation regulating the trade in corn. This was common in the 18c, but the most famous Corn Law was that enacted by Lord **LIVERPOOL**'s government in 1815. Passed at a time when market prices were dropping rapidly, it imposed prohibitively high duties on the import of foreign corn when the domestic price was lower than 80 shillings (£4) a quarter. Widely criticized by radical politicians as legislation designed to protect the landed interest at the expense of the ordinary consumer, the Corn Law was amended in 1828, with the introduction of a sliding scale, and duties were further reduced by **PEEL** in 1842. The Laws were repealed in 1846. ► **ANTI-CORN LAW LEAGUE**

**Cornwallis, Charles Cornwallis, 1st Marquis** (1738–1805)
British general and politician. He served in the **AMERICAN REVOLUTION**, although he was personally opposed to taxing the American colonists, accepting a command in the war. He defeated Gates at the Battle of **CAMDEN** (1780), but was forced to surrender at Yorktown (1781). In 1786 he became Governor-General of India, where he defeated **TIPPOO SAHIB** of Mysore, and introduced the series of reforms known as the Cornwallis Code. He returned in 1793, to be made marquis. He was Lord-Lieutenant of Ireland (1798–1801), and negotiated the Peace of Amiens (1802). Reappointed Governor-General of India (1804), he died at Ghazipur.

**coronelismo**
The Spanish term denoting the unfettered rule of a proprietor (frequently a trader) over a community, which was a natural result of the settlement of the vast interior of Brazil. Such men were often heads of extended families (*parentelas*) and were frequently nominated to public office, especially the National Guard, in recognition of their rule. Their position was vastly strengthened under **CAMPOS SALLES**, who encouraged the creation of one-party government in the states. Though many never held formal office in the Guard, the title *coronel* implied the ability to muster a substantial vote from local tenants and clients, and to produce *agregados* as personal militia in support of a state governor. The golden age of *coronelismo* ended with the **ESTADO NOVO** in 1937. ► **AGREGADO**; **PARENTELA**

**Corporation Act** (1661)
A British Act passed by the **CAVALIER PARLIAMENT** (1661–79) soon after the **RESTORATION** of **CHARLES II**. Office in municipal corporations was restricted to those who took the sacrament according to the usage of the Church of England. Part of the reassertion of Anglican supremacy represented by the **CLARENDON CODE**, the Act remained on the statute book until 1828.

**Corporations**
Fascist labour organizations in **MUSSOLINI**'s Italy. They were first established in 1926 to replace the old socialist-dominated unions and were to include both employers and employees. They were supposed to minimize industrial conflict and maximize efficiency. In practice, while not a disaster, the bargaining power of workers was greatly decreased, while grateful industrialists continued to do much as they pleased. In 1930 the National Council of Corporations was set up to act as a consultative body on the economy; in reality, its views were rarely canvassed and it was most important as a means of providing jobs for loyal party members.

**corregidor**
The Spanish term (literally, 'corrector') originally denoting Spanish government officials, first appointed by Alfonso XI of Castile in the 14c; the word was then applied to the short-term lieutenant-governors, nominated by viceroys, who headed the *cabildos* in all Spanish settlements, hearing appeal cases from the *alcaldes* (local magistrates). Often of **CREOLE** (American-born) origin, and sometimes known as *alcalde mayor*, in major cities such as Puebla in Mexico or Cuzco in Peru they were rarely strong enough to serve as a counterpoise to the **CABILDO**. The *corregidor de Indios* acted as the Viceroy's representative in Indian settlements or *corregimientos*, and was also known as alcalde mayor. He was responsible for the collection of taxes, organization of labour services and *repartimientos*; often closely linked to the **CONSULADO** traders, to whom he was generally indebted, the corregidor was supplanted by the *subdelegado* during the reign of **CHARLES III**.

**Corsica, Rebellions of**
In the 18c, Corsica was characterized by regular uprisings, first against Genoese rule (1729–68) and, after its acquisition by France, against its new French overlords. The main rebellions of the latter period were led by Pasquale de **PAOLI**, who ably resisted the French for over a year in 1768–9 and sought to turn the island into a British protectorate in 1793–5. Separatism was eventually crushed in the 1790s by the island's most famous son, Napoleon Bonaparte. ► **NAPOLEON I**

**Cortes**
The Spanish parliament. The late 12c Cortes of Leon is thought by many to have been the earliest of all

medieval parliaments, pre-dating the **MAGNA CARTA**. The Cortes exercised full democratic rights for the first time under the Second Republic of 1931–6. It continued to exist under the **FRANCO** regime of 1939–75, but only in a consultative capacity. In 1977 it was established as the lower chamber of a two-chamber parliament based on universal suffrage. With the Constitution of 1978 the Cortes's powers were extended. ► **REPUBLIC, SECOND** (Spain)

### Cortés, Hernán (1485–1547)

Spanish conqueror of Mexico. He studied at Salamanca, then accompanied Velázquez in his expedition to Cuba (1511). In 1519 he commanded an expedition against Mexico, fighting his first battle at Tabasco. He founded Veracruz, marched to Tlascala, and made allies of the natives. He then marched on the Aztec capital, capturing Emperor **MONTEZUMA II**, but the Mexicans rose and Cortés was forced to flee. He then launched a successful siege of the capital, which fell in 1521. He was formally appointed Governor and Captain-General of New Spain in 1522, but his authority was later superseded. He spent the years 1530–40 in Mexico, then returned to Spain. ► **EXPLORATION**

### Cortes of Cadiz (1810–13)

The first Spanish constituent legislature. During the War of Independence, the Cortes of Cadiz, initially called by the regency, staged an internal revolution by drawing up a liberal constitution. The Constitution of 1812 established a constitutional monarchy, embracing popular sovereignty, the division of powers, a unicameral Cortes, and the centralization of government. Although principally a liberal document, the Constitution did maintain Roman Catholicism as the state religion. The Cortes of Cadiz and the Constitution of 1812 became potent symbols of liberalism throughout southern Europe and Latin America. In Spain, the constitution was resurrected in 1820, 1837, 1854 and 1869.

### Cosgrave, William Thomas (1880–1965)

Irish politician. He joined the **SINN FÉIN** movement at an early age, and took part in the **EASTER RISING** (1916). He was elected a Sinn Féin MP (1918–22) and, after holding office as first President of the **IRISH FREE STATE** (1922–32), became Leader of the Opposition (1932–44). His son, Liam, was Leader of the **FINE GAEL** Party (1965–7) and Prime Minister (1973–7).

### Cossacks

Originally, members of semi-independent communities of fugitive peasants and military adventurers inhabiting the steppelands of South Russia and the Ukraine. Attempts to limit Cossack freedom led to several large-scale rebellions against the Russian government in the 17–18c. In the 18–19c Cossack horsemen were formed into military organizations (*hosts*), and earned a reputation for ferocious fighting.

### Costa, Afonso (1871–1937)

Portuguese politician. Born in the clerical Beira Baixa province, as Minister of Justice under the First Republic he led a vigorous anticlerical campaign culminating in the separation of Church and State in 1911. Between Jan 1913 and Feb 1914 Costa, a capable and energetic administrator, headed the most popular Portuguese Republican Party (PRP) government of the Republican era, being the only government to balance the budget. Costa's PRP was the vehicle of the urban lower middle classes, disenfranchising much of the working class by reducing the electorate by more than half to 400,000. The Costa government fell in 1914 partly through the internal divisions of the PRP and partly because it had alienated various interests, above all the army. Premier again (1916–17), Costa took Portugal into **WORLD WAR I** on the side of the Allies out of fear for its colonies in the post-war settlement. But the economic impact of the war and bad military losses paved the way for a coup (Dec 1917). Disenchantment with the Republic led Costa to go into exile in Paris in 1919. ► **REPUBLIC, FIRST** (Portugal)

### Costa, Joaquín (1846–1911)

Spanish reformer and historian. A prolific writer and campaigner, he was the most prominent member of the radical 'regenerationists'. This was a diffuse reform movement which emerged in late 19c Spain in reaction to the country's decline, a process that culminated in the loss of the final remnants of the Spanish empire in the 'Disaster of 1898'. A critic of the oligarchical **RESTORATION SYSTEM**, Costa constantly publicized the need for a development policy, drawing up detailed education, irrigation and agricultural plans for the modernization of Spain, while drawing on certain collective traditions. He co-founded the National League of Producers (1899), the National Union (1900), and in 1903 was elected as a deputy for the Republican Union. In his exasperation with the Restoration System, he advocated a 'revolution from above', endorsing the use of an 'iron surgeon' to carry out the necessary reforms. He failed, however, to articulate a coherent political doctrine. A unique publicist and reformer, Costa left a legacy of radical populism and corporatism, and all later regenerationists were to be in his debt.

### Costa, Manuel Pinto da (1937–)

São Tomé politician. In 1972 he founded the Movement for the Liberation of Sao Tomé and Príncipe (MLSTP) in Gabon, and in 1974, taking advantage of a military coup in Portugal, returned and persuaded the new government in Lisbon to recognize the MLSTP as the sole representative of the people and to grant independence a year later. He became President in 1975 and set his country on a politically non-aligned course. He was defeated in the 1991 presidential elections, the first after the restoration of multiparty politics.

### COSTA RICA   official name **Republic of Costa Rica**

The second smallest republic in Central America, bounded to the west by the Pacific Ocean; to the north by Nicaragua; to the east by the Caribbean; and to the south-east by Panama. Visited by **COLUMBUS** in 1502, it was named Costa Rica ('rich coast') in the belief that vast gold treasures existed. It gained independence from Spain in 1821, and was a member of the **CENTRAL AMERICAN FEDERATION** in 1824–39. During the 20c there was political unrest, with civil war in 1948, following which the army was disbanded. Under President **ARIAS SÁNCHEZ** (1986–90), attempts were made to formulate a peace plan for Central America, to end the civil wars in

neighbouring Nicaragua and in El Salvador, and the USA reduced its aid. During the 1990s there were outbreaks of industrial unrest and serious economic problems caused by falling prices for its main export commodities, but the latter have been largely overcome by diversification.

**CÔTE D'IVOIRE** official name **Republic of Côte d'Ivoire**, formerly known as (to 1986) **Ivory Coast**
A republic in West Africa, bounded to the south-west by Liberia; to the north-west by Guinea; to the north by Mali and Burkina Faso; to the east by Ghana; and to the south by the Gulf of Guinea. It was explored by the Portuguese in the 15c and came under French influence from 1842. Declared a French protectorate in 1889 and a French colony in 1893, it became a territory within French West Africa in 1904. It gained independence as a one-party republic in 1960, with Felix **HOUPHOUËT-BOIGNY** as President. He introduced a multiparty system for the first time in 1990, when the elections were won by his Democratic Party of the Côte d'Ivoire (PDCI). He was succeeded on his death in 1993 by Henri Konan-Bédié. The post-independence period of stability and religious and ethnic harmony ended in 1999 when Konan-Bédié was overthrown in a military coup. The disputed result of the 2000 presidential election led to fighting between different factions that lasted until 2003. **UN** peacekeepers were deployed but fighting broke out again when French peacekeeping forces retaliated against rebels following an attack on their troops.

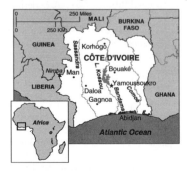

**Coty, René** (1882–1962)
French politician. A barrister, he was elected a Deputy in 1923, entered the Senate in 1935 and was Minister of Reconstruction in 1947. The last President of the French Fourth Republic (1953–9), after the constitutional crisis precipitated by the generals in Algeria (May 1958), he assisted the return to power of General de **GAULLE** and the consequent birth of the Fifth Republic (Jan 1959), with de Gaulle as his successor. ► **REPUBLIC, FIFTH** (France); **REPUBLIC, FOURTH** (France)

## Council of Europe
An association of European states, established in 1949. Its aim is to foster closer ties between member states in matters of economic, social, legal, scientific, educational and administrative affairs. It has a Committee of Ministers, comprising the member countries' foreign ministers, a representative Parliamentary Assembly, which meets in Strasbourg to discuss matters of common concern, and a European Court of Human Rights (a later addition). In 2004 it had 45 members.

## Counter-Reformation
A general movement of reform and missionary activity in the Roman Catholic Church from the mid-16c, stimulated in part by the Protestant **REFORMATION**. It included the revival of the monastic movement (eg Capuchins, 1528; Oratorians, 1575), especially the creation of the Jesuit Order. It provided for the enforcement of disciplinary measures by the Roman **INQUISITION**; its doctrinal formulations were made by the Council of **TRENT**; and liturgical and moral reforms were also introduced throughout the Church. There was a strong influence from mystics (eg John of the Cross, Teresa of Ávila) and devotional teachers (eg Francis of Sales). In a secular sense, the term also refers to the success of Roman Catholic powers in Europe in the late 16c and early 17c.

## Counter-Remonstrants
The name given to a party of orthodox Calvinist activists in the Dutch Republic in the early 17c. They opposed the **REMONSTRANTS** who had petitioned in 1610 for a more liberal Calvinist theology. The beliefs of the Counter-Remonstrants were enshrined in the canons of the Synod of **DORDRECHT**; they were also known as Gomarists, after their leader, Francis Gomarus.

## Coureurs du bois
The French-Canadian term for fur-traders who 'went Indian'. Indians began to realize that their identity was threatened through contact with settlements and trading posts. They also grew to understand that they were in a strong position to play off the French against English fur-traders from Albany. French-Canadian fur-traders therefore made annual trips into the hinterland or *pays d'en haut* to deal directly with the Indians, and frequently decided not to return to the settlements. ► **FUR TRADE**

## Court, Pieter de la (1618–85)
Dutch economist and publicist. Although trained as a lawyer, he worked as cloth manufacturer in Leiden before moving to Amsterdam in 1673. He published several important works, especially *Holland's Welfare* (1662), which were characterized by their support for political, religious, and especially economic liberty. He was a forerunner of Adam **SMITH**, and was closely linked with the party of Johan de **WITT**, leader of the merchant interest in the Dutch Republic, whose policies he articulated.

## Couthon, Georges (1756–94)
French revolutionary. A lawyer at the outbreak of the **FRENCH REVOLUTION**, he was elected to the National **CONVENTION**, where he demonstrated his hatred of the priesthood and the monarchy. In July 1793 he became a member of the Committee of **PUBLIC SAFETY**.

At Lyons he crushed the insurrection with merciless severity (1793), and helped to usher in the Reign of TERROR. ROBESPIERRE's fall brought down Couthon also; he was thrown into prison, freed by the mob with whom he was popular, recaptured by the soldiers of the Convention, and executed, with SAINT-JUST and Robespierre.

## Covenanters
Originally, signatories (and their successors) of the National Covenant (1638) and the SOLEMN LEAGUE AND COVENANT (1643) in Scotland, who resisted the theory of 'DIVINE RIGHT OF KINGS' and the imposition of an episcopal system on the Presbyterian Church of Scotland. When declared rebels, they resorted to open-air preaching. Until Presbyterianism was restored in 1690, they were savagely persecuted, with imprisonment, execution without trial, and banishment (eg to Holland or the USA).

## cowboys
Cattle herders in 19c USA who flourished on the trans-Mississippi plains during the 'open range' period of the cattle industry (c.1865–85). They were particularly important in the 'long drive' from Texas to the railheads in Missouri and Kansas. Cowboys included many Confederate veterans, as well as former slaves and Mexicans. Contrary to popular imagery, the cowboy's life was one of hard work and privation. In the popular mind the cowboy remains the embodiment of the American hero who stands for rugged self-sufficiency and frontier justice.

## Cowpens, Battle of (1781)
During the AMERICAN REVOLUTION, an engagement in South Carolina in which a small American army under Daniel Morgan (1736–1802) defeated a British force under Banastre Tarleton (1754–1833).

## Cox, Percy (1864–1937)
British diplomat. After receiving his military training, he served in India. During his time there, he left the army to work in the Indian political service in the Persian Gulf area; he was subsequently made Foreign Secretary in India but his major work was in Iraq, where he moved in 1914. He attended the CAIRO CONFERENCE of 1921 which resulted, on his returning to Iraq, in his supervision of the emergence by resolution of the Council of Ministers of the Amir Faysal, second son of Sharif HUSAYN IBN 'ALI of Mecca, as King of Iraq (as FAYSAL I), a resolution which was ratified by a referendum upon which Cox insisted. Given his military background, he was also tasked with supervising the creation of an army for the country, and with looking after its constitutional arrangements. His last act in Iraq was his signature on behalf of the British of a Protocol to the 1922 Anglo-Iraqi Treaty which, amongst other things, reduced the effective period of the Treaty to four years, a provision which was welcomed by the King and a majority of the politicians.

## Coxey's Army
A band of jobless men gathered together in 1894 by US businessman Jacob Sechler Coxey (1854–1951), who travelled from Ohio to Washington, DC in an attempt to highlight the need for government spending to relieve unemployment. Along the way the group increased in size from 100 to 500. Coxey hoped to persuade the government to embark on a new public works programme, but was arrested before he could finish his address on the Capitol steps (1894). Despite the publicity his 'army' received, the march had no apparent impact on government policy.

**CPP** ► CONVENTION PEOPLE'S PARTY

## Craig, James, 1st Viscount Craigavon (1871–1940)
Ulster politician. His early career was as a stockbroker. He was an MP in the UK parliament (1906–21), where he vigorously campaigned to preserve the Act of Union against the Irish nationalists. After Northern Ireland refused to join the South in 1921, he worked as its first Prime Minister (1921–40) to maintain order in the Province and then to develop social and educational services under powers devolved to STORMONT. His Unionist beliefs ensured that the interests of the Protestant majority in Northern Ireland would be paramount. He died suddenly while still in office. ► CARSON, EDWARD

## Craig, Sir James Henry (1748–1812)
British soldier and colonial administrator. He fought in the AMERICAN REVOLUTION, being wounded at the Battle of BUNKER HILL (1775) and serving with distinction in the invasion of the Hudson River Valley. After playing a prominent part in the capture of the Dutch colony of the Cape of Good Hope, he was made the colony's temporary governor from 1795 to 1797. After further commands in India, England and in the NAPOLEONIC WARS, he became Governor-General of Canada (1807–11). There, with the backing of London and the English-speaking Montreal merchants, he sought to Anglicize the province. To that end he dissolved the assembly and cashiered many French officers from the militia. In 1810 the printers and proprietor of the critical newspaper Le Canadien were arrested for treason and, when war broke out with the USA, he introduced a special Act which enabled him to suppress the newspaper altogether. This provoked both riots and the election of an increased number of radical French-Canadian deputies. The British government drew back from its policy and Craig was recalled. His name is still hated in the province, and the period of his governorship is known as the 'Reign of Terror'.

## Cranmer, Thomas (1489–1556)
Archbishop of Canterbury. His suggestion that HENRY VIII appeal for his divorce to the universities of Christendom won him the King's favour, and he was appointed a royal chaplain. He was made Archbishop of Canterbury in 1533, making allegiance to the pope 'for form's sake'. He later annulled Henry's marriages to CATHERINE OF ARAGON (1533) and to Anne BOLEYN (1536), and divorced him from ANNE OF CLEVES (1540). He was largely responsible for the Book of Common Prayer (1549 and 1552). On Henry's death, Cranmer rushed Protestant changes through. He had little to do with affairs of state, but agreed to the plan to divert the succession from Mary to Lady Jane GREY (1553), for which he was later arraigned for treason. Sentenced to death, he retracted the seven recantations he had been forced to sign, before being burnt alive. ► REFORMATION (England)

**Craxi, Bettino** (1934–2000)
Italian politician. After being active in the Socialist Youth Movement, he became a member of the Central Committee of the Italian Socialist Party (PSI) in 1957, a member of the National Executive (1965) and a Deputy Secretary (1970–6). In 1976 he became General-Secretary, and after the July 1983 election he became Italy's first socialist Prime Minister, successfully leading a broad-based coalition until 1987. He resigned his post as PSI General-Secretary in Feb 1993 following allegations of corruption, and chose self-imposed exile in Tunisia rather than face the charges brought against him.

**Crazy Horse**, Sioux name **Ta-Sunko-Witko** (c.1849–1877)
Oglala **SIOUX** chief, regarded as the foremost Sioux military leader. He defeated General **CUSTER** at the Battle of **LITTLE BIGHORN** (1876), leading a combined force of Sioux and **CHEYENNE**. He and his followers surrendered the following year, and he died in custody at Fort Robinson, Nebraska, stabbed in the back, according to a well-known Native American pictograph.

**Crécy, Battle of** (1346)
A battle between France and England in the **HUNDRED YEARS' WAR**. Using tactics perfected against the Scots, **EDWARD III** routed a larger French army, mainly cavalry, near Abbeville (Somme). It was a classic demonstration of the superiority over mounted knights of a coordinated force of dismounted men-at-arms, and archers providing offensive fire-power.

**Créditistes**
French-Canadian partner of the **SOCIAL CREDIT PARTY**. After a revival in their fortunes the party gained 26 seats in the 1962 federal elections but declined to 24 seats in 1963 when the Quebec representatives set up their own organization. Since then the party's popularity declined with the size of the rural population, and by 1980 it was eliminated.

**Crédit Mobilier Scandal** (1872)
A scandal involving a US finance company, the Crédit Mobilier Co, which was controlled by the Union Pacific Railroad Co, and to which fraudulent construction contracts were sold by Union Pacific for vast sums of money. The money included federal subsidies and land grants that were intended for the railway itself. **CONGRESS** ordered an investigation and found that 13 of its members were involved, two of whom were censured. Crédit Mobilier became a symbol of post-Civil War corruption and contributed to the worsening reputation of Ulysses S **GRANT**'s administration.

**Cree**
An Algonquian-speaking Native American group from the Canadian subarctic region, originally hunters and fishermen. With guns acquired from French fur-traders in the 17c, they began to expand and are now the largest and most widespread of their language group. In the mid-19c they split: one group, the Plains Cree, moved west, and became bison hunters, while the Woodland Cree remained in forested areas and continued to hunt there. Their population is currently c.8,000. ► **NATIVE AMERICANS**

**Creek**
Native North Americans originally organized in a confederacy living in Georgia and Alabama. Members of the Muskogean linguistic group, they were an agricultural people with a highly developed social system. During the colonial period they gave assistance to both the French and the British. They rose up in the Creek War of 1813–14 to stop white invasion of their territory, but were defeated and forced to cede much of their land. In the 1830s they were part of the 'removal' of the **FIVE CIVILIZED TRIBES** to Oklahoma, where many of the remaining c.50,000 Creeks continue to live today.

**creole**
In 20c usage, which varies widely between regions, the term generally denotes a native-born West Indian or Latin American of mixed European and African blood, or a French or Spanish native of the states surrounding the Gulf of Mexico. In its original 16–18c usage, the term was used specifically to denote a white person born in Spanish America of Spanish parents. In Spanish colonial America, creoles were discriminated against and ultimately led the revolutions that heralded the end of the colonial regime there in the early 19c.

**Crerar, Thomas Alexander** (1876–1975)
Canadian politician. Founder of the **PROGRESSIVE PARTY** when he bolted from the Liberals in protest against their high tariff budget of 1920, he led the party to second place in the 1921 elections with 65 seats. Preferring to hold the balance of power, he left official opposition to the Conservatives. Within a year he resigned as leader, at least in part because he insisted on conventional principles of party organization and representation in conflict with those of his Alberta and Ontario membership. He re-entered politics, becoming Minister of Railways and Canals in Mackenzie **KING**'s administration in 1929. Although he lost his seat in 1930, he won again with the Liberals in 1933, and served in the government as Minister of Mines and Resources. In 1945 he became a Senator, and resigned in 1966.

**Crespo, Joaquín** (1845–98)
Venezuelan soldier and politician. He was a supporter of Antonio **GUZMÁN BLANCO**, and served as a figurehead President under Guzmán Blanco's absolute rule in 1884–6. Four years after Guzmán Blanco had been deposed, Crespo led a revolution to depose President Andueza Palacio and set up his own dictatorship in 1892–4. Then he was elected to the presidency in 1894–8. During the 1890s a long-running dispute with Britain over the boundary between eastern Venezuela and western British Guiana (now Guyana) came to a head, and after appeals to the USA, the matter was decided by an international tribunal. The decision finally handed down favoured Britain, and Venezuela was denied access to gold that had been found in the border area.

**Crespy, Peace of** (1544)
An agreement between **FRANCIS I** of France and Emperor **CHARLES V**, under the terms of which France agreed to help Charles in his struggle against the Protestants, and Charles agreed to give up territory in either northern Italy or the Netherlands. By the

next year, circumstances had changed, and Charles saw no reason to maintain his offer of territory.

**Crete** ► GREECE

## Crimean War (1854–6)

A war fought in the Crimean Peninsula by Britain and France against Russia. Its origins lay in Russian successes in the Black Sea area and the British and French desire to prevent further expansion into the **OTTOMAN EMPIRE** by the Russians, since this would threaten the Mediterranean and overland routes to India. Major battles were fought in 1854 at the River Alma (20 Sep), **BALACLAVA** (25 Oct) and Inkerman (5 Nov). The war was notable both for the nursing exploits of Florence **NIGHTINGALE** at Scutari and the pioneer war reports of W H Russell in *The Times*. The fall of the Russian fortress at **SEVASTOPOL** (Sep 1855) led to peace negotiations. Under the treaty finally agreed at Paris (Mar 1856), Russia returned southern Bessarabia to neighbouring Moldavia and had to accept the neutralization of the Black Sea; **MOLDAVIA AND WALLACHIA** were soon to unite as an independent Romania. Shattered by its defeat in the war, Russia turned to overdue internal reform. ► **PARIS, CONGRESS OF**

## Cripps, (Richard) Stafford (1889–1952)

British barrister and politician. He made a fortune in patent and compensation cases. In 1930 he was appointed Solicitor-General in the second Labour government, and became an MP in 1931. During the 1930s he was associated with several extreme left-wing movements, and was expelled from the **LABOUR PARTY** in 1939 for his 'popular front' opposing Neville **CHAMBERLAIN**'s policy of **APPEASEMENT**. He sat as an independent MP during **WORLD WAR II**, was Ambassador to the USSR (1940–2), and in 1942 became Lord Privy Seal, and later Minister of Aircraft Production (1942–5). In the 1945 Labour government, he was readmitted to the party and appointed President of the Board of Trade. In 1947 he became Minister of Economic Affairs and then Chancellor of the Exchequer (1947–50), introducing a successful austerity policy. He resigned due to illness in 1950.

## Crispi, Francesco (1819–1901)

Italian politician. A member of the provisional government established in Palermo after the insurrection of Jan 1848, he was exiled from the Kingdom of the **TWO SICILIES** in 1849 and settled in Turin; in 1853 he was expelled from Piedmont for supporting a Mazzinian conspiracy in Milan. He helped to organize the Expedition of the **THOUSAND** to his native Sicily in 1860 and, as a member of the interim government established there by **GARIBALDI**, sought to prevent its annexation by Piedmont. After unification, he initially led the extreme Left in the Italian parliament but by 1865 had been converted to monarchism. In the 1870s he achieved fame by campaigning against parliamentary corruption, and in 1877–8 served as Interior Minister under **DEPRETIS**. He was Prime Minister twice (1887–91 and 1893–6), leaving politics between these two terms of office because of allegations of bigamy. As Prime Minister, his foreign policy was characterized by a loathing for the French and by a strengthening of ties with Germany and Austria. This forced him to neglect **IRREDENTISM**

and to concentrate on colonial expansion, culminating in the disaster of the Battle of **ADOWA** (1896), which brought his second government to an ignominious end. On the domestic front, his period of office was notable for violent anticlericalism (a response in large part to **LEO XIII**'s refusal to recognize the annexation of Rome) and the energetic and brutal suppression of peasant and worker unrest.

## Cristero Revolt (1927–9)

Rural guerrilla warfare against the Mexican government. Confined to the states of Guadalajara, Morelos, Colima, Jalisco, and Michoacán, the rebels fought under the banner 'Viva Christo Rey!'. Unlike their predecessors, they did not merely seek to restore the traditional pre-eminence of the Church in Mexico, but also to carry through social reforms; they thus presented a fundamental challenge to the revolutionary governments led by **CALLES** and **OBREGÓN**. By the end of 1927, Church and State were at stalemate; the Church suspended public worship and the State persecuted the clergy. In June 1929 the Vatican and US Ambassador Dwight Morrow achieved a compromise by which Church property was returned to the clergy and religious instruction was permitted in the churches.

## Critchlow, Hubert (1884–1958)

Guyanese trade unionist. In 1906, as an employee of Booker Brothers, he led an unofficial dockers' strike and became the mouthpiece of Guyanese labour. In Jan 1917 another 13-day strike resulted in a nine-hour day and increased wages for waterfront workers. Two years later Critchlow founded the British Guiana Labour Union, the first registered trade union in the British West Indies (1921), when unions were legalized. Although Critchlow and the BGLU lost some of their dynamism in the 1930s (when the sugar workers Manpower Citizens' Association became the dominant force in Guyanese labour), as 'father' of Guyanese unionism, he was honoured with the secretaryship of the British Guiana Trades Union Congress in 1941.

## Crittenden Compromise (1860)

An attempt in the months preceding the **AMERICAN CIVIL WAR**, by Kentucky Senator John J Crittenden, to resolve the crisis between North and South by the formal recognition of **SLAVERY** in territories south of 36°30' (the repealed **MISSOURI COMPROMISE** line). This proved unacceptable to Abraham **LINCOLN**, whose election as President encouraged secession by the slave-holding South.

## CROATIA    official name **Republic of Croatia**

A mountainous republic in eastern Europe, bounded to the south-west and west by the Adriatic Sea; to the north by Slovenia; to the north-east by Hungary; to the east and south-east by Serbia, Bosnia and Herzegovina and Montenegro. It includes the region lying between Bosnia and Hungary, called Slavonia, which was recorded as a kingdom in its own right in 1240 and was administered by the Hungarian King Béla IV as a *banovina* with its own *ban* (viceroy) within the Kingdom of Croatia in 1260. In the 13–14c, Slavonia was ruled by members of the ruling dynasty in Hungary, but was returned to the Croatian ban in 1476. The Slavonian *sabor* (parliament) was joined to that of Croatia in the mid-16c but Slavonia was then occupied by the Ottomans until the Treaty of **KARLOWITZ** (1699), when it passed to the Habsburg Emperor and was absorbed into the **MILITARY FRONTIER**. The Croatian people were originally Slav settlers who migrated (6–7c) from White Croatia in the Ukraine to the old Roman provinces of Pannonia and **DALMATIA**. Their independent kingdom, ruled by Croatian kings, existed from 910 until 1102, when the Croatian crown passed to the Hungarian Árpád Dynasty. From 1526 to 1918 the Croatian and Hungarian crowns were joined under the **HABSBURG DYNASTY**, but during the 15–16c the Croats became divided between three empires: the Croats in Croatia and Slavonia were subject to the Habsburgs; those in Dalmatia were subject to Venice; and those in Bosnia and Herzegovina to the Ottomans. In 1868 Croatia and Slavonia were made a joint crown land under Hungarian rule. Not until 1918 and the creation of the Kingdom of Serbs, Croats and Slovenes (later **YUGOSLAVIA**) were the Croats all subject to one government. During occupation by the **AXIS POWERS** in 1941–5, after the disintegration of Yugoslavia, part of Croatia and Bosnia and Herzegovina formed the Independent State of Croatia, a satellite state of the Axis Powers, which became subject to the brutal regime of Ante **PAVELIĆ**, the leader of the **USTAŠA** fascist movement. In 1945 Croatia became one of the constituent republics of the Socialist Federal Republic of Yugoslavia. In 1991 the Croatian President Franjo **TUDJMAN** declared Croatia's independence from the Yugoslav federation, which was followed by confrontation with the National Army and civil war; a ceasefire was declared in 1992 but fighting restarted in 1993 and by 1998 Croatian forces had established control over the whole country. From 1992 Croatian forces were involved in the war in Bosnia and Herzegovina where there is a large Croat population. Since the death of the authoritarian Tudjman in 1999, Croatia has been more outward looking. It has joined the **WORLD TRADE ORGANIZATION** and plans to join the **EU** in 2007. ➤ DUBROVNIK; FIUME; GAJ, LJUDEVIT; ILLYRIAN MOVEMENT; NAGODBA; SOUTH SLAVS; TRIALISM; TRIUNE KINGDOM; USTAŠA; YUGOSLAV COMMITTEE; YUGOSLAVISM

**Croce, Benedetto** (1866–1952)
Italian philosopher, historian, literary critic and politician. Although best remembered as a scholar, Croce had an active political life. Under the last **GIOLITTI** ministry he was Education Minister (1920–1), and as a Senator following the fascist seizure of power, he profited from the virtual immunity afforded by his enormous reputation to criticize the fascist regime constantly. In 1943 he played a prominent part in organizing the anti-fascists, and was a minister in both the **BADOGLIO** and **BONOMI** governments of 1944. He became President of the Italian Liberal Party in 1947 and a member of the Constituent Assembly; he became a Senator again in 1948.

**Crockett, Davy (David)** (1786–1836)
US frontiersman. He distinguished himself against the **CREEK** in Jackson's campaign of 1814, and was elected to the **HOUSE OF REPRESENTATIVES** from Tennessee (1827–31 and 1833–5). He died fighting for Texas at the Battle of the **ALAMO**. Highly embellished stories of his exploits have assumed mythological proportions.

**Croix de Feu, Ligue des**
A French political movement (1927–36), which was originally an organization of veteran soldiers of **WORLD WAR I**, under the leadership of Colonel de **LA ROCQUE**. It developed into a mass movement with a membership of about 250,000, campaigning for political change in a fashion which suggested that it could be a French version of **FASCISM**. That this was not really the case was shown when, uniformed **LEAGUES** having been prohibited in 1936, it transformed itself into a legal political party, the PSF (*Parti social français*, 'French Social Party').

**Cromer, Evelyn Baring, 1st Earl** (1841–1917)
British colonial administrator. He was private secretary to his cousin, Lord Northbrook, when Northbrook was Viceroy of India (1872–6), British Controller-General of Egyptian Finance (1879–80), Finance Minister of India (1880–83), and Agent and Consul-General in Egypt (1883–1907). Effectively the ruler of Egypt, he reformed its administration and agricultural policies, and put its finances on a good footing.

**Cromwell, Oliver** (1599–1658)
English soldier and statesman. A convinced Puritan, after studying law in London, he sat in both the **SHORT PARLIAMENT** and the **LONG PARLIAMENT** (1640), and when war broke out (1642) fought on the Parliamentary side at Edgehill (1642). He formed his unconquerable Ironsides, combining rigid discipline with strict morality, and it was his cavalry that secured the victory at the Battle of **MARSTON MOOR** (1644), while under **FAIRFAX** he led the **NEW MODEL ARMY** to decisive success at **NASEBY** (1645). He quelled insurrection in Wales in support of **CHARLES I**, and defeated the invading army of Hamilton. He then brought the King to trial, and was one of the signatories of his death warrant (1649). Having established the **COMMONWEALTH**, Cromwell suppressed the **LEVELLERS**, the Irish (1649–50), and the Scots (under **CHARLES II**) at **DUNBAR** (1650) and Worcester (1651). Using the power of the army, he dissolved the Rump of the Long Parliament (1653), and after the failure of a nominated **BAREBONE'S PARLIAMENT**, established a **PROTECTORATE** (1653). As Protector (1653–8), he refused the offer of the crown (1657). At home he extended religious toleration, and gave Scotland and Ireland parliamentary representation. Under him the Commonwealth became the head and champion of Protestant Europe. ➤ ENGLISH CIVIL WARS

**Cromwell, Richard** (1626–1712)
English statesman. The third son of Oliver **CROMWELL**, he served in the Parliamentary Army, sat in

parliament in 1654 and 1656, and was a member of the Council of State in 1657. In Sep 1658 he succeeded his father as Lord Protector, but he soon fell out with parliament, which he dissolved in 1659. He recalled the **RUMP PARLIAMENT** of 1653, but proved incapable of ruling, and was forced to abdicate in May 1659. After the **RESTORATION** (1660) he lived abroad, in France and Geneva, under the alias 'John Clarke', but returned to England in 1680.

**Cromwell, Thomas, Earl of Essex** (c.1485–1540)
English statesman, known as *malleus monachorum* ('the Hammer of the Monks'). He served as a soldier on the Continent (1504–12), then entered **WOLSEY**'s service in 1514, and became his agent and secretary. He arranged **HENRY VIII**'s divorce with **CATHERINE OF ARAGON**, and put into effect the Act of Supremacy (1534) and the dissolution of the monasteries (1536–9). He became Privy Councillor (1531), Chancellor of the Exchequer (1533), Secretary of State and Master of the Rolls (1534), Vicar-General (1535), Lord Privy Seal and Baron Cromwell of Oakham (1536), Knight of the Garter and Dean of Wells (1537), Lord Great Chamberlain (1539) and finally Earl of Essex (1540). In each of his offices, he proved himself a highly efficient administrator and adviser to the King; but Henry's aversion to **ANNE OF CLEVES**, a consort of Cromwell's choosing, led to his ruin. He was accused of treason, sent to the Tower and beheaded. ► **REFORMATION** (England)

**Cronje, Piet** (1835–1911)
Boer general. Born at Colesberg, South Africa, he was a leader in the **BOER WARS** (1881 and 1899–1900), defeated Methuen at Magersfontein, but surrendered to Lord Roberts at **PAARDEBERG** (1900). He died at Potchefstroom, Transvaal.

**Crosland, (Charles) Anthony (Raven)** (1918–77)
British politician. He taught in Oxford after serving in **WORLD WAR II**. Elected as a Labour MP in 1950, he became Secretary for Education and Science (1965–7), President of the Board of Trade (1967–9), Secretary for Local Government and Regional Planning (1969–70), Environment Secretary (1974–6) and Foreign Secretary (1976–7). A strong supporter of Hugh **GAITSKELL**, he was a key member of the revisionist wing of the **LABOUR PARTY** aiming to modernize socialist ideology, and wrote one of its seminal texts, *The Future of Socialism* (1956). ► **SOCIALISM**

**Crossman, Richard Howard Stafford** (1907–74)
British politician. He became a philosophy tutor at Oxford, and leader of the Labour group on Oxford City Council (1934–40). In 1938 he joined the staff of the *New Statesman*. In 1945 he became a Labour MP, and under **WILSON** was Minister of Housing and Local Government (1964–6), then Secretary of State for Social Services and head of the Department of Health (1968–70). He was editor of the *New Statesman* (1970–2). His best-known work is his series of political diaries, begun in 1952, keeping a detailed and frequently indiscreet record of the day-to-day workings of government and political life. They were published in four volumes (1975–81), despite attempts to suppress them. ► **LABOUR PARTY** (UK)

**Crow**
A Siouan-speaking Native American tribe of the Great Plains who inhabited the Yellowstone River area and the Rocky Mountains. They were skilled warriors and hunters on horseback, hunting buffalo for food and using buffalo rawhide for making moccasins, containers and shields. The only crop they produced was tobacco. They practised the 'Sun Dance' and were considered to be a 'tobacco society', believing that smoking their pipes provided them with a direct linkage to the Great Spirit. Many Crow still practise their traditional pipe ceremonies on their reservation in Montana. They separated from the **HIDATSA** and moved westwards in the early 18c, were enemies of the **SIOUX**, and allied with whites in the **INDIAN WARS** of the 1860s and 1870s; they were settled on reservations in Montana in 1868. Their population is currently c.13,000. ► **NATIVE AMERICANS**

**Crown Colony Government**
British imperial system of trusteeship government in which full executive power was vested in the Governor. Introduced into Trinidad and St Lucia in 1797 and 1803 respectively, 'the direct protection of the Crown of the unrepresented classes, which takes the place of representation' was meant to be a panacea to cure the evils of the **ASSEMBLIES**. The elective principle was absent from the constitution, the Governor's Executive Council being composed of his chief officials and the Legislative Council which, while it had nominated unofficial members, possessed an unofficial majority. The system was in place in most of the British West Indies by 1898 and, although reformist and impartial, it excluded the rising coloured middle-class from the decision-making process and was viewed as imposed, alien and paternalistic.

**Crusade, First** (1095–9)
Proclaimed by Pope **URBAN II** in 1095, this crusade was ostensibly in response to a request by the Byzantine Emperor **ALEXIUS I COMNENUS** for assistance against the Seljuk Turks whose encroachments in Anatolia had become ever more threatening since the catastrophic defeat some years previously of the Byzantine forces at **MANZIKERT** in 1071. Urban's preaching, insisting as it did on the liberation of Jerusalem from Muslim control, aroused such fervour that an ill-fated 'People's Crusade' under Peter the Hermit and Walter Sansavoir set out prior to the main body of the Crusade. This disorganized and motley crew were ferried across the Bosphorus, having created much mayhem on their passage through Europe; once in Anatolia, they were wiped out by the **SELJUKS** of Rum. The Crusade proper, however, inflicted a major defeat on the Turks at Dorylaeum (July 1097) and went on to establish a foothold in northern Syria at Antioch (1098). The capture of Jerusalem, accompanied by looting and massacre, was accomplished in 1099, crusading counties having been established in Edessa, Antioch and Tripoli. **GODFREY OF BOUILLON**, one of the leaders of the Crusade, became ruler of the new Latin Kingdom of Jerusalem and the crusade itself was distinguished from its successors by the presence of Adhemar of Le Puy as Papal Legate. The successful prosecution of the First Crusade was aided not a little by the disarray into which the petty Turkish princedoms of the Levant had fallen at this time.

## Crusade, Second (1147–9)

Proclaimed by Pope **EUGENIUS III**, this crusade was led by **LOUIS VII** of France and **CONRAD III** of Germany, and was launched in response to the capture (1144) of Edessa and the consequent discomfiture of the **FRANKS** at the hands of the Turkish Atabeg, 'Imad al-Din Zangi. After disastrous campaigns in Anatolia and in Syria, Damascus was unsuccessfully besieged. This achieved nothing apart from damage to the Crusaders' name as a power to be reckoned with in Palestine and Syria, and was a great disappointment to St **BERNARD OF CLAIRVAUX**, who had expended much effort in its promotion. ► **ZANGID DYNASTY**

## Crusade, Third (1189–92)

This was proclaimed by Pope Gregory VIII following the defeat by **SALADIN** of the field army of the Latin Kingdom of Jerusalem at the Battle of **HITTIN** (July 1187), and his subsequent capture of the Holy City itself (Oct 1187). Led by the three great rulers of Western Christendom, **FREDERICK I, BARBAROSSA, PHILIP II** of France and **RICHARD I, THE LIONHEART**, the Crusade promised much. It did not, in the event, live up to this promise. Barbarossa perished by drowning in the River Cydnus in Anatolia before even arriving in the Holy Land, with the consequent disintegration of the German effort; the leisurely outward progress of Philip and Richard, the pillaging and capture of Cyprus from their thoroughly disillusioned Byzantine co-religionists, and the scarcely veiled hostility between the French and English (which led to Philip's early return to France and Richard's subsequent preoccupation with affairs at home and his own departure (1192)) meant that the Crusade failed in its objective of regaining Jerusalem. It did, however, bring **GUY OF LUSIGNAN**'s siege of Acre to a successful close in 1191 and gained, if not an overwhelming, at least morale-lifting victory over Saladin's forces at Arsuf in the same year. Richard managed to achieve a compromise settlement whereby pilgrimage to the Holy Places was safeguarded and the Crusaders maintained their position on the Levantine littoral with the Muslims (in this case the **AYYUBID DYNASTY**) controlling the hinterland.

## Crusade, Fourth (1202–4)

Proclaimed by **INNOCENT III**, with the aim of recovering the Holy Places in Palestine, the Crusade faced financial difficulties over the provision of ships and finished up by being beholden to the Venetians, who diverted it to their own ends. First of all, Zara (the modern Zadar) in **DALMATIA** was taken, then, under Venetian pressure, attention was redirected to Constantinople. The latter was sacked and pillaged under the pretext of restoring Isaac II Angelus and his son, Alexius, to their positions of power in Byzantium. The ageing Doge, Enrico **DANDOLO**, played a leading part in the operation and in the subsequent establishment of a Latin Empire (which lasted until 1261) and particularly in the election of Baldwin of Flanders to be the first Latin Emperor of Constantinople as **BALDWIN I**. The **BYZANTINE EMPIRE**, although surviving for a further 200 years or so, was unable fully to recover from the blow. In consequence, such credibility as the Crusading enterprise had in the eyes of the Eastern Christians (which was precious little if we are to take the reactions of **ANNA COMNENA** as at all typical) evaporated. The original objectives of Innocent III were not addressed at all.

## Crusades, Later

These were mostly directed towards Egypt and North Africa, it having been supposed that the route to the control of Palestine was through the defeat of the Ayyubids (and subsequently the **MAMLUKS**) in Egypt. Failure in the Nile Delta by the Fifth and Seventh Crusades, despite initial success in the capture of Damietta by the former in 1219 and by the latter in 1249, prevented these crusades having a significant impact on the Holy Land. The Eighth Crusade (1270–2) had a limited success in the negotiation of a truce with the Mamluks by the future King **EDWARD I** of England and the treaty between **CHARLES OF ANJOU**, King of Naples and Sicily, with Tunis (although this last does seem to relate more to the interest of his twin realms than to any intention of assisting the Latins in Palestine). Of these later crusades only the so-called Sixth Crusade of the Emperor **FREDERICK II** (*Stupor Mundi*) made any considerable impact on the Holy Land itself. Frederick's negotiation of the peaceful cession to his rule of Jerusalem by the Ayyubid al-Kamil, while under excommunication by Gregory IX because of his delays in setting out on the Crusade (which meant that, in the eyes of the papacy, his gaining control of Jerusalem 'did not count'), serves to underline how futile much of the Crusading effort had been and was still to be. As a result of Frederick's negotiations, Jerusalem was again in the hands of the Latins from 1229 (when Frederick was crowned King of Jerusalem) until 1244, when the Latin forces were defeated by a joint Egyptian and Khwarizmian army. The Latins were finally driven from the Holy Land by Al-Ashraf Khalil, son of the Mamluk Sultan Qalawun (1291). ► **AYYUBID DYNASTY**

## CSCE (Conference on Security and Cooperation in Europe)

A series of conferences whose aim was to formalize the post-**WORLD WAR II** structure of Europe. Originally proposed by the **USSR** in the 1950s but deferred because of the **COLD WAR** until the early 1970s, talks started in Finland in 1972 between **NATO** and **WARSAW PACT** countries about a Conference on Security and Cooperation in Europe. The final stage of these talks produced the **HELSINKI FINAL ACT**, which set out the agreements reached, and several follow-up conferences took place, organized without any formal institutional structure. The CSCE became a permanent institution with its own infrastructure and secretariat in 1990. In 1995 its name was changed to the Organization for Security and Cooperation in Europe (OSCE) to reflect its changed status as an instrument for early warning, conflict prevention and crisis management and its major role in overseeing elections.

## CSU (*Christlich-Soziale Union*, 'Christian Social Union')

Bavarian political party. The successor to the pre-1933 Bavarian People's Party, the CSU functions as the Christian Democratic Party of Bavaria (within which the **CDU** does not organize). Founded in Jan 1946 it dominates Bavarian state politics by virtue of its

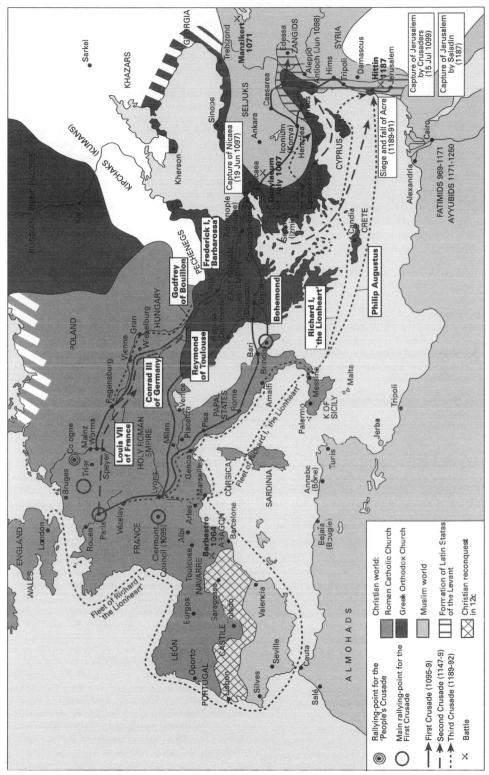

**The First, Second and Third Crusades (11–12c)**

absolute majority in the **LANDTAG** obtained in 1962 and operates in coalition with the CDU in the **BUNDESTAG**. Somewhat to the right of the CDU, it is a staunch exponent both of Bavarian particularist and all-German interests (with a European democratic federation as a long-term aim). Its membership is socially diverse, but is dominated by independent and salaried members of the middle classes. While leader of the CSU, the late Franz-Josef **STRAUSS** was a prominent advocate of right-wing Christian Democracy within Bavaria and Germany as a whole.

## cuartelazo

A Spanish pejorative term meaning 'barrack room coup': one which puts first the interests of the military, narrowly defined as the motivation for the coup. Such coups have often occurred when the incumbent government was judged to have accorded a high priority to health and education rather than military expenditure. Rulers in the 20c who owed their preeminence to *cuartelazos* include Chaves (Paraguay), Onganía and Videla (Argentina), Torrijos and Robles (Panama), Tinoco (Costa Rica) and **PÉREZ JIMÉNEZ** (Venezuela).

## Cuauhtémoc (c.1495–1525)

Last Aztec ruler. He was the successor to **MONTEZUMA II**, who resisted the Spaniards under **CORTÉS** at the siege of **TENOCHTITLÁN** (now Mexico City) in 1521. He was later executed while on an expedition with Cortés to Honduras.

---

**CUBA** official name **Republic of Cuba**

An island republic in the Caribbean Sea. It was visited by **COLUMBUS** in 1492, and was a Spanish colony until 1898. Spain relinquished its rights over Cuba following a US-supported revolution led by José **MARTÍ**. Cuba gained independence in 1902, with the USA retaining naval bases and reserving the right of intervention in domestic affairs. The struggle against the dictatorship of General **BATISTA** led by Fidel **CASTRO**, unsuccessful in 1953, finally succeeded in 1959, and a communist state was established. In 1961 an invasion by US-supported Cuban exiles was defeated at the **BAY OF PIGS**, and in 1962 the discovery of the installation of Soviet missile bases in Cuba prompted a US naval blockade. The collapse of the Soviet Union in 1991 meant that Cuba lost the commercial, military and economic support that it had enjoyed since 1960, and Castro was forced to reduce public services and introduce food rationing. In 1992 agreement was reached for the withdrawal of Russian troops. After emigration was permitted (1980), many Cubans settled in Florida, leading to the need for an agreement between Cuba and the USA (1994) to regulate the flow of asylum seekers. For over 30 years the USA has maintained a continually tightening economic

and political blockade of Castro's Cuba, but this has failed to destroy the economy, which has benefited in recent years from the relaxation of state controls and increased overseas investment and tourism. ► **CUBAN MISSILE CRISIS**; **CUBAN REVOLUTION**; **HELMS–BURTON ACT**

## Cuban Missile Crisis (Oct 1962)

A period of acute international tension and potential military confrontation between the USA and USSR, following the USA's discovery of Soviet nuclear missile sites in Cuba. President John F **KENNEDY** demanded the dismantling of the base and the return of the missiles, and threw a naval blockade around the island. The crisis ended on 28 Oct, when Soviet leader **KHRUSHCHEV** agreed to Kennedy's demands in return for the withdrawal of US missiles from Turkey.

## Cuban Revolution (1895–8)

Sometimes known as the War of Independence, the nationalist revolt against Spanish imperialism started in Apr 1895 when a force landed by **MARTÍ** and Gómez in Oriente province joined that of Maceo near Santiago. A provisional government was proclaimed and, although Martí was killed soon afterwards, Gómez and Maceo triumphed everywhere until 'Butcher' Weyler, the Spanish Commander-in-Chief, resorted to a policy of terror. Weyler's atrocities, however, provoked popular sympathy for the rebel cause in the USA and when the USS *Maine* blew up in Havana harbour (Feb 1898), the Americans blamed the Spanish authorities and instituted a military intervention, the **SPANISH–AMERICAN WAR** (1898). ► **MAINE, USS**

## Culloden, Battle of (16 Apr 1746)

A battle fought near Inverness, the last major battle on British soil, which marked the end of the Jacobite **FORTY-FIVE REBELLION** led by Charles Edward **STUART**. His force, mainly of Scottish Highlanders, was crushed by a superior force of English and lowland Scots under the Duke of **CUMBERLAND**. ► **JACOBITES**

## Culpeper's Rebellion (1677)

An uprising in the Albemarle section of North Carolina led by John Culpeper and George Durant against the group of proprietors who administered the colony. It was sparked off by the government's attempt to enforce the British **NAVIGATION ACTS**, which denied the colonists a free market outside England and imposed harsh taxes on goods. The rebels captured the acting governor Thomas Miller, who was also the customs collector, and set up their own parliament with Culpeper as Governor. They governed the colony for two years, and Culpeper went to England in an attempt to justify his activities. He was replaced as governor by a proprietorial nominee and tried for treason in 1680, but was acquitted with the help of the proprietors who saw him as a useful political ally.

## Cultivation System

An economic system introduced into Java in 1830 by Governor-General Johannes van den **BOSCH**. Using the traditional structures of deference and obligation within Javanese society, the Cultivation System coerced the rural population of Java into a remarkable expansion of the cultivation of tropical crops for export, notably sugar, coffee and indigo. The Dutch colonial state and many Dutch officials made huge profits from the system. Its impact on the Javanese themselves has long been a matter of great controversy, between those who have argued that the system brought impoverishment and economic stagnation and those who have argued that for many Javanese it secured an important advance in their material condition. Under fierce attack from liberal elements in Holland from the mid-19c, the Cultivation System began to be dismantled in the 1870s, although it did not finally disappear until 1918–19.

## Cult of Personality (1956)
The formula used to condemn Joseph **STALIN** and his dictatorship at the Twentieth Congress of the Communist Party of the USSR. It took some time after Stalin's death in 1953 for Nikita **KHRUSHCHEV** to establish himself and to build a suitable case against him. Many of Stalin's crimes were made known, but they were attributed to his being led astray, and not to the system that allowed him to act dictatorially. Khrushchev and his successors could, therefore, still be communists and run their country autocratically, so long as they steered clear of Stalin's excesses.

## Cultural Revolution (1966–76)
An abbreviation for the Great Proletarian Cultural Revolution, a radical Maoist mass movement in China initiated as a rectification campaign in 1966, which ended only with the death of **MAO ZEDONG** and the arrest of the **GANG OF FOUR** in the autumn of 1976. To prevent the Chinese revolution from stagnating and to avoid 'revisionism', Mao aimed at replacing the old guard, including Liu Shaoqi (died in prison in 1969), Peng Zhen and **DENG XIAOPING** (both disgraced in 1966), with a new generation of fervent revolutionaries. He appealed directly to the masses, in particular to young students, the **RED GUARDS**, who with the support of the **PEOPLE'S LIBERATION ARMY** overthrew not only party leaders but all so-called 'bourgeois reactionaries' and 'capitalist-roaders' in authority in schools, universities, factories and the administration. The ten years of social and political turmoil saw the closure of schools and universities, factories at a standstill, and millions of people sent to undertake manual labour in the countryside as re-education. ➤ **MAOISM**

## Culture System
A system of taxation in the Dutch East Indies, in general use 1830–70. Governor-General Johannes van den **BOSCH** first conceived the idea of making the colony more lucrative by imposing a tax in kind of about 20 per cent on the land and labour of the natives. These resources were used to cultivate crops such as coffee, tea, indigo and tobacco, which then became the property of the colonial regime. The profits of the system were transferred annually to the Dutch treasury, and were of considerable help to the home economy. After 1865, under pressure from economic and humanitarian liberalism, the system was gradually dismantled; it was much admired by other colonial powers, like Britain and Belgium.

## Cumberland, William Augustus, Duke of (1721–65)
British general. The second son of King **GEORGE II**, he adopted a military career, and in the War of the **AUS**-TRIAN SUCCESSION (1740–8) was wounded at Dettingen (1743) and defeated at Fontenoy (1745). He crushed Charles Edward **STUART**'s rebellion at the Battle of **CULLODEN** (1746), and by his harsh policies against the Highland clans thereafter earned the lasting title of 'Butcher'. In the **SEVEN YEARS' WAR**, he surrendered to the French (1757), and thereafter retired.

## Cunard, Sir Samuel (1787–1865)
Canadian ship-owner. Born in Halifax, Nova Scotia, he succeeded as a merchant and shipowner and emigrated to Great Britain in 1838. For the new steam rail service between the UK and the USA, he joined up with George Burns of Glasgow and David McIver of Liverpool to found (1839) the British and North American Royal Mail Steam Packet Company, later known as the Cunard Line. The first passage (1840) was that undertaken by the *Britannia* in 14 days 8 hours.

## Cunningham of Hyndhope, Andrew Browne Cunningham, 1st Viscount (1883–1963)
British naval commander. He joined the navy in 1898. He commanded a destroyer in **WORLD WAR I**, and in **WORLD WAR II** he was Commander-in-Chief of British naval forces in the Mediterranean (1939–43). He defeated the Italian navy at Taranto (1940) and Cape Matapan (1941), and was in command of Allied naval forces in the invasion of North Africa (1942), and Sicily and Italy (1942). Promoted Admiral of the Fleet in 1943, he was First Sea Lord from 1943 to 1946.

## Cuno, Wilhelm (1876–1933)
German politician. After an early career in the senior civil service and commerce (from 1918 Director-General of the Hamburg–America Shipping Line, Hapag), Cuno served as an economic adviser to the German government at the Treaty of **VERSAILLES** negotiations and at the subsequent **REPARATIONS** talks. In Nov 1922 he became Chancellor of Germany, despite belonging to no party, at the head of a pro-business government. His foreign and economic policies collapsed as a result of the crisis precipitated by the French occupation of the Ruhr in 1923, leading to his resignation on 12 Aug, after which he returned to the business world.

## Curtin, John Joseph Ambrose (1885–1945)
Australian politician. He was active in trade union work, and edited a Perth newspaper. In 1928 he entered parliament, and became leader of the **AUSTRALIAN LABOR PARTY** in 1935. As Prime Minister (1941–5), he appealed for support from the USA and organized national mobilization during the war against Japan. He died in office.

## Curzon, George Nathaniel, 1st Marquis Curzon of Kedleston (1859–1925)
British politician. He became an MP in 1886, and travelled widely in the East. He became Under-Secretary for India (1891–2), and for Foreign Affairs (1895), and in 1898 was made Viceroy of India and given an Irish barony. He introduced many social and political changes, establishing in the interests of imperial security a new North-West Frontier province (1901) under a Chief Commissioner responsible to the government of India alone. He also partitioned Bengal (1905). He resigned after a disagreement with Lord **KITCHENER** (1905), returning to politics in 1915 as

Lord Privy Seal. He became Foreign Secretary (1919–24), and was created a marquis in 1921. ➤ **CURZON LINE**

## Curzon Line

A line of territorial demarcation between Russia and Poland proposed in 1920 by the British Foreign Secretary, Lord **CURZON**. Poland rejected the proposal, subsequently gaining larger territories. In Sep 1939 a boundary similar to the Curzon Line became the border between German- and Soviet-occupied Poland, and in 1945 was recognized as the frontier between Poland and the USSR. ➤ **YALTA CONFERENCE**

## CUSFTA (Canada–US Free Trade Agreement)

An agreement between Canada and the USA ratified in 1988 and implemented in 1989 which allowed for the eventual elimination of all tariffs on trade between the two countries. It was superseded in 1994 by **NAFTA** but can be seen as a precursor of larger trade blocs in the Americas.

## Custer, George Armstrong (1839–76)

US army officer. He graduated from the US Military Academy at West Point (1861), and after a brilliant career as a cavalry commander in the **AMERICAN CIVIL WAR** served in the campaigns against the tribes of the Great Plains. His actions were controversial, but his gift for self-publicity made him a symbol of the cavalry. He and over 200 of his men were killed at the Battle of **LITTLE BIGHORN**, Montana (25 June 1876), by a combined force of **SIOUX** and **CHEYENNE**. ➤ **INDIAN WARS**

## Custozza or Custoza, Battles of (25 July 1848 and 24 June 1866)

Two of the most important battles of the **RISORGIMENTO**. In the first, the Piedmontese army of **CHARLES ALBERT** was routed by the Austrian army of **RADETZKY**. The second battle was part of the Italian campaign to seize Venetia. Once again, it resulted in Austrian victory, Archduke Albrecht defeating the Italian army commanded by **LA MARMORA** and **VICTOR EMMANUEL II**. ➤ **LISSA, BATTLE OF**; **SALASCO ARMISTICE**

## Cuza, Alexander Ioan (1820–73)

Hospodar (Governor) of Moldavia and Wallachia. Born into a boyar family, he studied in Paris and Bologna. In 1848 he led the meeting of liberal landowners at Jassy, where he put forward a programme of limited social and political reform, and in 1857 he emerged as a leading member of the Moldavian *divan ad hoc*. His election as hospodar by Moldavia (Jan 1859) and Wallachia (Feb 1859) effected the unification of the two Danubian Principalities. As hospodar, he worked for the administrative union of the two provinces, a goal which was achieved in 1862. With **KOGĂLNICEANU** as Prime Minister, he introduced a programme of social and economic change, issuing a civil code based on the **CODE NAPOLÉON**, sequestering the lands of the Dedicated Monasteries, giving land to peasants, abolishing payments and dues to landowners, and encouraging foreign investment. He roused opposition from the conservatives led by Ion **BRĂTIANU** and the liberals led by Constantin A **ROSETTI**, and in 1866 was forced by a group of army officers to abdicate. ➤ **MOLDAVIA AND WALLACHIA**; **ROMANIA**

## Cvetković, Dragiša (1893–1969)

Serbian politician. After studying law at Subotica, he entered politics as a member of the Serbian Radical Party and held a series of minor government posts until 1939, when he succeeded **STOJADINOVIĆ** as Prime Minister. Supported by Prince **PAUL KARAGEORGEVIĆ**, he negotiated the **SPORAZUM** with Vladko **MAČEK**, which led to a measure of cooperation between the Croats and the Yugoslav government. In Mar 1941 he and Cincar-Marković signed an agreement with the **AXIS POWERS** in which they pledged Yugoslavia's neutrality. A few days later, his government was overthrown in a coup led by General Dušan Simović. He went abroad in 1943, and eventually settled in France.

## CYPRUS  official name Republic of Cyprus

An island republic in the north-east Mediterranean Sea. Cyprus has a recorded history of 4,000 years, with its rulers including the Greeks, Ptolemies, Persians, Romans, Byzantines, **FRANKS**, Arabs, Venetians, Turks and British. Byzantine control of the island ended at the time of the Third **CRUSADE** when **RICHARD I, THE LIONHEART** conquered Cyprus on his way to Palestine and established **GUY OF LUSIGNAN** as King of Cyprus. This marked the beginning of a long period in which aspiring Crusaders could look on Cyprus as a relatively safe haven. St Louis's Crusaders, for instance, wintered in Cyprus in 1248–9, and as late as 1365 Peter I of Lusignan, titular King of Jerusalem, was King of Cyprus. In the 15c, because the piracy out of the island had remained a constant threat to Muslim seaborne trade in the eastern Mediterranean, the Circassian Mamluk, Sultan al-Ashraf Barsbay, mounted an attack and established Mamluk influence. Later, when Cyprus became effectively a protectorate of the Venetian empire, it still paid tribute to the Mamluk Sultan. The last vestige of Frankish influence in the eastern Mediterranean, the island fell to the Ottoman Sultan, **SELIM II**, in 1571 and remained under Ottoman control until occupied by the British in 1878. It became a British Crown Colony in 1925. Greek Cypriot demands for union with Greece (**ENOSIS**) led in the 1950s to guerrilla warfare against the British administration by **EOKA** under **GRIVAS** and **MAKARIOS III**, and a four-year state of emergency (1955–9). Cyprus achieved independence in 1960, with Britain retaining sovereignty over the military bases at Akrotiri and Dhekelia. There was Greek-Turkish fighting throughout the 1960s, with a **UN** peacekeeping force sent in 1964, and further terrorist activity in 1971. The 1974 Turkish invasion led to occupation of over one-third of the island, with displacement of over 160,000 Greek Cypriots; the island was divided into two parts by the Attila Line, from the north-west coast above Pomos to Famagusta in the east, cutting through Nicosia. Famagusta (the chief port prior to the 1974 Turkish invasion) remains under Turkish occupation, and has been declared closed by the Cyprus government. Turkish government members ceased to attend government in 1983, when the Turkish community declared itself independent (as the 'Turkish Republic of Northern Cyprus', recognized only by Turkey). Peace talks on reunification in the 1990s were inconclusive, and there were sporadic outbreaks of violence, but in 1993 Cyprus and Greece agreed upon a common defence policy, and Turkey affirmed its commitment to a political agreement with Cyprus. Impetus for reunification became greater as Cyprus's admission to the EU grew closer, and UN-sponsored talks from 1999 onwards resulted in 2004 in the Annan plan for a united republic with a two-state federal structure. This was accepted by the Turkish Cypriots but rejected by the Greek Cypriots, and only the southern part of the island joined the EU in May 2004. ► MAMLUKS

### Cyrankiewicz, Józef (1911–89)
Polish politician. He became Secretary of the Socialist Party in Krakow in 1935. Taken prisoner by the Germans (1939), he escaped and organized resistance, but was sent to AUSCHWITZ in 1941. In 1945 he became Secretary-General of the Socialist Party, and after two periods as Premier (1947–52 and 1954–70) became Chairman of the Council of State (1970–2) and of the All-Poland Peace Committee (1973).

### Czartoryski, Adam Jerzy (1770–1861)
Polish politician. The outstanding member of a famous family, he fought against Russia in the Polish insurrection of 1792. Sent in 1795 to St Petersburg to serve in the imperial civil service, he gained the friendship of the imperial Grand Duke Alexander and the confidence of Emperor PAUL, who made him ambassador to Sardinia. When ALEXANDER I ascended the throne, he appointed him assistant to the Minister of Foreign Affairs. As curator of the University of Wilno (1803), he strove to keep alive a spirit of nationality, and when some of the students were sent to Siberia, resigned his office. Disappointed with the treatment Poland received at the Congress of VIENNA (1814–15), he threw himself wholeheartedly into the Revolution of 1830. He was elected President of the provisional government and summoned a national diet; this declared (Jan 1831) the Polish throne vacant and elected him head of the national government. He immediately devoted half of his large estates to the public service; although he resigned his post (Aug), he continued to fight as a common soldier. After the suppression of the rising, excluded from the amnesty and with his Polish estates confiscated, he escaped to Paris, where he lived thereafter. During the 1848 revolutions he freed all his serfs in Galicia, and during the CRIMEAN WAR he endeavoured to induce the allies to identify the cause of Poland with that of Turkey. He refused the amnesty offered to him by ALEXANDER II, and died near Paris.

### Czech Baroque (17c and 18c)
One of the two most outstanding periods in Czech architecture and art, associated with important historical developments. The centre of Prague was particularly well endowed, with the ornate designs of many churches such as St Francis and St Nicholas, the Clementirium with its rich libraries, the Loretto and Strahov monasteries, and the town palaces of great noble families. The Czechs had finally lost their independence at the Battle of the WHITE MOUNTAIN and were subjected to the rigours of the Habsburg COUNTER-REFORMATION. But compensation came in financial and cultural investment that even Mozart could tolerate and benefit from. However, later nationalists tended to denigrate what appeared to them a 'period of darkness'.

### Czech Gothic (14–15c)
One of the two most outstanding periods in Czech architecture and art, associated with important historical developments. The centre of Prague was particularly well endowed, with the clean lines of the Cathedral and the Castle, the Charles Bridge, the Carolinum which was the seat of the University set up in 1348, the Old and the New Town Halls and many churches. The Czech lands were rich in agriculture and silver-mining, and formed a crossing-point for European trade. CHARLES IV made them the centre of the HOLY ROMAN EMPIRE for half a century, and Jan HUS gave them the leading place in reform of the Church for all of a century. It was to this period that Czech nationalists in the 19c looked back for inspiration.

### Czechoslovakia
A republic in central Europe from 1918, when the Czechs and Slovaks declared an independent state, until 1992, when it dissolved itself to form two separate states, the CZECH REPUBLIC and SLOVAKIA. It was partially dismembered when Germany annexed the SUDETENLAND in 1936, and came completely under German control from Mar 1939 as the BOHEMIAN PROTECTORATE, until liberated in 1945. In the post war period it was under communist rule, until the VELVET REVOLUTION in 1989. ► CZECHOSLOVAK INDEPENDENCE, DECLARATION OF; PRAGUE SPRING

### Czechoslovak Independence, Declaration of (1918)
The moment when the Czechs and Slovaks declared themselves free of Austria-Hungary and came together in a united state. Significantly, the declaration came out simultaneously in Geneva and Prague on 28 Oct, and on 30 Oct in Slovakia. Exiled politicians such as Tomáš MASARYK and Edvard BENEŠ played at least as great a role as those at home; and the Slovaks trailed behind the Czechs in their nationalist activities as in their economic development. Indeed, it was the Czechs abroad who pressed the case for union, with support from the Allied powers. And this has caused the union to be questioned at least twice, once following the MUNICH AGREEMENT, and the second time after the so-called VELVET REVOLUTION.

### Czechoslovak Legion
A corps of 30,000–40,000 Czech and Slovak volunteers and ex-prisoners of war in Russia, who fought briefly on the Eastern front and became embroiled with the BOLSHEVIKS (May 1918) while being transported home along the Trans-Siberian railway. They seized many towns along the railway and for a time controlled much of Siberia. Their activities intensified the RUSSIAN CIVIL WAR, but also helped Tomáš MASARYK to gain recognition from the Allied powers

for a provisional Czechoslovak government abroad.

**Czechoslovak–Soviet Alliance** (1935)
The treaty linking the two countries against the growing threat from Germany. Relations had been strained since 1917 and the involvement of the **CZECHOSLOVAK LEGION** in the **RUSSIAN CIVIL WAR**. It was 1934 before Czechoslovakia recognized the USSR *de jure*. However, things changed in 1935 when **HITLER** announced the reintroduction of conscription and the Franco-Soviet alliance was signed. But **BENEŠ** only agreed to the new treaty on condition that its operation would depend on the previous functioning of the Franco-Soviet alliance. This was to ensure that he would not be left to fight Hitler with **STALIN** as his sole ally. During the Munich crisis France reneged on its international obligations and Beneš did not attempt to activate his Soviet pact.

**Czechoslovak–Soviet Alliance** (1943)
The treaty linking the two countries against the proven threat from Germany. Relations had been strained since the **MUNICH AGREEMENT** and the **GERMAN–SOVIET PACT** but improved following the German invasion of the USSR in 1941. **BENEŠ** was anxious to liberate his country and prevent another Munich. **STALIN** wanted all possible allies to win the war and negotiate a satisfactory peace. So, in 1943 a new treaty replaced that of 1935. This time it was a direct alliance, not dependent upon a third party. In return, the USSR promised non-interference in Czechoslovakia's internal affairs. Unfortunately, similar treaties signed with Poland and other states were abused along with this one. The Soviet government did not interfere; but the Communist Party did.

**Czech Reformation** (15c)
One of the more important attempts to reform the medieval Christian Church before the 16c Protestant

**REFORMATION**. It arose from the intellectual and social ferment aroused in Bohemia and Moravia when **CHARLES IV** made his imperial seat in Prague and in 1348 founded a university there. It drew strength from the preachings and in 1415 the martyrdom of Jan **HUS** and a strong streak of anti-German feeling. It produced the Czech Brethren and other more extreme groups. But it declined as the Czech lands faded in prosperity and independence, and gave way first to Lutheranism and Calvinism and finally, after 1620, to the **COUNTER-REFORMATION**. But its spirit remained as an inspiration to Czech nationalists in the 19c.

## CZECH REPUBLIC

A landlocked republic in eastern Europe, bounded to the west by Germany; to the north and east by Poland; to the south-east by Slovakia; and to the south by Austria. It comprises the former provinces of **BOHEMIA**, **SILESIA** and Moravia, and from 1918 to 1993 it formed part of Czechoslovakia. It became an independent republic in 1993 following the dissolution of Czechoslovakia in 1992, and Václav **HAVEL**, formerly President of Czechoslovakia, became President. In Mar 1999 the Czech Republic was admitted to **NATO** and in 2004 it joined the **EU**. ► **SLOVAKIA**

**Dabrowski, Jan Henryk** (1755–1818)
Polish soldier. He fought against Russia with Tadeusz **KOŚCIUSZKO** (1794), then formed a Polish legion in the French army and played a distinguished part throughout the Napoleonic campaigns. On **NAPO-LEON**'s fall he returned to Poland, and was appointed by Emperor **ALEXANDER I** a general of cavalry and Polish senator. ► **NAPOLEONIC WARS**

**Dacca** ► **DHAKA**

**Dachau**
German **CONCENTRATION CAMP**. Founded on **HIM-MLER**'s orders on 20 Mar 1933 to accommodate political detainees under brutal conditions, Dachau was expanded during **WORLD WAR II** to hold detainees from throughout Europe. By the time it was liberated by US troops in Apr 1945 about 30,000 people had died there. ► **HOLOCAUST**

**Dacko, David** (1930–2003)
Central African politician. Educated in Brazzaville, he was a teacher and trade unionist before being elected to the territorial assembly in 1957, becoming successively Minister of Agriculture (1957–8), Minister of Administrative Affairs (1958), Minister of the Interior (1958–9) and Prime Minister (1959–60). He became the first President of the Central African Republic (1960) but was deposed in a coup, led by **BOKASSA**, in 1966 and was imprisoned until 1976, when he was appointed one of Bokassa's advisers. With the help of the French, he was responsible for removing Bokassa in 1979, becoming President, a post to which he was re-elected in 1981, but was then removed from office by a military coup led by André-Dieudonné Kolingba.

**Daendels, Herman Willem** (1762–1818)
Dutch soldier and colonialist. He joined the French revolutionary army as a general in 1793, and in 1796 entered Dutch service under a succession of governments. He was appointed Governor-General of the Dutch East Indies (1807–10). In 1815 he was made Governor of the Dutch colonies on the coast of Africa, where he died.

**Dahomey** ► **BENIN**

**Daigo II**, in full **Go-Daigo Tenno** (1288–1339)
Japanese Emperor (1318/39). He attempted to restore direct imperial rule after it had been eclipsed by the **KAMAKURA SHOGUNATE**. An abortive attempt to overthrow the shogunate in 1324 resulted in his banishment to the south-west. He escaped in 1333 and returned to the imperial capital, Kyoto, in triumph after the leader of the **SHOGUN**'s army, **ASHIKAGA TA-**

**KAUJI**, changed sides. Daigo then exercised personal rule, but his attempts to intervene directly in administration aroused the enmity of his erstwhile supporter, Ashikaga, who rose in revolt. Daigo fled to Nara prefecture, south of Kyoto, where he continued to maintain his claim to the throne in opposition to the new emperor (from another line of the imperial family) installed in Kyoto by Ashikaga. The two rival imperial families (known as the Northern and Southern Courts) were not to be reunited until 1392. No emperor after Daigo ever attempted to rule directly.

**Dáil Eireann**
The lower house of the parliament of the Republic of Ireland. Unlike the upper house, the Senate (*Seanad Eireann*), whose 60 members, except for the 11 chosen by the Prime Minister, are elected by various economic and cultural constituencies, the Dáil is elected by universal suffrage by proportional representation for a period of five years. It nominates the Prime Minister for appointment by the President. There are 166 members, who are called *Teachti Dála*.

**daimyo**
A Japanese feudal lord, equivalent to a medieval baron in Europe. Powerful under the **TOKUGAWA SHOGUNATE**, *daimyo* lost power at the **MEIJI RESTORATION**. They had responsibility for keeping the peace, and the amount of rice their domains produced showed their prestige. ► **FEUDALISM; SAMURAI**

**Dakota**
The largest division of the group of Native American tribes commonly called the **SIOUX**, which also includes the Nakota and Lakota. Like other Plains people cultures, the Dakota were nomadic buffalo hunters. Perhaps the most famous Dakota Sioux warrior was **SITTING BULL**. The Sioux now prefer to be referred to as Dakota. ► **NATIVE AMERICANS**

**Daladier, Édouard** (1884–1970)
French politician. In 1927 he became a leader of the **RADICAL PARTY**, and in 1933 Minister of War and Prime Minister of a short-lived government, a pattern which was repeated in 1934. In 1936 he was Minister of War in the **POPULAR FRONT** cabinet, and as Premier (1938–40) supported appeasement policies and signed the **MUNICH AGREEMENT**. On 20 Mar 1940 he resigned as Prime Minister, becoming successively War and Foreign Minister in **REYNAUD**'s cabinet, and on the fall of France was arrested and interned until 1945. He was one of the defendants in the **RIOM TRIAL** (1942) of Third Republic leaders. After the war he continued in politics until 1958. ► **REPUBLIC, THIRD** (France)

# Dance

Art & Literature

It is generally assumed that dance is as old as human society and that it has existed in all the continents from the very earliest times. The fact that various birds and animals perform dance-like movements, especially during courtship, gives further credence to the suggestion that a propensity for rhythmic movement and physical display is innate in humankind as in other species. Early human beings no doubt did dance purely for pleasure and entertainment, but their dancing in the main had a purpose and a context, and many of the forms of dancing that we now think of primarily as entertainment grew out of older, purposeful forms.

### The original functions of dance

Several functions are usually ascribed to early dance. It formed an important part of religious ritual: dancing was a form of worship, a way of propitiating or supplicating the gods, or ensuring the fertility of the earth and a good harvest. In places as far apart as Australia, the Amazon forests and northern Europe, tribal peoples danced around trees to worship them, to ensure their continued growth or magically to draw the strength of the tree into themselves. Maypole dancing is a survival of this.

Dancing also had a social function, especially in courtship. It ritualized a display of physical vigour and fitness for mating, as well as the actual process of wooing. It was a way of enacting social cohesion or of passing information from one generation to another. In Polynesia and Micronesia dancing accompanied the recital of poetry (concerned with genealogies and legends) to the accompaniment of drums, with the movements of hands, arms and heads providing additional meaning to the words. The dances of the Australian **Aboriginals** told of their mythical origins. Hunting dances in Africa and elsewhere passed on tribal lore concerning the behaviour of animals and the conduct of the hunt to the young. Dancing also represented and taught the manipulation of tools and weapons: net-casting, spear-throwing and similar activities. Morris dancing is said to derive from an early weapons dance.

Dancing also had a military function. Besides energizing the fighters before they went into battle, war dances were a way of signalling hostile intent and instilling fear into the enemy. As a display of controlled ferocity and extraordinary energy contained within disciplined movement, the stamping dances of Zulu warriors leave few spectators unmoved.

### Religion and dance

According to the biblical story told in the Book of Samuel, King David 'danced before the Lord with all his might' when bringing the Ark of the Covenant into his city. Samuel also recounts that 'Saul's daughter looked through a window and saw King David leaping and dancing before the Lord; and she despised him in her heart'.

Most early civilizations gave dance a place in religious ritual, and out of ritual dancing in both India and ancient Greece grew a variety of dramatic forms. Dances honouring Dionysus, the god of wine, are held to be the origin of Greek tragedy. Perhaps mindful of its religious associations, the Greeks generally held dancing in high esteem. It was one of the arts that philosophers recommended as worthy of teaching to the young. It was also a communal activity in which citizens were proud to take part.

Dance was appreciated less by the Romans, who tended to regard it as effeminate. All the dancing schools in Rome were closed in 150 BC. But though dancing was something that respectable Romans would not engage in themselves, its entertainment value was appreciated. Dance and pantomimes involving dance were popular spectacles, though the social status of public performers was low – a situation that was to persist in Europe for many centuries.

The Christian Church's attitude towards dance was on the whole that of Saul's daughter and the Romans. Dance did form a part of the worship of some early sects and was incorporated into the religious services of the Shakers (founded around 1750 in England and first appearing in the USA in 1774). Though only extreme puritans denounced the dancing of the peasantry or at court as sinful or attempted to outlaw it, there was no route from religious dancing into the cultural mainstream in the Christian world. The situation was much the same in Islam, where only the sect of the whirling dervishes, founded in 1273 by the Persian mystic and poet Jalal ad-Din ar-Rumi, used dance as a way of entering into a religious trance, as the shamans of many earlier societies had done.

### Indian classical dance

In India dance emphatically emerged out of religion into an artistic tradition of great variety and strength. Dance was used to enact the stories of the gods in temple worship. The principles guiding it were set down in the early Sanskrit theoretical treatise, the *Natyasastra* (c.100 BC–AD 100), which also served as a manual for early Indian drama and music. It specifies a large variety of expressive gestures for the head, the hands and other parts of the body, and gives them a particular meaning (there are over 4,000 such *mudras* – gestures or positions – in classical Indian dance), besides prescribing the correct training for performers and the psychological and spiritual preparation required for a performance.

Six schools of dance developed out of religious dance – the best-known and most closely linked to the *Natyasastra* being *bharata natyam*, famous especially for slow graceful and lyrical dances known as *padams* that illustrate and accompany love poems. *Bharata natyam*, especially in modern times, is usually performed by solo women dancers. *Kathakali* is a more vigorous – often explosively so – form of dance drama most often performed by men and originating in Kerala in the 17c. The performers wear elaborate costumes and make-up to portray stories of gods and heroes in mime. In general, the link between dance, **drama** and **music** in **theatre** was maintained in the East, while in the West the three elements developed separately.

Indian dance had a profound effect throughout South-East Asia in the period c.100–1000 AD. In Indonesia, Cambodia and Thailand, Indian principles and stories were merged with existing local traditions to produce distinctive forms of dance and drama that survive to the present day. In India itself, classical dance declined under Mughal and British rule but was revived in the late 19c and early 20c.

## Ballet

The **Renaissance** saw a revival of dance in Europe both as a courtly pastime and as an entertainment. Court banquets would sometimes be enlivened by appropriate interludes between courses: Neptune and his court ushering in the fish course, or Jason, the Argonauts and the golden fleece heralding the arrival of the lamb. When **Catherine de' Medici** went to France to marry the future King **Henry II**, she brought the tradition of court entertainment and a love of dance with her. In 1581 she employed the famous dancing master and violinist Balthazar de Beaujoyeulx to create the *Ballet comique de la reine* as the spectacle to end all spectacles: a five-and-a-half-hour wedding entertainment danced by the gentlemen and, unusually for the time, the ladies of her court. This spectacle, fully documented in a book that appeared the following year, is generally taken as the starting point for the history of ballet.

In the next century **Louis XIV**, who loved dancing, further encouraged the art. The Académie Royale de Danse was founded in 1661. Molière wrote *comédie-ballets* for the king, among them *Le Bourgeois gentilhomme* (1670), and Lully provided the music. The dancers in these pieces were the king and his court – until 1670, that is, when Louis decided he was too fat to dance and reluctantly retired from the scene. All his courtiers immediately gave up as well, leaving the field free for professional dancers.

The chief dancers in these early performances were men. It was acceptable for men to show their legs and they wore tights as part of their everyday costume; women were prevented from making high leaps and expansive leg movements by their long, heavy court dresses. During the 18c clothes became lighter and the famous dancer Maria Camargo (1710–70) shortened her skirts to calf length so that her rapid complex footwork could be more easily seen.

For much of the 18c, however, ballet remained mainly an episode or interlude in a larger work. The French ballet master and choreographer Jean-Georges Noverre (1727–1810) was foremost among those who proposed that ballet should be an independent dramatic art form, communicating a storyline and emotion through movement and gesture. The comic ballet *La Fille mal gardée* was first staged in 1789, but the classical repertoire of great ballets dates mainly from the 19c: *La Sylphide* (1832), *Giselle* (1841) and the ballets to Tchaikovsky scores in the 1880s and 1890s: *Swan Lake*, *The Sleeping Beauty* and *The Nutcracker*.

## Modern dance

Classical ballet produced some of its most famous works and scored some of its greatest triumphs in the early 20c, especially in productions by Sergei Diaghilev (1872–1929) for his Ballets Russes, starring the great Nijinsky (1890–1950), and productions for the Bolshoi and Kirov ballet companies during the Soviet era. During the same period a movement began to free stage dance from the conventions of classical ballet, particularly associated with two US women dancers: Isadora Duncan (1877–1927), who worked mainly in Europe, and Ruth St Denis, (1877–1968). Duncan advocated a free-flowing dance style inspired by ancient Greece, while St Denis was famous for an exotic blend of Eastern styles. In 1930 Martha Graham (1894–1991), who had earlier worked with Ruth St Denis, founded the Dance Repertory Theatre in New York City and trained a company in her own method, which was to use every aspect of the body and mind to dramatic purpose. Modern freely expressive dance continued to develop throughout the 20c, in turn influencing the ballet tradition from which it originally broke away.

## Social dancing

The older forms of social dancing in the European tradition usually involve couples dancing in a set. This holds true both for English country dancing, Scottish country dancing (where 'country' is really the French *contre* and implies two lines of dancers), American square dances and the stately court dances of Europe such as the minuet. The arrival of the waltz in around 1800, to be followed by the polka in the mid-19c, broke up the set as couples danced as couples independently of others. The waltz also began a tradition of new dances and was considered wild, uninhibited and morally dubious, until older people decided that they had no real option but to copy the young. Other dances involving the standard 'ballroom hold' (man's right hand in small of woman's back, woman's left hand on man's right shoulder, man's left and woman's right arms extended and hands clasped) evolved in the early 20c: the tango, the quickstep and the foxtrot. For the first 50 years or so of the century, these dances dominated the repertoire in the public ballrooms which had become popular places of entertainment in many parts of the world. The Charleston craze of the late 1920s introduced a form of dance in which couples danced together without actually clasping each other. The advent of the jitterbug in the USA in the 1930s kept couples as couples holding hands, but with each using the other almost as a piece of gymnastic equipment. The rock 'n' roll revolution of the 1950s made the jive – a less gymnastic version of the jitterbug – the standard dance of young people throughout most of the Western world. The 1960s craze, the twist, separated couples again, and the tendency in the latter half of the 20c – through disco dancing and beyond – has been to make the man-and-woman couple dancing together (with the man 'leading') a thing of the past, no longer in keeping with social realities. While almost all forms of dance referred to here still flourish, and dancing is still a social activity, dancing to the most popular music of the day is currently a form of self-expression rather than community in couples or groups.

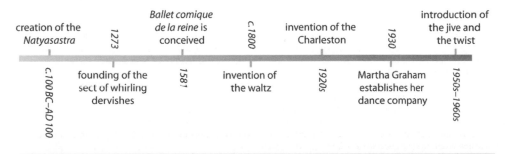

## Dalai Lama

The traditional religious and temporal head of **TIBET**, whose name literally means 'ocean-like guru', regarded as an incarnation of the Bodhisattva Avalokiteshvara. Tenzin Gyatso (1935– ), held to be the 14th incarnation, ruled in Tibet from 1940 to 1959. After temporarily fleeing Tibet (1950–1) during the Chinese invasion of the country, he escaped to India during a local uprising in 1959. Tibetans still regard him as their spiritual leader. He won the **NOBEL PEACE PRIZE** in 1989.

## Dalberg, Karl Theodore von (1744–1817)

Son of an important noble family, he studied canon law at Göttingen and Heidelberg before being made administrator of the Erfurt bishopric (1772). He supported the League of Princes and Frederick of Prussia in 1785 to promote German unity. In 1802 he became archbishop of Mainz and Arch Chancellor of the Empire. After the reorganization of the Empire in 1803, he was primate of Germany, controlling Mainz, Cologne and Trier. He supported **NAPOLEON I** to foster German unity and was made prince primate of the Rhine Confederation. As a result of Napoleon's changes to German territories in 1810, he became Grand Duke of Frankfurt. After Napoleon's defeat and the Congress of **VIENNA** (1814–15), he was left with only the Archbishopric of Regensburg.

## Daley, Richard Joseph (1902–76)

US politician. As Democratic mayor of Chicago (1955–76) and city boss, his political machine was so powerful that Democratic candidates at both the state and national level sought his backing. He became notorious during the 1968 Democratic Convention in Chicago, when the city's police force clubbed and gassed demonstrators protesting against the **VIETNAM WAR**. By 1972 his influence had waned as a result of reforms that increased the representation of women, blacks and other minorities in the Democratic Party.

## Dalhousie, James Andrew Broun Ramsay, 1st Marquis of (1812–60)

British politician and colonial administrator. He became an MP in 1837, was made Earl of Dalhousie in 1838, and President of the Board of Trade in 1845. As Governor-General of India (1847–56), he encouraged the development of railways and irrigation works. He annexed Satara (1847) and Punjab (1849), but the annexation of Awadh (Oudh) (1856) caused resentment, which fuelled the 1857–8 **INDIAN UPRISING**. He was made a marquis in 1849, and retired through ill health in 1856.

## Dalmatia

The name given since antiquity to the narrow strip of land and over 1,000 islands along the eastern Adriatic coast from the south end of Pag to Cavtat, south of **DUBROVNIK**. A Roman province inhabited by Illyrians, then settled by **SLAVS** (7c), in the Middle Ages Dalmatia was governed by the kings of Croatia and later those of Hungary. From the 14c, most of Dalmatia was ruled by the Republic of Venice and the towns, notably Zadar, Šibenik, Split and Dubrovnik, still show the influence of Venetian culture. Occupied by **NAPOLEON I**'s army and included in the **ILLYRIAN PROVINCES** (1809–13), following the Congress of Vienna (1814–15), Dalmatia was governed by Austria until 1918 when it became part of the Kingdom of Serbs, Croats and Slovenes, later Yugoslavia. Annexed by **MUSSOLINI**'s Italy in **WORLD WAR II**, in 1943 it was handed over to the **USTAŠA** regime of Ante **PAVELIĆ**. Since 1945 Dalmatia has been part of the Republic of Croatia.

## Dalton, (Edward) Hugh John Neale Dalton, Baron (1887–1962)

British politician. First elected as a Labour MP in 1924, he held the posts of Minister of Economic Warfare (1940–2) and then President of the Board of Trade (1942–5). In the post-war Labour government he was Chancellor of the Exchequer (1945–7), Chancellor of the Duchy of Lancaster (1948–50), Minister of Town and Country Planning (1950–1) and, briefly, Minister of Local Government (1951). He was elevated to the peerage in 1960. ▶ **LABOUR PARTY (UK)**

## Damascus, Capture of (1154)

In the early 12c Damascus had been held largely through the astute capacities of the Seljuk princeling Tughtegin against both Muslim and Crusaders alike, and towards the middle of the century became an objective of the Atabeg Imad al-Din Zangi. Zangi's death (1146), followed by his son **NUR AL-DIN'S** accession to control over Aleppo, in no way diminished the threat to Damascus which, although possessed of astute statesmen, was by this time ruled by the enfeebled Burid Dynasty. The effect of the Second **CRUSADE**'s attack on Damascus (1148) led to the Burid statesman Unur's appealing to Nur al-Din for assistance. The Second Crusade's abandoning of the siege of Damascus was in some respects a result of the threat posed by Nur al-Din, but it was now clear that Damascus was essential to the control of Syria. The death of Unur (1149) followed by a recognition by the citizenry of Damascus of the need for strong rule led to Nur al-Din's besieging army (1154) being admitted to the town by the Damascenes themselves and the fall of the last Burid. ▶ **ZANGID DYNASTY**

## Damaskinos, Demetrios Papandreou (1891–1949)

Greek archbishop and regent of Greece. After serving in the army during the **BALKAN WARS**, he was ordained priest (1917) and elected Bishop of Corinth (1922) and Archbishop of Athens (1938), but was exiled because of his opposition to **METAXAS**. Returning to Greece in 1941, he was able to give secret assistance to the British during the German occupation. After the withdrawal from Greece of German troops, Winston **CHURCHILL**, eager to establish peace between the warring factions and to settle the constitutional crisis, agreed to Damaskinos' appointment as regent until a plebiscite could be held over the issue of the monarchy (Dec 1944). When the Greeks voted for the return of their king, Damaskinos resigned as regent (Sep 1946) and continued his work as archbishop. ▶ **PLASTIRAS, NIKOLAOS**

## Danby, Thomas Osborne, 1st Earl of ▶ LEEDS, THOMAS OSBORNE, 1ST DUKE OF

## Dance ▶ See panel

## Dandolo, Enrico (c.1110–1205)

Doge of Venice (1192–1205). He sailed at the head of the Fourth **CRUSADE** in 1202. The Crusaders could not raise the sum that they had negotiated for the ships that the Venetians had supplied. Dandolo proposed that the debt be paid in military service to Venice. This resulted in the subjugation of Trieste and Zara, the coast of Albania and the Ionian Islands. Most notoriously, it led to the Sack of **CONSTANTI-NOPLE** in 1204, from which much of the plunder was carried off to Venice.

## Danegeld

In a narrow sense, the royal tax (Old English, *geld*) levied in England between 991 and 1012 according to hidage, but distinct from the ordinary geld, in order to buy peace from Danish invaders. After 1066, the term was used for the general geld, which was effectively abandoned in 1162. ➤ **DANELAW**; **ETHELRED THE UNREADY**; **VIKINGS**

## Danelaw

That part of England where Danish conquest and colonization in the late 9c left an imprint on not only legal and administrative practices, but on place names, language and culture. Danish-derived customs survived even the **NORMAN CONQUEST**, and in the 12c all eastern England from the Thames to the Tees was so designated. ➤ **VIKINGS**

## Danish–German War ➤ GERMAN–DANISH WAR

## Danish West Indies, Sale of (1917)

The result of an agreement reached in Jan 1916 between the governments of Denmark and the USA concerning the Danish West Indian colonies, the main islands being St Croix, St Jan and St Thomas, acquired in the 18c. The agreement stipulated that the US government would pay the Danish government US$25 million for the islands, which the USA considered part of its sphere of influence and of strategic importance after the opening of the Panama Canal. To the agreement was annexed a declaration in which the US government recognized the sovereignty of Denmark over the whole of Greenland. On 14 Dec 1916 a referendum about the agreement was held in Denmark with 64.3 per cent of the votes in favour of the sale and 35.7 per cent, a surprisingly high proportion, against. On 1 Apr 1917, five days before the USA declared war on Germany, the islands were handed over by the Danish government to the USA and renamed the 'Virgin Islands of the USA'.

## D'Annunzio, Gabriele (1863–1938)

Italian writer. One of Italy's most important literary figures of the late 19c and early 20c. He was a fervent supporter of the **TRIPOLITANIAN WAR** and an active advocate of Italian intervention in **WORLD WAR I**, during which he saw action as an airman. In Sep 1919 he occupied the disputed port of **FIUME** with a force of volunteer 'legionaries', where he introduced a constitution drafted by his syndicalist friend, Alceste **DE AMBRIS**. Expelled from Fiume by the Italian navy in Jan 1921, D'Annunzio then flirted with the fascist movement and in Aug 1921 was actually invited by Dino **GRANDI** and Italo **BALBO** to take over its leadership. Although D'Annunzio refused to usurp **MUSSO-LINI**'s position, the latter both admired him and considered him a threat to his dominance of the **FAS-CIST PARTY**, especially in the aftermath of the **MAT-TEOTTI** crisis. Such fears were unfounded, as D'Annunzio never sought to challenge Mussolini for power.

## Danquah, Joseph Boakye (1895–1965)

Ghanaian nationalist and politician. After pursuing his studies in London, where he qualified as a lawyer, he returned to Ghana and founded the *Times of West Africa* in 1931. He was a leader of the **UNITED GOLD COAST CONVENTION** (UGCC), which campaigned for independence, but he fell out with its successor, the **CPP**, and became leader of the opposition. He was imprisoned in 1961–2 and 1964–5 and died in prison.

## Danton, Georges Jacques (1759–94)

French revolutionary politician. He became a lawyer, and was practising in Paris at the outbreak of the **FRENCH REVOLUTION**. In 1790 he formed the **CORDE-LIERS' CLUB**, a rallying point for revolutionary extremists, and in 1792 became Minister of Justice. He voted for the death of **LOUIS XVI** (1793), and was one of the original members of the Committee of **PUBLIC SAFETY**. He tried to abate the pitiless severity of his own Revolutionary Tribunal, but lost the leadership to **ROBESPIERRE**. He was arrested and brought before the Tribunal, charged with conspiracy. Despite a heroic and eloquent defence, he was guillotined.

## Danubian Principalities ➤ MOLDAVIA AND WALLA-CHIA

## Dardanelles

Narrow strait in north-west Turkey, connecting the Aegean Sea and the Sea of Marmara, part of the important waterway linking the Mediterranean and the Black Sea. It was the scene of an unsuccessful Allied campaign in **WORLD WAR I**. Intending to overcome the Turks and come to the aid of Russia, the British War Council approved a naval expedition to capture Constantinople by forcing a route up the Dardanelles. Many of the Anglo-French battleships were destroyed during the attempted passage, and efforts were subsequently concentrated on the land attack at **GALLI-POLI**.

## Darfur

The largest and westernmost region of **SUDAN**, and the location of an ethnic conflict since the 1990s between nomadic Arab tribes, who are camel and cattle herders, and black African ethnic groups, who tend to be settled farmers. Conflict over resources, traditionally settled by mediation, was exacerbated in the late 1990s by prolonged drought and increasing desertification, which led to violence. In 2003, groups representing the black African peoples sought to share power with the Arab-dominated government, which responded by arming Arab militias, such as the *Janja-weed*, and permitting them to carry out mass executions and forcible depopulation in the region. Over 1.8 million people were displaced in 2003–4 and aid agencies struggled to alleviate starvation in refugee camps in Darfur because of government obstructiveness and repeated ceasefire violations. Observers accused the government of **ETHNIC CLEANSING** and even **GENOCIDE**, claims it denied, but it continued to resist international pressure to call off the militias and failed to keep agreements brokered by the **AFRI-CAN UNION** and the **UN**.

**Darlan, Jean Louis Xavier François** (1881–1942)
French admiral. He passed through the École Navale in 1899, became captain in 1918, and navy Commander-in-Chief in 1939. He served in the **VICHY** government as Minister of the Navy and Mercantile Marine, Vice-President of the Council of Ministers, and Secretary of State for Foreign Affairs and the Navy. He then commanded French forces in North Africa (1942), where he concluded an armistice with the Allies. He was killed by an anti-Vichy assassin in Algiers. ► **WORLD WAR II**

**Darnand, Joseph** (1897–1945)
French politician. A militant in extreme-right movements, he was involved in the 1938 *Cagoule* ('hooded men') conspiracy, all financed by **MUSSOLINI**, to murder left-wing Italian exiles in France. He collaborated with the Germans in **WORLD WAR II**, organizing the *Milice*, an auxiliary police force responsible for many atrocities. He fled to Germany, was captured, tried and executed. ► **VICHY**

**Darnley, Henry Stewart, Lord** (1545–67)
English nobleman. He was the second husband of **MARY, QUEEN OF SCOTS** and father of James VI of Scotland and I of England. He married Mary (his cousin) in 1565, and was made Earl of Ross and Duke of Albany. In Scotland, his debauchery and arrogance made him unpopular, and his part in the murder (1566) of the Queen's secretary, David Rizzio, caused his downfall. He became estranged from the Queen, and during an illness was killed at Edinburgh, when Kirk O' Field, the house in which he was sleeping, was destroyed by gunpowder (the result of a plot probably organized by the Earl of **BOTHWELL**, perhaps with Mary's knowledge). ► **JAMES VI AND I**

**Darrow, Clarence Seward** (1857–1938)
US civil liberties lawyer. In 1907 he successfully defended 'Big Bill' **HAYWOOD** and Charles Moyer of the Western Federation of Miners, implicated in the murder of Frank Steunenberg, ex-governor of Idaho. In 1924, his defence of Richard Loeb and Nathan Leopold in the most sensational murder trial of the age saved them from the death penalty; and in the Monkey Trial of 1925, at Dayton, Tennessee, he defended the high school biology teacher John Scopes who was charged under the Tennessee state law forbidding the teaching of Darwin's Theory of Evolution. Although Scopes was found guilty and fined US$100, Darrow demolished the views which lay behind the law and the arguments of the the prosecution, led by William Jennings Bryan, the elderly champion of Protestant fundamentalism. In 1934 Darrow was appointed to investigate Senator Gerald Nye's charge that the codes introduced by the National Recovery Board were favouring monopolies. His scathing report led eventually to the demise of price control.

**Das, Chitta Ranjan** (1870–1925)
Bengali patriot and politician. Called to the Bar in 1894, he soon acquired a reputation for skilfully representing nationalists, such as Aurobindo **GHOSH** (1908), accused of **TERRORISM** by the British colonial government in India. He participated in the campaign against the partition of Bengal, chaired the Bengal Provincial Congress (1917) and the **INDIAN NA-**TIONAL CONGRESS (1918), and renounced his legal practice and all his property to join M K **GANDHI**'s **NON-COOPERATION MOVEMENT** (1920). Imprisoned in 1921, he emerged (1922) to help form the **SWARAJ** Party to contest district and provincial council elections (then boycotted by the Indian National Congress). Opposed to Hindu **COMMUNALISM**, he was popular with both Muslim and Hindu communities in Bengal and with Congressmen in Bengal, the Swarajists winning a majority of seats in the Bengal Council elections of 1923–4, and Das being elected Mayor of Calcutta City Corporation in 1924. Soon after, he came to an agreement with Gandhi that allowed both Swarajists and Gandhians to campaign from the Congress platform. Although he himself rejected violence, many of his followers were either involved in terrorism or openly advocated the use of violence in opposition to colonial rule. A strong supporter of the trade union movement, Das campaigned on behalf of railway workers and labourers on the Assam tea plantations; he and his followers were thus a powerful force for radicalism within the Indian Nationalist movement, a radicalism that grew in the years following his death. Sadly, his achievements in forging unity between Hindus and Muslims in Bengal survived his death by only a few years: factionalism and violence led ultimately to the partition of the province on independence in 1947. ► **BENGAL, PARTITION OF; BOSE, SUBHAS CHANDRA**

**Dashkova, Ekaterina Romanovna** (1743–1810)
Russian princess and author. In 1759 she married Prince Dashkov. She was an intimate friend and leading supporter of the Empress **CATHERINE II, THE GREAT** in the conspiracy that deposed her husband, **PETER III**, in 1762. She travelled widely in Europe, and was director of the Academy of Arts and Sciences in St Petersburg (1783–96). She wrote several plays, and was the first President of the Russian Academy (1783). On Catherine's death in 1796 she was ordered by the new emperor, her son **PAUL**, to retire to her estates at Novgorod.

**Daudet, Léon** (1867–1942)
French writer and political activist, son of Alphonse Daudet. He studied medicine but turned to journalism, and in 1904 began to associate with the right-wing royalist *Ligue de l'action française* ('League of French Action'), whose newspaper, *L'Action française*, he edited from 1908 (jointly with Charles Maurras after 1917). He sat in the Chamber of Deputies as a leader of the extreme right from 1919 to 1924. He wrote several novels, but is best remembered for his numerous memoirs and critical works, especially *Le Stupide XIXe Siècle* (1922).

**Daughters of the American Revolution (DAR)**
A patriotic society organized in the USA in 1890; members must be directly descended from soldiers or patriots of the revolutionary period. It has three divisions: historical, educational and patriotic. ► **AMERICAN REVOLUTION**

**Dauphin**
The title of the eldest son of the reigning French monarch in the period 1350–1830, acquired in 1349 when the future King **CHARLES V** purchased the lands known as Dauphin.

**David I** (c.1085–1153)
King of Scots (1124/53). He was the youngest son of **MALCOLM III, CANMORE** and Queen (later St) **MARGARET**. Educated at the court of **HENRY I** of England, he became Earl of Huntingdon through his marriage to Maud de Senlis (c.1113). Once King, he emphasized his independence, systematically strengthened royal power, and firmly secured the foundations of the medieval Kingdom of Scotland. In 1136, as a nominal supporter of the claims of his niece, Empress Matilda, to the English crown, he embarked on wars of territorial conquest against Stephen. He was defeated in 1138 at the Battle of the Standard, near Northallerton, but from 1141 occupied the whole of northern England to the Ribble and the Tees.

**David II** (1324–71)
King of Scots (1329/71). The only surviving son of Robert **BRUCE**, he became King at the age of five. In 1334, after the victory of **EDWARD III** of England at the Battle of **HALIDON HILL** (1333), he fled to France. He returned in 1341, and later invaded England, but was defeated and captured at Neville's Cross, near Dunbar (1346), and was kept prisoner for eleven years. After his death at Edinburgh he was succeeded by his sister's son, **ROBERT II**.

**Davies, Clement Edward** (1884–1962)
British politician. Elected MP for Montgomeryshire in 1929, he held his seat until his death. Although offered a post as Education Secretary in Winston **CHURCHILL**'s 1951–5 government, he declined, and thus helped to preserve the independent existence of the **LIBERAL PARTY**, which he led from 1945 to 1956.

**Davis, Angela** (1944– )
US activist. In the late 1960s she became involved with the Student Non-violent Coordinating Committee and the **BLACK PANTHERS**, and in 1968 she joined the Communist Party. She was arrested on charges of conspiracy, kidnapping and murder in 1970, but after a ten-month trial she was acquitted of all charges.

**Davis, Jefferson** (1808–89)
US politician. After studying at the US Military Academy at West Point, he served in several frontier campaigns. He entered the **HOUSE OF REPRESENTATIVES** for Mississippi (1845), fought in the **MEXICAN WAR** (1846–7), and became Secretary of War (1853–7). In the **SENATE** (1847–51) he led the extreme States' Rights Party, and supported **SLAVERY**. President of the Confederate States of America at the close of the **AMERICAN CIVIL WAR** (1865), he was imprisoned for two years, then released on bail. Though indicted for treason, he was never brought to trial, and he was included in the amnesty of 1872.

**Davison, Emily** (1872–1913)
English suffragette. Born in Blackheath, she was educated first at London University and then at Oxford, where she gained a first in English. In 1906 she became a militant member of the Women's Social and Political Union (WSPU). Her activities included stone-throwing, setting letterboxes alight, and attacking a Baptist minister whom she mistook for **LLOYD-GEORGE**. Frequently imprisoned, she often went on hunger strike, and was repeatedly force-fed. In the 1913 Derby, wearing a WSPU banner, she tried to catch the reins of the king's horse, but she was

trampled underfoot and died several days later. ▶ **SUFFRAGETTES**

**Davitt, Michael** (1846–1906)
Founder of the Irish **LAND LEAGUE**. Before becoming a journalist, he worked in a cotton mill, where he lost an arm in an accident. In 1866 he joined the Fenian Movement, was arrested in 1870 for sending guns to Ireland, and sentenced to 15 years' penal servitude. Released in 1877, he began an anti-landlord crusade that culminated in the Land League (1879). During a further period of imprisonment, he was elected an MP (1882), but disqualified from taking his seat. A strong Home Ruler but opponent of **PARNELL**, he was twice more an MP (1892–3 and 1895–9). ▶ **FENIANS; HOME RULE**

**Davout, Louis Nicolas** (1770–1823)
French general. He was educated with **NAPOLEON I** at the military school of Brienne. As general he accompanied Napoleon to the East, and mainly secured the victory at the Battle of **ABOUKIR BAY** (1799). A Marshal of the Empire (1804), he acted a brilliant part at **AUSTERLITZ** (1805) and Auerstädt (1806), and was made Duke of Auerstädt (1808). As governor of Poland he ruled that country with the harshest despotism; after the retreat from Moscow he became Governor-General of the Hanse towns. On Napoleon's return from Elba in 1815, Davout was appointed War Minister; after the Battle of **WATERLOO** he received the command of the remnant of the French army under the walls of Paris. In 1819 he was made a peer of France. ▶ **JENA AND AUERSTÄDT, BATTLES OF**

**Dawes Plan** (1924)
A report on Germany's economic problems issued by a committee presided over by US banker Charles G Dawes (1865–1951). The plan laid down a schedule of annual German payments of **REPARATIONS**, outlined the reorganization of the German Reichsbank, and recommended a large foreign loan for Germany. A further report was drawn up in 1929 by an international commission chaired by US Corporation official Owen Young (1874–1962). ▶ **YOUNG PLAN**

**Dayan, Moshe** (1915–81)
Israeli general and politician. During the 1930s he joined the illegal Jewish defence organization, the **HAGANAH**, and was imprisoned by the British (1939–41), then released to fight with the Allies in **WORLD WAR II** (when he lost his left eye, thereafter wearing his distinctive black eye-patch). He became Chief of Staff (1953–8), joined the Knesset as a Labour member in 1959, but left the Labour Party in 1966 to set up the Rafi Party with David **BEN-GURION**. He won international acclaim as Defence Minister in 1967 when his heavily outnumbered forces triumphed over Egypt, Jordan and Syria in the **SIX-DAY WAR**, and he himself became a symbol of Israeli dash and courage. As Foreign Minister, he helped to secure the historic peace treaty with Egypt (1977). He resigned from the **BEGIN** government in 1979, and launched a new centre party in 1981, but died the same year.

**D'Azeglio, Massimo Tarpelli** (1798–1866)
Piedmontese politician, painter and novelist. Influenced by his friend Cesare **BALBO** and the exiled Vincenzo **GIOBERTI**, D'Azeglio published his famous

*Degli ultimi casi di Romagna* in 1846, in which he developed a moderate, patriotic programme. As well as developing the ideas of Balbo and Gioberti, he succeeded them as Piedmontese Prime Minister, replacing the latter in May 1849 and retaining the post until 1852. During his period of office, extensive anticlerical legislation was initiated which was to continue under his successor, CAVOUR. In 1860 D'Azeglio was made Governor of Milan after its acquisition from the Austrians, but he remained unenthusiastic about annexation of the south of Italy, judging the time not yet right.

## Dazhai

A production brigade in the Chinese province of Shanxi that was personally hailed by MAO ZEDONG in 1964 as a national model for agricultural development, embodying the ideals of self-help, egalitarianism and ideological correctness. Peasants in Dazhai were said to have transformed the barren hillsides into fertile terraced fields. After Mao's death in 1976, the achievements of Dazhai were increasingly called into question and its production figures were said to have been falsified.

## D-Day (6 June 1944)

The day when the Allies launched the greatest amphibious operation in history (codenamed 'Overlord'), and invaded German-occupied Europe. By the end of D-Day, 130,000 troops had been landed on five beach-heads along a 50mi/80km stretch of the coast of NORMANDY, at a cost of 10,000 casualties. ► NORMANDY CAMPAIGN; WORLD WAR II

## DDP (*Deutsche Demokratische Partei*, 'German Democratic Party')

German political party. The DDP was founded on 20 Nov 1918 from left-liberal elements who supported the transformation of post-WORLD WAR I Germany from a semi-absolutist monarchy to a parliamentary democracy. Until its dissolution in 1930, the DDP participated actively in Weimar coalition governments, particularly with the SPD and the CENTRE PARTY. Its middle-class supporters, however, became increasingly disenchanted with the republic and abandoned the DDP in large numbers. On 9 Nov 1930 the party was wound up and its remnants integrated in the small DSP (German State Party). ► WEIMAR REPUBLIC

## Deák, Ferenc (1803–76)

Hungarian politician. Born into the gentry class, he practised as an advocate, and entered the national Diet in 1832, playing a moderate liberal role. In 1848 he became Minister of Justice, dissociating himself from Lajos KOSSUTH's more extreme Magyar nationalism. In the restored Diet of 1860–1, he emerged as leader of moderate liberalism; his efforts helped Hungary to recover her constitution (1867), and on her behalf he negotiated the AUSGLEICH of 1867, establishing the Dual Monarchy of AUSTRIA-HUNGARY.

## Deakin, Alfred (1856–1919)

Australian politician. He entered the Victorian Legislative Assembly in 1879 and held various offices, including that of Chief Secretary (1886–90). Out of office after 1890, his political interests increasingly centred on FEDERATION. He was a member of the committees that drew up draft constitutions at both the National Australasian Convention in 1891 and the Federal Convention of 1897–8, and went to Britain with BARTON's delegation to present the draft constitution to the British parliament in 1900. He became Attorney-General in Barton's first federal government and was largely responsible for the immigration legislation that created the WHITE AUSTRALIA POLICY and the Judiciary Act that established the High Court. He became Prime Minister on Barton's retirement (1903), and held the office again in 1905–8 with the support of Labor. His second ministry created much of the distinctive structure of Australian government, including 'New Protection', which attempted to link wage rates to the new protective tariff. Although a lifelong social reformer, Deakin was wary of trade union power and the strict party discipline of Labor, and his third ministry (1909–10) was in coalition with Sir Joseph COOK's anti-socialists, marking a fundamental realignment in Australian politics. A nationalist, Deakin sought greater Australian influence in imperial affairs, criticizing the naval subsidy to Britain and promoting an Australian navy and compulsory military service. Yet he was also an imperialist, so effective as an advocate of imperial preference and closer union at the 1907 Imperial Conference that some British imperialists considered inviting him to lead an imperial party in Britain. Failing health forced his political retirement in 1913.

## De Ambris, Alceste (1874–1934)

Italian politician and trade unionist. After leading a long strike in the Parma region in 1908, he was forced into political exile, but in 1913 was elected to the Italian parliament. He campaigned for intervention in WORLD WAR I in the hope that it would trigger a revolution, and in 1919 he joined Gabriele D'ANNUNZIO in FIUME where he was responsible for drafting a bizarre, guild-based constitution that was later to inspire the fascist CORPORATIONS. He left Italy in 1922 after MUSSOLINI's seizure of power.

## Déat, Marcel (1894–1955)

French socialist politician. He left the United Socialist Party (SFIO) in 1933 as co-founder of the 'neo-socialist' *Parti socialiste de France* ('Socialist Party of France') which did not long survive. A visceral hatred of war led him from appeasement to COLLABORATION. In 1941 he created the RNP (*Rassemblement national populaire*, 'National Popular Assembly') in the zone of German occupation. In Mar 1944 German pressure forced LAVAL to accept him as Minister of Labour in the VICHY government; he fled to Germany, was sentenced to death *in absentia*, but evaded arrest until his death in Italy. ► SOCIALIST PARTY (FRANCE)

## De Beers Consolidated Mines Ltd

The diamond mining company formed by Cecil RHODES in 1887 from the amalgamation of several companies operating at Kimberley, Cape Province. The De Beers mine was one of the original diamond concessions named after the Boer farmer on whose land the diamonds were found. Rhodes and his associate Rudd formed the De Beers Mining Company in 1880 and set about the gradual acquisition of other mines. Kimberley became virtually a company town and by 1900 De Beers was contributing 50 per cent of all the exports of the Cape Colony. Rhodes used both his personal wealth derived from the Company and the Company's own finances to help to advance his interests on the Rand and to form the **BRITISH SOUTH AFRICA COMPANY** to pursue his dreams in Central Africa. De Beers developed the closed compound system for migrant black labourers that became a major feature of South African urban life, and remains one of the most powerful companies in South Africa.

**De Bono, Emilio** (1866–1944)
Italian soldier and politician. Present at the humiliating defeat of the Battle of **ADOWA** in 1896, De Bono commanded a corps in **WORLD WAR I**. After the war, he rallied to **FASCISM** and took part in the **MARCH ON ROME**. He was Director of Police and then Governor of Tripolitania from 1925. In 1935 he was placed in charge of the forces to invade Ethiopia but was quickly replaced by **BADOGLIO**. As early as 1940, De Bono began to have doubts over **MUSSOLINI**'s fitness to lead Italy in a war, worried by the latter's desire to control all policy personally. He was present at the meeting of the **FASCIST GRAND COUNCIL** of 25 July 1943 that toppled Mussolini, and was later put on trial and executed by the Republic of **SALÒ**.

**Debray, Régis** (1940–)
French Marxist theorist. Educated at the École Normale Supérieure, he gained international fame through his association with the Marxist revolutionary Ernesto Che **GUEVARA** in Latin America during the 1960s. His most influential writings have been *Revolution in the Revolution?* (1967) and *The Power of the Intellectual in France* (1979), the latter a broadside against the growing influence of 'mediacrats'.

**Debré, Michel Jean Pierre** (1912–96)
French politician. After taking part in the **RESISTANCE MOVEMENT**, he helped to set up of the *École Nationale d'Administration* (ENA, 'National School of Administration') in 1945, the training ground for France's governing élites in politics, industry and the civil service in subsequent years. He was elected to parliament as a member of the Gaullist Party (RPF) in 1948, and violently attacked the constitution of the Fourth Republic. In 1958 de **GAULLE** charged him with the task of producing the new constitution of the Fifth Republic, and made him its first Prime Minister (1959–62). ► **GAULLISTS**; **REPUBLIC, FIFTH** (France); **REPUBLIC, FOURTH** (France)

**Debs, Eugène Victor** (1855–1926)
US politician. He worked as a locomotive fireman, and in 1893 was founder and first President of the American Railway Union, in 1894 leading the **PULLMAN STRIKE** for higher wages. He helped to establish the Socialist Party of America, was imprisoned for labour agitation, and between 1900 and 1920 stood five times as socialist candidate for President. His indictment for violation of the Espionage Act brought him imprisonment (1918–21).

**Decatur, Stephen** (1779–1820)
US naval commander of French descent. He served against the French, and gained great distinction in the war with Tripoli (1801–5), burning the captured Philadelphia, and escaping under the fire of 141 guns. Promoted captain in 1804 and commodore in 1810, in the **WAR OF 1812** with England he captured the frigate *Macedonian*, but in 1814 surrendered to the British. He was killed in a duel at Bladensburg, Maryland.

**Deccani Sultanates**
Successors in the Deccan to the Bahmani Sultanate, comprising the Imad Shahi Dynasty of Berar (1484–1575), Barid Shahi Dynasty of Bidar (1492–1619), Qutb Shahi Dynasty of Golconda (1518–1687), Nizam Shahi Dynasty of Ahmadnagar (1490–1637) and Adil Shahi Dynasty of Bijapur (1489–1686). Usually disunited, the four sultans of Ahmadnagar, Bidar, Bijapur and Golconda united in 1565 to inflict a decisive defeat on Ramaraja, the Vijayanagari ruler. Shia Muslim by persuasion, they were the target of **AURANGZEB**'s Sunni orthodoxy and finally he eliminated them.

**December Ninth Movement** (1935)
A massive student demonstration in the Chinese capital of Beijing to protest against Japanese military incursions in north China, and to call upon the Chinese government of **CHIANG KAI-SHEK** to lead a campaign of national resistance. Although the demonstration was brutally suppressed, the movement provided many supporters for the Chinese Communist Party, increasingly perceived as the genuine representative of Chinese nationalism because of its call for an anti-Japanese war. ► **COMMUNIST PARTY, CHINESE**

**Decembrists**
A group of progressive-minded Russian army officers who had long been discussing constitutional reform, and who attempted a coup against the autocratic government of the new tsar **NICHOLAS I** (12 Dec 1825). The rebellion was quickly suppressed, five of its leaders hanged, and over 200 conspirators exiled to Siberia. They were later regarded as martyrs and founders of the 19c Russian revolutionary movement. ► **ROMANOV DYNASTY**

**Declaration of Independence** (1776)
The document adopted by the US **CONTINENTAL CONGRESS** to proclaim the separation of the 13 colonies from Britain. Drawn up by a committee of John **ADAMS**, Benjamin **FRANKLIN**, Thomas **JEFFERSON**, Robert R Livingston and Roger **SHERMAN**, it announced the right of revolution, detailing the Americans' reasons for the break, and asserted that American government should be based on a theory of natural law, and should respect the fundamental rights of individuals.

**Declaration of Rights** (1689)
An English statute which ended the brief interregnum after **JAMES VII AND II** quit the throne in Dec 1688, establishing **WILLIAM III** and Mary II as joint monarchs. The bill effectively ensured that monarchs must operate with the consent of parliament, and must not suspend or dispense with laws passed by that body. ► **BILL OF RIGHTS**

**Declaration of the Rights of Man and Citizen** (27 Aug 1789)
A declaration made by the French National Assembly, proclaiming liberty of conscience, of property, and of the press, and freedom from arbitrary imprisonment. It finally ended the privileged system of the **ANCIEN RÉGIME**. ► **FRENCH REVOLUTION**

**Declaratory Act** (1766)
A British Act passed by the **ROCKINGHAM** government.

After much opposition in the US colonies to the introduction of taxes by the preceding George GRENVILLE administration, Rockingham repealed the STAMP ACT (1765); but this legislation reasserted the British parliament's general right to legislate for the colonies 'in all cases whatsoever'.

### Defence of the Realm Act (DORA) (Nov 1914)

A British Act introduced to give the government greater controls over the activities of its citizens. The most important control related to restrictions on press reporting and other forms of censorship. The restrictions were increased as WORLD WAR I progressed.

### Defenestration of Prague (1618)

The dramatic gesture with which the Czech Protestants challenged the authority and religion of the Habsburg Emperors within the Czech lands. On an issue of church-building, a crowd of nobles and knights marched on Prague Castle and, after a dispute, threw two imperial councillors, the Counts Martinic and Slavata, and their secretary out of a high window. Falling on rubbish, the victims survived. But in due course the Czech estates proceeded to depose FERDINAND II from the thrones of Bohemia and Moravia and to replace him with FREDERICK V of the Palatinate. The course was set for the Battle of the WHITE MOUNTAIN and the end of Czech independence. ► HABSBURG DYNASTY

### De Gasperi, Alcide (1881–1954)

Italian politician. An Austrian subject until the end of WORLD WAR I, he was elected to the Austrian parliament in 1911 as a deputy for the Trentino and became known as an ardent defender of the interests of the Italian minority. In 1919, after Italian annexation of his native region, he attended the first congress of the POPOLARI at Bologna and in 1921 was elected to the Italian parliament. Although he originally backed MUSSOLINI's government, he soon withdrew his support and was arrested while trying to flee the country with false papers; he was sentenced to four years in prison but served only six months. On his release, he became Vatican Librarian, a post he held until the liberation of Rome. Made Secretary-General of the CHRISTIAN DEMOCRATIC PARTY (DC), he was Minister without Portfolio in the first BONOMI ministry, while PARRI made him Foreign Minister. In June 1946 he became Prime Minister, successfully supporting Italy's transition from monarchy to republic and signing the peace treaty with the Allies (Feb 1947). In Jan 1947 he formed a government with the support of both socialists and communists, but he soon jettisoned this alliance, excluding them from his government in May 1947. Foremost among his reasons for ending a policy of cooperation with the left was the heightening tension between the USA (on which Italy was heavily dependent for investment and aid) and the USSR, and increasing pressure from Pope PIUS XII, who had made it clear as early as June 1946 that he saw it as his 'main aim to fight communism'. Despite a narrower basis for his government, De Gasperi remained Prime Minister until July 1953, providing continuity even though he presided over eight separate governments. He remained Secretary-General of the DC until his death.

### De Geer, Louis Gerhard (1818–96)

Swedish politician. In 1858 he was appointed Minister of Justice, a post which made him in effect Prime Minister, and which he held until 1870. He was largely responsible for the replacement in 1866 of the Diet of four estates (nobles, clergy, burghers and peasants) with a parliament of two houses, one indirectly elected through county councils and one directly elected on a narrow franchise. He was appointed Prime Minister (the title being then accepted) in 1876, but resigned four years later after defeat in parliament.

### Degrelle, Léon (1906–94)

Belgian politician. From French-speaking Belgium, he founded the fascist REXISM movement in the 1930s, and achieved considerable support in the elections of 1936. During WORLD WAR II he collaborated with the German forces, commanding the Walloon (French-speaking Belgian) regiment on the Russian front, and was briefly put in charge of German-occupied Belgium towards the end of the war. He escaped in 1945 to Spain, and was condemned to death in his absence. In 1974 he was declared an undesirable alien in Belgium.

### Dekker, Eduard Douwes, pseudonym Multatuli (1820–87)

Dutch radical publicist and novelist. He served for many years in the Dutch civil service in Java, and in his novel *Max Havelaar* (1860), and in many bitter satires, he protested in particular against the abuses of the Dutch colonial CULTURE SYSTEM.

### de Klerk, F(rederik) W(illem) (1936–)

South African politician. Born into a prominent Nationalist family (his father was a cabinet minister and President of the Senate, his uncle the Prime Minister Johannes STRIJDOM), he graduated from Potchefstroom University and established a legal practice in Vereeniging, which he represented as a NATIONAL PARTY member in the South African parliament from 1972. He served in the cabinets of both B J VORSTER and P W BOTHA, but never in major positions. Elected National Party leader for the Transvaal in 1982, when TREURNICHT left to form the CONSERVATIVE PARTY OF SOUTH AFRICA, he used that position as the political base from which to replace Botha on his retirement in 1989. He was chiefly responsible for the public policy of ending APARTHEID, successfully winning elections in Sep 1989 (but with a reduced majority), creating an all-party Convention for a Democratic South Africa (CODESA), and winning a referendum supporting negotiations with the ANC, from which he removed the ban in Feb 1990. Although attacked from the right for betraying Afrikaner and white interests, and from the left for sanctioning state and Inkatha violence, his leadership of the white population towards an accord with blacks in South Africa was essential for the maintenance of peace during the handover to majority rule in South Africa. In 1993 a transitional constitution was adopted which extended the franchise to all South African adults, and de Klerk and MANDELA were joint recipients of the NOBEL PEACE PRIZE. When Mandela became President of South Africa in the country's first multiracial elections, de Klerk was appointed Second Deputy President, in which post he remained until 1996, when the National Party withdrew from the ruling coalition. He stood down as its leader in 1997.

## Delaney, Martin Robinson (1812–85)
US anti-**SLAVERY** activist. The grandson of slaves, he became a doctor and a journalist, his major work being *The Condition, Elevation, Emigration and Destiny of the Colored Peoples of the United States* (1852). By 1854, despairing of ever achieving black **CIVIL RIGHTS** in the North, he began to advocate emigration of blacks to Africa. This he abandoned after travelling in West Africa on the eve of the **AMERICAN CIVIL WAR**, resuming the struggle for racial equality within the USA, and becoming active in the Freedmen's Bureau.

## Delaware
An Algonquian-speaking Native American tribe who inhabited New Jersey, northern Delaware and eastern Pennsylvania in the early 17c, when they were at peace with the early European Quaker settlers. However, their numbers declined due to European diseases, relations with the colonists deteriorated, and after selling large areas of land the Delaware drifted south into Ohio, where they settled in the 1760s. They fought the English in **PONTIAC'S CONSPIRACY**, became British allies during the **AMERICAN REVOLUTION** and the **WAR OF 1812**, but opposed Anglo-Americans during the late 18c, until they ceded most of their land in the Treaty of **GREENVILLE** (1795). There are now Delaware reservations in Wisconsin, Oklahoma and Ontario, where most of the c.16,000 population live. ▶ **NATIVE AMERICANS**

## Delcassé, Théophile (1852–1923)
French politician. He was twice Foreign Minister (1898–1905 and 1914–15), during which time he promoted the **ENTENTE CORDIALE** with Britain (1904), and worked towards the **TRIPLE ENTENTE** with Britain and Russia.

## Delescluze, (Louis) Charles (1809–71)
French radical republican and journalist. His revolutionary politics drove him from France to journalism in Belgium (1835), but the **FEBRUARY REVOLUTION** (1848) brought him back to Paris. His writing made him popular, but brought him imprisonment (1849–53), and he was transported until 1859. He played a prominent part in the **PARIS COMMUNE**, and died on its last barricade.

## Delfim Neto, Antônio (1929–)
Brazilian economist and politician. The son of Italian immigrants, he is widely viewed as the typical technocrat, an econometrician who believed in rapid GDP growth and centralization as an antidote to the social problems of Brazil. He was Economic Secretary to São Paulo state (1966) and Planning Minister under Costa e Silva, becoming 'economic Tsar' under his successor, Emílio **MÉDICI**. Heavily reliant upon repression to curb the labour unions, he became the darling of the propertied class as the author of the 'Economic Miracle' of 1968–73 and was recalled to office (Aug 1979–Mar 1985). He attempted to sustain GDP and export growth as antidotes to soaring international oil prices, interest rates and a deteriorating balance of payments.

## Delgado, Humberto (1906–65)
Portuguese general and politician. Born into a modest military family, in the 1920s he keenly supported the counter-revolution as a junior officer. His vertiginous rise through the military ranks led him to become, at 46, the youngest general in the Portuguese armed forces. However, **SALAZAR** never entirely trusted Delgado, considering him too independent. Delgado's democratic experience abroad, especially in the USA (1953–7), caused him to reject the Salazar regime, and in Apr 1958 Delgado scandalized the dictatorship by standing against the official presidential candidate. His charismatic appeal led to huge demonstrations of support in Lisbon and Oporto, but a heavily rigged vote ensured his defeat. The humiliated Salazar soon got rid of direct presidential elections, restrictive as they had been. Delgado tried to stage three coup attempts in 1958, but failed on each occasion for lack of support. He left Portugal in 1959 and attempted unsuccessfully to win over the armed forces from abroad. He was murdered in Spain, near the Portuguese border, by the **PIDE** in mysterious circumstances.

## Delhi Sultanate (1200–1526)
The principal northern Indian Muslim kingdom between the 13c and 16c, in which Sultan **ILTUTMISH** (1211/36) made his permanent capital at Delhi. It became an imperial power under the Khalji Dynasty (1290–1320), but its power was much reduced under the **SAYYID** and **LODI** dynasties, and the sultanate was destroyed by **BABUR** at the Battle of **PANIPAT** in 1526. ▶ **MUGHAL EMPIRE**

## Deligiannis or Deliyannes, Theodoros (1824–1905)
Greek politician. From a prominent family of landowners, he entered politics as a Conservative, first serving as Foreign Minister (1878) and later as Prime Minister (1885, 1890 and 1895). An advocate of the **MEGALE IDEA**, he conducted an extravagant foreign policy intended to bring about the creation of Greater Greece. In Mar 1905 he was assassinated on the steps of the National Assembly.

## Delors, Jacques (1925–)
French politician. He served as social affairs adviser to Prime Minister Jacques Chaban-Delmas (1969–72). He joined the **SOCIALIST PARTY** in 1973 and served as Minister of Economy and Finance in the administration of President **MITTERRAND** (1981–4), overseeing a programme of austerity (*rigueur*). He became President of the European Commission in 1985 and was elected to a second four-year term as President in 1988, a position he held until 1995 when Jacques **SANTER** took over. As Commission President he oversaw significant budgetary reforms and the move towards the removal of all internal barriers in the **EC** in 1992, with increased powers residing in Brussels.

## Delta Works
Series of public works in the Netherlands to protect the coastline against storms, designed after the disastrous floods of Feb 1953. The Delta Plan (5 Nov 1957) laid down projects to strengthen the water defences by building new or improved dams, bridges and surge barriers in the south-west of the country, effectively closing off the sea-arms between Rotterdam

and Antwerp. The project cost enormous sums of public money, opened up the Dutch province of Zeeland to economic development, was generally successful in achieving its aims, and was officially completed in 1986.

### Dembiński, Henryk (1791–1864)
Polish soldier. He entered the Polish army in 1809 and fought under **NAPOLEON I** against Russia and at **LEIPZIG** (1813). In the Polish revolution of 1830 he eventually became Commander-in-Chief; in 1833 he entered the service of **MUHAMMAD 'ALI**. On the outbreak of the Hungarian insurrection in 1848, Lajos **KOSSUTH** appointed him Commander-in-Chief. He was hampered by the jealousy of **GÖRGEY**, and after the defeat of Kapolna (1849) was forced to resign. On Kossuth's resignation he fled to Turkey, but in 1850 returned to Paris.

### Demirel, Süleyman (1924– )
Turkish politician. He qualified as an engineer at Istanbul Technical University and worked on hydroelectric schemes in the USA and Turkey before making the transition from public service to politics. In 1964 he became President of the centrist Justice Party (JP), now subsumed in the True Path Party (TPP). He served three terms as Prime Minister from 1965, until a military coup in 1980 resulted in a three-year ban on political activity. He was placed in detention but released in 1983. He returned to power in the 1991 election and, upon the death of Torgut **ÖZAL**, became President in 1993, serving until 2000.

### democracy
A form of government in which the people govern themselves or elect representatives to govern them. This latter form, or representative democracy, is the only one feasible in large political units, although plebiscite procedures may preserve some of the features of the direct form in a representative democracy. The oldest democracies are identified as those that developed in some ancient Greek city-states in the 5c BC, especially Athens, in which assemblies of free adult males decided policy by open voting. In larger nation-states, democracy is representative, ie citizens elect representatives (such as MPs) to act and legislate on their behalf. It was not until the 20c, with the abolition of **SLAVERY** and the extension of voting to women, that 'the people' could be taken to mean the entire adult population of a country. Further necessary conditions are the legal equality of citizens, and freedom of information to ensure that citizens are in an equal and informed position to choose their rulers and hold them accountable. Some critics argue that economic equality is also necessary for all classes in society to take a full part in political life.

### Democracy Wall Movement (1978–9)
A protest movement in China against the excesses of the **CULTURAL REVOLUTION**, the corruption of the Chinese Communist Party, and infringement of human rights. Ironically, the movement initially may well have been unofficially encouraged by **DENG XIAOPING**, who was at the time intent on reducing the influence of his Maoist opponents. At the Third Party Plenum (Dec 1978), Deng succeeded in gaining approval for his economic reforms. Wall-posters started to appear in the centre of the city during the Third Plenum that not only criticized **MAO ZEDONG** and the Cultural Revolution, but also called into question the socialist system itself. Magazines were also published advocating greater democratic and artistic freedom. Many of the people involved were young urbanites, including workers, students, and former **RED GUARDS** disillusioned with the party. In Mar 1979 Deng Xiaoping, fearing that the protests had gone too far, ordered a clampdown and a number of dissidents were arrested. By the end of 1979 the movement had virtually come to an end; a limited number of wall-posters were allowed only to be displayed in a park far from the city centre. ➤ **MAOISM**

### Democratic Centralism (post-1906)
The term used by **LENIN** in 1906 to describe the operating principles that would govern the Communist Party and the Soviet state. Elections and accountability were mandatory, but it was also ordained that lower bodies must implement the decisions of higher bodies. This was used to eliminate whatever democracy the revolutionaries of 1917 might have envisaged and to institute dictatorship. It was implicit in the 1936 constitution, explicit in that of 1977. It continued as a party rule to the end and helps to explain why **COMMUNISM** was doomed as soon as open debate was allowed after 1985.

### Democratic Labour Party (DLP)
One of the two political parties that have shared power in Barbados since 1938. From that date, Grantley **ADAMS**'s Barbados Labour Party dominated politics until 1961, when the DLP, led by Errol **BARROW**, took a majority of seats in the legislature. The DLP was ousted in the 1976 election by the BLP, led by 'Tom' Adams, but with Adams's death in 1985, the DLP returned to power (under Barrow) in 1986. Barrow's death that year saw the leadership of the party pass into the hands of Erskine Sandiford, and Sandiford and the DLP were again victorious in the 1991 election. They remained in power until 1994, when they were again defeated by the BLP, this time led by Owen Arthur, but have not been in office since.

### Democratic Labor Party, Australian (ADLP)
Australian political party, formed in 1957 from anticommunist groups that had formerly been part of the **AUSTRALIAN LABOR PARTY** (ALP). The DLP was largely centred in Victoria, and drew most of its support from parts of the Catholic section of Australian society. At its height, in the late 1950s and through the 1960s, its importance lay in its ability to prevent the ALP from winning national government. Its policies were strongly anti-communist and pro-defence, and incorporated elements of Catholic teaching on social matters. No DLP representative has been elected to the national parliament since 1974.

### Democratic Party
US political party. It was originally composed in the late 18c of those opposed to the economic policies of Alexander Hamilton and in sympathy with France rather than Britain (during the Anglo-French Wars of the 1790s). Its first successful presidential candidate was Thomas **JEFFERSON**, and in the early 1800s it dominated its opponent, the **FEDERALIST PARTY**. During the 1830s, under Presidents Andrew **JACKSON** and Martin **VAN BUREN**, the party gained mass appeal

among the electorate through shrewd political management, and was identified as representative of the 'common man'. The party was split over **SLAVERY** and secession during the **AMERICAN CIVIL WAR**, and its position of national dominance was taken over by the **REPUBLICAN PARTY**. After the war the party became conservative, based in the South and West, achieving only intermittent success. It returned to a majority position in 1932, with Franklin D **ROOSEVELT**'s '**NEW DEAL**', and added large urban areas and ethnic, racial and religious support to its conservative Southern base. It also became associated with a more liberal stance on social reform and minority rights, especially in the 1960s. Since the early 1960s it has had great difficulty winning the presidency, with the exception of Jimmy **CARTER** (1977–81) and Bill **CLINTON** (1993–2000). Its traditional majorities in the **HOUSE OF REPRESENTATIVES** and **SENATE** fell to Republican resurgence in the 1990s, partly because its former total grip on the South collapsed as a result of the **CIVIL RIGHTS**' agitation, which drove white voters into a revived Southern Republican party. ► **WHIG PARTY**

**Democratic Party of the Left** ► PCI

**Democratic Unionist Party**
The political party formed in Northern Ireland in 1971 under the leadership of Rev Ian **PAISLEY** after a split in the Unionist Party over Protestant reaction to demands, both by Catholics in the province and from Westminster, for greater social and political equality. It has had strong appeal to many working-class Protestants, and during the 1980s attracted about one-third of the Unionist vote. Frequently suspicious in the 1970s and early 1980s that the official Unionists were less zealous in their support for Protestantism, the two Unionist parties agreed on concerted opposition to the **ANGLO-IRISH AGREEMENT** (1985), and agreed in the 1987 general election not to nominate candidates against one another, thus avoiding a split in the Unionist vote. Although both parties cautiously endorsed the 1993 **DOWNING STREET DECLARATION** and the resultant peace talks in 1994 (the DUP with extreme reluctance and scepticism), the Official Ulster Unionist Party, under the leadership of David **TRIMBLE** from 1995, willingly entered into the multiparty talks of 1997 that resulted in the **GOOD FRIDAY AGREEMENT** (1998); the DUP refused to join the talks and criticized the ambiguities of the agreement but took up its seats in the Northern Ireland Assembly elected in Jun 1998 although it refused to recognize the representatives of **SINN FÉIN**. In the Nov 2003 elections to the (suspended) Northern Ireland Assembly, the DUP won the most seats.

**Democrats 66** (*Democraten 66*, 'D66')
Dutch political party formed in 1966 on a programme of radical constitutional reform. It wished to break the mould of 'compromise politics' and **VERZUILING** in the Netherlands by introducing a directly elected President, and by changing pure proportional representation to a more district-based system. In other matters D66 is generally left-of-centre. It has formed part of every coalition government since 1994, except for a short-lived government in 2002.

**Deng Xiaoping (Teng Hsiao-p'ing)**, originally **Deng Xixian** (1904–97)
Chinese politician. Born in Sichuan Province, he joined the Chinese Communist Party (CCP) in 1925 as a student in Paris, where he met a fellow-student **ZHOU ENLAI**, and adopted the name Xiaoping ('Little Peace'). He later studied in Moscow (1926), where he became associated with **MAO ZEDONG**. By 1930 he had joined Mao's army in China, during the period of the **JIANGXI SOVIET**. He took part in the **LONG MARCH** (1934–6) and served as a political commissar to the **PEOPLE'S LIBERATION ARMY** (PLA) during the civil war (1937–49). He rose quickly: by 1954 he was Secretary-General of the Chinese Communist Party and in 1955 became a Politburo member, but reacted strongly against the excesses of the **GREAT LEAP FORWARD** (1958–9). When Mao launched the **CULTURAL REVOLUTION** (1966), Deng was purged along with **LIU SHAOQI**, but retained the confidence of Premier Zhou Enlai and was rehabilitated in 1973 and restored to power as Vice-Premier and Vice-Chairman of the Party in 1975. Again dismissed in 1976, after the death of Mao he was restored again. Working with his protégés **HU YAOBANG** and **ZHAO ZIYANG**, he proceeded to introduce a pragmatic new economic modernization programme, starting with decentralization, which abolished the communes of the 1950s, and led not only to the release of entrepreneurial energy and massive economic growth, but also, later, to provincial discontent engendered by unequal development and rising taxation and corruption. His reputation was tarnished by his imposition of martial law in China in May 1989 and his sanctioning of the army's massacre of around 3,000 unarmed pro-democracy demonstrators in **TIANANMEN SQUARE**, Beijing, the following month. Though devoid of any constitutional authority (he had retired from the Politburo in 1987), he remained in power by virtue of his extreme old age and position as a veteran of the Long March right up to his death.

**Denikin, Anton Ivanovich** (1872–1947)
Russian soldier. He entered the army at the age of 15, and rose to lieutenant-general in **WORLD WAR I**. After the **RUSSIAN REVOLUTION** of 1917 he led the White Army in the south against the **BOLSHEVIKS** (1918–20). He won the Ukraine, but was defeated by the **RED ARMY** at Orel (1919), and in 1920 resigned his command and escaped to Constantinople. Thereafter he lived in exile in France (1926–45) and the USA (1945–7), and wrote books on his military experiences.

**Denkyira**
A state developed in the mid-17c by one of the princelings of the Akan people in the western Gold Coast. Its power was based on gold and trade with Europeans on the coast. However, its ruler never developed an effective imperial administration and it was weakened and eventually destroyed by competition and conflict with its eastern neighbour, the **AKWAMU** state, in the early 18c. Akwamu in its turn was defeated by Akin and then by the **ASHANTI** in the 1730s and 1740s.

**DENMARK** official name **Kingdom of Denmark**
A kingdom in northern Europe, it is the smallest of the Scandinavian countries and consists of most of

the Jutland Peninsula, several islands in the Baltic Sea (the largest include Zealand, Fyn, Lolland, Faister and Bornholm), and some of the northern Frisian Islands in the North Sea. Greenland and the Faroes are self-governing regions of Denmark. It formed part of Viking kingdoms in the 8–10c and was the centre of the Danish Empire under CANUTE in the 11c. In 1389 it was joined with Sweden and Norway under one ruler, an arrangement formalized in the KALMAR UNION (1397); Sweden separated from the union in the 16c, as did Norway in 1814. Schleswig-Holstein was lost to Germany in 1864, but northern Schleswig was returned after a plebiscite in 1920. Denmark was occupied by Germany during WORLD WAR II. Iceland became independent of Danish rule in 1944, and Greenland and the Faroes remain dependencies. Denmark joined the EC in 1973 but rejected membership of the EURO ZONE in 2000. Its monarch, Queen MARGRETHE II, acceded to the throne in 1972. ► SCHLESWIG-HOLSTEIN PROBLEM; SOCIAL DEMO-CRATIC PARTY (Denmark)

### Denmark, German Invasion of (8–9 Apr 1940)

An adjunct to the German invasion of Norway that met with little or no resistance on the part of the Danish armed forces and government. The latter continued in office until dismissed by the German occupying authorities in 1943. ► NORWAY, GERMAN INVASION OF; WORLD WAR II

### Deoband

The 'House of Learning'. This leading Muslim theological centre of India was founded in 1867 by Muhammad Abid Husain in Saharanpur district in the state of Uttar Pradesh. Deoband has a puritanical and orthodox outlook, and prepares students mainly for religious leadership of the Muslim community. Students study jurisprudence, Quranic exegesis, Islamic traditions, scholastic theology and philosophy. Deoband enrols students from all parts of the Muslim world. It has a library which contains Arabic, Persian and Urdu manuscripts. It also has a mosque, lecture halls and student residences.

### Deodoro da Fonseca, Manuel (1827–92)

Brazilian general and politician. A TARIMBEIRO, he served in the front line in the War of the TRIPLE ALLIANCE and was promoted for valour. A traditional Conservative follower of the Marshal Duke of Caxias, he was eventually alienated by Liberal and Conservative politicians' insensitive treatment of the army during the 1880s; idolized by junior officers, he agreed to lead them against the Ouro Prêto cabinet on 15 Nov 1889, and was manoeuvered by republicans into declaring against PEDRO II. A sick man, his presidency

(1889–91) rested on the support of the armed forces. He was outmanoeuvred by Congress, but assumed dictatorial powers in early Nov 1891. A few weeks later he was toppled by a constitutionalist revolt under Floriano PEIXOTO.

### Department of Regional Economic Expansion (DREE)

Canadian federal department. In 1969 it became responsible for the administration of the Agricultural Rehabilitation and Development Act (ARDA) and the Fund for Rural Economic Development (FRED). Parliament gave the department extraordinary powers under the Regional Development Incentives Act. The choice of regions or firms that qualified for capital assistance grants was made by the minister appointed by Pierre TRUDEAU, Pierre Marchand. Up to C$12 million could be allotted to the projects of his choice and soon the department was involved in many different federal/provincial development schemes, so that by 1979 the department's expenditure had grown to half a billion dollars per year.

### dependency theory, also known as Prebisch–Singer theory

An economic theory concerning the terms of trade between industrialized 'core' economies and those on the 'periphery'. Arguing that the 'core' imposes 'underdevelopment' on dependent 'peripheries', it advocates import substitution industrialization (ISI) coupled with central planning, trade barriers and foreign exchange controls to allow developing nations to create a solid industrial base. Economic policies based on this theory were adopted in Latin America and India after WORLD WAR II, but although there were some early successes, lack of skilled workers and experienced management initially prevented these states from exploiting potential new export markets, while long-term trade barriers tended to protect inefficient domestic manufacturing practices. ISI cost too much in subsidies, often failed, and since the theory blocked the formation of trading communities and partnerships, severely hampered the competitiveness of these economies when they did re-enter global export markets, often with catastrophic economic and social results.

### Depretis, Agostino (1813–87)

Italian politician. A friend of both GARIBALDI and MAZZINI, he broke with the latter after the abortive Milanese insurrection of 1853. Depretis played a key part in the Expedition of the THOUSAND to Sicily in 1860, serving for a while as the island's 'prodictator'. Although he began his parliamentary career on the political left, he abandoned his earlier radicalism and achieved ministerial office in 1862 and 1866. He was to be Prime Minister for all but two years in the period 1876–87 and became the arch-exponent of TRASFORMISMO. Depretis played a key part in orientating Italy towards the TRIPLE ALLIANCE with Germany and Austria-Hungary.

### De Priest, Oscar Stanton (1871–1951)

US politician. Born in Alabama, he ran away from home to Chicago where he was the first black to be elected to the city council (as a Republican, in 1915). He became an alderman in 1927, and the first black congressman from the North in 1928. Holding office until 1934, when he was defeated by a black Democrat, he secured passage for a bill to reduce discrimination in the Civilian Conservation Corps.

### Derby, Edward Geoffrey Smith Stanley, 14th Earl of (1799–1869)
British politician. He entered parliament as a Whig in 1828, and became Chief-Secretary for Ireland (1830) and Colonial Secretary (1833), when he carried the Act for the emancipation of West Indian slaves. In 1834 he withdrew from the party and soon after joined the Conservatives, subsequently becoming party leader, 1846–68. In 1844 he entered the House of **LORDS** as a baron. He retired from the cabinet in 1845, when **PEEL** decided to repeal the **CORN LAWS**, and in 1846 headed the Protectionists in the Lords. In 1851 he succeeded his father as Earl of Derby. Leader of minority governments on three occasions (1852, 1858–9 and 1866–8), his third administration nevertheless passed the second Reform Act (1867). ► **CONSERVATIVE PARTY** (UK); **REFORM ACTS**; **TORIES**; **WHIGS**

### Dergue
The name, meaning 'committee', given to the Provisional Military Administrative Council (PMAC) in Ethiopia after the military's overthrow of Emperor **HAILE SELASSIE** in 1974 and chaired by Haile Mariam **MENGISTU**. Operating like a politburo, its members increasingly also came to fill governmental positions, and it was responsible for organizing the creation of the Worker's Revolutionary Party to advance its radical socialist policies.

### Déroulède, Paul (1846–1914)
French politician and poet. A fervent nationalist, founder of the *Ligue des patriotes* ('League of Patriots') in 1882, and the author of patriotic verses, his writings called for revenge on Germany, and he was active in the campaign against **DREYFUS**. In 1900 he was exiled for ten years for sedition, but returned in 1905.

### Desai, Morarji Ranchhodji (1896–1995)
Indian politician. Educated at Bombay University, he became a civil servant, entering politics in 1930. After various ministerial posts, he became a candidate for the premiership in 1964 and 1966, but was defeated by Indira **GANDHI**. He became Deputy Prime Minister but led a breakaway faction of Congress, the Congress (S), following the party's split in 1969. Detained during the state of emergency (1975–7), he was then appointed leader of the newly formed Janata Party, and elected Premier (1977–9). The Janata government was, however, characterized by internal strife and he was forced to resign in 1979.

### desamortización ► DISENTAILMENT

### desegregation
In the USA, the movement to end the **SEGREGATION** between black African-American citizens and whites. After the end of the **AMERICAN CIVIL WAR** many laws enforcing segregation were passed (the **JIM CROW LAWS**). The movement for desegregation began with the foundation of the National Association for the Advancement of Colored People (**NAACP**) in 1909, but met with fierce resistance, especially in the South. **WORLD WAR II** saw the US armed forces still basically segregated, but generated pressure for change. President **TRUMAN** set out to achieve racial integration in the services. During the 1950s and 1960s the **CIVIL RIGHTS MOVEMENT** gained strength. Although the Supreme Court had ruled in 1896 in the **PLESSY V FERGUSON** case that segregation in schools along the 'separate but equal' principle was legal, in 1954 its **BROWN V BOARD OF EDUCATION OF TOPEKA, KANSAS** decision marked the abolition of segregation in state schools and heralded the end of legal segregation everywhere. Together with the NAACP, Martin Luther **KING** and the **FREEDOM RIDERS** became noted leaders of the desegregation movement, and their efforts resulted in the **CIVIL RIGHTS ACTS**.

### Desert Rats
Members of the 7th British Armoured Division, which in 1940 took as its badge the jerboa or desert rat, noted for remarkable leaps. The media applied the name generally to all British servicemen in the **NORTH AFRICAN CAMPAIGN**, and it was readily adopted by those not entitled to wear the jerboa shoulder flash. ► **WORLD WAR II**

### Deshima
A small island in Nagasaki Bay, south-west Japan, the site of a Dutch trading factory between the 17c and 19c. The first Europeans to arrive in Japan were Portuguese and Spanish missionaries in the 16c, followed in the early 17c by Dutch and English traders. Suspicion of Christianity by the Japanese authorities, who perceived it as a political threat, led to the expulsion of the Spanish and Portuguese by the 1630s. The new **TOKUGAWA SHOGUNATE** officially proclaimed a policy of isolation (**SAKOKU**) after 1636, curtailing all foreign trade and contact. The one exception was the permission granted the Dutch to reside and trade at Deshima. It was through Japanese contact with the Dutch that Western learning was introduced into Japan in the 18c and early 19c. A small number of dedicated Japanese scholars translated Dutch texts on anatomy, medicine, shipbuilding, astronomy and gunnery, providing the foundation for early modernization. The significance of Deshima faded once Japan was opened up to Western trade after 1854.

### Desmoulins, (Lucie Simplice) Camille Benoist (1760–94)
French revolutionary and journalist. He studied law in Paris. He played a dramatic part in the storming of the **BASTILLE**. He was also an influential pamphleteer. A member of the **CORDELIERS' CLUB** from its foundation, he was elected to the National **CONVENTION**, and voted for the death of King **LOUIS XVI**. He actively attacked the **GIRONDINS**, but by the end of 1793 argued for moderation, thus incurring the hostility of **ROBESPIERRE**. He was arrested and guillotined. ► **FRENCH REVOLUTION**

### Dessalines, Jean Jacques (c.1758–1806)
Emperor of Haiti (1804/6). Born in the north of Haiti, he was bought at the age of about 30 by a free black named Dessalines, whose name he adopted. In the slave insurrection of 1791 he fought alongside **TOUSSAINT L'OUVERTURE** until the 'governor-general for life' was captured. When it became clear that Napoleon planned to reconquer Haiti and reintroduce slavery, he led an army that defeated the French, who

surrendered in 1803. He was created Governor-General and in Sep 1804 crowned Emperor as Jacques I. But his cruelty and debauchery alienated his adherents, and he was assassinated near Port-au-Prince.

### Destroyer–Bases Deal (1940)

An agreement made between US President Franklin D ROOSEVELT and UK Prime Minister Winston CHURCHILL in which the USA (at the time committed to 'all aid short of war') gave Britain 50 destroyers in return for the lease of eight bases on British territory, including the West Indies, Newfoundland and British Guiana (now Guyana). The destroyers were a vital resource in the early stages of WORLD WAR II, but were of World War I design and soon became obsolete.

### détente

An attempt to lower the tension between states as a means of reducing the possibility of war and of achieving peaceful coexistence between different social and political systems. A prominent feature of relations between the USA and USSR in the 1970s, it led to several agreements over arms (SALT) and security and cooperation (HELSINKI FINAL ACT). In the early 1980s, there was a cooling towards détente on the part of the USA, on the grounds that too many concessions had been made and that the USSR did not adhere to the spirit of such agreements; but there was a considerable improvement in relations in the later part of the decade. ► COLD WAR; CSCE

### Dettingen, Battle of (27 June 1743)

Fought during the War of the AUSTRIAN SUCCESSION on the banks of the River Main between British, Hanoverian and Austrian forces, under the nominal command of GEORGE II, and a French army under Marshal Noailles. The resulting French defeat was not followed up, reducing the battle's strategic importance. This was the last occasion on which a ruling British sovereign took command of troops in battle.

### de Valera, Éamon (1882–1975)

Irish politician. Born in the USA, but brought up in County Limerick, he became a teacher in Dublin, and was active in Gaelic revival and republican movements. A commandant of the Irish Volunteers in the EASTER RISING (1916), he was arrested but escaped the firing squad because of his US citizenship. He became a SINN FÉIN MP in 1917 and was leader of the party from 1917 to 1926. He was elected President of DÁIL EIREANN but resigned in opposition to the Anglo-Irish Treaty (1921) and supported the anti-treaty side in the IRISH CIVIL WAR. In 1926 he became leader of FIANNA FÁIL, his newly formed republican opposition party, which won the 1932 elections. As Prime Minister (1932–48, 1951–4 and 1957–9), he instituted social, industrial and agricultural reforms and was instrumental in framing the constitution of 1937, which established the IRISH FREE STATE as Éire. He was President of Ireland from 1959 to 1973.

### Devolution, War of (1667–8)

A Franco-Spanish conflict prompted by LOUIS XIV of France in pursuit of his wife's legal claims to the Spanish Netherlands. According to the laws of devolution of the provinces of BRABANT and Hainaut, females of a first marriage took precedence over males of a second with regard to property inheritance. To uphold the

claims of Queen MARIA THERESA, the elder daughter of PHILIP IV of Spain, Louis's armies overran Flanders, prompting the Dutch Republic, England and Sweden to negotiate the Triple Alliance (1668); to this, France responded with the invasion of Franche-Comté. When a secret treaty of compromise between Louis and the Emperor LEOPOLD I was signed in early 1668, France agreed to peace at the Treaty of Aix-la-Chapelle (2 May 1668).

### Devonshire, William Cavendish, 4th Duke of (1720–64)

British politician. His family connections enabled him to embark early upon a political career; he became a Whig MP in 1741, a Privy Councillor in 1751, and was appointed Lord Lieutenant and Governor-General of Ireland in 1754. He succeeded to the dukedom in 1755. He was appointed First Lord of the Treasury by GEORGE II in 1756 at the beginning of the SEVEN YEARS' WAR, largely because William PITT, THE ELDER, whose inclusion in a war ministry was considered vital, refused to serve under the Duke of Newcastle. He was ineffectual in the post, resigning after six months. He was Lord Chamberlain of the Household from 1757 to 1762.

### devşirme

In the OTTOMAN EMPIRE, the levy made every five years of one out of every four Christian boys aged between 10 and 20. The youths chosen were then educated and converted to Islam. Many became JANISSARIES but some, like SOKOLOVIĆ, attained high office at court, rising to the office of Grand Vizier. SKANDERBEG was also recruited into Ottoman service by this system. The practice of devşirme ended in the 17c.

### de Wet, Christian Rudolf (1854–1922)

Afrikaner politician and general. He became conspicuous in the Transvaal War of 1880–1, and in the war of 1899–1902 was the most audacious of all the Boer commanders. In 1907 he became Minister of Agriculture of the Orange River Colony, and in 1914 joined the South African insurrection, but was captured. Sentenced to six years' imprisonment, he was released in 1915. He died in Dewetsdorp district, South Africa. ► BOER WARS

### Dewey, George (1837–1917)

US admiral. He served with the Union naval forces in the AMERICAN CIVIL WAR (1861–5), and as Commodore in the SPANISH–AMERICAN WAR (1898) defeated the Spanish fleet at the Battle of MANILA BAY without losing a man.

### Dewey, Thomas Edmund (1902–71)

US politician. District attorney for New York County (1937) and Governor of New York State (elected 1942, 1946, 1950), he was the Republican nominee for President in 1944 and 1948. In 1948 he appeared to be a much stronger candidate than President Harry S TRUMAN, but spectacularly lost the election in one of the greatest presidential upsets in US history.

### DGB (Deutscher Gewerkschaftsbund, 'German Trade Union Federation')

Founded in the western zones of Germany in 1949, the DGB was the successor to the WEIMAR REPUBLIC's ADGB as well as its liberal and Christian trade unions. It embraces 16 individual unions, each representing a major sector of the economy, and by the 1990s had organized over 11.8 million employees, including 3.8 million from the former East Germany – about a third of the entire German workforce. The DGB is closely involved in most areas of economic and social policy-making and formulates its pay policy (*Tarifpolitik*) in the light of official assessments of Germany's economic health. Consensus rather than confrontation characterizes its actions.

## Dhaka

Capital of present-day Bangladesh. The town was adorned, as the prosperous capital of Bengal, with fine buildings by Shayista Khan, the Mughal Governor of Bengal (1664–77 and 1680–8). In 1668, the British **EAST INDIA COMPANY** started a factory in Dhaka, a centre for the purchase of fine cotton and muslin goods. Dhaka was ceded by the Dutch to the British in 1824. Subsequently, it became a hotbed of nationalist political activists such as the Bengali revolutionaries during the Indian freedom struggle. Following the partition of India in 1947, Dhaka became the capital of East Pakistan, and later following the formation of Bangladesh in 1971, its capital.
► **INDIA, PARTITION OF**

## Dharmapala, Anagarika (1864–1930)

Sri Lankan nationalist and religious reformer. He was born Don David Hewavitarana and took the name Anagarika Dharmapala as a result of his activities with the Buddhist Theosophical Society. He wrote and spoke as the champion of Buddhist reformism and the interests of the **SINHALA** people, but never formed or led any significant political grouping. Instead he devoted his attention in his later years to campaigning for the return into Buddhist hands of Buddhist sacred sites in North India.

## Dharmashastra

The 'Law Books', translated in 1776 from the original Sanskrit, first into Persian and only then into English at the orders of Warren **HASTINGS**, then Governor-General of Bengal under the British **EAST INDIA COMPANY**. These ancient codes of law are generally assigned to various ancient worthies, among whom Manu, who is the author of the law-book of Manu (*Manava Dharmashastra*), is generally regarded as the most important. The *Dharmashastras*, unlike the *Dharmasutras*, deal usually with formal law, and not so much with religious and ethical domestic duties. Amalgamated with English (and some Muslim) law, the *Dharmashastra* helped to frame the colonial legal system, which is still largely used in India today.

## Diane de Poitiers (1499–1566)

Mistress of **HENRY II** of France. She was married at 13, and left a widow at 32; she then won the affections of the boy **DAUPHIN**, already wedded to **CATHERINE DE' MEDICI**. On his accession (1547), Diane enjoyed great influence, and was made Duchess of Valentinois. After his death (1559), she retired to her Château d'Anet.

## diarchy

A system where political authority is divided; associated with constitutional reforms introduced by the British into India in 1919. Under the reforms, some departments of provincial government were under Indian control, while others, including finance and security, remained under British control. The reforms did not extend to central government, and the system was seen by some as a concession to 'moderate' Indian opinion in an attempt to seduce them into co-operation with the British Raj.

## Diaspora

The term (literally, 'scattering') used to describe the Jews scattered in the world outside the land of Israel, from either voluntary or compulsory resettlements, such as the Assyrian and Babylonian deportations in the 8c and 6c BC, or later dispersions in the Graeco-Roman period; also known as the Dispersion. The Babylonian Talmud and the Septuagint were important literary products of those Jews that had settled 'abroad'.

## Díaz, Armando, Duke (1861–1928)

Italian soldier. Wounded in Tripoli in 1913, he was promoted major-general in 1914. He replaced **CADORNA** after the disaster of **CAPORETTO** (Nov 1917) and led the Italian army to victory at **VITTORIO VENETO**. He served as War Minister in **MUSSOLINI**'s first cabinet (1922–4) and was made a marshal in 1927.

## Díaz, (José de la Cruz) Porfirio (1830–1915)

Mexican politician. A follower of Benito **JUÁREZ**, he fought against the conservatives and Emperor **MAXIMILIAN**'s French-imposed rule in 1864–7. He seized power in 1876 and was President until 1880, returning in 1884 to remain in office until 1911, when he was ousted by Francisco **MADERO**. His long period of office saw the impact of the changes brought about by the laws of La **REFORMA**, including the emergence of a wage-earning rural populace, the rise of a powerful northern economy, export-led economic growth stimulated by the railroad and extensive foreign investment. Though a master manipulator, his regime became a gerontocracy, and his patronage of the **CIENTÍFICOS**' attempt to 'whiten the nation' meant that he was open to the accusation of having betrayed Mexico to foreign, mainly Anglo-American, interests. Nonetheless, his regime (known as the Porfiriato) did much to stimulate material progress in Mexico. He died in Paris, in the midst of a revolution whose outcome was influenced by the changes he had fomented.

## Díaz del Castillo, Bernal (c.1492–1581)

Spanish soldier and historian. One of the handful of conquistadors who accompanied Hernán **CORTÉS** to Mexico in 1519, he is noted for his *Historia verdadera de la conquista de la Nueva España* (1632, Eng trans *The True History of the Conquest of New Spain*, 1908–16), written at the age of 84.

## Dictation Test

A method used by Australian governments (1902–58) to exclude certain classes of intending immigrants. Based on the example of Natal (1897), under the Immigration Act of 1901, immigrants received a test in a European language. Non-Europeans were the main target, but it was also used with those considered politically undesirable; the most celebrated case was the anti-fascist Egon Kisch (1885–1948), who was tested in Scottish Gaelic (1934). Kisch was eventually admitted when the High

Court decided that this was not a European language. ➤ **WHITE AUSTRALIA POLICY**

## dictatorship of the proletariat
A term used by Marx to describe the period of transition from capitalism to socialism, when the working class has seized political power either through revolution or through the use of democratic political institutions. Under the influence of **LENIN**, the term was transformed from its original use to that of a dictatorship imposed on behalf of, and ultimately on, the revolutionaries. ➤ **MARXISM–LENINISM**

## Diebitsch, Hans Karl Friedrich, Count (1785–1831)
German-born Russian soldier. He joined the Russian army in 1801, and was a major-general in the campaigns of 1805 and 1812–14. In the Russo-Turkish War of 1828–9 he won the surname of Zabalkanski ('Crosser of the Balkans'), and was promoted field marshal. He died of cholera while suppressing the Polish insurrection of 1830–1. ➤ **RUSSO-TURKISH WARS**

## Diefenbaker, John George (1895–1979)
Canadian politician. In 1940 he entered the Canadian Federal House of Commons, becoming leader of the Progressive Conservatives (1956) and Prime Minister (1957–63) after 22 years of **LIBERAL PARTY** rule. His government introduced important agricultural reforms, and extended the federal franchise to Canada's Amerindian peoples. He remained active in national politics until his death in Ottawa.

## Dien Bien Phu
A district capital in north-west Vietnam, some ten miles from the border with Laos, and the site of the major battle that brought an end to the French colonial presence in Vietnam. Dien Bien Phu is situated in a wide valley, surrounded by steep hills. In late 1953 it was reoccupied by French military forces, who intended to use it as a major base to disrupt **VIET MINH** operations. The Vietnam People's Army, under **VO NGUYEN GIAP**, surrounded the base with heavy artillery, dragged up into the hills by human and animal carriers – an extraordinary feat of endurance. The Vietnamese assault began on 13 Mar 1954 and on 7 May the French base was overrun, with over 10,000 prisoners being taken. It was a humiliating defeat for the French.

## Diggers
A radical group in England formed during the **COMMONWEALTH**, led by Gerrard Winstanley (1609–72), preaching and practising agrarian **COMMUNISM** on common and waste land. From Apr 1649 they established the Digger community at St George's Hill, Surrey, followed by colonies in nine other southern and Midland counties. The movement was suppressed and its communities dispersed by local landowners. ➤ **FIFTH MONARCHISTS**

## Diktat
The name given to the Treaty of **VERSAILLES** (1919) by its critics in Germany. Adolf **HITLER** and the **NAZI PARTY** in particular lambasted the republican parties for signing the *Diktat* which had, undoubtedly, triggered resentment and outrage across the political spectrum. The republicans, however, felt they had had no realistic choice but to sign under protest.

## Dimitrijević, Dragutin, alias Apis (1876–1917)
Serbian army officer. The son of a craftsman, he rose swiftly through the army to become a member of the Serbian General Staff (1901), Head of Intelligence (1913) and a colonel (1916). His reputation rests on his near prodigious enthusiasm for conspiracy: he took part in the assassination of King Alexander **OBRENOVIĆ** (1903); he founded the secret society the **BLACK HAND** (1911); he plotted at various times against the kings of Bulgaria and of Greece and Emperor **FRANCIS JOSEPH**; and he seems to have had a part in the fateful assassination of **FRANCIS FERDINAND**, Archduke of Austria, at Sarajevo (1914). Finally he was executed on a charge, probably trumped up by Nikola **PAŠIĆ**, of conspiracy against the Regent, **ALEXANDER I KARAGEORGEVIĆ** (1917).

## Dimitrov, Gemeto (1903–72)
Bulgarian politician. After studying medicine in Belgrade and Sofia, he began to take an active part in left-wing politics as a member of the Pladne Group of the Agrarian Union. Like many others during the dictatorship of **BORIS III**, he was arrested and tortured (1935). After the outbreak of **WORLD WAR II**, he organized opposition to the Tripartite Pact and had to flee to Turkey. He returned to Bulgaria in 1944 and began to reorganize the Agrarian Party. Placed under house arrest, with US assistance he escaped to the USA, where he founded the Bulgarian National Committee and the newspaper *Free and Independent Bulgaria*.

## Dimitrov, Georgi Mikhailovich (1882–1949)
Bulgarian politician. A leading figure in the Bulgarian Socialist Party before **WORLD WAR I**, he helped to found the Bulgarian Communist Party in 1919. After visiting Moscow, he returned to Bulgaria and led an uprising that earned him a death sentence (1923). He fled to Yugoslavia, then lived in Vienna and Berlin and worked for **COMINTERN**. One of the communist leaders accused of setting fire to the **REICHSTAG**, he conducted a brilliant defence against the charges engineered by the Nazi prosecution and was acquitted. He then went to Moscow and served as Secretary-General of the Executive Committee of Comintern (1935–43). Returning to Bulgaria in 1945, he was elected President of the Central Committee of the **FATHERLAND FRONT** and became Prime Minister after the elections in Oct 1946 that established communist rule. ➤ **KOSTOV, TRAICHO**; **VELCHEV, DAMIAN**

## Dingane (d.1843)
King of the Zulu (1828/40). The successor to **SHAKA**, he ruled at a time of increasing white penetration of Natal. He had good relations with the traders at Port Natal, but became alarmed at land concessions to whites in northern Natal. In Feb 1838 Piet **RETIEF**, one of the leaders of the Boer Voortrekkers, secured a grant of land, but he and his party were murdered on Dingane's orders on the same day. Retief was avenged at the Battle of **BLOOD RIVER**, when Andries **PRETORIUS** defeated Dingane. The latter was subsequently overthrown by his brother, Mpande (1840/72), and fled to Swaziland, where he was killed.

## Dingiswayo (d.1818)
Chief of the Mthethwa, one of the northern Zulu **NGUNI** tribe peoples. He is credited with laying the foundations of the Zulu state developed by **SHAKA** in the

1820s. Dingiswayo succeeded some time in the 1790s and set about a more centralized system among the northern Nguni, perhaps as a result of developing trade with Delagoa Bay or ecological problems in the region caused by a combination of rising population and severe drought. Dingiswayo began the military revolution taken up by the Zulu, particularly the development of age regiments, and abolished traditional ceremonies like circumcision. He was killed in 1818 following conflict with the rival Ndwandwe group, and was succeeded by Shaka.

### Ding Ling (Ting Ling) (1902–86)

Chinese feminist writer and Communist Party activist. From a landowning family, she went to Shanghai University in 1923–4 and published her first short story in 1927. She became increasingly politicized and joined the Chinese Communist Party in 1932, becoming active in the League of Left-Wing Writers. Arrested and placed under house arrest by the GUOMINDANG authorities (1933–6), she succeeded in escaping to the communist stronghold in the north-west. In 1942 Ding Ling was censured in a rectification campaign for a series of stories and essays expressing disillusion with the failure of communist ideals to be put into practice. One essay in particular criticized male party attitudes towards women. After 1949 she once again became a member of the literary establishment but in the 1957 anti-rightist campaign she again fell foul of party authorities. She was expelled from the Party and Writers' Union, sent to prison and then to a labour reform camp. She was finally rehabilitated in 1979.

### Dinka

Eastern Sudanic-speaking transhumant cattle herders of the Upper Nile in the Sudan Republic, occupying a vast area of low-lying and often swampy country. Lacking centralized political authority, they comprise many subgroups recognizing only the authority of religious chiefs.

### Diori, Hamani (1916–89)

Niger politician. He was educated in Dahomey and then at the William Ponty School in Dakar. A teacher and then instructor in the language school for colonial administrators (1938–46), he helped form the RASSEMBLEMENT DÉMOCRATIQUE AFRICAIN in 1946 and represented Niger in the French National Assembly (1946–51 and 1956–7). In 1956 he became Prime Minister of Niger and in 1960, at independence, its first President. Building on close relations with France, he ran one of the most stable countries in West Africa, being re-elected in 1965 and 1970, but opposition within his party (the Niger Progressive Party) led to his overthrow in Apr 1974 through a military coup. He was placed under house arrest for 13 years, before he left for Morocco, where he died.

### Diouf, Abdou (1935–)

Senegalese politician. He studied at Dakar and Paris universities before graduating with a law degree and returning to Senegal to work as a civil servant. After holding a number of posts, including that of Secretary-General to President SENGHOR, he became Prime Minister in 1970 and succeeded Senghor on the latter's retirement (1 Jan 1981). He was re-elected President of Senegal in 1983, 1988 and 1993, but was defeated in the 2000 election.

### Dipanagara (1785–1855)

Javanese prince and the central figure in a major revolt against Dutch colonial rule on Java in the early 19c. The eldest son of Sultan Hamengkubuwana III, but raised by his grandmother away from the court at YOGYAKARTA, Dipanagara strongly disliked the intrigue, decadence and corrupt European influence found at court. In his early twenties he underwent a profound religious experience which convinced him that he was to be, in the millenarian tradition, the divinely appointed saviour King of Java. Harsh economic conditions and violent conflict within the court in the early 1820s led Dipanagara into open rebellion. The Java War (1825–30) cost some 200,000 Javanese lives. In 1830, with the rebellion broken, Dipanagara was exiled from Java, eventually to Makasar, to live out his days.

### Directory

The government of the First Republic of France (1795–9), established in the Thermidorian reaction to the Reign of TERROR, with five executive Directors. Its limited franchise and narrow social base added to the difficulties of rampant inflation. After political conspiracies from Left and Right, it was overthrown by the coup of 18 Brumaire (9–10 Nov), bringing NAPOLEON I to power. ► BRUMAIRE COUP; FRENCH REVOLUTION; REPUBLIC, FIRST (France); THERMIDOR

### di Rudini, Antonio Starabba, Marquis (1839–1908)

Italian politician. Having taken part in the revolutionary uprising in his native Sicily before the arrival of GARIBALDI, di Rudini became Mayor (1864) and then Prefect (1866) of Palermo. He was made Prefect of Naples in 1868. Elected to parliament, he became Minister of the Interior (1869) and Prime Minister (1891–2 and 1896–8). He owed his second term of office to CRISPI's fall after the Battle of ADOWA (1896). He had to resign in 1898 after his extremely tough repression of strikers and left-wing protesters. ► BAVA BECCARIS, FIORENZO

### disarmament

Arms control that seeks to promote international security by a reduction in armed forces and/or weapons. The levels are set by agreement, and then opened up for inspection and enforcement by the other side or an independent inspectorate. General (applying to all countries) and comprehensive (applying to all categories of forces and weapons) disarmament was first attempted in 1927 and 1934 by the LEAGUE OF NATIONS, and by the UN in the 1950s, but such moves have not been successful. Disarmament is therefore limited to agreements between two or a few countries, and restricted to particular classes of weapons and troop levels. Problems arise in determining equivalences between different types of weapons held by different countries, and in verifying arms reduction treaties, especially in respect of nuclear weapons, largely because weapons can be reassembled. There is also the possibility of nuclear disarmament involving no agreement with other countries, used as a means of encouraging others to follow. Such unilateral action may also be taken for moral reasons and as a means of diminishing the chances of being attacked, particularly as regards nuclear and chemical weapons.

## disentailment

The modern process of disentailment (*desamortización*) in Spain, which aimed to bolster the royal finances and implement agrarian reform, began under CHARLES IV in 1798; by 1808, about one sixth of all Church property had been disentailed. Major ecclesiastical disentailment took place in 1833–43. The last and most important period was after the revolution of 1854, when roughly a third of all land changed hands. The beneficiaries were not the urban bourgeoisie, but those whose wealth derived from the State, Church and the land; later, bourgeois purchasers joined, rather than replaced, the old class. Although the process accelerated the commercialization of agriculture, it also produced appalling social hardship.

## Disraeli, Benjamin, 1st Earl of Beaconsfield (1804–81)

British politician. He made his early reputation as a novelist, publishing his first novel, *Vivian Grey*, in 1826. He is better known for his two political novels, *Coningsby* (1844) and *Sybil* (1845), which date from his period as a Romantic Tory, critical of industrial developments. He became leader of the 'Young England' movement which espoused these values, and came to prominence as a critic of PEEL's free-trade policies, especially the repeal of the CORN LAWS (1845–6). He became leader in the Commons of the Conservatives after the Peelites left the party, and was Chancellor of the Exchequer in DERBY's minority governments of 1852 and 1858–9. While Chancellor in the government of 1866–8, he piloted the 1867 Reform Bill through the Commons. He became Prime Minister on Derby's resignation in 1868, but was defeated the same year in the general election. His second administration (1874–80) was notable both for diplomacy and social reform, though much of the latter only consolidated legislation begun under GLADSTONE. During his administration, Britain became half-owner of the Suez Canal (1875), and the Queen assumed the title Empress of India (1876). His skilful diplomacy at the Congress of BERLIN (1878) contributed to the preservation of European peace after conflict between the Russians and the Turks in the Balkans. Defeated in 1880 by Gladstone and the Liberals, he then effectively retired, dying the following year. ► REFORM ACTS; TORIES; VICTORIA

## Disturbances (1935–8)

A series of strikes and riots which took place in the British West Indies, sometimes known as 'The Troubles'. These had their roots in post-1918 socio-economic deprivation and this was exacerbated by the GREAT DEPRESSION after 1929 and the lack of political representation in the Crown Colonies. Discontent surfaced first in Belize and Jamaica (1934), spread to the sugar workers in St Kitts and Guyana (1935) and culminated in serious disorder in Trinidad, Jamaica and Barbados (1937–8). In Trinidad BUTLER's oratory provoked the oilfield workers, in Barbados Clement Payne's deportation led to the deaths of 14 people, and in Jamaica the Jamaica Worker's Union of BUSTAMANTE brought rioting to the sugar estates and docks, and the arrest of 700 people. Stung into action by the degree of unrest, the imperial government set up the MOYNE COMMISSION.

## Divine, Father, originally George Baker (1877–1965)

US religious leader. In 1919 he founded the Peace Mission movement in New York, which stressed communal living, celibacy and complete racial equality. He also founded a series of settlements, at one time numbering more than 150, which were known as 'heavens', and achieved his greatest popularity during the GREAT DEPRESSION by offering nourishing 15-cent meals to the poor. He claimed to possess supernatural powers and once placed a curse on the New Jersey Turnpike after receiving a speeding ticket. Most of his followers believed that he was God, but after his death the movement faltered.

## divine kingship

The notion that rulers are descended from the gods and are therefore themselves deities first propounded in ancient Egypt. Diffusionists believed that this legitimating idea passed through the kingdom of Kush on the upper Nile to West, East and Central Africa, where there are many instances of states whose rulers underpin their power with this concept. More modern views see divine kingship as being a spontaneous and independent development in many different parts of the world.

## Divine Right of Kings

The concept of the divinely ordained authority of monarchs, widely held in the medieval and early modern periods, and often associated with the ABSOLUTISM of LOUIS XIV of France and the assertions of the House of STUART.

## Dix, Dorothea Lynde (1802–87)

US humanitarian and reformer. At the age of 19 she established her own school for girls in Boston (1821–35), and then lived in semi-retirement while she struggled to recover from tuberculosis. In 1841 she visited a Massachusetts prison and was shocked to find inmates confined because of insanity and subject to chaining, flogging and other forms of abuse. She began a lifelong crusade for specialized treatment of the mentally ill, and her efforts led to the founding of numerous state mental hospitals in the USA, Canada and Europe. She was also an advocate of prison reform, arguing for educational programmes and the separation of prisoners according to the severity of their crimes.

## Dixie

The name of the area of Southern states in the USA that constituted the Confederacy during the AMERICAN CIVIL WAR. It may have derived from the surname Dixon in MASON–DIXON LINE, a former demarcation on the Maryland–Pennsylvania borders that once separated the slave and free states, or from the fact that on the back of the US$10 bills issued by a New Orleans bank prior to the Civil War, the French word *dix* appeared; hence, the South, and most especially Louisiana, came to be called the land of the dixies ('the tens'), and thereafter Dixie Land. It was about this time (1859) that the minstrel songwriter David D Emmett composed the song 'Dixie', which became popular as a Confederate war melody.

## Dixiecrat

A member of a group of 35 Southern Democrats (officially calling themselves States' Rights Democrats) who stormed out of the 1948 Democratic National Convention to form a third party (officially called the States' Rights Party) because they opposed the **DEMOCRATIC PARTY**'s newly articulated policy of extending the reach of **CIVIL RIGHTS**. Caught in the middle of this catastrophic party split was President Harry S **TRUMAN**, who wanted to preserve the central tenets of Franklin D **ROOSEVELT**'s **NEW DEAL**. The 35 renegade Democrats later met in Birmingham, Alabama, to nominate South Carolinian Strom Thurmond as their Dixiecrat candidate for President of the USA. In the ensuing election, Thurmond managed to carry four states: South Carolina (of which he had been governor), Alabama, Louisiana and Mississippi. Thurmond received over 1 million popular votes, which translated into 39 electoral votes, or over 7 per cent of the total cast. Truman won re-election. However, the appearance of the Dixiecrats constituted one of the most significant assaults on the US two-party system in the history of the country, rivalled only in recent years by Ross Perot in the 1992 elections.

## DJIBOUTI   official name **Republic of Djibouti**

A republic in north-east Africa, bounded to the north-west by Eritrea, to the west and south by Ethiopia, to the south east by Somalia; and to the north by the Gulf of Aden. It was the object of French colonial interest in the mid-19c and became the capital of French Somaliland in 1892. Following **WORLD WAR II** it became a French Overseas Territory, and from 1967 was called the French Territory of the Afars and the Issas. It gained independence in 1977 under the rule of President Hassan **GOULED APTIDON** and the Popular Rally for Progress Party. In 1991 Afar discontent with the Issa domination of government under one-party rule led to civil war; introduction of a multiparty system in 1992 failed to resolve matters and the war continued until power-sharing was agreed in 1994. Some factions continued fighting until 2000, when a peace agreement was signed.

## Djilas, Milovan (1911–95)

Yugoslav politician and writer. Born in Montenegro, he was active in the outlawed Yugoslav Communist Party in the 1930s and was subsequently imprisoned (1933–6). He was, with **TITO**, a remarkable partisan leader during **WORLD WAR II**. In the post-war government, he was Vice-President of Yugoslavia but concern for doctrine led him to criticize the communist system practised in Yugoslavia. Expelled from the

party in 1954 and imprisoned (1956–61 and 1962–6), he was released under amnesty. He was formally rehabilitated by the Yugoslav authorities in 1989.

## Dmitri (1583–91)

Russian prince. The youngest son of Tsar **IVAN IV, THE TERRIBLE**, he appears to have been murdered. It was popularly believed at the time that his murderer was the regent, **BORIS GODUNOV**. In about 1603 Dmitri was impersonated by a runaway Moscow monk, Grigori Otrepiev. The latter, dubbed the 'false Dmitri', was crowned Tsar by the army in 1605 but killed in a rebellion the following year. Other subsequent pretenders suffered a similar fate.

## DNVP (*Deutschnationale Volkspartei*, 'German National People's Party')

German political party. Founded in late Nov 1918 by a coalition of conservative politicians, the DNVP came to represent much of the old, German imperial élite. It never accepted the legitimacy of the **WEIMAR REPUBLIC**, cooperated sporadically and unwillingly in coalition governments, and pursued particularly virulent campaigns against any compromise agreements between Germany and her erstwhile enemies. In Jan 1933 the DNVP entered a coalition with the **NAZI PARTY** that paved the way for **HITLER**'s overthrow of the republic, before dissolving itself in the middle of that year.

## Dobi, Istvan (1898–1968)

Hungarian politician. He spent the earlier part of his life as a day-labourer on various characteristically large estates. He had a brief experience as a soldier in the Hungarian Red Army in 1919, but it was not until 1935 that he joined the Independent Smallholders Party. During and after **WORLD WAR II**, he rose within its ranks and, as leader of its left wing, became Prime Minister within the predominantly communist government of 1949. He remained in office until 1952 during the worst of the Stalinist purges, and was President of the State Council through to 1967, including during the Hungarian Uprising of 1956.

## Dobrudja

The region lying between the Black Sea and the Danube, now divided between Bulgaria and Romania. Settled by the Greeks, Romans, Byzantines, Goths, Alani and Huns, and conquered by the Ottoman Turks, in the 18–19c it was the object first of Russian, then of Romanian and Bulgarian ambitions. ► **ROMANIA**

## Dobrynin, Anatoli Fedorovich (1919– )

Soviet diplomat and politician. He worked as an engineer at an aircraft plant during **WORLD WAR II**, then joined the diplomatic service in 1946. He served as Counsellor at the Soviet Embassy in Washington (1952–5), assistant to the Minister for Foreign Affairs (1955–7), Under-Secretary at the **UN** (1957–9) and head of the USSR's American Department (1960–1), before being appointed the Soviet ambassador to Washington (1962–86). Dobrynin played an important part in resolving the **CUBAN MISSILE CRISIS** in 1962 and was influential in promoting Soviet–US entente. A member of the Communist Party (CPSU) from 1945, he became a full member of its Central Committee in 1971. In 1986, the new Soviet leader,

Mikhail **GORBACHEV**, appointed him Secretary for Foreign Affairs and head of the International Department. He was an adviser to Gorbachev from 1988 to 1991.

**Doctors' Plot** (1952–3)
Alleged plot by nine doctors, seven of them Jewish and all paid by the USA, to get rid of several Soviet politicians. It was a fabrication by the secret police and was intended to prepare the ground for a public trial that would herald a new round of **STALIN**'s purges. Anti-Semitism and anti-Americanism were judged to be good bases on which to win support for removing Stalin's opponents. Fortunately Stalin died, and Nikita **KHRUSHCHEV** subsequently used this and other evidence to condemn his entire behaviour.

**Doe, Samuel Kenyon** (1951–90)
Liberian soldier and politician. He joined the army as a private in 1969, reaching the rank of sergeant in 1975. In Apr 1980 he led a coup by junior officers in which President **TOLBERT** was killed. In 1981 he made himself general and army Commander-in-Chief and established a party (the National Democratic Party of Liberia) in 1984 under whose aegis he narrowly won the 1985 presidential election. Widespread dissatisfaction with his rule generated several opposition groups and a virtual civil war erupted in 1989, which the **ECONOMIC COMMUNITY OF WEST AFRICAN STATES** (ECOWAS) attempted to mediate. Doe was killed in the ensuing internal struggle for power.

**Dogali Ambush** (1887)
A dramatic defeat for the Italian army in which 500 troops were massacred by Abyssinians resisting Italy's policy of forcing trade through the port of Massawa on the Red Sea (acquired by Italy in 1885). Public outcry led to an Italian blockade of Abyssinia, until Emperor **JOHN IV** agreed to pay compensation and to use Massawa as a trading post. Nonetheless, Dogali was seen as a major blow to national pride, which was to find an echo in the defeat at **ADOWA** nine years later.

**Doihara Kenji** (1883–1948)
Japanese army general. He served in China (1913–20) and in 1931 became Director of Military Intelligence at Mukden in Manchuria. Doihara was a key participant in the Japanese military's plans to overrun Manchuria, which culminated in the creation of the Japanese puppet-state of **MANZHUGUO** in 1933. He then became involved in a relentless campaign to expand Japan's influence in north China, a campaign that was ultimately to lead to full-scale war with China in 1937. In 1948 Doihara was executed as a Class A war criminal.

**Doi Takako** (1929–)
Japanese politician. After lecturing on the Japanese constitution at Doshisha University, she entered the Diet in 1969 and from 1986 to 1991 she was leader of the **JAPAN SOCIALIST PARTY** (now the Social Democratic Party of Japan), the first woman party leader in Japan. In 1989 she became the Leader of the Upper House, but resigned in 1991 following heavy losses in local elections. She held the position of Speaker in the Upper House from 1993 until 1996, when she returned as party leader, holding the latter post until her resignation in 2003.

**doken kokka**
A Japanese phrase meaning 'construction state', it refers to the bankers, builders and politicians who have backed public works, making construction rather than manufacturing or the service industries the core of the Japanese economy since **WORLD WAR II**. The sector employs over 6 million workers, and operates a welfare system similar to the US **NEW DEAL**. Although vital for post-war reconstruction, many recent projects have been condemned as unnecessary or dangerous and of benefit only to the **LIBERAL DEMOCRATIC PARTY** (LDP), the banks and the builders. Despite the economy's near-collapse by the late 1990s, the emphasis on public works did not diminish and by 2002 public debt was nearly 70 per cent of GDP. The systematic awarding of public works contracts to selected construction companies and the idea of building the country out of recession are considered to be policy mainstays of the LDP, in power almost without a break since 1955. Charges of corruption have been levelled at the government, most notably by the murdered politician Koki Ishii who was instrumental in uncovering a bribery scandal that embarrassed the administration headed by Junichiro Koizumi.

**Dolgikh, Vladimir Ivanovich** (1924–)
Soviet politician and engineer. Born in the Krasnoyarsk region and educated in Irkutsk, he worked in engineering for 20 years before being drawn into the party machine in 1969. He climbed the political ladder quickly in **BREZHNEV**'s command economy, and in 1972 became a secretary in the Central Committee, and in 1982 a candidate member of the **POLITBURO**. He appeared to be in line for further promotion, but in 1988 Mikhail **GORBACHEV** dismissed him and closed down the heavy industry section of the party secretariat as no longer relevant to a marketizing economy.

**Dolgorukova, Katarina, Princess Yurevskaya** (1847–1922)
Russian noblewoman. She was the mistress of Emperor **ALEXANDER II**, who married her in 1880 after his first wife's death. Under the pseudonym of Victor Laferté, she published *Alexandre II, Détails inédits sur sa vie intime et sa mort* (1882). Her *Mémoires* (1890) were suppressed by the Russian government.

**dollar diplomacy**
The US government's use of economic rewards (eg low-interest loans or outright grants) or punishments (eg placing a high tariff on a commodity a country exports to the USA) to influence the internal and/or external policies of a foreign nation, particularly with the aim of promoting US business interests overseas. Used after 1900, it was the motivation behind the **ROOSEVELT COROLLARY**, and was widely used in foreign affairs by President William **TAFT**. To some extent, it was replaced by Roosevelt's **GOOD NEIGHBOR POLICY** in 1933.

**Dolle Mina**
Dutch feminist movement, named after *Dolle* ('Wild') Wilhel*mina* Drucker (1847–1925), an early Dutch activist for the emancipation of women. Growing out of the political upheaval in the late 1960s, the name *Dolle Mina* was first used in 1970, when for a

few years the world saw a number of demonstrations designed to promote awareness of women's issues and rights, such as equal pay, child care, divorce and abortion. After 1972 membership declined.

**Dollfuss, Engelbert** (1892–1934)
Austrian politician. He studied in Vienna and Berlin, and became leader of the Christian Socialist Party. As Chancellor (1932–4), he suspended parliamentary government, drove the socialists into revolt and militarily crushed them (Feb 1934). In July 1934 an attempted Nazi putsch in Vienna culminated in his assassination. ▻ NAZI PARTY

**Domela Nieuwenhuis, Ferdinand** (1846–1919)
Dutch socialist and anarchist leader. He began his career as a Lutheran minister, but left the Church in 1879 when he became a socialist, founding the newspaper *Recht voor Allen* ('Rights for All'). He was Secretary of the Social-Democratic League, the first Dutch socialist party (1882–7), and was imprisoned in 1886–7 for treasonous newspaper articles, and elected to parliament in 1888–91. Thereafter he rejected the parliamentary way, and became an anarchist, co-founding the National Labour Secretariat in 1893 as a socialist trade union federation. Often ridiculed for his extreme views, he was nonetheless one of the founders of the modern Dutch socialist labour movement. He had numerous international socialist contacts, and the widespread emotional support he enjoyed amongst working people was shown at his funeral when tens of thousands poured into Amsterdam for the occasion.

**Domesday Book**
The great survey of England south of the Ribble and Tees rivers (London and Winchester excepted), compiled in 1086 on orders of WILLIAM I; sometimes spelled Doomsday Book. Information is arranged by county and, within each county, according to tenure by major landholders; each manor is described according to value and resources. Domesday is one of the greatest administrative achievements of the MIDDLE AGES, yet its central purpose remains unclear. Most probably it was to assist the royal exploitation of crown lands and feudal rights, and to provide the new nobility with a formal record and confirmation of their lands, thus putting a final seal on the Norman occupation. ▻ NORMAN CONQUEST

**Dominic, St** (c.1170–1221)
Spanish founder of the Order of Friars Preachers. He studied at Palencia, where he acquired such a name for piety and learning that he was made a canon in 1193. He led a life of rigorous asceticism, and was especially devoted to missionary work, notably among the ALBIGENSES of southern France. His preaching order was approved by Pope HONORIUS III in 1216. By the time of his death, at Bologna, his order occupied 60 houses, and had spread as far as England, where from their dress the monks were called Black Friars. He was canonized in 1234 by GREGORY IX.

**DOMINICA** official name **Commonwealth of Dominica**
An independent republic located in the Windward Islands, in the east Caribbean Sea. It was discovered by COLUMBUS in 1493, and there were attempts at co-

lonization by the French and British in the 18c. It became a British Crown Colony in 1805. It was part of the Federation of the West Indies from 1958 to 1962, and gained independence in 1978. Edison James became Prime Minister in 1995, ending the 15-year tenure of Dame Eugenia CHARLES, but his United Workers' Party lost the 2000 election to the Dominica Labour Party.

## DOMINICAN REPUBLIC

A republic of the West Indies, comprising the eastern two-thirds of the island of Hispaniola, and bordering Haiti to the west. It was discovered by COLUMBUS in 1492 and became a Spanish colony in the 16–17c; the eastern province of Santo Domingo remained Spanish after the partition of Hispaniola in 1697. Taken over by Haiti on several occasions, it gained independence in 1844 under its modern name, but was reoccupied by Spain in 1861–5. A long dictatorship at the end of the 19c was followed by revolution and bankruptcy. Dictatorships, revolutions and military coups continued through the 20c, with right-wing parties holding power for most of the 1970s, 1980s and early 1990s. Joaquín BALAGUER, who was President in 1966–78 and from 1986, was re-elected in 1994, but a political crisis arose amid allegations of fraud and corruption, and fresh elections were called. These resulted in the election in 1996 of Leonel Fernández, leader of the Liberation Party; he was defeated in 2000 but re-elected in 2004.

**Dominion of Canada**
Established on 1 July 1867, by the BRITISH NORTH AMERICA ACT of 29 Mar, the Dominion consisted of three provinces, Canada (now divided into Quebec and Ontario), Nova Scotia and New Brunswick, all united by the CONFEDERATION MOVEMENT. Desire for unification had intensified because of the need for improvements in transport and because of the proximity of the USA, which inspired emulation as well as fear. The ending of RECIPROCITY in 1866 and the failure of the USA to curb the FENIANS perhaps accentuated the provinces' link with the British crown, which was a distinguishing feature of the confederation (although the term 'Dominion' was chosen rather than 'Kingdom' in deference to US

republican sentiment). Manitoba joined the Dominion in 1870, British Columbia in 1871, Prince Edward Island in 1873, Alberta and Saskatchewan in 1905, and Newfoundland in 1949. ► **BROWN, GEORGE**; **CARTIER, GEORGE ÉTIENNE**; **COMPACT THEORY OF CONFEDERATION**; **MACDONALD, JOHN ALEXANDER**

## domino theory

A strategic theory first used by President **EISENHOWER** in 1954, reflecting the view that, as neighbouring states are so interdependent, the collapse of one will spread to the others. Originally referring to the belief that if one country became communist, others would follow, the theory relates to military collapse as well as insurgence, and has been used to justify intervention in a country not immediately threatened but whose neighbour is. It was an important element in the US policy of intervention in South-East Asia in the 1960s and 1970s, and in Central America in the 1980s. ► **VIETNAM WAR**

**DOM-TOM** (*Départements d'outre-mer* and *Territoires d'outre-mer*, 'Overseas Departments' and 'Overseas Territories')
French colonial possessions that are now treated as being an integral part of French metropolitan territory, electing representatives to the French National Assembly, etc. They were part of the **FRENCH UNION** (*Union française*), established in 1946, renamed the *Communauté* ('Community') in 1958, and are all that remained when the other colonies and associated states (protectorates) became independent.

**Donald III**, also called **Donald Bane** (1033–c.1100)
The younger son of **DUNCAN I**, he seized the throne on **MALCOLM III**'s death but his reign was short and turbulent. He was briefly supplanted by Malcolm's eldest son, **DUNCAN II**, whom he probably had murdered, and was finally overthrown in 1097 by an English army in support of the claim of Edgar, Malcolm's eldest surviving son by his second marriage to Queen (later St) **MARGARET**. Edgar (1097/1107) had him blinded, and he was buried on Iona.

## Donglin (Tunglin) Movement

A movement of political and moral reform led by scholars and officials in China during the 1620s. Associated with the Donglin Academy, established in 1604 in the city of Wuxi near Shanghai, they both advocated a return to classical Confucianism and condemned corruption at court. During the reign of Ming Tianqi (1620/7), Donglin followers gained official positions and became deeply involved in factional politics. Their criticism of misgovernment brought them into conflict with the powerful eunuch Wei Zhongxian (1568–1627), who launched a terror campaign against them. Most were dismissed from office and some were executed.

**Dönitz, Karl** (1891–1980)
German Nazi politician and naval commander. He entered the submarine service of the German navy in 1916, and became a staunch advocate of **U-BOAT** warfare. He planned **HITLER**'s U-boat fleet, was made its commander in 1936, and in 1943 became Commander-in-Chief of the German navy. Becoming *Führer* on the death of Hitler, he was responsible for the final surrender to the Allies, and in 1946 was sentenced to ten years' imprisonment for war crimes. ► **WORLD WAR II**

**Donner Party** (1846)
A group of 82 pioneers who hired, and were led by, George and Jacob Donner across the Sierra Nevada Mountains and on to the Sacramento Valley in California. The route took longer than anticipated, and the party were too late to cross the mountains before winter set in. They were snowbound for three months, and only 40 survived the ordeal. Because some of the survivors had resorted to cannibalism to survive, the Donner Party disaster entered US folklore as an emblem signifying a wide range of ideas, including the dangers of poor planning and incompetent leadership, and endurance in the face of nature's brutality.

## Donoughmore Commission

A committee sent by the British government to Ceylon in 1927 to examine the Ceylonese constitution and recommend reforms. These recommendations were reluctantly accepted by Ceylonese political leaders and served as the basis for the new constitution of 1931. The reforms replaced communal electorates by territorial constituencies and extended the franchise to all resident adults. An assembly or state council with legislative and executive powers was also established under the recommendations of the Donoughmore Commission. The new constitution was in effect until 1946.

**Dopolavoro** (*Opera Nazionale Dopolavoro*)
In Italy, the national network of clubs and other recreational and welfare centres established by the fascists in 1925. The membership of the *Dopolavoro* (literally, 'after work') expanded massively to include 4 million by 1939. The Dopolavoro provided bars, sports facilities, libraries, dances and concerts, as well as organizing holidays, and was undoubtedly one of the most successful and popular innovations of the fascist state. ► **BALILLA**; **FASCISM**; **FASCIST PARTY**

**Dordrecht** or **Dordt** or **Dort, Synod of** (13 Nov 1618–9 May 1619)
An important Church council held in the Dutch Republic to resolve the disputes between the **REMONSTRANTS** and the **COUNTER-REMONSTRANTS**. The Dutch Calvinists had been squabbling for some time over theology, and the Synod was a resounding victory for the orthodox Counter-Remonstrants, who silenced or banished their enemies. The Synod promulgated many of the documents that have been the foundation of Dutch Calvinism, and commissioned the great States Bible translation, comparable to the English Authorized Version. The Synod had a political impact; the Orangist party had supported the Counter-Remonstrants, and with their victory they were able to dispose of many enemies, and to relaunch the war with Spain, ending the **TWELVE YEARS' TRUCE**.

**Dorgon** (1612–50)
Manchu prince. The 14th son of **NURHACI**, he commanded the Manchu armies that invaded China in 1644. As regent for the first Manchu Emperor of China, Shunzhi (1644/61), Dorgon oversaw the completion of the Manchu conquest of China. He amassed

much personal power, alienating the other Manchu princes in the process. Although he was responsible for the forced imposition of the queue (or pigtail) amongst the Chinese as a sign of subservience to the Manchus, he also made use of Chinese officials in government and continued to rely on Chinese institutions. He died while on a hunting trip and was posthumously denounced for usurping power.

**Doria, Andrea** (c.1466–1560)
Genoese mercenary and admiral. After serving under various Italian princes, he was given command of the Genoese fleet, defeating the Turks in 1519. When the imperial faction came to power (1522), he transferred his allegiance to **FRANCIS I** of France, and commanded the French fleet, defeating Emperor **CHARLES V** in Italy and Provence. After a period of papal service, he rejoined the French, but in 1529, fearing Francis's power, he went over to Charles V, entered Genoa, and established an oligarchy under his domination. He continued to fight the Turks with many successes, but was defeated at Algiers (1541) and Djerba (1560). His family continued to rule at Genoa until the end of the 18c.

**Doriot, Jacques** (1898–1945)
French politician. A metalworker, communist Deputy (1924) and Mayor of St Denis, a working-class suburb of Paris, he was excluded from the **COMMUNIST PARTY** in 1934 for advocating a **POPULAR FRONT** before it was adopted as party policy. He then co-founded the *Parti populaire français* ('French People's Party'), regarded as the only fascist-type party in France to have much popular support. However, it had already entered a period of crisis in 1938. During **WORLD WAR II** he collaborated with the Germans, organizing the LVF (*Légion des volontaires français contre le bolchévisme*, 'League of French Volunteers against Bolshevism') to fight on the Eastern Front. At the liberation he fled to Germany, where he was killed in an Allied air raid. ► **COLLABORATION** (France)

**Dort, Synod of** ► **DORDRECHT, SYNOD OF**

**Dos Santos, José Eduardo** (1942–)
Angolan nationalist and politician. He joined the **MPLA** in 1961 and was forced into exile in Zaire (now Democratic Republic of Congo), where he founded the MPLA Youth League. In 1963 he went to the USSR to study petroleum engineering and telecommunications. He returned to Angola in 1970 to participate in the war of liberation, being responsible for the MPLA's medical services. A close confidant of Agostinho **NETO**, he became Foreign Minister on independence and First Deputy Prime Minister, Planning Minister and head of the National Planning Commission. When Neto died in 1979, he succeeded to the presidency and, conscious that the cost of fighting **UNITA** with its South African backers was destroying Angola, negotiated the withdrawal of Cuban and South African forces in 1989 and then a ceasefire between MPLA and UNITA. The ceasefire did not hold, however, and fighting, interspersed with peace talks, continued until 2002 when, after the death of their leader Jonah **SAVIMBI**, UNITA forces demobilized. He was re-elected head of the MPLA in 2003.

**Dost Muhammad** (1793–1863)
Ruler of Afghanistan (1826/38 and 1843/63). He lost

Peshawar from the Afghan state in 1834, and subsequently made claims to the British on Peshawar. He was ousted in 1839 by Shah Shuja, a descendant of Afghan kings, and the British, and following his defeat by British forces in 1840, he surrendered. Upon Lord Ellenborough's proclamation, he returned to the throne of Afghanistan in 1843, later becoming a British ally as a result of a treaty signed in 1855. He was assisted by the British in some subsequent battles against the Persians, and died at the age of 80 after recapturing Herat from them.

**Doubleday, Abner** (1819–93)
US general and alleged inventor of baseball. He served as a major-general of volunteer Union troops in the **AMERICAN CIVIL WAR**, fighting at **ANTIETAM**, **FREDERICKSBURG** and **GETTYSBURG**. He had been known for organizing team games during his boyhood, and in 1907 a commission reported that Doubleday had invented baseball at Cooperstown, New York, in 1839. This report has been discredited, and it is now known that a game similar to baseball was played in the USA and England long before Doubleday's time.

**Douglas**
A Scottish family that includes William the Hardy, Crusader, who harried the monks of Melrose and joined **WALLACE** in the rising against the English in 1297. His son, Sir James Douglas (c.1286–1330), called 'the Black Douglas' because of his swarthy complexion, effectively shared command with Robert **BRUCE** of Scottish forces victorious at the Battle of **BANNOCKBURN** (1314). The hero of 70 fights, he was slain in Andalusia. His son, William, died at the Battle of **HALIDON HILL**; and the next Lord of Douglas, Hugh, brother of James, made over the now great domains of the family in 1342 to his nephew, Sir William. ► **SCOTTISH WAR OF INDEPENDENCE**

**Douglas, Stephen Arnold** (1813–61)
US political leader. Appointed to the Illinois Supreme Court in 1841, he was elected to the **HOUSE OF REPRESENTATIVES**, where he served from 1847–61, and then to the **SENATE**, serving from 1847 to 1861. In 1858 he ran against Abraham **LINCOLN** in the senatorial race, participating in a number of debates that gained national attention for Lincoln. Douglas's position on **SLAVERY** in the territories was that each territory should decide for itself. In 1860 he was nominated for the presidency, but was defeated by Lincoln.

**Douglas, William Orville** (1898–1980)
US judge. Educated at Whitman College and Columbia University, he was a law professor at Yale, then a member (1936) and chairman (1937–39) of the Securities and Exchange Commission. A strong supporter of the **NEW DEAL** legislation, he was appointed to the Supreme Court in 1939 to replace Louis **BRANDEIS**. As a justice he strongly supported **CIVIL RIGHTS** and liberties, and guarantees of freedom of speech. He wrote *We the Judges* (1956), *A Living Bill of Rights* (1961), autobiographical works, and many books on his travels.

**Douglas-Home, Sir Alec** ► **HOME OF THE HIRSEL, BARON**

# *Drama*

*Art & Literature*

### Origins

Several origins have been proposed for drama: the ceremonies and
dances performed by hunter-gatherers to ensure a successful hunt and
initiate the young into the nature of the animals they hunted and the tactics used to kill them is one; dramatic story-
telling in which the narrator enacts different roles while telling the story is another; religious ritual, and the enactment of
religious stories at festivals, such as those conducted in ancient Egypt from before 2000 BC, is a third.

### Ancient Greek theatre

Western drama is usually taken to have begun in Greece with the institution of dramatic competitions at the spring
festival in honour of Dionysus in Athens in the 6c BC. The date traditionally given for the holding of the first competition
is 534 BC. The contests were specifically for tragedy; three dramatists competed each year, staging three plays each. The
subject matter of the plays was drawn from mythology, from epic poetry, and occasionally from history, and the
performances took place in the open air. A major role in Greek drama was taken by the chorus, a group of 15 men who
usually spoke or chanted in unison and danced as a group. It is possible that the original plays involved simply a chorus
and a single actor, since Aeschylus, the earliest of the great Greek tragedians whose work has survived, is traditionally
said to have introduced a second actor, and Sophocles a third. The small number of actors did not necessarily restrict the
number of parts in a play since the actors, who were all men, were always masked and played many parts.

    Comedy became part of the Athenian city festival in 486 BC. The comedies of Aristophanes, the only early Greek
comedies to survive, deal in a robustly satirical manner with topics and characters from contemporary life. Later Greek
comedy allocated a lesser role to the chorus and eventually dispensed with it altogether. Its plots centred on romantic
entanglements rather than political issues. The distinction in subject matter between tragedy and comedy, the former
drawing on myth and history for its high heroic themes and the latter concerned with everyday existence, romance, and
humanity's distinctly unheroic side, was to remain essentially intact through many centuries. Together with other
aspects of Greek dramaturgy, it was enshrined in Aristotle's *Poetics* (c.330 BC) and passed on to later generations of
playwrights throughout Europe who aspired to imitate the classical models.

### Roman and medieval theatre

The theatre of ancient Rome was heavily influenced by that of ancient Greece. Nevertheless, there is a distinctive Roman
style in the comedies of Plautus and Terence and the tragedies of Seneca that have survived. The Roman theatrical
tradition survived the fall of Rome and continued in the **Byzantine Empire**, and it is likely that a tradition of reading and
performing Roman comedies continued in the West through the so-called Dark Ages.

    Dramas on Christian themes were also performed in Byzantium, and there are records of large-scale open-air
performances of Biblical plays taking place from the 12c. The space in which the Biblical and allegorical plays were
performed was extensive, and the acting areas for different parts of the play were situated at various locations within it,
often symbolically, at the points of the compass. Whereas classical drama tended to be concise and Aristotle
recommended that a play show one action, performed in one place and preferably lasting only as long as the actual
performance, Christian drama often required a much larger canvas. Thus, in the famous cycles of mystery plays
performed at Corpus Christi, not only in England but across Europe, separate scenes were often performed on a
succession of pageant wagons and depicted the whole 'history' of humankind from the Fall to the Last Judgement.

### Traditional theatre in Asia

Theatrical performance dates back to very ancient times in India, China and other parts of Asia. The earliest surviving
plays in Sanskrit date from the 1–2c AD, and the *Natyasastra*, a text setting out the basic rules for theatre construction,
play writing, the training of actors and acting technique, is believed to have been compiled between c.100 BC and
AD 100. Traditional Indian drama contains a very strong element of **dance**. Plays were performed to celebrate religious
and court festivals, and most commonly depicted the heroic exploits or love story of a king or sage. Though Sanskrit
drama died out in northern India, a southern form of it, *kutiyattam*, continues to be performed in Kerala province to the
present day.

    Fully developed drama in China probably dates from around the 12c. Regional styles evolved in different parts of the
country. The earliest style originated in the south, but a northern style, *zaju*, which flourished especially in the 13–14c, is
generally regarded as representing the high point of Chinese drama. Peking Opera, the Chinese regional style that is best
known in the West and has a tradition that has lasted to the present day, dates from the end of the 18c. Besides the stylized
gestures and syncopated musical accompaniment common to all traditional Chinese theatre, it is notable for the
thrilling acrobatics that are a feature of its performances.

    The two main forms of traditional Japanese theatre are both comparatively late developments. Though its roots go
back to earlier times, *Noh* dates basically from the 14c. It is stark, simple and restrained, much influenced by Zen
Buddhism, and for most of its history, aimed at the **samurai** class. *Kabuki* dates from the 17c. From the beginning, it was
a more popular form with a broader appeal, with flamboyant costumes, gestures and acting style. The specifically
Japanese form of puppet theatre, *bunraku*, also developed in the 17c. Puppet theatre was and is an important and
popular art form not only in Japan, but also in Cambodia, Thailand and Indonesia.

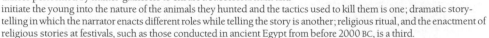

**Douglass, Frederick** (1817–95)
US abolitionist. Born into **SLAVERY**, he escaped in
1838, and in 1841 emerged as a major anti-slavery
force. He founded the abolitionist paper *North Star*
in Rochester in 1847 and edited it for 17 years. During
the **AMERICAN CIVIL WAR** he encouraged blacks to

join Union forces. He also supported the cause of
**WOMEN'S RIGHTS**, and became US Minister to Haiti.
➤ **ABOLITIONISM**

**Doumer, Paul** (1857–1932)
French politician. He was a working jeweller, journalist, Deputy (1888), and then Governor-General of

## Theatre buildings

Greek drama was performed in open-air amphitheatres with a semicircular auditorium arranged on a natural hillside overlooking a circular dance floor – the orchestra – backed by a low dressing room, the façade of which also served as a place to hang pieces of scenery. The Romans built free-standing semicircular auditoria, replaced the orchestra with a raised rectangular stage and backed it with an imposing architectural façade.

When permanent theatres began to be built again in Europe in the 16c, they were built both indoors and out. In England and Spain outdoor theatres were modelled on the courtyards and innyards where players performed before they acquired a permanent home. A thrust stage projected out from the dressing rooms into an open space filled with spectators; others watched from surrounding galleries. Europe's oldest surviving indoor theatre, the Teatro Olimpico in Vicenza, Italy, was completed in 1585. It was an attempt to recreate a Roman theatre inside a large hall and had a fixed architectural backdrop. The future, however, lay with stages built with a proscenium arch and a curtain to facilitate the use of movable scenery. The earliest example of a theatre with a proscenium arch is the Teatro Farnese in Parma, Italy, constructed between 1618 and 1628 specifically to stage opera. From Italy this design spread across Europe and eventually across the world, to become what many would still regard as the classic shape for a theatre. The possibilities of the proscenium-arch stage allowed for much greater realism in the presentation of scenes but tended to separate off the performers from the audience. From the end of the 19c a reaction against the proscenium-arch theatre set in, and modern theatre design frequently incorporates a thrust stage of the Elizabethan type or allows for theatre-in-the-round, in which the audience surrounds the acting area on all sides.

## Modern drama

Though the drama of imperial Spain, like other aspects of Spanish literature, drew stature from the complexities of a long era of relative decline, the golden age of a country's theatre often coincides with one of great vigour and achievement in its national life. The plays of Shakespeare and his great contemporaries were produced in the reigns of **Elizabeth I** and **James VI and I**, those of Molière and Racine in the reign of **Louis XIV** of France. Great verse drama, in particular, came to be regarded as a cornerstone of national culture just when it ceased to be the most appropriate form for future development.

As in other arts, the trend in drama from the late **Renaissance** to the end of the 19c was towards a greater realism: psychological, social and presentational. Serious drama, in which the protagonists were not kings and queens or great figures from history or mythology but ordinary bourgeois men and women speaking prose, is generally thought of as an 18c development. But the development of prose drama was set back by the discovery of Shakespeare by continental Europe and the desire of the Romantic movement to free itself from the shackles of French classicism by following the Shakespearean model. The great flowering of serious socially realistic prose drama came at the end of the 19c in the work of Ibsen and Chekhov. By this time the working classes, hitherto mainly represented in the theatre by servants and low-life characters in comedy, had also begun to have a serious voice in the theatre.

The 20c was eclectic in all the arts, and in drama no less than any other. Ever greater social realism on the one hand appeared alongside a return to older, simpler and less representational styles of play writing and staging, which were often backed up by technical wizardry, especially in the use of electric lighting, that earlier ages could only dream about. Experimental theatre, in which almost anything goes, exists alongside both theatre devoted to staging the classics of world literature and commercial theatre that earns a living mainly from musicals and plays within the realistic convention. The advent of the **cinema** and **television** has opened up new opportunities for writers, directors and actors, but there is no indication that the experience of live theatre, which has thrilled audiences for millennia, has lost any of its basic appeal. ➤ **Poetry; Prose**

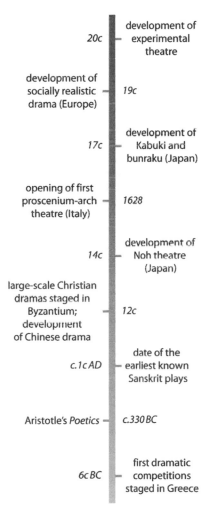

| | |
|---|---|
| 20c | development of experimental theatre |
| development of socially realistic drama (Europe) | 19c |
| | development of Kabuki and bunraku (Japan) |
| | 17c |
| opening of first proscenium-arch theatre (Italy) | 1628 |
| | development of Noh theatre (Japan) |
| | 14c |
| large-scale Christian dramas staged in Byzantium; development of Chinese drama | 12c |
| | date of the earliest known Sanskrit plays |
| | c.1c AD |
| Aristotle's *Poetics* | c.330 BC |
| | first dramatic competitions staged in Greece |
| | 6c BC |

French **INDOCHINA** from 1897 to 1902 (where he is credited with the creation of the modern French colonial state). Doumer was President of the Chamber (1905–6), of the Senate (1927–31), and of the Third Republic (1931–2). He was shot by a Russian émigré, Gorgalov. ➤ **REPUBLIC, THIRD** (France)

**Doumergue, Gaston** (1863–1937)
French politician and first Protestant President of the French Republic (1924–31). He was Prime Minister in 1913–14 and 1934 (when he failed to carry constitutional changes); and President of the Senate (1923–4). ➤ **REPUBLIC, THIRD** (France)

**Dover, Treaty of** (1670)
A treaty, some of whose terms were kept secret from the British parliament and some of the King's ministers, between **CHARLES II** of Great Britain and **LOUIS XIV** of France. Under its terms, Charles received French subsidies and agreed to maintain amity with France and, at an appropriate time, declare himself a convert to Roman Catholicism. Charles received almost £750,000 during the 1670s, a crucial supplement to inadequate income. Though the secret terms were not revealed until 1682, they were guessed by many in parliament in the later 1670s, doing much to sour relations with the King. ➤ **EXCLUSION CRISIS**; **POPISH PLOT**

**Dowding, Hugh Caswell Tremenheere Dowding, 1st Baron** (1882–1970)
British air chief marshal. He served in the Royal Artillery and the Royal Flying Corps in **WORLD WAR I**. As Commander-in-Chief of Fighter Command (1936–40), he organized the air defence of Britain during **WORLD WAR II**, which resulted in the victorious Battle of **BRITAIN** (1940). He retired in 1942 and was created a peer in 1943.

**Downing Street Declaration** (15 Dec 1993)
A framework for all-party peace talks agreed by the Prime Ministers of Ireland and the UK, Albert Reynolds and John **MAJOR**. It was a statement of principles and conditions to be followed in the renewed quest for peace in Northern Ireland, guaranteeing self-determination for its people and promising British government recognition of a unified Ireland if a majority of the province's people agreed. In 1994 a cessation of violence was announced by both the **IRA** and the Unionist paramilitary groups, but the requirement to disarm before talks could begin proved insurmountable and the ceasefire collapsed in Feb 1996. The so-called all-party talks began without **SINN FÉIN** in June 1996, but following a new ceasefire in 1997 Sinn Féin was allowed to participate in renewed negotiations. Though these resulted in the 1998 **GOOD FRIDAY AGREEMENT**, it subsequently became apparent that Sinn Féin did not share all the basic premises of the Declaration. ➤ **ANGLO-IRISH AGREEMENT**

**Dozsa, György** (d.1514)
Hungarian soldier. He was ennobled for his exploits in fighting the Turks as a member of the Belgrade garrison. In 1514 Archbishop Tamas Bakocz appointed him to command a crusade. However, fired by the grievances of the peasants who joined his army, and frustrated by the delaying tactics of the majority of the Hungarian nobles, he turned away from the Turks and marched against them instead. Despite his initial success and his heroism, he was defeated at Temesvár and cruelly put to death.

**Draft**
US **CONSCRIPTION**. It was introduced first in 1777 when the number of volunteers failed to meet the quotas demanded by the **CONTINENTAL CONGRESS**. During the **AMERICAN CIVIL WAR** it was enacted first by the South in 1862, followed by the North in 1863. Both acts caused great opposition, with a major riot taking place in New York, because the draft flouted the US tradition of voluntary service, while in the

South it was believed to be an abuse of **STATES' RIGHTS**. On both sides, provisions for substitution and exemption gave rise to the slogan 'a rich man's war and a poor man's fight'. The draft was introduced for **WORLD WAR I** with the passage of the Selective Service Act of 1917, and again in 1940 in anticipation of the USA's entry into **WORLD WAR II**, and again in various crises such as the invasion of Korea, the **BERLIN AIRLIFT**, and the **CUBAN MISSILE CRISIS**. Much of the opposition to the **VIETNAM WAR**, especially the student protest, centred on the draft. Eventually offenders numbered 570,000, so that under President Richard **NIXON** a fairer lottery system was introduced in 1969, with the draft itself being ended in 1973.

**dragonnades**
In France, a system of billeting troops on Protestant households in order to 'persuade' them to convert to Catholicism. It was instituted in 1681 and continued for the rest of the reign of **LOUIS XIV**.

**Drake, Sir Francis** (c.1540–1596)
English seaman and explorer. In 1567 he commanded the *Judith* in his kinsman John Hawkins's ill-fated expedition to the West Indies, and returned there several times to recover the losses sustained from the Spaniards, his exploits gaining him great popularity in England. In 1577 he set out with five ships for the Pacific, through the Straits of **MAGELLAN**, but after his fleet was battered by storm and fire, he alone continued in the *Golden Hind*. He then struck out across the Pacific, reached Pelew Island, and returned to England via the Cape of Good Hope in 1580 having circumnavigated the globe. The following year, Queen **ELIZABETH I** visited his ship and knighted him. In 1585 he sailed with 25 ships against the Spanish Indies, bringing home tobacco, potatoes and the dispirited Virginian colonists. In the battle against the Spanish **ARMADA** (1588), which raged for a week in the Channel, his seamanship and courage brought him further distinction. In 1595 he sailed again to the West Indies, but died of dysentery off Porto Bello. ➤ **EXPLORATION**

**Drama** ➤ *See panel*

**Drapeau, Jean** (1916–99)
Canadian politician. He became Mayor of Montreal in 1954, backed both by those wanting improved municipal services and those who demanded the elimination of gambling and prostitution. Drapeau sought more autonomy for the city and when he was thwarted by **DUPLESSIS** he became a strong critic of the provincial Premier. When the **OCTOBER CRISIS** occurred in 1970 Drapeau, along with the Montreal chief of police and Robert **BOURASSA**, asked the federal government to implement the **WAR MEASURES ACT**. When Pierre Laporte's body was found, Montreal public opinion was so hardened that Drapeau was given 92 per cent of the votes in the following city elections. His administration backed Expo 67 (when General de **GAULLE** delivered his notorious 'Vive le Québec libre' speech), and Montreal's successful bid to hold the 1976 **OLYMPIC GAMES**, and although the financial entanglements were still being unravelled in 1980, the increase in jobs certainly benefited the working population. He was mayor until 1986, then

went on to become Ambassador to UNESCO in Paris (1987–91).

## Dravida Munnetra Kazhagam (DMK)
A TAMIL regional nationalist party and now one of the two main political parties in the southern Indian state of Tamil Nadu. The DMK traces its origins to the Dravidian movement of the 19c, as well as to the Non-Brahmin movement of the 20c. It stands primarily for the promotion of Tamil regional cultural identity. After the death of its leader C N Annadurai in 1969, the DMK split into its two present offshoots, the DMK and the AIADMK. The AIADMK ruled Tamil Nadu from 1977 to 1987. The DMK was then briefly returned to power with Karunanidhi as Chief Minister, but lost heavily in the 1991 elections. In 1997 a commission of inquiry reported that the DMK was partly responsible for the assassination of Rajiv GANDHI in 1991; the Congress (I) Party demanded that the United Front oust the DMK from its multiparty coalition government but this demand was refused, whereupon Congress withdrew its external support (which had been promised, on the formation of the UF government in 1996, in exchange for the continuation of its policies), Prime Minister Gujral resigned and the government was dissolved. ► INDIAN NATIONAL CONGRESS

## Dred Scott v Sandford (1857)
US Supreme Court case in which the slave Dred Scott sued for his freedom on the grounds of residence in a free state (Illinois) and territory (Wisconsin) to which a former owner had taken him. The US Supreme Court Chief Justice Roger B TANEY ruled that slaves were not US citizens and therefore lacked standing in the court. Going beyond the case, the court also ruled that the MISSOURI COMPROMISE, which excluded SLAVERY from the northern territories, was unconstitutional. This decision and other remarks by Taney, such as his comment that blacks had no rights that a white man was bound to respect, increased sectional tension and helped to bring on the AMERICAN CIVIL WAR.

## Drees, Willem (1886–1988)
Dutch politician. After a short period working in a bank, he moved to the Hague as a government stenographer and then entered politics, joining the Socialist Democratic Workers' Party and becoming its chairman in 1911. He sat in the Second Chamber from 1933 until the German invasion of 1940, after which he played an important part in the resistance movement. In 1947, as Minister of Social Affairs, he introduced the state pension and then became Prime Minister (1948–58). A modest, puritanical man, he became one of the most durable figures in Dutch politics.

## Drees, Willem (1922–98)
Dutch economist and politician. The son of Willem DREES (1886–1988), after graduating at the Netherlands School of Economics, Rotterdam, he joined the INTERNATIONAL MONETARY FUND (IMF) in Washington (1947–50), and then worked in the Dutch Embassy in Jakarta (1950–5). He returned to the Netherlands as Director of the Budget in the Ministry of Finance (1956–69), later becoming Professor of Public Finance at the Netherlands School of Economics (1963–71).

## Dresden, Battle of (1813)
NAPOLEON I's last victory in Germany, fought outside the Saxon capital, Dresden, then a major French depot, against an allied force of Austrian, Prussian and Russian troops under Prince SCHWARZENBERG (1771–1820). The French, however, were denied complete success, being twice defeated by the Allies in the following ten days. ► NAPOLEONIC WARS

## Dresden, Treaty of (1745)
This treaty ended the second of the SILESIAN WARS in which FREDERICK II, THE GREAT of Prussia retained Silesia but had to recognize FRANCIS I as Holy Roman Emperor.

## Dreyfus, Alfred (1859–1935)
French Jewish army officer. An artillery captain on the General Staff, in 1893–4 he was falsely charged with delivering defence secrets to the Germans. He was court-martialled and transported to Devil's Island, French Guiana. The efforts of his wife and friends to prove him innocent provoked a vigorous response from militarists and anti-Semites, and deeply divided the French intellectual and political world. After the case was tried again (1899), he was found guilty but pardoned, and in 1906 the verdict was reversed. Proof of his innocence came when German military documents were uncovered in 1930.

## drugs, war on
A term describing US attempts to halt the importation and use of illegal drugs in the USA. Launched in the 1970s, the strategy has had little impact. Efforts to deal with the supply side of the drugs trade became increasingly political, encompassing both US domestic and foreign policy, and have been used as justification for intervention in the internal affairs of Latin American countries through the provision of financial aid and technical expertise, the extradition of suspected manufacturers and traffickers for trial in US courts, and military action such as the invasion of Panama in 1989. Critics maintain that disruption of supply is ineffective and that the US government should seek to reduce demand by addressing the economic and social problems that encourage drug abuse. ► REGIME CHANGE

## Druze
A religious faith that originated during the closing years of the Fatimid caliph al-Hakim (996–1021), who some extremist ISMAILIS regarded as a manifestation of the Divinity. The Druze, who survive in parts of Jordan, Lebanon and Syria, deviate considerably in belief and practice from the main Muslim body. They await the return from divine concealment of both al-Hakim and his disciple Hamza ibn Ali. They assemble on Thursdays, instead of the usual Fridays, reject many of the prescriptions of the Shari'a, affirm monogamous marriage, and believe in the transmigration of souls. Today they number c.600,000.

## Dual Alliance (1879)
A defensive alliance between the German and Austro-Hungarian Empires, assuring 'reciprocal protection' from direct Russian attack, and at least benevolent neutrality in case of an attack from any other power. It expanded to the TRIPLE ALLIANCE in 1882 by the inclusion of Italy, and remained the focus of German and Austro-Hungarian foreign policy

until 1918. ► AUSTRIA-HUNGARY, DUAL MONARCHY OF

**Duan Qirui (Tuan Ch'i-jui)** (1865–1926)
Chinese politician. He took up a military career, rising to prominence as a protégé of YUAN SHIKAI, becoming his Prime Minister and remaining in office after his death (1916). His aim was to reunite the country, but his resort to force and his increasing dependence on Japan proved highly unpopular in China, and the Northern generals facing the Southern Nationalist regime refused to fight. His decision to force them to obey plunged China into the successive civil wars of its 'period of warlordism' (1916–25), in which four groups fought for control. Defeated, he retired from politics in 1920, except for a brief return in 1924. ► WARLORDS

**Duarte, José Napoleón** (1925–90)
El Salvador politician. Trained as a civil engineer in the USA, he founded the Christian Democratic Party (PDC) in 1960. After serving as Mayor of El Salvador (1964–70), he was elected President in 1972 but was soon impeached and exiled for seven years in Venezuela. He returned, and in 1980 regained the presidency with US backing. He lost the 1982 election, and for two years witnessed a fierce struggle between right- and left-wing elements. He returned as President in 1984, but in 1988, stricken by terminal cancer, was forced to resign.

**Dubček, Alexander** (1921–92)
Czechoslovak politician. After living with his parents in the USSR from 1925 to 1938, he returned home and joined the Communist Party in 1939, worked underground during WORLD WAR II and took part in the Slovak uprising in 1944. He rose through various party and parliamentary offices to become a full member of the Presidium in 1963 and, on the forced resignation of Antonín NOVOTNÝ, First Secretary in Jan 1968. He began to introduce a series of far-reaching reforms, including the abolition of censorship and increased freedom of speech. His political liberalization policy during the PRAGUE SPRING provoked Soviet hostility to what he called SOCIALISM WITH A HUMAN FACE and led to the occupation of Czechoslovakia by WARSAW PACT forces (Aug 1968). In 1969 he was replaced as First Secretary by Gustáv HUSÁK. He became President of the Federal Assembly for a few months in 1969, but was then expelled from the Presidium and deprived of party membership in 1970. In 1989, following the popular uprising and the resignation of the communist government, he became Chairman of the new Federal Assembly. Not quite as radical as the post-1989 reformers, he did not play a prominent political role and before he could develop one, he died as the result of a car accident.

**Dubois, Guillaume** (1656–1723)
French prelate. The son of a poor apothecary, he was first tutor and then secretary to the Duke of Chartres; when the latter (Philippe, Duke of ORLÉANS) became Regent in 1715, Dubois was virtually all powerful. He was appointed Foreign Minister and Archbishop of Cambrai (1720), a cardinal (1721), and Prime Minister of France (1722).

**Du Bois, William Edward Burghardt** (1868–1963)
US CIVIL RIGHTS activist, historian and sociologist. He studied at Fisk, Harvard and Berlin, and in his writings explored the history and lives of black Americans. In politics he campaigned for full equality, opposing the tactics of Booker T WASHINGTON. He helped found the National Association for the Advancement of Colored People (NAACP), and in his later years lived in Ghana, where he died.

**Dubrovnik, Republic of**
A wealthy independent city state after 1358, when it ceased to acknowledge Venetian suzerainty, Dubrovnik was governed by an oligarchy of noble families. A flourishing centre of trade, literature and art, in 1667 it was almost totally destroyed in an earthquake. Occupied by NAPOLEON I's army in 1806, it lost its status as an independent republic in 1808, when it became part of the ILLYRIAN PROVINCES (1809–13). The Congress of VIENNA (1814–15) granted the republic to Austria and, as part of the province of DALMATIA, it remained subject to Vienna until 1918, when it became part of the Kingdom of Serbs, Croats and Slovenes (later Yugoslavia).

**Duce**
The Italian word (literally, 'leader') commonly applied to MUSSOLINI; it corresponds with HITLER's title, *Führer.*

**Dulles, John Foster** (1888–1959)
US politician. Educated at Princeton and the Sorbonne, he became a lawyer. During WORLD WAR II he advocated a world governmental organization, and in 1945 advised at the Charter Conference of the UN, thereafter becoming US delegate to the General Assembly. In 1953 he became US Secretary of State, and was known chiefly for his aggressive anti-communist rhetoric and his policy of brinkmanship.

**Duma**
The name given to various forms of political assembly in pre-revolutionary Russia, such as the medieval 'Boyars' Council'. Municipal *dumas* (town councils) similar to the rural *zemstvos* were introduced as part of local government reforms in 1870. After the Russian REVOLUTION OF 1905, the State Duma, a quasi-parliamentary body, was established with progressively limited constitutional powers. Four State Dumas were elected between 1906 and the 1917 revolution, when the institution was abolished. ► RUSSIAN REVOLUTION; ZEMSTVO

**Dumbarton Oaks Conference** (21 Aug–7 Oct 1944)
An international conference at a mansion called Dumbarton Oaks in Georgetown, Washington, DC at which US, British, Soviet and Chinese diplomats drafted the preliminary proposals for an international organization whose purpose would be 'the maintenance of international peace and security'. These proproposals became the basis for the UN Charter, which was formally drafted the following year at the San Francisco Conference.

**Dumouriez, Charles François du Périer** (1739–1823)
French general. In 1792 he defeated the Prussians at Valmy and the Austrians at Jemappes, but in 1793 lost to the Austrians at Neerwinden. His leanings towards the monarchy caused him to be denounced by the revolutionaries, and to save his head he went over to the

Austrians. He later settled in England. ► FRENCH RE-
VOLUTIONARY WARS

**Dunant, (Jean) Henri** (1828–1910)
Swiss philanthropist. He inspired the foundation of
the international **RED CROSS** after seeing the plight of
the wounded on the battlefield of **SOLFERINO**. His efforts brought about the conference at Geneva (1863)
from which came the **GENEVA CONVENTION** (1864),
and in 1901 he shared the first **NOBEL PEACE PRIZE**.

**Dunbar, Battle of** (27 Apr 1296)
The battle fought between English and Scottish forces
after Scottish magnates had deprived King John (**BAL-
LIOL**) of independent authority and had negotiated
alliances with France and Norway. **EDWARD I**
marched north and his victory resulted in Balliol's
resignation of the throne. He was taken to England
as prisoner. Scotland remained without a King until
Robert **BRUCE** was crowned in 1306. ► **SCOTTISH
WAR OF INDEPENDENCE**

**Dunbar, Battle of** (3 Sep 1650)
Fought between an English army under Oliver
**CROMWELL** and Scots forces supporting the recogni-
tion of **CHARLES II** after **CHARLES I**'s execution.
Hemmed in by Scottish forces under the Earl of **LE-
VEN**, Cromwell launched a surprise counter-attack
which was entirely successful. ► **ENGLISH CIVIL
WARS**

**Duncan I** (c.1010–1040)
King of Scots (1034/40). He was the grandson of
Malcolm II (1005–34) and the son of Bethoc and Crinan, Abbot of Dunkeld. He succeeded to Strathclyde
and probably ruled over most of Scotland except the
islands and the far north. He attempted southward
expansion, and a long and unsuccessful siege of Durham weakened his position. He was killed by **MAC-
BETH** at Pitgaveney, near Elgin.

**Duncan II** (c.1060–1094)
King of Scots (1094). The son of **MALCOLM III, CAN-
MORE** and Ingibjorg, he was held hostage by **WILLIAM
I** of England from 1072 but was released and knighted
by **WILLIAM II**. Aided by an English army, he overthrew **DONALD III**. Attempting to appease anti-
English feeling, he tried to rule without English support but only weakened his position and was killed
on 12 Nov 1094 by the mormaer of the Mearns, probably at the instigation of Donald. ► **DUNCAN I**

**Dundee, John Graham of Claverhouse, 1st Vis-
count** (c.1649–1689)
Scottish soldier, known as 'Bonnie Dundee' or
'Bloody Claverhouse'. In 1672 he entered the Prince
of Orange's horse guards, and at the Battle of Seneffe
saved the future **WILLIAM III**'s life. He returned to
Scotland in 1677, and defeated the **COVENANTERS** at
Bothwell Brig (1679). He was made a Privy Councillor
in 1683, and became Viscount Dundee (1688). Joined
by the Jacobite clans, he raised the standard for **JAMES
VII AND II** against William and Mary, but died from a
musket wound after his successful battle against
Mackay at the Pass of Killiecrankie. ► **JACOBITES**

**Dunois, Jean d'Orléans, Count**, known as **the Bas-
tard of Orléans** (1403–68)
French soldier. The illegitimate son of Louis, Duke of
Orléans, he was a general in the **HUNDRED YEARS'**

WAR. He defeated the English at Montargis (1427), defended Orléans with a small force until its relief by
**JOAN OF ARC** (1429), then inflicted further defeats on
the English, forcing them out of Paris, and by 1453
from Normandy and Guyenne.

**Dupleix, Joseph François** (1697–1763)
French colonial administrator. In 1741 he became
Governor-General of all the French Indies; his skilful
diplomacy among the native princes almost made
the Carnatic a French province. His power alarmed
the British **EAST INDIA COMPANY**. When war broke
out in Europe between France and England, several
engagements took place between the French and the
Nawab of the Carnatic, who endeavoured in vain to
seize Madras. Dupleix's science and courage were
displayed in the defence of Pondicherry, which Admiral **BOSCAWEN** attacked in vain for five weeks.
However, Dupleix's ambitious project of founding a
French empire in India on the ruins of the Mughal
monarchy was frustrated by **CLIVE OF PLASSEY**,
though the struggle continued until Dupleix's recall
in 1754. The French Company refused to reimburse
him for the vast sums he had spent out of his (alleged) private fortune, and he died in poverty and
neglect in 1763. ► **EAST INDIA COMPANY, FRENCH**

**Duplessis, Maurice le Noblet** (1890–1959)
Canadian politician. He led the **UNION NATIONALE** to
power in Quebec in 1936, gaining power through a
methodical exploitation of *nationalisme* and fear of
Anglicization; yet he encouraged further encroachments by US corporations on Quebec's economic
life. His campaign against radical reformers gained
him the support of the Roman Catholic Church,
which he retained almost throughout his political career. His attitude towards labour was expressed in the
notorious **PADLOCK ACT** (1937) that crippled the **CCF**,
but it was his antagonistic attitude towards federal
government (which he claimed was invading provincial rights through the **WAR MEASURES ACT**) that contributed most to his defeat in 1939, when Ernest
**LAPOINTE** and other French-Canadian ministers
threatened to resign if he was returned to office. He
did regain power in 1944, defeating both the incumbent Liberals under Adélard **GODBOUT** and the extremist **BLOC POPULAIRE**, and maintained his pre-war
policies. An alliance between labour, professionals,
academics and even some churchmen eventually
succeeded in demonstrating the scale of corruption
in his government and although Duplessis himself
died suddenly in 1959, the *Union Nationale* was defeated by the Liberals in 1960.

**Duquesne, Abraham, Marquis of** (1610–88)
French naval officer. He distinguished himself from
1637 to 1643 in the war with Spain. After serving
Sweden (1644–7), he returned to France, capturing
Bordeaux, which had declared for the **FRONDE**
(1650). He defeated the Dutch and the Spanish fleets
(1672–6). On the revocation of the Edict of **NANTES**,
Duquesne was the only Protestant excepted.

**Durando, Giacomo** (1807–94)
Italian soldier and politician. The brother of Giovanni
**DURANDO**, he was implicated in a plot in 1831; forced
to flee Sardinia-Piedmont, he lived in exile in Belgium, Portugal and Spain until 1848. He commanded

a corps in the war against the Austrians and was the aide-de-camp of **CHARLES ALBERT** at the Battle of **NOVARA** (1849). In 1855 he became Piedmontese Minister for War and from 1856 to 1861 was the Italian ambassador in Istanbul. In 1862 he entered the government again, this time as Foreign Minister. He presided over the Italian Senate from 1884 to 1887.

**Durando, Giovanni** (1804–69)
Italian soldier. Cashiered by **CHARLES FELIX** in 1821, he served in Portugal and Spain before returning to Italy in 1848. He became Commander-in-Chief of the papal army that was sent to assist the Venetian rising against the Austrians, before the **PAPAL ALLOCUTION** of Apr 1848 forbade him to continue his advance against fellow Catholics. Disregarding **PIUS IX**'s instructions, he retreated to Vicenza, where he was forced to surrender. He then entered Piedmontese service, fighting at the Battle of **NOVARA**, in the Crimean campaign and at **SOLFERINO** (1859).

**Durbar**
The audience-chamber or body of officials at the Indian royal court. In British India the term was applied to formal assemblies marking important state occasions to which leading Indians were invited, eg the Delhi Durbar of 1911 celebrating the visit of King **GEORGE V** and Queen Mary.

**Durcansky, Ferdinand** (1906–74)
Slovak Populist Party politician. Upset by the union of Czechs and Slovaks in a single state in 1918, he was active in the 1930s in trying to negotiate Slovak independence. After the **MUNICH AGREEMENT** he visited **GOERING** and others in Berlin, and was encouraged to make trouble for the rump Czechoslovak government in Prague. Eventually **HITLER** virtually ordered him and his superior, **TISO**, to declare independence; this was the signal for the Nazis to sweep into Prague in Mar 1939 and establish the **BOHEMIAN PROTECTORATE**. Durcansky was immediately made Slovak Foreign Minister, although about a year later he was dismissed as insufficiently compliant. He was condemned to death *in absentia* in 1947, and spent the remainder of his life abroad.

**Durham, John George Lambton, 1st Earl of** (1792–1840)
British politician. He served in the dragoons, and in 1813 became a Whig MP. In 1828 he was created Baron Durham. He became Lord Privy Seal (1830), and was one of those who drew up the Reform Bill. He was made an earl in 1833, and became Ambassador to St Petersburg (1835). As Governor-General of Canada (1838), his measures were statesman-like, but the House of **LORDS** voted disapproval of his amnesty to several of the French-Canadian rebels, and he resigned. His report on Canada (1839) advocated the union of Upper and Lower **CANADA**, which was accepted in 1841. ▶ **REFORM ACTS**; **WHIGS**

**Durham Report**
A British government report of 1839 recommending the union of Upper and Lower **CANADA** into a single political structure; produced by Lord Durham, the Governor-General of Canada, it called for the assimilation of French-Canadian into English-Canadian economic and linguistic culture. It also recommended responsible government.

**Dürnkrut, Battle of** (1278)
Refusing to accept defeat after his battle with **RUDOLF I** of Habsburg in 1276, Ottokar II of Bohemia began to prepare for battle again in 1278. In a pre-emptive strike, Rudolf attacked him with an army of 2,000 horsemen and the support of Ladislav of Hungary. Ottokar's army was put to flight and he himself was killed. The battle paved the way for the rise of the **HABSBURG DYNASTY**.

**Durruti, Buenaventura** (1896–1936)
Spanish revolutionary anarchist. He was the most prominent violent activist to emerge from the ferocious urban guerrilla warfare of 1919–23 in Barcelona between the employers (backed by the state) and the **CNT**. Exiled in Europe and South America during the period 1923–31, Durruti was the principal leader of the revolutionary **FAI**. During the Second Republic, he agitated for an immediate revolution from below, and was frequently jailed. He led the anarchist militia in the **SPANISH CIVIL WAR** until he was shot dead in Nov 1936 in mysterious circumstances, probably by a Nationalist sniper. His funeral procession in Barcelona was the last great demonstration of strength by the anarchist movement. ▶ **REPUBLIC, SECOND** (Spain)

**Dushan, Stephen** ▶ **STEPHEN DUSHAN**

**Dutch East Indies**
A name applied to Indonesia until 1945, when **SUKARNO** declared independence; the area included the islands of Java, Sumatra, the Celebes, most of Borneo, the Moluccas and Bali. The Dutch recognized Indonesia's independence in 1949.

**Dutch Revolt** ▶ **EIGHTY YEARS' WAR**

**Dutch West India Company**
The organization of Dutch merchants responsible for the settlement of New Netherland, now New York. The Company was established in 1621, and was dissolved in 1674. It was later reorganized as a trading venture.

**Dutra, Eurico Gaspar** (1885–1974)
Brazilian soldier and politician. Commissioned into the army in 1910, he rose to become a general in 1932, during which time he opposed all anti-government revolutionary activities, including the coup which brought Getúlio **VARGAS** to power in 1930. However, he supported Vargas during the São Paolo Revolt (1932), was appointed War Minister (1936–45), and helped Vargas to draft a new constitution for Brazil, the **ESTADO NOVO**, in 1937. After seizing power in a military coup in 1945, Dutra became President of Brazil (1946–51) at the head of the **PSD** (Social Democratic Party). He soon adopted a new constitution, restoring the country to constitutional democracy.

**Duvalier, François**, known as **Papa Doc** (1907–71)
Haitian politician. He held power from 1957 until his death, ruling in an increasingly arbitrary fashion. His regime saw the creation of the civilian militia known as the Tonton Macoute, and the exile of many people. He became President for life in 1964, and was succeeded in this post by his son, Jean-Claude ('Baby Doc') **DUVALIER**, whose regime lasted until 1986.

**Duvalier, Jean-Claude**, known as **Baby Doc** (1951– ) Haitian politician, son of François ('Papa Doc') **DU-VALIER**. After studying law at the University of Haiti, he followed his father into politics. At the age of 20 he became President for life, ruling, as had his father, through a private army. In 1986 he was deposed in a military coup led by General Henri Namphrey and went into exile in Grasse, in the south of France.

**DVP** (*Deutsche Volkspartei*, 'German People's Party') German political party. Founded in Dec 1918, the DVP represented the interests of right-wing liberalism and heavy industry in the **WEIMAR REPUBLIC**. Although its attitude to Weimar was equivocal, its leader, **STRESEMANN**, served continuously as German Foreign Minister from 1923 until his death in Oct 1929, in which post he did much to revise the more onerous provisions of the Treaty of **VERSAILLES**. During the early 1930s, the DVP lost most of its electoral support, and on 4 July 1933 the party was wound up.

**Dzerzhinsky, Felix Edmundovich** (1877–1926) Russian revolutionary, of Polish descent. In 1897 he was exiled to Siberia for political agitation, fought in the Russian **REVOLUTION OF 1905**, and in 1917, as one of the organizers of the coup d'état, became chairman of the secret police and a member of the Bolshevik Central Committee until his death. After 1921 he also reorganized the railway system, and was chairman of the Supreme Economic Council (1924–6), trying to combine industrialization with good relations with the peasantry.

**Dzungars**
Western **MONGOLS** (also known as Eleuthes or Kalmuks) who resisted the Manchu expansion into Central Asia during the 18c. A series of campaigns by the Manchu Emperor **QIANLONG** during the 1750s resulted in their destruction and the incorporation of their territory in Turkestan (henceforth known as Xinjiang) into the Qing Empire in 1759. ► **QING DYNASTY**

**EAM** (*Ethnikón Apeleftherotikón Métopon*, 'National Liberation Front')
A coalition of left-wing parties in Greece during **WORLD WAR II**, it was founded and dominated by the **KKE** (Communist Party of Greece) which hoped to take power upon liberation. EAM organized a military wing, **ELAS**, established a system of government, education, health care and justice in the areas it liberated, and in Mar 1944 created the Political Committee of National Liberation (PEEA), which challenged the Greek government-in-exile. By the end of the war, the EAM enjoyed support throughout Greece and, bitterly opposed to the return of **GEORGE II**, it continued to demand a plebiscite to decide the future constitution of Greece. By 1945, dissension among its various left-wing members weakened EAM and its role was superseded by the KKE, which remained the strongest party on the Left. With armed bands at their command, the communists, royalists and republicans embarked on civil war, which lasted until 1949. ➤
**EDES; EKKA; GREEK CIVIL WAR; KLARAS, ATHANASIOS; PLASTIRAS, NIKOLAOS; VAFIADIS, MARKOS; ZACHARIADIS, NIKOS; ZERVAS, NAPOLEON**

### Eanes, António dos Santos Ramalho (1935– )
Portuguese general and politician. For his role in quashing the far Left at the end of the Revolution of Apr 1974–Nov 1975, he was promoted from an unknown colonel to Chief of Staff. With his remote, austere and humourless manner, and his dark glasses, he often appeared to be a hangover from the **SALAZAR** regime. In 1976 he was elected President as the principal non-communist candidate. During his ten-year presidency, the laconic and enigmatic Eanes did much to uphold the new democratic regime amidst the debilitating squabbles of the political parties, and his essential honesty won him wide popular support. Politically, he proved to be left-of-centre (though he drifted rightwards), and was distrusted by the Right. From 1986 to 1987 he was leader of the Portuguese Democratic Renewal Party.

### Early, Jubal Anderson (1816–94)
US soldier. He commanded a Confederate brigade at **BULL RUN** (1861) and a division at **FREDERICKSBURG** (1862) and **GETTYSBURG** (1863). He was defeated three times (1864) by Philip **SHERIDAN** and George **CUSTER** on a raiding expedition down the Shenandoah Valley towards Washington, and was relieved of his command after a rout at Waynesboro. He fled to Canada, but returned in 1869 to his former profession as a lawyer in Virginia.

### Earp, Wyatt Berry Stapp (1848–1929)
US lawman and gunfighter. He served as assistant marshal in the Kansas cattle town of Dodge City, then moved (1878) to Tombstone, Arizona, where he worked as a messenger for **WELLS, FARGO & CO**, and later as a saloon guard, while his brother Virgil served as marshal. His falling-out with the Clanton gang led to the infamous shoot-out at the OK Corral (1881). Though they were represented in the stories of the Old West as the champions of law and order, Wyatt, his brothers and their associates were seen by the townspeople of Tombstone as little more than criminals.

### Earth Summit (UN Conference on Environment and Development)
A UN conference in Rio de Janeiro in 1992 that addressed the issues of poverty and excessive consumption, and the need to protect the environment and safeguard natural resources. The aims of the resulting Rio Declaration on Environment and Development were the eradication of poverty through sustainable economic development, and the protection of the environment and natural resources. Other outcomes of the summit were the UN Framework on **CLIMATE CHANGE**, the UN Convention on **BIOLOGICAL DIVERSITY, AGENDA 21**, and the Statement of Forest Principles, which recognized the importance of the world's forests and supported their sustainable management. The UN Commission on **SUSTAINABLE DEVELOPMENT** was created to monitor the Rio agreements. Five-yearly reviews of progress in these areas were held in New York in 1997 and at the World Summit on Sustainable Development in Johannesburg in 2002.

### East Bank
The region in Jordan, east of the River Jordan, which comprises the governorates of Amman, Al Balqa, Irbid, Al Karak and Maan. It corresponds roughly to the former Emirate of Transjordan.

### Eastern Question
A complex set of diplomatic problems affecting 18c, 19c and early 20c Europe. It was created by the slowly declining power of the **OTTOMAN EMPIRE**, the emergence of the Balkan nations and nationalism, and the ambitions in south-east Europe of the Great Powers, especially Russia and Austria (later Austria-Hungary).

### Eastern Rumelia
The region lying between the Balkan and Rhodope mountains which was created by the Treaty of Berlin (1878) from the Bulgarian lands remaining after the establishment of the autonomous principality of Bulgaria and the return of Thrace and Macedonia to the

Ottoman Empire. Eastern Rumelia was ruled by a governor appointed by the Ottomans and subject to the approval of the Great Powers. The separation of Eastern Rumelia from Bulgaria was temporary; in 1885 the two regions were united after a bloodless revolution.

### Easter Rising (24–9 Apr 1916)

A rebellion of Irish nationalists in Dublin, organized by the Irish Republican Brotherhood and **SINN FÉIN**. The focal point of the rebellion was the seizing of the General Post Office by the Irish Volunteers, led by Patrick **PEARSE**, and the Irish Citizen Army, led by James Connolly (1870–1916), where an Irish republic was declared. The rising was put down and several leaders were executed. Although initially the rising was not widely popular, the reprisals increased support for the nationalist cause in Ireland.

### East India Company, British

A British trading monopoly, established in India in 1600, which later became involved in politics. Its first 'factory' (trading station) was at Surat (1612), with others at Madras (1639), Bombay (1688) and Calcutta (1690). A rival company was chartered in 1698, but the two companies merged in 1708. During the 18c it received competition from other European countries, in particular France. The company benefited territorially from local Indian disputes and Mughal weakness, gaining control of Bengal (1757), and after the Battle of Baksar receiving the right to collect revenue from the Mughal emperor (1765). Financial indiscipline among company servants led to the 1773 Regulating Act and Pitt's 1784 India Act, which established a Board of Control responsible to Parliament. Thereafter it gradually lost its independence. Its monopoly was broken in 1813, and its powers handed over to the British crown in 1858. It ceased to exist as a legal entity in 1873.

### East India Company, Dutch (*Vereenigde Oost-indische Compagnie*)

A trading company founded in 1602 to protect trade in the Indian Ocean and assist in the war against Spain. It established 'factories' (trading stations) on the Indian subcontinent, but made little political/cultural contact there; it founded long-term colonies in South Africa, Ceylon, and especially the Indonesian archipelago. It was at the height of its prosperity during the 17c and was dissolved in 1799.

### East India Company, French (*Compagnie des Indes Orientales*)

A commercial/political organization, founded in 1664, which directed French colonial activities in India. It established major trading stations at Chandernagore, Pondicherry, and Mahé, and competed for power with the British during the 18c. Its governor, **DUPLEIX**, captured Madras (1746), but was defeated during the **SEVEN YEARS' WAR** (1756–63). The Company lost government support and ceased to exist during the **FRENCH REVOLUTION**. ► **EAST INDIA COMPANY, BRITISH**

### EAST TIMOR

Part of a mountainous island in South-East Asia, in the Sunda group. It was colonized by the Portuguese in the 16c, and after **WORLD WAR II**, when the western part of Timor passed from the Netherlands to Indo-

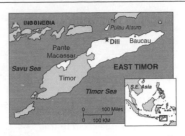

nesia, it remained an overseas province of Portugal until 1975 when, following the fall of the **SALAZAR** regime in Portugal, colonial rule was withdrawn from East Timor and the leftist Fretilin (*Frente Revolucionária de Timor Leste Independente*, the Revolutionary Front of Independent East Timor) emerged as the major domestic political force. It immediately declared East Timor independent as the Democratic Republic of East Timor, sparking off invasion by Indonesia, which alleged that Fretilin was a communist movement, and violent civil war ensued. The capital, Dili, was taken and East Timor was declared the 27th province of Indonesia (July 1976). It was administered as the province of Timor Timur, though the **UN** refused to recognize Indonesian sovereignty in East Timor and continued to regard it as a Portuguese colony. In 1991 pro-independence protesters were massacred by the Indonesian army in Dili, provoking international condemnation. Despite such forcible suppression, guerrilla struggles between Indonesian forces and Fretilin continued until the Indonesian government agreed to a plebiscite offering a choice between a special autonomous regime within Indonesia and independence. The vote, held in 1999, resulted in a large majority for independence, the Indonesian parliament recognized the result, and East Timor became independent on 20 May 2002 under President Xanana Gusmao, leader of Fretilin, which formed the post-independence government.

### Eban, Abba, originally Aubrey Solomon (1915–2002)

Israeli diplomat and politician. Born in South Africa, he was educated in England and taught oriental languages at Cambridge before serving as a liaison officer at Allied HQ during **WORLD WAR II**. In 1944 he worked in the Middle East Arab Centre in Jerusalem, and in 1948 was Israeli **UN** representative in New York and then ambassador in Washington (1950–9). He returned to Israel, where he won a seat in the Knesset and joined David **BEN-GURION**'s government. Between 1959 and 1974 he held several posts, under various prime ministers, and was Foreign Minister from 1966 to 1974. ► **MAPAI PARTY**

### Ebert, Friedrich (1871–1925)

German politician. He started life as a saddler, then became a journalist on a Social Democratic newspaper and a **REICHSTAG** member (1912). Chairman of his party (1913), he was a leader in the **REVOLUTION OF 1918**; his firm line against groups on the far left and deals with the old order to achieve this provoked much controversy. He was the first President of the German Republic (1919–25).

### Eboli, Ruy Gómez de Silva, Prince of (1516–73)

Portuguese nobleman. He became the adviser and confidant of **PHILIP II** of Spain from 1559 until his own death. Even more famous was his wife, Aña Mendoza de la Cerda (1540–91), whom he married in 1552 and who is featured in portraits with an eyepatch over one eye. She became involved in the intrigues of the King's secretary, Antonio PÉREZ, and was kept in confinement from 1579.

## EC (European Community)
A community of states in Western Europe created for the purpose of achieving economic and political integration. It comprised three communities, which merged to form the European Community in 1967. The first of these was the European Steel and Coal Community, established in 1952 under the Treaty of Paris by France, West Germany, Italy, Belgium, the Netherlands and Luxembourg. It created common institutions for regulating the coal and steel industries under a common framework of law and institutions, thereby producing the first breach in the principle of national sovereignty. In the early 1950s unsuccessful attempts were made to establish a European Defence Community and a European Political Community. In 1958, under the Treaty of Rome, the six states established the European Economic Community (EEC) and the European Atomic Energy Community, which provided for collaboration in the civilian sector of nuclear power. To develop and oversee the policies of economic and, increasingly, political integration, a number of supranational community institutions were set up, including the Commission, the Council of Ministers, the European Parliament, and the European Court of Justice. A further six members joined the original six: Denmark, Ireland, UK (1973), Greece (1981), Portugal and Spain (1986). These 12 states signed the Treaty of MAASTRICHT (1992), creating the European Union (EU) from 1 Jan 1993.

## Ecclesiastical Principalities
The states in the HOLY ROMAN EMPIRE ruled directly by Church officials. The rulers were elected by the cathedral chapters. Although unable to establish strong dynasties, the Church princes functioned in every other way as secular princes. Three were Electors: the Archbishops of Mainz, Cologne and Trier. Other prominent states were the bishoprics of Speyer, Worms, Würzburg and Bamberg, and the territories of the the Abbots of Fulda and Lorsch.

## Ecevit, Bülent (1925– )
Turkish politician. After working as a government official and a journalist, he became an MP for the centre-left Republican People's Party in 1957. He was Minister of Labour, then in 1966 became Secretary-General of his party and subsequently (1972) Chairman. He headed a coalition government in 1974 and during office ordered the invasion of Cyprus. He was Prime Minister again in 1977 and in 1978–9, when he imposed martial law on Turkey. After the military coup of 1980, he was imprisoned twice for criticizing the military regime. He was once again Prime Minister from 1999 to 2002.

## Echegaray y Eizaguirre, José (1833–1916)
Spanish dramatist, scientist and politician. Born of Basque descent in Madrid, he taught mathematics, held portfolios in various ministries (1868–74), then won literary fame with his many plays in prose and verse, notably *The Great Galeoto* (1881). He shared the Nobel Prize for Literature in 1904. In 1905 he returned to politics as Minister of Finance (1905), and to science as Professor of Physics at Madrid.

## ECLAC (Economic Commission for Latin America and the Caribbean)
A regional commission of the UN, founded as the Economic Commission for Latin America (ECLA) in 1948 to raise the level of economic activity in Latin America and to strengthen the economic ties of Latin American countries among themselves and internationally. The scope of ECLA was broadened to include the Caribbean in 1984. Its headquarters are in Santiago, Chile, and there are 41 member states, including several North American and European nations with historical ties to the region. Under its first executive secretary, Raul PREBISCH, ECLAC's policies encouraged governments to industrialize their economies by import substitution policies in line with the implications of DEPENDENCY THEORY. However, the pressure of western free-market globalization and the effects of economic downturns on the region's inefficient economies in the 1980s and 1990s led to recession, poverty and social unrest.

## Economic Community of West African States (ECOWAS)
An organization formed (May 1975) by 15 West African states through the Treaty of Lagos: Benin, the Gambia, Ghana, Guinea, Guinea-Bissau, Côte d'Ivoire, Liberia, Mali, Mauritania (withdrew 2002), Niger, Nigeria, Senegal, Sierra Leone, Togo and Upper Volta (now Burkina Faso). Cape Verde joined in 1977. It is based in Abuja, Nigeria. Its principal objectives are the ending of restrictions on trade between the signatories, the establishment of a common customs tariff, the harmonization of economic and industrial policies, and equalization of the levels of development of member states. In 1990 it set up a Standing Mediation Committee to mediate disputes between member states. It has also supported the free movement of peoples and has overseen collaborative military involvement through the ECOWAS Monitoring Group (ECOMOG) in Liberia, Guinea-Bissau and Sierra Leone.

## Economic Societies of Friends of the Country
The most active expression of the ENLIGHTENMENT in 18c Spain, they originated in the Basque country in a group formed in 1748 by the Count of Peñaflorida and others, which in 1765 took the name the Basque Society of Friends of the Country, receiving royal approval the following year. The societies functioned mainly as discussion groups, and published various proposals for economic and technical reform. The minister CAMPOMANES encouraged them, and in the 1770s some 60 were founded under royal patronage in the main cities of Spain. The society in Madrid commissioned Jovellanos to draw up his famous *Report on the Agrarian Law*. ➤ BASQUES

ECOWAS ➤ ECONOMIC COMMUNITY OF WEST AFRICAN STATES

ECUADOR official name **Republic of Ecuador**
A republic straddling the Equator in the north-west of South America. It is bounded to the north by Colombia; to the south and east by Peru; and to the west

by the Pacific Ocean, and includes the Galápagos Islands. Formerly part of the Inca Empire, it was taken by the Spanish in 1527 and included in the Viceroyalty of **NEW GRANADA**. On gaining independence in 1822, it joined Panama, Colombia and Venezuela as part of **GRAN COLOMBIA** until the union dissolved in 1830, when it became an independent republic. There were sporadic border disputes with Peru in the 1990s. The country was politically unstable throughout the 20c (there were 22 presidents between 1925 and 1948, none completing a term in office) and the instability has continued owing to economic difficulties since the 1990s which prompted reforms that provoked popular protests. In 2000 Ecudor adopted the US dollar in an effort to overcome inflation and stabilize the economy..

**Eda Saburo** (1907–77)
Japanese politician. Active in the pre-war Farmers' Movement, Eda joined the **JAPAN SOCIALIST PARTY** (JSP) in 1946 and was elected to the House of Councillors (upper house) in 1950. During the 1960s he served as Secretary-General of the JSP, when he incurred the wrath of the party's dominant left wing for suggesting a shift in the party's approach of confrontation with the existing capitalist system to one of promoting gradual change within the system.

**Edde, Émile** (1886–1949)
Lebanese nationalist and lawyer. A Maronite, he spent **WORLD WAR I** in France, having been sentenced to death *in absentia* by the Turks. After the war he was adviser to Picot's deputy, Robert Coulondre, thereby acquiring considerable prestige in the eyes of the Lebanese. Disagreement between the two meant, however, that this arrangement did not last long. Edde, though, was destined to play a leading part in Lebanese politics. In 1924 he was elected President of the Representative Council of Greater Lebanon, which was dissolved by the French High-Commissioner early the following year. By 1927 a rival to Edde's position had emerged in Bishara al-Khouri: where Edde was more at home with the French language and culture, al-Khouri, although a French-speaker, had excellent Arabic; where Edde was outspoken, al-Khouri tended to be reserved. Both politicians, however, regarded Lebanon as more a part of the Mediterranean culture than of a greater Arab world. Elected to the presidency again in 1936, Edde managed to survive, relying heavily on French support, until 1941; at this point, however, wartime shortages became too much for his already weak regime, and he was forced to resign. Edde was again active in public life from 1942, establishing his Francophile following

as the National Bloc. However, despite some sympathy amongst the Christian element of the population, Edde's stance put him out of touch with the country as a whole.

**Eden, (Robert) Anthony, 1st Earl of Avon** (1897–1977)
British politician. He became a Conservative MP in 1923, and was Foreign Under-Secretary (1931), Lord Privy Seal (1933), and Foreign Secretary (1935), resigning in 1938 over differences with Neville **CHAMBERLAIN**. In **WORLD WAR II** he was first Dominions Secretary, then Secretary of State for War, and Foreign Secretary (1940–5). Again Foreign Secretary (1951–5), he was involved with the negotiations in Korea and Indo-China, and the 1954 Geneva Summit Conference. He succeeded Winston **CHURCHILL** as Prime Minister (1955–7), and in 1956 ordered British forces (in collaboration with the French and Israelis) to occupy the Suez Canal Zone. His action was condemned by the **UN** and caused a bitter controversy in Britain which did not subside when he ordered a withdrawal. In failing health, he resigned abruptly in 1957. He was created an earl in 1961. ➤ **CONSERVATIVE PARTY** (UK); **SUEZ CRISIS**

**EDES** (*Ellínikos Dímokratikos Ethnikós Strátos*, 'National Republican Greek League')
One of the three major Greek resistance groups operating after the German invasion of Greece (6 Apr 1941). Formed during the winter of 1941–2, its leader in Greece was the republican Napoleon **ZERVAS**. It rivalled **EAM/ELAS** in power and influence, and was favoured by the British government as a counterweight to the communists. It cooperated with Special Operations Executive and EAM/ELAS in Sep 1942, cutting German supply lines over the Gorgopotamos viaduct and, following the National Bands Agreement (summer 1943), it took part in Operation Animals. With the withdrawal of the Axis forces, conflict between the rival resistance groups grew and EDES was forced from the field by EAM/ELAS. ➤ **EKKA**; **GREEKS**; **PLASTIRAS, NIKOLAOS**; **VAFIADIS, MARKOS**; **ZACHARIADIS, NIKOS**

**Edgar the Atheling** (c.1050–c.1125)
Anglo-Saxon prince, the grandson of **EDMUND II, IRONSIDE**. Though chosen as king by some influential Englishmen after the Battle of **HASTINGS**, he was never crowned. He submitted to **WILLIAM I, THE CONQUEROR** (by Dec 1066), but then rebelled and fled to Scotland (1068), where his sister Margaret married **MALCOLM III, CANMORE**. He was finally reconciled with King William in 1074. He was taken prisoner at the Battle of Tinchebrai (1106), fighting for Duke Robert of Normandy against **HENRY I** of England, and lived in obscurity after his release.

**Edinburgh, Duke of, Prince Philip** (1921– )
The husband of Queen Elizabeth II, the son of Prince Andrew of Greece and Princess Alice of Battenberg, born at Corfu. He became a naturalized British subject in 1947, when he was married to the Princess Elizabeth (20 Nov). In 1956 he began the Duke of Edinburgh Award Scheme to foster the leisure activities of young people. ➤ **ELIZABETH II**

**Edirne, Capture of** (1362)
Edirne (Adrianople), which was to be the Ottoman

capital from 1366 to 1453 (the year in which Constantinople fell), was lost to the Byzantines in 1362. This Turkish success formed a part of what was a systematic reduction of the Balkans. Achieved either right at the end of **ORHAN**'s reign or at the beginning of the reign of **MURAD I**, it paved the way for the Turkish control of the Balkans that stood them in such good stead when Asia Minor was overrun by **TIMUR**.

### Edmund II, Ironside (c.980–1016)
King of the English (1016). The son of **ETHELRED THE UNREADY**, he was chosen King by the Londoners on his father's death (Apr 1016), while **CANUTE** was elected at Southampton by the witan. Edmund hastily levied an army, defeated Canute, and attempted to raise the siege of London, but was routed at Ashingdon or possibly Ashdon, Essex (Oct 1016). He agreed to a partition of the country, but died a few weeks later, leaving Canute as sole ruler.

### Edo
The former name for Tokyo, capital of Japan. Edo became a castle town at the end of the 16c and the capital of the **TOKUGAWA SHOGUNATE** after 1603. Due to its administrative and economic importance, Edo became one of the most populous cities in the world during the 18c, with an estimated population of 1 million. With the overthrow of the Tokugawa in 1868 and the restoration of imperial rule (the **MEIJI RESTORATION**), the city was renamed Tokyo (Eastern Capital) and became the capital of the new Meiji state.

### Edo, Treaty of (29 July 1858)
An agreement between Japan and the USA that extended the rights given to the USA in the Treaty of **KANAGAWA** and marked the opening up of Japan to westernization. It was negotiated by the first US consul in Japan, Townsend Harris (1804–73). Diplomatic relations were established, a conventional tariff was accepted, trading rights were granted at five additional Japanese ports, and US citizens were granted extra-territorial rights in five treaty ports.

### Edward I (1239–1307)
King of England (1272/1307). The elder son of **HENRY III** and Eleanor of Provence, he married **ELEANOR OF CASTILE** (1254) and later Margaret of France, the sister of **PHILIP IV** (1299). In the **BARONS' WARS**, he at first supported Simon de **MONTFORT**, but rejoined his father, and defeated de Montfort at Evesham (1265). He then won renown as a crusader to the Holy Land, and did not return to England until 1274, two years after his father's death. In two devastating campaigns (1276–7 and 1282–3), he annexed north-west Wales, and ensured the permanence of his conquests by building magnificent castles. He reasserted English claims to the overlordship of Scotland when the line of succession failed, and decided in favour of John **BALLIOL** as King (1292). But Edward's insistence on full rights of suzerainty provoked the Scottish magnates to force Balliol to repudiate Edward and ally with France (1295), thus beginning the **SCOTTISH WAR OF INDEPENDENCE**. Despite prolonged campaigning and victories such as Falkirk (1298), he could not subdue Scotland as he had done Wales. He died while leading his army against Robert **BRUCE**. ► **WALLACE, WILLIAM; WESTMINSTER, STATUTES OF**

### Edward II (1284–1327)
King of England (1307/27). He was the fourth son of **EDWARD I** and **ELEANOR OF CASTILE**. In 1301 he was created Prince of Wales, the first English heir-apparent to bear the title, and in 1308 married **ISABELLA OF FRANCE**, the daughter of **PHILIP IV**. Throughout his reign, Edward mismanaged the barons, who sought to rid the country of royal favourites and restore their own place in government. The Ordinances of 1311 restricted the royal prerogative in matters such as appointments to the King's household, and demanded the banishment of Edward's favourite, Piers Gaveston, who was ultimately captured and executed (1312). Edward was humiliated by reverses in Scotland, where he was decisively defeated by Robert **BRUCE** at the Battle of **BANNOCKBURN** (1314). The Ordinances were formally annulled (1322), but the King's new favourites, the Despensers, were acquisitive and unpopular, and earned the particular enmity of Queen Isabella. With her lover Roger Mortimer, she toppled the Despensers (1326) and imprisoned Edward in Kenilworth Castle. He renounced the throne in 1327 in favour of his eldest son, **EDWARD III**, and was then murdered in Berkeley Castle, near Gloucester.

### Edward III (1312–77)
King of England (1327/77). The elder son of **EDWARD II** and **ISABELLA OF FRANCE**, he married Philippa of Hainaut in 1328, and their eldest child, Edward (later called **EDWARD, THE BLACK PRINCE**), was born in 1330. By banishing Queen Isabella from court and executing her lover, Roger Mortimer, he assumed full control of the government (1330), and began to restore the monarchy's authority and prestige. He supported Edward **BALLIOL**'s attempts to wrest the Scots throne from **DAVID II**, and his victory at the Battle of **HALIDON HILL** (1333) forced David to seek refuge in France until 1341. In 1337, after **PHILIP VI** had declared **GUYENNE** forfeit, he revived his hereditary claim to the French crown through Isabella, the daughter of **PHILIP IV**, thus beginning the **HUNDRED YEARS' WAR**. He destroyed the French navy at the Battle of **SLUYS** (1340), and won another major victory at the Battle of **CRÉCY** (1346). David II was captured two months later at the Battle of Neville's Cross, near Durham, and remained a prisoner until 1357. Edward was renowned for his valour and military skill. ► **WILLIAM OF WYKEHAM**

### Edward IV (1442–83)
King of England (1461/70 and 1471/83). He was the eldest son of Richard, Duke of York. His father claimed the throne as the lineal descendant of **EDWARD III**'s third and fifth sons (respectively Lionel, Duke of Clarence, and Edmund, Duke of York), against the Lancastrian King **HENRY VI** (the lineal descendant of Edward III's fourth son, **JOHN OF GAUNT**). Richard was killed at the Battle of Wakefield (1460), but Edward entered London in 1461, was recognized as King on Henry VI's deposition, and with the support of his cousin Richard Neville, Earl of **WARWICK**, decisively defeated the Lancastrians at Towton. He threw off his dependence on Warwick, and secretly married Elizabeth Woodville (1464). Warwick forced him into exile in Holland (Oct 1470), and Henry VI regained the throne. Edward

returned to England (Mar 1471), was restored to kingship (11 Apr), then defeated and killed Warwick at the Battle of Barnet (14 Apr), and destroyed the remaining Lancastrian forces at the Battle of TEWKESBURY (4 May). Henry VI was murdered soon afterwards, and Edward remained secure for the rest of his reign. ► LANCASTER, HOUSE OF; ROSES, WARS OF THE; YORK, HOUSE OF

### Edward V (1470–83)
King of England (Apr/June 1483). He was the son of King EDWARD IV and Elizabeth Woodville. Shortly after his accession, he and his younger brother, Richard, Duke of York, were imprisoned in the Tower by their uncle, Richard, Duke of Gloucester, who usurped the throne as RICHARD III. The two princes were never heard of again, and were most likely murdered (Aug 1483) on their uncle's orders. In 1674 a wooden chest containing the bones of two children was discovered in the Tower, and these were interred in Westminster Abbey as their presumed remains. ► ROSES, WARS OF THE

### Edward VI (1537–53)
King of England (1547/53). He was the son of HENRY VIII by his third queen, Jane SEYMOUR. During Edward's reign, power was first in the hands of his uncle, the Duke of Somerset, and after his execution in 1552, of John Dudley, Duke of Northumberland. Edward became a devout Protestant, and under the Protectors the English Reformation flourished. He died of tuberculosis, having agreed to the succession of Lady Jane GREY (overthrown after nine days by MARY I). ► REFORMATION (England)

### Edward VII (1841–1910)
King of the UK (1901/10). The eldest son of Queen VICTORIA, in 1863 he married Alexandra, the eldest daughter of CHRISTIAN IX of Denmark. They had three sons and three daughters: Albert Victor, Duke of Clarence; George; Louise, Princess Royal; Victoria; Maud, who married HAAKON VII of Norway; and Alexander. As Prince of Wales, his behaviour led him into several social scandals, and the Queen excluded him from affairs of state. As King, he carried out several visits to continental capitals which strove to allay international animosities. ► GEORGE V

### Edward VIII (1894–1972)
King of the UK (Jan/Dec 1936). He was the eldest son of King GEORGE V. He joined the navy and, during WORLD WAR I, the army, travelled much, and achieved considerable popularity. He succeeded his father in Jan 1936, but abdicated (11 Dec) in the face of opposition to his proposed marriage to Mrs Ernest Simpson, a commoner who had been twice divorced. He was then given the title of Duke of Windsor, and the marriage took place in France in 1937. The Duke and Duchess of Windsor lived in Paris, apart from a period in the Bahamas (1940–5), where he was Governor.

### Edward, the Black Prince (1330–76)
Eldest son of EDWARD III. He was created Earl of Chester (1333), Duke of Cornwall (1337) and Prince of Wales (1343). In 1346, though still a boy, he fought at the Battle of CRÉCY, and is said to have won his popular title (first cited in a 16c work) from his black armour. He won several victories in the HUNDRED YEARS' WAR, including the Battle of POITIERS (1356).

He had two sons, Edward (1365–70) and the future RICHARD II. In 1362 he was created Prince of Aquitaine and lived there until 1371, when a revolt forced him to return to England. A great soldier, he was a failure as an administrator.

### Edward the Confessor (c.1003–1066)
King of England (1042/66). He was the elder son of ETHELRED THE UNREADY and Emma of Normandy, and the last king of the Old English royal line. After living in exile in Normandy, he joined the household of his half-brother HARDAKNUT in 1041, and then succeeded him on the throne. Until 1052 he maintained his position against the ambitious Godwin family by building up Norman favourites, and in 1051 he very probably recognized Duke William of Normandy (later WILLIAM I) as his heir. However, the Godwins regained their ascendancy, and on his death-bed in London, Edward, who remained childless, nominated Harold Godwin (HAROLD II) to succeed, the NORMAN CONQUEST following soon after. Edward's reputation for holiness began in his lifetime, and he rebuilt Westminster Abbey, where he was buried, in the Romanesque style. His cult grew in popularity, and he was canonized in 1161.

### EEC (European Economic Community)
Established in 1958 after the Treaties of Rome (1957), and often referred to as the Common Market, the economic community was one of three European communities that merged in 1967 to form the European Community (EC) Its policies, regulations and institutions constitute the economic basis of the European Union (EU). It is essentially a customs union, with a common external tariff and a common market with the removal of barriers to trade among the members. In addition it has a number of common policies, the most important of which is the COMMON AGRICULTURAL POLICY, providing for external tariffs to protect domestic agriculture and mechanisms for price support. There are common policies for fisheries, regional development, industrial intervention, and economic and social affairs. A European Monetary System set up in 1979 to regulate exchange rate movements among the member states' currencies was superseded in 1998 by the European Monetary Union. In 1986 the Single European Act was passed, allowing for the completion of the process of creating a common market within the community by the beginning of 1993.

### Eelam
The name of the proposed independent state in north and east Sri Lanka demanded by some Tamil groups, including the militant LTTE.

### EFTA (European Free Trade Association)
An association originally of seven Western European states who were not members of the European Economic Community (EEC), intended as a counter to the EEC; it was established in 1959 under the Stockholm Convention. The members (originally Austria, Denmark, Norway, Portugal, Sweden, Switzerland and the UK) agreed to eliminate over a period of time trade restrictions between them, without having to bring into line individual tariffs and trade policies with other countries. Agriculture was excluded from the agreement, although individual arrangements

# Ancient Egyptian Civilization

*Culture & Society*

### Predynastic Period

Human occupation of the Nile Valley is evidenced by Palaeolithic flint implements found in Upper Egypt before 1200 BC. In the Neolithic period, the cultivation of crops and domestication of animals began. Certain localities have given their name to Predynastic cultures such as Badarian in Middle Egypt, where by c.4500 BC the transition from stone technology to the gradual introduction of copper termed 'Chalcolithic' had taken place. By c.4000 BC, a community at el-Amra (hence Amratian or Naqada I culture) produced pottery of red ware, which was burnished, often with a black rim or white painted incised decoration. The later Gerzean or Naqada II culture (from el-Gerza) began c.3500 BC and was characterized by buff-coloured pottery decorated with scenes in purplish paint. In the late Predynastic period there appear to have been two confederations consisting of local communities corresponding roughly to the later provinces of Egypt. The leaders of the two were 'kings' of Upper and Lower Egypt. In the century prior to c.3100 BC, Upper and Lower Egypt vied for supremacy until the conquest of the north by the south led to the unification under King Narmer and the start of the historic Dynastic period in Egypt.

### Early Dynastic Period (Archaic Period) (c.3100–c.2780 BC)

The period comprising the 1st and 2nd Dynasties, the formative era of Egyptian culture. A centralized administration was based on the newly founded capital of Memphis at the apex of the Delta. At the same time, a system of writing, hieroglyphic script, was devised in order to convey information on vital matters such as flood control and agricultural production. At this time, artistic conventions, craft methods and the lifestyle of the Egyptians quickly assumed the forms which were to become characteristic and remain little altered for centuries. The skill and resources of the people are shown by their rapid mastery of the working of stone, initially to make vessels but soon applied in architecture. Little is known of the internal activities of the country, but the prime concern was to counteract, by means of a strong central authority, the tendency of the newly created union of north and south to dissolve into scattered units.

### Old Kingdom (c.2780–c.2181 BC)

The period of pyramid building, when ancient Egypt had a central government under the absolute power of a god-king. Through the king, authority was delegated to officials (often members of his family). He controlled their training, granted them land and made provision for their burials and funerary endowments. The administrative structure included the treasury, the granaries, the public works department, the royal household and temple estates. Alongside the massive pyramids, there is in contrast the simple, elegant design of furniture, jewellery and burial equipment. During this period expeditions were sent to Sinai and Nubia, while trading for timber with western Asia was conducted by sea. Economic factors and the growing independence of local governors led to the breakdown of central control and the resulting confusion of the First Intermediate Period.

---

were permitted. The EEC was treated as a single member of EFTA, and there has been a free trade agreement between the EFTA countries and the European Community (**EC**), and considerable trade between the two groupings. In 1991 the EC and EFTA established a European Economic Area (EEA). The departure to the EEC from EFTA of the UK, Denmark (1973) and Portugal (1986), and to the European Union (**EU**) of Austria, Sweden and Finland (1995), left the future of EFTA in doubt, but it continues with Iceland, Liechtenstein, Norway and Switzerland as members.

### Eger, Golden Bull of (1213)

An agreement between the Holy Roman Emperor **FREDERICK II** and Pope **INNOCENT III**, repeating and formalizing the terms of an agreement made by **OTTO IV** at Speyer. It recognized the territorial aspirations of the papacy in full and emancipated the German Church from imperial control.

### Egidian Constitution (1357)

This political settlement takes its name from the warrior cardinal and constitutional lawyer, Egidio Albornoz. He imposed it on the **PAPAL STATES** after his skilful reconquest (with slender military means) of the petty tyrannies that had developed there, and it was to remain valid for virtually the entire history of these territories.

### Egmond, Lamoral, Count of and Prince of Gavre (1522–68)

Dutch soldier and political figure. As one of the fore-most nobles of the Netherlands, he accompanied the Emperor **CHARLES V** to Algiers in 1541 and in all his later campaigns, distinguishing himself at St Quentin (1557) and Gravelines (1558), for which he was made **STADHOLDER** of Flanders and Artois in 1559. He then sided with the party in the Netherlands that opposed **PHILIP II** of Spain's policies in the Low Countries, and left the Council of State. He went on a special mission to Spain in 1565 to tell the King of conditions in the Netherlands, and after the **IMAGE-BREAKING RIOTS** (1566), he distanced himself from the Prince of Orange and the '**BEGGARS**'. He seemed to have restored order and to have gained the confidence of the Duke of **ALBA**, by then (1567) Lieutenant-General to the Netherlands, but suddenly he was seized, condemned to death, and beheaded in Brussels.

---

**EGYPT** official name **Arab Republic of Egypt**

A republic in north-east Africa, bounded to the west by Libya; to the south by Sudan; to the east by the Red Sea; to the north-east by Israel; and to the north by the Mediterranean Sea. The history of Egypt can be traced as far back as c.6000BC, to Neolithic cultures on the River Nile. A unified kingdom embracing lower and upper Egypt was first created in c.3100BC, ruled by Pharaoh dynasties; the pyramids at El Giza were constructed during the Fourth Dynasty. Egyptian power was greatest during the New Empire period (c.1567–c.1085BC). It became a Persian province in the 6c BC and was conquered by Alexander the Great in the 4c BC. Ptolemaic Pharaohs ruled Egypt until 30BC. It was conquered by Arabs in AD672. From

### First Intermediate Period (c.2181–c.2040 BC)

The period covering the 7th to 11th Dynasties of the Egyptian chronicler Manetho. Following the collapse of the Old Kingdom, the country suffered civil wars, infiltration of the Nile Delta by **Bedouin**, plundering, a breakdown of central government, poverty and the ephemeral rule of many kings. The 7th and 8th Dynasties in Memphis had limited authority; the rest of Egypt was ruled by the nomarchs who became independent princes. By c.2160 BC the princes of Heracleopolis imposed their will over neighbouring nomes (governorates) and set up the 9th and 10th Heracleopolitan Dynasties in Middle Egypt. The warlike princes of Thebes later founded the 11th Dynasty in the south, overcame the Heracleopolitans and achieved the unification of the country c.2040 BC, leading to the Middle Kingdom.

### Middle Kingdom (c.2040–c.1786 BC)

The period covering the last 50 years of the 11th Dynasty up to the end of the 12th Dynasty. The founders were the princes of Thebes who extended their authority throughout Upper and Lower Egypt, reunifying the country with central government control in place of the disruption of the First Intermediate Period. Mines and quarries were again worked and trade renewed. Architecture and art regained their former high standard of design and crisp execution. In the 12th Dynasty, by strong government, the adoption of a co-regency to ensure the smooth transition from one ruler to another, and the establishment of an almost feudal system to obtain the support of the provincial governors, the kings put the country into a stable, prosperous condition. The conquest of Lower Nubia was undertaken with the boundary set at the 2nd Cataract on the Nile. Contacts were maintained with Western Asia, particularly the port of Byblos. The craftsmanship of the Middle Kingdom jewellers and goldsmiths was unsurpassed in taste, beauty of design and technical skill. The strength of the Middle Kingdom administration is demonstrated by its being continued for over a century by officials in the succeeding 13th Dynasty in spite of the short and ever weaker rule of a number of petty kings.

### Second Intermediate Period (c.1786–c.1567 BC)

The period covering the 13th to 17th Dynasties. For the 13th Dynasty, with its numerous kings of ever decreasing power, the breakdown of authority was cushioned through the efforts of government officials. Possibly simultaneously, the 14th Dynasty, of which little is known, exercised some control at Xois in the Delta. The weakened state of the country allowed Asiatics to move into the Delta where, under the leadership of the Hyksos, the 15th and 16th Dynasties came to power. The 15th or Great Hyksos had their capital at Avaris in the Delta by c.1675 BC, while the minor kings of the 16th Lesser Hyksos seem to have reigned concurrently, although no details are preserved. To the south at Thebes, the local princes formed the 17th Dynasty c.1650 BC. The early members of the family were confined to the Theban area, but later rulers challenged the Hyksos and, in a series of armed clashes, began the liberation of Egypt which was finally accomplished by Ahmose I of the 18th Dynasty.

### New Kingdom (c.1567–c.1085 BC)

The great era which began with the expulsion of the Hyksos (c.1567 BC). This was when Egypt became an imperial power, with a sphere of influence extending, at its height, from the 4th Cataract of the Nile in the south, to the Amanus

1798 until 1801, it was occupied by France under **NAPOLEON I**. The Suez Canal was constructed in 1869. A revolt in 1879 against the ruling Khedive was put down by British intervention in 1882. Egypt became a formal British protectorate in 1914, but declared its independence in 1922. It was used as a base for Allied forces during **WORLD WAR II**. King **FAROUK** was deposed by the army in 1952, and Egypt was declared a republic the following year. **NASSER** asserted his authority, negotiating the British withdrawal from the Suez base in 1955. In 1956 he nationalized the Suez Canal and survived a joint Anglo-French and Israeli invasion (**SUEZ CRISIS**). An attack on Israel, followed by Israeli invasion in 1967, resulted in the loss of the Sinai Peninsula and control of part of the Suez Canal (regained following negotiations in the 1970s). In 1981, President **SADAT** was assassinated, and relations with Arab nations were strained, but they im-

proved again during the 1980s. During the 1990s there were violent attacks and clashes between Muslim and Coptic Christians. Islamic fundamentalists (mainly the Islamic Group and al-Jihad organizations) grew increasingly violent in their campaign against the government and by the end of the decade foreign tourists as well as Egyptians were included among their victims. Sadat's successor, President Hosni **MUBARAK**, has followed a policy of moderation and reconciliation, playing an active role in the Middle East peace process to resolve the Arab–Israeli conflict in the 1990s, but has been unable to stem **TERRORISM** at home. The last free elections in Egypt were in 1950; since then it has been under martial law, although Mubarak's presidency has been approved by national referendum every six years since 1981. ➤ **ANCIENT EGYPTIAN CIVILIZATION**

### Ehrenburg, Ilya Grigorevich (1891–1967)

Soviet novelist and journalist. Born in Kiev, he was in exile in Paris before 1917 and returned to fight against the communists. Yet he was allowed back again in 1923 and wrote novels in praise of the system that were accepted abroad. In the **KHRUSHCHEV** period he wrote in favour of an East–West thaw and managed to open the eyes of the Soviet public to some genuine truths about the West.

### Eichmann, Karl Adolf (1906–62)

Austrian **SS** officer. A fanatical Nazi and anti-Semite, he became a member of the SS in 1932 and organized anti-Jewish activities, particularly their deportation to concentration camps. Captured by US forces in

Mountains of Anatolia in the north. The commitment of the early kings of the 18th Dynasty to a policy of expansion, with political control over Palestine and Syria, the exploitation of Nubia and the dedication of the spoils of war to Amun Re at Thebes as thanks offerings for their victories, was continued by succeeding ruling families. In the reign of Amenhotpe III, the country reached the peak of its achievements culturally, economically and politically. Following the religious and artistic revolution of the Amarna period under Akhenaten (Amenhotpe IV), the Ramesside kings attempted to reimpose Egypt's hold in western Asia. However, the balance among the neighbouring nations began to shift away from economies based on bronze to those using iron. This, combined with ethnic movements in the Mediterranean after 1200 BC and the ever-increasing power of the priesthood of Amun, led to a steady decline in Egypt's prestige and the end of the empire in the early 11c BC.

### Third Intermediate Period (c.1085–c.656 BC)
Post-imperial Egypt, a period when the country was divided and sometimes under foreign domination. The 21st Dynasty ruled from Tanis in the Delta, while at Thebes the High Priests of Amun controlled the south. The kings at Tanis were buried there with rich grave goods. The Amun priests were responsible for rescuing the plundered royal tombs of earlier kings and re-interring the remains. The 22nd Dynasty, of Libyan origin, assumed the throne c.945 BC and ruled from Tanis (and possibly also Bubastis). In spite of a successful campaign into Palestine and ending the hereditary position of the High Priests of Amun by appointing royal nominees such as Shoshenq I, conditions in Egypt were greatly disturbed. About 818 BC another line of kings, the 23rd Dynasty, was established in the Delta and ruled concurrently with the 22nd Dynasty, causing the country to fragment into smaller units. Following the Nubian invasion of Egypt (c.728 BC), order was restored, the short-lived 24th Dynasty ended with Tefnakhte, and thereafter the 25th Dynasty ruled until c.656 BC.

### Late Period (c.656–343 BC)
The period covering the 25th to 30th Dynasties. The 25th Dynasty (Nubian) kings were devoted to the worship of Amun and stressed the importance of the position of the Divine Adoratrice of the god at Thebes. This office was held by royal princesses, who were appointed by adoption. New buildings were erected and others restored, both in Egypt and Nubia. The dynasty ended with the invasions of the Assyrians in 671 BC and 663 BC. Princesses loyal to Ashurbanipal were installed in the Delta, with Thebes under the control of the Divine Adoratrice. The Prince of Sais was strong enough to unite the country and set up the 26th Dynasty. There was an upsurge in artistic and cultural expression inspired in particular by the best works of the Old Kingdom. Assyria was overwhelmed by Babylon (612 BC), and inevitably there followed a clash with Egypt. The Persians then conquered Babylon in 539–538 BC, and soon afterwards invaded Egypt (525 BC); under the 27th Dynasty the country became a satrapy of the Persian Empire. From this time onwards, frequent revolts to gain independence are recorded in Greek sources. Following the ephemeral 28th and 29th Dynasties, the last native kings formed the 30th Dynasty, but by 343 BC, Egypt was once more subject to Persia until the conquest of Alexander III, the Great.

---

1945, he escaped from prison some months later, having kept his identity hidden, and in 1950 reached Argentina. He was traced by Israeli agents and in 1960 was seized, taken to Israel, condemned for 'crimes against humanity' and executed.

### Eighth Route Army
The Chinese 'Red Army', formed by the communists in 1927. It was given this name in 1937 when it entered into an uneasy alliance with the Nationalist army of **CHIANG KAI-SHEK** against the Japanese invaders of China.

### 'Eight-Legged Essay' (baguwen)
The standard form of essay written in the Chinese **CIVIL SERVICE EXAMINATION SYSTEM** during the **MING DYNASTY** and **QING DYNASTY**. The introduction of this form, the composition of balanced prose in a rigid eight-part structure, coincided with a reduction in the scope of the examinations themselves; only approved classical interpretations of Confucian texts could be used and preparation increasingly came to rely on rote memorization. By the 18c, form and calligraphy assumed more importance than the presentation of original ideas. Handbooks on the writing of eight-legged essays were produced for potential examination candidates. The eight-legged essay was finally abolished in 1902 and replaced with a more topical dissertation. Three years later, the civil service examinations themselves were abolished.

### Eighty Years' War (1568–1648)
Uprisings and wars against Spanish Habsburg rule by

17 provinces in the Low Countries, also called the War of Independence, the Revolt of the Netherlands, and the Dutch Revolt. The provinces, previously separate principalities in the Burgundian sphere of influence, were finally united by **CHARLES V**, who was also King of Spain. His son, **PHILIP II**, pursued through his regents policies of centralization, increased taxation and persecution of non-Catholics; resistance to centralization and religious persecution began in the 1550s. The wars devastated the ten southern provinces retained by the Spanish. The rebels, led by William of Orange and his Protestant sea force of '**BEGGARS**', established themselves in the seven northern provinces, chiefly Holland, which were declared a republic in 1588, with the Orange family as stadholders. Independence was finally recognized by Spain in 1648. ➤ **BLOOD, COUNCIL OF**; **HABSBURG DYNASTY**; **STADHOLDER**; **WILLIAM I, THE SILENT**

### Einaudi, Luigi (1874–1961)
Italian politician. Professor of Public Finance in Turin (1902–49), he was a Senator (1915–45) and President of Italy (1948–55). His most important role was as Budget Minister (a post specially created for him in 1947 by **DE GASPERI**); he devised a rigorous deflationary policy of tight monetary control and high interest rates that was not abandoned until 1950. While this arguably slowed Italy's post-war industrial recovery and certainly contributed to high unemployment, it also helped to revive confidence in the lira and to lay the foundation for growth in the post-1950 era.

**Éire ►** IRELAND, REPUBLIC OF

**Eisenhower, Dwight David**, nicknamed **Ike** (1890–1969)
US general and 34th President. He graduated from the US Military Academy at West Point, and by 1939 had become chief military assistant to General Douglas **MACARTHUR** in the Philippines. In 1942 he commanded Allied forces for the amphibious descent on French North Africa. His ability to coordinate the Allied forces and staff led to his selection as Supreme Commander of the Allied Expeditionary Force that spearheaded the 1944 invasion of Europe. In 1950 he was made Supreme Commander of the **NATO** forces in Europe. In 1952 the popularity that he had gained as a war hero swept him to victory in the US presidential election, in which he ran as a Republican; he was re-elected in 1956. During his administration (1953–61) he negotiated a truce in the **KOREAN WAR** (1953) and continued US efforts to contain **COMMUNISM**. During his second term the administration became more active in **CIVIL RIGHTS** issues, sending troops to **LITTLE ROCK**, Arkansas to enforce a school **DESEGREGATION** order. ► **REPUBLICAN PARTY**; **WORLD WAR II**

**Eisenhower Doctrine** (1957)
The US declaration to protect the Middle East against communist aggression, intended to reassure the Western allies after the **SUEZ CRISIS**. Addressing **CONGRESS**, President **EISENHOWER** stated that the USA regarded the Middle East as vital to its security and that it should give economic and military aid to any country in the region that requested it.

**ejido**
A traditional form of communal landholding in Mexico; *ejido* lands existed in the Valley of Mexico at the time of the conquest and were areas claimed as common or **CABILDO** properties outside the settlement or village, which were to be protected from alienation to private holders. The idea of the ejido as a communal property was revived by the followers of Emiliano **ZAPATA**, who believed that title to lands should be vested in the village. Communal *ejidos* were created under Lázaro **CÁRDENAS**, who expropriated large integrated *haciendas* created under Porfirio **DÍAZ** as a means of forming loyal peasant communities immune to pressure from the Cristeros and supporting the PRM (*Partido de la Revolución Mexicana*). Some 41.5 million acres/16.8 million hectares were distributed. ► **HACIENDA**

**EKKA** (*Ethnike Kai Koinonike Apeleutherosis*, 'National and Social Liberation')
The smallest of the three major resistance groups in Greece during **WORLD WAR II**. Led by Colonel Dimitrios Psarros, its politics were liberal and republican. It took an active part in the resistance from summer 1943 onwards, but was forced from the field when its leader was murdered by **ELAS** (Apr 1944). ► **EAM**; **EDES**

**El Alamein, Battles of** (1942)
Two battles in **WORLD WAR II**, named after a village on Egypt's Mediterranean coast. In the first, inconclusive battle (1–27 Jul) the British 8th Army, under **AUCHINLECK**, halted the advance of **ROMMEL'S AFRIKA CORPS**. The second battle (23 Oct–4 Nov) ended in **MONTGOMERY'S** victory over Rommel and proved to be a turning point in the war in Africa. ► **NORTH AFRICAN CAMPAIGN**

**ELAS** (*Ethnikós Laïkós Apeleftherotikós Strátos*, 'National Popular Liberation Army')
The Greek resistance army founded in Dec 1941 as the military wing of the communist-dominated **EAM**. In the field from summer 1942, while fighting to liberate Greece from the Axis forces, its ultimate goal was the establishment of communist rule at the end of the war. It worked to eliminate rival resistance bands, cooperating with **EDES** only under the auspices of the British **SPECIAL OPERATIONS EXECUTIVE** (SOE). At the end of the war, with c.70,000 men, it controlled most of Greece and refused to cooperate with the British-backed government of George **PAPANDREOU**. Although it agreed to disarm in Feb 1945, the fighting between communists, republicans and royalists continued, erupting into the **GREEK CIVIL WAR** of 1946–9.

**El Dorado**
Literally 'the gilded one', the term refers to a powerful early colonial Spanish-American legend of a ruler coated in gold, believed to exist in **NEW GRANADA** (now Colombia). By extension, it came to mean a land of fabulous wealth. Sir Walter **RALEIGH** organized two expeditions (1595 and 1617) from England in search of El Dorado.

**Eleanor of Aquitaine** (c.1122–1204)
Queen consort of **LOUIS VII** of France (1137–52) and, after the annulment of this marriage, of the future **HENRY II** of England (1154–89). She was imprisoned (1174–89) for supporting the rebellion of her sons, two of whom became kings of England (**RICHARD I** in 1189 and **JOHN** in 1199).

**Eleanor of Castile** (c.1245–1290)
Queen consort of **EDWARD I** of England (1254/90). The daughter of **FERDINAND III**, she accompanied Edward to the Crusades, and is said to have saved his life by sucking the poison from a wound he had. She died at Harby, Nottinghamshire, and the 'Eleanor Crosses' at Northampton, Geddington, and Waltham Cross are survivors of the 12 erected by Edward at the halting places of her cortège. The last stopping place was Charing Cross, where a replica now stands. ► **CRUSADES, LATER**

**Electors**
Members of the electoral college that chose Holy Roman Emperors. By the 13c membership was limited to seven: the Duke of Saxony, King of Bohemia, Count Palatine of the Rhine, Margrave of Brandenburg, and Archbishops of Cologne, Mainz and Trier. The *Golden Bull* (1356) of Emperor **CHARLES IV** permanently granted the right of election to the seven. ► **HOLY ROMAN EMPIRE**

**Eliot, Sir John** (1592–1632)
English statesman. He entered parliament in 1614 and was knighted in 1618. He became a supporter of **CHARLES I'S** favourite, the 1st Duke of **BUCKINGHAM**, but in 1625 turned against him and moved his **IMPEACHMENT**. His policy of antagonism to the King led to his imprisonment on three occasions. He died

in the Tower, thus becoming a martyr to the parliamentary cause.

### Elizabeth, St (1207–31)

Hungarian princess. The daughter of Andreas II of Hungary, at the age of four she was betrothed to Louis IV, Landgrave of Thuringia. She was educated at his father's court, the Wartburg, near Eisenach, and at 14 she was married; a boy and two girls were the fruit of their union. Louis, who admired her for her piety and ceaseless alms-giving, died as a crusader at Otranto in 1227, whereupon Elizabeth was deprived of her regency by her husband's brother, and exiled on the plea that she wasted state treasures by her charities. After severe privations, she was received into the monastery of Kitzingen by the abbess, her aunt. Later she retired to a cottage near the castle of Marburg and lived in cloistered simplicity for the remainder of her days. She was canonized by Pope **GREGORY IX** in 1235.

### Elizabeth I (1533–1603)

Queen of England (1558/1603). She was the daughter of **HENRY VIII** by his second wife, Anne **BOLEYN**. On the death of **EDWARD VI** (1553), she sided with her Catholic half-sister, Mary, against Lady Jane **GREY** and the Duke of Northumberland, but her identification with Protestantism made Mary suspicious, and she was imprisoned for her alleged part in the rebellion led by Sir Thomas Wyatt (1554). Ascending the throne on **MARY I**'s death, she reduced animosities and promoted stability by engineering a moderate Protestant Church settlement, and it is from this time that a distinctive Anglican Church was effectively established. She made peace with France and Scotland, and strengthened her position by secretly helping Protestants in these countries. **MARY, QUEEN OF SCOTS**, was thrown into her power (1568) and imprisoned, causing numerous conspiracies among English Catholics. After the most sinister plot was discovered (1586), Elizabeth was reluctantly persuaded to execute Mary (1587); many other Catholics were persecuted in the 1580s and 1590s. Infuriated by this, and by Elizabeth's part in inciting the Netherlands against him, Philip of Spain attacked England with his 'invincible **ARMADA**' (1588), but England managed to repel the attack, though war continued until 1604. Of all Elizabeth's personal relationships, only one touched her deeply, that with Robert Dudley, Earl of **LEICESTER**, whom she would probably have married had it not been for her adviser **CECIL**'s remonstrances. A strong and astute, but sometimes cruel and capricious, woman, the 'Virgin Queen' was nevertheless popular with her subjects, becoming later known as 'Good Queen Bess'; and her reign is seen as a period of generally effective government and increased international status.

### Elizabeth II (1926–)

Queen of the UK (1952/ ) and Head of the **COMMONWEALTH OF NATIONS**. The elder daughter of King **GEORGE VI**, she was proclaimed Queen on 6 Feb 1952, and crowned on 2 June 1953. Her husband was created Duke of **EDINBURGH** on the eve of their wedding (20 Nov 1947), and styled Prince Philip in 1957. They have three sons, Prince **CHARLES**, Prince Andrew and Prince Edward, and a daughter, Princess Anne.

### Elizabeth Petrovna (1709–62)

Empress of Russia (1741/62). The daughter of **PETER I, THE GREAT** and **CATHERINE I**, she was passed over for the succession in 1727, 1730 and 1740, finally becoming empress on the deposition of Ivan VI. She was guided by favourites throughout her reign, some better than others. A war with Sweden was brought to a successful conclusion, but her animosity towards **FREDERICK II, THE GREAT** led her to take part in the War of the **AUSTRIAN SUCCESSION** and in the **SEVEN YEARS' WAR**, which helped to establish Russia as a European power. At home, she contributed considerably to the extension and entrenchment of serfdom.

### Ellenborough, Edward Law, 1st Earl of (1790–1871)

British politician. He became a Tory MP in 1813 and held office under several administrations, becoming Governor-General of India (1841). Parliament approved his Afghan policy in 1843, but his subsequent policy led to his early recall (1844). He was then created Viscount Southam and Earl of Ellenborough. He became First Lord of the Admiralty in 1846, and in 1858 was made Minister for India, but the publication of a dispatch in which he rebuked Viscount **CANNING** forced him to resign and he held no further office.

### Elphinstone, Mountstuart, 11th Lord Elphinstone (1779–1859)

British colonial administrator and historian. He entered the Bengal civil service in 1795, served with distinction on **WELLESLEY**'s staff (1803) at the Battle of Assaye, and was appointed Resident at Nagpur. In 1808 he was sent as the first British Envoy to Kabul; and as Resident from 1810 at Pune ended the Maratha War of 1817 and organized the newly acquired territory. He was Governor-General of Bombay (1819–27), where he founded the system of administration, and did much to advance state education in India. He returned to Britain in 1829, and, declining the governor-generalship of India, lived in comparative retirement until his death.

**EL SALVADOR** official name **Republic of El Salvador**

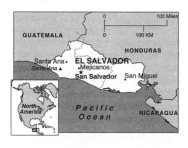

The smallest of the Central American republics, bounded to the north and east by Honduras; to the west by Guatemala; and to the south by the Pacific Ocean. Originally part of the Aztec kingdom, it was conquered by the Spanish in 1526, and achieved independence from Spain in 1821. A member of the **CENTRAL AMERICAN FEDERATION** until its dissolution in 1839, it became an independent republic in 1841. In the 20c it was ruled by dictatorships, suffered political unrest, and waged war with Honduras in 1965 and 1969. There was also considerable political unrest in the 1970s, with guerrilla activity directed against the US-supported government. Following the assassination of the Archbishop of San Salvador, Oscar Romero, in 1980, a civil war erupted in which 75,000 died and many became refugees. A peace agreement signed in 1992 recognized the extreme left-wing guerrilla group Frente Farabundo Marti de Liberación (FMLN) as a political party; it won a few seats in the 1994 elections in which the right-wing Alianza Republicana Nacionalista (ARENA) under President Armando Calderón Sol came to power. Since then, FMLN has increased its share of the vote, often being the largest party in parliament, but it has never held office, as ARENA has always formed coalition governments with smaller right-wing parties.

## Emancipation Acts
Statutes of imperial legislatures which freed colonial slaves. The bill to emancipate slaves in the BRITISH EMPIRE was introduced by Sir Thomas Buxton (1786–1845) and was passed in Aug 1833. It granted financial compensation to the slave owners and freed the slaves under a system of APPRENTICESHIP on 1 Aug 1834. On that date 750,000 slaves became free in the British West Indies, and it was reported that the expected trouble had not materialized and that the ex-slaves had spent the weekend in chapels and churches in thanksgiving. France freed its slaves in 1848, the Netherlands in 1863, the USA in 1865 and Spain in 1885.

## Emancipation Proclamation (1 Jan 1863)
A document issued by President Abraham LINCOLN during the AMERICAN CIVIL WAR, that declared the freedom of all slaves in areas then in rebellion against the US government. Originally set forth in a preliminary statement on 22 Sep 1862, it was intended as a war measure to reduce the reserves of manpower in the South. It freed the slaves in the Confederacy but did not free the slaves in areas that supported the US government (the Union).

## Emma, in full Adelheid Emma Wilhelmina Theresia (1858–1934)
Queen and Regent of the Netherlands (1879/98). The daughter of Prince George Victor of Waldeck-Pyrmont and Helena of Nassau-Weilburg, she became the second wife of the Dutch King WILLIAM III on 7 Jan 1879. In 1880 her daughter, the future Queen WILHELMINA, was born; Emma became Regent shortly before the death of her husband in Dec 1890 until her daughter came of age in 1898. After William III's unpopularity, Emma succeeded in restoring the esteem of the Dutch for their monarchy.

## Emmet, Robert (1778–1803)
Irish patriot. He left Trinity College, Dublin, to join the United Irishmen, and travelled on the Continent for the Irish cause, at one point meeting NAPOLEON I. In 1803 he plotted an insurrection against the English, but it proved a failure. He was captured and hanged in Dublin.

## Empecinado, El, real name Juan Martín Díaz (1775–1825)
Spanish soldier and patriot. El Empecinado (literally, 'the Stubborn One') acquired great distinction as a guerrilla leader against the French in the PENINSULAR WAR (1808–14). He became a general in 1814,

but for petitioning Ferdinand III to re-establish the CORTES was banished to Valladolid (1818). On the outbreak of the insurrection in 1820, he joined the Constitutionalists; and on the Absolutists' triumph in 1823 he was exhibited in an iron cage, and fatally stabbed by a soldier.

## Empire, First (France)
The system of government established by NAPOLEON I in 1804, which continued until his fall in 1814, restored for the HUNDRED DAYS in 1815, then abolished after his defeat at the Battle of WATERLOO.

## Empire, Second (France)
The system of government established by Louis Napoleon (NAPOLEON III) in 1852, which continued until he fell from power in Sep 1870.

## encomienda
A feudal-type tenure or grant, applied especially to the tenure of landed property, and known in Spain since the Middle Ages. The best-known encomiendas were those of the military orders, such as those of the Orders of ALCÁNTARA and SANTIAGO, their holders being known as encomenderos. In America, from the 16c the word encomienda was applied to the tenure or grant of the labour of native Indians, and was known also as a repartimiento.

## Encyclopedists
A collective term for the distinguished editors (Diderot and d'Alembert) and contributors (notably Voltaire, MONTESQUIEU, CONDORCET, Helvetius and ROUSSEAU) to the Encyclopédie, a major work of social and political reference published in France (1751–72), associated with the French ENLIGHTENMENT. ► PHILOSOPHES

## Engelbrekt Engelbrektsson (c.1390–1436)
Swedish rebel and military commander. He was born in Bergslagen of an iron-mining family of German ancestry. When the war between King ERIK OF POMERANIA and the HANSEATIC LEAGUE disrupted iron exports, he led a series of rebellions against the King, and in 1434 forced the Council of the Realm to retract its oath of loyalty to Erik. In the following year, at a meeting of the Estates at Arboga (often described as the first Swedish Parliament), he was appointed Commander-in-Chief of the realm. Within a few months the Council reversed its decision, but a year later Erik was again deposed, and Engelbrekt was appointed joint Commander-in-Chief with the noble KARL KNUTSSON. Shortly after this Engelbrekt was murdered, as the result of a personal quarrel, while travelling from his castle at Örebro to Stockholm. His reputation as a hero of national liberation has ensured him a place in literature, not least in the 'Song of Liberty' by Bishop Thomas of Strangnas, the greatest Swedish poem of the Middle Ages.

## Engels, Friedrich (1820–95)
German socialist philosopher, collaborator with Karl MARX, and founder of 'scientific socialism'. From 1842 he lived mostly in England. He first met Marx in Brussels in 1844 and collaborated with him on the Communist Manifesto (1848). He died in London, after spending his later years editing and translating Marx's writings. ► COMMUNISM; MARXISM; MARXISM–LENINISM; SOCIALISM

**Enghien, Louis Antoine Henri de Bourbon, Duke of** (1772–1804)
French soldier, the only son of Louis Henri Joseph, Prince of Condé. He commanded the émigré vanguard from 1796 to 1799. At the Peace of Lunéville (1801) he went to reside in Baden. Bonaparte, claiming that Enghien was involved in a conspiracy against him, violated the neutral territory of Baden, captured the duke and took him to Vincennes. In Mar 1804 he was shot in the castle moat. Boulay de la Meurthe said of this act that it was worse than a crime – it was a blunder, a saying often wrongly attributed to **FOUCHÉ** or to **TALLEYRAND**. ► **NAPOLEON I**

**ENGLAND**

The largest country within the United Kingdom, forming the southern part of the island of Great Britain. The area includes the Isles of Scilly, Lundy and the Isle of Wight. It was raided by Julius Caesar in 55BC and 54BC, conquered by the Romans in the 1c, and invaded by Nordic tribes in the 5c, when many Celtic groups were forced into Cornwall and Wales. England was unified in 924–39, and taken by **WILLIAM I, THE CONQUEROR** in 1066. The **MAGNA CARTA**, which began the nation's constitutional development, was signed during the reign of King **JOHN** in 1215. Under **EDWARD I** England succeeded in conquering Wales by 1283. The Wars of the **ROSES** from 1455 until 1485 resulted in the House of **TUDOR** becoming the ruling family until 1603. There was major colonial expan-

sion in the 16c. In the 17c there was a seven-year war between Royalists and Parliamentarians (the **ENGLISH CIVIL WARS**), at the end of which **CHARLES I** was executed (1649). In the 18c the first Act of **UNION** was signed in 1707, joining England in legislative union with Scotland; the second, which was signed in 1800, joined England and Scotland with Ireland, creating the United Kingdom (UK). ► **NORTHERN IRELAND**; **SCOTLAND**; **UNITED KINGDOM**; **WALES**

**Englandspiel** (1942–4)
The codename given to a highly successful German counter-espionage operation in the Netherlands during **WORLD WAR II**. The occupying German forces obtained the codes used by the Dutch resistance in radio contact with Britain, and by impersonating the resistance the Germans were able to capture 57 agents sent in from England, and to arrest hundreds of resistance personnel. Several English bombers were also brought down by them. ► **RESISTANCE MOVEMENT** (Netherlands)

**English Civil Wars** (1642–8)
The country's greatest internal conflict, between supporters of parliament and supporters of **CHARLES I**, caused by parliamentary opposition to what it considered growing royal power. Although the King left London in 1642, open hostilities between royalists and parliamentarians did not immediately break out. The prospect of compromise was bleak, but both sides, fearing the consequences of civil strife, moved

# The Enlightenment

Culture & Society

The Enlightenment was essentially an 18c phenomenon, though it had its
roots in the 17c. It is difficult to assign a starting date to it (the 'Glorious
Revolution' of 1688–9 in Britain is sometimes suggested), but it is generally taken to have ended after the outbreak of the
French Revolution in 1789. It was, however, a process, a movement, or a way of thinking as much as a historical period.
It affected all the countries of Europe to varying degrees as well as other parts of the world under European influence or
control, especially Britain's North American colonies. It had an impact not only on their cultural and intellectual life, but
on their political and social life as well, and its influence extended well into the following century and beyond.

### Characteristics of the Enlightenment

Nature, and nature's laws lay hid in night: God said, *Let Newton be!* and all was light.

Alexander Pope's famous epigram not only celebrates one of the great intellectual heroes of the age, it also illustrates the
sense of 'enlightenment', of momentous discovery and epochal change that inspired the people at the forefront of the
movement. It was not the case, however, that knowledge of Newton and his discoveries suddenly became public
property. 'Very few people read Newton …', wrote Voltaire, 'because you have to be very erudite to understand him'.
Those who did read and could understand, however, had a duty to pass on their knowledge to a wider public through
their own writings.

This was a fundamental characteristic of the Enlightenment. It was a top-down process and its spirit was nothing if
not didactic. The great figures of the Enlightenment, with a few notable exceptions, were energetic, prolific and
extremely polished writers rather than original thinkers: popularizers and publicists rather than discoverers
themselves. They were curious about everything; they analysed, compared and criticized, and above all they were expert
in presenting ideas in such a manner that their contemporaries could not only digest but actually enjoy them. They
believed that humanity had progressed, was progressing, and through the application of reason, science, tolerance and
benevolent goodwill, though many obstacles remained to be removed, it could progress still further.

### Precursors

Neither Montaigne, **Locke**, Bayle, **Spinoza**, **Hobbes**, nor Lord Shaftesbury … will ever cause as much
commotion in the world as the Cordeliers (Franciscans) once did about the shape of their sleeves and their
hoods.

Here Voltaire mentions in a single sentence several of the men whose rational and sceptical writings the **Philosophes**
referred to time and again, insists, perhaps disingenuously, on their harmlessness, and indicates the kind of darkness
from which enlightened people had emerged and which they still had to combat.

Besides Sir Isaac Newton, the list should also include the French philosopher René Descartes, who provided the
classic statement of the method to be adopted for rational philosophical enquiry: to doubt everything and believe
nothing to be true before establishing rational grounds for believing it to be true. In other words, the authority of the
Bible, the Fathers of the Church, or Aristotle would not suffice Descartes and his followers as it had many previous
thinkers.

Descartes, 'born to expose the errors of antiquity, but to replace them with his own' (Voltaire), believed that certain
ideas were present in the human mind from birth. John Locke, however, proved to the satisfaction of his contemporaries
that the human mind at birth was a blank sheet (*tabula rasa*), and that its ideas were obtained exclusively from sense
experience. The significance of this 'discovery' lay not only in the importance that it placed on education, but also in the

---

slowly towards the use of armed force. Charles finally
issued commissions of array (Jun 1642), and raised
his standard two months later at Nottingham. The
first major engagement took place at Edgehill in Oct.
It was inconclusive, but royalist forces then threatened London, the key parliamentary stronghold.
Royalist strategy in 1643 centred upon taking the
capital by a three-pronged attack from armies in the
north, the south-west and the Thames valley. By autumn the north and the west (apart from a garrison
in Gloucester) were in their hands, although parliament held back the tide in the (drawn) first Battle of
Newbury. The crucial event of 1643 was parliament's
alliance with the Scots in the **SOLEMN LEAGUE AND
COVENANT**, which strengthened its hand militarily
and threatened the King's forces on a new front. In
1644 parliament, assisted by the Scots, became a formidable foe. This was clear in July when its forces,
aided by Scottish invaders, inflicted a serious defeat
upon the royalists at the Battle of **MARSTON MOOR**.
The King's forces in the west fared better, with victories in the second Battle of Newbury, against the
combined forces of Essex, the Earl of Manchester,

and Sir William Waller. However, in 1645, strengthened by the creation of the **NEW MODEL ARMY**, parliament took control of the Midlands and the west, with
important victories at the Battles of **NASEBY** and Lang-
port. The First Civil War ended in 1646 when Charles
surrendered to the Scots at Newark in May, and his
stronghold of Oxford fell in June. He was handed over
to parliament's custody (Jan 1647) when the Scots
left for home, and in June was seized by the army.
From June 1646 to Apr 1648 there was an uneasy
peace and attempts at compromise. Negotiations between the King and parliament had begun as early as
1645, but they achieved little. The main sticking
points were religion, particularly parliament's disestablishment of the Church, and the King's prerogative
rights, many of which had been abolished by parliament. The climax came (Aug 1647) when the army
presented the King with the Heads of Proposals, calling for religious toleration, and parliamentary control of the armed forces. Charles made a secret
alliance with the Scots, promising to establish Presbyterianism in England, which parliament had failed
to do; they invaded England (Apr 1648), and were

implication that knowledge and belief were relative, ie dependent on the experiences that a particular individual had undergone. Locke's political writings also had a profound influence on the latter part of the 18c.

**Cultural relativism**

Increased knowledge of and interest in other countries, cultures and religions were vital to the intellectual life of the Enlightenment. The above quotations from Voltaire come from his *Philosophical Letters* or *Letters on the English*, a work mainly written during his exile in Britain in 1726–8; in it he intended to explain that Protestant, comparatively tolerant and enlightened country, including its major thinkers and writers, to his compatriots in Roman Catholic, and comparatively benighted, France. But the comparisons extended way beyond the borders of Europe. Noble savages (especially **Native Americans**) and sage Orientals are frequently invoked in works of the Enlightenment, often contrasting their beliefs and customs with those of Europeans and stressing their superior rationality and beneficence. A typical and seminal work of the time is the *Persian Letters* (1721) by the French writer Montesquieu, which purports to be the correspondence of two noble Persians travelling in France, and satirizes French social, political and religious institutions. Swift's *Gulliver's Travels* (1726) is a work with a similar satirical intention, though its traveller is a European and the countries he visits are imaginary.

**Religion**

The Church, especially the Roman Catholic Church, was the most frequent target of satirical and polemical attacks by the writers of the Enlightenment. The Church attempted to maintain a stranglehold on the intellectual life of Europe, and had the power to have the publication of unorthodox writings prohibited and their unorthodox writers imprisoned or exiled. Consequently, especially in its early stages, the Enlightenment was something of an underground movement. Works likely to prove controversial were often published in Holland, one of the most tolerant countries in Europe. Likewise, articles published in encyclopaedias on topics such as the Eucharist would be strictly orthodox, whereas less conspicuous articles, such as Diderot's entry on *Pain Béni* ('Consecrated Bread') in the *Encyclopédie* were not.

Though the Enlightenment was anticlerical, it was not irreligious. The great majority of its major figures believed in the existence of the 'Supreme Being'. Many, such as Voltaire, espoused or were strongly influenced by deism, a religious philosophy which rejected all revelation and 'superstitious' dogma, asserted a natural and universal human impulse to believe in a benign creator whose existence was discoverable through reason, and encouraged rationality, tolerance and brotherly love.

**The Encyclopédie**

If one work sums up the Enlightenment's didactic aims and achievements it is the *Encyclopédie* or *Dictionnaire raisonné des sciences, des arts et des métiers* ('Descriptive and Analytical Dictionary of the Sciences, Arts and Trades'), published in France between 1751 and 1780 in 35 volumes. Edited by Denis Diderot and Jean d'Alembert, it contains articles by most of the notable French writers of the time, including Montesquieu, Jean Jacques **Rousseau** and Voltaire. It built upon the work of previous encyclopaedists, in particular that of the Frenchman Pierre Bayle and the Englishman Ephraim Chambers. It is remarkable not only for its breadth and comprehensiveness, but for the extraordinary number of illustrations it contains. (Volumes of illustrations continued to appear when further publication of text was prohibited and the first 10 volumes were suppressed in 1759.) It encapsulates the spirit of the age, its inquisitiveness, its rationality, and not least its belief that it was possible for the rational and educated person to know almost everything there was to know or that was worth knowing.

**Enlightened despots**

Among those who were influenced by the Enlightenment were the sovereigns of a number of European states, notably **Frederick II, the Great** of Prussia, the Russian Empress **Catherine II, the Great** and the Holy Roman Emperor **Joseph**

---

repulsed only after the Battle of Preston (Aug). Bitterly fought, the second war earned Charles the epithet 'that man of blood' and, ultimately, his execution (30 Jan 1649). Possibly 100,000 died in the two wars: 1 in 10 of adult males. ► **CAVALIERS**; **COMMONWEALTH**; **COVENANTERS**; **CROMWELL, OLIVER**; **INDEPENDENTS** (England); **IRETON, HENRY**

**Enlightened Despots**

The misnomer for a number of European absolute monarchs who, under the influence of the ideas of the **ENLIGHTENMENT**, used their power to pursue comprehensive legal, social and educational reforms. However, while they acknowledged responsibility for the common good, political consultation and popular participation remained firmly ruled out. Best-known examples are **FREDERICK II, THE GREAT** of Prussia, **JOSEPH II** of Austria, **LEOPOLD II** (as Duke of Tuscany), **CATHERINE II, THE GREAT** of Russia and **CHARLES FREDERICK OF BADEN**.

**Enlightenment, The** ► *See panel*

**enosis**

The Greek term for the policy of seeking union with

Greece, first applied in the 1840s to the Cretans' agitation for union with the Kingdom of Greece. In Cyprus in the 1950s, demands for independence from Britain and *enosis* became insistent, giving rise to the underground movement **EOKA**. There followed a serious and long-running conflict amounting to civil war between the island's Greek and Turkish inhabitants, with the latter bitterly opposed to enosis. ► **GRIVAS, GEORGEIOS**; **KARAMANLIS, CONSTANTINE**; **MAKARIOS III**

**enragés**

Literally 'madmen', the term refers to a group of French revolutionary extremists, led by Jacques Roux. Enjoying popular support (1793), and dedicated to radical social and economic measures (eg controls on food), they were supplanted by the Hébertists (Sep 1793). Roux was executed by the Jacobin government. ► **FRENCH REVOLUTION**; **HÉBERT, JACQUES RENÉ**; **JACOBINS**

**Entente Cordiale**

A term first used in the 1840s to describe a close relationship between the UK and France; then given to

II. All were absolute rulers and none of them made any serious attempt to mitigate the **absolutism** of their rule, but all were touched to a greater or lesser extent by the spirit of the age and showed a measure of reformist zeal. Frederick the Great, himself a voluminous writer on political, historical and military subjects and a skilled flautist, corresponded with Voltaire, entertained him at the Palace of Sans-Souci, and later fell out with him. He was a tireless administrator, a promoter of new agricultural and manufacturing products, and re-codified Prussian law in favour of greater justice for all classes of society. Catherine the Great corresponded with both Voltaire and Diderot, and entertained the latter at her court, though after a flirtation with reform she reverted to more conservative policies later in her reign. Joseph II stringently curtailed the power of the Roman Catholic Church and the papacy within his domains, suppressed 700 convents, extended toleration to Protestants, and ended discrimination against Jews, besides abolishing serfdom and removing most forms of censorship. His reforms, however, provoked considerable resistance, and he was forced to revoke many of them before he died.

### Revolution

Two revolutions saw out the era. Some of the leaders of the movement for American independence, especially Benjamin Franklin, Thomas **Jefferson** and Thomas **Paine**, must also be counted as major representatives of the Enlightenment, and the **Declaration of Independence** is firmly based on Enlightenment principles. In particular it shows the influence of John Locke's *Two Treatises of Government* (1690), and the 'Commonwealth' tradition in British thought, with its stress on the contractual nature of the relationship between ruler and ruled. The **American Revolution** was welcomed and approved in many European countries apart from Great Britain, and its assertion of human rights, however belied by the survival of **slavery** in the USA, proved an important precedent.

Locke's thinking also influenced the political writings of Jean-Jacques Rousseau, a philosopher whose works point in general beyond the Enlightenment to the Romantic era that was to follow it. The ringing declaration that opens Rousseau's *Social Contract*, 'man is born free; and everywhere he is in chains', and its slogan '**Liberty, Equality, Fraternity**', were a major inspiration for the French Revolution, which in its early stages was also widely welcomed elsewhere. But the Reign of **Terror** which followed traumatized much of Europe, and appeared to belie the sense of inevitable progress and the intrinsic goodness in humanity that the Enlightenment had tried to foster. With the rise of a conservative Romantic culture, a 'revolt against the Enlightenment' set in.

The achievements of the Enlightenment were nonetheless real, and it represents a key stage in the development of the concept of a liberal, just, secular and humanitarian society that remains the ideal for many peoples in the world today.
► Encyclopedists; Enlightened Despots

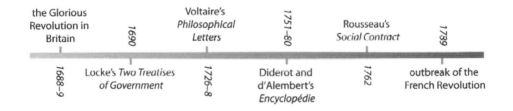

the Glorious Revolution in Britain — 1690 — Voltaire's *Philosophical Letters* — 1751-80 — Rousseau's *Social Contract* — 1739

1688-9 — Locke's *Two Treatises of Government* — 1726-8 — Diderot and d'Alembert's *Encyclopédie* — 1762 — outbreak of the French Revolution

---

a series of agreements in 1904 between the two countries dealing with a range of issues, in particular establishing the predominant role of the UK in Egypt and France's interests in Morocco.

### Enver Pasha (1881–1922)

Turkish soldier and politician. A leader in the 1908 revolution of **YOUNG TURKS**, in Aug 1914 as the pro-German Minister of War he steered the Turkish government into a secret alliance with Germany directed against Russia. After the Turkish surrender in 1918 at the end of **WORLD WAR I**, he fled to Russia and was killed in an insurrection in Turkestan.

### Environmental Awareness and Politics, Emergence of ► *See panel*

### EOKA (*Ethniki Organosis Kipriakou Agono*, 'National Organization of Cypriot Struggle')

A Greek-Cypriot underground movement which sought to end British rule and achieve **ENOSIS** (union with Greece). Founded in 1955 by a Greek army officer, Colonel Georgeios **GRIVAS**, and supported by Archbishop **MAKARIOS III**, it pursued a campaign of anti-British violence that came to a climax in

1956–7. EOKA declined and was disbanded after Makarios's acceptance in 1958 of independence for Cyprus rather than enosis. The organization resurrected unsuccessfully as EOKA B during the period 1971–4. ► **KARAMANLIS, CONSTANTINE**

### Eötvös, József, Baron (1813–71)

Hungarian author and politician. He became an advocate in 1833, but soon devoting himself to literature, published a work on prison reform, and the novels *The Carthusian* (1838–41), *The Village Notary* (1846) and others. In 1848 he was Minister of Religion and Public Instruction, and held the post again under **ANDRÁSSY** in 1867–71. He was responsible for some liberal legislation.

### Epirus

The region divided between Albania and Greece lying between the Pindos Mountains and the Ionian Sea. A kingdom in antiquity, the ruling family of the dominant Molossian tribe included Olympias, wife of Philip II of Macedon and mother of Alexander III, the Great; her brother Alexander became the first King of Epirus. Its most notable king was Pyrrhus

# The Emergence of Environmental Awareness and Politics

Culture & Society

Human settlement has always had an impact on the environment and on available resources. From the earliest times, human beings have hunted and gathered food, cut down trees for fire and shelter, and mined for minerals and other materials for tools. In hunter-gatherer societies, when local resources became exhausted or waste products accumulated, people moved on, allowing areas to regenerate. As societies become settled, agriculture and small-scale manufacturing had greater impacts on the environment, with woodland cleared for cultivation, stone quarried for building, etc. Even so, resource consumption and environmental pollution were still at a lower level than the Earth's natural regeneration rate, helped by the deliberate husbandry of natural resources by many societies, although it was possible for exceptionally dense populations, such as that of the Classical Mayan civilization, or rapidly growing populations in areas with poor soils, like parts of colonial New England, to over-exploit renewable resources to the point of crisis.

The global sustainability of the balance between consumption and regeneration started to shift in the 18c with the advent of the **Industrial Revolution**, a process which transformed the economies of many European countries and the USA by the end of the 19c and of Russia, China, India and many parts of Asia and South America in the 20c. **Industrialization** caused resources to be consumed and waste products to be created at a far greater rate than ever before, promoted **urbanization**, which concentrated populations in rapidly expanding cities, and polluted the air and drinking water of adjacent areas.

By the second half of the 20c the deleterious impacts on the environment of industrialization and lack of husbandry were beginning to become apparent. The consumption of natural resources at a greater than sustainable rate meant that the exhaustion of some non-renewable resources, such as fossil fuels, within a few generations could be predicted, while the fur trade and **overfishing** were bringing some species close to extinction. Industrial waste products were found to be causing atmospheric pollution, such as acid rain which poisons lakes and kills forests, while industrial chemicals were depleting the ozone layer; the use of artificial fertilizers and pesticides to improve agricultural yields (the **Green Revolution** of the 1960s and 1970s) was killing wildlife, either directly or by destroying their habitats; and discharges into rivers and seas were poisoning aquatic life.

It was not only wildlife that was suffering as a consequence of pollution. Atmospheric pollution, such as lead in vehicle emissions, water pollution from discharges and chemical contaminants, such as pesticide residues in crops, were found to cause serious health problems in humans. The discharge of mercury compounds into the sea by a Japanese company in the 1950s and 1960s contaminated seafood which subsequently poisoned hundreds of people. Public concern grew over agricultural practices that left chemical residues in crops and meat. Diseases have always occasionally mutated to jump species but fear that modern intensive farming might cause high incidences of disease in livestock and poultry, facilitating mutations enabling diseases to cross species, increased in Western countries in the 1990s, leading to the rapid growth of the market for organically farmed foodstuffs. This concern has also manifested itself in widespread consumer opposition to the introduction of genetically modified (GM) crops because of the perception that their human and environmental impacts could not be quantified.

Deforestation, whether as a consequence of pollution or to clear land for cultivation or building, contributes not only to the destruction of wildlife habitats, threatening biological diversity, but also to the reduction of the Earth's capacity to absorb the 'greenhouse gases' emitted by burning fossil fuels to generate electricity and fuel vehicles. The build-up of these gases, particularly carbon dioxide, is believed to have increased the Earth's annual average temperature (global warming) and caused global weather patterns to become increasingly erratic (climate change), with serious consequences for agriculture, especially in developing countries with low rainfall or facing encroaching desertification. Antarctica, with its continent-sized ice cap, has been shown to be the area with the fastest temperature increase and the highest ultraviolet levels on the Earth, which has potentially traumatic implications for its own ecosystems and the world's sea level and weather patterns.

---

(c.319–272BC). In 168BC it became part of the Roman province of Macedonia and was repeatedly invaded during the Middle Ages. Under Byzantine rule, it was divided, with centres at Dyrrachium (Durrës in modern Albania) and Acarnania. After 1204 it was established as a despotate, but it returned to Byzantine rule (1335) until it was taken by the Serbs (1348–86). During the 15c the Turks and Venetians occupied much of Epirus. The part under Turkish rule was freed in 1881 and, although the Greek Army occupied north Epirus during the **BALKAN WARS**, in 1913 most of Epirus went to form the newly independent Albanian state.

## Equal Rights Amendment

Proposed amendment to the **US CONSTITUTION** stating that equal rights shall not be denied on account of sex. First introduced in 1923, it was not approved by Congress until 1972. Although the adoption deadline

was extended from 1979 to 1982, the amendment fell just short of ratification by the required 38 states.

**EQUATORIAL GUINEA** official name **Republic of Equatorial Guinea**
A republic in western central Africa, comprising a mainland area (Río Muni) and several islands (notably Bioko and Annabón) in the Gulf of Guinea. The mainland is bounded to the north by Cameroon; to the east and south by Gabon; and to the west by the Gulf of Guinea. It was first visited by Europeans in the 15c. The island of Fernando Po (Bioko) was claimed by Portugal in 1494 and held until 1788. Occupied by Britain from 1781 until 1843, the rights to the area were acquired by Spain in 1844. It gained independence in 1968 and was ruled by President Macias Nguema until a military coup in 1979 led by his nephew, Obiang Nguema, put an end to his repressive regime. A new constitution was approved in 1991 and

The environmental impacts of industrialization have been compounded by rapid growth in the global population in the 20c. In industrialized and industrializing countries, economic growth improves nutrition, public health provision and access to medical care. Along with advances in medical science, these factors greatly increase survival rates and longevity. But more people, living for longer, increases further the demands on global resources and the impetus for poorer countries to industrialize in order to achieve economic growth. According to UN Population Division data, the world's estimated population grew from 3.0 billion in 1960 to 5.3 billion in 1990 and 6.2 billion in 2000; it is forecast to grow to 7.9 billion by 2025 and 8.9 billion by 2050.

The impact of rapid population growth on global resources was the first of these problems to be recognized, though more because of its economic than its environmental consequences; developing countries, many faced with poverty, **Third World debt**, wars or internal unrest in the post-colonial era, struggled to achieve a rate of economic growth that outstripped their population expansion. From the late 1940s onwards, UN agencies, non-governmental organizations such as international aid agencies, and national governments have sought to promote family planning for economic reasons. The Chinese government introduced in 1979 a policy requiring couples to limit their families to one child.

Initially, concerns about environmental deterioration and the exhaustion of natural resources tended to be raised by scientists, such as Rachel Carson, whose book *Silent Spring* (1962) caused many to question the cavalier way in which humans were treating the environment. These concerns were acted upon at grass-roots level by pressure groups formed in response to increasing public awareness of the problems. Many such groups were founded to address single issues but subsequently widened their remit as the interconnected nature of the problems became more apparent; the World-Wide Fund for Nature (founded in 1961 as the World Wildlife Fund) began by campaigning to save individual species from extinction and has since expanded its activities to address the destruction of habitats and global warming; **Greenpeace**, formed in 1971 to oppose nuclear testing, now campaigns against destruction of the rainforests, global warming, GM crops, commercial whaling, overfishing and nuclear power, and lobbies for increased waste reduction and recycling.

Local pressure groups concerned with environmental issues in a specific area have also sprung up, usually to protect local habitats and wildlife or resist plans for new roads, airports or other forms of development. Petitions and demonstrations gave way to more proactive protest methods in the 1990s, with protesters chaining themselves to threatened trees or tunnelling under habitat sites threatened by construction projects. With the advent of the internet, mass demonstrations started to attract international support from a variety of campaign groups, such as the attempts to disrupt the **Group of 8** summits.

Lobbying by environmentalists had some success in persuading national governments in developed countries to address certain environmental issues, such as reducing air pollution by banning or limiting emissions from domestic and industrial chimneys, or reducing soil and water pollution by restricting the types of artificial fertilizers and pesticides used in agriculture. However, the scope of such measures was often limited by opposition from industry, the financial burden of anti-pollution measures placing businesses at a disadvantage if their competitors were not similarly regulated. Their effectiveness was also limited in some cases by circumvention; industries in developed countries avoided the expense of treating hazardous waste products there by exporting the waste, and its attendant pollution problems, to developing countries.

The impact of national action was also limited by the supranational nature of the problems, the effects of pollution often being felt far from its source. For instance, traces of radioactive fallout from the **Chernobyl** disaster were reported in areas of North America and Western Europe, and the death of forests in Scandinavia and Germany was blamed on acid rain caused by emissions from British power stations.

International action to address the problems and ensure compliance with anti-pollution measures was slow to develop. U **Thant**, the Secretary General of the UN, sounded an alarm in 1969 when he said that if a global partnership did not begin to tackle the world's demographic and environmental problems within a decade, he feared that the problems would have grown to such proportions that they would be beyond control. His fears were reinforced by *Limits to Growth*, a report produced in 1972 by an international group of scientists, economists, businesspeople, international civil servants and politicians. *Limits to Growth* concluded that if the developed world continued to consume the Earth's

multiparty democracy was legalized in 1992. Even so Nguema's Equatorial Guinea Democratic Party (PDGE) has maintained its grip on power, most of the elections since 1992 being boycotted because of irregularities by the opposition parties, some of which have been banned. Opposition leaders were imprisoned in 2002 for allegedly taking part in an attempted coup, and another alleged coup by foreign nationals was suppressed in Mar 2004.

### Erfurt, Congress of (27 Sep–14 Oct 1808)
This settlement of European affairs between **NAPO-LEON I** and the Russian Tsar **ALEXANDER I** was also attended by the 34 princes of the **CONFEDERATION OF THE RHINE**. They were treated dismissively by Napoleon, but Alexander was able to achieve a reduction in Prussian **REPARATIONS** due to France from 140 to 120 million francs. In return for territorial gains in Eastern Europe (Finland, Moldavia, Wallachia), Russia agreed not to hinder the French war effort in Spain and to join France if the latter were attacked by Austria.

### Erfurt Programme (Oct 1891)
A programme formulated by the **SPD** in a conference

resources at its present rate, non-renewable resources would be exhausted in less than 100 years, and only an immediate limit on population, pollution and economic growth would avert the collapse of society.

The first global environmental meeting, the Stockholm Conference on the Human Environment, was held in 1972 and attended by 113 nations. These countries agreed to cooperate in the preservation and enhancement of the human environment, and the conference led to the establishment of the UN Environment Programme (UNEP).

In the 1980s international moves towards protecting the environment began to bear fruit. Measures to prevent further depletion of the Earth's ozone layer, a problem which had become apparent in the 1970s, were introduced by the **Vienna Convention** of 1985 and strengthened by the **Montreal Protocol** of 1987. The **Basle Convention** (1989) imposed an international regulatory regime intended to overcome circumvention of national anti-pollution measures and dumping of hazardous waste in developing countries.

In 1987 the UN's World Commission on Environment and Development published the report *Our Common Future*, which warned that the world would face human suffering and environmental damage if working practices remained unchanged. The main outcome of the report was the UN Conference on Environment and Development (the **Earth Summit**), at Rio de Janeiro in 1992. The summit linked economic growth with protection of the environment and natural resources, agreeing that development should be more globally sustainable and that its benefits should be more equitably distributed. The measures agreed at the Earth Summit covered climate change, biological diversity, forests, and consumption and sustainable development.

Internationally negotiated agreements have been the most significant moves yet towards addressing the impacts of human activity on the environment and natural resources. They do not, however, always command universal or whole-hearted support from the world's governments and whether widespread compliance will be achieved remains to be seen. Many developing countries have resented the developed world's insistence that they should comply with anti-pollution measures which have implications for their industrial development, perceiving these as attempts to limit their economic growth. This resentment is fuelled by the fact that the developed world has been responsible for much of global pollution and its own compliance is often laggardly, with targets routinely eased as it becomes apparent that they will not be met by the intended deadline. Nor have these governments always enforced compliance with environmental conservation measures; Japanese whalers are believed to have evaded the **International Whaling Commission**'s moratorium on commercial whaling, while objecting to the continuation of **aboriginal subsistence whaling**.

National interests have also proved an obstacle to progress. Some countries have refused to sign international agreements that they consider to run counter to their interests; the most notable example of this is the USA's repudiation in 2001 of the Kyoto Protocol to the UN Framework on **Climate Change**, on the grounds that developing countries are not required to share the burden of limiting emissions and that this gives them an unfair economic advantage.

Another obstacle to progress is scepticism in some quarters about the causes of environmental problems. There is a school of thought, particularly in the USA, that questions the theory of global warming, believing that the rise in the Earth's annual average temperature is within the parameters of previous global temperature changes, and so dismisses the concept of climate change and its influence on weather patterns, sea-level, desertification, etc. This thinking has influenced the policies of President George W **Bush**'s administration, as to some extent has the so-called 'religious right' in the USA, which believes that concern for the future of the planet is irrelevant, even if permanent damage to the environment brings about catastrophic collapse, because of the imminence of the second coming of Jesus Christ.

Possibly the greatest obstacle to change, however, is one of attitude. The Earth Summit affirmed the rights of people to development, acknowledging the benefits of economic growth and its importance in achieving the eradication of poverty. But the summit's Declaration on Environment and Development also emphasized the responsibility to make this economic development more sustainable if its impact on the environment is not to cause further damage and consequent human suffering. Much hinges on the readiness of developed countries to accept the consequences of achieving a more equitable distribution of economic benefits and of complying with environment protection measures where these harm their economic interests. ► **Sustainable Development, UN Commission on**; **Trade and Globalization**

---

which lent German social democracy an explicitly Marxist flavour. The SPD still subscribed to the principles of political liberty, but adopted a Marxist view of economics and future economic development that coexisted uneasily with the social reformist character of many of its day-to-day policies. ► **GOTHA, CONGRESS OF**; **MARXISM**

**Erhard, Ludwig** (1897–1977)

German economist and politician. Professor of Economics at Munich, he was appointed by the US authorities as Economic Director of the Bizone in 1948. In the following year he was elected to the Federal Parliament in **BONN** and made Economics Minister in the **ADENAUER** administration. He was a leading architect of the **SOCIAL MARKET ECONOMY**, a key element of the West German 'economic miracle' of recovery from wartime devastation. He succeeded **ADENAUER** as Chancellor (1963–6), but economic difficulties forced his resignation. ► **CHRISTIAN DEMOCRATS**

**Ericsson, Leif** ► **ERIKSSON, LEIF**

**Erie Railroad**

US railroad linking the Great Lakes with New York City. Its construction became a by-word for fraud, financial manipulation and political corruption by speculators Jim Fisk and Jay Gould, who also issued millions of dollars of watered stock in order to beat off a takeover bid from Cornelius **VANDERBILT** in 1868. The railroad collapsed under this burden of debt in the depression of 1893, but underwent several subsequent reorganizations and bankruptcies.

**Erik XIII** (of Sweden) ► **ERIK OF POMERANIA**

**Erik XIV** (1533–77)

King of Sweden (1560/9). He was the eldest son and successor of **GUSTAV I VASA**. Tutored by a German

Lutheran nobleman, his outlook was that of a **RE-NAISSANCE** prince. His temperament was, however, highly unstable. Suspicious of others to the point of paranoia, in 1563 he imprisoned his half-brother John, who had been conducting an independent foreign policy as Duke of Finland. In the same year Erik became involved in a seven-year war with the Denmark of **FREDERICK II**, Lübeck and Poland, which ended inconclusively with the Peace of Stettin (1570). Before it ended he had several members of the Sture family butchered on unjustified suspicion of having designs on the Swedish throne, and in 1568 married privately a lowly soldier's daughter, Karin Månsdotter. This provided a pretext for a rebellion amongst the nobles, led by his half-brothers John and Charles (IX), who in 1569 dethroned him in favour of John. Erik spent the rest of his days in captivity and probably died of arsenic poisoning, administered on **JOHN**'s orders. In his early years he was a suitor for the hand of both **ELIZABETH I** of England and **MARY, QUEEN OF SCOTS**.

### Erik Jedvarsson, St (d.c.1160)

King of Sweden (c.1158/60). The patron saint of Sweden, he is said to have led a Christian crusade for the conversion of the Finns, and to have been murdered at mass in Uppsala by a Danish pretender to his throne. He was married to Kristina, who was descended from a royal line of Swedish kings, and was the father of King Knut Eriksson (c.1173/96).

### Erik of Pomerania (1382–1459)

King of Sweden (1397/1438), Denmark (1397/1439) and Norway (1397/1442). The son of Duke Wratislaw VII of Pomerania and Maria, the niece of Queen **MARGRETHE I**, he was adopted as heir to the triple monarchy by his great-aunt in 1389, and crowned at Kalmar in Sweden in 1397, when the treaty of union between the three countries was formally sealed. In 1405 he married Philippa, the daughter of King **HENRY IV** of England. It was not until 1412, however, on Queen Margrethe's death, that he gained actual power. Aggressive commercial and military policies against the **HANSEATIC LEAGUE** that ultimately failed led to economic disasters that fomented rebellion, and he was deposed by all three countries one by one: Sweden in 1438, Denmark in 1439 and Norway in 1442. He was succeeded by his nephew, Christopher of Bavaria.

### Eriksson, Leif, also called Leif the Lucky (fl.1000)

Icelandic explorer and one of the first Europeans to reach America. He was the son of Erik the Red (Erik Thorvaldson). Just before the year 1000 he set sail from Greenland to explore lands to the west, reaching Baffin Land, Labrador, and an area he called '**VÍNLAND**' ('Land of Vines'), the coastline of which he explored extensively, perhaps as far as Cape Cod. The location of Vínland has defied precise identification, but remains of a Norse settlement have been found in Newfoundland, Canada. ➤ **EXPLORATION**

### ERITREA   official name State of Eritrea

A country in north-east Africa, bounded to the north and north-west by Sudan; to the west and south-west by Ethiopia; to the south by Djibouti; and to the east by the Red Sea. Taken by Italy in 1884, it became an Italian colony in 1890. It was used as a base for the

Italian invasion of Abyssinia in 1935, and became part of Italian East Africa in 1936. It was then taken by the British in 1941, federated with Ethiopia at the request of the **UN** in 1952, and made a province of Ethiopia in 1962. This galvanized into action the Eritrean Liberation Front (ELF), which had been founded as the Eritrean Liberation Movement in 1958 (it changed its name in 1961) and it waged guerrilla warfare against the government throughout the 1960s and 1970s. In 1970 a communist faction broke away to form the Eritrean People's Liberation Front (EPLF), which emerged during the 1980s as the dominant rebel group. Despite this division and much fighting between rebel groups, it managed, through support from the Eastern bloc and some Arab countries, to prevent its destruction both while **HAILE SELASSIE** was Emperor and when **MENGISTU** was President. When Soviet support waned, the EPLF joined with other Ethiopian rebel groups, including the Tigray People's Liberation Front, and overthrew the **DERGUE** in 1991. The EPLF immediately formed a separate provisional Eritrean government. A referendum on independence was held in Apr 1993, following which Eritrea was declared independent in May 1993, and the EPLF prepared to become the ruling political party by renaming itself the People's Front for Democracy and Justice in 1994. The post-independence regime has become increasingly authoritarian; elections scheduled for 2001 did not take place and have not been rescheduled. In 1998, Eritrea and Ethiopia began an armed struggle over border territory in **TIGRAY** and occasional clashes have continued. ➤ **ADOWA, BATTLE OF**

### Erlander, Tage Fritiof (1901–85)

Swedish politician. He became active in the Social Democratic Party while he was studying at the University of Lund, and was elected to parliament in 1933. He was minister without portfolio in the wartime coalition government from 1944, and was Minister for Ecclesiastical Affairs when chosen to succeed Per Albin **HANSSON** as party leader and Prime Minister in 1946. He made way for the younger Olof **PALME** in 1969. A moderate, his brand of consensual government was dubbed 'Harpsund democracy' after his country estate, where he consulted with leaders in all walks of society.

### Ershad, Hussain Muhammad (1930– )

Bangladesh soldier and chief martial law administrator. Appointed army Chief of Staff by President **ZIAUR RAHMAN** in 1978, he repeatedly demanded that the armed forces should be involved in the country's administration. In 1982 he led a bloodless military coup, becoming President the following year, and proceeded to introduce a new rural-orientated economic programme. He was re-elected in 1986 and lifted martial law, but he faced continued political opposition and demands for a full return to civilian rule until he resigned in 1990. In the 1996 general election he was elected to parliament as leader of the Jatiya Party. He was found guilty of corruption and imprisoned in Nov 2000

**Erskine, Thomas Erskine, 1st Baron** (1750–1823)
British jurist. He sought a career in the navy and army before studying law. Called to the Bar in 1778, his success was immediate and unprecedented, and he became a KC and MP (1783). His sympathy with the **FRENCH REVOLUTION** led him to join the 'Friends of the People', and to undertake the defence in many political prosecutions of 1793–4, notably of Thomas **PAINE**. He became a peer in 1806 and for a while acted as Lord Chancellor (1806–7), after which he retired into private life.

**Erzberger, Matthias** (1875–1921)
German politician. He became controversial when, as a leading member of the Centre Party, he began to advocate peace without annexations as early as 1917 and again (1918–19) when, as a member of the armistice delegation, he advocated acceptance, despite some fierce German opposition, of the terms of the Treaty of **VERSAILLES**. Finance Minister and Vice-Premier in 1919, he drastically reformed the tax system and nationalized the German railways. Unsuccessful in a libel action against an unscrupulous political opponent, he resigned in Feb 1921 and was assassinated in Aug of the same year by members of an extremist group (*Organisation Consul*) in the Black Forest.

**Erzerum, Treaty of** (1823, confirmed 1847)
More usually regarded as two treaties, the Treaty of Erzerum in its first manifestation was signed on 18 July 1823 and was expressly aimed at defining the frontier in lower Iraq between the territories of the Ottoman Sultan and those of the Qajar Shah of Persia. However, the disputes that had arisen over the frontier, centring on the foundation (1812) of the town of Muhammara at the mouth of the Karun River, were not effectively solved by the 1823 treaty. Both Sultan and Shah continued to claim the town, and the dispute led to the signing of the so-called 'Second' Treaty of Erzerum in 1847, by which Muhammara was granted to the Persians.

**Eshkol, Levi** (1895–1969)
Israeli politician. Born in the Ukraine to parents of traditional Jewish piety, he settled in Palestine as an agricultural worker in 1914. After Israeli independence in 1948, he supervised the founding of several hundred new villages to absorb immigrants. A member of the **MAPAI PARTY**, Eshkol served as Minister of Finance (1952–63) and as Prime Minister and Defence Minister (1963–9), transferring the latter post to Moshe **DAYAN** during the **SIX-DAY WAR** of 1967. Eshkol established diplomatic relations with West Germany and was also the first Israeli leader to visit the USA. Despite internal political difficulties in 1964–5, he remained Prime Minister until his death. ► **RESTITUTION AGREEMENT**

**Espartero, Baldomero** (1793–1879)
Spanish general and politician. He spent the period 1815–25 in South America, fighting the independence movements. After the accession of **ISABELLA II** in 1833, he played a leading role in defeating the Carlist supporters of her uncle, Don **CARLOS**, driving Don Carlos from Spain (1884) and being made Duke of Vitoria. In 1841 he was instrumental in forcing Isabella's mother, **MARÍA CRISTINA**, to leave Spain, becoming sole regent (1841/3). He was, therefore, Spain's first modern **CAUDILLO**. Driven out by Ramón **NARVÁEZ** in 1843, he lived abroad in England and in retirement in Spain, but in 1854, with Leopoldo **O'DONNELL**, led a successful revolution. In 1856 he resigned as head of the revolutionary government in favour of O'Donnell. In 1870 his name was put forward for the throne, which he refused; in 1875 he tendered his allegiance to **ALFONSO XII** after his accession.

**Esquilache, Leopoldo de Gregorio, Marquis of** (d.1785)
Spanish politician. Secretary of War and Finance under **CHARLES III** of Spain, he held the post of Minister of Finance in Naples before he came with the new monarch from Italy in 1759. He attempted a number of reforms in the Spanish fiscal system, but was frustrated by opposition and by a series of bad harvests (1760–6) that precipitated agitation in several cities. He was sacked (Mar 1766) after major riots in Madrid ('the Esquilache Riots'), apparently provoked by a new decree regulating dress. The Jesuits were blamed for the events and expelled. Esquilache returned to Naples the following month and was then appointed Spanish ambassador in Venice.

**Essex, Robert Devereux, 2nd Earl of** (1566–1601)
English soldier and courtier. He served in the Netherlands (1585–6), and distinguished himself at Zutphen. At court, he quickly rose in the favour of **ELIZABETH I**, despite his clandestine marriage in 1590 with Sir Philip Sidney's widow. In 1591 he commanded the forces sent to help **HENRY IV** of France, and took part in the sacking of Cadiz (1595). He became a Privy Councillor (1593) and Earl Marshal (1597). He alienated the Queen's advisers, and there were constant quarrels with Elizabeth (notably the occasion when he turned his back on her, and she boxed his ears). His six months' lord-lieutenancy of Ireland (1599) proved a failure; he was imprisoned and deprived of his dignities. He attempted to raise the City of London, was found guilty of high treason, and beheaded in the Tower.

**Estado Novo** (Brazil)
Literally 'New State', this was the name given by President Getúlio **VARGAS** to his authoritarian regime in Brazil (1937–45). The term was copied from the Estado Novo established in **SALAZAR**'s Portugal. The Estado Novo had a profound influence on the party political structure of Brazil until 1965. The political leadership of the various states imposed by Vargas in 1937 formed the backbone of the **PSD**, while the labour unions formed the 'nationalist' PTB (*Partido Trabalhista Brasileiro*). Francisco Campos and Carlos Medeiros Silva, architects of the Estado Novo, were brought back to reshape the constitution of 1946 in an authoritarian mould. ► **ESTADO NOVO** (Portugal)

**Estado Novo** (Portugal)
The authoritarian political system (literally, 'New State') under **SALAZAR** which ruled Portugal from the early 1930s to 1969. This entailed the abolition of political parties and trade unions, total censorship, the vesting of power in an all-powerful executive, and the glorification of the values of 'God, Country and Family'. Despite its fascist trappings and corporatist aspirations, the aim of the Estado Novo was mass depoliticization rather than mobilization within a single party totally identified with the state. The heavily centralized and authoritarian Estado Novo effectively allowed the old élite to retain political and social control.

**estancia**
A standard term used in Spanish America to denote a ranch. By the early 16c, *estancia* denoted a private landholding held by a Spaniard or **CREOLE**, supplying cattle to the towns and *encomenderos*. By the mid-17c they had absorbed Indian lands and were combined as *haciendas*. Estancias emerged in late 18c Río de la Plata as large tracts of open land owned by merchants of Buenos Aires, such as Juan Manuel de **ROSAS**, on which cattle were bred and driven for slaughter in coastal *saladeros* (salting plants). Enclosed by barbed wire a century later, their vast wealth supported the Argentine economy. The same development can be charted for the rise of analogous groups in Uruguay and Rio Grande do Sul, Brazil. ➤ **ENCOMIENDA**; **HACIENDA**

**Estates General** (*États-Généraux*) (France)
An assembly representing the different provinces of the French monarchy, called by the King primarily to grant taxes, roughly equivalent to the English parliament, beginning in 14c (the normally accepted date for its first meeting is 1347). Although it never met on such a regular basis as the English parliament, it appeared by 16c to be on the way to becoming a regular institution, but after the meeting of 1614 no more were called until 1789. In the intervening period the king ruled as an absolute monarch, although some provincial Estates continued to meet intermittently. Both the Estates General and the provincial Estates met and voted in three separate houses: the First Estate (the clergy), the Second Estate (the nobility) and the Third Estate (the commoners). Hence the Third Estate was the whole non-noble population, except for the clergy.

**Este** (1000–1875)
Italian family who became rulers of Ferrara towards the end of the 12c and maintained their hegemony over the city until 1598, when it was incorporated into the **PAPAL STATES**. Azzo D'Este (1205–64), the first marquess, had established his authority over the area by the time of his death, and the office of *signore* of Ferrara was made hereditary in the family during the time of his son, Obizzo (d.1293), and the territories of Modena and Reggio were annexed to it. Niccolò III (1383–1441) brought peace and security to the state during his long reign, while his sons and successors, Leonello (1407–50), Borso (1413–71) and Ercole (1431–1505), were notable patrons of the arts and of humanist scholarship, a tradition continued by Isabella (1474–1539) and Beatrice (1475–97), daughters of Ercole, who married respectively Fran-

cesco **GONZAGA** of Mantua and Lodovico **SFORZA** of Milan. Alfonso I (d.1534) quarrelled with Popes **JULIUS II** and **LEO X** and lost the family's papal fiefs in 1527, while his son, Ippolito (d.1572), erected the magnificent Villa d'Este at Tivoli. Although Ferrara was lost in 1598, the family retained the duchy of Modena until 1859, when Francis V (1819–75) resigned his territories to **VICTOR EMMANUEL II**.

**Esterházy**
A powerful Hungarian aristocratic family, which flourished in several branches between the 16c and 19c. Among its many members were Count Pál Esterházy of Frakno (1635–1713), the Habsburg field marshal who was made a Prince of the Empire in 1687 for promoting the dynasty's cause and for his successes against the Turks. Prince Miklós IV (1765–1833) fought against Napoleon, but by extravagance brought his vast estates into sequestration. Prince Pál Antal (1786–1866), represented Austria in London until 1842, and in 1848 was Minister of Foreign Affairs.

**Estigarribia, José Félix** (1888–1940)
Paraguayan general and war hero. He won fame as a brilliant commander in the **CHACO WAR** (1932–5), on the strength of which he became President (1939–40). He died in a plane crash near Asunción.

**ESTONIA**   official name **Republic of Estonia**

A republic in eastern Europe, bounded to the west by the Baltic Sea; to the north by the Gulf of Finland; to the east by Russia; and to the south by Latvia. Occupied by **VIKINGS** in the 9c, during its history it has been owned by Denmark, Sweden, Poland, Russia and the **TEUTONIC KNIGHTS** of Germany. For a time it was divided into two areas: northern Estonia and Livonia (southern Estonia and Latvia), but was ceded to Russia in its entirety by Sweden in the Treaty of **NYSTADT** in 1721. It achieved independence in 1918, became a Soviet Socialist Republic in 1940, and was occupied by Germany during **WORLD WAR II**. There was a resurgence of the nationalist movement in the 1980s and it declared its independence on the dissolution of the USSR in 1991. A new constitution was agreed the following year. Russian troops were withdrawn in 1994. Estonia joined the **EU** and **NATO** in 2004.

**Estrada Doctrine**
A non-interventionist stance first articulated in 1930 by the Mexican Foreign Minister Genaro Estrada. The doctrine recognizes unfettered national sovereignty and rejects the concept of diplomatic recognition as an interference in the domestic affairs of another nation. Its roots lie in previous doctrines regulating jurisdictional issues in the Americas, particularly the **MONROE DOCTRINE** (1823) and the Calvo Doctrine (1868) preventing legal disputes arising in Latin

American countries being adjudicated abroad, and its conception reflected deep-seated fears of US interference following the **MEXICAN REVOLUTION**. The doctrine's appeal to the states that have adopted it, such as the USA and the UK, is that in effect it allows governments to have dealings with more than one regime within a sovereign state without having to formally recognize or make choices between them.

### Estrada Palma, Tomás (1835–1908)

Cuban nationalist and politician. A commander in the **TEN YEARS' WAR**, he was captured by the Spanish in 1877 and on his release moved to New York where he became Principal of the Central High School for Boys and leader of the Cuban exiles in the USA. For his work for the struggle for Cuban independence in the USA, he was elected President of the new republic (1901 and 1905) but, after having to call in US troops in 1906 to put down a rebellion against his government, was forced into retirement.

### ETA (*Euskadi Ta Askatasuna*, 'Basque Homeland and Freedom')

The extremist Basque nationalist organization set up in 1959 to secure the independence of the Basque country. It was later influenced by Third World nationalism, **MARXISM**, and the use of violence, all of which led to much internal feuding and divisions. ETA initiated a campaign of armed struggle in 1968, which has led to over 700 assassinations. Its killing of Admiral **CARRERO BLANCO** in 1973 undoubtedly altered the course of the post-Francoist transition. The terrorist campaign continued throughout the 1990s when the ETA used blackmail and kidnap to raise 'revolutionary taxes' from businesses to fund its activities. The organization's political front, *Herri Batasuna* ('Popular Unity'), renamed *Euskal Herritarrok* ('Basque Citizens') in 1998, generally wins between 10 and 20 per cent of the vote in the Basque country, but was suspended by the Spanish parliament in 2002 and banned in 2003 because of its links with ETA.

### Ethelred the Unready (c.968–1016)

King of England (978/1016). The son of Edgar, he was aged about 10 when the murder of his half-brother, Edward the Martyr, placed him on the throne. In 1002 he confirmed an alliance with **NORMANDY** by marrying, as his second wife, Duke Richard's daughter Emma – the first dynastic link between the two countries. Renewed attacks by the **VIKINGS** on England began as raids in the 980s, and in 1013 **SVEIN I HARALDSSON, FORKBEARD** secured mastery over the whole country and forced Ethelred into exile in Normandy. After Svein's death (1014) he returned to oppose **CANUTE**, but the unity of English resistance was broken when his son, **EDMUND II, IRONSIDE**, rebelled. 'Unready' is a mistranslation of *Unraed*, not recorded as his nickname until after the **NORMAN CONQUEST**, which means 'ill-advised' and is a pun on his given name, Ethelred (literally, 'good counsel').

### ETHIOPIA  official name **Federal Democratic Republic of Ethiopia**, formerly **Abyssinia**

A landlocked republic in north-east Africa, bounded to the west and south-west by Sudan; to the south by Kenya; to the east and north-east by Somalia; and to the north by Djibouti and Eritrea. It is the oldest in-

dependent country in sub-Saharan Africa, and the first African country to be Christianized. Abyssinian independence was recognized by the **LEAGUE OF NATIONS** in 1923, but after the invasion of Italy in 1935 the country was annexed as Italian East Africa from 1936 to 1941, when Emperor **HAILE SELASSIE** returned from exile. A military coup led to the establishment of the Marxist Provisional Military Administrative Council (PMAC) or **DERGUE**, in 1974, and left-wing opposition was met by mass arrests and executions in 1977–8. In addition to conflict with Somalia over the **OGADEN** district during the 1970s and 1980s, there was internal division with separatist Eritrean and Tigrean forces, who secured victories over government troops in the early 1980s, while the country suffered severe famine. Eritrea secured independence in 1993. The PMAC dissolved in 1987, with the transfer of power to the People's Democratic Republic, but an attempted coup in 1989 was followed by the complete collapse of **MENGISTU**'s regime in 1991 and renewed famine in 1992. A transitional government ruled until a new federal system was established in 1995. Relative stability and economic growth slowly returned, although a border dispute with Eritrea over **TIGRAY** flared up in 1998 and occasional outbreaks of fighting have occurred since.

### ethnic cleansing

The removal from an area by a militarily superior ethnic group, either by extermination or forced migration, of members of another ethnic group or groups. The term was first used by Croat nationalists in the 1940s and came to particular notice in recent years with the outbreak of the war in **BOSNIA AND HERZEGOVINA** in 1992, the systematic clearance of Albanians from **KOSOVO** by Serbian troops in 1999, and Arab attacks on black African ethnic groups in **DARFUR** in 2003.

### Eto Shimpei (1834–74)

Japanese politician. From a lower-ranking **SAMURAI** family, he was a participant in the overthrow of the **TOKUGAWA SHOGUNATE** and was awarded a minor government post. In 1872, as Minister of Justice, he helped draft a new penal code. He resigned the following year in protest against the government's refusal to sanction a military expedition to Korea, and began to champion the disgruntled samurai in his home prefecture of Saga, most of whom had fallen on hard times following the political and social reforms of the new government. By 1874 Eto was calling for a national representative assembly, condemning the monopoly of power held by those from the former feudal domains of SATSUMA and CHOSHU. Following his attempted armed uprising in Saga in 1874, he was tried and executed.

## EU (European Union)

A community of states in Western Europe created in 1993 by the Treaty of MAASTRICHT. It is a further development in the political integration of the European Community (EC) member states, which had attained the economic integration initiated by the European Economic Community (EEC). The original members of the EC were joined by Austria, Finland and Sweden (1995), Cyprus, Czech Republic, Estonia, Hungary, Latvia, Lithuania, Malta, Poland, Slovakia and Slovenia (2004). In accordance with the agreement on European Monetary Union, the EURO ZONE was established in 2002, with the euro as a common currency in 12 member states. An EU constitution has been drafted and is scheduled to come into force, subject to approval in a series of national referenda, in 2006. ► MAASTRICHT, TREATY OF; NICE, TREATY OF

## Eugène of Savoy, Prince François Eugène de Savoie Carignan (1663–1736)

Austrian general. Born in Paris and brought up at the court of LOUIS XIV of France, he left when refused a commission and, at the age of 19, entered the service of Emperor LEOPOLD I. Having distinguished himself in the war against the Turks, he was appointed field marshal in 1694. On the outbreak of the War of the SPANISH SUCCESSION (1701), he was made commander of the imperial army in Italy, joined forces with MARLBOROUGH at the Danube in 1704, leading up to the decisive victory at BLENHEIM. Their cooperation was renewed in 1708 in the Netherlands, resulting in the victories of OUDENARDE (11 July 1708) and MALPLAQUET (1709). After Marlborough's recall, he succeeded to the allied supreme command but, abandoned by England, had to accept the terms of the Treaty of RASTATT (1714). By 1716 he was again in the field against the Turks, putting an end to their power in Hungary and capturing Belgrade (1718). Distrusted by Emperor CHARLES VI and plotted against at court, he retired from active service to devote himself to the arts and literature, and to the building of his palace of Belvedere in Vienna, where he died.

## Eugenius III, originally Bernardo Paganelli (d.1153)

Italian pope (1145/53). He was a Cistercian monk. His predecessor (Lucius II) having died during a rebellion against the papacy in Rome, he was obliged to flee to Viterbo immediately upon his election. Soon after his return, he was again driven out by a revolt initiated by ARNOLD OF BRESCIA, and turned his attention to promoting a second crusade in France. ► CRUSADE, SECOND

## Eugenius IV, originally Gabriele Condulmer (1383–1447)

Italian pope (1431/47). By birth a Venetian nobleman, he quarrelled with the Council of BASLE because it sought to limit papal power. In 1434 he was driven from Rome by the COLONNA and opened a new council which met at Ferrara, then Florence, where it achieved a fleeting reunion of the Greek and Latin Churches. He excommunicated the bishops at Basle, but the council there deposed him in 1439 and elected AMADEUS VIII, THE PEACEFUL of Savoy as Felix V.

## eunuchs

Castrated male attendants employed at the Chinese imperial court from the time of the Qin Dynasty (221–206BC). Initially introduced to wait upon the female members of the imperial family, eunuchs often became the personal confidants of the emperor, wielding enormous influence. During the later (Eastern) Han Dynasty (AD25–220) they were able to manipulate the dynastic succession, and by the time of the Tang Dynasty (618–907) had infiltrated every level of government. Most eunuchs were castrated before the age of ten and were either younger sons of poor families or children from non-Chinese frontier peoples. Their influence reached its height during the latter decades of the MING DYNASTY (1368–1644), when they controlled appointments and tax collection. Eunuch influence was greatly reduced during the succeeding QING DYNASTY (1644–1911).

## Eureka

In Australian history, an armed clash between goldminers and a combined police and military force at the Eureka Stockade, Ballarat, Victoria (1854), which cost the lives of 30 miners and five soldiers, with many others wounded. The miners had objected to the expensive mining licence imposed by the government. Public opinion swung behind the miners, juries refused to convict, and reforms to the goldfields were put into effect. The miners' rejection of government authority and use of a southern cross flag gave the incident symbolic significance for Australian democracy and national identity. ► AUSTRALIAN GOLD RUSH

## Eurocommunism

An attempt in the 1970s and 1980s by western European communist parties, led by the PCI (Italian Communist Party), to refashion MARXISM–LENINISM and follow a doctrine more appropriate to liberal democracies and market economies.

## European Community ► EC

## European Economic Community ► EEC

## European Union ► EU

## euro zone

The euro, of 100 cents, is the common EU currency introduced in Jan 2002, since when it has been used in the 12 member states (Austria, Belgium, Finland, France, Germany, Greece, Ireland, Italy, Luxembourg, the Netherlands, Portugal, Spain), that make up the euro zone. The MAASTRICHT TREATY established the European Monetary Union (EMU) and set economic convergence criteria for countries wishing to participate. The British government deferred participation in 1989 and the Danes rejected membership in a referendum in 2000. The European Central Bank was created in 1998, and notes and coins came into circulation on 1 Jan 2002, national currencies being withdrawn two months later.

## Evangelical Union

Suspicious of the intentions of MAXIMILIAN I, Duke of Bavaria, the Protestant German princes formed this

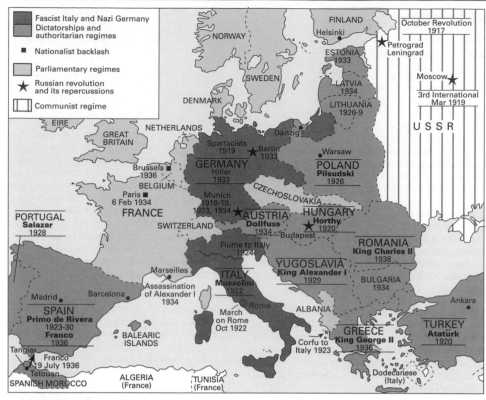

Legend:
- Fascist Italy and Nazi Germany
- Dictatorships and authoritarian regimes
- Nationalist backlash
- Parliamentary regimes
- ★ Russian revolution and its repercussions
- Communist regime

**European dictatorships, 1920–39**

Union in 1608. The Catholics, under Maximilian, reacted by forming the **CATHOLIC LEAGUE**. The Union was headed by the Elector Palatine, Frederick IV, a Calvinist, and was viewed with suspicion by many Lutherans. Initially allied with France and prepared for war in the **JÜLICH–CLEVES SUCCESSION CONFLICT**, the Union broke down after the assassination of **HENRY IV** of France (May 1610). Under **FREDERICK V**, the Union again appeared in the field early in the **THIRTY YEARS' WAR** but was finally destroyed at the Battle of the **WHITE MOUNTAIN** (1620).

**Evatt, Herbert Vere** (1894–1965)
Australian jurist and politician. He served in the state Assembly (1925–30), and was justice of the High Court of Australia (1930–40), when he entered federal politics. As Australian Minister of External Affairs (1941–9), he was a frequent visitor to Britain, at times attending Winston **CHURCHILL**'s war cabinet between 1941 and 1945. He was leader of the **AUSTRALIAN LABOR PARTY** in opposition (1951–60), and finally Chief Justice of New South Wales until his retirement in 1962.

**Ever-Normal Granaries**
A system of state regulation of grain supplies of imperial China dating from the reign of Han Wudi (141/87BC). With its aim of stabilizing grain supplies and prices, the system was underpinned by the assumption that the state had a duty to prevent private speculation and provide for the people's well-being. Surplus grain was purchased and stored by government agencies and sold whenever supplies were inadequate. Grain supplies might also be transported

to other regions experiencing shortages. The system remained virtually intact until the 19c, when increasing government weakness and corruption led to its breakdown.

**Evers, Medgar** (1925–63)
US **CIVIL RIGHTS** activist. Field Secretary of the **NAACP** with responsibility for registering black voters and organizing boycotts of establishments which practised racial discrimination, he was shot dead outside his home in Jackson, Mississippi. His murder illustrated the dangers faced by black civil rights activists working in the South. A white man, Byron de la Beckwith, boasted of and was indicted for his murder, but was freed after two trials ended in hung juries.

**'Ever-Victorious Army'**
A foreign-led Chinese army which assisted the Qing imperial forces in the suppression of the **TAIPING REBELLION** (1850–64) in its closing stages. It was first commanded by an American, Frederick Townsend Ward, and then, following his death, by Charles **GORDON**, a British artillery officer. The army made use of steam-driven gunboats and modern weapons. Although it played only a minor role in the suppression of the Taipings, its fighting efficiency prompted some Chinese provincial officials to advocate the introduction of Western technology (especially military) into China on a larger scale. ➤ **QING DYNASTY**

**Evian Agreements** (1962)
These agreements were the result of secret talks held at Evian, on the French shore of Lake Geneva, to end the war in Algeria. The government of General de **GAULLE** and representatives of the provisional government of

# *Exploration*

Transport & Travel

More is known about exploration that originated in Europe than anywhere else. Lack of documentation deprives us of detailed knowledge of non-European explorers like the Polynesians of the Pacific. An exception is the accounts we have of the seven expeditions into the Indian Ocean by fleets of junks sent by the **Ming Dynasty** of China under the Muslim Chinese Admiral **Zheng He** in the period between 1405 and 1433. However, after exploring the African coast, the Chinese abandoned nautical exploration, and the ensuing history of sea exploration grew out of the earliest developments in Mediterranean civilization. As centres developed and prospered, there was a need for trade between them, and the development of writing meant that some record was kept of travellers' discoveries.

According to Herodotus, Pharaoh Necho sent out a fleet that circumnavigated Africa (c.600 BC). The Phoenicians travelled from their cities of Sidon, Tyre and Carthage all around the Mediterranean and beyond, into the Atlantic. Hanno, a navigator from Carthage, went along the west coast of Africa and founded a colony there.

The founding of colonies was a prime reason for exploration. The Etruscans probably moved to Italy from Lydia around 900 BC after a famine. Citizens from Greek city-states, where land was in short supply and political dissent could be dangerous, founded settlements in Cumae (750 BC), Massilia (Marseilles, 600 BC), Neapolis (Naples, 600 BC, by refugees from Cumae), Syracuse (734 BC) and Byzantium (Istanbul c.660 BC).

Alexander III, the Great moved spectacularly beyond the bounds of the Mediterranean in 334 BC, taking his armies across the Hellespont to Asia Minor, on through Syria, Egypt, Mesopotamia and Persia, to lands unknown to most Europeans, to the Hindu Kush, Samarkand, Tashkent and Kashmir. His empire was succeeded in the west by the Romans, whose armies covered much of southern Europe and North Africa. In AD 84 Agricola's fleet circumnavigated the coast of Great Britain.

Nomadic invaders sweeping across Europe from the north from AD 238 to the sack of Rome in AD 410 sought plunder, not new lands in themselves. It was the sea-going Norsemen who were true explorers as well as raiders. Erik the Red (Erik Thorvaldson) explored the Greenland coast and founded colonies (985); his son Leif **Eriksson** landed in 'Vinland' (1000), thought to be America, possibly Newfoundland.

It was by sea that the most dramatic explorations were to be made. Long journeys had been made by land over the old trade routes, notably that to China described by Marco Polo in his writings c.1320, but improvements in boat design, the need to transport bulky materials more cheaply, the inexhaustible desire of European monarchs for riches for their treasuries, and above all a belief that a new trade route might be found to Asia, all gave impetus to the voyages of discovery.

In Portugal, a younger son of King John I of Portugal, Prince **Henry the Navigator**, encouraged exploratory voyages down the African coast. Portugal used its Jewish minority's access to Arab mathematics to develop tables to facilitate celestial navigation, and its captains discovered Madeira (1420), the Azores (1427) and the Cape Verde Islands (1456–60). In 1460 they sailed as far south as Sierra Leone, finding for a grateful Portuguese government the 'Gold Coast', the 'Ivory Coast' and the 'Slave Coast'. In 1488 Bartolomeu Dias rounded the Cape of Good Hope and entered the Indian Ocean. In 1498 Vasco da **Gama** reached India, to be followed by Pedro Cabral, who sighted Brazil in 1500 and landed at Mozambique.

The Spanish had money after the fall of Granada to sponsor an Italian, Christopher **Columbus**, to search for a westward or south-westward route to Asia. He found the Bahamas and explored Cuba in 1492, and returned to Cuba in 1493, believing it to be part of mainland China. In 1498 he found the Venezuelan coast, and in 1502 made the momentous discovery of the Panamanian isthmus, exploring the coasts of Honduras and Nicaragua, but believing himself to be in **Indochina**. Amerigo **Vespucci** followed in his path and explored the coast of Venezuela in 1499. His name was given to the Americas following a published (incorrect) report that he had landed on the mainland in 1491.

For the first half of the 16c Spanish explorers made one startling voyage after another, their aim to seize the wealth of the New World. In 1513 Juan **Ponce de León** explored and named Florida, and **Balboa** explored the isthmus of Panama and sighted the Pacific. Ferdinand **Magellan** penetrated into that ocean via the Strait of Magellan in 1519, but was killed in the Philippines. Rather than face the return journey the remaining ship, captained by Juan del Cano, continued to sail

---

Algeria, led by **BEN BELLA**, agreed to a ceasefire and to the establishment of an independent Algeria after a referendum. The agreements were given massive support in referenda in both France and Algeria, in spite of the attempts of the **OAS** (*Organisation de l'Armée Secrète*) to undermine them. ► **ALGERIAN WAR OF INDEPENDENCE**

### Exclusion Crisis (1678–81)
The name given to events, beginning with the **POPISH PLOT**, during a campaign in parliament to exclude **CHARLES II**'s brother, James, Duke of York (later **JAMES VII AND II**), from succession to the throne on grounds of his Roman Catholicism. Showing considerable political skill, the King outmanoeuvred his Whig opponents and undermined their power base. Many were arrested or fled abroad. ► **WHIGS**

**Exploration** ► *See panel*

### Extensive Development (post-1928)
The term used by Soviet-style economists to describe the massive, planned build-up of basic industries in backward societies like the early USSR. The emphasis was on production, not on producers or on consumers. The twin objectives were the creation of a national capital and the expansion of the working class. The technique was imposed on the states of Eastern Europe after **WORLD WAR II**, irrespective of their level of development. By the 1960s, the cry went up for intensive development, the establishment of consumer industries and the employment of new technologies. The fact that too little came too late seriously undermined Soviet-style **COMMUNISM** in the 1980s.

### Eyadéma, (Étienne) Gnassingbé (1937–)
Togolese soldier and politician. He joined the French army in 1953, serving outside Africa for many years, and became army Chief of Staff in 1965. He led a

west and circumnavigated the globe, returning to Spain in 1522. Most importantly for Spain, between 1519 and 1536, **Cortés** conquered Mexico, and Francisco **Pizarro** had taken Peru.

With the treasury full, Spain was able to outfit expeditions to the south of what is now the USA, to explore the Colorado River, and to trace the Amazon from its source to the Atlantic. From 1540 to 1542 Pedro de **Valdivia** explored Chile, while at the same time Francisco Vasquez de Coronado explored a large area of the south-west of North America, and he and his men were the first Europeans to see the Grand Canyon (1540). The lands explored and appropriated by the Spanish were by no means empty, but were not held by a Christian sovereign and had no allies.

The English, rivals of Spain, made their own effort in the second half of the century. One aim was to find a northern route to Asia. Richard Chancellor went round the north of Scandinavia and overland to Moscow (1553–4). Sir Francis **Drake** became the second captain to circumnavigate the globe (1577–80), and Sir Walter **Raleigh** explored the coast of Guinea, Trinidad and the Orinoco River (1585).

Martin Frobisher and Henry Hudson continued the search for a north-west passage to Asia, the first finding and naming Frobisher Bay (1576–8), and the second the Hudson River and Hudson Bay (1609–10). The French, too, were interested in the north, specifically for the **fur trade**, and Samuel de **Champlain** traced the course of the St Lawrence, founded and named Quebec, placed a colony in Nova Scotia, and explored Vermont where Lake Champlain is named after him (1603–13). Robert Cavalier, Sieur de **La Salle**, followed the course of the Mississippi to the Gulf of Mexico (1682).

The Dutch began to trade in the East Indies in 1595. They founded their **East India Company** in 1602, and created a base at Cape Town in 1652 to provision their ships. From the East Indies in 1642, Abel **Tasman** was sent on an expedition by the Governor-General, Anthony Van Diemen, and discovered Van Diemen's Land (now Tasmania) and New Zealand, but Holland did not establish colonies there. Many Dutch ships made landfall or were wrecked on the west coast of Australia; this they called New Holland, though it seemed a desert country. So it seemed too to William Dampier's expedition, funded by the English Admiralty in 1699.

The Age of Reason provided a climate in which scientific expeditions to gain knowledge and find new plants was encouraged. Captain James **Cook** made three voyages to the Pacific. The first, sponsored by the Royal Society in 1768, lasted three years and included the circumnavigation and charting of New Zealand, and the charting of the eastern coast of Australia, his botanists and artists recording what they found of flora, fauna and indigenous peoples. Impressed by the variety of plants, he named his Australian landfall Botany Bay and claimed the continent for King **George III**, ignoring any claims of its 250,000 Aboriginal inhabitants to ownership. He was given command of a second voyage to explore the shores of the Antarctic, and also visited Tahiti and the New Hebrides, and discovered and charted New Caledonia and other groups. On his third voyage he surveyed the coast of North America as far as the Bering Strait, but was killed in Hawaii when he was forced to turn back there after having left. The Pacific had been sailed before, by Polynesians in massive ocean-going canoes, navigating by the stars. They had been looking for new places to live, and gradually colonized the islands, reaching the two large islands of what is now New Zealand c.1000 AD. Cook's voyages provided Europeans with unrivalled new knowledge about Oceania.

The British were to concentrate their colonizing efforts on Australia, but the huge areas involved meant that the continent was not circumnavigated until 1802–3. Settlements were made in the south and west of Australia, and the first expedition to cross the interior of the continent, south to north, was made in 1860 by Robert O'Hara Burke and William John Wills, leading a team of 17 men and 26 camels (both leaders died of starvation on the return journey).

Similar vast distances in Africa were investigated by more countries: Britain, Germany, Belgium, Portugal, France and Italy had all staked their claims by the end of the 19c. The African slave trade reached its peak in the 18c, but land for colonization was also valuable, and the missionary societies were active too. Exploration for its own sake played a part in the activities of Scots such as James Bruce, who found the source of the Blue Nile (1772), Mungo **Park**, who went up the Gambia River and reached the Niger (1795), David **Livingstone**, who crossed southern Africa, exploring the Zambezi River and the Victoria Falls (1849–59), and the Welshman Sir Henry Morton **Stanley**, who surveyed Lake Tanganyika and traced the course of the Congo to the west coast (1874–89). Richard Burton explored Somalia and Ethiopia (1854–8), and Verney Lovett Cameron crossed equatorial Africa from east to west (1875).

Exploration of the American continents proceeded too from the growing settlements on the east coast. In 1793

---

bloodless military coup in 1967, deposing President Grunitsky. He banned all political parties until 1969, when he founded a new organization, the *Rassemblement du Peuple Togolais*, as a vehicle for the organization of support for the government. Despite opposition, he has survived and introduced a degree of democratization.

### Eylau, Battle of (1807)

The indecisive battle between Russian and French armies as **ALEXANDER I** tried to halt **NAPOLEON I**'s drive from Prussia through Poland. Casualties were high on both sides, but Alexander stuck to his anti-French alliance. His reaction was quite different a few months later after his army's defeat at **FRIEDLAND**.

### Eyre, Edward John (1815–1901)

British explorer and colonial governor. He emigrated to Australia in 1833, where he drove stock from Syd-

ney to Melbourne and Adelaide. From Adelaide in 1839–40 he made exploratory forays to the north, reaching Lake Eyre, and west across the Eyre Peninsula, but without finding a route out of South Australia. In 1841, with just his overseer, Baxter, and three **ABORIGINALS**, he set out to reach Albany in the west. On the way Baxter died and two Aboriginals deserted, but fresh supplies provided by a French whaler enabled Eyre to complete the first crossing from South to Western Australia. In 1841 he was appointed protector of Aboriginals at Moorundie, South Australia, returning to England in 1844. He became Lieutenant-Governor of New Zealand (1846), Lieutenant-Governor of St Vincent (1854), acting Governor (1861) and then Governor of Jamaica (1864). There, his severe repression of a Negro rebellion (1865) created a political storm in England and led to his recall and retirement.

Alexander Mackenzie, a Scots fur-trader, crossed from the Atlantic to the Pacific coast of north-western Canada, and George Vancouver explored the island off the Canadian coast that now bears his name. The **Lewis and Clark expedition** travelled overland along the Missouri and Columbia rivers to the Pacific Ocean (1804–6). Zebulon Montgomery Pike led expeditions to the headwaters of the Mississippi, Arkansas and Red rivers, sighting Pike's Peak (1806–7). They showed the way for the move to the western frontier.

By the end of the 18c, much that was possible to explore had been explored, although China and Russia still remained something of a mystery. Russians had ventured onto the American continent, settling on Kodiak Island for the fur trade and claiming the huge area of Alaska (which was sold to the USA in 1867), but few had ventured into Russia itself.

The cold wastes of the Arctic and Antarctic remained a wilderness to be mastered. Fridtjof **Nansen** attempted to reach the North Pole in 1893, but the successful expedition was made by Robert Peary in 1909. Roald Amundsen and Robert Falcon **Scott** competed to reach the South Pole, Amundsen arriving first in 1911. Scott and his party died after getting there in 1912. Other expeditions followed, for scientific study. There were inaccessible places remaining to be conquered in South America and Africa, but the ones to be pursued most diligently were the mountains of the Himalayas, the depths of the ocean and outer space. The summit of Mt Everest was reached by Edmund Hillary and Tenzing Norgay in 1953.

### Sea exploration
The ocean floor was first examined exhaustively by the British Challenger expedition (1872–6), which mapped depths, took core samples and discovered 4,417 new species of marine organisms. Since **World War II** echo-sounding techniques have been used to measure depths and increasingly sophisticated submersibles have allowed examination of vaster depths. In 1932 Charles Beebe and Otis Barton descended to approximately 2,953ft/900m off the coast of Bermuda in a bathysphere. In 1960 Jacques Piccard and Don Walsh descended to 35,800ft/10,912m in the Marianas Trench off Guam. Modern submersibles such as the US *Alvin* can descend to 12,832ft/4,000m, and robot submersibles to 19,685ft/6,000m, with television cameras, lights and specimen-gathering tools. Dives on Pacific ocean ridges have revealed hydrothermal vents producing plumes of very hot, fine, black sulphide precipitates, and forms of life previously unknown. However, the oceans have still to be thoroughly explored.

► Space Exploration

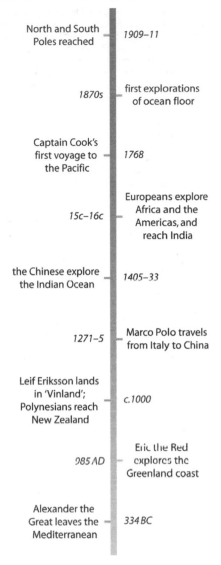

| | |
|---|---|
| North and South Poles reached | 1909–11 |
| 1870s | first explorations of ocean floor |
| Captain Cook's first voyage to the Pacific | 1768 |
| 15c–16c | Europeans explore Africa and the Americas, and reach India |
| the Chinese explore the Indian Ocean | 1405–33 |
| 1271–5 | Marco Polo travels from Italy to China |
| Leif Eriksson lands in 'Vinland'; Polynesians reach New Zealand | c.1000 |
| 985 AD | Eric the Red explores the Greenland coast |
| Alexander the Great leaves the Mediterranean | 334 BC |

---

### Eyskens, Gaston (1905–88)
Belgian economist and politician. After studying in Leuven and the USA, he became Professor of Economics at Leuven (1934–75). In 1939 he was elected MP for the **CHRISTIAN PEOPLE'S PARTY**, and in 1965 became a Senator in the Upper House. He was Minister of Finance in 1945 and in 1947–9, and from 1949 to 1950 was Prime Minister for the first time. In the mid-1950s he was Minister for Economic Affairs, and led the government again in 1958–61. Appointed Minister for Finance (1965–6), he became Prime Minister twice more (1968–72 and 1972–3). He led coalitions with both the Left and Right, and was one of the pivotal figures of post-war Belgian politics, playing a central role in the negotiations surrounding the abdication of King **LEOPOLD III**, the debate on education funding, and the decolonization of the Congo.

### EZLN (Ejército Zapatista de Liberación Nacional, 'Zapatista National Liberation Army')
A Mexican guerrilla movement, named after the revolutionary leader Emiliano **ZAPATA**, which launched a rebellion in the poor southern state of Chiapas in 1994. Its aim was to establish rights (health care, education, work, housing and food) for indigenous Maya Indians and to fight for greater democracy. A series of political reforms were agreed upon by the ruling Institutional Revolutionary Party (**PRI**), but despite these, and a military offensive against the EZLN in 1995, and various ceasefires and political treaties, fighting continued. In 1996 the FZLN (*Frente Zapatista de Liberación Nacional*, 'Zapatista National Liberation Front'), the EZLN's political wing, was set up to disseminate its demands. In a 1997 agreement the government committed itself to constitutional amendments granting greater rights to indigenous peoples, and the EZLN violence has diminished.

## Fabian Society
A socialist group established in 1884 which took its name from the Roman general, Fabius Maximus *Cunctator* ('the Delayer'), noted for his cautious military tactics. It adopts a gradualist approach to social reform, and sometimes 'Fabian' is applied to people who are not members of the society but who believe in reformist **SOCIALISM**. The society has remained a small select group, but has a close association with the British **LABOUR PARTY**, and has been a source of socialist ideas and arguments.

## Fabius, Laurent (1946– )
French socialist politician. He had a brilliant academic career and became economic adviser to the **SOCIALIST PARTY** leader François **MITTERRAND**, in 1976. Elected to the National Assembly in 1978, he was appointed Budget Minister when the party gained power in 1981, and Minister for Research and Industry in 1983. In 1984 he was appointed Prime Minister and introduced a more free-market economic programme, which had some success, but resigned following his party's electoral defeat in Mar 1986. A popular and moderate social democrat, he heads an influential faction within the party.

## Facta, Luigi (1861–1930)
Italian politician. As Prime Minister in Mar 1922, after the collapse of the **BONOMI** ministry, he made no real effort to resist the fascist seizure of power, even given the refusal of **VICTOR EMMANUEL III** to declare a state of emergency. His government collapsed (28 Oct 1922) and was replaced by that of **MUSSOLINI**. ➤ **MARCH ON ROME**

## Factory Acts
Legislation passed in Britain from 1802 onwards to regulate employment in factories. The early Acts were generally concerned to limit the hours of work of women and children in textile factories only. The 1833 Factory Act prohibited children under nine from working in textile mills, and was the first to appoint factory inspectors. A maximum 10-hour working day for women and older children was enacted in 1847. ➤ **CHILD LABOUR**

## Fagel, Gaspar (1634–88)
Dutch politician. A member of a prominent family in the Dutch Republic, he trained as a lawyer and set up practice in The Hague. In 1663 he became Pensionary of the town of Haarlem, through the influence of Johan de **WITT**. Fagel followed de Witt's anti-Orange policies, and in 1670 he became Secretary to the States General; in 1672 he changed sides to support the Stadholder **WILLIAM III, OF ORANGE**, and became his **GRAND PENSIONARY**. ➤ **STADHOLDER**

## Fahd ibn Abd al-Aziz al-Saud (1923– )
King of Saudi Arabia (1982/ ). As effective ruler since the assassination of his older half-brother **FAYSAL** in 1975, he became King on the death of his other half-brother, **KHALID**. A great promoter of the modernization of his country, he was also a central figure in the shaping of Saudi Arabia's foreign policy in the 1970s and 1980s, countering Soviet influence through financial assistance to moderate Arab states such as Egypt. He opposed the **CAMP DAVID ACCORDS** and demanded a **JIHAD** against Israel after its annexation in 1980 of East Jerusalem. Despite this, in 1981 he produced a plan for a Middle Eastern peace settlement, apparently recognizing Israel's right to secure boundaries. This plan, however, was never endorsed. In the months preceding the **GULF WAR**, Fahd accepted the support of a US-led coalition of Western and Arab forces to help protect Saudi oilfields from potential Iraqi invasion. The war itself incited criticism of his regime by pro-democracy activists, but he declared that his country was not suited to democracy and instead created in 1992 a 60-member Consultative Council that has a purely advisory function. He suffered a debilitating stroke in 1996 and many of his official functions are now carried out by his brother Crown Prince Abdullah.

## FAI (*Federación Anarquista Ibérica*, 'Iberian Anarchist Federation')
A semi-secret group of activists established in Spain in 1927 to preserve the purist and revolutionary anarchist tradition in reaction against the increasing syndicalism of the **CNT**. Though loosely organized, the FAI came to exercise great influence within the CNT during the Second Republic, being the major force in its split of 1932. The FAI also promoted the disastrous revolutionary risings of Jan and Dec 1933. During the **SPANISH CIVIL WAR**, the FAI became a bureaucracy within the CNT, playing an important role not only in the successful agrarian and industrial collectives, but also in the often ineffective anarchist militia. ➤ **REPUBLIC, SECOND** (Spain)

## Faidherbe, Louis Léon César (1818–89)
French general and colonial administrator. As Governor of Senegal (1854–61 and 1863–5), he greatly extended the frontiers of his province, laying the foundation of France's empire in Africa. In the **FRANCO-PRUSSIAN WAR**, he commanded the army of the North, but was defeated near St Quentin (1871). He was twice elected as a Deputy (1871 and 1879).

## Fair Deal

The name adopted by US President Harry S TRUMAN for his post-WORLD WAR II liberal and pro-labour domestic policies. ► NEW DEAL

## Fair Employment Practices Committee (FEPC)

Established (1941) by President Franklin D ROOSEVELT, the FEPC was created to eliminate racial discrimination in the war production industries and in government employment. President Harry S TRUMAN's efforts to establish permanent status for the committee were met with rejection by the SENATE in 1946. In 1964 the Fair Employment Opportunity Commission was established to prevent discrimination in employment. ► RANDOLPH, A(SA) PHILIP

## Fairfax, Thomas Fairfax, 3rd Baron (1612–71)

English parliamentary general. In the ENGLISH CIVIL WARS, he distinguished himself at the Battle of MARSTON MOOR (1644), and in 1645 was given command of the NEW MODEL ARMY, defeating CHARLES I at the Battle of NASEBY. He was replaced by CROMWELL in 1650 for refusing to march against the Scots, who had proclaimed CHARLES II king, and withdrew into private life. In 1660 he was head of the commission sent to The Hague to arrange for the King's return.

## fair trade

A political and social movement promoting products that guarantee a fair price for producers. Originating in Oxfam's Worldshop in 1959, the movement is now associated with promoting products sold in accordance with the UN Charter of Human Rights and INTERNATIONAL LABOUR ORGANIZATION agreements and which guarantee a fair price that covers production costs and facilitates social and economic development. By 2004 the movement had also begun to focus on the abolition of agricultural subsidies and commodity dumping by developed nations. Free trade economists view fair trade support as unsustainable in an interdependent global economy but the WORLD BANK has taken a more positive view, especially in relation to potential increases in employment and decreases in production costs. To counter false labelling of goods and overcome perception of fair trade as a niche market, a monitoring system was established in 2003 and a Fairtrade Mark was launched in 2004. ► BRANDT COMMISSION; NORTH–SOUTH DIVIDE; THIRD WORLD DEBT; UNCTAD

## Fakhr al-Din (1572–1635)

Member of the DRUZE sect which, at the time in question, was not even regarded as properly Muslim by the orthodox. The Druze, since the foundation of their sect in the early 11c by al-Darazi, an adherent of the Fatimid caliph al-Hakim bi-Amrillah, have wielded considerable influence in areas of Syria but more particularly Lebanon up to the present day. Fakhr al-Din was able to make himself master (1591–1613) of Lebanon and parts of northern Palestine, then part of the OTTOMAN EMPIRE. He treated independently with the European powers, having a certain amount of success particularly as regards commerce. The Ottomans procured his exile to Tuscany, but not to be so easily restrained, Fakhr al-Din organized his return to Lebanon in 1618 and his reinstatement as master of the territories in which he had previously held sway. Despite his considerable influence, particularly between 1623 and 1631, the replacement in Istanbul of a weak Ottoman regime by a strong one, led by Sultan MURAD IV, saw a speedy reduction in the power and influence of Faldhr al Din who was defeated by Ottoman forces and captured. He was taken to Istanbul and executed.

## Falange Española

The principal fascist movement (literally, 'Spanish Falange') of 20c Spain. Founded (Oct 1933) by José Antonio PRIMO DE RIVERA, the son of the military dictator of the 1920s, the Falange remained a small if vocal and violent movement during its first two years. In the general election of Feb 1936 it won a mere 0.7 per cent of the vote. Following the triumph of the Popular Front, the Falange grew rapidly as disillusioned middle-class youth deserted the mainstream right-wing parties. Party activists played a key role in the street-fighting that helped polarize the political climate in the spring and summer of 1936. The Falange also assisted in the military rebellion of July 1936 against the Republic. During the SPANISH CIVIL WAR, the Falange became the dominant political movement in the Nationalist zone and controlled the press and propaganda. But the mass influx into the Falange and the loss of its leadership (especially José Antonio, executed in Alicante jail in Nov 1936) diluted its radical spirit. The political fate of the Falange was sealed in Apr 1937 when General FRANCO, as the Nationalists' head of state and military leader, forcibly united it with the Carlists to become the *Falange Española Tradicionalista y de las JONS*. Under the Franco dictatorship of 1939–75 the Falange adopted a subordinate role, serving as the regime's dependent and clientelist administrative arm. It organized the labour force through the 'vertical syndicates', helped control the middle classes, and acted as the political cheerleader of the dictator.

## Falcón, Juan Crisóstomo (1820–70)

Venezuelan soldier and politician. He assumed power as a Liberal leader, and became President of Venezuela in 1863 during the 'Federalist Wars' between the Conservatives and Liberals. Despite his manifesto proclaiming federalism, democracy and social reform, political chaos ensued and he was deposed by the Conservatives in 1868. A civil war raged until in 1870 Falcon's Vice-President, Antonio GUZMÁN BLANCO, also a Liberal leader, assumed power for himself.

## Faliero, Marino (c.1274–1355)

Doge of Venice (1354/5). He is notorious for conspiring to replace the republic with a principate. His swift execution (before the public at large was aware of the crisis) enhanced the reputation of the Venetian constitution for stability and justice, though Faliero's fate inspired plays by Byron and Swinburne, and a painting by Delacroix.

## Falin, Valentin Mikhailovich (1926–)

Soviet specialist in international relations. Born in Leningrad and educated in Moscow, he held a range of Communist Party and Foreign Ministry postings from 1950 onwards. In 1968–71 he was head of the German department of the Foreign Ministry, and Ambassador to West Germany in 1971–8, the period when relations were 'normalized'. In the 1980s he was for a time influential in journalism, and in 1988 he succeeded **DOBRYNIN** as head of the international department of the party, but its days were numbered.

**Falkenhayn, Erich von** (1861–1922)
German military commander. Following a varied military career, he succeeded **MOLTKE** as Chief of the German General Staff in the autumn of 1914. He decided against a German retreat in the West, despite the French success at the first Battle of the **MARNE**, and during 1915 pursued limited objectives in the East. In 1916 he launched the offensive at the Battle of **VERDUN**, which sought to destroy the French army through a process of massive and rapid attrition. His failure here, and other setbacks, led to his replacement by **HINDENBURG** and **LUDENDORFF** in 1917. He brilliantly commanded the German forces in the occupation of Romania when it entered the war, and continued to serve successfully as a field commander. ► **WORLD WAR I**

**Falklands War** (Apr–June 1982)
A war between Britain and Argentina, precipitated by the Argentine invasion of the Falkland Islands (known to Argentines as the Malvinas). Britain had ruled the islands continuously since 1833, but Argentina claimed them by inheritance from the Spanish Empire and through their proximity to her shores. The British had been conducting talks with Argentina on sovereignty over the Falklands, involving either a leaseback arrangement or a joint administration. When these talks broke down, the government of General **GALTIERI** issued a warning to the British. The British government announced the withdrawal of HMS *Endurance* from the South Atlantic, and on 19 Mar scrap merchants landed on South Georgia, ostensibly to demolish a whaling station, but they also raised the Argentine flag. On the night of 1–2 Apr the full-scale invasion of the Falklands began. The 70 Royal Marines on the islands were overwhelmed, and the Governor was deported to Uruguay. The British immediately fitted out a task-force to retake the islands, and the Foreign Office team, including Lord **CARRINGTON**, resigned. The task-force consisted of almost 70 ships, including some 40 requisitioned merchantmen and some well-known passenger vessels such as the *Queen Elizabeth II*. A 200-mile maritime exclusion zone was declared around the Falklands, and on 2 May the Argentine cruiser *General Belgrano* was sunk by the nuclear submarine HMS *Conqueror*. This brought to an end peace initiatives conducted by the US Secretary of State, Alexander **HAIG**, and the Peruvian government. South Georgia was retaken (25 Apr); the destroyer HMS *Sheffield* was sunk by an Exocet missile (4 May); 5,000 British troops were landed at Port San Carlos (21 May); more troops were landed at Bluff Cove (6–8 June), an operation attended by much loss of life when the Argentine air force attacked the *Sir Tristram* and *Sir Galahad*. The British forces took Darwin and Goose Green on 28 May, and after the recapture of the capital, Port Stanley, the Argentinians surrendered (14 June). The war cost the British £700 million; 254 British and 750 Argentine lives were lost. Some political commentators claim that it did much to save the declining fortunes of the government of Margaret **THATCHER**.

**Fallières, Armand** (1841–1931)
French politician. He became an advocate and was a Deputy from 1876 to 1890. After a series of minor posts in **FERRY**'s Cabinet, he was Minister of the Interior under Charles Duclerc (1882–3) and then Prime Minister for a matter of weeks in 1883. A Senator from 1890 to 1906, he became President of the Senate (1899–1906), before becoming President of the Third Republic (1906–13). ► **REPUBLIC, THIRD** (France)

**Family Compact**
The high Tory political and social élite of Upper **CANADA**. The phrase was coined in 1828 by Marshall Spring Bidwell, speaker of the House of Assembly, but it described a situation that had been developing from the first years of the 19c. The regulations that governed land grants were not only complicated but designed to serve the 'well-affected and respectable classes' already established. The Family Compact also controlled the seats in the two councils and most of those in the elective assembly. Its members monopolized patronage and obtained canal and bank charters, as well as land. This political control also ensured that only the Anglican Church benefited from the **CLERGY RESERVES**, and denied financial support for the fledgling public education system. Reform agitation resulted in the expulsion of the leaders from the province, while the UK refused even to acknowledge petitions of protest. The resulting social tensions fuelled the radical leadership of William Lyon **MACKENZIE** and were a major cause of the rebellions of 1837. ► **BAGOT, SIR CHARLES**; **DURHAM REPORT**

**Fan Chung-yen** ► **FAN ZHONGYAN**

**Fanfani, Amintore** (1908–99)
Italian politician. A professor of political economy, he was elected as a Christian Democrat deputy in 1946 and held a number of ministerial posts until 1954, when he was elected General-Secretary of the party. He was Foreign Minister three times (1958–9, 1960–3 and 1965–8), a post which he twice combined with his six periods as Prime Minister (1954, 1958–9, twice in 1960–3, 1982–3 and 1987). Nominated a life Senator in 1972, he was President of the Italian Senate in 1968–73, 1976–82 and 1985. ► **CHRISTIAN DEMOCRATIC PARTY**

**Fang Li-chih** ► **FANG LIZHI**

**Fang Lizhi (Fang Li-chih)** (1936– )
Chinese astrophysicist and dissident. During the 1957 anti-rightist campaign he was dismissed from the Chinese Communist Party, but was rehabilitated during the late 1970s at a time of relative cultural freedom. As Vice-President of the University of Science and Technology in Hefei (Anhui province), he called for greater democracy and condemned party corruption. He supported student demonstrations in Dec 1986 and was once again expelled from the party for his advocacy of 'bourgeois liberalism'. In the wake of the brutal suppression of the democracy movement in 1989, Fang Lizhi was accused of being one of the ringleaders. He sought refuge in the US Embassy and was eventually allowed to leave for the West.

**Fanon, Frantz** (1925–61)
Martinique-born doctor and revolutionary. His study

of the Algerian revolution, *The Wretched of the Earth* (1961), became the inspiration and manifesto for liberation struggles throughout the Third World. Educated as a psychiatrist in France and sent to Algeria, Fanon changed sides and joined the rebels, but died of leukaemia before seeing the achievement of independence for Algeria.

## Fanti States

Separate traditional states, each under the authority of a royal chief, in southern Ghana. The Fanti are Kwa-speaking farmers and fishermen, but formerly they traded with the Europeans in coastal towns such as Elmina and Cape Coast.

## Fan Zhongyan (Fan Chung-yen) (989–1052)

Chinese reforming scholar-official of the **SONG DYNASTY**. He championed a Confucian activism in government in reaction against the otherworldly concerns of Buddhism, stressing the importance of Confucian scholars participating in public life and the need for social welfare projects. Fan is especially known for his promotion of the clan (a corporate organization bringing together related families in a particular region) as the ideal basis of society, providing for a stable and harmonious political order. He helped to devise clan rules that laid down standards for personal conduct and management of clan institutions such as schools and orphanages.

## FAO ► FOOD AND AGRICULTURE ORGANIZATION

## Fara'izi Movements

A religious sect founded in eastern Bengal in 1802 by Haji Shariatullah upon his return after 20 years from Mecca. Shariatullah asked the rural Muslims of Bengal to purge themselves of non-Muslim accretions, both Hindu and animist. He held that Muslims under the British lived in a land of war, where the Id and Friday prayers could not be held properly. His son, Dhadu Miyan, organized the sect on community lines and also started an agrarian movement against Hindu landlords, which was suppressed by the British.

## FARC–EP (*Fuerzas Armadas Revolucionarias de Colombia – Ejército del Pueblo*, 'Revolutionary Armed Forces of Colombia – People's Army')

The paramilitary wing of the Colombian communist party. Founded in 1964 and organized as a militia, it claims to represent Columbia's poor, particularly against right-wing paramilitary groups, and opposes US intervention in the country, the privatization of natural resources and **GLOBALIZATION**. As well as guerrilla action against political targets, the organization is involved in drug trafficking, extortion and kidnapping, and acts to protect its sources of funding as much as to further its political aims. It participated in peace talks with the government from 1998 to 2002 but these were broken off after the kidnapping of a presidential candidate. Recent governments have been unable to suppress it or reach a negotiated settlement. ► DRUGS, WAR ON

## Farel, Guillaume (1489–1565)

French reformer. He studied in Paris, and became a convert to Protestantism in 1521. He fled to Basle, and moved to Geneva in 1532. The severity of the ecclesiastical discipline imposed by **CALVIN** produced a reaction, so that in 1538 the two reformers were expelled from the city. He became a pastor in Neuchâtel in 1538, and worked there for the rest of his life.

## Fargo, William G(eorge) (1818–81)

US businessman. In 1844, with Henry Wells (1805–78) and Daniel Dunning, he founded Wells & Co, the first express company to operate west of Buffalo, New York. This merged with two other companies in 1850 to form the American Express Company, of which Fargo became secretary and, following other mergers and Wells' retirement, President (1868–81). In 1852 he and Wells founded **WELLS, FARGO & CO**, which handled express business initially between New York and California. Later, Fargo also became the owner of the **PONY EXPRESS** (1861) and the Overland Mail Co (1866). He served as Mayor of Buffalo (1862–6) but was unsuccessful in his bid to join the US **SENATE** (1871).

## Farinacci, Roberto (1892–1945)

Italian politician. One of the founding members of Italian **FASCISM** and perhaps the most intransigent **RAS**. He was a deputy (1921–2), Secretary-General of the **FASCIST PARTY** (1925–6), a member of the **FASCIST GRAND COUNCIL** (from 1935) and a Minister of State (1938). An ardent anti-Semite, he was ideologically much closer to Nazism than most other **GERARCHI**. In the famous meeting of the **FASCIST GRAND COUNCIL** (25 July 1943), he was one of the minority who voted for total loyalty to the alliance with Germany. At the end of the war he was captured and executed on the same day and by the same partisans as **MUSSOLINI**.

## Farini, Luigi Carlo (1812–66)

Italian revolutionary and politician. Involved in the Bologna uprising against papal rule in 1831, and expelled from the **PAPAL STATES** in 1843, Farini was summoned back to Rome by **PIUS IX** who appointed him Under-Secretary of State. When Pius fled to Gaeta after the murder of Pellegrino **ROSSI**, Farini followed but he was subsequently dismissed and exiled because of his liberal sympathies. He settled in Turin and collaborated with **CAVOUR** on *Il Risorgimento*, the latter's liberal and progressive journal. He became a minister in the **D'AZEGLIO** government and supported Cavour during the 1850s. In June 1859 he was appointed as Commissioner Extraordinary in Modena and the following year was recognized as 'dictator' in Parma and the Papal Legations as well; in Mar 1860 he orchestrated their transfer by plebiscite to the new united Italy. After the annexation of the Kingdom of the **TWO SICILIES**, he was made Lieutenant-General of Naples. He became Prime Minister on the resignation of **RATTAZZI** (Dec 1862), but resigned himself because of ill health in Mar 1863. His admiration and close cooperation with Cavour earned him the nickname 'Cavour's shadow'.

## Farnese, Alessandro (1545–92)

Italian general. He fought in the service of **PHILIP II** of Spain, who was his uncle, and distinguished himself against the Turks at the Battle of **LEPANTO** (1571). As Governor-General of the Spanish Netherlands (1578–92), he captured Antwerp (1585), and compelled **HENRY IV** of France to raise the siege of Paris (1590).

## Farnese Family

The ruling family of the Principality of Parma, with important Spanish links. Alessandro Farnese was one of the greatest generals of his day, serving with distinction in the Netherlands against the rebels. Elizabeth Farnese (1692–1766) was the Queen (1714/46) of **PHILIP V** of Spain, and played an active role in Spanish foreign policy. ➤ **FARNESE, ALESSANDRO**

## Faroe Islands, Possession of the

The group of islands lying between the Shetland Islands and Iceland, and subject to the Danish crown. The islands were settled from Norway and the Norse settlements in Scotland from the beginning of the 9c. They were converted to Christianity c.1000 and made tributary to the Norwegian crown c.1035. A bishopric was established at Kirkjubøur at the beginning of the 12c, but abolished in 1557 after the introduction of the **REFORMATION**. The islands were governed as a Danish province, but in the 17c were granted for long periods as a fief of the Danish crown. With the abolition of absolute monarchy in Denmark in 1848, the islands were granted a seat in both the upper and lower houses of the Danish parliament in Copenhagen, and a provincial assembly (*Lagting*) was set up in 1852. During **WORLD WAR II** the Faroes were occupied by British troops. A referendum held in 1946 voted for independence, but this was disallowed and home rule was introduced in 1948. When Denmark joined the **EEC** in 1973, the islands were excluded because of their special fishing interests. Plans for a referendum in 2001 were shelved after Denmark threatened to withdraw its annual subsidies if the result favoured independence.

## Farouk I (1920–65)

Last King of Egypt (1936–52). Born in Cairo, he was educated in England, and studied at the Royal Military Academy, Woolwich. After **WORLD WAR II** he turned increasingly to a life of pleasure. The defeat of Egypt by Israel (1948) and continuing British occupation led to increasing unrest, and General **NEGUIB**'s coup (1952) forced his abdication and exile. In 1959 he became a citizen of Monaco, and he died in Rome.

## Farragut, David Glasgow (1801–70)

US naval commander. He joined the navy in 1810 and saw service against the British in the **WAR OF 1812**, and against pirates in 1820. In the **AMERICAN CIVIL WAR** he served with the Union forces and commanded the armament fitted out for the capture of New Orleans (1862). He took part in the siege and capture of **VICKSBURG** (1863), and destroyed the enemy's gunboats in Mobile Bay, leading to the town's surrender. He was made Vice-Admiral, the rank being created for him by special Act of Congress, as was also that of Admiral (1866).

## Farrakhan, Louis, originally Louis Eugene Wolcott, formerly known as Louis X (1933– )

US leader of the Nation of Islam. He was born in New York City, and his tough upbringing led him to join **MALCOLM X**'s Black Muslim movement. In 1978 Farrakhan was excommunicated by the World Community of Islam and revived the name and principles of the Nation of Islam, promoting self-reliance, healthy eating and abstinence from drugs. More radical than the leaders of the **CIVIL RIGHTS MOVEMENT**, he has been widely criticized for his anti-Jewish rhetoric. The growing influence among African-Americans of his message of self-respect was demonstrated in the 1995 'Million Man March' in Washington, DC. In 1996 *Time* magazine included him in its list of the 25 most influential people in the USA. ➤ **BLACK MUSLIMS**

## Farroupilha Revolt

A separatist rebellion in the southern provinces of Brazil, especially Rio Grande do Sul. The rebels, known as *farropos* ('ragamuffins'), proclaimed an independent republic in 1836, but the south was restored to Brazil by 1845. The revolt was eventually brought to an end under the strong government of Luís Alves de Lima e Silva (who was later created Duke of Caxias) by a combination of his tactics and the conciliation of *estanciero* interests in an amnesty. The last major civil war under the Brazilian Empire, the divisions it left remained an integral part of **GAUCHO** politics to the 1970s.

## Fasci Siciliani

The first *fasci* (literally, 'bundles') were established in Sicilian towns in the late 19c as mutual-aid societies for workers and peasants, which could also operate as primitive trade unions. The leadership of the Fasci was very varied, often being run by anarchists but also by local gentry, academics, professionals and even *mafiosi*. In 1893 they began to gain widespread support among the Sicilian peasantry and were instrumental in coordinating a number of agricultural strikes. The traditional rural violence that accompanied some strike action was used as a pretext by the recently formed government of Francesco **CRISPI** to take repressive action. In Jan 1894 the Fasci were officially dissolved and martial law was declared in Sicily. Many members of the Fasci were arrested and sentenced to imprisonment; others were deported to nearby islands without trial. Crispi also used the disorder as an excuse to strike off the names of thousands of potential socialist or anarchist supporters from the electoral rolls.

## fascism

A term applied generically, and often inaccurately, to a variety of extremely nationalistic and authoritarian, populist movements that reached their pinnacle in the interwar years. The movement originated in Italy, centred on **MUSSOLINI**. It is hard to define the central tenets of fascism even in Italy, where it began as a republican, anti-capitalist, anticlerical movement with a strong syndicalist influence, and yet quickly switched to supporting the free market, the monarchy and the Church. However, all fascist movements (Oswald **MOSLEY**'s **BLACKSHIRTS** in Britain, the **IRON GUARD** in Romania, the **CROIX DE FEU** in France or any other of its manifestations across Europe) shared common features: an aggressive and unquestioning nationalism; a disrespect for democratic and liberal institutions, which did not, however, preclude using them to attain power; a profound hatred for **SOCIALISM**; an emphasis on a single charismatic leader; a strong association with militarism. There are many similarities between fascism and Nazism, the latter often being described as simply an extreme manifestation of the former. However, it should be stressed that, although xenophobic, there was nothing intrinsically anti-Semitic about Italian fascism, at least in its early stages. After the end of WORLD WAR II, fascism was largely discredited, although groups such as the ITALIAN SOCIAL MOVEMENT and the British and French National Fronts show many similarities.

**Fascist Grand Council** (*Gran Consiglio di Fascismo*)
Established in 1923 as a parallel fascist cabinet alongside the constitutional one, the *Gran Consiglio* did relatively little. Instead, MUSSOLINI created it primarily to provide apparently prestigious posts to occupy potentially dangerous RAS. By 1928 it had become, in theory, the most powerful organ of both party and state, composed almost entirely of ministers. In practice its powers were extremely limited: it was purely advisory and could only convene on the orders of Mussolini; he did not summon it at all between 1939 and July 1943. Despite his attempts to keep the Council as no more than a forum for careerists, nonentities and sycophants, it did eventually assert itself in the famous meeting of 25 July 1943 when it voted by a majority of 17 to 7 in favour of Dino GRANDI's motion to remove the DUCE from office: Mussolini was dismissed by King VICTOR EMMANUEL III and arrested the following day.

**Fascist Party** (*Partito Nazionale Fascista*, PNF)
The fascist movement was founded by MUSSOLINI at a meeting in Milan in Mar 1919. Originally it was no more than a fringe movement, associated with the 'futurists' and anticlerical, anti-capitalist and republican in philosophy. It contested elections in 1919 disastrously, and was not put on a formal party footing until Oct 1921, when the PNF was established. Its remarkable growth, both in membership and electoral support, has much to do with the chaotic political climate of the post-war years, the weakness of liberal institutions and widespread fear of COMMUNISM, but the PNF's ideology also changed, Mussolini realizing that if it were to appeal broadly it could not continue to be anticlerical, against the free market or hostile to the monarchy. By Oct 1922 it was already the most significant political force in Italy and by 1929 had effectively become the sole Italian political party, dominating an essentially totalitarian regime. However, the nature of the party also altered; largely as a result of purges undertaken by the DUCE it lost its revolutionary edge and became increasingly bureaucratic. By the 1930s membership was seen more as a prerequisite for advancement than a sign of genuine commitment to the ideals of FASCISM.

**Fashoda Incident** (1898)
The settlement of Fashoda (now Kodok) on the upper White Nile was the scene of a major Anglo-French crisis in this year. French forces under Captain Jean Baptiste Marchand had reached the Nile after an 18-month journey from Brazzaville. The British, who were in the process of retaking the Sudan, issued an ultimatum; France was not prepared to go to war, and Marchand was ordered to withdraw. The incident destroyed French ambitions for a transcontinental African empire, and confirmed British mastery of the Nile region. ➤ AFRICA, PARTITION OF; KITCHENER, (HORATIO) HERBERT, 1ST EARL KITCHENER OF KHARTOUM

**Fatah, al-**
The popular name (in Arabic, 'victory') for the Pales-

tine National Liberation Movement (PNLM), created in 1957 under the leadership of Yasser ARAFAT. It is the single biggest Palestinian movement, and operates under the umbrella of the PLO (Palestine Liberation Organization). It played a major role in establishing the 1993 peace agreement with Israel, but was beset by internal divisions during the negotiations between the PLO and Israel in 1995. Various factions, such as the al-Aqsa Martyrs Brigade, continue to carry out terrorist attacks in its name. ➤ PALESTINE

**Fateh Singh, Sant** (1911–72)
Sikh religious leader. A campaigner for Sikh rights, he was involved in religious and educational activity in Rajasthan, founding many schools and colleges there. In 1942 he joined the QUIT INDIA MOVEMENT, and was imprisoned for his political activities. During the 1950s he agitated for a Punjabi-speaking state, which was achieved once Haryana was created as a separate state in 1966.

**Fatherland Front**
The popular front organized by the communists in Bulgaria during WORLD WAR II. Formed (Jun 1942) from a combination of Social Democrats, ZVENO and the left-wing Pladne Agrarians, it was from the first dominated by its communist members. In Sep 1944 it organized strikes and prepared to take over the government. Through the Front, the communists held key positions in the pro-Western government of the right-wing Agrarian Kosta Muraviev. It attacked its opponents, organized a 'people's militia', and tried and executed members of past governments and the regents. In Mar 1945 Georgi DIMITROV was elected President of the Central Committee, and in Nov of the same year the Front won a majority in the elections through fraud. Its activities ensured that Bulgaria was completely under communist control by Nov 1947.

**Fatimid Dynasty**
An Arab dynasty tracing its descent from Fatima, daughter of the Prophet Muhammad, and her husband, 'Ali. The dynasty came to prominence through its leadership of the Isma'ili movement, a branch of Shia Islam which believed that the government of the Muslim community should reside in a series of divinely-guided *imams* drawn from the family of the Prophet. The first Fatimid publicly to proclaim himself was Ubayd Allah who, in 910, established himself as Caliph in North Africa with the support of the Berber Kutama people, taking the title al-Mahdi ('Rightly Guided One'). Al-Mu'izz (952/75) conquered Egypt and built a new capital at Cairo; he and his successors extended their rule to Palestine, Syria and the holy places of Mecca and Medina. The principal aim of the Fatimids was the establishment of a universal caliphate, to be attained both by military means and by the maintenance of a vast missionary network intended to subvert the rule of their 'Abbasid rivals and to propagate the Isma'ili faith throughout the Middle East. However, the Sunni Muslims and Coptic Christians who constituted the majority of the Egyptian population were left in relative peace, except during the turbulent reign of al-HAKIM (996/1021). That of al-Mustansir (1036/94) marked a turning point in Fatimid fortunes, with the independence of the Zirid

amirs in North Africa, and the loss of much of Syria to the Seljuks, while from 1099 Palestine was conquered by the Frankish Crusaders. By this time the caliphs, who were frequently minors, had fallen under the domination of viziers and generals, and in the course of the 12c, Egypt came under increasing pressure from the **FRANKS** of Jerusalem and **NUR AL-DIN**, the ruler of Muslim Syria, who recognized the religious authority of the 'Abbasids. In 1168 Egypt was occupied by a Syrian army and, on the death of al-'Adid (1171), the caliphate was abolished by Nur al-Din's general, **SALADIN**. ➤ **'ABBASID DYNASTY**

**Faure, Edgar Jean** (1908–88)
French politician. He entered politics as a radical, before becoming a Gaullist. He was Minister of Finance and Economic Affairs several times in the 1950s, becoming Premier for two short periods (1952 and 1955–6). He was later Minister of Agriculture (1966), Education (1968) and Social Affairs (1969), and President of the National Assembly (1973–8). He became a Member of the European Parliament in 1979.

**Faure, (François) Félix** (1841–99)
French politician. A merchant and shipowner in Le Havre, he became a Deputy for that town in 1881 and, after holding posts in several administrations, in Jan 1895 he succeeded **CASIMIR-PÉRIER** as President of the French Third Republic. He was a moderate republican, whose period in office was notable for the strengthening of links with Russia, and rocky diplomatic relations with the UK following the **FASHODA INCIDENT**. It was during his presidency that Madagascar was declared a French colony. ➤ **REPUBLIC, THIRD** (France)

**favela**
The original *favela* was erected on the Morro de Castelo in Rio de Janeiro by the families of soldiers returning from the **CANUDOS CAMPAIGN** of 1897, to beg for their salaries. Currently, the word is a generic term for shanty towns around Rio and the southern cities of Brazil. *Favelas* have their own distinctive political organizations and provide housing for the low paid, and support for populist politicians and popular religious sects alike.

**Favre, Jules Claude Gabriel** (1809–80)
French lawyer and politician. He took part in the **JULY REVOLUTION** of 1830, defended Felice **ORSINI** (the Italian revolutionary executed for his abortive attempt to assassinate Emperor **NAPOLEON III**), became a republican leader, and after the fall of Napoleon III became Foreign Minister in the Government of **NATIONAL DEFENCE**, and in **THIERS'** first government, in which capacity he negotiated the Treaty of Frankfurt in 1871.

**Fawcett, Dame Millicent** (1847–1929)
British **WOMEN'S RIGHTS** campaigner. Keenly interested in the higher education of women and the extension of the franchise to her sex, she was made President of the National Union of Women's Suffrage Societies (1897–1919).

**Fawkes, Guy** (1570–1606)
English conspirator. Born of Protestant parentage, he became a Catholic at an early age, and served in the

Spanish army in the Netherlands (1593–1604). He crossed to England at Robert Catesby's invitation, and became a member of the **GUNPOWDER PLOT** to blow up parliament. Caught red-handed, he was tried and hanged.

**Faysal I** (1885–1933)
King of Iraq (1921/33). He was the son of **HUSAYN IBN 'ALI**, King of the Hijaz. He played a major role in the **ARAB REVOLT** of 1916, and was for a short while King of Syria after **WORLD WAR I**. Installed as King of Iraq by the British, he became a leader of Arab nationalism. He died in Berne, Switzerland.

**Faysal II** (1935–58)
King of Iraq (1939/58). He was the great-grandson of **HUSAYN IBN 'ALI**, King of the Hijaz. He succeeded his father, King **GHAZI**, who was killed in an accident, and after an education at Harrow was installed as king. In Feb 1958 he concluded with his cousin, King **HUSSEIN** of Jordan, a federation of the two countries in opposition to the **UNITED ARAB REPUBLIC** of Egypt and Syria. In July 1958 he and his entire household were assassinated during a military coup, and Iraq became a republic.

**Faysal ibn 'Abd al-'Aziz** (1904–75)
King of Saudi Arabia (1964/75). Appointed Viceroy of the Hijaz in 1926, he became Minister for Foreign Affairs in 1930, Crown Prince in 1953, and succeeded his half-brother **IBN SAUD** as King. He was assassinated in the royal palace in Riyadh by his nephew, Faysal ibn Musayd.

**fazenda**
The term used to describe a large plantation in Brazil. In colonial times (16–18c), the term was identified with cattle ranching and the production of cotton or subsistence crops, especially in the north-east and Minas Gerais, often with the use of *caboclo* (part-Indian) and free black labour using huge tracts of land. Similar to ranches in other parts of Latin America, north-eastern *fazendas* employed very few slaves; only in Minas were slaves introduced to supply food for the mining camps. By the 1840s the word had become synonymous with the *fazenda do café* (coffee-estate), especially in the Valley of the Paraíba, using large-scale slave labour and **AGREGADOS**, displacing local *sitiantes*. Such fazendas became ever more mechanized and specialized; by 1900, they employed immigrant **COLÔNOS** and freedmen, and grew millions of coffee trees. Land-hungry, the fazendas surged across the high-quality western plateau of São Paulo into Paraná. By the 1980s the term applied to any large-scale extensive farming enterprise producing cash crops (such as the **HACIENDA**). The diminutive form of the word, *fazendola*, implies small-scale landholding, not producing significant cash crops. ➤ **SITIANTE**

**fazendeiro**
The owner of a **FAZENDA**; the head of the patriarchal family, exercising quasi-regal powers within its lands. These lands were often obtained by a combination of force – the dispossession of *posseiros* (squatters) or *sitiantes* (smallholders) – and possession of royal land grants (*sesmarías*). Generally, the term is synonymous with 'slaveowner', since slaves performed many functions in both pastoral, cotton and coffee

culture. Currently, *fazendeiros* exercise control over labour forces (*bois-frias*) in surrounding and tributary areas. This has generally been achieved by influence over *vendas*, or general stores, which offered credit to **COLÔNOS**, posseiros and sitiantes. ► **SITIANTE**

### Fazl al-Haq (1873–1962)
Bengali Muslim leader. Formerly a lawyer, teacher and journalist in Calcutta, the reunification of Bengal in 1912 saw Haq become a political leader of the Muslims. He became Secretary and then President of the **MUSLIM LEAGUE**, and was chiefly concerned with the political organization of rural interest groups. Haq was Chief Minister of Bengal from 1937 to 1943. After breaking with the Muslim League in 1941, he reconstructed his ministry with the help of Hindus. In Pakistan he was first Advocate-General of East Pakistan and then its Chief Minister, before being appointed Governor (1956–8).

### Fazl-i Husain (1877–1936)
Punjabi Muslim political leader. He participated in both Congress and **MUSLIM LEAGUE** activities in Punjab. Husain saw the 1919 reforms as advantageous to the Punjabi Muslims, for these would give the Muslims a Legislative Council majority. Thus, he opposed the non-cooperation boycott of the legislatures and was elected to the Punjab council. He served afterwards in various high offices in the Punjab government and in the government of India, handling education and revenue. Husain was a strong supporter of separate Muslim electorates and intervened successfully to prevent his fellow-Muslims from surrendering these during negotiations in 1930–1. ► **NON COOPERATION MOVEMENT**

### FBI (Federal Bureau of Investigation)
The US organization primarily concerned with internal security or counter-intelligence operations, although it also has responsibility for investigating violations of federal law not remitted by the federal government to any other organization. The FBI is a branch of the Department of Justice. ► **CIA**; **HOOVER, J EDGAR**

### FDP (*Freie Demokratische Partei*, 'Free Democratic Party')
German political party. Founded in the Federal Republic in Dec 1948, the FDP was the successor to previous German liberal parties. Initially a centre-right party with close links to business, the FDP adopted a centre-left slant in its Freiburg Theses (1971), which included support for economic democracy (**MITBESTIMMUNG**), equal opportunity in education and the fostering of individual political responsibility. The FDP has always been a minority party, typically gaining 10 per cent of the vote (and therefore 10 per cent of seats in the **BUNDESTAG**). However, this has enabled it to hold the balance of power for most of the period since 1949, thereby modifying the programmes and policies of both **CDU/CSU** and **SPD** governments. FDP politicians such as Hans-Dietrich **GENSCHER** have played a major role in German government.

### FEB (*Força Expedicionária Brasileira*, 'Brazilian Expeditionary Force')
The only Latin American troops to serve in the European theatre in **WORLD WAR II**, the 25,000-strong FEB fought alongside the US 5th Army in Italy in 1944–5, under the command of General Mascarenhas de Moraes. Trained in US bases, combat in Italy forged a group of officers who were strongly anti-communist and committed to democracy; they were also convinced that, in the short run, arbitrary government might be necessary. Veteran FEB officers formed key groups within both the high command and the Escola Superior da Guerra. They became a diehard opposition to Getúlio **VARGAS** in 1945 and **GOULART** in 1961–4, and formed the backbone of the 1964–7 **CASTELO BRANCO** government.

### February Revolution (Czechoslovakia; 1948)
The name given by the communists to their assumption of power in Czechoslovakia. The National Front government was divided down the middle in the approach to fresh elections due in Apr or May 1948, with communists and non-communists exchanging accusations of impropriety. East–West tension was also growing. The communists resorted to extra-parliamentary tactics, whereupon the non-communists resigned to try to force an earlier election; however, it was a minority resignation. The communists called out their militia, leaving President **BENEŠ** with little alternative but to ask Klement **GOTTWALD** to take power. However, it was hardly a revolution, and the communists soon changed their monopoly position.

### February Revolution (France; 22–4 Feb 1848)
The revolution in France which resulted in the abdication of King **LOUIS-PHILIPPE**, the proclamation of a republic, and the establishment of a provisional government. Although not the first of the European revolutions of 1848, it inspired subsequent revolutionary activity in Germany and Austria. ► **REPUBLIC, SECOND** (France); **REVOLUTIONS OF 1848–9**

### February Revolution (Russia; Feb–Mar 1917)
Popular demonstrations, strikes and military mutinies in Petrograd, Russia, resulting from pre-war misgovernment and wartime privation, which led to the abdication of Tsar **NICHOLAS II** and the collapse of the Tsarist government. The old regime was succeeded by a series of provisional governments composed of ostensibly liberal and moderate socialist ministers, and simultaneously by the establishment of the Soviet ('Council') of Workers' and Soldiers' Deputies. This 'dual power' prevented the emergence of decisive government and provided the opportunity for the **BOLSHEVIKS** to prepare for their revolution, which materialized in Oct/Nov of the same year. ► **APRIL THESES**; **JULY DAYS**; **MENSHEVIKS**; **OCTOBER REVOLUTION**

### Fedayeen
Derived from the Arabic *fidai*, 'one who sacrifices oneself' (for a cause or country), the term is now generally translated as 'commando' or 'guerrilla fighter'. A number of organizations, including the **PLO** (Palestine Liberation Organization), have trained military or paramilitary groups who are termed 'fedayeen'. The word first appeared in general use in the late 11c or early 12c, when the operatives of the **ASSASSINS** of Alamut and in Syria were known thus because of their willingness to sacrifice their own lives in pursuit of their murderous objectives.

**Federal Bureau of Investigation** ► FBI

**Federal Constitutional Convention** ► CONSTITU-TIONAL CONVENTION

**Federalist Papers**
A series of 85 essays defending the US CONSTITU-TION, most of which were published in New York newspapers between Oct 1787 and Aug 1788, and subsequently collected in book form. Under the pen name of 'Publius', Alexander HAMILTON and James MADISON were the major contributors, with John JAY writing five of the articles. The papers provide important insights into the objectives sought by the framers of the US Constitution. They discuss the importance of establishing a strong centralized government while preserving state and individual freedoms. Although written in an effort to win over the citizens of New York to the constitution, the Federalist essays have become one of the most important US contributions to democratic political philosophy. ► FEDERAL-IST PARTY

**Federalist Party**
US political party that favoured a strong centralized government. It was formed in support of the domestic policies of Secretary of the Treasury, Alexander HA-MILTON, who represented the interests of merchants and men of property, and President WASHINGTON's foreign policy. Washington (in office 1789–97) and John ADAMS were Federalist Presidents, but after Thomas JEFFERSON's victory in the 1800 election, the Federalists never again held the presidency, and the party's opposition to the WAR OF 1812 led to its demise. ► HARTFORD CONVENTION

**Federal Reserve System (FRS)**
The US central banking system, set up in 1913. Under the system, the USA is divided into 12 districts, each with its own Federal Reserve Bank. The system is supervised by a central board of governors called the Federal Reserve Board. Its responsibilities include maintaining credit and monetary conditions as well as monitoring member banks. Less than half of the c.3,400 banks in the USA are members of the 'Fed'.

**federation** (Australia)
In Australian history, the events leading up to the political union of the colonies (1 Jan 1901). The eastern states of Australia gained self-government in the 1850s, and Western Australia in 1890. By the 1880s colonial development raised the issue of intercolonial trade and internal tariff barriers, while the extension of European imperialism into the Pacific raised that of defence. A Federal Council was established in 1883 which New South Wales refused to join. The rivalry between free-trade New South Wales and protectionist Victoria was the greatest of the problems federationists had to overcome. Negotiations began in earnest after Sir Henry PARKES's speech at Tenterfield (1889), arguing that federation was essential to Australian defence, led to the Australasian Federation Conference (1890) and the National Australasian Convention (1891). Agreement was reached on the US model of federation which protected state rights, with a lower house based on population, a senate representing the states, and a high court to adjudicate on constitutional disputes. Discussions continued through the 1890s, culminating in the Federal Con-

vention of 1897–8 which amended the constitution drafted in 1891. Anti-federalist interests remained powerful, and it required two referendums and further amendments before the constitution was accepted by all states.

**Federation, Festival of** (14 July 1790)
A grandiose celebration of the first anniversary of the fall of the BASTILLE, attended by delegates from all over France. It epitomized the decentralizing and libertarian aspirations of the first period of the FRENCH REVOLUTION.

**Federation Riots** (1876)
An outburst of violence in Barbados provoked by the Governor's attempt to force the Assembly to join a federation of the Windward Islands. Hennessy, a maverick Irishman, angered by the reactionary nature of the Barbadian plantocracy's attitudes towards his reforms, threatened to 'raise up the blacks, if he could not bend the whites', and gave the black estate workers to understand that it was their masters' intransigence towards the proposed federation which was holding up land reform and wage increases. In Mar 1876 disorder broke out, eight people died and troops had to be brought in from Jamaica and Guyana. The planters blamed Hennessy, claiming he was attempting to deprive Barbados of its age-old 'representative' government. Hennessy was recalled, and Barbados never submitted to CROWN COLONY GOVERNMENT, successfully resisting incorporation into the Windwards federation.

**Fehrbellin, Battle of** (1675)
A battle in which FREDERICK WILLIAM, THE GREAT ELECTOR of Brandenburg, defeated a Swedish army allied with LOUIS XIV of France. He was unable to pursue this victory with a conquest of all of Swedish Pomerania because of additional French pressure.

**Fehrenbach, Konstantin** (1852–1926)
German politician. After an early legal career, Fehrenbach was elected to the Baden state parliament in 1885 and to the REICHSTAG in 1903. On the right of the CENTRE PARTY, Fehrenbach served as President of the National (constituent) Assembly in 1919 and as German Chancellor from June 1920 to May 1921. He played a leading role in REPARATIONS negotiations with the Allies, but his willingness to make concessions was undermined by the hostility of one of his partners in the ruling coalition, the DNVP.

**Feijó, Diogo Antônio** (1784–1843)
Brazilian Roman Catholic priest and politician. Appointed Brazilian deputy to the CORTES in Lisbon in 1822, he was a deputy to the Brazilian Cortes in 1822–3, and a senator from 1833. Following the amendment of the Brazilian constitution in 1834 to allow for the creation of provincial assemblies with local power and a sole regent to be elected every four years, he became Brazil's first regent (1835), but was forced to resign two years later.

**Feijoo, Benito Jerónimo** (1676–1764)
Spanish theologian. His career as a Benedictine monk and Professor of Theology at the University of Oviedo (Asturias) spanned four reigns, and he is commonly regarded as the 'father' of the Spanish ENLIGHTENMENT. Not until the age of 50 did he begin to produce

his seminal writings. Through the nine volumes of his *Teatro Crítico* (1726–39) and the five of his *Erudite Letters* (1742–60), he reached a Spanish public to whom he introduced Newtonian science and a spirit of criticism of superstition. His work provoked considerable attacks and controversy, but in 1750 **FERDINAND VI** prohibited any further attacks on his works, which were declared to enjoy royal favour. He continued writing until 1759. His work as an early diffuser of the Enlightenment in Spain was complemented by other writers, notably Mayans i Ciscar, but he enjoyed unrivalled popularity among the élite, and numerous editions of his works were issued in the generation after his death.

**Felix V ►** AMADEUS VIII, THE PEACEFUL

**Feng Guifen (Feng Kuei-fen)** (1809–74)
Chinese scholar-official. He helped defend his native district during the **TAIPING REBELLION** and became an administrative adviser to the powerful provincial official **LI HONGZHANG** in 1864. He is credited with being one of the first Chinese scholars to advocate administrative reform and the introduction of Western technology in what became known as the **SELF-STRENGTHENING MOVEMENT** of the 1860s and 1870s.

**Feng Guozhang (Feng Kuo-chang)** (1859–1919)
Chinese militarist. He trained at the Beiyang Military Academy, one of the military schools established during the last decades of the **QING DYNASTY**. On graduating, he entered the service of **YUAN SHIKAI**, Commander of the **BEIYANG ARMY**, China's first modern army. After the creation of a republic in 1912, he became one of a number of influential militarists known as the 'Beiyang Clique'. He served as a provincial military governor before becoming Acting President of the Chinese Republic (1917–18). During his one year in office China declared war on Germany.

**Feng Kuei-fen ►** FENG GUIFEN

**Feng Kuo-chang ►** FENG GUOZHANG

**Feng Yu-hsiang ►** FENG YUXIANG

**Feng Yuxiang (Feng Yu-hsiang)** (1882–1948)
Chinese warlord. Known as the 'Christian General', he rose through the ranks to command an independent force. In 1924 he took Beijing, and set up a government which included members of the Nationalist Party. He supported the Nationalist government in 1927, but became apprehensive of the growing personal power of **CHIANG KAI-SHEK**, and joined in two successive revolts, both of which failed. He left China in 1947 to visit the USA, and died in a ship fire on his return journey. **►** GUOMINDANG; WARLORDS

**Fenian Raids**
A series of attacks on Canada from 1866 to 1870 led by the Fenian Brotherhood. The **FENIANS** (mostly New York Irish immigrants) hoped to take advantage of the anti-British sentiment felt by many Northerners in the aftermath of the **AMERICAN CIVIL WAR**, and to invade Britain's North American possessions. Once established in Canada, the Fenians hoped to force Britain to negotiate the independence of Ireland. Although they did capture Fort Erie before withdrawing, divisions within the Fenian organization and the US authorities' hostility left no real pros-

pect of success. However, their threat did encourage support for the **CONFEDERATION MOVEMENT**, especially in the Maritime Provinces.

**Fenians**
Another name for the Irish Republican Brotherhood, a nationalist organization founded in New York in 1857. As well as its attacks on Canada (1866–70), in 1867 it staged a failed rising in Ireland and carried out violent raids in Manchester and London to rescue imprisoned supporters. The fatalities that occurred caused these to be called the 'Fenian Outrages'. It was active in planning the **EASTER RISING** but was thereafter superseded by the **IRA. ►** SINN FÉIN

**Ferdinand** (1865–1927)
King of Romania (1914/27). The nephew of King **CHARLES I** of Romania, he was named as heir to the throne in 1880. He married Princess Marie of Edinburgh, granddaughter of Queen **VICTORIA** and Tsar **ALEXANDER II**. He succeeded his uncle in Oct 1914 and led Romania into **WORLD WAR I** on the side of the Allies. Romania almost doubled in size at the end of the war, and in 1922 he was crowned King of Greater Romania at Alba Iulia. Distrusting his son, the future **CHARLES II** of Romania, he named his grandson, **MICHAEL**, as his successor.

**Ferdinand I** (1503–64)
Holy Roman Emperor (1556/64). The son of **PHILIP I, THE HANDSOME**, he was the brother and successor of Emperor **CHARLES V** who, as early as 1521, made over to him the Habsburg possessions in Germany. Married to the sister of Lewis II of Hungary and Bohemia, he claimed these kingdoms on his brother-in-law's fall against the Turks in 1526. However, while he succeeded without difficulty in Bohemia, there ensued a 12-year struggle over Hungary with a Magyar rival, John Zapolya (1487–1540), before the permanent union between Austria, Bohemia and Hungary was secured. Ferdinand advocated compromise with the Protestants and negotiated the religious Peace of **AUGSBURG** (1555). The creator of a unified administration in the Austrian lands, he died in Vienna, and was succeeded by his son, **MAXIMILIAN II**.

**Ferdinand I** (1751–1825)
King of Naples, as Ferdinand IV (1759/99, 1799/1806 and 1815/16), King of Sicily, as Ferdinand III (1759/1816) and King of the **TWO SICILIES** (1816/25). Until 1777 he was guided in most aspects of his rule by his able adviser, **TANUCCI**. With the latter's fall from favour, Ferdinand came almost solely under the influence of his wife, **MARIA CAROLINA**, and her half-English, half-French lover, John Acton. It was they who persuaded him to join the anti-French coalition of 1793 and to march on French-occupied Rome in 1796. In 1798–9 a French army led by Championnet counter-attacked and seized Naples; Ferdinand was forced to flee to Sicily and the **PARTHENOPEAN REPUBLIC** was established. The French satellite was, however, short-lived, overthrown by the **SANFEDISTI**. In 1801 Ferdinand signed the Armistice of Foligno with the French, but two years later he again declared war; defeated by **NAPOLEON I**'s armies, he was replaced on the throne of Naples by Napoleon's brother, Joseph (1806). Ferdinand again fled to Sicily, placing himself under British protection until 1815.

In return for providing him with continued safe haven, the British forced Ferdinand to send away his wife (1811) and to grant a constitution (1812). In 1815 he returned to Naples, surviving an attempted insurrection by **MURAT**. After his restoration, Ferdinand avoided the worst excesses of reaction, guided by the shrewd counsel of his able minister, Prince Luigi de' Medici. Medici, however, was no liberal; nor could he restrain ultra-reactionaries, such as Prince Antonio Canosa, Chief of Police. From his appointment in 1816, the latter waged an energetic campaign against the **CARBONARI** and other sects. Canosa's measures were probably counter-productive in the long run, since the Carbonari were heavily involved in the July 1820 revolution in Naples. Led by Guglielmo **PEPE**, this bloodless coup brought about the concession of a liberal constitution. However, Pepe, faced with both a separatist rising in Sicily and an army sent by **METTERNICH** to restore the old order, was defeated by the Austrians at the Battle of Rieti. After the collapse of the revolution, the Kingdom of the **TWO SICILIES** was brought much more firmly within the Austrian sphere of influence.

### Ferdinand I (1861–1948)

Prince and first King of modern Bulgaria (1887/1918). On the abdication of Prince Alexander of Battenberg, he accepted the crown, as Prince, in 1887. Dominated at first by the Premier Stephan **STAMBOLOV**, he later took increasing control of the government. After proclaiming Bulgaria independent of the Ottoman Empire in 1908, he took the title Tsar. In 1912 he joined the Balkan League against Turkey. Allying himself with the **CENTRAL POWERS**, he invaded Serbia in 1915. His armies routed, he abdicated in 1918, to be succeeded by his son, **BORIS III**. ► **BALKAN WARS**

### Ferdinand II (1578–1637)

Holy Roman Emperor (1619/37). The grandson of **FERDINAND I**, in 1596 he assumed the government in his paternal duchies of Styria, **CARNIOLA** and **CARINTHIA**, where he pursued a policy of recatholicization with great severity and success. Nominated head of the **HABSBURG DYNASTY**, he became King of Bohemia in 1617, of Hungary in 1618 and was elected Emperor in 1619. His rigorous Catholicism and absolutist tendencies sparked off a rebellion against him in Bohemia, which developed into the **THIRTY YEARS' WAR**. After a series of spectacular successes (thanks largely to his general, **WALLENSTEIN**), he issued the Edict of **RESTITUTION** (1629), which made even many Catholic princes suspicious of his aims. The subsequent intervention of Sweden and France, as well as Wallenstein's dismissal (1630) and murder (1634), turned the war against the Habsburg forces. The compromise Peace of Prague, two years before his death in Vienna, clearly marked the failure of Ferdinand's bid to restore uniform Catholicism and imperial supremacy in Germany.

### Ferdinand II (1810–59)

King of the **TWO SICILIES** (1830/59). Despite granting a political amnesty early in his reign, Ferdinand II was even more reactionary than his predecessor, **FRANCIS I**; when his first Minister of Police, Francesco Intoni, suggested moderate liberal reforms, he was promptly exiled. Together with Intoni's replacement, Francesco Delcarretto, Ferdinand managed to make his king-

dom one of the most reactionary states in Europe. Yet despite, perhaps because of, his terror of conspiracy and insurrection, his reign was characterized by frequent uprisings, most significantly in 1848–9. In Jan 1848 insurrection in Palermo, the capital of Sicily, heralded the beginning of revolutions throughout his territories. On the mainland he managed to check the revolutionary upheavals rather more rapidly, and soon re-established his authority in Naples. His ruthless bombardment of the Sicilian city of Messina (Sep 1848) earned him the sobriquet of 'Bomba'; he was finally able to restore complete order on the island in the summer of 1849. The 1850s witnessed renewed persecution by Ferdinand of any of those who advocated reform.

### Ferdinand II, the Catholic (1452–1516)

King of Aragon and King of Castile, as Ferdinand V (1479/1516), of Sicily as Ferdinand II and of Naples as Ferdinand III (1503/16). In 1469 he married Isabella of Castile, sister of Henry IV of Castile, and ruled jointly with her until her death. He introduced the **INQUISITION** (1478–80), and in 1492, after the defeat of the **MOORS**, the Expulsion of the **JEWS**. Under him, Spain gained supremacy following the discovery of the Americas, and in 1503 he took Naples from the French, with the help of the **HOLY LEAGUE**. To him and Isabella, Spain owed her unity and greatness as a nation and the foundation of her imperial influence. ► **ISABELLA I, THE CATHOLIC**

### Ferdinand III (1200–52)

King of **CASTILE** (1217/52) and of Leon (1230/52). From 1224 he devoted himself to a series of offensives against the weakened Almohad caliphate in Andalusia. After achieving a major breakthrough with the capture of Córdoba (1236), he went on to take Jaen, Seville, Cadiz and the surrounding territories, settling his conquests with Christian inhabitants. By the time of his death he had annexed more Muslim territory than any other Spanish king, and reduced the remaining Muslim states to vassal kingdoms of Castile.

### Ferdinand III (1608–57)

Holy Roman Emperor (1637/57). The son of Emperor **FERDINAND II**, he became King of Hungary in 1625 and of Bohemia in 1627. A more moderate representative of the **COUNTER-REFORMATION** than his father, he succeeded **WALLENSTEIN** as commander of the imperial armies in 1634 and headed a peace party at the imperial court. On his succession to the imperial crown, he sought to halt the fighting, but the struggle continued for another decade, ending only with the Peace of **WESTPHALIA** (1648). Interested in philosophy and the natural sciences, he was also an accomplished musician and a notable patron of the arts.

### Ferdinand VI (1711–59)

King of Spain (1746/59). Having succeeded his father, **PHILIP V**, he played no active role in the government of his country, which was occupied throughout the reign in resisting English aggression in both Europe and the colonies. He had the good fortune to be served by able ministers, notably Zenón de Somodevilla, Marquis de Ensenada, who from service in the military administration rose to become Chief Secretary of State (1743–54). Ensenada's term in office was, however, balanced by the appointment in 1746 as minister of José de Carvajal. Carvajal believed in a rapprochement with England which he carried through in 1750; after his death in 1754, his policies were continued by the Irishman Ricardo Wall. Ensenada, whose lasting historical monument is the great survey (*catastro*) of **CASTILE** carried out in 1749, was removed from power in 1754, shortly after Carvajal's death, as a result of English intrigues. In 1758 Ferdinand's wife, Bárbara of Braganza, died; the King was deeply affected, and died mad the following year. ► **BRAGANZA, HOUSE OF**

**Ferdinand VII** (1784–1833)
King of Spain (1808/33). The eldest son of **CHARLES IV** and Queen Maria Luisa, he intrigued against his parents and was banished from Madrid in 1807. When **NAPOLEON I** invaded Spain in 1808, Charles abdicated in favour of his son, but Ferdinand was brushed aside by the French emperor and replaced as king by Napoleon's brother, Joseph **BONAPARTE**. For six years Ferdinand lived in exile on the estate of the French Foreign Minister, **TALLEYRAND**, at Valençay, where the treaty was signed with Napoleon in 1813 that restored him to the throne. He refused to accept Napoleon's liberal Constitution of Cadiz (1812) and inaugurated a period of counter-revolutionary terror. A revolution in 1820 obliged Ferdinand briefly to recognize the 1812 constitution but repressive **ABSOLUTISM** was reinstated three years later with the aid of French troops. The second terror lasted until his death in 1833, which signalled the outbreak of the first Carlist War (1833–9).

**Fernández de Córdoba, Gonzalo**, known as **the Great Captain** (1453–1515)
Spanish soldier. He served with distinction against the **MOORS** of Granada, and afterwards in Portugal. Sent to assist **FERDINAND II, THE CATHOLIC** in his **HOLY LEAGUE** against the French (1495), he conquered the greater part of the Kingdom of Naples, and expelled the French. When the partition of Naples was determined upon in 1500, Gonzalo again set out for Italy, but first took Zante and Cephalonia from the Turks and restored them to the Venetians. He then landed in Sicily, occupied Naples and Calabria, and ultimately won a great battle (1503) at the Garigliano River. His victory secured Naples for Spain. Recalled in 1506, and treated by the King with neglect, Gonzalo withdrew to his estates in Granada.

**Ferraro, Geraldine Anne** (1935– )
US Democrat politician. The daughter of Italian Roman Catholic immigrants, she was educated at Marymount College, Fordham University and New York Law School and, after marrying wealthy businessman John Zaccaro in 1960, established a successful law practice (1961–74). She served as assistant district attorney for the Queens district of New York between 1974 and 1978, and worked at the Supreme Court from 1978, heading a special bureau for victims of violent crime, before being elected to the **HOUSE OF REPRESENTATIVES** in the same year. In **CONGRESS**, she gained a reputation as an effective, liberal-minded politician and was selected in 1984 by Walter Mondale to be the first female vice-presidential candidate of a major party, in an effort to add sparkle to the Democrat ticket. After the Demo-

crats' convincing defeat, she returned to private law practice and in 1992 unsuccessfully sought the New York Democratic nomination for US Senator. In 1994 and 1995 she served as US representative on the **UN** Human Rights Commission.

**Ferrer, Francisco** (1849–1909)
Spanish anarchist and educationist. A follower of the Republican **RUIZ ZORRILLA**, Ferrer participated in the abortive Villacampa rising of 1886, the last Republican rising for over 40 years. In 1901 he established the *Escuela Moderna* ('Modern School') in Barcelona, an influential secular and experimental school following libertarian principles. He was made a scapegoat for the popular rising of the **TRAGIC WEEK** in July 1909. His execution in Oct 1909 caused an international outcry, which contributed to the fall from power of the conservative Prime Minister Antonio **MAURA**.

**Ferry, Jules François Camille** (1832–93)
French politician. Secretary of the Government of **NATIONAL DEFENCE**, he was Mayor of Paris during the siege (1870–1) and incurred popular hostility. He became Minister of Public Instruction in 1879 and Prime Minister (1880–1). **GAMBETTA**'s death made him the undisputed leader of the moderate republicans, and his second period as Prime Minister (1883–5) saw major reforms. A modern education system was created (state primary education became free, compulsory and secular), constitutional reforms were voted, and a vast colonial empire acquired, in Madagascar and Indo-China. A trivial incident there (the Lang-son Incident, in which it was wrongly reported that the French army had suffered a major defeat at the hands of the Chinese) led to the fall of his government (Mar 1885); he never again held office, although he had just been elected President of the Senate, when he died. ► **PARIS, SIEGE OF**

**Fersen, Fredrik Axel von** (1719–94)
Swedish soldier and politician. A descendant of the Scottish Macphersons, he served successively in the French and Swedish armies and was made a field marshal in 1770. He was leader of the Hat Party in the 1750s and 1760s and, after the victory of the rival Caps in 1765, cooperated with the Court Party to work for an increase in royal power. This was achieved after the coup d'état of King **GUSTAV III** in 1771, but Fersen became disillusioned with the new monarch and joined the opposition to him.

**Fersen, Hans Axel von** (1755–1810)
Swedish soldier and politician. The son of Count Fredrik Axel von **FERSEN**, he fought as a volunteer with the French army in America during the War of Independence. On his return, he served at the French court, where he became closely attached to Queen Marie Antoinette. In 1791, disguised as a coachman, he drove the royal family on their flight to Varennes. He returned to Sweden in 1799, and in 1801 was appointed Earl Marshal. It was in this capacity that, in 1810, he rode in the funeral procession of Christian August of Augustenburg, the recently elected heir to the Swedish throne, and was murdered by a mob who suspected him of having poisoned the prince.

**Feudalism** ► *See panel*

# *Feudalism*

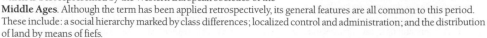

*Culture & Society*

### European feudalism

Feudalism refers to a system of social, political and economic control which is best represented by the Western European societies of the **Middle Ages**. Although the term has been applied retrospectively, its general features are all common to this period. These include: a social hierarchy marked by class differences; localized control and administration; and the distribution of land by means of fiefs.

### Feudal society

The essence of feudalism lay in the relationship between an overlord and his vassal, the latter proffering his services to the lord in return for a fief, an area of land variable in size. This land could in turn be sub-let to tenants, who would likewise perform tasks in accordance with their social position. The process by which an individual became a vassal was known as 'homage'. This symbolic act of surrender involved kneeling before a lord and giving over joined hands to be clasped by him. The vassal was also required to swear an oath of fidelity, or fealty, to the lord, promising to harm neither the lord nor his property. In return the vassal was handed an object representing his fief and the protection which the lord would bestow upon him.

Established upon the concept that all land was the divinely ordained property of the king, the feudal system encompassed a hierarchy of nobles, ranging from the top tier of large estate owners down to *seigneurs*, who were manor lords and vassals of those higher up the social ladder. The type of duty required of a knight in the service of his lord was originally one of either personal sacrifice or knight service. This could involve fighting on behalf of the lord or king, or recruiting fighters through other means. In the 12c this was replaced by *scutage*, the payment of a fee exempting one from active service. Yet service could theoretically be insisted upon by the king, leading to dissent among the increasingly powerful nobility. The **Magna Carta** of 1215 resulted in part from the attempts of **Richard I** to impose a standard scutage tax and extensive feudal duties on the English barons. The document, curtailing the powers of the monarch, was met with papal rebuke and provoked widespread baronial revolt.

The result of this system was a highly fragmented and localized society, in which a nobleman was answerable only to his overlord and wielded supreme authority over the workers on his land. While altering profoundly the relationship between lords and peasants, the feudal system also extended to the Church; lords influenced the appointments of bishops and abbots, who would offer prayers and supplication for their beneficiaries in return for employment and protection. Furthermore, the law courts were soon to become full of vassals, presiding over cases relating to their lords' estates. Indeed, these courts had supreme authority over minor and intermediate affairs, leaving the major offences to be dealt with by the Crown.

### Origins

An early form of feudalism existed in the Frankish lands of Western Europe in the 8c. All land was traditionally the property of the monarch, therefore prospective tenants had to petition the king for a *benefice*, or land grant, which lasted for one lifetime. Gradually the concept of providing land in return for acts of service emerged, allowing a king or lord to retain ownership of, and access to, the land they granted. Benefices were soon to disappear altogether, replaced by hereditary fiefs as royal power increasingly gave way to regional dynasties. The system spread south and east as it matured and became the dominant European social and military structure. The Crusades carried it as far as Jerusalem and the **Normans** brought it to all of the British Isles except the Gaelic west of Ireland.

### The manorial system

The decline of the Roman Empire in the West during the 4–5c led to much social instability and concern among the

---

### Feuillants, Club of the

An association of moderate Deputies and former members of the Jacobin Club, led by the Marquis of **LAFAYETTE**, Antoine **BARNAVE** and Jean **BAILLY**, who aimed at establishing a constitutional monarchy in France during the first stage of the Revolution (1791). ► **FRENCH REVOLUTION**; **JACOBINS**

### FFI (*Forces français de l'intérieur*, 'French Interior Forces')

The armed forces of the French Resistance within France, as distinct from the **FREE FRENCH** fighting overseas; they played an important part in the battle for the liberation of France, and were incorporated into the regular army in Nov 1944. ► **RESISTANCE MOVEMENT** (France); **WORLD WAR II**

### Fianna Fáil

Irish political party founded in 1926 by those opposed to the 1921 Anglo-Irish Treaty. It first came to power under **DE VALERA** in 1932, and has been the governing party for most of the period since. In the 1930s it emphasized separation from the UK, and has consistently supported the unification of Ireland.

In domestic issues its approach is more pragmatic than ideological.

### Fielding, William Stevens (1848–1929)

Canadian journalist and politician. Liberal Premier of Nova Scotia, he threatened to secede in 1886 if the federal government refused to lower tariffs and re-dress other provincial complaints. In 1896 he became the Finance Minister in **LAURIER**'s administration and introduced a two-tier tariff system that answered the needs of farmers for a low tariff while still maintaining some high rates to protect manufacturers. In 1910 he negotiated a trade agreement with the USA which, like his earlier system, took into account the needs of both agriculture and industry. While the US **CONGRESS** ratified it in the summer, the Conservatives under Robert Laird **BORDEN** filibustered the bill in the House of Commons. In response Laurier called an election, the government was defeated, and Fielding lost his seat. ► **LIBERAL PARTY** (Canada)

### Field of the Cloth of Gold (June 1520)

The ceremonial meeting in Picardy between **HENRY**

peasants for their security. As a result, seigneurs turned to the system adopted by Roman landowners of giving protection and accommodation to workers in exchange for their service, property or even freedom. These tenures would come in either free or unfree form, the various services conferred upon the tenant largely depending on his social position. This was known as the manorial system, the foundation upon which feudal society was based.

The free worker would be employed in a certain amount of agricultural service each year, called *socage*. In addition, there were certain conditions required by the landowner of those living under his authority. 'Relief' demanded a payment to the landowner upon the transfer of a fief to an heir while *'escheat'* meant the return of a fief to a lord when no heir was apparent. Payment and permission was also required when the tenant's daughter wished to be married.

The peasant class was generally prescribed an unfree tenure, or *villeinage*, where service was administered at the discretion of the lord. The villeins who performed this service were entirely at the mercy of their lord's will, having no power to leave their employment but every chance of being indiscriminately released from service. This practice was eventually removed in Britain, and replaced by copyheld tenure, which allowed peasants to pay rent rather than performing active service for their residency.

### Decline of the feudal system

As Britain moved into the 13–14c, society moved away from feudal control towards a more centralized state administration. With the increase in trade and communication came the prominence of large towns as economic and social centres. This posed a threat to the manorial system, which relied on its self-contained nature and mutually beneficial lord–peasant relationship for its continued existence. The wealth and opportunity present in the large towns proved alluring to both peasant and noble, offering employment for the former and a new market for the latter. Villeins were increasingly able to buy their freedom or forgo their duties by paying a basic rent to the overlord. Indeed the peasant class contributed to their emancipation by revolting during this period, signalling a rejection of their former subservient existence.

### Japanese feudalism

The origins of Japanese feudalism, which closely parallels that of its European equivalent, lie in the disintegration of imperial rule in 8c Japan. The growth of private estates, or *shoen*, caused a fragmentation of central administration as these estates gained increasing autonomy from imperial control. This situation promoted important families such as the **Fujiwara** to positions of local authority, weakening the Emperor's power in the process.

### Kamakura Shogunate

Central authority returned in the late 12c with the rise to power of Minamoto no Yoritomo (1147/99), who established his *bakufu* military administration in Kamakura. In 1192 Yoritomo's sovereignty was given imperial recognition and he became the first **shogun** general of the **Kamakura Shogunate**, a military dictatorship which was to remain in power until 1333. This period was characterized by the increasing prominence of the *shugo*, who were appointed by the shogun as military governors of local administrations. Initially their role included both the administration of troops and peace-keeping duties; this soon extended to the control of law and order, further undermining central imperial authority.

With time, however, the increasing power of the shugo threatened to usurp the existing shogunate authority. **Ashikaga Takauji**, a warrior leader, rebelled against his superiors and overthrew the Kamakura Shogunate, placing an emperor on the throne who would meet his every demand. Takauji subsequently became shogun in 1338.

### Ashikaga Shogunate

The period of Ashikaga rule from 1338 to 1573 saw the emergence of a new class of military leader: the **daimyo**, or feudal lord. Having been granted territorial powers by the shogunate, the daimyo exercised great control over their estates, granting fiefs to vassals who repaid them with military service. The vassals, later **samurai**, were the warrior class who lived under the **bushido** code of honour. This demanded absolute loyalty to the shugo master and viewed death as the

---

**VIII** of England and **FRANCIS I** of France. Francis was trying (in vain) to woo England away from its alliance with the Emperor **CHARLES V**. The lavish finery of the occasion gave the meeting its name, and enhanced the standing of the English monarchy.

**Fierlinger, Zdenek** (1891–1976)

Czechoslovak diplomat and politician. He was appointed ambassador in Moscow in 1937 and therefore played an important role in maintaining a liaison between Edvard **BENEŠ** and **STALIN** before, during and after the **MUNICH AGREEMENT**, and again following the Soviet entry into **WORLD WAR II**. A social democrat by persuasion, he inclined increasingly to the communist point of view, was Prime Minister in the interim post-war government 1945–6, and then Minister of Industry in Klement **GOTTWALD**'s coalition government between 1946 and 1948. In Feb 1948 he played a crucial role in persuading most of the social democrats to join the communists in taking over power and putting an end to traditional Czechoslovak democracy for more than 40 years. His influence declined particularly after Gottwald's death

in 1953, but he remained useful for propaganda purposes.

**Fieschi, Giovanni Luigi de, Count** (c.1523–1547)

Italian nobleman. He belonged to a Genoese noble line which by tradition feuded with the Doria, who had restored republican government in Genoa. In 1547 Fieschi and his brothers organized an unsuccessful plot to establish an oligarchy. However, Fieschi, stepping from one galley to another at night, fell overboard, and was drowned in the harbour. The scheme ended there, and the Doria returned to wreak merciless vengeance on the other plotters.

**Fifteen Rebellion**

The name given to the first of the Jacobite rebellions against Hanoverian monarchy to restore the Catholic Stuart Kings to the British throne. The rising began at Braemar (Sep 1715), with the Earl of Mar proclaiming James Edward **STUART** (the 'Old Pretender') as King. Jacobite forces were defeated at Preston in Nov, and the rebellion collapsed early in 1716. ➤ **JACOBITES**; **STUART, HOUSE OF**

honourable alternative to capture. In contrast to the pretensions of the shugo, theirs was a frugal existence which valued swordsmanship over material wealth.

The growing status of the daimyo was tempered by their limited sphere of influence, instilling a desire for expansion and conflict among the most powerful feudal lords. The most notable result of this was the **Onin War** of 1467–77, a dispute over the shogunal succession. The struggles continued into the 16c, causing the number of daimyo to fall dramatically as power became concentrated in the hands of a few. The period leading up to the establishment of the **Tokugawa Shogunate** in 1603 marked a determined military effort to suppress the daimyo. This was led by **Tokugawa Ieyasu** and achieved its aim of stripping power from the daimyo and uniting them under the authority of the new shogunate.

### Tokugawa Shogunate
The decisive Battle of **Sekigahara** in 1600 paved the way for Tokugawa Ieyasu to claim the title of shogun in 1603. The Tokugawa Shogunate was to be the most enduring and successful of the three military dictatorships, surviving for over 250 years until 1867. The relative harmony of this period was achieved through a combination of daimyo control and a policy of national exclusion. The resulting social order was surprisingly similar to the European feudal model, though on a national rather than a local scale.

Controlling daimyo activity was essential in the aftermath of the succession struggles of the late 16c, from which three distinct categories of daimyo emerged: *fudai*, the hereditary vassals who had supported the Tokugawa accession; *shimpan*, non-hereditary kinsmen; and *tozami*, those opposed to the new regime. While still exerting considerable authority at a local level, the daimyo were now forced to swear an oath of fealty to the shogun in exchange for land, the amount of which was controlled. A limited number of vassals were required to stay in the grounds of the daimyo's estate, whether as fief holders or salaried retainers. By comparison, the influence of the samurai was steadily growing during this period, as the shogunate officially acknowledged their status and allowed them to carry two swords, leaving them as the only weapon holders among the four hereditary classes of samurai, farmers, craftsmen and merchants.

In order to further limit daimyo autonomy, the shogunate established the **Alternate Attendance System** in the 17c. Daimyo were obliged to spend six months annually in Edo (now Tokyo), the Tokugawa capital. During the remaining months of the year the family of the daimyo were kept in Edo, providing both a financial and emotional burden on the daimyo and assuring his compliance with shogun rule. In addition to this system, Tokugawa law was established nationwide, removing local jurisdiction.

The Tokugawa policy of national exclusion, or **Sakoku**, was adopted in response to the worldwide spread of Christianity and the threat posed by this to the Japanese political set-up. The Sakoku policy was manifested in five directives from 1633 to 1639; these outlawed Christian missions and foreign trade, and had the additional aim of preventing daimyo from growing wealthy through foreign trade links. Nevertheless, some trading did occur with the Dutch, the Chinese and the Koreans, laying the foundations for a more open-minded approach to foreign affairs in the 18–19c.

### Downfall of the feudal system: the Meiji Restoration
The status of the daimyo diminished with the sanctions described above, and the rise of the samurai to positions of local and military authority left them increasingly powerless. A crisis in agriculture, their principal source of income, sounded the death knell for their extravagant lifestyles.

The growth of industry in 19c Japan established Edo, Osaka and Kyoto as urban trade centres, generating a centralization of power and administration which undermined local estates. As anti-Tokugawa feeling grew among the tozami estates, the return of centralized imperial power seemed increasingly likely. Choshu and Satsuma samurai revolted in 1867, causing the overthrow of the shogunate, and prepared the way for the **Meiji Restoration** of 1868.

---

### Fifth Amendment (1791)
Amendment to the **US CONSTITUTION** which protects against self-incrimination. This gained notoriety during the **COLD WAR** anti-communist investigations, when 'taking the Fifth' became synonymous with an admission of guilt. More important constitutionally, however, has been the amendment's clause prohibiting the deprivation of 'life, liberty, or property without due process of law'. Before the **AMERICAN CIVIL WAR** it was used to defend **SLAVERY** (**DRED SCOTT V SANDFORD**), and afterwards, when this clause was incorporated into the **FOURTEENTH AMENDMENT**, it was used as an argument (known as 'substantive due process') against economic regulation.

### fifth column
A popular expression from the early days of **WORLD WAR II** to describe enemy sympathizers who might provide active help to an invader. The name originally described the rebel sympathizers in Madrid in 1936 during the **SPANISH CIVIL WAR**, when four rebel columns were advancing on the city.

### Fifth Monarchists
A millenarian religio-political grouping in England in the 1650s which believed that the second coming of Christ was imminent. The name derived from the Bible (Daniel 2.44), adherents seeking a 'fifth monarchy' to succeed the empires of Assyria, Persia, Greece and Rome. Though radical Puritans, Fifth Monarchists did not form a coherent sect. They opposed the new Establishment represented by the **PROTECTORATE** of Oliver **CROMWELL** supported by the army after the dissolution of **BAREBONE'S PARLIAMENT** (1653). Under Thomas Venner, they mounted uprisings against both Cromwell (1657) and the restored monarchy of **CHARLES II** (1661); after the latter Venner was executed. ► **RESTORATION**

### 'Fifty-Four Forty or Fight'
US political slogan used by the **DEMOCRATIC PARTY** in the 1844 presidential election. It referred to the US claim to the Oregon country lying between the northern border of California (latitude 42°N) and the southern border of what is now Alaska (54° 40'N). The UK also claimed the region for similar reasons

of discovery and settlement. In spite of the expansionist arguments of Stephen Douglas and Lewis Cass in **CONGRESS**, and those of President **POLK** in his inaugural speech and his first annual message to Congress, a compromise was reached with Britain in 1846 drawing the frontier along the 49th parallel.

### Figueras, Estanislao (1819–82)
Spanish politician. For taking part in Republican plots in 1866 he was imprisoned but, after the expulsion of **ISABELLA II**, he became a member of the Republican government. On the abdication of King Amadeus I in 1873, he became President of the Spanish Republic, but soon resigned.

### Figueres (Ferrer), José Don Pepe (1906–90)
Costa Rican politician. In May 1948 he led a civilian rising against an attempt to annul the legal election of Otilio Ulate. Figueres headed a junta for 18 months, during which he carried through fundamental reforms of a social democratic nature: abolishing the armed forces; nationalizing the banking system; creating an electoral law and another law promoting rural cooperatives; and the modernization of the educational and social security systems. The constitution of 1949 embodied these reforms. He was President twice (1953–8 and 1970–4), and is commonly known as the person who created a regime strong enough to survive the buffeting of civil war in neighbouring Nicaragua and El Salvador. His son, José Maria Figueres Olsen, was President of Costa Rica from 1994 to 1998.

**FIJI** official name **Republic of Fiji**

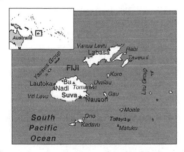

A Melanesian island group of 844 islands and islets in the south-west Pacific Ocean (c.100 permanently inhabited), forming an independent republic. Fiji was visited by **TASMAN** in 1643, and by **COOK** in 1774. It became a British colony in 1874, and gained independence within the **COMMONWEALTH OF NATIONS** in 1970. The growing size of the Indian population has been a cause of political instability in recent decades, with Fijians fearing the loss of political power. The 1987 election brought to power an Indian-dominated coalition, which led to military coups in May and Sep, and withdrawal of Fiji from the Commonwealth; a civilian government was restored in Dec. A new constitution upholding ethnic Melanesian political power was effected in 1990, but was attacked by opposition parties as racist. In 1997 the racist elements were taken out, and Fiji was readmitted to the Commonwealth. The 1999 election brought to power a multiracial coalition government headed by an ethnic Indian Prime Minister. He and most of the Cabinet were held hostage for several weeks in 2000 by indi-

genous Fijians; the military staged a coup and Fiji was again suspended from the Commonwealth. Although the courts upheld the illegality of the government installed by the military, the Great Council of Chiefs supported the interim government. In elections in 2001, the United Fiji Party won the most seats and an indigenous Melanesian government was formed.

### Filiki Etairia
Literally 'the Society of Friends', this Greek revolutionary organization was founded in Odessa in 1814 and drew its support from Greek merchants and professionals. Modelling themselves on the Freemasons, secretive and conspiratorial, its members aimed to liberate the Greeks from Ottoman rule. Hoping for Russian support, the society organized the revolt in the Danubian Principalities which marked the beginning of the **GREEK WAR OF INDEPENDENCE** (1821). ►
**MOLDAVIA AND WALLACHIA**

### Fillmore, Millard (1800–74)
US politician and 13th President. He educated himself, and became a lawyer. A member of the **HOUSE OF REPRESENTATIVES** from New York for eight years (1833–5 and 1837–43), he was elected Vice-President when Zachary **TAYLOR** won the 1848 election, becoming President (1850) on Taylor's death. A moderate on the **SLAVERY** issue, he signed the **COMPROMISE OF 1850** and tried to enforce the Fugitive Slave Act.

### Financial Action Task Force
An inter-governmental body that develops and promotes policies at national and international level to combat money-laundering. Set up in 1989 following a G7 summit, the Task Force now consists of 25 member countries and 27 international observer bodies and organizations. The Task Force's 'Forty Recommendations', launched in 1990 and revised in 1996 and 2003, outline systems and measures to deal with the threat posed by the misuse of international banking and financial institutions. In 2001, in response to the **SEPTEMBER 11 ATTACKS**, the Task Force produced a further 'Eight Special Recommendations' intended to deny terrorists and their supporters access to the international financial system. In 2000, 15 jurisdictions or countries were judged to be deficient or unwilling to co-operate with the Task Force, but by 2004 only six countries featured on its list of unco-operative nations. ► **GROUP OF 8**; **TERROR, WAR ON**

### finca
The term used to describe a substantial property in Colombia (the Chilean equivalent is *fundo*). The property, which is smaller than a **HACIENDA**, is often managed by an administrator (*mayordomo*) and produces cash crops for sale in the cities; it utilizes various forms of labour, including tenant farmers (*arrendatarios*) and day-labourers.

### Fine Gael
Irish political party created out of the pro-Anglo-Irish Treaty (1921) wing of **SINN FÉIN**. It was known as *Cumann na nGaedheal* from 1923 until it changed its name in 1933. The first government of the **IRISH FREE STATE**, it has largely been in opposition since the 1930s, and has never held power on its own. It supports the unification of Ireland by peaceful means.

**Finkenstein, Treaty of** (4 May 1807)
An agreement negotiated between France and Persia, which provided for French cooperation with Persia by way of the supply of material and aid by military advisers, in an attempt to force the Russians to leave Georgia. The Persian side of the agreement was the provision of assistance to France should she decide to invade India.

---

**FINLAND** official name **Republic of Finland**

A republic in northern Europe, bounded to the east by Russia; to the south by the Gulf of Finland; to the west by the Gulf of Bothnia and Sweden; and to the north by Norway. Finland was ruled by Sweden from 1157 until its cession to Russia in 1809. In the 19c it became an autonomous grand duchy of the Russian tsar, and a nationalist movement developed. It became an independent republic in 1917 and its parliamentary system was created in 1928. It was invaded by the USSR in 1939 and 1940 in the RUSSO-FINNISH WAR, and lost territory to the USSR after 1944. Finland has remained neutral since WORLD WAR II. It joined the EC in 1995 and the EURO ZONE in 1998. ►
CONTINUATION WAR

**Finlandization**
Supposedly the policy of influencing the internal politics and foreign policy of a small neighbouring country by bringing pressure to bear on it. The notion refers specifically to the Soviet trade and diplomatic sanctions applied to Finland in 1958 because the Finnish government formed after the elections did not contain any communist members, although they had won a quarter of the seats. The sanctions were effective; a number of ministers resigned and a government more acceptable to the USSR was formed. But, in general, Finland retained a great freedom of action in return for unimportant concessions.

**Finnbogadóttir, Vigdís** (1930–)
Icelandic politician. Born in Reykjavik, she studied French language and literature in France and returned to Iceland to teach French in secondary school and French drama at the University of Iceland in Reykjavik. The first woman to be elected head of any state, she was first elected President against three male candidates (1980), and was re-elected three times, serving until 1996.

**Finnish–Soviet War** ► RUSSO-FINNISH WAR

**Firmian, Carlo (Karl Gotthard), Count of** (1718–82)
Austrian nobleman, administrator and diplomat. Born in Trento, Firmian became an Aulic Councillor at the remarkably young age of 22. As a young man, he travelled extensively in Europe and most especially in Italy. In 1752, he benefited from the patronage of KAUNITZ and was sent on a diplomatic mission to Naples. Then, in 1759, he was made Governor of the important Austrian province of Lombardy, where he proved an able and reforming administrator; under his administration the tax system was made more equitable and rationalized, economic restrictions were removed, and many Church privileges were abolished. Firmian's mild and tolerant rule created fertile ground for the lively academic debate epitomized in the publication of Cesare Beccaria's masterpiece; *Dei delitti e delle pene* (1764, Eng trans *On Crimes and Punishments*, 1880).

**First Fleet**
In Australian history, the name given to the 11 ships that left Portsmouth, England carrying the first European settlers to eastern Australia (1787). The fleet carried officials, 212 marines and their families, and 759 convicts plus provisions. The fleet's captain, Arthur PHILLIP, decided that BOTANY BAY was unsuitable and proceeded north to Sydney Cove, Port Jackson, where he hoisted the British flag (26 Jan 1788).

**Firuz Shah Tughlaq** (1305–88)
Tughlaq ruler of the Kingdom of Delhi (1351/88). As the third Tughlaq ruler of the kingdom, Firuz Shah restored peace and order to his realm, encouraged agriculture, and implemented irrigation schemes (traces of his canals still remain). He indulged a passion for building and founded a new capital, Firuzabad, which is part of present-day Delhi. Firuz Shah embarked on various military missions, with mixed results. During his reign there was a disastrous attempt to transfer the capital from Delhi to Daulatabad.

**Fisher, Andrew** (1862–1928)
British-born Australian politician. A coalminer from the age of 12, he emigrated to Queensland in 1885. From mining, he gradually moved into trade union activity and politics, entering the Queensland state assembly in 1893 and the first federal parliament in 1901. He became AUSTRALIAN LABOR PARTY (ALP) leader in 1907 and then Prime Minister (1908–9, 1910–13 and 1914–15). At the start of WORLD WAR I he made the dramatic promise to support the war effort 'to the last man and the last shilling'. He was Australian High Commissioner in London (1916–21).

**Fisher, John Arbuthnot Fisher, 1st Baron** (1841–1920)
British admiral. He joined the navy as a boy in 1854, and rose to be First Sea Lord (1904–10 and 1914–15). His major reforms of the Royal Navy prepared the country for WORLD WAR I, including the introduction of the 'Dreadnought' battleship and 'Invincible' cruiser. He was made a peer in 1909.

**FitzGerald, Garrett Michael** (1926–)
Irish politician. He became a barrister and a lecturer in political economy (1959–73). In 1969 he was elected FINE GAEL member of the Irish parliament for Dublin South-East and was leader of the Fine Gael

Party (1977–87). He became Minister for Foreign Affairs (1973–7) and Prime Minister (1981–2 and 1982–7).

## Fiume (Rijeka)
Port in Croatia of mixed Slav and Italian population. Although not included in the areas promised to Italy by the Treaty of **LONDON** (1915), Fiume was claimed by the Italian delegation at the **PARIS PEACE CONFERENCE**. Italian claims were rejected and the port was afforded free city status, but in Sep 1919 it was seized by the Italian poet Gabriele **D'ANNUNZIO** and a band of nationalist 'legionaries' who ran it as an independent 'Italian producers' republic'. By the Treaty of **RAPALLO** (12 Nov 1920), Yugoslavia and Italy agreed that Fiume should regain free city status and in Jan 1921 D'Annunzio was ejected by the Italian navy. Free city status was, however, never restored, the terms of Rapallo being abandoned on **MUSSOLINI**'s seizure of power. In Jan 1924 Yugoslavia recognized Fiume as Italian, although the adjoining harbour of Susak remained under Yugoslavian control. At the end of **WORLD WAR II**, it became part of the Republic of Croatia within the Socialist Federal Republic of Yugoslavia.

## Five Civilized Tribes
The native tribes (Chickasaws, Creeks, Choctaws, Cherokees, Seminoles) who originally inhabited the present south-east USA, so called because they adapted relatively easily to the European way of life. Nevertheless, they were forced to leave the area under the Removal Act of 1830, and were relocated west of the Mississippi River. Large numbers of **NATIVE AMERICANS** died as a result of exposure, disease and the hardships suffered en route and in the new **INDIAN TERRITORY**. The name given to the **CHEROKEE** ordeal, the '**TRAIL OF TEARS**', sums up the fate of these tribes. ➤ **CHICKASAW**; **CREEK**; **CHOCTAW**; **SEMINOLE**

## Five Dynasties and Ten Kingdoms Period ➤ CHINESE DYNASTIES PRE-1000AD

## Five-Year Plans
Independent India adapted this model (initiated in the USSR under **STALIN** in 1928) for organizing the economy during the 1950s. The Indian Planning Commission was set up in 1950 to enable the government to supervise economic development. The commission was asked to assess development resources, formulate a national five-year plan, and assess progress; the first plan was implemented during the period 1951–6. The plans covered the activities of both central and state governments, although states controlled their own plans.

## Flandin, Pierre Étienne (1889–1958)
French politician. From 1914 to 1940 he was President of the *Alliance démocratique* ('Democratic Alliance'), a moderate republican group. He frequently held cabinet office, notably as Finance Minister (1931–2); as Prime Minister (1934–5) he vainly tried to solve the economic crisis by deflation, and to counterbalance the German threat by joining with Italy in the Stresa front. He supported appeasement, and voted for **PÉTAIN** in 1940. He was briefly in office under **VICHY** (14 Dec 1941), which ended his active political career.

## Flemish Movement
A cultural and political emancipation movement in Belgium, aimed at the recognition of the rights of the Dutch-speaking inhabitants of the northern part of the country (Flanders) as opposed to the interests of the French-speaking inhabitants of southern Belgium (Wallonia) and, increasingly, of the capital Brussels. Born of the Belgian Revolution, it was originally a cultural movement concerned principally with the recognition of Flemish (the Belgian form of Dutch) as a language in literature, education and politics. Many petitions and pressure-groups resulted in a number of language laws in the 1870s and 1880s which recognized the existence of Flemish; as the suffrage was widened in 1893 beyond the Francophone bourgeoisie, the movement gained political power and achieved an 'Equality Law' in 1898, giving the two languages equal status. There followed a long dispute over the University in Ghent, which the movement wanted as a Dutch-language institution; this was finally agreed in 1930. During both World Wars, elements of the Flemish Movement chose to work with the German authorities in the hope of achieving their aims; this brought the movement into some temporary disrepute. Since then, the Flemish Movement has ridden on the rising economic power of coastal Flanders, and has contributed to the political federalization of Belgium, culminating in 1993 in the amendment of the constitution to create a federal state. Belgium now consists of three autonomous regions: the Walloon Region (Wallonia), the Flemish Region (Flanders) and the bilingual Brussels-Capital Region.

## Fleury, André-Hercule de ('1653–1/43)
French prelate and politician. Replacing the Duke de Bourbon as Chief Minister (1726), he was made cardinal, and effectively controlled the government of **LOUIS XV** until 1743. Through skilful diplomacy he limited French involvement in the War of the **POLISH SUCCESSION** (1733–8), restoring the country's prestige as a mediator.

## FLN (*Front de Libération Nationale*, National Liberation Front)
An organization founded in the early 1950s which campaigned and fought for Algerian independence from France, under the leadership of Ahmed **BEN BELLA**. The war with the FLN led to the collapse of the French Fourth Republic in 1958, and the return to power of de **GAULLE**. France's inability to defeat the FLN led to the Evian conference in 1962, and complete Algerian independence. ➤ **OAS**; **REPUBLIC, FOURTH** (France)

## Flodden, Battle of (9 Sep 1513)
A victory of the English over the Scots, fought in Northumberland. King **JAMES IV** of Scotland, allied with France, invaded England in Aug, but was defeated by English forces under Thomas Howard, Earl of Surrey. The Scottish dead included James, 13 earls and three bishops; the battle ended the Scottish threat for a generation.

## Flood, Henry (1723–91)
Irish politician. He became leader of the popular party in the Irish parliament after his election in 1759. In 1775 he became Vice-Treasurer of Ireland,

but was removed in 1781 as a strong nationalist. In 1783 he was returned for Winchester, and in 1785 for Seaford, but he failed to make a great mark at Westminster.

**Floquet, Charles Thomas** (1828–96)
French lawyer and radical politician. He opposed the Second Empire, and was elected to the National Assembly in 1871 as a republican. Having resigned in Apr 1871, he sought to mediate between the government and the **PARIS COMMUNE**. He was elected to the Chamber of Deputies in 1876, was President of the Chamber (1885–8, 1889–93) and Prime Minister (1888–9). Floquet opposed 'Boulangism' and wounded the movement's leader, Georges **BOULANGER**, in a duel in 1888. His political influence waned after his implication in the Panama scandal of 1893, although he was later a Senator (1894–6). ► **EMPIRE, SECOND** (France)

**Flores, Juan José** (1801–64)
Ecuadorean politician. One of **BOLÍVAR**'s principal aides, he fought with distinction in the **SPANISH-AMERICAN WARS OF INDEPENDENCE** and became the first President of Ecuador (1830–5 and 1839–43) after the collapse of **GRAN COLOMBIA**. Illiterate and capricious, he imposed an autocratic constitution in 1830. As the representative for conservative Quito, he alternated in government with his Liberal opponent, Vicente Rocafuerte (1835–9), returning in 1839 and retaining power until 1845. He eventually sided with Gabriel **GARCÍA MORENO** against the Liberals of Guayaquil, under Guillermo Franco, to create a conservative state in 1860.

**Floridablanca, Count of** (1728–1808)
Spanish administrator and minister. A leading member of the group of civil servants and ministers under **CHARLES III** that aimed to modernize the monarchy. A cautious and conservative civil servant, he planned the road system radiating from Madrid. He was also the architect of the French alliance, the cornerstone of Spain's foreign policy until the war with France in 1793. Chief Minister (1777–92) during the last years of Charles III's reign, his hostility to revolutionary France hastened the end of his ministerial career because he was unable to resolve Franco-Spanish relations.

**Floris V** (1254–96)
Count of Holland (1256/96). He was the son of Count William II (1227–56), who was murdered when Floris was a baby. A regency ensued, first by his uncle, Floris the Guardian (c.1228–1258), and then by his aunt, Aleidis of Holland (d.1284), who was replaced in 1263 by Otto II of Gelre (c.1200–1271). In 1266, at the age of 12, he was declared of age, and succeeded to his title in order to escape the Gelre influence. In c.1270 he married Beatrix, daughter of the Count of Flanders. Floris was responsible for an expansion of the Count's power within his own territory, and also for territorial gain, mainly at the expense of the Bishop of Utrecht and the West Frisians, whom he finally defeated in 1289. As King **EDWARD I** of England's principal ally on the Continent against the French, he won the English wool staple for the Holland town of Dordrecht in 1295, but then changed sides to support the French.

This resulted in his kidnap by some of his nobles, who intended to send him to England; he was, however, murdered when others tried to effect his release.

**Flourens, Gustave** (1838–71)
French republican politician. He distinguished himself by his book, *La Science de l'homme* (1865); as an ardent republican, he took part in the Cretan insurrection against the Turks (1866), and fell fighting for the **PARIS COMMUNE** (1871).

**FNLA** (*Frente Nacional de Libertação de Angola*, 'National Front for the Liberation of Angola')
Formed in 1962, the FNLA established a government in exile under Holden Roberto in Zaire (now Democratic Republic of Congo) and, with US assistance, was active in northern Angola, especially after the Portuguese left the country. Poor leadership and reduced US support weakened its effectiveness and it ceased operations in the early 1980s.

**Foch, Ferdinand** (1851–1929)
French marshal. He taught at the École de Guerre, proved himself a great strategist at the Battle of the **MARNE** (1914), Ypres, and other **WORLD WAR I** battles, and became Allied Commander-in-Chief in Mar 1918. He quarrelled with the Prime Minister, **CLEMENCEAU**, about the peace settlement, regarding it as not providing adequately for French security.

**Foix, Gaston** (1489–1512)
French nobleman and soldier, nephew of **LOUIS XII** of France. He became Duke of Nemours in 1505. He twice overthrew the Swiss, at Como and Milan (1511); chased the papal troops from Bologna; seized Brescia from the Venetians (1512); and defeated the Spaniards at Ravenna, where he was killed.

**Folketinget**
Literally 'the People's Thing', the parliament of Denmark located at Christiansborg Palace in Copenhagen. It has 179 members, of whom two are elected in the Faroe Islands and two in Greenland, both self-governing regions of the Kingdom of Denmark. The members of the *Folketinget* are elected for periods of four years by universal adult suffrage. The system of voting is proportional representation. Folketinget was established by the Danish constitution of 5 June 1849 as a result of popular pressure for democratic reforms following the **FEBRUARY REVOLUTION** in France and the death of the absolute monarch, King **CHRISTIAN VIII** in 1848. The 1849 Danish parliament, *Rigsdagen*, consisted of two chambers: a lower chamber, Folketinget, and an upper chamber, *Landstinget*. In 1901 a Danish political consensus was reached to the effect that a government could not continue if a majority of the members of the Folketinget was against it, thus giving priority to the more democratically elected of the parliament's two chambers. In 1915 female suffrage was introduced in Denmark. On 5 June 1953, as part of a revision of the Danish constitution, the upper chamber of the Rigsdagen was abolished and the name Folketinget was carried on as the name of the Danish parliament as such.

**Fontenoy, Battle of** (1745)
A battle in which French forces under **LOUIS XIV** of France and Maurice, Count of **SAXE**, decisively defeated an Anglo-Dutch-Austrian army commanded

by William Augustus, Duke of **CUMBERLAND**. Fought in Hainaut in the Austrian Netherlands, the battle ensured the French conquest of Flanders in the War of the **AUSTRIAN SUCCESSION**, and was the last major military victory for a French army until the French Revolution.

### Food and Agriculture Organization (FAO)
A **UN** agency established in 1945 with the aim of improving nutritional standards and the production and distribution of food and farm products, especially to developing countries, and providing financial support in emergency situations.

### Foot, Michael Mackintosh (1913–)
British Labour politician. He joined the staff of the *Tribune* in 1937, becoming editor (1948–52 and 1955–60). He was also acting editor of the *Evening Standard* (1942–4) and a political columnist on the *Daily Herald* (1944–64). He became an MP in 1945, serving until 1992, and was Secretary of State for Employment (1974–6), Deputy Leader (1976–80) then Leader (1980–3) of the **LABOUR PARTY**, resigning after his party's heavy defeat in the 1983 general election. A prominent figure on the party's left and a pacifist, he has long been a supporter of the Campaign for Nuclear Disarmament (**CND**). A prolific writer, his best-known work is his biography of Aneurin **BEVAN**.

### Football War (July 1969)
A lightning war fought over several days between Honduras and El Salvador, which was rapidly halted by international pressure. It was provoked by the wave of migration from overpopulated Salvador to the unoccupied territories of Western Honduras, and was so named because recriminations between the two Central American states came to a head during the qualifying matches for the 1970 World Cup.

### Force Acts
In the USA, various Acts passed to enforce the federal law. In 1833 President Andrew **JACKSON** passed a Force Bill to counteract **NULLIFICATION**, and in 1870–1 three Force Acts were passed: the first (31 May 1870) enforced the Fifteenth Amendment, which gave every US citizen, regardless of race, the right to vote; the second (28 Feb 1871) augmented the first and placed congressional elections under national control in towns of populations exceeding 20,000; and the third, also called the **KU KLUX KLAN** Act (20 Apr 1871), outlawed paramilitary organizations like the Ku Klux Klan.

### forced labour camp
A prison camp where those regarded as politically undesirable or of an unwanted nationality are deported to carry out forced labour on behalf of the state. In the modern world they date back to 1918 in Soviet Russia, where millions of citizens regarded with suspicion by the authorities were sent for 'correction' in the 1920s, 1930s and 1950s. The camps were used more as a means of punishment and social control than of political correction, and most inmates died in the camps. It is estimated that at its peak there were between 12 and 15 million people in Soviet camps. **HITLER** also established forced labour camps. The camps in what was the USSR have largely disappeared since Mikhail **GORBACHEV**'s time.

### Ford, Gerald Rudolph (1913–)
US politician and 38th President. Educated at the universities of Michigan and Yale, he served in the US Navy during **WORLD WAR II**. He became a Republican member of the **HOUSE OF REPRESENTATIVES** (1949–73), and on the resignation of Spiro **AGNEW** in 1973 became the first appointed Vice-President. He became President (1974–6) when Richard **NIXON** resigned because of the **WATERGATE** scandal. The full pardon he granted to Nixon the same year, combined with an economic recession and inflation, made him unpopular, and he was defeated in the 1976 presidential election by Jimmy **CARTER**. ► **REPUBLICAN PARTY**

### Foreign Legion
The élite formation of the French army, recruited from non-French nationals. 'La Légion étrangère' was first raised in 1831, and has seen action almost wherever French arms have been engaged. Always the subject of romance and adventure, the legion retains its reputation for toughness.

### Formigny, Battle of (1450)
The decisive defeat near Bayeux (Calvados) during the **HUNDRED YEARS' WAR** of an army sent by the English government, then bankrupt and bereft of allies, to stem French advances in Normandy. Having lost their previous tactical superiority, the English were bombarded out of their positions by artillery, and routed by infantry. The French reconquest of Normandy was swiftly completed.

### Fornovo, Battle of ► ITALIAN WARS

### Forrest, John Forrest, 1st Baron (1847–1918)
Australian explorer and politician. From 1865 he was a colonial surveyor. In 1869 he explored inland from Perth; in 1870 he reached South Australia from the west along the south coast and in 1874 made the eastward journey across the centre. Surveyor General for the colony from 1883, he was the first Premier of Western Australia (1890–1901), exploiting the rise in wealth and population from the gold-rush boom of the decade to develop the port of Freemantle and provide basic services throughout the colony. An active but cautious federalist, he moved to federal politics in 1901 and was, in turn, Minister for Defence, Home Affairs and five times Treasurer in various governments (1901–18). He died at sea, off Sierra Leone.

### Forrest, Nathan Bedford (1821–77)
American Confederate general. A wealthy Mississippi cotton planter and slave trader, he joined the Confederate Army at the outbreak of the **AMERICAN CIVIL WAR**. He raised his own cavalry force, served at Shiloh and Chickamauga, and later carried out raids behind Union lines. Considered a military genius, he tarnished his reputation with the massacre of 300 blacks at Fort Pillow in Tennessee on 12 Apr 1864, but nevertheless he became a lieutenant-general in 1865. After the war he was the leading organizer and the first Grand Wizard of the **KU KLUX KLAN**, but on seeing the widespread use of violence of other members, he sought in vain to disband the organization (1869).

### Forster, William Edward (1819–86)
English politician. Born of Quaker parentage, he became Liberal MP for Bradford in 1961, rose to Cabinet

# Fortification

War & Warfare

The earliest forms of fortification were simple uses and augmentations of existing natural features. Examples of this include the hill-fort, earthwork ramparts and ditches on eminences dating from the second millennium BC, and the *crannog*, a Celtic community built on supports in a lake from the Bronze Age onwards. As building skills developed, more complex fortified structures appeared, including the ancient Greek acropolis, or citadel, and the Iron Age Scottish *broch*, a drystone tower used as a fortified home.

The building of walls to keep invaders out was another early development, notably in Mesopotamia, where in the fourth millennium BC the inhabitants built the Median Wall between the Tigris and the Euphrates, and in China, where the Great Wall, over 2,150mi/3,460km long, was begun in the 3c BC to repel attacks from the Jung and Ti nomads to the north.

The ancient Assyrians were so formidable in battle that their enemies, rather than meet them in the field, preferred to fortify their cities with thick walls of brick and stone. The Assyrian attackers had to develop siege-warfare techniques to counter this, and are recorded as using scaling-ladders and battering-rams. The ancient Egyptians protected their frontiers with fortresses, typically employing a dry moat, battlements, and balconies from which defenders could fire down at besiegers.

Roman legions on the march built fortified camps, complete with ramparts, palisades and ditches, both as safe bases in which to pass the night and as places of retreat should they be hard-pressed in battle. This pattern was copied by Charlemagne (742–814) in the fortresses he built to secure his frontiers and control unruly territories, situating them carefully on hills near rivers.

In France, Charles the Bald (823–77) built castles along the major rivers to stand against the depredations of Scandinavian raiders. The fortified Ile de la Cité in Paris was important in the successful resistance of the Viking siege of 885–6. Around the same period in England, Alfred the Great (849–99) used forts in much the same manner to combat the Danes.

The **Normans** were great masters of strategic fortification, and by the middle of the 11c they had perfected the 'motte and bailey' castle. The motte was a mound on which a wooden stockade surrounded a keep which served as the home of a baron and his family. This in turn was surrounded by a ditch. The bailey was a forecourt, originally for livestock, which was also protected by a stockade and ditch. A drawbridge could be raised to cut off access. In time, wooden keeps gave way to those made of stone, thereby countering the risk of being set on fire by attackers.

Siegecraft was slow to match the improvements in fortification, but as such weapons as bows and stone-throwing devices became more powerful, castle builders responded with great curtain walls (low walls outside the main defences) and multiple baileys, while mottes and keeps became smaller and less important. Besieging armies of this period tended to rely on starving out the defenders or undermining the walls.

This all changed, however, with the advent of cannon. As more powerful and accurate guns evolved, fortifications hitherto considered impregnable now fell to bombardment, such as in 1415 when the artillery of **Henry V** broke down the walls of Harfleur. After the devastation of medieval defences in Italy during French invasions, 16c Italian military engineers developed artillery-resistant defences. Fortifications built in the 16c were often constructed partly underground with relatively low upper structures to provide less of a target for gunners. Walls were made thicker to withstand the strike of cannonballs, covered ways were built, and outworks were reinforced. Defenders also made use of cannon and other firearms, and walls were built with bastions and *redans* (salient points with parapets) from which fire could rake attackers from numerous angles. The *glacis*, a long open slope which assault troops would have to cross under fire, was also in widespread use.

The greatest exponents of both fortification and siegecraft in the late 17c and early 18c were the French military engineer, Sébastien de **Vauban**, and his Dutch rival Menno van **Coehoorn**. Coehoorn devised a system of fortification ideally suited to the flat lands of the Netherlands, and for the violent storm tactics he used in sieges he developed a bronze mortar that later became known as the Coehoorn mortar. Vauban used ramparts of earth to absorb the impact of

---

rank, and in 1870 carried the Elementary Education Act. Under the **GLADSTONE** administration of 1880 he was Chief Secretary for Ireland. He was attacked unceasingly in parliament by the Irish members, and his life was threatened by the 'Invincibles' for his measures of coercion. A strong opponent of **HOME RULE**, he was a severe critic of Charles Stewart **PARNELL** and, determined to re-establish law and order, had him and other Irish leaders arrested. When in 1882 a majority of the Cabinet determined to release the 'suspects', Forster and Lord Cowper (the Lord Lieutenant) resigned.

## Fortescue, Sir John (c.1385–c.1479)
English jurist. He was called to the Bar, and became Lord Chief Justice of the King's Bench (1442). He sided with the Lancastrians, fled with **MARGARET OF ANJOU** and her son to Scotland, and in 1463 em-

barked with them for Holland. During exile he wrote his *De Laudibus Legum Angliae* (1537, 'In Praise of the Laws of England') for the instruction of Prince Edward, a work which came to be of great value to later jurists. After the defeat of the Lancastrians at the Battle of **TEWKESBURY**, he submitted to Edward IV. ► **LANCASTER, HOUSE OF**

## Fortification ► *See panel*

## Fort Knox
A US army post established in Kentucky in 1917. Since 1937 it has been the site of the US Bullion Depository.

## Fort Stanwix, Treaties of (1768, 1784)
Two agreements in the USA between whites and Native American tribes, the first of which established a boundary between British Crown lands and the **IROQUOIS CONFEDERACY**. The second, forced upon the

cannonballs, and the use of angled rather than rounded shapes, such as in bastions, to ensure that no area of approach was not commanded by defending fire. Vauban also used extended outworks, such as *ravelins* (two-sided embanked salients) or *demilunes* (crescent-shaped salients) in a dry moat, to compel besiegers to begin their work at a distance.

In siegecraft, Vauban introduced the method of digging trenches parallel to the perimeter of the defences and connected by zigzag-trenches to approach the enemy walls, thereby ensuring that defending fire could not be concentrated at any single point. He commanded many successful sieges, especially in the Low Countries, and his methods of both constructing and attacking fortifications remained standard practice until the latter part of the 19c, when the increasing range of artillery compelled change.

Non-European societies also developed fortification traditions. The Turks were great exponents of siege artillery, as evidenced by the manner of the Capture of **Constantinople** in 1453. The **Mughal Empire**, which had Central Asian Turkic origins, employed heavy artillery, and used massive fortifications such as the Red Fort (Lal Quila) in Delhi, built in the 17c by the Emperor **Shah Jahan**. Significantly, his successor **Aurangzeb** built a protective barbican to shield the Lahore Gate from siege guns.

In both Japan and China truly colossal fortifications were built – so huge as to pose problems even for 20c artillery. In Japan between 1570 and 1630, some 200 new fortresses of stone – with bastions, citadels and moats – were built as a response to the spread of Western-type guns. Ironically, the establishment of the **Tokugawa Shogunate** in early 17c Japan ushered in over 250 years of internal peace.

The construction of battlefield trenches was the next major development in fortification. Trench warfare was developed by the Maoris in the **Maori Wars** against the British in the 19c, and was next seen extensively in the **American Civil War**, the **Russo-Japanese War**, and especially in **World War I**. Particularly on the Western Front, the construction of well-protected systems of trenches by both the Allies and the Germans led to stalemate. Reinforced underground dugouts and bunkers largely nullified the effects of artillery barrages that were expected to clear a way for advancing infantry who had to penetrate great fields of barbed wire while under fire from machine-gun posts.

Drawing on the lessons of this conflict, between the wars the French constructed a line of fortifications (the **Maginot Line**) along their border with Germany which would have been formidable to the attacking methods of 1918. The Germans built a similar line, the **Siegfried Line**. However, this type of fortification assumed that warfare would be largely static, and proved vulnerable to the German **Blitzkrieg**, with such methods as circumvention of strong points, aerial bombardment, and attacks by tanks and paratroops. The development of air-raid bunkers and reinforced concrete pill-boxes typified fortification in **World War II**. These constructions proved serious obstacles to attacking troops, such as in the US recapture of the Pacific Islands from the Japanese (the **Pacific War**), and new weapons such as the flame-thrower had to be employed.

In the late 20c the most notable development was the deep underground bunker, constructed as a defence against the ultimate destructive power of nuclear weapons. ► Artillery; Warfare

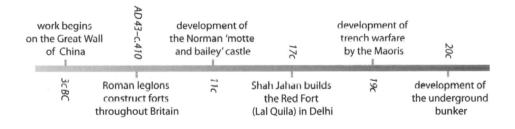

Iroquois after their defeat in the **AMERICAN REVOLU-TION**, made them yield their lands west of the Niagara River, but it was rejected by the tribes of the Ohio County. The treaties are named after the colonial military stronghold situated between Wood Creek and the Upper Mohawk River where they were signed, itself named after General John Stanwix.

**Fort Sumter** (12–13 Apr 1861)
The US federal installation in Charleston (South Carolina) harbour, bombarded in the first military engagement of the **AMERICAN CIVIL WAR**. Shortly after President Abraham **LINCOLN**'s inauguration, the fort's commanding officer, Captain Robert Anderson, informed the Union government that he had only enough supplies to last until early Apr. On 6 Apr 1861 Lincoln informed the Governor of the seceded state of South Carolina that he intended to provision the

garrison. Confederate General Pierre **BEAUREGARD** issued an ultimatum to surrender, which Anderson refused. On 12 Apr the fort came under fire, and Union troops departed two days later for lack of ammunition. The Confederate states thus having opened hostilities, Lincoln issued a call to the states for troops and began to blockade Southern ports.

**Fort Ticonderoga**
A fortress situated between Lake Champlain and Lake George in New York, USA. It was built in 1755 by the French (as Fort Carillon), and during the **FRENCH AND INDIAN WAR** resisted attack in 1758, but the following year was captured by the British under **AMHERST** and renamed. During the **AMERICAN REVO-LUTION** it succumbed to a surprise attack in 1775 by the **GREEN MOUNTAIN BOYS** led by Ethan **ALLEN**, but was recaptured by **BURGOYNE** in 1777. Following the

British surrender at the Battle of **SARATOGA** that year, it was recovered by the Americans. Now restored, it is a tourist attraction and museum.

**Forty-Five Rebellion** (1745–6)
The Jacobite rebellion which aimed to restore the Catholic Stuart kings to the British throne and displace the Hanoverians. It began in July 1745 when Charles Edward **STUART** (the 'Young Pretender') arrived in Scotland and proclaimed his father King James III. Support came mainly from the Scottish Highland clans, and there were some early successes. The Jacobite forces reached as far south as Derby, but the rebellion lost support, and was crushingly defeated at the Battle of **CULLODEN** in 1746. After the '45, the Hanoverian regime brutally suppressed the clan system. ► **JACOBITES**; **STUART, HOUSE OF**

**forty-niners**
Adventurers who swarmed to California in 1849, after the discovery of gold there the previous year. Their number may have been as high as 100,000. ► **GOLD RUSH**

**Forty-Seven Ronin, Incident of the** (1701–3)
An incident that took place in Japan which provided a potent symbol of self-sacrificing loyalty for later generations. Following a quarrel, a minor feudal lord wounded a powerful official at the **SHOGUN**'s court in **EDO**. He was ordered to commit suicide and his domain was confiscated for this breach of etiquette. The lord's **SAMURAI** retainers then became *ronin* (masterless samurai) with their status much diminished. Forty-seven of these ronin vowed to take vengeance for their former lord, and after biding their time for two years they succeeded in killing the shogunal official in 1703, knowing full well they would have to die themselves for such an act. For their unflinching loyalty to their lord, the 47 ronin became heroes.

**Foscari, Francesco** (c.1370–1457)
Doge of Venice (1423/57). His warlike policies on the Italian mainland were vital to the creation of a territorial state under Venetian rule. However, his princely style of government and his promotion of the interests of his family resulted in his deposition, and to his death from rage and grief soon afterwards. His career is the subject of a play by Byron.

**Foster, William Z(ebulon)** (1881–1961)
US labour leader and politician. A committed socialist, he joined the **INDUSTRIAL WORKERS OF THE WORLD** in 1909 and as an American Federation of Labor leader was involved in organizing steelworkers during the strike of 1919. In 1921 his Trade Union Educational League (founded 1920) was designated the US Communist Party, and Foster was made its Secretary-General. He stood as a presidential candidate in 1924, 1928 and 1932. In 1932 Foster suffered a heart attack and the leadership passed to Earl Browder, but he was restored as chairman in 1945–56.

**Fouché, Joseph, Duke of Otranto** (1763–1829)
French revolutionary politician. A member of a Catholic teaching order before 1789, he was elected to the National **CONVENTION** (1792), and became an extreme revolutionary, being noted for his zealous support of attacks on the Christian religion, and for

his part in the bloody suppression of opposition at Lyons. He then turned against **ROBESPIERRE**, being one of the main organizers of the **THERMIDOR** coup. Appointed Chief of Police in 1799, he helped to bring **NAPOLEON I** to power, and retained the post until 1815, surviving all the rapid changes of 1814–15. The First Empire gave him his titles of nobility, and great wealth. He was banished in 1816. ► **EMPIRE, FIRST** (France); **FRENCH REVOLUTION**; **JACOBINS**

**Fould, Achille** (1800–67)
French financier and politician. Elected in 1842 to parliament, after the revolution of 1848 he served the Provisional Government. During the presidency of Louis Napoleon (**NAPOLEON III**), he was four times Minister of Finance, during which time he stabilized the country's finances. He resigned (1852) on the confiscation of the property of the Orléans family, but again served as Minister of Finance from 1861 to 1867. ► **ORLÉANS, HOUSE OF**

**Foulques V** ► **FULK V**

**Founding Fathers**
American statesmen who played a significant role during the **AMERICAN REVOLUTION** and/or the period of confederation. The term is most often used for the 55 delegates of the **CONSTITUTIONAL CONVENTION** of 1787, who created the **US CONSTITUTION** and made possible the federal union. Present at the Convention were George **WASHINGTON**, who became its President, Benjamin **FRANKLIN** and James **MADISON**.

**Fouquet, Nicolas** (1615–80)
French politician. Cardinal **MAZARIN** made him *Procureur-Général* to the parliament of Paris (1650) and Superintendent of Finance (1653). He became extremely rich, and was ambitious to succeed Mazarin, but **LOUIS XIV** himself took up the reins of power on Mazarin's death, and Fouquet was arrested for embezzlement (1661). He was sentenced to life imprisonment in the fortress of Pignerol, where he died.

**Fouquier-Tinville, Antoine Quentin** (1747–95)
French revolutionary politician. He was Public Prosecutor to the Revolutionary Tribunal from 1793. He superintended all the political executions during the Reign of **TERROR** until July 1794, sending his friends, among them **ROBESPIERRE**, **DANTON** and **HÉBERT**, to execution as cheerfully as he sent their enemies; in the end he himself was guillotined. ► **FRENCH REVOLUTION**

**Fourah Bay College**
A college in Sierra Leone founded as a missionary establishment as early as 1814, the first institution of Western education in West Africa. In 1827 it became a training college for teachers and missionaries, and in 1876 became affiliated to the University of Durham for the award of degrees. Many of the members of the élite of West Africa were educated there, and the first nationalist movements were founded by its former students.

**Four Freedoms** (1941)
Four basic human rights proclaimed in an annual message to Congress by President Franklin D **ROOSEVELT** as basic human rights. They included freedom of speech and worship, and freedom from want and fear.

## Four Modernizations, The

This refers to the long-term policy aim of the Chinese Communist Party to achieve advanced development in the fields of agriculture, industry, science and technology, and national defence. Coined by Premier **ZHOU ENLAI** at the Third National People's Congress (1964), the phrase was downplayed during the **CULTURAL REVOLUTION** when ideological correctness took precedence over strictly economic development. After **MAO ZEDONG**'s death in 1976 the term was revived by **DENG XIAOPING**, and at the Third Plenum of the Party's Eleventh Central Committee (Dec 1978) priority was given to the implementation of the Four Modernizations. Although ambitious targets set in 1978 had to be modified subsequently, the policy has led to free-market reforms in the countryside, more autonomy being granted to urban enterprises, increasing professionalization of the army, and encouragement of foreign investment and more extensive trade with the West.

## Fourteen Points

A peace programme outlined by US President Woodrow **WILSON** in a message to **CONGRESS** in 1918, towards the end of **WORLD WAR I**. The programme offered the possibility of an acceptable peace to the **CENTRAL POWERS**, and as a result Wilson came to be perceived as a moral leader. It was largely instrumental in bringing about the surrender of Germany and the beginning of peace talks. Several of the points, however, were compromised or defeated in the actual treaty.

## Fourteenth Amendment (1868)

US constitutional amendment adopted during **RECONSTRUCTION** after the **AMERICAN CIVIL WAR** to guarantee equality before the law to blacks and whites alike. Its first section defined federal and state citizenship for all American-born or naturalized persons specifically to include the ex-slaves, and it prohibited the states from abridging their 'privileges and immunities' and denying them the 'equal protection of the laws'. Judicial interpretation of the amendment soon turned it to purposes for which it was never intended. Since corporations were legal 'persons', the amendment became used as a shield against state regulation, particularly of railroads and working conditions. Its negative wording was also taken to allow individual discrimination, while the 'separate but equal' argument even gave the amendment's sanction to formal legislative segregation. This flagrant abuse was reversed during the 1950s and 1960s. In the 1970s, 1980s and 1990s it was sometimes used with success by conservatives against policies of **AFFIRMATIVE ACTION** and **POSITIVE DISCRIMINATION**. ► **BROWN V BOARD OF EDUCATION OF TOPEKA, KANSAS**; **PLESSY V FERGUSON**

## Fox, Charles James (1749–1806)

British politician. He became an MP at 19, and two years later was a junior Lord of the Admiralty. He supported Lord **NORTH**, but in 1772 resigned over American policy. Foreign Secretary in 1782 and 1783, he became Secretary of State after North's downfall, and formed a coalition with him, which held office for a short period in 1783. He supported the **FRENCH REVOLUTION**, and strongly opposed the war with France. After **PITT, THE YOUNGER**'s death (1806) he

was recalled to office as Foreign Secretary, but died soon afterwards.

## Fox (Quesada), Vicente (1942– )

Mexican industrialist and politician. Describing himself as a man of the people and promising to end government corruption and improve the economy, he was elected President in 2000, ending the **PRI**'s 71-year monopoly of the presidency. His centre-right National Action Party (PAN) supports free-market economics and conservative values and is closely associated with the Roman Catholic Church. His political inexperience resulted in slow progress, government disarray and widespread disillusionment. Opponents accused his administration of betraying the **ESTRADA DOCTRINE** in its attempts to improve relations with the USA, particularly over emigration, and by voicing criticism of Cuba, a long-standing ally.

## Fraga Iribarne, Manuel (1922– )

Spanish politician and academic. As Minister of Information and Tourism under **FRANCO** (1962–9), he liberalized the regime, above all through the Press Law of 1966. By contrast, he was a hardline Minister of the Interior in 1975–6. In Sep 1976 he founded *Alianza Popular*, which became the main opposition party to the **PSOE** in 1982 and was renamed the **PP** in 1987. A conservative of authoritarian temperament, he was a dynamic, if abrasive, leader of *Alianza* in 1979–86 and was elected again in 1989. In 1990 Fraga was elected President of the regional government of Galicia, his home region.

## FRANCE  official name **Republic of France**, ancient name **Gallia**

A republic in western Europe, bounded to the north and north-east by the English Channel, Belgium, Luxembourg and Germany; to the east by Switzerland, Italy and Monaco; to the south by the Mediterranean Sea, Spain and Andorra; and to the west by the Bay of Biscay. There is evidence of prehistoric settlement in France, as revealed in Paleolithic carvings and rock paintings (eg at Lascaux) and in Neolithic megaliths (eg at Carnac). Celtic-speaking Gauls were dominant by the 5c BC. The country was part of the Roman Empire from 125BC to the 5c AD, and was invaded by several Germanic tribes in the 3–5c. The **FRANKS** inaugurated the Merovingian epoch in the 5c. Clovis I was the first Merovingian king to control large parts of Gaul; the last to hold significant power was Dagobert I (died 638), though the royal dynasty survived until Childeric III's deposition in 751. The Carolingian ruling dynasty ultimately replaced the Merovingians when Pepin III, the Short became King of the Franks in 751. The power of the Carolingian kings came to a peak in the 8c, with the succession of Charlemagne. A feudal monarchy was founded in 987 by Hugh Capet; this was the third Frankish royal dynasty (the **CAPETIAN DYNASTY**), which ruled France until 1328. The Plantagenets of England acquired several French territories in the 12c, but lands were gradually recovered during the **HUNDRED YEARS' WAR** (1337–1453), apart from Calais (regained in 1558). The Capetian dynasty was followed by the **VALOIS** and **BOURBON** dynasties, from 1328 and 1589 respectively. In the 16c there was ongoing rivalry between **FRANCIS I** and Emperor **CHARLES V**, then

the Wars of **RELIGION** took place from 1562 until 1598. In the 17c the power of the monarchy was restored, reaching its peak under **LOUIS XIV**. However, the **FRENCH REVOLUTION** of 1789 dismantled the **ANCIEN RÉGIME** in the name of liberty, equality and fraternity, and the First **REPUBLIC** was declared in 1792. The **FIRST EMPIRE** (1804–14) was ruled by **NAPOLEON I**, before the restoration of the monarchy for a period between 1814 and 1848. The Second **REPUBLIC** (1848–52) was followed by the Second **EMPIRE** (1852–70), ruled by Louis Napoleon (**NAPOLEON III**), and the Third **REPUBLIC** lasted from 1870 to 1940. There was great political instability between the World Wars, with several governments holding office for short periods. The country was occupied by Germany from 1940 until 1944, with the pro-German government at **VICHY** and the **FREE FRENCH** in London under the conservative and nationalist de **GAULLE**. The Fourth **REPUBLIC** began in 1946; shortly afterwards there was war in Indochina (1946–54), and conflict in Algeria (1954–62). The Fifth **REPUBLIC** began in 1958 under President de Gaulle. That same year, France became a founding member of the **EEC**. Presidents **POMPIDOU** and **GISCARD D'ESTAING** had policies not unlike de Gaulle's, but in 1981 France's first socialist President for 35 years, François **MITTERRAND**, was elected. He was succeeded in 1995 by the right-wing Jacques **CHIRAC**, who was re-elected in 2002 following a second round run-off with the extreme right-wing candidate Jean-Marie **LE PEN**. ► **PLANTAGENET DYNASTY; SOCIALIST PARTY** (France)

### Francesco IV d'Este (1779–1846)

Duke of Modena (1815/46). He was an extremely reactionary ruler of the restoration period who served as the model for Stendhal's Enrico IV in *La Chartreuse de Parme*. He harboured ambitions for the Piedmontese throne in 1821 and seems to have briefly flirted with the idea of cooperating with liberal revolutionaries, who hoped to persuade him to lead a nationalist insurrection (1829–30). He was responsible for the summary execution of Ciro **MENOTTI**. ► **MISLEY, ENRICO**

### Franchet d'Esperey, Louis Félix Marie François (1856–1942)

French soldier. He was made commanding general of the French 5th Army in 1914, gaining success at the Battle of the **MARNE**. In 1918 he was appointed Commander-in-Chief of Allied armies in Macedonia, where from Salonica he overthrew Bulgaria and advanced as far as Budapest; only the end of the war prevented his dash for Berlin. He was made Marshal of France in 1922. He had some links to the French extreme Right but refused to support **PÉTAIN** in 1940. ► **WORLD WAR I; WORLD WAR II**

### Francia, José Gaspar Rodríguez de (1766–1840)

Paraguayan dictator. Educated in Paraguay and Argentina in theology and law, he assumed a prominent role in Paraguay's movement for independence. Francia ('El Supremo') held absolute power from 1814 until his death, adopting a policy of isolating Paraguay from the outside world.

### Francis I (1494–1547)

King of France (1515/47). He was Count of Angoulême and Duke of Valois before succeeding **LOUIS XII** as King and marrying his daughter, Claude. He combined many of the attributes of medieval chivalry and a **RENAISSANCE** prince, the dominant feature of his reign being his rivalry with Emperor **CHARLES V**, which led to a series of wars (1521–6, 1528–9, 1536–8 and 1542–4). After establishing his military reputation against the Swiss at Marignano (1515) in his first Italian campaign, he later suffered a number of reverses, including his capture at PAVIA (1525) and imprisonment in Madrid. Though he avoided religious fanaticism, he became increasingly hostile to Protestantism after 1534. ► ITALIAN WARS; VALOIS DYNASTY

**Francis I** (1708–65)
Holy Roman Emperor (1745/65). He was the eldest son of Leopold, Duke of Lorraine, whom he succeeded in 1729. However, he resigned his dominions in return for French recognition of his claim to the German imperial throne upon his marriage to the Habsburg heiress, MARIA THERESA, in 1736. Awarded the Grand Duchy of Tuscany in compensation, he was finally elected Holy Roman Emperor in 1745. This office gave him little political influence, though, and in spite of being made co-regent of Austria, affairs of state remained firmly in the hands of his wife.

**Francis II** (1544–60)
King of France (1559/60). He was the eldest son of HENRY II and CATHERINE DE' MEDICI. In 1558 he married MARY, QUEEN OF SCOTS. His short reign was dominated by the Guise family, in their struggle against the Protestants. ► GUISE, HOUSE OF; RELIGION, WARS OF

**Francis II** (of Austria) (1768–1835)
Holy Roman Emperor (1792/1806). He was also, as Francis I, first Emperor of Austria (1804/35), and King of Hungary (1792/1830) and Bohemia (1792/1836). Defeated on several occasions by NAPOLEON I (1797, 1801, 1805 and 1809), he made a short-lived alliance with him, sealed by the marriage of his daughter, MARIE LOUISE, to the French Emperor. Later he joined with Russia and PRUSSIA to help win the Battle of LEIPZIG (1813). By the Congress of VIENNA (1814–15), thanks to METTERNICH, he recovered several territories (including Lombardy-Venetia and DALMATIA). ► NAPOLEONIC WARS

**Francis II** (1836–94)
King of the TWO SICILIES (1860/1). A weak and cowardly monarch, he was often referred to by his nick name, 'Bombino' (the diminutive form of 'Bomba', the sobriquet of FERDINAND II). In July 1860 he restored the 1848 constitution in a vain attempt to win public support in the face of the threat posed by GARIBALDI, who had seized Sicily and crossed to the mainland of the Kingdom of the Two Sicilies. He fled in the face of Garibaldi's advance and capitulated at Gaeta (13 Feb 1861). He played a small part in trying to stimulate unrest in his former territories during the GRANDE BRIGANTAGGIO.

**Franciscans**
Religious orders founded by St Francis of Assisi in the early 13c. The first order, of Friars Minor, is now divided into three groups: the Observants (OFM), the Conventuals (OFMConv) and the Capuchins (OFMCap). These lead active lives preaching to the poor and needy. The second order is made up of nuns, known as the Poor Clares (PC). The third order is a lay fraternity. Together, they constitute the largest religious order in the Roman Catholic Church, notable for missionary and social work.

**Francis Ferdinand** (1863–1914)
Archduke of Austria, nephew and heir-apparent

(from 1896) to the Emperor FRANCIS JOSEPH. On a visit to Sarajevo (in modern Yugoslavia) in June 1914, he and his wife, Sophie, were assassinated by the BLACK HAND, a group of young Serbian nationalists, among whom was the perpetrator, Gavrilo PRINCIP. Austria, encouraged by Germany, used the incident as a pretext for attacking Serbia, which precipitated WORLD WAR I.

**Francis Joseph** (1830–1916)
Emperor of Austria (1848/1916) and King of Hungary (1867/1916). He was the grandson of Emperor Francis I of Austria (Holy Roman Emperor FRANCIS II). During his reign the aspirations of the various nationalities of the empire were rigorously suppressed. He was defeated by the Prussians in 1866, and established the Dual Monarchy of AUSTRIA-HUNGARY in 1867. His annexation of Bosnia and Herzegovina in 1908 agitated Europe and especially Russia, and his government's attack on Serbia in 1914 precipitated WORLD WAR I.

**Franco, Francisco**, in full **Francisco Paulino Hermenegildo Teódulo Franco Bahamonde** (1892–1975)
Spanish general and dictator. He graduated from Toledo military academy in 1910, rising rapidly through the ranks in Spanish Morocco, to become Europe's youngest general in 1926. He oversaw the repression of the Asturias miners' revolt (1934), and during 1935 served as Chief of Staff. In 1936 he joined, at the last moment, the conspiracy against the Popular Front government (elected Feb 1936) which was launched on 17–18 July; the rebellion led to the SPANISH CIVIL WAR. Franco's leadership of the vital Army of Africa, and his close relations with the rebels' Italian and German allies, led to his becoming (Sep 1936) generalíssimo of the rebel forces and chief of the Nationalist state. Between Oct 1936 and Apr 1939, he led the Nationalists to victory, and presided over the construction of an authoritarian regime that endured until his death. During WORLD WAR II, he wanted to join Germany and Italy, but HITLER was not prepared to pay his price of France's north African territories, at Hendaye (Oct 1940). Franco therefore kept Spain out of the war, but sent the Blue Division to fight in the USSR, and provided the Germans with logistical and intelligence support. During the 1950s, his anticommunism made possible a rapprochement with the Western powers, the Bases Agreement of 1953 with the USA providing Franco with his breakthrough. The greatest paradox of Franco was that he oversaw the modernization of the Spanish economy in the 1950s and 1960s which undermined the political foundations of his police state and prepared it for the transition to democracy. In 1969 he announced that upon his death the monarchy would return in the person of JUAN CARLOS, grandson of Spain's last ruling king. Franco died in Madrid, and within two years almost every vestige of his dictatorship had disappeared.

**Franco-German Treaty of Cooperation** (Jan 1963)
The treaty signed by President de GAULLE and Chancellor ADENAUER signalling a rapprochement and the ending of centuries of conflict. It made provisions for regular summit meetings, and cooperation and consultation in foreign, economic, and cultural affairs. A

symbol of the new, post-war order in Europe, the treaty also underpinned the EEC.

**Franco-Prussian War** (1870–1)
The conflict occasioned by the Hohenzollern candidature for the Spanish throne and the Ems telegram, and caused by the changing balance of power in Europe. It resulted in crushing defeats for France at the Battles of SEDAN and Metz by MOLTKE's reformed Prussian army, the Siege of PARIS, and the humiliating Treaty of Frankfurt. ▶ HOHENZOLLERN DYNASTY

**Franco-Russian Alliance** (1894)
The treaty under which Russia guaranteed France against Germany or Italy, France guaranteed Russia against Germany or Austria, and both agreed to mobilize if all three of Germany, Austria and Italy did so. It was largely the result of a change in German policy towards Russia from friendly reassurance to careless disregard. Already smarting from Germany's triumph in 1870, France was ready to provide loans when opportunity offered from 1887 onwards and to make military and naval overtures soon after WILLIAM II dismissed BISMARCK in 1890. The treaty overcame a tradition of hostility stretching back to Napoleon Bonaparte's invasion of Russia and retreat from Moscow, and helped prepare the setting for WORLD WAR I.

**Frangipani**
A noble Roman family which figured in the Guelf and Ghibelline quarrels of the 12c and 13c, causing a schism in the Church and the election of an antipope, Gregory VIII. ▶ GHIBELLINES; GUELFS

**Franjiyeh, Süleyman** (1910–92)
Lebanese politician. President of Lebanon (and thus a Maronite) from 1970 to 1976, he presided over Lebanon at a particularly tense time, in that Palestinian guerrillas ejected from Jordan in 1970–1 began conducting their operations from Palestinian refugee camps in Lebanon. He was President when the civil war broke out in 1975 and demitted office in 1976, the year of the Syrian invasion. He was, however, still active in Maronite politics in 1978 when, as a result of his pro-Syrian stance (which lasted until 1984), a split occurred in Maronite ranks and Phalangist militiamen murdered his son, Tony Franjiyeh, and other members of his family.

**Frank, Anne** (1929–45)
Dutch Jewish girl. Her family went into hiding in Amsterdam to evade capture by the occupying German forces during WORLD WAR II. The diary she kept of her life during this period (1942–4) was published in 1947 and is probably the most moving single testament against oppression and persecution. The family was betrayed, and Anne died in a German CONCENTRATION CAMP in 1945. ▶ HOLOCAUST

**Frankfurter, Felix** (1882–1965)
Austrian-born US law teacher and judge. Educated at the College of the City of New York and at Harvard, he taught at the Harvard Law School (1914–39) and served as an associate justice of the US Supreme Court (1939–62). He was a noted supporter of civil liberties and helped found the AMERICAN CIVIL LIBERTIES UNION, although in court he advocated judicial restraint in opposing legislative and executive

policy. In constitutional cases he claimed that judges should consider whether legislators could reasonably have enacted such a law.

**Frankfurt Ghetto**
The Jewish quarter of Frankfurt. It was destroyed in 24 hours on 14 June 1711 by one of the largest fires in German history prior to the present century.

**Frankfurt Parliament**
An elected assembly convened following the German revolutions of Mar 1848 to draft a liberal constitution for all of Germany. It represented every state in the GERMAN CONFEDERATION, but proved to be disunited and powerless. After its offer of the imperial crown to the King of PRUSSIA was repudiated by Austria and rejected by the King himself, the parliament disintegrated. ▶ REVOLUTIONS OF 1848–9

**Franklin, Benjamin** (1706–90)
US politician, author and scientist. He set up a printing house in Philadelphia, bought the *Pennsylvania Gazette* (1730), and built a reputation as a journalist. In 1736 he became Clerk of the Pennsylvania legislature, in 1737 Deputy Postmaster of Philadelphia, and in 1753 Deputy Postmaster-General for the colonies, and was sent on various diplomatic missions to England. In 1748 he began his research into electricity, proving that lightning and electricity are identical, and suggesting that buildings be protected by lightning conductors. In 1776 he was actively involved in framing the DECLARATION OF INDEPENDENCE. A skilled negotiator, he successfully won Britain's recognition of US independence (1783). He was US Minister in Paris until 1785, three times President of the State of Pennsylvania, and a member of the CONSTITUTIONAL CONVENTION. In 1788 he retired from public life. ▶ ALBANY CONGRESS

**Franks**
Germanic peoples, originally from the lower Rhine region. Clovis I led the Salian and Ripuarian Franks and founded a kingdom embracing much of Gaul; Charlemagne, their greatest ruler, attempted to revive the Roman Empire in the West. They gave their name to Francia and to Franconia, which by the 13c stood for what is now France, but earlier had diverse territorial connotations, reflecting the vicissitudes of Frankish royal power. ▶ SALIC LAW

**Franz Josef** ▶ FRANCIS JOSEPH

**Fraser, (John) Malcolm** (1930– )
Australian politician. In 1955 he became the youngest MP in the House of Representatives. He was Minister for the Army (1966–8), Defence (1969–71), and Education and Science (1968–9, 1971–2). He became Leader of the LIBERAL PARTY OF AUSTRALIA in 1975, and was Prime Minister in a Liberal–National Country coalition from the same year, retiring from politics after his government's defeat in 1983.

**Fraser, Peter** (1884–1950)
British-born New Zealand politician. In 1910 he emigrated to New Zealand, and became involved in trade union organization. A founder-member of the New Zealand Labour Party (1916), he was imprisoned during WORLD WAR I for opposing conscription. He entered parliament in 1918, became Deputy Party Leader in 1933, and Leader and Prime Minister in

1940, holding office until 1949, when his government was defeated.

## Fraser, Simon (1776–1862)

Canadian fur-trader and explorer. In 1792 he joined the North-West Company as a clerk, becoming a partner in 1801. In 1805 he was given responsibility for the company's operations beyond the Rockies, and established the first settlements in New Caledonia, now central British Columbia. Hoping to discover a water route which would cut the company's transport costs, in 1808 he braved the dangerous reach now known as the Fraser River Canyon. In 1815 he was arrested with other company officers at Fort William in retaliation for the Seven Oaks Incident (a North West Company attack on the HUDSON'S BAY COMPANY's Red River Settlement). The charges could not be sustained and Fraser had retired to Upper CANADA by the time his trial took place.

## Fratricide, Law of

This law was promulgated by the Ottoman Sultan MEHMED II, THE CONQUEROR: 'To whichever of my sons the Sultanate may be granted, it is proper for him to put his brothers to death, to preserve the order of the world'. The law was designed to provide a stable regime and prevent dynastic conflicts for the succession to the throne. For a century and a half, each new sultan had his brothers strangled by a silken bowstring. The last such killings were in 1595, when Sultan Mehmed III ordered the execution of his 19 brothers. After this, the succession went to the eldest male member of the Ottoman house. The system of sending Ottoman princes to govern provinces of the Empire and so learn how to rule, now came to an end. Instead, they spent their lives in the *kafe* or cage, a group of buildings in the royal palace. There, surrounded by concubines, they lived lives of luxurious imprisonment, from which they emerged only to rule or when they were dead. The result was a marked decline in the quality of the sultans, who were often feeble in mind or body, a serious deficiency in a state where all power was in the hands of the Sultan.

## Frederick I (1249–68)

Duke of Austria. The son of Count Hermann of Baden and Gertrude, widow of Leopold of Austria, after the death of his father (1250) he was forced to relinquish Austria to Ottokar of Bohemia and fled to Bohemia. There he became friendly with CONRADIN OF SWABIA and went with him to Italy in 1267 to reconquer the Hohenstaufen lands. He was captured at the Battle of Tagliacozzo and was beheaded in Naples along with Conradin, at the insistence of King Ottokar. ► HOHENSTAUFEN DYNASTY

## Frederick I (1371–1440)

Elector of Brandenburg. As Frederick VI, Count of Nuremberg, he was the founder of the Brandenburg line of the HOHENZOLLERN DYNASTY. In 1410 he was instrumental in having SIGISMUND elected German King and as a reward was made Governor of Brandenburg (1411) and confirmed as Elector and Margrave in 1417. He led the imperial army against the HUSSITES (1422 and 1427–31) but his lack of success led him to support the peace negotiated in the pacts of Prague (1433) and Iglau (1436). ► ELECTORS; HUSSITE WARS

## Frederick I (1471–1533)

King of Denmark (1523/33) and Norway (1524/33). He was the son of CHRISTIAN I and uncle of CHRISTIAN II and, as Duke of Holstein, was chosen king when Christian II, who had just lost Sweden to GUSTAV I VASA, was dethroned in 1523 by a rebellion in Denmark. In 1531–2 he fended off an invasion of Norway by the ex-king; he then tricked him into accepting safe-conduct for a parley in Copenhagen, and imprisoned him for life instead. Frederick died soon afterwards, on the verge of accepting Lutheranism, and was succeeded by his son, CHRISTIAN III.

## Frederick I (1657–1713)

Elector of Brandenburg (1688/1713) and King in Prussia (1701/13). He was the son of FREDERICK WILLIAM, THE GREAT ELECTOR, whom he succeeded in 1688 (as Frederick III of Brandenburg). In 1701 he assumed the title of King in Prussia, the only part of the Hohenzollern dominions outside the HOLY ROMAN EMPIRE. His foreign policy was generally supportive of the Habsburgs, and during the War of the SPANISH SUCCESSION he took part in the Grand Alliance against France. Unlike his predecessors and most of his successors, his main interests were not military. Instead, he maintained a splendid court life and was a great patron of the arts and of learning. ► HABSBURG DYNASTY; HOHENZOLLERN DYNASTY

## Frederick I, Barbarossa (c.1123–1190)

German King and Holy Roman Emperor (1152/90). Born of the HOHENSTAUFEN DYNASTY, he succeeded his uncle, CONRAD III, in 1152. His reign was a continuous struggle against unruly vassals at home, the city-republics of Lombardy, and the papacy. He went on several campaigns in Italy, and though severely defeated at LEGNANO (1176), he quelled HENRY THE LION of Bavaria, and asserted his feudal superiority over Poland, Hungary, Denmark and Burgundy. He led the Third CRUSADE against SALADIN (1189), and was victorious at Philomelium and Iconium. ► LOMBARD LEAGUE

## Frederick II (1194–1250)

German King (1212/50) and Holy Roman Emperor (1215/50). The grandson of FREDERICK I, BARBAROSSA, he was the last Emperor of the Hohenstaufen line. He was also King of Sicily (1198) and of Germany (1212). He keenly desired to consolidate imperial power in Italy at the expense of the papacy, and devoted himself to organizing his Italian territories, but his plans were frustrated by the Lombard cities and by the popes. Embarking on the Fifth Crusade in 1228, he took possession of Jerusalem, and crowned himself King there (1229). Returning to Italy, he continued his struggles with the papacy until his death, at Fiorentino. ► CRUSADES, LATER; HOHENSTAUFEN DYNASTY; LOMBARD LEAGUE

## Frederick II (1534–88)

King of Denmark and Norway (1559/88). He was the son and successor of CHRISTIAN III. In the early years of his reign he was engaged in a seven-year war against the Sweden of the deranged ERIK XIV, which was brought to an inconclusive ending with the Treaty of Stettin (1370). The remainder of his reign was a period of peace and prosperity. A pleasure-loving monarch, he built the magnificent RENAIS-

**SANCE** castle of Kronborg at Elsinore, to which he brought English musicians to provide entertainment, and was a patron of the astronomer Tycho Brahe and other scientists. He was succeeded by his young son, **CHRISTIAN IV**. His daughter, **ANNE OF DENMARK**, married King James VI of Scotland and I of England. ► **JAMES VI AND I**

### Frederick II, the Great (1712–86)
King of Prussia (1740/86). He was the son of **FREDERICK WILLIAM I** and Sophia Dorothea, daughter of **GEORGE I** of England. He developed an early devotion to French culture and his desire for independence resulted in bitter conflict with, and permanent alienation from, his despotic father. Almost immediately on his accession to the throne, he invaded the Austrian province of Silesia which he managed to hold on to through three wars, although Prussia was brought to the brink of annihilation more than once. In domestic affairs he continued his father's policy of centralization and personal **ABSOLUTISM**, but redefined the king's role as that of the first servant of the state. However, his promotion of agriculture, commerce and industry proved meddlesome in many respects. Committed to religious tolerance he had, on the other hand, little regard for civil and national self-determination, and in 1772 became involved in the first partition of Poland. A misanthropist and recluse in his last years, Frederick left Prussia a great power when he died at Potsdam. ► **AUSTRIAN SUCCESSION, WAR OF THE**; **AUSTRO-PRUSSIAN DUALISM**; **SEVEN YEARS' WAR**; **SILESIAN WARS**

### Frederick III (1415–93)
King of Germany (1440/93), and Holy Roman Emperor (1452/93). His reign was turbulent, and he lost his hold on many territories. Although he succeeded in diffusing the long-running controversy over the power of the papacy and that of the Church's councils with the religious settlement known as the Concordat of Vienna (1448), he failed to oppose the Turkish invasions of 1469 and 1475. Nevertheless, by the marriage (1477) of his son, **MAXIMILIAN I**, to Mary, daughter of **CHARLES THE BOLD**, Duke of Burgundy, he laid the foundation of the subsequent greatness of the **HABSBURG DYNASTY**. ► **BASLE, COUNCIL OF**

### Frederick III (1609–70)
King of Denmark and Norway (1648/70). He was the son and successor of **CHRISTIAN IV**. The first half of his reign was taken up with costly wars against Sweden, but after the peace settlement of 1660 he established absolute hereditary monarchy over Denmark, Norway and Iceland, embodied in the Royal Law (*Kongelov*) of 1665. He was an enlightened patron of scientific and antiquarian studies, and founded the Royal Library in Copenhagen.

### Frederick III (1831–88)
German Emperor and eighth King of **PRUSSIA**. The only son of **WILLIAM I**, in 1858 he married Victoria, Princess Royal of England. As Crown Prince of Prussia (from 1861), he protested against **BISMARCK**'s reactionary policy in relation to constitutional questions and the press. In the **FRANCO-PRUSSIAN** War he commanded the 3rd Army and was made field marshal (1870). In 1871 he became Crown Prince of the German Empire. In 1878, when the Emperor was wounded by an assassin, the Crown Prince was appointed provisional Regent. When, in 1888, Emperor William I died, Frederick was already ill, with cancer of the throat. He was proclaimed emperor as Frederick III, but he died at Potsdam. His son, **WILLIAM II**, succeeded him. Frederick had a great horror of war, intensely disliked autocratic ideas, and sought to liberalize German institutions.

### Frederick V (1596–1632)
Elector of the Palatinate (1610/23) and King of Bohemia (as Frederick I, 1619/20). Born at Amberg in the Upper Palatinate, he was the leading Calvinist prince of Germany and was married to Elizabeth, the daughter of James VI of Scotland and I of England. As head of the **EVANGELICAL UNION** he was offered, and accepted, the Bohemian crown when the estates rose in rebellion against **FERDINAND II**. Swiftly defeated by the imperial forces at the Battle of the **WHITE MOUNTAIN** outside Prague (1620), the 'Winter King' went into exile in Holland, eventually losing the Palatinate as well as Bohemia. ► **JAMES VI AND I**

### Frederick VI (1768–1839)
King of Denmark (1808/39) and Norway (1808/14). He was the son of **CHRISTIAN VII**. During his reign, Frederick supported liberal measures; feudal serfdom was abolished, the criminal code amended, and the slave trade prohibited in the Danish colonies. However, he refused to join Britain against Napoleon, and after the war lost Norway to Sweden (1814). The state became bankrupt in 1813, and did not recover for many years. In 1831 he granted a more liberal constitution to his subjects. ► **NAPOLEONIC WARS**

### Frederick VII (1808–63)
King of Denmark (1848/63). He was the son and successor of **CHRISTIAN VIII**, and the last of the Oldenburg line. In 1849 he promulgated a new and liberal constitution, abolishing monarchical **ABSOLUTISM**. He died childless, and was succeeded by **CHRISTIAN IX**.

### Frederick VIII (1843–1912)
King of Denmark (1906/12). He was the son and successor of **CHRISTIAN IX**, and brother of Queen Alexandra of Britain. In 1907 he made a state visit to Iceland to celebrate the granting of home rule there (1904). He married Princess Louise of Sweden, and was well-liked for his simple lifestyle. His second son, Prince Carl, became King **HAAKON VII** of Norway. He was succeeded by his eldest son, **CHRISTIAN X**.

### Frederick IX (1899–1972)
King of Denmark (1947/72). The son and successor of **CHRISTIAN X**, he trained as a naval officer (rising to rear-admiral in 1946), and was Crown Prince from 1912. During **WORLD WAR II** he assisted his father in resistance to the German occupation, and was held under house arrest (1943–5). He granted home rule to the Faroes in 1948, and in 1953 a new constitution provided for female succession to the throne. In 1935 he had married Ingrid, daughter of King **GUSTAV VI ADOLF** of Sweden; their eldest daughter now became crown princess and succeeded him as Queen **MARGRETHE II** in 1972. Their youngest daughter, Anne-Marie, married King **CONSTANTINE II** of Greece, who was later dethroned.

## Frederick Augustus, Duke of York and Albany (1763–1827)

Duke of York. He was the second son of King **GEORGE III** of Great Britain. A soldier by profession, he was unsuccessful both in the field in the Netherlands (1793–9) and as British Commander-in-Chief (1798–1809), and earned the nickname of the 'grand old Duke of York' in the nursery rhyme. However, his painstaking reform of the army proved of lasting benefit, especially to **WELLINGTON**. In 1809 he resigned because of the traffic in appointments conducted by his mistress, Mary Anne Clarke, but he was exonerated and reinstated in 1811.

## Frederick Augustus I (1750–1827)

Elector, as Frederick Augustus III (1763/1827), and first King of Saxony (1806/27). Under his rule Saxony recovered rapidly from the **SEVEN YEARS' WAR**, but fared less well during the Napoleonic era. Defeated alongside **PRUSSIA** at the Battles of **JENA AND AUERSTÄDT** by France in Oct 1806, Frederick Augustus subsequently allied with **NAPOLEON I** and remained loyal to him almost to the end. Although confirmed on his throne by the Congress of **VIENNA** (1814–15), Saxony lost much territory to Prussia as a result of his alliance with France.

## Frederick Henry (1584–1647)

**STADHOLDER** of the United Provinces (1625/47). The son of **WILLIAM I, THE SILENT** and Louise de Coligny, he led the Dutch Republic after 1625, when he became Stadholder of the provinces of Holland, Zeeland, Utrecht, Gelderland and Overijssel. In 1640 Groningen and Drente also elected him. As military leader of the northern Dutch territories in their revolt against Spain (the **EIGHTY YEARS' WAR**), he had considerable success, especially in **BRABANT** and Limburg. Although not a hereditary monarch, he set up a court and, after 1640, applied a dynastic foreign policy, marrying off his children (by Amalia of Solms-Braunfels) to the royal families of England and Germany.

## Fredericksburg, Battle of (13 Dec 1862)

In the **AMERICAN CIVIL WAR**, a fruitless attempt by a Northern army of well over 100,000 to capture the town of Fredericksburg, Virginia, from a Southern army that was heavily outnumbered.

## Frederick William, the Great Elector (1620–88)

Elector of Brandenburg (1640/88). On his accession, Brandenburg was at its weakest, but ruthless manoeuvring during the last stages of the **THIRTY YEARS' WAR** enabled him to make considerable territorial gains in the Peace of **WESTPHALIA** (1648), and in 1660 he acquired full sovereignty in **PRUSSIA**. His designs on Swedish Pomerania were frustrated, though, when French intervention invalidated Brandenburg's victory at **FEHRBELLIN** (1675). This prompted the diplomatic orientation towards Austria that was to dominate Hohenzollern foreign policy until 1740. Keeping a small standing army to serve foreign policy as well as domestic purposes, he established the rule of princely **ABSOLUTISM** by breaking the traditional tax voting rights of the estates. The Junker nobility were compensated for their loss of political influence with social privileges over the peasantry. With a view to the economic development of his dominions, he offered asylum to large numbers of Huguenot refugees. ► **HOHENZOLLERN DYNASTY**

## Frederick William I (1688–1740)

King of Prussia (1713/40). He was the son of **FREDERICK I**, whom he succeeded. Known as the 'Soldier King', his reign saw everything and everybody being subordinated to the push for a massive increase of the army. The enforcement of strict discipline gave even the civil service a decidedly military character. His suppression of the estates' influence and the creation of a centralized administrative directory (1723) transformed the scattered dominions of the **HOHENZOLLERN DYNASTY** into a unified state, albeit one resembling a large barracks. In many ways he can be regarded as the real creator of Prussia, and although his foreign policy was peaceful throughout, it was he who laid the foundation for his country's subsequent expansion.

## Frederick William II (1744–97)

King of Prussia (1786/97). He was the nephew and successor of **FREDERICK II, THE GREAT**. Although some of the latter's more unpopular measures were revoked, no comprehensive reforms were undertaken and Prussia became increasingly ossified. A weak character, he relied on the suggestions of mistresses and favourites, and under the influence of a mystic sect ordered a reactionary clampdown in religious and educational matters. Under him, Prussia became involved in the wars of the European coalition against revolutionary France, and in the second and third partitions of Poland (1792 and 1795).

## Frederick William III (1770–1840)

King of Prussia (1797/1840). He was the son of **FREDERICK WILLIAM II**. At first cautiously neutral towards **NAPOLEON I**'s conquests, he eventually declared war (1806) and was severely defeated at the Battles of **JENA AND AUERSTÄDT**, with the loss of all territory west of the Elbe. To further Prussia's recovery, he sanctioned the liberalizing reforms of **HARDENBERG** and **STEIN** and the military reorganization of **SCHARNHORST** and **GNEISENAU**, sharing in the decisive victory at the Battle of **LEIPZIG** with Tsar Alexander I (1813). By the Congress of **VIENNA** (1814–15) he recovered many of his possessions, gained vital new territories on the Rhine and Ruhr, and thereafter tended to support the forces of conservatism. ► **NAPOLEONIC WARS**

## Frederick William IV (1795–1861)

King of Prussia (1840/61). The son of **FREDERICK WILLIAM III**, he began his reign by granting minor reforms and promising radical changes, which were never implemented. He opposed the popular movement of 1848, but was forced to grant a representative parliament (1850). In 1857, afflicted with insanity, he resigned the administration to his brother.

## Frederikshamn, Peace of (1809)

The treaty ending the Russo-Swedish War of 1808–9 and transferring the Grand Duchy of Finland from Swedish to Russian rule. This completed the expansion of Russia towards the Baltic, giving it control of strategic Finnish fortresses. It also began the gradual process of undermining the supremacy of the Swedish élite within Finland, by cutting it off from its mother country and by recognizing the privileges of

# *Freemasonry*

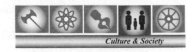

Culture & Society

### Origins

The origins of Freemasonry are shrouded in mystery. It is generally accepted, however, that some degree of continuity exists between guild-type organizations of stonemasons in the **Middle Ages** and the Masonic lodges of the 17–18c to the present day. Medieval masons had lodges (huts on the sites where they were working in which they could store their tools and hold meetings), they elaborated legends concerning the history of their craft, had initiation rites, and employed secret signs and rules of secrecy concerning matters discussed in the lodge. They were 'free' most probably in the sense that they were bound to no single employer and were itinerant, though it has also been suggested that 'Freemason' is a shortening of freestone-mason or a corruption of 'frère' (brother) mason.

It is sometimes argued that the mysterious lore and practices of Freemasonry cannot be adequately explained by lineal descent from guilds of medieval stone workers. Two frequently suggested additional sources for them are the Knights Templar and the Rosicrucians, either or both acting as a channel for the ancient esoteric wisdom of the Near East into Freemasonry. The **Templars** were a military and religious order founded c.1120 to protect pilgrims to the Holy Land, who, after acquiring great wealth over the next two centuries, were accused of heresy and practising secret rites, and bloodily suppressed by King **Philip IV, the Fair** of France in 1307. The Rosicrucians were a secret order founded, according to their own legend, by a German, Christian Rosenkreuz, who travelled to the East at the end of the 14c to study its secret wisdom. While influence from either source is possible, neither connection has been established to the satisfaction of most historians.

Before 1600, lodges in Scotland began to admit members who were not trained and practising stonemasons. As a two-grade mystery, Freemasonry was invented in 16c Scotland by a blend of operative masons' club traditions and **Renaissance** neo-platonic mysticism which attracted upper-class adherents. The King's Master of Works was the earliest Grand Master, being succeeded by members of the Sinclair or St Clair family of Rosslyn, who had a long history of association with the Knights Templar. By the middle of the 17c Freemasonry had spread to England and later Ireland. Records of English Freemasonry from the late 17c show the induction of men like Elias Ashmole (1617–92), the antiquary with an interest in alchemy and Rosicrucianism, whose collection formed the basis of the Ashmolean Museum in Oxford. These men were known as 'accepted' or 'adopted' Masons.

Gradually a distinction began to be drawn between 'operative' lodges, consisting of practising artisans, and 'speculative' lodges, whose members joined for social reasons or because of their interest in the history and mystique of the Craft. By the early 18c 'speculative' lodges were probably in the majority. In 1717 four London lodges joined together to found a Grand Lodge, which soon became the Grand Lodge of England. The history of modern Freemasonry starts from this point, though the Grand Lodges of Scotland and Ireland remained important autonomous bodies.

### The eighteenth century

During the 18c, English-style, three-degree Freemasonry spread rapidly throughout Europe and beyond. The first authentically documented lodge in France was established c.1725. Freemasonry was widespread in the British Army, and lodges were frequently established while the Army was on service abroad. The first officially warranted American lodge was established in Boston in 1733. The spirit of brotherliness in Freemasonry, together with its myth of a universal religion older than the great established religions of the world, chimed in with the new spirit of toleration. Many 18c members of the organization took their membership extremely seriously and Masonic ideals inspired their work, a notable example being the composer Mozart, especially in his opera *The Magic Flute*. Freemasonry was undoubtedly a

the Finnish estates which were at that time a Swedish preserve but eventually became a target for Finnish nationalists. A century later the same nationalists were to turn against Russia.

### Free Coloured

The intermediate class which resulted from unsanctified unions between members of the white plantocracy and its slaves and which became an economic force in the British West Indies c.1800. Varying from Mustifino (15/16 white) to Sambo (1/4 white), these illegitimate offspring were often emancipated by their fathers and had property settled upon them. While the group grew in economic importance after 1750, its members becoming craftsmen, merchants, professionals and even planters and slave owners, it was excluded by law from any role in the legal and political process. Its disabilities were removed by 1830 and after that date prominent coloured men, such as George William Gordon and Edward Jordan in Jamaica, and Samuel Prescod Jackson and Conrad Reeves in Barbados, were to be found as legislative councillors and magistrates. Known as *affranchis* in the French colonies, the group played a key role in the outbreak of the Haitian Revolution.

**Freedom and People's Rights Movement** (*Jiyu minken undo*)

A political movement in early Meiji Japan during the 1870s and 1880s calling for a national representative assembly along Western lines. The movement originated in 1873 with a split in the new Meiji government over whether to send a punitive expedition to Korea. Some members, like **ITAGAKI TAISUKE**, resigned when the decision was taken not to send an expedition. He founded political societies in his own domain of Tosa, denouncing the monopoly of power by leaders from **CHOSHU** and **SATSUMA** and calling for a nationally elected assembly. At first comprising dissident **SAMURAI**, the movement spread nationwide and obtained the support of landowners and wealthy farmers; these political societies formed the *Jiyuto* (Liberal Party) in 1881. The ideology of the movement was influenced by Anglo-Saxon liberalism, although more radical members were influenced by **ROUSSEAU**'s concept of popular sovereignty. Government suppression and the internal rift between moderates and radicals severely hampered the movement and, after a series of violent incidents (1882–4), the government dissolved the Jiyuto. The

major vehicle for the values of the **Enlightenment**, and like the Enlightenment, it was élitist.

Exposures of Masonic ritual were published around 1730, and attempts to suppress Freemasonry on the part of governments or the Church began around the same time. Police action against Freemasonry was taken in Holland in 1735, in Sweden in 1736 and in France in 1737, and in 1738 a papal bull was issued forbidding all Roman Catholics to become Freemasons on pain of excommunication. However, the great Roman Catholic monarchies regarded this as beyond papal authority, and lodges flourished in them, often with regular or secular clergy as members, until the **French Revolution**. The effect of this measure was to strengthen the tie between Freemasonry and enlightened opposition to the Church and the authoritarian regimes it bolstered. It also helped to foster the reputation of the Freemasons as a subversive organization. Freemasons were prominent in the struggle for American independence (George **Washington** and Benjamin **Franklin** were both active Masons), in the French Revolution (**Danton**, **Desmoulins**) and in the movement for the unification of Italy in the next century (**Garibaldi**, **Mazzini**). The notion of Freemasonry as a vast international, revolutionary and anticlerical conspiracy seems to have been exacerbated by an ultra-conservative interpretation of the French Revolution as entirely the result of a Masonic plot.

### Later developments

Freemasonry continues as a fraternal and charitable organization worldwide, and its members over the last two centuries have included many very eminent and powerful men. Its later history – its charitable and educational work apart – has mainly concerned further efforts to suppress or expose it, or to suggest that Masonic loyalties take precedence over official duties or a strict regard for justice, where Masons are members of organizations such as the police or the armed forces. A specifically **Anti-Masonic Party** existed in the USA between 1827 and 1835. It was formed during the furore that followed the alleged abduction and murder by Masons of a former Mason who threatened to publish a book revealing the organization's secrets. The Anti-Masonic Party won seats in the New York state legislature and **Congress**, and entered a candidate for the presidential elections of 1832. Most of its leading members later joined the **Whig Party**, the ancestor of the modern **Republican Party**. In the 20c the conspiratorial accusations against the movement were revived by the Nazi Party to justify its banning in Germany in 1933.

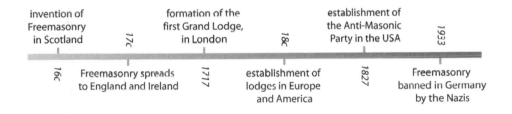

movement, however, hastened the government's own plans for a constitution, which was promulgated in 1889. ► **MEIJI CONSTITUTION**

### Freedom Charter

The policy document adopted by the Congress Alliance (June 1955), when 3,000 opposition delegates from all regions of South Africa met to coordinate policies, and which was issued by the **ANC** (African National Congress) itself in 1956, setting out its non-racial policy for South Africa, emphasizing its Fabian principles as well as its commitment to racial equality.

### Freedom Riders

In the USA, an inter-racial group of non-violent activists, mainly from the North, who rode on buses through the Southern USA in the 1960s to challenge segregationist policies. They sometimes incurred violent attacks from Southern racists but their actions succeeded in heightening public knowledge and support of the **CIVIL RIGHTS** campaign.

### Free French

Frenchmen who answered General de **GAULLE**'s appeal, broadcast from London (18 June 1940), to reject the impending armistice between France and Germany, and join him in fighting on. He became leader of the Free French forces, and the 2nd French Armoured Division helped to liberate Paris (25 Aug 1944). ► **RESISTANCE MOVEMENT** (France); **WORLD WAR II**

### Freemasonry ► *See panel*

### Free Officers

In Egypt, a small group of army officers formed after the fiasco of the 1948 war, who were bent on the expulsion of the British from Egypt and the removal of the politicians in power at the time. In the aftermath of the riots of **BLACK SATURDAY** (Jan 1952), the Free Officers, fearing that King **FAROUK** might be about to have them arrested, rose and forced Farouk into abdication (July 1952). The Free Officers (with **NEGUIB** nominally at their head, but actually led by Gamal Abd al-**NASSER**) took control of the country; Nasser went on to run the country until his death in 1969. The Free Officers played a leading role in Egypt throughout the period until the June War (**SIX-DAY WAR**) of 1967 when, with the growing rift between Abd al-Hakim **AMER** and Nasser, and the former's subsequent suicide, the solidarity of the Free Officers was broken.

### Free Officers' Movement (Libya)

Libya became an independent country in 1951 with the Sanusi leader, Amir Idris, as King. His regime was, however, soon condemned by students and young army officers as corrupt, and for being dependent on foreign support. Inspired by the pan-Arab and socialist doctrines of Gamal Abd al-NASSER and the BA'ATH PARTY, the Free Officers' Movement, consisting of middle-ranking officers and NCOs and led by Muammar GADDAFI, seized power. They set up a Revolutionary Command Council and established a military dictatorship. Foreign banks and businesses were nationalized, and political parties and trade unions were outlawed.

### free silver

A demand made within the US DEMOCRATIC PARTY in 1895 for the unlimited coinage of silver at a ratio of 16:1 with gold. Intended as a reflationary solution for agrarian economic problems, in the 1896 presidential election, free silver became a major plank of the Democratic Party platform. But after Democrat William Jennings BRYAN lost to Republican William MCKINLEY, interest in the issue faded.

### Free-Soil Party (1848)

A US political party whose slogan was 'free soil, free speech, free labor, and free men'. Opposed to the expansion of SLAVERY into territories annexed after the MEXICAN WAR, it ran former President Martin VAN BUREN as its presidential candidate in 1848. Van Buren lost, but the slavery issue was later taken up by the REPUBLICAN PARTY.

### Frei (Montalva), Eduardo (1911–82)

Chilean politician. He became one of the leaders of the Social-Christian Falange Party in the late 1930s, and of the new Christian Democratic Party after 1957. His presidency (1964–70) saw an ambitious programme of social reform, which brought Chile substantial international support. His initial scepticism of the PINOCHET regime turned into outright opposition. By the time of his death, he was widely seen as the father of opposition to the dictatorship.

### Freikorps

German paramilitary organizations. Formed in late 1918 and 1919 by military officers who recruited demobilized soldiers, sailors, students and members of the unemployed, the Freikorps (literally, 'volunteer corps') played an equivocal and often violent role in the early history of the WEIMAR REPUBLIC. Sanctioned by the Social Democratic Army Minister, Noske, their initial purpose was to suppress extreme left-wing insurgency and subsequently to defend Germany's eastern frontier, particularly in Upper Silesia, against Polish irregular forces. However, they were strongly anti-republican in spirit and engaged in a campaign of terror and assassination against prominent republican figures as well as attempting to topple the republic in the KAPP PUTSCH of 1920. Despite their official dissolution in 1920, the Freikorps maintained a clandestine existence and were involved in HITLER's failed 1923 putsch. Subsequently quiescent, many Freikorps officers later resurfaced as leaders of the SA of the NAZI PARTY. ▸ MUNICH PUTSCH

### Frelimo (Frente de Libertação de Moçambique, 'Mozambique Liberation Front')

Founded in 1962, it was led by Eduardo MONDLANE and was based in Dar es Salaam. When Mondlane was assassinated, the leadership passed to Samora MACHEL and Frelimo waged a successful guerrilla war against the Portuguese, establishing liberated zones in which rudimentary governmental structures were established. At independence in 1975, it became the only legal party in Mozambique. It adopted Marxist–Leninist policies and sought to repair the country's economy, but was opposed by the brutal and destructive dissident group RENAMO, which by the end of the 1980s had caused 100,000 deaths and created one million refugees. Following negotiations between Renamo and President CHISSANO, Frelimo and Renamo signed a peace agreement in 1992 and Renamo became a legitimate political party. Frelimo won Mozambique's first multiparty elections in 1994.

### Frémont, John Charles (1813–90)

US explorer and politician. In 1843 he crossed the Rocky Mountains (where a peak is named after him), and found an overland route across the continent. He explored the Great Salt Lake (1843), fought in the MEXICAN WAR (1846), then went to California, where he made a fortune in the GOLD RUSH, and became a Senator. In 1856 he was the first presidential candidate of the new REPUBLICAN PARTY, losing to James Buchanan, but receiving one million votes and making the party a major force in national politics. He later became Governor of Arizona (1878–83).

### French, Sir John Denton Pinkstone, Earl of Ypres (1852–1925)

British field marshal. He joined the navy (1866), then the army (1874), and distinguished himself in the Sudan (1884–5) and South Africa (1899–1901). Chief of Imperial General Staff (1911–14), he held supreme command of the British Expeditionary Force in France (1914–15), but was criticized for indecision, and resigned. He was made a viscount (1915) and earl (1921), and was Lord-Lieutenant of Ireland (1918–21). ▸ WORLD WAR I

### French and Indian War (1756–63)

The last of the 18c wars between France and Britain for the control of North America. France accepted final defeat at the Treaty of PARIS (1763). ▸ SEVEN YEARS' WAR

### French Community

A grouping of some former French colonies which under the constitution of the Fifth Republic (1958) opted to stay closely associated with France. The member states had full internal autonomy, but many matters, including currency, defence, and foreign affairs remained the responsibility of the Community, which in effect meant France. Some 12 overseas territories opted to join. Pressures for full independence continued to build up, and in 1960 it became possible to be fully independent within the Community, thus rendering it of no practical relevance. ▸ FRENCH UNION; REPUBLIC, FIFTH (France)

### French Republican Calendar

A calendar introduced during the FRENCH REVOLUTION by the National CONVENTION to herald the beginning of a new epoch for France and for humanity in general, and to further the anticlerical campaign for de-Christianization. The structure and nomenclature were devised by a committee under the Deputy Fabre d'Eglantine, Year 1 dating from the abolition of the monarchy and the declaration of the First Republic (22 Sep 1792). Twelve 30-day months were introduced and divided into three 10-day weeks of *decadi*, eliminating Sundays. They were given names derived from nature, notably from the seasons: Vendémiaire, Brumaire, Frimaire, Nivôse, Pluviôse, Ventôse, Germinal, Floréal, Prairial, Messidor, **THERMIDOR** and Fructidor. The system was abolished under **NAPOLEON I** (1805). ▶ **BRUMAIRE COUP**; **VENDÉMIAIRE, 12TH AND 13TH**

### French Revolution (1789)
A complex upheaval, profoundly affecting every aspect of government and society, and therefore considered a significant turning-point in French history. Although its causes have been subject to conflicting interpretation, conventionally the start was the summoning of the **ESTATES GENERAL** (spring 1789), which became the National Assembly when its three houses combined; it is also known as the Constituent Assembly. It responded to public pressure, such as the storming of the **BASTILLE** (14 July 1789), with wide-ranging political, social and economic measures (1789–91). These included the abolition of feudal, aristocratic and clerical privileges, a **DECLARATION OF THE RIGHTS OF MAN AND CITIZEN** (1789), the establishment of a constitutional government, the confiscation of Church property, and a reorganization of Church–State relations in the **CIVIL CONSTITUTION OF THE CLERGY** (1790). Thus, the **ANCIEN RÉGIME** was effectively dismantled in the name of 'LIBERTY, EQUALITY, FRATERNITY'. Meanwhile, the royal family had been removed from Versailles to Paris (Oct 1789), but after their flight to Varennes (June 1791) their fate was sealed. A **LEGISLATIVE ASSEMBLY** was elected; however, after an insurrection on 10 Aug 1792, France was declared a republic (1792), and a new assembly (the National **CONVENTION**) was effected in Sep 1792. At the same time, the September Massacres occurred. The Paris crowd, in panic at the advance of invading armies, and incited by demagogues, entered the prisons and massacred thousands of innocent victims. **LOUIS XVI** and his queen, **MARIE ANTOINETTE**, were executed (1793). The Revolution then entered more dramatic phases, marked by political extremism and bitter rivalry between **GIRONDINS** and **JACOBINS** (the latter led by **ROBESPIERRE**). Although the Jacobins seized control of the Committee of **PUBLIC SAFETY** (July 1793) and instituted the dictatorship of the Reign of **TERROR**, Robespierre's short-lived triumph ended with his execution (1794). The Convention suppressed opponents from both sides, Jacobins and royalists, with military force before establishing the government of the **DIRECTORY** (1795), which was in turn overthrown by Napoleon Bonaparte (**NAPOLEON I**) in the **BRUMAIRE COUP** (1799). Under the **CONSULATE** (1799–1804) and the First Empire (1804–15), many of the ideas of the Revolution, such as popular sovereignty and civil equality, were disseminated in those areas of Europe subjected to French rule. ▶ **CHOUANS**; **EMPIRE, FIRST** (France); **FRENCH REPUBLI-**

**CAN CALENDAR**; **FRENCH REVOLUTIONARY WARS**; **MOUNTAIN, THE**; **PLAIN, THE**; **SANS-CULOTTES**

### French Revolutionary Wars (1792–9)
A series of campaigns between France and neighbouring European states hostile to the **FRENCH REVOLUTION** and to French hegemony, merging ultimately into the **NAPOLEONIC WARS** (1799–1815). Starting with France's declaration of war on Emperor **FRANCIS II**, Prussia and Sardinia, which precipitated the War of the First Coalition (1792–7), French forces attacked the Rhine, the Netherlands and Savoy, after checking an initial Austro-Prussian advance at Valmy (1792). France later extended hostilities to Britain, Holland and Spain (1793); after successfully invading the Netherlands (1794), the French broke the Coalition (1795–6), isolating Britain (1797). A Second Coalition (1798) expelled French forces from Italy and the Rhinelands, before suffering defeat by **NAPOLEON I** (1799–1800). ▶ **DUMOURIEZ, CHARLES FRANÇOIS (DU PÉRIER)**; **MURAT, JOACHIM**

### French State (*État français*) (1940–4)
The name given to the regime established after the French defeat in 1940, in which all power was placed in the hands of **PÉTAIN**, to emphasize the break made with the Third Republic; Pétain was given power to promulgate a new constitution, but one was never drawn up. The French State is also known unofficially as the **VICHY** regime, from its capital in the zone not originally occupied by the German army; it was abolished upon the liberation of occupied France, by an ordinance of Aug 1944. ▶ **COLLABORATION** (France); **REPUBLIC, THIRD** (France); **WORLD WAR II**

### French Union (*Union française*)
A term for the French Empire introduced by the constitution of the Fourth Republic in 1946. Former colonies were reclassified as departments of France or overseas territories; trust territories became overseas territories; and former protectorates became associated states. The latter had all become independent when the Union was renamed the *Communauté* ('community') in 1958; the former colonies rapidly gained their independence also, leaving only a few small overseas departments and territories (**DOM-TOM**). ▶ **REPUBLIC, FOURTH** (France)

### Frère-Orban, Hubert Joseph Walthère (1812–96)
Belgian politician. He trained as a lawyer, and was one of the most prominent Francophone liberal leaders in Belgium of the 19c. He took part in most liberal cabinets from 1847 onwards, and was Prime Minister (1867–70 and 1878–84). His liberalism was primarily economic, and aimed against restrictions on entrepreneurial freedom; in political matters his liberalism was moderate or 'doctrinaire', not extending to universal suffrage or social reforms.

### Frescobaldi
One of several banking families in 14–15c Florence with European-wide interests. Their clients included **EDWARD II** of England, whose wars with Scotland they financed in exchange for customs revenues. The royal default on debts led to a crisis for the Frescobaldi bank in 1311. ▶ **BARDI AND PERUZZI**

**Freyberg, Bernard, 1st Baron Freyberg** (1889–1963)
New Zealand soldier. Born in London, he was educated at Wellington College, New Zealand. At the outbreak of WORLD WAR I he enlisted in England and served in Gallipoli and France, winning the Victoria Cross at Beaumont Hamel. In WORLD WAR II he was given command of the New Zealand forces in the Middle East. He commanded Commonwealth forces in ill-fated operations in Greece and Crete (1941) and in the Sahara. He commanded the New Zealand Corps in Italy (1944–5) and was Governor-General of New Zealand (1946–52).

**Freycinet, Charles Louis de Saulces de** (1818–1923)
French politician. An engineer, in 1870 he was called by GAMBETTA to the War Department where he rendered great services. He was a Senator from 1876 to 1920, and his ministerial career spanned the years 1877 to 1916, during which he was four times Prime Minister (1879–80, 1882, 1886 and 1890–2). He was Prime Minister and Foreign Minister at a crucial moment, in 1882, when French withdrawal from a proposed joint expedition led to British control of Egypt: his major contribution was at the Ministry of War (1888–93).

**Friedland, Battle of** (June 1807)
A battle fought in northern Prussia between French and Russian forces. It resulted in a complete, if costly, victory for NAPOLEON I, forcing the Russians to sue for peace, which was signed the next month under the terms of the Treaty of Tilsit. It was one of the crucial encounters in the collapse of the Fourth Coalition (Britain, Russia and Prussia) against France. Prussia suffered most; Russia, although defeated, strengthened its position as a major European power since Tsar ALEXANDER I reached a number of ruler-to-ruler agreements with Napoleon. ►TILSIT, TREATIES OF

**Friedman, Milton** (1912–)
US economist. The foremost exponent of MONETARISM, he argued that a country's economy can be controlled through its money supply. He was awarded the 1976 Nobel Prize for Economics, and was a policy adviser to the REAGAN administration (1981–8). His ideas were applied in the UK, with almost messianic zeal, by the Conservative government of Margaret THATCHER.

**Friends, Society of**
A Christian sect founded by George Fox and others in mid-17c England, and formally organized in 1667; members are popularly known as Quakers, possibly because of Fox's injunction 'to quake at the word of the Lord'. Persecution led William PENN to establish a Quaker colony (Pennsylvania) in 1682. Belief in the 'inner light', a living contact with the divine Spirit, is the basis of its meetings for worship, where Friends gather in silence until moved by the Spirit to speak. They emphasize simplicity in all things, and are active reformers promoting tolerance, justice and peace. Today most meetings have programmed orders of worship, though meetings based on silence (unprogrammed) still prevail in the UK and parts of the USA.

**Frihedsråd**
Literally 'Freedom Council', a coordinating body established in Denmark (Sep 1943) in order to regulate and escalate the country's resistance against the Nazi occupation (1940–5). The formation of the *Frihedsråd* came in response to the dismissal of the Danish government by the German occupation force (29 Aug 1943), following extensive strike action and several acts of sabotage in Danish towns and cities. The Frihedsråd gathered all factions of the Danish resistance movement, from Communists to Conservatives. By definition, the organization carried no official authority, but it played a vital role in organizing the growing sabotage campaign, and in the formation and command of a Danish underground army numbering 43,000 men at the time of the German capitulation. The Frihedsråd was supported by the Allied nations, particularly the UK, and its activities contributed greatly to the recognition of Denmark as an Allied nation after WORLD WAR II. During the war, the Frihedsråd was also involved in formulating the broadly democratic political direction that peacetime Denmark was to follow. Several of its members took office in the first Danish post-war government, formed in May 1945, immediately after the liberation of Denmark by Allied forces. ►DENMARK, GERMAN INVASION OF

**Frolov, Ivan Timofeevich** (1929–)
Soviet philosopher, ideologist and journalist. He had a long education in Moscow before turning to journalism in the 1960s and 1970s, when he had two spells on the *World Marxist Review* in Prague divided by a turn as editor of *Problems of Philosophy* in Moscow. In the latter case he had some disagreements with orthodox views that made him a target for Mikhail GORBACHEV's recruiting policy. In 1986 he was appointed editor of *Communist*, in 1989 editor-in-chief of *Pravda*, and in 1990 a member of the POLITBURO. However, Gorbachev's role was all but past.

**Fronde, The** (1648–53)
A series of civil revolts in France during the regency of ANNE OF AUSTRIA, caused by economic grievances and opposition to Cardinal MAZARIN and the central government. The disturbances, named after a contemporary street urchins' game, developed into two phases: the *Fronde Parlementaire* (1648–9), and that of the Princes (1650–3). After the declaration of LOUIS XIV's majority (1651), the Princes' opposition was slowly undermined; royal forces under TURENNE recovered Paris (1652) and the provinces (1652–3), ending the most serious threat to the central government during the ANCIEN RÉGIME.

**Front de Libération de Québec** (FLQ, 'Quebec Liberation Front')
Canadian terrorist organization set up in the early 1960s with the aim of separating Quebec Province from Canada. On the extreme left wing and anticapitalist, it targeted the prosperous English-speaking sector of Quebec society. The FLQ had little formal organization, although arrangements were made for its members to train with the PLO. It gave the impression of being a much larger conspiracy than it actually was, for its name was simply appropriated by small independent groups to indicate responsibility for terrorist attacks. The arrest of Pierre Vallière and

Charles Gagnon, two of the movement's theorists, set off its most active period which culminated in the OCTOBER CRISIS of 1970. ► PARTI QUÉBECOIS

**Frontenac, Louis de Buade, Count of** (1622–98)
French-Canadian politician. He served in the army, and in 1672 was appointed Governor of the French possessions in North America. He was recalled for misgovernment in 1682, but was sent out again in 1689. He extended the boundaries of NEW FRANCE down the Mississippi, launched attacks on New England villages, repulsed the British siege of Quebec (1690), and broke the power of the Iroquois (1696).

**frontier thesis**
The theory proposed by US historian Frederick Jackson Turner (1861–1932) in his essay 'The Significance of the Frontier in American History' (1893). Turner argued that the existence of a western frontier area throughout most of the USA's history had a profound effect on the nation's character, and that US society had been spared massive social unrest because citizens unhappy with their lot in life could always begin anew by moving to the frontier. In effect, frontier life fostered the individualism and democratic spirit that made the USA unique among nations.

**Frundsberg, Georg von** (1473–1528)
German soldier. He was the founder and leader of German *Landsknechte* during the ITALIAN WARS of Emperors MAXIMILIAN I and CHARLES V. He fought in 20 pitched battles, and the victory at PAVIA (1525) was largely due to him.

**Frunze, Mikhail Vasilevich** (1885–1925)
Russian revolutionary and professional soldier. Frunze exercised profound influence upon Soviet military doctrine. A Bolshevik from 1904, active in both the 1905 and 1917 events, he rose to prominence in the RUSSIAN CIVIL WAR with successful commands on the eastern and southern fronts. But he was soon engaged in debate with TROTSKY, Commissar for War, about creating a RED ARMY fit for the future. In 1925 he displaced him but died during an operation, often claimed to have been a medical murder. But his concept of unified command and policy won through. ► BOLSHEVIKS

**Fuad I** (1868–1936)
King of Egypt (1922/36). The son of Khedive ISMA'IL PASHA, he was Sultan of Egypt from 1917, and became King when the British protectorate was ended. His position in Egypt was not helped by the fact that his father had been responsible for the sale (at a farcically low price) of Egyptian Suez Canal shares to Britain, or his brother Tawfiq's incapacity as a ruler, which had led to the British occupation of 1883. The Egyptian nationalists of the WAFD PARTY despised his dispensation, and his acquisition and flaunting of conspicuous wealth, coupled with his corrupt entourage of hangers-on, provoked adverse comment. In an attempt to control the party, he suspended the constitution in 1931, but was forced to restore it in 1935. He was succeeded by his son, FAROUK I, who was to be the last King of Egypt.

**Fuad Pasha, Mehmed** (1814–69)
Turkish politician and littérateur. He was the son of the poet Izzet-Mollah, became an Admiralty physi-

cian, but in 1835 took up history and politics. After diplomatic service in London and Madrid, he became Grand Interpreter to the Porte, Minister of Foreign Affairs (1852 and 1855), and Grand Vizier (1861–6). To him Turkey owed the hatti-sherif of 1856.

**Fuchs, (Emil) Klaus (Julius)** (1912–88)
British spy and physicist. Born in Rüsselsheim, Germany, he escaped from Nazi persecution to the UK in 1933, was interned during WORLD WAR II, then naturalized in 1942. From 1943 he worked in the USA on the atom bomb, and in 1946 became head of the theoretical physics division at Harwell, UK. He was sentenced in 1950 to 14 years' imprisonment for disclosing nuclear secrets to the Russians, but was released (1959) and worked in the nuclear research centre of East Germany until 1979.

**fuero**
A traditional Spanish (and Spanish-American) term for a set of legal privileges and immunities attaching to a specific group, such as the clergy or the army, or to a region, most notably the Basque country.

**Fugger**
A south German family of merchants and bankers who reached their greatest importance during the late 15c and early 16c. Weavers by origin and settled at Augsburg since 1367, they rose to prominence through a series of judicious marriages and success in the spice and cloth trade. Their business interests spread over much of central, southern and eastern Europe, culminating in the financing of the imperial election of CHARLES V, who subsequently elevated one of their number, Jakob II, the Rich (1459–1525), to the rank of imperial count. The latter was also responsible for setting up the still extant Fuggerei, a charitable foundation providing houses for the poor of Augsburg. From the late 16c, the family's influence declined.

**Fugitive Slave Laws** (1793 and 1850)
US federal legislation requiring the return of runaway slaves who fled to states where SLAVERY had been abolished. Enforcement was hindered by the 'personal liberty laws' of several Northern states, which allowed runaway slaves the benefit of a trial by jury, and sometimes by popular 'rescues' of captured runaways. The laws were repealed in 1864. ► COMPROMISE OF 1850

**Fujimori, Alberto Kenyo** (1939–)
Peruvian politician. He founded and led the conservative Cambio '90 ('Change '90') Party, and, promising reform, succeeded Alan GARCÍA PÉREZ to become President in 1990. Within two years he had dismantled the existing order in Peru by dismissing Congress (1992), sacking senior judges, imposing order through an 'Emergency National Reconstruction Government', and changing the constitution. His administration was dogged throughout by violence from the Maoist SENDERO LUMINOSO ('Shining Path') guerrilla group. In 2000, he fled to Japan to avoid corruption charges and was stripped of the presidency.

**Fujiwara Family**
An influential Japanese courtier family during the HEIAN ERA (794–1185). The Fujiwara achieved

prominence through intermarriage with the imperial family; as the fathers of empresses, Fujiwara family heads were able to exercise *de facto* authority. In the 9c they often assumed the post of regent (*sessho*) for child emperors, controlling finances and appointments. One of the most influential of Fujiwara family heads was Fujiwara no Michinaga (966–1028), the father of four empresses and grandfather of three emperors, who dominated the court for 30 years. The family's influence gradually waned as increasingly ambitious military families in the provinces began to encroach on its vast landholdings, the basis of Fujiwara economic power.

**Fukoku-Kyohei ('Wealthy Country and Strong Army')**
A slogan used in Japan by government leaders after the MEIJI RESTORATION in 1868 to describe national policy. Priority was given to a programme of industrial and military modernization to strengthen the country against the perceived threat of Western imperialism. Such a programme, it was hoped, would also convince the Western powers to treat Japan on an equal basis and revise the unequal treaties signed under the TOKUGAWA SHOGUNATE in the 1850s and 1860s.

**Fukuda Takeo** (1905–95)
Japanese politician and financier. He worked at the Ministry of Finance (1929–50) and was Deputy Vice-Minister (1945–6), Director of the Banking Bureau (1946–7), and Director of the Budget Bureau (1947–50). A member of the House of Representatives from 1952, he served as Minister of Finance (1965–6, 1968–71 and 1973–4). In 1974 he became Deputy Prime Minister and Director of the Economic Planning Agency, until his appointment as Prime Minister (1976–8). He was President of the LIBERAL DEMOCRATIC PARTY in 1966–8 and 1976–8.

**Fukuzawa Yukichi** (1835–1901)
Japanese political thinker and educator. From a lower-ranking SAMURAI family, he was an avid student of the West and was a member of the first official Japanese missions to the USA (1860) and Europe (1862). After the MEIJI RESTORATION (1868), Fukuzawa championed the virtues of individualism, cosmopolitanism and a scientific spirit, arguing that only a reformed people would achieve national wealth and strength. He also played a crucial role in the development of higher education and a modern press.

**Fulani Emirates**
Muslim states formed by the Fulbe or Peul Fula-speaking peoples of the Sahel zone of West Africa. The pastoral Fulani established their authority over the agricultural Hausa in a series of holy wars in the early 19c. The kingdoms were subsequently conquered by the British, and in the early 20c they became one of the prototypes of the INDIRECT RULE system.

**Fulbright, James William** (1905–95)
US politician. Educated at the University of Arkansas, and George Washington University Law School, he was a Rhodes scholar at Oxford, and taught law in Washington and Arkansas. He was elected to the HOUSE OF REPRESENTATIVES as a Democrat in 1942 and to the SENATE in 1944. He sponsored the Fulbright Act (1946), which established an exchange scholarship system for students and teachers between the USA and other countries. As Chairman of the Senate Foreign Relations Committee, he became a major critic of the escalation of the VIETNAM WAR. He lost his Senate seat in 1974. ► DEMOCRATIC PARTY

**Fulk V** (1095–1143)
Count of Anjou (1109/31) and King of Jerusalem (1131/43). He was proposed by LOUIS VI, THE FAT of France, to be King of Jerusalem at the request of King BALDWIN II, who had no male heirs. Fulk arrived in the Holy Land in May 1129 and moved to Jerusalem where he married Melisend, one of Baldwin's four daughters. On Baldwin's death (1131), Fulk and Melisend were crowned King and Queen of Jerusalem. Fulk's accession was the occasion for an outburst of the internal rivalries that so bedevilled the Latin Kingdom. More serious problems, however, were in store as, after a period of damaging internecine strife amongst the Muslim princelings in the Levant, the Turkish Atabeg, 'Imad al-Din Zangi, was setting in train the harnessing of Muslim effort against the FRANKS in the north, and in 1136 the Damascenes also went on the offensive. Fulk was, however, capable of handling the Muslims both in the military and diplomatic spheres and when, later, Damascus itself was threatened by Zangi, it was an alliance with Fulk that saved the city. Thus, despite problems internally with his fellow Franks and externally with the Muslims, by 1140 King Fulk was securely established in his own kingdom.

**Fuller, (Sarah) Margaret** (1810–50)
US feminist and journalist. She became part of the Transcendentalist circle that centred around Ralph Waldo Emerson, and despite a lack of higher education was known as one of its brightest stars. Her *Woman in the Nineteenth Century* (1845) is the earliest major piece of US feminist writing. She died in a shipwreck while returning to the USA after taking part in the abortive Italian revolution of 1848.

**Fuller, Melville Weston** (1833–1910)
US jurist. He practised law in Chicago from 1856 and became active in the DEMOCRATIC PARTY, befriending Grover CLEVELAND, who in 1888 appointed Fuller Chief Justice of the Supreme Court. Although he lacked a national reputation at the time of his appointment, he soon won praise for his skilful leadership of the court and his ability to engineer compromises. He sought to protect traditional civil liberties and tended towards a strict interpretation of the Constitution. In 1895 he wrote two important decisions weakening the Sherman Anti-Trust Act and striking down the first personal INCOME TAX passed by CONGRESS. ► ANTI-TRUST ACTS

**Funan** ► SOUTH-EAST ASIA PRE-1000AD

**Fundamental Orders of Connecticut** (1639)
US colonial charter. An agreement for self-government adopted by the Connecticut towns of Hartford, Windsor and Wethersfield, and extended to other towns. It was replaced by a royal charter in 1662.

**Funding Loan**
This term refers to the loan of £10 million contracted (June 1898) between CAMPOS SALLES and the Rothschilds to enable Brazil to meet its external obligations

for 12 years, and thus prevent a formal declaration of state bankruptcy. Guaranteed by the Rio Customs receipts, it enabled the government to stabilize the exchange rate and control expenditure, introduce sales taxes in Rio, raise excise taxes, dramatically reduce the money supply, and lease railroads to international firms. The measure consolidated financial institutions, and stimulated the cartelization of coffee exports and the growth of industry; opposition to it was met by the imposition of one-party rule in the states. At the outset of **WORLD WAR I**, another loan (of £15 million) was negotiated; this operation terminated in 1927.

## fuorusciti

The Italian word (literally, 'exile', 'outlaw', 'émigré') often applied to political opponents of the fascist regime who fled, or were forced to leave, Italy during the 1920s and 1930s. Many served in the republican armies in the **SPANISH CIVIL WAR** and consequently fought against Italian troops sent by **MUSSOLINI** to assist **FRANCO**. They achieved a famous victory over Italian fascist 'volunteers' at the Battle of Guadalajara (Mar 1937). ➤ **FASCISM**

## fur trade

The history of the fur trade in North America is inextricably linked with the exploration of the continent and the struggle between France and Britain for its control. The trade was first centred along the St Lawrence River and the Atlantic coast around Newfoundland and **ACADIA** during the late 16c and early 17c. The furs were brought to the fishing stations by **NATIVE AMERICANS** attracted by the exchange for relatively cheap trinkets and other manufactured goods. In 1608 Samuel de **CHAMPLAIN** established a base at Quebec and contacts with the **ALGONQUIN** and **HURON** tribes, whom he assisted against their traditional enemies, the Iroquois. With the advance of settlement and the opening up of trading routes into the interior, it became clear by the late 17c that the French were caught between the British colonies to the south and the **HUDSON'S BAY COMPANY** (set up in 1670 as the result of information from two disaffected French traders) to the north and west. While the Iroquois acted as middlemen bringing the trade into British hands at Albany, the French re-established a forward position with the chain of forts and trading posts that controlled the Great Lakes region and the upper Mississippi and Ohio valleys until the cession of **NEW FRANCE** to Britain in 1763. In the late 18c and early 19c the north-western fur trade was bitterly contested between the independents, who organized themselves as the **NORTH WEST COMPANY** (opening up new routes to the Pacific seaboard, where they found John Jacob **ASTOR**'s Pacific Fur Company already established), and the Hudson's Bay Company. After the amalgamation of the two Canadian companies in 1821, the HBC organized the trade on a continental basis, ceding its lands to the Dominion in 1869 but continuing as the most important economic force in the north. ➤ **IROQUOIS CONFEDERACY**

## Furtseva, Yekaterina Alexeevna (1910–74)

The first woman member of the Soviet Communist Party's **POLITBURO**. After a technical education, she became a party worker and rose to be district secretary in Moscow in 1942 and a member of the Central Committee in 1956. A supporter of Nikita **KHRUSHCHEV**, she was brought into the Politburo in 1957 in the aftermath of the **ANTI-PARTY PLOT**. Hardly a major political figure, she was pushed out in 1961. However, from 1960 until her death she was Minister of Culture and apparently had no difficulty in insisting on ever greater conformity.

## Futa Jalon and Futa Toro

Regions in West Africa, respectively the highlands near the source of the River Senegal and the valley of the lower Senegal, where a sequence of jihads or holy wars broke out among the Fulani herdsmen in the 17–18c. These wars produced Islamic states that were the forerunners of their more significant 19c successors. West African history became essentially a conflict of two imperialisms, African-Islamic and European.

# G

## GABON  official name **Gabonese Republic**

A republic in west equatorial Africa, bounded to the south, east and north-east by the Congo; to the north by Cameroon; to the north-west by Equatorial Guinea; and to the west by the Atlantic Ocean. Gabon was visited by the Portuguese in the 15c and was under French control from the mid-19c. A slave ship was captured by the French and the liberated slaves formed the settlement of Libreville in 1849. The country was occupied by France in 1885, and became one of four territories of French West Africa in 1910. It gained independence in 1960 under President **M'BA**, and in 1991 a new constitution was introduced allowing a multiparty system. President Omar **BONGO**, in power since M'ba's death in 1967, retained his position on being re-elected in the multiparty presidential elections in 1993 and was re-elected for a fifth term in 1998. His *Parti Démocratique Gabonais* ('Gabonese Democratic Party') has remained the ruling party under the multiparty system, although the government includes opposition party members.

## Gaddafi, Muammar (1942–)

Libyan political and military leader. He abandoned his university studies in favour of military training in 1963, and went on to form the **FREE OFFICERS' MOVEMENT** which overthrew King Idris in 1969. He became Chairman of the Revolutionary Command Council, promoted himself to colonel (the highest rank in the revolutionary army) and became Commander-in-Chief of the Libyan Armed Forces. As *de facto* head of state, he set about eradicating colonialism by expelling foreigners and closing down British and US bases. He also encouraged a religious revival and return to the fundamental principles of Islam. A somewhat unpredictable figure, Gaddafi has openly supported violent revolutionaries in other parts of the world while ruthlessly pursuing Libyan dissi-

dents both at home and abroad. He waged a war in Chad, threatened other neighbours, and in the 1980s saw his territory bombed and aircraft shot down by the USA. In the 1990s his refusal to extradite for trial two Libyan men suspected of organizing the bombing of a PanAm aircraft over Lockerbie, Scotland, in 1988, led to the imposition of sanctions by the **UN** Security Council in 1992. Eventually, with the help of a deal brokered by Nelson **MANDELA**, he agreed in Apr 1999 to a trial in the Netherlands, and sanctions were lifted. Since 2003 he has made further moves to end Libya's isolation, and in 2004 promised to allow UN nuclear weapons inspections.

## Gadsden Purchase (1853)

A strip of land in south Arizona and New Mexico bought by the USA from Mexico for US$10 million. The purchase was negotiated by the minister to Mexico, James Gadsden (1788–1858), as a feasible route for a southern railroad to the Pacific.

## Gage, Thomas (1721–87)

British general. In 1760 he became Military Governor of Montreal, in 1763 Commander-in-Chief of the British forces in America, and in 1774 Governor of Massachusetts. In 1775 (18 Apr) he sent a force to seize a quantity of arms at Concord; the next day the skirmish of Lexington took place which began the **AMERICAN REVOLUTION**. After the Battle of **BUNKER HILL** (June 1775) he resigned, and returned to England, where he died. ➤ **LEXINGTON AND CONCORD, BATTLES OF**

## Gairy, Sir Eric Matthew (1922–97)

Grenadian politician. In 1950 he founded the country's first political party, the left-of-centre Grenada United Labour Party (GULP) and was soon a dominant figure in Caribbean politics. He held the posts of Chief Minister in the Federation of the West Indies (1957–62), Premier of Grenada (1967–74) and, on independence in 1974, Prime Minister. He was ousted by the left-wing leader Maurice **BISHOP** in 1979 and GULP was defeated in the 1990 election by the National Democratic Congress of Nicholas Brathwaite. ➤ **WEST INDIES, FEDERATION OF THE**

## Gaitskell, Hugh Todd Naylor (1906–63)

British politician. He became a socialist during the 1926 **GENERAL STRIKE**. He became an MP in 1945, he was Minister of Fuel and Power (1947) and of Economic Affairs (1950), and Chancellor of the Exchequer (1950–1). In 1955 he was elected Leader of the Opposition by a large majority over **BEVAN**. He bitterly opposed **EDEN**'s Suez action (1956), and refused to accept a narrow conference vote for uni-lateral disarmament (1960). This caused a crisis of leadership in which he was challenged by Harold **WILSON** (1960) and Arthur Greenwood (1961), but he retained the loyalty of most Labour MPs. ► **BUTS-KELLISM**; **LABOUR PARTY** (UK); **SUEZ CRISIS**

**Gaj, Ljudevit** (1809–72)
Croatian nationalist. Inspired in his youth by the ro-mantic nationalism of Kollár, Šafarík and Herder, his belief in the common nationality of the **SOUTH SLAVS** (whom he referred to as Illyrians) led him to formu-late a standard South Slav literary language and found a Croatian newspaper. Through his literary activities, he became increasingly involved in opposition to Hungarian and German political and cultural influ-ence in Croatia. To counter the pro-Hungarian party in Croatia, in 1841 he founded the Illyrian National Party, which espoused the ideas of the **ILLYRIAN MOVEMENT** and championed Croatian state-right. Ever hopeful for the support of Vienna against the Hungarian nationalists, he concluded a pact with the Hungarian conservatives in a move designed to gain the confidence of the Austrian minister **METTERNICH** (1845). Under the government of *Ban* Josip **JELAČIĆ**, in Mar 1848 Gaj led a delegation to Vienna and pre-sented the Emperor with the Croats' requests for the reorganization of the Habsburg Monarchy as a fed-eration. Later that year he was elected to the Croatian *sabor* (parliament), but shortly afterwards was ob-liged to leave political life, following his apparent in-volvement in a financial scandal with the Serbian prince Miloš **OBRENOVIĆ**. ► **STROSSMAYER, JOSIP JURAJ**; **YUGOSLAVISM**

**Galawdewos** (d.1559)
Emperor of Ethiopia (1540/59). With Portuguese aid he defeated the Muslims who, under **AHMAD GRAN**, (Ahmad ibn Ibrahim al-Ghazi) had dominated Ethiopia in the early years of the 16c. He strength-ened the authority of the monarchy and reformed the cultural and religious institutions of the empire. Towards the end of his reign he was preoccupied with the migration of Galla tribesmen but, despite various successes in battle (1554–5), was unable perma-nently to check their advance.

**Galdan** (c.1632–1697)
Chief of the western **MONGOLS**, or **DZUNGARS**. He re-sisted the encroachment of the Manchu **QING DY-NASTY** and, following the Qing subjugation of the eastern Mongols in 1675, took the offensive. By the late 1670s Galdan had taken control of several central Asian oases, such as Kashgar and Turfan. The Qing Emperor **KANGXI** had to undertake three campaigns in the 1690s before defeating Galdan at the Battle of Jao Modo (Outer Mongolia) and forcing him to com-mit suicide.

**Galileo**, properly **Galileo Galilei** (1564–1642)
Italian astronomer and mathematician. He entered the university at Pisa as a medical student in 1581. He became Professor of Mathematics at Padua (1592–1610), where he improved the refracting tele-scope (1610), and was the first to use it for astronomy. His realization that the ancient Aristotelian teachings were unacceptable brought severe ecclesiastical cen-sure, and he was forced to retract before the **INQUISI-TION**. ► **SCIENCE**; **SCIENTIFIC REVOLUTION, THE**

**Gall**, original name **Pizi** (c.1840–1894)
Native American **SIOUX** chieftain. Orphaned at an early age, he was cared for as a younger brother by the Sioux chief **SITTING BULL**, whose war chief he be-came. With Sitting Bull and **CRAZY HORSE**, Gall played an instrumental role in the Battle of the **LITTLE BIG-HORN** (1876), where General **CUSTER** and his 200-strong force were annihilated. Gall and Sitting Bull went to Canada, but there was nowhere to live and no buffalo left to hunt, so Gall left again, gave himself up to the US Army and settled on a reservation in South Dakota. From 1881 he encouraged his people to be more friendly towards the whites. In 1889 he became a judge at the Indian Agency's Court of In-dian Offences. That same year he was persuaded to sign the treaty that ceded much of the Sioux territory to white settlers. ► **NATIVE AMERICANS**

**Gallatin, Albert** (1761–1849)
US financier and politician. In 1793 he was elected a senator, in 1795 a member of the **HOUSE OF REPRE-SENTATIVES**, and from 1801 to 1813 was US Secretary of the Treasury. He played an important part in the peace negotiations with Great Britain in 1814, and signed the Treaty of **GHENT**.

**Gallegos, Rómulo** (1884–1969)
Venezuelan politician. In his country's first demo-cratic elections (1948), Gallegos became President. However, his **LIBERALISM** displeased the military and certain powerful elements in the USA, and he was deposed within a few months. He lived in exile until 1958, when he was welcomed back as an hon-oured hero.

**Gallicanism**
A French religious doctrine, emphasizing royal or episcopal authority over matters pertaining to the French Church at the expense of papal sovereignty. It emerged during **PHILIP IV**'s struggle with **BONIFACE VIII** (1297–1303), and remained a traditional, though controversial force in France, invoked to defend established liberties against **ULTRAMONTANISM** and papal interference.

**Galliéni, Joseph Simon** (1849–1916)
French soldier. He served in the war of 1870–1, also in West Africa and Tonkin, and was Governor of Upper Senegal from 1886, and Governor-General of Mada-gascar (1897–1905). As Minister for War, and Milit-ary Governor of Paris from 1914, he saw to its fortifications and contributed to the victory of the **MARNE** (1914) by his foresight and planning. He was posthumously created Marshal of France in 1921.

**Gallipoli Campaign** (1915–16)
A major campaign of **WORLD WAR I**. With stalemate on the Western Front, the British War Council advo-cated operations against the Turks to secure the **DAR-DANELLES** and aid Russia. The land campaign began with amphibious assaults on the Gallipoli Peninsula (Apr 1915). Australian and New Zealand forces were heavily involved; the beach where they landed is still known as Anzac Cove. Allied casualties were 250,000 out of 480,000 engaged. The operation was aban-doned as a costly failure, with successful evacuations of all remaining troops in Jan 1916. ► **ANZAC**

**Galt, Sir Alexander Tilloch** (1817–93)
Canadian politician. In 1844–55 he was High Commissioner of the British American Land Company, which made huge profits from lands obtained through its influence with the Château Clique and in London. As a business leader of the English-speaking community in **CANADA EAST**, his signature on the **ANNEXATION MANIFESTO** in 1849 reflected fears for its future in markets no longer protected by the British **NAVIGATION ACTS**. However, he recognized that **RECIPROCITY** would only be of benefit with a more integrated Canadian economy, and in 1858 he was persuaded by **MACDONALD** and George Étienne **CARTIER** (with whom he was involved in the Grand Trunk Railway) to enter politics, on the understanding that they would work towards confederation. As Finance Minister in the Macdonald–Cartier administration, he introduced the high tariffs of 1859, and he served in the 'great coalition' of 1864 that negotiated the terms of confederation. In 1880 he became the first Canadian High Commissioner in London. ▶ **CONFEDERATION MOVEMENT**

**Galtieri, Leopoldo Fortunato** (1926–2003)
Argentine soldier and politician. After training at the National Military College, he was commissioned in 1945 and progressed steadily to the rank of lieutenant-general in 1979, when he joined the junta which had been in power since the military coup that ousted Isabelita **PERÓN** in 1976. In 1981 the leader of the junta, General Viola, died and Galtieri succeeded him as President. The state of the Argentine economy worsened and, to counter mounting domestic criticism, in Apr 1982 Galtieri ordered the invasion of the long-disputed Malvinas (Falkland) Islands. Their recovery by Britain, after a brief and humiliating war, brought about his downfall. He was court-martialled in 1983 and sentenced to 12 years' imprisonment for negligence in starting and losing the **FALKLANDS WAR**. He was released in 1989.

**Gama, Vasco da** (c.1469–1525)
Portuguese navigator. Born in Sines, Alentejo, he led the fleet which, in the wake of Bartolomeu Dias' rounding of the Cape of Good Hope (1488), made the first direct voyage from Lisbon to the Malabar coast of south-west India. In 1502–3 he led a squadron of ships to Calicut to avenge the murder of a group of Portuguese explorers left there by Pedro Cabral, and in 1524 he was sent as viceroy to India but died shortly after. ▶ **EXPLORATION**

**Gambetta, Léon Michel** (1838–82)
French politician. A republican, he was one of the opposition deputies in 1869. After the surrender of **NAPOLEON III**, he helped to proclaim the Third Republic (1870), became Minister of the Interior in the Government of **NATIONAL DEFENCE**, made a spectacular escape from the Siege of Paris in a balloon, and for five months ruled France as leader of the Tours Delegation until the armistice of 28 Jan 1871. Re-emerging as leader of the republicans, his role was important in the voting of the constitutional laws of 1875, and in the defeat of **MACMAHON**'s abortive coup in 1877. The jealousy of other republican politicians, and fear of the role that could be played by such a popular and strong leader, meant that he was subsequently virtually excluded from office, only forming a weak and

brief ministry in 1882, before his early accidental death. ▶ **PARIS, SIEGE OF**; **REPUBLIC, THIRD** (France)

**GAMBIA, THE**    official name **Republic of The Gambia**

A republic in west Africa, bounded on all sides by Senegal except for the Atlantic Ocean coastline in the west. Visited by the Portuguese in 1455, it was settled by the English in the 17c and became an independent British Crown Colony in 1843. It joined the **COMMONWEALTH OF NATIONS** in 1965 and became a republic in 1970 under the presidency of Sir Dawda Kairaba **JAWARA**. Between 1982 and 1989 the Gambia and Senegal joined to form the Confederation of **SENEGAMBIA**. In 1994 Jawara was ousted in a military coup and replaced by Yahya Jammeh, who was elected President in 1996 and re-elected in 2001. His Alliance for Patriotic Reorientation and Construction party won the 2002 election, which was boycotted by opposition parties.

**Gamelin, Maurice Gustave** (1872–1958)
French soldier. He attained lieutenant-colonel's rank in 1914, but no divisional command until 1925. In 1935 seniority brought him the post of Chief of Staff of the army and membership of the *Conseil supérieur de la guerre* ('Supreme War Council'); but his unfitness for overall command was exposed in his pronouncement that 'To attack is to lose'. In 1940 he refused to rethink his outmoded defensive strategy of 'solid fronts', which crumbled under the German **BLITZKRIEG**. He was hurriedly replaced by General **WEYGAND**, tried and imprisoned (1943–5). ▶ **RIOM TRIAL**

**Gandhi, Indira Priyadarshini** (1917–84)
Indian politician. The daughter of Jawaharlal **NEHRU**, she was educated at Visva-Bharati University (Bengal) and Oxford, and in 1942 married Feroze Gandhi (d.1960). She became President of the Indian Congress Party (1959–60), Minister of Information (1964) and Prime Minister (1966–77) after the death of Shastri. After her conviction for election malpractices, she declared a state of emergency (1975–7), was defeated in elections by the Janata Party, and was Premier again (1980–4). She achieved a considerable reputation through her work as a leader of the developing nations, but was unable to stem sectarian violence at home. She was assassinated in New Delhi by Sikh extremists who were members of her bodyguard, and succeeded by her elder son, Rajiv **GANDHI**. ▶ **INDIAN NATIONAL CONGRESS**

**Gandhi, M(ohandas) K(aramchand)** (1869–1948)
Indian nationalist leader. He studied law in London, and in 1893 went to South Africa, where he spent 21 years opposing discriminatory legislation against Indians. In 1914 he returned to India, where he supported the Home Rule movement, and became

leader of the **INDIAN NATIONAL CONGRESS**, advocating a policy of non-violent non-cooperation to achieve independence. Following his first major non-cooperation and **CIVIL DISOBEDIENCE** campaign (1919–22), he was jailed for conspiracy (1922–4). In 1930 he led a 200-mile march to the sea to collect salt in symbolic defiance of the government monopoly; this marked the beginning of the second major campaign of civil disobedience. On his release from prison (1931), he attended the London Round Table Conference on Indian constitutional reform. In 1946 he negotiated with the Cabinet Mission which recommended the new constitutional structure. After independence (1947), he tried to stop the Hindu–Muslim conflict in Bengal, a policy which led to his assassination in Delhi by Nathuram Godse, a Hindu fanatic. ► **NON-COOPERATION MOVEMENT**; **ROUND TABLE CONFERENCES**; **SWARAJ**

**Gandhi, Rajiv** (1944–91)
Indian politician. As the eldest son of Indira **GANDHI** and the grandson of **NEHRU**, he was born into a Kashmiri-Brahmin family which governed India for all but four years in the first four decades after independence. He was educated at Doon School (Dehra Dun) and Cambridge University, where he failed his engineering degree. In contrast to his younger brother, Sanjay (1946–80), he exhibited little interest in politics and became a pilot with Indian Airlines. Following Sanjay's death in an air crash, he assumed the family's political mantle, being elected to his brother's Amethi parliamentary seat (1981) and appointed a General-Secretary of the Congress (I) Party (1983). After his mother's assassination in 1984, he became Prime Minister and secured a record majority in the parliamentary elections later that year. He attempted to cleanse and rejuvenate the Congress (I) Party, inducting new technocrats and introducing a free-market economic programme. Congress (I), however, suffered heavy losses in the Nov 1989 general election, and he was forced to resign as Premier after this defeat. He was assassinated by **TAMIL** terrorists during a subsequent election campaign in May 1991.

**Gandhi, Sonia** (1946–)
Italian-born Indian politician. She married Rajiv **GANDHI**, son of Indira **GANDI**, in 1968 and has two children. She became an Indian citizen in 1983. After her husband's assassination in 1991, Congress (I) officials tried to persuade her to succeed him but she distanced herself from politics until 1998, when she became President of the Congress (I) Party. In 1999 she was elected to parliament in the general election, although the party was heavily defeated by the BJP. Her tireless campaigning before the 2004 general election helped the party and its allies to a surprise victory. Despite the urging of the party she declined the premiership, recognizing the prejudice against her as a foreigner, but remained Congress Party leader, managing the coalition government, with Manmohan Singh as Prime Minister.

**Gang of Four**
A description given by **MAO ZEDONG** to the Shanghai-based hard-core radicals of the Chinese **CULTURAL REVOLUTION**: Zhang Chunqiao, Yao Wenyuan, Wang Hongwen and Jiang Qing. Zhang and Yao were veterans of the Shanghai party machine. Wang emerged as a workers' leader in the Shanghai 'January Revolution' of 1967. Jiang, Mao's wife, enjoyed his trust and was the acknowledged leader of the Gang. All were members of the politburo when they were arrested and disgraced in 1976.

**Gao Gang (Kao Kang)** (c.1902–1955)
Chinese political leader. In the mid-1930s he was in charge of a small independent communist area at Baoan, Shaanxi, where the **LONG MARCH** led by **MAO ZEDONG** ended. Mao and Gao Gang became close political allies, and he later became Chief Party Secretary of Manchuria (1949). He set the national pace in economic development, but in 1955 was accused of attempting to set up a 'separate kingdom'. He apparently committed suicide. ► **COMMUNIST PARTY, CHINESE**

**Gapon, Georgei Apollonovich** (1870–1906)
Ukrainian priest and reformer. In 1902 he became leader of the so-called Union of Russian Factory Workers. Without his knowledge, this seems to have been financed by the Tsarist police as a means of penetrating and controlling the working-class movement. However, with deteriorating economic conditions, its numbers grew; and in Jan 1905 Gapon was quite happy to lead them in a procession to the Winter Palace in the sincere belief that the Tsar **NICHOLAS II** would accede to their demands. The result was **BLOODY SUNDAY**. Thereafter, idealists like Gapon could exercise less and less influence on Russian developments.

**Garang, John** (1945–)
Sudanese soldier. After studying agricultural economics in the USA, he returned to Sudan, where he joined the army. Another period in the USA, for military training, was followed by a post at the Military Research Centre in Khartoum. In 1983 he formed the Sudanese People's Liberation Movement in southern Sudan. Backed by Marxists in Ethiopia, the movement grew out of Garang's belief that the resources of southern Sudan were being exploited by the country's northerners. Waging a relentless guerrilla campaign, the organization has posed a considerable threat to the stability of the Sudan. Involving conflict with the regular Sudanese army, the movement's activities have done much to increase the sufferings of the people in a country already racked by famine.

**Garašanin, Ilija** (1812–74)
Serbian politician. Having supported the constitutionalists during the 1830s, in 1842 he took part in the deposition of Prince Michael **OBRENOVIĆ**. He became prominent in the pro-constitution government under **ALEXANDER KARAGEORGEVIĆ** and was Minister for Internal Affairs (1843–52), organizing the police and bureaucracy. Very conservative, in 1844 he wrote the **NACERTANIJE** for the guidance of the Prince, believing that Serbia would be the core around which the other **SOUTH SLAVS** would unite. He remained a prominent minister after the return of Michael Obrenović (1860/8), but lost his pre-eminence when the prince changed direction in foreign affairs. After the succession of Milan **OBRENOVIĆ**, he retired into private life.

**García Moreno, Gabriel** (1821–75)
Ecuadorean dictator. Born in Guayaquil in Ecuador,

he studied theology and witnessed the **REVOLUTIONS OF 1848–9** in Europe. Elected Mayor of Quito, he seized power in 1860 with the support of Juan José **FLORES**, and was President from 1861 to 1865 and from 1869 to 1875. He was assassinated on the eve of re-election. García Moreno proclaimed two constitutions, both of which were theocratic structures; citizenship was limited to Catholics and all others were stripped of **CIVIL RIGHTS**. These survived his death, enduring until 1895.

## García Pérez, Alan (1949– )

Peruvian politician. After studying law in Lima, he continued his education in Guatemala, Spain and France. He returned to Peru in 1978 and was elected to the National Congress, for the moderate, left-wing APRA Party, which he had joined as a youth. Four years later he became Secretary-General of the party, and in 1985 succeeded Fernando **BELAÚNDE** as President, becoming the first civilian to do so in democratic elections. He inherited an ailing economy, which forced him to trim his socialist programme. By 1991 the economy was in tatters, and García was a prisoner of the deepening struggle between the **SENDERO LUMINOSO** and the armed forces in the Andes and a conservative Congress in Lima. He was succeeded by the conservative Alberto **FUJIMORI**, and sought political asylum in Colombia in 1992, returning to Peru in 2001.

## García y Iñigues, Calixto (1839–98)

Cuban lawyer, soldier and revolutionary. In the struggle for independence from Spain, he was a leader in the **TEN YEARS' WAR** (1868–78) and in 1898 went on to lead the Cuban force, in support of the USA, at El Caney in the **SPANISH–AMERICAN WAR**.

## Garfield, James A(bram) (1831–81)

US politician and 20th President. He was a farm-worker, teacher, lay preacher and lawyer before being elected to the Ohio state senate in 1859. He fought in the **AMERICAN CIVIL WAR** until 1863, when he entered the **HOUSE OF REPRESENTATIVES**, eventually becoming a leader of the **REPUBLICAN PARTY**. After his election as President (a post he held only from Mar to Sep 1881), he alienated the '**STALWARTS**', a major faction of the Republican Party, by passing them over for federal appointments. On 2 July 1881, he was shot in the Washington railroad station by a disappointed office-seeker, Charles Guiteau, and died two months later.

## Garibaldi, Giuseppe (1807–82)

Italian revolutionary, soldier and politician. The greatest hero of the **RISORGIMENTO**, he was a member of **YOUNG ITALY** and took part in an abortive Mazzinian insurrection in Genoa in 1834. He subsequently fled to South America, where he fought in defence of the Rio Grande do Sul republic against the Brazilian Empire, and in Uruguay against the Argentine dictator de **ROSAS**. He returned to Italy (1848) and offered his services to **CHARLES ALBERT** against the Austrians but was rejected. Instead, he took part in the government and defence of the Roman Republic, before attempting to relieve the Venetian republic of Daniele **MANIN**. After the **REVOLUTIONS OF 1848–9** he visited America, before settling on the island of Caprera. In 1856 he backed the **ITALIAN NATIONAL SOCIETY** and

played a minor but brilliant part in the 1859 campaign against the Austrians. In 1860 he set sail from Genoa with his **THOUSAND** volunteers to assist the anti-Bourbon rebellion that had broken out in Sicily. Having seized control of the island, he crossed to the mainland of the Kingdom of the **TWO SICILIES** and overran much of the **MEZZOGIORNO** before handing it over to **VICTOR EMMANUEL II**. In 1862 he attempted to march on Rome but was stopped by Piedmontese troops at **ASPROMONTE**; a similar attempt to seize the papal capital was blocked by French forces at **MENTANA** in 1867. He fought with limited success against the Austrians in 1866, and in 1870 he offered his services to the French after the Battle of **SEDAN**. In 1870 he was elected a deputy at the Bordeaux Assembly. He passed his last years as a farmer on Caprera.

## Garneau, Francis Xavier (1809–66)

Canadian historian. His *Histoire du Canada* (1845–8) was written to rebut Lord **DURHAM**'s assertions that French-Canadians had neither a history nor a culture of any significance. His work provided Quebec nationalism with an intellectual basis and a body of material on which later writers drew freely.

## Garner, John Nance (1868–1967)

US politician. He served as a Democratic congressman for Texas (1903–33) and became Speaker of the House in 1931. As Vice President (1933–41) under Franklin D **ROOSEVELT**, Garner steered much **NEW DEAL** legislation through **CONGRESS** during his first two terms.

## Garnet, Henry Highland (1815–82)

US abolitionist. He was a former slave who, with Frederick **DOUGLASS**, helped promote racial pride and dispel popular stereotypes of blacks. A persuasive and witty speaker, he argued at the National Convention of Coloured Citizens in 1843 that a slave was justified in using violence to gain his freedom. By the 1850s, like another anti-**SLAVERY** activist Martin **DELANEY**, he despaired of achieving racial justice and advocated the emigration of blacks to Africa. ► **ABOLITIONISM**

## Garnier-Pagès, Louis Antoine (1803–78)

French politician. A member of the Chamber of Deputies (1842–8), he led the extreme Left. Mayor of Paris (1848) and Finance Minister of the Provisional Government, he was a member of the *Corps Législatif* in 1864, and of the Provisional Government in 1871. He wrote *Histoire de la Révolution de 1848* (1861–2) and *L'Opposition et l'Empire* (1872).

## Garrison, William Lloyd (1805–79)

US abolitionist. Educated informally, he emerged in 1830 as one of the foremost anti-**SLAVERY** voices in the USA. His newspaper, *The Liberator*, argued the case for immediate abolition, and his American Anti-Slavery Society drew thousands of people to the cause. ► **ABOLITIONISM**

## Garvey, Marcus Moziah Aurelius (1887–1940)

Advocate of black nationalism. Born and brought up in poverty in Jamaica, he promoted self-help for blacks and black pride, and in 1914 founded the Universal Negro Improvement Association. Two years later he left Jamaica for New York, his arrival in New York coinciding with the wave of black migration into Harlem. Despite little formal education, he proved to be a gifted writer and speaker. It was in the ghettos of the northern cities that he found his greatest following, reaching blacks through his weekly, *Negro World*, and greatly expanding his Association, a forerunner of the black nationalist movement. However, his call for a return to Africa attracted little interest. He founded such enterprises as the Black Factories Corporation and the Black Star Line, a steamship line owned and operated by blacks, which, however, collapsed in 1921 due to mismanagement. In 1923 he was convicted of mail fraud, imprisoned, and later deported. After he left the country, his black nationalist movement went into decline. He died in obscurity in London.

## Gaspée
A British customs schooner set on fire and destroyed by colonists after it went aground near Providence, Rhode Island (9 June 1772). The schooner had been stationed off the coast to counter the profitable smuggling trade of the region. A subsequent investigation by the British into the incident ended in failure.

## Gastarbeiter
A German term for the foreign, usually Mediterranean, workers who have been employed in large numbers in the German (West German, to 1990) economy since the 1960s. The term (literally, 'guest workers') belies the fact that many of these migrants have settled in Germany with their families, and that their presence is indispensable to the German economy. However, only a few have become German citizens and many return to their country of origin after completing a predetermined period of employment.

## Gates, Horatio (1728–1806)
British-born US general. He joined the British Army, served in America in the SEVEN YEARS' WAR (1756–63), and then settled in Virginia. In the AMERICAN REVOLUTION he sided with his adoptive country and fought for its cause. In 1777 he took command of the Northern department, and forced the British Army to surrender at the Battle of SARATOGA. In 1780 he commanded the Southern department, but his army was routed by CORNWALLIS at the Battle of CAMDEN, and he was superseded. He returned to Virginia, but in 1790 emancipated his slaves and then settled near New York City.

## GATT (General Agreement on Tariffs and Trade)
An international treaty to promote trade and economic benefits, signed in 1947. Its aim was to encourage free trade by the imposition of trade rules and reduction of tariffs among its nations. The 'Uruguay' or eighth round of talks involved seven years of complex negotiation (1986–93) and met much opposition, particularly from French farmers. It cut many tariffs by 40 per cent and created the WORLD TRADE ORGANIZATION (WTO) to take over as the authoritative body on international commerce.

## Gau
A National Socialist administrative district created initially to organize the NAZI PARTY during the WEIMAR REPUBLIC and coordinate electoral and other work. The *Gau* became a form of administration parallel to the traditional one in Nazi Germany. The *Gaue* were retained after HITLER's takeover, each headed by a *Gauleiter* who was a party official answerable to

Hitler, not the civil authorities. In this way, the Nazis created a regional administrative structure which operated parallel to the traditional one and allowed the party to bypass the civil service when it so desired. Needless to say, conflict developed between the party and civil authorities over their precise areas of competence.

## gaucho
A nomadic, fiercely independent mestizo horseman of the Argentine pampa, first appearing in the 17c. With the advent of ranches, railways and settled government in the 19c, the gaucho vanished, though gaucho skills live on among the rural population of Argentina and Uruguay. The gaucho myth tradition suffuses Argentine political and social life; enshrined in the tango, echoed in PERONISM, it is both elemental and conservative. The inhabitants of Rio Grande do Sul in Brazil are known as gauchos; their distinctive politics – their support of a series of charismatic political leaders and resort to war – have given 'gaucho politics' a specific tenor.

## Gaulle, Charles André Joseph Marie de (1890–1970)
French general and politician. Born into a devout Catholic and conservative family, he was educated by the Jesuits and at Saint-Cyr military college, and fought with distinction in WORLD WAR I. Only a colonel in 1940, he was known as the author of several books on military and historical topics, especially one advocating mechanized warfare. He was promoted temporary General of Brigade (1 June 1940), and four days later entered the government as Under-Secretary at the Ministry of National Defence. Refusing to accept the armistice, he fled to England, where (18 June 1940) he appealed to the French people to continue the struggle. As the leader of the FREE FRENCH, he fought many diplomatic battles against President ROOSEVELT to ensure that France was treated as a co-belligerent, thus emerging in 1944 as head of the provisional government. He organized the election of an assembly to draw up a new constitution, but resigned in protest at the trend of its deliberations (Jan 1946), thus consigning himself to the political sidelines until 1958, when the Algerian crisis led to his recall to power as the last Prime Minister of the Fourth Republic. He used this position to draw up a new constitution for the Fifth Republic, which embodied the presidential system he had wanted in 1946. It was approved by a referendum (Sep 1958) and he became its first President (1959–69). He defeated two attempted coups, launched by supporters of a French Algeria, and negotiated Algerian independence (1962). France's colonies were also granted independence, while he concentrated on winning France a leading place in Europe by excluding Britain from the EC (European Community) and by signing an historic reconciliation treaty with Germany (both 1963). He developed a French nuclear deterrent, and removed France from its military obligations under NATO (1965). His supporters won by a big majority in the elections following the 'events' of 1968, but he lost a referendum on constitutional reform in 1969, and resigned. ► NATIONAL DEFENCE, GOVERNMENT OF; REPUBLIC, FIFTH (France); REPUBLIC, FOURTH (France)

**Gaullist Party ► GAULLISTS**

**Gaullists**
Supporters of General de **GAULLE**, more specifically members of political parties which followed him in his lifetime, and claimed to embody his legacy after his death. Their names have changed frequently. The principal ones are RPF (*Rassemblement du Peuple Français*, 'Assembly of the French People') (1947–54), UNR, later UNR–UDT (*Union pour la Nouvelle République*, 'Union for the New Republic') (1958–67), UDR (*Union des démocrates pour la Ve République*, 'Union of Democrats for the Fifth Republic') (1967–76), and RPR (*Rassemblement pour la République*, 'Assembly for the Republic') from 1976 until 2002, when it was absorbed into the UMP (*Union pour un Mouvement Populaire*). Gaullists emphasize the need for a strong foreign policy, and have become one of the two main constituents of the right wing. **► INDEPENDENT REPUBLICAN PARTY**

**Gaylani, Rashid Ali al-** (1892–1965)
Iraqi politician. He was Prime Minister of Iraq in 1933, 1936–8 and 1940–1. An opponent of Nuri al-**SAʿID** and a fervent nationalist, he eventually fell in with the prevailing Iraqi opinion, which resented the British presence in the country; after initially permitting British reinforcement in Iraq, he was later implicated in supporting Iraqi armed resistance to the British and was expelled after the surrender of the Iraqi army. He returned to Iraq but, accused of plotting against Abd al-Krim **QASSIM**, fled and died in exile.

**gay rights movement**, also called **gay liberation movement**
A movement whose ultimate goal is society's acceptance or tolerance of homosexuality. More specifically, it aims to eliminate the laws that make homosexual sex between consenting adults illegal, and to prevent discrimination against homosexuals in such areas as employment, housing and health. Since the 1980s gay rights activists have also worked to heighten awareness about AIDS and to support victims of the disease. The first organization to promote homosexual rights was founded in 1897 in Germany; it spread rapidly but ended with the rise of Nazism in the 1930s. Meanwhile, other groups sprang up in the UK and USA throughout the 20c. The first violent incident took place in June 1969 when rioting broke out amongst homosexuals resisting police raiders at the Stonewall Inn in Greenwich Village, New York. By the end of the 20c, the UK (in 1967) and about half of the US states had decriminalized homosexual acts between consenting adults. However, the gay rights movement has been less successful in most of Latin America, several African countries and the Muslim Middle Eastern nations, who all remain relatively intolerant.

**Gaza Kingdom**
One of the kingdoms established by the northern **NGUNI** people (of whom the Zulu are the most famous) after their dispersal in southern Africa known as the *Mfecane*. After the defeat of Zwide by Shaka in 1819, Shoshangane (d.1858), one of Zwide's military leaders, led his followers across the Limpopo and established his sovereignty over the Tsonga people in Mozambique. The state became a thorn in the side of the Portuguese and was not fully subdued until the 19c. The 'Shangaans' of the Gaza state became celebrated as labour migrants in the gold mines of the **WITWATERSRAND**.

**Gaza Strip**
The 140 sq mi/363 sq km coastal area inhabited by 1,324,991 Arabs and an estimated 5,000 Israeli settlers (2004), and bounded to the north, east and south by Israel, to the south-west by Egypt (though with an Israeli-controlled corridor lying parallel to the Egyptian border) and to the west by the Mediterranean Sea.. It was administered by Egypt from 1949 until lost to the Israelis in the 1967 war, and was under Israeli military administration until 1994. In 1993 the **OSLO ACCORDS** between Israel and the **PLO** led to Palestinian self-government from May 1994 in the Gaza Strip and the Jericho area of the **WEST BANK**. The Palestinian National Authority, whose first chairman was Yasser **ARAFAT**, faced the problems of high unemployment, rising population, inadequate sewage and water services, and the fact that over half the population of the Gaza Strip live in refugee camps. After the fall of the **NETANYAHU** government in 1999, improvements were made to airport and sea port facilities, and in building direct links with the West Bank. Since Ariel **SHARON**'s election in 2001, both airport and sea port have been closed and the airport runway destroyed. Closures of the border with Israel, in response to terrorist attacks in Israel and the second **INTIFADA**, have damaged the economy and caused high unemployment. **► PALESTINIAN AUTONOMOUS AREAS**

**Gdańsk** (formerly **Danzig**)
Industrial port and capital of Gdańsk voivodship, north Poland. A German city, it passed to Poland in 1466, on the Peace of Thorn, but was regained by **PRUSSIA** (1793–1919). It became a free city within the Polish tariff area in 1919 and its annexation by Germany in 1939 precipitated **WORLD WAR II**. Its German population fled, or were expelled, at the end of the war in 1945. In the 1980s the city's Lenin shipyard was the scene of much labour unrest in support of **SOLIDARITY**.

**Gdlyan, Telman Khorenovich** (1940– )
Soviet lawyer. Of Armenian extraction, he, along with **IVANOV**, exposed misdemeanours in Uzbekistan involving the late Leonid **BREZHNEV**'s son-in-law. He then proceeded to attack other figures such as Yegor **LIGACHEV**, but encountered hostility even among Mikhail **GORBACHEV**'s supporters. Both Gdlyan and Ivanov were very popular with the general public, and they certainly undermined communist credibility.

**Geisel, Ernesto** (1908–96)
Brazilian general and dictator. Prominent in both the **QUADROS** and **CASTELO BRANCO** administrations, his ascendancy in 1973–4, largely a result of his brother Orlando's control of the military, marked the re-emergence of Golberi de Couto e Silva, nemesis of the hardliners, such as Air Force Minister Sousa e Melo and Navy Minister Rademakr, who believed in an uncompromising dictatorship. During Geisel's presidency (1974–9), he and Golberi successfully

masterminded a return to a regime in which the military acted in their traditional role as a moderating power. Geisel's imperial style allowed him subsequently to play a discrete role in politics. His support for Tancredo **NEVES** in early 1985 was decisive in persuading the army to acquiesce in a return to civilian rule.

**Gelasius II**, originally **John of Gaeta** (1058–1119)
Italian pope (1118/19). He was formerly cardinal and chancellor under **URBAN II** and Paschal II. On the death of the latter in 1118, he was chosen pope by the party hostile to the Emperor **HENRY V**. Gelasius fled to Gaeta to escape the advancing imperialists, and excommunicated Henry and Gregory VIII, the antipope he had set up. Shortly after he was able to return to Rome, but in the same autumn had to flee to France, where he died in the monastery at Cluny.

**Gemayel, Amin** (1942– )
Lebanese politician. The son of Pierre **GEMAYEL**, he trained as a lawyer and supported his brother, Bashir **GEMAYEL**, in the 1975–6 civil war, becoming President (1982–8) after the latter's assassination. Politically more moderate, his policies initially proved no more successful in determining a peaceful settlement of the problems of Lebanese government.

**Gemayel, Bashir** (1947–82)
Lebanese army officer and politician. The youngest son of Pierre **GEMAYEL**, he joined the militia of his father's Phalangist Party and came to be the party's Political Director in the Ashrefieh sector of East Beirut, where he was an active leader of the Christian militia in the civil war of 1975–6. By the systematic elimination of rivals, he came to command the military forces of East Beirut. He distanced his party from Israeli support, and aimed to expel all foreign influence from Lebanese affairs. Having twice escaped assassination, he was killed in a bomb explosion while president-elect, ten days before he was due to take office. His brother, Amin **GEMAYEL**, was elected President in his stead one week later.

**Gemayel, Pierre** (1905–84)
Lebanese politician. A member of the Maronite Christian community of Lebanon, he was educated in Beirut and Paris, and trained as a pharmacist. In 1936 he founded the Kataeb or Phalangist Party, modelled on the Spanish and German fascist organizations, and in 1937 became its leader. He was twice imprisoned (1937 and 1943), held various ministerial posts (1960–7), and led the Phalangist militia in the 1975–6 civil war. ► **GEMAYEL, AMIN; GEMAYEL, BASHIR**

**General Agreement on Tariffs and Trade** ► **GATT**

**Generalitat**
The Catalan autonomous government; an institution of medieval origin restored under the Second Republic of 1931–6 by the Catalan Autonomy Statute of Sep 1932. Dominated by the Catalan Left, it clashed repeatedly with the right-wing administration in Madrid. In Oct 1934 it joined the left-wing rising against the central government by declaring a Catalan Republic within a Federal Republic of Spain. Following its defeat, the Generalitat was suspended until the victory of the Popular Front in Feb 1936. At the beginning of the **SPANISH CIVIL WAR**, it shared power with the **CNT**-dominated Anti-Fascist Militia Committee, but lost a great deal of power to the central government after the CNT and **POUM** had been crushed in the May Days of 1937. Dissolved under **FRANCO**, the Generalitat was re-established after his death. ► **CATALAN AUTONOMY STATUTES; REPUBLIC, SECOND** (Spain)

**Generality Lands**
The name given to buffer-territories between the northern Dutch Republic and the southern (Spanish/Austrian) Netherlands during and after the **EIGHTY YEARS' WAR**. In 1648 they included northern **BRABANT**, Dutch Limburg and Zeeland Flanders, which had been conquered by the Dutch in the wars against Spain; in 1713 part of Gelderland was added. The districts were governed by the Dutch States General, in which they had no voice; they were also punitively taxed. They now form part of the modern Dutch state, and remain distinct by being Catholic, whereas the rest of the country is either Protestant or of mixed religion.

**General Strike** (4–12 May 1926)
A national strike in Britain, organized by the Trades Union Congress (TUC) in support of an existing miners' strike to resist wage cuts. The government organized special constables and volunteers to counter the most serious effects of the strike, and issued an anti-strike propaganda journal, *The British Gazette*. The TUC called off the strike, though the miners' strike continued fruitlessly for three more months.

**Geneva Convention**
An international agreement on the conduct of warfare, first framed in 1864 and ratified in 1906. It is chiefly concerned with the protection of the wounded and the sanctity of the **RED CROSS**, while prohibiting methods of war (such as the use of 'dumdum' bullets, which expand on impact) that might cause unnecessary suffering. The terms were extended in 1950, and again in 1978, to confirm the prohibition of attacks on non-defended civilians, reprisals against civilians, and the prisoner-of-war rights of guerrilla fighters.

**Geneva Peace Conference** (1973)
The conference, arranged by Henry **KISSINGER** under the auspices of the **UN**, to discuss the disengagement of Israeli and Arab forces and to achieve a peace settlement after the **YOM KIPPUR WAR**. Despite its failure to achieve substantial results, the conference (convened 21 Dec 1973), was remarkable for its efforts towards getting Egypt, Jordan and Israel together. The USA and USSR attended in what was really an observational capacity, but the actual ceasefire arrangements were achieved by Kissinger in his so-called 'shuttle' diplomacy.

**Genghis Khan** (c.1162–1227)
Mongol conqueror. He succeeded his father, a Mongol chief, at the age of 13 and had to struggle hard for years against hostile tribes. His ambition awakening with his continued success, he spent six years in subjugating the Naimans and in conquering Tangut. From the Turkish Uighurs, who voluntarily submitted, the **MONGOLS** derived their civilization, alphabet and laws. In 1206 he dropped his name

Temujin for that of Genghis (Jingis or Chingis) Khan ('Universal Ruler'). He overran the empire of northern China (Khitai) in 1217, and the following year he attacked the powerful empire of Khwarazm, took Bokhara, Samarkand, Khwarazm and other chief cities, returning home in 1225. Two of Genghis's lieutenants penetrated northwards from the southern shore of the Caspian Sea through Georgia into southern Russia and the Crimea, everywhere routing and slaying, and returned by way of the Volga. Meanwhile, in the Far East, another of his generals had completed the conquest of all northern China (1217–23) except Hunan. After a few months' rest, Genghis set out once again; he died after thoroughly subduing the kingdom of the Tanguts. Genghis was not only a warrior and conqueror, but a skilful administrator and ruler; having conquered empires stretching from the Black Sea to the Pacific, he organized them into khanates, some of which lasted until the 17c.

## Genoa Economic Conference (Apr–May 1922)

A conference of 34 states hosted by Italy to promote European economic reconstruction and to discuss the restoration of economic and diplomatic relations with the USSR. Presided over by Luigi FACTA, the conference achieved little on either front. Instead, it served to bring together Soviet and German delegates who took the opportunity to arrange closer military collaboration, signing the Treaty of RAPALLO (16 Apr 1922).

## genocide

The deliberate mass extermination of a population, usually an ethnic group, on cultural or biological grounds. The most nefarious historical example was the slaughter, in specially constructed extermination camps, of almost six million Jews by the Nazis during WORLD WAR II. Combining anti-Semitism and racial science theories of SOCIAL DARWINISM, the Nazis justified such extermination according to an extreme hierarchical view of humankind. Genocide was one of the principal charges brought against the defendants at the NUREMBERG TRIALS, and in 1948 in its approval of the Convention on the Punishment of the Crime of Genocide, the UN classified genocide as a crime under international law. ► NAZI PARTY

## genro

The unofficial term (literally, 'senior statesman') for influential Japanese leaders who had spearheaded the MEIJI RESTORATION (1868) and continued to serve the Emperor as chief advisers. Originally seven in number (with two added in 1912), they were mostly middle- or lower-ranking SAMURAI from the two former domains of CHOSHU and SATSUMA. The three most significant genro were ITO HIROBUMI, YAMAGATA ARITOMO and MATSUKATA MASAYOSHI. They oversaw political, military and economic reforms in the 1870s and 1880s and, after the adoption of the MEIJI CONSTITUTION in 1889, either served as Prime Minister or collectively chose one. The genro were a force for stability and continuity, and with their passing the political system became more unstable as competing institutions (the Diet, the military, and the Imperial Household Ministry) jostled for pre-eminence.

## Genscher, Hans-Dietrich (1927–)

German politician. He trained as a lawyer, studying at Leipzig before he moved to West Germany in 1952. He became Secretary-General of the Free Democratic Party (FDP) in 1959, and was Minister of the Interior for five years before becoming, in 1974, Vice-Chancellor and Foreign Minister in SCHMIDT's coalition government. In the same year, he became Chairman of the FDP, a post to which he was re-elected in 1982. He retained his cabinet post after 1982 in the coalition between the FDP and the CHRISTIAN DEMOCRATS. He played a crucial role in the maintenance and furtherance of the OSTPOLITIK after the fall of the Social Democratic Party (SPD).

## Gentile, Giovanni (1875–1944)

Italian philosopher and politician. Unlike his friend Benedetto CROCE, Gentile became a firm supporter of FASCISM, being chosen by MUSSOLINI to serve as Education Minister in 1922. He twice served as a member of the FASCIST GRAND COUNCIL (1923–4 and 1925–9) and rallied to the DUCE in the autumn of 1943, when he established the fascist Republic of SALÒ. He was killed in Florence by anti-fascist partisans.

## Gentiloni, Vincenzo Ottorino, Count (1865–1916)

Italian politician. President of the 'Catholic Electoral Union', he urged that good Catholics reject their traditional hostility to the Italian state and that they participate actively in Italian political life. In 1913 he made the so-called 'Gentiloni Pact' with GIOLITTI, in which Catholic votes were promised to liberal candidates on condition that they would not pursue anti-clerical policies.

## Gentlemen's Agreement (1907)

An informal pact between the USA and Japan under which Japan agreed to limit Japanese migration to the USA in return for a promise by President Theodore ROOSEVELT not to discriminate against the Japanese.

## Genyosha

A Japanese ultra-nationalist organization (literally, 'Black Ocean Society') created by ex-SAMURAI from Fukuoka prefecture in 1881. Dissatisfied with their lot and critical of the new Meiji state, the ex-samurai promoted conservative values at home and vigorous expansion abroad. The Genyosha was responsible in the 1880s for several terrorist attacks on government ministers thought to be 'soft' in their dealings with the West, and engaged in conspiratorial activity in Korea and Manchuria. While some members of the Genyosha sought genuine cooperation with Asian revolutionaries, most supported the aggressive actions of the Japanese military during the 1930s. The Genyosha was forcibly disbanded in 1945.

## geopolitics

The study of geographical factors as a basis of the power of nations. It is a combination of political geography and political science, and its considerations include territory, resources, climate, population, social and political culture, and economic activity.

## George I (1660–1727)

King of Great Britain and Ireland (1714/27). Born in Hanover, he was the great-grandson of James I of England, and was proclaimed King on the death of

Queen **ANNE**. Elector of Hanover since 1698, he had commanded the Imperial forces in the **MARLBOR-OUGH** wars. He divorced his wife and cousin, the Princess Dorothea of Zell, imprisoning her in the castle of Ahlden, where she died (1726). He took relatively little part in the government of the country. His affections remained with Hanover, and he lived there as much as possible. ► **JACOBITES**; **JAMES VI AND I**; **WALPOLE, ROBERT**

### George I (1845–1913)
King of Greece (1863/1913). The second son of King **CHRISTIAN IX** of Denmark, he served in the Danish navy. On the deposition of King **OTHON** of Greece, he was elected king by the Greek National Assembly. In 1867 he married the Grand Duchess Olga, the niece of Tsar **ALEXANDER II** of Russia. His reign saw the consolidation of Greek territory in **THESSALY** and **EPIRUS**, and the suppression of a Cretan insurrection in 1896–7. Involved in the **BALKAN WARS** (1912–13), he was assassinated at Salonica, and was succeeded by his son, **CONSTANTINE I**.

### George II (1683–1760)
King of Great Britain and Ireland (1727/60) and Elector of Hanover. Born in Hanover, he was the son of **GEORGE I**. In 1705 he married Caroline of Anspach (1683–1737). Though he involved himself more in the government of the country than his father had, the policy pursued during the first half of the reign was that of Robert **WALPOLE**. In the War of the **AUSTRIAN SUCCESSION**, he was present at the Battle of **DETTINGEN** (1743), the last occasion on which a British sovereign commanded an army in the field. His reign also saw the crushing of Jacobite hopes at the Battle of **CULLODEN** (1746), the foundation of British India after the Battle of **PLASSEY** (1757), the beginning of the **SEVEN YEARS' WAR** and the capture of Quebec (1759). ► **QUEBEC, BATTLE OF**; **STUART, CHARLES**

### George II (1890–1947)
King of Greece (1922/3 and 1935/47). The son of **CONSTANTINE I** and grandson of **GEORGE I** of Greece, he succeeded to the throne on his father's second abdication in 1922, but was deposed the following year by a military junta. Restored to the throne by plebiscite in 1935, he worked closely with his dictatorial Prime Minister, Ioannis **METAXAS**. When Greece was overrun by the Germans, after the country had successfully resisted the Italian invasion of 1940–1, he withdrew to Crete and then England. In 1946 he was restored to the throne, again by plebiscite. He was succeeded by his brother, **PAUL I**.

### George III (1738–1820)
King of Great Britain and Ireland (1760/1820), and Elector (1760/1815) and King (1815/20) of Hanover. The eldest son of Frederick Louis, Prince of Wales (1707–51), his father predeceased him, and he thus succeeded his grandfather, **GEORGE II**. Eager to govern as well as reign, he did not lack ability but was not politically adept and caused considerable friction. With Lord **NORTH** he shared in the blame for the loss of the American colonies, and popular feeling ran high against him for a time in the 1770s. In 1783 he called **PITT, THE YOUNGER** to office, an important stage in reducing the political influence of a small group of established Whig families. In 1810 he suf-

fered a recurrence of a mental derangement, and the Prince of Wales was made Regent. He died insane and blind. ► **AMERICAN REVOLUTION**

### George IV (1762–1830)
King of the United Kingdom and of Hanover (1820/30). The eldest son of **GEORGE III**, he became Prince Regent in 1810 because of his father's insanity. Rebelling against a strict upbringing, he went through a marriage ceremony with Mrs Fitzherbert, a Roman Catholic, in 1785, thus forfeiting his title to the crown. The marriage was later declared invalid, and in 1795 he married Princess Caroline of Brunswick, whom he tried to divorce when he was King. Her death in 1821 ended a scandal in which the people sympathized with the Queen. A frequently vilified and always extravagant monarch, he was responsible for the building of the pavilion at Brighton.

### George V (1865–1936)
King of the United Kingdom (1910/36). He was the second son of **EDWARD VII**. He served in the navy, travelled in many parts of the Empire, and was created Prince of Wales in 1901. His reign saw the creation of the Union of South Africa (1910), **WORLD WAR I**, the **IRISH FREE STATE** settlement (1922) and the **GENERAL STRIKE** (1926). His consort, Mary (1867–1953), married him in 1893; she organized women's war work (1914–18), and continued with many public and philanthropic activities after the death of her husband. They had five sons and one daughter.

### George VI (1895–1952)
King of the United Kingdom (1936/52). The second son of **GEORGE V**, he served in the Grand Fleet at the Battle of **JUTLAND** (1916). In 1920 he was created Duke of York, and married in 1923. He played at Wimbledon in the All-England tennis championships in 1926. He ascended the throne on the abdication of his elder brother, **EDWARD VIII**. During **WORLD WAR II** he continued to reside in bomb-damaged Buckingham Palace, visited all theatres of war, and delivered many broadcasts, for which task he mastered a speech impediment. He and his wife, Elizabeth (*née* Elizabeth Bowes-Lyon), had two children, Princess Elizabeth (later Queen **ELIZABETH II**) and Princess Margaret.

### George of Podiebrad (1420–71)
King of Bohemia (1458/71). Born into the Czech nobility in Podiebrad, he became an adherent of the moderate reformist followers of Jan **HUS**, the so-called Utraquists. In the interregnum and civil strife following the death of Albert II in 1439, Podiebrad gradually emerged as leader of the Utraquists, seized Prague in 1448, and finally and officially had himself made regent for the new young king, Ladislav Posthumus in 1453. Following Ladislav's death in 1457, Podiebrad was crowned his successor (1458). He succeeded for a while in allaying the bitternesses of religious controversy. But in 1462 he inevitably refused to abolish the *compactata* of Prague (1433), which legitimized the Utraquists; this angered Pope **PIUS II**, but the Emperor restrained him from excommunicating Podiebrad. The next pope (Paul II), however, excommunicated him in 1466. King **MATTHIAS I, CORVINUS** of Hungary took the field to enforce the ban and to make a bid for the Czech crown, but

Podiebrad captured him and forced him into a truce at Vilémov (1469). When Matthias was nevertheless invited to be King of Bohemia by the Catholic nobles, Podiebrad persuaded the Czech estates to offer the succession instead to the Polish prince Władysław Jagiełło. This was typical of his diplomatic moves intended to help preserve Czech independence. So was the proposal he made, unsuccessfully, in the years 1462–4 for a league of European princes to keep the peace.

**GEORGIA**   official name **Republic of Georgia**

A republic in eastern Europe, occupying central and western Transcaucasia. It is bounded to the southeast by Azerbaijan; to the south by Armenia and Turkey; to the west by the Black Sea; and to the north by Russia. It was proclaimed a Soviet Socialist Republic in 1921, and formed the Transcaucasian Republic with Armenia and Azerbaijan before becoming a constituent republic of the USSR in 1936. In 1990 the Communist Party's monopoly of power was abolished and in multiparty elections Zviad Gamsakhurdia was elected President. Georgia declared its independence in May 1991. Armed opposition to Gamsakhurdia's government led to civil war, resulting in his deposition and the suspension of parliament in Jan 1992. In Mar 1992 a State Council took control and Eduard **SHEVARDNADZE** became chairman; in Sep he was appointed President and set about restoring stability to the nation, although civil conflict continued throughout 1993. In addition, there was fighting by secessionists in the regions of Abkhazia, to whom Shevardnadze agreed in 1994 to give a measure of autonomy, and South Ossetia. Shevardnadze was forced to resign in Nov 2003 after massive demonstrations over alleged electoral fraud, and the presidential election in 2004 was won by the pro-Western Mikhail Saakashvili. Georgia joined the CIS (Commonwealth of Independent States) in 1993.

**gerarchi**
The Italian word (literally, 'hierarch') applied by MUS-SOLINI to the leading figures of the FASCIST PARTY; hence the name of the party periodical, *Gerarchia*.

**Gerhardsen, Einar** (1897–1987)
Norwegian politician. Of working-class origin, he rose to prominence in the Norwegian Labour Party between the wars but was not a member of the Labour government that was in power when the German invasion of Norway took place in 1940. This, together with his active participation in the Resistance, made him well qualified to lead the first post-war government in Norway. He was Prime Minister (1945–51, 1955–63 and 1963–5), leading Norway into membership of NATO in 1949 and presiding over a long period of economic growth and social welfare legislation. ➤ NORWAY, GERMAN INVASION OF

**German Confederation**
A Central European state system created at the Congress of VIENNA (1814–15) to fill the void left by NA-POLEON I's destruction (1801–6) of the HOLY ROMAN EMPIRE. Dominated until after 1848 by Austria, it was rendered unstable by the subsequent rising power of PRUSSIA, and was dissolved in 1866 following the AUSTRO-PRUSSIAN WAR. ➤ NORTH GERMAN CONFEDERATION

**German–Danish War** (1864)
The Schleswig-Holstein question was reopened in Nov 1863 by the death of King **FREDERICK VII** of Denmark, followed by the promulgation of a new constitution by his successor, **CHRISTIAN IX**, which altered the status of the duchy of Schleswig in contravention of the London Protocol of 1852. German nationalist outrage against Denmark was exploited by Otto von **BISMARCK**, Minister President of Prussia. Prussia, Austria and other German states carried out a 'federal execution' against Denmark on behalf of the GERMAN CONFEDERATION. In Dec 1863 German troops entered the duchy of Holstein and the Danes withdrew their forces into Schleswig. Following a Danish refusal to withdraw from Schleswig, German forces entered the duchy and hostilities began (1 Feb 1864). The Danes retreated to the fortified position of Dybböl, which guarded the approach to the island of Als and thus the route to the Danish capital, Copenhagen. Dybböl was under intense bombardment (2–18 Apr 1864) before being stormed by Austrian and Prussian troops, who outnumbered the defenders six to one. An armistice came into force and an attempt was made to reach a negotiated settlement at the London Conference (May–June 1864) but, in the vain hope of obtaining active British support, the Danes rejected a compromise agreement (22 June). When the war was resumed, German forces captured Als and occupied most of the Jutland Peninsula. A new armistice was signed (20 July) and in the Treaty of Vienna (30 Oct 1864) Denmark surrendered Schleswig-Holstein to Prussia and Austria. The duchies came under Prussian control following the AUSTRO-PRUSSIAN WAR of 1866.

**German–Danish Wars** (1848–50)
Wars which resulted from the clash of German and Danish nationalisms in the duchies of Schleswig and Holstein during the REVOLUTIONS OF 1848–9. Both duchies had mixed German and Danish populations; both were ruled by the Danish crown, but Holstein was also part of the GERMAN CONFEDERATION. Following a declaration (Mar 1848) that Schleswig was to be brought into a closer relationship with the Kingdom of Denmark, a provisional government for Schleswig-Holstein was formed at Kiel and appealed to Prussia for assistance. Prussian troops crossed the border of Holstein (4 Apr 1848) and the Danish army was obliged to retreat but managed to hold a line on the Jutland Peninsula, while Danish naval forces blockaded Prussian ports. A seven-month armistice concluded at Malmö (26 Aug 1848) was regarded as a betrayal of the German national cause by the delegates assembled at the FRANK-FURT PARLIAMENT. War between Denmark and the government of Schleswig-Holstein, again backed by Prussian and other German forces, was resumed in

the spring of 1849 and led to further Danish setbacks which were ended by the defensive victory at Fredericia (6 July 1849). The third and final round was fought in July 1850 between Denmark and Schleswig-Holstein, this time without official support from the German states, and ended with a Danish victory at Isted (25 July 1850). The Schleswig-Holstein question was formally settled by the London Protocol of 8 May 1852. ► GERMAN DANISH WAR

## German East Africa Company
The company established by the Germans to exploit its newly acquired territory of Tanganyika. It acquired a charter on the British model in 1885 after Carl Peters and his associates in the Society for German Colonization had collected treaties from East African chiefs. However, the charter was lost by 1892 because Peters's company proved unable to cope with Swahili and African resistance to its rule.

## Germanías
Revolutionary movements (literally, 'brotherhoods') which were active between 1519 and 1523 in Valencia and Mallorca, at the same time as the COMUNEROS in CASTILE. Led in Valencia by Juan Llorens, an artisan, and then after his death in battle by Vicent Peris, a more radical figure, the Germanías represented the interests of the guilds and middle sectors against the upper aristocracy. They were also hostile to the MU-

DEJARS of the province and forced them to baptize. Peris was executed (Mar 1522) and a harsh repression took place. In Mallorca a violent Germania was led eventually by Juan Colom, and not crushed until Mar 1523.

## German South West Africa Company
A company formed to exploit the German colony in South West Africa proclaimed by Bismarck in 1884 out of the trading positions of Adolf Luderitz. The company was never chartered and was always under-capitalized. In the 1890s it faced competition from a more financially secure British company, the South West Africa Company.

## German–Soviet Pact (23 Aug 1939)
Following Germany's failure to gain British support for, or even toleration of, her expansionist plans after 1938, and following difficulties surrounding the conclusion of a British–French–Soviet pact of mutual assistance directed against Germany, the German and Soviet governments moved swiftly to settle their differences. The respective Foreign Ministers, RIBBENTROP and MOLOTOV, signed an agreement (including a Secret Protocol) which defined territorial interests in Eastern Europe (effectively partitioning the region between them), renounced the use of force against one another, guaranteed friendly relations and allowed extensive economic relations to develop.

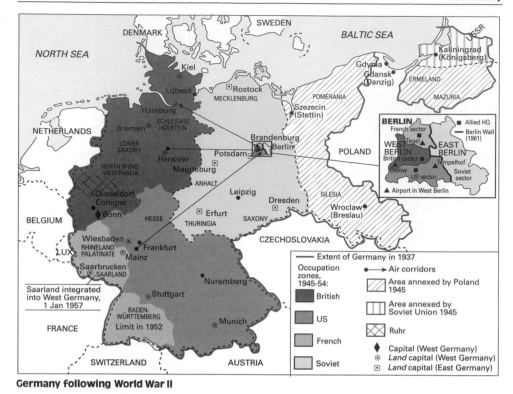

**Germany following World War II**

The fate of Poland was thereby sealed, but **HITLER**'s attack on the USSR in June 1941 ended what was always an opportunistic and cynical agreement.

### Germantown, Battle of (4 Oct 1777)

During the **AMERICAN REVOLUTION**, an attack made by George **WASHINGTON** and his forces on the British troops who had occupied Philadelphia and were stationed at Germantown. Despite their recent defeat at **BRANDYWINE**, the Americans attempted to surprise the British, but their plans were thwarted by bad weather and bad coordination of the planned four-pronged attack, and they suffered heavy losses. Over winter they retreated to **VALLEY FORGE**. Despite the outcome of the battle, Washington's strategic ability was obvious, and it helped to convince the French that they should join the war in support of America.

### GERMANY official name **Federal Republic of Germany**

A central European state formed by the political unification of West Germany and East Germany in 1990. It is bounded to the east by Poland and the Czech Republic; to the south by Austria and Switzerland; to the west by France, Luxembourg, Belgium and the Netherlands; and to the north by the North Sea, Denmark and the Baltic Sea. It was the location of the union of the ancient Germanic tribes within the Frankish empire of Charlemagne in the 8c and of an elective monarchy after 918 under Otto I, with the **HOLY ROMAN EMPIRE** divided into several hundred states. Many reforms and territorial changes took place during the Napoleonic era, and after the Congress of **VIENNA** (1814–15) a **GERMAN CONFEDERATION** of 39 states under Austria was formed. Under **BISMARCK**, **PRUSSIA** succeeded Austria as the leading German power

and excluded her from the **NORTH GERMAN CONFEDERATION**. The union of Germany and foundation of the Second **REICH** (1871), with the King of Prussia as hereditary German Emperor, gave rise, from around 1900, to an aggressive foreign policy which eventually led to **WORLD WAR I**. After the German defeat, the Second Reich was replaced by the democratic **WEIMAR REPUBLIC** and, in 1933, political power passed to the **NAZI PARTY**. **HITLER**'s acts of aggression as Chancellor and Leader (*Führer*) of the totalitarian Third Reich, eventually led to **WORLD WAR II** and a second defeat for Germany, with the collapse of the German political regime. The area of Germany was subsequently reduced, and occupied by the UK, USA, France, USSR and Poland, whose zone is now recognized as sovereign Polish territory. This Western occupation softened with the creation of the Federal Republic of Germany (1949) out of the three western zones, and a socialist German Democratic Republic (East Germany) out of the Soviet-occupied zone. Western forces continued to occupy West Berlin, which became a province of West Germany, while East Germany was governed on the communist Soviet model, with the Socialist Unity Party (**SED**) guaranteed a pre-eminent role. Anti-Soviet demonstrations in East Germany were put down in 1953, and both republics were recognized as sovereign states the following year. In 1958 West Germany was a founder-member of the **EEC**. The flow of refugees from East to West Germany continued until 1961, but was largely stopped by the building of the **BERLIN WALL**. East Germany was accorded diplomatic recognition and membership of the **UN** after signing a treaty with West Germany in 1973. In East Germany the movement for democratic reform, as well as mounting economic crisis, culminated (Nov 1989) in the opening of the Berlin Wall and other border crossings to the West, and a more open government policy. Free elections (Mar 1990) led first to economic union with West Germany (July) and then full political unification (Oct), in which West Germany's federal system of government, built around 10 states (*Länder*) with considerable powers, absorbed East Germany as five additional states. Germany is a leading industrial and trading nation, and a dominant force in the European Union (**EU**) and the **EURO ZONE**, but modernization of the former East German economy has been a lengthy and costly process and since 1991 Germany has experienced increasing economic problems, such as low growth and high employment. There have also been outbreaks of racial violence by the far Right. Chancellor Helmut **KOHL** and the **CDU** (Christian Democratic Union) held power for 16 years from 1982, and were defeated in 1998 by the **SPD** (Social Democratic Party) led by Gerhard Schröder.

**Geronimo**, Apache name **Goyathlay** (1829–1909)
Mexican-born Chiricahua **APACHE** chief. The best known and most fearsome of all Apaches, he led numerous raiding parties in Mexico and Arizona following the massacre of his family by Mexican soldiers. He forcibly resisted the internment of his people on a reservation, escaping from white control on several occasions, but made a final surrender in 1886. In his old age he became a Christian and a figure in public spectacles, including President Theodore **ROOSEVELT**'s inauguration parade. ▶ **INDIAN WARS**

**gerrymander**
A term describing the redrawing of electoral districts so as to benefit the party in power in forthcoming elections. It was first coined in the USA in 1812 by combining the last name of Elbridge Gerry (1744–1814), then Governor of Massachusetts, with salamander, the shape of which animal the newly created electoral district was said to resemble.

**Gestapo**
An abbreviation of *Geheime Staatspolizei*, the political police of the German Third **REICH**, founded in 1933 by **GOERING** on the basis of the Prussian political police. It soon extended throughout Germany, and from 1936 came under the control of **HIMMLER**, as head of the **SS**. ▶ **NAZI PARTY**

**Gettysburg, Battle of** (1–3 July 1863)
Marking the turning point in the **AMERICAN CIVIL WAR**, the Gettysburg campaign began in June 1863. It consisted of a major series of engagements in Pennsylvania between the army of north Virginia (Confederate) and the army of the Potomac (Union), after Robert E **LEE**, the Southern commander, decided to take the war into the North. The Battle of Gettysburg ended with a Union victory, but with heavy losses on both sides (Union 23,000; Confederate 25,000). On 4 July, Lee's severely reduced troops retreated, with the defeat ending any prospect of foreign recognition for the Confederacy.

**Gettysburg Address** (19 Nov 1863)
A speech given by President **LINCOLN** during the **AMERICAN CIVIL WAR**, at the dedication of a war cemetery in Pennsylvania on the site of the Battle of **GETTYSBURG**. Ill-regarded at the time, it is now thought of as one of the masterpieces of US oratory, from its often-quoted opening, 'Fourscore and seven years ago our fathers brought forth on this continent a new nation', to its memorable conclusion, 'that government of the people, by the people, for the people, shall not perish from the earth'.

**Geyl, Pieter** (1887–1966)
Dutch historian and patriot. He was educated in The Hague, at Leiden and in Italy. After serving as London correspondent of the *Nieuwe Rotterdamsche Courant* (1913–19), he was appointed the first Professor of Dutch Studies at London University (1919–36) and Professor of Modern History at Utrecht (1936–58). During **WORLD WAR II**, he was imprisoned in **BUCHENWALD** and other Nazi concentration camps. He was a believer in a 'greater Netherlands', always mourning the loss of Dutch-speaking Flanders and **BRABANT** during the **EIGHTY YEARS' WAR** in the late 16c. As a historian, however, he was a climatologist and environmentalist, arguing that the outcome of the Dutch revolt against Habsburg Spain was dictated by movements of rivers and water-currents rather than religion or economics. His multi-volume history of the Eighty Years' War and its sequels were published in the 1930s, translated into English as *The Revolt of the Netherlands* and *The Netherlands Divided*, while his struggle against Hitlerian domination of Europe is reflected in his *Napoleon, For and Against* (1944). He was also a poet and essayist, debating with numerous living and dead historians, and was the leading interpreter of the Dutch past to his country and the world.

**Ghadr Party and Movement**
Originally an organization of Indian migrants, especially Punjabis, settled in British Columbia and on the west coast of the USA, it derived its name from the title of its journal, *Ghadr* (Urdu, 'revolution'). Influenced by the activities of Irish radicals and Russian revolutionaries, a highly organized conspiracy was hatched at the start of **WORLD WAR I**, the Indian–Berlin Committee of the 'Hindustan Ghadr Party' offering money and arms to help raise a revolt against the British in India. Accordingly, large numbers of Ghadrites returned to the subcontinent. Many were arrested, but by late 1914 a substantial body of party members and suppporters was established in the Punjab. Led by men such as Rashbehari Bose and Sachin Sayal, attempts were made to foster mutiny in the Indian army; bombs were manufactured, robberies committed and arsenals raided in order to raise arms and supplies for a general uprising. However, the British pre-empted this plan, arresting large numbers of Ghadrites in Punjab, Bengal, Singapore and elsewhere. A series of trials, including the 1915 Lahore Conspiracy Case, resulted, in which Ghadrites and others accused of revolutionary activities were prosecuted under the Defence of India Act; 46 people were hanged and 194 were imprisoned. A total of 145 revolutionaries were hanged or killed by the police, and some 306 sentenced to transportation. Later, further trials of Ghadrites were held in the USA, whilst in India those revolutionary cells still active were riven by factionalism. Attempts to revive

the Ghadr Movement in India after 1919 failed due to the growing popularity and success of the Gandhian Congress, although in the 1930s and 1940s returning Ghadrites, having served out their term in prison, often became activists once again in the Indian Communist movement.

### Ghaffar Khan, Abd al- (1891–1988)

Muslim Indian politician. He was from North-West Frontier Province, where in 1921 he formed *Khudai Khidmatgar* ('Servants of God') to act as an agent of social welfare and peaceful political change in the mostly Muslim province. Because of his close links with the **INDIAN NATIONAL CONGRESS** and his strict adherence to M K **GANDHI**'s technique of **SATYAGRA-HA**, he became popularly known as the 'Frontier Gandhi'. Due to the close co-operation of Khudai Khidmatgar and the Congress, North-West Frontier province became the only one with a Muslim majority to be controlled by the Congress after the 1937 national election. Abd al-Ghaffar boycotted the July 1947 referendum on the issue of North-West Frontier province's accession to Pakistan, and this led to his political decline and that of his party. His later demands for an independent Pathan state resulted in repeated imprisonment in Pakistan and eventual exile in Afghanistan.

**GHANA** official name **Republic of Ghana**

A republic in West Africa, bounded to the west by the Côte d'Ivoire; to the north by Burkina Faso; to the east by Togo; and to the south by the Gulf of Guinea. Ghana was discovered by Europeans in the 15c, and became the centre of the slave trade in the 18c. The modern state was created by the union of two former British territories, British Gold Coast (Crown Colony in 1874) and British Togoland, in 1957, the name being taken from the ancient Kingdom of Ghana. It gained independence in 1957, the first British colony in Africa to do so, and became a republic within the **COMMONWEALTH OF NATIONS** in 1960. Kwame **NKRUMAH**, who had led the nationalist movement and had been Prime Minister when Ghana became independent, became the first President in 1960, but was later deposed. Jerry **RAWLINGS** seized power from President Hilla **LIMANN** in a military coup in 1981 and was elected President in 1992, when a multiparty constitution was approved. John Kufuor

was elected President in 2000, Ghana's first peaceful democratic transfer of power, and in 2002 he set up a reconciliation commission to investigate human rights abuses during military rule. ➤ **GHANA, KING-DOM OF**

### Ghana, Kingdom of

An African kingdom in the western Sudan which may have its origins as early as the 5–6c, but which certainly flourished in the 8–11c. It probably derived its name from the title of its king, and bears no geographical relationship to the modern state of Ghana, which lies further to the south and east. It was one of a series of states on the margin between the savanna and the desert, controlling the trade of the Sahara. Its capital was sacked by the **ALMORAVIDS** c.1076 and its power broken, though it lingered on until the 13c. ➤ **BERBERS**

### Ghazi (1912–39)

King of Iraq (1933/9). The son of King **FAYSAL I**, he proved not to be of his father's calibre and was seen as inadequate when faced with the duties required of the King of Iraq. Despite, or possibly because of, his popularity with Iraqi army officers (educated, as he himself had been, in the UK), his reign saw a general increase in anti-British sentiment throughout his country.

### Ghaznevids

The dynasty founded by Sebuktigin, son of Alptegin, a Turkish slave of the Samanids who had attained to a position of great influence in Samanid government circles. The most famous member of the dynasty was Sebuktigin's son, Mahmud (999/1030). Ghazna, situated high in Afghanistan overlooking the plain of what is now Pakistan, to which access could be gained through the valley of Kabul, enabled Mahmud in the early 11c to annex the Punjab, Multan and part of Sind. Mahmud's westward expansion extended to capturing most of Persia from the **BUYIDS**. He thus established control over a wide empire, and, with the riches therefrom accruing, he was able to beautify his capital and play patron to men of science, learning and the arts, notable among whom was the poet Firdawsi, author of the *Shahnama*, the Persian national epic, to name but one. After the death of Mahmud, the dynasty soon began to show signs of decay. Various powers in east and west gradually gained control of elements of the Ghaznevid Empire and the last Ghaznevid finally fell in 1186 in Lahore at the hands of the Ghurids.

### Ghegs

The northern Albanians who, until **WORLD WAR II**, retained their strong tribal organization and lived in isolated communities in the mountains. Under Ottoman rule, they were Sunni Muslims. They speak Gheg, one of the Albanian dialects.

### Ghent, Pacification of (8 Nov 1576)

The peace treaty signed by almost all the provinces of the northern and southern Netherlands in the early stages of the **EIGHTY YEARS' WAR** against Spain. It agreed to stop all religious persecution (except against the Catholics in Holland and Zeeland) and to leave the religious question to be decided by the States General; confiscated property was to be returned and political prisoners released. **WILLIAM I** of

Orange was recognized as **STADHOLDER** of Holland and Zeeland. This was a highpoint of the revolt: all the Netherlands provinces united against Spain, with freedom of religion. Two years later, however, the Union of **ARRAS** broke ranks, and the southern Netherlands drifted back to Spain.

### Ghent, Treaty of (1814)
The treaty between the USA and Britain that ended the **WAR OF 1812**, without any resolution of the major issues from which the conflict had grown. These had included maritime rights and military control of the Great Lakes.

### Gheorghiu-Dej, Gheorghe (1901–65)
Romanian politician. A railway worker, he joined the Romanian Communist Party (RCP) in 1930 and was imprisoned in 1933 for his role in the Griviţa railway strike. On his release in 1944, he became Secretary-General of the RCP and Minister of Communications (1944–6), and in 1945 was instrumental in the ousting of the coalition government of Nicolae Rădescu (1874–1953) and the establishment of a communist regime. He then served in a variety of economic posts (1946–52) and as Prime Minister (1952–5), before becoming state President in 1961. A Stalinist, he nonetheless retained the support of Nikita **KHRUSHCHEV**'s Moscow, while developing increasingly independent policies during the 1950s and 1960s. ► CEAUŞESCU, NICOLAE

### Ghibellines
The pro-imperial party in Italian cities of the 13–14c, favouring the involvement of the Holy Roman Emperor in Italian politics, even after the decline of the Hohenstaufen state from 1266. They supported the invasion of Emperor **HENRY VII** in 1308, although the power and status of the Empire had much diminished by that date. ► GUELFS; HOHENSTAUFEN DYNASTY

### Ghosh or Ghose, Aurobindo (1872–1950)
Bengali nationalist and poet. He started the philosophy of cosmic salvation through spiritual evolution. Educated in Christian convents in India and at Cambridge, he took administrative and professorial posts in India, and then turned to the study of Indian culture. A teacher in Baroda, Ghosh showed only a passing interest in nationalist politics through the writing of a few articles prior to 1905. Coincident with the partition of Bengal, however, he returned to Calcutta to become Principal of the National College, and became prominent in the **SWADESHI** movement. Taking editorial control of the newspaper *Bande Mataram*, he wrote and published articles that greatly increased Hindu nationalist fervour in the Bengali contingent of Congress. Acquitted of a charge of sedition in 1908, he became an acknowledged leader of the so-called 'extremist' group within the Bengal Congress. He started a new journal, *Karmayogin*, in 1910 but fled Bengal soon afterward to escape government surveillance. He went to the French colony of Pondicherry near Madras, where he founded Auroville, an international centre for spiritual development. ► BENGAL, PARTITION OF

### Ghost Dance
A Native American messianic cult inspired in 1889 by the Paiute Indian religious leader **WOVOKA**. He promised that if **NATIVE AMERICANS** lived peacefully and performed the Ghost Dance ritual (which involved dancing for days until a trance-like state was attained), whites would disappear, the buffalo would return, and the dead would rise. It had followers among many of the Plains peoples, especially the **SIOUX**, but after the massacre at **WOUNDED KNEE** (1890), when many were killed wearing 'ghost shirts' from which they expected supernatural protection, the movement came to an end.

### Gia Long, also called **Nguyen Phuoc Anh** (1762–1820)
Vietnamese emperor, the founder of the Nguyen Dynasty. In a series of military campaigns in the 1790s, he extended and consolidated the authority of the Nguyen clan, taking advantage of the disintegration of the existing, Tay Son, order. Final victory was achieved in 1802 and, for the first time in Vietnam's history, a single court (at Hue) could claim authority over the whole territory: from the border with China in the north to the Mekong delta in the south. Emperor Gia Long's reign sought to secure Nguyen power within a highly centralized administration. His law code, promulgated in 1815 and drawing heavily on Chinese models, greatly strengthened the position of the ruling élite.

### Gibraltar
The narrow peninsula rising steeply from the lowlying coast of south-west Spain at the eastern end of the Strait of Gibraltar, which is an important strategic point of control for the western Mediterranean. Settled by the Moors in 711, Gibraltar was taken by Spain in 1462, and ceded to Britain in 1713, becoming a British Crown Colony in 1830. It played a key role in Allied naval operations during both World Wars. A proposal to end British rule was defeated by a referendum in 1967; a proposal for joint British-Spanish sovereignty was rejected in an unofficial referendum in 2002. The frontier with Spain was closed from 1969 until 1985, and Spain continues to claim sovereignty.

### Gierek, Edward (1913–2001)
Polish politician. He lived in France (1923–34) during the **PIŁSUDSKI** dictatorship, and joined the French Communist party in 1931. He was deported to Poland in 1934, but moved to Belgium (1937–48), becoming a member of the Belgian resistance. On his return to Poland in 1948, he joined the ruling Polish United Workers' Party (PUWP), being inducted into its Politburo in 1956 and appointed party boss of Silesia. He became First Secretary and leader of the PUWP in 1970 when **GOMUŁKA** resigned after strikes and riots in Gdansk, Gdynia and Szczecin. Head of the party's 'technocrat faction', he embarked on an ambitious industrialization programme which, with foreign loans, also involved high consumer spending. This plunged the country heavily into debt and, following a wave of strikes in Warsaw and Gdansk, spearheaded by the **SOLIDARITY** free trade union movement, he was forced to resign in 1980.

### Giers, Nikolai Karlovich (1820–95)
Russian diplomat and politician. He gained wide experience serving in various diplomatic posts in the Balkans and the Middle East before becoming

Deputy Foreign Minister in 1875 and Foreign Minister in 1882. Concerned to protect his country against its traditional rivals, France and Britain, he was inclined to lean towards Germany. He struggled hard to retain the special German connection both before and after **BISMARCK**'s dismissal in 1890. Initially he resisted the **FRANCO-RUSSIAN ALLIANCE** signed in 1894, but he was forced to recognize changing circumstances.

## Gilded Age
A derogatory term for a period in the latter part of the 19c in the USA. Taken from the title of a novel by Mark Twain (1835–1910) and Charles Dudley Warner (1829–1900), it referred to the widespread political corruption and scandals of the time.

## Gil Robles, José María (1898–1980)
Spanish politician and academic. As a young and pugnacious leader of the **CEDA**, he was the principal figure of the Right during the Second Republic. Effectively dominating the governments of Nov 1933–Dec 1935, as Minister of War he prepared the army for the rising of July 1936. Exiled as a member of the monarchist opposition to the **FRANCO** regime (1936–53 and 1962–5), he was the founder and first President of the Popular Democratic Federation, and also created the Christian Social Democratic Party. However, in the 1977 general election his party was annihilated. ► **REPUBLIC, SECOND** (Spain)

## Ginkel, Godert de (1630–1703)
Dutch general. He accompanied **WILLIAM III** to England in 1688, and fought at the Battle of the **BOYNE** (1690). As Commander-in-Chief in Ireland, he defeated the remaining rebels, and was created Earl of Athlone (1692). He later led the Dutch troops under the Duke of Marlborough.

## Gioberti, Vincenzo (1801–52)
Piedmontese writer and politician. Ordained in 1825 and expelled from Piedmont in 1833 because of his outspoken defence of the Polish cause, he wrote extensively on Italian history and politics. His most important work, *Del primato morale e civile degli italiani* ('On the Moral and Civil Primacy of the Italians'), written in exile in Brussels and published in 1843, called for an Italian Confederation under papal presidency. His dreams seemed to have been realized with the election of the apparently liberal **PIUS IX** in 1846 and the outbreak of revolution in 1848. Briefly Prime Minister of Piedmont (Dec 1848–Mar 1849), he became disillusioned with, and retired from, politics and was condemned by an increasingly reactionary Pius. ► **BALBO, CESARE**; **CHARLES ALBERT**; **D'AZEGLIO, MASSIMO**

## Giolitti, Giovanni (1842–1928)
Italian politician. An astute and unprincipled parliamentary manager, Giolitti entered parliament in 1882 as a liberal. He became **CRISPI**'s Minister of Finance in 1889. Prime Minister from 1892 to 1893, he was brought down by a banking scandal. He returned to politics as Interior Minister under **ZANARDELLI** in 1901, becoming Prime Minister again from 1903 to 1909, except for a brief spell out of office in 1905–6. As Prime Minister, he sought to combat leftist strikes and disorders through economic policy rather than confrontation; in foreign policy he strengthened Italy's ties with Austria and Germany. During his fourth

spell as Prime Minister (1911–14), he brought Italy into the **TRIPOLITANIAN WAR**, gaining Libya, Rhodes and the Dodecanese. However, the war resulted in unpopular tax increases. A general strike forced him from office in 1914. In opposition, he urged neutrality in 1915. His fifth ministry (1920–1) failed to cope with post-war disorder or the violence of the **SQUADRISTI**, and he was unable to block **MUSSOLINI**'s ascent to power.

## Giraud, Henri Honoré (1879–1949)
French soldier. Commander of the 7th and 9th Armies in 1940, he was captured by the Germans, but escaped. Reaching North Africa in 1942, he joined the Allied cause, and was imposed by the USA as joint chairman with de **GAULLE** of the committee of National Liberation. Rapidly outmanoeuvred by the latter, he resigned and played no further political role of any consequence. ► **WORLD WAR II**

## Girondins or Girondists
A group of deputies in the **LEGISLATIVE ASSEMBLY** (1791–2) and French Convention (1792–5), led by Jean Roland, Charles **DUMOURIEZ** and Jacques **BRISSOT**. Their name derived from the Gironde region of south-western France. They aroused the hostility of **ROBESPIERRE** and the 'MOUNTAIN' in the Convention, many being executed during the Terror (1793). ► **CONVENTION, NATIONAL**; **FRENCH REVOLUTION**; **PLAIN, THE**; **TERROR, REIGN OF**

## Giscard d'Estaing, Valéry (1926– )
French politician. He entered the Ministry of Finance as a civil servant and was appointed Finance Minister in 1962. He led that faction of the **INDEPENDENTS** who remained loyal to de **GAULLE** after Algerian independence, and turned them into a new political party, the **INDEPENDENT REPUBLICAN PARTY**. He returned to the Finance Ministry in 1969, defeated **MITTERRAND** and the Gaullist candidate to become President in 1974, and was then beaten by Mitterrand in 1981. In 1984 he was re-elected to the National Assembly and was the influential leader of the *Union pour la démocratie française* ('Union for French Democracy'), a centre-right grouping which he formed in 1978, until 1996. In 1989 he resigned from the National Assembly to play, instead, a leading role in the European Parliament.He chaired the Convention on the Future of Europe that drafted the **EU** constitution. ► **GAULLISTS**

## Giulio de' Medici ► CLEMENT VII

## Gladstone, W(illiam) E(wart) (1809–98)
British politician. He entered parliament in 1832 as a Conservative, working closely with **PEEL**. From 1834 he held various junior posts, becoming President of the Board of Trade (1843–5). He was Chancellor of the Exchequer in **ABERDEEN**'s coalition (1852–5) and then again under **PALMERSTON** and **RUSSELL** (1859–66). In 1867 he became leader of the **LIBERAL PARTY**, and soon after served his first term as Prime Minister (1868–74). In a ministry notable for administrative reform, he disestablished and disendowed the Irish Church, reformed the Civil Service and established a system of national elementary education (1870). Frequently in office (1880–5, 1886 and 1892–4) until his resignation in 1894, he succeeded in carrying out a scheme of parliamentary reform

(1884) which went a long way towards universal male suffrage. In his last two ministries he introduced bills for Irish **HOME RULE**, but both were defeated. ▸ **CONSERVATIVE PARTY** (UK)

### Glanvill, Ranulf de (d.1190)
Chief Justiciary of England (1180–9). He was adviser to **HENRY II** and reputed author of the earliest treatise on the laws of England. In 1174 he raised a body of knights and captured **WILLIAM I, THE LION**, of Scotland. He joined the Third **CRUSADE** and died during the siege of Acre.

### glasnost
A Russian term, usually translated as 'openness', describing the changes in attitude on the part of leaders of the former USSR following Mikhail **GORBACHEV**'s rise to power in 1985. These brought about a wider and franker dissemination of information, and the opportunity for genuine debate both within Soviet society and in Soviet relations with foreign powers. The policies of glasnost and **PERESTROIKA** ('restructuring') were intended to work together to bring about political liberalization and a reduction in Soviet inefficiency; in reality they contributed to the economic discontent and nationalist uprisings that precipitated the collapse of the Soviet Union in 1991 and the toppling of the once dominant Communist Party.

### Glemp, Józef (1929– )
Polish ecclesiastic. He became Bishop of Warmia in 1979 and succeeded Cardinal Stefan **WYSZYNSKI** as Archbishop of Gniezno and Warsaw, and Primate of Poland, after the latter's death in 1981. A specialist in civil and canonical law, Glemp was a prominent figure during Poland's internal political unrest, attempting with some success to moderate hardline communist attitudes. He was made a cardinal in 1983.

### Glendower, Owen (c.1354–c.1416)
Welsh chief. He studied law at Westminster, and became esquire to the Earl of Arundel. In 1401 he rebelled against **HENRY IV**, proclaimed himself Prince of Wales, established an independent Welsh parliament, and joined the coalition with Harry Percy (Hotspur), who was defeated at the Battle of Shrewsbury (1403). He continued to fight for Welsh independence until his death. ▸ **PERCY**

### Gleneagles Agreement (1977)
An undertaking entered into by Commonwealth heads of government, meeting at Gleneagles in Scotland, to discourage sporting links with South Africa as a symbol of disapproval of **APARTHEID**.

### Glistrup, Mogens (1926– )
Danish politician. From 1956 to 1963 he was a member of the Faculty of Law at Copenhagen University. In 1972 he founded the anti-tax Progress Party (*Fremskridtspartiet*), which after the general election in 1973 became a right-wing force in Danish politics. He was a member of the Danish parliament (**FOLKETINGET**) in 1973–83 and 1987–90.

### Glorious First of June, Battle of the (1794)
A naval battle fought off the Isle d'Ouessant (near Brest) between British and French navies. The victory for Admiral Richard **HOWE** resulted in the capture of a third of the French ships, and confirmation of British naval supremacy. ▸ **FRENCH REVOLUTIONARY WARS**

### Glorious Revolution (Dec 1688–Feb 1689)
The name given to the events during which **JAMES VII AND II** fled from England, effectively abdicating the throne, and **WILLIAM III** and Mary II were established by parliament as joint monarchs. The title, coined by **WHIGS** who in the long term benefited most from it, celebrates the bloodlessness of the event, and the assertion of the constitutional importance of parliament.

### Gloucester, Humphrey, Duke of (1391–1447)
Youngest son of **HENRY IV**, and protector during the minority of **HENRY VI** (1422–9). He greatly increased the difficulties of his brother, **BEDFORD**, by his greed, irresponsibility, and factious quarrels with their uncle, Cardinal Henry **BEAUFORT**. In 1447 he was arrested for high treason at Bury St Edmunds and five days later was found dead in bed (apparently from natural causes). His patronage of literature led to his nickname 'the Good Duke Humphrey'.

### Glubb, Sir John Bagot, known as Glubb Pasha (1897–1986)
British soldier. Educated in Cheltenham and the Royal Military Academy, Woolwich, he served in **WORLD WAR I**, and became the first organizer of the native police force in the new state of Iraq (1920). In 1930 he was transferred to British-mandated Transjordan, organizing the Arab Legion's Desert Patrol, and becoming Legion Commandant (1939). He had immense prestige among the Bedouin, but was dismissed from his post in 1956 following Arab criticism. Knighted in 1956, he then became a writer and lecturer.

### Glyndwr, Owain ▸ GLENDOWER, OWEN

### Gneisenau, August Wilhelm Anton, Count Neithardt von (1760–1831)
Prussian general. In 1786 he joined the Prussian army, fought at Saalfeld and **JENA AND AUERSTÄDT** (1806), helped to reorganize the army after its defeat by **NAPOLEON I** (1807), and in the war of liberation gave distinguished service at the Battle of **LEIPZIG** (1813). In the **WATERLOO** campaign, as chief of **BLÜCHER**'s staff, he directed the strategy of the Prussian army. ▸ **NAPOLEONIC WARS**; **PRUSSIA**

### Gobind Singh (1666–1708)
Last of the 10 Sikh Gurus (1675/1708). He completed the process by which the Sikhs developed from the quietist faith propagated by Guru Nanak to a militant creed. Coming to the leadership on the execution by the Mughals of his father, Guru Tegh Bahadur (1664/75), he was implacably hostile to them, and in the final years of the 17c established a small Sikh state in the Punjab foothills by military means. At the Baisakhi festival in 1699 he instituted the Khalsa, the new Sikh brotherhood marked by a new code of discipline, the 'Five Ks' (visible symbols, including the uncut hair and beard), and common adoption of the name Singh for males and Kaur for females. Following **AURANGZEB**'s death in 1707, there were moves toward an accommodation between Sikhs and Mughals, ended by Gobind Singh's death the following year at the hands of Pathan assassins. Traditionally, Gobind Singh declared on his death-bed that

guruship would henceforth reside in the Sikh scripture (*Guru Granth*) and the Sikh community (*Guru Panth*), his sons having already died in battle or been executed by the Mughals.

**Godbout, Adélard** (1892–1956)
Canadian politician. He became Liberal Premier of Quebec in 1939, defeating Maurice **DUPLESSIS** and the **UNION NATIONALE**. In 1944 his administration placed the Montreal Light, Heat and Power Company in public ownership, the first move in breaking free from the English-speaking community's hold on the economy of Quebec. ► **LIBERAL PARTY** (Canada)

**Goderich, Frederick John Robinson, Viscount, and 1st Earl of Ripon** (1782–1859)
British politician. He entered parliament as a Tory MP in 1806, becoming President of the Board of Trade (1918–23 and 1841–3) and Chancellor of the Exchequer (1823–7). He was associated with financial reforms to reduce government debt and promote greater freedom of trade. His success earned him the sobriquet 'Prosperity Robinson'. He was Secretary of State for War and the Colonies (1827) under George **CANNING**, whom he succeeded. His weak leadership was soon exposed and he resigned willingly before meeting parliament as Prime Minister (1827–8), the only Premier to do so. Briefly changing parties, he served in **GREY**'s Whig governments as Secretary for War and the Colonies (1830–3) and Lord Privy Seal (1834–5). His last government office was under **PEEL** as President of the Board of Control (1843–6), and he introduced the Bill to repeal the **CORN LAWS** (1846). His extensive governmental career testifies to administrative competence but not to leadership. ► **TORIES**; **WHIGS**

**Godfrey of Bouillon** (c.1061–1100)
French Crusader. Duke of Lower Lorraine from 1089 to 1095, he was elected one of the principal commanders of the First **CRUSADE**. After the capture of Jerusalem (1099) he was proclaimed King, but he refused the crown, accepting only the title 'Defender of the Holy Sepulchre'. He died at Jerusalem.

**Godolphin, Sidney Godolphin, 1st Earl of** (1645–1712)
English statesman. He entered parliament (1668), visited Holland (1678), and was made head of the Treasury and a baron (1684). He stood by **JAMES VII AND II** when William of Orange landed (1688), and voted for a regency; yet in 1689 William reinstated him as First Commissioner of the Treasury. He was ousted in 1696, but made Lord High Treasurer by Queen **ANNE** (1702) and created earl (1706). His able management of the finances helped **MARLBOROUGH** in the War of the **SPANISH SUCCESSION** (1700–13); but court intrigues led to his dismissal in 1710. ► **WILLIAM III, OF ORANGE**

**Godoy, Manuel de** (1767–1851)
Spanish court favourite and Chief Minister (1792–1808) under **CHARLES IV**. An obscure guards officer, he achieved dictatorial power at the age of 25 through the favour of the Queen, Maria Luisa, whose lover he was. In 1795 he assumed the title 'Prince of the Peace', following Spain's defeat by Revolutionary France; in 1796 he allied with France against England – a disastrous move that turned Spain into a virtual

French satellite, and contributed massively to her losing her American empire. In 1808 he was overthrown, spending the rest of his life exiled in Rome and in Paris, where he died.

**Godwin** (d.1053)
Earl of Wessex. He was probably the son of the South Saxon Wulfnoth. Godwin became powerful under King **CANUTE**, and in 1042 helped to raise **EDWARD THE CONFESSOR** to the throne, marrying him to his daughter, Edith. He led the struggle against the King's foreign favourites, which Edward revenged by confining Edith in a monastery and banishing Godwin and his sons (1051). In 1052 Godwin landed in England, received the support of the people, and was reinstated. His son, **HAROLD II**, was, for a few months, Edward's successor.

**Goebbels, (Paul) Joseph** (1897–1945)
German Nazi politician. A deformed foot absolved him from military service, and he attended several universities, obtaining his doctorate at Heidelberg. He became **HITLER**'s enthusiastic supporter, led the **NAZI PARTY** in Berlin from 1926 and was appointed head of the Ministry of Public Enlightenment and Propaganda in 1933. A political radical and bitter anti-Semite, his gift of mob oratory made him a powerful exponent of Nazi philosophy. Wartime conditions greatly expanded his role as a propagandist, and from 1943 Goebbels did much to squeeze every last effort from the population and economy. He retained Hitler's confidence to the last, being appointed Plenipotentiary for the Pursuit of Total War in July 1944. In the Berlin bunker, he and his wife committed suicide after taking the lives of their six children. His diaries now constitute a major historical source. ► **WORLD WAR II**

**Goerdeler, Carl** (1884–1945)
German politician. He served under **HITLER** as Commissar for Price Control (1934), but resigned from his mayoralty of Leipzig in 1937 and became one of the leaders who opposed Hitler. This opposition culminated in **STAUFFENBERG**'s unsuccessful bomb plot of 20 July 1944, for which Goerdeler was executed together with a number of generals.

**Goering, Hermann Wilhelm** (1893–1946)
German Nazi politician. In **WORLD WAR I** he fought on the Western Front, then transferred to the air force, and commanded the famous 'von Richthofen Squadron'. In 1922 he joined the **NAZI PARTY** and was given command of **HITLER**'s stormtroopers (**SA**) until the unsuccessful 1923 putsch. In exile until 1927, he became President of the **REICHSTAG** in 1932, and joined the Nazi government in 1933 with responsibility for **PRUSSIA** and air travel. He founded the **GESTAPO**, and set up the concentration camps for political, racial and religious suspects. In 1935 he took charge of the reconstituted **LUFTWAFFE** and in 1936 became director of the Four Year Plan, renewed in 1940, to prepare the economy for war. He played a major part in the **ANSCHLUSS** with Austria (1938) and in the annexation of the **SUDETENLAND** (1938). In 1940 he was made Marshal of the **REICH**, the first and only holder of the rank, but his political influence and personal drive declined as his wish for aggressive diplomacy was superseded by open warfare. As **WORLD WAR II**

went against Germany and the *Luftwaffe* failed to meet expectations, his prestige waned further. In 1945 he attempted a palace revolution, was condemned to death, but escaped, to be captured by US troops. In 1946 he was sentenced to death at the **NUREMBERG TRIALS**, but before his execution could take place he committed suicide.

**Gökalp, Ziya**, pseudonym of **Mehmet Ziya** (c.1875–1924)

Turkish thinker. He owed his education, in the major Islamic languages (Arabic and Persian in addition to his native Turkish) and in the sciences both religious and secular, to his uncle. His career was spent in an intellectual attempt to contain the contrasting and not infrequently conflicting influences of orthodox religion, mysticism and modern science with which he had come into contact. Initially a thorn in the flesh of the authorities in Istanbul with his liberal and re-volutionary views, he was arraigned in 1897 and in due course exiled to his native Diyarbakir. By 1908 he was recognized as a prominent liberal writer and lecturer in his home province, and in course of time returned to Istanbul where he lived from 1912 to 1919. During this period he emerged as the propoun-der of a nationalist ideology for the Turks, which in-volved a reorientation of Turkish leanings emphasizing a Western approach. Exiled to Malta by the British after **WORLD WAR I**, he occasioned no sur-prise when, after his release in 1921, he associated himself with Mustafa Kemal **ATATÜRK** and his na-tional movement. Gökalp died with a reputation throughout his country as a thinker who had prepared the ground for the emergence of modern Turkey.

**Gokhale, Gopal Krishna** (1866–1915)

Indian social reformer and nationalist. He founded the Servants of India Society (1905) to work for the relief of the underprivileged, and in the same year, was elected President of the **INDIAN NATIONAL CON-GRESS**. He advocated moderate and constitutional methods of agitation and gradual reform, and died in Pune.

**Golden Bull**

Any document whose importance was stressed by authentication with a golden seal (Latin, *bulla*). Spe-cifically, the term is used for the edict promulgated by Emperor **CHARLES IV** in 1356 to define the German constitution. It formally affirmed that election of an emperor was by a college of seven princes, and recog-nized them as virtually independent rulers.

**Golden Fleece, Order of the**

The exclusive chivalric order founded in 1430 by **PHILIP THE GOOD**, Duke of Burgundy, in order to in-crease the dependence of his highest nobles on his leadership; in this sense it was comparable to the English Order of the Garter. Later, the order passed from the House of **BURGUNDY** to the **HABSBURG DY-NASTY**, and so to the royal houses of Spain and Aus-tria. The knights could only be tried by their sovereign and fellow knights, and were members of the Council of State; it was thus an order of great po-litical significance and prestige. The derivation of the order's name is uncertain: it might refer to the object of the quest of Jason and the Argonauts, or to Gideon's fleece.

**Golden Horde**

A feudal state, constituting at its height from the mid-13c to the end of the 14c the western part of the Mon-gol Empire, and occupying most of central and southern Russia and western Siberia. Its capital was first at Sarai Batu and then at Sarai Berbe on the River Volga. The Russian princes were vassals of the Khan of the Golden Horde, and paid regular tribute. The state was weakened by the Black Death (1346–7) and then soon overthrown by the Grand Princes of Moscow. ► **MONGOLS**

**Golden Spurs, Battle of the** (11 July 1302)

A great victory by Flemish foot-soldiers over a French army of knights; about 1,000 French nobles perished, and their golden spurs gave the battle its name. After the Matins of **BRUGES**, the whole of Flan-ders rose up against France, and pinned down the French forces near Kortrijk. A great French army came to relieve the town and punish the Flemings, but was heavily defeated by the citizens' army from the Flemish industrial towns. The victory granted temporary independence to Flanders from France, and increased the democratic factor in Flemish urban politics.

**Goldie, Sir George Taubman** (1846–1925)

British soldier and trader. After service as an army of-ficer, he became a trader in West Africa. He foresaw the developing Partition of **AFRICA** and believed that British interests must be secured against the French in the Oil Rivers region and along the Niger as a great commercial highway to the interior. By 1884 he had amalgamated all the British companies as the Na-tional Africa Company and set out to secure treaties from chiefs throughout the Niger Delta and in north-ern Nigeria. In 1886 he secured a charter for his re-named **ROYAL NIGER COMPANY** and effectively ruled the Niger regions until 1898. Frederick Lugard joined his employ and conquered the emirates of Northern Nigeria.

**Goldman, Emma**, known as **Red Emma** (1869–1940)

US anarchist, feminist and birth-control advocate. Her Jewish family left Russia for Germany to avoid persecution and, in 1885, she migrated to the USA, where she began her anarchist career. Imprisoned during **WORLD WAR I** for opposing government pol-icy, she was deported to the USSR and eventually settled in France.

**Gold Rush**

A burst of enthusiasm for mining, following the dis-covery of gold deposits in Sutter's Mill, California, in 1848. Major rushes of prospectors included Califor-nia (1849), Colorado (1858–60), Idaho (1861–4), Montana (1862–4), South Dakota (1876–8) and Yu-kon territory (1896). ► **KLONDIKE GOLD RUSH**

**gold standard**

A monetary standard or system according to which a country's unit of currency has a precise value in gold, and the country can exchange its currency for gold at that particular price at any time. Countries who be-longed to the gold standard had fixed exchange rates, and their monetary authorities had to hold a reserve of gold at all times. The first country to introduce an official gold standard was Britain (1821); all major countries had followed suit by 1900. The 'full' gold standard, whereby the population dealt in gold coins, was superseded in the 1920s by the gold-exchange standard, which required monetary authorities alone to be able to convert currency and enabled them to supplement their gold reserves with US dollars. The gold standard collapsed during the **GREAT DEPRESSION** of the 1930s, but it was restored again after **WORLD WAR II** with a new system that 'pegged' currencies either to the US dollar or to gold. After 1971 the dollar and other paper currencies replaced gold completely and it was no longer officially used in international exchange.

**Goldwater, Barry Morris** (1909–98)
US politician. Educated at the University of Arizona, he became a US Senator for that state in 1952. In 1964 he gave up his **SENATE** seat to become the Republican nominee for the presidency, but was overwhelmingly defeated by Lyndon B **JOHNSON**. He returned to the Senate in 1969, serving until 1987, and was one of the architects of the conservative revival within the **REPUBLICAN PARTY**.

**Göllheim, Battle of** (1298)
The decisive encounter between King **ADOLF OF NASSAU** and the anti-king **ALBERT I** of Habsburg, in which Adolf was defeated and killed.

**Gombos, Gyula** (1886–1936)
Hungarian politician. An army officer during **WORLD WAR I**, he found himself fighting Béla **KUN**'s Soviet Republic alongside Admiral **HORTHY** in 1919. Following Hungary's reduction in size and status in the post-war settlement, he drifted further to the right. He became Minister of Defence (1929) and was Prime Minister (1932–6). He strengthened the totalitarian tendencies in Hungarian politics; and in foreign policy he flirted with Italy and Germany. In 1933 he was one of the first foreign statesmen to visit **HITLER** and congratulate him on his coming to power.

**Gomes, Albert** (1911–78)
Trinidadian politician, trade unionist and novelist. He edited an anti-establishment periodical, *The Beacon*, and founded (1937) the Federated Workers' Union. A member of the Port of Spain City Council, he attacked the colonial government and maintained this criticism when elected to the Legislative Council in 1946. However, on becoming Minister of Labour (1950), with a policy of 'industrialization by invitation', he lost his earlier radicalism and quickly became less influential after the nationalist upsurge of 1956. Gomes was Deputy Leader of the Democratic Labour Party in the federation elections of 1958.

**Gómez, Juan Vicente** (1857–1935)
Venezuelan dictator. A rancher with no formal education, he became Vice-President under Cipriano **CASTRO** in 1899. He deposed Castro in 1908, and his dictatorial rule (1908–35) witnessed the dramatic expansion of the oil industry, mainly Standard Oil and Anglo-Dutch Shell, in the Maracaibo region. He played off the major multinationals and the army benefited accordingly.

**Gompers, Samuel** (1850–1924)
British-born US labour leader. After migrating to the USA in 1863, he followed his father's trade as a cigar maker, joining a union the following year. Self-educated, he studied and rejected **MARXISM** and **SOCIALISM**, developing instead the US practice of non-political trade unionism. He helped found (1886), and was long-time President of, the American Federation of Labor (AFL), and with the AFL's triumph as the main force in organized labour he became a major public figure. ► **AFL–CIO**

**Gomułka, Władysław** (1905–82)
Polish political leader. A professional trade unionist, in 1943 he became Secretary of the outlawed Communist Party. He was Vice-President of the first post-war Polish government (1945–8), but his criticism of the USSR led to his expulsion from the party in 1949 and his imprisonment from 1951 to 1954. He returned to power as Party First Secretary in 1956. In 1970, following a political crisis, he resigned office, and spent his remaining years largely in retirement.

**Gondomar, Diego Sarmiento de Acuña, Count of** (1567–1626)
Spanish diplomat. As Ambassador in England (1613–18 and 1620–2), he worked to arrange the marriage of Prince Charles (later **CHARLES I**) with the Infanta. He had great influence over **JAMES VI AND I**, but caused public hostility in England. He was recalled to Spain in 1622, and lost influence after the Anglo-Dutch alliance of 1624.

**Gong (Kung)** (1833–98)
Manchu Prince. The sixth son of the Manchu Qing Emperor Daoguang (1821/51), he was given the task of signing the Convention of Beijing (1860) with invading British and French forces. The convention, which ratified the 1858 Treaty of **TIANJIN**, guaranteed as a treaty port, and gave Britain a lease on Kowloon. Originally anti-foreign, Prince Gong after 1860 advocated conciliation and the use of diplomacy. In 1861 he became Head of the *Zongli Yamen* (*Tsungli Yamen*), a government institution created to deal with the foreign powers. Following the death of Emperor Xianfeng (1851/62) and the accession of a boy-emperor, Tongzhi (1862/74), Prince Gong assisted the two Empress-Dowagers in regency government. His authority was increasingly diminished after 1875 with the growing influence of Empress-Dowager **CIXI**, and in 1884 he was stripped of his official positions.

**Gonzaga**
A princely northern Italian family who ruled Mantua for three centuries, from 1432 as marquises, from 1530 as dukes. They championed imperial interests and were often at war with the **VISCONTI** of Milan. In the 15c, and to a lesser extent in the 16c, the Gonzaga presided over one of the most splendid of **RENAISSANCE** courts. The last Gonzaga duke died in 1627, opening the so-called Mantuan phase of the **THIRTY YEARS' WAR**. The duchy itself survived until 1708, when the 10th and last duke was deprived of his estates and sent into exile by the Emperor Joseph I. A branch of the family became Dukes of Montferrat.

**González Márquez, Felipe** (1942–)
Spanish politician. He practised as a lawyer, and in 1962 joined the Spanish Socialist Workers' Party (**PSOE**), then an illegal organization. The Party regained legal status in 1977, three years after he became Secretary-General. He persuaded the PSOE to

adopt a more moderate policy, and in the 1982 elections they won a substantial majority. González then became Prime Minister in the first left-wing administration since 1939, remaining in power until 1996.

**Good Friday Agreement**, formal title **Belfast Agreement**

A Northern Ireland peace agreement resulting from multiparty talks between the UK and Irish governments and representatives of Unionist, nationalist and other groups, which was signed on Good Friday (10 Apr) 1998. The agreement's three strands addressed Northern Ireland's institutions, relations between Northern Ireland and the Republic of Ireland, and relations between both parts of Ireland and the rest of the UK. The Agreement was flawed, most crucially in decoupling talks on a political settlement from those on disarmament, and disputes, particularly over weapons decommissioning and prisoner release, delayed implementation, contributing, along with **STORMONTGATE**, to the suspension of the Northern Ireland Assembly and the return to direct rule in 2002. Hopes of renewed progress were raised in late 2004 when the **IRA** appeared to agree to decommission its weapons, but collapsed in Dec 2004 when an IRA raid on a bank discredited it and Sinn Féin's commitment to the peace process.

**Good Neighbor Policy**

A term coined in the 1930s to describe a change in US policy regarding its relationships with Latin American countries. The USA revamped its policy from one in which it had used **DOLLAR DIPLOMACY** and gunboat diplomacy to enforce its will on weaker countries, to one in which the USA pledged to treat other countries like equals. President Franklin D **ROOSEVELT** promised that the USA would be a 'good neighbor', withdrawing US marines from Latin American countries and annulling the **PLATT AMENDMENT**, but subsequent history indicates that the USA continued to rely on the dollar and the gunboat to get its way in the Caribbean, Central America and South America.

**Gorbachev, Mikhail Sergeevich** (1931– )

Soviet politician. Educated at the Law Faculty of Moscow State University and Stavropol Agricultural Institute, he began work as a machine operator (1946), and joined the Communist Party in 1952. He held a variety of senior posts in the Stavropol city and district Komsomol and Party organizations (1956–70), and was elected a deputy to the USSR Supreme Soviet (1970) and a member of the Party Central Committee (1971). He became Central Committee Secretary for Agriculture (1979–85); candidate member of the **POLITBURO** (1979–80) and full member (1980–91) of the Central Committee (1979–80); and, on the death of **CHERNENKO**, General-Secretary of the Party (1985–91). In 1988 he also became Chairman of the Presidium of the Supreme Soviet, ie head of state, and in 1990, the first Executive President of the USSR. On becoming General-Secretary he launched a radical programme of reform and restructuring (**PERESTROIKA**) of the Soviet economic and political system. A greater degree of political participation, civil liberty, public debate, and journalistic and cultural freedom were allowed under the policy of **GLASNOST** (openness). In defence and foreign affairs he reduced mili-

tary expenditure and pursued a policy of détente, disarmament and arms control with the West. He ended the Soviet military occupation of Afghanistan (1989) and accepted the break-up of **COMECON** and the **WARSAW PACT**, the withdrawal of Soviet troops from Eastern Europe and the reunification of Germany. But he failed to fulfil his promise to reform the economy and improve the living standards of the Soviet people, and proved unable to cope with the rising tide of nationalism. Following the unsuccessful coup against him in Aug 1991, he lost power to Boris **YELTSIN** despite accepting the demise of the Communist Party. In Dec 1991 he felt obliged to resign from the presidency as the USSR itself collapsed into 15 separate republics.

**Gorbachev, Raisa Maximovna** (1932–99)

Wife of Mikhail **GORBACHEV**, and the first ever wife of a Soviet leader to play a public role. Born of a railway family in the Altai region, she graduated from Moscow University and pursued a career in sociological research and lecturing. A woman of considerable intelligence and obvious charm, she had standing in her own right before 1985 when, as the General-Secretary's wife, she began to appear with him on important occasions, including overseas tours. In an unsettled society she attracted criticism, but abroad she added to her husband's political and popular prestige and did a great deal to make a success of East–West arms talks.

**Gorchakov, Prince Alexander Mikhailovich** (1798–1883)

Russian politician. A cousin of Prince Mikhail **GORCHAKOV**, he was ambassador at Vienna (1854–6), then succeeded **NESSELRODE** as Foreign Minister. He was, until **BISMARCK**'s rise, the most powerful minister in Europe. He secured Austrian neutrality in the Franco-German War of 1870, and in 1871 the freeing of Russia from the Black Sea neutralization clauses of the Treaty of Paris (1856). After the conclusion of the Russo-Turkish War (1878), the repudiation of the Treaty of **SAN STEFANO**, and the signing of the treaty negociated at the Congress of **BERLIN**, his influence began to wane, and he retired in 1882.
➤ **PARIS, CONGRESS OF**; **RUSSO-TURKISH WARS**

**Gorchakov, Prince Mikhail** (1793–1861)

Russian soldier. A cousin of Prince Alexander **GORCHAKOV**, he served against the French in the Napoleonic campaign of 1812–14, and in the Russo-Turkish War of 1828–9. He helped to suppress the Polish revolution of 1831 and took part in the capture of Warsaw, and he assisted in the suppression of the Hungarian insurrection in 1849. On the outbreak of the **CRIMEAN WAR** (1854–6) he commanded in the Danubian Principalities, but as Commander-in-Chief in the Crimea (1855) he was defeated on the Chernaya, although he recovered his laurels by his gallant defence of **SEVASTOPOL**. He was military governor of Poland from 1856 to 1861. ➤ **RUSSO-TURKISH WARS**

**Gordon, Charles George** (1833–85)

British general. He joined the Royal Engineers in 1852, and in 1855–6 fought in the **CRIMEAN WAR**. In 1860 he went to China, where he crushed the **TAIPING REBELLION**, for which he became known as 'Chinese

Gordon'. In 1877 he was appointed Governor of the Sudan. He resigned in poor health in 1880, but returned in 1884 to relieve Egyptian garrisons which lay in rebel territory. He was besieged at Khartoum for ten months by the Mahdi's troops, and was killed there two days before a relief force arrived.

## Gordon Riots

Anti-Catholic riots in London which caused a breakdown of law and order in parts of the capital for several days in early June 1780. They occurred after Lord George Gordon (1751–93), leader of the Protestant Association, had failed in his attempt to have clauses in the 1778 Catholic Relief Act (removing restrictions on the activities of priests) repealed. ► CATHOLIC EMANCIPATION

## Gore, Al(bert), Jr (1948– )

US politician. He was educated at Harvard, and at Vanderbilt University, where he studied law and divinity. He worked as an investigative reporter for *The Tennessean* (1971–6), and in 1976 was elected as a Democrat from Tennessee to the HOUSE OF REPRESENTATIVES, a position he held for eight years. He became a US Senator in 1984. Four years later he mounted an unsuccessful campaign for President, but in 1992 made a successful bid for Vice-President on the Democratic ticket with Bill CLINTON. In the 2000 presidential election he lost narrowly, and controversially, to George W BUSH. An ardent environmentalist, he is the author of *Earth in the Balance* (1992).

## Gorée Island

A small island off the Cape Verde Peninsula, Senegal. Throughout the 18c and early 19c, when Gorée was first a French, and then a British colony, it was a major centre of slave storage before shipping to the Americas.

## Görgey, Artúr (1818–1916)

Hungarian rebel soldier. During the revolt of 1848 he compelled Jelačić and his 10,000 Croats to capitulate at Ozora. As Hungarian Commander-in-Chief, although often in dispute with Lajos KOSSUTH, he relieved Komorn by inflicting a series of severe reverses on the Austrians, practically driving them out of the country. In 1849 he was repeatedly defeated, and in Aug surrendered to the Russians with his army of 24,000 men, at Világos near Arad. Görgey was imprisoned at Klagenfurt, but was eventually set free in 1867 and returned to Hungary in 1868.

## Göring, Hermann ► GOERING, HERMANN

## Gorky, Maxim (1868–1936)

Russian and Soviet writer and revolutionary. Born in Nizhni Novgorod, subsequently rechristened after him, he had little formal education and learned most from his frequent wanderings. From the turn of the century his inclinations were revolutionary, and in 1905 he officially joined the BOLSHEVIKS. However, he was in and out of friendship with LENIN and disapproved of what the Bolsheviks did in the years 1917–18, but he was on good and influential terms in the years 1918–21 before going abroad for his health. He returned in 1931 to preside over the new Writers' Union and sing the praises of much of what STALIN was doing. This was in the spirit of the socialist realist

philosophy he helped create. He died less happy in 1936, and in 1991 his birthplace took back its old name.

## Gorshkov, Sergei Georgievich (1910–88)

Soviet admiral. He joined the navy in 1927 and, after graduating from the Frunze Naval Academy in 1931, he served in the Black Sea and in the Far East. From 1940 to 1955 he served mostly in the Black Sea fleet. His wartime exploits won him great fame, and by 1951 he commanded the fleet. He was appointed Commander-in-Chief of the entire Soviet navy by Nikita KHRUSHCHEV in 1956, with the brief to cut back expenditure. However, after the CUBAN MISSILE CRISIS in 1962 and Khrushchev's ousting in 1964, the new Soviet leader, Leonid BREZHNEV, pressed for naval expansion to enable the USSR to project itself globally. Gorshkov supported this view and oversaw a massive naval build-up, both surface and underwater, creating a force capable of challenging the West's by the 1970s. He remained in command of the navy until his death, although his influence declined rapidly after Mikhail GORBACHEV came to power in 1985.

## Gorton, Sir John Grey (1911–2002)

Australian politician. He was a Liberal Senator for Victoria (1949–68) and a member of the House of Representatives (1968–75). He served in the governments of Sir Robert MENZIES and Harold HOLT, and succeeded Holt as Prime Minister in 1967. In 1971 he was defeated on a vote of confidence and resigned in favour of William McMahon. ► LIBERAL PARTY OF AUSTRALIA

## Goshi ('Rural Samurai')

A lower-ranking status group in feudal Japan, which before the late 16c included all retainers expected to support themselves from income of the land granted to them as fiefs. The *goshi* became a distinct group after the 1590s, when most SAMURAI were separated from the land and expected to serve their lord on a full-time basis in the castle town. During the 18c and early 19c the goshi increasingly saw themselves as a rural élite (wealthy village-heads were often awarded goshi rank), and were hostile to the status, pretensions and privileges of the urban samurai. Many goshi participated in the anti-Tokugawa movement of the 1860s. ► TOKUGAWA SHOGUNATE

## Gosplan

The State Planning Commission in the former USSR. Established in 1921, it had overall responsibility for state and regional planning, translating general economic objectives into specific blueprints. Its responsibilities varied over the years, but in the end it proved to be a liability as its bureaucratic functions prevented the Soviet economy from responding to new needs.

## Gotha, Congress of (22–7 May 1875)

This conference saw the union of the General German Workers' Association and the Social Democratic Workers' Party to form the Socialist Workers' Party, which was the direct forerunner of the SPD. The new party adopted a programme that demanded a democratic political order in Germany and a socialist society to be achieved 'by all legal means'. In Oct 1891 the Gotha Programme was replaced by the ERFURT PROGRAMME.

**Goto Shojiro** (1838–97)
Japanese politician. He came from Tosa, one of the domains in the forefront of the **MEIJI RESTORATION**. After 1868 Goto became a government minister, but resigned in 1873 after the government's refusal to sanction a military expedition to Korea. With another ex-**SAMURAI** from Tosa, **ITAGAKI TAISUKE**, Goto began to petition for a representative assembly, charging that the government was monopolized by leaders from **SATSUMA** and **CHOSHU**. In 1881 he helped form Japan's first political party, the *Jiyuto* (Liberal Party), but like many party politicians of the time succumbed to the temptations of government bribes. He eventually abandoned the Jiyuto and joined the government as Communications Minister and then Minister for Agriculture and Commerce.

**Gottwald, Klement** (1896–1953)
Czechoslovak politician. In **WORLD WAR I** he fought with the Austro-Hungarian army. A Marxist, he helped to establish the Communist Party in 1921 and became its Secretary-General in 1929. He opposed the **MUNICH AGREEMENT** of 1938 and later went to Moscow, where he was prepared by the Party for eventual office. In 1945 he became Vice-Premier in the Czechoslovak provisional coalition government. Prime Minister following elections in 1946, he pursued a pro-Soviet line and in Feb 1948 took advantage of his opponents' divisions to stage a coup d'état which averted a defeat for the Party at the polls; in June 1948 he became President. Strong in his support for **STALIN**, whose line he followed closely, he established a complete dictatorship that eliminated many of his Communist colleagues. Ironically, he died of an illness contracted while he was attending Stalin's funeral.

**Gouin, Sir (Jean) Lomer** (1861–1929)
Canadian politician. The Liberal Premier of Quebec from 1905 to 1920, he was considered by many to be dominated by the English-speaking business community who controlled the hydroelectric power, transport and manufacturing industries. He became federal Minister of Justice in the administration of Mackenzie **KING**. ► **LIBERAL PARTY** (Canada)

**Goulart, João Belquior Marques** (1918–76)
Brazilian politician. Born in Rio Grande do Sul, he became the wealthy landowning neighbour of Getúlio **VARGAS**. He was linked with the PTB in the late 1940s and, as Vargas' protégé, became Minister of Labour in 1954. He became leader of the PTB in 1960 and, having been accused by the army of nurturing pro-communist sympathies, was elected Vice-President against military hostility; the army reluctantly agreed to allow him to become President of a parliamentary regime in 1961. A weak and vacillating leader in 1963–4, he alienated moderate opinion by flirting with nationalist and left-wing groups. Goulart was ejected by a coup (Mar 1964) engineered by the army and supported by powerful conservative politicians in the UDN. The coup was precipitated by his insistence on recruiting support among non-commissioned officers in the army and navy.

**Gouled Aptidon, Hassan** (1916–)
Djiboutian politician. While serving as a representative of French Somaliland in France, he became in-creasingly active in the independence movement and in 1967 founded the African People's League for Independence (APLI). Djibouti achieved self-government in 1977 and he became the country's first President, later merging the APLI with other groups to form the country's only political party, the People's Progress Party. His policy of neutralism in a war-torn region of the continent ensured his continuing popularity and he was re-elected in 1987 and 1993. He retired from his post in May 1999.

**Gourlay, Robert Fleming** (1778–1863)
Canadian reformer. A Scottish immigrant, he was disappointed by his failure to secure a large land grant and incensed by the bitterness of settlers at the Crown and **CLERGY RESERVES** of Upper **CANADA**, the lack of an emigration policy and the exclusion of Americans from settlement, complaints of which he learnt through replies to a questionnaire he had circulated to gather material for an emigrant's guide. Calling a convention of town delegates and agitating for reform, he was arrested and imprisoned when he refused to obey an order of banishment.

**Government of India Acts**
Measures passed by the British Parliament to regulate the government of India (1883–1935). They included the 1858 Act which transferred British **EAST INDIA COMPANY** powers to the British crown, and the 1919 and 1935 Acts which introduced limited constitutional change. Motivated in part by the need for retrenchment and increased taxation in the wake of India's involvement in **WORLD WAR I**, the 1919 Act attempted to seduce moderate Indian politicians into cooperating with the colonial regime by offering a say in local and provincial government to a small proportion of the population from among the wealthier and more influential sections of society. The 1935 Act went further, although it still fell well short of a universal franchise, and led to the establishment of elected Congress ministries in most of the Indian provinces. Although these provincial governments had no say in matters of security, and the British governors retained a right of veto over both candidates and legislation, they were nonetheless a successful experiment in self-government, persuading some colonial officials that they could perhaps live with democracy. Unfortunately, representatives of minority political parties were largely excluded from the Congress governments, fuelling communal divisions in the country, whilst many officials merely saw provincial government as an undesirable concession, forced upon them by M K **GANDHI**'s civil disobedience movement of 1930–2. The ministries resigned *en masse* in 1939, following Viceroy Linlithgow's declaration of war with Germany without prior consultation with Indian politicians. ► **COMMUNALISM**; **INDIA ACTS**; **MONTAGU–CHELMSFORD REFORMS**; **SCHEDULED CASTES AND TRIBES**

**Gowon, Yakubu** (1934–)
Nigerian soldier and politician. A Christian in a Muslim area, he was educated at a CMS missionary school and then Government College, Zaria. His military training began in Ghana and continued in the UK where he attended the Royal Military Academy, Sandhurst, among other institutions. He was commissioned into the Nigerian army in 1956,

serving with the UN force in the Congo (1960–1). He became Adjutant-General in 1963 and Chief of Staff in 1966. The ethnic conflicts in the country precipitated a coup on 15 Jan 1966, led by IGBO officers, and Gowon headed a counter-coup (July 1966). He then became head of the Federal Military Government and Commander-in-Chief. Unable to prevent a civil war, he fought to retain BIAFRA (the Eastern Region) within a single Nigeria, while acceding to ethnic concerns by increasing the number of states; with the assistance of both the USA and the USSR, he prevailed. However, his retarded return to democracy encouraged another military coup; he was deposed in 1975 and went into exile.

## Graaf, Sir de Villiers, Bt (1913–99)

South African politician. Educated in South Africa, the UK and the Netherlands, he saw military service in WORLD WAR II. Elected a United Party MP in 1948, he became party leader in 1956, remaining so until 1977, when he transferred his allegiance to the New Republic Party. The political heir to Jan SMUTS, his opposition to the NATIONAL PARTY was too gentlemanly to challenge its hegemony and too conservative to build a new coalition across the race divide. He epitomized the failure of well-meaning liberalism in these years.

## Graeco-Roman Heritage, The ▶ See panel

## Graeco-Turkish War (1921–2)

This war was ostensibly provoked by Greek fears for the safety of the Greeks in the Izmir region of Anatolia in the face of growing Turkish nationalism. By the Treaty of Sèvres (1920), Greece had received the right to administer Izmir and its hinterlands for five years. When, in Dec 1920, CONSTANTINE I returned to Greece, he determined to bolster his position by championing the cause of the Anatolian Greeks. In July 1921 the government ordered 100,000 troops into Anatolia to attack Kemal ATATÜRK's men. The Turks withdrew and the Greeks foolishly advanced with the intention of taking Ankara, but became bogged down in Sep 1921. No attempt was made to evacuate the Greek troops and, in Aug 1922, they were defeated by the Turks, who entered Izmir and destroyed the town. By the Treaty of LAUSANNE, Greece lost the major gains made after WORLD WAR I and some 1.3 million Greeks were forced to leave Anatolia, while 380,000 Turks were expelled from Greece. Utterly discredited, Constantine I abdicated and was succeeded by GEORGE II.

## Grafton, Augustus Henry Fitzroy, 3rd Duke of (1735–1811)

British politician. He became an MP in 1756, succeeding to his peerage the following year. He was a prominent opponent of BUTE in 1762–3 and became Secretary of State for the Northern Department (1765–6) under ROCKINGHAM. He accepted office under PITT, the Elder, as First Lord of the Treasury (1766–70) and took over leadership of the administration on his resignation (1768–70). His administration was weak and divided. He wished to pursue a more liberal policy towards the American colonies than his colleagues would allow and he handled WILKES's expulsion from the Commons ineptly. Soon after his resignation, he resumed office under Lord

NORTH as Lord Privy Seal (1771–5) but resigned when war broke out with the colonies. He served in the same office under Rockingham (1782–3) before retirement from politics when he became increasingly sympathetic to evangelicalism. ▶ GEORGE III

## Gramsci, Antonio (1891–1937)

Italian journalist, politician and political thinker. Born in Sardinia of a humble family, he was educated at Turin University, where he was drawn into political activity in the Socialist Party. A founder-member of the PCI (Italian Communist Party) in 1921, he was Italian delegate at the Third International in Moscow (1922). In 1924 he became leader of the communists in parliament. He was one of a number of outspoken communist critics of the fascist regime to be arrested in 1928 and was sentenced to 20 years' imprisonment; he died a prisoner. His reputation rests primarily on his *Prison Notebooks*, a collection of thoughts and reflections written while in confinement and published posthumously.

## Granada, Conquest of (2 Jan 1492)

The conquest was achieved by FERDINAND II, THE CATHOLIC and ISABELLA I, THE CATHOLIC after ten years of campaigning. Splits among the Muslim leadership helped the Christians; a key role was played by BOABDIL, last King of Granada, who overthrew his father but refused to surrender the city, which underwent a nine-month siege and then capitulated on terms which assured respect for Muslim property and the Islamic faith. The campaigns helped to strengthen the Spanish monarchy by stimulating the emergence of regular military forces, and encouraged religious zeal under the form of a 'crusade'. The pope in 1494 rewarded Ferdinand and Isabella with the title 'the Catholic Monarchs'. The Kingdom of Granada, however, suffered through the death or emigration of about half of its Muslim population.

## Granby, John Manners, Marquis of (1721–70)

British army officer. He was the eldest son of the Duke of Rutland. His reputation was made in the SEVEN YEARS' WAR, when he led the British cavalry in a major victory over the French at Warburg (1760). He became a popular hero, and in 1763 was appointed Master-General of the Ordnance.

## Gran Chaco

The lowland plain covering part of northern Argentina, western Paraguay and southern Bolivia. Historically Bolivian, its ownership was disputed in the 1932–5 CHACO WAR between Paraguay and Bolivia. Paraguay wished to vindicate its losses in the war with Brazil, Uruguay and Argentina, which had led to the loss of lands in the Chaco; Bolivia sought to regain access to the sea, which had been lost in the War of the PACIFIC (1879–84). Bolivia eventually ceded 20,000 sq mi/52,000 sq km in Paraguay in 1938. ▶ TRIPLE ALLIANCE, WAR OF THE

## Gran Colombia

Literally 'Greater Colombia', this is the name given by historians to the union of Venezuela, New Granada and Quito (Ecuador) formed in 1819 by Simón BOLÍVAR and known by him as Colombia. The union dissolved in 1830, and the name Colombia was later adopted by New Granada.

# *The Graeco-Roman Heritage*

*Culture & Society*

### Historical background

Ancient Greek civilization reached its widest influence during the reign of Alexander the Great (336/323 BC), which spread Hellenistic culture over the known world from Egypt to India. Increasing Roman intervention in the affairs of this Hellenistic world, after the disintegration of Alexander's empire, finally led to its absorption into the Roman Empire.

Rome had expelled the last of its kings in 510 BC to become a republic in which power lay in the hands of the patricians, or landed aristocracy, and their ruling assembly, the Senate. Over time the plebs, or common people, claimed a greater role in the state, and the patrician families declined in influence. The armies of the republic conquered many provinces under their great generals, and the increasing power and rivalry of these commanders led to the civil wars that disrupted the last century of the republic. The rule of Julius Caesar (c.100–44 BC) as dictator was ended by his assassination by republicans, and out of the succeeding struggle for power Octavian emerged as victor, taking the title of Augustus and becoming the first Roman emperor in 27 BC.

The imperial system founded by Augustus was based on the old republican institutions, such as the Senate, but with a more powerful aristocracy and a supreme monarchic ruler at its head. The security brought about by Augustus's rule helped Rome expand its empire, for example in Western Europe and Asia. Under succeeding emperors Rome came to rule a great swathe of territory centred around the Mediterranean, from Mesopotamia in the east to Spain in the west, and from Egypt in the south to Britain in the north.

In AD 395 the Emperor Theodosius divided the Roman Empire into two parts: the eastern empire, based in Constantinople, and the western empire, based in Rome. When Rome fell to Germanic invaders, the eastern city became the capital of the whole empire, which its rulers strove to reunite. Despite the reconquest of part of Italy by the Emperor Justinian, this reunification was never achieved and the eastern empire, in the form of the **Byzantine Empire**, continued alone as the bulwark of Roman culture and the Christian religion.

### The heritage

The legacy of Graeco-Roman culture and achievements has had great influence on the development of European civilization, leaving its mark on such areas as language, law, literature, architecture, philosophy, mathematics and government. This influence has waxed and waned at different periods, as various generations have 'discovered' their debt to the ancients.

Europe in the 5–6c is traditionally known as the 'Dark Ages', as they followed the fall of Rome and the domination by 'uncivilized' Germanic tribes of the former western empire. However, Graeco-Roman culture was kept alive in this period by the Christian Church, particularly in the centres of scholarship, the monasteries.

The fact that the Christian world still looked to the Roman Empire as the model for society is shown by the crowning of Charlemagne by Pope Leo III as Emperor of the West in 800. Even more explicitly, the Christian lands in central Europe that Charlemagne ruled became known as the **Holy Roman Empire**, as medieval popes sought to create a state that would be a true successor to the empire of Rome. In time the title bore little relation to the actual extent and *raison d'être* of the empire.

Although the **Middle Ages** had cultivated Latinity and preserved classical texts, the **Renaissance**, which began in the 14c, saw a greatly heightened interest in classical scholarship and art. In architecture Brunelleschi drew inspiration from Roman examples for his churches in Florence. The sculptor Donatello was greatly influenced by classical works in the creation of his *David* and his equestrian monument to Gattamelata. In literature classical writings were the inspiration of poets such as Dante and Petrarch. Dramatists studied works by such classical playwrights as Terence and Seneca, whose influence on Elizabethan and Jacobean drama became particularly strong. Although vernacular languages began increasingly to be used, Latin continued to be the language of scholars and scientists. Renaissance Latinists were purists

---

### Grand Alliance, War of the (1805–7)

A phase in the **NAPOLEONIC WARS**. A third coalition of states (Britain, Austria, Russia, Sweden and **PRUSSIA**) was formed to attack France by land and sea. Despite Britain's success at the Battle of **TRAFALGAR** (1805), the coalition was undermined by spectacular French victories at Ulm, **AUSTERLITZ** (1805), and **JENA AND AUERSTÄDT** (1806). The Treaties of **PRESSBURG** (1805) and **TILSIT** (1807) ended hostilities.

### Grand Army of the Republic (GAR)

US veterans organization. Established in 1866 by ex-Union soldiers, the GAR became an important force in post-**AMERICAN CIVIL WAR** politics.

### Grand Council (*Junjichu*)

A ruling institution in **QING DYNASTY** China whose origins date from 1726 when the Yongzheng Emperor (1722/35) was preparing for a military expedition against the **DZUNGARS**. As a compact, secret and informal group of trusted confidants that transcended the formal bureaucracy, the Grand Council greatly fa-

cilitated the consolidation of imperial autocracy. Grand Councillors transmitted important imperial edicts directly to provincial officials, while the latter were able to send secret memorials on local affairs to the Grand Council.

### Grande Brigantaggio

The term commonly used to describe the civil war in the south of Italy after unification. The 'Great Brigandage' was a euphemism, adopted by the military and political authorities of the newly united Kingdom of Italy to conceal the political and social origins of discontent in the **MEZZOGIORNO**. There, large sections of the gentry and perhaps the majority of the peasantry showed little liking for the policies of **PIEMONTIZZAZIONE** adopted by the government in Turin. The use of martial law and violent repression, legalized by the so-called **PICA LAW** of 1863, enabled order to be effectively restored by 1865.

### grandfather clause

US political manoeuvre. It was a device used by

who scorned the modified ecclesiastical Latin that had evolved in the medieval period. They consciously tried to return to Roman norms in Latin, especially the prose style of Cicero.

In the 17–18c, because educated Western élites from Austria to Virginia were raised on classical literature, the republicanism of ancient Rome, with its rhetoric of 'Liberty, sustained by Virtue, and threatened by Corruption', became a common, incipiently radical creed, even in the mouth of the conservative George **Washington**. Roman models also informed much of the political thought of the **French Revolution**; it was as First Consul, a revival of the Roman term, that **Napoleon I** came to exercise supreme power in France. Like Augustus, he consolidated his position as sole ruler by becoming emperor, and like the Roman legions his regiments were issued with eagle standards.

In the politics of the 19c, bourgeois liberals harked back to ancient Greek rather than Roman ideas of democracy in their efforts to broaden the base of political power. However, the full democracy of the ancient city state, with the whole populace meeting regularly to make decisions, was impracticable in a populous modern state, and what came to be established was far from pure democracy, with representatives rather than the people themselves participating in government. It was with the inspiration of classical Greece, rather than an idea of what modern Greece was or could be, that Hellenophiles from Western Europe, like Byron, took part in the **Greek War of Independence** (1821–8). Similarly, the perceived ideals of ancient Greece were the motivating force behind the movement that established the modern **Olympic Games** in 1896. Sanitized concepts of ancient Greek architecture and sculpture became icons by the mid-19c, and the ancient Greeks were regarded as having invented 'European Civilization'.

In the 20c the Italian dictator **Mussolini** not only adopted the Roman *fasces*, bundles of bound rods signifying authority, as the symbol of his fascist movement, but also aspired to the creation of a new Italian empire.

It has been argued, however, that while the heritage of Graeco-Roman culture has certainly had a profound influence on many areas of European culture, much of what is seen as deriving from that heritage owes as much to modern interpretations as to the original inspiration. An example of this is the 18c poets' writing of 'Imitations' of classical poets like Horace or Juvenal in order to address contemporary issues, or Pope's *Iliad*, that is as much Pope as Homer. There appears to have been a need to identify the ancient Greeks and Romans as our forefathers – a way, almost, of legitimizing modern ideas and institutions, even to the point of ascribing contemporary ideals to the ancients before claiming them as our own. Such feelings no doubt motivated the historian Geoffrey of Monmouth to claim in his *Historia Regum Britanniae* (c.1135) that Britain had been founded by Brutus, a grandson of Aeneas.

The heritage has always been ambiguous. Ancient Rome was a symbol of empire, but its early history could also be used as a paradigm of republican virtue and what threatened it. Ancient Greece could have fantasies of a cosmopolitan Eurasian Empire projected on it if Alexander the Great were emphasized, but the history of 'democratic' republican Athens could be used by Victorian liberals to give their own politics a spuriously lengthy ancestry. ► **Middle East, The Heritage of the**

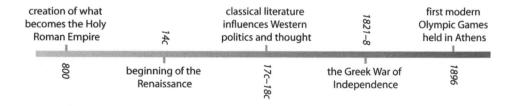

| creation of what becomes the Holy Roman Empire | | classical literature influences Western politics and thought | | first modern Olympic Games held in Athens |
|---|---|---|---|---|
| | *14c* | | *1821–8* | |
| *800* | beginning of the Renaissance | *17c–18c* | the Greek War of Independence | *1896* |

Southern US states between 1895 and 1910 to keep blacks from voting. It exempted from literacy requirements persons who were eligible to vote on 1 Jan 1867 or their descendants, thus excluding former slaves, who had not been given the right to vote by that date. It was ruled unconstitutional by the Supreme Court in 1915. ► **CIVIL RIGHTS**

**Grandi, Dino, Count** (1895–1988)
Italian politician. A powerful **RAS** who in 1921, disillusioned with **MUSSOLINI**, unsuccessfully offered the leadership of the fascist movement to Gabriele **D'AN-NUNZIO**. He was a quadrumvir in the **MARCH ON ROME**. Foreign Minister (1929–32) and Ambassador to London (1932–9), he became extremely anglophile and warned Mussolini about the likely hostile reaction of the British to his proposed Conquest of **ABYSSINIA**. Minister of Justice and President of the 'Chamber of Fasces and Corporations' (1939–43), he grew increasingly worried about the **DUCE**'s enslavement to **HITLER**'s policies and moved the motion in the **FASCIST GRAND COUNCIL** (25 July 1943) that

full constitutional powers be restored to **VICTOR EMMANUEL III**. In 1944 he was sentenced to death *in absentia* by the Republic of **SALÒ**. After liberation, he retired from politics and spent most of the rest of his life in Brazil.

**Grand Pensionary** (*Raadspensionaris*)
The leader of the provincial sovereign assemblies or states in the Dutch Republic. Each province had its own Pensionary, sometimes under another title (eg Secretary, Syndic), whose official job was to provide legal advice to the government. By far the most important was the Pensionary of Holland, who chaired the meetings of the states and executed its decisions, acting as Prime Minister and Foreign Minister. He led the Holland deputation to the States General, and the dominance of the province of Holland in the republic meant that the Holland Grand Pensionary was often effectively the leader of the republic; naturally this caused periodic conflict with the holder of the other great Dutch office, the **STADHOLDER**. Famous pensionaries were Jan van **OLDENBARNEVELDT**, Jacob

CATS, Johan de WITT, Gaspar FAGEL, Anthony HEIN-SIUS and Simon van SLINGELANDT. The title was also given to Rutger Jan SCHIMMELPENNINCK as leader of the BATAVIAN REPUBLIC in 1805–6.

## Grand Remonstrance
The statement of CHARLES I of England's abuses, and of reforms made by the LONG PARLIAMENT in 1640–1; passed by 11 votes in the House of COM-MONS (22 Nov 1641), and thereafter published as an appeal for support. The close vote reflected the formation of roughly equal parties of 'royalists' and 'parliamentarians'.

## Granger Movement
A US organization of farmers, officially known as the Patrons of Husbandry, founded in 1867, which adopted a radical stance towards farmers' problems and big business. The name stems from the title *grange* (or farm) adopted by local units. The organization still exists. ➤ POPULIST PARTY

## Grant, Ulysses S(impson), originally Hiram Ulysses Grant (1822–85)
US general and 18th President. After graduating from the US Military Academy at West Point in 1843, he fought in the MEXICAN WAR (1846–8), and later settled as a farmer in Missouri. On the outbreak of the AMERICAN CIVIL WAR (1861), he rejoined the army and by 1862 was promoted to the rank of major general, leading Union forces to victory, first in the Mississippi Valley, then in the final campaigns in Virginia. He accepted Confederate general Robert E LEE's surrender at APPOMATTOX COURT HOUSE (1865), and was made a full general in 1866. President from 1869 to 1877, he presided over the RECONSTRUCTION of the South, but his administration was marred by scandal.

## Granvelle, Antoine Perrenot (1517–86)
French-born Spanish prelate and diplomat. The son of the jurist and diplomat Nicholas Granvelle, in 1540 he was appointed Bishop of Arras and Secretary of State to Emperor CHARLES V. On the latter's abdication in 1556, he transferred his services to PHILIP II of Spain. In 1559 he became Prime Minister to MARGARET OF PARMA in the Netherlands, in 1560 Archbishop of Malines, and the following year cardinal. His policy provoked such hostility in the Low Countries, however, that at the King's advice he retired in 1564 to Franche-Comté. In 1570 he represented Spain in Rome at the drawing-up of a treaty of alliance with Venice and the Papal See against the Turks. From 1570 to 1575 he was Viceroy of Naples and from 1579 to 1586 was Chief Minister of Spain.

## Grattan, Henry (1746–1820)
Irish politician. In 1775 he entered the Irish parliament, where his oratory made him the leading spokesman for the patriotic party. He secured Irish free trade in 1779, and legislative independence in 1782. He was returned for Dublin in 1790, and in 1805 was elected to the House of COMMONS, where he fought for CATHOLIC EMANCIPATION.

## Gravelotte, Battle of (1870)
A critical engagement of the FRANCO-PRUSSIAN WAR. The French Army of the Rhine under Marshal Bazaine, though inflicting heavy casualties on the Germans, failed to break von MOLTKE's troops, and retreated to nearby Metz; the decision led to MAC-MAHON's attempt to relieve Metz, and the French disaster at SEDAN.

## Graziani, Rodolfo, Marquis of Neghelli (1882–1955)
Italian soldier. He served in Libya in 1913 and on the Italian front during WORLD WAR I. In 1930 he became Vice-Governor of Cyrenaica and in 1936 was given command of the Italian forces on the Somalian front during the Conquest of ABYSSINIA. He succeeded BA-DOGLIO as Viceroy of Ethiopia. In July 1940 he was placed in charge of the Italian forces in North Africa but was replaced (Mar 1941) after a series of defeats. In Sep 1943 he accepted MUSSOLINI's invitation to become Defence Minister of the Republic of SALÒ. He was captured at the end of the war and put on trial for war crimes (Oct 1948). In 1950 he was sentenced to 25 years, but was released the same year. He was active in the ITALIAN SOCIAL MOVEMENT until his death.

## Great Awakening
The widespread 18c Christian revival movement in the USA, which reached its high point in the 1740s in New England. Jonathan Edwards and George WHITEFIELD were among its leaders.

## Great Depression
The worldwide slump in output and prices, and the greatly increased levels of unemployment, which developed between 1929 and 1934. It was precipitated by the collapse of the US stock market (the WALL STREET CRASH) in Oct 1929. This ended US loans to Europe and greatly reduced business confidence worldwide. A major Austrian bank also collapsed, producing destabilization in much of Central and Eastern Europe.

## Greater East Asia Co-Prosperity Sphere
The term applied to Japan's empire in East and South-East Asia after 1942. It implied the creation of a politically and economically integrated Asia under Japanese leadership and free of Western colonial domination. The concept had originated in 1938 with Japan's proclamation of a New Order in East Asia following her invasion of China in 1937. The New Order was designed to create an autarchic bloc comprising Japan, China and Manchuria that would be free of Anglo-Saxon liberalism and Soviet COMMUNISM. Japan's rapid conquest of South-East Asia in 1942 meant that no detailed preparation had been carried out on the future of the Greater East Asia Co-Prosperity Sphere. Even its geographical boundaries remained vague (with some Japanese leaders including India and/or Australia). Although a Greater East Asia Ministry was created in 1943, it had little centralized control over the separate Japanese military administrations in South-East Asia. Long-term policy was sacrificed to the immediate needs of Japan's war economy, ultimately alienating Asian opinion which had initially welcomed the Japanese as liberators. Despite the granting, or promise, of independence to some South-East Asian countries (Burma, Philippines, Indonesia), the Sphere ended in ignominy with Japan's defeat in 1945.

## Great Exhibition
An exhibition held (May–Oct 1851) in Hyde Park,

London. Intended to celebrate the 'Works of Industry of all Nations', in reality it symbolized Britain's mid-19c industrial supremacy. Prince **ALBERT** helped to organize the Exhibition, for which the Crystal Palace was constructed.

## Great Leap Forward

A movement in China, initiated in 1958, which aimed at accelerating both industrial and agricultural progress, 'walking on two legs'. Abandoning Russian models, it planned the creation of 'communes' in a true collective system. It failed miserably.

## Great Northern War (1700–21)

A war in which Sweden under King **CHARLES XII** fought against a coalition of its neighbours, who were seeking to deprive it of the territories in the Baltic and northern Germany that it had won during the previous century. Denmark was forced to withdraw early in the struggle, and the army of **PETER I, THE GREAT** of Russia was defeated by a far smaller Swedish force at Narva in 1700. But Charles failed to pursue his advantage and became involved in an attempt to dethrone Augustus of Saxony, King of Poland, who had also attacked him. After forcing Augustus to renounce the throne, Charles turned once more against Peter, but was defeated by him at the Battle of **POLTAVA** in the Ukraine (1709). This led to the re-formation of the anti-Swedish coalition, joined also by Brandenburg-Prussia and Hanover. By Charles's death (1718) Sweden had lost most of its Baltic possessions, and a series of treaties in 1720 and 1721 left Russia as the leading Baltic power, with Sweden reduced to one of second rank.

## Great Patriotic War (1941–5)

The name given by **STALIN** to the war against **HITLER**. His communist ideology had allowed him to make the 1939 **GERMAN–SOVIET PACT**, but what he faced after 1941 was Hitler's determination to destroy the USSR and its Slav peoples. What he also discovered was that these peoples made incredible efforts to defend their country, not the system that **COMMUNISM** had impressed on it. He therefore encouraged all forms of patriotic feelings; even the Patriarchate of Moscow was reinstated. However, after 1945 it was more or less back to Soviet communism. ► **WORLD WAR II**

## Great Schism (1378–1417)

The 14c was a period of deep crisis for the papal monarchy. Seven successive popes resided at Avignon between 1309 and 1377. In 1378 the Church divided between supporters of Pope Urban VI in Rome and those of Pope **CLEMENT VII** in Avignon, and the European monarchies took sides according to their own rivalries. The rival popes hurled anathemas at each other, and the crisis deepened in 1409 when the Council of Pisa, which had met to heal the schism, elected the scandalous **CONDOTTIERE** Baldassare Cossa as **JOHN XXIII** as a third pope. Only in 1417, with the election of **MARTIN V** at the Council of Constance, did the schism come to an end.

## Great Society

The name given to a legislative programme called for by US President Lyndon B **JOHNSON** ('LBJ') on 19 Jan 1965, which committed his administration to vigorous action on health insurance, education, housing and urban renewal. The opportunity and mandate for federal initiatives in what had previously been local responsibilities came from the extraordinary 1964 election results, which returned LBJ as President in his own right, with a larger percentage of the popular vote (61 per cent) than ever before achieved, together with a two-thirds Democratic majority in both houses of **CONGRESS**.

## Great Trek

The movement of parties of Boers (*Voortrekkers*) which made them the masters of large tracts of the interior of southern Africa. Objecting to British suzerainty, they began to leave Cape Colony in 1835 in separate trekking groups. Two parties were wiped out by black African resistance and malaria, when they headed for Delagoa Bay in Mozambique. Some settled in the Transvaal, where they were threatened by the **NDEBELE**. One party in Natal was massacred by the **ZULU**, an event avenged by the Battle of **BLOOD RIVER** in 1838. When the British annexed Natal in 1843, the majority of the Boers returned to the interior. The British made several unsuccessful attempts to resolve the divisions in the area, but when the region was reunited it was largely under Boer control. ► **AFRIKANERS; BOER WARS**

## Grechko, Andrei Antonovich (1903–76)

Soviet marshal and politician. He fought in the cavalry during the **RUSSIAN CIVIL WAR** and held several cavalry commands in the first half of **WORLD WAR II**. As Commander-in-Chief in East Germany in 1953 he helped put down the Berlin rising, and he was Commander-in-Chief of the **WARSAW PACT** when the **BERLIN WALL** was erected in 1961. He became Minister of Defence in 1967 and a **POLITBURO** member in 1973. In the debate about East–West détente he was regarded as a hardliner.

**GREECE** official name **The Hellenic Republic**, ancient name **Hellas**

A republic in south-eastern Europe, occupying the southern part of the Balkan peninsula and numerous islands in the Aegean and Ionian seas. It is bounded to the north by Albania, the Former Yugoslav Republic of **MACEDONIA** and Bulgaria; to the east by Turkey and the Aegean Sea; to the south by the Mediterranean Sea; and to the west by the Ionian Sea. Greece has been inhabited since Palaeolithic times, and its prehistoric civilization culminated in the remarkable Minoan culture of Crete (3400–1100BC). The Dorians (a sub-group of Hellenic peoples) invaded from the north in the 12c BC, and Greek colonies were established along the north and south Mediterranean coasts and on the shores of the Black Sea. In the

8–6c BC the Greeks settled throughout the eastern Mediterranean, establishing colonies along the shores of Asia Minor and the adjoining islands. There were many city states on the mainland, notably Sparta and Athens. In the southern part of the Balkan Peninsula, a distinctive Greek culture has persisted unbroken since antiquity; the Slav and Avar invaders who arrived in waves in the 6c and later settled in the southern part of the Balkan Peninsula were Hellenized and assimilated into the original population. In the 5c BC Persian invasions were repelled at Marathon, Salamis, Plataea and Mycale, and Greek literature and art flourished. Conflict between Sparta and Athens (the Peloponnesian War, 431–404BC) weakened the country, which was overwhelmed by the Macedonians (4c BC) under Philip II of Macedon, who unified the Greek city states under their hegemony. Military expeditions under his son, Alexander III, the Great, penetrated Asia and Africa. Macedonian power was broken by the Romans in 197BC, and Greece and Crete then formed part of the Greek-speaking BYZANTINE EMPIRE which stretched deep into Asia Minor and the Middle East. The Byzantine Age (330–1204) was a period of political and cultural hegemony for the Greeks in the Balkans and eastern Mediterranean. After the sack of Constantinople (1204), the Balkan Greeks fell prey to the ambitions of the FRANKS and Venetians, and finally to the Turks who occupied Greece from 1460 to 1830. Crete was purchased by the Venetian Republic in 1210 and enjoyed an artistic renaissance, but after it too fell to the Ottomans (1669), it went into a long decline. The Greek national revival began in the late 18c, and led to the GREEK WAR OF INDEPENDENCE (1821–8) against the Turks. By the end of the war Greece, though ravaged, was a free state, and it gained formal recognition of its independence from the Ottoman Porte in 1832. During the war, the Cretans joined the insurgents but were quickly crushed and made subject to the Egyptian Viceroy ALI PASHA. Under Ottoman control again from 1840, Cretan demands for ENOSIS grew apace with revolts (1858, 1866–9 and 1895), but these were handled cautiously by the Greek government lest it antagonize the Ottoman Porte. After a brief military campaign, Crete was declared independent under a High Commissioner appointed by the Great Powers (1898). The Cretan assembly declared its enosis in 1908, but not until the Treaties of LONDON (1913) was it joined to the Kingdom of Greece. Following independence, Greek society was riddled with divisions, the 19c seeing continuous arguments over the constitution and form of government. In the 20c the Greeks were at war from 1912 to 1922, and from 1940 to 1949: first the BALKAN WARS, then WORLD WAR I, both of which brought substantial territorial gains, and then the disastrous war against the Turks in Anatolia (1919–22) during which c.30,000 Christians were killed in Izmir (Smyrna) in Sep 1922, and over a million Greeks were forced to leave Asia Minor. The Greek Republic was established in 1924 and the monarchy restored in 1935. Meanwhile, Crete became a stronghold of support for its native son, Eleuthérios VENIZÉLOS, and rebelled against METAXAS (1938). During WORLD WAR II, Greece and Crete were occupied by the Germans, and Greece was afterwards ravaged by the bloody GREEK CIVIL WAR (1944–9). Following a tentative period of democracy, a military coup in 1967 led to the right-wing dictatorship of the GREEK COLONELS (1967–74). The monarchy was formally abolished and democracy restored in 1974, since when there has been relative peace and stability. Greece joined the EC in 1981 and the EURO ZONE in 2000. ► CONSTANTINOPLE, PATRIARCHATE OF; EAM; EDES; EKKA; ELAS; EOKA; EPIRUS; FILIKI ETAIRIA; GREEK WAR OF INDEPENDENCE; KLEPHTS; LAUSANNE, TREATY OF; MEGALE IDEA; NAVARINO BAY, BATTLE OF; PASOK

## Greek Civil War (1944–9)

Rooted in the struggle between communist and monarchist partisans for control of Greece, the conflict erupted as the Axis forces retreated at the end of WORLD WAR II. Britain sent troops to back the monarchist forces, while the USSR supported the communists. With US financial aid, the British were able to remain in Greece after 1945, and helped to re-establish the monarchy. The rupture between Yugoslavia and Russia in 1948 also helped to weaken communist resistance and an end to hostilities was declared in Oct 1949.

## Greek Colonels (1967–74)

The name given to the right-wing military regime established in Greece after the coup led by Colonel George PAPADOPOULOS, Colonel Nikolaos Makarezos and Brigadier Stylianos Pattakos (21 Apr 1967). Militantly anti-communist, the regime imprisoned its political opponents, frequently on island camps, where torture was widely used. Strikes were forbidden during this period, and there was strict censorship of the arts and media. In 1973 Papadopoulos declared the monarchy abolished and had himself elected President for eight years. He was ousted in a counter-coup (Nov 1973) but the new regime under General Dimitrios Ioannidis was yet more conservative, and no attempt was made to restore constitutional rule. In July 1974 the regime backed an attempt to depose Archbishop MAKARIOS in Cyprus and to declare ENOSIS; Greece was on the brink of war with Turkey. Another military coup followed, in which Ioannidis was ousted and KARAMANLIS was brought back from exile. Leading members of the 'Colonels' regime' were put on trial and imprisoned for life.

## Greek War of Independence (1821–8)

The struggle of the Greeks to gain independence from the OTTOMAN EMPIRE. The revolt against the Ottoman Turks broke out in the Peloponnese and on several islands in 1821. At first the Turks were unable to retake the areas controlled by the rebels but, with the aid of Egyptian forces, in 1825 they invaded the Peloponnese, capturing Missolonghi (1826), and advanced to take Athens. Britain, Russia and eventually France came to the aid of the Greek rebels, destroying the Egyptian fleet at NAVARINO BAY (1827). By the Treaty of ADRIANOPLE (1829), the allies guaranteed Greek independence. The Ottoman Porte formally recognized Greek independence by the Treaty of Constantinople (1832). ► ALI PASHA

## Greeley, Horace (1811–72)

US journalist and politician. The founder of the *New*

*York Tribune*, he was the most influential Republican journalist of his day, combining support for economic development ('Go West, Young Man') with vigorous anti-**SLAVERY** attitudes. It was in response to his 1862 plea for emancipation, the 'Prayer of Twenty Million', that **LINCOLN** emphasized that the aim of the **AMERICAN CIVIL WAR** was to preserve the union, not to destroy slavery. In 1864 he undertook an unofficial and unsuccessful effort at peacemaking. By 1872 he was advocating a general amnesty for ex-Confederates and this won him an unexpected presidential nomination in that year by the splinter Liberal Republican Party and the **DEMOCRATIC PARTY**.

## greenback

A popular term for paper currency in the USA, particularly in the **AMERICAN CIVIL WAR** and **RECONSTRUCTION** eras, which saw strong debate about the place of currency in the monetary system. The Greenback Party was a minor party which sought a reflationary paper currency to solve the problems of farmers and working people. It ran presidential candidates in 1876, and (as the Greenback Labor Party) in 1880 and 1884. In 1892 it supported the **POPULIST PARTY**.

## Greene, Nathanael (1742–86)

American soldier. At the Battle of **BRANDYWINE** (Sep 1777), he commanded a division and saved the American army from complete destruction. In 1780 he succeeded Horatio **GATES** in command of the army of the South, which had just been defeated by Charles **CORNWALLIS**, and improved its condition. Although defeated by Cornwallis at Guilford Courthouse (Mar 1781), he conducted a masterly retreat into South Carolina which, with Georgia, was rapidly retaken. He lost every battle, yet won the war in the South.

## Green Gang (*Qingbang*)

A Chinese underworld organization active in Shanghai during the 1920s, with its headquarters in the French Concession area. Green Gang leaders were often businessmen or had links with financial circles and were involved in prostitution, gambling and opium rackets. The Nationalist leader, **CHIANG KAI-SHEK**, also formed close ties with the Green Gang, and after he gained control of Shanghai (Mar 1927) during the **NORTHERN EXPEDITION**, he used it to attack communist-led labour unions in the city, often with the connivance of foreign concession authorities and the National Revolutionary Army. Ironically, following the brutal suppression of the labour unions, Chiang then turned against the very bourgeoisie who had supported the suppression; Green Gang members launched a campaign of terror against wealthy businessmen, forcing them to buy government bonds and extend loans to Chiang's regime.

## Green Line

A phrase used of a demarcation boundary between disputants. It was first adopted following riots in **CYPRUS** in 1963 when a line showing the position of a buffer zone between Turkish and Greek Cypriots was marked on a map of Nicosia in green ink and the zone became known as the Green Line. It was also used of the area separating Muslim and **DRUZE** West Beirut from **MARONITE** East Beirut during the 1975–91 war in Lebanon, because of the grass and trees that grew in the abandoned area. The term is also applied colloquially to the 1949 Armistice line that mapped out the internationally recognized borders of **ISRAEL**, the **WEST BANK** and the **GAZA STRIP** after the war following the creation of the state of Israel in 1948.

## Green Mountain Boys

The movement of landowners and speculators who created the state of Vermont from territory disputed between New York and New Hampshire. They defied the authority of New York's government and harassed New York settlers. Of many rural insurrections in early America, the Green Mountain Boys was the only one that succeeded. During the **AMERICAN REVOLUTION**, they redirected their energies and helped capture for the colonists the British **FORT TICONDEROGA**, on Lake Champlain (1775). The cannon taken were important in the successful American siege of occupied Boston. ➤ **ALLEN, ETHAN**

## Greenpeace

An international environmental pressure group which began in Canada and the USA in 1971, and was set up in the UK in 1976. It campaigns by direct action (non-violent passive resistance) against commercial whaling and seal culling, the dumping of toxic and radioactive waste at sea, the testing of nuclear weapons, and so on. ➤ **RAINBOW WARRIOR**

## Green Revolution

A popular term for the improvements in agricultural productivity in some Third World countries that resulted from the development of new high-yielding strains of cereal crops, and the use of fertilizers and pesticides. It occurred in some developing countries in the 1960s and 1970s, and was largely the result of Norman Borlaug's plant-breeding research in Mexico, which produced high-yielding dwarf wheat varieties, and work at the International Rice Research Institute in the Philippines, which produced similarly improved strains of rice. Success with these new varieties depended on an integrated crop-management system, the application of high levels of fertilizers and pesticides, and adequate water supplies. For this reason it tended to benefit only the most prosperous farmers, and was too costly for farmers living in poorer areas, where an increase in agricultural productivity was most urgently needed. ➤ **AGRICULTURE**

## Greens, The (*Die Grünen*)

German political party. This coalition of ecologist, pacifist, anti-nuclear and other special interest groups was established as a federal party in 1980 and dominates environmental politics in Germany. It has held seats in various **LAND** (state) parliaments and has been represented in the **BUNDESTAG** since 1983 and in the European Parliament since 1984. Internally it is divided between *Realos* ('Realists') prepared to work with conventional parties (especially the **SPD**) and *Fundis* ('Fundamentalists') who are not, with the Realos in the ascendant. The Greens have formed part of every coalition government since 1998.

## Greenville, Treaty of (1795)

The treaty concluded between the USA and the **DELAWARE**, Shawnee and Miami Confederacy **NATIVE AMERICANS** after the victory of General Anthony **WAYNE** at the Battle of Fallen Timbers (Ohio). The

Native Americans ceded their lands east of the Wabash River (which Britain had hoped to use as a buffer zone between the USA and Canada), thus allowing safe white settlement throughout most of Ohio and south-east Indiana and encouraging immigration into the North West Territories.

**Grégoire, Henri** (1750–1831)
French prelate and revolutionary. His *Essai sur la régénération des juifs* (1789) became widely popular. He was sent to the **ESTATES GENERAL** of 1789 as a Deputy of the clergy. He was the first of his order to take the oaths of loyalty to the new constitution, and was elected 'Constitutional Bishop' of Loir-et-Cher. The **CONCORDAT** (1801) forced him to resign his bishopric. He died unreconciled with the Church. Among his works are *Histoire des sectes religieuses* (1814) and *L'Église gallicane* (1818). ➤ **FRENCH REVOLUTION**

**Gregory VII, St**, originally **Hildebrand** (c.1020–1085)
Italian pope (1073/85). He became a cardinal in 1049. As pope, he worked to change the secularized condition of the Church, which led to conflict with the German Emperor **HENRY IV**, who declared Gregory deposed in a diet at Worms (1076), but then yielded to him after excommunication. In 1080 Henry resumed hostilities, appointing an anti-pope (Clement III), and after a siege took possession of Rome (1084). Gregory was freed by Norman troops, but was forced to withdraw to Salerno, where he died.

**Gregory IX**, originally **Ugo** or **Ugolino de Segni** (1155–1241)
Pope (1227/41). A powerful advocate of papal supremacy, he was a strong supporter of the **FRANCISCANS** and the Dominicans. After an initial phase of uneasy collaboration with the Emperor **FREDERICK II**, in which the pope supported the emperor in his relations with the Lombard cities, while the emperor supported the pope against opposition in Rome, a ferocious conflict broke out over Frederick's Constitutions of Melfi, which subjected Sicily to his will. Rome itself was under siege when the aged pope died.

**Gregory XIII**, originally **Ugo Buoncompagni** (1502–85)
Italian pope (1572/85). A professor of law from Bologna, he became one of the theologians at the Council of **TRENT**, then in 1565 a cardinal and legate to Spain. He displayed extraordinary zeal for the promotion of education and endowed many of the colleges in Rome. His pontificate is notable for the correction of the **CALENDAR** and the introduction of the Gregorian Computation in 1582, but his reputation was sullied by his ordering a *Te Deum* for the slaughter of French protestants in the **ST BARTHOLOMEW'S DAY MASSACRE** in 1572.

**Gregory XVI**, originally **Bartolomeo Alberto Mauro Cappellari** (1765–1846)
Pope (1831–46). Elected when the **PAPAL STATES** were in the midst of liberal revolt, he quickly demonstrated himself to be a reactionary with marked sympathy for the Jesuits. Under pressure from the powers, he and his Secretary of State, Cardinal Tommaso Bernetti, did initiate some reforms on paper, but in practice they often remained a dead letter or simply masked conservative intentions. ➤ **CENTURIONI**

**GRENADA** also called **Isle of Spice**

An independent constitutional monarchy of the West Indies and the most southerly of the Windward Islands, in the eastern Caribbean Sea. It was discovered by **COLUMBUS** in 1498, and named Concepción. Settled by the French in the mid-17c, it was ceded to Britain in 1763 by the Treaty of **PARIS**, but retaken by France in 1779, and ceded again to Britain in 1783. It became a British Crown Colony in 1877 and gained independence in 1974 under Prime Minister Eric **GAIRY**. A popular people's revolution was successfully mounted in 1979 by Maurice **BISHOP**, who became Prime Minister but was killed during a further uprising in 1983. US troops invaded the island in Oct 1983 to restore stable government, which was maintained during the administration of Herbert **BLAIZE** (1984–9). In 1995 the New National Party led by Keith Mitchell defeated the National Democratic Congress government under Prime Minister Nicholas Brathwaite, and came to power. ➤ **GRENADA INVASION**

**Grenada Invasion** (25 Oct 1983)
The 'police' action by the USA in the Caribbean, provoked by the fear that the lives of 1,000 US citizens were at risk following the murder of Prime Minister Maurice **BISHOP** and the subsequent army takeover. It was claimed that the USA had been asked for help by the Organization of East Caribbean States. This invasion of a member of the British **COMMONWEALTH OF NATIONS** received widespread criticism from the USA's Western allies.

**Grenville, George** (1712–70)
British politician. He practised as a lawyer and was first an MP in 1741, becoming Lord of the Admiralty (1744–7), Lord of the Treasury (1747–54) and Treasurer of the Navy (1754–5 and 1756–62). He was briefly Secretary of State for the Northern Department (1762–3) and then became Prime Minister (1763–5). During his period in office, Wilkes was arrested for seditious libel under a general warrant for his attack on the King's speech (1763). The closer supervision of revenue collection (1764–5) and the **STAMP ACT** (1765) began the process of alienating the American colonies from British rule. His lack of tact and maladroit handling of arrangements to cover a possible regency during **GEORGE III**'s first serious illness (1765) led to his dismissal by the King and he remained in opposition for the rest of his life. ➤ **BUTE, JOHN; PELHAM, HENRY; PELHAM, THOMAS PELHAM-HOLLES, 1ST DUKE OF NEWCASTLE**

**Grenville, Sir Richard** (1542–91)
British naval commander. A cousin of Sir Walter

RALEIGH, he fought in Hungary and Ireland (1566–9) and was knighted c.1577. He commanded, in 1585, the seven ships carrying Raleigh's first colony to Virginia. In 1591, as commander of the *Revenge*, he fought alone against a large Spanish fleet off the Azores, and died of wounds on board a Spanish ship.

### Grenville, William Wyndham Grenville, 1st Baron (1759–1834)

British politician. The son of George GRENVILLE, he studied at Eton and Oxford and entered parliament in 1782. He became Paymaster-General in 1783, Home Secretary in 1790 and Foreign Secretary in 1791. He resigned with PITT, THE YOUNGER, in 1801 on the refusal of GEORGE III to agree to CATHOLIC EMANCIPATION. In 1806–7 he formed the coalition government of 'All the Talents', which abolished the slave trade. ► SLAVERY

### Grévy, François Paul Jules (1807–91)

French politician. Vice-President of the Constituent Assembly of 1848, he opposed Louis Napoleon (NAPOLEON III), and after the coup d'état retired from politics. In Feb 1871 he was elected President of the National Assembly, and in 1879 he became President of the Republic. Re-elected in 1885, he resigned in Dec 1887 after a financial scandal involving his son-in-law.

### Grey, Charles Grey, 2nd Earl (1764–1845)

British politician. He became a Whig MP in 1786, and was a leading supporter of parliamentary reform in the 1790s. In 1806 he became First Lord of the Admiralty, Foreign Secretary and Leader of the House of COMMONS. In 1807 he succeeded his father as 2nd Earl Grey. In 1830 he formed a government promising peace, retrenchment and reform, and after considerable difficulties secured the passage of the 1832 Reform Bill. In the new parliament he carried the Act for the abolition of SLAVERY in the colonies, but was forced to resign in 1834 following disagreement over the Irish question. ► REFORM ACTS; WHIGS

### Grey, Sir George (1812–98)

British colonial governor and Premier of New Zealand. He explored in Western Australia (1837–9), and became successively Governor of South Australia (1841), New Zealand (1845) and Cape Colony (1854). Again Governor of New Zealand (1861–8), he brought the MAORI WARS to a close. As Premier of New Zealand (1877–9), he had much influence with the MAORIS, and wrote on Polynesian culture. He returned to Britain in 1894.

### Grey, Lady Jane (1537–54)

Queen of England for nine days in 1553. She was the eldest daughter of Henry Grey, Marquis of Dorset, and great-granddaughter of HENRY VII. In 1553 the Duke of Northumberland, foreseeing the death of EDWARD VI, aimed to secure the succession by marrying Jane (against her wish) to his fourth son, Lord Guildford Dudley. Three days after Edward's death (9 July), she was named as his successor, but was forced to abdicate in favour of MARY I, who had popular support. She was imprisoned in the Tower of London, and beheaded.

### Gribeauval, Jean-Baptiste Vaquette de (1715–89)

French military officer. As Inspector-General of artillery from 1776 onwards, he reformed French artillery equipment and operational practice, to make it the most effective in the world for a century. One of his early officer pupils was Napoleon Bonaparte. ► NAPOLEON I

### Griboyedov, Alexander Sergeevich (1795–1829)

Russian writer and diplomat. He wrote *Gore ot Uma* (1822–4, 'The Mischief of Being Clever'), a comedy in rhymed iambics, which satirized the contemporary Moscow society so aptly that it has provided household phrases for the Russian people. Though sympathizing with the Decembrist Revolution, he was cleared, and in 1828 became Russian ambassador to Persia, where he had previously served in a lesser capacity. He was killed in an anti-Russian demonstration at the Embassy in Tehran.

### Griffith, Arthur (1872–1922)

Irish nationalist politician. He worked as a compositor, then as a miner and journalist in South Africa (1896–8), before editing *The United Irishman* (1899). In 1905 he founded the newspaper *Sinn Féin*, editing it until 1914, and directed the early development of SINN FÉIN. He was twice imprisoned (1916–17 and 1920–1), and became an MP (1918–22). He headed the delegation which signed the Anglo-Irish Treaty (Dec 1921) and was President of DÁIL EIREANN (1922).

### Griffith, Samuel Walker (1845–1920)

Welsh-born Australian judge. Emigrating to Australia in 1854, he studied at Sydney University. From 1867 he practised law in Queensland, entered the state legislature in 1872 and was state Premier (1883–8 and 1890–3). He was an active proponent of FEDERATION and as chairman of the Constitutional Committee of the National Australasian Convention in 1891 had a major role in drafting what became, in amended form, in 1900 the Australian Commonwealth Constitution. Chief Justice of Queensland from 1893, he was first Chief Justice of the High Court of Australia (1900–19).

### Grimaldi

A noble Genoese house; from 1419, lords of the Principality of Monaco.

### Grimké, Sarah Moore (1792–1873) and Angelina Emily (1805–79)

US abolitionists and feminists. Born into a major slaveholding family, the sisters rejected their family's way of life and joined the Quakers, who were officially anti-SLAVERY. They moved to Philadelphia and lived quietly until, in 1836, Angelina published a letter in the anti-slavery newspaper *The Liberator*. They became public figures, and Angelina undertook an unprecedented speaking tour. She resisted efforts to silence her, but gave up public life after her marriage to the abolitionist Theodore Weld (1803–95). Sarah lived with the couple thereafter, and the two remained committed to social change. ► ABOLITIONISM

### Griqua

People of mixed race who spoke Dutch and established stock-raising, hunting and trading communities under patriarchal leadership on the frontier of Cape Colony in the late 18c and early 19c. Their peoples are now integrated into what was formerly called the **CAPE COLOURED** community.

**Grishin, Viktor Vasilevich** (1914–92)
Soviet politician. He was a supporter of Leonid **BREZHNEV**, whom he expected to succeed. A railwayman, he only took up party work during **WORLD WAR II**. From 1956 to 1967 he was head of the Soviet trade unions and managed to keep them firmly in line. In 1967 he became First Secretary of the Moscow party and succeeded in making it toe the line for 18 years. In 1985 Mikhail **GORBACHEV** replaced him almost immediately and put Boris **YELTSIN** in his place, an obvious sign of reform.

**Grivas, Georgeios Theodoros** (1898–1974)
Greek-Cypriot nationalist leader. He commanded a Greek army division in the Albanian campaign of 1940–1, and led a secret ultra right-wing organization called 'X' (Khi) during the German occupation of Greece. An ardent nationalist, in 1955 he became head of the underground campaign against British rule in Cyprus; as founder and leader of **EOKA**, he began to call himself 'Digenis Akritas' after a legendary Greek hero. In 1959, after the Cyprus settlement, he left Cyprus and was promoted general in the Greek army. In 1971 he returned secretly to Cyprus and, as leader of EOKA-B, directed a terrorist campaign for **ENOSIS** (union with Greece) until his death, at Limassol. He was accorded a hero's funeral.

**Groener, Wilhelm** (1867–1939)
German military commander and politician. A prominent member of the German General Staff during **WORLD WAR I**, General Groener led army negotiations with the Social Democratic government in Nov 1918 to guarantee the old army's survival in the republic. Successful in this, he later held various ministerial posts in Weimar governments, serving as Army Minister and as Interior Minister under **BRÜNING**. His failure to sustain a ban on the **SA** of the **NAZI PARTY**, coupled with the fall of Brüning's government, ended his political career in May 1932. **— WEIMAR REPUBLIC**

**Groen van Prinsterer, Guillaume** (1801–76)
Dutch historian and politician. After studying law and classics at Leiden University, he became Secretary to the King's cabinet and archivist to the Dutch royal family. Having converted to orthodox Calvinism c.1828, he advocated a Christian approach to political affairs, rejecting both reactionary conservatism and secular liberalism. In 1847 he published a seminal critique of the **FRENCH REVOLUTION**, *Ongeloof en Revolutie* ('Unbelief and Revolution'), which became the classic statement of a renascent Calvinist political movement in the Netherlands. This gave rise to the **ANTI-REVOLUTIONARY PARTY**, in defence of constitutional monarchy and parliamentary rights, which later joined with the Christian Historical Union to form the Dutch **CHRISTIAN DEMOCRATIC APPEAL** (CDA). He was a member of the Second Chamber of parliament (1849–57 and 1862–6). His spiritual and political heir was Abraham **KUYPER**.

**Gromyko, Andrei Andreevich** (1909–89)
Soviet politician and diplomat. He studied agriculture and economics, and became a research economist at the Soviet Academy of Sciences. In 1939 he joined the staff of the Russian Embassy in Washington, becoming Ambassador in 1943; after **WORLD WAR II** he was permanent delegate to the **UN** Security Council (1946–8) and then Deputy Foreign Minister for most of the period 1949–57. The longest-serving Foreign Minister (1957–85), he was responsible for conducting Soviet relations with the West during the **COLD WAR**, presenting an austere and humourless public demeanour for which he became notorious in diplomatic circles. Mikhail **GORBACHEV** promoted him to the largely honorific and mainly domestic post of President in 1985, but he retired from office following the 19th Party Conference in 1988, when he was replaced in a much stronger presidency by Gorbachev himself.

**Gronchi, Giovanni** (1888–1978)
Italian President. One of the founders of the **POPOLARI**, he entered **MUSSOLINI**'s first government as Under-Secretary of State for Industry and Commerce, but in 1923 he moved into opposition and led his party in the **AVENTINE SECESSION**. He took part in the resistance and was elected to the post-war Constituent Assembly as a Christian Democrat. He was President of Italy from 1955 to 1962. **— CHRISTIAN DEMOCRATIC PARTY**

**Grósz, Károly** (1930–96)
Hungarian politician. The son of a steelworker, he began his career in 1946 as a printer and rose to be a newspaper editor (1958–61). Having joined the ruling Hungarian Socialist Workers' Party in 1945, he moved to Budapest in 1961 to work in the agitprop department, becoming its deputy head in 1968 and its head in 1974. Grósz served as Budapest Party chief (1984–7) and was inducted into the Politburo in 1985. He became Prime Minister in 1987 and succeeded János **KÁDÁR** as Party leader in 1988, giving up his position as Prime Minister six months later. He moved pragmatically with the times and, following the lead given by Mikhail **GORBACHEV** in Moscow, became an apparently committed and frank-speaking reformer in both the economic and political spheres, seeking to establish in Hungary a new system of 'socialist pluralism'. However, when the Party reconstituted itself as the new Hungarian Socialist Party in Oct 1989, he was replaced as leader by Rezsö Nyers, a more radical ex-communist.

**Grotius, Hugo**, also called **Huig de Groot** (1583–1645)
Dutch jurist, politician, diplomat, poet and theologian. He studied at Leiden, practised in The Hague, and in 1613 was appointed Pensionary of Rotterdam. He was a political champion of the **REMONSTRANTS**, and in 1618 religious and political conflicts led to his imprisonment. In 1621 he escaped in a trunk from Loevestein Castle to Paris, where **LOUIS XIII** for a time gave him a pension. In 1625 he published his great work on international law, *De Jura Belli et Pacis* ('On the Law of War and Peace'). He also led diplomatic missions for Sweden, where he died. He is honoured as one of the founders of international law.

**Grouchy, Emmanuel, Marquis of** (1766–1847)
French Napoleonic soldier. He greatly distinguished himself in Italy (1798), and fought at Hohenlinden, **EYLAU**, **FRIEDLAND** (1807), **WAGRAM** and in the Russian campaign of 1812. On **NAPOLEON I**'s escape from Elba, he destroyed the Bourbon opposition in the

south of France, and helped to rout **BLÜCHER** at Ligny, but failed to play an effective part at the Battle of **WATERLOO** due to misleading orders (1815). He retired to the USA, returning in 1819, and was reinstated as marshal in 1831.

### Groulx, Abbé Lionel (1878–1967)
French-Canadian nationalist historian and novelist. In reaction to the more moderate interpretations of the early 20c, he depicted French-Canadian history as an unremitting struggle against English domination, and in such works as *Notre maître le passé* (1944) he celebrated the clerical and agrarian elements of that past, although he never explicitly advocated separatism.

### Group of Eight also known as G8
An informal forum for major industrial nations to meet annually and discuss economic issues. Established in 1975 by President Valery **GISCARD D'ESTAING**, the original group of five nations (France, Germany, Japan, UK and USA) expanded in 1977 to include Canada and Italy, when it became known informally as the G7, and in 2002 to include Russia. The G8 experts' groups on organized crime (Lyon Group) and international terrorism (Roma Group) were amalgamated in 2001 following the **SEPTEMBER 11 ATTACKS**. Since the late 1990s G8 summits have attracted protests, sometimes violent, by organizations concerned about the environment and the effects of global **CAPITALISM**. ► **FINANCIAL ACTION TASK FORCE**; **TERROR, WAR ON**

### Groza, Petru (1884–1958)
Romanian politician. During the 1930s he led the Ploughmen's Front, which drew its support from the Transylvanian peasantry. When Romania entered **WORLD WAR II** in 1944, he joined the communist front organization, the National Democratic Front (FND). In Nov 1944, together with his fellow 'home Communist' **GHEORGIU-DEJ**, he represented the FND in the government of Sănătescu. In Feb 1945 **STALIN** approved his appointment as presiding minister in the FND government, a post he held until 1952 when he became President of the Presidium of the Romanian Communist Party.

### Grundherrschaft
A system of landlordship which developed in medieval Germany. It necessarily included public authority and aristocratic rule as opposed to simple estate ownership (*Gutsherrschaft*). At the centre of the system was the lord's hall or court (*Hof*), from which the lord exercised his economic and political powers in his estates.

### Grundtvig, Nicolaj Frederik Severin (1783–1872)
Danish theologian, historian, poet and educator. He dedicated his life to the spiritual regeneration of Denmark during the years following the **NAPOLEONIC WARS**. Strongly influenced by his visits to England in 1829–31, Grundtvig worked for political and religious freedom, but above all for the enlightenment of the common people. He was the inspiration behind the folk high school movement, begun in 1844, which provided adults with education in both practical subjects and the humanities, and which contributed to the transformation of rural life in Denmark in the aftermath of the **GERMAN–DANISH WAR**.

### Grunwald (Tannenberg), Battle of (1410)
A crushing defeat inflicted on the Teutonic Order under Grand Master Ulrich von Jungingen by King Ladislav of Poland and his cousin, Witold of Lithuania. The Grand Master of the Order, all but one of its commanders and 205 of its knights died in the battle and the conquest of the Order's lands was only prevented by Henry of Plauen's vigorous defence of them. The battle marked the end of the Order's military dominance in north-east Europe and the decline of its political and financial authority quickly followed. ► **HERMANN OF SALZA**; **TEUTONIC KNIGHTS**; **WINRICH OF KNIPRODE**

### Gruppi d'Azione Patriottica
Anti-German and anti-fascist urban guerrillas during **WORLD WAR II**. Usually attached to the communists, the so-called *Gappisti* were especially active in the closing stages of the war, where their daring and ruthless actions often elicited brutal German reprisals.

### Guadalcanal, Battle of (1942)
A battle in the South Pacific in **WORLD WAR II**. Following the attacks on **PEARL HARBOR** and Singapore (7–8 Dec 1941), Japan advanced into the South Pacific, reaching Guadalcanal in the Solomon Islands in May 1942. US forces reinvaded and after six months of bitter fighting, in one of the crucial actions of the war, they halted the Japanese advance.

### Guadalupe, Sentence of (1486)
The judgement decreed by **FERDINAND II, THE CATHOLIC** as arbiter in the long-running dispute between the Catalan *remensa* ('redemption') peasants and their lords. The remensa peasants in Catalonia were so called because of the custom obliging them to buy their freedom if they wished to move from their lord's land; their position was one of serfdom. By his judgement, Ferdinand abolished this custom, confirmed their right to liberty, and ended other feudal customs known as the *malos usos* ('evil usages'), in exchange for a payment to be made to the lords. The sentence brought freedom to the Catalan peasantry but did not improve their condition.

### Guadalupe Hidalgo, Treaty of (2 Feb 1848)
The agreement that settled the **MEXICAN WAR**, with Mexico yielding all of Texas, Arizona, Nevada, California and Utah, and parts of New Mexico, Colorado and Wyoming. The USA paid US$15 million, and assumed US$3.25 million worth of Mexican debts.

### Guandong (Kwantung) Army
The Japanese military force that protected the leasehold territory on the Liaodong Peninsula (southern Manchuria) and the South Manchuria Railway, acquired by Japan in 1905 as a result of the **RUSSO-JAPANESE WAR**. During the 1920s, at a time when China was in turmoil, the Guandong Army began to act independently of the civilian government in Tokyo in pursuit of Japanese interests in the region, a situation helped by the fact that the army's commander reported directly to the General Staff rather than to the Prime Minister. In 1931 the Guandong Army exploited a sabotage incident on the South Manchuria railway to justify a full-scale offensive in Manchuria, and by 1932 had created the puppet-state of **MANZHUGUO**. The Guandong Army henceforth exercised dominant political control in Manchuria, calling

for a mobilization of all resources to counter the USSR, which it perceived as Japan's main threat. Tokyo's decision in 1941 to advance towards South-East Asia, however, precluded any decision to go to war with the USSR. Six days after the USSR itself declared war on Japan (9 Aug 1945), the Guandong Army had to surrender to Soviet forces. Thousands were sent to labour camps in the USSR, and the survivors were not repatriated until the mid-1950s.

### Guangxu (Kuang-hsu) (1871–1908)
Emperor of China (1875/1908). A ruler of the **QING DYNASTY**, with the personal name Zai Tian (Tsai T'ien), he was a nephew of the Empress-Dowager **CIXI** and ascended the throne as a minor in 1875. Cixi acted as regent until his majority in 1889 but continued to exercise influence thereafter. In 1898 Guangxu seized the opportunity to assert himself by supporting a programme of reform (the **HUNDRED DAYS OF REFORM**) and issued a series of reforming edicts. However, Cixi, with the support of conservatives at court, rescinded the reforms and placed the hapless Guangxu under virtual house arrest until his mysterious death one day before the death of the Empress-Dowager. ► **KANG YOUWEI**

### GUATEMALA   official name **Republic of Guatemala**

The northernmost of the central American republics, bounded to the north and west by Mexico; to the south-west by the Pacific Ocean; to the east by Belize and the Caribbean Sea; and to the south-east by Honduras and El Salvador. Mayan and Aztec civilizations flourished before the Spanish conquest of 1523–4. Guatemala gained independence in 1821 as part of the **CENTRAL AMERICAN FEDERATION**, which was officially dissolved in 1840, since when the country has had a series of dictatorships broken by short periods of representative government. In 1985 civilian rule was restored. Guatemala's long-standing dispute regarding its claim to Belize ended in 1991 with the recognition of Belize's independence. In 1996, after 35 years of fighting between left-wing Guatemalan National Revolutionary Unity guerrillas and the government, a peace agreement was signed, ending Latin America's longest civil war.

### Guchkov, Alexander I (1862–1936)
Russian politician. From a business family, he believed in gradual constitutional change and helped to found the Octobrist Party, which based itself on the representation promised in **NICHOLAS II**'s 1905 **OCTOBER MANIFESTO**. But he became disillusioned with a powerless **DUMA** and eventually with Nicholas, who would not prosecute the 1914 war seriously. In 1917, although he regretted the passing of the **ROMANOV DYNASTY** with Nicholas's abdication, he became Minister of War in the **RUSSIAN PROVISIONAL GOVERNMENT** in the hope of promoting moderate change. But his advocacy of continuing the war and his opposition to far-reaching land reform undermined his position and he was forced out of office in May, even before the main assault by the **BOLSHEVIKS** in Oct 1917.

### Guderian, Heinz Wilhelm (1888–1953)
German general and creator of the German Panzer (armoured) forces. He was a career soldier from his first commission in 1908. After serving in **WORLD WAR I**, he stayed in the small army allowed to Germany by the Treaty of **VERSAILLES**, and was an ardent pioneer of mechanized warfare. Created general of Panzer troops in 1938, he advocated the idea of fast-moving '**BLITZKRIEG**' warfare which he later put into brilliant effect, commanding forces in France and the USSR. He had a stormy relationship with **HITLER**, being dismissed and reinstated several times. ► **WORLD WAR II**

### Guelfs
The pro-papal, anti-imperial party in Italian cities in the 13–14c, opposed to the power of the Holy Roman Emperors, and successful in resisting the authority of the **HOHENSTAUFEN DYNASTY**, whose power was eclipsed after 1266. Allied with the papacy, the Guelfs resisted the claims of potential successors, and dominated Florentine politics. ► **GHIBELLINES**; **HOLY ROMAN EMPIRE**; **WELFS**

### Guernica
Historic Basque town. As a traditional meeting place for the **BASQUES**, Guernica is a symbol of Basque sovereignty. After the Autonomy Statute was approved in Oct 1936, the Basques' first President (or *Lendakari*) was chosen in Guernica. On 26 Apr 1937, a market day, the town was decimated by the German Condor Legion (**LUFTWAFFE**) on the orders of the Spanish High Command. Guernica's destruction became synonymous with the atrocities committed by the Nationalists and their fascist allies during the **SPANISH CIVIL WAR**. The bombing was immortalized in Picasso's painting, 'Guernica'. ► **BASQUE AUTONOMY STATUTES**

### Guerra González, Alfonso (1940–)
Spanish politician. A close friend of Felipe **GONZÁLEZ MÁRQUEZ** from the early 1960s, Guerra was largely responsible for the transformation of the **PSOE** in the 1970s into a major political organization. He complemented the charismatic appeal of González through his outstanding administrative abilities, though his control of the party machine was heavily personalized and intolerant of dissent. A deputy in every election since 1977, he was Deputy Prime Minister from 1982 until his major split with González in 1991. A ruthless, sarcastic and demagogic politician, specializing in inflammatory attacks on opponents, he made many enemies both inside and outside the Socialist Party.

### guerrilla
A member of a small, independent, often politically

motivated armed force making surprise attacks, eg against government troops. The term was invented in the 16c Spanish colonial wars in Chile, and then applied in the **PENINSULAR WAR** to Spanish and Portuguese resistance fighters. Guerrilla techniques were used during **WORLD WAR II** (eg by the **CHETNIKS** and **TITO**'s partisans in Yugoslavia, and the National Liberation Front in Greece), and in the **VIETNAM WAR** (by the **VIET CONG**). National liberation groups, militant extremists, and freedom fighters in many countries have favoured guerrilla warfare, both the traditional method of harrying and attacking the enemy in open countryside, and the more recent tactic of mounting attacks in built-up areas (so-called urban-guerrilla warfare). ► **ARAUCANIANS**

**Guesclin, Bertrand du** (c.1320–1380)
French knight. A military leader during the **HUNDRED YEARS' WAR**, he entered royal service on the eve of **CHARLES V**'s accession. After becoming Constable of France in 1370, he assumed command of the French armies, reconquering Brittany and most of southwestern France. He died while besieging Château-neuf-de-Randon in the Auvergne.

**Guesde, Jules Bazile** (1845–1922)
French politician. A supporter of the **PARIS COMMUNE**, he was sentenced *in absentia*, and fled abroad, where he was converted to **MARXISM**. On his return to France (1876) he was a leading figure in the first attempts to create a workers' movement. In 1882 he founded his own party, the POF (*Parti ouvrier français*, 'French Workers' Party'), which he led until it was incorporated in the United Socialist Party (SFIO) in 1905. The united party accepted Guesde's rigid Marxism in theory, but in practice **JAURÈS**'s parliamentary tactics had greater influence. Guesde was a Deputy (1893–8 and 1906–22), and accepted office during **WORLD WAR I**. He did not join the **COMMUNIST PARTY** in 1920. ► **SOCIALIST PARTY** (France)

**Guevara, Che**, properly **Ernesto Guevara de la Serna** (1928–67)
Argentine revolutionary leader. He trained as a doctor (1953), and played an important part in the Castro revolution (1956–9), after which he held government posts under Fidel **CASTRO**. He left Cuba in 1965 to become a guerrilla leader in South America, and was captured and executed in Bolivia. His career was important as an inspiration to a variety of left-wing groups throughout the continent, and his failure to stimulate peasant revolt in Bolivia indicated that the Cuban experience of revolution could not be repeated elsewhere.

**Guicciardini, Francesco** (1483–1540)
Italian historian and diplomat. He was Professor of Law at Florence and also practised as an advocate. As a diplomat he served as Florentine ambassador to the court of **FERDINAND II, THE CATHOLIC** of Aragon (1512–14), then travelled widely in papal service, acting as Governor of Modena (1516) and Reggio (1517) before retiring in 1534. He secured the election of Cosimo I de' **MEDICI** as Duke of Florence, then withdrew to Arcetri, where he produced the phenomenal contemporary history *Storia d'Italia* ('History of Italy'), an account of events in Italy in the period 1494–1534.

**Guillaume de la Mark**, known as **Wild Boar of the Ardennes** (d.1485)
Liège politician. He opposed those Prince-Bishops of Liège supported by the House of **BURGUNDY** in its attempts to unite the Low Countries; in this he was aided by the French King **LOUIS XI**. In 1483 he ruled Liège as regent, and had his son elected bishop, but was defeated by the forces of neighbouring **BRABANT** at the Battle of Hollogne in 1483; in the same year the pope appointed Jean de Hornes as bishop instead. Hostilities were ended, but Jean de Hornes's brother, the Count of Montigny, captured Guillaume and took him to Maastricht, where he was condemned and beheaded.

**Guillotin, Joseph Ignace** (1738–1814)
French physician and revolutionary. He proposed that the Constituent Assembly, of which he was a Deputy, should use a decapitating instrument as a means of execution. This was adopted in 1791 and named after him, though a similar apparatus had been used earlier in Scotland, Germany and Italy.

**GUINEA** official name **Republic of Guinea**, formerly (1979–84) **People's Revolutionary Republic of Guinea**, and (1890–1979) **French Guinea**

A republic in West Africa, bounded to the north-west by Guinea-Bissau; to the north by Senegal and Mali; to the east by Côte d'Ivoire; to the south by Liberia and Sierra Leone; and to the south-west by the Atlantic Ocean. Part of the Mali empire in the 16c, it became a French protectorate in 1849 and was governed with Senegal as Rivières du Sud. It became a separate colony in 1893, and a constituent territory within French West Africa in 1904. It reverted to separate colonial status as an Overseas Territory in 1946, and became an independent republic in 1958 under President Ahmed Sékou **TOURÉ**. Following Touré's death in 1984, Lansana **CONTÉ** led a bloodless coup and became President, establishing a Military Committee for National Recovery. Following the introduction of a multiparty system in 1992 Conté was elected President and has retained office in subsequent elections.

**GUINEA-BISSAU** official name **Republic of Guinea-Bissau**, formerly (to 1974) **Portuguese Guinea**
A republic in West Africa, bounded to the east and south by Guinea; to the north by Senegal; and to the west by the Atlantic Ocean. Discovered by the Portuguese in 1446, it became a Portuguese colony in 1879. After becoming an Overseas Territory of Portugal in 1952, it gained independence in 1973, with Luís de Almeida **CABRAL** as President from 1974. He was deposed by a military coup led by João **VIEIRA** in 1980,

and the constitution was changed in 1984 to make Vieira President. A multiparty system was introduced in 1991. The first multiparty elections were held in 1994; they were won by the ruling party and Vieira was re-elected. In May 1999, Vieira was ousted in a military coup which developed into a civil war that was ended only with **ECOWAS** intervention. Kumba Yala was elected President in Jan 2000 but deposed in 2003 in a military coup. ECOWAS persuaded to the military to accept a form of constitutional government, with Henrique Rosa as president.

### Guiscard, Robert (c.1015–1085)
Norman adventurer. The son of Tancred de Hauteville, he campaigned with his brothers against the Byzantine Greeks, and created a duchy comprising southern Italy and Sicily. In 1059 the papacy recognized him as Duke of Apulia, Calabria and Sicily. He ousted the Byzantines from Calabria by 1060, then conquered Bari (1071) and captured Salerno (1076). In 1081 he crossed the Adriatic, seized Corfu, and defeated the Byzantine Emperor **ALEXIUS I COMNENUS** at Durazzo. He died while advancing on Constantinople. ► **NORMANS**

### Guise, Charles of (1525–74)
French prelate and Archbishop of Reims, created Cardinal of Guise in 1547. He was the son of Claude of Lorraine, 1st Duke of Guise and brother of Mary of Guise and Francis, 2nd Duke of **GUISE**, with whom he became all-powerful in the reign of **FRANCIS II** (of France). He introduced the **INQUISITION** into France and exerted a great influence at the Council of **TRENT**. ► **GUISE, HOUSE OF**

### Guise, Claude of Lorraine, 1st Duke of (1496–1550)
French nobleman and soldier. He fought under **FRANCIS I** (of France) at Marignano in Italy in 1515 and defeated the Imperial army at Neufchâteau. He was Regent during the captivity of Francis I by **CHARLES V** (1525–7). For suppressing the peasant revolt in Lorraine (1527), Francis created him Duke of Guise. He was the father of Mary of Guise, who married **JAMES V** of Scotland and became mother of **MARY, QUEEN OF SCOTS**. ► **GUISE, HOUSE OF**

### Guise, Francis, 2nd Duke of, called La Balafré ('the Scarred') (1519–63)
French soldier and politician, son of Claude of Lorraine, 1st Duke of **GUISE**. In 1556 he commanded the expedition against Naples, and took Calais (1558), bringing about the Treaty of Château Cambrésis (1559). He and his brother, Cardinal Charles of **GUISE**, shared the chief power in the state during the reign of **FRANCIS II** (of France). Heading the Roman Catholic Party, they firmly repressed Protestantism. Guise and **MONTMORENCY** won a victory over the **HUGUENOTS** at Dreux (1562), and Guise was besieging Orléans when he was assassinated by a Huguenot. ► **GUISE, HOUSE OF**

### Guise, Henry, 3rd Duke of (1550–88)
French soldier and politician, son of Francis, 2nd Duke of **GUISE**. He was one of the contrivers of the **ST BARTHOLOMEW'S DAY MASSACRE** (1572), and was the head of the **HOLY LEAGUE** against the Bourbons (1576). ► **BOURBON, HOUSE OF**; **GUISE, HOUSE OF**

### Guise, Henry, 5th Duke of (1614–64)
French prelate and soldier, grand-nephew of Henry, 3rd Duke of **GUISE**. Having opposed **RICHELIEU**, he was condemned to death, but fled to Flanders. He put himself at the head of **MASANIELLO**'s revolt in Naples, but was taken by the Spanish (1647) and carried to Madrid. After another attempt to win Naples (1654) he settled in Paris. His *Mémoires* were published in 1669. ► **GUISE, HOUSE OF**

### Guise, House of
The French ducal house of Lorraine, named after the town of Guise. Members of the house were prominent as staunch leaders of the Catholic party during the 16c civil wars, through their relationship with the royal houses of **STUART** and Valois. The first duke was Claude of Lorraine, 1st Duke of Guise (1496–1550), who served under **FRANCIS I** of France in Italy and was given the ducal title in 1528. Henry, 3rd Duke of Guise, instigated the murder of **COLIGNY** in the **ST BARTHOLOMEW'S DAY MASSACRE** (1572). On the death of the seventh duke, Francis Joseph (1675), the estates reverted to Mary of Lorraine, on whose death the line became extinct. ► **RELIGION, WARS OF**; **VALOIS DYNASTY**

### Guizot, François Pierre Guillaume (1787–1874)
French historian and politician. He studied law in Paris, but in 1812 he became Professor of Modern History at the Sorbonne. A member of the *Doctrinaires* (a group of moderate constitutional liberals who elevated their policy of the *juste milieu*, or 'middle road', to a complete political philosophy), he was elected to the Chamber (1830), became Minister of the Interior (1830), and then of Public Instruction (1832). As **LOUIS-PHILIPPE**'s chief adviser (1840), he relapsed into reactionary methods of government, and was forced to escape with him to London in 1848. After 1851 he gave himself up entirely to his historical publications.

### Gulag
The acronym of *Glavnoye Upravleniye Ispravitelno-Trudovykh Lagerey* ('Main Administration of Corrective Labour Camps'). From 1930 this was the Soviet secret police department that administered the system of forced labour camps for those found guilty of what were known as crimes against the state (and which were very broadly defined). Many Soviet dissidents were 'punished' in this way and many innocent victims died. The system was exposed by Alexander **SOLZHENITSYN** in his *Gulag Archipelago*, which was finally published in 1973.

## Gulf Cooperation Council (GCC)

An organization which provides for cooperation between the states surrounding the Persian Gulf. It was established in 1981 by Bahrain, Kuwait, Oman, Qatar, Saudi Arabia and the United Arab Emirates.

## Gulf of Tonkin Resolution (1964)

The US constitutional authorization to escalate the VIETNAM WAR, passed at the request of President Lyndon JOHNSON by an overwhelming majority in CONGRESS, after two US destroyers had reportedly been attacked by North Vietnamese torpedo boats. Its repeal in 1970, the result of mounting opposition to the war and doubts as to the wisdom of giving such discretion to the President, was unopposed by President Richard NIXON, who believed that he had the necessary authority to achieve US aims in the war by virtue of his powers as Commander-in-Chief.

## Gulf War (1980-8) ► IRAN–IRAQ WAR

## Gulf War (16 Jan–27 Feb 1991)

A war which followed the invasion of Kuwait by Iraq in Aug 1990. A rapid air and land campaign, codenamed 'Desert Storm', was mounted by a US-led international coalition based in Saudi Arabia on the authority of President George H W BUSH after Iraq failed to withdraw from Kuwait by the UN deadline. The Bush administration gained its highest popular approval ratings during the crisis, largely due to the President's impassioned attacks on the Iraqi leader, Saddam HUSSEIN. Iraqi forces were expelled from Kuwait and a large part of Iraq's military resources was destroyed. US casualties were set at 79 killed, 213 wounded, 45 missing and 9 captured. Casualty figures for Iraq are unavailable, although they have been estimated at 35,000 killed, 175,000 captured.

## Gulistan, Treaty of (Oct 1813)

The peace treaty between Russia and Persia signed at Gulistan in the Caucasus. The actual date of the signing of the treaty is the subject of some dispute, but is given somewhere between 12 Oct and 24 Oct 1813. In any event, the treaty, achieved through the mediation of Britain as represented by Sir Gore Ouseley, resulted in the cession of several formerly Persian regions to Russia, in the recognition of Russia's sole rights to navigation in the Caspian Sea, and in the granting to Russia of the right to intervention in the support of nominated heirs to the throne of the Qajars. The treaty, which was the result of Persia's having to sue for peace after defeats at the hands of the Russians in 1812, presaged increased Russian (and British) intervention in Persia later in the 19c.

## Gunpowder Plot

A conspiracy by Catholic gentry, led by Robert Catesby, to blow up the English parliament. It failed when Guy FAWKES, who placed the explosives, was arrested (5 Nov 1605). The plot failed because one conspirator, Francis Tresham, warned his brother-in-law, Lord Monteagle, not to attend; and Monteagle reported the matter to the government. The scheme reflected Catholic desperation after the failure of previous plots to remove JAMES VI AND I in 1603; peace with Spain in 1604, which ended the prospect of foreign support; and new sanctions against recusant Catholics, resulting in 5,000 convictions in the spring of 1605.

## Guomindang (Kuomintang, KMT)

The Chinese Nationalist Party, founded by SUN YAT-SEN in 1919 and later led by CHIANG KAI-SHEK. It ruled China from Nanjing (Nanking) in 1927–37 and 1945–9, and from Chonqing during the war with Japan (1937–45). It retreated to Taiwan in 1949.

## Guo Songdao (Kuo Sung-tao) (1818–91)

Chinese official and diplomat. He took an active part in the resistance against the TAIPING REBELLION and was an enthusiastic advocate of the use of a steamship fleet on the Yangzi River. In 1863 he was Provincial Governor of Guangdong and in 1875 a provincial judicial commissioner in Fujian. In 1876 Guo was appointed Minister to England, becoming China's first diplomatic representative abroad. In 1878 he was also appointed Minister to France. His positive appraisal of Western political institutions and his promotion of railways and telegraphs incurred the wrath of conservatives back home and he was recalled at the end of 1878. Thereafter, he withdrew from official life.

## Gupta ► INDIA, PRE-ISLAMIC

## Gurkhas

An élite infantry unit of the British Army recruited from the hill tribes of Nepal. Their characteristic weapon, the Kukri fighting knife with its curved blade, has contributed to their fame, in battles from the North-West Frontier of India in the 19c, via the Western Front in WORLD WAR I, to the Burma and Italian campaigns of WORLD WAR II. Gurkha infantry also took part in the FALKLANDS WAR of 1982, and were deployed as part of the British contribution to the UN peacekeeping force in EAST TIMOR in 1999.

## Gursel, Cemal (1895–1966)

Turkish general. He emerged as leader of the rebel grouping, the 1960 revolution, against the Menderes government, ending the period of control by the Democratic Party by arresting Menderes himself (who was later executed) and other members of his cabinet. Gursel and a group of officers formed a National Unity Committee and assumed control of the country. A new constitution was drawn up by a national constituent assembly and this was ratifed by popular vote in 1961. Gursel was President of the Turkish Republic from 1961 until his death.

## Gush Emmunim

An Israeli pressure group set up after the 1973 elections, dedicated to an active settlement policy in territories such as the WEST BANK, occupied by the Israelis after the 1967 war. The name is Hebrew, meaning 'Bloc of the faithful'. ► ARAB–ISRAELI WARS

## Gustav I Vasa (1496–1560)

King of Sweden (1523/60). The founder of the VASA DYNASTY, he was born into a gentry family at Lindholmen in Uppland. In 1518 he was taken to Denmark as a hostage on the orders of King CHRISTIAN II, but managed to escape. After the death of his father in the STOCKHOLM BLOODBATH, he led an uprising against Christian. He captured Stockholm in 1523 and was elected King by the Diet, effectively ending the KALMAR UNION. Despite several rebellions against him, Gustav strengthened monarchical power, and his long reign was a peaceful one.

**Gustav II Adolf** (1594–1632)
King of Sweden (1611/32). He was the son of CHARLES IX of Sweden. After ascending the throne, he brought to an end the wars which he had inherited, with Denmark (1613) and Russia (1617), and set out to drive Poland from the eastern Baltic. Having carried the war to Poland itself (1626), he concluded in 1629 the six-year Truce of Altmark with that power, in order to have his hands free to enter the THIRTY YEARS' WAR in Germany in 1630. After establishing a bridgehead in Pomerania and winning a decisive victory over the opposing Catholic forces at Breitenfeld in Saxony (1631), he began a triumphal march through central and southern Germany, which carried him almost to the gates of Vienna. He was, however, drawn back to Saxony by the Imperial commander, WALLENSTEIN, and was killed during the Swedish victory at LÜTZEN. Working closely with his Chancellor, Axel OXENSTIERNA, Gustav reformed Sweden's central and local administration, and made Stockholm the administrative capital for the first time. He was himself a brilliant military commander and made the Swedish army one of the most formidable in Europe.

**Gustav III** (1746–92)
King of Sweden (1771/92). He was the son and successor of King ADOLF FREDERICK and LOVISA ULRIKA. Reared by his mother in the spirit of the ENLIGHTENMENT, he was at home with the most celebrated thinkers and artists of his day. On ascending the throne, he set about ending the party squabbles and noble oligarchy of the AGE OF LIBERTY, and in 1772 arrested the Council in a coup d'état and introduced a new constitution which restored a degree of royal power. He then set about a series of reforms which purged the bureaucracy, improved the state's finances, reformed the penal code and introduced a measure of religious toleration. His court became a northern Versailles, with the foundation of the Royal Opera House (1782), the Swedish Academy (1786) on the French model, and the Royal Dramatic Theatre (1788). But his reforming zeal ran out of steam after 1780, and his increasingly autocratic style of government alienated many nobles. When, in 1788, he launched an attack on Russia from Finland, he found himself faced with a mutiny of noble officers. This, however, brought an anti-noble reaction and enabled him to assume well-nigh absolute powers. Peace was made with Russia in 1790, and Gustav became involved with plans for the restoration of royal power in France, whose culture he much admired. He encouraged Count Hans Axel von FERSEN to attempt the rescue of the French royal family in the abortive 'Flight to Varennes' (June 1792) and planned to land a Russo-Swedish army in Normandy for a march on Paris. But in Mar 1792 he was shot by a former army officer, Johan Jakob ANCKARSTRÖM during a masked ball in the Royal Opera House, dying a lingering death. Married to Sofia Magdalena of Denmark, he was succeeded by his young son, GUSTAV IV ADOLF.

**Gustav IV Adolf** (1778–1837)
King of Sweden (1792/1809). He was the son and successor of GUSTAV III. During his minority, the regent was his uncle Charles, Duke of Södermanland. In the first years of his reign as an absolute monarch, he did much to improve Swedish agriculture with a General Enclosure Act (1803). But his aversion to NAPOLEON I induced him to abandon Swedish neutrality and declare war on France in 1805. When Russia changed sides as a result of the Treaty of Tilsit (1807) and became an ally of Napoleon, the Swedes were driven from Pomerania, their last German possession. In 1808 Sweden was attacked by France's ally, Denmark, and Finland was invaded by the Russia of ALEXANDER I. Tactless and autocratic by nature, Gustav spurned an offer of help from a British force under Sir John Moore which was anchored off Gothenburg, and Finland was occupied by Russia in 1809. He was arrested by noble bureaucrats in Stockholm before he could escape to the south, and was forced to abdicate. He was exiled with his wife, Queen Frederika of Baden, and their children. After divorcing his wife (1812), he spent 25 years wandering in Europe before his death in St Gallen in Switzerland, as 'Colonel Gustafsson'. He was succeeded on the throne by his uncle as King CHARLES XIII under a new constitution which limited the power of the monarch. ► TILSIT, TREATIES OF

**Gustav V** (1858–1950)
King of Sweden (1907/50). The son and successor of OSCAR II, he was the longest-reigning king in Swedish history. Shy and reserved by nature, he disliked pomp and spectacle and refused a coronation ceremony, thus becoming the first 'uncrowned king' on the Swedish throne. Nevertheless, he sought to assert the personal power of the monarchy and, in 1914, in his famous 'Courtyard Speech' to a farmers' rally, challenged the Liberal government with a call for greater spending on defence. The government resigned in protest, but demands for his abdication were stilled by the outbreak of WORLD WAR I, when Sweden mobilized but remained neutral. Thereafter he reigned as a popular constitutional monarch, and in WORLD WAR II came to symbolize the unity of the nation. He continued, however, to exercise political influence, and his threat to abdicate in 1941 was a factor in persuading the Swedish government to give way to German demands. He married Princess Viktoria, daughter of the Grand Duke of Baden and great-granddaughter of GUSTAV IV ADOLF, thus uniting the reigning house of Bernadotte with the former royal house of Vasa. His nephew was Count Folke BERNADOTTE. He was succeeded by his son, GUSTAV VI ADOLF. ► VASA DYNASTY

**Gustav VI Adolf** (1882–1973)
King of Sweden (1950/73). The son and successor of GUSTAV V, he was a respected scholar and archaeologist, and an authority on Chinese art. In 1905 he married Princess Margaret (the grand-daughter of Queen VICTORIA), by whom he had four sons and a daughter. In 1923 he married Lady Louise Mountbatten, the sister of Earl MOUNTBATTEN of Burma. His eldest son, Gustav Adolf, having been killed in an air-crash (1947), he was succeeded by his grandson, CHARLES XVI GUSTAV.

**Gu Weijun (Ku Wei-chun)**, also known as **Wellington Koo** (1888–1985)
Chinese diplomat. He studied in the USA and joined the Ministry of Foreign Affairs in 1912. As a member of the Chinese delegation to the PARIS PEACE

CONFERENCE (1919), he refused to sign the ensuing treaty in protest against the powers' decision to allow Japan to retain control of the Qingdao (Tsingtao) Peninsula, Germany's former leasehold territory in China. Gu was China's chief delegate at the first meeting of the **LEAGUE OF NATIONS** assembly (1920), helping to draft the League Covenant. He gained renown in 1932 when, as China's delegate to the League of Nations, he forcefully condemned Japanese aggression in Manchuria. In June 1945 Gu represented China at the signing of the **UN** Charter, of which China was the first signatory.

**GUYANA** official name **Cooperative Republic of Guyana**, formerly (to 1966) **British Guiana**

A republic on the northern coast of South America, bounded to the east by Suriname; to the west by Venezuela; to the south by Brazil; and to the north by the Atlantic Ocean. It was sighted by **COLUMBUS** in 1498 and settled by the Dutch in the late 16c. Several areas were ceded to Britain in 1815, and the areas were consolidated as British Guiana and formally came under British rule in 1831. Following racial disturbances in 1962, Guyana gained independence in 1966 and in 1970 became a republic, led by President Forbes **BURNHAM**. He was succeeded on his death in 1985 by Desmond **HOYTE**, whose **PEOPLE'S NATIONAL CONGRESS** Party was defeated in 1992 by the People's Progessive Party under Cheddi **JAGAN**. After Jagan's death in Mar 1997, his widow, Janet Jagan, was elected President (Dec 1997), serving until 1999, when she resigned. She was succeeded by Bharrat Jagdeo, who was elected President in 2001.

**Gu Yanwu (Ku Yen-wu)** (1613–82)
Chinese scholar and official. He is celebrated for his loyalty to the **MING DYNASTY** and his refusal to serve the succeeding Manchu **QING DYNASTY**. He participated in the Ming resistance movement against the Manchus in the late 1640s and later led the life of an independent scholar, rejecting all offers by the Qing authorities to enter officialdom. Gu was to serve as an inspiration for early 20c anti-Manchu revolutionaries.

**Guyenne (Guienne)**
A medieval duchy, including Gascony, in southwestern France, bounded to the west by the Bay of Biscay. The rump of Aquitaine, it remained a possession of the English crown after **NORMANDY** and other French territories were lost in 1204–5. The claim of the kings of England to be independent rulers of Guyenne was one of the causes of the **HUNDRED YEARS' WAR**. It was finally conquered by the French in 1453. The area is now occupied by the departments of Gironde, Dordogne, Lot, Aveyron, Tarn-et-Garonne and Lot-et-Garonne. ► **ANGEVINS**

**Guy of Dampierre** (c.1226–1305)
Count of Flanders and Namur. The second son of William of Dampierre, the death of his elder brother (1251) brought Guy the County of Flanders in 1278, his second marriage, in 1265, to Isabella of Luxembourg having brought him Namur. In Flanders he strove to restore the Count's power, some of which had been lost to the rich and powerful industrial-commercial towns. In foreign policy, Guy allied himself with the English against King **PHILIP IV** of France, who was trying to extend his influence over Flanders. In 1300 France occupied the County and Guy was forced to surrender; a general revolt broke out, leading to the Matins of **BRUGES** and the Battle of the **GOLDEN SPURS**, but Guy died in French captivity.

**Guy of Lusignan** (d.1194)
French Crusader. He became King of Jerusalem in 1186 as consort of Sibylla, daughter of Amalric I, but was defeated and captured at the Battle of **HITTIN** (1187) by **SALADIN**, who overran most of the kingdom. On the death of his wife in 1190, the throne passed to **CONRAD OF MONTFERRAT**, but as compensation Guy received Cyprus, where his family ruled until 1474.

**Guzmán Blanco, Antonio** (1829–99)
Venezuelan dictator. Educated in Europe, he was violently anticlerical, and a bitter opponent of José Antonio **PÁEZ**. He was Vice-President from 1863 to 1868, when he was driven from office. He then headed a revolution which restored him to power in 1870, and became dictator, holding the presidency on three occasions (1873–7, 1879–84 and 1886–8). He was prevented from returning from a visit to Paris by a rising in Caracas and died in exile.

**Gwyn** or **Gwynn** or **Gwynne, Nell Eleanor** (c.1650–1687)
English actress, and mistress of **CHARLES II**. Born of humble parents, she lived precariously selling oranges before establishing herself as a comedienne at Drury Lane, London, especially in breeches parts. 'Pretty, witty Nell's' first protector was Lord Buckhurst, but the transfer of her affections to Charles II was genuine. She had at least one son by the king – Charles Beauclerk, Duke of St Albans – and James Beauclerk was allegedly a second.

**Haakon IV** ► HAAKON THE OLD

**Haakon VII** (1872–1957)
King of Norway (1905/57). Born Prince Carl of Denmark, the second son of King **FREDERICK VIII**, he was elected King of Norway when the country voted for independence from Sweden. In 1896 he married Princess Maud, youngest daughter of King **EDWARD VII** of Britain. Known as the 'people's king', he dispensed with much of the pomp of royalty. When Germany invaded Norway in 1940 he refused to abdicate, and when further armed resistance was impossible, carried on the resistance from England, returning in triumph in 1945. He was succeeded by his son, **OLAV V.** ► NORWAY, GERMAN INVASION OF

**Haakon the Old** (1204–63)
King of Norway (1217/63). The illegitimate grandson of the 'usurper' **SVERRIR SIGURDSSON**, he was placed on the throne as a boy of 13 by his powerful and ambitious uncle, Duke Skúli, who acted as regent. Eventually Skúli tried to rebel against his nephew, but was defeated and killed in 1240. Haakon strengthened relationships with the Church, and was ceremoniously crowned in 1247. A great empire-builder, he annexed Iceland and Greenland to the Norwegian crown (1262), but in the following year, on an expedition to the Western Isles of Scotland to reassert Norwegian power there, he suffered a setback at the Battle of Largs against **ALEXANDER III** of Scotland and died at Kirkwall in the Orkneys on his way back to Norway.

**Habash, George** (1925–)
Palestinian guerrilla leader. A radical, it was his Damascus-based Popular Front for the Liberation of Palestine (PFLP), created in 1967, which carried out the first Middle East airliner hijackings. Attacks carried out by the PFLP included the May 1972 incident at Lod Airport (Tel Aviv), when 27 civilians were killed by Japanese Red Army gunmen who opened fire in the terminal building, and the June 1976 hijacking of an Air France airliner to Entebbe Airport in Uganda (which resulted in a successful Israeli commando rescue raid during which four civilians died). He consistently demanded Palestinian control of the **GAZA STRIP** and the **WEST BANK**, so there was common ground between him and his old enemy, Yasser **ARAFAT.** ► PALESTINE

**habitants**
The peasant settlers of **NEW FRANCE** (Canada). Since the feudal customs transplanted from France were not suited to pioneering conditions, the *habitants* gained certain advantages such as the reduction of the *corvée* (the forced labour duty) to six days or a commutation. Another benefit they gained (though only after government pressure) was the use of the *seigneur's* mill. Whilst the *seigneurs* still retained a certain status, their economic distinctions became increasingly less marked.

**Habré, Hissène** (c.1930–)
Chadian nationalist and politician. The son of a desert shepherd, he worked as a clerk for the French army before becoming an administrator. He joined the FAN guerrillas in the early 1970s but, having made his peace with President Malloum in 1978, he was appointed Prime Minister. When Goukouni seized power in 1979, he became Defence Minister. However, supported by the **CIA**, he fought against Goukouni and took power himself in 1982. With French military assistance and support from African heads of state, he forced Libya to withdraw from northern Chad and, although uneasily, retained power until ousted in a coup by Idriss Déby in 1990.

**Habsburg Dynasty**
A major European dynasty whose origins lie in the Upper Rhine region. The name is derived from the Habichtsburg ('Hawk's Castle') in what is today Switzerland, built c.1020 by Bishop Werner of Strassburg. The title Count of Habsburg does not occur until 1090 but, by the time **RUDOLF I** gained the German crown in 1273, the Habsburgs had accumulated a considerable mass of Swiss, Swabian and Alsatian possessions. The acquisition, in 1278, of Austria initiated the crucial shift of their power from the south-west to the south-east of the **HOLY ROMAN EMPIRE**, whose crown they were to hold with few interruptions (1292–8, 1308–1437 and 1742–5) until its fall. The international expansion of the House of Habsburg started in the late 15c when **MAXIMILIAN I** married the heiress of Burgundy and the Netherlands, with Spain added one generation later in the same way and followed by the conquest of Bohemia and Hungary in 1526. Including the Spanish colonies overseas, **CHARLES V** could thus truly claim to be the ruler of 'an empire on which the sun never sets'. After his abdication (1556), the Habsburg dominions were divided between the Spanish line, which died out in 1700, and the German line, whose members continued to rule over a varying collection of territories until 1918, having adopted the title of Emperor of Austria in 1804. In 1867 the venture of Archduke Maximilian (the title of all Habsburg princes since 1359) to establish himself as Emperor of Mexico ended with his execution. ► PRAGMATIC SANCTION

## HABSBURG DYNASTY

| Regnal Dates | Name |
| --- | --- |
| 1273/91 | Rudolf I |
| 1298/1308 | Albert I |
| 1314/22 | Frederick I |
| 1438/9 | Albert II |
| 1440/93 | Frederick III |
| 1493/1519 | Maximilian I |
| 1519/58 | Charles V |
| 1558/64 | Ferdinand I |
| 1564/76 | Maximilian II |
| 1576/1612 | Rudolf II |
| 1612/19 | Matthias |
| 1619/37 | Ferdinand II |
| 1637/57 | Ferdinand III |
| 1658/1705 | Leopold I |
| 1705/11 | Joseph I |
| 1711/40 | Charles VI |
| 1740/2 | Interregnum |
| 1742/5 | Charles VII |
| 1745/65 | Francis I |
| 1765/90 | Joseph II |
| 1790/2 | Leopold II |
| 1792/1835 | Francis II |
| 1835/48 | Ferdinand I |
| 1848/1916 | Francis Joseph |
| 1916/18 | Charles I |

**Habsburg Serfs, Emancipation of the** (1781 and 1849)
A revolutionary social and economic transformation with political consequences for the Habsburg Empire. The practice of serfdom came under increasing criticism during the spread of the European **EN-LIGHTENMENT**. Peasant risings became more frequent and bitter; and serfs proved to be poor labourers and worse soldiers. In 1781 **JOSEPH II** abolished serfdom, although most peasants were still obliged to provide labour service or to make payments in lieu. It was not until 1849 that **FRANCIS JOSEPH** abolished the remaining obligations as a means of ensuring that the peasants in his dominions would not join the other rebels in the **REVOLUTIONS OF 1848-9**. Emancipation accelerated the **INDUSTRIAL REVOLUTION** by freeing peasant labour, but as they crowded into the cities and factories they became the backbone of national and socialist movements.

**Habyarimana, Juvenal** (1937–94)
Rwandan soldier and politician. He was educated at a military school, joined the National Guard and rose rapidly to become its Chief of Staff (1963–5), then Minister of Defence and police Chief of Staff (1965–73), and a major-general in 1973. In the same year, as fighting between the Hutu and Tutsi tribes restarted, he led a bloodless coup against President Gregoire Kayibanda and established a military regime. He founded the National Revolutionary Development Movement (MRND) as the only legal party and promised an eventual return to constitutional government, gradually introducing a degree of democracy into the one-party system. In 1992 the country held its first multiparty elections and elected a Prime Minister. However, in 1993 tribal tensions flared up and the Rwanda Popular Front, consisting of Tutsi rebels, demanded a share of government in return for a peace pact. Returning from peace talks in Tanzania, Habyarimana died when his plane was shot down.

**Hácha, Emil** (1872–1945)
Czechoslovak lawyer and politician. He became President of Czechoslovakia in Oct 1938 on **BENEŠ**'s resignation following the German annexation of Sudetenland; under duress, he made over the state to **HITLER** in Mar 1939. He was puppet President of the subsequent German protectorate of Bohemia and Moravia. Arrested after liberation in 1945, he died in prison.

**hacienda**
The standard Spanish-American term for a large landed estate, usually worked by a resident population of tenant-labourers cultivating small plots of land and subject to labour obligations of various kinds. *Haciendas* emerged in the late 17c and early 18c due to the growth of local markets for their produce. By the mid-18c they had become clusters of buildings, including housing plus *estancias*, often held piecemeal. By the late 18c prominent families in Mexico and Peru owned strings of haciendas, organized as one substantial enterprise. These supplied an entire range of goods for domestic consumption and export. They were complemented by smaller ranchos, held by mestizo peasant farmers. A century later their position was strengthened with the growth of wage labour. ► **ESTANCIA**

**Hadrian IV** ► **ADRIAN IV**

**Hafstein, Hannes Pétursson** (1861–1922)
Icelandic politician. He studied law in Copenhagen and returned to Iceland in 1887 to head the Independence Party in the campaign to secure home rule from Denmark. As Prime Minister (the first after the granting of home rule by the Danish crown) in 1904–7 and 1912–14, he was responsible for reforms in education and health, and inaugurated a telegraph and telephone system. He was also a distinguished lyric poet.

**Haganah**
The Jewish underground militia in **PALESTINE**, founded in the 1920s during the period of the British Mandate in response to nationalist Arab attacks on Jewish settlements. Banned by the British authorities, the *Haganah* ('self-defence') maintained a policy of restraint, opposing the **TERRORISM** of the **IRGUN** and others. However, this changed when the British sought to limit Jewish immigration after **WORLD WAR II**. The Haganah comprised a part-time membership, but 1941 saw the creation of a full-time striking force, the *Palmach*. After the War of Independence in 1948, in which it played a central role, the Haganah became the Israel Defence Force, the official Israeli army. ► **IRGUN**; **ISRAEL**; **JEWISH AGENCY**; **LIKUD**; **STERN GANG**

**Hague Peace Conferences**
Two conferences at The Hague, the Netherlands, in 1899 and 1907. The first met on the initiative of Count Muravyov, the Russian Foreign Minister, to discuss the limitation of armaments, but the 26 countries represented made little progress. A permanent court of arbitration was set up for states in dispute wishing to use its services. The second met on the initiative of

President Theodore **ROOSEVELT**, sat under the chairmanship of Tsar **NICHOLAS II** and, with 44 countries represented, produced a series of conventions to try to limit the horrors of war.

**Haidar Ali** (1722–82)
Indian Muslim ruler of Mysore (1766/82). Having conquered Calicut and fought the Marathas, he waged two wars against the British, in the first of which (1767–9) he won several gains. In 1779 he and his son, **TIPPOO SAHIB**, again attacked the British, initially with great success; but in 1781–2 he was defeated. He died at Chittoor.

**Haig, Alexander Meigs, Jr** (1924– )
US general and administrator. Educated at the US Military Academy at West Point and at Georgetown, he held a number of staff and field positions, serving in the **VIETNAM WAR**. A full general by 1973, he then retired from the army to become White House Chief of Staff during the last days of Richard **NIXON**'s presidency. Returning to active duty, he became supreme **NATO** commander before returning again to civilian life. He served President Ronald **REAGAN** as Secretary of State in 1981–2, and sought the Republican nomination for the presidency in 1988.

**Haig, Douglas Haig, 1st Earl** (1861–1928)
British field marshal. He obtained a commission in the 7th Hussars, and served in Egypt, South Africa and India. In 1914 he led the 1st Army Corps in France, and in 1915 became commander of the **BRITISH EXPEDITIONARY FORCE**. He waged a costly and exhausting war of attrition, for which he was much criticized, but led the final successful offensive in front of Amiens (Aug 1918). In post-war years he devoted himself to the care of ex-servicemen, organizing the Royal British Legion. His earldom was awarded in 1919. ▶ **WORLD WAR I**

**Haile Selassie I**, previously **Prince Ras Tafari Makonnen** (1892–1975)
Emperor of Ethiopia (1930/5 and 1941/74). He led the revolution in 1916 against Lij Eyasu and became regent and heir to the throne, becoming Emperor in 1930. He set about westernizing the institutions of his country, but was driven out when the Italians occupied Ethiopia in 1935 and settled in England. Restored in 1941 by the British, he became a father-figure of African nationalism and was central to the establishment of the **ORGANIZATION OF AFRICAN UNITY**, whose headquarters were in Addis Ababa. His authoritarian rule, however, built up centres of opposition, both among the élite and among non-Amharic peoples. He survived an attempted coup in 1971, but the famine of 1973 led to economic crisis, industrial strikes and ultimately a mutiny in the army and he was deposed (12 Sep 1974). He died a year later at army headquarters.

**Hailsham, Quintin McGarel Hogg, 2nd Viscount**, also called **Baron Hailsham of St Marylebone** (1907–2001)
British politician. He became a Conservative MP in 1938 and succeeded to the viscountcy in 1950. He was First Lord of the Admiralty (1956–7), Minister of Education (1957), Lord President of the Council (1957–9 and 1960–4), Chairman of the **CONSERVATIVE PARTY** (1957–9), Minister for Science and Tech-

nology (1959–64), and Secretary of State for Education and Science (1964). In 1963 he renounced his peerage and re-entered the House of **COMMONS** in an unsuccessful bid to become Leader of the Conservative Party. In 1970 he was created a life peer and was twice Lord Chancellor (1970–4 and 1979–87), retiring in 1987.

**HAITI** official name **Republic of Haiti**

A republic in the West Indies. It occupies the western third of the island of Hispaniola in the Caribbean Sea. Hispaniola was discovered by **COLUMBUS** in 1492, and Haiti was created when the western third of the island was ceded to France in 1697. In 1791–1804 the Haitian Revolution, the only successful slave revolution in the New World, took place; it culminated in the independence of Haiti (1804). A white–coloured confrontation was superseded in Aug 1791 by a slave insurrection, prominent in which were **TOUSSAINT L'OUVERTURE** and Jean-Jacques **DESSALINES**. Maitland's British expeditionary force (1798) was expelled, the white and coloured armies overcome by 1800 and, in 1801, an independence constitution was sent to Paris. By then, France was under **NAPOLEON**'s control and he despatched an army to crush the black **JACOBINS**. Toussaint was captured by trickery but the 20,000-strong French force was defeated and withdrew (Nov 1803), leaving **DESSALINES** to proclaim himself Emperor of an independent Haiti (1804). Haiti had an Emperor until 1859, when it became a republic. From 1822 to 1844 Haiti was united with Santo Domingo (Dominican Republic); from 1915 to 1934 it was under US occupation; and from 1957 to 1986 the **DUVALIER** family had absolute power, their rule being enforced by a civilian militia known as the Tonton Macoute. Jean-Claude **DUVALIER** fled in 1986, leaving the country under military control. In 1990 Jean-Bertrand Aristide was elected President but he was deposed in a military coup in 1991; the **UN** imposed a trade embargo on Haiti which had a severe effect on the economy. Under military rule the Tonton Macoute were revived under the name *attachés*. Following US-led negotiations with the military leaders, Aristide was restored to power in 1994, but he lost the 1995 election and René Préval became President in 1996. Aristide was re-elected President in 2000 but faced with accusations of government corruption and mounting protests, he went into exile in Feb 2004 and was replaced by an interim president, Boniface Alexandre.

**Hajduks**
South Slav bandits who resisted the Ottoman Turks, made a distinctive contribution to the Serbs' struggle for independence from the **OTTOMAN EMPIRE** and, like the Greek **KLEPHTS**, were celebrated in folklore.

**Hájek, Jiří** (1913–93)
Czechoslovak academic, diplomat, politician and

dissident. A political scientist and social democrat, he was imprisoned in a **CONCENTRATION CAMP** for much of **WORLD WAR II**. On the left wing of his party, he joined with the communists in 1948 and soon began to rise: ambassador in London (1955–8); Deputy Foreign Minister (1958–62); Ambassador to the **UN** (1962–5); and Minister of Education (1965–8). In 1968 Alexander **DUBČEK** appointed him Foreign Minister, in which post he tried to act as broker between the USSR and the West and, after the Soviet invasion in Aug, tried to condemn the Soviet action by flying to the UN in New York. But he was summoned home and soon deprived of all his positions and privileges. In 1977 he was one of the founders of **CHARTER 77** and was frequently harassed thereafter. Thoroughly disillusioned by the communist subversion of socialism, he had the satisfaction of witnessing the so-called **VELVET REVOLUTION** in 1989.

### Hakim, al- (985–1021)
Fatimid Caliph of Egypt (996/1021). He succeeded his father, al-'Aziz, at the age of 11, and the early part of his reign was characterized by the persecution of the Christian and Jewish minorities and the destruction of thousands of churches, including the Holy Sepulchre in Jerusalem. His extreme Shiite policies in Muslim affairs aroused the antagonism of the predominantly Sunni population. From 1017, he became convinced of his own divinity, which was publicly preached by his followers Hamza and al-Darazi, and in the midst of a growing crisis the caliph disappeared in mysterious circumstances. His cult became the basis of the **DRUZE** religion which took root in the Lebanon, Syria and Galilee.

### Hakka
A people from north China who settled in southern China in the 12–13c and remained unassimilated. During the 18–19c they were involved in feuds over land, and many eventually migrated to other areas, including Taiwan, Hong Kong, Indonesia, Malaysia and Singapore.

### Haldane, Richard Burdon Haldane, 1st Viscount (1856–1928)
British politician, philosopher and lawyer. He entered parliament in 1879 as a Liberal. As Secretary of State for War (1905–12), he remodelled the army and founded the Territorials; British mobilization took place in 1914 on the basis of his plans. He was Lord Chancellor (1912–15) and again in 1924 following his move to the **LABOUR PARTY**. He also wrote on the philosophical aspects of relativity, and helped to found the London School of Economics (1895). ➤ **LIBERAL PARTY** (UK)

### Hale, Nathan (1755–76)
American Revolutionary War hero. Born in Coventry, Connecticut, he joined the Continental Army in 1775 and a year later volunteered for a dangerous information-gathering mission behind British lines on Long Island. He was captured and before being hanged as a spy reportedly stated, 'I regret that I have but one life to lose for my country.'

### Halidon Hill, Battle of (19 July 1333)
A battle between England and Scotland during the **SCOTTISH WAR OF INDEPENDENCE**. **EDWARD III** of England turned from besieging Berwick-upon-Tweed, and inflicted a massive defeat on the Scottish relief army. ➤ **DAVID II**

### Halifax, Charles Montagu, 1st Earl of (1661–1715)
English politician. A Whig, he became MP for Maldon (1688) and a Lord of the Treasury (1692), establishing the National Debt and the Bank of England (1694). As Chancellor of the Exchequer (1694–5), he introduced a new coinage. In 1697 he was First Lord of the Treasury and Leader of the House of **COMMONS**, but resigned when the **TORIES** came to power in 1699, and became Baron Halifax. On Queen **ANNE**'s death he was made a member of the Council of Regency, and on **GEORGE I**'s arrival (1714) became an earl and Prime Minister. He was also a patron of letters and a poet. ➤ **WHIGS**

### Halifax, Edward Frederick Lindley Wood, 1st Earl of (2nd creation) (1881–1959)
British politician. He became a Conservative MP (1910–25), and held a range of political posts before becoming (as Baron Irwin, 1925) Viceroy of India (1926–31). He was Foreign Secretary (1938–40) under Neville **CHAMBERLAIN**, whose '**APPEASEMENT**' policy he implemented, and Ambassador to the USA (1941–6). He was created an earl in 1944. ➤ **CONSERVATIVE PARTY** (UK)

### Halifax, George Savile, 1st Marquis of (1633–95)
English statesman. He was created viscount (1668) for his share in the **RESTORATION**, and in 1672 was made a marquis and Lord Privy Seal. On the accession of **JAMES VII AND II** (1685), he became President of the Council, but was dismissed soon after. He was one of the three Commissioners appointed to treat with William of Orange (later **WILLIAM III**), after he landed in England (1688). He gave allegiance to William and resumed the office of Lord Privy Seal; however, joining the opposition, he resigned his post in 1689.

### Hall, Ben(jamin) (1837–65)
Australian bushranger. The son of an English convict, he was arrested for armed robbery in 1862 but was acquitted. Rearrested on suspicion of involvement in the Eugowra gold robbery with Frank Gardiner, he was again released, but returned home to find his farm burnt down by the police. The most glamorous of the Australian bushrangers, between 1863 and 1865 he led a series of audacious raids, most notably on Bathurst and the Sydney–Melbourne road. After the shooting of two policemen, Hall went into hiding, but was betrayed and killed in a police ambush (May 1865).

### Hallstein Doctrine
Federal German foreign policy stance, named after the State Secretary for Foreign Affairs, Dr Walter Hallstein. Following **ADENAUER**'s visit to Moscow in 1955, which saw the opening of diplomatic relations between the USSR and the Federal Republic of Germany, the West German government declared that it would not maintain diplomatic relations with any state (other than the USSR) which maintained relations with East Germany. Relations were accordingly severed with Yugoslavia in 1957, but the Hallstein Doctrine fell into abeyance during the late 1960s and more particularly in the early 1970s with the inception of **OSTPOLITIK**.

**Halsey, William Frederick, Jr**, known as **Bull Halsey** (1884–1959)
US naval officer. He served in the White Fleet (1908–9), and held destroyer commands during **WORLD WAR I**. He distinguished himself throughout the **PACIFIC WAR** (1941–5), latterly as commander of the Third Fleet in the battles for the Caroline and Philippine islands, and for carrier attacks on the Japanese mainland. In Oct 1944 he defeated the Japanese navy at the Battle of **LEYTE GULF**. He retired as Fleet Admiral in 1949.

**Hamaguchi Osachi** (1870–1931)
Japanese politician. He began his career as a Finance Ministry bureaucrat and was elected to the lower house of the Diet in 1915. In 1927 he assumed the presidency of the Minseito, one of the two main political parties of the time, and became Prime Minister of a Minseito government in 1929. Renowned for his incorruptibility and dogged determination, he adopted a policy of domestic financial austerity and better relations with the USA and UK. He aroused the bitter hostility of the navy when, in 1930, he pushed through the Diet ratification of the London Naval Treaty, which placed restrictions on Japan's naval development. In assuming sole responsibility for the ratification of the treaty and ignoring the opinions of the navy, Hamaguchi was accused by both the military and ultra-nationalists of infringing the Emperor's prerogative of supreme command. In Nov 1930 he was shot by a right-wing fanatic and died the following year.

**Hamas** (*Harakat-al-Muqawima al-Islamiyya*, 'Islamic Resistance Movement')
A militant Islamic organization that opposes the attempted peaceful settlement between Israeli and **PLO** leaders. Founded in 1987 by the **MUSLIM BROTHERHOOD** together with some of the PLO's religious factions, it urges Palestinians to participate in **JIHAD** (holy war) in order to prevent the occupation of **PALESTINE** by non-Muslims, and it was responsible for inciting the first **INTIFADA** (1987–93). Following the first of the **OSLO ACCORDS** signed in 1993, its terrorist campaign to halt the peace process was intensified and included the use of suicide bombers.

**Hamburg**
The history of Germany's largest port began in 825 with the construction of the Mammaburg, a small moated castle between the Alster and Elbe rivers. After Lübeck, Hamburg was the premier Hanseatic town. Hamburg profited from the emigration of prosperous Dutch merchants to the Lower Elbe during the **EIGHTY YEARS' WAR**. Its fortifications spared it from the ravages of the **THIRTY YEARS' WAR**. The Treaty of Gottorp (1768) created it an Imperial town, freeing Hamburg from the titular rule of Denmark which had existed since 1459. It was annexed by Napoleon's French Empire in 1810 but became a free city again in 1815.

**Hamilton, Alexander** (1755–1804)
US politician. Educated at King's (now Columbia) College, New York, he fought in the **AMERICAN REVOLUTION**, becoming George **WASHINGTON**'s aide-de-camp (1777–81). After the war, he studied law, and in 1782 was returned to **CONGRESS**. He was instru-

mental in the movement to establish the USA in its present political form. As Secretary of the Treasury (1789–95), his policy of funding a national debt and assuming the state debts restored the country's finances to a firm footing. He was the real founder and a leader of the **FEDERALIST PARTY** until his death. His successful effort to thwart the ambition of his rival, Aaron **BURR**, led to a duel in Weekauken, New Jersey, in which Hamilton was killed.

**Hamilton, James, 1st Duke of** (1606–49)
Scottish royalist commander during the **ENGLISH CIVIL WARS**. He fought during the **THIRTY YEARS' WAR**, leading an army in support of **GUSTAV II ADOLF** (1631–2), and later played a conspicuous part in the contest between **CHARLES I** and the **COVENANTERS**. Created duke in 1643, he led a Scottish army into England (1643), but was defeated by Oliver **CROMWELL** at the Battle of **PRESTON**, and beheaded.

**Hammarskjöld, Dag Hjalmar Agne Carl** (1905–61)
Swedish politician. He was the son of Hjalmar Hammarskjöld, Conservative Prime Minister of Sweden during the early years of **WORLD WAR I**. He became in 1933 an assistant professor at the University of Stockholm, in 1935 State Secretary of Finance, and from 1941 to 1948 was Chairman of the Bank of Sweden. He was a cabinet minister from 1951 to 1953, when he became Secretary-General of the **UN**. Hammarskjöld, who once described himself as 'the curator of the secrets of 82 nations', played a leading part in the setting up of the UN Emergency Force in Sinai and Gaza in 1956, in conciliatory moves aimed at securing peace and stability in the Middle East in 1957–8 and in sending observers to Lebanon in 1958. He was awarded the **NOBEL PEACE PRIZE** in 1961, after his death in an air crash near Ndola in Zambia while he was attempting to resolve the Congo crisis.

**Hammer, Armand** (1898–1991)
US financier and philanthropist. Using his Russian origins and business contacts, he became an intermediary between five Soviet general-secretaries and US presidents from Franklin D **ROOSEVELT** to Richard **NIXON**. With **STALIN**'s accession to power, Hammer left Russia, taking with him many Russian paintings which he used to found the Hammer Galleries in New York City. Retiring to Los Angeles after building a second fortune, in 1961 he bought Occidental Petroleum, a company near bankruptcy, and by 1965 had made it a major force in the oil industry. Convicted of making illegal contributions to Nixon's re-election fund, he was put on a year's probation and fined US\$3,000. President George H W **BUSH** pardoned him in 1989.

**Hampden, John** (1594–1643)
English parliamentarian and patriot. He became a lawyer, and in 1621 an MP. His opposition to **CHARLES I**'s financial measures led to his imprisonment (1627–8), and in 1634 he became famous for refusing to pay Charles's imposed levy for outfitting the navy ('ship money'). A member of both the **SHORT PARLIAMENT** and the **LONG PARLIAMENT**, he was one of the five members whose attempted seizure by Charles (1642) precipitated the **ENGLISH CIVIL WARS**. He fought for the Parliamentary Army at

Edgehill and Reading, but was killed at Thame.

## Hampi

The site of the former Hindu capital of Vijayanagar, near the south-western Indian village of Hampi. The city was founded in the 14c, and remained the centre of a vast and powerful Hindu empire until 1565, when it was sacked. It remains an important religious and tourist centre, and is a World Heritage Site.

## Hampton Roads Conference (3 Feb 1865)

An unsuccessful peace conference organized by President Abraham LINCOLN's wartime adviser, Francis Preston Blair, which was intended to mark a negotiated end to the AMERICAN CIVIL WAR. The talks between the President, the Secretary of State William H SEWARD, and three Confederate spokesmen took place on a steamer moored at Hampton Roads, Virginia. They failed because the Union rejected the Confederacy's plea to be treated as a sovereign state, offering instead a settlement that demanded reunion, the abolition of SLAVERY and the disbandment of Confederate troops; however, the Confederacy would accept nothing short of independence. The war ended two months later at APPOMATTOX COURT HOUSE.

## Hancock, John (1737–93)

American revolutionary and political leader. He graduated from Harvard and became a merchant in Boston. He opposed the STAMP ACT, and in 1768 his sloop *Liberty* was seized by the British for smuggling. As President of the CONTINENTAL CONGRESS (1775–7) he was the first to sign the DECLARATION OF INDEPENDENCE, writing his name in a bold hand. He remained in the Congress until 1780, when he was elected Governor of Massachusetts.

## Han Dynasties ► CHINESE DYNASTIES PRE-1000AD

## Hanlin Academy

A central government institution in imperial China whose members lectured to the emperor on the CONFUCIAN CLASSICS, prepared imperial edicts and officiated at ritual ceremonies. Originating in the 8c as a loosely organized group of littérateurs, it acquired status as a regular central government agency during the YUAN DYNASTY (1264–1368). Only the top metropolitan degree-holders were appointed, and so membership of the Hanlin Academy often brought with it important official posts. A State Historiographer's Office within the Academy prepared a chronicle of each reign, made public after the reigning emperor's death.

## Hanna, Mark, also known as Marcus Alonzo Hanna (1837–1904)

US businessman and politician. He served in the Union Army (1864) and, starting in partnership with his father in coal and iron, made the most of the great post-war expansion. He helped organize the Union National Bank, bought the Cleveland Opera House, invested in Cleveland street-railways, and moved into politics to protect business interests, backing Ohio candidates for the presidency, both successfully (James A GARFIELD, 1880; William MCKINLEY, 1896) and unsuccessfully (John Sherman, 1888). He transformed local and state Republican boss systems into a massively organized national fighting force for

the 1896 election, carrying campaign finance to unprecedented lengths. He refused cabinet office, but accepted a seat in the SENATE in 1897.

## Hannes Pétursson Hafstein ► HAFSTEIN, HANNES PÉTURSSON

## Hanover, House of

### HOUSE OF HANOVER

| Regnal Dates | Name |
|---|---|
| 1714/27 | George I |
| 1727/60 | George II |
| 1760/1820 | George III |
| 1820/30 | George IV |
| 1830/7 | William IV |
| 1837/1901 | Victoria |

A branch of the Guelf Dynasty, more specifically the Brunswick-Lüneburg line which, in 1692, acquired the Electoral dignity for Hanover. On the death of Queen ANNE in 1714, the Elector Georg Ludwig, who was descended through the female line from Princess Elizabeth, the sister of CHARLES I, became King of Great Britain and Ireland, as GEORGE I, thus securing the Protestant succession. Monarchs from the House of Hanover ruled their British and German dominions in personal union until the death of WILLIAM IV in 1837. Thereupon, the British crown went to Queen VICTORIA who was, however, disqualified under the SALIC LAW from succession in Germany. In consequence, her uncle, the Duke of Cumberland, became King of Hanover under the name of Ernest Augustus. While the family name of the British dynasty changed to SAXE-COBURG-GOTHA when Victoria married Prince ALBERT in 1840, the Hanoverians continued to rule their native country until 1866, when it was annexed by Prussia for siding with Austria in the preceding war. A descendant of the last King of Hanover succeeded to the Duchy of Brunswick in 1913, after the Brunswick-Wolfenbüttel line had become extinct, but was toppled by the revolution of 1918.

## Hanover, State of

Originally the principality of Brunswick-Calenberg-Göttingen, created in 1638, the state took its name from its largest city, Hanover. In 1692 Duke Ernest Augustus was made an elector by Emperor LEOPOLD I. It was merged with the Duchy of Lüneburg in 1705. Ernest Augustus married SOPHIA ALEXEEVNA of the Palatinate, granddaughter of JAMES VI AND I of Britain. In 1714, Sophia's son, George Louis, became GEORGE I of Britain, after which the electorate was ruled by a minister of the British monarch. Britain lost claim to the electorate, which recognized only male rulers, when VICTORIA came to the British throne (1837).

## Hanseatic League

A late medieval association of 150 north German towns, including Bremen, Hamburg and Lübeck. It had its origins in the practice of early medieval merchants from individual towns travelling together for safety. The development of the Hansa, as it was also known, was given a great impetus by German colonization of Eastern Europe. It facilitated the exchange of raw materials from the east and manufactured goods from the west, dominated trade from the Atlantic to the Baltic, and fought successful wars against neighbours between 1350 and 1450. It declined because of internal divisions, English and Dutch competition, and the growth of princely power.

## Hansson, Per Albin (1885–1946)

Swedish politician. He rose to prominence in the Social Democratic youth movement and was elected to parliament in 1918. He served as Minister of Defence in Social Democrat administrations in 1918–25 under Hjalmar **BRANTING**, whom he succeeded as leader of the party (1925). Hansson became Prime Minister of a minority Social Democrat government in 1932, but secured the support of the Agrarians in the so-called 'cow deal' the following year and, apart for a brief period in 1936, was in office from then until his death. He presided over the foundation of the modern welfare state in Sweden and guided his country's successful policy of neutrality during **WORLD WAR II**.

## Hara Kei (1856–1921)

Japanese politician. From a **SAMURAI** family, he worked as a newspaper editor before joining the Ministry of Foreign Affairs (1882). He resigned from government service to join the **SEIYUKAI**, a political party formed in 1900, and shortly afterwards gained a seat in the lower Diet. As Home Minister in various nonparty cabinets (1906–8, 1911–12 and 1913–14) and leader of the *Seiyukai*, Hara was able to advance the party's interests by appointing pro-Seiyukai provincial governors and promoting regional economic development. As the head of the majority party in the Diet, he became Prime Minister in 1918 and presided over the first party cabinet since the establishment of the **MEIJI CONSTITUTION**. He proved to be a conservative premier, however, moving cautiously on political and social reform. Although he expanded the electorate by lowering tax qualifications, he did not endorse the principle of universal manhood suffrage. He was assassinated by an ultra-nationalist fanatic.

## Harald III Sigurdsson ➤ HARALD HARDRADA

## Harald Hardrada (1015–66)

King of Norway (1045/66). The half-brother of **OLAF II** (St Olaf), he was present at the Battle of Stiklestad in 1030 where St Olaf was killed, and sought refuge in Kiev at the court of his kinsman, Prince Jaroslav the Wise, together with his nephew, **MAGNUS I, THE GOOD**. He had a lurid career as a Viking mercenary with the Varangian Guard in Constantinople, and returned to Norway in 1045 to demand, and receive, a half-share in the kingdom from his nephew. He became sole king on his nephew's death in 1047, and earned the nickname Hardrada ('Hard-Ruler'). After long and unrelenting wars against King **SVEIN II ULFSSON** of Denmark, he invaded England in 1066 to claim the throne after the death of **EDWARD THE CONFESSOR**, but was defeated and killed by **HAROLD II** at Stamford Bridge.

## Hardaknut (1018–42)

King of Denmark (1035/42) and of England (1040/2). He was the son of **CANUTE** and Emma (the widow of King **ETHELRED THE UNREADY**), and was Canute's only legitimate heir. He inherited Denmark on his father's death in 1035, but was unable to come to England immediately to claim the throne there. The English elected his half-brother, **HAROLD I, HAREFOOT** regent in his stead, and then confirmed Harold as King in 1037. Hardaknut mounted an expedition to invade England to claim the crown, but Harold died in Mar 1040, before he arrived. Hardaknut was thereupon elected King, and promptly punished the English by imposing a savage fleet-tax to pay for his expedition. His reign was universally disliked; he died of convulsions at a drinking party.

## Hardenberg, Karl August, Prince von (1750–1822)

Prussian politician. After holding appointments in Hanover, Brunswick, Ansbach and Bayreuth, he became a Prussian minister in 1791, and Chief Minister in 1803. In 1806, under **NAPOLEON I**'s influence, he was dismissed, but later appointed Chancellor and Chief Minister (1810–22). In the war of liberation he played a prominent part, and after the Treaty of Paris (1814) was made a prince. He reorganized the Council of State (1817), of which he was appointed President, and continued the work of von **STEIN**, carrying out many reforms in the army, social structure, culture and education. ➤ **PARIS, TREATIES OF; PRUSSIA**

## Hardie, (James) Keir (1856–1915)

British politician. He worked in the mines between the ages of seven and 24, and was victimized as the miners' champion. He became a journalist and the first Labour MP, entering parliament for East Ham in 1892. He founded and edited *The Labour Leader*, and was Chairman of the **INDEPENDENT LABOUR PARTY** (founded 1893). Instrumental in the establishment of the Labour Representation Committee, Hardie served as Chairman of the **LABOUR PARTY** (1906–8). His strong pacifism led to his becoming isolated within the party, particularly once **WORLD WAR I** had broken out.

## Harding, Warren G(amaliel) (1865–1923)

US politician and 29th President. He became a successful journalist, gained a seat in the Ohio State Senate (1899) and the lieutenant-governorship (1902), after which he returned to journalism until 1914, when he was elected to the US Senate. Emerging as a power in the **REPUBLICAN PARTY**, he won its nomination. As President (1921–3), he campaigned against US membership of the **LEAGUE OF NATIONS**. ➤ **PROHIBITION; TEAPOT DOME SCANDAL**

## Hardinge, Henry Hardinge, 1st Viscount (1785–1856)

British soldier and colonial administrator. After service in the **PENINSULAR WAR**, he became an MP (1820–44) and Secretary of War (1828–30 and 1841–4). In 1844 he was appointed Governor-General of India, and after the first Sikh War was created a viscount (1846). Returning in 1848, he succeeded **WELLINGTON** as Commander-in-Chief of the British Army (1852), but was demoted following the disasters early in the **CRIMEAN WAR** (1854–6). ➤ **SIKH WARS**

## harijan

The name (Hindi, 'children of God'), proposed by M K **GANDHI** for the untouchables. ➤ **CASTE**

## Harley, Robert, 1st Earl of Oxford (1661–1724)

British politician. He became a lawyer, and a Whig MP in 1689. In 1701 he was elected Speaker, and in 1704 became Secretary of State. Shortly after, he became sympathetic to the **TORIES**, and from 1708 worked to undermine the power of the **WHIGS**. In 1710 **GODOL-PHIN** was dismissed, and Harley made Chancellor of the Exchequer, head of the government, and (1711) Earl of Oxford and Lord High Treasurer. The principal Act of his administration was the Peace of **UTRECHT** (1713). In 1714 he was dismissed, and after the Hanoverian succession spent two years in prison. He then retired from politics. ➤ **HANOVER, HOUSE OF**

**Harold I, Harefoot** (d.1040)
King of England (1037/40). He was the younger son of **CANUTE** and his English mistress, Ælfgifu of Northampton. On Canute's death, the English elected Harold regent for his half-brother **HARDAK-NUT**, King of Denmark, the legitimate heir to the throne, who could not leave Denmark to claim the crown. In 1037 Harold was elected King; he died (Mar 1040) just as Hardaknut was poised to invade England to claim back the throne.

**Harold II** (c.1022–1066)
Last Anglo-Saxon King of England (1066). The second son of Earl Godwin, by 1045 Harold was Earl of East Anglia, and in 1053 succeeded to his father's earldom of Wessex, becoming the right hand of **ED-WARD THE CONFESSOR**. After Edward's death (Jan 1066), Harold, his nominee, was crowned as King. He defeated his brother **TOSTIG** and **HARALD HARD-RADA** , King of Norway, at Stamford Bridge, Yorkshire (Sep 1066), but Duke William of Normandy (**WIL-LIAM I, THE CONQUEROR**) then invaded England, and defeated him at the Battle of **HASTINGS** (14 Oct 1066), where he died, shot through the eye with an arrow.

**Harpers Ferry Raid** (1859)
An attack on the federal arsenal in Virginia, led by abolitionist John **BROWN**, designed to launch a slave insurrection. The raiders were captured, and Brown was executed amidst great publicity. ➤ **ABOLITION-ISM**

**Harriman, William Averell** (1891–1986)
US politician and diplomat. Educated at Yale, he became Ambassador to the USSR (1943) and to Britain (1946), Secretary of Commerce (1946–8), and special assistant to President **TRUMAN** (1950–1), helping to organize **NATO**. He was Director of the Mutual Security Agency (1951–3), Governor of New York (1955–9), ambassador-at-large (1961 and 1965–8) and US representative at the Vietnam peace talks in Paris (1968). He negotiated the partial **NUCLEAR TEST-BAN TREATY** between the USA and USSR in 1963, and continued to visit the USSR on behalf of the government, making his last visit there at the age of 91. ➤ **VIETNAM WAR**

**Harris, Sir Arthur Travers**, nicknamed **Bomber Harris** (1892–1984)
English air force officer. Born in Cheltenham, Gloucestershire, he emigrated to Rhodesia in 1910. He served with the 1st Rhodesian Regiment in South West Africa (1914–15) and with the Royal Flying Corps in France and in defence of London. On the formation of the Royal Air Force (Apr 1918), he received a permanent commission. He commanded No 4 Group Bomber Command (1937–8) and RAF Palestine and Transjordan (1938–9). He was Deputy Chief of Air Staff (1940–1) and head of the RAF Delegation in the USA (1941). As Commander-in-Chief Bomber Command RAF (1942–5), he organized mass bombing raids on German cities. This 'area bombing' earned him his nickname, but he did not break German morale.

**Harrison, Benjamin** (1833–1901)
US politician and 23rd President. In 1854 he became a lawyer in Indianapolis, and during the **AMERICAN CIVIL WAR** fought in **SHERMAN**'s Atlanta campaign. He was elected US Senator from Indiana in 1881. In 1888 he defeated Grover **CLEVELAND** on the free-trade issue, and was President from 1889 to 1893. Failing to gain re-election, he returned to his law practice in Indianapolis, Indiana, where he died.

**Harrison, William Henry** (1773–1841)
US general and 9th President. He fought against the **NATIVE AMERICANS**, and when Indiana Territory was formed (1800) he was appointed Governor, serving for 12 years. He tried to avoid further **INDIAN WARS**, but was compelled to quell **TECUMSEH**'s uprising, which ended in the Battle of **TIPPECANOE** (1811). In the **WAR OF 1812** he defeated the British in the Battle of the **THAMES** (1813). In 1816 he was elected to the **HOUSE OF REPRESENTATIVES**, and in 1824 he became a Senator. With the slogan 'Tippecanoe and Tylertoo', he was elected to the presidency in 1840, but died in Washington a month after his inauguration. His grandson was Benjamin **HARRISON**.

**Harris Treaty** ➤ **EDO, TREATY OF**

**Hartford Convention** (1814–15)
A gathering at Hartford, Connecticut, of delegates from the New England states to oppose the **WAR OF 1812** and to propose changes in the **US CONSTITU-TION**. The Treaty of **GHENT**, ending the war, and US victory at New Orleans, discredited both the Convention and the **FEDERALIST PARTY**, with which the Convention was associated.

**Hartling, Poul** (1914–99)
Danish politician. He represented the Liberal Party (*Venstre*) and was Danish Foreign Minister (1968–71) and Prime Minister (1973–5). From 1978 to 1985 he was the **UN** High Commissioner for Refugees.

**Harvester Judgement** (1907)
A landmark decision of the Australian Conciliation and Arbitration Court made by Justice H B **HIGGINS** under the Excise Tariff Act (1906), which allowed firms paying fair wages to claim exemption from excise duty. Giving judgement on the claim of the harvester manufacturer, H V Mackay, Higgins calculated the fair wage for an unskilled labourer on the basis of need, establishing the principle of the minimum or family wage tied to the cost of living. It remained a central feature of the Australian industrial system until the end of the 1960s.

**Haryana**
The northern Indian state carved out of the erstwhile state of Punjab in 1966. Haryana's population is largely Hindi-speaking. There remain disputes between Punjab and Haryana over the transfer of Chandigarh, their joint capital, to Punjab, and the transfer, in return, of Hindi-speaking areas to Haryana. Haryana,

like Punjab, is a predominantly agricultural state, though industries have grown up in the last few decades. It has sites like Kurukshetra and **PANIPAT** where historic battles have been fought. Politics in Haryana is dominated dualistically by the Congress Party and the opposition **LOK DAL** which, under various guises, allies from time to time with the BJP and Congress fragments.

### Haselrig, Sir Arthur (d.1661)
English parliamentarian. In 1640 he sat in the **LONG PARLIAMENT** and **SHORT PARLIAMENT** for his native county, Leicestershire, and he was one of the five members whose attempted seizure by **CHARLES I** in 1642 precipitated the **ENGLISH CIVIL WARS**. He commanded a parliamentary regiment, and in 1647 became Governor of Newcastle. After the **RESTORATION**, he was imprisoned and died in the Tower of London.

### Hasluck, Sir Paul Meernaa Caedwalla (1905–93)
Australian politician and historian. A journalist on the *West Australian* (1922–38), he was lecturer in history at the University of Western Australia (1939–40). Seconded during **WORLD WAR II** to the Australian Department of External Affairs, he became head of the Australian mission to the United Nations, returning to the university in 1948. He entered federal politics in 1949, and was successively Minister for Territories (1951–63), for Defence (1963–4) and for External Affairs (1964–9). He was Governor-General of Australia (1969–74).

### Hassan II (1929–99)
King of Morocco (1961/99). Educated in France, Crown Prince Hassan served his father as head of the army and, on his accession as King in 1961, also became Prime Minister. He suspended parliament and established a royal dictatorship in 1965 after riots in Casablanca. Despite constitutional reforms in 1970 and 1972, he retained supreme religious and political authority. His forces occupied Spanish (Western) Sahara in 1957. He mobilized a large army to check the incursion of **POLISARIO** guerrillas across his western Saharan frontier from 1976 to 1988. Unrest in the larger towns led Hassan to appoint a coalition 'government of national unity' under a civilian Prime Minister in 1984. He was succeeded by his son, Muhammad VI. ► **WESTERN SAHARA**

### Hastings, Battle of (14 Oct 1066)
The most decisive battle fought on English soil, which led to the successful **NORMAN CONQUEST** of England. Norman cavalry overcame the resolute defence of the Anglo-Saxon army fighting on foot, and **HAROLD II**'s death in battle cleared the way for Duke William of **NORMANDY**'s coronation. Not until 1092 (the capture of Carlisle) were the **NORMANS** masters of all England. ► **WILLIAM I, THE CONQUEROR**

### Hastings, Warren (1732–1818)
British colonial administrator. Educated at Westminster, he joined the British **EAST INDIA COMPANY** in 1750, and by 1774 was Governor-General of Bengal. Carrying out several reforms, he made the Company's power paramount in many parts of India. However, wars (1778–84) interfered with trade, and damaged his reputation, and on his return to England in 1784 he was charged with corruption. After a

seven-year trial, he was acquitted. The Company made provision for his declining years, which he spent as a country gentleman in Worcestershire, England.

### Ha-Tinh Uprising ► NGHE-AN/HA-TINH UPRISINGS

### Hatoyama Ichiro (1883–1959)
Japanese politician. He was first elected to the Diet in 1915 and became a prominent leader of the **SEIYUKAI** in the 1930s. As Education Minister (1931–4), he clamped down hard on liberal university teachers who questioned the nature of the Japanese state. In 1946 he organized the conservative Japan Liberal Party (*Nihon Jiyuto*), which gained a victory in the elections of that year. On the verge of becoming Prime Minister, he was purged from official life by the US occupation authorities for his role in supporting the military cabinets of the 1930s. Although he was rehabilitated in 1951, he found that leadership of the Liberal Party was now firmly in the hands of **YOSHIDA SHIGERU**. He formed a new conservative party, the Japan Democratic Party (*Nihon Minshuto*), which successfully ousted Yoshida from power (Dec 1954), when Hatoyama became Premier. During Hatoyama's premiership (1954–6), relations with the USSR were normalized, thus paving the way for Japan's entry into the UN in 1956, and the two conservative parties were merged to form the **LIBERAL DEMOCRATIC PARTY** (LDP).

### Hat Party (Sweden) ► AGE OF LIBERTY

### Hatt-i Humayun (1 Feb 1856)
The second edict of reform decreed in Istanbul as a result of pressure from the Western powers (Britain, France and Austria). The object of the edict was essentially to insist on internal reforms in Turkey to protect Christian subjects of the Ottomans, and hence to bolster the effect of the peace treaty after the **CRIMEAN WAR** by depriving Russia of pretexts for interfering in the internal affairs of the **OTTOMAN EMPIRE**.

### Haughey, Charles James (1925– )
Irish politician. He became a **FIANNA FÁIL** MP in 1957. From 1961 he held posts in the Ministries of Justice, Agriculture, and Finance, but he was dismissed in 1970 after a quarrel with the Prime Minister, Jack **LYNCH**. He was subsequently tried and acquitted on a charge of conspiracy to import arms illegally. After two years as Minister of Health and Social Welfare, he succeeded Lynch as Premier (1979–81), was in power again for a nine-month period in 1982, and again from 1987 to 1992, after defeating Garrett **FITZGERALD** in the 1987 elections. He resigned after allegations of illegal telephone-tapping led his Progressive Democrat coalition allies to withdraw their support.

### Hausa ► FULANI EMIRATES

### Haussmann, Georges Eugène, Baron (1809–91)
French financier and town planner. He entered public service, and under **NAPOLEON III** became prefect of the Seine (1853), improving Paris by widening streets, laying out boulevards and parks, and building bridges. He was made a baron and senator, and was elected to the Chamber of Deputies in 1881.

**Havel, Václav** (1936–)
Czechoslovak dramatist and reluctant but distinguished politician. Educated at the Academy of Dramatic Art in his native Prague, he began work in the theatre as a stagehand and became resident writer for the Prague 'Theatre on the Balustrade' (1960–9). Having been chairman of the Writers' Union during the **PRAGUE SPRING**, his work was then judged subversive. He was one of the founders of **CHARTER 77** in 1977 and was subsequently imprisoned several times, his plays only being performed abroad. During the so-called **VELVET REVOLUTION** in Dec 1989, which ended **COMMUNISM** in Czechoslovakia, he was elected President by direct popular vote. Although he subsequently opposed the division of Czechoslovakia into two separate states, he nevertheless stood for the presidency of the Czech Republic, a post he held from 1993 to 2003.

**Havelock, Sir Henry** (1795–1857)
British soldier. A lawyer by training, he joined the army a month after the Battle of **WATERLOO**, and went out to India in 1823. He distinguished himself in the Afghan and **SIKH WARS**, and in 1856 commanded a division in Persia. On the outbreak of the **INDIAN UPRISING** (1857–8), he organized a column of 1,000 Highlanders and others at Allahabad with which to relieve Cawnpore and Lucknow, engaged and broke the rebels at Fatehpur, and, driving them before him, entered Cawnpore. Next, crossing the Ganges, he fought eight victorious battles, but through sickness in his little army had to retire to Cawnpore. In Sep **OUTRAM** arrived with reinforcements, and Havelock again advanced, Outram waiving his superior rank, and serving under Havelock as a volunteer. The relieving force fought their way to the Residency, where they in turn were besieged by the determined rebel forces until Nov, when Sir Colin Campbell forced his way to their rescue. A week after the relief, Havelock died of dysentery. ► **AFGHAN WARS**; **LUCKNOW, SIEGE OF**

**Havlícek Borovský, Karel** (1821–56)
Czech political journalist. In the early days of the 1848 revolt in Prague, he established *National News*, a newspaper devoted to the nationalist cause. It was closed down by the Habsburg authorities in 1849 but he started another, *The Slav*, in 1850. Late in 1851 he was arrested and exiled to Austria, where he could not undertake political journalism. Released in 1855, he returned home to find his wife dead; he died himself a year later. His contemporary impact was slight, but he served as a model to others who came after him.

**Haw-Haw, Lord** ► **JOYCE, WILLIAM**

**Hawke, Bob (Robert James Lee)** (1929–)
Australian politician. He worked for the **AUSTRALIAN COUNCIL OF TRADE UNIONS** for over 20 years, before becoming an MP in 1980. His **AUSTRALIAN LABOR PARTY** defeated the **LIBERAL PARTY OF AUSTRALIA** in the 1983 election, only one month after adopting him as leader. The most successful Labor Prime Minister in Australian history, he won four general elections, the last in 1990. He was challenged and replaced by Paul Keating in 1981.

**Hawke, Edward Hawke, 1st Baron** (1705–81)
British admiral. As a young commander he fought against the French and Spanish, for which he was knighted (1747). His major victory was against the French at Quiberon Bay (1759), which caused the collapse of their invasion plans. He also became an MP (1747), First Lord of the Admiralty (1766–71) and a baron (1776).

**Hawkyns, Sir John** (1532–95)
British sailor. He was the first Englishman to traffic in slaves (1562) between West Africa and the West Indies, but on his third expedition his fleet was destroyed by the Spanish (1567). He became navy treasurer (1573), and was knighted for his services against the Spanish **ARMADA** in 1588. In 1595, with his kinsman **DRAKE**, he commanded an expedition to the Spanish Main, but died at Puerto Rico.

**Hawley–Smoot Tariff Act** (17 June 1930)
US legislation which imposed tariffs on imported goods, including farm products and industrial items, in a misguided attempt by President **HOOVER** to help US farmers. As a result, many European exports were excluded from the US market, and before long retaliatory tariffs had been imposed on US exports, stifling the struggling world trade even further.

**Hay, John Milton** (1838–1905)
US politician and writer. Educated at Brown University, he became a lawyer, and private secretary to President **LINCOLN**. After Lincoln's death (1865), he served as a diplomat in Paris, Vienna and Madrid. He returned to the USA and to journalism in 1870, and went on to write poetry, fiction and a multi-volume biography of Lincoln. He became Assistant Secretary of State (1879), Ambassador to Britain (1897) and Secretary of State (1898), serving under Presidents **MCKINLEY** and **ROOSEVELT**. ► **OPEN DOOR POLICY**

**Haya de la Torre, Víctor Raúl** (1895–1979)
Peruvian politician and political thinker. Educated in Lima, he was the founder (1924) of APRA (*Alianza Popular Revolucionaria Americana*), known as the Aprista Party, the voice of radical dissent in Peru. Imprisoned (1931–3) after standing against Colonel Luis Sánchez Cerro, he was released on the latter's assassination (1933), and went into hiding (1934–45). The Aprista Party changed its name to the *Partido del Pueblo* ('People's Party') in 1945, and supported the successful candidate, José Luis Bustamante; control of the government, however, lay in Haya's hands. On Bustamante's overthrow (1948), Haya sought refuge in the Colombian Embassy in Lima and later (1954) left for Mexico. He returned to Peru when constitutional government was restored (1957) and fought the bitter 1962 election campaign which, after army intervention, he lost to Fernando **BELAÚNDE** Terry. Haya was instrumental in drafting the constitution of 1979 restoring parliamentary democracy, but died before the People's Party finally gained power in 1985 under Alan **GARCÍA PÉREZ**.

**Hayashi Razan** (1583–1657)
Japanese Confucian scholar and ideologist. He served as adviser to the **TOKUGAWA SHOGUNATE**. As the promoter of Neo-Confucianism, with its emphasis on loyalty and its assumption that a hierarchical and harmonious polity reflected the natural order, Hayashi provided ideological support for the shogunate and the political ascendancy of the warrior class.

**Hay-Bunau-Varilla Treaty** (1903)
An agreement between the USA and Panama creating the Panama Canal Zone under US sovereignty, and giving the USA the right to build and operate the Canal, in return for a US$10 million fee and US$250,000 annual rent. The chief parties involved were US Secretary of State John **HAY**, and Philippe **BUNAU-VARILLA**, representing Panama. ► **HAY-HERRAN TREATY**

**Hayden, Bill (William George)** (1933–)
Australian politician. He entered the federal parliament in 1961, serving under Gough **WHITLAM** whom he replaced as **AUSTRALIAN LABOR PARTY** leader in 1977. In 1983 he surrendered the leadership to the more charismatic Bob **HAWKE** and was Foreign Minister in his government (1983–8). From 1989 to 1996 he was Governor-General of Australia.

**Hayek, Friedrich August von** (1899–1992)
Austrian economist. He studied law, economics and psychology in Vienna. With Ludwig von Mises he founded the Austrian Institute of Economic Research in 1927; their 'Austrian School' favoured *laisser faire* and minimal government using monetary policy to smooth out the business cycle. At the London School of Economics from 1931, he became a British citizen in 1938. He then held a position in the University of Chicago (1950–62) and at the University of Freiburg, Germany, from 1968. He won the Nobel prize for economics in 1974. Although his early works were influential, *The Pure Theory of Capital* (1941) was published too late to reverse the growing influence of J M **KEYNES**. His hostility to socialism and conviction that free politics could only be sustained by free markets attracted renewed attention in the 1980s and 1990s, influencing the British Prime Minister Margaret **THATCHER** and the US presidents Ronald **REAGAN** and George W **BUSH**.

**Hayes, Rutherford B(irchard)** (1822–93)
US politician and 19th President. He practised law in Cincinnati (1849–61), served in the **AMERICAN CIVIL WAR**, entered **CONGRESS** (1865–7) as a Republican, and was elected Governor of Ohio three times (1867, 1869, 1875). The contested 1876 presidential election between Hayes and Samuel J Tilden was finally resolved in Hayes's favour, with concessions made to the Southern states in the Compromise of 1877. Hayes supported civil service reform but was unsuccessful in his efforts to prevent freer coinage of silver. ► **REPUBLICAN PARTY**

**Hay-Herrán Treaty** (1903)
An agreement between the USA and Colombia giving the USA the right to build a canal across the isthmus of Panama, then part of Colombia. Its rejection by the Colombian Senate led to the Panamanian revolt for independence, with US sponsorship. The parties involved were US Secretary of State John **HAY**, and Tomás Herrán, Colombian chargé d'affaires based in Washington. ► **HAY-BUNAU-VARILLA TREATY**

**Haykal, Muhammad Hasanayn** (1923–)
Egyptian journalist and author. Early in his career he covered the 1948 War and the **KOREAN WAR**. He had contacts with the **FREE OFFICERS** before the 1952 coup, and his subsequent career has spanned the period from Gamal Abd al-**NASSER**'s presidency to that of Hosni **MUBARAK**. The most influential journalist of his generation, Haykal became editor of the respected Cairo newspaper, *al-Ahram*, in 1957, writing on subjects including Nasser's relations with world leaders such as Nikita **KHRUSHCHEV** and Lyndon B **JOHNSON**, in addition to other Arab heads of state. He also had contacts with guerrilla leaders, including Che **GUEVARA**. Removed from the editorship in 1974 following his criticism of Anwar **SADAT**'s conduct of the **YOM KIPPUR WAR**, Haykal was briefly held under arrest in 1981 when Sadat, ostensibly to deal with the religious extremism of the **MUSLIM BROTHERHOOD**, extended his purge to include journalists and opposition party leaders.

**Haymarket Square Riot** (4 May 1886)
A clash between police and demonstrators at a labour union rally in Chicago, at which a bomb exploded, killing seven police and injuring some 70 others. Four persons were executed by the state of Illinois for their involvement. Violent labour disputes, fuelled by anarchist elements within the movement and culminating in the riot, led to a loss of public support for the union movement.

**Hay-Pauncefote Treaties** (1900–1)
Agreements between the USA and Britain that ended the British claim to joint rights to build and operate a canal across Central America. The chief parties involved were US Secretary of State John **HAY** and British Ambassador Lord Pauncefote.

**Haywood, William Dudley**, known as **Big Bill** (1869–1928)
US labour leader. After working as a miner, homesteader and cowboy, he joined the Western Federation of Miners in 1896, and quickly achieved prominence. In 1905 he helped to found the **INDUSTRIAL WORKERS OF THE WORLD** (IWW), which was committed to revolutionary labour politics and to the organization of all workers in one big union. An active socialist, he was convicted of sedition in 1917 for his opposition to **WORLD WAR I**. He fled from the USA in 1921, and took refuge in the USSR, dying in Moscow.

**Hearst, William Randolph** (1863–1951)
US newspaper publisher. He took over the *San Francisco Examiner* in 1887 from his father. Invading the territory of Joseph Pulitzer, he acquired the *New York Morning Journal* (1895), launching the *Evening Journal* a year later. He revolutionized journalism with the introduction of banner headlines, lavish illustrations and other sensational methods, nicknamed by critics 'the yellow press', and designed to win readers away from Pulitzer's *New York World*. In 1897–8 he published exaggerated and fabricated reports on the Cuban struggle for independence, which boosted circulation enormously and incidentally helped bring about the **SPANISH-AMERICAN WAR**. He made himself the head of a national chain of newspapers and periodicals which included the *Chicago Examiner, Boston American, Cosmopolitan* and *Harper's Bazaar*. He was a member of the **HOUSE OF REPRESENTATIVES** (1903–7), but failed to become mayor and governor of New York. By the end of his life his business empire was virtually bankrupt and his fabulous art collection had to be sold.

**Heath, Sir Edward Richard George**, also called **Ted Heath** (1916– )
British politician. He served in **WORLD WAR II**, and became a Conservative MP in 1950. Following a career in the Whips' office (1951–9), he was Minister of Labour (1959–60), then Lord Privy Seal (1960–3) and the chief negotiator for Britain's entry into the European Common Market (**EEC**). He became the **CONSERVATIVE PARTY**'s first elected leader in 1965, and remained Leader of the Opposition until the 1970 election, when he became Prime Minister (1970–4). After a confrontation with the miners' union in 1973, he narrowly lost the two elections of 1974, and in 1975 was replaced as leader by Margaret **THATCHER**. He continued to play an active part in politics, being particularly critical of his successor's policies, until he retired from Parliament in 2001.

**Heaven and Earth Society**
A Chinese secret society, also known as the Triads (*tiandihui*), that originated in the 1670s during the early years of the **QING DYNASTY** as a group pledging loyalty to the previous **MING DYNASTY**. The Triads first emerged in Taiwan, then spread to the southern provinces of Fujian, Guangdong and Guangxi, initially drawing recruits from seamen and poor urban-dwellers. Spawning a wide variety of local branches with different names, the Triads engaged in smuggling, racketeering and robbery, in addition to organizing armed uprisings, particularly during the 19c. With its blood oath rituals and appeal to brotherhood, the society provided an attractive refuge for the homeless and destitute, but its conservative ideology, harking back to a restoration of the Ming Dynasty, made it increasingly irrelevant amidst the far-reaching political changes of the 20c. The Triads remain active today in Hong Kong and overseas Chinese communities.

**Hébert, Jacques René**, also called **Père Duchesne** (1757–94)
French revolutionary. An extremist, he represented the aspirations of the **SANS-CULOTTES**. He became a popular political journalist, assumed the pseudonym 'Le père Duchesne' after launching a satirical newspaper of that name (1790), and joined both the Cordelier and Jacobin clubs. He had a major part in the September Massacres and the overthrow of the monarchy. After denouncing the Committee of **PUBLIC SAFETY** for its failure to help the poor, he tried to incite a popular uprising, but having incurred the suspicion of **DANTON** and **ROBESPIERRE**, he and 17 of his followers ('Hébertists') were guillotined. ► **CORDELIERS' CLUB**; **FRENCH REVOLUTION**; **GIRONDINS**; **JACOBINS**

**Heian Era** (794–1185)
The period in Japanese history which began with the removal of the imperial capital from Nara to Heian (present-day Kyoto) and ended with the ascendancy of the warrior class and the establishment of the **KAMAKURA SHOGUNATE**. The Heian period is seen as the apogee of the aristocratic age in Japan, when the imperial capital was the political, social and cultural centre. During this period an attempt was made to implement an emperor-dominated political system based on the Chinese model. After the mid-10c, however, a rising warrior class and the emergence of private landed estates (*shoen*), which became the principal form of landholding, vitiated such efforts.

**Heights of Abraham, Battle of the** ► **PLAINS OF ABRAHAM, BATTLE OF THE**

**Heimwehren**
Austrian volunteer defence leagues. These were organized after **WORLD WAR I** to protect Austria's southern (Yugoslav) frontier. By the late 1920s, the *Heimwehren* were explicitly anti-socialist and anti-republican, receiving financial aid and encouragement from right-wing Austrian governments and from fascist Italy. Involved both in the crushing of the Austrian Socialists (Feb 1934) and of the Austrian Nazis (July 1934), the Heimwehren were subsequently disbanded by the **SCHUSCHNIGG** government in 1936. ► **NAZI PARTY**

**Hein, Piet** (1577–1629)
Dutch naval commander. After an adventurous career as a galley-slave of the Spanish and a merchant captain, in 1623 he became a Vice-Admiral under the Dutch. In 1624 he defeated the Spaniards near San Salvador in Brazil, and again in 1626 off Bahia, returning with an immense booty. In 1626, near Cuba, he captured the Spanish silver flotilla, valued at 12 million guilders; in 1629 he was made Lieutenant-Admiral. He died in a sea battle against the **PRIVATEERS** of Dunkirk.

**Heinemann, Gustav** (1899–1976)
West German politician. He practised as an advocate from 1926 and lectured on law at Cologne (1933–9). After the war he was a founder of the Christian Democratic Union (**CDU**), and was Minister of the Interior in **ADENAUER**'s government (1949–50), resigning over a fundamental difference over defence policy; being a pacifist, he opposed Germany's rearmament. He formed his own neutralist party, but later joined the Social Democratic Party (**SPD**), was elected to the **BUNDESTAG** (1957) and was Minister of Justice in **KIESINGER**'s 'Grand Coalition' government from 1966. In 1969 he was elected President but resigned in 1974.

**Heinsius, Anthony** (1641–1720)
Dutch politician. He was appointed Pensionary of Delft in 1672, and became an increasingly important friend and agent of the **STADHOLDER** William III. When William left for England in 1688 (to become King **WILLIAM III**), Heinsius was left in charge as **GRAND PENSIONARY** of Holland in 1689.

**Hekmatyar, Gulbuddin** (1947– )
Afghan guerrilla leader. Formerly an engineer, in the 1970s he opposed the republican government of General Muhammad Daud Khan, and rose to prominence during the 1980s in the fight to oust the Soviet-installed communist regime in Afghanistan. As leader of one of the two factions of the *Hizb-i Islami* ('Islamic Party'), he was seen as the most intransigently fundamentalist, refusing to join an interim 'national unity' government with Afghan communists as the USSR began to wind down its military commitment. He was injured in a car bomb attack on his group's headquarters in Peshawar in 1987, and in 1988 briefly served as President of the seven-party **MUJAHIDIN** alliance. He was Prime Minister of

the Republic of Afghanistan from 1993 to 1996.

**Hellespont ►** DARDANELLES

**Helms–Burton Act (The Cuban Liberty and Democratic Solidarity (Libertad) Act)** (1996)
US legislation tightening the 40-year US embargo on trade and financial transactions with Cuba. It seeks international sanctions against the government of Fidel **CASTRO**, specifies US policy toward a post-communist Cuba and aimed to protect the interests of US nationals who owned assets in Cuba before the 1959 revolution by allowing lawsuits in US courts to be brought against foreign companies trading in Cuba. To avoid damaging trade disputes, this third provision has been routinely waived by the **CLINTON** and **BUSH** administrations. The Act, promoted by Senator Jesse Helms and Representative Dan Burton, effectively locked US policy towards Cuba into the direction desired by the powerful, vehemently anti-Castro Cuban diaspora in Florida, a politically key swing state. It is an example of a recent trend for US governments to use legislation, such as the Iran-Libya Sanctions Act (1996), to try to change the political climate of another country. ► **REGIME CHANGE**

**He Long (Ho Lung)** (1896–1977)
Chinese Red Army general. The son of a lowly army officer and with little formal education, he was active as a bandit during the 1910s in his home province of Hunan, before enrolling in the provincial army. He Long joined the **GUOMINDANG** in 1926 and became a commander in the National Revolutionary Army. He was a participant in the Nanchang army uprising against the Guomindang on 1 Aug 1927, a date that is now considered by the Chinese Communist Party to mark the birth of the Red Army. During the **SINO-JAPANESE WAR** (1937–45) he became a divisional commander in the communist **EIGHTH ROUTE ARMY** and was elected a member of the party's Central Committee in 1945. Always a firm believer in party control of the army, he was made Marshal of the People's Republic of China (1955) and elected to the Politburo in 1956.

**Helsinki Final Act** (1 Aug 1975)
The concluding act of a conference on security and cooperation in Europe, held in Helsinki and attended by the heads of 35 states, including the USA and USSR, with the objective of forwarding the process of **DÉTENTE** through agreements on economic and technological cooperation, security, disarmament and human rights. These were set out in the Final Act within the principles of sovereignty and self-determination and existing frontiers. There have been several follow-up conferences, and a permanent organization called the Conference on Security and Cooperation in Europe (**CSCE**) was set up; this became the Organization for Security and Cooperation in Europe (OSCE) in 1994.

**Henderson, Arthur** (1863–1935)
British politician. Several times Chairman of the **LABOUR PARTY** (1908–10, 1914–17 and 1931–2), he was elected an MP in 1903, served in the coalition cabinets (1915–17), and became Home Secretary (1924) and Foreign Secretary (1929–31) in the first Labour governments. He was President of the World Disarmament Conference in 1932, won the **NOBEL PEACE PRIZE** in 1934, and also helped to establish the **LEAGUE OF NATIONS**. ► **MACDONALD, RAMSAY**

**Heng Samrin** (1934– )
Cambodian (Kampuchean) politician. He served as a political commissar and commander in **POL POT**'s **KHMER ROUGE** (1976–8) but, alienated by his brutal policies, led an abortive coup against him, then fled to Vietnam. Here he established the Kampuchean People's Revolutionary Party (KPRP) and became head of the new Vietnamese-installed government in Cambodia in 1979. He remained in *de facto* control of Cambodia until Vietnam's withdrawal of its troops in 1989, when his influence began to wane. In 1991 he stepped down as head of state in favour of Prince (later King) **SIHANOUK**.

**Henlein, Konrad** (1898–1945)
Sudeten German politician. A bank clerk and then gymnastics teacher, he was the leader from 1935 onwards in the agitation and conspiracy that led, in 1938, to Germany's seizure of Sudetenland from Czechoslovakia, and in 1939 to the institution of its Protectorate of Bohemia and Moravia and the dissolution of Czechoslovakia. *Gauleiter* of Sudetenland in 1938–9 and Civil Commissioner for the Protectorate from 1939 to 1945, he committed suicide when in US hands.

**Henry I** (c.1008–1060)
King of France (1031/60). He was the son of Robert II. He was involved in struggles with **NORMANDY** and with **BURGUNDY**, which he had unwisely granted to his rival brother, Robert. Several of his conflicts were with William of Normandy (later **WILLIAM I, THE CONQUEROR**).

**Henry I** (1068–1135)
King of England (1100/35) and Duke of Normandy (1106/35). He was the youngest son of **WILLIAM I, THE CONQUEROR**. Under Henry, the Norman empire attained the height of its power. He conquered Normandy from his brother Robert Curthose at the Battle of Tinchebrai (1106), maintained his position on the Continent, and exercised varying degrees of authority over the King of Scots, the Welsh princes, the Duke of Brittany, and also the Counts of Flanders, Boulogne and Ponthieu. His government of England and **NORMANDY** became increasingly centralized and interventionist, with the overriding aim of financing warfare and alliances, and consolidating the unity of the two countries as a single cross-Channel state. His only legitimate son, William Adelin, was drowned in 1120, and in 1127 he nominated his daughter, Empress Matilda, widow of Emperor **HENRY V** of Germany, as his heir for both England and Normandy. But Matilda and her second husband, Geoffrey of Anjou, proved unacceptable to the King's leading subjects. After Henry's death, the crown was seized by **STEPHEN**, son of his sister Adela. ► **ANGEVINS**

**Henry II** (1133–89)
King of England (1154/89). He was the son of Empress Matilda, **HENRY I**'s daughter and acknowledged heir, by her second husband, Geoffrey of Anjou. Already established as Duke of Normandy (1150) and Count of Anjou (1151), and as Duke of Aquitaine by marriage to **ELEANOR OF AQUITAINE** (1152), Henry invaded England in 1153, and was recognized (Treaty of

Wellingford) as the lawful successor of **STEPHEN**. He founded the Angevin or **PLANTAGENET DYNASTY** of English kings, and ruled England as part of a wider Angevin empire. Henry restored and transformed English governance after the disorders of Stephen's reign. His efforts to restrict clerical independence caused conflict with his former Chancellor, Thomas **BECKET**, Archbishop of Canterbury, which was ended only with Becket's murder (1170). Henry led a major expedition to Ireland (1171), which resulted in its annexation. The most serious challenge to his power came in 1173–4 when his son, the young Henry, encouraged by Queen Eleanor, rebelled in alliance with **LOUIS VII** of France, **WILLIAM I** of Scotland and Count Philip of Flanders. All parts of the King's dominions were threatened, but his enemies were defeated. In 1189 he faced further disloyalty from his family when his sons **JOHN** and **RICHARD I** allied with **PHILIP II** of France, who overran Maine and Touraine. Henry agreed a peace which recognized Richard as his sole heir for the Angevin empire, and he died shortly afterwards at Chinon. ► **ANGEVINS**; **CLARENDON, CONSTITUTIONS OF**

### Henry II (1519–59)

King of France (1547/59). The second son of **FRANCIS I**, he became heir to the throne in 1536. In 1533 he married **CATHERINE DE' MEDICI**; although he had ten children by her, his mistress, **DIANE DE POITIERS**, was treated virtually as his consort. She was an ardent Catholic, favouring the Guise family, and her influence at court contributed to the oppression of his Protestant subjects. Through the influence of the Guises he formed an alliance with Scotland, and declared war against England, which ended in 1558 with the taking of Calais. He continued the long-standing war against Emperor **CHARLES V**, gaining Toul, Metz and Verdun, but suffered reverses in Italy and the Low Countries, which led to the Treaty of **CATEAU-CAMBRÉSIS** (1559). He was killed accidentally while taking part in a tournament to celebrate the signing of the Treaty. ► **GUISE, HOUSE OF**

### Henry II, the Holy (973–1024)

German King and Emperor of the West. Although originally intended for a life in holy orders, he was elected Duke of Bavaria on the death of his father, Henry the Wrangler, in 995, and crowned King of Germany in 1002. He waged several campaigns against the Christian Polish king Bolesław I, in alliance with the heathen Liutitians, and against Arduin of Ivrea, who claimed the Italian throne. He was crowned Emperor in 1014 and fought Greeks and Lombards in southern Italy at the request of the pope. His main achievement was the elaboration of the so-called Ottonian system of government in Germany, ruthlessly using the Church as a tool of imperial authority. He was canonized in 1146. ► **OTTONIANS**

### Henry II Jasomirgott (1114–77)

Duke of Austria. The second son of Leopold III, he was originally Count Palatine of the Rhine, and succeeded his younger brother, Leopold IV, as Margrave of Austria and Duke of Bavaria (1141). He married Theodora, the niece of the Byzantine Emperor **MANUEL I COMNENUS**, in 1149. Unable to hold Bavaria, he surrendered it to the **WELFS** in 1156; as compensation, Austria was made into a dukedom and the

rights he received, the Privilegium minus, made it a semi-independent principality. He was a loyal supporter of **FREDERICK I, BARBAROSSA**.

### Henry III (1017–56)

Holy Roman Emperor (1039/56). The son of Conrad II, he became Duke of Bavaria (1027), Duke of Swabia (1038), sole King of the Germans (1039) and Holy Roman Emperor (1046). He resolutely maintained the imperial prerogatives of power and made great use of **MINISTERIALES** to secure his authority. In 1046 he put an end to the intrigues of three rival popes by deposing them all and appointing Clement II in their stead. He promoted learning and the arts, founded monastic schools, and built many great churches. ► **HOLY ROMAN EMPIRE**

### Henry III (1207–72)

King of England (1216/72). He was the elder son and successor, at the age of nine, of **JOHN**. He declared an end to his minority in 1227, and in 1232 stripped the justiciar, Hubert de **BURGH**, of power. His arbitrary assertion of royal rights conflicted with the principles of **MAGNA CARTA**, and antagonized many nobles. Although he failed to recover Poitou (northern Aquitaine) in 1242, he accepted the Kingdom of Sicily (1254). This forced him to seek the support of the barons, who under the leadership of the King's brother-in-law, Simon de **MONTFORT**, imposed far-reaching reforms by the Provisions of **OXFORD** (1258), which gave them a definite role in government. When Henry sought to restore royal power, the barons rebelled and captured him at Lewes (1264), but were defeated at Evesham (1265). The Dictum of Kenilworth (1266), though favourable to Henry, urged him to observe Magna Carta. Organized resistance ended in 1267, and the rest of the reign was stable. Henry was succeeded by his elder son, **EDWARD I**. ► **BARONS' WARS**

### Henry III (1551–89)

King of France (1574/89). The third son of **HENRY II**, in 1569 he gained victories over the **HUGUENOTS**, and took an active part in the **ST BARTHOLOMEW'S DAY MASSACRE** (1572). In 1573 he was elected to the crown of Poland, but two years later succeeded his brother, **CHARLES IX**, on the French throne. His reign was a period of almost incessant civil war between Huguenots and Catholics. In 1588 he engineered the assassination of Henry, 3rd Duke of **GUISE**, enraging the Catholic League. He joined forces with the Huguenot leader Henry of Navarre (**HENRY IV**), and while marching on Paris was assassinated by a fanatical priest. The last of the Valois line, he named Henry of Navarre as his successor. ► **GUISE, HOUSE OF**; **HOLY LEAGUE** (1576); **RELIGION, WARS OF**; **VALOIS DYNASTY**

### Henry IV (1050–1106)

King of the Germans (1056/1106). He succeeded his father, **HENRY III**, with his mother acting as Regent. He tried to break the power of the nobles; but his measures provoked a rising of the Saxons. After defeating them at Hohenburg (1075), he repressed both secular and ecclesiastical princes. This brought the intervention of Pope **GREGORY VII** and several years of conflict with the papacy, during which he appointed an anti-pope, Clement III, who crowned him Emperor in 1084. In his later years, he faced a further rebellion, in which his sons Conrad and Henry took part. He was compelled to abdicate, escaped, and found safety at Liège, where he died. ► CANOSSA; TRIBUR, PRINCES' MEETING AT

**Henry IV** (c.1367–1413)
King of England (1399/1413). The first king of the House of LANCASTER, he was the son of JOHN OF GAUNT (who was the fourth son of EDWARD III). In 1397 he supported RICHARD II against the Duke of GLOUCESTER, and was created Duke of Hereford, but was banished in 1398. After landing at Ravenspur, Yorkshire, Henry induced Richard, now deserted, to abdicate in his favour. During his reign, rebellion and lawlessness were rife, and he was constantly hampered by lack of money. Under Owen GLENDOWER the Welsh maintained their independence, and Henry's attack on Scotland in 1400 ended in his retreat with no victories won. The Scots were, however, defeated by a force led by the Percies at Homildon Hill (1402), and it was partly annoyance at the King's apparent ingratitude that led the Percies to support the Scots and Welsh against Henry, which in turn led to the King's victory against them at Shrewsbury (1403). Henry was a chronic invalid in later years, and only rarely asserted himself in power struggles between the Prince of Wales and Archbishop Arundel, who was supported by Henry's second son, Thomas. ► PERCY

**Henry IV (Henry of Navarre)** (1553–1610)
First Bourbon King of France (1589/1610). The third son of Antoine de Bourbon, he was brought up a Calvinist. He led the Huguenot army at the Battle of Jarnac (1569) and became leader of the Protestant Party. Henry married Margaret of Valois in 1572, but this marriage was annulled in 1599, and in 1600 he married MARIE DE' MEDICI. After the ST BARTHOLOMEW'S DAY MASSACRE (1572), he was spared by professing himself a Catholic, and spent three years virtually a prisoner at the French court. In 1576 he escaped, revoked his conversion, and resumed command of the army in continuing opposition to the Guises and the Catholic HOLY LEAGUE (1576). After the murder of HENRY III, he succeeded to the throne. In 1593 he became a Catholic, thereby unifying the country, and by the Edict of NANTES (1598) Protestants were granted liberty of conscience. His economic policies, implemented by his minister SULLY, gradually brought new wealth to the country. He was assassinated in Paris by a religious fanatic. ► BOURBON, HOUSE OF; GUISE, HOUSE OF; HUGUENOTS; RELIGION, WARS OF; VALOIS DYNASTY

**Henry V** (1081–1125)
German King (1099/1125) and Holy Roman Emperor (1111/25). In 1106 he allied himself with the nobility and dethroned his father, HENRY IV. His reign was dominated by the issues involved in the INVESTITURE CONTROVERSY and his power struggle with the princes, whose support he alienated by favouring the MINISTERIALES and the towns. In 1111 he agreed with Pope Paschal II to give up his rights to invest bishops in return for coronation as Emperor and the return of the royal insignia. This agreement was rejected by the German bishops and princes, whereupon Henry took the pope prisoner and forced him to concede both coronation and rights of investiture (1111). This concession was later withdrawn and Henry was excommunicated. Finally, negotiations with Pope CALIXTUS II led to the end of the Investiture Controversy in the Concordat of Worms, in which the princes, rather than the Emperor, took the initiative. ► WORMS, CONCORDAT OF

**Henry V** (1387–1422)
King of England (1413/22). The eldest son of HENRY IV, he fought against GLENDOWER and the Welsh rebels (1402–8), and became Constable of Dover (1409) and Captain of Calais (1410). To this time belong the exaggerated stories of his wild youth. The main effort of his reign was his claim, through his great-grandfather, EDWARD III, to the French crown. In 1415 he invaded France, and won the Battle of AGINCOURT against great odds. By 1419 Normandy was again under English control, and in 1420 was concluded the 'perpetual peace' of Troyes, under which Henry was recognized as heir to the French throne and Regent of France, and married CHARLES VI's daughter, Catherine of Valois. ► HUNDRED YEARS' WAR

**Henry VI** (1165–97)
Holy Roman Emperor (1190/7). The son of FREDERICK I, BARBAROSSA, he married Constance, the aunt and heiress of William II of Sicily (1186), and succeeded his father in 1190. He was opposed by the papacy, the GUELFS, RICHARD I, THE LIONHEART and Constance's illegitimate brother, TANCRED, who had been elected King by the Sicilian barons on the death of William. This hostile coalition collapsed when Richard fell into the hands of Leopold V of Austria, who turned his captive over to Henry. On the death of Tancred (1194) he overran Sicily, where Constance bore him a son, FREDERICK II. Emperor since 1191 and now King of Sicily, he was regarded by contemporaries as the most powerful man on earth, although he was unsuccessful in his plans to make the empire hereditary. Still a young man, he died at Messina, probably of malaria, while engaged in preparations for a crusade.

**Henry VI** (1421–71)
King of England (1422/61 and 1470/1). He was the only child of HENRY V and Catherine of Valois. During Henry's minority, his uncle John, Duke of BEDFORD, was Regent in France, and another uncle, Humphrey, Duke of GLOUCESTER, was Lord Protector of England. Henry was crowned King of France at Paris in 1431, two years after his coronation in England. But once the Burgundians had made a separate peace with CHARLES VII (1435), Henry V's French conquests were progressively eroded, and by 1453 the English retained only Calais. Henry had few kingly qualities, and from 1453 suffered from periodic bouts of insanity. Richard, Duke of York, seized power as Lord Protector in 1454, and defeated the King's army at St Albans (1455), the first battle of the Wars of the ROSES. Fighting resumed in 1459, and although York himself was killed at Wakefield (1460), his heir was proclaimed King as EDWARD IV after Henry's deposition (1461). In 1464 Henry returned from exile in Scotland to lead the Lancastrian cause, but was captured and imprisoned (1465–70). Richard Neville, Earl of WARWICK, restored him to the throne (Oct 1470), his nominal rule ending when Edward IV

returned to London (Apr 1471). After the Yorkist victory at the Battle of TEWKESBURY (May 1471), where his only son was killed, Henry was murdered in the Tower. ► HUNDRED YEARS' WAR

**Henry VII** (1274–1313)
Holy Roman Emperor (1308/13) and King of Germany. Originally Count of Luxembourg, a French-speaking minor prince from the extreme west of the empire, he was elected Emperor in 1308 as an alternative candidate to CHARLES OF VALOIS, mainly due to the skilful diplomacy of his brother Baldwin, Archbishop of Trier. His family soon rose to great power with the marriage of his son John to Elizabeth, heiress of Bohemia (1311). In 1310 Henry led an army to Italy, where he remained with the aim of restoring imperial authority, but made little progress against the opposition of King Robert of Naples and the Guelf cities. The imperialist cause collapsed when he died near Siena, probably of malaria.

**Henry VII** (1457–1509)
King of England (1485/1509). The founder of the Tudor Dynasty, he was the grandson of Owen Tudor, who married Queen Catherine of Valois, the widow of HENRY V. After the Lancastrian defeat at the Battle of TEWKESBURY (1471), Henry was taken to Brittany, where several Yorkist attempts on his life and liberty were frustrated. In 1485 he landed unopposed at Milford Haven, and defeated RICHARD III at the Battle of BOSWORTH FIELD. As King, he restored peace and prosperity to the country, which was helped by his marriage of reconciliation with Elizabeth of York. He was also noted for the efficiency of his financial and administrative policies. He dealt efficiently with Yorkist plots, such as those surrounding the pretenders Lambert SIMNEL and Perkin WARBECK. Peace was concluded with France (1492), and the marriage of his elder son and heir, Arthur, to CATHERINE OF ARAGON, cemented an alliance with Spain. He was succeeded by his second son, as HENRY VIII. ► TUDOR, HOUSE OF

**Henry VIII** (1491–1547)
King of England (1509/47). The second son of HENRY VII, soon after his accession he married CATHERINE OF ARAGON, his brother Arthur's widow. As a member of the HOLY LEAGUE (1510), he invaded France (1512), winning the Battle of the SPURS (1513); and while abroad, the Scots were defeated at the Battle of FLODDEN. In 1521 he published a book defending the Catholic sacraments in reply to LUTHER, receiving from the pope the title 'Defender of the Faith'. From 1527 he determined to divorce Catherine, whose children, except for Mary (later MARY I), had died in infancy. This policy directly precipitated the Reformation in England. He tried to put pressure on the pope by humbling the clergy, and in defiance of Rome was privately married to Anne BOLEYN (1533). Using parliamentary statute to strengthen his actions against the Roman Catholic Church, it was enacted in 1534 that his marriage to Catherine was invalid, and that the King was the sole head of the Church of England. The policy of suppressing the monasteries followed (1536–9). In 1536 Catherine died, and Anne Boleyn was executed for infidelity. Henry then married Jane SEYMOUR, who died leaving a son, afterwards EDWARD VI. In 1540 ANNE OF CLEVES became

his fourth wife, in the hope of attaching the Protestant interest of Germany; but dislike of her appearance caused him to divorce her speedily. He then married Catherine HOWARD (1540), who two years later was executed on grounds of infidelity (1542). In 1543 his last marriage was to Catherine PARR, who survived him. His later years saw further war with France and Scotland, before peace was concluded with France in 1546. He was succeeded by his son, Edward VI. ► CROMWELL, THOMAS; MORE, THOMAS; REFORMATION (England); WOLSEY, THOMAS

**Henry, Patrick** (1736–99)
US politician. After training as a lawyer, he entered the colonial Virginia House of Burgesses, where his oratorical skills won him fame and before whom he delivered his famous lines 'Give me liberty or give me death'. He was outspoken in his opposition to British policy towards the colonies, particularly on the subject of the STAMP ACT (1765), and he made the first speech in the CONTINENTAL CONGRESS (1774). In 1776 he became Governor of Virginia, and was four times re-elected. ► AMERICAN REVOLUTION

**Henry of Navarre** ► HENRY IV (of France)

**Henry Raspe** (c.1204–1247)
Landgrave of Thuringia and German anti-king. He was the last of the Ludovinger to rule Thuringia, which he received from the Emperor c.1231. Although he was excommunicated (1240) for his support of the Emperor against the papacy, he went over to the papal side in 1245 and was elected King in 1246 by the clerical princes and supporters in Thuringia. He defeated CONRAD IV (to whom he had been appointed as Regent (1246)) near Frankfurt in 1246 and died, without heir, the following year, never having been crowned.

**Henry the Lion** (1129–95)
Duke of Saxony (1142/80) and Bavaria (1156/80). The head of the GUELFS, he pursued a vigorous policy of expansion in the north-east, conducted a crusade against the Wends and promoted trade by refounding Lübeck and setting up a series of trade agreements. In 1158 he founded Munich. His ambitious designs roused against him a league of princes in 1166, but he retained power through an alliance with Emperor FREDERICK I, BARBAROSSA. After breaking with Frederick in 1176, he was deprived of most of his lands, and exiled. Ultimately he was reconciled to Frederick's successor, HENRY VI.

**Henry the Navigator** (1394–1460)
Portuguese prince. He was the third son of John I, King of Portugal, and Philippa, daughter of John of Gaunt, Duke of Lancaster. He set up court at Sagres, Algarve, and erected an observatory and school of scientific navigation. He sponsored many exploratory expeditions along the West African coast, and the way was prepared for the discovery of the sea route to India. ► EXPLORATION

**Hepburn, Mitchell Frederick** (1896–1953)
Canadian politician. A farmer who came to power as the Liberal Premier of Ontario (1934–42) with the promise of a 'swing to the left' and a fight in favour of the 'dispossessed and oppressed', he soon began to fight the CIO, which was asked in to help organize

the General Motors plant at Oshawa in 1937, branding them as 'foreign agitators' and communists. After Mackenzie KING refused to send in the MOUNTIES, Hepburn organized his own anti-labour force, nicknamed 'Hepburn's Hussars' or the 'Sons of Mitch's', and attacked the federal government for its 'cowardice'. Although the strikers won company recognition, Hepburn gained increased electoral support, winning 75 per cent of the seats in the subsequent election. Hepburn continued his feud with the federal administration of Mackenzie King over both provincial rights (wrecking the 1941 conference on the recommendations of the ROWELL–SIROIS COMMISSION) and its war policies, but this fight ruined his party and destroyed his health. Resigning from office in 1942, he lost his seat in the election of 1945 in which the LIBERAL PARTY was decimated. ► AFL–CIO

### Herero Revolt (1907)
A resistance movement by Bantu-speaking peoples in Namibia, crushed by the Germans with great brutality. They participated in the struggle for Namibian independence against South African rule.

### Hereward the Wake (d.c.1080)
Anglo-Saxon thegn. He returned from exile to lead in East Anglia the last organized English resistance against the Norman invaders. He held the Isle of Ely against WILLIAM I, THE CONQUEROR for nearly a year (1070–1), then disappeared from history, and entered medieval outlaw legend as a celebrated opponent of the forces of injustice. ► NORMAN CONQUEST

### hermandad
Literally 'brotherhood', this Spanish term refers to a popular 'vigilante' peacekeeping organization in medieval Castilian towns; it was adapted by the Castilian crown in the late 15c to act as local police and judiciary. These organizations lost much of their power and prestige during the 16c, and now the term is used only of ceremonial religious brotherhoods.

### Hermann, Count of Salm (d.1088)
German anti-king. Elected as the successor to the anti-king RUDOLF OF RHEINFELDEN (1080), he defeated Frederick I of Swabia and was formally crowned in Goslar in 1081. However, his support evaporated and he fled from the Emperor's army to Denmark. With the support of Welf IV, he was able to undertake renewed campaigns in Germany but died storming a castle in 1088. No new anti-king was elected after his death.

### Hermann of Salza (1170–1239)
Grand Master of the Teutonic Order. Born into a family of MINISTERIALES, he became Grand Master in 1209. Under his leadership, the Order responded to Conrad of Masowia's appeal for help against the Prussians and he laid the basis of the Order's later power there. He was one of FREDERICK II's closest advisers, acting as a diplomat in his service. His good relations with the pope allowed him to mediate in the dispute between the empire and the papacy, and he was able to use his position to gain many important concessions for the Teutonic Order. ► TEUTONIC KNIGHTS

### Hermannsson, Steingrímur (1928– )
Icelandic politician. He trained as an electrical engineer in the USA, returning to pursue an industrial career. He became Director of Iceland's National Research Council (1957–78) and then made the transition into politics, becoming Chairman of the Progressive Party (PP) in 1979. He became a minister in 1978 and then Prime Minister, heading a PP–Independence Party (IP) coalition (1983–7), after which he accepted the Foreign Affairs portfolio in the government of Thorsteinn Pálsson. He was Prime Minister again from 1988 to 1991.

### Herrin Massacre (22 June 1922)
The tragic outcome of a labour dispute in southern Illinois, USA. During a miners' strike, one mining company decided to try to operate a mine using non-union labourers. The striking miners rounded up the non-unionized miners, assuring them of their safety, and marched them to a place near Herrin. There, as their captives ran for cover, the striking miners opened fire, killing more than 20 and wounding many others. A grand jury returned 214 indictments for murder and other offences, but local influence prevented any convictions.

### Herriot, Édouard (1872–1957)
French politician. Mayor of Lyons from 1905 until his death, he became Minister of Transport during WORLD WAR I. A radical, he was three times Premier (1924–5, 1926 (for two days) and 1932), and was on several occasions President of the Chamber of Deputies. In 1942 he became a prisoner of the Nazis. After WORLD WAR II he was President of the National Assembly (1947–53). ► NAZI PARTY

### Herstigte Nasionale Party ► HNP

### Hertzog, J(ames) B(arry) M(unnik) (1866–1942)
South African politician. He was a Boer general (1899–1902), and in 1910 became Minister of Justice in the first Union government. In 1913 he founded the Nationalist Party, advocating complete South African independence. As Premier, in coalition with Labour (1924–9), and with SMUTS in a United Party coalition (1933–9), he pursued a legislative programme that destroyed the African franchise, created job reservation for whites, and also tightened land segregation. He renounced his earlier secessionism, but at the outbreak of WORLD WAR II declared for neutrality, was defeated, and in 1940 retired.

### Herzen, Alexander Ivanovich (1812–70)
Russian nobleman, political thinker and active propagandist. A brilliant student, he was arrested and exiled in 1834 and again in 1841 for his revolutionary ideas. In 1847 he left Russia for Paris but settled in London in 1851, becoming a powerful liberal socialist propagandist by his novels and treatises, and by the smuggling into Russia of his influential journal Kolokol ('The Bell'). He died in Paris.

### Herzl, Theodor (1869–1904)
Hungarian Zionist leader. He moved to Vienna at the age of 18, where he trained as a lawyer and pursued a career as a journalist and author. In Paris as a newspaper correspondent (1891–5), he covered the DREYFUS trial in 1894 and was deeply affected by its anti-Semitism. He became convinced that the only adequate Jewish response was a political one. In 1895 he published Der Judenstaat ('The Jewish State'), in

which he argued that the Jews should have their own state, which would receive Jews from those parts of the world where they experienced rejection or persecution. In 1897, in Basel, he convened the First Zionist Congress, which declared its goal to be the founding of a national Jewish home in **PALESTINE** and established the **WORLD ZIONIST ORGANIZATION** to that end. Herzl spent his remaining years strengthening this organization and seeking support for its aims from influential European leaders, and succeeded in moulding it into an efficient institution. While not original in his ideals, Herzl's efforts have rendered his name inseparable from the emergence of political **ZIONISM** in the modern period. ► **BEN-GURION, DAVID**

**Heselrige, Sir Arthur** ► HASELRIG, SIR ARTHUR

**Heseltine, Michael Ray Dibdin Heseltine, Baron** (1933– )
British politician. He built up a publishing business before becoming a Conservative MP in 1966. After holding junior posts in Transport (1970), Environment (1970–2), and Aerospace and Shipping (1972–4), he was appointed Secretary of State for the Environment (1979–83), and then Defence Secretary (1983–6). He resigned from the government in dramatic fashion by walking out of a cabinet meeting over the issue of the takeover of Westland helicopters. His challenge to Margaret **THATCHER**'s leadership of the **CONSERVATIVE PARTY** directly led to her resignation (Nov 1990) but he was defeated by John **MAJOR** in the election to succeed her. In Major's cabinet, he served as President of the Board of Trade, in which position in 1992–3 he planned the closure of several of Britain's collieries, and then Deputy Prime Minister (1995–7), a reward for persuading his followers to back Major in the 1995 leadership contest.

**He Shen (Ho Shen)** (1750–99)
The son of a minor Manchu nobleman in China, he became the personal favourite of Emperor **QIAN-LONG**. He attracted the interest of the Emperor in 1775 while serving as a member of the Imperial Bodyguard. Thereafter, he was given important government posts and by 1778 was in charge of the Beijing gendarmerie and superintendent of customs. He used his influence with the Emperor to intervene in official appointments and amass a huge personal fortune, thus contributing to the depletion of the treasury and the spread of corruption throughout the bureaucracy. Shortly after Qianlong's death, He Shen was arrested and forced to commit suicide.

**Hess, (Walter Richard) Rudolf** (1894–1987)
German Nazi politician, **HITLER**'s deputy as party leader. Educated at Godesberg, he fought in **WORLD WAR I**, then studied at Munich. He joined the **NAZI PARTY** in 1920, and became Hitler's close friend and (in 1934) deputy. In 1941, on the eve of Germany's attack on the USSR, he flew alone to Scotland to plead the cause of a negotiated Anglo-German peace. He was temporarily imprisoned in the Tower of London, then placed under psychiatric care near Aldershot. At the **NUREMBERG TRIALS** (1946) he was sentenced to life imprisonment, and remained in Spandau prison, Berlin (after 1966, as the only prisoner), until his death. ► **WORLD WAR II**

**Hesse**
Established as an independent landgravate in the late 13c, the area experienced many problems until reunited by the Landgrave (1509–67) **PHILIP THE MAG-NANIMOUS**, who introduced Lutheranism in 1526 and founded the first Protestant University at Marburg (1527). The various subdivisions between subsequent heirs produced Hesse-Kassel and Hesse-Darmstadt. The former was allied with Sweden in the **THIRTY YEARS' WAR**. Frederick, son of Landgrave Charles (1654–1730) became Frederick I, King of Sweden in 1720. Hesse-Kassel became an electorate in 1803.

**Heuss, Theodor** (1884–1963)
West German politician and President. Educated at Munich and Berlin, he became editor of the political magazine *Hilfe* (1905–12), professor at the Berlin College of Political Science (1920–33), and an MP (1924–8 and 1930–2). A prolific author and journalist, he wrote two books denouncing **HITLER**, and when the latter came to power in 1933, he was dismissed from his chair and his books publicly burnt. In 1946 he became a founder-member of the Free Democratic Party (**FDP**), and helped to draft the new federal constitution. He was the first President of the Federal Republic of Germany (1949–59).

**He Xiangning (Ho Hsiang-ning)** (1880–1972)
Chinese revolutionary and feminist. Educated in Hong Kong and Japan, she married fellow revolutionary **LIAO ZHONGKAI** in 1905 and was an active advocate of links with the communists and Russia. Her husband was assassinated in 1925, and when two years later **CHIANG KAI-SHEK** broke with the communists, she returned to Hong Kong and was an outspoken critic of his leadership. She returned to Beijing in 1949 as head of the overseas commission. He Xiangning was one of the first Chinese women to cut her hair short and publicly to advocate nationalism, revolution and female emancipation.

**Heydrich, Reinhard**, nicknamed **the Hangman** (1904–42)
Prominent Nazi functionary and Deputy Chief of the **GESTAPO**. As a youth, he joined the **FREIKORPS** ('Volunteer Corps'), and was later a naval sub-lieutenant; in 1931 he had to quit the navy and entered the **SS**, rising to be second-in-command of the secret police, and charged with pacifying occupied territories. In 1941 he was made protector of Bohemia and Moravia, but the following year was killed by Czech assassins parachuted in from the UK. In the murderous reprisals, Lidice village was razed and every man put to death.

**Heyn, Piet** ► HEIN, PIET

**Hezbollah** or **Hezbullah**
The umbrella organization in south Beirut of militant Shiite Muslims with Iranian links; the name means 'Party of God'. It came to world attention after the TWA hijacking in Cairo in 1985, and the subsequent taking of hostages. It fought Israeli forces occupying southern Lebanon until Israel's withdrawal in 2000, when it switched to attacks, often suicide bombings, against Israeli citizens and armed forces inside Israel. ► **SHIITES**

**Hiawatha**, originally **Haionhwat'ha ('He makes Rivers')** (fl. c.1570)
Native American leader (perhaps legendary). A chieftain of the MOHAWK or of the Onondaga people, he is said to have been a founder of the League of the Five Nations of the Iroquois (known as the IROQUOIS CONFEDERACY), uniting the Mohawk, Oneida, Onondaga, Cayuga and SENECA tribes. According to legend, he joined Huron mystic Deganawida in a plan to end warfare among NATIVE AMERICANS in what is now New York State, travelling from tribe to tribe to negotiate the alliance and build a confederacy governed by elected representatives.

**Hickok, Wild Bill**, originally **James Butler Hickok** (1837–76)
US frontier marshall. He became a stagecoach driver on the Santa Fé and Oregon Trails, a fighter of NATIVE AMERICANS, and a Union Army scout during the Civil War. He gained fame as the gambling, ready-to-kill marshall of Hays (1869) and Abilene (1871), Kansas. After touring briefly with William F CODY's Wild West Show (1872–3) and teaming up with Calamity Jane, in Deadwood, Dakota, he was shot dead by Jack McCall during a poker game.

**Hidalgo (y Costilla), Miguel** (1753–1811)
Mexican revolutionary. The son of a poor farmer, he became a curate in several parishes. He was known to the INQUISITION as an avid reader of ROUSSEAU, and was banished to Dolores outside Mexico City. He led a rising against the Spanish authorities (16 Sep 1810), with the cry of 'Long live our Lady of Guadalupe, death to bad government and the Spaniards'. His following, a 'horde' some 60,000 strong, sacked Guanajuato, but his 'war of revenge' terrified wealthy creoles into support for the colonial authorities. Executed at Chihuahua, he remains a symbol of nationalism, and is often known as 'the Father of Mexican independence'.

**Hidatsa**
A Siouan-speaking Native American tribe that occupied what is now eastern North Dakota. They settled in villages and depended on farming for subsistence, constructing earth lodges of log frames covered with sod and thatch; when they left their villages to hunt bison in winter, however, they used tepees made of hide. The Hidatsa separated from the CROW in the early 18c and merged with the Mandan and Arikara tribes in defence against frequent SIOUX raids. The Fort Berthold Reservation was established in 1870 for the Three Affiliated Tribes, as the Hidatsa, Mandan and Arikara came to be known. In 1931 they shared a US$2 million land claims settlement. After WORLD WAR II, construction of the Garrison Dam took their best land, diminishing cattle-raising and farming, and leaving reservation life at near-subsistence level. The population of the combined tribes on the reservation numbered about 3,500 in the early 21c. ➤ NATIVE AMERICANS

**Higgins, Henry Bournes** (1851–1929)
Irish-born Australian politician and judge. His family emigrated to Melbourne in 1870 and he went on to become a successful lawyer, entering the Victorian assembly in 1894. He was a state representative at the Federal Convention (1897–8), where he criticized the powers reserved to the states and the rigidity of the federal constitution. As a supporter of Irish HOME RULE, and opposing both the terms of FEDERATION and Australian participation in the BOER WARS, he lost his seat in the Victorian elections of 1900, although he remained popular with the Labor movement. In 1901 he entered Commonwealth politics as a Liberal, but became Attorney-General in the brief Labor administration of 1904. In 1906 he was appointed to the High Court, and in 1907 became President of the Commonwealth Conciliation and Arbitration Court. A firm believer in state intervention in industrial relations, he had, with KINGSTON, been responsible for the conciliation and arbitration provisions of the constitution. As President of the Arbitration Court he made the HARVESTER JUDGEMENT, which established the principle of the minimum wage. He fought for the Commonwealth's right to arbitrate in the High Court, and resigned in protest against the interference of Prime Minister William HUGHES in 1921. By then arbitration had become an integral part of the Australian industrial system.

**Highland Clearances** (c.1810–20)
The often violent eviction of thousands of crofting families in the Scottish Highlands by landlords who wanted to use the land themselves for farming sheep. The Highland cottages were usually burned and the peasants were resettled in crofts by the coast where they had to turn to fishing and gathering kelp to survive. The situation was exacerbated by the need for more food by the growing population in the Highlands in the early 19c, and by the potato famine during the 'hungry forties'. The clearances marked the beginning of rural depopulation in the region which has continued ever since.

**Hijaz Railway**
The railway, running between Damascus and Medina, which was built between 1901 and 1908, when the area was under Ottoman domination. The construction and subsequent operation of the railway was the province of a subdepartment of government later to become the Hijaz Railway Ministry. Financed by popular subscription and grants from the central treasury, the railway was constructed with German technical assistance. Its strategic importance to the Turkish military effort in the Hijaz during WORLD WAR I made it an immediate target after the proclamation of the ARAB REVOLT by Sharif HUSAYN IBN 'ALI of Mecca in 1916. The Amir, Faysal and British officers (among whom was T E LAWRENCE) successfully destroyed the railway as an effective transport system and were thus able to wrest control of Mecca and Jedda from the Ottomans, at the same time as isolating those Ottomans then in the Yemen. ➤ FAYSAL I

**Hill, James Jerome** (1838–1916)
US railway magnate. Born near Guelph, Canada, he moved to St Paul, Minnesota, in 1856, where he entered the transportation business. He took over the St Paul–Pacific line (1878), extending it to link with the Canadian system, and founded the Great Northern Railway Co in 1890 to unite all his properties. To reduce competition he acquired control of competing lines, including the Northern Pacific Railroad, which financier Edward H Harriman tried in turn to wrest from him in a stock exchange battle that caused

a panic on Wall Street in 1901. That same year Hill established an even larger holding company, the Northern Securities Co, which violated the Sherman Anti-Trust Act and was dissolved by the Supreme Court in 1904. He was later active in the construction of the Canadian Pacific Railroad. ► ANTI-TRUST ACTS

**Hill, Joe**, originally **Joel Emmanuel Hägglund** or **Joseph Hillstrom** (c.1872–1915)
US labour organizer and songwriter. Born in Sweden, he was a seaman who went to the USA in about 1901 and became an active member of the radical labour union the **INDUSTRIAL WORKERS OF THE WORLD**. For them, he wrote popular pro-union songs such as 'Coffee An', 'The Rebel Girl' and 'The Preacher and the Slave' (which includes the phrase 'pie in the sky'). He became a legend and a martyr of the union movement after he was arrested for murder (1914), convicted on circumstantial evidence, and, despite calls for a retrial by President Woodrow **WILSON** and the Swedish government, was executed.

**Hillery, Patrick John** (1923– )
Irish politician. Following his election as an MP (1951), he held ministerial posts in Education (1959–65), then Industry and Commerce (1965–6), and Labour (1966–9), then became Foreign Minister (1969–72). Before becoming President of the Irish Republic (1976–90), he served as the **EEC** Commissioner for Social Affairs (1973–6).

**Himmler, Heinrich** (1900–45)
German Nazi politician and Chief of Police. He joined the **NAZI PARTY** in 1925, and in 1929 was made head of the **SS**, which he developed into **HITLER's** personal bodyguard into a powerful party weapon. In 1933 he commanded the Bavarian political police and in 1934 took over the secret police (**GESTAPO**) in **PRUSSIA**. Chief of Police from 1936, he later initiated the systematic liquidation of Jews. In 1943 he became Minister of the Interior, and in 1944 Commander-in-Chief of the home forces. He was captured by the Allies, and committed suicide at Lüneburg. ► HOLOCAUST; WORLD WAR II

**Hincks, Sir Francis** (1807–85)
Canadian politician. Editor of the *Examiner*, the **CANADA WEST** reform party newspaper founded in 1837, he united with Louis H **LAFONTAINE** in the campaign for **RESPONSIBLE GOVERNMENT** which Lord Sydenham sought to evade. He became Prime Minister in 1851, and was primarily responsible for initiating **RECIPROCITY** negotiations with the USA. He was also a sponsor of the Grand Trunk Railway, but some dubious financial dealings forced him out of office in 1854.

**Hindenburg, Paul Ludwig Hans Anton von Beneckendorff und von** (1847–1934)
German general and President (1925–34). Educated at Wahlstatt and Berlin, he fought in the **FRANCO-PRUSSIAN WAR** (1870–1), rose to the rank of general (1903), and retired in 1911. Recalled at the outbreak of **WORLD WAR I**, he won victories over the Russians (1914–15), and later directed the creation of strategic fortifications on the Western Front (the Hindenburg Line). A national hero, he became the second President of the German Republic in 1925 despite his known anti-republican views. He was re-elected in

1932 to block **HITLER's** candidacy, but in 1933 appointed Hitler as Chancellor.

**Hinduism** ► RELIGION

**Hindu Mahasabha**
An Indian socio-political organization concerned with advancing Hindu nationalism. It started in Punjab in 1907 and claimed that the Congress and its concern for Hindu–Muslim unity would endanger Hindus. Within the Mahasabha, there was a divide between those who sought social reforms and those who were orthodox. The organization expanded under the leadership of **LAJPAT RAI** and **MALAVIYA**, who kept it linked with the Congress. Under Savarkar, it broke completely with the Congress in 1937 and strengthened links with the **RSS**. Its members included Nathuram Godse, M K **GANDHI's** assassin. Mahasabha electoral support declined after 1952 as its Hindu nationalist themes were pre-empted by the **JAN SANGH**.

**Hirata Atsutane** (1776–1843)
Japanese scholar and theologian. As an extreme chauvinist, he condemned Buddhist and Confucian influences in Japanese culture and insisted that the Japanese were superior to all other peoples. By elevating those **SHINTO** beliefs in the divine character of the imperial institution, Hirata's teachings helped to undermine the legitimacy of the shogunate, influencing the imperial loyalist movement that was ultimately to overthrow the **TOKUGAWA SHOGUNATE**.

**Hirohito** (1901–89)
Emperor of Japan (1926/89). The 124th emperor in direct descent, his reign was marked by rapid militarization and the aggressive wars against China (1931–2 and 1937–45) and Britain and the USA (1941–5). The latter ended with the dropping of atomic bombs on **HIROSHIMA** and **NAGASAKI**. Under US occupation, Hirohito in 1946 renounced his mythical divinity and most of his powers, and became a democratic constitutional monarch. ► AKIHITO; WORLD WAR II

**Hiroshima, Atomic Bombing of** (6 Aug 1945)
Hiroshima, the capital of Hiroshima prefecture, South Honshu Island, Japan, was chosen as the target for 'Little Boy', the first atomic bomb ever dropped, because of its importance as a centre of military and supply bases, shipyards and industrial plants. Approximately 150,000 people were killed or wounded as a result, and 75 per cent of the city's buildings were destroyed or severely damaged.

**Hirota Koki** (1878–1948)
Japanese diplomat and politician. He had close links with the ultra-nationalist **GENYOSHA** and served in diplomatic posts in China, Britain, the USA and the USSR before becoming Foreign Minister in various non-party cabinets (1933–4 and 1934–6). He championed an assertive foreign policy to protect Japan's interests in China, and in 1935 laid down principles to guide Sino-Japanese relations: the formation of a Japan–China–Manchuria economic bloc, suppression of all anti-Japanese activities in China, and the creation of a Sino-Japanese front against **COMMUNISM**. As Prime Minister (1936–7), he increased the military budget and signed the **ANTI-COMINTERN**

PACT with Germany and Italy, thus alienating Japan even further from the Anglo-Saxon powers. Appointed Foreign Minister again (1937–9), Hirota supported Japan's full-scale invasion of China in 1937. After the war, he was tried as a Class A war criminal and executed in 1948, the only civilian to be so sentenced.

## Hiss, Alger (1904–96)
US civil servant. He reached high office as a State Department official, then stood trial twice (1949, 1950) on a charge of perjury, having denied before a Congressional Un-American Activities Committee that in 1938 he had passed secret state documents to Whittaker Chambers, an agent for an international communist spy ring. The case roused great controversy, but he was convicted at his second trial, and sentenced to five years' imprisonment. He did not return to public life after his release. The justice of his conviction continues to be disputed. ► HUAC; MCCARTHY, JOSEPH

## Histadrut
Israeli Zionist labour organization, formed in 1920, incorporated into the International Confederation of Free Trade Unions. Comprising both industrial and agricultural workers, its remit nonetheless includes activities beyond those normally associated with trade unions. Histadrut is involved in marketing and distribution, banking, building programmes, irrigation, healthcare, education and entertainment, as well as in traditional negotiations on working conditions and wages. Of considerable economic importance, Histadrut is run by an elected executive whose leaders have had strong ties with the MAPAI PARTY. ► JEWISH LABOUR MOVEMENT IN PALESTINE; WORLD ZIONIST ORGANIZATION; ZIONISM

## Hitler, Adolf (1889–1945)
German dictator and leader of the NAZI PARTY. The son of a minor customs official, he was educated at Linz and Steyr, attended art school in Munich, but failed to pass into the Vienna Academy. He lived on his family subventions in Vienna (1904–13), yet inhabited hostels and did a variety of menial jobs. In 1913 he emigrated to Munich, where he found employment as a draughtsman. In 1914 he served in a Bavarian regiment, became a corporal, was decorated, and was wounded in the last stages of WORLD WAR I. In 1919 he joined a small political party which in 1920 he renamed as the National Socialist German Workers' Party. In 1923, with other extreme right-wing factions, he attempted to overthrow the Bavarian government as a prelude to a 'March on Berlin' in imitation of MUSSOLINI's 'MARCH ON ROME', but was imprisoned for nine months in Landsberg jail, during which time he dictated to Rudolf HESS his political testament Mein Kampf (1925, Eng Trans 'My Struggle', 1939). He expanded his party greatly in the late 1920s, won important parliamentary election victories in 1930 and 1932, and though he was unsuccessful in the presidential elections of 1932 against HINDENBURG, he was made Chancellor in 1933. He then suspended the constitution, silenced all opposition, exploited successfully the burning of the REICHSTAG building, and brought the NAZI PARTY to power, having dozens of his opponents within his own party and the SA murdered by his bodyguard, the SS, in the

NIGHT OF THE LONG KNIVES (1934). He openly rearmed the country (1935), established the Rome–Berlin 'axis' with Mussolini (1936) and pursued an aggressive foreign policy which culminated in WORLD WAR II (3 Sep 1939). His domestic policy traded off social and economic improvements for political dictatorship enforced by the Secret State Police (GESTAPO). His government established concentration camps for political opponents and Jews, over 6 million of whom were murdered in the course of World War II. With his early war successes, he increasingly ignored the advice of military experts and wantonly extended the war with his long-desired invasion of the USSR in 1941. The tide turned in 1942 after the defeats at EL ALAMEIN and STALINGRAD. He miraculously survived the explosion of the bomb placed at his feet by Colonel STAUFFENBERG (July 1944), and purged the army of all suspects. When Germany was invaded, he retired to his Bunker, an air-raid shelter under the Chancellory building in Berlin. All available evidence suggests that Hitler and his wife, Eva BRAUN, committed suicide and had their bodies cremated (30 Apr 1945).

## Hitler–Stalin Pact ► GERMAN–SOVIET PACT

## Hitler Youth (Hitler-Jugend)
The organization, set up by Adolf HITLER in 1933, designed to inculcate Nazi principles in German youths. By 1935, membership accounted for almost 60 per cent of German boys. It became (1 July 1936) a state agency that all young 'Aryan' Germans were expected to join. On his tenth birthday, after various investigations (especially for 'racial purity'), a German boy would enter the Deutsches Jungvolk ('German Young People'). At 13, he was eligible to join the Hitler Youth, in which he remained until the age of 18, living an austere life, dominated by Nazi theory, generally with minimum parental guidance. When he was 18, he became a member of the Nazi Party, serving in the state labour service and the armed forces until at least the age of 21. A parallel organization, the Bund Deutscher Mädel ('League of German Girls'), trained girls for domestic duties and motherhood.

## Hittin, Battle of (4 July 1187)
This battle saw the destruction by the Sultan SALADIN of the field army of the Latin Kingdom of Jerusalem and led directly to his capture of Jerusalem (2 Oct 1187). An ill-advised march from Sepphoris, with Tiberias as its objective, led to GUY OF LUSIGNAN's Crusaders being caught at a disadvantage on hostile terrain by Saladin's combined muster, including as it did forces deriving from Egypt and the entire Fertile Crescent. The defeat of the Crusaders at Hittin, the capture of their nobility, and the destruction of the Latin field army, coupled with the subsequent loss of Jerusalem, constituted the proximate cause of the Third CRUSADE.

## HIV/AIDS
The human immunodeficiency virus (HIV) is a retrovirus that causes acquired immune deficiency syndrome (AIDS) and thereby exposes victims to a high risk of attack by a spectrum of serious medical conditions. HIV infection occurs through contact with certain types of bodily fluids from an infected person, thereby making the new host HIV-positive. This is

not the same as AIDS, but it is the condition from which AIDS usually develops. A collapse in the number of a certain type of white blood cell in the subject signals the suppression of the body's immune system. AIDS victims do not die of AIDS but of opportunistic conditions and infections taking advantage of the body's defencelessness when its immune system becomes depressed. AIDS may have originated from an animal source in Africa, and came to public attention during the 1980s, when it first appeared in the West and seemed to affect only homosexual men (the 'gay plague') but it subsequently presented in women and heterosexual men, often intravenous drug users or recipients of blood transfusions. The virus was isolated and identified in 1984, but the limited availability and effectiveness of anti-HIV drugs threw the emphasis in the 1980s onto prevention of infection, with public health campaigns promoting 'safe sex', needle-exchange programmes for intravenous drug users and restrictions on blood donation. Public health campaigns have been more successful in some countries than others; by 2003 rates of HIV infection in the USA and UK were less than 1 per cent but were much higher in Africa and particularly southern African countries, reaching 38.8 per cent of adults aged 15–49 in Swaziland. Such high rates of infection, largely the consequence of unsafe sexual practices and the refusal of some governments to admit the existence of the problem, are a growing demographic, economic and social disaster for the countries most affected. Their economies are deprived of the contributions of a significant proportion of the economically active workforce while faced with the rising costs of treatment for sufferers and the care of the many orphaned children. Since 2003 cheap generic copies of anti-HIV drugs have become available in developing countries but their availability has yet to have an impact on infection or death rates. International efforts to address the problems are headed by UNAIDS, a joint **UN** programme involving several UN agencies, which supports affected countries by providing technical support and training health workers. The **WORLD HEALTH ORGANIZATION**'s '3 by 5' campaign aims to treat 3 million HIV/AIDS sufferers by 2005. The **WORLD BANK**'s Multicountry AIDS Programme has allocated over US$1 billion in assistance in sub-Saharan Africa and over US$150 million for Caribbean countries.

**Hlinka, Andrei** (1864–1938)
Slovak priest and politician. As a young man he was attracted by the political stance of the Slovak National Party and by the concern for the peasants of the Magyar Populist Party. In 1905 he established the Slovak Populists Party as a compromise, but he was soon being harassed by the Hungarian authorities. In 1918 he supported the creation of Czechoslovakia but he was subsequently disappointed with centralist rule from Prague and his own non-involvement in governing his countrymen. In the 1920s and 1930s he built up his party and secured some political concessions from Prague. But in the middle of 1938 he used the opportunity of **BENEŠ**'s discomfiture to demand autonomy for Slovakia. However, he died in Aug and left **TISO** to develop a treasonable relationship with Germany.

**HNP** (*Herstigte Nasionale Party*, 'Reconstituted National Party')
Founded in 1969 by dissidents from the **NATIONAL PARTY**, the HNP sought to preserve **APARTHEID** undiluted, the Afrikaans language, and a public policy based upon Calvinist principles. It allied with the Conservative Party in the late 1980s to embarrass the National Party in individual constituencies, occasionally defeating its candidates. It continues to exist as a small minority party.

**Hoa Hao** ▶ CAO DAI/HOA HAO

**Hoare–Laval Pact**
An agreement concluded in 1935 by the British Foreign Secretary Samuel Hoare and the French Prime Minister Pierre **LAVAL**, aimed at the settlement of a dispute between Italy and Abyssinia. By this pact, large parts of Abyssinia were ceded to Italy. A public outcry against the pact led to its repudiation by Britain and to Hoare's resignation. ▶ ABYSSINIA, CONQUEST OF

**Hobbes, Thomas** (1588–1679)
English political philosopher. He wrote several works on government, and in 1646 became mathematics tutor to the Prince of Wales (the future **CHARLES II**) at the exiled English court in Paris, where he wrote his major work on political philosophy, *Leviathan* (1651). In it he argues that human beings are wholly selfish, and enlightened self-interest explains the nature and function of the sovereign state; we are forced to establish a social contract in which we surrender the right of aggression to an absolute ruler, whose commands are the law. *Leviathan* offended the royal exiles in Paris and the French government with its hostility to Church power and religious obedience, and in 1652 Hobbes returned to England, made his peace with **CROMWELL** and the Parliamentary regime, and settled in London. He was welcome at the court of the restored Charles II after 1660.

**Hoche, Lazare** (1768–97)
French revolutionary soldier. Promoted from corporal to general, he defended Dunkirk against **FREDERICK AUGUSTUS, DUKE OF YORK AND ALBANY**, and drove the Austrians out of Alsace (1793), ended the civil war in La Vendée (1795), commanded the attempted invasion of Ireland (1796) and defeated the Austrians at Neuwied (1797). ▶ VENDÉE, WARS OF THE

**Ho Chi Minh**, originally **Nguyen That Thanh** (1892–1969)
Vietnamese politician. From 1912 he visited London and the USA, and lived in France from 1918, where he was a founder-member of the Communist Party. From 1922 he was often in China and then Moscow. He led the **VIET MINH** independence movement from 1941, and directed the successful military operation against the French (1946–54). Prime Minister (1954–5) and President (1954–69) of North Vietnam, he was the leading force in the war between North and South Vietnam during the 1960s. ▶ VIETNAM WAR

**Höchstädt, Battle of** (1703)
The battle won by the Elector of Bavaria over the Imperial general Styrum in the War of the **SPANISH**

SUCCESSION. The Battle of BLENHEIM (1704) is sometimes referred to as the Second Battle of Höchstädt as the latter is the nearest large town to the village of Blenheim.

**Hodza, Milau** (1878–1944)
Slovak politician. A Lutheran, he worked with Catholics such as HLINKA before WORLD WAR I in order to secure some kind of autonomy for Slovakia. He hoped for improvement within Austria-Hungary but failing that, he favoured a Czech-Slovak solution, which is what came in 1918. He never abandoned his Slovak sentiments, though he became mostly a convinced Czechoslovak and was appointed Czechoslovak Premier in 1935. The strain of dealing with HITLER and HENLEIN from 1937 to 1938 put his loyalties to test, and there is evidence that he was talking out of turn both to the Germans and to disloyal Slovaks at the height of the pre-Munich crisis. In the final days before the MUNICH AGREEMENT, he was dropped from the premiership, and even abroad during WORLD WAR II his political contribution was slight.

**Høegh-Guldberg, Ove** (1731–1808)
Danish politician. Of humble Jutland origin, he studied theology at the University of Copenhagen, and in 1761 was appointed Professor at the Noble Academy in Sorø. In the same year, he also became the tutor of Prince Frederick, son of the late King Frederick V and his second wife, the powerful Queen Dowager, Juliane Marie. On 16 Jan 1772, Juliane Marie was the leader of a palace revolution that overthrew the self-appointed, progressive-minded dictator Johann Friedrich STRUENSEE, who since the summer of 1770 had filled the power gap created by the mental illness of King CHRISTIAN VII. After the palace revolution, Høegh-Guldberg became Denmark's most influential politician, for 12 years pursuing his cautious policies from his power base, the King's 'court cabinet', of which he was the Secretary. Høegh-Guldberg's court rule culminated in the years 1780 to 1784. In 1784 his regime was overturned by another coup d'état led by Crown Prince Frederick, son of King Christian VII, and by Høegh-Guldberg's principal political adversary, Andreas Peter BERNSTORFF. After this, Høegh-Guldberg became a civil servant in the provincial town of Aarhus, where he loyally implemented the progressive policies of the new regime.

**Hofer, Andreas** (1767–1810)
Tyrolese patriot leader and innkeeper. In 1808 he called the Tyrolese to arms to expel the French and Bavarians, and defeated the Bavarians at the Battle of Isel Berg (1809). The Treaty of VIENNA between Austria and France after the Battle of WAGRAM (July 1809) left Tyrol unsupported. The French again invaded; but in eight days Hofer routed them and retook Innsbruck, and for the next two months was ruler of his native land. By the Peace of Vienna (Oct) Austria again left Tyrol at the mercy of her enemies. Hofer once more took up arms, but this time the French and Bavarians were too strong for him; Hofer had to disband his followers and take refuge in the mountains. Two months later he was betrayed, captured and taken to Mantua, where he was tried by court martial and shot.

**Hoffa, Jimmy (James Riddle)** (1913–75)
US labour leader. He was a grocery warehouseman when he joined the TEAMSTERS' UNION in 1931. He proceeded to reorganize it, strengthening central control, and was elected President in 1957. In the same year the Teamsters were expelled from the AFL–CIO for repudiating its ethics code. Hoffa negotiated the Teamsters' first national contract in 1964, but following corruption investigations by the Attorney-General, Robert F KENNEDY, was imprisoned in 1967 for attempted bribery of a federal court jury. His sentence was commuted by President NIXON and he was given parole in 1971, on condition that he resigned as Teamsters' leader. In 1975 he disappeared and is thought to have been murdered.

**Hoffman, Abbie (Abbot)** (1936–89)
US political activist. Following a university education in which he received two psychology degrees, he was active in the CIVIL RIGHTS MOVEMENT before organizing in 1968 the Youth International Party (YIP) or YIPPIES. Following the riot at the Democratic Convention in Chicago in 1968, Hoffman was convicted of crossing state lines with intent to riot, but the conviction was later overturned. He and Rubin were later expelled as YIP leaders for failing to share the money they had earned through speaking engagements.

**Hofkapelle**
As early as the Carolingian period, all written work in the royal chancellory was undertaken by clerics. These clerics were referred to as the Kapelle ('chapel') and were under the direction of a head chaplain. From c.854 the chaplain was entrusted with the leadership of the Chancellory, and from 975 the office of Chancellor was always held by the Archbishop of Mainz. The clerics in the Hofkapelle (literally, 'court chapel') also undertook political and diplomatic missions, and many, particularly in the Ottonian period, attained important feudal positions. Its importance declined from the 11c onwards, although the chancellor was a cleric until the 15c. ► OTTONIANS

**Hofmeyr, Jan Hendrik** (1845–1909)
South African politician. He took to journalism, as 'Onze Jan', rose to be political leader of the Cape Dutch, and dominated the AFRIKANER BOND. He represented the Cape at the Colonial Conferences of 1887 and 1894. After the JAMESON RAID (1895) he parted from RHODES, and thereafter worked outside parliament. His nephew, Jan Hendrik (1894–1948), was Deputy Premier to SMUTS and advocated a liberal policy towards the Africans.

**Hogendorp, Gijsbert Karel** (1762–1834)
Dutch politician. A member of a patrician family, he studied law and became active in politics as a champion of the House of Orange during the revolutionary PATRIOT MOVEMENT in the 1780s. He became Pensionary of Rotterdam, but was out of office during the period of French domination of the Netherlands (1795–1813). As the French were withdrawing in 1812, he was instrumental in arranging the return of William of Orange (who became King WILLIAM I), and chaired the committee which drew up the new Dutch constitutions in the post-Napoleonic period. He was Foreign Minister (1813–14), and Vice-President of the Council of State (1814–16), but disagreed

with King William and spent the years 1816–25 as an MP highly critical of the government. His writings on political economy had considerable impact in the Netherlands, promoting both political and economic liberalism.

### Hohenlinden, Battle of (1800)

A confused but crucial battle in the closing stage of the French Revolutionary War, causing the Austrians to abandon the Second Coalition by the Armistice of Steyr. It was fought near Munich between the French, commanded by General Moreau, and Archduke John's Austrian forces, the latter suffering heavy casualties. ➤ FRENCH REVOLUTIONARY WARS

### Hohenlohe-Schillingsfürst, Chlodwig Karl Victor, Prince von (1819–1901)

Prussian politician and Chancellor. A supporter of BISMARCK's unification policies and a noted conservative, he served as a diplomat in Paris and Alsace-Lorraine, before becoming Chancellor (1894–1900) and Prime Minister of PRUSSIA.

### Hohenstaufen Dynasty

The German royal dynasty named after the castle of Staufen in north-eastern Swabia. From 1138 to 1254 its members wore the crown of the HOLY ROMAN EMPIRE, starting with CONRAD III and ending with CONRAD IV, the dynasty reaching its zenith under FREDERICK I, BARBAROSSA and FREDERICK II. They were also kings of Germany and of Sicily. The Hohenstaufen period is associated with a flowering of German courtly culture.

## HOHENSTAUFEN DYNASTY

| Regnal Dates (as Holy Roman Emperor) | Name |
|---|---|
| 1138/52 | Conrad III |
| 1152/90 | Frederick I, Barbarossa |
| 1190/7 | Henry VI |
| 1198/1208 | Philip of Swabia |
| 1198/1214 | Otto IV |
| 1215/50 | Frederick II |
| 1250/4 | Conrad IV |

### Hohenzollern Dynasty

The German ruling dynasty of Brandenburg-Prussia (1415–1918) and Imperial Germany (1871–1918). Originating in Swabia in the 9c, one branch of the family became Burgraves of Nuremberg; a descendant, Frederick VIII, was rewarded by the Emperor with the title of Elector of Brandenburg (1415). After the THIRTY YEARS' WAR, the Hohenzollerns pursued a consistent policy of state expansion and consolidation, generating a long-standing rivalry with the HABSBURG DYNASTY (1740–1871), from which BISMARCK ensured that the Hohenzollerns emerged successfully with the imperial title (1871). WORLD WAR I ruined Hohenzollern militarism, and forced the abdication of the last Emperor, WILLIAM II (1918). ➤ FREDERICK I (of Prussia); FREDERICK II, THE GREAT; FREDERICK III (of Germany); FREDERICK WILLIAM, THE GREAT ELECTOR; FREDERICK WILLIAM III; HOLY ROMAN EMPIRE; WILLIAM I (Emperor)

### Ho Hsiang-ning ➤ HE XIANGNING

### Hojo Family

A Japanese warrior family during the KAMAKURA

## HOHENZOLLERN DYNASTY

| Regnal Dates | Name |
|---|---|
| ➤ *Electors of Brandenburg* | |
| 1417/40 | Frederick I |
| 1440/70 | Frederick II |
| 1470/86 | Albert Achilles |
| 1486/99 | John Cicero |
| 1499/1535 | Joachim I |
| 1535/71 | Joachim II |
| 1571/98 | John George |
| 1598/1608 | Joachim Frederick |
| 1608/19 | John Sigismund |
| 1619/40 | George William |
| 1640/88 | Frederick William (The Great Elector) |
| ➤ *Kings of Prussia* | |
| 1701/13 | Frederick I (Frederick III as Elector of Brandenburg, 1688/1713) |
| 1713/40 | Frederick William I |
| 1740/86 | Frederick II, the Great |
| 1786/97 | Frederick William II |
| 1797/1840 | Frederick William III |
| 1840/61 | Frederick William IV |
| ➤ *Emperors of Germany* | |
| 1871/88 | William I (King of Prussia, 1861/88) |
| 1888 | Frederick III |
| 1888/1918 | William II |

SHOGUNATE, whose members became hereditary regents virtually ruling Japan for more than a century. The patriarch of the family, Hojo Tokimasa (1138–1215), was the father-in-law of the first Kamakura SHOGUN, Minamoto no Yoritomo (1147–99). After his death, Hojo exercised control over the shogunate, becoming regent in 1203; thereafter, the post became hereditary. Under the fifth Hojo regent, Hojo Tokimune (1268/84), the Mongol invasions of 1274 and 1281 were successfully repelled. The last effective Hojo regent, Hojo Takatoki (1316/26), frustrated Emperor DAIGO II's two attempts to overthrow the shogunate and restore direct imperial rule. With the overthrow of the Kamakura Shogunate in 1333 by ASHIKAGA TAKAUJI, the Hojo regency was abolished and the family ordered to commit suicide. ➤ MINAMOTO FAMILY

### Holkeri, Harri Hermanni (1937–)

Finnish politician. A political activist in his teens, he joined the youth league of the centrist National Coalition Party in 1959 and was its Information, Research and National Secretary between 1962 and 1971. Holkeri was elected to Helsinki City Council in 1969, entered Parliament the following year and was Prime Minister from 1987 to 1991. He was Speaker of the UN General Assembly in 2000–1, and head of the UN Mission in Kosovo (UNMIK)

### Holmes, Oliver Wendell (1841–1935)

US judge. Known as the 'Great Dissenter', he was the son of the writer Oliver Wendell Holmes (1809–94). Educated at Harvard, he became a lawyer, and served in the Union Army in the AMERICAN CIVIL WAR. From 1867 he practised law in Boston, became co-editor of the *American Law Review*, and was Professor of Law at Harvard (1882). He became Chief Justice (1899–1902) of the Supreme Court of Massachusetts, and Associate Justice of the US Supreme Court

## HOLY ROMAN EMPERORS

| Regnal Dates | Name | Regnal Dates | Name | Regnal Dates | Name |
|---|---|---|---|---|---|
| 800/14 | Charlemagne (Charles I) | 1081/93 | Hermann[2 4] | 1346/78 | Charles IV |
| 814/40 | Louis I, the Pious | 1093/1101 | Conrad[2 4] | 1378/1400 | Wenceslas[4] |
| 840/3 | Civil War | 1106/25 | Henry V | 1400/10 | Rupert I[4] |
| 843/55 | Lothair I | 1125/37 | Lothair II | 1410/37 | Sigismund |
| 855/75 | Louis II | 1138/52 | Conrad III[4] | 1438/9 | Albert II[4] |
| 875/7 | Charles II, the Bald | 1152/90 | Frederick I, Barbarossa | 1440/93 | Frederick III |
| 877/81 | Interregnum | 1190/7 | Henry VI | 1493/1519 | Maximilian I[4] |
| 881/7 | Charles III, the Fat | 1198/1214 | Otto IV | 1519/56 | Charles V[4] |
| 887/91 | Interregnum | 1198/1208 | Philip of Swabia[2 4] | 1556/64 | Ferdinand I[4] |
| 891/4 | Guido of Spoleto | 1215/50 | Frederick II | 1564/76 | Maximilian II[4] |
| 892/8 | Lambert of Spoleto[1] | 1246/7 | Henry Raspe[2 4] | 1576/1612 | Rudolf II[4] |
| 896/9 | Arnulf[2] | 1247/56 | William, Count of Holland[2 4] | 1612/19 | Matthias[4] |
| 901/5 | Louis III | | | 1619/37 | Ferdinand II[4] |
| 905/24 | Berengar I | 1250/4 | Conrad IV[4] | 1637/57 | Ferdinand III[4] |
| 911/18 | Conrad I[2 4] | 1254/73 | Great Interregnum | 1658/1705 | Leopold I[4] |
| 919/36 | Henry I, the Fowler[4] | 1257/72 | Richard[2 4] | 1705/11 | Joseph I[4] |
| 936/73 | Otto I, the Great | 1257/75 | Alfonso (Alfonso X of Castile)[2 4] | 1711/40 | Charles VI[4] |
| 973/83 | Otto II | | | 1740/2 | Interregnum |
| 983/1002 | Otto III | 1273/91 | Rudolf I[4] | 1742/5 | Charles VII[4] |
| 1002/24 | Henry II | 1292/8 | Adolf[4] | 1745/65 | Francis I[4] |
| 1024/39 | Conrad II | 1298/1308 | Albert I[4] | 1765/90 | Joseph II[4] |
| 1039/56 | Henry III | 1308/13 | Henry VII | 1790/2 | Leopold II[4] |
| 1056/1106 | Henry IV | 1314/26 | Frederick (III)[3 4] | 1792/1806 | Francis II[4] |
| 1077/80 | Rudolf of Rheinfelden[2 4] | 1314/46 | Louis IV, the Bavarian | | |

*Notes*
[1] Co-emperor
[2] Rival
[3] Co-regent
[4] Ruler not crowned at Rome; therefore, strictly speaking, only King of Germany

(1902–32). He earned his nickname because he frequently dissented from the conservative court's majority opinions, especially as the court moved to dismantle social legislation, particularly relating to regulation of the economy.

## Holocaust

The attempt by Nazi Germany to destroy systematically European Jews. From the inception of the Nazi regime in 1933, Jews were deprived of CIVIL RIGHTS, persecuted, physically attacked, imprisoned, pressurized to emigrate, and murdered. With the gradual conquest of Europe by Germany, the death toll increased, and a meeting at Wannsee (Jan 1942) made plans for the so-called 'final solution'. Jews were herded into concentration camps, slave labour camps, and extermination camps. By the end of WORLD WAR II in 1945, more than 6 million Jews had been murdered out of a total Jewish population of 8 million in those countries occupied by the Nazis. Of these the largest number, 3 million, were from Poland. Other minorities (gypsies, various religious sects, homosexuals) and millions of Soviet prisoners were also subject to Nazi atrocities, but the major genocide was against the Jewish people. ► BABI YAR; CONCENTRATION CAMP; NAZI PARTY

## Holstein

A county, then (1474) a duchy of the HOLY ROMAN EMPIRE. After the Peace of Prague (1866) it was incorporated into Prussia with Schleswig as the province of Schleswig-Holstein, both of which had large Danish minorities.

### Holt, Harold Edward (1908–67)

Australian politician. He entered the House of Representatives in 1935, becoming Deputy Leader of the LIBERAL PARTY OF AUSTRALIA (1956), and Leader and Prime Minister when Robert MENZIES retired (1966). During the VIETNAM WAR he strongly supported the USA with the slogan 'all the way with LBJ'. He died in office while swimming at Portsea, near Melbourne.

### Ho Lung ► HE LONG

### Holy Alliance (20 Nov 1815)

The alliance concluded after the final defeat of NAPOLEON I between Austria, Britain, Prussia and Russia, which was designed to ensure the exclusion of the House of Bonaparte from power in France and to guarantee the monarchist order in Europe. Each power made specific military commitments in the event of war with France; however, royalist France itself joined the alliance at the Congress of Aachen (Aix-la-Chapelle) in 1818.

### Holy League (1510)

An alliance of the papacy under JULIUS II with Venice, Aragon and England against France. ► ITALIAN WARS

### Holy League (1571)

An alliance of three Catholic powers, Venice, Spain and the papacy, after protracted negotiations by Pope PIUS V (1570–1), to counter Turkish supremacy in the eastern Mediterranean. The League's fleet, commanded by Don JOHN OF AUSTRIA, smashed the Turks at the Battle of LEPANTO (1571), before disagreements divided the

# *The Holy Roman Empire*

*Culture & Society*

The title Holy Roman Empire, *sacrum Romanum imperium*, was first used in 1254. The political institution to which it refers, however, came into being over 400 years earlier. Its establishment is usually dated to the coronation of Charlemagne (742–814) in 800 as Emperor over most of Christian Western Europe. It was known as the Roman Empire and the Holy Empire before its full title was adopted. After the Carolingian period it was always based principally in the territory of modern-day Germany, though its full extent fluctuated considerably. It was at its zenith in the early **Middle Ages**, between the coronation of Otto I in 962 and the death of **Frederick II** in 1250, but remained officially in existence until 1806. In Nazi terminology it was the first *Reich*, succeeded by the German empire of the Hohenzollerns and their own imperially minded state.

### Origins

From the outset, the Empire was to some extent a backward-looking institution. It originated in the desire of the papacy to recreate the Roman Empire in the West as a protector of the Church and a counterweight to the **Byzantine Empire**. The Byzantine emperors had maintained an unbroken rule and upheld the Roman and Christian tradition in the East throughout the period of migrations and upheavals that followed the fall of Rome itself. They also retained at least a nominal sovereignty over the Roman Empire's former western dominions. By the 7–8c, however, their political influence in the West was waning and they had serious doctrinal differences with successive popes. The popes' spiritual influence was increasing but they felt vulnerable in an often hostile environment in Italy and in Rome itself. This led them to consider establishing a temporal authority co-extensive with their spiritual one. Lacking the political and military power to set up an empire of their own, they turned to what was, at that time, the predominant political force in Western Europe, the Kingdom of the **Franks**, and decided to bestow imperial status on it and its rulers.

By the time of the accession of Charlemagne as their king in 771, the Franks ruled all of modern France except Brittany, the Rhineland and much of central and south-western Germany. Moreover, from the time of the conversion of King Clovis in 496, they had been faithful and effective defenders of the Roman Catholic Church and Christendom. Clovis defeated the Visigoth Alaric II, an Arian heretic, at Vouillé in 497. Charles Martel, Charlemagne's grandfather, defeated Muslim invaders from Spain at Poitiers in 736. Charlemagne again fought the Muslims at Roncesvalles in 778 and established a buffer zone beyond the Pyrenees to protect the western flank of Christendom. By conquering and converting the heathen Saxons and finally overthrowing the northern Italian Kingdom of Lombardy, which the popes had long perceived as a threat to them, Charlemagne further enhanced his claims to the imperial title. It was bestowed on him in Rome by Pope Leo III on Christmas Day 800.

Charlemagne was outlived by only one of his sons so that, despite the Frankish custom of dividing up the ruler's territory between his surviving heirs, at least for administrative purposes, the Empire was passed on intact to Louis I, who reigned from 814 to 840. Dissension between Louis' sons, however, led to the division of Frankish territory into three parts and, in particular, to the loss of most of the territory of present-day France to the Empire thereafter.

### Emperor versus pope

The next significant imperial dynasty came from the East Frankish or German section of Charlemagne's former realm and established the tradition that the king of the Germans almost automatically became the emperor. The career of Otto I, the Great, in some ways mirrors that of Charlemagne. He succeeded his father, Henry the Fowler, as King in 936 and continued his work of bringing the German tribal duchies under royal control. He entered northern Italy to defend

---

allies; by 1573 Spain continued the struggle alone.

### Holy League (1576)

An association of militant French Catholics, led by Henry, 3rd Duke of **GUISE**, until his death in 1588. One of its members, a monk, assassinated **HENRY III** (of France), after which the League proclaimed the Cardinal de Bourbon king as 'Charles X'; however, **HENRY IV** managed to impose himself as king by renouncing Protestantism ('Paris is worth a mass'). ► **BOURBON, HOUSE OF; GUISE, HOUSE OF**

### Holy League (1684)

The union of the empire, Poland, Venice and the papacy against Turkey, following the imperial repossession of Vienna (1683). Pope **INNOCENT XI** planned further crusades in Hungary, Greece and Moldavia; the latter failed (1686), but after several years' fighting (1683–99) the League recovered most of Hungary for the Habsburgs, and began the reconquest of Greece (1685–7). ► **HABSBURG DYNASTY**

### Holyoake, Sir Keith Jacka (1904–83)

New Zealand politician. A successful farmer who represented New Zealand's agricultural industry over-

seas, he sat in the House of Representatives as its youngest member (1932–8). Re-elected in 1943, he became Deputy Leader of the National Party in 1947, Deputy Prime Minister in 1949 and, briefly, Party Leader and Prime Minister in 1957. He was Prime Minister (1960–72) and Governor-General of New Zealand (1977–80).

### Holy Roman Empire, The ► *See panel and table*

### Home Guard

A British home defence militia raised during the summer of 1940, when the German armies seemed poised to complete the conquest of Western Europe by invading Great Britain. At first called the Local Defence Volunteers, the name was changed at Prime Minister Winston **CHURCHILL**'s urging to the more evocative title of 'Home Guard'. The force was finally stood down in 1945. ► **WORLD WAR II**

### Homelands ► **APARTHEID**

### Home of the Hirsel, Baron, formerly Sir Alec (Alexander Frederick) Douglas-Home, 14th Earl of Home (1903–95)

British politician. He became a Conservative MP in

Queen Adelaide of Lombardy against a usurper, married her, became ruler of her territories, defeated the pagan Magyars decisively at the Battle of Lechfeld in 955, and returned to Italy to assist and protect Pope John XII against the people of Rome. He was rewarded by being crowned emperor in 962.

Otto, his immediate successors, and the Salian and Hohenstaufen dynasties that followed them, extended and consolidated the territory of the Empire until by the 13c it covered all of central Europe from Holstein in the north to Sicily in the south, and from Lyons in the west to Vienna and beyond in the east. They frequently faced revolts within Germany and on their borders, but the main source of political trouble for them lay in Italy and, in particular, in their relationship with the papacy.

A prime cause of dissension was the question of who had the right to invest members of the higher clergy, bishops and abbots, in their offices, but behind that lay the much larger issue of whose authority was supreme in Christendom, that of the emperor or that of the pope.

Early emperors used ecclesiastical appointments to consolidate their power in Germany and were powerful enough to depose popes with impunity, if it suited them. By the time of the Emperor **Henry IV**, the then pope, **Gregory VII**, felt he was on strong enough ground doctrinally and politically to mount a sustained challenge to the emperor. Gregory refused to ratify some ecclesiastical appointments made by Henry in Milan. Henry impulsively declared Gregory deposed. Gregory responded by excommunicating Henry and absolving his subjects from their allegiance. When Henry's enemies in Germany took advantage of this to discuss the election of a new king, he was forced to reconcile himself with Gregory and did penance for three days in the snow at **Canossa** in 1077. Though Henry later renewed the conflict and appointed a new pope, his act of submission had a powerful symbolic significance. Later emperors, such as **Frederick I, Barbarossa** and **Frederick II**, spent large amounts of time in Italy attempting and often succeeding in asserting their authority and extending their possessions there and battling with the popes. But after Frederick II's death in 1250, the tide turned decisively against them.

### Guelfs and Ghibellines

The **Guelfs** and **Ghibellines** were political factions in Italy in the 13–14c. Their opposition arose directly out of the emperors' involvement in Italian politics and disputes with the pope. The Guelfs supported the pope against the Empire and were to some extent an Italian nationalist party; the Ghibellines supported the Empire against the pope. Large cities with an independent municipal tradition tended to be Guelf, the great nobles tended to be Ghibelline. Likewise northern Italy tended to be Ghibelline and central Italy Guelf. The conflict was particularly intense in Florence from which the Ghibellines were expelled in 1266. A later conflict between two factions of the Guelfs there resulted in the banishment of the poet Dante Alighieri from his native city in 1309.

### Electors

By ancient tradition the kings of the Germans were elected to their office. This procedure was adopted into the Empire. A college of electors was definitively established after 1250. Its membership and the members' rights were defined by the **Golden Bull** of 1356. From 1356 there were seven **Electors**: the archbishops of Trier, Mainz and Cologne, the Duke of Saxony, the Count Palatine of the Rhine, the Margrave of Brandenburg and the King of Bohemia. In the 17c the Duke of Bavaria was added to the list, and also the Duke of Brunswick-Lüneburg who became the Elector of Hanover. Elections were held in the cathedral of Frankfurt am Main, and from 1562 imperial coronations were held there too. The last emperor to be crowned by the pope in Rome was **Frederick III** in 1452. The Empire had an assembly, the **Imperial Diet**, most famously convened at Worms in 1521 by **Charles V** to pronounce on Martin Luther and his writings.

### The Habsburgs

**Rudolf I** was the first **Habsburg** King of Germany, elected in 1273, but he was never actually crowned as emperor. In

1931 and was Neville **CHAMBERLAIN**'s Secretary during the negotiations with **HITLER** and beyond (1937–40). He became Minister of State at the Scottish Office (1951–5), succeeded to the peerage as 14th Earl of Home (1951), was Commonwealth Relations Secretary (1955–60), and Foreign Secretary (1960–3). After **MACMILLAN**'s resignation, he surprisingly emerged from the process of consultation as Leader of the **CONSERVATIVE PARTY** and, thus, Premier (1963–4). He made history by renouncing his peerage and fighting a by-election, during which, although Premier, he was technically a member of neither House. After the 1964 defeat by the **LABOUR PARTY**, he was Leader of the Opposition until replaced in 1965 by Edward **HEATH**, in whose 1970–4 government he was Foreign Secretary. In 1974 he was made a life peer.

it is often seen by its supporters as a precursor of independence. Ther term was first applied to policies for **IRELAND**, Irish Home Rule Bills being introduced and defeated in 1886 and 1893. Two other Bills were passed, in 1912 and 1920, but the first was suspended by the outbreak of World War I, and the 1920 legislation became operative only within **NORTHERN IRELAND** (1922–72); the rest of Ireland became virtually independent **IRISH FREE STATE** by treaty in 1921. Scottish Home Rule was a Scottish Liberal cause from the 1880s, but was achieved only in 1999 when referenda endorsed devolution for **SCOTLAND** and (more contentiously) for **WALES**. The restoration of self-government in Northern Ireland, introduced in 1998 but suspended in 2002, has proved difficult to achieve. ► **GOOD FRIDAY AGREEMENT; IRA; PLAID CYMRU; SCOTTISH NATIONAL PARTY**

### Home Rule

A term used in British politics for the handing down of certain legislative powers and administrative functions, previously exercised by a higher authority, to an elected body within a geographically defined area; usually put forward as an alternative to separatism,

### Homestead Act (1862)

A US law aimed at increasing the agricultural development of the West. It granted 160 acres/65 hectares of public land to settlers who agreed to stay five years and to cultivate their land. Homesteaders had to be US citizens or to have filed for citizenship, and either

addition to his original lands in Swabia, Rudolf acquired the dukedom of Austria which was to be the basis of his descendants' territory and power for the next six centuries. **Albert I**, his son, succeeded him after a short intermission, but was assassinated by his nephew in 1308. The imperial crown then passed out of the Habsburg line until 1437. From then, with a brief interruption in 1742–5, the Habsburg family provided all the Holy Roman Emperors until the title was abolished in 1806.

The Habsburgs' international expansion began in the late 15c through a series of dynastic alliances. **Maximilian I** married the heiress of Burgundy and the Netherlands, and later married his son to the daughter of the King of Spain. **Bohemia** and Hungary were also annexed to Austria through a marriage treaty arranged by him which took effect shortly after his death. His grandson and successor, **Charles V**, was both Holy Roman Emperor and King of Spain, and, as master of the Spanish colonies in America and elsewhere, could truly claim to be the ruler of 'an empire on which the sun never sets'. After Charles's abdication in 1556, the Habsburg dominions were divided again between a Spanish line, which died out in 1700, and a German one which continued to rule as Holy Roman Emperors, and subsequently as Emperors of Austria, until 1918.

### Decline

International entanglements had throughout the history of the Empire frequently diverted the emperor's attention away from one of his main tasks: the maintenance of his authority over the disparate states of Germany. Electors sometimes chose a weak Emperor in the hope of achieving greater independence; conversely, strong emperors preferred to keep the states weak and disunited to avoid any threat to their power. The upheavals of the **Reformation** during the reign of Charles V further complicated the situation by leaving some German states and towns, especially those in the north, Protestant, and others Catholic. The Empire remained Catholic and, under the Habsburgs, was based in the south-east. The **Thirty Years' War** in the next century pitted the emperor against the Protestant princes allied with Sweden and France, devastated Germany and seriously weakened the Empire. After the Peace of **Westphalia** in 1648, it lost all but nominal authority over the German states, and France became the dominant power in Europe. The 18c saw the rise of **Prussia** to the point where it was Austria's military and political equal within Germany. It was finally the threat that **Napoleon I**, already crowned Emperor of the French, might attempt to appropriate the Holy Roman title in an attempt to establish a European hegemony that led **Francis II** to abolish it in 1806 and restyle himself Emperor of Austria. ► **Habsburg Dynasty**; **Hohenstaufen Dynasty**; **Hohenzollern Dynasty**; **Salians**

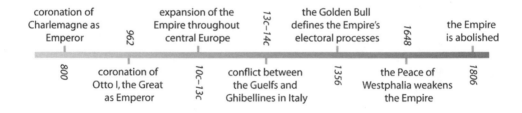

heads of families or over 21 years of age.

### Homestead Steel Strike (1892)

A five-month strike, one of the bitterest industrial disputes in US labour history, which seriously weakened organized labour in the steel industry at the Carnegie Steel Company, near Pittsburgh, USA. When the union would not agree to a wage cut, the manager, Henry Frick, refused to negotiate except with individual employees. He then recruited strike-breakers and hired 300 Pinkerton detectives to protect them. The union seized the works, and an armed battle broke out when the Pinkertons attempted to break in, in which several men were killed or injured. Control of the factory was regained only when the **NATIONAL GUARD** was sent in at Frick's request by the Governor of Pennsylvania. ► **PINKERTON, ALAN**

### Honda Toshiaki (1744–1821)

Japanese political economist and navigator. He learnt Dutch in order to acquire knowledge of the West and, after surveying Japan's northern island of Hokkaido in 1801, he advocated a programme to bring about wealth and power, focusing on the manufacture of gunpowder and metals, the encouragement of ship-

ping, and the colonization of Hokkaido. Honda's programme envisaged an end to the traditional policy of isolation and the promotion of state-sponsored foreign trade, thus anticipating developments after the **MEIJI RESTORATION** (1868).

**HONDURAS** official name **Republic of Honduras**

A republic in Central America, bounded to the south-west by El Salvador; to the west by Guatemala; to the east and south-east by Nicaragua; to the north by the Caribbean Sea; and to the south by the Pacific Ocean. The centre of Maya culture in the 4–9c, it was settled by the Spanish in the early 16c, and became a province of Guatemala. Honduras gained independence from Spain in 1821 and joined the CENTRAL AMERICAN FEDERATION. It became an independent sovereign state in 1838. There were several military coups in the 1960s and 1970s, and in 1981 the first civilian government for over 100 years took office. During the 1980s it was the base for rebels (CONTRAS) fighting against the government of Nicaragua. Honduras became dependent on help from the USA, which supported the rebels. The Contra war ended in 1990, but internal unrest continued throughout the 1990s and raised concerns about human rights abuses. In Oct 1998 the economy was devastated by the impact of the unprecedented Hurricane Mitch.

### Honecker, Erich (1912–94)
East German politician. Active in the communist youth movement from an early age, he was involved in underground resistance to HITLER, and was imprisoned for ten years. Released by Soviet forces, he became the first Chairman of the Free German Youth in the German Democratic Republic (1946–55). He first entered the Politburo in 1958, oversaw the building of the BERLIN WALL in 1961, and was elected party chief in 1971, becoming head of state from 1976 to 1989. Although prepared to deal with the West, he maintained a tight grip on East Germany. He was dismissed as a consequence of the anti-communist revolution. Manslaughter charges, instigated against him for the deaths of those fleeing East Germany who fell victim to his regime's 'shoot-to-kill' policy at her borders, were dropped in Jan 1993, after it was revealed that he was terminally ill. ► REVOLUTION OF 1989

**HONG KONG**

A special administrative region of the People's Republic of China, formerly (to 1997) a British Crown Colony. It is situated off the coast of south-east China, on the South China Sea. Britain first occupied Hong Kong during the first Opium War in 1841, and it was officially ceded to Britain by China the following year in one of the terms of the Treaty of NANJING; in addition to paying an indemnity, opening five TREATY PORTS to foreign trade, and abolishing the COHONG, China was compelled to cede the island of Hong Kong 'in perpetuity' to Britain. Under British rule, Hong Kong became a free-trade entrepôt, attracting migrants from the nearby province of Guangdong. The Kowloon Peninsula on the adjoining mainland was added to the colony in 1860, following the second of the OPIUM WARS (1856–60). Hong Kong was occupied by the Japanese in WORLD WAR II, but reoccupied by the British in 1945. The New Territories had been leased to Britain for 99 years in 1898, and, under the Sino-British Declaration initialled in 1984 by which Britain agreed to cede the whole of Hong Kong at the end of the lease, the region was restored

to China in July 1997. Tung Chee-Hwa was appointed the first chief executive of the new Hong Kong Special Administrative Region and pledged to abide by the 'one country, two systems' plan which was also outlined in the 1984 declaration to preserve the existing way of life. In 1990, China's Congress passed the Basic Law, Hong Kong's constitution, which guarantees that its social and economic systems will remain unchanged for 50 years.

### Hong Rengan (Hung Jen-kan) (1822–64)
Distant cousin and close associate of HONG XIUQUAN, leader of the TAIPING REBELLION. Left at home to look after family affairs when Xiuquan launched the rebellion (1850), he later went to Hong Kong, became a Christian, and studied Western culture. In 1859 he succeeded in reaching the rebel capital at Nanjing (Nanking), where he tried to introduce a programme of political, religious and military reforms. His aims were frustrated by the increasing madness of Xiuquan, the opposition of the rebellion's leaders, and the hostility of the British Minister to China. After the recapture of Nanjing by the Imperial forces (1864), he was caught and executed.

### Hong Xiuquan (Hung Hsiu-ch'üan) (1813–64)
Chinese revolutionary. Leader of the TAIPING REBELLION in China, and self-styled Divine Sovereign of the Heavenly Kingdom of Transcendent Peace. The son of a poor Guangdong farmer of HAKKA stock, during an illness he had religious visions which led him to preach a new Christian revelation in China. In 1843 he and two cousins began to preach and to destroy idols, arousing the opposition of Imperial forces. In 1851 he proclaimed a theocratic kingdom, and by 1853 his movement, half a million-strong, had taken Nanjing (Nanking). By 1855 the war against the Manchus had reached stalemate, and there were internal dissensions within his movement. In 1864 the troops of ZENG GUOFAN broke into Nanjing and massacred the Taipings within. Hong was already dead, either by his own hand or as a result of the siege. ► HONG RENGAN

### Honorius III, originally Cencio Savelli (d.1227)
Pope (1216/27). Unanimously elected as successor to INNOCENT III, his pontificate was at first dominated by the need to involve FREDERICK II in crusade. Concessions to achieve this aim were exploited by the Emperor for his own ends. Honorius then devoted his energies to the suppression of heresy within the boundaries of Christendom and the extension of those boundaries in the Baltic and Spain.

### Hood, Samuel Hood, 1st Viscount (1724–1816)
British admiral. He joined the navy in 1741, and fought during the AMERICAN REVOLUTION, when he defeated the French in the West Indies (1782), for which he was made a baron in the Irish peerage. In 1784 he became an MP, and in 1788 a Lord of the Admiralty. In 1793 he directed the occupation of Toulon and the operations in the Gulf of Lyons. He was made viscount in 1796.

### Hooks, Benjamin Lawson (1925–)
US CIVIL RIGHTS leader. A minister and lawyer, he was appointed by President NIXON to the Federal Communications Commission (FCC) in 1972 and became the first black American to serve there. After

leaving the FCC in 1977, he took over the leadership of the **NAACP**, a position he held until 1993.

**Hoover, Herbert Clark** (1874–1964)
US politician and 31st President. During **WORLD WAR I** he was associated with food and relief efforts in Europe. In 1921 he became Secretary of Commerce. As President (1929–33), his belief in spontaneous economic recovery made him reluctant to provide massive federal assistance for the unemployed after the stock market crash of 1929. This unpopular position led to his defeat by Franklin D **ROOSEVELT** in 1932. Following **WORLD WAR II**, he assisted **TRUMAN** with the various US European economic-relief programmes. ► **GREAT DEPRESSION**; **REPUBLICAN PARTY**

**Hoover, J(ohn) Edgar** (1895–1972)
US public official. Director of the **FBI**, his length of service, from 1924 until his death (because President Lyndon B **JOHNSON** exempted him from civil service retirement regulations) has been interpreted both as a tribute to his national importance in the fight against crime and as a recognition that he had learnt too much about the politicians. In the early days, his force was at a disadvantage in dealing with the gangsters of **PROHIBITION**, but with the **LINDBERGH** kidnapping case the FBI's powers were considerably strengthened. His selection and training of the 'G-Men' created an effective and efficient organization. The application of modern scientific techniques enabled him to develop counter-espionage methods of value not only during **WORLD WAR II** and the **COLD WAR**, but also in operations against the **MAFIA** and the **KU KLUX KLAN**. Highly sensitive to criticisms of the FBI, Hoover responded angrily to the strictures contained in the Warren Commission's report on the assassination of President **KENNEDY**, but he then used the urban riots of the 1960s with great political skill to increase the Bureau's powers and funding. A fanatical anti-communist, he saw much **CIVIL RIGHTS** protest in this light and flagrantly abused his powers in some investigations of the civil rights and anti-**VIETNAM WAR** movements (notably that of Martin Luther **KING**, Jr).

**Hoovervilles**
Shantytowns built by the unemployed during the **GREAT DEPRESSION**. They proliferated on the outskirts of cities and near rail junctions, where jobless men gathered to jump freight trains in search of a free ride to another part of the country in the hope of finding work. The name derives from President Herbert **HOOVER** (1929–33), whom many contemporaries blamed for failing to act decisively in the face of the USA's worst economic disaster.

**Hopkins, Harry Lloyd** (1890–1946)
US administrator. He was federal emergency relief administrator in the 1933 **GREAT DEPRESSION**, became Secretary of Commerce (1938–40), and supervised the Lend–Lease programme in 1941. A close friend of Franklin D **ROOSEVELT**, he undertook several important missions to Russia, Britain and other countries during **WORLD WAR II**. ► **LEND–LEASE AGREEMENT**; **NEW DEAL**

**Hore-Belisha, (Isaac) Leslie Hore-Belisha, 1st Baron** (1893–1957)
British barrister and politician. He became a London journalist, and a Liberal MP (1923). In 1934, as Minister of Transport, he gave his name to the 'Belisha' beacons, drafted a new highway code, and inaugurated driving tests for motorists. As Secretary of State for War (1937–40), he carried out several army reforms, and introduced conscription in 1939. He received a peerage in 1954. ► **LIBERAL PARTY** (UK)

**Horn, Arvid Bernhard** (1664–1742)
Swedish politician. Born in Finland, he began his career in the army, and on the outbreak of the **GREAT NORTHERN WAR** (1700) was a major-general. He won the favour of King **CHARLES XII** of Sweden, who in 1705 appointed him to the Royal Council and five years later made him Chancellor. Apart for a brief period under Queen **ULRIKA ELEONORA**, he held this office until the victory of his opponents, the Hat Party, in 1738. He dominated Swedish political life during the first two decades of the **AGE OF LIBERTY**, conducting a policy of peaceful reconstruction after the strains of the Great Northern War.

**Horrocks, Sir Brian Gwynne** (1895–1985)
British general. He joined the army in 1914, and served in France and Russia. In 1942 he commanded the 9th Armoured Division and then the 13th and 10th Corps in North Africa, where he helped to defeat **ROMMEL**. Wounded at Tunis, he headed the 30th Corps during the Allied invasion (1944). Horrocks was well known as a military journalist and broadcaster. ► **NORTH AFRICAN CAMPAIGN**; **WORLD WAR II**

**Hortense**, originally **Eugénie-Hortense de Beau-harnais** (1783–1837)
Queen of the Kingdom of Holland (1806/10). The daughter of General Alexandre **BEAUHARNAIS** and the future French Empress **JOSEPHINE**, she married **NAPOLEON I**'s brother **LOUIS NAPOLEON** in 1802, and so became Queen of Holland (the present-day Netherlands). She took many lovers and had several children of uncertain fatherhood, including the future Emperor **NAPOLEON III**, who was said to be the child of a Dutch admiral. In 1810 she divorced her husband and went to Paris as the Duchess of Saint-Leu.

**Horthy, Miklós Nagybányai** (1868–1957)
Hungarian sailor, politician and regent (1920/44). He became commander of the Austro-Hungarian fleet in 1918, and was then Minister of War in the counter-revolutionary 'white' government in 1919, opposing and suppressing Béla **KUN**'s communist regime in 1920. He became regent, presiding over a resolutely conservative, authoritarian system. In 1937 he became politically more active, and in **WORLD WAR II** he supported the **AXIS POWERS** until Hungary was overrun by the Germans in 1944. He was imprisoned by the Germans, but released by the Allies in 1945. He lived thereafter in Portugal, where he died.

**Horton, James Africanus** (1835–83)
Sierra Leonean doctor and surgeon-major. He served in the British Army and was the author of *West African Countries and Peoples* (1868). He acted as an adviser to traditional chiefs in the Gold Coast, and is regarded as one of the intellectual founders of modern West African nationalism.

**Horváth, Mihály** (1809–78)
Hungarian historian, prelate and revolutionary.

Professor at the University of Vienna (1844) and Bishop of Csanád (1848), he took an active part in the revolution of 1848 and then became Minister of Education in **KOSSUTH**'s government. After the revolution was crushed in 1849, he lived in exile, but returned under the amnesty of 1867.

**Ho Shen** ► HE SHEN

## Hospitallers
Members (priests or brother knights subject to monastic vows) of the Order of the Hospital of St John of Jerusalem, originally a purely charitable organization to care for sick pilgrims to the Holy Land. The warrior element developed and became predominant, and from the 12c they played a prominent role in the Crusades as an international religious-military order. After the loss of Acre in 1291, they transferred their headquarters to Limassol, Cyprus (1292), then Rhodes (1309), but were expelled by the Ottoman Turks in 1523. They moved to Malta (1530), which they held until dislodged by **NAPOLEON I** in 1798. The Sovereign Order is now based in Rome. It is known also as the Order of the Hospital of St John of Jerusalem, the Knights of Rhodes, the Knights of Malta or the Knights of St John of Jerusalem.

## hospodar
The title given to the governors of the Danubian Principalities under Ottoman rule. The office was at first filled by native princes, but after 1709 it was monopolized by the **PHANARIOTS**, who grew rich on the taxes raised from the Provinces. The Treaty of **ADRIANOPLE** (1829) decreed that hospodars were to be elected for life and this was confirmed by the **ORGANIC STATUTES**. In 1849 Russia and the Porte agreed to cooperate in the appointment, rather than the election, of the hospodars. The separate offices of Hospodar of Moldavia and Hospodar of Wallachia were first united in the person of Alexander **CUZA** and through him evolved into the office of Prince, and finally King, of Romania. ► **MOLDAVIA AND WALLACHIA**

## Hot Autumn of 1969
The term (in Italian, *Autunno caldo*) applied to the period of workers' sit-ins and strikes in Italy that represent the climax of student and worker demonstrations and agitation, begun in 1967.

## Hotta Masayoshi (1810–64)
Japanese feudal lord (**DAIMYO**). He became Senior Chief Councillor of the **TOKUGAWA SHOGUNATE** in 1855, at a time when the Western powers, particularly the USA, were pressing for new treaties that would open more of Japan's ports to foreign trade. He negotiated a full commercial treaty with the USA (Feb 1858), allowing a US minister to reside at the shogunal capital and open four more ports to foreign trade (in addition to the two opened in an 1854 treaty). In an attempt to silence critics of the treaty, Hotta took the unprecedented step of personally seeking imperial approval of the treaty. The Emperor and his advisers, however, continued to favour seclusion, and an imperial decree, while recognizing that foreign policy was the responsibility of the shogunate, did not specifically approve the treaty, thus damaging the shogunate's credibility. Hotta was shortly thereafter replaced as the regime's senior official by **II NAOSUKE**.
► **TREATY PORTS**

**Hottentots** ► KHOISAN

## Houphouët-Boigny, Felix (1905–93)
Ivorien politician. The son of a chief, he was educated in Côte d'Ivoire and at Dakar, and was a medical assistant and planter before turning to politics. He was President of the *Syndicat Agricole Africain* in 1944 and a founder of the *Parti Démocratique de la Côte d'Ivoire* (PDCI). Elected to the French Constituent Assembly (1945–6) and then National Assembly (1946–58), he held a series of ministerial posts. He became Prime Minister of Côte d'Ivoire in 1959 and President, at independence, in 1960. His paternalistic rule, which also combined close relations with France and support for capitalist enterprises, saw Côte d'Ivoire initially develop more successfully than most other West African countries, but economic decline and profligacy, especially the building of a palace and cathedral at Yamoussoukro, reduced his popularity.

## House of Representatives
In the USA, one of the two chambers of **CONGRESS**, in which, under the Constitution, legislative power is vested. The 435 members of the House are elected from Congressional districts according to population, although each state has at least one representative. Many state legislatures also have a House of Representatives. Although many bills are acted on by both the **SENATE** and the House, all revenue bills must originate in the House.

## Houston, Sam(uel) (1793–1863)
US politician. A former Governor of Tennessee, he moved to Texas in 1833 and led the force which overwhelmed the Mexican army under **SANTA ANNA** at San Jacinto and won Texan independence in 1836. After Texas was admitted to the Union in 1845, he served as US Senator and later became its Governor (1859). A consistent unionist, he refused in 1861 to convene the legislature to vote on secession. Texas was therefore the last state to secede and Houston was deposed for refusing to swear allegiance to the Confederacy.

## Howard, Catherine (c.1520–1542)
Queen of England. She was the fifth wife of **HENRY VIII**, and was a granddaughter of the 2nd Duke of Norfolk. She became Queen in the same month that **ANNE OF CLEVES** was divorced (July 1540). A year later she was charged by **CRANMER** with intercourse before her marriage with a musician and a kinsman, and was beheaded for treason.

## Howard, Charles, 1st Earl of Nottingham (1536–1624)
English admiral. A cousin of Queen **ELIZABETH I**, he commanded the English fleet against the Spanish **ARMADA** (1588). He succeeded to his father's title (Baron Howard of Effingham) in 1573, and became Lord High Admiral in 1585. For his role in the Cadiz expedition (1596) he was created an earl, and in 1601 he quelled **ESSEX**'s rising.

## Howard, Thomas, 3rd Duke of Norfolk (1473–1554)
English statesman. The brother-in-law of **HENRY VII**, he held several high offices under **HENRY VIII**. He was the uncle of Anne **BOLEYN** and Catherine **HOWARD**, after whose execution (1542) he lost power. The father of the Earl of Surrey, who was executed for

treason by Henry VIII, he would himself have been executed as an accessory but for Henry's own death. He remained in prison during the reign of **EDWARD VI**, but was released by the Catholic **MARY I**.

### Howe, Clarence Decatur (1886–1960)
Canadian businessman and politician. In 1936 he was appointed Minister of Transport in the Liberal government of Mackenzie **KING** and played a major role in establishing Trans-Canada Airlines (later Air Canada). He proved to be a superb administrator during **WORLD WAR II**, as Director of the Wartime Prices and Trade Board and Minister for Munitions and Supply. Faced with the refusal by private companies to produce synthetic rubber, he set up the Polymer Corporation as a crown company. Its success, both financial and in research and development, enabled the government to refuse its competitors' demands to close it down. Although he always had little patience with politics and politicians, Howe became Minister of Reconstruction in **SAINT LAURENT**'s administration in 1951, when the Defence Production Act gave him such wide economic powers that he became known as the 'Minister of Everything'. However, his management of the Trans-Canada Pipeline project, which he rammed through parliament in 1956 over outspoken opposition and charges that he had sold out the public interest to private US companies, marked the beginning of the end of more than 20 years of Liberal federal government and allowed the Conservatives a platform of reform on which they won the 1957 election. ➤ **LIBERAL PARTY** (Canada)

### Howe, Joseph (1804–73)
Canadian politician. In 1836 he entered Nova Scotia's assembly where he mobilized the reform party. His open letters to Lord John **RUSSELL**, making the case for **RESPONSIBLE GOVERNMENT**, were instrumental in winning it for Nova Scotia in 1848. As fishery commissioner, Howe was out of politics during the **CONFEDERATION MOVEMENT** (which he opposed). He was Premier of Nova Scotia in 1860–3 and, after federation, entered the first Canadian government at Ottawa. In 1869 John A **MACDONALD** persuaded him to join the Dominion cabinet (and increased the province's subsidy). His public opposition to administration policy caused some embarrassment and he resigned in 1873.

### Howe, Julia Ward (1819–1910)
US abolitionist and reformer, author of the 'Battle Hymn of the Republic', adopted as a rally song by the Union side in the **AMERICAN CIVIL WAR**. A respected writer, poet and lecturer, she was an early leader in the American women's suffrage movement. ➤ **ABOLITIONISM**

### Howe, Richard Howe, 1st Earl (1726–99)
British admiral. The brother of William, 5th Viscount **HOWE**, he entered the navy at 13, and distinguished himself in the **SEVEN YEARS' WAR**. He became a Lord of the Admiralty (1763), Treasurer of the Navy (1765), First Lord of the Admiralty (1783) and earl (1788). In 1776 he was appointed commander of the British fleet during the American War of Independence and, in 1778, defended the American coast against a superior French force. On the outbreak of war with France (1793), he took command of the Channel Fleet,

defeating the French off Ushant at the Battle of the **GLORIOUS FIRST OF JUNE** (1794). ➤ **FRENCH REVOLUTIONARY WARS**

### Howe, William Howe, 5th Viscount (1729–1814)
British soldier. The brother of Richard, 1st Earl **HOWE**, he joined the army in 1746 and served under General James **WOLFE** at **LOUISBOURG** (1758) and **QUEBEC** (1759), where he led the famous advance to the **PLAINS OF ABRAHAM** (1759). He became an MP in 1758. He was a commander in North America during the **AMERICAN REVOLUTION**, when his victories included Bunker Hill (1775), the capture of New York City (1776, with naval support provided by his brother) and **BRANDYWINE** Creek (1777). After his failure at **VALLEY FORGE** (1778), he was superseded by Sir Henry Clinton. He returned to England and was made a viscount in 1799.

### Howe of Aberavon, (Richard Edward) Geoffrey Howe, Baron (1926–)
British politician. He became a Conservative MP in 1964. Knighted in 1970, he became Solicitor-General (1970–2), Minister for Trade and Consumer Affairs (1972–4), Chancellor of the Exchequer (1979–83) and then Foreign Secretary (1983–9). A loyal supporter of Margaret **THATCHER**, in 1989 he was made Deputy Prime Minister, Lord President of the Council, and Leader of the House of **COMMONS**, but resigned from the government (Nov 1990) because of Thatcher's hostility towards European Monetary Union. His resignation speech set in train the events that led to her resignation. ➤ **CONSERVATIVE PARTY** (UK)

### Hoxha, Enver (1908–85)
Albanian politician. Born into a middle-class Muslim family, he joined the French Communist Party while he was living in France (1930–6). Returning home during **WORLD WAR II**, he joined the Albanian Labour Party (Puna), becoming provisional Secretary-General in 1941. With Mehmet **SHEHU**, he was a leader of the Albanian National Liberation Movement which began in 1942 under the direction of the Yugoslav partisans of **TITO**, and he became Chief Political Commissar of the National Liberation Army. In 1946, after Albania was declared a People's Republic, Hoxha held office as Prime Minister, Foreign Minister and Minister of Defence until 1954 when, as First Secretary of the Albanian Communist Party, he preferred to rule through the party. He presided over the most doctrinaire and rigid of post-war communist governments. A Stalinist, he broke with Yugoslavia (1948), then the USSR (1960) and finally China (1978), denouncing them as revisionists and imperialists. With each turn in foreign policy, he eliminated his rivals and opponents, but the late purge (1981–2) and the mysterious suicide of Shehu (1981) show he never succeeded in entirely destroying his critics. ➤ **ALIA, RAMIZ**; **XOXE, KOCI**

### Hoysala ➤ INDIA, PRE-ISLAMIC

### Hoyte, (Hugh) Desmond (1929–2002)
Guyanese politician. After studies at London University and the Middle Temple, he taught in a boys' school in Grenada (1955–7) and then practised as a lawyer in Guyana. He joined the socialist People's National Congress (PNC) Party and in 1968, two years after Guyana achieved full independence, was elected to

the National Assembly. He held a number of ministerial posts before becoming Prime Minister under Forbes **BURNHAM**. On Burnham's death, in 1905, he succeeded him as President, remaining in office until 1992.

### Hrushevsky, Mikhail S (1866–1934)
Ukrainian writer and political thinker. Russian-born and trained as a historian, he was appointed Professor of Ukrainian History in the University of Lvov, Galicia, in 1894, at a time of intensifying Russian nationalism. Since Galicia was then ruled by Austria, he was in a position to take up the Ukrainian case. He founded the Ukrainian National Democratic Party in exile, and he wrote extensively in Ukrainian which he helped to transform from a language of the peasantry to a medium for culture and for politics. He was able to return to Kiev in the **DUMA** period, without, however, having much impact, but in 1917–18 he was among the founders of the short-lived Ukrainian Republic.

### HUAC (House Un-American Activities Committee)
A committee of the **HOUSE OF REPRESENTATIVES**, it became a permanent committee in 1938 under the chairmanship of Democrat Martin Dies, with the purpose of investigating subversive activities. After the Republicans took control of the House of Representatives in 1946, the committee's focus became largely anti-communist. In the 1950s, when it became associated with Republican Senator Joseph **MCCARTHY**, it targeted alleged communists in the theatre, the movie industry, government and the trades. HUAC was notorious for basing its charges on loose gossip and for bullying witnesses. The committee was dissolved in 1975.

### Hua Guofeng (Hua Kuo-feng) (1921– )
Chinese politician. He was Vice-Governor of Hunan (1958–67), but came under attack during the **CULTURAL REVOLUTION**. A member of the Central Committee of the Party from 1969 and of the Politburo from 1973, he became Deputy Prime Minister and Minister of Public Security (1975–6), and was made Prime Minister (1976–80) and Chairman of the Central Committee. Under him, China adopted a more pragmatic domestic and foreign policy, with emphasis on industrial and educational expansion, and closer relations with Western and Third World countries. He resigned as Chairman in 1981. ▶ **MAO ZEDONG**

### Huai-hai, Battle of (1948–9)
A crucial battle of the **CHINESE CIVIL WAR** (1946–9) between the Communists and Nationalists. By the summer of 1948, communist armies already controlled Manchuria and much of the north China countryside. In order to open the way to the Yangzi River in central China, **MAO ZEDONG** launched a mass offensive (Oct 1948) against the Nationalist-held railway junction of Xuzhou (Hsuchow), which fell in Dec 1948. By the time the Battle of Huai-hai ended (Jan 1949), the Nationalists had lost 200,000 men; thereafter they were unable to prevent rapid communist advances throughout central and southern China.

### Hua Kuo-feng ▶ HUA GUOFENG

### Huang Hsing ▶ HUANG XING

### Huang Tsung-hsi ▶ HUANG ZONGXI

### Huang Xing (Huang Hsing) (1871–1916)
Chinese revolutionary leader. He helped to overthrow the **QING DYNASTY** and bring the Chinese Empire to an end. In 1905 he fled to Japan, where he organized a revolutionary group which joined **SUN YAT-SEN** as the Alliance Society. When the Republic was founded in 1912, he devoted himself to turning the society into a parliamentary party, a policy frustrated by President **YUAN SHIKAI**. Huang joined Sun Yat-sen in armed opposition to the President, but was defeated and fled to Japan. He returned to China in 1916 after the death of Yuan Shikai, but died later the same year in Shanghai.

### Huang Zongxi (Huang Tsung-hsi) (1610–95)
Chinese scholar. He was celebrated for his opposition to the Manchu **QING DYNASTY** and in 1644 joined the resistance movement in the south, loyal to the previous **MING DYNASTY**. However, he retired to a life of scholarship after 1649, refusing to accept an official position from the new dynasty. His critique of imperial **ABSOLUTISM**, written in 1662, exerted a considerable influence on early 20c Chinese reformers and revolutionaries.

### Huáscar, in full Inti Cusi Huallpa Huáscar ('Sun of Joy') (d.1532)
Inca chieftain. On his father's death in 1527 he succeeded to the larger, southern part of the empire, which he ruled from Cuzco, while his younger half brother **ATAHUALPA** was left about one-fifth in the north, **QUITO**. He tried to resist an armed rebellion by Atahualpa, who was determined to rule the whole kingdom, but was overwhelmed and captured in 1532. That year Francisco **PIZARRO** arrived to conquer Cuzco, and Huáscar was assassinated by order of Atahualpa, who seemed to think that Pizarro might restore him to his rightful place on the throne.

### Hudson's Bay Company
A London-based corporation which was granted a Royal Charter to trade (principally in furs) in most of north and west Canada (Rupert's Land) in 1670. It annexed its main competitors, the **NORTH WEST COMPANY**, in 1821, and developed extensive sea-based trade in otter pelts along the coast of British Columbia. Rupert's Land was purchased by the Canadian Government in 1870.

### Huerta, Victoriano (1854–1916)
Mexican dictator. Born into a Huichol family, he joined the Mexican army and advanced to the rank of general during the dictatorship of Porfirio **DÍAZ**. After Díaz went into exile, Huerta became an ally of liberal President Francisco **MADERO**, commanding the federal forces that suppressed the uprisings of Emiliano **ZAPATA** (1911) and others. In 1913, however, he overthrew Madero's regime and declared himself President of Mexico, dissolving the legislature and violently suppressing all opposition. When the US government withdrew its support and revolutionaries such as Zapata, Venustiano **CARRANZA** and Pancho **VILLA** joined together to fight him, Huerta was forced into exile (1914).

## Huggins, Godfrey Martin, 1st Viscount Malvern (1893–1971)

Rhodesian politician. Born in England, he emigrated to Southern Rhodesia in 1911 as a doctor but was soon drawn into politics, being elected at the first election after internal self-government. He was catapulted into the premiership of Southern Rhodesia in 1933, a post he held until his elevation to the premiership of the CENTRAL AFRICAN FEDERATION, of which he was one of the chief architects. He retired in 1956. Although the Central African Federation proved short-lived and Huggins's readiness to respond to nationalist pressures was too limited, he established a liberal base in Southern Rhodesia where class was deemed more significant than race. The combined forces of African nationalism and white reaction squeezed such liberals into positions of no power in the 1960s, but the development of the state which Zimbabwe's politicians inherited owes a great deal to Huggins's leadership in difficult economic conditions in the 1930s, 1940s and 1950s.

## Hughes, Charles Evans (1862–1948)

US politician and jurist. Elected Governor of New York State (1907) after exposing huge frauds in the insurance industry, he served as an Associate Justice of the Supreme Court (1910–16). He resigned to run as the Republican candidate in the presidential election of 1916, when he narrowly lost to Woodrow WILSON. He was appointed Secretary of State in 1921 by President Warren HARDING, and served until 1925.

## Hughes, William Morris (1862–1952)

British-born Australian politician and Prime Minister (1915–23). He emigrated to Australia in 1884, and entered the New South Wales legislature in 1894 and federal politics in 1901. He was Attorney-General (1908–9, 1910–13 and 1914–15), succeeding Andrew FISHER as Labor Leader and Prime Minister in 1915. A long-standing supporter of compulsory military service, he returned from a visit to Britain in 1916 to campaign for conscription. The referendum was lost, but Hughes and his followers were expelled from the AUSTRALIAN LABOR PARTY. He formed the Nationalist Party in 1917, retained office and represented Australia at the PARIS PEACE CONFERENCE of 1919. After the election of 1922, the Country Party held the balance of power and forced his retirement in favour of Stanley Melbourne BRUCE (1923). He engineered the overthrow of the Bruce–Page government in 1929, for which he was expelled from the Nationalist Party. Involved in the foundation of the United Australia Party, he held various offices during the 1930s and was briefly party leader in 1941. He remained in parliament until his death in 1952. ► NATIONAL PARTY OF AUSTRALIA

## Huguenots

French Calvinist Protestants whose political rivalry with Catholics (eg the House of GUISE) led to the French Wars of RELIGION (1562–98). Their leader, Henry of Navarre (HENRY IV), succeeded to the throne (1589), granting them important concessions on his conversion to Catholicism (Edict of NANTES, 1598); these were later revoked by LOUIS XIV (1685), resulting in persecution and emigration. ► ST BARTHOLOMEW'S DAY MASSACRE

## Hu Hanmin (Hu Han-min) (1879–1936)

Chinese politician. An early leader of the Chinese Nationalist Party, he was a founder-member of the Alliance Society created (1905) in Tokyo by SUN YAT-SEN, from which the Party later developed. After Sun's death (1925) he lost influence, and broke with CHIANG KAI-SHEK in 1931. He was imprisoned briefly for his opposition, and thereafter played little part in politics. ► GUOMINDANG

## Hukbalahap or Huk

Filipino peasant movement, concentrated in central Luzon. The term in fact refers to two related organizations: the People's Anti-Japanese Army, which was the most prominent of the indigenous resistance groups during the Japanese occupation of the Philippines; and the People's Liberation Army, which mounted a rising (the Huk Rebellion) against the newly independent Filipino Republic from late 1946. The origins of the rebellion lay in the severe deterioration of agrarian relations in central Luzon from the 1930s, arising from the increasingly harsh treatment of tenant farmers by the big landowners, many of whom had collaborated with the Japanese during the war years. The Communist Party of the Philippines was sometimes aligned with, and occasionally provided leadership within, the Huks. However, the rebellion remained essentially a rural one. By 1953 it had been broken, by a combination of effective military operations and changes in government policy which appeared to offer an alleviation of rural grievances.

## Hull, Cordell (1871–1955)

US politician. He became Secretary of State under ROOSEVELT in 1933, and served for the longest term in that office until he retired in 1944, having attended most of the great war conferences. He was a strong advocate of maximum aid to the Allies. He helped to organize the UN, for which he received the NOBEL PEACE PRIZE in 1945.

## humanism

The philosophy espoused by Kenneth KAUNDA and based upon Julius NYERERE's philosophy of UJAMAA, it aimed to find a specifically African conception of man's place in society and the economy, in which human dignity and equality were the central principles. It was never taken as seriously as Nyerere's writings as a blueprint for public policy.

## Humanists

Those scholars who, from the 14c onwards, worked to recover the pure language of the classical past, removing the glosses and errors generated in the centuries which separated the new era from the ancient world ('the *medium aevum*' and hence 'MIDDLE AGES'). The early humanists tended to find their ideal in the works of Cicero, but by the mid-15c there was a new interest in Greek learning, especially in the works of Plato. The application of humanist techniques to the text of the Bible by scholars such as Lorenzo Valla prepared the way for 'Christian humanists', most significantly Erasmus, who urged reform of the Church according to the principles of the Scriptures, an approach which links the RENAISSANCE to the REFORMATION. In sum, the Italian Renaissance gave people who were not clerics a new sense of their creative powers. Moreover, the specific developments in the visual arts and humanism identified above all with perspective and with a more refined sense of history, gave Europeans a new sense of space and time at precisely the moment when Europe was beginning to make its impact on the rest of the globe in the age of the great oceanic discoveries.

### Human Rights, Universal Declaration of ► UNIVERSAL DECLARATION OF HUMAN RIGHTS

### Humayun (1508–56)
Mughal Emperor of India (1530/42 and 1554/6). He became the second Mughal Emperor of India upon the death of his father, **BABUR**. The early part of his reign was spent fighting Sher Khan, an Afghan, by whom he was defeated in 1542. Sher Khan became Emperor **SHER SHAH** and founded the Sur Dynasty. From 1539 to 1554, Humayun was in exile when his son, **AKBAR THE GREAT**, was born. In 1544 Humayun captured and ruled southern Afghanistan for some time. Sher Shah having died in 1545, in 1554 Humayun marched from Kabul to Lahore and defeated Sikandar Shah at Sirhind (1555), eventually recapturing the Delhi throne. He died the following year, after a fall from his library stairs.

### Hume, Allan Octavian (1829–1912)
British colonialist and naturalist. After studying medicine, Hume joined the Bengal Civil Service in 1849. He became Commissioner of Customs for the North West Provinces, and Director-General of Agriculture. Having served in the **INDIAN UPRISING** of 1857–8, he carried with him a morbid fear of the repetition of these events. In order to provide an outlet for educated opinion, therefore, he organized the first National Congress in India, in Bombay in 1885, remaining the Secretary of this organization until 1908.

### Hume, Joseph (1777–1855)
British radical politician. He studied medicine at Edinburgh, and then in 1797 became assistant surgeon under the East India Company. After returning to England (1808), he sat in parliament (1812 and 1819–55), where his reform campaigns included the legalizing of trade unions, freedom of trade with India, and the abolition of army flogging, naval impressment, and imprisonment for debt. ► **EAST INDIA COMPANY, BRITISH**

### Humphrey, Hubert Horatio (1911–78)
US politician. He became Mayor of Minneapolis in 1945, and was elected Senator in 1948. He built up a strong reputation as a liberal, particularly on the **CIVIL RIGHTS** issue, but, as Vice-President from 1965 under Lyndon B **JOHNSON**, alienated many of his supporters by defending the policy of continuing the **VIETNAM WAR**. Although he won the Democratic presidential nomination in 1968, a substantial minority of Democrats opposed him, and he narrowly lost the election to Richard **NIXON**. He then returned to the **SENATE**. ► **DEMOCRATIC PARTY**

### Hundred Associates
The French colonization company organized by Cardinal **RICHELIEU** in 1627. Its aim was to settle 4,000 colonists in **NEW FRANCE** within 15 years and to support them for three years after their arrival. In return the Associates were given a monopoly of the **FUR TRADE** and a claim to the North American continent from the Arctic circle down to Florida. Their first two fleets were both captured by privateers and Quebec was lost in 1629. The profitable fur trade had to be sublet to another company and only 2,500 settlers had been sent out when the Associates' charter was revoked in 1663.

### Hundred Days (Mar–June 1815)
An interlude between **NAPOLEON I**'s escape from Elba and his defeat at the Battle of **WATERLOO**, during which he returned to Paris and tried to reconstitute the First Empire. He was finally exiled to St Helena. ► **EMPIRE, FIRST** (France)

### Hundred Days of Reform (1898)
A reform movement in China, which lasted for just over a hundred days. During this period **KANG YOU-WEI** and his supporters succeeded in securing Emperor **GUANGXU**'s approval of radical reforms affecting the constitution, administration, army and education. All were rescinded on the intervention of Empress-Dowager **CIXI**. Six leading reformers were executed, and Kang fled abroad. ► **QING DYNASTY**

### Hundred Flowers Campaign (1956–7)
A campaign in China which encouraged freedom of expression, under the slogan 'Let a hundred flowers bloom and a hundred schools of thought contend', in art and literature as well as political debate. By June 1957 a clampdown was imposed on the violent criticism of the Communist Party, and an anti-rightist campaign was launched.

### Hundred Years' War
A series of wars between England and France dated by convention 1337–1453. They formed part of a longer contest which began when England was linked with **NORMANDY** (1066), then with Anjou and Aquitaine (1154). In the 13c the Capetians redoubled their efforts to rule all France, but when **EDWARD III** claimed the French throne – from 1340 styling himself 'King of England and France' – traditional rivalries exploded into a dynastic struggle. Under **HENRY V** (1415/22) the English turned from raiding to territorial conquest, a task ultimately beyond their resources. Eviction from Guyenne (1453) reduced England's French territories to Calais (lost in 1558) and the Channel Islands, but the title of King of France was abandoned only in 1801. ► **AGINCOURT, BATTLE OF**; **ANGEVINS**; **CAPETIAN DYNASTY**

### HUNGARY    official name **Hungarian People's Republic**

A landlocked state in the Danube basin, central Europe, bounded to the north by Slovakia; to the east by the Ukraine and Romania; to the south by Serbia; to the south-west by Croatia; and to the west by Slovenia and Austria. The Magyars probably settled the Hungarian plain in the 9c and a kingdom was formed under St STEPHEN I in the 11c. This was conquered by Turks in 1526 and became part of the HABSBURG Empire in the 17c. Austria and Hungary were reconstituted as the Dual Monarchy of AUSTRIA-HUNGARY in 1867. The year 1869 was declared the Hungarian Millennium to celebrate the 1,000th anniversary of the Magyars' original settlement. It was used by the Hungarian government within Austria-Hungary to celebrate undoubted political and economic achievements in the course of the previous half century. It was also used as an anti-Habsburg demonstration and marked an intensification of the attempt to Magyarize Hungary's subject nationalities. Protests were made by the Magyar poor, as well as by SLAVS and Romanians. After WORLD WAR I Hungary became a republic, but a communist revolt introduced a new regime in 1919. A nominally monarchical constitution under a regent, Admiral Miklós HORTHY, was restored in 1920, but after the failure of its policy of alliance with Germany in WORLD WAR II, a new republic under communist government was formed in 1949. In 1956 there was a national insurrection known as the Hungarian Uprising, which followed the denunciation of STALIN at the 20th Congress of the Soviet Communist Party for his oppressive rule. Rioting students and workers pulled down statues of Stalin and demanded radical reform. When the new Prime Minister Imre NAGY announced, among other things, plans for Hungary's withdrawal from the WARSAW PACT, he was replaced by János KÁDÁR and Soviet troops and tanks crushed the uprising. Many were killed, thousands fled abroad, and Nagy was executed. Reform was set back for more than a decade. In 1989 pressure for political change was led from within the Communist Party; the same year Hungary was declared a democratic state and in 1990 multiparty elections were held. Since the elections of 1994, when the Hungarian Democratic Forum (MDF) were ousted by a Hungarian Socialist Party-led coalition under Prime Minister Gyula Horn, Hungary has experienced gradual economic growth. Hungary joined NATO in 1999 and the EU in 2004.

**Hung Hsiu-ch'üan ▸ HONG XIUQUAN**

**Hung Jen-kan ▸ HONG RENGAN**

**Hunt, Henry**, known as **Orator Hunt** (1773–1835)
British radical agitator. He was a well-to-do farmer who in 1800 became a staunch radical, and spent the rest of his life advocating the repeal of the CORN LAWS, democracy and parliamentary reform. In 1819, on the occasion of the PETERLOO MASSACRE, he delivered a speech which cost him three years' imprisonment. He became an MP in 1831.

**Hunyadi, János Corvinus** (c.1387–1456)
Hungarian statesman and warrior. Apparently a Wallach by birth, he was knighted and in 1409 presented by Emperor SIGISMUND with the Castle of Hunyad in Transylvania. His life was one unbroken crusade against the Turks, whom he defeated in several campaigns, notably in the storming of Belgrade (1456). During the minority of Ladislas V he acted as Governor of the Kingdom (1446–53). He died in Belgrade, of plague, shortly after his victory there. One of his

sons, **MATTHIAS I, CORVINUS**, became King of Hungary in 1458.

**Hurd of Westwell, Douglas Richard Hurd, Baron** (1930– )
British politician. He followed a career in the Diplomatic Corps (1952–66) before moving to work in the Conservative Research Department (1966–70). A Conservative MP from 1974 to 1997, he was Northern Ireland Secretary (1984–5), Home Secretary (1985–9) and Foreign Secretary (1989–97). He was an unsuccessful candidate for the CONSERVATIVE PARTY leadership (Nov 1990). He was made a life peer in 1997. ▸ THATCHER, MARGARET

**Huron**
Iroquoian-speaking Native North Americans, who settled in large towns and farming villages in Quebec and Ontario in the 16–17c. They supplied furs to French traders, competing with tribes of the IROQUOIS CONFEDERACY. Defeated by the Iroquois in 1649, many were driven to the west, and eventually settled on land in Ohio and Michigan, where they were known by the British as the Wyandots. In 1867 they were moved to the INDIAN TERRITORY in Oklahoma, where many still live.

**Hurtado de Mendoza, Diego** (1503–75)
Spanish politician of Basque origin. The great-grandson of Iñigo López de MENDOZA, he was entrusted by CHARLES V with the conduct of his Italian policy and the representation of his views at the Council of TRENT. He inherited his ancestor's gifts as a statesman and man of letters. His *War of Granada* is a masterpiece of prose. ▸ BASQUES

**Hus, Jan** (c.1372–1415)
Bohemian religious reformer. He was born at Husinec, from which his name derives. At the relatively new and intellectually lively University of Prague, he became a bachelor of arts in 1393, master of arts in 1396 and was elected dean of the faculty in 1401. He was influenced by the writings of Wycliffe among others. His preaching won him both royal and popular Czech support but in 1410 he was excommunicated by the Archbishop of Prague. He continued to preach even when, in 1412, the pope issued a papal bull against him and put Prague under an interdict. He was, therefore, called before a General Council at Constance and, despite a guarantee of safe conduct from Emperor SIGISMUND, he was burned after refusing to recant. The anger of his followers in the Czech lands led to the HUSSITE WARS, which lasted almost until the mid-15c and for a time guaranteed Czech independence. Hus's ideas exerted an important influence on the Protestant reformers in the 16c. ▸ HUSSITES; REFORMATION

**Husák, Gustáv** (1913–91)
Czechoslovak politician. He trained as a lawyer, joined the Communist Party in 1939 and became a member of the resistance movement during WORLD WAR II. After the war he was a parliamentary deputy and Party official, and became Minister of Agriculture in 1948–9 before being imprisoned, as an alleged Slovak bourgeois nationalist, in 1951. Rehabilitated in 1960, he worked at the Academy of Sciences (1963–8) until he became First Secretary of the Slovak Communist Party and Deputy Premier during the

**PRAGUE SPRING**. After the 1968 Soviet invasion, of which he approved, he replaced Alexander **DUBČEK** as General-Secretary of the entire Czechoslovak Communist Party in 1969. His task was to restore public order, 'cleanse' the Party and introduce a new federal constitution. He became state President in 1975 and, pursuing a policy of minimal economic reform, remained the dominant figure in Czechoslovakia until his retirement from his post as General-Secretary, under pressure, in 1987. He was finally replaced as state President by Václav **HAVEL** in Dec 1989 in the course of the so-called **VELVET REVOLUTION**.

## Husayni, Amin al- (1897–1974)
Arab nationalist leader. Educated in Jerusalem, Cairo and Istanbul, he went on to serve in the Turkish artillery. In 1921 the British, under their Mandate for **PALESTINE**, appointed him Mufti of Jerusalem and Permanent President of the Supreme Muslim Council, the most important Palestinian Muslim body. In 1930, in an attempt to attract outside support for the Arab cause in Palestine, he told the German representative in Jerusalem that the Palestinians were in sympathy with the new Germany. This search for support had been prompted by the **PEEL COMMISSION**'s report, which recommended the partition of Palestine and was rejected by the Palestinian Arabs. A thorn in the side of the British, al-Husayni spent his life in an unsuccessful attempt to avert the partition of Palestine. His collaboration with Nazi Germany, his call for Egyptian aid for German and Italian troops, and his support of Japan after **PEARL HARBOR**, were more than enough to cast him in the darkest light in the eyes of the Allies. In 1945 he was captured by the French and kept under house arrest near Paris. By mid-1946, however, he had escaped to Damascus and was cordially greeted later the same year in Egypt by the Prime Minister, Isma'il Sidqi. He continued to work for the Palestinian cause from Gaza as leader of the 'All Palestine Government', recruiting guerrillas for raids into Israel. After 1956, however, with the growing influence of al-**FATAH**, his own power declined. ► **PLO**

## Husayn ibn 'Ali (1856–1931)
Sharif of Mecca (1908/16) and King of the Hijaz (1916/24). The founder of the modern Arab Hashemite Dynasty, when **WORLD WAR I** began and the British tried to persuade him to rise up against the Turks, he negotiated with Sir Henry McMahon, British High Commissioner in Egypt, and proposed that Britain should accept as independent an area that included the present states of Syria, Lebanon, Iraq, Jordan and the Arabian Peninsula, except for Aden. McMahon accepted most of his demands but the British were making other agreements which conflicted with the promises made to Husayn, such as the **SYKES–PICOT AGREEMENT** with France (May 1916). Husayn began his revolt in June 1916, soon captured Mecca, and in 1917 moved out of the Hijaz and supported **ALLENBY** as he advanced into **PALESTINE**. At the end of the war, he was frustrated and bitter, as the Allies recognized him only as King of the Hijaz, and he was driven from there after a conflict (1919–24) with **IBN SAUD**. His sons, Faysal and Abdullah, became respectively King of Iraq and of Transjordan, but Husayn felt betrayed by Britain and France, who had left only Arabia as a truly independent Arab area. ► **ABDULLAH IBN HUSAYN**; **ARAB REVOLT**; **FAYSAL I**; **HUSAYN–MCMAHON CORRESPONDENCE**

## Husayn–McMahon Correspondence
The notorious correspondence between Sharif **HUSAYN IBN 'ALI** of Mecca and Sir Henry McMahon, the British High Commissioner in Egypt, initiated in 1915. It resulted in Husayn's becoming convinced that Britain supported the emancipation of the Arabs from Ottoman rule, and the establishment of a Greater Arab Kingdom in the Arabian Peninsula and parts of the Fertile Crescent. This conviction derived from an assurance dispatched by McMahon in Oct 1915 that Britain was 'prepared to recognize and support the independence of the Arabs' in accordance with Husayn's demands, subject to three reservations. Despite these reservations (which concerned those parts of the Levant 'west of the districts of Damascus, Homs, Hama and Aleppo' as not being wholly Arab, an exclusion with regard to British interests in lower Iraq, and an allusion to the 'interests of her (Britain's) ally France'), this correspondence was (and remains) a major source of irritation amongst the Arabs where their relations with Britain are concerned. It undoubtedly played a decisive part in encouraging the 1916 **ARAB REVOLT**, and the conflict between the tenor of the correspondence with the **SYKES–PICOT AGREEMENT**, coupled with the absence of any specific mention in the correspondence of the status of **PALESTINE** (despite McMahon's much later avowal that he had always thought of Palestine as being excluded from the territories promised to the Arabs), has done nothing to promote cordial relations between Britain and the Arabs.

## Huskisson, William (1770–1830)
English politician. He entered parliament for Morpeth in 1796 as a supporter of **PITT, THE YOUNGER**; returned for Liskeard in 1804, he became Secretary of the Treasury, and held the same office under William Bentinck, 3rd Duke of **PORTLAND** (1807–9). In 1814 he became commissioner of the Woods and Forests, in 1823 President of the Board of Trade and Treasurer of the Navy, and in 1827 Colonial Secretary, and resigned office finally in 1828. He obtained the removal of restrictions on the trade of the colonies with foreign countries, the removal or reduction of many import duties and relaxation of the navigation laws, and was an active pioneer of free trade.

## Huss, John ► **HUS, JAN**

## Hussein (ibn Talal) (1935–99)
King of Jordan (1952/99). Educated in Alexandria, and at Harrow and Sandhurst in England, he steered a middle course in the face of the political upheavals inside and outside his country, favouring the Western powers, particularly Britain, and pacifying Arab nationalism. After the 1967 war with Israel, the **PLO** (Palestine Liberation Organization) made increasingly frequent raids into Israel from Jordan; their power developed to such an extent that he ordered the Jordanian army to move against them and, after a short civil war (1970), the PLO leadership fled abroad. His decision to cut links with the **WEST BANK** (1988) prompted the PLO to establish a government in exile. He was married four times; his second wife was an

Englishwoman, by whom he had an heir, Abdullah, in 1962.

## Hussein, Saddam (1937– )

Iraqi soldier and President. He joined the Arab BA'ATH PARTY in 1957, and was sentenced to death in 1959 for the attempted assassination of General Abd al-Krim QASSIM, but escaped to Egypt. He played a prominent part in the 1968 revolution, and became Vice-President of the Revolutionary Command Council in 1969. On the retirement of his colleague, President al-BAKR, he became sole President (1979/2003). His attack on Iran in 1980, to gain control of the Strait of Hormuz, led to a war of attrition which ended in 1988. His invasion of Kuwait in Aug 1990 led to the 1991 GULF WAR, but by Feb that year he had been defeated by an Allied Force backed by the UN. However, he defied UN ceasefire resolutions imposed on Iraq and made further raids on Iran in 1993, inciting a US military response. His refusal to cooperate fully with UN weapons inspectors in 1997–9 led to renewed attacks, and in 2003 to the IRAQ WAR that toppled his regime. As Allied troops advanced, he went into hiding but was captured in Dec 2003 and went on trial in Iraq in Jul 2004 accused of crimes against humanity.
➤ IRAN–IRAQ WAR

## Hussites

Followers of Jan HUS, who in early 15c Bohemia initiated a movement for the reform of the universal Church. They failed in their main purpose but, together and in various sects, they anticipated the 16c REFORMATION by demanding the moral reform of the clergy, free preaching of the Word of God, and the availability of the Eucharist for all believers in two species or kinds (ie bread and wine).

## Hussite Wars (1419–36)

The burning at the stake of Jan HUS aroused enormous religious and national unrest in Bohemia and led to the formation of a Hussite League. The movement spread rapidly under King WENCESLAS IV and open war broke out under SIGISMUND, whom the Bohemians held responsible for Hus's death. In 1420 the pope called for a crusade against the HUSSITES. The Emperor suffered serious defeats, and raids into Silesia, Austria and as far as Danzig spread fear of the Hussites. For the first time, an imperial tax was levied to fund the war against them. Continued Hussite successes led to a diplomatic solution being reached in the pacts of Prague (1433) and Iglau (1436).

## Hu Yaobang (Hu Yao-pang) (1915–89)

Chinese politician. Born into a poor peasant family in Hunan province, he joined the Red Army in 1929 and took part in the LONG MARCH. He held a number of posts under DENG XIAOPING before becoming Head of the Communist Youth League (1952–67). During the CULTURAL REVOLUTION he was purged as a 'capitalist roader' and 'rusticated'; briefly rehabilitated (1975–6), he did not return to high office until 1978, when, through his patron Deng, he joined the Communist Party's Politburo. From Head of the Secretariat, he was promoted to Party Leader in 1981, but dismissed in 1987 for his relaxed handling of a wave of student unrest. Popularly revered as a liberal reformer, his death triggered an unprecedented wave of pro-democracy demonstrations.

## Hu Yao-pang ➤ HU YAOBANG

## Huysmans, Camille (1871–1968)

Belgian politician. After studying at Liège University, he became a teacher (1893–7). He subsequently worked as a journalist and trade unionist, and was a socialist MP from 1910 to 1965. Active in the Second International, and also in the FLEMISH MOVEMENT, Huysmans was especially concerned that Dutch be made the language of instruction at Ghent University. He was involved in municipal politics in Antwerp (of which he was Mayor, 1933–40 and 1944–6) and in Brussels; he held several national cabinet posts and from 1946 to 1947 was Prime Minister. His party dropped him in 1965 (when he was in his nineties); he set up his own socialist group but was not elected.

**IAEA** ▸ INTERNATIONAL ATOMIC ENERGY AGENCY

**Iași, Treaty of** ▸ JASSY, TREATY OF

**Ibárruri (Gómez), Dolores**, known as **La Pasionaria** (1895–1989)
Spanish communist orator and politician. Born into a Catholic mining family in the Basque country, she became a member of the Central Committee of the Spanish Communist Party (1930), served as Spanish delegate to the Third International (1933 and 1935), and was elected Deputy to the Spanish **CORTES** (1936). With the outbreak of the **SPANISH CIVIL WAR** (1936), she became the Republic's most emotional and effective propagandist. After the war she took refuge in the USSR, becoming Secretary-General (1942–60) and then (1960) President of the Spanish Communist Party in exile. In 1977 she returned to Spain as Communist Deputy for Asturias.

**Ibbetson, Denzil** (1847–1948)
British Lieutenant-Governor of Punjab. Educated at Cambridge, he entered the **INDIAN CIVIL SERVICE** in 1870 and was posted to Punjab. During his career, he held various posts, including Superintendent of Census, Financial Commissioner, and Secretary to the Government of India in the Department of Revenue and Agriculture. He was also a retired member of the Viceroy's Executive Council, India. Ibbetson published the *Census Report of Punjab* in 1883 and the *Gazetteer of Punjab* in 1883–5.

**Ibn Khaldun** (1332–1406)
Arab philosopher, historian and politician, born in Tunis. He was widely involved in political intrigues before he turned to history, eventually becoming a college president and judge in Cairo. He wrote a monumental history of the Arabs, best known by its *Muqaddima*, or introduction, in which he explains the rise and fall of states by the waxing and waning of the spirit of *asabiya* ('solidarity'). He died in Cairo.

**Ibn Saud**, in full **Ibn Abd al-Rahman al-Saud** (1880–1953)
First King of Saudi Arabia (1932/53). Seeking exile with his family in 1890, he was brought up in Kuwait. In 1901 he succeeded his father, and set out to reconquer the family domains from the Rashidi rulers, an aim which he achieved with British recognition in 1927. He changed his title from Sultan of Nejd to King of Hijaz and Najd in 1927, and in 1932 to King of Saudi Arabia. After the discovery of oil (1938), he granted substantial concessions to US oil companies. He died in Ta'if, Saudi Arabia. His son, Saud (1902–69) had been Prime Minister for three months when he suc-

ceeded his father in 1953. In 1964 he was peacefully deposed by the Council of Ministers, and his brother **FAYSAL** became king, as well as remaining Prime Minister and Minister of Foreign Affairs.

**Ibo** ▸ IGBO

**Ibrahim Pasha** (1789–1848)
Viceroy of Egypt. Born at Kavalla, Rumelia, he was the son (or adopted son) of **MUHAMMAD 'ALI**. In Egypt from 1805, he became Governor of Cairo, and later commanded the army. In 1833 he invaded Syria, but European intervention forced his withdrawal in 1840. He succeeded his father as Viceroy when the latter became senile, but predeceased him, dying in Cairo after only 40 days in office.

**IBRD** ▸ INTERNATIONAL BANK FOR RECONSTRUCTION AND DEVELOPMENT

**ICELAND** official name **Republic of Iceland**

An island state lying between the northern Atlantic Ocean and the Arctic Ocean, south-east of Greenland and 550mi/900km west of Norway. It was settled by the Norse in the 9c, and in the 10c was the seat of the world's oldest parliament, the **ALTHING**. It united with Norway in 1262, and with Denmark in 1380. In 1918 Iceland became an independent kingdom with the same sovereign as Denmark, and since 1944 it has been an independent republic. The extension of the fishing limit around Iceland in 1958 and 1975 precipitated the 'Cod War' disputes with the UK. Subsequent attempts to restrict fishing in Icelandic waters were successful under the right-wing coalition government of Davíd Odsson, which came to power in 1991, but problems in the fishing industry led to a worsening economic situation in the early 1990s. Olafur Ragnar Grimsson was elected to succeed Vigdís **FINNBOGADÓTTIR** as President in 1996.

**Ichikawa Fusaye** (1893–1981)
Japanese politician and feminist. Starting her working

life as a teacher, she then became involved in politics and feminism, helping to found the New Women's Association (c.1920), which successfully fought for women's right to attend political meetings. During her time in the USA (1921–4), she was impressed by the US suffrage movement, and in 1924 formed the Women's Suffrage League in Japan. Following **WORLD WAR II** she became head of the New Japan Women's League, which secured the vote for women in 1945, and went on to fight for their wider rights. She campaigned against legalized prostitution and served in the Japanese Diet (1952–71), where she continued to press for an end to bureaucratic corruption. After defeat in 1971 she was triumphantly returned to parliament in 1975 and 1980.

**ICJ ► INTERNATIONAL COURT OF JUSTICE**

## iconoclasm

Literally 'image breaking', this Greek terms refers to the extreme rejection of the veneration of images. The practice was justified as an interpretation of the second of the Ten Commandments, and was supported by the Byzantine (or eastern Roman) emperor in the 8c, and again by certain reformers in the 16c.

**Iconoclastic Riots ► IMAGE-BREAKING RIOTS**

**IDA ► INTERNATIONAL DEVELOPMENT ASSOCIATION**

## Idris Aloma (d.c.1600)

Ruler of Bornu (c.1569/c.1600). He was a warrior-king and the dominant figure in the central Sudan. During his reign, and those of his sons, the Karini peoples of **BORNU** became a distinct, unified nation.

## Igbo

A people of eastern Nigeria, living in many small and traditionally autonomous communities, with a common culture (present-day population c.13 million). They dominated agricultural trade in Nigeria, and produced the earliest bronze art in the region. They established the short-lived state of Biafra (1960–70), during which time the genocide of Igbo living in other parts of Nigeria occurred.

## Iglesias, Pablo (1850–1925)

Spanish politician and trade union leader. He was the founder and father figure of both the Spanish Socialist Party and its trade union movement, the **UGT**. The Socialist movement was dominated by him until his later years, when he was incapacitated by ill health. He was a highly moralistic, austere and cautious character who preached revolutionary ideas, while practising a pragmatic reformism. His twin obsessions were building up the Socialists' organizations and educating the working class. He became the Socialists' first Deputy to the **CORTES** through the alliance with the Republicans in 1910, though the **PSOE** never surpassed seven seats before his death in 1925.

## Ignatiev, Nikolai Pavlovich, Count (1832–1908)

Russian diplomat. He entered the diplomatic service in 1856 and, arriving as Ambassador in Beijing in 1859, he used guile and foreign military pressure to induce the Chinese to accept the Treaty of **BEIJING**, which gave Russia most of the Amur province that it wanted, including the site for Vladivostok. In 1864 he became Ambassador at Constantinople where, as an enthusiast for the Slav cause as well as for Russia's imperial interests, he encouraged the Balkan **SLAVS**, and took a principal part in the diplomacy before and after the Russo-Turkish War of 1878. He was primarily responsible for the Treaty of **SAN STEFANO**, which was then largely undone at the Congress of **BERLIN**. He was appointed Minister of the Interior in 1881, but was dismissed the following year for expressing excessively liberal, if somewhat impractical, ideas. ► **RUSSO-TURKISH WARS**

## Iguala Plan (Plan de Iguala) (1821)

A plan for the constitution of Mexico as devised by the **CREOLE** landowner and leader of the independence movement, Agustín de **ITURBIDE**. Proclaimed in the Mexican town of Iguala, it stated that Mexico would be an independent state ruled by a Bourbon monarch, that the state religion would be Roman Catholicism, and that all people would have equal rights, ie that anyone could hold office regardless of race. The plan was approved by most of the country's influential groups, who saw that it would free them from the Spanish government. The next stage was the signing in Aug 1821 by Iturbide and the Spanish Viceroy of the Convention of Córdoba, by which Spain acquiesced in the Iguala Plan and agreed to withdraw its troops, but the following year the Spanish government refused to accept the Convention. By then, however, seeing the lack of a European prince available to rule Mexico, Iturbide had already made himself emperor and discarded the plan.

## Ii Naosuke (1815–60)

Japanese feudal lord. He was Chief Counsellor, or Elder (tairo), of the **TOKUGAWA SHOGUNATE** in 1858–60. Ii took the initiative in signing a commercial treaty with the USA (July 1858) despite strong pro-seclusionist feelings both at the imperial court and amongst many feudal lords and **SAMURAI**. He instituted repressive measures against his critics and was eventually assassinated by the retainers of one domain (Mito) that had borne the brunt of his repression.

## Ikeda Hayato (1900–65)

Japanese politician and economic expert. Educated in Kyoto, he became Finance Minister (1949) of the Liberal-Democratic (Conservative) Party, and introduced an 'income doubling policy' of economic growth and higher living standards. As Prime Minister (1960–4), he was a supporter of the **US–JAPAN SECURITY TREATY** (1960), and developed a low-key style in international relations during the post-war recovery period.

## Ilbert Bill

The bill, introduced in 1883 by Courtney Ilbert, according to which the privilege enjoyed by every British subject in India to be tried only by a magistrate of his own race was to be withdrawn. However, in deference to strong expressions of European public opinion, this privilege was withdrawn merely to the extent of conferring jurisdiction in such cases on all magistrates of whatever race as well as on justices of the peace, who were European British subjects and also the highest magistrates. This stirred up resentment amongst Indians, including early nationalist politicians, who felt that a racial privilege was being perpetuated, and that a slur was being cast upon Indian magistrates.

## ILGWU (International Ladies Garment Workers Union)

US labour organization. Founded in 1900, it saw conflict in its early years as different ethnic and political groups and skilled and unskilled workers vied for control. Massive strikes in 1909–11 in New York led to a settlement with dress manufacturers that included the 'Protocol of Peace'. Negotiated under the aegis of Louis D **BRANDEIS**, the protocol offered improved wages and working conditions in exchange for a ban on strikes and lock-outs, and imposed impartial arbitration as a means of ending disputes. By the 1920s the presence of a strong communist faction had caused the union's fortunes to decline, but David Dubinsky's election as President in 1932, coupled with **NEW DEAL** legislation favourable to labour, helped it regain strength. Membership continued to grow at a rapid pace until the 1960s, but later fell with the gradual decline of the labour unions. The ILGWU's advanced social welfare programmes, which included such benefits as medical and disability insurance and unemployment compensation, provided a model for other unions.

## Ili Crisis (1879–81)

This term refers to the tense situation between Russia and China following the Russian occupation of the Chinese prefecture of Ili in northern Xinjiang (Chinese Turkestan) near the border of Russian Turkestan. Xinjiang had been conquered as a military colony by the **QING DYNASTY** in 1759, but the region's Turkic-speaking Muslims (Uighurs) remained hostile. A Muslim rebellion in 1864 was quickly exploited by an adventurer from neighbouring Khokand, Yakub Beg, who by 1870 had imposed his control over all of Xinjiang. The Russians then occupied the strategically important and mineral-rich Ili region to protect trading privileges obtained there in 1851. A promise to evacuate the region once the Qing had restored its authority was not fulfilled after Qing armies had defeated Yakub Beg and retaken Xinjiang (1877). Relations between China and Russia became extremely tense in 1879 when the Treaty of Livadia, signed by a Chinese diplomatic mission to Russia, allowed the latter to remain in effective control of Ili; in Beijing, officials denounced the treaty and called for war. A second mission was sent (1881), resulting in the Treaty of St Petersburg (24 Feb 1881), by which Russia finally agreed to hand back Ili to Chinese control. The resolution of the crisis gave a moral boost to hardline Chinese officials who advocated greater resistance to foreign encroachment.

## Iliescu, Ion (1930–)

Romanian politician. He joined the Communist Youth Union in 1944 and the Communist Party in 1953, and from 1949 to 1960 served on its Central Committee. In 1965 he began a three-year term as head of Party Propaganda, and as a member of the Central Committee again from 1968 held office as First Secretary and Youth Minister (1967–71), and First Secretary of Jassy County (1974–9). In 1984 he withdrew from office but, in the wake of the 1989 revolution and the execution of Nicolae **CEAUȘESCU**, he returned to politics, becoming President of the National Salvation Front (Dec 1989) and, two months later, of its successor, the Provisional Council for National Unity. In May 1990 he was elected President and resigned his party posts. Discontent with the economic situation resulted in protests against his government in late 1990 and early 1991, although he was still re-elected in 1992, serving until 1996 and again from 2000 to 2004.

## Ilinden Uprising (2 Aug 1903)

**VMRO**, hoping to provoke the Great Powers to intervene, organized a rebellion among the peoples of Macedonia against Ottoman rule. The uprising was badly planned, its leader, Gotse Delchev, was captured and executed before it began, and the Great Powers avoided involvement. The Ottoman authorities' brutal suppression of the revolt did, however, prompt Emperor **FRANCIS JOSEPH** and Tsar **NICHOLAS II** to force the Ottoman government to pay compensation and to allow foreign advisers into Macedonia.

## Ilkhanid Dynasty

A Mongol dynasty, the Ilkhans ruled in Iran and the central Islamic lands after the capture of Baghdad by Hulagu in 1258. Hulagu adopted Maragha as his capital, while his son, Abaqa, preferred Tabriz. However, it was generally from what is now north-western Iran (or Iranian Azerbaijan) that the Ilkhans conducted their affairs. There was considerable internecine strife between the various Mongol groupings and with the Turks. Despite this, by the time of Ghazan, who took control after the execution of Baidu (4 Oct 1295), the economic position of the lands under Ilkhanid dispensation was healthy. This was particularly true of agriculture, which had benefited from Ghazan's reforms. Learning and scholarship also flourished. While Ghazan's predecessor, Baidu, had been a Christian, Ghazan, who was a Buddhist, ultimately converted to Islam. He then overthrew Baidu and brought to a close a curious interlude when the foremost ruler in the central Islamic lands was not a Muslim. Decay and collapse, however, soon followed; while details surrounding the fall of the Ilkhans is obscure, it seems that with the death of Togha-Temur in 1353, the Ilkhanid state ceased to exist.

## Illyrian Movement

The cultural and political movement among the Croats which, after 1830, aspired to Croatian independence and the unification of the **SOUTH SLAVS** who inhabited the region known in antiquity as Illyria. Under the leadership of Ljudevit **GAJ** and Count Janko Drašković, it drew its support from the Croatian bourgeoisie. Identified with Croatian romanticism and the first phase of Croatian nationalism, after the **REVOLUTIONS OF 1848–9** the Illyrian Movement faded away but its programme re-emerged in the **YUGOSLAVISM** of **STROSSMAYER**.

## Illyrian Provinces (1809–13)

The name given by **NAPOLEON I** to the province which he formed from **DALMATIA**, Croatia, **CARNIOLA** and **CARINTHIA**. Marshal **MARMONT** was appointed Governor of the Provinces, and Ljubljana, now in modern Slovenia, was chosen as the administrative capital. ► **ISTRIA**

**ILO** ► **INTERNATIONAL LABOUR ORGANIZATION**

## Ilorin

A state lying to the north of Yorubaland in central Nigeria which resisted European missionary and trading encroachment in the 19c, but was conquered by the **ROYAL NIGER COMPANY** and acted as a further springboard for the conquest of the northern emirates. Muslim Ilorin was an outlier of the Sokoto caliphate. It was annexed to British rule in 1896 when Sir George **GOLDIE** undertook a campaign against it and its neighbour **NUPE**.

## Iltutmish (d.1236)

Delhi Sultan of the Mamluk ('Slave') Dynasty (1211/36). The son-in-law and foremost slave of **QUTB-UD-DIN AIBAK**, he held fiefs under Aibak, whom he succeeded in 1211 after defeating Aram Shah, the latter's son. Iltutmish recovered Punjab, captured Sind and Bihar, and established his authority in Bengal. In Feb 1229, Iltutmish became Sultan of India as per the patent of the 'Abbasid Caliph of Baghdad. He also recaptured Gwalior and invaded Malwa and Ujjain successfully. The greatest of the Slave kings, on his death he named his daughter **RAZIYA** as his successor. ► **'ABBASID DYNASTY; MAMLUKS**

## Ilyushin, Sergei Vladimirovich (1894–1977)

Soviet aircraft designer. Born of a peasant family in the Vologda region, he found his way to the military Aviation Academy in Moscow, and by about 1930 was already working on new aeroplane designs. These were used to equip the wartime and post-war Soviet air force, and increasingly to provide aircraft for Aeroflot, the Soviet civilian airline.

## Image-breaking Riots (1566)

Generally, the violent destruction of high-church statues and valuables, such as that carried out in England by the soldiers of Oliver **CROMWELL**; however, the most famous outburst was in the Low Countries almost a century before. The riots of 1566 began in Aug in Steenvoorde in Flanders, where a mob smashed the decorations of a Catholic convent church; within a month the destruction had spread right through the Netherlands northwards to Groningen. The leadership was unidentified and much of the popular support was spontaneous; however, Calvinist preachers were usually the immediate instigators. Besides the obvious anti-Catholicism, the movement was motivated by economic crisis and frustration that the Dutch Revolt against Spain seemed to be achieving little. The result of the riots was a hardening of Spanish attitudes; **PHILIP II** decided to send the Duke of **ALBA** to restore order, and his harsh conduct signalled the start of the **EIGHTY YEARS' WAR** (1568).

## imam

(1) A religious leader and teacher of a Sunni Muslim community, who leads worship in the mosque. (2) A charismatic leader among Shiite Muslims, who believe that in every generation there is an imam who is an infallible source of spiritual and secular guidance. The line of imams ended in the 9c, and since then the Ayatollahs serve as the collective caretakers of the office until the return of the expected imam. ► **SHIITES; SUNNIS**

## Imam Ahmad (d.1962)

Imam Ahmad of the Yemen succeeded his father, the Imam Yahya, who was assassinated in 1948, and ruled the country until his death in 1962, when with the backing particularly of Egypt, the Yemen Arab Republic (YAR) was proclaimed. A protracted civil war ensued, with Egyptian troops being sucked into what was for them a particularly undesirable conflict insofar as the so-called 'royalists', who supported Ahmad's son, the Imam Muhammad al-Badr, and were backed by the Saudis (who naturally had no wish to see a left-of-centre republican regime on their back doorstep), were familiar with the mountainous terrain of the country, a terrain which was totally alien to the Egyptian forces sent to support the Republican cause.

## IMF ► **INTERNATIONAL MONETARY FUND**

## Immigration and Nationality Act (1965)

US legislation that laid the foundation of modern US immigration policy and began the largest wave of immigration to the USA in a century. It abolished the national quota system established in the 1920s in favour of a system based on family reunification and required skills, and placed a ceiling on immigration from the Western Hemisphere. Between the 1970s and the 1990s the number of immigrants doubled to over 9 million, 80 per cent coming from Latin America, the Caribbean and Asia. In an attempt to control numbers, an amendment in 1978 abolished hemisphere quotas and instituted an annual quota of 290,000 immigrants worldwide (reduced to 270,000 in 1980), with a maximum of 20,000 from any one country. A series of further acts and amendments has attempted to control numbers more closely, especially illegal immigration, by instituting amnesties and penalizing employers of illegal immigrants.

## impeachment

A legal process for removing public officials from office. Originating in medieval England, the process was revived in that country in the 17c when the **RUMP PARLIAMENT** voted to bring **CHARLES I** to trial, resulting in his conviction and beheading. In the USA, the constitution provides that the **HOUSE OF REPRESENTATIVES** may move to impeach for 'high crimes and misdemeanors'. The case is then tried by the **SENATE**, where a two-thirds majority is required for conviction. It is generally agreed that impeachment is a cumbersome method because of the problem of defining unacceptable behaviour and crimes. The move to impeach President Richard **NIXON** in 1974 did, however, have the effect of forcing his resignation. Earlier, impeachment proceedings against President Andrew **JOHNSON** in 1867, which were politically inspired, resulted in his acquittal. The impeachment in 1999 of President Bill **CLINTON**, who had attempted to cover up his extra-marital affair with Monica Lewinsky by allegedly perjurious means, also resulted in acquittal.

## Imperial Aulic Court (*Reichshofrat*)

The Aulic Court was designed by **MAXIMILIAN I** in 1498 to be the Empire's highest executive and judicial body. The court was reorganized by **FERDINAND I** in 1559. Thereafter, it balanced the **IMPERIAL CAMERAL TRIBUNAL**, which dealt with judicial matters and litigation, providing the Emperor with advice on foreign and domestic affairs. The court accompanied the Emperor's person and eventually made its permanent residence with him in Vienna.

## Imperial British East Africa Company

A British company founded and chartered to rule a large area of East Africa in 1888. It was designed to ward off the German and French threats to the area, and maintain British access to Lake Victoria, Uganda and the upper Nile. However, it was seriously under-capitalized, and could not find the resources to develop the region, create an infrastructure, or withstand African resistance. It was wound up in 1894, and its territories became the protectorates (later Crown Colonies) of Kenya and Uganda.

## Imperial Cameral Tribunal (*Reichskammergericht*)

Between 1495 and the Empire's end in 1806, the Cameral Tribunal was the highest court in the Empire. After reforms in 1555 it was composed of men trained in law, and it was instrumental in introducing Roman law throughout the Empire. The court sat at Speyer until 1693 and thereafter at Wetzler. It dealt with civil cases; criminal cases were usually referred to the **IMPERIAL AULIC COURT**.

## Imperial Conferences

The consultative arrangements devised in 1907 by which the British and Dominion governments met on a regular basis. A permanent secretariat was established and meetings at four-year intervals were organized. The Canadian Prime Minister, Sir Wilfred **LAURIER**, was suspicious of both the title and its implications, but he wished to challenge the London government's right to decide the foreign policy of the empire as a whole and thereby commit Canada without proper consultation. The 1911 conference provided the first occasion for at least some briefing by the imperial government, when Sir Edward Grey gave the prime ministers a cagey description of the European situation. By 1926 the conference at last accepted the principle that the dominions were independent nations. In the 1920s **BALFOUR** recommended a new constitutional framework for the Empire in which the dominions became 'autonomous communities within the **BRITISH EMPIRE**, equal in status' but still 'united by a common allegiance to the crown', and this was embodied in the Statute of **WESTMINSTER**. However, there were limits to the British government's readiness to see the dominions as equal partners. At the 1930 conference it refused to consider the Canadian Prime Minister R B **BENNETT**'s plea for imperial preferential tariffs. By 1944, however, the Imperial Conference had become a genuine means by which the prime ministers discussed problems and suggested mutually acceptable solutions.

## Imperial Diet (*Reichstag*)

The Diet was the assembly of the **HOLY ROMAN EMPIRE** (c 1100–1806). After 1489, the Diet was divided into three chambers or colleges. Seven lay and ecclesiastical princes (**ELECTORS**) formed the electoral college and were charged with electing a new emperor. The second college, also of princes, was composed of the other noble rulers, lay and ecclesiastical. The third college represented delegates from the Imperial towns. With the collapse of central authority during the **THIRTY YEARS' WAR**, the Diet lost its legislative powers and became a largely ceremonial body.

## Imperial Federation League (1884–94)

A British pressure group, with branches in Canada, working towards federation for the British Empire. Its members saw this as answer to the challenge of industrial powers such as Germany and the USA, to Britain's isolation within Europe, and to the rivalry with other imperial powers that emerged after 1880. The British league split over the tariff in 1893 and was succeeded by the British Empire League; but this, with its Canadian counterpart, dwindled away in the early 1900s.

## imperialism

The extension of the power of the state through the acquisition, normally by force, of other territories, which are then subject to rule by the imperial power. Many suggest that the motivation behind imperialism is economic, through the exploitation of cheap labour and resources and the opening up of new markets. Others suggest that non-economic factors are involved, including nationalism, racism and the pursuit of international power. The main era of imperialism was the 1880s to 1914, when many European powers sought to gain territories in Africa and Asia. Imperialism of the form associated with the establishment of European empires has in large measure disappeared, but the term is now often applied to any attempts by developed countries to interfere in underdeveloped countries. There is also increasing interest in the idea of *neo-colonialism*, where certain countries are subjugated by the economic power of developed countries rather than through direct rule. ➤ **INDIRECT RULE**

## Imperial Maritime Customs

A Chinese government institution under foreign management during the late 19c and early 20c in charge of collecting customs duties accruing from foreign trade. In 1854 the Chinese Superintendent of Trade at Shanghai fled the city following its occupation by secret society rebels (Small Sword Society). UK and US consuls then assumed responsibility for collecting the maritime customs and remitting them to the Chinese governments, and this arrangement was extended to other **TREATY PORTS**. In 1861 the Chinese government formally appointed Horatio Lay, a British subject, Inspector-General of Imperial Maritime Customs, and the institution remained under foreign direction until its abolition in 1945. The most celebrated Inspector-General was Robert Hart, who served in the post from 1863 to 1908. Chinese nationalists cite the institution as an example of Western imperialism in China, while some Western historians underline its contribution to China's modernization.

## Imperial Rescript on Education (30 Oct 1890)

The rescript issued in the name of the Japanese **MEIJI EMPEROR** that sought to provide the basic aims of education, emphasizing the importance of inculcating traditional values of loyalty to the Emperor, filial piety and concern for the common welfare. It represented a conservative reaction to the westernizing reforms of the 1870s and 1880s, which were thought to have encouraged individualism and materialism. The close relationship between the Emperor and his subjects, described as existing since time immemorial, was the central focus of the rescript. Copies were displayed in every school, where children had to recite the rescript every day. After **WORLD WAR II**, US occupation authorities condemned the rescript for having contributed to the emergence of fanatical emperor-worship, ultra-nationalism and militarism during the late 1930s, and ordered its replacement by new educational aims to encourage a democratic spirit in Japan.

**Imperial Rescript to Soldiers and Sailors** (4 Jan 1882)

The rescript issued in the name of the Japanese **MEIJI EMPEROR** to provide a code of ethics for the military services. It was issued at a time when a national conscript army had only recently been formed (1873) and against a background of **SAMURAI** discontent with modernizing reforms, which had led to several uprisings in the late 1870s. The support of the military services were therefore essential for the new Meiji government. The rescript described service to the state in terms of absolute loyalty to the Emperor and called for a spirit of patriotism, discipline and simplicity amongst the military (harkening back to traditional ethics of the samurai class). At the same time, all servicemen were to eschew politics, an injunction that was to be broken in the 1930s when ultra-nationalist army officers attempted a military takeover of government. Like the **IMPERIAL RESCRIPT ON EDUCATION**, this rescript has been regarded since 1945 as providing the moral underpinning for the pre-war ideology of fanatical emperor-worship and extreme nationalism.

**Imperial Rule Assistance Association (IRAA)**

An umbrella organization created in Japan (Oct 1940) to promote a New Order whereby all interests in society would be united behind mobilization for war and the national interest. Launched by the Prime Minister **KONOE FUMIMARO** in the summer of 1940, the IRAA was originally intended to be the nucleus of a mass-based reformist party that would absorb all existing political parties and occupational groups, thereby challenging the political, bureaucratic and economic élites. It was supported by army officers who wanted to see a controlled economy as well as intellectuals attracted to models of European fascism. In practice, however, the IRAA soon came under the control of the bureaucracy (in particular the Home Ministry) and became merely an instrument of government control. Although political parties were formally abolished, former party élites continued to exercise leadership in the Diet, while business élites were able to obstruct all attempts to impose total state control of the economy.

**Imperial Towns** (*Reichsstädte*)

Cities in the **HOLY ROMAN EMPIRE** directly ruled by the Emperor. The term is often confused with Free Imperial City (*freie Reichsstadt*), though the latter is correctly applied only to the seven cities which had won freedom from ecclesiastical control: Basle, Strasbourg, Speyer, Worms, Mainz, Cologne and Regensburg. Most of the Imperial towns were in South Germany. The largest grouping of them was the **HANSEATIC LEAGUE**. After the Peace of **WESTPHALIA** (1648) their representatives made up the third college of the Imperial Diet. Many smaller towns lost their Imperial privileges; the number declined from over 80 in 1521 to 51 in 1789. Most were governed by oligarchies through a town council (*Rat*).

**Imperial Way Faction** (*Kodo-ha*)

Japanese army faction in the 1930s which stressed the importance of the **SAMURAI** spirit and mystic devotion to the emperor. The faction comprised ultranationalist junior officers who denounced corruption amongst political and business élites (who were seen as insensitive to the economic hardships of the people as a result of the **GREAT DEPRESSION**) and advocated direct action to sweep away the civilian establishment and achieve national renovation in preparation for what they saw as an inevitable war with the USSR. In Feb 1936 the faction attempted a coup in Tokyo but it was suppressed by the army senior command.

**Imrédy, Béla** (1891–1946)

Hungarian financier and politician. He was Director of the national bank from 1932 to 1935 and thereafter its President. Between 1932 and 1935 he was also Minister of Finance, and from May 1938 to Feb 1939 Prime Minister. Internally he supported authoritarian rule and externally he supported **HITLER's** policies, particularly after the **MUNICH AGREEMENT** in Sep 1938. During the Nazi occupation (1944–5) he acted as Minister of Economic Affairs. After the war he was executed as a war criminal.

**IMRO** ► **VMRO**

**Incas** ► **PRE-COLUMBIAN CIVILIZATIONS**

**income tax**

A tax levied on an individual's personal income or on a business income. The first income tax was levied in Britain in 1799 by the government of William **PITT, THE YOUNGER**, specifically to fund the war against the French. It was repealed in 1816 but reintroduced by **PEEL** since government revenue had declined due both to moves towards free trade, which had lowered indirect taxation, and the penny post, which had lowered postal service income. The tax originally applied only to the wealthiest citizens, but was gradually applied to most full-time employees right down the social scale. David **LLOYD GEORGE's** 'people's budget' of 1909 was the first to introduce different rates of income tax according to the ability to pay. In the USA a federal income tax was imposed in 1862 to help finance the **AMERICAN CIVIL WAR** and was eventually made permanent in 1913, when the 16th Amendment to the Constitution was ratified; by then most of the US states had already begun to impose their own taxes.

**Indentured Labour, Indian**

Workers from India, imported in the period 1838 to 1917 into those British West Indies colonies which lost their labour force after the emancipation of slaves. After 1834, British West Indies governments set up emigration offices in Bombay, Calcutta and Madras and offered a five-year indenture, rations, housing and a free passage home. The latter condition was dropped after 1854 and when their term of indenture was completed many immigrants chose to stay, buying up cheap crown land and putting down roots. It is calculated that some 370,000 Indian labourers went to Jamaica, Trinidad and Guyana prior

to 1917; their descendants make up half the population in Trinidad and Guyana today.

## indentured servants

The name given to Europeans who were contracted to serve as field labourers mainly in St Kitts and Barbados prior to the **SUGAR REVOLUTION**. In those colonies the native population was hostile or nonexistent and a source of labour was found in the 'rejects' of England and France: common criminals, beggars and rebels, although some penurious gentlemen also served. The contract provided passage, board and lodging, and the promise of land or a passage home after the three- to seven-year period of indenture was completed. The civil unrest in England and Ireland between 1640 and 1660 resulted in many deportations, and Barbados alone received 23,000 servants in the period 1645–60. As conditions were very harsh and mortality high, many indentured servants took to buccaneering, the most notable being Henry **MORGAN**. ► **BUCCANEERS**

## indentured servitude

A system of contract labour, developed to attract immigrants to the early American colonies, offering poor Englishmen Atlantic passage in exchange for a term of service. After serving their terms (generally four years, during which, in contrast to slaves, they retained legal rights), most indentured servants became wage-labourers on plantations or farms, although a few did succeed in becoming landowners. Through most of the 17c, some 1,500 indentured servants were brought to the Chesapeake Bay colonies every year. In the late 17c, however, the numbers declined significantly as large numbers of slaves were imported.

## Independent Labour Party (ILP)

British political party formed in 1893 with the objective of sending working men to parliament. It was so-

cialist in aim, but wished to gain the support of working people whether they were socialist or not. One of its leading figures was Keir **HARDIE**. Many of its leaders played a major part in founding the Labour Representation Committee (1900), which became the **LABOUR PARTY** in 1906. It was affiliated to the Labour Party but put up its own candidates, and was disaffiliated in 1932. It continued to have a few members of parliament up to 1950. ► **SOCIALISM**

## Independent Republican Party

French political party. Those members of the CNI (*Centre national des indépendants*, 'National Centre of Independents') who continued to support de **GAULLE** after 1962 and who formed a new party in 1966, led by **GISCARD D'ESTAING**. At first little more than a weak adjunct to the Gaullist Party, it emerged as an equal partner with its leader's election as President in 1973, and became one of the two main right-wing parties. In 1978 it was incorporated in the UDF (*Union pour la démocratie française* ('Union for French Democracy'), an electoral coalition, with various small centre groups. Often referred to as Giscardiens, after their leading figure. ► **GAULLISTS**; **INDEPENDENTS** (France)

## Independents (England)

The name given to those Puritans in favour of religious toleration who rejected a Presbyterian establishment in England during the 1640s and who founded their own independent congregations. From these developed Congregationalism. The term is also used to distinguish those parliamentarians who favoured an all-out war against **CHARLES I** involving, if necessary, his deposition from 'Presbyterians' who wanted a defensive war and accommodation with the King. The leadership of the **NEW MODEL ARMY** from 1645 reflected 'independent' objectives. ► **CROMWELL, OLIVER; ENGLISH CIVIL WARS; PURITANISM**

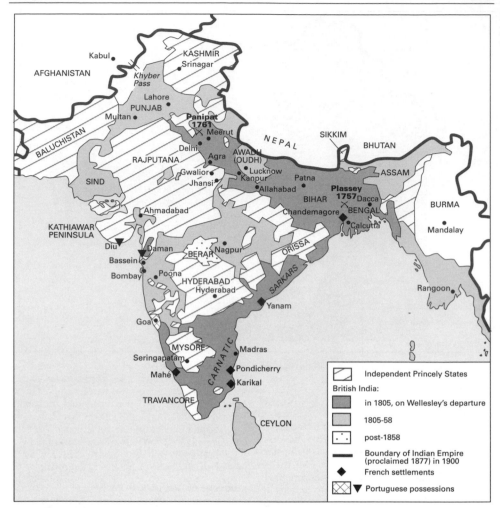

**India, 1753–1890**

---

**Independents** (France)
French political party, officially known as the CNI (*Centre national des indépendants*, 'National Centre of Independents' or 'Independents'). The party was organized in 1948, and was the successor to the pre-**WORLD WAR II** parties known collectively by the name *Modérés* ('**MODERATES**'). In 1951 it incorporated the *Parti paysan* ('Peasant Party'), and in 1952 many former **GAULLISTS**. It was led by Antoine Pinay and supported de **GAULLE** in 1958, but its opposition to his Algerian policy led to its collapse in 1962. A small faction, led by **GISCARD D'ESTAING**, remained loyal to de Gaulle's government, and resurrected the party as the **INDEPENDENT REPUBLICAN PARTY** in 1966.

**INDIA** official name **Republic of India**
A federal republic in southern Asia, bounded to the north-west by Pakistan; to the north by China, Nepal and Bhutan; to the east by Myanmar and Bangladesh; to the south-east by the Bay of Bengal; and to the south-west by the Arabian Sea. The Indus civilization, which emerged in c.2500BC, was destroyed in 1500BC by the Aryans, who developed the Brahminic caste system. The Mauryan Emperor Asoka unified most of India, and established Buddhism as the state religion in the 3c BC. Hinduism spread in the 2c BC,

and there were Muslim influences during the 7–8c AD, with a sultanate established at Delhi. Delhi was captured by **TIMUR** in 1398 and the **MUGHAL EMPIRE** was established by **BABUR** in 1526, and extended by **AKBAR THE GREAT** and **AURANGZEB**. The Portuguese, French, Dutch and British had footholds in India in the 18c, which led to conflict between France and Britain in 1746–63. The development of British interests was represented by the British **EAST INDIA COMPANY**, and British power was established after the **INDIAN UPRISING** (1857) was crushed. A movement for independence arose in the late 19c, and the Government of India Act in 1919 allowed the election of Indian ministers to share power with appointed British governors; a further Act in 1935 allowed the election of independent provincial governments. Passive resistance campaigns led by Mahatma **GANDHI** began in the 1920s, and independence was granted in 1948, on the basis of partition which established a Muslim state (Pakistan). Indian states were later reorganized on a linguistic basis. There was a Pakistan–India war over disputed territory in Kashmir and Jammu in 1948; this unresolved issue underlay further India–Pakistan conflict in 1965 and 1971 (the **INDO-PAKISTAN WARS**), as well as periods of

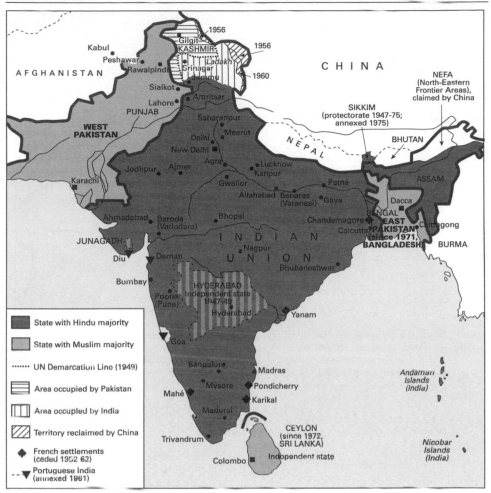

**Partition of India (1947)**

tension in 1999 and 2000–2 that were heightened by the fact that both countries now possessed nuclear weapons. There has been sporadic Hindu Muslim hostility internally too, notably in 1978, but also in 1992 and 2002, when the mosque at Ayodhya was the focus of violent rioting that claimed many lives. Separatist movements continue, especially that of the Sikhs' demand for an independent Sikh state in the Punjab. The suppression of the militant Sikh movement in 1984 led to the assassination of Indira **GANDHI**. Also that year a major gas leak at the city of **BHOPAL** caused c.2,500 deaths. Rajiv **GANDHI**, leader of the Congress (I) Party, was assassinated during the 1991 general election. Increasing tension generally resulted in inter-communal violence and the declaration in 1993 of a national state of emergency. The Congress (I) Party was heavily defeated in the 1996 elections, and a period of political instability followed in which there were several general elections and allegations of widespread corruption in public life. Economic reforms, begun in the early 1990s, continued and India became a global centre for information technology skills. The Congress (I) Party, eclipsed by the Hindu nationalist Bharatiya Janata Party (BJP) in the 1990s, won a surprise victory in the 2004 general election under Sonia **GANDHI**; she refused the prem-

iership and Manmohan Singh became Prime Minister, the first Sikh to hold the office. ► **INDIAN NATIONAL CONGRESS**; **KASHMIR PROBLEM**

**India, Partition of** (1947)
Under the Indian Independence Act of July 1947, the formerly British-ruled Indian sub-continent was partitioned on 14–15 Aug into two independent countries, a predominantly Hindu India and a predominantly Muslim Pakistan. There was a lot of communal violence at this time which had started in the spring of 1947. Many Muslims migrated from India to Pakistan and many Hindus from Pakistan to India, resulting in a refugee population of some 6 million Muslims (in Pakistan) and 4.5 million Sikhs and Hindus (on the Indian side of the border). In places there was a total collapse of law and order, before, during and after the partition. The violence that accompanied the migration resulted in what is believed to have been near to a million deaths – although the official total was 180,000. All princely states in the Indian subcontinent were left to choose their own fate but were advised to integrate with either India or Pakistan according to the religious affiliations of their peoples and their geographical positions. The state of Kashmir, however, remains in dispute. ► **KASHMIR PROBLEM**

# Pre-Islamic India

*Culture & Society*

### Indus Valley Civilization
The earliest known South Asian civilization, which flourished
c.2300–c.1750 BC across half a million square miles around the River
Indus in Pakistan. Over 100 sites have been identified with important urban centres at Mohenjo-daro and Harappa
(Pakistan), and Kalibangan and Lothal (western India). There were uniform principles of urban planning, with streets set
out in a grid pattern and public drainage systems. Weights and measures were standardized, and there was widespread
trade with western Asia. A common writing system was used, which remains undeciphered. Great granaries on citadel
mounts suggest the existence of priest-kings or a priestly oligarchy. There is no firm explanation for the decline of the
civilization.

### Vedic Age
A period (c.1500–c.600 BC) which began with the migration of Indo-European tribes (Indo-Aryans) to northern India.
It was a period of transition from nomadic pastoralism to settled village communities, with cattle representing the major
form of wealth. There was religious worship of personified forces of nature and abstract divinities, centred on a ritual of
sacrifice.

### Magadha
One of the greatest empires of ancient India. The capital was originally Rajagriha and was later shifted to the River
Ganges at Pataliputra. The geographical position of Magadha gave it control over the lower Ganges plain, including the
river, supplying it with revenue from river trade. The first important king of Magadha was Bimbisara, a man of
determination and political foresight, who reigned in the second half of the 6c BC. He was murdered (491 BC) by his son,
Ajatashatru, who was impatient to rule. After Ajatashatru's death (461 BC), Magadha was ruled by a succession of weak
kings until 413 BC, when the Shishunaga Dynasty assumed the throne and ruled for half a century.

### Nanda
A dynasty described as the first empire-builders of India. Mahapadma Nanda founded the dynasty in the mid-4c BC. He
was Emperor of Magadha and succeeded in gaining control of Kalinga and of other parts of Deccan. The Nandas were the
first of a number of non-Kshatriya dynasties. The Nandas built up a vast army anticipating the Greek invasion but never
had the opportunity to use the army against them since the campaign of Alexander III, the Great, terminated in Punjab.
The dynasty made a methodical collection of taxes, and land revenue became a substantial source of income. They also
built canals and carried out irrigation projects. The possibility of an imperial structure based on an essentially agrarian
economy began to germinate in the Indian mind. The further development of the Nandas was cut short, however, by
Chandragupta Maurya, who usurped the Nanda throne in 321 BC.

### Maurya
A powerful north Indian kingdom (c.321–c.185 BC) which stretched from Afghanistan to southern India, and is the
earliest example in the subcontinent of a state system. Its third ruler, Ashoka (c.269/232 BC), was famous for his
conversion to Buddhism and for the many edicts he had engraved on rocks and pillars detailing his policies of rule by
*dharma* (a code of conduct based on social responsibility).

### Satavahana
An early Hindu dynasty, which ruled over the North Deccan (1c BC to 3c AD) prior to the rise of the Gupta Dynasty. The
area of origin of the Satavahanas is a matter of some dispute, but while in power they were centred on the Krishna Valley.
The Satavahanas had a loose confederation of chiefdoms rather than a centralized empire. Ties were based on kinship

---

**India, Pre-Islamic** ► *See panel*

### India Acts
Passed by the British parliament, the Regulating Act
of 1773 and India Act of 1784 attempted to reform
the corrupt and inefficient administration of the British **EAST INDIA COMPANY** over the developing Indian
empire, whilst avoiding the necessity for Parliament
to have to take direct responsibility for governing
the newly acquired territories. The 1773 Act set up
the post of Governor-General and a Governing
Council in India, and that of 1784 established a Board
of Control in London, made up of members of the
cabinet, to decide on strategic questions concerning
the government of India. The Acts were intended to
meet criticism amongst the English establishment of
the all too evident speculation of Company funds,
seen in the growing number of 'Nabobs' (merchants
and Company employees returning from India with
vast fortunes who then bribed their way into positions of influence), as well as the maladministration
of Bengal (which resulted in the death of one-third
of the population in the famine of 1770) and the war-

mongering of Warren **HASTINGS** (Governor-General,
1773–85). Subsequent Acts in 1813 and 1830 deprived the East India Company of its monopoly of
the East Indies trade and then of its trading functions
altogether, allowing it to concentrate entirely on the
business of administration. During this later period,
the so-called 'era of reform', zealous attempts were
made to improve the Company's administration
along utilitarian lines, as well as to impress the mark
of British rule on the Indian population. The result
was the **INDIAN UPRISING** of 1857 and the abolition
of the Company the following year. ► **GOVERNMENT
OF INDIA ACTS**

### Indian Civil Service (ICS)
Formerly known as the Covenanted Civil Service
because its nominated members entered into coven-
ants originally with the British **EAST INDIA COMPANY**,
and afterwards with the Secretary of State in council,
ICS members filled the higher posts in the government
secretariats in various departments. Under a decree
dating 1853, the ICS was opened to all natural-born
British subjects, regardless of race, who would be ap-

and socio-religious connections; the Satavahana rulers were Brahma-Kshatriyas. Their main sources of revenue were products of the land, and both regional and international trade. While not a naval power, the Satavahana appear to have taken over much of the coastal and high-seas trading after the decline of Rome's Far Eastern merchant navy. The Satavahana Dynasty saw the rise of urbanism in South India. Although Hindu, the Satavahana were tolerant of both Jainism and Buddhism in order not to prejudice trade with societies of those faiths.

### Kushana
The chief tribe of the Yueh-chi people of China, the Kushanas ruled over much of north India, Afghanistan and Central Asia in the 1–3c AD; their empire extended southwards as far as Sanchi, and to the east as far as Benares, with Mathura almost having the status of a second capital. The Kushana were Buddhist and also patronized some Hindu sects. The history of northern India under the Kushanas was closely associated with events in Central Asia. Kujula Khadhises and his son, Vima, were the first Kushanas; they came from Central Asia and gained control of north-west India in the 1c. Vima Kadphises was succeeded by Kanishka. It was under the latter that the Kushana Dynasty flourished, and this period ranks as one of the significant phases in the cultural development of northern India. Although Kanishka's successors ruled for 150 years, Kushana power gradually diminished after his reign.

### Vakataka
A dynasty which rose to power in the second half of the 3c AD, emerging after the collapse of the Satavahana kingdom, and which was spread over present-day Madhya Pradesh, Maharashtra and north-west Andhra Pradesh. Pravarsena I, ruling in the early 4c, conquered large parts of the western Deccan and central India. The Vakataka kingdom was divided into four parts under the successor of Pravarsena I. This weakened the state but at the same time prevented the complete takeover of the kingdom by Samudragupta, since he was content to obtain the homage of the Vakataka feudatories in central India and did not harass the main line of the Vakataka kings. Their survival after the Gupta campaigns gave them the opportunity to rearrange their territory which dominated the Deccan. A marriage alliance with the Gupta made the Vakataka kingdom virtually a part of the Gupta Empire.

### Gupta
A decentralized state system (AD 320–540) covering most of northern India, with provinces (*desa*) and districts (*pradesa*). It was materially prosperous, especially in urban areas, and is known as India's 'Classical' or 'Golden' Age, when norms of Indian literature, art, architecture and philosophy were established, and Hinduism underwent a revival.

### Pallava
The Pallavas ruled from the 4c to the end of the 9c, when their territories were annexed by the Chola kings of **Thanjavur** (Tanjore). The Pallava period in south India saw the growth of the Aryan institutions in the south. Amongst the later group of Pallava rulers, Mahendra-Varman I (600/30) was responsible for the growing political strength of the Pallavas and during his reign some of the finest rock-cut temples, including the famous one sited at Mahabalipuram, were built. Another famous Pallava king, who ruled for 40 years, was Narsimha-Varman II. The Pallavas developed a navy, built dockyards at Mahabalipuram and Nagapattinam, and conducted extensive maritime trade with South-East Asia.

### Maitraka
The Indian dynasty that ruled Gujarat and Saurashtra from the 5c to the 8c. Its founder, Bhatarka, was a Gupta general who took advantage of the decline of the Gupta Empire to establish Valabhi (present-day Vala) as his capital. Under Shiladitya I (c.6c), the kingdom extended into Malwa and Rajasthan, but later suffered at the hands of Harsha and the Chalukyas. After Harsha's death (c.647), the dynasty revived until c.780, when the last Maitraka king, Shiladitya VI, was killed and his capital razed by the Arabs. The Maitraka Empire played a significant role in the history of Jainism and Buddhism.

pointed as civil servants subject to their performance in a competitive examination held in England. The first Indian, the poet Tagore's brother, Satyendranath Tagore, entered the ICS in 1864. At independence, the ICS was renamed as the Indian Administrative Service (IAS).

**Indian National Congress**, also called **Congress Party** or **Congress (I) Party**
A broad-based political organization, it was founded in 1885 and became a nationwide political party in 1920. It spearheaded the nationalist movement for independence from Britain under the leadership of charismatic figures such as M K **GANDHI** and Jawaharlal **NEHRU**. An uneasy alliance of Left and Right, business and rural interests, it has been the dominant political party in India since 1947; exceptions to its rule occurred in the periods 1977–80, when the Janata Party ruled, 1989–91, when the **JANATA DAL** and Janata Dal (S) ruled, and from 1996–2004, when a United Front coalition ruled. After Nehru's death the party split and a younger, more radical faction emerged under the leadership of Indira **GANDHI**. In 1978, while in opposition, she renamed the party the 'real' Indian National Congress, or Congress (I) (where I stands for Indira). After her assassination in 1984, her son Rajiv **GANDHI** assumed the leadership, until he too was assassinated (1991). P V Narasimha Rao became leader and served as Prime Minister until the party's worst ever election defeat in 1996, after which he resigned. Sitaram Kesri was leader until he resigned in 1998 to allow Rajiv Gandhi's widow, Sonia **GANDHI**, to take over the leadership. She was nominanted as Prime Minister when the party won the 2004 general election but declined the office, although remaining the party's President. ► **NON-COOPERATION MOVEMENT; QUIT INDIA MOVEMENT**

**Indian Territory**
The land designated by the US government as a 'permanent' homeland for **NATIVE AMERICANS** who were forced to give up their land in the south-east, which had been guaranteed by federal treaties, and relocate in the west in compliance with the Indian Removal Act of 1830. The boundaries of what was to be inviol-

**Chalukya**

An Indian ruling dynasty which flourished in two main branches. The Western Chalukyas controlled Deccan (543–757 and c.975–c.1189), with capitals at Vatapi and Kalyani. The Eastern Chalukyas ruled what is present-day Andhra Pradesh from Vengi (c.624–c.1070).

**Pala**

One of the three dynasties vying with one another for supremacy in north India in the 8–10c. Established by Gopala (supposedly elected by the people) in the mid-8c in Bengal, the dynasty soon came into conflict with the Pratiharas over control of **Kanauj**. In decline in the mid-10c, the kingdom recovered under Mahipala I (c.975/1027); Rampala (1072/1126) successfully put down the Kaivarta rebellion (recorded in Sandhyakaranandin's *Ramacarita*). Buddhists by persuasion, the Palas encouraged the development of great Buddhist monasteries as educational centres, but never themselves had a permanent seat of government.

**Pratihara**

The most important of the Gurjara kingdoms which sprang up in the 7c in western India. The first major ruler, Nagabhata I, made his mark by repelling the Arabs of Sind when they attempted to overrun Rajasthan and Malwa (c.725). The next ruler, Vatsaraja (c.778/792), campaigned successfully against the Palas but was himself invaded and defeated by the Rashtrakuta ruler; these were the opening moves in a triangular contest for dominance in north India which lasted for more than a century. Employing a markedly decentralized administration, the greatest of their rulers was Mihira Bhoja (c.835/c.888), who had successes against both the Palas and Rashtrakutas.

**Rashtrakuta**

An Indian dynasty which produced a long line of warriors and successful administrators. It was founded by Dantidurga, who overthrew the Chalukyas in 750 and established his capital at Malkhed near modern Sholapur. The Rashtrakutas soon dominated the entire area of northern Maharashtra. They also contested with the Pratiharas for the control of Gujarat and Malwa. The Rashtrakutas constantly fought the eastern Chalukyas of Vengi, the Pallavas of Kanchi and the Pandyas of Madurai. The greatest Rashtrakuta rulers were Indra III (915/27) and Krishna III (939/65). The Rashtrakuta rule in Deccan lasted for almost 200 years until the end of the 10c. The Rashtrakuta rulers were tolerant in their religious views and patronized not only Shaivism and Vaishnavism, but Jainism as well. The famous rock-cut temple of Shiva at Ellora was built by one of the Rashtrakuta kings, Krishna I, in the 9c. The Rashtrakuta kings were great patrons of arts and letters. In their courts, we find not only Sanskrit poets but scholars who wrote in Prakrit and Kannada.

**Chola**

An ancient **Tamil** dynasty which ruled much of southern India between the 8c and 13c. The height of power was under Rajaraja (985/1014) and Rajendra (1014/44), who extended the kingdom to include Ceylon (now Sri Lanka). It introduced highly developed revenue administration, village self-organization, and irrigation systems. Tamil architecture and literature flourished.

**Chandella**

A North Indian dynasty prominent in the 10–12c as one of the successor states to their former overlords, the Pratiharas. The first major reigns of Harsha (c.900/c.925) and Yashovarman (c.925/c.950) saw their rise at the expense of the Pratiharas, as well as the start of their notable temple building at their early capital, Khajuraho (later to become a purely religious centre), in a distinctive and highly ornate style. Their main rivals were the neighbouring dynasty, the Kalachuris of Tripuri. The last significant ruler was Paramardi (1165/1202), the latter half of whose reign saw prolonged conflicts with the Chahamanas of Shakambhari (Chauhans) and the plundering of their later capital, Mahoba, in 1182. The

able territory based on new treaties signed in the 1830s were redefined several times, beginning in 1834. The original area included most of Oklahoma and parts of Kansas and Nebraska. The passage of homestead and land allotment acts opened up parts of the area to white homesteaders and developers. The northern section was lost in 1854 when Kansas and Nebraska became territories, and by the end of the century most of the remaining Indian Territory had been absorbed into what is now Oklahoma. ► **FIVE CIVILIZED TRIBES**

**Indian Uprising** (1857–8)

A serious rebellion against British rule, triggered off partly by the belief among Indian **SEPOY** troops in British **EAST INDIA COMPANY** service that new cartridges had been greased with animal fat – something which would have been abhorrent to both Hindus and Muslims. At the same time, there was resentment among the old governing class, especially in the recently annexed Kingdom of Awadh, over the reduction in their power and Western innovations. The sepoy mutiny at Meerut (10 May 1857) spread throughout Bengal army units in northern India, with both urban and rural populations rising in support of the revolt. Delhi quickly fell, and Kanpur and Lucknow garrisons were besieged. The British finally regained full control in mid-1858 after a final phase of struggle in Central India. The immediate result was the transfer of government from the British **EAST INDIA COMPANY** to the British crown (1858), but the long-term result, apart from much racial bitterness, was to make British policy in India much more conservative and reluctant to alienate or provoke Indian religious traditions or the surviving Indian princes. The rising had proto-national aspects, albeit on a regional and racial basis, so the old terms for it, 'Indian Mutiny' or 'Sepoy Mutiny', are clearly inadequate. Modern scholars are moving towards 'Great Rebellion of 1857' as a term which recognizes its breadth and depth without exaggerating its modernity. ► **LUCKNOW, SIEGE OF**

**Indian Wars** (1622–1890)

In American history, the process of invasion and conquest by which white people settled the present USA.

dynasty was overthrown in the Muslim conquest of North India with the capture of their stronghold, Kalanjara, in 1202 by **Qutb-ud-Din Aibak**.

### Chauhans (Chahamanas) of Shakambhari

A prominent dynasty of North India, originally from the 8c feudatory to the Pratiharas, but emerging as independent rulers in the 11–12c. They were Rajputs, a feudal warrior nobility of obscure, possibly immigrant origin, assimilated into Kshatriya status. Several related branches of the family ruled other small states in Rajasthan. Vigraharaja IV (1150/63) captured Delhi from the Tomaras, and from then on the dynasty was involved in conflict with the Muslims by now established in the Punjab. Prithviraja III (1177/92) is famous for his conflicts both with the Gahadavalas (Gahrwals) of Kanauj and with **Muhammad Ghuri**, whom he defeated in the first Battle of Tarain in 1191; the second Battle of Tarain (1192) was a decisive victory for the Muslims and spelt the end of this branch of the Chauhans. These events are celebrated in the bardic chronicle, the *Prithviraj Rasau* of Chand Bardai, one of the earliest works of Rajasthani literature.

### Hoysala

A family of petty hill chiefs of the Western Ghats who carved out of the dismembered Chalukya state a southern Indian state (11–14c) in present-day Mysore. The most important Hoysala rulers were Vira Ballala II (1173/1220), Vira Someswara, their greatest ruler (1233/64), and Vira Ballala III. The Hoysalas started declining after c.1335. At the fall of the Hoysala state, some Hoysala officers founded the Vijayanagar kingdom. The Hoysalas made important contributions to South Indian art and architecture.

### Yadava

Originally the name of a late Vedic tribe which settled in the Mathura area in northern India, the name was used of a dynasty which ruled in northern Deccan (Aurangabad region) from 900 to 1300, whose contribution to the final disintegration of the Chola Dynasty was significant. In 1296 **Ala al-Din Khalji** attacked the city of Deogiri, the Yadava capital. He defeated the Yadavas, and the Yadava king was forced to pay a vast amount of gold to Ala al-Din as part of the ensuing peace treaty. Between 1327 and 1330 **Muhammad bin Tughlaq** moved his capital from Delhi to Deogiri and renamed it Daulatabad. Yadavas patronized the Marathi language and played an important part in establishing Marathi as the language of intellectual communication.

### Pandya

The South Indian dynasty which, along with the Chola Dynasty, began to dominate the east coast after the turn of the 1c BC and was associated with the emergence of **Tamil** culture. The Cheras, Cholas and Pandyas were continually at war with one other. From the mid-6c, South India was ruled by the Pallavas of Kanchi, Chalukyas of Badami, and the Pandyas with their capital at Madurai. The Pandyas had established their position in the area of the south of Tamil-nadu, and were to remain in control of this region for many centuries. The conflict between these warring states persisted for several centuries, and in the 9c the Pallavas succumbed to a combined attack from the Pandyas and the Cholas. By the 13c the Pandyas had superseded the Cholas as the dominant power in the Tamil country and might well have maintained this position in the subsequent century had it not been for the attacks from Turkish rulers from the north and the threat of interference from the northern Deccan, which was virtually in the hands of the **Delhi Sultanate**.

### Vijayanagar

The last great medieval Hindu state, located in southern India (1336–1565) and named after its capital, 'the city of victory'. It served as a barrier against invasion by North Indian Muslim sultanates, and created the conditions for creative productivity in which Sanskrit and regional literatures thrived. It was finally overthrown by an alliance of four Muslim rulers, the **Deccani Sultanates**, in 1565.

---

The Europeans set out to remake the New World in the image of the Old, if possible by persuasion, if necessary by force. The result was the destruction of the indigenous population, cultures and economies. Through European diseases to which the **NATIVE AMERICANS** had no natural resistance, the imposition of white culture, and warfare, the native population of North America was reduced from perhaps 4 million at first contact to about 250,000 by 1900. The list of specific Indian wars is very long, most of them being actual skirmishes between a local tribe and the white settlers usurping their land. They are generally accepted to have begun with the revolt of the **POWHATAN CONFEDERACY** against settlers at **JAMESTOWN**, Virginia in 1622, and to have ended with the massacre at **WOUNDED KNEE** in 1890. Specific early conflicts include the **PEQUOT WAR** (1637) and **KING PHILIP'S WAR** (1676) in New England, and the Pueblo Revolt (1680–92) led by Popé against Spanish settlements in what is now New Mexico and Arizona. From 1689 to 1763, Native American warfare was bound up with the struggle between France and Britain for control of the continent, the **FRENCH AND INDIAN WAR**. The AL-

GONQUIN tribes sided with the French. The English, eventually victorious, enjoyed the support of the **IROQUOIS CONFEDERACY** of western New York, important both for their internal strength and for their control of the Mohawk Valley and Lake Ontario plain, the only natural break in the Appalachian Mountains. Further west, the **OTTAWA** chief **PONTIAC** seized almost all the British fur trading posts from upper Michigan to New York State before the French cut off their supplies. By 1830 the US government had formalized a policy of denying Indian rights and removing tribes from the lands east of the Mississippi to unsettled lands in the west. Despite resistance, the **FIVE CIVILIZED TRIBES** of the south-east and others were forced to move west and settle in **INDIAN TERRITORY**. The **SEMINOLE** people of Florida, whose number included escaped black slaves, fought for over 30 years, accepting defeat in 1842 when nearly all were lost. Some finally moved west, but a small group survived by living in the Everglades. The Indian wars generally followed the progress of white settlers as they moved their frontier westward. On the plains, the US Cavalry fought the **SIOUX** and the **CHEYENNE**, under such leaders as **SIT-**

TING BULL and CRAZY HORSE. These 'Sioux Wars' lasted over 30 years until finally ended by the incident at Wounded Knee (1890). The massacre of warriors, women and children by the Cavalry at Sand Creek, Colorado (1864) inflamed ARAPAHO, COMANCHE, Kiowa and Cheyenne already fighting to avoid being placed on reservations. In the south-west, the NAVAJO conflict ended with their mass imprisonment (1864–8) at Fort Sumpter, while the APACHE, under such leaders as COCHISE and GERONIMO, fought on until 1900. At the same time Nez Percé, under Chief JOSEPH, and the Modoc fought for their lands in the north-west until their eventual defeat. Throughout the wars, the NATIVE AMERICANS fought at material and numerical dis-advantage. They were disadvantaged as well by their own concept of warfare, for they understood it in wholly different terms from their foes. Finally they were handicapped by their own lack of unity. Specific tribes approached each war in terms of their own friendships and enmities. This gave some, such as the Iroquois, more power to shape their own futures. But only on a few occasions did such confederacies surmount tribal boundaries. ► LITTLE BIGHORN, BATTLE OF THE; PONTIAC'S CON-SPIRACY

## indirect rule

A form of colonial rule especially characteristic of British rule in Africa during the interwar years. In general terms it involved the use of existing political structures, leaders, and local organs of authority. Thus, local political élites enjoyed considerable autonomy, although they still had to keep in accord with the interests of the colonial power. It was adopted on grounds of its cheapness and to allow for independent cultural development, but was in-creasingly criticized for its failure to introduce a modernizing role into colonial administration, and was gradually given up after 1945. ► FULANI EMI-RATES; LOZI STATE

## Indochina

The term, as currently used, refers to the present-day states of Vietnam, Laos and Cambodia. French Indo-china, the Indochinese Union, was established in 1887, and comprised the protectorates of Cambodia, Laos, Tonkin and Annam, together with the colony of COCHIN-CHINA. French Indochina as a political unit ceased to exist in 1954, following the conclusion of the Geneva Agreements and the withdrawal of the French.

INDONESIA official name **Republic of Indonesia**, formerly **Netherlands Indies, Dutch East Indies, Netherlands East Indies** and **United States of In-donesia**

A republic in South-East Asia comprising the world's largest island group. It includes the island group of the Moluccas, also called the Spice Islands; Kaliman-tan, a group of four provinces in the Indonesian part of Borneo; Sumatra, which is the fifth-largest island in the world and was the centre of the Buddhist king-dom of Srivijaya in the 7–13c, and was discovered by Marco POLO in the 13c; and the mountainous island of Timor. Since the independence of Indonesia in 1945, all these places have developed separatist movements of varying intensity. The eastern part of Timor was colonized by the Portuguese in the 16c and the western part by the Dutch in the 17c, and it was divided between Portugal and Holland in 1859. West Timor (former Dutch Timor) was included in Indonesia at independence, and is administered as part of the province of Nusa Tenggara Timur. Colonial administration withdrew from EAST TIMOR in 1975 and the region declared itself independent as the Democratic Republic of East Timor. Violent civil war broke out and East Timor was annexed by Indonesia in 1976, but this annexation was not recognized by the UN and was reversed by popular plebiscite in 1999 after a long nationalist struggle against Indone-sian ascendancy. Irian Jaya was granted a degree of autonomy in 2002, but fighting continues with se-paratists in the north Sumatran province of Aceh, although this was suspended in Dec 2004 when Su-matra, and in particular Aceh, was devastated by the Indian Ocean tsunami, which killed over 200,000 people in Indonesia. Indonesia was settled in early times by Hindus and Buddhists whose power lasted until the 14c. Islam was introduced in the 14–15c. Portuguese settlers arrived in the early 16c, and the Dutch EAST INDIA COMPANY was established in 1602. Occupied by the Japanese in WORLD WAR II, In-donesia declared its independence in 1945, under Dr SUKARNO. The 1945 constitution established a 1,000-member People's Consultative Assembly. The federal system was replaced by unified control in 1950. The expulsion of Dutch citizens led to a breakdown of the economy, causing hardship and unrest. Sukarno's rule became increasingly authoritarian and was op-posed by the Communist Party; there was an unsuc-cessful military coup in 1965 but the ensuing disarray enabled General SUHARTO to purge the Communist Party, depose Sukarno (1967) and make himself President. Following his re-election in 1988,

# *Industrialization*

*Culture & Society*

Industrialization can be broadly defined as the evolution from an agrarian economy in which goods are made individually by craftsmen to an economy in which manufacturing is mechanized under a factory system using skilled and semi-skilled labour. The process is generally characterized by an accelerated pace of economic change, associated with technical innovation, and leads to the emergence of mass markets for manufactured goods. It usually promotes **urbanization** and a wider social distribution of wealth, which stimulate rapid growth in population, and a desire for greater popular participation in government. Industrialization depends upon the availability and exploitation of new materials (eg cotton, linen, steel), new energy sources (eg coal, coke, steam, petroleum products), new and more efficient machines to produce new products (eg the spinning jenny and the power loom in cloth production), new working methods (eg the division and specialization of labour in the factory system), fast transportation systems (eg canals, railways, steamships, motor vehicles, aircraft) and efficient communications (eg telecommunications, radio, computers).

The prototype of the process was the **Industrial Revolution**, which began in Britain in the second half of the 18c, spread to Europe and the USA during the 19c, and to most of the rest of the world in the 20c. The 18c in Britain was a period of technical and mechanical innovation that coincided with the right conditions, in terms of demographic patterns, availability of natural resources and development of faster transportation systems, to revolutionize the centuries-old working practices. **Agriculture** in Britain had undergone a revolution in methods and technology from the beginning of the 18c, and greatly improved efficiency and mechanization for the first time allowed much greater numbers of people to be supported than were directly involved in food production, creating a pool of available workers for the manufacturing centres that developed from the 1770s. For with the advent of machines such as the spinning jenny (c.1764) and the spinning frame for cotton (1768) that greatly speeded up textile output, it became more efficient to concentrate machines and workers in one building, and the first 'manufactory', a water-powered spinning factory, was opened by Richard Arkwright (1732-92) in 1771. With this innovation, manufacturing began to move away from home-working to factories, which enabled mass production, and to draw former textile home-workers and the surplus agricultural workforce to the factories. By 1850, almost half of the British population lived in cities, many of which had been only small towns or villages 100 years before.

Those centres that flourished in the early stages of industrialization, the cotton and woollen towns of Lancashire, central Scotland and the West Riding of Yorkshire, were those in close proximity to the resources they needed: raw materials (wool), or the ports through which they were imported (cotton); fast, running water to power the earliest generation of machines; and coal mines to provide fuel for the steam-powered machines, such as the power loom patented in 1785 by Edmund Cartwright (1743-1823), which accelerated the development of the factory system.

Steam power depended on coal, the ready availability and cheapness of which was the result of the development in the early 18c of a steam engine to pump water out of mines, allowing deeper seams to be worked. The resulting expansion in production stimulated the building of canals to transport the coal from the mines into the cities, providing a ready-made network for the bulk transport of raw materials and finished manufactured goods between the growing manufacturing areas and domestic markets and the ports.

Technological innovation was not the sole impetus for industrialization on the scale experienced in Britain between 1760 and 1830. The rise in demand for coal and iron was stimulated in part by considerations of strategic military supply in a period that saw the **American Revolution**, the **French Revolutionary Wars** and the **Napoleonic Wars**. Demand could be met because innovations such as the substitution of coke for charcoal in iron-smelting (c.1709) and the development of the crucible process of steelmaking (c.1740) had improved iron and steel production. Although slower to develop, the mechanization of heavy industry sustained the Industrial Revolution in its second phase from c.1830.

Industrialization accelerated social change. Ownership of land ceased to be the sole source of wealth and status with the expansion of a middle class whose wealth was based on entrepreneurship and profit from trade. Wealth increased

---

Suharto instituted a New Order policy to revolutionize the country's economy, but his period in office was dogged by Islamic fundamentalist uprisings, ethnic violence, and by the long-running civil war in East Timor. Following an economic collapse and calls for political reform, the Suharto regime collapsed. In May 1998 Suharto was replaced by his deputy, B J Habibie, but Habibie's cautious reforms proved incapable of placating an aroused public. The debacle in East Timor further damaged government prestige and in June 1999, in the first democratically held elections for 44 years, Habibie was succeeded as President by Abdurrahman Wahid. Wahid was impeached in 2001 and replaced by the Vice-President, Megawati Sukarnoputri, Sukarno's daughter. An **AL-QAEDA** bombing at a nightclub in Bali in 2002 caused heavy casualties, especially among tourists.
► **SOUTH-EAST ASIA PRE-1000 AD**

**Indo-Pakistan Wars** (1947–9, 1965 and 1971)
The conflict between Hindus and Muslims that first led to partition at independence in 1947 and the creation of India and Pakistan has been kept alive since for a number of reasons, including resentment at the bloodshed that accompanied partition, and the contentious manner with which the boundary between the two countries was delineated by the British, under huge pressures in the months before their departure. The boundary has been a cause of dispute ever since. The fate of various nominally still independent Princely states had also not been decided at the time of partition. The British applied massive pressure, exploiting residual loyalty to **GEORGE VI** on the part of their rulers, to force them into joining one of the new nations. Nevertheless, problems remained. The ruler of Hyderabad, a Muslim, wanted to declare his mainly Hindu state independent; India successfully invaded it. In Kashmir, on the border between India and Pakistan, the Raja, Hari Singh, was in a dilemma since, although himself a Hindu, the majority of his population were Muslim. An uprising in

throughout the initial phase of industrialization owing to the continuing expansion of production and trade, made possible by the development of the steam engine. Colonies and overseas trade routes established in the 18c ensured that foreign markets supplemented domestic ones, and improved communications and transport systems allowed manufactured goods to be moved efficiently. Steam not only powered the machines in the mills and mines, but also the means of transporting goods, such as the railways and steamships. The development of both private and government credit structures founded upon stable political institutions, and the economics of comparative regional advantage preached by Adam **Smith**, encouraged financial risk-taking on a global scale. The rewards in an era of **laissez-faire** economics, which prioritized low taxation, could be very great, and fortunes were made by the growing class of industrialists. The **Great Exhibition** of 1851 was the high point of Britain's industrial dominance but industrial techniques were easily exportable and by the 1860s that dominance was eroding fast.

Industrialization was not without its negative aspects. Mechanization of the textile industry between 1780 and 1860 cut production costs, by as much as 50 per cent in some cases, but its most immediate impact was to cause widespread unemployment (80 per cent fewer men and women were needed in the overall process) and to change the nature of the workforce from skilled to unskilled labour. Wages fell as unemployment created a greater pool of potential workers and the unskilled, especially women and children, became cheaper to employ than semi-skilled men. The rapidly growing urban working class faced squalid living conditions, high mortality rates and exploitation at work, but the concentration of workers in workplaces enabled labour to become organized and to campaign for better working conditions and social reforms. The changes in society also stimulated demand for political change, particularly political representation for the working and middle classes, especially in the industrial centres, many of which were without parliamentary representation until the Reform Act of 1832. The franchise in the UK was gradually extended throughout the 19c, although universal adult suffrage was not achieved until the early 20c.

Industralization spread rapidly throughout most of Europe and the USA in the 19c, and the first global industrial system based on textiles, steam and steel was established by 1914. European factories were able to capitalize on Britain's pioneering of new methods and technology, accelerating their own mechanization. As early as 1817 Belgium had developed machine shops at Liège and, like Britain, its early industrialization was based on its native textile, iron and coal industries. German industrialization developed early from a strong pre-1800 textile base into mechnization and the coal, iron and steel industries of the Ruhr and Silesia. With victory in the **Franco-Prussian War** followed by German unification in 1870, Germany progressed so rapidly that its industrial production had overtaken that of Britain by 1900. Across the Atlantic, the abundance of natural resources, particularly coal and water, and land for expansion, and a free-market economy coupled with the expansionist philosophy of **Manifest Destiny** turned the USA into an industrial powerhouse by the beginning of the 20c. The development of steel-making, exploitation of precisely engineered interchangeable parts, the refinement of the combustion engine and electrification formed the basis of this second phase of industrialization.

The global spread of industrialization was rapid throughout the 20c. Except in the USA, it tended not to be solely the result of free-market capitalism but rather a government-sponsored policy achieved through protectionist, authoritarian or centralized methods. Tsarist Russia had built up substantial industrial capacity, using much foreign capital, but the USSR's **Five-Year Plans**, initiated under **Stalin** in 1928, aimed to build up basic industries, using domestic investment, and were made possible by abundant natural resources and the electrification of the country in the 1930s. The plans are an example of **extensive development** and the technique was extended to the Eastern European states of the Soviet bloc in the second half of the 20c, although after Stalin's death the Soviet government increasingly sought to pursue **intensive development**, diversifying the economy to produce consumer goods and introducing new materials and technologies. However, this change of emphasis was undermined by the inflexibility of central economic planning.

When India adopted the Five-Year Plan system in the 1950s, the government supervised the growing economy but avoided some of the problems of central planning by permitting individual states a degree of control over implementation. China's **Great Leap Forward** (1958-61) abandoned the Soviet model, instead attempting

---

the west of the country decided the matter for him, forcing him to turn to India for help, which was afforded only on the condition that Kashmir joined the Indian union. This decision, made without consulting the population, was contested by Pakistan, which supported the insurgents against the Indian army, the fighting in Kashmir only being brought to an end in 1949 after the UN arranged a ceasefire, pending a plebiscite to decide the fate of the territory. This plebiscite was never held, and fighting broke out between India and Pakistan again in 1965, a ceasefire being brokered by the Soviet Premier Alexei KOSYGIN after an arms embargo was imposed by the USA and USSR. In 1971 a third war was occasioned by the uprising in East Pakistan that led to the foundation of the independent state of Bangladesh. This time it was India that intervened in support of Sheikh MUJI-BUR RAHMAN and the AWAMI LEAGUE; fighting also occurred on the western frontier between India and Pakistan, and in Kashmir, where the 1949 ceasefire

line dividing the Indian and Pakistani-controlled areas of Kashmir became known as the Line of Control (LOC). On this occasion, the superior size of the Indian army outmatched the Pakistanis and an uneasy peace reigned. In the 1980s the rearming of Pakistan by the USA following the Soviet invasion of Afghanistan accelerated the arms race between the two countries, both sides acquiring the capacity to manufacture nuclear weapons (the first test explosion of an Indian bomb occurring in 1974). The foundation of the South Asian Association for Regional Cooperation in 1986 (comprising India, Pakistan, Bangladesh, Bhutan, Nepal, the Maldives and Sri Lanka) has helped to relieve tension in subsequent years, but the unresolved situation in Kashmir continues to cause tension between the two countries and brought them to the brink of war in 2001-2. ► **INDIA, PARTITION OF**; **KASHMIR PROBLEM**; **PRINCELY STATES, INDIAN**

**Indo-Sri Lankan Peace Accord** (1987)

An agreement signed by Rajiv GANDHI, Prime Minis-

industrialization though the creation of communes but resulted only in a famine that killed millions. Successful industrialization began in China only with economic liberalization under **Deng Xiaoping** in the 1980s but a significant industrial base and transport infrastructure was then constructed in 20 years, and only a shortage of resources such as oil is likely to inhibit continuing growth.

Japan began industrializing in 1868 during the **Meiji Restoration**, when new leaders imported technology and experts from the West in a deliberate attempt to copy the development of Britain and Germany. The rise of the **zaibatsu** and the close relationship between these conglomerates and the government allowed Japan to become the first eastern industrialized power. Recovery after World War II was overseen by **MITI** and contributed to the growth of a government-led economic bureaucracy, creating one of the most important global economies of the late 20c.

In the late 20c, primary industrial activities began to migrate from the former core industrial nations to the developing world. Steel production and ship-building moved from Europe and the USA to Korea, where the authoritarian regime of **Park Chung-hee** created an export-led industrial base, and manufacturing capacity moved from Europe to China and India, and from the USA to Mexico. The attraction was the ready availability of a non-unionized workforce, the lower wage expectations and low production costs, the same conditions that had facilitated the Industrial Revolution 200 years earlier, although in this case the existence of these conditions was often the result of a government's financial support as a part of its industrialization strategy. However, the trend towards manufacturing in the developing world also typified a third phase of global industrialization. New technology is exploited, most notably the silicon chip and resultant computer technology within factories, while new materials, particularly plastics, are used to create products. Although some goods are sold in the country of manufacture to a growing new acquisitive middle class, most are exported to the developed world, the bulk of the profits going often to foreign investors or a new super-rich indigenous group.

In the leading economies that experienced the shrinkage or export of their manufacturing base, primary industrial activities were mostly replaced by service industries dealing mainly in services to consumers rather than producing goods for consumption; examples include retailing (including food), franchising and the provision of entertainment, news media and leisure services. The service sector economic model allows most economic activity to be described as services to people, however, so although many large companies continue to make goods, such as vacuum cleaners or computer hardware, the supply of business solutions has replaced manufacturing as the focus of their business. Advances in information technology have allowed for the identification and customization of products within niche markets instead of a reliance on mass production standardized for the assembly line. The communications revolution has allowed the movement of goods in the supply chain 'just in time', removing the need for large stockholdings. As a result of niche marketing and customization, services sector production can be defined by the value added, rather than the actual physical product; indeed, in some sectors of the service economy, there may be no discernable product.

These economies are often referred to as 'post-industrial', a term popularized by sociologist Daniel Bell in *The Coming of Post-Industrial Society* (1973). He postulated that information and scientific technologies would become the primary sources of wealth and social development in developed economies, which would be run by meritocracies. Broadly speaking, a post-industrial society is one in which most workers are not involved in either agriculture or manufacturing. In post-industrial society, information, knowledge and creativity are the sources of energy. It is characterized by a highly educated, skilled and flexible workforce, often self-employed and well-remunerated, though no longer guaranteed long-term employment or offered permanent contracts. Certainly the shift of manufacturing to the developing world has not diminished the economic strength of the original industrial powers, as ownership of finance, innovation, research and design continues to remain their preserve. However, the service sector model as a description of current trends in the developed world is criticized as futuristic, and there is continuing debate as to whether it is possible to develop a model for long-term wealth creation without the inclusion of 'old-fashioned' industrialized product manufacture.

---

ter of India, and J R **JAYAWARDENE**, the President of Sri Lanka. An attempt by Gandhi to impose a solution to Sri Lanka's **TAMIL** secessionist problem, the Accord collapsed due to a lack of support from all sections of Sri Lankan society. Troops from the Indian Peace-keeping Force (IPKF) were quickly embroiled in conflict with the militants of the **LTTE**, while Jayawardene's government was threatened by violent protests led by the **JVP**.

**Industrialization** ► *See panel*

**Industrial Revolution**

A term usually associated with the accelerated pace of economic change, the associated technical and mechanical innovations, and the emergence of mass markets for manufactured goods, beginning in Britain in the last quarter of the 18c with the mechanization of the cotton and woollen industries of Lancashire, Central Scotland, and the West Riding of Yorkshire. After the harnessing of steam power, cot-

ton and woollen factories were increasingly concentrated in towns, and there were hugely increased rates of **URBANIZATION**. A rapid population increase, stimulated by greater economic opportunities for early marriage, is also associated with this type of economic growth. The mechanization of heavier industries (iron and steel) was slower, but sustained the Industrial Revolution in its second phase from c.1830. ► **INDUSTRIALIZATION**

**Industrial Workers of the World (IWW)**

US radical labour organization movement, whose members were known as Wobblies. An offshoot of the Western Federation of Miners, it was founded in 1905 by a group which opposed the craft unionism of the AFL and proposed instead a union of both skilled and unskilled workers. The movement was soon splintered because of the radical ideology of its leader, 'Big Bill' **HAYWOOD**, who called for the destruction of capitalism and the formation of a new society and maintained that employers' violence must be met in kind. He was less interested in negotiation than in striking and sabotage. Lack of organization and funds meant that the IWW had few successes in industrial conflicts although its membership reached a peak of at least 60,000. It declined rapidly after the RED SCARE of 1919–20. ► AFL–CIO

## Indus Valley Civilization ► INDIA, PRE-ISLAMIC

## INF (Intermediate Nuclear Force) Treaty
A treaty signed (Dec 1987) in Washington by US President Ronald REAGAN and Soviet General-Secretary Mikhail GORBACHEV, involving the elimination of 1,286 missiles from Europe and Asia, and over 2,000 warheads. It was noted for its inclusion of the most comprehensive, stringent and intrusive verification procedures ever seen in an arms control treaty, including short notice on-site verification, and was a major break in the arms race and a step forward in arms control generally, leading to later agreements in both the nuclear and conventional fields. ► SALT; START

## Inkatha Freedom Party
A South African Zulu political organization founded in the Black homeland of KwaZulu in 1975 by Chief Gatsha BUTHELEZI. In the 1970s and 1980s it offered an opposition voice to APARTHEID but then it became the vehicle for Zulu nationalism and a sometimes violent antagonist to the ANC (African National Congress), for which it received clandestine support from the police and, as revealed in 1991, from government sources as well. The movement became a political party in 1990 and is thought to have had over 2 million members during the 1990s. In the first multiracial elections in South Africa (1994), Inkatha polled 10.5 per cent of the vote, gaining 43 seats in the new national assembly, and Buthelezi was made Home Affairs Minister. In the second multiracial elections (1999), it polled only 8.3 per cent and its share of the vote declined further in 2004.

## INLA (Irish National Liberation Army)
The military wing of the IRISH REPUBLICAN SOCIALIST PARTY, a small paramilitary group committing relatively few but particularly ruthless terrorist attacks. Probably created by former members of the Provisional IRA disenchanted with the 1972 ceasefire, it was responsible for the killing of the Conservative MP Airey Neave (Mar 1979). Its impact lessened with internal feuds in the 1980s, and in Aug 1998 it announced a ceasefire in the aftermath of the bombing of Omagh.

## Innocent III, originally Lotario de' Conti di Segni (1160–1216)
Italian pope (1198/1216). His pontificate is regarded as the high point of the temporal and spiritual supremacy of the Roman see. He judged between rival emperors in Germany, and had OTTO IV deposed. He laid England under an interdict and excommunicated King JOHN for refusing to recognize Stephen LANGTON as Archbishop of Canterbury. Under him the fourth Lateran Council was held in 1215. ► LATERAN COUNCILS

## Innocent IV, originally Sinibaldo Fieschi (d.1254)
Italian pope (1243/54). Genoese by birth and trained in the canon law at Bologna, Innocent IV took a view of papal supremacy very similar to that of INNOCENT

III. He was unscrupulous in the construction of his own power network through the exercise of patronage, and his pontificate brought the struggle between the papacy and Emperor FREDERICK II to its climax. At Frederick's death (1250), he sought to establish papal overlordship in Sicily. This was acknowledged by Frederick's illegitimate son, MANFRED, who nevertheless led a revolt in 1254. Innocent also put the INQUISITION on a permanent basis in Italy.

## Innocent X, originally Giambattista Pamfili (1574–1655)
Italian pope (1644/55). An unscrupulous man, he was notorious for his nepotism. Scarcely had he been elected than he began systematic attacks on the Barbarini, relatives of his predecessor, Urban VIII. He was quickly forced to desist from this persecution when his victims fled to France and successfully appealed to Cardinal MAZARIN for protection. When the latter threatened to annex the papal enclave of Avignon, Innocent backed down. In international affairs, Innocent's condemnation of the Peace of WESTPHALIA served only to demonstrate the growing impotence of the papacy, while his support for Spanish claims to Portugal (which had regained its independence again in 1640) proved equally fruitless. Even the Bull *Cum Occasione* (1653) condemning Jansenist views on grace, rather than restoring unity to the Church, merely sparked over a century of internal religious controversy.

## Innocent XI, originally Benedetto Odescalchi (1611–89)
Italian pope (1676/89). Elected pope despite the opposition of LOUIS XIV of France, he took over an empty treasury and an inefficient administration. To counter these, he embarked on a policy of retrenchment (including the abolition of many sinecures and a campaign against luxury) and tried, with some success, to end the practice of nepotism; he also sought financial aid from Catholic princes. The consequence of these reforms was that he was able to put papal finances on a sufficiently sound footing to aid JOHN III SOBIESKI of Poland and the Holy Roman Emperor LEOPOLD I to break the Turkish siege of Vienna (1683). However, in other areas he was less successful, most notably in his dealings with LOUIS XIV. Poor from the start, his relations with the French King further deteriorated because of his reluctance (like CLEMENT X) to see the implementation of Louis's edict of 1673, which empowered the King to seize the revenue of vacant sees. Matters came to a head when Louis summoned a French synod that, under royal pressure, published the so-called Four or Gallican Articles (*Déclaration du clergé de France*), which fiercely affirmed the limitations of papal authority within France. In retaliation, Innocent refused to confirm the promotion of any French clergy involved in the synod. In 1685 he further angered the French monarch by condemning his treatment of the HUGUENOTS and, in 1688, by opposing his candidate for the archbishopric of Cologne; Louis's response was to occupy the papal enclave of Avignon. In theological matters, Innocent was far from unsympathetic to Jansenist views, but he drew the line at the Quietist doctrines of his friend, the Spaniard Miguel de Molinos, whom he had tried and imprisoned.

**Innocent XII**, originally **Antonio Pignatelli** (1615–1700)
Italian pope (1691/1700). Jesuit-educated, he was papal ambassador to Tuscany, Poland and Austria before becoming a cardinal in 1681. It was he who brought an end to the poor relations between **LOUIS XIV** of France and the papacy by persuading the latter to withdraw the Gallican Articles of 1682 and to relinquish the occupied papal enclave of Avignon. In return for this, Innocent championed the candidacy of Philippe of Anjou (Louis XIV's grandson) as the heir to the Spanish throne and acknowledged the French monarch's right to administer vacant sees. In theological matters, he condemned both **JANSENISM** (1696) and Quietism (1699), while in ecclesiastical and domestic affairs he carried on the struggle against nepotism, which he condemned in the Bull *Romanum decet pontificem* (1692). ▶ **INNOCENT XI**

**Innocent XIII**, originally **Michelangelo dei Conti** (1655–1724)
Italian pope (1721/4). A former papal ambassador to Switzerland and Portugal, and a cardinal from 1706, in 1721 he invested the Holy Roman Emperor **CHARLES VI** with sovereignty over Naples. He recognized James Francis Edward **STUART** (the Old Pretender) as King of England and promised him subsidies if he returned England to Roman Catholicism. Although he was hostile towards the Jansenists – he confirmed the Bull *Unigenitus* in 1722 – he was also distrustful of the Jesuits, taking particular issue with the modified 'Chinese rites' which they employed with some success to attract converts in Asia.

**Inönü, Ismet**, originally **Ismet Paza** (1884–1973)
Turkish soldier and politician. He fought in **WORLD WAR I**, then became **ATATÜRK**'s Chief of Staff in the war against the Greeks (1919–22), defeating them twice at Inönü. As the first Premier of the new republic (1923–37), he introduced many political reforms, and was elected President in 1938 on Atatürk's death. From 1950 he was Leader of the Opposition, and held office as Premier again from 1960 to 1965, when he resigned.

**Inoue Kaoru** (1836–1915)
Japanese politician and elder statesman (**GENRO**). From a **SAMURAI** family in **CHOSHU**, he took an active part in the overthrow of the **TOKUGAWA SHOGUNATE**, purchasing arms from England and playing a key role in arranging the Chosu–**SATSUMA** alliance (1866) against the Tokugawa regime. In the new Meiji government (1868–87) he served as Minister of Public Works, Minister of Agriculture and Commerce, Minister of Finance and Minister of Foreign Affairs. He was a keen advocate of economic modernization and developed close ties with business interests. As Foreign Minister (1879–87) he negotiated with the Western powers over treaty revision, but was unable to obtain their agreement to end the foreign privilege of extraterritoriality in Japan.

**inquilino**
This Spanish term refers to tenants attached to the land by unilateral agreements, a practice which evolved during the colonial period in Chile. The *inquilino* provided some 240 days of labour, received nominal wages, a plot, a small house and the right to pasture stock on unused land. The growth of agro-industrial businesses and the cities has partially eroded *inquilinaje*, which was strongest during the late 19c and proved the bedrock of the family groups ruling Chilean society.

**Inquisition**
A tribunal for prosecuting heresy, first created on a local and temporary basis in 13c France and Germany. In Spain, this medieval Inquisition existed in the realm of **ARAGON**, with its chief seat in Tarragona. It was, however, superseded in the late 15c by the new Castilian or Spanish Inquisition, founded by papal bull in 1478 and set up in 1480; this was devoted primarily to investigating the orthodoxy of the cultural minorities that since 1492 (Jews) and 1502 (Muslims of **CASTILE**) had been forced to accept the Catholic faith. Of the 16 permanent tribunals of peninsular Spain, 11 were founded by 1500, three between 1505 and 1526, and one (Santiago) in 1574; the last, established in 1640, was that of Madrid. A contemporary estimated that in its first ten years it burnt 2,000 people and punished 15,000 others. Portugal, like Castile, had no medieval Inquisition, and attempts by the authorities to introduce one on the Castilian model foundered until a tribunal was created temporarily in 1539; it was not until a papal bull was promulgated (July 1547) that the Inquisition was fully introduced. The Inquisition of Portugal was introduced into Goa in 1560, and into Brazil later that century; in the metropolis it held its last **AUTO-DA-FÉ** in 1765 and was eventually abolished by decree in 1821. The Spanish Inquisition was established in Peru in 1570 and in Mexico the following year; in Spain it survived until the early 19c, until its abolition in 1834.

**Institución Libre de Ensenañza ('Free Educational Institute')**
Spanish secular educational association. Beginning in 1875 as a small private school renowned for its excellence and defiance of catholic norms, the Institución greatly influenced liberal culture in Spain. The college it established at Madrid University became an important focus of liberal intellectual life, and it was also instrumental in the creation of various leading state research bodies.

**integralismo**
A Brazilian fascist movement of the 1930s. Its supporters were noted for their green shirts and aggressive street actions. The Brazilian Integralists Party, led by Plinio Salgado, was suppressed after a vain attack on the presidential Catete Palace in Rio de Janeiro (10 May 1938). The party had been used as a tool by Getúlio **VARGAS** against liberals and the communist-led *Aliança Nacional Libertadora* (ANL) headed by Luís Carlos Prestes, a leading *tenente* in the struggle against the old republic.

**Intelligentsia** (19c)
A peculiarly Russian phenomenon, a small educated class, interested in ideas, but separated both from its social peers and those lower down the scale. In a population of millions they numbered only thousands. In a Tsarist autocracy, ideas drove them to read and write about opposition, even revolution, and this split them from the nobility and the new class of businessmen. Although towards the end of the century

some groups participated in movements to the people, they had few genuine contacts with ordinary peasants. However, they developed a debate that helped to produce the political parties of the period 1894–1917.

### intendentes

This Spanish term (literally, 'intendants') refers to well-salaried colonial officials with significant staff, responding directly to the Spanish crown. The intendant system, instituted by the House of Bourbon in Spain, was transplanted from Spain to Cuba in 1764, the Viceroyalty of La Plata in 1782, Peru in 1784, Mexico in 1786, and in other regions in 1790. Military officers appointed for more than ten years, in Hispanic America they were in charge of administration, finance, the military and justice; they were effectively a response to the growth and maturity of colonial society and larger changes in the international economy, principally the growth of English economic weight. Nevertheless, the system achieved centralization and rationalization, financing the growth of full-scale military forces in the Americas.

### Intensive Development (post-1953)

The term used by Soviet-style economists to describe the second stage of growth following initial industrialization, itself entitled **EXTENSIVE DEVELOPMENT**. After **STALIN**'s death, Nikita **KHRUSHCHEV** and later Leonid **BREZHNEV** tried to diversify the economy of the USSR by expounding the production of consumer durables and introducing new materials and technologies. Other communist countries followed suit. Largely because of too much central planning, the communist world lagged behind the West, a fact which sapped confidence in the regimes and contributed to their downfall in the period 1989–91.

### interdependency theory

A neo-liberal theory developed in the 1970s, which describes the ways that a group, whether a nation state, a multinational company or a non-governmental organization, deals with international issues and emphasizes economic and political inter-relationships. It challenges the Realist analysis that security dilemmas inevitably lead to conflict, postulating instead that differences can be overcome through cooperation; more cooperation leads to increased interaction and greater security. The theory has been criticized for underplaying the impact of domestic politics on international decision-making, neglecting the ethnic or religious aspects of national identity and underestimating the importance of security issues, especially in relation to public policy decisions.

### International

An abbreviation originally of International Working Men's Association, the name given to successive organizations attempting to establish international cooperative mechanisms for socialist, communist and revolutionary groups. The First International was created in London in 1864 and its leadership was initially assumed by **MARX**, but it slowly disintegrated, not least because of differences between him and **BAKUNIN**. The Second International was formed in Paris in 1889, but it largely collapsed in 1914 as socialist parties took sides in **WORLD WAR I**. The Third International (**COMINTERN**) was founded by **LENIN** in Mos-

cow in 1919 and represented mainly communist parties. It became, in effect, a tool of **STALIN**'s foreign policy until he abolished it in 1943 during **WORLD WAR II**. There was a brief attempt in the 1930s by **TROTSKY** to launch a Fourth International, which came into existence in Périgny in France in 1938 but remained merely an umbrella for miscellaneous left-wing groups of no particular importance. ▸ **COMMUNISM**

### International Atomic Energy Agency (IAEA)

A specialized agency of the **UN** founded in 1957, it promotes research into and development of the non-military uses of nuclear energy, and oversees a system of safeguards and controls that restrict the use of nuclear materials for military purposes. ▸ **IRAQ**; **IRAQ WAR**

### International Bank for Reconstruction and Development (IBRD)

A specialized agency of the **UN** founded in 1945, it was set up to provide funds and technical assistance to help raise the standards of living in developing countries. It is closely affiliated to the **INTERNATIONAL DEVELOPMENT ASSOCIATION** and part of the World Bank Group, based in Washington, DC.

### International Brigades

In the **SPANISH CIVIL WAR**, foreign volunteer forces recruited by the **COMINTERN** and by individual communist parties to assist the Spanish Republic. Almost 60,000 volunteers, mostly workers, fought in Spain between Oct 1936 and the brigades' withdrawal in Oct 1938, playing a particularly important role in the defence of Madrid.

### International Court of Justice (ICJ)

Set up under the **UN** Charter of 1945, the International Court of Justice was established in 1946, taking over from its predecessor, the Permanent Court of International Justice. The court was set up for the purpose of hearing international law disputes and is the principal judicial organ of the UN. Hearings usually take place in The Hague, the Netherlands, and are presided over by 15 judges appointed by the UN Security Council and the General Assembly.

### International Criminal Court (ICC)

An international court instituted in 2002 with jurisdiction over individuals accused of genocide, crimes against humanity and war crimes. It replaces ad-hoc **UN** tribunals and makes it possible to initiate prosecutions referred by any member state or the UN Security Council. The Court is located in The Hague, the Netherlands, and its 18 judges are legal experts representing the world's principal legal systems. China, Russia, India, Israel and the USA are opposed to its jurisdiction.

### International Development Association (IDA)

A branch of the World Bank Group, it is affiliated to, but distinct from, the **INTERNATIONAL BANK FOR RECONSTRUCTION AND DEVELOPMENT** (IBRD), based in Washington, DC. It was set up in 1960 to provide help to the world's 50 poorest countries by giving them aid on more preferential terms than the IBRD.

### International Energy Agency

An intergovernmental agency within the **OECD**, set up in 1974 in response to the oil crisis that arose in 1973 when Arab members of OPEC refused to supply countries that had supported Israel in the YOM KIPPUR WAR. IEA member countries coordinate their energy policies to secure energy supplies, promote economic growth and coordinate the development of alternative forms of energy. It is located in Paris and has 26 members.

### International Labour Organization (ILO)
An autonomous agency associated with the LEAGUE OF NATIONS, which became the first specialized agency of the UN in 1946. A tripartite body representing governments, employers and workers, it is concerned with industrial relations and the pay, employment and working conditions of workers.

### International Monetary Fund (IMF)
A specialized agency of the UN, first conceived at the BRETTON WOODS CONFERENCE, established in 1945, and affiliated to the UN in 1947, it was set up to promote international monetary cooperation, the expansion of international trade and exchange rate stability, and to give financial assistance to states in need.

### International Whaling Commission (IWC)
The Commission was established by the International Convention for the Regulation of Whaling (1946) in an attempt to conserve whale stocks while maintaining a viable whaling industry, as large-scale commercial whaling had brought some species close to extinction. In 1975 the IWC limited catches and in 1982 it imposed a moratorium on commercial whaling of all varieties of whale with effect from the 1985–6 season. The moratorium has not been universally observed; some members, such as Iceland, Japan and Norway, are thought to have used the IWC's permits to catch whales for research purposes as a means of evading the moratorium. A Revised Management Procedure for commercial whaling was adopted in 1994 but has yet to be implemented. ►
ABORIGINAL SUBSISTENCE WHALING

### Interprovincial Conferences (Canada)
A governmental consultative process. The first, in 1887, was convened by Honoré MERCIER, and was essentially a convention of provincial Liberals. It passed resolutions against the federal government's disallowing power and for increases in provincial subsidies. In the short term Ottawa reacted to the resolutions in a limited way, refraining from disallowing a contentious Quebec law and introducing subsidies for Nova Scotia's iron and steel industry. With the growing complexity and interdependence of the Canadian government and economy from the late 19c onwards, inter-governmental conferences (both federal-provincial and interprovincial) have become an increasingly important aspect of policy making and administration. The some 158 federal-provincial and 30 interprovincial bodies now in existence focus mainly on economic and constitutional matters, headed by a First Ministers' Conference, with various ministerial conferences and Continuing Committees feeding up to them. Since 1960 there has also been an annual meeting of provincial premiers.

### interregnum
A period between rulers; normally, in British history, the period between CHARLES I's execution (30 Jan

1649) and the RESTORATION of CHARLES II (5 May 1660); also, the period between the departure of JAMES VII AND II (22 Dec 1688) and the accession of WILLIAM III and Mary II (23 Feb 1689; in Scotland 20 Apr 1689).

### Interregnum (1254–73)
The term used to describe the period when the German throne was held by puppet kings appointed by the princes, which marks the end of the HOHENSTAUFEN DYNASTY and the beginning of the rise of the HABSBURG DYNASTY. After the deaths of CONRAD IV (1254) and the anti-King WILLIAM, COUNT OF HOLLAND (1256), the princes elected two foreigners as kings of Germany: Richard of Cornwall and ALFONSO X, THE WISE, of Castile. Neither spent much time in Germany, leaving the princes and towns free to pursue their own ends. The Interregnum was the culmination of a long period of decline in the power of the monarchy in Germany.

### intifada
The term used to describe uprisings in the Israeli-occupied Palestinian territories of the WEST BANK and GAZA STRIP. The first intifada, the 'war of stones', began in late 1987 and continued until the first of the OSLO ACCORDS was signed in 1993. It took the form of demonstrations, strikes, rock-throwing and civil disobedience such as the refusal to pay taxes. The second, or al-Aqsa, intifada followed a visit by Ariel SHARON to the Temple Mount, location of the al-Aqsa mosque, in Israeli-occupied east Jerusalem in Sep 2000 during which he proclaimed the sensitive area to be Israeli territory. Riots broke out the following day. When Sharon became prime minister in Feb 2001, his government took a hard line against the intifada and the violence escalated. Suicide bombings by movements such as HAMAS have contributed to the high fatality rate in Israel, whose military has retaliated with extreme force. Deaths have been numerous on both sides. To prevent suicide bombings, in June 2002 Israel started building a high wall between Israeli and Palestinian territories, effectively partitioning the country and causing great hardship to some Palestinian communities, despite international opposition and legal moves to prevent construction.

### Intolerable Acts (1774)
The American name for laws passed by parliament in London to punish Massachusetts for the BOSTON TEA PARTY (1773). They were called the Boston Port Act, the Massachusetts Government Act, the Administration of Justice Act, and a Quartering Act. The QUEBEC ACT, though addressing a different problem, was also taken by colonists to add insult to the injury of the Intolerable Acts.

### Inuit
The indigenous peoples of the Arctic regions of Alaska, Canada, Greenland and Chukotka, Russia; they were known as Eskimos until 1977, when the name Inuit was adopted. There are three languages, all of the same family, so different groups can communicate verbally, but there is no common written form of the languages. Before contact with Europeans, Inuit people lived in family groups of five or six people within hunting groups of six to ten families. They hunted seal and whale by the coast in winter, and

some moved inland in summer to hunt caribou. Contact with Europeans generally began with Christian missionaries; in Greenland, Lutheran missionaries encouraged literacy in the Inuit language and it became the country's official language. From the 19c, contact with European whalers and fur traders began to change the Inuit way of life as they remained by the coast all year to work in the whaling industry. Exploitation of Arctic gas and oil reserves during the 1950s began to destabilize some Inuit communities. Some remain nomadic hunters and gatherers, but increasing numbers live in established settlements with schools, medical facilities and airstrips. In Canada, the Inuit Tapirisat of Canada (ITC) was established in 1972 to preserve Inuit culture through voluntary separation from white communities, and in 1999 the autonomous Inuit region of Nunavut was created. Internationally, Inuit are represented by the Inuit Circumpolar Conference, which promotes Inuit interests and meets every four years to discuss matters of common interest, such as pollution and the creation of a common written language. ➤ ABORIGINAL SUBSISTENCE WHALING

## Inukai Tsuyoshi (1855–1932)

Japanese politician. He was a newspaper reporter before helping to form a political party, the *Kaishinto* (Progressives), in 1882. Inukai was elected to the first Diet in 1890 and was re-elected a further 18 times. He became known for his strong opposition to clique-government and his championing of constitutionalism. During the 1920s he was associated with the largest political party in the Diet, the SEIYUKAI, becoming its President in 1929. He became Prime Minister in 1931 at a time of economic hardship at home and independent Japanese military action in Manchuria to sever the region from China. He aroused the anger of ultra-nationalists when he attempted to reassert civilian control of the army in Manchuria and reach a compromise settlement with China. In May 1932 he was assassinated in an abortive army coup. His death marked the end of party cabinets in Japan until after WORLD WAR II.

## Investiture Controversy (1075–1122)

A conflict between reforming popes and lay rulers, notably the German emperor, over the leadership of Christian society. It was named after the royal practice of investing a newly appointed bishop or abbot with a ring or pastoral staff, the symbols of his spiritual office. This was condemned in 1075 by Pope GREGORY VII as epitomizing secular domination of the Church, and the ensuing power struggle between the emperors and the papacy led to the permanent weakening of the German monarchy in favour of the princes. ➤ CANOSSA; HENRY IV

## Ionescu, Take (1858–1922)

Romanian politician. First a liberal, then a conservative, he was a founder and leader of the Conservative–Democratic Party in 1907. As Foreign Minister during WORLD WAR I, he agreed (1916) to the entry of Romania on the side of the Allies. He was delegate to the peace conference at VERSAILLES (1919) and worked for the creation of the LITTLE ENTENTE. He was, briefly, President from 1921 to 1922.

## Iorga, Nicolae (1871–1940)

Romanian politician and historian. As editor (1903–6) of *Sămănătorul* ('The Sower'), he advocated conservative and patriotic values. Active in political life, he was elected to the Romanian parliament (1907) and founded the National Democrat Party. As Prime Minister and Minister of Education (1931–2), he supported CHARLES II of Romania. With the establishment of the ANTONESCU regime, he was one of several leading figures in Romanian political and cultural life who were murdered in the years 1940–1.

## Iqbal, Sir Muhammad (1875–1938)

Indian poet and philosopher. He was educated at Lahore, Cambridge (where he read law and philosophy) and Munich. On his return to India, he achieved fame through his poetry, whose compelling mysticism and nationalism caused him to be regarded almost as a prophet by Muslims. His efforts to establish a separate Muslim state eventually led to the formation of Pakistan. He was knighted in 1923, and died at Lahore, Punjab.

## iqta

Land granted to army officials in the Islamic empire of the Caliphs for limited periods instead of a regular salary. The *iqta* system was established in the 9c. Land subject to the iqta was originally owned by non-Muslims and thus subject to a special property tax, the *kharaj*. While the land remained legally the property of its owner, the iqta was a grant of appropriation to a Muslim officer entitling him to collect the kharaj from the owner. Out of this, the officer was to pay a small tax, but could keep the rest as his salary.

## IRA (Irish Republican Army)

An anti-British paramilitary guerrilla force established in 1919 by Irish nationalists to combat British forces in Ireland. It opposed the Anglo-Irish Treaty of 1921 because the Irish Free State was a dominion and the six counties of the North of Ireland remained part of the UK, but it was suppressed by the Irish government after being defeated in the IRISH CIVIL WAR and banned by Éamon DE VALERA in 1936. Continuing to hold out for a united republican Ireland, it became an underground organization but remained largely inactive until the late 1960s, when it re-emerged during the civil rights agitation in Northern Ireland. In 1969, a major split in its ranks led to the formation of the Provisional IRA alongside the Official IRA. The Official IRA has been virtually inactive since 1972, and generally supports political action to achieve Irish unity. The Provisionals became the dominant republican force, responsible for shootings and bombings in Northern Ireland, Britain and Western Europe. Targets were mainly security and military personnel and establishments, although many civilians were victims of sectarian killings and attempts to disrupt civilian life. The uneasy truce in Northern Ireland after 1998 hinged on political negotiations, but was as much the product of military deadlock and the growing power of very similar Loyalist paramilitaries as of any major change of heart by the IRA. The SEPTEMBER 11 ATTACKS inhibited any IRA inclination to break the ceasefire because shifts in US attitudes meant that any indiscriminate terrorism would lose it US funding and support. The IRA's refusal to decommission its weapons was a major obstacle to progress on the

**GOOD FRIDAY AGREEMENT**, but the hopes raised by its apparent change of heart in late 2004 were dashed by its alleged responsibility for a bank raid in Dec 2004, a crime which cast doubt on the sincerity of its commitment to a settlement in Northern Ireland. ► **SINN FÉIN**

**IRAN**  official name **Islamic Republic of Iran**, formerly (to 1935) **Persia**

A republic in south-west Asia, bounded to the north by Armenia, Azerbaijan, Turkmenistan and the Caspian Sea; to the east by Afghanistan and Pakistan; to the south by the Gulf of Oman and the Arabian Gulf; to the south-west by Iraq; and to the north-west by Turkey. Iran was an early centre of civilization and its dynasties include the aggressive Sassanids (from 3c) and its first royal house, the Achaemenids (from 7c). It was ruled by the Arabs, Turks and **MONGOLS** until the **SAFAVID DYNASTY** in the 16–18c and the **QAJAR DYNASTY** in the 19–20c. A military coup in 1921 led to independence in 1925 under Reza Shah Pahlavi, who abdicated and was succeeded as Shah by his son Muhammad Reza Shah **PAHLAVI** in 1941. Protests against the Shah's regime in the 1970s led to a revolution in 1978. The Shah went into exile and an Islamic Republic was proclaimed under Ayatollah **KHOMEINI** in 1979. Following the ex-Shah's admission to the USA for medical treatment, the US Embassy in Tehran was seized for over a year in 1979–81, with the revolutionary government demanding his return to Iran. The **IRAN–IRAQ WAR** in 1980–8 claimed possibly one million Iranian lives. On Khomeini's death in 1989, there was a political struggle for power, out of which emerged Hashemi **RAFSANJANI**. He remained President until 1997, when he was defeated by Ayatollah Muhammad Khatemi. Although Khatemi's supporters won a majority in the 2000 elections and Khatemi was re-elected in 2001, reformist legislation was blocked and in 2004 the reformists lost their parliamentary majority. During the **GULF WAR** and the **IRAQ WAR**, Iran remained neutral. During the 1990s relations between Iran and the West, particulary the USA, were strained due to its lack of cooperation during the Middle East peace process and its rumoured involvement in both international **TERRORISM** and the development of nuclear weapons. In 2002 US President George **BUSH** declared Iran to be one of the countries in his **AXIS OF EVIL**, and in the aftermath of the Iraq War there were concerns that Iran might become the next target of the war on **TERROR** because it had started to build a nuclear reactor in 2002. The **IAEA** reported in 2003 that there was no evidence that Iran was developing nuclear weapons, and in Nov 2004 Iran agreed with the **EU** to suspend its uranium enrichment programme.

**Iran, Anglo-Soviet Invasion of** (Aug 1941)
Suspicions that Reza Shah was sympathetic to the Germans in **WORLD WAR II** resulted in the Anglo-Soviet invasion of Iran in Aug 1941, although it is possible that a desire to protect oil supplies among other things was as much of a motive for the invasion on the British side as any inklings of pro-German leanings in the Shah. The invasion and subsequent occupation forced the abdication of Reza Shah in favour of his son, Muhammad Reza, and the presence of the Soviets allowed a brief reappearance of the Tudeh Party. The military occupation lasted until 1946.

**Iran–Contra Affair** (1986)
A major US political scandal. It grew out of the **REAGAN** administration's efforts to obtain the release of US hostages held in Lebanon by groups friendly to Iran, by secretly supplying arms to Iran's strongly anti-American government. **NATIONAL SECURITY COUNCIL** officials (notably, Colonel Oliver North) had been involved in the diversion of the proceeds of the arms sales to Iran to Nicaragua, to support the anti-government Contra rebels, even though **CONGRESS** had banned the supplying of arms to the **CONTRAS**. Congressional hearings in 1987 centred on the legality of the arms-for-hostages deal and on whether Colonel North had acted on his own as the Administration claimed, or whether top government officials, including President Reagan himself, were involved. The issues have not been satisfactorily resolved.

**Iran Hostage Crisis** (1979–81)
On 4 Nov 1979 the US Embassy in Tehran, Iran, was seized by a mob and its staff of 52 were taken hostage. The action was approved by the Ayatollah **KHOMEINI** who, like many Iranians, hated Americans for the role of the **CIA** in the overthrow of the Mossadegh government (1953) and for their training of Shah Muhammad Reza **PAHLAVI**'s secret police. The price demanded for the release of the hostages was the return of the Shah and all his wealth. Neither **UN** appeals nor President Jimmy **CARTER**'s move to freeze all Iranian assets induced Iran to release the hostages. In 1980 an attempted helicopter rescue operation using US marines failed, causing the Carter administration great political embarrassment. The crisis preoccupied Carter during his last months in office and may well have been the single most important factor in his defeat by Ronald **REAGAN** in the 1980 election. After 444 days of captivity, the hostages were released on the day President Reagan was inaugurated, and Iranian assets were unfrozen.

**Iranian Revolution**
The 1979 revolution in Iran which deposed the Shah (15 Jan) and led to the triumphant return (1 Feb) from his French exile of the Ayatollah **KHOMEINI**. Khomeini appointed Dr Mehdi Bazargan as Prime Minister (1979–80), although real power was to remain with Khomeini's 15-man Islamic Revolutionary Council. Revolutionary forces took control of the country, and Khomeini announced the establishment of the Islamic Republic.

**Iran–Iraq War** (1980–8)
Although the 1975 peace agreement with Iran ended Iraq's Kurdish revolt, Iraq still wanted a readjustment of its borders with Iran. After the Islamic revolution in Iran, the Iranians accused Baghdad of fomenting demands for autonomy by the Arabs of Iran's Khuzestan province. In addition, Iraq feared Iranian provocation of its own 60 per cent Shiite population. After some border fighting in 1980, Iraqi forces advanced into Iran (22 Sep). By the time a peace was agreed (1988), the war had cost about half a million lives on both sides, and presented a serious threat to shipping in the Gulf. Iraq accepted Iran's pre-war boundary terms in Aug 1990. ➤ **KURDS**; **SHIITES**

---

**IRAQ**   official name **Republic of Iraq**

A republic in south-west Asia, bounded to the east by Iran; to the north by Turkey; to the north-west by Syria; to the west by Jordan; to the south-west and south by Saudi Arabia; and to the south-east by Kuwait and the Arabian Gulf. Iraq was part of the **OTTOMAN EMPIRE** from the 16c until **WORLD WAR I**. It was captured by British forces in 1916 and became a British-mandated territory in 1921. It gained independence under the Hashemite Dynasty in 1932, and the monarchy was replaced by military rule in 1958. Since the 1960s, Kurdish nationalists in the north-east have been fighting to establish a separate state. Saddam **HUSSEIN** came to power as President in 1979. His invasion of Iran in 1980 led to the **IRAN–IRAQ WAR**, which lasted until 1988. The invasion of Kuwait in 1990 led to **UN** sanctions, the **GULF WAR** in 1991, and Iraqi withdrawal. Tension in the area remained, and Iraqi attacks on Kurds and Shiites continued. UN sanctions remained in place owing to Iraq's refusal to allow verification of the destruction of its weapons of mass destruction (**WMD**), and in 2003 a US-led military force invaded and occupied the country (**IRAQ WAR**), toppling Saddam Hussein, who was captured in Dec 2003. From May 2003 onwards, an insurgency developed with the apparent aim of destabilizing the country; this included attacks on the UN headquarters and the **RED CROSS** in Baghdad, frequent suicide bombings and shootings, particularly of Iraqi police and army personnel, and the abduction and murder of Western aid and reconstruction workers. Despite deteriorating internal security, sovereignty was handed over to an interim government headed by Iyad **ALLAWI** in Jun 2004, and elections for a Transitional National Authority were held in Jan 2005.

**Iraq War** (20 Mar–1 May 2003)
A war precipitated by the perceived failure of Iraq to comply with the **UN**'s proposed inspections and monitoring of its arms programme following the 1991 **GULF WAR**. Although a 1998 bombing campaign was believed to have destroyed Iraq's remaining nuclear, chemical and biological weapons, by 2002 US President George W **BUSH** and British Prime Minister Tony **BLAIR** believed President Saddam **HUSSEIN** was again secretly stockpiling illegal weapons. On 20 Mar 2003 a US-led coalition of 35 countries invaded Iraq. Baghdad fell to coalition forces on 9 Apr and on 1 May President Bush announced the end of 'major combat'; an insurgency then developed that claimed more lives than the war. No weapons of mass destruction (**WMD**) were found but Saddam Hussein was captured in Dec 2003. The Iraq War can be seen as a campaign in the war on **TERROR** declared by President Bush after the **SEPTEMBER 11 ATTACKS**. The war polarized public opinion worldwide, and was a major issue in the 2004 US presidential election campaign.

**Ireland, Lordship of**
The part of Ireland, mostly Munster and Leinster, under English rule from the 12c to the 16c. Anglo-Norman barons invited to Ireland in 1167 by the Gaelic king of Leinster, who wanted their support in expanding his territory, brought much of the south of the island under their own control. **HENRY II**, fearing intervention by the barons in English affairs, crossed to Dublin in 1171, reasserted his authority over them and assumed the 'lordship of Ireland'. Though its expansion was curbed later by a Gaelic resurgence, the Lordship covered a much larger area than just the **PALE**. The kingdom of Ireland superseded the Lordship as a political entity in the mid 16c when **HENRY VIII** was declared 'king of Ireland' (1541) by an Irish parliament. This title implied a claim to direct jurisdiction over the whole island, including the autonomous Gaelic principalities of the west and north, which drew later Tudor monarchs into war.

---

**IRELAND, REPUBLIC OF**   also called (since 1948) **Irish Republic** (Irish, **Éire**)

A republic occupying southern, central and north-western Ireland. It is separated from Great Britain by the Irish Sea and St George's Channel, and is bounded to the north-east by Northern Ireland, part of the UK. It was occupied by Goidelic-speaking Celts during the Iron Age, and a high kingship was established c.200AD, its capital being at Tara (Meath). Following conversion to Christianity by St Patrick in

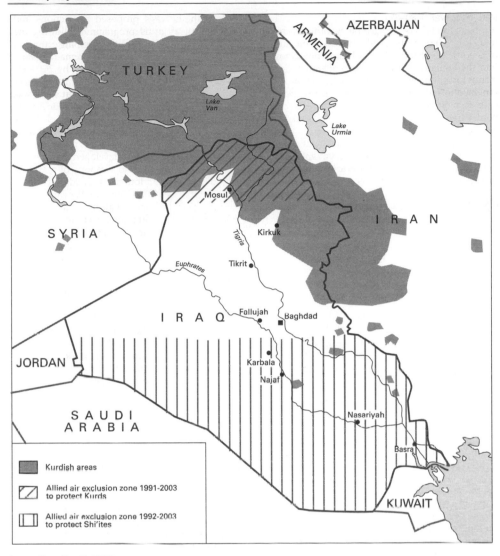

**Iraq after the Gulf War**

the 5c, Ireland became a centre of learning and missionary activity. The south-east was attacked by Vikings from c.800. **HENRY I** of England declared himself Lord of Ireland in 1171, and Anglo-Norman expansion created a Lordship of **IRELAND** which at one point dominated much of the island before being pushed back into Munster and Leinster by a Gaelic revival in 14–15c. **HENRY VIII** took the title 'King of Ireland' in 1542, but direct Crown rule was confined to the area around Dublin known as the **PALE**, though the Anglo-Norman vassals of the Crown ruled over much more. Elizabethan conquest finally unified the island under English control, which was shaken by a Catholic rebellion during the War of the Three Kingdoms in the 1640s. Parliamentary forces under Oliver **CROMWELL** reconquered Catholic Ireland in 1649–50. The Protestant communities in Ulster continued to survive this turmoil, as they did later when supporters of the deposed Catholic King **JAMES VII AND II** were defeated by **WILLIAM III** at the Battle of the **BOYNE** (1690). Following a century of suppres-

sion, the struggle for Irish independence developed in the 18–19c, including such revolutionary movements as Wolfe **TONE**'s Society of **UNITED IRISHMEN** (1796–8), and later **YOUNG IRELAND** (1848) and the **FENIANS** (1866–7). The Act of **UNION**, uniting Ireland and Britain, came into effect in 1801; the Catholic Relief Act (1829) effected **CATHOLIC EMANCIPATION**, enabling Catholics to sit in Parliament; and **LAND ACTS** (1870–1903) attacked Irish rural discontent (prior to these acts, the **IRISH FAMINE** in 1845–7 had drastically reduced the population). Two Home Rule Bills (1886, 1893) were defeated, and a third, passed in 1912, never came into effect because of **WORLD WAR I**. In 1916 there was an armed rebellion against British rule (the **EASTER RISING**), and in 1919 a republic was proclaimed by **SINN FÉIN**. A Home Rule Act of 1920 was largely ignored by Irish republicans, but was put into effect in Northern Ireland. In 1921 a treaty gave Ireland dominion status as the **IRISH FREE STATE**, subject to the right of Northern Ireland to opt out; this right was exercised, and a frontier was agreed in 1925. The Irish constitution of 1937 re-named the country Éire and declared the country a sovereign, independent and democratic state with a directly elected President, a restored but weakened Senate, and a **DÁIL EIREANN** elected by proportional representation. All constitutional links between the Irish Republic and the UK were severed with the declaration of the republic in 1948. This came into effect in 1949 with the Republic of Ireland Act, which changed the relationship between Ireland and Britain. The republic retained special citizenship arrangements and trade preference with Britain, but left the **COMMONWEALTH OF NATIONS**. The Westminster parliament passed the Ireland Act (1949) which confirmed a special relationship of Irish citizens in the UK, but declared that Northern Ireland would remain part of the UK until its citizens declared otherwise. Since 1973 the Irish Republic has been a member of the **EC**. During the 1990s Irish prime ministers Albert **REYNOLDS** (1992–4), John Bruton (1994–7) and Bertie Ahern (1997– ) were involved in the Northern Ireland peace process. The President of Ireland from 1990 was Mary **ROBINSON**. She was succeeded in 1997 by Mary McAleese. ► **DE VALERA, ÉAMON**; **HOME RULE**; **IRA**

**Ireton, Henry** (1611–51)
English soldier. At the outbreak of the **ENGLISH CIVIL WARS** he fought for parliament, and served at Edgehill, **NASEBY** and the siege of Bristol. **CROMWELL**'s son-in-law from 1646, he was one of the most implacable enemies of **CHARLES I**, and signed the warrant for his execution. He accompanied Cromwell to Ireland, and in 1650 became Lord Deputy. He died of the plague during the siege of Limerick.

**Irgun (Zvai Leumi)**
The terrorist organization operating in **PALESTINE** during the British Mandate and seeking the establishment of a Jewish state. Formed in 1931 after disagreement with the **HAGANAH** and reconstituted in 1937, it accepted **JABOTINSKY**'s ideology and engaged in armed conflict with Arabs and the British. Led by Menachem **BEGIN** from 1943, Irgun bombed Jerusalem's **KING DAVID HOTEL** in 1946, hanged two British sergeants in 1947 in response to the execution of its members, and attacked the Arab village of Deir Yassin in 1948. Condemned for this by the **JEWISH AGENCY**, the Irgun became the nucleus of the right-wing Herut Party in Israel after 1948.

**Irigoyen, Hipólito** ► **YRIGOYEN, HIPÓLITO**

**Irish Civil War** (1922–3)
A conflict in the newly independent **IRISH FREE STATE** between supporters and opponents of the Anglo-Irish Treaty (Dec 1921). Republicans, led by **DE VALERA**, refused to accept the treaty and in Jun 1922 conflict broke out between republican 'Irregulars' and government forces ('Staters') commanded by Michael **COLLINS**. The war was far bloodier than the preceding war for independence, the government taking ruthless measures against its opponents. A ceasefire in May 1923 was ambiguous, as the republicans still refused to recognise the validity of the treaty, but it marked the defeat of their challenge to democratic politics in the south of Ireland.

**Irish Famine**
The widespread starvation of Irish peasantry which followed the potato blight in 1845–7, and the consequent destruction of the crop. Because of starvation and emigration (to Britain and the USA), the population of Ireland fell by almost 25 per cent between 1845 and 1851. The British government was widely blamed by the emigrants for the scale of the disaster. ► **PEEL, ROBERT**

**Irish Free State**
Established by the Anglo-Irish Treaty (Dec 1921) with Dominion status under the British crown. Accordingly, 26 counties (excluding the six of Northern Ireland) became self-governing and in effect independent. The treaty was ratified by a small majority in the **DÁIL EIREANN** and power was transferred from Westminster (Mar 1922). Republicans, led by **DE VALERA**, refused to accept the authority of the crown and the **IRISH CIVIL WAR** (1922–3) ensued. The name 'Irish Free State' was retained until Dominion status was dismantled with the new constitution of 1937. ► **COLLINS, MICHAEL**; **GRIFFITH, ARTHUR**

**Irish Republic** ► **IRELAND, REPUBLIC OF**

**Irish Republican Socialist Party**
A political party formed in 1974 largely as a break-away group from the official **SINN FÉIN**, disagreeing with its political strategy and the ceasefire. Its most prominent member was Bernadette McAliskey. It was involved in a feud with the Official **IRA** in the 1970s, and subsequently moved closer to the Provisional Sinn Féin. ► **INLA**

**ironclad**
A warship developed in Europe and the USA in the mid-19c which was built of wood with iron plates to protect the hull. During the **CRIMEAN WAR** (1854–6) the French and British mounted guns on ironclad barges which had to be towed. The first actual steam-powered warship was the French *Gloire* (1859). The first British ironclad was the *Black Prince* (1861), which displaced 9,210 tons and could travel at 14.5 knots. The first battle between ironclads took place during the **AMERICAN CIVIL WAR** between the *Monitor* and the *Merrimack* off Hampton Roads, Virginia, in 1862. ► **MONITOR, USS V CSS MERRIMACK**

**Iron Curtain**
A term formerly used to describe the separation of certain East European countries from the rest of Europe by the **COLD WAR** and in particular the political and military domination of the USSR. It was first used by Nazi Propaganda Minister **GOEBBELS** in 1943, and became widely known after Winston **CHURCHILL** used it in a speech in 1946.

**Iron Guard**
The name commonly applied to the Legion of the Archangel Michael, a movement with a fascist ideology which in the 1930s, under the leadership of Corneliu Zelea **CODREANU**, established a mass following in Romania. Founded in 1927, the Legion was at first a quasi-religious organization encouraging moral regeneration. Chauvinist and anti-Semitic, it founded its military section, the Iron Guard, to combat the communists. First dissolved by the Romanian government in 1933, it operated under a front, 'All for

the Fatherland'. In 1938 the Guard was again disbanded and Codreanu shot. Ion **ANTONESCU** established links with the Guard and its new leader, Horia Sima, but in 1941 the movement was crushed with German support. ► **CHARLES II**

**Ironsi** ► **AGUIYI-IRONSI, JOHNSON**

**Ironside, William Edmund, 1st Baron** (1880–1959)
British field marshal. He served as a secret agent disguised as a railwayman in the **BOER WARS**, held several staff appointments in **WORLD WAR I**, and commanded the Archangel expedition against the **BOLSHEVIKS** (1918). He was Chief of the Imperial General Staff at the outbreak of **WORLD WAR II**, and placed in command of the Home Defence Forces (1940). The 'Ironsides', fast light-armoured vehicles, were named after him. He was made a peer in 1941.

**Iroquois Confederacy**
A confederation of Iroquois tribes during the 17–18c in northern New York State, consisting of the **MOHAWK**, Oneida, Onondaga, Cayuga and **SENECA**, later joined by the Tuscarora. Also known as the Iroquois League or the 'Six Nations', they were united largely for control of the **FUR TRADE** and for war. Numbering close to 16,000, they defeated many of their Native American rivals in the mid-17c, but were less successful thereafter. The league broke up during the **AMERICAN REVOLUTION** when the tribes took sides; the four groups siding with the British were defeated in 1779. Today most of the c.80,000 Iroquois live in upstate New York, although some live on reservations elsewhere in the USA and Canada.

**irredentism**
In the new nations of 19–20c Europe, the acquisition, by negotiation or more usually conquest, of 'unredeemed' territory. The term is most commonly applied to the Italians. The term *Italia irredenta* ('unredeemed Italy'), was used from the late 19c of those lands, such as Trieste, Istria, Gradisca and Trentino, which had Italian populations but remained under Austrian rule. The 'irredentists' were those who sought to regain these regions either by negotiation or war. By extension, the term came to be applied to similar cases of new nations claiming lands inhabited by compatriots but under foreign rule. Greek irredentists, for example, sought to incorporate Greek-speaking, Turkish-controlled areas into the new Greek kingdom. ► **ENOSIS; MEGALE IDEA; RISORGIMENTO**

**Isaac I Comnenus** (d.1061)
Eastern Roman Emperor in Constantinople (1057/9). He established the finances of the empire on a sounder footing, laid the clergy under contribution at the tax collections, and repelled the Hungarians attacking his northern frontier; and then, resigning the crown (1059), retired to a monastery, where he died.

**Isaacs, Sir Isaac Alfred** (1855–1948)
Australian jurist and politician, the son of a Jewish tailor. He became a barrister and, as Attorney-General for Victoria, helped prepare the federal constitution (1897–9). He sat in the federal parliament (1901–6), was a justice of the High Court (1906–30), and Chief Justice (1930–1). From 1931 to 1936 he was Governor-General, the first Australian to hold that office.

**Isabella I, the Catholic** (1451–1504)
Queen of **CASTILE** (1474/1504). The daughter of John II, King of Castile and Leon, in 1469 she married Ferdinand V of Aragon (**FERDINAND II, THE CATHOLIC**), with whom she ruled jointly from 1479. During her reign, the **INQUISITION** was introduced (1478), the Conquest of **GRANADA** completed (1482–92) and the Jews expelled (1492). She sponsored the voyage of Christopher **COLUMBUS** to the New World. ► **JEWS, EXPULSION OF THE; RECONQUEST**

**Isabella II** (1830–1904)
Queen of Spain (1833/68). The elder daughter of **FERDINAND VII** and **MARÍA CRISTINA** of Naples, she succeeded to the throne as an infant, with her mother and later (1840–3) General **ESPARTERO**, as Regent. Her succession was disputed by her uncle, Don **CARLOS**, and not until the Carlists' defeat in the First Carlist War (1833–40) was she secure. Her reign was characterized by acute political instability and repeated military intervention. Her own meddling in politics, together with her scandalous private life following an unsatisfactory marriage (1846) to Prince Francisco de Asís, weakened the Crown, and led to her overthrow in the 1868 Revolution. Although her son, **ALFONSO XII**, was restored to the throne in 1874, she spent the rest of her life in exile.

**Isabella of France** (1292–1358)
Queen consort of **EDWARD II** of England. The daughter of **PHILIP IV, THE FAIR** of France, she married Edward in 1308 at Boulogne. She became the mistress of Roger Mortimer, with whom she overthrew and murdered the King (1327). Her son, **EDWARD III**, had Mortimer executed in 1330, and Isabella was sent into retirement, eventually to join an order of nuns.

**Isa ibn Sulman** (1933–99)
Ruler of Bahrain (1971/99). Despite encouragement from Britain to maintain a federal connection with the Arab Emirates further down the Persian Gulf, he declared his island's full independence in 1971; in this he adopted much the same attitude as the ruler of Qatar, Khalifa ibn Hamad al-**THANI**. He also made a show of attempting a democratic approach to government, but after little more than a year dissolved the elected assembly and full powers reverted to the Shaykh and his family.

**Isandhlwana, Battle of** (1879)
A serious reverse for the British in the **ZULU WAR** of 1879. One of three British columns advancing into Zulu territory was caught by surprise by the main Zulu army and when its ammunition ran out was virtually destroyed by the Zulus using their traditional tactics. It caused considerable public alarm in Britain, allayed only by the victory at Ulundi later in the same year.

**Ishibashi Tanzan** (1884–1973)
Japanese politician. In the 1930s he was an economic journalist and vociferous critic of the militarists. He joined the Liberal Party (*Nihon Jiyuto*) after the war and served as Finance Minister in 1946. In 1951 Ishibashi became head of **MITI**, a powerful government ministry created in 1949 to promote economic development. He served briefly as Prime Minister for two months in 1956 before illness forced him to retire. Ishibashi was a keen supporter of the **NORMALIZA-**

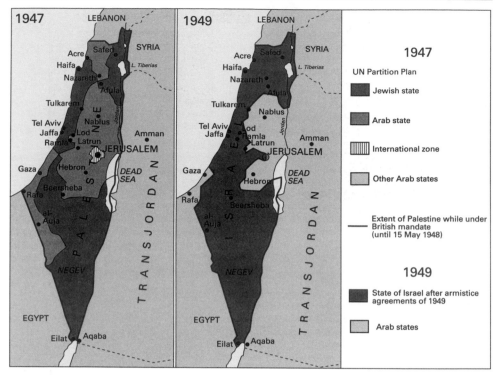

**Creation of the State of Israel**

---

**TION** of relations between Japan and communist China during the 1950s and 1960s.

### Ishiwara Kanji (1889–1949)

Japanese army officer. He graduated from the prestigious Army War College in 1918 and lectured there (1925–8). Influenced by the apocalyptic doctrines of the Japanese medieval Buddhist monk **NICHIREN**, Ishiwara believed in the inevitability of a final conflict between East and West, as represented by Japan and the USA. To prepare for this conflict, he maintained that Japan needed to harness resources in East Asia (especially Manchuria). After 1929, as an operations officer attached to the Japanese army (**GUANDONG ARMY**) that protected Japan's interests in south Manchuria and along the South Manchuria railway, Ishiwara helped plan the campaign in 1931 (without reference to the civilian government in Tokyo) that resulted in the transformation of Manchuria into the Japanese puppet-state of **MANZHUGUO**. On his return to Japan (1932), his abrasiveness and independent way of thinking brought him into conflict with his military superiors. In 1937, especially, he criticized Japan's invasion of China, fearing that a long drawn-out war of attrition would sabotage Japan's efforts in building a national defence state. He was forced out of the army in 1941.

### Islam ► RELIGION

### Isma'il (1645–1727)

Sultan of Maghrib (Morocco) (1672/1727). He consolidated the authority of the state and took firm control of piracy, which he turned into a state enterprise. He also established an élite corps of black slaves (*abid al-Bukhari*), who owed personal devotion to the Sultan.

### Isma'il I (1487–1524)

Safavid Shah of Iran (1501/24). He was the founder of the **SAFAVID DYNASTY** in Persia. Despite not having been accorded the renown of his illustrious successor, Shah **'ABBAS I, THE GREAT**, his achievement was nonetheless considerable. Isma'il, a Turkish-speaker from Tabriz, was astute enough to realize that the original quietist, Sunni Sufi Safavid order would not impart sufficient ideological impact to motivate Iranians against the Ottoman Turks. He therefore made a point of establishing Twelver Shiism as his state religion, thus converting his lands from the Sunni to the Shiite sect of Islam, to lend credibility to his confrontation with the Ottoman Turks, who were **SUNNIS**. Despite Isma'il's Turkic origins and the fact that he chose Tabriz for his capital, the language of his administration was Persian.

### Ismailis

Adherents of a secret Islamic sect, one of the main branches of the Shiites; also known as the 'Seveners'. It developed from an underground movement (c.9c), reaching political power in Egypt and North Africa in the 10–12c. It distinguished between inner and outer aspects of religion, was critical of Islamic law, and believed that in the eventual new age of the seventh imam, a kind of universal religion would emerge that was independent of the laws of all organized religions. Thus, it welcomed followers of other religions, but retained its own secret traditions and rites.

### Isma'il Pasha (1830–95)

Khedive of Egypt (1867/79). The second son of Ibrahim Pasha, he was educated at Saint-Cyr, France. In 1863 he became deputy of the Ottoman Sultan, and

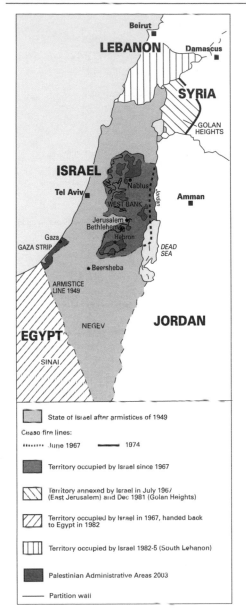

**Israel and her neighbours since 1949**

Map key:

State of Israel after armistices of 1949

Cease fire lines:
········ June 1967     ——— 1974

Territory occupied by Israel since 1967

Territory annexed by Israel in July 1967
(East Jerusalem) and Dec 1981 (Golan Heights)

Territory occupied by Israel in 1967, handed back
to Egypt in 1982

Territory occupied by Israel 1982-5 (South Lebanon)

Palestinian Administrative Areas 2003

——— Partition wall

was granted the title of Khedive in 1867. His massive development programme included the building of the Suez Canal, which was opened in splendour in 1869. The accumulation of a large foreign debt led to European intervention; he was deposed by the Ottoman Sultan, and replaced by his eldest son, **TEWFIK PASHA**. He died in exile in Istanbul.

### isolationism

A foreign policy strategy of withdrawing from international affairs as long as the country's interests are not affected. It is a means of avoiding involvement in international conflicts, and implies neutrality in most cases. It was practised most notably by the USA, which kept out of the **LEAGUE OF NATIONS** and **WORLD WAR II** until attacked by the Japanese.

**ISRAEL** official name **State of Israel**

A democratic republic in the Middle East, with Jerusalem as its capital, bounded to the north by Lebanon; to the north-east by Syria; to the east by Jordan; to the south-west by Egypt; and to the west by the Mediterranean Sea. Zionists settled in **PALESTINE** in the 1880s when it was under Ottoman rule, and the British declared support for a Jewish 'national home' there in 1917. However, Zionist ambitions were never satisfied under the **LEAGUE OF NATIONS** mandate given to Britain (1918–47), although Jewish immigration in the 1930s and 1940s increased greatly due to Nazi persecution. The British evacuated Palestine after **WORLD WAR II**, unable to control a new flood of Jewish immigration heavily supported by the USA. Tension between Arabs and Jews led the UN in 1947 to support the formation of two states in Palestine, one Jewish and the other Arab. When the Arab side rejected this, David **BEN-GURION** announced the creation of the independent State of Israel on 14 May 1948. Military conflict with surrounding countries ensued in which Israeli forces were victorious. Further wars took place in 1956 (**SUEZ CRISIS**) and 1967 (**SIX-DAY WAR**), when Israel gained control of the **GAZA STRIP**, the Sinai Peninsula as far as the Suez Canal, the **WEST BANK** of the River Jordan including the eastern sector of Jerusalem, and the Golan Heights in Syria; these areas have since been referred to as the 'occupied territories'. Wars also broke out in 1973 (**YOM KIPPUR WAR**) and in 1982 (Lebanon War), which forced the **PLO** to leave Beirut in 1982-5. In contrast, a peace agreement between Israel and Egypt's President Anwar **SADAT** was reached in 1979. During the 1990s there were several attempts to launch peace talks to resolve the Israeli–Palestinian conflict. The **OSLO ACCORDS** (1993) led to the establishment of the **PALESTINIAN AUTONOMOUS AREAS**, and Israel and Jordan signed a peace treaty in 1994. However, violence continued, with suicide bombings in Israeli cities, an armed struggle in south Lebanon, and more fighting between West Bank Palestinians and Israeli forces; a major issue was the government's policy of building Jewish settlements in Arab areas. In 1999 **NETANYAHU**'s Likud Party was defeated by the Labour Party led by Ehud Barak, who withdrew Israeli forces from Lebanon but failed to reach agreement with the Palestinians on various issues not settled by the Oslo Accords. In Sep 2000 a second **INTIFADA** began, against which **SHARON**'s Likud government took a hard line after coming to power in 2001, including

building a wall between Israeli and Palestinian areas despite international protests and the risk of endangering the **ROADMAP PEACE PROCESS**. Yasser **ARAFAT**'s death in Nov 2004 ended the deadlock in negotiations with the Palestinians, which resumed with the new leader, Mahmoud Abbas. ➤ **BALFOUR DECLARA-TION**; **HAMAS**; **IRGUN**; **MAPAI PARTY**; **WORLD ZIONIST ORGANIZATION**; **ZIONISM**

## Istria

The peninsula at the north end of the Adriatic, divided between the republics of Slovenia and Croatia. Under Byzantine rule (538–787) and with Venice part of the Ravenna exarchate, it was settled by **SLAVS** in the 7c. By the 15c Istria was divided between the Austrian Habsburgs and the Republic of Venice, with the latter holding about three-quarters of the area. After **NAPOLEON I** took Venice in 1797, the French included the whole peninsula in the **ILLYRIAN PRO-VINCES** (1809–13). Austrian forces took Istria in 1813 and Habsburg possession was confirmed at the Congress of **VIENNA** (1814–15). In 1921 it was annexed by **MUSSOLINI**'s Italy, and the fascist government tried to suppress all expression of Slovene and Croatian national identity. After **WORLD WAR II**, in 1947, it was formally ceded to the Socialist Federal Republic of Yugoslavia and was divided between the republics of Croatia and Slovenia. ➤ **HABSBURG DY-NASTY**

## Itagaki Seishiro (1885–1948)

Japanese army officer. Along with **ISHIWARA KANJI**, he was a key player in the Japanese military conquest

of Manchuria. He became Army Minister in 1937 and then Chief of General Staff of the China Expeditionary Army in 1939. After **WORLD WAR II** he was tried as a war criminal and executed.

## Itagaki Taisuke (1837–1919)

Japanese politician. The leader of the **FREEDOM AND PEOPLE'S RIGHTS MOVEMENT** in the 1870s, he came from an upper **SAMURAI** family in Tosa domain and was a participant in the **MEIJI RESTORATION**. Although he entered the government in 1869, he resigned in 1873 when proposals for a military expedition to Korea were rejected. Condemning the monopoly of power held by those from the former domains of **CHOSHU** and **SATSUMA**, from 1874 he began calling for a national representative assembly, drawing on ideas from Western liberalism. In 1881 he formed Japan's first political party, the *Jiyuto* (Liberals), which attracted the support of former **SA-MURAI** and wealthy landowners. Due to government harrassment and internal rivalries, the party was disbanded in 1884, but was revived in time to contest the country's first elections for a national diet in 1890. In 1898 Itagaki, in alliance with the *Shimpoto* (Progressives) of **OKUMA SHIGENOBU**, formed Japan's first party cabinet but it only lasted four months before internal bickering brought an end to the experiment. Thereafter, Itagaki retired from active politics.

## Italian National Society (*Società Nazionale Italiana*)

Nationalist organization established by Giorgio Pallavicino (1796–1878), Daniele **MANIN** and Giuseppe

LA FARINA in July 1857. It channelled the backing of many former republicans and Mazzinians, including GARIBALDI, into the moderate, monarchist camp that sought unification through Piedmontese expansion. It also played an important role in preparing the ground in northern and central Italy for annexation by VICTOR EMMANUEL II. ► RISORGIMENTO

**Italian Social Movement** (*Movimento Sociale Italiano*)
The post-war Italian neo-fascist movement that stands on the extreme right of Italian parliamentary politics. It is a fringe party which has never received more than 10 per cent of the national vote. However, it remains strong in some regions such as the Alto-Adige, where it is seen as defending the interests of the Italian-speaking population against the privileged German population and their *Südtiroler Volkspartei*. Its most able leader was Giorgio Almirante (1915–88). In 1993 the movement was renamed the National Alliance (*Alleanza Nazionale*).

**Italian Wars** (1494–1559)
A long series of conflicts often described in terms of the rivalry between the French VALOIS DYNASTY and the HABSBURG DYNASTY, but which in many ways form a continuity between the struggles of popes and emperors in the Middle Ages and the religious wars of the REFORMATION era. The first war was prompted by CHARLES VIII's decision in 1494 to activate the Angevin claim to Naples, dormant since the SICILIAN VESPERS of 1282. His invasion was triumphant, but on their return northward the French had to face a powerful Italian alliance at Fornovo on the Taro and performed wonders to cut their way through it. In 1499 LOUIS XII pressed the claims of his house (Orléans) to Milan, but was drawn south by the apparent disregard of FERDINAND II, THE CATHOLIC of partition arrangements made at the Treaty of Granada (1500). In 1503 Gonzalo FERNÁNDEZ DE CÓRDOBA won decisive victories over the French at Cerignola and on the Garigliano. Franco-Spanish rivalry in Italy was effectively institutionalized and reached new heights during the long conflict between FRANCIS I of France and Emperor CHARLES V. ► CAMBRAI, LEAGUE OF; CAMBRAI, TREATY OF; CATEAU-CAMBRÉSIS, TREATY OF; CRESPY, PEACE OF; MADRID, TREATY OF; ORLÉANS, HOUSE OF

**ITALY** official name **Italian Republic**
A republic in southern Europe, comprising the boot-shaped peninsula extending south into the Mediterranean Sea, as well as Sicily, Sardinia and some smaller islands. It is bounded to the north-west by France; to the north by Switzerland and Austria; and to the north-east by Slovenia. In pre-Roman times, Italy, which was not a concept covering the racially mixed Po Valley, was inhabited by Etruscans in the north, Latins in the centre of the country and Greeks in the south. Most regions were part of the Roman Empire by the 3c BC; barbarian tribes invaded in the 4c AD, and the last Roman emperor was deposed in AD476. Italy was later ruled by the Lombards and by the FRANKS under Charlemagne, who was crowned Emperor of the Romans in 800. It became part of the HOLY ROMAN EMPIRE under Otto I, the Great in 962, and conflict between popes and emperors continued throughout the MIDDLE AGES. There were disputes

between GUELFS and GHIBELLINES in the 12c. Italy was divided amongst five main powers during the 14–15c (Kingdom of Naples, Duchy of Milan, republics of Florence and Venice, and the papacy). The country made a major contribution to European culture through the RENAISSANCE. Four satellite republics were set up after a successful French invasion during the wars of the FRENCH REVOLUTION, and NAPOLEON I was crowned King of Italy in 1805. The 19c saw an upsurge of liberalism and nationalism (the RISORGIMENTO); unification was achieved by 1870 under VICTOR EMMANUEL II of Sardinia, aided by CAVOUR and GARIBALDI; colonies were established in Eritrea (1870–89) and Somaliland (1889), but the attempt to secure a protectorate over Abyssinia was defeated at the Battle of ADOWA (1896). During WORLD WAR I, Italy fought alongside the Allies. The fascist movement brought MUSSOLINI to power in 1922, and he led the Conquest of ABYSSINIA (1935–6) and occupation of Albania (1939). The alliance with HITLER in WORLD WAR II led to the end of the Italian Empire. Political instability has resulted in over 45 governments in power since the formation of the democratic republic in 1946. Italy was a founding member of the EEC in 1958 and of the EURO ZONE. Following corruption scandals in the early 1990s, a right-wing government led by Silvio BERLUSCONI was elected in 1994, causing fears in Europe about a resurgence of the extreme Right. However, in 1996 the elections were won by a left-wing coalition led by Prime Minister Romano Prodi, who in 1999 resigned to become President of the European Commission. In 2001 Berlusconi returned to power at the head of a centre-right coalition government that became increasingly eurosceptic and aligned itself with the USA and UK in the IRAQ WAR. ► FASCISM

**Ito Hirobumi** (1838–1909)
Japanese politician. He was Premier (1885–8, 1892–6, 1898 and 1900–1). Ito visited Europe and the USA on several occasions, drafted the MEIJI CONSTITUTION (1889), and played a major role in abolishing Japanese FEUDALISM and building up the modern state. He was assassinated at Harbin by a supporter of Korean independence.

**Iturbide, Agustín de** (1783–1824)
Mexican general and politician. Born in Valladolid of a Spanish father and CREOLE mother, he fought as part of Calleja's forces against HIDALGO (Y COSTILLA) and MORELOS (Y PAVÓN), defeating the latter. He seized the moment in 1821, when Mexican conservatives were caught off balance by the radical liberal regime in Spain, to group together the military, aristocracy and clergy in support of Mexican independence. His manifesto, the IGUALA PLAN, attracted support from conservatives and rebels alike; it guaranteed the status of Roman Catholicism, independence under a Bourbon monarch, and equality between creoles and Spanish-born. He proclaimed himself Emperor as Agustín I (1822/3), after the Bourbons failed to provide the prince required by the plan. However, beset with political and financial problems, he was forced to abdicate by a revolt of which one of the leaders was SANTA ANNA. He then travelled in Europe and, on his return to Mexico, was executed, having been sentenced *in absentia*.

**Ituzaingó, Battle of** (1827)
The only significant land battle of the Argentine–Brazilian War of 1825–8. The battle, in the Argentine province of Corrientes, was a tactical stalemate, the organization of the Argentine forces being offset by the skill of the Brazilians.

**Ivan I, Moneybag** (d.1341)
Grand Prince of Moscow (1328 or 1332/41). A skilful diplomat and careful administrator, he expanded Moscow's territory and developed its economy. He also made Moscow the capital of Russia by transferring the metropolitan cathedral from Kiev in 1326. His two sons, Simeon the Proud (1341/53) and Ivan II, the Meek (1353/9), reigned after him, continuing the tradition he had started.

**Ivan III, the Great** (1440–1505)
Grand Prince of Moscow (1462/1505). Building on his predecessors' work, he succeeded in ending his principality's subjection to the **MONGOLS**, and gained control over several important Russian principalities, notably Novgorod and Tver. In 1493 he assumed the title of 'Sovereign of all Russia' (including Kiev) and, upon marrying the Byzantine Princess Sofia, he acquired the emblem of the two-headed eagle of the **BYZANTINE EMPIRE**. In many respects he was the real founder of Russia and won it international acceptance. ► **GOLDEN HORDE**

**Ivan IV, the Terrible** (1530–84)
Grand Prince of Moscow (1533/84). He was the first prince to assume the title of 'tsar' (from Latin, *Caesar*), indicating the power of Russia and asserting his own authority. He subdued Kazan and Astrakhan, made the first inroads into Siberia, and established commercial links with England. The first half of his reign was one of autocratic benevolence as he took account of the needs of his people. However, after the death in 1560 of his first wife, Anastasia, he lost his sense of balance and saw treachery everywhere. He embarked on a ghastly reign of terror, directed principally at the feudal aristocracy (**BOYARS**), and killed his eldest son and heir, Ivan, in 1581. He nonetheless did much for Russian culture and commerce, not least in his moments of guilt and remorse.

**Ivanov, Nikolai Veniaminovich** (1952– )
Russian lawyer. He was the junior partner of **GDLYAN** in proving corruption in high places during the last years of Leonid **BREZHNEV**'s dictatorial rule. He helped Gdlyan in the 'Uzbek affair' and then in attacking senior Muscovite communists. With Gdlyan, he attracted both official disapproval and popular encouragement.

**Ivashko, Vladimir Antonovich** (1932–94)
Ukrainian politician. He became First Secretary of the Ukrainian Communist Party in 1989 and Deputy General-Secretary of the Soviet Communist Party in 1990, only to see the party as a whole dissolved a year later. He was engineer, lecturer and, more particularly, party official who rose to the top quickly when the hardline and ageing **SHCHERBITSKY** died and Mikhail **GORBACHEV** seized the reform opportunity. He certainly appointed Yegor **LIGACHEV**, but he was not particularly liberal and in any case did not have long to make an impact on a conservative USSR.

**Ivory Coast** ► **CÔTE D'IVOIRE**

**Iwakura Tomomi** (1825–83)
Japanese court noble. He supported the anti-Tokugawa movement and helped restore direct imperial rule in 1868. He helped formulate the **CHARTER OATH**, the manifesto of the new government's modernization drive. Between 1871 and 1873 he led a mission to the USA and Europe with the original aim of negotiating a revision of the treaties signed in the 1850s and 1860s, in particular the abolition of the foreign privilege of extraterritoriality in Japan. The Western powers were reluctant to countenance any change and Iwakura returned to Japan convinced more than ever of the need for internal modernization. ► **MEIJI RESTORATION**; **TOKUGAWA SHOGUNATE**

**Iwasaki Yataro** (1835–85)
Japanese entrepreneur. The son of a farmer who claimed **SAMURAI** descent, Iwasaki became the financial agent for his domain (Tosa), taking over its interests in shipping and coal-mining. In 1873 he founded the Mitsubishi Trading Company and developed close personal links with the new Meiji government, receiving government subsidies and contracts. By 1877 Iwasaki owned over 80 per cent of all ships in Japan and monopolized the coastal trade, having successfully defeated his US and UK rivals. Mitsubishi became one of the largest **ZAIBATSU** (financial combines), with interests in banking, insurance and mining.

**Iwo Jima**
The most important and largest of the Japanese Volcano Islands, situated in the western Pacific Ocean. A major battle of **WORLD WAR II** took place on the island in 1944–5, when the heavily fortified Japanese air base was taken in a three-month campaign. The island was occupied by the USA from 1945 until it was returned to Japan in 1968.

**IWW** ► **INDUSTRIAL WORKERS OF THE WORLD**

**Iyasu I, the Great** (d.1706)
Emperor of Ethiopia (1682/1706). He succeeded to the throne in 1682 and proved to be a brave and far-sighted ruler. A modernizer and patron of the arts, he made a determined effort to reunify the kingdom following the wholesale migration of Galla tribesmen into the empire, and to reform its institutions after a period of decline during the 17c. He was assassinated by a kinsman of his wife.

**Izetbegović, Alija** (1925–2003)
Bosnia and Herzegovinian politician. Born in Bosanski Samac, he was educated at the University of Sarajevo. In 1945, following the creation of the Yugoslav Federation, he was imprisoned for three years for promoting Bosnian nationalist policies. On his release he wrote several books on Islamic politics and in 1988 became leader of the Party of Democratic Action. With the break-up of Yugoslavia he became President of Bosnia and Herzegovina (1990) and the inspirational leader of the Bosnian Muslims in the civil war that followed. From 1996 to 2000 he was a member of the federal presidential triumvirate introduced under the provisions of the Dayton Peace Accord.

**Izvolski, Alexander Petrovich** (1856–1919)
Russian diplomat and politician. He served as an envoy in Europe and Japan before becoming Foreign Minister in 1906. He negotiated the **ANGLO-RUSSIAN ENTENTE** in 1907 and also tried to improve relations with Austria and simultaneously strengthen the Russian hold on Turkey. However, in 1908 Austria did not honour the understanding that he believed he had with it, unilaterally annexed Bosnia and Herzegovina and left him inadequately prepared diplomatically to get the Straits opened for Russian warships. From 1910 to 1917 he acted as ambassador in Paris, where he helped to strengthen the **FRANCO-RUSSIAN ALLIANCE** of 1894.

**Jabotinsky, Vladimir** (1880–1940)
Jewish writer and Zionist, born in Odessa. Realizing that **WORLD WAR I** would spell the end of the **OTTOMAN EMPIRE**, Jabotinsky and others persuaded the British government to allow Jewish involvement in the fight for **PALESTINE**. The result was a Jewish transport unit which fought in the **GALLIPOLI CAMPAIGN** but was disbanded in 1916. However, Jabotinsky was instrumental in convincing the British to sanction the more substantial Jewish Legion which took recruits from Britain, North America and, towards the end of the war, Jews from Palestine. Thereafter, the Legion became the basis for the **HAGANAH**. Unlike that of others, Jabotinsky's **ZIONISM** was right-wing and hostile to socialism. This led him to found in 1925 the Zionist Revisionist Movement, later renamed the New Zionist Organization. With growing resistance to Jewish immigration to Palestine under the British Mandate, Jabotinsky supported terrorist activities by the **IRGUN**.

**Jackson, Andrew**, nicknamed **Old Hickory** (1767–1845)
US politician and 7th President. He trained as a lawyer, and became a member of the **HOUSE OF REPRESENTATIVES** for Tennessee (1796), its Senator (1797), and a judge of its Superior Court (1798–1804). In the **WAR OF 1812**, he was given command of the South, and became famous for his defence of New Orleans (1814–15). Regarded as a folk hero, he won the presidency in 1828 in a campaign that gave him a large majority in the popular vote. His emphasis on the importance of the popular vote came to be known as '**JACKSONIAN DEMOCRACY**'. His presidency (1829–1837) was significant for its use of executive power, most notable in the **NULLIFICATION** issue and in the **BANK WAR**.

**Jackson, Jesse Louis** (1941– )
US **CIVIL RIGHTS** leader and minister. As Martin Luther **KING**'s lieutenant, he established a strong branch of the **SCLC** in Chicago. In 1967 he initiated Operation Breadbasket, which aimed to create jobs by attracting business investment in black enterprises in the cities. In 1971 he became the executive director of Operation PUSH (People United To Serve Humanity). These two projects helped get him national attention, and in 1983 he became a candidate for the Democratic presidential nomination. His 'Rainbow Coalition' attracted a good deal of media attention, but without an organized political base, he had little chance of success. He was the first black American to mount a serious campaign for the office.

He was a candidate again in 1987, but was again unsuccessful in gaining the nomination.

**Jackson, Robert H(oughwout)** (1892–1954)
US jurist. A supporter of Franklin D **ROOSEVELT**'s **NEW DEAL** policies, he became a general counsel for the US Bureau of Internal Revenue in 1934, then served as Solicitor-General (1938–9) and Attorney-General (1940–1) of the USA. In the latter position in 1940 he drafted an opinion defending the **DESTROYER–BASES DEAL** for Roosevelt. From 1941 to 1954 he was an associate justice of the US Supreme Court, during which time he took leave from the bench to be chief US prosecutor at the **NUREMBERG TRIALS** (1945–6).

**Jackson, Thomas Jonathan**, known as **Stonewall Jackson** (1824–63)
US Confederate general. In 1851 he became a professor at the Virginia Military Institute. During the **AMERICAN CIVIL WAR**, he became a Confederate general. He commanded a brigade at **BULL RUN**, where his firm stand gained him his nickname. He showed tactical superiority in the campaign of the Shenandoah Valley (1862), and won several victories, notably at Cedar Run, Manassas and Harpers Ferry. He was accidentally killed by his own troops at Chancellorsville.

**Jacksonian Democracy**, also called **Jacksonianism**
A political movement or approach associated with the administration of Andrew **JACKSON** (1829–37). His election marked a turning point in US history and a triumph for political democracy because it was the first time a US President had won by appealing directly to the mass of the voters rather than by relying on a recognized political organization for support. Consequently, egalitarianism and equal opportunity became more important than ever before; this attitude was reflected in the political reform that widened the franchise. The standards that Jackson introduced for measuring candidates and making decisions were adopted as a yardstick in US politics for the remainder of the 19c.

**Jacoba of Bavaria** ► JACQUELINE OF HOLLAND

**Jacobins**
A radical political group in the **FRENCH REVOLUTION**, originally the Club Breton in Versailles, but renamed after transferring to the premises of the Dominican or 'Jacobin' fathers in Paris (1789). After successive purges, the club became the instrument of the Terror under **ROBESPIERRE**'s dictatorship (1793–4), the name being associated thereafter with left-wing

extremism. ► TERROR, REIGN OF

## Jacobites
Those who supported the claim of the Catholic JAMES VII AND II of England, and his successors, to the British throne. The Jacobites launched two major rebellions, in 1715 (the FIFTEEN REBELLION) and 1745 (the FORTY-FIVE REBELLION), against the Protestant Hanoverian succession, and in the period 1714–60 some British Tory politicians had Jacobite sympathies. ► TORIES

## Jacqueline of Holland (1401–36)
Dutch noblewoman. The only child of Count William VI of Holland and Zeeland and Duke of Bavaria, and of Margaret of Burgundy, she made a series of marriages which caused her much trouble. She married, first (1415), Prince John of Touraine, DAUPHIN of France, who died in 1417, the year in which Jacqueline succeeded her father. She waged war against John of Bavaria for the right to succeed to her father's title there, then in 1418 married her cousin, Duke John IV of BRABANT, who mortgaged Holland and Zeeland to John of Bavaria. Repudiating the marriage, she went to England, where she married (with debatable legality) Humphrey, Duke of Gloucester, in 1422. Deserted by him during an invasion to regain her lands in Hainaut, she surrendered to PHILIP THE GOOD of Burgundy in 1428, and in 1433 relinquished to him her claims to sovereignty. In 1432 she was married once more, this time to Frans van Borsele, a Zeeland nobleman.

## Jacquerie (1358)
Originally, a serious peasant rebellion in northeastern France, noted for its savagery. Started by mercenaries following the English victory at Poitiers (1356), it degenerated (May 1358) into bitter violence between the oppressed peasantry, aggrieved Parisians, and their noble overlords; the latter massacred the insurgents indiscriminately at Meaux and Clermont-en-Beauvaisis (June 1358). The term then came to be used for any peasant rising.

## Jagan, Cheddi Berrat (1918–97)
Guyanese socialist politician and writer. With BURNHAM, he led the nationalist People's Progressive Party (PPP) in demanding self-government in the early 1950s. The Jagan–Burnham alliance won the 1953 election but the Governor, accusing Jagan of 'communist' policies, suspended the constitution, dismissed Jagan and his cabinet and called in British troops. He came to power with the PPP again in 1957, but an austerity budget and Jagan's desire to hasten the end of imperial rule led to racial rioting and a long general strike in Georgetown only ended by further British military intervention (1961–4). In the 1964 election, based on a British-devised proportional representation constitution, Burnham's PEOPLE'S NATIONAL CONGRESS was victorious, and Jagan became the leader of the official opposition. He held this position for 28 years, before becoming President from 1992 until his death.

## Jagat Seths
The title of the heads of the Hindu banking house of the Seths, awarded to them by Nawab Alivardi Khan of Bengal in the mid-18c. The Seths financed the large transit and foreign trade of Bengal in the early 18c. As lenders, they became politically influential and conspired with the British to remove Nawab SIRAJ UD-DAULA, who had insulted them. In the 1760s the Seths were removed by Mir Kasim from Murshidabad to the new capital, Monghyr. In 1763 Mir Kasim put to death the two leading members of the house, suspecting them of complicity with the British EAST INDIA COMPANY.

## Jagiełłon Dynasty
The ruling dynasty of Poland-Lithuania, Bohemia and Hungary, which dominated east central Europe from the Baltic to the Danube in the 15–16c. It was founded when Jagiełło, Grand-Duke of Lithuania, married Queen Jadwiga of Poland and so became King of Poland from 1386 to 1434, as Władysław II. The dynasty flourished under his acquisitive successors until SIGISMUND II AUGUSTUS (1548/72) died without heirs. In between times, Władysław III was also King of Hungary (1440/4), and a later Władysław ruled both Bohemia (1471/1516) and Hungary (1490/1516).

## Jahangir (1569–1627)
Mughal Emperor (1605/27). The son of AKBAR THE GREAT, he was named Salim and took the title of Jahangir on his accession. The earlier part of his reign was a period of peace and great prosperity for the empire, with a steady growth of trade and commerce and a great flowering of the arts. The latter part of the reign was characterized by continual rebellions against his rule, principally on behalf of his various sons, and he was only able to survive as ruler by dint of the courage and vigour of the empress, NUR JAHAN. He was, however, a just and tolerant man, and a consistent patron of the arts.

## Jahn, Friedrich Ludwig (1778–1852)
Prussian physical educationist, known as the 'Father of gymnastics' (Turnvater). In 1811 he started the first gymnasium (Turnplatz) in Berlin and his methods soon became very popular. An ardent nationalist, he commanded a volunteer corps in the NAPOLEONIC WARS (1813–15); after the peace of 1815, he resumed his teaching and published Die deutsche Turnkunst (1816, Eng trans A Treatise on Gymnastics, 1828). The gymnasia began to witness political gatherings which attracted students and intellectuals; these meetings were too liberal to please the Prussian government, and they were closed in 1818. Jahn, who had taken a prominent part in the movement, was arrested in 1819, and suffered five years' imprisonment. He was elected to the Frankfurt National Assembly in 1848.

## Jaime I, the Conqueror (1208–76)
Count of Barcelona and King of Aragon, Valencia and Mallorca (1213/76). Possibly the greatest of the rulers of the Catalan lands, he spent his infancy in France with Simon de MONTFORT. Soon after, he succeeded to the throne of Aragon and committed himself to a campaign of military expansion against the Muslim powers in the Iberian Peninsula. His capture of Mallorca in 1229 was followed by the subjugation of the remaining Balearic Islands. From 1232 he commenced the campaigns that culminated in 1238 with the capture of Valencia. Catalan expansion threatened the already expanding Kingdom of CASTILE, and a treaty to define their respective limits was

signed in 1244. In 1266 he conquered Murcia but handed it over to Castile. The marriage of his son, Peter, to the Princess of Sicily began Catalan expansion further into the Mediterranean. Under him, the first Catalan code of maritime law, the *Llibre del consolat de Mar*, was drawn up, and the key figures of early Catalan culture, Ramon Penyafort and Ramon Llull, were active.

## Jainism

An indigenous religion of India which regards Vardhamana Mahavira (599–527BC), said to be the last *Tirthankara* ('ford-maker'), as its founder. Jains believe that salvation consists in conquering material existence through adherence to a strict ascetic discipline, thus freeing the soul from the working of karma for eternal all-knowing bliss. Liberation requires detachment from worldly existence, an essential part of which is the practice of *ahimsa*, non-injury to living beings, an ideal also used by M K **GANDHI** in his campaigns against British rule in India.

## Jai Singh, Mirza Raja (d.1743)

King of Amber, in present-day Rajasthan (1699/ 1743). He was a vassal and prominent general of the Mughal Emperor **AURANGZEB**, on whose behalf he brought the troublesome **SHIVAJI** to heel after the latter's raid on the town of **SURAT**. In 1708 Jai Singh rebelled against Bahadur Shah, Aurangzeb's son and successor. He was subsequently pardoned by him and, in 1722, was made Viceroy of Agra, where he succeeded in subduing the Jats. He was later made Viceroy of Malwa by the Mughal Emperor Farrukh-siyar. However, in later years, he could not restrain the Marathas. It was Jai Singh who founded Jaipur, and built still extant astronomical observatories at Delhi and Jaipur.

## Ja Ja of Opobo (1821–91)

West African merchant prince. An ex-slave, he established a highly successful trading operation in the Niger Delta before the Partition of **AFRICA**. He founded his kingdom in 1869, when he led many of the constituent houses of the Kingdom of Bonny to his new capital to command the palm oil trade. He shipped oil directly to Britain and resisted European encroachments upon his trade. However, he aroused the enmity of other traders, of missionaries and of British consuls. In 1885, without any authorization from London, Consul Sir Harry Johnston deposed him, a significant move in the development of total British command of the Niger Delta.

## Jakeš, Miloš (1922–)

Czechoslovak politician. Originally an electrical engineer, he joined the Communist Party of Czechoslovakia in 1945 and studied at the Higher Party School in Moscow (1955–8). He supported the Soviet invasion of Czechoslovakia in 1968 and later, as head of the Party's Central Control Commission, oversaw the purge of reformist personnel. He became a member of the Central Committee in 1977 and of the Politburo in 1981, and in Dec 1987 replaced Gustáv **HUSÁK** as Party leader. Although enjoying close personal relations with the Soviet leader, Mikhail **GORBACHEV**, he emerged as a cautious reformer who made it clear that restructuring (*prestavba*) in Czechoslovakia would be a slow and limited process. He was forced

to step down as CCP leader in Nov 1989, following a series of pro-democracy rallies.

**Jallianwalla Bagh Massacre ►** AMRITSAR MASSACRE

## Jamaat-i Islami

The party founded in 1941 by Maulana Abu'l Ala **MAUDUDI**, to voice his opposition to the **MUSLIM LEAGUE**'s demands for Pakistan, which he regarded as not properly Islamic and liable to encourage Hindu nationalism. Following the Partition of **INDIA** in 1947, Maududi moved to Pakistan and the party became a persistent critic of the government. Banned in 1953 for fomenting trouble over the Ahmadiyyas, it later staged a comeback. An Indian successor party, established in 1948, was banned by the Indian government in 1992 following the Ayodhya disturbances.

### JAMAICA

An island nation of the West Indies in the Caribbean Sea. It was visited by **COLUMBUS** in 1494 and settled by the Spanish in 1509. From 1640 West African slave labour was imported for work on the sugar plantations. Jamaica was occupied by the British in 1655. Self-government was introduced in 1944, and independence was achieved in 1962 under Prime Minister Alexander **BUSTAMANTE**, leader of the conservative **JAMAICA LABOUR PARTY** (JLP). The JLP and the People's National Party (PNP), founded in 1938 by Norman **MANLEY**, have dominated post-independence politics. The 1972 election was won by the PNP led by Michael **MANLEY**, but his socialist policies, his troubles with the **INTERNATIONAL MONETARY FUND** (IMF) and his inability to stimulate the economy saw the return of the JLP under Edward **SEAGA** in 1980. Seaga reversed many of the PNP policies but the JLP's reliance on capitalism fared no better in creating economic stability, and the PNP won the 1989 election. In 1993 the JLP disputed a landslide victory by the PNP (led from 1992 by Percival J Patterson) and boycotted the government. Relations between the two parties, often fraught, degenerated into violence, which continued for some years and still occasionally mars political life. The economy remains weak, and there are high levels of crime and violence, largely associated by drugs. **►** RASTAFARIANISM

## Jamaica Labour Party (JLP)

One of the two major political parties which have shared power in Jamaica since independence in 1962, **BUSTAMANTE**'s JLP, founded in 1943, grew out of his Industrial Trade Union. Although the PNP dominated politics from 1957 to 1962, Bustamante won the election of that year and the JLP retained power until 1972 under, successively, Bustamante, Donald Sangster and Hugh Shearer. Ousted in the 1972 general election by the PNP, the JLP returned to power under Edward SEAGA in 1980. However, the JLP's reliance on capitalism fared no better that the PNP's socialism in creating economic stability, and Manley and the PNP were returned in the 1989 election. In 1993 the JLP disputed a landslide victory by the PNP (led from 1992 by Percival J Patterson) and boycotted the government; it has been in opposition since.

### James I (1394–1437)
King of Scots (1406/37). His father, ROBERT III, sent him for safety to France, but he was captured at sea (1406), held prisoner in England for 18 years, and did not begin to rule until his release in 1424. An accomplished poet, he wrote *The Kingis Quair* to celebrate his romance with Joan Beaufort, a cousin of HENRY V of England, whom he married in 1424. He was acquisitive and vindictive, and his ruthlessness towards the descendants of ROBERT II's second marriage led to his murder at Perth.

### James I (of England) ▶ JAMES VI AND I

### James II (1430–60)
King of Scots (1437/60). The son of JAMES I of Scotland, he came to the throne at the age of six, and took control of the government in 1449. The early years of his personal rule were dominated by his efforts to curb the power of the mighty Douglases, whom he eventually defeated in 1455. He later attempted to recover Roxburgh Castle from the English, and was killed during the siege. ▶ DOUGLAS

### James II (of England) ▶ JAMES VII AND II

### James III (1452–88)
King of Scots (1460/88). The eldest son of JAMES II of Scotland, he came to the throne at the age of eight, and took control of the government in 1469. His marriage in that year to Margaret of Denmark led to the incorporation of Orkney and Shetland within the Scottish realm (1472). He was defeated and killed by rebel nobles at the Battle of Sauchieburn, near Stirling.

### James IV (1473–1513)
King of Scots (1488/1513). The eldest son of JAMES III of Scotland, he became active in government at his accession, at the age of 15, and gradually exerted his authority over the nobility. In 1503 he married MARGARET TUDOR, the eldest daughter of HENRY VII: an alliance which led ultimately to the union of the crowns. However, he adhered to the French alliance when HENRY VIII joined the HOLY LEAGUE against France, and was induced to invade England by the French. He was defeated and killed, along with the flower of his nobility, at the Battle of FLODDEN.

### James V (1512–42)
King of Scots (1513/42). The son of JAMES IV of Scotland, and an infant at his father's death, he grew up amid the struggle between the pro-French and pro-English factions in his country. In 1536 he visited France, marrying Magdeleine, the daughter of FRANCIS I (1537), and after her death, Mary of Guise (1538). War with England followed from the French alliance (1542), and after an attempt to invade England, he was routed at Solway Moss. He retired to Falkland Palace, Fife, where he died soon after the birth of his daughter, Mary (later, MARY, QUEEN OF SCOTS).

### James VI and I (1566–1625)
King of Scotland (1567/1625) as James VI and, as James I, the first Stuart King of England and Ireland (1603/25). He was the son of MARY, QUEEN OF SCOTS, and Henry, Lord DARNLEY. On his mother's forced abdication, he was proclaimed King, and brought up by several regents. When he began to govern for himself, he ruled through his favourites, which caused a rebellion, and a period of imprisonment. In 1589 he married Princess ANNE OF DENMARK. Hating Puritanism, he managed in 1600 to establish bishops in Scotland. On ELIZABETH I's death, he ascended the English throne because of his descent from MARGARET TUDOR, wife of JAMES IV of Scotland. At first well received, his favouritism again brought him unpopularity. ▶ ADDLED PARLIAMENT

### James VII and II (1633–1701)
King of Scotland, as James VII, and of England and Ireland, as James II (1685/8). The second son of CHARLES I of England, he escaped to Holland nine months before his father's execution. At the RESTORATION (1660) he was made Lord High Admiral of England, and commanded the fleet in the ANGLO-DUTCH WARS; but after converting to Catholicism he was forced to resign his post. The national ferment caused by the POPISH PLOT (1678) became so formidable that he had to retire to the Continent, and several unsuccessful attempts were made to exclude him from the succession. During his reign his actions in favour of Catholicism raised general indignation, and William, Prince of Orange, his son-in-law and nephew, was finally asked by leading clerics and landowners to invade. Deserted by ministers and troops, James escaped to France, where he was warmly received by LOUIS XIV. He made an ineffectual attempt to regain his throne in Ireland, which ended in the Battle of the BOYNE (1690), and remained at St Germain until his death.

### James, C(yril) L(ionel) R(obert) (1901–89)
Trinidadian writer, lecturer, political activist and cricket enthusiast. James's aim was the freedom of the black race through MARXISM and revolution. For his Trotskyite writings he was deported from the USA, while in Trinidad his former pupil, Eric WILLIAMS, the Prime Minister, put him under house arrest. His most influential book was *The Black Jacobins: Toussaint L'Ouverture and the San Domingo Revolution* (1938). ▶ TOUSSAINT L'OUVERTURE

### James, Jesse Woodson (1847–82)
US WILD WEST outlaw. Born in Clay County, Missouri, he joined a band of pro-Confederate guerrillas as a teenager, and at the war's end he and his brother Frank turned to robbery, leading a gang of outlaws from 1866. They carried out numerous bank and train robberies over a period of 15 years, until a large price was put on Jesse's head and he was shot by Robert Ford, a member of his own gang seeking the reward. Frank gave himself up and after his release lived the rest of his life on the family farm. Jesse became a legendary figure, celebrated in ballads and dime novels, and latterly in Hollywood films.

### Jameson, Sir Leander Starr, 1st Baronet (1853–1917)
South African politician. After studying medicine, he

set up in practice in Kimberley (1878). Through Cecil **RHODES**, 'Dr Jim' engaged in pioneer work, was in 1891 made administrator for the South Africa Company at Fort Salisbury, and won popularity among the whites for his lack of administrative scruple. In 1895 he withdrew the British South African Police from Mashonaland to Bechuanaland (Botswana) to support a supposed uprising of Uitlanders in Johannesburg. He invaded the Transvaal (the **JAMESON RAID**) on 29 Dec 1895, but the expected rising failed to materialize. At Krugersdorp, Jameson and his men were overpowered by a force of Boers, and after a sharp fight were compelled to surrender (2 Jan 1896). Handed over to the British authorities (July), Jameson was condemned in London to 15 months' imprisonment, but was released in Dec. In 1900 he was elected to the Cape Legislative Assembly, and in 1904–8 was (Progressive) Premier of Cape Colony. Made a baronet in 1911, he retired from politics the following year.

**Jameson Raid** (Dec 1895–Jan 1896)
An expedition against the South African Republic, which was supposed to link up with a revolt by white workers on the Rand and topple the government of President **KRUGER**. Leander Starr **JAMESON**, administrator for the South Africa Company at Fort Salisbury, led a detachment of British South Africa Police into the Transvaal, but they were easily defeated and arrested. The German Emperor, **WILLIAM II**, sent a telegram of congratulation to Kruger, and the incident caused a major government crisis in Britain as well as contributing to the tensions that led to the Boer War. ➤ **BOER WARS**

**Jamestown** (USA)
A deserted town, 15mi/24km inland from Chesapeake Bay, Virginia, USA, the site of the first successful British settlement in America. Excavated archaeologically (1934–56), it was founded in 1607 by 105 settlers as James Fort, but after 1699 was superseded as the capital of Virginia by Williamsburg, and abandoned.

**Janata Dal**
A minority Indian political party, led by V P **SINGH**, which governed India with the support of the BJP and CPIM during the period Dec 1989–Oct 1990. A faction of the Janata Dal, the Janata Dal (S), then held power, with Chandra Shekhar as Prime Minister, with the support of the much larger Congress (I) Party. It led a coalition government from 1996 to 1998, but the series of splits that followed have weakened its influence.

**Janata Vimukti Peramuna (People's Liberation Front)** ➤ **JVP**

**Janissaries**
An élite force of soldiers in the Turkish army established by **MURAD I** during the 14c. Originally recruited from among prisoners of war, they were later raised by **DEVŞIRME** (levy) from among the Christian subjects of the **OTTOMAN EMPIRE**. The recruits, who constituted a 'New Force' (*Yeni Çeri*, whence Janissary) of infantry, were converted to Islam, educated and given a military training. Always potentially mutinous and involved in power struggles at the Porte, they were finally disbanded after a revolt in Constantinople in 1826. ➤ **JANISSARIES, MASSACRE OF THE**

**Janissaries, Massacre of the** (June 1826)
Also known as the 'Auspicious Incident', the massacre was the result of a revolt of the **JANISSARIES** against the formation of the élite Eskinciyan corps, which they perceived as the usurper of their own privileged position. The Ottoman Sultan, **MAHMUD II**, had been paving the way for the dissolution of the Janissaries; over time, the corps had acquired a power out of all proportion to its original status and was riddled with corruption. By appointing personnel loyal to himself within the Janissary corps, winning over the religious hierarchy and establishing a popular perception of himself as a moderate reformer, Mahmud was able to muster sufficient force against the Janissaries to force them to retreat to their barracks. In the ensuing siege, the gates of the barracks were destroyed and troops moved in; those Janissaries in the open were slaughtered and the buildings of the depot were set ablaze, the Janissaries within perishing. Janissaries elsewhere in the empire were hunted down and the corps was abolished. ➤ **OTTOMAN EMPIRE**

**Jan Sangh**
'The Hindu People's Party' was the major Hindu nationalist political party until the rise of the BJP (Bharatiya Janata Party). It was formed in 1951 by Syama Prasad Mookerjee and leaders of the **RSS** (*Rashtriya Swayamsevak Sangh*), a militant Hindu cultural organization, in order to promote and represent Hindu political interests more effectively in government. It was most specifically designed to offer a national alternative to the secularist Congress Party of Jawaharlal **NEHRU**, from which Mookerjee himself had resigned in 1947. The Jan Sangh's support came primarily from the merchant and middle classes of the north Indian states. It is considered by its detractors to be a communal anti-Muslim political party with fascistic inclinations. This charge its members have always denied, although it has consistently demanded the maintenance of traditional Hindu institutions, replacement of English by Hindi as the sole official language of India, and has opposed concessions to Muslims. These, it has argued, are legitimate and appropriate policies in a predominantly Hindu society. On economic issues, it supported liberalization. The Jan Sangh merged into the Janata Party which ruled India under the leadership of Morarji **DESAI** in 1977–9, but broke away in the early 1980s to emerge as the BJP, the main opposition party from 1991 until it led a coalition government in 1998–9. ➤ **HINDU MAHASABHA**

**Jansenism**
A heretical movement in the Roman Catholic Church in France and Holland in the 17c and 18c. It followed the teaching of Cornelius Jansen, who adopted the theology of St Augustine, particularly on predestination, and promulgated a rigorous and ascetic way of life. Condemned by the Papal Bull *Unigenitus* (1713), which was accepted in France in 1720, Jansenism was nevertheless defended by a party in the French Church and protected by the *Parlements*, who had their revenge on the Jesuits, seen as the chief agents of the papal campaign against Jansenism, in 1764,

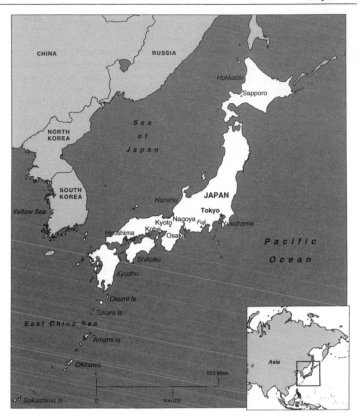

with the expulsion of the Jesuits from France. It has also survived in the Netherlands in the **OLD CATH-OLIC CHURCH**. ➤ **PARLEMENT**

## JAPAN

An island state off the east coast of Asia. It comprises the four large islands of Hokkaido, Honshu, Kyushu and Shikoku, and many small islands. Originally occupied by the Ainu, in the 4c the country developed from individual communities into small states; by the 5c, the Yamato Dynasty was the most dominant. Its culture was strongly influenced by China (8–12c). It was united and ruled by shoguns from 1603 by the Tokugawa Dynasty of military dictators, who tamed the feudal lords. Contact with the West was severely restricted until the visit of the US Commodore Matthew **PERRY** in 1853. After the **MEIJI RESTORATION** in 1868, successful wars were waged with China in 1894–5, and Russia in 1904–5. Japan annexed Korea in 1910, occupied **MANCHURIA** in 1931–2 and entered **WORLD WAR II** with a surprise attack on the US fleet at **PEARL HARBOR**, Hawaii, in 1941. It occupied British and Dutch possessions in South-East Asia (1941–2), but was pushed back during 1943–5. Atomic bombs were dropped on **HIROSHIMA** and **NAGASAKI** in 1945. There was strong economic growth in the 1960s, which was severely affected by the international oil crisis in the 1970s. Investment in other countries led to increased economic success and a trade surplus with most trading partners, but Japan suffered in the global recession of the 1990s, its huge banking sector being particularly hard hit by a massive slump, and in the 1997 Asian economic crisis, and its economy has since been in deep trouble. In 1993 the **LIBERAL**

**DEMOCRATIC PARTY** (LDP) lost power for the first time since 1955, but after three short-lived coalition governments in 1993–5, the LDP's Ryutaro Hashimoto became Prime Minister of a new coalition in 1996. Following a sharp downturn in the economy, he was replaced in 1998 by Keizo Obuchi, who was replaced in turn in 2001 by Junichiro Koizumi, who promised to transform the economy. ➤ **DOKEN KOKKA**; **KEIRETSU**; **ZAIBATSU**

**Japan Communist Party** (JCP; *Nihon Kyosanto*) Formed in July 1922 as a branch of the **COMINTERN**, it was to remain a small and illegal organization until 1945. Severe government repression in the late 1920s and in the 1930s resulted in many members being imprisoned. With Japan's defeat in 1945 and the ensuing US occupation, the JCP was legalized and played a leading role in the workers' movement of the late 1940s. In the 1946 elections the party garnered 2.1 million votes, obtaining five seats in the lower house. The suppression of the left-wing movement that coincided with the outbreak of the **KOREAN WAR** in 1950 forced the JCP underground and some of its members resorted to terrorist tactics. After the mid-1950s, under the leadership of Miyamoto Kenji, the JCP adopted a gradualist approach and regained parliamentary ground. In 1980 the party won 29 lower house seats with nearly 10 per cent of the popular vote. Communist-backed candidates were also elected mayors of several cities. The JCP remains one of Japan's largest political parties in terms of active membership and has increasingly adopted a nationalist orientation.

**Japan Socialist Party** (JSP; *Nihon Shakaito*), now

## JAPANESE EMPERORS

The first 14 emperors (to Chuai) are regarded as legendary, and the regnal dates for the 15th to the 28th emperor (Senka), taken from the early Japanese chronicle *Nihon Shoki* are not considered to be authentic. The reign of an emperor is known by a name that is not necessarily the emperor's personal name.

| Regnal Dates | Name | Regnal Dates | Name | Regnal Dates | Name |
|---|---|---|---|---|---|
| 660/585BC | Jimmu | 749/58 | (Empress) Koken** | 1274/87 | Go-Uda |
| 581/549BC | Suizei | 758/64 | Junnin | 1287/98 | Fushimi |
| 549/511BC | Annei | 764/70 | (Empress) Shotoku** | 1298/1301 | Go-Fushimi |
| 510/477BC | Itoku | 770/81 | Konin | 1301/8 | Go-Nijo |
| 475/393BC | Kosho | 781/806 | Kammu | 1308/18 | Hanazono |
| 392/291BC | Koan | 806/9 | Heizei | 1318/39 | Go-Daigo |
| 290/215BC | Korei | 809/23 | Saga | 1339/68 | Go-Murakami |
| 214/158BC | Kogen | 823/33 | Junna | 1368/83 | Chokei |
| 158/98BC | Kaika | 833/50 | Nimmyo | 1383/92 | Go-Kameyama |
| 97/30BC | Sujin | 850/8 | Montoku | ▶*Northern Court* | |
| 29BC/AD70 | Suinin | 858/76 | Seiwa | 1331/3 | Kogon |
| 71/130 | Keiko | 876/84 | Yozei | 1336/48 | Komyo |
| 131/90 | Seimu | 884/7 | Koko | 1348/51 | Suko |
| 192/200 | Chuai | 887/97 | Uda | 1352/71 | Go-Kogon |
| 270/310 | Ojin | 897/930 | Daigo | 1371/82 | Go-Enyu |
| 313/99 | Nintoku | 930/46 | Suzaku | 1382/1412 | Go-Komatsu |
| 400/5 | Richu | 946/67 | Murakami | 1412/28 | Shoko |
| 406/10 | Hanzei | 967/9 | Reizei | 1428/64 | Go-Hanazono |
| 412/53 | Ingyo | 969/84 | En-yu | 1464/1500 | Go-Tsuchimikado |
| 453/6 | Anko | 984/6 | Kazan | 1500/26 | Go-Kashiwabara |
| 456/79 | Yuryaku | 986/1011 | Ichijo | 1526/57 | Go-Nara |
| 480/4 | Seinei | 1011/16 | Sanjo | 1557/86 | Ogimachi |
| 485/7 | Kenzo | 1016/36 | Go-Ichijo | 1586/1611 | Go-Yozei |
| 488/98 | Ninken | 1036/45 | Go-Suzaku | 1611/29 | Go-Mizuno-o |
| 498/506 | Buretsu | 1045/68 | Go-Reizei | 1629/43 | (Empress) Meisho |
| 507/31 | Keitai | 1068/72 | Go-Sanjo | 1643/54 | Go-Komyo |
| 531/5 | Ankan | 1072/86 | Shirakawa | 1654/63 | Go-Sai |
| 535/9 | Senka | 1086/1107 | Horikawa | 1663/87 | Reigen |
| 539/71 | Kimmei | 1107/23 | Toba | 1687/1709 | Higashiyama |
| 572/85 | Bidatsu | 1123/41 | Sutoku | 1709/35 | Nakamikado |
| 585/7 | Yomei | 1141/55 | Konoe | 1735/47 | Sakuramachi |
| 587/92 | Sushun | 1155/8 | Go-Shirakawa | 1747/62 | Momozono |
| 592/628 | (Empress) Suiko | 1158/65 | Nijo | 1762/70 | (Empress) |
| 629/41 | Jomei | 1165/8 | Rokujo | | Go-Sakuramachi |
| 642/5 | (Empress) Kogyoku* | 1168/80 | Takakura | 1770/9 | Go-Momozono |
| 645/54 | Kotoku | 1180/3 | Antoku | 1779/1817 | Kokaku |
| 655/61 | (Empress) Saimei* | 1183/98 | Go-Toba | 1817/46 | Ninko |
| 662/71 | Tenji | 1198/1210 | Tsuchimikado | 1846/66 | Komei |
| 671/2 | Kobun | 1210/21 | Juntoku | 1867/1912 | Meiji |
| 673/86 | Temmu | 1221 | Chukyo | 1912/26 | Taisho |
| 686/97 | (Empress) Jito | 1221/32 | Go-Hirakawa | 1926/89 | Shōwa |
| 697/707 | Mommu | 1232/42 | Shijo | 1989/ | Heisei |
| 707/15 | (Empress) Gemmei | 1242/6 | Go-Saga | | |
| 715/24 | (Empress) Gensho | 1246/59 | Go-Fukakusa | | |
| 724/49 | Shomu | 1259/74 | Kameyama | | |

*Same empress although reigns have different names
**Same empress although reigns have different names

called the **Social Democratic Party of Japan** (SDPJ)

Japan's largest opposition party. Socialism was introduced to Japan at the end of the 19c and the country's first socialist party was formed in 1901, but was banned by the government two days later. Although several anti-communist 'proletarian' parties did emerge during the 1920s and contested Diet elections, they were all banned in the 1930s, except for the Socialist Masses Party (*Shakai Taishuto*), which supported the aggressive nationalism of the Japanese militarists. The JSP was formed in Nov 1945, winning a plurality of seats in the 1947 elections for the lower house. The party then led a coalition government (1947–8) under **KATAYAMA TETSU**, the only time the JSP had been in power, before economic crisis and internal rivalries led to its downfall. The party has been plagued by a left–right division; in 1951–5 it split over the 1951 Security Treaty with the USA, while in 1959 a right-wing faction withdrew to form the Democratic Socialist Party. Despite losing public support in the 1960s and 1970s, the JSP remained the largest opposition party, and championed neutralism and a non-nuclear defence policy. After 1986, under the leadership of **DOI TAKAKO**, the JSP gained additional public support, making important gains in the 1989 and 1990 elections. The party suffered a setback in 1991 local elections, however, and Doi was replaced by Masashi Ishibashi. From 1993 it took part in coalition governments, and in 1994–6 supplied Japan's first socialist Prime Minister since 1948, Murayama Tomiichi. The party has been known as the Social Democratic Party of Japan since 1996. In 1998 it lost many members to the newly formed Democratic Party of Japan, leaving it Japan's smallest political party.

### Jarring, Gunnar (1907–2002)
Swedish diplomat. He was appointed a special representative to the **UN**, with responsibilities for the Middle East, in late 1965. However, despite many visits to the Middle East in the period 1967–9, he was unable to generate any real enthusiasm amongst either Israelis or Arabs in his attempts to gain acceptance of UN Resolution 242, aimed at a Middle Eastern settlement, with the Israeli return of territories occupied in the wake of the **SIX-DAY WAR** of 1967. After the civil war in Jordan in late 1970, he was again involved in trying to broker a peace settlement in the area.

### Jarrow March (Oct 1936)
A march to London by unemployed workers in the Durham shipbuilding and mining town, to put the unemployed case. Jarrow was among the towns worst affected by the Depression, and the march took place at a time when the economy was recovering in much of the rest of the country. It alerted the more prosperous South and Midlands to the intractable problems of depressed areas.

### Jaruzelski, Wolciech Witold (1923– )
Polish general and President. He took part in the Soviet liberation of Poland from German occupation in 1944–5. Afterwards he rose to become Chief of the General Staff in 1965, Minister of Defence in 1968, a full member of the Politburo in 1971, and First Secretary of the Communist Party and Prime Minister in 1981. In Dec of that year, in order to end the power of the free trade union, **SOLIDARITY**, to prevent the break-up of **COMMUNISM** in Poland and to obviate Soviet intervention, and, at the same time, to promote moderate economic reform, he introduced martial law, which he only partially lifted a year later. His many attempts to find a middle way proved unsuccessful and in 1988 he had to negotiate a reform package with Solidarity. The communists lost power in the consequent elections that year, and Jaruzelski became a token President until Lech **WAŁESA** was ready to run for election himself in 1990. Although a sad figure at the end, he did not entirely fail. It was probably largely due to him that the USSR did not invade Poland in 1981 and that the eventual transfer of power was essentially peaceful.

### Jassy, Treaty of (1792)
This treaty confirmed the terms of the 1774 Treaty of **KUCHUK KAINARJI** and ended the Russo-Turkish War of 1787–92. The war had begun as a combined Russo-Austrian assault on the **OTTOMAN EMPIRE**, intended to partition it. Austria, however, quickly withdrew,

and **CATHERINE II, THE GREAT** had to abandon her 'Grand Plan'. Nevertheless, under General **SUVOROV**'s command, Catherine's armies conquered the entire northern shores of the Black Sea. Under the treaty, Russia extended her lands to the Dniester River, but returned Bessarabia and **MOLDAVIA AND WALLACHIA** to Ottoman rule. ► **RUSSO-TURKISH WARS**

### Jaszi, Oszkar (1875–1957)
Hungarian politician and scholar. Before **WORLD WAR I** he held an appointment at the Ministry of Agriculture, but he was too radical in his views to progress far in administration or in politics. He was close to the Social Democrats in opposing vestiges of feudalism and in supporting minority rights against the prevailing policy of Magyarization; but in 1914 he founded his own Radical Party. After the war he tried to woo the minority peoples, but in the wake of the peace settlement this proved unpopular with the Magyars. In 1919 he left for the USA where he wrote extensively on Central Europe.

### Jaurès, (Auguste Marie Joseph) Jean (1859–1914)
French political leader, writer and orator. He lectured on philosophy at Toulouse, then became a moderate republican deputy in 1885. Defeated in 1889, he returned to parliament as a socialist; defeated again in 1898, he campaigned on behalf of **DREYFUS**, and founded the *Parti socialiste français* ('French Socialist Party'), which, unlike its rival the *Parti socialiste de France* ('Socialist Party of France'), led by Jules **GUESDE**, supported Dreyfus and ministerial participation. Jaurès was persuaded to drop the latter policy as the price to pay for unification of the two factions in the United Socialist Party, known officially as the SFIO (*Section française de l'Internationale ouvrière*, 'French Section of the Workers' International') in 1905, but he retained much influence in parliament until his assassination in 1914. He helped to found the socialist newspaper *L'Humanité* (1904), and wrote in it frequently; the need to avert a war between the Great Powers was a major theme. ► **SOCIALIST PARTY** (France)

### Jawara, Alhaji Sir Dawda Kairaba (1924– )
Gambian politician. Educated at a Muslim primary school, Methodist Boys' GS Bathurst and Achimota College (Ghana), he continued his veterinary studies at Glasgow and Edinburgh universities. He returned to the Gambia as a veterinary officer (1954–60), before entering politics as leader of the People's Progressive Party, becoming Minister of Education (1960–2) and Prime Minister at independence in 1963. On the Gambia becoming a republic in 1970 he became President. He was re-elected in 1972, 1977, 1983 and 1987, despite an abortive coup against him in 1981, which was put down by Senegalese troops and paved the way for the creation of the short-lived confederation of **SENEGAMBIA**. He was overthrown in another coup in 1994.

### Jay, John (1745–1829)
US politician and jurist. Educated at King's (now Columbia) College, New York, he was admitted to the Bar in 1768. He was elected to the **CONTINENTAL CONGRESS** (1774–5), becoming its President in 1778. He helped negotiate (1781–3) peace with Great Britain under the Treaty of Paris, and he served as

Secretary for Foreign Affairs (1784–9). Jay contributed to the **FEDERALIST PAPERS** in an effort to secure ratification of the Constitution. He became the first Chief Justice of the Supreme Court (1789–95), and in that capacity negotiated **JAY'S TREATY**. From 1795 to 1801 he was Governor of New York. ► **AMERICAN REVOLUTION**

**Jayatilaka, Sir Baron** (1868–1944)
Ceylonese lawyer and official representative of the Ceylon government in India. Educated in Colombo and Oxford, Jayatilaka became an advocate at the Supreme Court of Ceylon in 1913. He was a member of the Legislative Council of Ceylon from 1924 to 1931. During his career he held office as the Vice-Chairman of the Board of Ministers, the Leader of the State Council, and the Minister of Home Affairs, Ceylon. Jayatilaka also revised and edited a number of old Sinhalese works.

**Jayavarman VII** (c.1120–c.1218)
Ruler of the Cambodian kingdom of Angkor (1181/ c.1218). His reign was marked by vigorous building construction, notably of the city of **ANGKOR THOM** and of its central shrine, the Bayon. These are among the most remarkable constructions in the ancient world, although the demands which their erection placed upon the resources of Angkor may well have exhausted the state. Certainly, his successors did not undertake any further monumental constructions. Jayavarman VII also extended the authority of Angkor, making claims over parts of Burma (now Myanmar) and the Malay Peninsula.

**Jayawardene, J(unius) R(ichard)** (1906–96)
Sri Lankan politician. After studying law in Colombo, he became a member of the State Council (1943) and the House of Representatives (1947). Honorary Secretary of the Ceylon National Congress (1940–7), he went on to hold office as Minister of Finance (1947–53), Vice-President of the **UNP** (United National Party) and Deputy Leader of the Opposition (1960–5). As Leader of the Opposition after the 1970 election defeat, he rebuilt the UNP's organization and led it to a landslide victory in 1977, when he became Prime Minister. The following year he became the country's first Executive President under a new constitution and he won a second term of office in 1982. In 1988 he retired and was succeeded by his Prime Minister, Ranasinghe **PREMADASA**. His period as head of state was marked by his pro-Western 'open economy' policies and by deteriorating relations between the **SINHALA** and **TAMIL** communities, culminating in the 1987 **INDO-SRI LANKAN PEACE ACCORD** and the second **JVP** (People's Liberation Front) insurrection of 1987–9.

**Jay's Treaty** (1794)
An agreement between the USA and Britain to end the British occupation of military posts in the northwestern parts of US territory, and for altering the terms of US commerce with Britain and its colonies. Negotiated by John **JAY**, it was very unpopular with the US public, largely because of the restrictions it imposed on US trade with the West Indies.

**jaziyah**
The 'poll tax' levied upon non-Muslims in India by Islamic rulers who tolerated idolatry on payment of tribute. According to strict Islamic law, this poll tax was payable only by Jews and Christians, but these rulers claimed it from their Hindu subjects as commutation money for not embracing Islam. The *jaziyah* was abolished in Kashmir by Zain-ul-Abidin in the early 15c, and **AKBAR THE GREAT** abolished it in 1579. However, **AURANGZEB** reimposed the jaziyah in 1679, forcing many poor Hindus to convert to Islam in order to escape payment. **MUHAMMAD SHAH** proclaimed but abandoned the poll tax in 1720, and declined later to levy it.

**Jebtsundamba Khutuktu**
Literally 'living Buddha', this was the title given to the head of the Tibetan Buddhist (Lamaist) Church in outer Mongolia between the 17c and the early decades of the 20c. The installation of the *Jebtsundamba Khutuktu* took place at a time when the **QING DYNASTY** was extending its control throughout Mongolia and promoting the Yellow Sect of the Tibetan Lamaist Church there. The eighth, and last, Jebtsundamba Khutuktu (1870–1924) was a Tibetan who was enthroned as head of state (*bogdo-khan*) in 1912 when a republican revolution in China that overthrew the Qing Dynasty enabled Outer Mongolia to break free from Chinese control. The Mongolian People's Party, founded in 1921 with the support of the USSR, declared a republic in 1924, and on the Jebtsundamba Khutuktu's death the same year no successor was chosen.

**Jefferson, Thomas** (1743–1826)
US politician and 3rd President. He became a lawyer (1767) and a member of the Virginia House of Burgesses. A delegate to the Second **CONTINENTAL CONGRESS** (1775), he drafted the **DECLARATION OF INDEPENDENCE**. Jefferson was Governor of Virginia (1779–81), Minister to France (1785) and Secretary of State (1790). He served as Vice-President under John **ADAMS** (1797–1801) and as President (1801–9). Important events of his administration include the **LOUISIANA PURCHASE** (1803) and the Embargo Act of 1807. After he retired to Monticello, he founded the University of Virginia.

**Jeffreys, George, 1st Baron Jeffreys of Wem** (1648–89)
English judge. Called to the Bar in 1668, he was knighted (1677) and became Recorder of London (1678). He was active in the **POPISH PLOT** prosecutions, became Chief Justice of Chester (1680), baronet (1681) and Chief Justice of the King's Bench (1683). In every state trial he proved a willing tool of the crown, and was raised to the peerage by **JAMES II** (1685). His journey to the West country to try the followers of **MONMOUTH** earned the name of the 'BLOODY ASSIZES' for its severity. He was Lord Chancellor (1685–8), but on James's flight was imprisoned in the Tower of London, where he died.

**Jelačić, Josip** (1801–59)
Croatian politician and soldier. The Croatian national hero in the struggle against the Magyars, he was appointed Ban (Viceroy) of Croatia in 1848 by the Vienna government, which hoped he would secure Croatian support for Austria in the impending clash with the Magyar nationalists. He led the Croatian *sabor* (parliament) in its declaration of independence

from Hungary, a move which temporarily lost him his office (Jun 1848). He was reinstated later the same year and, at Scwechat, defeated the Hungarian troops of Artúr **GÖRGEY** which were marching on Vienna. Within Croatia, he oversaw the liberation of the serfs. He was made a count in 1855.

### Jellicoe, John Rushworth Jellicoe, 1st Earl (1859–1935)

British admiral. He became Third Sea Lord (1908), and was Commander-in-Chief, Grand Fleet at the outbreak of **WORLD WAR I**. His main engagement was the inconclusive Battle of **JUTLAND** (1916), for which at the time he was much criticized. Promoted First Sea Lord, he organized the defences against German submarines, and was made Admiral of the Fleet (1919). He later became Governor of New Zealand (1920–4). He was created an earl in 1925.

### Jemappes, Battle of (6 Nov 1792)

Fought between the Austrians and the French in present-day Belgium during the **FRENCH REVOLUTIONARY WARS**, the battle was decisively won by the French General **DUMOURIEZ**. For the Austrian southern Netherlands (now Belgium) the French victory was crucial, because in 1793 they were annexed as part of revolutionary France.

### Jena and Auerstädt, Battles of (1806)

French military victories of the **NAPOLEONIC WARS**, both fought in Saxony on 14 Oct 1806 between two French armies under **NAPOLEON I** and **DAVOUT** and combined Prussian-Saxon forces The French smashed the obsolete Prussian army inherited from **FREDERICK II, THE GREAT**, enforcing the reduction of **PRUSSIA** to half its former size. ➤ **GRAND ALLIANCE, WAR OF THE; TILSIT, TREATIES OF**

### Jenkins, Roy Harris, Baron Jenkins of Hillhead (1920–2003)

British politician. He became a Labour MP in 1948, and was Minister of Aviation (1964–5), Home Secretary (1965–7), Chancellor of the Exchequer (1967–70), Deputy Leader of the **LABOUR PARTY** in opposition (1970–2) and again Home Secretary (1974–6). He resigned as an MP in 1976 to take up the presidency of the European Commission (1977–81). Upon his return to Britain, he co-founded the **SOCIAL DEMOCRATIC PARTY** (1981), and became its first leader, standing down after the 1983 election in favour of David **OWEN**. Defeated in the 1987 election, he was given a life peerage and also became Chancellor of Oxford University ➤ **LIBERAL PARTY** (UK)

### Jenkins' Ear, War of

A war between Britain and Spain starting in 1739, and soon merging into the wider War of the **AUSTRIAN SUCCESSION** (1740–8). Some of the violent anti-Spanish indignation in Britain that provoked the war was due to Captain Robert Jenkins, who claimed to have had an ear cut off by Spanish coastguards in the Caribbean.

### Jesuits' Estates Act (1888)

A Quebec statute by which Honoré **MERCIER**'s administration disposed of the compensation for Jesuit property sequestrated by the crown when the Order was suppressed in the late 18c. After its re-establishment in Quebec (1842), successive governments had been unable to solve the question of how to allot the compensation, which had to be spent on education. The property was valued at C$400,000 and the Act granted C$70,000 to the province's Protestant schools while the rest was to be divided within the Catholic community at the pope's discretion. In Quebec this seemed a sensible solution, but in Ontario the **ORANGE ORDER** was enraged, and charged Mercier with inviting the pope to intervene in Canadian affairs. John A **MACDONALD**, however, refused to disallow the Act as it fell clearly within provincial powers over education.

### Jewish Agency

The executive body of the **WORLD ZIONIST ORGANIZATION**, established in 1922 as the Jewish Agency for Palestine. The shorter title was adopted in 1929 and, until 1948, the Jewish Agency regulated the **YISHUV**'s relations with world Jewry and the British authorities. The latter recognized its oversight of Jewish affairs in **PALESTINE** and its role as negotiator for the Zionist position. Although many of its functions passed to the Israeli government after 1948, the Agency continued to be involved in immigration and agricultural settlement, as well as in education abroad. With headquarters in Jerusalem and New York, the Agency was reconstituted in 1971 to take account of relations with non-Zionists. ➤ **BALFOUR DECLARATION**

### Jewish Labour Movement in Palestine

Labour was an issue which preoccupied many Jewish settlers in **PALESTINE** in the late 19c and early 20c, including David **BEN-GURION**. This stemmed from Zionist-socialist critiques of the situation of Russian and European Jewry, who were experiencing both emancipation and anti-Semitism. Their aim was to create a Jewish homeland to whose economy Jews themselves would contribute through a complete range of occupations. Numerous trade unions and political parties resulted in the early 1900s. Most of the unions combined in 1920 to form the **HISTADRUT**, while the **MAPAI PARTY** became the main socialist party of the **YISHUV** and, after 1948, the State of Israel. ➤ **ALIYAH; ZIONISM**

### Jewish National Fund

The fund established (Dec 1901) by the **WORLD ZIONIST ORGANIZATION**, with the aim of buying land in **PALESTINE**. Although initially based in Vienna, its headquarters were in Jerusalem by 1922. The fund spent most of its first 45 years acquiring land in Palestine for Jewish settlement, so that by 1947 it possessed 234,000 acres/95,000 hectares. It operated leases of 49 years to its lessees, based on Leviticus 25:10, 23–4. Since Israeli independence in 1948, the Fund has concentrated on land improvement, irrigation and afforestation. Supported by worldwide Jewish contributions, it is headed by a board of directors. ➤ **JEWISH AGENCY**

### Jews, Expulsion of the (31 Mar 1492)

This decree, expelling Jews from Spain, was issued by King **FERDINAND II, THE CATHOLIC** and Queen **ISABELLA I, THE CATHOLIC**. It was influenced in part by the Spanish **INQUISITION**, which believed that the presence of Jews encouraged **CONVERSOS** to practise Judaism. Jews were given four months to accept baptism or leave the country; the edict was in fact one of conversion and not of expulsion. A high proportion converted, including important community leaders, and others returned even after leaving, so that the final number of expulsions was probably less than 50,000. Those who left went mainly to Portugal (where a forced conversion was decreed in 1497), North Africa and Italy; there is no evidence of emigration to Turkey until much later. The expulsions had no significant impact on the economy of Spain, since Jews had been a small and persecuted minority with no access to commerce or the major professions. Some Spanish leaders criticized the decree, and in the early 17c there were proposals, considered seriously by the Count-Duke of OLIVARES, to allow the émigrés back to Spain.

### Jiang Jieshi ► CHIANG KAI-SHEK

### Jiang Jing'guo (Chiang Ching-kuo) (1910–88)
Taiwanese politician. The son of CHIANG KAI-SHEK, he studied in the USSR during the early 1930s, returning to China with a Russian wife in 1937 at the time of the Japanese invasion. After the defeat of Japan in 1945, he held a number of government posts before fleeing with his father and the defeated GUO-MINDANG forces to Taiwan in 1949. He became Defence Minister (1965–72), and then Prime Minister (1972–8). He succeeded to the post of Guomindang leader on his father's death (1975) and became state President in 1978. Under his stewardship, Taiwan's post-war 'economic miracle' continued, but in the political sphere there was repression. During the closing years of his life, with his health failing, he instituted a progressive programme of political liberalization and democratization which was continued by his successor, LEE TENG-HUI.

### Jiang Qing (Chiang Ch'ing) (1914–91)
Chinese politician. She trained in drama and literature, and then became an actress in Shanghai. In 1936 she went to Yenan to study Marxist–Leninist theory, met MAO ZEDONG and became his third wife in 1939. She was attached to the Ministry of Culture (1950–4), and in the 1960s began her attacks on bourgeois influences in the arts and literature. One of the leaders of the CULTURAL REVOLUTION, she was elected to the Politburo (1969), but after Mao's death (1976) was arrested with three others – the GANG OF FOUR – imprisoned, expelled from the Communist Party and tried in 1980. She was sentenced to death, but the sentence was later suspended.

### Jiangxi (Kiangsi) Soviet
The most important rural base area under the control of the Chinese Communist Party (CCP) between 1930 and 1934. It had its origins in MAO ZEDONG's decision to abandon the cities and create a peasant-based Red Army controlling the countryside. Emphasis henceforth was on 'protracted revolution', in which liberated rural base areas would eventually surround the cities. Mao began (Feb 1930) organizing a rural soviet in the southern province of Jiangxi, which was to become the most important of several such soviets established in this region with control over an estimated 3 million inhabitants. In Nov 1931 the First National Congress of the Chinese Soviet Republic formally established a soviet government under Mao. After 1932, however, when the Moscow-trained urban party leadership came to Jiangxi, Mao lost influence. His flexible attitude towards rich peasants was condemned, while his guerrilla tactics were replaced by a strategy of conventional warfare to confront the series of encirclement campaigns launched against the soviet by CHIANG KAI-SHEK's Nationalist armies. By the end of 1933, the Jiangxi Soviet had to be abandoned and the communists embarked on the LONG MARCH that would take them to the far north-west of China.

### Jiang Zemin (Chiang Tse-min) (1926–)
Chinese politician. The son-in-law of former President LI XIAN'NIAN, after university he began a career as an electrical engineer and trained in the USSR. He was Commercial Counsellor at the Chinese Embassy in Moscow (1950–6) and during the 1960s and 1970s held a number of posts in the heavy and power industry ministries. Elected to the Chinese Communist Party (CCP)'s Central Committee in 1982, he was appointed Mayor of Shanghai in 1985. Here he gained a reputation as a cautious reformer, loyal to the party line. He was inducted into the CCP's Politburo in 1987 and in June 1989, following the TIANANMEN SQUARE massacre and the dismissal of ZHAO ZIYANG, was elected Party Leader, a post he held until 2002. He was President from 1993 to 2003, and was succeeded by Hu Jintao. Fluent in English and Russian, Jiang, a compromise figure, maintained China's 'open door' economic strategy.

### jihad
Literally meaning 'striving' in Arabic, the term is often used with the specific sense of struggling against enemies of Islam in 'holy war'. According to the Quran, Muslims have a duty to oppose those who reject Islam, by armed struggle if necessary, and jihad has been invoked to justify both the expansion and defence of Islam.

### Jim Crow Laws
A term used to characterize US state laws passed from the 1890s onwards, to segregate blacks from whites in the south in schools, public transport, housing and other areas. They were gradually abolished from the mid-20c, largely because of the CIVIL RIGHTS MOVEMENT, which led to Supreme Court decisions and changes in Federal policies. ► PLESSY V FERGUSON

### Jin (Chin) Dynasty ► CHINESE DYNASTIES PRE-1000AD

### Jin (Jurchen) Dynasty
A dynasty in northern China (1122–1234) founded by the Jurchen tribe that captured (1126) Kaifeng, the capital of the SONG DYNASTY. Following this success, a frontier was established with the southern Song along the Huai River. It was finally destroyed by the MONGOLS in 1234.

### Jinggangshan (Ching-Kang shan)
The mountain stronghold on the border between the central Chinese provinces of Hunan and Jiangxi where MAO ZEDONG took the survivors of his armed force that had participated in one of the abortive AUTUMN HARVEST UPRISINGS in 1927. During the ensuing year, Mao began the task of building a Red Army,

recruiting from amongst vagrants and bandits as well as agricultural labourers and poor peasants. Mao also carried out a radical land redistribution policy, although he later adopted a more flexible policy towards rich peasants. He was forced to abandon Jinggangshan in 1928 following repeated Nationalist attacks, and moved to south-east Jiangxi where he was to create the first rural soviet. ► JIANGXI SOVIET

### Jinnah, Muhammad Ali (1876–1948)
Indian Muslim politician and founder of Pakistan. Educated in Bombay and London, he was called to the Bar in 1897, and practised in Bombay. He became a member of the INDIAN NATIONAL CONGRESS (1906) and the MUSLIM LEAGUE (1913), and supported Hindu–Muslim unity until 1930, when he resigned from the Congress following disagreement over the demands attached to M K GANDHI's programme of CIVIL DISOBEDIENCE. His advocacy of a separate state for Muslims led to the creation of Pakistan in 1947, and he became its first Governor-General.

### Joan of Arc, St, known as the Maid of Orléans (c.1412–1431)
French patriot and martyr. She halted the English ascendancy in France during the HUNDRED YEARS' WAR. Born into a peasant family, at the age of 13 she heard the voices of Saints Michael, Catherine and Margaret bidding her rescue France from English domination. She was taken to the DAUPHIN, and eventually allowed to lead the army assembled for the relief of Orléans. Clad in a suit of white armour and flying her own standard, she entered Orléans (1429), forced the English to retire, and took the Dauphin to be crowned CHARLES VII at Rheims. She then set out to relieve Compiègne, but was captured and sold to the English by John of Luxembourg. Put on trial (1431) for heresy and sorcery, she was found guilty by an English-dominated court, and burnt. She was canonized in 1920.

### Joan the Mad (Juana La Loca) (1479–1555)
Countess of Flanders and Queen of Castile (1505/55) and Aragon (1516/55). The daughter of FERDINAND II, THE CATHOLIC and ISABELLA I, THE CATHOLIC, she became the wife of PHILIP I, THE HANDSOME, of Flanders in 1495. The couple settled in Ghent and had several children, of whom the eldest was the future Emperor CHARLES V. On her mother's death (1504), she became Queen of Castile and she and Philip moved to Spain in 1506. Philip died the same year and Joan, who suffered from severe melancholia, was declared unfit to govern and was shut away under close watch in Tordesillas, while her father assumed the government of Castile (1510). Although Ferdinand died in 1516, Joan's son Charles, now King of Spain, did not release her and she remained incarcerated, along with her youngest daughter, Catalina, until her death.

### Jodl, Alfred (1890–1946)
German general and Nazi collaborator. An artillery subaltern in WORLD WAR I, he became HITLER's close associate. General of Artillery in 1940, he was the planning genius of the German High Command and Hitler's chief adviser. He was found guilty of war crimes at the NUREMBERG TRIALS (1946), and executed. ► WORLD WAR II

### Joffre, Joseph Jacques Césaire (1852–1931)
French general. He joined the army in 1870, and rose to be French Chief of Staff (1914) and Commander-in-Chief (1915), carrying out a policy of attrition against the German invaders of France. He retired as Commander-in-Chief and was made Marshal of France (1916). ► WORLD WAR I

### Jogjakarta ► YOGYAKARTA

### Johan III (of Sweden) ► JOHN III

### John ('John Lackland') (1167–1216)
King of England (1199/1216). The youngest son of HENRY II of England, he was one of the least popular monarchs in English history. He tried to seize the crown during RICHARD I's captivity in Germany (1193–4), but was forgiven and nominated successor by Richard, who thus set aside the rights of Prince ARTHUR, the son of John's elder brother Geoffrey. Arthur's claims were supported by PHILIP II of France, and after Arthur was murdered on John's orders (1203), Philip marched against him with superior forces and conquered all but a portion of Aquitaine (1204–5). In 1206 John refused to receive Stephen LANGTON as Archbishop of Canterbury, and in 1208 his kingdom was placed under papal interdict. He was then excommunicated (1209), and finally conceded (1213). His oppressive government, and failure to recover NORMANDY, provoked baronial opposition, which led to demands for constitutional reform. The barons met the King at Runnymede, and forced him to seal the Great Charter (MAGNA CARTA) (June 1215), the basis of the English constitution. His repudiation of the Charter precipitated the first Barons' War (1215–17). ► BARONS' WARS

### John I (c.1255–1294)
Duke of Brabant. As the second son of Henry III, he succeeded to the Duchy on the death of his older brother, Henry VI, in 1267. In 1270 he married Margaret of France (the daughter of LOUIS IX), and in 1271 Margaret, daughter of GUY OF DAMPIERRE. He increased the power of the Duchy of BRABANT, and obtained the Duchy of Limburg for his family as well.

### John II, the Good (1319–64)
King of France (1350/64). The son of PHILIP VI, in 1356 he was taken prisoner by EDWARD, THE BLACK PRINCE at the Battle of POITIERS (1356), and transported to England. After the Treaty of Brétigny (1360) he returned home, leaving his second son, the Duke of Anjou, as a hostage. When the duke broke his parole and escaped (1363), John chivalrously returned to London, and died there.

### John II Casimir Vasa (1609–72)
King of Poland (1648/68). The son of King SIGISMUND III VASA of Sweden, he was elected king to succeed his brother, WŁADYSŁAW IV VASA, in 1648. Throughout his reign he was faced with external and internal threats, sometimes combined, a sign of Poland's growing weakness. A successful Swedish invasion in 1655 forced him to take refuge in Silesia while moves were made to elect CHARLES X GUSTAV of Sweden in his place. John Casimir returned to Poland in 1656 with widespread support but hostilities continued until the Peace of Oliwa (1660). On his return, he had solemnly promised to alleviate the plight of the

Polish serfs and he made a strenuous effort to introduce constitutional reform (1660–1). However, all reformist legislation was opposed by conservative opponents and, when he persisted, they raised a bloody rebellion under their leader, Jerzy Lubomirski (1665–6). Although Lubomirski admitted defeat, John Casimir finally abdicated in 1668 and ended his life as a pensioner of LOUIS XIV in Paris.

### John II Comnenus (1088–1143)
Byzantine Emperor (1118/43). He succeeded his father, ALEXIUS I COMNENUS. In government he relied on trusted servants rather than his immediate family, some of whom, such as his sister ANNA COMNENA and brother Isaac, intrigued against him and were deprived of their positions. Apart from an abortive attempt to curtail the trading privileges of the Venetians, his energetic rule was distinguished by military and diplomatic success. In the Balkans his victory over the Patzinaks (1122) effectively ended a long-standing threat to the empire and was thereafter commemorated by a public holiday; in the east he recovered territory in Cilicia and asserted Byzantine overlordship over the Normans of Antioch (1137). He was killed in a hunting accident while on campaign. ► BYZANTINE EMPIRE

### John III (1300–55)
Duke of Brabant and of Limburg. He was the son of John II and Margaret of York, the daughter of King EDWARD I of England. At the start of the HUNDRED YEARS' WAR John tried to walk a tightrope between France and England; in 1338 he decided to secure the English wool staple at Antwerp by supporting England. When the staple was moved to Bruges in 1340, he switched to France.

### John III (1537–92)
King of Sweden (1569/92). He was the second son of King GUSTAV I VASA by his second wife, Margareta Leijonhufvud, and the half-brother and successor to ERIK XIV. Having been made Duke of Finland by his father, he married the Polish princess Katarina Jagełłonica, and embarked on his own pro-Polish foreign policy, which led to his imprisonment by King Erik. On his release, apparently reconciled to Erik, he joined his younger brother Charles (later, King CHARLES IX) in a rebellion which ended in Erik's deposition and John's accession to the throne. He brought the Seven Years' War with Denmark and Lübeck to an end with the Treaty of Stettin (1570) and thereafter fought against Russia in Livonia, side by side with his brother-in-law, SIGISMUND II AUGUSTUS of Poland, driving Tsar IVAN IV, THE TERRIBLE from the Baltic. An avid student of theology, he negotiated with the pope for the return of Sweden to the Catholic fold and introduced (1577) a Catholic liturgy (the 'Red Book'). His son, who was raised as a Catholic, was elected King of Poland in 1587 as SIGISMUND III VASA, and succeeded his father on the Swedish throne.

### John III Sobieski (1629–96)
King of Poland (1674/96). A military commander, or hetman, he defeated the Turks at Choczim in 1673, and was elected King the following year. He had ambitions in Germany but he was constantly plagued by Turkish incursions. In 1683 he raised the Turkish

siege of Vienna in a famous victory but, although he won European fame, he got little thanks from Austria. His later campaigns against the Turks were not equally successful. Domestic unrest and especially financial and religious difficulties clouded the last years of his reign.

### John (João) IV (1604–56)
King of Portugal (1640/56). As Duke of Braganza, he was the leading aristocrat and greatest landowner in Portugal. When the country freed itself from Spanish rule in 1640, he became King of the newly independent Portugal. Despite alliances with France, Sweden and the Dutch, and with Portugal's ancient ally, England, he was unable to secure Spanish recognition of independent Portugal during his lifetime.

### John IV (1831–89)
Emperor of Ethiopia (1868/89). He succeeded Emperor Theodore, who committed suicide after the Napier invasion of Ethiopia in 1867–8. Although John wielded even greater power in Ethiopia than his predecessor, his authority was threatened in the 1880s by the Italians in Eritrea, the Mahdist forces in the Sudan and King MENELIK of Shoa to the south. In 1882 John came to terms with Menelik, accepting him as his successor. He was killed in battle with the Mahdists in 1889. ► THEODORE, KASSAI

### John VI (1535–1606)
Count of Nassau-Dillenburg. The direct ancestor of the royal house of the Netherlands (Orange-Nassau), he was the eldest of the younger brothers of WILLIAM I, THE SILENT, Prince of Orange. He supported his brother during the EIGHTY YEARS' WAR against Spain, and became STADHOLDER of Gelderland in 1578, which he proceeded forcibly to convert to Calvinism. He did not always see eye to eye with his brother William, and returned to Germany in 1580. He was married three times and had 24 children.

### John XXII, originally Jacques Duèse (c.1249–1334)
French pope (1316/34). One of the most celebrated of the popes of Avignon, he intervened in the contest for the Imperial Crown between Louis of Bavaria and Frederick of Austria, supporting the latter. A long contest ensued both in Germany and Italy between the Guelf (papal) party and the Ghibelline (imperial) party. In 1327 Louis entered Italy, was crowned Emperor at Rome, and deposed the pope, setting up an anti-pope (1328). Although Guelf predominance at Rome was later restored, John died at Avignon. ► GHIBELLINES; GUELFS

### John XXIII, originally Baldassare Cossa (d.1419)
Anti-pope (1410/15). A scandalous and corrupt figure, he came to the papacy because of the conviction that his military skills were essential if Rome were to be won back from the dominion of Naples. He was one of three claimants to the papal throne, a rivalry which brought the GREAT SCHISM to its point of crisis. The Council of Constance eventually forced him to abdicate on grounds of simony, perjury and sodomy, and swear not to renege on the decision.

### John XXIII, originally Angelo Giuseppe Roncalli (1881–1963)
Italian pope (1958/63). Relatively old when he was elected pope and thought by many to be a stopgap,

he caused surprise in 1962 by calling an Ecumenical Council of the Roman Catholic Church, known as the Second **VATICAN COUNCIL** or Vatican II. This considered the position of the Church in the modern world, and one of its outcomes was the use of vernacular languages in the mass. He promoted social reform and cooperation with other religions, breaking new ground in 1960 when he met the Archbishop of Canterbury, Geoffrey Fisher, the first formal meeting between a pope and a head of the Anglican Church since the **REFORMATION**. He was beatified in 2000.

### John, Patrick (1937– )
Dominican politician. In the period before full independence he served in the government of Chief Minister Edward LeBlanc, and succeeded him in 1974. On independence in 1978 he became the country's first Prime Minister. His increasingly authoritarian style of government led to the loss of his assembly seat in 1980 and his replacement as Prime Minister by Eugenia **CHARLES**. The following year he was arrested for alleged complicity in a plot to overthrow Charles but was acquitted. A subsequent trial, in 1985, found him guilty and he was given a 12-year prison sentence.

### John Birch Society
A moderately sized, extreme right-wing pressure group in the USA which promotes conservative ideas and policies, and is strongly patriotic and anticommunist. Founded in 1958, it was named after a US missionary and intelligence officer who was killed by Chinese communists on 25 Aug 1945 and considered the first hero of the **COLD WAR**.

### John Frederick I, the Magnanimous (1503–54)
Elector of Saxony (1532/54). A Lutheran, he was involved in Imperial politics and the **SCHMALKALDIC LEAGUE** before he became Elector. He vacillated between support for Philip of Hesse and Emperor **CHARLES V**. He came near to war with his relative, **MAURICE**, Duke of Saxony, in 1541. Shortly after war broke out between Charles V and the Schmalkaldic League, John Frederick was placed under the Imperial ban. He was captured at the Battle of **MÜHLBERG** (24 Apr 1547) and held until May 1552. He was stripped of the electorate, a loss he accepted in the Treaty of Naumburg (Feb 1554).

### John George I (1585–1656)
Elector of Saxony. He succeeded his elder brother, Christian II, in 1611. A leading Lutheran prince, his native conservatism and his strong distaste for Calvinism made him an unsteady defender of Protestantism. During the **THIRTY YEARS' WAR** he at first supported the Catholic emperor **FERDINAND II**, before agreeing in 1631 to head a defensive Protestant alliance. His support for the cause remained lukewarm and in 1635 he signed the separate Peace of Prague with the emperor.

### John Lackland ► JOHN ('JOHN LACKLAND')

### John of Austria, Don (1547–78)
Spanish soldier. The illegitimate son of Emperor **CHARLES V**, he defeated the **MOORS** in Granada (1570) and the Turks at the Battle of **LEPANTO** (1571). In 1573 he took Tunis, and was then sent to Milan and (1576) to the Netherlands as Viceroy. He planned to marry **MARY, QUEEN OF SCOTS**, but died of typhoid at Namur.

### John of Gaunt (1340–99)
Duke of Lancaster. He was the fourth son of King **EDWARD III** of England, and ancestor of Kings **HENRY IV**, **V** and **VI** of England. In 1359 he married his cousin, Blanche of Lancaster, and through her succeeded to the dukedom in 1362. After her death (1369), he married Constance, daughter of **PEDRO THE CRUEL** of Castile, and assumed the title of King of Castile, though he failed by his expeditions to oust his rival, Henry of Trastámare. In England he became highly influential as a peacemaker during the troubled reign of **RICHARD II**. He was made Duke of Aquitaine by Richard (1390), and sent on several embassies to France. On his second wife's death (1394) he married his mistress, Catherine Swynford, by whom he had three sons; from the eldest descended **HENRY VII**.

### John of Nepomuk, St (c.1345–1393)
Catholic patron saint of Bohemia. He studied at the University of Prague, and became Vicar-General to the Archbishop of Prague. For crossing King **WENCESLAS IV**, who wished to create a new bishopric, he was tortured and drowned in the Vltava. He was canonized in 1729 as part of the Habsburg and Jesuit campaign to ensure that there was an appropriate Catholic martyr to set against popular veneration for the reformist martyr Jan **HUS**.

### John Paul II, originally Karol Józef Wojtyła (1920–2005)
Polish pope (1978/2005). The first non-Italian pope in 456 years, he was educated and ordained in Kraków in 1946, received further education in Rome and Lublin, and became Professor of Moral Theology at Lublin and Kraków. Archbishop and Metropolitan of Kraków (1964–78), he was created cardinal in 1967. Noted for his energy and analytical ability, his pontificate has seen many foreign visits, in which he has preached to huge audiences. In 1981 he survived an assassination attempt, when he was shot and wounded in St Peter's Square by a Turkish national, Mehmet Ali Agca, possibly at Bulgarian instigation. A champion of economic justice and an outspoken defender of the Church in communist countries, he has been uncompromising on moral issues. In the 1980s his visits to Poland and his meetings with Mikhail **GORBACHEV** were of great assistance to **SOLIDARITY** in promoting Polish independence, achieved in 1989. ► **POPE**

### John the Fearless (1371–1419)
Duke of Burgundy, the eldest son of **PHILIP THE BOLD**. His father's death in 1404 left him in possession of **BURGUNDY**, Flanders and Artois. He opposed Louis, Duke of **ORLÉANS**, brother of the periodically insane **CHARLES VI, THE FOOLISH**, whose assassination (1407) led to civil war between the Burgundian party and Orléans's supporters, the Armagnacs. John gained, lost and regained control of Paris, the King, and the government, but was murdered during a conference at Montereau-Faut-Yonne, probably at the instigation of the **DAUPHIN**, the future **CHARLES VII**. ► **ORLÉANS, HOUSE OF**

### John Zapolya ► ZAPOLYA, JOHN

**Johnson, Andrew** (1808–75)
US politician and 17th President. With little formal schooling, he became alderman and Mayor in Greeneville, Tennessee, and a member of the legislature (1835), state Senate (1841) and CONGRESS (1843). He was Governor of Tennessee (1853–7), and a US Senator (1857–62). During the AMERICAN CIVIL WAR he was made Military Governor of Tennessee (1862), and became Vice-President when Abraham LINCOLN was re-elected in 1864. On Lincoln's assassination (1865), he became President (1865–9). A Democrat, his RECONSTRUCTION policies were opposed by the Republican Congress, who wished to make reconstruction of the Southern states dependent on a measure of protection for black CIVIL RIGHTS. After he vetoed the CIVIL RIGHTS ACTS of 1866, his popularity declined rapidly. Politically motivated IMPEACHMENT proceedings were brought against him, but fell short of conviction by one vote. ► DEMOCRATIC PARTY

**Johnson, Hiram Warren** (1866–1945)
US lawyer and politician. He practised law in Sacramento and then from 1902 in San Francisco. A Progressive Republican, he was Governor of California in 1911–17, during which time he helped to organize the PROGRESSIVE PARTY and stood unsuccessfully as Theodore ROOSEVELT's running mate in 1912. He was then elected to the SENATE (1917–45) and became known for his isolationist views, strongly opposing the LEAGUE OF NATIONS and US involvement in the UN.

**Johnson, Lyndon B(aines),** known as **LBJ** (1908–73)
US politician and 36th President. Educated at Southwest Texas State Teachers College, he was a teacher and congressman's secretary before becoming a Democratic member of the HOUSE OF REPRESENTATIVES in 1937. He became a Senator in 1949, and later an effective Democratic majority leader (1954). Vice-President under John F KENNEDY in 1961, he assumed the presidency after Kennedy's assassination, and was elected to the office in 1964 with the biggest majority ever obtained in a presidential election until that time. His administration (1963–9) passed the Civil Rights Act of 1964 and the VOTING RIGHTS ACT of 1965, and his GREAT SOCIETY programme to reduce poverty, eliminate racial discrimination, provide medical care, and improve education. However, the escalation of the VIETNAM WAR led to large-scale marches and protests and to his growing unpopularity, and he decided not to seek re-election in 1968. ► CIVIL RIGHTS ACTS; DEMOCRATIC PARTY

**Johnston, Sir Harry H(amilton)** (1858–1927)
British administrator, explorer and artist. He played a significant part in the Partition of AFRICA. Trained as an artist, he also developed scientific and linguistic interests and in 1879 he went to Tunis to paint and explore. Later he travelled in Angola, the Congo and (1884) the Kilimanjaro region of East Africa, where he collected treaties with local chiefs. He subsequently served the Foreign Office in West Africa (1885–9), Lisbon (1889), Mozambique (1889–91), British Central Africa (Malawi, 1891–6), Tunis (1897–9) and Uganda (1899–1901). He is generally credited with inventing the phrase 'Cape to Cairo'.

**Joinville, Jean, Sire de** (c.1224–1317)
French historian. He took part in the unfortunate Seventh Crusade of LOUIS IX (1248–54) and was imprisoned at Acre, and ransomed. He returned with Louis to France, and lived partly at court and partly on his estates. Throughout the crusade he kept notes on events, which he later wrote up in his *Histoire de Saint Louis* (completed by 1309). ► CRUSADES, LATER

**Jonathan, Chief (Joseph) Leabua** (1914–87)
Lesotho chief and politician. Educated in mission schools before working in South African mines and then in local government in Basutoland, he entered politics in 1952. He joined the Basutoland National Council in 1956 and in 1959 founded the Basutoland National Party, which favoured a free enterprise economy and cordial relations with South Africa. He was elected to the Legco in 1960 and became Prime Minister in 1965 but he suspended the constitution in 1970. Parliamentary government was restored in 1973 and elections held regularly until 1985, when they were cancelled. He was overthrown in a military coup (Jan 1986).

**Jones, (John) Paul** (1747–92)
Scottish-born American naval commander. Originally named John Paul, he was apprenticed as a cabin boy, made several voyages to America, and in 1773 inherited property in Virginia. He joined the navy at the outbreak of the AMERICAN REVOLUTION, and performed a number of daring exploits off the British coast, capturing and sinking several ships. Outmanned and outgunned in the famous battle against the Serapis, he refused to surrender, declaring 'I have not yet begun to fight' and through sheer grit emerged victorious.

**Jones, J Raymond** (1900–91)
US politician. The first black 'boss' of TAMMANY HALL. From his base in the Carver Democratic Club, Jones had run Harlem since the 1920s and formed an alliance with Adam Clayton POWELL. When Tammany's image became tarnished by scandal in the 1950s, Jones split with Powell and backed Robert Wagner Jr for Mayor of New York in 1957. In return, Wagner placed him in charge of patronage, and he took over Tammany in 1964. This was a significant gain for the black community, and Jones became one of the major power brokers within the DEMOCRATIC PARTY, until the machine all but collapsed under the pressure of black protest and Jones was challenged by Robert KENNEDY. In 1967 the 'Harlem Fox' (as Jones was known) retired to the West Indies, leaving among his protégés the first black to become Mayor of New York, David Dinkins. ► POLITICAL MACHINE

**Jones, Mary Harris**, known as **Mother Jones** (1830–1930)
Irish-born US labour activist. She migrated to the USA via Canada, lost her family in an epidemic in 1867, and thereafter devoted herself to the cause of labour. An effective speaker, she travelled to the scenes of major strikes, especially in the coal industry, and continued to work as a labour agitator almost until her death.

**Jón Sigurdsson** ► SIGURDSSON, JÓN

**JORDAN** official name **Hashemite Kingdom of Jordan**

A kingdom in the Middle East, bounded to the north by Syria; to the north-east by Iraq; to the east and south by Saudi Arabia; and to the west by Israel. Jordan was part of the Roman Empire, and came under Arab control in the 7c. It was the centre of Crusader activity in the 11–12c, and part of the Turkish Empire from the 16c until WORLD WAR I, after which the area was divided into PALESTINE (west of the River Jordan) and Transjordan (east of the River Jordan), both administered by Britain. Transjordan gained independence in 1946, and the British mandate over Palestine ended in 1948, with the newly created State of Israel fighting to control the WEST BANK area. An armistice in 1949 left Jordan in control of the West Bank, and the West and East Banks united within Jordan in 1951. However, Israel took control of the West Bank after the SIX-DAY WAR in 1967. Following attempts by the Jordanian army to expel Palestinian guerrillas from the West Bank in 1970–1, civil war erupted; an amnesty was declared in 1973, and claims to the West Bank were ceded to the PLO (Palestine Liberation Organization) in 1974; Jordan formally renounced sovereignty over the West Bank and East Jerusalem in 1999. A ban on political parties in Jordan was ended in 1991 and the first multiparty elections since 1956 took place in 1993. The monarch, who is head of state and of government, was King HUSSEIN from 1952 to 1998. On his death he was succeeded by his son, Abdullah II, who has instituted economic reforms in association with the INTERNATIONAL MONETARY FUND. In 2000 Jordan joined the WORLD TRADE ORGANIZATION.

**Jordan, Vernon Eulion, Jr** (1935– )
US CIVIL RIGHTS leader. After earning a law degree from Harvard University (1960), he became a field secretary for the NAACP, and in 1970 director of the United Negro College Fund. He was President of the NATIONAL URBAN LEAGUE (1972–81), and became an influential voice in politics for black concerns.

**Jørgensen, Anker** (1922– )
Danish politician. He worked his way up through the organizations of the Danish labour movement and has been a member of the Danish parliament (FOLKETINGET) since 1964. From 1972 to 1987 he was leader of Denmark's SOCIAL DEMOCRATIC PARTY and was Prime Minister in 1972–3 and again in 1975–82. From 1982 to 1993 he was chairman of the Danish delegation in the Nordic Council.

**Josel von Rosheim** (c.1478–1554)
Leader of the German Jewish community under Emperors MAXIMILIAN I and CHARLES V. He used his political skills and contacts at court to protect the Jews from persecution through his efforts as a *shtadlan* (advocate).

**Joseph II** (1741–90)
Holy Roman Emperor (1765/90). The son of Emperor FRANCIS I and MARIA THERESA, until his mother's death (1780) he was co-regent, and his power was limited to the command of the army and the direction of foreign affairs. A sincere enlightened despot, he was known as 'the revolutionary emperor' for his programme of modernization. He was determined to assert Habsburg leadership, but some of his ambitious plans were thwarted variously by the diplomatic obstruction of France, Prussia, the United Provinces and Britain, by war (with Prussia in 1778–9 and Turkey in 1788) and by insurrection (in the Netherlands in 1787, Hungary 1789 and the Tyrol 1790). ➤ HABSBURG DYNASTY

**Joseph, Chief** (c.1840–1904)
Leader of the Nez Percé NATIVE AMERICANS, born in the Wallowa Valley of Oregon. The Nez Percé had agreed to settlement on a reservation, but when whites overran their territory and the government wanted to claim even more land, they resisted. Chief Joseph opposed any conflict, but helped lead his people on a gruelling fighting retreat from US troops through approximately 1,500 mi/2,400 km of wilderness. They were finally overwhelmed and forced to surrender close to the Canadian border. Chief Joseph died on a reservation in Washington State.

**Joseph, Père**, originally **François Joseph le Clerc du Tremblay** (1577–1638)
French diplomat and mystic. He became a Capuchin in 1599, and Cardinal RICHELIEU's secretary in 1611. His byname, *L'Éminence Grise* (or 'Grey Eminence') derives from his contact with Richelieu (the 'Red Eminence'), for whom he went on several important diplomatic missions, especially during the THIRTY YEARS' WAR.

**Josephine**, née **Marie Josèphe Rose Tascher de la Pagerie** (1763–1814)
First wife of Napoleon Bonaparte, and French Empress. In 1779 she married Alexandre, Viscount of BEAUHARNAIS, who was executed during the FRENCH REVOLUTION (1794). She married Napoleon in 1796, and accompanied him on his Italian campaign, but soon returned to Paris. At Malmaison, and afterwards at the Luxembourg and the Tuileries, she attracted round her the most brilliant society of France. The marriage, being childless, was dissolved in 1809. She retained the title of Empress. ➤ NAPOLEON I

**Josephinism**
The series of policies and reforms which Emperor JOSEPH II tried to introduce after the death of his mother, MARIA THERESA, in 1780. He attempted to reform the Imperial structure, control the clergy (by severing all effective ties with Rome), introduce conscription and remove burdens on the peasants. Revolts in Tyrol and the Netherlands and a threatened uprising in Hungary forced him to reverse the entire reform programme.

**Joubert, Piet**, also called **Petrus Jacobus Joubert** (1834–1900)
Boer soldier and politician. Born in Cango, Cape

Colony, he fought against the British in the Transvaal (1880–1), and became Vice-President under **KRUGER** (1883). He organized the initial Boer successes of the second Boer War (1899–1902), but died in Pretoria after a short illness. ➤ **BOER WARS**

**Jouhaux, Léon** (1879–1954)
French trade union leader. He became General-Secretary of the **CGT** (*Confédération générale du travail*, 'General Confederation of Labour') in 1909, remaining until 1947. Originally an advocate of revolutionary syndicalism, he soon adopted a more moderate position, supporting the French government during **WORLD WAR I**, and rejecting **COMMUNISM** in 1920. Nevertheless, he supported the reunification of the trade union movement in 1936, which rapidly led to communist domination of the CGT under his ineffective presidency. In Dec 1947 this led to his resignation from the CGT, and to his becoming President of the anti-communist trade union federation (CGT–FO).

**Jovellanos, Gaspar Melchor de** (1744–1811)
Asturian politician, historian and writer. One of the leading figures of the Spanish **ENLIGHTENMENT**, he trained as a lawyer and entered the bureaucracy. In 1797 he was appointed Secretary of Justice, but was subsequently sacked by Manuel de **GODOY**. He is best known for his writings on the themes of justice, the rights of the Crown against the Church and the **INQUISITION**, reform of the universities, and economic liberalism. His most famous report, on the *Agrarian Law* (1795), proposed reforms in agriculture. He was imprisoned in 1801 by Godoy, but freed in 1808. After his release he withdrew to Asturias but refused to join the reforming **AFRANCESADOS** who supported Joseph Bonaparte.

**Joyce, William**, known as **Lord Haw-Haw** (1906–46)
British traitor. As a child, he lived in Ireland and in 1922 his family emigrated to England. In 1937 he founded the fanatical British National Socialist Party, and fled to Germany before war broke out. Throughout **WORLD WAR II**, he broadcast from Radio Hamburg propaganda against Britain, gaining his byname from his upper-class drawl. He was captured by the British at Flensburg, and was tried and executed in London.

**Joyeuse Entrée** (*Blijde Inkomst*)
A processional entry into a town in the later Middle Ages to celebrate the accession or marriage of a ruler, especially in the Low Countries. Reminiscent of the Roman triumphal entries, they involved ceremonial arches, plays and decorated floats. One *Joyeuse Entrée* in particular is remembered as the quasi-constitution of the Duchy of **BRABANT**. It was granted on 3 Jan 1356 by Johanna of Brabant and Wenzel of Luxembourg, and allowed the Brabantines some say in their own government. The document was used in the protests and revolts against the Spanish King **PHILIP II** (the **EIGHTY YEARS' WAR**) and the Austrian Emperor **JOSEPH II** (**BRABANT REVOLUTION**), and also in drawing up the Belgian constitution of 1831.

**Juan Carlos I** (1938–)
King of Spain (1975/ ). The son of Don Juan de Borbón y Battenberg, Count of Barcelona, and the grandson of **ALFONSO XIII**, who went into exile in 1931, he was educated in Switzerland, and from 1948, by

agreement between his father and General **FRANCO**, in Spain. He earned commissions in the army, navy and air force, and studied at the University of Madrid before marrying (1962) Princess Sophia of Greece. In 1969 Franco named him as his eventual successor, and he was proclaimed King on Franco's death in 1975. Instead of upholding the Franco dictatorship (as had been intended), he decisively presided over Spain's democratization, helping to defeat a military coup (1981) and assuming the role of a constitutional monarch.

**Juan José of Austria** (1629–79)
Spanish politician and soldier. The natural son of **PHILIP IV** of Spain and the actress Maria Calderón, he served as Viceroy of Naples from 1648 to 1651. After suppressing the revolt there, in 1650 he commanded the armies in Catalonia and received the surrender of Barcelona (1652). He was Viceroy of Catalonia (1652–6) and of the Netherlands (1656–9), and commander of forces fighting Portugal (1661–4). On the accession of **CHARLES II** of Spain, he was involved in power struggles to control the government against the King's mother, the Regent Mariana, and her confessor, Father Nithard. He eventually succeeded in obtaining power in 1676, as Chief Minister, but died suddenly three years later. A man of culture and vision, he patronized new trends in scientific thought.

**Juárez, Benito Pablo** (1806–72)
Mexican national hero and politician. A Zapotec Indian, he was a clerk and lawyer and then Governor of Oaxaca (1847–52). Exiled by conservatives under **SANTA ANNA** (1853–5), he then returned to join the new Liberal government. Proposing fundamental change, he abolished the *fueros*, seized control of Church lands, and passed the anticlerical and liberal constitution of 1857. During the civil war of 1857–60, he assumed the presidency, upholding a free church in a free state. He was elected President on the Liberal victory (1861), a post he held until his death. The French invasion under **MAXIMILIAN** forced him to the far north, from where he directed resistance until Maximilian's defeat in 1867. He then restored republican rule, creating the basis for the regime of Porfirio **DÍAZ**.

**Jubilee 2000**
An international debt-cancellation campaign inspired by the beginning of the third millennium, in particular a drive by major religious groups and non-religious organizations to declare 2000 a 'jubilee' in the Old Testament sense of 'release from servitude'. In 1996 the **GROUP OF 8** countries agreed to write off half of the official debt of 40 countries under the highly indebted poor country (HIPC) initiative, provided certain conditions were met. Jubilee 2000 advocated the cancellation of the entire debt of 52 countries, arguing that this would increase global stability and cost the debt-holders relatively little. Critics argued that debt relief must be combined with measures that would prevent a repetition of the debt cycle. Successor bodies have continued to call for total cancellation of the debt of the poorest countries with refinancing as necessary by international financial institutions. ➤ **THIRD WORLD DEBT**

**Jubogha, Jubo** ➤ **JA JA OF OPOBO**

**Judaism** ► RELIGION

**Jugnauth, Sir Aneerood** (1930–)
Mauritian politician. After qualifying as a barrister in London (1954), he returned to Mauritius and was elected to the Legco in 1963. In 1970 he helped found the socialist Mauritius Militant Movement, but broke from it to form his own Mauritius Socialist Party. He became Prime Minister (1982) in a coalition government, altered the name of his party to the Mauritius Socialist Movement and retained leadership of the coalition after elections in 1983, 1984, 1987 and 1991. In 1995 he was succeeded as Prime Minister by Navin Ramgoolam. He served as Prime Minister again from 2000 to 2003, when he became President.

**Juin, Alphonse Pierre** (1888–1967)
French soldier. He passed out top of his class, which included Charles de GAULLE, at the Saint-Cyr military academy and fought in WORLD WAR I. As divisional commander in the 1st French Army, he was captured by the Germans in 1940, but was later released (Jun 1941) and became Military Governor of Morocco. After the Allied invasion of Tunisia, he changed sides, helped to defeat von Arnim's AFRIKA CORPS remnants and distinguished himself in the subsequent Italian campaign. He was resident-general in Morocco (1947–51) and served in senior NATO commands. He broke with de Gaulle in 1960 over his Algerian policy, and retired. ► WORLD WAR II

**Juliana**, in full **Juliana Louise Emma Marie Wilhelmina** (1909–2004)
Queen of the Netherlands (1948/80). The daughter of Queen WILHELMINA and Prince Hendrik, she was educated at Leiden University and became a lawyer. In 1937 she married Prince BERNHARD LEOPOLD; they had four daughters. On the German invasion of Holland (1940), Juliana escaped to Britain and later resided in Canada. She returned to Holland in 1945, and became Queen on the abdication of her mother in 1948. In 1980 she herself abdicated in favour of her eldest daughter, BEATRIX, and once more took the title of Princess.

**Jülich–Cleves Succession Conflict**
A dispute over rival claims to the duchy upon the death, without issue, of Duke John William in 1609. The duchy was claimed by Philip Louis, Count Palatine of Neuburg, John Sigismund, Elector of Brandenburg, and the Elector of Saxony, among others. The assassination of HENRY IV of France and the death of the leader of the EVANGELICAL UNION, Frederick IV, prevented a war. France and the Union supported Philip and John, while the Holy Roman Emperor RUDOLF II and the CATHOLIC LEAGUE supported the Saxon Duke. The Treaty of Xanten (1614) averted another war by awarding Jülich and Berg to John, while Philip's successor, Wolfgang William, a convert to Catholicism, received the rest. In the 18c another crisis arose when the extinction of the Neuburg line allowed FREDERICK WILLIAM I of Prussia to claim (after agreeing to the PRAGMATIC SANCTION) the duchy. Prussia abandoned its claim in 1742 and the duchy passed to Sulzbach, thence to Bavaria (1799).

**Julius II**, originally **Giuliano della Rovere** (1443–1513)
Italian pope (1503/13). His public career was mainly devoted to re-establishing papal sovereignty in its ancient territory, and removing foreign domination in Italy. His participation in the League of CAMBRAI (1508) restored the PAPAL STATES, but the HOLY LEAGUE (1510) with Spain and England against LOUIS XII of France was less successful. A liberal patron of the arts, he employed Bramante for the design of St Peter's, begun in 1506, and commissioned works from Raphael and Michelangelo.

**Julius III**, originally **Giovanni Maria Ciocchi del Monte** (1487–1555)
Italian pope (1550/5). He was one of the three delegates to the Council of TRENT, which he reopened after his election. He sent Cardinal Reginald POLE to organize with MARY I the reunion of England with the Church of Rome.

**July Days** (16–20 July 1917)
Largely spontaneous anti-government demonstrations in Petrograd in Russia, marking growing popular dissatisfaction with the Provisional Government's record since the beginning of the Revolution. Demonstrators demanded that Russia withdraw from WORLD WAR I, the actual overthrow of the Provisional Government, and the transfer of 'All power to the Soviets'. LENIN initially opposed the demonstrations, judging the time for a proletarian–socialist revolution to be premature, but he eventually gave half-hearted support. Despite several hundred deaths, nothing was achieved except a slight swing to the right within the Provisional Government. Lenin was more convinced than ever of the need for a highly organized revolutionary party and carefully directed revolution of the kind he had advocated since first establishing the BOLSHEVIKS. ► APRIL THESES; FEBRUARY REVOLUTION (Russia); OCTOBER REVOLUTION

**July Revolution** (1830)
A three-day revolt in Paris which ended the Bourbon Restoration, forcing the abdication of the reactionary CHARLES X. It resulted in the establishment of a more liberal regime dominated by the wealthy bourgeoisie, the so-called 'July Monarchy', under the Orléanist LOUIS-PHILIPPE, 'King of the French'. ► BOURBON, HOUSE OF

**Jumblatt, Kemal** (1919–77)
Lebanese politician and hereditary DRUZE chieftain. He founded the Progressive Socialist Party in 1949, held several Cabinet posts (1961–4) and was Minister of the Interior (1969–70). The Syrian intervention on the side of the Christians in 1976 was a response to the increasing power of his authority in partnership with the Palestinians. He was assassinated in an ambush outside the village of Baaklu in the Chouf Mountains. His son, Walid, became leader of the Druze after his death.

**June Days** (1848)
A violent episode in the French FEBRUARY REVOLUTION (1848), when working-class radicals resisted the dissolution of the NATIONAL WORKSHOPS in Paris. They were crushed by the NATIONAL GUARD and troops of the republican government under the direction of General Louis Eugène CAVAIGNAC, thus exacerbating class divisions in France for generations.

**June War ▶ ARAB–ISRAELI WARS**

**Jung Bahadur** (1816–77)
Nepali politician. He was Prime Minister and virtual ruler of Nepal from 1846 to 1877. He visited Britain in 1850–1 and his closeness to that country was exemplified by his assistance in providing the British with a body of **GURKHAS** during the **INDIAN UPRISING** of 1857–8; this led to the tradition of Gurkha military service in the British Army. Jung Bahadur was the founder of the Rana Dynasty, which provided a line of prime ministers for the country until 1951, when the last hereditary Prime Minister, Mohun, retired.

**Junín, Battle of** (1824)
A major cavalry battle of the **SPANISH-AMERICAN WARS OF INDEPENDENCE**, fought at nearly 4,300 m/14,000 ft in the Peruvian Andes. It was the last major victory of Simón **BOLÍVAR**.

**Junker**
Prussian aristocrats whose power rested on their large estates, situated predominantly to the east of the River Elbe, and on their traditional role as army officers and civil servants. Their position came increasingly under threat in late 19c Germany as a result of industrialization, but they jealously safeguarded their privileges and power. The loss of lands east of the rivers Oder and Neisse in 1945 and the confiscation of their estates in East Germany destroyed their basis. ▶ **PRUSSIA**

**junta**
An administrative council, especially in Italy and Spain. The term is now commonly applied to a military leadership that has taken control of a country, particularly in Latin America.

**Jurchen ▶ JIN (JURCHEN) DYNASTY**

**juros**
In Spain, annuities paid out of state income for loans to the Crown. The practice was begun systematically by **FERDINAND II, THE CATHOLIC** and **ISABELLA I, THE CATHOLIC** as a means of raising funds for the wars against Granada, and assumed overwhelming importance in the 16c and 17c, when the Crown had to borrow to cover its commitments. The loans yielded interest of about seven per cent in the 16c, which made them attractive to all investors as a form of national debt. Repayment consumed in 1556 some 68 per cent of normal state revenue, and in 1565 some 84 per cent; by the 17c, their repayments exceeded available revenue. The system continued until the mid-19c.

**justicialismo**
This was the populist doctrine, lying midway between **CAPITALISM** and **COMMUNISM**, espoused by the followers of Juan Domingo **PERÓN** between 1946 and 1970. It was a combination of **CREOLE** nationalism, support for the *descamisados* ('shirtless masses'), and the massive extension of state power into every aspect of Argentine social and economic life. It also entailed government controls over employment and social security provision. Industrial and trading corporations were designed to maintain the descamisados as passive support to Perón, while destroying opposition groups, whether the Church, British investors or trade unions. After he was ousted in 1955, *justicialismo* became the official doctrine of the Peronists. ▶ **PERONISM**

**Jutland, Battle of** (31 May–1 June 1916)
A sea battle of **WORLD WAR I** (and the first major challenge to British naval supremacy since the Battle of **TRAFALGAR** in 1805), in which Admiral **JELLICOE** led the British Grand Fleet from Scapa Flow and intercepted the German High Seas Fleet off the west coast of Jutland, Denmark. Though the battle itself was inconclusive, German naval chiefs withdrew their fleet to port, and turned to unrestricted submarine warfare as a means of challenging British command of the sea.

**JVP** (*Janata Vimukti Peramuna*, 'People's Liberation Front')
Left-wing Sri Lankan political group, founded in the late 1960s by Rohan Wijeweera and other left-wing activists from the small group of Sri Lankan Maoists. In 1971 Wijeweera was detained just before the JVP launched an insurrection against the government of Sirimavo **BANDARANAIKE**. After a brief period of legality in the late 1970s, the party was again proscribed after the 1983 anti-**TAMIL** riots, but re-emerged to lead the opposition to the 1987 **INDO-SRI LANKAN PEACE ACCORD**. Between 1987 and 1989 huge numbers died in the JVP's clash with the government's security forces, which eventually ended with the capture and killing of Wijeweera. In 1994 the JVP returned to peaceful politics, gradually building up electoral successes until in 2004 it entered government as a minority partner to the People's Alliance in the United People's Freedom Alliance coalition.

## Kabaka Yekka

Literally 'the King Alone', this was a neo-traditionalist movement in Buganda organized round allegiance to, and support of, the *Kabaka* (or 'King') of Buganda in the 1960s. It disintegrated when the Kabaka was forced into exile in 1966.

## Kabila, Laurent Désiré (1939–2001)

Congolese politician and soldier. He received a university education in France and at Dar es Salaam, Tanzania, where he met Yoweri MUSEVENI. In 1960 Kabila became a youth leader in a political party allied to Patrice LUMUMBA's government, which was overthrown by MOBUTU in 1961. Kabila then took part in an opposition movement which was eventually suppressed by Mobutu in 1965. In 1967 he founded the People's Revolutionary Party, which established a Marxist region in eastern Zaire and survived by mining gold and trading ivory until the 1980s, when Kabila took to trading gold in Dar es Salaam. In 1996 he grouped together various opposition groups to form the Alliance of Democratic Forces for the Liberation of Congo-Zaire (ADFL) and with an army consisting mainly of Tutsis from eastern Zaire, supported by Rwanda, Angola and Uganda, led them in a civil war against Mobutu's corrupt and oppressive regime. On 17 May 1997, with Mobutu having fled Kinshasa, Kabila installed himself as President and renamed the country the Democratic Republic of the Congo, but was unable to exercise control over the entire country, although fighting with rebel factions lessened after a ceasefire in 1999. Kabila was assassinated in 2001 and succeeded as President by his son, Joseph.

## Kabir (1440–1518)

Indian mystic and poet. He tried to unite Hindu and Muslim thought, preached the essential unity of all religions and was a forerunner of SIKHISM, which was established by his disciple, Nanak. Kabir was brought up by a Muslim weaver and later influenced by a Hindu ascetic, Ramananda. He took the best tenets of both Hinduism and Islam and preached his own religion called *sahaja-yoga* ('simple union'): from Hinduism, he took the ideas of transmigration and the law of karma, but rejected idolatry, asceticism and CASTE; from Islam, he accepted the idea of one God and the equality of all men before God.

## Kabra Bassa

A major dam and hydroelectric plant in Mozambique. Kabra Bassa was a set of cataracts on the Zambezi just above the town of Tete which were seen by David LIVINGSTONE on his second African journey between 1858 and 1863. In the late 1960s, the Portuguese rulers of Mozambique embarked upon the building of a dam, funded by foreign investment, which would supply electricity to South Africa and create a vast lake which would provide irrigation for new areas of white settlement in the Zambezi Valley. FRELIMO saw it as a symbol of continuing white domination and from 1968 began a campaign to sabotage it. They failed, but pinned down Portuguese troops in its defence. South African military and air forces were also involved.

## Kabyle

A Berber people of Algeria. Organized into different castes with serfs, they speak Kabyle, a Hamito-Semitic language, and are predominantly Muslims. They live in villages, grow grains and olives, and herd goats. Population c.2 million. ► BERBERS

## Kadalie, Clements (c.1095–1951)

Nyasaland (Malawian) trade union leader. A migrant, he founded in 1919 the Industrial and Commercial Workers' Union of South Africa, the first large-scale trade union for black people. Kadalie started the union in the Cape, where he led a series of dock strikes. By 1923 it had become a mass movement reaching a peak of membership of 86,000 in 1928. However, it declined rapidly from 1929 onwards and was defunct by 1933, failing because Kadalie led it into political action, split it into moderate and radical factions, expelled the Communists and forced the creation of a separate organization in Natal. It never secured a large membership among the workforce of the Rand gold mines and failed to gain international recognition.

## Kádár, János (1912–89)

Hungarian politician. He joined the illegal Communist Party in 1931, and was arrested several times. He became a member of its Central Committee (1942) and of the Politburo (1945). As Minister of the Interior from 1948 to 1951, he organized the trial of László RAJK, but he was arrested and imprisoned for his anti-Stalinist views (1951–4). When the anti-Soviet Hungarian Uprising broke out in 1956, he was a member of the 'national' government of Imre NAGY, but he then formed a puppet government which invited measured Soviet intervention and helped to suppress the uprising. He resigned in 1958, becoming Prime Minister again in 1961. His long reign as Party Secretary ended in 1988, and during that time he did manage to introduce elements of reform into the Hungarian economy. However, by the mid-1980s he had become comparatively conservative, and reform petered out, to the immediate advantage of Hungarian COMMUNISM. ► STALIN, JOSEPH

**Kadets** (1905–18)
The short name for the Russian Constitutional Democratic Party that was established in the Russian REVOLUTION OF 1905 to represent liberal non-Marxist interests. The main plank in their programme was their demand for a constituent assembly completely to reform Russia's political structure. This was unacceptable to NICHOLAS II; and even though they were the largest group in the first DUMA, their numbers dropped in the succeeding three, which were in any case powerless assemblies. Eventually in 1917 they participated in the RUSSIAN PROVISIONAL GOVERNMENT, with Pavel MILIUKOV as Foreign Minister, but they were already falling behind popular cries for change. When the RUSSIAN CONSTITUENT ASSEMBLY was finally elected in Nov, they had a mere 15 out of 703 representatives. When it was disbanded in Jan 1918, they were declared illegal.

**Kaganovich, Lazar Moiseyevich** (1893–1991)
Soviet politician. He joined the Communist Party in 1911 and, after participating actively in the 1917 RUSSIAN REVOLUTION, became First Secretary of the Ukrainian Party in 1925. In 1928 he moved to the secretariat of the All-Union Party and in 1930 became a full member of the POLITBURO, as well as serving for five years as First Secretary of the Moscow Party. He played a prominent role in the brutal, forced collectivization programme in the early 1930s, and in the great purges of 1936–8. He also served as Commissar for Railways and was responsible for building the Moscow metro. A close ally of STALIN, he survived the latter's death in 1953 but, having fallen foul of Nikita KHRUSHCHEV and participated in the ANTI-PARTY PLOT, was dismissed in 1957, being posted to a managerial position in a Siberian cement works. He retired into obscurity in Moscow, to die just as the USSR was about to collapse.

**Kagawa Toyohiko** (1888–1960)
Japanese social reformer and evangelist. A convert to Christianity, he was educated at the Presbyterian College in Tokyo, and Princeton Theological Seminary in the USA. Returning to Japan, he became an evangelist and social worker in the slums of Kobe. He became a leader in the Japanese labour movement, helping to found the Federation of Labour (1918) and the Farmers' Union (1921), as well as to establish agricultural collectives. In 1928 he founded the Anti-War League and after WORLD WAR II was a leader in the women's suffrage movement, and helped with the process of democratization.

**Kaiser**
The title assumed (Dec 1870) by the Prussian King WILLIAM I following the unification of Germany and the creation of the German Empire. He was succeeded on his death in 1888 by his son FREDERICK III, who survived him by only three months, and then by his grandson WILLIAM II, who ruled until his enforced abdication in 1918.

**Kalashnikov, Mikhail Timofeevich** (1919–)
Soviet military designer. He invented the famous Soviet rifle also used extensively by foreign armies and international terrorists. Born of peasant stock in the Altai area, he joined the army in 1938. Seriously wounded in 1941, he began experimenting with what was to be the famous AK-47 assault rifle taken into Soviet service in 1949. Other versions were produced later. He was a deputy of the USSR Supreme Soviet (1950–4, 1966–9).

**Kalinin, Mikhail Ivanovich** (1875–1946)
Soviet politician. He was the formal head of state after the 1917 Revolution and during the years of STALIN's dictatorship (1919–46). A peasant and metalworker, he entered politics as a champion of the peasant class, and won great popularity. He became President of the Soviet Central Executive Committee (1919–38), and of the Presidium of the Supreme Soviet (1938–46). A member of the POLITBURO from 1926 onwards, he was an influential figure; but he was sufficiently pliable to survive the purges in the late 1930s and to die a natural death.

**Kallay, Miklós** (1887–1976)
Hungarian politician. A big landowner, he became Lord Lieutenant of Szabolcs county. To the right in politics, he was Minister of Agriculture from 1932 to 1935. During WORLD WAR II he served as Prime Minister (Mar 1942–Mar 1944). Initially he cooperated with Germany but after the Battle of STALINGRAD he tried to make a separate settlement with the Allies, only to be imprisoned in Nov 1944 in Mauxhaussen CONCENTRATION CAMP. He subsequently settled in the USA.

**Kalmar Union**
The dynastic union of Denmark, Norway and Sweden achieved at Kalmar in Sweden in 1397, when ERIK OF POMERANIA was crowned king of all three kingdoms. It came about partly as a result of previous dynastic marriages, partly to satisfy the interests of nobles with landed property in more than one country, but principally to present a more united front against the threat of dominance by the German HANSEATIC LEAGUE. Many Swedish nobles came to resent what they saw as infringements of their rights by a king residing in Copenhagen and, on several occasions in the course of the 15c, broke away from the Union under their own head of state, until finally under GUSTAV I VASA Sweden withdrew from the Union altogether (1523). Norway, however, with a much weaker nobility, remained united with Denmark until 1814. ► KARL KNUTSSON; STURE, STEN, THE ELDER

**Kalmuks** ► DZUNGARS

**Kalonga** (mid-17–18c)
The dynastic title of the paramount chiefs of the Maravi kingdoms of central southern Africa. *Kalonga* Muzura in the mid-17c allied himself with the Portuguese. A formidable warrior, he was able to subjugate the lesser kingdoms of the area, but by the beginning of the 18c the empire was collapsing from fragmentation amongst the ruling group and from competition from the subject-peoples, particularly the Chewa kingdom whose rulers, the Undi, replaced the *Kalonga* as the dominant political authority in the area during the 18c.

**Kamakura Shogunate** (1192–1333)
Japan's first warrior government, established by Minamoto no Yoritomo (1147/99). In 1192 the Emperor,

recognizing his paramount position, bestowed on Minamoto the title of **SHOGUN** (military generalissimo), although Minamoto had already in 1180 established a military government (*bakufu*) in Kamakura (south of Tokyo). Minamoto used his power to appoint military governors and estate stewards, principally in the eastern part of the country. There were altogether nine Kamakura shoguns, although from the 13c onwards effective power was in the hands of members of the **HOJO FAMILY**, who occupied the hereditary post of regent. The Kamakura Shogunate was overthrown in 1333 by **ASHIKAGA TAKAUJI**. ➤ **ASHIKAGA SHOGUNATE**

## KAMAKURA SHOGUNATE

| Regnal Dates | Name |
| --- | --- |
| 1192/9 | Minamoto Yoritomo |
| 1202/3 | Minamoto Yoriie |
| 1203/19 | Minamoto Sanetomo |
| 1226/44 | Fujiwara Yoritsune |
| 1244/52 | Fujiwara Yoritsugu |
| 1252/66 | Munetaka Shinno |
| 1266/89 | Koreyasu Shinno |
| 1289/1308 | Hisaaki Shinno |
| 1308/33 | Morikuni Shinno |

**Kamenev, Lev Borisovich**, originally **Lev Borisovich Rosenfeld** (1883–1936)
Soviet politician. He was an active revolutionary throughout Russia and abroad from 1901 onwards, associating with **LENIN**, **TROTSKY** and **STALIN**, and was exiled to Siberia in 1915. Liberated after the **FEBRUARY REVOLUTION**, he was active as a Bolshevik throughout 1917, became the first Chairman of the Central Executive Committee of the All Russian Congress of Soviets and subsequently held various Party, government and diplomatic appointments. Expelled from the Party as a Trotskyist in 1927, he was readmitted the next year but again expelled in 1932. The same happened in 1933–4. He was finally executed for allegedly conspiring against **STALIN**. Like many others falsely accused, he was rehabilitated in 1988 during the **GORBACHEV** years.

**kamikaze**
A Japanese term (literally, 'divine wind') identifying the volunteer suicide pilots of the Japanese Imperial Navy, who guided their explosive-packed aircraft into enemy ships in **WORLD WAR II**. They emerged in the last year of the **PACIFIC WAR**, when Allied forces were closing on the Japanese homeland.

**Kanagawa, Treaty of** (31 Mar 1854)
The first agreement signed between Japan and a Western nation. It was instigated by Commodore Matthew **PERRY**, who in 1853 sailed a fleet of warships into Tokyo Bay and requested access to Japanese ports for supplies, then departed to allow the Japanese government time to think the matter over. Following Perry's return, a treaty was signed in Mar 1854 giving US ships access (from 22 June 1855) to Shimoda and Hakodate, and allowing a US consul at Shimoda. The treaty was supplemented by others, such as the Treaty of **EDO**, negotiated by Townsend Harris.

**Kanaris, Constantine** (1790–1877)
Greek admiral and politician. He was one of several merchant-captains who provided their own ships for service in the struggle for Greek independence. He used fireships to blow up the Turkish flagship in the Strait of Chios (1822), repeated the feat in the harbour of Tenedos, and in 1824 burnt a Turkish frigate and some transport ships. He held high commands, and was made a senator in 1847. He was Prime Minister of Greece on three occasions between 1848 and 1877, and took part in the revolution that put **GEORGE I** on the throne in 1863.

**Kanauj**
An ancient city in the state of Uttar Pradesh in India. Kanauj rose after the Gupta period during Harsha's time and was the capital of the kingdom of the Gurjara Pratiharas c.1000AD in north India. It was taken by **MAHMUD OF GHAZNI** c.1018. A later Gahrwal ruler, Jayachandra, is said initially to have been allied to **MUHAMMAD GHURI** whose forces, led by **QUTB-UD-DIN AIBAK**, later destroyed Kanauj in 1193. Kanauj became part of the kingdom of Jaunpur and later became part of the Lodi kingdom. In 1540 **SHER SHAH** defeated **HUMAYUN** at Kanauj, and built a fort there. After his death, Kanauj was taken by the Mughals.

**Kandyan Kingdom**
The last independent kingdom in Sri Lanka. It was based in the city of Kandy in the mountainous interior of the country and was founded in the late 15c and early 16c, after the demise of the great classical kingdoms of **ANURADHAPURA** and **POLONNARUWA**, and as their successors in the south-west of the country were threatened by the Portuguese. For most of its existence the kingdom had to deal with a hostile European presence in the lowlands, first the Portuguese, then the Dutch, and finally the British, who captured the kingdom in 1815 with the assistance of a conspiracy against the king by the leading aristocratic families.

**Kanem**
West African kingdom situated to the north-east of Lake Chad under the Sefuwa Dynasty, which survived from the 10c to the 19c. The strength of Kanem was based on its position between the forest and the desert and its ability to trade salt and copper from the north with forest goods and cottons from the south. Kanem's power was replaced by that of Bornu in the 15c.

**K'ang-hsi** ➤ **KANGXI**

**Kanghwa, Treaty of** (27 Feb 1876)
Korea's first treaty with a foreign power (Japan), signed after considerable pressure from the new Meiji government in Tokyo. Following the **MEIJI RESTORATION** (1868), the Japanese government sent envoys to the Korean court to seek diplomatic relations and bilateral trade. With the Korean court dominated (until 1873) by the xenophobic regent **TAEWON-GUN**, Japan's requests were rejected. When three Japanese gunboats were fired upon off the coast of Kanghwa Island (near the Korean capital of Seoul) in 1875, Japan used this as a pretext to demand a commercial treaty, a demand backed up by the sending of an armed naval force to Korea. The resulting treaty established formal diplomatic relations between the two countries and opened three ports for trade in which Japanese consuls were stationed. The treaty

was to encourage the Western powers to seek similar concessions, beginning a process of ending Korea's traditional isolation and its long-established dependence on China as its vassal state.

## Kang Sheng (K'ang Sheng) (1899–1975)
Chinese politician. He studied Soviet security and intelligence techniques in Moscow during the early 1930s. He was a prominent member of the Chinese Communist Party during the 1960s, and exercised considerable behind-the-scenes influence in his capacity as Head of Party Security. During the CULTURAL REVOLUTION he was associated with the radical-left group led by MAO ZEDONG's wife, JIANG QING. Since Mao's death in 1976, Kang's role in the persecution of party members and intellectuals during the Cultural Revolution has been condemned.

## KaNgwane
A former national state or non-independent Black homeland in eastern Transvaal, South Africa, created in 1977 by the APARTHEID system for Swazi people not living in the independent nation of Swaziland. In 1994 it was reincorporated into South Africa and is now part of Mpumalanga province.

## Kangxi (K'ang-hsi) (1654–1722)
Emperor of China (1661/1722). The third son of the first Manchu Qing Emperor, he presided over the consolidation of Manchu rule in China. He suppressed the Rebellion of the THREE FEUDATORIES in the south and captured Taiwan from Ming loyalist forces in 1682. In order to gain the support of the scholar class, Kangxi patronized Confucian learning and promoted himself as the ideal Confucian monarch, embarking on a series of extensive tours of the country. His secret palace memorial system, allowing certain provincial officials to report directly to him on confidential matters without going through official channels at the capital, allowed Kangxi to exercise personal supervision over the bureaucracy. The last years of his reign were marked by factional struggles over the succession. His fourth son, Yongzheng (1722/36), eventually succeeded. ► QING DYNASTY

## Kang Youwei (K'ang Yu-wei) (1858–1927)
Chinese reformer and leader of the HUNDRED DAYS OF REFORM in China (1898). In 1895 he organized thousands of young scholars to demand drastic national reforms. The young Emperor GUANGXU summoned him to implement reforms as the first step to creating a constitutional monarchy, but the movement was ended when CIXI seized the Emperor, executed six of the young reformers, and punished all who had supported them. Kang and his disciple LIANG QICHAO escaped to Japan with foreign help. He returned to China in 1914, and died at Tsingtao, Shandong.

## K'ang Yu-wei ► KANG YOUWEI

## Kanpur, Massacre of (1857)
The native cavalry of the garrison of Kanpur (Cawnpore), based in Uttar Pradesh in northern India, rebelled against their British masters on 4 June 1857 and the garrison, led by Sir Hugh Wheeler, was besieged for three weeks. On 27 June members of the garrison were offered a safe passage to Allahabad on thatched barges. However, as they were leaving, the barges came under gunfire and were set ablaze. The survivors, including women and children, were later transferred to a small house called the Bibighar, where they were killed on 15 July by the NANA SAHIB'S men.

## Kansas–Nebraska Act (1854)
A bill passed by the US CONGRESS in 1854 to establish the territories of Kansas and Nebraska. Because it opened up the possibility of extending SLAVERY into western territories, by allowing popular sovereignty, it led to bitter debates. The ensuing protests contributed to the formation of the REPUBLICAN PARTY, which was hostile to the expansion of slavery.

## KANU (Kenyan African National Union)
The party which led Kenya to independence in 1963. It was founded in 1960 as a successor to the Kikuyu Central Association of 1929 and the Kenya African Union of 1947. The Kenya African Democratic Union (KADU) was a rival body which represented mainly non-Kikuyu groups. KANU won the first Kenyan election, with President Kenyatta becoming the leader of independent Kenya, although he tried to bring KADU into a coalition. KANU was the sole legal party from 1982 until 1991, and remained in power afterwards, allegedly through electoral fraud and corruption, until the 2002 elections.

## Kao Kang ► GAO GANG

## Kapodistrias, Ioannis Antonios (1776–1831)
Greek national leader. An Ionian nobleman born on Corfu, he entered the service of Tsar ALEXANDER I and from 1816 was joint Foreign Minister of Russia. In 1828 he became President of the new Greek state. Authoritarian and paternalistic, he attempted to create a national army, administrative bureaucracy and education system. He tried to revive the economy, which had been wrecked by the GREEK WAR OF INDEPENDENCE, but his plan to create a stable landowning peasantry was frustrated by powerful clan leaders. In 1831, in the course of a feud, he was assassinated at Nafplion by members of a local clan seeking revenge.

## Kapp Putsch (Mar 1920)
An unsuccessful coup by some FREIKORPS units against the SPD-dominated German government led by extreme right-wing politicians and a small number of army commanders. Scheduled reductions in the size of Germany's armed forces under the terms of the Treaty of VERSAILLES led one of the affected commanders, von Lüttwitz, to order forces loyal to him to seize Berlin and force a change in policy. The government fled rather than comply, leading to the creation of a rebel government under Wolfgang Kapp, a civil servant, which lasted three days. He was toppled by a general strike organized by the ADGB and by passive resistance from the Civil Service and the national bank. Significant was the failure of the army to oppose the coup, even if it did not actively support it.

## Kapwepwe, Simon (1922–89)
Zambian nationalist leader and politician. Educated in mission schools before becoming a teacher, he helped found the Northern Rhodesian African National Congress in 1946. After a period of study in India, he returned to be Treasurer and then helped

form the breakaway United National Independence Party (**UNIP**) of which he became Treasurer (1960–7). After holding several ministerial posts in the early days of independence, including the vice-presidency, he resigned from UNIP to form his own party, the United Progress Party, in 1971 in order to oppose Kenneth **KAUNDA**. The party was banned in 1972, when Zambia became a one-party state, and Kapwepwe was detained. He rejoined UNIP in 1977.

### Karadžić, Radovan (1945– )
Politician and leader of the Serbian Democratic Republic of Bosnia and Herzegovina. He became prominent in politics in 1990 on the creation of the Serbian Democratic Party (SDS), the main Serbian party in Bosnia. As the self-styled President of Serb-controlled Bosnia from 1992 to 1996, he signed the Vance–**OWEN** Peace Plan in May 1993, and the Dayton Peace Agreement in Dec 1995. However, with the aim of uniting all the Serbs in the former Yugoslavia into one Greater Serbia, his militias drove over one million Muslims from their homes, killing many thousands. He was indicted by the **UN** war crimes tribunal in 1996 and forbidden from standing for re-election. He has not yet been apprehended and brought to trial.

### Karadžić, Vuk Stefanović (1787–1864)
Leader of the Serb national revival. Born in a remote village in western Serbia, he is said to have been taught to write with ink made from gunpowder and water. During the first Serbian Uprising (1804), he was secretary to a leader of the **HAJDUKS**. The next year he studied briefly at Sremski Karlovci, then in southern Hungary. He returned to teach in Belgrade, but fled to Vienna when the Turks reoccupied the city and crushed the uprising of 1813. Influenced by the ideas of Herder and Kopitar, he was persuaded by Goethe to collect Serbian folk poetry and folklore. Among his many literary and scholarly achievements, he tried to create a standard Serbian orthography, grammar and dictionary based on the dialect used in Herzegovina, compiled a Serbian–German dictionary (1818) and translated the New Testament into Serbian (published 1869). ➤ **KOSOVO, BATTLE OF**; **OBRADOVIĆ, DOSITEJ**; **SERBIAN UPRISINGS**

### Karageorge, originally George Petrović (c.1768–1817)
Serbian national leader. The leader of the Serbian Uprising in 1804, he was elected Governor of Serbia in 1808. After the Turks regained control of Serbia in 1813, he fled to Austria but was murdered on his return in 1817 with the connivance of his rival, Prince Miloš **OBRENOVIĆ**. He was founder of the Karageorgević Dynasty. ➤ **SERBIAN UPRISINGS**

### Karakhan Manifesto (25 July 1919)
A declaration issued by the Soviet Assistant Foreign Commissar Leo Karakhan, renouncing all former Tsarist rights and privileges in China. A similar declaration had been issued the year before by the Foreign Commissar G V Chicherin. Although the Soviet government in 1920 insisted that such a declaration had not implied handing over the **CHINESE EASTERN RAILWAY** without compensation (it remained, in fact, under Soviet control until 1935, when it was sold to

Japan), the Karakhan Manifesto had a profound effect on young Chinese radicals, convincing them that the new Soviet state was the only foreign country willing to treat China as an equal.

### Karamanlis, Constantine (1907–98)
Greek politician. A lawyer, he was elected to parliament in 1935, became Minister of Public Works (1952), then in 1955 succeeded Alexander **PAPAGOS** as Prime Minister and reconstituted the right-wing Greek Rally as the National Radical Union. Confronting the Cyprus dispute and sensitive to US and **NATO** anxiety over the activities of **EOKA**, in 1959 he signed a treaty with the Greek and Turkish Cypriot communities whereby Cyprus would become an independent republic in the British **COMMONWEALTH OF NATIONS**. After his party's election defeat in 1963, he left politics and lived abroad. He returned to become Prime Minister again in 1974, when he supervised the restoration of civilian rule after the collapse of the Colonels' dictatorship (1967–74), and drafted a new constitution introducing the office of President. He then served as President from 1980 to 1985, and from 1990 until his retirement in 1995. ➤ **GREEK COLONELS**

### Karami, Rashid (d.1987)
Lebanese politician. The son of Abd al-Hamid Karami, he succeeded to the leadership, albeit disputed, of the Muslims in the Tripoli area of Lebanon while still a young man. In the 1950s Karami established himself, along with Sa'ib Salam, as a politician with pro-**NASSER** sympathies, and became a member of the newly formed National Front, which constituted a concentration of all Camille **CHAMOUN**'s opponents. After Chamoun's departure following the disturbances of 1958, and Chehab's assumption of the presidency, Karami formed a predominantly National Front cabinet. A subsequent Christian strike drove home the fact that some Phalange and pro-Christian elements would have to be included and, accordingly, a new and more representative cabinet was formed. During the civil war in the 1970s, Karami was himself called upon to become Prime Minister. He was confronted with the problem of trying to ensure stability while, on the one hand, negotiating with the President to bring an end to the fighting and, on the other hand, having to recognize that, in the environs of Tripoli, Tony Franjiyeh's ultra-right Zghorta Liberation Army was at daggers drawn with his own supporters. Much later Karami, who must be regarded as amongst those Lebanese politicians who strove to save the country, headed the coalition government formed by President Amin **GEMAYEL** in 1984. Karami was assassinated in 1987.

### Kara Mustafa (d.1683)
Turkish Grand Vizier. He was brought up in the family of Grand Vizier Mehmet **KÖPRÜLÜ**, whose daughter he married. On the death of Fazil Ahmed **KÖPRÜLÜ** in 1676, Kara Mustafa became Grand Vizier and in 1682 he conquered the whole of upper Hungary while gathering a huge army for an assault upon Vienna. The Austrians, reinforced by the Polish King **JOHN III SOBIESKI**, forced the Ottomans to retreat, and Kara Mustafa was dismissed and executed in Belgrade.

**Karamzin, Nikolai Mikhailovich** (1766–1826)
Russian historian. In 1790–2 he wrote the *Moscow Journal*; in 1802 he began publishing the *Messengers of Europe*; and in 1804 he started compiling his *History of Russia*, which appeared in 12 volumes. In the years of the war against **NAPOLEON I** he helped to shape Russian patriotism. He also argued in favour of modernizing the language as a means of linking Russia with European ideas. Yet in his *Memorandum on Ancient and Modern Russia* in 1811, while attacking ministries, he still supported aristocracy. In short, he defended Tsarism while enabling its critics to have access to the ideas that would destroy it.

**Karavelov, Ljuben** (1834/5–79)
Bulgarian revolutionary and writer. Influenced by the Russian Slavophils and radical socialists he met while studying in Odessa, he joined the Bulgarian revolutionary organizations active in Serbia (1867) and founded the Bulgarian Revolutionary Committee with Khristo **BOTEV** and Vasil Levski in Bucharest (1871). He published the two journals *Freedom* (1869–72) and *Independence* (1873–4), and in his novels and memoirs attacked both the Greeks and the Turks as the Bulgarians' oppressors. ► **SLAVOPHILS AND WESTERNERS**

**Kardelj, Edvard** (1910–79)
Yugoslav (Slovene) politician. A schoolteacher, he joined the Communist Party and was among the many imprisoned during the dictatorship of **ALEXANDER I**. He lived in the USSR and joined **TITO** as a partisan during **WORLD WAR II**, becoming Vice-President of **AVNOJ** and in 1946 Foreign Minister and Deputy Prime Minister. With **DJILAS** he went to Moscow in 1948 to face **STALIN**'s criticism of Yugoslavia's independent foreign policy and stood firm with Tito in demonstrating that Yugoslavia would not become merely a Soviet satellite. He was the prominent theoretician of Tito's post-war regime, drawing up the federal constitution and leading the search for a **MARXISM** purified of all Stalinist accretions.

**Karen**
Heterogeneous peoples, found in parts of Lower Burma, along the Thai–Burmese border and in north-west Thailand. At present, over 90 per cent of the estimated 3 million Karen live in Burma. It is generally accepted that the Karen first appeared in the territory of present-day Burma c.500AD, thus preceding Burman, Thai and **MON**. From the 1820s, US Baptist missionaries found large numbers of converts among the Karen, thus encouraging further a distinct Karen identity, and the National Karen Association was founded in 1881. In granting Burma independence in 1948, the British refused Karen appeals for the creation of a separate Karen state and the following year the Karen National Union declared a rebellion against Rangoon. Although the Karen forces were driven back, their demands for autonomy continue.

**Karl VIII** (of Sweden) ► **KARL KNUTSSON**

**Karl XVI Gustav** ► **CHARLES XVI GUSTAV**

**Karl Knutsson** (1408–70)
King of Sweden (1448/57, 1464/5 and 1467/70) and of Norway (1449/50). A powerful Swedish magnate,

he was appointed guardian of the realm after the rebellion of **ENGELBREKT ENGELBREKTSSON** and during the reign of Christopher III (Christopher of Bavaria) he was given large fiefs in Finland. On Christopher's death in 1448, he was elected King of Sweden by his fellow nobles. In 1457 he was driven from Sweden by an insurrection in favour of **CHRISTIAN I** of Denmark, but was twice recalled by factions opposed to the **KALMAR UNION**.

**Karlowitz, Treaty of** (1699)
The peace settlement which was concluded at the end of the so-called Vienna War (1684–99) between the Ottoman Sultan Mustafa II and Emperor **LEOPOLD I** with his allies in the **HOLY LEAGUE** (Poland, Venice and the papacy). The Emperor gained all the liberated Croatian and Hungarian lands (except the Banat of **TEMESVÁR**) and Transylvania. The Republic of Venice gained the Peloponnese and regained the Dalmatian coast. Poland regained Podolia and a part of the Ukraine but surrendered its conquests in Moldavia. The treaty marked the beginning of the Ottoman retreat from Europe.

**Karmal, Babrak** (1929–96)
Afghan politician. Educated at Kabul University, where he studied law and political science, he was imprisoned for anti-government activity during the early 1950s. In 1965 he formed the Khalq ('Masses') Party and, in 1967, the breakaway Parcham ('Banner') Party. These two groups merged in 1977 to form the banned People's Democratic Party of Afghanistan (PDPA), with Karmal as deputy leader. After briefly holding office as President and Prime Minister in 1978, he was forced into exile in Eastern Europe, returning in 1979, after the Soviet military invasion, to become head of state. Karmal's rule was fiercely opposed by the **MUJAHIDIN** guerrillas and in 1986 he was replaced as President and PDPA leader by Sayid Muhammad **NAJIBULLAH**.

**Kärnten** ► **CARINTHIA**

**Károlyi, Mihályi, Count** (1875–1955)
Hungarian politician. In 1901 he classified himself a liberal, but from 1906 an independent. Despite his aristocratic background he struggled for democratic reforms, and during **WORLD WAR I** he opposed the alliance with Germany. In 1918 he was briefly Prime Minister, and President from Jan to July 1919. His well-known willingness to accommodate the subject nationalities won him the wrath of most of his fellow Magyars and he was forced into exile. Before and during **WORLD WAR II** he won an international reputation as a champion of democratic Hungary, and he served as Ambassador in Paris (1947–9). With the triumph of **COMMUNISM**, he was once more compelled to flee abroad.

**Károlyi, Sandor, Baron** (1668–1743)
Hungarian landowner, soldier and politician. Lord-Lieutenant of Szatmár county, he became a leading general in Ferenc **RÁKÓCZI**'s army revolting against Austrian rule in the period 1703–11. Without Rákóczi's consent he concluded the compromise peace of Szatmár. He was subsequently successful in institutionalizing this compromise so that the Hungarian diet enjoyed privileges not granted to others in the Habsburg Empire. He also began textile

manufacturing on his estates, assisting his country's recovery from its long wars. ► HABSBURG DYNASTY

### Kartini, Raden Adjeng (1879–1904)

Javanese aristocrat, one of the first to advocate equal opportunities for Indonesian women. Her ideas and aspirations, as expressed in letters to a Dutch pen-friend, were published as *Door duisternis tot licht* (1911, 'Through Darkness into Light'). She set up a school in her house in 1903, with the blessing of the Education Minister. She later started another school with her husband, the Regent of Renbang, but died soon after giving birth to her first child.

### Karume, Sheikh Abeid (1905–72)

Zanzibari politician. A sailor, he became active in local politics in the 1940s, was elected a town councillor in 1954 and helped found the Afro-Shirazi Party in 1957. Following the 1964 coup that deposed the Sultan of Zanzibar, he became President of the Revolutionary Council. When Zanzibar united with Tanganyika in 1964 to form Tanzania, he became Vice-President, but his expressed opposition to democratic changes made him enemies and he was assassinated in 1972.

### Kasavubu, Joseph (1910–69)

Zairean politician. Educated locally in a seminary, he worked as a teacher and civil servant in the Belgian colonial administration before entering politics. He was Mayor of Leopoldville in 1957 and, supported by the UN in his struggle for power against Patrice LUMUMBA, became President of the Republic of the Congo in 1960. In the ensuing civil war he first defeated MOBUTU's challenge and recaptured the presidency, but was later deposed by Mobutu, whom he had appointed as Commander-in-Chief.

### Kashmir Problem

In 1947, at the time of the partition of India, Kashmir was a largely Muslim-populated state with a Hindu ruler. In Oct 1947 there was an uprising of Muslims in western Kashmir, supported from across the border in Pakistan. Kashmir appealed to India, which sent troops in exchange for the accession of the kingdom to the Indian Union. After fighting had continued for several months, the UN intervened in 1949, establishing along the ceasefire line a provisional demarcation line which left most of Kashmir with India. India and Pakistan fought a second war over Kashmir in 1965, with a truce being agreed at Tashkent the following year. After the 1971 Bangladesh War, both countries accepted, under the terms of the 1972 Simla Agreement, that the Kashmir problem ought to be settled bilaterally. Subsequent years have witnessed further turmoil in Kashmir, with some Kashmiris demanding an independent nation, and in 1999 serious violence broke out again when a force of around 600, allegedly organized by the Pakistan army, crossed the Line of Control (LOC), to which India responded with air strikes directed at the newly occupied areas. An Indo-Pakistan summit in Jul 2001 failed to reach an agreement. Despite US urging, Pakistan failed to control the militants at the time of the AFGHAN WAR (2001), and Kashmiri attacks on the Kashmiri assembly in Oct 2001 and the Indian parliament in Dec exacerbated tensions to the point that war seemed imminent until in Jan 2002 President Pervez MUSHARRAF of Pakistan called for a negotiated settlement and said that Kashmiri fighters would no longer be able to operate from Pakistan. Tension remained high in 2003, with frequent exchanges across the LOC between Indian and Pakistani troops; a ceasefire was announced in Nov 2003. Diplomatic talks between the two countries began in Jun 2004, raising hopes for peace talks.

### Katanga

The southernmost province of the Democratic Republic of the Congo (previously Zaire), rich in minerals. In 1960, when the Congo achieved independence from Belgium, Katanga (called Shaba since 1972) attempted to secede under the leadership of Moïse TSHOMBE. In the ensuing chaos the government of Patrice LUMUMBA was overthrown. Lumumba was assassinated in 1961, and the unitary state was later re-created under the military leadership of President MOBUTU.

### Katayama Tetsu (1887–1978)

Japanese politician. A Christian socialist, he helped form the Socialist People's Party (*Shakai Minshuto*) in 1926, one of a number of 'proletarian parties' founded during the 1920s. In 1945 Katayama emerged as the leader of the newly created JAPAN SOCIALIST PARTY, which achieved a plurality of votes in the first elections held under the 1947 Peace Constitution. He headed a coalition government in 1947–8, the country's first and, to date, only socialist Prime Minister. Katayama's government created a new Ministry of Labour, enacted the Anti-Monopoly Law, and presided over the dissolution of the ZAIBATSU, the pre-war financial combines. The government became increasingly unpopular, however, when economic crisis forced it to impose price and wage controls. After his resignation in 1948, Katayama became identified with the party's right wing. In 1960 he joined a breakaway group that formed the moderate Democratic Socialist Party, which, unlike the larger Socialist Party, supported the 1951 Security Treaty with the USA.

### Katholieke Volkspartij ► CATHOLIC PEOPLE'S PARTY (NETHERLANDS)

### Katkov, Mikhail Nikiforovich (1818–87)

Russian journalist. He was Professor of Philosophy at Moscow from 1845 to 1850, when the teaching of his subject was stopped, and after 1861 he was editor of the *Moscow Gazette*. He was at first an advocate of reform, a vaguely Pan-Slav liberal, but he was converted by the Polish rising of 1863 into a crudely chauvinist Russian, increasingly supportive of reactionary Tsarist government. Because of his success as a publicist, he accordingly did great damage to the cause of moderate reform in 19c Russia.

### Kato Takaaki, also called Kato Komei (1860–1926)

Japanese politician. He initially worked for the firm of Mitsubishi, marrying the daughter of its founder, IWASAKI YATARO. He studied in England (1883–5) and was to remain an enthusiastic Anglophile throughout his life. As Minister to Britain (1894–1900), he supported the idea of an ANGLO-JAPANESE ALLIANCE. Elected to the Diet in 1902 he joined a political party, the *Doshikai* (Constitutional Association of Friends) in 1913, soon becoming its leader. While Foreign Minister (1914–16), Kato attempted to follow a policy free from the interference of the **GENRO**. He engineered Japan's entrance into **WORLD WAR I** on the side of the Allies in 1914 as a means of expanding Japan's influence in China. As leader of the moderately progressive **KENSEIKAI**, which became the largest single party in the 1924 elections, Kato became Prime Minister (1924–6). During his premiership, universal male suffrage was enacted (1925), but attempts to reform the upper house (House of Peers) failed. In order to placate conservative critics, Kato's government also enacted the Peace Preservation Law (1925) to restrict left-wing thought. He died in office. ➤ **PEACE PRESERVATION LAWS**

## Katsura Taro (1847–1913)
Japanese army general and politician. A member of the **CHOSHU** clique, he was a general in the **SINO-JAPANESE WAR** (1894–5), Governor-General of Japan's colony of Taiwan (1896–8) and Army Minister, before serving as Prime Minister on three occasions (1901–6, 1908–11 and 1912–13). He helped reorganize the army on the German model, and during his terms as Prime Minister Japan became a major imperialist power, forging an alliance with Britain (1902), defeating Russia (1905) and annexing Korea (1910). In 1912 he came under increasing attack in and outside the Diet for his increased military expenditures and his attempts to stay in power by creating his own party (*Doshikai*) to rival the majority party, the **SEIYUKAI**. He resigned in Feb 1913 and died shortly afterwards.

## Katyn Massacre (May 1940)
A massacre of more than 10,000 Polish army officers in the Katyn forest near Smolensk, Belorussia. The officers were shot and buried, and their mass graves were discovered by German occupying forces in 1943. Soviet authorities persistently denied responsibility for the massacre, blaming it on the Germans. In 1989 the Soviet–Polish Historical Commission (set up in 1987 to establish the truth) reported that the crime was most probably committed by the Soviet security service (NKVD). This was later confirmed by the Soviet authorities. ➤ **WORLD WAR II**

## Kaufmann, Konstantin Petrovich (1818–82)
Russian general and administrator. He distinguished himself at the successful siege of Kars (1855) during the **CRIMEAN WAR**, and from 1867 to 1882 was Governor of Turkestan. In 1868 he occupied Samarkand, and in 1873 conducted the campaign against Khiva. He effectively brought the three khanates of Bukhara, Khiva and Kokand under the control of the Russian Empire.

## Kaunda, Kenneth David (1924–)
Zambian nationalist leader and politician. Educated in mission schools and Munali Secondary School, he became a teacher and welfare officer before entering politics and becoming Secretary-General of the (Northern Rhodesian) **ANC** in 1953, breaking away from it to form the Zambian African National Congress in 1958. After a spell in prison as a result of his nationalist activities, he replaced Mainza Chona as leader of the United National Independence Party (**UNIP**) in 1960 and, after UNIP won elections in

1961, he was made Minister of Local Government and Social Welfare (1962–3) in the first black African government and then, on independence in 1964, he became President. A close friend of Julius **NYERERE**, he espoused a version of African socialism called **HUMANISM**, made UNIP the sole legitimate party and oversaw a steady decline in the country's economic position and political liberalism. Forced by the democratic movement elsewhere in the world and internal pressures, he called an election in 1991 and was defeated. He was implicated in a plot to overthrow his successor, Frederick Chiluba, in 1997 and placed under house arrest until charges against him were dropped in 1998.

## Kaunitz-Rietberg, Wenzel Anton, Prince von (1711–94)
Austrian statesman. He distinguished himself in 1748 at the congress of Aix-la-Chapelle, and as Austrian ambassador at the French court from 1750 to 1752 converted old enmity into friendship. In 1753 he was appointed chancellor, and for almost 40 years directed Austrian politics. Active in the ecclesiastical reforms of **JOSEPH II**, he was a liberal patron of arts and sciences.

## Kautsky, Karl Johann (1854–1938)
German socialist leader. In 1883 he founded and edited *Die Neue Zeit*. A disciple of **MARX**, he wrote a study of Marxist economic theory (1887), and of Sir Thomas More and his *Utopia* (1888). He also wrote against Bolshevism in *Die Diktatur des Proleteriats* (1918, trans 1931). ➤ **MARXISM**

## Kawakami Hajime (1879–1946)
Japanese economist. He played a significant role in popularizing **MARXISM** in Japan after 1918. As Professor of Economics at Kyoto University (1908–28), Kawakami placed most emphasis on the moral aspects of Marxism, and drew the public's attention to the poverty-stricken conditions of Japanese workers and tenant farmers. He was forced to resign his university post in 1928 as part of the government's campaign against left-wing thought. After an unsuccessful attempt to run for the Diet in 1930, he joined the **JAPAN COMMUNIST PARTY** (1933). He was arrested shortly afterwards and imprisoned until 1937.

## Kawawa, Rashidi Mfaume (1926–)
Tanzanian trade unionist, nationalist leader and politician. From an early age he was involved in labour politics, becoming President of the Tanganyika African Civil Servants' Association. He joined the Tanganyika African Association (1951–6) and was a founder-member, and later Secretary-General and President of the Tanganyika Federation of Labour. From 1957 he was a member of the Tanganyika Legislative Council and, when Julius **NYERERE** resigned as Prime Minister (1962), Kawawa briefly replaced him. He became first Vice-President (1962–4) and was re-elected after the amalgamation of Tanganyika and Zanzibar until 1972, when he was once again appointed Prime Minister. As a result of his overly zealous commitment to the **TANGANYIKA AFRICAN NATIONAL UNION** guidelines set forth in the **ARUSHA DECLARATION**, he was demoted to Minister of Defence and National Service in 1977, but returned to

the office of President in 1980. He lost status in government when **MWINYI** replaced Nyerere, but he was re-elected almost unanimously as Secretary-General of **CHAMA CHA MAPINDUZI** (CCM) in the 1987 Congress, a position he held until 1993.

**KAZAKHSTAN** official name **Republic of Kazakhstan**, also spelled **Kazakstan**

A republic in western Asia, bounded to the north by Russia; to the south by Turkmenistan, Uzbekistan and Kyrgyzstan; to the east by China; and to the west by the Caspian Sea. Formerly the home of nomadic Kazakhs and ruled by Mongol khans, it was taken over by Tsarist Russia during the 19c. In the early 20c a nationalist movement was violently suppressed. The country became the Kazakh Autonomous Soviet Socialist Republic and joined the USSR in 1936. In 1991 it became an independent republic under President Nursultan **NAZARBAEV**, leader of the Socialist Party, the renamed former Communist Party, and became a founding member of the **CIS** (Commonwealth of Independent States). In 1993 it ratified **START** I and began a process of economic reform. It has huge oil reserves, exported through a pipeline to the Black Sea opened in 2001.

**Kazembe, Kingdom of**
Central African kingdom founded in the mid-18c by one of the dynasties that were offshoots of the Lunda empire, and situated in the Luapula Valley between Lake Mweru and Katanga. It occupied a strategic position rich in resources of salt, iron and copper, and attracted the interest of the Portuguese. However, it was divided in the late 19c between King **LEOPOLD II** of the Belgians and Cecil **RHODES' BRITISH SOUTH AFRICA COMPANY**.

**Kearny, Philip** (1814–62)
US general. He began his military career as a second lieutenant of cavalry on the Western frontier under the command of his uncle, Colonel Stephen Watts **KEARNY**. He later fought in the Mexican War, losing an arm, and in 1859 he went to France to serve with **NAPOLEON III**. He became the first American to earn the cross of the French Legion of Honour but returned to the USA at the outbreak of the **AMERICAN CIVIL WAR** and became a brigadier-general of Union forces. A popular commander, he played an important role in the **PENINSULAR CAMPAIGN**, earning him promotion to major-general. He was killed during a reconnoitring mission in Virginia.

**Kearny, Stephen Watts** (1794–1848)
US general. He enlisted in the US army at the outbreak of the **WAR OF 1812**, and spent much of the next 35 years on frontier duty. As brigadier-general of the army of the West during the **MEXICAN WAR**, he used diplomacy to occupy Sante Fe, New Mexico, in 1846, then proceeded with a small force to California,

which was thought to have been pacified by Commodore Robert F Stockton but which was in fact still the scene of vigorous resistance by the Mexican-Californians. A conflict of authority with Stockton led to the arrest of John Charles Frémont, who had been named Governor of California by Stockton, and Kearny remained as military governor of the territory. He then became Governor-General of Veracruz and Mexico City (1848).

**Keating, Paul John** (1944– )
Australian Labor politician. Born in Sydney, he entered politics in 1969 as Labor MP for Blaxland. A committed republican, he opposed Australia's continuing links with the British Royal family and made it his party's policy to end them. In 1991 he was elected Prime Minister and produced proposals to turn Australia into a republic by the end of the century. Although the policy attracted wide support, he was defeated in the 1996 general election and announced that he was leaving politics. He was succeeded as party leader by Kim Beazley.

**Kefauver, (Carey) Estes** (1903–63)
US political leader. He was elected by his home state to the **HOUSE OF REPRESENTATIVES** (1939–49) and the **SENATE** (1949–63). A Democrat, he supported the **NEW DEAL** and fought monopolies. He was noted for conducting televised Senate hearings concerned with the investigation of organized crime (1950–1).

**keiretsu**
A Japanese term describing a loose conglomeration of companies organized around a single bank and holding shares in other companies. These developed in Japan after **WORLD WAR II** when anti-trust legislation was introduced to break up **ZAIBATSU**. After 1948, and especially during the **KOREAN WAR**, an economically strong, capitalist Japan was considered essential, and so a modified form of *zaibatsu* was encouraged. *Keiretsu* are usually either horizontally or vertically organized. The largest horizontal *keiretsu* span a wide range of industries; the 'big six' (DKB, Fuyo, Mitsubishi, Mitsui, Sanwa and Sumitomo) are of this sort. Newer, vertical *keiretsu* are typical of large manufacturing company groups and are usually more closely connected to the original industry; examples include the vehicle manufacturers Toyota, Nissan and Honda and the electronics firms Hitachi, Toshiba and Sanyo. Economic downturns have loosened the ties binding together these conglomerates.

**Keita, Modibo** (1915–77)
Mali politician. Educated at William Ponty School, Dakar, he helped to found the **RASSEMBLEMENT DÉMOCRATIQUE AFRICAIN** in 1946 and was elected to the territorial assembly in 1948. He was a deputy in the French Assembly (1956–9) before becoming President of the Mali Federation (1959–60) and at independence President of Mali (1960–8). A radical who looked to **NKRUMAH** for leadership, he was overthrown by the military in 1968 and was imprisoned until his death.

**Keitel, Wilhelm** (1882–1946)
German field marshal and Nazi collaborator. He joined the army in 1901, and became an artillery staff officer in **WORLD WAR I**. An ardent Nazi and close associate of **HITLER**, he was made Chief of the Supreme

Command of the Armed Forces (1938). In 1940 he signed the Compiègne armistice with France, and in 1945 was one of the German signatories of surrender in Berlin. He was convicted of war crimes at the **NUREMBERG TRIALS**, and executed. ► **NAZI PARTY**; **WORLD WAR II**

### Kekkonen, Urho Kaleva (1900–86)

Finnish politician. After studying law at Helsinki University and fighting against the **BOLSHEVIKS** in 1918, he entered the Finnish parliament as an Agrarian Party deputy, holding ministerial office in 1936–9 and 1944. He was Prime Minister on four occasions in the early 1950s before being elected President (1956), in succession to Juho **PAASIKIVI**. Although Kekkonen had always been hostile to Stalinist Russia, as President he encouraged a policy of cautious friendship with the USSR. At the same time his strict neutrality ensured that he retained the confidence of his Scandinavian neighbours. He supported Finland's membership of **EFTA** (1961) and in 1975 was host to the 35-nation European Security Conference in Helsinki. Five years later he accepted a Lenin Peace Prize. His popularity in Finland led to the passage of special legislation enabling him to remain in office until 1984, but his health gave way and he resigned in 1981. ► **STALINISM**

### Kellogg–Briand Pact (27 Aug 1928)

A proposal made by French Foreign Minister Aristide **BRIAND** to US Secretary of State Frank B Kellogg (1856–1937) that the two countries should sign a pact renouncing war as an instrument of national policy. At Kellogg's suggestion, a Paris conference in 1928 formally condemned recourse to war, and the pact was subsequently signed by 65 states (the Pact of Paris). However, no provision was made for the punishment of aggressors.

### Kelly, Ned (1855–80)

Australian bushranger, the son of an Irish convict. Brought up in an environment of lawlessness, stock theft and conflicts with the police, Kelly was arrested four times between 1869 and 1871, served three years in prison for horse-stealing (1871–4), and began horse-stealing again in 1876. In 1878 the attempt to arrest his brother, Dan, also for horse-stealing, led to allegations that Ned, Dan, Mrs Kelly and two others had tried to murder a trooper named Fitzpatrick. Mrs Kelly was sentenced to three years' imprisonment, and Ned and Dan went into hiding where they were joined by Steve Hart and Joe Byrne. At Stringybark Creek, three of the four policemen in pursuit were killed by the gang, which then robbed banks at Euroa and Jerilderee. Kelly's plan to lure the police into a trap and derail their train at Glenrowan backfired when the police were warned. Trapped in the Glenrowan Hotel, three of the gang were killed and Kelly, despite his body armour and headgear, was shot and captured. He was hanged in Melbourne in 1880. By far the most famous of the bushrangers, his feats and defiance of authority made him a legendary figure.

### Kennan, George Frost (1904–2005)

US diplomat and historian. After graduating from Princeton in 1925 he joined the US foreign service. During **WORLD WAR II** he served in diplomatic posts in Berlin, Lisbon and Moscow, and in 1947 was appointed director of policy planning by Secretary of State George C **MARSHALL**. He advocated the policy of '**CONTAINMENT**' of the USSR by political, economic and diplomatic means, which was adopted by Secretaries of State Dean **ACHESON**, and John Foster **DULLES**. Kennan subsequently served as US Ambassador in Moscow (1952–3) and Yugoslavia (1961–3). From 1956 to 1974, as Professor of History at the Institute for Advanced Study at Princeton, he revised his strategic views and called for US 'disengagement' from Europe.

### Kennedy, Edward Moore, also called Ted Kennedy (1932– )

US politician. The younger brother of John F **KENNEDY** and Robert F **KENNEDY**, he was educated at Harvard and the University of Virginia. He was called to the Bar in 1959, and elected a Democratic Senator in 1962. In 1969 he became the youngest-ever majority whip in the **SENATE**, where he has established a notable record on advancing liberal issues. But his involvement the same year in a car accident at Chappaquiddick, in which a companion (Mary Jo Kopechne) was drowned, dogged his subsequent political career. In 1979 he was an unsuccessful candidate for the presidency; the nomination went to Jimmy **CARTER**, who became President in 1980.

### Kennedy, John F(itzgerald) (1917–63)

US politician and 35th President. Educated at Harvard, he joined the US Navy in 1941 and became a torpedo boat commander in the Pacific. Elected to the **HOUSE OF REPRESENTATIVES** as a Democrat in 1947, he became Senator from Massachusetts in 1952 and President in 1960. He was the first Catholic, and the youngest person, to be elected President. His domestic policies called for a 'new frontier' in social legislation, involving a federal **DESEGREGATION** policy in education, and **CIVIL RIGHTS** reform. Although criticized for his handling of the **BAY OF PIGS**, he later displayed firmness and moderation in foreign policy. In 1962 he induced the USSR to withdraw its missiles from Cuba, and he negotiated a partial **NUCLEAR TEST-BAN TREATY** with the Soviets the following year. On 22 Nov 1963, he was assassinated by rifle fire while being driven in an open car through Dallas, Texas. The alleged assassin, Lee Harvey **OSWALD**, was himself shot and killed two days later, during a jail transfer. ► **CUBAN MISSILE CRISIS**; **DEMOCRATIC PARTY**; **KENNEDY, ROBERT F**

### Kennedy, Joseph Patrick (1888–1969)

US businessman and diplomat. The grandson of an Irish Catholic immigrant, he was educated at Harvard. During the 1930s, as a strong supporter of **ROOSEVELT** and the '**NEW DEAL**', he was rewarded with minor administrative posts, and the ambassadorship to Great Britain (1937–40). He had political ambitions for his sons, and placed his large fortune at their disposal for that purpose. The eldest, Joseph Patrick (1915–44), was killed in a flying accident while on naval service in **WORLD WAR II**. The others achieved international political fame. ► **KENNEDY, EDWARD M**; **KENNEDY, JOHN F**; **KENNEDY, ROBERT F**

### Kennedy, Robert Francis (1925–68)

US politician. Educated at Harvard and the University

of Virginia, he served in the US Navy during **WORLD WAR II**, was admitted to the Bar (1951), and became a member of the staff of the **SENATE** Select Committee on Improper Activities (1957–60). He managed the presidential campaign of his brother, John F **KENNEDY**, and as his Attorney-General (1961–4) and closest adviser, actively sought to enforce laws that guaranteed blacks **CIVIL RIGHTS**. In 1964 he was elected Senator for New York. On 5 June 1968 he was shot after winning the Californian primary election, and died the following day. His assassin, Sirhan Sirhan, was later convicted of murder.

### Kenseikai

The Japanese political party (literally, 'Constitutional Association') formed in 1916 by **KATO TAKAAKI**, calling for moderate reform and constitutional government. In 1924 the *Kenseikai* became the majority party in the Diet and joined with other parties to bring down a **GENRO**-chosen non-party cabinet. Kato then became Prime Minister of a Kenseikai-dominated coalition government (1924–6). This government promoted international cooperation, normalized relations with the USSR, reduced the number of army divisions and enacted universal male suffrage. In 1927 the Kenseikai fell from power and shortly thereafter became the *Rikken Minseito* ('Constitutional Democratic Party').

### Kentucky and Virginia Resolutions (1798 and 1799)

Declarations by two state legislatures that the **ALIEN AND SEDITION ACTS** violated the **US CONSTITUTION**. This laid the foundation for the future development of the doctrine of 'state sovereignty' and the state's right to nullify Federal law. The resolutions were written by Thomas **JEFFERSON** (Kentucky) and James **MADISON** (Virginia).

---

**KENYA** official name **Republic of Kenya**

A republic in East Africa, bounded to the south by Tanzania; to the west by Uganda; to the north-west by Sudan; to the north by Ethiopia; to the north-east by Somalia; and to the east by the Indian Ocean. Anthropologists have found fossils of very early hominids in the region. The coast was settled by Arabs in the 7c, and the country came under Portuguese control in the 16–17c, and under British control as an East African Protectorate in 1895. After it became a British colony in 1920, an independence movement led to the **MAU MAU** rebellion in 1952–60. Led by **KANU**, it gained independence in 1963 under Prime Minister Jomo **KENYATTA**, who became President when Kenya became a republic in 1964. He was suc-

ceeded on his death in 1978 by Daniel Tarap **MOI**. In 1991 a multiparty system was legalized. Moi won the elections of 1992 and 1998, amid allegations of electoral fraud, and during the 1990s there were sporadic outbreaks of violent unrest fuelled by demands for constitutional change. In the 2002 elections, Moi's chosen successor as president, Uhuru Kenyatta, was beaten by Mwai Kibaki, whose National Rainbow Coalition won the legislative elections.

### Kenyatta, Jomo, originally Kamau Ngengi (1891–1978)

Kenyan nationalist and politician. Educated by Scots missionaries, he joined the Young Kikuyu Association in 1922 and politics thereafter dominated his life. He edited the Kikuyu Central Association's newssheet, *Mwigwithania*, and played a major role in representing progressive black Kenyan opinion in the 1930s, visiting London on more than one occasion to lobby government. He visited the USSR several times and got to know most of the anti-colonial lobby in the UK, where he worked throughout **WORLD WAR II**. He attended the famous Fifth Pan-Africanist Conference at Manchester (1945) and, on his return to Kenya in 1946, he was elected President of the Kenyan African Union, becoming the country's major spokesman for the anti-colonial movement. On the outbreak of the **MAU MAU** uprising and the subsequent emergency, he was tried, found guilty on what later proved to be perjured evidence and was detained until 1961. Chosen *in absentia* to be President of the Kenyan African National Union (**KANU**) in 1960, he was elected in 1962 to the Legco and then, after the independence elections, became Prime Minister in 1963 and President when Kenya became a republic in 1964. A remarkable mixture of Kikuyu nationalist, pragmatic politician and father-figure (he was known as *Mzee* or 'old man'), he surprised observers by leading Kenya into a period of economic growth and unexpected tribal harmony.

### Kérékou, Mathieu Ahmed (1933– )

Benin soldier and politician. The son of a soldier, he joined the colonial army, being trained in France, whose army he served. He joined the Dahomey army at independence in 1961, rising to command it in 1966. He took part in the 1967 coup that overthrew President Soglo but returned to the army, while remaining Vice-President of the Military Revolutionary Council (CNR). In 1972 he led a further coup, establishing a National Council of Revolution and espousing 'scientific socialism'. He renamed Dahomey 'Benin', and began to return the country to democracy, being first elected to the presidency in 1980 and re-elected in 1984 and 1989. He dissolved the CNR and finally resigned from the army in 1987 as a gesture of his commitment to democracy. He announced his abandonment of **MARXISM** in 1991, and his intention to stand in open elections to be held that year. Defeated, he handed over power to a national conference, but was re-elected President in 1996 and again in 2001.

### Kerensky, Alexander Fyodorovich (1881–1970)

Russian socialist. He studied law in St Petersburg and made a name for himself as counsel for the defence in Tsarist times in several leading political trials. He was a critical but reasonable member of the third and fourth Dumas. In the 1917 **RUSSIAN REVOLUTION** he became Minister of Justice in Mar, Minister of War in May, and Prime Minister in July in the Provisional Government. Though crushing **KORNILOV**'s military revolt in Aug, he found it increasingly difficult to put through moderate reforms in a deteriorating political situation, and in Oct was swept away by the **BOLSHE-VIKS**, and fled to France. In 1940 he went to Australia and in 1946 to the USA, writing several books on the Revolution. He died in New York City. He was a talented, well-meaning politician, possibly too superficial and flamboyant to deal with a turbulent society and dedicated revolutionaries. ► **MENSHEVIKS**; **OCTOBER REVOLUTION**

**Kerr, Sir John Robert** (1914–91)
Australian administrator. Born in Sydney, he became a QC in 1953 and after a number of senior legal and judicial appointments, became Chief Justice of New South Wales in 1972, and Lieutenant-Governor in the following year. He was sworn in as Governor-General of the Commonwealth of Australia in 1974, and the next year made Australian constitutional history; the coalition opposition had refused to pass the government's budget bill unless a federal election was called. The private banks declined to release funds to enable the business of government to be conducted. To resolve this impasse he exercised his vice-regal 'reserve powers' and dismissed the Prime Minister, Gough **WHITLAM**, asking the Leader of the Opposition, Malcolm **FRASER**, to form a caretaker government and to call an immediate election. At that election, Kerr's actions were endorsed by the voters, who elected a new coalition government, led by Fraser. Stepping down as Governor-General in 1977, he was named Australian ambassador to **UNESCO** in 1978, but the ensuing controversy obliged him to resign without taking up the appointment.

**Kesselring, Albert** (1885–1960)
German air commander and field marshal in **WORLD WAR II**. He led the **LUFTWAFFE** attacks on France and (unsuccessfully) on Britain. In 1943 he was made Commander-in-Chief in Italy, and in 1945 in the West. Condemned to death as a war criminal in 1947, he had his sentence commuted to life imprisonment, but was released in 1952. ► **NAZI PARTY**

**Keynes, John Maynard Keynes, 1st Baron** (1883–1946)
English economist. Born in Cambridge, he was educated at Eton and King's College, Cambridge. In both World Wars he was an adviser to the Treasury. The unemployment crisis inspired his two great works, *A Treatise on Money* (1930) and the revolutionary *General Theory of Employment, Interest and Money* (1936). He argued that full employment was not an automatic condition, expounded a new theory of the rate of interest, and set out the principles underlying the flows of income and expenditure. His views on a planned economy influenced Franklin D **ROOSEVELT**'s **NEW DEAL** administration. In 1943 he proposed the international clearing union, and in 1944–6 he played a leading part in the formulation of the Bretton Woods agreements, the establishment of the **INTERNATIONAL MONETARY FUND** (IMF), and the troublesome, abortive negotiations for a continuation of the **LEND–LEASE AGREEMENT**. ► **BRETTON WOODS CONFERENCE**

**KGB** (*Komitet Gosudarstvennoy Bezopasnosti*, 'Committee for State Security')
From 1953 to 1991 one of the Soviet Union's two secret police organizations with joint responsibility for internal and external order, and security and espionage. Its tasks included the surveillance of key members of the Communist Party, the administration, and the military; the monitoring and regulation of dissidents and the population at large; and espionage and subversion abroad.

**Khalid ibn Abd al-Aziz al-Saud** (1913–82)
King of Saudi Arabia (1975/82). The fourth son of the founder of the Saudi Dynasty, he ascended the throne after the assassination of his brother **FAYSAL**. His caution and moderation served as a stabilizing factor in the Middle East; Khalid's personal influence was seen in the halting of the Lebanese Civil War (1975–6), and in his country's disagreement with the other members of **OPEC** over oil price increases. He died at Ta'if, Saudi Arabia.

**Khaljis**
A Turkish tribe, long-settled in Afghanistan, which ruled the kingdom of Delhi for 30 years from 1290, when Firuz Khalji, a Balban noble, ascended the throne. Firuz's nephew, **ALA AL-DIN KHALJI**, treacherously slew Firuz and proclaimed himself King in 1296. In 1304 and 1306, invading Mughal armies were defeated by Ala al-Din's forces. Further expeditions in 1310 plundered the Hoysalas and the Pandyas. Ala al-Din died in 1316 and his son, Mubarak, seized the throne. Mubarak quelled rebellions in Gujarat and Deogir, but was treacherously killed in 1320 by his Chief Minister, Khusrau Khan, who proclaimed himself King and wiped out the Khaljis.

**Khalkas**
The collective name for tribes in eastern Mongolia who allied with the Manchu **QING DYNASTY** during the 18c, helping the dynasty to extend its control over western Mongolia.

**Khama** (c.1837–1923)
King of the Ngwato, one of the Tswana peoples occupying the north of modern Botswana (1875/1923). He was a successful modernizing ruler, who avoided the direct conquest of his kingdom by seeking an accommodation with Europeans. In the late 19c Khama tried to protect his state from the **NDEBELE** to the north and the Boers to the east by securing the protection of missionaries and of British imperial rule. He first sought the protection of Queen **VICTORIA** in 1876, but a protectorate was not granted until 1885 and imperial rule not fully established until 1891. He succeeded in avoiding control by the **BRITISH SOUTH AFRICA COMPANY**, which had secured a charter to rule in Rhodesia. Khama had already become a Christian, insisting on the conversion of his entire people when he did so. He issued laws to reform African traditional customs such as bride-price and initiation ceremonies and banned the brewing of strong liquor in his kingdom. He visited London in 1895 on the occasion of the centenary of the founding of the London Missionary Society.

## Khama, Sir Seretse (1921–80)

Botswana Chief and politician. He was educated at Fort Hare College and London, where he trained as a lawyer. The heir to the chieftainship of the Ngwato, he only inherited the title in 1963. He was banned by the colonial authorities from returning to Bechuanaland because of his marriage to a white woman. When he was permitted to return as a private citizen in 1956, he founded the Bechuanaland Democratic Party, won a seat to Legco in 1965 and became President of the Republic of Botswana from its independence in 1966 to his death in 1980. Plagued by health problems, he nevertheless managed to steer Botswana with great skill along a democratic path in the shadow of South Africa.

## Khan, Abdul Qadeer (1935–)

Pakistani scientist. Born in India, he moved to Pakistan in 1952 and was educated there and in West Germany and Belgium. From 1972 to 1975 he worked at a uranium enrichment plant in Amsterdam run by the Dutch-British-German consortium URENCO. After his return to Pakistan in 1976 he became involved in Pakistan's nuclear weapons programme, reporting directly to the Prime Minister's office. Despite constraints on nuclear technology and limited resources, he succeeded in acquiring both uranium enrichment technology and bomb-making capability by 1988. During the 1990s he was suspected of selling uranium enrichment technology to Middle Eastern countries and President **MUSHARRAF** dismissed him in 2001, possibly under pressure from the USA. Following investigations in 2004 he admitted selling nuclear technology to Iran, Libya and North Korea. After this he was reportedly confined to his home but appears to have avoided legal action by cooperating with the authorities. ► **AXIS OF EVIL**; **TERROR, WAR ON**

## khedive

An ancient Persian title acquired from the Ottoman Sultan by the effectively independent Viceroy of Egypt, **ISMA'IL PASHA**, in 1867. It was used until Egypt became a British protectorate (1914).

## Khilafat Movement

A protest campaign by Indian Muslims (1919–24) against British policy towards the Sultan of Turkey, who was also Caliph of Islam. It joined forces with the **NON-COOPERATION MOVEMENT** for Indian independence. However, it was weakened by the Turks' own deposition of the Sultan (1923) and the abolition of the Caliphate (1924).

## Khitan (Ch'i-tan)

A federation of proto-Mongolian nomadic tribes that dominated north China in the 10–12c. Their ruler, Yelu Abauji (Yeh-lu A-pao-chi) (872–926) proclaimed himself Emperor of the Liao Dynasty (916–1125), which held sway over inner Mongolia and north China. Attempts by the Chinese **SONG DYNASTY** to dislodge them failed, and from the 11c the Song was forced to pay annual tribute to pacify the Khitan. Unlike many non-Chinese conquest dynasties, the Khitan Liao resisted sinicization, preserving its nomadic and shamanist practices, and treating the Chinese under its rule as an inferior caste. The Khitan were conquered by a forest-hunting tribe from east-

ern Manchuria, the Jurchen, who established their own dynasty, the Jin (Chin) (1122–1234), in northern China. ► **JIN (JURCHEN) DYNASTY**

## Khmer Empire

An empire in mainland South-East Asia, founded in the 7c, with its capital at **ANGKOR THOM** from 802 onwards. In the 11–12c it extended to South Laos and a large part of Thailand. It was eventually overthrown by the Thais in the 15c.

## Khmer Rouge

A Cambodian communist guerrilla force, which opposed the right-wing government that deposed Prince **SIHANOUK** in 1970 and the subsequent US invasion of eastern Cambodia. After gaining control of the country in 1975, its government, led by **POL POT**, set about a drastic transformation of 'Democratic Kampuchea', involving the mass forced evacuation from the towns to the countryside, the creation of agricultural cooperatives, and the execution of thousands of 'bourgeois elements'. In late 1978, Vietnam invaded Cambodia, and the Khmer Rouge were ousted, retiring to the Thai–Cambodian border region. Following the Vietnamese withdrawal from Cambodia in 1989, they mounted a major offensive, especially in the western and southern provinces. Western intelligence estimates suggest that the force at that time consisted of 20,000–35,000 armed men, with 50,000–100,000 refugees in Khmer Rouge-controlled camps along the border and in Thailand. As the Party of Democratic Kampuchea, it refused to take part in the multiparty elections in 1993 and continued violently to oppose the elected government. However, in 1996 it suffered internal divisions; a splinter group escaped from the Khmer Rouge to join the Cambodian government and the force appeared to be breaking up. Pol Pot, who was regarded as the overall leader, was put through a show trial in 1997 and sentenced to life imprisonment; he died in 1998. Other senior personnel included the deputy leader Ieng Sary (1930– ), who defected to the government in 1996, guerrilla commander Son Sen (1930–97), who was executed at Pol Pot's behest, and Khieu Samphan (1931– ), the leader of Khmer Rouge delegations at international conferences, who eventually pledged allegiance to the government in 1998.

## Khoisan

Groups of peoples inhabiting the Cape of Good Hope and encountered by the Dutch when landing at the Cape to trade and after their settlement of 1652. They are made up of the Khoikhoi (Hottentots) and San (Bushmen) people. The Khoikhoi were pastoralists, while the San were hunter-gatherers. However, there was a great deal of marital and economic interaction between them and they are generally grouped together. They spoke a language with distinctive click sounds which survives among the San and has lent its clicks to the Bantu language of the **NGUNI** people. The Dutch at first traded amicably with the Khoisan, but relations soon became bitter and violent. The Khoi, whose decentralized political system made it difficult for them to combine for military success, were devastated by war, the loss of their cattle through drought and raids, and outbreaks of smallpox. Under the **APARTHEID** regime, the Khoi were one element in the GATE COLOURED community while the San were marginalized in the Kalahari Desert. In 18c Europe, the word 'Hottentot' was used to mean any uncivilized person.

**Khomeini, Ayatollah Ruhollah**, originally **Ruhollah Musawi** (1900–89)
Iranian religious and political leader. A Shiite Muslim who was bitterly opposed to the pro-Western regime of Shah Muhammad Reza **PAHLAVI**, he was exiled to Turkey and Iraq in 1964, and from Iraq to France in 1978. He returned to Iran amid great popular acclaim in 1979 after the collapse of the Shah's government, and became virtual head of state. Under his leadership, Iran underwent a turbulent 'Islamic Revolution' in which a return was made to the strict observance of Muslim principles and traditions. In 1979 a new Islamic constitution was sanctioned, into which was incorporated his leadership concept of the *Vilayet-i faqih* ('Trusteeship of the Jurisconsult'). This supreme religious and political position was recognized as belonging to Khomeini, as was the title *Rahbar* ('Leader'). In 1989 he provoked international controversy by publicly commanding, through the issue of a fatwa, the killing of Salman **RUSHDIE**, author of the novel *The Satanic Verses* (1988).

**Khrushchev, Nikita Sergeevich** (1894–1971)
Soviet politician. Coming from a poor background and with little education but a sharp intellect, he joined the Communist Party in 1918, fought in the **RUSSIAN CIVIL WAR** and rose rapidly in the Party organization through working with **KAGANOVICH** and **STALIN**. In 1939 he was made a full member of the **POLITBURO** and of the Presidium of the Supreme Soviet. During **WORLD WAR II** he served as a senior political officer on the Ukrainian front. In 1953, on the death of Stalin, he became First Secretary of the **COMMUNIST PARTY OF THE SOVIET UNION**, though his position was not secure until 1955. In 1956, at the 20th Party Congress, he denounced **STALINISM** and the 'personality cult' in a well-known secret speech that fundamentally altered the course of Soviet history. Among the events of his administration were the 1956 Poznan Riots that he quietened down, the Hungarian Uprising that he crushed, and the failed attempt to install missiles in Cuba (1962). The latter, and his inability fundamentally to improve the Soviet economy, led to his being deposed in 1964 and replaced by Leonid **BREZHNEV** and Alexei **KOSYGIN**. He died in retirement in Moscow. ► **CUBAN MISSILE CRISIS**

**Khuen-Héderváry, Károly** (1849–1918)
Ban (Governor) of Croatia (1883–1903). A Hungarian landowner, he was supported by the Unionist Party which sought closer ties between Zagreb and Budapest. As ban, he established a Hungarian-dominated regime which ignored the historical rights of the Kingdom of Croatia and exploited antagonism between the Serbs, whom he conspicuously favoured, and the Croats over Bosnia and Herzegovina. In 1903 he left Croatia to become Prime Minister of Hungary (1903 and 1910–12). ► **NAGODBA**; **STARČEVIĆ, ANTE**

**Kiakhta, Treaty of** (1728)
A treaty signed by Tsarist Russia and **QING DYNASTY**

China, which attempted to solve border disputes and provide more trading opportunities between the two countries. The earlier Treaty of **NERCHINSK** (1689) had provided for Qing control of the Amur River region (in north Manchuria); the Treaty of Kiakhta drew a line between Kiakhta (south of Lake Baikal in Siberia) and the Argun River (flowing south from the Amur). The treaty also allowed Russia to trade at Kiakhta and other border settlements. The Russians were also permitted to maintain an Orthodox Church and hostel in Beijing for the benefit of visiting Russian merchants, the first time foreigners were allowed a permanent official presence in the Chinese capital.

**Kiangsi Soviet** ► **JIANGXI SOVIET**

**Kidd, William**, known as **Captain Kidd** (c.1645–1701)
Scottish merchant and privateer. Born in Greenock, Strathclyde, he worked as a successful sea captain with a small fleet of trading vessels, based in New York, in the 1680s. During the War of the League of **AUGSBURG** against France (1689–97), he fought as a privateer to protect Anglo-American trade routes in the West Indies. In 1695 he went to London and was given command of an expedition against pirates in the Indian Ocean. He reached Madagascar early in 1697, but instead of attacking pirates began to sanction attacks on merchant ships. After a two-year cruise he returned to the West Indies to find that he had been proclaimed a pirate. He sailed to Boston, where he surrendered on promise of a pardon (1699), but was sent as a prisoner to London, where he was convicted of piracy and hanged.

**Kido Koin**, also called **Kido Takayoshi** (1833–77)
Japanese **SAMURAI** politician. He played a prominent part in the **MEIJI RESTORATION** (1868) and helped cement the anti-Tokugawa alliance between his own domain of **CHOSHU** and that of **SATSUMA** in 1866. After 1868 Kido became one of the architects of the new centralized state. He was a member of **IWAKURA TOMOMI**'s mission to the West (1871–3) and, on his return, was the first Japanese leader to propose a constitution for Japan, based on the German model. ► **TOKUGAWA SHOGUNATE**

**Kiesinger, Kurt Georg** (1904–88)
West German politician. Educated at Berlin and Tübingen, he then practised as a lawyer (1935–40), and served during **WORLD WAR II** at the Foreign Office on radio propaganda. Interned after the war until 1947, he was exonerated of Nazi crimes. In 1949 he became a member of the **BUNDESTAG**, and succeeded **ERHARD** as Chancellor (1966). A Christian Democrat and long a convinced supporter of **ADENAUER**'s plans for European unity, he formed with Willy **BRANDT** a government combining the Christian Democratic Union (**CDU**) and the Social Democrats (**SPD**). He was Chancellor from 1966 to 1969, when, following election defeat, he was succeeded by Brandt.

**Kiev Rus** (c.882–1240)
The first settled Russian state, famed for princes such as Oleg, Igor, Sviatoslav, Vladimir, Jaroslav and Vladimir Monomakh, but also for periods of civil war. At times it extended towards the Baltic and Black seas, but it was frequently threatened by other tribes on the move; in the end it succumbed to the **MONGOLS**.

It arose around Kiev on the strength of trade routes and declined as the routes shifted to the Mediterranean. Possibly its most important contribution to history was its conversion to Christianity in 988 or thereabouts. This guaranteed that Russia would be neither Muslim nor Judaic and would become part of Europe. Kiev Rus has also been one of the bases for Ukrainian nationalism, requited in 1991.

## Kiheitai

A volunteer militia unit (literally, 'irregular militia') organized by the Japanese domain of CHOSHU in 1863 at a time when the Western powers were threatening to take military action in response to attacks on foreigners in the TREATY PORTS. Significantly, it recruited from amongst all social classes, including peasants, thus breaking with the tradition whereby military functions were monopolized by the SAMURAI class. The unit was equipped with modern rifles and its leaders were chosen on the basis of ability rather than hereditary status. It played a part in the overthrow of the TOKUGAWA SHOGUNATE. Although the Kiheitai was disbanded in 1869, it served as a model for the 1873 Conscription Law, which provided for a national army drawing on all ranks in society.

## Kikuyu Central Association (KCA)

A society founded in Kenya in 1922 under the leadership of Harry Thuku. Jomo KENYATTA, the future nationalist leader and President of Kenya, became Secretary-General of the KCA, which became the basis of African politics in the British colony. It took up African grievances such as the European occupation of Kikuyu lands in the 'White Highlands' and the missionary campaign to abolish female circumcision. It established the Kikuyu leadership of nationalism in Kenya, but was banned during WORLD WAR II. The Kenya African Union emerged as its successor in 1944.

## Kilwa

A great trading town on the coast of southern Tanzania, which acted as the major entrepôt of the trade of the interior of East-Central Africa with the Middle East and the Indian Ocean. Kilwa owed its rise to the migration of Shirazi merchants from the Persian Gulf in the 12c. By the early 14c it had supplanted Mogadishu as the greatest port on the coast, the southern limit of the Arab traders who used the annual monsoons to connect Africa to Asia. It flourished for the succeeding two centuries until sacked by the Portuguese. Its remaining ruins are testimony to its magnificence in its heyday with palaces, mosques and warehouses built of coral. It became a slaving port in the 18c.

## Kimberley, Siege of (1899–1900)

One of the three sieges of the second Boer War, in which Boer forces attempted to pen up their British opponents and secure control of vital lines of communication. The siege lasted from the middle of Oct 1899 until Feb 1900, when the town was relieved by General John FRENCH. ➤ BOER WARS

## Kim Chong-il (Kim Jong II) (1942– )

North Korean politician. The eldest son of the North Korean communist leader KIM IL SUNG, he was born in the USSR, where his mother had retreated from the Korean anti-Japanese guerrilla base in Manchuria. Kim Chong-il played a leading part in ideological and propaganda work, helping to create the cult that surrounded his father. In 1980 he became First Secretary of the Party's Central Committee. From 1982, frequently referred to as the 'dear leader', he was regarded as heir-apparent, and he officially succeeded his father in 1998.

## Kim Dae Jung (1925– )

South Korean politician. A Roman Catholic, he was imprisoned by communist troops during the KOREAN WAR. He challenged General PARK for the presidency in 1971 and was later imprisoned (1976–8 and 1980–2) for alleged 'anti-government activities'. He lived in exile in the USA (1982–5) and on his return successfully spearheaded an opposition campaign for democratization. In the 1987 presidential election he was defeated by the government nominee, ROH TAE WOO. In 1995 he formed the National Congress for New Politics (NCNP), and in 1997, partly by creating a strategic alliance with the United Liberal Democrats (ULD), became the first opposition candidate to win the presidential election. In 2000 he took part in groundbreaking talks with North Korea and was awarded the NOBEL PEACE PRIZE.

## Kim-Il Sung, originally Kim Song-ju (1912–94)

North Korean soldier and politician. He founded the Korean People's Revolutionary Army in 1932, and led a long struggle against the Japanese. He proclaimed the Republic in 1948, and remained effective head of state until his death. He was re-elected President in 1982, having named his son, KIM CHONG-IL, as his eventual political successor. Throughout his long dictatorship he isolated his country by working against Western interests wherever he could and by being hostile towards South Korea; he also refused to agree to inspection of his nuclear arsenal and threatened to pull out of the NUCLEAR NON-PROLIFERATION TREATY. At home he dealt ruthlessly with anyone who dared to oppose him and developed a personality cult that pervaded every aspect of North Korean life. His death in 1994 was greeted by scenes of massive public grief.

## Kim Jong II ➤ KIM CHONG-IL

## Kim Ok-kyun (1851–94)

Korean revolutionary. From a prominent family, he served in the government of King Kojong (1864/1907) and, after visiting Japan in 1882, promoted modernization on the Japanese model and an end to Korea's traditional tributary relationship with China. His reform proposals, however, were blocked by the family of the King's consort (the Min), who dominated the court. In 1885, with the connivance of the Japanese Minister and the assistance of Japanese troops stationed in the Korean capital, Kim staged a palace coup. A new cabinet was formed with Kim as Finance Minister, but two days later Chinese troops intervened and he fled to Japan. He was assassinated by a Korean government agent in Shanghai.

## Kim Yong-sam (1927– )

South Korean politician. After election to the National Assembly in 1954, he was a founder-member of the opposition New Democratic Party (NDP), becoming its President in 1974. His opposition to the **PARK** regime resulted in his being banned from all political activity. In 1983 he staged a 23-day pro-democracy hunger strike and in 1985 his political ban was formally lifted. In that year he helped form the New Korea Democratic Party (NKDP) and in 1987 the centrist Reunification Democratic Party (RDP). In his 1987 bid for the presidency he came second, behind the governing party's candidate, **ROH TAE WOO**. In 1990 he merged the RDP with the ruling party to form the new Democratic Liberal Party (DLP), and in 1993 was elected President. Upon election he immediately launched an anti-corruption campaign but his popularity suffered, and in the election of 1995 the DLP won only five of the top 15 posts. His term in office ended in 1997.

### King, (William Lyon) Mackenzie (1874–1950)

Canadian politician. He studied law at Toronto, and became an MP (1908), Minister of Labour (1909–11), **LIBERAL PARTY** leader (1919) and Prime Minister (1921–6, 1926–30 and 1935–48). His great ability to find common ground among differing political views made a major contribution to the Liberal domination of national politics for a whole generation, and his view that the dominions should be autonomous communities within the **BRITISH EMPIRE** resulted in the Statute of **WESTMINSTER** (1931). He resigned from office in 1948. ► **ROWELL–SIROIS COMMISSION**

### King, Martin Luther, Jr (1929–68)

US **CIVIL RIGHTS** leader. The son of a Baptist minister, he studied at Morehouse College and Boston University, and set up his first ministry in Montgomery, Alabama. In 1957 he helped found the **SCLC** (Southern Christian Leadership Conference) as a base for coordinating efforts in the struggle for racial equality. Embracing M K **GANDHI**'s message of achieving change through non-violent resistance, he mobilized the black community to challenge segregation laws in the South through non-violent marches and demonstrations, boycotts and freedom rides, and broadened support for the 1964 Civil Rights Act. His voter registration drive in Alabama, culminating in the Selma march, led to the passage of the Voting Rights Act in 1965. In 1968, he was assassinated in Memphis, Tennessee, by James Earl Ray. ► **CIVIL RIGHTS MOVEMENT**

### King–Crane Commission

A commission composed of two US members, Henry King and Charles Crane, which carried out its work in Jun, Jul and Aug 1919. Its remit – to ascertain local reactions to the proposed Middle Eastern mandatory arrangements – resulted in their reporting opposition to separation from **PALESTINE** and to the proposal for a French mandate in Syria. The commission also found that the Zionist programme for Palestine could not, at least in its extreme form, be reconciled with the **BALFOUR DECLARATION** in which the rights of the non-Jewish population of Palestine were enshrined. The Commission's report was published in 1922 and its findings were all but disregarded.

### King David Hotel, Bombing of the (22 July 1946)

The attack by the **IRGUN** on a wing of the King David Hotel in Jerusalem, the headquarters of British rule in **PALESTINE**. It took place as part of a wider campaign by the Irgun and others in response to opposition from the British Labour government to Jewish immigration into Palestine. ► **JEWISH AGENCY**; **ZIONISM**

### King George's War ► AUSTRIAN SUCCESSION, WAR OF THE

### King Philip's War (1675–6)

US colonial war. An attempt by the **NATIVE AMERICANS** of central New England to stop further white expansion. It was led by Metacom, King **PHILIP**, or chief of the Wampanoags, who tried to build an inter-tribal coalition. The Native Americans lost, and were killed or enslaved, but not before killing hundreds of colonists. ► **INDIAN WARS**

### Kingston, Charles Cameron (1850–1908)

Australian politician. A lawyer, he entered South Australian politics in 1881, and was state Attorney-General (1884–5 and 1887–9), Chief Secretary (1892) and Premier (1893–9). His ministry was the first in Australia to give votes to women (1894), and to introduce state conciliation and arbitration (1894). A leading figure in the **FEDERATION** movement, he attended the National Australasian Convention in 1891 and the Federal Convention of 1897–8, at which, with H B **HIGGINS**, he included conciliation and arbitration powers in the federal constitution. He entered federal politics in 1901, and was Minister of Trade and Customs in **BARTON**'s government. Disputes with his colleagues over the scope of his conciliation and arbitration Bill led to his resignation in 1903, and although an arbitration Act was passed in 1904, ill health prevented any return to office.

### King William's War (1689–97)

The first of the great wars between France and England for the control of North America. Known in Europe as the War of the League of **AUGSBURG**, it was settled by the Treaty of **RIJSWIJK** (1697). ► **WILLIAM III**

### Kinnock, Neil Gordon Kinnock, Baron (1942–)

British politician. He became a Labour MP in 1970, joined the **LABOUR PARTY**'s National Executive Committee (1978), and was chief opposition spokesman on education (1979–83). He was elected party leader in 1983, following Michael **FOOT**. During the 1980s he reorganized the party and led successful attacks on its left-wing influence and on **MILITANT TENDENCY**. He resigned the Labour Party leadership in 1992, following his defeat by John **MAJOR** in the general election of Apr 1992. He was a member of the European Commission from 1995 to 2004.

**KIRIBATI** official name **Republic of Kiribati**

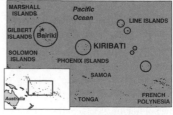

A nation comprising 33 low-lying atolls in three main groups, the Gilbert Islands, Phoenix Islands and Line Islands, scattered across c.1.2 million sq mi/3 million sq km of the central Pacific Ocean, north-east of New Zealand. Inhabited for over 2,000 years, the islands were settled by Samoans, Fijians and Tongans. The Gilbert and Ellice Islands (see TUVALU) were proclaimed a British Protectorate in 1892 and annexed in 1916 as the Gilbert and Ellice Islands Colony, which subsequently incorporated the Line Islands and Phoenix Islands. The colonies separated in 1975, and the Gilbert, Phoenix and Line Islands became independent as Kiribati in 1979. Kiribati is threatened by rising sea levels – two atolls were reported submerged in 1999 – and in 2002 Kiribati, with TUVALU and the MALDIVES, began legal action against the USA over its refusal to sign the Kyoto Protocol.

### Kirk, Norman Eric (1923–74)
New Zealand politician. While working as an engine-driver, he joined the Labour Party and became involved in local, then national politics, becoming President of the party in 1964. He entered parliament in 1957, was Leader of the Opposition (1965–72) and became Prime Minister in 1972, at a time when his country's economy was in difficulties. Forced by Britain's entry into the EEC and the USA's disengagement in Asia, he sought a more independent regional role for New Zealand, opposed French nuclear testing in the Pacific and sent ships into the test area. He died in office.

### Kirov, Sergey Mironovich (1886–1934)
Russian revolutionary and politician. In and out of prison from 1905 onwards, he played an active part in the OCTOBER REVOLUTION and RUSSIAN CIVIL WAR, and during the 1920s held a number of leading provincial Party posts. He had been elected a full member of the Central Committee by 1923, and in 1934 he became a full member of the POLITBURO at the 17th Party Congress and was elected as a secretary of the Central Committee. Later that year he was assassinated at his Leningrad headquarters, possibly at the instigation of STALIN, who then used his death as the pretext for a widespread campaign of reprisals.
▶ BOLSHEVIKS; BUKHARIN, NIKOLAI IVANOVICH; COMMUNISM; TROTSKY, LEON

### Kisan Sabhas
'Peasant associations' in India. The first All-India Kisan Congress of Apr 1936 brought together regional groups which had developed during the CIVIL DISOBEDIENCE movement of 1930–4. After the second congress (Dec 1936), relations between the Congress and the Kisan Sabha movement were strained; after the Sabha's demands for radical agrarian reform became very insistent, Congress forbade (1938) its members from joining any Sabhas. During WORLD WAR II the Sabha came increasingly under communist control and went underground soon after independence. It re-emerged as part of the Communist Party of India in 1952, but its strength varied from region to region.

### Kiselev, Pavel Dmitriyevich, Count (1788–1872)
Russian general and politician. An efficient and not inhumane soldier, he was Governor of the Danubian Principalities following the Treaty of ADRIANOPLE of 1829, until in 1836 he was put in charge of a new Fifth Department to look after the state peasantry, who comprised about a third of the Russian population. Over the next 20 years he introduced several reforms affecting everything from landholding to health and education; these were some of the better aspects of NICHOLAS I's autocratic reign. However, Kiselev's concentration was on administration, and his reforms were often ignored or simply spoiled by malpractices at local level.

### Kishi Nobusuke (1896–1991)
Japanese politician. The brother of SATO EISAKU, he took the name of Kishi when he was adopted into his uncle's family. He entered the Ministry of Agriculture and Commerce (1920) and during the interwar years was identified as one of the 'new bureaucrats' (shinkanryo), who championed more extensive economic planning. While he served in the Japanese puppet-state of MANZHUGUO (1936–9), Kishi worked closely with the military in developing heavy industry. On returning to Japan, he became a Vice-Minister of Commerce and Industry, helping to place the economy on a war footing. He then served in the wartime cabinet of TOJO HIDEKI. After the war, he was imprisoned by the US occupation authorities but was released in 1948. Kishi was one of the architects, in 1955, of the LIBERAL DEMOCRATIC PARTY (LDP), formed when the two major conservative parties merged. A controversial Prime Minister (1957–60), he ensured ratification of the renewed US–JAPAN SECURITY TREATY (1960) in the face of an opposition boycott in the Diet and massive public demonstrations. He resigned shortly afterwards, but remained influential within the LDP.

### Kissinger, Henry Alfred (1923– )
US political scientist and politician. His family emigrated from Germany to the USA in 1938, to escape the Nazi persecution of Jews. He was educated at Harvard, served in WORLD WAR II, and subsequently joined the Harvard faculty. He became President Richard NIXON's adviser on national security affairs in 1969, was the main US figure in the negotiations to end the VIETNAM WAR, and became Secretary of State in 1973, serving under Nixon and FORD. His 'shuttle diplomacy' during the Arab–Israeli War of 1973 helped bring about a ceasefire, and resulted in a notable improvement in Israeli–Egyptian relations. He left public office in 1977.

### Kita Ikki (1883–1937)
Japanese national socialist. A promoter of a Japanese-led Pan-Asianism, in 1919 he wrote An Outline Plan for the Reorganization of Japan in which he argued that a radical reordering of Japanese society was required in order for Japan to take her rightful place as leader of Asia. He called for a military coup that would sweep away the constitution and civilian political establishment and establish direct rule under the Emperor. Kita also advocated nationalization of industry, confiscation of all excess wealth, and land reform. His ideas influenced the radical army officers of the IMPERIAL WAY FACTION. When they staged an abortive coup in 1936, Kita was arrested as an accomplice and executed.

### Kitchen Cabinet
Term used in US politics to describe an informal group of advisers surrounding a US President. It

originated in the mid-19c in the administration of President Andrew **JACKSON**.

### Kitchener, (Horatio) Herbert, 1st Earl Kitchener of Khartoum (1850–1916)

British field marshal and statesman. He joined the Royal Engineers in 1871, and served in Palestine (1874), Cyprus (1878) and the Sudan (1883). By the final rout of the Khalifa at **OMDURMAN** (1898), he won back the Sudan for Egypt, and was made a peer. Successively Chief of Staff and Commander-in-Chief in South Africa (1900–2), he brought the Boer War to an end, and was made viscount. He then became Commander-in-Chief in India (1902–9), Consul-General in Egypt (1911) and Secretary for War (1914), for which he organized manpower on a vast scale ('Kitchener armies'). He was lost with HMS *Hampshire*, mined off the Orkney Islands. ► **BOER WARS**; **WORLD WAR I**

### KKE (*Kommunistikon Komma Ellados*, 'Communist Party of Greece')

Founded in 1918 as the Socialist Workers' Party of Greece by Greek socialists, the character of the KKE changed after 1924 as Moscow-trained communists started to 'bolshevize' and take control of the party. The most 'westernized' of Greek political parties, at least a quarter of its support came from the urban middle classes as well as industrial workers and peasants, but particularly among refugees from Anatolia after the **GRAECO-TURKISH WAR**. In the 1926 election, the KKE gained ten seats in parliament, although total party membership did not exceed 2,000. In 1936, the KKE's plans for a general strike on 5 Aug were foiled when the **METAXAS** regime arrested all leading members on the preceding day – a black day, still not forgotten, in the history of Greek communism. Until 1939 the KKE was incapable of action, with its members in prison or having been released after signing 'declarations' denouncing the party. The government infiltrated and manipulated the party so that, in 1940, there were no less than three central committees. During **WORLD WAR II** the KKE was the dominant force behind the **EAM** (National Liberation Front); it tried to seize power during the German occupation, and again in Dec 1944 after the German withdrawal and during the **GREEK CIVIL WAR**. After a reformist faction left the party in 1991, the extreme left-wing KKE was reduced in size and importance. The main representative of the left in modern Greek politics is now the left-of-centre Panhellenic Socialist Movement (**PASOK**), opposed on the right by the New Democracy (ND).

### Klapka, György (1820–92)

Hungarian soldier and patriot. He became a lieutenant-general in the Austrian army, but in the Hungarian Uprising of 1848–9 he fought valiantly against the Austrians, holding Komárom for eight weeks after the rest of Hungary had submitted. Although he later conducted anti-Austrian activities abroad, he was permitted under the amnesty of 1867 to return from exile, and he died in Budapest.

### Klaras, Athanasios, also known as Aris Veloukhiotis (1905–45)

Greek resistance leader; he was the leader of **ELAS** resistance bands in Greece during **WORLD WAR II**. He took part in the settlement of Greek refugees from Asia Minor (1922) and joined the Greek Communist Party (1924). Under the dictatorship of Ioannis **METAXAS** he was interned (1936–9), but was released after retracting his communist convictions. After the German occupation of Greece (Apr 1941), he was impatient to organize resistance but it was not until Mar 1942 that he received orders from **EAM**, the communist-led National Liberation Front, to form guerrilla bands and to take to the mountains. Committed to the establishment of a communist regime, he organized communist-led self-administration in the liberated regions, oversaw the brutal coercion of the often recalcitrant local population and waged war against the other resistance organizations. He attacked **EKKA** (May 1943) and, with the agreement of EAM, launched a campaign against **EDES**, led by his cousin, Napoleon **ZERVAS** (Oct 1943). Opposed to any compromise, however expedient, he condemned the EAM leaders for their compliance with the Allies and the Greek government-in-exile at the Lebanon Conference (May 1944) and at Varkiza (Feb 1945). For the sake of party unity, he formally agreed to the demobilization of ELAS, but withdrew with sections of his followers to the mountains. At its Apr 1945 plenum, the Greek Communist Party, now led by Nikos **ZACHARIADIS**, condemned Veloukhiotis who, hounded from village to village by the communists and Greek government officials, committed suicide.

### Kléber, Jean Baptiste (1753–1800)

French general. He served in the Austrian army (1776–82), became an architect, and then joined the **NATIONAL GUARD** (1792). He commanded in the Vendéan War, but was recalled for leniency. He later won victories at Fleurus (1794) and Altenkirchen (1796), and he accompanied Bonaparte to Egypt, was wounded at Alexandria, and won the Battle of Mount Tabor (1799). When Napoleon Bonaparte left Egypt, Kléber was left in command. He attempted to reconquer Egypt, but was assassinated by a Turkish fanatic at Cairo. ► **NAPOLEON I**

### Kleist, Ewald von (1881–1954)

German military commander. He joined the army in 1900 and served as a cavalry officer during **WORLD WAR I**. During **WORLD WAR II** he commanded an armoured group in the French campaign (1940) and from 1942 to Mar 1944 commanded an army group on the Russian front. Promoted field marshal in 1943, he was later dismissed by **HITLER** and was subsequently taken prisoner by the Allies. He died in captivity in the USSR.

### Klephts

Greek folklore celebrated the Klephts as bandits who robbed the rich to give to the poor, and for their ability to worst the Ottoman Turks. While the heroic image presented in folk-songs was grounded in fact, it should not be forgotten that many Klephts were simply brigands and opportunists.

### Klondike Gold Rush

A flood of prospectors (largely US) when gold was discovered in Canada's Yukon Territory in 1896. The rush lasted for five years, generated an estimated US$50 million in gold, established the town of Dawson, and invigorated the economies of British

Columbia, Alberta, Alaska and Washington State.

**Knights of Labor** (1878–93)
An early US labour organization. It tried to organize all workers in support of a large-scale political and social programme, regardless of their age, race or colour. Its membership peaked at around 700,000 in 1886, but then declined.

**Know-Nothings** (1856)
US political party. A popular name for the short-lived anti-immigrant American Party. It was so called because of the response members were instructed to give to questions from outsiders: 'I know nothing'.
► NATIVISM

**Knox, John** (c.1513–1572)
Scottish Protestant reformer, born near Haddington, Lothian. A Catholic priest, he acted as notary in Haddington (1540–3), and in 1544 was influenced by George WISHART to work for the Lutheran Reformation. After Wishart was burned (1546), Knox joined the reformers defending the castle of St Andrews, and became a minister. After the castle fell to the French, he was kept a prisoner until 1549, then became a chaplain to EDWARD VI, and was consulted over the second Book of Common Prayer. On the accession of MARY I (1553), he fled to Dieppe, and then to Geneva, where he was much influenced by CALVIN. He returned to Scotland in 1555 to preach, and then again in 1559, where he won a strong party in favour of reform, and founded the Church of Scotland (1560). He played a lasting part in the composition of *The Scots Confession, The First Book of Discipline* and *The Book of Common Order*. He died in Edinburgh. ► MARY, QUEEN OF SCOTS; REFORMATION (Scotland)

**Knox, Philander Chase** (1853–1921)
US lawyer and politician who served in the cabinets of Presidents William MCKINLEY, Theodore ROOSEVELT and William TAFT. As Attorney-General of the USA (1901–4), he drew up the legislation for the new US Department of Commerce and Labor in 1903, and as US Secretary of State (1909–13) under Taft he promoted foreign policy based on DOLLAR DIPLOMACY. He also served two terms as a US Senator (1904–9, 1917–21) and strongly opposed the LEAGUE OF NATIONS.

**Knut Sveinsson** ► CANUTE

**Kobayashi Takaji** (1903–33)
Japanese revolutionary. A literary activist and prominent leader of the proletarian literature movement in the late 1920s, he participated in strikes while his short stories and novellas (all censored or banned outright until after 1945) championed the heroic struggle of the working class against oppression and exploitation. Forced to go underground after 1929, Kobayashi was eventually arrested, tortured, and executed in 1933.

**Kogălniceanu, Michael** (1817–91)
Romanian politician and historian. With Ion BRĂTIANU he led the Liberal Party and was appointed Prime Minister by Alexander CUZA (1862). He presided over a period of economic and social reform, sequestering the lands of the Dedicated Monasteries which were controlled by the PHANARIOTS, introducing a civil code based on the CODE NAPOLÉON, reorganizing local government and establishing more schools. He lost the support of Cuza, however, and was dismissed in 1865. He later served in the Liberal government (1876) and strongly supported Prince Charles (later King CHARLES I of Romania).

**Kohl, Helmut** (1930– )
German politician. Educated in Frankfurt and Heidelberg, he became a lawyer, and joined the CHRISTIAN DEMOCRATS. In 1976 he moved to BONN as a member of the Federal Parliament, became leader of the opposition, and his party's candidate for the chancellorship. After the collapse of the SCHMIDT coalition in 1982, Kohl was installed as Chancellor (1982–98), and in the elections of 1983 he formed a government which adopted a central course between political extremes. Following the REVOLUTION OF 1989 in East Germany, Kohl played a decisive part in ensuring the integration of the former communist state within the Federal Republic of Germany. In 1991, six weeks after united Germany's first national elections, he announced a coalition government that, while maintaining CDU/CSU dominance in the key Defence and Labour and Social Affairs Ministries, reflected the strength of the vote for the Free Democrats, with the FDP's Hans-Dietrich GENSCHER remaining as Foreign Secretary. The Kohl era ended in 1998 with the election victory of the Social Democrats, led by Gerhard Schröder.

**Koht, Halvdan** (1873–1965)
Norwegian politician and historian. He was a Professor of History at Oslo University from 1910 to 1935, when he became Foreign Minister under the Labour government (1935–40). A prolific writer on Norwegian history and literature, he was also a highly controversial figure in Norwegian political life. Koht was strongly criticized for his failure to anticipate the German invasion of Norway (Apr 1940) and was replaced as Foreign Minister in the government-in-exile by Trygve LIE. ► NORWAY, GERMAN INVASION OF

**Koivisto, Mauno Henrik** (1923– )
Finnish politician. A Social Democrat, he served as Minister of Finance in 1966–7, and Prime Minister in 1968–70 and 1979–81. As Governor of the Bank of Finland after 1968 (retaining office while serving as Prime Minister, with another politician serving as acting governor), he presided over a period of tight monetary policy which helped to consolidate the country's economic growth. As President (1982–94), he had a more relaxed political style than his predecessor, Urho KEKKONEN, although he maintained the latter's policy of close cooperation with USSR until its demise in 1991.

**Kokovtsov, Vladimir Nikolaevich, Count** (1853–1943)
Russian politician. He had two spells as Finance Minister before becoming Prime Minister following STOLYPIN's assassination in 1911. He was good at reducing budget expenditure and resisting right-wing corruption, at raising French loans and giving sound advice to NICHOLAS II. However, he exercised little power and was replaced in 1914 by someone more conservative and compliant.

## Kokutai

A Japanese term, meaning 'national essence', used to denote the country's unique polity, in particular the role of an unbroken imperial line descended from the gods. The term was first used during the TOKUGA-WA SHOGUNATE (1603–1867) as a reaction against Chinese influence on Japanese culture. From the 1890s onwards, the idea of Japan as a family-state in which the close relationship between the Emperor and his subjects was likened to that of a father and his children increasingly took hold. During the 1920s and 1930s, protection of the *kokutai* was used as justification for the suppression of dissident thought. With the dismantling of the Emperor-centred state after WORLD WAR II, the term was no longer used and it has little meaning in today's Japan.

## Kolchak, Alexander Vasilevich (1874–1920)

Russian naval commander. In WORLD WAR I he was in command of the Black Sea fleet. After the RUSSIAN RE-VOLUTION of 1917, he went to Omsk as War Minister in an anti-Bolshevik government. He cleared Siberia in cooperation with DENIKIN and other leaders of the White Army, styling himself latterly 'supreme ruler of Russia'. In 1919 Omsk fell to the BOLSHEVIKS; Kolchak was betrayed, and shot.

## Kolettis, Ioannis (1774–1847)

Greek politician. A Vlach doctor from EPIRUS, he served at the court of ALI PASHA. He joined the civilian government of George Kountouriotes at Kranidi before becoming, with Agostino Kapodistrias and Theodoros KOLOKOTRONIS, joint head of the administration established after the assassination of Ioannis KAPODISTRIAS (1831). While serving as Greek representative in Paris, he was influenced by French political thought and became leader of the 'French Party' in Greece during the 1840s. He played an important role in drawing up the 1844 Greek constitution, which was inspired by the French July Monarchy and which established Greece as a constitutional monarchy. From 1845 until his death, he led the government and won wide support for King OTHON, formulating the programme of Greek territorial expansion known as the MEGALE IDEA. ► MAV-ROKORDATOS, ALEXANDER

## Kollár, Jan (1793–1852)

Slovak writer. He was one of the early formative group of Czech and Slovak intellectuals who helped to give their peoples a sense of being and purpose. He wrote about the SLAVS in general and was anxious to promote unity among them. Though a Slovak, he worked in the Czech lands and also wrote in Czech, determined to bring the two groups together. After the failure of the 1848–9 rebellions, he was seduced into working with the authorities in Vienna in the hope of influencing them to defend Slovakia against Hungarian pressure. He gained nothing and lost respect. The Slovak national movement lost its unity and impetus for some years to come.

## Kollontai, Alexandra Mikhailovna (1872–1952)

Russian feminist and revolutionary. The world's first female ambassador, she was born in St Petersburg into an upper-class family, but rejected her privileged upbringing and became interested in socialism. Married to an army officer, she nevertheless joined the Russian Social Democratic Party and, for her revolutionary behaviour and the radical views she expressed at the First All-Russian Congress of Women, was exiled to Germany in 1908. In 1915 she travelled widely in the USA, begging the nation not to join WORLD WAR I, and urging the acceptance of socialism. In 1917, following the RUSSIAN REVOLUTION, she returned to Russia, becoming Commissar for Social Welfare. In this post she agitated for reforms, including collective childcare and easier divorce proceedings. Partly because her private liaisons and aggressive feminist advocacy shocked the Party, she was appointed Minister to Norway, Mexico and Sweden, becoming ambassador in 1943. She played a vital part in negotiating the termination of the CON-TINUATION WAR (1944).

## Kolokotronis, Theodoros (1770–1843)

Greek military leader. The captain of a band of KLEPHTS in the Morea, he played an important role in the GREEK WAR OF INDEPENDENCE. Inspired by the ideals of the FRENCH REVOLUTION, he was recruited to the FILIKI ETAIRIA and supported Alexander YPSILANTI (1783–1828) in his bid to head the revolutionary government (1821). He refused to support Kountouriotes' government at Kranidi and organized raids against it from his base at Nauplion. In 1824 he was bribed into surrender and lent his support to Ioannis KAPODISTRIAS, whom he succeeded in 1831, heading an administration with Agostino Kapodistrias and Ioannis KOLETTIS. Conservative and Orthodox in outlook, he led the 'Russian Party'.

## Komeito

The 'Clean Government' Party of Japan, which achieved the power of veto over the traditional ruling LIBERAL DEMOCRATIC PARTY by winning 20 seats in the Upper House in the 1989 elections, following revelations about government corruption. *Komeito* is an offshoot of *Soka Gakkai*, a born-again Buddhist cult founded in 1930 but based on the teachings of the 13c holy man NICHIREN. In WORLD WAR II, Soka Gakkai's leader was jailed by Japan's thought police and starved to death. The organization was unbanned in 1964 and formed Komeito as its political wing, but six years later the party broke its religious links to broaden its appeal. Together with the Social Democratic Party of Japan (formerly JAPAN SOCIALIST PARTY) it remains one of the main opposition parties in Japanese politics.

## Komenský, Jan Ámos ► COMENIUS, JOHN AMOS

## Komorowski, Tadeusz Bór (1895–1966)

Polish soldier. As 'General Bór' he led the heroic but unsuccessful Warsaw rising against the occupying Germans in 1944, and settled in England after WORLD WAR II.

## Komsomol

The All-Union Leninist Communist League of Youth, founded in 1918, incorporating the majority of persons between the ages of 14 and 28. Its purpose being the socialization of youth in the thought and ways of the COMMUNIST PARTY OF THE SOVIET UNION, it served as a recruiting ground for Party membership until 1991.

## Kong ► GONG

## Kongo, Kingdom of

An African kingdom situated to the south of the River Congo which by the 15c had a coastline of 150 mi/ 240 km and reached inland for 250 mi/400 km. It was already involved in trade in ivory, copper and slaves when the Portuguese arrived in the area in 1482. Some of its kings accepted Christianity, but it was disrupted by the stepping up of the slave trade, and declined during the 18c when the Portuguese turned their attention southwards to Angola.

## Kong Xiangxi (K'ung Hsiang-hsi) ► K'UNG, H H

## Koniev, Ivan Stepanovich (1897–1973)

Soviet military commander. Born into a peasant family, he was drafted into the Tsarist army in 1916, and joined the **RED ARMY** and the Communist Party in 1918. For some time he was a political commissar, but after graduating from the Frunze Military Academy in 1934 he held various commands, including in the Far East, before the USSR was drawn into **WORLD WAR II**. In the years 1941–5 he served with great distinction on several sections of the Western front. Made Marshal of the USSR in 1944, he was Commander-in-Chief, Ground Forces in 1946–50, First Deputy Minister of Defence, and, in 1956–60, Commander-in-Chief of the **WARSAW PACT** forces, which he built into an effective fighting force. ► **RUSSIAN CIVIL WAR**

## Königgrätz-Sadowa, Battle of (3 July 1866)

The decisive Prussian victory in the 1866 war against **AUSTRIA**. The battle itself was hard-fought and close-run, but by the next day it was apparent that the Austrians (who suffered much higher casualties) were in full retreat and the Prussian pursuit began. Diplomatic intervention by the French Emperor **NAPOLEON III** led to the Peace of **NIKOLSBURG**. ► **AUSTRO-PRUSSIAN WAR; PRUSSIA**

## Königsberg

A city in East Prussia (now Russia) which arose around a Teutonic castle built in 1255. In 1340 it became a Hansa town. From 1547 it was the seat of the Grand Master of the **TEUTONIC KNIGHTS** and then (1525–1618) the Dukes of Prussia. Albert I created a Lutheran university in Königsberg in 1544. It was viewed as the royal city of the Prussian dukes and kings.

## Konoe Fumimaro (1891–1945)

Japanese politician. From an aristocratic family, he inherited the title of prince from his father. Konoe was a prominent member of the Upper House (House of Peers), before becoming Prime Minister for the first time in 1937. He favoured the growth of Japanese influence in Asia, criticizing what he felt was an Anglo-American attempt to preserve the status quo. During his first term as Premier (1937–9) he led Japan into full-scale war with China in an attempt to create a New Order in East Asia. During his second term (1940–1) Japan's relations with the USA worsened, especially after his government signed a military alliance with the **AXIS POWERS** (Tripartite Pact) in Sep 1940. He resigned when his offer of a summit meeting with President **ROOSEVELT** was rebuffed. Although Konoe was a member of the first post-war government (1945), he was indicted as a war criminal by the US occupation authorities. He committed sui-

cide on the day he was to turn himself in for confinement and trial.

## Koo, Wellington ► GU WEIJUN

## Köprülü (late 17c)

The name of three Turkish Grand Viziers who effectively controlled the Ottoman government for most of the late 17c. Mehmet Köprülü (d.1661) was an Albanian by birth who rose from working in the imperial kitchen to become Grand Vizier in 1656 when he was in his seventies. He ruthlessly consolidated his power and rebuilt the Ottoman fleet for service against the Venetians. He retired shortly before his death in 1661 in favour of his son, Fazil Ahmed Köprülü (d.c.1676), who, during his 15 years as Grand Vizier, built upon the foundation laid down by his father. He personally led the army against Austria, securing advantageous terms at the Peace of Vasvár (Eisenberg) in 1664, and against Crete which was taken in 1669. He died of dropsy and his place was taken by his foster-brother **KARA MUSTAFA**, who brought the Ottomans to the gates of Venice. Fazil Ahmed's younger brother, Fazil Mustafa Köprülü (d.1691), became Grand Vizier in 1689. Like his predecessors, he reformed the administration and reorganized the army. He showed particular concern for non-Muslim subjects in the Balkans. He was killed in battle near Karlowitz.

## KOREA, DEMOCRATIC PEOPLE'S REPUBLIC OF

also called **North Korea**

A socialist state in eastern Asia, in the northern half of the Korean Peninsula, bounded to the north by China; to the north-east by Russia; to the west by Korea Bay and the Yellow Sea; and to the east by the Sea of Japan. It is separated from South Korea to the south by a demilitarized zone of 487 sq mi/1,262 sq km. The peninsula was united in the 7c by the Silla Dynasty, which was succeeded by the Koryo Dynasty in 935 and then the **YI DYNASTY**, which ruled (1392–1910) as a vassal of China. In 1910 it was formally annexed by Japan, and after Japan's defeat in **WORLD WAR II** it was partitioned along the 38th parallel (latitude 38°N), being occupied in the north by communist Soviet troops and in the south by non-communist US troops. The **KOREAN WAR** (1950–3) was fought between these communist and non-communist forces. Reunification talks between North and South Korea in 1980 were broken off by North Korea, though there were further talks with South Korea in 1990, 1997–9 and 2000. Power in North Korea lies in the hands of the Korean Workers'

(Communist) Party, whose leader is the President. **KIM-IL SUNG** was President from 1972 until his death in 1994, and since 1998 his son **KIM CHONG-IL** has held power. Acute food shortages caused by a combination of natural disasters and economic mismanagement left the country dependant on international aid in the late 1990s. During the 1990s Western nations became increasingly concerned about North Korea's covert development of nuclear weapons. In 1994 North Korea agreed to freeze its nuclear development programme in return for aid, but it became clear in 2002 that it had reactivated the programme and it announced in 2003 that it had sufficient material to produce nuclear weapons. Talks between North Korea and the USA, mediated by China, to resolve the nuclear issue began in 2003 and continue. ▬ AXIS OF EVIL

---

**KOREA, REPUBLIC OF** also called **South Korea**

A republic in eastern Asia occupying the southern half of the Korean Peninsula, bounded to the west by the Yellow Sea; to the east by the Sea of Japan; to the south by the Korean Strait; and to the north by North Korea, from which it is separated by a demilitarized zone. It was united in 668 by the Silla Dynasty, which was succeeded by the Koryo Dynasty (918–1392) and the **YI DYNASTY** (1392–1910), which ruled as a vassal of China. It was formally annexed by Japan in 1910, and on the defeat of Japan after **WORLD WAR II** in 1945 the country was entered by Russia (from the north) and the USA (from the south) to enforce the Japanese surrender, dividing the country at the 38th parallel of latitude. In a bid to unite the country, North Korean forces invaded in 1950, sparking off the **KOREAN WAR** (1950–3). There was a military coup in 1961, led by **PARK CHUNG-HEE**, who formed a government but was assassinated in 1979. South Korea's economy was transformed in the latter part of the 20c, mainly by the development of heavy industry and electronics. Reunification talks with North Korea took place in 1980, 1990, 1997–9 and 2000, but tensions remain because of the North's nuclear programme and concern over its weak economy and the prospect of US troop withdrawals from the demiliatarized zone. ▬ CHAEBOL

**Korean War** (1950–53)
A war between communist and non-communist forces in Korea, which had been partitioned along the 38th parallel in 1945 after Japan's defeat in

**WORLD WAR II**. The communist North invaded the South in 1950 after a series of border clashes, and a **UN** force intervened, driving the invaders back to to the Chinese frontier. China then entered the war and, together with the North Koreans, occupied Seoul. The UN forces counter-attacked, and by 1953, when an armistice was signed, had retaken all territory south of the 38th parallel. ▬ MACARTHUR, DOUGLAS

**Kornilov, Lavr Georgevich** (1870–1918)
Russian general. With previous intelligence and diplomatic experience, he was a divisional commander in **WORLD WAR I**, tried to turn the tide against the Germans by an offensive in June 1917 and, in Aug 1917, marched on Petrograd (St Petersburg), in an attempt to set up a military directorate. He was forced to surrender by **KERENSKY**, but subsequently escaped. Kornilov then organized a Cossack force against the **BOLSHEVIKS**, but fell in battle. ▬ KORNILOV AFFAIR

**Kornilov Affair** (1917)
A military attempt to prevent the **BOLSHEVIKS** coming to power. The failure of the Brusilov offensive in July 1917 greatly weakened the **RUSSIAN PROVISIONAL GOVERNMENT**. **KERENSKY** appointed the adventurous General **KORNILOV** as Commander-in-Chief, but he apparently succumbed to right-wing influence and in Aug attempted a military coup by sending cavalry to Petrograd (St Petersburg). He failed and simply increased support for the Bolsheviks. ▬ BRUSILOV OFFENSIVES

**Korošec, Anton** (1872–1940)
Slovene politician. He studied theology at Maribor and was ordained a priest, taking a leading role in the Slovene People's Party before **WORLD WAR I**. An advocate of **TRIALISM**, he became President of the coalition of South Slav members in the Austrian parliament (1917) and President of the National Council of Slovenes, Croats and Serbs in Zagreb (Oct 1918). After the creation of the Kingdom of Serbs, Croats and Slovenes (later Yugoslavia), he served as Vice-Premier (1919). Conservative and opportunistic, he continued to represent the interests of the Slovenes and was the only non-Serb interwar Prime Minister and Minister of the Interior (Jul 1928–Jan 1929). During the dictatorship of **ALEXANDER I**, he was interned on the island of Hvar (1933) but was released during the regency to serve again as Minister of the Interior (1935–8).

**Koryo, Kingdom of**
The kingdom in the Korean Peninsula ruled by the Koryo Dynasty (918–1392), founded by Wang Kon, and which had its capital at Kaesong (Songdu). ▬ KOREA, DEMOCRATIC PEOPLE'S REPUBLIC OF; KOREA, REPUBLIC OF

**Kościuszko, Tadeusz Andrzej Bonawentura** (1746–1817)
Polish soldier and patriot. He was trained in the military academies in Warsaw and Paris. In 1776 he went to North America, where he fought for the colonists in the **AMERICAN REVOLUTION** and was eventually promoted to brigadier-general and became a US citizen. He returned to Poland in 1784; and when Russia attacked his country in 1792, he held Dubienka for five days, with 4,000 men against 18,000. In 1794, after initial hesitation, he took charge of a national

uprising in Kraków, being appointed dictator and Commander-in-Chief. In spite of his defeat of a greatly superior force of Russians at Racławice, he had to withdraw to Warsaw, winning popular support by suspending serfdom. He conducted a difficult but brilliant defence of the city but, overpowered by superior numbers in the Battle of Maciejowice (10 Oct 1794) and wounded, he was taken prisoner. Two years later Emperor **PAUL I** of Russia had him freed. He went first to England, then to America, and in 1798 to France. In 1806 he refused to support **NAPOLEON I**'s plan for the restoration of Poland, the Grand Duchy, because it would not secure genuine independence; similarly, in 1815 he refused to support **ALEXANDER I**'s so-called Congress Poland. He settled in Switzerland in 1816, and died when his horse fell over a precipice.

### Kosice Programme (Apr 1945)

The political programme on which post-1945 Czechoslovakia was based. It consisted of a compromise between 'westernizers' and communists, the pre-war ministries who had accompanied **BENEŠ** to exile in London and Klement **GOTTWALD** and his colleagues coming home from Moscow. It was based on the hope that good East–West relations would continue after the war; and while it excluded some parties and concentrated on socializing the economy, it meant nationalizing much of industry, but stipulated free elections and did not contemplate collectivizing agriculture. However, Kosice in Slovakia was liberated by the **RED ARMY** and when the **COLD WAR** got under way, the compromise was abandoned in 1948 to fit the objectives of **COMMUNISM**.

### KOSOVO

A region of the Republic of Serbia, bounded to the west and south by Montenegro, Albania and Macedonia. The heart of medieval Serbia, it encompasses many sites of religious significance for the Serbs as well as the scene of their defeat by the Ottoman Turks (1389). Settled by Albanians as well as Serbs, it has long been the cause of friction between the two nations. In the 19c it was the centre of the Albanian national revival, but was granted to Serbia when the first Albanian state was established (1913). During **WORLD WAR II** it was included within Albania by the Italian fascists and its future was a contentious issue between Albanian resistance movements. Returned to Yugoslavia in 1945, it became an autonomous pro-

vince within the Socialist Federal Republic of Serbia, with Albanian and Serbian as its official languages. In 1981 Albanian students led demands for the establishment of Kosovo as the seventh Yugoslav republic and the ensuing riots led to the declaration of a state of emergency. Since then there has been constant unrest, exacerbated by Serb nationalism after the rise to power in Serbia of Slobodan **MILOŠEVIĆ**. In 1989 he removed the province's autonomous status, forcing Kosovo to cede its legislative powers to Serbia; this resulted in widespread rioting by ethnic Albanians, who make up 90 per cent of the population. In a 1991 referendum Kosovo voted decisively for independence from both Serbia and Yugoslavia, and the nationalists won the general election. However, the Serbian-dominated Yugoslav government refused to recognize either result, declaring them illegal, and tightened its control of Kosovo. The fighting between Kosovo's nationalists and Serbian government forces reached its peak in the late 1990s. In Jan 1999 a brutal and systematic process of **ETHNIC CLEANSING** by the Serbs drove the Kosovo Albanians from their homes, prompting the intervention in Mar of **NATO** forces who mounted heavy air-strikes on Milošević's military resources in an attempt to force him to stop the atrocities. Ten weeks later the Serbs did withdraw and a NATO peacekeeping force entered the region to oversee the dismantling of land-mines and the return of thousands of refugees to their homes. Kosovo has since been administered by the **UN** Mission in Kosovo (UNMIK), with security provided by the NATO-commanded Kosovo Force (KFOR). Talks on Kosovo's final status are scheduled for 2005. ► **BALLI KOMBËTAR**; **KOSOVO, BATTLE OF**; **LNC**; **PRIZREN, LEAGUE OF**

### Kosovo, Battle of (28 June 1389)

The Ottoman Turks' victory over the Serbs on the Kosovo plain marked the end of the medieval Kingdom of Serbia. The battle was the subject of Serbian ballads in the oral tradition including the celebrated *Maiden of Kosovo*. ► **KRALJEVIĆ, MARKO**; **LAZAR, HREBELJANOVIĆ**

### Kossuth, Lajos (1802–94)

Hungarian revolutionary. Part Slovak, part local German, he was born into a poor but noble family near Zemplén. He practised law for a time and in 1832 was a deputy at the Diet of Pressburg. He edited a journal which, owing to the law, could not be printed, but only transcribed and widely circulated. The issue of a lithographed paper led, in 1837, to imprisonment. Freed in 1840, he became editor of the twice-weekly *Pesti Hirlap*, advocating extreme Liberal, and somewhat chauvinistic, views. In 1847, sent by the county of Pest to the Diet, he became leader of the radical opposition; and in Mar 1848, after the **FEBRUARY REVOLUTION** in France, he demanded an independent government for Hungary. In Sep 1848, pushing aside the more conservative nobility and heading the Committee of National Defence, he prosecuted the war with extraordinary energy, and in Apr 1849 induced the National Assembly at Debrecen to declare that the **HABSBURG DYNASTY** had forfeited the throne. Appointed Provisional Governor of Hungary, he sought in vain to secure the intervention of the Western powers; and finding that the dissensions between himself and his generals were damaging the national cause, he resigned his dictatorship in favour of Artúr GÖRGEY. After the defeat at Temesvár (9 Aug 1849), he fled to Turkey, where he was made a prisoner but not extradited. In Sep 1851, liberated by British and US influence, he went to England, where, as subsequently in the USA, he was received with respect and sympathy, but no more. From 1852 he lived mainly in England until, on the Franco-Italian War with Austria in 1859, he proposed to NAPOLEON III to arrange a Hungarian rising against Austria. The Peace of Villafranca bitterly disappointed Kossuth; and in 1861 and in 1866 he again tried in vain to bring about a rising against Austria. When in 1867 DEÁK effected the reconciliation of Hungary with the dynasty, Kossuth retired from active political life, and afterwards lived mostly in Turin. In 1867 he refused to avail himself of the general amnesty. ► REVOLUTIONS OF 1848–9; VILLAFRANCA ARMISTICE

### Kostov, Traicho (c.1897–1949)

Bulgarian politician. He studied law and joined the Bulgarian Communist Party (BCP) in 1920. Tortured and imprisoned under the regime of BORIS III, he was left a cripple. During WORLD WAR II, a 'home' rather than a 'Moscow' communist, he served in the postwar FATHERLAND FRONT government as Secretary of the Central Committee of the BCP (1944–8), Deputy Prime Minister (1946–9) and Minister for Electrification (1947–9). After criticizing the terms of economic deals with the USSR, he was summoned with the Yugoslavs KARDELJ and DJILAS to justify himself before STALIN (1948). In 1949 he was tried on charges of wartime collaboration with the police and the British and plotting to assassinate Georgi DIMITROV. He was executed in Dec 1949, a victim of Stalin's purges of 'home communists' and 'Titoists'. However, he was posthumously rehabilitated and decorated (1956). ► TITO; VELCHEV, DAMIAN

### Kosygin, Alexei Nikolaievich (1904–80)

Soviet politician. A textile worker by training, he owed his advancement in the 1930s to the vacancies resulting from STALIN's purges. Elected to the Supreme Soviet (1938), he held a variety of political industrial posts, and became a member of the Central Committee in 1939 and of the POLITBURO in 1948. He had a chequered career in the post-WORLD WAR II period, falling in and out with both Stalin and Nikita KHRUSHCHEV. It was only when, in 1964, he succeeded the latter as Chairman of the Council of Ministers (or Prime Minister) that he could attempt serious, if decentralizing, reforms. However, he was blocked in the late 1960s by the Party machine and the caution of Leonid BREZHNEV. He soldiered on until 1980, when he resigned because of ill health, and he died soon after, having failed to rescue the economy from over-centralization and -planning.

### Kotoku Shusui (1871–1911)

Japanese socialist and anarchist. In 1898 he joined the newly founded Society for the Study of Socialism (Shakai shugi Kenkyukai) and in 1901 helped to form Japan's first social democratic party, which was quickly outlawed by the government. Kotoku became a fierce critic of Japanese imperialism, opposing the RUSSO-JAPANESE WAR (1904–5). His paper, Heimin shimbun ('Common People's Newspaper') published the first Japanese translation of the Communist Manifesto in 1904. By 1906 Kotoku had abandoned parliamentary tactics and adopted an anarcho-syndicalist position, calling for direct action and a general strike. He was arrested for supposed involvement in a plot to assassinate the MEIJI EMPEROR in 1910 and executed the following year.

### Kountche, Seyni (1931–87)

Niger soldier and politician. Trained in France, he served with the French army in Indochina and Algeria. He joined the Niger army at independence in 1961, undertaking further military training in France before becoming Chief of Staff in 1973. He led the military coup against Hamani DIORI in 1974 and established a military government. However, he set about restoring the country's economy and a return to civilian rule, but died in Paris while undergoing surgery.

### Koxinga, originally Zheng Chenggong (Cheng Ch'eng-kung) (1624–62)

Chinese warrior general. Born of a Japanese mother, his father was a pirate and trader along China's east coast during the last years of the MING DYNASTY, before being made an official. The young Zheng was given the imperial surname, and was thus known as Kuo-hsing yeh ('Lord of the Imperial Surname'), from whence came the Dutch derivation of Koxinga. Although his father submitted to the Manchu QING DYNASTY in 1646, Zheng himself resisted Manchu rule, continuing to support a Ming loyalist movement, controlling much of the south-eastern coast around Amoy. After an abortive attack on Nanjing in 1659, he retreated to Taiwan where he expelled the Dutch from their fortress of Zeelandia. Although he died later in the same year (1662), his sons continued to monopolize trade between Taiwan and the mainland until Qing forces captured the island in 1683.

### Kozlov, Frol Romanovich (1908–65)

Soviet politician. Graduating in 1936 from what later became the Leningrad Polytechnic, he held Communist Party functions in various parts of the country before returning to Leningrad in 1949 to work his way up to be First Secretary there. In 1957 he became a member of the POLITBURO in the wake of the ANTI-PARTY PLOT. Thereafter he held two brief ministerial posts before becoming Second Secretary to Nikita KHRUSHCHEV in the Soviet party as a whole. As such he tried to restrain Khrushchev's reforms in the interests of conservative forces and was reputed to be behind an unsuccessful coup in 1963, but that year he suffered a stroke and had to leave the field to Leonid BREZHNEV.

### KPD (Kommunistische Partei Deutschlands, 'Communist Party of Germany')

German political party. Founded at New Year 1919, the KPD was, initially, a coalition of left-wing Social Democrats within the Spartacus League (Spartakus Bund) and various anarcho-syndicalist groupings which opposed the WEIMAR REPUBLIC. At first an independent-minded party led by Rosa LUXEMBURG and Karl LIEBKNECHT, the KPD later came increasingly under Russian control and became virulently hostile to the SPD by the mid-1920s. Cooperation with the SPD, which it branded 'Social Fascist', or with other republican parties to defend the Weimar Republic during the early 1930s was therefore out of the question. Its relationship with the **NAZI PARTY**, however, although highly violent, became more and more equivocal. When the organization was banned by the Nazis (Mar 1933), many members left politics or even switched to the Nazi Party or **SA**, but a minority put up sustained, if low-level, passive resistance until the end of the Third **REICH**. After **WORLD WAR II**, the revived KPD in eastern Germany forced the SPD there into a merger to form the **SED**, the ruling party of the German Democratic Republic. Soon afterwards it was banned in the Federal Republic. During Weimar, the KPD failed to gain a significant foothold in the trade union and working-class cultural movement and towards the end of Weimar relied on the unemployed and marginalized working-class groups for its growing, if minority, support. ► **COMMUNISM**; **SPARTACISTS**

### Krag, Jens Otto (1914–78)
Danish politician. He was Minister of Foreign Affairs (1958–62), when he became Leader of Denmark's **SOCIAL DEMOCRATIC PARTY**, which he led until 1972. During this time he had two periods as Prime Minister (1962–8 and 1971–2). In 1972 he led Denmark into the Common Market, but after the **EEC** referendum (Oct 1972), which showed 63.3 per cent of the votes in favour of membership and 36.7 per cent against, he surprisingly decided to resign and was succeeded by Anker **JØRGENSEN**.

### Krain ► CARNIOLA

### Kraljević, Marko (1335–94/5)
Serbian Prince. The ruler of a small principality within Serbia, he fought with Prince **LAZAR** at the Battle of **KOSOVO** (1389). Later he became a vassal of the Turks and died fighting for Sultan **BAYEZID I** against the Wallachians led by **MIRCEA THE OLD** at the Battle of Rovine. He is celebrated in Serbian epic poetry for his prodigious strength and supernatural powers and, like many folk heroes, is said not to have died but to be asleep, ready to rescue his country in its hour of need.

### Kramar, Karel (1860–1937)
Czechoslovak politician. He almost became a professor, but took up politics in the 1890s as a member of the Young Czech Party that wished to improve the lot of all **SLAVS** within Austria-Hungary. He was also pro-Russian, and at the beginning of **WORLD WAR I** he tried to float a scheme that would make Bohemia and Moravia a kingdom with a Russian prince. He was accordingly imprisoned by the Austrian authorities for much of the war but emerged at the end as provisional Prime Minister in **MASARYK**'s government. He was then very active, pressing the Czechoslovak case during the Versailles peace conference. However, in the middle of 1919, he lost his place in the government as too conservative for the majority. Although he remained in parliament, his influence waned; he had been overtaken by history.

### Krasin, Leonid Borisovich (1870–1926)
Soviet politician, diplomat and engineer. Expelled from St Petersburg Technological Institute in 1888 for radical political activity, he graduated from Khar-

kov Technological Institute in 1900 and continued thereafter to be both practising engineer and occasional revolutionary activist. He took part in the negotiations leading up to the Treaty of **BREST-LITOVSK** in 1918; and as Commissar for Foreign Trade (1920–6), he was deeply involved in most of the negotiations leading to the **NORMALIZATION** of Soviet relations with other European states. Increasingly pragmatic in his approach, he died shortly after being appointed Ambassador to Britain.

### Krausism
Spanish cultural movement. Based on the ideas of the German idealist Karl Krause, Krausism had a major impact on educational, religious, political and ethical thought in Spain. As interpreted in Spain, Krausism contributed to liberalism by stressing harmonious social development through reason. Its advocates became a secular priesthood for ethical progress.

### Kreisau Circle (*Kreisauer Kreis*)
A German anti-Nazi resistance group, founded by Count Helmuth von Moltke in 1940, which met on his estate at Kreisau. The Circle drafted a Christian–conservative political programme for post-war Germany. Von Moltke was arrested in Jan 1944, after which most of his colleagues attached themselves to von **STAUFFENBERG**'s group which tried, unsuccessfully, to kill **HITLER** in July 1944.

### Kreisky, Bruno (1911–90)
Austrian politician. Educated at Vienna University, he joined the Social Democratic Party of Austria (**SPÖ**) as a young man and was imprisoned for his political activities from 1935 until he escaped to Sweden in 1938. He returned to Austria and served in the Foreign Service (1946–51) and the Prime Minister's office (1951–3). He was increasingly active in party politics and in 1970 became Chancellor in a minority SPÖ government. He steadily increased his majority in subsequent elections but in 1983, when that majority disappeared, he refused to serve in a coalition and resigned.

### Kremlinology
The once essential art of deducing by 'reading between the lines' from various, often indirect, sources what was happening in Soviet politics. The need arose from the 'monolithic unity' presented by Soviet leaders to their own people and the outside world, hiding their conflicts and divisions through strict control of the media. Under Mikhail **GORBACHEV**, **GLASNOST** lessened the need for Kremlinology to the point where the supply of information became as abundant as elsewhere.

### Kriegel, Frantisek (1908–79)
Czechoslovak politician. Active in the Communist Party from the 1930s, and a doctor by training, he practised his profession in both the **SPANISH CIVIL WAR** and **CHINESE CIVIL WAR** from 1936 until 1945. He subsequently held a series of party and government appointments and acted as health adviser in Cuba in the years 1960–3. In 1968 he played an important role as Chairman of the National Front and he was abducted to Moscow along with Alexander **DUBČEK** and others after the invasion. The Soviet authorities initially refused to release him, and he never signed the protocol that was extracted in Moscow;

that and his subsequent outspokenness lost him all his positions and privileges.

**Krishnadevaraya** (d.1529)
Ruler of the Hindu empire of Vijayanagar (1509/29). A warrior king, he spent much of his reign at war with the Sultan of Bijapur, inflicting a severe defeat upon the Muslims at the Battle of Raichur in 1520. A poet himself, he was a liberal patron of writers in the Telugu language of the region.

**Krishna Menon, Vengalil Krishnan** (1896–1974)
Indian politician. He was educated at the Presidency College, Madras, and at London University. He went to Britain in 1924 and became a history teacher and a London barrister. In 1929 he became Secretary of the India League and the mouthpiece of Indian nationalism in Britain. When India became a Dominion in 1947, he became India's High Commissioner in London. In 1952 he became leader of the Indian delegation to the **UN**, bringing Jawaharlal **NEHRU**'s influence to bear on international problems as leader of the Asian 'uncommitted' and 'neutralist' bloc. During the first 1956 **SUEZ CRISIS** on the nationalization of the Canal, he formulated a plan to deal with it. As Defence Minister (1957–62) he came into conflict at the UN with Britain over Kashmir. He was Minister of Defence Production for a short time in 1962.

**Kristallnacht** (9–10 Nov 1938)
A **POGROM** against the Jews in National Socialist Germany unleashed by the **SA** and **NAZI PARTY** members following a provocative speech by Joseph **GOEBBELS**. The ostensible reason was the murder in Paris of a German official by a Polish Jew. The result was the massive destruction of Jewish property in Germany, the death of 91 Jews, and subsequently heightened pressure on Jews to emigrate from the country combined with the further isolation and persecution of those remaining.

**Krofta, Kamil** (1876–1945)
Czechoslovak historian and diplomat. A professor at Charles University in Prague, he entered diplomatic service as Ambassador to the Vatican (1920–2), and then held postings in Vienna and Berlin. He became Deputy Foreign Minister in 1927 and Foreign Minister in 1936. It was not easy to follow **BENEŠ** or even to serve him when he was elected President, but Krofta proved both able and loyal in the pre-Munich struggle to preserve Czechoslovakia. He was imprisoned in a **CONCENTRATION CAMP** during **WORLD WAR II** and died just after he was set free.

**Kronstadt Rebellion** (Mar 1921)
An uprising of sailors from the Baltic fleet stationed at Kronstadt in the Gulf of Finland. Protesting against the dictatorial Bolshevik policy of 'war communism', the mutineers demanded political and economic reforms under the slogan of 'free Soviets', and established a revolutionary commune on the orders of **LENIN**. The rising was crushed by **RED ARMY** units after fierce fighting and heavy losses on both sides. But at the Tenth Communist Party Congress in the same month, Lenin was sensitive enough to introduce his '**NEW ECONOMIC POLICY**', which at least improved the material conditions of the Soviet people. ► **BOLSHEVIKS**

**Kropotkin, Prince Peter** (1842–1921)
Russian geographer, savant, radical and anarchist. In 1857 he entered the corps of pages. After five years' service and exploration in Siberia, he returned to Moscow to study mathematics, while acting as Secretary to the Geographical Society. In 1871 he explored the glacial deposits of Finland and Sweden; but in 1872, critical of the limited nature of reform in Russia, he associated himself with the extremist section of the International Working Men's Association. Arrested in 1874 and imprisoned in Russia, he escaped to England in 1876. At Lyons he was condemned in 1883 to five years' imprisonment for anarchism; but, released in 1886, he settled in England until the **RUSSIAN REVOLUTION** of 1917 took him back to Russia. Well-known for his *Memoirs of a Revolutionist* (1900), he wrote widely and contributed both to the revolutionary ferment in his own country and to criticism abroad of its political backwardness.

**Kruchina, Nikolai Yefimovich** (1928–91)
Soviet politician. Graduating as an agronomist in 1952, he was a **KOMSOMOL** official from then until 1962 when he was transferred to the Communist Party proper. From 1978 to 1983 he was second-in-command of the agricultural section of the Central Committee and came into close contact with Mikhail **GORBACHEV**. He was then made chief administrator of party affairs, a post that gave considerable financial responsibility. Suddenly in 1991, as the **AUGUST COUP** crumbled, he committed suicide, suggesting corruption as well as disloyalty among Gorbachev's former lieutenants.

**Kruger, Paul**, in full **Stephanus Johannes Paulus Kruger**, known as **Oom ('Uncle') Paul** (1825–1904)
Afrikaner politician. He took part in the **GREAT TREK** of the 1830s, becoming leader of the independence movement when Britain annexed Transvaal (1877). In the first Boer War (1881), he was head of the Provisional Government, and subsequently became President of the South African Republic (1883–1902). During the second Boer War (1899–1902), he came to Europe to seek (in vain) alliances against Britain, making his headquarters at Utrecht. He died at Clarens, Switzerland. ► **BOER WARS**

**Krupskaya, Nadezhda Konstantinova** (1869–1939)
Russian revolutionary, and wife and widow of **LENIN**. A Marxist activist before she met Lenin in 1894, she was sentenced to exile about the same time as he was and allowed to join him in Siberia in 1898 on condition that they got married. Thereafter they were inseparable, and Krupskaya acted as his agent, organizer and fellow-thinker in both Europe and Russia. She disliked the political limelight and, following the Bolshevik **RUSSIAN REVOLUTION**, she was mainly active in promoting education and the status of women. As Lenin's widow she at first opposed **STALIN** but subsequently supported some of his policies, and was accordingly exploited. She left a rather brief *Reminiscences of Lenin.* ► **BOLSHEVIKS**

**Kryuchkov, Vladimir Alexandrovich** (1924– )
Soviet lawyer, diplomat and secret policeman. Born and educated in Volgograd (Stalingrad), he immediately threw himself into local Communist Party work. However, in 1954 he was recruited into the diplomatic

service and became Third Secretary in Budapest, where Yuri **ANDROPOV** was serving as ambassador. Thereafter he went everywhere with Andropov, to the Central Committee as a sector head in 1957 and to the **KGB** in a similar posting in 1967. From 1974 to 1988 he was deputy chairman, mainly responsible for foreign intelligence; but in 1988, under Mikhail **GORBACHEV**, he became chairman. Obviously expected to support reform, he was brought into the **POLITBURO** in 1989 and transferred to the presidential council in 1990. But in 1991, disenchanted or ambitious, he helped organize the attempted **AUGUST COUP** that led to his own imprisonment and Boris **YELTSIN**'s advancement. He was released on amnesty in 1994.

### Kuang-hsu ► GUANGXU

### Kubitschek (de Oliveira), Juscelino (1902–76)

Brazilian politician. The grandson of a Czech immigrant, he studied medicine in Belo Horizonte, Minas Gerais, and went on to become mayor of the city (1940–5). He was elected to Congress by the **PSD** (*Partido Social Democrático*) in 1945 and was Governor of Minas Gerais in 1951–5. As President (1956–61), his ambitious *Programa de Metas* ('Programme of Goals') emphasized transport, energy, manufacturing and the building of Brasília rather than social measures, and was the blueprint for subsequent programmes during military rule. The political necessity for high GDP growth rates hampered effective counter-inflationary policies and the achievement of a *modus vivendi* with international creditors, bequeathing massive problems to subsequent **QUADROS/GOULART** and **CASTELO BRANCO** administrations. He was a candidate for the presidency in 1965 when he was exiled by Castelo Branco.

### Kublai Khan (1214–94)

Mongol Emperor of China (1279/94). He was the grandson of **GENGHIS KHAN**. An energetic prince, he suppressed his rivals, adopted the Chinese mode of civilization, encouraged men of letters and made Buddhism the state religion. He established himself at Cambaluc (modern Beijing), the first foreigner ever to rule in China, and ruled an empire that extended as far as the River Danube. The splendour of his court was legendary.

### Kučan, Milan (1941– )

Slovenian politician. During the late 1980s, as the communist President of Slovenia, he resisted pressure from Belgrade to stifle the emergence of opposition parties in his republic, long the most liberal in the Yugoslav Federation. In 1990, after the Slovenes held the first free elections anywhere in Yugoslavia since **WORLD WAR II**, he was re-elected as non-communist President of Slovenia. He declared Slovenia's secession from the Yugoslav Federation on 25 July 1991. With the backing of Serbia's President, Slobodan **MILOŠEVIĆ**, Yugoslav Federal army units attacked Slovenia, but Milošević was obliged to withdraw and to accept Slovenia's independence.

### Kuchuk Kainarji, Treaty of (21 July 1774)

The treaty signed at the end of the Russo-Turkish War of 1768–74, **CATHERINE II, THE GREAT**'s first war against the **OTTOMAN EMPIRE**. The war had begun when Sultan Mustafa III, egged on by his French and Austrian allies, made a pre-emptive attack on Russian forces. Following several notable victories, Russia greatly improved its strategic position on the Black Sea by gaining control of the estuaries of the Don, Dnieper and Bug rivers. The treaty gave the Russians the right to represent the Sultan's Orthodox subjects in **MOLDAVIA AND WALLACHIA** and the Aegean Islands, and marked the first stage in the establishment of Russian interests in the Danubian Principalities. Russia was also granted trading privileges throughout the Ottoman Empire, free passage through the Straits and the right to set up consulates throughout the empire. Among other terms, Greek merchants gained the right to sail under the Russian flag. The treaty marked a turning-point for Russia; henceforward, Tsarist policy moved from domestic consolidation to foreign conquest. ► **RUSSO-TURKISH WARS**

### Ku Klux Klan

US white supremacist organization. The first klan was founded after the **AMERICAN CIVIL WAR** to oppose **RECONSTRUCTION** and the new rights being granted to blacks. The members, disguised in white robes and hoods, engaged in whippings, lynchings and cross burnings to terrorize blacks and their sympathizers in the rural areas of the South. The Klan declined in influence after federal laws were passed against it, but was re-established after **WORLD WAR I**. This time its influence was felt far beyond the South, and its targets were enlarged to include Catholics, foreigners and Jews as well as blacks. It declined during the 1930s, but was revived by the fear of **COMMUNISM** in the 1950s. In the 1960s its violent opposition to the **CIVIL RIGHTS MOVEMENT** led to a federal government crackdown, and the prosecution of key members. Subsequently the Klan moved toward working through traditional political channels in order to further its agenda.

### kulaks

The most progressive stratum of the late 19c and early 20c Russian peasantry. The kulaks became significant after the final emancipation of the serfs in 1905, building up successful medium-sized farms with encouragement from the Tsarist government, which was anxious to broaden its very narrow support. During the collectivization of agriculture in the 1930s, **STALIN** 'liquidated' the kulaks as a class, asserting that they were enemies of the revolution. In fact he eliminated an important source of agricultural wealth that his successors tragically lacked. ► **RUSSIAN SERFS, EMANCIPATION OF THE**

### Kulikov, Viktor Georgevich (1921– )

Soviet commander. He rose to be Chief of Staff of a tank brigade during **WORLD WAR II**, then worked his way up until in 1969 he became the commander of Soviet forces in Germany. His subsequent promotion was even quicker: Chief of the General Staff and First Deputy Defence Minister in 1971; and Commander-in-Chief of the **WARSAW PACT** and Marshal of the USSR in 1977. He was therefore deeply involved in Leonid **BREZHNEV**'s military build-up and opposed Mikhail **GORBACHEV**'s cutbacks. He was relieved of his appointment in 1989 not long before the disbandment of the Warsaw Pact, the two events obviously being connected.

## Kulturkampf

In the German Empire, a 'cultural conflict' between the Prussian state and the Roman Catholic Church. It was inspired by liberal suspicion of Catholics' extra-German loyalties, and involved discriminatory legislation against the Church's position within **PRUSSIA**. Exploited by **BISMARCK** to consolidate his position, it was most intense during the period 1870–8, but gradually subsided following the election of Pope **LEO XIII** (1878), and effectively ended by 1886.

## Kumaratunga, Chandrika Bandaranaike (1945– )

Sri Lankan politician. The daughter of S W R D **BANDARANAIKE** and Sirimavo **BANDARANAIKE**, she was educated in Colombo and Paris. From 1972 to 1976 she was Principal Director of the Sri Lankan Land Reforms Commission. She married Vijaya Kumaratunga in 1978 and has two children. Following her husband's assassination in 1988, she became a Research Fellow at the Institute of Commonwealth Studies in London. After returning to Sri Lanka, she was elected Chief Minister of the Western Provincial Council in May 1993, representing the **SLFP**. In 1994 she was elected first Prime Minister and then President of Sri Lanka, appointing her mother Prime Minister. Although injured by a **TAMIL** suicide bomber, she was re-elected president in 1999. Her opponent, Ranil Wickramasinghe, was elected Prime Minister in 2001. She opposed his moves towards ending the long conflict with the **LTTE**, considering them too lenient. Her party won the 2004 parliamentary elections.

## Kumazawa Banzan (1619–91)

Japanese **SAMURAI** administrator and Confucian scholar. The son of a masterless samurai (*ronin*), Kumazawa entered the service of the **DAIMYO** (feudal lord) of Bizen, where he was instrumental in promoting administrative reforms. His writings stressed the importance of empirical knowledge of the external world and of the need to adopt practical solutions to changing circumstances. Kumazawa's thought influenced later samurai activists of the early 19c dissatisfied with the rigidities of the status quo.

## Kun, Béla (1886–1939)

Hungarian political leader and revolutionary. He was a journalist and social democrat, who was conscripted into the Austro-Hungarian army and became a prisoner of war in Russia in 1916. In 1917 he sympathized with the **BOLSHEVIKS**, and in 1918 founded the Hungarian Communist Party. In Mar 1919 he organized a communist revolution in Budapest and set up a Soviet republic that succeeded **KÁROLYI**'s post-**WORLD WAR I** government. His policy of nationalization and other socialist measures failed, however, to gain popular support, and he was forced to flee for his life in Aug of that year. After escaping to Vienna, he returned to Russia where, in 1921, he became a member of the Executive Committee of the **COMINTERN**. He then fell victim to the Stalinist purges of the late 1930s. ► **STALIN, JOSEPH**

## Kunaev, Dimmukhamed Akhmedovich (1912–93)

Kazakh politician. A metallurgist by occupation and communist by inclination, he worked his way up the Kazakh party ladder in the 1940s and 1950s, coming into close contact with Leonid **BREZHNEV** and being made First Secretary in 1960. He was demoted by Nikita **KHRUSHCHEV** in 1962, but reappointed in 1964 by Brezhnev, who also brought him into full membership of the **POLITBURO**. This gave Brezhnev his personal support. His inclusion in the Politburo also conciliated opinion in Kazakhstan; inevitably, it meant his dismissal by Mikhail **GORBACHEV** in 1986. His ousting led to riots in Alma Ata but these were countered by charges of extensive corruption.

## Kunersdorf, Battle of (12 Aug 1759)

A battle, during the **SEVEN YEARS' WAR**, in which **FREDERICK II, THE GREAT** suffered a tremendous defeat at the hands of an Austro-Russian force commanded by Loudon and Soltykov. The engagement resulted in immense loss of life and the near ruin of Frederick's army.

## K'ung, H H, in full K'ung Hsiang-hsi (Kong Xiangxi) (1881–1967)

Chinese politician and banker. He came from a family of traditional bankers and received a missionary education in China before studying in the USA (1901–7). Through marriage, K'ung developed close ties with **SUN YAT-SEN** and **CHIANG KAI-SHEK** (their wives were sisters), joining the **GUOMINDANG** in 1924 and becoming Minister of Industry and Commerce of the new Nationalist government in 1928. As Governor of the Bank of China and Minister of Finance (1933–44), K'ung attempted to increase the government's financial control of the modern sector. Through control of the four major banks, the government floated more bond issues to finance its military projects. K'ung's abandonment of the silver standard in favour of a managed paper currency in 1935 was to lead ultimately to hyperinflation in the 1940s. During the war against Japan, K'ung was instrumental in obtaining US loans and was China's representative at the **BRETTON WOODS CONFERENCE** (1944). He moved to the USA permanently in 1948.

## Kuomintang (KMT) ► GUOMINDANG

## Kuo Sung-tao ► GUO SONGDAO

## Kurds

A nationalistic West Iranian-speaking ethnic group settled in neighbouring mountainous areas of Anatolia, Iraq, Iran and Turkey (including some in Syria and Armenia), an area which they call Kurdistan, and numbering 9–10 million. They were originally pastoral nomads with some agriculture, but the creation of national boundaries after **WORLD WAR I** restricted their seasonal migrations, and most are now urbanized. They have been Sunni Muslims since the 7c AD. In Turkey they are politically oppressed, and there has been fighting in the Kurdish regions there since 1984 between government forces and the separatist PKK (Marxist Kurdish Workers' Party). The fighting flared up in 1992 and led to the bombing of PKK bases in Iraq and Syria. In Iran the Kurds have suffered religious persecution, especially after the **IRANIAN REVOLUTION** of 1979. In Iraq the Kurds' failure to achieve autonomous status for Kurdistan during the 1970s, despite promises by the Ba'athist government, resulted in hostilities between Kurds and government forces, and the union of the Patriotic Union of Kurdistan (PUK) and the Kurdish Democratic Party (KDP). Further unrest resulted in the use of chemical weapons by Saddam **HUSSEIN** which killed thousands of Kurds. Another 1.5 million were forcibly moved from their mountain homes and put in townships. A revolt following the 1991 **GULF WAR** was brutally suppressed, causing hundreds to flee, until the **UN** intervened, and in 1996 Iraqi forces launched further attacks against the Kurds. Elections had been held for an Iraqi-Kurdistan National Assembly in 1992, but these were inconclusive due to internal strife between the PUK and KDP. In Feb 1999 the Turks' capture of the Kurdish guerrilla leader Abdullah Ocalan sparked off demonstrations and attacks by Kurds, mainly on Greek embassies, in over 20 European cities. Ocalan was tried in Turkey and sentenced to death, although the sentence was commuted to life imprisonment in 2002. During the **IRAQ WAR**, Kurdish leaders refused to allow Turkish troops to take part in the US military campaign in northern Iraq but Kurdish fighters fought alongside US troops, taking control of the northern cities of Kirkuk and Mosul. The PUK and KDP united with other parties to form a United Kurdistan Coalition to contest the election held in Iraq in Jan 2005.

## Kuril Islands, Dispute over the
A territorial dispute between the USSR and Japan over ownership of the southern group of Kuril Islands. During the 18c Russia began settling the northern and central Kurils, while the **TOKUGAWA SHOGUNATE** laid claim to the southern islands, an arrangement that was formalized by the Treaty of Shimoda (7 Feb 1855). With the Treaty of St Petersburg (7 May 1875), Russia surrendered its claim to the northern and central Kurils (in return for which Japan gave up her claims to Sakhalin Island), and the islands were then administered by Japan as part of Hokkaido (1875–1945). The Kurils were occupied by Soviet forces shortly after the USSR declared war on Japan (9 Aug 1945) and were formally declared Soviet territory. Since Japan insisted on the return of the southern Kurils (Kunashiri, Etorofu, Shikotan, Habomai islands), which it regards as inalienable Japanese territory (and are referred to as the Northern Territories), a Soviet–Japanese peace treaty was never signed, although relations were normalized in 1955. Even with the dismantling of the USSR in 1991, the dispute remains unresolved.

## Kuropatkin, Alexei Nikolaievich (1848–1925)
Russian general. He was Russian Chief of Staff under **SKOBELEFF** in the Russo-Turkish War of 1877–8, and Commander-in-Chief in Caucasia (1897). As Minister of War (1898–1904) and Commander-in-Chief in Manchuria (1904–5), his record against the victorious Japanese was at best mediocre. He commanded the Russian armies on the northern front Feb–Aug 1916, and then was Governor of Turkestan until the **RUSSIAN REVOLUTION** in 1917. ➤ **RUSSO-TURKISH WARS**

## Kushana ➤ INDIA, PRE-ISLAMIC

## Kusunoki Masashige (d.1336)
Japanese warrior chieftain. Celebrated for his loyalty to Emperor **DAIGO II**, Kusunoki supported Daigo's abortive attempt to restore direct imperial rule (1333–6), but was defeated in battle by the forces of **ASHIKAGA TAKAUJI**, who supported a rival claimant

to the throne. Kusunoki committed suicide shortly afterwards. He became a folk hero in later centuries and in school textbooks of the 1930s was eulogized for his faithful devotion to the throne and his spirit of self-sacrifice. ➤ **ASHIKAGA SHOGUNATE**

## Kut al-Amara, Battles of (28 Sep 1915 and 29 Apr 1916) and Siege of (1915–16)
Kut al-Amara, on the west bank of the Tigris, some 100 mi/160 km from Baghdad, was taken first by the British under Major-General Charles Townshend in Sep 1915. Townshend later over-reached himself and was forced to fall back on Kut al-Amara, having suffered a reverse near the site of the ancient Ctesiphon. The Turks laid siege to Kut in Dec 1915 and, despite attempts to relieve Kut by British forces in Iraq, Townshend was forced to ask for terms. Townshend's proposals for terms were refused by the Turks and he surrendered, having first obtained a guarantee for his troops, in 1916.

## Kutuzov, Mikhail Ilarionovich, Prince of Smolensk (1745–1813)
Russian field marshal. He distinguished himself in Poland and in the **RUSSO-TURKISH WARS**, and from 1805 to 1812 he commanded against the French. In 1812, as Commander-in-Chief, he fought **NAPOLEON I** obstinately at the Battle of **BORODINO**, and later obtained a great victory over **DAVOUT** and **NEY** at Smolensk. His army pursued the retreating French out of Russia into Prussia, where he died.

## Kuusinen, Otto Vilgelmovich (1881–1964)
Finnish-born Soviet politician. An active Bolshevik in both the 1905 and 1917 Russian Revolutions, he founded the Finnish Communist Party in 1918, but emigrated to Moscow when it was outlawed in 1930. He had already been working there as Secretary of the **COMINTERN** Executive Committee, a function he performed until 1939. He was then briefly Chairman of the Presidium of the so-called Karelo-Finnish Republic, which won him membership of the Soviet Party's Central Committee. A survivor, he was selected by Nikita **KHRUSHCHEV** in 1957 to be a member of the **POLITBURO** in the aftermath of the **ANTI-PARTY PLOT**. However, he died before it could be known how he would fare with Leonid **BREZHNEV**.

## KUWAIT official name State of Kuwait

An independent state at the head of the Arabian Gulf, bounded to the north and west by Iraq; to the south by Saudi Arabia; and to the east by the Arabian Gulf. The port was founded in the 18c, and the state has been ruled since 1756 by the **SABAH FAMILY**. Britain became responsible for Kuwait's foreign affairs in 1899. It became a British protectorate in 1914, and fully independent in 1961. The invasion and annexation by Iraq in Aug 1990 led to the **GULF WAR** in Jan–Feb 1991, with severe damage to Kuwait City and the infrastructure of the country. The Kuwait government went into exile in Saudi Arabia until the country was liberated in 1991. Major post-war problems included large-scale refugee emigration, the burning of oil wells by Iraq (all capped by Nov 1991) and the pollution of Gulf waters by oil. In 1992 the port of Umm Quasr and part of an oilfield were passed to Kuwait when the boundary between Iraq and Kuwait was moved by 600 m/1,970 ft. In 2003 Kuwait was a base for the build-up of forces for the **IRAQ WAR**.

**Ku Wei-chun** ► GU WEIJUN

**Ku Yen-wu** ► GU YANWU

**Kuyper, Abraham** (1837–1920)
Dutch theologian and politician. As a clergyman, founder of the Free University of Amsterdam (1880), member of the Dutch parliament and Prime Minister (1900–5), Kuyper sought to develop a Christian world-view of society. He founded and edited two newspapers and wrote numerous books, few of which have been translated into English, apart from *Lectures on Calvinism* (1898), *Principles of Sacred Theology* (1898) and *The Work of the Holy Spirit* (1900). His theology of common grace, the kingdom of God, and the 'sphere-sovereignty' of the Church and other social institutions, offer a Calvinistic version of Social Christianity. In the Netherlands he is remembered as the emancipator of the orthodox Calvinists and as the founder of the **ANTI-REVOLUTIONARY PARTY**.

**Kuznetsov, Vasili Vasilevich** (1901–90)
Soviet politician. He joined the Communist Party in 1927, and managed to steer so clear of trouble that in 1952 he became a member of the **POLITBURO**. Although he held various second-level political posts, he achieved little. Mikhail **GORBACHEV** took the first opportunity to get rid of him in 1986 in order to free the system and make room for new blood.

**Kwantung Army** ► GUANDONG ARMY

**KwaZulu**
National state or non-independent Black homeland in Natal province, eastern South Africa, during the **APARTHEID** era. Situated close to the Indian Ocean between the Transkei and Durban, it was granted self-governing status in 1971, and reincorporated into South Africa in 1994.

**KYRGYZSTAN** official name **Kyrgyz Republic**, formerly (1936–91) **Kirghizia**

A mountainous republic in north-east Central Asia, bounded to the north by Kazakhstan; to the west by Uzbekistan; to the south and south-west by Tajikistan; and to the south-east and east by China. It was proclaimed a constituent republic within the USSR in 1936, and in 1991 gained independence under President Askar Akayev and became a member of the **CIS** (Commonwealth of Independent States). A constitution introduced in 1993 advocated respect for the international and moral principles of law and human rights, and for the beliefs of Islam, but Akayev's re-election in 2000 was regarded as flawed. The first multiparty elections were held in 1995. The country has implemented market reforms, but not without difficulties, including inflation of over 700 per cent in 1993, the suspension of privatization (resumed in 1998) because of fears that assets were being sold too cheaply, high levels of unemployment and widespread malnutrition.

## Labadie, Jean de (1610–74)

French ex-Jesuit Protestant reformer. A former member of the Jesuits, he became a Calvinist convert in 1650 and was minister at Middelburg in the Netherlands from 1666. He became increasingly pietistic, and preached a return to primitive Christianity. He was suspended by the Dutch Church in 1669, whereupon he moved his Labadist colony to Germany, where he died.

## Labourers' Statute (1351)

A law passed in an endeavour to stabilize the English economy in the wake of the Black Death. It represented the first-ever attempt to control wages and prices by freezing wages and the prices of manufactured articles, and by restricting the movement of labour. Like most subsequent attempts, it failed abysmally to achieve its aims and contributed largely to the 1381 PEASANTS' REVOLT.

## Labour Party (Netherlands) (*Partij van de Arbeid*, PvdA)

Dutch political party, founded in 1946 to replace the Social Democratic Workers' Party (*Sociaal-Democratische Arbeiders Partij*, SDAP), founded in 1894 in Amsterdam. The SDAP was originally a Marxist socialist party, although there were always debates between Marxists and revisionists. In 1918 the Marxists, led by Pieter TROELSTRA, launched an abortive coup attempt. Thereafter, the labour unions gained a greater role in the party; in the 1930s the Dutch socialists fully embraced the Plan Socialism of Hendrik de MAN. In 1939 the socialists first joined the government. After WORLD WAR II, in 1946, in an attempt to create a broad-left party, the PvdA was formed to replace the SDAP, and indeed a number of liberals and confessionals joined for a short time; however, in the long run there was little change. The PvdA, as the second most popular party, joined the Catholics (the largest) in a long spell of coalitions after the war (1945–58); after another stint of government (1965–6), the party underwent considerable radicalization, with the emergence of a New Left movement. In 1973 the socialists again formed a government with the confessionals, but it fell because of internal strife in 1977; in the ensuing election Labour increased its vote, but was unable to find any coalition partners. It spent the 1980s out of office, but returned to power in 1989 (again with the confessionals), by then reformed along social-democratic lines. After the 1994 election, in which Labour emerged as the largest party in parliament, its leader Wim Kok became Prime Minister of a coalition government that held office until 2002. The party lost ground in the 2002 election, but recovered in 2003.

## Labour Party (Norway)

Despite the pioneering activities of Marcus THRANE, working-class political organization did not develop on a large scale in Norway until the beginnings of rapid industrialization at the end of the 19c. The Norwegian Labour Party was founded in 1884. Following the enactment of male suffrage (1898), four Labour candidates were elected to the *Storting* (parliament) in 1904, and by 1915 the party had won 32 per cent of the vote. Initially a moderate, reformist party, Labour moved sharply to the left during WORLD WAR I. Its youth movement was represented at the Zimmerwald Conference in 1915 and established links with BUKHARIN. Led by Martin Tranmæl, the Left gained control at the 1918 Party Congress. In 1919 the Norwegian Labour Party became the second foreign party (after the Bulgarian) to join the COMINTERN. The right wing of the party split away in 1920 to form the Social Democratic Party. In 1923 the party broke with the Comintern; the Left then broke away to form the Norwegian Communist Party. The Social Democrats rejoined the party in 1927; in the elections of that year it became the largest single party in the country and in Jan–Feb 1928 formed a short-lived minority government under Christopher Hornsrud. Committed to parliamentarism and measures to combat the depression, Labour obtained 40 per cent of the vote in 1933 and a deal with the Agrarian Party enabled it to form a government under Johan Nygaardsvold in 1935. Despite its achievements in social reform, the Labour government neglected defence and was forced into exile in London (Jun 1940) following the German invasion of Norway. Labour won an absolute majority in the first post-war elections with a programme of extensive economic reconstruction and nationalization. Einar GERHARDSEN was Prime Minister from 1945 to 1951 and again from 1955 to 1965. The defection of part of its left wing to form the Socialist People's Party deprived Labour of its majority in 1961, and from 1965 to 1971 Norway was ruled by a coalition of non-socialist parties. Labour returned to office under Trygve Bratteli, but his government resigned when the Norwegian electorate rejected EEC membership in the referendum of Oct 1972. In the election of 1973 the party's vote fell to 35 per cent but it remained in office through the support of the Socialist Electoral Alliance (anti-EEC socialists). In 1976 the leadership passed from Bratteli to Odvar Nordli, who was in turn succeeded briefly as Prime Minister by Gro Harlem

**BRUNDTLAND** in 1981. After a period of minority conservative and centre-right coalition government, Brundtland returned to power in 1986 and remained in office for ten years, apart from when Jan P Syse was Prime Minister in 1989–90. Thorbjørn Jagland took over from her as leader in 1996, and in 1997 the Labour government was forced to resign in favour of a new centre coalition government. When this government fell in 2000, Labour formed a minority government until the 2001 election, in which it won the greatest number of seats but was kept out of power by another centre coalition, headed by Kjell Magne Bondevik. ► **KOHT, HALVDAN**; **LIE, TRYGVE**; **NORWAY, GERMAN INVASION OF**

**Labour Party** (UK)
A British socialist/social democratic political party, originally formed in 1900 as the Labour Representation Committee to represent trade unions and socialist societies as a distinct group in parliament. In 1906, 26 MPs were elected and the name changed to the Labour Party. In 1922 it overtook the Liberals as the main opposition party, and the first minority Labour government was elected in 1924, lasting 11 months. The first majority Labour government under Clement **ATTLEE** (1945–51) established the welfare state and carried out a significant nationalization programme. Since then Labour has been in office 1964–70, 1974–9 and from 1997. The breakaway **SOCIAL DEMOCRATIC PARTY** of the 1980s hurt the party's electoral chances throughout that decade. Outside parliament, the annual conference and the National Executive Committee share policymaking, though their influence is greater in opposition. The leader and deputy leader are elected annually when in opposition by an electoral college composed of trade unions, constituency parties and the parliamentary Labour Party. The British Labour Party has been little influenced by **MARXISM**, unlike the corresponding parties in Europe, and with the dominance of 'New Labour' under Tony **BLAIR**, its socialism has been greatly moderated. ► **SOCIALISM**

**Lacoste, Robert** (1898–1989)
French socialist politician. He began his career as a civil servant, becoming a trade union official. In **WORLD WAR II** he began the first trade union Resistance group. In 1944 he was Minister of Industrial Production, and was Minister for Industry and Commerce in 1946–7 and again in 1948. From 1956 to 1958 he was resident minister in Algeria, and was accused of allowing the military authorities to use torture and other ruthless measures against the rebels. He was Senator for the Dordogne (1971–80). ► **RESISTANCE MOVEMENT** (France)

**Ladislas IV** (of Poland) ► **WŁADYSŁAW IV VASA**

**Ladysmith, Siege of** (1899–1900)
One of the three sieges of the second Boer War in which Boer forces attempted to pen up their British opponents, and around which many of the actions of the war took place. An attempt to relieve the town was frustrated at the Battle of **SPION KOP** (Jan 1900), but General Sir Redvers Buller (1839–1908) succeeded in raising the siege on 28 Feb 1900. ► **BOER WARS**; **KIMBERLEY, SIEGE OF**; **MAFEKING, SIEGE OF**

**La Farina, Giuseppe** (1815–63)
Italian revolutionary and writer. In 1837 La Farina was forced to leave his native Sicily and settled in Florence; he returned when revolution broke out in 1848 and joined the Provisional Government. After the failure of the **REVOLUTIONS OF 1848–9**, he went to live first in Paris and then in Turin. By 1853 he had come to believe in the idea of Italian unification under the King of Sardinia-Piedmont and in 1856 he founded the **ITALIAN NATIONAL SOCIETY**. In 1859 he helped to instigate and orchestrate a number of liberal/nationalist revolutions in central Italy which were used by **CAVOUR** as a pretext for subsequent annexation by Piedmont. The following year he sent by Cavour to Sicily, to try to prevent **GARIBALDI** exerting too much influence over the course of events on the island, but poor relations with the great military hero led to La Farina's withdrawal.

**Lafayette, Marie Joseph Paul Yves Roch Gilbert du Motier, Marquis of** (1757–1834)
French soldier and revolutionary. After a period at court, he fought in the USA against the British during the **AMERICAN REVOLUTION** (1777–9 and 1780–2), and became a hero and a friend of George **WASHINGTON**. A liberal aristocrat, in the National Assembly of 1789 he presented a draft of a Declaration of the Rights of Man, based on the US **DECLARATION OF INDEPENDENCE**. Hated by the **JACOBINS** for his moderation, he defected to Austria, returning to France during the **CONSULATE**. During the Restoration he sat in the Chamber of Deputies (1818–24), became a radical Leader of the Opposition (1825–30), and commanded the **NATIONAL GUARD** in the 1830 **JULY REVOLUTION**. ► **DECLARATION OF THE RIGHTS OF MAN AND CITIZEN**

**Laffitte, Jacques** (1767–1844)
French financier and politician. He acquired great wealth as a Paris banker, and in 1814 became Governor of the Bank of France. He was elected to the Chamber of Deputies in 1817. In 1830 his house was the headquarters of the **JULY REVOLUTION**, and he supplied a great part of the funds needed. In Nov 1830 he formed a cabinet, but he only held power until Mar 1831. From the ruins of his fortune he founded a Discount Bank in 1837. In 1843 he was elected President of the Chamber of Deputies.

**Lafitte** or **Laffite, Jean** (c.1780–c.1826)
French pirate. He and his band of smugglers preyed on Spanish ships in the Gulf of Mexico, and they aided US authorities during the **WAR OF 1812** by revealing British attack plans and manning US artillery during the Battle of **NEW ORLEANS** (Dec 1814–Jan 1815). After the war Lafitte returned to piracy, based at Galveston in Texas, and succeeded in scuttling a US merchant ship in 1820. His headquarters were then raided and destroyed, perhaps burned by Lafitte himself, and he moved his men to plague the seas off Spanish America (the Spanish Main) instead.

**La Follette, Robert Marion, Sr** (1855–1925)
US politician. Three times Progressive Governor of Wisconsin, he began his political career by winning election as a district attorney after exposing corruption in the **POLITICAL MACHINE** of the local **REPUBLICAN PARTY**. From 1885 to 1891, he served in the

HOUSE OF REPRESENTATIVES. As Governor of Wisconsin, he reformed the primary election process and the civil service, strengthened the railroad commission and introduced measures for workers' compensation and the conservation of natural resources. His widely publicized and imitated reforms became knowns as the 'Wisconsin Idea'. He would have been the PROGRESSIVE PARTY presidential candidate in 1912 but for the re-entry into politics of ex-President Theodore ROOSEVELT; in 1924 he became the nominee. Although he failed in his presidential bid, he received nearly five million votes.

### Lafontaine, Sir Louis Hippolyte (1807–64)

Canadian lawyer and politician. He recognized that French-Canadian culture would best be served by full French-Canadian participation in politics and by achieving RESPONSIBLE GOVERNMENT. Although a follower of PAPINEAU, he opposed the rebellion of 1837, and went to London to request constitutional reform. As the leader of the French-Canadians of CANADA EAST, he joined in a coalition with CANADA WEST's reform leaders, Robert BALDWIN and Francis HINCKS. The British government had sought to assimilate the French-Canadians by insisting on equal representation in the provincial legislature and on the use of English as the language of debate. The French-Canadians, however, became more politically cohesive and were able to unite with the English-speaking reformers to form an alliance which became the majority party. With the arrival as Governor-General of the realist Sir Charles BAGOT in 1842, Lafontaine and Baldwin were eventually accepted as the leaders of a ministry. They therefore not only introduced a semblance of a responsible government, but demonstrated the potential of bi-cultural cooperation. There was a short interruption to reform when Sir Charles METCALFE replaced Bagot, but with the introduction of free elections in 1848, the Baldwin–Lafontaine coalition came into office and served until 1851.

### Lafontaine, Oskar (1943–)

West German politician. Educated at BONN University, he became leader of the Saar regional branch of the Social Democratic Party (SPD) in 1977 and served as Mayor of Saarbrücken (1976–85). He gained a reputation for radicalism and was variously dubbed 'Red Oskar' and the 'Ayatollah of the SAARLAND'. He began to mellow, however, after his election as Minister-President of the Saarland state parliament in 1985. In 1987 he was appointed a deputy chairman of the SPD's federal organization and served as the SPD's unsuccessful Chancellor-candidate in the 1990 BUNDESTAG elections after surviving an assassination attempt. In Oct 1998 he was sworn in as Finance Minister in Gerhard Schröder's SPD-led coalition government, but his unpopular fiscal policies led to his resignation in Mar 1999.

### La Guardia, Fiorello Henry (1882–1947)

US politician. He became Deputy Attorney-General (1915–17) and served seven terms in the HOUSE OF REPRESENTATIVES as a Republican (1917–21 and 1923–33). Three times Mayor of New York City (1934–46), he was a popular and effective leader who initiated broad reforms in public services, fought corruption, and undertook a major rebuilding programme. New York's La Guardia Airport is named after him. ► REPUBLICAN PARTY

### La Hogue, Battle of (13–17 May 1692)

A naval victory in the English Channel, won by an Anglo-Dutch force after a five-day running battle over a numerically inferior French fleet. The defeat seriously reduced COLBERT's navy, ended French hopes of invading England, and gave the Allies control of the seas for the duration of the Nine Years' War (1689–97).

### laissez-faire

An economic doctrine (literally, 'leave alone') advocating that commerce and trade should be permitted to operate free of government controls. It was a popular view in the mid-19c and is still part of modern-day conservative political thinking. The phrase originated with the French 18c free-trade economists.

### Lajpat Rai, Lala (1865–1928)

Indian politician and writer. He was a follower of the ARYA SAMAJ and when it split in 1893, he and Hans Raj led the moderate 'college faction' which concentrated on building up a chain of 'Dayanand Anglo-Vedic colleges'. At the same time, Lajpat Rai developed a somewhat sporadic interest in Congress politics, as well as a more sustained involvement in SWADESHI enterprises. In two articles published (1901) in the *Kayastha Samachar*, Lajpat Rai advocated technical education and industrial self-help and criticized the Congress as being a gathering of English-educated élites. He also argued that Congress should openly and boldly base itself on the Hindus alone. He led the wave of so-called extremist nationalism in Punjab between 1904 and 1907. The Congress split in the Surat session in 1907 and Lala Lajpat Rai formed the famous 'extremist' trio of Lal, Pal and Bal, with Bipin Chandra PAL and Bal Gangadhar TILAK. Deported on charges of instigating the peasants, he led the NON-COOPERATION MOVEMENT in Punjab in 1921.

### Lake Erie, Battle of (10 Sep 1813)

A major US naval victory in the WAR OF 1812 in which six British ships were defeated by a US fleet of nine ships led by Oliver Perry (1785–1819, elder brother of Matthew PERRY). This victory reversed the course of the north-west campaign, forcing the British to abandon Fort Detroit and ensuring that they would have no claim to the north-west at the end of the war. It also opened the way for the US forces to enter Canada and made Oliver Perry a national hero; his report of the battle ('We have met the enemy and they are ours') became famous.

### Lake George, Battle of (8 Sep 1755)

A battle of the FRENCH AND INDIAN WAR which took place south of Lake George in north-eastern New York State. The colonial forces under Colonel William Johnson defeated the French and Indian forces led by Baron Ludwig August Dieskau.

### Lakshmibai (d.1858)

Maratha Rani (Queen) of Jhansi. The state of Jhansi was absorbed in 1853 by the British under the annexation policy made by Lord DALHOUSIE. According to this policy, all 'dependent' Indian states without direct heirs were to lapse to the British. In 1857 Jhansi was besieged and taken by the British despite desperate resistance from the Rani. The Rani then went first to Kalpi, and then to Gwalior with Tantia Tope, where after proclaiming the Nana as Peshwa, she died fighting in 1858. She is regarded by some as the best and bravest military leader of the Indian forces during the INDIAN UPRISING.

### La Marmora, Alfonso Ferrero (1804–78)

Piedmontese soldier and politician. He fought in the campaign against Austria in 1848 and was involved in the suppression of the Genoese revolt of 1849. During the 1850s he was instrumental in reforming the Piedmontese army, which formed the basis of the Italian army after 1860. In 1855 he commanded the Italian contingent in the CRIMEAN WAR, and in 1860 he became Prime Minister on the resignation of CAVOUR. In 1860 he was made Governor of recently annexed Milan and the following year took the same job in Naples. He was Prime Minister again in 1864 and, as Foreign Minister, concluded the 1866 alliance with Prussia which was to lead to the Italian acquisition of Venetia. In 1870 he was once again made a royal governor, this time of Rome, just seized from the papacy. He subsequently retired from public life.

### Lamartine, Alphonse Marie Louis de (1790–1869)

French poet, politician and historian. His best-known work was his first volume of lyrical poems, *Méditations poétiques* (1820). He became a member of the Provisional Government after the 1848 JULY REVOLUTION, and acted as Minister of Foreign Affairs. He then devoted himself to literature, publishing several historical and other works.

### Lambert, John (1619–84)

English general. He studied law, then joined the Parliamentary Army in the ENGLISH CIVIL WARS, commanding the cavalry at the Battle of MARSTON MOOR (1644), and participating in several victories. He headed the army group which overthrew Richard CROMWELL (1659), and virtually governed the country with his officers as the 'Committee of Safety'. After the RESTORATION (1660) he was tried, and imprisoned on Drake's Island, Plymouth, until his death.

### Lambing Flat Riots (1860–1)

In Australian history, a series of anti-Chinese riots on the Burrangong goldfields (Young, New South Wales) which expelled the Chinese and destroyed their camps. Police intervention led to further rioting in which one miner was killed. The riots reflected the racial and economic hostility to the Chinese that was general on Australian goldfields, leading to immigration restrictions and ultimately the WHITE AUSTRALIA POLICY.

### Lamennais, Félicité Robert de (1782–1854)

French priest and writer. He began in 1816 his famous *Essai sur l'indifférence en matière de religion* (1818–24), a denunciation of private judgement and toleration, which was favourably received in Rome. However, notions of popular liberty began to change his outlook, and *L'Avenir*, a journal founded by him in 1830 with MONTALEMBERT and others, was condemned by the pope in 1832. The *Paroles d'un croyant* (1834) brought about complete rupture with the Church, and revolutionary doctrines in his later work got him a year's imprisonment. Active in the 1848 FEBRUARY REVOLUTION, he sat in the Assembly until the

coup d'état. At his death he refused to make peace with the Church.

### Lampião, originally Virgulino Ferreira da Silva (d.1938)

Brazilian bandit. Dubbed the 'King of the Cangaçeiros', he began his career in 1921. His fame rested on the size of his band, some 40–50 men on routine raids, who attacked large properties and even interior cities within the states of north-eastern Brazil. His brother's savage attack on Sousa (Paraíba) in 1924 and his equivocal role in combating the Prestes Column (a group of young soldiers, led by Luís Carlos Prestes, which was in conflict with the federal government under President Washington Luís from 1926 to 1928) stimulated the growth of federal rule in the interior, limiting the control previously exercised by *coroneis*. Nevertheless, he was regarded as a popular hero in the country at large, and was the subject of a vast popular literature. ► CANGAÇO; CORONELISMO

### Lancaster, House of

The younger branch of the PLANTAGENET DYNASTY, founded by Edmund 'Crouchback', the younger son of HENRY III and 1st Earl of Lancaster (1267–96), whence came three kings of England: HENRY IV, HENRY V and HENRY VI. ► EDWARD IV; ROSES, WARS OF THE; YORK, HOUSE OF

## HOUSE OF LANCASTER

| Regnal Dates | Name |
| --- | --- |
| 1399/1413 | Henry IV |
| 1413/22 | Henry V |
| 1422/61 | Henry VI |
| 1461/70 | Yorkist rule |
| 1470/1 | Henry VI (restored) |

### Lancaster House

The London venue for various conferences preparing the way for independence in several parts of the British empire. It is most noted for the 1961 conference, which paved the way to Kenyan independence and the 1989 conference in which the British Foreign Secretary, Lord CARRINGTON, managed to forge agreement for an independence constitution for Zimbabwe and procedures to end the civil war in that country.

### Land

A constituent 'state' in the German (and also the Austrian) Federation. The majority of the Federal (West) German *Länder* (the plural form of the word) were set up by the Allied occupation authorities before the Federation (BUND) was created. Most *Land* constitutions are strongly plebiscitary in nature and envisage the democratization of broad aspects of society. The *Länder* enjoy sovereign rights in defined fields and are further strengthened in German constitutional life by the fact that the upper house of the federal parliament (the BUNDESRAT) consists of nominees of the Land governments. However, in practice the *Bund* has considerable influence over the shape of legislation at Land level. ► BASIC LAW

### Land Acts, Irish

A succession of British Acts passed in 1870, 1881, 1903 and 1909 with the objective first of giving tenants greater security and compensation for improvements, and later of enabling tenants to buy the estates they farmed. The Acts also aimed to reduce nationalist grievances and agitation. ► **LAND LEAGUE**

## Landdrost
Full-time officials and magistrates of the Dutch **EAST INDIA COMPANY** in South Africa, who administered the interior regions of the colony. They were normally strangers to their areas, and were assisted by a secretary, a messenger and a number of soldiers. They managed all legal matters, border conflicts and wars, and frequently came into conflict with the Boer citizens of their districts.

## Länder ► LAND

## Landfriede
An imperial measure (literally, 'country-wide peace') to restrict private warfare. This institution is linked to the **TREUGA DEI**, which originated in France, but it was not limited to specific feast days or times. The first imperial *Landfriede* was promulgated by **HENRY IV** in Mainz, with the aim of regulating feuds between princes. Breach of the peace was punishable by imperial sanctions and the policy was vigorously pursued by **FREDERICK I**, reaching a high point in the Mainz imperial Landfricde of 1235. It made a significant contribution to securing law and order in the empire. There were also parallel local *Landfrieden*, the first of which was enacted for Bavaria in 1094.

## Land League
An association formed in Ireland in 1879 by Michael **DAVITT** to agitate for greater tenant rights, in particular the 'three Fs': *fair rents*, to be fixed by arbitration if necessary; *fixity of tenure* while rents were paid; and *freedom* for tenants to sell rights of occupancy. **GLADSTONE** conceded the essence of these demands in the 1881 Land Act. ► **LAND ACTS, IRISH**

## landmine ban treaty
An international campaign to ban anti-personnel landmines began in 1992, with the support in particular of Diana, Princess of Wales. In 1996 the Canadian government announced that it would prepare a treaty, and the text of the Convention on the Prohibition of the Use, Stockpiling, Production and Transfer of Anti-Personnel Mines and on their Destruction, known as the Ottawa Convention, was agreed in Sep 1997 and became binding in 1999. It also assists landmine victims and works for the destruction of stockpiles and clearance of minefields, although there has been little interest in clearance because of the cost. The Convention was signed by 121 states but some countries, including China, Russia and the USA, refused to sign on the grounds that they consider landmines necessary.

## Landsknechte
German mercenary troops of the 16c first raised by **MAXIMILIAN I**. The term originally differentiated them from the more numerous Swiss mercenaries, whose reputation declined after the Battles of Marignano and Padua. The *Landsknechte* were the mainstay of the Imperial and German armies and fought on both sides of the **THIRTY YEARS' WAR**. Their organizational structure formed the pattern of the later regimental system, still in use at the present time.

## Landtag
Literally 'state diet' or 'parliament', this term describes the parliament of German (and Austrian) states (*Länder*). ► **BASIC LAW; BUND; LAND**

## Lange, David Russell (1942–)
New Zealand politician. After studying law at Auckland University and qualifying as a solicitor and barrister, he worked as a crusading lawyer for the underprivileged in Auckland. Elected to the House of Representatives in 1977, he became Deputy Leader of the Labour Party in 1979 and Leader in 1983. He won a decisive victory in the 1984 general election on a non-nuclear defence policy, which he immediately put into effect, despite criticism from other Western countries, particularly the USA. Re-elected in 1987, he resigned the premiership in 1989, following bouts of ill health and disagreements within his party.

## Langevin, Sir Hector-Louis (1826–1906)
Canadian lawyer, journalist and politician. Mayor of Quebec in 1856, and Solicitor-General in the coalition ministry that achieved confederation, he replaced George Étienne **CARTIER** as the French-Canadian representative in the cabinet of John A **MACDONALD**. However, he was an extremist Catholic, gaining much of his support from the intolerant ultramontane wing of the Church, and Macdonald found it necessary to balance his power by inviting into the cabinet the Grand Master of the **ORANGE ORDER**, Mackenzie **BOWELL** and later Joseph Adolphe **CHAPLEAU**. Langevin was forced to resign in the railway scandal of 1891. ► **CONFEDERATION MOVEMENT**

## Langton, Stephen (c.1150–1228)
English prelate and Archbishop of Canterbury. Pope **INNOCENT III** made him a cardinal (1206) and Archbishop (1207), but King John refused to accept his appointment, and Langton was kept out of the see until 1213. He took sides with the barons against John, and his name is the first of the subscribing witnesses of **MAGNA CARTA**. ► **JOHN ('JOHN LACKLAND')**

## Lansbury, George (1859–1940)
British politician. Active as a radical since boyhood, he became a convinced socialist in 1890 and a Labour MP in 1910, resigning in 1912 to stand in support of women's suffrage. He was defeated and not re-elected until 1922. He founded and edited the *Daily Herald* (1912–22), and became Commissioner of Works (1929) and leader of the **LABOUR PARTY** (1931–5). ► **MACDONALD, (JAMES) RAMSAY; SOCIALISM**

## Lansdowne, Henry Charles Keith Petty-Fitzmaurice, 5th Marquis of (1845–1927)
English statesman. As British Foreign Secretary from 1900 to 1905 he promoted arbitration treaties with the USA, the **ENTENTE CORDIALE** with France, and the **ANGLO-JAPANESE ALLIANCE**. As Unionist leader in the Lords from 1903, he sat (without portfolio) in **ASQUITH**'s coalition Cabinet (1915–16), advocating peace by negotiation in 1917.

## Lansing–Ishii Agreement (2 Nov 1917)
The name given to the exchange of diplomatic notes

between the Japanese ambassador to the USA, Ishii Kikujiro, and the US Secretary of State, Robert Lansing, which agreed on a set of principles concerning policy towards China. The agreement helped soothe tensions between the two countries at a time when the USA was becoming increasingly critical of Japan's attempts to enhance its influence in China. Respect for China's territorial integrity and commitment to the **OPEN DOOR POLICY** (ie that all powers should have equal economic opportunities in China) were confirmed; at the same time, the USA recognized that Japan had special interests in China because of 'territorial propinquity'. The agreement was superseded by the Washington Treaties of 1921–2, which committed all the powers to respect China's independence.

**LAOS** official name **Lao People's Democratic Republic**

A landlocked republic in South-East Asia, bounded to the east by Vietnam; to the south by Cambodia; to the west by Thailand and Myanmar; and to the north by China. It was discovered by Europeans in the 17c, dominated by Thailand in the 19c, and became a French protectorate in 1893. Occupied by the Japanese in **WORLD WAR II**, it gained independence from France in 1949. From 1953 to 1975 civil war raged between the Lao government, supported by the USA, and the communist-led Patriotic Front (**PATHET LAO**, now the Lao People's Revolutionary Party, LPRP), supported by North Vietnam. In 1975 the monarchy was abolished and a communist republic was established in 1975 with the Pathet Lao leader, Prince **SOUPHANOUVONG**, as President until he retired in 1986. The LPRP is the only political party, although approved non-partisan candidates have been elected to the National Assembly. Although still officially a communist state, Laos initiated market reforms in 1986 and joined the **ASSOCIATION OF SOUTH EAST ASIAN NATIONS** (ASEAN) in 1997. Bombings and armed attacks in 2003 were attributed to insurgents from the Hmong people.

### La Pérouse, Jean François de Galaup, Count of (1741–88)
French navigator. In 1785, in command of an expedition of discovery, he visited the north-west coast of America, explored the north-east coasts of Asia, and sailed through La Pérouse Strait between Sakhalin

and Yezo. In 1788 he sailed from Botany Bay, and his two ships were wrecked north of the New Hebrides.

### Lapointe, Ernest (1876–1941)
Canadian politician. As a Liberal with Rouge tendencies, he was very critical of **BORDEN** and **MEIGHEN**'s stand against the **WINNIPEG GENERAL STRIKE**. In 1921 he was appointed to a minor position in the Mackenzie **KING** administration, but it was as an adviser on French-Canadian affairs and attitudes that the Prime Minister valued him. In 1924 he became Minister of Justice. Like King, he believed the unity of the country was the foremost issue and therefore put his concern for social reform to one side (accepting, for instance, the notorious anti-communist **PADLOCK ACT** in Quebec). Although he opposed conscription, he played an important role in generating support within Quebec for Canada's participation in **WORLD WAR II**, and when Maurice **DUPLESSIS** challenged the **WAR MEASURES ACT**, Lapointe's threat to resign was an effective contribution to the return of a more amenable provincial administration. ► **LIBERAL PARTY** (Canada); **ROUGES**

### Lapua Movement
A semi-fascist political movement which originated in the Finnish town of Lapua in 1929. Composed mainly of small farmers who were influenced by Lutheran pietism and who were fiercely both nationalist and anti-communist, the movement agitated for the suppression of the Finnish Communist Party (which had been formally illegal in Finland since 1919). Its pressure on parliament and acts of violence led to the banning of the Communist Party's front organizations in 1930. The Lapua Movement was itself declared illegal in 1932 following an abortive armed uprising against the government. However, during its short period of existence Lapua was one of the most significant manifestations of right-wing extremism in interwar Europe. ► **COMMUNIST PARTY** (Finland)

### Largo Caballero, Francisco (1869–1946)
Spanish trade union and socialist leader. Secretary-General of the **UGT** from 1918 to 1936, his corporativist aspirations led him to collaborate with the dictatorship of **PRIMO DE RIVERA** of 1923–30. As Minister of Labour (1931–3) under the Second Republic, he altered the exploitative economic and social relations of rural Spain. From 1934 to 1935 he was the leader of the socialists' increasingly revolutionary left wing as the Right reversed the reforms of 1931–3. His revolutionary stance contributed significantly to the polarization of the Republic in 1936. Appointed Prime Minister (Sep 1936) after the **SPANISH CIVIL WAR** broke out, he proved a conservative and rigid war leader, curtailing the social revolution and re-establishing state authority. He was nonetheless ousted by the communists in May 1937 for opposing the suppression of the **CNT** and **POUM**. First detained in exile by the **VICHY** French and then, in Feb 1943, by the **GESTAPO**, he was liberated from a **CONCENTRATION CAMP** in Apr 1945. ► **REPUBLIC, SECOND** (Spain)

### Lari Massacre (26 Mar 1953)
A notorious incident during the **MAU MAU** emergency in Kenya in which over 100 Kikuyu of the loyal chief Luka were killed by insurgents of the secret society.

As with the assassination of the senior chief, Waruhiu, in the previous year, the massacre revealed the extent to which the emergency was in one of its aspects a Kikuyu civil war.

## La Rochefoucauld, François, 6th Duke of (1613–80)

French writer. An active member of the opposition to Cardinal **RICHELIEU**, he was forced to live abroad (1639–42). He then joined in the revolts known as the **FRONDE** (1648–53), and was wounded at the siege of Paris. He retired to the country in 1652, returning to the court on **MAZARIN**'s death in 1661. His major works were written while in retirement: *Mémoires* (1664) and the epigrammatic collection *Réflexions*, which is commonly known as the *Maximes* (1665).

## La Rocque, François, Count of (1886–1946)

French regular army officer. He resigned from the army in 1928 to enter business; in 1931 he became leader of the Ligue des **CROIX DE FEU** which expanded its membership very rapidly under him. In 1936 he became leader of the *Parti social français* ('French Social Party') which replaced the *Croix de Feu*. During **WORLD WAR II** he supported the **RESISTANCE MOVEMENT**.

## La Salle, (René) Robert Cavelier, Sieur de (1643–87)

French explorer and pioneer of Canada. Born in Rouen, he later settled as a trader near Montreal, Canada, and descended the Ohio and Mississippi to the sea (1682), claiming lands for France which he named Louisiana after **LOUIS XIV**. In 1684 an expedition set out to establish a French settlement on the Gulf of Mexico, but La Salle spent two years in fruitless journeys searching for the Mississippi Delta. His followers mutinied and he was murdered. ► **EXPLORATION**

## Las Casas, Bartolomé de (1474–1566)

Spanish missionary priest. Dubbed the 'Apostle of the Indians', he sailed in the third voyage of **COLUMBUS** (1502) to Hispaniola, was ordained (1512), and travelled to Cuba (1513). His desire to protect the natives from **SLAVERY** led him to visit the Spanish court on several occasions. Appointed Bishop of Chiapa, he was received (1544) with hostility by the colonists, returned to Spain, and resigned his see (1547).

## Lassalle, Ferdinand (1825–64)

German socialist. He studied philosophy at Breslau, Berlin and Paris, and in 1846 engaged in eight years of divorce litigation on behalf of the Countess Hatzfeld, for which he received a pension. He took part in the **REVOLUTION OF 1848**, and was imprisoned for six months for an inflammatory speech. He lived in the **RHINELAND** until 1857, developing his theories of **SOCIALISM**, much influenced by **MARX**. He then returned to Berlin, and at Leipzig in 1863 founded the Universal German Workers' Association to agitate for universal suffrage. He was killed in a duel over a love affair, at Geneva. ► **MARXISM**

## Lateran Councils

A series of councils of the Church held at the Lateran Palace, Rome, between the 7c and the 18c. Those held in 1123, 1139, 1179 and especially 1215 are the most significant. The Fourth or Great Council defined the doctrine of the Eucharist ('transubstantiation'), and represents the culmination of medieval papal legislation.

## Lateran Pacts (Feb 1929)

The name given to agreements, between the Italian fascist state and the papacy, reached after negotiations between **MUSSOLINI** and Pius XI's Secretary of State, Cardinal Gaspari. The pacts brought an end to the Church–State conflict which had been raging in Italy since the **RISORGIMENTO**. By them, Italy recognized the sovereignty of the Vatican City, gave substantial compensation to the papacy for the loss of its territories during the Risorgimento, and guaranteed religious education at all levels of state schooling. In return, the Church recognized the Italian state for the first time. The pacts were confirmed in the constitution of 1948.

## Latimer, Hugh (c.1485–1555)

English Protestant reformer and martyr. He was appointed a university preacher in 1522. Converted to Protestantism, he was one of the divines who examined the lawfulness of **HENRY VIII**'s marriage, and declared on the King's side. In 1535 he was made Bishop of Worcester, but opposed the Six Articles of Henry VIII, for which he was imprisoned in 1536, 1546 and 1553. He became known as a preacher under **EDWARD VI**, but under **MARY I** was tried for heresy and was burnt. ► **REFORMATION** (England)

## Lattre de Tassigny, Jean de (1889–1952)

French soldier. He commanded an infantry battalion during **WORLD WAR I**, and in 1940 he commanded the 14th Division; he was then sent by the **VICHY** government to command in Tunisia. He was recalled for sympathy with the Allies and arrested in 1942. He escaped from Riom prison via North Africa to London in 1943. As commander of the French 1st Army he took a brilliant part in the Allied liberation of France (1944–5), signing the German surrender. He was responsible for the reorganization of the French army and was appointed Commander-in-Chief of Western Union Land Forces under **MONTGOMERY** in 1948. In 1950, as Commander-in-Chief in French Indo-China, for a time he turned the tide against the **VIET MINH** rebels. He was posthumously made a Marshal of France in 1952. ► **RIOM TRIAL**

**LATVIA** official name **Republic of Latvia**

A republic in north-eastern Europe, bounded to the west by the Baltic Sea; to the north-west by the Gulf of Riga; to the north by Estonia; to the east by Russia; to the south-east by Belarus; and to the south by Lithuania. Incorporated into Russia in 1721, it became an independent state in 1918, but was proclaimed a Soviet Socialist Republic in 1940. It was occupied by Germany during **WORLD WAR II**. In the 1980s a new nationalist movement grew up, and in 1990 independence talks began with the USSR. Independence was declared in 1991 under President Anatolijs Gorbunovs, and the last Russian troops left Latvia in 1994, but tensions remain between the Russian and Latvian communities. Latvia joined **NATO** and the **EU** in 2004. ► **VIKE-FREIBERGA, VAIRA**

**Laud, William** (1573–1645)
Archbishop of Canterbury. He was ordained in 1601. His learning and industry brought him many patrons, and he rapidly received preferment, becoming King's Chaplain (1611), Bishop of St David's (1621), Bishop of Bath and Wells and a Privy Councillor (1626), Bishop of London (1628) and Archbishop of Canterbury (1633). With **STRAFFORD** and **CHARLES I**, he worked for **ABSOLUTISM** in Church and State. In Scotland, his attempt (1635–7) to Anglicize the Church led to the **BISHOPS' WARS**. In 1640 the **LONG PARLIAMENT** impeached him. He was found guilty, and executed on Tower Hill.

**Lauderdale, John Maitland, Duke of** (1616–82)
Scottish statesman. He was an ardent supporter of the **COVENANTERS** (1638), and in 1643 became a Scottish Commissioner at Westminster. Made earl in 1645, he was taken prisoner at Worcester (1651), and imprisoned. At the **RESTORATION** (1660) he became Scottish Secretary of State. A Privy Councillor, he was a member of the **CABAL** advisers to **CHARLES II**, and was created duke in 1672. ► **ENGLISH CIVIL WARS**

**Lauenburg**
A duchy associated with Holstein and Denmark. Duke Magnus I (d.1543) introduced the **REFORMATION** to the Duchy. The extinction of the ruling house in 1689 resulted in claims by John George III, Elector of Saxony, and George William, Duke of Brunswick, among others. George William prevailed and, after an indemnity, was recognized as Duke by the Saxon Elector. His nephew, George Louis, Elector of Hanover, later **GEORGE I** of Britain, became Duke in 1692. The duchy was occupied (1803) by France, reverted to Hanover (1813) and was eventually ceded to Prussia (1816).

**Laurier, Sir Wilfrid** (1841–1919)
Canadian politician. He became a lawyer, a journalist and a member of the Quebec Legislative Assembly. He entered federal politics in 1874, and became Minister of Inland Revenue (1877), leader of the **LIBERAL PARTY** (1887–1919), and the first French-Canadian and Roman Catholic to be Prime Minister of Canada (1896–1911). A firm supporter of self-government for Canada, in his home policy he was an advocate of compromise and free trade with the USA. ► **'COMMERCIAL UNION'; IMPERIAL CONFERENCES**

**Lausanne, Treaty of** (1923)
After the **GRAECO-TURKISH WAR**, it replaced the Treaty of Sèvres and granted considerable concessions to the Turks, freeing them from paying the reparations imposed on them as a defeated power at the end of **WORLD WAR I**. The Turks retained their lands in Anatolia and Thrace, while Greece lost most of its major war gains: Eastern Thrace, the Smyrna region, and the

Imvros and Tenedos islands. The Turkish minister **INÖNÜ** and the Greek Eleuthérios **VENIZÉLOS** agreed to the exchange of populations that led to the uprooting of 380,000 Turks from Greece and 1.3 million Greeks from Anatolia. The treaty also confirmed the British annexation of Cyprus.

**Lausanne Conference** (1932)
The conference held between the Allied powers and Germany to discuss the question of German reparation payments, which had been suspended by the moratorium imposed by the unilateral decision of US President Herbert **HOOVER** in 1931, after the onset of the **GREAT DEPRESSION**. A final reparation payment by Germany was agreed, but the Lausanne convention was never ratified, and no more payments were actually made.

**Laval, Pierre** (1883–1945)
French politician. He became a lawyer, Deputy (1914), and Senator (1926), before serving as Premier (1931–2, 1935–6). From a position on the extreme left of the **SOCIALIST PARTY**, he moved rightwards during the 1920s and 1930s, and in the **VICHY** government was **PÉTAIN**'s deputy (1940). He was removed from office in Dec 1940 but restored with much greater power in Apr 1942. Again Prime Minister in 1942–4, he openly collaborated with the Germans. Fleeing after the liberation to Germany and Spain, he was brought back, charged with treason, and executed in Paris. ► **WORLD WAR II**

**La Vallière, Louise Françoise de la Baume le Blanc, Duchess of** (1644–1710)
Mistress of **LOUIS XIV** of France. She was maid of honour to Henrietta Anne of England, Duchess of Orléans, before becoming the royal mistress (1661–7). She bore the King four children, and remained at court reluctantly after Mme de **MONTESPAN** superseded her (1667). Eventually she was allowed to retire to a Carmelite nunnery in Paris (1674), where she died.

**Lavigerie, Charles Martial Allemand** (1825–92)
French prelate. As Primate of Africa and Archbishop of Algiers (1884) he became well-known for his missionary work, and founded the order of the White Fathers (1868). In 1888 he founded the Anti-Slavery Society. In 1890 his 'toast of Algiers' launched Pope **LEO XIII**'s campaign to persuade French Catholics to rally to the republic. ► **SLAVERY**

**Lavrentev, Mikhail Alexevich** (1900–80)
Soviet mathematician. He held several influential academic appointments in both Moscow and Kiev, and during and after **WORLD WAR II** came into close contact with Nikita **KHRUSHCHEV**. He was a full member of the Soviet Academy of Sciences from 1946, a deputy in the Supreme Soviet from 1958, and a candidate member of the Central Committee from 1961. This enabled him to build Akademgorodok, or Academic City, in Novosibirsk, designed to educate generations of super-brains and promote outstanding research. His creation partly achieved its purpose but it also helped to expand the intellectual frustration that built up under Leonid **BREZHNEV**.

**Law, (Andrew) Bonar** (1858–1923)
British politician. He was an iron merchant in

Glasgow, became a Unionist MP in 1900, and in 1911 succeeded **BALFOUR** as Unionist leader. He acted as Colonial Secretary (1915–16), became a member of the war cabinet, Chancellor of the Exchequer (1916–18), Lord Privy Seal (1919), and from 1916 Leader of the House of **COMMONS**. He retired in 1921 through ill health, but returned to serve as Premier for several months in 1922–3.

### Lawrence, Sir Henry Montgomery (1806–57)
British soldier and colonial administrator. In 1823 he joined the Bengal Artillery and took part in the first Burmese War (1828), the first of the **AFGHAN WARS** (1838), and the **SIKH WARS** (1845–6 and 1848–9). In 1856 he pointed out the danger of reducing the British Army, and the latent germs of rebellion. The following year he was appointed to Lucknow, and did all he could to restore contentment there, but the **INDIAN UPRISING** broke out in May. It was owing to his foresight that it was possible for 1,000 Europeans and 800 Indians to defend the Residency for nearly four months against 7,000 rebels. He was mortally injured during this defence. ➤ **LUCKNOW, SIEGE OF**

### Lawrence, John Laird Mair Lawrence, 1st Baron (1811–79)
British colonial administrator. He joined the Indian Civil Service in Delhi, and became Commissioner, then Lieutenant Governor, of the Punjab. He carried out many economic and social reforms, for which he was nicknamed 'the Saviour of the Punjab'. After helping to put down the **INDIAN UPRISING** of 1857–8, he was made a baronet, and in 1863 became Governor-General of India. He returned to England in 1869, was made a baron, and died in London.

### Lawrence, T(homas) E(dward) known as Lawrence of Arabia (1888–1935)
British soldier and author. Before **WORLD WAR I** he travelled in the Middle East, studying Crusader castles and participating in the excavation of Carchemish. In 1914 he joined military intelligence and was sent to Cairo, where he became a member of the Arab Bureau. In 1916 he was appointed the British liaison officer to the **ARAB REVOLT**, led by **FAYSAL**, the son of Sharif **HUSAYN IBN 'ALI** of Mecca, and was present at the taking of Aqaba (1917) and of Damascus (1918). He was an adviser to Faysal at the **PARIS PEACE CONFERENCE** and a member of the Middle East Department at the Colonial Office (1921). His account of the Arab Revolt, *Seven Pillars of Wisdom*, abridged by himself as *Revolt in the Desert*, became one of the classics of war literature. His exploits received so much publicity that he became a legendary figure, and so he attempted to escape his fame by enlisting in the ranks of the RAF (1922) as J H Ross, in the Royal Tank Corps (1923) as T E Shaw, and again in the RAF in 1925. He retired in 1935 and was killed in a motorcycling accident the same year.

### Lawson, Nigel, Baron Lawson of Blaby (1932– )
British politician. He worked for various newspapers and for television (1956–72), including editing the *Spectator* (1966–70), before being elected to parliament in 1974. When the Conservatives returned to office he became Financial Secretary to the Treasury (1979–81), Energy Secretary (1981–3) and Chancellor of the Exchequer (1983–9). During his time at the Exchequer, Britain saw lower direct taxes, but high interest rates and record trade deficits. ➤ **CONSERVATIVE PARTY** (UK)

### Lazar, Hrebeljanović (1329–89)
Prince of Serbia (1371/89) and Serbian national hero. He led his people into battle against the Ottoman Turks, repulsing Sultan **MURAD I** at Pločnik (1386) but was captured and executed by the Turks at the Battle of **KOSOVO**, which marked the end of the medieval Kingdom of Serbia (1389). He was buried in the monastery at Ravenica but was later reburied at Vrdnik (1683) and finally at Belgrade, in the Orthodox cathedral built by Miloš **OBRENOVIĆ** (1845). ➤ **KRALJEVIĆ, MARKO**

### League of Nations
A former international organization whose constitution was drafted at the **PARIS PEACE CONFERENCE** in 1919 and incorporated into the Treaty of **VERSAILLES**. The main aims were to preserve international peace and security by the prevention or speedy settlement of disputes and the promotion of disarmament. With its headquarters in Geneva, the League operated through a Council, which met several times a year, and an annual Assembly. Its original members included the victorious Allies of **WORLD WAR I**, except for the USA, which refused to join, and most of the neutral nations. Germany joined in 1926, and the USSR in 1934, but Germany and Japan withdrew in 1933, and Italy in 1936. Although the League succeeded in settling some minor disputes, it became increasingly ineffective in the later 1930s, when it failed to stop major acts of aggression by Japan, Italy and Germany. In 1946 it transferred its functions to the UN. ➤ **WILSON, THOMAS WOODROW**

### leagues (*ligues*)
The name given to French political movements, which, while being in some ways akin to political parties, also had an extra-parliamentary dimension, which made them appear proto-fascist. The most important were the *Ligue des patriotes* ('League of Patriots', 1882), and *Ligue de la patrie française* ('League of the French Fatherland', 1899), the *Ligue de l'action française* ('League of French Action', 1899) and the Ligue des **CROIX DE FEU** (1927).

### Learn from the PLA Campaign (1963–4)
A political campaign in China which began within the **PEOPLE'S LIBERATION ARMY** (PLA), aiming to stress the importance of service to the Communist Party and commitment to socialist ideals. A key aspect of the campaign was to elevate the position of **MAO ZEDONG** and his thought at a time when his influence within the party had waned following the disasters of the **GREAT LEAP FORWARD**. With the active support of **LIN BIAO**, appointed by Mao in 1959 as Defence Minister and head of the PLA, a compilation of Mao's sayings (*Quotations from Chairman Mao*, known as the 'Little Red Book') was studied and memorized throughout the PLA, thereby initiating the cult of Mao that was to attain grotesque proportions during the **CULTURAL REVOLUTION**. By the end of 1963, Mao was calling upon the entire country to 'learn from the PLA', implying that it was the army rather than the party that incarnated the spirit of self-sacrifice and dedication to collective values. The

campaign marked the beginning of the PLA's increasing involvement in politics (army personnel were assigned to work in various government organizations) and Mao's attack on the party hierarchy.

**Lease, Mary Elizabeth** (1853–1933)
US reformer. She spoke out in favour of women's suffrage, prohibition of alcohol and other causes. Nicknamed the 'Kansas Pythoness' for the strength of her populist rhetoric, her command to 'raise less corn and more hell' became the Populist Party's slogan. ► **PROHIBITION**

**LEBANON** official name **Republic of Lebanon**

A republic on the eastern coast of the Mediterranean Sea, south-west Asia, bounded to the north and east by Syria, and to the south by Israel. From the 16c until after **WORLD WAR I**, it was part of the **OTTOMAN EMPIRE**. After the massacre of Roman Catholic **MARONITES** by Muslim **DRUZE** in 1861, the Maronite area around Jabal Lubnan was granted special autonomous status. In 1920 the state of Greater Lebanon, based upon Maronite Christian Jabal Lubnan, was created under French mandate, and incorporated the Muslim coastal regions despite great opposition. Lebanon became a constitutional republic in 1926 and gained independence in 1941. Palestinian resistance units were established in Lebanon by the late 1960s, despite government opposition, and Palestinian raids into Israel were followed by Israeli reprisals. Several militia groups developed in the mid-1970s, notably the Shiite Muslim Afwaj al-Muqawama al-Lubnaniya (**AMAL**) and the Muslim Lebanese National Movement (LNM). Palestinian firepower was used to back up the political struggle of the LNM against the Maronite Christian and Sunni Muslim establishment. Muslim and Christian differences grew more intense and from 1975 Lebanon was beset by civil disorder as rival political and religious factions sought to gain control. Palestinian commandos joined the predominantly leftist Muslim side, and the Syrian-dominated Arab Deterrent Force (ADF) was created to prevent Palestinian fighters gaining control. In 1976 Palestinian forces moved from Beirut to southern Lebanon, where the ADF was unable to deploy. West Beirut, also outside government control, became the scene of frequent conflict between opposing militia groups. Meanwhile, Christian militias, backed by Israel, sought to regain control in East Beirut and areas to the north. Following Palestinian terrorist attacks, Israel invaded southern Lebanon in 1978 and 1982, when the Israeli siege of Palestinian and Syrian forces in Beirut led to the withdrawal of Palestinian forces. The unilateral withdrawal of Israeli forces brought clashes between the Druze (backed by

Syria) and the Christian Lebanese militia. A ceasefire was announced in late 1982 but was broken many times, and international efforts to achieve a political settlement were unsuccessful. In the mid-1980s rival groups began taking foreigners as hostages, who were gradually released in the early 1990s. Syrian troops entered Beirut in 1988 in an attempt to restore order but were attacked in 1989 by Lebanese troops under General Michel Aoun. The **LEAGUE OF ARAB STATES** proposed a peace plan, the **TA'IF ACCORD**, which reduced the domination of Maronite Christians in government. A timetable for militia disarmament was introduced in 1991 and government elections took place in 1992, though they were boycotted by many Maronite Christian parties. The Amal and **HEZBOLLAH** parties gained the most seats and Rafiq al-Hariri became Prime Minister and made plans to rebuild the economy. Clashes between Israeli troops, or the Israel-backed South Lebanon Army (SLA), and Hezbollah guerrillas continued in southern Lebanon throughout the 1990s but the SLA collapsed after Israel withdrew its forces in 2000. Under the terms of the constitution, the President must be a Maronite Christian, the Prime Minister a Sunni Muslim, and the 108-member parliament is equally divided between Christians and Muslims.

**Lebeau, Joseph Jean Louis** (1794–1865)
Belgian politician. Trained as a lawyer and active as a journalist in liberal opposition to the government of King **WILLIAM I**, after the Belgian Revolution of 1830 Lebeau helped draw up the constitution of the new state of Belgium, and became an MP and (briefly) Foreign Minister in 1831. He was Minister for Justice (1832–4) and Governor of Namur (1834–40); he formed the first purely liberal Belgian government (without the Catholics) in 1840, in which he was himself Foreign Minister (1840–1).

**Lebensraum**
An expansionist concept (literally, 'living space') developed by the Nazis (especially **HITLER**) from the early 1920s onwards, which planned to extend German control far into the USSR to provide land for colonization. Hitler argued that Germany was overpopulated, and needed more agriculturally productive land to guarantee future food supplies for an expanded German population. The alleged inferiority of East European peoples was used to justify this, parallels being made with European/British colonialism in America and Australia. ► **NAZI PARTY**; **WORLD WAR II**

**Lebowa**
National state or non-independent Black homeland in northern Transvaal province, north-east South Africa, during the **APARTHEID** era. Situated north-east of Pretoria, it was granted self-governing status in 1972, and reincorporated into South Africa in 1994.

**Lebrun, Albert** (1871–1950)
French politician and President (1932–40). He became a Deputy in 1900, was Minister for the Colonies (1911–14), for Blockade and Liberated Regions (1917–19), Senator (1920), and President of the Senate (1931). The last President of the Third Republic, he surrendered his powers to **PÉTAIN** in 1940. ► **REPUBLIC, THIRD** (France)

## Leburton, Edmond (1915–97)
Belgian politician. He studied at Liège University and in 1946 became an MP for the **BELGIAN SOCIALIST PARTY**. From 1954 to 1971 he held numerous cabinet posts with economic and social portfolios; in 1973–4 he was Prime Minister.

## Le Chapelier, Isaac René Guy (1754–94)
French revolutionary politician. He is best known for the law he introduced in June 1791, and known by his name, forbidding associations of members of the same trade, and thus banning trade unions and strikes as well as employers' associations. It was the keystone of economic liberalism. He was executed in 1794.

## Le Clerc (de Hauteclocque), Jacques Philippe (1902–47)
French soldier. After fighting in 1940, he joined the **FREE FRENCH** forces under de **GAULLE** in England. He became military commander in French Equatorial Africa, and led a force across the desert to join the British 8th Army, in 1942. He commanded the French 2nd Armoured Division in **NORMANDY**, and received the surrender of Paris in 1944. ► **NORMANDY CAMPAIGN; WORLD WAR II**

## Ledru-Rollin, Alexandre Auguste (1807–74)
French republican politician. In 1841 he was elected Deputy for Le Mans. At the **FEBRUARY REVOLUTION** (1848) he became Minister of the Interior in the Provisional Government. As candidate for the presidency against Louis Napoleon (**NAPOLEON III**) he was beaten, and an unsuccessful attempt to provoke an insurrection in June 1849 drove him to England. He was amnestied in 1870, and after his return was elected to the National Assembly (1871).

## Le Duc Tho, originally Phan Dinh Khai (1911–90)
Vietnamese politician. He joined the Indo-Chinese Communist Party in 1929 and was exiled to the penal island of Con Dia by the French in 1930. Released in 1937, he became head of the Nam Dinh revolutionary movement, but was re-arrested and imprisoned (1939–44). After **WORLD WAR II**, he worked for the Communist Party of Vietnam (CPV), entering its Politburo in 1955. As leader of the Vietnamese delegation to the Paris Conference on Indo-China (1968–73), he was awarded the 1973 **NOBEL PEACE PRIZE**, jointly with Henry **KISSINGER**, but he declined to accept it. He retired from the Politburo in 1986.

## Lee, 'Jennie' (Janet), Baroness Lee of Asheridge (1904–88)
British politician. The daughter of a Scottish miner, she made her own way in socialist politics, becoming the youngest elected woman MP (1929–31). She married Aneurin **BEVAN** in 1934. Re-elected to parliament in 1945, she became Minister for the Arts (1967–70), and was given the task of establishing the Open University. She retired from the House of **COMMONS** in 1970 and was made a life peer. ► **LABOUR PARTY (UK); SOCIALISM**

## Lee, Robert E(dward) (1807–70)
US general. Educated at the US Military Academy at West Point, he received a commission in the Engineer Corps. He fought in the **MEXICAN WAR** and later became Superintendent of West Point. He commanded the US troops that captured John **BROWN** at Harpers Ferry. When the Southern states seceded from the Union, he resigned from the US Army so he would be free to serve his native state of Virginia. In 1861 he accepted the position of Commander-in-Chief of the Confederate Army of Virginia. His achievements are central to the history of the **AMERICAN CIVIL WAR**. He was in charge of the defences at Richmond, and halted federal forces in the **SEVEN DAYS' BATTLES** (1862). His forces were victorious in the second battle of **BULL RUN**. His first northern invasion was stopped at the Battle of **ANTIETAM**. His troops repulsed the Union side in the Battle of **FREDERICKSBURG** and were victorious at the Battle of Chancellorsville. His second northern invasion ended in defeat at the Battle of **GETTYSBURG** (1863). In the **WILDERNESS** campaign (1864) Lee's forces were badly battered. In Feb 1865 Lee became Commander-in-Chief of all of the Southern armies, but the Confederate cause was hopeless at that point and two months later he surrendered his army to General Grant at **APPOMATTOX COURT HOUSE**, Virginia. After the war, Lee became President of Washington College at Lexington.

## Leeds, Thomas Osborne, 1st Earl of Danby and 1st Duke of (1631–1712)
English politician. He became MP for York in 1665. After opposition to **CLARENDON**, he was appointed Treasurer of the Navy (1668) and Privy Councillor (1673). He became Lord Treasurer in 1673, succeeding Clifford as King **CHARLES II**'s Chief Minister until his fall during the **EXCLUSION CRISIS** (1679). He was successively Baron Osborne and Viscount Latimer (1673), Earl of Danby (1674), Viscount Osborne of Dunblane (1675), Marquis of Carmarthen (1689) and Duke of Leeds (1694). Under Charles, he increased the yield from taxes and thus the King's financial independence. He also worked for the marriage of Mary, daughter of James, Duke of York, to **WILLIAM III, OF ORANGE** (1677). He was impeached on charges of secret financial dealings with **LOUIS XIV** of France on Charles's behalf, and imprisoned in the Tower (1684). During **JAMES VII AND II**'s reign, he opposed the King's Catholic policies. His negotiations with the Dutch were part of a process which culminated in William of Orange's arrival in England (1688) and assumption of the crown. He was rewarded with the Presidency of the Council (1689–99) but further **IMPEACHMENT** proceedings, for taking a bribe to secure a charter for a new East India Company (1695), ended his career as Chief Minister. In semi-retirement during Queen **ANNE**'s reign, he supported the **TORIES**, especially defending the Church of England. ► **EAST INDIA COMPANY, BRITISH; POPISH PLOT**

## Lee Kuan Yew (1923–)
Singaporean politician. Born into a wealthy Chinese family, he studied law at Cambridge and qualified as a barrister in London before returning to Singapore in 1951 to practise. He founded the moderate, anti-communist People's Action Party (PAP) in 1954, and entered the Singapore Legislative Assembly in 1955. He became the country's first Prime Minister in 1959, a position he held until 1990. He acquired a formidable reputation for probity and industry, and oversaw

the implementation of a successful programme of economic development. His son, Brigadier-General Lee Hsien Loong (1952– ), became Prime Minister in 2004.

### Lee Teng-hui (1923–)
Taiwanese politician. Educated at universities in the USA and Japan, he taught economics at the National Taiwan University before becoming Mayor of Taipei in 1979. A member of the ruling GUOMINDANG and a protégé of JIANG JING'GUO, he became Vice-President of Taiwan in 1984 and state President and Guomindang leader on Jiang's death in 1988. The country's first island-born leader, he is a reforming technocrat who significantly accelerated the pace of liberalization and 'Taiwanization'. He was defeated in the 2000 presidential election.

### Left-Republicans
Spanish political parties. In the 1920s two new Republican parties emerged in reaction against the old-style populism and patronage politics of Alejandro LERROUX'S RADICAL REPUBLICAN PARTY: Republican Action in 1925 and the Radical–Socialist Party in 1929. They aimed to provide the Republican movement with a more progressive and modern content, their most coherent and articulate representative being Manuel AZAÑA. Under the Second Republic, the Left-Republicans dominated the liberal reformist administrations of 1931–3, but were devastated in the general election of Nov 1933. They were nonetheless central to the creation of the Popular Front coalition that won the election of Feb 1936. However, the Left-Republicans' vacillatory leadership during the spring and summer of 1936 not only contributed to the polarization of the political climate, but also was critical in the conversion of the military rising of July 1936 into a civil war. ➤ REPUBLIC, SECOND (Spain); SPANISH CIVIL WAR

### Lega Lombarda ('Lombardy League')
The main party of the *Lega Nord* ('Northern League'), a coalition of north Italian political parties seeking autonomy from Rome, which became an increasingly potent political force in the early 1990s. Its appeal is based on traditional CAMPANILISMO and north–south hostility (which have been exacerbated by anxieties over immigration, both from the MEZZOGIORNO and from outside Italy) and on the premise that politicians in Rome are too ready to tax the prosperous north to provide for the backward and endemically criminal south. Under the leadership of Umberto Bossi, the Lega Nord won over 50 seats in the 1992 general election and won control of Italy's industrial heartland in the local elections of 1993. After the collapse of the traditional party system, it also had considerable success in 1994 when it entered a short-lived coalition government led by Silvio BERLUSCONI. Despite a split in the League that year, the campaign continued for secession of a northern Italian state which Bossi called Padania.

### Legien, Carl (1861–1920)
German trade union leader. Active in the trade union movement from 1886, he became Convener of the General Trade Union Commission in 1890 and Convener of the ADGB in 1919. He was also an active member of the SPD from 1885, sitting in the REICHSTAG in 1893–8 and 1903–20. His aim was to shape the pro-SPD unions into a powerful bargaining force for German labour and his efforts were crowned by the Stinnes–Legien Agreement (Nov 1918) under which German employers recognized the trade unions as sole legitimate bargaining partners. Months before his death, Legien organized the general strike which toppled the KAPP PUTSCH. Many of his achievements were overturned by the employers after his death.

### Legislative Assembly (1791–2)
In France, the first assembly elected under the constitution drawn up by the revolutionary Constituent Assembly. It was dispersed after the rising of 10 Aug 1792, and was replaced by the National CONVENTION.

### Legitimists
In France, the supporters of CHARLES X and of his heir, as opposed to the ORLÉANISTS, supporters of the Orléans branch of the French royal house. The division between the two factions was an important cause of the eclipse of royalism in late 19c France, especially in the National Assembly (1871–5), where the two royalist groups together had a majority, but which nevertheless established the Third Republic. ➤ ORLÉANS, HOUSE OF; REPUBLIC, THIRD (France)

### Legnano, Battle of (1176)
This was the decisive victory of the Italian communes of the LOMBARD LEAGUE over the armies of the Emperor FREDERICK I, BARBAROSSA. As a result, Frederick was forced to acknowledge the liberty of the Italian cities and to come to terms with Pope ALEXANDER III in the Treaty of Venice (1177).

### Leicester, Robert Dudley, Earl of (c.1532–1588)
English nobleman. The favourite of ELIZABETH I, he became Master of the Horse, Knight of the Garter, a privy councillor, baron, and finally Earl of Leicester (1564). He continued to receive favour in spite of his unpopularity at court and a secret marriage in 1578 to the widow of Walter, Earl of Essex; yet Elizabeth was only temporarily offended. In 1585 he commanded the expedition to the Low Countries, but was recalled for incompetence in 1587. He was nonetheless appointed in 1588 to command the forces against the Spanish ARMADA, and died later that year.

### Leipzig, Battle of (1813)
The overwhelming defeat of NAPOLEON I's forces by the armies of the Fourth Coalition, also called the Battle of the Nations. Heavily outnumbered by the Allied force of Austrians, Prussians, Russians and Swedes, Napoleon tried to withdraw, but his troops were badly mauled; he effectively surrendered French control east of the Rhine. ➤ NAPOLEONIC WARS

### Leipzig Manifesto (1631)
This manifesto was designed to establish a neutral, third force in Germany during the THIRTY YEARS' WAR. Protestant Saxony and Brandenburg wanted some means of driving all foreign armies (eg the Swedes) from the Empire while working to relax the EDICT OF RESTITUTION which was aimed at reintroducing Catholicism. The manifesto doomed Swedish hopes for a rising by the Protestant princes against the Emperor in support of the invading Swedish troops.

**Leisler, Jacob** (1640–91)
American rebel. He emigrated from Germany to New Amsterdam (later New York) in 1660 and became a successful merchant. After the English took over control of the colony from the Dutch in 1664, the original colonists grew resentful and strongly resisted the unification of New England and New York – called the Dominion of New England – imposed by **JAMES VII AND II** in 1685. When James was deposed, Leisler led an insurrection ('Leisler's Rebellion') in 1689 against the British Crown's agent, Governor Francis Nicholson, who fled to England, leaving Leisler to head a revolutionary government for the next 18 months. Though he declared loyalty to the new king, **WILLIAM III**, Leisler resisted the authority of the new governor of the province, Colonel Henry Sloughter, who arrived in 1691, and was captured, charged with treason and hanged.

**Lena Goldfields Strike** (1912)
A landmark on the road to the unrest that led to the **RUSSIAN REVOLUTION** (1917). In the British-owned goldfields about 5,000 workers protested against poor living conditions in the difficult climate of Eastern Siberia; their complaints were ignored. When they went on strike, troops opened fire and killed over 200. The **DUMA**, the public and foreign observers were equally distressed. Improvements were promised but did not materialize. The number of strikes then increased year by year down to the outbreak of **WORLD WAR I**.

**Lenart, Jozef** (1923–2004)
Slovak politician. He fought in the **SLOVAK UPRISING**, then gained industrial experience in the Bata shoe concern. He rose quite suddenly to the premiership in 1963 while Czechoslovakia experienced industrial stagnation; and as a pragmatic reformer he achieved important results in the next few years. However, discontent increased with the **NOVOTNÝ** regime and Lenart found himself turning away from reform. When the **PRAGUE SPRING** eventually broke out in 1968 he lost the premiership.

**Lenclos, Anne**, known as **Ninon de Lenclos** (1620–1705)
French courtesan, poet and feminist. Born in Paris, she started her long career at the age of 16, founding a salon which favoured Jansenists. Among her lovers were two marquises, two marshals, the 'Great Condé', and the dukes of **LA ROCHEFOUCAULD** and Sévigné. Her behaviour cost her a spell in a covent in 1656 at the behest of **ANNE OF AUSTRIA**, but her popularity ensured a swift release, and afterwards she wrote *La Coquette vengée* (1659, 'The Coquette Avenged') in her own defence. ► **CONDÉ, LOUIS II OF BOURBON, PRINCE OF**

**Lend–Lease Agreement** (1941)
The arrangement by which the USA lent or leased war supplies and arms to Britain and other Allies during **WORLD WAR II**. It was a measure in which President **ROOSEVELT** took a close personal interest. The Lend–Lease Act was passed by Congress in Mar 1941, when British reserves were almost exhausted. By the time the agreement terminated in 1945, the allies had received about £5,000 million worth of materials.

**Lenin, Vladimir Ilyich**, originally surnamed **Ulyanov** (1870–1924)
Russian Marxist revolutionary and political leader. He was educated at the universities of Kazan and St Petersburg, where he graduated in law. From 1895 to 1897 he was in prison, and from 1897 to 1900 he was exiled to Siberia for participating in underground revolutionary activities; there he used his time to study and write extensively about **MARXISM**. At the Second Congress of the Russian Social Democratic Labour Party (1903) he caused the split between what came to be called the Bolshevik and Menshevik factions. Apart from the frustrating period of the Russian **REVOLUTION OF 1905**, he spent the entire period until 1917 abroad, developing and publicizing his political views. Following the **FEBRUARY REVOLUTION** in 1917, he returned to Petrograd from Zurich, and urged the early seizure of power by the proletariat under the slogan 'All Power to the Soviets'. In Oct 1917 he initiated the Bolshevik revolution and became head of the first Soviet government. He made peace with Germany at **BREST-LITOVSK** in order to concentrate on defeating the Whites in the ensuing **RUSSIAN CIVIL WAR** (1918–21) and then changed tactics again by switching from a ruthless centralized policy of 'war communism' to the **NEW ECONOMIC POLICY**, which his critics in the Party saw as a 'compromise with capitalism' and a retreat from strictly socialist planning. On his death, his body was embalmed and placed in a mausoleum in front of the Moscow Kremlin, where it still lies. In 1924 Petrograd (formerly St Petersburg) was renamed Leningrad in his honour. Much was subsequently done in his name by **STALIN** and others, some of which he would not have approved of. But the nature of the USSR and the reasons for its final collapse in 1991 owed much to him; and it was not altogether surprising that the citizens of Leningrad voted for their city to resume the name of St Petersburg. ► **APRIL THESES; BOLSHEVIKS; MENSHEVIKS; OCTOBER REVOLUTION; RUSSIAN REVOLUTION**

**Leningrad, Siege of** (1941–4)
One of the more heroic incidents in Soviet and world history. The Soviet Union's second city, formerly Tsarist Russia's capital, St Petersburg, was besieged for 28 months and lost over a third of its population from the fighting or from starvation. It received less help than it might have from **STALIN** though it played a large part in the defeat of **HITLER**; it survived largely on the will of its people. Memories of the siege influenced many Leningraders to object to the reversion to the former name of St Petersburg in 1991.

**Leninism** ► **MARXISM–LENINISM**

**Lenshina, Alice Mulenga** (1924–78)
The leader of a millenarian movement, the Lumpa Church, which from 1964 led opposition to the newly independent regime in Zambia. The church and its followers embodied rural and traditional resistance to the urban politics of the new African élite, and became a major focus of opposition to the regime of Kenneth **KAUNDA**.

**Leo X**, originally **Giovanni de' Medici** (1475–1521)
Italian pope (1513/21). 'Let us enjoy the papacy!' he is said to have remarked on his elevation, and he set about so doing, with consequences which he could

scarcely have imagined. His vast project for the re-building of St Peter's made it necessary to preach an indulgence in order to raise funds to do so and this provoked Martin LUTHER's 95 theses. Leo's failure to respond either promptly or effectively helped to increase the REFORMATION's early momentum.

**Leo XIII**, originally **Vincenzo Gioacchino Pecci** (1810–1903)
Pope (1878/1903). Elected on the death of PIUS IX, he was less reactionary than his predecessor and his more conciliatory stance was instrumental in ending the so-called KULTURKAMPF in Germany and getting the French clergy to accept the republic. However, nominally at least, he continued Pius IX's policy of refusing to recognize the Italian state. ► LATERAN PACTS

**Leopold I** (1640–1705)
Holy Roman Emperor (1658/1705). The second son of FERDINAND III and the Infanta Maria Anna, he was elected to the crowns of Hungary (1655) and Bohemia (1657), and succeeded to the Imperial title in 1658. In 1666 he married his niece, Margaret Theresa, second daughter of PHILIP IV of Spain. After her early death (1673), he took a second Habsburg bride, Claudia Felicitas, before his third marriage (1676) to Eleonore of Palatinate-Neuburg, by whom he had two sons, the future Emperors Joseph I and CHARLES VI. Committed throughout his long reign to the defence of the power and unity of the House of Habsburg, he faced constant external threats from the Ottoman Turks and the King of France, in addition to the hostility of the Hungarian nobility. Treaties of neutrality (1667, 1671) between Leopold and LOUIS XIV of France gave way to military conflict over the Rhine frontier (1674–9 and 1686–97), as the issue of the Spanish inheritance loomed closer. To substantiate the rights of his son, Charles, against the French claimant, Leopold took the Empire into the Grand Alliance (1701). He died in Vienna while his armies were still deeply involved in the War of the SPANISH SUCCESSION and the Hungarian revolt of Rákóczi (1703–11). ► HABSBURG DYNASTY

**Leopold I** (1790–1865)
First King of the Belgians (1831/65). The son of Francis, Duke of Saxe-Coburg, he was the uncle of Queen VICTORIA. He distinguished himself in the wars against NAPOLEON I, and in 1816 he married Charlotte, daughter of the future GEORGE IV of England; he lived in England after her death in 1817. He declined the crown of Greece (1830), but the following year became King of the Belgians. His second marriage in 1832 to Marie Louise of Orléans, daughter of LOUIS-PHILIPPE, ensured French support for his new kingdom against the Dutch. He was an influential force in European diplomacy prior to BISMARCK's ascendancy.

**Leopold II** (1747–92)
Holy Roman Emperor (1790/2). The third son of Emperor FRANCIS I and MARIA THERESA, he succeeded his father as Grand-Duke of Tuscany in 1765, and his brother, JOSEPH II, as Emperor in 1790. He succeeded in pacifying the Netherlands and Hungary, and was led by the downfall of his sister, MARIE ANTOINETTE, to form an alliance with Prussia against France. He

died before the joint Austro-Prussian attack on France that launched the cycle of FRENCH REVOLUTIONARY WARS.

**Leopold II** (1835–1909)
King of the Belgians (1865/1909). The son of LEOPOLD I, in 1853 he married Maria of Habsburg. His chief interest was the expansion of Belgium abroad. In 1879 he founded a company to develop the Congo, in 1885 became King of the Congo Free State, and presided over the infamous 'Red Rubber Regime' there; the Belgian state was forced to annex the colony in 1908.

**Leopold III** (1901–83)
King of the Belgians (1934/51). The son of ALBERT I, in 1926 he married ASTRID of Sweden, and after her death Liliane Baels in 1941. On his own authority he ordered the capitulation of the Belgian army to the Germans (1940), thus opening the way to Dunkirk. He then remained a prisoner in his own palace at Laeken until 1944, and afterwards in Austria. After returning to Belgium in 1945, he was forced to abdicate in 1951 in favour of his son, BAUDOUIN I. ► WORLD WAR II

**Leopoldovna, Anna** (1718–46)
Regent of Russia. Born Elisabeth Katharine Christinem, she was the daughter of Charles Leopold, Duke of Mecklenburg Schwerin, and the niece of the Empress ANNA IVANOVNA. In 1739 she married Prince Anton Ulrich, Duke of Brunswick. Their son, Ivan, was declared Emperor of Russia at the age of eight weeks on the death of Anna Ivanovna, and Anna Leopoldovna was appointed regent. A year later, however, Ivan was deposed by the Empress ELIZABETH PETROVNA, and Anna was thrown into prison, where she died.

**Lepanto, Battle of** (7 Oct 1571)
The naval battle fought by the forces of the Christian HOLY LEAGUE against those of the OTTOMAN EMPIRE, off the coast of Greece. The Christian forces were raised by the papacy, Venice, the Italian states and Spain, and commanded by Don JOHN OF AUSTRIA, with 208 warships. The Turks mustered 230 warships. At stake was the security of Western Europe, threatened by successful Ottoman expansion. The battle was a clear victory for the Christians, who lost 10 galleys and 8,000 men. On the Turkish side, the commander, Ali Pasha, was killed; all but 30 of the galleys were destroyed or captured; 30,000 casualties were sustained and 3,000 men taken prisoner. Although a decisive watershed in the Christian–Muslim conflict in the Mediterranean, the victory did not stop the Ottomans from putting to sea with a further fleet the following year.

**Le Pen, Jean-Marie** (1928– )
French politician. The son of a Breton fisherman, he served in the 1950s as a paratrooper in Indochina and Algeria. In 1956 he was elected as a right-wing Poujadist Deputy. During the 1960s he had connections with the extremist OAS (*Organisation de l'Armée Secrète*), before forming the National Front in 1972. This party, with its extreme right-wing policies, emerged as a new 'fifth force' in French politics, winning 10 per cent of the national vote in the 1986 Assembly elections. A controversial figure and noted

demagogue, he unsuccessfully contested the presidency in 1988. In Apr 1998 he was convicted of assaulting a Socialist candidate during the 1997 elections and, following an appeal, was barred from holding office for one year. The National Front split in Jan 1999 following his power struggle with Bruno Mégret, but he was its candidate in the 2002 presidential election, when he was second-placed in the first round of voting, ahead of Prime Minister Lionel Jospin, but was beaten in the second round run-off by the incumbent Jacques **CHIRAC**.

### Lerma, Don Francisco Gómez de Sandoval y Rojas, Duke of (1553–1625)

Spanish politician. The minister and confidant of **PHILIP III** of Spain, during the period 1598–1618 he played an important role in government policy. A peaceful foreign policy was being pursued at this time: various treaties were signed with the French (1598), English (1604) and Dutch (1609, the **TWELVE YEARS' TRUCE**); and there was a rapprochement with France (the marriage, in 1615, of Philip to Elizabeth of France). In domestic affairs, he was notable in having influenced the transfer of the court from Madrid to Valladolid (1601–6), and the decree expelling the **MORISCOS** (1609). Created cardinal in 1618, he was dislodged by a palace coup the same year, and was forced to give up some of his accumulated wealth.

### Lerroux, Alejandro (1864–1949)

Spanish politician and journalist. During the first decade of the 20c he was the highly innovative and audacious populist leader of Barcelona. In forging a new basis for collaboration between the working class and republicanism, he formed the first modern party in Spain. Mythologized by his fiery anticlerical demagogy, the charismatic Lerroux was known as the 'Emperor of the Parallel' (a working-class thoroughfare). After he founded the **RADICAL REPUBLICAN PARTY** in 1908, he became increasingly conservative, even offering in 1923 to become the civilian figurehead of **PRIMO DE RIVERA'S** dictatorship. Although he also dedicated more and more time to his own varied business interests, Lerroux retained an extraordinary hold over his party. During the Second Republic, he led the Radicals as the principal source of opposition to the progressive Republican–Socialist coalition of 1931–3, having left the government in Dec 1931. He was crucial to the formation of the alliance with the non-Republican Right, which ruled Spain from Nov 1933 to Oct 1935 and which polarized the regime to an unprecedented degree. During this period he headed five administrations before falling from power through a bribery scandal. Despite backing the Nationalists during the **SPANISH CIVIL WAR**, he was prevented from returning to Spain from his exile in Portugal until 1947 because of his earlier involvement with **FREEMASONRY**. ► **REPUBLIC, SECOND** (Spain)

### Lesage, Jean (1912–80)

Canadian politician. He became the Liberal Premier of Quebec in 1960, carried into power on a wave of nationalist fervour, although the Liberals won only 50 out of the 95 seats. He then introduced the **QUIET REVOLUTION** against corruption, the Catholic Church's involvement in lay issues such as education, welfare and health, and against the economic domination of the USA and of anglophone Canadians in Quebec. His demands for a more active governmental role in the province, because of its special situation within the Confederation, began to cause unease among other Canadian provinces, especially when he asked for an increased share of tax revenue. In 1966 his government was defeated by the **UNION NATIONALE**. He remained leader of the Provincial Party until his retirement in 1970. ► **LIBERAL PARTY** (Canada)

---

**LESOTHO** official name **Kingdom of Lesotho**

An African kingdom completely bounded by South Africa. Lesotho was originally inhabited by hunting and gathering San (Bushmen). Bantu peoples arrived in the 16c, and the nation of the Basotho was organized in 1824 by **MOSHOESHOE I**. After fighting both the **AFRIKANERS** and the British, Moshoeshoe put his country under British protection as Basutoland in 1868, and it was administered until 1880 from Cape Colony. In 1884 it came under direct control of the British government as a British High Commission Territory. The Kingdom of Lesotho gained independence in 1966 as a hereditary monarchy within the **COMMONWEALTH OF NATIONS** and with Chief **JONATHAN** as Prime Minister. Fearing defeat in the 1970 election, Chief Jonathan declared a state of emergency and the country was ruled by a Military Council until 1993 when the military rulers were ousted. Democratic rule was restored in 1994 and in 1995 King **MOSHOESHOE II** returned from the exile imposed on him by the Military Council in 1990, the throne passing to his eldest son Letsie III after his death in 1996. Protests after the 1998 election lead to the revision of the constitution before the 2002 election, which was again won by the Lesotho Congress for Democracy. Lesotho has one of the world's highest levels of **HIV/AIDS** infection.

### Lesseps, Ferdinand Marie, Viscount of (1805–94)

French engineer. After holding several diplomatic posts in Europe, in 1854 he began to plan the Suez Canal, finally built 1860–9. He was knighted, and received several other honours. In 1881 work began on his scheme for a Panama Canal; but in 1892–3 the management was charged with breach of trust, and Lesseps and his son, Charles, were found guilty.

### Le Tellier, Michel (1603–85)

French politician. A lawyer, and government official, specializing in military supply, he was loyal to **MAZARIN** during the **FRONDE**, and became one of the principal advisers of **LOUIS XIV**. Together with his son, **LOUVOIS**, he was the creator of Louis XIV's army; he was a great rival of **COLBERT**; his last act was to draw up the revocation of the Edict of **NANTES**.

## Lettow-Vorbeck, Paul Emil von (1870–1964)
Prussian officer. He commanded the German forces in East Africa in **WORLD WAR I**. These forces, largely composed of black troops recruited from warlike peoples in Tanganyika, were expanded and reorganized by him, and raided the Uganda railway early in the war. He failed to hold the Kilimanjaro area, where most German settlers were located, and fell back to the Tanganyika Central Railway. In 1916 the railway was captured by forces led by General Jan **SMUTS** and he moved south to the Rufiji. He subsequently invaded Portuguese East Africa and Northern Rhodesia and surrendered after the Armistice at Abercorn (now Mbala, Zambia) on 25 Nov 1918.

## lettres de cachet
A royal order of the French kings, sealed with the monarch's private seal, issued for the arrest and imprisonment of individuals during the **ANCIEN RÉGIME**. The practice was abolished in the **FRENCH REVOLUTION** (1790).

## Levant, The
A general name formerly given to the eastern shores of the Mediterranean Sea, from western Greece to Egypt. The Levant States were Syria and Lebanon, during the period of their French mandate (1920–41). ► **MANDATES**

## Levellers
A radical political movement during the **ENGLISH CIVIL WARS** and the **COMMONWEALTH**. It called for the extension of male franchise to all but the poorest, religious toleration, and the abolition of the monarchy and the House of **LORDS**. Led by John **LILBURNE**, Richard Overton (c.1631–1664) and William Walwyn (1600–80), it was supported by 'agitators' in the Parliamentary Army (1647–9), and was defeated at Burford (May 1649).

## Leven, Alexander Leslie, 1st Earl of (c.1580–1661)
Scottish general. He became Field Marshal of Sweden under **GUSTAV II ADOLF**. Recalled to Scotland in 1639, he took command of the Covenanting Army in the **BISHOPS' WARS** against **CHARLES I**, who made him an earl in 1641 in the hope of winning his allegiance. He fought for the Parliamentary Army in the **ENGLISH CIVIL WARS**, and received Charles's surrender at Newark. After the execution of the King, he supported **CHARLES II**, was captured in 1651, and imprisoned until 1654. ► **DUNBAR, BATTLE OF** (1650)

## Lévesque, René (1922–87)
Canadian politician. He founded the **PARTI QUÉBECOIS** in 1968 after **LESAGE**'s defeat and the refusal of the **LIBERAL PARTY** to become more nationalist. By uniting the majority of francophones who wished greater autonomy for Quebec and those who wanted complete political independence for the province, he won a stunning victory in 1976, with 41 per cent of the vote. He then introduced electoral and labour reforms, pressed hard for the completion of the huge Quebec Hydro scheme and initiated legislation to place foreign-owned and other corporations under public ownership. More controversial were Bill 101, which legislated for a unilingual province, and a referendum law on the question of Quebec's future.

With the other provinces refusing to commit themselves to economic relationships with Quebec, and with Prime Minister Pierre **TRUDEAU**'s full involvement in the campaign, the Quebeckers voted against secession. Lévesque then began to demand enhanced provincial powers, along with Alberta's Premier, Peter Lougheed. In 1981 Quebec became increasingly isolated, with Lévesque refusing to endorse Trudeau's constitutional reforms, which challenged not only Bill 101 but also Lévesque's demand for compensation from Ottawa if the province opted out of federal socio-economic programmes. The party became deeply divided over the secession issue, but in 1985 Lévesque maintained his leadership with a 75 per cent vote.

## Lewis, John L(lewellyn) (1880–1969)
US labour leader. Born the son of a Welsh coalminer, he grew up to hold the presidency of the Union of United Mineworkers from 1920 to 1960. When its membership was reduced by the **GREAT DEPRESSION** to 150,000 in 1933, fearing a communist takeover, Lewis led a vigorous recruitment drive that increased the membership to 500,000. When, in 1935, he was unsuccessful in his attempts to change the AFL's traditional exclusion of industrial workers, he reacted by founding the Committee for Industrial Organizations, which became the CIO after its expulsion from the AFL in 1938. He took the coal miners out on several strikes during **WORLD WAR II**, and his fiery personality and stubborn drive led to clashes with Presidents Franklin D **ROOSEVELT** and Harry S **TRUMAN**. Although he swung the vote of organized labour behind Roosevelt in 1936, he reverted to his original Republicanism in 1940, and was a member of the isolationist **AMERICA FIRST COMMITTEE**. ► **AFL–CIO**

## Lewis and Clark Expedition (1804–6)
The first American transcontinental journey, named after its leaders Meriwether Lewis and William **CLARK**, and commissioned by Thomas **JEFFERSON** to explore the area made accessible by the **LOUISIANA PURCHASE** (1803). The expedition started in St Louis on 14 May 1804 and sailed up the Missouri River to spend the winter in what is now North Dakota. Then they journeyed westwards, through Montana, to cross the Continental Divide at Lemhi Pass in Idaho, from where they went north along the Clearwater, Snake and Columbia rivers to reach the Pacific Ocean in Nov 1805. There they built Fort Clatsop, where they spent the winter, and the following spring set out on the return journey for St Louis, arriving on 23 Sep 1806. As instructed, the leaders returned with diaries and maps which greatly advanced the knowledge of the area. ► **EXPLORATION**

## Lexington and Concord, Battles of (19 Apr 1775)
The first battles of the **AMERICAN REVOLUTION**, fought in Massachusetts after British troops tried to seize supplies stored at the village of Concord, and were confronted by colonial militia.

## Leyte Gulf, Battle of (1944)
A battle during **WORLD WAR II**, when the Japanese fleet converged on the US 3rd and 7th Fleets protecting Allied landings on Leyte in the central Philippines. The Japanese suffered irreplaceable losses of 300,000 tonnes of combat ships, compared to US

losses of 37,000 tonnes. The way was opened for further US gains in the Philippines and on islands nearer Japan.

**L'Hôpital, Michel de** (1507–73)
French politician. In 1554 he became Superintendent of Finances, in 1560 Chancellor of France. He strove to pacify the religious quarrel by staying the hand of the Catholic persecutors, but resigned in 1568 and retired to his estate near Etampes.

**Liang Ch'i-ch'ao** ► LIANG QICHAO

**Liang Qichao (Liang Ch'i-ch'ao)** (1873–1929)
Chinese reformer and intellectual. He was a student and follower of KANG YOUWEI, with whom he served during the HUNDRED DAYS OF REFORM (1898). He escaped to Japan, thereafter devoting himself to journalism, through which he became the most influential political writer of his generation. Liang returned to China in 1912, and was influential in creating the Progressive Party, which supported YUAN SHIKAI in the hope of maintaining national unity. However, the violence and corruption prevalent under Yuan led him to despair of the possibility of democracy in China, and he retired from politics to study Buddhism.

**Liang Shuming (Liang Shu-ming)** (1893–1981)
Chinese rural reformer. While teaching at Beijing University (1917–24), he argued that Confucianism, with its stress on harmony and adaptation to nature, was relevant to the modern world as an antidote to the materialism and aggressive individualism associated with Western culture. During the 1930s Liang was involved in the rural reconstruction movement, an attempt to create model villages based on economic cooperation and the harmonization of social relations. In 1945–6 he was Secretary-General of the CHINA DEMOCRATIC LEAGUE, formed in 1944 to represent a 'third force' in Chinese politics independent of both the Communists and Nationalists. Liang stayed on in China after the Communist victory in 1949, and during the early 1950s was an outspoken critic of party politics towards the peasants.

**Liao Chung-k'ai** ► LIAO ZHONGKAI

**Liao Zhongkai (Liao Chung-k'ai)** (1878–1925)
Chinese politician. Born into an overseas Chinese family in the USA, he studied in Japan before becoming the GUOMINDANG's leading financial expert after 1912. Associated with its left wing, he supported the United Front with the communists in 1923, advocating a planned economy along socialist lines. In 1924 he played an important role in setting up both the workers and peasant departments under Guomindang auspices as part of its new strategy of mass mobilization. As the leading Guomindang representative at the Whampoa Military Academy, Liao also laid the basis for the political commissar system that was to be used throughout the National Revolutionary Army. He aroused opposition from right-wing members of the Guomindang who opposed the United Front, and who may have been involved in his assassination.

**Liaquat Ali Khan** (1895–1951)
Pakistani politician. After leaving Oxford he became a member of the Inner Temple. He joined the MUSLIM LEAGUE in 1923, and became Prime Minister of Pakistan in 1947. He was assassinated in 1951.

**Liberal Democratic Party** (LDP; *Jiyu minshuto*)
The conservative party that ruled continuously in Japan from its formation in Nov 1955 until its defeat in Aug 1993. It was created by the merger of the two principal conservative parties established after 1945. The party gained the support of business groups because of its commitment to economic growth, the free enterprise system and traditional values, while its policy of subsidizing domestic rice production proved popular with the farmers. Until the late 1960s, the party won every Diet election with substantial margins (although never achieving the two-thirds majority required for any revision of the 1947 PEACE CONSTITUTION which some LDP members desired). From the 1970s, its popularity dipped and its share of the popular vote never exceeded 50 per cent, but the fragmentation of the opposition ensured its position as the majority party until 1993. Bribery scandals and the increasing importance of money politics, whereby factions expended huge sums of money to get their candidates elected, tarnished the LDP's reputation. In 1992 a group of rebel LDP MPs formed the Japan New Party (JNP) and brought down the government in a vote of no confidence (June 1993). Two further groups of rebel MPs formed the Japan Renewal Party (JRP) and the Sakigake (Harbinger) Party, and the LDP lost its majority in the general election that followed. These three new parties then formed a coalition with several other existing parties, and the new government came into power in Aug 1993, but it and its successor both collapsed. In 1994 the LDP returned to power in a coalition with the Social Democratic Party (SDP) of Japan and the Sakigake Party under a socialist Prime Minister, Tomiichi Murayama. In 1996 it formed a new coalition, this time under LDP president Ryutaro Hashimoto. It remains the largest party in the parliament, but for over a decade it has failed to achieve a majority and governs only by forming coalitions.

**Liberal Democratic Party** (Netherlands) ► DEMOCRATS 66

**liberalism**
As a political philosophy, liberalism developed in Europe in the 18–19c and was associated with the new middle classes who challenged the traditional monarchical, aristocratic and religious views of the state. Classical liberalism argues for limited government, and the values traditionally espoused are those of freedom (of the individual, religion, trade and economics, and politics). In the 20c, it came to occupy the centre ground in the political spectrum.

**Liberal Party** (Belgium)
After playing an important role in events during the French revolutionary period and in the Belgian Revolution, Belgian liberals first formed a party in June 1846. Besides embracing the general liberal principles of personal, constitutional and economic liberty, the Belgian liberals were particularly anticlerical. There were liberal governments in Belgium in 1847–55, 1857–70 and 1878–84; they dominated politics in the third quarter of the 19c. Two factors caused their decline: internal splits between progres-

sive radicals and 'doctrinaire' conservatives, and universal male suffrage (1893 in Belgium). However, on a smaller scale, liberalism has continued to be a force in Belgian politics. It has now dropped its anticlericalism, and tends to represent employers' viewpoints. In 1961 the Liberal Party split into two wings, the French-speaking *Parti pour la Liberté et le Progrès*, and the Flemish *Partij voor Vrijheid en Vooruitgang*. In 1971 these two wings separated and decided to act independently with their own programmes. The Francophone wing joined part of the **RASSEMBLEMENT WALLON** in 1976 to form the *Parti des Reformées et des Libertés Wallones*.

## Liberal Party (Canada)

This party evolved from the reform groups of **CANADA EAST** and **CANADA WEST** in the late 1840s and early 1850s, joined by the **CLEAR GRITS** in 1855 and the **ROUGES** after confederation. The party's early lack of cohesion and its failure to organize at a federal level meant that it was easily distracted by provincial issues and without the Conservatives' ability to distribute patronage it could not attract new members or erode Conservative support. After the 1871 Treaty of **WASHINGTON**, however, Liberals had the necessary issues to unite their provincial groups and were ready, under the leadership of Alexander **MACKENZIE**, to take advantage of the railway scandal of 1873 to win power. Their failure to negotiate a reciprocity agreement with the USA in 1874 and refusal to adopt a higher tariff policy, combined with the effects of depression and the accusation of atheism levelled by Quebec's Catholic Church, lost them the 1878 election and they remained in opposition under the leadership of Edward **BLAKE** in the 1880s. It was not until the end of the century that the party developed a formula for success, which essentially followed the example of the Conservatives. This was an anglofrancophone coalition, tempering reform with pragmatism, and cemented by a new emphasis on patronage. Sir Wilfrid **LAURIER** led the party to success in 1896, and by recruiting provincial premiers to his cabinet he increased the government's appeal to the provinces. The party was severely damaged by the defection of Clifford **SIFTON** (over reciprocity in 1911) and Henri **BOURASSA** (over naval policy), and joined the union government of R L **BORDEN** to bring in conscription during **WORLD WAR I**. After Laurier's death, W L Mackenzie **KING** led the party back into office in 1921, adding to the old formula a unique ability to blur political issues that enabled distinctly antagonistic groups to remain within the Liberal fold, and which kept them in power (with Progressive Party allies) until 1930, and from 1935 until his retirement in 1948. His successor, Louis **SAINT LAURENT** was not able to maintain this unity and the party began to alienate itself from Western Canada, resulting in the defeat of 1957. Although Lester **PEARSON** led the party back into minority government in 1963, it was not until Pierre **TRUDEAU** took the leadership that the party was successful in re-establishing itself nationally. It was out of office from 1984 until 1993, when it regained power under the leadership of Jean **CHRÉTIEN**, who became Prime Minister. It was re-elected in 1997 with a reduced majority and retained power in the 2000 and 2004 elections.

## Liberal Party (Netherlands)

Liberalism was first found in the Netherlands at the end of the 18c in the **PATRIOT MOVEMENT**, but became politically mature as an opposition group to the government of King **WILLIAM I**. The most prominent liberal was Johan **THORBECKE**, who was responsible for the new constitution of 1848 and formed several governments in the third quarter of the 19c. Despite their domination and the usual splits between left and right, there was no formal parliamentary party until 1885 when the Liberal Union (*Liberale Unie*) was formed as a loose association. There were several splinter-actions in the 1890s, caused by dissent over the issue of universal suffrage; in 1901 the less conservative liberals formed the Progressive Democratic League (*Vrijzinnig Democratische Bond*), which in 1938 became the National Liberal Party (*Liberale Staatspartij*). This became the Party of Freedom (*Partij van de Vrijheid*) in 1946, which after another merger in 1948 became the present liberal party, the People's Party for Freedom and Democracy (*Volkspartij voor Vrijheid en Democratie*, VVD). The Dutch liberals are now the party of the employers; they were in government with the Christian Democrats in the 1980s, when they commanded nearly a fifth of the vote. In the 1990s they formed part of the coalition governments headed by Wim Kok and have served in all subsequent coalitions.

## Liberal Party (Sweden)

Formed in 1900 to fight for parliamentary government and an extension of the franchise, it is the oldest of Sweden's modern political parties. It formed an administration for the first time in 1905 under Karl Staaff. Divided in 1924 over the question of prohibition, it was reunited in 1934. Under its leader Ola Ullsten, it participated in the non-socialist government formed in 1976 and, when this collapsed in 1978, Ullsten was briefly Prime Minister at the head of a minority administration. It returned to power in the coalition governments of 1991–4 but has remained in opposition since.

## Liberal Party (UK)

One of the two major political parties in the UK in the 19c and early 20c. It developed from the aristocratic Whig Party in the middle years of the 19c when, especially under **GLADSTONE**'s leadership, it appealed to the rapidly growing urban middle classes, to skilled working men and to religious nonconformists. Many of its landowning supporters and also radical imperialists were alienated by Gladstone's Irish **HOME RULE** policy from the mid-1880s. Based on values of economic freedom and, from the late 19c, social justice, the last Liberal government enacted in the decade before **WORLD WAR I** many important social reforms which anticipated the welfare state. Internal splits and the challenge of a reorganized **LABOUR PARTY** weakened it from 1918 onwards and by the end of the 1920s the Liberals were clearly a minority third party on the centre-left of British politics, a position they have not been able to escape despite revivals in the 1970s and alliance with the **SOCIAL DEMOCRATIC PARTY** in the 1980s. The party became known as the Liberal Democrats after the decision to merge with the Social Democrats in 1987. The Liberal Democrats increased their share of the vote under the leadership of Paddy **ASHDOWN** (1988/99) and Charles Kennedy (1999/ ) and remain the third party in the UK parliament. In Scotland they have been partners in the coalition government with Labour since the inception of the Scottish parliament in 1999. ► **CONSERVATIVE PARTY** (UK); **TORIES**; **WHIGS**

### Liberal Party of Australia
Australia's largest conservative party, formed by **MENZIES** in 1944–5 from existing conservative groups. It built up a mass following in the late 1940s, and was victorious in 1949. It governed from 1949 to 1972 and again from 1975 to 1983, sometimes in coalition with the Country/National Party. As the major anti-Labor grouping in Australian politics, the party is the descendant of **DEAKIN**'s Liberal Party in the early years of **FEDERATION**, **HUGHES**'s Nationalist Party (1917) and the United Australia Party (1931). Organized through branches in federal and state electorates, the party stands for individual liberty, private enterprise and economic competition, law and order, the family and state rights. Out of office from 1983 to 1996, it returned to power in a coalition with the National Party led by Liberal Prime Minister John Howard. While it does not hold power in any of the state or territory governments, its majorities in the Lower House and Senate increased in the 2004 federal elections. ► **NATIONAL PARTY OF AUSTRALIA**

### liberation theology
A style of theology originating in Latin America in the 1960s, and later becoming popular in many developing countries. Accepting a Marxist analysis of society, it stresses the role and mission of the Church to the poor and oppressed in society, of which Christ is understood as liberator. Its sympathy for revolutionary movements led to clashes with established secular and religious authorities.

### Liberation Tigers of Tamil Eelam ► LTTE

### LIBERIA official name **Republic of Liberia**

A tropical republic in West Africa, bounded to the north-west by Sierra Leone; to the north by Guinea; to the east by the Côte d'Ivoire; and to the south by the Atlantic Ocean. Mapped by the Portuguese in the 15c, it originated as a result of the activities of the philanthropic **AMERICAN COLONIZATION SOCIETY** wishing to establish a homeland for former slaves. The country was first settled in 1822, and constituted as the Free and Independent Republic of Liberia in 1847. A military coup and the assassination of the President in 1980 established a military government, the People's Redemption Council, with a chairman (Samuel **DOE**) and a cabinet. Doe's National Demo-

cratic Party of Liberia formed the government in the mid-1980s under a new constitution, and Doe became President in 1986. Dissatisfaction with Doe's autocratic and corrupt rule resulted in civil war in 1990 and the intervention of an ECOWAS (**ECONOMIC COMMUNITY OF WEST AFRICAN STATES**) peacekeeping force. A ceasefire was agreed in 1990, and peace agreements were signed in 1993 and 1995, but fighting continued until 2003 when all factions signed the Comprehensive Peace Agreement. A transitional power-sharing government, led by Gyude Bryant, was set up to work towards elections in 2005, and the UN Mission in Liberia (UNMIL) was established to supervise the peace process.

### Liberman, Yevsesi Grigorevich (1897–1983)
Soviet economist. Born and educated in Kharkov, he spent all his working life practising there as an academic economist. In 1962 he published an article in *Pravda* entitled 'Plan, Profit, Bonuses', which in a mild way advocated something of a market mechanism. Though far short of Mikhail **GORBACHEV**'s ideas, this was the basis for the reforms introduced by **KOSYGIN** in 1965 but undermined by the **BREZHNEV** hardliners after the **PRAGUE SPRING** in 1968.

### 'Liberty, Equality, Fraternity'
The motto of the French Republic; adopted in June 1793, it remained the official slogan of the state until the Bourbon Restoration (1814). It was re adopted during the Second Republic (1848–51), and has remained the national slogan from 1875 to the present day, except during the German occupation (1940–4). ► **FRENCH REVOLUTION**; **REPUBLIC, SECOND** (France)

### Liberty Federation ► MORAL MAJORITY

### LIBYA official name **Great Socialist People's Libyan Arab Jamahiriya**

A north African state, bounded to the north-west by Tunisia; to the west by Algeria; to the south-west by Niger; to the south by Chad; to the south-east by Sudan; to the east by Egypt; and to the north by the Mediterranean Sea. Controlled at various times by Phoenicians, Carthaginians, Greeks, Vandals and Byzantines, Libya came under Arab domination during the 7c. It was under Turkish rule from the 16c until the Italians gained control in 1911, and was named Libya by them in 1934. It suffered heavy fighting during **WORLD WAR II**, then came under British and French control. It became the independent Kingdom of Libya in 1951. A military coup established a republic under Muammar **GADDAFI** in 1969, and it was governed by a Revolutionary Command Council. Foreign military installations were closed down in the early 1970s, and government policy since the revolution has been based on the promotion of Arab unity and the furtherance of Islam. Relations with other countries have been strained by controversial activities, including the alleged organization of international **TERRORISM**: diplomatic relations were severed by the UK after the murder of a policewoman in London in 1984; Tripoli and Benghazi were bombed by the US Air Force in response to alleged terrorist activity in 1986; two Libyan fighter planes were shot down by US aircraft off the north African coast in 1989; and sanctions were imposed by the **UN** Security Council against Libya in 1992 following its refusal to extradite for trial two men suspected of organizing the bombing of a PanAm aircraft over Lockerbie in 1988. Sanctions were suspended in 1999 after the suspects were handed over for trial under Scottish law in the Netherlands, and lifted in 2003 after Libya admitted responsibility for the bombing and paid compensation. Since 2003, Gaddafi has sought to end Libya's international isolation, abandoning its weapons of mass destruction (**WMD**) programmes and promising in 2004 to allow UN nuclear weapons inspections.

**Li-chia System** ► LIJIA SYSTEM

**Li Chih** ► LI ZHI

**Li Dazhao (Li Ta-chao)** (1888–1927)
Chinese revolutionary. One of the founders of the Chinese Communist Party, whose interpretation of **MARXISM** as applied to China had a profound influence on **MAO ZEDONG**. Appointed Head Librarian of Beijing University and Professor of History (1918), he had the young Mao as a library assistant, and founded one of the first of the communist study circles which in 1921 were to form the Communist Party. In 1927, when the Manchurian military leader Zhang Zuolin (Chang Tso-lin), then occupying Beijing, raided the Soviet Embassy, Li was captured and executed.

**Lidice, Destruction of** (1942)
A Nazi-German act of savage revenge on innocent Czech villagers. In late May resistance fighters fatally wounded Reinhard **HEYDRICH**, the **GESTAPO** officer who was in charge of the **BOHEMIAN PROTECTORATE**. Heydrich had a nasty reputation, but that was quickly overshadowed by actions to avenge his death. The worst of these was in June when, as an example, the village of Lidice was destroyed, its almost 200 males shot, its 200 females sent off to Ravensbrück **CONCENTRATION CAMP**, and its 100 children dispersed, many to their deaths. However, the tragedy was to stiffen the Czech resistance and convince the Allies of the need to expel the Germans from Czechoslovakia after the war.

**Lie, Trygve Haldvan** (1896–1968)
Norwegian lawyer. After becoming an MP, he was appointed Minister of Justice and of Shipping before fleeing to Britain with other members of the Norwegian Government in 1940, where he acted as Foreign Minister until the end of **WORLD WAR II**. In 1946 he was elected **UN** Secretary-General, but resigned in 1952. He served as Minister for Industry (1963–4) and for Commerce and Shipping until his death.

**Liebknecht, Karl** (1871–1919)
German barrister and politician. The son of Wilhelm **LIEBKNECHT**, he was a member of the **REICHSTAG** (1912–16). During **WORLD WAR I** he was imprisoned as an independent, anti-militarist, social democrat. He was a founder-member with Rosa **LUXEMBURG** of the German Communist Party (**KPD**) in 1918–19 and led an unsuccessful revolt in Berlin, the 'Spartacus Rising', in Jan 1919, during which he and Rosa Luxemburg were killed by army officers. ► **SPARTACISTS**

**Liebknecht, Wilhelm** (1826–1900)
German politician. He studied at Giessen, Marburg and Berlin, became a lawyer (1847), and developed an interest in **SOCIALISM**. For his part in the Baden insurrection (1848–9), he had to take refuge in Switzerland and in England, where he worked closely with **MARX**. He returned to Germany in 1862 and during a two-year imprisonment was elected to the **REICHSTAG** (1874). A co-founder of the German Social Democratic Party (**SPD**) (1875), he became one of its leading spokesmen. ► **MARXISM**

**LIECHTENSTEIN**   official name **Principality of Liechtenstein**

A small independent alpine principality in central Europe, lying between the Austrian state of Voralberg to the east and the Swiss cantons of St Gallen and Graubünden to the west. Originally the medieval counties of Vaduz and Schellenberg, this small territory came into the hands of the princes of Liechtenstein between 1699 and 1712. A principality of the **HOLY ROMAN EMPIRE** from 1719, Liechtenstein became a member of the **CONFEDERATION OF THE RHINE** in 1806 and of the **GERMAN CONFEDERATION** from 1815 to 1866. In 1862 it became a constitutional state and from 1866 was fully independent. It is ruled by the hereditary princes of the House of Liechtenstein, since 1989 Prince Hans Adam II, although he passed on day-to-day responsibilities to his son Prince Alois in 2004. A 2003 referendum approved constitutional changes giving the monarch greater powers over the government and judiciary. Close economic and political ties have existed at different times with Austria and Switzerland.

**Ligachev, Yegor Kuzmich** (1920–)
Soviet politician. After graduating as an engineer in 1943, he worked in the Urals region before joining the Communist Party in 1944. From then until 1961 he worked in his native Novosibirsk as an official first of **KOMSOMOL** and then of the local Party. As Party Chief of the new 'science city' of Akademgorodok, he gained a reputation as an austere opponent of

corruption. He was brought to Moscow by Nikita **KHRUSHCHEV** in 1961 but, after the latter was ousted in 1964, he was sent to Tomsk, where he was regional party boss for 18 years. However, he became a full member of the Central Committee in 1976, and in 1983 he was promoted to the Secretariat by Yuri **ANDROPOV**, becoming Ideology Secretary in 1984. With the accession to power of Mikhail **GORBACHEV** in 1985, Ligachev was brought into the **POLITBURO**. He initially served as Gorbachev's deputy, but they became estranged over the issue of reform and in 1988 he was demoted to the position of Agriculture Secretary. As Gorbachev became more radical, Ligachev became more conservative, and in 1990 he was expelled from the Central Committee as well as the Politburo. He remained an anti-reform critic even after the USSR collapsed.

### Li Hongzhang (Li Hung-chang) (1823–1901)
Chinese scholar and soldier. He rose to prominence in the resistance to the **TAIPING REBELLION**, and became the most influential Chinese statesman of the late 19c. A protégé of **ZENG GUOFAN**, he was the chief representative of China in its relations with foreign powers, and supported limited industrialization at home.

### Li Hsien-nien ► LI XIAN'NIAN

### Li Hung-chang ► LI HONGZHANG

### Lijia (Li-chia) System
This term refers to a sub-bureaucratic level of government in imperial China inaugurated by the founder of the **MING DYNASTY**, **MING HONGWU**. It represented an attempt to extend the government's reach below the district (*xian*), the lowest level of the formal bureaucracy. A community (*lt*), comprising 110 households, was subdivided into units (*jia*) of ten households. The heads of the ten wealthiest households were to be responsible for population registration and the levying and collection of taxes, each head serving a one-year term. The system continued to be used during the succeeding **QING DYNASTY**, although its functions were increasingly blurred with those of the **BAOJIA SYSTEM**.

### Likud
The coalition of right-wing political parties in Israel, named *Likud Liberalim Leumi* in full ('National Union of Liberals'). The coalition was composed mainly of the Herut Party and Liberal Party. The former was constructed in 1948 out of the **IRGUN** and **HAGANAH**, while the latter was created in 1961. Formed in 1973 in opposition to the Israel Labour Party, Likud governed Israel from 1977 to 1992 under Menachem **BEGIN** and Yitzhak **SHAMIR**; this included the period 1984–90 in coalition with the Israel Labour Party. Shamir was replaced as leader in 1993 by Binyamin **NETANYAHU**, who led the Likud coalition to power again in 1996, but failed to repeat this achievement in 1999. He was replaced by Ariel **SHARON**, who became Prime Minister at the head of Likud coalitions in 2001, retaining power after the 2003 election. To maintain a working majority, Likud has sometimes negotiated the support of small parties, which have been influential beyond their size as a result. ►
**MAPAI PARTY**

### Lilburne, John (c.1614–1657)
English revolutionary. Imprisoned by the **STAR CHAMBER** in 1638 for importing Puritan literature, he rose in the Parliamentary Army, but resigned from it in 1645 over the Covenant. He became an indefatigable agitator for the **LEVELLERS** during the **ENGLISH CIVIL WARS**, thought Cromwell's republic too aristocratic, and demanded greater liberty of conscience and numerous reforms. He was repeatedly imprisoned for his treasonable pamphlets.

### Li Lisan (Li Li-san) (1900–67)
Chinese politician. Chinese Communist Party leader and effective head of the Party (1928–30), he enforced what subsequently became known as the 'Li Lisan line', in which the Party's weak and undeveloped military forces were used in futile attempts to capture cities. His authoritarian methods alienated his fellow leaders. He was demoted in 1930, and lived in the USSR until 1945. Thereafter, he was employed by the Chinese Communist Party in various minor roles.

### Lima, Declaration of (1938)
An agreement made during the F D **ROOSEVELT** administration which provided for pan-American consultation in case of a threat to the 'peace, security or territorial integrity' of any state.

### Limann, Hilla (1934–98)
Ghanaian diplomat and politician. He was educated in Ghana and then at the LSE and the Sorbonne, where he earned a doctorate. He was a teacher before joining the Ghanaian diplomatic service as Head of Chancery at Lomé (1968–71). Limann then served his country at many international gatherings while being his country's counsellor at its permanent mission to the **UN** in Geneva (1971–5) and senior officer Ministry of Foreign Affairs (1975–9). In 1979 he was chosen to lead the People's National Party and was its successful presidential candidate in the 1979 elections, becoming President until his removal from office (31 Dec 1981) as a result of a military coup led by Flt-Lt Jerry **RAWLINGS**.

### limpieza de sangre
'Blood purity' (signifying purity from Jewish origins) was a requirement of some institutions in Spain from the late 15c onwards. Apparently first introduced by the University College of St Bartolomé in Salamanca in 1482, the requirement was a symptom of anti-Semitism in Spanish society, and discriminated against **CONVERSOS**. Several bodies subsequently adopted statutes of *limpieza*, among them the Jeronimite Order (1486) and the Cathedral of Seville (1515). The tendency gained force when in 1547 Siliceo, Archbishop of Toledo, forced through a statute in his cathedral. However, by the late 16c there was widespread criticism of the social implications of limpieza, and prominent figures including the Spanish Inquisition began attempts to abolish the practice. Despite this, statutes of limpieza remained in force in many parts of Spain until the 19c.

### Lin Biao (Lin Piao) (1907–71)
Chinese military leader. He was one of the leaders of the Chinese Communist Party and a Marshal of the Red Army. Lin became Minister of Defence in 1959, and in 1968 replaced the disgraced **LIU SHAOQI** as heir-apparent to **MAO ZEDONG**. He was one of the

promoters of the **CULTURAL REVOLUTION**, and appears to have been a patron of extreme left-wing factions. In 1971, after a political struggle, he was killed in a plane crash in Mongolia, apparently in the course of an attempt to seek refuge in the USSR.

**Lincoln, Abraham** (1809–65)
US politician and 16th President. Elected to the Illinois legislature in 1834, he became a lawyer in 1836. A decade later, he was elected to a single term in **CONGRESS**, where he spoke against the extension of **SLAVERY**, and in 1860 was elected President as the **REPUBLICAN PARTY**'s candidate on a platform of hostility to slavery's expansion. When the **AMERICAN CIVIL WAR** began (1861), he defined the issue in terms of national integrity, not anti-slavery, a theme he restated in the **GETTYSBURG ADDRESS** (1863). Nonetheless, in his Emancipation Proclamation that same year, he announced his intention of freeing all slaves in areas of rebellion. He was re-elected in 1864; after the final Northern victory he proposed to reunite the nation on the most generous terms, but on 14 Apr 1865 he was shot at Ford's Theater, in Washington, DC, by an actor, John Wilkes **BOOTH**, and died next morning. He immediately became a national hero, and is regarded as one of the finest symbols of American democracy.

**Lindbergh, Charles Augustus** (1902–74)
US aeronaut. His 1927 flight from New York to Paris, taking 33.5 hours in his monoplane *Spirit of St Louis*, won him a prize of US$25,000 for the first solo transatlantic flight, and instant fame. To this was added national sympathy when his son was abducted and murdered in 1932. In 1940 he became a member of the isolationist **AMERICA FIRST COMMITTEE**, and his popularity was seriously damaged in 1941 because of his suggestion to negotiate a settlement with **HITLER**'s Germany.

**Linlithgow, Victor Alexander John Hope, 2nd Marquess of** (1887–1952)
British politician. He served during **WORLD WAR I** on the Western Front. He was Chairman of the Royal Commission on Agriculture in India (1926–8) and was also a member of the Select Committee on Indian Constitutional Reform. In 1936 he became Viceroy of India, in succession to Lord Willingdon, and held the post until 1943, thus becoming the longest holder of that office. In 1939, he declared war against Germany before consulting the Indian political parties; the Congress Party was offended by this step, and provincial Congress ministries resigned in protest. Although he suppressed opposition to British rule in India during **WORLD WAR II**, under him provincial autonomy functioned smoothly. He was responsible for jailing the Congress leaders of the **QUIT INDIA MOVEMENT** in 1942–3.

**Lin Piao** ► LIN BIAO

**Lin Tse-hsü** ► LIN ZEXU

**Lin Zexu (Lin Tse-hsü)** (1785–1850)
Chinese politician. He was regarded in China as the first great patriot to resist the incursions of foreign powers into China. Lin was appointed Imperial Commissioner to deal with the problem of the increase in illegal imports of opium. At Guangzhou (Canton) he

held members of the British community hostage in their warehouses until they surrendered their stocks of opium, thus precipitating a British punitive expedition. When China suffered defeat, he was exiled to Chinese Turkestan, but later recalled. ► **OPIUM WARS**; **TAIPING REBELLION**

**Lion of Janina** ► ALI PASHA

**Li Peng (Li P'eng)** (1928–)
Chinese politician. He was the son of the radical communist writer Li Shouxun, who was executed by the **GUOMINDANG** in 1930. Adopted by **ZHOU ENLAI** on his mother's death (1939), he trained as a hydroelectric engineer and was appointed Minister of the Electric Power Industry in 1981. He became a vice-premier in 1983, was elevated to the Politburo in 1985 and made Prime Minister in 1987. As a cautious, orthodox reformer, he sought to retain firm control of the economy and favoured improved relations with the USSR. In 1989 he took a strong line in facing down the student-led, pro-democracy movement, becoming in the process a popularly reviled figure. His period in office ended in 1998.

**Li Shih-tseng** ► LI SHIZENG

**Li Shizeng (Li Shih-tseng)** (1881–1973)
Chinese anarchist, educator and prominent member of the **GUOMINDANG**. From an influential official family, Li went to France in 1902 to study. While there he became attracted to anarchism and founded a journal, *Xin Shiji* ('New Century'). This not only called for the overthrow of the **QING DYNASTY** but also condemned Confucian social institutions, such as the family, for stifling the individual and entrenching sexual inequality. As an enthusiastic Francophile, Li organized a work-study programme for Chinese students in France (1919–21). He championed work-study as part of his vision to create a harmonious and cooperative society, in which class divisions would be dissolved through education and the integration of intellectual and manual labour. Ironically, many work-study students later became prominent members of the Chinese **COMMUNIST PARTY**. Li's hostility to **COMMUNISM** and his close personal ties with **SUN YAT-SEN** and **CHIANG KAI-SHEK** drew him into the Guomindang and he became a member of the party's supervisory committee in 1924. In the 1950s he was a policy adviser to Chiang Kai-shek's regime in Taiwan.

**Lissa, Battle of** (20 July 1866)
The clash between the Italian and Austrian navies, in which, despite possessing a marked superiority in numbers and quality of vessels, the Italian admiral, Count Carlo di Persano, contrived through his own incompetence to turn probable victory into defeat.

**List, (Georg) Friedrich** (1789–1846)
German political economist. A disciple of Adam **SMITH**, he was charged with sedition in 1824, went to the USA, and became a naturalized citizen. He was US consul at Baden, Leipzig and Stuttgart successively. A strong advocate of protection for new industries, he did much by his writings to form German economic practice.

**Líster, Enrique** (1907–94)
Spanish Communist leader and general. During the **SPANISH CIVIL WAR** he became commander of the

Republic's famous 5th Regiment. Exiled in the USSR, he fought with the Soviet army in **WORLD WAR II**, reaching the rank of general. A member of the Spanish Politburo from 1946, he was expelled in 1970. In 1973 he founded the Spanish Workers' Communist Party (PCOE), and returned to Spain in 1977, where his party made little impact.

**Listone**
The Italian word (literally, 'big list') used to describe the fascist-approved candidates put forward by **MUSSOLINI** when contesting the Apr 1924 Italian elections. It included not only members of the **FASCIST PARTY** but also nationalists, right-wing liberals (including **ORLANDO**, **SALANDRA** and De Nicola) and even a few **POPOLARI**. Indeed, of the 374 victorious candidates on the *Listone*, under two-thirds were genuine fascists. The Listone was remarkably successful, bringing Mussolini a comfortable parliamentary majority.

**Li Ta-chao** ► **LI DAZHAO**

**LITHUANIA**  official name **Republic of Lithuania**

A republic in north-eastern Europe, bounded to the north by Latvia, to the east and south-east by Belarus, to south-west by Poland and the Russian enclave of Kaliningrad, and to the west by the Baltic Sea. It was united with Poland from 1385 to 1795. Intensive Russification led to revolts in 1905 and 1917. Occupied by Germany in both World Wars, it was proclaimed a republic in 1918 but annexed by the USSR in 1940. The growth of a nationalist movement in the 1980s led to a declaration of independence in 1990 under President Vytautas Landsbergis, who was succeeded in 1993 by Algirdas Brazauskas. Rolandas Paksas was elected President in 2003 but was impeached by parliament in Apr 2004 over allegations of corruption, and Valdas Adamkus, president from 1998 to 2003, was re-elected President in Jun. Lithuania joined **NATO** and the **EU** in 2004.

**Little Bighorn, Battle of the** (25–6 June 1876)
The famous battle, popularly called 'CUSTER's Last Stand', between US cavalry, under General **CUSTER**, and the **SIOUX** and **CHEYENNE**, under **SITTING BULL** and **CRAZY HORSE**. The **NATIVE AMERICANS** destroyed Custer's force. Issues behind the battle included Custer's bloody dawn attack on a Cheyenne village at the Washita in 1868, and the white invasion of the Black Hills, sacred to the Sioux. ► **INDIAN WARS**

**Little Entente**
A system of alliances between Czechoslovakia and Yugoslavia (1920), Czechoslovakia and Romania (1921), and Yugoslavia and Romania (1921), consolidated into a single treaty signed in Belgrade in 1929. The alliances aimed to maintain post-1919 boundaries in central Europe, and prevent a Habsburg

restoration. ► **HABSBURG DYNASTY**

**Little Rock**
The capital city of Arkansas, USA, which was the scene of rioting over **DESEGREGATION** in 1957. Following the US Supreme Court decision in 1954 that declared desegregation unconstitutional, the Central High School was included in a gradual desegregation plan by the city school board. However, the state's governor, Orval Faubus, mobilized the state militia, ostensibly to prevent violence but in reality to block the admission of nine black students. An injunction forbade Faubus to block the students' admission, and the guardsmen were duly withdrawn, but rioting among the whites broke out, resulting in US army troops being sent to Little Rock by President Dwight D **EISENHOWER** to enforce the desegregation law and keep order.

**Litvinov, Maxim Maximovich** (1876–1951)
Soviet revolutionary and diplomat. He was an early critic of Tsarist rule and joined the Social Democratic Party in 1898. He was soon exiled abroad and joined the Bolshevik faction after 1903. Having lived in Britain for over a decade, he was appointed Bolshevik Ambassador in London (1917–18), and held various roving commissions before becoming Deputy Commissar (1921), then Commissar (1930) for Foreign Affairs. Until **STALIN** dismissed him in the spring of 1939, he was the chief architect of improved relations between the USSR and the West in the face of **HITLER**. He did not return to favour until after Hitler's attack in 1941, when he became Ambassador to the USA (1941), and Vice-Minister of Foreign Affairs (1942–6). A strong advocate of cooperation between the USSR and the West even at the onset of the **COLD WAR**, he died in Moscow. ► **BOLSHEVIKS**; **LITVINOV PROTOCOL**

**Litvinov Protocol** (1999)
The term used to describe Soviet attempts to improve security by working with Western proposals. Maxim **LITVINOV**, Soviet Deputy Foreign Commissar, had been attempting to normalize relations with neighbouring states and to secure guarantees against Germany. When the US Secretary of State, Frank B Kellogg, proposed the renunciation of war as the core of a new international treaty (**KELLOGG–BRIAND PACT**), Litvinov managed to persuade the USSR's Western neighbours to adhere to his protocol, also renouncing war, as a kind of Eastern alliance against Germany.

**Li Tzu-ch'eng** ► **LI ZICHENG**

**Liu Shao-ch'i** ► **LIU SHAOQI**

**Liu Shaoqi (Liu Shao-ch'i)** (1898–1969)
Chinese politician. A leading figure in the Chinese communist revolution, he attended university in Moscow in 1921, returned to China in 1922 and became a communist trade union organizer. In 1939 he joined **MAO ZEDONG** at Yan'an, where he emerged as the chief party theorist on questions of organization. In 1943 he became Party Secretary, and succeeded Mao in 1959. After the **CULTURAL REVOLUTION**, the extreme Left made Liu their principal target, and in 1968 he was stripped of all his posts and dismissed from the party. He was rehabilitated in 1980. ►
**GREAT LEAP FORWARD**

## Liverpool, Robert Banks Jenkinson, 2nd Earl of (1770–1828)

British politician. He entered parliament in 1790, and was a member of the India Board (1793–6), Master of the Royal Mint (1799–1801), Foreign Secretary (1801–4), Home Secretary (1804–6 and 1807–9), and Secretary for War and the Colonies (1809–12). He succeeded his father as Earl of Liverpool in 1807. As Tory Premier (1812–27), he oversaw the final years of the NAPOLEONIC WARS, the war of 1812–14 with the USA, and a difficult and lengthy process of readjustment to peace. His administrations adopted trade liberalization policies in the 1820s. He resigned after suffering a stroke early in 1827. ► TORIES

## Livingstone, David (1813–73)

Scottish missionary and traveller. He trained as a physician in Glasgow and was ordained in the London Missionary Society in 1840. He worked for several years in Bechuanaland (now Botswana), then travelled north (1852–6) and discovered Lake Ngami and the Victoria Falls. He led an expedition to the Zambezi (1858–63) and discovered Lake Shirwa and Lake Nyasa. In 1866 he returned to Africa to establish the sources of the Nile, but the river he encountered proved to be the Congo. On his return to Ujiji, after severe illness, Livingstone was found by Henry Morton STANLEY, sent to look for him by the New York Herald. He again set out to find the sources of the Nile, but died in Old Chitambo (now in Zambia). ► EXPLORATION

## Livonian Knights

Brothers of the Knighthood of Christ in Livonia, commonly known as the Sword-Brothers, their order was founded c.1202 to support the Bishop of Riga in his missionary work among pagan Latvians. They achieved significant successes against the Estonians (1211 and 1217) but were unable to establish a secure power base. After a crushing defeat in battle against the Lithuanians (Saule, 1236), the remnants of the order formed part of the Livonian branch of the TEUTONIC KNIGHTS. By the 14c they controlled the eastern Baltic lands of Courland, Estonia and Livonia. However, in 1561 they disbanded in the face of threats from Russia.

## Li Xian'nian (Li Hsien-nien) (1909–92)

Chinese politician. Born into a poor peasant family in Hubei province, he worked as a carpenter before serving with the GUOMINDANG forces (1926–7). After joining the Chinese Communist Party (CCP) in 1927, he established the Oyuwan Soviet (People's Republic) in Hubei, participated in the LONG MARCH and was a military commander in the war against Japan and in the CHINESE CIVIL WAR. He was inducted into the CCP Politburo and secretariat in 1956 and 1958, but fell out of favour during the CULTURAL REVOLUTION. He was rehabilitated, as Finance Minister, by ZHOU ENLAI in 1973, and later served as state President in the 'administration' of DENG XIAOPING (1983–8).

## Li Yuanhong (Li Yuan-hung) (1864–1928)

Chinese militarist. As the commander of the army division in central China whose mutiny (Oct 1911) against the QING DYNASTY signalled the collapse of the monarchy and creation of a republic, Li served briefly and reluctantly as the overall leader of the revolutionary army. He failed to curb the growing influence of the northern (Beiyang) militarists during his two terms as President of the Chinese Republic (1916–17 and 1922–3) and was a virtual figurehead.

## Li Yuan-hung ► LI YUANHONG

## Li Zhi (Li Chih) (1527–1602)

Chinese iconoclast during the MING DYNASTY. After serving as a minor government official (1555–81), he led the life of a Buddhist recluse. He aroused the ire of officials and scholars with his radical critique of traditional Confucian morality and condemnation of enforced conformity. He considered selfishness and profit to be respectable motivations, advocated free choice in marriage, and insisted that Confucianism, Buddhism and Daoism all had equal truth and value. Li was arrested in 1602 and committed suicide in jail. His unorthodox views form part of a significant dissident tradition in imperial China.

## Li Zicheng (Li Tzu-ch'eng) (1605–45)

Chinese bandit. The leader of a peasant rebellion that overthrew the MING DYNASTY, he came from a peasant family in north-west China (Shaanxi province) and was a soldier before resorting to banditry in the 1620s. By the spring of 1644, he had amassed a huge peasant army with his promotion of tax relief and distribution of goods, and controlled much of north and north-west China. He captured Beijing in Apr 1644 and the last Ming Emperor committed suicide. Although Li proclaimed a new dynasty (Shun), he was forced to evacuate Beijing (June 1644) by invading Manchu forces from the north-east, who gained the support of Chinese military commanders appalled by the disorder and cruelty of Li's regime. He was killed one year later. ► QING DYNASTY

## Ljotić, Dimitrije (1891–1945)

Serbian lawyer. He held a number of minor offices under King ALEXANDER I then, during WORLD WAR II, working for the collaborationist government of General Milan NEDIĆ, he led the Serbian fascist movement, Zbor, and its youth movement, the White Eagle. Serb-nationalist in ideology, Zbor aspired to the creation of a corporate regime on the model of MUSSOLINI's Italy. Ljotić was killed while trying to escape from Yugoslavia at the end of the war.

## Lliga

Catalan regionalist party. Originally founded in 1901 as the Lliga Regionalista, it became the principal representative of the Catalan bourgeoisie. It was instrumental in the creation of the Mancomunitat, a limited form of autonomous government, in 1913. However, the Lliga's principal aim was to establish the Catalan bourgeoisie as the ruling class within Spain. The general strike of 1917 led the Lliga to withdraw into an alliance with the central government, thereby gravely undermining the opposition to the monarchy. The party split in 1922. Rebuilt by Francesc CAMBÓ under the Second Republic as the Lliga Catalana, it was overshadowed throughout the regime by the Esquerra (Catalan Left). ► REPUBLIC, SECOND (Spain)

## Lloyd-George (of Dwyfor), David Lloyd George, 1st Earl (1863–1945)

British politician. Born in England of Welsh parentage,

he became a solicitor, and in 1890, as a strong supporter of **HOME RULE**, a Liberal MP for Caernarvon Boroughs (a seat he was to hold for 55 years). He was President of the Board of Trade (1905–8), and Chancellor of the Exchequer (1908–15). His 'people's budget' of 1909–10 was rejected by the House of **LORDS**, and led to a constitutional crisis and the Parliament Act of 1911, which removed the Lords' power of veto. He became Minister of Munitions (1915), Secretary for War (1916), and superseded **ASQUITH** as coalition Prime Minister (1916–22), carrying on a forceful war policy. After **WORLD WAR I**, he continued as head of a coalition government dominated by Conservatives. He negotiated with **SINN FÉIN**, and conceded the **IRISH FREE STATE** (1921), a measure which helped to precipitate his downfall. Distrusted as mendacious and unscrupulous, he failed to revive a divided **LIBERAL PARTY** and, following the 1931 general election, he led a 'family' group of Independent Liberal MPs. He was made an earl in 1945. ► **BOER WARS**

## Llywelyn

The name of two Welsh princes. Llywelyn ap Iorwerth or Llywelyn the Great (d.1240) successfully maintained his independence against King **JOHN** and **HENRY III**, and gained recognition of Welsh rights in the **MAGNA CARTA** (1215). Llywelyn ap Gruffydd (d.1282) helped the English barons against Henry III, and opposed **EDWARD I**, who forced his submission. He was slain near Builth, at which point Wales lost her political independence.

## LNC (Lufta Nacional Çlirimtare, 'National Liberation War')

Dominated from its inception by the communists, this Albanian movement also included members from other political parties. Closely supervised by the Yugoslav resistance, it was forced by **TITO** to abandon any hope of acquiring **KOSOVO**, and reached an agreement with the other Albanian resistance group, **BALLI KOMBËTAR**. In May 1944, following the Yugoslav example of **AVNOJ**, the LNC met at Përmët and founded an Anti-Fascist Council of National Liberation with Enver **HOXHA** as leader. When the regime in Tirana collapsed following the withdrawal of German forces (Nov 1944), the LNC quickly established its authority, trying and executing members of the former government and eliminating all opposition to the establishment of a communist regime. Renamed the Democratic Front, in Dec 1945 it alone fielded candidates in the elections and in Jan 1946 it declared Albania a people's republic.

## Lobengula (c.1836–1894)

King of the **NDEBELE** or Matabele people of Zimbabwe (1870/94). After a two-year succession crisis, he succeeded his father, **MZILIKAZI**, to rule directly over **MATABELELAND**. He frequently raided and established authority over many of the chieftaincies of the Shona people in Mashonaland. During his reign many Europeans, prospectors, hunters, missionaries, traders and concession-seekers, reached his kingdom from the south. He became embroiled in complex diplomatic negotiations and set out to protect his kingdom with great astuteness. However, Cecil **RHODES** succeeded in securing key concessions for mining and land alienation in Mashonaland which enabled him

to secure a charter for his **BRITISH SOUTH AFRICA COMPANY** and invade Mashonaland (1890). Lobengula attempted to maintain a peaceful coexistence with the white settlers, but was forced into war in 1893. The Ndebele were defeated and Lobengula died, possibly of smallpox, while fleeing north to the Zambezi. He left a number of sons who were claimants to the throne of Matabeleland, but the region was incorporated into Southern Rhodesia. The Ndebele rose in revolt in 1896 and made Nyamanda king, but they sued for peace later the same year. Their chieftaincies survive and they now constitute 20 per cent of the population of Zimbabwe.

## Locarno Pact (Oct 1925)

The international agreement, made at Locarno, Italy, guaranteeing the post-1919 frontiers between France, Belgium and Germany, and the demilitarization of the Rhineland. The treaty was guaranteed by Italy and Britain as well as signed by the three states directly concerned, France, Germany and Belgium. At the same time, Germany agreed to arbitration conventions with France, Belgium, Poland and Czechoslovakia, and France signed treaties of mutual guarantee with Poland and Czechoslovakia.

## Locke, John (1632–1704)

English empiricist philosopher. His two treatises *On Government*, published anonymously in 1690, constitute his reply to the patriarchal, divine right theory and also to the **ABSOLUTISM** of Thomas **HOBBES**. The *Treatises* present a social contract theory that embodies a defence of natural rights and a justification for constitutional law, the liberty of the individual and the rule of the majority: if the ruling body offends against natural law it must be deposed. This sanctioning of rebellion had a powerful influence on the American and the French revolutions. ► **AMERICAN REVOLUTION; DIVINE RIGHT OF KINGS; FRENCH REVOLUTION**

## Lockheed Scandal

A political scandal in Japan that revealed the close links between the **LIBERAL DEMOCRATIC PARTY** (LDP) and business interests. It broke in 1976, when **TANAKA KAKUEI** (who had resigned as Prime Minister in 1974 amidst allegations of shady financial dealings) was named during US **SENATE** hearings into the bribery of foreign officials by US multinationals. The US Lockheed Aircraft Corporation was alleged to have paid Tanaka, as Prime Minister, 500 million yen to ensure the purchase of its planes by a Japanese civil airline. Subsequent investigations in Japan highlighted the extent of bribes and kickbacks involved, and several businessmen and politicians, including Tanaka, were prosecuted. In 1983 Tanaka was sentenced to four years in prison but was released on bail pending appeal; the case was still dragging on when he died ten years later. Significantly, however, Tanaka remained a Diet member and his faction continued to be influential within the LDP during the 1980s.

## Lodge, Henry Cabot (1850–1924)

US politician, historian and biographer. He became a Republican Senator from Massachusetts in 1893, and after **WORLD WAR I** led the opposition to the Treaty of **VERSAILLES** (1919). The treaty was not ratified,

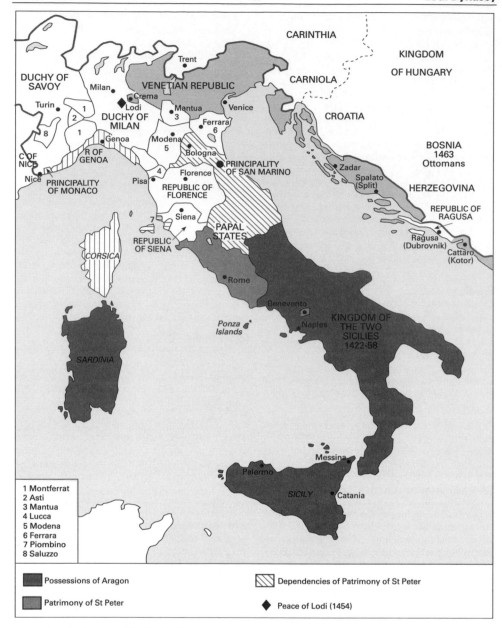

1 Montferrat
2 Asti
3 Mantua
4 Lucca
5 Modena
6 Ferrara
7 Piombino
8 Saluzzo

Possessions of Aragon      Dependencies of Patrimony of St Peter

Patrimony of St Peter      ◆ Peace of Lodi (1454)

**Italy after the Peace of Lodi (1454)**

preventing the USA from joining the **LEAGUE OF NA-TIONS** in 1920.

### Lodi, Peace of (1454)

The Capture of **CONSTANTINOPLE** in 1453 inspired the pope to act as peacemaker between the warring states of Italy, and the league formed at Lodi was to defend Italy against the Turkish threat. Its principal result was to define the spheres of influence of the dominant Italian powers: Venice, Milan, Florence, Naples and, more indirectly, the papacy. Although there remained overlaps and sources of friction, the treaty was more or less effective until the outbreak of the **ITALIAN WARS**.

### Lodi Dynasty

After the Timurid invasion in 1398, a new dynasty, the

Sayyid, arose in Delhi. A number of Afghan generals established themselves in Punjab, the most important of whom was Bahlul Lodi. He checked the growing power of the Khokhars, a fierce tribe which lived in Salt Ranges, and soon dominated the entire Punjab. Called in to help the ruler of Delhi against an impending attack by the ruler of **MALWA**, Bahlul Lodi stayed on. Before long, his men took over the control of Delhi. Bahlul formally crowned himself in 1451 when the ruler of Delhi died in exile. The Lodis dominated the upper Ganges Valley and Punjab from the mid-15c. As distinct from early Delhi rulers, who were Turks, the Lodis were Afghans. The most important of the Lodi Sultans was Sikandar Lodi (1489/1517), an efficient administrator who laid great emphasis on justice. During his reign all the highways of the empire

**Long March (Oct 1934–Oct 1935)**

were made safe from robbers and bandits. It was he who selected the site for the city of Agra in 1506, which in the course of time became the second capital of the Lodis. The Lodi Dynasty came to an end with the defeat of Ibrahim Lodi by **BABUR** at the Battle of **PANIPAT** (1526).

## Lok Dal

An agrarian-based Indian political party, started as the Bharatiya Lok Dal (BLD) in 1969 under the leadership of Charan **SINGH**. Its supporters belonged mainly to the so-called backward or middle-status peasant castes. The BLD merged into the Janata Party towards the end of the 'Emergency'. The Janata government collapsed in 1979 when the BLD re-emerged as the Lok Dal, ruling India briefly with Charan Singh as Prime Minister. Upon Charan Singh's death in 1987, the party split into two and his son, Ajit Singh, presided over one faction. The two factions merged into the **JANATA DAL**, which ruled briefly from 1989, but soon parted company in 1990 when the Janata Dal government fell. Both factions continue as minority parties.

## Lollards

A derisive term applied to the followers of the English theologian John **WYCLIFFE**. The movement, responsible for the translation of the Bible into the vernacular,

was suppressed; however, it continued among the enthusiastic but less literate of society, generally anticlerical in attitude, and in some ways anticipated the **REFORMATION** in England.

## Lombard League

A coalition of northern Italian cities, established in 1167 to assert their independence as communes (city-republics) confronting the German Emperor **FREDERICK I, BARBAROSSA**. The league, of which new versions were later formed, set a model for inter-city alliances, and underlined the rising political importance of urban communities in the medieval West.

## Lombardy-Venetia, Kingdom of

The title given to the Habsburg Kingdom in northern Italy established by the Vienna Settlement and administered as part of the Austrian Empire. Although ruled with a fair degree of efficiency, there were major anti-Austrian insurrections in the kingdom in 1848–9. Lombardy was lost by the Austrians to **VICTOR EMMANUEL II** of Piedmont after the war of 1859 and Venetia was acquired by the newly united Kingdom of Italy in 1866. ► **PLOMBIÈRES, AGREEMENT OF**; **REVOLUTIONS OF 1848–9**

## Lomé Convention

A series of agreements, named after the capital of Togo where the first Convention was signed, between the **EC** and a number of developing nations in Africa, the Caribbean and the Pacific (ACP). It came into force on 1 Apr 1976 and was intended to provide preferential trading arrangements for ACP countries within the Common Market, such as duty-free access for exports on a non-reciprocal basis. The Convention was renewed at five-year intervals from 1979 until it was replaced in 2000 by the Cotonou Agreement, which has a wider scope that includes human rights and governance issues.

**London, Treaties of** (1827, 1830, 1913 and 1915)
By the 1827 treaty, France, Britain and Russia agreed to work for Greek autonomy and to mediate between the rebels and the Ottoman Porte. By the 1830 treaty, the Great Powers agreed to Greek independence and established the boundaries of the new Greek kingdom. By the 1913 treaty at the end of the **BALKAN WARS**, it reduced Ottoman possessions in Europe to the area around Constantinople, while Crete was ceded to Greece and Bulgaria gained Adrianople. The 1915 treaty secured Italian entry into **WORLD WAR I** on the side of the Allies and promised the Italians the South Tyrol, Trentino, Gorizia, Gradisca, **TRIESTE**, **ISTRIA**, part of **DALMATIA**, Saseno and Vlorë in Albania, as well as continued possession of the Dodecanese Islands and a share in the Turkish and German colonies.

**London Convention** (1884)
A convention agreed between President Paul **KRUGER** and the British Government which revised the **PRETORIA CONVENTION** of 1881. The British secured the definition of the western border of the Transvaal which laid the way open to their annexation of Bechuanaland and the maintenance of the 'road to the north', while in exchange Kruger persuaded the British to reduce the republic's debt, remove the British resident from Pretoria, recognize the name 'South African Republic' and abolish the Queen's suzerainty except in respect of specific powers.

**Long, Huey Pierce** (1893–1935)
US politician. Flamboyant, astute and ambitious, he used the grievances of poor whites and his record as Public Service Commissioner to win the governorship of Louisiana, and then (1928–31) proceeded to build one of the most effective political machines in the history of US politics. His programme of extensive public spending on roads, educational institutions and hospitals not only reformed and developed Louisiana's public services, but also mitigated the impact of the Depression upon the state. Although a ruthless manipulator of the state legislature and judiciary, Long refused to use race as a political issue. Aiming at a national audience, he developed the 'Share Our Wealth' plan for income redistribution. A Democratic US Senator from 1931, by 1935 he claimed to have a following of 7.5 million for the plan. Initially supportive of the **NEW DEAL** and President Franklin D **ROOSEVELT**, he became a vehement critic of the President and planned to run against him as a third-party candidate in 1936. However, he was widely feared and reviled as a potential dictator, and was assassinated in Sep 1935.

**Long March** (1934–5)
The long trek in China, covering over 5,000 mi/

8,050 km, made by approximately 100,000 communists under **MAO ZEDONG** to reach their base in Shaanxi from the **JIANGXI SOVIET**, which had been encircled by nationalist government troops.

**Long Parliament**
An English parliament called (Nov 1640) by **CHARLES I** after his defeat by the Scots in the second of the **BISHOPS' WARS**. It was legally in being 1640–60, but did not meet continuously. It attacked prerogative rights and alleged abuses of power by the King and his ministers, and abolished the Court of **STAR CHAMBER**, the Councils of the North and for Wales, and the Ecclesiastical Court of High Commission (1641), the bishops and the Court of Wards (1646), and the monarchy and the House of **LORDS** (1649). Moderates were eliminated in **PRIDE**'s Purge (Dec 1648), and the remaining **RUMP PARLIAMENT** was dismissed by **CROMWELL** in 1653. The Rump was recalled in the death-throes of the **PROTECTORATE** (May 1659), and all members in Dec 1659.

**Longueville, Anne, Duchess of** (1619–79)
French noblewoman. Known as the 'soul of the **FRONDE**', she exerted a considerable influence on politics, in which she first began to interest herself as the mistress of the Duke of **LA ROCHEFOUCAULD**. In the first war of the Fronde (1648) she sought in vain to win over her brother, 'the Great Condé'. In the second she won over both him and **TURENNE**. After the death of her husband and her desertion by La Rochefoucauld, she entered a convent but continued to have influence at court. ► **CONDÉ, LOUIS II OF BOURBON, PRINCE OF**

**Lopes, Francisco Higinio Craveiro** (1894–1964)
Portuguese politician. Born into a distinguished military family, Lopes was educated at the Military School in Lisbon and fought in the expeditionary force in Mozambique in **WORLD WAR I**. As a full colonel, in 1942 he entered negotiations for cooperation with the Allies and was responsible for the modernization of the Portuguese air force. In 1944 he entered parliament, in 1949 was promoted to general, and was President of Portugal from 1951 to 1958.

**López, Carlos Antonio** (1790–1862)
Paraguayan dictator. He was President of Paraguay (1844–62) and although his regime was authoritarian and corrupt, he improved the internal structure of the country by building roads and railways, and by revamping the judicial system and the army. He also created government monopolies to bolster the economy. In foreign affairs he ended the isolation of the country but became involved in disputes with the USA and UK, and with the Argentine civil war of 1845–6, when Argentina refused to recognize Paraguay's independence.

**López, Francisco Solano** (1826–70)
Paraguayan dictator. He was the son of Carlos Antonio **LÓPEZ**, the dictator of Paraguay from 1844 to 1862. On his father's death, he succeeded him in power, leading his country into internecine war with Brazil, Argentina and Uruguay. He himself died in action at Cerro Corá, Paraguay, in the last battle of the War of the **TRIPLE ALLIANCE**.

**López Rodó, Laureano** (1920–2000)
Spanish politician, academic and lawyer. He was the most influential **OPUS DEI** technocrat to serve in a **FRANCO** government. As Secretary-General of the Presidency and Commissar of the Plan of Development, he formed part of the Opus Dei group which undertook the economic modernization of Spain from the late 1950s onwards. An intimate ally of Admiral **CARRERO BLANCO**, he became one of Franco's closest associates, being the dominant minister in the cabinet from 1965 to 1973. He was also Minister of Foreign Affairs (1973–4) and Ambassador to Austria (1974–7). He played an important role in persuading Franco to accept the candidacy of **JUAN CARLOS I** as heir to the throne. After Franco's death, he joined the *Alianza Popular* on its foundation in 1976, being elected as a deputy for Barcelona in 1977. He left the party in 1979.

**Lords, House of**
The non-elected house of the UK legislature. Traditionally, its membership has included hereditary peers and life peers (including judicial members, the *Lords of Appeal in Ordinary*); also the two archbishops and certain bishops of the Church of England. The House can no longer veto, though it can delay, bills passed by the House of **COMMONS**, with the exception of a bill to prolong the duration of a parliament. Its functions are mainly deliberative, its authority based on the expertise of its membership. The House of Lords also constitutes the most senior court in the UK. Appeals heard by the House are confined to matters of law and dealt with by the Lords of Appeal in Ordinary. Under the Labour government of Tony **BLAIR**, the House faced sweeping but vague plans for reform in 1999, beginning with the abolition of the hereditary peers' right to vote. The proposal was temporarily modified to allow a minority of hereditary peers to continue to vote for a period, but it became clear that the central problem was government reluctance to accept a genuinely rationalized second chamber which might use its powers vigorously as the result of an electoral mandate.

**Loris-Melikov, Mikhail Tariyelovich** (1825–88)
Russian general and political reformer. Having made a name for himself during the Russo-Turkish War of 1877–8, he was appointed in 1880 to head a supreme commission to suppress revolution and advise on its causes. He came up with a proposal for limited representative participation in government. **ALEXANDER II** was examining this favourably when he was assassinated in 1881. On the conservative intervention of Konstantin **POBEDONOSTSEV, ALEXANDER III** rejected the idea (which did not surface again until 1905), and so Loris-Melikov resigned. ➤ **RUSSO-TURKISH WARS**

**Lothair III, of Supplinburg** (c.1075–1137)
German King (1125/37) and Holy Roman Emperor (1133/7). He succeeded to extensive lands in Saxony and was involved in an uprising against **HENRY IV** in 1088. His marriage to the heiress Richenza (1110) made him the most powerful noble in Germany. As a reward for supporting **HENRY V** against Henry IV, he was made Duke of Saxony (1106) but he was soon involved in revolts against the King (1112–15). He was elected King on Henry's death (1125) and his reign was dominated by a long struggle against

Frederick and Conrad Hohenstaufen, which was finally resolved at the Diet of Bamberg (1135). ➤ **CONRAD III**

**Louis I, the Great** (1326–82)
King of Hungary (1342/82) and Poland (1370/82). He succeeded his father, **CHARLES ROBERT**, as King of Poland in 1342 and until 1356 his reign was mostly devoted to campaigns against Queen Johanna of Naples, who was implicated in the murder (1344) of her husband Andrew, Louis's younger brother. Louis's ultimate lack of success in Italy was compensated for by the conquest of **DALMATIA** (including the port of Dubrovnik) from Venice, recognized in the Peace of Zara (1358); and in 1370 he became King of Poland on the death of Casimir III. A notable patron of the arts, Louis founded the first Hungarian university at Pécs in 1367.

**Louis IV, the Bavarian** (c.1283–1347)
Holy Roman Emperor (1328/47), a younger son of Louis, Duke of Upper Bavaria. He was elected King of Germany in 1314, opposed by a rival candidate, Frederick II, Duke of Austria, whom he eventually defeated in battle at Mühldorf (1322). Pope **JOHN XXII**, however, refused to recognize his title, referring to him only as 'Louis the Bavarian', a name which stuck. In 1328 he received the imperial crown from the people of Rome, but was forced to leave Italy the next year. Thereafter, Louis remained mostly in Germany, maintaining his position against internal opposition with the financial support of the cities. He waged a war of propaganda against the papacy with the help of Marsilius of Padua, William of **OCKHAM**, and the Spiritual Franciscans; he invaded Italy (1327–30), captured Rome and set up an anti-pope, Nicholas V (1328/30), in opposition to Pope John. In 1338, at the Diet of Rense, the electoral princes precipitated a Church/State division by declaring that the Emperor did not require papal confirmation of his election. His energetic policy of family aggrandizement, however, cost him his alliance with the House of Luxembourg, who raised up a rival emperor, **CHARLES IV**, a year before Louis met his death while hunting.

**Louis VI, the Fat** (1081–1137)
King of France (1108/37). He succeeded his father **PHILIP I** in 1108. Despite an inclination to gluttony and a corpulence which left him unable to mount a horse after the age of 46, he was one of the most active of the House of Capet, and greatly increased the power and prestige of the monarchy. ➤ **CAPETIAN DYNASTY**

**Louis VII** (c.1120–1180)
King of France (1137/80). The second son of **LOUIS VI, THE FAT**, in 1137 he became King, married Eleanor, heiress of Aquitaine, and continued the consolidation of royal authority begun by his father. The marriage was annulled in 1152, whereupon Eleanor married Henry Plantagenet, Count of Anjou, who became King of England in 1154 as **HENRY II**. Faced with a vast agglomeration of power on both sides of the Channel, Louis succeeded in staving off the Angevin threat, enlisting the aid of the papacy and fomenting discord within Henry's family. ➤ **ANGEVINS**; **ELEANOR OF AQUITAINE**

**Louis VIII, the Lion** (1187–1226)
King of France (1223/6). The son of **PHILIP II** and

Isabella of Hainaut, his short reign was marked chiefly by his acquisition of the Montfort claim to the County of Toulouse (1224) and the resumption of the Albigensian Crusade in the south in 1226. This led to the submission of Count Raymond VII to his widow, Blanche of Castile (1229), and the eventual absorption of all Languedoc into the royal domain. ► ALBIGENSES; CRUSADES, LATER

**Louis IX, St** (1214–70)
King of France (1226/70). He was the son of LOUIS VIII, THE LION. By his victories he compelled HENRY III of England to acknowledge French suzerainty in GUYENNE (1259). He led the Seventh Crusade (1248), but was defeated in Egypt, taken prisoner, and ransomed. He embarked on a new, eighth, crusade in 1270, but died of plague at Tunis. He was canonized in 1297.

**Louis X, the Quarrelsome** (1289–1316)
King of Navarre (1305/16) and of France (1314/16). The son of PHILIP IV, THE FAIR, during his brief reign, which was marked by unrest among his barons, he was guided in his policy by his uncle CHARLES OF VALOIS.

**Louis XI** (1423–83)
King of France (1461/83). The eldest son of CHARLES VII, THE VICTORIOUS, he made several unsuccessful attempts against his father's throne, and had to flee to Dauphiné. His severe measures as king led to a coalition against him (1465), which he survived. During his reign he added to his lands, defeated CHARLES THE BOLD, Duke of Burgundy (1477), and actively encouraged trade and industry.

**Louis XII** (1462–1515)
King of France (1498/1515). He was the son of Charles, Duke of Orléans, to whose title he succeeded in 1465. He commanded the French troops at Asti during CHARLES VIII's invasion of Italy (1494–5) before succeeding him to the French throne (1498) and marrying the King's widow, ANNE OF BRITTANY. His forces were driven from Italy (1512) and then defeated by an Anglo-Imperial alliance at the Battle of Guinegate (1513). To guarantee peace, Louis married Mary Tudor, sister of HENRY VIII (1514), but died shortly afterwards. ► TUDOR, HOUSE OF

**Louis XIII** (1601–43)
King of France (1610/43). The eldest son of HENRY IV and MARIE DE MÉDICI, he succeeded to the throne on the assassination of his father (1610). He was, however, excluded from power, even after he came of age (1614), by the Queen Regent. In 1617 Louis took over the reins of government, and exiled Marie de Médici to Blois (1619–20). By 1624 he was entirely dependent upon the political acumen of RICHELIEU, who became his Chief Minister. Louis's later years were enhanced by French military victories in the THIRTY YEARS' WAR against the Habsburgs. ► HABSBURG DYNASTY; HUGUENOTS

**Louis XIV**, also known as **the Great** and **the Sun King** (1638–1715)
King of France (1643/1715). He was the son of LOUIS XIII, whom he succeeded. During his minority (1643–51) France was ruled by his mother, ANNE OF AUSTRIA, and her Chief Minister, Cardinal MAZARIN. In 1660 Louis married the Infanta Maria Theresa,

elder daughter of PHILIP IV of Spain, through whom he was later to claim the Spanish succession for his second grandson. In 1661 he assumed sole responsibility for government, advised by various royal councils. His obsession with France's greatness led him into aggressive foreign and commercial policies, particularly against the Dutch. His patronage of the Catholic Stuarts also led to the hostility of England after 1689; but his major political rivals were the Austrian Habsburgs, particularly LEOPOLD I. From 1665 Louis tried to take possession of the Spanish Netherlands, but later became obsessed with the acquisition of the whole Spanish inheritance. His attempt to create a Franco-Spanish Bourbon bloc led to the formation of the Grand Alliance of England, the United Provinces, and the Habsburg Empire, and resulted in the War of the SPANISH SUCCESSION. In his later years Louis was beset by other problems. His determination to preserve the unity of the French state and the independence of the French Church led him into conflict with the Jansenists, the HUGUENOTS and the papacy, with damaging repercussions. His old age was overshadowed by military disaster and the financial ravages of prolonged warfare. Yet Louis was the greatest monarch of his age, who established the parameters of successful absolutism. In addition, his long reign marked the cultural ascendancy of France within Europe, symbolized by the Palace of Versailles, where he died, to be succeeded by his great-grandson as LOUIS XV. ► BOURBON, HOUSE OF; COLBERT, JEAN BAPTISTE; FOUQUET, NICOLAS; FRONDE, THE; HABSBURG DYNASTY; JANSENISM; STUART, HOUSE OF

**Louis XV**, known as **the Well-Beloved** (1710–74)
King of France (1715/74). He was the son of Louis, Duc de Bourgogne and Marie-Adelaide of Savoy, and the great-grandson of LOUIS XIV, whom he succeeded. Until he came of age (1723), he was guided by the Regent, Philippe d'Orléans, and then by the Duc de Bourbon, who negotiated a marriage alliance with Maria Leczczynska, daughter of the deposed King Stanisław I of Poland. In 1726 Bourbon was replaced by the King's former tutor, the elderly FLEURY, who skilfully steered the French state (État français) until his death (1744). Thereafter, Louis vowed to rule without a First Minister, but allowed the government to drift into the hands of ministerial factions, while indulging in secret diplomatic activity, distinct from official policy, through his own network of agents. This system (le secret du roi) brought confusion to French foreign policy in the years preceding the Diplomatic Revolution (1748–56), and obscured the country's interests overseas. Instead, France was drawn into a trio of continental wars during Louis's reign, which culminated in the loss of the French colonies in America and India (1763). Among innumerable mistresses, the two who were most famous and influential were the Countess du BARRY and Madame de POMPADOUR. In 1771 Louis tried to introduce reforms, but these came too late to staunch the decline in royal authority. He was succeeded by his grandson, LOUIS XVI. ► AUSTRIAN SUCCESSION, WAR OF THE; SAVOY, HOUSE OF; SEVEN YEARS' WAR

**Louis XVI** (1754–93)
King of France (1774/93). He was the third son of the

DAUPHIN Louis and Maria Josepha of Saxony, and the grandson of **LOUIS XV**, whom he succeeded in 1774. He was married in 1770 to the Archduchess **MARIE ANTOINETTE**, daughter of the Habsburg empress **MARIA THERESA**, to strengthen the Franco-Austrian alliance. He failed to give consistent support to ministers who tried to reform the outmoded financial and social structures of the country, such as **TURGOT** (1774–6) and **NECKER** (1776–81). He allowed France to become involved in the **AMERICAN REVOLUTION** (1778–83), which exacerbated the national debt. To avert the deepening social and economic crisis, he agreed in 1789 to summon the **ESTATES GENERAL**. However, encouraged by the Queen, he resisted demands from the National Assembly for sweeping reforms, and in Oct was taken with his family from Versailles to Paris as hostages to the revolutionary movement. Their attempted flight to Varennes (Jun 1791) branded the royal pair as traitors. Louis reluctantly approved the new constitution (Sep 1791), but his moral authority had collapsed. In Aug an insurrection suspended Louis's constitutional position, and in Sep the monarchy was abolished. He was tried before the National **CONVENTION** for conspiracy with foreign powers, and was guillotined in Paris. ► **FRENCH REVOLUTION**

## Louis (Charles) XVII (1785–95)
Titular King of France (1793/5). He was the second son of **LOUIS XVI** and heir to the throne from June 1789. After the execution of his father (Jan 1793), he remained in the Temple prison in Paris. His death there dealt a blow to the hopes of royalists and constitutional monarchists. The secrecy surrounding his last months led to rumours of his escape, and produced several claimants to his title. ► **FRENCH REVOLUTION**

## Louis XVIII, in full Louis Stanislas Xavier, Count of Provence (1755–1824)
King of France, in name (1795/1824) and in fact (1814/24). The younger brother of **LOUIS XVI**, he fled from Paris (June 1791), finally taking refuge in England, and becoming the focal point for the royalist cause. On **NAPOLEON I**'s downfall (1814) he re-entered Paris, and made promise of a Constitutional Charter. His restoration was interrupted by Napoleon's return from Elba, but after the Battle of **WATERLOO** (1815) he again regained his throne. His reign was marked by the introduction of parliamentary government with a limited franchise. The system of constitutional monarchy practised in France under the Restoration, a system in which the King was more than a mere figurehead ('the King governs as well as reigns'), was defended by François **GUIZOT** and the *Doctrinaires*. ► **FRENCH REVOLUTION**

## Louisbourg, formerly spelled Louisburg
A town on the east coast of Cape Breton Island in Nova Scotia, Canada, which was founded by the French in 1713 and where a fortress of the same name, built in 1720, became one of France's chief North American strongholds. In 1745, when Britain was fighting France in the War of the **AUSTRIAN SUCCESSION**, it was successfully besieged by a force from New England led by Sir William Pepperell. The Treaty of Aix-la-Chapelle restored it to France in 1748. During the **SEVEN YEARS' WAR**, the fortress was besieged

in 1758 by a British force led by Jeffrey **AMHERST**, and its defeat, as the last French stronghold in **ACADIA**, enabled Britain to attack Quebec the following year using Louisbourg as a base. The fortifications were destroyed in 1760.

## Louisiana Purchase (1803)
The sale by France to the USA of an area between the Mississippi River and the Rocky Mountains for US$15 million. The purchase gave the USA full control of the Mississippi Valley.

## Louis Napoleon (1778–1846)
King of Holland (1806/10). He was the younger brother of the French Emperor **NAPOLEON I**. A marriage was arranged in 1802 between him and **HORTENSE** de Beauharnais, and in 1808 the future Emperor **NAPOLEON III** was born, although there is some doubt about his father's identity. In 1806 Napoleon I put his brother on the throne of the Kingdom of Holland (present-day Netherlands), intending to make it a satellite state of France. Louis Napoleon, however, took his kingship seriously, learned the Dutch language, and was generally well-liked by his new subjects, often defending them against the demands of the French; for this he was dethroned by his brother in 1810, who annexed the Netherlands to France. Louis left for England, where he wrote an apology for his reign in Holland.

## Louis Napoleon ► NAPOLEON III

## Louis of Male (1330–84)
Count of Flanders, Nevers and Rethel. The son of **LOUIS OF NEVERS**, he became Count of Flanders in 1346. In 1357 he also became Duke of **BRABANT** through his wife Margaret's family. He expanded his County with Walloon Flanders (1369), and also inherited Artois and Franche-Comté through his mother. Internationally he tried to remain neutral, and to keep the trading connection open with England; in Flanders he tried to limit the growing power of the industrial towns, which brought him into conflict with Philip van **ARTEVELDE**, who defeated him at Beverhoutsveld in 1382.

## Louis of Nassau (1538–74)
German nobleman. A younger brother of **WILLIAM I**, Prince of Orange (and of **JOHN VI**, Count of Nassau), he played a significant role in the early years of the **EIGHTY YEARS' WAR** in support of his brother William and the Dutch against Spain. He led a military expedition from Germany into Groningen in 1568, and was active in the Huguenot struggles against France, where he abandoned Lutheranism for Calvinism. In 1572 he captured Mons from the Spanish (though it was lost again the same year), and died in the Battle of Mokerheide.

## Louis of Nevers (c.1304–1346)
Count of Flanders, Nevers and Rethel. He was brought up at the French court, married Margaret, daughter of the French King **PHILIP V**, and supported France heavily when he became Count in 1322. This meant cutting off Flanders from England (and English wool) in the **HUNDRED YEARS' WAR**, which, together with heavy taxation, caused a general revolt in Flanders led by Jacob van **ARTEVELDE**. Louis left his county to fight for the French against England,

and died in the Battle of **CRÉCY**. His successor was his son, **LOUIS OF MALE**.

## Louis-Philippe (1773–1850)
King of the French (1830/48). Known as the 'Citizen King', he was the eldest son of Louis Philippe Joseph, Duke of **ORLÉANS** (Philippe Égalité). At the **FRENCH REVOLUTION** he entered the **NATIONAL GUARD**, and with his father renounced his titles to demonstrate his progressive sympathies. He joined the Jacobin Club (1790), and fought in the Army of the North before deserting to the Austrians (1793). He lived in exile and married Marie Amélie, daughter of **FERDI-NAND I** of the **TWO SICILIES**. He returned to France (1814), but fled to England again in the **HUNDRED DAYS**. On the eve of **CHARLES X**'s abdication (1830) he ruled with the title of King of the French. He strengthened his power by steering a middle course with the help of the upper bourgeoisie; but political corruption and industrial and agrarian depression (1846) caused discontent, and united the radicals in a cry for electoral reform. The dominant figure in his governments from 1840 to 1848 was François **GUIZOT**. When the Paris mob rose (1848), he abdicated, and escaped to England with Guizot. ► **BOURBON, HOUSE OF**; **FEBRUARY REVOLUTION** (France); **JACOBINS**; **JULY REVOLUTION**

## Louvois, François Michel le Tellier, Marquis of (1641–91)
French politician. The son of Michel **LE TELLIER**, he was Secretary of State for War under **LOUIS XIV**. He reformed and strengthened the army, and was recognized as a brilliant administrator and the King's most influential minister in the years 1683–91. ► **NANTES, EDICT OF**

## Lovisa Ulrika (1720–82)
Queen of Sweden. Born in Berlin, she was the daughter of **KING FREDERICK WILLIAM I** of Prussia and the sister of **FREDERICK II, THE GREAT**. In 1744 she married **ADOLF FREDERICK**, heir to the Swedish throne. After her husband came to the throne in 1751, she worked tirelessly to increase royal power and formed a Court Party in the Diet to struggle for this. She saw her dreams realized after the accession of her son, **GUSTAV III**, in 1771, but relations between them cooled and they were reconciled only just before her death.

## Lowell, Francis Cabot (1775–1817)
US industrialist and founder of the cotton industry. Based on his observations of textile mills in England, he established and built (with the help of mechanical designer Paul Moody) a cotton spinning and weaving mill, in Waltham, Massachusetts, which was the first factory in the world to process raw cotton and manufacture it into cloth. Lowell, Massachusetts, is named after him.

## Loyalists
Colonial Americans who remained loyal to Britain during the **AMERICAN REVOLUTION**. Britain defined the term carefully, since loyalists were eligible for compensation. It was not enough to have been born or been living in the American colonies at the onset of revolution; it was necessary to have served the British cause in some substantial manner and to have left the USA before or soon after the termination of hostili-

ties. During the revolution special corps were established for over 19,000 loyalist troops. Half of the 80,000–100,000 refugees went to Canada, especially to the Maritime Provinces, and their presence contributed to the creation of Upper **CANADA** in 1791. Their influence was not insubstantial in the establishment of governmental, social, educational and religious institutions. In 1789 Lord Dorchester ordained that both they and their children were entitled to add the letters 'UE' after their names, indicating their belief in the Unity of Empire. They then became known as the United Empire Loyalists. ► **CARLETON, GUY, 1ST BARON DORCHESTER**; **UNITED EMPIRE LOYALIST**

## Loyola, Ignatius de, properly Iñigo López de Recalde (1491 or 1495–1556)
Spanish theologian and founder of the Jesuits. He became a soldier, was wounded, and while convalescing read the lives of Christ and the saints. In 1522 he went on a pilgrimage to Jerusalem, studied in Alcalá, Salamanca and Paris, and in 1534 founded with six associates the Society of Jesus. Ordained in 1537, he went to Rome in 1539, where the new order was approved by the pope. The author of the influential *Spiritual Exercises*, he was canonized in 1622.

## Lozi State
A state formed by a cluster of Bantu-speaking agricultural and cattle-herding people of western Zambia, living in the flood-plain of the upper Zambesi. It was penetrated by hunters, traders and missionaries in the late 19c and, under King Lewanika, peacefully accepted colonial rule. During the colonial period, the state was known as Barotseland and was controlled by **INDIRECT RULE**, so that their kingship and distinctive institutions survived.

## LTTE (Liberation Tigers of Tamil Eelam)
Also known as the 'Tigers' or the 'Tamil Tigers', the Sri Lankan secessionist group which has been fighting to establish a separate **TAMIL** state (**EELAM**) in the north and east of the country. The group was founded in Jaffna in the mid-1970s and gradually grew in size and effectiveness, particularly after the anti-Tamil violence of the early 1980s. A reluctant partner to the **INDO-SRI LANKAN PEACE ACCORD** overseen by Rajiv **GANDHI**, it soon found itself fighting the Indian Peace-keeping Force (IPKF) and it was widely believed to have been responsible for Gandhi's assassination in Tamil Nadu in 1991. The violent civil war between the LTTE rebels and the government forces claimed thousands of military and civilian lives throughout the 1990s. Peace talks between the LTTE and the government began in 2002 but stalled in 2003 and violence has resumed, although on a lesser scale than before.

## Luba-Lunda Kingdoms
A succession of African states occupying territory in what is now the Democratic Republic of Congo. They were powerful by the 17c, involved in slave and ivory trading with the Portuguese and later with Zanzibar. The Luba states were relatively unstable, but the Lunda Empire seems to have consolidated its power through trade. The central Lunda state did not survive the ending of the Angolan slave trade in the 1840s, and the others fell to European imperialism.

**Lubbers, Ruud (Rudolf Franz Marie)** (1939– )
Dutch politician. After graduating from Erasmus
University, Rotterdam, he joined the family engineering business of Lubbers Hollandia. He made rapid
progress after entering politics, becoming Minister
of Economic Affairs in 1973 and, in 1982, at the age
of 43, Prime Minister, leading a **CHRISTIAN DEMO-
CRATIC APPEAL** (CDA) coalition. He remained in office until 1994. In 2001 he became **UN** High
Commissioner for Refugees.

**Lublin, Union of** (1569)
An Act uniting Poland and the Grand Duchy of
Lithuania. The Union, separately confirmed by the
Polish and Lithuanian assemblies (*sejms*), completed
the formal unification of the two states begun in the
14c. It established a common political system and
currency, and a commonwealth headed by a king
jointly elected by the Polish and Lithuanian aristocracy. This greatly enlarged Poland and brought
it increasingly into conflict with an expanding
Russia.

**Lucknow, Siege of** (1857–8)
The siege of the Lucknow garrison began on 1 July
1857. On 25 Sep, Henry Havelock's forces broke
through the siege and reinforced the garrison. Additional British forces under Sir Colin Campbell broke
through on 18 Nov, and women, children, the sick
and the wounded were removed to safety. Two days
later Havelock died and Campbell left for Kanpur.
During Campbell's absence, Tantia Tope attacked the
garrison, forcing Campbell to return to Lucknow.
Campbell defeated Tantia on 6 Dec and went to Kanpur from where he returned with a large army on 28
Feb 1858 and succeeded in repossessing Lucknow
for the British on 21 Mar. ► **INDIAN UPRISING**

**Luddites**
The name given to the group of workers who destroyed newly introduced textile machinery in Nottingham, Yorkshire, and Lancashire (1811–12). Their
fear was that the output of the equipment was so
much faster than the output of a hand loom operator
that many jobs would be lost. Known as 'the Ludds',
after their leader, Ned Ludd, the movement ended
with a mass trial in York in 1813 when many were
hanged or transported to Australia. The term has
since been used to describe any resistance to technological innovation.

**Ludendorff, Erich** (1865–1937)
German general. He and **HINDENBURG** defeated the
Russians at the Battle of Tannenberg (1914). In 1916
he became Chief of Staff under Hindenburg and con-
ducted the 1918 spring offensives on the Western
Front. In 1923 he was a leader in the unsuccessful
**HITLER** putsch at Munich, but was acquitted of
treason. He became involved with the **NAZI PARTY**,
but from 1925 led a minority party of his own. ►
**WORLD WAR I**

**Ludwig I** (1786–1868)
King of Bavaria (1825/48). His lavish expenditure on
pictures, public buildings and favourites, and by
taxes and reactionary policy, provoked active discontent in 1830, and again in 1848, when he abdicated in
favour of his son, Maximilian II.

**Ludwig II** (1845–86)
King of Bavaria (1864/86). The son of Maximilian II,
on his accession he devoted himself to patronage of
Wagner and his music. In the 1870–1 **FRANCO-
PRUSSIAN WAR** he threw Bavaria on the side of **PRUSSIA**,
and offered the imperial crown to **WILLIAM I**, though
he took no part in the war, and lived the life of a recluse. He was almost constantly at feud with his ministers and family, mainly on account of his insensate
outlays on superfluous palaces, and was declared insane in 1886. A few days later he was found drowned,
with his physician, in the Starnberger Lake near his
castle of Berg. It is not known whether his death was
suicide, murder, or simply accidental.

**Ludwig Wilhelm I** (d.1709)
Margrave of Baden. The Imperial general at the Battle
of Heilbronn (1693), he commanded Imperial troops
against the French in the War of the **SPANISH SUCCES-
SION**.

**Luftwaffe**
The correct name for the German air force, re-
established in 1935 under **GOERING**, in contravention of the Treaty of **VERSAILLES**. Dominant in the
early years of German victory in **WORLD WAR II**, the
*Luftwaffe* suffered production shortfalls and poor
central leadership which led to defeat in the Battle of
**BRITAIN**. It had all but ceased to exist by 1945, having
lost some 100,000 aircraft. The Federal Republic of
Germany's air force, also known as the Luftwaffe,
was re-established in 1956, and today is a critical
element in **NATO**, operating over 300 combat aircraft.
► **BRITAIN, BATTLE OF**

**Lugard, Frederick John Dealtry Lugard, 1st Baron**
(1858–1945)
British soldier and colonial administrator. In 1878 he
was commissioned as an army officer, serving in the
Sudan against **MOHAMMED AHMED**, the **MAHDI**
(1885), and in Burma (now Myanmar) after the fall
of King Thibaw (1886), and commanded an expedition against slavers in Nyasaland (1888). His activities in rough-and-ready Uganda peacekeeping led
to its being made a British protectorate in 1894. Appointed Commissioner in the Nigerian hinterland by
Joseph **CHAMBERLAIN** (1897), he kept a French challenge at bay and kept the peace. Britain having declared a protectorate over Northern and Southern
Nigeria, Lugard was high commissioner for the North
(1900–7), and established administrative paternalistic control with minimal force. He was Governor of
Hong Kong from 1907, helping to establish its University in 1911. He returned to Nigeria as Governor
of the two protectorates, becoming Governor-
General (1914–19) on their amalgamation. His principle was one of use of existing tribal institutions as
the infrastructure for British rule.

**Lukács, György** (1885–1971)
Hungarian Marxist philosopher, critic and politician.
From a wealthy Jewish family, he studied in Budapest,
Berlin and Heidelberg. He published two important
early works of literary criticism, *Soul and Form*
(1910) and *The Theory of the Novel* (1916). In 1918 he
joined the Hungarian Communist Party, but after the
defeat of the uprising in 1919 he lived abroad in Vienna (1919–29) and Moscow (1930–44). He returned to

Hungary after **WORLD WAR II** as professor at Budapest; he came in for political criticism in the early 1950s and, more or less inevitably, joined **NAGY**'s short-lived revolutionary government in 1956 as Minister of Culture. After the Russian suppression he was briefly deported and interned but returned to Budapest in 1957. His major book on **MARXISM**, *History and Class Consciousness* (1923), was repudiated as heretical by the Russian Communist Party and in the 1950s, in abject public confession, by Lukács himself. His situation and influence grew in the 1960s as his works were published.

**Lukashenka, Alyaksandr** (1954–)
Belarusian politician. After service in the Soviet Army, he became manager of a collective farm. In 1990, he was elected to the Belarusian parliament where he was noted for hardline authoritarian views, including opposition to the **USSR**'s dissolution, and attacks on corruption and the privileges of Soviet **NOMENKLATURA**. In 1994 he won the first democratic presidential election, promising uncorrupt government and greater integration between Russia and Belarus, while opposing privatization and market reforms. Lack of economic reform led the **WORLD BANK** and **IMF** to suspend lending to Belarus in 1995 and caused domestic unrest. A threat to impeach him prompted him to call a referendum in 1996 to extend his term to seven years, following which he disbanded parliament. He has become increasingly dictatorial and has been accused of human rights abuses. In 1998 he blamed foreign governments for an economic crisis that halved the value of the rouble and expelled seven ambassadors. He claimed a landslide victory in the 2001 presidential election, described by international observers as 'failing to meet international standards'.

**Lukyanov, Anatoli Ivanovich** (1930–)
Soviet lawyer, bureaucrat and political conspirator. Born in Smolensk and educated in Moscow, he held a series of legal positions within the Soviet and the party. A moderate reformer, he began to rise very quickly first with Yuri **ANDROPOV** and then with Mikhail **GORBACHEV**. In 1989 he was elected deputy chairman under Gorbachev's chairmanship of the new Supreme Soviet, and in 1990, when Gorbachev was elevated to the presidency, Luykanov became chairman. In 1991 it was to save his vision of the USSR that he participated in the **AUGUST COUP** to oust Gorbachev; but he achieved quite the opposite of what he wanted and landed in prison.

**Lula**, properly **Luis Inácio Lula da Silva** (1944–)
Brazilian labour leader and politician. He came to national prominence as leader of the Metalworker's Union of São Bernardo, a São Paulo industrial zone housing key industries, especially in motor vehicles. Forced by the military regime's labour legislation to concentrate on local issues, Lula led strikes in the Saab–Scania plant in May 1978 and 1979 involving 500,000 workers and making the employers concede higher wages through direct negotiations rather than via government-led labour courts. In Oct 1979 he founded the PT (*Partido dos Trabalhadores*), to achieve representation for workers in Congress; it has drawn support from a range of traditional radical movements and the left wing of the Church. Elected to

Congress in 1986, he was unsuccessful in the 1989 presidential race, but won the presidential election in 2002.

**Lumey, William of** (c.1542–1578)
Nobleman from the southern Netherlands and a leader of the Dutch Revolt against Spain. A great-grandson of **GUILLAUME DE LA MARK**, he was active in opposition to the town authorities at an early age. In the **EIGHTY YEARS' WAR** he joined the revolt against Spain, and became admiral of the Sea-**BEGGARS**, leading the attack on the port of Brielle in Apr 1572. However, **WILLIAM I, THE SILENT** considered his violent persecution of Catholics a liability and had him imprisoned in 1573; in 1574 he left for Germany.

**Lumumba, Patrice Hemery** (1925–61)
Congolese politician. Educated at mission schools, both Catholic and Protestant, he was a post office clerk and then director of a brewery. He helped form the *Mouvement National Congolais* in 1958 to challenge Belgian rule and, when the Congo was granted independence, he was made its first Prime Minister (1960). A major symbolic figure in the African history of the period, he sought a unified Congo and opposed the secession of **KATANGA** under Moïse **TSHOMBE**. He was arrested by his own army in Sep 1960, handed over to the Katangese and murdered. His name, however, remains significant as the embodiment of African nationalism and the opponent of Balkanization manipulated by ex-colonial countries and their allies.

**Lunacharsky, Anatoli Vasilevich** (1875–1933)
Russian philosopher and revolutionary. As a student and writer he dabbled in **MARXISM**. He was imprisoned several times for his political activities and spent much time associating with émigrés in Western Europe. In 1917 he offered his services to **LENIN** who made him in effect the Minister of Education, a function he performed none too well until 1929 when he took up a somewhat similar party post. He died on his way to becoming ambassador to Spain, and was perhaps fortunate not to have had to face the purges of the 1930s.

**Lundy's Lane, Battle of** (1814)
The only Canadian engagement in the **WAR OF 1812** which was not simply a skirmish. Casualties were high on both sides, with the Americans suffering more fatalities. The Americans retreated and were unable to continue their campaign in the Niagara district.

**Luns, Joseph Marie Antoine Hubert** (1911–2002)
Dutch politician. After studying law, he joined the Dutch diplomatic service (1940–52). In 1952 he became Minister without Portfolio for the Dutch **CATHOLIC PEOPLE'S PARTY**, and from then on was inextricably bound up with Dutch foreign affairs. For the whole of the period 1957–71 he was Foreign Minister, and from 1971 to 1984 he was Secretary-General of **NATO**. He was integrally involved in the formation and consolidation of the **EC**, and was a central figure in international relations during the days of the **COLD WAR**.

**Lupescu, Magda**, originally **Magda Wolff** (1902–77)
Mistress and second wife of King **CHARLES II** of Romania. Her Jewish descent as much as her dissolute

behaviour earned her the disapproval of Romanian society, itself notorious for its profligacy. Because of the scandal surrounding their affair, Charles renounced his claim to the throne and when he returned to Romania in 1930 it was on condition that she remain abroad. When she also returned and took up residence in the palace, the Prime Minister, Iuliu **MANIU**, resigned. Upon her marriage in 1947 to Charles, she took the name Princess Elena and lived in exile with the former king.

### Lusitania, Sinking of the (May 1915)

A Cunard passenger liner torpedoed by a German submarine off the Irish coast while in transit from New York to Liverpool, with 128 Americans among those lost. The German government had announced (Feb 1915) that any passenger ship caught within a designated war zone around the British Isles would be sunk without warning. President Woodrow **WILSON** declared he would hold Germany accountable for such deaths in the future. Although the German authorities argued that the *Lusitania* was carrying war munitions for the Allies, they did eventually make **REPARATIONS**. However, any US sympathy toward Germany up to this point disappeared, and many called for a declaration of war.

### Luther, Hans (1879–1962)

German politician. After an early career in local government, Luther entered national government in 1922. He served in various cabinets and, as Finance Minister, succeeded in re-establishing a stable German currency (the *Rentenmark*) after the Great Inflation of 1923. He became Chancellor in Jan 1925 at the head of the centre-right coalition that concluded the **LOCARNO PACT** with the Allies. He resigned in 1926, but served as President of the National Bank between 1930 and Mar 1933 and then as Ambassador to Washington until 1937. He held various public and academic offices in the Federal Republic and published a number of books.

### Luther, Martin (1483–1546)

German religious reformer. He spent three years in an Augustinian monastery, obtained his degree at Erfurt, and was ordained in 1507. His career as a reformer began after a visit to Rome in 1510–11 and after witnessing the preaching and selling of indulgences, to raise money (for St Peter's Basilica and the Elector/Archbishop of Mainz), by the monk Tetzel in lands around Saxony. In 1517 he drew up 95 theses on indulgences, which he nailed on the church door at Wittenberg. Violent controversy followed, and he was summoned to Rome to defend his theses, but did not go. He then began to attack the papal system more boldly, and publicly burned the papal bull issued against him. An order was issued for the destruction of his books; he was summoned to appear before the Diet at Worms, and was put under the ban of the Empire. In 1525 he married a former nun, Katharina von Bora. The drawing up of the Augsburg Confession, where he was represented by **MELANCHTHON**, marks the culmination of the German **REFORMATION** (1530). His translation of the Bible became a landmark of German literature. ➤ **REFORMATION**

### Luthuli, Albert John Mvumbi (1898–1967)

South African nationalist. He qualified as a teacher and taught for 15 years before succeeding to the chieftainship of Groutville, the community in Natal in which he had been raised, in 1935. He joined the **ANC** (African National Congress) in 1946, became President of the Natal branch and led a campaign of passive resistance against **APARTHEID**, for which he was deposed from his chieftainship by the South African government. He became President of the ANC in 1952, reflecting the 'colour-blind' traditions of the party, but was repeatedly 'banned', and was imprisoned (1956–7). He was awarded the **NOBEL PEACE PRIZE** in 1960.

### Lützen, Battle of (1632)

A battle during the **THIRTY YEARS' WAR**, fought near Leipzig in Saxony between forces led by King **GUSTAV II ADOLF** of Sweden and an Imperial army commanded by Albrecht von **WALLENSTEIN**. Wallenstein withdrew into Bohemia after the battle, during which Gustav was slain.

### Lützen, Battle of (1813)

A battle of the **NAPOLEONIC WARS** between **NAPOLEON I**'s advance guard and Russo-Prussian armies. It resulted in heavy casualties, but was inconclusive.

### Luwum, Janani (1922–77)

Ugandan bishop. The son of a Christian, he became a teacher and was converted in 1948. He was ordained into the Anglican Church and, despite his evangelicalism which disturbed more conventional Christians in Uganda, he became a theological college principal, Bishop of Northern Uganda and was then elected Archbishop of Uganda in 1974. He spoke out fearlessly against the atrocities committed during Idi **AMIN**'s period of rule, as a result of which he was murdered. So concerned was the Amin government that a memorial service for him was forbidden.

---

**LUXEMBOURG**   official name **Grand Duchy of Luxembourg**

An independent constitutional monarchy in northwestern Europe, bounded to the east by Germany; to the west by Belgium; and to the south by France. After being occupied by the Romans and then the **FRANKS** (in the 5c), Luxembourg came under the control of the House of Luxembourg in the 11c. The first Count of Luxembourg was created in 1060; the family, which owned lands in the area between the Maas and the Mosel from the 13c, took its name from the Castle of Lützelburg, and came to prominence when **HENRY VII** was elected Holy Roman Emperor in 1308. Although they lost the imperial throne after Henry's death, his son John gained control of Bohemia and the Luxemburgers' power grew comparable with that of the Habsburgs. Their most important representative was Emperor **CHARLES IV**, who elevated Luxembourg to a duchy in 1354. From 1346 until 1437 (when the dynasty died out in the male line with the death of **SIGISMUND**), all but one of the German kings came from the House of Luxembourg. The country of Luxembourg was controlled by various European powers (Burgundy 1443–77, Habsburgs 1477–1555, Spain 1555–1684, France 1684–97) before returning to Habsburg control after the War of the **SPANISH SUCCESSION**, and being made a Grand Duchy and passed to the Netherlands following the Congress of **VIENNA** in 1815. In 1830 much of Luxembourg joined the Belgians in the revolt against **WILLIAM I**; this resulted in the division of the country, with the western, French-speaking region joining Belgium. The remaining Grand Duchy was granted political autonomy in 1838, and recognized as a neutral independent state in 1867. Occupied by Germany in both World Wars, it entered into economic union with Belgium in 1921, joined the **BENELUX** economic union in 1948, and abandoned neutrality on joining **NATO** in 1949. The head of state is the Grand Duke or Grand Duchess, currently Grand Duke Henri, who succeeded in 2000 when his father, Grand Duke Jean, abdicated. Luxembourg was a founding member of the **EEC** in 1958 and the **EURO ZONE**. ► **HABSBURG DYNASTY**

**Luxemburg, Rosa** (1871–1919)
German social democrat. She emigrated to Zurich in 1889, where she studied law and political economy, and subsequently became a German citizen in 1895. A radical, she and the German politician Karl **LIEBKNECHT** formed the Spartacus League (1916), which later became the German Communist Party (**KPD**, 1919). She was arrested and murdered during the 'Spartacus Rising' in Berlin. ► **MARXISM**; **SPARTACISTS**

**Lvov, Giorgiy Yevgenievich, Prince** (1861–1925)
Russian liberal politician. Educated in Moscow, he joined the imperial civil service, then entered local government and became a member of the **DUMA**. In effect, he was Prime Minister in the first and second provisional governments after the **FEBRUARY REVOLUTION** of 1917, but his moderate policies and his determination to continue the war against Germany and Austria led to the collapse of his government. He was succeeded by **KERENSKY**, and subsequently arrested by the **BOLSHEVIKS**, but he escaped to Paris, where he died. ► **RUSSIAN REVOLUTION**

**Lyautey, Louis Hubert Gonzalve** (1854–1934)
French marshal and colonial administrator. He held administrative posts in Algeria, Tonkin and Madagascar, and became resident Commissary-General in Morocco (1912–16 and 1917–25), and also War

Minister (1916–17). He was made a Marshal in 1921.

**Lynch, Jack**, popular name of **John Mary Lynch** (1917–99)
Irish politician. Following a career in the Department of Justice (1936), he was called to the Bar (1945). Elected an MP in 1948, he held ministerial posts in Lands (1951), the Gaeltacht (1957), Education (1957–9), Industry and Commerce (1959–65) and Finance (1965–6), before becoming Prime Minister (1966–73 and 1977–9). Perceived as a strong supporter of the Catholic minority in Northern Ireland, he drew criticism from both Northern Ireland and mainland Britain. In 1979 he resigned both as Prime Minister and from the leadership of **FIANNA FÁIL**. He retired from politics in 1981. ► **HAUGHEY, CHARLES**

**Lyons, Joseph Aloysius** (1879–1939)
Australian politician. He became a teacher, entering politics in 1909 as Labor member in the Tasmanian House of Assembly. He held the posts of Treasurer, Minister of Education and Railways (1914–16), and was Premier (1923–8). Then in the federal parliament (1929–39), he was in turn Postmaster-General and acting Treasurer. Lyons favoured balanced budgets and reduced public expenditure to meet the Depression and when these were rejected, left the **AUSTRALIAN LABOR PARTY** to found the **UNITED AUSTRALIA PARTY**; he became Prime Minister (1932–9) after the election of Dec 1931.

**Lyons, Treaty of** (1601)
In 1599 in an attempt to define and defend the frontiers of France, **HENRY IV** laid claim to the Marquisate of Saluzzo, which brought him into conflict with Savoy and its Spanish allies. Through the mediation of Pope Clement VIII, agreement was reached at Lyons in 1601. France ceded Saluzzo in return for Bresse, Bugey, Gex, Valromey and financial compensation. For an additional sum, the Duke of Savoy was allowed to use routes connecting Savoy with the Franche-Comté. France, however, was not well-placed to sustain any of its allies who might be threatened from the Spanish power base in Lombardy.

**Lysenko, Trofim Denisovich** (1898–1976)
Soviet agronomist. He first became famous in 1929 for 'vernalization', making possible the spring sowing of winter wheat, a technique of beating nature which appealed to **STALIN** and, later, Nikita **KHRUSHCHEV**. He began to produce attractive theories to transform agricultural production, he discredited genetics and had geneticists imprisoned or shot, and he dominated the scene as President of the Soviet Academy of Agricultural Sciences (1938–56 and 1961–2). Although an investigation in 1965 proved his innovations useless, he continued to exert some influence until his death.

## Maastricht, Treaty of

An agreement signed (7 Feb 1992) in Maastricht, Netherlands, by the 12 nations of the **EC** to create the European Union (**EU**). Particularly controversial sections were the Social Chapter and European Monetary Union (EMU). Britain initially 'opted out' of the former when it was signed (Dec 1989) by the other 11 countries, although this decision was later reversed and its directives were incorporated into the Treaty of Amsterdam (2 Oct 1997). In May 1998, 11 of the 15 member states were chosen to join the first stage of European Monetary Union, and on 1 Jan 1999 fixed their exchange rates against the 'euro'.
▶ EURO ZONE

## Macanaz, Melchor Rafael de (1670–1760)

Spanish legist and politician. A leading protagonist of Bourbon absolutism in Spain, he came to prominence during the War of the **SPANISH SUCCESSION**, when he was appointed Intendant in Valencia and then in **ARAGON**, where he helped to abolish the *fueros* of these realms and to establish the new Bourbon authority. In 1714 he was appointed *fiscal* (Attorney-General) of the Council of **CASTILE**, and drew up several reform plans, including one for the reform of the **INQUISITION**. Conflict with the latter, and the coming of Elizabeth Farnese as queen, led to his exile in France. While in exile, he carried out several diplomatic missions for the Spanish government, and on the accession of a new king he was in 1748 allowed to return to Spain. He was, however, arrested on his arrival, and kept in prison until shortly before his death. ▶ BOURBON, HOUSE OF ; FARNESE FAMILY

## Macao, Portuguese Settlement of

The settlement in the Pearl river delta on the southern coast of China acquired by Portugal in 1557. It was used as a base for Catholic missionaries in the 17c and 18c as well as being a port of call for British traders on their way to Canton in the early 19c. Until the 19c, Macao was a flourishing trade centre, but the silting of its harbour and increasing competition from Hong Kong led to its decline. With the overthrow of the **SALAZAR** dictatorship in Portugal in 1975 and the new government's commitment to decolonization, China exercised more influence in the colony. In 1987 it was agreed that Macao be formally returned to Chinese control in 1999 under the same arrangements applying to the British return of Hong Kong to China in 1997 (ie that the capitalist system should remain in place).

## MacArthur, Douglas (1880–1964)

US general. Educated at the US Military Academy at West Point, he joined the US Army, and in **WORLD WAR I** served with distinction in France. In 1941 he became commanding general of the US armed forces in the Far East, and, after losing the Philippines, from Australia directed the recapture of the south-west Pacific (1942–5). He formally accepted the Japanese surrender, and commanded the occupation of Japan (1945–51). In 1950 he led the **UN** forces in the **KOREAN WAR**, defeating the North Korean army, but was relieved of command when he tried to continue the war against China.

## Macartney, George Macartney, 1st Earl (1737–1806)

Irish diplomat. In 1764 he was sent as an envoy to Russia, from 1769 to 1772 was Chief Secretary of Ireland, and in 1775 was Governor of Grenada. There (an Irish baron from 1776) he was taken prisoner by the French in 1779. Governor of Madras (1781–5), in 1792 he was made an earl and headed the first diplomatic mission to China. After a mission to **LOUIS XVIII** at Verona (1795–6), he went out as Governor to the Cape (1796), but returned in ill health in 1798.

## Macbeth (c.1005–1057)

King of Scots (1040/57). He was probably a grandson of Kenneth II (971/95), son of Findleach, Mormaer of Moray, and nephew of Malcolm II. Macbeth overthrew and killed **DUNCAN I** in 1040 and defeated a challenge to his kingship from Crinan, father of Duncan I, in 1045. Despite his malign Shakespearean image, he seems to have ruled wisely, avoiding expensive and debilitating raids on England. He was a benefactor of the Church and went on pilgrimage to Rome (1050). He was defeated and killed by **MALCOLM III, CANMORE**, son of Duncan I, at Lumphanan on 15 Aug 1057 after an invasion from England aided by Earl Siward of Northumbria.

## McCarran Act (23 Sep 1950)

A US Act which created the Subversive Activities Control Board to register all communist individuals and organizations. The act ensured that no communist was allowed to participate in US defence work, and no current or previous member of a communist or fascist organization could enter the USA. In 1964 and 1965 the Control Board was accused of violating certain guarantees in the Fifth Amendment (ie the right of freedom to travel by denying passports to communists, and guarantees against self-incrimination by forcing communists to be registered), and it was abolished in 1973.

**McCarran–Walter Act** (30 June 1952)
A US Act which amended the National Origins Act and allowed immigration by Chinese, Japanese and other Asian people. It retained the quota system and provided for selective skills-based immigration, but limited immigration from eastern and south-eastern Europe and devised ways of weeding out communists from potential immigrants so that they could be denied entrance to the USA, or even deported if they had already gained residency.

**McCarthy, D'Alton** (1836–98)
Canadian politician. From an Ulster Protestant background, he rose to be one of John A MACDONALD's lieutenants, but when Macdonald refused to disallow Quebec's JESUITS' ESTATES ACT, he established the Equal Rights Association. The association's title was curiously inappropriate since it sought to limit the use of French in Ontario's schools and to annul Ottawa's acceptance of French as an official language in the North West Territories. The McCarthyites' assertion that they were ready to use force to maintain Anglo-Saxon Protestantism destabilized the Conservative Party, in which moderates argued that confederation required tolerance of French rights. French-Canadians also began to question the old alliance between the BLEUS and the Ontario Tories. One of the results of his campaign was the enactment of the MANITOBA SCHOOLS ACT.

**McCarthy, Joseph Raymond** (1909–57)
US politician. Educated at Marquette University, Milwaukee, he became a circuit judge in 1939, and after war service was elected Senator in 1946. He achieved fame for his unsubstantiated accusations in the early 1950s that communists had infiltrated the State Department, and in 1953 became chairman of the SENATE permanent sub-committee on investigations. By hectoring cross-examination and damaging innuendo, he arraigned many innocent citizens and officials, overreaching himself when he came into direct conflict with the army. This kind of anti-communist witchhunt became known as 'McCarthyism'. His power diminished after he was formally condemned by the Senate in 1954. ► HUAC

**McClellan, George B(rinton)** (1826–85)
US general. Educated at the US Military Academy at West Point, when the AMERICAN CIVIL WAR began he drove Confederate forces out of West Virginia, and was called to Washington to reorganize the Federal Army of the Potomac. His Virginian campaign ended disastrously at Richmond (1862). He forced LEE to retreat at the Battle of ANTIETAM, but failed to follow up his advantage, and was recalled. In 1864 he opposed LINCOLN for the presidency, and in 1877 was elected Governor of New Jersey.

**McCulloch v Maryland** (1819)
US Supreme Court decision which prevented a state interfering with the exercise of a legitimate federal power. McCulloch was a clerk in the Baltimore branch of the Bank of the United States who appealed against an indictment for his failure to affix a state tax stamp on US banknotes. The court sustained his appeal with Chief Justice John MARSHALL, declaring that although sovereignty was divided between the national government and the states, the former was supreme 'within its sphere of action'.

**Macdonald, Flora** (1722–90)
Scottish heroine. After the FORTY-FIVE REBELLION, she conducted the Young Pretender, Charles Edward STUART, disguised as 'Betty Burke', to safety in Skye. For this she was imprisoned in the Tower of London, but released in 1747. She married in 1750, and in 1774 emigrated to North Carolina, where her husband fought in the AMERICAN REVOLUTION. When he was captured (1779), Flora returned to Scotland, to be rejoined there in 1781 by her husband. They settled at Kingsburgh, Skye.

**Macdonald, John Alexander** (1815–91)
Scottish-born Canadian politician. His family emigrated to Canada in 1820, and he was educated in law at Kingston. Entering politics in 1843, he became leader of the Conservative Party and joint Premier in 1856. Prime Minister in 1857–8 and 1864, he played an important role in bringing about the confederation of Canada, and in 1867 formed the first government of the new dominion. The PACIFIC SCANDAL brought down his government in 1873, but he regained the premiership in 1878, retaining it until his death in office. ► DOMINION OF CANADA; JESUITS' ESTATES ACT; TARIFF POLICY (Canada)

**Macdonald, John Sandfield** (1812–72)
Canadian politician. From an Irish background, he became Solicitor-General in Robert BALDWIN's ministry (1849–51), but Francis HINCKS passed him over and he, like George BROWN, became a bitter critic of the government. When George Étienne CARTIER was defeated in 1862, Macdonald was asked to form a ministry. As a reformer and a Catholic, he believed in the 'double-majority' principle, requiring a government to hold majorities within each half of the province, in order to contain both Protestants and Catholics within the party. However, as Reform Premier in 1862–4 he forgot his principles and voted for a Separate School bill against the wishes of his Protestant supporters. He was Premier of Ontario (1867–71).

**MacDonald, (James) Ramsay** (1866–1937)
British politician. He had little formal education, worked as a clerk, then joined the INDEPENDENT LABOUR PARTY in 1894, eventually becoming its leader (1911–14 and 1922–31). He became an MP in 1906, and was Prime Minister and Foreign Secretary of the first British Labour government (1924). Prime Minister again (1929–31 and 1931–5), he met the financial crisis of 1931 by forming a largely Conservative 'National' government, most of his party opposing, and reconstructed it the same year after a general election. Defeated by Shinwell in the 1935 general election, he returned to parliament in 1936, and became Lord President. He died on his way to South America. ► LABOUR PARTY (UK)

**MacDougall, William** (1822–1905)
Canadian politician. He was the first Governor of the North West Territories in 1869. A Clear Grit before confederation, he became Minister of Public Works in the MACDONALD cabinet of 1867. Exploration of the North West Territories had established the agricultural potential of the 64,000 sq mi/166,000 sq km belt beyond the Red River along North

Saskatchewan to the mountains. MacDougall was one of the negotiators for the purchase of these **HUDSON'S BAY COMPANY** lands, but the **MÉTIS** of the Red River colony were not informed either of this fact or of his appointment as Governor. Thus, his entry was blocked, and the rebellion began. ► **CLEAR GRITS**; **RED RIVER REBELLION**

---

**MACEDONIA** official name **Former Yugoslav Republic of Macedonia**, abbreviation **FYR Macedonia**

A republic in southern Europe, bounded to the west by Albania; to the south by Greece; to the east by Bulgaria; and to the north by Serbia. The area of ancient Macedonia (consisting of the present region of Macedonia in northern Greece and the Former Yugoslav Republic of Macedonia) was inhabited by Macedonians who spoke a Slav language closer to Bulgarian than Serbo-Croat. Through the centuries many tribes and nations settled in Macedonia and its ethnic composition is accordingly complex; the French *macédoine* is a synonym for 'medley' or 'mixture'. Slav tribes arrived in the 7c and mixed with the Greek and romanized Illyrians and Thracians, while the Byzantine rulers established settlements of Scythians and christianized Turks. In the 9c the Bulgars conquered Macedonia but the region returned to Byzantine rule until the Ottoman conquest (1355). Under the Turks, Sasi, Tartars, Čerkezi, Gypsies and Jews all settled and mixed with the local population. At the end of the 19c, a Macedonian nationalist movement emerged, its members insisting that the Macedonians were neither Bulgars nor Serbs, but a distinct Slav nation with its own language; this was a claim which the neighbouring Serbs, Bulgars and Greeks, nations all bent on territorial expansion, were determined to discount. After the **BALKAN WARS** in 1913, Macedonia was divided between Greece and Serbia. It is the Serbian part that was given to Yugoslavia by the Treaty of **NEUILLY** in 1919, an act confirmed by the treaties signed at the **PARIS PEACE CONFERENCE** in 1947, when the region was named the Republic of Macedonia within the Federal Republic of Yugoslavia. Despite claims to parts of it by Albania and Bulgaria, and deteriorating relations with Greece (which claims that its region called Macedonia is the only one entitled to the name), Macedonia formally seceded from Yugoslavia in 1991 and was admitted to the **UN** in 1993 as the Former Yugoslav Republic of Macedonia; Greece recognized it and lifted its trade blockade in 1995. UN and US peacekeeping forces arrived in 1992 and 1993 to maintain borders and prevent the conflict in Bosnia and Herzegovina spreading to Macedonia; the UN force withdrew in 1998 as China vetoed the renewal of its mandate owing to Macedonia's recognition of Taiwan. There was ongoing tension and sporadic violence between ethnic Albanians and Macedonians throughout the 1990s, and when instability in neighbouring Kosovo spilled over into Macedonia in 2001, there was an uprising by ethnic Albanians aggrieved at their lack of civil rights and equality. Peace talks were facilitated by international bodies and resulted in the Orhid Agreement giving Albanians greater recognition within Macedonia and recognizing Albanian as an official language. **NATO** handed over peacekeeping duties to the **EU** in 2003. The first post-independence president was Kiro Gligorov, elected in 1991, who, despite serious injury in an assassination attempt in 1995, remained in power until 1999. His successor, Boris Trajkovski, was killed in an aircraft accident in 2004 and Prime Minister Branko Crvenkovski was elected President. ► **ILINDEN UPRISING**; **SAMUEL**; **SOUTH SLAVS**; **VMRO**

**Maček, Vladko** (1879–1964)
Croatian politician. A doctor of law, he served in the Austrian army during **WORLD WAR I**. As a member of the Croatian Peasant Party in Yugoslavia, he was imprisoned in 1924 with its leader, Stjepan **RADIĆ**, becoming party leader himself in 1928. Again imprisoned in 1933, on charges of treason, he was released the following year under the regency of Prince **PAUL KARAGEORGEVIĆ**. In 1939 he signed the **SPORAZUM** with **CVETKOVIĆ**, thus securing Croatian participation in government, and became Vice-President of Yugoslavia, continuing in this position under General Dušan Simović who seized power in a coup (27 Mar 1941). He refused **RIBBENTROP**'s offer of assistance in creating an independent Croatia and at first urged the Croats to support the **USTAŠA** regime of **PAVELIĆ**. He retired from political life shortly afterwards and was interned on his farm until the end of **WORLD WAR II**, when he went into exile in France and the USA.

**Machel, Samora Moises** (1933–86)
Mozambique nationalist leader and politician. He trained as a medical assistant before joining **FRELIMO** in 1963, soon becoming active in the guerrilla war against the Portuguese colonial power. Commander-in-Chief in 1966, he succeeded **MONDLANE** on the latter's assassination in 1969 and was President of Mozambique from its independence in 1975 until his death in an air crash. Avowedly a Marxist, his success at politicizing the peasantry in northern Mozambique during the liberation war led him to believe in the dominant role of the party but, after the flight of white Portuguese in 1974 and the economic failure of his policies, he became more pragmatic, turning to the West for assistance, advising **MUGABE** to temper principle with prudence, and began establishing more harmonious relations with South Africa.

**Machiavelli, Niccolò di Bernardo dei** (1469–1527)
Italian statesman and political theorist. He travelled on several missions in Europe for the Florentine republic (1498–1512). On the restoration of the **MEDICI**, he was arrested on a charge of conspiracy (1513) and, although pardoned, was obliged to withdraw from public life. He devoted himself to literature, writing historical treatises, poetry, short stories and comedies. His masterpiece is *Il Principe* (1532, 'The Prince'), whose main theme is that all means

may be used in order to maintain authority, and that the worst acts of the ruler are justified by the treachery of the governed. It was condemned by the pope, and its viewpoint gave rise to the adjective 'Machiavellian'.

**machine** ► POLITICAL MACHINE

**Macía, Francisco** (1859–1933)
Catalan leader. The leader and founder, in 1922, of *Estat Català*, the Catalan nationalist party, he was a central figure in the Catalan struggle to achieve autonomy. After **PRIMO DE RIVERA**'s dictatorship collapsed, Macía forged a coalition of the Catalan Republican Party and his own *Estat Català*, creating the Republican Left of Catalonia. He was the first President of Catalonia under the autonomy statute of 1932 granted by the Second Republic. His Republican Left was defeated in the elections of 1933 and Macía died a few weeks later. ► **CATALAN AUTONOMY STATUTES**; **REPUBLIC, SECOND** (Spain)

**Mackenzie, Alexander** (1822–92)
Canadian politician. A Clear Grit before confederation and leader of the **LIBERAL PARTY** afterwards, he came to the fore when George **BROWN** retired from public life and Oliver Mowat restricted his political ambitions to Ontario. Mackenzie lacked sufficient support in parliament when he tried to form a government after the railway scandal of 1872–3 and he opted for a general election. A good majority established him as Prime Minister, but his tenure was cautious and inept. His go-slow public construction of the Canadian Pacific Railway (for which he took personal responsibility as Minister of Public Works), nearly lost British Columbia to the USA, while his inability to deal with the severe depression and his refusal to raise the tariff lost him the election of 1878. In 1880 the party threatened to rebel and he was succeeded by Edward **BLAKE**. ► **CLEAR GRITS**; **PACIFIC SCANDAL**

**Mackenzie, William Lyon** (1795–1861)
Canadian politician. He emigrated to Canada in 1820, established the *Colonial Advocate* in 1824, and entered politics in 1828. In 1837 he published in his paper the 'Declaration of the Toronto Reformers' (modelled on the US Declaration of Independence), headed a band of reform-minded insurgents, and after a skirmish with a superior force fled to the USA, where he was imprisoned. He returned to Canada in 1849, becoming a journalist and MP (1851–8). ► **CANADA, UPPER**; **REBELLIONS OF 1837**

**McKinley, William** (1843–1901)
US politician and 25th President. He served in the **AMERICAN CIVIL WAR**, then became a lawyer. As a Republican, he was elected to the **HOUSE OF REPRESENTATIVES** in 1877, and in 1892 was elected Governor of Ohio, despite his name being identified with the unpopular high protective tariff carried in the McKinley Tariff Act of 1890. During the presidential election of 1896 he secured a large majority as an advocate of the **GOLD STANDARD**. During his term as President (1897–1901), the **SPANISH–AMERICAN WAR** (1898) broke out, culminating in the acquisition of Cuba and the Philippines. He was re-elected in 1900, but his second term ended when he was shot by an anarchist in Buffalo, New York. ► **REPUBLICAN PARTY**

**Mackinnon, William** (1823–93)
Scottish merchant and shipowner. A significant late 19c imperialist figure, he went to India in 1847 and founded a prosperous general mercantile company in Calcutta with his partner, Robert Mackenzie. In 1856 he formed the Calcutta and Rangoon Steam Navigation Company (later renamed the British India Steam Navigation Company), which became one of the largest shipping companies in the world. Mackinnon developed an interest in East Africa and secured (1877) a concession from Barghash, Sultan of Zanzibar, to develop the mainland territories of Zanzibar. The British government refused to support Mackinnon, but once German competition had become a real threat in the area a charter was granted to Mackinnon's **IMPERIAL BRITISH EAST AFRICA COMPANY** (1888). The chartered company ruled Kenya and Uganda for only a few years but failed through lack of capital and the costs of suppressing African resistance. The territories were taken over by the British government in 1893.

**Maclean, Donald Duart** (1913–83)
British double agent. He studied at Cambridge at the same time as **BURGESS** and **PHILBY**, and was similarly influenced by **COMMUNISM**. He joined the diplomatic service in 1935, serving in Paris, Washington (1944–8), and Cairo (1948–50), and from 1944 acted as a Soviet agent. He became head of the US Department of the Foreign Office, but by 1951 was a suspected traitor, and in May of that year, after Philby's warning, disappeared with Burgess to the USSR. He died in Moscow.

**McLean, John** (1785–1861)
US jurist. He was trained as a lawyer in Ohio and served as a member of **CONGRESS** (1812–16) and a judge of the Ohio Supreme Court. As Postmaster-General (1823–9) he reformed the entire US postal system and instituted a system of appointments based on merit. He served on the Supreme Court from 1829 and is remembered for his dissenting opinion in the Dred Scott case, in which he argued that **SLAVERY** has no fundamental legal sanction in the USA. ► **DRED SCOTT V SANDFORD**

**MacMahon, Marie Edmé Patrice Maurice de, Duke of Magenta** (1808–93)
French marshal and President of the Third Republic. He was descended from an Irish Jacobite family. In the **FRANCO-PRUSSIAN WAR** (1870–1) he was defeated at Wörth and surrendered at **SEDAN** (1870). After the war he suppressed the **PARIS COMMUNE** (1871), and succeeded **THIERS** as head of state (1873). Failing to assume dictatorial powers, he resigned in 1879, thus ensuring the supremacy of parliament. ► **REPUBLIC, THIRD** (France)

**Macmillan, Sir (Maurice) Harold, 1st Earl of Stockton** (1894–1986)
British politician. He became a Conservative MP in 1924. He was Minister of Housing (1951–4) and Defence (1954–5), Foreign Secretary (1955), Chancellor of the Exchequer (1955–7), and succeeded **EDEN** as Premier (1957–63). He became popular and respected during a period of economic boom, earning the sobriquet 'Supermac'. He was re-elected in 1959. After several political setbacks, and a major scandal

(the **PROFUMO** Affair), he resigned through ill health in 1963, and left the House of **COMMONS** in 1964. He became Chancellor of Oxford University in 1960, and an earl in 1984. ► **CONSERVATIVE PARTY** (UK)

**McNamara, Robert Strange** (1916– )
US politician and businessman. After service in the air force (1943–6), he worked his way up in the Ford Motor Company to the office of President by 1960. A Democrat, in 1960 he joined the J F **KENNEDY** administration as Secretary of Defense, being particularly involved in the **VIETNAM WAR**. He resigned in 1968 to become President of the World Bank (a post he held until 1981). In the 1980s he emerged as a critic of the nuclear arms race. ► **DEMOCRATIC PARTY**

**Macquarie, Lachlan** (1761–1824)
British soldier and colonial administrator. He became Governor of New South Wales in 1810 after the deposition of **BLIGH**. He raised the colony to a state of lawfulness and prosperity, but his liberal policies towards ex-convicts united his opponents, and caused his resignation. He returned to Britain in 1822.

---

**MADAGASCAR**   official name **Republic of Madagascar**

An island republic in the Indian Ocean, separated from East Africa by the Mozambique Channel. It was settled by Indonesians in the 1c AD and by African traders in the 8c. The French established trading posts in the late 18c and claimed the island as a protectorate in 1885. After becoming an autonomous overseas French territory (the Malagasy Republic) in 1958, it gained independence in 1960 and was named Madagascar again in 1975. Following anti-government riots, in 1992 a new constitution was approved which reduced the powers of the President, Didier Ratsiraka, who had held office since 1975. He was defeated in 1993 but returned to office in 1997 after winning the 1996 elections. In the 2001 presidential election there were allegations of vote-rigging on both sides and the ensuing civil unrest brought the country close to civil war. A recount showed that Marc Ravalomana had won but Ratsiraka refused to accept the result and violence continued until Jul 2002, when Ratsiraka went into exile and his supporters surrendered.

**Madariaga y Rojo, Salvador de** (1886–1978)
Spanish diplomat and writer. Educated in Madrid and

Paris, he became a journalist in London (1916–21), a member of the **LEAGUE OF NATIONS** secretariat (1922–7), Professor of Spanish Studies at Oxford (1928–31), and Spanish Ambassador to the USA (1931) and France (1932–4). During 1934 he was briefly Minister of Education and Justice under the Spanish Second Republic. An opponent of the **FRANCO** regime, he was in exile from 1936 to 1976. The author of many historical works, especially on Spain and Spanish America, he died at Locarno, Switzerland. ► **REPUBLIC, SECOND** (Spain)

**Madero, Francisco Indalécio** (1873–1913)
Mexican revolutionary and politician. The son of a wealthy landowner, groomed in Paris and educated in the USA, he was no social revolutionary, although he greatly improved the *peons'* condition on his own estates. He unsuccessfully opposed Porfirio **DÍAZ**'s local candidates in 1904, and in 1908, when Díaz was quoted as saying that he would not seek another term, Madero took the dictator at his word and launched his own presidential campaign. A spiritualist, vegetarian and practitioner of homoeopathic medicine, he was an unlikely challenger, and at first was not taken seriously. But his popularity grew rapidly and Díaz turned to repression, imprisoning Madero and many of his supporters. He escaped to the USA, from where he directed a military campaign. His supporters, including **VILLA**, captured Ciudad Juárez, where he established his capital (May 1911), and the dictatorship crumbled. Once elected President (Oct 1911), Madero's moderate political reform programme pleased no one and he faced a succession of revolts by Emiliano **ZAPATA** and others demanding land reform, as well as by supporters of the old dictatorship. On the night of 23 Feb 1913, he and his Vice-President were murdered following a military coup led by General Victoriano **HUERTA**, planned with the assistance of US ambassador Henry L Wilson. ► **PEON**

**Madison, James** (1751–1836)
US politician and 4th President. He entered Virginia politics in 1776, played a major role in the **CONSTITUTIONAL CONVENTION** of 1787, which framed the federal **US CONSTITUTION**, and collaborated in the writing of the **FEDERALIST PAPERS**. He served as a Congressman from Virginia (1789–97) in the first federal **CONGRESS**, and was a strong advocate of the Bill of Rights. He was Secretary of State under **JEFFERSON**, and President himself for two terms (1809–17). His period in office was dominated by the **WAR OF 1812** with Britain.

**Madiun Rebellion** (Sep–Oct 1948)
A rebellion by major elements in the Indonesian Communist Party (**PARTAI KOMUNIS INDONESIA**, PKI) against the Indonesian government, at a time when the peoples of Indonesia were still engaged in their violent post-war struggle to prevent the restoration of Dutch colonial rule. The rebellion was primarily driven by deep disagreements with other forces in Indonesia over the ways in which the struggle with the Dutch should be pursued and over the aims of the revolution. It was fiercely crushed by government forces, with much loss of life. In launching the rebellion against the government, the PKI provoked the charge, long-sustained, of treachery against the

revolution. The defeat of the communists, however, opened the way for stronger US support for the Indonesian government, which was crucial in effecting the final Dutch withdrawal in 1949–50.

## madrasahs
Islamic schools which concentrate on theology and linguistics, as well as teaching Islamic science, history, poetry and literature. They originated in the Middle East in the medieval period and then spread throughout the Islamic world, including India. The schools were attached to mosques and, as with similar institutions linked to Hindu temples, an emphasis was placed on religious training. Madrasahs were state-financed, and it is estimated that during the Tughlaq period in India there were as many as a thousand madrasahs in Delhi alone. To this day, madrasahs remain an important part of Indian life, as elsewhere in the Islamic world.

## Madres de la Plaza Mayo
A group of women whose silent protests publicized the human rights abuses of Argentina's military regime in the 1970s and early 1980s. Emerging in 1977 as an informal group of 14 women trying to discover the fate of family members kidnapped by the military junta, *Las Madres de la Plaza Mayo* ('The Mothers of the May Plaza'). by 1982 involved around 2,500 women in its weekly silent protests in central Buenos Aires against a system of state-sponsored terrorism that had 'disappeared' tens of thousands of its citizens. It acted as a catalyst for the re-emergence of civil society after 1983 and has developed into a broader social movement.

## Madrid, Treaty of (Jan 1526)
The treaty signed by King **FRANCIS I** of France while a prisoner of **CHARLES V** in Madrid, after the former had been captured by the Imperial forces at the Battle of **PAVIA** (Feb 1525). Under the treaty, Francis was to surrender **BURGUNDY** to Charles, but on his release he refused to honour his promise. At the time a small town, Madrid was in 1561 adopted by **PHILIP II** as capital of Spain.

## Madvig, Johan Nicolai (1804–86)
Danish politician and classical scholar. He was Professor of Latin at Copenhagen (1829–70), and Inspector of Higher Schools (from 1848). He was one of the chief speakers of the national Liberal Party, was Minister of Religion and Education (1848–51), and was repeatedly President of the Danish parliament.

## Mafeking, Siege of (Oct 1899–May 1900)
The most celebrated siege of the second Boer War, during which Colonel Robert **BADEN-POWELL** and a detachment of British troops were besieged by the Boers. The news of their relief aroused public hysteria in Britain, the celebrations being known as 'mafficking'. The truth about the siege was rather different from the heroic action depicted by the British press. It is now known that the white garrison survived in reasonable comfort as the result of appropriating the rations of the blacks, who were faced either with starvation or with running the gauntlet of the Boers by escaping from the town. ► **BOER WARS**; **KIMBERLEY, SIEGE OF**; **LADYSMITH, SIEGE OF**

## Mafia
Literally meaning 'boldness' in Italian, the secret society has its origins in the 9c, when the Arabs conquered Sicily and its inhabitants took to the hills, where they lived by banditry. This way of life created a network of criminal families which by the 19c pervaded the whole island. In the late 1800s immigrants took the network to the USA, where it formed the subculture *Cosa Nostra*, the underworld of gangsters and racketeers who controlled prostitution, drug trafficking and gambling during the Depression. It has never had a coherent overall structure in its native Sicily, making it more difficult to eradicate, whereas in the USA the national linkages of recognized crime 'families' made the Italian-American Mafia vulnerable to intensive **FBI** offensives in the late 20c.

## Magadha ► INDIA, PRE-ISLAMIC

## Magellan, Ferdinand (c.1480–1521)
Portuguese navigator. He was born near Villa Real in Tras os Montes, served in the East Indies and Morocco, then laid before **CHARLES V** a scheme for reaching the Moluccas by the west. Sailing from Seville on 10 Aug 1519 with five ships and 270 men, he coasted Patagonia, passing through the strait which bears his name (21 Oct–28 Nov), and reached the ocean which he named the Pacific. He was later killed by local people in the Philippine Islands, but his ship, the *Victoria*, was taken safely back to Spain on 6 Sep 1522, to complete the first circumnavigation of the world. ► **EXPLORATION**

## Magenta, Battle of (4 June 1859)
French victory in the Franco-Piedmontese campaign against Austria. The battle was marked by extremely high casualties on both sides.

## Magersfontein, Battle of (1899)
An engagement of the second Boer War in which British forces were defeated by the Boers. It followed on the defeat of the British at **MODDER RIVER** several days previously, both actions taking place a few miles from Kimberley as part of the British attempts to relieve that town. ► **BOER WARS**; **KIMBERLEY, SIEGE OF**

## Maghreb or Maghrib
An area of north-west Africa including the countries of Morocco, Algeria and Tunisia; largely occupied by sedentary and nomadic **BERBERS** of the Kabyle, Shluh and Tuareg groups. In Arabic, the word refers to Morocco only.

## Maginot Line
French defensive fortifications stretching from Longwy to the Swiss border, named after André Maginot (1877–1932), French Minister of Defence (1924–31). The line was constructed (1929–34) to act as protection against German invasion, but Belgium refused to extend it along her frontier with Germany. The German attack of 1940 through the Low Countries largely by-passed the Maginot Line, whose name became synonymous with passive defence and defeatism. ► **WORLD WAR II**

## Magna Carta
The 'Great Charter', imposed (June 1215) by rebellious barons on King **JOHN** of England, it was designed to prohibit arbitrary royal acts by declaring a body of defined law and custom which the King must

respect in dealing with all his free subjects. The principle that kings should rule justly was of long standing, but in Magna Carta the first systematic attempt was made to distinguish between kingship and tyranny. While failing to resolve all the problems raised by the nature of the English crown's relations with the community, it endured as a symbol of the sovereignty of the rule of law, and was of fundamental importance to the constitutional development of England and other countries whose legal and governmental systems were modelled on English conventions.
► BARONS' WARS

### Magnus I, the Good (1024–47)
King of Norway (1035/47) and of Denmark (1042/7). The illegitimate son of King OLAF II (St Olaf), he was named after Emperor Charlemagne (Carolus Magnus). After St Olaf's death at the Battle of Stiklestad in 1030, the boy was given refuge at the court of Prince Jaroslav the Wise in Kiev, and was brought back by popular acclaim in 1035 to assume the Norwegian throne. In 1042 he inherited the Danish throne, and in the following year won a notable victory over the Wends at Lürschau Heath in southern Jutland. In 1045 he agreed to share the throne of Norway with his uncle HARALD HARDRADA, and died two years later during a campaign in Denmark.

### Magnus III, Barelegs ('Barfot') (c.1074–1103)
King of Norway (1093/1103). The son of King OLAF III, THE PEACEFUL, he was one of the last of the Norse Viking sea-kings bent on strengthening Norway's hold over her North Sea territories. He harried the Orkneys and Shetland (1098–9), and in 1102–3 led another punitive naval expedition west to Scotland and Ireland; he took Dublin, and built new fortifications in the Isle of Man, but was killed in an ambush in Ulster. He earned his nickname because he abandoned Norse trousers in favour of the Scottish kilt.

### Magnus V Erlingsson (1156–84)
King of Norway (1162/84). The son of Earl Erling the Crooked, he was raised to the throne as a child under his father's regency; in 1164 he was crowned by Archbishop Eystein at a church ceremony in Bergen, the first religious coronation in Norway. After his father's death in 1179 he was engaged in a long war against a rival claimant to the throne, the Faroese-born 'usurper', SVERRIR SIGURDSSON. He was forced to flee to Denmark for safety, and lost his life in a naval battle in an attempt to regain his kingdom.

### Magnus VI, the Law-Mender (1238–80)
King of Norway (1263/80). The son of HAAKON THE OLD, he succeeded to the throne when his father died in the Orkneys on his return to Norway after the Battle of Largs (1263). He made peace with King ALEXANDER III of Scotland and ceded the Western Isles and the Isle of Man. He revised and standardized the laws of the land in a series of legal codes, from which he earned his nickname, and which were based on the 'four sisters' of Mercy, Truth, Fairness and Peace.

### Magnus Eriksson (1316–74)
King of Sweden (1319/65) and, as Magnus VII, of Norway (1319/55). He was the son of Duke Erik Magnusson of Sweden and Ingeborg, the daughter of King Haakon V of Norway. He inherited the throne of Norway from his grandfather and was elected to the Swedish throne in the same year on the deposition of his uncle, Birger Magnusson. In 1335 he married Blanche of Namur, by whom he had two sons. In 1355 he handed over the crown of Norway to his younger son, Haakon VI, and in the following year was deposed in Sweden by his elder son, Erik. Magnus regained the throne in 1359, but lost the island of Gotland to Valdemar IV Atterdag of Denmark and was again deposed in 1365 in favour of his nephew, Albrekt of Mecklenburg. He died in a shipwreck. He is associated with a code of law which covered the whole of Sweden and which remained in force until the 18c.

### Magnússon, Skúli (1711–94)
Icelandic reformer. He was the first Icelander to hold the important post of treasurer (landfógeti) on the island (in 1749). He worked hard to develop industry and fought against the abuses committed by the Danish merchants who enjoyed a monopoly of trade with Iceland.

### Magnús Stephensen ► STEPHENSEN, MAGNÚS

### Mahathir bin Muhammad (1925– )
Malaysian politician. He practised as a doctor (1957–64) before being elected to the House of Representatives as a United Malays' National Organization (UMNO) candidate. He won the support of UMNO's radical youth wing through his advocacy of 'affirmative action' in favour of bumiputras (ethnic Malays). Following sharp attacks on the then Prime Minister, Tunku Putra ABDUL RAHMAN, in the wake of the 1969 race riots, he was expelled from UMNO. He was, however, subsequently readmitted and, after holding several ministerial posts, was appointed UMNO leader and Prime Minister in 1981. He immediately launched a 'look east' economic policy which sought to emulate East Asian industrialization. Despite severe divisions within UMNO, he saw off all challengers and led the ruling alliance to successive electoral victories until his retirement in 2003.

### Mahdi
The name (literally, 'divinely-guided one') given by Sunni Muslims to those who periodically revitalize the Muslim community. SUNNIS look forward to a time before the Last Day when a Mahdi will appear and establish a reign of justice on earth. SHIITES identify the Mahdi with the expected reappearance of the hidden Imam. Many Muslim leaders have claimed the title, such as MOHAMMED AHMED, who established a theocratic state in the Sudan in 1882. His great-grandson, Sadiq al-Mahdi, was Prime Minister of the Sudan in 1986–9.

### Mahdi's Revolt
MOHAMMED AHMED, the MAHDI of the Sudan, joined the Samaniyya dervish order, but c.1872 he proclaimed privately that he was al-Mahdi al-Muntazar ('the awaited or expected Mahdi'), who promised believers that a new order was imminent. He made a tour of the Sudan from Dongola to Sennar, from the Blue Nile to Kordofan, and convinced himself of the people's disaffection and discontent with the established order. In 1881 he made his first public appearance as Mahdi, and Mahdism spread from Kordofan

and Bahr al-Ghazal to the eastern Sudan, despite the dispatch of several fruitless and occasionally disastrous (as in the case of Hicks Pasha) expeditions against him. In 1884 he laid siege to Khartoum and in 1885 the governor, General Charles (Chinese) **GORDON**, was killed. Mohammed Ahmed died later in 1885 but the Sudan was to remain under Mahdist control until **KITCHENER** reduced the Sudan in the following decade, finally defeating the Mahdists at **OMDURMAN**.

### Mahican ► MOHICAN

### Mahmud II (1785–1839)
Ottoman Sultan (1808/39). His reign was marked by the cession of Bessarabia to Russia (1812), Greece's successful struggle for independence (1820–8), a disastrous war with Russia (1828–9), and the triumphs of **MUHAMMAD 'ALI**. He shattered the power of the **JANISSARIES** by a massacre in 1826, introduced many domestic reforms, and did much to westernize Turkey. He died in Constantinople.

### Mahmud of Ghazni (971–1030)
Muslim Afghan conqueror of India. The son of Sebuktigin, a Turkish slave who became ruler of Ghazni (modern Afghanistan), he succeeded to the throne in 997. He invaded India 17 times between 1001 and 1026, and created an empire that included Punjab and much of Persia. A great patron of the arts, he made Ghazni a remarkable cultural centre.

### Maichew or Mai Ceu, Battle of (31 Mar 1936)
The decisive battle of the Italian invasion of Abyssinia, in which the Emperor **HAILE SELASSIE** was defeated and the Italian commander, Marshal Badoglio, prepared for the final advance on Addis Ababa. The Emperor decided that, instead of withdrawal, he would attack the Italian camp at Maichew with forces which consisted of the Imperial Guard and large numbers of Galla under feudal chiefs. The Italians had forewarning of the attack, harried the Ethiopians with air power, and were able to repulse the Ethiopian forces with superior artillery. It became Selassie's last despairing gesture before he fled into exile and the Italians were able to complete their conquest. Ethiopian resistance passed from the traditional leaders to the guerrilla Patriots. ► **ABYSSINIA, CONQUEST OF**

### Maine, USS (15 Feb 1898)
A US battleship which was blown up and sunk whilst in Havana harbour, where it had been sent in Jan 1898 to protect US citizens during the rioting caused by the Cuban struggle for independence from Spain (which had begun three years before). The explosion that destroyed the ship and took 260 lives was never explained; the US naval report said it was caused by an underwater mine, while the Spanish inquiry claimed there was an explosion in the ship's magazine. Whatever the cause, it served to precipitate the **SPANISH–AMERICAN WAR**.

### Maintenon, Madame de, properly Françoise d'Aubigné, Marchioness of Maintenon (1635–1719)
Second wife of **LOUIS XIV** of France. In 1652 she married the crippled poet Paul Scarron, and on his death was reduced to poverty. In 1669 she took charge of the King's two sons by Madame de **MONTESPAN**, and moved with them to the court in 1673. By 1674 the

King's generosity enabled her to purchase the estate of Maintenon, near Paris, which was converted to a marquisate. After the Queen's death (1683) Louis married her secretly. On the King's death (1715) she retired to the educational institution for poor girls which she had founded at Saint-Cyr (1686).

### Mainz Republic
The government established (1793) in Mainz by the occupying armies of Revolutionary France which had ousted the Elector. The vote to ratify the changes and the new relationship with France was almost totally boycotted by the citizens of Mainz.

### Maipú or Maipó, Battle of (1818)
A decisive battle of the **SPANISH-AMERICAN WARS OF INDEPENDENCE**, fought near Santiago. A notable victory for the Argentine general José de **SAN MARTÍN**, it secured the final liberation of Chile from Spanish rule.

### Maitraka ► INDIA, PRE-ISLAMIC

### Majapahit
A Javanese state of the 14c and 15c. Majapahit was a Hindu–Buddhist kingdom, by far the most important of the pre-Islamic states of Indonesia. It was both a land-based trading empire and an important naval power. Majapahit's authority was said to extend to Sumatra, the Malay Peninsula, Kalimantan and the islands of the eastern Indonesian archipelago, although given difficulties of communication over that vast area, it would rarely have been effectively exercised. Majapahit also maintained relations with Cambodia, Siam, Burma and Vietnam and sent missions to China. The capital was witness to great annual religious festivals.

### Maji Maji (1905)
A rising against German rule which took place in southern Tanganyika. People from a variety of ethnic backgrounds rose against harsh tax exactions and compulsory cotton growing. Priests and messengers moved from village to village urging people to rise, and claiming that they had a medicine which would turn bullets into water or *maji*. German administration broke down for several months, but the rising was put down with great brutality, causing a famine, in which a million people died, and a major ecological disaster in the region.

### Major, John (1943– )
British politician. He had a career in banking before becoming a Conservative MP in 1976. He rose to become Chief Secretary to the Treasury, was unexpectedly made Foreign Secretary in Margaret **THATCHER**'s cabinet reshuffle in 1989, and soon after replaced Nigel **LAWSON** as Chancellor of the Exchequer. He won the leadership contest following Thatcher's resignation, and served as Prime Minister (1990–7). He unexpectedly won the 1992 general election, but upon losing to the **LABOUR PARTY** in the landslide victory of 1997, Major immediately resigned the leadership and was succeeded by William Hague. ► **CONSERVATIVE PARTY** (UK)

### Majuba Hill, Battle of (1881)
An engagement which ended the first Boer War. In 1877 the British had attempted to federate the British and Boer territories of South Africa by invading and annexing the Transvaal. The latter was successfully

accomplished, but the plan was destroyed by the British victory at Ulundi in the ZULU WAR of 1879. With the Zulu threat removed, the Boers resolved to reestablish their independence. The British suffered several small reverses, culminating in their defeat at Majuba Hill. GLADSTONE's government restored a limited independence to the Orange Free State and the Transvaal under the PRETORIA CONVENTION, subsequently modified by the LONDON CONVENTION of 1884. Disagreements about the interpretation of these Conventions were to increase tensions later in the 19c. ► BOER WARS; JAMESON RAID

### Makarios III, originally Mihail Khristodoulou Mouskos (1913–77)

Cypriot political and religious leader. He was ordained priest in 1946, elected Bishop of Kition in 1948, and Archbishop and Primate of the Orthodox Church of Cyprus in 1950. He reorganized the ENOSIS (union) movement, was arrested and detained in 1956, but returned to a tumultuous welcome in 1959 to become chief Greek-Cypriot minister in the new Graeco-Turkish provisional government. Later that year he was elected President (1960–74 and 1974–7).

### Malan, Daniel F(rançois) (1874–1959)

South African politician. Educated at Stellenbosch and Utrecht universities, in 1905 he joined the ministry of the Dutch Reformed Church but in 1915 left to become editor of Die Burger, the Nationalist newspaper. Elected an MP in 1918, he held the portfolios of Interior, Education and Public Health by 1924. He helped reform the NATIONAL PARTY with HERTZOG and became leader of the Opposition to SMUTS's United Party. He led the National Party to its decisive electoral victory in 1948 and oversaw the initial implementation of the policy of APARTHEID. He retired in 1954.

### Malatesta

Lords of the state of Rimini in north-east Italy from the 13c to the 16c; among the most durable of several families of signori who dominated political life in the Italian RENAISSANCE. Originally the political 'vicars' of the papacy, the Malatesta state was overthrown in 1500 by a coalition of the papacy and the French. ► PAPAL STATES

### Malaviya, Madan Mohan (1861–1946)

Indian politician and journalist. A nationalist, he joined the Congress in 1886 and was a prominent member of the Uttar Pradesh Legislative Council and the Central Legislature. Mainly concerned with the furtherance of Hindu interests, Malaviya campaigned for the use of Hindi and was the dominant force in the creation of the Benares Hindu University in 1916. He was an important member of the HINDU MAHASABHA, from which he broke away in 1928, although he remained the chief Hindu spokesman within Congress. He opposed the Communal Award of 1932, which created separate electorates representing different religious and social groups, and left the Congress to form a new party to fight the award, which he regarded as 'communal'. ► COMMUNALISM

### MALAWI   official name Republic of Malawi, formerly (to 1964) Nyasaland

A republic in south-eastern Africa, bounded to the south-west and south-east by Mozambique; to the

east by Lake Nyasa (Lake Malawi); to the north by Tanzania; and to the west by Zambia. It was discovered by the Portuguese in the 17c, and European contact was established by David LIVINGSTONE in 1859. Scottish church missions were established in the area, and it was claimed as the British Nyasaland Districts Protectorate in 1891, and then called the British Central Africa Protectorate in 1893. It was established as the British colony of Nyasaland in 1907, and in the 1950s it joined with Northern and Southern Rhodesia (now Zambia and Zimbabwe) to form the Federation of Rhodesia and Nyasaland. After gaining independence in 1964, it became a republic in 1966 under President Hastings BANDA. As a result of international pressure and growing unrest within the country, a referendum was held in 1993 in which the population voted for a multiparty system. Banda was voted out of office the following year and was replaced by Bakili Muluzi, who served until 2004, when he was succeeded by Bingu wa Mutharika. Malawi faces serious problems because of the high level of HIV/AIDS infection among the population.

### Malawi Congress Party (MCP)

Founded in 1959, this party grew out of the Nyasaland African National Congress. It was the only legal party in Malawi until 1993 and had as its Life President Hastings BANDA. The popularity of the MCP and Banda declined in the 1990s as demands for multiparty democracy grew and they were voted out of office in 1994 in the first all-party elections. Also that year Banda resigned the MCP leadership in favour of Gwanda Chakuamba. The party has remained in opposition since.

### MALAYSIA   official name Federation of Malaysia

An independent federation of states situated in South-East Asia. It is divided into two parts separated by the South China Sea: Peninsular or West Malaysia, and East Malaysia. East Malaysia comprises the states of Sabah and Sarawak on the island of Kalimantan

(Borneo), and West Malaysia (formerly the Federation of Malaya) occupies the southern part of the Malay Peninsula. Malaysia formed part of the Srivijaya Empire in the 9–14c and experienced Hindu and Muslim influences in the 14–15c. From the 16c, Portugal, the Netherlands and Britain vied for control. Singapore, Malacca and Penang were formally incorporated into the British Colony of the **STRAITS SETTLEMENTS** in 1826. British protection, which extended over Perak, Selangor, Negeri Sembilan and Pahang, was constituted into the Federated Malay States in 1895, and protection treaties with several other states (Unfederated Malay States) were agreed in 1885–1930. The region was occupied by the Japanese in **WORLD WAR II**, after which Sarawak became a British colony, Singapore became a separate colony, the colony of North Borneo was formed, and the Malay Union was established, uniting the Malay states and the Straits Settlements of Malacca and Penang. In 1948 the British set up the Federation of Malaya. Growing resentment by the Chinese-dominated Malayan Communist Party (MCP) of Malay dominance within the Federation led to an insurrection led by the MCP against British rule. The insurrection and the campaign to crush it became known as the Malayan Emergency. Following growing MCP violence, including the murder of European estate managers, on 18 June 1948 the British administration declared a state of emergency throughout Malaya. In the early years of the insurrection, the MCP achieved a number of notable successes, including the assassination of the High Commissioner, Sir Henry Gurney, in Oct 1951. However, by the mid-1950s, through a combination of fierce military measures, substantial resettlement of the Chinese rural population (which had provided much of the MCP's support) and the introduction of political initiatives that clearly would soon take Malaya to independence, the insurrection was broken, although, officially, it did not end until 31 July 1960. Malaya gained independence in 1957 and the constitutional monarchy of the Federation of Malaysia came into existence in 1963. Two years later Singapore withdrew from the Federation. The head of state is a monarch elected for five years by sultans. In 2003 Abdullah Ahmad Badawi became Prime Minister, replacing **MAHATHIR BIN MOHAMAD**, who had served for 22 years. Parts of the country were devastated by the Indian Ocean tsunami on 26 Dec 2004.

**Malcolm III, Canmore**, from Gaelic **Ceann-mor ('Large-headed')** (c.1031–1093)
King of Scots (1058/93). He was the son of **DUNCAN I**, who was slain by **MACBETH** in 1040. He returned from exile in 1054 and conquered southern Scotland; but he did not become king until he had defeated and killed Macbeth (1057), and disposed of Macbeth's stepson, Lulach (1058). He first married Ingibjorg, daughter of the Earl of Orkney, by whom he had a son, **DUNCAN II**, briefly King of Scots (1094). His second marriage was to the English Princess Margaret (later St **MARGARET**), sister of **EDGAR THE ATHELING**. He launched five invasions of England between 1061 and died in a skirmish near Alnwick, Northumberland.

**Malcolm IV, the Maiden** (c.1141–1165)
King of Scots (1153/65). He was the grandson and successor of **DAVID I**. Compelled to restore the northern English counties to **HENRY II** in return for the earldom and honour of Huntingdon (1157), he served on Henry's expedition to Toulouse (1159), and was then knighted. Malcolm continued to implement David I's Normanizing policies, despite native opposition. He defeated Fergus, Lord of Galloway, in 1161, and in 1164 Somerled, Lord of Argyll, was vanquished and slain at Renfrew. His byname was coined in the 15c, in recognition of his well-attested reputation for chastity.

**Malcolm X** (1925–65)
US militant black activist, who became the most effective spokesman for **BLACK POWER**. Born Malcolm Little, he took the name 'X' to symbolize the stolen identities of the generations of black slaves. After an adolescence of violence, narcotics and petty crime, he came under the influence of Elijah **MUHAMMAD** while in prison for burglary and after his release in 1952 became Muhammad's chief disciple within the **BLACK MUSLIMS**, greatly expanding the organization's following. In 1963 Malcolm was suspended from the Nation of Islam after disagreements with Muhammad and gained the deep hatred of the leader's loyal followers. Malcolm founded the Organization for Afro-American Unity, dedicated to the alliance of American blacks and other non-white peoples. In the last year of his life, following a pilgrimage to Mecca, Malcolm announced his conversion to orthodox Islam and put forward the belief in the possible brotherhood between blacks and whites. Malcolm's extreme stance and the inflammatory nature of his oratory had scared many whites, appealed to many northern blacks in the urban ghettos, and had been met with criticism by moderate **CIVIL RIGHTS** leaders who deplored his violent message. In 1965 Malcolm was the victim of Black Muslim assassins who retaliated against the man they viewed as a traitor.

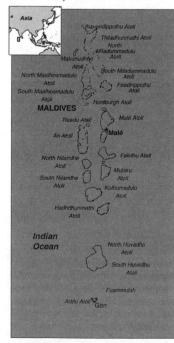

**MALDIVES** official name **Republic of Maldives**, formerly **Maldive Islands**

A republic consisting of an island archipelago in the Indian Ocean. A former dependency of Ceylon (now Sri Lanka), it was a British protectorate from 1887 until 1965, when it gained independence. It became a special member of the **COMMONWEALTH OF NATIONS** in 1982 and a full member in 1985. Its sultanate was abolished in 1968 when it became a republic under President Ibrahim Nasir. He was succeeded in 1978 by Maumoon Abdul Gayoom, who was re-elected for a sixth term in 2003. A state of emergency was declared in 2004 after pro-democracy demonstrations became violent; President Gayoom promised to introduce reforms, encourage political parties (there are none at present) and limit the presidential term. Much of the low-lying state was devastated by the Indian Ocean tsunami on 26 Dec 2004.

**Malenkov, Giorgiy Maximilianovich** (1902–88)
Soviet politician. He joined the **RED ARMY** in 1919 and the Communist Party in 1920, and by 1925 he was a Central Committee official. He was very closely involved in the collectivization of agriculture and the purges of the 1930s under **STALIN**. Malenkov became a member of the Central Committee in 1939 and of the **POLITBURO** in 1946; he became Deputy Premier in the same year, succeeding Stalin as Party General-Secretary and Premier in 1953. However, he was very quickly forced out of his Party post and, under pressure from Nikita **KHRUSHCHEV**, in 1955 he resigned as Premier, admitting responsibility for the failure of Soviet agricultural policy. Having participated in the so-called **ANTI-PARTY PLOT** in 1957, he was sent by Khrushchev to Kazakhstan as manager of a hydro-electric plant. He died an obscure pensioner in Moscow. ► **COMMUNISM**

**Malesherbes, Chrétien (Guillaume de Lamoignon) de** (1721–94)
French politician. In 1744 he became a counsellor of the **PARLEMENT** of Paris, and in 1750 was made chief censor of the press. At **LOUIS XVI**'s accession (1774) he was made Secretary of State for the royal household, instituting prison and legal reforms in tandem with **TURGOT**'s economic improvements. He resigned in 1776 on the eve of Turgot's dismissal. Despite his reforming zeal, he was mistrusted as an aristocrat during the **FRENCH REVOLUTION**. Arrested as a royalist (1794), he was guillotined in Paris.

**MALI** official name **Republic of Mali**

A landlocked republic in West Africa, bounded to the north-east by Algeria; to the north-west by Mauritania; to the west by Senegal; to the south-west by Guinea; to the south by the Côte d'Ivoire; to the south-

east by Burkina Faso; and to the east by Niger. Between the 13c and 15c the medieval Kingdom of Mali flourished in the Western Sudan, dominating the the trade routes of the Sahara with North Africa. The kingdom reached its peak in the 14c and declined in the 15c. Although it had a quasi-Islamic ruling group, it was dominated by Muslim merchants, and it became an important factor in the Islamicization of West Africa. Mali was governed by France from 1881 to 1895 and was a territory of French Sudan (part of French West Africa) until 1959, when it entered a partnership with Senegal as the Federation of Mali. It achieved independence as a separate nation in 1960. Its first President, Modibo **KEITA**, was overthrown in 1968 in a military coup led by Moussa Traoré, who held power until his arrest in 1991 following pro-democracy rioting. In 1992 a new multiparty constitution was approved in a referendum and the elections were won by the Alliance for Democracy in Mali Party (ADEMA) and President Alpha Oumar Konaré. This government resigned in 1993 after popular protests and was replaced by a succession of short-lived governments, either formed by ADEMA or ADEMA-led coalitions. In 2002, Moussa Traoré regained the presidency and the Spirit 2002 coalition won the legislative elections. In the early 1990s, there was a rebellion against the government by Tuareg tribesmen (the Tuareg Unified Movements and Fronts of Azawad) in the north of the country, concluded by a peace agreement in 1994.

**Malik, Jakub Alexandrovich** (1906–80)
Soviet politician. Having been educated and having practised as an economist in the Ukraine until 1935, he studied at the Diplomatic Institute in Moscow from then until 1937, when he entered the Foreign Service. Said to be one of **STALIN**'s favourite 'juniors', he was ambassador to Japan from 1943 to 1945 and Deputy Foreign Minister with particular responsibility for Far Eastern affairs in 1946–53. From 1948 to 1952 he was also Soviet spokesman at the **UN**, succeeding Andrei **GROMYKO**. Ambassador to Britain in 1953–60, from 1960 he was again Deputy Foreign Minister, serving a second term as Ambassador to the UN in 1968 to 1976.

**Malinovsky, Rodion Yakovlevich** (1898–1967)
Soviet general. He was a corporal in **WORLD WAR I**, when, after the Russian collapse, he escaped via Siberia and Singapore to fight in a Russian brigade in France. He joined the **RED ARMY** in 1919 after the **RUSSIAN REVOLUTION**, built up experience as a military adviser and instructor, and was major-general at the time of the Nazi invasion in 1941. He commanded the forces which liberated Rostov, Kharkov and the Dnieper basin and led the Russian advance on Budapest and into Austria (1943–5). When Russia declared war on Japan, he took a leading part in the Manchurian campaign and after **WORLD WAR II** he held important commands in the Far East. In Oct 1957 he succeeded **ZHUKOV** as Nikita **KHRUSHCHEV**'s Minister of Defence and remained in that post under **BREZHNEV** until his death. He therefore bore considerable responsibility for the great Soviet build-up of the 1960s.

**Malou, Jules** (1810–86)
Belgian politician. He was MP for Ypres (1841–86), Minister for Finance (1847–8), and Prime Minister

and Finance Minister (1871–8 and 1884). A leader of the Catholics in their struggle for state-sponsored Catholic education, he is remembered for his work with Belgium's finances and its railways. ► **SCHOOLS QUESTION (BELGIUM)**

### Malplaquet, Battle of (1709)
A bitter military engagement of the War of the **SPAN- ISH SUCCESSION** between the French army led by Marshals Villars (1653–1734) and Boufflers (1644–1711) and the Grand Alliance army com- manded by **MARLBOROUGH** and Prince **EUGÈNE OF SAVOY**. Malplaquet, a very costly victory for the Allies, stiffened French resistance and swung English opinion behind the **TORIES'** peace policy.

### Malraux, André Georges (1901–76)
French politician and novelist. He studied oriental languages and spent much time in China, where he worked for the **GUOMINDANG** and was active in the 1927 revolution. He also fought in the **SPANISH CIVIL WAR**, and in **WORLD WAR II** escaped from a prison camp to join the French Resistance. He was Minister of Information in de **GAULLE'S** government (1945–6) and Minister of Cultural Affairs (1960–9). He is known for his novels, notably *La Condition humaine* (1933), winner of the Prix Goncourt, and *L'Espoir* (1937). ► **RESISTANCE MOVEMENT (FRANCE)**

---

### MALTA    official name **Republic of Malta**

An archipelago republic in the central Mediterranean Sea. Malta has at various times been controlled by Phoenicia, Greece, Carthage and Rome. It was con- quered by Arabs in the 9c, and later by Spain, and under Emperor **CHARLES V** it was given to the Knights **HOSPITALLERS** in 1530. Captured by the British dur- ing the **NAPOLEONIC WARS**, and a Crown Colony from 1815, it was an important strategic base in both World Wars. In 1942 Malta was awarded the George Cross for its resistance to heavy air attacks. It achieved inde- pendence in 1964, and became a republic in 1974. The British Military Facilities agreement expired in 1979. Malta joined the **EU** in 2004.

### Malthus, Thomas Robert (1766–1834)
English economist. Born near Dorking, Surrey, in 1798 he published anonymously his *Essay on the Principle of Population*. In it he maintained that there is a natural tendency of population to increase faster than the means of subsistence. The problem had been handled by Benjamin **FRANKLIN**, David Hume and many other writers, but Malthus crystallized the views of those writers, and presented them in sys- tematic form with elaborate proofs derived from his- tory, calling for positive action to cut the birth-rate, by sexual abstinence or birth control.

### Malwa
Situated on the high plateau between the Narmada and Tapti rivers in central India. The earliest mention of Malwa in history is made in the context of the 6c BC empire of Avanti (modern Ujjain). Another great an- cient Indian dynasty to rule Malwa was the Shaka who remained in this region until 5c AD. By the sec- ond half of the 10c, the Pawars had established their control over Malwa with their capital in Dhar near In- dore. During the period 1400–1525 Malwa com- manded the trunk routes between Gujarat and northern India and also between north and south India. During the 15c the kingdom of Malwa reached the height of its glory. The capital was shifted from Dhar to Mandu. Here the rulers of Malwa constructed a large number of buildings, the ruins of which are still impressive. One of the early rulers of Malwa, Hushang Shah, adopted a broad policy of religious tolerance. Mahmud Khalji (1436/69), who is consid- ered as the most powerful of Malwa rulers, fought nonetheless with almost all of his neighbours. This feuding with neighbouring territories continued after his death until Malwa was taken over by Rana Sanga of Mewar in 1517.

### Mamaev Kurgan (Mamai Hill)
An area in the heart of Volgograd, USSR, and the scene of the most severe conflict during the Battle of **STALINGRAD** (1942–3).

### Mamelukes ► **MAMLUKS**

### Mamluks
Slave soldiers who constituted the army of the Ayyu- bid sultanate established in Egypt by **SALADIN** in the 1170s. Their commanders (*Amirs*) created a profes- sional army of high quality. In 1250 they overthrew the Ayyubids, and established Muslim dynasties until conquered by the Turks in 1516–17. They continued to rule in Egypt with Ottoman blessing until their massacre by **MUHAMMAD 'ALI** in 1811. ► **OTTOMAN EMPIRE**; *See panel*

### Man, Hendrik de (1885–1953)
Belgian politician. He took a doctorate at Leipzig Uni- versity in economic history, and was appointed to a chair at Frankfurt University in 1929. In 1933 he was forced to leave Germany, and entered active politics in his native Belgium. He rejected **MARXISM**, and de- veloped his own socialist theory, laid out in his La- bour Plan (*Plan du Travail*) of 1934. This non- revolutionary socialism, working with the bour- geoisie and using the democratic state as the instru- ment of socialism, was highly influential in Europe in the 1930s. De Man served as a cabinet minister (1935–8), and was chairman of the **BELGIAN SOCIAL- IST PARTY** from 1939. When the Germans invaded, he entered into collaboration with the New Order, and dissolved his Socialist Party. He escaped to Swit- zerland in 1942, where he died in a traffic accident; in Belgium he was convicted *in absentia* in 1945.

### Manchu
Originally a people of Tartar stock from Manchuria (an area that included present-day Liaoning, Jilin and Heilongjiang), they ruled all China from 1644 to 1911 under the **QING DYNASTY**. (Both *Qing* and *Man* mean 'pure'.)

## MAMLUKS

| Regnal Dates | Name | Regnal Dates | Name |
|---|---|---|---|
| ▶ *Bahri Line* | | 1389 | al-Salih Hajji II (2nd reign) |
| 1250 | Shajar al-Durr | ▶ *Burji (Circassian) Line* | |
| 1250/7 | Aybak | 1382/9 | Barquq (1st reign) |
| 1257/9 | 'Ali | (1389/90) | al-Salih Hajji II) |
| 1259/60 | Qutuz | 1390/9 | Barquq (2nd reign) |
| 1260/77 | Baybars I | 1399/1405 | Faraj (1st reign) |
| 1277/80 | Baraka Khan | 1405 | al-Mansur 'Abd al-'Aziz |
| 1280 | Salamish | 1405/12 | Faraj (2nd reign) |
| 1280/90 | Qala'un | 1412 | al-'Adil al-Musta'in |
| 1290/4 | Khalil | 1412/21 | al-Mu'ayyad Shaykh |
| 1294/5 | al-Nasir Muhammad (1st reign) | 1421 | al-Muzaffar Ahmad |
| 1295/7 | Kitbugha | 1421 | Tatar |
| 1297/9 | Lajin | 1421/2 | al-Salih Muhammad |
| 1299/1309 | al-Nasir Muhammad (2nd reign) | 1422/37 | Barsbay |
| 1309 | Baybars II | 1437/8 | Yusuf |
| 1309/40 | al-Nasir Muhammad (3rd reign) | 1438/53 | al-Zahir Jaqmaq |
| 1340/1 | Abu Bakr | 1453 | 'Uthman |
| 1341/2 | Kujuk | 1453/61 | Inal |
| 1342 | Ahmad | 1461 | al-Mu'ayyad Ahmad |
| 1342/5 | Isma'il | 1461/7 | Khushqadam |
| 1345/6 | Sha'ban I | 1467/8 | Bilbay |
| 1346/7 | Hajji I | 1468 | Timurbugha |
| 1347/51 | al-Nasir al-Hasan (1st reign) | 1468/96 | al-Ashraf Qa'it Bay |
| 1351/4 | Salih | 1496/8 | al-Nasir Muhammad |
| 1354/61 | al-Nasir al-Hasan (2nd reign) | 1498/1500 | Qansuh |
| 1361/3 | al-Mansur Muhammad | 1500/1 | Janbalat |
| 1363/76 | Sha'ban II | 1501 | al-'Adil Tuman Bay |
| 1376/82 | al-Mansur 'Ali | 1501/17 | Qansuh al-Ghawri |
| 1382/9 | al-Salih Hajji II (first reign) | 1517 | al-Ashraf Tuman Bay |
| (1382/9) | Barquq) | | |

## Manchukuo ▶ MANZHUGUO

## Manchuria

A former region of north-east China. A mountainous area, sparsely populated by nomadic tribes, this was the home of the Manchus, who overthrew the MING DYNASTY to become the last Chinese emperors as the QING DYNASTY. Rich in natural resources (timber, coal, iron, magnesite, oil, uranium and gold), Manchuria came under Russian military control in 1900. Captured by Japan in 1932, it became part of the puppet-state of MANZHUGUO, until liberated by Russian troops in 1945. Subsequently, it was one of the bases for the successful Chinese communist offensive that destroyed the GUOMINDANG regime in China. The border area with Russia remains a continuing focus of political tension. ▶ PUYI

## Mandalay

The last capital of the last dynasty of Burma. Situated in the dry central plains, Mandalay was founded by King MINDON in 1857. Like most Burmese capitals, it was designed to represent the ordered structures of the Buddhist universe. During the brief third Anglo-Burmese War in late 1885, much of Mandalay was destroyed; its records and treasures were looted and the last king of the dynasty, Thibaw, was deposed and exiled. ▶ ANGLO-BURMESE WARS

## Mandal Commissions

The name commonly given to the Backward Classes Commission, appointed by India's Janata government in 1978 (under President Morarji DESAI) to examine the position of the former 'untouchable' castes and other low status groups within Indian society. The Commission, under Janata Party member Bindeshwari Prasad Mandal, was asked to report on the effectiveness of the measures taken since independence (1947) to end discrimination against the so-called 'backward classes' and to recommend means by which anti-discriminatory policies could be improved. Following a national survey, the report was published in 1980, but later the same year the Congress Party, under Indira GANDHI, was returned to power, and its proposals were never implemented. It was viewed by some, particularly on the political right, as a divisive political initiative, and Mandal himself resigned from the Janata Party soon after publication of the report. After the defeat of the Congress Party in 1989, the Commission's proposals were revived by the new Prime Minister, V P SINGH, in an attempt to boost the popularity of his minority government. Subsequent attempts to increase the reservation of student places in higher education and appointments in the government service for members of the backward classes proved highly controversial, provoking widespread rioting and unrest in the towns and cities of northern India. The agitation was led mostly by students and younger members of high-caste groups, who adopted self-immolation as a means of protest. The widespread outrage this provoked, together with the controversy over attempts by Hindu fundamentalist groups, backed by the Janata Party, to demolish a Muslim shrine at Ayodhya in northern India to make way for the construction of a Hindu temple on the site, led ultimately to the collapse of V P Singh's government (Nov 1990). In practice, the Commission's proposals would have proved of little benefit to the untouchables; nor did they pose much of a threat to the upper castes. However, the implementation of the recommendations caused widespread opposition amongst the increasingly desperate, unemployed, educated youth of north India. After the restoration of the Congress Party to power (May 1991), new proposals were discussed for the modification of **POSITIVE DISCRIMINATION**, placing more emphasis on economic rather than social disadvantage and thus avoiding the issue of **CASTE**. In 1993 the National Commission for Backward Classes was set up to consider issues of social inclusion and reservation but, as critics have continued to point out, despite legislation and the creation of such bodies, the lot of the lower castes in terms of education, health provision and real employment opportunities has not greatly improved and cynics have dismissed the whole exercise as a vote-gathering tactic.

### Mandarins (Scholar-Official Class)
A 19c Western term used to refer to the class of officials in imperial China who obtained their appointment through success in the **CIVIL SERVICE EXAMINATION SYSTEM** based on the **CONFUCIAN CLASSICS**. Since the number of government posts was always less than the total number of degree-holders, officials were part of a much larger scholarly élite (sometimes referred to in English as 'the gentry') that derived its status from being representatives of the Confucian moral order.

### Mandate of Heaven (Tianming/T'ien-ming)
An important doctrine in imperial China first introduced by the Zhou Dynasty to justify its overthrow of the preceding Shang Dynasty. Early Zhou leaders claimed that rulers were entrusted to rule by Heaven (tian), an impersonal but all-powerful presence that dominated the cosmos. Since the last Shang ruler had been corrupt, Heaven had commanded the Zhou to remove the Shang. To symbolize the mandate to rule granted by heaven, the first Zhou king (and all subsequent rulers) came to be known as the Son of Heaven. The Confucian philosopher Mencius provided a further moral imperative to the doctrine, implying that any ruler who failed to attend to the needs of the people could justifiably be overthrown. Throughout subsequent Chinese history, a popular insurrection or even a natural calamity might be interpreted as a sign of Heaven's displeasure with the ruler, while the leader of a rebellion who succeeded in establishing a new dynasty would legitimize his rule by claiming that the Mandate of Heaven had been withdrawn from the previous dynasty. ► **CHINESE DYNASTIES PRE-1000**AD

### mandates
A system under which former territories of the German and Ottoman empires were to be administered by the victorious powers of **WORLD WAR I** under international supervision. The mandates were granted by the **LEAGUE OF NATIONS**, and annual reports had to be submitted to its Permanent Mandates Commission. Britain and France acquired mandates in the Middle East (Palestine, Iraq, Transjordan, Syria, Lebanon) and Africa (Tanganyika, Togo, Cameroon)

while Belgium acquired Ruanda-Urundi, South Africa acquired South West Africa, and Australia and New Zealand acquired New Guinea and Western Samoa. The functions of the Commission were later taken over by the Trusteeship Council of the **UN**.

### Mandela, Nelson Rolihlahla (1918–)
South African nationalist leader. Educated at Fort Hare College (1938–40), he practised law in Johannesburg before joining the **ANC** (African National Congress) in 1944 and founding the Congress Youth League. For the next 20 years he was at the forefront of black opposition to **APARTHEID**, being 'banned' (1956–61) and sentenced to life imprisonment in 1964 for his leadership of the ANC. He spent most of the next 25 years in prison on Robben Island before being released, on President F W **DE KLERK**'s orders, on 11 Feb 1990. He was elected Deputy President of the ANC by the party in exile (Apr 1990) and in July 1991, in Durban, at the party's first congress inside South Africa for a quarter of a century, he was elected President. In 1993 he was awarded the **NOBEL PEACE PRIZE** jointly with de Klerk for their work in the process of reform, and on 10 May 1994 he was inaugurated as South Africa's first black President. In 1999 he was succeeded as party leader and President by Thabo **MBEKI**.

### Mandelstam, Osip Yemilevich (1891–1938)
Russian poet. Born of Jewish parents in Warsaw, he was brought up in St Petersburg. His early success with *Kamen* (1913, Eng trans *Stone*, 1981), *Tristia* (1922, 'Sad Things'), and *Stikhotvorenia 1921–25* (1928, 'Poems') was followed by suspicion and arrest (1934) by the Soviet authorities. His death was reported from Siberia in 1938. His *Sobraniy sochineniy* (Eng trans, *The Complete Poetry*, 1973) were published in three volumes (1964–71). His wife, Nadezhda, wrote their story in *Hope Against Hope* (1970).

### Manfred (1232–66)
King of Sicily (1258/66). The illegitimate son of Emperor **FREDERICK II**, he was made Prince of Tarentum. He bravely defended the interests of the empire for his nephew **CONRADIN OF SWABIA** against the aggression of Pope **INNOCENT IV**. However, the pope compelled Manfred to flee to the **SARACENS** for shelter. With their aid he defeated the papal army, and in 1257 he became master of the kingdom of Naples and Sicily. On the false rumour of Conradin's death (1258) he was crowned King at Palermo, but was killed in the Battle of **BENEVENTO**.

### Mangu Khan (1251/9)
Great Khan of the Mongol Empire. He was the grandson of **GENGHIS KHAN**. During his rule the **MONGOLS** began their offensive against **SONG DYNASTY** China. He died while campaigning, and the conquest of China was completed by his brother **KUBLAI KHAN**.

### Manhattan Project
The codename for the most secret scientific operation of **WORLD WAR II**, the development of the atomic bomb, undertaken successfully in the USA from 1942 onwards. The project culminated in the detonation of the first atomic weapon near Alamogordo, New Mexico (16 July 1945).

## Manifest Destiny

A term for US expansion throughout North America in the mid-19c, used particularly to rationalize the conquest of Native American and Mexican lands and southern and western settlements. The phrase was coined by the editor of the *United States Magazine and Democratic Review*, John O'Sullivan, who, in 1845, stated that it was the country's 'manifest destiny to overspread the continent allotted by Providence for the free development of our yearly multiplying millions'.

## Manila Bay, Battle of (1 May 1898)

An engagement in the SPANISH-AMERICAN WAR which contributed to the final US victory. Under Commodore George DEWEY, the US Asiatic squadron attacked the Spanish fleet moored in Manila Bay, and succeeded in destroying the entire fleet without losing any of its own men. The squadron then bombarded Manila, which surrendered and was occupied by the US Army from 13 Aug. The victory established the USA as a major Pacific power and made Dewey a popular hero at home.

## Manila Galleon

A collective term applied to the Spanish vessels which sailed across the Pacific between Manila and Acapulco from 1565 to 1815. Carrying rich cargoes of silver from Mexico and Peru, and goods from China, the vessels were an attraction for pirates, particularly English.

## Manin, Daniele (1804–57)

Venetian lawyer and politician. Arrested with Niccolò Tommaseo (1802–74) in Jan 1848 because of his demands that the Austrian government of the Kingdom of LOMBARDY-VENETIA undertake extensive reforms and concede greater autonomy to the Italian population, he was freed (Mar 1848) after an anti-Habsburg insurrection broke out in Venetia. He rapidly emerged as the leader of the revolution, proclaiming the restoration of the Republic of Saint Mark and being elected its President. The pressing need to resist Austria obliged him to cooperate with the revolutionary government in Milan and CHARLES ALBERT of Sardinia-Piedmont. In July 1848, following widespread support for fusion with Lombardy and Piedmont among the population of the Venetian *Terraferma*, he allowed the Venetian assembly to vote on whether the republic should become part of a greater north Italian kingdom. He resigned over the assembly's pro-fusion stance, but by Aug had returned to power and continued to resist the Austrians, despite growing tension with more radical elements led by Giuseppe Sirtori. After the defeat of King Charles Albert by the Austrians at Novara, Manin continued the heroic defence of Venice, assuming virtually dictatorial powers (Aug 1849) until typhus, bombardment and food shortages forced the city's eventual surrender later that month. He fled Venice and settled in Paris, where he gradually shifted from his republican and essentially Venetian stance, towards a position as a monarchist and Italian patriot. In 1856 he supported LA FARINA in his creation of the ITALIAN NATIONAL SOCIETY. His ashes were returned to Venice in a public ceremony in 1868.

## Manin, Ludovico (1726–1802)

Last Doge of Venice. Elected in Mar 1789, during his rule the Venetian Republic ill-advisedly antagonized the French revolutionary regime by allowing émigrés sanctuary, but declined to join the league of Italian states advocated by VICTOR AMADEUS III to counter the growing French threat. The republic was forced to capitulate in 1797 in the face of overwhelming French military superiority. ▶ CAMPO FORMIO, TREATY OF

## Manitoba Schools Act (1890)

Canadian educational legislation. Passed by the Manitoba provincial assembly under pressure from the campaign of D'Alton MCCARTHY, it established a non-sectarian educational system and reversed the act under which Manitoba had been admitted to the Confederation with denominational schools specified. Popular outrage among Catholics, especially in Quebec, challenged the act in the courts, but the Privy Council found in favour of the law. After the Supreme Court had declared remedial legislation to be within federal jurisdiction, the Conservative administration reluctantly introduced it, but not in time to be carried before the election of 1896. When the Liberals won the election, LAURIER ensured that the matter was settled by negotiation rather than coercion. While separate schools were not re-established, denominational religious instruction was accepted, as was bilingual teaching where there were more than ten pupils with a native language other than English. This solution satisfied all except the Catholic Church, which eventually relented after Vatican approval had been sought by the Liberals.

## Maniu, Iuliu (1873–1953)

Romanian politician. The leader of the National Party, he directed the provisional government in Transylvania which proclaimed union with Romania (Dec 1918). Later, as leader of the National Peasant Party, he served as Prime Minister and tried to carry out agrarian reform (1928–30) but resigned from office when King CHARLES II of Romania introduced his mistress, Magda LUPESCU, into the Romanian court. He was again Prime Minister (1932–3) and his electoral alliance with the IRON GUARD was an expediency aimed at curbing the King's power (1937). He played a major role in the coup (Aug 1944) and was a minister without portfolio in General Sănătescu's national government which declared war on Germany. The post-war communist regime, in a move intended to destroy the Peasant Party, had him arrested, accused of conspiring with US intelligence agents. He received a life sentence (1947) and died in prison.

## Manley, Michael Norman (1924–97)

Jamaican politician. The son of Norman MANLEY, he was educated in Jamaica, served in the Royal Canadian Air Force in WORLD WAR II, and then studied at the London School of Economics (1945–9). He worked as a journalist in Britain before returning to Jamaica, where he became a leader of the National Workers' Union in the 1950s, sat in the Senate (1962–7) and was then elected to the House of Representatives. In 1969 he became Leader of the People's National Party (PNP) and, in 1972, Prime Minister. He embarked on a radical, socialist programme, cooling relations with the USA and forming links with Cuba, and despite rising unemployment was re-elected in 1976. He was decisively defeated in 1980 and 1983, but returned to power in 1989 with a much more moderate policy stance. However, he was forced to resign in 1992 due to poor health.

**Manley, Norman Washington** (1893–1969)
Jamaican politician. A Rhodes scholar at Oxford, he was called to the Bar and then became a respected QC. In 1938 he won fame by successfully defending his cousin, and political opponent, Alexander **BUSTA-MANTE**, who was then an active trade unionist, on a charge of sedition. In the same year Manley founded the People's National Party (PNP) and in 1955, seven years before Jamaica achieved full independence, became Chief Minister. He handed over leadership of the PNP to his son, Michael **MANLEY**, in 1969.

**Mannerheim, Carl Gustav Emil, Baron** (1867–1951)
Finnish soldier and politician. When Finland declared her independence (1918), he became Supreme Commander and Regent. Defeated in the presidential election of 1919, he retired into private life, but returned as Commander-in-Chief against the Russians in the **RUSSO-FINNISH WAR** of 1939–40. He continued to command the Finnish forces until 1944, when he became President of the Finnish Republic until 1946. He died at Lausanne, Switzerland. ► **WORLD WAR II**

**Mannix, Daniel** (1864–1963)
Irish-born Australian Catholic archbishop. He was appointed Coadjutor-Archbishop of Melbourne in 1912 and Archbishop in 1917, and campaigned strongly for the rights of Catholics in Australian society, especially state aid for Church schools. After the **EASTER RISING** in Ireland (1916) he became an outspoken supporter of Irish **HOME RULE**, and opposed **HUGHES** demands for conscription in 1916–17. His position verged on a populist identification with the working classes, with whom he enjoyed an immense prestige which he never lost; the social establishment demanded his deportation. In 1920, returning to Europe, he was fêted in the USA, but refused entry to Ireland by the British government. His social views involved a hostility to **CAPITALISM** that for many years made him close to the **AUSTRALIAN LABOR PARTY**, but increasingly he came to regard **COMMUNISM** as the greater threat, and he supported the **DEMOCRATIC LABOR PARTY** after the Labor Party split of the mid-1950s. His involvement with the Catholic laity and combative nature made him a powerful force in Australian society and politics for half a century.

**Mansabdar**
The name (literally, 'holder of an office') given to a member of the military/civil hierarchy created by the Mughal emperor **AKBAR THE GREAT**. All *mansabdars* owed direct allegiance to the emperor and were liable to contribute a contingent to the Mughal army, thus augmenting the size of the army at the emperor's disposal. Akbar drew his mansabdars from all ethnic groups – Irani and Turani, native Muslim, Rajput and other Hindus – which served to weaken the parochialism and factional interests then rife. Every office was graded and assigned one of 33 ranks, from the lowest rank (*mansab*) of 10 to the highest of 7,000. Each officer was assigned a pair of numbers: the *zat*,

a personal rank which determined the person's status and thus salary, was in Akbar's time usually the same as or higher than the *sawar* rank, which indicated the number of cavalrymen – and an appropriate number of infantry and so on – that the mansabdar was required to maintain. Mansabdars were paid handsomely (although they were of course expected to maintain their contingent out of their revenue) by *jagirs*, assignments of land revenue in lieu of salary (the territory assigned for this purpose being regularly changed: the 'rotation of jagirs').

**Mansfeld, Ernst, Count** (1580–1626)
German soldier of fortune in the **THIRTY YEARS' WAR**. The illegitimate son of Peter Ernst Mansfeld, he refused his father's possessions, the promised reward for his brilliant services in Hungary and elsewhere, and went over to the Protestant princes. After he defended the Count Palatine Frederick for a time (1618–20), he was driven by the disaster of the Weissenberg to retreat to the Palatinate, from which he carried on for two years a predatory war on the imperialists, defeating **TILLY** in 1622. Thereafter, he served the United Netherlands, beating the Spaniards at Fleurus (1622). At **RICHELIEU**'s solicitation he raised an army of 12,000 men (mostly in England), but in 1626 he was crushed by **WALLENSTEIN** at Dessau. He died near Sarajevo in Bosnia, when marching to join Gabriel **BETHLEN** of Transylvania.

**Mansfield, William Murray, 1st Earl** (1705–93)
British judge. He became Solicitor-General (1742), an MP, Attorney-General (1754), Chief Justice of the King's Bench (1756), a member of the cabinet, and baron. He was impartial as a judge, but his opinions were unpopular, and during the **GORDON RIOTS** of 1780 his house was burnt. Made earl in 1776, he resigned office in 1788.

**Mansfield Judgement** (1772)
The name given to the ruling by Lord Justice **MANS-FIELD** in a case involving a runaway black slave that **SLAVERY** was neither allowed nor approved under English law, and which effectively abolished slavery in England and Wales.

**Manstein, Fritz Erich von** (1887–1973)
German soldier. At the outset of **WORLD WAR II** he became Chief of Staff to **RUNDSTEDT** in the Polish campaign and later in France, where he was the architect of **HITLER**'s **BLITZKRIEG** invasion plan. In 1941 he was given command of an army corps on the Eastern Front and though not trained in armoured warfare handled his panzers with great resource in the Crimea. After the disaster of **STALINGRAD**, he contrived to extricate the right wing in sufficient strength to stage a successful counter-attack at Kharkov, though he failed to relieve **PAULUS**'s 6th Army. After being captured in 1945, he was imprisoned as a war criminal but released in 1953. A strong advocate of fluid defence for preventing the enemy from exploiting an advantage, he embodied his theories and an account of his military career in his *Lost Victories* (trans 1959).

**Mansur, al-**, originally **Ibn Abi Amir** (940–1002)
Ruler of Córdoba (978/1002). He rose from humble origins to become one of the greatest political and military figures of medieval Spain. From 981 he was effective ruler of the Caliphate of Córdoba and won a

series of impressive victories which earned him the sobriquet *al-Mansur bi-llah* ('Victorious through Allah'). In some 20 years he undertook 50 successful expeditions against the Christians, the most famous being the sacking in 997 of Santiago de Compostela, the key Christian shrine.

**Mantua, Duchy of** ► CHERASCO, PEACE OF; GONZA-GA

**Manuel I Comnenus** (c.1122–1180)
Byzantine Emperor (1143/80). He was the youngest son of **JOHN II COMNENUS**. His initial successes against the Turks and the Normans were halted by the massive defeat of his army at the hands of the **SEL-JUKS** at Myriokephalon (1176), which marked the beginning of the downfall of the empire. ► **BYZANTINE EMPIRE**

**Manuel I, the Great** (1469–1521)
King of Portugal (1495/1521). He consolidated royal power, and his reign, marred only by persecution of the Jews, was the golden age of Portugal. He prepared the code of laws that bears his name, and made his court a centre of chivalry, art and science. He sponsored the voyages of Vasco da **GAMA**, Cabral, and others, which helped to make Portugal the first naval power of Europe and a world centre of commerce.

**Manuel II** (1889–1932)
King of Portugal (1908/10). On the assassination of his father, King Charles (Carlos) I, and Crown Prince Luis, on 1 Feb 1908, he became king, but was forced to abdicate at the revolution of 3 Oct 1910. He subsequently settled in England.

**Manuel II Palaeologus** (1350–1425)
Byzantine Emperor (1391/1425). He was the son of John V Palaeologus (1341/91). For much of his reign, Manuel was besieged in Constantinople by the Turks. At one point he was relieved by the advance of **TIMUR** into Asia Minor, but he failed to profit from this diversion and was overwhelmed.

**Manzhuguo**
A Japanese puppet-state established in 1932 in Manchuria, which Japanese forces had invaded in 1931. **PUYI**, the last Qing Emperor, was its nominal head. The regime ended with the defeat of Japan in 1945. ► **QING DYNASTY; SINO-JAPANESE WAR**

**Manzikert, Battle of** (1071)
The Byzantine Emperor Romanus IV Diogenes (1068/71) tried to extend his empire into Armenia but was defeated at Manzikert near Lake Van by the Seljuk Turks under **ALP ARSLAN** (1063/72), who then launched a full-scale invasion of Anatolia.

**Mao Dun (Mao Tun)**, pseudonym of **Shen Yanbing (Shen Yen-ping)** (1896–1981)
Chinese writer. Educated at Beijing University, he became one of the foremost left-wing intellectuals and writers in China, adopting the pseudonym Mao Dun. In 1926 he joined the Northern Expedition as a propagandist, but had to go underground in Shanghai as a communist activist. In 1930 he helped to organize the influential League of Left-Wing Writers. After the communists came to power in 1949, he was China's first Minister of Culture (1949–65), and was founder-editor of the literary journal *People's Literature*

(1949–53). During the **CULTURAL REVOLUTION** he was kept under house arrest in Beijing (1966–78).

**Maoism**
Specifically, the thought of **MAO ZEDONG**, and more broadly a revolutionary ideology based on **MARX-ISM–LENINISM** and adapted to Chinese conditions. Maoism shifted the focus of revolutionary struggle from the urban workers or proletariat to the countryside and the peasantry. There were three main elements: strict Leninist principles of organization; Chinese tradition; and armed struggle as a form of revolutionary activity. Mao gained political power in 1949 through a peasant army, his slogan being 'Political power grows through the barrel of a gun'. While there were attempts to take account of the views of the masses, the Chinese Communist Party was organized along strict centralist, hierarchical lines, and increasingly became a vehicle for a personal dictatorship. In domestic terms, Mao pursued a radical and far-reaching attempt to transform traditional Chinese society and its economy, using thought reform, indoctrination and the psychological transformation of the masses. Maoism was regarded in the 1960s, at the height of the **CULTURAL REVOLUTION**, as a highly radical form of Marxism–Leninism that was distinct from the bureaucratic repression of the USSR, and had a strong appeal among the New Left. Since his death, his use of the masses for political purposes, his economic reforms and his conception of political power have been increasingly criticized inside and outside China as seriously misguided and too rigid.

**Maoris**
Polynesian people who were the original inhabitants of New Zealand. The first of them arrived, probably from the Marquesas, about 800, bringing with them dogs and rats, and some cultivated plants, including the kumara (sweet potato). They also ate fern roots, fish and birds, including the large flightless moa, which they hunted to extinction. By 1200 they had explored the whole country, and by 1800 numbered over 100,000. They were skilful carvers of wood and greenstone (jade). Politically they were divided into loose tribes linked by trade and sporadic warfare, and ruled by hereditary chiefs. In the 19c they came to be outnumbered and dominated by European (*pakeha*) settlers. Their culture declined; they lost most of their land; and by 1896 their population had shrunk to 42,200. There has been some improvement in the 20c. Numbers have risen (c.500,000 in 2001), and since the 1970s they have become politically more assertive. The Maori language has been officially encouraged, and they have obtained the return of some of their land. ► **MAORI WARS**

**Maori Wars**
A succession of conflicts (1843–7 and 1860–72) in which the Maori people attempted, unsuccessfully, to resist the occupation of New Zealand by British settlers. The wars, both in the 1840s and the 1860s, concerned the settlers' demands for land and the growing opposition of a section of Maori opinion to land sales, with the colonial government caught between them, but in practice favouring the settlers. The fighting involved the contrasting slow, methodical sieges of efficiently defended Maori strongholds and widespread guerrilla conflict as Maori resistance

# *Maps and Charts*

Transport & Travel

On the basis of encounters with non-literate peoples who either possess maps or have learnt to draw sketch maps, it has been suggested that the idea of making and using graphical guides for travellers or graphical representations of localities goes back a very long way in human history. The earliest maps still in existence are Babylonian, dating from around 2300 BC. They are *cadastral* maps – land surveys for the purposes of taxation – made on clay tiles. The ancient Egyptians used geometrical methods to produce similar plans so that property boundaries could be re-established after Nile floods.

Regional maps still in existence are of somewhat later date. An Assyrian map of part of northern Mesopotamia – also on a clay tablet – dates from around 500 BC, while the Chinese produced regional maps on silk in the 2c BC. The Incas and Aztecs were also skilled map-makers; the Incas had maps cut in stone that showed some geographical features in relief, and **Montezuma II** is said to have presented Hernán **Cortés** with a map of the Gulf of Mexico drawn on cloth.

### Ancient Greek cartography
The first known map of the world was produced in the 6c BC by Anaximander. Perhaps influenced by Babylonian models, he showed the earth as a flat, circular disc surrounded by the ocean, with the Aegean at its centre. Scientific progress associated with the late-6c BC school of Pythagoras, however, led to the acceptance of the idea that the earth is a sphere. This, combined with observations of the sun's apparent movement along the ecliptic – the route it follows between the tropics of Cancer and Capricorn in the course of the year – enabled maps to begin to be made on mathematical principles and incorporating (however crudely) lines of latitude and longitude. The first map-maker to do this was Eratosthenes (c.276–194 BC), who became head of the great library in Alexandria and measured the angle of the ecliptic and the circumference of the earth with considerable accuracy. His world map extends from England to India and south to Libya. One of his successors in Alexandria, Ptolemy (Claudius Ptolemaeus, c.90–168 AD), is frequently cited as the greatest and most influential geographer of the ancient world. In the 2c AD he published his *Geography*, which is both a collection of maps drawn using accurate conical projection, and a treatise on how such maps should be drawn. By modern standards the maps of Ptolemy, his predecessors and most of his successors for the next 1,500 years are woefully inaccurate. But it is a moot point whether Ptolemy should be censured for showing Scotland jutting eastward from the northern extremity of England, for overestimating the size of the island of Sri Lanka, and for making the longitudinal extent of the Mediterranean 20° greater than it is in reality, or whether he should be congratulated for knowing as much as he did.

### From the Romans to the Middle Ages
The Romans made no effort to improve on Greek achievements in scientific cartography. They preferred the disc model for the earth as it made maps easier to draw. The maps they produced tended to be practical aids to officials making journeys by road. A late copy of a road map of the Roman Empire exists in the form of a long narrow roll – a kind of strip map in effect. It should be remembered that written itineraries were as important, if not more important, to early travellers than actual maps. A map of the type indicated above – like the much later road maps of Britain produced by John Ogilby in 1675 – might be thought of as a representation of an itinerary in graphic form.

After the fall of the Roman Empire, all knowledge of scientific map-making on the Greek model was lost and few maps appeared in the West. Those that were produced frequently made geographical knowledge subject to Christian doctrine – Jerusalem, for instance, was taken to be the centre point of the world, as Delphi had been for some of the less scientific of the ancient Greeks. Arabian scholars, however, knew and revered the work of Ptolemy. Al-Idrisi (or Edrisi), the geographer to King **Roger II** of Sicily, produced a world map and geographical survey of the known world in around

was often localized and tribal. Nevertheless, time and numbers were on the side of the Europeans; Maori resistance was worn down, and they were forced to surrender or retreat to the wilder central North Island where pursuit was both difficult and unnecessary. An uneasy stand-off was reached by the early 1870s but peace was not formalized until 1881.

**Mao Tse-tung** ► MAO ZEDONG

**Mao Tun** ► MAO DUN

**Mao Zedong (Mao Tse-tung)** (1893–1976)
Chinese political leader. He was the leading theorist of the Chinese communist revolution which won national power in China in 1949. The son of a farmer, at the age of 12 he sought an education in Changsha, where he was introduced to Western ideas. After graduating from a teachers' training college there, he went to Beijing, where he came under the influence of **LI DAZHAO**. He took a leading part in the **MAY FOURTH MOVEMENT**, then became a Marxist and a founding member of the Chinese Communist Party (CCP) (1921). During the first United Front with the

Nationalist Party, he concentrated on political work among the peasants of his native province, and advocated a rural revolution, creating the **JIANGXI SOVIET**. After the break with the Nationalists in 1927, the Communists were driven from the cities, and with the assistance of **ZHU DE**, he evolved the guerrilla tactics of the 'people's war'. In 1934 the Nationalist government was at last able to destroy the Jiangxi Soviet, and in the subsequent **LONG MARCH** the Communist forces retreated to Shaanxi to set up a new base. When in 1936, under the increasing threat of Japanese invasion, the Nationalists renewed their alliance with the Communists, Mao restored and vastly increased the political and military power of his party. His claim to share in the government led to civil war; the regime of **CHIANG KAI-SHEK** was ousted from the Chinese mainland; and the new People's Republic of China was proclaimed (1 Oct 1949) with Mao as both Chairman of the CCP and President of the Republic. He followed the Soviet model of economic development and social change until 1958, then launched his **GREAT LEAP FORWARD**, which encouraged the establishment of rural industry and

1154. Al-Idrisi's work was based on his own travels and on accounts brought back by travellers sent out by the king on journeys of exploration. This aptly illustrates the way in which over the centuries accounts by travellers such as Marco **Polo** were used by geographers and map-makers to fill in the blanks on existing maps and to correct and amplify previous knowledge. Arabian knowledge also found its way into southern Spain, where the Catalan school of highly skilful map-makers developed during the 14c. Abraham Cresques, a Jew from Palma Majorca, produced an atlas (the Catalan atlas) for the King of Aragon in 1375, which shows Asia more accurately than any previous Western map and is marked with many of the features described by Marco Polo in his account of his travels.

### Early sea charts

As early travellers probably used written itineraries, early sailors who generally kept within sight of the coast used written records – known in English as pilots' *rutters* – containing useful information on seamarks and hazards. As aids to navigation, star charts probably preceded sea charts, and many early civilizations made them. A tradition of Arab, Indian and Chinese navigation that used azimuthal star charts and determined latitude by measuring the altitude of the pole star probably dates from very ancient times. The **Pawnee** of North America are also known to have used star charts for navigation on land during their seasonal migrations.

The first recorded use of a sea chart in European waters was in 1270, when King **Louis IX** of France was shown one on his way to fight in a Crusade. The compass had been first used in Europe about a century earlier (though its use in China is recorded a century before that). Maps of the Mediterranean dating from around 1275 carry a compass rose showing north and incorporate compass bearings between ports. These charts – known as *portolan* charts or *portolanos* – represented a considerable advance on anything previously produced by medieval mapmakers in Europe, and were adopted into the maps produced by the Catalan school. Because of the short distances involved in Mediterranean sailing, the curvature of the earth did not greatly affect courses plotted along the straight 'rhomb' lines representing compass bearings on the portolan charts.

### The Renaissance and the Age of Exploration

Ptolemy's map and his *Geography* became available in the West again in the early 15c. His maps were reissued – often with improvements and additions – and from this period onwards maps could be engraved and printed. The known world extended east and was beginning to extend south along the coast of Africa; sailing westward, it could only be assumed that by travelling far enough one would reach the coast of Asia. It was with this belief that **Columbus** set sail.

From around 1500 charts and maps begin to appear showing sections of the New World. In 1529 Diego Ribero, a Portuguese chart-maker working in Spain, incorporated information brought back from **Magellan's** circumnavigation of the globe in a chart that shows something of the true extent and position of the Pacific Ocean. In 1569 Gerardus Mercator produced the first map drawn using the method of projection that bears his name. In it lines of longitude are shown an equal distance apart over the whole of the map, and the path of a ship following a constant compass bearing can be represented by a straight line. Though extremely useful in enabling a sailor to plot a course as a straight line without distortion due to the earth's curvature, Mercator's projection distorts distance and the size of landmasses in the higher latitudes, where lines of longitude converge on a globe. Modern equal-area projections provide a more accurate picture, but no flat map can avoid distortion. For this reason large globes were often preferred in the 16–17c.

The concepts of latitude and longitude had been understood and used from the days of the ancient Greeks. Whereas the equator provided the obvious prime parallel, there was no similarly obvious prime meridian; 0° of longitude was not finally fixed at Greenwich by international agreement until 1884. Though the determination of latitude by astronomical observation with the aid of tables was comparatively simple, the accurate determination of longitude presented a more difficult problem; it was finally solved by the invention of a reliable marine chronometer by John Harrison in the 1760s. If the chronometer was set to show the time at 0°, then the difference between local time at noon and 0°, time enabled navigators to calculate their longitude accurately – four minutes of time difference being equal to one degree of longitude.

---

the use of surplus rural labour to create a new infrastructure for agriculture. The failure of the Great Leap lost him most of his influence, but by 1965, with China's armed forces securely in the hands of his ally, **LIN BIAO**, he launched a **CULTURAL REVOLUTION**, and the Great Leap strategy was revived (though with new caution) when the left wing was victorious in the ensuing political struggles (1965–71). He died in Beijing after a prolonged illness, which may well have weakened his judgement during his last years. A strong reaction set in against the excessive collectivism and egalitarianism that had emerged, but his anti-Stalinist emphasis on rural industry and on local initiative was retained and strengthened by his successors. ► **COMMUNISM**; **MAOISM**

### Mapai Party

Acronym for the Hebrew *mifleget poalei eretz yisrael* ('Party of the Workers of the Land of Israel'). A political party created in 1930 from two already existing parties by David **BEN-GURION** among others, Mapai aimed to establish a national Jewish homeland in **PALESTINE** built on socialist principles and became

the main party in the **YISHUV**. During **WORLD WAR II**, Mapai opposed British policy in Palestine but supported the war against the Nazis; after 1948 it maintained a dominant position within Israeli politics. Mapai combined with two other socialist parties in 1968 to form the Israel Labour Party (Hebrew, *mifleget ha-avodah ha-yisraelit*), which remained in power until 1977 when the rival **LIKUD** coalition came to power. Since then the two have operated in a two-party system. ► **JEWISH AGENCY**; **LIKUD**

### Mapillas

Descendants of early Arab settlers in many of the coastal towns of peninsular India. Arabs visited India long before the days of Muhammad, and there is evidence of small Muslim communities from the 8c. Unlike the Roman traders, the Arabs settled permanently in the coastal regions of south India, where they were welcomed as traders and given land for their trading stations; they were free to practise their religion. The Malabar Muslims, being mainly traders, were not concerned with converting others to Islam, and therefore coexisted peacefully with

## National maps

France was the first nation to carry out a full-scale national survey based on triangulation (calculated from the meridian of Paris). This was begun in 1744 by César François Cassini, continued by his son, Jacques Dominique, and not finally completed until 1818. The British Ordnance Survey was officially established (as the Trigonometrical Survey) in 1791, following British cooperation in surveying the Channel area for the Cassini project. The first four sheets of the one inch to the mile survey were published in 1801, and covered Kent and part of Essex and London. Other countries soon established their own surveys, and in the course of the 19c most of the countries of Europe were mapped. In 1879 a Geological Survey was organized in the USA for the purpose of mapping the entire country, and a land survey was established in Japan in 1888. In 1891 the International Geographical Congress proposed the mapping of the entire world on a scale of 1:1,000,000. The project started slowly, and though the rate of progress increased after **World War II** it is still incomplete.

## Modern developments

Aerial photography, begun in **World War I**, has been of enormous assistance to modern map-makers. So too has the use of artificial satellites for surveying. Beginning in 1966, the USA has been involved in a complete geodetic survey of the surface of the earth by satellite. The satellite-based Global Positioning System (GPS), originally funded by the US Department of Defense, also enables the latitude, longitude and altitude of any point on the earth's surface to be accurately determined. Of equal importance are geographic information systems (GISs) that have the ability to overlay additional information on existing data, a feature fundamental to modern mapping.

Maps of the seabed began to be made in the 19c when the first submarine cables were laid down. The use of echo-sounding devices, first used for hydrographic surveying during the 1920s, has made such maps and navigational charts far more accurate.

Photography has also played an important part in the production of modern and accurate star atlases, and the mapping of the northern skies to modern standards was completed in the 1950s. Finally, and on an even grander scale, projects such as the Hubble Space Telescope open the prospect of mapping the universe, a task that Ptolemy undertook in addition to his maps of the earth back in the 2c AD.

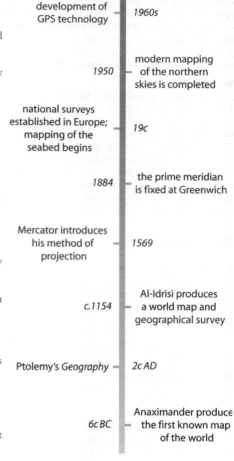

| | |
|---|---|
| development of GPS technology | 1960s |
| 1950 | modern mapping of the northern skies is completed |
| national surveys established in Europe; mapping of the seabed begins | 19c |
| 1884 | the prime meridian is fixed at Greenwich |
| Mercator introduces his method of projection | 1569 |
| c.1154 | Al-Idrisi produces a world map and geographical survey |
| Ptolemy's *Geography* | 2c AD |
| 6c BC | Anaximander produces the first known map of the world |

local society. However, social and economic changes under British rule and the poverty that resulted, as well as instances of favouritism by police and the local administration, provoked a succession of up-risings in the 19c and early 20c, which often took on a 'communal' or sectarian character. The most serious outbreak was that of 1921, that was marked not only by murder and mayhem, but attempts at the forcible conversion of Hindus. The price for this was paid during the pacification campaigns of the British and the famine that stalked the country in this part of India for many years afterwards. A wider significance of these events lay in the way in which they helped to undermine the cooperation between Muslims and Hindus that had characterized the early years of the Indian independence movement.

**Maps and Charts** ► *See panel*

## Maquiladoras

A Spanish term used in Mexico (literally, 'assembly') signifying foreign-owned industrial assembly plants built on the US border, in order to take advantage of lower wage rates and less onerous labour legislation in Mexico. The growth of *maquiladora* industries was most rapid in the 1960s, as both the US and Mexican authorities sought to limit the flight of the *braceros* to California and Texas, while major multinational manufacturing firms sought to take advantage of tax-breaks conceded under Mexican legislation designed to stimulate industrial growth and exports. Their effective contribution to Mexican growth is hotly debated, while their existence is also unpopular with US labour unions. ► **BRACERO**

## Maquis

The local name given to the dense scrub in Corsica; adopted in German-occupied France by groups of young men who hid in the hills and forests to escape forced labour in Germany. Organized into Resistance groups, they led the national rising against the Germans on and after **D-DAY**. ► **RESISTANCE MOVEMENT** (France); **WORLD WAR II**

## Marat, Jean Paul (1743–93)

French revolutionary politician. He studied medicine at Bordeaux, and lived in Paris, the Netherlands and London. At the Revolution he became a member of the **CORDELIERS' CLUB** and established the radical paper *L'Ami du peuple* ('The Friend of the People'). His virulence provoked hatred, and he was several times forced into hiding. Elected to the National **CONVENTION**, he became a leader of the **MOUNTAIN**, and advocated radical reforms. After **LOUIS XVI**'s death he was locked in a struggle with the **GIRONDINS**, and was fatally stabbed in his bath by a Girondin supporter, Charlotte **CORDAY**; thereafter he was hailed as a martyr. ► **FRENCH REVOLUTION; GIRONDINS**

## Maratha Kingdom

A west Indian regional power, founded by the Maratha warrior-leader **SHIVAJI** (1627–80), which filled the vacuum left by Mughal decline. It later became a confederacy of leading families (Bhonsle, Gaekwad, Holkar, **SINDIA**) under hereditary chief ministers (Peshwas). The kingdom was defeated by the Afghans at the Battle of **PANIPAT** (1761). Internal disputes caused the Peshwa to seek British protection at one stage, but the kingdom was finally destroyed by the British in the last of three wars, fought in 1775–82, 1803–5 and in 1818.

## Maravi, Kingdom of

An African kingdom situated north of the Zambezi and south of Lake Malawi, which has given its name to the modern Malawi. It was a rather loose confederation of chiefdoms under a titular head which occupied territory spanning land in Malawi, Zambia and Mozambique. Its peoples were involved in long-distance trade, and in the 17c its power reached the eastern African coast; but it was disrupted by the migrations of the Ngoni in the early 19c.

## Marbury v Madison (1803)

The first US Supreme Court decision declaring a federal law unconstitutional. William Marbury had received a minor judicial appointment as one of the last acts of President John **ADAMS**'s administration. James **MADISON**, the new Secretary of State, refused to deliver the commission and Marbury took legal action. Chief Justice John **MARSHALL** admonished Madison but found that the clause of the Federal Judiciary Act (1789) under which Marbury brought his case was contrary to the **US CONSTITUTION**. In a classic assertion of the doctrine of judicial review he argued that 'it is emphatically the province and duty of the judicial department to say what the law is'.

## March, Juan (1884–1962)

Spanish business magnate. If Barcelona was the nexus of his financial empire, Mallorca (where he was born) became his own personal fiefdom. Imprisoned for fraud by the Second Republic, he retaliated by aiding the military rebellions of 1932 and July 1936. During the **SPANISH CIVIL WAR** he was a key backer of the Nationalists. He died the richest person in modern Spain, allegedly the seventh in the world. ► **REPUBLIC, SECOND** (Spain)

## Marchais, Georges René Louis (1920–97)

French communist politician. A former metalworker, he joined the French **COMMUNIST PARTY** (PCF) in 1947, becoming its Secretary-General in 1972. Under his leadership the PCF pledged its commitment to the 'transition to socialism' by democratic means, and joined the **SOCIALIST PARTY** (PS) in a new 'Union

of the Left'. This union was, however, severed by Marchais in 1977 and the party returned to an orthodox 'Moscow line', although PCF ministers participated in the **MITTERRAND** government (1981–4). He unsuccessfully contested the 1981 presidential election and stepped down as PCF leader in 1994.

## Marchand, Jean Baptiste (1863–1934)

French soldier and explorer. He explored the White Nile, and caused a Franco-British crisis by hoisting the tricolour at Fashoda in 1898. As a general he distinguished himself in **WORLD WAR I**. ► **FASHODA INCIDENT**

## Marchenko, Anatoli Tikhonovich (1938–86)

Soviet dissident. One of the small group of prominent Soviet dissidents whose continuing courage did much to bring down the communist system. As a young worker and writer, he was first imprisoned in 1960 for attempting to travel abroad and spent 18 of his remaining 26 years in jails or camps for championing his rights. He wrote the first detailed account of Buzhnev labour camp in *My Testimony* in 1968, and died in prison on hunger strike but in suspicious circumstances.

## March First Movement (1919)

A non-violent protest in Korea led by religious groups (both Buddhist and Christian) in response to the failure of the **PARIS PEACE CONFERENCE** to grant Korea independence from Japan (Korea had been a colony since 1910). The timing of the demonstration coincided with funeral ceremonies for the former Korea king, Kojong (1864/1907). Mourners signed a declaration of independence amidst rumours that Kojong had been poisoned for having refused to sign a statement supporting permanent unity with Japan. Japanese troops responded with violence and hundreds of Koreans were killed (553 according to Japanese figures at the time; 7,189 according to later Korean figures). Colonial control was relaxed for a time during the 1920s by party governments in Japan anxious to atone for the incident, but with the emergence of military-led cabinets in the 1930s Japanese policy in Korea once more became oppressive.

## March on Rome (Oct 1922)

The largely symbolic march on the Italian capital by several thousand fascists. Although **MUSSOLINI** subsequently liked to portray the event as a glorious seizure of power, he had already successfully negotiated and bullied his way into office before his supporters actually arrived in the capital. He did not reach Rome himself until he was already certain of success in his bid for power and had been invited to form a government by **VICTOR EMMANUEL III**.

## March through Georgia (1864)

A campaign in the American Civil War by the Northern army under General **SHERMAN**, resulting in devastation of the area between Atlanta and the ocean. In military terms it completed the task of splitting the Confederacy on an East–West line. ► **AMERICAN CIVIL WAR**

## March to the Sea ► MARCH THROUGH GEORGIA; SHERMAN, WILLIAM TECUMSEH

## Marco Polo ► POLO, MARCO

**Marco Polo Bridge Incident** (7 July 1937)
A clash between Chinese and Japanese troops near the Marco Polo Bridge, south-west of Beijing, that was to lead to full-scale war between China and Japan (1937–45). Exercising their right under the Boxer Protocol (1901), which allowed foreign troops to be stationed in the vicinity of Beijing, Japanese soldiers were engaged in manoeuvres when skirmishes with local Chinese forces took place. Although a local ceasefire was arranged (11 July 1937), the Japanese Prime Minister, **KONOE**, announced plans to mobilize five divisions for north China. The head of the Chinese Nationalist government, **CHIANG KAI-SHEK**, reversing the appeasement policy he had followed regarding persistent Japanese attempts to remove north China from Chinese central government control, responded by reinforcing Chinese forces. Chiang's unyielding stand was prompted by the anti-Japanese united front agreement he had been compelled to sign in 1936 with the communists. On 29 July 1937 Japanese troops attacked and occupied Beijing, signalling the start of the war between the two countries.

**Marcos, Ferdinand Edralin** (1917–89)
Filipino politician and President (1965–86). He trained as a lawyer, and as a politician obtained considerable US support as an anti-communist. His regime as President was marked by increasing repression, misuse of foreign financial aid, and political violence (notably, the assassination of Benigno **AQUINO** in 1983). He declared martial law in 1972. Overthrown in 1986 by a popular revolt led by Cory **AQUINO**, he went into exile in Hawaii, where he and his wife, Imelda, fought against demands from US courts investigating charges of financial mismanagement and massive corruption. He died in Honolulu.

**Marengo, Battle of** (14 June 1800)
The important, but narrow, French victory over the Austrians, fought in northern Italy during the War of the Second Coalition. It enabled **NAPOLEON I** to ensure his restored hegemony in northern Italy, to guarantee the re-establishment of the **CISALPINE REPUBLIC** and to assert his political authority in France. ► **NAPOLEONIC WARS; WARS OF THE COALITION**

**Margai, Sir Albert Michael** (1910–80)
Sierra Leone politician. The son of a trader and the brother of Sir Milton **MARGAI**, he was educated in Roman Catholic schools before becoming a nurse and pharmacist. He studied law in London (1944–7) and was elected a member of Legco in 1951, when he was appointed Minister of Education, Welfare and Local Government. A member of the Sierra Leone People's Party from 1951–8, he helped found the People's National Party and became Minister of Finance at independence. When his brother died, he succeeded him as party leader and Prime Minister (1964–7). Following the military coup led by Siaka **STEVENS** in 1967, he went into exile in London.

**Margai, Sir Milton Augustus Strieby** (1895–1964)
Sierra Leone nationalist leader and politician. The elder brother of Sir Albert **MARGAI**, he was educated in Roman Catholic mission schools, Fourah Bay College and in the UK, where he qualified as a doctor. Appointed a member of the Protectorate Assembly

in 1940, he was elected to Legco in 1951, when he helped found the Sierra Leone People's Party and played a major role in pressing for independence. He was Chief Minister (1954–8) and, on independence, Prime Minister until his death in 1964.

**Margaret I, Margaret II** (of Denmark) ► **MARGRETHE I, MARGRETHE II**

**Margaret, Maid of Norway** (1283–90)
Infant Queen of Scotland (1286/90). The granddaughter of **ALEXANDER III** of Scotland, she was the only child of Alexander's daughter Margaret (who died in childbirth) and King Erik II of Norway. When Alexander III died in 1286, Margaret was the only direct survivor of the Scottish royal line. In 1289 she was betrothed to the infant Prince Edward (the future **EDWARD II** of England), son of **EDWARD I**, but she died at sea the following year on her way from Norway to the Orkneys.

**Margaret, St** (c.1045–1093)
Scottish Queen. Born in Hungary, she came to England, but after the **NORMAN CONQUEST** fled to Scotland with her boy brother, **EDGAR THE ATHELING**. She married the Scottish king **MALCOLM III, CANMORE** and did much to civilize the realm, and to assimilate the old Celtic Church into the rest of Christendom. She was canonized in 1250.

**Margaret I, Margaret II** (of Denmark) ► **MARGRETHE I, MARGRETHE II**

**Margaret of Angoulême** ► **MARGARET OF NAVARRE**

**Margaret of Anjou** (1429–82)
Queen Consort of **HENRY VI** of England (1445/82). She was the daughter of René of Anjou. Because of Henry's madness, she became deeply involved in political life, and during the Wars of the **ROSES**, was a leading Lancastrian. Defeated at the Battle of **TEWKESBURY** (1471), she was imprisoned in the Tower for four years, until ransomed by **LOUIS XI** of France. She then retired to France, where she died. ► **LANCASTER, HOUSE OF**

**Margaret of Austria** (1480–1530)
Duchess of Savoy and Regent of the Netherlands. The daughter of the Emperor **MAXIMILIAN I** and **MARY OF BURGUNDY**, in 1497 she married, first, the Infante Juan of Spain, who died within a few months, and then in 1501, Philibert II, Duke of Savoy. In 1507 her father appointed her Regent of the Netherlands and guardian of her nephew, the future Emperor **CHARLES V**. In 1519 she was appointed Regent again, by Charles V, and proved herself an effective and capable stateswoman. She was convinced of the importance of the Low Countries to Habsburg interests, and was a great patron of the arts. ► **HABSBURG DYNASTY**

**Margaret of Navarre** (1492–1549)
Queen of Navarre. The sister of **FRANCIS I** of France, in her youth she was known as Marguerite d'Angoulême. In 1509 she was married to the Duke of Alençon, who died in 1525; and in 1527 to Henri d'Albret, titular King of Navarre. Their daughter, Jeanne d'Albret, was the mother of **HENRY IV** of France. A patroness of humanism and literature in

the **RENAISSANCE** tradition, she sheltered religious reformers at her court in Angoulême.

## Margaret of Parma (1522–86)

Regent of the Netherlands. The illegitimate daughter of the Emperor **CHARLES V**, she married first Alessandro de' **MEDICI** (1536) and second Ottavio Farnese, Duke of Parma (1538), to whom she bore Alessandro **FARNESE** (later Duke of Parma) in 1545. From 1559 to 1567 she was Regent of the Netherlands, masterful, able, and a staunch Catholic. She rapidly restored peace after the **IMAGE-BREAKING RIOTS** (1566), but was replaced by the Duke of **ALBA**. While her son Alessandro was governor of the Netherlands (1578–86), later ruling as regent for **PHILIP II** of Spain, Margaret was made head of the civil administration for a time.

## Margaret Tudor (1489–1541)

Queen of Scotland. The elder daughter of **HENRY VII** of England, she became the wife of **JAMES IV** of Scotland (1503) and the mother of **JAMES V**, for whom she acted as Regent. After James IV's death in 1513 she married twice again, to the Earl of Angus (1514) and Lord Methven (1527). She was much involved in the political intrigues between the pro-French and pro-English factions in Scotland, but lacking Tudor shrewdness, she was discredited (1534). Her great-grandson was **JAMES VI AND I.** ► **TUDOR, HOUSE OF**

## Margrethe I (1353–1412)

Queen of Denmark (1375/1412), Norway (1380/1412), and Sweden (1388/1412). She became Queen of Denmark in 1375, on the death of her father, Valdemar IV, without male heirs. On the death of her husband, Haakon VI, in 1380, she became ruler of Norway; and in 1388 she aided a rising of Swedish nobles against their King, Albrekt of Mecklenburg, and became Queen of Sweden. She had her infant cousin, **ERIK OF POMERANIA**, crowned King of the three kingdoms at Kalmar in 1397, but remained the real ruler of Scandinavia until her death at Flensburg. ► **KALMAR UNION**

## Margrethe II (1940– )

Queen of Denmark (1972/ ). The daughter of **FREDERICK IX**, whom she succeeded, she is an archaeologist, and was educated at the universities of Copenhagen, Aarhus and Cambridge, the Sorbonne, Paris, and the London School of Economics. In 1967 she married a French diplomat, Count Henri de Laborde de Monpezat, now Prince Henrik of Denmark. Their children are the heir-apparent, Prince Frederik André Henrik Christian, and Prince Joachim Holger Valdemar Christian.

## Maria Carolina (1752–1814)

Queen of Naples. The daughter of **MARIA THERESA** of Austria, she married Ferdinand IV of Naples (**FERDINAND I**) in 1768 and rapidly came to dominate him. She appointed her English lover, John Acton, Prime Minister and brought Naples into the Austro-British coalition against revolutionary France. She fled to Sicily with her husband during the uprising that led to the establishment of the **PARTHENOPEAN REPUBLIC** and again in 1806 when the French invaded Naples. However, the British forces defending Sicily thought her a danger and had her exiled to Austria, where she spent the remainder of her life.

## María Cristina (1806–78)

Queen Consort and Regent (1833/40) of Spain. She was the daughter of Francis I, King of the **TWO SICILIES**, and fourth wife of **FERDINAND VII** of Spain. On his death (1833), she became Regent for their daughter, **ISABELLA II**. A Carlist war broke out, and in 1836 she was forced to grant a constitution; in 1840 she resigned the regency and fled to France, but returned in 1843. Her share in the schemes of **LOUIS-PHILIPPE** over the marriage of her daughter in 1846, and her reactionary policy, made her unpopular. In 1854 a revolution drove her again to France, where, except for a time in Spain (1864–8), she lived thereafter.

## Maria II da Gloria (1819–53)

Queen of Portugal (1826/8 and 1834/53). Proclaimed Queen under a regency following the death of her grandfather, John VI, in 1826, Maria was overthrown by her uncle, Miguel, in 1828. A civil war between Liberals and Absolutists ensued (1832–4), returning Maria to the throne. In Nov 1836 she tried to engineer a coup d'état against a leftist government. Similarly, the civil war of 1846–7 was caused by Maria's imposition of the conservative Saldanha as Prime Minister. Although Maria was forced to abdicate, the English and Spanish enforced the Peace of Gramido (June 1847), which restored her to power until her death in childbirth. Through both her interference and her favouritism, she undoubtedly exacerbated the political instability of the years 1836–51, being personally responsible for several crises.

## Maria Theresa (1717–80)

Archduchess of Austria and Queen of Hungary and Bohemia (1740/80). The daughter of Emperor **CHARLES VI**, in 1736 she married Francis, Duke of Lorraine, and in 1740 succeeded her father in the hereditary Habsburg lands. Her claim, however, led to the War of the **AUSTRIAN SUCCESSION**, during which she lost Silesia to Prussia. In 1741 she received the Hungarian crown, and in 1745 her husband was elected Holy Roman Emperor (**FRANCIS I**). Although her Foreign Minister, **KAUNITZ**, tried to isolate Prussia by diplomatic means, military conflict was renewed in the **SEVEN YEARS' WAR**, and by 1763 she was finally forced to recognize the status quo of 1756. In her later years she strove to maintain international peace, and reluctantly accepted the partition of Poland (1772). Of her ten surviving children, the eldest son, **JOSEPH II**, succeeded her. ► **FREDERICK II, THE GREAT; HABSBURG DYNASTY**

## Marie Antoinette, in full Josèphe Jeanne Marie Antoinette (1755–93)

Queen Consort of France (1774/93). She was the daughter of Maria Theresa and Emperor **FRANCIS I** of Austria, and sister of **JOSEPH II** and **LEOPOLD II**. Married in 1770 to the **DAUPHIN** (later **LOUIS XVI**), in order to strengthen the Franco-Austrian alliance, she exerted a growing influence over him. Capricious and frivolous, she aroused criticism by her extravagance, disregard for conventions, devotion to the interests of Austria, and opposition to reform. From the outbreak of the **FRENCH REVOLUTION**, she resisted the advice of constitutional monarchists such as **MIRABEAU**, and helped to alienate the monarchy from the people. In June 1791 she and Louis tried to escape from the Tuileries to her native Austria, but were apprehended at Varennes and imprisoned in Paris. After the King's execution, she was arraigned before the Revolutionary Tribunal and guillotined.

**Marie de' Medici** (1573–1642)
Queen Consort of **HENRY IV** of France. The daughter of Francesco de' Medici, Grand Duke of Tuscany, she married Henry in 1600, following his divorce from his first wife, Margaret of Valois. She gave birth to a son (later **LOUIS XIII**) in 1601 and, after her husband's death (1610), she acted as Regent. Confined in Blois when Louis assumed royal power (1617), she intrigued against him, becoming the figurehead for an aristocratic revolt in 1619. She was reconciled with the King through the mediation of **RICHELIEU**, formerly her protégé and now the King's adviser. She lived at court from 1621 until her attempts to discredit Richelieu failed following another coup attempt in 1630. Exiled to Compiègne, she escaped to Brussels (1631) and her last years were spent in poverty.

**Marie-Louise** (1791–1847)
Empress of France (1811/14). The daughter of Emperor **FRANCIS II** of Austria, she married **NAPOLEON I** in 1810, after his divorce from **JOSEPHINE**. In 1811 she bore him a son, who was created King of Rome and who became **NAPOLEON II**. On Napoleon's abdication, she returned to Austria. By the Treaty of Fontainebleau (1814), she was awarded the Duchies of Parma, Piacenza and Guastalla in Italy.

**Marinheiro**
The pejorative name (literally, 'sailor') often used to describe a Portuguese in 19c Brazil. The Portuguese frequently dominated the retail trades in the major cities and were often accused of cartelizing trade. *Mata Marinheiro* ('Death to the Portuguese') was a popular slogan of the 1830s, and was used by the revolutionaries of 1848 in Recife. Anti-Portuguese sentiment fomented riots in the 1870s and 1890s, particularly in Rio de Janeiro, and Pará, where they were led by the Jacobins.

**Marion, Francis**, known as **the Swamp Fox** (c.1732–1795)
American Revolutionary general. Born in Winyah, South Carolina, he first saw action against the **CHEROKEE** in 1759, and he joined the Revolutionary Army in 1776. After American forces were defeated at **CHARLESTON** and **CAMDEN**, South Carolina, the state was almost entirely in British hands, but Marion gathered a rough militia (1780) and led a series of guerrilla attacks on British troops. His nickname referred to his skill in retreating to seemingly impassable swamps where the British could not follow. He was promoted to brigadier-general in 1781, and in Sep of that year he won an important victory at Eutaw Springs.

**Maritsa River, Battle of** (1371)
At this battle, the Ottoman Turks defeated the Serbs and overran Macedonia and southern Serbia, forcing the Serbian Prince, Marko **KRALJEVIĆ** to become a vassal of Sultan **MURAD I**.

**Marj Dabiq, Battle of** (1516)
This battle, between the Ottoman Turks of Sultan **SELIM I, THE GRIM** and the **MAMLUKS** of Qansawh, resulted in a crushing defeat for the Mamluks and the death of Qansawh himself. It was during the reign of **BAYEZID II** (1481/1512) that the Ottomans began to pose a serious threat to Mamluk influence in northern Syria. After various provocations, the promise of support for Shah Isma'il the Safavid on the part of Qansawh proved too much for the Ottomans and despite Qansawh's attempts while on a visit to Aleppo to appear to be acting merely as an intermediary between Isma'il and Selim, Selim's intelligence had told him of Qansawh's inclination towards Isma'il. By murdering the attendants of Qansawh's envoy, Selim left Qansawh in no doubt as to his intentions. The Battle of Marj Dabiq ensued; after his victory, Selim was popularly acclaimed in Aleppo as a liberator from the harshness of Mamluk rule. The battle also opened up Syria to Sultan Selim and the Ottoman Turks.

**market economy**
An economic system where prices, wages, and what is made and sold are determined primarily by market forces of supply and demand, with no state interference. The contrast is with a command economy, where the state takes most, if not all, economic decisions. Most Western economies these days are mixed, with varying degrees of state control or intervention.

**Markievicz, Constance Georgine, Countess** (1868–1927)
Irish nationalist. The daughter of Sir Henry Gore-Booth of County Sligo, she married the Polish count Casimir Markievicz. She fought in the **EASTER RISING** (1916), and was sentenced to death but reprieved. Elected the first British woman MP in 1918, she did not take her seat, but was a member of the **DÁIL EIREANN** from 1923.

**Marković, Ante** (1924– )
Yugoslav politician. He joined the Communist Youth Movement in Yugoslavia in 1940 and fought in **TITO**'s partisans, becoming a member of the Communist League of Yugoslavia in 1943. He was a member of the Central Committee of the League of Communists of Croatia (1982–6) and, as Prime Minister of the Socialist Federal Republic of Croatia, introduced a programme of economic reform. A member of the Central Committee of the League of Communists of Yugoslavia from 1986, he succeeded Branko Mikulić as Prime Minister of Yugoslavia (Mar 1989). A liberal and pro-Western, he was hailed as 'man of the year' by the popular Croatian magazine *Danas* (1990). After six months of civil war between the Serbs and Croats, he announced his resignation as Prime Minister of Yugoslavia (Dec 1991).

**Marlborough, John Churchill, 1st Duke of** (1650–1722)
English general. Commissioned as an ensign in the Guards (1667), he fought in the Low Countries. In 1678 he married Sarah Jennings, a close friend and attendant of Princess Anne, and was further promoted. On **JAMES VII AND II**'s accession (1685), he was elevated to an English barony and given the rank of general. He took a leading part in quelling **MONMOUTH**'s rebellion at Sedgemoor but, concerned for the integrity of the Anglican Church under James, in

1688 he deserted to the Prince of Orange (later **WILLIAM III**), and served the Protestant cause in campaigns in Ireland and Flanders. Under Queen **ANNE**, he was appointed Supreme Commander of the British forces in the War of the **SPANISH SUCCESSION**, and he became Captain-General of the Allied armies. His military flair and organization skills resulted in several great victories – Donauwörth and **BLENHEIM** (1704), **RAMILLIES** (1706), **OUDENARDE** and the capture of Lille (1708) – for which he was richly rewarded with Blenheim Palace and a dukedom. Forced by political interests to align himself with the Whig war party (1708), his influence waned with theirs after 1710. When his wife fell from royal favour, the **TORIES** pressed for his downfall. Dismissed on charges of embezzling, he left England for continental Europe (1712), returning after **GEORGE I**'s accession (1714), when he was restored to his former offices. ➤ **WHIGS**

### Marmont, Auguste Frédéric Louis Viesse de (1774–1852)

French soldier. He went with **NAPOLEON I** to Italy, and fought at Lodi, in Egypt, and at **MARENGO** (1800). He was sent to Dalmatia in 1805, defeated the Russians there, and was made Duke of Ragusa. He was next Governor of the **ILLYRIAN PROVINCES**, and in 1811 succeeded **MASSÉNA** in Portugal. In 1813 he fought at **LÜTZEN**, Bautzen and Dresden. In 1814 he deserted to the Allies, compelling Napoleon to abdicate, and earning Marmont from the Bonapartists the title of traitor. At the **JULY REVOLUTION** (1830) he endeavoured to reduce Paris to submission, and finally retreating with a few faithful battalions, conducted **CHARLES X** across the frontier, living thereafter in exile.

### Marne, Battle of the (1914)

A battle early in **WORLD WAR I**, in which General **JOFFRE**'s French armies and the **BRITISH EXPEDITIONARY FORCE** halted German forces which had crossed the Marne and were approaching Paris, thus ending German hopes of a swift victory. The German line withdrew across the River Aisne, dug in, and occupied much the same positions until 1918.

### Marnix, Philippe de, Lord of St Aldegonde (c.1540–1598)

Netherlands politician and writer. He studied under **CALVIN** and Beza at Geneva, and was active in the **REFORMATION** in the Netherlands, and in 1566 in the revolt against Spain. An intimate friend of **WILLIAM I, THE SILENT**, he represented him at the first meeting of the Estates of the United Provinces, held at Dordrecht in 1572, and was sent on special missions to the courts of France and England. As burgomaster of Antwerp, he defended the city for 13 months against the Spaniards; but having then capitulated, he incurred so much ill-will that he retired from public life. He is said to have written the patriotic 'Wilhelmus' song, the prose satire *The Roman Beehive* (1569), a metrical translation of the Psalms (1580) and part of a prose translation of the Bible.

### Maronites

Under the influence of Monotheletism, the 'Syrian' Christians of Lebanon became the separate Maronite Church in the 8c. They united with Rome towards the end of the 12c, though retaining a separate liturgy and practice, and as a result of the influence of Rome from the late 15c, the Maronite Christians of Lebanon became distinctly westward-leaning. In modern Lebanon, the constitution has stipulated that the President should be a Christian (which, in Lebanese terms, means a Maronite Christian) and the Prime Minister a Muslim. The privileged position accorded to the Maronites (largely as a result of the French occupation) was built on the fiction of there being a Christian majority in the country or, at least, equal numbers of Christians and Muslims. The **TA'IF ACCORD** of 1989 addressed the constitutional majority enjoyed by the Christians (Maronites) in Lebanon. They number c.2 million.

### Maroons

Name derived from the Spanish *cimarrones* for runaway slaves who fled the estates for the refuge of the mountains (*cima* meaning 'summit'). Maroon communities existed in Hispaniola, Dominica, St Vincent and St Lucia but the best-known and documented are the Maroons of Jamaica. Living in the rugged interior of the island in a number of separate settlements, they were a constant threat to British rule and the plantations which they occasionally raided. In the 18c there were two Maroon Wars. The first (1734–8) was concluded by a peace treaty in which the Maroon chief of Trelawny Town, Cudjoe, agreed to assist in the defence of the island and hand over runaway slaves in return for sovereignty over 1,500 acres/610 hectares of land. The Second Maroon War (1795–6) led to the deportation of 556 Maroons to Nova Scotia and then to Sierra Leone.

### Marprelate Tracts

Seven pamphlets covertly published in London in 1587–9. The pseudonymous author, 'Martin Marprelate', satirized the Elizabethan Church and bishops, and favoured a Presbyterian system. One alleged author, John Penry, was executed; another, John Udall, died in prison; a third, Job Throckmorton, successfully refuted the accusations. The Tracts led to statutes against dissenting sects and sedition (1593).

### Marranos

A derogatory word used since at least the 15c in Spain and Portugal to describe Jews or, more specifically, those **CONVERSOS** who secretly continued to practise their Jewish faith. The word was, and is, commonly used as a synonym for 'pig', although its etymological origins are obscure.

### Marryshow, Albert (1885–1958)

Grenadian champion of a federation of the British West Indies. In 1913 he founded a newspaper, *The West Indian*, which campaigned for greater West Indian unity and for an extension of the franchise, based on his belief that the 'People's Parliament' should be founded on universal adult suffrage. Marryshow lived long enough to sit in the Federation of the **WEST INDIES** for which he had so long struggled, but not long enough to see it dissolved four years later.

### Marshall, George Catlett (1880–1959)

US general and politician. Educated at the Virginia Military Institute, he became Chief of Staff (1939–45), and directed the US Army throughout

**WORLD WAR II**. After two years in China as special representative of President **TRUMAN**, he became Secretary of State (1947–9), originating the **MARSHALL PLAN** for the post-war reconstruction of Europe, and Secretary of Defense (1950–1). He retired (Sep 1951) after nearly 50 years of military and civilian service, and was awarded the **NOBEL PEACE PRIZE** in 1953.

**Marshall, John** (1755–1835)
US jurist. The foremost Chief Justice in the history of the US Supreme Court, in the 1790s he became a supporter of the Federalist measures of George **WASHINGTON** and Alexander **HAMILTON**, and was named Chief Justice by the outgoing President, John **ADAMS**, in 1801. From then until his death he dominated the Supreme Court, establishing the US doctrine of Supreme Court judicial review of federal and state legislation. ➤ **AMERICAN REVOLUTION**; **MARBURY V MADISON**; **MCCULLOCH V MARYLAND**

**Marshall, Thurgood** (1908–93)
US jurist. Associate justice of the US Supreme Court and **CIVIL RIGHTS** advocate. Educated at Lincoln and Howard universities, he joined the legal staff of the National Association for the Advancement of Colored People (**NAACP**), and argued many important civil rights cases. He served as a judge of the US Court of Appeals (1961–5), and as Solicitor-General of the United States (1965–7), before becoming the first black Associate Justice of the US Supreme Court, a post he held until his retirement in 1991.

**MARSHALL ISLANDS** official name **Republic of the Marshall Islands**

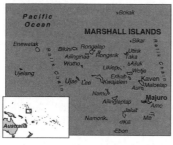

An independent archipelago republic in the central Pacific Ocean. Originally inhabited by Micronesians, it was explored by the Spanish in 1529 and became a German protectorate in 1886. After **WORLD WAR I** it came under Japanese control, and after **WORLD WAR II** it became a **UN** Trust Territory (1947–78), administered by the USA. Between 1946 and 1962 US nuclear weapon tests were held on the Bikini and Enewetak atolls. After the Marshall Islands became a self-governing republic in 1979, a compact of free association with the USA was signed in 1982, and came into force in 1986; a renegotiated compact was signed in 2003. By this the USA retained control of external security and defence and gave financial help. The trusteeship ended in 1990, and full independence was gained in 1991 under President Amata Kabua. Kessai Note became President in 2000 and was re-elected in 2003.

**Marshall Plan**
The popular name for the European Recovery Program, a scheme for large-scale, medium-term US aid to war-ravaged Europe, announced in 1947 by US Secretary of State George **MARSHALL**. 'Marshall Aid' was rejected by the USSR and the Eastern bloc, but during the period 1948–50 it materially assisted Western Europe's economic revival.

**Marsilius of Padua** (c.1275–c.1342)
Italian political theorist and philosopher. He was rector of the University of Paris from 1313, where he lectured on natural philosophy, engaged in medical research, and involved himself actively in Italian politics. In 1324 he completed *Defensor Pacis*, a political treatise much influenced by Aristotle's *Politics*, which argued against the temporal power of clergy and pope and developed a thoroughgoing, secular theory of the state based on popular consultation and consent and on natural rights. When the authorship of the work became known he was forced to flee Paris (1326). Excommunicated by Pope **JOHN XXII**, he took refuge at the court of **LOUIS IV, THE BAVARIAN** in Munich, and remained under his protection till his death.

**Marston Moor, Battle of** (2 July 1644)
A major conflict in the first of the **ENGLISH CIVIL WARS**, in which a force of 27,000 parliamentary and Scottish troops defeated 18,000 royalists near York. The royalist cavalry was led by Prince **RUPERT**; the parliamentary horse by Oliver **CROMWELL**. The defeat led to the fall of the royalist stronghold of York, and the virtual collapse of **CHARLES I**'s cause in the north.

**Martens, Wilfried** (1936–)
Belgian politician. Educated at Louvain University, he was adviser to two governments, in 1965 and 1966, before becoming Minister for Community Problems in 1968. He was President of the Dutch-speaking Social Christian Party (CVP) from 1972 to 1979, when be became Prime Minister at the head of a coalition. He continued in office, apart from a brief break in 1981, heading no fewer than six coalition governments. In 1994 he led the European People's Party (PPE) in the European Parliament.

**Martí, José Julián** (1853–95)
Cuban national hero. Educated in Havana, Madrid and Saragossa, he devoted his life to the liberation of Cuba from Spain. Much of his adult life was spent in exile, and he became famous for his journalism, plays and poems. In 1892 he helped to found the Cuban Revolutionary Party (*Partido Revolucionario Cubano*), which in 1895 mounted an armed rebellion in the island, during which he was killed near Dos Ríos. The independence of Cuba was achieved seven years after his death. ➤ **CUBAN REVOLUTION**

**Martin V**, originally **Oddone Colonna** (1368–1431)
Italian pope (1417/31). Through his election, during the Council of Constance, the **GREAT SCHISM**, which had begun in 1378, was finally extinguished. He died in Rome, just after calling the Council of **BASLE**.

**Martinet, Jean** (d.1672)
French army officer. He won renown as a military engineer and tactician, devising forms of battle manoeuvre, pontoon bridges, and a type of copper assault-boat used in **LOUIS XIV**'s Dutch campaign. He also achieved notoriety for his stringent and brutal forms of discipline, and was 'accidentally' killed by his troops at the siege of Duisberg.

**Martínez Barrio, Diego** (1883–1962)
Spanish politician. Under the Second Republic he was Minister of Communications (Apr–Dec 1931) and caretaker Prime Minister (Oct–Dec 1933). A leading Freemason, he was national Grand Master from 1931 to 1934. His opposition to the alliance with the non-Republican Right led him to split with the **RADICAL REPUBLICAN PARTY** in May 1934, taking up to a quarter of the party with him. After the Popular Front victory of Feb 1936, he was elected President of the **CORTES** and, on the outbreak of the military rising of July 1936, tried to form a government of conciliation. A man of immense integrity and reserve, he was President of the republic in exile until his death. ➤ **REPUBLIC, SECOND** (Spain)

**Marwaris**
One of the largest trading communities in India. The Marwaris, originally from Marwar in Rajasthan, started to establish their reputation as merchants in medieval India. In this period some communities specialized in wholesale trade and others in retail trade; the former being called *seth* or *bohra* and the latter *beoraris* or *bania*. The wealthy merchants lived in an ostentatious manner and adopted the manners of the nobles.

**Marx, Karl Heinrich** (1818–83)
German founder of modern international **COMMUNISM**, the son of a Jewish lawyer. He studied law at **BONN** and Berlin but took up history, Hegelian philosophy and Feuerbach's materialism. He edited a radical newspaper in the **RHINELAND**, and after it was suppressed, moved to Paris (1843) and Brussels (1845). There, with **ENGELS** as his closest collaborator and disciple, he reorganized the Communist League, which met in London in 1847. In 1848 he finalized the *Communist Manifesto* (1848), which attacked the state as the instrument of oppression, and religion and culture as ideologies of the capitalist class. He was expelled from Brussels, and in 1849 settled in London, where he studied economics, and wrote the first volume of his major work, *Das Kapital* (1867). He died with this work unfinished. ➤ **CAPITALISM**; **MARXISM**; **MARXISM–LENINISM**; **SOCIALISM**

**Marx, Wilhelm** (1863–1946)
German politician. A member of the **CENTRE PARTY**, Marx pursued a varied legal and political career before serving in the National (constituent) Assembly (1919–20) and then as Chairman of the Centre Party (1922–8). He served as Chancellor between Nov 1923 and Jan 1925 at the head of a centre-right coalition which renegotiated Germany's **REPARATIONS** obligations with the Allies (**DAWES PLAN**). In Mar 1925 he was, as the republican candidate, narrowly defeated by **HINDENBURG** in the presidential elections. After this he held further ministerial posts, including that of Chancellor (Jan 1927–May 1928). He withdrew from public life in 1932.

**Marxism**
The body of social and political thought informed by the writings of Karl **MARX**. It is essentially a critical analysis of capitalist society contending that such societies are subject to crises which create the conditions for proletarian revolutions and the transformation to **SOCIALISM**. Much of Marx's writing, especially *Das Kapital*, was concerned with the economic dynamics of capitalist societies, seeing the state as an instrument of class rule supporting private capital and suppressing the masses. Because of private capital's need to earn profits or extract surplus value, wages have to be kept to a subsistence minimum. This produces economic contradictions, because it restricts the purchasing power of workers to consume the goods produced. **CAPITALISM** is, therefore, inherently unstable, being subect to crises of booms and slumps. Marx's view was that these crises would become increasingly worse, and eventually lead to revolution, whereby the working class would seize the state and establish a dictatorship of the proletariat, productive power would be in public hands and class differences would disappear (socialism). This classless society would eventually lead to the withering away of the state, producing a communist society. Marxism has sought to popularize and extend this method of analysis to contemporary conditions. In particular, Western Marxism has examined the impact of state intervention in smoothing out the crises of capitalism and establishing a legitimacy for the existing capitalist order through its control over education and the media. In non-industrialized societies Marxism has been adapted to account for revolution in countries where there is no extensive development of capitalism, in contrast to Marx's view of history. It is generally recognized that his writings regarding the transformation to, and the nature of, socialism lacked detail. Consequently, Marxism has adopted a wide range of interpretations. ➤ **MARXISM–LENINISM**

**Marxism–Leninism**
A distinct variant of **MARXISM** formulated by **LENIN** who, prior to the Bolshevik Revolution, argued for direct rule by the proletariat, defined as workers and poor peasants, and in the circumstances of Russia after 1905 advocated direct democracy through the soviets (councils). In practice, the Bolshevik Revolution did not produce a democratic republic, but gave a 'leading and directing' role to the Communist Party, seen as the vanguard of a working class which had insufficient political consciousness to forge a revolution. Such a well-organized and disciplined party, operating according to the principles of democratic centralism, would be able to exploit the revolutionary situation and create a new socialist society. Leninist principles of a revolutionary vanguard became the central tenet of nearly all communist parties. They were organized according to the idea of democratic centralism that afforded the leadership, on the grounds of its revolutionary insight, the right to dictate party policy, to select party officials from above, and to discipline dissenting party members. In addition, Lenin modified **MARX**'s theory of historical materialism, contending that revolutionary opportunities should be seized when they arose, without waiting for the social and economic crisis of bourgeois **CAPITALISM** leading to proletarian revolution. He also developed a theory of imperialism which held that it was the last stage of a decaying capitalism. This was used to justify revolution in feudal Russia, because it was an imperial power, and subsequently to justify communist intervention in underdeveloped countries as part of the struggle between

SOCIALISM and IMPERIALISM. Serious doubts were cast upon Lenin's views by the many failures of the socialism they led to and eventually by the collapse of the USSR in 1991. ► MAOISM; RUSSIAN REVOLUTION

## Mary I (1516–58)

Queen of England and Ireland (1553/8). She was the daughter of HENRY VIII of England by his first wife, CATHERINE OF ARAGON. A devout Catholic, during the reign of her half-brother, EDWARD VI, she lived in retirement, refusing to conform to the new religion. Despite Northumberland's conspiracy to prevent her succession on Edward's death (1553), she relied on the support of the country, entered London and ousted Lady Jane GREY. Thereafter she proceeded cautiously, repealing anti-Catholic legislation and reviving Catholic practices, but her intention was to restore papal supremacy with the assistance of Cardinal POLE, and to cement a Catholic union with PHILIP II of Spain. These aspirations provoked a rebellion led by the Protestant Sir Thomas Wyatt (1554), followed by the execution of Lady Jane Grey and the imprisonment of Mary's half-sister, Elizabeth (later ELIZABETH I), on suspicion of complicity. Mary's unpopular marriage to Philip (1554) was followed by the persecution of some 300 Protestants, which earned her the name of 'Bloody Mary' in Protestant hagiography, though her direct responsibility is unproven. Broken by childlessness, sickness, grief at her husband's departure from England, and the loss of Calais to the French, she died in London. ► CRANMER, THOMAS; LATIMER, HUGH; REFORMATION (England); RIDLEY, NICHOLAS

## Mary, Queen of Scots (1542–87)

Queen of Scots (1542–67) and Queen Consort of France (1559/60). She was the daughter of JAMES V of Scotland by his second wife, Mary of Guise. Queen of Scotland at a week old, her betrothal to Prince Edward (later EDWARD VI) of England was annulled by the Scottish parliament, precipitating war with England. After the Scots' defeat at PINKIE (1547), she was sent to the French court and married (1558) the DAUPHIN (later FRANCIS II), but was widowed at 18 (1560) and returned to Scotland (1561). A Catholic with a clear dynastic claim, she was ambitious for the English throne, and in 1565 she married her cousin, Henry Stuart, Lord DARNLEY, a grandson of MARGARET TUDOR, but disgusted by his debauchery, was soon alienated from him. The vicious murder of RIZZIO, her Italian secretary, by Darnley and a group of Protestant nobles in her presence (1566) confirmed her insecurity. The birth of a son (the future JAMES VI AND I) failed to bring a reconciliation. When Darnley was found, strangled, after an explosion at his residence (1567), the chief suspect was the Earl of BOTHWELL, who underwent a mock trial and was acquitted. Mary's involvement is unclear, but she consented to marry Bothwell, a divorcee with whom she had become infatuated. The Protestant nobles under Morton rose against her; she surrendered at Carberry Hill, was imprisoned at Loch Leven, and compelled to abdicate. After escaping, she raised an army, but was defeated again by the confederate lords at Langside (1568). Placing herself under the protection of Queen ELIZABETH I, she found herself instead a prisoner for life. Her presence in England stimulated numerous plots to depose Elizabeth. Finally, after the BABINGTON conspiracy (1586) she was brought to trial for treason, and executed in Fotheringay Castle, Northamptonshire. ► MORAY, JAMES; MORTON, JAMES

## Mary of Burgundy (1457–82)

Daughter of Duke CHARLES THE BOLD of BURGUNDY and Isabella of Bourbon, she inherited all the Burgundian possessions in France and the Netherlands, as Duchess, in 1477. France repossessed Burgundy and Picardy while the Netherlands rose up against her; Mary married Emperor MAXIMILIAN I of Austria who restored order in Mary's dominions. By this means the Burgundian possessions came into Habsburg hands; Mary's son PHILIP I, THE HANDSOME, succeeded her in 1482 when she fell from her horse while out hunting and died.

## Mary of Hungary (1505–58)

Queen of Hungary and Bohemia. The daughter of PHILIP I, THE HANDSOME and JOAN THE MAD, she married Louis II of Hungary, thus becoming Queen of Hungary and Bohemia. In 1531 her brother, Emperor CHARLES V, confident of her administrative capabilities, asked her to act as regent in his Low Countries possessions, which she did from 1531 to 1555. Despite her patronage of the arts and her efficient government, Mary's rule subjugated the interests of the Netherlands provinces to those of Spain and the empire, which, along with the persecution of Protestant heretics, helped lay the ground for the EIGHTY YEARS' WAR.

## Mary of Modena (1658–1718)

Queen of Great Britain and Ireland (1685/8). The only daughter of Alfonso IV, Duke of Modena, she married the future James VII of Scotland and II of England, as his second wife, in 1672 when he was Duke of York. They lost five daughters and a son in infancy, but in 1688 she gave birth to James Francis Edward STUART (the future 'Old Pretender'). When William of Orange (the future WILLIAM III) landed in England later that year at the start of the 'GLORIOUS REVOLUTION', she escaped to France with her infant son, to be joined there later by her deposed husband. She later gave birth to a daughter and spent the rest of her life at St Germain. ► JAMES VII AND II

## Masaniello, properly Tommaso Aniello (1623–47)

Neapolitan patriot. A fisherman of Amalfi, he led the successful revolt of the Neapolitans against Spanish rule in July 1647. However, the revolt degenerated into murder and massacre, and Masaniello was assassinated by agents of the Spanish viceroy.

## Masaryk, Jan (1886–1948)

Czechoslovak diplomat and politician. The son of Tomáš MASARYK, after a youth of travelling and developing a variety of skills, he entered the diplomatic service in 1918, and from 1925 to 1938 was Czechoslovak envoy in London. There, his fluent English and personal charm won him many friends, but proved inadequate to prevent CHAMBERLAIN imposing the MUNICH AGREEMENT on his country. He became a popular broadcaster during the war. In July 1941 he was appointed Foreign Minister of the Czechoslovak government in exile, returning with President BENEŠ to Prague in 1945 and remaining in office in the hope of bridging the growing gap between East and West in the developing **COLD WAR**. On 10 Mar 1948, following the Communist takeover of power in Czechoslovakia, his body was found beneath the open window of the Foreign Ministry in Prague, and it is generally believed that he killed himself in protest at the Stalinization of his homeland. ➤ **STALIN, JOSEPH**

### Masaryk, Tomáš Garrigue (1850–1937)
Philosopher, politician and first President of the Czechoslovak Republic. Half Czech and half Slovak, he received his university education in Vienna and Leipzig, read and travelled widely, and married an American before becoming Professor of Philosophy at the newly authorized Czech University of Prague in 1882. Entering politics in the nationalistic atmosphere of the 1880s and 1890s, he made his name as an independent of courage and common sense through his many writings and his intervention in several fraught disputes. A deputy in the Czech and Austrian Imperial parliaments off and on after 1891, he was variously a 'realist' and a 'progressive'; but his main political contribution came after 1914 when he travelled abroad to France, Britain, Russia and the USA to win support and recognition for an independent state, first Czech, then Czechoslovak. He became its first President in 1918 and was regularly re-elected until he retired in 1935. His character and authority were crucial in developing a prosperous, democratic republic which, tragically, Britain and France helped Germany to destroy in 1938–9 after his death. ➤ **CZECHOSLOVAK INDEPENDENCE, DECLARATION OF**

### Masire, Sir Quett Ketumile Joni (1995– )
Botswanan journalist and politician. A journalist, he was Director of *African Echo* in 1958 before founding, with Sir Seretse **KHAMA**, the Botswana Democratic Party in 1962, whose Secretary-General he became. Deputy Prime Minister in 1965, he was Minister of Finance in 1966 and Vice-President 1966–80, taking over the presidency on Sir Seretse Khama's death in 1980. He continued his predecessor's policy of non-alignment and helped Botswana become one of the most politically stable nations in Africa. He retired from the presidency in 1998.

### Mason–Dixon Line
The border between Maryland and Pennsylvania, drawn in 1763–7 by the British astronomer Charles Mason (1730–87) and his colleague Jeremiah Dixon (of whom little is known). It is regarded as the boundary of 'the South'.

### Massachusetts Bay Company
A joint stock company established in 1629 by royal charter to promote trade and colonization along the Merrimack and Charles rivers in New England. Its Puritan stockholders won the right to acquire all of the company's stocks. The company became self-governing, and it elected John Winthrop its first governor. Puritan settlers began what would become the Great Puritan Migration. The first group arrived in Salem in 1630, and later established a settlement in Boston. The company and the Massachusetts Bay Colony were one and the same, but in 1684 the company lost its charter, and two years later the colony became part of the Dominion of New England.

### Massasoit (c.1590–1661)
Grand Sachem (inter-tribal chief) of the Wampanoag, a Native American people who inhabited parts of present-day Massachusetts and Rhode Island, particularly the coastal areas. After the **PLYMOUTH COLONY** was established by the **PILGRIM FATHERS** in 1620, Massasoit negotiated peace with the settlers in 1621 and remained on friendly terms with them for the rest of his life. After his death tensions grew between the European settlers and the **NATIVE AMERICANS** whose lands they were taking, and Massasoit's second son, Metacom (King **PHILIP**), became involved in the bloody **KING PHILIP'S WAR**.

### Masséna, André (1758–1817)
The greatest of **NAPOLEON I**'s marshals, he distinguished himself in Napoleon's Italian campaign (1796–7) when he defeated the Russians, led by Count **SUVOROV**, at Zurich (1799), and successfully defended Genoa (1800). Created Marshal of the Empire in 1804, he commanded the army in Italy and was made Duke of Rivoli (1807). After the Austrian campaign (1809) he was made Prince of Essling. However, forced to retreat in the Iberian Peninsula by **WELLINGTON**'s forces, he was relieved of his command in 1810.

### Massey, Charles Vincent (1887–1967)
Canadian politician and diplomat. In 1952 he became the first native-born Governor-General. In 1925 Mackenzie **KING** invited him to join his cabinet but he failed to win a seat in 1926 and he was appointed instead as Canada's first minister to the USA. He was chairman of the 1949 Royal Commission on National Development in the Arts, Letters and the Sciences which inquired into the federal cultural agencies, such as the Canadian Broadcasting Corporation, the National Film Board, the National Gallery and the National Research Council. Its report, submitted in 1951, suggested that a Canadian Council for the 'Encouragement of the Arts, Letters, Humanities and Social Sciences be established' and that Canada's cultural institutions be supported in order to limit US influence.

### Massey, William Ferguson (1856–1925)
Irish-born New Zealand politician. He emigrated to New Zealand (1870), where he became a farmer. Elected to the House of Representatives (1894), he became Leader of the Opposition (1903) and, in 1912, Prime Minister. The creator of the Reform Party, Massey represented small property owners' fears of **SOCIALISM** and crushed the industrial unrest of 1912–13. During **WORLD WAR I**, he formed a coalition government (1915–19) with Sir Joseph **WARD**, but remained Prime Minister until his death.

### Matabele ➤ **NDEBELE**

### Matabeleland
The name given to the region of western and southern Zimbabwe, between the Zambezi and Limpopo rivers. It was named after the Matabele or **NDEBELE**, a **NGUNI** tribe (related to the Zulu) originally located in Natal and the Transvaal. Acquired by the **BRITISH SOUTH AFRICA COMPANY** in 1893, it became part of Southern Rhodesia in 1923.

**Mata Hari**, stage name of **Margaretha Gertruida Zelle** (1876–1917)
Alleged Dutch spy. She became a dancer in France (1903), had many lovers, several in high military and governmental positions (on both sides during and before **WORLD WAR I**) and, found guilty of espionage for the Germans, was shot in Paris.

**Mataram**
A major Javanese kingdom, in south-central Java, which rose to prominence towards the end of the 16c. Mataram reached the height of its power under Sultan Agung (1613–46) in a series of strikingly successful military campaigns. However, its domination was short-lived, partly because its expansion soon brought it into conflict with the Dutch **EAST INDIA COMPANY** but also because internal rebellion within its territories could not be long suppressed. Under Sultan Agung's incompetent son, Amangkurat I (1646/77), Mataram came close to complete collapse. In the late 17c and the first half of the 18c, the Mataram court was torn apart by internal rivalries, while the Dutch became increasingly influential in the Javanese interior. Finally, under the Giyanti settlement of 1755, Mataram was divided.

**Mather, Cotton** (1662–1728)
US colonial minister. The son of Increase **MATHER**, he was educated at Harvard, and became the foremost Puritan minister in New England during his time. A polymath, he reported on American botany, and was one of the earliest New England historians. But his reputation suffered lasting disfigurement because of his involvement in the **SALEM WITCH TRIALS** of 1692.

**Mather, Increase** (1639–1723)
US clergyman. Born in Dorchester, Massachusetts, he graduated from Harvard in 1656, and from Trinity College, Dublin, in 1658. His first charge was Great Torrington in Devon, England, but in 1661, finding it impossible to conform, he returned to the USA, and from 1664 until his death was pastor of the Second Church, Boston. From 1685 to 1701 he was also President of Harvard. Sent to England in 1689 to lay colonial grievances before the king, he obtained a new charter from **WILLIAM III**. He published 136 works, including *Cases of Conscience Concerning Evil Spirits* (1693), which helped to calm the atmosphere following the **SALEM WITCH TRIALS** of 1692.

**Mathura**
Situated in the state of Uttar Pradesh and popularly known as the birthplace of Lord Krishna, Mathura is a famous centre of pilgrimage for Hindus. It features prominently in the history of the Indo-Greeks, and the Central Asian empires of India.

**Matica Slovenská** (1861)
Slovak cultural-nationalist organization. Modelled on the **MATICE ČESKÁ**, this was meant to raise funds to publish Slovak works of an essentially political character. It quickly became the centre of the nationalist movement, so much so that the Hungarian authorities closed it down in 1875 and refused to open it despite repeated requests. Other secret bodies took its place from time to time, and it remained a symbol of frustrated nationalism.

**Matice Česká** (1831)
Czech cultural-nationalist organization. The Czech Foundation was established by František **PALACKÝ** and other writers to publish books in Czech about the Czech people. By 1848 its membership had risen from essentially a handful to over 2,000. However, in due course other organizations took over its leading nationalist role.

**Matilda of Tuscany** (c.1046–1115)
The 'Great Countess' of Tuscany. She was a devoted supporter of the papacy and, in particular, **GREGORY VII**, even taking the field at the head of her troops to aid him in his struggle against the **HOLY ROMAN EMPIRE**. In 1077 it was at her stronghold of **CANOSSA** that the Emperor **HENRY IV** did barefoot penance to the pope. After Gregory's death in 1085 her lands were ravaged by the Emperor's allies, but she refused to make peace or recognize the anti-pope Clement III. Instead she steadfastly supported Pope **URBAN II** until his death in 1099.

**Matsudaira Sadanobu** (1758–1829)
Japanese feudal lord (**DAIMYO**). He was Chief Senior Councillor of the **TOKUGAWA SHOGUNATE** from 1787 to 1793, at a time of growing financial crisis for the regime and **SAMURAI** indebtedness to an emerging merchant class. Matsudaira imposed draconian sumptuary laws to curb merchant extravagance and cancelled the debts of shogunal retainers. His attempt to reinforce the traditional hierarchy (which placed samurai at the top and merchants at the bottom) ultimately failed to stem the tide of social and economic change.

**Matsukata Masayoshi** (1835–1924)
Japanese **GENRO** (senior statesman). He was a member of the **SATSUMA** clique of former **SAMURAI** (which included **SAIGO TAKAMORI** and **OKUBO TOSHIMICHI**) who had all played an important role in the **MEIJI RESTORATION** and rose to prominence in the new government after 1868. As Finance Minister in the 1880s and 1890s, Matsukata tackled the serious problem of inflation by pursuing a deflationary policy: withdrawing inconvertible paper notes, increasing indirect taxes and cutting administrative expenditures. He also established the Bank of Japan in 1882 with the monopoly right of convertible note issue, and sold off government enterprises to private entrepreneurs to build up the government's specie reserves. Although Matsukata's policies are credited with putting the Japanese economy on a sound footing (Japan adopted the **GOLD STANDARD** in 1897), they also contributed to hardship in the countryside, where many small landowners were forced into tenancy as a result of falling prices and increased taxes. Matsukata served twice as Prime Minister (1891–2 and 1896–8).

**Matsuoka Yosuke** (1880–1946)
Japanese diplomat and politician. After studying in the USA, Matsuoka joined the diplomatic service (1904) and attended the **PARIS PEACE CONFERENCE** (1919) as a member of the Japanese delegation. As Vice-President, and later President, of the South Manchuria Railway, he supported the expansion of Japan's interests in Manchuria. Matsuoka led the withdrawal of the Japanese delegation from the

LEAGUE OF NATIONS in 1933 in response to the league's adoption of the Lytton Commission report, which had criticized the actions of the Japanese military in Manchuria. As Foreign Minister (1940–1), Matsuoka sought to strengthen Japan's position in the Far East and counter US hostility to its war in China by concluding the Tripartite Pact with Germany and Italy (27 Sep 1940) and signing a neutrality pact with the USSR (13 Apr 1941). Matsuoka's grand scheme ultimately failed; HITLER's invasion of the USSR brought the latter into the allied camp, while US hostility to Japan's war in China (1937–45) merely intensified. In 1946 he was indicted as a Class A war criminal, but died before the trial was concluded.

### Matteotti, Giacomo (1885–1924)

Italian politician. As a talented young deputy, belonging to Filippo TURATI's moderate Socialist Unity Party, Matteotti bravely and openly denounced the corruption and intimidation practised by the FASCIST PARTY in the 1924 elections, only to be murdered by thugs acting on the orders of MUSSOLINI. The murder resulted in widespread hostility and disgust towards Mussolini and a wave of anti-fascist feeling, which briefly threatened to bring an end to his rule.

### Matthias (1557–1619)

Holy Roman Emperor (1612/19). He was the third son of Emperor MAXIMILIAN II. A tolerant man in religious matters, he favoured a policy of moderation towards German Protestants although, as Governor of Austria, he was responsible for suppressing risings of Protestant peasants (1594–7). Elected Emperor on his brother RUDOLF II's death, he continued to pursue a conciliatory policy which aroused the antagonism of other Catholic princes, including his nephew and heir, Ferdinand (later FERDINAND II), whose more rigid policy was instrumental in provoking the THIRTY YEARS' WAR in 1618.

### Matthias I, Corvinus (c.1440–1490)

King of Hungary (1158/90). He was the second son of János HUNYADI. He drove back the Turks, and made himself master of Bosnia (1462), MOLDAVIA AND WALLACHIA (1467), Moravia, Silesia and Lusatia (1478), Vienna, and a large part of Austria proper (1485). He greatly encouraged the arts and letters, founded the Corvina Library and the Pozsony Academy, promoted industry, and reformed finances and the system of justice. However, his rule was arbitrary and his taxes heavy, and in the end he had to compromise with the nobility who feared for the loss of their privileges.

### Maududi, Maulana Abu'l Ala (1903–79)

Muslim revivalist thinker and founder of the JAMAATI ISLAMI Party. Beginning as a journalist, he became known as an opponent of both Pakistani and Indian nationalism. After India gained its independence, he was several times imprisoned by the Pakistan government.

### Mau Mau

The phrase used by the colonial authorities for the uprising in Kenya, largely among the Kikuyu, which caused a state of emergency in the early 1950s. Its aims were anti-colonial and anti-settler (especially in the formerly Kikuyu 'White Highlands'), rather than self-consciously nationalist, and much of its violence was directed against fellow Kikuyu who were thought to be collaborating with the colonial authorities. But the disruption it caused hastened the transition to independence. However, very few of those who fought for Mau Mau benefited materially from the transfer of power.

### Maura, Antonio (1853–1925)

Spanish politician. As the leader of a regenerationist movement within the Conservative Party, he sought a revolution from above. Autocratic and clerical, he was, however, unable to implement his nebulous ideas because of opposition from both Right and Left. In 1903 he tried, as Prime Minister, to replace *caciquismo* with an indirect, corporate franchise, but was dismissed the following year by King ALFONSO XIII. His second period in office was from 1907 to 1909; he fell from power after the TRAGIC WEEK, a popular revolt in Barcelona against conscription. Four years later, he organized a proto-fascist party. Appointed Premier again in 1913, he hoped to become the 'iron surgeon' of the national government, but the Cabinet fell that same year. He headed a further two governments in 1919 and 1921–2.

### Maurice (1521–53)

Duke (1541/53) and Elector (1547/53) of Saxony. A Protestant, he sided with Emperor CHARLES V and refused to join the SCHMALKALDIC LEAGUE when promised the electorship then held by his relative, JOHN FREDERICK I, THE MAGNANIMOUS. Made Elector in 1547, Maurice was wary of Charles's Catholic goals; he changed sides and forced the Emperor to accept the Lutheran position in the Treaty of PASSAU (1552). He then returned to the Imperial camp and was killed, at the Battle of Sieverhausen (1553), fighting against Albert II Alcibiades of Brandenburg, who had refused to accept the Passau accord.

### Maurice (1567–1625)

Stadholder of the United Provinces (1585/1625). The son of WILLIAM I, THE SILENT, he was elected STADHOLDER of Holland and Zeeland in 1585 and later (1589 onwards) of Utrecht, Overijssel and Gelderland, also becoming in 1587 Captain-General of the armies of the United Provinces during their War of Independence from Spain. During this period he was probably the leading soldier in Europe. He checked the Spanish advance, and by his steady offensive (1590–1606) liberated the northern provinces of the Netherlands from Spain. During the TWELVE YEARS' TRUCE he entered into domestic political conflict with OLDENBARNEVELDT, and won the day at the Synod of DORDRECHT in 1618–19. In the renewed conflict with the Habsburgs in 1621, he commanded the republic, with help from England and France, this time with rather less military success. ► EIGHTY YEARS' WAR; HABSBURG DYNASTY; UNITED PROVINCES OF THE NETHERLANDS

### Maurice (1696–1750)

Marshal of Saxony. He was an illegitimate son of Elector Frederick Augustus I of Saxony (King AUGUSTUS II, THE STRONG of Poland). In 1711 he was created Count of Saxony. He served with the French against his half-brother, King AUGUSTUS III of Poland, in the War of the POLISH SUCCESSION. In 1744 he was put in charge of Louis IV's force set to invade Britain in support to Charles Edward **STUART**, the Young Pretender. The wreck of the fleet in a storm forced the plan to be abandoned. He was then promoted to field marshal. He won France's last great military victory before the Revolution at **FONTENOY** when he defeated the Duke of **CUMBERLAND** (11 May 1745) during the War of the **AUSTRIAN SUCCESSION**.

---

**MAURITANIA**    official name **Islamic Republic of Mauritania**

A republic in north-west Africa, bounded to the south-west by Senegal; to the south and east by Mali; to the north-east by Algeria; to the north by **WESTERN SAHARA**; and to the west by the Atlantic Ocean. Discovered by the Portuguese in the 15c, it became a French protectorate within French West Africa in 1903 and a French colony in 1920. It gained independence in 1960. When the Spanish withdrew from Western Sahara in 1976, Mauritania and Morocco divided between them a large area in the south under the name of Tiris el Gharbia. However, after conflict with the **POLISARIO** Front guerrillas, Mauritania renounced all rights to the region in 1979, leaving Morocco to annex it. There were military coups in 1978 and 1984, and a new constitution was adopted in 1991 with the approval of multiparty elections. In 1989 violent disturbances broke out on the border with Senegal which resulted in the frontier being closed until diplomatic relations with Senegal were restored in 1992. During the 1990s there was ethnic tension and internal unrest by groups in opposition to the government, exacerbated by several years of drought which left much of the population facing food shortages. Civil disturbances and an attempted coup in 2003 were followed by further fighting and suppression of coup plots.

---

**MAURITIUS**    official name **Republic of Mauritius**

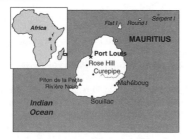

A small island nation in the Indian Ocean, east of Madagascar. It was visited by Arabs in the 10c and discovered by the Portuguese in the 16c. The Dutch took

possession in 1598–1710, followed by the French in 1710–1810, and the British in 1810. It was formally ceded to Britain by the Treaty of Paris in 1814, and governed jointly with the Seychelles as a single colony until 1903. It became an independent sovereign state within the **COMMONWEALTH OF NATIONS** in 1968 and an independent republic in 1992. Cassam Uteem was elected to the largely ceremonial role of President in 1992. The Mauritian Socialist Party (MSM) under Sir Anerood **JUGNAUTH** held power from 1982 to 1995, when they were defeated by an opposition alliance led by Navin Ramgoolam. The 2000 election was won by a coalition of the MSM and Mauritian Militant Movement under Jugnauth. Jugnauth became President in 2003, and was succeeded as Prime Minister by Paul Berenger.

**Mauroy, Pierre** (1928– )
French politician. He was a teacher before becoming involved with trade unionism and socialist politics, and was prominent in the creation of a new French **SOCIALIST PARTY** in 1971. He became Mayor of Lille in 1973, and was elected to the National Assembly the same year. A close ally of **MITTERRAND**, Mauroy acted as his spokesman during the socialists' successful election campaign. He was Prime Minister from 1981 to 1984.

**Maurras, Charles** (1868–1952)
French royalist journalist and political theorist. He was early influenced by the ideas of Auguste Comte. By 1894 he was established as an avant-garde journalist and a proponent of monarchism. From 1908, in the newspaper *Action française*, his articles wielded a powerful influence on the youth of the country. In 1936 he was imprisoned for violent attacks on the government. At the fall of France (1940) he supported the **VICHY** government, and in 1945 was sentenced to life imprisonment, but released on medical grounds in 1952. ► **COLLABORATION** (France); **WORLD WAR II**

**Maurya** ► **INDIA, PRE-ISLAMIC**

**Mavrokordatos, Alexander** (1791–1865)
Greek politician. From one of the 11 Phanariot families, during the **GREEK WAR OF INDEPENDENCE** he headed the Senate which governed the newly liberated areas of western Greece. In 1822 he helped to draft the provisional constitution known as the Epidaurus Constitution. Under King **OTHON**, he led the 'English Party' which favoured constitutional rule. He was briefly the Greek representative in London but was recalled to become, briefly, Foreign Minister and alternate President of the Council (1841). He again held office in 1844 but was replaced by **KOLETTIS**. During the Russo-Turkish War (1854–7) when the Piraeus was occupied by British and French troops, he was appointed to form a new administration which would maintain Greek neutrality. ► **KOLOKOTRONIS, THEODOROS**; **PHANARIOTS**; **RUSSO-TURKISH WARS**

**Mavrokordatos, Constantine** (1711–69)
Alternately Hospodar (Governor) of Wallachia and Moldavia (1730–69). From a Greek Phanariot family, in 1730 he was chosen by the clergy and boyars to succeed his father as Hospodar of Wallachia; in 1733 he was chosen as Hospodar of Moldavia. He

cooperated with the Ottoman Porte in resisting the spread of Habsburg and Russian influence into the Danubian Principalities. Mavrokordatos introduced a wide-ranging programme of reform, easing the tax burden on the peasantry and abolishing serfdom in Wallachia (1746) and Moldavia (1749). He built schools throughout the provinces and founded the academies at Bucharest and Jassy. In his foreign policy he achieved the reintegration of OLTENIA into Wallachia (1739). During the Russo-Turkish War (1768–74) he was seized by the Russians, and died in captivity. ► MOLDAVIA AND WALLACHIA; PHANAR-IOTS; RUSSO-TURKISH WARS

## Max, Adolphe (1869–1939)
Belgian politician and patriot. First a journalist, then an accountant, he became Burgomaster of Brussels in 1909. When the German troops approached Brussels in Aug 1914, he boldly drove to meet them and opened negotiations. He defended the rights of the Belgian population against the invaders, and in Sep was imprisoned by the Germans, later refusing an offer of freedom on condition that he went to Switzerland and desisted from anti-German agitation. In Nov 1918 he returned to Belgium, was elected to the House of Representatives, and became a minister of state.

## Maximilian, in full Ferdinand Maximilian Joseph (1839–67)
Emperor of Mexico (1864/7). Born in Vienna, he was the younger brother of Emperor FRANCIS JOSEPH, and was an archduke of Austria. In 1863, supported by the French, he accepted the offer of the crown of Mexico, falsely believing that he had the general support of the people of Mexico. This offer was in fact the result of conniving between those conservative Mexicans who sought the overthrow of the government of Benito JUÁREZ and the French Emperor NAPOLEON III, who wished to further his own interests in Mexico. When the French troops were forced, under US pressure, to withdraw from Mexico, Maximilian refused to abdicate, seeing this as the desertion of his people. He made a brave defence at Querétaro, but his forces were starved into surrender. He was captured and executed, despite petitions for clemency by many European monarchs.

## Maximilian I (1459–1519)
Holy Roman Emperor (1493/1519). Born Archduke of Austria at Weiner Neustadt, he was the eldest son of Emperor FREDERICK III and Eleanor of Portugal. Elected King of the Romans (1486), he inherited the Habsburg territories and assumed the imperial title in 1493. He pursued an ambitious foreign policy, based on dynastic alliances, with far-reaching results for Habsburg power. His marriage to MARY OF BUR-GUNDY (1477) brought his family the Burgundian inheritance, including the Netherlands, of which he was twice regent (1482/93 and 1506/7). This was followed by union with the Spanish kingdoms of Castile and Aragon, when the Spanish crown passed to his grandson, subsequently CHARLES V (1516). A double marriage treaty between the Habsburgs and the Jagiełłon Dynasty (1506) eventually brought the union of Austria-Bohemia-Hungary (1526). He was involved in conflict with the Flemish, the Swiss, the German princes, and especially with the Valois kings

of France. Financial difficulties weakened his campaigns, and he was later forced to cede Milan (1504) to LOUIS XII. He incurred the hostility of the Venetians, and despite the League of CAMBRAI (1508), suffered defeat. He died, leaving his extended empire to his grandson, Charles V. ► HABSBURG DYNASTY; HOLY ROMAN EMPIRE; VALOIS DYNASTY

## Maximilian I (1573–1651)
Duke (1598/1651) and Elector of Bavaria (1623/51). Educated at the Jesuit college at Ingolstadt, on his succession to the dukedom (1598) he instituted energetic reforms of the country's inefficient bureaucracy and disordered finances. He placed himself at the head of the CATHOLIC LEAGUE in 1609 and pledged his support to Emperor FERDINAND II in the THIRTY YEARS' WAR, obtaining as a reward the confiscated lands of FREDERICK V of the Palatinate. By the Peace of WESTPHALIA (1648), the Palatinate was returned to Frederick's heir, Charles Louis, but Maximilian retained the electoral title. The foremost Catholic prince in Germany after the Emperor, Maximilian was a keen defender of German liberties and resisted imperial attempts to turn the empire into a centralized Habsburg monarchy.

## Maximilian I Joseph (1756–1825)
King of Bavaria (1806/25). Elector, as Maximilian IV Joseph (1799/1806), and first Wittelsbach King of Bavaria (1806/25). In 1795 he succeeded his brother as Duke of Zweibrücken after having served in a French regiment in Alsace from 1777 to 1789. Austria forced him to attack France in 1799 but he signed a separate peace in 1801. He acceded to the Bavarian throne in Dec 1805 and, advised by his minister Montgelas, succeeded in consolidating Bavaria's territory. He supported NAPOLEON I but switched to Austria after Napoleon's defeat in Russia and was thereby able to retain his kingdom. He created a liberal state, granting a constitution in 1808 and establishing a bicameral parliament in 1818. ► NAPOLEONIC WARS

## Maximilian II (1527–76)
Holy Roman Emperor (1564/76). The eldest son of Emperor FERDINAND I and Anna of Bohemia and Hungary, he became King of Bohemia in 1548 and Emperor in 1564. An intelligent, tolerant and cultivated man who considered himself 'neither Catholic nor Protestant but a Christian', he embarrassed his family by his Protestant leanings and was obliged in 1562 to swear to live and die within the Catholic Church. As Emperor he secured considerable religious freedom for Austrian Lutherans and deplored the intolerance of the Catholic reaction in Spain and France. A patron of the arts and sciences, he set out to make Vienna a centre of European intellectual life.

## Maximilian II Emmanuel (1662–1726)
Elector of Bavaria (1679/1726). A military leader, he distinguished himself at the capture of Belgrade (1688). He was Governor of the Spanish Netherlands (1692) while fighting for the Habsburgs against LOUIS XIV of France. He supported the French in the War of the SPANISH SUCCESSION and lost his lands as a result (after Blenheim). He was restored to his former possessions after the Treaty of UTRECHT (1713). ► HABSBURG DYNASTY

**Maximilian III Joseph** (1727–77)
Elector of Bavaria (1745/77). The son of **CHARLES VII**, he renounced all claim to the Imperial throne and made peace with **MARIA THERESA**. In return, he was able to recover his state, which the Austrians had occupied. His capitulation to Maria complicated the plans of **FREDERICK II, THE GREAT** for checking Austrian power.

**Mayakovsky, Vladimir Vladimirovich** (1893–1930)
Russian poet. He began writing at an early age, and was regarded as the leader of the Futurist school. Involved in underground activity before the **RUSSIAN REVOLUTION** (1917) and deeply committed to its success, he emerged as the propaganda mouthpiece of the Communist Party but also wrote satirical plays. Travelling abroad frequently in the 1920s, he became critical of the regime and eventually committed suicide in Moscow.

**Mayas** ► PRE-COLUMBIAN CIVILIZATIONS

**Mayflower Compact** (1620)
An agreement to establish a 'civil body politic', signed aboard the ship *Mayflower* by members of the Pilgrim party about to settle in the Cape Cod region.

**May Fourth Movement** (1919)
A student demonstration in Beijing which crystallized the political and cultural aspirations of those who struggled for a new China. Originally a protest against the Japanese takeover of Germany's rights in Shandong (agreed by the Western powers at the Versailles Peace Conference), the movement spread nationwide, rallying students and intellectuals across a broad political spectrum. ► **VERSAILLES, TREATY OF**

**May Thirtieth Movement** (1925)
The large-scale anti-imperialist demonstrations in China which resulted in increased membership for both the Chinese **COMMUNIST PARTY** and the **GUO-MINDANG**. On this day, a crowd of workers and students in Shanghai protesting against the earlier killing of a Chinese worker in a Japanese textile mill was fired upon by the British-led international settlement police force. The incident, during which 13 died and many more were injured, led to nationwide strikes and boycotts. The most significant of these was the 15-month boycott against the British colony of Hong Kong following the killing of 52 demonstrators by British and French troops in Canton (23 June 1925). The movement clearly revealed the strength of opposition to foreign privilege in China. The powers, adapting to the new situation, began discussions in 1925 on the return to China of tariff autonomy.

**Mazarin, Jules, Cardinal**, originally **Giulio Mazarini** (1602–61)
Neapolitan cleric, diplomat and politician. He became Papal Nuncio to the French court (1634–6) and entered the service of **LOUIS XIII** in 1639. Through the influence of **RICHELIEU** he was elevated to cardinal, succeeding his mentor as First Minister in 1642. After Louis's death (1643), he retained his authority under the Queen Regent, **ANNE OF AUSTRIA**. Blamed by many for the civil disturbances of the **FRONDE**, he twice fled the kingdom, and returned to Paris in 1653 after the nobles' revolt had been suppressed. His foreign policy was more fruitful: he concluded the Peace of **WESTPHALIA** (1648), whose terms increased French prestige, and negotiated the Treaty of the Pyrenees (1659), ending the prolonged Franco-Spanish conflict. ► **BOURBON, HOUSE OF**

**Mazeppa, Ivan Stepanovich** (c.1644–1709)
Russian nobleman, and hetman of the Cossacks. Having become a page at the court of Poland, he was involved in an intrigue with a nobleman's wife, and was sent home bound naked upon his horse. Mazeppa now joined the Cossacks, and in 1687 was elected hetman of the Ukraine. He won the confidence of **PETER I, THE GREAT**, who made him Prince of the Ukraine; but when Peter curtailed the freedom of the Cossacks and seemed in any case likely to be defeated by his Swedish enemy **CHARLES XII**, Mazeppa entered into treasonable negotiations. However, his hopes of an independent crown for the Ukraine perished in the disaster of **POLTAVA** (1709), and he fled with Charles to Bender, where he died.

**Mazzini, Giuseppe** (1805–72)
Italian patriot. Initiated into the **CARBONARI** as a young man, he was arrested by the Piedmontese police and exiled to France, where in 1833 he founded his own movement, **YOUNG ITALY**. Expelled from France, he travelled widely in Europe, calling for republican insurrection. During the **REVOLUTIONS OF 1848–9** he took part first in the Lombard revolt against Austrian rule and, subsequently, in the governing triumvirate of the Roman Republic established after **PIUS IX** fled the city. A number of abortive Mazzinian insurrections during the 1850s (notably that of Pisacane) and a growing support for the moderate views embodied by the **ITALIAN NATIONAL SOCIETY** largely discredited Mazzini. In the final decade of his life he continued to preach republicanism and women's emancipation and played a small part in the establishment of the First International, but never managed to reconcile his ideas to those of socialism.

**M'ba, Léon** (1902–67)
Gabon politician. Educated in Catholic schools, he was in turn accountant, journalist and administrator. He was elected for the **RASSEMBLEMENT DÉMOCRA-TIQUE AFRICAIN** to the Gabon Assembly in 1952 and, in the French tradition, used the mayoral position (of Libreville) to enhance his political ambitions. He was Head of Government (1957–60) and President from Gabon's independence until his death in 1967.

**Mbande, Jinga** ► NZINGA

**Mbeki, Thabo Mvuyelwa** (1942–)
South African politician. Born in Transkei, the son of Govan Mbeki (1910–2001), who was imprisoned with Nelson **MANDELA** in 1964, he was active in the African National Congress (**ANC**) from his student days and was briefly imprisoned in 1962. Following his release he studied in England and the USSR, and on his return to South Africa took a leading role in the ANC, becoming its chairman in 1989. As such, he played a significant part in the negotiations with F W **DE KLERK** that led to the dismantling of **APART-HEID**. In 1994 he was appointed Vice-President of South Africa and took over from Nelson Mandela as President in May 1999. He was re-elected in 2004.

# *Medicine*

Science & Technology

From the earliest times, all societies seem to have had some knowledge of herbal remedies and to have practised folk medicine. Invariably, illness was deemed to have a supernatural cause, so that the patient was treated with the aim of propitiating the gods or releasing evil from the body. The earliest civilizations also bequeathed evidence of their use of drugs to treat illness; in Egypt and Mesopotamia, for example, the practical application of salves was part of a medical tradition that included divination to obtain a prognosis and incantation to help the patient. Indian physicians made clinical descriptions of many of the commonly occurring illnesses, used some drugs still exploited by modern medicine, and also performed surgery, including skin grafts. Religious belief forbade the cutting of dead bodies, however, and knowledge of physical anatomy was rudimentary.

The prohibition on desecration of the dead was also a feature of early Chinese society, and as a consequence Chinese ideas of physiology do not rest on observational analysis. However, a well-developed medical tradition has flourished in China from the earliest times to the present day, with special attention given to the pulse as a means of diagnosis. The aim is to balance the *yin* (the negative, dark, feminine, cold, passive element) and the *yang* (the positive, light, masculine, warm, active element). The pharmacopoeia for doing this is vast: vegetable, animal and mineral. Of equal importance is acupuncture, which uses needles to vary the flow of *ch'i* (energy) that is deemed to travel along invisible channels in the body (meridians). The efficacy of acupuncture is most visibly apparent in its use in anaesthesia.

In the West, medicine was originally an aspect of religion, but then was partially rationalized by the Greek philosophers. Sick people would go to the temple of the god Asclepius for incubation – a sleep during which the god would visit them in a dream, and the dream would be interpreted by priests who would then give a diagnosis or advice. Later, Empedocles conceived the idea that there are four elements – fire, air, earth and water, which in terms of the human body became blood, phlegm, yellow bile and black bile – which must be kept in balance. This concept was adopted by Aristotle (384–322 BC) and remained a tenet of Western medicine until the 18c. Aristotle observed the world as a biologist, performing dissections of animals and learning something of anatomy and embryology. After him, the centre of Greek learning was Alexandria, where the principles expounded by Hippocrates (c.460–c.377 BC) were upheld. He rejected the idea that illness was sent from the gods, and made his diagnosis and prognosis after careful observation and consideration. Hippocrates is regarded as the 'father of medicine', and parts of the oath attributed to him are still used in medical schools.

Another major influence on Western medicine was Galen (c.130–201 AD), a Greek doctor who studied at Alexandria and later went to Rome. He gathered up all the existing writings of Greek physicians, and stressed the importance of anatomy. As dissection of the human body was illegal, he used apes. Despite this, he was wrong on many anatomical points, including the transport of blood, which he stated ebbed and flowed. It is worth noting that at this time Rome had an excellent regard for public health, with clean drinking water, sewage disposal and hospitals. Such benefits for ordinary citizens did not become widely available again in the West until the 20c.

After the fall of the Roman Empire, medical care in the West resided in the infirmaries of the monasteries. In the Islamic Empire, Persian and Arab physicians developed medicine and drug treatment, with much of their knowledge based on translations of the Greek classics lost to the West until the 15c. The most renowned of these physicians was Avicenna (980–1037), whose medical system was to be the standard in many medical schools until the 17c.

The first medical school in Europe was established at Salerno in the 12c. Other European schools followed: at Montpellier, Paris, Bologna and Padua. It was at Bologna that Mondino dei Liucci (c.1270–1326) published the first manual of anatomy, after carrying out his own dissections. But it was the Flemish anatomist Andreas Vesalius (1514–64) who significantly advanced the science of anatomy with his detailed descriptions and drawings published in 1543, correcting the mistakes of Galen. He was sentenced to death by the **Inquisition** for performing the dissections, but there was a new spirit of enquiry abroad that could not be held back. The improved knowledge of anatomy led to an improvement in surgical technique, and surgeons, long despised as inferior practitioners by physicians, began to organize and be recognized. The great increase in the sizes of European armies in the 16c and 17c led to enhanced demand for effective military surgery. In France, Ambroise Paré (1510–90) reformed surgical practice, stopping the cauterizing of wounds. In England and Scotland, companies were formed which later became the Colleges of Surgeons.

In the 17c William Harvey's experiments produced the theory of the circulation of the blood (1628), reinforced by the work of Marcello Malpighi, but it was more than a hundred years later, following the work of the French chemist Antoine Lavoisier (1743–94), that the reason for its circulation, to transport oxygen, was understood. Other key developments over that time were the growth of microscopal studies, and a new scientific approach to obstetrics. The end of the 18c saw the introduction to Europe of vaccination against smallpox, the beginnings of a drive against the disease that would see it eradicated in the 20c.

The 19c saw practical improvements to aid diagnosis, the invention of the stethoscope and the use of percussion of

---

**Mboya, Tom (Thomas Joseph)** (1930–69)
Kenyan trade unionist and politician. Educated at Catholic mission schools and Ruskin College, Oxford, he was an employee of the Nairobi City Council when he became Treasurer of the Kenyan African Union in 1953. He was elected Secretary-General of the Kenyan Federation of Labour in 1955 and a member of Legco in 1957. Mboya was a founder-member, and Secretary-General (1960–9) of the Kenyan African National Union (**KANU**). His reformist instincts brought him into conflict with his fellow Luo, Oginga **ODINGA**, but he eventually won out, forcing Odinga out of KANU after the party's conference at Limuru (1966), thus binding himself closer to Jomo **KENYATTA**. He was Minister of Labour (1962–3), Minister of Justice and Constitutional Affairs (1963–4), Minister for Economic Planning and Development (1964–9) when his essentially

the chest. At the same time, scientific research produced new knowledge about physiology. Even more important was the work of Louis Pasteur (1822–95), which established the germ theory of disease transmission. From his work developed the field of bacteriology, and the concept of antisepsis introduced by Joseph Lister (1827–1912). This was of great importance to all surgical patients, and in the field of obstetrics, where women had died regularly from puerperal fever before it was realized that doctors were transmitting bacteria from diseased patients to healthy ones.

Another major advance in surgery was the discovery of anaesthetic gases: ether was first used in the USA in 1846 and chloroform in Edinburgh, Scotland, in 1847. This not only saved patients pain but enabled longer, more complicated surgical procedures to take place.

The 19c was a time of serious research and discoveries in all fields. Many conditions were recognized and described in detail for the first time. The finding that diseases were transmitted by insect bites enabled precautions to be taken to stop the spread of malaria and yellow fever. At the very end of the century, the discovery of X-rays by Röntgen, and that of radium by Marie and Pierre Curie, provided new diagnostic tools. At around the same time, Freud began his work in psychological analysis.

Progress in the 20c was marked by the growth of advanced technology and the development of new drug treatments. The first discoveries of bacteria-killing organisms were made haphazardly, most notably Alexander Fleming's discovery of penicillin in 1928. Sulfonamides were then discovered, and later streptomycin, the first antibiotic to be effective against tuberculosis. Research also led to the discovery of insulin, enabling treatment for diabetes, until then a fatal disease.

Improved public health measures, nutrition and living conditions, combined with advances in immunology and state programmes to immunize children, led to the demise in the West of typhoid, tetanus, diphtheria, tuberculosis, measles, whooping cough and polio. Similarly, the discovery of vitamins early in the century, and the understanding of their importance, also led to the elimination of rickets and scurvy in the West, and to the mitigation of beriberi in Africa and Asia. Drugs were also found to treat malaria, yellow fever and leprosy.

Now that people live longer than ever before, the chief causes of death in the Western world are heart disease and cancer. New treatments for cancer by surgery, chemotherapy and radiation therapy have improved the prognosis for some sufferers, and in cardiology too, new treatments have been developed, notably angiograms, open-heart surgery and heart transplants. The techniques of organ transplants have been extended to lungs, livers and kidneys, and artificial joints for the hips and knees have been repeatedly improved.

For those wishing to plan their families or avoid conception, methods of contraception became more reliable than ever before with the development, in the 1960s, of the oral contraceptive pill for women. Abortion, too, became safer and was legalized in many countries. On the other hand, for those willing and yet unable to conceive, fertility drugs and *in vitro* fertilization provided a possible way to start a family.

The ability of doctors to do so many things previously considered impossible has led many to the expectation that every illness and disease has a cure. But some, such as types of cancer, continue to defy research, and new diseases continue to emerge; AIDS is one example, ebola virus another. The escalating costs of medical care, the power of pharmaceutical companies, and the responsibility of funding health services have all been central social issues in recent times, and treatments such as access to organ transplants have caused much social dissent.

Although the Western model of medicine is the most globally pervasive, for various reasons folk and herbal treatments have not disappeared. In non-Western societies, particularly in rural areas, Western medicine has simply not made inroads into traditional medical practices. However, even in the West, under the umbrella 'complementary medicine' are a multitude of different approaches, including aromatherapy, auto-suggestion, chiropractic, hydrotherapy, homoeopathy and osteopathy. Many of the complementary approaches have long histories, and some, such as acupuncture, have even been incorporated into Western orthodox medical practice.

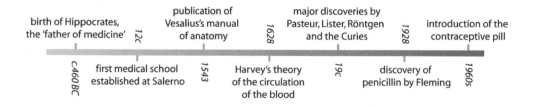

Fabian philosophy established the 'free enterprise with state regulation' economic system which Kenya epitomizes. He was assassinated in 1969.

## Meade, George Gordon (1815–72)
US soldier. Born in Cadiz, Spain, he trained at West Point and served against the Seminoles and in the MEXICAN WAR. In the AMERICAN CIVIL WAR he fought at BULL RUN and ANTIETAM, after which he was pro-moted to major-general of volunteers. He led troops at FREDERICKSBURG and at Chancellorsville, and in 1863 he was given command of the Army of the Potomac. He defeated Robert E LEE at GETTYSBURG but was criticized for failing to press his advantage.

## Mecca and Medina, Capture of (1803–4)
The holy city of Mecca was vacated in 1803 by Ghalib, the Sharif; thereupon, Saud ibn Abd al-Aziz with his

**WAHHABIS** entered and destroyed everything which, in the Wahhabi view, smacked of idolatrous practices, executing all those suspected of being involved in them. Unsuccessful in his attempts to take Medina and Jedda, Saud withdrew and his garrison in Mecca was massacred by the native Meccans. An unsuccessful attempt to mount an attack on the Wahhabis from Baghdad gave Saud the opportunity to return to campaigning in the Hijaz, where he took Medina in 1804, Mecca in 1806, and subsequently Jedda.

## Mecklenburg

A region which first came under German control in 1160. It converted to Lutheranism during the **REFORMATION**. Mecklenburg sided with Denmark and Sweden in the **THIRTY YEARS' WAR** and ceded part of its territory, Wismar, to Sweden in the Peace of **WESTPHALIA** (1648), which was not returned until 1803. The area, divided into two duchies, joined Napoleon's Rhine Confederation (1808). The Congress of **VIENNA** (1814–15) recognized the two as Grand Duchies. The University of Rostock was founded in Mecklenburg in 1419.

## Medicare (30 July 1965)

A programme in the USA, under the direction of the Social Security Administration, that reimburses physicians and treatment centres for medical expenses incurred by qualified patients 65 years of age or older or by qualified disabled patients. Together with Medicaid, which provides medical insurance for the poor, it was enacted as an amendment to the Social Security Act (1965) during Lyndon B **JOHNSON**'s administration as part of his **GREAT SOCIETY** reforms, and came into effect in 1966.

## Medici

A family which made its wealth through banking and which ruled Florence from 1434 to 1494, though without holding formal office. They were overthrown at the start of the **ITALIAN WARS** in 1494, but they returned to power in 1512. They became hereditary Dukes of Florence in 1537 and Grand Dukes of Tuscany from 1569. By that stage, however, their dynastic power base had shifted away from Florence, first to Rome when Giovanni (1475–1521) became Pope **LEO X** in 1513 and then when Catherine, the niece of another Medici pope, **CLEMENT VII**, was married to the heir to the throne of France who became **HENRY II. ► CATHERINE DE' MEDICI**

## Medici, Cosimo de', the Elder (1389–1464)

Florentine financier, statesman and philanthropist. His father, Giovanni de Bicci de' Medici, appears to have created the Medici wealth, and Cosimo was to use it to fuel the machine of his own power in Florence. He was exiled by the ascendant Albizzi faction in 1433, having opposed the imposition of taxes for what proved a disastrous war. He returned in 1434 and stifled family faction while maintaining the façade of republican government with a mixture of ruthlessness and urbanity. He employed some of his wealth in patronage of the arts, including Europe's first public library, though his encouragement of the platonic revival among humanists may have been designed to make them espouse the contemplative life and stay out of politics. He was posthumously commemorated as 'Pater Patriae'.

## Medici, Cosimo I de', the Great (1519–74)

Duke of Florence (1537/74) and Grand Duke of Tuscany (1569/74). A skilled soldier, he annexed the republic of Siena in 1555, and doubled the territory of Tuscany during his rule. He devoted his considerable energies to developing the trade and agriculture of Tuscany and to the expansion of its military. He was a notable patron of the arts and a great collector of Etruscan antiquities.

## Médici, Emílio Garrastazú (1905–90)

Brazilian military dictator. A career military officer, he was Chief of Staff to Artur da Costa e Silva in the late 1950s, Military Academy Commander in 1964 and Head of the SNI (National Information Service, the military intelligence operation attached to the presidency) during Costa's government. Nominated President by the military junta in 1969, he governed until 1974, using a military-technocratic team to balance repression and rapid economic growth. He manipulated elections and liquidated guerrillas in major cities as well as Araguaía in Goías and Pará, at the cost of creating an almost autonomous security apparatus, and stimulated settlement of Amazonia.

## Medici, Lorenzo de', the Magnificent (1449–92)

Florentine ruler, son of Piero de' **MEDICI** and grandson of Cosimo de' **MEDICI**. He succeeded as head of the family upon the death of his father in 1469, and was an able, if autocratic, ruler who made Florence the leading state in Italy. In 1478 he showed courage and judgement in thwarting an attempt by malcontents, with the encouragement of Pope **SIXTUS IV**, to overthrow the Medici, although the rising led to the assassination of Lorenzo's brother, Giuliano (1453–78). Lorenzo was a distinguished lyric poet as well as being, in the words of **MACHIAVELLI**, 'the greatest patron of literature and art that any prince has ever been'.

## Medici, Piero de', the Gouty (1416–69)

Ruler of Florence (1464/8). The son of Cosimo de' **MEDICI** and father of Lorenzo de' **MEDICI**, he revealed his abilities as prince in surmounting a notable constitutional crisis by the judicious use of force. The illness which killed him so young was also to claim Lorenzo.

## Medici, Piero de', the Unfortunate (1471–1503)

Florentine ruler. The eldest son of Lorenzo de' **MEDICI**, he succeeded his father in 1492, but his disregard of republican forms made him unpopular. With the invasion of Italy by **CHARLES VIII** of France in 1494, Piero was obliged to surrender key Florentine forces to the aggressor, a step strongly resented by the civic authorities, who banished the Medici from the state. Piero died fighting against the French in the **ITALIAN WARS**.

## Medicine ► See panel

## Medina Sidonia, Alonso Pérez de Guzmán el Bueno, 7th Duke of (1550–1619)

Spanish naval commander and Captain General of Andalusia. He was a distinguished administrator with a good record in the conquest of Portugal. Appointed to command the Great Armada in the Enterprise of England on the death of the Marquis of Santa Cruz (1588), he led the Armada successfully up the

English Channel to rendezvous with Parma off the Dutch coast. He was, however, thwarted by the latter's failure to break out, action by the English fleet and adverse weather. He returned to Spain north-about round Britain, and continued in royal service. He was one of the wealthiest and most influential men in Spain. ► ARMADA, SPANISH

## Medvedev, Roy Alexandrovich (1925–)

Soviet historian, dissident and politician. Although remaining a Marxist, he was highly critical of STALIN and other communist leaders. In 1968 he was expelled from the Communist Party and denied employment in academic bodies. However, he continued writing as a private individual, publishing his best book, *Let History Judge*, in 1971. In this way he helped to sustain ideological criticism of Leonid BREZHNEV's dictatorship. Under Mikhail GORBACHEV he was able to enter politics. He was readmitted to the party and elected to the Congress and the Supreme Soviet in 1989. His twin brother, Zhores MEDVEDEV, also suffered as a critic of Brezhnev.

## Medvedev, Zhores Alexandrovich (1925–)

Soviet geneticist and dissident. Like his twin brother, Roy MEDVEDEV, he became an opponent of the communist system through his scientific studies. As a reputable geneticist, he was particularly critical of the damage LYSENKO had done with political support. In 1970 he was confined to a psychiatric hospital but was released as a result of protests from abroad. On visiting Britain in 1973, he was deprived of his Soviet citizenship and he stayed on working as a gerontological researcher. His publications include *The Rise and Fall of Lysenko*, helping to set the Soviet scientific record straight.

## Meech Lake Accord (1987)

Canadian constitutional amendment, which recognized French-speaking Quebec as a 'distinct society', in response to the province's demands for special status within the confederation. The agreement was concluded in 1987 but did not receive enough support from the English-speaking provinces to be ratified. The failure of the Accord intensified Quebec separatism and also fuelled resentment among the native INUIT and Indians at their own lack of representation. The Charlottetown Agreement, balancing concessions of greater autonomy for Quebec and the Inuit and Amerindian populations with other constitutional reforms aimed at the Western provinces, was put to a referendum on 26 Oct 1992. This was defeated by 54.4 per cent to 44.6 per cent.

## Megale Idea

Literally, 'the Great Idea', this describes the programme of Greek expansion which was first formulated in the 1840s by Ioannis KOLETTIS and which aspired to the revival of the BYZANTINE EMPIRE. With Constantinople as its capital, this new Greek empire was to embrace EPIRUS, THESSALY, Macedonia, THRACE, the Aegean Islands, Crete, Cyprus, the west coast of Asia Minor and EASTERN RUMELIA, and all other areas which were Hellenized. This programme of IRREDENTISM was to dictate the course of Greek foreign policy well into the 20c and had a staunch advocate in Eleuthérios VENIZÉLOS. At the end of

WORLD WAR I, the Treaty of Sèvres (1920) brought Greece closer to realizing the Megale Idea but after the Anatolian debacle it forfeited its territorial gains by the Treaty of LAUSANNE (1923). ► DELIGIANNIS, THEODOROS; ENOSIS; RIGAS, VELESTINLIS PHERAIOS

## Mehemed-Pasha Sokollu, Sokolović (c.1505–1579)

Grand Vizier of the OTTOMAN EMPIRE. Born to a Serb family and recruited by DEVŞIRME, he was trained as a janissary and entered the service of the Sultan. Enjoying the trust of SÜLEYMAN I, THE MAGNIFICENT, he was appointed dragoman of the Ottoman fleet (1546) and *beglerbeg* (Governor) of RUMELIA (1549). After a series of military victories, he rose from Third to Grand Vizier (1555–65). He accompanied Süleyman on his Hungarian campaign and directed operations at the siege of Sigetvár, keeping secret the death of the Sultan lest it demoralize the troops. Under SELIM II (1566/74) he enjoyed great authority, overseeing the rebuilding of the fleet after the Battle of LEPANTO (1571). Under MURAD III (1574/95) opposition to him mounted and he was murdered. ► JANISSARIES

## Mehmed I (c.1387–1421)

Ottoman Sultan (1413/21). His reign marks the beginning of the recovery from the devastating effects of the conquests of TIMUR. He was the father of Sultan MURAD II.

## Mehmed II, the Conqueror (1432–81)

Ottoman Sultan (1451/81). The founder of the OTTOMAN EMPIRE, he was born in Adrianople. He succeeded his father, MURAD II, in 1451, and took Constantinople in 1453, renaming it Istanbul, thus extinguishing the BYZANTINE EMPIRE and giving the Turks their commanding position on the Bosphorus. Checked by János HUNYADI at Belgrade in 1456, he nevertheless annexed most of Serbia, all Greece, and most of the Aegean Islands. He threatened Venetian territory, was repelled from Rhodes by the Knights of St John (1479), took Otranto in 1480 and died in a campaign against Persia.

## Mehmed III (1566–1603)

Ottoman Sultan (1595/1603). He was the son of MURAD III, whom he succeeded. On his accession to the throne, he invoked the Law of FRATRICIDE by which the sultan could have his brothers put to death. All 19, of whom the eldest was only 11, were accordingly executed by strangulation.

## Mehmed IV (1642–93)

Ottoman Sultan (1648/87). He succeeded his deposed father, Ibrahim I, as a child, in the middle of a long war with Venice (1645–64). Anarchy in the country was quelled by the appointment of able viziers, Mehmet KÖPRÜLÜ (1656) and his son Fazil Ahmed (1661) and foster son KARA MUSTAFA (1676). In 1664 the Turks were defeated by the Austrians under Montecucculi at the Battle of St Gotthard; in a war with Poland (1672–6) the Turks were twice defeated by King JOHN III SOBIESKI, but gained Polish Ukraine, which they lost to Russia in 1681. In 1683 the Turks, under Kara Mustafa, laid siege to Vienna, which was relieved by John Sobieski. After defeat at the second Battle of Mohács (1687), Mehmed was deposed, and replaced by SÜLEYMAN II.

## Mehmed V (1844–1918)

Ottoman Sultan (1909/18). He was Turkey's first 'constitutional monarch', having gained his elevation through the victory of the **YOUNG TURKS** and their deposition of **ABD UL-HAMID II**. A pious and mild man, Mehmed reigned under the control of the Unionist Party, whose power became total in 1913. He was constrained to proclaim a holy war (*jihad*) against the Entente Powers in 1914, but this did not greatly influence his Muslim subjects. As a constitutional monarch, he was unable to wield effective power and as a result it was not he, but initially his Grand Vizier and subsequently Unionist leaders such as **ENVER PASHA** and **TALAT PASHA**, who controlled affairs. Significantly, it was Enver's German sympathies which turned Turkey's initially neutral stance into a German alignment at the outbreak of **WORLD WAR I** in 1914.

## Mehmed VI (1861–1926)

Last Ottoman Sultan (1918/22). He was the brother of **MEHMED V**. Unsuccessful in suppressing the nationalists led by Mustafa Kemal **ATATÜRK**, he died in exile.

## Mehta, Sir Pherozeshah (1845–1915)

Indian political leader and lawyer. A Parsee from Bombay, he came under the influence of Dadabhai **NAOROJI**, a successful businessman and nationalist politician, in the late 1860s and early 1870s. Along with **TILAK** and **GOKHALE**, he was one of the founder-members of the **INDIAN NATIONAL CONGRESS**. Mehta started taking a more active interest in the Congress from 1889 and was a prominent leader of the 'moderate' or right-wing faction of the Congress movement, playing an important role in the so-called 'split' in the Congress at a famous session in Surat in 1907. A pioneering journalist and a member of the Bombay Legislative Council from 1886, Mehta was also a member of the Imperial Legislative Council after 1898, until ill health forced him to retire in 1902. He devoted himself in later years not only to Congress politics (of which he became increasingly suspicious), but also to business education and municipal reform, for which he was knighted in 1904.

## Meighen, Arthur (1874–1960)

Canadian lawyer and politician. A Conservative, in 1913 he became Solicitor-General in Robert **BORDEN**'s Union government and was the architect of much of its strategy during **WORLD WAR I**: railway nationalization, conscription and the deeply-resented Wartime Elections Act. It was Meighen who also orchestrated the government's draconian response to the **WINNIPEG GENERAL STRIKE** (1919), insisting that organized labour was revolutionary. Both the Immigration Act and the criminal code were amended so that strike leaders would face either deportation or long prison sentences. In 1920 Meighen succeeded Borden as Prime Minister and his high tariff policy was a major factor in the defeat of the Conservative Party in 1921. He became Prime Minister again in 1925 but when the Progressives deserted him, the Governor-General allowed him to dissolve parliament, a mechanism which had not been afforded to Mackenzie **KING** in a similar situation. King won the election by promising to prevent such imperial intervention. Meighen then resigned as Conservative leader a few months later, and was replaced by R B

**BENNETT**. In 1940 the Conservatives invited him to lead the party again but he failed to win a seat and retired from politics.

## Meiji Constitution (1889)

Promulgated by the Japanese **MEIJI EMPEROR** on 11 Feb 1889, this constitution was to remain in effect until 1947. It was the result of a long debate that had begun with the **MEIJI RESTORATION** (1868), when the new government promised greater public participation in the political process. By the 1870s some government leaders like **KIDO KOIN** were advocating a written constitution on the Western model as a means of unifying the country and to enhance Japan's credentials as a modern state (and thereby persuade the Western powers to revise their unequal treaties with Japan). There was disagreement, however, over the timing and scope of such a constitution. In order to deflect the more radical demands of the **FREEDOM AND PEOPLE'S RIGHTS MOVEMENT**, an imperial rescript (12 Oct 1881) promised a parliament by 1890. **ITO HIROBUMI**, who had led an investigative mission to Europe in 1882, was charged with drafting a constitution. Influenced by the ideas of German constitutional theorists (whom Ito had met while in Europe) the constitution, presented as a gift by the Emperor to the people, was an authoritarian, if ambivalent, document. Article One stated that sovereignty lay with the Emperor; at the same time, he was to be above the political fray and rule only through his ministers. In line with the notion of 'transcendental' cabinets, such ministers were responsible solely to the Emperor and not to the Diet, which comprised two houses: an appointed upper house and a lower house to be elected on a limited franchise. The Diet could not initiate legislation, although it could veto the government's budget. Basic rights were guaranteed, but could be modified by law. Like cabinet ministers, the military, Imperial Household Ministry, and Privy Council were not subject to Diet control and were directly responsible to the Emperor. The Meiji constitutional system was therefore inherently unstable since each of these institutions could claim to represent the imperial will, while in time political parties in the Diet would demand more power and influence.

## Meiji Emperor (Mutsuhito) (1852–1912)

Emperor of Japan (1867/1912). He became the symbol of Japan's modernization. He is commemorated by the Meiji Shrine and the Meiji Memorial Picture Gallery, Tokyo, and a large mausoleum at Momoyama, near Kyoto. ➤ **MEIJI RESTORATION**; **TOKUGAWA SHOGUNATE**

## Meiji Restoration (1868)

An important point in Japanese history, when the last **SHOGUN** was overthrown in a short civil war, and the position of the **MEIJI EMPEROR** was restored to symbolic importance. Powerful new leaders set about making Japan into an industrial state; the four hereditary classes of Tokugawa Japan were abolished; and new technology and technical experts were brought from the West. ➤ **DAIMYO**; **SAMURAI**; **TOKUGAWA SHOGUNATE**; *See map*

## Meir, Golda (1898–1978)

Israeli politician. Born in Kiev, she emigrated with her

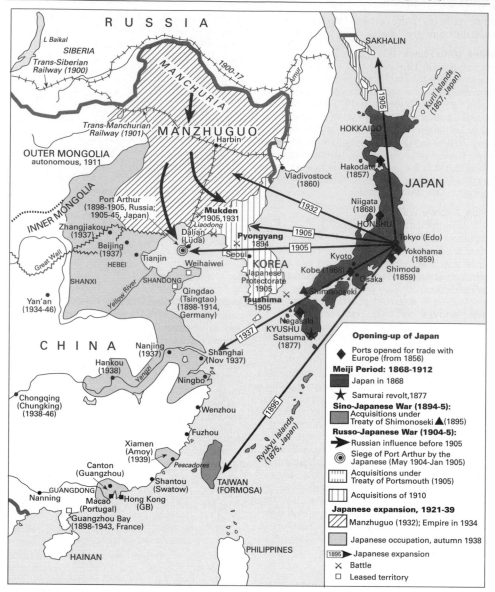

**Japan, 1868–1939**

family to Milwaukee, USA, when she was eight. She married in 1917 and settled in **PALESTINE** in 1921. She was Israeli Ambassador to the USSR (1948–9), Minister of Labour (1949–56), and Foreign Minister (1956–66). As Prime Minister (1969–74), her efforts for peace in the Middle East were halted by the fourth Arab–Israeli War (1973). ► **ARAB–ISRAELI WARS**; **MAPAI PARTY**

**Melanchthon, Philipp**, originally **Philipp Schwartzerd** (1497–1560)
German religious reformer, whose name is a Greek translation of his German surname, 'black earth'. Educated at Heidelberg and Tübingen, he became Professor of Greek at Wittenberg in 1516 and **LUTHER**'s fellow worker. His *Loci Communes* (1521) is the first great Protestant work on dogmatic theology, and he composed the Augsburg Confession (1530).

**Melbourne, William Lamb, 2nd Viscount** (1779–1848)
British politician. He became a Whig MP in 1805, and Chief Secretary for Ireland (1827–8). Succeeding as second viscount (1828), he became Home Secretary (1830–4) under **GREY**. Prime Minister in 1834 and 1835–41, he formed a close, almost avuncular, relationship with the young Queen **VICTORIA**. Defeated in the election of 1841, he resigned and thereafter took little part in public affairs. His wife (1785–1828) wrote novels as Lady Caroline Lamb, and was notorious for her nine months' devotion (1812–13) to Lord Byron. ► **CHARTISTS**; **WHIGS**

**Melgarejo, Mariano** (1818–71)
Bolivian general and politician. He deposed José María de Achá to become President of Bolivia in 1865, and by the end of his presidency in 1871 had not only given away much of Bolivia's claim to the

nitrate resources in the Atacama Desert but had reduced the country to financial ruin.

**Méline, (Félix) Jules** (1838–1925)
French politician. He was a Deputy (1872–1903) and Senator (1903–25), and famous as the champion of the peasantry. He was several times Minister of Agriculture (1883–5, 1896–8 and 1915–16) and campaigned for increases in tariffs on both agricultural and industrial products, which he imposed by the law of 1892 (the Méline tariff). He was Prime Minister (1896–8) of a moderate republican ministry, supported by the *Ralliés*, Catholics who had accepted the republic; in this position he refused to allow the reopening of the **DREYFUS** case.

**Mellon, Andrew William** (1855–1937)
US financier, philanthropist and politician. Born in Pittsburgh, Pennsylvania, he trained as a lawyer and entered his father's banking house in 1874. He took over in 1882, soon establishing himself as a banker and industrial magnate. Entering politics, he was Secretary of the Treasury from 1921 to 1932 under Presidents Warren G **HARDING**, Calvin **COOLIDGE** and Herbert **HOOVER**, and made controversial fiscal reforms, drastically reducing taxation of the wealthy. He was ambassador to the UK from 1932 to 1933.

**Menchú, Rigoberta Tum** (1959– )
Guatemalan activist. Born near San Marcos, she worked as a domestic servant and as a cotton-field labourer. Her campaign for human rights began when she was a teenager, and she had to flee to Mexico when her brother and parents were killed by security forces in 1980. In 1983 her book *I Rigoberta Menchú* was published, and her cause was taken up by Danielle Mitterrand, wife of President **MITTERRAND** of France. In 1986 Menchu narrated the film *When the Mountains Tremble*, which portrays the difficulties experienced by the native Quiche people. In 1992 she helped to organize opposition to celebrations of the 500th anniversary of the arrival of Christopher **COLUMBUS** in America, and that same year was awarded the **NOBEL PEACE PRIZE**.

**Menderes, Adnan** (1899–1961)
Turkish politician. Though educated for the law, he became a farmer, and entered politics in 1932, at first in opposition, then with the party in power under Kemal **ATATÜRK**. In 1945 he was one of the leaders of the new Democratic Party and became Prime Minister when it came to power (1950). He was deposed (1960) in an army coup, put on trial, and hanged at Imrali.

**Mendès-France, Pierre** (1907–82)
French politician. He entered parliament in 1932 as a member of the **RADICAL PARTY**, in 1941 escaping to join the **FREE FRENCH** forces in England. He was Minister for National Economy under de **GAULLE** in 1945. As Prime Minister (1954–5), he ended the war in Indo-China, but his government was defeated on its North African policy. A firm critic of de Gaulle, he lost his seat in the 1958 election.

**Mendoza, Antonio de** (c.1490–1552)
Spanish colonial governor and aristocrat. Appointed first viceroy of New Spain (Mexico) by Emperor **CHARLES V** (Charles I of Spain) in 1535, he provided the new colony with leadership for nearly 15 years. He improved relations between the Spaniards and the native Indians by alleviating the exploitation of the latter, encouraging agriculture and mining, building schools and churches, improving education, and introducing the first printing press to the New World (1535). He also sponsored expeditions to explore what are now New Mexico and Colorado. In 1551 he was appointed viceroy of Peru, but he died soon after taking office in Lima.

**Mendoza, Iñigo López de** (fl.1450)
Spanish statesman and poet. The father of Pedro González de **MENDOZA** and great-grandfather of Diego Hurtado de Mendoza, he was created Marquis of Santillana by John II of Castile in 1445 for his services in the field. Mendoza was a wise statesman, a sturdy patriot, and an admired poet of Petrachan sonnets, lyrics, allegories and didactic poems. He left an excellent account of the Provençal, Catalan and Valencian poets, and was an early folklorist and collector of popular proverbs.

**Mendoza, Pedro González de** (1428–95)
Spanish prelate and statesman. The son of Iñigo López de **MENDOZA**, he was created a cardinal in 1473 and was later made Chancellor of Castile. As Archbishop of Castile, in 1474 he helped Isabella of Castile gain the throne (as **ISABELLA I, THE CATHO-LIC**). He became the Archbishop of Toledo and Primate of Spain in 1482, and was a trusted minister of Isabella and her husband, **FERDINAND II, THE CATHOLIC**.

**Menelik** (1015–1913)
Emperor of Ethiopia. The King of Shoa, he succeeded **JOHN IV** when the latter was killed (1889) in battle with the Mahdists in the Sudan. Menelik had conquered the Galla and Somali people, adding the Ogaden to the Ethiopian state, and had cultivated Europeans, particularly the Italians. He was probably the most powerful indigenous ruler in Africa, but he faced threats from a number of quarters: Egyptian imperialism from the North, the Mahdists in the Sudan, and the Italians in Eritrea and Somalia. He concluded the Treaty of Wichale or Ucciali with the Italians, interpreting this as a sign of diplomatic friendship. The Italians considered that it gave them a protectorate over Ethiopia and advanced into the interior to make good their claims. However, Menelik had supplied himself with modern arms and the Italians were defeated at the Battle of **ADOWA** in 1896, perhaps the greatest success of Africans against Europeans in the Partition of **AFRICA**. **MUSSOLINI**'s invasion of Ethiopia in 1936 was a conscious act of revenge.

**Menem, Carlos Saúl** (1930– )
Argentine politician. While training for the legal profession, he became politically active in the Peronist (Justice Party) movement, founding the Youth Group in 1955. In 1963 he was elected President of the party in La Rioja and in the same year unsuccessfully contested the governorship of the province, eventually being elected in 1983 and re-elected in 1987. In 1989 he defeated the Radical Union Party (UCR) candidate and became President of Argentina, a position he held until 1999. A highly pragmatic ruler, he rapidly

jettisoned inflammatory rhetoric to move towards discussion of the Falklands/Malvinas issue, and to begin an ambitious privatization policy.

**Menéndez de Avilés, Pedro** (1519–74)
Spanish sailor and colonist. After going to sea aged 14, he was appointed by Emperor **CHARLES V** to protect Spain from pirates in 1549, and in 1554 became Captain-General of the Indies fleet, in which position he made three trips to America. Courageous, impetuous and brutal, he made many enemies and was imprisoned in 1563, but was restored to royal favour two years later and charged with the exploration and colonization of Florida. There in 1565 he founded St Augustine, where he built a fortress, and in Sep he attacked the French Protestant colony of Fort Caroline, allegedly explaining that he massacred the entire population 'not as Frenchmen, but as heretics'. He thus firmly established Spanish dominance in Florida. He built other forts along the Atlantic coast before being recalled to Spain to set up a fleet to fight the English.

**Menéndez y Pelayo, Marcelino** (1856–1912)
Spanish Catholic thinker. Spanish conservatism owed him a great debt as an ardent and prolific defender of Spanish orthodoxy and tradition. He attacked the ideas of the **ENLIGHTENMENT** and even praised the work of the **INQUISITION**. He represented the Conservative Party in both the **CORTES** and the Senate.

**Mengistu, Haile Mariam** (1937– )
Ethiopian soldier and politician. He trained at Guenet Military Academy and took part in the attempted coup against Emperor **HAILE SELASSIE** in 1960, but was not put on trial. He was a member of the Armed Forces Coordinating Committee (**DERGUE**) which helped overthrow Haile Selassie in 1974. He manipulated himself into the chairmanship of the Dergue and became undisputed leader and head of state in 1977. Allying himself with the USSR and modelling himself upon Cuba's **CASTRO**, he sought a socialist transformation for Ethiopia, while retaining its territorial borders intact. Mismanagement, drought and internal war weakened his hold on the country and he fled from Addis Ababa in 1991, travelling to Zimbabwe where he was offered political asylum. In 1994 he was tried in *absentia* in Ethiopia and found guilty of genocide and war crimes.

**Mennonites**
The Dutch and Swiss **ANABAPTISTS** who later called themselves Mennonites after one of their Dutch leaders, Menno Simons (1496–1559). They adhere to the Confession of Dordrecht (1632), baptize on confession of faith, are pacifists, refuse to hold civic office, and follow the teachings of the New Testament. Most of their one million adherents live in the USA.

**Menotti, Ciro** (1798–1831)
Italian revolutionary. He was involved, with Enrico **MISLEY**, in an attempt to create a united Italian state. However, his attempt to launch an insurrection in the Duchy of Modena resulted in his arrest and summary execution by **FRANCESCO IV D'ESTE**.

**Mensheviks**
In Russian literally 'minority-ites', the members of the moderate faction of the Marxist Russian Social Democratic Labour Party, led by L Martov, which split with **LENIN**, who engineered a false majority for his supporters (hence called **BOLSHEVIKS** or 'majority-ites') at the Party's Second Congress in 1903. The Mensheviks particularly opposed Lenin's policy of organizing a small disciplined party dedicated to promoting and provoking revolution. In 1917 some Mensheviks joined the Provisional Government; but from 1918 onwards they were subject to increasing persecution, their leaders forced abroad in 1921 and many one-time members put on trial in 1930–1. ► **RUSSIAN REVOLUTION**

**Menshikov, Alexander Danilovich** (1673–1729)
Russian field marshal and politician. Born of poor parents in Moscow, he entered the army, distinguished himself at the Siege of Azov, and afterwards accompanied **PETER I, THE GREAT** in his travels to Holland and England. During the war with Sweden (1702–13) he played an important part at **POLTAVA** (Peter made him a field marshal on the spot), Riga, Stettin and elsewhere. At the capture of Marienburg the girl who became **CATHERINE I** fell into Menshikov's hands, and was through him introduced to the Tsar. Towards the end of Peter's reign, Menshikov lost favour owing to extortions and suspected duplicities. But when Peter died, he secured the succession of Catherine, and during her reign and that of her young successor, **PETER II**, he governed Russia with almost absolute authority. He was about to marry his daughter to the young tsar when the jealousy of the old nobility led to his banishment to Siberia and the confiscation of his estates.

**Menshikov, Alexander Sergeevich** (1789–1869)
Russian soldier. The great-grandson of Alexander Danilovich **MENSHIKOV**, he rose to the rank of general in the Napoleonic campaigns of 1812–15. Seriously wounded at Varna in the Turkish campaign of 1828, he was made head of the Russian navy. His overbearing behaviour and incompetent diplomacy as ambassador at Constantinople contributed greatly to the outbreak of the **CRIMEAN WAR**. He commanded at Alma and Inkerman with no great skill, and defended **SEVASTOPOL**, but in 1855 was recalled because of illness. ► **NAPOLEONIC WARS**

**Mentana, Battle of** (3 Nov 1867)
The defeat of **GARIBALDI** at the hands of French troops rushed to Italy by **NAPOLEON III** to defend Rome. Garibaldi's ill-organized and diplomatically ill-considered attempt to march on the papal capital resulted in the return of the French garrison, which had been withdrawn (Dec 1866) under the terms of the so-called September Convention.

**Menzies, Sir Robert Gordon** (1894–1978)
Australian politician. He practised as a barrister, entering the Victoria parliament in 1928. In 1934 he moved to federal politics as member for Kooyang. He was Attorney-General (1935–9), Prime Minister (1939–41) and Leader of the Opposition (1943–9), during which time he rebuilt the conservative elements in Australian politics from the disintegrating **UNITED AUSTRALIA PARTY** into the formidable **LIBERAL PARTY OF AUSTRALIA**. Successful in the 1949 election, he became Prime Minister again, holding office

for 16 years until his retirement in 1966. Old-fashioned in his regard for British traditions, Menzies was also strongly anti-communist and supported US involvement in the Pacific. He led Australia into SEATO (**SOUTH-EAST ASIA TREATY ORGANIZATION**), the **ANZUS** pact and actively supported the USA in the **VIETNAM WAR**. He shrewdly exploited the **AUSTRALIAN LABOR PARTY**'s divisions over **COMMUNISM** in the 1950s, but failed in his attempt to ban the Australian Communist Party. The 'Menzies Era' was one of economic growth and prosperity which made Australia briefly 'the lucky country'. In 1956 he headed the Five Nations Committee which sought to come to a settlement with Gamal Abd al-**NASSER** on the question of the **SUEZ CRISIS**.

### Mercier, Désiré Joseph (1851–1926)
Belgian Roman Catholic primate and theologian. He took holy orders in 1874 and was appointed to a chair at Leuven (Louvain) University in 1882. In 1906 he was appointed Archbishop of Mechelen (Malines) and primate of Belgium; he received a cardinal's hat in 1906. In Flanders (northern Belgium) he was often disliked for his opposition to the **FLEMISH MOVEMENT**, and to the use of the Flemish language in Catholic schools in particular. His social Catholicism also won him much support.

### Mercier, Honoré (1840–94)
Canadian politician. Leader of the Quebec liberals, he revived the **PARTI NATIONAL** in response to the execution of **RIEL** in 1885, bringing both **ROUGES** and conservatives into a 'united front' to preserve French-Canadian rights. In 1887 he became Premier of Quebec, and sought the support of the Catholic Church with the passage of the **JESUITS' ESTATES ACT**. Realizing that a majority of the English-speaking provinces also sought a greater measure of autonomy, he called an **INTERPROVINCIAL CONFERENCE** in 1887 which supported **COMPACT THEORY OF CONFEDERATION**. His popular premiership was curtailed by charges of corruption in 1891, when the Lieutenant-Governor removed him from office. The charges were unproven but the party was badly beaten in the following year and he only just retained his seat.

### MERCOSUR (Mercado Común del Sur, 'Southern Common Market')
A South American trade organization comprising Argentina, Brazil, Paraguay and Uruguay, which was founded in 1991 and officially inaugurated on 1 Jan 1995. Under the terms of the Protocol of Ouro Prêto (signed in Dec 1994), tariffs on about 90 per cent of goods traded between member states were abandoned, a common tariff averaging 12 per cent for goods imported from elsewhere was erected, and express passport lanes for nationals travelling between member states were set up. Both the **EU** and the **ANDEAN GROUP** agreed to negotiate free-trade zones with MERCOSUR, and a pact with the latter, now the Andean Community (**CAN**), was signed in 2004. Bolivia, Chile, Colombia, Ecuador, Mexico and Venezuela are associate members.

### Meredith Incident
US **CIVIL RIGHTS** incident. When James Howard Meredith (1933– ) was rejected by the University of Mississippi, which had admitted only whites during its

114-year history, he filed a lawsuit against them with the aid of the **NAACP** and won admission for his senior year in the fall of 1962. His appearance on campus in 1962 provoked rioting that resulted in two deaths, but he enrolled and completed the year under federal guard and became the University's first African-American graduate in 1963.

### Merriman, John Xavier (1841–1926)
English-born South African politician. He went early to South Africa, where his father was Bishop of Grahamstown. He was a member of various Cape ministries from 1875, and Premier (South African Party) from 1908 to 1910.

### Merritt, William Hamilton (1793–1862)
Canadian entrepreneur. He built the Welland Canal, bypassing the Niagara cataract, to provide a major route for exports and imports into the American–Canadian interior. The canal was completed by 1829 but essential improvements were not completed until 1848, when the US railways provided a satisfactory alternative which Canadians were ready to use. Merritt was also one of the foremost proponents of **RECIPROCITY**. ► **CANALS**

### Mesopotamia Campaign
This campaign in **WORLD WAR I** represented an effort by the British to safeguard both the route to India and the newly discovered oilfields of Persia. The Ottomans had declared for the German interest in the war and it was thus essential, for the realization of the above two aims, that British arms prevail in Iraq. After the catastrophe of **KUT AL-AMARA** earlier in the war, a regrouped British offensive under General Maude took Kut early in 1917 and entered Baghdad in Mar of the same year. Further operations on the River Euphrates and the River Tigris as far as Mosul resulted in a complete British occupation of Mesopotamia.

### Mesta
The Spanish guild of sheepowners, instituted in 1273 by **ALFONSO X**, the Mesta was given extensive privileges to protect the country's biggest industry, wool. It was granted rights to pasture its more than 2 million sheep across lengthy tracts (cañadas) of countryside, and the right to have its own officials and judges to protect it in the courts; in return, it paid substantial taxes to the Castilian crown. Flourishing in the early 16c, the Mesta decayed later when the country's trade and industry declined. It was fiercely attacked by reforming ministers in the 18c, notably **CAMPOMANES**, to whom its bad reputation is chiefly due, and was eventually abolished in 1836.

### Metacom or Metacomet ► PHILIP, KING

### Metaxas, Ioannis (1870–1941)
Greek general and dictator. He fought against the Turks in 1897, studied military science in Germany, and in 1913 became Chief of the General Staff. On the fall of King **CONSTANTINE I** in 1917 he fled to Italy, but returned with him in 1921. In 1935 he became Deputy Prime Minister, and as Premier in 1936 established a fascist dictatorship. He led the resistance to the Italian invasion of Greece in 1940. He remained in office until his death, which, it was rumoured, was brought about by poison administered by agents of **HITLER**.

## Metcalfe, Charles Theophilus Metcalfe, Baron (1785–1846)

British colonial official. He went in 1808 as an envoy of Lord **MINTO** to the Sikh ruler **RANJIT SINGH** of Lahore, in order to cement the cracks in the East India Company's north-western front. After heading the Delhi Residency (1811–18), he was Resident in Hyderabad (1820–5), where he exposed irregularities in the Nizam's financial relations with the House of Palmer and Co., in whose Hyderabad branch Lord **HASTINGS**, the then Governor-General, was personally interested. Serving continuously in India from 1800, he was Lord William **BENTINCK**'s right-hand man during most of his government and, following his retirement (1835), acted as Governor-General until the arrival of his permanent successor. He resigned from the service in 1837 and became Governor-General of Jamaica (1839) and Governor-General of Canada (1843). Having succeeded Sir Charles **BAGOT** in 1843, he attempted to reverse the trend towards **RESPONSIBLE GOVERNMENT** and reassert his independence of ministers. On his pressing the Crown's right to make all appointments, the ministry, including Robert **BALDWIN** and **LAFONTAINE**, resigned, and the assembly showed their support for them in a vote of no confidence. Metcalfe then dismissed the government and, in the following bitterly fought election campaign, appealed to the country for support; he won, but with a dangerously narrow margin. His ministers were weak and unpopular, although they managed to remain in power for two years. With the end of the mercantile system and repeal of the **CORN LAWS**, the need to maintain the colonies in political dependence was diminished and in 1845 Metcalfe resigned, to allow for the introduction of responsible government.

## métis

Canadians of Native American and white stock (both French and Scottish, but especially the former). They thought of themselves as a separate people, with a culture which blended their French heritage with Aboriginal skills. Living a semi-nomadic life and dependent on buffalo-hunting, the semi-military structure of their society enabled them to resist the pressures of new settlements. However, the failures of the rebellions in Red River (1869–70) and Saskatchewan (1885) meant that the *métis* either sank further into poverty or were absorbed into the city, for they did not benefit even from the slender privileges which treaties bestowed on the **NATIVE AMERICANS**. ► **RED RIVER REBELLION**

## Metternich, Klemens Wenzel Nepomuk Lothar, Prince of (1773–1859)

Austrian politician. He studied at Strasbourg and Mainz, was attached to the Austrian Embassy at The Hague, and became Austrian Minister at Dresden, Berlin and Paris. In 1809 he was appointed Foreign Minister, and negotiated the marriage between **NAPOLEON I** and **MARIE LOUISE**. He took a prominent part in the Congress of **VIENNA** (1814–15), and between 1815 and 1848 was the most powerful influence for **CONSERVATISM** in Europe. His suppression of liberal and nationalist movements contributed much to the tension that produced the upheaval of 1848. After the fall of the Imperial government in that year, he fled to England, and in 1851 retired to his castle of Johannesburg on the Rhine. ► **REVOLUTION OF 1848**

## Mexican Revolution (1910–20)

A period of political turmoil in Mexico which was fomented by the dictatorial regime of Porfirio **DÍAZ**, and began while he was President (1876–80, 1884–1911). When Díaz indicated his determination to perpetuate his rule, Francisco **MADERO** set himself up at the head of an Anti-Re-electionist movement and won widespread support, particularly from the growing urban middle-class and labour groups who had remained unacknowledged in national politics. However, Díaz imprisoned him and declared himself the winner of a mock election, until Madero, released from prison, directed a military coup from the USA which forced Díaz to resign. Madero became President in 1911, but was too moderate to satisfy anyone's demands, even those of his one-time supporter Emiliano **ZAPATA**, and was assassinated in a counter-revolutionary coup led by Victoriano **HUERTA** in 1913. In 1914 several revolutionary groups, led by Zapata, Pancho **VILLA**, Venustiano **CARRANZA** and Álvaro **OBREGÓN**, combined successfully to oust Huerta, making Carranza briefly President, but the groups then split into two separate factions – the Conventionists led by Zapata and Villa, who aimed to follow the radical proposals of the 1914 convention of Aguascalientes, and the Constitutionists led by Carranza and Obregón, who aimed to restore the 1857 liberal constitution – and civil war ensued. The USA's support of Carranza incited attacks by Villa's forces on US towns, including Columbus in New Mexico, and led in 1916 to an invasion by US troops under General John **PERSHING**, who failed to capture Villa. In 1917 Carranza returned to the presidency, officially accepting the new radical constitution. In practice, however, he ignored the constitution, gradually lost virtually all his supporters, and was deposed and assassinated in 1920. Adolfo de la Huerta became Interim President until Obregón was elected in Nov. Although 1920 is generally considered to mark the end of the Mexican Revolution, it is argued that since factional fighting continued, including the **CRISTERO REVOLT** (1927–9) in which Christian forces rebelled against the state, the revolution did not really end until around 1940 when the reformist presidencies of Lázaro **CÁRDENAS** (1934–40) and Ávila Camacho (1940–6) achieved peace and consolidation.

## Mexican War (1846–8)

A war between Mexico and the USA, declared by the US **CONGRESS** after it received a message from President **POLK** calling for war. The culmination of a decade of friction resulting from the secession of Texas from Mexico in 1835, the war began with General Zachary **TAYLOR**'s advance into the area between the River Nueces and the Rio Grande. US troops assaulted Mexico City in Sep 1847 and Mexico was subsequently forced to cede most of the present-day south-west USA. This 'national catastrophe' provided the basis for the subsequent struggle between conservatives under **SANTA ANNA** and liberals under **JUÁREZ**. ► **GUADALUPE HIDALGO, TREATY OF**; **WILMOT PROVISO**

## Mexican War (1862–7)

The Mexican government having suspended interest payments on its foreign debt to France, Spain and Britain, **NAPOLEON III** tried to use this default as a pretext for intervention designed to turn Mexico into a client state of France. A joint expedition of the three European powers in 1862 was followed by a larger French force in 1863, and the proclamation of the Austrian Archduke **MAXIMILIAN** as Emperor of Mexico. The end of the **AMERICAN CIVIL WAR** forced the French to withdraw their troops, Maximilian was captured and executed. The war had always been unpopular in France, and the outcome was seen as a humiliation.

## MEXICO official name United Mexican States

A federal republic in the south of North America, bounded to the north by the USA; to the west by the Gulf of California; to the west and south-west by the Pacific Ocean; to the south by Guatemala and Belize; and to the east by the Gulf of Mexico. It was at the centre of Mesoamerican civilizations for over 2,500 years: the Gulf Coast Olmecs were based at La Venta; Zapotecs at Monte Albán near Oaxaca; Mixtecs at Mitla; Toltecs at Tula; Mayas in the Yucatán; and Aztecs at **TENOCHTITLÁN**. The Spanish arrived in 1516, and in 1519 **CORTÉS** came ashore near Veracruz, destroying the powerful Aztec capital within two years and establishing the Viceroyalty of **NEW SPAIN**. The struggle for independence began in 1810 and Mexico became a federal republic in 1824. In all it lost nearly a third of its territory to the USA in 1836 and following the **MEXICAN WAR** (1846–8). There was civil war in 1858–61, and another **MEXICAN WAR** in 1862–7 during which French forces occupied Mexico City in 1863, declaring Archduke **MAXIMILIAN** of Austria to be Emperor of Mexico. The French withdrew and Maximilian was executed in 1867. The Mexican Revolution began in 1910 while Porfirio **DÍAZ** was President, largely fomented by his dictatorial regime, and did not end until 1920 and the establishment of a constitutional republic. Radicalism within the new one-party regime dominated by the Institutional Revolutionary Party (PRI) became more rhetoric than reality by the 1940s, but the second half of the 20c was rendered difficult due to economic problems, only partially relieved by mass emigration to the USA. Mexico became part of **NAFTA** in 1994, and in the same year Ernesto Zedillo Ponce de León became President. The PRI's domination of Mexican politics ended in 1997 when the party failed to gain the majority of seats in parliament for the first time since 1929, although the PRI regained the majority from the National Action Party (PAN) in the 2003 election. The PAN candidate, Vicente **FOX**, was elected President in 2000. Armed revolts by the Zapatista National Liberation Army (**EZLN**) in the southern state of Chiapas (Jan–Aug 1994, Dec 1994–Feb 1995) caused a political crisis but talks were broken off in 1998. In early 2001 hundreds of Zapatistas marched from Chiapas to Mexico City in support of a bill of indigenous rights, which was enacted in May 2001, but the Zapatistas broke off negotiations with the government, claiming that the bill's provisions had been watered down.► **PRE COLUMBIAN CIVILIZATIONS; SPANISH-AMERICAN WARS OF INDEPENDENCE**

## Mezzogiorno

The Italian word (literally, 'midday') used to describe Italy to the south of Rome, usually in contrast to the more developed north and centre of the country.

## Michael (1921–)

King of Romania (1927/30 and 1940/7). The son of **CHARLES II** of Romania, he first succeeded to the throne on the death of his grandfather, **FERDINAND**, his father having renounced his own claims in 1925. In 1930 he was supplanted by Charles, but was again made King in 1940 when the Germans gained control of Romania. In 1944 he played a considerable part in the overthrow of the dictatorship of Ion **ANTONESCU**. He announced the acceptance of the Allied peace terms, and declared war on Germany. His attempts after the war to establish a broader system of government were foiled by the progressive communization of Romania. In 1947 he was forced to abdicate and lived in exile. He was allowed to re-enter the country in 1997.

**Michael** (of Portugal) ► **MIGUEL**

**Michael VIII Palaeologus** (c.1225–1282)
Eastern Roman Emperor (1259/82) and founder of
the last dynasty to rule in the **BYZANTINE EMPIRE**. He
distinguished himself as a soldier, and was made regent for the heir to the throne, John Lascaris, whom
he ultimately deposed and blinded. His army took
Constantinople in 1261, thus re-establishing the Byzantine Empire. He was responsible for the abortive
reunion of the Church of Constantinople with that
of Rome (Council of Lyons, 1274).

**Michael Romanov** (1596–1645)
Tsar of Russia (1613/45). The great-nephew of **IVAN IV,
THE TERRIBLE**, he was the founder of the **ROMANOV
DYNASTY** that ruled Russia until the revolution of
1917. He was elected by a remarkably widely representative **ZEMSKI SOBOR** after a successful revolt
against the Poles, when Russia was also threatened
with invasion from Sweden. Michael brought to an
end the **TIME OF TROUBLES** that had plagued Russia
since the death of **BORIS GODUNOV** in 1605. He concluded peace with Sweden (1617) and Poland (1618),
but he left the business of government largely in the
hands of his father, the extremely able Patriarch Fila-
ret (Fedor Nikitch Romanov). The latter reorganized
the army and industry with the help of experts from
abroad and consolidated the system of serfdom,
although raising enough money to fund the state remained a serious problem.

**Michael the Brave** (1558–1601)
Hospodar (Governor) of Wallachia. Threatened by
the Ottoman Turks, he submitted to the suzerainty of
Sigismund Báthory, Prince of **TRANSYLVANIA**, and
achieved two victories over the Turkish forces
(1595). He then pledged his loyalty to the Habsburg
Emperor **RUDOLF II** and made peace with the Turks
(1598), before turning against his erstwhile protector, Báthory, in 1599. He proclaimed himself Prince
of Transylvania and went on to conquer Moldavia
(1600) taking the title 'Prince of Ungro-Wallachia,
Transylvania and Moldavia' but was forced into retreat by the Emperor, whom he then helped to crush
a Hungarian rebellion at Gorăslău (1601). His swift
changes of allegiance in the past made his loyalty suspect again and he was put to death on the orders of
one of Rudolf's generals. Having briefly united the
Romanian lands of Transylvania, **MOLDAVIA AND
WALLACHIA**, in the 19c he was hailed by the Romanian nationalists as the father of their nation. ► **RO-
MANIA**

**Michurin, Ivan Vladimirovich** (1855–1935)
Soviet agronomist. In 1875 he started improving fruit
varieties by stock-scion grafting on his plot in Kozlov.
It was **LENIN** who drew attention to him in 1920, and
**STALIN** then exploited him as an example of what
could be done through collectivization. He never developed any theories, but after his death **LYSENKO**
claimed to be his scientific heir and managed in this
way to raise his own respectability. In 1932 Kozlov, in
the Soviet manner, was renamed Michurinsk.

**Mickiewicz, Adam Bernard** (1798–1855)
National poet of Poland. Born near Navahrudak, Russia (now Belarus), he was educated in Vilna and published his first poems in 1822. He was arrested for his
revolutionary activities, and after the failure of the

Polish revolt of 1830–1 he had to flee to the West.
After travelling in Germany, France and Italy he wrote
his masterpiece, the epic *Pan Tadeusz* (1834). He
taught at Lausanne and Paris. Generally he tried to
keep the Polish spirit alive through his writings, and
in 1853 he went to Italy to organize a Polish legion. He
died in Constantinople, his country still not free, but
eternally in his debt. ► **NAPOLEON III**

---

**MICRONESIA**  official name **Federated States of
Micronesia**

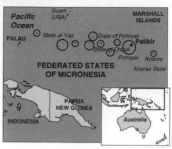

A republic consisting of a group of islands divided
into four states in the western Pacific Ocean: Yap,
Chuuk (formerly Truk), Pohnpei (formerly Ponape)
and Kosrae. Micronesia was probably first settled by
eastern Melanesians in 1500BC. The Spanish colonized it in the 17c and sold it to Germany in 1898.
From 1914 to 1944 it was occupied by the Japanese,
then was taken by US forces and in 1947 became part
of the **UN** Trust Territory of the Pacific Islands, administered by the USA. From 1965 there was a growing
campaign for independence, and Micronesia became
a self-governing federation in 1979. A compact of free
association was signed with the USA in 1982 which
made the USA responsible for Micronesia's internal
security and defence. The USA continued to adminis-
trate until 1986, when full independence was
achieved. Micronesia was admitted to the UN in
1991. A renegotiated compact of free association was
signed in 2003.

**Middle Ages**
The period of European history between the collapse
of the Roman Empire in the West and the **RENAIS-
SANCE** (c.500–c.1500); sometimes, however, the
term is restricted in its use to the four or five centuries
after the year 1000. By the early 16c, humanists regarded the civilization that followed the fall of Rome
as distinctly different from the classical culture that
preceded it and the classical revival of their own day.
The notion of a separate but inferior medieval civilization has since been transformed into a more positive appreciation of the age and its achievements,
notably the emergence of national states, the vigour
of cultural life, and the spiritual attainments of the
Church in what was above all an age of faith. Though
quite a well-defined period between ancient and
modern times, it has no obvious beginning, still less
an obvious end.

**Middle East, The Heritage of the** ► *See panel*

**Midway, Battle of** (1942)
US naval victory. Admiral Chester **NIMITZ**, fore-
warned of Japanese intentions by the breaking of
their naval codes, reinforced Midway Island and

# *Heritage of the Middle East*

*Culture & Society*

### Historical background

The Middle East is usually taken to mean the lands around the eastern
Mediterranean and the Arabian Peninsula, along with Turkey and Iran.
This was the site of the first great urban civilizations and was fought over by many warring cultures, who saw possession
of the Fertile Crescent, the well-watered lands stretching from Armenia to Arabia, as the prize. In Mesopotamia the
Sumerians had built several large cities by 3000 BC, such as Ur and Uruk. Subsequent empires rose and fell in the region,
including that of Sargon of Akkad, the Babylonians, and the Assyrians, and it was eventually absorbed into even greater
empires, such as that of Cyrus II of Persia (d. 530 BC).

Cyrus' successors, the Achaemenid Dynasty, expanded the empire and ruled until defeat by Alexander the Great
(356–323 BC) led to their replacement by the Macedonian Seleucid Dynasty (312–64 BC). The Romans brought the
Seleucid Empire to an end, and the Parthians ruled much of the Middle East until they too were displaced by the
Sassanians (AD 224).

Above all, the Middle East was the cradle of the three great Abrahamic religions: Judaism, Christianity and Islam.
Under the later Roman or **Byzantine Empire**, the region was held under the hegemony of the Eastern Orthodox Church,
albeit with much restiveness from alternative creeds like the Coptic Church, with its pope in Alexandria. The Arab
conquest of the Middle East in the 7c brought the area under Islamic rule and the **'Abbasid Dynasty** held sway from 749
to 1258, establishing its capital at Baghdad. This city was sacked by the **Mongols** as they extended their empire
westwards until they in turn were checked by the **Mamluks**, who ruled the region until they were ousted by the Ottoman
Turks in 1517.

At its height, the **Ottoman Empire** ruled over an area extending westward to Austria and eastward to Persia, but
centuries of decline and loss of territory to such powers as Russia culminated in its break-up after **World War I**.
Individual Middle Eastern states emerged from this, such as Iraq, Lebanon and Syria, and the modern state of Israel was
eventually formed from the British mandate of **Palestine**.

### The heritage

The Middle East was part of the Hellenistic world that was brought into being by the conquests of Alexander the Great,
and was therefore important in the influence of the **Graeco-Roman Heritage** on Europe. However, the most obvious
significance of the region for Western culture is that it was the birthplace of the Christian religion. The collection of the
most sacred and divinely authoritative writings of Christianity, the Bible, was written there in Hebrew, Aramaic and
Greek. The Jewish scriptures that make up the Old Testament ingrained the names of Middle Eastern places and people,
such as Canaan, Judah, Babylon, Solomon and Sennacherib, on the minds of worshippers throughout the Christian
world. The New Testament described the life, death and resurrection of Jesus taking place in what was to be known as the
Holy Land, and promulgated the elements of Christian belief that distinguished it from Judaism.

It was the Roman Empire that helped further the spread of Christianity from its Middle Eastern origins, and it was the
Empire's division into eastern and western empires that led to the East–West schism between the Orthodox and
Western Churches in 1054. The fact that Palestine was under the control of Muslims was not perceived as being of great
importance to the West until the Seljuk Turks began to hinder Christian pilgrimage to holy sites in the 11c. The ultimate
effect of this was to trigger the series of papal-inspired military expeditions known as the Crusades, with the goal of
establishing Christian rule in the Holy Land. Jerusalem was taken in 1099, and a Latin Kingdom was established in the
region that endured in various forms until 1291.

The legacy of the Crusades, and the settlement by Westerners in what they called Outremer, was complex, and
included the exacerbation of Muslim–Christian hostility, especially after several massacres of Muslims by Crusaders.

---

forced the Japanese to withdraw with the loss of four
aircraft-carriers. This was the first battle in which the
use of aircraft enabled engagement beyond visual
range, and together with the Battle of the Coral Sea,
saved Australia and Hawaii and stemmed the Japanese push into the Central Pacific.

### Miguel (1802–66)

King of Portugal (1828/34). The third son of King
John VI, he plotted (1824) to overthrow the constitutional form of government granted by his father, but
was banished with his mother, his chief abettor. On
John's death in 1826, the throne devolved upon Miguel's elder brother, **PEDRO I**, Emperor of Brazil; he,
however, resigned it in favour of his daughter, **MARIA
II DA GLORIA**, making Miguel regent. Miguel then
summoned a **CORTES**, which proclaimed him King
in 1828. In 1832 Pedro captured Oporto and Lisbon,
and Charles Napier destroyed Miguel's fleet off Cape
St Vincent (1833). The following year Maria was restored, and Miguel withdrew to Italy.

### Mihailović, Draža (1893–1946)

Serbian soldier. He rose to the rank of colonel in the
Yugoslav army, and in 1941 remained in Yugoslavia
after the German occupation, forming groups (**CHET-
NIKS**) to wage guerrilla warfare. He later allied himself with the Germans and then with the Italians to
fight the communists. He was executed in Belgrade
by the **TITO** government for collaboration. ▶ **WORLD
WAR II**

### Mikołajczyk, Stanisław (1901–67)

Polish politician. He was born the son of an émigré
miner in Westphalia and, returning to independent
Poland at the end of **WORLD WAR I**, he soon entered
politics and became leader of the Peasant Party
(1931–9). From 1940 to 1943 he held office in the exiled Polish government in London and, following
General **SIKORSKI**'s death, became Prime Minister
(1943–4). After the German defeat, he became
Deputy Premier in the new coalition government in
Warsaw, promoted by the USSR and accepted by
the Western Allies. With a large peasant following,
he hoped to resist a total takeover by the pro-
Soviet communists. However, following rigged
elections in 1947 he had no alternative but to flee to

The romanticized exploits of the Christian warriors provided literary themes for centuries afterwards, not least in Tasso's epic poem *Jerusalem Delivered* (1581). Eastern influences made their way west with returning Crusaders, including greater bodily cleanliness, more advanced medical and surgical techniques (the writings of the Arab philosopher Avicenna greatly influenced medieval European **medicine**), the use of spices in cooking, the art of glass-blowing, and religious ideas like Manichaeism. Eastern goods also travelled in greater quantities to Europe, such as Persian carpets, damask wall hangings, ivory carvings and Chinese porcelain. The two military religious orders founded in the Holy Land, the Knights **Hospitallers** and the Knights **Templars**, were to play important roles in European history long after the fall of Jerusalem in 1187.

In the late 18c and early 19c, the Romantic movement, with its emphasis on the exotic and the sublime, along with its rejection of classicism, aroused new interest in the Middle East. The *Turkish Letters* of Lady Mary Wortley Montagu, who had been the wife of the British Ambassador to Constantinople, attracted great interest when they were published in 1763, and motivated new travellers to venture east. The collection of Arabic stories known as the *Arabian Nights* had been popular in Europe in the 18c and was revived in English translation in 1839–41, and again in 1885–8 by Sir Richard Burton. Byron's journeys in Ottoman Greece and Albania inspired many of his earlier works, including his 'Turkish Tale' *The Bride of Abydos* and *The Corsair*. Edward FitzGerald's version of the Persian poet Omar Khayyam's *Rubaiyat* (1859) helped set the introspective, melancholy tone of late Victorian writing.

In the 19c many archaeologists, seeking to substantiate details of the histories recounted in the Bible, excavated in the Middle East, and important finds were made, particularly in Mesopotamia, that attested to the greatness of the Biblical cities such as Nineveh and Babylon. This work continued into the 20c and involved, among others, the young T E Lawrence (1888–1935), whose interest in the culture of the Arab tribes reflected a growing contemporary Western trend. Lawrence's part in the Arab revolt against the Ottoman rulers (1916–18), and his account of it in *Seven Pillars of Wisdom*, earned him the romantic epithet of 'Lawrence of Arabia'.

It is significant that Western romanticism concerning the Islamic Middle East has failed entirely to incorporate such huge realities as the Shia culture of Iran and much of Mesopotamia or Iraq. The inability to internalize a fantasized version of Iranian culture led to a Western tendency to demonize leading figures in the **Iranian Revolution** of 1979, including Ayatollah Ruhollah **Khomeini**. Bedouin sheikhs could be handled more easily however, as evidenced by the roles played by Rudolf Valentino, the first great male movie heart-throb and screen lover, in highly successful performances in *The Sheikh* (1921) and *The Son of the Sheikh* (1926). Neither film bore any relation to reality.

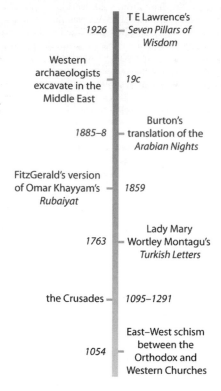

| | |
|---|---|
| 1926 | T E Lawrence's *Seven Pillars of Wisdom* |
| Western archaeologists excavate in the Middle East | 19c |
| 1885–8 | Burton's translation of the *Arabian Nights* |
| FitzGerald's version of Omar Khayyam's *Rubaiyat* | 1859 |
| 1763 | Lady Mary Wortley Montagu's *Turkish Letters* |
| the Crusades | 1095–1291 |
| 1054 | East–West schism between the Orthodox and Western Churches |

the West, where he settled in the USA.

### Mikoyan, Anastas Ivanovich (1895–1970)

Soviet politician. Educated in a seminary, he became a Bolshevik in 1915 and was active in the Caucasus. A candidate member of the Central Committee from 1922 and of the **POLITBURO** from 1926, he supported **STALIN** against **TROTSKY** in the 1920s and survived the former's purges in the 1930s. He held various ministerial posts connected with trade, doing much to improve Soviet standards of living and introducing several ideas from the West. Mikoyan survived Stalin and allied with Nikita **KHRUSHCHEV**. He was Vice-Chairman of the Council of Ministers (1955–64) and President of the Presidium of the Supreme Soviet (1964–5). An extremely versatile politician, he helped Khrushchev survive the **ANTI-PARTY PLOT** in 1957, and in 1962 persuaded Fidel **CASTRO** to accept the withdrawal of Soviet missiles from Cuba.

### Militant Tendency

A British political group which came to prominence in the 1980s. Ostensibly, *Militant* is a newspaper published by **LABOUR PARTY** members espousing Marxist positions. In practice, critics argued, the newspaper is a front for a 'party within a party', a separate organization of revolutionary Trotskyists who have entered the Labour Party (*entryism*) to use its organizational base for its own political ends. To all intents and purposes Militant is a cover for the Revolutionary Socialist League, the original British section of the Fourth International. In the 1980s its supporters infiltrated a number of local Labour parties and the Young Socialists (its youth wing). Fearing the adverse electoral publicity resulting from Militant activities, the Labour Party moved to expel members of Militant on the grounds that they were members of a separate political party, which is against the party's constitution. Many of those expelled took the party to court, but their cases were not upheld. Since then, Militant's influence has declined.

### Military Frontier (*Militärgrenze*; *Vojna Krajina*)

The broad stretch of borderland which the Habsburgs maintained from the 16c as a militarized buffer zone between their lands and the **OTTOMAN EMPIRE**. First established along the Croatian–Ottoman border, it was later extended through the Banat of **TEMESVÁR** and **TRANSYLVANIA**. It was directly under the control of the War Council in Vienna until 1881 when it was dissolved. **▪▶ HABSBURG DYNASTY**

### Military Service Act (1917)

Canadian conscription legislation. It was introduced because Canada's voluntary militia had been unable to fulfil the commitment to provide four full divisions on the Western Front. Robert Laird **BORDEN**'s Minister for Militia, Sir Sam Hughes, had deterred many French-Canadians from volunteering by his Ulster Protestant prejudices. The Act was particularly unpopular in Quebec, where many believed they were being asked to fight for the empire while being denied equal rights at home. With **WORLD WAR II** the government tried to maintain a policy of 'no conscription' to ensure national unity, despite continuous pressure from the English-speaking provinces, especially after the fall of France. In response Mackenzie **KING** held a referendum which showed that although 80 per cent of the English-speaking population wished to free the government from its pledge, 72 per cent of French-Canadians were against doing so. King therefore retained the policy and sacked his Defence Minister when he was advised that there were not enough volunteers to maintain the Canadian commitment after the Normandy landings in 1944. But with the failure of the policy to enlist home defence draftees, King was forced to reintroduce conscription. Protestation from French-Canadians, both among civilians and in the forces, was fierce, while one French-Canadian minister resigned from the government and 34 Quebec Liberals voted against it in a vote of confidence. Even so, King managed to survive the election of 1945, albeit with a reduced majority.

### Militia Bill (1862)

Canadian legislation to provide better protection against incursions from the USA during the **AMERICAN CIVIL WAR**, and from **FENIAN RAIDS**. The first bill proposed a force of 50,000 at a cost of C$1 million per year. Its rejection in favour of a cheaper alternative was seen by the British government as Canadian reluctance to assume their defensive responsibilities, but it was countered by the insistence that Canadians had the right to determine their own defence and how much they would allocate to it. This argument indicated the colony's progress towards autonomy.

### Miliukov, Pavel Nikolaevich (1849–1943)

Russian historian and politician. As a professor of history in Moscow he wrote extensively on the condition of the people and was almost inevitably drawn into criticizing the Tsarist regime. During the Russian **REVOLUTION OF 1905** he campaigned for the establishment of a constituent assembly. In the Dumas that followed he led the Constitutional Democrats or **KADETS**, whose aim remained the eventual establishment of a constituent assembly. That became the official policy of the **RUSSIAN PROVISIONAL GOVERNMENT** in 1917 in which Miliukov was Minister of Foreign Affairs. Unfortunately his wish that Russia should continue the war cost him his job in May and helped to undermine the government that might have made his assembly a reality. It was easy for **LENIN** to dismiss the one and only **RUSSIAN CONSTITUENT ASSEMBLY** in Jan 1918. **▪▶ DUMA**

### Millerand, Alexandre (1859–1943)

French politician. He entered parliament (1885) and was Minister of Commerce (1899–1902), the first socialist to hold ministerial office. However, in 1905 he refused to join the SFIO and moved towards the right, holding office as Minister of Works (1909–10) and of War (1912–13 and 1914–15), when he resigned on complaints of deficiency of supplies. His chief critic, **CLEMENCEAU**, later appointed him *commissaire général* in Alsace–Lorraine (1919). As Prime Minister (1920), he formed a right-wing coalition (**BLOC NATIONAL**) and gave support to the Poles during the Russian invasion of 1920. He became President in 1920 and resigned in 1924 in face of opposition from the **CARTEL DES GAUCHES** under **HERRIOT**. He later entered the Senate. **▪▶ SOCIALIST PARTY** (France)

### millet

An administrative unit within the **OTTOMAN EMPIRE**. The subjects of the Ottoman Sultan were divided into millets, according to religious affiliation. There were five major millets or divisions, each under its own religious leaders: Muslim; Orthodox; Jewish; Roman Catholic; and Gregorian Armenian. Tax collection, education and legal matters were organized within each millet.

### Milner, Alfred Milner, 1st Viscount (1854–1925)

British politician and colonial administrator. He established his reputation in Egypt and was appointed Governor of the Cape and High Commissioner in South Africa (1897). There he became convinced that the British position was endangered by the South African Republic (Transvaal), and set about the political rationalization of the region through the **BOER WARS**. He hoped to encourage sufficient English-speaking immigration to outnumber the Boers in a South African dominion. He additionally became Governor of the Transvaal and Orange River Colony in 1901, but was forced to resign in 1905 as a result of irregularities over Chinese labour he had introduced for the Rand gold mines. He was Secretary for War (1916–19) and Colonial Secretary (1919–21), and died in Kent, England.

### Milorg

Abbreviated form of *Militær Organisasjonen*, the secret resistance force formed in Norway following the German invasion of the country in Apr 1940. **▪▶ NORWAY, GERMAN INVASION OF**

### Milošević, Slobodan (1941– )

Serbian politician. He joined the Communist League in 1959 while a student. In 1966 he entered government service as an economic adviser to the Mayor of Belgrade and later held senior posts in the Yugoslav federal banks and gas industry (1969–83). Appointed President of the Serbian League of Communists in 1984, he became President of Serbia in 1989. Both a Serbian nationalist and a hardline Communist Party leader in the pre-**PERESTROIKA** mould, he removed **VOJVODINA**'s autonomous status and won immediate popularity by similarly disenfranchising the Albanian majority in **KOSOVO** province, and went on to survive the republic's 1990 multiparty elections that removed the communist leadership in Croatia and Slovenia. Bitterly opposed to the break-up of Yugoslavia, he agitated for the Yugoslav federal army to be sent into Slovenia and Croatia, after each declared its independence in 1991, and later (1992) into Bosnia and Herzegovina. An unrepentant champion of a 'Greater Serbia', he did nothing to prevent the fighting in Bosnia, led by avowedly 'independent' Serbian militias bent on joining the greater part of the newly independent Republic of Bosnia to the Republic of Serbia and eliminating all non-Serb residents through 'ETHNIC CLEANSING'. In 1995 he took part in the peace talks in Dayton, Ohio, negotiating on behalf of the Bosnian Serbs. A treaty was signed and sanctions against the country were lifted. In 1996 Milošević was re-elected amidst accusations of vote rigging, but, constitutionally barred from seeking another term as President of Serbia, in 1997 became instead President of the whole Federal Republic of Yugoslavia. The government clampdown on Kosovo following the province's 1991 referendum in favour of independence led to fighting against Kosovo nationalists and the start of a brutal and systematic process of ethnic cleansing by the Serbs. Milošević refused to stop the atrocities, despite diplomatic efforts by the international community, and in Mar–June 1999 NATO forces bombed Serbia. During the conflict the UN war crimes tribunal indicted Milošević for human rights atrocities in Kosovo and after his arrest on corruption charges in Apr 2001, he was extradited to The Hague and put on trial for war crimes in 2002. ► KUČAN, MILAN; TUDJMAN, FRANJO

**Milyutin, Vladimir Petrovich** (1884–1937)
Russian economist. Menshevik, turned Bolshevik, turned practical economist, he joined the Russian Social Democratic Party in 1903 when only 19; but by 1917 he was as well schooled in prisons as in splits in the party. He tended to waver in his politics, which may have turned him to economics, a discipline in which the communists were short of specialists. He held various posts, including Commissar for Agriculture (1919–22) and Vice-Chairman of Gosplan (1929–37). ► BOLSHEVIKS; MENSHEVIKS

**Min** (1851–95)
Consort of the Korean King, Kojong (1864/1907). She was the leader of a powerful faction at court, mainly comprising members of her own family, which was strongly opposed to increased Japanese influence in Korea. Min was assassinated in a palace coup instigated by the Japanese Minister to Korea, Miura Goro, in an attempt to secure control over the Korean King. The plot misfired, however; Miura was cashiered by his own government while King Kojong increasingly looked to China for protection.

**Minamoto Family**
An important Japanese family that dominated politics for most of the HEIAN ERA (794–1185). The family was an offshoot of the imperial line when Emperor Saga (809/23) gave the surname Minamoto to 33 of his 50 children. They were treated as ordinary nobles and in time comprised individual lineages that were only loosely unified. Most members of the Minamoto clan remained in the capital as high civil officials. Others distinguished themselves in the eastern provinces as warrior chieftains, of whom the most notable was Minamoto no Yoritomo (1147/99). After defeating his rivals in 1185, Minamoto no Yoritomo established a military government in eastern Japan, which

became the basis of the KAMAKURA SHOGUNATE, the first of the warrior governments that dominated Japan until the 19c.

**Mindon** (1814–78)
Burmese king of the Konbaung Dynasty. Mindon came to the throne in Feb 1853, having launched a revolt against his half-brother, King Pagan Min, in the final stages of the second Anglo-Burmese War. Quickly bringing that war to an end, Mindon sought throughout his long reign to prevent a further extension of British power at his kingdom's expense. He established comparatively cordial relations with the British (important commercial treaties were concluded). Burmese diplomatic missions were sent to a number of the other European powers, in an attempt to secure arms and alliances, and domestic reforms were undertaken, notably the improvement of internal communications. In 1857 he established a new capital at Mandalay. Mindon gave Burma 25 years of comparative peace, but the fundamental internal and external problems facing Burma could not be solved. His death led to a bloody succession struggle at the court and Burma entered a new period of extreme instability, leading to the third Anglo-Burmese War (1885) and the final collapse of Burmese independence. ► ANGLO-BURMESE WARS

**Mindszenty, József** (1892–1975)
Roman Catholic Primate of Hungary. He became a priest in 1915, Archbishop of Esztergom and Primate in 1945, and Cardinal in 1946. He then acquired international fame in 1948 when he was charged with treason by the communist government in Budapest. He was sentenced to life imprisonment the following year, but in 1955 was released on condition that he did not leave Hungary. At the end of the Hungarian Uprising in 1956 he was granted asylum in the US legation, where he remained as a voluntary prisoner until 1971, when conditions in Hungary eased and he was allowed to go abroad. He spent his last years in a Hungarian religious community in Vienna.

**Ming Dynasty** (1368–1644)
The last indigenous Chinese dynasty, founded by MING HONGWU, and finally replaced by the Manchu QING DYNASTY after peasant rebels had sacked Beijing and driven the last emperor to commit suicide. Its capital was shifted from Nanjing (Nanking) to Beijing in 1421 by the Yongle Emperor, who was responsible for building such monuments as the Forbidden City and the Temple of Heaven.

**Ming Hongwu (Ming Hung-wu)** (1328–98)
Emperor of China (1368/98). This was the reign title of Zhu Yuanzhang (Chu Yuan-chang), founder of the Chinese MING DYNASTY. The son of a peasant, he became a leader of the Red Turbans, one of a number of Buddhist and Daoist-inspired millenarian sects that rose in revolt against the Mongol YUAN DYNASTY during the 1340s. In 1356 he captured Nanjing and during the next few years disposed of his rivals to establish his own dynasty, the Ming. His reign was marked by the consolidation of imperial power (the post of Senior Chancellor was abolished and all central government organs were placed directly under the Emperor), agrarian reconstruction (low land taxes, reforestation, and resettlement of abandoned

land) and intimidation of the landed and scholarly élites, a reflection of Zhu Yuanzhang's commoner origins.

### Ming Yongle (Ming Yung-lo) (1360–1424)

Emperor of China (1402/24). The reign title of Zhu Di (Chu Ti), the third Emperor of the Chinese **MING DYNASTY**. The fourth son of **MING HONGWU**, he had been enfeoffed as the Prince of Yan (Yen), present-day Beijing. When he was passed over in the succession for his nephew, Ming Jianwen (1398/1402), he rose in revolt, eventually seizing the throne for himself. In 1421 Ming Yongle transferred the capital from Nanjing to Beijing, where it has remained ever since, and began the construction of the Imperial Forbidden City. Ming Yongle's reign also witnessed the expansion of China's land frontiers and an attempt to assert China's influence in South-East Asia with the maritime expeditions organized by the court eunuch **ZHENG HE**.

### Ming Yung-lo ► MING YONGLE

### Ministeriales

A group of court officials who were originally unfree retainers. In the 9–10c German kings looked increasingly to this group for their warriors and officials in order to curb the power of the nobility. They came to be of great political importance, particularly in the 12c when they became the chief instruments in the attempts of the **HOHENSTAUFEN DYNASTY** to rebuild the power of the monarchy after the **INVESTITURE CONTROVERSY**.

### Minitari ► HIDATSA

### Minobe Tatsukichi (1873–1948)

Japanese constitutional scholar. A member of the House of Peers (Upper House of the Diet), he was accused by the military in 1935 of lèse-majesté for his views on the Emperor. A supporter of party cabinets and democratic constitutionalism, Minobe asserted that the Emperor was an 'organ' of the state, a notion that was seen as an attack on the sacred nature of the imperial institution. Amidst growing calls during the 1930s by both the military and civilian ultranationalists for the elimination of 'dangerous thoughts', Minobe was forced to resign from the House of Peers and many of his works were banned.

### Minto, Gilbert John Murray Kynynmond-Elliot, 4th Earl of (1845–1914)

British colonial administrator. After serving in the Scots Guards (1867–70) and working as a journalist in Spain and Turkey (1874–7), he fought in the second Afghan War (1879) before going to Canada. As Governor-General (1898–1905) he was an intermediary between the Prime Minister, Wilfrid **LAURIER**, and Joseph **CHAMBERLAIN**, the British Colonial Secretary. As Viceroy of India (1905–10) in succession to Lord **CURZON**, he found an associate in John Morley, the radical Secretary of State. Both were convinced that something must be done to associate articulate Indian opinion more closely with the government. The two men, though different in their origins and natures, made an effective team. Among the problems tackled by Minto and Morley were the securing of better representation of important Indian interests and the enlargement of the powers of the existing legislative councils. The Indian Councils Act,

the core of which is generally known as the **MORLEY–MINTO REFORMS**, became law in 1909. As a result of a campaign by a Muslim delegation for representation of Muslim interests through special constituencies, this law introduced the principle of communal representation. Six special Muslim constituencies of land-holders were created for the Imperial Legislative Council, and others in some other provinces. This measure is considered as the official germ of Pakistan.

### Mintoff, Dom(inic) (1916–)

Maltese Labour statesman. Trained as an engineer, in 1947 he joined the Malta Labour Party and in the first Malta Labour government that year he became Minister of Works and Deputy Prime Minister. As Prime Minister (1955–8), his demands for independence, and the accompanying political agitation over the transfer of the naval dockyard to a commercial concern, led directly to the suspension of Malta's constitution in Jan 1959. He resigned to lead the Malta Liberation Movement, became Leader of the Opposition in 1962, and was elected premier again (1971–84).

### Minutemen

Militiamen, particularly in New England, who were prepared to take up arms at very short notice. They were important in the first months of the **AMERICAN REVOLUTION**, before the creation of a regular Continental Army under George **WASHINGTON**. ► **BUNKER HILL, BATTLE OF**; **LEXINGTON AND CONCORD, BATTLES OF**

### mir

A peasant commune in pre-revolutionary Russia (also known as *obshchina*). Its origins and functions were disputed, but after the emancipation of the serfs in 1861 it exercised collective authority of an economic and quasi-judicial nature over the peasants. Among its most important functions were the periodic redistribution of land allotments among its members and the collection and payment of taxes and redemption dues. ► **RUSSIAN SERFS, EMANCIPATION OF THE**

### Mirabeau, Honoré Gabriel Riqueti, Count of (1749–91)

French revolutionary politician and orator. Elected to the **ESTATES GENERAL** by the Third Estate of Marseilles (1789), his political acumen made him a force in the National Assembly. He advocated a constitutional monarchy on the English model, but failed to convince **LOUIS XVI**. As the popular movement progressed, his views were also rejected by the revolutionaries. He died in Paris before the climax of the Revolution. ► **FRENCH REVOLUTION**

### Mirambo (c.1840–1884)

King of the Nyamwezi. He was the most important of the warrior kings of the Nyamwezi people of Tanzania, who became traders connecting the East African coast to the interior in the 19c. Mirambo created military bands of followers called *ruga-ruga*, who were influenced by the age-regiment system of the Ngoni people, and by the 1870s was able to control the Swahili traders conveying ivory and slaves to the coastal ports.

**Miranda, Francisco de**, known as **the Precursor** (1750–1816)

Venezuelan revolutionary. After serving in the Spanish army, he fled in 1783 to the USA, and travelled widely in Europe. Actively plotting for Spanish-American independence, he organized (from New York) a disastrous expedition to Venezuela (1806). In 1810 he returned to Venezuela to take part in the struggle for independence then under way. Two years later, having been given dictatorial powers, he was captured by royalists and sent to Spain, where he died in prison in Cádiz. ► **SPANISH-AMERICAN WARS OF INDEPENDENCE**

**Mircea the Old** (1386/1418)

Prince of Wallachia. Threatened by the Ottoman Turks in the south and by the Hungarians in the north, he preserved the independence of his principality through a mixture of diplomacy and warfare. His alliance with Władysław II Jagiełłon of Poland deterred the Hungarians from further advance (1389) so that, as the Ottomans approached yet closer, he was able to conclude a defensive alliance with the Hungarian King **SIGISMUND** (1395). He extended his territory to rule over Muntenia, **OLTENIA**, Banatul, Severinuliu, **DOBRUDJA** and Moldavia as far as the River Prut. His fortunes changed after the accession of Sultan **MEHMED I** (1413/21) and after 1415 he was obliged to pay tribute to the Porte and to surrender Dobrudja. ► **MOLDAVIA AND WALLACHIA**; **ROMANIA**

**Mishima Yukio**, pseudonym of **Hiraoka Kimitake** (1925–70)

Japanese writer. He passionately believed in the chivalrous traditions of Imperial Japan, became expert in the martial arts, and in 1968 founded the Shield Society, a group of a hundred youths dedicated to a revival of **BUSHIDO**, the **SAMURAI** knightly code of honour. The most extreme expression of his élitist right-wing views was in an essay *Sun and Steel* (1970); in the same year he committed suicide by performing hara-kiri after a carefully staged token attempt to rouse the nation to a return to pre-war nationalist ideals.

**Misley, Enrico** (1801–63)

Italian revolutionary. Having been introduced to Italian nationalist ideas as a young man, he conceived the bizarre plan of persuading one of the most reactionary rulers in Italy, **FRANCESCO IV D'ESTE**, to put himself at the head of a liberal, nationalist movement. Francesco seems initially to have been flattered by the plans but he had no love for liberalism and in 1829 Misley (who it has been suggested may have been a paid *agent provocateur*) left Italy for France. In 1832 he published a shrill and mendacious attack on Austrian hegemony in Italy. He spent most of the rest of his life in Spain, where he pursued a successful career as a financier and industrialist.

**Missouri Compromise** (1820)

An agreement to admit Missouri, with **SLAVERY**, and Maine (formerly part of Massachusetts), without it, to statehood simultaneously, in order to preserve a sectional balance in the US **SENATE**. The compromise also forbade slavery in the rest of the **LOUISIANA PURCHASE** lands, north of 36°30'. It was in effect until

1854, when it was repealed by the **KANSAS–NEBRASKA ACT**.

**mita**

A Spanish word (originally meaning 'turn') which refers to a forced labour system, instigated by the Spanish crown in 1574, which provided a regular trained workforce for its great colonial mining complexes in the Andes. First used in Inca times for rotary labour, the term was then applied to labour recruitment under the **ENCOMIENDA** and, later, to repartimiento labour. Under Spanish rule, each year one seventh of all adult males in Indian communities were sent to work in the mines and refining mills; these *mitayos* worked one week in three at fixed wages, hiring themselves out as free labourers (*mingados*) for the other two weeks. Mitayos provided a subsidy for the vast Spanish mining operation in the 17c, but were displaced by free labour by 1812, when labour tributes were abolished.

**Mitakshara**

A commentary on the lawbook of Yajnavalkya, written by Vijnaneshvara, a medieval jurist, who was at the court of the great Chalukya emperor Vikramaditya VI (1075–1127). There are two great schools of family law, Mitakshara, and Dayabhaga. Most families of Bengal and Assam followed the rules of Dayabhaga, while the rest of India generally followed Mitakshara. These two schools became the basis of civil law and were to remain so until very recently. They deal with property rights in a Hindu joint-family system. Both systems refer among other things to property held jointly by the male members of the family. According to the Dayabhaga school it is only on the death of the father that the sons can claim rights to the property, whereas in the Mitakshara school the sons can claim this right during the lifetime of the father. In either case the father does not have absolute rights over property.

**Mitbestimmung**

As early as 1848, German working-class organizations had demanded their rights of *Mitbestimmung*, or co-determination, in the workplace. However, effective employee rights of co-determination (as against mere consultation) only came into being with the establishment of the Federal Republic. The 1952 Factory Constitution Law (or *Betriebsverfassungsgesetz*) allowed co-determination in social matters, but similar rights across a broad range of company affairs was introduced in the iron, steel and coal industries at that time and universally in larger firms in 1976. Elected workers' and staff representatives sit on the upper board (*Aufsichtsrat*) of German companies where they enjoy equal rights with shareholders' representatives in defined key areas. Co-determination is not unrestricted in Germany, but the contemporary system is regarded by the trade unions and the **SPD** as an important element of the democratic order.

**Mitchell, Sir James Fitzallen** (1931–)

St Vincent and the Grenadines politician. He trained and worked as an agronomist (1958–65) and then bought and managed a hotel in Bequia, St Vincent. He entered politics through the St Vincent Labour Party (SVLP) and in the pre-independence period served as Minister of Trade (1967–72). He was then

Premier (1972–4), heading the People's Political Party (PPP). In 1975 he founded the New Democratic Party (NDP) and, as its leader, served as Prime Minister from 1984 to 2000.

### Mitchell Commission, formally The Sharm El-Sheikh Fact-Finding Commission

The Commission, chaired by former US senator George Mitchell, was set up in 2000 following a conference in Sharm el-Sheikh, Egypt, to examine the causes of the second **INTIFADA** and to consider how to prevent recurrences of the violence. Its report in Apr 2001 recommended that Israel stop all new settlement activity, including 'natural growth' of existing settlements, in the **WEST BANK** and **GAZA STRIP** and lift economic restraints on Palestinian areas; that the Palestinian Authority prevent Palestinian attacks on Israelis; and that Israel limit its use of lethal force against Palestinians. Although accepting the report's findings, Palestinians felt that the implementation process was not clear, while Israel was unwilling to prevent the natural growth of settlements. The Commission report failed to gain support from the US government and there was no attempt at implementation.

### MITI (Ministry of International Trade and Industry)

The powerful Japanese government ministry created in 1949 to formulate and implement trade and industrial policy. The initial aim was to provide unified control over industrial recovery and export growth so as to end dependence on US aid. Until the mid-1960s MITI exercised total control over imports and exports, and allocated imported technology, investment funds and resources to those sectors (coal, steel, shipbuilding) deemed crucial for industrial growth. After the mid-1960s, in response to foreign accusations of protectionism, MITI relaxed its controls and began to liberalize foreign trade, although it continued to exercise influence over the economy through informal 'administrative guidance', encouraging rationalization of industry (such as mergers) and recommending loans for chosen institutions. In 2001 it was reorganized and renamed the Ministry of Economy, Trade and Industry. As a key component of the 'economic bureaucracy', MITI played a crucial role in Japan's post-war recovery and its attainment of economic superpower status. On retirement, many of its officials become executives of leading private corporations, illustrating the close ties that exist between government and business.

### Mitre, Bartolomé (1821–1906)

Argentine politician. Exiled by General Juan Manuel de **ROSAS**, he returned to the country as a follower of General Justo José de **URQUIZA** after the Battle of Monte Caseros, which brought about Rosas's downfall. He became Governor of Buenos Aires in 1860. As President (1862–8), he created a national administrative structure in Buenos Aires, set about the construction of railroads and encouraged immigration, while eliminating *caudillos*. He was defeated by Domingo **SARMIENTO** in the 1868 presidential elections. In 1870 he founded the newspaper *La Nación*, and in 1874 attempted a coup against Sarmiento's choice for President, Nicolás Avellanada. Mitre failed, however, to rally support among the *estancieros*, and was jailed.

He made another bid for the presidency in 1891 as the candidate for the *Unión Cívica*, but withdrew in favour of the Conservative candidate.

### Mitsotakis, Costas (Constantine) (1918– )

Greek politician. Leader of the New Liberals, a party on the centre-right founded in 1977 which claims to be the successor to the Liberal Party of his uncle, Eleuthérios **VENIZÉLOS**. From 1990 to 1993 he served as Prime Minister and Minister for the Aegean in the government of Constantine **KARAMANLIS**.

### Mitterrand, François Maurice Marie (1916–96)

French politician. Having served in the French army (1939–40) and been taken prisoner, he escaped from captivity and was active in the **RESISTANCE MOVEMENT**. Elected a Deputy in 1946, and at once appointed a cabinet minister, he continued to hold office frequently for the rest of the Fourth Republic. He belonged to none of the major parties, but was a member of a tiny faction, the UDSR (*Union démocratique et socialiste de la Résistance*, 'Democratic and Socialist Union of the Resistance'). In 1958 he was a stubborn opponent of de **GAULLE**, and of the new constitution, which he characterized as being semi-fascist in a book entitled *Le Coup d'État permanent* (1964). He worked assiduously to unify the Left, standing unsuccessfully as the left-wing candidate in the 1965 presidential elections. After the collapse of the Left in 1968, and its very poor showing in the 1969 presidential elections, in which he was not a candidate, he achieved this aim in 1971 when the SFIO (**SOCIALIST PARTY**) merged with various left-wing groups, including Mitterrand's own, to form the new Socialist Party of which he was at once elected leader. This was followed by agreement with the French Communist Party on a common programme (1972). Although this was later denounced by the communists, the two parties remained close allies. After he was elected President in 1981, a coalition government that included communists was formed (1981–4), which embarked on a major programme of nationalization and job creation. In 1983 this produced economic crisis, and had to be abandoned. The Right won the parliamentary elections of 1986, opening a period of 'cohabitation', in which his powers as President were restricted, but Mitterrand won the presidential elections of 1988, and managed to achieve in the parliamentary elections of the same year an assembly with no overall majority, but in which it was possible to form left-wing cabinets, thus restoring his political authority. In 1992 the Socialist Party suffered a crushing defeat and, despite Mitterrand's peacemaking efforts in Bosnia the same year, the combination of France's recession, unemployment situation and Socialist Party scandals resulted in the loss of the presidency to Jacques **CHIRAC** in 1995. ► **REPUBLIC, FOURTH** (France)

### Mixtecs ► PRE-COLUMBIAN CIVILIZATIONS

### Mlada Bosna

The revolutionary organization (literally, 'Young Bosnia') opposed to **TRIALISM** and to the Austrian annexation of Bosnia (1908). Its members were drawn from the Bosnian Serb intelligentsia.

### Mlynar, Zdenek (1930–97)

Czechoslovak politician. Coming of age in communist

Czechoslovakia, educated in law in Moscow in the last years of **STALIN** and the first years of **KHRUSHCHEV**, and then observing the slow stagnation of the **NOVOTNÝ** years in Czechoslovakia, he became a reformer through disillusionment. During the period of the **PRAGUE SPRING**, when he became a secretary of the purged Communist Party Central Committee, he made a major contribution to Alexander **DUBČEK**'s action programme and was one of the leaders abducted to Moscow following the Soviet invasion. Released with the others, he quickly lost his party function and eventually, when he signed **CHARTER 77**, he lost his employment and went to Austria, teaching politics in Innsbruck. He returned to Czech politics in the 1990s as a member of the reform communist group Left Bloc and stood for parliament in 1996 without success.

**Mobutu Sese Seko Kuku Ngbendu Wa Za Banga**, originally **Joseph Désiré Mobutu** (1930–97)
Zairean soldier and politician. After army training and a period of study in Brussels, he joined the Belgian *Force Publique* in 1949. By 1956 he was a colonel. He joined Patrice **LUMUMBA**'s *Mouvement National Congolais* in 1958 and was Chief of Staff in 1960 at the time of independence. The indecisiveness of government in Leopoldville led him to take over the government to deal with the problem of Katanga's secession but he handed power back to civilians within five months. After the 1963–5 civil war, he intervened again, this time permanently. He renamed the country Zaire in place of the Belgian Congo and imposed a degree of stability on the country that had hitherto been unknown. Backed by US money and the power of the army, his regime became increasingly corrupt and unpopular. By 1993 Zaire was in a state of financial collapse; meanwhile, Mobutu lived in splendour, having amassed a fortune from his country's resources. He was forced to abandon democratic elections and ruled through a military council. In May 1997 he was forced into exile by Laurent **KABILA** and died four months later in Rabat, Morocco.

**Modder River, Battle of** (1899)
One of the engagements of the second Boer War through which the British hoped to relieve the Siege of **KIMBERLEY**. The Boers had command of a hilltop, a traditional Boer tactic, but as this made them vulnerable to modern artillery, they gave up the hilltop and dug trenches by the river. The British failed to take the positions, and were defeated two weeks later at **MAGERSFONTEIN**, putting back the relief of Kimberley by three months. ➤ **BOER WARS**

**Moderate Party** (*Partido Moderado*)
The party which dominated Spanish party politics from 1834 to 1868, together with the **PROGRESSIVE PARTY**. The Moderate Party was more conservative than its chief rival, though their differences were more of degree than principle. The representative of the large landowners and aristocrats, loosely organized and venal, the Moderate Party dominated the period 1843–50 under Ramón **NARVÁEZ**, supported the rule of the Liberal Union in 1858–63, and returned to power under Narváez again in 1863–8. The constitution of 1845 best embodied its principles. The Moderates' oligarchical style of rule was revived under the **RESTORATION SYSTEM** of 1875–1923.

**Moderates** (*Modérés*)
French political grouping. The name applied for most of the Third Republic to the more conservative part of the republicans, as opposed to the radicals and socialists. Originally known as the **OPPORTUNISTS**, and then as the Progressists, between 1900 and 1940 they were usually known as the Moderate Republicans, or simply as the Moderates. They were organized in two factions: the *Alliance démocratique* ('Democratic Alliance'), more to the left, and the *Fédération républicaine* ('Republican Federation'), more to the right. The heirs to this tradition were the **INDEPENDENTS** (1948–62) and then (since 1966) the **INDEPENDENT REPUBLICAN PARTY**. ➤ **REPUBLIC, THIRD** (France)

**Moderate Unity Party** (Sweden)
The name adopted in 1969 by the party of Swedish Conservatives, previously called 'The Right', whose origins can be traced back to 1904. It last formed an administration in 1928–30 under Arvid Lindman, but has participated in non-socialist coalitions since **WORLD WAR II**. In the person of Carl Bildt it provided a Prime Minister for the 1991–4 administration before returning to its position as the main opposition party to the **SOCIAL DEMOCRATIC PARTY**.

**Moeller van den Bruck, Arthur** (1876–1925)
German writer. A radical right-winger, he was strongly opposed to Weimar's parliamentary order and toyed with Bolshevik as well as right-wing and racist ideas. In 1923 he published *The Third Reich* whose title was subsequently adopted by the National Socialists to describe the successor state to the **WEIMAR REPUBLIC**. ➤ **BOLSHEVIKS**; **NAZI PARTY**; **REICH**

**Mohács, Battle of** (1526)
A significant Turkish victory in Europe, when the army of the Ottoman Sultan **SÜLEYMAN I, THE MAGNIFICENT** annihilated a Hungarian force one fifth its size under King Louis II outside Buda. Louis was killed, Hungary was plunged into civil war, and the way was opened for a long period of Turkish and particularly Habsburg domination of the old Hungarian kingdom. Since Louis was simultaneously King of Bohemia/Moravia, the Czech throne was also made vacant and was likewise occupied by the Habsburg Archduke Ferdinand, marking the beginning of an Austrian rule that lasted until 1918. ➤ **HABSBURG DYNASTY**

**Mohammed Ahmed** (1844–85)
The **MAHDI**. Born in Dongola, he was for a time in the Egyptian civil service, then a slave trader, and finally a relentless and successful rebel against Egyptian rule in the eastern Sudan. He made El Obeid his capital in 1883, and defeated Hicks Pasha and an Egyptian army. In 1885 Khartoum was taken, and General **GORDON** killed. He died later that year, at **OMDURMAN**.

**Mohammed Nadir Shah** (c.1880–1933)
King of Afghanistan (1929/33). As Commander-in-Chief to **AMANULLAH KHAN** (ruler and later King of Afghanistan from 1926) he played a prominent role in the third of the **AFGHAN WARS** against Britain (1919), which secured the country's full independence

in 1922. He subsequently fell into disfavour and was forced to live in exile in France. In 1929, with British diplomatic support, he returned to Kabul and seized the throne, immediately embarking on a programme of economic and social modernization. These reforms, however, alienated the Muslim clergy and in 1933 he was assassinated. He was succeeded by his son, Mohammed **ZAHIR SHAH**.

## Mohawk

An Iroquoian-speaking Native American tribe who originally inhabited north-eastern New York State. The name Mohawk means 'man-eater', and was given to them by their neighbours; the Mohawks referred to themselves as the *Ganiengehaga*, meaning 'people of the flint'. As the easternmost of the Five Nations, they were considered the 'keepers of the eastern door', and in the 17c they instigated the **IROQUOIS CONFEDER-ACY** to control trade routes. The women harvested corn, beans and squash, while the men cleared fields and hunted. The Mohawks traced their kinship through the female line. For males, war was a traditional means of gaining prestige and honour; many religious ceremonies focused on warfare, and the introduction of firearms by the Dutch and English increased the Mohawk chances of victory. Under the leadership of Joseph **BRANT**, the Mohawks supported the British in the **AMERICAN REVOLUTION**, after which many moved to Canada. Today, they live along the US Canadian border near the St Lawrence River, numbering c.27,000 on the Canadian side and c.7,000 in the USA. ➤ **NATIVE AMERICANS**

## Mohican

An Algonquian-speaking Native American tribe who inhabited the Upper Hudson River Valley and Housatonic River Valley in New York and Connecticut. They were defeated by the **MOHAWK** in the late 17c and were forced to abandon their eastern lands. Their decline inspired James Fenimore Cooper's novel *The Last of the Mohicans* (1826). Most surviving Mohicans had migrated to western Pennsylvania and Indiana by 1730. Part of this society was assimilated into the **DELAWARE** confederation; another group settled near Stockbridge, Massachusetts; additional Mohican and other Algonquian-speaking tribes joined the Stockbridge colony and moved west to a reservation in north central Wisconsin. Descendants of the Mohican (who numbered c.1,500 in 2001) live in the Stockbridge–Munsee Indian community next to the Menominee Reservation in Wisconsin. ➤ **NATIVE AMERICANS**

## Moi, Daniel T arap (1924– )

Kenyan politician. Educated in local schools he was a primary school, and unqualified, teacher (1946–56). He entered Legco in 1957 and then was elected for the Baringo constituency which he represented 1963–78. Chairman of the Kenyan African Democratic Union (KADU) in 1960–1, he was Minister of Education in the coalition pre-independence government (1960–1) and, after KADU had merged with the Kenyan African National Union (**KANU**), he was made Minister of Home Affairs (1964–7). He became Vice-President of Kenya in 1967 and succeeded Jomo **KENYATTA** on the latter's death in 1978. He shifted the ethnic balance of central politics away from the Kikuyu towards the Kalenjin peoples of the Rift Valley

and cracked down hard on dissidents and opponents, reducing the already limited opportunities for meaningful political participation available to Kenyans. He survived an attempted coup in Aug 1982 and won successive elections until 2002, when he was constitutionally barred from re-election and KANU was defeated for the first time since independence.

## Moldavia and Wallachia, also known as **the Danubian Principalities**

Two independent Balkan principalities formed in the 14c: Moldavia lies in north-eastern Romania, south-west of the River Prut; Wallachia lies in southern Romania, south of the Transylvanian Alps. In the 16c they were incorporated into the **OTTOMAN EMPIRE**, but the **RUSSO-TURKISH WARS** during the 18–19c weakened Turkish control of the Balkans, and the two states gained autonomy under a Russian protectorate by the Treaty of **ADRIANOPLE** (1829). In 1862 Moldavia and Wallachia merged to form the unitary Principality of Romania; Russian Moldavia (now Moldova) became a Soviet Socialist Republic in 1940.

**MOLDOVA** official name **Republic of Moldova**, formerly (1940–91) **Moldavia**

A republic in eastern Europe, bounded to the west by Romania, and to the north, east and south by the Ukraine. Between the 15c and 1812 Moldavia also included the region to the east called **BESSARABIA**, the ownership of which was disputed between Russia and the **OTTOMAN** Turks. In 1812 Bessarabia, together with the eastern part of Moldavia, was ceded to Russia, and the two areas assumed the one name, Bessarabia. Although officially autonomous in 1812–28, Bessarabia thereafter came under Russian rule. Meanwhile the Danubian Principalities joined together to form the Principality of Romania in 1862. Following a nationalist movement, Bessarabia declared its independence from Russia in 1918 and united with Romania, but in 1940 Romania was forced to cede Bessarabia to the USSR, and it was incorporated with another small strip of land as the Moldavian Soviet Socialist Republic. Moldavia achieved independence from the USSR as the Republic of Moldova in 1991 and became a member of the **CIS** (Commonwealth of Independent States). Ethnic tension has grown in the country due partly to independence movements in the Dnestr and Gagauz regions, which have large Russian and Ukrainian populations, and also to a movement advocating unification with Romania. The Gagauz region was granted a degree of autonomy in 1994 and the Dnestr region in 1995, but Russian peacekeeping forces remained in the Dnestr region while talks continue. In 2004 the government withdrew from talks on the status of Dnestr and imposed economic sanctions on the region. ► MOLDAVIA AND WALLACHIA

**Molé, Louis Matthieu, Count** (1781–1855)
French politician and writer. His father was guillotined during the Terror. In his *Essai de morale et de politique* (1806) he vindicated NAPOLEON I's government on the ground of necessity, and was made a count. LOUIS XVIII made him a peer and minister for the navy; and LOUIS-PHILIPPE made him Foreign Minister and, in 1836, Prime Minister, but his regime was unpopular. He left politics after the coup d'état of 1851. ► TERROR, REIGN OF

**Molinos, Miguel de** (1640–97)
Spanish divine. Ordained in 1652, in 1675 he published his *Spiritual Guide*. He was arrested for his views, which embodied an exaggerated form of Quietism, and after a public retraction, was condemned to life imprisonment.

**Mollet, Guy Alcide** (1905–75)
French socialist politician. A schoolteacher and member of the SOCIALIST PARTY, in 1946 he became Mayor of Arras, a Deputy in the National Assembly, Secretary-General of the Socialist Party and a cabinet minister in the Léon BLUM government. He survived the international crisis over the Anglo-French intervention in Suez (Nov), but fell from office in May 1957. In 1959 he was elected a Senator, remaining leader of the SFIO until its absorption into the new Socialist Party in 1971, which ended his political influence.

**Molly Maguires**
A secret organization of (primarily) Irish miners, involved in industrial disputes in Pennsylvania, USA, during the 1870s. The prosecution of their leaders led to hangings and imprisonments, which crushed the group.

**Molotov, Vyacheslav Mikhailovich**, originally **Vyacheslav Mikhailovich Skriabin** (1890–1986)
Soviet politician. Of middle-class origin and a student at Kazan University, he became a Bolshevik in 1906 and was close to LENIN and STALIN during the RUSSIAN REVOLUTION in 1917. He subsequently acted as Stalin's right-hand man, first in domestic politics and, from 1939 onwards, as Foreign Minister, in foreign affairs. Holding office until 1949, he negotiated the Nazi–Soviet Pact with RIBBENTROP and was then Stalin's chief adviser at the TEHRAN CONFERENCE and YALTA CONFERENCE, and was present at the founding of the UN (1945). After WORLD WAR II, he emerged as the uncompromising champion of Soviet ambition; his *nyet* ('no') at meetings of the UN became a byword, and helped to foster the COLD WAR. He was less in favour in Stalin's last years, but became Foreign Minister again in 1953 until he was forced out by Nikita KHRUSHCHEV in 1956. He was then a leading figure in the failed ANTI-PARTY PLOT in 1957, but was gracefully allowed to occupy two further official posts before retiring in 1962. ► BOLSHEVIKS; COMMUNISM; GERMAN–SOVIET PACT

**Molotov cocktail**
A bottle filled with petrol, kerosene and tar, first used by Finnish soldiers as an anti-tank weapon during the RUSSO-FINNISH WAR with the USSR. Originally the fuse was a rag ignited with a match, but eventually ampules of sulphuric acid were used. With little armour themselves, the Finns used their Molotov cocktails with devastating effect. The name 'Molotov' was that of the Soviet Foreign Minister. ► MOLOTOV, VYACHESLAV MIKHAILOVICH

**Moltke, Helmuth Karl Bernhard, Count von** (1800–91)
Prussian field marshal. He entered Prussian service in 1822, and became Chief of the General Staff in Berlin (1858–88). His reorganization of the Prussian army led to the successful wars with Denmark (1863–4), Austria (1866) and France (1870–1). ► AUSTRO-PRUSSIAN WAR; FRANCO-PRUSSIAN WAR; PRUSSIA

**Momoh, Joseph Saidu** (1937–2003)
Sierra Leone soldier and politician. Educated in secondary school in Freetown and military academies in Ghana, Britain and Nigeria, he was commissioned into the Sierra Leone army in 1963. He was a battalion commander by 1968 and was appointed a minister of state in 1975. When Siaka STEVENS announced his retirement in 1985, Momoh, who had been hand-picked to be Stevens's successor, was endorsed by the country's only political party, the All People's Congress, as the sole presidential candidate. Having won the election, he sought to distance himself from his predecessor's policies in an attempt to restrain corruption and reform the economy. He was deposed in 1992.

**Mon**
An agricultural people of Burma (now Myanmar) and Thailand, thought to have come originally from western China, establishing a kingdom in Burma in about the 9c. They introduced Buddhism and Pali writing into Burma, and were subjugated by the Burmans by the 18c. They speak an Austro-Asiatic language, also known as Tailang. Population now c.1.1 million.

**Mon, Alejandro** (1801–82)
Spanish politician and administrative reformer. As Minister of Finance in 1844–5, he created the tax system that was the basis of government finance for the rest of the 19c. Accordingly, he has been dubbed 'the Peel of Spain'. ► PEEL, SIR ROBERT

**MONACO**     official name **Principality of Monaco**
A small principality on the Mediterranean Riviera, close to the Italian frontier with France. In 1297 the GRIMALDI family won Monaco from the Genoese, who had held it since 1191, but they did not secure full possession until 1419. Though the Grimaldis were allies of France (except when they were under Spanish protection in 1524–1641), Monaco was formally annexed by France in 1793 during the French Revolutionary regime. It has been under French protection ever since, apart from a period under Sardinia in 1815–61. Monaco is governed by the reigning Prince

of Monaco (Prince Rainier since 1949) and a Council of Government appointed by him.

**Monagas, José Tadeo** (1784–1868)
Venezuelan general and politician. He fought in the SPANISH-AMERICAN WARS OF INDEPENDENCE (1810–26) under Simón BOLÍVAR, and at the time of the dissolution of the union of GRAN COLOMBIA in 1830 he was the military leader of Venezuela. In the midst of a political struggle between the Conservative government and new Liberal Party, Monagas defeated José Antonio PÁEZ to become President in 1847. Though he had been elected a Conservative, he appointed Liberal Ministers and ruled by dictatorship (1847–50, 1855–8), as did his brother, José Gregorio Monagas, whom he placed in the President's office in 1851–5. Though the Monagas brothers passed liberal laws, they were not implemented, and shortly after José Tadeo Monagas revised the constitution in 1857 to his own advantage he was overthrown and banished (1858). He returned as leader of a faction in 1868, but died soon afterwards.

**Monash, Sir John** (1865–1931)
Australian soldier. He practised as a civil engineer and also held a commission in the Australian Citizen Force (1887), rising to command the 13th Infantry Brigade by 1913. He commanded the 4th Australian Infantry Brigade at Gallipoli (1914–15), the 3rd Australian Division in France (1916), and the Australian Corps as Lieutenant-General (1918). Recognized as one of the outstanding generals of WORLD WAR I, he was noted for the meticulous preparation and planning of his operations. After the war, he was chairman of the Victorian State Electricity Commission. ► GALLIPOLI CAMPAIGN

**Monck, George, 1st Duke of Albemarle** (1608–70)
English general. He fought in the Low Countries, and with the royalists in Scotland, then joined the COMMONWEALTH cause and served successfully in Ireland, Scotland, and (1652–4) in the first of the ANGLO-DUTCH WARS. He feared a return to civil war during and after Richard CROMWELL's regime (1658–9), and was instrumental (as commander of the army in Scotland) in bringing about the RESTORATION of CHARLES II, for which he was created Duke of Albemarle. ► ENGLISH CIVIL WARS

**Mondlane, Eduardo** (1920–69)
Mozambiquan nationalist leader. Educated in mission schools, he furthered his training at Fort Hare College and Lisbon University and developed into a respected sociologist with research posts in the USA and with the UN. He returned to Mozambique in 1961 to form FRELIMO and launched the guerrilla war against Portuguese colonialism in 1964. He was murdered by a parcel bomb in Dar es Salaam.

**monetarism**
The theory or practice of controlling an economy by using the supply of money in circulation. The essence of the theory, whose main exponent is the US economist Milton FRIEDMAN, is that if the money supply is allowed to rise too quickly, prices will rise, resulting in inflation. To curb these inflationary pressures, governments may feel the need to reduce the money supply and raise interest rates. Monetarism emerged in the 1960s and 1970s and was a major influence on economic policy in Britain during the THATCHER administration (1979–90), in the USA under REAGAN (1981–9), and in Chile under PINOCHET (1974–90).

**Mongkut** (1804–68)
The 4th King of the CHAK(K)RI DYNASTY of Thailand. Passed over for the throne on the death of his father in 1824, Mongkut entered the monkhood. By the late 1830s he had emerged as, in effect, the leader of a reformist order, the *Thammayutika*. Mongkut ascended the throne in 1851. His reign, which lasted until his death in 1868, is perhaps most noted for the opening of the kingdom to political and commercial intercourse with the Western powers, a process marked by the signing of the Bowring Treaty between Thailand and Britain in 1855. Mongkut also undertook a limited measure of internal reform, and he paid close attention to the education and training of his son, CHULALONGKORN, who succeeded him in 1868.

MONGOLIA   official name **People's Republic of Mongolia**, formerly **Outer Mongolia**

A landlocked republic in eastern central Asia, bounded to the north by Russia and on other sides by China. Originally the homeland of nomadic tribes, which united under GENGHIS KHAN in the 13c to become part of the great Mongol Empire, Mongolia was assimilated into China, and divided into Inner and Outer Mongolia. Inner Mongolia remains an autonomous region of China, but Outer Mongolia declared itself an independent monarchy in 1911 when China's imperial regime collapsed. In 1921, Mongolian revolutionaries formed what became the Mongolian People's Revolutionary Party (MPRP) and, with the support of the RED ARMY, removed Chinese and Tsarist forces from Mongolia and formed a government. The Mongolian People's Republic, aligned with the USSR, was formed in 1924, but was not recognized by China until 1946. Following pro-democracy demonstrations, a multiparty system was introduced in 1990, but the MPRP has continued to dominate politics. Although it lost power in 1996 to an alliance of nationalists and social democrats, the alliance became the subject of corruption scandals and its free-market policies caused widespread social disruption; in 1997 the MPRP leader, Natsagiyn Bagabandi, was elected President and in 2000 the

MPRP won the legislative elections. ▸ MONGOLS

## Mongols

The general name applied to the linguistically related tribes of Central Asia and southern Siberia who effected the violent collapse of the 'Abbasid Empire before converting to Islam. United under GENGHIS KHAN in 1206, they spread into what are now Iran and Russia and then conquered China under his grandson KUBLAI KHAN, who ruled as first emperor of the YUAN DYNASTY. After Kublai's death they began splitting up, and over the next two to three centuries they were gradually pushed back to the territories they now inhabit. ▸ 'ABBASID DYNASTY; GOLDEN HORDE; MONGOLIA

## Monitor, USS v CSS Merrimack (8 Mar 1862)

A sea battle during the AMERICAN CIVIL WAR which took place off Hampton Roads, Virginia. It was the first battle between ironclad, steam-powered warships and changed the nature of naval combat. The 10-gun CSS *Virginia* – a former Union ship that had been captured and converted into an ironclad by the Confederacy but was still commonly called by her first name, *Merrimack* – sank two and captured one of the five blockading USA warships. However, the *Merrimack* was then forced back into harbour by the USS *Monitor* commanded by Lieutenant Lorimer Worden, where she was scuttled two months later when Norfolk was evacuated.

## Monkey Trial ▸ DARROW, CLARENCE

## Monmouth, Battle of (1778)

An engagement in New Jersey between British and American troops during the AMERICAN REVOLUTION. It was notable for Washington's suspension of General Charles Lee (1731–82) from command, and for the discipline of American troops under fire. ▸ WASHINGTON, GEORGE

## Monmouth, James, Duke of (1649–85)

Illegitimate son of CHARLES II of England. He was created Duke of Monmouth in 1663, and became Captain-General in 1670. He had substantial popular support, and as a Protestant became a focus of opposition to Charles II. After the discovery of the RYE HOUSE PLOT (1683), he fled to the Low Countries. In 1685 he landed at Lyme Regis, and asserted his right to the crown. He was defeated at the Battle of SEDGEMOOR, captured, and beheaded. ▸ JAMES VII AND II

## Monnet, Jean (1888–1979)

French political economist and diplomat. He introduced in 1947 the Monnet Plan for the modernization of French industry. He was President of the European Coal and Steel High Authority (1952–5), and of the Action Committee for the United States of Europe (1956–75). ▸ EC; EEC

## Monroe, James (1758–1831)

US politician and 5th President. After serving in the AMERICAN REVOLUTION, he entered politics, becoming a member of the SENATE (1790–4), Minister to France (1794–6), Governor of Virginia (1799–1802), Minister to England and Spain (1803–7), and Secretary of State (1811–17), before becoming President in 1817. During his 'era of good feeling' he signed the MISSOURI COMPROMISE, acquired Florida, and set forth the principles of the MONROE DOCTRINE. He won an easy re-election in 1820.

## Monroe Doctrine

A major statement of US foreign policy, proclaimed in 1823, attributed to President James MONROE, but written by Secretary of State John Quincy ADAMS. The doctrine was issued after renewed interest in the Americas by European powers, especially Britain and Russia, following the Spanish-American revolutions for independence. It announced (1) the existence of a separate political system in the Western Hemisphere, (2) US hostility to further European colonization or attempts to extend European influence, and (3) non-interference with existing European colonies and dependencies or in European affairs.

## Montagu–Chelmsford Reforms

After a report (Apr 1918) by the Secretary of State for India, E S Montagu, and the Viceroy, Lord Chelmsford, the British agreed the 1919 Government of India Act. Promising progressive moves towards Indian self-government within the British Empire, it provided as a first step enlarged electorates, and partial provincial autonomy whereby responsibility for certain aspects of government was transferred to elected Indian ministers; at the centre a bicameral legislature comprising a Council of State and a Legislative Assembly with increased powers. The number of Indians on the central executive council was also enlarged; the Indian government gained a larger degree of independence from the control of Whitehall. It was rejected by many Indians, and its promise of future progress was resisted by some British Conservatives, but a further step was taken, with full provincial autonomy under Indian control, in 1935. ▸ GOVERNMENT OF INDIA ACTS

## Montalembert, Charles René Forbes de, Count of (1810–70)

French historian and politician, the eldest son of a noble French émigré and his English wife. In 1830 he eagerly joined the Abbé LAMENNAIS and Henri Lacordaire in *L'Avenir*, a Catholic liberal newspaper. Montalembert, who had succeeded to his father's peerage, pleaded with great eloquence the cause of religious liberty, in spite of the papal condemnation of *L'Avenir*. A famous protest against tyranny was his great speech (Jan 1848) upon Switzerland. After the FEBRUARY REVOLUTION (1848) he was elected a member of the National Assembly; and he supported Louis Napoleon (NAPOLEON III) until the confiscation of the Orléans property, when he became a determined opponent of the imperial regime. He visited England in 1855, and wrote *De l'Avenir politique de l'Angleterre*, and many other works on medieval Church history, and on contemporary political topics; he sought, in vain, to reconcile Catholicism and liberalism.

## Montcalm (de Saint Véran), Louis Joseph de Montcalm-Grozon, Marquis of (1712–59)

French general. During the SEVEN YEARS' WAR, he took command of the French troops in Canada (1756), and captured the British post of Oswego and Fort William Henry. In 1758 he defended FORT TICONDEROGA, and proceeded to the defence of QUEBEC, where he died in the battle against General

James **WOLFE** on the **PLAINS OF ABRAHAM**.

## Montefeltro

Lords of Urbino in north-east Italy in the **RENAIS-SANCE**. Federigo (d.1484) was the ideal prince: a successful **CONDOTTIERE**, politician, and patron of the arts. The most famous Renaissance handbook for courtiers, by **CASTIGLIONE**, was based on the author's experience of the Montefeltro court of Federigo's son, Guidobaldo, c.1504. ➤ **PAPAL STATES**

## MONTENEGRO

A central European republic federated with the republic of Serbia, a mountainous region bounded to the south-west by the Adriatic Sea; to the north-west by Bosnia and Herzegovina; to the north-east by Serbia; and to the south-east by Albania. The area was part of the Roman province of Illyria, settled by **SLAVS** in the 7c and established as the independent province of Zeta. In the late 12c it was incorporated into the Serbian empire. Montenegrin independence was recognized at the Congress of **BERLIN** (1878), although border disputes with Albania continued. The country retained its independent monarchy until 1918, when King Nicholas was deposed and Montenegro absorbed into Serbia. Of the six republics that made up Yugoslavia as established in 1945 (Croatia, Slovenia, Bosnia and Herzegovina, Macedonia, Montenegro and Serbia), only Serbia and Montenegro remained as the Federal Republic of Yugoslavia, declared on 27 Apr 1992. This was restructured with effect from Feb 2003 into a loose federation of the two republics, with the federation responsible for defence, foreign and economic affairs, while each republic is responsible for internal matters. Parties associated with President Milo Djukanović won the 2002 elections, demonstrating Montenegran approval for the new structure. Djukanović stepped down as president to become Prime Minister and was replaced as President in 2003 by the former Prime Minister Filip Vujanovic.

## Montesa, Order of

A military order founded in the crown of **ARAGON** by King Jaime II, to replace the Order of **TEMPLARS**, abolished by the pope in 1312. It derived its name from the Castle of Montesa in Valencia, formerly a Templar stronghold. Granted approval by the pope in 1317, it came to possess extensive estates (*encomiendas*). Members were in theory subject to semi-monastic discipline. ➤ **ENCOMIENDA**

## Montespan, Françoise Athénaïs de Rochechouart, Marchioness of (1641–1707)

Mistress of **LOUIS XIV**. She replaced Mlle de La Vallière as the king's mistress c.1667, and after her marriage was annulled (1674) received official recognition of her position. She bore the king seven children who were legitimized (1673). Supplanted first by Mlle de Fontanges and later by Mme de **MAINTENON**, she left court in 1687 and retired to the Convent of Saint-Joseph, Paris, eventually becoming the Superior.

## Montesquieu, Charles-Louis de Secondat, Baron of la Brède and of (1689–1755)

French philosopher and jurist. Educated at Bordeaux, he became an advocate, but turned to scientific research and literary work. He settled in Paris (1726), then spent some years travelling and studying political and social institutions. His best-known work is the comparative study of legal and political issues, *De l'esprit des lois* (1748), which was a major influence on 18c Europe.

## Montezuma I (c.1390–1464)

Aztec Emperor of Mexico (c.1437/1464). His reign is notable for the annexation of Chalco and the crushing of the Tlascalans. ➤ **PRE-COLUMBIAN CIVILIZATIONS**

## Montezuma II (1466–1520)

The last Aztec Emperor of Mexico (1502/20). A distinguished warrior and legislator, he died at **TENOCHTITLÁN** during the Spanish conquest. One of his descendants was Viceroy of Mexico from 1697 to 1701. ➤ **CORTÉS, HERNÁN; PRE-COLUMBIAN CIVILIZATIONS**

## Montfort, Simon de, Earl of Leicester (c.1208–1265)

English politician and soldier. In 1238 he married **HENRY III** of England's youngest sister, Eleanor, and as the King's deputy in Gascony (1248) put down disaffection with a heavy hand. He returned to England in 1253, became the leader of the barons in their opposition to the king, and defeated him at Lewes (1264). He then became virtual ruler of England, calling a parliament in 1265; but the barons soon grew dissatisfied with his rule, and the king's army defeated him at Evesham, where he was killed. ➤ **BARONS' WARS**

## Montgomery, Bernard Law, 1st Viscount Montgomery of Alamein (1887–1976)

British field marshal. Commissioned into the Royal Warwickshire Regiment (1908), in **WORLD WAR II** he gained renown as arguably the best British field commander since **WELLINGTON**. A controversial and outspoken figure, he was nevertheless a 'soldier's general', able to establish a remarkable rapport with his troops. He commanded the 8th Army in North Africa, and defeated **ROMMEL** at the Battle of **EL ALAMEIN** (1942). He played a key role in the invasion of Sicily and Italy (1943), and was appointed Commander-in-Chief, Ground Forces, for the Allied **NORMANDY CAMPAIGN** (1944). On his insistence, the invasion frontage was widened, and more troops were committed to the initial assault. Criticized for slow progress after **D-DAY**, he uncharacteristically agreed to the badly-planned airborne landings at Arnhem (Sep 1944), which resulted in the only defeat of his military career. In 1945 German forces in north-western Germany, Holland and Denmark surrendered to him on Lüneburg Heath. Appointed field marshal (1944) and viscount (1946), he served successively as Chief of the Imperial General Staff (1946–8) and Deputy Supreme Commander of **NATO** forces in Europe (1951–8). ► **NORTH AFRICAN CAMPAIGN**

**Montgomery Bus Boycott** (1955–6)
The first major instance of black activism during the **CIVIL RIGHTS MOVEMENT**. It began after a black woman, Rosa Lee **PARKS**, was arrested for sitting in the white section of a bus. Mobilized by Martin Luther **KING**, the black community boycotted the bus service in Montgomery, Alabama, for 381 days until the bus company was persuaded by a 65 per cent drop in revenue, and a Supreme Court decision that declared bus segregation unconstitutional, to integrate its seating (21 Dec 1956). The event also marked the beginning of King's rise as a **CIVIL RIGHTS** leader.

**Montluc, Blaise de** (1502–77)
French soldier. He fought in Italy, and as governor of **GUYENNE** treated the **HUGUENOTS** with great severity. His *Mémoires* were called 'la bible du soldat' by **HENRY IV** (of France).

**Montmorency, Anne, 1st Duke of** (1493–1567)
Marshal and Constable of France. He distinguished himself under his childhood friend, **FRANCIS I** of France, at Marignano (1515) and became Constable (1538); suspected by the king of siding with the **DAUPHIN**, he was banished from court in 1541. He was restored to his dignities by **HENRY II** (1547), commanded at the disaster of St Quentin (1557), and was taken prisoner by the Spaniards. He opposed the influence of **CATHERINE DE' MEDICI** and commanded against the **HUGUENOTS** at Dreux (1562). In 1563 he drove the English out of Le Havre. He again engaged the Huguenot leader, Louis I of Bourbon, Prince of **CONDÉ** at St Denis (1567), where he received his death-wound.

**Montoire sur Loir**
A village in central France, where **LAVAL**, and two days later **PÉTAIN**, met **HITLER** (22–4 Oct 1940) to define the policy of Franco-German **COLLABORATION**.

**Montoneros**
Argentine urban guerrillas claiming allegiance to **PERONISM** and (from 1970) staging terrorist actions against the military regime then in power. Repudiated by Juan Domingo **PERÓN** himself (1974), the Montoneros renewed their attacks on the regime installed in 1976, meeting with severe repression. Their activities encouraged the Argentine military to embark on the 'Dirty War' against the urban guerrillas, culminating in the Malvinas (Falklands) imbroglio. ► **MADRES DE LA PLAZA MAYO**

**Montreal Protocol on Substances that Deplete the Ozone Layer** (1987)
An agreement setting out schedules for phasing out ozone-depleting chemicals. Following the adoption of the **VIENNA CONVENTION FOR THE PROTECTION OF THE OZONE LAYER** in 1985, it became apparent that the depletion of the Earth's ozone layer was advan-

cing more rapidly than previously realized, requiring stronger measures to curtail the production and consumption of ozone-depleting chemicals. The Montreal Protocol was adopted in 1987 and came into force in 1989. The 1990 (London) Amendment established a multilateral fund to provide financial and technical assistance to help developing countries comply with their obligations. Other amendments were adopted in 1992 (Copenhagen), 1995 (Vienna), 1997 (Montreal) and 1999 (Beijing) to speed up the phasing-out process and to expand the range of chemicals covered.

**Montreux Convention** (1936)
This agreement revised the terms of the Treaty of **LAUSANNE** (1923) and allowed Turkey to remilitarize the Straits. Turkey was given absolute control of the waterway and could regulate the passage of warships through it in times of conflict, and in peacetime if it felt threatened. These generous concessions are explained by Britain's desire to prevent Turkey allying itself with **HITLER**.

**Montrose, James Graham, 1st Marquis of** (1612–50)
Scottish general. He helped to draw up the Covenant in support of Presbyterianism, and served in the Covenanter army in 1640, but transferred his allegiance to **CHARLES I**, and led the royalist army to victory at Tippermuir (1644). After the royalist defeat at the Battle of **NASEBY** (1645), his army became disaffected, and his remaining force was defeated at Philiphaugh. He fled to Europe, returning to Scotland after Charles's execution to avenge his death. His army was largely lost by shipwreck, and the remnant defeated at Carbisdale (1650). He was taken prisoner, and hanged in Edinburgh. ► **COVENANTERS**; **ENGLISH CIVIL WARS**

**Montseny, Federica** (1905–94)
Spanish anarchist writer and leader. She fought for **WOMEN'S RIGHTS** within both the **CNT** and the **FAI**. Montseny strongly supported anarchist participation in the Popular Front elections of Feb 1936. She became Minister of Public Health in the Republican government of Sep 1936–May 1937, the first woman in Spain to achieve a ministerial portfolio. Exiled to France in 1939, she remained active in anarchist circles, returning to Spain in 1975.

**Montt, Manuel** (1809–80)
Chilean politician. A member of Congress from 1840 to 1851, before being appointed President in 1851, he served as Minister of Interior and of Justice under President Bulnes (1841–51) and founded the University of Chile (1843). His ten-year presidency was authoritarian and conservative in style, which angered both conservatives and liberals alike, but brought about many improvements in education, communication, transport and law reform, and the colonization of the area south of the Bío Bío River. In 1861 he gave up the presidency to the moderate José Joaquín Pérez (his first choice of successor having resulted in an armed revolt by the liberals) and became President of the Supreme Court, in which office he remained until he died.

**Moonje, Balakrishna Shivaram** (1872–1948)
Indian nationalist. A reputed eye surgeon who joined

the Indian freedom struggle. He studied at Hislop College, Nagpur and at Grant Medical College, Bombay. He attended the Bombay Congress session and adopted TILAK as his guru. He subsequently gave up his medical practice to enter politics. He worked for the SWADESHI boycott and took a prominent part in the Home Rule Movement. He was elected President of the Central Legislature in 1926, but resigned the post at the call of Congress. He represented HINDU MAHASABHA on the joint parliamentary committee and in 1937 formed a Hindu Military Education Society and started the Bhonsle Military School. He wrote a new Manusmriti which was never published. He received the popular title Dharmavira for his religious activities and was nicknamed Field Marshal Moonje for his military qualities.

## Moore, Sir John (1761–1809)
British general. From 1794 he served in many countries in Europe, and in the West Indies, but is remembered for his command of the English Army in Spain (1808–9), where he was forced to retreat to La Coruña. There he defeated a French attack, but was mortally wounded. ► PENINSULAR WAR

## Moors
The name applied in Spanish to Muslims from North Africa who conquered the Iberian Peninsula in the 8c. The Hispanic Christian kingdoms (CASTILE, above, all) fought wars of RECONQUEST, which by the mid-13c eliminated the Moors from all but the small southern Kingdom of Granada. Granada was conquered in 1492, and in 1502 all professed Muslims were expelled by order of ISABELLA I, THE CATHOLIC. ► GRANADA, CONQUEST OF

## Moplahs ► MAPILLAS

## Moral Majority
A US pressure group founded by Rev Jerry Falwell in 1979 which campaigns for the election of morally conservative politicians and for changes in public policy in such areas as abortion, homosexuality, and school prayers. It is associated with Christian fundamentalists who in the 1980s played a prominent role in US politics. It changed its name to the Liberty Federation in 1986.

## Morant Bay Rebellion (1865)
Black uprising against the colonial government in Morant Bay, St Thomas, Jamaica. Infuriated by the violence of the local militia's response to a peaceful demonstration, a group of black smallholders led by Paul Bogle, a charismatic Baptist preacher, fired the Court House and in the ensuing riot 30 people of both sides were killed. The Governor, Edward John Eyre, blamed the discontent on George William Gordon, a coloured landowner and ex-magistrate. Gordon was tried, convicted and hanged for high treason in Kingston, Bogle and 400 other 'rebels' were executed, and 600 people were flogged in St Thomas. Embarrassed by Eyre's savage reaction to this 'African uprising', London recalled the Governor (although many in Britain continued to regard him as the saviour of the island). Gordon and Bogle are now revered as nationalist heroes in Jamaica.

## Morat, Battle of (22 June 1476)
A decisive battle in the war between the Burgundians under CHARLES THE BOLD and the Swiss Confederation (1474–6). A crushing defeat was inflicted on the Burgundians who lost c.11,000 men, against Swiss losses of only c.410.

## Moravian Brethren
A Protestant movement descended from the so-called Unity of Czech Brethren formed in Bohemia in 1457 by Petr Chelčický among others and subsequently at the centre of the CZECH REFORMATION in its struggle with the Austrian COUNTER-REFORMATION. Most were driven out of Bohemia and Moravia by FERDINAND II after his victory at the Battle of the WHITE MOUNTAIN in 1620, but some survived until 1725, when CHARLES VI completed their expulsion. The survivors found refuge in Saxony where they became known as Moravians. Some spread across Europe and on to North America where, in 1734, they established the Moravian Church.

## Moraviantown, Battle of ► THAMES, BATTLE OF THE

## Moray, James Stuart, 1st Earl of (1531–70)
Regent of Scotland (1567/70). He was the illegitimate son of JAMES V of Scotland, and half-brother of MARY, QUEEN OF SCOTS. He acted as Mary's chief adviser (1560), but supported John KNOX and opposed Mary's marriage to DARNLEY. After an attempted coup, he was outlawed and took refuge in England (1565). Pardoned the following year, he became regent for Mary's baby son when she abdicated (1567), and defeated her army at Langside (1568). His Protestant and pro-English policies alienated some Scots nobles, and he was killed at Linlithgow by one of Mary's supporters.

## Morazán, Francisco (1792–1842)
Central American politician. He was instrumental in organizing the government of the newly independent Honduras (1821), and led the Liberal Party in revolts in 1827 against Manuel José Arce, the first President of the United Provinces of Central America (also called the CENTRAL AMERICAN FEDERATION, established 1823), and in 1829 in the capital, Guatemala City. As the elected President of the United Provinces of Central America from 1830, he passed laws to limit the power of the Roman Catholic Church, spent much time quashing revolts, and ultimately failed to retain the unity of the federation. Forced by a Conservative-backed rebel army to flee to Peru in 1840, he amassed an army and in 1842 invaded Costa Rica in a bid to restore the federation, but was captured and shot.

## More, Sir Thomas, also known as St Thomas More (1478–1535)
English statesman. He became a lawyer, then spent four years in a Carthusian monastery to test his vocation for the priesthood. He did not take holy orders, and under HENRY VIII of England became Master of Requests (1514), Treasurer of the Exchequer (1521), and Chancellor of the Duchy of Lancaster (1525). On the fall of WOLSEY (1529), he was appointed Lord Chancellor, but resigned in 1532 because of his opposition to Henry's break with Rome. On refusing to recognize Henry as head of the English Church, he was imprisoned and beheaded. A leading humanist

scholar, as revealed in his Latin *Utopia* (1516) and many other works, he was canonized in 1935. ➤ **REFORMATION** (England)

**Morelos (y Pavón), José María** (1765–1815)
Mexican revolutionary. Born in Michoacán, New Spain. A mestizo, his early life was spent as a muleteer before he entered the priesthood. He then joined **HIDALGO (Y COSTILLA)** in the struggle for Mexican independence as the leader in the south and reorganized the insurgents in the period 1810–13. A brilliant guerrilla leader, he regrouped opposition to Spanish rule in 1811 under a supreme junta. In opposition to the Spanish Constitution of Cádiz, he convened a 'sovereign congress' at Chilpancingo which, though beleaguered, declared independence at Apatzingán (22 Oct 1814). This first Mexican constitution was republican, and abolished the fuero and **SLAVERY**. Isolated and trapped by the royalist forces under Viceroy Felix Calleja, he was captured, defrocked and executed in Mexico City. He was one of the founders, with Vicente Guerrero, Guadalupe Victoria and Juan Álvarez, of the radical liberal tradition of Mexican politics.

**Moreno, Mariano** (1778–1811)
Argentine lawyer and revolutionary political leader. He held various posts in the Spanish colonial administration and came to notice with his essay *Representación de los hacendados* (1809, 'Landowners' Petition') which argued for Argentina's right to trade freely with other nations and led the viceroy to relax some of the severe restrictions imposed by the Spanish Navigation Acts. The following year the Spanish bureaucrats in Buenos Aires, including the viceroy, were ousted by a provisional junta, and Moreno became Secretary for Political and Military Affairs and, later, leader. He was an ardent advocate of full independence for Argentina and encouraged the spread of revolution. When his views proved too radical for the Conservative members of the junta, he was forced to resign (1810). He was given a diplomatic mission to Brazil and the UK, but died at sea.

**Morgan, Sir Henry** (c.1635–1688)
British buccaneer. Morgan's 'Brethren of the Cross' terrorized Spanish settlements in the Caribbean between 1655 and 1671. Welsh-born, Morgan went to Barbados as an indentured servant but later joined the cosmopolitan **BUCCANEERS** in St Domingue. In 1655 he took part in the capture of Jamaica and Mansfield's raid on Cuba. Provided with letters of marque by the Governor of Jamaica, Thomas Modyford, Morgan made daring, brutal and profitable attacks on Puerto Bello (1668), Maracaibo (1669) and Rio de la Hacha and Panama (1670–1). When buccaneering was outlawed by the Treaty of Madrid (1670), Morgan returned to Port Royal and was twice made Deputy Governor of Jamaica. ➤ **INDENTURED SERVANTS**

**Morgan, J(ohn) (P)ierpont** (1837–1913)
US banker, financier and art collector. The son of the financier John Spencer Morgan, he built his father's firm into the most powerful private banking house in the USA. He acquired a controlling interest in many of the country's principal railroads, and in 1901 he bought out Andrew **CARNEGIE** and formed the US Steel Corporation, at that time the world's largest corporation. In the public mind he came to represent the manipulative forces of the 'money trust'. He compiled one of the greatest private art collections of his day, which he bequeathed to the Metropolitan Museum of Art in New York. He was also noted for his extensive philanthropic benefactions.

**Morgarten, Battle at the Pass of** (1315)
The decisive battle between Duke Leopold of Austria and the Swiss cantons. Leopold suffered a crushing defeat while attempting to impose the imperial ban on the cantons and reassert Habsburg rights there. As a result of their victory, the cantons renewed the Confederation and had their rights recognized by **LOUIS IV, THE BAVARIAN**, while Habsburg lands in the area were confiscated by the Emperor. ➤ **HABSBURG DYNASTY**

**Mori Arinori** (1847–89)
Japanese politician. From a **SATSUMA** samurai family, Mori studied in Britain and the USA (1865–8) and on his return became a vigorous proponent of westernization, advocating the abolition of traditional customs and even the replacement of the Japanese language by English. He was Japan's first envoy to the USA (1871–3) and Vice-Foreign Minister (1878–9) before heading the newly established Education Ministry in 1885. He created a centralized and secular education system with emphasis on practical instruction and service to the state. A series of higher schools, culminating in the prestigious Tokyo Imperial University, were also founded to train a governing élite. Mori was assassinated by a religious fanatic on the same day the **MEIJI CONSTITUTION** was promulgated (11 Feb 1889).

**Morínigo, Higinio** (1897–1985)
Paraguayan general and military dictator. Following the death in an air crash of President **ESTIGARRIBIA** (1940), Morínigo was appointed President and immediately imposed an authoritarian regime which persecuted the Blancos in favour of the Colorados, but improved housing and public health. In 1947 the Blancos and other groups rebelled, instigating a devastating civil war that led to the deposition of Morínigo in 1948. He fled to exile in Argentina.

**Moriscos**
The name given to Spanish Muslims and their descendants who accepted Christian baptism. They came into existence on a large scale when the Castilian government in 1502 ordered Muslims in Granada and **CASTILE** to choose between baptism and expulsion. The Muslims of the crown of **ARAGON** were not forced to convert until 1526. *Moriscos* formed a high proportion of the Mediterranean population of Spain, and most resisted all attempts to convert them effectively. In Granada they were responsible for a major uprising in the Alpujarra region (1569). They were eventually expelled *en masse* in 1609–14, to a total of some 300,000. The economic effects of their departure were serious in certain areas. ➤ **ALPUJARRAS, REVOLTS OF**

**Morlaks**
Originally the Venetian term for non-urban **SLAVS** and Vlachs living along the Dalmatian coast, the name came to be used erroneously as a synonym for **HAJDUKS**.

## Morley–Minto Reforms

The popular name given to the 1909 Indian Councils Act. They broadened the basis of Indian government, allowed Indians to sit on the Imperial Legislative Council, introduced direct elections for non-official seats in provincial legislative councils, and granted separate or communal electorates to minorities. They were not intended to progress to full parliaments, and were soon criticized for holding up administration, dividing Muslims and Hindus, and failing to appease Indian opinion. ► MINTO, GILBERT JOHN MURRAY KYNYNMOND-ELLIOT, 4TH EARL OF

## Mormons

The name given to the religious groups that base their beliefs on the Book of Mormon. The largest was founded by Joseph SMITH as the Church of Jesus Christ of Latter-Day Saints in Fayette, New York (1830), and is now based in Salt Lake City, Utah, where it was led by Brigham YOUNG in 1846–7. Smith claimed to have been led to a hidden gospel written on golden plates and buried 1,000 years before on a hill near Palmyra, New York. Transcribed as the Book of Mormon, it tells of an ancient American people to whom Christ appeared after his ascension, and teaches Christ's future establishment of the New Jerusalem in America. Mormons also take their doctrine from the King James Version of the Bible, but they believe that humans can become gods, and that Jesus's incarnation was unique only because it was the first.

## Mornay, Philippe de, Lord of Plessay-Marly
(1549–1623)
French Huguenot leader and polemicist. Converted to Protestantism in 1560, he was nicknamed the 'Pope of the HUGUENOTS' for his role in the Wars of RELIGION (1562–98). A trusted counsellor of Henry of Navarre (HENRY IV), he undertook many embassies for the Protestant cause; however, he lost the King's favour after Henry's conversion to Catholicism (1593) and played no further part in national affairs.

## Morny, Charles Auguste Louis Joseph, Duke of
(1811–65)
French nobleman, believed to be the son of Queen HORTENSE and the Count of Flahaut, and so half-brother of NAPOLEON III. In 1838 he became a manufacturer of beet sugar and was mixed up in all sorts of speculations. Chosen a Deputy in 1842, he quickly became prominent in financial questions. After 1848 he supported Napoleon, took a leading part in the coup d'état, and became Minister of the Interior. From 1854 to 1865 he was President of the *Corps Législatif*, and was Ambassador to Russia in 1856–7. He is the 'Duc de Mora' in Alphonse Daudet's *Le Nabab* (1877).

## Moro, Aldo (1916–78)
Italian politician. A leading figure in the CHRISTIAN DEMOCRATIC PARTY (DC), he served twice as Prime Minister (1963–8 and 1974–6) and was Foreign Minister (1970–2). During the 1970s he was one of the DC moderates who sought to cooperate with BERLINGUER. He was one of several important figures to die at the hands of the RED BRIGADES.

**MOROCCO** official name **Kingdom of Morocco**
A kingdom in North Africa, bounded to the south-west by WESTERN SAHARA; to the south-east and east

by Algeria; to the north by the Mediterranean Sea; and to the west by the Atlantic Ocean. From the 12c BC the northern coast was occupied by Phoenicians, Carthaginians and Romans. Arabs invaded in the 7c AD, and Europeans began to establish an interest in the region in the 19c. The Treaty of Fez in 1912 established Spanish Morocco (capital, Tétouan) and French Morocco (capital, Rabat), and the international zone of Tangier was created in 1923; the protectorates gained independence in 1956, and HASSAN II acceded as King of Morocco in 1961. Hassan died in 1999 and was succeeded by his son, Muhammad VI; since his accession, Morocco has been moving away from absolute monarchy. When Spain withdrew from the former Spanish Sahara (WESTERN SAHARA) in 1975, the territory came under the joint control of Morocco and Mauritania; in the face of conflict with the POLISARIO Front independence movement, Mauritania withdrew in 1979 and the area was annexed by Morocco. Moroccan sovereignty is not recognized by the UN, but peace talks are deadlocked and a proposed referendum on the territory's future, although agreed by both parties, has yet to take place.

## Morrill Land Grant Act (1862)
US educational legislation. The act (sponsored by Representative Justin Morrill of Vermont) provided for the sale of public lands to establish 'land-grant' colleges in every state. The majority of these were agricultural and technical colleges, many of which have grown into the state universities. The act was a major precedent for the provision of federal aid for education in the 20c.

## Morris, Robert (1734–1806)
US merchant and politician. He was born in England and went to America in 1747, where he made a fortune in merchant shipping. He emerged as an important Whig leader when he joined the CONTINENTAL CONGRESS (1775–8), and he signed the DECLARATION OF INDEPENDENCE (1776). During the AMERICAN REVOLUTION he was instrumental in raising money for George WASHINGTON's army, becoming known as the 'financier of the Revolution'. The leading organizer of America's first national commercial bank, the Bank of North America (1781), he later declined the position of first Secretary of the Treasury and became instead Senator for Pennsylvania (1789–95). Late in life he suffered bankruptcy after speculating in Western lands, and spent three years in a debtor's prison until his release was permitted by the first Bankruptcy Act (1800).

**Morrison of Lambeth, Herbert Stanley Morrison, 1st Baron** (1888–1965)
British politician. Largely self-educated, he helped to found the London LABOUR PARTY of which he became Secretary (1915). First elected an MP in 1923, he was Minister of Transport (1929–31), Minister of Supply (1940) and Home Secretary (1940–5). He served in the war cabinet from 1942, and became a powerful post-war figure, acting as Deputy Prime Minister (1945–51), but was defeated by GAITSKELL for the leadership of the Labour Party in 1955. He was made a life peer in 1959.

**Morton, James Douglas, 4th Earl of** (c.1525–1581)
Regent of Scotland (1572/8). Although a Protestant, he was made Lord High Chancellor by MARY, QUEEN OF SCOTS (1563), yet he was involved in the murders of RIZZIO (1566) and DARNLEY (1567), and played an important part in the overthrow of the Queen. He joined the hostile noble confederacy, leading its forces at Carberry Hill and Langside, and succeeded MORAY as regent for JAMES VI AND I. However, his high-handed treatment of the nobles and Presbyterian clergy caused his downfall (1581). He was arraigned for his part in Darnley's murder, and executed at Edinburgh.

**Morton, John** (c.1420–1500)
English statesman and cardinal. He practised as a lawyer, and adhered with great fidelity to HENRY VI, but after the Battle of TEWKESBURY made his peace with EDWARD IV, and became Master of the Rolls (1473) and Bishop of Ely (1479). RICHARD III imprisoned him (1483), but he escaped, and after the accession of HENRY VII was made Archbishop of Canterbury (1486), Chancellor (1487), and Cardinal (1493). ► ROSES, WARS OF THE

**Mosaddeq, Muhammad** (1880–1967)
Iranian politician. He held office in Iran in the 1920s, returned to politics in 1944, and directed his attack on the Anglo-Iranian Oil Co., which, by his Oil Nationalization Act of 1951 (in which year he became Prime Minister), he claimed to have expropriated. His government was overthrown by a royalist uprising in 1953, and he was imprisoned. He was released in 1956.

**Mosaic Theory of Ethnicity**
Canadian social theory. The concept emerged in the 1920s to describe the pluralism of Canadian society. The analogy facilitated the description of each racial group, its status and influence within the whole society as well as its cultural and institutional contributions to the nation. In 1965 John Porter suggested the refinement of a vertical mosaic, with status and prestige indicated by layers, so that some ethnic groups were heavily represented in the upper strata whilst others, without power, remained in the lower strata. He believed the idea of the mosaic (as opposed to that of the melting pot) impeded social mobility, and thus encouraged the persistence of conservative traits within Canadian society.

**Mościcki, Ignacy** (1867–1946)
Polish politician and scientist. Opposed to Tsarist rule as a young man, he spent many years in Switzerland, where he became a chemist. He later returned to Poland, where he was Professor of Chemistry at Lvov (1912–26). In 1926, as part of his coup d'état, Józef PIŁSUDSKI made him President of Poland, a respectable figure hiding a virtual dictatorship. In 1939 he fled to Romania and then retired to Switzerland, where he died.

**Moshoeshoe I** (c.1786–1870)
King of the southern Sotho people. He was the founder of the state that has survived as the independent Lesotho, surrounded by South Africa. Moshoeshoe was the son of a small chieftain who succeeded in creating a congeries of people to protect themselves from the marauding NGUNI flooding out of northern Natal in the diaspora known as the *Mfecane*. From his stronghold at Thaba Bosiu he was able to build his power and play off the rivalries of Boer and Briton in the 1840s and 1850s. He invited French Protestant missionaries to his kingdom and, although he himself was never baptized, he adapted some traditional customs to missionary demands. In turn he used the missionaries as his protectors and go-betweens. In 1868 he persuaded the British to annex his kingdom to avoid further encroachments and attacks from the Boers. After a brief period when Basutoland, as Lesotho was then known, was administered from the Cape, Moshoeshoe's state was placed directly under the British Colonial Office in 1880 and, like Swaziland, escaped incorporation in the white-dominated Union of South Africa in 1909.

**Moshoeshoe II**, originally **Constantine Bereng Seeiso** (1938–96)
King of Lesotho (1966/90 and 1995/6). Educated at Roma College, Ampleforth and Corpus Christi College, Oxford, he was installed as Paramount Chief of the Basotho in 1960 and then proclaimed King when Lesotho became independent in 1966. His political involvement resulted in his being twice placed under house arrest and in 1970 he spent eight months of exile in Holland. He returned on the understanding that he would behave as a constitutional monarch. He remained King after the military coup in Jan 1986, but was exiled (1990–2) to England and did not take up Major-General Lekhanya's invitation to return to Lesotho. In Nov 1990 his eldest son succeeded to the throne as King Letsie III, although Letsie abdicated in favour of his father who was restored to the throne in Jan 1995, a position he held until his death in a car crash.

**Mosley, Sir Oswald Ernald, 6th Baronet** (1896–1980)
British politician. He was successively a Conservative, Independent and Labour MP, and a member of the 1929 Labour government. He resigned from the LABOUR PARTY, and founded, first, the New Party (1931), and then, following a visit to Italy, the British Union of Fascists, of which he became leader, and which is remembered for its anti-Semitic violence in the East End of London and its support for HITLER. Detained under the Defence Regulations during WORLD WAR II, he founded another racialist party, the UNION MOVEMENT, in 1948. He died in Orsay, near Paris, where he mainly lived after the war. ► BLACKSHIRTS

**Mosquera, Tomás Cipriano de** (1798–1878)
Colombian politician. Born into a prominent colonial

family, he served under **BOLÍVAR** as a boy. A brigadier at 30, he was 'an unreliable friend and an implacable enemy'. Well-travelled and pragmatic, he was instrumental in repressing a revolt led by religious interests against constitutionalist measures in 1839–42. By the time of his presidency of New Granada (1845–9), he had begun to move to the conservative camp, favouring centralist rule, supported by his brother, the Archbishop of Bogotá, and the army. A beneficiary of increasing prosperity and international trade, he switched towards a conservative liberal view, becoming President of Colombia for a second time (July 1861). Architect of the anticlerical, liberal and ultra-federalist constitution of 1863, he manipulated a shifting alliance of Radicals, Liberals and Independents against the ever-present Conservatives. Elected to a further term in 1865, he assumed dictatorial powers, and was toppled and exiled in 1867.

**Motlana, Nthato Harrison** (1925– )
South African doctor and politician. Educated at Kilnerton High School and Fort Hare College where he came into contact with the **ANC** (African National Congress) Youth league, he qualified as a doctor at the University of the **WITWATERSRAND**. Involved in establishing a network of ANC branches on the Witwatersrand, he was banned in 1953 for five years. By the mid-1970s he had became a leading figure in Soweto and played a major role in the 1976 uprising, helping to establish the Soweto Committee of Ten, which developed into the Soweto Civil Association, of which he is chairman. One of the few leading political figures to have lived in the townships and retained the respect of ordinary citizens, he became an articulate spokesman for black interests in the 1980s while the ANC was still banned.

**Motoda Eifu** (1818–91)
Japanese Confucian scholar. As tutor to the **MEIJI EMPEROR**, his call for a return to traditional values during the 1880s represented a conservative backlash against the westernizing trends of the 1870s. Appointed Court Adviser in 1886 and a member of the Privy Council in 1888, Motoda helped draft the **IMPERIAL RESCRIPT ON EDUCATION** (30 Oct 1890), which emphasized the inculcation of patriotism and reverence for the emperor.

**Motoori Norinaga** (1730–1801)
Japanese scholar. He championed the superiority of Japan's ancient culture and beliefs as a reaction against the influence of rational Chinese thought. Condemning Japan's deference to Chinese civilization, Motoori reaffirmed **SHINTO** myths portraying Japan as the 'Land of the Gods' and highlighted the uniqueness of Japan's sacred imperial institution (an unbroken line of emperors descended from the gods) in contrast to the succession of dynasties that prevailed in China. Known as *Kokugaku* ('National Learning'), Motoori's ideas were to influence the imperial loyalist movement of the 19c that overthrew the **TOKUGAWA SHOGUNATE** and to provide the basis of ultra-nationalist ideology in the 1930s.

**Mott, Lucretia** (1793–1880)
US abolitionist and feminist. A Quaker, she became deeply involved in anti-**SLAVERY** agitation in the 1830s, helping to organize the Philadelphia Female Anti-Slavery Society (1833). She was one of the driving forces at the world's first **WOMEN'S RIGHTS** convention, held at Seneca Falls, New York, in 1848. ► **ABOLITIONISM; SENECA FALLS WOMEN'S RIGHTS CONVENTION**

**Mountain, The**
A group of Jacobin extremist Deputies in the French Convention, led by **ROBESPIERRE**, so-called because they sat on the highest tiers of seats in the chamber, where they overlooked their political opponents, the **GIRONDINS**, and the uncommitted majority who were known collectively as 'the Plain'. ► **CONVENTION, NATIONAL; FRENCH REVOLUTION; JACOBINS; PLAIN, THE**

**mountain men**
In the USA, fur-trappers and traders living in the frontier wilderness of the Rocky Mountains from the 1820s to the 1840s, when the drop in beaverskin prices forced them to leave. Two of the most famous were Jim Bridger (1804–81), director of the Rocky Mountain Fur Company, a scout and guide for exploring and surveying expeditions and the first white man to see the Great Salt Lake (1824), and Kit **CARSON**, an expert trapper and hunter who later served as a frontier guide, most notably for John **FRÉMONT**'s three western expeditions (1842, 1843, 1845). Carson's exploits made him a folk hero, and he was glorified in songs and stories.

**Mountbatten, Lord Louis Francis Albert Victor Nicholas, 1st Earl Mountbatten of Burma** (1900–79)
British Admiral of the Fleet and statesman. He was the younger son of Prince Louis of Battenberg (later Louis Mountbatten, Marquess of Milford Haven) and Princess Victoria of Hesse, the granddaughter of Queen **VICTORIA**. Having joined the Royal Navy in 1916, in **WORLD WAR II** he became chief of **COMBINED OPERATIONS COMMAND** (1942), and played a key role in preparations for **D-DAY**. In 1943 he was appointed Supreme Commander, South-East Asia, where he defeated the Japanese offensive into India (1944), and worked closely with **SLIM** to reconquer Burma (1945). He received the Japanese surrender at Singapore, and in 1947 was sworn in as last Viceroy of India prior to independence. Created an earl in 1947, he returned to the Admiralty, and became First Sea Lord (1954) and Chief of the Defence Staff (1959). Retiring in 1965, he remained in the public eye, and was assassinated by Irish terrorists while fishing near his summer home in the Irish Republic.

**Mounties (The Royal Canadian Mounted Police)**
The force was founded as the Royal North-West Mounted Police in 1873 by Lt Col George Arthur French who was the first commissioner, recruited mainly from the British Army and retaining its red jackets and pillbox hats. Organized on strictly military lines, the Mounties established tight control over the new territories as compared with law enforcement in the American West. Policing was only one of their many roles in the North West until 1953, when the Department of Northern Affairs took over most of their civic duties. In the other provinces the Mounties were amalgamated with the federal Dominion Police in 1920 and became the Royal Canadian Mounted

Police. In 1928 Saskatchewan became the first province to contract the RCMP to provide a police force, followed by Alberta and other provinces in the later decades. Ontario and Quebec have not followed their example.

## Moyne Commission (1940)

A royal commission of the British government set up after the **DISTURBANCES** to investigate the social and economic conditions prevailing in the British West Indies. Headed by the Lord Moyne, its members toured the British Caribbean colonies (1938–9) and its recommendations were made public in 1940, although because of its critical nature, the full report was not published until 1945. It attributed social discontent to the current appalling socio-economic conditions and recommended the creation of an imperially financed Colonial Development and Welfare Fund to encourage spending on health, education and housing projects. The Commission also supported the growth of trade unions, but was ambivalent towards constitutional progress.

## Moynihan, Daniel Patrick (1927–2003)

US politician. Educated at the City College of New York and Tufts University, he taught at Syracuse, Harvard, and the Massachusetts Institute of Technology. He served in the administrations of Presidents **JOHNSON** and **NIXON**, acquiring notoriety as the author of *The Negro Family: The Case for National Action* (1965). He became Ambassador to India (1973–4), and won a seat in the **SENATE** as a Democrat from New York in 1976. ► **DEMOCRATIC PARTY**

**MOZAMBIQUE** official name **People's Republic of Mozambique**

A republic in south-eastern Africa, bounded to the south by Swaziland; to the south and south-west by South Africa; to the west by Zimbabwe; to the north-west by Zambia and Malawi; to the north by Tanzania; and to the east by the Mozambique Channel and the Indian Ocean. The country was originally inhabited by Bantu peoples from the north in the 1–4c. By the late 15c the coast had been settled by Arab traders and discovered by Portuguese explorers. Administered as part of Portuguese India from 1751, Mozambique acquired separate colonial status as Portuguese

East Africa in the late 19c, and became an overseas province of Portugal in 1951. An independence movement formed in 1962, the *Frente de Libertação de Moçambique* (**FRELIMO**), which took up arms against colonial rule. Independence was gained in 1975 and Mozambique became a socialist one-party state. A brutal civil war erupted between the ruling party Frelimo and the opposition group **RENAMO** until in 1992 a peace agreement was signed which made Renamo a legitimate political party. A new constitution under a multiparty system was implemented in 1990, and in 1994 the first multiparty elections were won by Frelimo. In 1986 Mozambique's first President, Samora **MACHEL**, was killed in an air crash and was succeeded by Joaquim **CHISSANO**. Armando Guebuza became President following elections in Dec 2004. The long civil war, severe drought and devastating floods in 2000 and 2001 have left Mozambique one of the world's poorest countries.

## Mozarabs

The term, derived from Arabic, designating Christians who lived under Muslim rule in Spain. *Mozarabs* were given their own administration and their religion was tolerated, but they had to live in separate areas. Under later Muslim rulers in Spain, such as the **ALMORAVIDS** and especially the **ALMOHADS**, they were frequently persecuted. Toledo was regarded as their chief city. The term *mozarab* is also used of their culture, in particular their traditional church liturgy.

## MPLA (*Movimento Popular de Libertação de Angola*, 'Popular Movement for the Liberation of Angola')

Formed in 1975, under the leadership of Agostinho **NETO**, by the merger of several nationalist groups, the organization faced opposition from **UNITA** and the **FNLA** which could not be defused through negotiation, and civil war ensued. The Marxist-Leninist MPLA received support from Cuba and the Soviet Union, while UNITA was supported by South Africa and the USA, with the situation further complicated by the Angolan backing for the Namibian independence movement **SWAPO**. The MPLA abandoned its Marxist policies and ceased to be the sole political party in 1992, though it still won the majority of seats in the multiparty election in 1992. Despite UNITA's involvement in the political process since 1992, fighting has continued, and the MPLA has remained in power.

## MRP (*Mouvement républicain populaire*, 'Popular Republican Movement')

French political party, founded in 1944 by a group of Catholics, led by **BIDAULT**, who were active in the **RESISTANCE MOVEMENT**. It was heir to the tradition of Christian democracy that had found expression before **WORLD WAR II** in the *Parti démocrate populaire* ('Popular Democratic Party'), founded in 1924. It won nearly a quarter of the vote in 1945–6, and was one of the three pillars of the coalition government (Tripartism) of 1945–7. However, its support declined rapidly, being halved in the 1951 elections. It supported Charles de **GAULLE** in 1958, but was divided by his Algerian policy, as some of its leaders, notably Bidault, opposed Algerian independence. Other members of the MRP objected to de Gaulle's opposition to European integration, and it withdrew from the government in 1962. Its electoral support continued to decline, and it merged in a new political formation, the *Centre démocrate* ('Democratic Centre') in 1963.

## Mubarak, Hosni (1928–)
Egyptian politician. A pilot and flying instructor who rose to become Commander of the Egyptian Air Force, he was Vice-President under Anwar SADAT from 1975 until the latter's assassination in 1981. The only candidate for the presidency, Mubarak pledged to continue Sadat's domestic and international policies, including firm treatment of Muslim extremists and the peace process with Israel. During the GULF WAR, he was the Arab leader most critical of Saddam HUSSEIN, and reasserted his credentials with Israel by denouncing the Iraqi missile attacks on Haifa and Tel Aviv. In 1993, he was involved in the events leading to the signing of a peace accord between the Palestine Liberation Organization (PLO) and Israel.

## muckrakers
A derogatory term coined in 1906 by President Theodore ROOSEVELT for crusading journalists, authors and critics whose accounts of social evils were attracting widespread attention. Among the most important were Ida M Tarbell (1857–1944), Lincoln Steffens (1866–1936), Ray Stannard Baker (1870–1946) and Upton Sinclair (1878–1968).

## Mudejars
The MOORS remaining, mostly as peasants or craftsmen, in regions of medieval Spain reconquered for Christianity. Many were expelled during the final stages of RECONQUEST in the 15c.

## Mudros Armistice (30 Oct 1918)
The armistice which took the Ottomans out of WORLD WAR I, signed at Mudros, a harbour on the Aegean island of Lemnos. The principal participants were Huseyn Rauf Bey, the Ottoman Navy Minister, and Vice-Admiral Calthorpe, commander of the British forces in the Aegean, representing the Entente Powers. The armistice provided for an immediate end to hostilities, demobilization of the Ottoman land forces, surrender of the Ottoman fleet, the withdrawal of Ottoman troops from certain specified territories, and the breaking of all contact with the Austro-Hungarian and German empires. This break in relations was to be accompanied by the expulsion of all nationals of the two central Powers. The agreement also covered the opening of the DARDANELLES and Bosphorus, the stationing of appropriate personnel in strategic positions and access to all Ottoman naval and military facilities. Despite the theoretically provisional nature of the armistice, the British handling of it left suspicions of British intent in the minds of both the French and the Turks. Calthorpe had been ordered by the British government to exclude the French from the talks, and the British approach to enforcing the terms of the armistice, particularly regarding demobilization and the surrender of important positions, led the Turks to suspect that the British intention was no less than a piecemeal dismemberment of what remained of the OTTOMAN EMPIRE in Thrace and Anatolia. Although the Nationalists were able successfully to oppose some of the armistice provisions, the British handling of

## MUGHAL DYNASTY

| Regnal Dates | Name |
| --- | --- |
| 1526/30 | Babur |
| 1530/56 | Humayun |
| 1556/1605 | Akbar I, the Great |
| 1605/27 | Jahangir |
| 1627/58 | Shah Jahan |
| 1658/1707 | Aurangzeb (Alamgir) |
| 1707/12 | Bahadur Shah I (Shah Alam I) |
| 1712/13 | Jahandar Shah |
| 1713/19 | Farrukh-siyar |
| 1719 | Rafi-ud-Darajat |
| 1719 | Rafi-ud-Daulat |
| 1719 | Neku-siyar |
| 1719 | Ibrahim |
| 1719/48 | Muhammad Shah |
| 1748/54 | Ahmad Shah |
| 1754/9 | Alamgir II |
| 1759/1806 | Shah Alam II |
| 1806/37 | Akbar II |
| 1837/57 | Bahadur Shah II |

the matter did little for future relations between the two countries.

## Mugabe, Robert Gabriel (1924–)
Zimbabwean nationalist leader and politician. Educated in Catholic missions schools and Fort Hare College, he was a teacher successively in Southern Rhodesia, Northern Rhodesia and Ghana before returning to Southern Rhodesia in 1960 as Publicity Secretary to the National Democratic Party. He was Deputy Secretary-General of ZAPU in 1961 before being detained and then imprisoned, but co-founded ZANU in 1963. He was detained again (1964–74) during which period he replaced Ndabaningi SITHOLE as President of ZANU and qualified as a lawyer. Released in 1974, he went to Mozambique to oversee the guerrilla war against the white regime. United uncomfortably with Joshua NKOMO's ZAPU in the PATRIOTIC FRONT to press for black majority rule, Mugabe essentially retained his independence and, to the surprise of many, led ZANU (PF), as the combined party was called, to a decisive victory in 1980; hence, he became Prime Minister in the first government of independent Zimbabwe. In 1987 he persuaded parliament to agree to combine the roles of head of state and head of government, and he became the country's first Executive President. In 1988 ZANU and ZAPU merged to make Zimbabwe effectively a one-party state, under Mugabe's leadership. Criticized for an increasingly autocratic style of leadership, he was re-elected in 1996 and again in 2002 in elections whose integrity was questioned. His support for the illegal appropriation of white farmers' lands, which began in 2000, counteracted the Supreme Court's attempts to uphold the rule of law. The appropriations caused an agricultural collapse that left Zimbabwe in need of international food aid.

## Mughal Empire
An important Indian Muslim state (1526–1857), founded by BABUR. It temporarily declined under HUMAYUN (1530–40), who lost control to the Afghan chieftain, Sher Shah (1540–5). His son, AKBAR THE GREAT, defeated the Afghan challenge at PANIPAT (1556) and extended the empire to include territory

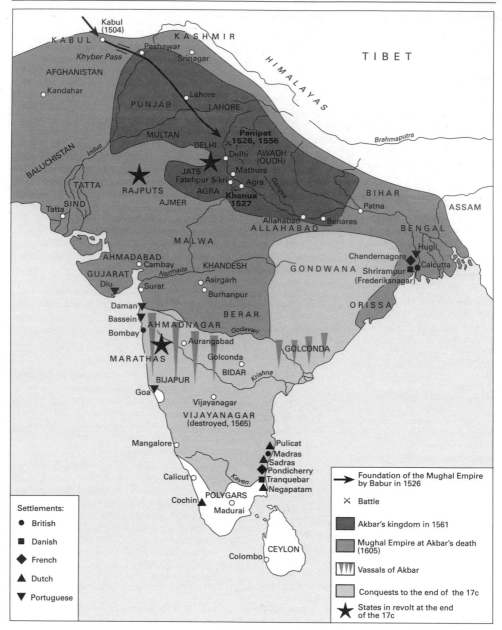

Foundation of the Mughal Empire by Babur in 1526

×  Battle

Akbar's kingdom in 1561

Mughal Empire at Akbar's death (1605)

Vassals of Akbar

Conquests to the end of the 17c

★ States in revolt at the end of the 17c

Settlements:
● British
■ Danish
◆ French
▲ Dutch
▼ Portuguese

**Mughal Empire**

between Afghanistan and Deccan. This was a period of religious freedom, in which a policy of conciliation was pursued with the Rajput states. Akbar was succeeded by **JAHANGIR** (1605–27) and **SHAH JAHAN** (1627–58). Its last great emperor was **AURANGZEB** (1658–1707), who extended the limits of the empire further south. However, religious bigotry alienated non-Muslim supporters and undermined the empire's unity. The empire disintegrated under Maratha and British pressure. By the mid-18c it ruled only a small area around Delhi, but its administrative forms and culture continued to have great influence. Its last emperor, Bahadur Shah II (1837–57) was exiled by the British to Rangoon after the 1857–8 **INDIAN UP-RISING**. ➤ **MARATHA KINGDOM**; *See map*

**mugwump**

US political epithet used to describe an Independent Republican in the US election of 1884 who, preferring reform to party discipline (particularly on the question of ending the **SPOILS SYSTEM**), supported the Democrat Grover **CLEVELAND**, rather than the Republican James **BLAINE**. The name is said to derive from an Algonquian word meaning 'chief'. ➤ **REPUBLICAN PARTY**

**Muhammad, Elijah** (1897–1975)

US black leader. Born Elijah Poole, he moved to Detroit from Georgia in 1923, where eight years later he came into contact with Wali Farad, the founder of the **BLACK MUSLIMS**. In 1934 Muhammad became the leader of the movement as 'Messenger of Allah'. During

**WORLD WAR II** he was arrested and imprisoned for discouraging his followers from registering for the **DRAFT**. After his release he initiated a period of fast expansion for the Black Muslims. ➤ **MALCOLM X**

## Muhammad, Murtala Ramal (1937–76)
Nigerian soldier. A Muslim Hausa from Northern Nigeria, he trained at Sandhurst and the Royal School of Signals before returning to Nigeria and then serving in the **UN** Congo operations in 1960. He commanded the Nigerian 2nd Battalion at the start of the **BIAFRAN WAR** and was made federal Commissioner of Communications in 1974. When General **GOWON** was deposed in 1975, he became head of state, but he was himself assassinated in an unsuccessful uprising on 13 Feb 1976.

## Muhammad 'Ali (c.1769–1849)
Viceroy of Egypt (1805/48). An Albanian military officer, he was sent to Egypt with a Turkish–Albanian force on the French invasion in 1798. After the French left, he supported the Egyptian rulers in their struggles with the **MAMLUKS**, and became the chief power in Egypt (1805). He formed a regular army, improved irrigation, and also introduced elements of European civilization. He extended Egyptian territory, routing the Ottoman army at Koniya (1832), but the Quadruple Alliance of 1840 compelled him to limit his ambition to Egypt. In 1848 he became insane, and was succeeded by his adopted son, Ibrahim.

## Muhammadan Educational Association
The body founded by Sir Sayyid **AHMAD KHAN** to disseminate elements of European knowledge to Indian Muslims. In 1872 Khan was instrumental in the establishment of a select committee which discussed the educational needs of the various classes within Muslim society. The Committee's report led to the concept of a school that was intended to serve all Muslims and cut across sectarian differences. A number of Hindus donated to his cause, and after 1873 Hindus were expected to participate in the student body. In June 1875 the Muhammadan Anglo-Oriental College (now Aligarh Muslim University) was opened. The institution enrolled students at the elementary level and adopted the standard government curriculum under an English headmaster within a carefully constructed Islamic environment. Between 1882 and 1902 the College sent up 220 Muslim graduates. Aligarh élites formed a very important section of the Muslim intelligentsia and played a crucial role in the formation of the **MUSLIM LEAGUE**.

## Muhammad bin Tughlaq (c.1290–1351)
Sultan of Delhi (1325/51). The son of Ghiyas-ud-Din Tughlaq, he is best remembered as a ruler who undertook a number of bold experiments. He was a scholar in his own right and spent a lot of time in theological and philosophical debates. He was a secular ruler and was accused by many orthodox theologians of being a 'rationalist', ie someone unwilling to accept religious beliefs as a matter of faith. Tughlaq had a reputation of being hasty and impatient and many of his experiments failed. The best-known of his misadventures was his transfer of the capital from Delhi to Deogiri. Deogiri had been a base for the expansion of Muslim rule in south India. He wanted to make Deogiri a second capital so that he might be able to control southern India better, and so he ordered many of the officers and leading men, including many Sufi saints, to shift to Deogiri, which he renamed Daulatabad. The transfer of the capital, however, proved traumatic for many involved and in the end the effort failed. Another failed experiment was the introduction of token currency.

## Muhammad Ghuri (d.1206)
Conqueror of North India. Assigned Ghazni by his elder brother, Ghiyas-ud-Din, after its capture in 1173, Muhammad used it as a base for expansion into India, starting with a successful attack on Multan in 1175–6 and establishing himself in the Punjab in 1186. Conflicts with various Rajput dynasties culminated in his victory at the second Battle of Tarain in 1192, giving him control of all north India as far as Delhi; after the battle, Muhammad returned to Khurasan, leaving the conduct of the campaign to **QUTB-UD-DIN AIBAK**, who secured all north India, except Gujarat and Rajasthan, by 1203.

## Muhammad Shah (1702–48)
Mughal ruler (1719/48). During his ineffectual rule, the **MUGHAL EMPIRE** continued to decline (with the Marathas making large gains) and Delhi was sacked by Nadir Shah in 1739, although **AHMAD SHAH DURRANI** was repelled in 1748.

## Mühlberg, Battle of (1547)
The battle at which the Duke of **ALBA** defeated the forces of the **SCHMALKALDIC LEAGUE**. The victory was the highwater mark of the power of Emperor **CHARLES V.**

## Muiscas ➤ **PRE-COLUMBIAN CIVILIZATIONS**

## Mujahidin or Mujahideen
Muslim guerrillas (literally, 'holy warriors') who resisted the Soviet occupation of Afghanistan after the invasion (Dec 1979). Based in Iran and Pakistan, they formed various armed bands united by their common aim of defeating the invaders, and the conflict was proclaimed a **JIHAD** ('holy war'). The Russians withdrew from Afghanistan in 1989, and the Mujahidin subsequently experienced much internal dissent and conflict over their role in the country's future.

## Mujibur Rahman, known as Sheikh Mujib (1920–75)
Bangladesh politician. Born in Tungipara, into a landowning family, he was educated in Calcutta and Dhaka University, from which he was expelled for political activities. In 1949 he co-founded the **AWAMI LEAGUE**, campaigning for autonomy for East Pakistan (Bangladesh), became its leader in 1953, and led it to electoral victory in 1970. In 1972, after the civil war between East and West Pakistan, he became Prime Minister of newly independent Bangladesh. He introduced a socialist economic programme but became increasingly intolerant of opposition, establishing a one-party state. In Aug 1975 he and his wife were assassinated in a military coup. ➤ **WAJED, HASINA**

## Mukhitdinov, Nuritdin Akramovich (1917– )
Soldier and apparatchik, the first central Asian to achieve prominence in Soviet politics. Having fought during **WORLD WAR II**, he rose to be First Secretary of the Communist Party in Uzbekistan in 1955. Nikita **KHRUSHCHEV** then made him a candidate member of the **POLITBURO** in 1956 and a full member in 1957,

essentially to boost his own support, but also to secure backing from beyond the Slav states. But he failed to measure up and was dismissed in 1961.

**Mukhopadhyay, Ashutosh** (1864–1924)
Indian legal figure. After a brilliant academic career, he obtained his doctorate in law in 1894. Made a judge in the Calcutta High Court in 1904, he was a member of the Legislative Council and the Vice-Chancellor of Calcutta University for ten years. He was the President of the Asiatic Society of Bengal, and a chairman and trustee of the Indian Museum and the Council of Imperial (now National) Library.

**Muldoon, Sir Robert David** (1921–92)
New Zealand politician. He served as an infantryman in WORLD WAR II before becoming an accountant. He was elected to parliament in 1960 as an MP for the New Zealand National Party, was Minister of Finance (1967–72) and briefly Prime Minister (1972) when the government was defeated. He became Party Leader and Leader of the Opposition (1974) and was Prime Minister (1975–84). He resigned the party leadership in 1984, and became Shadow Foreign Affairs spokesman (1986–92).

**Mulroney, (Martin) Brian** (1939–)
Canadian politician. The son of an Irish immigrant, he studied law and then practised as a labour lawyer in Montreal, while becoming increasingly active in the Progressive Conservative Party. In 1976 he failed to wrest the party leadership from Joe CLARK and returned to business as President of a US-owned iron-ore company. In 1983 he replaced Clark and in 1984 became Prime Minister, with a landslide victory over the Liberals. He initiated a number of radical measures, including the MEECH LAKE ACCORD, settling disputes between the provinces and the centre, and negotiated the NAFTA free-trade agreement with the USA. Decisively re-elected in 1988, he resigned abruptly from office in 1993. ► CONSTITUTION ACT OF 1982

**Multatuli** ► DEKKER, EDUARD DOUWES

**Munich Agreement** (29 Sep 1938)
One of the more infamous acts in history that has come to stand for a betrayal for the worst of reasons and with the worst of consequences. After a long period of pressurizing Czechoslovakia to make whatever concessions its Sudeten German subjects demanded, the Prime Ministers of Britain and France, CHAMBER-LAIN and DALADIER, met the two fascist dictators of Italy and Germany, MUSSOLINI and HITLER, and, in the absence of BENEŠ, they agreed to the country's virtual dismemberment, allegedly in the interest of European peace. But the peace Chamberlain and Daladier bought at the price of Czechoslovakia only encouraged Hitler and Mussolini and, a year later, they had to go to war in worse circumstances for the sake of Poland.

**Munich Putsch** (1923)
The abortive attempt by HITLER to overthrow the state government of Bavaria, as a prelude to a march on Berlin and the establishment of a Nazi regime in Germany. It was supported by General LUDENDORFF, but badly planned, and it disintegrated in the face of firm Bavarian police action. Hitler was tried for treason, and sentenced to five years' imprisonment. ► NAZI PARTY

**Muñoz Marín, Luis** (1898–1989)
Puerto Rican politician and architect of the modern state. Son of the nationalist Muñoz Rivera, and educated in the USA, he took up the cause of the peasant in 1938 and founded the Popular Democratic Party that took power in that year. Muñoz, with the aid of the last US Governor, Guy Rexford Tugwell, introduced social reforms and industrialization and was the creator of 'Operation Bootstrap'. He was elected Governor himself in 1948 and held the post until his retirement (1960). Previously a supporter of Puerto Rican independence, in 1950 he devised the status of commonwealth (associated free statehood) for the island in its relationship with the USA.

**Munro, Sir Thomas** (1761–1827)
British colonial administrator. A British EAST INDIA COMPANY official of humble Scottish origins, he contributed significantly to early British knowledge of, and authority over, its subject population in India. He was associated with the introduction, in the early 19c, of the Ryotwari system of land revenue collection, which advocated settlement direct with the cultivator. As with many of his other innovations, Ryotwari grew out of Munro's understanding of Indian traditions and problems acquired through many years of service both as a soldier and administrator. During his governorship of Madras, the Ryotwari system became a rule, although it only acquired its modern methodical form after 1885.

**Münster, Capture of** (1535)
A city in north-western Germany originally called Mimigernaford. The name was changed to Münster in 1068. It was chartered in 1137 and later joined the HANSEATIC LEAGUE. It was seized by Anabaptist radicals in 1534 who began a programme of change meant to make the city the 'New Jerusalem'. When it was obvious that a combined Catholic–Protestant army was to move against Münster, many ANABAPTISTS rallied to the city. The city was taken in 1535 and three of its leaders (including Jan BOKELSON) were executed (1536). The city was later the site of the negotiations which produced the Peace of WESTPHALIA (1645–8).

**Münster, Treaty of** (30 Jan 1648)
The peace treaty which brought to an end the EIGHTY YEARS' WAR between the Dutch Republic and Spain, and part of the Peace of WESTPHALIA. In the treaty Spain recognized the sovereign independence of the Dutch Republic of the UNITED PROVINCES OF THE NETHERLANDS; both sides recognized each other's current possessions in Europe and the colonies, the Dutch were permitted to close the Scheldt River to trade, and both countries granted freedom of conscience to each other's citizens. It represented the victory of the Dutch Republic, and the final split between the northern and southern Netherlands.

**Müntzer, Thomas** (c.1489–1525)
German preacher and Anabaptist. He studied theology, and in 1520 began to preach at Zwickau, but his socialism and mystical doctrines soon brought him into conflict with the authorities. In 1525 he was

elected pastor of the **ANABAPTISTS** of Mülhausen, where his communistic ideas soon aroused the whole country. A leader of the **PEASANTS' WAR** (1524–5), he was captured at the Battle of Frankenhausen, and executed at Mülhausen.

## muqti

A governor under the **DELHI SULTANATE** (1200–1526). The sultanate was divided into provinces, each under a *muqti*, who was responsible for the administration of the province and the collection of revenue from those peasants who paid their tax directly to the state. From the share that he received, the muqti was required to maintain a quota of horses and foot soldiers which were at the sultan's disposal. The muqti's appointment was not permanent, and he could be transferred at any time to another part of the kingdom.

## Murad I (c.1326–1389)

Ottoman Sultan (1360/89). The son of **ORHAN**, his main achievement lay in his being the first of the Ottomans to carry Ottoman arms into Europe. Details of his campaigns are difficult to disentangle reliably from the sources, but in broad outline western Thrace was conquered and raids were mounted into western Bulgaria. Murad established Adrianople (Edirne) as the European capital of the Ottomans (1366) and the Byzantine Emperor John V Palaeologus submitted to him as a vassal. There is little doubt that the Ottomans derived advantage from the Byzantine–Bulgar animosities at this time. Later (c.1371) the Turks checked a Serbian advance and were able, as a result, to establish themselves in Macedonia. Further conquests followed, with Murad's troops taking Sofya and Niš in the mid-1380s, thereby securing a firm foothold for the Ottomans in the Balkans. Murad also campaigned in Anatolia, and his leniency there provoked friction amongst the Serbs in his army. It is suggested that this in some way contributed to the general growth in feeling against the Turks among the Serbs as a whole, which led to the defeat (1388) of a Turkish force at Pločnik by a combined force of Serbs and Bosnians. This defeat caused Murad himself to move against the Serbs, and the Battle of **KOSOVO** in 1389 cost Murad his life, although the Ottoman forces emerged victorious under the leadership of **BAYEZID I**, Murad's successor. Murad's reign represents the transition in the role of the Ottoman ruler from being one of a group of warring princelings in Asia Minor to being the ruler of a state of a size and consequence requiring complexities of government and administration not hitherto associated with the minor Turkish dynasties of Anatolia.

## Murad II (c.1401–1451)

Ottoman Sultan (1421/44 and 1446/51). The son of **MEHMED I**, he was faced initially with two pretenders supported by the Byzantine Emperor **MANUEL II PALAEOLOGUS**. Having dealt with both, he began the Siege of **CONSTANTINOPLE** (1422). He was, however, again beset by the problem of rivals, who caused him to raise the siege, and it was not until 1425 that Murad II was safely ensconced upon his throne. The death of Manuel (1424) and the accession of John VIII Palaeologus enabled Murad to negotiate a peace and the Ottomans were able once again to turn their attention to problems on their frontiers. They captured Thessalonika (1430) and took fortresses in Epirus and Albania, and mounted raids into Serbia and, in 1438, into Hungary. In 1440 they unsuccessfully laid siege to Belgrade. A reaction, represented by a crusading army under János **HUNYADI**, resulted in defeat for the Turks, but Murad was able to conclude a peace in 1444 which effectively represented a recognition of the *status quo ante* as far as the geographical extent of Ottoman political influence was concerned. The brief period (1444–6) following Murad's abdication in favour of his son, **MEHMED II, THE CONQUEROR**, ended with Hungarian aggression in contravention of the peace treaty. The remaining years of Murad's reign were spent largely in campaigns in the Balkans. Despite the necessity of warlike dispositions to consolidate and maintain his rule, his policies were essentially of a peaceful nature, and he is the first of the Ottoman rulers to have maintained a court where letters, the arts, poetry and science flourished.

## Murad III (1546–95)

Ottoman Sultan (1574/95). He appears to have had no great taste for politics and the affairs of state, preferring to trust his viziers and only becoming involved when rivalries between groups threatened to get out of hand. Factions in the palace were responsible for war with Safavid Persia (1578–90) and the start of the 'Long War' (1593–1606) between the Ottomans and the Habsburgs. Foreign policy was also under the control of viziers and, at times, a harem clique; there were contacts with Venice, France, and even Queen **ELIZABETH I** of England. Murad is remembered as a generous sultan, who was particularly fond of his harem. A cultivated ruler, he both patronized and involved himself in letters and the arts, and under his rule architecture flourished, notable among his architects being the great Sinan.

## Murad IV (c.1611–1640)

Ottoman Sultan (1623/40). Until 1632, he was under the influence of those who had engineered his preferment and the Ottoman state itself was perceived (correctly) as weak by its enemies, who included the Safavid Shah **ABBAS I, THE GREAT** (d.1629), who took Baghdad and Iraq, except for Mosul and Basra. It was, however, uprisings among the soldiery and divisions among the rebellious troops that gave Murad the chance to assert his authority. This he did ruthlessly by hunting down all rebels and having them executed. Discipline was restored by 1635, corruption (which had been rife) eradicated, and Murad's rule was enforced by a network of informers who served to alert the Sultan to any impending problems. His major achievement in foreign affairs was to bring to a close the hostilities with Safavid Persia, which had lasted for well over a century, by creating the conditions for the signature of a peace treaty between the two countries (1639). Iraq was thenceforward to be in the Ottoman sphere of influence, with Erevan and parts of the Caucasus remaining under Safavid control. By the time of his death, Murad had, in eight years, successfully returned the **OTTOMAN EMPIRE** from a state of enfeebling anarchy to some semblance of stability and its former glory.

## Murat, Joachim (1767–1815)

French soldier and King of Naples (1808/15). Having

# *Music*

*Art & Literature*

Musical instruments are among the oldest artefacts. In fact, it is difficult to imagine a human society, however primitive, in which the creation of rhythmic or melodious sounds had no part. All societies have evolved their own kind of music, and all civilizations have developed music as an art form, formalizing and sophisticating it and thus generally creating a distinction – but not usually an unbridgeable gulf – between the music of court, ceremony and religious ritual, and that of the common people.

### Mesopotamia to Rome

The earliest representations of music-making as part of high culture are found in relics of the Sumerian civilization dating from around 3000 BC. The principal instruments seem to have been the harp and lyre, simple percussion instruments, pipes and possibly trumpets. Very similar instruments are depicted in ancient Egyptian paintings and variants of them still form the basis of music-making in ancient Greece. What the West borrowed from ancient Greece – as in so many other spheres – was a systematization, a theory.

Pythagoras is generally credited with establishing the mathematical bases of music. The Greeks evolved a method of tuning the lyre to give perfect intervals and tuning it to different 'modes': scales or sequences with different starting notes and a different ordering of tones and semitones that give the melodies produced in them a particular musical and, by extension, emotional quality. They were also assumed to exercise a particular effect on the listener.

Like all other early civilizations, the Greeks used music in religious ceremonies. They also used it in the performance of plays, and considered the study of music an essential element in the development of the mind, debating its ethical effects and social usefulness. Pythagoras and his followers went further and speculated that the cosmos as a whole could be understood as being governed by mathematical and musical relationships – a sort of religion of numbers – forming a perfect and literally harmonious whole.

From the Etruscans the Romans seem to have adopted a particular interest in and skill with wind instruments. Perhaps the main contribution of the Roman period to musical history lies in the development of a greater array of brass instruments, trumpets and tubas used for military purposes and often at funerals, and in the invention of the organ. Hydraulic organs – the air for the pipes being compressed by a weight of water – were in use by at least 90 BC. An organ with a keyboard (as opposed to a set of slides to admit air to the pipes) is mentioned in a text of the 1c AD, and the organ is known to have been played as an accompaniment to gladiatorial contests and in the theatre during imperial times.

### The Eastern musical tradition

Ancient Chinese and Indian writers shared with the Greeks a belief in the transcendental significance and power of music. Confucius (551–479 BC) opposed the use of music exclusively for entertainment on the grounds that its proper use was to dispel the passions and contribute to the general harmony of the universe. Consequently, though music was in favour with most Chinese dynasties – under the Zhou (Chou) Dynasty (c.1122–256 BC) it was one of the four subjects set to be studied by the sons of the nobility; Ming Ti, one of the Han emperors (AD 58–75), had three court orchestras comprising 829 musicians; and the Tang emperor Tang Tai-tsung had 10 comprising 1,400 musicians – it was denounced as an idle pastime under the Qin (Ch'in) Dynasty (221–206 BC) and almost all musical instruments, books and manuscripts were ordered to be destroyed. Most Chinese music is based on a five-tone scale. Among the important early instruments in China were flutes, panpipes, the *sheng*, a type of mouth organ, and various types of percussion instruments, with a special place reserved for the *qin* or long zither, an instrument requiring great subtlety and refinement in performance, and the favoured instrument of scholar musicians. Music has always played a very important role in Chinese drama; the best-known style in the West, Peking Opera, is a late one which first developed in the late 18c and early 19c.

Indian classical music, like Indian classical drama, can trace its origins back to a very early Sanskrit theoretical treatise called the *Natyasastra*. The Muslim invasions of the 15c resulted in a split between northern and southern traditions.

---

enlisted in the cavalry on the eve of the Revolution, he was promoted to general during **NAPOLEON I**'s Egyptian campaign of 1799. He helped the latter become First Consul and subsequently married his sister, Caroline. In 1808 he replaced Napoleon's brother, Joseph, as King of Naples, where he introduced a number of reforms. He commanded Napoleon's cavalry during the 1812 invasion of Russia but resigned his commission in 1812 and returned to Naples. After Napoleon's defeat at **LEIPZIG** (1813), Murat sought to keep his throne by a treaty with the Austrians, but when Napoleon escaped from Elba, Murat rallied to his cause, hoping to conquer the whole of Italy. Defeated by the Austrians at Tolentino (3 May 1815), he fled to France and then Corsica; in Sep 1815 he sailed for Calabria, intending to reclaim his old kingdom, but was captured and executed by the troops of **FERDINAND I**.

**Muraviev-Amursky, Nikolai Nikolaevich, Count** (1809–81)
Russian politician. Appointed Governor-General of Siberia in 1847 by **NICHOLAS I**, he was strongly supported by him and latterly by **ALEXANDER II** in his determined efforts to explore and then control the Amur River, formally under Chinese rule. By 1859 he was in an unassailable position, and it was left to the diplomats to secure the territory from China by the Treaty of **BEIJING** in 1860. Vladivostok became Russia's open declaration of Pacific ambition.

**Murray, Sir James** (1721–94)
British soldier and administrator. Military commander in Canada after the death of General James **WOLFE**, he was responsible for the application of the 1763 Proclamation that excluded Catholics from holding public office. It was impossible for the very few Protestants to supply an Assembly, and it was

Both are monophonic (they consist of an unharmonized melody) and both are based on *ragas*: basic sequences of notes, deriving from scales or modes, on which the performer improvises with greater or less freedom. Indian music is usually performed by a melody instrument, the voice, the sitar or a similar stringed instrument, together with a number of instruments providing a rhythmic accompaniment or a drone.

The ancient Shinto religion of Japan had and still retains a special 'god music' (*kagura*) to praise and entertain the gods. The court music of Japan (*gagaku*) was heavily influenced by Chinese and Korean music in the 5–10c. It was based on a five-tone scale and usually performed by orchestras consisting of woodwind, stringed and percussion instruments. For chamber music and solo performance the *koto*, a 13-stringed zither, and the *samisen*, a flat-backed lute, were the instruments of choice. A musical accompaniment is also an essential part of the best-known forms of traditional Japanese theatre, *Noh* and *Kabuki*.

The ancient gong and drum ensembles of Indonesia, of which the best known are the *gamelan* orchestras of Java and Bali, have their origins in religious rituals, and were originally played to honour the ancestors and ensure good harvests. Like all the music of the East it has a theoretical underlay and a highly developed performance practice.

### Jewish, Christian and Islamic music

Psalm 150, which exhorts the people to praise the Lord with the sound of the trumpet, the psaltery and harp, the timbrel and dance, with stringed instruments and organs, and with loud and high-sounding cymbals, seems to conjure up the splendour and exuberance of the music accompanying not only ancient Hebrew religious ritual, but the rituals of other faiths. The chanting of sacred texts by specially trained musicians was a feature of Jewish temple worship from at least the 5c BC. The tradition of chanting liturgical texts and singing hymns was adopted and developed by the early Christian Church. Gregorian chant, the traditional monophonic form of chanting used for the offices of the Western Church and still heard in monasteries and churches to the present day, evolved from the time of Gregory I, the Great, who was pope from 590 to 604, though Gregory's role in instituting it, let alone devising it, is disputed. The Roman model of chant gradually spread across Europe by oral transmission; the first indications of written musical notation do not reappear until the middle of the 9c.

Early followers of Muhammad claimed that he had regarded music as a 'forbidden pleasure' and secular music was for a time banned. Although the chanting of prayers and hymns was practised, this was not considered to be 'music' as such. From the late 7c onwards, however, music began to flourish, heavily influenced by Persian and Byzantine practice, at the courts of the Umayyad and 'Abassid caliphs. The classic form of Arab music, based around the tuning of the two-stringed Persian lute in fourths, developed in the 9–10c.

### Musical notation

Alphabetical notation – the use of letters of the alphabet to denote musical notes – was used in ancient Greece and elsewhere. The earliest form of notation in Christian music consisted of *neumes*: handwritten marks that appear in Byzantine texts from the 8c, and indicate rises or falls in pitch, ultimately deriving from signs indicating how written texts were to be read aloud. Neumes appear in Western texts from the 9c and gradually began to indicate duration as well as rise and fall. A staff line was added, followed by additional lines, until by about 1200 the familiar five-line stave had evolved. The development of the stave meant that pitch could be indicated accurately; the next step was to develop different shapes to indicate different note lengths. This occurred during the 13c. Time signatures first appeared in France in the 14c. By the middle of the 15c, when white notes (notes with unfilled heads) were added to black notes, something akin to modern notation was already in existence. The key signature evolved as a result of the fundamental change that took place in Western music around the beginning of the 17c in which modes, deriving originally from Greek music, were replaced by diatonic scales. By this time music was being printed and the standardization of notation proceeded apace. From the 18c instructions as to the speed and manner of performance began to be added (usually in Italian), becoming much more elaborate in the 19c. The standard form of notation thus evolved persisted throughout the 20c, although both jazz performers and some composers of modern classical music have found the system too restrictive.

### The Western classical tradition

There is nothing else in world music to compare with the 1,000-year and more development of Western classical music

---

also dangerous to retain the judiciary within the control of such a small number. Murray, therefore, had to make adjustments in order to establish a stable government. Already on bad terms with the English-speaking merchants (he thought them subversive, while they disliked military rule), Murray modified the proclamation to allow Catholics to sit on juries and to practise law, and introduced French legal customs into the judicial system. These concessions, as well as the lack of *habeas corpus*, angered the English-speaking merchants, who petitioned London for his replacement. In 1766 he was recalled, although the QUEBEC ACT later adopted many of his administrative arrangements, and was one of the factors which prevented the colony from joining the AMERICAN REVOLUTION.

### Muscovy Company

An English trading company granted a charter in 1554 allowing it to monopolize trade between England and Russia. In 1568 Tsar IVAN IV, THE TERRIBLE allowed the company to conduct trade with the Orient via the River Volga. Political intrigues led to the expulsion of the company's agents from Russia in 1649, after which it ceased to exist.

### Museveni, Yoweri Kaguta (1944– )

Ugandan revolutionary leader and politician. A graduate of Dar es Salaam University, he was Assistant Secretary for Research in President OBOTE's office until Idi AMIN's coup of 1971. He returned to Dar es Salaam as an exile and headed the Front for National Salvation against Amin while teaching at the Cooperative College, Moshi. He led the attack on Mbarar, with Tanzanian troops, and participated at the forefront of the fighting that drove Amin from power. Museveni became Minister of Defence in the governments of Yusuf Lulu and Godfrey Binaisa

from, for example, the simple plainsong setting of the Latin hymn *Veni Creator Spiritus* ('Come, Creator spirit') to its setting in the first movement of Gustav Mahler's *Eighth Symphony* (1907). This is scored for such colossal vocal and orchestral forces that it is frequently known by the nickname 'Symphony of a Thousand'. From the 16c to the latter part of the 18c, the centre and seedbed of European musical life was Italy, where opera was invented around the beginning of the 17c. During the lifetime of Mozart (1756–91) the centre shifted to the German-speaking countries, with Vienna having the best claim to be the musical capital of the Western world during the fabulous century and a half which saw the flourishing of the genius Mozart himself, as well as Haydn, Beethoven, Schubert, Brahms, Wagner and Mahler, and the beginnings of the 20c break with the tonal tradition in the work of Schoenberg, Berg and Webern. Though Italy and Germany were the centres of excellence, so to speak, musical culture flourished and great music was written in almost all the countries of Europe.

Over the centuries musical instruments have become continually more powerful in tone, more versatile and more varied, so that by the end of the 20c it was possible to argue the need for 'authentic' performances on original instruments of the music of Brahms (1833–97), let alone that of J S Bach (1685–1750), the supreme genius of the Baroque era, Claudio Monteverdi (1567–1643), the first great composer of Italian opera, or earlier masters. Until the 18c music tended to be heard in a religious, ceremonial or theatrical context, or enjoyed privately. From the 18c the public concert came into being, having a tremendous effect on the type of music written. Up to the time of Mozart, a group of performers would usually be directed by a soloist or one of the leading instrumental players. From the time of Beethoven, a conductor was usually needed to keep the ensemble together. Individual performers, for example the Italian opera singers employed by Handel (1685–1759), had always enjoyed considerable fame, often across Europe. The combination of public performances and the reverence paid to creative and interpretive artists, from the time of the Romantic movement in the early 19c, greatly increased their celebrity. There was a classical music industry run by concert impresarios before the invention of sound recording at the end of the 19c. The 20c saw that industry grow, though it was comparatively small in comparison to that intrinsically 20c phenomenon, the popular music industry.

### Popular music

For centuries the music of ordinary folk, whatever culture they belonged to, was folk music, religious music – in the Christian West especially hymns – and songs that 'filtered down' from high culture. What is now known as popular music is largely a creation of the 19c and early 20c: sentimental ballads written to be sung to the piano, the songs of Stephen Foster imitating black slave songs, dance music, comic songs written for the music hall, and then jazz.

Jazz has very little to do with traditional African music (though the latter's influence on Latin American music is much greater). Its roots are in spirituals, in the blues, in military marches and in syncopated banjo and piano playing that found a compositional outlet in ragtime, before ragtime in its turn influenced the jazz proper that emerged in New Orleans around the turn of the 20c. Jazz was born among the black people of the southern USA. It has its own history; the original New Orleans style was an ensemble style. Virtuoso soloists such as Louis Armstrong (1901–71) and Duke Ellington (1899–1974) greatly increased the expressive range and technical complexity of jazz. The big band era of the late 1920s and 1930s was succeeded by bebop in the 1940s and the sparer, more complex forms of modern jazz from the 1950s.

From its becoming more widely known (the first jazz recording was made in 1917), jazz has exerted an influence not only on the music of shows and films but also on classical music. Later it contributed to the birth of 'pop'. Pop, generally defined as popular music aimed at young people, which usually has a strong rhythmic beat and electronically amplified instrumentation, emerged as a distinct genre in the 1950s, with its emergence forever associated with the name of Elvis Presley (1935–77). Presley combined white country-and-western and black rhythm-and-blues music with a smouldering, sexually suggestive performance style which made many of his successors – the Beatles for example – look sedate. Presley opened the breach, as it were, but musically he did not take things very far, whereas a comparison of the early recordings of the Beatles with their later recordings indicates the degree of sophistication possible within the pop idiom. Indigenous forms of popular music sprang up in response to earlier forms of the Western variety, but pop has become an international genre and the driving force behind an enormous money-making industry.

---

(1979–80) but he fell out with Obote on the latter's return to power. When the Tanzanian troops left in 1982 a virtual civil war ensued until 1986, when Museveni's forces prevailed and Obote once again fled the country. Museveni has since attempted to follow a policy of national reconciliation, and won re-election in 1996 and 2001.

### Musharraf, Pervez (1943–)

Pakistani general and politician. A liberal Muslim, he was born in India but his family moved to Pakistan at the **PARTITION OF INDIA** in 1947. He was commissioned in the Pakistani army in 1964 and by 1998 had risen to the rank of general. He overthrew the government in a bloodless coup in 1999 after attempts were made to remove him from command, and became head of the government. In 2000 he also assumed the presidency, to which he was elected for a five-year term by referendum in 2002 following an agreement, which he did not keep, to resign his army post by the end of 2004 and become a civilian president. His early policies included recognition of Afghanistan's **TALIBAN** regime, support for Kashmiri insurgents and the reservation of Pakistan's 'first strike' nuclear capacity in any potential conflict with India. His support was indispensable to the USA and its allies during the **AFGHAN WAR** (2001) although it angered militant factions at home and he has been the target of several assassination attempts. He is viewed in the west as progressive and modernizing, although concerns have been raised by recent disclosures about the sale of Pakistan's nuclear technology and uncertainty about his intentions when his term of office ends. ▶ **KHAN, ABDUL QADEER; TERROR, WAR ON**

**Music** ▶ *See panel*

### Muslim Brotherhood

An Islamic movement, founded in Egypt in 1928 by

an Egyptian schoolteacher, Hasan al-**BANNA**. Its original goal was the reform of Islamic society by elimination of Western influences and other decadent accretions. Subsequently, it became more radical, and its goal of a theocratic Islamic state found support in many other Sunni countries. ▶ **SUNNIS**

## Muslim League

Founded in 1906 by politicized Muslims, many of whom were active in the Muhammadan Educational Conference established by Sir Sayyid **AHMAD KHAN**, the league saw itself as the spokesman for all Muslims in British India. By the 1930s, it had begun to articulate a Muslim nationalism expressed through the concept of Pakistan, a separate Muslim state. In 1927 the league split over the question of the Simon Commission. Muslim fear of a Hindu-dominated post-independence government led to the reorganization of the league under Muhammad Ali **JINNAH** in 1934. The search for a positive programme led the league in two directions. The first was that of safeguards; Muslims welcomed federation as it gave provinces greater freedom and thus tended to safeguard Muslims in their majority areas. They sought to reduce the scope of the centre as much as possible. The second direction was towards autonomy in the Muslim majority areas. In 1930 **IQBAL** suggested the union of the Frontier Province, Baluchistan, Sind and Kashmir as a Muslim state within a federation. Choudhari Rahmat Ali Khan developed the concept of a separate Muslim state at Cambridge and invented the term Pakistan in 1933. The ideology of Iqbal and the vision of Rahmat Ali Khan were turned into a practical programme by Jinnah, the future President of Pakistan, and the Muslim League was the dominant party in Pakistan after 1947. However, it gradually lost power, split into factions and by the 1970s had disappeared. ▶ **INDIA, PARTITION OF**

## Mussert, Antoon Adriaan (1894–1946)

Dutch politician. He made his early career as a hydraulic engineer in Dutch government service, but under the influence of fascism and Nazism he founded the **NATIONAL SOCIALIST MOVEMENT** (*Nationaal Socialistische Beweging*, NSB), the main Dutch fascist party. During the German occupation of the Netherlands he collaborated fully, and was given the title of 'Leader of the Dutch People'; however, he had little real power. After the war he was captured, sentenced to death and executed by firing squad.

## Mussolini, Benito (1883–1945)

Italian politician. The son of a blacksmith and a schoolteacher, he fled Italy in 1902 to avoid military service. In 1904 he returned to Italy as editor of the socialist newspaper *Avanti!*, but resigned in 1914 because of his refusal to support Italian neutrality. He was wounded while serving at the front and began to edit his own nationalist paper, *Il Popolo d'Italia*. In Mar 1919 Mussolini established the fascist movement, borrowing ideas from Gabriele **D'ANNUNZIO** and the 'futurists'; in Oct 1921 he converted this into the **FASCIST PARTY**. Profiting from the economic and political instability of post-war Italy and the support of paramilitary **SQUADRISTI** and local **RAS**, as well as a readiness to ally with politicians of differing ideologies, he was able first to take control of a number of provincial cities and then present himself as the only

man capable of restoring order to a country that seemed to be slipping ever more rapidly into political chaos. In Oct 1922 he was asked by **VICTOR EMMANUEL III** to form a government and the following month assumed dictatorial powers. His rule came under serious threat only once after the ill-judged murder of **MATTEOTTI** (1924) and during the course of the mid-1920s he was able to consolidate power. Using a mixture of intimidation, patronage and propaganda, he was able to turn Italy into a totalitarian state by 1929. Despite his early aggression of the **CORFU INCIDENT** (1923) and his fierce nationalism, his foreign policy was not marked by overt expansionism or aggression until the mid-1930s. However, in 1935 he launched the Conquest of **ABYSSINIA**, which was followed by large-scale intervention in the **SPANISH CIVIL WAR** on the side of **FRANCO**. During this period he moved increasingly towards cooperation with **HITLER**, which culminated in the Pact of **STEEL** and eventually in the invasion of France in 1940. In 1939 Mussolini annexed Albania but (Oct 1940) failed to seize Greece. The arrival of German troops to assist in the conquest of Greece signalled the beginning of his dependence on Hitler, and henceforth his actions were dictated largely by the needs of Berlin. Dissatisfaction with this policy and a realization of the likely victory of the Allies persuaded many of his **GERARCHI** to oppose him, and at a meeting of the **FASCIST GRAND COUNCIL** (25 July 1943) it became clear that he had lost the support of most of his closest associates. The following day he was arrested after being summoned by **VICTOR EMMANUEL III**, but was subsequently rescued by German paratroopers. In Sep 1943 he was established at the head of the puppet Republic of **SALÒ** in German-occupied northern Italy but was no more than an impotent quisling. On 28 Apr 1945 he was captured by partisans and shot while trying to flee Italy. ▶ **DUCE**

## Mutesa I (c.1837–1884)

Long-reigning Kabaka (King) of Buganda (1856/84). Under his rule the power of the monarch and the extent of the kingdom on the northern shore of Lake Victoria were greatly increased. Mutesa was fascinated by the Muslim Zanzibari traders who visited his court and was eager to supply himself with modern firearms. His court developed Islamic practices, but Mutesa was also beset with Christian Europeans. In 1876 a religious persecution created Muslim martyrs. He invited both Catholic and Protestant missionaries to Buganda to try to balance them against each other and also encouraged the restoration of indigenous religion. His successor, Mwanga, inherited a religious powder keg.

## Mutesa II, known as King Freddie (1924–69)

Kabaka (King) of Buganda (1939/53 and 1955/66). Mutesa was educated in England and was an honorary captain in the Grenadier Guards. He succeeded as Kabaka during **WORLD WAR II** and set about safeguarding the position of his kingdom within Uganda, even attempting to lead it to separate independence. At the centre of several controversies relating to the independence and post-colonial politics of Uganda, Mutesa was exiled (1953–5) by the Governor, Sir Andrew Cohen, for opposing British plans for unitary decolonization. On independence, he was briefly

President of Uganda with Milton **OBOTE** as his Prime Minister, but in 1966 Obote overthrew him in a coup. Mutesa escaped to London, where he died.

## mutilated victory

The term (in Italian, *vittoria mutilata*) coined originally by Gabriele **D'ANNUNZIO** to describe the consequences of Italy's treatment by its allies after **WORLD WAR I**. Italy, having been brought into war by promises of extensive territorial and colonial gains, suffered among the greatest human and material losses of any of the Western states. However, the Italian delegates at the **PARIS PEACE CONFERENCE** were virtually ignored by those of Britain, France and the USA. While most of the territory promised by the Treaty of **LONDON** (1915) was handed over, Italian claims for colonies and mandates were disregarded (doubly offensive given the readiness to allow Australia and South Africa control of mandated territory) and the Dalmatian littoral was given to Yugoslavia. This not entirely unfounded sense of being cheated played a large part in stimulating aggressive nationalist sentiment which helped contribute to the growth of **FASCISM**.

## Muzorewa, Abel Tendekayi (1925– )

Zimbabwean cleric and politician. Educated in Methodist schools in Southern Rhodesia and at theological college in the USA, he was ordained in 1963 and became a bishop of the United Methodist Church in Southern Rhodesia in 1968. Founder President of the African National Council in 1971, he failed to hold together the differing elements of the nationalist movement and chose the path of an 'internal settlement' rather than guerrilla war. After the **ANC** won the first universal suffrage election in 1979, he was Prime Minister of 'Zimbabwe–Rhodesia' for a few months before the 1980 election swept Robert **MUGABE** into power. In 1996 his request for Zimbabwe's 'unfair electoral rules' to be changed was rejected by the Supreme Court, and he withdrew his candidacy for the presidential election, which was won by Mugabe.

## MVSN (*Milizia Volontaria per la Sicurezza Nazionale*, 'National Security Militia')

The fascist militia set up in Jan 1923 by **MUSSOLINI**. Recruited mainly from ex-**SQUADRISTI**, paid out of state funds and answerable only to Mussolini himself, the militia was established primarily to keep the fascist movement under the **DUCE**'s own control. By organizing the members of the fascist squads, Mussolini was able to prevent powerful **RAS** from mustering their own private armies and to prevent also the worst excesses of *squadrismo*, so fostering his image as the one man able to keep order. However, the MVSN served little real military or policing purpose.

## Mwata Yamvo (1600–mid-19c)

The dynastic title of the paramount chiefs of the Lunda empire of central Africa. The empire expanded steadily from its inception c.1600 so that by the mid-19c as many as 36 great chiefs of the region were reputed to pay tribute to the *Mwata Yamvo*.

## Mwene Mutapa

The dynastic title of the kings of northern Zimbabwe with whom Portuguese traders established close relations in the 16c. Gatsi Rusere (d.1622) appealed to the Portuguese for aid in suppressing a rebellion, ceding in return the mineral wealth of the kingdom to his 'brother-in-arms', the king of Portugal. Towards the end of his reign relations with the Europeans deteriorated although the king received Christian baptism on his death-bed. His son Nyambo Kapararidze broke openly with the Portuguese and placed himself at the head of an uprising in 1631. He was defeated in battle in 1633 and then replaced by the puppet-king Mavura (d.1652), after which the dynasty survived only in subordination to the Portuguese.

## Mwinyi, (Ndugu) Ali Hassan (1925– )

Tanzanian politician. Having trained as a teacher, he taught in Zanzibar (1954–61) before going to the UK to study for two years. On his return, he joined the Zanzibar Ministry of Education and then the Zanzibar State Trading Corporation. In 1969 he became a Minister of State in the office of President Julius **NYERERE** and thereafter Minister of Health and Home Affairs, Minister of Natural Resources and Tourism, and Minister of State in the Vice-President's Office. In Apr 1984 he was elected President of Zanzibar and in Oct 1985 he succeeded Nyerere as President of Tanzania. He attempted to loosen the state's control over the country's economy while retaining a faith in the single party, the **CHAMA CHA MAPINDUZI** (CCM), but in the first multiparty presidential and parliamentary elections in 1995, Mwinyi lost the presidency to Benjamin Mkapa.

## Myall Creek Massacre (1838)

In Australian history, the massacre of 28 **ABORIGINALS** in north-east New South Wales by a party of assigned convicts for an alleged attack on cattle. Seven of the men charged with the massacre were found guilty and hanged, the first whites executed for murdering Aboriginals. The accused attracted considerable support from other colonists, who regarded Aboriginals as less than human; thereafter the murder of Aboriginals was carefully concealed.

**MYANMAR** official name **Union of Myanmar**, formerly (to 1988) **Socialist Republic of the Union of Burma**

A republic in South-East Asia, bounded to the north and north-east by China; to the east by Laos and Thailand; to the north-west by India; to the west by Bangladesh; and to the south and west by the Bay of Bengal and the Andaman Sea. The country was first unified in the 11c by King Anawrahta. **KUBLAI KHAN** invaded in 1287. A second dynasty was established in 1486, but it was plagued by internal disunity and wars with Siam from the 16c. A new dynasty under King **ALAUNGHPAYA** was founded in 1752. Burma was annexed to British India in 1886 following the **ANGLO-BURMESE WARS** of 1824–85. It separated from India in 1937 and was occupied by the Japanese in **WORLD WAR II**. It gained independence as the Union of Burma under Prime Minister U **NU** in 1948, who was overthrown in a military coup in 1962 led by U **NE WIN** in 1962. Ne Win became chairman of the revolutionary council and then state President when the country became a single-party socialist republic in 1974. In 1988 there was another military coup, led by General Saw Maung, who seized power, imposed martial law, changed the country's name to Myanmar and placed **AUNG SAN SUU KYI**, the leader of the National League for Democracy (NLD) party, under house arrest. The 1990 election, the country's first multiparty election for 30 years, was won by the NLD but the result was ignored by the military rulers and persecution of pro-democracy demonstrators has continued despite international protests. Saw Maung was replaced by his deputy, General Than Shwe, in 1992. Aung San Suu Kyi took part in **UN**-brokered talks with the government in 2000, but the NLD boycotted a constitutional convention held in 2004 and their leader remained under house arrest.

There has been fighting since independence with armed insurgent groups, mostly derived from ethnic groups. Since 1992, 15 ethnic groups have signed ceasefire agreements following offensives against them by the government, although the largest, the Kayin (Karen), and their allies continue to fight; the **UN** and the **EU** have expressed concern about human rights abuses against the ethnic minorities. ▶ **PAGAN**

**My Lai incident** (Mar 1968)
The massacre of several hundred unarmed inhabitants of the South Vietnamese village of My Lai by US troops, an incident exposed by *Life* magazine photos in 1969. The officer responsible, Lieutenant Calley, was court-martialled in 1970–1. ▶ **VIETNAM WAR**

**Mzilikazi** (c.1790–1868)
Chief of the **NDEBELE** (c.1820/1868). The Ndebele were one of the **NGUNI** groups which clashed with **SHAKA**, King of the Zulu. In the early 1820s, Mzilikazi led his people over the Drakensberg on to the high veld, where he attacked a number of peoples and finally settled in what is now the western Transvaal. The missionary Robert Moffat made contact with him and they established a close relationship. Mzilikazi came into conflict with the Boer **VOORTREKKERS** and was defeated by a Boer commando under Hendrik Potgieter in 1837 near the modern Pretoria. He and his people then moved northwards, settling in what is now south-western Zimbabwe. There he established his power over many of the Shona peoples and succeeded in keeping whites at bay until his death.

## NAACP (National Association for the Advancement of Colored People)

US **CIVIL RIGHTS** organization established in 1910. This biracial association developed from the National Negro Committee Conference, held in 1909 in the aftermath of riots in Springfield, Illinois, in which eight people had died. Though Booker T **WASHINGTON** refused to join the association, its founding members included Jane **ADDAMS**, William Monroe Trotter and W E B **DU BOIS**, who became editor of its magazine, *Crisis*. The NAACP's aim was to 'make 11,000,000 Americans physically free from peonage, mentally free from ignorance, politically free from disenfranchisement and socially free from insult', through educating public opinion, lobbying for legislative reform and sponsoring court action. Its first major success came in 1915 when the Supreme Court ruled the **GRANDFATHER CLAUSE** to be unconstitutional, and a series of victories over aspects of segregation culminated in **BROWN V BOARD OF EDUCATION OF TOPEKA, KANSAS** (1954). The membership of the movement grew from 6,000 in 1914 to 650,000 in the mid-1990s. During the 1990s it was harmed by financial scandals involving its top officers and was more than US$3 million in debt. It was also criticized for seeking alliances with extremist groups like the Nation of Islam. ➤ **BLACK MUSLIMS**

## Nabuco (de Araújo), Joaquim Aurélio (1849–1912)

Brazilian politician and abolitionist. Born into a major Liberal political dynasty, he was a diplomat, then became a deputy (1878–80, 1885 and 1887–9). He founded the Brazilian Society for the Abolition of Slavery and led the campaign to abolish **SLAVERY** through the legislature and the courts, rather than by extrajudicial means. He triumphed, largely as a result of the slave insurrections in São Paulo in 1887–8, the refusal of the Cabinet to face possible civil war, and the acceptance of abolition as a *fait accompli* by the Chamber of Deputies in May 1888. An admirer of **PEDRO II**, he left public life after the former's deposition (Nov 1889), returning as a special envoy and ambassador to the USA.

## Nacertanije (1844)

Literally 'outline', the term describes the Serbian national programme presented by Ilija **GARAŠANIN** to Alexander **KARAGEORGEVIĆ**. It advocated the creation of Great Serbia, which was to include Serbia, Montenegro, Bosnia and Herzegovina and, for the sake of a corridor to the sea, north Albania. Serbian foreign policy continued to be informed by the *Nacertanije* throughout the 19c. After the creation of the Kingdom of Serbs, Croats and Slovenes (later Yugoslavia) at the end of **WORLD WAR I**, the continued desire of many Serbs for the Great Serbia of the Nacertanije bedevilled their relations with the other nations within Yugoslavia.

## Nadir Shah (1688–1747)

King of Persia (1736/47). Born in Khurasan, he expelled the Afghan rulers of Persia, defeated the Turks (1731), conquered Afghanistan, and ravaged the north-west of India, taking Delhi. His domestic policy led to revolts, especially on religious matters, and he was assassinated at Fathabad.

## NAFTA (North American Free Trade Agreement)

An agreement between the USA, Mexico and Canada, ratified in 1993 and implemented in 1994, allowing for the progressive lifting of tariffs and the elimination of most import and export restrictions between the three countries.

## Nagano Osami (1880–1947)

Japanese naval officer. Educated at the Naval Academy, Etajima, he studied law at Harvard and served as naval attaché in Washington (1920–3). Promoted rear-admiral in 1928, he was superintendent of the Naval Academy (1928–9). As head of the Japanese delegation to the 2nd London Naval Conference (1935–6), he advocated the expansion of Japanese naval power. He was Navy Minister (1936–7), Commander-in-Chief Combined Fleet (1937) and Chief of Naval General Staff (1941–4). He planned and ordered the Japanese attack on **PEARL HARBOR** (Dec 1941) and died while on trial for war crimes.

## Nagasaki

The capital of Nagasaki prefecture, western Kyushu, Japan, it was the target for the second atomic bomb of **WORLD WAR II** (9 Aug 1945) which killed or injured c.75,000 people and destroyed over a third of the city.

## Nagodba (1868)

Literally 'compromise', this term describes the agreement which regulated Croatia's status within the Dual Monarchy of **AUSTRIA-HUNGARY**. After the **AUSGLEICH** (1867), **DALMATIA** and **ISTRIA** came under the Austrian half of the Dual Monarchy, while Croatia and Slavonia were joined and placed under Hungarian jurisdiction. The *Nagodba* recognized Croatia as a distinct political unit within Hungary and allowed the Croats to elect their own *sabor* (parliament) and to have a measure of control over their internal affairs; however, in matters concerning external affairs, finance, defence and trade, they were subject to the joint parliament at Pest. The overall effect of the

Nagodba was to effect Croatia's subordination to Hungary; the Croats were then left without direct access to the central government of the empire and their *ban* (governor) was chosen by the Hungarian Prime Minister and the Emperor, a provision which led to the appointment of the much-reviled **KHUEN-HÉDERVÁRY**. In Sep 1868 the *sabor*, which had fallen prey to Hungarian gerrymandering, accepted the Nagodba, which remained in force until the collapse of the Habsburg Empire (1918).

### Naguib, Mohammed ► NEGUIB, MOHAMMED

### Nagy, Imre (1896–1958)

Hungarian politician. Born into a poor peasant family, he came into contact with Bolshevism as a prisoner in Russia in **WORLD WAR I** and, after returning to Hungary, he held a minor post in the Béla **KUN** revolutionary government in 1919. He fled to the USSR for two years, but returned to participate in the illegal Hungarian communist movement until 1929, when he again had to flee. Returning with the **RED ARMY** in 1944, he held various ministerial posts in a chequered career until he became Prime Minister. As a moderate he was ousted in 1955 and brought back during the Hungarian Uprising the following year. His decision to declare Hungary neutral and to appeal to the **UN** for help provoked Soviet suppression of the uprising. He was displaced by János **KÁDÁR** and executed in 1958. What was regarded as his martyrdom was avenged with the overthrow of the communists in 1989. ► **RUSSIAN REVOLUTION**

### Nahayan, Sheikh Zayed bin Sultan al- (1918–2004)

Amir of Abu Dhabi. He was governor of the eastern province of Abu Dhabi, one of seven Trucial States on the southern shores of the Persian Gulf and the Gulf of Oman which were under British protection, until in 1969 he deposed his brother, Sheikh Shakhbut, and became Amir. When the States decided to federate as the United Arab Emirates in 1971 he became President of its Supreme Council and held this office until his death. Under his rule the UAE ceased to be a collection of medieval emirates and emerged as an efficient modern state with one of the highest per capita incomes in the world.

### Nahhas, Mustafa al- (1879–1965)

Egyptian politician. He was the leader of the **WAFD PARTY** in Egypt in 1923 and Premier in 1928, 1930 and 1950. In addition, al-Nahhas acted as regent for King **FAROUK** in his early years and, despite their being dismissed by Farouk in 1938, the Wafd were brought back in 1941 at Britain's behest. The damage done to the reputation of the Wafd by their cooperation with the British was irreparable. Although al-Nahhas became Premier again in 1950 after the Wafd's victory in the elections, and despite his endeavours to regain credibility for the Wafd by giving the party an anti-British bias, they were again dismissed by Farouk in 1952. Al-Nahhas then left the political stage, charged with but not tried for corruption, and in the same year (1952) King Farouk was deposed by General **NEGUIB** on behalf of the **FREE OFFICERS**. The Wafd Party was dissolved in 1953.

### Naicker, E V Ramaswami (1879–1973)

Indian social reformer. A fiery anti-Brahmin crusader, he was responsible for reorganizing the Justice Party, a rival of the **INDIAN NATIONAL CONGRESS**, into the **DRAVIDA MUNNETRA KAZHAGAM** (DMK), an exclusively **TAMIL** party. He began his public career as an exponent of social equality and became a crusader against 'untouchability' – the synonym for the range of prejudices (particularly acute in the south of India) which were directed against low-caste members of Indian society. He was elected Chairman of Erode Municipal Council and joined the Congress in the 1910s. Naicker participated in the **NON-COOPERATION MOVEMENT** and courted arrest in 1922. In 1925 he launched the Self-Respect Movement and, in 1933, led his first anti-Hindu march. He was elected President of the Justice Party in 1938 and reorganized it into the DMK in 1944. He denounced Hinduism, the **CASTE** system and child marriage, and opposed the imposition of Hindi, the northern language, on the population of southern India, the 'Dravidians'. ► **BRAHMINS**

### Naidu, Sarojini (1879–1949)

Indian feminist, politician and poet. Educated at Madras, London and Cambridge, she became known as 'the Nightingale of India' as the author of three volumes of lyric verse between 1905 and 1915. She lectured widely on feminism and campaigned for the abolition of purdah, and in 1925 became the first President of M K **GANDHI**'s **INDIAN NATIONAL CONGRESS**. She was imprisoned several times for **CIVIL DISOBEDIENCE**, and took a leading part in the negotiations that led to her country's independence in 1947, when she was appointed Governor of the United Provinces, now Uttar Pradesh.

### Najibullah, Sayid Muhammad (1947–96)

Afghan politician. He became active in the Moscow-inspired People's Democratic Party of Afghanistan (PDPA) in the mid-1960s, and was twice imprisoned for his political activities. After King Mohammed **ZAHIR SHAH** was deposed in a military coup and abdicated (1973), he rose rapidly in the party hierarchy, and as a member of the PDPA's Central Committee, played a key role in the negotiations that led to the 1978 Treaty of Friendship with the USSR that served as a pretext for the Russian invasion the following year, when he was made Information Minister. He was admitted to the Afghan Politburo in 1981, and became President in 1987. Strong guerrilla resistance by the members of the National Islamic Front continued, and insistence by the Russian army, in the wake of continued attacks by Pakistani **MUJAHIDIN** guerrillas on the Kabul–Soviet border, that Najibullah's regime should continue to be funded despite the USSR's own economic difficulties, was a factor in the resignation in Dec 1990 of Foreign Minister Eduard **SHEVARDNADZE**. In 1991 the **UN** renewed its call for elections in Mujahidin-controlled territories with a view to replacing Najibullah's regime with a democratically elected government. Najibullah finally agreed to resign, handing over power to a coalition of Mujahidin leaders in May 1992, but was unable to leave Kabul and took refuge in a UN compound. Four years later he was dragged out by **TALIBAN** guerrillas, shot dead, and his body suspended from a pole outside the presidential palace.

### Nakasone Yasuhiro (1918–)

Japanese politician. Educated at Tokyo University, he

was a junior naval officer in **WORLD WAR II**, and entered the Ministry of Home Affairs in 1945. Elected to the Diet at the age of 29 for the Liberal-Democratic (Conservative) Party, he held a range of ministerial posts from 1959 to 1982. As Prime Minister (1982–7), he supported the renewal of the **US–JAPAN SECURITY TREATY**, and maintained close relations with US President Ronald **REAGAN**.

### Nakaz (1767)

Literally the 'instruction' from **CATHERINE II, THE GREAT** to the Legislative Commission she summoned to discuss and reshape the laws of Russia that had last been codified in 1649. It took her 18 months to prepare and she drew heavily on the works of Montesquieu and other writers of the European **ENLIGHTENMENT**. However, she modified their ideas to suit her own autocratic purposes. The commission excluded the largest segment of the population, the serfs, and in the course of a year and a half of discussion it became divided along interest group lines. Catherine dismissed it without its achieving other than the accumulation of papers useful to administrators and historians. Yet it did help to establish her prestige in Russia and abroad.

### Namboodiripad, E M S (1909–98)

Indian politician. Hailing from Kerala, he was educated in Victoria College, Palghat and St Thomas College, Trichur. He was Chief Minister of Kerala in 1957–9 and again in 1967–9. Acting General-Secretary of the Communist Party in 1962–3, he became its Secretary-General in 1978 and went on to hold the post of Secretary-General of the **COMMUNIST PARTY OF INDIA (MARXIST)** (CPM). He also wrote on various Indian political and economic issues.

**NAMIBIA**   official name **Republic of Namibia**, formerly (to 1968) **South West Africa**, earlier **German South West Africa**

A republic in south-western Africa, bounded to the north by Angola; to the north-east by Zambia; to the east by Botswana; to the south by South Africa; and to the west by the Atlantic Ocean. Pre-colonial Namibia was inhabited by Bantu tribes and San (Bushmen). It became the German protectorate of South West Africa in 1884, and from 1904 the Germans waged near-genocidal wars to crush the Herero and Nama peoples. Occupied by South African troops in 1914, it was mandated to South Africa by the **LEAGUE OF NATIONS** in 1920. South Africa continued to administer the area as South West Africa, but the **UN** challenged South African rule from 1966, changing the name to

Namibia in 1968, and recognizing the South West Africa People's Organization (**SWAPO**) as representative of the Namibian people. After guerrilla warfare and the withdrawal of its forces in Mozambique, South Africa installed an interim administration in 1985, and Namibia gained full independence in 1990 under President Sam **NUJOMA**. In 1994 the Walvis Bay area, a major port and South African enclave, was returned to Namibia. Hifikepunye Pohamba won the presidential election in 2004. Namibia faces the problems associated with high levels of **HIV/AIDS** infection.

### Nana Sahib, properly Brahmin Dundhu Panth (c.1820–59)

Indian rebel. The adopted son of the ex-Peshwa of the Marathas, he became known as the leader of the 1857–8 **INDIAN UPRISING**. On its outbreak, he was proclaimed Peshwa, and was held responsible for the massacres at Cawnpore (Kanpur). After the collapse of the uprising he escaped into Nepal. ► **KANPUR, MASSACRE OF**

### Nanda ► PRE-ISLAMIC, INDIA

### Nanjing, Treaty of (29 Aug 1842)

Signed at the conclusion of the first Opium War between China and Britain, it was to be the first of a series of unequal treaties that gave extensive privileges to the foreign powers in China. Five **TREATY PORTS** were opened for British residence and trade; British consuls were to be stationed permanently in these ports; the **COHONG** monopoly system was abolished; a huge indemnity was imposed on the Chinese government to compensate for the opium confiscated in 1839 and to cover the expenses of the British military expedition; and the island of Hong Kong was ceded to Britain 'in perpetuity'. A supplementary treaty (1843) fixed tariff rates, thus infringing on China's tariff autonomy, and stipulated a 'most-favoured nation' clause: any privileges or immunities granted to the nationals of other foreign countries were to be automatically extended to those of Britain. The USA and France concluded similar treaties with China in 1844; additional privileges granted included the enjoyment of extraterritoriality (foreigners in the treaty ports to be subject to the jurisdiction of their own consuls) and the right of missionaries to build churches and proselytize in the treaty ports. While the **QING DYNASTY** regarded such concessions as minor irritants, by the turn of the century Chinese nationalists were to view the Nanjing Treaty as the opening move in a full-scale imperialist onslaught on China. ► **OPIUM WARS**

### Nansen, Fridtjof (1861–1930)

Norwegian explorer, scientist and statesman. Educated at Oslo and Naples, in 1882 he travelled into the Arctic regions, and in 1888 made an east–west journey across Greenland. His greatest scheme was to reach the North Pole by grounding his specially built ship, the *Fram*, on the ice in the Kara Sea in 1893 and successfully drifting with the current across the Arctic Ocean to Svalbard. Nansen left the ship and attempted to reach the North Pole on foot during the three-year voyage, but failed. During the union crisis with Sweden (1905) he was one of the leading spokesmen for Norwegian independence

and Norway's unofficial representative in Britain. In 1906–8 he was the first ambassador of independent Norway in London and played an active part in the negotiations leading to the Norwegian integrity treaty of 1907. During **WORLD WAR I** he headed a trade delegation to the USA which led to a war trade agreement in Apr 1918. As Norway's first delegate to the **LEAGUE OF NATIONS** (1920), Nansen became deeply engaged in post-war relief work. He was appointed League Commissioner for Refugees, and thousands of displaced persons were issued with special 'Nansen passports'. In 1921 he organized relief for the victims of famine in Russia, saving 1.5–2 million people from death by starvation. In 1922 he was awarded the **NOBEL PEACE PRIZE** in recognition of his relief efforts.
► **EXPLORATION**

**Nantes, Edict of** (1598)
A law promulgated by **HENRY IV** of France granting religious and civil liberties to his Huguenot subjects at the end of the Wars of **RELIGION**. **RICHELIEU** annulled its political clauses (1629) as a threat to the integrity of the state, and the same motive led **LOUIS XIV** to order the revocation of the edict (1685). ► **HU-GUENOTS**

**Naoroji, Dadabhai** (1825–1917)
Indian politician. He became Professor of Mathematics at Elphinstone College, Bombay, and was later a member of the Legislative Council. From 1892 to 1895 Naoroji represented the London constituency of Finsbury in the House of **COMMONS** – the first Indian MP – and was also President of the **INDIAN NATIONAL CONGRESS**. He was particularly renowned for his economic critiques of British rule in India, despite his admiration for the British system of education and the country's tradition of liberal political philosophy.

**Napier, Sir Charles James** (1782–1853)
British general and colonial administrator. He fought in the **PENINSULAR WAR** from 1808 to 1811, against the USA (1812), and in 1842 was sent to India to take command of the war in Sind. He defeated the Amirs at Miani (1843), and was made Governor of the province. In 1847 he returned to England, but went back to India before the end of the second of the **SIKH WARS** to command the army. He left India in 1851.

**Napier, Robert Cornelis, 1st Baron Napier of Magdala** (1810–90)
British field marshal. Born in Ceylon, he joined the army in 1826 and distinguished himself at the siege of **LUCKNOW** (1857–8). He carried out successful expeditions during the Chinese War (1860) and in Abyssinia (1868), and became Commander-in-Chief in India (1870), Governor of Gibraltar (1876–82) and Constable of the Tower of London (1887). Created a baron in 1868, he died in London. ► **INDIAN UPRISING**

**Napoleon I**, also called **Napoleon Bonaparte** (1769–1821)
French general and Emperor (1804/15). He entered the military schools at Brienne (1779) and Paris (1784), commanded the artillery at the siege of Toulon (1793) and was promoted Brigadier-General. In 1796 he married **JOSEPHINE**, widow of the Viscount of **BEAUHARNAIS**, and soon after left for Italy, where

he skilfully defeated the Piedmontese and Austrians, and made several gains through the Treaty of **CAMPO FORMIO** (1797). Intending to break British trade by conquering Egypt, he captured Malta (1798), and entered Cairo, defeating the Turks; but after the French fleet was destroyed by **NELSON** at the Battle of the Nile, he returned to France (1799), having learnt of French reverses in Europe. The **BRUMAIRE COUP** followed (9 Nov 1799), in which Napoleon assumed power as First Consul, instituting a military dictatorship. He then routed the Austrians at **MARENGO** (1800), made further gains at the Treaty of Lunéville (1801), and consolidated French domination by the **CONCORDAT** (1801) with Rome and the Treaty of **AMIENS** with Britain (1802). Elected consul for life, he crowned himself Emperor in 1804. His administrative, military, educational and legal reforms (notably the **CODE NAPOLÉON**) made a lasting impact on French society. War with Britain was renewed, and extended to Russia and Austria. Forced by the British naval victory at **TRAFALGAR** (1805) to abandon the notion of invasion, he attacked the Austrians and Russians, gaining victories at Ulm and **AUSTERLITZ** (1805). Prussia was defeated at **JENA AND AUERSTÄDT** (1806), and Russia at **FRIEDLAND** (1807). After the Treaties of **TILSIT**, he became the arbiter of Europe. He then tried to cripple Britain with the Continental System, ordering the European states under his control to boycott British goods. He sent armies into Portugal and Spain, which resulted in the bitter and ultimately unsuccessful **PENINSULAR WAR** (1808–14). In 1809, wanting an heir, he divorced Josephine, who was childless, and married the Archduchess **MARIE LOUISE** of Austria, a son being born in 1811. Believing that Russia was planning an alliance with Britain, he invaded, defeating the Russians at **BORODINO** (1812), before entering Moscow, but he was forced to retreat, his army broken by hunger and the Russian winter. In 1813 his victories over the allied armies continued at **LÜTZEN**, Bautzen and Dresden, but he was routed at the Battle of **LEIPZIG**, and France was invaded. Forced to abdicate, he was given the sovereignty of Elba (1814). The unpopularity which followed the return of the Bourbons motivated him to return to France in 1815. He regained power for a period known as the **HUNDRED DAYS**, but was defeated by the combination of **WELLINGTON**'s and **BLÜCHER**'s forces at **WATERLOO**. He fled to Paris, abdicated, surrendered to the British, and was banished to St Helena, where he died. ► **BOURBON, HOUSE OF**; **FRENCH REVOLUTION**; **NAPOLEONIC WARS**; *See map*

**Napoleon II**, originally **François Charles Joseph Bonaparte** (1811–32)
King of Rome. He was the son of **NAPOLEON I** by the Empress **MARIE LOUISE**. Styled King of Rome at his birth, after his father's abdication in 1814 he was brought up in Austria and in 1818 given the title of the Duke of Reichstadt, though allowed no active political role. Bonapartists proclaimed him Napoleon II in Paris in 1815, but he was formally deposed five days later.

**Napoleon III**, originally **Charles Louis Napoleon Bonaparte** (1808–73)
President of the Second French Republic and Emperor of the French (1852/70). Born in Paris, the third

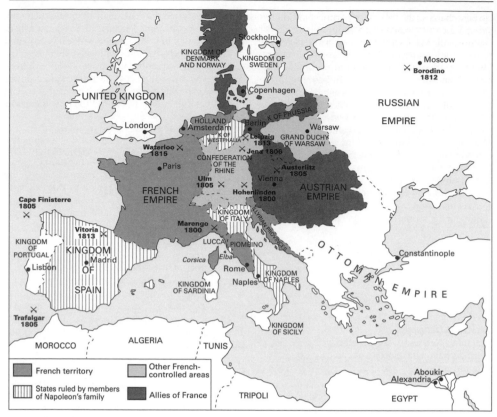

**Napoleonic Europe, c.1812**

son of Louis Bonaparte, King of Holland (the brother of **NAPOLEON I**) and **HORTENSE** (de Beauharnais), he was brought up in Switzerland. On the death of the Duke of Reichstadt (**NAPOLEON II**) in 1832, he became head of the Napoleonic dynasty. He made two abortive attempts on the French throne (1836 and 1840), for which he was imprisoned at Ham, near Amiens. He escaped to England (1846), but when the Bonapartist tide swept France after the **FEBRUARY REVOLUTION** (1848) he was elected first to the Assembly and then to the Presidency (1848–52). He carried out a coup d'état in 1851 and assumed the title of Emperor (1852); in 1853 he married Eugénie de Montijo de Guzmán (1826–1920), a Spanish countess, who bore him a son, the Prince Imperial (1856). He actively encouraged economic expansion and the modernization of Paris. His search for prestige in foreign affairs was at first successful in the **CRIMEAN WAR** (1854–6) and in the war against Austria (1859), which brought France Nice and Savoy (1860); it also led, not in accordance with his plans, to the unification of Italy. Outside Europe, he joined with Britain in expeditions to open China to commerce (1857–60), and acquired colonies in Senegal and Indo-China, but his ill-starred intervention in Mexico (1862–5) ended in disaster. Encouraged by the Empress Eugénie, he unwisely declared war on Prussia in 1870 and suffered humiliating defeat, culminating in the Battle of **SEDAN**. Confined at Wilhelmshohe until 1871, he went into exile in England, where he lived until his death. ► **EMPIRE, SECOND** (France); **FRANCO-PRUSSIAN WAR**; **HAUSSMANN, GEORGES**

**EUGÈNE, BARON**; **MEXICAN WAR**

**Napoleon Bonaparte** ► **NAPOLEON I**

**Napoleonic Wars** (1800–1)
The continuation of the **FRENCH REVOLUTIONARY WARS**, fought to preserve French hegemony in Europe. They increasingly became a manifestation of **NAPOLEON I**'s personal ambitions. The wars began with Napoleon's destruction of the Second Coalition (1800); after a peaceful interlude (1802–3) Britain resumed hostilities, prompting Napoleon to prepare for invasion, and encouraging the formation of a Third Coalition (1805–7). While Britain retained naval superiority (1805), Napoleon established territorial domination, sustained by economic warfare, resulting in the invasions of Spain (1808) and Russia (1812). Gradually the French were overwhelmed by the Fourth Coalition (1813–14); the **HUNDRED DAYS'** epilogue ended with the Battle of **WATERLOO** (1815). ► **AUSTERLITZ/COPENHAGEN/LEIPZIG/MARENGO/TRAFALGAR/WAGRAM, BATTLES OF**; **CONFEDERATION OF THE RHINE**; **GRAND ALLIANCE, WAR OF THE**; **PARIS, TREATIES OF**; **PENINSULAR WARS**; **TILSIT, TREATIES OF**; **VIENNA, CONGRESS OF**

**Narayan, Jaiprakash**, also known as **JP** (1902–79)
Indian freedom fighter and politician. He was educated in a village primary school and abandoned his studies in 1921 to join the **NON-COOPERATION MOVEMENT**. He went to the USA on a scholarship and obtained a masters degree from the University of Ohio. Influenced by Marxist ideas, he joined the communist movement. He accepted, however, **NEHRU**'s offer

to take charge of the Labour Department in Congress, joined the **CIVIL DISOBEDIENCE** movement after the failure of the M K **GANDHI**–Irwin talks and was jailed. One of the founders of the Congress Socialist Party in 1934, he advocated the abolition of the Zamindari system and the nationalization of heavy industries. The author of a number of books and booklets on social, political and economic problems, he took an active part in the **QUIT INDIA MOVEMENT** of 1942, but gave up politics after India gained independence and joined the **BHOODAN** movement of Vinoba **BHAVE**. Later, he was closely involved in the protest movement against the Chinese policy on **TIBET** and also toured the tribal areas of Nagaland in an attempt to bring about a rapprochement between the rebel Nagas and the government of India. He organized famine relief for the affected people of Bihar in 1967 and persuaded several dacoits of Madhya Pradesh to surrender their arms in 1972. He led the movement for restoration of democracy and liberties after the imposition of the 'emergency' by Indira **GANDHI** in 1975, for which he was arrested. Released in 1977, he led the Janata Party to victory in the general election of that year.

**Narodna Obrana**
Literally 'National Defence', this term refers to the Serbian nationalist society which was founded after the annexation of Bosnia and Herzegovina by Austria (1908).

**Narodniki**
Russian populists, revolutionaries who turned their backs on intellectual arguments and looked to an awakened peasantry as the hope for political and social change. The movement really got under way in the early 1870s as young people, mostly the privileged and educated from the towns, went into the countryside to harangue the frequently baffled peasants. Many were arrested, and following mass trials in 1877–8, many were exiled to Siberia. Thereafter, the movement became more conspiratorial and turned to **TERRORISM** and assassination. The first group to emerge was 'Land and Liberty'; and it was an offshoot of this, 'The People's Will', that organized **ALEXANDER II**'s assassination in 1881. Populism and terrorism in various forms continued until 1917.

**Narváez, Pánfilo de** (c.1478–1528)
Spanish conquistador, colonial official and explorer. He was one of the early settlers in Jamaica and then served in Diego Velázquez's campaign to conquer Cuba (1511). In 1520 he was sent to arrest Hernán **CORTÉS** in Mexico on a charge of treason but was captured and imprisoned for over a year. In 1527 he sailed from Spain with about 600 soldiers, sailors and colonists under the orders of Emperor **CHARLES V** to colonize the area west of Florida. About 140 deserted the expedition in Santo Domingo, and another 50 perished in a hurricane in Cuba. The expedition arrived in Florida in 1528 and began a treacherous overland journey northwards. They were not rejoined by their original ships and had to construct new boats before setting sail for Mexico. All but four men were lost at sea, including Narváez.

**Narváez, Ramón María** (1800–68)
Spanish soldier and politician. A supporter of **ISABEL-**

**LA II**, he defeated the Carlists in 1836, and then took part in an unsuccessful insurrection against **ESPARTERO** in 1840 and fled to France, where he was joined by **MARÍA CRISTINA**. In 1843 he led a Republican insurrection in Madrid that drove Espartero from power, and became virtual dictator. He lost power temporarily in 1851, and was briefly exiled as special ambassador to France, but from 1856 he was Premier again several times.

**Naseby, Battle of** (14 June 1645)
A major conflict of the **ENGLISH CIVIL WARS** in Northamptonshire. The royalist forces of **CHARLES I**, outnumbered by two to one, were defeated by parliament's **NEW MODEL ARMY** led by **FAIRFAX**, with **CROMWELL** commanding the cavalry. Royalist cavalry, led by Prince **RUPERT**, left the main battle, fatally weakening Charles's forces.

**Nash, Sir Walter** (1882–1968)
British-born New Zealand politician. Nash went to New Zealand in 1909. From 1919 to 1960 he served on the national executive of the New Zealand Labour Party, encouraging the adoption of a moderate reform programme in the Christian socialist tradition. A member of parliament from 1929, he held numerous ministerial appointments from 1935 onwards and in **WORLD WAR II** was Deputy Prime Minister to Peter **FRASER**, although from 1942 to 1944 he headed a special mission to the USA. He was Prime Minister (1957–60), retiring from the party leadership in 1963.

**Nasir al-Din Shah** (1831–96)
Qajar Shah of Persia (1848/96). He visited England in 1873 and 1889, introduced some European ideas into Persia, granted trade concessions to Britain and Russia, and was shot near Tehran by an assassin. He was succeeded by his second son, Muzaffar al-Din.

**Nasriddinova, Yadgar Sadykovna** (1920– )
Soviet bureaucrat and politician. Born in Uzbekistan and educated in the Tashkent Institute of Railway Engineering, she rose through various party and government offices, eventually becoming Chairman of the Soviet of Nationalities in Moscow (1970–4). Her corruption was such, however, that she had to be demoted to a ministry in 1974; it was not until 1988 that she could be removed from the party itself.

**Nassau**
A Burgundian noble family, who rose as servants of the Habsburgs, then rebelled against their authority in the Low Countries. They were made *stadholders* of Holland, Zeeland, and Friesland, Counts of Nassau, and Princes of Orange by Emperor **CHARLES V**. The heirs to the titles, William of Orange (1533–84), and his brother Louis (1538–74), Count of Nassau, supported and led the revolt against their former masters that developed into the **EIGHTY YEARS' WAR** (1566–1648). ► **HABSBURG DYNASTY; STADHOLDER; WILLIAM I, THE SILENT**

**Nassau Agreement** (Dec 1962)
An agreement made between UK Prime Minister Harold **MACMILLAN** and US President John F **KENNEDY**, under which the USA supplied Polaris missiles for British nuclear submarines to replace the cancelled Skybolt air-launched missile system. It angered European leaders, particularly Charles de **GAULLE**,

and led to France vetoing Britain's entry into the **EEC** (29 Jan 1963).

## Nasser, Gamal Abd al- (1918–70)

Egyptian politician. An army officer, he became dissatisfied with the corruption of the regime of King **FAROUK**, and was involved in the military coup of 1952. He became Prime Minister (1954–6) and then President (1956–70), deposing his fellow officer, General Mohammed **NEGUIB**. During his term of office, he nationalized the Suez Canal, which led to Israel's invasion of Sinai and the intervention of Anglo-French forces. He aimed to build a North African Arab empire, and in 1958 created a federation with Syria, the **UNITED ARAB REPUBLIC**, from which Syria withdrew in 1961. After the Arab–Israeli **SIX-DAY WAR** (1967), heavy losses on the Arab side led to his resignation, but he was persuaded to stay on, and died while still in office in Cairo.

## Natchez

A Muskogean-speaking Native American tribe who lived on the east side of the lower Mississippi River. Living in five towns and numbering c.4,000, they subsisted on corn, melons, squash and tobacco, supplemented by deer and fish. Having engaged in frequent warfare with the French, the Natchez were forced across the river and settled at Sicily Island, Louisiana, where they were ravaged by disease and death. Some joined the **CHICKASAW**; others fled to the Coosa River; the rest moved to Indian Territory. Today, their population has all but disappeared. ► **NATIVE AMERICANS**

## Nation, Carry Amelia (1846–1911)

US temperance advocate, born in Kentucky. After the death of her first husband from alcoholism, she moved to Kansas, where she took up the temperance cause. She gained notoriety as a prohibitionist following her numerous saloon-smashing expeditions, for which she was frequently arrested for disturbance of the peace, and during which this large and powerful woman wielded a hatchet to destroy bars and the alcohol they contained.

## National American Woman Suffrage Association (NAWSA)

A US feminist organization. Founded in 1890, it united the National Woman Suffrage Association (for which the suffrage was only one cause amongst others) with the American Woman Suffrage Association (for which the suffrage was the only cause). Elizabeth Cady **STANTON** was President of the new organization for the first two years, followed by Susan B **ANTHONY** until 1900. By 1912, under the leadership of Carrie Chapman **CATT**, the movement had become increasingly staid in contrast with the more militant National Women's Party organized by Alice **PAUL**. Nevertheless, its policy of intense lobbying was instrumental in achieving passage of the 19th Amendment, giving women the vote, which was finally ratified in June 1919, and went into effect in Aug 1920.

## National Defence, Government of (1870–1)

In France, the government that replaced the Second Empire on 4 Sep 1870. As its name indicates, its primary task was seen as continuing the war against Prussia. It consisted of republicans, and continued in office until replaced by a government under **THIERS**, appointed by the National Assembly elected in Feb 1871. ► **EMPIRE, SECOND** (France)

## National Front (NF)

A strongly nationalist political party in Britain which centres its political programme on opposition to immigration, and calls for the repatriation of ethnic minorities even if they were born in the UK. The party was created in 1960 by the merger of the White Defence League and the National Labour Party, and in its early years was a small neo-Nazi grouping. In the mid- and late 1970s it had some minor impact in elections and its membership grew. It tried to develop a more respectable face and recruited some members from the right of the **CONSERVATIVE PARTY** to widen its base beyond hardline neo-fascists. Its political appeal declined with the election of a Conservative government in 1979. It has since been supplanted by the neo-Nazi **BRITISH NATIONAL PARTY**, formed by NF chairman John Tyndall in 1982.

## National Guard (France)

The body created (13 July 1789) in France to replace the royal troops that the National Assembly refused to allow to enter Paris. Other towns followed the example, and soon most towns had their own guard under the control of the municipal council. It consisted of active (richer) citizens, and played a prominent part in the revolutionary events of 1792–3. Having shown royalist sympathies in 1795, it was suppressed; revived in a different form under the First Empire, and reorganized again in 1815, it became a bastion of the 'bourgeois' monarchy of **LOUIS-PHILIPPE**. The refusal of some elements of the Paris National Guard to defend the regime in Feb 1848 was the signal for the **FEBRUARY REVOLUTION**. It was virtually suspended during the Second Empire, but the Paris National Guard was enormously expanded and transformed in 1870 in a vain attempt to defeat the Prussian invader. Its revolt (Mar 1871) was the catalyst of the **PARIS COMMUNE**, in which many of its rank and file perished. It was finally suppressed after the defeat of the Commune. ► **EMPIRE, FIRST** (France); **EMPIRE, SECOND** (France)

## National Guard (USA)

The military reserves of each of the 50 US states, equipped by the US government but controlled by the states, and subject to federal or state call-up in times of emergency. Originally a state militia composed of volunteers, it was created by **CONGRESS** in 1916 to serve as an auxiliary to the regular US Army. Armed and trained by the federal government at US Army bases, during wartime the Guard is subject to federal control and can be called to serve in a war zone. For political reasons, Guard units were rarely sent abroad and in the decades before the suspension of the draft in the 1970s, many men enlisted in the National Guard to avoid serving in the regular army. The demise of the draft caused a major shrinkage in Guard membership. Its units, however, were an essential component of the US military presence in Iraq after the **IRAQ WAR**. In peacetime the Guard is headed by state governors, who have the power to call its members to serve during times of emergency, such as natural disasters or widespread civil unrest. ► **DRAFT**

## National Labor Relations Act (1935)

US labour legislation. Instigated and steered through CONGRESS by Senator Robert WAGNER, the act sought to find an effective means of guaranteeing the right of collective bargaining. It established a National Labor Relations Board with legal powers to ensure compliance by employers, especially in allowing employees to elect their own bargaining agent without fear of discrimination. It also prohibited company unions and opened the way for a huge expansion in union membership. ➤ LEWIS, JOHN L; TAFT–HARTLEY ACT; UNITED AUTOMOBILE WORKERS

## National Party (NP)

A party formed in South Africa, in 1912, to reflect the Boer (AFRIKANER) interest. Over the years it absorbed smaller parties like the Afrikaner Party and developed an explicit programme of Afrikaner advancement and separation of the races. It gained power in 1948 and retained it until 1994. Originally an almost exclusively Afrikaner party, it later began to lose some Afrikaners to more specifically nationalist organizations while gaining the support of conservative English-speaking white South Africans. Under the leadership of F W DE KLERK, the party orchestrated the transfer of power from whites to a more democratic political base and oversaw the dismantling of APARTHEID. These reforms culminated in 1994 in the country's first multiracial elections, when the NP was defeated but retained a significant presence in the new government of national unity led by the ANC, until it was withdrawn from the governing coalition in 1996. De Klerk stepped down as leader in 1997 and was replaced by Marthinus van Schalkwyk, who renamed it the New National Party (NNP). South Africa's second multi-race elections were disastrous for the NNP, which won only 7.4 per cent of the vote and even lost its Western Cape stronghold to the ANC, and its fortunes declined further in the 2004 elections. Van Schalkwyk, having aligned the NNP with the ANC and been made Minister of Environmental Affairs and Tourism, announced in Aug 2004 that he would be applying to join the ANC, and its membership was expected to do the same.

## National Party of Australia

The third largest party in Australia, it grew out of the Australian Country Party formed in 1920. Renamed the National Country Party in 1975, it took its present title in 1982, but except in Queensland it remains sectional in both its support and its policies. Socially conservative, favouring low tariffs and support for agriculture, it has generally acted in coalition with the major anti-Labor grouping of the time, most notably the LIBERAL PARTY OF AUSTRALIA. Only in Queensland, where the National Party title was adopted in 1974, has the party been able to rule in its own right.

## National Republican Party

US political party. It emerged in the winter of 1824–5 from remnants of the US Democratic-Republican Party. Opposed to Andrew Jackson and centred on John Quincy ADAMS (President, 1825–9) and Henry CLAY, his Secretary of State, the National Republicans espoused active intervention in the economy. By 1836 they were absorbed into the WHIG PARTY. ➤ REPUBLICAN PARTY

## National Revolution (1940)

In France, the name given by the supporters of PÉTAIN and the VICHY regime to the abolition of Third Republic; it symbolized their political programme, also epitomized in the national motto, *Travail, Famille, Patrie* ('Work, Family, Fatherland'), that was imposed in place of the republican 'LIBERTY, EQUALITY, FRATERNITY'. ➤ COLLABORATION (France); REPUBLIC, THIRD (France); WORLD WAR II

## National Road

A road built in the early 19c from Cumberland, Maryland, to Vandalia, Illinois, and eventually to St Louis, Missouri. Its construction and repair were financed initially by government sales of land, but in the 1830s this became the responsibility of the states through which it passed. The National Road played an important role in the expansion of the West.

## National Security Council (NSC)

A body created by CONGRESS in 1947 to advise the US President on the integration of domestic, foreign and military policies relating to national security. It was designed to achieve effective coordination between the military services and other government agencies and departments, and is composed of the President, Vice-President, Secretary of State, Secretary of Defense, Secretary of the Treasury and the National Security Adviser. The Chairman of the Joint Chiefs of Staff and the Director of Central Intelligence are advisers.

## National Socialist Movement (*Nationaal Socialistische Beweging*, NSB)

Dutch fascist party. Founded in 1931 by A A MUSSERT and C van Geelkerken (1901–76), the party attracted some support in the Netherlands in the 1930s, achieving eight per cent of the votes in the local elections of 1935. During the German occupation in WORLD WAR II there were 87,000 members, but the German authorities gave the leaders of the NSB very little real power. After the war NSB members were widely persecuted, interned, tried and imprisoned; several of the leaders, such as Mussert, were executed.

## National Urban League

US CIVIL RIGHTS organization. Founded in 1911 by professional blacks and progressive whites, it aimed to provide for rural blacks arriving in Northern cities the same services as those provided to white arrivals by settlement houses and charities. The definition of its aims demonstrates the influence of Booker T WASHINGTON: 'to promote, encourage, assist and engage in any and all kinds of work for improving the industrial, economic, social and spiritual condition among Negroes'.

## National Workshops (1848)

Set up in France after the FEBRUARY REVOLUTION of 1848, the name suggested an attempt to create a state-supported cooperative system of production, advocated by Louis BLANC in his book *L'Organisation du travail* (1839). In reality, they amounted to little more than a scheme of unemployment pay, and were soon seen as impossible to continue because of the huge cost. Restriction of entitlement to the payments led to the rising of the Parisian workers known as the JUNE DAYS.

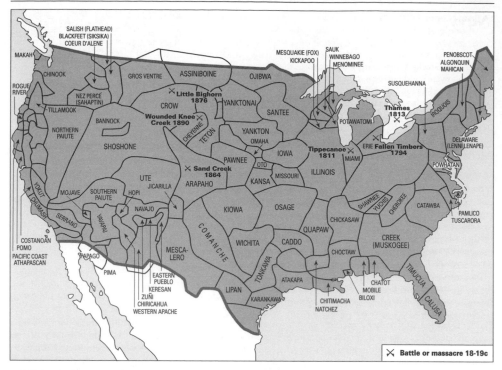

**Native Americans: Location of tribes at the time of discovery**

**Nation of Islam ► BLACK MUSLIMS**

**Native Americans** (American Indians)
The original inhabitants of the Western Hemisphere who arrived during the last Ice Age, estimated at 20,000 to 40,000 years ago. They came in several migrations over a land bridge connecting Alaska with Siberia, and spread gradually throughout the Americas. In what is now the USA, the Native Americans developed ways of life that suited the area in which they lived. Those of the north-west coast lived off the sea; those living on the buffalo-rich Great Plains were hunters and gatherers; those in the warm and abundant south-east were skilled farmers and fishermen. **COLUMBUS**, mistakenly believing he had reached India, called the indigenous people he encountered 'Indians'. Friendships with the Native Americans were indispensable to the survival of the early European settlers, who were shown how to grow native crops and where to hunt and fish, saving them from almost certain starvation. The Europeans unwittingly brought diseases to which the native people had no immunity, wiping out thousands and nearly destroying whole tribes. In addition, as more Europeans came and spread further west, Native American resistance to the encroachment of white settlers increased and the long conflict known as the **INDIAN WARS** began. The numerous tribes with their diverse languages lacked the cohesion to repel the influx of well-supplied, determined settlers. Since Native American land was increasingly in demand, most of the tribes east of the Mississippi River were pushed west. But as western land was opened to settlers, the Native Americans were forced onto reservations in hostile terrain and far from their original lands, sometimes close to traditional tribal enemies. With their affairs administered by the federal government,

they lost control over their lives and were not granted US citizenship until 1924. Of the current population of almost 2.4 million, more than half live off reservations in metropolitan areas. Over 50 languages are spoken among the more than 500 tribes. As a group, Native Americans are among the poorest in the nation and continue to contend with both the prejudice and the romanticized images of the past. Throughout the second half of the 20c they have been pressing for increasing self-determination, striving to balance their economic and political survival against the preservation of their cultural and spiritual identities. ► *See map*

**nativism**
US anti-immigrant attitude, generally expressed by native-born white Protestants. From the early 19c, a major focus of anti-immigrant feeling was directed toward Irish Catholics, who were accused by nativists of bringing the papacy into US politics. Nativist antagonism was also extended to other immigrant groups. Between 1854 and 1858, the nativist movement made significant political gains with the American Party, popularly known as the **KNOW-NOTHINGS**. Nativism began to diminish in importance as the **SLAVERY** issue became a dominant American concern. With the renewal of immigration in the late 19c and early 20c, nativist sentiment resurfaced and contributed largely to the passage of the Immigration Act of 1924, which eventually brought a sharp curtailment to immigration by establishing immigration quotas.

**NATO (North Atlantic Treaty Organization)**
An organization established by a treaty signed in 1949 by Belgium, Canada, Denmark, France, Iceland, Italy, Luxembourg, the Netherlands, Norway, Portugal, the UK and the USA; Greece and Turkey acceded

# *Navy*

*War & Warfare*

The ancient Greeks were the first to develop organized navies. By the 7c BC they were building true warships which had specially strengthened bows designed for ramming enemy vessels and decks from which marines could fire missiles and launch boarding attacks. Sails were used for cruising when the wind was favourable, but oars were the main propelling force. The Greek *trireme*, with three banks of oars on each side, was a fast and manoeuvrable ship that dominated the eastern Mediterranean for two centuries.

Greek naval prowess was vital in staving off Persian invasion, and it was the victory of the Athenian fleet at Salamis (480 BC) that made conquest impossible for the Emperor Xerxes. Athens' reliance on her navy led to neglect of her army, contributing to her eventual defeat in the Peloponnesian War in 404 BC.

The power of the Romans was based on their army, although they proved able to raise and operate fleets when necessary, such as in the wars against the great naval power of Carthage. The Roman general Pompey (106–48 BC) proved himself a capable admiral when he swept the Mediterranean of pirates, but neglect of the Roman navy cost Rome abiding control of the seas.

Galleys were important to the navy of the **Byzantine Empire**; their large fighting *dromon* had 100 oars in two banks. In their struggle against the pirates who threatened their trade routes and the ever-encroaching Turks, the Byzantines had the advantage of better-built ships as well as the secret weapon of Greek fire: an incendiary mixture launched at enemy vessels from a tube or a ballista.

In the West, the **Vikings** used specialized war vessels to mount raids and eventually conquer territory. The Viking longship used sails for distance travel and oars when fighting. It carried crews of up to 200 men, and with its shallow draught could sail up rivers and navigate coastal waters. To combat this menace, Alfred the Great (849–99) built up the first major English fleet of vessels, based on the longship design.

The 15c saw an important advance in ship construction with the development of square-rigged ships armed with cannon. Specialized warships maintained by the Crown remained rare, for the bigger merchant ships could be pressed into the line of battle. In the following century, an English Navy Royal came into existence on a permanent basis, with **Henry VII** establishing Portsmouth as the base of the navy and building the first dry dock. Under **Henry VIII**, English ships pioneered the gunport cut in the ship's side to allow heavy broadside cannon to be mounted in large numbers, as opposed to carrying them in wooden castles at bow and stern. The Spanish navy, although committed to galley fleets in the Mediterranean, increasingly took up this design for its Atlantic operations.

The leading seaman of the galleon era was Sir Francis **Drake**, who led expeditions attacking Spain's communications with her colonies and preying on the richly laden ships sailing from the Americas. As open confrontation with Spain became inevitable, the Elizabethan navy was built up, and when in 1588 the Spanish **Armada** was launched, the English navy met it with a mixture of royal galleons and private ships. The fleet of smaller English vessels was able to outmanoeuvre the Spaniards and disperse their fleet with fire ships so that they were torn apart by storms on their flight around the north of Scotland. In the long term, however, no state could maintain naval supremacy.

In the Mediterranean, the Spanish soldier Don **John of Austria** commanded the Christian fleet that defeated the Turks at the Battle of **Lepanto** (1571). Lepanto was a galley fight, though the galleys fought with big bow-mounted cannon. The Turks never quite recovered from the losses of ships and trained men, though they did, of course, rebuild a galley navy.

The 17c saw naval rivalry between the English and the Dutch. Oliver **Cromwell** continued **Charles I**'s policy of building up the navy, and the first warships with three decks of guns were introduced. Under **Charles II** the English fleet

in 1952, West Germany in 1955, Spain in 1982, the Czech Republic, Hungary and Poland in 1999, and Bulgaria, Estonia, Latvia, Lithuania, Romania, Slovakia and Slovenia in 2004. In 1966, France withdrew all its forces from NATO command, but it remains a member. NATO is a permanent military alliance originally established to defend Western Europe against Soviet aggression. The treaty commits the members to treat an armed attack on one of them as an attack on all of them, and for all to assist the country attacked by such actions as are deemed necessary. The alliance forces are based on contributions from the member countries' armed services and operate under a multi-national command. The remit includes the deployment of nuclear, as well as conventional, weapons. Its institutions include a Council, an International Secretariat, the Supreme Headquarters Allied Powers, Europe (SHAPE), and various committees to formulate common policies. In the 1970s and 1980s, NATO policy of a first-strike nuclear attack to fend off a Soviet conventional attack became controversial in Western Europe, where many thought it increased the possibility of nuclear war.

After the 1989 changes in Eastern Europe, a NATO summit in London (July 1990) began the process of redefining NATO's military and political goals, and these became more political than military, concentrated on maintaining peace within Europe. In 1997 tension between Russia and the West was relaxed when Russia was granted a formal voice in NATO affairs in exchange for NATO's expansion in eastern Europe. Nato's first military attack was carried out in 1994 when it launched air strikes against Bosnian Serb forces entering UN-designated 'safe areas' during the war in Bosnia and Herzegovina. In 1999 its forces were again deployed to stop the Serbs from achieving the **ETHNIC CLEANSING** of Albanians from **KOSOVO**. In 2003, NATO took over command of the International Security Assistance Force in Afghanistan. ► **NUCLEAR WEAPONS**

**NAURU** official name **Republic of Nauru**
An island nation in the west-central Pacific Ocean, 26 mi/42 km south of the Equator and 2,500 mi/4,000 km north-east of Sydney, Australia. It was administered until 1914 by Germany, which annexed it in 1888, and then administered by Australia under a

was given the title of the Royal Navy, and many reforms were introduced by Samuel **Pepys** in his capacity as naval administrator. The Royal Navy was never totally able to overcome the Dutch, but fiscal exhaustion led to a decline in Dutch naval power after 1700. In the 18c French warships usually had finer lines and more speed than their British counterparts but they were less solidly built and expensive to maintain, despite the general adoption of protective copper-sheathed bottoms by European navies by the end of the century. By 1700 combat navies were almost exclusively formed of state-owned specialist warships.

In the era of the **French Revolution** and the **Napoleonic Wars**, the Royal Navy won a series of major sea victories against their French and Spanish foes, notably the **Glorious First of June** in the Atlantic (1794), **Cape St Vincent** (Feb 1797), **Camperdown** (Oct 1797), **Aboukir Bay** (1798) and **Trafalgar** (1805). Under such able commanders as **Nelson**, Britain was established as the greatest sea power, restricting **Napoleon I** to land campaigning.

During the 19c steam power gradually replaced sail. The first vessel powered by a propeller (the *Princeton*) was launched in 1843 by the USA. Britain's first screw-driven ship (the *Dauntless*) followed in 1844, and by 1870 the Royal Navy had abandoned sail altogether. Ironclads – ships protected by iron armour – were the next major development, and they saw service in the **American Civil War**. That conflict also saw the first use of semi-submersible vessels with the Confederate craft *David* launching torpedo attacks on Union vessels.

The late 19c saw many advances in warship design and weaponry, and the German navy in particular expanded rapidly in an attempt to challenge the supremacy of the Royal Navy. The rival navies never really tested each other in **World War I**, with only one major fleet engagement, the indecisive Battle of **Jutland** in 1916, taking place. German submarines, or U-boats, posed a threat to British merchant shipping as well as naval vessels, a role they were to repeat in **World War II**. It was during that war that the aircraft-carrier came to prominence, particularly in dominating the Pacific battles between the US and Japanese fleets.

After World War II the nuclear submarine became increasingly important as part of a deterrent strike force, and during the **Cold War**, Russian and **NATO** submarine fleets, armed with ever more destructive missiles, constantly patrolled within launching range of enemy targets. The Royal Navy necessarily played a prominent role in the **Falklands War** in 1982 when a task-force of warships and aircraft-carriers was despatched to eject the Argentine forces. Both the British and Argentine navies lost vessels in the fighting, to attacks from submarines, missiles or carrier-based aircraft. The **Gulf War** and **Iraq War** underlined the enduring importance of naval capability, not only as an effective logistical tool for power projection, but also as a platform for air power in the shape of carrier-based aircraft and ship and submarine-launched missiles. ► **Air Force**; **Army**; **Ships**

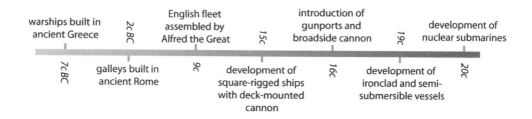

| | | | | |
|---|---|---|---|---|
| warships built in ancient Greece | 2c BC | English fleet assembled by Alfred the Great | 15c | introduction of gunports and broadside cannon | 19c | development of nuclear submarines |

| 7c BC | galleys built in ancient Rome | 9c | development of square-rigged ships with deck-mounted cannon | 16c | development of ironclad and semi-submersible vessels | 20c |

**LEAGUE OF NATIONS** mandate from 1919 and, following the end of Japanese occupation during World War II, as a **UN** trust territory from 1947. It gained its independence in 1968, becoming the world's smallest independent republic both in size and population. Nauru's future is uncertain as its phosphate reserves are running out, mining has ruined much of the island and its population relies for water on stored rainfall and desalination plants.

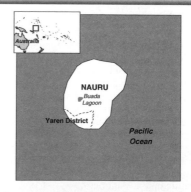

### Navajo or Navaho

Athabascan-speaking Native North Americans. They are thought to have migrated to the south-west some time around 1000AD. With a population numbering over 260,000, they are one of the largest Native American groups in the USA. In the 18c they carried out raids on Spanish settlers and **PUEBLO** in the area, but were themselves eventually defeated by US troops led by Kit **CARSON** in 1863–4. They settled in 1868 on a reservation covering much of Arizona and some of New Mexico and Utah. The Navajo Reservation and their government-allotted land in these states today measures some 26,000 sq mi/67,000 sq km. Tribal income is derived from the raising of sheep and horses, metalworking, weaving, and some mining of gas, uranium and oil resources found on their reservation, but the land is generally poor and thousands earn their living by becoming casual labourers elsewhere. The Navajo remain among the poorest of **NATIVE AMERICANS**.

### Navarino Bay, Battle of (1827)

A battle fought when the British and French (with the

agreement of the Russians) destroyed the Turkish and Egyptian fleets off south-west Greece. The outcome was an important factor in the achievement of Greek independence from the **OTTOMAN EMPIRE**, which was formally recognized in 1828.

### Navarre, Kingdom of
A former kingdom of northern Spain, co-extensive with the modern province of Navarre. It was an early centre of resistance to the **MOORS** and united with **CASTILE** in 1515.

### Navas de Tolosa, Battle of Las (1212)
The key battle of the medieval Spanish **RECONQUEST**, won by Alfonso VIII of Castile at the head of a joint army from Castile, France, Aragon, Navarre and Portugal, which routed the Almohad rulers, checked the Muslim advance permanently and prepared the way for the further extension of Christian territory. ► **AL-MOHADS**

### Navigation Acts (1650–96)
Protective legislation in Britain, designed to increase England's share of overseas-carrying trade. The laws stated that all imports to England had to be in English ships or in those of the country of origin. The laws were frequently contentious in the 18c, adding to the 13 American colonies' sense of grievance against the mother country. These Acts were not repealed until 1849. ► **AMERICAN REVOLUTION**

### Navy ► See panel

### Naxalites
An extremist group which broke away from the Communist Party of India in 1969, with the aim of forming a truly revolutionary Marxist–Leninist party; their name derived from the 1967 Naxalbari revolts in west Bengal. Influenced and approved by the Chinese Communist Party, their intention was to seize power by violent means, rather than through parliamentary channels. In the early 1970s the group was involved in political violence, including murder, in a number of Indian states. Most members were subsequently arrested, and what had been a serious threat to law and order was removed.

### Nayaks
Telugu chieftains of the Vijayanagari empire, often at odds with their overlords; some of them founded small kingdoms of their own at Ikkeri, Jinji (Gingee), **THANJAVUR** (Tanjore) and Madurai, which became more prominent after the sack of Vijayanagara in 1565. These Nayak dynasties were in conflict not only with one another but with the **DECCANI SULTANATES**, the Mughals and the European powers of the British and the French. The greatest of the Madurai Nayaks was Tirumala Nayak (1623/59), known both for his military campaigns and for his rebuilding of the great Minakshi Temple at Madurai.

### Nazarbaev, Nursultan Abishevich (1940– )
Kazakhstan politician. Originally a metalworker, he turned to party duties in 1969 and rose steadily in the 1970s and dramatically in the 1980s. By 1984 he was Chairman of the Kazakhstan Council of Ministers, and by 1989 he had been selected as First Secretary of the Kazakh Communist Party. In 1990 he was chosen for the Soviet **POLITBURO** and became President of the Kazakh Supreme Soviet. As elected President of Kazakhstan in 1991 he took his republic out of the USSR but kept it in the Commonwealth of Independent States (**CIS**).

### Nazi Party (NSDAP)
A German political party which originated as the German Worker's Party (DAP), founded in 1919 as a patriotic working-man's party to protest against the German surrender of 1918 and the Treaty of **VERSAILLES**, and renamed the *Nationalsozialistische Deutsche Arbeiterpartei* ('National Socialist German Workers' Party', NSDAP or Nazi Party) in 1920. Adolf **HITLER** became the party's leader the following year. Its ideology was a blend of imperialist nationalism, racism, **SOCIALISM** and more traditional ideas. Nazi ideology maintained that the world was divided into a hierarchy of races; Aryans, of whom Germans were the purest example, were the supreme culture-bearing race, while the Jews were the lowest. It was also contended that the Jews were intent on world conquest through infesting the Aryan race. This set of ideas was set out by Hitler in *Mein Kampf* (1925), although public opinion forced the NSDAP to play down this theme until after 1933. It was not until the 1930s, with the onset of economic crisis, that the Nazi Party gained a position of significant support; in 1932 with 37.3 per cent of the vote it became the largest party in the **REICHSTAG**. Support came from people of all backgrounds, although its electorate was strongly Protestant and its membership young. In 1933 Hitler was appointed Chancellor in a coalition government, a position from which he was able to build up a personal dictatorship, through legal measures, terror and propaganda. Once in power, the Nazis ruthlessly crushed opposition, initiated a vigorous job-creation programme, from 1935 engaged in extensive rearmament, and in the late 1930s invaded Austria and the **SUDETENLAND** (1938), and Bohemia-Moravia and Memel (1939) as a strategic and economic prerequisite for the conquest of Eastern Europe to obtain land (**LEBENSRAUM**) for the 'master race'. During **WORLD WAR II**, Nazi policies included slave labour, plunder, and mass extermination, leading to the **NUREMBERG TRIALS** of 1946. Nazism as a political ideology is now viewed as a terrifying combination of populism and technocracy with inhumanity, Social-Darwinistic imperialism, and almost nihilistic amorality. ► **ANSCHLUSS**; **HOLOCAUST**

### Nazi–Soviet Pact ► GERMAN–SOVIET PACT

### Ndebele
A Bantu-speaking people of south-western Zimbabwe and northern South Africa. They originated in the 19c as an offshoot of **NGUNI** groups who moved north, conquering some of the indigenous Shona peoples, and established a highly stratified state. In the 1890s they resisted white pioneers' encroachment on their land, but were ruthlessly suppressed. Today they constitute 17 per cent of the population of Zimbabwe. ► **ZULU KINGDOM**; **MATABELELAND**

### Ndongo
A kingdom to the south of the Congo mouth which the Portuguese first encountered in the late 15c. Its ruler was known as the Ngolo and gave his name to Angola. The Portuguese attempted to turn Ndongo

into a major slaving partner and also embroiled it in wars with the kingdom of Kongo. A new kingdom known as Matamba emerged from it in the 16c, but like its neighbours it was eventually subsumed within the Portuguese colony.

**Nechaev, Sergei Gennadievich** (1847–82)
Russian revolutionary. The schoolteacher son of a workman, he left St Petersburg for Geneva in 1869 at the age of 21 and teamed up with **BAKUNIN** to write a book called *Revolutionary Cathechism* on how to be a professional revolutionary. He returned home before the end of the year to found a small organization, the 'People's Reckoning', which achieved notoriety for killing one of its members, allegedly a police spy. He immediately escaped to Zurich, but in 1872 he was extradited and imprisoned in St Petersburg. From the Peter and Paul Fortress he kept in touch with his fellow revolutionaries until his death ten years later.

**Necker, Jacques** (1732–1804)
French politician and financier. Initially a banker's clerk, he moved to Paris (1762), founded a bank, and became a wealthy speculator. By 1776–7 he became Director of the French Treasury and Director-General of Finances. He attempted some administrative reforms, but tried to finance French involvement in the **AMERICAN REVOLUTION** by heavy borrowing, while concealing the large state deficit. He was dismissed in 1781, but recalled in 1788 to deal with the impending financial crisis. He summoned the **ESTATES GENERAL**, but his proposals for social and constitutional change aroused royal opposition. He was dismissed and hastily recalled (1789), but finally resigned in 1790. He retired to his estate near Geneva, where he died. ► **LOUIS XVI**

**Nedić, Milan** (1877–1946)
Serbian politician and soldier. Chief of Staff and Minister of War during the 1930s, he collaborated with the German occupation during **WORLD WAR II** and was President of the puppet government in Belgrade from 1941 to 1944. At the end of the war, he was imprisoned and committed suicide. ► **LJOTIĆ, DIMITRIJE**

**Negrín (López), Juan** (1892–1956)
Spanish politician. He studied medicine in Germany, and became Professor of Physiology at the University of Madrid (1923–31). As a moderate Socialist, he was a parliamentary deputy throughout the Second Republic (1931–6). During the **SPANISH CIVIL WAR** he served as Finance Minister (1936–7) and Prime Minister (1937–9) and for a time was also Defence Minister. As Premier he adopted a pro-Soviet, pro-communist but anti-revolutionary position, aimed at winning the Western democracies' support for the Republic, but his 'Thirteen Points' (1938) failed to impress Britain and France. In 1939, shortly before the end of the civil war, he was overthrown by an anti-communist coup. He died in exile in France. ► **REPUBLIC, SECOND** (Spain)

**negritude**
Associated above all with francophone writers, such as Aimé Cesaire and Léopold **SENGHOR**, negritude was a philosophy which valued the contribution of black people and held that black people had a special intellectual approach which was less rational than the Graeco-Roman tradition and more instinctual.

**Neguib, Mohammed** (1901–84)
Egyptian leader. As general of an army division in 1952 he carried out a coup d'état in Cairo which banished King **FAROUK I** and initiated the 'Egyptian Revolution'. Taking first the offices of Commander-in-Chief and Prime Minister, he abolished the monarchy in 1953 and became President of the republic. He was deposed in 1954 and succeeded by Colonel Gamal Abd al-**NASSER**.

**Nehru, Jawaharlal**, known as **Pandit ('Teacher')** (1889–1964)
Indian politician. Educated at Harrow and Cambridge, he became a lawyer, and served in the Allahabad High Court. He joined the Indian Congress Committee (1918), became an admirer and follower, if sometimes a critic, of M K **GANDHI**, and was imprisoned several times by the British. In 1929 he was elected President of the **INDIAN NATIONAL CONGRESS**. From 1947 to 1964 he was India's first Prime Minister and Minister of External Affairs, following a policy of neutrality during the **COLD WAR**. He introduced a policy of industrialization, reorganized the states on a linguistic basis, and brought the dispute with Pakistan over Kashmir to a peaceful, though not final, solution.

**Nehru, Motilal** (1861–1931)
Indian nationalist leader, lawyer and journalist. The father of Jawaharlal **NEHRU**, he became a follower of M K **GANDHI** in 1919, founded the *Independent* of Allahabad and became the first President of the reconstructed **INDIAN NATIONAL CONGRESS**. In the 1920s he co-headed the **SWARAJ** Party (with Chitta Ranjan **DAS**) in which members of the Congress entered the legislatures, and wrote a report as a basis for Indian constitutional development and to solve the political differences between Hindus and Muslims. The report was not, however, acceptable to members of the All-India **MUSLIM LEAGUE**, led by Muhammad Ali **JINNAH**.

**Nejedly, Zdenek** (1878–1962)
Czechoslovak communist ideologue. A professor of music in the Charles University, Prague, from before **WORLD WAR I**, he joined the Communist Party during the depression in 1929, and emigrated to Moscow with other leaders during **WORLD WAR II**. In post-war National Front governments until 1953 he held ministerial posts, usually education, and in 1952 he became chairman of the Academy of Sciences. A man of many words but simple thoughts, he restricted the education of a whole generation of Czechoslovaks to narrow Marxist ideas; however, he was very popular with sympathizers abroad.

**Nelken, Margarita** (1896–1968)
Spanish politician and feminist. The daughter of German Jews, she was born in Madrid but did not achieve Spanish nationality until 1931. During her early years she was a painter, exhibiting her works in Paris and Vienna as well as Spain, but following a severe eye-illness dedicated herself to literary criticism. She was also active on behalf of **WOMEN'S RIGHTS**, publishing *The Social Condition of Women* (1922), as well as being involved in land reform movements in Estremadura and Andalusia. Under the Second

Republic (1931–6) Nelken was successful in all three general elections as a deputy for the Socialist Party (**PSOE**). She agitated for land reform, was active in the national arbitration boards, and formed part of the National Committee of Women against War and Fascism. Her impatience with the parliamentary process led her to become one of the most radical Socialist deputies. During the **SPANISH CIVIL WAR** (1936–9) she led various campaigns for the mobilization of women. In 1937 she joined the Communist Party (**PCE**). After the civil war, she was exiled in Paris, Moscow and finally Mexico, where she died. ► **REPUBLIC, SECOND** (Spain)

### Nelson, Horatio Nelson, Viscount (1758–1805)

British admiral. He joined the navy in 1770, and was sent to the West Indies (1784) to enforce the **NAVIGATION ACTS** against the newly independent USA. There he married Frances Nisbet, and in 1787 retired with her to Burnham Thorpe. In 1794 he commanded the naval brigade at the reduction of Bastia and Calvi, where he lost the sight of his right eye, and in an action at Santa Cruz had his right arm amputated. In 1798 he followed the French fleet to Egypt, destroying it at the Battle of **ABOUKIR BAY**. On his return to Naples, he fell in love with Emma, Lady Hamilton, and began a liaison with her that lasted until his death. In 1801 he was made rear-admiral, and led the attack on Copenhagen. Previously created a baron, he then became a viscount, and Commander-in-Chief. In 1805 he gained his greatest victory, against the combined French and Spanish fleet at the Battle of **TRAFALGAR**. During the battle he was mortally wounded on his flagship, HMS *Victory*. His body was brought home and buried in St Paul's Cathedral, London. ► **HOOD, SAMUEL; NAPOLEONIC WARS**

### Nemanja or Nemanjić Dynasty (1168–1372)

The Serbian ruling family which rose to prominence in **RAŠKA**. In 1168 the Byzantine emperor **MANUEL I COMNENUS** granted **STEPHEN I NEMANJA** and his brothers great tracts of land which they held as vassals. These estates were part of the core of the medieval state of Serbia. In 1372, with the death of Uroš V, the son of **STEPHEN DUSHAN**, the dynasty died out.

### Nenni, Pietro (1891–1980)

Italian politician. As editor of the socialist paper *Avanti!* he was exiled by the fascists in 1926, and served as a political commissar for the International Brigades during the **SPANISH CIVIL WAR**. He became Secretary-General of the Italian Socialist Party (PSI) in 1944, Vice-Premier in the **DE GASPERI** coalition (1945–6) and Foreign Minister (1946–7). In 1963–8 he once again served as Vice-Premier in the four-party left-centre coalition headed by Aldo **MORO**. In Dec 1968 he accepted the post of Foreign Minister but resigned in July 1969.

### Neo-Confucianism

A reassertion of Confucian political and moral values in China during the **SONG DYNASTY** in reaction against the otherworldly concerns of Buddhism, which had been influential in China since the 6c. Neo-Confucian scholars refocused attention on the traditional **CONFUCIAN CLASSICS** and promoted the virtues of public service and social welfare activism. Only through active engagement in society, they argued, could one bring one's own self-cultivation to fruition. In order to rival Buddhist metaphysics, Neo-Confucian scholars also constructed a metaphysical system of their own, claiming that correct relationships prescribed by Confucian thought (eg within the family, or between ruler and ruled) were manifestations of abstract principles (*li*) immanent in the cosmos. The commentaries on the classics written by Zhu Xi (1130–1200), the most important Neo-Confucian thinker, became accepted orthodoxy from the 14c and were designated as the only correct interpretations to be used in education and the **CIVIL SERVICE EXAMINATION SYSTEM**.

### neoconservatism

A pejorative phrase originally coined to describe former left-wingers who move to the political right in national politics, but more recently applied to journalists, policy advisers and institutions associated with the American Enterprise Institute and the Project for the New American Century and publications supporting their aims. Neoconservatism's basic tenets propose that the USA should use its status to promote democratic values, in particular advocating an aggressive foreign policy to oppose state-sponsored terrorism, including unilateral and preemptive action and **REGIME CHANGE**; that the USA should support Israel unconditionally while seeking to democratize the Arab Middle East; and that the USA should maintain unchallenged its position in the world. Neoconservatism has greatly influenced US foreign policy under Republican administrations since the 1980s and especially that of President George W **BUSH**.

### NEPAL   official name **Kingdom of Nepal**

A landlocked independent kingdom lying along the southern slopes of the Himalayas in central Asia, bounded to the north by the Tibet region of China, and to the east, south and west by India. Nepal was ruled from about the 4c to the 10c by the Licchavi Dynasty, then from the 10c to 18c by the Malla Dynasty, under which Hinduism became the dominant religion. Modern Nepal was formed from a group of independent hill states that were united in the 18c. In 1769 the current ruling dynasty came to power following an invasion by Gurkhas, who moved the capital to Kathmandu. A parliamentary system was introduced in 1959, but was replaced in 1960 by a party-less system of *panchayats* (village councils). Nepal is a constitutional monarchy ruled by a hereditary King. King **BIRENDRA BIR BIKRAM** (1972–2001), the Queen and other members of the royal family were killed in Jun 2001 by Crown Prince Dipendra, who then shot himself; after his death a few days later, King Birendra's brother, Gyanendra, became king. A period of unrest in 1990 was followed by a reduction of the King's powers and the introduction of a new constitution with a multiparty parliamentary system.

But the factionalized nature of the country's politics have led to frequent changes of government, and the instability has been exacerbated by the Maoist insurrection that began in 1996, spreading from the remote west to most of the rest of the country. The government attempted to suppress the insurgents by often brutal methods but with little success. After a brief ceasefire in 2001 (Jul–Dec), fighting intensified and a state of emergency was declared in Nov. A second ceasefire in 2003 also failed and clashes between the insurgents and the security forces continued; both insurgents and the police have been implicated in human rights abuses and atrocities.

**Nerchinsk, Treaty of** (7 Sep 1689)
China's first treaty with a foreign country (Russia) which was regarded as an independent state rather than a vassal. It settled, for the time being, border disputes between Tsarist Russia and QING DYNASTY China in the wake of Russian expansion eastwards across Siberia. By the 1640s Russian traders were moving south into the Amur River region (northern Manchuria) demanding tribute from tribes that owed allegiance to the Qing. Following a siege of the Russian stockade at Albazin (on the Amur River) by Qing forces in 1686, both countries decided on a peace settlement since each was fearful that the other would ally with neighbouring Mongol tribes to the west. Envoys met at Nerchinsk (founded by the Russians in 1658) and the resulting treaty provided for Qing control of the Amur River region in exchange for which Russia was allowed to send trading caravans to the Chinese capital at Beijing. The treaty held good until the mid-19c when further Russian expansion in the Amur region led to territorial concessions being wrung from an enfeebled Qing Dynasty. ▶ BEIJING, TREATY OF

**Nesselrode, Karl Robert Vasilevich, Count** (1780–1861)
Russian politician. He was born in Lisbon, the son of a diplomat. After experience in the army, the navy and the foreign service, he represented Russia at the Congress of VIENNA (1814–15), and was one of the most active diplomats in the subsequent HOLY ALLIANCE. He became Foreign Minister in 1822, and dominated Russian foreign policy on behalf of ALEXANDER I and NICHOLAS I for 30 years. His Balkan policy of trying to extend Russia's influence over the OTTOMAN EMPIRE at the expense of Britain and France contributed to the outbreak of the CRIMEAN WAR in 1854.

**Netanyahu, Binyamin** (1949–)
Israeli LIKUD politician. He was born in Israel and educated at the Massachusetts Institute of Technology in the USA. Between 1967 and 1972 he served in the Israeli Defence Forces, and in 1976 became a director of the Jonathan Institute, a foundation that studies counter-terrorism. In 1982 he was appointed Israel's ambassador to the UN, and in 1988 was elected to the Knesset as a member of the right-wing Likud Party. Having served as Deputy Foreign Minister (1988–91) and Deputy Prime Minister (1991–2), he contested the 1996 general election and was elected Prime Minister. In contrast to his predecessor, Yitzhak RABIN, he pursued a more cautious policy in implementing the 1993 OSLO ACCORDS with the

Palestinians. He failed to win re-election in 1999, losing to the Labour Party candidate, Ehud Barak. He later served in Ariel SHARON's coalition governments, first as Foreign Minister and then as Finance Minister.

**NETHERLANDS, THE** also known as **Holland**, official name **Kingdom of the Netherlands**

A maritime kingdom in north-western Europe, bounded to the west and north by the North Sea; to the east by Germany; and to the south by Belgium. It was part of the Roman Empire until the 4c AD, and part of the Frankish Empire by the 8c before being incorporated into the HOLY ROMAN EMPIRE. The Netherlands passed to the Dukes of BURGUNDY in the 15c and then to PHILIP II, who succeeded to Spain and the Netherlands in 1555. Attempts to stamp out Protestantism led to rebellion in 1572. The seven northern provinces united against Spain in 1579. These UNITED PROVINCES OF THE NETHERLANDS achieved independence, finally recognized by Spain in 1648 at the end of the EIGHTY YEARS' WAR, and so founded the modern Dutch state. Between 1795 and 1813 it was overrun by the French, who established the BATAVIAN REPUBLIC. Thereafter, it was united with Belgium as the Kingdom of the United Netherlands, until Belgium broke away to form a separate kingdom in 1830. Although the country was neutral in WORLD WAR I, it was invaded by the Germans in 1940 and occupied during WORLD WAR II. The Netherlands joined with Belgium and Luxembourg to form the BENELUX economic union in 1948, and was a founding member of the EEC in 1958. In the late 1940s there were conflicts over the independence of Dutch colonies in South-East Asia, particularly Indonesia. In 1980 Queen BEATRIX acceded to the throne. Recent years have seen controversy over the attitude of Islamic immigrants to the traditional liberalism of the Dutch.

**Neto, (Antonio) Agostinho** (1922–79)
Angolan nationalist and politician. The son of a Methodist missionary, he was educated in a Methodist school in Luanda before studying medicine in Portuguese universities. He returned to Angola to work in the colonial medical service and joined the MPLA. He was imprisoned several times (1952–62) but escaped from the Cape Verde Islands to Zaire (now Democratic Republic of Congo), where he soon became President of the MPLA and its leader in the guerrilla war against Portuguese colonialism. His close ties with CASTRO gave him both Cuban and Soviet backing, and this assistance enabled him to prevail in the civil war which followed the Portuguese retreat from Angola. He became the first President of Angola in 1974, holding the post until his death.

**Neuilly, Treaty of** (27 Nov 1919)
This agreement dictated the terms to be paid by Bulgaria as a defeated power at the end of **WORLD WAR I**. Bulgaria surrendered to Greece the gains it had made in Western Thrace after the **BALKAN WARS** and ceded to Serbia four regions of strategic significance. The Bulgarians were also to pay an indemnity of US$450 million, about a quarter of the national wealth, and a great quantity of their livestock. The size of the Bulgarian army, police force and border guard was greatly reduced. ➤ **BORIS III; STAMBOLISKI, ALEXANDER; THRACE**

**Neutrality Acts**
A series of US acts passed in the 1930s which aimed to prevent the USA becoming involved in the escalating European conflict. The 1935 Act authorized a temporary embargo on arms shipments to all belligerents; the 1936 Act outlawed loans or credits to belligerents; and the 1937 Act forbade munitions shipments to either side in the **SPANISH CIVIL WAR**. By the time of the attack on **PEARL HARBOR**, the bans had been lifted and the neutral course had been abandoned.

**Neva, Battle of the** (1240)
A battle between Russian and Swedish forces on the River Neva, where Russian troops led by Prince Alexander of Novgorod (subsequently referred to as **ALEXANDER NEVSKY**) attacked and defeated Swedish forces under cover of fog. The victory thwarted Sweden's attempts to control the northern end of the trade route from the Baltic to the Black Sea. Two years later Alexander won a famous victory over the **TEUTONIC KNIGHTS** at Lake Peipus, proving that in the end the emerging Russian society could resist German as well as Swedish incursions.

**Neves, Tancredo de Almeida** (1910–85)
Brazilian politician. He was a local politician in the 1930s and became a federal deputy for the **PSD** in the 1950s. Justice Minister under Getúlio **VARGAS** in 1953–4, he was head of the Banco do Brasil under **KUBITSCHEK (DE OLIVEIRA)** (1956–8) and first Prime Minister and Justice Minister under João **GOULART**. Neves was a master of **CONCILIAÇÃO**, both as architect of the 1961 compromise, which allowed President Goulart to assume office under a 'parliamentary regime', and the referendum of Jan 1963, which restored traditional powers to the President. His inability to cobble together cross-party support for moderate policies was a leading factor in the coup of 1964. A man of moderate centrist views, he managed to gain the confidence of conservative groups in the 1970s for the transition to civilian rule. As **PMDB** Governor of Minas Gerais (1982–4), he articulated the 'Democratic Alliance' which won the presidential nomination in 1985, with José **SARNEY (COSTA)** as running-mate. Overtaken by illness a few hours before he was to take office, he remained the 'President who never was'.

**Newcastle, Duke of** ➤ **PELHAM, THOMAS PELHAM-HOLLES, 1ST DUKE OF NEWCASTLE**

**New Deal** (Canada)
The name given to the legislation influenced by US President **ROOSEVELT**'s New Deal, passed in 1935 by the Conservative administration of R B **BENNETT**, after the failure of more orthodox measures to solve the problems of the Depression. It established a social insurance plan, maximum hours and minimum wages, a marketing board for natural products, and farm credit provisions. This programme, and the fears of several Conservative supporters that the government would involve itself in economic planning and price-fixing, led to a split in the party and the formation of the Reconstruction Party, which let in the Liberals under Mackenzie **KING** with a landslide victory in the 1935 elections. Bennett's New Deal measures were declared unconstitutional in 1937, but they served as a basis for the **LIBERAL PARTY** programme after constitutional amendment. ➤ **NEW DEAL** (USA); **PRICE SPREADS COMMISSION; STEVENS, HENRY H**

**New Deal** (USA)
The administration and policies of US President Franklin D **ROOSEVELT**, who pledged a 'new deal' for the country during the campaign of 1932. He embarked on active state economic involvement to combat the **GREAT DEPRESSION**, setting the tone in a hectic 'first hundred days'. Although some early legislation was invalidated by the Supreme Court, the New Deal left a lasting impact on US government, economy and society, not least by the effective creation of the modern institution of the presidency. Major specific initiatives included the National Recovery Act (1933), the **TENNESSEE VALLEY AUTHORITY** (1933), the Agricultural Adjustment Act (1933), the National Youth Administration (1935), the **NATIONAL LABOR RELATIONS ACT** or Wagner Act (1935) and the Social Security Act (1935). The 'first New Deal' (1933–4), concerned primarily with restarting and stabilizing the economy, is sometimes distinguished from the 'second New Deal' (1935), aimed at social reform. Although Roosevelt was triumphantly re-elected in 1936 (losing only two states), his reform programme slowed considerably after his failure to reorganize the Supreme Court (1937), growing opposition to government spending and taxes, and the worsening situation in Europe, which increasingly directed Roosevelt's attention to foreign affairs.

**New Democratic Party (NDP)**
Canadian political party. It was established in 1961 by the merger of the **CCF** and the **CLC**. Whilst it did not attract much support in the Atlantic provinces, it presented a much wider appeal to the urban electorate of British Columbia, Saskatchewan, Ontario and Manitoba. Under the leadership of T C (Tommy) Douglas the party won 19 seats in the federal elections of 1962, while in 1969 it was elected into government in Manitoba. In the early 1970s a group of Trotskyites, the 'Waffle' group, seized power until they were expelled from the party in 1972. Later that year the NDP managed to win 30 seats in the federal elections and was able to keep the Liberals in power, giving its support in return for policies of economic nationalism. By the 1980s the NDP had become more centrist because the Liberals had taken over its characteristic policies. In 1984, however, under the leadership of Ed Broadbent the party was still able to muster 19 per cent of the vote and 30 seats in the legislature; in 1997 it gained 11 per cent of the vote and 21 seats. Subsequent leaders have been Audrey McLaughlin

(1989–95), Alexa McDonough (1995–2003) and Jack Layton (2003– ). The greatest contribution of the NDP to Canadian political life has been to present the country with an alternative to the major parties and exert a constant pressure from the left, which has ensured that social issues have retained political importance.

## New Economic Policy (NEP)

A partly experimental economic system introduced by **LENIN** in the USSR in 1921. Its main objective was to help the country recover from the ravages of the **RUSSIAN CIVIL WAR** and the diseconomies of the policy of 'war communism', but it also emerged from a dispute about the best way to organize economic development in the new society. The system privatized some small-scale business, decentralized major parts of industry and encouraged foreign investment. **STA-LIN** abandoned it in 1928 after Lenin's death and as part of his battle with **TROTSKY**. He forged ahead instead with the collectivization of agriculture and forced industrialization.

## New England Confederation (1643–84)

An agreement of the American colonies of Massachusetts, Plymouth, Connecticut and New Haven aiming to establish a common government for the purposes of war and Native American relations. The confederation declined in importance after 1664.

## New Fourth Army Incident (4 Jan 1941)

The military clash in central China between the communist New Fourth Army and Nationalist forces that effectively ended the second of the **UNITED FRONTS** forged in 1937 to counter Japanese aggression. The New Fourth Army had been created (1937) from communist remnants in south China and had been allowed to operate south of the Yangzi River against the Japanese. Tension grew, however, as the army expanded its operations north of the Yangzi, leading to frequent clashes with Nationalist troops. **CHIANG KAI-SHEK**, fearing an expansion of communist influence, ordered an attack on the headquarters force of the New Fourth Army at Maolin (Anhui province) in Jan 1941 as it was evacuating the region in accordance with an agreement reached the previous year. Most of the force was annihilated and the New Fourth Army was dissolved. This, together with Chiang's economic blockade of the Communists' principal base in the north-west, signified the end of any cooperation between the Communists and Nationalists for the remainder of the **SINO–JAPANESE WAR**.

## New France

Technically, this name was given to all the North American territories claimed by France between 1524 and 1803. Generally, however, it is used for the north-eastern colonies. In 1534 a cross was planted on the shores of the Gaspée by Jacques **CARTIER**, who thus claimed the territory for the King of France. However, it was Quebec, founded in 1608 by **CHAMPLAIN** as a base for exploration and fur-trading, that became the centre of the French colony. By 1663 the colony had become a royal province with a governor responsible for foreign relations and defence, an intendant to administer justice, and a bishop to impose spiritual discipline. It was therefore not given the opportunity to develop the early expressions of political responsibility and the sense of community that characterized the English colonies. It was, however, one of the early intendants, Jean Talon, who encouraged fishing, farming, lumbering, ship-building and the production of tar and potash, to ensure the colonies' economic development. **► FUR TRADE**

## New Freedom

The political programme on which US President Woodrow **WILSON** was elected in 1912. It was directed against the acceptance of large-scale enterprise by his opponent, Theodore **ROOSEVELT**, and was intended to return the spirit of free enterprise to the market-place, restoring an open society that would benefit individual entrepreneurs, immigrant minorities and women. The chief architect of Wilson's central argument that trusts and monopolies should be broken up by the federal government was Louis **BRANDEIS**, but the domestic record of Wilson's administration showed a very partial adherence to these principles. **► NEW NATIONALISM**

## New Frontier

The administration and policies of US President John F **KENNEDY** (1961–3). The programme was characterized by a high international profile and a liberal domestic stance. **► PEACE CORPS**

## New Granada (Nueva Granada)

The official name in the Spanish-American Empire for the area now covered by the Republic of Colombia. It was also the name (1739–1810) of a Spanish viceroyalty embracing Venezuela and Quito in addition to New Granada.

## New Guard

In Australian history, an extreme right-wing organization formed in New South Wales in 1932 by Eric Campbell, which claimed 100,000 members by 1933. Its principal achievement was the disruption of the official opening of Sydney Harbour Bridge (1932). In some respects a fascist organization, the Guard was defunct by 1935.

## Ne Win, U, also known as Maung Shu Maung (1911–2002)

Burmese politician. He was an active anti-British nationalist in the 1930s. In **WORLD WAR II** he became Chief of Staff in the collaborationist army after the Japanese invasion of Burma (now Myanmar), but joined the Allied forces later in the war. He held senior military and cabinet posts after Burma's independence (1948), before becoming caretaker Prime Minister (1958–60). In 1962, following a military coup, he ruled the country as chairman of the revolutionary council and became state President in 1974. After leaving this office in 1981, he continued to dominate political affairs as chairman of the ruling Burma Socialist Programme Party (BSPP). He followed an isolationist foreign policy and a unique domestic 'Burmese Way to Socialism' programme, a blend of **MARXISM**, Buddhism and Burmese nationalism. In 1988, with economic conditions rapidly deteriorating and riots in Rangoon, he was forced to step down as BSPP leader although he remained a formidably powerful political figure.

## New Left

A neo-Marxist movement which espoused a more

libertarian form of **SOCIALISM** compared to orthodox **MARXISM**. In part, it was inspired by the earlier writings of Marx, which were essentially humanistic, and the ideas of Italian politician Antonio **GRAMSCI** regarding the importance of ideological hegemony. It also drew on dialectical sociology and radical forms of existentialism. It is, however, difficult to pinpoint any central ideas specific to the New Left. The movement had some influence in the 1960s, particularly in student politics and in opposition to the **VIETNAM WAR**, but it never became an effectively organized political force. Its importance in the 1980s declined, and it gave way in part to the **NEW RIGHT**.

### New Liberal Club (*Shin Jiyu Kurabu*)
The Japanese political party formed in 1976 when six members of the ruling **LIBERAL DEMOCRATIC PARTY** (LDP) broke away to form their own party in protest at government corruption. Although only ever gaining a handful of parliamentary seats, the New Liberal Club formally entered into a coalition with the LDP following the 1983 election, in which the LDP had fallen short of a majority (the only time the LDP has entered a coalition with another party). The LDP's renewed parliamentary strength after 1983, plus the fact that New Liberal Club members always tended to support government policy, made the party's existence increasingly redundant. It was quietly disbanded in 1985 and its members rejoined the LDP.

### New Model Army
An English army established by Parliament (15 Feb 1645) to strengthen its forces in the first civil war against royalists. The county and regional armies of Essex, Manchester and Waller were merged into a successful national force. The cavalry and artillery were augmented, the battle tactics of **GUSTAV II ADOLF** adopted, discipline and pay improved, and religious toleration introduced. ► **ENGLISH CIVIL WARS**; **NASEBY, BATTLE OF**

### New Nationalism
The US political programme outlined by ex-President Theodore **ROOSEVELT** in a speech at Osawatomie, Kansas in Aug 1910, and on which he campaigned as the **PROGRESSIVE PARTY**'s candidate in the election of 1912. Roosevelt advocated such policies as graduated income and inheritance taxes, compensation for employee accident, closer supervision of female and child labour, and more effective corporate regulation. Greatly influenced by Herbert Croly's *The Promise of American Life*, the programme was essentially a call for government intervention to achieve social justice, and it later influenced such **NEW DEAL** brains trusters as Raymond Moley. ► **NEW FREEDOM**

### New National Party ► NATIONAL PARTY (NP)

### New Netherland
A Dutch colony in the Hudson River Valley. The first settlement was Fort Orange (Albany), founded in 1617; Nieuw Amsterdam (New York City) followed in 1624. Conquered by the English and named New York in 1664, it was restored by treaty to the English in 1674 after a second brief period of Dutch rule. Initially established on feudal social lines, the colony prospered on the basis of the **FUR TRADE**.

### New Orleans, Battle of (Dec 1814–Jan 1815)
An military engagement during the **WAR OF 1812** which occurred 15 days after peace had been made at the Treaty of **GHENT** (Dec 1814). Andrew **JACKSON**'s leadership of the US forces, which successfully repelled the British attempt to take New Orleans, made Jackson a national hero and improved public opinion of the US Army.

### New Right
A wide-ranging ideological movement associated with the revival of conservatism in the 1970s and 1980s, particularly in the UK and USA. Its ideas are most prominently connected with classical liberal economic theory from the 19c. It is strongly in favour of state withdrawal from ownership, and intervention in the economy in favour of a free-enterprise system. There is also a strong moral conservatism: an emphasis on respect for authority, combined with a strong expression of patriotism and support for the idea of the family. Politically, the New Right adopts an aggressive style that places weight on pursuing convictions rather than on generating a consensus. In the USA in the 1980s it was associated with the emergence of Christian fundamentalism (eg the **MORAL MAJORITY**) in the USA, and its influence could be seen in the **REAGAN** and **THATCHER** administrations.

### New Spain (Nueva España)
The formal title of the Spanish viceroyalty covering the area of modern Mexico.

## NEW ZEALAND

An independent state comprising a group of islands in the Pacific Ocean to the south-east of Australia. The two principal islands, North and South, are separated by the Cook Strait. It was settled by the **MAORIS** from South-East Asia before 1350. The first European sighting was made by Abel **TASMAN** in 1642, and he named it Staten Landt. It later became known as Nieuw Zeeland, after the Dutch province. Captain **COOK** sighted it in 1767, and the first settlement was established in 1792. The country remained a dependency of New South Wales until 1841. Outbreaks of war in the 1840s and 1860s between immigrants and Maoris (the **MAORI WARS**) were disastrous for the Maoris, much of whose land was taken. The country became the self-governing Dominion of New Zealand in 1907, and an active member of the **COMMONWEALTH OF NATIONS**. During the 1990s Maori activists demanded compensation for the land that the European settlers had taken from their people, and the government agreed either to pay compensation to certain tribes or to give them areas of land. The chief of state remains the British monarch, represented by a Governor-General.

### Ney, Michel, Duke of Elchingen (1769–1815)
French marshal. He fought in the FRENCH REVOLUTIONARY WARS, became a General of Division in 1799, and a Marshal of the Empire. He commanded the 3rd Corps of the Grand Army in the Russian campaign (1813), for which he received the title of Prince of Moskowa. After NAPOLEON I's abdication in 1814 he accepted the Bourbon restoration, but instead of obeying orders to retake Bonaparte (1815), Ney deserted to his side and led the centre at the Battle of WATERLOO. On LOUIS XVIII's second restoration, he was condemned for high treason and shot in Paris. ► BOURBON, HOUSE OF; NAPOLEONIC WARS

### Nghe-An/Ha-Tinh Uprisings (1930–1)
A fierce revolt against French colonial rule, which took place in the northern ANNAM provinces of Nghe-An and Ha-Tinh. The precise causes of the revolt are a matter of considerable scholarly dispute but important elements would include the markedly harsh agricultural conditions of that region, the burden of colonial taxation, social disintegration and the organizational skills of the INDOCHINA Communist Party. For a short period the rebels were able to seize power. However, French repression, including the bombing of demonstrations from the air, broke the revolt. Approximately 2,000 Vietnamese were killed.

### Ngo Dinh Diem (1901–63)
Vietnamese political leader. He became Prime Minister of the State of Vietnam in June 1954. This was the territory south of the 'temporary' demarcation line, established at the 1954 Geneva Conference. Ngo Dinh Diem quickly consolidated his position, securing the abdication of BAO DAI and suppressing the political-religious sects. He allied himself strongly with the USA, which saw in him an instrument by which the reunification of Vietnam, under the communists, might be prevented. However, by the beginning of the 1960s, Ngo Dinh Diem's internal position was weakening, largely because his encouragement of Catholic interests greatly angered the Buddhist majority. His violent treatment of Buddhist protest lost him US support. Ngo Dinh Diem was assassinated on 2 Nov 1963, in the course of a military coup that had, at the very least, tacit US approval.

### Nguni
A group of Bantu-speaking peoples of southern Africa. They originally occupied present-day Natal and Transkei, and in the 19c they carried out a series of migrations. The main groups today include the Zulu, Swazi and Xhosa of South Africa and Swaziland, the NDEBELE of Zimbabwe, and the Ngoni of Zambia, Malawi and Tanzania.

### Nguyen Van Thieu (1923–2001)
Vietnamese army officer and political leader. His military career began in the late 1940s and by 1963 he was Chief of Staff of the Armed Forces of the Republic of Vietnam (South Vietnam), becoming Minister of Defence and Deputy Premier in the following year. In 1965 he became head of state. Under a new, US-style presidential constitution, he was President

from 1967 until the collapse of the Saigon regime in 1975. During those years, his relationship with the USA, and with US public opinion, was central to his survival. He was roundly condemned in the West for his authoritarian, commonly corrupt, methods; he, in turn, felt betrayed by the US withdrawal from Vietnam, agreed with his northern enemies in Paris in early 1973. With the communist victory in 1975, he went into exile, first in Taiwan, then in the UK and finally in the USA.

### Niagara Movement
US CIVIL RIGHTS MOVEMENT. Founded in 1905 by W E B DU BOIS and others to resist the public acceptance of segregation advocated by Booker T WASHINGTON, and to agitate for 'every single right that belongs to a freeborn American, political and social'. The movement was superseded by the establishment of the NAACP.

### Nian Rebellion (1852–68)
A peasant insurrection in north-central China. Armed bandit gangs, known as Nian (literally, 'twist'; this may either be a reference to the twisted paper torches they used or a description of them as tightly knit outlaw bands), had been active in the region since the 1790s. Amidst the worsening economic situation in the 1850s and the turmoil caused by the TAIPING REBELLION, the Nian rebels gained control over entire villages, from where they conducted seasonal plundering expeditions. Unlike the Taipings, the Nian had no systematic ideology and no organization, although one leader, Zhang Luoxing (Chang Lo-hsing) declared himself leader of a Nian confederacy in 1852. After 1864, when they were dislodged from their fortified bases, the Nian resorted to mobile cavalry warfare until they were finally suppressed in 1868 by Qing forces carrying out a strategy of blockade. ► QING DYNASTY

### Nicaea, Conquest of (1331)
One of the Byzantine towns of Asia Minor, Nicaea (Iznik) came under threat from the nascent Ottoman state in the early 14c. A Byzantine relief army was defeated at Philocrene in 1330 and Nicaea fell to the Ottomans under ORHAN on 2 Mar 1331.

### Nicaea, Empire of
The successor state of the BYZANTINE EMPIRE, established after the Latins had conquered Constantinople (1204). It was founded by Theodore Lascaris, whose court at Nicaea (modern Iznik, Turkey) maintained the traditions of Byzantine administration and culture. MICHAEL VIII PALAEOLOGUS, co-emperor with John Lascaris at Nicaea, recovered Constantinople (1261) and restored the Byzantine Empire.

### NICARAGUA official name Republic of Nicaragua
The largest of the Central American republics, bounded to the north by Honduras; to the east by the Caribbean Sea; to the south by Costa Rica; and to the west by the Pacific Ocean. The Pacific coast was colonized by the Spaniards in the early 16c. Nicaragua gained independence from Spain in 1821 and left the CENTRAL AMERICAN FEDERATION in 1838. The plains of eastern Nicaragua, the Mosquito Coast, remained largely undeveloped and were under British protection until 1860. In the early 20c the country was ruled (1893–1909) by the dictatorial José Santos

Zelaya, who was overthrown in 1907 by a coup supported by the USA. The USA continued to exert its influence until the 1930s, when another dictator, Anastasio **SOMOZA (GARCÍA)** came to power in 1938; he ruled until his assassination in 1956. He was succeeded by first one son, Luis Somoza Debayle, and then another, Anastasio Somoza Debayle, the latter ruling from 1967 until the **SANDINISTA NATIONAL LIBERATION FRONT** (FSLN) seized power in 1979 and established a socialist junta of national reconstruction. The former supporters of the Somoza government (the **CONTRAS**), based in Honduras and supported by the USA until 1989, carried out guerrilla activities against the junta from 1979 until ceasefires and disarmament were agreed in 1990 and 1994. The ceasefires were a result of the Sandinistas' unexpected defeat in the 1990 elections by a coalition led by Violeta Chamorro, who became President in place of Daniel **ORTEGA**. Since the late 1990s, governments have been liberal or liberal-dominated coalitions, keeping the FSLN from power even though it is often the largest party in the National Assembly.

## Nicaraguan Revolution

A period of ongoing political and social turmoil in Nicaragua, which came to a head in 1979 when the **SANDINISTA NATIONAL LIBERATION FRONT** seized power from Anastasio Somoza Debayle (second son of Anastasio **SOMOZA**). ► **IRAN–CONTRA AFFAIR; NICARAGUA; ORTEGA, DANIEL**

## Nice, Treaty of (2001)

An agreement signed (26 Feb 2001) in Nice by the 15 nations of the **EU** to enable EU institutions to function smoothly after enlargement to 25 member states in 2004. The overall numbers of EU commissioners and European Parliament seats were increased but redistributed to accommodate the representatives of the new member states, and the scope of the national veto in the Council of Ministers was reduced, making more decisions subject to qualified majority voting (QMV) and redistributing the balance of votes used in QMV according to population. The Treaty was ratified by all the member states except initially for Ireland, which rejected it in a referendum in 2001 but voted in favour in 2002. The Treaty entered into force on 1 Feb 2003.

## Nichiren (1222–82)

Japanese Buddhist priest. He founded his own sect in 1253, condemning all other sects as evil. The fanatical zeal of his sect often led to violent clashes between his followers and the members of other sects. The na-

tionalist tone of Nichiren's teachings, emphasizing that Japanese Buddhism was the one true Buddhism, made him a hero to some ultra-nationalist ideologies of the 1930s and 1940s. ► **KOMEITO**

## Nicholas I (1796–1855)

Emperor of Russia (1825/55). The third son of **PAUL I**, he was an absolute despot, whose first action was ruthlessly to suppress the **DECEMBRISTS** and whose subsequent domestic policy was scrupulously devoted to preventing subversion. In 1830–1 he crushed the rising in Congress Poland and abolished its constitution, and then attempted to Russianize all the inhabitants of the empire. He helped to quell the 1848–9 Hungarian insurrection on Austria's behalf, and drew closer the alliance with Prussia. The re-establishment of the French Empire confirmed these alliances, and led him to intensify his policy of southwards expansion aimed particularly at dominating Turkey; but the opposition of Britain and France brought on the **CRIMEAN WAR**, during which he died. Ironically, Russia's defeat in 1856 strengthened the pressure for social and political change and precipitated the emancipation of the serfs under **ALEXANDER II** in 1861. ► **NAPOLEON III; NESSELRODE, KARL; RUSSIAN SERFS, EMANCIPATION OF THE**

## Nicholas I (1841–1921)

Prince and King of Montenegro (1860/1918). As the autocratic ruler of a backward state, he introduced a measure of reform calculated not to diminish his authority. He reorganized the state in 1879, issued a new law code (1888), reformed the army, issued a constitution (1905) and declared Montenegro a kingdom (1910). His foreign policy was determined by his dependence on subsidies from Russia and Austro-Hungary and he made a series of marriage alliances with Russia, Serbia and Italy. During **WORLD WAR I**, when the Habsburg army overran Montenegro, he fled to Italy (1916). He was declared deposed by the Montenegrin National Assembly (Nov 1918) and Montenegro then became part of the Kingdom of Serbs, Croats and Slovenes (later Yugoslavia). ► **PETROVIĆ-NJEGOŠ DYNASTY**

## Nicholas II (1868–1918)

Last Emperor of Russia (1895/1917). He was the son of **ALEXANDER III**. In foreign affairs his reign was marked by a switch from cooperation with Austria and Germany to an alliance with France, an entente with Britain, the disastrous **RUSSO-JAPANESE WAR** (1904–5) and, eventually, involvement in **WORLD WAR I**. Inadequate industrialization and insufficient social change helped precipitate the Russian **REVOLUTION OF 1905**. His failure to concede any real power to the assembly (**DUMA**), instituted in 1906, and also his incompetence as commander of the army against the Central Powers, in turn helped to precipitate the 1917 **RUSSIAN REVOLUTION** that led to his immediate abdication and to the murder of him and his family by Red Guards at Ekaterinburg in 1918.

## Nicholas V, originally Tommaso Parentucelli (1397–1455)

Italian pope (1447/55). He prevailed on the anti-pope, Felix V (**AMADEUS VIII, THE PEACEFUL**) to abdicate in 1449, and thus restored the peace of the Church. A liberal patron of scholars, he rebuilt the

Vatican and restored St Peter's and the Vatican Library. He vainly endeavoured to arouse Europe to the duty of succouring the Greek empire.

### Nicomedia, Conquest of (1337)
Nicomedia (Izmit) was taken by the Ottoman **ORHAN** after a siege lasting six years in 1337. (It was at Nicomedia that Orhan set up the first Ottoman madrasah to establish a name for himself as a credible Muslim prince by demonstrating his care for learning.) ▸ **MADRASAHS**

### Nicopolis, Battle of (1396)
A disastrous attack by Christians against the Turks, conquerors of much of Eastern Europe since the early 14c. The battle centred on the major fortress on the River Danube. The Christian forces were led by King **SIGISMUND** of Hungary (later Holy Roman Emperor) and **JOHN THE FEARLESS** (1371–1419), Duke of Burgundy. John was captured by the Turks and ransomed for a huge sum.

### Niemöller, Martin (1892–1984)
German theologian and resistance figure. After serving as a **U-BOAT** commander in **WORLD WAR I**, Niemöller entered the Lutheran Church and held various positions, most notably as Pastor in Berlin-Dahlem from 1931. He was a prominent member of the anti-Nazi **CONFESSING CHURCH**, for which he was arrested in 1937 and sent to Sachsenhausen and **DACHAU** concentration camps. Freed in 1945, he resumed his church career and adopted outspoken views on current affairs, most notably on German reunification and nuclear disarmament. ▸ **CONCENTRATION CAMP**

### Nien Rebellion ▸ NIAN REBELLION

**NIGER** official name **Republic of Niger**

A landlocked republic in West Africa, bounded to the north-east by Libya; to the north-west by Algeria; to the west by Mali; to the south-west by Burkina Faso; to the south by Benin and Nigeria; and to the east by Chad. Inhabited, according to archaeological evidence, during the Palaeolithic period, it was ruled by the Tuaregs from the 11c, the Zerma from the 17c, and the Hausa from the 14c, who ousted the Tuaregs in the 18c, but were themselves ousted by the Fulani. The first European occupiers were the French from 1883. Niger became a territory within French West Africa in 1904, and gained independence in 1960. There was a military coup in 1974 and political activity was not legalized again until 1989. Civil unrest in 1990 led to the approval of a multiparty constitution in 1992. Ma-

hamane Ousmane was elected President the following year, remaining in power until he was ousted by a military coup in 1996. Pressure from France resulted in a presidential election, following which the military leader Ibrahim Baré Maïnassara came to power. In 1999, following a coup in which the unpopular Maïnassara was assassinated, a new constitution was approved and Mamadou Tandja (the unsuccessful candidate in 1993 and 1996) was elected president; he was re-elected in 2004. In the 1990s there was ethnic unrest caused by Tuareg rebels fighting government forces in the north, until a peace agreement was reached in 1995. ▸ **FULANI EMIRATES**

**NIGERIA** official name **Federal Republic of Nigeria**

A republic in West Africa, bounded to the west by Benin; to the north by Niger; to the north-east by Chad; to the east by Cameroon; and to the south by the Gulf of Guinea and the Bight of Benin. There are over 250 tribal groups, notably the Hausa and Fulani in the north, Yoruba in the south, and **IGBO** in the east. Nigeria was at the centre of the Nok culture in 500BC–AD200. Several African kingdoms developed throughout the area in the Middle Ages (eg the Hausa and Yoruba), and Muslim immigrants arrived in the 15–16c. European settlers arrived and participated in the gold and slave trades. A British colony was established at Lagos in 1861, and protectorates of North and South Nigeria were created in 1900. These were amalgamated as the Colony and Protectorate of Nigeria in 1914, which became a federation in 1954 and gained independence in 1960. Nigeria was declared a federal republic in 1963 under President **AZIKIWE**. A military coup took place in 1966, and the Igbo people in the east formed the Republic of **BIAFRA** in 1967, resulting in the **BIAFRAN WAR** and eventually the surrender of Biafra in 1970. There were further military coups in 1983 and 1985, after which military rule was broken only temporarily, in 1993. In 1995 political activity was legalized, but Nigeria was suspended from the **COMMONWEALTH OF NATIONS** following the execution of nine pro-democracy activists. In Feb 1999 Olusegun **OBASANJO** was elected President in a transition from military to civilian rule, and Nigeria was readmitted to the Commonwealth in May that year. In the 2002 elections, the first civilian-run elections in 20 years, Obasanjo was re-elected President and the People's Democratic Party retained its parliamentary majority. The adoption of Shari'ah (Islamic) law in some northern states has exacerbated tensions between Christians and Muslims, and there have been sporadic, violent clashes in which hundreds have died; many Christians have left the northern states. ► FULANI EMIRATES

**Nightingale, Florence** (1820–1910)
English nurse and hospital reformer. She trained as a nurse at Kaiserswerth (1851) and Paris, and in 1853 became superintendent of a hospital for invalid women in London. In the CRIMEAN WAR she volunteered for duty and took 38 nurses to Scutari in 1854. She organized the barracks hospital after the Battle of Inkerman (5 Nov 1854) and by imposing strict discipline and standards of sanitation, drastically reduced the hospital mortality rate. She returned to England in 1856, and a fund of £50,000 was subscribed to enable her to form an institution for the training of nurses at St Thomas's and at King's College Hospital. She devoted many years to army sanitary reform, to the improvement of nursing, and to public health in India.

**Night of the Long Knives** (30 June–1 July 1934)
The event which took place in Germany when the SS, on HITLER's orders, murdered RÖHM and other leaders of the SA (Stormtroopers). The aim was to crush the political power of the SA, reassure the German establishment which was worried by SA excesses and settle old political scores. It has been estimated that up to 150 of Hitler's political opponents and rivals were killed, including von SCHLEICHER, the former Chancellor.

**nihilism**
A term made popular by Ivan Turgenev's *Fathers and Sons* (1861), referring to any outlook that denies the possibility of justifying moral values. It was a caricature but it came to characterize several members of the Russian radical intelligentsia, including Nikolai CHERNYSHEVSKY and particularly Dmitri Pisarev (1840–68), who advocated the total rejection of all existing institutions as well as moral values in the name of an unrestricted individual freedom intended to improve the lot of the Russian people.

**Nijmegen, Treaties of** (1678–9)
A peace settlement ending the Dutch War (1672–8) between the Netherlands and France and their allies, effectively recognizing French supremacy in Western Europe. Negotiations began in 1676, but fluctuated with the fortunes of war. The Dutch and Spanish governments acceded to LOUIS XIV of France's territorial demands, Spain being the principal loser (1678). After further military defeats, the Emperor LEOPOLD I concluded a separate treaty (1679). ► ANGLO-DUTCH WARS

**Nikolaevna, Klavdiya Ivanovna** (1893–1944)
Russian and Soviet WOMEN'S RIGHTS activist. Born in St Petersburg, a bookbinder by trade, she was early involved in revolutionary activities and frequently arrested from 1908 onwards. After 1917 she organized women's groups in St Petersburg and in 1924 she was appointed head of *Zhenotdel*, the Communist Party's women's section. In 1926 she was dismissed for supporting ZINOVIEV but survived to hold various lower rank appointments until her death.

**Nikolai Nikolaevich, Grand-Duke** (1859–1929)
Russian general. The nephew of ALEXANDER II, in WORLD WAR I he was the not particularly successful Russian Commander-in-Chief until he was displaced in 1915 by Tsar NICHOLAS II himself, who was

particularly unsuccessful. Transferred to be commander in the Caucasus (1915–17), he fared rather better. He was inclined to favour some concessions in politics but after 1915 he had no influence. He was able to die peacefully in France.

**Nikola Petrović** ► NICHOLAS I (of Montenegro)

**Nikolsburg, Peace of** (26 July 1866)
The provisional peace settlement after the Battle of KÖNIGGRÄTZ-SADOWA between PRUSSIA and Austria and, days later, Prussia and the north German states, which ended the AUSTRO-PRUSSIAN WAR and secured Prussian dominance in Germany. The Prussian Minister-President, BISMARCK, succeeded in creating a NORTH GERMAN CONFEDERATION in which Prussia was pre-eminent, in excluding Austria from German affairs, and in gaining French acceptance of this major shift in the European balance of power. The south German states remained independent until after the FRANCO-PRUSSIAN WAR (1870–1).

**Nikon** (1606–81)
Russian religious leader and reformer. Having made a name for himself as Metropolitan of Novgorod, he achieved the highest office in the Russian Church (that of Patriarch) in 1652, and immediately began to rectify mistakes that had crept into texts and rituals. Although he was attacked by many priests, he won the backing of a series of Church councils. Those who would not agree split off to become the OLD BELIEVERS. But Nikon then exceeded his powers by asserting that the Church stood above the state, just as the sun was greater than the moon. Tsar ALEXEI MIKHAILOVICH quarrelled with him in 1658 and a Church council deposed him in 1667.

**Nile, Battle of the** ► ABOUKIR BAY, BATTLE OF (Aug 1798)

**Nimeri, Gaafar Muhammad al-** (1930–)
Sudanese soldier and politician. Educated at Sudan Military College in Khartoum, he joined the army, and continued his training in Egypt, where he became a disciple of Gamal Abd al-NASSER. In 1969, with the rank of colonel, he led the military coup that deposed the civilian government and established a Revolutionary Command Council (RCC). In 1971, under a new constitution, he became President. Although twice re-elected, by the 1980s his regional policies and his attempts to impose strict Islamic law had made his regime unpopular and in 1985, while visiting the USA, he was deposed by an army colleague, General Swar al-Dahab.

**Nimitz, Chester William** (1885–1966)
US admiral. He trained at the US Naval Academy, served mainly in submarines, and by 1938 had become rear-admiral. Chief of the Bureau of Navigation during 1939–41, he then commanded the US Pacific Fleet, his conduct of naval operations contributing significantly to the defeat of Japan. He was made Fleet Admiral (1944) and Chief of Naval Operations (1945–7). ► WORLD WAR II

**Ninety-Two Resolutions** (1834)
Canadian political reform demands. The list of complaints against the government of Upper CANADA was drawn up by a committee of reformers led by William Lyon MACKENZIE. The system of patronage,

the dispensation of the **CLERGY RESERVES** and various economic policies were all attacked and coupled with the demand for an elective legislature.

### Ninomiya Sontoku (1787–1856)

Japanese rural moralist. His conservative teachings (emphasizing frugality, obedience, harmony and self-help) were used by the state in the late 19c and early 20c to reinforce social order in the countryside. Statues of Ninomiya were erected in every elementary school and national ethics textbooks of the 1930s portrayed him as a model of virtue.

### Nisei

The term used to describe US citizens of Japanese descent. Technically the term should be restricted to the second generation, the first being called *Issei*, and the third *Sansei*. The first generation, mainly market-gardeners and farmers who had settled in Hawaii and California, were legally prohibited from applying for US citizenship. They numbered less than 25,000 at the beginning of the 20c, but their rapid increase led to President Theodore **ROOSEVELT** concluding a 'gentleman's agreement' with the Japanese government in 1907 to discourage further immigration. California and other states passed laws preventing them from owning or leasing real estate. After **PEARL HARBOR**, President Franklin D **ROOSEVELT** ordered the *Issei* and the *Nisei*, even though the latter had been born with US citizenship, to be removed to concentration camps, and there was little protest from the rest of US society. In 1988 it was recognized by the federal government that these *Nisei* internees had been subjected to racial injustice and those still alive were awarded compensation of US$20,000 each.

### Nishihara Loans

The secret loans (totalling 145 million yen) made by the Japanese government to the Chinese Premier **DUAN QIRUI** between 1917 and 1918. Named after Nishihara Kamezo (1873–1954), who personally represented the Japanese Prime Minister, Terauchi Masatake, in Beijing, the loans were ostensibly granted for China's economic development. In reality they were used to keep Duan Qirui in power, in exchange for which Duan recognized Japan's retention of the former German leasehold territory in China it had occupied in 1914. The loan agreements were signed without the knowledge of the Chinese parliament; when details became known in 1919 they helped ignite the **MAY FOURTH MOVEMENT** student demonstrations. The loans were not recognized by subsequent Chinese governments and were never repaid.

### Nishio Suehiro (1891–1981)

Japanese labour leader and politician. A moderate trade union leader in the 1920s, Nishio was first elected to the Diet in 1928 as a member of the *Shakai Minshuto* (Social Masses Party), a proletarian party founded in 1926 that subsequently supported the military cabinets of the 1930s. He joined the **JAPAN SOCIALIST PARTY** (JSP) in 1945 and was a member of **KATAYAMA TETSU**'s socialist cabinet in 1947. Condemning the party's left-wing bias, in particular its opposition to Japan's security treaty with the USA, Nishio left the JSP in 1959 to form the Democratic Socialist Party, of which he remained Chairman until 1967.

### Nithsdale, William Maxwell, 5th Earl of (1676–1744)

Scottish Jacobite. In 1699 he married Lady Winifred Herbert, the youngest daughter of the Marquis of Powis. A Catholic in 1715, he joined the English **JACO-BITES** and was taken prisoner at Preston, tried for treason, and sentenced to death. The night before his execution he escaped from the Tower in woman's clothes, through the heroism of his countess. They settled at Rome, where he died.

### Nitti, Francesco Saverio (1868–1953)

Italian politician and professor. A deputy of radical and socialist sympathies from 1904, he grew closer to **GIOLITTI** in whose 1911–14 government he served as Minister of Agriculture and Industry. After **CAPOR-ETTO**, he became **ORLANDO**'s Finance Minister, before replacing him as Prime Minister (1919). A victim of fascist attacks on account of his consistent and outspoken attacks on **MUSSOLINI**, he went into self-imposed exile but returned to Italy after the war and remained active in politics until his death.

### Nivelle, Robert (1857–1924)

French soldier. He was an artillery colonel in Aug 1914, and made his name when in command of the army of Verdun by recapturing Douaumont and other forts (Oct–Dec 1916). He was Commander-in-Chief from Dec 1916 to May 1917, when his Aisne offensive failed and he was superseded by **PÉTAIN**. ▶ **VERDUN, BATTLE OF**; **WORLD WAR I**

### Nixon, Richard Milhous (1913–94)

US politician and 37th President. He became a lawyer, then served in the US Navy. A Republican, he was elected to the **HOUSE OF REPRESENTATIVES** in 1946, where he played a prominent role in **HUAC**. He became Senator in 1950 and Vice-President under **EI-SENHOWER** for two terms (1953–61). He lost the 1960 presidential election to John F **KENNEDY** but won in 1968. As President he sought to bring an end to the **VIETNAM WAR**, but did so only after the US invasion of Cambodia and Laos and the heaviest US bombing of North Vietnam of the entire conflict. He had diplomatic successes with China and the USSR. In his domestic policy he reversed many of the social programmes that had come out of the previous Democratic administrations. He resigned in 1974 under the threat of **IMPEACHMENT** after several leading members of his staff had been found guilty of involvement in the **WATERGATE** affair, and because he was personally implicated in the cover-up. He was given a full pardon by President Gerald **FORD**.

### Nkomati Accord

Essentially this was a non-aggression treaty signed between Mozambique and South Africa in 1984, in which the former agreed not to support the **ANC** (African National Congress) militarily and the latter agreed not to support **RENAMO** militarily. In practice, the superior power of South Africa meant that the agreement was implemented unilaterally.

### Nkomo, Joshua Mqabuko Nyongolo (1917–99)

Zimbabwean nationalist and politician. Educated in Natal and at Fort Hare College, where he joined the **ANC** (African National Congress), he returned to Bulawayo as a social worker and became General-Secretary of the Rhodesian Railway African Employees Association in 1951. Elected Chairman of the (Southern Rhodesian) African National Congress in 1951, he became its President in 1957, leaving the country for exile in 1959. When the ANC was banned, he became President of its successor, the National Democratic Party, but that, too, was banned. He then helped form the Zimbabwe African People's Union (**ZAPU**) of which he became President. His non-confrontationist tactics and tendency to spend time outside Rhodesia led to a more radical group breaking away to form the Zimbabwe African National Union (**ZANU**). ZANU and ZAPU, with different international patrons and separate military wings, competed for the representation of African opinion but were persuaded to unite to form the **PATRIOTIC FRONT** in 1976. ZAPU, however, was increasingly an **NDEBELE** party and in the 1980 elections won only 20 seats. Nkomo, who still saw himself as the father of Zimbabwean nationalism, was disappointed to be offered only the post of Minister of Home Affairs, from which he was dismissed in 1981. Violence in **MATABELELAND** encouraged him into a period of further exile, but he returned and agreed to integrate his party into ZANU, a union ratified in Apr 1988. He became Vice-President of the new party and was one of three senior members in the President's office forming in effect a 'super cabinet'.

### Nkrumah, Kwame (1909–71)

Ghanaian politician. Educated in a Catholic primary school and Achimota College, he then went to Lincoln and Pennsylvania universities in the USA. He studied law in London (1945–7) and was co-chairman of the famous Fifth Pan-African Congress held in Manchester in 1945. He returned to the Gold Coast as Secretary-General of the **UNITED GOLD COAST CONVENTION**, but broke with it to form the **CONVENTION PEOPLE'S PARTY** (CPP) in 1949. Imprisoned briefly (he was elected to Legco while in prison), he became leader of government business (1951), Prime Minister (1952–7) and continued in that post on independence until Ghana became a republic in 1960, when he became President. A radical Pan-Africanist, for which he was widely admired throughout much of the continent, he created considerable opposition within Ghana, most of which was repressed; however, the military intervened, overthrowing him in 1966 while he was abroad, symbolically on a visit to Beijing. He spent his years of exile in Guinea, where Sékou **TOURÉ** gave him the status of co-head of state. He died in Bucharest.

### Nkumbula, Harry Mwaanga (1916–83)

Zambian nationalist. Educated in local schools, he became a teacher before studying at Makerere College and the London School of Economics (1946–50). He was elected President of the Northern Rhodesian African National Congress (1951) and he was imprisoned briefly for his political activities. His support for a moderate independence constitution cost him the support of **KAUNDA**, who left the **ANC** to form **UNIP** in 1959. He was a member of the pre-independence coalition government but was leader of the opposition during the First Republic, being restricted for a while in 1970. With the one-party state Second Republic, he joined UNIP in 1973 but remained outside politics in his last years.

### NMD (National Missile Defense)

A system intended to protect the USA and some of its allies from ballistic missile attack. Overseen by the Ballistic Missile Defense Organization set up in 1993, NMD is a scaled-down version of **SDI**, work on which was terminated in 1993. In a speech in 2001, President George W **BUSH** made deployment of ballistic missile defenses a major goal of his presidency and in 2002 abrogated the **ABM TREATY** under which the development of this weaponry would be illegal. The first ground-based interceptor, one of six underground silos, was put in place at Fort Greely, Alaska, in Jul 2004.

### Nobel Peace Prize

A prize awarded annually (providing a suitable candidate is identified) since 1901 from the income of a trust fund established by the will of Swedish chemist and industrialist Alfred Nobel (1833–96). The prize, which is given to an individual or to an institution for important contributions to peace, consists of a gold medal and a sum of money, and is presented in Oslo on 10 Dec, the anniversary of Nobel's death. ► *See table*

### Noboru Takeshita (1924–2000)

Japanese politician. The son of an affluent sake brewer, he trained as a **KAMIKAZE** pilot during **WORLD WAR II**. After university and a brief career as a schoolteacher, he was elected to the House of Representatives as a **LIBERAL DEMOCRATIC PARTY** (LDP) deputy in 1958, rising to become Chief Cabinet Secretary (1971–2) to Prime Minister **SATO** and Minister of Finance (1982–6) under Prime Minister **NAKASONE**. Formerly a member of the powerful 'Tanaka faction', he founded his own faction, the largest within the party, in 1987, and three months later was elected LDP President and Prime Minister. Although regarded as a cautious, consensual politician, he pushed through important tax reforms. His administration was undermined by the uncovering of the Recruit-Cosmos insider share dealing scandal, which, though dating back to 1986, forced the resignation of senior government ministers, including, eventually, Takeshita himself (June 1989).

### Noli, Fan Stylian (1882–1965)

Albanian bishop and politician. Born into an Orthodox family in Thrace, he was educated in Greece and taught at a Greek school in Egypt, where he first encountered the Albanian national movement. After studying law at Harvard, he was ordained a priest and became a bishop in the Albanian Orthodox Church (1908). In 1920 he returned to Albania to represent the US-Albanians at the National Assembly held in Lushnjë. Left-wing and known as the 'Red Bishop', he was Foreign Minister in the 1921 Popular Party regime, but he criticized the conservative policies of **ZOG** and went on to form his own opposition party. After Zog fled (1924), Noli formed a government and tried to establish constitutional rule. He introduced agrarian reforms, tried to minimize Italian influence in Albania and made steps towards recognizing the Soviet regime. However, his government collapsed after only seven months, when Zog invaded the country. In 1930 Fan Noli retired from political life and resumed his religious duties in the USA. ► **WILLIAM OF WIED**

## NOBEL PEACE PRIZE WINNERS

| Year | Name | Year | Name |
|---|---|---|---|
| 1901 | (Jean) Henri Dunant; Frédéric Passy | 1959 | Philip Noel-Baker |
| 1902 | Élie Ducommun; Charles Albert Gobat | 1960 | Albert Lutuli |
| 1903 | Sir William Cremer | 1961 | Dag Hammarskjöld |
| 1904 | Institute of International Law | 1962 | Linus Pauling |
| 1905 | Bertha von Suttner | 1963 | International Red Cross Committee; |
| 1906 | Theodore Roosevelt | | League of Red Cross Societies |
| 1907 | Ernesto Teodoro Moneta; Louis Renault | 1964 | Martin Luther King, Jr |
| 1908 | Klas Pontus Arnoldson; Fredrik Bajer | 1965 | United Nations Children's Fund (UNICEF) |
| 1909 | Baron d'Estournelles de Constant; | 1966–7 | no award |
| | Auguste Beernaert | 1968 | René Cassin |
| 1910 | International Peace Bureau | 1969 | International Labour Organization |
| 1911 | Tobias Asser; Alfred Fried | 1970 | Norman Borlaug |
| 1912 | Elihu Root | 1971 | Willy Brandt |
| 1913 | Henri La Fontaine | 1972 | no award |
| 1914–16 | no award | 1973 | Henry Kissinger; Le Duc Tho (declined) |
| 1917 | International Red Cross Committee | 1974 | Seán MacBride; Eisaku Sato |
| 1918 | no award | 1975 | Andrei Sakharov |
| 1919 | Woodrow Wilson | 1976 | Mairead Corrigan; Betty Williams |
| 1920 | Léon Bourgeois | 1977 | Amnesty International |
| 1921 | Karl Branting; Christian Lous Lange | 1978 | Menachem Begin; Anwar al-Sadat |
| 1922 | Fridtjof Nansen | 1979 | Mother Teresa |
| 1923–4 | no award | 1980 | Adolfo Pérez Esquivel |
| 1925 | Sir Austen Chamberlain; Charles G Dawes | 1981 | Office of the United Nations High |
| 1926 | Aristide Briand; Gustav Stresemann | | Commissioner for Refugees |
| 1927 | Ferdinand Buisson; Ludwig Quidde | 1982 | Alva Myrdal; Alfonso García Robles |
| 1928 | no award | 1983 | Lech Wałesa |
| 1929 | Frank B Kellogg | 1984 | Desmond Tutu |
| 1930 | Nathan Söderblom | 1985 | International Physicians for the |
| 1931 | Jane Addams; Nicholas Murray Butler | | Prevention of Nuclear War |
| 1932 | no award | 1986 | Elie Wiesel |
| 1933 | Sir Norman Angell | 1987 | Oscar Arias Sánchez |
| 1934 | Arthur Henderson | 1988 | United Nations Peacekeeping Forces |
| 1935 | Carl von Ossietzky | 1989 | HH the Dalai Lama of Tibet |
| 1936 | Carlos Saavedra Lamas | 1990 | Mikhail Gorbachev |
| 1937 | Viscount Cecil of Chelwood | 1991 | Aung San Suu Kyi |
| 1938 | Nansen International Office for Refugees | 1992 | Rigoberta Menchú Tum |
| 1939–43 | no award | 1993 | Nelson Mandela; F W de Klerk |
| 1944 | International Red Cross Committee | 1994 | Yasser Arafat; Shimon Peres; Yitzhak Rabin |
| 1945 | Cordell Hull | 1995 | Joseph Rotblat; Pugwash Conferences |
| 1946 | Emily Greene Balch; John R Mott | | on Science and World Affairs |
| 1947 | American Friends Service Committee (USA); | 1996 | Carlos Filipe Ximenes Belo; |
| | Friends Service Council (UK) | | José Ramos-Horta |
| 1948 | no award | 1997 | Jody Williams and the International |
| 1949 | Lord Boyd-Orr | | Campaign to Ban Landmines |
| 1950 | Ralph Bunche | 1998 | John Hume; David Trimble |
| 1951 | Léon Jouhaux | 1999 | Médecins Sans Frontières |
| 1952 | Albert Schweitzer | 2000 | Kim Dae Jung |
| 1953 | George Catlett Marshall | 2001 | The United Nations and |
| 1954 | Office of the United Nations High | | Secretary-General Kofi Annan |
| | Commissioner for Refugees | 2002 | Jimmy Carter |
| 1955–6 | no award | 2003 | Shirin Ebadi |
| 1957 | Lester Bowles Pearson | 2004 | Wangari Maathai |
| 1958 | Dominique Georges Pire | | |

**Nomenklatura** (post-1930)

A list of official positions in the Communist Party of the USSR, and in Soviet government at most levels, and of people suited to fill them, predominantly communist. It was originally intended to identify good candidates in a developing society, but it was gradually abused first to support dictatorship and then to create and perpetuate an élite. By 1985 a corrupt system had paradoxically made reform essential in party and state and at the same time difficult to implement,

as Mikhail **GORBACHEV** found to his cost.

**Nomonhan Incident** (May–Sep 1939)

A military clash between Japanese and Soviet troops on the border between north-west Manchuria and Outer Mongolia. When the Japanese **GUANDONG ARMY** engaged in hostilities with Mongolian troops on the border at Nomonhan, Soviet troops intervened under the terms of a mutual defence treaty with Outer Mongolia. A full-scale border war ensued involving the use of aircraft and armoured divisions. Soviet mechanized units under Georgii **ZHUKOV** inflicted a heavy defeat on the Japanese forces (17,450 dead or missing). Japan's humiliation at Nomonhan convinced Tokyo that war with the USSR (which the Guandong Army had consistently advocated) was to be avoided, and led to the signing of the Japan–USSR Neutrality Pact in 1941.

## Non-Aligned Movement

A movement of states in the early years of the **COLD WAR** which positively espoused the cause of not taking sides in the major division within world politics between the USA and the USSR. Non-alignment was different from neutralism in that it was associated with moves to mediate between the **SUPERPOWERS**, and aimed to make a direct contribution to the achievement of peace. It was particularly associated with countries like India and statesmen like **NEHRU**. Attempts by Mediterranean, African and Asian countries in the 1960s to give renewed impetus to the movement were badly shaken by continuing superpower hostility. However, despite the end of the Cold War, conferences were still being held as recently as 2003.

## Non-Cooperation Movement

A nationalist campaign (1919–22) led by M K **GANDHI** and Congress in protest at the **AMRITSAR MASSACRE** and the **MONTAGU–CHELMSFORD REFORMS**, and to force the British to grant Indian independence. Locally, it took up many issues, and was linked, especially by Gandhi, with the **KHILAFAT MOVEMENT**. The movement marked M K **GANDHI**'s rise to preeminence in the Congress. It involved the boycott of Government institutions and foreign goods, and was abandoned when the protest became violent.

## non-violent resistance

The use of non-violent means to resist occupation by a foreign power or for other political purposes. It can involve an appeal to wider world opinion, as well as various forms of peaceful political resistance, such as general strikes and **CIVIL DISOBEDIENCE**. Damage to property is not necessarily ruled out. Non violent resistance is most famously associated with M K **GANDHI**'s resistance to British rule in India, and was popular with the **CIVIL RIGHTS** movements of the 1960s.

## Nootka Sound Incident (1789–90)

A dispute caused by the seizure in 1789 of four British trading ships at Nootka Sound, an inlet on the western side of Vancouver Island, Canada, which had been visited by Juan Pérez in 1774 and by Captain **COOK** in 1778, and was claimed by Spain. In response to Spain's claim to the whole north-western coast of America, Britain argued that the area had to be occupied to be owned by Spain, and threatened war. However, war was averted by the Nootka Sound Convention (28 Oct 1790) at which Spain, recognizing the superior strength and Prussian backing of Britain, agreed to Britain's demands and gave up her monopoly on trade and settlement in north-west America, thus opening up the West Pacific coast to British settlement.

## Noriega, Manuel Antonio (1934–)

Panamanian military leader. The ruling force behind the presidents of Panama in the period 1983–9, he had been recruited by the **CIA** in the late 1960s and was supported by the US government until 1987. Alleging his involvement in drug trafficking, the US authorities ordered his arrest in 1989; 13,000 US troops invaded Panama to support the 12,000 already there. He surrendered in Jan 1990 after taking refuge for ten days in the Vatican nunciature, and was taken to the USA for trial. In 1992 he was convicted of drug trafficking and racketeering, and sentenced to 40 years' imprisonment, reduced in 1999 to 30 years.

## normalization

A term used to describe the restoration of previously ostensibly friendly relations between states or other political organizations after a period of tension or conflict. It was more specifically applied to what was frankly the reimposition of Soviet-style **COMMUNISM** on those East European socialist states, such as Czechoslovakia in 1968, that had attempted to modify Soviet forms to suit their own conditions. ► **DÉTENTE**

## Norman Conquest

A fundamental watershed in English political and social history, though some of its consequences are much debated. It not only began the rule of a dynasty of Norman kings (1066–1154), but entailed the virtual replacement of the Anglo-Saxon nobility by **NORMANS**, Bretons and Flemings, many of whom retained lands in northern France. Moreover, between 1066 and 1144 England and **NORMANDY** were normally united under one king-duke, and the result was the formation of a single cross-Channel state. The Angevin conquest of Normandy (1144–5) and takeover of England (1154) ensured that England's fortunes would continue to be linked with France even after the French annexation of Normandy in 1204. ► **ANGEVINS**; **DOMESDAY BOOK**; **HASTINGS, BATTLE OF**; **HENRY I** (of England); **HUNDRED YEARS' WAR**; **WILLIAM I, THE CONQUEROR**; **WILLIAM II, RUFUS**

---

### NORMAN DYNASTY

| Regnal Dates | Name |
|---|---|
| 1066/87 | William I, the Conqueror |
| 1087/1100 | William II, Rufus |
| 1100/35 | Henry I |
| 1135/54 | Stephen* |

* Right to throne disputed by Matilda/Maud, daughter of Henry I; after her death, her son recognized Stephen as king for life and then succeeded him as Henry II

---

## Normandy

Former duchy and province in north-western France, along the littoral of the English Channel between Brittany and French Flanders; now the regions of Haute-Normandie and Basse-Normandie. A leading state in the **MIDDLE AGES**, its ruler, **WILLIAM I, THE CONQUEROR**, as Duke of Normandy, conquered England in 1066. Captured by France in 1204, its ownership was disputed between France and England in the **HUNDRED YEARS' WAR** until it became part of France in 1449. In 1944 it was the scene of the Allied invasion of occupied France. ► **NORMANDY CAMPAIGN**

## Normandy Campaign (1944)

A **WORLD WAR II** campaign which began on **D-DAY** (6 June 1944). Allied forces under the command of General **EISENHOWER** began the liberation of Western Europe from Germany by landing on the **NORMANDY** coast between the Orne River and St Marcouf. Artificial harbours were constructed along a strip of beach so that armoured vehicles and heavy guns could be unloaded. Heavy fighting ensued for three weeks, before Allied troops captured Cherbourg (27 June). Tanks broke through the German defences, and Paris was liberated (25 Aug), followed by the liberation of Brussels (2 Sep), and the crossing of the German frontier (12 Sep).

## Normans

By the early 11c, a label (derived from 'Northmen', ie **VIKINGS**) applied to all the people inhabiting **NORMANDY**, a duchy (and later province) in northern France, though probably only a small element was actually of Scandinavian descent. During the second half of the 11c and the first decade of the 12c, their achievements, especially as conquerors, were remarkable. They completed the conquest and aristocratic colonization of England and a large part of Wales, established a kingdom in southern Italy and Sicily, and founded the Norman principality of Antioch. They also fought against the Muslims in Spain and settled peacefully in Scotland. ► **GUISCARD, ROBERT**

## Norodom I (1838–1904)

King of Cambodia (1860/1904). When Norodom succeeded his father as king in 1860, Cambodia fell into civil war. Norodom fled to Bangkok, having spent much of his childhood at the Siamese court. On his return to Cambodia in 1863, he was approached by the French, recently established in **COCHIN-CHINA**, who offered him protection in exchange for commercial rights. Eager to escape from the influence of Siam, Norodom accepted. However, this action simply secured French domination, and Cambodia became a French protectorate. Until the 1880s, Norodom retained considerable freedom but from the middle of that decade the French greatly tightened their control.

## North, Frederick, 8th Lord North (1732–92)

British politician. He became a Lord of the Treasury (1759) and Chancellor of the Exchequer (1767), and as Prime Minister (1770–82) brought **GEORGE III** a period of political stability. He was widely criticized both for failing to avert the **DECLARATION OF INDEPENDENCE** by the North American colonies (1776) and for failing to defeat them in the subsequent war (1776–83). He annoyed the King by resigning in 1782, then formed a coalition with his former Whig opponent, **FOX** (1783), but it did not survive royal hostility. After this coalition was dismissed (1783), he remained an opposition politician until his death. ► **AMERICAN REVOLUTION**

## North African Campaign (1940–3)

A campaign fought during **WORLD WAR II** between Allied and Axis troops. After an initial Italian invasion of Egypt, Italian forces were driven back deep into Libya, and **ROMMEL** was sent to North Africa with the specially trained **AFRIKA CORPS** to stem a further Italian retreat. The British were driven back to the Egyptian border, though they defended Tobruk. They counter-attacked late in 1941, and fighting continued the following year, with Rommel once more gaining the initiative, but being halted at the inconclusive first Battle of **EL ALAMEIN** (Jul 1942). In Oct, British troops under **MONTGOMERY** defeated Rommel at the second Battle of El Alamein, and drove the German troops back once more. In Feb 1943 the Germans attacked US troops in Tunisia, were driven back, and finally 250,000 Axis troops, half of them German, were caught in a pincer movement by Allied forces advancing from the east and west. ► **AXIS POWERS**

## North Atlantic Treaty Organization ► NATO

## Northern Expedition (1926–8)

The military expedition undertaken by the Chinese Nationalists (**GUOMINDANG**) and their Communist allies to defeat provincial **WARLORDS** and reunify the country. Under the command of **CHIANG KAI-SHEK**, the National Revolutionary Army marched northwards from south China (Jul 1926) and had reached the Yangzi River (central China) by early 1927. At this point the left wing of the Guomindang, with the support of the Communists, established its own government at Wuhan, while the right wing under Chiang Kai-shek, after taking Shanghai (Apr 1927), embarked on a campaign of terror against Communists and their labour supporters. By Jun 1927 the left-wing Guomindang government had collapsed, effectively ending the United Front between Nationalists and Communists. Chiang then proceeded northwards, capturing Beijing (1928). Although a Nationalist government was formally proclaimed (with the capital at Nanjing), Chiang's control over the country was tenuous. Most warlords had simply enrolled under the Nationalist banner and continued to exercise control of their own armies. Furthermore, although the Communists' urban base had been destroyed during the Northern Expedition, they developed rural bases after 1928 that were ultimately to engulf the entire country. ► **UNITED FRONTS**

## NORTHERN IRELAND also called Ulster

A constituent division of the United Kingdom of Great Britain and Northern Ireland, occupying the north-eastern part of Ireland. A separate parliament to the rest of Ireland (**STORMONT**) was established in 1920, with a House of Commons and a Senate. There is a Protestant majority in the population, generally supporting political union with Great Britain; many of the Roman Catholic minority look for union with the Republic of **IRELAND**. Violent conflict between the communities broke out in 1968 (the **ULSTER 'TROUBLES'**). After appeals from Catholic politicians, the British government sent a British Army peacekeeping force. Sectarian murders and bombings continued both within and outside the province, and as a result of the disturbances the Northern Irish parliament was abolished in 1972. A 78-member Assembly was formed in 1973, which was replaced by a Constitutional Convention in 1975. The Assembly reformed in 1982, but nationalist members did not take their seats. Under the 1985 **ANGLO-IRISH AGREEMENT**, the Republic of Ireland was given a consultative role in the government of Northern Ireland and all Northern Ireland MPs in

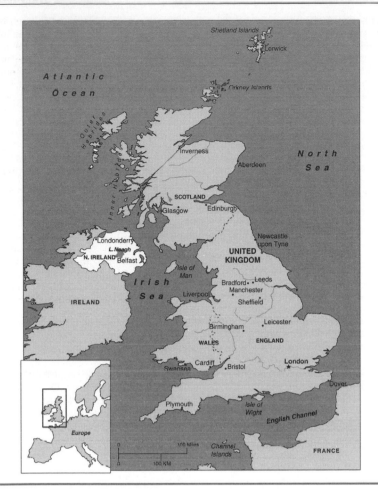

the British Parliament resigned in protest in 1986. Direct negotiations between the political parties took place in Belfast in 1991 and 1992, leading to the **DOWNING STREET DECLARATION** by UK and Irish governments in 1993. An **IRA** ceasefire was in place in 1994–6, but there was renewed violence in 1996–7 until the ceasefire recommenced in 1997. Further cross-party talks resulted in the **GOOD FRIDAY AGREEMENT** in 1998 under which a Northern Ireland Assembly was established in 1999 with limited powers devolved from the Secretary of State for Northern Ireland. Power-sharing collapsed following the **STORMONTGATE** scandal and led the British government to suspend the Assembly in Oct 2002. Although elections to the Assembly were held in Nov 2003, cross-party talks on the resumption of power-sharing have been unsuccessful and the Secretary of State retains responsibility for Northern Ireland departments. ► **ENGLAND**; **SCOTLAND**; **UNITED KINGDOM**; **WALES**

## North German Confederation

The state system and constitutional arrangement created in 1866 by **BISMARCK**, Minister President of **PRUSSIA**, following the Prussian defeat of Austria and the dissolution of the **GERMAN CONFEDERATION**. Utterly dominated by Prussia, the new confederation was itself dissolved with the creation of the German Empire in 1871. ► **AUSTRO-PRUSSIAN WAR**

## north–south divide

A geographical description of the economic differences between the industrialized 'First World' nations, mainly found in the northern hemisphere, and the developing 'Third World' nations, generally located in the southern hemisphere. Divisions of equity and sustainability between north and south arise from the more rapid growth of 'southern' populations, economic migration, 'northern' ecological degradation, trade imbalances and the gulf between standards of living. The Club of Rome's *Limits to Growth* (1972) did much to heighten awareness of the interconnection of global issues, although its solutions (slower growth in the north and abandonment of full economic development in the south) were widely criticized. Although running counter to the aims of trade organizations such as the **OECD**, the **BRANDT COMMISSION** was the earliest attempt to address the problems of north–south trade imbalance, advocating solutions such as **THIRD WORLD DEBT** relief and **FAIR TRADE** initiatives. ► **JUBILEE 2000**

## North West Company

Canadian fur-trading association. Established in 1779, it set up a string of trading partnerships and achieved a remarkable record of exploration. The Montreal partners managed finance and marketing, meeting the 'wintering' partners once a year in Fort William to collect the furs and make policy decisions.

The 'wintering' partners in turn organized the trappers and canoeists. In 1821, however, the company was absorbed into the **HUDSON'S BAY COMPANY**, with which it had been conducting bitter and often violent competition. ► **FRASER, SIMON**; **FUR TRADE**

## Northwest Ordinance of 1787

An Act of the American **CONTINENTAL CONGRESS** establishing procedures by which newly settled Western territories could become states on the basis of full political equality with the original states. It was one of several Northwest Ordinances passed in 1784–7.

## North-West Rebellion (1885)

Canadian revolt. The **MÉTIS** of the Saskatchewan, like those of Red River, had suffered from the encroachments of English-speaking settlers without any governmental assurances or safeguards. Although they had an effective leader in Gabriel Dumont, they appealed to Louis **RIEL**, who returned from the USA to lead them. When two Indian tribes also gave their support it began to look as if the North West was about to explode, but a large body of militia crushed the revolt. Dumont escaped but Riel was captured and later executed. The speed with which the militia were able to get from Ottawa to Winnipeg (six days instead of the two months taken in 1870 by the Wolseley expedition) showed the value of the Canadian Pacific Railway, encouraging the government to lend it the money essential for its completion. ► **RED RIVER REBELLION**

**NORWAY** official name **Kingdom of Norway**

A kingdom in north-west Europe, bounded to the north by the Arctic Ocean; to the east by Sweden, Finland and Russia; to the west by the North Sea and Norwegian Sea; and to the south by the Skagerrak. A noble family from Sweden settled itself in southern Norway in the 7c, and the establishment of Norway as a united kingdom was achieved c.900 by Harald the Fair-Haired. **CANUTE** brought Norway under Danish rule in 1028 but on his death the throne reverted to **MAGNUS I, THE GOOD**. It was united with Sweden and Denmark in 1397 in the **KALMAR UNION** and remained under Danish rule until 1814, when Sweden was allowed to annex Norway as a reward for its assistance against **NAPOLEON I**. Growing nationalism resulted in independence in 1905. Norway declared neutrality in both World Wars, but was occupied by Germany in 1940–4. Norway joined **NATO** in 1949 and was a founder members of **EFTA** in 1960, but referendums in 1972 and 1994 have kept it out of the **EC/EU**.

## Norway, German Invasion of (8–9 Apr 1940)

A daring sea-borne operation, undertaken in defiance of British naval superiority, which was carried out as a preliminary to the German invasion of France and in order to protect Germany's supply of iron ore from northern Sweden. It brought all major Norwegian cities, including Oslo, Bergen, Trondheim and Narvik under German control within a single night. Refusing to capitulate or to hand over authority to **QUISLING**, the Norwegian government and King **HAAKON VII** maintained a resistance to the Germans which lasted, with British and French support, until June 1940. ► **WORLD WAR II**

## Notables, Assemblies of the (1787–8)

In France, the name originated with consultative assemblies called by the monarchy in 15–17c. They fell into disuse until **CALONNE** convoked such a meeting in 1787, hoping that these representatives of the privileged orders would agree to the ending of their exemption from certain taxes. They refused, and the first assembly was dissolved, leading to Calonne's fall. In 1788 **NECKER**, who replaced him, called a second assembly to advise on the method of calling the **ESTATES GENERAL**.

## Nothomb, Jean Baptiste (1805–81)

Belgian politician. Trained as a lawyer, he was active as a journalist-editor, and in political opposition to the union between the northern and southern Netherlands (present-day Netherlands and Belgium, 1815–30). After the Belgian Revolution he became a member of the National Congress and helped draft the constitution. He served as an MP (1831–48), Minister for Public Works (1837–40) and Minister for Home Affairs (1841–5), when he also led the government. He then became Belgian ambassador to Berlin.

## Notting Hill Riots (1958)

A series of violent demonstrations in north-west London. Directed at non-white immigrants living there, they brought immigration into the British political arena for the first time.

## Novara, Battle of (23 Mar 1849)

The defeat by **RADETZKY** of the Piedmontese forces under the command of the Polish General Chrzanowsky, which led to the abdication of **CHARLES ALBERT**.

## Novikov, Nikolai I (1744–1818)

Russian Freemason. Like other phenomena of the **ENLIGHTENMENT**, **FREEMASONRY** spread to the imitative Russia of **CATHERINE II, THE GREAT**. From 1779 to 1791, Novikov was active as publisher and journalist in Moscow. His main interests were education and philanthropy, and initially he had widespread support from fellow nobles and from Catherine. But particularly following the **FRENCH REVOLUTION**, she began to object to the criticism inherent in Novikov's activities. In 1791 she suspended his publications and in 1792 imprisoned him without trial. The idea of secret societies working for reform (one aspect of Freemasonry) revived in the 1820s and helped shape the activity of the **DECEMBRISTS**.

**Novi Pazar** ► **SANDŽAK OF NOVI PAZAR**

## Novosiltsev, Nikolai Nikolaeva, Count (1761–1836)

Russian bureaucrat. He was one of the 'unofficial

committee' of four friends and advisers of Tsar **ALEXANDER I**, who helped him to make a liberal start to his reign in the years 1801–3. In 1805 he headed a special mission to Britain, and the resulting treaty brought Alexander into the alliance against **NAPOLEON I**. In 1815 he became imperial commissioner in Warsaw, generally supervising the so-called Congress Kingdom of Poland. In 1820 he presented the Tsar with the definitive form of his Constitutional Charter of the Russian Empire, which advocated something approaching a federation of 12 provinces. Alexander favoured it but implemented it only marginally. With **NICHOLAS I**'s accession, however, Novosiltsev lost influence.

## Novotný, Antonín (1904–75)

Czechoslovak politician. He became a communist at the age of 17 and held various party jobs in the years before **WORLD WAR II**. Arrested in 1941, he survived four years in a Nazi **CONCENTRATION CAMP**. After his release, he rose rapidly in the Czechoslovak Communist Party, becoming Regional Secretary in Prague in 1945 and a member of the Central Committee in 1946. He played a leading part in the communist takeover of the Czechoslovak government in 1948. Novotný became all-powerful First Secretary of the Party in 1953 and from 1958 to 1968 he was also President of the republic. He was essentially a Soviet-style communist, so much committed to **CENTRAL PLANNING** and the needs of heavy industry that by 1961 there was an economic recession. His unpopularity forced him to make token concessions from 1962 onwards, especially in the hope of placating the Slovaks, but these empty gestures failed to satisfy his critics within the Party. He was therefore forced out, and succeeded as First Secretary by the reformist Slovak Alexander **DUBČEK** in Jan 1968, and was also forced to resign the presidency two months later. However, his negative and protracted tenure of office lost the Czechoslovak reform movement more time than it could make up in the course of the **PRAGUE SPRING**. ► **STALINISM**

## NPD (Nationaldemokratische Partei Deutschlands, 'National Democratic Party of Germany')

German political party. Founded in 1964 through the amalgamation of extreme right-wing splinter parties, notably the German Reich Party (DRP) and German Party (DP), the NPD became increasingly radical, especially under von Thadden's leadership from 1967. In its internal structure, politics and membership the NPD showed some disturbing parallels with the **NAZI PARTY**, but although it gained seats temporarily in various **LAND** (state) parliaments, it failed to enter the **BUNDESTAG** and by the mid-1970s had, to all intents and purposes, collapsed.

## NSDAP ► NAZI PARTY

## Nu, U, originally Thakin Nu (1907–95)

Burmese politician. He became a teacher, and in 1934 came to prominence through the student political movement. Imprisoned by the British for sedition (1940), he was released by the Japanese and served in Ba Maw's puppet administration. In 1946 he became President of the Burmese Constituent Assembly, and on independence in 1948 the first Prime Minister of the independent Union of Burma (1948–56, 1957–8, 1960–2). He was overthrown by a military coup led by General **NE WIN** in 1962, and imprisoned, but released in 1966. He then lived abroad, organizing resistance to the military regime, but returned to Burma (now Myanmar) in 1980 to become a Buddhist monk.

## Nuclear Non-Proliferation Treaty (NPT)

A treaty signed in 1968 by the USA, the USSR, the UK and 59 other states, now an open-ended list of 187 signatory countries. The treaty became effective in 1970 and was due to last initially for 25 years, but in 1995 it was extended indefinitely by 174 countries that voted on the matter at the **UN** headquarters. The other two declared nuclear powers, China and France, signed the treaty in 1992. The treaty sought to limit the spread of nuclear weapons, those possessing them agreeing not to transfer the capability to produce them, and those not possessing them agreeing not to acquire the capability. The treaty permits only five countries to possess nuclear weapons – China, France, Russia, the UK and the USA – but a number of other states are believed to have produced, or be close to producing, their own nuclear arms, including Iran and North Korea, which revoked its signature of the treaty in 1993. The only countries that have not signed the treaty, India, Israel and Pakistan, have all developed nuclear arms.

## Nuclear Test-Ban Treaty (1963)

A treaty prohibiting the testing of nuclear weapons on or above the surface of the earth, put forward by the USA and the USSR as an indirect means of slowing down the proliferation of countries with nuclear weapons. Though it was quickly signed by more than 100 governments, it was boycotted by two nuclear nations, France and China, and apparently did not prevent a number of nations, including Israel and Pakistan, from attempting to develop, or from developing, a nuclear capability. France carried out some tests in the Pacific in 1995–6 but then declared that it would do so no more and, together with China, Russia, the UK and the USA, agreed to sign a permanent test-ban treaty (1996). ► **NUCLEAR NON-PROLIFERATION TREATY; SALT; START**

## nuclear weapons

Bombs, missiles or other weapons of mass destruction (**WMD**) deriving their destructive force from the energy released during nuclear fission or nuclear fusion. According to their size and the means of delivery, they may be classified as tactical short-range weapons (for use on the battlefield), theatre medium-range weapons (for use against deep military targets), or strategic long-range weapons (for use against enemy cities and command centres). ► **CND**; **DISARMAMENT**; **NUCLEAR NON-PROLIFERATION TREATY; WARFARE**

## Nujoma, Sam Daniel (1929– )

Namibian nationalist. Educated at a Finnish missionary school in Windhoek, he was a railway worker and clerk until entering politics as the co-founder of the South West Africa People's Organization (**SWAPO**). He was exiled in 1960, set up a provisional headquarters in Dar es Salaam and led SWAPO's armed struggle from 1966 until 1989, when he returned to Namibia for the pre-independence elections, which his party won. He became the first President of Namibia in Mar 1990 and was re-elected in 1994 and 1999, standing down after completing his final term of office.

## nullification

A US political doctrine that a state has the power to render laws of the federal government void within its borders. It was tested by South Carolina during the 'Nullification Crisis' in 1832, over the issue of enforcing a federal tariff. That immediate issue was resolved by the **JACKSON** administration's Force Bill, authorizing the President to use armed forces to enforce the laws of **CONGRESS**. However, in larger terms the problem was not resolved until the **AMERICAN CIVIL WAR**, and in some ways continued through the **CIVIL RIGHTS MOVEMENT**.

## Núñez, Rafael (1825–94)

Colombian politician. Trained as a lawyer, he rose to prominence as a Liberal leader in the 1870s but, influenced by radical Spencerian ideas, such as the 'survival of the fittest', turned to conservatism. Governor of Bolivar, he was elected President (1880–2) with the support of moderate Liberals and Conservatives. Returned to office (1884–94), he fought the Liberals, assuring centralized government in the constitution of 1886, which lasted until 1936. He restored the power of the Church, and the Jesuits returned to dominate the education system. His governments were also marked by attempts at modernization. The secession of Panama in 1903 partially resulted from Núñez's centralization of administration in Bogotá, and his concern for the interests of his birthplace, Cartagena, the historic rival to Panama.

## Nupe

An Islamic state in central Nigeria which resisted the encroachments of Europeans in the 19c. It was conquered in 1896 by Sir George **GOLDIE** and forces of the **ROYAL NIGER COMPANY**. The southern half of the emirate was ceded to the British and a new Emir was installed likely to be sympathetic to the company. It was subsequently incorporated into the colony of Nigeria.

## Nur al-Din (1118–74)

Sultan of Egypt and Syria (1146/74). Also known as al-Malik al-Adil ('the Just Ruler'), he was the son of the Turkish Atabeg Zangi, whom he succeeded as ruler of Aleppo in 1146. He devoted himself to the **JIHAD**, the holy war against the Christian **FRANKS** of the Crusader states, defeating and killing Prince Raymond of Antioch (1149) and completely extinguishing the most exposed Frankish state, the county of Edessa (1146–51). He saw the unification of the Muslim Middle East as the key to his aim, and worked to bring about the conquest of Damascus (1154) and Mosul (1170), while through his generals Shirkuh and **SALADIN** he took control of Egypt and abolished the Fatimid caliphate. Nur al-Din's empire began to fall apart soon after his death, and it was left to Saladin, who by this time had made himself independent, to carry on his mission.

## Nuremberg Laws (1935)

Two racial laws promulgated in Nuremberg at a **REICHSTAG** meeting held during the **NAZI PARTY** Congress of that year. The first deprived of German citizenship those not of 'German or related blood'; the second made marriage or extra-marital relations illegal between Germans and Jews. Following on earlier arbitrary terror, the laws were the first formal steps in the process of separating off Jews and other 'non-Aryans' in Nazi Germany.

## Nuremberg Trials

Proceedings held by the Allies at Nuremberg after **WORLD WAR II** to try Nazi war criminals, following a decision made in 1943. An International Military Tribunal was set up in Aug 1945, and sat from Nov 1945 until Oct 1946. Twenty-one Nazis were tried in person, including **GOERING** and **RIBBENTROP** (who were sentenced to death), and **HESS** (who was given life imprisonment). ► **NAZI PARTY**

## Nurhaci (1559–1626)

Manchu (Jurchen) leader. He unified the tribes on China's north-eastern frontier, laying the foundations for the eventual Manchu conquest of China in 1644. Nurhaci belonged to a clan whose forebears had owed allegiance to the Chinese **MING DYNASTY**, but his policy of unifying the tribes through warfare and marriage ties, and his assumption of the title of Khan (ruler) in 1616 symbolized open defiance of the Ming. The creator of the **BANNER SYSTEM**, he developed a sophisticated military and bureaucratic organization, employing Chinese advisers and devising a Manchu written script. After his death, following an unexpected setback to his offensive on China, his sons and grandsons completed the task of conquest to establish the **QING DYNASTY**.

## Nur Jahan (fl.1611–27)

Wife of **JAHANGIR**, the eldest son of Emperor **AKBAR THE GREAT**. In 1611 her first husband, Sher Afghan, died in a clash with the Mughal Governor of Bengal. Nur Jahan's father, Itimad-ud-Daula, was made joint Diwan by Jahangir in the first year of his reign and, after Jahangir's marriage to Nur Jahan, he was raised to the office of Chief Diwan; furthermore Nur Jahan's brother, Asaf Khan, was appointed Khan-i-saman, a post reserved for nobles in whom the emperor had full confidence. Along with her father and brother, and in alliance with Khurram (**SHAH JAHAN**), Nur Jahan formed a group or *junta* which 'managed' Jahangir and his political activities. This led to the division of the court into two factions. Although her precise political role in this period is not clear, Nur Jahan was a dominant figure in the royal household and set new fashions based on Persian traditions.

## Nyamwezi

A people of the highlands of north-central Tanzania, south of Lake Victoria. In the 18c they created a trading network between the East African coast and some of the states of Uganda. Later they extended their commercial influence to the Kazembe kingdom in Zambia. Coastal Swahili and Europeans were in touch with them in the 19c, particularly during the reign of Chief Mirambo. ► **BUGANDA**; **LUBA-LUNDA KINGDOMS**; **SWAHILI**

**Nye Committee**, official name **the Senate Munitions Investigating Committee** (1934–6)
A US **SENATE** committee chaired by Senator Gerald Nye of North Dakota which investigated the political role and profits of the US armaments industry before

and during **WORLD WAR I**. The findings revealed that arms manufacturers, who had gained vast profits, seemed to have helped manoeuvre the USA into the war and that they generally showed a marked hostility to disarmament. This indictment of the munitions industry increased public support of **ISOLATIONISM** to such an extent that **CONGRESS** was persuaded to pass a series of **NEUTRALITY ACTS** (1935–9).

## Nyerere, Julius Kambarage (1922–99)

Tanzanian nationalist leader and politician. While working as a schoolteacher, he became President of the Tanganyika African Association (1953). He left the profession to co-found (1954) the **TANGANYIKA AFRICAN NATIONAL UNION** (TANU), of which he became President, and led the movement to independence. After a brief spell as a nominated member of Legco (from which he resigned), Nyerere was elected (1958) in his own right, becoming Chief Minister (1960–1) and, on independence, Prime Minister. He resigned from the post to reorganize the party and returned to central politics as President, negotiating the union of Tanganyika and Zanzibar in 1964. His idealism, reflected in the **ARUSHA DECLARATION**, dominated Tanzania's public policy and the country's reputation abroad. He resigned the presidency in 1985, but retained the presidency of his party, now **CHAMA CHA MAPINDUZI**, until 1990.

## Nyoro

A Bantu-speaking agricultural people of western Uganda. The original feudal kingdom of Bunyoro-Kitara was founded in the 14–15c with a pastoralist ruling class (*Hima*) and farming peasants (*Iru*). It was the most powerful kingdom in the area during the 19c, but was destroyed by the British in the 1890s. The kingship was abolished by the Ugandan government in 1966.

## Nystadt, Treaty of (1721)

The Russo-Swedish treaty, signed at Nystadt, Finland, ending the **GREAT NORTHERN WAR** and recognizing Russia's total victory. The cost of the war to Russia in terms of money and manpower was immense. However, so was the profit from the treaty: the area now occupied by Estonia, Latvia and Lithuania, and the south-east corner of post-**WORLD WAR I** Finland, above all the fortress of Vyborg. In this way, Russia was ensured permanent access to the Baltic Sea. The treaty marked the emergence of Russia as a major European power. ▶ **PETER I, THE GREAT**

## Nzinga (c.1582–1663)

Queen of Matamba. A royal princess of the Ndongo (a small kingdom adjoining the Portuguese colony of Angola), she fought to establish a kingdom independent of the Portuguese, free from war and the depredations of the slave trade. In 1623 she went personally to Angola to negotiate with the governor and was baptized a Christian as Dona Aña de Souza. Driven out of Ndongo by Portuguese troops the following year, she created the new kingdom of Matamba. Here she trained military élites to resist the Portuguese and allied herself with the Dutch following their capture of Luanda, the Angolan capital, in 1641. Although she had abandoned Christianity, she reconverted towards the end of her life, by which time Matamba had become a successful commercial kingdom (largely through acting as a broker in the Portuguese slave trade).

## OAPEC (Organization of Arab Petroleum Exporting Countries)

An organization formed under the umbrella of the Organization of Petroleum Exporting Countries (**OPEC**) in 1968 by Saudi Arabia, Kuwait and Libya, with its headquarters in Kuwait. By 1972 all the Arab oil producers had joined.

## OAS (*Organisation de l'Armée Secrète*, 'Secret Army Organization')

The clandestine organization of French Algerians, led by rebel army generals Jouhaud and Raoul **SALAN**, active (1960–2) in resisting Algerian independence. It caused considerable violence in Algeria and metropolitan France until thrown into rapid decline by the Franco-Algerian ceasefire (Mar 1962), Salan's capture (Apr 1962) and Algerian independence (Jul 1962). ► **ALGERIAN WAR OF INDEPENDENCE**; **FLN**

## Oastler, Richard (1789–1861)

British social reformer. A Tory humanitarian, he attacked the employment of children in factories and advocated a shorter working day, in campaigns resulting in the Factory Act (1833) and Ten Hours Act (1847). He was a strong opponent of **LAISSEZ-FAIRE** political economy, and campaigned against the implementation of the Poor Law Amendment Act (1834), which he believed reduced paupers to the status of slaves. His *Fleet Papers*, attacking the Poor Law and criticizing the government, were edited from prison, where he had been placed for debts owing to his former employer. ► **FACTORY ACTS**; **POOR LAWS**; **TORIES**

## Oates, Titus (1649–1705)

English conspirator. The son of an Anabaptist preacher, he took Anglican orders but was dismissed from his curacy for misconduct. In 1677 he concocted the **POPISH PLOT**, based partly on details he had picked up when he had passed himself off as a Catholic and infiltrated Jesuit seminaries. In 1678 he told a magistrate, later found dead, of a Catholic plot to massacre Protestants, burn London, and assassinate **CHARLES II**, replacing him with his brother James, Duke of York (**JAMES VII AND II**). Oates was considered a hero, and his evidence led to 35 executions. But after two years a reaction set in. In 1683 Oates was fined £100,000 for calling the Duke of York a traitor, he was imprisoned, and in May 1685 was found guilty of perjury and imprisoned for life. He was set free in the **GLORIOUS REVOLUTION** of 1688–9.

**Oba** ► BENIN, KINGDOM OF

## Obasanjo, Olusegun (1937– )

Nigerian soldier and politician. Educated at Abeokuta Baptist High School and Mons Officers' School, he joined the Nigerian army in 1958, training in both the UK and India, specializing in engineering. He served with the Nigerian unit in the **UN** Congo operations and was military commander of the federal forces during the **BIAFRAN WAR** (1967–70). He was made federal Commissioner of Works and Housing (1975) as well as Chief of Staff. After the short interim military rule led by Murtala **MUHAMMAD**, he became head of state (1976–9) overseeing the transfer back to civilian rule. He has played an important role on the international stage, especially within the **COMMONWEALTH OF NATIONS**, and as founder and leader of the African Leadership Forum, and in Feb 1999 was elected President, ending 15 years of military rule in Nigeria. He was re-elected in 2003.

## Obote, (Apollo) Milton (1924– )

Ugandan politician. Educated in mission schools and Makerere College, he worked in Kenya (1950–5), being a founder-member of the Kenyan African Union. He kept his political links with his home country and was a member of the Uganda National Congress (1952–60), being elected to Legco in 1957. He helped form the Uganda People's Congress in 1960, became its leader and then leader of the opposition during the Kiwanuka government of 1961–2. The 1962 elections resulted in a coalition between Obote's UPC and the neo-traditionalist **KABAKA YEKKA** and he became Prime Minister. When fundamental differences between himself and the Kabaka could not be mediated, he staged a coup in 1966, deposing the Kabaka and establishing himself as Executive President. In 1971, however, his government was overthrown in a military coup, led by Idi **AMIN**. He went into exile in Tanzania and returned to Uganda with the Tanzanian army in 1979, regaining the presidency after elections in 1980. But he was once more overthrown by the military (July 1985) and went into exile again, this time in Zambia.

## Obradović, Dositej (1743–1811)

Leading figure in the Serbian national revival. Born into a Serbian family in the Banat of **TEMESVÁR**, as an Orthodox monk he travelled widely in the Near East, England, France and Germany. On his travels he absorbed the ideas of the **ENLIGHTENMENT** and became fiercely anticlerical. During the **SERBIAN UPRISINGS**, he was responsible for education in the administration of **KARAGEORGE**. ► **KARADŽIĆ, VUK STEFANOVIĆ**

**Obregón, Álvaro** (1880–1928)
Mexican general and politician. Born near Álamos, Mexico, he was a planter in Sonora who gained prominence fighting against the revolutionaries, first in the service of Francisco **MADERO** in 1912, and then in aid of Venustiano **CARRANZA** against Pancho **VILLA** and Emiliano **ZAPATA** in 1915. Five years later he overthrew President Carranza and was himself elected as President of Mexico. In office from 1920 to 1924, he carried out agrarian, labour and educational reforms, struggled against US oil companies, and sought to limit the power of the Catholic Church. Re-elected in 1928, he was assassinated by a fanatical Roman Catholic before his term began.

**Obrenović, Alexander** (1876–1903)
King of Serbia (1889/1903). The son of Milan **OBRENOVIĆ**, he became King after his father's abdication (1889), the last of the Obrenović Dynasty. Governing at first through a regency, he used the army to take control of the country in 1893 and introduced some limited reform, reinstating the 1869 constitution which allowed more power to the executive (1894). He lacked popular support and his marriage in 1897 to a widow of ill-repute undermined yet further his authority. In June 1903 a group of Serbian army officers staged a coup and brutally murdered the King and Queen with the Prime Minister, War Minister and the Queen's brothers. ► **PAŠIĆ, NIKOLA**

**Obrenovic, Michael** (1822–1868)
Prince of Serbia (1839/42 and 1860/8). The second son of Miloš **OBRENOVIĆ**, he succeeded his father and governed through a regency until 1842, when he was overthrown and replaced by **ALEXANDER KARA-GEORGEVIĆ**. He succeeded his father as Prince once again in 1860. Well-educated and a clever politician, he looked to expand the Serbian state on the lines of Ilija **GARAŠANIN**'s **NACERTANIJE**. He increased and improved the army, created a War Ministry and built up a system of alliances with the other Balkan states against the **OTTOMAN EMPIRE**. While maintaining the form of the constitution, he controlled the assemblies and concentrated supreme power in his own hands. He was assassinated in June 1868.

**Obrenović, Milan** (1854–1901)
Prince (1868/82) and King (1882/9) of Serbia. In 1868 he succeeded his cousin, Michael **OBRENOVIĆ**, and governed through a regency. In 1869 he issued a new constitution which gave the assembly a stronger role, but his rule was both authoritarian and ineffectual. In 1889 he abdicated in favour of his son, Alexander **OBRENOVIĆ**. ► **RISTIĆ, JOVAN**

**Obrenović, Miloš** (1780–1860)
Prince of Serbia (1830/42 and 1858/60). The founder of the Obrenović Dynasty, in 1815 he led the second stage of the **SERBIAN UPRISINGS** and was ruler of the semi-independent Serbian state, before finally becoming the first Prince of autonomous Serbia (1830). Eliminating his rivals, including **KARA-GEORGE**, he ruled autocratically and amassed a great fortune. He considered that the so-called Turkish Constitution (1838) placed too many limitations on his authority and he left Serbia. After the fall of the constitutionalist regime of **ALEXANDER KARAGEORGEVIĆ**, he returned to Serbia and ruled as an absolute prince.

**O'Brien, William** (1852–1928)
Irish journalist and nationalist. He became editor of the weekly *United Ireland*, and sat in parliament as a Nationalist (1883–95). Several times prosecuted, and imprisoned for two years, he later returned to parliament (1900–18), and founded the United Irish League (1898) and the All-for-Ireland League (1910).

**O'Brien, William Smith** (1803–64)
Irish nationalist. He entered parliament in 1826, joining Daniel **O'CONNELL**'s Repeal Association (1843), but withdrew in 1846 after disputes over the use of force. Leader of the **YOUNG IRELAND** movement, he organized an unsuccessful rebellion in 1848, and was given a death sentence, commuted to transportation for life. In 1854 he was released, on condition of his not returning to Ireland, and in 1856 he received a free pardon.

**Occupied Territories** ► **GAZA STRIP**; **WEST BANK**

**Ockham** or **Occam, William of**, nicknamed **the Venerable Inceptor** (c.1285–c.1349)
English philosopher, theologian and political writer. Born in Ockham, Surrey, he entered the Franciscan order, studied theology at Oxford as an 'inceptor' (beginner), but never obtained a higher degree – hence his nickname. He was summoned to Avignon by Pope **JOHN XXII** to answer charges of heresy, and became involved in a dispute over Franciscan poverty, which the pope had denounced on doctrinal grounds. He fled to Bavaria (1328), was excommunicated, and remained under the protection of Emperor **LOUIS IV, THE BAVARIAN** until 1347. He died in Munich, probably of the Black Death. He published many works on logic and also published several important political treatises in the period 1333–47, generally directed against the papal claims to civil authority, including the *Opus nonaginta dierum* ('Work of 90 Days').

**O'Connell, Daniel** (1775–1847)
Irish political leader. He became a lawyer, and in 1823 formed the Catholic Association, which successfully fought elections against the landlords. His election as MP for County Clare precipitated a crisis in **WELLINGTON**'s government, which eventually granted **CATHOLIC EMANCIPATION** in 1829, enabling him to take his seat in the Commons. In 1840 he founded the Repeal Association, and agitation to end the union with Britain increased. In 1844 he was imprisoned for 14 weeks on a charge of sedition. In conflict with the **YOUNG IRELAND** movement (1846), and failing in health, 'the Liberator' left Ireland in 1847, and died in Genoa.

**O'Connor, Feargus Edward** (1794–1855)
Irish Chartist leader. He studied at Dublin, became a lawyer, and entered parliament in 1832. Estranged from **O'CONNELL**, he devoted himself to the cause of the working classes in England. His Leeds *Northern Star* (1837) became the most influential Chartist newspaper. He attempted, without great success, to unify the Chartist movement via the National Charter Association (1840), and presented himself as leader of the Chartist cause. Elected MP for Nottingham in 1847, in 1852 he became insane. ► **CHARTISTS**

**O'Connor, Sandra Day** (1930– )
US lawyer and jurist. She studied at Stanford, and after practising law she entered Arizona politics as a Republican, becoming majority leader in the state Senate before moving to the state bench. In 1981 President **REAGAN** named her to the US Supreme Court. She was confirmed, becoming the first woman in that position. ➤ **REPUBLICAN PARTY**

**October Crisis** (1970)
Terrorist crisis in Quebec. After the arrest of Pierre Vallière and Charles Gagnon, the **FRONT DE LIBÉRA-TION DE QUÉBEC** (FLQ) changed its tactics from bombing to kidnapping. One plan was foiled, but on 5 Oct the group kidnapped the British Trade Commissioner in Quebec, James Cross. A ransom of C$500,000 was demanded, along with the release of a number of 'political prisoners'. There was to be no police pursuit, transport out of the country was to be provided for the gang and the FLQ manifesto was to be broadcast on radio and television. The last two demands were accepted, and the Attorney-General of Quebec promised to support parole for a number of 'political prisoners'. Cross was not released, however, and on 10 Oct the Minister of Labour and Immigration, Pierre Laporte, was also kidnapped. Three days later students began a campaign of rallies and sit-ins, and the **PARTI QUÉBECOIS** began to put pressure on Premier Robert **BOURASSA** to form an emergency coalition government. Instead, he brought in the army to back up the police and the **WAR MEASURES ACT** was implemented to round up FLQ sympathizers. Although over 450 were arrested, only 20 were convicted in the 62 cases brought. Protest against the Act died down after Laporte's murder on 17 Oct. Cross was discovered and his release obtained after safe passage to Cuba was guaranteed to the kidnappers. Later that month the murderers of Laporte were apprehended and imprisoned.

**October Manifesto** (17 Oct 1905)
The proclamation issued by **NICHOLAS II** at the height of the Russian **REVOLUTION OF 1905**, promising the Russians freedom of speech and assembly and the election of a legislative body. This took the steam out of the opposition, but gradually the freedoms were ignored, while the Dumas that were elected were increasingly unrepresentative and powerless. This breach of promise was one of many factors decreasing Tsarism's chances of survival. ➤ **DUMA**

**October Revolution** (1917)
The overthrow of the Russian Provisional Government by Bolshevik-led armed workers (Red Guards), soldiers and sailors (25–6 Oct 1917 old style; 7–8 Nov new style). The revolution was organized by the Military Revolutionary Committee of the Petrograd Soviet, but was based on **LENIN**'s tactical exploitation of the Provisional Government's failure to provide effective leadership in a rapidly escalating crisis. The members of the government were arrested and it was replaced by the Soviet of People's Commissars (*Sovnarkom*), chaired by Lenin. This first Soviet government then proceeded to totally reorganize the economy and polity of Russia on lines that lasted for over 70 years. ➤ **APRIL THESES**; **BOLSHEVIKS**; **FEBRUARY REVOLUTION** (Russia); **JULY DAYS**

**October War** ➤ **ARAB–ISRAELI WARS**

**Octobrists** (1905–18)
The short name for the Union of 17 October, those Russian liberals who, in contrast with the **KADETS**, accepted the Tsar's **OCTOBER MANIFESTO** in 1905 as a basis on which to achieve moderate reform. Their numbers were greatest in the third and fourth Dumas for which the franchise was most biased, but they still achieved little. In 1911 their leader, Alexander **GUCHKOV**, was elected **DUMA** President but could not even exercise influence upon **NICHOLAS II**. Although Guchkov was Minister of War in the **RUSSIAN PROVISIONAL GOVERNMENT** of 1917, they were even more out of touch than the Kadets with the changing public mood and had virtually no representation in the **RUSSIAN CONSTITUENT ASSEMBLY** in 1918.

**Oda Nobunaga** (1534–82)
Japanese warrior. The first of the three great historical unifiers of Japan, followed by **TOYOTOMI HIDEYOSHI** and **TOKUGAWA IEYASU**, born into a noble family near Nagoya. He became a general, and occupied the old capital, Kyoto, in 1568, destroying the power of the Buddhist Church and favouring Christianity as a counter-balance. He built Azuchi Castle, near Kyoto, as his headquarters. He was assassinated by one of his own generals, in Kyoto.

**Oder–Neisse Line**
The new Polish–German border, drawn by the **WORLD WAR II** Allies in a series of conferences and negotiations in 1944–5, and involving the transfer to Poland of a sizable area of the Third **REICH**. The decision was partly based on historical arguments but also facilitated the transfer of territory in the east of Poland claimed by the USSR. A source of contention between the Federal Republic of Germany on the one hand and the German Democratic Republic and Poland on the other, the border was finally recognized by the Federal Republic in 1970 and by the reunited Germany in 1990.

**Odinga, (Ajuma) Oginga** (1911–94)
Kenyan nationalist and politician. Educated at Alliance High School and Makerere College, he was a schoolteacher when he became active in local Luo politics. He was elected to Legco in 1957 and was Vice-President of **KANU** (1960–6), during which period he pressed unflinchingly for independence, his apparent extremism being contrasted with the moderation of **MBOYA**. He was Minister of Home Affairs (1963–4) and then Vice-President (1964–6). At the Limuru Party Conference in 1966, Mboya managed to remove Odinga from positions of authority and he soon resigned to form the Kenya People's Union. He was re-elected on the KPU ticket in the Little General Election of 1966 and provided a charismatic figure round whom dissidents might congregate. Consequently, the party was soon banned and Odinga spent the next 25 years in and out of detention.

**O'Donnell, Leopoldo** (1809–67)
Spanish soldier and politician. Descended from an Irish family, he was born in Tenerife. He supported the infant Queen **ISABELLA II** against her uncle, Don **CARLOS**, and later supported her mother, the regent **MARÍA CRISTINA**, but was forced into exile with her in 1840. In 1843 his intrigues against **ESPARTERO**

were successful, and as Governor-General of Cuba he amassed a fortune. He returned to Spain in 1846, was made War Minister by Espartero in 1854, but in 1856 supplanted him as Prime Minister by a coup d'état. After only three months in office, he was succeeded by **NARVÁEZ**, but in 1858 returned to power. In 1859 he led a successful campaign against the Moors in Morocco and was made Duke of Tetuan. He was Prime Minister again in 1863 and 1865, but in 1866 his government was upset by Narváez.

### Odo of Bayeux (c.1036–1097)

Anglo-Norman prelate. He was Bishop of Bayeux. The half-brother of **WILLIAM I, THE CONQUEROR**, he fought at the Battle of **HASTINGS** (1066) and was created Earl of Kent. He played a conspicuous part under William in English history, and was regent during his absences in Normandy, but left England after rebelling against **WILLIAM II, RUFUS**. He rebuilt Bayeux Cathedral, and may have commissioned the Bayeux Tapestry.

### OECD (Organization for Economic Cooperation and Development)

An international organization set up in 1961 to assist member states to develop economic and social policies aimed at high and sustained economic growth with financial stability. As at 2004, its members included Australia, Austria, Belgium, Canada, the Czech Republic, Denmark, Finland, France, Germany, Greece, Hungary, Iceland, Republic of Ireland, Italy, Japan, Republic of Korea, Luxembourg, Mexico, the Netherlands, New Zealand, Norway, Poland, Portugal, Slovakia, Spain, Sweden, Switzerland, Turkey, the UK and the USA. Its headquarters are in Paris.

### Official Nationality (1833)

A crude analysis of the domestic policy of Tsar **NICHOLAS I** that gradually became his government's doctrine. It was originally propounded in 1833 by Count Sergei Uvarov, then Minister of Education, who held that the three fundamental elements were the following: Orthodoxy (the attitudes and practices of the **RUSSIAN ORTHODOX CHURCH**), Autocracy (maintaining the absolute authority of the Tsars) and Nationality (maintaining the singular loyalty of the Russian people to their Church, their Tsars and their heroic past). Nicholas was by nature dictatorial and fundamentally opposed to change. The new doctrine helped him to resist it until his death and therefore made his successor's task all the more difficult.

### Official Secrets Acts

British legislation intended to prevent disclosure of confidential government information to potential enemies. The original Act was passed in 1911, with sections 1 and 2 being rushed into force when war appeared imminent. The scope of Section 2 was long considered too broad, allowing governments to suppress disclosures even where these could cause no harm to the national interest, only official embarrassment, and the draconian nature of the Act made convictions difficult to secure. The Official Secrets Act 1989 abolished Section 2 of the 1911 Act. It narrows the range of people to whom the Section 2 provisions apply and specifies how different classes of information should be treated, clarifying the legal protection of official information. Successful prosecution hinges on whether a disclosure of information has damaged the national interest. Although less draconian, the 1989 Act is still very broad and convictions are still rare.

### Ogaden

The disputed region of south-eastern Ethiopia which became part of Abyssinia in 1890 and part of Italian East Africa from 1936 to 1941. It is largely inhabited by Somali-speaking nomads and was claimed by Somalia in the 1960s. The Somalis invaded in 1977, but were repulsed by Ethiopian forces. Fighting continued throughout the 1980s with Cuban and Soviet backing, and into the 1990s, when the number of refugees who fled the drought and war for Somalia exceeded one million. The problems of drought and resource allocation remain.

### Ogarkov, Nikolai Vasilievich (1917–94)

Soviet military adviser and politician. Son of a peasant, he joined the **RED ARMY** in 1938 and rose through wartime experience and subsequent commands to become First Deputy Chief of the General Staff in 1968 and a full member of the Communist Party Central Committee in 1971. From 1977 to 1984 he was Chief of Staff and Deputy Defence Minister. For over a decade he helped to strengthen and expand the Soviet forces. But his advocacy of further improving conventional forces met opposition even from Leonid **BREZHNEV** and certainly from Yuri **ANDROPOV**. His removal in 1984 got rid of an obstacle to East–West arms control talks.

### Ogedei (1186–1241)

Mongol ruler. Third son of the Mongol conqueror **GENGHIS KHAN**, he was elected by the Mongol nobility in 1229 to succeed his father. Ogedei continued with his father's expansionist policy, seizing north China in 1234 and initiating a western campaign that took the **MONGOLS** to the borders of Hungary and Poland. His construction of a new, permanent capital at Karakorum (Outer Mongolia) and his use of Chinese-educated advisers to establish a civilian administration signified a growing concern with settled government rather than periodic plunder.

### Oglethorpe, James Edward (1696–1785)

English general and colonial settler. Born in London, he served with Prince **EUGÈNE OF SAVOY**, and from 1722 to 1754 sat in parliament. He suggested a colony in America for debtors from English jails and persecuted Austrian Protestants. Parliament contributed £10,000, while **GEORGE II** gave a grant of land, called Georgia after him, and in 1732 Oglethorpe went out with 120 emigrants and founded Savannah. In 1735 he took out 300 more, including Charles and John **WESLEY**, and in 1738 he was back again with 600 men. After war with Spain was declared in 1739, Oglethorpe invaded Florida (1740), and in 1742 repulsed a Spanish invasion of Georgia. He left Georgia permanently in July 1743. Promoted major-general he was criticized for an insufficently vigorous pursuit of Prince Charles Edward **STUART**'s Jacobite army as it retreated from England in the winter of 1745–6. He was an MP until 1768.

### O'Higgins, Bernardo (1778–1842)

Chilean revolutionary. The son of Ambrosio O'Higgins, an Irish-born Governor of Chile and Viceroy of Peru, he was educated in Peru and England. He played the major role in the Chilean struggle for independence, having been influenced by others involved in the struggle for Latin American independence, especially Francisco **MIRANDA**. He became the first leader ('supreme director') of the new Chilean state in 1817. However, his reforms aroused antagonism, particularly in the Church and among the aristocracy and business community, and he was deposed in 1823, thereafter living in exile in Peru, where he died.

### Ohira Masayoshi (1910–80)

Japanese politician. A Finance Ministry bureaucrat, Ohira was first elected to the Diet in 1952 and later went on to serve as Foreign Minister and Finance Minister in **LIBERAL DEMOCRATIC PARTY** (LDP) cabinets of the 1970s. He became LDP President (and Prime Minister) in 1978 under new party election rules that aimed to give a greater role to the party rank and file in the constituencies. During his premiership, Ohira hosted the 1979 Tokyo economic summit of developed countries. Following a no-confidence vote against him in 1980, when rival LDP factions joined the opposition, Ohira dissolved the Diet. He died ten days before new elections, but the LDP won handsome majorities in both houses.

### Ojibwa

An Algonquian-speaking Native American tribe who originally inhabited the northern Great Lakes region around Lake Superior and Lake Huron. Traditionally hunters, they were skilled woodworkers, developed a form of picture-writing, and were successful in the **FUR TRADE**. Powerful warriors, they defeated the **IROQUOIS** and the Santee **SIOUX** in separate battles, and in the 17c expanded their territory and became one of North America's most populous indigenous peoples. Today many Ojibwa live on reservations across the upper Midwestern states from Montana to Michigan, and in Canada in the provinces of Ontario, Manitoba and Saskatchewan. The population of the tribe was c.190,000 in the early 21c. ► **NATIVE AMERICANS**

### Ojukwu, Chukwenmeka Odumegwu (1933– )

Nigerian soldier and politician. Educated in church schools in Lagos, Epsom College and Lincoln College, Oxford, he joined the Nigerian army in 1957. After attending military college in England, he served with the Nigerian force in the **UN** Congo operations and was named Military Governor of the mainly **IGBO**-speaking Eastern Region of Nigeria after the military coup of Jan 1966. He proclaimed the Eastern Region the independent Republic of Biafra in May 1967, thus precipitating the **BIAFRAN WAR**, and for three years acted as Head of Government and Supreme Commander. When his forces were finally defeated in 1970, he fled to Côte d'Ivoire. He returned to Nigeria in 1982 but an attempt to return to politics led to his imprisonment. He was released two years later but was banned from standing for President in the 1993 elections, and was an unsuccessful candidate in the 2003 presidential election.

### Okawa Shumei (1886–1957)

Japanese ultra-nationalist. He was involved in several right-wing plots against the civilian government. A fierce critic of Western colonialism in Asia, Okawa founded societies to protect the **KOKUTAI** ('national essence') and promote renovation of the state. Unlike **KITA IKKI**, Okawa was willing to work with military and bureaucratic élites, and lectured to the Army Academy on the need for Asian unity and struggle against the West. He was imprisoned in 1932 for his participation in an abortive military coup but was released in 1934. Okawa was indicted by allied authorities as a Class A war criminal in 1945 (the only person to be so indicted who was not a military or government figure). Judged to be insane, however, Okawa was never brought to trial.

### Okhranka (1881–1917)

The secret police in the last decades of Tsarist rule. With the assassination of **ALEXANDER II** in 1881, following the abolition of the Third Section, **ALEXANDER III** felt it essential to find an alternative. From a law on state protection, all sorts of far-reaching powers were conferred on government agents: to send people into exile without a trial, for example. In this way much opposition was controlled, but some went underground and became, like the **BOLSHEVIKS**, more dangerous. Eventually the Okhranka brought Tsarism into widespread disrepute.

### Okinawa

The largest and most populous of the Ryukyu Islands in the western Pacific Ocean. Regarded as a key US objective during **WORLD WAR II** because it commanded the approach to Japan, it was taken by the USA after a gruelling compaign with heavy casualties on both sides (Apr–Jun 1945). The USA returned the island to Japan in 1972 but kept some of its military bases there. In the 1990s there were calls to close the bases down, and in 2004 the two governments started to discuss redeploying some of the US forces.

### Okubo Toshimichi (1830–78)

Japanese **SAMURAI** official. He participated in the overthrow of the **TOKUGAWA SHOGUNATE** and became one of the most powerful members of the new Meiji government after 1868. His commitment to modernization was reinforced after his visit to the West with the **IWAKURA TOMOMI** mission (1871–3). As Head of the newly created Home Ministry, Okubo laid the foundations for a national police force. In 1877 he commanded the new imperial conscript army which defeated the samurai rebellion led by **SAIGO TAKAMORI**. Considered a traitor by many disgruntled samurai, he was assassinated in 1878.

### Okuma Shigenobu (1838–1922)

Japanese politician. He came from a **SAMURAI** family

in Saga domain, one of the four domains (along with **CHOSHU, SATSUMA** and Tosa) that took the lead in the overthrow of the **TOKUGAWA SHOGUNATE** (1868). He became a councillor in the new Meiji government and was a keen advocate of industrial development. He aroused the ire of his government colleagues in 1881 when he proposed the immediate establishment of constitutional government based on the British parliamentary system. He was purged from government and, in the following year, he created Japan's second political party, the *Rikken Kaishinto* (Constitutional Reform Party), which gained support amongst the urban educated and mercantile classes. In 1898 Okuma joined with **ITAGAKI TAISUKE**, leader of the *Jiyuto* (Liberal Party) to form Japan's first party cabinet, but it collapsed within four months due to internal rivalries. In 1914 Okuma was chosen by the **GENRO** to head a non-party cabinet but his aggressive attempt to enhance Japan's influence in China brought him into conflict with the more cautious *genro* and he was forced to resign.

**Olaf II**, also known as **St Olaf** (c.995–1030)
King of Norway (1015/30). He fought in England (1009–11), became a Christian, and completed the work of conversion begun by Olaf I Trygveson. His reforms provoked dissension, and he was killed by a rebel army at Stiklestad. He later became the patron saint of Norway.

**Olaf III, the Peaceful** (d.1093)
King of Norway (1067/93). He was at the Battle of Stamford Bridge in Yorkshire (1066) when his father, **HARALD HARDRADA**, was defeated and killed by King **HAROLD II** of England. He was, however, allowed to return to Norway with the survivors of the Norwegian invasion force, and assumed the throne of Norway the following year. His long reign was marked by unbroken peace and prosperity in Norway. He was succeeded by his illegitimate son, **MAGNUS III, BARELEGS**.

**Olav V** (1903–91)
King of Norway (1957/91). A keen sportsman and Olympic gold medallist, Crown Prince Olav escaped from Oslo with his father, King **HAAKON VII**, following the German invasion in Apr 1940, accompanying him into exile in Britain (June 1940). He participated actively in the war effort and from 1944 to 1945 served as chief of the Norwegian armed forces. He succeeded his father as King in 1957, but performed a mainly ceremonial role as monarch. ► **NORWAY, GERMAN INVASION OF**

**Old Believers** (1653)
Those who split from the **RUSSIAN ORTHODOX CHURCH** because of the reforms introduced by Patriarch **NIKON** in 1652. Among the first and most famous to protest was the Archpriest Avvakum, who in 1653 accused Nikon of heresy. However, when a series of Church councils supported Nikon it was Avvakum and his like who were persecuted as heretics. Avvakum was burned at the stake in 1682, but the Old Believers survived, generating many sects in the 18c and 19c, varying in their beliefs from being upholders of ancient Russian practices to being social and political rebels.

**Oldcastle, Sir John** (c.1378–1417)
English Lollard leader and knight. After serving in the Scottish and Welsh wars, and becoming an intimate of **HENRY V** when Prince of Wales, he was tried and convicted on charges of heresy in 1413. He escaped from the Tower, and conspired with other **LOLLARDS** to capture Henry V at Eltham Palace, Kent, and take control of London. The rising was abortive. Oldcastle remained free until caught near Welshpool in 1417, and was hanged and burnt. Shakespeare's character, Falstaff, is based partly on him.

**Old Catholic Church**
An independent religious denomination in the Netherlands (and parts of Germany and Switzerland), founded in 1723 as a result of a dispute with the Roman Catholic Church. The Old Catholics maintained that the **REFORMATION** and **EIGHTY YEARS' WAR** had not destroyed the Catholic Church in the Netherlands; the Jesuits denied this, and accused the Old Catholics of **JANSENISM**. In 1725 the Old Catholics founded their own seminary at Amersfoort. The Church still thrives in the Netherlands today in small numbers, rejecting many Roman Catholic dogmas such as the Immaculate Conception, papal infallibility, celibacy for priests and the use of Latin in church services.

**Oldenbarneveldt, Jan van** (1547–1619)
Dutch politician and lawyer. As adviser to Prince **MAURICE**, Stadholder of the United Provinces, he opposed his warlike schemes and in 1609 concluded a truce with Spain. This caused a political rift which eventually resulted in his being represented as a secret friend of Spain. He was illegally arrested, condemned as a traitor, and executed. Of his two sons, the elder escaped to Antwerp and the younger was executed.

**Oldenburg**
A city and duchy in north-western Germany, lying near the North Sea district of East Frisia (Ostfriesland). The city received its charter in 1345 and was the capital of the Duchy of Oldenburg. The Duchy was neutral in the **THIRTY YEARS' WAR**. In 1667 it passed to the Danish crown, thence to Emperor **PAUL I** of Russia in 1773. He ceded it to Frederick Augustus who also controlled the neighbouring bishopric of Lübeck. It became a grand duchy in the 19c.

**Old Pretender** ► **STUART, JAMES FRANCIS EDWARD**

**Olivares, Guzmán y Pimentel, Count-Duke of** (1587–1645)
Spanish statesman. The favourite and Chief Minister of **PHILIP IV** of Spain from 1623 to 1643, he cultivated the arts, and tried to modernize Spain's anachronistic administration and to build up military resources. However, his introduction of the **UNION OF ARMS** brought revolts in Portugal and Catalonia (1640–3). He took Spain into renewed conflict with the United Provinces, challenged France over the Mantuan succession (1628–31) and was **RICHELIEU**'s great opponent in the **THIRTY YEARS' WAR**. After the Spanish fleet was destroyed at the Battle of the Downs (1639) and Roussillon was overrun by the French, he was dismissed (1643), and died mad in exile at Toro. ► **HABSBURG DYNASTY**

**Ollivier, Émile** (1825–1913)
French politician. One of the five republican opposition deputies elected to parliament in 1857, from 1864 he came closer to the regime, as one of the members of the 'third party'. **NAPOLEON III** charged him to form a constitutional ministry (Jan 1870), but 'with a light heart' he rushed his country into war with Prussia. He was overthrown on 9 Aug 1871.

**Olmecs** ► PRE-COLUMBIAN CIVILIZATIONS

**Oltenia**
Part of western Wallachia, sometimes known as the County of Severin. It was subject to the Habsburg Emperor after the Treaty of **PASSAROWITZ** (1718) but was returned to Wallachia by the Peace of Belgrade (1739). Its chief town is Craiova. ► **MOLDAVIA AND WALLACHIA**; **ROMANIA**

**Olympic Games** ► *See panel*

**Olympio, Sylvanus** (1902–63)
Togolese politician. Educated at the London School of Economics, he returned to Africa as District Manager of the United Africa Company. He was President of the Togolese Assembly in 1946 and then led the country's government from 1958 to 1960 when, on independence, he became President. He was killed on 13 Jan 1963 in a military coup.

**OMAN** official name **Sultanate of Oman**, formerly **Muscat and Oman**

An independent state in the extreme south-eastern corner of the Arabian Peninsula. It is bounded to the north-east by the Gulf of Oman; to the east and south-east by the Arabian Sea; to the south-west by Yemen; to the west by Saudi Arabia; and to the north-west by the United Arab Emirates. Oman was a dominant maritime power of the western Indian Ocean in the 16c. It suffered internal dissension in 1913–20 between supporters of the Sultanate and members of the Ibadhi sect who wanted to be ruled exclusively by their religious leader. A separatist tribal revolt in 1964 led to a police coup that in 1970 installed a new sultan from the ruling family, **QABOOS BIN SAID**, who became both head of state and premier. The state is a hereditary absolute monarchy. Moves were made in the 1990s towards the establishment of constitutional principles and political and legal systems.

**Omar Pasha**, properly **Michael Latas** (1806–71)
Croatian-born Ottoman general. He served in the Austrian army but in 1828 he deserted, fled to Bosnia, and became a Muslim. He was appointed writing-master to **ABD UL-MAJID I**, on whose accession to the Ottoman throne (1839) Omar Pasha was made colonel, and, in 1842, Governor of Lebanon. From 1843 to 1847 he suppressed insurrections in Albania, Bosnia and Kurdistan. On the invasion of the Danubian Principalities by the Russians in 1853, he defeated the Russians in two battles. In the **CRIMEAN WAR** he repulsed the Russians at Eupatoria (Feb 1855) but was sent too late to relieve Kars. He was Governor of Baghdad (1857–9); in 1861 he again pacified Bosnia and Herzegovina, and overran Montenegro in 1862.

**Omdurman, Battle of** (1898)
An engagement outside Khartoum, across the Nile, which confirmed the British reconquest of the Sudan. The British campaign under **KITCHENER** had been authorized in 1895, and instituted with powerful Anglo-Egyptian forces in 1896. The overwhelming defeat of the massed forces of the Khalifa (the successor of the **MAHDI**), with many casualties, illustrated the power of modern weapons. ► **FASHODA INCIDENT**; **MOHAMMED AHMED**

**O'Neill, Hugh, 2nd Earl of Tyrone** (c.1540–1616)
Irish rebel. Born in Dungannon, the son of an illegitimate son of Conn O'Neill (c.1484–c.1559), a warlike Irish chieftain who was made Earl of Tyrone on his submission to **HENRY VIII** in 1542, he was invested with the title and estates c.1597, but soon plunged into intrigues with the Irish rebels and the Spaniards against **ELIZABETH I**. As 'the O'Neill', he spread insurrection all over Ulster, Connaught and Leinster. Despite Spanish support he was defeated in 1601–2 by Charles Blount, 8th Lord Mountjoy, at Kinsale, and badly wounded. He intrigued with Spain against **JAMES VI AND I**, and in 1607 fled to the Spanish Netherlands. He died in Rome.

**O'Neill, Terence Marne, Baron O'Neill of the Maine** (1914–90)
Ulster politician. He served in the Irish Guards during **WORLD WAR II**. A member of the Northern Ireland parliament (1946–70), he held junior posts before becoming Minister for Home Affairs (1956), Finance (1956–63), and then Prime Minister (1963–9). A supporter of closer cross-border links with the Irish Republic, he angered many Unionists. Following a general election in 1969, dissension in the Unionist Party increased, and he resigned the premiership soon after. Made a life peer in 1970, he continued to speak out on Northern Ireland issues. ► **DEMOCRATIC UNIONIST PARTY**

**Onin War** (1467–77)
The long drawn-out struggle in Japan between rival **DAIMYO** (feudal lords), named after the Onin Era (1467–9) in which it began. The *daimyo* had been granted territorial powers by the **ASHIKAGA SHOGUNATE** and by the end of the 14c had considerable autonomy. The political situation became increasingly unstable from the mid-1460s when rival *daimyo* took sides in a shogunal succession dispute. Full-scale war broke out in the Kyoto region, lasting for ten years. The Ashikaga Shogunate was permanently weakened, continuing in name only to 1573, and there ensued a period of disunity and periodic warfare that was essentially to last until the end of

# Olympic Games

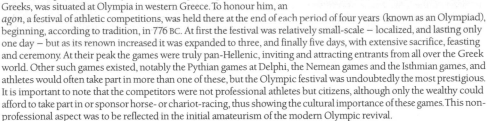

## Classical games

The most important sanctuary of Zeus, the supreme god of the ancient Greeks, was situated at Olympia in western Greece. To honour him, an *agon*, a festival of athletic competitions, was held there at the end of each period of four years (known as an Olympiad), beginning, according to tradition, in 776 BC. At first the festival was relatively small-scale – localized, and lasting only one day – but as its renown increased it was expanded to three, and finally five days, with extensive sacrifice, feasting and ceremony. At their peak the games were truly pan-Hellenic, inviting and attracting entrants from all over the Greek world. Other such games existed, notably the Pythian games at Delphi, the Nemean games and the Isthmian games, and athletes would often take part in more than one of these, but the Olympic festival was undoubtedly the most prestigious. It is important to note that the competitors were not professional athletes but citizens, although only the wealthy could afford to take part in or sponsor horse- or chariot-racing, thus showing the cultural importance of these games. This non-professional aspect was to be reflected in the initial amateurism of the modern Olympic revival.

Among the range of competitions, which included athletics, boxing and wrestling, the premier event was the *stadion*, a foot race along one length of the stadium at Olympia, approximately 656ft/200m. This was a component of the pentathlon, which also included the long jump, the discus, the javelin and wrestling. Some events were significantly more demanding than others, notably a foot race run in full hoplite armour, reflecting the military training that citizens were often obliged to undergo, and the fiercely competitive chariot race of around 8.7mi/14km, in which many entrants failed to complete the course through injury or damage to their vehicles. There were separate events for boys and men – who competed naked – and women took part in one competition only, a shortened version of the *stadion*.

Competitors did not contend for rich prizes. The sole reward for the victors was to be crowned with a simple olive wreath, but the status they gained among their fellow citizens was enormous. Invariably, they would be further rewarded by their home city with privileges, free food and drink for life, and, sometimes, gifts of money. Their feats might also be celebrated in poetry specially commissioned by a wealthy aristocratic patron. The victory odes composed by Pindar (c.518–c.438 BC), detailing the subject's prowess and linking this to appropriate elements of the city's mythology, are a prime example of this genre. While winning was considered to bring great honour to both the competitor and his city, it seems to have been considered shameful to take part and be defeated.

The Olympic games continued during the Hellenistic Age (323–30 BC) that followed the rule of Alexander III, the Great (356–323 BC), and survived into the period of Roman domination of Greece. However, as the Christianization of the Roman emperors drove them to eradicate the pagan elements in their dominions, the association of the festival with the worship of Zeus became increasingly unacceptable and the games were ended by order of Emperor Theodosius I, the Great in AD 393.

## The modern games

The modern revival of the Olympic Games came about largely at the instigation of the French educationist Baron Pierre de Coubertin (1863–1937). He believed that physical education and participation in sport were vital to the formation of individual character, and that friendly competition between countries would help promote the cause of international peace. In 1894 he helped set up the International Olympic Committee (IOC), which still formulates policy and decides on venues, with its headquarters in Lausanne, Switzerland.

Like the ancient games, the modern festival was to take place every four years, with events open to all amateurs. Athens was chosen as the first venue in 1896, symbolizing the link with the ancient Greek ideal. Thereafter, a different nation has staged each subsequent festival, although some cities have played host more than once, such as Paris (1900 and 1924), London (1908 and 1948) and Athens (1896 and 2004). Competition to host the Olympics is intense and led to corruption scandals in the 1990s over gifts and hospitality lavished on IOC delegates by potential host cities. The opening

the 16c, when a new military hegemony under the **TOKUGAWA SHOGUNATE** began to take shape.

## OPEC (Organization of Petroleum Exporting Countries)

An international economic organization set up in 1960 with its headquarters in Vienna; the longest-surviving major cartel. It consists of 11 oil-producing countries: the founder-members were Iran, Iraq, Kuwait, Saudi Arabia and Venezuela; they have since been joined by Algeria, Indonesia, Libya, Nigeria, Qatar and the United Arab Emirates (formerly Abu Dhabi). Ecuador joined in 1973 but left in 1992, and Gabon joined in 1975 but left in 1994. OPEC's purpose is to coordinate the petroleum policy of members to protect their interests, especially in relation to the fixing of prices for crude oil and the quantities to be produced. It rose to prominence in 1973 when it raised oil prices by 70 per cent and refused to supply some of the Western nations who had backed Israel in the **YOM KIPPUR WAR**. OPEC's importance declined

slightly during the 1980s as consumer countries began to exploit their own oil reserves and other means of energy production.

## Open Door Policy

US foreign policy towards China, formulated in response to the weakness of the later **QING DYNASTY**. Announced in Mar 1900 by Secretary of State John **HAY**, the Open Door policy sought to preserve Chinese integrity and US trade rights by opposing the development of spheres of influence dominated by Britain, Germany, Russia, France, Italy and Japan.

## Opium Wars

Two wars (1839–42 and 1856–60) between Britain and China, fought over the question of commercial rights in China, specifically relating to the opium trade. The British were victorious on each occasion, and gained increased access to China through the Treaties of **NANJING** (Nanking) (1842) and **TIANJIN** (Tientsin) (1858). ► **ARROW WAR; TREATY PORTS**

ceremony traditionally includes the lighting of an Olympic flame by a torch carried by relays of runners from Olympia.

The range of events chosen for the modern festival echoed the ancient games in including athletics, wrestling and gymnastic competitions, but added such modern disciplines as cycling, fencing, shooting and lawn tennis. The ancient pentathlon was given a modern equivalent, this time consisting of cross-country running, swimming, shooting, fencing and equestrianism. Ancient disciplines such as the discus and the javelin were also to be found.

Women first took part, in athletics, in the 1928 games. A separate Winter Olympics was set up in 1924 to be held every four years, at first in the same year as the summer festival but the IOC changed the schedule in 1986 so that since 1994 the Winter Olympics has been held two years after each summer games. Another offshoot has been the Special Olympics, intended for competitors who have physical or mental disabilities.

With every successive Olympiad the number of events has increased, with practically every recognized sport, from soccer to judo to synchronized swimming, being represented. Increasing professionalism amongst the competitors, though improving record performances, has greatly eroded the original amateur ideal. In the era of the **Cold War**, between 1948 and 1990 in particular, the Communist regimes fielded teams of 'amateurs' paid to be full-time competitors by holding nominal positions in such bodies as national armed forces, while US competitors were often the product of heavily endowed college scholarship programmes for athletes. The IOC recognized that the rules requiring amateur status discriminated against athletes without sponsorship or other forms of funding and the amateur status rules have been gradually relaxed since the 1970s and 1980s, although no money may to be received during the games. This is contrary to the aims of the founders, as is the highly influential part often played by politics. For example, the Nazis planned to use the 1936 Berlin Olympics as a stage for a demonstration to the world of German (and Aryan) superiority. In fact they were often discomfited by the results on the field, not least the four gold medals won by the black US runner Jesse Owens.

World wars in the 20c led to the cancellation of three Olympiads (in 1916, 1940 and 1944) and meetings have been marred by mass boycotts staged by one international bloc or another in order to make a political point. Other political manifestations have included the **Black Power** salutes given by black US medallists in Mexico (1968) and the terrorist massacre of hostages, including Israeli athletes, at the Munich games in 1972.

A growing problem in recent years has been the use of performance-enhancing drugs by athletes. The IOC banned the use of such drugs in 1968, and sanctions against their use include suspending athletes from competition, sometimes for life, and stripping them of any medals they have won. Despite this, there has been widespread flouting of the ban and of the international drugs testing regime, leading the IOC to set up the World Anti-Doping Agency in 1999 to coordinate drug testing.

**Oppenheimer, Sir Ernest** (1880–1957)
South African mining magnate, politician and philanthropist. Born in Friedberg, Germany, he was the son of a Jewish cigar merchant. At the age of 16 he worked for a London firm of diamond merchants and, sent out to Kimberley as their representative in 1902, soon became one of the leaders of the diamond industry. In 1917, with J P Morgan, he formed the Anglo-American Corporation of South Africa, and at the time of his death his interests covered 95 per cent of the world's supply of diamonds. He was Mayor of Kimberley (1912–15), raised the Kimberley Regiment and was MP for Kimberley (1924–38).

**Oppenheimer, John Süss** (1698/99–1738)
A prominent financier in the Palatinate and Hesse. He was also Chief Minister under Charles Alexander (Duke, 1733–7). He established various monopolies and was involved in the programme of the Duke, a Catholic, to break his subjects' Lutheranism by a system of harsh taxation. He was so disliked that he was executed soon after the Duke's death.

**Oppenheimer, (Julius) Robert** (1904–67)
US nuclear physicist. Born in New York City, he studied at Harvard, Cambridge and under Max Born at Göttingen University, Germany, where he received his doctorate in 1927. He returned to the USA and established schools of theoretical physics at Berkeley and the California Institute of Technology (Caltech). During **WORLD WAR II** he was selected as leader of the atomic bomb project, set up the Los Alamos laboratory and brought together a formidable group of scientists. After the war he became director of the Institute for Advanced Studies at Princeton University and continued to play an important role in US atomic energy policy from 1947, promoting peaceful uses of atomic energy and bitterly opposing development of the hydrogen bomb. In 1953 he was declared a security risk and was forced to retire from political activities.

**Opportunists**
French political tendency. The more conservative

tendency among the republicans, the name was coined in 1874, and was applied to the supporters of **GAMBETTA**, and **FERRY**, who ruled for most of the period 1880–5; after that time the term went out of use, being replaced first by Progressists, and then by **MODERATES**.

## Opus Dei

Established in Spain in 1928 by an Aragonese priest, José María Escrivá, Opus Dei (literally, 'the Work of God') is a lay order within the Catholic Church which has sought secular power through the recruitment of leading professionals. With its ultra-conservative theology and its severely traditional view of women, the sodality has moved in the opposite direction to most other orders within the Church. Under the **FRANCO** regime Opus Dei, dubbed 'the Holy Mafia', rose rapidly to a position of considerable power. It orchestrated Spain's economic modernization from the late 1950s and remained the major force within the government until 1973. The three ministers involved in the most notorious scandal of the Franco regime, the Matesa affair of 1969, were all Opus Dei members. Elsewhere, Opus has been linked to numerous dictatorial regimes in Latin America, often in collaboration with the **CIA**. Under Pope **JOHN PAUL II**, Opus Dei became the most powerful order in the Roman Catholic Church. Its operational secretiveness, its unique semi-autonomous status, and its wealth have combined to produce what is, in effect, a powerful conservative pressure group within the Church.

## Orán, Conquest of (1509)

The most spectacular of the several conquests by Christians of Muslim forts on the North African coast. After the easy capture in 1508 of the fort of Peñon de Vélez de Gomera, attempts were made to seize other forts. In May 1509 Cardinal Cisneros personally financed and led an expedition which sailed from Cartagena with 90 ships, and captured Orán on 18 May. The fort was unsuccessfully besieged several times in later years by Muslim forces.

## Orange Order

An association that developed from the Orange Society, which had been formed in 1795 to counteract growing Catholic influence in Ireland and 'to maintain the laws and peace of the country and the Protestant constitution'. The name was taken from the Protestant Dutch dynasty represented by **WILLIAM III, OF ORANGE**. Organized in 'lodges', it was bitterly criticized by a parliamentary enquiry of 1835 and went into voluntary dissolution. It experienced popular revival in late-19c Ulster and provided the backbone of resistance to **HOME RULE** proposals from the mid-1880s, and has been central to organized Protestantism in Northern Ireland since partition.

## Orange Order (Canada)

The First Grand Lodge was established in Canada in 1830, and the order had grown to 2,000 lodges with 100,000 members by the 1980s. Its growth and activities have made it one of the most powerful pressure groups in Canadian politics. Not only did Orangemen reinforce the pro-British and Tory sentiments of the loyalists, they introduced the rigid hostilities nurtured in the old country, transferring their antagon-

ism from Irish Catholics to the French-Canadian 'Papists'. In 1848 **LAFONTAINE** introduced a Secret Societies Bill to counteract their activities, but this only incited the Orangemen of Upper **CANADA** to further demonstrations. During a visit by the Prince of Wales in 1860 they attempted, by various ruses, to force him to acknowledge a relationship between the order and the monarchy. This he managed to refuse, but John A **MACDONALD** apologized to the order for him. The murder of the Orangeman Thomas **SCOTT** during the **RED RIVER REBELLION** led indirectly to the campaign of D'Alton **MCCARTHY** and the **MANITOBA SCHOOLS ACT**. The murder of another Orangeman, which occurred in Montreal during a provocative 12 July parade in 1877, also incensed the order, and Macdonald was able to use this anger to swing it behind the Conservatives to win the next election. In 1878 he included the Grand Master, Mackenzie **BOWELL** in his cabinet.

## Ordinance of 1787 ► NORTHWEST ORDINANCE OF 1787

## Ordzhonikidze, Gregori Konstantinovich (1886–1937)

Georgian politician. The son of a small landowner, he had already joined the **BOLSHEVIKS** before graduating as a director at Tiflis in 1905. Between then and 1917 he was in and out of prison and in and out of Russia for his revolutionary activities. In 1920–1 he helped establish Soviet rule in Georgia and Armenia, and by 1930 he was a **POLITBURO** member and Chairman of the Council for Soviet Economy. However, as friends and relatives were shot in **STALIN**'s purges, he lost heart and took his own life.

## Oregon Boundary Dispute

A disagreement between the British and US governments over the frontier between respective possessions on the west coast of North America. Britain claimed the north-west basin of the Columbia River to its mouth at Fort Vancouver, while the USA sought a boundary farther north. The Oregon Treaty (1846) settled the US–Canadian boundary on the 49th parallel, dipping south at Juan de Fuca Strait to maintain British claims to Vancouver Island. Residual disputes over the disposition of the Gulf/San Juan Islands in the strait were settled by arbitration in 1872.

## Oregon Trail

The main route for emigration to the far west of the USA during the 1840s. The trail began at Independence, Missouri, crossed the Rockies at South Pass in Wyoming, and terminated at the mouth of the Columbia River. Extending some 2,000 mi/3,200 km in length, it took approximately six months to travel it by wagon train.

## Organic Acts

Statutes of the US **CONGRESS** which laid down the relationship of Puerto Rico to the USA between 1900 and 1950. The First Organic Act of 1900 (the Foraker Act) effectively made Puerto Rico a US dependency in that supreme power was vested in the US governor and a nominated executive council. The Second Organic Act of 1916 (the Jones Act) conferred universal male suffrage and made Puerto Ricans citizens of the USA. The Public Law Act of 1950 allowed the new Commonwealth (a status devised by **MUÑOZ**

MARÍN) to draft its own constitution.

## Organic Statutes (1831–2)
These statutes regulated the government in the Danubian Principalities, introducing similar highly centralized administrations into **MOLDAVIA AND WALLACHIA**. Political power rested in the hands of the high boyars who sat in the legislative assembly and from whose ranks the hospodars were to be elected for life. The statutes acknowledged the boyars as the owners of their land, strengthened their hold over the peasantry and confirmed their exemption from taxation. Drawn up under Russian supervision, the Organic Statutes gave Russia a large measure of influence over internal affairs in the Principalities. ➤ **AKKERMAN, CONVENTION OF; STURDZA, MIHAIL**

## Organization for Security and Cooperation in Europe ➤ CSCE

## Organization of African Unity (OAU)
An organization founded in 1963 by representatives of 32 African governments, which reflected the views of the moderate leaders, such as **NYERERE**, rather than radicals such as **NKRUMAH**. By protecting territorial integrity, the organization accepted the artificial boundaries bequeathed by the colonial powers and preserved individual self-interest over continental political and economic unity. It remained, however, the main forum for the African continent to express its political views and, through its Liberation Committee, assisted the decolonization of southern Africa. It supported sanctions to effect the end of **APARTHEID** in South Africa and admitted that nation as its 53rd member in 1994. It had some success at mediation, but its lack of sanctions resulted in its inability to solve problems where major African powers disagreed. In 2002 it was replaced by the **AFRICAN UNION**.

## Organization of American States (OAS)
A regional agency established in 1948 to coordinate the work of a variety of inter-American departments recognized within the terms of the UN Charter. The organization was formed to promote peace, economic cooperation, and social advancement in the Western hemisphere. Traditionally anti-communist, it suspended Cuba's membership in 1962. Its central organ, the General Secretariat, is housed in Washington, DC, and consists of one representative from each member country. Thirty-five countries within the Americas are members. Its most recent members include Canada (1990), Belize (1991) and Guyana (1991). ➤ **PAN-AMERICAN UNION**

## Organization of Central American States
An agency established in 1951 by Costa Rica, El Salvador, Guatemala, Honduras and Nicaragua (Panama refused to join) to promote economic, social and cultural cooperation. In 1965 this was extended to include political and educational cooperation. The Organization has also been involved in legal reform.

## Organization of the Islamic Conference (OIC)
An organization whose 57 members are Islamic nations in the Middle East, north and west Africa, central Asia and the Indian subcontinent. It has permanent delegation status with the UN. Its aims are to safeguard the interests of Muslims worldwide, to protect the Muslim holy places and to fight discrimination against Muslims. The OIC was established in 1969 in response to an arson attack earlier that year on the al-Aqsa mosque in Jerusalem, Islam's third most holy site. Its headquarters are in Jeddah, Saudi Arabia.

## Orhan (1288–1360)
Ottoman Sultan (1324/60). The son of **OSMAN I**, he took Bursa in his father's time, and afterwards reduced Nicaea and Mysia. He organized the state and established the Ottoman bridgehead in Europe. ➤ **OTTOMAN EMPIRE**

## Orlando, Vittorio Emanuele (1860–1952)
Italian politician. Professor of Law at Palermo University, he was elected to parliament in 1897. He served as Minister of Education, before becoming Minister of Justice in 1916. At the height of the **CAPORETTO** crisis he became Prime Minister, remaining in office until June 1919. His inability to force Woodrow **WILSON** and **CLEMENCEAU** to honour the terms of the Treaty of **LONDON** (1915) at the **PARIS PEACE CONFERENCE**, coupled with post-war economic dislocation and growing political violence, brought about his downfall. He made little attempt to resist **MUSSOLINI** and appeared on the fascist **LISTONE** in the Apr 1924 election. He belatedly adopted a more openly anti-fascist stance in 1925. After **WORLD WAR II** he became a Senator.

## Orléanists
Supporters of the Orléans branch of the French royal house, which reigned in the person of **LOUIS-PHILIPPE** (1830–48). Rivalry between them and the **LEGITIMISTS**, supporters of **CHARLES X** and of his heir, the Count of **CHAMBORD**, was an important factor in the eclipse of the royalist cause, especially in the National Assembly (1871–5), in which the two royalist factions together had a majority, but which nevertheless established the Third Republic. The death of the legitimist claimant in 1883 reunited the monarchists. ➤ **ORLÉANS, HOUSE OF; REPUBLIC, THIRD** (France)

## Orléans, House of
The junior branch of the **VALOIS** and Bourbon dynasties in France, the title of which fell to four individual lines: Philippe de Valois, created Duke in 1344 but died without issue; Louis I de Valois (1372–1407), whose descendants held the title until 1544; Gaston (1608–60), the Bourbon third son of **HENRY IV**, made Duke in 1626; and **LOUIS XIV**'s younger brother Philippe (1640–1701), from whom descended the Regent Orléans (1674–1723), Louis Philippe Joseph, Duke of **ORLÉANS**, 'Philippe Égalité' (1747–93), who died in the **FRENCH REVOLUTION**, and **LOUIS-PHILIPPE** (1773–1850), 'King of the French'. The latter's son was the last to hold the ducal title. ➤ **BOURBON, HOUSE OF**

## Orléans, Louis Philippe Joseph, Duke of, also called Philippe Égalité (1747–93)
French Bourbon prince. The cousin of King **LOUIS XVI** and father of **LOUIS-PHILIPPE**, he inherited his father's title in 1785. At the **FRENCH REVOLUTION** he proved a strong supporter of the Third Estate against the privileged orders, and in 1792 renounced his title of nobility for his popular name. At the National **CONVENTION** he voted for the King's death but was

himself arrested after the defection of his eldest son to the Austrians (1793), and guillotined. ► ESTATES GENERAL; MARIE ANTOINETTE

## Orléans, Philippe, Duke of (1674–1723)
Regent of France during the minority of LOUIS XV, son of the first duke Philippe, and grandson of LOUIS XIII. He had been appointed Regent by LOUIS XIV's will, but with limited powers as President of a REGENCY Council. He persuaded the PARLEMENT to override the will, thus acquiring full powers, but at the expense of restoring the authority of the *Parlement*, which he later tried to restrict. He entrusted the conduct of foreign affairs to the Abbé DUBOIS, who formed the Quadruple Alliance with the Netherlands, Britain and Austria (1718), defeating Spain and producing the fall of ALBERONI (1719). His adoption of John Law's scheme led to financial disaster. In 1720 he accepted the Papal Bull *Unigenitus*, condemning JANSENISM. His power ended when Louis XV came of age in 1723.

## Orléans, Siege of (Oct 1428–May 1429)
The English blockade of the main stronghold still loyal to CHARLES VII of France, during the HUNDRED YEARS' WAR. Orléans was relieved by troops inspired by JOAN OF ARC. Anglo-Burgundian forces, who already controlled most of northern France, were prevented from pressing south, but the event was less of a turning point in the war than the Franco-Burgundian rapprochement of 1435. ► PHILIP THE GOOD

## Orlov
A Russian family that rose to eminence when one of its members, Gregory (1734–1783), an officer in the Imperial Guards, succeeded King STANISŁAW II AUGUST PONIATOWSKI of Poland as the favourite of CATHERINE II, THE GREAT. It was he who planned the murder of PETER III, and his brother Alexis (1737–1808) who committed the deed (1762). The legitimate line of Orlov became extinct, but Feodor, a brother of Gregory and Alexis, left four illegitimate sons, one of whom, Alexis (1787–1862), distinguished himself in the French and Turkish wars. He negotiated the Treaty of Unkiar-Skelessi with the OTTOMAN EMPIRE in 1833, in 1844 became head of NICHOLAS I's secret police, the Third Department, and frequently acted in the role of senior diplomat as, for example, at the Congress of PARIS in 1856. His last appointment was under ALEXANDER II as chairman of a committee to consider the abolition of serfdom.

## Ormonde, James Butler, 12th Earl and 1st Duke of (1610–88)
Anglo-Irish general. In the ENGLISH CIVIL WARS he commanded the royalist army in Ireland (1641–50), and was compelled to retire to France. At the RESTORATION he was rewarded by the ducal title of Ormonde, and twice became Lord-Lieutenant of Ireland.

## Orsini
A powerful Roman noble family which periodically dominated papal politics and appointments (including the election of family members to the papacy itself) from the 11c. In the 1400s, 'by custom', one Orsini, along with a French and a Venetian cardinal, was entitled to sit in the College of Cardinals. The family intermarried with the MEDICI of Florence in the same period. ► POPE

## Orsini, Felice (1819–58)
Italian patriot, revolutionary and follower of MAZZINI. Elected to the Roman Constituent Assembly in 1848, he took part in the defence of the city under the command of GARIBALDI. In Jan 1858, after a decade of agitation and exile, he went to Paris to try to assassinate NAPOLEON III whom he considered to have betrayed the Italian cause. In the attempt, ten people were killed but the Emperor survived unharmed. Orsini was sentenced to death, but before his execution he wrote a personal appeal to Napoleon begging him to assist the Italian struggle. It is possible that fear of further attempts on his life or the passion of Orsini's plea contributed to Napoleon's readiness to meet with CAVOUR at PLOMBIÈRES and to declare war on Austria in 1859.

## Ortega (Saavedra), Daniel (1945–)
Nicaraguan military leader. Educated in Managua, he became active in his teens in the resistance movement against the Somoza regime, and in 1963 joined the SANDINISTA NATIONAL LIBERATION FRONT (FSLN). He became National Director of the FSLN in 1966, was imprisoned for seven years for urban guerrilla bank raids, and then, in 1979, played a major part in the overthrow of Anastasio Somoza Debayle. A junta led by Ortega established a provisional government, and in 1985 he became President, but US-backed counter-revolutionary forces, the 'CONTRAS', threatened his government's stability. By 1989, however, there were encouraging signs of peace being achieved. He surprisingly lost the 1990 general election to Violeta Chamorro, and supervised the peaceful handover of power.

## Ortega y Gasset, José (1883–1956)
Spanish politician, philosopher and journalist. From a well-to-do family of newspaper proprietors, he studied philosophy in Germany before becoming a professor at the Central University of Madrid. He promoted the cultural regeneration of Spain through his voluminous journalistic and other writings, his extensive speech-making, and the foundation of cultural institutions and numerous publications, such as the League of Political Education of Spain (1914), the leading liberal newspaper *El Sol* (1917), and the cultural journal *Revista de Occidente* (1923). In the process, he became one of the most influential makers of public opinion. With the advent of the Second Republic in 1931, he founded the Group at the Service of the Republic, was elected as one of its deputies, but soon became disillusioned, dissolving the group in 1932 and abandoning politics altogether in 1933. He spent the SPANISH CIVIL WAR in France, estranged from either side. After the war, he continued to publish a great deal and lectured widely, both in Europe (including Spain) and America. He returned to Spain in 1955 to die. ► REPUBLIC, SECOND (Spain)

## Oscar I (1799–1859)
King of Norway and Sweden (1844/59). He was the only son and successor of CHARLES XIV JOHN. Born in Paris, he accompanied his father to Sweden when the latter was elected heir to the Swedish throne in

1810. A liberal by temperament, he sought to conciliate nationalist feelings in Norway, encouraged social and economic development but opposed any attempts to limit his political power. He took a particular interest in foreign policy. He favoured the political union of the Scandinavian monarchies and nearly involved Sweden in the **CRIMEAN WAR** in the hope of regaining Finland. He married Josephine of Leuchtenberg, the daughter of Empress **JOSEPHINE**'s son, Eugène de Beauharnais. Oscar suffered from a brain tumour during the last two years of his reign, during which his eldest son acted as regent, succeeding him as **CHARLES XV**.

### Oscar II (1829–1907)
King of Sweden (1872/1907) and of Norway (1872/1905). He was the younger son of **OSCAR I** and brother of **CHARLES XV**, whom he succeeded. A vigorous, intelligent and highly cultured man, his foreign policy was marked by admiration of the new German Empire of Otto von **BISMARCK**. His reign saw growing tension between his Norwegian and Swedish subjects until in 1905 he was compelled to surrender the crown of Norway to Prince Carl of Denmark, elected King of Norway as **HAAKON VII**. The sacrifice saddened the last years of Oscar's life. He was married to Sofia of Nassau, by whom he had four sons, of whom **GUSTAV V** succeeded him as King.

### OSCE ► CSCE

### Osceola (c.1804–1838)
American **SEMINOLE** Native American leader. He refused to accede to US government demands in 1835 that the Seminoles give up their lands in the Florida Everglades and move to the West. He fought for many months in the Everglades, but in 1837 he was tricked by a false peace overture to come out and have talks with General Thomas S Jesup. He was captured and died in prison in South Carolina.

### Oslo Accords
A series of agreements in the Middle East peace process. The first agreement, the Declaration of Principles on Interim Self-Government Arrangements, was initialled in Oslo on 20 Aug 1993 by representatives of **ISRAEL** and the **PLO** and signed at the White House on 13 Sep in a ceremony attended by President **CLINTON**, Yitzhak **RABIN** and Yasser **ARAFAT**. Subsequent agreements included the Cairo Agreement on the Gaza Strip and the Jericho Area (1994), the Washington Declaration, the Agreement on Preparatory Transfer of Powers and Responsibilities between Israel and the PLO (1994), the Interim Agreement on the West Bank and the Gaza Strip ('Oslo 2') signed in 1995, the Protocol on Redeployment in Hebron (1997) and the Wye River Memorandum (1998). The initial agreement granted self-government to the Palestinians of the **GAZA STRIP** and the **WEST BANK** town of Jericho from 1994, extended to a further seven towns and 450 villages by 'Oslo 2', and stipulated a phased withdrawal of Israeli forces. These agreements were for an interim period of five years, during which time the permanent status of the area was to be resolved. Other contentious issues, such as Jewish settlements on the West Bank, the future of Jerusalem and Palestinian refugees, security and borders, were not part of the initial agreements.

Following the 1996 Israeli general election, implementation of the agreements slowed as Binyamin **NETANYAHU**'s government took a more cautious approach and with the election of Ehud Barak's government in 1999 talks with the Palestinians broke down completely, undermined principally by the lack of a timetable for the withdrawal of Israeli forces and Israel's reluctance to ban Jewish West Bank settlement. Implementation of the Oslo Accords effectively ended in autumn 2000 when the second **INTIFADA** started.

### Osman I (1259–1326)
Founder of the **OTTOMAN EMPIRE**. Born in Bithynia, the son of a border chief, he founded a small Turkish state in Asia Minor called Osmanli (or Ottoman). On the overthrow of the Seljuk sultanate of Iconium in 1299 by the **MONGOLS**, he gradually subdued a great part of Asia Minor.

### Osman Nuri Pasha (1832–1900)
Turkish general. He fought in the **CRIMEAN WAR** (1853–56) and numerous other campaigns, and became a national hero for his defence of Plevna against the Russians, in 1877.

### Ossory
An ancient Irish kingdom, co-extensive with the diocese of Ossory (seat, Kilkenny), conquered by Anglo-Norman invaders in the late 12c. The most powerful families in the area were the Marshals, Earls of Pembroke, Wales, and Lords of Leinster (1199–1245), and the Butlers, created Earls of Ormonde (1328) and Ossory (1528).

### Ostend Manifesto (1854)
A statement presented by the US ministers to Great Britain, France and Spain, effectively asserting US claims over the then Spanish colony of Cuba. It stated that if Spain refused to sell Cuba, then the USA was justified in taking it by force. Although repudiated by the US government, the manifesto gave notice of future US interest in Cuba and in the Caribbean.

### Ostpolitik
The policy initiated in West Germany in the 1960s as part of the process of détente to normalize relations with communist countries that recognized the German Democratic Republic (GDR) and with the GDR itself. It led to treaties with Poland and the USSR, the recognition of the Polish border (the **ODER–NEISSE LINE**) and, most significantly, the recognition of the GDR. Largely masterminded by Willy **BRANDT**, the policy sought to prevent, and even reverse, the deepening schism between the Federal Republic and GDR and had the broader aim of generally improving relations between West and East. It culminated in German reunification in 1990.

### Oswald, Lee Harvey (1939–63)
US alleged assassin of President John F **KENNEDY**. Born in New Orleans, he was a Marxist and former US marine who had lived for some time in the USSR (1959–62). On 23 Nov 1963 he was charged with the murder of President Kennedy, whom he was alleged to have shot from the sixth floor of the Texas School Book Depository, as the President passed by in a motor cavalcade. Two days later, Oswald was shot dead by Jack Ruby, who claimed to be avenging

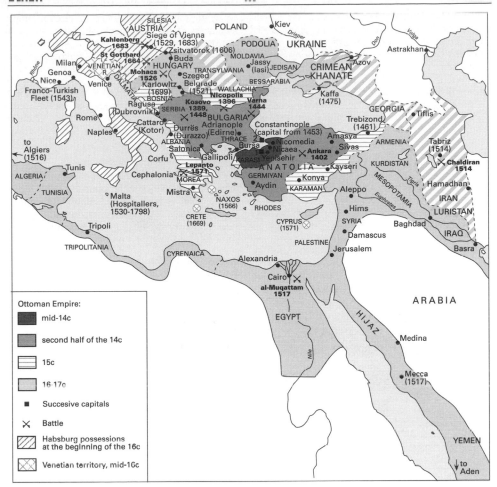

**Formation of the Ottoman Empire**

Ottoman Empire:
- mid-14c
- second half of the 14c
- 15c
- 16-17c
- ■ Successive capitals
- ✕ Battle
- Habsburg possessions at the beginning of the 16c
- Venetian territory, mid-16c

Jacqueline Kennedy. Claims were made that Oswald had links with the US secret service and with the **MAFIA**. In 1979, the House Assassinations Committee decided that Kennedy 'was probably assassinated as a result of a conspiracy'.

**Othon**, also called **Frederick Otto of Wittelsbach** (1815–67)
King of Greece (1832/62). The son of King **LUDWIG I** of Bavaria, in 1832 he was chosen by the Great Powers to rule the newly independent Greek kingdom. At first he governed through a regency appointed by his father but, after assuming full control, he showed himself increasingly inclined to rule as an absolute monarch, surrounding himself with Bavarian advisers. The growing frustration of many Greek politicians at the domination of their country by a German oligarchy culminated in a coup (1843), after which Othon was forced to form a new government and to accept a new constitution (1844). He was driven from Greece after another coup in 1862 and retired to Bavaria. ➤ **KOLETTIS, IOANNIS**; **MAVRO-KORDATOS, ALEXANDER**

**Otis, James** (1725–83)
US politician. A leading Boston attorney, Otis was advocate general in 1760, when royal revenue officers demanded his assistance in obtaining from the Mas-

sachusetts Superior Court general search warrants allowing them to enter any man's house in quest of goods that violated the Sugar Act of 1733. Otis refused and argued powerfully before the court against taxation without representation and violation of the rights of colonists. In 1761, elected to the Massachusetts assembly, he became a radical opponent of British rule. In 1769 he was beaten in an altercation with revenue officers and received a head injury from which he never fully recovered.

**Ottawa**
An Algonquian-speaking Native American tribe who originally inhabited the area around Lake Huron, where Samuel de **CHAMPLAIN** encountered them in 1615. They are traditionally thought to have been part of the same tribe as the **OJIBWA** and the Potawatomi. Threatened by the **IROQUOIS**, they began in 1649 to migrate eastwards. In the 1680s they were important fur-trappers and traders. Their only real resistance to Anglo-American expansion was in **PONTIAC'S CONSPIRACY**, and they fought as British allies in the **AMERICAN REVOLUTION** and the **WAR OF 1812**. After living for many years in the Great Lakes area, in the 19c they settled on reservations in Oklahoma, and around the Great Lakes. Their population is currently c.14,000. ➤ **NATIVE AMERICANS**

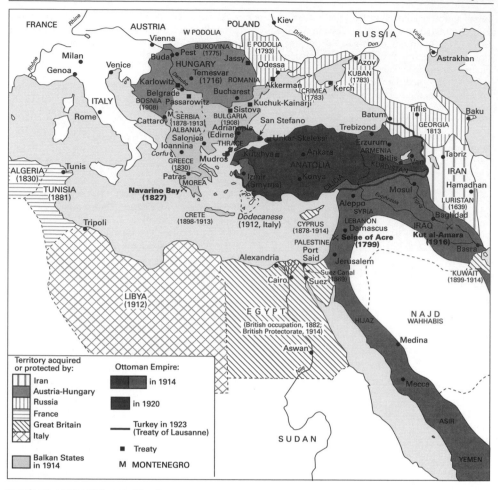

**Break-up of the Ottoman Empire**

## Ottawa Conferences (1894, 1932)

British **IMPERIAL CONFERENCES**. The main topic in 1894 was the development of communications between the individual units of the **BRITISH EMPIRE**. Underlying the conference was a realization that the nature of imperial relationships had altered and that a new way of dealing with them had to be found. A major evolution was evident by 1932 in the agreements at the Ottawa economic conference held between Britain and its dominions at the height of the world depression. The conference negotiated a limited amount of imperial preference following the adoption of a new protective tariff by the British government earlier that year.

## Otto III (980–1002)

German King and Holy Roman Emperor (983/1002). The son of Otto II, he came to the throne at the age of three. His mother, Empress Theophano, ruled as regent until her death in 991; thereafter his grandmother, Adelaide, widow of Otto I, the Great, was regent until his accession in 996. Under the influence of Adalbert of Prague, he undertook a campaign against the heathen **SLAVS** on the Elbe (997) and promoted the cult of Charlemagne in an attempt to enhance the standing of the Western Empire. In his brief reign he managed to engineer into the papacy

first his cousin, Gregory V, and then his tutor, **SYLVESTER II**. He lived most of his short life in Rome and tried to make it the capital of the empire, but was driven out by the hostility of the people in 1002.

## Otto IV (c.1174–1218)

German King and Holy Roman Emperor (1198/1214). The son of **HENRY THE LION** and Matilda, the daughter of **HENRY II** of England, he grew up at the court of his uncle **RICHARD I** of England, who created him Count of Poitou. He was elected King in 1198 in opposition to **PHILIP OF SWABIA**, against whom he struggled for supremacy for ten years. Philip's murder in 1208 left the way free for his coronation as Emperor (1209), but his subsequent invasion of Sicily lost him the support of Pope **INNOCENT III** who raised up Philip's nephew **FREDERICK II** as a rival, and Otto's cause finally collapsed after his defeat by **PHILIP II** of France at **BOUVINES** in 1214.

## Ottoman Empire

A Muslim empire founded c.1300 by Sultan **OSMAN I**, and originating in Asia Minor. Ottoman forces entered Europe in 1345, conquered Constantinople in 1453, and by 1520 controlled most of south-eastern Europe, including part of Hungary, the Middle East and North Africa. Following the 'golden age' of **SÜLEYMAN I, THE MAGNIFICENT** (1520/66), the empire began a protracted decline. During the 19c and early 20c, Ottoman power was eroded by the ambitions of Russia and Austria in south-east Europe, the ambitions of France, Britain and Italy in North Africa, the emergence of the Balkan nations, and internal loss of authority. It joined the Central Powers in 1914, and collapsed with their defeat in 1918. ► YOUNG TURKS; *See maps and table*

## OTTOMAN DYNASTY

| Regnal Dates | Name |
|---|---|
| 1281/1324 | Osman I |
| 1324/60 | Orhan |
| 1360/89 | Murad I |
| 1389/1402 | Bayezid I |
| 1403/13 | Interregnum |
| 1413/21 | Mehmed I |
| 1421/44 | Murad II (1st reign) |
| 1444/6 | Mehmed II, the Conqueror (1st reign) |
| 1446/51 | Murad II (2nd reign) |
| 1451/81 | Mehmed II, the Conqueror (2nd reign) |
| 1481/1512 | Bayezid II |
| 1512/20 | Selim I, the Grim |
| 1520/66 | Süleyman I, the Magnificent |
| 1566/74 | Selim II |
| 1574/95 | Murad III |
| 1595/1603 | Mehmed III |
| 1603/17 | Ahmed I |
| 1617/18 | Mustafa I (1st reign) |
| 1618/22 | Osman II |
| 1622/3 | Mustafa I (2nd reign) |
| 1623/40 | Murad IV |
| 1640/8 | Ibrahim |
| 1648/87 | Mehmed IV |
| 1687/91 | Süleyman II |
| 1691/5 | Ahmed II |
| 1695/1703 | Mustafa II |
| 1703/30 | Ahmed III |
| 1730/54 | Mahmud I |
| 1754/7 | Osman III |
| 1757/74 | Mustafa III |
| 1774/89 | Abd ul-Hamid I |
| 1789/1807 | Selim III |
| 1807/8 | Mustafa IV |
| 1808/39 | Mahmud II |
| 1839/61 | Abd ul-Majid I |
| 1861/76 | Abd ul-Aziz |
| 1876 | Murad V |
| 1876/1909 | Abd ul-Hamid II |
| 1909/18 | Mehmed V |
| 1918/22 | Mehmed VI |
| 1922/4 | Abd ul-Majid II (Caliph only) |

## Ottonians

German royal dynasty. Also known by their family name, the Liudolfinger, the family was founded in the 9c. They ruled Germany from 919 until 1024 under the kings Henry I, Otto I, the Great, Otto II, OTTO III (hence the name Ottonians) and HENRY II, THE HOLY, and completed the transformation of the eastern Frankish kingdom into the German kingdom. They supported Church reform and pursued a policy of elevating churchmen as a counterbalance to the ambitions of the nobility. They reannexed Lotharingia and established the principle that the country could not be divided by inheritance. Their support of the Church led to the so-called Ottonian RENAISSANCE, with notable achievements in architecture, literature and the arts.

## Oudenarde, Battle of (1708)

A Grand Alliance victory in Flanders during the War of the SPANISH SUCCESSION. While laying siege to Oudenarde, the French under the Duke of Vendôme and Burgundy were surprised by Allied troops commanded by Prince EUGÈNE OF SAVOY and the Duke of MARLBOROUGH. A bitter contest followed, and later (1709) the French withdrew to their frontier.

## Oudinot Expedition

The French military expedition under the command of General Nicolas-Charles Oudinot sent, with the backing of Louis Napoleon Bonaparte (later NAPOLEON III), to crush the Roman Republic and to restore Pope PIUS IX. Having finally overcome the republic's forces commanded by GARIBALDI, a French garrison was left in Rome to protect the pope. ► ROMAN QUESTION

## Outram, Sir James (1803–63)

British general and political officer. He joined the Bombay native infantry in 1819, and became political agent in Gujarat (1835–8). He fought in the first of the AFGHAN WARS (1838–42), and took part in the relief of Lucknow (1857–8). Known as 'the Bayard of India' because of his reputation for chivalry, he was made a baronet in 1858. ► INDIAN UPRISING; LUCKNOW, SIEGE OF

## overfishing

During the second half of the 20c traditional fishing practices worldwide were replaced by large-scale 'factory' fishing that harvested enormous quantities of fish. As catches grew dramatically fish stocks declined to a level at which extinction became a risk in many fishing grounds. A moratorium on cod fishing on the Newfoundland Banks was introduced in 1992 with devastating effects on the local economies of eastern Canada but a decade later cod stocks had not recovered and other species were in decline. Numerous reports and consultations within the industry rarely produced any concerted action nationally or internationally. Some governments' unilateral attempts to protect their national fisheries resulted in disputes with other countries, such as the 'cod wars' between Iceland and the UK (1958, 1972-3, 1975-6). The EEC's common fisheries policy (CFP) was introduced in 1983 to address the problem but a 1992 review showed that its half-hearted measures had not arrested the decline in Europe's fish stocks and further restrictions were equally ineffective because quotas were still set at levels too high to maintain stocks; a revised CFP was introduced in 2003 in the hope of improving stock management.

## ÖVP (Österreichische Volkspartei, 'Austrian People's Party')

Austrian political party. Founded in 1945, the ÖVP represented the key Christian (Catholic) political groupings of interwar Austria and identifies with contemporary European Christian Democracy. It has played a major role in most Austrian governments since 1945, sometimes in coalition with the SPÖ. In 1986–7 it became embroiled in the controversy surrounding Kurt **WALDHEIM**'s candidacy for the Austrian presidency.

## OVRA
In Italy, the mysterious name given to **MUSSOLINI**'s secret police force. Never really an integral part of the **FASCIST PARTY** machinery, the OVRA was little more than a slightly expanded version of the old secret branch of the Ministry of the Interior police.

## Owen, David Anthony Llewellyn Owen, Baron (1938– )
British politician. He trained in medicine, then became an MP (1966) and Under-Secretary to the Navy (1968). He was Secretary for Health (1974–6), and Foreign Secretary (1977–9). One of the so-called 'Gang of Four' who formed the **SOCIAL DEMOCRATIC PARTY** (SDP) in 1981, he succeeded Roy **JENKINS** as its leader in 1983. Following the Alliance's disappointing result in the 1987 general election, he opposed Liberal leader David **STEEL** over the question of the merger of the two parties. In 1988, after the SDP voted to accept merger, Owen led the smaller section of the party to a brief independent existence. He retired from parliament in 1992 and went on to become, along with Cyrus Vance, a peace-broker in the troubles that erupted after the disintegration of Yugoslavia.

## Owen, Robert (1771–1858)
Welsh social and educational reformer. The son of a saddler, by the age of 19 he had risen to be manager of a cotton mill in Manchester. In New Lanark, Scotland, he established a model community with improved housing and working conditions, and built an Institute for the Formation of Character, a school (including the world's first day-nursery and playground, and also evening classes) and a village store, the cradle of the cooperative movement. In 1813 he formed New Lanark into a new company with Jeremy **BENTHAM** and others. In *A New View of Society* (1813) he argued that character was formed by the social environment, and went on to found several cooperative Owenite communities, including one at New Harmony in Indiana (1825–8), but they were unsuccessful.

## Oxenstierna, Axel Gustafsson, Count (1583–1654)
Swedish statesman. He was born in Uppland into one of Sweden's leading noble families. Trained abroad for the Church, he entered royal service in 1605 and was instrumental in achieving the smooth accession of **GUSTAV II ADOLF** in 1611. From then on, he was Gustav's Chancellor, responsible for administrative reform and Sweden's relations with foreign powers. He implemented a thorough reform of central and local administration, setting up new 'colleges' headed by the great officers of state. The Diet of four estates was also given a defined membership and procedure. After the King's death in 1632, Oxenstierna became regent for his young daughter, **CHRISTINA**, and directed Sweden's war effort in Germany. He set up the Heilbronn league of German princes in 1633 and after control of southern Germany was lost in 1635, he returned to Sweden to persuade his fellow councillors to fight on until the country's war aims had

been achieved. He continued as Chancellor after Christina came of age in 1644, but thereafter lost influence to the Queen's own favourites.

## Oxford, Provisions of (1258)
A baronial programme imposing constitutional limitations on the English crown. **HENRY III** of England had to share power with a permanent council of barons, parliaments meeting three times a year, and independent executive officers (chancellor, justiciar, treasurer). In 1261 the pope absolved Henry from his oath to observe the Provisions. ► **BARONS' WARS**

## Oyama Iwao (1842–1916)
Japanese soldier and prince. In the **SINO-JAPANESE WAR** of 1894–5 he took Port Arthur and Wei-hei-Wei from China, and in the **RUSSO-JAPANESE WAR** of 1904–5 defeated General Alexei **KUROPATKIN** in several encounters.

## Oyo, Kingdom of
The dominant Yoruba (Nigeria) state of the 17c and 18c. Both the Oyo Dynasty and those of the other kingdoms of the Yoruba were said to have been founded by descendants of a King of Ife, and their peoples were notably town dwellers. The success of Oyo was based on its cavalry, which extended the kingdom south-westwards and also jostled for power with its neighbouring savanna states Borgu and **NUPE**. Its expansion was based on securing the salt trade and trading routes to the coast associated with European slaving. In the 18c it came into conflict with Dahomey and won the war of 1726–30. In the early 19c, Oyo became a victim of the jihads or holy wars of the period. Its northern territory became the Fulani emirate of **ILORIN**, and the state broke up into a series of small states competing with each other in incessant rivalries and warfare. ► **JIHAD**

## Ozaki Yukio (1859–1954)
Japanese politician. A journalist before he turned to politics, Ozaki participated in the formation of the *Rikken Kaishinto* (Constitutional Reform Party) in 1882 and was elected to the first Diet in 1890 (he was to be elected a further 24 times). Ozaki remained a consistent advocate of party government and expansion of the suffrage. Outspoken, he maintained an independent stance even during **WORLD WAR II**, criticizing the dictatorial style of Prime Minister **TOJO HIDEKI**. He retired from politics in 1953.

## Özal, Turgut (1927–93)
Turkish politician. Educated at Istanbul Technical University, he entered government service and in 1967 became Under-Secretary for State Planning. From 1971 he worked for the World Bank, in 1979 joined the office of Prime Minister Bülent **ECEVIT**, and in 1980 was Deputy to Prime Minister Bülent Ulusu, within the military regime of Kenan Evren. When political pluralism returned in 1983, Özal founded the Islamic, right-of-centre Motherland Party (ANAP, *Anavatan Partisi*) and led it to a narrow but clear victory in the elections of that year. In the 1987 general election he retained his majority, and in 1989 became Turkey's first civilian President for 30 years.

**Paardeberg, Battle of** (1900)
The first major British victory of the second Boer War, following the relief of the Siege of **KIMBERLEY**. The Boers abandoned the position they had held at **MAGERSFONTEIN**, and moved east to defend Bloemfontein. Their defeat at Paardeberg opened the way for the full-scale attack on the Orange Free State and the Transvaal, and the taking of the Boer cities. ► **BOER WARS**

**Paasikivi, Juho Kusti** (1870–1956)
Finnish politician. He became Conservative Prime Minister after the civil war in 1918. He recognized the need for friendly relations with Russia, and took part in all Finnish–Soviet negotiations. He sought to avoid war in Sep 1939, conducted the armistice negotiations and became Prime Minister again in 1944. He succeeded Carl Gustav **MANNERHEIM** as President (1946–56). ► **CONTINUATION WAR**; **RUSSO-FINNISH WAR**

**Pacific, War of the** (1879–84)
A war fought between Chile on the one hand and Peru and Bolivia (in alliance since 1873) on the other, arising out of Chilean grievances in the Atacama Desert, then Bolivian-held. Chile won command of the sea in the early months of the war, and sent large expeditions to Peru, occupying the capital, Lima (Jan 1881). Peace treaties gave Chile large territorial gains.

**Pacific Islands Forum** ► **SOUTH PACIFIC FORUM**

**Pacific Scandal** (1872–3)
A political scandal in Canada which toppled Prime Minister John **MACDONALD**'s Conservative administration. In 1871, following an agreement that a transcontinental railway would be built within ten years, British Columbia agreed to join the **DOMINION OF CANADA**. In 1872 a contract for the railway was awarded to a syndicate led by shipowner and financier Sir Hugh **ALLAN**, who was also a major financial supporter of the Conservative Party. A general election that year returned the Conservatives to power, and the defeated Liberals accused Macdonald of having given the contract to Allan as a reward. Macdonald was forced to resign, the contract was cancelled, and a election was called in 1874, which the Conservatives lost. The Canadian Pacific Railway was finally completed in 1885.

**Pacific War** (1941–5)
Following the bombing by Japan of the US naval base at **PEARL HARBOR**, the USA entered into war against all the **AXIS POWERS** (Germany, Italy and Japan) and

**WORLD WAR II** spread into the Pacific. Japan, which had Thailand as an ally and had set up bases in Vichy-controlled Indochina, quickly occupied the Philippines, most of South-East Asia and Burma (now Myanmar), the Netherlands East Indies (now Indonesia), and several Pacific Ocean islands. Meanwhile, US land forces worked with the British and Chinese on the Asian mainland; naval and amphibious forces advanced through the islands that would give them access to Japan; and General Douglas **MACARTHUR** planned a counter-attack from Australia. Despite all the early victories, Japan lost the crucial Battle of **MIDWAY** of 3–6 June 1942, a US victory that marked a turning point in the war. The long battle on **GUADALCANAL** and Tulagi in the Solomon Islands (Aug 1942–Feb 1943) also resulted in US victory, and was followed by the recapture of Bougainville and New Britain (Papua New Guinea), New Guinea and the Mariana Islands (July 1944). The Battle of **LEYTE GULF** effectively demolished what remained of Japanese naval power, while on land Burma was successfully reoccupied by **SLIM**'s army. In 1945 Manila (Mar) and **OKINAWA** (Apr–June) were recaptured by the USA, and the Japanese finally surrendered in Aug following the dropping of atomic bombs on **HIROSHIMA** and **NAGASAKI**.

**Paderewski, Ignacy Jan** (1860–1941)
Polish pianist, composer and patriot. He studied in Warsaw, becoming a professor in the Conservatoire (1878), and a virtuoso pianist, appearing throughout Europe and the USA. During **WORLD WAR I** he used his popularity abroad to argue the case, particularly in the USA, for Poland regaining its independence, and in 1919 he became for a time Prime Minister of Poland in order to establish a sense of political unity. But he soon retired from politics, lived in Switzerland, and resumed concert work. He was elected President of Poland's provisional parliament abroad in 1940, though poor health prevented him pursuing an active role. He died in New York City.

**Padilla, Juan de** (1490–1521)
Leading noble of Toledo. He emerged as one of the principal leaders of the Revolt of the **COMUNEROS** in 1520, but his forces were eventually defeated at the Battle of **VILLALAR** (1521) and he and his companions were beheaded. His wife, Maria (d.1531), held Toledo against the royal forces from 1521 to 1522, and then fled to Portugal.

**Padlock Act** (1937)
Canadian anti-communist legislation. Enacted by **DUPLESSIS**'s **UNION NATIONALE** administration in

# Painting

Art & Literature

The oldest examples of painting to have survived are the Palaeolithic cave paintings found in south-western France and northern Spain, created c.15,000 BC. Realistic depictions of animals were painted on the walls, the paint medium being a mixture of coloured earths and animal fats. In some cases a compound of powdered earth and charcoal was blown at the wall through hollow bones.

Paintings are also found on Egyptian tomb walls (stylized representations of the deceased and his servants, c.3000 BC), in frescoes in the excavations of Minoan Crete (depicting the culture and the environment, notably the dolphins at Knossos), murals in rock caves at Ajanta, India (illustrations of Buddha's life in a more naturalistic style than is seen in later Indian art, c.5c AD), and the vivid Maya murals at Bonampak, Mexico, from around the 8c AD (prisoners being displayed to a ruler). Such frescoes reveal what was important to each civilization, and reveal also the value placed on an ability to record life in this two-dimensional way.

While all societies expressed themselves in visual arts, not all societies made use of painting. Where they did, the artists were usually craftsmen in the service of the rulers, not creative individuals expressing themselves in the manner they wished.

It is known that wall paintings existed in ancient Greece but none has survived. The arts of the Roman Empire, however, were preserved in the buried buildings of Pompeii and Herculaneum. The artists allowed themselves freedom in representation, creating the images of fantastic buildings as well as using perspective to create illusions of reality. These paintings were a secular decoration, like the mosaic floors that adorned many a Roman villa. The Romans took the next step from painting on walls to painting on wooden panels, and developed portraiture, partly for funerary purposes (at the same time as their portraits in sculpture). Small painted panels became the norm for the religious works of the Eastern Church. Byzantine icons were stylized portraits of holy figures, always painted from the frontal view. The stylization was carried to extremes after the iconoclasm of Leo III (c.750–816), who forbade the veneration of images. The artists established a convention of light and dark patterns on a flat surface to avoid the impression of a real body.

In the Western Church a more realistic style prevailed, though still flat. The Church was the foremost patron of artists and craftsmen, followed by rich and powerful rulers and states. Paintings were commissioned on wood for altarpieces, and on the walls of churches, monasteries and town halls. Italy was the centre for the development of painting styles: in Rome, the home of the pope, and in the city-states of Venice, Padua, Florence, Siena, Bologna and Pisa, where money was available to devote to great works. In Siena the town hall was decorated with frescoes depicting 14c city life, with one of the city's heroes painted larger than life on the wall of the council chamber. In Padua and Florence the works of Giotto (c.1267–1337) showed a move away from the flat Gothic style to a greater realism.

Florence was the starting point for the art **Renaissance** in Italy. The key to the new look that was to move out from Italy over the whole of Europe was the use of a one-point perspective to create a three-dimensional effect. This, with the use of foreshortening, brought an increased drama to painting. Frescoes remained the most important means for an artist to express himself, but oil painting on wood and canvas was also used.

Italy in the 16c produced artists of immense talent. Chief among them was Michelangelo (1475–1564), a sculptor as well as painter, whose master works are still to be seen on the ceiling and walls of the Sistine Chapel. The fresco work of Raphael (1483–1520) is also to be seen in the Vatican. He excelled in portraiture, which he also executed on the easel, and he was profoundly influenced by another giant of the Renaissance, Leonardo da Vinci (1452–1519). Leonardo spent so much time on his scientific experiments that he left few paintings, but his *Last Supper* is regarded as a masterpiece even though it started to deteriorate soon after its completion because of the experimental method he used (oil on dry plaster rather than the traditional *buon 'fresco* application of pigments to a damp surface). Titian (c.1488–1576) revolutionized painting in oils and has been described as the founder of modern painting.

The importance of the great Renaissance artists was not only in the value of their art, but the effect it had on future generations of artists and the view of art in the Western world. A very different view prevailed in other cultures, where painting was not an end in itself but an aid to other arts. In the Islamic world, where the representation of the human figure was forbidden in religious art, a secular tradition of highly decorative manuscript illustration developed. Beginning in Tabriz in the 14c, Persian miniature painting developed through the next century and was the chief painting style throughout the Middle East, as well as in the **Mughal Empire** in India. Mughal art developed a remarkable miniature tradition which eventually fused Persian manuscript illustration with indigenous Hindu styles and European art, including individual portraiture and elements of perspective. By the 17c, trade contacts had made examples of European art freely available in India. In Hindu India the art of sculpture predominated over painting, but from the

---

Quebec, it authorized the closure of any premises that were suspected of producing communist propaganda. Since the term 'communist' was not properly defined, the government was able to hinder the growth of the **CCF** and also to use it against trade unions. The law was declared unconstitutional by the Supreme Court in 1957.

**Padmore, George** (1902–59)
Trinidadian international revolutionary and Pan-Africanist. He spent most of his life campaigning against colonialism in Africa and preaching African

**SOCIALISM** and unity; his memory is revered in West Africa.

**Páez, José Antonio** (1790–1873)
Venezuelan general and politician. He commanded the forces of *llaneros* ('cowboys') during the **SPANISH-AMERICAN WARS OF INDEPENDENCE** as principal lieutenant of Simón **BOLÍVAR**. On the break-up of **GRAN COLOMBIA**, he became President of Venezuela (1831) and ruled the country until the late 1840s, again assuming power in 1861–3. He died in exile in New York City.

classical Gupta and the wall-paintings at Ajanta, there developed a continuous tradition of brightly coloured devotional painting, often expressed as ephemera on paper.

In Islamic art there was no attempt or desire to evoke the emotional response achieved by the generation of Western painters that followed the Renaissance masters. The dynamism of their compositions and the emotional response they evoked was intensified by the next generation of painters. El Greco (1541–1614), a Crete-born Spanish painter who studied in Italy (possibly under Titian), developed a portrait style that combined Italian Mannerism and Baroque rhythm in an intensely emotional approach. The lessons of the Italian Renaissance spread out across Europe, exhibited in the realistic treatment of the human form by Albrecht Dürer (1471–1528) in Germany, the characterful portraits of **Henry VIII** and Sir Thomas **More** by Hans Holbein (1497–1543) in England, and the depictions of Flemish peasant life by Pieter Brueghel, the Elder (c.1520–1569). The artist was now his own boss and could diverge from the general style. The nightmarish visions of Hieronymous Bosch (c.1450–1516) were quite unlike anything produced by his contemporaries as well as being unlike his own more conventional work. Nonetheless, they were accepted by the local churches that commissioned them, and later collected by **Philip II** of Spain, forming an inspiration for the Surrealist movement in the 20c.

Drama was the keynote in the Baroque style that developed in art in the 17c. This was achieved by composition, movement and the use of *chiaroscuro* (contrast of light and shadow), as in the works of Caravaggio (1573–1610). The intense realism of paintings such as *The Flagellation of Christ* influenced the powerful work of the Flemish Peter Paul Rubens (1577–1640) and that of the greatest of Northern painters, Rembrandt (1606–69), in Holland. Rembrandt refined the use of chiaroscuro, introducing a subtlety in its use to large canvases such as *The Night Watch* (1640–2) and to portraits, especially self-portraits, with psychological insights.

Northern Europe produced other painters of note, not always recognized at the time. Jan Vermeer (1632–75), in Holland, created detailed portrayals of everyday life and domestic interiors, but made little attempt to sell his paintings. In contrast, the Flemish Sir Anthony Van Dyck (1599–1641) made his success at the court of **Charles I** of England. His flattering portrait studies influenced both English portraiture in the 18c (notably the successful Thomas Gainsborough, 1727–88, and Sir Joshua Reynolds, 1723–92) and posterity's view of the Stuart monarchy.

In France the style moved from the Baroque to the Rococo, employing more delicacy and less muscle. Antoine Watteau (1684–1721) specialized in elegantly dressed young people posing in fantasies of pastoral scenes. This somewhat frivolous style was countered by the ideals of Neoclassicism and the **French Revolution**, embodied in the works of Jacques Louis David (1748–1825) and his pupil Jean Auguste Ingres (1780–1867). Ingres was the leading exponent of the classical tradition in France in the 19c, interested more in draughtsmanship than in facial characteristics or colour.

The austerity of the classical form was challenged by the Romantics, who wanted to portray drama and heroism, as in *The Raft of the Medusa* by Théodore Géricault (1791–1824). At the same time, landscape assumed a new importance. From being a mere backdrop to figures, it became the subject in its own right, as in the works of Camille Corot (1796–1875). Where figures were included, usually peasants, they were presented as symbols of the pure, unspoiled life.

In England John Constable (1776–1837) was painting his poetic vision of the English countryside, aided by his scientific observations and notes on cloud formations and the light produced by different weather conditions. His view of nature was tranquil, whereas J M W Turner (1775–1851) depicted natural drama – storms and tempests, dramatic use of light and shade, and colour gradations – that foreshadowed the Impressionists.

The Impressionist movement in France was in part a revolt against the standards of the Academies that ruled the art world, but it was also a continuation of that realistic thread – the examination of character through art – that had started in the 17c. The subject matter was the life to be seen wherever the artist lived, rather than mythological or historical figures. The style was a departure from the accepted norm; slabs, sweeps and patches of colour were used to create a mood, with little detail. At first these artists were rejected and reviled by the art world. A group of them, Camille Pissaro (1830–1903), Alfred Sisley (1839–99), Pierre Auguste Renoir (1841–1919) and Claude Monet (1840–1926), staged their own exhibition in 1874, but Monet, triumphant in the 20c, had his work rejected for 20 years. In an important departure from traditional practice, the painters worked in the open air rather than in the studio; they also worked together and often painted the same landscape scene. Exotic influences also made their mark, notably Japanese art.

In Japan painting had always been the most important of the visual arts. Like other aspects of Japanese culture it had developed from Chinese influences. Chinese painting had begun with tomb illustration around 300 BC, which favoured legends of heroes. However, a strong landscape tradition, heavily influenced by Taoism, emerged around AD 200, long before it arose in Western art. Landscape painting dominated the tradition, with two styles evident: the monumental and the minimal. In keeping with the cultural respect for the perfections of the past, later painters were mostly content to follow the artists of the **Song Dynasty**, rather than innovate. In both Japan and China, calligraphy was developed to the highest standard, and the disciplined brush was important in their respective painting traditions. The quick sparse brush strokes had initially been employed to depict scenes from nature on the paper screens that separated rooms in a

## Pagan

The capital of the first Burman state, located in the dry plains of central Burma (now Myanmar), at the point where the great Irrawaddy River turns towards the East. The state of Pagan emerged in the middle of the 9c. In the 11c, under Anawrahta, it extended its authority both to the north and to the south, the latter securing important access to the port cities on the Gulf of Martaban and the Kra Isthmus, and thus to their commercial and cultural connections. The most important physical legacy of Pagan was its astound-ing programme of temple construction. The ruins of over 2,000 temples, within an area of 26 sq mi/67 sq km, still stand. Pagan began to weaken in the 13c, initially probably as a result of the heavy and continuous religious donations of the state in the form of skilled labour and irrigated rice fields. A Mongol invasion and Shan incursions at the end of the century brought about its final collapse.

## Page, Sir Earle Christmas Grafton (1880–1961)

Australian politician. He practised medicine and sat in the federal parliament from 1919 until his death.

Japanese house. In the Edo period, scenes from Japanese classical literature were popular, then coloured woodblock prints became the chief style. The works that so influenced the Impressionists were created by Katsushika Hokusai (1760–1849) and Ando Hiroshige (1797–1858). Hokusai specialized in 'pictures of the floating world' that treated commonplace subjects in an expressionist manner. This school of painting had not previously included landscapes, and his treatment of nature was new. Hiroshige's landscapes in the same genre were freer and less austere, mostly striking compositions of rain, snow and mist. The relationship between Impressionist paintings and these works is immediately apparent.

They were also important to the work of Post-Impressionists, particularly Vincent Van Gogh (1853–90) and Henri Toulouse-Lautrec (1864–1901). Van Gogh received no recognition in his own lifetime, and committed suicide. The dark palette of his early masterpieces was brightened by his move to France and friendship with Toulouse-Lautrec and Paul Gauguin (1848–1903). Gauguin had been inspired by the colours and the scenes of the Pacific, living first in Martinique, then in Tahiti and the Marquesas. He was the first to direct attention to 'primitive' art as aesthetic expression, and so influenced most of the fields of artistic expression that came after him. Toulouse-Lautrec's special contribution was his use of quick sketches of people in action to form his paintings. His subjects were the clientele of cafés and bars, and the prostitutes and barmaids of Montmartre.

The painter Paul Cézanne (1839–1906), with his structural style, influenced the Cubism developed by Pablo Picasso (1881–1973) and Georges Braque (1882–1963), with its emphasis on formal, geometrical criteria, and its attempt to express the three-dimensional, without perspective, on the flat surface. Picasso was associated with several art movements in a long, innovative career working in many media. Before focusing on Cubism he had been associated with *les fauves* ('wild beasts'), a group that included Henri Matisse (1869–1954) and Maurice de Vlaminck (1876–1958), who were also influenced by primitive, particularly African, art.

African art was also the inspiration for the Expressionists, who aimed to show emotional rather than external realities. The full flowering of this movement occurred in Germany, with two groups, *Der Blaue Reiter* ('The Blue Rider') and *Die Brücke* ('The Bridge'), although the style was also embraced elsewhere, for instance in *The Scream* (1913) by the Norwegian Edvard Munch (1863–1944).

From here Western painting began to move in completely new directions. Out of Cubism developed Abstract Art, which relies entirely on lines, shapes and colours for its aesthetic appeal, with no dependence on natural appearances. The accepted criteria of the art world were challenged by the shock tactics of a Swiss group calling themselves *Dada* ('rocking horse', a name chosen at random from a dictionary). Their methods were taken up by the Surrealists, whose aim was to free the artist from the demands of logic and to penetrate behind consciousness to the 'super-reality'. The theories of Sigmund Freud (1856–1939) were important here, and dream-like landscapes were created with familiar objects juxtaposed in an unfamiliar way, or having undergone a strange transformation, as in *The Persistence of Memory* (1931) by Salvador Dalí (1904–89). Other leading painters include René Magritte (1898–1967), Joan Miró (1893–1983) and Max Ernst (1891–1976), and their influence is seen in the work of many more, as well as in **cinema** and advertising.

Many Surrealists crossed the Atlantic to the USA during and after **World War II**, and many of the innovations of the 1940s and 1950s were made there. Abstract Impressionism, as in the works of Jackson Pollock (1912–56), who dripped paint on canvas in a random way, was followed by Op Art (relying on optical illusion for its effect) and Pop Art (representational pictures of the ephemeral aspects of 20c suburban life), with Andy Warhol (1926–87) and Roy Lichtenstein (1923–97) as its chief representatives.

A number of styles developed alongside each other in the second half of the 20c, both abstract and realist, with an increasing tendency for painters to create multi-media works employing sound and video, and often requiring spectator participation. ► **Architecture**; **Sculpture**

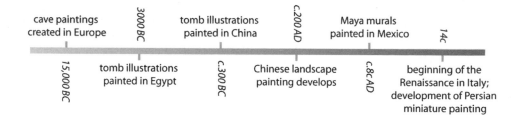

cave paintings created in Europe — 3000 BC — tomb illustrations painted in China — c.200 AD — Maya murals painted in Mexico — 14c

15,000 BC — tomb illustrations painted in Egypt — c.300 BC — Chinese landscape painting develops — c.8c AD — beginning of the Renaissance in Italy; development of Persian miniature painting

He became Leader of the Country Party in 1921 and Deputy Prime Minister and Treasurer in the Bruce–Page coalition government of 1923–9. He was Deputy Prime Minister (1934–9) and briefly Prime Minister in 1939. In 1941 he became Australian minister in London, representing Australia on war cabinet committees. Minister of Health in 1949, he retired to the backbenches in 1956. ► **NATIONAL PARTY OF AUSTRALIA**

**Pahlavi, Muhammad Reza** (1919–80)
Shah of Persia (1941/79). He succeeded on the abdi-

cation of his father, Reza Shah, in 1941. His reign was for many years marked by social reforms and a movement away from the old-fashioned despotic concept of the monarchy, but during the later 1970s the economic situation deteriorated, social inequalities worsened, and protest at Western-style 'decadence' grew among religious fundamentalists. After several attempts at parliamentary reform the Shah, having lost control of the situation, left the country, and a revolutionary government was formed under Ayatollah **KHOMEINI**. The ex-Shah having been admitted to the

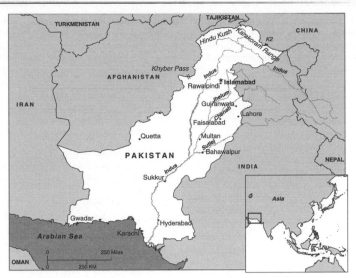

USA for medical treatment, the Iranian government seized the US Embassy in Tehran and held many of its staff hostage for over a year, demanding his return to Iran. He made his final residence in Egypt at the invitation of President Anwar **SADAT** and died there.

**Paine, Thomas** (1737–1809)
Anglo-American political writer. In 1774 he sailed for Philadelphia, where his pamphlet *Common Sense* (1776) argued for complete independence from Britain. He served with the American army, and was made Secretary to the Committee of Foreign Affairs. In 1787 he returned to England, where he wrote *The Rights of Man* (1791–2) in support of the **FRENCH REVOLUTION**. Indicted for treason, he fled to Paris in 1792, where he was elected a Deputy to the National **CONVENTION**, but imprisoned for his proposal to offer the King asylum in the USA. At this time (1794–5) he wrote *The Age of Reason*, in favour of deism. Released in 1796, he returned to the USA in 1802.

**Painting** ► *See panel*

**Paisley, Ian Richard Kyle** (1926– )
Northern Ireland militant Protestant clergyman and politician. An ordained minister since 1946, he formed his own Church (the Free Presbyterian Church of Ulster) in 1951, and from the 1960s became deeply involved in Ulster politics. He founded the Protestant **DEMOCRATIC UNIONIST PARTY** and stood as its MP for four years until 1974, since when he has been the Democratic Unionist MP for North Antrim, although he resigned briefly in protest at the **ANGLO-IRISH AGREEMENT** of 1985. He was a member of the European Parliament from 1979 until 2004. A rousing orator, he is strongly in favour of maintaining the Union with Britain, and fiercely opposed to the **IRA**, Roman Catholicism and the unification of Ireland. He participated in the all-party peace process of 1995–6, only with deeply held misgivings, and opposed the **GOOD FRIDAY AGREEMENT** (1998), becoming a trenchant critic of its shortcomings. He was elected to the Northern Ireland Assembly in 1998 and re-elected in 2003, when his party won the greatest number of seats, making him the leading Protestant Unionist negotiator in the talks on restoring

devolved government. He vetoed a deal with **SINN FÉIN** late in 2004 owing to doubts about its sincerity that turned out to be well-founded.

**PAKISTAN** official name **Islamic Republic of Pakistan**
An Asian state, bounded to the east by India; to the west by Afghanistan and Iran; and to the north by China. The disputed area of Jammu and Kashmir lies to the north. Pakistan's walled cities at Mohenjo-Daro, Harappa and Kalibangan are evidence of civilization in the Indus Valley over 4,000 years ago. Muslims ruled the region under the **MUGHAL EMPIRE** from 1526 to 1761, and the British ruled most areas from the 1840s. Pakistan was separated from India to form a state for the Muslim minority in 1947, consisting of West Pakistan (Baluchistan, North-West Frontier, West Punjab, Sind) and East Pakistan (East Bengal), which are physically separated by 1,000 mi/1,600 km. Conflict with India broke out over Jammu and Kashmir in 1949. The successful Indian occupation of most of the disputed territory was the cause of wars in 1965 and 1971 (the **INDO-PAKISTAN WARS**) as well as periods of tension in 1999 and 2000–2, the latter heightened by the knowledge that both countries possessed nuclear weapons. Pakistan was proclaimed an Islamic republic in 1956. Differences between East and West Pakistan developed into civil war in 1971, resulting in East Pakistan becoming an independent state (Bangladesh). A military coup led by General **ZIA UL-HAQ** took place in 1977, and former Prime Minister Zulfikar Ali **BHUTTO** was executed in 1979, despite international appeals for clemency. In 1991 there was increased violence within the country, particularly in Sind, and during the 1990s there were several changes of government amid allegations of corruption. In 1999 the government was overthrown in a military coup by General Pervez **MUSHARRAF**, who became head of the government and then, in Jun 2001, also assumed the presidency. After the **SEPTEMBER 11 ATTACKS**, President Musharraf aligned Pakistan with the USA's war on **TERROR**, providing indispensable support to the allies in the **AFGHAN WAR**, which angered militant factions and opponents have used procedural disruptions to prevent the

National Assembly from functioning properly since the 2002 elections. International concerns were raised in 2004 by disclosures about Pakistan's sale of its nuclear technology to other countries. ► **INDO-PAKISTAN WARS**; **KASHMIR PROBLEM**; **KHAN, ABDUL QADEER**

### Pal, Bipin Chandra (1858–1932)

Indian nationalist and freedom fighter. Though born into an orthodox **ZAMINDAR** family in Sylhet (in present-day Bangladesh), he opposed traditional orthodoxy and religious practices. He entered politics in 1877 and his association with the great reformist **BRAHMO SAMAJ** leader Keshab Chandra Sen drew him into this movement in 1880. He was also greatly influenced by B G **TILAK**, Lala **LAJPAT RAI** and Aurobindo **GHOSH**. In 1898 he went to England on a scholarship for theological studies and, on his return, launched a weekly journal, *Young India* (1902), through which he championed the complete freedom of India. He campaigned for the boycott of British goods and also advocated a policy of passive resistance and non-cooperation. A member of the famous Congress trio 'Lal, Pal and Bal', he spent the years 1908–11 in England, where he worked for India's freedom and published *Swaraj*. In the later stages of the freedom movement, he withdrew from political life, although he continued to write on national matters. ► **NON-COOPERATION MOVEMENT**; **SWARAJ**

### Pala ► INDIA, PRE-ISLAMIC

### Palach, Jan (1948–69)

Czech philosophy student. As a protest against the invasion of Czechoslovakia by **WARSAW PACT** forces (Aug 1968) and its subsequent '**NORMALIZATION**', he burnt himself to death in Wenceslas Square in Prague in Jan 1969. He became a hero and symbol of hope, and was mourned by thousands. Huge popular demonstrations marking the 20th anniversary of his death were held in Prague in 1989.

### Palacký, František (1798–1876)

Czech historian and a leading light in the Czech national revival. Politically he argued the case before and during the 1848–9 revolutionary outburst in the Habsburg Empire for the restoration of Czech autonomy. Subsequently, and particularly after the **AUSGLEICH** of 1867 recognized the equality of Hungary alongside Austria, he became more radical in looking towards eventual independence. However, his greatest contribution was his mammoth *History of Bohemia* (1836–67), which established the historical case for the burgeoning national movement.

### Palafox y Melzi, José de (1780–1847)

Spanish patriot. Nominally head of the heroic defence of Saragossa (Jul 1808–Feb 1809), he was carried prisoner to France, and not released until 1813. He was made Duke of Saragossa (1836) and Grandee of Spain (1837).

### Palatinate, The

A German Rhenish principality, with Heidelberg as its capital. Acquired by the Wittelsbach family (1214), it was elevated to an imperial electorate by the **GOLDEN BULL** of 1356, and became increasingly wealthy and important in the 13–15c. After the introduction of Calvinism by Frederick III (1559/76), it was the leading Protestant German state and head of the Protestant Union (1608), before its division and systematic devastation in the **THIRTY YEARS' WAR** (1618–48) and later by France (1685). In the 18c it lost significance, being successively reunified as a single state (1706), linked dynastically with Bavaria (1777), and occupied by the French (1793–4). Shared between Baden and Bavaria (1815), it was finally absorbed into the German Reich (1871).

### Pale (Ireland)

That part of the Lordship of **IRELAND** under the direct control of the Dublin administration. Defined in 1464 as the four counties of Dublin, Kildare, Louth and Meath, it was used to raise revenue for the administration and to support the retinues of magnates attending a parliament when one was held in Dublin.

### Pale, The (Russia)

In the 19c and early 20c, the area within which the bulk of the Jewish population of imperial Russia was forced to live. This was fairly broadly defined in **ALEXANDER I**'s time, but following the assassination of **ALEXANDER II** in 1881 it was restricted to the narrow confines of what had been eastern Poland plus part of south-west Russia. In typical anti-Semitic fashion it was alleged by Konstantin **POBEDONOSTSEV**, Procurator of the Holy Synod, and others that Jews had been involved in the assassination and were enemies of the state. There were frequent pogroms within the Pale, and Jews were officially discriminated against throughout Russia. The result was that more Jews did become involved in opposition activities and that some contributed to the emergence of the Zionist movement; most Jews were forced to follow those occupations they were accused of monopolizing. ► **POGROM**

### Palestine

A region bordering the east Mediterranean, historically settled by Philistines then Israelites. During the 20c it has been disputed by Jewish and Arab interests. Palestine was viewed by the Jews as the 'Promised Land', but it also contains Islamic holy sites associated with the prophet Muhammad. After **WORLD WAR I** a mandate was granted to the UK by the **LEAGUE OF NATIONS** to administer the territory (1920–48). The **BALFOUR DECLARATION** supported the establishment of a Jewish homeland. After **WORLD WAR II** the UN recommended that there should be separate Jewish and Arab states in Palestine. When the Arabs rejected this, David **BEN-GURION** announced the creation of the independent State of Israel in May 1948. The new state was immediately invaded by its Arab neighbours, but in the ensuing conflict the Israelis were victorious, and gained more land than had been allotted to them under the UN plan. Over 700,000 Arab refugees left the Israeli-occupied areas. The **PLO** was recognized by the **ARAB LEAGUE** in 1974 as the official voice of Palestinian Arabs. Attempts by Palestinians to achieve greater political freedom were unsuccessful, provoking civil disobedience and violent clashes such as the first **INTIFADA**, until the 1990s, when Israel under Yitzhak **RABIN** seemed to accept the concept of a Palestinian state. Israeli and Palestinian leaders signed the first of the **OSLO ACCORDS** in 1993, granting Palestinian self-government in the **PALESTINIAN AUTONOMOUS AREAS**. Talks on the final status of Palestinian areas stalled in the late 1990s and became deadlocked when Israel and the USA refused to negotiate any longer with Yasser **ARAFAT**. His death in Nov 2004 and the election in Jan 2005 of a moderate successor, Mahmoud Abbas, has led to renewed talks with Israel.

## Palestinian Autonomous Areas

The Palestinian Autonomous Areas comprise the **GAZA STRIP** and parts of the occupied **WEST BANK** that have self-government under the **OSLO ACCORDS**. Self-government was intended to be for a five-year interim period during which time the permanent status of the area should have been resolved. The first areas, the Gaza Strip and the West Bank town of Jericho, were handed over to representatives of the Palestinian National Authority in 1994. An 88-member Palestine Legislative Council and a president, Yasser **ARAFAT**, were elected in 1996. Talks on the final status of the areas stalled in the late 1990s when right-wing parties held power in Israel but were revived by the **ROADMAP PEACE PLAN**, which also sought political reforms in the Palestinian National Authority. The Authority was criticized for the limited nature of its civil institutions and its failure to decentralize, and Arafat's administration was accused of police brutality and corruption, failures that Arafat was unwilling or unable to address. Violence in the area increased as the second **INTIFADA** escalated. Arafat's death in Nov 2004 was felt to improve the likelihood of reaching a successful settlement of the issues, and the election in Jan 2005 of Mahmoud Abbas (also known as Abu Mazen) as Arafat's successor was welcomed by Israel and the USA.

## Pallava ➤ INDIA, PRE-ISLAMIC

## Palme, (Sven) Olof (1927–86)

Swedish politician. He graduated in law from the University of Stockholm in 1951 and became private secretary to the Social Democratic Prime Minister Tage **ERLANDER** in 1954. He was elected to parliament four years later and was appointed minister without portfolio in 1963. He succeeded Erlander as Prime Minister on the latter's resignation in 1969. Palme lost power in 1976, but returned at the head of a minority government in 1982. He was shot dead by an unknown assailant in the centre of Stockholm after a visit to the cinema with his wife. His leadership of the Social Democratic Labour Party saw a left-ward swing in its policies, and he was an outspoken critic of US policy in the **VIETNAM WAR**.

## Palmer Raids

A series of mass arrests of communists, leftists and labour union organizers, carried out the orders of US Attorney-General A Mitchell Palmer (1872–1936) during the **RED SCARE** of 1919–20. Thousands of supposed Bolsheviks and subversives were arrested and jailed, and hundreds were deported. Most of the arrests, imprisonments and deportations were unconstitutional, but they nonetheless effectively stifled leftist movements in the USA until the **GREAT DEPRESSION**.

## Palmerston (of Palmerston), Henry John Temple, 3rd Viscount (1784–1865)

British politician. He became a Tory MP in 1807, served as Secretary of War (1809–28), joined the **WHIGS** (1830), and was three times Foreign Secretary

(1830–4, 1835–41 and 1846–51). His brusque speech, assertive manner, and robust defences of what he considered to be British interests abroad made him a controversial figure and secured him the name of 'Firebrand Palmerston'. He was unpopular with Queen **VICTORIA** and many of his political colleagues, but cultivated public opinion. Home Secretary in **ABERDEEN**'s coalition (1852), he became Premier in 1855, when he vigorously prosecuted the **CRIMEAN WAR** with Russia. He remained in office until 1858, and was Prime Minister again in 1859–65. ➤ **LIBERAL PARTY** (UK); **TORIES**; **WELLINGTON, DUKE OF**

## Pan-Africanism

An ideal and a movement, drawing its ideas from black American and West Indian writers and activists. In part, it reflects a pride in the African continent and Africanness (and thus has some similarities with **NEGRITUDE**) and, in part, a commitment to self-rule. Although the pull towards continental unity is strong in rhetoric and emotion, Pan-Africanism has failed ultimately to provide a strong enough ideology to transcend local self-interest and rivalries, nor has its political manifestation, the **ORGANIZATION OF AFRICAN UNITY**, managed to provide the institutional framework for continental unity, although the OAU's successor, the **AFRICAN UNION**, does aim to introduce continental institutions.

## Pan-Africanist Congress (PAC)

A South African political party and offshoot of the **ANC** (African National Congress), the PAC was formed in 1959 as a movement rejecting the multiracial assumptions of the ANC as well as its communist and Soviet links. It was banned in 1960 and its leaders went into exile, organizing opposition to the **APARTHEID** regime in South Africa from Zambia. The ban was lifted in 1990, and it remains a smaller, but perhaps more closely knit, party than the ANC, despite its leadership problems in the years of exile. In the first multiracial elections in 1994, the PAC won 1.2 per cent of the vote and five seats in the National Assembly. Its share of the vote did not improve in the 1999 and 2004 elections.

**PANAMA** official name **Republic of Panama**

A republic occupying the south-eastern end of the isthmus of Central America, bounded to the north by the Caribbean Sea; to the south by the Pacific Ocean; to the west by Costa Rica; and to the east by Colombia. It was visited by **COLUMBUS** in 1502 and quickly gained strategic importance as a centre of Spanish trade movement, a vital link between the Caribbean and Pacific. It remained under Spanish colonial rule until 1821, when it gained its independence and joined the union known as **GRAN**

**COLOMBIA.** The US-inspired revolution of 1903 led to a break from the Colombian union. Under the terms of a 1977 agreement, Panama assumed sovereignty of the **PANAMA CANAL**, previously administered by the USA, in 1999. In 1984 General Manuel **NORIEGA** seized control of the country and instituted a period of military rule that lasted until Dec 1989, when US forces invaded Panama City after allegations of corruption and drugs trafficking against Noriega had led to strict US sanctions and heightened tensions in the area; Noriega was deposed, tried and convicted for drugs offences in the USA. In 1991, Panama introduced a new constitution that abolished its armed forces. Mireya Moscoso was elected President in 1999. He was succeeded in 2004 by Martín Torrijos, the son of a former dictator.

**Panama Canal**
A canal bisecting the Isthmus of Panama and linking the Atlantic and Pacific oceans. It is 51 mi/82 km long, and 490 ft/150 m wide in most places; built by the US Corps of Engineers (1904–14). In 1979 US control of the Panama Canal Zone (5 mi/8 km) of land flanking the canal on either side passed to the Republic of Panama, which guaranteed the neutrality of the waterway itself when control of the canal was passed over on 31 Dec 1999. ▶ **BUNAU-VARILLA, PHILIPPE JEAN; CANALS; HAY–BUNAU-VARILLA TREATY; HAY–HERRÁN TREATY; PANAMA**

**Panama Congress** (1826)
Attended by delegates from Mexico, Peru, Gran Colombia and the **CENTRAL AMERICAN FEDERATION** at the invitation of Simón **BOLÍVAR** (who did not himself attend). The treaty of Spanish-American confederation agreed at the meeting had no practical effect, but the Congress remains a symbol of the quest for Latin American unity.

**Pan-American Union**
An organization founded in 1890 (and first called the International Bureau for American Republics) to foster political and economic cooperation among American states, and to draw North and South America closer together. Until **WORLD WAR II** the Union concluded many agreements covering trade, migration and neutrality zones around their coasts, despite fears among many members of domination by the USA. In 1948 it became part of the wider **ORGANIZATION OF AMERICAN STATES** (OAS), and now forms its permanent administrative and advisory machinery. It has four departments: economic and social affairs; international law; cultural affairs; and administrative services.

**Pan-Arabism**
The belief that Arabs should unite to form one nation had its origins in the Arab nationalist movement before **WORLD WAR I**. With the collapse of the **OTTOMAN EMPIRE** in that war and the foundation of separate Arab states after it, the belief in a single Arab nation declined. It was revived in the late 1930s when the Palestinian Arabs, revolting against Jewish colonization and British rule, appealed to Arabs everywhere for support. Egypt took up Pan-Arabism as a means of asserting Egyptian leadership in the Middle East. In 1945 the League of **ARAB STATES** was formed with its headquarters in Cairo, but it was unable to prevent

the formation of the State of Israel. In the 1950s the cause of Arab unity was taken up by Gamal Abd al-**NASSER** in Egypt and by the **BA'ATH PARTY** in Syria, in order to oppose Israel and domination by foreign powers. There was a short-lived union of Syria and Egypt (1958–61) but the rivalries of Egypt, Syria and Iraq prevented Arab unification. With the defeat of Arab states by Israel in the 1967 war, Nasser's leadership was discredited and the idea of Pan-Arabism lost its appeal.

**Panchayati Raj**
A form of local self government in rural India initially advocated by M K **GANDHI** which proposed rule by village councils and other rural local bodies. It was promoted by the central government as a matter of national policy from 1957 to 1963, when the state governments were pressured to adopt some form of democratic decentralization and to involve people down to village level directly in the planning process. By the mid-1960s, however, support for Panchayati Raj had declined, even in its stronghold of Maharashtra and Gujarat. In 1977 the Janata government began to reopen the question of the importance and relevance of Panchayati Raj institutions, an issue which has since become important in the national political debate.

**Pandit, Vijaya Lakshmi** (1900–90)
Indian politician and diplomat. The sister of Jawaharlal **NEHRU**, she was the leader of the Indian **UN** delegation (1946–8 and 1952–3), and also held several ambassadorial posts (1947–51). In 1953 she became the first woman President of the UN General Assembly and from 1954 to 1961 she was Indian High Commissioner in London.

**Pandya** ▶ **INDIA, PRE-ISLAMIC**

**Panipat, Battles of** (1526, 1556 and 1761)
Three battles which took place 50 mi/80 km north of Delhi, India. The first (1526), between **BABUR** and the Sultan of Delhi, represented the beginning of the **MUGHAL EMPIRE**. The second (1556) marked the restoration of Mughal power when **AKBAR THE GREAT** defeated the Afghan challenge. The third (1761) saw the defeat of Maratha forces by the Afghan **AHMAD SHAH DURRANI**, which paved the way for British supremacy.

**Pan-Islamism**
A movement to unite all Muslims against the threat from Christian states. It was born in the 1860s and 1870s among the Young Ottomans, who criticized the Ottoman government for failing to help the Central Asian Khans, who had been overrun by the Russians. A militant supporter of Pan-Islamism was Jamal al-Din al-**AFGHANI**, who criticized reformers such as Sir Sayyid **AHMAD KHAN** for weakening loyalty to Islam by making concessions to infidel imperialists in India. Muhammad **ABDUH** was another leading figure in the intellectual revival of Islam, regarding nationalism with suspicion as it weakened the religious ties which bound Muslims together. 'He who professes the Muslim faith ... ceases to concern himself with his race or nation', he wrote. Yet liberalism and nationalism overshadowed religion among the radical élites who identified Islam with social conservatism and political backwardness. In

Turkey the success of **ATATÜRK** in obtaining a negotiated peace on his own terms at Lausanne (1923) gave a great boost to secular nationalism among young army officers in Arab lands in the 1920s and 1930s. After **WORLD WAR II**, there was a great revival of Islamic beliefs and movements, which responded to the feelings of the suppressed lower classes, opposed to their westernized rulers. The **MUSLIM BROTHERHOOD** in Egypt was the most successful of these movements until the revolution that brought the Ayatollah **KHOMEINI** to power in Iran in 1979. In the 1980s military, secular regimes were struggling to hold on to power by resisting the tide of Islamic fundamentalism, and in the early 1990s in Algeria the Islamic Salvation Front (*Front Islamique du Salut*, FIS) was on the verge of being elected to power when the government resigned and an interim military regime cancelled the elections and took over; the country soon degenerated into civil war between Islamic groups and the government.

**Pankhurst, Emmeline** (1858–1928)
British suffragette. In 1905 she organized the Women's Social and Political Union, and fought for women's suffrage by violent means, on several occasions being arrested and going on hunger strike. After the outbreak of **WORLD WAR I**, she worked instead for the industrial mobilization of women. Of her daughters and fellow workers, Dame Christabel turned later to preaching Christ's Second Coming, and Sylvia diverged to pacifism, internationalism and Labour politics. ► **SUFFRAGETTES**; **WOMEN'S RIGHTS**

**Pan-Turkism**
A movement which sought to unite all Turks. In the late 19c it was strongest among the Turkish peoples of the Russian Empire. The Ottoman Turks at first rejected Pan-Turkism, as it would disrupt their multinational empire but, as the **OTTOMAN EMPIRE** lost its provinces in Europe, many sought a new unity in joining all Turks together. Sultan **ABD UL-HAMID II** suppressed these ideas but, after the Young Turk revolution of 1908, the desire to unite the Turkish peoples of Central Asia with those of Anatolia spread. This seemed possible with Russia's defeat in **WORLD WAR I**, but **ATATÜRK** rejected Pan-Turkism to concentrate on ruling the new Turkish Republic that arose after the collapse of the Ottoman Empire. ► **YOUNG TURKS**

**Pao-chia System** ► BAOJIA SYSTEM

**Paoli, Pasquale de** (1725–1807)
Corsican patriot. He returned from exile in 1755 to take part in the struggle against the island's Genoese overlords. After Corsica's purchase by the French in 1768, he led a renewed rebellion but was defeated and fled to England. With the **FRENCH REVOLUTION** he was made Governor of his native island. However, he again grew dissatisfied with French rule and launched an insurrection against the Convention. This too failed and in 1796 he returned to live in exile in England.

**papacy** ► POPE

**Papadopoulos, George** (1919–99)
Greek soldier and politician. He underwent army

training in the Middle East and fought in Albania against the Italians before the German occupation of Greece in **WORLD WAR II**. A member of the resistance during the occupation, he then rejoined the army, reaching the rank of colonel. In 1967 he led a coup against the government of King **CONSTANTINE II** and established a virtual military dictatorship. In 1973, following the abolition of the monarchy, he became President under a new republican constitution, but before the year was out he was himself ousted in another military coup. In 1974 he was arrested, tried for high treason and convicted, but his death sentence was commuted.

**Papagos, Alexandros** (1883–1955)
Greek soldier and politician. After a brilliant military career involving service in the **BALKAN WARS** (1912–13) and the Greek invasion of Turkey (1919–22), he was made Minister of War in 1935 and Chief of Staff the following year. In 1940, as Commander-in-Chief, he repelled the Italian attack on Greece, pushing the enemy forces back into Albania. Less successful against a German attack in Apr 1941, he was captured and taken as a hostage to Germany. After his release at the end of **WORLD WAR II**, he led the campaign in Greece against the communist guerrillas. He was made field marshal in 1949, but resigned as Commander-in-Chief two years later in order to concentrate on a political role. He formed a new political party, the Greek Rally, and was Prime Minister of an exclusively Greek Rally government from 1952 until his death in 1955.

**Papal Allocution** (Apr 1848)
The formal message delivered by **PIUS IX** in which he made it clear that he would not back war against Austria. It marked the point where Pius IX ceased to be the darling of Italian patriots and showed his true reactionary colours.

**Papal States**
The 'States of the Church', straddling rural, mountainous areas of central Italy, comprising territories received by treaties and donations in the **MIDDLE AGES**. The papal government was often ineffective, and relied upon local lords (Malatesta of Rimini, Montefeltro of Urbino) who were appointed as 'vicars in temporal matters'. Annexed in 1870, the papacy refused to recognize their loss until the **LATERAN PACTS** (1929), which established the Vatican papal state.

**Papandreou, Andreas George** (1919–96)
Greek politician. The son of George **PAPANDREOU**, before entering active politics he had an impressive academic career, holding professorial posts at universities in the USA and Canada. He became a US citizen in 1944, but returned to Greece as Director of the Centre for Economic Research in Athens (1961–4) and Economic Adviser to the Bank of Greece, and resumed his Greek citizenship. His political activities led to imprisonment and exile after the military coup led by **PAPADOPOULOS** in 1967. He returned to Greece in 1974 and threw himself wholeheartedly into national politics, founding the Panhellenic Liberation Movement, which later became **PASOK** (the Panhellenic Socialist Movement). He was leader of the opposition from 1977 and in

1981 became Greece's first socialist Prime Minister. Re-elected in 1985, in 1988 a heart operation and news of his impending divorce, following his association with a young former air stewardess, created speculation about his future. The 1989 general election produced no clear result and, after unsuccessful attempts to form a new government, he resigned and was succeeded by Tzannis Tzannetakis. His party was returned to power in 1993, although he was in poor health throughout his last premiership and resigned in 1996.

**Papandreou, George** (1888–1968)
Greek politician. A lawyer by training, he moved into politics in the early 1920s. The monarchy had been temporarily removed in 1923 and reinstated by the army in 1925, but Papandreou, a left-of-centre republican, held office in several administrations including the brief period when the monarchy was temporarily removed (1923–5) and in the following decade. In 1942 he escaped from Greece during the German occupation and returned in 1944 to head a coalition government, but, suspected by the army because of his socialist credentials, remained in office for only a few weeks. He remained an important political figure, founding the Centre Union Party (1961), and returning as Prime Minister (1963 and 1964–5). A disagreement with the young King **CONSTANTINE II** in 1965 led to his resignation, and in 1967, when a coup established a military regime, he was placed under house arrest. His son, Andreas **PAPANDREOU**, was to carry forward his political beliefs.

**Papen, Franz von** (1879–1969)
German politician and Nazi collaborator. He was military attaché in Mexico and Washington, Chief of Staff with a Turkish army, and in 1921 joined the **CENTRE PARTY**. He was Chancellor (1932), playing a major part in undermining the **WEIMAR REPUBLIC**, **HITLER**'s Vice-Chancellor (1933–4), and Ambassador to Austria (1936–8) and Turkey (1939–44). Taken prisoner in 1945, he was acquitted at the **NUREMBERG TRIALS**.

**Papineau, Louis-Joseph** (1786–1871)
French-Canadian politician. The speaker of Lower **CANADA**'s House of Assembly (1815–37), he opposed union with Upper **CANADA**, and agitated for a greater degree of governmental independence from Britain. His leadership of the *Patriotes* during the **REBELLIONS OF 1837** led to charges of treason. He escaped to Paris, but returned to Canada after a general amnesty was granted in 1844.

**PAPUA NEW GUINEA** official name **Independent State of Papua New Guinea**

An independent island group in the south-west Pacific Ocean. Possibly inhabited by South-East Asians

who came to Papua New Guinea via Indonesia many thousands of years ago, it was visited by the Portuguese and the Spanish in the 16c before being colonized by the British and Dutch in the late 18c. In 1884 Britain proclaimed a protectorate in the south-east, while Germany proclaimed the north-east quadrant to be a German protectorate. German New Guinea was established in the north-east in 1899. The German colony was overrun by Australia in **WORLD WAR I**, and in 1920 Australia was mandated to govern the British and German areas. These were combined in 1949 as the **UN** Trust Territory of Papua and New Guinea, which gained independence within the **COMMONWEALTH OF NATIONS** in 1975. The British monarch is head of state, represented by a Governor-General. Border areas are sometimes affected by the overspill from fighting between separatists and government forces in the neighbouring Indonesian province of Irian Jaya. In 1989 fighting began on the island of Bougainville between separatists led by the Bougainville Revolutionary Army and government forces. Fighting lasted until a ceasefire came into effect in 1998, following which further talks led to the signing of a peace agreement in 2001 that provides autonomy for the island.

**PARAGUAY** official name **Republic of Paraguay**

A landlocked country in central South America, bounded to the north-west by Bolivia; to the north and east by Brazil; and to the south-west by Argentina. Originally inhabited by Guaranís, it was settled by the Spanish after 1537, and by Jesuit missionaries who arrived in 1609. It gained independence from Spain in 1811. During the disastrous War of the **TRIPLE ALLIANCE** (1864–70) against Brazil, Argentina and Uruguay, Paraguay lost over half of its population. In 1935 it regained territory disputed with Bolivia after the three-year **CHACO WAR**. Civil war broke out in 1947, and in 1954 General Alfredo **STROESSNER** seized power, with US backing, and was appointed President, but he lost US support over time and was forced to stand down following a coup in 1989. The first multiparty elections, held in 1993, were won by the centre-right National Republican Association-Colorado Party (formerly led by Stroessner) and its candidate, Juan Carlos Wasmosy, became President. The party has won all subsequent elections and retained the presidency, but splits in the party have contributed to the instability that has prevailed since the 1990s, with several attempted coups and widespread corruption.

**Paraguayan War** ► **TRIPLE ALLIANCE, WAR OF THE**

## parcería

The system of 'sharecropping' unsuccessfully attempted by major coffee producers in São Paulo in the 1850s. Immigrants would be contracted to work on *fazendas* against a *'parceria* contract'. These contracts were of two types: those where payment was dependent on the coffee market and those where it was independent of it. In the first case, the profits from the crop were divided; in the second, a price was fixed in advance. The system failed, mainly because *fazendeiros* saw the effective working of a labour market as a threat to their overall control of their fazendas, many of which were not only undivided but also largely worked by slave-labour until 1887–8. The mistreatment of *parceiros* led European governments to discourage, if not prohibit, emigration to Brazil until the 1890s. ➤ **FAZENDA**; **FAZENDEIRO**

## parentela

A term used in Brazil meaning 'extended family', including all relatives (*parentes*) by blood, marriage and ritual, generally living in a number of households. Colloquially, the term is understood as a plethora of obedient kin, and élite *parentelas* have crucial national significance. The practice of endogamous marriage conserved patrimony (especially on *fazendas*) within the family group by preventing the dividing-up of property among legitimate heirs entailed by inheritance laws. *Patria potestas* – the authority of the head of the household – denied wives the right to alienate landed property without their husband's consent. By no means limited to the élite, parentelas explain the preponderance of **CORONELISMO** throughout Brazil, especially in the northeast. ➤ **FAZENDA**

## Paris, Congress of ('1856)

The peace conference which ended the **CRIMEAN WAR**. In the resulting Treaty of Paris (30 Mar 1856), Russia gave up southern Bessarabia (acquired in 1813), which cut her off from the mouth of the River Danube, to Moldavia (now Moldova) and Kars to Turkey. The Straits Convention of 1841, which did not allow any warships to pass through the Bosphorus, was re-affirmed. The most serious clause for Russia was that neutralizing the Black Sea: neither Russia nor Turkey was allowed warships or naval bases there. Russia regarded this as a serious threat to her security in the south, as in wartime British and French warships could rapidly enter an undefended Black Sea. She took advantage of France's defeat in the **FRANCO-PRUSSIAN WAR** (1870–1) to repudiate this clause. Russia also gave up her claim to act as protector of the Orthodox Christians in the **OTTOMAN EMPIRE**, and under **ALEXANDER II** embarked upon its first serious programme of domestic reform.

## Paris, Louis Philippe, Count of (1834–94)

French nobleman, grandson of King **LOUIS-PHILIPPE**, and pretender to the French throne. He returned to France in 1871 and renounced his claim to the throne in favour of the Count of **CHAMBORD**; the latter's death in 1883 made him head of the House of Bourbon. ➤ **BOURBON, HOUSE OF**

## Paris, Pact of (27 Aug 1928) ➤ **KELLOGG–BRIAND PACT**

## Paris, Siege of (1870–1)

The siege of Paris carried out by the Prussian army. Attempts by the **NATIONAL GUARD** from inside the city, and by the new armies raised by **GAMBETTA** south of the River Loire, failed to lift the siege. Food shortages forced the Government of National Defence to ask for an armistice. The hysterical atmosphere of the siege, and the existence of the **NATIONAL GUARD**, which was not disarmed by the terms of the armistice, were important causes of the insurrection of 18 Mar, leading to the **PARIS COMMUNE**. ➤ **NATIONAL DEFENCE, GOVERNMENT OF**

## Paris, Treaties of (1814–15)

Successive peace settlements involving France and the victorious coalition of Britain, Austria, Prussia, Russia, Sweden and Portugal, restoring the Bourbon monarchy to France in place of the Napoleonic Empire, before and after the **HUNDRED DAYS** (1815). In 1815 a large indemnity and army of occupation replaced the generous terms of 1814. ➤ **BOURBON, HOUSE OF**; **NAPOLEONIC WARS**

## Paris, Treaty of (1763)

The peace settlement ending the **SEVEN YEARS' WAR** (1756–63), signed by Britain, France and Spain. Spain surrendered Florida to the British, but received the Louisiana Territory and New Orleans from France, and Havana and Manila from Britain. In exchange for minor concessions, France ceded Canada, America east of the Mississippi, Cape Breton and the St Lawrence Islands, Dominica, Tobago, the Grenadines and Senegal to Britain. In the short term, Britain was isolated by the French determination for revenge, but the final consequence was British colonial supremacy.

## Paris, Treaty of (10 Feb 1947)

This treaty exacted indemnities from nations allied with Germany during **WORLD WAR II**. Italy was obliged to surrender the Dodecanese Islands to Greece.

## Paris Club

An informal group of 19 creditor nations that meets regularly to discuss debt relief and rescheduling for countries with the most intractable debt problems. Founded in 1956 and with headquarters in France, it has no legal status but operates under rules and guidelines which stipulate, for example, that no creditor can profit from debt rescheduling and that relief can only be offered to countries prepared to implement reforms, usually approved by the **IMF**. Although it provides the economic framework for rescheduling debt, each member state must negotiate the particulars bilaterally with the debtor nation. ➤ **THIRD WORLD DEBT**

## Paris Commune (18 Mar–28 May 1871)

An uprising that followed France's humiliating defeat in the **FRANCO-PRUSSIAN WAR** (1870–1). A bungled attempt to disarm the **NATIONAL GUARD** produced an uprising and the election of a municipal council, which took the name of Commune, with its revolutionary associations. The government, headed by the veteran Orléanist **THIERS**, retreated to Versailles, where the monarchist National Assembly refused all compromise, as did the Commune. When a sufficient military force had been assembled, Paris was recaptured with huge loss of life. Members of the National

Guard fighting for the Commune were massacred in thousands, and others were sentenced to long terms of imprisonment, leaving an unprecedented legacy of bitterness. ► ORLÉANISTS

**Paris Pacts** (1954)
A series of amendments and protocols to the Treaty of Brussels and the Brussels Treaty Organization. Italy and the Federal Republic of Germany became members of what became known as the WESTERN EUROPEAN UNION. Germany agreed not to manufacture atomic, bacteriological or chemical weapons, thus clearing the way for its rearmament and membership of NATO.

**Paris Peace Conference** (1919–20)
A meeting of 32 'allied and associated powers' who met in Paris to draw up a peace settlement after WORLD WAR I. Five treaties were concluded: with Germany (Treaty of VERSAILLES, 1919), Austria (Treaty of ST GERMAIN, 1919), Hungary (Treaty of TRIANON, 1920), Bulgaria (Treaty of NEUILLY, 1919) and Turkey (Treaties of Sèvres, 1920, and LAUSANNE, 1923).

**Paris Peace Conference** (1946–7)
Meetings of the five members of the Council of Foreign Ministers representing the main WORLD WAR II allies (USA, Russia, UK, France and China), and delegates from 16 other nations involved against the AXIS POWERS. It drew up peace treaties with Bulgaria, Finland, Hungary, Romania and Italy. Despite repeated divisions, agreement was finally reached and the treaties signed in the spring of 1947.

**Park, Mungo** (1771–1806)
Scottish explorer. He became a surgeon in Edinburgh, and in 1792 served on an expedition to Sumatra. In 1795–6 he made a journey along the Niger River, recounted in *Travels in the Interior of Africa* (1799). He settled as a surgeon in Peebles, Scotland, but in 1805 undertook another journey to the Niger. His expedition reached Boussa, where he was drowned following an attack by natives. ► EXPLORATION

**Park Chung-hee** (1917–79)
South Korean soldier and politician. Educated at a Japanese military academy, he fought with the Japanese forces during WORLD WAR II. Park joined the South Korean army in 1946, becoming a major-general by 1961, when he ousted the civilian government of Chang Myon in a bloodless coup. He formed the Democratic Republican Party (DRP) and was elected state President in Dec 1963. He embarked on an ambitious, and remarkably successful, programme of export-led industrial development, based on strategic government planning and financial support, which attained 'miracle' annual growth rates of 10–20 per cent during the 1960s and 1970s. However, he ruled in an austere and authoritarian manner, imposing martial law (Oct 1972) and introducing restrictive 'emergency measures' (May 1975). In Oct 1979, during a brief economic downturn, he was assassinated by the head of the Korean Central Intelligence Service. ► CHAEBOL

**Parkes, Sir Henry** (1815–96)
Australian politician. He emigrated to New South

Wales in 1839, and became a well-known journalist in Sydney. A member of the colonial parliament in 1854, his early career was interrupted by the financial difficulties that troubled him for most of his life. He was five times Premier of New South Wales between 1872 and 1891. During his last ministry he displayed a new interest in FEDERATION, his speech at Tenterfield (Oct 1889) reviving the question and leading to the Australasian Federation Conference (1890) and the National Australasian Convention in 1891, in which he played a leading role. He was knighted in 1877.

**Parks, Rosa Lee** (1913–)
US CIVIL RIGHTS protester. Her action as a black woman who refused to give up her seat to a white man on a bus in Montgomery, Alabama, led in 1955 to the MONTGOMERY BUS BOYCOTT by the black community. The boycott led to the Supreme Court decision in 1956 that declared bus segregation unconstitutional. Parks became an inspiration to other blacks and a symbol of the non-violent protest advocated by the CIVIL RIGHTS MOVEMENT.

**parlamentarismo**
A political term used in Brazil, which denotes a belief that presidential power should be checked by an executive directly responsible to the lower house of Congress. Since such an executive functioned under the imperial constitution and opponents of Floriano PEIXOTO espoused this ideal, it has largely been seen as conservative. Certainly, politicians from Rio Grande do Sul and Minas Gerais, such as Raúl Pilla and Afonso Arinos de Melo Franco, repeatedly held this sort of viewpoint, especially during the constitutional crisis of the 1960s and the redemocratization of the late 1980s. On the other hand, pragmatists like Tancredo NEVES called for a parliamentary regime as a way of checking chief executives (such as GOULART or SARNEY (COSTA)) and bringing about a CONCILIAÇÃO between the army and civilian politicians. The chaotic experience of 1961–3 indicated to many that political parties lacked the discipline to implement such a system and Sarney managed to prevent the PMDB leadership and the more conservative PSD from imposing it in 1987–8.

**Parlement**
The French court of law in ANCIEN RÉGIME France, originally a single institution, the *Parlement* of Paris, which developed from the medieval king's court or *curia regis*, and subsequently assumed both political and judicial functions. Between the 14c and 17c a network of provincial Parlements emerged, but all were abolished in 1790. In the 18c (especially 1763–89) the Parlements assumed the role of opposition to the monarchy, and as a result were abolished by Maupeou in 1771. Their restoration on the accession of LOUIS XVI in 1774 is often seen as a fatal mistake on the part of the monarchy.

**Parnell, Charles Stewart** (1846–91)
Irish politician. He studied at Cambridge, and in 1875 became an MP, supporting HOME RULE, and gaining great popularity in Ireland by his audacity in the use of obstructive parliamentary tactics. In 1879 he was elected President of the Irish National LAND LEAGUE, and in 1886 allied with the Liberals in support of

GLADSTONE's HOME RULE Bill. He remained an influential figure until 1890, when he was cited as co-respondent in a divorce case, and was forced to retire as leader of the Irish nationalists. ➤ LIBERAL PARTY (UK)

**Parr, Catherine** (1512–48)
Queen of England (1543/7). The daughter of Sir Thomas Parr of Kendal, she married first Edward Borough, then Lord Latimer, before becoming Queen of England (1543), as the sixth wife of HENRY VIII. A learned, tolerant and tactful woman, she persuaded Henry to restore the succession to his daughters, and showed her stepchildren much kindness. Very soon after Henry's death (1547) she married a former suitor, Lord Thomas Seymour of Sudeley, and she died in childbirth the following year.

**Parri, Ferruccio** (1890–1982)
Italian politician. Imprisoned for helping Fillipo TURATI to escape from fascist Italy, he was one of the founders of the PARTY OF ACTION. Briefly Prime Minister in 1945, he remained a constant champion of left-wing cooperation and solidarity throughout the 1950s and 1960s.

**Partai Komunis Indonesia (PKI)**
The Indonesian Communist Party. The mid-1910s saw the establishment of a small social-democratic movement in the Netherlands East Indies, entirely Dutch in its membership. By the beginning of the 1920s, the movement had evolved into a communist organization and the membership had become predominantly Indonesian. It took the name Partai Komunis Indonesia in 1924. In 1926–7 the PKI launched an ill-planned rebellion against the Dutch, and was fiercely crushed, re-emerging as a major political force in 1945, as the Indonesian rebellion against the post-war return of the Dutch got underway. In 1948 elements within the PKI launched a rebellion at Madiun against the republican government. This rebellion was also quelled, leaving the PKI open to the charge that it had threatened the revolution. The PKI rose again in the late 1950s and early 1960s, developing as a very powerful political force in SUKARNO's 'Guided Democracy'. But its power was broken in 1965–6 when, in the aftermath of an attempted coup, hundreds of thousands of PKI members and sympathizers were slaughtered.

**Parthenopean Republic** (1799)
The short-lived satellite republic established in Naples by an uprising assisted by the French revolutionary armies under the control of General Championnet. The republic was brought down by the SANFEDISTI of Cardinal RUFFO. ➤ FERDINAND I; MARIA CAROLINA

**Parti National**
Canadian political party. Originally formed in 1871 by young liberals in Quebec who wished to assert their devotion to the Church, it was revived as an alliance of Liberals and rebel Conservatives who deeply resented the execution of Louis RIEL. Under Honoré MERCIER's leadership, the party managed to oust Quebec's Conservative government in 1886, but scandal brought an early end to its administration in 1891.

**Parti Québecois**
Canadian political party. Formed by LÉVESQUE after the LIBERAL PARTY under LESAGE was defeated in 1966, essentially for refusing to be more nationalistic. The party members (or *Péquistes*) gained support from all classes and from organized labour as well as from the business community. The major aim of the party has been to attain sovereignty-association for Quebec, that is, parity of status with the federal government. The pressure for this, however, has had to be balanced against the wish of the majority of Québecois to remain within Canada. As a result, the parliamentary party lost the support of its more radical *indépendentistes* in 1984. It was swept from power in the 1985 elections but returned to favour with the rise of separatism in the 1990s and formed a government after winning the 1994 provincial election, remaining in office until 2003. In 1995 it issued another referendum to gauge popular feeling over secession from Canada, and the proposal was rejected by only a very narrow margin. ➤ SÉPARATISME

**Party Cadres** (post-1920)
Highly trained, dedicated communist or communist-model party functionaries whose task was to win and maintain support for policies decided from above and to ensure absolute party loyalty. STALIN developed the idea during his rise to power in the 1920s and was fond of saying that 'cadres decide everything'. They became somewhat less important in the more sophisticated society of the 1970s and 1980s, and in the 1990s in China some were accused of misuse of public funds and corruption.

**Party Congress** (post-1898)
The supreme policy-making body of Soviet and other communist-model parties. The first to meet was that of the All-Russian Social Democratic Party in Minsk in 1898. The second was in Brussels and London in 1903 and witnessed the split between the BOLSHEVIKS and the MENSHEVIKS. At the seventh in 1918 the party changed its name to Communist Party. From then until the 16th in 1930, Soviet Party Congresses saw genuine and often fierce debates. STALIN summoned only three between 1934 and 1952, using them to rubber-stamp his policies. Nikita KHRUSHCHEV used the 20th in 1956 to attack the dead Stalin and begin a very slow process of reform; but Leonid BREZHNEV again made them dull adulatory performances. Mikhail GORBACHEV used the 27th in 1986 to launch his more rapid reform programme. The 29th, scheduled for the autumn of 1991 and intended to radicalize the Soviet party, never met; the party had already been abolished following the failed AUGUST COUP. The experience of most East European communist-model parties was similar.

**Party of Action** (*Partito d'Azione*)
The underground Italian anti-fascist movement founded in July 1942, formed of a broad coalition of left-wing liberals, republicans and radicals, most of whom came from the educated and professional classes. The *Azionisti* remained outside both the 'United Freedom Front' established by BONOMI and its successors, the COMMITTEES OF NATIONAL LIBERATION (CLNs). It was, however, actively involved in the creation of local CLNs and fiercely supported the COMMITTEE FOR THE LIBERATION OF UPPER

ITALY: in Nov 1944 it published an open letter to other anti-fascist parties urging the strengthening of both as instruments of popular democracy. The Action Party played a key role in the anti-German risings in the north of Italy in Apr 1944, but was too radical and idealistic to win substantial electoral support after the end of the war. Among the most prominent *Azionisti* was Ferruccio PARRI.

## pasdaran

A name applied since 1979 to the revolutionary guards of the Islamic Republic of Iran. ► IRANIAN REVOLUTION

## Pašić, Nikola (c.1846–1926)

Serbian politician. He was condemned to death in 1883 for his part in the plot against King MILAN OBRENOVIĆ, but survived to be Prime Minister of Serbia (five times, from 1891) and later of Yugoslavia (1921–4 and 1924–6), which he helped to found.

## Paskevich, Ivan Feodorovich (1782–1856)

Russian general. He served against the French in 1805, and against the Turks, and took a prominent part in the campaign of 1812. In 1827, conquering Persian Armenia and taking Yerevan, he was made Count of Yerevan; in 1828–9 he made two campaigns against the Turks in Asia, taking Kars and Erzerum. In 1831 he suppressed the rising in Poland, and was made Prince of Warsaw. Under his governorship Poland was incorporated with Russia (1832). In 1848, sent to the support of Austria, he defeated the insurgent Hungarians. In 1854 he commanded the Russian army on the Danube, was wounded at Silistria and retired to Warsaw, where he later died. A loyal imperial servant and trusted by NICHOLAS I, he was typical of those who helped to expand Russia territorially and to suppress it politically.

## PASOK (*Panellinion Socialistikou Kinema*, 'Panhellenic Socialist Movement')

Established in 1974 under the leadership of Andreas PAPANDREOU, its original programme was based on socialization, decentralization and worker self-management. In foreign policy it advocates neutrality: it opposed Greece's entry into the EEC (1979); it remains hostile to NATO, and is opposed to the establishment of US military bases in Greece. It first came to power in the 1981 election, when Papandreou became Greece's first socialist Prime Minister. PASOK was voted out of office in 1989 but returned in 1993. Papandreou was succeeded as PASOK leader and Prime Minister in 1996 by Constantine ('Costas') Simitis, who led the party to two more election victories before resigning in Jan 2004. His replacement as leader was George Papandreou, son of Andreas, but even the power of that name could not prevent PASOK losing the election a few months later.

## Passarowitz, Treaty of (1718)

The treaty signed at Požarevac in modern Serbia which established peace after the Austro-Turkish and Venetian-Turkish wars (1716–18). Venice surrendered the Morea to the Ottomans, while the Habsburg Emperor gained Belgrade and parts of liberated Serbia, Oltenia and the Banat of TEMESVÁR. The subjects of the Emperor also gained favourable terms for trade within the OTTOMAN EMPIRE.

## Passau, Treaty of (1552)

The treaty forced upon Emperor CHARLES V by the rebellion of MAURICE, Elector of Saxony. Charles V had to acknowledge the position of Lutheranism in the HOLY ROMAN EMPIRE. It marked the effective failure of his plan to reintroduce Catholicism to the empire by force of arms.

## Passchendaele, Battle of (31 July–10 Nov 1917)

The third battle of Ypres during WORLD WAR I; a British offensive which was continued despite no hope of a breakthrough to the Belgian ports, the original objective. It was notable for appallingly muddy conditions, minimal gains, and British casualties of at least 300,000. In the final action, Canadians captured the village of Passchendaele, six miles north-east of Ypres.

## Pasternak, Boris Leonidovich (1890–1960)

Russian poet, translator and novelist. Before and after the 1917 RUSSIAN REVOLUTION he established his reputation as a poet. It was because of political pressure during the STALIN years that he became the official translator into Russian of several major authors, such as Shakespeare, Verlaine and Goethe. His major work, *Dr Zhivago* (completed in 1956), caused a political furore and was banned in the USSR, but was an international success after its publication in Italy in 1957. Expelled by the Soviet Writers' Union, he was compelled to refuse the Nobel Prize for Literature in 1958. *Dr Zhivago* was finally published in the USSR in 1988, a clear indication of how Mikhail GORBACHEV had changed official attitudes.

## Pasvanoglu, Osman Pasha (1758–1807)

Balkan rebel leader. He was one of the most important rebel bandit leaders in the Balkans during the late 18c. In 1795 he declared himself and his lands independent from the Sultan. From his base at Vidin on the Danube he waged a constant rebellion against the Ottoman Porte and gained control of extensive territories in the area of modern Bulgaria and Romania.

## Patel, Vallabhbhai Jhaverbhai, also called Sardar (1875–1950)

Indian politician and lawyer. A Gujarati peasant leader, described as M K GANDHI's right-hand man. By background a staunch Hindu, conservative and broadly identified with the interests of the business community, he was a lawyer by training and began his political career after being elected as a municipal councillor in Ahmadabad (1917). Soon after, he joined the Gujarat Sabha, a political body of great assistance to M K Gandhi during his political campaigns. Patel distinguished himself during India's independence struggle by his leading role in the Kheda peasants' SATYAGRAHA (1918) and the Bardoli Satyagraha (1928), both launched in opposition to the colonial government's attempts to raise the land tax on peasant farmers. Following the successful conclusion of these campaigns, he was given the honorific title Sardar ('Leader') by Gandhi. He joined the Salt Satyagraha of 1930, the individual CIVIL DISOBEDIENCE movement of 1940–1 and the QUIT INDIA MOVEMENT of 1942, following each of which he spent long periods in prison. A great party organizer, he was also, along with Jawaharlal NEHRU, a key negotiator on behalf of the **INDIAN NATIONAL CONGRESS** during the talks leading to the transfer of power from the British in 1947. As Deputy Prime Minister of independent India, Patel assumed responsibility for the Indian States as well as Home Affairs and Information and Broadcasting, and was responsible for persuading, or coercing, the nominally independent Indian **PRINCELY STATES** into joining the Indian Union soon after independence. In tackling these and many other problems of post-partition India, he acted with thoroughness and ruthless efficiency.

**Pathet Lao**
Laotian nationalist movement (literally, 'Land of Lao') founded in 1950. In alliance with the **VIET MINH** of North Vietnam, it employed armed resistance to French rule in Indochina. After the country's civil war, the movement (officially renamed the Lao People's Liberation Army in Oct 1965), took part in the coalition government set up in 1974; early the following year it assumed effective control of the country. In Dec 1975 it abolished the monarchy in Vientiane and made its leader, Prince **SOUPHANOUVONG**, President of the newly proclaimed Lao People's Democratic Republic.

**Patiño, José** (1667–1736)
Spanish politician. Chief Minister of Spain in 1726–36, he rose to prominence during the War of the **SPANISH SUCCESSION**. In 1726 he was Minister of the Navy and Finance, and subsequently took charge of War (1730) and Foreign Affairs (1733), an area he had in practice controlled for some time. The first notable minister of the Bourbon monarchy in Spain, Patiño's efforts were centred on three fields: the armed forces, the economy and foreign policy. His lasting achievement was the creation of the Spanish navy. He pursued the interests of the royal family in Italy, particularly the rights of Elizabeth Farnese's son, Don Carlos, to the Duchy of Parma (1731). Thanks to the first Family Pact (1733), which ensured agreement between the Bourbon states of France and Spain against Austria, Spanish forces ensured the succession (1734) of Carlos to the Kingdom of Naples. Spain was obliged, however, to cede Parma to Austria, a failure which was severely criticized in Madrid, where a pamphlet war was unleashed against the minister and embittered his last years. ➤ **BOURBON, HOUSE OF**

**Patiño, Simón Ituri** (1862–1947)
Bolivian industrialist and diplomat. He developed Bolivia's tin mines, and by the early 1900s controlled over half of the country's tin production, making himself a vast fortune. He was influential in government circles, and served as ambassador to Spain (1920–6) and France (1926–41). Though he allegedly financed the Bolivian war against Paraguay in 1932–5, he was criticized for not investing his wealth in Bolivia itself.

**Patriarchate of Moscow, Establishment of** (1589)
The establishment of the Patriarchate was one of the most significant achievements of **BORIS GODUNOV**, acting as regent for the young Tsar Theodore. He obtained the consent of Jeremiah the Patriarch of Constantinople, and all the Eastern Patriarchs in effect to upgrade the **RUSSIAN ORTHODOX CHURCH** and to make it the symbol and support of Moscow and Tsarism. This not only contributed in due course to ending the **TIME OF TROUBLES**, it was the base upon which the **ROMANOV DYNASTY** duly built.

**Patriot Act** (2001)
A controversial piece of US legislation signed by President George W **BUSH** in Oct 2001 in the wake of the **SEPTEMBER 11 ATTACKS**. A complex act incorporating provisions of earlier anti-terrorist legislation, it was passed through Congress in a matter of weeks without the normal procedural processes. Although it contains provisions colloquially known as 'sunset clauses' for sections of the Act to be reviewed and amended or deleted in 2006, the new powers it granted to the **FBI** and **CIA** were criticized for being without the usual legal checks and balances; by Jan 2004, one section had been ruled unconstitutional. An attempt in 2003 to extend the provisions of the Act even further and on a permanent basis by a Patriot Act II provoked such a violent outcry that the legislation proved abortive, but it has been alleged that some of that Act's more controversial proposals were smuggled through Congress in the nominally fiscal Intelligence Authorization Act 2004. ➤ **TERROR, WAR ON**

**Patriotic Front (PF)**
A Zimbabwean movement formed by the merging of the Zimbabwe African National Union (**ZANU**), led by Robert **MUGABE**, and the Zimbabwe African People's Union (**ZAPU**), led by Joshua **NKOMO**, in 1976. It was intended to unite the major exiled nationalist movements in a concerted opposition, both political and military, to Ian **SMITH**'s white minority regime. In the elections held under the Lancaster House Agreement in 1980 the PF won an overwhelming victory In the post-independence period, however, the Front broke up when Nkomo, whose principal power base was among the **NDEBELE** people in **MATABELELAND**, and Mugabe, who represented the majority Shona people, became estranged. Later they were reconciled as moves were made to create a one-party state.

**Patriot Movement**
A late 18c Dutch political movement that called for a role for the wealthy middle classes in politics, until then dominated by patricians and aristocrats. Reliant on rationalism and other **ENLIGHTENMENT** ideologies, the Patriots can be seen as the Dutch version of the French revolutionaries, and as the precursors of Dutch liberals. They took the name 'Patriot' from their insistence that policy should benefit the entire nation (*patria*), rather than just the élite classes. Their efforts were directed against the government of the **STADHOLDER**; one of the main activists was Joan Derk van der **CAPELLEN TOT DEN POLL**. In the confusion after the fourth of the **ANGLO-DUTCH WARS** (1780–4), the Patriots gained a measure of political power in certain regions; in 1787 **WILLIAM V** was restored to power with Prussian military help. The Patriots fled to France, returned with the French revolutionary troops in 1795, and played a significant role in several of the governments of the French period (1795–1814), notably the **BATAVIAN REPUBLIC**.

**Patrons of Husbandry** ➤ **GRANGER MOVEMENT**

**Patton, George Smith**, also called **Old Blood and Guts** (1885–1945)
US general. Patton trained at the US Military Academy at West Point and became one of the most daring and flamboyant US combat commanders in **WORLD WAR II**. An excellent strategist and proponent of mobile tank warfare, he played a key role in the Allied invasion of North Africa (1942–3), led the US 7th Army in its assault on Sicily (1943), commanded the 3rd Army in the invasion of France, and contained the German counter-offensive in the Ardennes (1944). He was fatally injured in a motor accident near Mannheim, and died at Heidelberg. ► **BULGE, BATTLE OF THE**; **NORMANDY CAMPAIGN**

**Pauker, Ana** (1893–1960)
Romanian politician. The daughter of a Moldavian rabbi, she joined the Social Democrat Party in 1915 and took part in revolutionary movements in Romania (1917–18). She married Marcel Pauker (1920) and with him joined the Communist Party, becoming a member of the Central Committee in 1922. She was arrested in 1925, but escaped to the USSR where she worked for **COMINTERN**. She returned to Romania in 1934 and was again arrested. A 'Moscow communist' who spent **WORLD WAR II** in the USSR, she returned home after the overthrow of Ion **ANTONESCU** (Sep 1944). Summoned to Moscow with **GHEORGIU-DEJ** (Jan 1945), she was instructed by **STALIN** to establish a government under the control of the National Democratic Front, the communist front in Romania. She entered the Foreign Ministry in 1947 and took part in organizing the collectivization of all land. With Stalin's consent, she was relieved of her offices in 1952.

**Paul, Alice** (1885–1977)
US feminist. Involved with the British suffragette movement while living in England, on her return to the USA (1912) she became the leader of the **NATIONAL AMERICAN WOMAN SUFFRAGE ASSOCIATION** (NAWSA) congressional committee and organized a march of several thousand women in Washington (1913). Although her tactics generated much publicity, they proved too militant for most members of NAWSA and she left the organization to found the National Women's Party. After the Nineteenth Amendment (1920) gave women the right to vote, she turned her efforts to working for other **WOMEN'S RIGHTS**. ► **PANKHURST, EMMELINE**; **SUFFRAGETTES**

**Paul I** (1754–1801)
Emperor of Russia (1796/1801). He was the second son of **PETER III** and **CATHERINE II, THE GREAT**. A man of highly unstable temperament, he reversed many of his mother's policies (and, in time, many of his own), thereby arousing hostility from the nobility and army. His foreign policy, first attacking and then supporting France, won him considerable military successes but led to Russia's isolation. His officers conspired against him, and he was assassinated in St Petersburg, being succeeded by his son, **ALEXANDER I**.

**Paul I** (1901–64)
King of Greece (1947/64). In 1922 he served with the Greek navy against the Turks; but in 1924, when a republic was proclaimed, went into exile. In 1935 he returned to Greece as Crown Prince. In **WORLD WAR II** he served with the Greek general staff in the Albanian campaign, and was in exile in London (1941–6). His reign covered the latter half of the **GREEK CIVIL WAR** and its difficult aftermath; during the early 1960s his personal role, and that of his wife Queen Frederika, became sources of bitter political controversy.

**Paul III**, originally **Alessandro Farnese** (1468–1549)
Italian pope (1534/49). The first of the popes of the **COUNTER-REFORMATION**, in 1538 he issued the bull of excommunication and deposition against **HENRY VIII** of England, and also the bull instituting the Order of the Jesuits in 1540. He also summoned the Council of **TRENT** (1545).

**Paul IV**, originally **Giampietro Carafa** (1476–1559)
Italian pope (1555/9). As a bishop, he showed rigorous opposition to heresy and was instrumental in the re-establishment of the **INQUISITION** in Rome and Italy. As pope, he sought to enforce discipline among the clergy, established censorship and a full *Index* of forbidden books. His Neapolitan origins helped to make him ferocious in his hatred of things Spanish. He was an opponent of the Jesuits, and declared war on Emperor **CHARLES V** in 1555 on the grounds that the Emperor could not abdicate his title without papal permission. Defensive of papal authority, he was also opposed to a reconvening of the Council of **TRENT**.

**Paul V**, originally **Camillo Borghese** (1552–1621)
Italian pope (1605/21). He became nuncio in Spain and cardinal prior to his election as pope. In 1606 he issued a decree of excommunication against the Doge and Senate of Venice, and placed the republic under Interdict. The crisis, and the fierce anti-papal propaganda of the Venetian Paolo Sarpi, prompted the English ambassador to suggest that Venice might become a Protestant state, but it ended in a messy compromise.

**Paul Karageorgević** (1893–1976)
Prince Regent of Yugoslavia (1934/41). The son of Arsen and brother of King **PETER I KARAGEORGEVIĆ**, he became regent for King **PETER II** of Yugoslavia after the assassination of the latter's father, King **ALEXANDER I**. Although he upheld the constitution of the previous dictatorial regime, his regency marked the beginning of a more relaxed period in the government of Yugoslavia. He worked closely with **STOJADINOVIĆ** and his right-wing party, the Yugoslav Radical Union (1935–9), and with **CVETKOVIĆ** and **MAČEK** played a leading role in bringing about the **SPORAZUM** (1939). In foreign affairs he developed relations with Germany and Italy so that at the outbreak of **WORLD WAR II** Yugoslavia, although officially neutral, was in the Axis camp. After signing the Tripartite Pact with **HITLER** and Benito **MUSSOLINI**, the regency was overthrown in a coup led by General Dušan Simović (Mar 1941). He left Yugoslavia for Kenya and later settled in Paris.

**Paulus, Friedrich** (1890–1957)
German field marshal and tank specialist. He capitulated to the Soviets with the remnants of his army at the siege of Stalingrad in 1943. Released from captivity in 1953, he became a lecturer on military affairs under the East German government. ► **STALINGRAD, BATTLE OF**; **WORLD WAR II**

**Pavel, Josef** (1908–73)
Czechoslovak soldier, politician and reformer. Joining the Communist Party in the depression in 1929, he studied with the COMINTERN in Moscow in 1935–7, fought in the SPANISH CIVIL WAR in 1937–8 and in the West in 1939–45. He then rose to be commander of the people's militia that gave their backing to the FEBRUARY REVOLUTION (1948) and acted as deputy to the Minister of the Interior until his arrest (1950). Because of his service in the West he was viewed as suspect by the puppets who did STALIN's dirty work in Prague and was sentenced to 25 years in prison. Released in 1955, he did little until he became Minister of the Interior during the PRAGUE SPRING. His attempt to make the political police responsible won him enemies and soon after the Soviet invasion he was dismissed. Experiences such as his were one of the ingredients that made for the revulsion against COMMUNISM expressed in Europe in 1989.

**Pavelić, Ante** (1889–1959)
Croatian fascist leader. A member of the extreme nationalist wing of the Croatian Party of Right (ie state-right) established by STARČEVIĆ, he left Yugoslavia for Italy where, with Benito MUSSOLINI's support, he organized the USTAŠA, the Croatian fascist movement. Chosen by Mussolini to run the puppet-government of the Independent State of Croatia (1941–5), he instituted a reign of terror. At the end of the war, he escaped with the retreating German army and settled in Argentina.

**Pavia, Battle of** (1525)
A Habsburg victory over French forces laying siege to Pavia during the ITALIAN WARS. The assailants were commanded by FRANCIS I of France, and taken prisoner after an abortive French cavalry attack on the garrison. The defeat temporarily checked the French threat in Italy, which had seen them take Milan in 1524. ► HABSBURG DYNASTY

**Pawnee**
A Native American people, members of the Caddoan linguistic group, who migrated from south-eastern Texas to the Platte River in Nebraska, and lived in permanent villages there from the 16c to the late 19c. They acquired horses in the 17c and 18c, and became seasonal buffalo hunters. Although they fought many of the PLAINS INDIANS, they had peaceful relations with the whites and served as scouts for the US Army. They gradually gave up their lands in Nebraska during the 19c (the last in 1876) and moved to Oklahoma, where in 2000 there were around 3,000 Pawnee living on or near their reservation. ► NATIVE AMERICANS

**Paxton Boys Massacre** (14 Dec 1763)
The murder at Lancaster County jail of seven men, five women and eight children of the Christian Conestoga Native American tribe by a group of 57 Scots-Irish frontiersmen from Paxton, Pennsylvania, led by Lazarus Stewart. Although the murderers' main motive was to avenge the deaths of fellow whites in PONTIAC'S CONSPIRACY, the incident was symptomatic of growing antagonism between NATIVE AMERICANS and white settlers, and of the frontiersmen's need for defence and for political representation of their grow-

ing colonies. Following the massacre, in Jan 1764 a group of 600 armed frontiersmen marched on Philadelphia where they were placated by Benjamin FRANKLIN and others who offered them an official hearing of their grievances. None of the Paxton Boys was ever tried for the massacre.

**Paz Estenssoro, Víctor** (1907–2001)
Bolivian revolutionary and politician. He was the founder of the left-wing *Movimiento Nacionalista Revolucionario* (MNR, 'National Revolutionary Movement') in 1941, going on to become its principal leader. Following the 1952 revolution, he served as President (1952–6) and held office again from 1960 to 1964, when he was ousted by a military coup. He went into exile in Peru, returning to Bolivia in 1971 as an adviser to the government of President Hugo Banzer Suárez. He failed to win election in 1979, but in 1985, after no candidate managed to achieve a majority, Congress elected him President. His main achievement in office (1985–9) was to reduce the raging inflation that had crippled Bolivia's economy.

**Pazmany, Peter, Cardinal Archbishop** (1570–1637)
Hungarian religious leader. Born into a Protestant family, he became a Jesuit and was elevated to the archbishopric of Esztergom in 1616. He helped convert many of his fellow nobles, and during the THIRTY YEARS' WAR he steadily supported the Austrian Habsburg cause in Europe. His religious writings were very influential, as was the university he founded at Nagyszombal, north-west of Estergom, in 1635. ► HABSBURG DYNASTY

**PCE** (*Partido Comunista de España*, 'Spanish Communist Party')
Established in 1920, the PCE was of little significance in the 1920s. Under the Second Republic of 1931–6 it played a minor role in the Asturias rising of Oct 1934 and, as part of the Popular Front coalition, won a total of 16 parliamentary seats in the Feb 1936 general election. However, once the SPANISH CIVIL WAR broke out, the PCE soon became the dominant force in the Republic. This was because the USSR, in the absence of support from Britain and France, was the Republic's principal backer. The Communists opposed all other tendencies within the Republican camp, partly in order to meet the needs of STALIN's foreign policy, and partly because of its authoritarian nature. This policy culminated in the May Days of 1937, when the CNT and POUM were defeated by the Communists. Under the FRANCO dictatorship (1939–75), the PCE emerged as the leading opposition force, due in great measure to the CCOO (*Comisiones Obreras*). After Franco, the party failed to capitalize on its widespread support during the last years of the regime, despite evolving from neo-Stalinism to, in 1978, EUROCOMMUNISM. Having won 23 seats in the 1979 election, it was reduced to a mere four in 1982. The PCE subsequently split into various factions, the official party forming the backbone of the *Izquierda Unida* ('United Left') coalition. ► PSOE; REPUBLIC, SECOND (Spain)

**PCI** (*Partito Comunista Italiano*, 'Italian Communist Party')
Established in 1921 after the split in the socialist ranks that followed the decision of the majority to

join the Third International, the party was driven underground during the fascist regime. However, at the end of **WORLD WAR II** it emerged as the most active force in the resistance, dominating the partisan struggle against the Germans and the Republic of **SALÒ**. Under the leadership of **TOGLIATTI**, it initially sought to work together with the other anti-fascist parties but found itself increasingly at loggerheads with the **CHRISTIAN DEMOCRATIC PARTY**. It remained, however, consistently the second-biggest party in parliament, reaching its pinnacle under the leadership of **BERLINGUER** during the 1970s. In the course of the 1980s it declined, losing direction completely with the collapse of Eastern European **COMMUNISM** after 1989. It changed its name in 1991 to *Partito Democratico della Sinistra* (PDS, 'Democratic Party of the Left'), with a more militant splinter group calling itself *Rifondazione Comunista*. Although both performed poorly in the Apr 1992 elections, the PDS emerged as Italy's largest party and came to power in 1996 at the head of the 'Olive Tree' coalition led by centrist Romano Prodi. In 1998 the PDS, along with various smaller parties, formed *Democratici di Sinistra* (DS, 'Democrats of the Left'), and members of the *Rifondazione Comunista* formed a new Italian Communist Party (PdCI).

**PDS** (*Partido Democrático Social*, 'Social Democratic Party')

The heir to a long tradition of Brazilian conservatism, the immediate progenitor of this party was the UDN (*União Democrática Nacional*) formed in 1945 to challenge the power of Getúlio **VARGAS**, and it is arguably the descendant of the Brazilian Empire's Liberal Party (1831–89). The UDN had conspired with the army to break the natural majority achieved by the PDS and PTB (*Partido Trabalhista Brasileiro*), which were both Vargas's creations, in the 1950s; it supported **CASTELO BRANCO** in 1964 and in 1965 united with a conservative PDS faction to form the ARENA (*Aliança Renovadora Nacional*) Party. The Figueiredo government's attempt (1979–85) to reshuffle political groupings to divide the opposition created the PDS, in turn, as the successor to ARENA. The PDS became notorious as the personal vehicle for wealthy beneficiaries of the military regime, such as Paulo Salim Maluf, whose bid for the presidency divided the party in 1985, forcing a major faction to form the PFL (*Partido do Frente Liberal*). Ostracized during the mid-1980s, the PDS formed part of the conservative coalition supporting President **COLLOR DE MELLO**, but ceased to exist from 1993 as it merged with the PDC (*Partido Democrata Cristão*) to form the PPR (*Partido Progressista Reformador*), which in turn merged with the PP (*Partido Progressista*) in 1995 to form the PPB (*Partido Progressista Brasiliero*).

**Peabody, George** (1795–1869)

US merchant, financier and philanthropist. Born in South Danvers, Massachusetts, now called Peabody, he became a partner in a Baltimore dry-goods store in 1815. In 1837 he established himself in London as a merchant and banker, raising loans for US causes. In his lifetime he gave away a fortune for philanthropic purposes. He endowed the Peabody Institutes in Baltimore and Peabody, and the Peabody Museums at Yale and Harvard. He also set up the Peabody Educa-

tion Fund for the promotion of education in the southern USA, and built working men's tenements in London.

**Peace Constitution** (1947)

The name given to the post-**WORLD WAR II** Japanese constitution that replaced the authoritarian **MEIJI CONSTITUTION** (1889). Based on the draft imposed (Feb 1946) on the Japanese cabinet by US occupation authorities, the constitution attributed sovereignty to the people rather than the Emperor, who was now to be considered merely as a symbol of state. (In Jan 1946 **HIROHITO** had renounced his divinity.) In contrast to the 1889 constitution, an elected bicameral Diet, to which cabinets were collectively responsible, was to be the sole law-making organ of the state; furthermore, the lower house (House of Representatives) clearly had precedence over the upper house (House of Councillors) since it could override any veto by the upper house by repassing a disputed bill by a two-thirds majority. Prime ministers were to be chosen by the Diet (and hence the majority party), thus enshrining the principle of party government so fiercely opposed by governing élites in the pre-war period, while most cabinet ministers had to be both civilians and members of the Diet. The constitution also provided for an extensive guarantee of **CIVIL RIGHTS** and freedoms (including women's suffrage), which could not be limited by law. The most controversial aspect of the constitution was Article 9 (Peace Clause), which renounced war as a sovereign right of the nation and provided for permanent disarmament. Subsequent interpretations of this article, however, led to the creation of the Self-Defence Forces, an army in all but name, to be used solely for defence of the homeland. The constitution could be amended by a two-thirds majority of both houses followed by approval from a majority of voters. It was formally promulgated by Emperor Hirohito on 3 Nov 1946 and came into effect on 3 May 1947. The constitution has never been amended.

**Peace Corps**

A corps of volunteers created during the Kennedy administration in 1961 to assist and educate people in developing countries. In 1966 alone there were over 15,000 volunteers working in 52 countries, and by 1993 over 135,000 volunteers had worked in over 100 countries. The volunteers are assigned to tasks according to their skills, given about three months' training, and expected to work in their designated country for two years. The programme concentrates on education, health, agriculture and public works, and emphasizes self-sufficiency. ► **KENNEDY, JOHN F**

**Peace Preservation Laws**

The repressive legislation in pre-**WORLD WAR II** Japan that sought to clamp down on all strands of dissident thought. The first Peace Preservation Law was passed in 1887 to restrict the activities of the **FREEDOM AND PEOPLE'S RIGHTS MOVEMENT**, and led to the arrest and internal exile of many activists calling for the election of a national assembly. The Peace Preservation Law of 1925 outlawed any association calling for an alteration of the **KOKUTAI** ('national essence') or denying the system of private property. Although the law was applied to both rightists and leftists, it was primarily used to detain suspected communists, of whom 66,000 were arrested between 1928 and 1941. The law was repealed in Oct 1945.

**Pearl Harbor**
US naval base on the island of Oahu, Hawaii. On 7 Dec 1941, the bombing of the base by the Japanese, before any declaration of war, brought the USA into **WORLD WAR II**. Nineteen US ships were sunk or disabled in the surprise attack, and over 2,000 lives were lost.

**Pearse, Patrick (Pádraic) Henry** (1879–1916)
Irish writer, educationist and nationalist. A barrister, he was a leader of the Gaelic League, and editor of its journal. Having commanded the insurgents in the **EASTER RISING** (1916), he was proclaimed President of the Provisional Government. After the revolt had been quelled, he was court-martialled and shot, along with his brother, William.

**Pearson, Lester Bowles** (1897–1972)
Canadian politician. Educated in Toronto and at Oxford, he was leader of the Canadian delegation to the **UN**, becoming President of the General Assembly in 1952–3. Secretary of State for External Affairs (1948–57), his efforts to resolve the **SUEZ CRISIS** were rewarded with the **NOBEL PEACE PRIZE** in 1957. As Prime Minister (1963–8), he introduced a comprehensive pension plan, socialized medicine and sought solutions to the growing separatist feeling in Quebec. ► **BILINGUALISM AND BICULTURALISM, ROYAL COMMISSION ON**

**Peasants' Land Bank** (1883)
The Russian government bank intended to help free peasants or communes to buy land in order to produce a peasantry loyal to the existing order. It was established by the Minister of Finance, Nikolai **BUNGE** and was, comparatively speaking, so successful during its first two years that a Nobles' Land Bank also had to be instituted, with a lower rate of interest, to prevent impoverished aristocrats losing too much of their land. The Peasants' Bank was even more successful after the Russian **REVOLUTION OF 1905**, once the peasants were wholly free. It loaned almost five times as much in the following decade as in the previous two.

**Peasants' Revolt** (June 1381)
An English popular rising, among townsmen as well as peasants, based in Essex, Kent and London, with associated insurrections elsewhere. It was precipitated by the three oppressive poll taxes of 1377–81, the underlying causes being misgovernment, the desire for personal freedom, and an assortment of local grievances. It was quickly suppressed. ► **POLL TAX**

**Peasants' War** (1524–5)
Probably the largest peasant uprising in European history, raging through Germany, from the Rhineland to Pomerania. It sought to defend traditional agrarian rights against lords and princes, and appealed to notions of divine law fostered by the Lutheran **REFORMATION**. It was denounced by **LUTHER**, and brutally suppressed by the princes.

**Peć, Patriarchate of**
The seat of the Serbian Orthodox Church was moved c.1345 from Žiča to Peć in modern **KOSOVO**. It remained there after the Ottoman conquest of Serbia (1389) until Sultan Mustafa III abolished the Serbian Patriarchate (1766), at which point the Serbian Church fell under the control of the Greek **PHANARIOTS**. The Sultan restored the autonomy of the Serbian Orthodox Church in 1830 when Serbia was established as an autonomous state. ► **BULGARIAN EXARCHATE; CONSTANTINOPLE, PATRIARCHATE OF; SAVA, ST**

**Pedro I** (1798–1834)
First Emperor of Brazil (1822/31). Born in Lisbon, he was the second son of John VI of Portugal. He fled to Brazil with his parents on **NAPOLEON I**'s invasion, and became Prince Regent there when his father returned to Portugal (1821). Liberal in outlook, he declared for Brazilian independence in 1822, and was crowned as Pedro I. His failure to hold Montevideo, Brazilian fears for his involvement in Portugal after the death of his father, and the army's defeat in the **ARGENTINE-BRAZILIAN WAR** (1825–8) all contributed to his abdication in favour of his son, **PEDRO II**, on 7 Apr 1831. He withdrew to Portugal, having become Pedro IV of Portugal on the death of his father (1826). He abdicated the Portuguese throne in favour of his daughter, **MARIA II DA GLORIA**, within months and died in Lisbon.

**Pedro II** (1825–91)
Emperor of Brazil (1831/89). The son of **PEDRO I**, he came to the throne as a minor following his father's abdication, and assumed full power in 1840. His reign is generally divided into a period of consolidation (1831–49), **CONCILIAÇÃO** (1850–68) and decline (1868–89). By supporting, in turn, Liberal and Conservative governments (he presided over almost 40 cabinets during his reign), he exercised a moderating influence. Gradualist in the extreme, he manipulated the system of patronage to achieve the consolidation of the empire and to implement strategic reforms, including the emancipation of slaves. The two regencies of his daughter, Izabel, in 1871–2 and 1887–8 witnessed the passage through parliament of the first emancipation law and the abolition of **SLAVERY**. In Nov 1889 he was toppled by a military coup against the reform cabinet of Ouro Prêto, and went into exile, dying in Paris.

**Pedro the Cruel** (1334–69)
King of Castile and Leon (1349/69). The attempts of both Pedro and his father, Alfonso XI, to assert strong monarchic government aroused resentment among the nobility, who found a leader in Pedro's illegitimate brother, Henry of Trastámara. A revolt in 1354 was suppressed and Henry fled to France, but returned in 1366 with French and Aragonese support. With the help of **EDWARD, THE BLACK PRINCE**, Pedro defeated his rival at Najera (1367) but, after Edward's departure from Spain, Pedro was finally routed and killed by Henry at Montiel (1369).

**Peel, Sir Robert** (1788–1850)
British politician. He became a Tory MP in 1809. He was made Secretary for Ireland (1812–18), where he displayed a strong anti-Catholic spirit, and was fiercely attacked by **O'CONNELL**, earning the nickname 'Orange Peel'. As Home Secretary (1822–7 and 1828–30), he carried through the **CATHOLIC EMANCIPATION** Act (1829) and reorganized the London police force ('Peelers' or 'Bobbies'). As Prime Minister

(1834–5 and 1841–6), his second ministry concentrated upon economic reforms, but his decision to phase out agricultural protection by repealing the CORN LAWS (1846) split his party and precipitated his resignation. He remained in parliament as leader of the 'Peelites' (1846–50). ▶ TORIES; WHIGS

## Peel Commission

The report of this commission (issued 7 July 1937) is famous (or notorious) for being the first formal recommendation of the partition of PALESTINE into separate states, Arab and Jewish, with the retention by the British of a corridor to the Mediterranean. Serious rioting by the Arabs, directed against the Jews, had led Stanley BALDWIN, the British Prime Minister, to appoint a royal commission to enquire into the working of the British mandate under the chairmanship of Earl Peel. Despite the commission's evident recognition that there was an intractable problem in Palestine (a situation which had been foreseen by Henry King and Charles Crane nearly two decades before) and their earnest endeavour to find a solution of some sort, the commission's recommendations found favour with only some Arabs and Zionists, and was rejected by the British House of LORDS. ▶ KING–CRANE COMMISSION

## Peixoto, Floriano Vieira (1839–95)

Brazilian military leader. He was educated in the Escola Militar in Rio and fought in the War of the TRIPLE ALLIANCE (or Paraguayan War). As Adjutant-General, he refused to order troops against forces under DEODORO DA FONSECA on 15 Nov 1889. A Liberal in politics, Peixoto was virtual Minister of War under the Republic, and promoted young radical officers (Jacobins) to power. As Vice-President (1891–3), he defeated both the federalist and naval revolts. Haunted by fears of the restoration of the monarchy and European intervention, his government was both antiforeign and highly arbitrary. He cultivated a sphinx-like cult among young military officers and urban society, which inspired attacks on subsequent regimes and still prevails.

## Pei-yang Army ▶ BEIYANG ARMY

## Pelham, Henry (c.1695–1754)

British politician. He became a Whig MP in 1717 and regularly supported WALPOLE and TOWNSHEND, his relatives by marriage. His political advance was steady: he became Lord of the Treasury (1721–4), Secretary for War (1724–30) and Paymaster-General (1730–42). After Walpole's fall, he refused to serve under Wilmington, but replaced him as First Lord of Treasury in Aug 1743, a post he held until his death, acting also as Chancellor of the Exchequer. He admitted several TORIES to his ministry (1744), which became colloquially known as the 'Broad Bottom', and defeated a challenge to his leadership by CARTERET and the Prince of Wales (1746). His ministry presided over the peace negotiations ending the War of the AUSTRIAN SUCCESSION (1748). Buttressed by a secure parliamentary majority largely achieved through a deployment of patronage considered by his opponents as corrupt, Pelham provided GEORGE II with secure, if unimaginative, government until his death in London while still in office. ▶ SEVEN YEARS' WAR

## Pelham, Thomas Pelham-Holles, 1st Duke of Newcastle (1693–1768)

English politician. He became Earl of Clare in 1714 and Duke of Newcastle in 1715. A Whig and a supporter of WALPOLE, in 1724 he became Secretary of State, and held the office for 30 years. He succeeded his brother, Henry PELHAM as Premier (1754–6), and was extremely influential during the reigns of GEORGE I and II. In 1757 he was in coalition with PITT, THE ELDER during the SEVEN YEARS' WAR, but resigned in 1762 after hostility from the new King, GEORGE III. ▶ WHIGS

## Pelikán, Jiří (1923–99)

Czechoslovak student politician and media reformer. An underground member of the Communist Party in WORLD WAR II, he was President of the Czechoslovak Students Union in 1948 and became President of the International Union of Students for the period 1953–63. He then switched to another political appointment as Director of Czechoslovak state television. In the course of the PRAGUE SPRING this brought him into the forefront of the reform movement, for the opening of television had an important impact within Czechoslovakia and abroad. But after the events of Aug 1968, he had to leave the country, much to the detriment of Czech broadcasting for some 20 years. In exile in Italy, he joined the Italian Communist Party (PCI) and was elected to the European parliament in 1979.

## Pelloux, Luigi Girolamo (1839–1924)

Italian general and politician. A patriot who took part in all the major wars for Italian unification, he was a deputy from 1880 and twice served as Minister of War (1891–3 and 1896–7). In 1898 he briefly became Prime Minister and Interior Minister following the fall of DI RUDINI. He pursued a policy of harsh repression against the parties of the left, but a poor showing in the general elections of 1900 forced him to resign.

## Peloponnesus

The southern Balkan Peninsula joined to mainland Greece by a narrow isthmus at Corinth. Dominated in antiquity by Sparta, in 146BC it became the Roman senatorial province of Achaea. Invaded by the Goths (267), by Alaric I (395) and the Ostrogoths (549), it was settled by the SLAVS and Avars in the 6c. Known as the Morea, it became a theme in Byzantium in 805. After the fall of Constantinople (1203) it was subject to barons from France, Flanders and Burgundy, and to the Neapolitan House of Angevin (1318–83). It was held continuously by the Ottoman Turks from 1460 to 1828 except for an interlude of Venetian government (1699–1718), the Venetians having had trading interests there since the 11c. A centre of insurgence in the GREEK WAR OF INDEPENDENCE, in 1828 it became part of the Kingdom of Greece. Apart from Corinth, the main city was Nauplia, the capital of Ottoman Morea after 1540 and of the newly independent Kingdom of Greece until 1834. ▶ KARLOWITZ, TREATY OF; OTHON; PASSAROWITZ, TREATY OF

## Pelshe, Arvid Yanovich (1899–1983)

Latvian politician. He joined the BOLSHEVIKS in 1915, participated in the Petrograd Soviet in 1917, and failed with others to establish COMMUNISM in Latvia in 1919. He then drifted through various jobs until the

USSR seized Latvia in 1941. From then on he rose within the Latvian Communist Party. By 1959 he was its First Secretary; in 1966 he was called to the **POLITBURO** in Moscow of which he was still a member when he died at the age of 84. He acquired a reputation as illiberal but corrupt, which did little to endear his fellow Latvians to communism.

## PEMEX (Petróleos Mexicanos)
One of the largest state-owned corporations in Latin America, and a virtual state within a state in Mexico, the oil company was created in 1938 by President Lázaro **CÁRDENAS**. He seized the assets of foreign (mainly British) multinationals as a result of the failure to implement the wage rates decreed by the 1917 Constitution's *junta de arbitraje y conciliación*, invoked by Cárdenas to rule on labour practices; the companies received compensation in Mexican bonds. PEMEX was charged with the management, regulation and production of oil found on Mexican soil. A logical outcome of the Criollo nationalism enshrined in the constitution, PEMEX was free from other ministries; only after the 1982 debt crisis was its autonomy curtailed.

## Penal Laws
Collectively, statutes passed in the 16–17c against the practice of Roman Catholicism in Britain and Ireland, when Catholic nations were perceived as a threat. They prevented Catholics from voting and holding public office. Fines and imprisonment were prescribed for participation in Catholic services, while officiating priests could be executed. The laws were repealed in stages, from the late 18c, the last not until 1926. ► **CATHOLIC EMANCIPATION**

## penal settlements
Places of secondary punishment in Australia where convicts found guilty of serious offences were sent; also used for colonial criminals sentenced to **TRANSPORTATION**, and (after 1842) for British convicts transported for life. About 10 per cent of the 162,000 convicts transported to Australia spent some time in these settlements, which were mainly at Newcastle (1801–24), Port Macquarie (1821–30), Moreton Bay (1824–39), Macquarie Harbour (1822–33), Port Arthur (after 1830) and Norfolk Island (after 1825). Life in these settlements varied from hard to savage, with hard labour and frequent and severe floggings; the last three named had deservedly fearsome reputations.

## Pendleton Civil Service Reform Act (16 Jan 1883)
A US Act that provided for the open selection of government employees and guaranteed the right of citizens to compete for federal appointment without regard to politics, religion, race or national origin. It stated that the selection would be made by means of civil service examinations devised by a new three-person Civil Service Commission, and it thus outlawed the previous **SPOILS SYSTEM** that gave out appointments based on political party affiliations, which had led not only to corruption and incompetence, but also to the assassination of President James A **GARFIELD** by a disappointed office-seeker in 1881. At first only about a tenth of positions were covered by the new law, but this had increased to over 90 per cent of positions by 1980.

**P'eng Chen ►** PENG ZHEN

## Peng Dehuai (Peng Te-huai) (1898–1974)
Chinese communist general. He fought in the **SINO-JAPANESE WAR** (1937–45), became second-in-command to **ZHU DE**, and led the Chinese 'volunteer' forces in the **KOREAN WAR**.

**P'eng P'ai ►** PENG PAI

## Peng Pai (P'eng P'ai) (1896–1929)
Chinese rural revolutionary. From a landlord family, Peng studied in Japan before joining the Chinese **COMMUNIST PARTY** and organizing rural tenants in his home district of Haifeng in the southern province of Guangdong. In 1923 he succeeded in establishing a peasants' association, which campaigned for lower rents, led anti-landlord boycotts, and organized welfare activities. When the association was crushed by a local warlord in 1924, Peng fled to the **GUOMINDANG** base at Canton, where he became Secretary of the Peasants' Bureau and Director of the Peasant Movement Training Institute. By 1925 Peng had helped form the Guangdong Provincial Peasant Association, which claimed 200,000 members. During the **NORTHERN EXPEDITION** (1926–8) Peng returned again to his home district and organized China's first rural soviet. In the wake of **CHIANG KAI-SHEK**'s counter-revolution against the communists, however, Peng's soviet was crushed in 1928. Peng was captured and executed by the Guomindang the following year.

**Peng Te-huai ►** PENG DEHUAI

## Peng Zhen (P'eng Chen) (1902–97)
Chinese politician. He joined the Chinese **COMMUNIST PARTY** aged 21, and in 1929 was jailed for six years for organizing anti-government protests. Leader of the Party and Mayor of Beijing (1951–66), he was accused by **MAO ZEDONG** of protecting party intellectuals who had been critical of the policies of his **GREAT LEAP FORWARD**. He was the first high-ranking party member to be purged during the **CULTURAL REVOLUTION**, and disappeared from public view in 1966. He was not rehabilitated until 1979, three years after Mao's death. He was reappointed to the party's Central Committee and was instrumental in establishing a legal system and drafting a new constitution. He became known as a hardliner opposed to **DENG XIAOPING**'s free-market reforms, but was appointed head of the National People's Congress in 1983. Although he retired in 1988, he remained a significant force in politics into the 1990s.

## Peniakoff, Vladimir, nicknamed Popski (1897–1951)
Belgian soldier and author. Born in Belgium of Russian parentage, he was educated in England. He joined the British Army and from 1940 to 1942 served with the Long Range Desert Group and the Libyan Arab Force. In Oct 1942, with the sanction of the army, he formed his own force, Popski's Private Army, which carried out spectacular raids behind the German lines. He rose to the rank of lieutenant-colonel and was decorated for bravery by Britain, France and Belgium.

## Peninsular Campaign (1862)
In the **AMERICAN CIVIL WAR**, an extended attempt by the Union Army under General McClellan to take

Richmond, Virginia (the Confederate capital), by moving up the peninsula between the James and York rivers. Although Union troops won most of the battles, McClellan acted overcautiously, failed to take the offensive, and instead slowly moved his troops away from the capital. ► SEVEN DAYS' BATTLES

**Peninsular War** (1808–14)
The prolonged struggle for the Iberian Peninsula between the occupying French and a British army under Sir Arthur Wellesley (subsequently the Duke of **WELLINGTON**), supported by Portuguese and Spanish forces. Known in Spain as the 'War of Independence' and to Napoleonic France as 'the Spanish ulcer', it started as a Spanish revolt against the imposition of **NAPOLEON I**'s brother Joseph **BONAPARTE** as King of Spain, but developed into a bitter conflict, as British troops repulsed **MASSÉNA**'s Lisbon offensive (1810–11) and advanced from their base behind the Torres Vedras to liberate Spain. Following Napoleon's Moscow campaign (1812), French resources were over-extended, enabling Wellington's army to invade south-west France (1813–14). ► NAPOLEONIC WARS

**Penn, William** (1644–1718)
English Quaker leader and founder of Pennsylvania. Expelled from Oxford for his Puritan leanings, he joined the Quakers in 1666, was imprisoned for his writings (1668), and while in the Tower of London wrote the most popular of his books, *No Cross, No Crown*. In 1681 he obtained a grant of land in North America, which was called Pennsylvania in honour of his father. In 1682 he was granted land that later became Delaware. He referred to Pennsylvania as a 'Holy Experiment', where religious and political freedom could flourish. ► FRIENDS, SOCIETY OF

**Pensionary** ► GRAND PENSIONARY

**Pentagon**
The central offices of the US military forces and the Defense Department, in Arlington, Virginia. The complex was built in 1941–3, covers 35 acres/14 hectares, and is composed of five five-storey, concentric, pentagonal buildings.

**Pentagon Papers**
A 47-volume history of US involvement in Indochina from **WORLD WAR II** to May 1968, commissioned in 1967 by Defense Secretary Robert **MCNAMARA**. In 1971 parts of the top-secret document were leaked to the *New York Times* by one of its compilers, Daniel Ellsberg, whose initial support of US involvement in South-East Asia had turned to strong opposition. The US government managed to obtain a temporary restraining order, but the Supreme Court eventually ruled in favour of publication and the Pentagon Papers were released. Highly embarrassing to the **NIXON** administration of the time, they revealed acts of deception and miscalculation, unauthorized military attacks, and details about the still-controversial intensification of US action in the **VIETNAM WAR**.

**peon**
A day-labourer (originally a foot-soldier), the lot of the *peon* has long been the subject of travellers' accounts, novels and histories. *Peonaje* (peonage or debt servitude) emerged between 1870 and 1930 in many regions, especially in Mesoamerica and the Amazon, where massive capital investment and technological change combined with the absence, or resistance, of local sources of labour to make debt-peonage a viable form of operation. In general, major property owners used labour contractors (*enganchadores*), paternalistic measures, wage increases and advances to attract the labour needed on *haciendas*, *fincas, fazendas, usinas* or *estancias*. The 'golden age' of peonage came to an end in the 1940s, with the advent of significant population growth in many agricultural regions of Latin America. ► ESTANCIA; FAZENDA; HACIENDA

**People's Democracy**
A term applied by the former communist regimes (other than the USSR) to themselves. It correctly indicated that in theory they had some form of machinery enabling mass participation in government. However, since there was only one political party or so-called popular front and no secret ballot, there were no democratic elections, and the description was therefore a misnomer. ► COMMUNISM

**People's Liberation Army (PLA)**
The Chinese army, numbering over 2.4 million troops. It is a significant political as well as military force, although in recent years its political role has been somewhat reduced. ► CULTURAL REVOLUTION

**People's Liberation Front** (Sri Lanka) ► JVP

**People's National Congress (PNC)**
The major political party in Guyana, which provided the government from 1964 to 1992. Founded in 1955 by Forbes **BURNHAM** as a breakaway African party after a split in Cheddi **JAGAN**'s People's Progressive Party (PPP), it took Guyana to independence in 1966 and generally implemented socialist policies. After Burnham's death in 1985, the PNC retained power under the leadership of Desmond **HOYTE** until defeated by the PPP in 1992.

**People's National Movement**
The major political party in Trinidad, which provided the government of that state from its inception in 1956 until 1986. The personal party of Eric **WILLIAMS**, its founder, until his death in 1981, its rivals, the People's Democratic Party of Bhadase Maraj and the Democratic Labour Party of Dr Rudranath Capildeo, never mounted an effective challenge to its monopoly of power. In 1986 it was ousted by the National Alliance for Reconstruction led by Arthur Robinson, but returned to power in the election of 1991. In the election of 1995 it secured the same number of seats as the United National Congress (UNC), led by Basdeo Panday, but refused to form a coalition and had to step aside for a government made up of the UNC and National Alliance for Reconstruction. It returned to government in 2002 under Patrick Manning.

**People's Party** ► POPULIST PARTY

**Pepe, Florestano** (1778–1851)
Italian patriot and general. He was the brother of Guglielmo **PEPE** and served the **PARTHENOPEAN REPUBLIC**, Joseph **BONAPARTE** and Joachim **MURAT**. In 1811 he was made a general and in 1815 became Governor of Naples. He was an important member of the revolutionary government established by the liberal insurrection of 1820, but fiercely opposed the Sicilian

rebels who sought independence and the restoration of the **BENTINCK** constitution.

## Pepe, Guglielmo (1783–1855)
Italian patriot and general. The brother of Florestano **PEPE**, he saw service with the Italian legion attached to French forces in 1800 and tried to seize Naples in 1802. Like his brother, he served both Joseph **BONAPARTE** and Joachim **MURAT**. In 1810 he was made a baron by Murat and, in 1815, a lieutenant-general. He led the Neapolitan insurrection of July 1820 but was defeated at the Battle of Rieti (7 Mar 1821) by Austrian troops sent to restore the full powers of **FERDINAND I**. Condemned to death, he managed to flee abroad, returning to Naples in 1848 when the city was once again in the hands of liberal revolutionaries. He was sent by the new constitutional government to assist **CHARLES ALBERT** of Sardinia-Piedmont in his efforts to drive the Austrians from the north of Italy. When, after a conservative monarchist coup d'état, the Neapolitan forces were recalled, Pepe decided to carry on the patriotic struggle and went to assist the Venetian Republic of Daniele **MANIN**. After the collapse of the **REVOLUTIONS OF 1848–9**, he settled in Piedmont. ► **NAPOLEON I**

## Pepys, Samuel (1633–1703)
English diarist and Admiralty official. After the **RESTORATION**, he rose rapidly in the naval service and became Secretary to the Admiralty in 1672. He lost his office and was imprisoned on account of his alleged complicity in the **POPISH PLOT** (1679), but was reappointed in 1684. His celebrated Diary, which ran from 1 Jan 1660 to 31 May 1669, is interesting both as a personal record and for the vivid picture it gives of contemporary life, including naval administration and court intrigue. The highlights are probably the accounts of the three disasters of the decade – the Great Plague (1665–6), the Great Fire of London (1666) and the sailing up the Thames of the Dutch fleet (1665–7). The Diary was written in cipher and not decoded until 1825.

## Péquistes ► PARTI QUÉBECOIS

## Pequot War (1637)
Colonial North American War between English settlers and the Pequot tribe of Connecticut. After the Pequots murdered an English trader, the settlers retaliated with the aid of their allies, the Mohegans and the Narrangansetts. They attacked the main Pequot town on the Mystic River and slaughtered hundreds of men, women and children, effectively destroying the tribe.

## Perceval, Spencer (1762–1812)
British politician. He became an MP in 1796 and went on to become Solicitor-General (1801), Attorney-General (1802) and Chancellor of the Exchequer (1807). He was Premier from 1809 until 1812, when he was shot dead while entering the lobby of the House of **COMMONS** by a bankrupt Liverpool broker, John Bellingham. An efficient administrator, he had succeeded in establishing a firm Tory government. ► **TORIES**

## Percy
A noble family from the north of England, whose founder, William de Percy (c.1030–1096), went to

England with **WILLIAM I, THE CONQUEROR**. The best-known member of the family was Henry (1364–1403), the famous 'Hotspur', who fell fighting against **HENRY IV** at Shrewsbury. His father, who had helped Henry of Lancaster to the throne, was dissatisfied with the King's gratitude, and plotted the insurrection with his son.

## Peres, Shimon (1923– )
Israeli politician. He emigrated with his family from Poland to Palestine as a child in 1934, and was raised on a kibbutz, but received most of his education in the USA, studying at New York and Harvard universities. In 1948 he became Head of Naval Services in the new state of Israel, and later Director-General of the Defence Ministry (1953–9). In 1959 he was elected to the Knesset. He was Minister of Defence (1974–7), and in 1977 became Chairman of the Labour Party and leader of the opposition until 1984, when he entered into a unique power-sharing agreement with the leader of the **LIKUD** Party, Yitzhak **SHAMIR**. Under this agreement, Peres was Prime Minister from 1984 to 1986, when Shamir took over. After the inconclusive 1988 general election, Peres eventually rejoined Shamir in a new coalition. However, the second coalition collapsed in 1990 and a government was formed by Shamir. In 1992 Peres was defeated as Labour leader by Yitzhak **RABIN**, and Rabin went on to become Prime Minister that year. When Rabin was assassinated in 1995, Peres took over the premiership, but was defeated in elections in May 1996 by Binyamin **NETANYAHU**. ► **MAPAI PARTY**

## perestroika
The process of 'reconstructing' the Soviet economy and society through a programme of reforms gradually introduced after 1985 by General-Secretary Mikhail **GORBACHEV**. These reforms, meant to be consistent with the ideals of the Bolshevik Revolution, were directed at relaxing control over the economy, reducing the power of the bureaucracy and eliminating its corruption, and in due course democratizing the **COMMUNIST PARTY OF THE SOVIET UNION** itself. Unfortunately from Gorbachev's point of view, they exposed the failings of the previous regime without removing enough of them, and actually worsened the state of the Soviet economy. Challenged first by the conservatives and then by the radicals, Gorbachev was swept from power in Dec 1991, his reconstruction still incomplete. ► **BOLSHEVIKS**; **GLASNOST**

## Pérez, Antonio (1540–1611)
Spanish statesman. Secretary to **PHILIP II** of Spain, he was a close confidant of the King during the period 1566–79. Pérez became even more powerful when in 1573 his patron, Ruy Gómez, Prince of **EBOLI**, died and he assumed influence at court over the Eboli faction, headed by Ruy Gómez's widow, the Princess of Eboli. In 1578 he arranged the murder of a political rival, Juan de Escobedo, and obtained the King's complicity in it. When Philip learnt the full story, however, he ordered (1579) the arrest and imprisonment of Pérez and the Princess. In 1590 Pérez escaped from prison and went to Aragon, where he was a key figure in the troubles of Saragossa (1591). He then fled to France and to England, where he was befriended by the Earl of **ESSEX** and inspired several plots against

Philip. His writings, notably his *Relations*, served to inflame public opinion against the person and policies of Philip II.

**Pérez de Cuéllar, Javier** (1920– )
Peruvian diplomat. After graduating from Lima University, he embarked on a career in the Peruvian diplomatic service and represented his country at the first UN assembly in 1946. He succeeded the openly ambitious Kurt WALDHEIM as UN Secretary-General in 1982, his quiet, modest approach contrasting sharply with that of his predecessor. His patient diplomacy secured notable achievements, particularly in his second term, including a ceasefire in the IRAN–IRAQ WAR and the achievement of independence for Namibia. His work enhanced not only his own reputation but that of the UN as well. He was succeeded as Secretary-General in 1992 by Boutros BOUTROS-GHALI.

**Pérez Jiménez, Marcos** (1914–2001)
Venezuelan soldier and politician. He joined the ruling military junta after the coup of 1948, and was appointed President in 1952 following the assassination of the incumbent, Carlos Delgado Chalbaud. Upon taking power, he embarked on a massive building programme which personally earned him a fortune. He encouraged police oppression, closed the university, silenced the press, and did little to counter Venezuela's mounting unemployment and inflation. In 1958 he was ousted by opposition parties, and fled to the USA, from where he was extradited in 1963 and imprisoned for five years for embezzlement of government funds.

**Perkins, Frances** (1882–1965)
US politician. She was the first woman to hold cabinet rank, as Secretary of Labor (1933–45) in President Franklin D ROOSEVELT's cabinet. This appointment recognized her reputation as a social reformer, especially concerned with child labour and factory legislation. In 1945 she resigned from President Harry S TRUMAN's cabinet, and became a member of the Civil Service Commission (1946–52). Her memoir, *The Roosevelt I Knew* (1946), was the first, and in many ways remains one of the best, recollections of the NEW DEAL.

**Permanent Revolution** (post-1918)
TROTSKY's adaptation of MARXISM and Bolshevism in Russia in the wake of WORLD WAR I. When communist revolutions did not materialize in Germany and other advanced countries, Trotsky pronounced that Marxist revolution was a continuous process and ought to be supported everywhere in the world, including in backward countries. This contrasted with LENIN's and STALIN's adoption of SOCIALISM IN ONE COUNTRY, Russia, and exacerbated the quarrel that led to his exile and death. ► BOLSHEVIKS

**Perón, (Maria) Eva Duarte de**, known as **Evita** (1919–52)
Argentine political figure. The second wife of Juan PERÓN, she was a radio and screen actress before her marriage in 1945. She became a powerful political influence and a mainstay of the Perón government. Idolized by the poor, after her death in Buenos Aires support for her husband waned. Her body was stolen, taken to Europe, and kept in secret until 1976.

**Perón, Isabelita**, popular name of **María Estela Martínez de Perón** (1931– )
Argentine political figure. A dancer, she became the third wife of Juan PERÓN in 1961. She lived with him in Spain until his return to Argentina as President in 1973, when she was made Vice-President. She took over the presidency on his death in 1974, but her inadequacy in office led to a military coup in 1976. She was imprisoned for five years, and on her release settled in Madrid, and in 1988 returned to Argentina.

**Perón, Juan Domingo** (1895–1974)
Argentine soldier and President. He took a leading part in the army coup of 1943, gained widespread support through his social reforms, and became President (1946–55). He derived immense popularity by cultivating the support of the urban working and middle classes of Buenos Aires, expanding government expenditure in the wake of an export boom. He was deposed and exiled in 1955 when the boom burst, having antagonized the Church, the armed forces and many of his former Labour supporters. He resumed the presidency in triumph in 1973, and won an overwhelming electoral victory, but died the following year. ► PERÓN, EVITA; PERÓN, ISABELITA; PERONISM

**Peronism**
A heterogeneous Argentine political movement formed in 1945–6 to support the successful presidential candidacy of Juan PERÓN and his government thereafter. The movement later underwent division, some left-wing Peronists forming the MONTONEROS guerrilla group, but it survived Perón's death (1974). Despite continued internal disputes, the party made a good showing in the congressional elections of 1986. The ideology of Peronism (formally labelled Justicialism (JUSTICIALISMO) in 1949) has proved difficult to describe, and can perhaps best be viewed as a unique amalgam of nationalism and social democracy, strongly coloured by loyalty to the memory of Perón.

**Perry, Matthew Calbraith** (1794–1858)
US naval officer. The brother of Oliver Hazard Perry (who defeated the British at the Battle of LAKE ERIE in the WAR OF 1812), in 1837 he was appointed commander of the *Fulton*, one of the first naval steamships. He was active in suppression of the slave trade on the African coast in 1843, and in the MEXICAN WAR (1846–8) he captured several towns and took part in the siege of Veracruz. From 1852 to 1854 he led the naval expedition to Japan that forced it to open diplomatic negotiations with the USA and grant the first trading rights with Western powers. ► KANAGAWA, TREATY OF

**Perry Convention** ► KANAGAWA, TREATY OF

**Pershing, John Joseph**, known as **Black Jack** (1860–1948)
US general. He trained at the US Military Academy at West Point, and served in several INDIAN WARS (1886–91), in the SPANISH–AMERICAN WAR (1898), in the Philippines (1899–1903), in the RUSSO-JAPANESE WAR (1904–5), and in Mexico (1916). In 1917 he commanded the American Expeditionary Forces in Europe, and after the war became Chief of Staff (1921–4). His book *My Experiences in the World*

*War* (1931) won a Pulitzer Prize. ▶ **WORLD WAR I**

**Persigny, Jean Gilbert Victor Fialin, Duke of** (1808–72)

French politician. He secured the favour of Louis Napoleon (**NAPOLEON III**), and had the chief hand in the abortive attempts on the French throne of Strasbourg (1836) and Boulogne (1840), where he was captured and condemned to 20 years' imprisonment. Released in 1848, he strongly supported his patron then and in 1851. He was Minister of the Interior (1852–5 and 1860–3), Ambassador to England (1855–60), and a Senator until the fall of the Second Empire. ▶ **EMPIRE, SECOND** (France)

---

**PERU**  official name **Republic of Peru**

A republic on the west coast of South America, bounded to the north by Ecuador; to the north-east by Colombia; to the east by Brazil and Bolivia; and to the south by Chile. Peru had a highly developed Inca civilization in the 15c. The Spanish arrived in 1531, and the Viceroyalty of Peru was established. Gold and silver mines made Peru the principal source of Spanish power in South America. After declaring its independence in 1821, Peru entered into frequent border disputes during the 19c (eg the War of the **PACIFIC** in 1879–84). Clashes between Ecuador and Peru continued into the late 20c. There were also several military coups, and drug-related violence and terrorist activities resulted in large areas being declared under a state of emergency. In 1992–3 the constitution was suspended to allow President Alberto **FUJIMORI** absolute power to implement reforms and deal with **TERRORISM**, and the government succeeded in capturing Abimael Guzmán, leader of the **SENDERO LUMINOSO** guerrilla movement, in 1992 and his successor, Oscar Ramirez, in 1999. President Fujimori was re-elected in 1995 but resigned in 2000 and fled to Japan to escape corruption charges. His successor, elected in 2001, was Alejandro **TOLEDO**, the first President of Quechuan (native Peruvian Indian) descent.

**Peruzzi** ▶ **BARDI AND PERUZZI**

**Pétain, (Henri) Philippe** (1856–1951)

French soldier and politician. During **WORLD WAR I** he became a national hero for his defence of **VERDUN** (1916), and was made Commander-in-Chief (1917) and Marshal of France (1918). When France collapsed in 1940, the National Assembly voted him full powers to negotiate the armistice with Germany and

Italy, and made him Chief of State, with his government at **VICHY**. His aim to unite France under the slogan 'Work, Family and Country', and keep it out of the war, involved active **COLLABORATION** with Germany. After the liberation, he was tried in the French courts, his death sentence for treason being commuted to life imprisonment on the Ile d'Yeu, where he died. His role remains controversial, and some still regard him as a patriot rather than a traitor. ▶ **FRENCH STATE**; **WORLD WAR II**

**Peter I, the Great** (1672–1725)

Tsar (1682/1721) and Emperor (1721/5) of Russia. The son of Tsar **ALEXEI MIKHAILOVICH** and his second wife, Natalia Naryshkina, he was joint tsar with his mentally retarded half-brother, Ivan (V), under the regency of their sister, **SOPHIA ALEXEEVNA** (1682/9). On Ivan's death (1696), he became sole Tsar, and embarked on a series of sweeping military, fiscal, administrative, educational, cultural and ecclesiastical reforms. Many of these were based on Western European models, pulled Russia into the mainstream of European history, and provided the economic and political basis on which Peter and his successors could defend and expand their dominions. However, all classes of society felt the impact of the changes and the frequent brutality of their implementation; his own son, Alexei, died under torture (1718), suspected of leading a conspiracy against his father. Peter encouraged expansion eastwards towards China, fought major wars with the **OTTOMAN EMPIRE**, Persia, and in particular Sweden, which he defeated in the **GREAT NORTHERN WAR**. All this established Russia as a major power, and specifically gained it a maritime exit on the Baltic coast, where Peter founded his new capital, St Petersburg. Whether what Peter achieved was worth the cost then and later is a subject still much debated by historians. The fact that he died without naming his successor contributed to the loss of direction which followed his reign. ▶ **ROMANOV DYNASTY**

**Peter I Karageorgević** (1844–1921)

King of Serbia (1903/18) and King of the Serbs, Croats and Slovenes (1918/21). The son of Prince **ALEXANDER KARAGEORGEVIĆ**, he fought in the French army in the **FRANCO-PRUSSIAN WAR** (1870–1), and was elected King of Serbia by the Serbian parliament in 1903. In **WORLD WAR I** he accompanied his army into exile in Greece in 1916. He returned to Belgrade in 1918 and was proclaimed titular King of the Serbs, Croats and Slovenes until his death, although his second son, Alexander (later **ALEXANDER I KARAGEORGEVIĆ**), was regent.

**Peter II** (1715–30)

Tsar of Russia (1727/30). The grandson of **PETER I, THE GREAT** and son of the tsarevich Alexei (1690–1718), he succeeded to the throne on the death of his step-grandmother, **CATHERINE I**. He died of smallpox on the day designated for his wedding and was succeeded by Empress **ANNA IVANOVA**, daughter of Peter the Great's half-brother and co-tsar, Ivan V. Peter II was too young and his reign was too short for him to do other than allow faction-fighting around the tsar to become more or less an established tradition.

**Peter II** (1923–70)

King of Yugoslavia (1934/45). The son of **ALEXANDER I KARAGEORGEVIĆ**, he was at school in England when his father was assassinated in 1934. His uncle, Prince **PAUL KARAGEORGEVIĆ** was regent until 1941, when he was ousted by pro-Allied army officers, who declared King Peter of age and the latter assumed sovereignty. The subsequent German attack on Yugoslavia forced the King to go into exile within three weeks. He set up a government in exile in London, but lost his throne when Yugoslavia became a republic in 1945. From then on the ex-king lived mainly in California.

**Peter II Petrović** (1812–51)

Prince-Bishop of Montenegro. He succeeded his uncle, Peter I, in 1830 and tried to introduce a measure of modernization into his backward, isolated country. A cultured man with a knowledge of German, French, Latin and Russian, he wrote poetry that is still highly acclaimed, his most famous work being *The Mountain Wreath* (1847).

**Peter III** (1728–62)

Tsar of Russia (1762). He was the grandson of **PETER I, THE GREAT**, the son of Peter's youngest daughter, Anna, and Charles Frederick, Duke of Holstein-Gottorp. In 1742 he was declared heir-presumptive to his aunt, Empress **ELIZABETH PETROVNA** (the daughter of Peter the Great and **CATHERINE I**), and in 1745 he married Sophia Augusta von Anhalt-Zerbst (the future empress **CATHERINE II, THE GREAT**). An unstable and violent man, and a great admirer of **FREDERICK II, THE GREAT**, he withdrew Russia's forces from the **SEVEN YEARS' WAR** as soon as he succeeded to the throne (Jan 1762), and restored East Prussia to Frederick. This enraged the army and aristocracy, and in June of that year Peter was deposed by a group of nobles inspired by his ambitious wife, Catherine, and led by her lover, Count **ORLOV**. He was strangled in captivity a few days later, and Catherine was proclaimed Empress. His main domestic act had longlasting unfortunate consequences; he freed the gentry from their obligation to serve the state, while in no way diminishing the obligation of the serfs to serve the gentry.

**Peterloo Massacre** (1819)

The name given to the forcible break-up of a mass meeting about parliamentary reform held at St Peter's Fields, Manchester. The Manchester Yeomanry charged into the crowd, killing 11 people. The incident strengthened the campaign for reform. 'Peterloo' was a sardonic pun on the **WATERLOO** victory of 1815. ► **REFORM ACTS**

**Peter the Hermit**, also called **Peter of Amiens** (c.1050–1115)

French monk and a preacher of the First **CRUSADE**. When **URBAN II** launched the First Crusade at a council in Clermont (France) in 1096, Peter traversed Europe, producing extraordinary enthusiasm. He rallied an army of 20,000 peasants, and led one section of the crusading army to Asia Minor, where it was utterly defeated by the Turks at Nicaea.

**Pétion de Villeneuve, Jérôme** (c.1756–1794)

French revolutionary. In 1789 he was elected Deputy to the Third Estate. He was a prominent member of the Jacobin Club, and became a great ally of **ROBE-**

**SPIERRE**. He was one of those who brought back the royal family from Varennes (1791) and advocated the deposition of King **LOUIS XVI**. He was elected Mayor of Paris and was the first President of the National **CONVENTION**. He voted at the King's trial for death, but headed an unsuccessful attack on Robespierre. Proscribed on 2 June 1793, he escaped to Caen, and thence, on the failure of the attempt to make armed opposition against the Convention, to the Gironde, where his body was later found, partly devoured by wolves. ► **ESTATES GENERAL**; **JACOBINS**

**Petkov, Nikola** (1893–1947)

Bulgarian politician. The son of Prime Minister Dimitŭr Petkov, he studied law in Paris and was later attached to the embassy there. After the military coup which overthrew **STAMBOLISKI** (June 1923), he remained in exile in France until 1931, when he returned to Bulgaria and led the left-wing Pladne group of the Bulgarian Agrarian National Union. During **WORLD WAR II** he worked with the **FATHERLAND FRONT** and was interned (1942–4). He was a minister without portfolio in the Provisional Government (Sep 1944–July 1945) and then edited the *National Agrarian Banner* (1945–7), leading the pro-Western opposition to full communist rule. After the 1946 elections, he attacked Georgi **DIMITROV** as a Soviet puppet. Dimitrov waited until the USA had ratified the Bulgarian peace agreement (June 1947) before executing Petkov after a farcical show trial.

**Petöfi, Sándor** (1823–49)

Hungarian poet. He was successively actor, soldier and literary hack, but by 1844 had secured his fame as a genuine poet, his most popular work being *János vitéz* (1845, 'Janos the Hero'). An admirer of France and its successive revolutions, he threw himself into the revolutionary cause in 1848, somewhat to the discomfiture of the gentry leader, Lajos **KOSSUTH**. He wrote numerous war songs, and fell in battle at Segesvár, possibly to a Russian bullet. He was ever after regarded as a martyr in the cause of popular nationalism; in the Hungarian Uprising in 1956, for example, one of the revolutionary centres was the Petöfi Circle. ► **REVOLUTIONS OF 1848–9**

**Petrakov, Nikolai Yakovlevich** (1937– )

Soviet reform economist. A brilliant graduate of Moscow University in 1959, he joined the party and became the Deputy Director of the Institute of Mathematical Economics in 1965. He joined Mikhail **GORBACHEV**'s team of advisers in 1985 and was appointed personal assistant in 1990. But in the autumn of that year he failed to persuade him to adopt serious economic reforms, which proved to be part of Gorbachev's undoing.

**Petri, Olaus** (c.1493–1552)

Swedish reformer and statesman. After his return in 1519 from Wittenberg, where he had become a follower of Martin **LUTHER**, he gained the ear of King **GUSTAV I VASA**, who made him Chancellor in 1531. His directness, however, brought him into disfavour and in 1539 he was charged with high treason and condemned to death. He was pardoned and in 1543 made First Pastor of Stockholm.

**Petrov Affair**

The defection by Soviet Embassy Third Secretary,

Vladimir M Petrov, in Canberra (Apr 1954); he was granted political asylum by the Australian government. The Soviet government tried to fly Petrov's wife back to Moscow, but the aircraft was intercepted at Darwin, and she too was granted asylum. Later the Petrovs revealed they had been spying in Australia, and in one of their documents they implicated two members of the staff of Dr H V **EVATT**, the federal leader of the **AUSTRALIAN LABOR PARTY** opposition. Evatt defended his staff before a Royal Commission (1954–5), but it refused to clear them. The affair exacerbated the split in the Labor Party over **COMMUNISM** during the 1950s. ▶ **DEMOCRATIC LABOR PARTY**

## Petrović-Njegoš Dynasty

The ruling house of Montenegro (1696–1918), founded by Prince-Bishop Danilo (1670–1735). Its principal members were the Prince-Bishops Peter I (1784–1830), Peter II Petrović-Njegoš (1813–51), Prince Danilo (1826–60) and **NICHOLAS I** (Nikola Petrović), Prince and King of Montenegro.

## Phalange Party

The *Phalanges Libanaises* (Arabic, *kata'ib*) were founded in Lebanon in 1936 by Pierre **GEMAYEL**, a young Maronite Christian, to counteract the provocative activities of Muslim elements seeking union with Syria. Originally a Christian youth movement, the Phalanges Libanaises then crystallized into a political party under the leadership of Gemayel, adding yet another factor to the Lebanese political equation. This factor was to have a destabilizing influence some four decades later when the Phalange aimed at the eradication of the **PLO** (Palestine Liberation Organization) in Lebanon. Gemayel himself played a leading part in the Lebanese politics of the 1960s and led the Phalange militia in the 1975–6 civil war. Gemayel's son Amin subsequently became leader of the Maronite Christians and was able to gain support also from the Sunni Muslims. President of Lebanon from 1982 to 1988, Amin **GEMAYEL** was no friend of extremists as his relations with Shiite factions and the more headstrong elements of the Phalanges bear witness.

## Phanariots

A small Greek élite of 11 families which in the 18c rose to prominence in the administration of the **OTTOMAN EMPIRE**, first as interpreters, then in the 19c as hospodars of the Danubian Principalities, Dragoman (or Interpreter) of the Fleet and Grand Dragoman (a post equivalent to Minister of Foreign Affairs). Their name was derived from the Phanar district of Constantinople where they lived. ▶ **HOSPODAR; MAVROKORDATOS, CONSTANTINE; MOLDAVIA AND WALLACHIA; PEĆ, PATRIARCHATE OF**

## Phan Boi Chau (1867–1940)

Vietnamese nationalist. Together with **PHAN CHAU TRINH**, he dominated the anti-colonial movement in Vietnam in the early 20c. Born into a Confucian scholar family, he was in essence a Confucian revolutionary. In 1905 he went to Japan where, working under the supervision of the exiled **LIANG QICHAO**, he wrote a history of Vietnam's loss of independence to the French, copies of which were then smuggled back to Vietnam. In 1912, now in China, he was involved with other Vietnamese in the establishment of the 'Revival Society' (*Quang Phuc Hoi*) which sought to bring about a democratic republic in Vietnam. Forces were raised which launched, from South China, poorly-organized attacks on French units (1915). In 1925 Phan Boi Chau was arrested by French agents in Shanghai and returned to Vietnam. Brought before the Criminal Commission (Nov 1925), he was sentenced to life imprisonment. The ensuing widespread public outcry led to his release and he spent the rest of his life, in gently guarded retirement, at Hue.

## Phan Chau Trinh (1871–1926)

Vietnamese nationalist. Along with **PHAN BOI CHAU**, he was a leading figure in the anti-colonial movement in Vietnam in the early 20c. In contrast to Phan Boi Chau's commitment to a revolutionary monarchism, Phan Chau Trinh advocated Western-style republicanism. Between 1911 and 1925 he was in France, spending some of that time in prison. From France he launched strong attacks on the Vietnamese monarchy. Phan Chau Trinh's funeral in 1926 was held in Saigon, provoking unprecedented mass demonstrations and student strikes. This heralded a new phase in the anti-colonial struggle in Vietnam, one that would involve greater popular participation.

## Phibunsongkhram (1897–1964)

Thai military and political leader. Of humble origin, Phibun was educated at the Thai Military Academy and then, on a government scholarship, at the French Artillery School. In France he came into contact with a group of Thai students who were disaffected with the absolute monarchy in Bangkok and became involved in the coup which brought down the absolute regime (24 June 1932). Phibun gathered increasing authority in the first constitutional governments, becoming Prime Minister in 1938. During that premiership, he cultivated a close relationship with Japan, in late 1941 agreeing to allow Japanese forces to pass through his country in order to attack the British in Burma and Malaya. However, when the war turned against Japan, Phibun fell from office (July 1944). He returned as Prime Minister in 1947, this time aligning Thailand closely with the USA. Phibun remained in office until Sep 1957, when he was overthrown in a **SARIT THANARAT** coup. He died in exile in Japan.

## Philby, Kim, properly **Harold Adrian Russell Philby** (1912–88)

British double agent. He was educated at Cambridge, where, like **BURGESS**, **MACLEAN** and **BLUNT**, he became a communist. Already recruited as a Soviet agent, he was employed by the British Secret Intelligence Service (MI6) from 1944 to 1946 as head of anti-communist counter-espionage. He was First Secretary of the British Embassy in Washington, working in liaison with the **CIA** (1949–51), and from 1956 worked in Beirut as a journalist. In 1963 he disappeared to the USSR, where he was granted citizenship.

## Philike Heitaria ▶ FILIKI ETAIRIA

## Philip, King, originally **Metacom** or **Metacomet** (c.1639–76)

Native American chief of the Wampanoag. He was born on the Wampanoag lands (part of present-day

Massachusetts and Rhode Island), and in 1662 he succeeded his older brother as chief. He was called Philip or King Philip by the English. His conflicts with the colonists over land led to **KING PHILIP'S WAR** (1675–6), which raged throughout New England and cost the lives of thousands. The war ended with the defeat of the **NATIVE AMERICANS** at Kingstown (now Kingston) and the killing of Philip by a scout working with a colonial patrol. Philip's head was displayed on the fort at Plymouth for 25 years.

**Philip I** (1052–1108)
King of France (1067/1108). The son of **HENRY I**, his reign marked a low point in the prestige of the Capetian monarchy, largely due to his elopement with Bertrada, wife of Fulk of Anjou, a scandal which led to his excommunication. ▶ **CAPETIAN DYNASTY**

**Philip I, the Handsome** (1478–1506)
King of Castile (1506). He was the son of Emperor **MAXIMILIAN I** and **MARY OF BURGUNDY**. As Archduke of Austria and Duke of Burgundy, he married (1496) the Infanta of Spain, **JOAN THE MAD**, daughter of **FERDINAND II, THE CATHOLIC** of **ARAGON** and **ISABELLA I, THE CATHOLIC**. Isabella's death in 1504 made Joan the legal heiress to Castile, but Ferdinand promptly declared himself her regent. In 1506 Philip went to claim the throne, but died in the same year; Joan lost her reason and was put into confinement. Their children were Emperor **CHARLES V** and his successor, **FERDINAND I**.

**Philip II** (1165–1223)
King of France (1179/1223). The son of **LOUIS VII**, his reign formed a key period in the development of the medieval kingdom of France. He embarked on the Third **CRUSADE** in 1190, but returned the following year to concentrate on attacking the continental lands of the Angevin kings of England. When he died, Capetian power was firmly established over most of France. ▶ **ANGEVINS; CAPETIAN DYNASTY**

**Philip II** (1527–98)
King of Spain (1556/98) and (as Philip I) King of Portugal (1580/98). He was the only son of Emperor **CHARLES V** and Isabella of Portugal. Following the death of his first wife, Maria of Portugal, in childbirth (1545), he married **MARY I** (1554), becoming joint sovereign of England. Before Mary's death (1558) he had inherited the Habsburg possessions in Italy, the Netherlands, Spain and the New World. To seal the end of Valois–Habsburg conflict, he married Elizabeth of France (1559), who bore him two daughters. His brief fourth marriage to his cousin, Anna of Austria (1570), produced another son, the future **PHILIP III** of Spain. As the champion of the **COUNTER-REFORMATION**, he tried to destroy infidels and heretics alike. He sought to crush Protestantism, first in the Low Countries (from 1568), then in England and France. The destruction of the **ARMADA** (1588) and the continuing revolt of the Netherlands, along with domestic economic problems and internal unrest, suggest a reign marked by failure. However, among his political achievements were the curbing of Ottoman sea-power after the Battle of **LEPANTO** (1571) and the conquest of Portugal (1580). ▶ **ALBA, FERNANDO ÁLVAREZ DE TOLEDO, 3RD DUKE OF**; **EIGHTY YEARS' WAR**; **HABSBURG DYNASTY**; **VALOIS DYNASTY**

**Philip III** (1578–1621)
King of Spain (1598/1621). The son and successor of **PHILIP II** of Spain, he reacted against his dominating father by choosing his own advisers, notably the Duke of Lerma. A pious Catholic, he was actively concerned to restore the military fortunes of Spain. He was, however, uninterested in politics, and delegated administration to his advisers, Juan de Idiáquez and Lerma, preferring to travel elsewhere in the country. His reign was thus distinguished by a renewed role for administrative bodies such as the councils and the **CORTES**. After Lerma's fall in 1618, Philip played an increased role in government, but died shortly thereafter. It was during his reign that the **MORISCOS** were expelled.

**Philip III, the Bold** (1245–85)
King of France (1270/85). He was with his father **LOUIS IX** (St Louis) at his death in Tunis (1270), and fought several unlucky campaigns in Spain, the last of which, the attack on Aragon, caused his death.

**Philip IV** (1605–65)
King of Spain (1621/65). The son and successor of **PHILIP III**, he was an active scholar and patron of the arts. He took a close interest in politics, supporting the government of his mentor, the Count-Duke of **OLIVARES**, but turned against him when the latter's policies collapsed. His reign experienced serious reverses which confirmed Spain's decline as a European power. In 1640 both Catalonia and Portugal rebelled, and in 1647 Naples followed suit. The Dutch Netherlands won their independence at the Peace of **WESTPHALIA** (1648), and the war with France (1635) ended with the cession of northern Catalonia and part of the Spanish Netherlands in the Treaty of the **PYRENEES** (1659). He was succeeded by his only surviving child, the sickly **CHARLES II**.

**Philip IV, the Fair** (1268–1314)
King of France (1285/1314). He succeeded his father, **PHILIP III**, in 1285. By his marriage with Queen Joanna of Navarre he acquired Navarre, Champagne and Brie. He overran Flanders, but was defeated by the Flemings at Courtrai (1302). His struggle with Pope **BONIFACE VIII** arose from his attempts to tax the French clergy. The King's reply to the Papal Bull *Unam Sanctam* was to send his minister William de Nogaret to seize Boniface, who escaped but died soon afterwards (1303). After the short pontificate of Benedict XI, Philip procured the elevation of the pliant Frenchman **CLEMENT V** (1305), who came to reside at Avignon, thus beginning the 70 years' 'Babylonish captivity' of the papacy. Coveting the wealth of the **TEMPLARS**, Philip forced the pope to condemn and dissolve the order, whose property he appropriated (1314).

**Philip V** (1683–1746)
First Bourbon King of Spain (1700/46). He occupied the throne twice, abdicating briefly in 1724 in favour of his son, Luis I, who died within a few months. King at the age of 17, Philip was never given the opportunity to assert himself as a ruler. At the beginning of his reign, dominated by the War of the **SPANISH SUCCESSION**, policy was determined by his grandfather, **LOUIS XIV** of France. On the death of his first wife, Marie Louise of Savoy (1714), Philip married Elizabeth

Farnese of Parma. She was an imperious woman, who completely changed the political complexion of the court, placing in charge of affairs her confidant, the priest Giulio **ALBERONI**. For the rest of the reign, Farnese effectively imposed on ministers her obsession with securing the dynastic interests of her family in her native Italy and specifically in Parma. Philip's reign marked an important phase of readjustment to Spain's new role in Europe, and the importation of foreign tastes showed itself in the construction of new royal palaces in Madrid and Aranjuez.

### Philip V, the Tall (1293–1322)
King of France (1316/22). The second son of **PHILIP IV**, he succeeded his brother, **LOUIS X**, in 1316. The main achievements of his reign were the ending of the war with Flanders (1320), and his attempt to unify the coinage.

### Philip VI (1293–1350)
First Valois King of France (1328/50). The nephew of **PHILIP IV**, he became king on the death of **CHARLES IV**. His right was denied by **EDWARD III** of England, son of the daughter of Philip IV, who declared that females, though excluded by the **SALIC LAW**, could transmit their rights to their children. The **HUNDRED YEARS' WAR** with England thus began (1337), and in 1346 Edward III landed in **NORMANDY**, defeating Philip at the Battle of **CRÉCY**, just as the Black Death was about to spread through France. ► **VALOIS DYNASTY**

### Philip of Swabia (c.1177–1208)
German King (1198/1208). The youngest son of **FREDERICK I, BARBAROSSA**, he succeeded his brother Conrad as Duke of Swabia in 1196. After the death of **HENRY VI**, he became embroiled in a struggle for the throne with **OTTO IV**, who had been elected King with English support in 1198. Despite being temporarily excommunicated (1201) by Pope **INNOCENT III**, who wanted to weaken the Hohenstaufen position in Italy, he came to a settlement with Otto IV and was formally recognized in 1207. He was assassinated in 1208. ► **BOUVINES, BATTLE OF; HOHENSTAUFEN DYNASTY**

### PHILIPPINES, THE   official name **Republic of the Philippines**
A republic consisting of an archipelago of more than 7,100 islands and islets, situated to the north-east of Borneo and to the south of Taiwan. The Philippines was claimed for Spain by **MAGELLAN** in 1521 but ceded to the USA after the **SPANISH–AMERICAN WAR** of 1898. It became a self-governing Commonwealth in 1935, was occupied by the Japanese during **WORLD WAR II**, and achieved independence in 1946. During the period 1945–53 the communist-dominated Huk rebellion was suppressed. Ferdinand **MARCOS** seized power in 1965 and imposed martial law in 1972. His regime became increasingly repressive, corrupt and violent, and was believed responsible for the assassination of the exiled political leader Benigno **AQUINO** on his return to Manila in 1983. Aquino's death provoked mass demonstrations against the Marcos regime which caused its collapse in 1986 when Aquino's widow, Cory **AQUINO**, was elected president. She instituted a new constitution in 1987, but political unrest continued. Having survived six at-

tempted military coups, she refused to stand for re-election and was succeeded in 1992 by Fidel Ramos. Ramos' successor, Joseph Estrada, elected in 1998, resigned in 2001 following corruption allegations and was succeeded by Vice-President Gloria Arroyo, who was re-elected in 2004. Muslim and Communist insurgencies began in various parts of the Philippines in the 1960s. A 1996 agreement with the Moro National Liberation Front, Muslim separatists in the southern islands, created an autonomous Muslim region in Mindanao and three other islands ended their activities. This agreement was not accepted by the Moro Islamic Liberation Front, which reached a comprehensive peace agreement with the government in 2002 although the ceasefire was breached in 2003. Clashes with communist insurgents continued until peace talks, suspended in 1999, were resumed in 2004. After the **SEPTEMBER 11 ATTACKS**, Abu Sayyaf, an Islamic group suspected of links with **AL-QAEDA**, emerged on the island of Jolo. ► **HUKBALAHAP**

### Philip the Bold (1342–1404)
Duke of Burgundy (1364/1404). The youngest son of John the Good, King of France, he fought at **POITIERS** (1356), and shared his father's captivity in England. He married Margaret, heiress of Flanders in 1369, subdued a Flemish rebellion at Roosebeke (1382), and gained that country in 1384–5. Following the insanity of his nephew, the French king **CHARLES VI**, he became virtual ruler of France.

### Philip the Good (1396–1467)
Duke of Burgundy (1419/67). The grandson of **PHILIP THE BOLD**, he at first recognized **HENRY V** of England as heir to the French crown, but concluded a separate peace with the French in 1435. Philip created one of the most powerful states in later medieval Europe. A committed crusader, he maintained a fleet for operations against the Ottoman Turks. ► **OTTOMAN EMPIRE**

### Philip the Magnanimous (1504–67)
Landgrave of Hesse. He was converted to Lutheranism in 1524 and was a major driving force in the Protestant **SCHMALKALDIC LEAGUE** of 1531. He established Hesse as a sovereign state where the Protestant Church was prominent in the provision of state schools and hospitals. Despite pressure from radical **ANABAPTISTS**, Hesse maintained a tolerant

# Philosophy

*Culture & Society*

The history of philosophy is notoriously complex, primarily because its focus and concerns do not remain static over time. Despite this, it is still possible to outline the features of the world's main philosophical traditions, bearing in mind that the philosophy of any one period is determined by factors such as the philosophical climate and social context within which it is written.

### Western philosophy

The Western tradition of philosophy was born in the 6c BC in the Greek-speaking region around the Aegean Sea and southern Italy. Beginning with Thales of Miletus (c.620–c.555 BC), the first Western philosophers were cosmologists in that their subject of enquiry was the nature and origin of all things. What marks them as philosophers is that their speculations, unlike those of their predecessors, were naturalistic and made without recourse to myth or legend. The Greek tradition blossomed with Plato (c.428–c.348 BC) and Aristotle (384–322 BC) – both of whom remain highly influential – and between them they probed virtually every area of knowledge; there was as yet no distinction between theology, philosophy and science.

As Christianity became an important social force in Europe and North Africa (2–5c), apologists including St Augustine of Hippo (354–430) began to synthesize ancient philosophy with the Christian world-view, a process that continued with St Thomas Aquinas (1225–74), and throughout the **Middle Ages**. With the **Scientific Revolution** of the 16–17c, the physical sciences began to separate from philosophy and theology, and rationalist philosophers, including Descartes (1596–1650), began to assess the philosophical implications of the new scientific results. In the 18c the search for the foundations of knowledge produced the empiricism of John **Locke** and David Hume (1711–76), and by the turn of the century, a synthesis of rationalism and empiricism was made by Immanuel Kant (1724–1804). The 19c saw the development of positivist philosophy based entirely upon scientific method, as well as American pragmatism, and the competing political philosophies of **Marxism** and Utilitarianism. Existentialism, which became popular with Jean-Paul Sartre (1905–80) in the 20c, was prefigured in the writings of Sören Kierkegaard (1813–55), and by the late 19c and early 20c, psychology had established itself as a discipline distinct from philosophy.

By the 20c philosophy had fragmented into numerous strands: philosophy of science, philosophy of religion, philosophy of mind, and so on. In very general terms, however, the focus was on analytic or linguistic philosophy, due in no small part to the impact of Ludwig Wittgenstein (1889–1951). The century also saw the emergence of post-modernism, an eclectic and iconoclastic movement that rejects all meta-narratives.

### Indian philosophy

Speculation about the nature of the world and human existence occurred in India from very early times, with the composition of the Vedas (1200–800 BC). The beginnings of systematic thought is found in the Upanishads (800–400 BC), which laid the foundations for the later philosophical systems, and provided some of the texts upon which philosophical commentaries were written.

Indian philosophies have traditionally been divided into six orthodox systems (*astika*) and three heterodox systems (*nastika*). The six astika systems are: *Samkhya, Yoga, Purva Mimamsa, Vedanta, Nyaya* and *Vaisheshika*. The nastika

---

religious regime that accommodated pastors of different Protestant persuasions and where no one was executed for religious reasons. In 1539 Philip developed syphilis and in 1540 contracted a bigamous marriage with Margaret van der Saale. This moral ambiguity, and his long imprisonment after the Schmalkaldic War (1547–52), lessened his influence in European affairs.

## Phillip, Arthur (1738–1814)

English naval commander. Born in London, he trained at Greenwich and joined the navy in 1755. In 1787 he was appointed commander of the **FIRST FLEET**, carrying convicts to Australia. He landed on 26 Jan 1788 (subsequently celebrated as Australia Day), founded his penal colony settlement at Sydney, and explored the Hawkesbury River. He was founder and first Governor of New South Wales. He left in 1792 and was promoted Vice-Admiral in 1810.

## Phillips, Wendell (1811–84)

US abolitionist. He graduated from Harvard in 1831, and was called to the Bar in 1834. By 1837 he was the chief orator of the anti-**SLAVERY** party, closely associated with William Lloyd Garrison. He also championed the causes of **PROHIBITION**, women's suffrage, organization of labour, and currency reform. ▶ **ABOLITIONISM**

## Philosophes

The leaders of the French **ENLIGHTENMENT** (often political commentators, writers and propagandists) who were critical of the **ANCIEN RÉGIME** and advocates of rational criteria. Their great collective work was the *Encyclopédie* (1751–72). ▶ **ENCYCLOPEDISTS**

## Philosophy ▶ *See panel*

## Phoenix Park Murders (6 May 1882)

The murder in Dublin of the recently appointed Chief Secretary for Ireland, Lord Frederick Cavendish, brother of Spencer Compton **CAVENDISH**, 8th Duke of Devonshire, and his Under-Secretary, Thomas Henry Burke, by a terrorist nationalist group called 'The Invincibles'. More murders followed during the summer. The British government responded with a fierce Coercion Act, which permitted trials for treason and murder to take place before a judicial tribunal and without a jury, and gave police extensive additional search powers. Five of the Phoenix Park murderers were arrested and hanged.

## Photography ▶ *See panel*

## Phule, Jyotirao (1827–90)

Indian social reformer. He led the anti-Brahmin campaign in Maharashtra in the late 1800s and wrote

systems are materialism or scepticism, Buddhism and Jainism. Vedanta, represented primarily by Shankara (788–820), has been a pervasively influential school, though equally important for Indian philosophy as a whole has been the development of logic in the Nyaya school, founded by Gautama (fl.1c).

Indian philosophical traditions developed in specific schools through oral debates. The principal tenets of the schools were codified into short aphorisms (*sutras*) which were commented upon by later philosophers in the tradition. Generally, the highest value has been freedom or liberation (*moksha*), rather than an ethical absolute or good. There has also been a tendency to accept the doctrine of rebirth or reincarnation and karma, although not all schools accepted these ideas. Of particular importance has been speculation upon the nature of language, greatly enhanced by the early development of linguistics or Sanskrit grammar, and the nature of knowledge and its acquisition.

In recent times, Indian philosophy has been strongly influenced by its Western counterpart. In the 19c, the social philosophies of the utilitarian school inspired a number of religious and political movements, including the **Brahmo Samaj**. In the 20c Anglo-American linguistic philosophy formed the basis of much research, and European phenomenology was also influential, most notably in the work of K C Bhattacharya.

### Chinese philosophy
Philosophy first made its appearance in China during the Zhou Dynasty (1122–256 BC), a period of extreme political and social turmoil. From this turmoil emerged what became known as the Hundred Schools, competing philosophies each offering a solution to the ills of the day. These included Confucianism, Taoism, Yin-yang and Legalism.

During the short-lived Qin Dynasty (221–206 BC), Legalism became the first state ideology, emphasizing state power and a strict system of rewards and punishments. A number of its precepts were incorporated into official orthodoxy after this period, although it never regained its supremacy. State ideology was predominantly Confucian during the Han Dynasty (206 BC–AD 220), and the **Confucian Classics** became the basis of the Chinese **Civil Service Examination System**. For the next six centuries, Neo-Taoist and Buddhist philosophy prevailed, promoting a distinctly metaphysical philosophy. The Neo-Taoists concerned themselves with the relationship between Being and Non-Being, and the particular and the universal, and in this climate the recently imported Indian Buddhism engaged with these issues, eventually giving rise to distinctly Chinese schools.

The period between the 10c and 19c, known as the Neo-Confucian period, was marked by a reassertion of Confucian political and moral values. **Neo-Confucianism** refocused attention on the traditional Confucian Classics and promoted the virtues of public service and social welfare activism. Only through active engagement in society, they argued, could one bring one's own self-cultivation to fruition. In order to rival Buddhist metaphysics, they constructed a metaphysical system of their own, claiming that correct relationships prescribed by Confucian thought (eg within the family, or between ruler and ruled) were manifestations of abstract principles (*li*) immanent in the cosmos.

In the 20c Chinese philosophy became subject to Western influence, most notably with the introduction of Marxism as the official political philosophy. At the same time, a New Confucian movement emerged, attempting to synthesize the traditions of the West and the East, combining traditional Confucian values with Western democracy and science.

### Arabic philosophy
Arabic philosophy constitutes that philosophy produced in the Arabic language from the 9c to the present day by writers in the Islamic world, stretching from Andalusia to India. The tradition began in Iraq, with al-Kindi (d.873), who improved upon existing Arabic translations of Greek treatises and brought them to the attention of Arabic intellectuals.

---

*Ghulam Giri* (1872), which exposed the evils of a caste-based society. His organization, *Satyashodhak Samaj* (1873), proclaimed the need to save the lower castes from the hypocritical Brahmanas and their opportunistic scriptures. The Satyashodhak movement contained both an elite-based conservative trend and a more genuine mass-based radicalism, and struck some roots among the Maratha peasantry. ▸ **BRAHMINS; CASTE**

### Physiocrats
A group of French economic and political thinkers of the later 18c, led by François Quesnay, and committed to *a priori* principles of reason and natural law. Their theories made them critics of internal trade barriers and controls, and advocates of reform, to produce a system of economic liberalism.

### Piast Dynasty
The first rulers of Poland, a line of princes descended from a legendary Polish ploughman named Piast (fl. c.870), whose name was only applied to the dynasty 800 years later. Piast's son, Siemowit, was first of the new line of princes of Gniezno (Gnesen), commencing the loose consolidation of Great Poland which was to culminate in the great-great-grandson of Piast, Bolesław I, the Brave, being crowned king shortly before his death in 1025. Bolesław's great-grandson, Bo-

leslaw II, the Bold, briefly won back the title of king after it had fallen into abeyance, but after his death (1079) his successors lost it once more, Bolesław III, the Wry-Mouthed restoring lost lands to include the territories of Pomerania, Silesia and Little Poland (first held under Mieszko I, christianizer of Poland and father of Bolesław I). Bolesław III divided the lands among his descendants, resulting in constant struggles among the cousins and attempts at unification. Bolesław III's great-great-grandson, Przemysł II of Great Poland, was crowned king in 1295, but died in 1296. But the kingship then passed to his Bohemian son-in-law, Wenceslas (or Wacław) II (1300/5). It then passed to the Mazovian Piast line from Władysław I, the Short who became king in 1320, and consolidated his situation by marriage alliances with Hungary and Lithuania. His son, Casimir III, the Great, reigned from Władysław's death in 1333 until his own in 1370, during which time he finally relinquished Silesia and Pomerania but annexed Galicia, modernized its state and army administration, strengthened its economy and founded the university at Kraków (1364), also codifying the Polish laws. His death marked the end of the Piast Dynasty as he was succeeded by his nephew, Louis I (d'Anjou) of Hungary, from whom eventually descended the **JAGIEŁŁON DYNASTY**.

His work was developed by al-Farabi (d.950), who in addition to producing numerous commentaries on Aristotelian texts and broadening the scope of rational inquiry, established the first distinctly Islamic political theology, providing the basis for the philosophy produced in Islamic Spain during the 12c. Al-Farabi's influential writings also extended to Iran, where they formed the rudiments of Avicenna's (980–1037) philosophical training. However, the achievement of Avicenna was much greater in that his work established the first proper school of Arabic philosophy, the Peripatetic, and moulded much of Arabic philosophy from then on, with its emphasis on employing philosophical as opposed to theological criteria in argumentation, and in its use of logic. Moreover, his works were translated into Latin and deeply influenced the corpus of Western scholasticism.

Two further schools have developed within Arabic philosophy since Avicenna. First, the Illuminationist, represented by as-Suhrawardi (d.1193), which attempts to synthesize philosophy with mysticism, and the Metaphysical school, centred almost exclusively on the issue of Being, and represented by Mir Damad (d.1632) and his pupil Molla Sadra (d.1640).

European incursions into the Arab world from the time of **Napoleon I**'s invasion of Egypt (1798) promoted Western philosophy throughout the area, although at the same time they provoked a backlash in certain circles, and a call for a return to a more politically oriented philosophy to counter foreign domination. In other areas, attempts have been made to merge both traditions.

### African philosophy

Exactly what constitutes African philosophy is a matter of some debate, and the definition that is attached to the term dictates the origin of the history of the subject. For example, a number of scholars apply the term to the communal values, beliefs and world-views of traditional African oral cultures, highlighting the long and rich tradition of indigenous African philosophy, or more accurately African philosophies, stretching back in time throughout the continent. Features often cited as characteristic of these traditions include supernaturalism and communally derived ethics.

Critics of this approach claim that communal beliefs of this nature represent folk- or ethno-philosophy, and not philosophy as it is normally understood. Some, therefore, restrict the term to the thought produced by individuals within indigenous traditions who question, critically analyse and apply reasoning to their traditionally held beliefs. Others restrict the term still further, and trace the history of African philosophy to the work carried out by the modern-day, professional African scholar. However, this definition is rejected by those who hold that African scholars who are trained in Western philosophical methodologies simply do not produce African philosophy. Finally, there are those who limit the term to political philosophies from the post-colonial era that owe little or nothing to the Western tradition. These include the **humanism** proposed by Kenneth **Kaunda** in Zambia, the philosophy of **ujamaa** espoused by Julius **Nyerere** in Tanzania, and the concept of **negritude** promoted by Léon Damas, Aimé Cesaire and Léopold **Senghor** in Senegal.

What is certain is that unlike the Western, Chinese, Arabic and Indian traditions, there is very little in the way of a literary African philosophical tradition before the modern period. One exception is the Ethiopian tradition, represented most notably by Zar'a Ya'eqob (1599–1692), who produced the philosophical discourse *Hatata*, and formalized a system of ethics. However, if African philosophy is simply that which is produced on the continent of Africa, then the literary philosophical tradition can be traced back to the 4–5c Christian apologists in North Africa, including St Augustine of Hippo, and if the definition allows, even to the writings of the ancient Egyptians.

---

### Pica Law

The title, derived from the name of moderate Deputy Giuseppe Pica, given to emergency measures adopted in Italy in Aug 1863 to deal with the **GRANDE BRIGANTAGGIO**. Effectively, it did no more than legalize the existing policy of reprisals and martial law which had already been adopted by the military authorities in the **MEZZOGIORNO**.

### Piccolomini, Ottavio, Duke of Amalfi (1599–1656)

Italian soldier. He entered the Spanish service and, sent to aid the Emperor **FERDINAND II**, fought against the Bohemians (1620), in the Netherlands, and against Wallenstein's army at **LÜTZEN** (1632), and contributed to the fall of Wallenstein. He won great distinction at Nördingen (1634) and next year was sent to aid the Spaniards in the Netherlands to drive out the French. In 1640 he stopped the advance of the Swedes for a time, but he was worsted by them in Silesia. In 1643 he commanded the Spanish armies in the Netherlands, and after the Peace of **WESTPHALIA** (1648) was created field marshal.

### Pichegru, Charles (1761–1804)

French soldier, a labourer's son. He enlisted in 1783, and by 1793 was a General of Division. With **HOCHE**, he drove back the Austrians and overran the Palatinate; then defeating the Austrians at Fleurus in 1794,

he entered Amsterdam in 1795. Recalled by the Thermidorians, he crushed an insurrection in Paris. In 1797 he became President of the Council of Five Hundred, but as a result of his Bourbon intrigues, he was deported to Cayenne. Escaping next year, he made his way to London, and thereafter lived in Germany and England until the Bourbon conspiracy of **CADOUDAL** for the assassination of **NAPOLEON I**. The pair reached Paris but were betrayed; Pichegru was imprisoned and later found strangled in bed. ► **BOURBON, HOUSE OF**; **THERMIDOR**

### Pichincha, Battle of (1822)

A decisive battle of the **SPANISH-AMERICAN WARS OF INDEPENDENCE**, fought on the slopes of Mount Pichincha overlooking the city of Quito. It secured the liberation of Quito (now Ecuador) from Spanish rule.

### Pichon, Stéphen Jean Marie (1857–1933)

French politician and journalist. He served on **CLEMENCEAU**'s newspaper *La Justice* before entering the Chamber of Deputies in 1885. Becoming a diplomat, he served in Port-au-Prince, San Domingo, Rio de Janeiro, Beijing and Tunis; he represented the powers in negotiations with China during the Boxer Rebellion. He was Minister of Foreign Affairs twice (1906–11 and 1917–20), after which he joined *Le Petit Journal*

# *Photography*

*Art & Literature*

The first true photographs were created in France in 1827 by the physicist Nicéphore Niepce (1765–1833) and were called *heliographs*. It had been known for some time that some chemicals, such as silver chloride or silver iodide, were sensitive to light and Niepce made use of this. He exposed paper coated with silver chloride to make prints of images, but as he had no means of permanently fixing the prints the whole area of the treated paper would eventually darken. In 1824 he began to work with the inventor and painter Louis Daguerre (1789–1851), who produced images on silver plates that had been treated with silver iodide. These, however, were still impermanent.

The English physicist and inventor William Fox Talbot (1800–77) was responsible for the next step forward – establishing a method of fixing images. He did this by treating an exposed image with sodium chloride, which destroyed the light-sensitivity of the areas of silver iodide that had not taken the image, thus avoiding the gradual darkening of the whole surface. Daguerre used this process to make permanent photographs on silver plates, which became known as *daguerrotypes*.

Fox Talbot, meanwhile, evolved a different method, the *calotype* process, which used paper treated with silver iodide to create a negative. He fixed the image using sodium thiosulphite and used the negative to make prints.

It was in this era that photography began to impinge upon the wider public, especially in the field of portraiture. Rather than going through the long and expensive process of having a portrait painted, those who could afford it could now have a photograph taken in one sitting at the studio of a professional portrait photographer. People could now display, or carry around, perfect images of their families and loved ones.

In the 1840s and 1850s British and French inventors and photographers began to use glass plates to make negatives. The most popular method was to coat the glass plate with a light-sensitive substance suspended in *collodion*, a glutinous liquid made by dissolving pyroxylin in alcohol and ether. This type of wet negative had to be developed right away before the chemicals could dry out and this meant that immediate access to a darkroom was a prerequisite. Some enterprising photographers used mobile darkrooms, but it was only with the introduction of dry negatives in the 1870s that photography was released from the professional studio.

It was in 1889 that true mobility became possible for the photographer, when the US inventor George Eastman (1854–1932) produced film on a roll of cellulose nitrate, thus removing the need to carry around the heavy glass plates. This helped make smaller, cheaper cameras available for both the enthusiastic amateur and the world of business.

The idea of moving photographic images was also being explored in the late 19c. In 1872 the English-born US photographer Eadweard Muybridge (1830–1904) took a sequence of photographs of a galloping horse using 24 cameras that were each triggered by the horse breaking a thread as it passed. This demonstrated the way in which an illusion of actual movement could be generated from a series of photographs taken quickly one after another and was, in essence, the idea behind cine-photography. It also, for the first time ever, established the way a horse's legs move as it gallops. Their speed had hitherto defied the human eye, as earlier paintings of horses in rapid motion show.

The first real moving-picture camera was patented in 1889 by the English photographer William Friese-Green (1855–1921), using strips of celluloid. Friese-Green was able to show his film by projecting it, but the first truly practical projector was invented in 1895 by another Englishman, Robert W Paul. In France the Lumière brothers invented the *cinematograph*, a combined camera, printer and projector in 1895, and began to show their films to the public. **Cinema**

---

as its political editor. He was always seen as Clemenceau's protégé, and abandoned control of foreign policy to him in 1917–20. ► **BOXER RISING**

**PIDE** (*Policia Internacional de Defensa do Estado*, 'International Police for State Defence')
Portuguese secret police. With the establishment in 1933 of the PVDE ('Police of Vigilance and State Defence'), the secret police in Portugal became the most feared institution of the **ESTADO NOVO** under **SALAZAR**. The Salazar dictatorship, in common with other authoritarian regimes, created an unscrupulous secret police force to safeguard its interests. In the 1930s the PVDE drew on the police state techniques of Nazi Germany and Fascist Italy. The creation of a nationwide network of spies and informers effectively banned the discussion of politics in public for almost half a century. In 1945 the secret police was renamed the International Police for State Defence (PIDE). With even greater powers than those of its predecessor, the PIDE lasted until the end of the Salazar era, reaching the height of its influence during the 1960s. Not only did it have a leading role in the colonial war being fought in Portuguese Africa (launching vicious dirty tricks campaigns), but it also dealt a devastating blow to the opposition through

the murder of General **DELGADO** in 1965. The PIDE was undoubtedly the most loathed of all the state institutions of the Salazar dictatorship. In 1969 it was re-christened the General Directorate of Security (DGS) and its powers were curtailed.

**Pieck, Wilhelm** (1876–1960)
East German politician. The son of a labourer, he initially worked as a carpenter and was active from an early age in socialist politics. In 1915 he helped found the Spartacus League and in 1918–19 the German Communist Party (**KPD**), leading the unsuccessful 'Spartacus Uprising' in Berlin in 1919. During the **WEIMAR REPUBLIC**, Pieck was elected as a communist to the **REICHSTAG** in 1928, but was forced into exile in 1933 when **HITLER** came to power. He fled to Moscow where he became, in 1935, Secretary of the **COMINTERN**. In 1945 he returned to Berlin in the wake of the **RED ARMY** and created, in 1946, the dominant Socialist Unity Party (**SED**) out of the former KPD and Social Democratic Party (**SPD**). From 1949 he served as President of the German Democratic Republic, the post being abolished on his death. ► **SPARTACISTS**

**piemontizzazione**
The Italian term used to describe the policy adopted

developed rapidly and soon became the predominant and universal form of 20c entertainment.

In the early 20c the use of photographs expanded away from portraiture and the world of art, and found ever more applications, especially in journalism, where their immediacy and truth-to-life were ideal, and in advertising. In **World War I** photographs from the front brought the conditions of modern war home to the public as in no previous conflict.

Most photography was still based on the black-and-white image, but pioneering work in colour photography had been carried out by the Scottish physicist James Clerk Maxwell (1831–79). The Lumière brothers experimented with a colour process and colour images were being produced by a complicated multi-exposure technique by the turn of the century. By the 1930s colour film and transparencies were introduced.

The trend in cameras continued towards ever smaller, hence more portable, and cheaper varieties that could be mass-produced. On the technical side, great advances were made in the manufacture and use of specialized lenses, such as magnifying lenses and telephoto lenses, and in flash photography.

After **World War II** photography became one of the most popular hobbies and spread throughout society, even if only at the level of annual holiday snaps. One major innovation was the invention of a camera, the Polaroid Land Camera, that could produce an instant print without the need of an external developing process. Scientific applications continued to be found and special techniques evolved, such as infrared and ultraviolet photography, and the diagnostic use of X-ray photography in medicine. Specially designed cameras were made for use underwater, and photography followed humankind's ventures into space and onto the moon.

As movie cameras followed the trend in still cameras to become smaller and less expensive, more and more members of the public were able to acquire them and 'home movies' of holidays and special occasions became common. This type of camera was superseded in the 1980s, however, with the popularization of video. Commercial filming by recording images directly onto video cassette tapes, with no processing of film required, was cheaper and easier than using film cameras and the **television** industry was quick to exploit the new technology. The mass availability of home video cassette recorders (VCRs) was soon followed by portable VCRs or camcorders. The advent of digital cameras and camcorders allowed users to share pictures easily with family and friends using computer technology and the Internet, making the filming of life's events an everyday pastime.

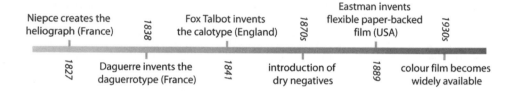

Niepce creates the heliograph (France) — 1827
1838
Daguerre invents the daguerrotype (France)
Fox Talbot invents the calotype (England) — 1841
1870s
introduction of dry negatives
Eastman invents flexible paper-backed film (USA) — 1889
1930s
colour film becomes widely available

by the government in Turin after 1859 to extend Piedmontese laws, institutions and often personnel to the territories newly annexed by **VICTOR EMMANUEL II**. The practice was extended to all of the peninsula with the exception of Tuscany, which briefly enjoyed considerable autonomy. In the **MEZZOGIORNO** it caused much ill-will and was an important contributory factor in the outbreak of the **GRANDE BRIGANTAGGIO**.

## Pierce, Franklin (1804–69)

US politician and 14th President. He studied law and was admitted to the Bar in 1827. From 1829 to 1833 he was a Democratic member of the state legislature, was elected to the **HOUSE OF REPRESENTATIVES**, and in 1837 to the **SENATE**. Returning to his private law practice in 1842, he volunteered for the **MEXICAN WAR** (1846–8), where he was made brigadier general. In 1852 he was nominated as a compromise candidate for the presidency against Winfield **SCOTT**, the Whig nominee, and elected. As President (1853–7), he favoured an expansionist policy, succeeding in the purchase from Spain of a significant strip of land in the south-west. On the issue of **SLAVERY**, he had supported the **COMPROMISE OF 1850**, but then signed the **KANSAS–NEBRASKA ACT**, which kindled a flame that ultimately led to the **AMERICAN CIVIL WAR**.

Because of the unpopularity of this act, he was not renominated, and he retired from politics in 1857.

## Pierlot, Hubert (1883–1963)

Belgian politician. After training and practising as a lawyer, he became a senator in 1926. He served as Minister for Internal Affairs (1934–5) and Agriculture (1936–8), and formed a government in Apr 1939. After the surrender of the Belgian forces in June 1940, he led the government in exile in London, leaving King **LEOPOLD III**, who had decided to stay with the army. His negative attitude to the King continued during his post-war government (1944–5), but his **CHRISTIAN PEOPLE'S PARTY** in general supported the King, so he retired from public life in 1945.

## Pietism

Originally, a movement within Lutheranism in the 17c and 18c stressing good works, Bible study, and holiness in Christian life. It was a reaction against rigid Protestant dogmatism, and influenced other groups, such as Moravians, Methodists and Evangelicals.

## Pig War (1906–11)

The name given to the period of 'economic warfare' between the Habsburg government and Serbia. In

1905 Serbia and Bulgaria had agreed to closer economic ties that would lead to eventual economic union. To force Serbia to break this agreement, the government in Vienna banned the import of all Serbian livestock (chiefly pigs) into the Habsburg Empire. The embargo, combined with the annexation of Bosnia and Herzegovina (1908), caused Austro-Serb relations to deteriorate yet further and drove Serbia closer to France and Russia.

## Pi i Margall, Francesc (1824–1901)
Spanish politician and thinker. Emerging as a leading political activist in the revolution of 1854, he was an anti-absolutist and anti-Catholic radical democrat. In 1868 he was elected to the constituent **CORTES** before becoming head of the Federal Republican Party. After he became President of the First Republic in Apr 1873, the Cortes voted for a federal regime. He resigned in July 1873, unable to resolve the clash between the cantonalists and the anti-federal democrats. He not only became the chief theoretician of federalism but was also widely regarded as a secular saint for his doctrinal purity and incorruptibility.
**►► CANTONALIST RISINGS; REPUBLIC, FIRST** (Spain)

## Pilgrimage of Grace (Oct 1536– Jan 1537)
A major Tudor rebellion in England, a series of armed demonstrations in six northern counties. It was directed against the policies and ministers of **HENRY VIII**, and combined upper-class and popular discontent over religious and secular issues, especially the Dissolution of the Monasteries. It was led by Lord Thomas Darcy, Robert Aske, and 'pilgrims' carrying banners of the Five Wounds of Christ. Darcy and Aske were subsequently executed for treason.

## Pilgrim Fathers
The English religious dissenters who established Plymouth Colony in America in 1620, after crossing the Atlantic on the *Mayflower*. The men, women and children included Puritan separatists and non-separatists. Before disembarking the adult males aboard signed the **MAYFLOWER COMPACT**.
**►► PLYMOUTH COLONY**

## Piłsudski, Józef (1867–1935)
Polish marshal and politician. Born near Vilna in Russian Poland, he was educated at the University of Kharkov. Imprisoned several times by the Tsarist authorities for his activities in the cause of Polish independence, he was the founder and leader of the Polish Socialist Party (1892). He formed a band of troops that fought on the side of Austria against Russia for part of **WORLD WAR I**, but in 1917 he was imprisoned in Germany. Freed the following year, he was in a good position to declare Poland's independence and to become head of state and Commander-in-Chief. Still anti-Russian, he was not unhappy to lead his country in the Polish–Soviet War in 1920–1 and to emerge with considerable territorial gains. In 1922 he was pushed out of power by more moderate politicians, but in 1926 he organized a coup d'état to become Prime Minister, Minister of War and leader of an authoritarian, right-wing nationalist regime until his death.

## Pimen, Patriarch (1910–90)
Russian Orthodox patriarch. Ordained a priest in 1932, he spent the later **STALIN** years in jail. However,

in Nikita **KHRUSHCHEV**'s time, in 1957, he was consecrated a bishop and in Leonid **BREZHNEV**'s time, in 1971, became the Patriarch. He supported Soviet peace initiatives and was a member of the World Peace Committee. Finally, in 1988, he met Mikhail **GORBACHEV** and secured his permission to celebrate the millennium of Christianity in Russia.

## Pinckney, Charles Cotesworth (1746–1825)
US statesman. Educated at Oxford, he became a lawyer. He was Washington's aide-de-camp at **BRANDYWINE** and **GERMANTOWN**, but was taken prisoner at the surrender of **CHARLESTON** (1780). He was a member of the convention that framed the **US CONSTITUTION** (1787). His refusal to pay bribes solicited by French agents brought the **XYZ AFFAIR** into the open. He was twice Federalist candidate for the presidency (1804 and 1808). **►► AMERICAN REVOLUTION**

## Pindling, Sir Lynden Oscar (1930–2000)
Bahamanian politician. Educated in the Bahamas and at London University, he practised as a lawyer before becoming centrally involved in politics, eventually as leader of the Progressive Liberal Party (PLP). He became Prime Minister in 1969 and led his country to full independence, within the **COMMONWEALTH OF NATIONS**, in 1973. The PLP, under Pindling, was re-elected in 1977, 1982 and 1987. He was defeated in the 1992 general election by Hubert Alexander Ingraham.

## Pinkerton, Allan (1819–84)
Scottish-born US detective. He was a Chartist who in 1842 settled at Dundee, Illinois, became a detective and deputy sheriff, and in 1850 founded the Pinkerton National Detective Agency. He headed a federal intelligence network for General **MCCLELLAN** during the **AMERICAN CIVIL WAR**, and his agency later took a leading part in breaking up the **MOLLY MAGUIRES** and in policing other labour disputes.

## Pinkie, Battle of (10 Sep 1547)
A battle fought between the English and the Scots at Musselburgh, east of Edinburgh. The English forces under Protector Somerset were victorious, but the aim of the war, of 'rough wooing' (to secure **MARY, QUEEN OF SCOTS** as a bride for **EDWARD VI**), was frustrated. Mary and Scotland formed an alliance with the French, and England was forced to evacuate by the Treaty of Boulogne (1550). **►► SEYMOUR, EDWARD, 1ST DUKE OF SOMERSET**

## Pinochet (Ugarte), Augusto (1915– )
Chilean dictator. A career army officer, he led the military coup overthrowing the government of Salvador **ALLENDE** (1973), establishing himself at the head of the ensuing military regime. In 1980 he enacted a constitution giving himself an eight-year presidential term (1981–9). A plebiscite held in 1988 rejected his continuation as President beyond 1990. Free elections were held in late 1989 and the Christian Democrat Patricio Aylwin was installed as President. Pinochet officially retired as army Commander-in-Chief in Mar 1998. In 1997 he was indicted in Spain on charges of genocide and crimes against humanity in connection with the deaths of Spanish nationals following the 1973 military coup. A campaign to have Pinochet extradited from Britain (where he had gone for medical treatment) to face trial in Spain on

charges of torture and conspiracy to torture failed and Pinochet returned to Chile, where he also avoided charges until in 2004 the Supreme Court stripped him of his immunity from prosecution.

**Pintasilgo, Maria de Lourdes** (1930–2004)
Portuguese politician. From 1970 to 1974 she was the Chairwoman of the National Committee on the status of women. After the 1974 revolution she was made Minister for Social Affairs, legislating above all on WOMEN'S RIGHTS. In 1976–9 she was Ambassador to UNESCO, and from 1979 to 1980 acted as caretaker Prime Minister. She also wrote widely on international affairs and women's issues.

**Pinzón, Vicente Yáñez** (c.1460–c.1524)
Spanish discoverer of Brazil, from a wealthy Andalusian family. He commanded the *Nina* in the first expedition of Christopher COLUMBUS (1492), and his brother Martin commanded the *Pinta*. In 1499 he sailed on his own account, and in 1500 landed near Pernambuco on the Brazil coast, which he followed north to the Orinoco. He was made Governor of Brazil by FERDINAND II, THE CATHOLIC and ISABELLA I, THE CATHOLIC.

**Pirogov, Nikolai I** (1810–81)
Russian surgeon. He was in charge of the medical service during the Siege of SEVASTOPOL and performed virtual miracles in improving appalling hospital conditions. He had the assistance of a sister-in-law of the Tsar, the Grand Duchess Elena Pavlovna, who organized 250 nurses into the Community of the Elevation of the Cross. Subsequently he played an important part in developing medical education. He also contributed more widely to higher education and took steps, for example, that eventually led to the establishment of the University of Odessa. His liberal ideas led to the loss of his last public appointment in 1866.

**Pisacane, Carlo** (1818–57)
Italian revolutionary. An ex-officer in the Bourbon army, he served in the French FOREIGN LEGION and took part in the defence of the Roman Republic in 1849. In 1857 he tried to launch an insurrection in the Kingdom of the TWO SICILIES, but was captured and killed by peasants.

**Pitt, William, 1st Earl of Chatham, the Elder** (1708–78)
British politician and orator. He joined the army (1731) and then entered parliament for the family borough, Old Sarum (1735). He led the young 'Patriot' WHIGS, and in 1756 became nominally Secretary of State, but virtually Premier. The enmity of GEORGE II led him to resign in 1757, but public demand caused his recall. Again compelled to resign when his cabinet refused to declare war with Spain (1761), he vigorously attacked the peace terms of the Treaty of PARIS (1763) as too generous to France. He formed a new ministry in 1766, but ill health contributed to his resignation in 1768. He collapsed during a debate in the House of LORDS in Apr 1778 and died the following month. His eldest son, John, 2nd Earl of Chatham (1756–1835), commanded the luckless Walcheren Expedition (1809). ► PITT, WILLIAM, THE YOUNGER; SEVEN YEARS' WAR

**Pitt, William, the Younger** (1759–1806)
British politician. The second son of William PITT, THE ELDER, he studied law, but then became an MP (1781), his first post being Chancellor of the Exchequer under SHELBURNE (1782). He became First Lord of the Treasury (1783), and was confirmed as Prime Minister at the election of 1784. During his long first ministry (1783–1801), he carried through important administrative and financial reforms, his policy being influenced by the political economy of Adam SMITH. He negotiated coalitions against France (1793 and 1798), but these had little success. After the Irish rebellion of 1798, he proposed a legislative union which would be followed by Catholic emancipation. The union was effected in 1800, but Pitt resigned office in 1801 rather than contest GEORGE III's hostility to emancipation. He resumed office in 1804. He drank very heavily, and this contributed to his early death while still in office. ► NAPOLEONIC WARS

**Pittsburgh Agreement** (1918)
The agreement between MASARYK, the future President of Czechoslovakia, and Czech and Slovak immigrants to the USA, setting out the possible lines of a Czechoslovak constitution. As leader of the exiles struggling to win support from the Allied Powers in WORLD WAR I, Masaryk wanted the immigrants' backing and promised the Slovaks that, to ensure the autonomy of Slovakia, it might be possible to create a federal state. When a unitary state emerged, the Slovaks in the USA felt betrayed and, particularly in the 1930s, worked hard to secure the separation of Slovakia that transpired in 1939 when HITLER occupied the Czech Lands and set up a puppet Slovakia.

**Pius II**, originally **Eneo Silvio de Piccolomini** (1405–64)
Italian pope (1458/64). He was employed on diplomatic missions before taking orders and becoming Bishop of Trieste (1447) and a cardinal (1456). As pope, he attempted to organize an armed confederation of Christian princes to resist the Turks, following their victory at Constantinople (1453). One of the most eminent humanist scholars of his age, his works are chiefly historical.

**Pius IV**, originally **Giovanni Angelo de' Medici** (1499–1565)
Italian pope (1559/65). He brought to a close the deliberations of the Council of TRENT. In many ways, this signalled an end to the conflict between the principles of papal monarchy and conciliarism: the council endorsed its declaration of faith as the Creed of Pius IV, even though it is still known as the Tridentine Creed, which connects it to the council.

**Pius V, St**, originally **Michele Ghislieri** (1504–72)
Italian pope (1566/72). As pope, he implemented the decrees of the Council of TRENT (1545–63), excommunicated Queen ELIZABETH I (1570), and inspired the HOLY LEAGUE (1571) against the Turks. The league's campaign culminated in the great victory of the Christian fleet under Don JOHN OF AUSTRIA at the Battle of LEPANTO in the Gulf of Corinth.

**Pius VI**, originally **Giovanni Angelo Braschi** (1717–99)
Italian pope (1775/99). His long pontificate saw the papacy confronted with repeated threats and crises:

# Plagues and Epidemics

Culture & Society

Then the angel of the Lord went forth and smote in the camp of the
Assyrians a hundred and fourscore and five thousand: and when they
arose early in the morning, behold, they were all dead corpses.

The destruction of the host of Sennacherib, recorded in the Book of Isaiah, is only one of a number of occasions in the
Old Testament when God is said to have visited a pestilence upon the enemies of His chosen people or upon that people
themselves. Outbreaks of pestilence are also referred to in works predating the biblical text: in the Babylonian *Epic of
Gilgamesh*, dating from around 2000 BC, and in an Egyptian text from the same period. A very early Chinese text dating
from about 1300 BC also shows a familiarity with the disastrous effects of epidemics.

Often described as 'plagues', such outbreaks may or may not have been caused by 'the plague' itself. However,
precisely what disease or diseases were involved in these and many other recorded outbreaks cannot be known with any
great certainty, although diseases such as smallpox and measles may have been involved. What can be said with some
confidence is that such epidemics were usually caused by new diseases against which the affected population had no
resistance. Epidemic diseases tended to be brought in from elsewhere; in fact, the victims were often able to see the
dreadful scourge advancing towards them or were able to trace its progress after the event. Thucydides (c.460–400 BC)
recounts that the disease that struck Athens in 430–429 BC was a new one and that its source was Ethiopia, from whence
it proceeded into Egypt, Libya and Persia, making its first appearance in Athens in the port of Piraeus, a clear indication
that it came by sea.

Modern 'flu epidemics give some indication of how the process works; they start – from the European perspective –
in some faraway place (Asian 'flu, Hong Kong 'flu), are carried across continents as sufferers travel abroad by air or sea,
then spread like wildfire among the population among which they alight. The influenza virus is highly unstable, which is
why 'flu epidemics continue to recur, and resistance acquired against last year's variety confers no immunity against this
year's. In the case of diseases such as measles, smallpox or mumps (the Greek physician Hippocrates records an
epidemic of mumps on the island of Thasos in the 4c BC), the population of Europe over the centuries has acquired a
considerable degree of immunity through prolonged exposure. As a result these have become essentially diseases of
childhood – serious enough for the individual sufferer, but unlikely to break out and decimate the adult population.

## The plague
The plague proper is caused by a bacillus carried by a flea parasitic on rodents, especially the brown rat, and occurs in
three related forms: bubonic, pneumonic and septicaemic. Bubonic plague, which produces swellings in the groin and
armpits, is fatal if not treated for between one-third and three-quarters of cases; pneumonic and septicaemic plague are
almost always fatal.

The first outbreak of plague in Europe that can be positively identified as such occurred in the reign of the (Eastern
Roman) Emperor Justinian in AD 542–3. The historian Procopius reports that at its height the plague was killing 10,000
people a day in Constantinople and that it raged there for four months before moving on to affect the whole
Mediterranean area and beyond.

The most famous and terrible outbreak of plague in European history was the Black Death. Beginning among the
troops of a Mongol invading army in the Crimea in 1346, the epidemic spread inexorably, reaching Sicily late in 1347 and
the Italian mainland early the following year. By the end of 1348 almost all of France was infected and the disease had
gained a foothold in the British Isles. By the end of 1350, when the first onset of the pestilence finally ran its course, the
infection had spread throughout Scandinavia and eastward along the Baltic coast into Russia.

It is impossible to know with any accuracy how many people died. Some areas were afflicted far more seriously than
others and some areas escaped unscathed; Florence suffered terribly whereas Milan was virtually unaffected. It is
generally accepted that about a third of the population in the affected areas of Europe died between 1346 and 1350.
Many graphic accounts of the passage of the Black Death have been left, perhaps the most notable that given by
Boccaccio in the preface to the *Decameron* (1358), and he also describes the immediate consequences of the epidemic
and the breakdown of normal social life and human relations.

Having swept through Europe so ferociously in the 14c, the plague did not simply disappear. It made more localized
reappearances, especially in seaports, for several centuries thereafter. London was often infected and in Shakespeare's
time the theatres were periodically closed due to plague, one instance of the basic preventive measures adopted by
governments. The quarantining of infected people or ship's companies was another. The Great Plague of London in
1665–6 also spread to other parts of the country and was one of the last major outbreaks in Western Europe. It was by no

the growth of anticlerical **ENLIGHTENMENT** thought;
the increasing tendency of monarchs to ignore the
papacy and view the Church only in terms of their
own interests and from a national context; and, above
all, the devastating changes brought by the **FRENCH
REVOLUTION** and subsequent European wars. Pius
VI was ill-suited to cope with so stormy a period
and, from the outset, was beset with problems. Under
Bourbon pressure to continue the anti-Jesuit policies
of his predecessor, **CLEMENT XIV**, he sought vainly to
dissuade **CATHERINE II, THE GREAT** of Russia and

**FREDERICK II, THE GREAT** of Prussia from offering the
Jesuits refuge, while simultaneously having to cope
with rumours among ultra-conservative **ZELANTI**
that he was secretly sympathetic towards the outlawed society. In 1781 he faced another blow to papal
authority when **JOSEPH II** of Austria published his
Edict of Toleration, which not only allowed greater
rights to non-Catholics but also constituted a broad
assault on the privileges, property and status of
the Church within the Habsburg Empire. Although
Joseph's death in 1790 meant an effective end to the

means the last outbreak elsewhere in the world. In 1894 the plague broke out again in China, ravaging Canton and Hong Kong, and from there proceeded to most of the major seaports of the world. The infection was for the most part contained, except in India where over the following ten years some six million people died of it. By 1894, however, the science of bacteriology was taking root. Scientists were able to study the disease, identify the causative bacillus and establish its method of transmission.

### The consequences of epidemics

The consequences of particular epidemics are difficult to pin down. Even in the case of a cataclysm of the magnitude of the Black Death, there is little agreement as to what the precise economic and social consequences were or how long it took the European nations to recover. There were psychological and intellectual consequences as well. The arrival of the Black Death was almost universally attributed to the wrath of God against sinful humanity. The sinfulness of the ecclesiastical establishment was part and parcel of the general ill, and the Black Death has been distantly and tenuously linked to the movement for reform of the Church that culminated in the **Reformation** nearly 200 years later.

In other instances the influence of an epidemic for the course of history is more clearly visible. It has been convincingly argued that the ease with which small Spanish forces were able to conquer two populous and well-established empires in South America in the 16c had a great deal to do with the effect on the numbers, health and morale of the population of the diseases carried by the invaders. The Spaniards were hardened against smallpox, measles, typhoid, typhus and dysentery, but the Aztecs and Incas were not. For thousands of years they had been quarantined from Old World viruses, and therefore had virtually no resistance. The armies that overthrew the Aztecs were composed mainly of Amerindian subjects revolting against the cruel Aztec regime. It was the death of almost nine indigenous people out of ten, due to viral massacres, which enabled the Spaniards to cheat their allies and establish their own ascendancy. In Peru, Spanish ascendancy was assisted by the death through disease of perhaps half the indigenous population.

These viral massacres in Central and South America following the Spanish incursions seem to have been matched by viral holocausts, less well recorded, among the **Native Americans** of North America. These facilitated early English settlement in New England, and went on into the 18c. By the time of Captain **Cook**'s voyages of exploration among the Pacific Islands, intelligent men like Cook grasped the high likelihood of a repetition of the disasters in the Americas, at least to the relatively isolated Polynesian islanders. They and the Aboriginal population of Australia were scythed down by diseases to which, due to lack of prior contact with Europeans, they had no resistance.

### Later epidemics and countermeasures

New diseases, particularly cholera and typhus, periodically ravaged the expanding cities of Europe in the 19c. By this time, however, the authorities were in a better position to control disease. The history of outbreaks of cholera in Britain in the 19c is closely linked to the progress of public health legislation. The first outbreak in 1832 led to the establishment of local boards of health. The next, in 1848, anticipated more than a year in advance because of reports of the disease from Asia, provoked the establishment of a central and more powerful Board of Health that promoted much-needed sanitation measures, such as the provision of piped water-borne sewerage systems and clean drinking water.

The 20c saw the fight against epidemic diseases continued on an international level with the establishment of an International Office of Public Hygiene in Paris in 1909, the forerunner of the Health Section attached to the **League of Nations** and to the **World Health Organization**, founded in 1948. Scientific and medical advances, including the discovery of antibiotics and the development of insecticides for use, for example, against malaria-carrying mosquitoes, made possible the virtual elimination of some of the worst scourges of previous centuries. But the 20c had serious epidemics of its own. The influenza pandemic of 1918–19 is estimated to have claimed 20 million victims worldwide, making it comparable with the worst outbreaks of previous ages. **HIV/AIDS**, originally confined in the West to certain sections of the population, notably the gay community and intravenous drugs-users, has become a devastating problem in parts of Africa, with serious demographic, economic and social consequences. Modern transport systems enable disease to spread much more quickly; severe acute respiratory syndrome (SARS) first appeared in southern China in Nov 2002, spread rapidly as some people who had contracted the disease travelled great distances before becoming ill, and by Mar 2003 it had become a global problem.

Although great advances were made in the containment of epidemics and treatment of disease in the 20c, research in the late 20c and early 21c has revealed the ability of bacteria to evolve, often rapidly, to develop new strains of disease or resistance to treatments. The growing resistance to antibiotic treatments of diseases such as tuberculosis (TB) has led to fears of a resurgence in the illness, and the development of antibiotic-resistant strains of bacteria, such as MRSA (Methicillin Resistant *Staphylococcus aureus*), can complicate treatment of other medical conditions. Consequently, 'plagues' and epidemics continue to be a threat to human health despite the progress of medical science.

---

Josephist anticlerical experiment, it was by this stage a trifling worry for Pius compared with the problems posed by events in France. The French Civil Constitution of 1790 struck a crippling blow to the Church, forcing Pius to denounce the revolution openly the following year. In 1796, however, Napoleon invaded the **PAPAL STATES** at the head of a revolutionary army and, two years later, the Holy City was occupied and Pius expelled. In 1799 Rome was formally seized by France; Pius died the same year, a defeated and dejected prisoner.

**Pius VII**, originally **Luigi Barnaba Chiaramonti** (1742–1823)

Italian pope (1800/23). He was responsible for the CONCORDAT (1801) with NAPOLEON I, and was forced in 1804 to consecrate him as Emperor. When the French occupied the **PAPAL STATES** in 1809, Pius was taken to France and made to sign a new Concordat sanctioning their annexation. The fall of Napoleon in 1814 allowed his return to Rome and the restoration of the Papal States. ► CONSALVI, ERCOLE

**Pius IX**, originally **Giovanni Maria Mastai Ferretti** (1792–1878)
Italian pope (1846/78). Originally hailed as the patriot pope longed for by **GIOBERTI**, his early reforms and apparently anti-Austrian stance evaporated in the face of the growing radicalism of the **REVOLUTIONS OF 1848–9**. After the **PAPAL ALLOCUTION** of Apr 1848 it became clear that he was embarking on an increasingly conservative course. On the assassination of Pellegrino **ROSSI** he fled Rome, returning only after the **OUDINOT EXPEDITION** had enabled the restoration of his full temporal powers. He was violently opposed to the unification of Italy which was accomplished through the annexation by **VICTOR EMMANUEL II** of the **PAPAL STATES** (1860–70), and refused to recognize the new united Kingdom of Italy. His ever more reactionary stance was manifest in the **SYLLABUS OF ERRORS** (1864) and the decree of Papal Infallibility of the first Vatican Council (1870). He spent the last years of his life in self-imposed 'imprisonment' in the Vatican City.

**Pius XII**, originally **Eugenio Pacelli** (1876–1958)
Italian pope (1939/1958). Under his leadership, the Vatican did much humanitarian work during **WORLD WAR II**, notably for prisoners of war and refugees. There has been continuing controversy, however, over his attitude to the treatment of the Jews in Nazi Germany. Some critics argue that he could have used his influence with Catholic Germany to prevent the massacres, whereas others suggest that any attempt to have done so would have proved futile and might possibly have worsened the situation. In the post-war years the plight of the persecuted churchmen in the communist countries, and the fate of Roman Catholicism there, became his personal concern.

**Pizarro, Francisco** (c.1478–1541)
Spanish conquistador. He served in Italy, and with the expedition which discovered the Pacific (1513). In 1526 he and **ALMAGRO** sailed for Peru, and in 1531 began the conquest of the Incas. He killed King **ATAHUALPA**, then worked to consolidate the new empire, founding Lima (1535) and other cities. Dissension between Pizarro and Almagro led to the latter's execution; in revenge, Almagro's followers assassinated Pizarro at Lima.

**Pizarro, Gonzalo** (c.1506–1548)
Spanish conquistador. The half-brother of Francisco **PIZARRO**, he accompanied him in the conquest of Peru, and did good service when the Indians besieged Cuzco (1535–6), and in the conquest of Charcas. In 1539 he undertook an arduous expedition to the east of Quito. One of his lieutenants, Francisco de Orellana, sent ahead for supplies, deserted his starving comrades, discovered the whole course of the Amazon, and returned to Spain. Only 90 out of 350 Spaniards returned with Pizarro in Jun 1542. In 1544 the new viceroy, Vela, arrived in Peru to enforce the 'New Laws'. The Spaniards, dismayed, entreated Pizarro to protect their interests. He mustered 400 men, entered Lima (Oct 1544), and was declared Governor of Peru; Vela was defeated and killed in battle (1546). When news of this revolt reached Spain, Pedro de la Gasca, an able ecclesiastic, was sent to Peru as President to restore order, and landed at Tumbes in Jun 1547. Pizarro defeated a force sent against him, and met Gasca near Cuzco (Apr 1548). However, his forces deserted him, he gave himself up and was beheaded.

**PKI** ► **PARTAI KOMUNIS INDONESIA**

**Plaatje, Sol Tshekisho** (1876–1932)
South African journalist, politician and literary figure. One of the founders of black nationalism, he first worked as a Post Office messenger and later a magistrates' court interpreter in Kimberley. He was in the town throughout the siege during the Boer War and kept a lively diary of those events. After the war he founded and edited newspapers, wrote books (including *Native Life in South Africa*), translated Shakespeare into his native tongue, Tswana, and was one of the founders of the South African Native National Congress, later the **ANC** (African National Congress).

**Place, Francis** (1771–1854)
English radical and reformer. Born in London, a self-educated tailor, he was a champion of radicalism and the right to form trade unions, and contrived the repeal of the anti-union **COMBINATION ACTS** in 1824. He was a leading figure in the agitation which brought about the passing of the Reform Act of 1832. Drafter of the People's Charter, and a pioneer of birth-control study, he wrote *The Principle of Population* (1822). ► **REFORM ACTS**

**Plagues and Epidemics** ► *See panel*

**Plaid Cymru**
The Welsh National Party, founded in 1925, with the aim of achieving independence for Wales. It stands for election throughout Wales, but finds support mainly in the north and west of the country. It had four MPs following the 1997 general election, and 17 seats in the elections for the Welsh Assembly in 1999. In the 2003 Welsh Assembly elections, its representation was reduced to 12 seats.

**Plain, The**
Known in French as the *Marais*, the term refers to the majority of deputies in the French revolutionary National **CONVENTION**, politically uncommitted to a particular faction although broadly aligned with the **GIRONDINS**. They were ultimately outmanoeuvred by extremists, the **JACOBINS** of the **MOUNTAIN**. ► **FRENCH REVOLUTION**

**Plains Indians**
A name given to various Native American groups who lived on the Great Plains between the Mississippi River and the Rocky Mountains in the USA and Canada. Most were nomadic or semi-nomadic buffalo hunters living together in small bands. Their lives were changed by the introduction of horses by the Spanish, which led to intensified warring between groups, and hunting over much greater expanses. Eventually the buffalo were exterminated, and white settlers finally destroyed the Plains Indians' power, placing the survivors in reservations. ► **ARAPAHO**; **CHEYENNE**; **COMANCHE**; **CREE**; **CROW**; **DAKOTA**; **GHOST DANCE**; **NATIVE AMERICANS**; **SIOUX**

**Plains of Abraham, Battle of the** (1759)
The site of a battle in Quebec City, Canada, in which British forces under James **WOLFE** defeated a French/ Canadian force under **MONTCALM** and **VAUDREUIL**,

and gained control over Quebec. Wolfe and Montcalm were both killed in the battle.

**Plantagenet Dynasty**
The name given by historians to the royal dynasty in England from HENRY II to RICHARD II (1154–1399), then continued by two rival houses of younger lines, Lancaster and York, until 1485. The dynasty was so called because, allegedly, Henry II's father Geoffrey of Anjou, sported a sprig of broom (Old French, *plante genêt*) in his cap. ► ANGEVINS; EDWARD I; EDWARD II; EDWARD III; HENRY III; JOHN ('JOHN LACKLAND'); LANCASTER, HOUSE OF; RICHARD I, THE LIONHEART; YORK, HOUSE OF

## PLANTAGENET DYNASTY

| Regnal Dates | Name |
|---|---|
| 1154/89 | Henry II |
| 1189/99 | Richard I, the Lionheart |
| 1199/1216 | John, Lackland |
| 1216/72 | Henry III |
| 1272/1307 | Edward I |
| 1307/27 | Edward II |
| 1327/77 | Edward III |
| 1377/99 | Richard II |

**Plantations in Ireland**
The term 'plantation' originally described settlements established in the 1550s to give a friendly hinterland and supply area to the English forts set up in the Irish midlands. An Elizabethan attempt at wider plantation in Munster was defeated by rebellion and war. Better-known is the proposed plantation of Ulster after 1608, which was intended to clear the native population off the land so that it could be tenanted by immigrant Scots and English. But immigrants were relatively few and landlords were unenthusiastic since untenanted land was useless to them, so there was mingling of native and newcomer but little clearance. By the time most Scots immigrants reached Ulster in the 1690s, as refugees from famine, plantation was a discredited and obsolete policy.

**Plassey, Battle of** (1757)
The decisive victory of Robert CLIVE OF PLASSEY over SIRAJ UD-DAULA, Nawab of Bengal, India. Clive's success was aided by the treachery of the Nawab's general, Mir Jafar, whom the British subsequently placed on the throne. The victory was an important step in the British acquisition of Bengal. ► EAST INDIA COMPANY, BRITISH

**Plastiras, Nikolaos** (1883–1953)
Greek politician. A Republican close to VENIZÉLOS, he organized the 1922 coup d'état following the humiliation of the Greek army by Kemal ATATÜRK in Anatolia. Determined to be seen to punish those responsible for the debacle, he contrived the execution of six politicians and military commanders, charging them with treason. After the Republicans' election defeat (1933), he organized another coup which failed and fled with Venizélos to France. Remaining in exile during WORLD WAR II, he was recognized as nominal leader of EDES. In 1945, during the regency of DAMAS-KINOS, he replaced George PAPANDREOU as Prime Minister. After the GREEK CIVIL WAR, he led the National Progressive Union (EPEK) and was again

Prime Minister in one of the many coalition governments during 1951.

**Platov, Matvei Ivanovich, Count** (1757–1818)
Russian soldier. He served in the Turkish campaign of 1770–1, and in 1801 was named by ALEXANDER I 'Hetman of the Cossacks of the Don'. He took part in the campaigns against the French (1805–7), and hung on their retreat from Moscow with pitiless pertinacity (1813), defeating Lefebvre at Altenburg, gaining a victory at Laon, and making his name memorable by the depredations of his fierce horsemen.

**Platt, Thomas Collier** (1833–1910)
US politician. He was a member of the HOUSE OF REPRESENTATIVES in 1873–7 and became a Senator in 1881, but resigned together with his political associate Roscoe CONKLING, after disagreeing with President GARFIELD over the appointment of reform Republicans to civil service positions. Again a Senator in 1897–1909, Platt helped Theodore ROOSEVELT to become Governor of New York in 1898 and supported his bid for the vice-presidency two years later, apparently in a bid to put a stop to Roosevelt's campaign against corruption in state politics.

**Platt Amendment** (1902)
Appendage to the Cuban independence constitution after the SPANISH–AMERICAN WAR (1898) which gave the USA the right to 'intervene for the preservation of Cuban independence'. Such interventions took place in 1906, 1912 and 1920 and, while the Platt Amendment was annulled in 1934, the USA's lease of the naval base at Guantanamo Bay was retained. The Reciprocal Trade Treaty of 1903 continued to allow the USA to dominate the Cuban economy, particularly under the BATISTA administration. The CASTRO revolution of 1959 can be seen as a response to that alien control while the US response (the BAY OF PIGS invasion of 1961) was another manifestation of the rights claimed under the Platt Amendment.

**Plekhanov, Georgei Valentinovich** (1856–1918)
Russian Marxist philosopher, historian and journalist. Dubbed 'the Father of Russian MARXISM', he left Russia in 1880, having already been involved in revolutionary action, and in 1883 founded the first Russian Marxist organization, the Liberation of Labour Group, in Geneva, where he remained until 1917. Arguing against the traditional idea of a peasants' revolt, and propounding the case for a bourgeois, followed by a proletarian, revolution, he was a major intellectual influence on the young LENIN. However, in 1903 he sided with the MENSHEVIKS against Lenin's BOLSHEVIKS, and in 1917 he denounced the OCTOBER REVOLUTION. He then moved to Finland, where he died. ► RUSSIAN REVOLUTION

**Plessy v Ferguson** (1896)
US Supreme Court decision that opened the way to racial segregation under the US CONSTITUTION by upholding the concept of 'separate but equal'. Homer Plessy was appealing against his conviction for refusing to leave a railroad car reserved for whites. The court ruled that if the facilities offered blacks were equal to those for whites, there was no infringement of the FOURTEENTH AMENDMENT. Justice John M Harlan dissented with the prescient warning that the

ruling was 'inconsistent with civil freedom' and would support prejudice. The decision came to underpin the whole structure of segregation in the Southern states during the first half of the 20c, eventually being overturned by **BROWN V BOARD OF EDUCATION OF TOPEKA, KANSAS** (1954).

**Pleve, Vyacheslav Konstantinovich** (1846–1904)
Russian police chief and politician. A lawyer by training, he was director of state police by the age of 35. He attacked the relatively conservative zemstvos, confiscated Armenian Church lands, and regularly persecuted Jews, Finns and Poles. He became Minister of the Interior after the assassination of the incumbent in 1902 by a socialist revolutionary, and was himself murdered the same way in 1904. He acquired notoriety for urging **NICHOLAS II** to fight Japan since what Russia needed was 'a small victorious war', which of course it lost. His repressive activities gave Tsarism an evil press in Russia and abroad. ► **ZEMSTVO**

**PLO (Palestine Liberation Organization)**
An organization that consists of several of the Palestinian groups opposed to Israel. Founded in 1964, its charter denied the right of Israel to exist and called for **PALESTINE** to be liberated by armed conflict. In 1974 the Arab summit in Rabat, Morocco, recognized the PLO as the sole legitimate representative of the Palestinian people. In 1982 its forces in Lebanon were attacked and expelled by Israel, with the support of the US **REAGAN** administration; many US servicemen and diplomats in Lebanon were killed as a result. Secret talks in Norway (1991–3) between the Israeli Prime Minister Yitzhak **RABIN** and the PLO led to the agreement signed in Washington, DC (13 Sep 1993) by Rabin and PLO leader Yasser **ARAFAT** on mutual recognition and limited self-rule in the **PALESTINIAN AUTONOMOUS AREAS**. Further peace talks in 1995 allowed for the expansion of Palestinian self-rule. However, changing Israeli governments, the second **INTIFADA** and Israel's growing anger with Arafat led to a deadlock in the peace process that ended only with Arafat's death in Nov 2004 and the election of a moderate, Mahoud Abbas, as his successor.

**Plojhar, Josef** (1902–81)
Czechoslovak politician. A member of the People's Party and an active Catholic priest, he agreed to support the communists in their takeover of power in 1948 and be a member of the new National Front government. He became Minister of Health and remained such until 1968 when the reformers removed him. Archbishop **BERAN** banned him from preaching, but his clerical collar gave his government some degree of respectability in foreign parts.

**Plombières, Agreement of** (July 1858)
A secret accord negotiated by **CAVOUR** with **NAPOLEON III**, in which the latter promised extensive military and financial assistance to Sardinia-Piedmont to drive the Austrians from the Kingdom of **LOMBARDY-VENETIA**. In return, France was to receive Savoy and probably Nice, while Clotilde, daughter of **VICTOR EMMANUEL II** was to marry Jerome Napoleon. The agreement provided the basis for a defensive–offensive alliance concluded on 18 Jan 1859, war eventually breaking out in Apr of the same year.

**Plunkitt, George Washington** (1842–1924)
US politician. Tammany leader of the New York Fifteenth Assembly District, Sachem of the Tammany Society and chairman of the Election Committee of **TAMMANY HALL**, he was at various times an assemblyman, state senator, police magistrate, county supervisor and alderman. At one time he held four public offices and drew salaries from three of them simultaneously, a fact of which he was inordinately proud. He was immortalized in a series of 'Very Plain Talks on Very Practical Politics', recorded by the journalist William L Riordon, and published under the title *Plunkitt of Tammany Hall* in 1905. It was a cheerfully ingenuous defence of machine politics, and has become a minor classic of US political science. ► **POLITICAL MACHINE**

**pluralism**
Both a description of and prescription for circumstances where political power is widely dispersed, so that no one interest group or class predominates. The principal conditions for pluralism are free elections, many and overlapping interests, low barriers to ways of organizing pressure on government, and a state that is responsive to popular demands. The term is commonly applied to liberal democracies, where it is argued that the large number of pressure groups complement electoral politics in allowing citizens to get their preferences reflected in government decisions. However, the argument that pluralism is democratic is criticized by some on the grounds that social and economic inequalities make political competition unequal.

**Plymouth Colony**
The American colony established by the *Mayflower* Pilgrims in 1620, comprising the south-east corner of modern Massachusetts. It existed as a separate entity until 1686, when it was absorbed into the Dominion of New England. In 1691 it became part of Massachusetts Bay. ► **PILGRIM FATHERS**

**PMDB** (*Partido do Movimento Democrático Brasileiro*, 'Brazilian Democratic Movement Party')
The political party created in Brazil (1979) by opposition groups in response to the military government's attempts to dissolve the two-party system created in the aftermath of the 1964 military coup. This system pitted ARENA (*Aliança Renovadora Nacional*), heir to the conservative UDN (*União Democrática Nacional*) and **PDS**, against the MDB (*Movimento Democrático Brasileiro*), itself the successor to **VARGAS'** PSD (pro-**KUBITSCHEK (DE OLIVEIRA)**) and the pro-**GOULART** PTB (*Partido Trabalhista Brasileiro*). By 1979, the strength of the PMDB in the cities and industrial zones of Brazil meant that it could outflank the Figueiredo government. Although the regime did succeed in dividing the PMDB between adherents to **BRIZOLA'S** PDT (*Partido Democrático Trabalhista*), a rump PTB, **LULA'S** PT (*Partido dos Trabalhadores*) and Tancredo **NEVES'** *Partido Popular*, the PMDB gained decisive victories in 1982. It provided the platform for Neves' presidential campaign in 1984–5, and was an uneasy supporter of **SARNEY (COSTA)** in the gubernatorial contest of 1986. Its identification with Sarney and the 'old politics' lost it the presidential campaign of 1989 to Fernando **COLLOR DE MELLO**. However, in the 1994 election, which was won by Fernando

# Poetry

*Art & Literature*

The origins of poetry are generally agreed to be in song, and the
connection between verse and music has remained strong throughout
history. It is nevertheless evident from the earliest surviving examples of poetry, and from poems passed down through an
oral tradition that may date back to pre-literate times, that the musical potential of words, their rhythms and ability to
sound together, soon developed an importance independent of any musical accompaniment. The formality of verse, and
its sense of being language raised above the level of the everyday, made it a natural choice for religious ritual. On the other
hand, the ability of verse to stick in the memory, still often exploited in the advertising jingle, gave it a great many humbler
uses: as a medium for entertaining or teaching small children or for passing down stories from one generation to the next.

### Epic poetry – the folk epic

There is still a tradition among some African peoples that on public occasions the chief should have a praise singer to go
before him announcing his great deeds and great qualities. It is suggested that the origins of epic or heroic poetry in pre-
literate societies may lie in the songs sung to encourage warriors preparing to go into battle, celebrating their courage
and exploits or those of their ancestors. Whatever the initial purpose and occasion for such poetry, many early societies
built up and maintained a tradition of bards reciting tales of heroes and gods in verse from memory, and passing them
down from one generation to the next. In ancient Japan noble families employed reciters whose job was to chronicle the
myths, legends and history of the family and recite them at banquets. Bards who recited unwritten epic tales were still
active in the Balkans in the early 20c.

The earliest extant epic poetry comes from Mesopotamia. The Sumerian predecessors of the Babylonians left epic
fragments dating from about 3000 BC, including part of the *Epic of Gilgamesh* written down on clay tablets in about
2000 BC in Babylonia and constituting the earliest known great poetic work of humankind. The story of King Gilgamesh,
who quarrels with the goddess Ishtar, befriends the wild man sent by Ishtar to overthrow him, undertakes many
adventures with him and, when his friend is killed, seeks the secret of immortality from a survivor of the Flood, is
thought to have influenced both parts of the Old Testament and of Homer. Other epics thought to have grown out of an
oral tradition are the Indian *Mahabharata* ('Great Story') and *Ramayana* ('Story of Rama') – the former composed
between 300 BC and AD 300, the latter thought of as slightly later from its rather more literary style – and poems from
northern Europe such as the Anglo-Saxon *Beowulf* (8c AD) and the *Nibelungenlied* ('Song of the Nibelungs'), written
down in Middle High German in the 13c. The Finnish national epic, the *Kalevala*, after centuries of oral transmission
was finally written down in the 19c.

Typical features of folk epic are standardized descriptions, for example of banquets or battles, and stock descriptive
epithets that attach themselves to characters or objects, presumably as aids to the reciter's memory. The *Iliad* and the
*Odyssey* of Homer, especially the former, contain such material in abundance: the 'wine-dark sea', 'rosy-fingered dawn',
and so on. It has long been a matter of dispute whether Homer ever existed, whether the poems are to be attributed to
collective or folk authorship, or whether a single individual was responsible for taking traditional material and putting it
into its present form. It is generally agreed, however, that the stories of a crucial episode during the siege of Troy and of
Odysseus's wanderings home after the end of the siege were written in Ionia in around the 8c BC. It is also beyond
dispute that the influence of the Homeric epics on the whole of Western literature has been enormous.

### The literary epic

The literary epic is a conscious effort by an individual poet to create a long heroic poem of similar scope and grandeur to
the folk epic. The Roman poet Virgil (70–19 BC) picked up the thread from Homer in making his hero, Aeneas, a survivor
of the siege of Troy. He went further in making the *Aeneid* (29–19 BC) a Roman national epic, not merely chronicling the
adventures of the legendary ancestor of the founders of the city, but celebrating its particular virtues and spirit.

---

Henrique Cardoso of the Party of Brazilian Social
Democracy (PSDB), the PMDB, still the largest party,
managed to increase its number of governorships
from seven to nine. Four years later its support had
dwindled, and only six of its governors were returned,
but it remains the third largest party in Congress.

**PNC ►** PEOPLE'S NATIONAL CONGRESS (Guyana)

**PNV** (*Partido Nacionalista Vasco*, 'Basque Nationalist
Party')
Founded in 1895, the PNV (or *Eusko Alderdi Jeltzalea*
in Basque), was the first political party to defend
Basque nationalism. Under the Second Republic of
1931–6 it was the leading party in Basque politics,
though it never had a majority. With the outbreak of
the SPANISH CIVIL WAR (Jul 1936), the PNV backed
the Republic in exchange for an autonomy statute,
which was passed in Oct 1936. Under the dynamic
leadership of José Antonio AGUIRRE, the PNV gained
control of the autonomous government. During the
Basque government's exile of 1939–75 the PNV pro-

vided most of its leadership. Since 1980 the PNV has
led the regional government of the Basque country,
but splits in the 1980s reduced its share of the Basque
vote to 22 per cent in 1987. It increased its share of the
vote to 28 per cent in the elections of 1998. In 2004
the PNV was a co-founder of the European Democratic Party. ► BASQUE AUTONOMY STATUTES;
REPUBLIC, SECOND (Spain)

**Pobedonostsev, Konstantin Petrovich** (1827–
1907)
Russian jurist and politician. Tutor, and later adviser,
to ALEXANDER III and NICHOLAS II, he became Professor of Civil Law at Moscow in 1858 and, as a member of a judicial commission in 1863, favoured liberal
reforms in the law. However, after becoming Procurator of the Holy Synod in 1866, he reacted against
this, becoming strongly opposed to any westernizing
changes in Russia and the most influential as well as
the most uncompromising champion of the autocracy and of the supremacy of the RUSSIAN ORTHO-
DOX CHURCH. He was eventually forced to resign in

Later writers endeavoured to emulate Virgil in writing a national epic, notably the Portuguese poet Camões, whose *Lusiads* was published in 1572. But the greatest successor to Virgil, Dante Alighieri, took the epic in a very different direction. His *Divine Comedy*, begun around 1307, is a vision of hell, purgatory and heaven, through which the author is led on what is both a personal quest and a general survey of human character and of the society of his time. Epics of chivalry and romance were written in the **Renaissance** by the Italian writers Ariosto and Tasso, and by the English poet Edmund Spenser, and in the 17c John Milton produced his great Christian epic of the Creation and Fall, *Paradise Lost*. After that the epic and heroic tradition of telling a great story in elevated verse largely died out. It is more appropriate to call long poems written later by some other name. A tradition of mock epic, in which the conventions of epic poetry are turned on their head and heroic grandeur is contrasted with contemporary bathos, remained strong throughout the 18c. A notable example is Alexander Pope's *The Rape of the Lock* (1712).

The part played by great poets such as Dante and Camões in developing their own vernacular languages should also be noted. They demonstrated the capacity of modern languages to support literary achievement, on a par with that of the ancient world. The poet who first gave England a literary voice was Geoffrey Chaucer. Writing in the latter part of the 14c he was a master of the art of narrative verse, creating an unforgettable collection of characters in his *Canterbury Tales*, and establishing the southern dialect as the literary language of England.

### Lyric poetry

For the Western tradition, subjective lyric poetry begins in ancient Greece with the work of Alcaeus and Sappho in the 7c BC, and Pindar in the 5c BC. Their work, as the name 'lyric' suggests, was intended to be sung. It inspired Roman writers such as Catullus and Horace. In turn, a continuing tradition of late Latin lyrical writing inspired the troubadours and Minnesänger, who established a vernacular tradition of love poetry, sung to the harp or recited in the courts of medieval Europe. The lyric as a verse form without a musical accompaniment is a creation of the Renaissance. The sonnets of Petrarch in particular, written in the 14c, inspired imitators in France, England and beyond.

Of equal importance as a source to the Western poetic tradition are the Hebrew Psalms, probably composed as a number of independent collections and later collated between 1300 BC and 500 BC. The lyric poem is as much a vehicle for spirituality and religious devotion as for the expression of earthly love. A tradition of Christian devotional poetry and hymn writing in the West began with the Latin hymns of the early Fathers and continued in a wide variety of forms. The **Reformation** and the **Counter-Reformation** produced a great deal of mystical religious poetry, some of it reaching the highest levels. Included in this are works by the Anglican dean John Donne (1572–1631) and the great Spanish mystics Fray Luis de León (1527–91) and St John of the Cross (1542–91).

Other cultures have their own lyric traditions. There is a great tradition of lyrical poetry in Arabic, for example, dating even from before the composition of the *Quran*. In Persia in the 13–14c, there was a flowering of the *ghazal*, a form used by poets such as Hafez and Rumi both for love poems and poems of religious mysticism. Chinese poetry, dating from the first collection around the 6c BC, the *Shih Ching*, is almost exclusively lyric, meditative and elegiac. The *haiku*, a poem consisting of 17 syllables, was perfected in Japan in the 17c and represents what many consider to be the essence of poetry: experience condensed into a short burst of evocative or passionate language. The hymns and poems of the Marathi mystics after 1400 played a key role in sustaining Hindu revivalism in the face of Muslim expansion in India.

The lyric tradition continues down to the present day. Indeed, it is difficult for a modern poet, at least in the West, to admit to anything other than a personal lyrical inspiration. The difficulties for a modern poet in fulfilling a public role and a praising or chronicling function, or speaking for anyone but himself or herself, are evident whenever the British poet laureate is called upon to celebrate a royal event.

### Dramatic verse

From the time of ancient Greeks to the 18c, verse was used as the medium for almost all tragedy, and for some comedy, in the Western tradition. Aeschylus, Sophocles, Euripides, Corneille and Racine, for example, deserve to be remembered as among the greatest poets of their respective ages, as well as great playwrights. Shakespeare holds a special place among

---

1905 in the midst of the revolution of that year, but he had by then done immeasurable damage to the progress of normal constitutional change. ➤ **REVOLUTION OF 1905**

**Pocahontas**, Powhatan name **Matoaka** (1595–1617) Native American princess, the daughter of a chief, Powhatan, who is said to have saved the life of Captain John **SMITH**, leader of a group of colonists who settled in Chesapeake Bay in 1607. She was captured and taken to Jamestown in 1612, where she embraced Christianity, was baptized Rebecca, married an Englishman, John Rolfe (1585–1622), and went to England with him in 1616. She embarked for Virginia the following year, but died of smallpox off Gravesend in England, leaving one son. ➤ **POWHATAN CONFEDERACY**

**Podgorny, Nikolai Viktorovich** (1903–83) Soviet politician. Born in the Ukraine, the son of a foundry worker, he worked in the sugar industry and in due course held managerial, educational and mi-

nisterial posts connected with food. In 1930 he joined the Communist Party, and after **WORLD WAR II** took a leading role in the economic reconstruction of the liberated Ukraine. He held various senior posts (1950–65), becoming a full member of the **POLITBURO** in 1960. Following the dismissal of Nikita **KHRUSHCHEV** (1964), he became Chairman of the Presidium and therefore titular head of state in 1965. He was relieved of this office in 1977 and replaced by Leonid **BREZHNEV**, partly because his performance was lacklustre, but mainly because Brezhnev wanted to be head of state as well as General-Secretary of the Party. ➤ **COMMUNISM**

**Poetry** ➤ *See panel*

**pogrom**
A violent racialist assault on a minority ethnic or religious group, especially Jews. The first great outbreak of pogroms was in Russia in 1881–2 following the assassination of Tsar **ALEXANDER II**, for which Jews were falsely blamed. Despite the findings of a

them, not only for the number and variety of his verse dramas, but also for producing a body of lyrical work, particularly his 154 sonnets. Shakespeare may also be credited with keeping poetic **drama** from going beyond its historical sell-by date. The discovery of Shakespeare on the continent of Europe in the late 18c and early 19c gave it a new lease of life under the Romantic movement when the tide was beginning to run towards **prose**. Verse dramas were written in the 20c and enjoyed some success, but there are no signs at present that verse is likely to recapture its former status in the **theatre**.

### Ballads

The origins and authorship of ballads – apparently simple, narrative, folk poems – are as much in dispute as those of folk epic, some scholars arguing for collective, some for individual authorship. Ballads from many cultures exist. It is impossible to trace traditional ballads in Europe further back than the **Middle Ages**. Besides being repositories of traditional tales and romances, from the early 16c ballads also took on a contemporary function as spreaders of news and comment about current events among the common people. The execution of a notorious murderer or highwayman, a battle, or any event out of the ordinary, might be recorded in simple verse and printed as a ballad. This tradition continued into the 19c.

Traditional ballads began to be collected and published during the 18c. Their simplicity and directness was a world away from the prevailing poetic fashion of the time, in which classical elegance and a refined and rather artificial diction predominated. In both Germany and England the poets of the early Romantic period, such as Goethe, Wordsworth and Coleridge, seized on the ballad tradition as a way of instilling new life into literary verse and bringing it back more into the realm of ordinary people.

### Poetry in modern times

Great poetry was written in many languages during the course of the 20c. There is a general sense, however, that the readership for poetry has diminished and that, unlike the novel, it plays very little part in the ordinary lives of the majority of people. The language of poetry is never quite the same as the language of ordinary life, and poetic fashion has frequently veered between a mode of expression that was consciously different from that of ordinary speech and one that consciously strove to imitate it. Much Western poetry in the early 20c was felt to be 'difficult' – difficult to understand and difficult to appreciate because it often diverged from traditional forms. In the late 20c, however, there was a conscious effort on the part of some writers to bring poetry back to a wider, and especially a young, public, emphasizing the spoken aspect of poetry – poetry as something to be heard rather than read. Performance poets, as they are known, are in this sense going back to the very roots of the poetic tradition and joining hands with the epic reciters and ballad singers of old in order to give poetry a popular, as well as a literary, future.

the *Epic of Gilgamesh* is written down (Sumeria) — *7c BC*

the Anglo-Saxon epic *Beowulf* is written down — *14c*

the haiku perfected (Japan) — *18c–19c*

*c.2000 BC*

first Western lyric poetry (Greece) — *8c AD*

Dante Alighieri's *Divine Comedy* (Italy) — *17c*

traditional ballads collected and published in Europe

commission in 1883–8 that Russian Jews were sinned against rather than sinning, pogroms and anti-Semitism in general grew more widespread and in fact provoked many Jewish intellectuals into revolutionary activities.

**Poincaré, Raymond Nicolas Landry** (1860–1934)
French politician. He studied law, becoming a Deputy (1887) and Senator (1903), holding office as Minister of Public Instruction (1893 and 1895), of Finance (1894–5 and 1906), and of Foreign Affairs (1912–13 and 1922–3). Elected Prime Minister (1912–13) and President (1913–20), he sought to play a more direct-ive role than previous incumbents. He had some success at first, especially in foreign affairs, but when **CLEMENCEAU** became Prime Minister in 1917, he found himself sidelined, and was unable to influence decisions at the post-war peace conference. As Prime Minister once again (1922–4) he sought to enforce the terms of the Treaty of **VERSAILLES** (notably the payment of reparations) against a recalcitrant Germany by occupying the Ruhr (1923–4). Although

Germany was thus forced to negotiate, Poincaré had by then been defeated in the 1924 elections, and his successor as Prime Minister, **HERRIOT**, bowing to British and US pressure, conceded much of what Poincaré had hoped to achieve. He was brought back to power (1926–9), as Prime Minister and Finance Minister, to deal with a financial crisis; he stabilized the franc, inaugurating a brief period of prosperity before France succumbed to the **GREAT DEPRESSION**.

**Poindexter, John Marlan** (1936–)
US naval officer and political adviser. The son of a bank manager, he was educated at the US Naval Academy and California Institute of Technology (Caltech), where he obtained a doctorate in nuclear physics. He became chief of naval operations during the 1970s and was deputy head of naval educational training from 1978 to 1981. In 1981 he joined President **REA-GAN**'S **NATIONAL SECURITY COUNCIL** (NSC), becoming National Security Adviser in 1985. He resigned, together with his assistant, Lieutenant-Colonel Oliver North, in 1986 in the aftermath of the **IRAN–**

**CONTRA AFFAIR**. Poindexter retired from the navy in 1987, and in 1990 was convicted by a Federal court on charges of obstructing and lying to **CONGRESS**. He was sentenced to six months in prison, but his sentence was overturned by the federal appeals court in 1991. In 2002 he was appointed Director of the Information Awareness Office of the Pentagon.

### Point Four Program (1949–53)

A US policy that provided technical assistance and economic aid to underdeveloped countries, named after the fourth point in President Harry S **TRUMAN**'s 1949 inaugural address. It was merged with other foreign-aid programs in 1953.

### Poissy, Synod of (1561)

A meeting of theologians called by the French Regent **CATHERINE DE' MEDICI**, and her adviser Michel de **L'HÔPITAL**, in an attempt to reconcile Catholics and Protestants. It failed due to the intransigence of both sides on the question of transubstantiation.

### Poitiers, Battle of (19 Sep 1356)

A battle between England and France during the **HUNDRED YEARS' WAR**. The English forces, under **EDWARD, THE BLACK PRINCE** (son of **EDWARD III**), were victorious and King **JOHN II** of France was captured. The battle had important consequences, the French King agreeing to return all possessions in France which had been held by **HENRY II** of England. When the French nobility resisted these terms, Edward III invaded France and laid siege to Paris. The Treaty of Bretigny (1360), which ceded much territory in France to Edward III together with a large ransom for King John, represented one of the high-water marks of English success during the war.

---

**POLAND**   official name **Republic of Poland**

A republic in central Europe, bounded to the north by Russia and the Baltic Sea; to the west by Germany; to the south-west by the Czech Republic; to the south by Slovakia; to the south-east by the Ukraine; and to the north-east by Belarus and Lithuania. Poland was inhabited from 2000BC or earlier and became an independent kingdom in the 9c. The Poles under the **PIAST DYNASTY** emerged as the most powerful of a number of Slavic groups in 1025. Towards the end of Jagiełłon rule Poland formed a union with Lithuania (1569), at which point it stretched from the Baltic to the Black Sea. This Commonwealth was weakened by attacks from Russia, Brandenburg, Turkey and Sweden, and eventually in 1772, 1793 and 1795 Poland was partitioned between Prussia, Russia and Austria, and was deprived of its independent statehood; Russia gained the lion's share of its territories. Following the 1815 Congress of **VIENNA**, Poland became a semi-

independent state called the Congress Kingdom of Poland, but was incorporated into the Russian Empire under **ALEXANDER I**. The Poles constantly struggled for national liberation, and there were uprisings in 1830, 1846–9 and 1863, which led to the kingdom being fully absorbed and subjected to a repressive campaign of Russification. However, the struggle continued and was eventually won at the end of **WORLD WAR I** in 1918 when an independent Polish state emerged. Germany invaded Poland in 1939, precipitating **WORLD WAR II**, and Poland was partitioned between Germany and the USSR in the same year. During the war a major resistance movement developed, and a government in exile was set up. In 1944 a People's Democracy was established under Soviet influence, and by 1947 communists controlled the government. The late 1970s saw the rise of an independent trade union known from 1980 as **SOLIDARITY**. Its leaders were detained in 1981–3, and a state of martial law was imposed. The economic situation worsened, and there was continuing unrest in the 1980s. In 1989 multiparty politics were legalized and elections were held: the communist government lost support and Solidarity had major successes. Solidarity's leader Lech **WAŁESA** became President of Poland in Dec 1990, but was defeated in 1995 by the former communist Aleksander Kwasniewski, who was re-elected in 2000. The transition to a **MARKET ECONOMY** in the 1990s was accompanied by popular discontent, political difficulties and recession, but nevertheless a private sector developed within the economy. In 1997 another new constitution was adopted which eradicated all signs of the former communist system and a Solidarity-led government was formed under Jerzy Buzek. In the 2001 elections, Solidarity failed to win any seats in the lower house of parliament and a coalition government led by the Democratic Left Alliance took office. Poland joined **NATO** in 1999 and the **EU** in 2004. ► **JAGIEŁŁON DYNASTY**

### Pole, Reginald (1500–58)

English Roman Catholic churchman and Archbishop of Canterbury. He received several Church posts, and was at first high in **HENRY VIII**'s favour, but after opposing the King on his divorce, he left for Italy, and lost all his preferments. In 1536 the pope made him a cardinal, and in 1554, in the reign of the Catholic Queen **MARY I**, he returned to England as papal legate. He became one of the most powerful advisers, returned the country to Rome, and became Archbishop of Canterbury. ► **REFORMATION** (England)

### Polignac, Auguste Jules Armand Marie, Prince of (1780–1847)

French politician. An exponent of papal and royal authority, he received the title of prince from the pope in 1820 and became in 1829 head of the last Bourbon ministry. He promulgated the St Cloud Ordinances that cost **CHARLES X** of France his throne (1830). He was imprisoned until 1836, then lived in exile in England, returning in 1845 to Paris. ► **BOURBON, HOUSE OF**; **JULY REVOLUTION** (1830)

**Polisario** (*Frente Popular para la Liberación de Saguia el Hamra y Río de Oro*, 'Popular Front for the Liberation of Saguia el Hamra and Río de Oro')

This is a movement of tribesmen from what is now

called **WESTERN SAHARA**, which aims to resist the attempts to absorb these areas into Morocco. This move on the part of King Hasan followed Spain's granting of independence to the region (its former colony), and the division of the region between Morocco and Mauritania. Hostilities in 1975 and Polisario's establishment (1976) of a 'government-in-exile' of the so-called Sahrawi Arab Democratic Republic (SADR) was the prelude to Mauritania's renouncing the portion of the former Spanish Sahara it had shared with Morocco. Polisario guerrillas put up armed resistance from bases in Algeria, where they were supplied with arms by both Algeria and Libya, thereby provoking a Moroccan response which included the building of defensive works on the 'borders'. In 1988 the **UN** proposed a referendum to enable the indigenous population to choose between the area becoming an independent state under Polisario or becoming part of Morocco, but following disagreements on both sides, the referendum has yet to be held. A UN-brokered ceasefire have been in force since 1991.

## Polish Corridor
An area of formerly Polish territory, acquired by Prussia at the time of the Partitions and transferred from Germany to Poland by the Treaty of **VERSAILLES** (1919). It linked the Polish heartland with the free city of Danzig (or Gdansk) and the Baltic Sea, but divided East Prussia from the rest of Germany. Its recovery was one of **HITLER**'s aspirations during the late 1930s, providing him with a pretext for his aggression against Poland.

## Polish Succession, War of the (1733–8)
Upon the death of the Polish King **AUGUSTUS II, THE STRONG** (1 Feb 1733), France and Spain opposed the Austrian- and Russian-backed claimant to the throne, Frederick Augustus II, Elector of Saxony. The ensuing war engulfed much of Europe and was ended by the Treaties of **VIENNA** (1735 and 1738) which recognized the claim of Frederick Augustus (**AUGUSTUS III** of Poland). The principal results of the war though were a redistribution of Italian territories and an increase in Russian power in Poland. France also agreed conditionally to accept the **PRAGMATIC SANCTION** of Emperor **CHARLES VI**. ► **STANISŁAW LESZCZYŃSKI**

## Politburo
The Political Bureau of the Central Committee of the **COMMUNIST PARTY OF THE SOVIET UNION**, at various times known as the Presidium. It was the highest organ of the Party, and, therefore, of the entire Soviet political system. Formally elected by the Central Committee, there were latterly about 15 members plus about seven candidate members who had no votes; in practice, though, membership was decided by the Politburo itself under the General-Secretary, who presided over it. Its functions might be compared to those of a cabinet, though its authority varied over the years. It was seldom questioned by the Party Congress or even by the Central Committee; in turn, it could only question the General-Secretary at times of crisis. Most other communist parties adopted the Soviet model.

## political action committee (PAC)
In the USA, a committee organized to raise funds to elect or defeat candidates for political office in order to promote certain policies or legislation, often in support of special interests. The first PAC was formed in 1944 to raise money for the re-election of President Franklin D **ROOSEVELT**; by 1994 more than 4,000 PACs were registered. There are three sorts: those sponsored by corporations (eg Microsoft, Coca-Cola), which account for almost half of all PACs; ideological PACs (eg Emily's List, the National Rifle Association); and 'leadership' PACs, formed by politicians to help elect other politicians to office. The Federal Election Commission requires PACs to be registered and strict rules govern how much money may be donated. There have long been calls for tighter regulation but a 1996 reform bill failed to pass through Congress. The Enron scandal in 2001 underlined how easily the power of corporate contributions could corrupt the democratic process.

## political machine
A term used to describe the US urban political organization developed in the late 19c in response to the constitutional decentralization of local politics intersecting with the flood of immigration into northern cities such as New York, Philadelphia and Boston at a time of very rapid physical growth. Hierarchically structured from the city level, down through the ward to the precinct, the machine depended on the ability of the 'boss' to respond to the individual needs of constituents who voted at his direction in return, thus allowing him to control nominations and to discipline office holders. Developed by both parties and sizable ethnic groups, political machines have been characterized by endemic corruption and inefficiency, and many contemporary observers regard them as a degradation of democratic politics.

## Polk, James K(nox) (1795–1849)
US politician and 11th President. He was admitted to the Bar in 1820, served in the **HOUSE OF REPRESENTATIVES** as a Democrat (1825–39), and was Governor of Tennessee (1839–41). Polk ran for President in 1844 as a 'dark horse' candidate who favoured the annexation of Texas. He became an activist President (1845–9) and a strong leader who set himself major objectives and achieved them. They included reducing the tariff, restoring the independent treasury system, settling the Oregon boundary dispute with Great Britain, and bringing Texas and California (which was under Mexican rule) into the Union. Texas was admitted to the Union in 1945. Unable to acquire California by peaceful negotiations, Polk ordered US troops to advance to the Rio Grande, precipitating war with Mexico. After the **MEXICAN WAR** (1846–8) the USA acquired California, New Mexico and most of the south-west. ► **'FIFTY-FOUR FORTY OR FIGHT'**

## Pollock, Sir George (1786–1872)
British soldier. Entering the British **EAST INDIA COMPANY**'s army in 1803, he was engaged at the siege of Bhartpur (1805) and in other operations. Pollock saw service in the Nepal (Gurkha) campaigns of 1814–16, and was promoted colonel in the first Burmese War (1824–6). In 1838 he was made major-general. After the massacre of General Elphinstone in Afghanistan, the Indian government sent him to the relief of Sir Robert Sale in Jelalabad. In Apr 1842 he forced his way through the Khyber Pass and reached

Sale, pushed on to Kabul, defeated the Afghan army, and recovered 135 British prisoners. He conducted the united armies back to India, and was rewarded with a political appointment at Lucknow. He returned to England in 1846, was Director of the East India Company from 1854 to 1856 and was created a field marshal in 1870.

## poll tax

A fixed tax levied on each individual member of a population. In the Southern states of the USA it was used by the **DEMOCRATIC PARTY** as a precondition of the right to vote, thereby disenfranchising poor people who were unable to pay. This use of the poll tax was declared unconstitutional in 1964. The poll tax was levied in 1377–81 in England, and was widely blamed for sparking off the **PEASANTS' REVOLT** led by Wat **TYLER**. Reintroduced in Scotland in 1989 and elsewhere in the UK in 1990 by Margaret **THATCHER** as the 'community charge', a replacement for local property rates, it was met with widespread unpopularity, riots and severe administrative difficulties.

## Polo, Marco (1254–1324)

Venetian merchant and traveller. Born into a noble Venetian merchant family, he accompanied his father and uncle on their second journey (1271–5) to the court of **KUBLAI KHAN** in China. Marco became an envoy in Kublai's service, and served as Governor of Yang Chow. He left China in 1292, and after returning to Venice (1295), fought against the Genoese, but was captured. During his imprisonment he compiled an account of his travels, *Il milione* ('The Million', translated as 'The Travels of Marco Polo'). ➤ **EXPLORATION**

## Polonnaruwa

A city in northern Sri Lanka and the centre of the island's second great Buddhist kingdom after the demise of **ANURADHAPURA**. The city was established by members of the invading south Indian Chola Dynasty, but was retained as the centre of government by the Sri Lankan kings who successfully fought them off during the 12c and 13c. The kingdom reached its zenith during the reigns of King Parakramabahu I (1153/86) and Nissanka Malli (1187/96), but rapidly declined after further attacks from south India and, possibly, the effects of malaria in the surrounding area.

## Pol Pot, also known as Saloth Sar (1925–98)

Cambodian (Kampuchean) politician. After working on a rubber plantation in his early teens, he joined the anti-French resistance movement during the early 1940s, becoming a member of the Indo-Chinese Communist Party and Cambodian Communist Party in 1946. During the 1960s and early 1970s he led the communist **KHMER ROUGE** in guerrilla warfare against the governments of Prince **SIHANOUK** and Lieutenant-General Lon Nol. After the destruction of the Lon Nol regime in 1975, he became Prime Minister. He proceeded brutally to introduce an extreme regime which resulted in the loss of perhaps more than 2,500,000 lives. The regime was overthrown by Vietnamese troops in Jan 1979 and Pol Pot took to the resistance struggle once more. Guerrilla activity continued into the 1990s. However, in 1996 a splinter group escaped to join the Cambodian government and the Khmer Rouge appeared to be breaking up.

Another faction put Pol Pot through a show trial in 1997 and he died whilst under house arrest.

## Poltava, Battle of (1709)

The famous Russian victory in the **GREAT NORTHERN WAR**. The Russians outnumbered the Swedes by two to one in soldiers and artillery (although at the Battle of Narva, in 1700, they had enjoyed better odds, yet had been beaten). The difference now was the quality of **PETER I, THE GREAT**'s army and of his own generalship. The war dragged on for another 12 years, but its outcome had in fact already been decided.

## Polyansky, Dmitri Stepanovich (1917– )

Ukrainian politician. Of peasant stock, he graduated in agriculture in Kharkov in 1939 and immediately became a Communist Party functionary. However, in 1958 his career blossomed when Nikita **KHRUSHCHEV** made him chairman of the Russian Council of Ministers. In 1960 he became a member of the **POLITBURO**. Even under Leonid **BREZHNEV** he held several other ministerial posts, but in 1976 he was dropped from all but ambassadorial appointments as he was no longer in favour.

## polycentrism

A political term, first used by the Italian Communist Party (**PCI**) leader Palmiro **TOGLIATTI** after the 20th Congress of the Soviet Communist Party in Feb 1956 to describe and support the growing independence of other communist parties from the Soviet party after the **STALIN** era. The trend was forced on Yugoslavia when it was expelled from the **COMINFORM** in 1948. It became more difficult to believe in after the Soviet suppression of the Hungarian Uprising in Oct 1956, but it reasserted itself in the late 1950s and early 1960s. It was no longer used after the Soviet invasion of Czechoslovakia in 1968. ➤ **MARXISM–LENINISM; STALINISM**

## Pomaks

Bulgarian Muslims who converted to Islam during the Ottoman occupation. In 1970 there were c.170,000 Pomaks still in Bulgaria, predominantly in the Meglen district of Macedonia. They use the Bulgarian language, but with many Turkish words. During the 1970s and 1980s they were subject to a programme of forced assimilation, which included changing their Islamic surnames for Slav ones.

## Pombal, Sebastião José de Carvalho e Mello, Marquis of (1699–1782)

Portuguese statesman. He became Ambassador to London (1739) and Vienna (1745), and Secretary for Foreign Affairs (1750). He showed great resourcefulness in replanning the city of Lisbon following the disastrous earthquake of 1755, and was made Prime Minister in 1756. He opposed Church influence, reorganized the army, and improved agriculture, commerce and finance. He was made count (1758) and marquis (1770), but fell from office on the accession of Maria I (1777).

## Pomerania

A region of north-central Europe along the Baltic Sea from Stralsund to the River Vistula in Poland. It was a disputed territory in the 17–18c, and was divided among Germany, Poland and the free city of Danzig in 1919–39. It was divided again, between East

Germany and Poland, in 1945.

### Pompadour, Madame de, in full Jeanne Antoinette Poisson, Marchioness of Pompadour (1721–64)

Mistress of **LOUIS XV**. A woman of remarkable grace, beauty and wit, she attracted the eye of the King at a ball. Installed at Versailles (1745), and ennobled as Marquise de Pompadour, she assumed the entire control of public affairs, and for 20 years swayed state policy, appointing her own favourites. She was a lavish patroness of architecture, the arts and literature. ► **SEVEN YEARS' WAR**

### Pompidou, Georges Jean Raymond (1911–74)

French politician. He trained as an administrator, joined Charles de **GAULLE**'s staff in 1944, and held various government posts from 1946. He helped to draft the constitution for the Fifth Republic (1959), and negotiate a settlement in Algeria (1961) and in the student-worker revolt of 1968. Prime Minister from 1962 to 1968, he was elected President, as the socialist candidate, after de Gaulle's resignation in 1969, and died in office. ► **REPUBLIC, FIFTH** (France)

### Ponce de León, Juan (1460–1521)

Spanish explorer. Born in San Servas, he was a court page, served against the Moors and became Governor, first of part of Hispaniola, then (1510–12) of Puerto Rico. On a quest for the fountain of perpetual youth, he landed on the coast of Florida in Apr 1513, and was made Governor. Failing to conquer his new subjects, he retired to Cuba, and died there from a wound inflicted by a poisoned arrow. ► **EXPLORATION**

### Poniatowski, Józef Antoni (1763–1813)

Polish patriot and French marshal. The nephew of King **STANISŁAW II AUGUST PONIATOWSKI**, he trained in the Austrian army, then commanded Polish armies against the Russians in the wars of the Second and Third Partitions of Poland. In 1807–9 he commanded Polish troops in Napoleon's Duchy of Warsaw, invading Galicia in 1809, hoping on both occasions to liberate his country. However, he was drowned while covering the French retreat at the Battle of **LEIPZIG**, thus losing his life as well as his cause. ► **NAPOLEONIC WARS**

### Poniatowski, Stanisław (1676–1762)

Polish soldier and official. He was the father of **STANISŁAW II AUGUST PONIATOWSKI**, the last King of Poland. He joined **CHARLES XII** of Sweden in supporting **STANISŁAW LESZCZYŃSKI** for the vacant Polish throne in the 1700s but later under **AUGUSTUS II** and **III** he was appointed to several administrative posts in Lithuania and Poland. He conspired deeply with Russia in securing his son's eventual election in 1764. Interested in promoting the future of a reformed Poland, he found little alternative but to work within the national and international system.

### Poniatowski, Stanisław II August ► STANISŁAW II AUGUST PONIATOWSKI

### Ponomarev, Boris Nikolaevich (1905–95)

Soviet ideologue. He joined the Communist Party at 14, and at 21 became an official propagandist. His subsequent appointments included spells at the **COMINTERN** and at the Institute of **MARXISM–LENINISM**.

In 1955 he became director of the international department of the Central Committee and was only moved when Mikhail **GORBACHEV** came to power in 1985. Throughout 30 years he was a conservative influence, asserting the ideological aspects of foreign policy.

### Pontiac (c.1720–1769)

Native American leader. Born near Maumee River in Ohio, he became chief of the **OTTAWA**. In 1763 he headed a widespread rising against the British garrisons, conducting an extended and ultimately unsuccessful siege of Detroit. Although Pontiac's forces captured several other forts, they were unable to match mounting British reinforcements, and the rebellion faltered by 1764. Pontiac was later murdered by a Native American from Illinois, causing a bitter inter-tribal war. ► **PONTIAC'S CONSPIRACY**

### Pontiac's Conspiracy (1763)

An attempt by Native Americans of the Ohio and Great Lakes country to drive whites out of the area, led by **PONTIAC**, chief of the Ottawa tribe, in retaliation against the English treatment of the **NATIVE AMERICANS** and the threat of expanding white settlements. The movement reached its peak with an unsuccessful siege of Detroit, and a final peace was signed in 1766. ► **INDIAN WARS**

### Pony Express (1860–1)

Mail transport by horse relays from St Joseph, Missouri, to Sacramento, California, from 1860 to 1861. A relay system of riders and ponies to cover the vast distance (2,000 mi/3,200 km) from St Joseph, across the Great Plains and Rocky Mountains, to Sacramento. The journey took about two weeks. Although the Pony Express was almost immediately made obsolete by the telegraph, it lives on in US legend as an emblem of American inventiveness and daring.

### Poona Sarvajanik Sabha

An Indian association, run by intellectuals and the middle class, which played an important role in the country's early freedom struggle. It came to prominence in 1896–7, when famine conditions in Deccan Maharashtra led to a demand for revenue remissions under the famine code – a demand which the government rejected. The *Poona Sarvajanik Sabha* sent agents into the countryside between Oct 1896 and Apr 1897 to popularize the legal rights of Raiyats in a famine situation. Along with the Indian Association, it also took up other issues, including the first all-India agitations on the Civil Service and the Press Act (1877–8).

### Poor Laws

Legislation in Britain originally formulated in 1598 and 1601, whereby relief of poverty was the responsibility of individual parishes under the supervision of Justices of the Peace and the administration of Overseers. Funds were provided by local property rates. As the population grew and rates rose at the end of the 18c, the Poor Laws were increasingly criticized. The Poor Law Amendment Act of 1834 radically changed the system, aiming to make application for poor relief less attractive and instituting a centralized poor law commission. The laws continued to operate into the 20c.

## POPES

Antipopes (who claimed to be pope in opposition to those canonically chosen) are given in square brackets.

| Dates of Pontificate | Name | Dates of Pontificate | Name | Dates of Pontificate | Name |
|---|---|---|---|---|---|
| until c.64 | Peter | [498 and 501/5 | Laurentius] | 827 | Valentine |
| c.64/c.76 | Linus | 514/23 | Hormisdas | 827/44 | Gregory IV |
| c.76/c.90 | Anacletus | 523/6 | John I | [844 | John] |
| c.90/c.99 | Clement I | 526/30 | Felix IV (or III) | 844/7 | Sergius II |
| c.99/c.105 | Evaristus | 530/2 | Boniface II | 847/55 | Leo IV |
| c.105/c.117 | Alexander I | [530 | Dioscorus] | 855/8 | Benedict III |
| c.117/c.127 | Sixtus I | 533/5 | John II | [855 | Anastasius (III)] |
| c.127/c.137 | Telesphorus | 535/6 | Agapetus I | 858/67 | Nicholas I |
| c.137/c.140 | Hyginus | 536/7 | Silverius | 867/72 | Adrian II |
| c.140/c.154 | Pius I | 537/55 | Vigilius | 872/82 | John VIII |
| c.154/c.166 | Anicetus | 556/61 | Pelagius I | 882/4 | Marinus I |
| c.166/c.175 | Soter | 561/74 | John III | 884/5 | Adrian III |
| 175/89 | Eleutherius | 575/9 | Benedict I | 885/91 | Stephen V (or VI) |
| 189/98 | Victor I | 579/90 | Pelagius II | 891/6 | Formosus |
| 198/217 | Zephyrinus | 590/604 | Gregory I | 896 | Boniface VI |
| 217/22 | Calixtus I | 604/6 | Sabinian I | 896/7 | Stephen VI (or VII) |
| [217/c.235 | Hippolytus] | 607 | Boniface III | 897 | Romanus |
| 222/30 | Urban I | 608/15 | Boniface IV | 897 | Theodore II |
| 230/5 | Pontian | 615/18 | Deusdedit | 898/900 | John IX |
| 235/6 | Anterus | | (or Adeodatus I) | 900/3 | Benedict IV |
| 236/50 | Fabian | 619/25 | Boniface V | 903 | Leo V |
| 251/3 | Cornelius | 625/38 | Honorius I | [903/4 | Christopher] |
| [251/c.258 | Novatian] | 640 | Severinus | 904/11 | Sergius III |
| 253/4 | Lucius I | 640/2 | John IV | 911/13 | Anastasius III |
| 254/7 | Stephen I | 642/9 | Theodore I | 913/14 | Lando |
| 257/8 | Sixtus II | 649/55 | Martin I | 914/28 | John X |
| 259/68 | Dionysius | 654/7 | Eugenius I[1] | 928 | Leo VI |
| 269/74 | Felix I | 657/72 | Vitalian | 928/31 | Stephen VII (or VIII) |
| 275/83 | Eutychian | 672/6 | Adeodatus II | 931/5 | John XI |
| 283/96 | Caius | 676/8 | Donus | 936/9 | Leo VII |
| 296/304 | Marcellinus | 678/81 | Agatho | 939/42 | Stephen VIII (or IX) |
| 308/9 | Marcellus I | 682/3 | Leo II | 942/6 | Marinus II |
| 310 | Eusebius | 684/5 | Benedict II | 946/55 | Agapetus II |
| 311/14 | Miltiades | 685/6 | John V | 955/64 | John XII |
| 314/35 | Sylvester I | 686/7 | Conon | 963/5 | Leo VIII |
| 336 | Mark | [687 | Theodore] | 964/6 | Benedict V |
| 337/52 | Julius I | [687/92 | Paschal] | 965/72 | John XIII |
| 352/66 | Liberius | 687/701 | Sergius I | 973/4 | Benedict VI |
| [355/65 | Felix (II)] | 701/5 | John VI | [974 | Boniface VII |
| 366/84 | Damasus I | 705/7 | John VII | | (1st pontificate)] |
| [366/7 | Ursinus] | 708 | Sisinnius | 974/83 | Benedict VII |
| 384/99 | Siricius | 708/15 | Constantine | 983/4 | John XIV |
| 399/401 | Anastasius I | 715/31 | Gregory II | [984/5 | Boniface VII |
| 402/17 | Innocent I | 731/41 | Gregory III | | (2nd pontificate)] |
| 417/18 | Zosimus | 741/52 | Zacharias | 985/96 | John XV (or XVI) |
| 418/22 | Boniface I | 752 | Stephen II[2] | 996/9 | Gregory V |
| [418/19 | Eulalius] | 752/7 | Stephen II (or III) | [997/8 | John XVI (or XVII)] |
| 422/32 | Celestine I | 757/67 | Paul I | 999/1003 | Sylvester II |
| 432/40 | Sixtus III | [767/9 | Constantine II] | 1003 | John XVII (or XVIII) |
| 440/61 | Leo I, the Great | [768 | Philip] | 1004/9 | John XVIII (or XIX) |
| 461/8 | Hilarius | 768/72 | Stephen III (or IV) | 1009/12 | Sergius IV |
| 468/83 | Simplicius | 772/95 | Adrian I | [1012 | Gregory (VI)] |
| 483/92 | Felix III (or II) | 795/816 | Leo III | 1012/24 | Benedict VIII |
| 492/6 | Gelasius I | 816/17 | Stephen IV (or V) | 1024/32 | John XIX (or XX) |
| 496/8 | Anastasius II | 817/24 | Paschal I | 1032/44 | Benedict IX |
| 498/514 | Symmachus | 824/7 | Eugenius II | | (1st pontificate) |

## pope

The title of the Bishop of Rome as head or Supreme Pontiff of the Roman Catholic Church; also, the title given to the head of the Coptic Church. The Bishop of Rome is elected by a conclave of the College of Cardinals, his authority deriving from the belief that he represents Christ in direct descent from the Apostle Peter, said to be the first Bishop of Rome. After the decline of the ancient churches of the Eastern Roman Empire, resulting from the spread of Islam, the Pope

## POPES *continued*

Antipopes (who claimed to be pope in opposition to those canonically chosen) are given in square brackets.

| Dates of Pontificate | Name | Dates of Pontificate | Name | Dates of Pontificate | Name |
|---|---|---|---|---|---|
| 1045 | Sylvester III | 1227/41 | Gregory IX | 1523/34 | Clement VII |
| 1045 | Benedict IX | 1241 | Celestine IV | 1534/49 | Paul III |
|  | (2nd pontificate) | 1243/54 | Innocent IV | 1550/5 | Julius III |
| 1045/6 | Gregory VI | 1254/61 | Alexander IV | 1555 | Marcellus II |
| 1046/7 | Clement II | 1261/4 | Urban IV | 1555/9 | Paul IV |
| 1047/8 | Benedict IX | 1265/8 | Clement IV | 1559/65 | Pius IV |
|  | (3rd pontificate) | 1271/6 | Gregory X | 1566/72 | Pius V |
| 1048 | Damasus II | 1276 | Innocent V | 1572/85 | Gregory XIII |
| 1049/54 | Leo IX | 1276 | Adrian V | 1585/90 | Sixtus V |
| 1055/7 | Victor II | 1276/7 | John XXI[4] | 1590 | Urban VII |
| 1057/8 | Stephen IX (or X) | 1277/80 | Nicholas III | 1590/1 | Gregory XIV |
| [1058/9 | Benedict X] | 1281/5 | Martin IV | 1591 | Innocent IX |
| 1059/61 | Nicholas II | 1285/7 | Honorius IV | 1592/1605 | Clement VIII |
| 1061/73 | Alexander II | 1288/92 | Nicholas IV | 1605 | Leo XI |
| [1061/72 | Honorius (II)] | 1294 | Celestine V | 1605/21 | Paul V |
| 1073/85 | Gregory VII | 1294/1303 | Boniface VIII | 1621/3 | Gregory XV |
| [1080 and | Clement (III)] | 1303/4 | Benedict XI | 1623/44 | Urban VIII |
| 1084/1100 |  | 1305/14 | Clement V | 1644/55 | Innocent X |
| 1086/7 | Victor III | 1316/34 | John XXII | 1655/67 | Alexander VII |
| 1088/99 | Urban II | [1328/30 | Nicholas (V)] | 1667/9 | Clement IX |
| 1099/1118 | Paschal II | 1334/42 | Benedict XII | 1670/6 | Clement X |
| [1100/2 | Theodoric] | 1342/52 | Clement VI | 1676/89 | Innocent XI |
| [1102 | Albert] | 1352/62 | Innocent VI | 1689/91 | Alexander VIII |
| [1105/11 | Sylvester (IV)] | 1362/70 | Urban V | 1691/1700 | Innocent XII |
| 1118/19 | Gelasius II | 1370/8 | Gregory XI | 1700/21 | Clement XI |
| [1118/21 | Gregory (VIII)] | 1378/89 | Urban VI | 1721/4 | Innocent XIII |
| 1119/24 | Calixtus II | [1378/94 | Clement (VII)] | 1724/30 | Benedict XIII |
| 1124/30 | Honorius II | 1389/1404 | Boniface IX | 1730/40 | Clement XII |
| [1124 | Celestine (II)] | [1394/1423 | Benedict (XIII)] | 1740/58 | Benedict XIV |
| 1130/43 | Innocent II | 1404/6 | Innocent VII | 1758/69 | Clement XIII |
| [1130/8 | Anacletus (II)] | 1406/15 | Gregory XII | 1769/74 | Clement XIV |
| [1138 | Victor (IV)][3] | [1409/10 | Alexander (V)] | 1775/99 | Pius VI |
| 1143/4 | Celestine II | [1410/15 | John (XXIII)] | 1800/23 | Pius VII |
| 1144/5 | Lucius II | 1417/31 | Martin V | 1823/9 | Leo XII |
| 1145/53 | Eugenius III | [1423/9 | Clement (VIII)] | 1829/30 | Pius VIII |
| 1153/4 | Anastasius IV | [1425/30 | Benedict (XIV)] | 1831/46 | Gregory XVI |
| 1154/9 | Adrian IV | 1431/47 | Eugenius IV | 1846/78 | Pius IX |
| 1159/81 | Alexander III | [1439/49 | Felix (V)] | 1878/1903 | Leo XIII |
| [1159/64 | Victor (IV)][3] | 1447/55 | Nicholas V | 1903/14 | Pius X |
| [1164/8 | Paschal (III)] | 1455/8 | Calixtus III | 1914/22 | Benedict XV |
| [1168/78 | Calixtus (III)] | 1458/64 | Pius II | 1922/39 | Pius XI |
| [1179/80 | Innocent (III)] | 1464/71 | Paul II | 1939/58 | Pius XII |
| 1181/5 | Lucius III | 1471/84 | Sixtus IV | 1958/63 | John XXIII |
| 1185/7 | Urban III | 1484/92 | Innocent VIII | 1963/78 | Paul VI |
| 1187 | Gregory VIII | 1492/1503 | Alexander VI | 1978 | John Paul I |
| 1187/91 | Clement III | 1503 | Pius III | 1978/2005 | John Paul II |
| 1191/8 | Celestine III | 1503/13 | Julius II | 2005/ | Benedict XVI |
| 1198/1216 | Innocent III | 1513/21 | Leo X |  |  |
| 1216/27 | Honorius III | 1522/3 | Adrian VI |  |  |

*Notes*
[1] Elected during the banishment of Martin I
[2] Although not actually consecrated, he is variously regarded and disregarded as pope; the numbering of subsequent popes named Stephen has, accordingly, been somewhat confused
[3] Different individuals
[4] There was no John XX

---

in Rome became the undisputed centre of the Christian Church, and enjoyed considerable political power as the temporal sovereign of extensive PAPAL STATES in Europe (now restricted to the Vatican City in Rome). The claim to infallibility was formalized at the First Vatican Council in 1870. ► *See table*

**Popiełuszko, Jerzy Alfons** (1947–84)
Polish priest. Serving in several Warsaw parishes after ordination, and inspired by the faith of his

compatriot St Maximilian Kolbe, he became an outspoken supporter of the **SOLIDARITY** trade union, especially when it was banned in 1981 with the introduction of martial law. His sermons at 'Masses for the Country' regularly held in St Stanisław Kostka Church were widely acclaimed. He ignored harassment and resisted official moves to have him silenced, but was kidnapped and murdered by the secret police in Oct 1984, more than a year after the lifting of martial law. It was probably this tragedy more than any other event that, in a profoundly Catholic country, spelt the eventual demise of the Communist Party. His grave and his church became a place of national pilgrimage.

## Popish Plot

An apocryphal Jesuit conspiracy in 1678 to assassinate **CHARLES II** of England, burn London, slaughter Protestants, and place James, Duke of York (later James VII of Scotland and II of England), on the throne. Created by opportunist rogues Titus **OATES** and Israel Tonge, it resulted in 35 executions, bills in three parliaments for the exclusion of James from the succession, and the fall of the Danby government. ➤ **JAMES VII AND II**

## Popolari

Members of the Italian Popular Party (*Partito Popolare Italiano*) which briefly emerged as a major force in Italian politics in the period between **WORLD WAR I** and the fascist seizure of power. It appealed basically to the Catholic voter and helped undermine the traditional liberal parties which could no longer guarantee Catholic support simply by promising not to introduce anticlerical measures. It ceased to exist under **FASCISM**, but many of its leaders subsequently played a part in the formation of the **CHRISTIAN DEMOCRATIC PARTY**.

## Popov, Gavril Kharitonovich (1936– )

Soviet economist and politician. Of Greek ethnic background, he graduated in economics in Moscow and joined the Communist Party in 1959. He was appointed Dean of the Faculty of Economics in 1971 and, with official backing, proceeded to introduce management studies. He blossomed on Mikhail **GORBACHEV**'s accession to power. In 1989 he was elected to the Congress of Deputies and in 1990 became Mayor of Moscow. A fierce critic of the slow pace of change, he left the party in 1990, survived Gorbachev's downfall in 1991 and resigned as Mayor in 1992.

## Popular Front

A strategy of the communist movement begun in the 1930s as a means of fostering collaboration among left and centre parties to oppose the rise of right-wing movements and regimes, most obviously fascist ones. There were Popular Front governments in France, Spain and Chile. The strategy virtually died with the signing of the **GERMAN–SOVIET PACT** (1939), but re-emerged after **HITLER** had invaded the USSR.

## populism

Essentially a political outlook or mentality rather than an ideology, identified by a popular reaction to dramatic change, such as rapid industrialization. People feel that events are beyond their control, which is blamed on some conspiracy of foreigners, ethnic groups, economic interests, or intellectuals. The populist reaction is to 'regain' control from the suggested centres of power, usually through some form of participation, and to seek revenge and redemption. Beyond that, populism is an obscure and variable outlook, and has failed to establish political parties successfully. It is often found in underdeveloped countries as a reaction against more developed countries.

## Populist Party

US political party. It was founded in 1892 by farmers and labourers in the West who had become disenchanted with the economic and commercial policies imposed by the East. Running on a programme of economic and political reform, its first presidential candidate, James B Weaver, took more than 1 million votes in 1892, but at the next election (1896), the populists endorsed the Democratic nominee, William Jennings **BRYAN**, and by the end of the century the party had disappeared as a political entity.

## Portales, Diego (1793–1837)

Chilean politician. A major trader in Valparaíso, he acquired a major interest in national affairs in 1824 when he was awarded the government monopoly on the sale of tobacco, tea and alcoholic beverages in return for servicing a British loan. A pragmatist, he was principally concerned with power, discipline, stability and directed order and, as Chief Minister (1830–2 and 1835–7), he was the key figure in creating a new and stable political system. He imposed the conservative constitution of 1833, which lasted until 1925, and created a centralized state, dominated by the Church and the landed classes. By 1835 he was effectively a dictator, having evolved a government of merchants and powerful landowners, whose *inquilinos* served as an effective military force. He was murdered near Valparaíso by a group of soldiers during the war against General Andrés **SANTA CRUZ**'s Peru–Bolivian Confederation, which was seen as a direct threat to the country. ➤ **INQUILINO**

## Porte, The Sublime

Originally the ministerial department of the Grand Vizier of the **OTTOMAN EMPIRE**, it was finally established under the name *Bab-i Ali* ('Sublime Porte') in 1718 during the sultanate of **AHMED III**. The Porte (or Gate) was used to refer to the buildings housing the central offices of government in Istanbul, including the Ministries of the Interior and Foreign Affairs and the Council of State. By extension, the term then came to be used of the government itself.

## porteño

This Spanish term describes an inhabitant of the city of Buenos Aires. The early history of Argentina can be seen as a struggle between *unitarios*, who saw Buenos Aires as the dominant force in the Platine Basin, and federalists, who viewed the interests of up-river states such as Entre Ríos, the province of Buenos Aires or Santa Fé as more important. The high profile assumed by Buenos Aires after 1810 stimulated cities of the interior to struggle against *porteños*, such as liberal-centralist Bernardino **RIVADAVIA**, intent on the rapid creation of a modern state. The tyranny of **ROSAS** epitomized the pre-eminence of provincial **CAUDILLO**

and **GAUCHO** over the civilized urban liberal; the porteños finally regained influence under **MITRE** and
**SARMIENTO** in the 1860s. By 1880 their economic supremacy was secure and the city of Buenos Aires was
brought under congressional rule.

### Portland, William Henry Cavendish Bentinck, 3rd Duke of (1738–1809)

British politician. He became an MP in 1761, succeeding to the dukedom in 1762. His first cabinet post was
as Lord Chamberlain of the Household under **ROCK-
INGHAM** (1765–6). Along with other aristocratic
**WHIGS**, he maintained connection with Rockingham
which kept him in opposition until 1782, when he
was Lord Lieutenant of Ireland. Portland was nominal
head of the ministry (Apr–Dec 1783) usually known
as the **FOX–NORTH** coalition which **GEORGE III** hated
and rapidly dismissed. He led the Whigs in opposition to **PITT, THE YOUNGER** until 1794 when he agreed
to join him in a coalition government to provide
order and stability and to meet the challenge of the
**FRENCH REVOLUTIONARY WARS**. Some have seen the
Pitt–Portland coalition as the foundation of the modern Tory (later Conservative) Party. He served as
Home Secretary (1794–1801) during a period of considerable radical disturbance in England and rebellion in Ireland (1798) and as Lord President of the
Council under Addington (1801–3). In Pitt's last
ministry he was successively Lord President
(1804–5) and Minister without Portfolio (1805–6).
He was summoned by **GEORGE III** in 1807 to head an
administration of Pittites after the fall of the 'Ministry
of all the Talents'; by now old, frail and gouty, he was
little more than titular leader until his death in office.
► **TORIES**

### Port Royal

A French religious and intellectual community occupying the former convent of Port-Royal-des-Champs,
near Paris. It was associated with the Jansenist movement, and founded by the Abbé de Saint-Cyran
(1637), a friend and admirer of the theologian Cornelius Jansen, himself a devotee of Augustinian philosophy. The community was dispersed in 1665, and
the convent destroyed (1710–11). ► **JANSENISM**

### Portsmouth, Treaty of (5 Sep 1905)

The treaty, signed in Portsmouth, New Hampshire
(USA), which concluded the **RUSSO-JAPANESE WAR**.
Japan acquired south Sakhalin from Russia as well as
the Russian leasehold in south Manchuria (Liaodong
Peninsula) and the Russian-built South Manchuria
Railway. Japan's predominant position in Korea was
also confirmed, enabling Tokyo to declare a protectorate over Korea and then to annex it as a formal
colony (1910). The Japanese demand for an indemnity, however, was abandoned when Russia ada-
mantly refused, a compromise that provoked angry
public demonstrations in Tokyo. This treaty marked
the beginning of Japanese expansion on the Chinese
mainland, which was increasingly to arouse the suspicion of the USA.

---

**PORTUGAL**   official name **Republic of Portugal**
A country in south-western Europe on the western
side of the Iberian Peninsula, bounded to the north
and east by Spain; and to the south and west by the
Atlantic Ocean. It became a kingdom under Alphon-

so I in 1139. The Portuguese Empire began in the 15c,
a time of major world exploration by the Portuguese.
Portugal came under Spanish domination from 1580
to 1640, and was invaded by the French in 1807. The
monarchy was overthrown and the First Republic established in 1910. A military coup took place in 1926,
and in the early 1930s the country came under the **ES-
TADO NOVO** regime of Dr António **SALAZAR**, whose
dictatorship of over 35 years (1932–68) was safeguarded by the feared **PIDE**. A military coup in 1974
was followed by ten years of political unrest under
15 governments. Full civilian government was restored in 1982. Macao, Portugal's last overseas territory, was transferred to Chinese sovereignty in 1999.
Portugal joined the **EC** in 1986. ► **REPUBLIC, FIRST**
(Portugal)

### Portugal, Revolt of (1640–68)

The union of the crowns of Spain and Portugal in
1580 led to increasing dissatisfaction in Portugal,
principally because of the failure of Spain to protect
the vulnerable Portuguese overseas empire. In 1640
the troubles in Catalonia encouraged a group of Portuguese to rally round the Duke of Braganza, proclaimed by them as King **JOHN (JOÃO) IV**. An uprising
in Lisbon (1 Dec 1640) ended with the murder of the
viceroy, Miguel de Vasconcellos, a confidant of the
Spanish minister **OLIVARES**. Spain's commitments,
especially in Catalonia, made it difficult to deal with
the national rising, which soon gained the support of
France, which sent naval and military help. In 1660
the marriage of Princess **CATHERINE OF BRAGANZA**
to **CHARLES II** of England ensured English help. Repeated failures by Spanish troops to subdue the rebellion ended with the Treaty of Lisbon (Feb 1668),
which recognized Portugal's independence. ► **BRAG-
ANZA, HOUSE OF**

### Porvoo, Diet of (1809)

The meeting of the Finnish estates convened by Tsar
**ALEXANDER I** at Porvoo (Borgå) following the Russian conquest of Finland (hitherto part of the Swedish kingdom) in 1808–9. On this occasion the Tsar
guaranteed the rights enjoyed by the Finns under
Swedish rule, thus allowing Finland considerable
autonomy within the Russian Empire. The Diet has
generally been regarded as marking the emergence

of Finland as a modern state.

## positive discrimination

A policy using systems of quotas and targets to help groups who have historically been disadvantaged within majority communities because of race, ethnicity, nationality or gender. India's constitution outlines three main areas of positive discrimination: political reservation, in which a number of seats in the national parliament and the state legislatures are reserved for 'scheduled castes'; employment reservation, which principally applies to government jobs; and education reservation, which makes places available for scheduled castes in schools and universities. In the USA, the policy of **AFFIRMATIVE ACTION** was originally articulated in 1961 and by the 1970s included elaborate but often undisclosed means of assessment for quotas and targets, particularly in education and employment. This became highly contentious and the legality of positive discrimination was challenged in 1978 by the **BAKKE CASE**, which alleged 'reverse discrimination' in a case concerning university entrance admissions requirements.

## Potemkin (1905)

The Russian warship immortalized in Sergei Eisenstein's 1926 film for mutinying in the course of the Russian **REVOLUTION OF 1905**. The crew put to sea and resisted the attempts of loyal ships to capture them but eventually surrendered to the Romanian authorities. There were subsequent mutinies in the naval bases of Kronstadt and Sevastopol. Tsar **NICHOLAS II** rode out the revolution, but disaffection in his forces was an ominous sign of what was to unseat him in 1917.

## Potemkin, Grigori Alexandrovich (1739–91)

Russian field marshal and statesman. He entered the Russian army, attracted the attention of **CATHERINE II, THE GREAT** and became her intimate and most enduring favourite, heavily influencing Russian foreign policy in particular. There is some reason to believe they were secretly married. He distinguished himself in the **RUSSO-TURKISH WARS** (1768–74 and 1787–92), during which Russia gained the Crimea and the northern coast of the Black Sea. He also helped to develop Catherine's unsuccessful Greek project which would have replaced the **OTTOMAN EMPIRE** with a new Greek Empire based on Constantinople. Within Russia he became famous for the Potemkin villages, apparently prosperous artificial centres quickly built ahead of Catherine's carriage-routes and subsequently dismantled.

## potlatch

A custom among **NATIVE AMERICANS** of the northwest Pacific coast which involved status-seekers trying to affirm or reaffirm their position, or to outdo their rivals, by giving ever more lavish gifts. The gifts were given out according to the social rank of the recipients, and since the ceremony was accompanied by feasting and speech-making, there were many witnesses to the rank of the recipients and, most importantly, to the generosity and social status of the host and his family.

## Potsdam Conference (17 July–2 Aug 1945)

The last of the great **WORLD WAR II** strategic conferences, following the **TEHRAN CONFERENCE** and **YALTA CONFERENCE**. During this period Winston **CHURCHILL** (and later Clement **ATTLEE**), **STALIN** and **TRUMAN** met to discuss the post-war settlement in Europe. Soviet power in Eastern Europe was recognized *de facto*, and it was agreed that Poland's western frontier should run along the **ODER–NEISSE LINE**. The decision was also made to divide Germany into four occupation zones. The political differences that began to emerge between the USA and the USSR could be said to have marked the start of the **COLD WAR**.

## Poujade, Pierre (1920–2003)

French right-wing political leader. A small shopkeeper in a tiny town, in 1951 he was elected a member of the Saint Cére municipal council, and in 1954 he organized his Poujadist movement, the UDCA (union for the defence of tradesmen and artisans), as a protest against the French tax system. His party had successes in the 1956 elections to the National Assembly, but disappeared in 1958. Jean-Marie **LE PEN**, leader of the National Front, was first elected as a Poujadist Deputy in 1956.

## POUM (*Partido Obrero de Unificación Marxista*, 'Workers' Marxist Unification Party')

Independent Spanish Marxist party. The POUM, founded in Sep 1935, never had a mass following, but its outstanding thinkers led it to exert considerable influence. Its leading figures were the Marxist theoreticians Joaquín Maurín, the originator of the *Alianza Obrera* ('United Workers' Front'), and Andreu Nin. The POUM's defence of a revolutionary war effort and general independence during the **SPANISH CIVIL WAR** resulted in its persecution by the Communist Party (**PCE**) in the May Days of 1937. It was vigorously repressed thereafter until the end of the war.

## Powell, Adam Clayton, Jr (1908–72)

US clergyman and politician. Pastor of the Abyssinian Baptist Church in Harlem, he was a charismatic community leader. In 1941 he was elected as a Democrat to the City Council of New York and the following year he founded the *People's Voice*. Elected to the **HOUSE OF REPRESENTATIVES** in 1945, he was chairman of the House Committee on Education and Labor from 1951, though persistent absenteeism did inhibit his effectiveness. It was Powell who first used the phrase '**BLACK POWER**' (at Howard University in 1966), and who acted as convenor of the first National Conference on Black Power. In 1967 he was expelled from the House of Representatives for misusing public funds and for unbecoming conduct. Re-elected in 1968, he had the satisfaction of a Supreme Court ruling in favour of his appeal against expulsion, but he lost his seat in 1970. ► **JONES, J RAYMOND**

## Powell, Colin Luther (1937–)

US soldier and politician. The son of Jamaican immigrants, he was raised in New York and educated at George Washington University. A professional soldier for 35 years, in the 1980s he held posts at the Pentagon and as deputy to the head of National Security Affairs, Frank Carlucci, whom he succeeded in 1987. In 1989 he took charge of the Army Forces Command, was promoted to four-star general and then became the first African-American chairman of the Joint Chiefs of Staff. He played leading roles in planning the invasion of **PANAMA** (1989) and the **GULF WAR** (1991). After his retirement from the army in 1993 he became active in politics and, disinclined to run for president despite his widespread popularity, became the first African-American Secretary of State in 2001, holding the position for President George W **BUSH**'s first term until his resignation in 2004. Widely viewed as a moderate, he was respected for his attempts to find international consensus and build support for US actions following the **SEPTEMBER 11 ATTACKS** and to mediate between Israel and the Palestinians, but his moderation was out of step with the prevailing **NEOCONSERVATISM** of the administration and he was sidelined in the run-up to the **IRAQ WAR**.

### Powell, (John) Enoch (1912–98)
British politician. He was Professor of Greek at Sydney (1937–9), and became a Conservative MP in 1950. He held several junior posts before he became Minister of Health (1960–3). His outspoken attitude on the issues of non-white immigration and racial integration came to national attention in 1968, and as a consequence of this he was dismissed from the shadow cabinet. He was elected as an Ulster Unionist MP in Oct 1974, losing his seat in 1987. ▶ **CONSERVATIVE PARTY** (UK)

### Powhatan Confederacy
A group of Algonquian-speaking Native North American tribes inhabiting the Tidewater region of Virginia at the time of the first white settlements. Named after Chief Powhatan, the group was initially receptive to the settlers, but grew suspicious of the newcomers, and in 1622 and 1644 launched massive attacks on them. They were defeated on both occasions. Scattered descendants of these tribes are still found in Virginia. ▶ **INDIAN WARS; POCAHONTAS**

### Poynings' Law (1495)
A statute enacted by a parliament in Ireland at the direction of the English Lord Deputy Sir Edward Poynings. It confirmed that a parliament could only meet with the approval of the king, who must be told what legislation he was being asked to approve by prior submission to him in council. It was not designed to muzzle opinion but to stop local magnates from abusing the royal authority in parliament to their private advantage, and above all to stop another attempt such as Lambert **SIMNEL**'s to use a parliament to legitimize a usurping bid for the throne. It survived unaltered until abolished in 1782. ▶ **ROSES, WARS OF THE**

### Pozzo di Borgo, Carlo Andrea, Count (1764–1842)
Corsican-born Russian diplomat. He practised as an advocate in Ajaccio. In 1790 he joined the party of Paoli, who made him President of the Corsican Council and Secretary of State, but in 1796 he was obliged to seek safety from the Bonapartes in London. In 1798 he went to Vienna and effected an alliance of Austria and Russia against France. In 1803 he entered the Russian diplomatic service. Though he resigned over the Treaty of Tilsit in 1807, he returned in 1812 and laboured strenuously to unite **NAPOLEON**'s enemies against him, seduced Marshal Bernadotte from the Napoleonic cause, and urged the allies to march on Paris. He represented Russia in Paris, at the Con-

gress of **VIENNA** (1814–15) and the Congress of Verona, and was ambassador to London from 1834 to 1839, when he settled in Paris, where he died. ▶ **CHARLES XIV JOHN; TILSIT, TREATIES OF**

### PP (Partido Popular, 'Popular Party')
Spanish conservative party. It was founded in 1976 as *Alianza Popular* (AP, 'Popular Alliance') and headed by 'the magnificent seven', all former Francoists under the leadership of Manuel **FRAGA IRIBARNE**. The party defended **LAISSEZ-FAIRE** capitalism alongside more traditional Spanish conservative values. In the 1977 election AP won only 16 seats, but in 1982 it came second to the Socialist Party with a quarter of the vote cast. In 1989 the party was renamed *Partido Popular*, and in 1990 Manuel Fraga stepped down as leader and was succeeded by José María Aznar. During the 1990s the PP absorbed several smaller parties to become a major political force, and came to power at the head of a coalition of nationalist parties after the 1996 election, with Aznar as Prime Minister. Its Mar 2004 electoral defeat by the **PSOE** was due to its support for the **IRAQ WAR** and its attempt to make political capital out of the **AL-QAEDA** railway bombings in Madrid shortly before the election by blaming them on **ETA**.

### Pragmatic Sanction
A Habsburg family law devised in 1713 by Emperor **CHARLES VI** to alter an earlier pact in favour of the undivided succession of his heirs, male or female, to the Habsburg lands (1713). Later, much effort was deployed in achieving internal and international guarantees for his daughter **MARIA THERESA**'s claims, though these were repudiated by **FREDERICK II, THE GREAT** of Prussia (1740). ▶ **HABSBURG DYNASTY**

### Prague Spring (1968)
The name given to the events associated with the attempt made to reform **COMMUNISM** in Czechoslovakia and to create instead what Alexander **DUBČEK** called '**SOCIALISM WITH A HUMAN FACE**'. The action programme anticipated many of Mikhail **GORBACHEV**'s subsequent reforms in the USSR and attracted widespread popular support. But the thought that Czechoslovakia might develop a political system with several parties in which the communists could be defeated at the polls and themselves divided on Czech/Slovak ethnic grounds did not occur to Leonid **BREZHNEV**, who saw his control over Eastern Europe and within the USSR itself threatened. Hence the Soviet invasion in Aug, the Dubček Doctrine, and the removal of Dubček and his colleagues, who had not had quite enough time to dispose of conservative opposition. The whole area lost a great opportunity.

### Prajadhipok (1893–1941)
The 7th King of the **CHAK(K)RI DYNASTY** of Thailand, and the last absolute monarch in that line. He was educated in England, at Eton and the Woolwich Military Academy. Prajadhipok ascended the throne in 1925. His apparent instincts for political reform were smothered by an older generation of ministers and advisers. In June 1932 the absolute monarchy was overthrown in a bloodless coup. Prajadhipok remained as a constitutional monarch until Mar 1935, when he abdicated. He then lived in England until his death.

# *Pre-Columbian Civilizations*

*Culture & Society*

The term pre-Columbian civilizations denotes the cultures that developed in parts of Mexico and Central America (Mesoamerica) and western South America (Andean region) prior to European incursions into the continent from the 16c.

## Mesoamerica

### Early history
Extensive human habitation of the Mesoamerican region dates from around 8000 BC. At this time, grazing mammals were hunted for their meat, hides and bones. With the climatic change around 7000 BC, and perhaps also because of over-hunting, the herds disappeared, and the inhabitants initiated the process of becoming sedentary agriculturists, growing maize, beans and squashes. Archaeological evidence suggests that by 1500 BC this process was almost complete.

### Olmecs
Members of a highly elaborate culture on the Mexican Gulf coast at its height in 1200–600 BC. The Olmec influenced the rise and development of the other great civilizations of Mesoamerica. They probably had the first large planned religious and ceremonial centres, at San Lorenzo, La Venta, and Tres Zapotes, where the resident élite and their families lived, served by much larger populations dispersed throughout the lowland area. The centres had temple mounds, monumental sculptures, massive altars, and sophisticated systems of drains and lagoons. They were probably also the first people in the area to devise glyph (symbolic character) writing and the 260-day Mesoamerican **calendar**.

### Zapotecs
A civilization of southern Mexico (300 BC–AD 300), influenced by Olmec culture. It was centred on Monte Albán, a ceremonial site located on a high ridge in the Valley of Oaxaca. The Zapotec worshipped a pantheon of gods headed by the rain god Cosijo, and religious rites, including human sacrifice, were presided over by a priestly hierarchy.

### Mayas
The best-known civilization of the classic period of Mesoamerica (AD 250–900), the Maya rose to prominence c.300 in present-day southern Mexico, Guatemala, northern Belize and western Honduras. Inheriting the inventions and ideas of earlier civilizations, such as the Olmec and Teotihuacán, they developed astronomy, calendrical systems, pictographic writing and ceremonial architecture, including pyramid temples. The tropical rainforest area was cleared for agriculture, and rain water was stored in numerous reservoirs. They also traded with other distant people, clearing routes through jungles and swamps. Most people farmed, while centres such as Tikal and Bonampak were largely ceremonial and political, with warrior kings and an élite of priests and nobles ruling over the countryside. Mayan urban civilization started to decline, for complex reasons including over-exploitation of the environment, drought and destructive wars, c.900, although some peripheral centres still thrived, possibly influenced by the Toltec warrior culture from adjacent Mexico.

### Mixtecs
A people who can be traced to the 7c, by which time they had already achieved a high degree of civilization. They were famed for their skill in metallurgy, particularly in their use of gold, copper and silver, and for their jewellery and ceramics. By the 14c they had moved from the mountains into the Valley of Oaxaca, where they occasionally mixed or clashed with the Zapotec, occupying Zapotec centres including Monte Albán. In the 15c the Mixtec and Zapotec fought alongside in an attempt to fend off Aztec invasion, but eventually succumbed, becoming tribute-bearing vassals to their Aztec masters.

### Toltecs
A people (or peoples) who controlled most of central Mexico between c.900 and 1170, and were the last such dominant culture prior to the Aztecs. According to Aztec records, the ten kings of the Toltec ruled from 980 to 1168. Thus, they are transitional between the Maya of the classical period and the Aztec dominance. They had a variation on the usual Mesoamerican pantheon, and a priesthood, but in a form appropriate for people led by an imperialistic warrior caste. War gods took some precedence over gods of fertility in the orientation of worship, and human sacrifice increased

---

**Prasad, Rajendra** (1884–1963)
Indian politician. Having been active in Bihari politics, he left legal practice to become a supporter of M K **GANDHI**, helped found the *Searchlight* newspaper, and was President of the **INDIAN NATIONAL CONGRESS** on several occasions between 1934 and 1948. In 1946 he was made Minister for Food and Agriculture, and was India's first President (1950–62). He died at Patna.

**Prat de la Riba, Enric** (1870–1917)
Catalan nationalist and conservative theorist of the Catalan bourgeoisie. A founder in 1901 of the *Lliga Regionalista* (which sought autonomy within the Spanish state), he was Secretary of the party. His ideas on autonomy contributed to the creation of a regional government, the Mancomunitat, in 1914. He served as President of the Mancomunitat until his death, undertaking numerous projects to strengthen Catalan culture. ► **LLIGA**

**Pratihara** ► **INDIA, PRE-ISLAMIC**

**Prazos**
Estates granted by the Portuguese crown on the basis of African concessions to estate-holders (*prazeros*) in the Zambezi Valley of south-central Africa in the 17c and 18c. These were designed to promote settlement and develop Portuguese trade with the region. Regulations to prohibit absenteeism and pluralism, and to encourage Portuguese women to emigrate were generally ignored and the estates

considerably. Their capital was at Tula, 50mi/80km north of Mexico City. Impressive ruins at Chichen Itzá in Yucatán are Mayan, but may show the last survival of Toltec influences after their eclipse in their homelands.

## Aztecs

Arriving in the Mexico Valley in the 13c, the Aztecs became the most powerful people of Mesoamerica during the 15–16c. Their main city, **Tenochtitlán** (on the site of present-day Mexico City), near Lake Texcoco, became the most densely populated city of the region. They built up a great and powerful despotic ascendancy, with a strong military force, subjugating nearly all the people of central Mexico, and eventually ruling 400–500 smaller tribute-paying units (probably 5–6 million people), which provided them with raw materials and produce. People captured in wars were offered for human sacrifice to the Aztec gods. The Aztecs were famous for their agriculture, developing elaborate irrigation systems and cultivating all available land to feed their increasing population. Their best-known ruler was **Montezuma II**. Like other peoples of the region, they recorded their history in books written in a pictographic script; most of these were destroyed by the Spanish. They developed a complex calendar system, and built famous pyramids and temples. The Aztec empire was finally destroyed by a revolt of subject peoples taking advantage of the invasion of the Spanish under **Cortés** in 1521.

## Andean region

### Pre-Inca history

Prior to the domination of the Inca, a number of cultures inhabited the coastal and highland regions of the Andes. The first evidence of sedentary life in the region is found c.2500 BC, with settlements of between 50 and 1,000 inhabitants. Pottery was introduced c.1800 BC, and with the predominance of a new style of pottery throughout the region from 1400 BC, the Chavín, the first indications of a unifying political élite. For the most part, political élites continued to predominate in the region from then on. These include the Huari (7–11c), centred near what is now Ayacucho, and the Chimú (12–15c), the last civilization to dominate the region prior to the Inca, with their capital at Chan Chan near modern-day Trujillo.

### Chibchas or Muiscas

The inhabitants of the central highlands of Colombia from about 1200, they were centred near what is now Bogotá and developed the most extensive political system in the area, made up of small units under hereditary chiefs. They were great traders, extremely prosperous, and were never conquered by the Incas, from whom they were separated by mountains and jungles, but they were overrun by the Spanish in the 16c, and were plundered and subjugated within the new Kingdom of Granada.

### Incas

Originally a small group of Quechua-speaking Indians living in the Cuzco Basin of the central Andean highlands, in the 11c the Inca established their capital at Cuzco, the Sacred City of the Sun, where they built huge stone temples and fortresses, and occasionally covered important buildings in sheets of gold. While Aztec civilization was based on maize, Inca achievement depended on their equivalent crop, potatoes, which was to be Peru's most important gift to Europe. During the 15c, they brought together much of the Andean area, stretching along the entire western length of South America, from near the present Ecuador–Columbia border to south central Chile, and occupied much of the Andean region of Bolivia as well. The Incas succeeded in creating an organizational structure that could hold a vast area together, and were able to extract from it the resources necessary to support armies of conquest and a sizable state apparatus. They used former rulers as regional administrators (provided they were loyal) but these were denied any independence, and Inca culture, language (Quechua), and the cult of the Sun were forcibly imposed. The Inca emperor was a despotic ruler of a highly stratified society, and a quasi-religious figure thought to be a direct descendant of the sun god, Inti. The population of the empire has been variously estimated between 5 and 10 million in 1500. The Incas were not innovative; they merely expanded and intensified existing practices, such as in agriculture. They had a system of more than 9,320mi/15,000km of **roads**, and hundreds of way stations and administrative centres that provided an essential infrastructure for communication, conquest and control. They also had impressive storage facilities, such as the food warehouses at the administrative city of Huanuco Pampa in central Peru. In 1532, Spanish invaders under **Pizarro** encountered the Incas. They captured the emperor, **Atahualpa**, whom they later murdered, and seized control of the empire. By the 1570s Inca power, probably already past its peak and over-extended and disintegrating when the Spanish arrived, was totally destroyed.

---

became progressively Africanized, by the 19c becoming African chieftaincies with only vestiges of Portuguese culture.

### Prchlik, Václav (1922–)

Czechoslovak general and politician. He joined the forces and the Communist Party at the end of **WORLD WAR II**, rose through various official appointments to be political administrator of the army from 1955 to 1968, and in Jan 1968 apparently foiled an attempt by some of his colleagues to suppress the reform movement before it began. During 1968 he began a purge of the top security services and prepared to transfer the political responsibility for them from the party to parliament. After the Soviet invasion in Aug, which he was prepared to resist, he was dismissed,

and in fear of the secret police returned to Czechoslovakia.

### Prebisch, Raúl (1901–86)

Argentinian economist. He studied economics and was professor of political economy at the University of Buenos Aires (1925–7). Like many contemporaries, he originally supported neoclassical economic theories but the **GREAT DEPRESSION** profoundly affected his thinking and he became increasingly critical of the way in which what he described as the 'core' industrialized nations dominated and manipulated the 'periphery' of undeveloped nations. After holding several senior posts in the public sector, including heading the Argentine Central Bank, he became the executive secretary of ECLA in 1948.

During his 15 years in this post he won support for economic policies based on his **DEPENDENCY THEORY**. He was committed to protecting independent development that would simultaneously lift undeveloped economies out of poverty and place them among the world's developed nations. From 1965–9 he was the secretary-general of **UNCTAD** and then became director-general of the UN Latin American Institute for Economic and Social Planning. He is viewed by some as the most influential economist shaping Latin American development policy in the second half of the 20c. ► **ECLAC**

## Pre-Columbian Civilizations ► *See panel*

## Premadasa, Ranasinghe (1924–93)
Sri Lankan politician. The first Sri Lankan head of government to have emerged from the urban working classes rather than the traditional élite families, he began his political career attached to the Ceylon Labour Party. He formed a temperance group dedicated to moral uplift, then joined the **UNP** (United National Party) in 1950 and became Deputy Mayor of the Colombo municipal council (1955). Elected to Sri Lanka's parliament in 1960, he served, successively, as UNP Chief Whip (1965–8 and 1970–7), the Minister of Local Government (1968–70) and Leader of the House (1977–8), before becoming Prime Minister, under President **JAYAWARDENE**, in 1978. During ten years as Prime Minister, Premadasa implemented a popular housebuilding and poverty-alleviation programme, which provided the basis for his election as President (Dec 1988). He was assassinated by a suicide bomber in Colombo.

## Prempeh (d.1931)
Last King of the **ASHANTI** (1888/96). He was deposed by the British, imprisoned at Elmina, and exiled to the Seychelles. He was allowed to return in 1924, with chief's rank from 1926.

## Prem Tinsulanonda (1920–)
Thai soldier. Educated at the Chulachomklao Royal Military Academy, Bangkok, he entered the army as a sub lieutenant in 1941 and rose to become Commander-General of the 2nd Army Area in 1974, and Assistant Commander-in-Chief of the Royal Thai Army in 1977. During the administration of General Kriangsak Chomanam (1977–80) he served as Deputy Minister of the Interior and, from 1979, as Defence Minister. He was appointed Prime Minister (Mar 1980). Prem then formally relinquished his army office and established a series of civilian coalition governments. He withstood coup attempts in Apr 1981 and Sep 1985, and ruled in a cautious manner, retaining the confidence of key business and military leaders. Under his stewardship, 'newly industrializing' Thailand achieved annual growth rates in excess of nine per cent. He retired, on 'personal grounds', in July 1988.

## Premyslids (8c–early 14c)
The native dynasty ruling more or less the area of the present Czech lands in their formative period. Its origin is attributed to the marriage between a princess Libuse and a peasant Premysl. It came to an end with the death of Václav III in 1306. In the meantime, the dynasty presided over a highly successful development. This did not simply embrace the foundation of the bishopric of Prague in 973 or the acquisition of a permanent royal title by Otakar I (1197–1230), but also the growth of a prosperous agricultural community interspersed with highly successful trading towns. In addition, the Premyslids left a legacy of involvement in Germany, and vice versa, which made subsequent Czech history both glorious and disastrous, as in the period of Jan **HUS** and the **HUSSITE WARS**.

## Preobrazhensky, Yevgeny Alexandrovich (1886–1937)
Soviet economist. The son of a priest in the Urals, he developed revolutionary tendencies quite early in life. After the 1917 **RUSSIAN REVOLUTION** he spent some time in his home territory, but mainly he was active in Moscow, drafting, amongst other things, the 1919 party programmes. He associated with **TROTSKY** and **BUKHARIN** and joined with the latter in publishing the *ABC of Communism*, thereby incurring **STALIN**'s anger. He died in prison in 1937. His writings have now attracted renewed interest.

## Pressburg, Treaty of (1491)
An agreement concluded by the Habsburgs, securing their rights to the Hungarian succession on King Vladislav II's death without heirs. ► **HABSBURG DYNASTY**

## Pressburg, Treaty of (1805)
A treaty following **NAPOLEON I**'s victories at Ulm and **AUSTERLITZ**, which imposed harsh terms on Austria, effectively ending the **HOLY ROMAN EMPIRE** and establishing a ring of French client states. ► **NAPOLEONIC WARS**

## Prester John
Mythical Christian priest-king of a vast empire in Central Asia. Reports of his existence, wealth and military might, substantiated by a famous letter purporting to have come from him in 1165, raised the morale of Christian Europe as it faced the Muslim threat. The story almost certainly related to the Christian kingdom of Ethiopia, which had been cut off by the Islamic conquest of Egypt. 'Prester' comes from Old French *prestre*, 'priest'.

## Preston, Battle of (17–19 Aug 1648)
A series of engagements between the English Parliamentary Army under **CROMWELL** and **LAMBERT** and a numerically superior Scottish force in support of **CHARLES I** under the Duke of **HAMILTON**. Hamilton's inability to concentrate his forces enabled them to be picked off piecemeal. The defeat ended the Second Civil War. Hamilton was captured and executed (1649). ► **ENGLISH CIVIL WARS**

## Pretoria Convention (1881)
The agreement which brought to an end the first Boer War, establishing limited independence for the Boers in the Transvaal. In 1877 the Secretary of State for the Colonies, Lord Carnarvon, and the High Commissioner in South Africa, Sir Bartle Frere, resolved to attempt to reunite the two British colonies and two Boer states in southern Africa. The Transvaal was invaded and annexed by Sir Theophilus Shepstone in an attempt to place its bankrupt finances on a sound footing, but after the British suffered reverses in the **ZULU WAR** in 1879, the Boers set about re-establishing

their independence. The British were defeated at a number of small engagements in the eastern Transvaal, notably **MAJUBA HILL** where the British commander, General Sir George Colley, was killed. **GLADSTONE**'s Cabinet resolved to abandon imperial responsibilities in return for a vague declaration of suzerainty, under which the British would control Boer foreign policy. The interpretation of the extent of such 'suzerainty' bedevilled relations between British and Boer up to the Boer War of 1899–1902. ► **BOER WARS**

**Pretorius, Andries Wilhelmus Jacobus** (1799–1853)
Afrikaner leader. Born at Graaff-Reinet, Cape Colony, he was a prosperous farmer, who joined the **GREAT TREK** of 1835 into Natal, where he was chosen Commandant-General. He later accepted British rule, but after differences with the Governor he trekked again, this time across the Vaal. Eventually the British recognized the Transvaal Republic, later the South African Republic, whose new capital was named Pretoria after him.

**Pretorius, Marthinus Wessel** (1819–1901)
Afrikaner soldier and politician. The son of Andries **PRETORIUS**, he succeeded his father as Commandant-General in 1853, and was elected President of the South African Republic (1857–71), and of the Orange Free State (1859–63). He fought against the British again in 1877, until the independence of the Republic was recognized (1881), then retired, and died at Potchefstroom. ► **BOER WARS**

**PRI** (*Partido Revolucionario Institucional*, 'Institutional Revolutionary Party')
Mexican political party, previously known as the PRN (*Partido Revolucionario Nacional*, 'National Revolutionary Party') and the PRM (*Partido de la Revolución Mexicana*, 'Mexican Revolutionary Party'). Founded by Plutarco **CALLES** in 1929, in the wake of the **MEXICAN REVOLUTION** (1910–20), as an instrument for change through the achievement of unified and dictatorial centralism, the party has dominated Mexican political life ever since. The PRN was a coalition of local military chiefs, officeholders and CROM, the largest labour organization, and owed its strength to Calles' steady erosion of the autonomy of the states. **CÁRDENAS**, Calles' successor, created the succeeding PRM by replacing regional chiefs with military, labour, peasant and popular groups; labour and peasant organizations were seen as an effective counterpoise to the military, while the resolution of conflict lay in the hands of the President. By the time the PRM became the PRI (in 1945, under Ávila Camacho), the military sector had been disbanded, other interest groups had been included and the state organization strengthened. The party's political monopoly remained unchallenged until the late 1970s when opposition parties began to win congressional seats; the 1988 elections saw the PRI's first-ever loss of Senate seats, and in 1989 the PRI state governorship monopoly was broken for the first time. In the 1997 elections the PRI suffered major losses and for the first time no longer had a majority in the Chamber of Deputies. This pattern continued in 2000, but the party recovered ground in the 2003 elections.

**Pribičević, Svetozar** (1875–1936)
Serbian politician. Head of the Serbian Independent Party, which represented the Serbs within the Habsburg Empire, during **WORLD WAR I** he advocated union with Serbia to form a South Slav state. Soon disillusioned with the organization of the Kingdom of Serbs, Croats and Slovenes (later Yugoslavia) under the arch-Serbian nationalists Nikola **PAŠIĆ** and King Alexander I, in 1919 he led the Democratic Party, a breakaway group from the Serbian Radical Party. He was Minister of Education (1921–2). After 1927 he advocated the reorganization of the Kingdom of Yugoslavia as a federation. He was imprisoned during the royal dictatorship but was released to seek medical treatment in Czechoslovakia, where he died. ► **KOROŠEC, ANTON; MAČEK, VLADKO; RADIĆ, STJEPAN**

**Price, George** (1919– )
Belize politician. Educated in Belize City and the USA, he was elected to the Belize City Council in 1947 and in 1950 founded the People's United Party (PUP), a left-of-centre grouping which grew out of the People's Committee, a smaller group calling for the independence of Belize. Partial self-government was achieved in 1954 and Price became Prime Minister, continuing to lead his country until it achieved full independence in 1981. In 1984 PUP's 30 years of uninterrupted rule ended when the general election was won by the United Democratic Party (UDP), led by Manuel Esquivel, but Price unexpectedly returned to power in 1989 and remained there until 1993.

**Price Spreads Commission** (1934)
Canadian governmental inquiry. Instituted by the Ministry of Trade and Commerce to investigate the retail trade, the Commission found that retailers, especially the large department and chain stores, made their employees work very long hours for very low wages. Premier R B **BENNETT** went public with its findings, condemning employers for their exploitation. His radio addresses on 'the state of the times' upset many of his conservative adherents, but Bennett insisted on the reforms, such as the Wages and Hours Bill and Unemployment Insurance, which had been suggested by the commission. Employers who broke the new laws were to be punished as criminals, not civil offenders. It was the controversy over the commission that led Henry H **STEVENS** to resign from the cabinet to lead the Reconstruction Party of disaffected conservatives in the 1935 election. ► **NEW DEAL** (Canada)

**Pride, Sir Thomas** (d.1658)
English army officer during the **ENGLISH CIVIL WARS**. Little is known of his early life. He commanded a regiment at the Battle of **NASEBY** (1645), and served in Scotland. When the House of **COMMONS** betrayed a disposition to effect a settlement with **CHARLES I**, he was appointed by the army (1648) to expel its Presbyterian royalist members ('Pride's Purge'). He sat among the King's judges, and signed the death warrant. He was knighted by **CROMWELL** in 1656. ► **LONG PARLIAMENT**

**Pridi Phanomyong** (1900–83)
Thai politician. Trained as a lawyer, notably in France in the 1920s, Pridi was a leading civilian figure in the

# *Printing*

Science & Technology

The earliest forms of printing – the making of a meaningful impression of something on a surface – included the use of seals and signet rings to transfer an image to a receptive material such as clay or hot wax. The first recorded printing of text, however, took place in China, where paper had been invented in the 2c AD. Wooden blocks were carved with the characters of a text, inked, and then used to make multiple copies. In this way Buddhist scriptures were being printed by the 9c, the first authenticated work being the *Diamond Sutra*. Similar wooden blocks were used in Europe in the **Middle Ages**, again mainly for religious purposes such as printing copies of portraits of saints.

In the 1450s printing in Europe was revolutionized by the introduction of movable type, or type made up of individual characters. This meant that, instead of type being permanently fixed and usable only to print copies of a single text, the same type could be broken up and reassembled for printing completely different matter. The Chinese and Koreans had experimented with movable characters made of wood and baked clay, and the Koreans were the first to cast movable type in bronze at the turn of the 15c. European printers such as the Dutchman Laurens Janszoon (c.1370–1440) had also tried to use movable wooden type, but it was the German Johannes Gutenberg (1400–68) who took the process forward by inventing a mould for casting movable metal type, the first printing press, and a type of ink that would allow paper to be printed on both sides of a sheet. Gutenberg used these innovations to produce his first printed work, a version of the Bible.

The English printer and translator William Caxton (c.1422–91) produced the first printed text in English (*Recuyell of the Historyes of Troye*) at Bruges in 1474, two years before setting up the first printing press in Britain, at Westminster. He went on to print at least 100 books, many of which he translated himself from French.

Until this time copies of texts could only be made by painstaking transcription by hand, a costly and time-consuming process that had changed little since Roman times when slaves were used to copy scrolls. Now multiple printed copies could be produced much more cheaply and rapidly and this had an enormous influence on the communication of knowledge. While religious texts continued to be the mainstay of the growing printing trade, secular works increasingly came to be produced and distributed.

The basic techniques of printing remained largely unchanged until the 19c but refinements were made over the years, improving the efficiency of the process. Typefounders all over Europe, especially in Italy, created ranges of different, more legible typefaces, and new methods of printing illustrations were brought in, such as lithography. This was printing using a flat plate (originally of stone, as the name suggests, later of metal) instead of a surface in relief, like set type. The printed image was created by making some parts of the plate receive ink while others repelled it. Presses remained hand-operated, with a wooden screw being turned that lowered a sheet of dampened paper onto the type before pressing it down to take the impression.

The great industrial and mechanical advances of the 19c made their mark on the printing trade with the introduction of many new methods that made the process less laborious and slow. Progress went hand-in-hand with the expansion of mass literacy, creating an ever-growing demand for the printed word. Mechanical presses were invented, including steam-driven varieties. Examples included the platen press, in which a *platen* (a flat metal plate) pressed the paper against the type; the cylinder press, in which a rotating drum pressed paper against a flat assembly of type; and the rotary press, in which type mounted on a rotating cylinder was brought into contact with paper on another rotating drum. The

---

coup group which overthrew the absolute monarchy in June 1932. He was then a prominent, but also highly controversial, government minister for much of the rest of the 1930s. In 1933 he drafted a National Economic Plan. This radical initiative, widely seen as communist, created a storm in Bangkok and forced Pridi into a brief exile in France. During the Japanese occupation (1941–5) Pridi acted as Regent for the absent King Ananda but also, towards the end of that period, as a clandestine leader of the anti-Japanese 'Seri Thai' movement, codename 'Ruth'. He was briefly Prime Minister in 1946. However, he remained a highly controversial figure in Thai politics. He left Thailand for exile in 1949, never to return, living first in China and then, from 1970, in France.

**Prieto, Indalécio** (1883–1962)
Spanish socialist leader. He served under the Second Republic first as Minister of Finance in 1931 and then as an innovative Minister of Public Works from 1931–3. The outstanding parliamentary orator of the Socialist Party, Prieto was also the leader of its moderate wing. He was unable to take up the premiership in May 1936 because of the opposition of **LARGO CABAL-LERO**, the leader of the party's left wing. Such a move may have thwarted the military rising of July 1936

which led to civil war. During the **SPANISH CIVIL WAR**, he proved a defeatist Minister of the Navy and Air Force (Sep 1936–May 1937) and Minister of Defence (May 1937–Apr 1938). He was forced to resign because of his opposition to the Communist Party. After the war, he tried to unite the socialists with the Republicans and even the monarchists in an effort to overthrow the **FRANCO** regime. ► **REPUBLIC, SECOND** (Spain)

**Prim (y Prats), Juan** (1814–70)
Spanish soldier. As a Progressive he opposed the dictatorship of **ESPARTERO**, and was exiled (1839), but came back and defeated him in 1843. He was Captain General of Puerto Rico from 1847 to 1848, and deputy in the **CORTES** (1850–6). Failing in an insurrectionary attempt in 1866, he fled to England and Brussels, and from there guided the revolution that in 1868 overthrew **ISABELLA II**. He was War Minister under **SERRANO**, but soon became a virtual dictator. Prim secured the election of Amadeus I of Savoy as King in 1870, but was later shot by an assassin.

**primary**
In US politics, a preliminary election to determine which candidates for public office are to appear on the ballot for a general election. There are various

method known as offset was also invented, in which the printed impression was first made from the type onto an intermediate surface, usually a rubber sheet, from which it was then transferred to the paper. A further important development was the introduction of continuous rolls of paper in the place of individual sheets. This was particularly useful in the expanding newspaper industry, in which large numbers of copies had to be produced in a short time.

The technology of typesetting also made great strides in the 19c. Before this period type had been set by hand, with the individual metal characters being picked out from cases and set precisely into place one at a time. In the hands of an experienced compositor this could be speedy, but now machines were becoming available that were faster still. At a linotype machine a typesetter worked with a keyboard, the end product being whole lines of type in individual metal slugs. A process known as stereotyping allowed metal (and later rubber) printing plates of complete pages to be cast from pages of standing type, thus enabling several presses to print copies of a text at the same time.

Manufacturing processes were also mechanized, with guillotines to trim the printed sheets and binders to enclose and secure the pages between stiff covers. However, as with many crafts, this applied mainly to mass-produced items and traditional hand techniques continued to be used for smaller, high-quality editions.

The printing of illustrations was also refined, with metal blocks replacing the wooden ones. Photographic processes allowed such innovations as half-tone, in which illustrations could be reproduced for printing through breaking them up into tiny dots by photographing them through fine screens. Photography was also used to make lithographic printing plates and greatly facilitated the colour separations needed for colour printing.

Printers and technologists in the 20c continued both to speed up and clean up the basic printing process with such innovations as filmsetting. This allowed type to be set by exposing individual letters on film which could then be used to make a printing plate. The latter part of the century saw the increased use of computers, leading to the consolidation of many of the traditionally separate techniques. By the 1990s, editing, typesetting and the preparation of graphics could all be handled by computer and printing plates could be created directly from the files. Technological developments mean that it is now economic to print small numbers on demand as well as very large quantities. ► **Books**

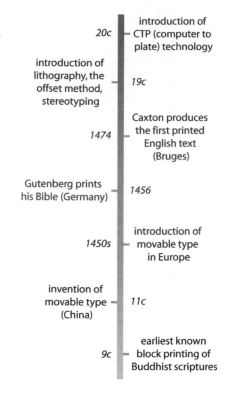

| | |
|---|---|
| 20c | introduction of CTP (computer to plate) technology |
| introduction of lithography, the offset method, stereotyping | 19c |
| 1474 | Caxton produces the first printed English text (Bruges) |
| Gutenberg prints his Bible (Germany) | 1456 |
| 1450s | introduction of movable type in Europe |
| invention of movable type (China) | 11c |
| 9c | earliest known block printing of Buddhist scriptures |

forms of primary, the most common being the closed primary, in which any voter who has registered with a particular party can vote for that party's respective candidate.

### Primo de Rivera, José Antonio (1903–36)
Spanish fascist leader. The son of the dictator General Miguel **PRIMO DE RIVERA**, he was an aristocratic playboy turned charismatic political leader. He founded the **FALANGE ESPAÑOLA**, a totalitarian and nationalistic movement, in Oct 1933. After the Falange fused with the *Juntas de Ofensiva Nacional Sindicalista* (JONS) in Feb 1934, he was elected leader. Detained in Mar 1936 by the Popular Front, he supported the rising of July 1936 against the Republic. He was shot on 20 Nov 1936 in Alicante jail. The cult of 'the absent one' became a central myth of the **FRANCO** regime.

### Primo de Rivera (y Orbaneja), Miguel (1870–1930)
Spanish dictator. He served in Cuba, the Philippines and Morocco, and in 1923 led a military coup, inaugurating a dictatorship which lasted until 1930. During 1928–9 he lost the support of the army, the ruling class, and the King, **ALFONSO XIII**, and in 1930 gave up power. He died in Paris. His son, José Antonio **PRIMO DE RIVERA** founded the Spanish Fascist Party, **FALANGE ESPAÑOLA**, in 1933, and was executed by the

Republicans in 1936. ► **FASCISM**; **SPANISH CIVIL WAR**

### Princely States, Indian
Before the colonial period, India was composed of various independent kingdoms, with only the north of the country being dominated by the **MUGHAL EMPIRE**. With the slow collapse of this empire, many of its constituent parts broke off to become effectively independent states (such as Hyderabad). With the rise of British colonial rule, many of these newly emergent successor states, as well as others with much longer histories, succeeded in maintaining their independence by entering into treaties with the British. Those that resisted, such as Mysore, were often crushed, but even those that were defeated, such as Gwalior and Holkar, having been deprived of much of their territory, continued as nominally independent rulers. This meant that, although the British dominated the subcontinent by the 19c, they never directly administered more than two-thirds of the country. Under Lord **DALHOUSIE**'s notorious policy of lapse, some independent states (such as Jhansi) were taken over in the 1850s; others, such as Awadh (Oudh), were too wealthy a prize to be resisted and were annexed without a pretext. Such high-handedness, however, caused resentment, which was a factor

in the **INDIAN UPRISING** of 1857–8. Subsequently, the British propped up the Indian aristocracy wherever possible, provided they were willing to serve as loyal collaborators. The rewards for this loyalty were sumptuous, giving many rulers fabulous wealth which, combined with a lack of real power, earned them a reputation for decadence. On independence in 1947, the governments of independent India and Pakistan saw the Indian princes as a relic of colonial rule and had little use for them. Some, such as Hyderabad, Kashmir and Junagadh, made a bid for independence, but all were sooner or later annexed. Some ex-rulers went on to enjoy successful political careers but, following the abolition of aristocracy and all its privileges by Indira **GANDHI** in 1971, the majority sank into obscurity. ► **COMMUNALISM; INDIA, PARTITION OF**

### Princip, Gavrilo (1895–1918)

Serbian nationalist and revolutionary. He was a member of the secret Serbian terrorist organization known as the **BLACK HAND**, dedicated to the achievement of independence for the South Slav peoples from the Austro-Hungarian Empire. He and a group of young zealots assassinated **FRANCIS FERDINAND**, Archduke of Austria, and his wife Sophie on a visit to Sarajevo (28 June 1914). The murder precipitated **WORLD WAR I**, after Austria declared war on Serbia (28 July 1914). Princip died in an Austrian prison.

### Printing ► *See panel*

### privateers

Quasi-legal European freebooters who attacked Spanish shipping and settlements in the Caribbean in the period 1520–1650. Some were simply pirates; others were issued with letters of marque by their home governments which gave their captains the right to raid Spanish treasure ships and towns as instruments of war in periods of conflict with Spain. The most infamous were the French corsairs Jean Ango, François Le Clerc and Jacques de Sore operating in the period 1530–55, the Englishmen Hawkins and **DRAKE** in the period 1562–96, and the Dutchman Piet Heyn in the 1620s.

### Privilegium Maius (1358–9)

The most important of the documents forged by **RUDOLF IV OF HABSBURG** to secure a position for Austria in the Electoral College. Rudolf was not one of the **ELECTORS** named in the *Golden Bull* (1356) and to remedy this he forged several documents, which he claimed dated as far back as Julius Caesar and had been ratified by **HENRY IV**. These were rejected by **CHARLES IV**, on the advice of Petrarch, but ratified by **FREDERICK III**. They were not exposed as forgeries until 1852. ► **GOLDEN BULL**

### Prizren, League of

Its founding in 1878 at Prizren in southern **KOSOVO** marked the first stage in the creation of an Albanian state. The original aim of its members was to defend the Albanian national lands from expansionist foreign powers; at the Congress of **BERLIN** (1878) they advocated the maintenance of the **OTTOMAN EMPIRE** and autonomy and unification for the districts of Janina, Monastir, Üskub and Shkodër. Organized by the leading Albanian nationalist, Abdul Frashëri, its members were mainly Gheg landlords and notables,

with a few southern **TOSKS**. By 1880 the autonomists had control of the League and in Apr 1881 the movement was crushed by Sultan Abdul Hamit II. ► **GHEGS**

### Proclamation of 1763 (8 June 1763)

An attempt by the British crown at the end of the **FRENCH AND INDIAN WAR** to halt Anglo-American encroachment on Native American territory by creating a western limit to frontier settlement. On hearing news of the start of **PONTIAC'S CONSPIRACY**, **GEORGE III** proclaimed that the crest of the Appalachian Mountains would constitute the 'Proclamation Line', although several groups of settlers and **NATIVE AMERICANS** already lived on the 'wrong' side, and others had been promised land to the west of it. Subsequent agreements, including the first treaty of Fort Stanwix, pushed the Proclamation Line west to the benefit of the white settlers. ► **FORT STANWIX, TREATIES OF**

### Profumo, John Dennis (1915–)

British politician. He became a Conservative MP in 1940, and held several government posts before becoming Secretary of State for War in 1960. He resigned in 1963 after admitting that he had been guilty of a grave misdemeanour in deceiving the House of **COMMONS** about the nature of his relationship with Christine Keeler, who was at the time also involved with a Soviet diplomat. He later sought anonymity in social and charitable services. ► **CONSERVATIVE PARTY** (UK)

### Progressive Era (1890–1914)

A period in US history characterized by the campaigns and achievements of the Progressive movement, which was sparked off by the suffering caused by the agrarian, financial and industrial depression that began in the 1890s. Presidents Theodore **ROOSEVELT** and Woodrow **WILSON** in different ways espoused many of the concerns of the Progressive movement, eg popular government, free trade, **ANTITRUST** legislation, the popular election of senators, social reforms including the improvement of working conditions, and **PROHIBITION**. Among the main protagonists of progressivism were Jane **ADDAMS** and Robert **LA FOLLETTE**. ► **PROGRESSIVE PARTY; SOCIAL GOSPEL**

### Progressive Party (Canada)

The political party established in 1920 with the support of the farming community, it fought the 1921 federal election on a platform of lower tariffs and a reciprocity agreement with the USA. When it won 65 seats it became the second largest group in the Commons, to the surprise of the country. Its leader, Thomas **CRERAR**, chose not to make the party the official opposition and over the next few years Mackenzie **KING** was able to cut away the farmers' support, so that by 1926 the party had all but disappeared.

### Progressive Party (Spain; *Partido Progresivo*)

The Spanish political party which dominated the period 1834–68 along with the **MODERATE PARTY**. The more liberal of the two parties, the Progressive Party supported the legitimacy of revolution and national rather than monarchical sovereignty. The constitution of 1837 was its classic statement. The party ruled

1835–40, drawing on the authoritarian General **ESPARTERO** to remain in power from 1840 to 1843 and in 1854–6. The party declined thereafter until its collapse in 1868.

**Progressive Party** (USA) (1912–16, 1924 and 1948)
US political parties. The name was used by three separate third-party political initiatives. The first, essentially a breakaway from the **REPUBLICAN PARTY**, centred on former President Theodore **ROOSEVELT**, who was its presidential candidate in 1912. The second developed in 1924 from Midwestern farmer and labour discontent. Its presidential candidate, Senator Robert **LA FOLLETTE** of Wisconsin, won 4 million votes. In the 1948 election, Democrats opposed to President Harry S **TRUMAN**'s cold war policy ran Henry A **WALLACE**, who received only 1 million popular votes. ► **NEW NATIONALISM**

**Prohibition** (1920–33)
An attempt to forbid the manufacture, transportation and sale of all alcoholic drinks in the USA, authorized by the 18th Amendment to the **US CONSTITUTION** (1919). Building on 19c temperance movements and the powerful lobbying of the Anti-Saloon League, **CONGRESS** passed the national legislation as a wartime emergency measure. Its enforcement, through the Volstead Act, gave rise to one of the great political controversies of the 1920s, and led to various '**BOOT-LEGGING**' operations that created new opportunities for organized crime. It also gained celebrity for J Edgar **HOOVER** and his 'G-Men'. It was repealed in 1933 by the 21st Amendment. ► **CAPONE, AL**

**Prokopovich, Feofan** (1681–1736)
Russian prelate and politician. He was educated at Kiev Orthodox Academy (where in 1711 he was appointed rector), and Rome. In St Petersburg in 1716 his sermons and theories for Church reforms brought him to the notice of **PETER I, THE GREAT**, who made him his adviser and Bishop of Pskov, and in 1724 Archbishop of Novgorod. He was responsible for a new Spiritual Regulation which included setting up a Holy Synod instead of the existing patriarchate (which Peter had kept vacant since 1700). This consisted of ten, and later twelve, clerics presided over by a lay procurator, and by and large ensured Tsarist control of the Orthodox Church.

**pronunciamiento**
Spanish army rising. The 'pronouncement' of the army (or a section thereof) for a particular regime amounted to an attempted coup d'état. Its origins lay in the role of the army in the administration of the 18c and the clashes of the War of Independence between soldiers and politicians. In the 19c, when there were numerous *pronunciamientos*, it became the instrument of liberal revolution. Although there were far fewer in the 20c, those of 1923, 1936 and 1981 had far-reaching consequences.

**Prose** ► *See panel*

**Protectorate**
A regime established by the Instrument of Government (1653), the work of army conservatives, England's only written constitution. The Lord Protectors, Oliver **CROMWELL** (1653/8) and his son Richard **CROMWELL** (1658/9), issued ordinances

and controlled the armed forces, subject to the advice of a Council of State and with parliament as legislative partner. It failed to maintain support, and its collapse led to the **RESTORATION**. ► **COMMONWEALTH**

**Protocols of the Elders of Zion**
A fraudulent document, originally printed in Russia (1903) and much translated, ostensibly reporting discussions among Jewish elders of plans to subvert Christian civilization and erect a world Zionist state. Exposed as forgeries in *The Times* (1921), the 'Protocols' have nevertheless been, and remain, a staple of right-wing, anti-Semitic propaganda. ► **ZIONISM**

**Proudhon, Pierre Joseph** (1809–65)
French socialist and political theorist. In his first important book, *Qu'est-ce que la propriété?* (1840), he affirmed the bold paradox 'property is theft', because it involves the exploitation of the labour of others. He then published his greatest work, the *Système des contradictions économiques* (1846). During the **FEBRUARY REVOLUTION** (1848), the violence of his utterances brought him three years' imprisonment, and after further arrest (1858) he retired to Belgium. Amnestied in 1860, he was seen by Karl **MARX** as his chief rival in the international socialist movement.

**Prussia**
A North European state, originally centred in the East Baltic region as a duchy created by the **TEUTONIC KNIGHTS**, but later owing suzerainty to Poland. Inherited by the German House of Brandenburg in the early 17c, Brandenburg-Prussia was consolidated and expanded, and Polish sovereignty thrown off, by **FREDERICK WILLIAM, THE GREAT ELECTOR**. The Kingdom of Prussia was founded in 1701; under **FREDER-ICK WILLIAM I** and **FREDERICK II, THE GREAT**, it acquired western Prussia and **SILESIA**, and gained considerable territory in western Germany at the Congress of **VIENNA** (1814–15). During the 19c it emerged as the most powerful German state, and was ultimately the focus of German unification. Within the federated German Empire (1871–1918) it was dominant, and within the **WEIMAR REPUBLIC** (1919–33) it retained considerable autonomy and influence. As a legal entity, Prussia ceased to exist with the post-1945 division of Germany and the establishment of a revised East German–Polish frontier. ► **AUSTRO-PRUSSIAN WAR**; **FRANCO-PRUSSIAN WAR**; **FREDERICK WILLIAM III**; **GERMAN CONFEDERATION**; **NORTH GERMAN CONFEDERATION**; **ZOLLVEREIN**

**Prussian Law Code** (*Allgemeines Preussisches Landrecht*) (1794)
The code was drawn up by Johann H C Carmer (1721–1801). It was Germany's first legal code and it combined traditional German laws with Roman law and elements of natural law.

**Prynne, William** (1600–69)
English Puritan pamphleteer. In 1633 his *Histrio-Mastix: the Players Scourge* appeared, which contained an apparent attack on Queen Henrietta Maria, wife of **CHARLES I**; for this he was tortured, fined and imprisoned. Released in 1640 by the **LONG PARLIAMENT**, he prosecuted **LAUD** (1644), and became an MP (1648). Purged from the House in 1650, he was again imprisoned (1650–2). After **CROMWELL**'s death he returned to parliament as a royalist, for which he

# Prose

Art & Literature

In contrast to **poetry**, prose is a medium whose use is far from exclusively literary. Indeed, though the obvious medium of choice for writing for a practical purpose, and for chronicles, histories, books of law, instruction and the like, prose tended to be something of a poor relation of verse for imaginative literature until the modern era. Major canonical religious texts like the Old Testament or the Quran are often poetical in format, and some languages, including Scots Gaelic, developed very little prose, as distinct from poetical literature, before the late 18c.

### Rhetoric

While poets, according to Horace, are born and not made, the art of writing prose, especially prose speeches, has always been considered to lie within the realm of the teachable. The establishment of democratic institutions in ancient Athens made public speaking a necessary skill for all who wished to play a serious part in the political process. As a consequence, schools of rhetoric arose, and the Sophists who ran them claimed to be able to teach the pupils to be able to present the weaker side of an argument just as forcibly as the stronger. They were vigorously attacked by Socrates and Plato for their moral relativism and cynical unconcern for truth. Nevertheless, teachers of rhetoric, many of Greek origin, flourished in ancient Rome, and rhetoric became one of the seven liberal arts later taught at medieval universities. While the teaching of rhetoric and interest in it as a subject declined from the 18c onwards, modern lawyers and politicians, in particular, still need many of the same skills that their distant predecessors learned from the Sophists.

### Ornate versus plain

In everyday use, the word rhetoric suggests an elaborate use of language full of 'figures of speech'. In both poetry and prose, fashion has alternated between the ornate and stylized, and the deliberately plain. In setting out to translate the Bible into German in the 1520s, Martin **Luther** announced that he intended to take his cue from 'the old woman in the market place'; direct, contemporary, even homespun. The translators and revisers who prepared the Authorized Version of the Bible in English also wrote with the intention of simplicity of style in mind. Much of Elizabethan and 17c English prose, however, is self-consciously literary, ornate and obscure.

Towards the end of the 17c, Bishop Thomas Sprat in his *History of the Royal Society* (1667) recommended a 'close, naked and natural way of style' to its members as most suitable for intellectual productions of all kinds. This is wholly in keeping with the spirit of the **Enlightenment**, then in its early stages, in which books were to be written for a wider audience; for polite society in general rather than for the scholarly or literary few. The essays of Addison and Steele, first in the *Tatler* (1709–11) and subsequently in the *Spectator* (founded 1711), became models for most of the 18c, not only of clarity and simplicity but also of gentlemanly elegance in prose. The author was a gentleman writing for other gentlemen. This was the prevailing spirit of the age in the century that saw the first flowering of the novel in English.

### Tales

Among the earliest imaginative writings in prose that survive from ancient civilizations are collections of tales and fables. The most ancient of recorded tales are from Egypt and date from 2000 BC. Ancient India was particularly rich in them. The *Jatakas*, a collection of Buddhist fables written in Pali, a language derived from Sanskrit, are presumed to date from the 4c BC. Motifs originating from this and later Sanskrit collections, such as the *Panchatantra* (4c AD) are found throughout many collections of stories in other Indo-European languages and Arabic, for example in the fables of Aesop (6c BC), which in their present form derive mainly from versions made in the 1c AD. A feature of some Sanskrit collections is their use of a framing narrative within which the individual tales are set. This technique was borrowed and used to brilliant effect in the *Thousand and One Nights* (the *Arabian Nights*), fragments of which survive in a version dating from around AD 800, but which reached its full form in around 1400. The same framing technique is used in the greatest collection of prose stories from the European late **Middle Ages**, Boccaccio's *Decameron*, written between 1348 and 1353. In this instance a group of friends escapes from Florence during an outbreak of the plague to a country villa, where they entertain each other with stories over a period of ten days.

### The novel

Works sometimes described as novels were produced during both the Hellenistic period in ancient Greece, and in

---

was made Keeper of the Tower Records. ➤ **PROTECTORATE**; **PURITANISM**

**PSD** (*Partido Social Democrático*, 'Social Democratic Party')
The Brazilian party, formed in 1945, as a coalition of rural *coroneis* and urban leaders, including industrialists who had benefited substantially from the rule of **VARGAS**, yet could not readily support his own PTB (*Partido Trabalhista Brasileiro*, 'Brazilian Labour Party'). The PSD effectively retained control of Vargas' political machine in 1945, electing Eurico Gaspar **DUTRA** as President, and receiving nearly 43 per cent of the vote. The party's 'natural alliance' with the PTB came to the fore during the 1950 presidential election, when the bulk of its leaders supported Vargas rather than its 'own' candidate. The blend of populist

politics espoused by the PTB and the **CORONELISMO** of the countryside provided a powerful base for **KUBITSCHEK (DE OLIVEIRA)**'s *Programa de Metas*, but foundered under the weak leadership of João **GOULART**. Much of the PSD merged with the ARENA party after 1965, inexorably delivering the rural vote to the military government.

**PSOE** (*Partido Socialista Obrero Español*, 'Spanish Socialist Workers' Party')
Spanish political party, founded in 1879, which established itself slowly, limited both by organizational rigidity and theoretical shortcomings. Although the party proclaimed a revolutionary rhetoric, it remained wedded to reformist practices, even to the extent of collaborating with the dictatorship of Miguel **PRIMO DE RIVERA** (1923–30). Under the Second

ancient Rome, notably Petronius's *Satyricon* (1c AD) and Apuleius's *The Golden Ass* (1c AD). The first novel proper is reckoned by many scholars to be *The Tale of Genji* written in the 11c by a lady of the Japanese court known as Murasaki Shikibu. This work, however, remained unknown in the West until recent times. In China – where there is a long and rich literary tradition of prose – novels, often in a vernacular style, appeared from the 16c, including Wu Ch'eng-en's *Hsi-yu chi*, commonly translated as 'Monkey' in English editions. In the 18c, Ts'ao Chan's *Hong Lou Meng* ('Dream of the Red Chamber') was published, perhaps the finest Chinese prose ever written. The tradition of the novel in European languages, which eventually influenced the writing of fiction throughout the rest of the world, dates essentially from the late 16c and early 17c. The word itself comes from the Italian *novella*, the word used by Boccaccio to describe his tales in the *Decameron*.

From Spain in the 16c came the picaresque or rogue novel, not so much a collection of tales as a collection of amusing or outrageous incidents experienced by the hero whose character provided the connecting thread linking the whole. From Spain also came what is generally reckoned to be the first great European novel, Cervantes' *Don Quixote* (1605–15). In satirizing prose romances of chivalry, which his hero takes to be factually true, Cervantes is also pointing to another ancestor of the novel form. In contrasting the grandiose folly of the hero's imaginings with the social realities in which he actually lives, he may be said to be exploring, comically, the troubled relationship between the individual and society, the theme of so many later works in this same genre.

The growth of the reading public during the 18c led to an increasing demand for both novels of a kind that truly reflected and sensitively commented on contemporary life, and those of a more escapist kind. It is perhaps doubtful whether in 1800, despite the number of excellent writers who had already used the form, anyone would have spoken of a classic novel or the great tradition of the novel, or felt that the achievements of prose fiction rivalled those of poetry and **drama**. The great novelists of the 19c – Stendhal, Balzac, Dickens, George Eliot, Melville, Tolstoy and Dostoyevsky, to name but a few – demonstrated that in scope and depth the novel could equal any other genre. The great age of novel writing continued into the 20c, and though its death as a literary form has been frequently predicted, it continues as a vehicle of both serious literature and popular entertainment to the present day.

**The short story**
The literary short story, as opposed to the prose tale, is a form that developed alongside the novel. It dates essentially from the early 19c, partly as a response to the demand from editors of popular and literary magazines for material to fill their pages.

The German writers Heinrich von Kleist and E T A Hoffmann were among its early exponents. The latter strongly influenced the American writer Edgar Allen Poe, whose influence on succeeding generations of mystery and detective writers was enormous. Many great novelists produced short stories, among them Tolstoy, Henry James and D H Lawrence. A few writers produced all or most of their best work in this form, notably Guy de Maupassant, Katherine Mansfield and Franz Kafka in the early 20c. Besides being an important literary genre in its own right, the short story, with its demand for concentration, economy, and the creation of character and action in few words and a short space, provides an excellent training ground for aspiring writers.

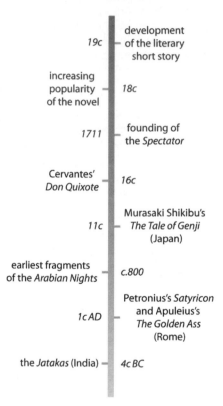

| | | |
|---|---|---|
| | 19c | development of the literary short story |
| increasing popularity of the novel | 18c | |
| | 1711 | founding of the *Spectator* |
| Cervantes' *Don Quixote* | 16c | |
| | 11c | Murasaki Shikibu's *The Tale of Genji* (Japan) |
| earliest fragments of the *Arabian Nights* | c.800 | |
| | 1c AD | Petronius's *Satyricon* and Apuleius's *The Golden Ass* (Rome) |
| the *Jatakas* (India) | 4c BC | |

Republic of 1931–6 the PSOE was the leading political force on the Left, forming the backbone of the reformist Republican–Socialist administrations of 1931–3. However, the reversal of reform after the electoral victory of the Right in Nov 1933 rapidly radicalized the PSOE, culminating in the Asturian rising of Oct 1934. The insurrection's defeat divided the party between the 'revolutionary' stance of **LARGO CABALLERO** and the moderate Indalécio **PRIETO**. After the **SPANISH CIVIL WAR** broke out, Largo Caballero was made Premier in Sep 1936, but in May 1937 he was ousted by the Communists to be replaced by Juan **NEGRÍN**, a socialist who supported communist policies. In Apr 1938, Negrín removed Indalécio Prieto, the last obstacle to communist domination. As the Republic plunged to defeat, the PSOE collapsed and during **FRANCO**'s dictatorship PSOE opposition was negligible. However, it played an important role during the transition to democracy. In 1982 the PSOE won an overall majority in the general election; it remained in power, led by Prime Minister Felipe **GONZÁLEZ**, until defeated by the *Partido Popular* (**PP**) in 1996. The PSOE in power did much to modernize Spain and raise its international profile, though it proved intolerant of dissent, lost the support of the trade unions, and was discredited by corruption scandals. Its fortunes revived in 2004 when it ousted the **PP** government and José Luis Zapatero became Prime Minister. ► REPUBLIC, SECOND (Spain)

**Public Against Violence** (1989)
The Slovak offshoot and equivalent of Czech **CIVIC FORUM** that united most of the anti-communist groups in Slovakia in Nov 1989 to help bring down

the Czechoslovak communist government. There was no bloodshed and the 'party' won more seats than any other in the June 1990 election. But it subsequently split on the issue of relations with the Czech lands. Even Jan Carnogursky, Slovak Prime Minister and leader of the rump 'party', had inevitably to talk in nationalist terms.

## Public Safety, Committee of

French revolutionary political body, set up in the war crisis (Apr 1793) to organize defence against internal and external enemies. Its members, elected by the National **CONVENTION**, came to exercise dictatorial powers during the Reign of **TERROR**, particularly under **ROBESPIERRE**'s leadership. After his downfall (July 1794), its powers were strictly limited. ► **FRENCH REVOLUTION**

## pueblo

Means both 'the village' and 'the village dwellers' or 'the people'. Underlines the enormous importance attached to local ties in Spanish life. National unity came late to Spain, the persistence of the 'pueblo' providing the most significant yardstick.

## Pueblo

Native American peoples of the south-west who live in settlements called *pueblos* in multi-storied, permanent houses made of clay. Culturally and linguistically diverse, they are divided into eastern and western Pueblo, the latter including the Hopi and the Zuni. They are famed for their weaving, basketry, sand paintings and pottery. Their population is currently c.70,000. ► **NATIVE AMERICANS**

## Pugachev, Emelyan (c.1742–1775)

Russian Don Cossack. He fled to the Urals, from where he launched a mass rebellion against **CATHERINE II, THE GREAT**. This was neither the first nor the last such insurrection based on the simmering discontent of an exploited peasantry and led by a largely free Cossack. Pugachev carried his revolt to the Volga, proclaimed himself to be Peter III, Catherine's murdered husband, and promised to restore ancient freedoms. The rebellion was marked by great ferocity on both sides, and Pugachev's name later became a byword for the spirit of peasant revolution in Russia. He was captured in 1774 and taken to Moscow, where he was tortured and executed. Catherine's handling of the episode was in stark contrast to her allegedly enlightened social philosophy and only contributed in the long run to the downfall of Tsarism. ► **COSSACKS**; **RAZIN, STENKA**

## Pułaski, Kazimierz (1747–79)

Polish nobleman and soldier. One of the few who fought successfully against Russia, he was outlawed at the First Partition of Poland (1772). In 1777 he went to America, and for his conduct at **BRANDYWINE** was given command of a brigade of cavalry. In 1778 he organized 'Pułaski's legion', and in May 1779 entered Charleston and held it until it was relieved. He was mortally wounded at the siege of Savannah. ► **AMERICAN REVOLUTION**

## Pullman Strike (1894)

A US labour conflict. During the depression of 1894 the Pullman Palace Car Company in Chicago cut workers' wages by 25–40 per cent, but maintained their high rents in the residential town founded by the company. The workers were members of the newly formed American Railway Union, which retaliated by refusing to handle Pullman cars, and thereby interfering with the mail service. Despite pleas from Governor John Altgeld, President Grover **CLEVELAND** ordered federal troops to the site and after much violence, the strike was broken. The Attorney-General's court injunction, which forbade interference with the mail and interstate commerce, established the principle that a strike could violate the Sherman Anti-Trust Act. ► **ANTI-TRUST ACTS**; **DEBS, EUGENE**

## Pulszky, Ferenc Aurelius (1814–97)

Hungarian politician and author. He studied law, travelled, and published (1837) a successful book on England. In 1848 he became **ESTERHÁZY**'s factotum, but, having joined the revolution, went to London in 1849 to plead for help, which was never given. He stayed on to become a journalist. When Lajos **KOSSUTH** came to England, Pulszky became his companion and went with him to America. He was condemned to death in 1852, but after living in Italy (1852–66) and being imprisoned in Naples as a Garibaldian, he was pardoned in 1867 at the time of the **AUSGLEICH**. He returned to Hungary, sat in parliament and was Director of Museums.

## Puritanism

The belief that further reformation was required in the Church of England under **ELIZABETH I** and the Stuarts. It arose in the 1560s out of dissatisfaction with the 'popish elements', such as surplices, which had been retained by the Elizabethan religious settlement. It was not always a coherent, organized movement; rather, a diverse body of opinions and personalities, which occasionally came together. It included the anti-episcopal Presbyterian movement of John Field and Thomas Cartwright in the 1570s and 1580s; the separatist churches that left England for Holland and America from 1590 to 1640; the 'Presbyterian', 'independent', and more radical groups which emerged during the **ENGLISH CIVIL WARS** and **INTERREGNUM**; and the nonconformist sects persecuted by the **CAVALIER PARLIAMENT**'s '**CLARENDON CODE**' under **CHARLES II**. ► **REFORMATION**; **RESTORATION**; **STUART, HOUSE OF**

## Putin, Vladimir (1952– )

Russian politician. Born in Leningrad (now St Petersburg), he studied law at Leningrad State University and then worked for the KGB from 1975 to 1991, mostly in East Germany. After the USSR's collapse he worked for the mayor of St Petersburg before moving to the presidential administration in 1996 and in 1998 becoming Federal Security Bureau chief. President **YELTSIN** appointed him acting Prime Minister in Aug 1999, and he became acting President when President Yeltsin resigned in Dec 1999. He won the presidential election in 2000 and was re-elected in 2004. His United Russia party won the parliamentary election in 2003. He imposed control over the Russian media, and limited the power of the oligarchs who built up vast business interests in the energy and media sectors in the 1990s. He has countered violent attacks by separatists with overwhelming force in **CHECHNYA**, defying Western criticism by portraying the separatists as part of the global terror network. Concern that Putin favours central control rather than democracy increased in 2004 when he proposed that regional governors should no longer be directly elected but appointed by Moscow.

**Puyi (P'u-i)** (1906–67)
Last Emperor of China (1908/12) and the first of MANZHUGUO (1934/5). This was the personal name of Hsuan T'ung. Emperor at the age of two, after the CHINESE REVOLUTION (1911) he was given a pension and a summer palace. Known in the West as Henry Puyi, in 1932 he was called from private life by the Japanese to be provincial dictator of Manzhuguo, under the name of Kang Teh. Taken prisoner by the Russians in 1945, he was tried in China as a war criminal (1950), pardoned (1959) and became a private citizen. The story of his life was made into a film, *The Last Emperor*, in 1988.

**Pyat, Félix** (1810–89)
French journalist and revolutionary. He signed LEDRU-ROLLIN's appeal to the masses to arm in 1849, escaped to London, and became a member of the 'European revolutionary committee'. Returning to Paris on amnesty in 1870, he was a leader of the communards, and again escaped to London. He was condemned to death, *in absentia*, in 1873, but pardoned in 1880.

**Pym, John** (1584–1643)
English politician. He left Oxford without taking a degree, studied law, and entered parliament (1614). In 1641 he took a leading part in the IMPEACHMENT of STRAFFORD, helped to draw up the GRAND REMONSTRANCE, and in 1642 was one of the five members whom CHARLES I singled out by name. He stayed in London during the ENGLISH CIVIL WARS, and died soon after being appointed Lieutenant of the Ordnance.

**Pyramids, Battle of the** (1798)
A battle fought between French forces under NAPOLEON I and the Mamluk rulers of Egypt. The battle enabled Napoleon to take Cairo and establish control of Egypt. The Egyptian campaign aimed at strangling British lines of communication with India. ➤ MAMLUKS

**Pyrenees, Treaty of the** (7 Nov 1659)
The peace treaty between France and Spain ending the hostilities of the THIRTY YEARS' WAR. It followed a series of Spanish Habsburg defeats since 1643 (the Austrian Habsburgs made a separate peace in the Treaty of WESTPHALIA, 1648). The French King, LOUIS XIV, had ambitions in the Low Countries, and this treaty gave him part of the Spanish Netherlands: nearly all Artois, Grevelingen, and several other parts. The French, for their part, withdrew from most of Italy. The treaty also arranged Louis's marriage to PHILIP IV of Spain's daughter, MARIA THERESA. The treaty brought to an end the war in the southern Netherlands (now Belgium) and marked the end of Spanish military and political dominance in Western Europe. ➤ HABSBURG DYNASTY

### Qaboos bin Said (1940–)

Sultan of Oman (1970/ ). The son of Sa'id bin Taimur, he is the 14th descendant of the ruling dynasty of the Albusaid family. Educated in England, where he was trained at Sandhurst, the Royal Military Academy, he disagreed with the conservative views of his father and in 1970 overthrew him in a bloodless coup and assumed the sultanship. He proceeded to pursue more liberal and expansionist policies, while maintaining an international position of strict non-alignment.

### Qadhdhafi, Mu'ammar ➤ GADDAFI, MUAMMAR

### Qajar Dynasty

A Turcoman tribe which furnished Persia with a dynasty which ruled from 1795 to 1924. Qajar authority over Persia was established by Aqa Muhammad Khan at the expense of the Zand Khans whom he ousted. Murdered in 1797, Aqa Muhammad Khan was succeeded by his nephew, Fath Ali Khan, then Governor of Fars, who reigned with the title of Fath Ali Shah. The period of Qajar rule saw a great increase in the influence in Persia of both the British and the Russians, interference by which latter in the internal affairs of Persia was established in the Treaty of **GULISTAN** which gave the Tsar the right not only to recognize the Prince nominated as heir to the Qajar throne, but also to intervene on his behalf should there be dissension over his accession. The absolute nature of Qajar rule, coupled with the affectation of ostentatious luxury on the part of some Qajar Shahs, led to many disturbances, and this coupled with foreign interference led to difficulties with the religious hierarchy. A coup d'état in the early 1920s at the instigation of Reza Khan led in due course to the deposition of the last Qajar ruler, Ahmad Shah, and the coronation of Reza as Reza Shah Pahlavi.

### Qarakhanid Dynasty

A Turkish dynasty which ruled in Central Asia from the 10c to the early 13c. Initially a tribal confederation which, in the 10c, was instrumental in bringing down the Samanid Dynasty in Transoxiana, the Qarakhanids after an initial period of cordiality had hostile relations with **MAHMUD OF GHAZNI**. In the early 11c the Qarakhanids accepted Sunni Islam and the spiritual suzerainty of the 'Abbasid caliph. In the mid-11c the khanate split into an eastern and a western branch, the eastern branch being situated in Semirechye and adjoining territories, the western situated in Transoxiana until the early 13c when, caught between the Khwarazm-Shahs and the Qara-Khitay, the last Qarakhanid, 'Uthman Khan, succumbed to the Khwarazm-Shah Ala al-Din Muhammad, who captured Samarkand and had 'Uthman executed. Adopting Persian and Islamic values, both cultural and religious, the Qarakhanids patronized architecture, the arts and scholarship, while at the same time not losing sight of their own Turkish identity. ➤ 'ABBASID DYNASTY

### Qara-Qoyunlu

The so-called 'Black Sheep' Turcomans ruled over portions of Eastern Anatolia, Iraq and much of Iran in the second half of the 14c and for much of the 15c. The first Qara-Qoyunlu leader to achieve prominence was Bayram Khoja, who, by the time of his death (1380), had brought the territories from Mosul to Erzerum under the sway of his tribe. His successors, Qara-Mehmet and Qara-Yusuf, both had to contend with **TIMUR**, but it was Qara-Yusuf who established the reputation of the Qara-Qoyunlu, bequeathing territories stretching from Erzinjan (Erzincan) to Qazvin and from Shirvan to Basra. Amongst those whose hostility he faced was Shah-Rukh the Timurid. However, after Qara-Yusuf's death, Shah-Rukh, realizing that he would not be able completely to reduce the Qara-Qoyunlu, supported individual members of the ruling family; his declaration in 1434 of Jihan-Shah as leader of the Qara-Qoyunlu led subsequently to the development of Qara-Qoyunlu lands into an empire. After Shah-Rukh's death, Jihan-Shah was able to take Rayy and Isfahan, and extend his rule to Kerman and Fars. However, a disastrous expedition against Uzun Hasan Beg of the Aq-Qoyunlu (or 'White Sheep' Turcomans) resulted in Jihan-Shah's death in 1467. By 1469, the authority of the Qara-Qoyunlu was almost completely in the hands of the Aq-Qoyunlu.

### Qashqais

A Turkish people living in Iran in the province of Fars. A relatively recent community (the earliest mention of them dates from the 18c), the nomadic Qashqais have a history of clashes with central authority in Iran. They were, for instance, disarmed by Reza Shah in 1930, and in **WORLD WAR II** they refused to surrender German agents who had sought asylum amongst them. In 1963 land reforms were imposed on the territories of the Qashqais and their attempts to resist were forcibly put down; their tribesmen were disarmed and the ruling family of khans forced into exile.

### Qassim, Abd al-Krim (1914–63)

Iraqi soldier and revolutionary. The son of a carpenter, he joined the army and by 1955 had risen to the rank of brigadier. In 1958 he led the coup which resulted in the overthrow of the monarchy and the deaths of King **FAYSAL II**, his uncle Prince Abdul Ilah, and the pro-Western Prime Minister General Nuri al-**SA'ID**. Qassim suspended the constitution and established a left-wing military regime with himself as Prime Minister and head of state, but soon found himself increasingly isolated in the Arab world. He survived one assassination attempt, but failed to crush a Kurdish rebellion (1961–3) and was killed in a coup led by Colonel Salam **AREF**, who reinstated constitutional government.

---

**QATAR**   official name **State of Qatar**

A low-lying state on the east coast of the Arabian Peninsula, comprising the Qatar Peninsula and numerous small offshore islands. It is bounded to the south by Saudi Arabia and the United Arab Emirates, and elsewhere by the Arabian Gulf. Under the suzerainty of Bahrain for most of the 19c, Qatar was then ruled by the Turks before becoming a British protectorate after the Turkish withdrawal in 1916. It declared its independence in 1971. Qatar is a hereditary monarchy, with an Emir who until 1996 was both head of state and Prime Minister. Sheikh Khalifa bin Hamad al-**THANI** ruled from 1972 until 1995, when he was deposed by his son, Sheikh Hamad bin Khalifa al-Thani. The latter's liberal reforms led to an attempted coup by Sheikh Khalifa in 1996. Reforms have included extending the franchise to women (1999) and introducing a new constitution (2004) that provides for a consultative council some of whose members are directly elected.

**Qianlong (Ch'ien-lung)** (1711–99)
Emperor of the Manchu **QING DYNASTY** (1736/96). During his reign the Chinese empire attained its zenith of power and prosperity. Tibet and Mongolia were incorporated into the empire and neighbouring states (eg Korea, Burma, Annam) regularly sent tribute missions to Qianlong's court. The supreme confidence in China's superiority and self-sufficiency as the Middle Kingdom was dramatically illustrated by Qianlong's rejection of requests made by the Macartney mission (1793) for increased Sino-British trade. Peace and stability at home, however, led to a huge increase in population that outstripped the availability of land, while Qianlong's final years were marked by bureaucratic complacency and widespread corruption. When he abdicated in 1796 (so as not to reign longer than his grandfather, **KANGXI**) government financial resources were depleted, official mor-

ale was low, and the efficiency of Manchu military forces much impaired, all of which boded ill for the dynasty's ability to meet internal and external threats from the early 19c onwards.

**Qin Dynasty ▶ CHINESE DYNASTIES PRE-1000AD**

**Qing Dynasty** (1644–1911)
The last dynasty of imperial China, it was founded by the Manchus following their conquest of China in 1644. **KANGXI** (1661/1722) made concerted attempts to suppress corruption and reduce taxation and was also a great patron of the arts and sciences. During his reign, Jesuit missionaries from France were allowed to settle in China and, with his permission, they were responsible for the first geographical survey of the empire in 1718. Much of the reign was taken up with military matters, the Rebellion of the **THREE FEUDATORIES** and wars with the **MONGOLS** and with Russia. The early years of **QIANLONG**'s long reign (1736/96) were peaceful and prosperous, but the latter half was marred by corruption at court. Military conquests and the suppression of internal rebellions, especially the White Lotus Rebellion (1796–1807), were a considerable drain on the treasury. He formally abdicated in 1796, although he continued to 'instruct' his son on the conduct of national affairs until his death. The dynasty entered a period of decline in the 19c as China fell more and more under the domination of the European powers but did not finally collapse until the **CHINESE REVOLUTION** in 1911, when China became a republic.

**Qishan (Ch'i-shan)** (d.1854)
Manchu official of the Chinese government. He was appointed Imperial Commissioner at Canton in 1840 to negotiate with the British expeditionary force during the first of the **OPIUM WARS**. Qishan's attempt to compromise with the British led to the signing of the Chuenpi Convention (Jan 1841), which proposed the cession of Hong Kong to Britain and the reopening of the port of Canton to foreign trade. The convention was disowned by both the Qing Emperor (for having ceded too much) and by the British government (which felt it had not granted enough). Qishan was dismissed and the war dragged on until 1842.

**Qiu Jin (Ch'iu Chin)** (1875–1907)
Chinese feminist and revolutionary. In 1904 Qiu Jin abandoned her family to study in Japan, where she became actively involved in radical Chinese student associations calling for the overthrow of the Manchu **QING DYNASTY**. On her return to China in 1906, she founded a women's journal in which she argued that the liberation of women was an essential prerequisite for a strong China. In 1907 Qiu Jin was implicated in an abortive anti-Manchu uprising and was executed by the Qing authorities.

**Qiying (Ch'i-ying)** (d.1858)
Chinese official. A member of the Imperial clan, he held a succession of senior posts in central government (1823–36), and in 1842 was sent to Nanjing (Nanking) to defend the city against the British. He negotiated the Treaty of **NANJING**, followed by similar treaties with the USA, France, and other countries, and pursued a policy of conciliation until recalled in 1848. In 1858, when the Chinese had again been defeated by the British, he was sent to join in the

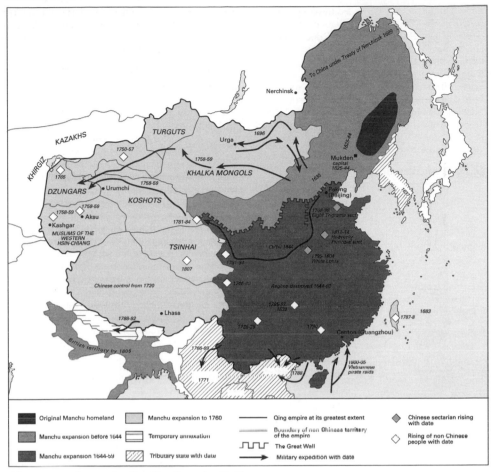

**China's expansion under the Qing Dynasty, 17–18c**

negotiations for the Treaty of TIANJIN, but the British representatives confronted him with evidence of the insincerity of his former protestations of friendship. He left his post in despair and against orders, and was commanded by the Emperor to commit suicide.

## Quadrilateral

The defensive position on the borders of Lombardy and Venetia formed by the four fortified cities of Verona, Mantua, Peschiera and Legnano. Following the CINQUE GIORNATE (1848), the Austrian commander, RADETZKY, retreated to the Quadrilateral and used it as the basis for his eventual recapture of the rebellious Italian provinces of the Habsburg Empire. During the war of 1859, the difficulty in dislodging the Austrians from the Quadrilateral seems to have played a large part in persuading NAPOLEON III to seek peace after the Battles of SOLFERINO and MAGENTA (1859); it fell into Italian hands only in 1866.
► HABSBURG DYNASTY

## Quadros, Jânio da Silva (1917–92)

Brazilian politician. Trained as a teacher, he was elected to the municipal council of São Paulo in 1947. He was a masterful campaigner and orator, with a unique personal style; as the 'man of destiny', he won election to the São Paulo State Assembly, Prefecture and Governorship between 1951 and 1955. He began preparing for the presidential race in 1960, as

the only hope of the UDN (União Democrático Nacional), mobilizing popular support in the process. He defeated his PSD opponents and assumed the presidency in 1961, determined to overcome the economic crisis bequeathed by KUBITSCHEK (DE OLIVEIRA). This he did by exercising near-dictatorial prerogatives to temper crisis economic measures with a strongly nationalist foreign policy. He incurred the wrath of Congress and the far Right, led by Carlos Lacerda, and resigned (25 Aug 1961), pitching the country into crisis. Banned from political life in 1965, he returned to politics in 1985 as Prefect of São Paulo, failing in another bid for the presidency in 1989.

## Quadruple Alliance (1718)

A treaty signed by Britain, France, and the Habsburg Emperor CHARLES VI, to which the Dutch were expected to accede, to ensure the principle of collective security in Western Europe. It provided for mutual guarantees of titles, possessions, and rights of succession, despite Spain's hostility to Italian territorial provisions, and secured peace for a generation (1718–33).

## Quakers ► FRIENDS, SOCIETY OF

## Quantrill, William Clarke, also known as Charley Hart (1837–65)

American Confederate guerrilla. In 1861, after the outbreak of the AMERICAN CIVIL WAR, he served briefly with the Confederate Army, then put together a notorious band known as Quantrill's Raiders that repeatedly slipped through Union lines in the mid-west to raid army camps and plunder civilians. Although they were declared outlaws by the Union forces, the Confederacy made the Raiders an official troop, with Quantrill as captain. In Aug 1863 they set fire to Lawrence, Kansas, killing at least 150 people, and in Oct, dressed as Union soldiers, they defeated a Union cavalry unit and slaughtered those they took captive. Quantrill died from wounds sustained in a raid in Kentucky.

**Quayle, (James) Dan(forth)** (1947–)
US politician. Born in Indianapolis, Indiana, he was educated at DePauw and Indiana universities, then served as a captain in the Indiana **NATIONAL GUARD** (1970–76). He worked as a lawyer, journalist and public official, becoming a member of the **HOUSE OF REPRESENTATIVES** (1977–81) and **SENATE** (1981–8) representing the state of Indiana. He was elected Vice-President under George H W **BUSH** in 1988. As Vice President he was a proponent of political con-servatism and of a business community unhindered by federal regulation.

**Quebec, Battle of** (13 Sep 1759)
A battle fought during the **SEVEN YEARS' WAR** between British forces under General James **WOLFE** and French forces defending Quebec under the Marquis of **MONTCALM**. It followed an audacious plan by Wolfe to transport British troops from the St Law-rence River up steep, wooded cliffs. British victory led to speedy capture of Quebec and the subsequent collapse of French power in Canada. Both Wolfe and Montcalm were killed in the battle.

**Quebec Act** (1774)
British statute enacted to remedy the anomalous situation of Quebec within the empire. In 1769 the Board of Trade advised the extension of British insti-tutions to the new colony and suggested that the French should participate in the government of the colony. Sir Guy **CARLETON** took a different view of the problem, believing that the French seigniorial system should be maintained and that **RESPONSIBLE GOVERNMENT** should be withheld. The Board of Trade report was suppressed and the Quebec Act, which reversed the established principle of colonial rule through British institutions, was passed. The gover-nor was to rule with the assistance of a council which included the French seigniors; the seigniorial system of tenure continued and the position of the Catholic Church was maintained. The Act showed generosity to a conquered people but omitted to consider the expectations of either the **HABITANTS** or the English-speaking settlers who were unhappy at the retention of the civil law embodied in the custom of Paris and the absence of *habeas corpus*. The Act was superseded by the Constitutional Act of 1791.

**Queen Anne's War** (1702–13)
The second of the four intercolonial wars waged by Britain and France for control of colonial North America, known in Europe as the War of the **SPANISH SUCCESSION**. Both sides made considerable use of Native American allies. Settled by the Peace of **UTRECHT** (1713), the war resulted in British control

of Newfoundland, **ACADIA** and Hudson's Bay. Britain also gained the Asiento, allowing trade with Spanish America.

**Queenston Heights, Battle of** (1812)
Military engagement in the **WAR OF 1812**. A victory for the British regular army, it reassured Canadians who doubted Britain's commitment to their defence, while pro-Americans were forced to reconsider their loyal-ties. A monument was erected as a memorial to Isaac Brock, the British commanding officer, killed while charging somewhat injudiciously up the face of the Heights.

**Queipo de Llano, Gonzalo, Marquis of Queipo de Llano y Sevilla** (1875–1951)
Spanish soldier. After military service in Cuba and Morocco, he was promoted to the rank of major-general in the Republican army, but went over to the rebel side at the beginning of the **SPANISH CIVIL WAR**. In July 1936 he led the forces which captured Seville, and became Commander-in-Chief of the Southern Army. In his many propaganda broadcasts from Seville, he drew on General Emilio Mola's phrase '**FIFTH COLUMN**', as used to describe the rebel sup-porters inside Madrid, who were expected to add their strength to that of the four columns attacking from outside. In Apr 1950 he was given the title of marquis.

**Quezon (y Molina), Manuel Luis** (1878–1944)
President of the Commonwealth of the Philippines. He studied in Manila, served with **AGUINALDO** during the insurrection of 1899, and in 1905 became Gover-nor of Tayabas under the US regime. In 1909 he went to Washington as one of the resident Filipino com-missioners. President of the Filipino Senate (1916–35), he played a major role in the negotiation of Filipino independence in the early 1930s, and was elected first President of the Filipino Commonwealth (1935). Here he established a highly centralized gov-ernment verging on 'one-man' rule. Quezon dis-played great courage during the Japanese onslaught from Dec 1941, refusing to evacuate to the USA until President **ROOSEVELT** intervened.

**Quiet Revolution** (1960–6)
Quebec reform programme. Pursued by Jean **LE-SAGE**'s Liberal government of Quebec with the slo-gan, *Il faut que ça change* ('Things must change'), it sought to counteract the influence of the Catholic Church in civic spheres such as education and pro-moted state activism to 'decolonize' Quebec's econo-my from the influence of American and English-speaking institutions. It also began to participate in the federal/provincial shared-cost programmes, though previously shunned by **DUPLESSIS** and the **UNION NATIONALE**, to provide the range of social ser-vices available elsewhere in Canada. However, the re-sulting huge increases in the size of the provincial civil service and the tax burden gave the Union Na-tionale a platform for their return to power under Daniel Johnson. ► **LIBERAL PARTY** (Canada)

**Quinet, Edgar** (1803–75)
French writer and politician. Appointed Professor of Literature in 1839, he began the lectures which formed his brilliant *Du génie des religions* (1842); then he joined Michelet in attacking the Jesuits. His

lectures caused so much excitement that the government suppressed them in 1846. After the **FEBRUARY REVOLUTION** (1848), he was elected to the National Assembly and voted with the extreme left. Following the coup d'état he was exiled to Brussels and Switzerland, and after the downfall of **NAPOLEON III**, he returned to Paris and was elected to the National Assembly (1871).

### Quisling, Vidkun Abraham Lauritz Jonsson (1887–1945)

Norwegian fascist leader. He embarked on a military career, graduating from the military academy with high honours in 1911, and went on to serve as a military attaché in Russia and Finland (1918–21) and to work with Fridtjof **NANSEN** as a relief administrator in the USSR (1922–6). Quisling entered politics in 1929 and was Minister of Defence in 1931–2. In May 1933 he founded a new party, *Nasjonal Samling* ('National Union') in imitation of the German National Socialist Party. However, the party met with little electoral success and disintegrated after 1936. He then turned to Germany and in Dec 1939 made contact with the Nazi leader Alfred Rosenberg and the head of the German navy, Admiral **RAEDER**, as well as with **HITLER** himself. Following the German invasion of Norway (Apr 1940), Quisling declared himself head of a government but won no support and was forced to step down six days later. It was from this point onward that his name became synonymous with 'traitor'. The German occupation authorities reluctantly allowed Quisling to head a puppet government from May 1942 onwards. At the end of **WORLD WAR II** he was arrested and put on trial, and executed by firing squad on 24 Oct 1945. ▶ **FASCISM**; **NORWAY, GERMAN INVASION OF**

### Quit India Movement

A campaign launched (Aug 1942) by the **INDIAN NATIONAL CONGRESS** calling for immediate independence from Britain, and threatening mass nonviolent struggle if its demands were not met. M K **GANDHI** and other Congress leaders were arrested, and the movement was suppressed, though not without difficulty. It was described by the Viceroy, Lord Linlithgow, as 'by far the most serious rebellion since that of 1857'; 57 army battalions had to be used to help restore order and there were more than 1,000 deaths. It contributed significantly to the eventual decision by Britain to withdraw from India soon after the end of **WORLD WAR II**. ▶ **INDIAN UPRISING**

### Quito

The capital of Ecuador, situated in the northern central part of the country at an altitude of 9,350 ft/2,850 m. From the 11c until 1487 it was ruled by the Shyris, sovereigns of the Cara Indians, and it was then joined to the Inca Empire and became its capital. In 1530 it was ruled by **ATAHUALPA** who used it as a base from which to conquer the rest of the country, which belonged to his half-brother, **HUÁSCAR**. Soon afterwards Quito was captured by the Spanish; it remains the centre of all political, cultural and social affairs, but was surpassed by Guayaquil as an economic centre in the 20c.

### Qutb-ud-Din Aibak (d.1210)

Founder of the **DELHI SULTANATE**. A former slave become general, he was entrusted by **MUHAMMAD GHURI** with the continuation of his conquest of north India after 1192. Following Muhammad's death in 1206, Qutb-ud-Din declared himself Sultan of Muhammad's Indian possessions (1206/10), throwing off subordination to the Ghurids and establishing the so-called 'Slave' or Mamluk Dynasty of the Delhi Sultanate. He was succeeded, briefly, by his son, Aram Singh, and then by his son-in-law, **ILTUTMISH**. ▶ **MAMLUKS**

### Quwwatli, Shukri al- (1891–1967)

He was early a member of the Young Arab Association, which was founded in Paris but later moved to Syria. This group aimed originally to free Arabs from Turkish rule, while at the same time discouraging the Western powers from interfering in Arab affairs. Al-Quwwatli went on to become a leader of the **SYRIAN NATIONAL BLOC**, which distinguished itself by winning the first elections permitted by the French (1943). However, despite a declaration of independence in 1944, full independence was not achieved until 1946. Al-Quwwatli had a resurgence of political influence when he returned to power after the election of 1955, but this only lasted until the following year, when the government fell. He was President in 1958 and, with Gamal Abd al-**NASSER**, proclaimed the short-lived **UNITED ARAB REPUBLIC** (effectively the creation of Salah al-Din **BITAR** of the Syrian **BA'ATH PARTY**).

### QwaQwa

National state or non-independent Black homeland in **APARTHEID** South Africa, granted self-governing status in 1974. Abolished in 1994, when it was reincorporated into South Africa.

### Rabin, Yitzhak (1922–95)

Israeli soldier and politician. After studies at a school of agriculture, he embarked on an army career, completing his training in Britain. He fought in the 'War of Independence' (1948–9) and represented the Israeli Defence Forces (IDF) at the armistice in Rhodes. In the IDF he rose to become Chief of Staff in 1964, heading the armed forces during the successful SIX-DAY WAR of 1967. After serving as Ambassador to the USA (1968–73), he moved decisively into the political arena, becoming Labour Party leader and Prime Minister (1974–7), and Defence Minister (1984–90). Rabin won back the leadership of the Labour Party and in 1992 was again Prime Minister of a centre-left government that favoured Palestinian self-government. In 1993, he signed the first of the OSLO ACCORDS with the PLO, granting self-rule to the Palestinians of Gaza and Jericho and stipulating a phased withdrawal of Israeli forces. In 1994 he signed a peace treaty with Jordan; the same year he was awarded the NOBEL PEACE PRIZE jointly with Shimon PERES and Yasser ARAFAT. In 1995 he signed a second accord agreeing to further troop withdrawals from the WEST BANK and further expansion of Palestinian self-rule in the area. These concessions aroused extreme and often violent opposition in Israel and he was assassinated by a young Israeli extremist while attending a peace rally in Tel Aviv. He was succeeded as Prime Minister by his old rival Shimon Peres. ➤ ARAB–ISRAELI WARS; MAPAI PARTY

### Rabuka, Sitiveni (1948– )

Fijian soldier and politician. He completed his army training at Sandhurst Military College in England, and then served with a UN peacekeeping force in the Lebanon, before returning to Fiji with the rank of colonel. When the 1987 elections produced an Indian-dominated coalition government, he engineered a coup that deposed the Prime Minister, Kamisese Mara, and established his own provisional administration. In Dec 1987 he declared the country a republic and reinstated Mara as Premier, while retaining control of the security forces and of internal affairs. He became Deputy Prime Minister in 1991, and was Prime Minister from 1992 to 1999.

### Races, The Origins and Spread of ➤ See panel

### Radek, Karl Berngardovich (1885–1939)

Russian revolutionary and politician. Educated in Kraków and Bern, and left-wing in his views, he became a journalist in Germany and Switzerland. He was active in Petrograd (now St Petersburg) following the Bolshevik Revolution and participated ob-

liquely in the unsuccessful German revolution. Returning to the USSR, he became a leading member of the Communist International, but lost standing with his growing distrust of extremist tactics. He was charged as a supporter of TROTSKY, and expelled from the Party (1927–9). He was readmitted after recanting, but in 1937 he was a victim of one of STALIN's show trials, being sentenced to ten years in prison, where he is believed to have been murdered by fellow-prisoners two years later. ➤ BOLSHEVIKS; COMMUNISM; RUSSIAN REVOLUTION

### Radetzky von Radetz, Joseph, Count (1766–1858)

Austrian general. He saw action against the Turks (1788–9) and French (1792–1815). In 1831 he became Commander-in-Chief of the Austrian forces in Italy. Forced from Milan after the famous CINQUE GIORNATE of street fighting in 1848, he took refuge in the QUADRILATERAL, before rallying his forces and defeating the Piedmontese army at CUSTOZZA (25 July 1848). When CHARLES ALBERT once again invaded Lombardy in 1849, Radetzky's forces routed them at the Battle of NOVARA (23 Mar 1849), resulting in the Piedmontese king's abdication. It was Radetzky who negotiated with the new King, VICTOR EMMANUEL II, at Vignale the following day; contrary to popular tradition, he did not demand the abolition of the STATUTO. Following the collapse of the REVOLUTIONS OF 1848–9, Radetzky became Governor-General and military commander of the Kingdom of LOMBARDY-VENETIA until he retired in 1857.

### Radhakrishnan, Sir Sarvepalli (1888–1975)

Indian philosopher and politician. Educated in Madras, he taught at Mysore and Calcutta universities, and became Professor of Eastern Religions and Ethics at Oxford (1936–52). In 1946 he was chief Indian delegate to UNESCO, becoming its chairman in 1949. A member of the Indian Assembly in 1947, he was Indian Ambassador to the USSR (1949), Vice-President of India (1952–62) and President (1962–7). He was knighted in 1931.

### Radić, Stjepan (1871–1928)

Croatian politician. An admirer of the Czech leader Tomáš MASARYK, he and his brother Antun founded the Croat People's Peasant Party (HPSS, Hrvatska Pučka Seljačka Stranka) in 1904. A member of the National Council which represented the SOUTH SLAVS of the Habsburg monarchy in the months before the creation of the Kingdom of Serbs, Croats and Slovenes (Dec 1918), he was deeply suspicious of the motives of Nikola PAŠIĆ and of the Serbs in general. After unification, he and the HPSS maintained their vehement opposition to the new Belgrade-based government. Imprisoned in Mar 1919, on his release (Dec 1920) he sought foreign support for an autonomous Croatian republic. He visited Moscow (1924) and affiliated the HPSS with the Communist Peasant International. The Belgrade government charged him with cooperation with **COMINTERN** and imprisoned him and the other HPSS leaders until 1925 when, in an apparent volte-face, he accepted the constitution and agreed to cooperate with the Serbian Radical Party. He alternately sat and withdrew from the Belgrade parliament until 1928, when he and his nephew, Pavle Radić, were shot by a Montenegrin deputy during a parliamentary sitting. His death shortly afterwards brought an end to any semblance of Croat–Serb cooperation and precipitated the establishment of the royal dictatorship. ► **ALEXANDER I KARAGEORGEVIĆ; KOROŠEC, ANTON; MAČEK, VLADKO; PRIBIČEVIĆ, SVETOZAR**

### radicalism

Any set of ideas, normally of the Left but not exclusively so, which argues for more substantial social and political change than is supported in the political mainstream. What is radical is a matter of judgement, and so the term is very widely applied. In a number of countries there are radical parties that are left-of-centre.

### Radical Party (Argentina)

Formed in 1891 as the Radical Civic Union (*Unión Cívica Radical*), it commanded wide support in the early 20c, remaining a leading Argentine party thereafter, though at times divided into two separate branches. The party gained its great strength from the support of the lower middle classes in Buenos Aires, and from the ability of the first **YRIGOYEN** administration (1916–22) to secure their loyalty against the lower classes. Radicals won the Argentine presidency in 1916, 1922, 1928, 1958, 1963, 1983 and 1999. In 2001, in alliance with the smaller and more left-wing *Frepaso*, it became the second-largest party in the Chamber of Deputies.

### Radical Party (France)

Political party founded in 1901. Radicalism as a political tendency came into existence around 1840, and after 1870 the term designated the left-wing faction of the republicans, as opposed to the **OPPORTUNISTS** or **MODERATES**. However, an organized political party only appeared in 1901, with the title *Parti républicain radical et radical-socialiste* ('Republican Radical and Radical-Socialist Party'). It at once became the largest political party in France, and had representatives in office throughout the remainder of the Third Republic. Its most important leaders were **CAILLAUX, HERRIOT** and **DALADIER**. Paradoxically **CLEMENCEAU**, the most important representative of the radical tendency before 1901, was never close to the organized party. It was always loosely organized and undisciplined, and was discredited by the collapse of the Third Republic. It was revived after **WORLD WAR II**, but was much reduced in strength; its most important leader in that period was **MENDÈS-FRANCE**, Prime Minister in 1954–5. After 1958 it faded even more, and was eventually absorbed in other political formations. ► **REPUBLIC, THIRD** (France)

**Radical Republican Party** (*Partido Republicano Radical*, PRR)

Spanish political party. Founded in 1908, the Radical Party soon moved away from its revolutionary working class origins in Barcelona to become a federation of largely middle class regional parties centred on the charismatic figure of the populist leader Alejandro **LERROUX**. By the advent of the Second Republic, the Radical Party was not only the most historic Republican party, but also by far the largest. It had also become staunchly conservative. From 1931 to 1933 it was the most formidable source of opposition to the reforms of the progressive Republican-Socialist administrations under Manuel **AZAÑA**. From 1933 to 1935 the Radical Party was the principal element in a succession of right-wing coalition governments formed in alliance with the non-Republican Right (resulting in a major internal party split in May 1934), which overturned the reforms of the first two years and thereby polarized the Republic to an unprecedented degree. The resulting breakdown of the regime culminated in the **SPANISH CIVIL WAR** of 1936–9. ► **REPUBLIC, SECOND** (Spain)

### Radishchev, Alexander Nikolaevich (1749–1802)

Russian noble, official and writer. He exposed the hollowness of **CATHERINE II, THE GREAT**'s profession of enlightened views. Influenced by his studies at Leipzig, he was critical of much that he then observed in Russia. In 1790 he published *A Journey from St Petersburg to Moscow*, an account of the evils of serfdom and the iniquities of the bureaucracy told in the form of a genuine traveller's tale. What might have been acceptable to Catherine when she issued her **NAKAZ** in 1767, was anathema in the wake of the **FRENCH REVOLUTION**. She had Radishchev arrested and sentenced to death; in the end, he was exiled to Siberia. The *Journal* remains a testament to the true state of Catherine's Russia.

### Radowitz, Joseph von (1797–1853)

Prussian soldier. In 1813 he entered the Westphalian army, in 1823 the Prussian, and in 1830 became Chief of the Artillery Staff. Connected by marriage with the Prussian aristocracy, he headed the anti-revolutionary party during and after 1848, and was **FREDERICK WILLIAM IV**'s adviser. After 1848 the abortive Prussian scheme of a German constitution by means of the alliance of the three kings was largely his work. He wrote political treatises. ► **PRUSSIA**

### Raeder, Erich (1876–1960)

German grand admiral. He joined the navy in 1894, and became a Chief of Staff during **WORLD WAR I**. In 1928 he was made Commander-in-Chief of the Navy, a Grand Admiral in 1939, and in 1943 head of an anti-invasion force. At the **NUREMBERG TRIALS** (1946), he was sentenced to life imprisonment, but released in 1955. ► **WORLD WAR II**

### Raffles, Sir (Thomas) Stamford (1781–1826)

British colonial administrator. He became the Lieutenant-Governor of Java (1811–16), where he reformed the administration during that British **INTERREGNUM**. In 1816 ill health brought him home to England, where he was knighted. As Lieutenant-Governor of Benkoelen (1818–23), he established a British settlement at Singapore, which rapidly grew

# The Origins and Spread of Races

Culture & Society

Some researchers in the field of anthropology advance the theory that modern human beings developed in distinct groups independently in several different parts of the world. However, it is true to say that most physical anthropologists believe that humankind evolved in Africa around 4 million years ago and spread from there to other areas of the globe. It is believed that the earliest form of man to migrate from Africa was *Homo erectus*, a primitive apelike creature formerly classified as *Pithecanthropus*, that appeared around 1.5 million years ago. These early ancestors of human beings spread northwards into Europe and from there into Asia, where their fossil remains have been found. Migration into the Americas was made possible by a now submerged land-bridge which existed between Siberia and Alaska, and accounts for the similarities between the Mongoloid peoples of Asia and the **Native Americans**.

The spread of humankind was affected by the ice ages or glacial periods that occurred periodically during the Pleistocene epoch. As primitive humans had no clothing other than ill-fitting animal skins, they could not survive in areas that were covered by the ice sheets, but during interglacials – periods of comparative warmth between glaciations – they were able to migrate to new lands. Glacials – periods during which the polar ice cap spread southwards – also helped facilitate migration in that they contributed to the creation of land suitable for primitive man to live on. The advancing glaciers would spread over areas of land that had been covered with dense forest, and were thus inhospitable for human habitation. Once the ice had retreated, these regions developed warm grasslands – ideal environments for herds of bison, deer and other animals that prehistoric humans hunted for meat, skins and bones. Glacials also increased available land by turning large masses of seawater into ice, which brought about a fall in sea levels, exposing new land for settlement and creating land bridges over which migration could take place, such as those between the Malay Peninsula and the Indonesian Islands.

Originating from common ancestors, primitive human beings who migrated began to diversify and develop different physical characteristics. The main groupings into which humankind has traditionally been divided are Caucasoid (the light-skinned peoples of Europe, North Africa and south-western Asia), Mongoloid (peoples with a medium skin pigmentation, a fold of skin over the inner canthus of the eye, and straight black hair, such as most Asians, Native Americans and **Inuit**), Negroid (brown- or black-skinned peoples with tightly-curled hair and broad noses, such as indigenous Africans), and Australoid (the dark-skinned indigenous peoples of Australia, the Pacific Islands and southern Asia). Various theories attempt to account for the development of races amongst human beings. One is based on the concepts of the geographical race and the local race. The former is a population group contained within a distinct geographical area that is bounded in some way, such as a continent or island surrounded by seas or an area enclosed by

into one of the more important trading centres in the East. He was closely involved in the establishment of the Zoological Society of London in the early 1820s.
► **EAST INDIA COMPANY, BRITISH**

## Rafsanjani, (Ali Akbar) Hashemi (1934– )
Iranian cleric and political leader. He trained as a mullah under Ayatollah Ruhollah **KHOMEINI** at the holy city of Qom, from 1950. His friendship with Khomeini led him into opposition against Shah Muhammad Reza **PAHLAVI** and brief imprisonment in 1963. During the 1970s he became wealthy through the construction business in Tehran, but continued to keep in close touch with the exiled Khomeini. Following the 'Islamic Revolution' of 1979–80 he became Speaker of the Iranian parliament (Majlis), emerging as an influential and pragmatic power-broker between fundamentalist and technocrat factions within the ruling Islamic Republican Party (which he helped to found), and playing a key role in securing an end to the **IRAN–IRAQ WAR** (1980–8). In Aug 1989, soon after the death of Ayatollah Khomeini, Rafsanjani became state President and *de facto* national leader. He stepped down as President in 1997 but remains a powerful political figure.

## Raglan, Fitzroy James Henry Somerset, 1st Baron (1788–1855)
British general. He joined the army in 1804, fought at the Battle of **WATERLOO** (1815), became an MP, and was made a baron in 1852. In 1854 he led an ill-prepared force against the Russians in the **CRIMEAN WAR**, but though victorious at Alma he did not follow up his advantage. His ambiguous order led to the

**CHARGE OF THE LIGHT BRIGADE** (1854) at Balaclava. He died at **SEVASTOPOL**. His name was given to the raglan sleeve, which came into use in the 1850s.

## Railroad, Central Pacific
An American company organized in 1861 by Leland Stanford, Collis P Huntington, Charles Crocker and Mark Hopkins to build the Central Pacific Railway. The railway was begun in 1863 and was built eastwards from Sacramento to join up with the Union Pacific Railroad which was begun in 1865 and built westwards from Omaha. Both companies received government subsidies in the Pacific Railway Act of 1862. The Central Pacific Railroad had to negotiate the Sierra Nevada Mountains and blast nine tunnels, while the Union Pacific had to contend with the Rocky Mountains and attacks by **NATIVE AMERICANS**. The country's first transcontinental line (1,800 mi/ 2,900 km) was completed when the lines joined at Promontory Point, near Ogden, Utah, on 10 May 1869. ► **RAILROAD, TRANSCONTINENTAL**; **RAILWAYS**

## Railroad, Transcontinental
The first transcontinental system in the USA, formed when the Central Pacific and Union Pacific railroads were connected in 1869. The route surveys undertaken during the 1850s all had serious sectional implications and not until after the Republican victory in 1860 was the central route chosen. This had the advantage of being straight and using the lowest mountain passes; however, building was still delayed by Native American attacks and high costs. The two railroads joined at Promontory Point near Ogden, Utah, in 1869. Both had received huge land-grants in order

mountains. This type of physical delimitation would ensure that a people would be isolated from their neighbours and so be compelled to interbreed over the course of many generations, establishing particular racial characteristics. Examples of geographical races would include the Amerindian, Polynesian, Asiatic and African. A local race is a subdivision of a geographical race, limited to a fairly narrow group of people.

The Darwinian idea of natural selection is also considered important, that is, the process by which only the creatures best adapted to their environment survive and reproduce, thus establishing their characteristics as dominant in subsequent generations. This would affect humankind especially in terms of climatic adaptation in such characteristics as the colour of skin and eyes. Melanin, a pigment in human skin and eyes that protects against sunburn and skin cancer, would be particularly necessary in hot, sunny regions, and people who had this in larger quantities would tend to be naturally selected in such areas. Similarly, the development of lighter skin and eye coloration in northern regions can be seen as natural selection. As the human body needs vitamin D to help in the absorption of calcium, and exposure to sunlight assists in the natural production of vitamin D in the body, people living in climates with winters of long dark nights would have to be able to absorb as much vitamin D as possible during the hours of available sunlight and paler skin is conducive to this.

Another form of adaptation is the development of lungs that are able to hold more air; this occurs amongst peoples living at high altitudes, where the level of oxygen in the atmosphere is lower. It is also thought that tightly curled hair became dominant in hot climates as it afforded a higher degree of protection to the head from the rays of the sun. The narrower nose of northern races is believed to have evolved as it would be more efficient in warming cold air before it entered the lungs than a broader nose. Similar processes would also be involved in the development of other racial characteristics such as facial structure, shapes of eyes, body weight, and proportion of fat in the body.

Another theory maintains that many differences between races are genetic, that is, inherited through genes, as a product of people mating exclusively within a particular gene pool (the sum of the genes found in any interbreeding population). For example, a particular blood group may be more dominant in one population group than in another for no more complex a reason than that the group's ancestors happened to belong to that blood group.

In the period of recorded history there have been great movements and mixtures of races. For example, the racial structure of India was greatly changed by the invasion from Persia (beginning around 2000 BC) by Aryan peoples, supplanting the aboriginal Dravidians. In more recent times, the European discovery of the Americas in 1492 introduced Caucasoid peoples to that region as well as Negroid peoples, the latter initially as slaves. With modern forms of transportation making migration ever easier, the movement and intermixture of races around the world has been accelerated. Australia, for example, now has a predominantly Caucasoid population, but the high incidence of skin cancer among these people indicates that they are genetically better adapted for the climatic conditions of the northern hemisphere.

---

to finance the project, but Leland Stanford and his associates of the Central Pacific used their economic power as much for their own private financial gain as for national economic objectives. Their evasion of taxes and their discriminatory freight charges were largely responsible for the establishment of the Interstate Commerce Commission (1887) and the move toward regulation by the Populist and Progressive reformers of the late 19c and early 20c. ► **RAILROAD, CENTRAL PACIFIC; RAILWAYS**

**Railways** ► *See panel*

**Rainald of Dassel** (c.1120–1167)
Archbishop of Cologne. He became state Chancellor in 1156 and was one of Frederick I's most influential advisers, staunchly asserting imperial rights against those of the papacy. He was responsible for the canonization of Charlemagne in Cologne in 1165, the model for Frederick's administration during Rainald's chancellorship. His death marked the end of Frederick's policy of military aggression. ► **FREDERICK I, BARBAROSSA**

**Rainbow Warrior**
Part of Greenpeace's fleet used for environmental direct action campaigns. The first ship called *Rainbow Warrior* was in Auckland, New Zealand, on 10 Jul 1985 on its way to disrupt French nuclear tests at Mururoa atoll in the Pacific Ocean when two mines attached to the ship exploded, killing Fernando Pereira, a Greenpeace photographer. The French government originally denied involvement but later admitted that it had carried out the bombing and two French secret service officials were convicted

and imprisoned for manslaughter and arson.

**Rais** or **Raiz, Gilles de Laval, Baron** ► **RETZ, GILLES DE LAVAL, BARON**

**Rajagopalachari, Chakravarti** (1878–1972)
Indian political leader. The first Governor-General of independent India, he was educated at Central College, Bangalore, and Presidency and Law Colleges, Madras. He joined the Bar in 1900 and practised until 1919 at Salem. Rajagopalachari joined the Non-Cooperation and **SATYAGRAHA** movements and was elected Congress General-Secretary in 1921–2. He was a member of the Congress Working Committee in 1922–42, 1946–7 and 1951–4. Prime Minister of Madras from 1937 to 1939, he was a member of the interim government in 1946–7, Governor of West Bengal in 1947–8, acting Governor-General of India (Nov 1947), and then Governor-General from Jun 1948 to Jan 1950. He was Chief Minister of Madras between 1952 and 1954 and founded the **SWATANTRA PARTY** in 1959. ► **NON-COOPERATION MOVEMENT**

**Rajk, László** (1908–49)
Hungarian politician. An early convert to **COMMUNISM**, he was expelled from Budapest University for his political activities and became a building worker. Leader of the left-wing faction of his union, he organized an important building workers' strike in 1935 but then deemed it wise to go abroad. He was Party Secretary to the Hungarian battalion of the **INTERNATIONAL BRIGADES** during the **SPANISH CIVIL WAR** but was eventually imprisoned in France. He returned to Hungary in 1941 to become a secretary to the Communist Party Central Committee, but he was first

# *Railways*

Transport & Travel

### Beginnings

The ancestors of modern railways were the wagonways or tramroads (a 'tram' originally being a coal wagon) which were developed in central Europe from the 16c or earlier in mining and quarrying districts to assist with the transport of heavy loads. It was found that laying down a track made of parallel lengths of wood enabled wagons to move at greater speeds and with heavier loads than was possible over muddy or uneven ground. Wooden crosspieces were soon added to keep the main timbers in place. Iron plates were fastened to the timbers to prevent them wearing down, and the first cast-iron rails were produced in Britain at Coalbrookdale Ironworks in 1767. A flange to prevent the wagons from slipping off was either incorporated into the track or fitted to the wagon wheels.

Typically, the earliest railways were laid between mines or quarries, and a wharf on the bank of a river, canal or seaport, from which coal or stone could be transported elsewhere. An extensive system of plateways (plated wooden tracks) or railways existed on the lower Tyne in England by the end of the 18c to convey coals to the riverside. The trucks were usually drawn by horses or manhandled. On slopes, wagons would descend by gravity often with a brakeman riding behind, or an 'inclined plane' would be used on which the descending wagon drew another wagon up. From the late 18c, stationary steam engines were employed to haul wagons up gradients. Finally, in 1804, Richard Trevithick (1771–1833) constructed the first practical steam locomotive for a colliery line from Merthyr Tydfil to Abercynon in Wales.

Another legacy left to modern railways from the early tramroads is the standard gauge, in use throughout the USA, Canada, and most of Europe of 4ft 8½in/143.51cm. The early wagons generally had axles 5 ft/152.4 cm long. This, taking the width of the wheels into consideration, meant that the rails had to be 4ft 8½in apart.

### Early public railways

The first public railway project in Britain approved by Parliament (1801) was for part of a line to run from London to Portsmouth, and the first authenticated instance of passenger transport on a railway was between Swansea and Oystermouth in Wales around 1806. The first public railway in the world to make regular use of a steam locomotive to pull trains, however, was the Stockton to Darlington Railway, which was constructed as a colliery line and opened to traffic in 1825. Its first locomotive was the *Locomotion*, designed and built by George Stephenson. Its passenger transport was a sideshow, operated by local road carriers not by the railway company itself, and many of the passenger trains were still horse-drawn.

The Liverpool and Manchester Railway took the process one stage further. It was constructed with the intention of carrying large-scale passenger traffic. There was still debate about the best method of hauling trains, and the directors of the company originally intended to use stationary engines. They were persuaded, however, to change their minds in favour of steam locomotives. Trials were held at Rainhill in 1829, the contest being won by George Stephenson's *Rocket*. Seven more Stephenson engines were ordered for the line's official opening in 1830.

### Railway boom

The enormous success of the Liverpool and Manchester Railway immediately created a desire for other, longer railways in Britain. The railway age was also beginning in other countries. The first railway charter in the USA was granted in 1827 and the first 13-mile stretch of the **Baltimore and Ohio Railroad** opened in 1830. The first railway in France was opened between Lyons and St Étienne in 1832. Engineering techniques pioneered in Europe in the construction of **canals** were adapted for the surveying and construction of railway lines, which began to spread rapidly. In Britain between 1835 and 1837, Acts of Parliament were passed authorizing the construction of 1,600 mi/2,600 km of railway. Construction costs varied widely depending on the type of terrain to be covered and often ran way beyond original estimates. This first boom was followed by a slump, but between 1844 and 1846 railway mania revived again. In 1846 alone, parliamentary approval was given for a further 4,540 mi/7,300 km of line (by no means all of which was necessarily built). By 1850 Britain possessed 6,084 mi/9,790 km of railway line and a network that served most of the well-populated areas of the country.

Large fortunes were made, and not infrequently lost, by men such as George Hudson of York, the 'Railway King', who invested in the new lines and the companies that operated them. The biggest fortunes of all were made in the USA by men such as Cornelius **Vanderbilt**, who controlled the New York Central Railroad, and Collis Potter Huntington, one of the founders of the Central Pacific Railroad which established the westward end of the Trans-continental Railroad.

### Opening up the interior

In the USA the railway played a vital part in the opening up of the West. The California **Gold Rush** of 1849 stimulated public demand for a transcontinental rail link, which had first been proposed in 1836. Railroads gradually reached out from the East. The **American Civil War** provided a final stimulus to complete the project, and the tracks built by the Union Pacific and Central Pacific Railroads eventually joined together at Promontory, Utah, in 1869. The first railways were opened in Australia in 1854, in South Africa in 1860 and in New Zealand in 1863. In Russia the Trans-Siberian railway was begun in 1891 and completed seven years later, linking Vladivostok and the far eastern provinces to

---

interned by the Hungarians and then imprisoned by the Germans. He rose rapidly after 1945, becoming a full member of the Central Committee, Minister of the Interior, then Foreign Minister. In 1949 he was arrested and tried on trumped-up charges during the Stalinist purges and, like many others who had first-hand experience of the West, was executed. In 1955 he was rehabilitated, but his fate had much to do with under-

mining communism in Hungary. ➤ **STALINISM**

### Rajputs

Descended either from the Huns settled in northern and western India or from those tribes and peoples who had entered India along with the Hun invaders, the Rajputs rose to political importance in the 9c and 10c, when they were divided into a number of clans, of which four claimed a special status. These four –

Moscow. In many parts of the world railways were built not merely to facilitate travel and trade, but to open up remote areas, to enhance national prestige and to consolidate political control. The provision of railway links to neighbouring states by Prussia and Piedmont was part of their strategy for becoming the dominant powers in a unified Germany and Italy respectively. Cecil **Rhodes**' grandiose idea for a railway linking the Cape to Cairo (across British-held territory) was inspired by a similar aim.

## Impact

The emergence of the railway as the principal transporter of freight heralded the demise of the canals, particularly in the UK and the USA. Rail transportation was far quicker, wagons could carry far greater volume than canal barges, and as railway routes became more widespread and national networks were established, the canals could not compete. In both countries, railway proprietors also bought up canals in order to shut them down, thereby securing a stranglehold on transportation that remained until the arrival of the motor engine.

### Underground railway

An underground railway system for London was first proposed in 1843. Work began on constructing the Metropolitan Railway in 1860 by the 'cut and cover' method (excavating a large trench along an existing road and roofing it over). The line opened between Farringdon and Paddington in 1863 using steam locomotives to pull trains. The first electrically-hauled underground line in London was the City and Southern which opened in 1900.

Other cities followed London's example. An underground railway opened in Budapest in 1898, the same year that construction of the Paris Métro began. Boston had the first subway in the USA, which was constructed between 1895 and 1897. The subway in New York City opened in 1904. Urban underground and surface railway transport systems continued to expand throughout the 20c, even as mainline traffic declined, becoming faster, more integrated, and more sophisticated. The Bay Area Rapid Transportation (BART) in San Francisco opened in 1976 as the first fully automated urban railway system.

### The 20c

The railway network and railway traffic worldwide are generally reckoned to have reached a peak around the time of **World War I**. The vast majority of railway trains at this time were still steam-hauled. Electrification of surface railways began in the USA in 1895, after electric traction had proved its viability in street railways. The Paris to Orléans line was electrified in 1900. Electrification began late in Britain, being adopted by the Southern Railway during the 1930s. A diesel railcar began operating in Sweden in 1913 and the first diesel-electric shunting locomotive came into service in the USA in 1925. After the middle of the century, electric and diesel-electric locomotives rapidly began to replace steam locomotives as the main form of traction. Overall, however, in the developed world railway traffic showed a steep decline in the latter part of the century in the face of competition from the private motor car, road haulage for freight, and **aircraft** for long-distance travel. Rationalization of the often unrealistically expanded networks inherited from the pre-1914 era became commonplace. In the UK it was associated with the Beeching Plan of the early 1960s, which involved extensive line closures.

High-speed trains were first introduced in Japan in 1964 and in France in 1981. Greater speeds, of up to 310 mph/500 kph, should be attained by maglev (magnetic levitation) trains, which float on a magnetic field about $\frac{1}{2}$ in/10 mm above a guideway. A maglev service between Shanghai's airport and city centre opened in 2003, the 18.5 mi/30 km journey taking 8 minutes at speeds up to a maximum of 270 mph/430 kph.

High-speed trains have had some success in wresting back the initiative from air travel, and commuters in large cities still depend heavily on rail travel. Wherever congestion and pollution are major problems, railways are promoted as an environmentally friendly form of transport. In this perhaps lies their main hope for the future. ► **Railroad, Central Pacific**; **Railroad, Transcontinental**

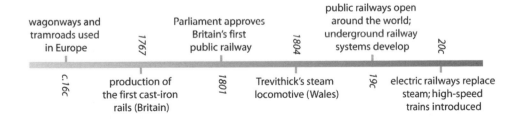

wagonways and tramroads used in Europe — *1767* — Parliament approves Britain's first public railway — *1804* — public railways open around the world; underground railway systems develop — *20c*

*c.16c* — production of the first cast-iron rails (Britain) — *1801* — Trevithick's steam locomotive (Wales) — *19c* — electric railways replace steam; high-speed trains introduced

the Pratiharas, the Chauhans, the Chalukyas (or Solankis) and the Parmaras (or Pawars) – claimed descent from a mythical figure which arose out of a vast sacrificial fire pit near Mount Abu in Rajasthan. These clans, which came to be known as the Agnikula or Fire Family, dominated early Rajput activities; other Rajput clans, claiming descent from the solar and lunar races, established themselves as local kings in various parts of western and central India. ► **PRE-ISLAMIC INDIA**

### Rákóczi, Ferenc, II (1676–1735)

Hungarian Prince of Transylvania (1704/11). An energetic and cultured member of a famous family, in 1703 he led a revolt of Hungarian nobles against Austrian Habsburg rule, and in 1704 was officially elected Prince of Transylvania. He struggled hard but was defeated by the Austrians at Trencsén in 1708 and had to leave the country after the Hungarian–Austrian Treaty of Szatmár in 1711. Although he sought help in Poland until 1712, in France until 1717, and finally in Turkey, he could not reactivate the struggle against Austria. All that he left was inspiration for later generations.

**Rákosi, Mátyás** (1892–1971)
Hungarian politician. He was already active in the labour movement before **WORLD WAR I**. Conscripted in 1914, he spent most of the war years as a prisoner in Russia and moved further to the left, joining the Hungarian Communist Party on his return home. He was commander of the Red Guard in Béla **KUN**'s Soviet Republic in 1919 and then fled to the USSR where he became Secretary of the Communist International. Returning to Hungary in 1924, he spent the years 1925–40 in prison until he was released to return to Moscow. He led the Hungarian communist émigrés there and came back to Budapest in 1945 as their General-Secretary. Rákosi was then responsible for many of the changes introduced and was deeply implicated in the Stalinist purges. He was much criticized after **STALIN**'s death, but in 1955 he attempted to reinstate Stalinist practices, thus helping to provoke the 1956 Hungarian Uprising. He was then removed from office and, in 1962, expelled from the party. ► **STALINISM**

**Raleigh** or **Ralegh, Sir Walter** (1552–1618)
English courtier, navigator and author. He became prime favourite of Queen **ELIZABETH I**. He was knighted in 1584, and that year sent the first of three expeditions to America. After the arrival of the Earl of **ESSEX** at court, he lost influence, and spent some years in Ireland. On his return, Elizabeth discovered his intrigue with Bessy Throckmorton, one of her maids-of-honour, and he was committed to the Tower of London. On his release, he married Bessy, and lived at Sherborne. He took little part in the intrigues at the close of Elizabeth's reign, but his enemies turned **JAMES VI AND I** against him, and he was imprisoned (1603), his death sentence being commuted to life imprisonment. While in the Tower, he wrote his *History of the World* (1614), and several other works. Released in 1616, he made an expedition to the Orinoco in search of a goldmine, which was a failure. His death sentence was invoked, and he was executed. ► **EXPLORATION**

**Ralliement**
French political movement, launched on behalf of Pope **LEO XIII** by Cardinal **LAVIGERIE** in 1890, and confirmed by the encyclical *Inter innumeras sollicitudines* (1892), appealing to Catholics to accept the Third Republic, and to stop supporting the monarchist Right. It was hoped that it would be met by a new attitude on the part of the moderate republicans, who would abandon their anticlericalism, thus allowing some realignment in French politics. It had some success, although it was rejected by many Catholic politicians, and produced the conservative **MÉLINE** government (1896–8). However, any chance it might have had of leading at that time to a reconciliation between the Catholic Church and the republic was destroyed by the **DREYFUS** affair. ► **REPUBLIC, THIRD** (France)

**Rama V** ► **CHULALONGKORN, PHRA PARAMINDR MAHA**

**Ramadan War** ► **ARAB–ISRAELI WARS**

**Ramananda** (fl.14c)
Indian religious reformer. He was a Vaishnava and was associated with the Bhakti movement. He tried to abolish the **CASTE** system among his followers and like other Bhakti movement saints, he introduced a more personal element into Hindu religious activities.

**Ramaphosa, (Matamela) Cyril** (1952–)
South African trade unionist. He became chairman of the all-black South African Students' Organization in 1974. After 11 months of detention in 1974–5, he became an articled clerk in Johannesburg and was active in the BPC (Black People's Convention). He was detained again in 1976 but, after graduating from the University of South Africa with a law degree in 1981, he joined CUSA as an adviser in its legal department. He became General-Secretary of the National Union of Mineworkers in 1982 and led (Sep 1984) the first legal strike by black mineworkers. He brought the NUM into COSATU (Congress of South African Trade Unions) and was elected Secretary-General of the **ANC** in 1991 at the party's congress in Durban.

**Rambouillet, Catherine de Vivonne, Marquise de** (1588–1665)
French noblewoman. At the age of 12 she was married to the son of the Marquis de Rambouillet, who succeeded to the title in 1611. She disliked the morals and manners of the French court, and for 50 years she gathered together in the famous Hôtel de Rambouillet the talent and wit of the French nobility and literary world, including Condé, François de Malherbe and Pierre Corneille. Although later satirized by Molière for its preciosity, her salon helped to set the standard for correct and elegant language. ► **CONDÉ, LOUIS II OF BOURBON, PRINCE OF**

**Ramgoolam, Sir Seewoosagur** (1906–86)
Mauritian doctor and politician. Educated in Mauritius and London University, he practised as a doctor before becoming a member of Legco (1940–48) and then the Executive Council (1948–58). He was Ministerial Secretary to the Treasury (1958–60), then Minister of Finance (1961–5), and also Prime Minister (1965–80). After retirement, he was Governor-General of Mauritius from 1984 until his death.

**Ramillies, Battle of** (1706)
A spectacular victory in the War of the **SPANISH SUCCESSION** won by **MARLBOROUGH** over **LOUIS XIV** of France's army commanded by Marshal Villeroi. The French suffered heavy casualties. The forces of the Grand Alliance overran large areas of the northern and eastern Spanish Netherlands, but were unable to exploit their success to force France to make peace.

**Ram Mohan Roy, Raja** (1774–1833)
Indian religious reformer. He did much to awaken the Hindu social conscience and, indirectly, the birth of nationalism. Of high Brahmin status, he came early to question his ancestral faith, and studied Buddhism in Tibet. He published various works, with the aim of uprooting idolatry, and supported the British wish to outlaw suttee. In 1828 he began the **BRAHMO SAMAJ**

association, and in 1830 was given the title of Raja.

**Ramon Berenguer III, the Great** (1082–1131)
Count of Barcelona (1096/1131). He was born only a few days after the murder of his father, Ramon Berenguer II. As ruler, he was actively at war with the **ALMORAVIDS** to the south of his lands, and distinguished himself in his expedition (1114–5) to the islands of Ibiza and Mallorca, which he captured and held for a while. In 1112 he married, as his third wife, Douce of Provence, who brought him as a dowry the county of Provence. In 1117 he also inherited the county of Cerdaña, and in 1118 restored the metropolitan see of Tarragona as the central see of the Catalan lands.

**Ramphal, Sir Shridath Surrendranath**, also known as **Sir Sonny Ramphal** (1928–)
Guyanese and Commonwealth lawyer and diplomat. After studying law in London, he was called to the Bar in 1951. He returned to the West Indies, and from 1952 held increasingly responsible posts in Guyana and the West Indies before becoming Guyana's Foreign Minister and Attorney-General in 1972, and Justice Minister in 1973. During much of this time he sat in the Guyanese National Assembly. From 1975 to 1989 he was Secretary-General of the **COMMONWEALTH OF NATIONS**.

**Ranade, Mahadev Govind** (1842–1901)
Indian lawyer and reformer. He is popularly known for his association with the *Prarthana Samaj* ('Prayer Society') in the Marathi-speaking western part of India. This society, founded in Pune in 1869, initially had a vague, undeveloped set of ideas. Ranade actively participated in its activities and helped to re-shape it into a patriotic association espousing a reinterpretation of Hindu tradition. His position as a subordinate judge in Pune prevented him from joining the **INDIAN NATIONAL CONGRESS** when it was formed in 1885. However, as an active sympathizer, he encouraged many others, including Gopal Krishna **GOKHALE**, to join and to take a leading role in the early Indian independence movement.

**Randolph, A(sa) Philip** (1889–1979)
US labour organizer, socialist and **CIVIL RIGHTS** activist. Initially a supporter of Marcus **GARVEY**, he opposed the idea of economic separatism in his journal, *The Messenger*. In 1925 he organized the Brotherhood of Sleeping Car Porters, the first black union to gain major successes, such as recognition by the Pullman Company. In 1941 he organized a march on Washington to demand equal employment opportunities for blacks in the defence industries, and racial **DESEGREGATION** in the armed forces. The march was called off after President Franklin D **ROOSEVELT** established the **FAIR EMPLOYMENT PRACTICES COMMITTEE**, but the tactic was revived during the **CIVIL RIGHTS MOVEMENT** of the 1960s, when he became the director of the March on Washington for Jobs and Freedom (28 Aug 1963).

**Ranjit Singh** (1780–1839)
Sikh ruler (1801/39). Known as the 'Lion of the Punjab', he succeeded his father as ruler of Lahore (now in Pakistan). He fought to unite all the Sikh provinces and, with the help of a modernized army trained by Western soldiers, became the most powerful ruler in India. In 1813 he procured the Koh-i-noor diamond from an Afghan prince, as the price of assistance in war. He died in Lahore.

**Rankin, Jeannette** (1880–1973)
US feminist and pacifist, the first female member of **CONGRESS**. Educated at Montana University and the New York School of Philanthropy, she went on to work as a social worker in Seattle (1909), where she became involved in the fight for **WOMEN'S RIGHTS**. In 1914 she was appointed Legislative Secretary of the **NATIONAL AMERICAN WOMAN SUFFRAGE ASSOCIATION**, and in 1916 was elected to the **HOUSE OF REPRESENTATIVES** as a Republican, the first woman in the Western world to become an elected member of a national legislature. During her two terms there (1917–19 and 1941–3) she consistently voted against US participation in both World Wars, promoted women's welfare and rights, and was instrumental in the adoption of the first bill granting married women independent citizenship. Continuing to campaign for women's issues throughout her career, she worked for the National Council for the Prevention of War from 1928 to 1939, and led the Jeannette Rankin March (1968) in which 5,000 women gathered on Capitol Hill, Washington, to protest against the **VIETNAM WAR**.

**Ranković, Aleksander** (1909–83)
Yugoslav politician. He joined the Communist Party in 1928 and was imprisoned during the dictatorship of King **ALEXANDER I KARAGEORGEVIĆ**. During **WORLD WAR II** he fought with **TITO** and the partisans, and in 1945 became director of the secret police, overseeing the ruthless elimination of all opposition to communist rule. He was also Minister of the Interior (1946–53) and Vice-President of Yugoslavia (1963). After 'bugging' Tito's home, he was accused of abusing his authority and was forced to resign (Jul 1966).

**Rapallo, Treaty of** (12 Nov 1920)
The treaty of friendship and neutrality bringing together a defeated Germany and an ostracized Russia. It recognized Istria as Italian and **FIUME** (Rijeka) as a free city; it also made provision for future economic accords and stressed a mutual obligation to uphold the Treaties of Trianon and St Germain. The countries both gained diplomatically and economically. Their military cooperation was of particular benefit to the USSR, whose communist revolution was never seriously challenged thereafter; Allied intervention in Russia finally ended the same year. It was a triumph for the conciliatory policy of **CHICHERIN**, then Foreign Minister, and was echoed in the **GERMAN–SOVIET PACT** of 1939.

**Rapallo, Treaty of** (16 Apr 1922)
The treaty signed by Germany and the Russian Federation during the World Economic Conference in Genoa. German fears of an agreement between the Western Allies and the USSR on German **REPARATIONS** payments and a Russian desire to escape economic and diplomatic isolation led to this agreement which, first, saw both parties renounce all claims arising from **WORLD WAR I** and, second, saw economic and trade links established on a 'most favoured nation' basis. The treaty was extended to the whole of

the USSR and was a significant blow against the post-World War I settlement. German–Soviet military and diplomatic cooperation subsequently became more extensive.

## ras

Derived from the Arabic word for 'head', used in Abyssinia to denote a feudal warlord, this term was adopted and used in Italy to describe local fascist bosses in the 1920s. Amongst the *ras* numbered many figures who were to play a key role in the development of the FASCIST PARTY, such as FARINACCI, Italo BALBO and Dino GRANDI. After attaining power in 1922, however, MUSSOLINI felt it essential to check the power of the ras and to control the excesses of the SQUADRISTI, both because his position was threatened by other charismatic fascist leaders and because he needed to prove that he could restore order to an Italy scarred by political violence. Some ras consequently fell victim to purges, while others were brought within the Establishment and given important jobs in the party and government.

## Rashtrakuta ► INDIA, PRE-ISLAMIC

## Rasin, Alois (1867–1923)

Czechoslovak politician. He took part in a famous student riot in 1893 and became involved in serious radical politics in the later 1890s. Rasin was imprisoned during WORLD WAR I and was then the first Finance Minister of the new Czechoslovak Republic. His tight monetary policies were, however, unpopular with particular groups and he was assassinated in 1923. Despite his unpopularity, it was Rasin who had set the new state on its feet economically, both domestically and internationally.

## Raška

The medieval name for the Serbian state derived from Rasa, the seat of the bishopric founded by Christianized Serbs and first mentioned in 1020. ► SERBIA

## Rasputin, Grigoriy Efimovich (1871–1916)

Russian peasant and self-styled religious 'elder' (*starets*). A member of the schismatic sect of *Khlysty* ('flagellants'), he was introduced into the royal household, where he quickly gained the confidence of Tsar NICHOLAS II and the Empress ALEXANDRA FEODOROVNA by his apparent ability to control through hypnosis the bleeding of the haemophiliac heir to the throne, Tsarevich Alexei. He was a notorious lecher and drunkard, and created a public scandal through the combination of his sexual and alcoholic excesses, and his political influence in securing the appointment and dismissal of government ministers. His influence was particularly baneful during WORLD WAR I, especially when the Tsar was away from St Petersburg commanding his army; it helped destroy cooperation between the Tsar and the DUMA that might have won the war and prevented the 1917 RUSSIAN REVOLUTION. He was murdered by a clique of aristocrats, led by Prince Felix Yusupov, a distant relative of the Tsar.

## Rassemblement Démocratique Africain (RDA)

Established in 1944, the RDA was a cross-national political party with branches in most parts of the French African empire, which sent members to the National Assembly in Paris. Its major figure was Felix HOUPHOUËT-BOIGNY.

## Rassemblement Wallon (RW)

Belgian political party of Walloon (French-speaking southern Belgian) nationalist-separatists. Formed in 1968 from a number of small Walloon groupings in reaction to increasing FLEMISH MOVEMENT activity, it elected 14 MPs in 1971, and took part in the government coalition in 1974–7. The Francophone wing of the liberals joined the RW in 1976 to form the *Parti des Reformées et des Libertés Wallones*, which gained only four seats in the 1978 election. In 1993 its main goal was realized in the political federalization of Belgium and the establishment of a separate regional government for Wallonia.

## Rastafarianism

A religious movement from Jamaica, followed by c.1 million people. It largely derives from the Old Testament and the thought of Jamaican political activist Marcus GARVEY, who advocated a return to Africa as a means of solving the problems of black oppression. When HAILE SELASSIE I was crowned Emperor of Ethiopia in 1930, he came to be viewed as the Messiah, with Ethiopia seen as the promised land. Rastafarians follow strict taboos governing what they may eat (eg no pork, milk, coffee); ganja (marijuana) is held to be a sacrament; they usually wear their hair in long dreadlocks, and cultivate a distinctive form of speech.

## Rastatt, Congress of (1797–9)

This congress was convened under the articles of the Treaty of CAMPO FORMIO to conclude a peace between the German states and France. The process failed when France refused to compensate the Germans for territories which they were expected to cede in an attached secret protocol.

## Rastatt, Treaty of (6 Mar 1714)

Emperor CHARLES VI signed this personal treaty ending hostilities that had lingered after the Peace of UTRECHT (1713), which had closed the War of the SPANISH SUCCESSION. The Emperor renounced his claim to Spain but did not recognize the Bourbon claimant, PHILIP V, until 1720. The Treaty of BADEN (Sep 1714) concluded an official peace between the entire Empire and France.

## Rathenau, Walther (1867–1922)

German industrialist and politician. He organized German war industries during WORLD WAR I, and in 1921, as Minister of Reconstruction, and after Feb 1922 as Foreign Minister, dealt with REPARATIONS. His attempts to negotiate a reparations agreement with the victorious Allies, and the fact that he was Jewish, made him extremely unpopular in nationalist circles, and he was murdered by extremists in the summer of 1922.

## Ratsiraka, Didier (1936–)

Malagasy naval officer and politician. Educated in Madagascar and then at naval college in France, he served in the navy (1963–70) before becoming military attaché in Paris (1970–2). A coup brought him to the centre of power in 1972, when he became Minister of Foreign Affairs and then, in 1975, President of the Supreme Revolutionary Council. He established a political party, the Advanced Guard of the Malagasy Revolution, and remained in office as President until 1993. He was elected President again in 1997, but in the election of 2001 a disputed result led to fighting in which his faction was defeated and he went into exile.

### Rattazzi, Urbano, Count (1808–73)

Italian politician. Elected deputy in the Piedmontese parliament in 1848, he led the centre-left anticlericals. Minister first of Education and then of Justice, he opposed the armistice with Austria in Mar 1849. In 1852 he brought the centre-left into an alliance with CAVOUR, the so-called CONNUBIO. Restored to government, he was first given his old position as Justice Minister (1853) and then became Interior Minister, a post he held from 1855 to 1858. The *Connubio* was based on an anticlerical policy (typified by the 1855 project to suppress all contemplative orders), which was in the end its undoing. As Cavour recognized the need to enlist the support of NAPOLEON III to drive the Austrians from northern Italy, he also realized that he would have to moderate his anticlerical stance to calm the French Emperor's fears about domestic Catholic opinion. The sweeping successes of clerical candidates in the elections of Nov 1857 gave Cavour the opportunity he needed to relocate the basis of his support, and in the new year Rattazzi was made to resign. Rattazzi returned to office in LA MARMORA's 1859 government, and was himself Prime Minister twice (Mar–Dec 1862 and Apr–Oct 1867).

### Rau, Johannes (1931–)

West German politician. He began his career as a salesman for a church publishing company before being attracted to politics as a follower of Gustav HEINEMANN. He joined the Social Democratic Party (SPD) and was elected to the parliament of his home state, the country's most populous, North Rhine Westphalia, in 1958. He served as chairman of the SPD's parliamentary group (1967–70), and as Minister of Science and Research in the state parliament (1970–8) before becoming its Minister-President in 1978. His successful record as state leader, his moderate policy outlook, and his optimistic and youthful personality persuaded the SPD to elect him federal party deputy chairman in 1982 and Chancellor-candidate for the 1987 BUNDESTAG election. However, the party was heavily defeated, and after this setback he concentrated on his work as state Premier. In 1999 he was elected German President, serving until 2004.

### Rawlings, Jerry (John) (1947–)

Ghanaian soldier and politician. Educated at Achimota College and the University of Ghana, he joined the air force. He led an unsuccessful coup in 1979, was imprisoned and then escaped to mount a successful one later the same year. He headed the Armed Forces Revolutionary Council, returning power to an elected government, led by Hilla LIMANN, in that year, when he retired from the air force. However, he re-entered the political scene in Dec 1981 when he led another successful coup and remained head of government, despite attempts to overthrow him in 1983 (twice) and 1987. After a referendum in 1992 voted for the return of constitutional government, Rawlings was elected President in multiparty elections. Re-elected in 1996, he retired from office in 2001.

### Rayburn, Sam(uel Taliaferro) (1882–1961)

US legislator. He grew up on a Texas farm and studied law with the intention of entering politics. He was elected to the HOUSE OF REPRESENTATIVES as a Democrat in 1913 and remained in CONGRESS until his death, serving a record 17 years as Speaker of the House (1940–7, 1949–53, 1955–61). Though he did not consider himself an orator, he wielded political influence through a network of personal contacts and was influential in passing Franklin D ROOSEVELT's NEW DEAL.

### Razin, Stenka, also known as Stepan Timofeevich Razin (c.1630–1671)

Russian Don Cossack, freebooter and rebel leader. He was the leader of a Cossack and peasant revolt in 1670–1 directed against the BOYARS and landowning nobility, at a time when the tsars were extending their authority. At one point he had as many as 200,000 rebels under his command. However, they were no match for the Tsar's well-trained troops. In Apr 1671 he was captured, taken to Moscow and publicly executed. He became a folk-hero celebrated in later legend and song as the embodiment of popular rebellion against authority. ► COSSACKS; PUGACHEV, EMELYAN

### Raziya (1236/40)

First woman ruler of the Delhi Sultanate. She was named by her father, ILTUTMISH, as his successor, none of her brothers being considered worthy of the throne. The nomination of a woman in preference to a man was a novel step and, in order to assert her claim, Raziya had to contend with the hostility of her brothers as well as that of powerful Turkish nobles. In the event, she retained the throne for only four years. However, though brief, her rule had a number of interesting features. It marked the beginning of a power-struggle between the monarchy and the Turkish chiefs, sometimes called 'the forty' or the *chahalgani*. She put up a brave defence against these hostile forces, discarding female apparel and holding court with her face unveiled, hunting and leading the army. This behaviour, coupled with her attempt to create her own party and to raise non-Turks to high positions was, however, found unacceptable; a powerful group of provincial nobles banded against her and, despite a spirited defence, she was defeated and killed.

### Reagan, Ronald Wilson (1911–2004)

US politician and 40th President. He began his career as a radio sports announcer, then went to Hollywood in 1937, where he acted in more than 50 films, and served as President of the Screen Actors Guild (1947–52 and 1959). Originally a Democrat and supporter of liberal causes, he became actively involved in politics as a union leader and increasingly anticommunist. He registered as a Republican in 1962. Governor of California for two terms (1967–75), he campaigned unsuccessfully for the Republican presidential nomination in 1968 and 1976. He was elected President in 1980, defeating Jimmy CARTER, and, with George H W BUSH as his running mate, won the second term in 1984. Reagan's popularity enabled him to make sweeping changes in social and economic policy, including cuts in social services, the deregulation of many industries, and a tax cut that mainly benefited the wealthy. His foreign policy was dominated by a strong anti-communist stand, which led to a massive increase in defence spending and the introduction of the Strategic Defense Initiative (**SDI**), or 'Star Wars'. During his second term, when his attitude toward the USSR became less confrontational, largely as a result of President Mikhail **GORBACHEV**'s policy of **PERESTROIKA**, he reached a major accord on nuclear arms reduction. The **IRAN–CONTRA AFFAIR** (Irangate) tarnished the reputation of his administration in its last two years. Instead of the balanced budget Reagan had sought, 'Reaganomics' left behind a huge federal deficit.

## Reaya

In the **OTTOMAN EMPIRE** the term was first applied to both Muslim and non-Muslim subjects, usually tradesmen and peasants; according to the model of the ideal Islamic society propounded by Nasireddin Tusi, they were the 'men of negotiation' and the 'men of husbandry'. From the 16c onwards, the term was customarily applied only to the non-Muslim subjects of the Sultan who were all liable to pay the capitation tax.

## Rebellions of 1837

(1) A rebellion in Quebec in Lower **CANADA** generated by a stalemate between the legislative council and the appointed executive council over control of provincial revenues. Led by **PAPINEAU** and his *Parti Patriote*, it sought to dissolve the unsatisfactory imperial tie with Britain. It was crushed by British government troops after several brief confrontations. (2) Later in 1837, a rebellion in Ontario in Upper **CAN-ADA**, which opposed the oligarchical control exercised by the **FAMILY COMPACT**, and the position of preferment enjoyed by the Church of England. Armed radicals led by **WILLIAM MACKENZIE** marched on Toronto to seize the government, but were repulsed by pro-government troops and volunteers. Mackenzie and Papineau both fled to the USA.

## reciprocity

A movement begun in British North America during the 1840s for the bilateral reduction of tariffs between the British colonies and the USA; it resulted in the Reciprocity Treaty of 1854. The treaty negotiations represented an important step in the growth of Canadian political autonomy. Arrangements became a source of discord in Washington, however, and the treaty was dissolved by the USA in 1866. Attempts to renew reciprocity failed up to 1911, when the idea was finally shelved. ► **BLAKE, EDWARD**; '**COMMERCIAL UNION**'; **DOMINION OF CANADA**; **MERRITT, WILLIAM**

## Reconquest

The term (in Spanish, *Reconquista*) applied to the campaigns by Christian forces in medieval Spain to recover territory from the Muslims, who had begun to overrun the peninsula in 711. The Reconquest is normally said to have begun with the victory of the Christian chieftain Pelayo from his base in the cave of Covadonga (718) in the Asturias. By the 10c, the successful advance of the Christian frontier led to the creation of the Kingdom of Leon. Occupation of the valley of the Duero led to the creation at the end of the 10c of the county of **CASTILE**, and a decisive step forward was then made with the capture of Toledo

(1085). The last great victory of the Reconquest was Las **NAVAS DE TOLOSA** (1212), which opened the way to Andalusia and the occupation in less than 40 years of the whole valley of the Guadalquivir (Córdoba in 1236 and Seville in 1248). On the Mediterranean side of the peninsula, the Aragonese and Catalan forces moved south into Valencia. By the end of the 13c the main drive of the Reconquest was at an end, leaving only the Kingdom of Granada under Muslim rule. Two centuries passed before that finally fell in 1492. The Reconquest had important social consequences, since it cultivated a warrior ethic among Spaniards, and emphasized the notion of religious crusade. ► **GRANADA, CONQUEST OF**

## Reconstruction

The period following the **AMERICAN CIVIL WAR** when the South, reeling from the physical and economic devastation it had sustained, was moving toward recovery and the status of the former Confederate states and the process of integration of the freed slaves was yet to be determined. President Andrew **JOHNSON** favoured a conciliatory approach toward the region, but radical Republicans took a hard line against what they viewed as recalcitrant Southern legislators dedicated to maintaining the power of the old order and determined to limit blacks' rights by evading the spirit of the Thirteenth Amendment by passing restrictive **BLACK CODES**. The Republican-controlled **CONGRESS** responded by passing four Reconstruction Acts, two **CIVIL RIGHTS ACTS**, and the Fourteenth and Fifteenth Amendments. Military law was established throughout the South. Eventually, however, Republican control of the area was weakened due in large part to corruption in the federal government, and Southern states were slowly readmitted to the Union. The **KU KLUX KLAN**, founded in 1866, gained in power, and the era ended with the Compromise of 1877, when a bargain among politicians gave a disputed presidential election to the Republican candidate Rutherford B **HAYES** in return for 'home' (ie white) rule in the South. Once white rule was fully restored, a policy of racial segregation evolved to keep black people firmly subordinate.

## Recopilación de las leyes de los reinos de las Indias

Published in four volumes in Madrid in 1681, the 'Compilation of the Laws of the Kings of the Indies' was the most famous of all attempts to compile all the laws and orders pertaining to each section of the Spanish royal government which dealt with its overseas dominions. This and similar colonial compilations became the bases for law in the successor states (eg *Ordenações Filipinas* for the dominions of the Portuguese crown). Iberian laws did not shape events; rather, they approximated historical events, or commented upon them. Law and regulations were better developed in some parts of the continent than others; they also varied in their substance and timing.

## Red Army

The Red Army of Workers and Peasants (RKKA, *Raboche Krest'yanskaya Krasnaya Armiya*), the official name of the army of the USSR from 1918 to 1945. It was built around the original Bolshevik Red Guards from 1917, but was the most important land force engaged in the defeat of Nazi Germany in the period

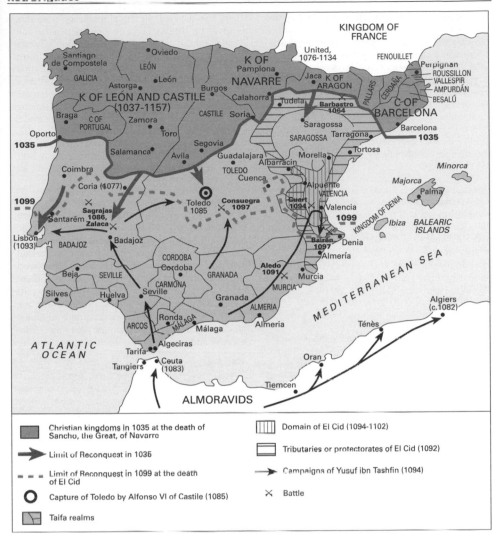

Reconquest of Spain, 11c

**Map legend:**

Christian kingdoms in 1035 at the death of Sancho, the Great, of Navarre

Limit of Reconquest in 1035

Limit of Reconquest in 1099 at the death of El Cid

O Capture of Toledo by Alfonso VI of Castile (1085)

Taifa realms

Domain of El Cid (1094-1102)

Tributaries or protectorates of El Cid (1092)

Campaigns of Yusuf ibn Tashfin (1094)

X Battle

---

1941–5. The epithet 'Red' gave it a political connotation which it never lost, even when 'Red' was changed to 'Soviet' in 1946. ▸ **BOLSHEVIKS**

**Red Brigades** (*Brigate Rosse*, BR)
An Italian left-wing terrorist organization founded in 1970 by Alberto Franceschini, Renato Curcio and Margherita Cagol. Its early years were marked by little real violence, but by 1974 the organization had hardened. The BR was at its most active in the period 1976–80, its energies directed at the killing and kidnapping of judges, politicians, businessmen and journalists. Lack of public sympathy and a more efficiently coordinated anti-terrorist campaign (based on using former BR members as informers) led to widespread arrests and a virtual end to its activities by the early 1980s. ▸ **MORO, ALDO**

**Red Cloud**, Sioux name **Mahpiua Luta** (1822–1909)
Native American leader, chief of the Oglala **SIOUX**. He led resistance to the Bozeman Trail, which crossed Native American lands in Nebraska, Wyoming and Montana, and was responsible for the Fetterman Massacre at which 82 whites were slain (1866). By carrying out raids on soldiers at frontier forts, he and his warriors forced the US government to abandon the trail in 1868. He signed a treaty with the USA in 1869 and thereafter lived at peace with whites, ending his days on a reservation in South Dakota. ▸ **NATIVE AMERICANS**

**Red Crescent** ▸ **RED CROSS**

**Red Cross**
An international agency founded by the **GENEVA CONVENTION** (1864) to assist those wounded or captured in war. There are national branches; the British Red Cross performs relief duties throughout the world; the US Red Cross also runs a blood supply service. All branches use the symbol of the red cross on a white ground, except Muslim branches, which use the red crescent, and Iran, which uses a red lion and sun.

**Red Front** (*Roter Frontkampferbund*, RFB)
German paramilitary league. This organization was founded by the Communist Party (**KPD**) in July 1924 as a counter-weight to the monarchist **STAHLHELM** and the republican **REICHSBANNER SCHWARZ-**

**ROT-GOLD**. Its membership grew to 100,000, but it was banned by the authorities in May 1929 after bloody clashes between it and the police in Berlin. It nonetheless continued to operate and was involved in violent confrontations with the Nazi **SA** in the early 1930s. After **HITLER**'s takeover it ceased to function effectively and some of its members deserted to the SA.

### Red Guards
Young radical Maoist activists (mostly students) who spread the **CULTURAL REVOLUTION** across China, destroying whatever was 'old', and rebelling against all 'reactionary' authority. The first Red Guards were a group formed in Qinghua University in Beijing on whom **MAO ZEDONG** bestowed his blessing (18 Aug 1966) at a mass rally in the capital. ► **MAOISM**

### Redmond, John Edward (1856–1918)
Irish politician. He entered parliament in 1881. A champion of **HOME RULE**, he was Chairman of the Nationalist Party in 1900. He declined a seat in **AS-QUITH**'s coalition ministry (1915), but supported **WORLD WAR I**, deplored the Irish rebellion, and opposed **SINN FÉIN**.

### Redondo, Nicolás (c.1927– )
Spanish trade union leader. He helped revive the Spanish Socialist Party (the **PSOE**) in the late 1960s and early 1970s. Redondo was arrested 13 times during the period 1951–73, but in 1971 he became the leader of the **UGT**. In 1974 he was effectively offered the leadership of the PSOE, but turned it down. From 1984 he was increasingly critical of the socialist government, breaking with it in 1988. In the same year he organized Spain's first general strike since 1934.

### Red River Rebellion (1869–70)
An uprising among the **MÉTIS**, caused by the failure of the Canadian government to treat their problems seriously after it had assumed sovereignty from the **HUDSON'S BAY COMPANY**. Bitter resentment was generated by the government's square survey system, which brought into doubt the land titles of the *métis* whose boundaries were based on river-front lots. The settlement of Manitoba by waves of Anglo-Protestant immigrants from Canada and the USA also brought huge problems, including the destruction of the buffalo on which the métis depended. The métis organized a 'National Committee' with Louis **RIEL** as its Secretary, prevented Lieutenant-Governor **MACDOU-GALL** from entering the settlement, seized Upper Fort Garry and invited both English- and French-speaking inhabitants to discuss a 'List of Rights'. Some Canadians organized themselves to resist the committee, but Riel, now head of the Provisional Government, ordered their imprisonment. The committee issued the 'Declaration of the People of Rupert's Land and the North West'. Meanwhile the government decided to delay the transfer of sovereignty from the Hudson's Bay Company and sent a delegation to meet with the committee and negotiate the territory's entrance into the confederation. When some of the imprisoned Canadians escaped and attempted to raise support among the Scots of the area, the métis captured them and also court-martialled Thomas Scott, an obstreperous Orangeman, whom they executed. News of an amnesty for all rebels

arrived four days later. Riel freed the other prisoners and sent representatives to Ottawa. They reached agreement with the Canadian government and as a result the Manitoba Act was passed, granting the métis 1,400,000 acres/567,000 hectares and bilingual rights. However, only verbal assurances of amnesty were given. When Ontario's Orangemen maintained pressure to punish Scott's executioners, the government sent in a military force and Riel fled to the USA.

### Red Scare (1919–20)
A period in US history characterized by an intense distrust of radicals and foreigners, and marked by the **PALMER RAIDS**. Perhaps due to the general fear of foreigners engendered by **WORLD WAR I** and the foundation of the Third International or **COMINTERN** in 1919, American fear of radicals was such that labour unrest, a series of bombings and strikes, including the steelworkers strike of 1919, and the attempted murder of John D **ROCKEFELLER**, Oliver Wendell **HOLMES** and Attorney-General A Mitchell Palmer, were all thought to have been communist-inspired. Many innocent people were imprisoned and some were deported, but the scare died down within the year when the communist threat was perceived not to exist after all.

### Red Shirts
The name given to the volunteer forces which served under **GARIBALDI** and which adopted their leader's distinctive red smock as a uniform. Red Shirts played a key part in the events of 1848–9, 1859–60 and 1866, as well as in a number of other minor campaigns.

### Reeves, William Pember (1857–1932)
New Zealand politician and writer. Trained in law and journalism, he became an MP (1887–96), and as a cabinet minister under Ballance and **SEDDON**'s government (1891–6) introduced important reforms in industrial legislation, especially the innovative Conciliation and Arbitration Act of 1894 (the first in the world to be compulsory), which he hoped would stimulate trade unionism. He moved to England in 1896 as Agent-General, and was Director of the London School of Economics (1908–19).

### Reforma, La
The name given to the period of Liberal rule in Mexico from 1855 to 1860 and its major reforming measures, which were generally associated with the governments of Benito **JUÁREZ** and Sebastián Lerdo de Tejada. The reforms included the abolition of military and ecclesiastical *fueros*, the secularization of education and the constitution of 1857. These changes not only sparked off the War of the Reforma (1857–60) but legitimized gradual changes taking place in the Mexican countryside as *haciendas* encroached on collective lands and wage labourers emerged in more prosperous zones of the country. It created the legal basis for the dramatic transformations achieved during the presidency of Porfirio **DÍAZ** (the period known as the Porfiriato). ► **FUERO**; **HACIENDA**

### Reform Acts
Legislation in Britain which altered parliamentary constituencies and increased the size of the electorate. The main Acts were: 1832, which gave the vote

to almost all members of the middle classes, and introduced a uniform £10 franchise in the boroughs; 1867, which gave the vote to all settled tenants in the boroughs, thus creating a substantial working-class franchise for the first time; 1884, which extended a similar franchise to rural and mining areas; 1885, which aimed to create parliamentary constituencies of broadly equal size; 1918, which created a universal male suffrage and gave the vote to women of 30 years and over; 1928, which gave the vote to all adult women; and 1969, which lowered the minimum voting age from 21 years to 18. The 1832 Reform Act was the subject of furious controversy, and was preceded by widespread agitation.

## Reformation

The Protestant reform movements in the Christian Church, inspired by and derived from Martin **LUTHER**, John **CALVIN**, and others in 16c Europe. A complex phenomenon, various factors are common to all reforms: a Biblical revival and translation of the Word of God into the vernacular; an improvement in the intellectual and moral standards of the clergy; emphasis on the sovereignty of God; and insistence that faith and scriptures are at the centre of the Christian message. Non-religious factors aiding the spread of the Reformation included the invention of the printing press, the political, social and economic uncertainties of the age, and a general feeling of revival caused by the **RENAISSANCE**. In Germany, Luther's '95 theses' (1517) questioned the authority of the Church and led to his excommunication. The Lutheran Church then spread rapidly, in Switzerland under **ZWINGLI** and later under Calvin, neither of whom allowed any form of worship or devotion not explicitly warranted by scripture. The authority of scripture, the cornerstone of the Reformation, required a degree of ecclesiastical authority (and power) to justify and maintain it. The doctrine of the priesthood of all believers and the importance placed on preaching the Word of God led to an educated clergy, and decentralized church communities were better able to prevent abuse of ecclesiastical privilege. ➤ **COUNTER-REFORMATION**; **REFORMATION** (England); **REFORMATION** (Scotland)

## Reformation (England)

The process by which the English Church rejected the authority of the Roman Catholic Church and established its own doctrine and liturgy. The English Reformation, unlike that of most European countries, was not predominantly doctrinal in origin. It was precipitated by **HENRY VIII** after the Church refused to permit his divorce from **CATHERINE OF ARAGON** in order to marry Anne **BOLEYN** with the intention of producing a male heir. Henry's response was to use parliament to pass statutes distancing the English Church from Rome. The English clergy were permitted to recognize Henry, rather than the pope, as Supreme Head of the Church in 1531, and the Act of Supremacy (1534) ended the pope's formal authority in England. Monasteries were dissolved during the later 1530s and their treasures forfeit to the Crown. Catholic doctrine was upheld by the 'Six Articles' (1539) but, during the reign of **EDWARD VI**, Protestant usages were promoted in two Acts of Uniformity (1549 and 1552). During the reign of **MARY I**, England

was formally reunited with Rome but the succession of **ELIZABETH I** (1558) confirmed England as a non-Catholic country. The Act of Uniformity (1559) and the 39 Articles of Religion (1563) were recognizably Protestant although Elizabeth's Church Settlement rejected extreme Protestantism. Elizabeth's control over the Church as 'Supreme Governor' was established by the Act of Supremacy (1559). ➤ **CRANMER, THOMAS**; **CROMWELL, THOMAS**; **PILGRIMAGE OF GRACE**; **REFORMATION** (Scotland)

## Reformation (Scotland)

The term used to describe the religious changes whereby the authority of the pope was repudiated and Protestant forms of doctrine and worship established. Following a period of toleration for Protestants under the Regent, Mary of Guise, in the 1550s, 'Lords of the Congregation' asserted their intention to overthrow Roman Catholicism (1557). The Regent's attempts to suppress Protestantism (1558–9) failed but **ELIZABETH I**'s intervention in Scotland was decisive. The Protestant party, aided by John **KNOX**, gained control. Catholicism was repudiated at a meeting of the Estates in 1560 ('Reformation Parliament') and celebration of Mass proscribed. One third of ecclesiastical revenues were appropriated to pay ministers of the Reformed Church and to augment royal finances (1562). **MARY, QUEEN OF SCOTS** did not ratify the religious changes, which were finally confirmed by **MORAY**, Regent for James VI, in 1567. Controversy between Presbyterians (led by Andrew Melville), who insisted on equality of ministers, and Episcopalians, who upheld the hierarchy of bishops, continued within the Church in the late 16c and 17c. ➤ **JAMES VI AND I**; **REFORMATION** (England)

## Reformatio Sigismundi

An anonymous pamphlet, probably written in 1439 during the Council of **BASLE**. It was drawn up in the name of Emperor **SIGISMUND** and shows the influence of Hussite ideas. It demanded the reform of both ecclesiastical and lay society, including the abolition of slavery, tithes and taxes. The pamphlet was widely disseminated and its demands echoed during the **PEASANTS' WAR**.

## reformism

Any doctrine or movement that advocates gradual social and political change rather than revolutionary change; most commonly applied to **SOCIALISM**. The underlying premise is that democratic procedures provide the most suitable means through which to build social change.

## Reform League (1863)

An organization of middle-class radicals and skilled trade unionists by working-class radicals to extend male suffrage, whose 1866 demonstrations against the fall of the Liberal Reform Bill was a factor in persuading the subsequent Conservative administrations of Lord **DERBY** and Benjamin **DISRAELI** to introduce their own reform proposals. It won the support of the Liberals in their 1868 election campaign, but was dissolved soon afterwards. ➤ **REFORM ACTS**

## Regalia

In German history, the privileges reserved, in the first instance, for the king, especially taxation, coinage, the right to establish markets and to forests, fishing, hunting and mining. In the Middle Ages the regalia formed the core of royal finances. Later, they were devolved into the hands of landowners. In a narrower sense, regalia also refers to the secular rights of bishops, and the rights of the king to appoint bishops and endow them with these rights were at the centre of the **INVESTITURE CONTROVERSY**.

## Regat

The name given to **MOLDAVIA AND WALLACHIA**, the core of the pre-**WORLD WAR I** Kingdom of Romania. ► **ROMANIA**

## Regency

The period of **LOUIS XV** of France's minority (1715–23) during which the country was ruled by a Regency Council presided over by Philippe, Duke of **ORLÉANS**. The main events of this period were the financial disaster of John Law's scheme (1719–20) and the acceptance in France of the Papal Bull *Unigenitus*, condemning **JANSENISM** (1720). The Regent entrusted foreign affairs to the Abbé **DUBOIS**, who formed the Quadruple Alliance with the Netherlands, Britain and Austria, and went to war with Spain. The Regency was notorious for the extravagance and debauchery of its ruling group.

## regime change

Military intervention by one state or group of states in the political affairs of another sovereign state to bring about a desired change in government. Rationales for intervention usually fall into four categories: violation of human rights, civil war, state-sponsorship of terrorism, or actual or suspected possession of weapons of mass destruction (**WMD**). Examples of attempted or actual regime change include the **BAY OF PIGS** invasion (1961), the US invasion of Panama City to arrest of General Manuel **NORIEGA** (1990), US intervention in Haiti to replace the military junta with an elected president (1994) and allied intervention in **AFGHANISTAN** (2001) and **IRAQ** (2003). The former USSR intervened in the Hungarian Uprising (1956) and the **PRAGUE SPRING** in Czechoslovakia (1968) to suppress reform and restore communist rule.

## Regulator Movements

In America, rural insurgencies in South Carolina (mid-1760s) and North Carolina (militarily defeated in 1771) shortly before independence. In both disputes the small farmers of the interior protested against excessive taxes and dishonest officials, and against the fact that the government was dominated by the slaveholding seaboard. The ensuing east–west bitterness fed into the **AMERICAN REVOLUTION**, but the causes and outcomes of each were different. The term 'regulator' was also used elsewhere in early America to describe popular insurrectionary movements.

## rehabilitation

The (usually posthumous) restoration to Party favour, and even membership, of communists who had been purged under a previous leadership. It was most prominently applied to Soviet communist leaders executed under **STALIN**, but was also a common practice in Eastern Europe. It was noticeable, however, that it usually remained selective; not all the innocents were rehabilitated. ► **COMMUNISM**

## Rehnquist, William H(ubbs) (1924– )

US jurist. Educated at the universities of Stanford and Harvard, he became a law clerk to Justice Robert H **JACKSON** in the US Supreme Court before entering private practice. He served as Assistant Attorney-General from 1968 to 1971, became head of the Office of Legal Counsel of the Justice Department, and challenged many laws protecting the rights of defendants, such as Miranda v Arizona, giving him the reputation of a protector of law enforcement. In 1971 he was named Associate Justice of the Supreme Court by President Richard **NIXON**. He was chosen by President Ronald **REAGAN** in 1986 to succeed Warren E **BURGER** as Chief Justice of the Supreme Court, a controversial nomination due to his history of extremely conservative opinions. As Chief Justice, he has presided over a Supreme Court that has followed a conservative trend away from the more liberal **WARREN** Court.

## Reich

The term used to describe the German Empire and the German national state between 1918 and 1945. The **HOLY ROMAN EMPIRE** was regarded as the First Reich, and unified Germany after 1870 was referred to as the Second Reich (*Kaiserreich*). After 1933, the enlarged Germany envisaged in **HITLER**'s plans was known as the Third Reich. The term is no longer used. ► **KAISER**

## Reichsbanner Schwarz-Rot-Gold

German paramilitary league (literally, 'National Flag Black-Red-Gold'). Founded in Feb 1924, the republican *Reichsbanner* sought to provide a counter-attraction to the monarchist leagues for Weimar military veterans and youth. Organized by the **DDP**, **CENTRE PARTY** and **SPD**, but dominated by the last, its membership exceeded 3.5 million by 1932, although with just 400,000 activists. It fought the Nazi **SA** and, occasionally, the communist **RED FRONT** and monarchist **STAHLHELM** on the streets during the early 1930s, but was ineffective against the dismantling of republican democracy and **HITLER**'s eventual takeover. It dissolved itself in Mar 1933.

## Reichsdeputationshauptschluss (24 Mar 1803)

Following the loss of German territories west of the Rhine to France (1795, 1797–9 and 1801), the remaining secular states sought compensation through the secularization of the extensive Church lands (in return for financial compensation) and the absorption of most self-governing imperial cities. This was achieved, ending papal involvement in and Catholic predominance in German affairs, but further wars with France delayed the full implementation of these agreements until 1815.

## Reichskristallnacht ► KRISTALLNACHT

## Reichstag

Literally 'imperial diet', the term refers to three German political institutions: (1) The lower, elected house of the German parliament (1871–1918). Seen by **BISMARCK** as a symbolic concession to national and liberal sentiment, the *Reichstag*, although elected by universal male suffrage, possessed very limited functions in Imperial Germany where power rested primarily with the Crown and the Emperor's ministers. However, it could block legislation and budgets and, as parties seeking an extension of parliamentary power gained a majority in the Reichstag, in 1912 a constitutional crisis, delayed by **WORLD WAR I**, developed. (2) The lower, elected house of the German parliament (1920–33). In this period (the **WEIMAR REPUBLIC**), governments were formed by dominant coalitions in the Reichstag, but political polarization and the growing strength of anti-republican parties (**NAZI PARTY, KPD**) necessitated the conduct of government under Article 48 of the constitution (presidential emergency powers) from 1930 to 1933. (3) An assembly dominated by the Nazi Party in the Third **REICH** (1933–45). **HITLER** periodically addressed the Reichstag, but real power had passed to Hitler, his ministers and to party officials.

### Reichstag Fire (27 Feb 1933)

The deliberate burning down of Germany's parliament building, shortly after the Nazi accession to power. A deranged Dutch ex-communist, van der Lubbe, was accused of arson and executed. The new Nazi government, insisting that the act was evidence of a wider communist conspiracy, used the situation to ban and suppress the German Communist Party (**KPD**). Communist conspiracy was certainly not behind the fire; nor were the Nazis themselves, though it was long believed to be so. It is now agreed that, however convenient the fire may have been to the regime, van der Lubbe acted alone. ► **NAZI PARTY**

### Reichswehr

Literally 'national defence', this is the term used to describe the armed forces of Germany in the period 1919–35. Consisting of 100,000 soldiers and 15,000 sailors, the *Reichswehr* was a professional force with junior ranks serving 12 years and officers 25 years. Relations between the Reichswehr and the republic were equivocal. The officers were opposed to any open, violent challenge to the state, but secretly supported anti-republican paramilitary leagues in Germany and undertook secret rearmament in collaboration with the USSR. Allegedly 'above politics', senior Reichswehr officers such as **GROENER** and **SCHLEICHER** were active in late Weimar government affairs and did much indirectly to pave the way for **HITLER**'s takeover. In 1935, with rearmament, the Reichswehr, by now bound by oath of personal loyalty to Hitler, was reorganized as the **WEHRMACHT**.

### Reid, Sir George Houstoun (1845–1918)

British-born Australian politician. He arrived in Melbourne with his parents in 1852, and in 1858 moved to Sydney, where he obtained a post with the Colonial Treasury. He studied law, and in 1878 became Secretary to the Attorney-General of New South Wales. A strong supporter of free trade, in 1880 he was elected to the Legislative Assembly of New South Wales, and in 1891 succeeded Sir Henry **PARKES** as Leader of the Opposition, becoming Premier of the state from 1894 to 1899. A cautious supporter of **FEDERATION**, he moved to the first federal parliament in 1901, still representing his old constituency, and became Leader of the Opposition in the House of Representatives. He was Prime Minister of Australia (1904–5) and retired from politics in 1908. In 1909 he was appointed Australia's first High Commissioner to London, a post he held with distinction until 1916. He then took up the seat for Hanover Square in the

British House of **COMMONS**, which he held until his death.

### Reign of Terror ► **TERROR, REIGN OF**

### Religion ► *See panel*

### Religion, Wars of (1562–98)

A series of religious and political conflicts in France, caused by the growth of Calvinism, noble factionalism and weak royal government. After 1559 there were a number of weak and/or young Valois kings whose mother, **CATHERINE DE' MEDICI**, attempted abortive compromises. Calvinist or 'Huguenot' numbers increased from the 1550s, fostered by the missionary activities of Geneva. The noble factions of Bourbon, Guise and Montmorency were split by religion as well as by family interests. Civil wars were encouraged by **PHILIP II** of Spain's support of the Catholic Guise faction and by **ELIZABETH I** of England's aid to the **HUGUENOTS**. They ended when the Huguenot Henry of Navarre (**HENRY IV**) succeeded to the throne (1589), converted to Catholicism (1593), crushed the Guise Catholic League (1589–98), and by the Edict of **NANTES** (1598) granted Protestants freedom of conscience. ► **BOURBON, HOUSE OF**; **GUISE, HOUSE OF**; **VALOIS DYNASTY**

### Remonstrants

Christians adhering to the Calvinistic doctrine of Jacobus Arminius (17c Netherlands), whose followers were also known as Arminians. They were named after the 'Remonstrance', a statement of Arminian teaching dating from 1610, and lost their theological and political case against the Counter-Remonstrants at the Synod of **DORDRECHT** (1618–19). Small in number, they have been influential among Baptists, and in Methodism and Calvinism.

### Rémusat, Charles François Marie, Count of (1797–1875)

French aristocrat. He early developed liberal ideas, and took to journalism. He signed the journalists' protest that brought about the **JULY REVOLUTION** (1830), was elected Deputy for Toulouse, in 1836 became Under-Secretary of State for the Interior and in 1840 Minister of the Interior. Exiled after the coup d'état of 1848, he devoted himself to literary and philosophical studies, until, in 1871, **THIERS** appointed him Minister of Foreign Affairs, which he remained until 1873.

### Renaissance

From the French for 'rebirth', the term is applied to several significant revivals of interest in the classical past which punctuate European history. One such revival is identified with the age of the Emperor Charlemagne (hence 'Carolingian Renaissance'), another with the Emperor Otto I, the Great in the 10c ('Ottonian Renaissance') while the '12c Renaissance' was marked by the fusion of Christian learning with the rediscovered works of Aristotle in the great intellectual synthesis known as scholasticism. Most famously, however, the term is applied to the cultural achievements of the Italians in the 14c and 15c. In turn, the absorption of Italian values in a general European context in the 16c then paved the way for the **SCIENTIFIC REVOLUTION** of the 17c and the **ENLIGHTENMENT** of the 18c. The idea was first formulated by

# *Religion*

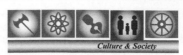

*Culture & Society*

The five major religious traditions in the world – Buddhism, Christianity, Hinduism, Islam and Judaism – have had such influence and enduring impact that they are commonly referred to as 'world religions'.

## BUDDHISM

A tradition of thought and practice originating in India around 2,500 years ago, derived from the teaching of Buddha (Siddhartha Gautama). The teaching of Buddha is summarized in the 'Four Noble Truths', the last of which affirms the existence of a path leading to deliverance from the universal human experience of suffering. A central tenet is the law of *karma*, by which good and evil deeds result in appropriate reward or punishment in this life or in a succession of rebirths.

### Divisions

There are two main traditions within Buddhism, dating from its earliest history. Theravada Buddhism adheres to the strict and narrow teachings of the early Buddhist writings: salvation is possible for only the few who accept the severe discipline and effort necessary to achieve it. Mahayana Buddhism is more liberal, and makes concessions to popular piety; it teaches that salvation is possible for everyone, and introduced the doctrine of the *bodhisattva* (or personal saviour). As Buddhism spread, other schools grew up, among them Chan or Zen, Tendai, **Nichiren**, Pure Land and Soka Gakkai.

### Theravada Buddhism in South and South-East Asia

While it largely died out in its original home of India, Theravada Buddhism is a significant religious force in the states of Burma, Cambodia, Laos, Sri Lanka and Thailand. According to tradition, Buddhism was introduced into the area by missions from the Indian emperor Ashoka in the 3c BC. Evidence is sparse but it appears that up to the 10c, various branches of the Hindu and Buddhist traditions were present in South-East Asia in scattered proportions. From the 11c to 15c, Theravada Buddhism grew in influence and there were significant contacts with Sri Lanka, where the movement was outward-looking. Buddhist states arose in Burma (now Myanmar), Cambodia, Laos, Java and Thailand, including the Angkor state in Cambodia and the **Pagan** state in Burma. In the modern period, with the exception of Thailand which was never colonized, Theravada Buddhism in South-East Asia was challenged by imperial occupation, Christian missionaries and the Western world-view.

### Mahayana Buddhism in North and Central Asia

The form of Buddhism commonly practised in China, Tibet, Mongolia, Nepal, Korea and Japan, Mahayana dates from about the 1c, when it arose as a more liberal development within Buddhism in northern India, emphasizing various forms of popular devotion.

### Tibetan Buddhism

In Tibet, orthodox Mahayana Buddhism and Vajrayana Buddhism (a Tantric form of Mahayana Buddhism) were transmitted through missionaries invited from India during the 8c. The popular Tibetan Buddhism of today emphasizes the appeasement of malevolent deities, pilgrimages and the accumulation of merit. However, since the Chinese invasion in 1959 and the **Dalai Lama**'s exile in India, Buddhism has been severely repressed.

### Chinese Buddhism

Buddhism first entered China from India in the 1c AD via the central Asian oases along the Silk Route, and by the end of the Han Dynasty (AD 220) it had established a reasonable presence in China. By the 9c, it had become so successful that the Tang Dynasty saw it as 'an empire within the empire' and persecuted it in 845, after which only the Chan and Pure Land schools remained strong. They drew closer together and became more harmonized. An attempt was made by the Marxist government of **Mao Zedong** (1949 onwards) to subdue Buddhism and other religions in China, and its lands were nationalized and its monks forced to engage in secular employment. Since 1978, however, Buddhism and other religions have been reviving in China.

## CHRISTIANITY

A world religion centred on the life and work of Jesus of Nazareth in 1c Palestine, and developing out of Judaism. The earliest followers were Jews who believed Jesus to be the Messiah or Christ, promised by the prophets in the Old Testament, and in unique relation to God, whose Son or 'Word' (*Logos*) he was declared to be. During his life he chose 12 men as disciples, who, after his death by crucifixion and his resurrection from the dead, formed the nucleus of the Church as a society or communion of believers. They gathered together to worship God through the risen Jesus Christ, believing he would return to earth and inaugurate the 'kingdom of God'. Through the witness of the 12 earliest leaders

---

the Florentine Vasari in his *Lives of the Artists* (c.1550). He identified three great eras of creativity: the first, c.1300, identified above all with Giotto; the second, around 1400, with the architect Brunelleschi, the sculptor Donatello and the painter Masaccio; while the climax, he thought, was reached in his own time in the work of Michelangelo. Vasari's vision was confined to achievements in the visual arts and within them he laid particular stress on the unique achievements of the Florentines. Subsequently, particularly since the work of Michelet and Burckhardt in the

19c, the application of the term has broadened to take in intellectual and social developments and other centres of creativity, notably Rome and Venice.

**Renamo** (*Resistencia Nacional Mozambicana*, 'Mozambiquan National Resistance')
An armed movement set up in 1976, first with Rhodesian and later with South African support, to oppose the **FRELIMO** government of Mozambique that came to power on independence in 1975. Although lacking a clear political aim, it managed to disrupt

(Apostles) and their successors, the Christian faith, despite sporadic persecution, quickly spread through the Greek and Roman world, and in AD315 was declared by Emperor Constantine to be the official religion of the Roman Empire. It survived the break-up of the Empire and the 'Dark Ages' through the life and witness of groups of monks in monasteries, and formed the basis of civilization in the **Middle Ages** in Europe.

## The Bible
The Christian Scriptures are divided into two testaments: the Old Testament (which corresponds roughly to the canon of Jewish scriptures), and the New Testament. The Old Testament, or Hebrew Bible, is a collection of writings originally composed in Hebrew, except for parts of Daniel and Ezra that are in Aramaic. These writings depict Israelite religion from its beginnings to about the 2c BC. The New Testament, written in Greek, is so called in Christian circles because it is believed to constitute a new 'testament' or 'covenant' in the history of God's dealings with his people, centring on the ministry of Jesus and the early development of the apostolic churches.

## Denominations
Major divisions in the Christian Church have developed as a result of differences in doctrine and practice. They are the Eastern or Orthodox Churches, the Roman Catholic Church, which acknowledges the Bishop of Rome (the **pope**) as head, and the Protestant Churches stemming from the split with the Roman Church in the **Reformation**. The impetus to spread Christianity to the non-Christian world in missionary movements, especially in the 19–20c, resulted in the creation of numerically very strong churches in the developing countries of Asia, Africa and South America. There are over 1,500 million Christians throughout the world. They observe an annual cycle of seasons (e.g. Advent, Lent), festivals (e.g. Easter, Christmas) and other holy days, such as saints' days.

### HINDUISM
The Western term for a religious tradition developed over several thousand years and intertwined with the history and social system of India. Hinduism does not trace its origins to a particular founder, has no prophets, no set creed, and no particular institutional structure. It emphasizes the right way of living (*dharma*) rather than a set of doctrines, and thus embraces diverse religious beliefs and practices. There are significant variations between different regions of India, and even from village to village. There are differences in the deities worshipped, the scriptures used, and the festivals observed. Hindus may be theists or non-theists, revere one or more gods or goddesses, or no god at all, and represent the ultimate in personal (eg *Brahma*) or impersonal (eg *Brahman*) terms. There are over 500 million Hindus.

## Beliefs
Common to most forms of Hinduism is the idea of reincarnation or transmigration. The term *samsara* refers to the process of birth and rebirth continuing for life after life. The particular form and condition (pleasant or unpleasant) of rebirth is the result of *karma*, the law by which the consequences of actions within one life are carried over into the next and influence its character. The ultimate spiritual goal of Hindus is *moksha*, or release from the cycle of *samsara*.

## Literature
There is a rich and varied religious literature, and no specific text is regarded as uniquely authoritative. The earliest extant writings come from the Vedic period (c.1500–c.500 BC), and are known collectively as the *Veda*. Later (c.500 BC–AD 500) came the religious law books (*dharma sutras* and *dharma shastras*) which codified the classes of society (*varna*) and the four stages of life (*ashrama*), and formed the basis of the Indian **caste** system. To this were added the great epics, the *Ramayana* and the *Mahabharata*. The latter includes one of the most influential Hindu scriptures, the *Bhagavad Gita*.

## Caste
Caste is central to Hinduism. When the Aryans came to India they brought with them a three-tiered social structure of priests (*brahmanas*), warriors (*kshatriyas*), and commoners (*vaishyas*), to which they added the serfs (*shudras*), the indigenous population of India which itself was probably hierarchically structured. This class (*varna*) system is given sanction by the Rig Veda (10.90), which describes each of the classes coming from the body of the sacrificed primal person (*purusha*). The class system, and the caste system which derives from it, is therefore regarded as a sacred structure by orthodox Hindus, in harmony with natural or cosmic law (*dharma*). The class system developed into the caste (*jati*) system which we know today. There are thousands of castes within India based on inherited profession and ideas of purity and pollution. The higher castes are regarded as ritually more pure than the lower. Although the practice was legally outlawed in 1951, some castes are so 'polluting' that their members are still called 'untouchables'. Marriage between castes is strictly forbidden and transgressors are severely punished.

## Gods
Brahma, Vishnu and Shiva are the chief gods of Hinduism, and together form a triad (the *Trimurti*). There are numerous

---

Mozambique's economy and transport system and was responsible for pressurizing the government into signing the **NKOMATI ACCORD**. By the end of the 1980s its violent activities had not only threatened the country's infrastructure but resulted in 100,000 deaths and 1 million refugees. In 1989 President **CHISSANO** agreed to meet its leader, Afonso Dhlakama. A new constitution was drafted, peace talks took place, and in 1992 Renamo and Frelimo signed a peace accord. Renamo became a legitimate political party and in 1994 Mozambique had its first multiparty elections (won by Frelimo).

**René, France-Albert** (1935– )
Seychelles politician. Educated locally, and in Switzerland and at King's College, London, he was called to the Bar in 1957. He returned to the Seychelles and entered politics, founding the socialist Seychelles People's United Party in 1964, which he led. A member of the National Assembly since 1965, he formed a coalition at independence in 1976 with his opponent James Mancham, who became President while René

lesser deities, including the goddesses Maya and Lakshmi. Pilgrimage to local and regional sites is common, and there is an annual cycle of local, regional and all-Indian festivals.

## ISLAM
The Arabic word for 'submission' to the will of God (Allah), and the name of the religion which originated in Arabia during the 7c through the prophet Muhammad. Islam teaches that since the beginning of time God has sent prophets, including Moses and Jesus, to provide the guidance necessary for the attainment of eternal reward, and the culmination of this succession is the revelation to Muhammad of the *Quran*, the perfect Word of God.

### Beliefs and traditions
There are five essential religious duties known as the 'pillars of Islam'.
1. The *shahadah* (profession of faith) is the sincere recitation of the two-fold creed: 'There is no god but God' and 'Muhammad is the Messenger of God'.
2. The *salat* (formal prayer) must be performed at fixed hours five times a day while facing towards the holy city of Mecca.
3. Alms-giving through the payment of *zakat* ('purification') is regarded primarily as an act of worship, and is the duty of sharing one's wealth out of gratitude for God's favour, according to the uses laid down in the *Quran*.
4. There is a duty to fast (*saum*) during the month of *Ramadan*.
5. The *Hajj* or pilgrimage to Mecca is to be performed if at all possible at least once during one's lifetime. *Shariah* is the sacred law of Islam, and applies to all aspects of life, not just religious practices. It describes the Islamic way of life, and prescribes the way for a Muslim to fulfil the commands of God and reach heaven. There is an annual cycle of festivals, including *Hijra* (*Hegira*), the beginning of the Islamic year, and *Ramadan*, the month in which Muslims fast during the hours of daylight.

### Divisions
There are two basic groups within Islam. **Sunnis** are in the majority, and they recognize the first four caliphs as Muhammad's legitimate successors. The **Shiites** comprise the largest minority group, and regard the imam as the principal religious authority. There are a number of subsects, including the Shiite **Ismailis** (one group of which, the Nizaris, regard the Aga Khan as their imam), and the puritanical Sunni **Wahhabis**, a reform movement begun in the 18c. There are over 700 million Muslims throughout the world.

## JUDAISM
The religion of the Jews, central to which is the belief in one God. The Hebrew Bible is the primary source of Judaism. Next in importance is the *Talmud*, which consists of the *Mishnah* (the codification of the oral *Torah*) and a collection of extensive early rabbinical commentary. Various later commentaries and the standard code of Jewish law and ritual (*Halakhah*) produced in the late Middle Ages have been important in shaping Jewish practice and thought.

### Communal life
However varied their communities, all Jews see themselves as members of a community whose origins lie in the patriarchal period. This past lives on in its rituals, and there is a marked preference for expressing beliefs and attitudes more through ritual than through abstract doctrine. The family is the basic unit of Jewish ritual, though the synagogue has come to play an increasingly important role. The Sabbath, which begins at sunset on Friday and ends at sunset on Saturday, is the central religious observance. The synagogue is the centre for community worship and study. There is an annual cycle of religious festivals and days of fasting. The first of these is *Rosh Hashanah*, New Year's Day; the holiest day in the Jewish year is *Yom Kippur*, the Day of Atonement. Other annual festivals include *Hanukkah* and *Pesach*, the family festival of Passover.

### Divisions
Modern Judaism is rooted in rabbinic Judaism, and its historical development has been diverse. Today most Jews are the descendants of either the **Ashkenazim** or the **Sephardim**, each with their marked cultural differences. There are also several branches of Judaism. Orthodox Judaism (19c) seeks to preserve traditional Judaism. Reform Judaism (19c) represents an attempt to interpret Judaism in the light of modern scholarship and knowledge, a process carried further by Liberal Judaism. Conservative Judaism attempts to modify orthodoxy through an emphasis on the positive historical elements of Jewish tradition.

    Anti-Semitic prejudice and periods of persecution have been a feature of the Christian culture of Europe; these increased with the rise of European nationalism, and culminated in the Nazi **Holocaust**. Its effect has been incalculable, giving urgency to the Zionist movement, established by the **World Zionist Organization** for the creation of a Jewish homeland, and remains pivotal in all relations between Jews and non-Jews today. There are over 14 million Jews.

---

became Prime Minister. When Mancham was abroad in 1977, René staged a coup, created a one-party state (1979–91) and made himself Executive President. He subsequently followed a policy of non-alignment and resisted attempts to remove him. He was elected in 1979 and re-elected regularly until he stepped down in 2004.

## René I, the Good (1409–80)
Duke of Anjou, Count of Provence and Piedmont. He was known as the 'Last of the Troubadours'. Having failed in his efforts (1438–42) to make good his claim to the crown of Naples, he married his daughter, **MARGARET OF ANJOU**, to **HENRY VI** of England (1445). In his last years, he devoted himself to Provençal poetry and agriculture at Aix.

## Rennenkampf, Pavel Karlovich von (1853–1918)
Russian cavalry officer. Of Baltic German origins, he commanded a force in the **RUSSO-JAPANESE WAR** (1904–5) and earned a reputation as a tough soldier, restoring order westwards from Harbin along the

Trans-Siberian Railway. In **WORLD WAR I**, in command of the 1st Army, he defeated the German 8th Army at Insterburg and Gumbinnen (Aug 1914), but was decisively defeated by **HINDENBURG** in the wake of the Battle of **TANNENBERG** a few days later. He was appointed Governor of Petrograd in 1915, and Commander-in-Chief of the northern front in 1916. After the **OCTOBER REVOLUTION** he was shot by the **BOLSHEVIKS**.

### Renner, Karl (1870–1950)
Austrian politician. He trained as a lawyer, joined the Austrian Social Democratic Party (**SPÖ**), and became the first Chancellor of the Austrian Republic (1918–20). Imprisoned as a socialist leader following the brief civil war (Feb 1934), he was Chancellor again (1945) after **WORLD WAR II**, and first President of the new republic (1945–50).

### reparations
Payments imposed on the powers defeated in war to cover the costs incurred by the victors. For example, they were levied by the Allies on Germany at the end of **WORLD WAR I**, though the final sum of £6,000 million plus interest was not fixed until Apr 1921. The Dawes (1924) and Young (1929) Plans revised the payment schedule and reduced the scale of the payments, which were finally abandoned after 1932, because of the Depression. ► **DAWES PLAN, YOUNG PLAN**

### Republic, First (France)
The regime that was established in France in Sep 1792, and which lasted officially until **NAPOLEON I** proclaimed himself Emperor in 1804 (although the period 1795–9 is usually referred to as the **DIRECTORY**, and the period 1799–1804 as the **CONSULATE**).

### Republic, First (Portugal) (1910–26)
The transition from the oligarchical rule of the monarchy to the pluralistic democracy of the new regime produced acute political instability because of a weak party system enhanced by the 1911 constitution. The reforms of the Republic largely benefited the urban lower middle classes, its main constituency, spurning the aspirations of the urban working class, women, and the rural peasants and labourers. For example, the labourers' strike in Alentejo of 1911–12 was brutally suppressed. Political uncertainty, a lack of resources, and the exclusivity of the Republicans all combined to prevent change. Military discontent and Republican divisions resulted in a conservative dictatorship (Jan– May 1915). Back in power, the Republican politicians entered **WORLD WAR I** in 1916 on the side of the Allies. Rocketing prices, food shortages, and heavy losses in France led to a coup under Bernardino Sidónio Pais (5 Dec 1917); this young charismatic man became the first Republican dictator of the 20c. The so-called New Republic was a forerunner of the authoritarian and corporatist state created by **SALAZAR** in the 1930s. Unable to secure his power base and thrown into crisis by the Allied victory of Nov 1918, Sidónio Pais was assassinated in Lisbon on 14 Dec 1918. From 1918 to 1926 the Republic was more unstable than ever. In 1919 there were four governments and in 1920, nine. Civil war broke out in northern Portugal, the economy collapsed and violence mounted. Several Republican politicians

were murdered, including Antonio Machado Santos, the leading figure of the 1910 revolution. The failure to maintain public order and protect living standards, and the political stranglehold of the Portuguese Republican Party (PRP) (preventing the emergence of other parties), alienated many of the Republic's own supporters. Though the internecine party warfare seemed remote, it reflected wider economic conflicts. The progressive governments of Dec 1923–July 1925 further consolidated the rapidly growing forces of counter-revolution. A marked swing to the right took place in the 1920s. Following the abortive coups of Apr and July 1925, the Republic was finally overthrown by a military rising on 28 May 1926.

### Republic, First (Spain) (1873–4)
The first period of Republican rule in Spain may be divided into four phases. The **FIGUERAS** government sought a unitary regime based on a presidential system. Its failure led to a rising of the provinces when scores of city-states, or cantons, declared their independence and pursued primitive **COMMUNISM**. Under **CASTELAR** the cantonalists were crushed by the army and a unitary republic was partially restored. Political in-fighting led to a coup in Jan 1873 and the rule of the aristocratic General **SERRANO** until a further coup in Dec 1874 brought the republic to an end and the monarchy was restored. ► **CANTONALIST RISINGS**

### Republic, Second (France)
The regime established in France after the **FEBRUARY REVOLUTION** (1848), which lasted until the proclamation of the Second **EMPIRE** in 1852.

### Republic, Second (Spain) (1931–6)
Spain's first democratic regime in nearly 60 years was established (14 Apr 1931) amidst great popular expectation following the disastrous policies of the monarchy. The Left-Republican–Socialist administrations of 1931–3 under Manuel **AZAÑA** made the most determined effort yet to transform Spain from a reactionary and backward society into a modern and progressive 'European' state. The failure of reform was partly due to the lack of unity and expertise within the governmental coalition, but more so to a scarcity of resources and the world depression. Above all, reform proceeded slowly because of the hostility of the traditional ruling classes to meaningful change, especially the landowners. The course of the Republic was fundamentally altered by the general election of Nov–Dec 1933. A parliamentary alliance was formed between the **RADICAL REPUBLICAN PARTY** and the Catholic **CEDA**. The Centre-Right administrations of Dec 1933 to Oct 1935 moved steadily to the right while demolishing the reforms of the first two years. This led to a major Radical schism (May 1934) and to mounting socio-economic conflict. The entry of three members of the proto-fascist CEDA into the government (4 Oct 1934) resulted in a Socialist general strike, a declaration of Catalan independence, and an armed rising in Asturias. The brutal repression of the October protest polarized the Republic to an unprecedented extent. As the CEDA gained more and more power at the expense of the Radicals throughout 1935, so the previously divided Left rallied to the banner of the Popular Front. In the general election of Feb 1936 the Popular Front won a

narrow victory. The political climate became increasingly volatile as the weak Left-Republican governments, now bereft of Socialist support, proved unable to impose themselves. The military rising of 17–18 July 1936 resulted in a civil war that lasted until Apr 1939. The origins of the SPANISH CIVIL WAR were overwhelmingly domestic in nature, embracing not one but several conflicts, ranging from social and political tensions to religious and regional ones.

**Republic, Third** (France)
The regime established in France on 4 Sep 1870, which lasted until the National Assembly voted full powers to PÉTAIN on 10 July 1940; it remains by far the longest French regime since 1789.

**Republic, Fourth** (France)
The regime established unofficially in France in 1944 on the country's liberation; it was, however, only legally confirmed by the referendum of 13 Oct 1946, which approved the new constitution by a small majority. The republic was brought down by the Algerian crisis of 13 May 1958, which led, first, to de GAULLE being voted into office as the last Prime Minister of the Fourth Republic and, second, to its replacement by the Fifth Republic on 5 Oct 1958. ► REPUBLIC, FIFTH (France)

**Republic, Fifth** (France)
The regime established in France by the referendum of 28 Sep 1958, approving the new constitution embodying the political ideas of de GAULLE.

**Republican Party**
US political party. It was formed in 1854 by Northern anti-SLAVERY factions of the existing Whig and Democratic Parties who opposed the Fugitive Slave Act (1850) and the KANSAS–NEBRASKA ACT (1854). The party's presidential candidate, Abraham LINCOLN, won the 1860 election, precipitating secession and the AMERICAN CIVIL WAR. With the exception of four terms, the Republicans continued to hold the presidency until the GREAT DEPRESSION, which set the stage for the election of Franklin D ROOSEVELT in 1932 and 20 years of Democratic Presidents. Although the Republicans had espoused isolationism before WORLD WAR II, they won the 1952 presidential election with the popular war hero Dwight D EISENHOWER. The next 40 years saw a series of split governments on the national level, with the Republicans often winning the presidency while the Democrats held majorities in CONGRESS. The WATERGATE scandal, which led to the first resignation of an American President, Richard M NIXON, was a black mark for the party, but it regained the presidency with the election of Ronald REAGAN in 1980 and, apart from Bill CLINTON's two-term administration, held it for the rest of the 20c through the presidencies of George H W BUSH and his son George W BUSH. The party has traditionally been identified with big business rather than with labour, and favoured STATES' RIGHTS, limited government regulation, free-market economic policies, and (in the COLD WAR period that followed World War II) a strong military and firm anticommunistic stance. It has generally had the support of voters of high socio-economic status and of white Anglo-Saxons rather than of ethnic minorities. However, Ronald Reagan managed to broaden the party's

historical base, drawing in many so-called Reagan Democrats, who were disillusioned with the policies of Democratic President Jimmy CARTER, and including right-wing conservatives and religious fundamentalist groups as well. ► MUGWUMP; NATIONAL REPUBLICAN PARTY; PROGRESSIVE PARTY (USA); SECESSION, RIGHT OF

**Resistance Movement** (Belgium, Het Weerstand)
Clandestine opposition to the German occupation of Belgium during WORLD WAR II, which took on serious proportions after the severe winter of 1940–1. Aid was provided to escaped prisoners of war and to Allied airmen, and there was also a lively underground press. Alongside there were sabotage and guerrilla groups, ranging from right-wing nationalist to communist; the largest was the Independence Front, with its own armed units (Patriotic Militias). The government in exile in London provided financial help; the Belgian resistance made an important contribution to the country's liberation in 1944. ► RESISTANCE MOVEMENT (France); RESISTANCE MOVEMENT (Netherlands)

**Resistance Movement** (France)
There was very little active resistance for the first two years of the German occupation during WORLD WAR II, but it developed rapidly from the summer of 1942. A great number of different organizations existed, covering the whole range of political opinion from left to right, although after the German invasion of the USSR communist recruitment was especially high. De GAULLE sought to coordinate the different groups from London and then, after the Allied invasion of North Africa, from Algiers; his delegate, Jean Moulin, was able to bring them all together in the *Conseil national de la résistance* ('National Council of the Resistance') before being murdered by the Germans. As well as guerrilla warfare against the occupying forces, there was a large political dimension to the Resistance, and elaborate and idealistic programmes were drawn up; only some of these found any embodiment after 1944. ► RESISTANCE MOVEMENT (Belgium); RESISTANCE MOVEMENT (Netherlands)

**Resistance Movement** (Netherlands, Het Verzet)
Also known as the 'Illegality' and the 'Underground', most Dutch resistance to the German occupation during WORLD WAR II was clandestine. Only a few strikes, notably on the railways from Sep 1944, and limited actions by individual students, doctors and churchmen in particular, were public displays of resistance. The underground resistance was active, however, especially in producing and distributing newspapers, and looking after the several hundred thousand people, many of them Jewish, trying to evade the German authorities. Help was also provided for Allied airmen, and espionage work was carried out, though not always with success. Finance was provided by the National Support Fund (*Nationaal Steunfonds*). ► ENGLANDSPIEL; FRANK, ANNE; RESISTANCE MOVEMENT (Belgium); RESISTANCE MOVEMENT (France)

**Responsible Government**
A Canadian adaptation of British parliamentary practice. Developed by Robert BALDWIN, the doctrine held that the government of the Province of Canada

should be exercised by a ministry chosen from the elected representatives of the people, and that it should be replaced if defeated in the elective legislature. Recommended in the **DURHAM REPORT**, it was several years before its practical implications were fully understood, and not until 1848 with the Baldwin–**LAFONTAINE** ministry in Canada and the Uniacke ministry in Nova Scotia did it come into operation.

### Resquesens y Zúñiga, Luis de (1528–76)
Spanish soldier and political figure, and Regent of the Spanish Netherlands (1573/6). He was already a sick man when he succeeded the Duke of **ALBA** as regent; his military achievements in the Low Countries were few and the country's finances remained chaotic. He tried to follow a more conciliatory line than his predecessor, announcing a general pardon in 1574 (excluding heretics), and abolishing the Council of **BLOOD** and the hated **TENTH PENNY** tax. He died in Brussels; the lack of an immediate successor led to a general uprising against Spanish authority in the **EIGHTY YEARS' WAR**.

### Restitution, Edict of (29 Mar 1629)
The imperial edict promulgated by Emperor **FERDINAND II** during the **THIRTY YEARS' WAR**, which decreed that all ecclesiastical property confiscated since the Treaty of **PASSAU** in 1552 (including archbishoprics, bishoprics and monasteries) should be restored to those people who owned it in 1555. In this way, Ferdinand hoped to recover all the lands which had been lost to Protestantism in the intervening years. The edict also stipulated that only adherents of the **AUGSBURG CONFESSION** were to have free exercise of religion and that all other 'sects' were to be broken up. Habsburg and Wittelsbach nominees were imposed on many bishoprics, and the edict was enforced by **WALLENSTEIN'S** 100,000-strong army. After Wallenstein's dismissal, the edict was enforced less strenuously and was superseded, in 1635, by the Peace of Prague. ➤ **HABSBURG DYNASTY**

### Restitution Agreement (Sep 1952)
The settlement reached between representatives of the State of Israel and Chancellor **ADENAUER** of the Federal Republic of Germany. Signed in Luxembourg, the agreement committed Germany to make material reparations to Israel, deemed to represent the Jewish people, and to another Jewish body representing the Diaspora, for persecutions suffered by the Jews under the Third **REICH**. As a result, and despite some opposition in both Israel and Germany, large sums of money were paid out to Israel and to individual survivors of **WORLD WAR II** in subsequent years. ➤ **HOLOCAUST**; **ISRAEL**

### Restoration
The return of **CHARLES II** to England (May 1660) at the request of the Convention Parliament, following the collapse of the **PROTECTORATE** regime. Many royal prerogative powers and institutions were not restored. The bishops and the Church of England returned, but parliament took the lead in passing the **CLARENDON CODE** (1661–5) outlawing dissent from the Book of Common Prayer (1662).

### Restoration System (1875–1923)
Spanish political system. The rotation in power of the

two dynastic parties – the Liberal-Conservatives and the Liberals – through an institutionalized form of electoral corruption. Election results were fixed by the Minister of the Interior through the local party bosses (or *caciques*). This was known as the *turno pacífico* ('peaceful rotation'). Although it quelled the interventionism of the army and brought a measure of political stability, it effectively excluded the non-monarchical opposition from the political process. The system was dismantled by the dictatorship of **PRIMO DE RIVERA** in 1923, though the caciques continued to exercise considerable influence under the Second Republic. ➤ **REPUBLIC, SECOND** (Spain)

### Retief, Piet (1780–1838)
One of the leaders of the Boer Trek which left the Cape in the 1830s to escape British rule. In 1837 Retief, originally from Stellenbosch but later resident in Grahamstown, published an explanatory manifesto and left the colony with about one hundred followers. His manifesto indicated that the British had disrupted proper white–black, master–servant relations and offended the law of God. He entered the Transvaal, crossed the Drakensberg into Natal and was killed by **DINGANE**, King of the Zulu, in 1838 when attempting to negotiate a land concession. ➤ **GREAT TREK**

### Retz, Gilles de Laval, Baron (1404–40)
Breton nobleman. He fought by the side of **JOAN OF ARC** at Orléans, but soon retired to his estates, where for over ten years he is alleged to have indulged in satanism and the most infamous orgies. He was hanged and burnt at Nantes, after being tried and condemned for heresy.

### Retz, Jean François Paul de Gondi, Cardinal (1614–79)
French prelate. He plotted against **MAZARIN**, and exploited the **FRONDE** (1648) to further his own interests and the power of the Church. After transferring his allegiance between the rebel factions and the Crown, he was made a cardinal, though in 1652 he was imprisoned on **LOUIS XIV'S** personal orders. After making peace with Louis in 1662, he received the abbacy of St Denis. ➤ **RICHELIEU, CARDINAL**

### Reuter, Paul Julius Reuter, Baron von, originally Israel Beer Josaphat (1816–99)
British journalist. Born in Kassel, Germany, he was the founder of the first news agency. He changed his name to Reuter in 1844, and in Aachen in 1849 formed an organization for transmitting commercial news by telegraph and pigeon post. In 1851 he fixed his headquarters in London, and gradually his system spread to the remotest regions.

### Réveil
A revival movement in early 19c northern European Protestantism, especially in the Netherlands, but also in Switzerland and France, with strong literary connections and political influence. It was a reaction to the rationalizing effects of the **ENLIGHTENMENT** on religion, and as a deeply romantic movement it looked back in nostalgia to before the French revolutionary upheavals, and in the Dutch case to the Golden Age of the 17c. The theology was orthodox Calvinist, but with an emphasis on personal piety; much practical work was also achieved in education

and social work. Leading figures in the Netherlands included Willem Bilderdijk (1756–1831). The Réveil's orthodox Calvinist political legacy was enacted by GROEN VAN PRINSTERER (who became a member in 1830) and the ANTI-REVOLUTIONARY PARTY.

### Revels, Hiram Rhodes (1822–1901)
US politician and educator. Born in North Carolina, he was chaplain of a Union black regiment in the AMERICAN CIVIL WAR, and later settled in Mississippi and served in the state Senate. Elected to the US SENATE in 1869, he was the first black American to serve in that body. He founded a school for former slaves, and became President of Alcorn College, a newly formed state college for blacks.

### Reventlow, Christian Ditlev (1748–1827)
Danish civil servant. He was the driving force behind a number of agricultural reforms carried out by the Danish government during the last 13 years of the 18c. The aims of the reforms were to increase agricultural productivity and dampen a growing dissatisfaction among Danish peasants with the feudal conditions under which they lived, particularly with the considerable amount of day-labour they were obliged to provide for their feudal lord. In 1786 Reventlow influenced Denmark's *de facto* ruler, Crown Prince Frederick (later King FREDERICK VI), to set up the Great Agricultural Commission whose work (Jun 1788) led to the abolition of serfdom which had hitherto bound the peasant to the land of the lord. This reform, however, caused the break-up of the government, resulting in a more cautious, landowner-friendly reform policy during the 1790s.

### Revere, Paul (1735–1818)
US patriot. He served as a lieutenant of artillery in the FRENCH AND INDIAN WAR, then followed the trade of silversmith and copperplate printer. He was one of the party that destroyed the tea in Boston harbour, and was at the head of a secret society formed to watch the British. On 18 Apr 1775, the night before LEXINGTON AND CONCORD, Revere rode from Charleston to Lexington and Lincoln, rousing the MINUTEMEN as he went. His ride was immortalized in a poem by Longfellow. ► AMERICAN REVOLUTION; BOSTON TEA PARTY

### Revolutionary Party of Tanzania ► CHAMA CHA MAPINDUZI (CCM)

### Revolution of 1830 (Germany)
The overthrow of the Bourbon monarchy in France led to liberal and populist revolts in many parts of Germany. In a number of German states constitutions were renewed or granted, but the monarchies of the key German powers, PRUSSIA and Austria, were not challenged effectively, and in 1834 the Vienna Conference of Ministers restored monarchist rule in most of Germany. ► BOURBON, HOUSE OF; JULY REVOLUTION (1830)

### Revolution of 1848 (Germany)
Following the overthrow of the Orléanist monarchy in France, revolution broke out in most German states. By the end of Mar 1849, the monarchs, including those of PRUSSIA and Austria, had agreed to the formation of liberal-dominated constituent assemblies, while in Frankfurt-am-Main a German parlia-

ment sought to draft a national and liberal constitution for all Germany. By the end of 1849 the revolution had failed, however. The Austrian monarchy retained control of its army which, area by area, suppressed the revolution in the Habsburg lands. Non-German minorities and German radicals refused to accept Frankfurt's writ and, since the new parliament had insufficient military forces, it relied heavily on the monarchist Prussian army. A successful counter-revolution in Prussia and the refusal of the Prussian King, FREDERICK WILLIAM IV, to accept the German crown offered by Frankfurt therefore finished the revolution. The political self-confidence of the German middle classes was dealt a severe blow, but limited constitutional concessions by the German monarchs paved the way for the Prussian constitutional crisis of 1861 and, subsequently, German unification under BISMARCK. ► FEBRUARY REVOLUTION (France); HABSBURG DYNASTY; ORLÉANS, HOUSE OF

### Revolution of 1905
A series of nationwide strikes, demonstrations and mutinies in Russia, given added stimulus by the massacre by soldiers of workers demonstrating peacefully in St Petersburg on what came to be called 'BLOODY SUNDAY' (9 Jan 1905 new style). Faced with continuing popular unrest, Tsar NICHOLAS II was forced to make some marginal concessions, including the legalization of most political parties, and qualified elections to a form of national assembly, the DUMA. ► RUSSIAN REVOLUTION

### Revolution of 1918 (Germany)
In the hour of Germany's defeat in WORLD WAR I, attempts to preserve the monarchy failed in the face of growing civil disorder. On 9 Nov a republic was declared by the SPD leader SCHEIDEMANN and a provisional government of majority and independent socialists formed. Although the Workers' and Soldiers' Councils, which were established spontaneously at this time, bore a superficial resemblance to the Russian soviets, the former supported the principle of parliamentary government in Dec 1918 and a National Assembly met in Weimar on 19 Jan 1919 to draft a constitution. Controversy has raged over how far the Social Democrats were wise to restrict major socio-economic change and changes in non-parliamentary institutions (army, civil service, judiciary) at this point, as well as relying on monarchist and right-radical military forces to restrain the radical Left. The survival of many monarchist institutions and grandees was subsequently to weaken the WEIMAR REPUBLIC.

### Revolution of 1989 (Germany)
Once the Soviet government under Mikhail GORBACHEV had declared it would not intervene in the affairs of its Eastern European allies, the future of East Germany (German Democratic Republic) was in doubt. Militarily dependent on the USSR and economically dependent on the Federal Republic of Germany and the USSR, East Germany's economy and society were wracked by increasing difficulties. During the summer of 1989, East German tourists in Hungary spilled across the recently demilitarized border into Austria and also invaded Federal German embassies in Prague and Warsaw. As East Germany's

population haemorrhaged, widespread civil unrest broke out within the country and culminated in the storming of the **BERLIN WALL** on 9 Nov. The communist regime collapsed and unification with the Federal Republic of Germany followed in 1990.

### Revolutions of 1848-9

A succession of popular uprisings in various West and Central European countries during 1848–9, some fuelled by political and economic grievances against established governments, often inspired by liberal and socialist ideas, others by demands for national independence from foreign rule, as in the Italian states, Bohemia and Hungary. In Italy particularly, a growing distaste for Austrian rule in the Kingdom of **LOMBARDY-VENETIA** and for Habsburg hegemony elsewhere in the peninsula combined with incipient liberalism and nationalism and separatist and economic grievances to stimulate protest and revolt. The granting of concessions by many rulers simply served to encourage greater demands from the populace and briefly most Italian states fell under some form of constitutional or republican control. However, regional and ideological differences, the fear of the propertied classes of radical social change and the re-establishment of conservative governments in Paris and Vienna led to the suppression of revolt and the restoration of the old order in almost every state. Only in the Kingdom of **SARDINIA** was there any significant change, the **STATUTO** granted by **CHARLES ALBERT** being retained as the basis for constitutional government. In France the abdication of Louis Philippe was followed by the Second Republic and the socialist experiment of **NATIONAL WORK SHOPS**; liberal constitutions were granted in Austria and in many German states; Britain experienced Chartism. The revolutions collapsed from internal weakness or military suppression, and aroused reaction, but they presaged the ultimate triumph of nationalism, if not liberalism. ➤ **CHARTISTS**; **REPUBLIC, SECOND** (France)

### Rexism

Belgian fascist political movement, founded by Léon **DEGRELLE**, and named after his publishing firm. Rexism grew out of right-wing Roman Catholic circles in Walloon (French-speaking) Belgium in the 1930s. In 1936 the Rex Party contested the national elections, and gained several seats in both chambers. During the late 1930s the party became increasing fascist and authoritarian, and during **WORLD WAR II** collaborated fully with the Nazi occupation forces. By 1944 it had lost all its support.

### Reynaud, Paul (1878–1966)

French politician. Elected a Deputy in 1919, he sat as an independent on the centre-right, frequently holding office, notably as Finance Minister (1930 and 1938–40) and Colonial Minister (1931–2). During his second term as Finance Minister he instigated a remarkable recovery from the economic crisis in which France found herself after the **POPULAR FRONT** experiment. He was influenced by de **GAULLE**'s advocacy of armoured warfare, and opposed appeasement. His appointment as Prime Minister (Mar 1940) was seen as a move towards a more vigorous prosecution of the war, but he had achieved little before the German onslaught led to his fall and

replacement by **PÉTAIN**, who asked for an armistice, which Reynaud had refused to do. He was imprisoned by the Germans during the war, re-entering politics after 1944, but without regaining his former influence. ➤ **INDEPENDENTS** (France); **WORLD WAR II**

### Reynolds, Albert (1932–)

Irish politician. His early career was as an entrepreneur in the entertainment and food-manufacturing industries. He became **FIANNA FÁIL** MP for Longford-West Meath (1977) and was Minister for Industry and Commerce (1987–9) and Finance (1989–91). Dismissed after an unsuccessful challenge to Charles **HAUGHEY** (1991), he nevertheless won the party leadership by a large majority after Haughey's resignation (Feb 1992) and became Prime Minister (1992–4). In 1993 he entered into talks concerning the future of Northern Ireland with British Prime Minister John **MAJOR**. Reynolds resigned after the coalition between Fianna Fáil and Labour broke up in 1994, and was succeeded as party leader by Bertie Ahern.

### Rhee, Syngman (1875–1965)

Korean politician. Imprisoned (1897–1904) for his part in an independence campaign, he later went to the USA, returning to Japanese-annexed Korea in 1910. After the unsuccessful rising of 1919, he became President of the exiled Korean Provisional Government. On Japan's surrender (1945) he returned to become the first elected President of South Korea (1948). Re-elected for a fourth term (1960), he was obliged to resign after only one month, following major riots and the resignation of his cabinet. He died, in exile, in Honolulu.

### Rhenish Federation (Rheinbund)

The Federation was established (1658) to preserve the Peace of **WESTPHALIA** (1648). Headed by Johann Philip von Schönborn, Elector of Mainz, the Federation was generally supportive of France and included both Catholic and Protestant princes.

### Rhenish League (1254–7)

A league of Rhineland towns which began in Mainz and Worms. After two years it included over 70 cities from Lübeck in the north to Zurich in the south. Many lay and ecclesiastical princes also joined. Its founder and administrator was Wolpode Arnold (d.1268). The purpose of the league was to secure law and order in the face of the breakdown of central power and to protect property, commerce, trade and the rights of the estates. It was recognized by **WILLIAM, COUNT OF HOLLAND** in 1255 but foundered on differences between its members caused by the disputed elections of 1257. ➤ **INTERREGNUM**

### Rhense, Electoral Assembly at (1338)

A meeting of the **ELECTORS** to discuss Emperor **LOUIS IV**'s conflict with the papacy. They formed an alliance for the defence of the empire, the first instance of the Electors acting together politically other than when electing the king. At the same time, they declared it was a traditional right that whoever was elected by the Electors was entitled to call himself King and to rule the empire, and that papal approval was not necessary.

## Rhineland

German territory largely to the west of the River Rhine, demilitarized and occupied by the victorious Allies from 10 Jan 1920. Governed by an Inter-Allied High Commission based in Koblenz, a customs frontier was established between the Rhineland and the rest of Germany. French attempts to establish a separate Rhine Republic failed and the occupation forces withdrew between 1926 and 1930. In Mar 1936 **HITLER** violated the area's demilitarized status (Treaty of **VERSAILLES; LOCARNO PACT**) when troops were ordered back into the territory.

## Rhodes, Cecil John (1853–1902)

South African politician. After studying in Oxford, he entered the Cape House of Assembly, securing Bechuanaland as a protectorate (1885) and the charter for the **BRITISH SOUTH AFRICA COMPANY** (1889), whose territory was later to be named after him, as Rhodesia. In 1890 he became Prime Minister of Cape Colony, but was forced to resign in 1896 because of complications arising from the **JAMESON RAID**. He was a conspicuous figure during the second Boer War of 1899–1902, when he organized the defences during the Siege of **KIMBERLEY**. He died at Muizenberg, Cape Colony, and in his will founded scholarships at Oxford for Americans, Germans and colonials ('Rhodes scholars'). ➤ **BOER WARS**

## Rhodesia Crisis

The series of events that began with the declaration by Prime Minister Ian **SMITH** of a Unilateral Declaration of Independence (11 Nov 1965), following the Rhodesian government's failure to agree with successive British administrations on a constitutional independence settlement that ensured the continuance of white supremacy. The British Government was successful in gaining **UN** support for sanctions while ruling out the use of force and, in 1966 and 1968, Smith engaged with Prime Minister Harold **WILSON** in (ultimately unsuccessful) attempts to resolve the crisis. An agreement was reached with Edward **HEATH**'s Conservative Government in 1971, but was ruled out after an independent fact-finding mission determined that it would be unacceptable to the black majority. The growing influence of the **ANC** (African National Congress), and the withdrawal of the Portuguese from Angola and Mozambique, served to remind Smith of his isolation, and in 1977 he announced that he was willing to enter into new talks on a one-man, one-vote basis, and released nationalist leaders Ndabaningi **SITHOLE** and Joshua **NKOMO** as a sign of good faith. However, they initially refused to participate in negotiations, and the escalation of terrorist activities continued unabated despite Smith having attained in 1978 an internal settlement, thus providing for multiracial government, with the moderate Sithole and Bishop Abel **MUZOREWA**. The return of a Conservative government in the UK in 1979 provided the springboard for fresh talks and a new settlement, leading to elections in 1980 that were won by the former Marxist guerrilla leader Robert **MUGABE**.

## Rhodesian Front (RF)

The Rhodesian political party formed in 1962 to oppose the relatively liberal United Federal Party, with Winston Field as its leader. Ian **SMITH** replaced him in a putsch in 1964 and led Rhodesia to its **UDI** (Unilateral Declaration of Independence). The RF, which gained a majority of seats in the 1962 general election, made a clean sweep of all contested seats thereafter and sought to preserve white political and economic dominance in the country. In 1977, however, under pressure of civil war and outside influence, it accepted the principle of universal adult suffrage and attempted to devise an 'internal settlement'. At independence in 1980, it changed its name to Republican Front and soon afterwards to Conservative Alliance of Zimbabwe.

## Ribbentrop, Joachim von (1893–1946)

German Nazi politician. He became a member of the **NAZI PARTY** in 1932, and as **HITLER**'s adviser in foreign affairs, was responsible in 1935 for the Anglo-German naval pact. He became Ambassador to Britain (1936) and Foreign Minister (1938–45). Captured by the British in 1945, he was condemned and executed at the **NUREMBERG TRIALS**. ➤ **WORLD WAR II**

## Ribot, Alexandre (1842–1923)

French politician. A member of parliament from 1878 to 1923, he was a quintessential moderate republican, opposed to excesses of either right or left. In a very long political career, he occupied high office on several crucial occasions, notably as Prime Minister (1892–3, 1895, 1914 and 1917), Minister of Foreign Affairs (1890–3, when he was largely responsible for the Franco-Russian alliance, and 1917, at a very difficult period of **WORLD WAR I**), and as Minister of Finance (1895 and 1914–17).

## Ricasoli, Bettino, Baron (1809–80)

Italian politician. A Tuscan aristocrat who participated in the national movement of 1848, he became the leader of the Tuscan moderates. He accepted **CAVOUR**'s vision of Italian unity and played a large part in smoothing the process of Tuscan annexation by **VICTOR EMMANUEL II**. He was elected a deputy in the new Italian parliament and became Prime Minister on Cavour's death (1861–2), holding the office again five years later (1866–7). As Prime Minister for the second time, he wanted to continue the war against Austria but was forced to consent to peace.

## Ricci, Matteo (1552–1610)

Italian founder of the Jesuit missions in China. He studied in Rome, then travelled to India, where he was ordained (1580), and went on to China in 1582. He so mastered Chinese as to write works which received much commendation from the Chinese literati, and met with great success as a missionary. He died in China.

## Richard, Cœur de Lion ➤ RICHARD I, THE LIONHEART

## Richard I, the Lionheart (1157–99)

King of England (1189/99). Known also as Richard, Cœur de Lion, he was the third son of **HENRY II** of England and **ELEANOR OF AQUITAINE**. Of his ten-year reign, he spent only five months in England, devoting himself to crusading and defending the Angevin lands in France. Already recognized as an outstanding soldier, he took Messina (1190), Cyprus and Acre (1191) during the Third **CRUSADE**, and advanced to within sight of Jerusalem. On the return journey, he was arrested at Vienna (1192), and remained a prisoner of the German Emperor **HENRY VI** until he agreed to be ransomed (1194). The rest of his reign was occupied in warfare against **PHILIP II** of France, while the government of England was conducted by the justiciar Hubert **WALTER**. Richard was mortally wounded while besieging the castle of Châlus, Aquitaine. ➤ **ANGEVINS**

### Richard II (1367–1400)

King of England (1377/99). He was the younger son of **EDWARD, THE BLACK PRINCE**, and succeeded his grandfather, **EDWARD III** of England, at the age of ten. He displayed great bravery in confronting the rebels in London during the **PEASANTS' REVOLT** (1381), but already parliament was concerned about his favourites, and the reign was dominated by the struggle between Richard's desire to act independently and the magnates' concern to curb his power. He quarrelled with his uncle, **JOHN OF GAUNT**, and his main supporters were found guilty of treason in the 'Merciless Parliament' of 1388. After Richard had declared an end to his minority in 1389, he built up a stronger following, and in 1397–8 took his revenge by having the Earl of Arundel executed, the Duke of Gloucester murdered, and several lords banished, the exiles including Gaunt's son, Henry Bolingbroke (later **HENRY IV** of England). His final act of oppression was to confiscate the Lancastrian estates after Gaunt's death (1399). Having failed to restrain the King by constitutional means, the magnates resolved to unseat him from the throne. Bolingbroke invaded England unopposed, and Richard was deposed in his favour (Sep 1399). He died in Pontefract Castle, Yorkshire, possibly of starvation. ➤ **LANCASTER, HOUSE OF**

### Richard III (1452–85)

King of England (1483/5). He was the youngest son of Richard, Duke of York. Created Duke of Gloucester by his brother, **EDWARD IV**, in 1461, he accompanied him into exile (1470), and played a key role in his restoration (1471). Rewarded with part of the Neville inheritance, he exercised viceregal powers in northern England, and in 1482 recaptured Berwick-upon-Tweed from the Scots. When Edward died (1483) and was succeeded by his under-age son **EDWARD V**, Richard acted first as protector; but within three months, he had overthrown the Woodvilles (relations of Edward IV's Queen, Elizabeth Woodville), seen to the execution of Lord Hastings, and had himself proclaimed and crowned as the rightful King. Young Edward and his brother Richard were probably murdered in the Tower on Richard's orders. He tried to stabilize his position, but failed to win broad-based support. His rival, Henry Tudor (later **HENRY VII**), confronted him in battle at **BOSWORTH FIELD**, and Richard died fighting bravely against heavy odds. Though ruthless, he was not the absolute monster Tudor historians portrayed him to be. Nor is there proof he was a hunchback.

### Richelieu, Armand Jean du Plessis, Cardinal and Duke of (1585–1642)

French politician. A protégé of the Queen Mother **MARIE DE' MEDICI**, he became Minister of State in 1624 and, as Chief Minister, was the effective ruler of France from then until 1642. His chief adviser and agent between 1624 and 1630 was a Capuchin friar,

François Joseph de Tremblay, known as Père **JOSEPH** and nicknamed *L'Éminence Grise*. Richelieu's twin aims – to secure obedience to the Bourbon monarchy within France and enhance French prestige abroad – were achieved at the expense of recalcitrant groups in French society. His principal achievement was to check Habsburg power, ultimately by sending armies into the Spanish Netherlands, Alsace, Lorraine and Roussillon. ➤ **BOURBON, HOUSE OF**; **HABSBURG DYNASTY**; **LOUIS XIII**

### Ridgway, Matthew B(unker) (1895–1993)

US general. Educated at the US Military Academy at West Point, he commanded the 82nd Airborne Division in Sicily (1943) and Normandy (1944). He commanded the 18th Airborne Corps in the North-West Europe campaign (1944–5) and the US 8th Army in **UN** operations in Korea (1950). He succeeded Douglas **MACARTHUR** in command of US and UN forces (1951), and was supreme allied commander Europe in succession to **EISENHOWER** (1952–3) and Army Chief of Staff (1953). He received the Presidential Medal of Freedom in 1986.

### Ridley, Nicholas (c.1500–1555)

English Protestant martyr. He was ordained c.1524, and studied in Paris and Louvain (1527–30). He then held a variety of posts, including chaplain to Thomas **CRANMER** and **HENRY VIII**, and Bishop of Rochester (1547). An ardent reformer, he became Bishop of London (1550), and helped Cranmer prepare the Thirty-Nine Articles. On the death of **EDWARD VI** he espoused the cause of Lady Jane **GREY**, was imprisoned, and executed at Oxford. ➤ **REFORMATION** (England)

### Rieger, František Ladislav (1818–1903)

Czech politician. A lawyer by training and son-in-law of František **PALACKÝ**, he took part in the unsuccessful constituent assembly in 1848–9 and had to lie low in the 1850s. But he re-emerged in 1861 in alliance with the provincial nobility to demand the restoration of the old Czech state. The Emperor **FRANCIS JOSEPH** would not yield and Rieger led his so-called Old Czech Party into a policy of abstention which was also unsuccessful except as a backdrop to the first great popular outburst of national feeling. By the late 1870s abstention was clearly discredited and Rieger joined the return to the Czech estates and the imperial parliament. Among concessions won in 1881 was the division of the Charles University, Prague, into two, a small German and a much larger Czech. Thereafter, Rieger's influence declined and the Young Czech Party and other new parties took over.

### Riel, Louis (1844–85)

Canadian politician. The leader of the **MÉTIS** during both the **RED RIVER REBELLION** and **NORTH-WEST REBELLION**, he fled to the USA when the federal government sent a military force into the Red River settlement in 1870. He returned to live there quietly, although Ontario Orangemen had offered a reward for his capture as the murderer of Thomas Scott. He was still regarded by French-speaking Canadians as a hero. When the USA threatened Manitoba with another of the **FENIAN RAIDS** in 1871, he mustered a *métis* cavalry force in defence and received public (though anonymous) thanks from the governor.

John A **MACDONALD** provided him with funds in the hope that he might return to exile, but in 1873 he was elected to the House of Commons in Ottawa. After his re-election in 1874, a motion was introduced by Mackenzie **BOWELL** demanding his expulsion from the House. He was finally granted amnesty in 1875 on condition of a further five years' exile. By this time he had suffered a nervous breakdown and was detained in a mental asylum in Quebec. In 1878 he had recovered sufficiently to leave for the USA where he became a schoolteacher. In 1884 Riel responded to the pleas of the métis in Saskatchewan and so became involved in his second rebellion. However, he provoked opposition by his religious manias, while his claims against the government for C\$35,000 also gave his motivation a mercenary cast. When he surrendered he was charged with treason, but he refused to let his defence counsel enter a plea of insanity. With a verdict of guilty the jury also recommended clemency, but after several reprieves and an assessment of his sanity, he was hanged. His body was interred in front of St Boniface Cathedral. French-Canadian outrage at his execution helped Honoré **MERCIER** to gain power in 1886.

### Rienzi or Rienzo, Cola di (1313–54)
Italian patriot. In 1347 he incited the citizens of Rome to rise against the rule of the nobles. The senators were driven out, and he was made tribune. Papal authority then turned against him, and he fled from Rome. He returned in 1354, and tried to re-establish his position, but was killed in a rising against him. Wagner's opera on his story was completed in 1840.

### Rif or Riff
A cluster of Berber agricultural and herding groups of north-east Morocco. Famed as warriors, in the 1920s they defeated the Spanish, but were eventually conquered by combined French and Spanish forces in 1926. They later served in the French and Spanish regiments in Morocco. ► **ABD AL-KRIM, MUHAMMAD**; **BERBERS**

### Rigas, Velestinlis Pheraios (1757–98)
Greek national hero, writer and revolutionary. Well-educated, he worked for the **PHANARIOTS** in Constantinople and the Danubian Principalities. Inspired by the ideals of the **ENLIGHTENMENT** and the **FRENCH REVOLUTION**, he translated various French works into vernacular Greek and wrote many revolutionary pamphlets. In Vienna in 1796 he began publishing revolutionary literature, including the *Declaration of the Rights of Man*, and he issued a map of the Balkan Peninsula and Asia Minor that anticipated the Greater Greece of the **MEGALE IDEA**. He drew up proposals for a Greek constitution and composed the *War Hymn* for which he is now best remembered. Involved in many conspiracies, he was arrested by the Austrian government, handed over to the Ottoman authorities and executed. ► **MOLDAVIA AND WALLACHIA**

### Rijeka ► FIUME

### Rijswijk, Treaty of (1697)
A settlement ending the Nine Years' War or the War of the League of **AUGSBURG** (1688–97), mediated by Sweden, between plenipotentiaries of **LOUIS XIV** of France on the one hand, and on the other **CHARLES II** of Spain, **WILLIAM III** of Britain (also representing the Netherlands), and the Emperor **LEOPOLD I**. Although the treaty ostensibly checked French expansionism, peace was short-lived; it freed Louis XIV to concentrate on the War of the **SPANISH SUCCESSION**.

### Rio de Janeiro Treaty (1947)
The Inter-American Treaty of Reciprocal Assistance, signed in Rio, which enshrines principles of hemispheric defence laid down during **WORLD WAR II**, especially a US–Brazilian alliance. It provides for certain types of mutual assistance in the case of an armed attack on any American state from outside the region and for mutual consultation in the event of any aggression between them or warlike action affecting territories situated outside them. It was the first permanent collective defence treaty signed by the USA and has remained the cornerstone of its military commitment to Latin America and the institutional basis for its hegemony. It has been applied on 16 occasions since 1948, in all cases to long-standing inter-American disputes, and to incidents within the Caribbean and Central American regions. It was not, however, invoked during the Falklands/Malvinas conflict. Directed mainly against Cuba, Latin American diplomats have argued that it has disguised, but not modified, the extent of US hegemony in Latin America. Since the break-up of the USSR, its purpose has become more questionable. ► **FALKLANDS WAR**

### Riom Trial (1942)
The trial by the **VICHY** regime of General **GAMELIN** and the leading figures of France's pre-war governments, notably **BLUM** and **DALADIER**, held responsible for the defeat of 1940; it was abandoned when it proved embarrassing for the military and for many who were in positions of authority under Vichy, but the defendants remained imprisoned, and were later handed over to the Germans. ► **WORLD WAR II**

### Riot Act
Legislation in Britain concerned to preserve public order, first passed at the beginning of the Hanoverian era in 1714. When 12 or more people were unlawfully assembled and refused to disperse, they were, after the reading of a section of this Act by a person in authority, immediately considered felons having committed a serious crime.

### Ripka, Hubert (1895–1958)
Czechoslovak journalist and politician. Prominent in the National Socialist Party (totally different from **HITLER**'s of the same name), he was given a place in **BENEŠ**'s government in exile during **WORLD WAR II**. Returning to Czechoslovakia in 1945, he became Minister of Foreign Trade until Feb 1948 when he joined the group of democratic politicians who tried to force an election by resigning. Since they constituted a minority, the **FEBRUARY REVOLUTION** went the other way. Ripka found himself, like others, forced once again to flee abroad.

### Rishon Massacre (Mar 1991)
The murder, at a labour market in Rishon le Zion, of seven Arab workmen from the **GAZA STRIP** by a 22-year-old Israeli, Ami Popper, served to refocus political attention on the conditions of Palestinians under Israeli occupation after the distraction of the 1991 **GULF WAR**.

## Rising in the North (1569–70)

A rebellion (sometimes known as the 'Rebellion of the Northern Earls') against **ELIZABETH I** by the Earls of Northumberland and Westmoreland. It was motivated by strong support for Catholicism in the north of England and precipitated by the arrival of **MARY, QUEEN OF SCOTS** in England (1568). A general rising was aborted when the Duke of Norfolk refused to lead it and the northern rising, beginning in Nov 1569 and centring on Durham, was confused and aimless, collapsing by Feb 1570. Westmoreland fled to the Netherlands but Northumberland was captured in Scotland and executed (1572). Despite its outcome, the rising demonstrated the limited impact of the Reformation in northern England. ► **REFORMATION** (England)

## Risorgimento

The Italian term (literally, 'resurgence') applied to the 19c movement by which Italy achieved unity. Although its origins lay in the administrative reforms and **ENLIGHTENMENT** ideas of the 18c and the Napoleonic period, it is usually held to have started properly in the decades after the Congress of **VIENNA** (1814–15). In its early stages it is associated with the insurrections of 1820–1 and the early 1830s, and the **REVOLUTIONS OF 1848–9**, as well as with the growing nationalist and anti-Austrian feelings expressed by thinkers such as **MAZZINI** and the more moderate **GIOBERTI**. After the failure of the popular revolts of the 1848–9 period, the *Risorgimento* came to fruition with the wars of unification (1859–70) and the creation of a single state under **VICTOR EMMANUEL II**. Since the 19c many historians have mythologized the Risorgimento, stressing the wide support for unification and ignoring both the excesses perpetrated in the name of the new Italian state and the complete absence of nationalist feeling among much of the population. ► **CAVOUR, CAMILLO; CHARLES ALBERT; GARIBALDI, GIUSEPPE; GRANDE BRIGANTAGGIO; MAZZINI, GIUSEPPE; THOUSAND, EXPEDITION OF THE; YOUNG ITALY**

## Ristić, Jovan (1831–99)

Serbian politician. In charge of Serbia's foreign policy at the outbreak of the Bosnian revolt (1875–8), he was briefly out of office but returned in 1876 to lead the government, which took Serbia into war against the Ottoman Porte in support of the Bosnians. The Serb army was all but destroyed and the Treaty of **SAN STEFANO** (1878), which established Bulgaria, shocked the Serbs, marking as it did the end of Russian support for Serbia. Still head of the Liberal government, Ristić set about the reconstruction of Serbia's diplomatic relations. He turned to the Habsburg government and later in 1878 concluded an agreement which secured Vienna's support in return for favourable trading arrangements. When Vienna tried to dictate terms for the extension of Serbia's railways, Ristić became disillusioned with the Serb–Habsburg concord and resigned (Oct 1880). ► **OBRENOVIĆ, MILAN**

## Rites Controversy

The dispute between the Vatican and the **QING DYNASTY** between 1693 and 1705 over interpretation of Chinese rites to honour Confucius and family ancestors. The Jesuits, who had begun to enter China at the end of the 16c and who were anxious to gain the support of the Chinese **MANDARINS**, adopted a tolerant approach to indigenous elements of Chinese culture, insisting that the rites were social ceremonies of respect rather than acts of idolatrous worship. Their approach was criticized as too lax by Jesuit leaders in Europe and other Catholic missionaries (Dominicans, Franciscans) in China. In 1704 the papacy decided in favour of the Jesuits' opponents, insisting that the rites had to be condemned. The papacy's attempt to enforce this decision in China was viewed as unwarranted interference by the Qing Emperor **KANGXI**, who reversed his previous policy of toleration towards missionaries. Under his successor, Yongzheng (1722/35), Christianity was formally proscribed.

## Rivadavia, Bernardino (1780–1845)

Argentine politician. A well-read **PORTEÑO**, he fought in the patriot militia that evicted the British in 1807. He supported the independence movement from Spain in 1810 and dominated the first revolutionary triumvirate in 1811. Rivadavia was greatly influenced by the reforms of **CHARLES III** of Spain (which created the **INTENDENTES**) and by the French radicals, and was a convinced Benthamite. Once in power, a torrent of legislation decreed the end of the **AUDIENCIA** and the slave trade, liberalized commerce and standardized the currency. When he returned to Argentina in 1821, after several years in Europe, he became a minister and propounded schemes to encourage immigration, abolished ecclesiastical privileges (*fueros*) and founded the University of Buenos Aires. His land law of 1874 established the system of landholding that has prevailed to the present, and encouraged large amounts of public land to fall into the hands of the few able to rent them; by 1827 over 6,500,000 acres/2,630,000 hectares had been rented to 112 corporations. Elected President in 1826, he was forced to resign in the wake of the inconclusive conflict with Brazil and provincial reaction to his centralist constitution. He was exiled to Paris, where he died. ► **ARGENTINE-BRAZILIAN WAR; FUERO**

## Rivas, Angel de Saavedra, Duke of (1791–1865)

Spanish politician and writer. Educated in Madrid, he served in the Civil War. He lived in exile (1823–34), became Minister of the Interior in 1835, and was soon exiled again. In 1837 he returned, became Prime Minister, and later was ambassador in Naples, Paris (1856) and Florence (1860).

## Rivera, José Fructuoso (c.1788–1854)

Uruguayan general and politician. He served under José **ARTIGAS** and was among his '33 *orientales*' who freed Uruguay. He served as the country's first President (1830–5), and was succeeded by Manuel Oribe, whom he at first supported but then overthrew (1838), and became President again until 1842. From 1843 to 1851 civil war erupted between his followers, the Colorado Party, who were based in Montevideo and were supported first by France and England and then by Brazil, and Oribe's followers, the Blanco Party, who controlled the interior and were supported by Argentine forces. Eventually defeated by the Argentine General Justo José de **URQUIZA** at the Battle of Inida Muerta (1845), Rivera fled to Brazil. He was appointed co-administrator of a provisional government in 1853 but died the next year.

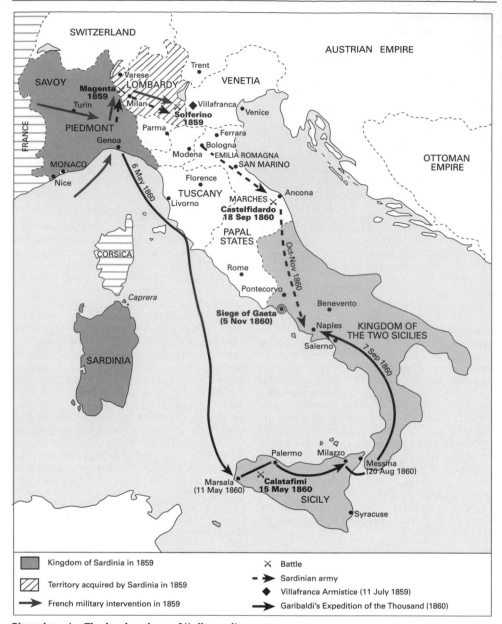

**Risorgimento: The beginnnings of Italian unity**

### Rizal, José (1861–96)

Filipino patriot and writer. He studied medicine in Madrid. He went on to publish political novels, *Noli me tangere* (1886) and *El Filibusterismo* (1891), which had a strong anti-Spanish tone. On his return to the Philippines, he was exiled to Mindanao. He returned to Manila just as an anti-Spanish revolt was erupting. Accused of instigating it, he was publicly shot.

### Rizzio, David (c.1533–1566)

Italian courtier and musician. He entered the service of **MARY, QUEEN OF SCOTS** in 1561, and rapidly becoming her favourite, was appointed Private Foreign Secretary in 1564. He negotiated Mary's marriage (1565) with **DARNLEY**, with whom he was at first on friendly terms, but the Queen's husband soon became jealous of his influence over Mary and of his

strong political power, and entered with other nobles into a plot to kill him. Rizzio was dragged from the Queen's presence and brutally murdered at the palace of Holyrood.

### roadmap peace plan

A plan to resolve the Israel–Palestine conflict proposed by the 'Middle East quartet' of the USA, Russia, the **EU** and the **UN**. The principles were announced by President George W **BUSH** in 2002. The three phases, each with a projected implementation date, included the end of violence and creation of an independent Palestinian state (2003), peace agreements between Israel and Arab states, and the resolution of issues not covered by the **OSLO ACCORDS** (2004-5). Implementation stalled because of the US and Israeli refusal to negotiate with Yasser **ARAFAT**, the continuing

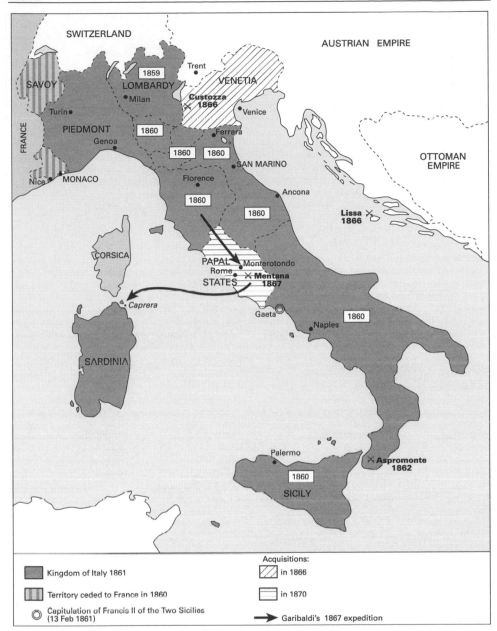

Risorgimento: Italy, 1860–70

Map legend:

Kingdom of Italy 1861

Territory ceded to France in 1860

Capitulation of Francis II of the Two Sicilies (13 Feb 1861)

Acquisitions:

in 1866

in 1870

Garibaldi's 1867 expedition

**Risorgimento: Italy, 1860–70**

**INTIFADA** and the opposition of key players to the **IRAQ WAR**. But the Israeli parliament's vote in Oct 2004 to withdraw most Jewish settlements from the **GAZA STRIP** and the death of Yasser Arafat in Nov 2004 led to a revival of talks about the plan's implementation.

**Roads** ► *See panel*

**Roanoke** (North Carolina)
The site of Sir Walter **RALEIGH**'s two attempts to found an English colony in North America. The first, in 1585, ended after trouble with the island's native inhabitants and the threat of an attack from Spanish forces. The second, an expedition of 117 men, women and children in 1587, had disappeared without trace by 1591 when a relief force found the town of

'Ralegh' deserted. The failures demonstrated that colonization was too expensive an enterprise for one individual to support, even with the monarch's blessing; and that settlements had to be defensible, Roanoke being an exposed island without a good harbour.

**'Robber Barons'**
US political epithet. First applied to railroad magnates like Jay Gould and Jim Fisk who exploited both national and local government, shareholders and the public in their ruthless operations, it was later extended to those like Cornelius **VANDERBILT**, Andrew **CARNEGIE** and John D **ROCKEFELLER** who developed large-scale enterprises by coercive horizontal and vertical integration.

# Roads

Transport & Travel

### Early roads

The earliest roads probably developed as soon as human beings began to
live in settled communities, established any kind of routine in their
existence, and needed to communicate with each other. The earliest long-distance roads in northern Europe tended to
run along high ground – like the Fosse Way, Icknield Way and Ridgeway in the UK – partly in order to avoid marshy
ground. Where bogs had to be traversed, trackways were constructed out of transverse logs laid on longitudinal logs or
beds of brushwood. A system of such trackways discovered in the Somerset levels in south-western England dates from
around 2500 BC.

Early civilizations usually had at least one royal road to carry communications from the capital to outlying areas. The
Persian Royal Road, which came into existence c.3000–300 BC, ran from the capital Susa, near the Persian Gulf, via
Nineveh and Ankara to reach the Mediterranean at Ephesus and Smyrna, a distance (from Susa to Smyrna) of 1,775 mi/
2,857 km. It had many staging posts and a messenger was said to be able to reach Ephesus from Susa in nine days. The
Inca Royal Road, built in the 15c, ran along the slopes of the Andes for a total distance of 3,250 mi/5,200 km. Though
paved only at the entrances to towns, the road was expertly surveyed and engineered, with retaining walls, drainage,
stairways cut into mountain sides, and rope bridges across gorges. The Incas did not have the wheel or use horses;
trained runners operating in relays carried messages and took five days to travel from Cuzco, the capital, to Quito,
approximately 1,250mi/2,000km away.

### Early paved roads

It is generally accepted that the invention of the wheel, somewhere around 3000 BC, first made necessary the
construction of roads overlaid with a hard surface. Wheeled vehicles tend to break up the surface of earthen tracks worn
by the feet of people and animals. The cities of the Indus Valley civilization, flourishing c.3000–1000 BC, had brick-
paved streets. Processional highways leading between temples and palaces in the ancient cities of Nineveh and Babylon
were paved with cut stone, as were the stairways that took the imperial roads of China across mountainous regions. It can
be safely assumed that all early civilizations provided a hardened surface for some city thoroughfares and some sections
of longer roads. The 1c BC Greek historian Diodorus relates that the Persian road between Susa and Ecbatana, some 200
mi/320 km long, was paved. The first civilization that constructed metalled roads on a large scale and as a matter of
policy, however, was that of the Roman Empire.

### Roman roads

The total distance of the roads constructed by Romans has been estimated at 53,000 mi/85,000 km. At its fullest extent
the Roman network covered the whole empire, circling the Mediterranean and extending deep into Asia and northwards
across Europe and Britain. Roman roads were not constructed to an absolutely standard pattern, but were adapted to
local conditions. A classic Roman road, however, was built above ground level with a cambered surface and drainage
ditches on either side. It had a compacted earth footing, a foundation layer, often of heavy stones, a rubble layer, and
surface layer of fitted stone blocks. Roman roads tended to be straight, the surveyors marking out a straight line between
one high point and the next. The first such road to be built was the Appian Way linking Rome and Capua, constructed in
312 BC on the initiative of the Censor Appius Claudius. First the Republic, and then the Empire, extended the network.
The Romans fully appreciated the advantages of well-made roads and the good communications that the roads
provided, not only for military purposes, but for purposes of general administration and trade, and for giving a sense of
cohesion to the Empire as a whole. The central government could rely on urgent messages carried by the imperial post
travelling 100 mi/160 km a day. A traveller under the late Roman Empire could make the entire journey from York in
northern England to Jerusalem on good, safe roads – something that was not possible again until the 20c.

### The Dark Age of roads

After the break-up of the Roman Empire, over 1,000 years were to elapse before any serious attempt was made to emulate
the Romans' achievements in Europe. During the intervening centuries, efforts were mainly directed at keeping the
roads in a state that was just about usable. They were dusty and rutted in summer, muddy quagmires in winter, and beset
with robbers at all times of the year. The Romans entrusted the maintenance of roads to local communities, and
possessed a central authority with the power to ensure that the necessary work was carried out. Later states lacked the
will or the power to do the same, nor did they have the Romans' technical expertise.

Attempts were made by French administrations of the 17c to use local forced labour to build and maintain roads, with
limited success. From 1633 the turnpike system was introduced into England under which private trusts were
authorized to maintain sections of road and charge tolls on people who used them. Eventually some 20,000 mi/32,000

---

**Robert II** (1316–90)
King of Scots (1371/90). He was the son of Walter,
hereditary Steward of Scotland. Robert acted as sole
regent during the exile and captivity of **DAVID II**; on
the latter's death, he became King by right of his descent from his maternal grandfather, Robert **BRUCE**,
and founded the Stuart royal dynasty. ► **STUART,
HOUSE OF**

**Robert III** (c.1340–1406)
King of Scots (1390/1406). The eldest son of **ROBERT
II** by his first marriage, during his reign the issue of
guardianship dominated politics as he was a perma-

nent invalid, the result of a kick from a horse. The
main contenders were his brother, Robert, Duke of
Albany (c.1340–1420), and his elder son, David,
Duke of Rothesay (c.1378–1402). Rothesay's fall
(1402), imprisonment and subsequent death at Falkland Castle brought Albany to an unrivalled position
of power, which was further increased by the imprisonment in England of many Scots nobles captured
at Homildon Hill (1402). Robert, anxious for the
safety of his younger son, James (the future **JAMES I**),
sent him to France, but Robert died shortly after news
arrived of James's capture by the English.

km of British roads were administered by turnpike trusts, resulting in considerable improvements and the development, towards the end of the 18c, of a fairly fast and reliable mail-coach service. Nevertheless, the increase in the movement of goods generated by the **Industrial Revolution** stimulated a flurry of canal-building rather than road-building. And when the poet John Keats travelled from London to Exeter by the regular coach in 1818, the journey still took 27 hours, and when he fell ill on a tour of Scotland later in the same year and needed to return home to London from Edinburgh as quickly as possible, he went by sea.

### Roads revived

The science of road engineering was effectively revived in France in the early years of the 18c. The *Corps de Ponts et Chaussées* ('Department of Bridges and Roadways') was established in 1716, and in 1747 it opened its own civil engineering school. The first major road-builder of the modern age was Pierre Trésaguet, who became Inspector-General of the *Corps de Ponts et Chaussées* in 1775, having previously been the chief civil engineer in Limoges. Trésaguet insisted on proper drainage and built his roads on a base layer of heavy stones topped by layers of progressively smaller stones. Two Scottish civil engineers, Thomas Telford and John McAdam, carried Trésaguet's work further in Britain in the late 18c and early 19c. Telford, like his French predecessor, favoured a deep excavation and heavy stone base. McAdam relied on a bed of compacted soil to bear the weight of the carriageway, considerably cutting costs. All three relied on the metal tyres of horse-drawn vehicles to crush the small stones of the top layer of the road into a smooth hard surface.

### The automobile age

Even on good new roads, however, there were no vehicles that could match the speed of trains, the main mode of transport for goods and passengers during the 19c. Agitation for further improvements to roads came at the end of the century – at first from the cycling lobby. With the invention of the internal-combustion engine and the gradual growth of motorized transport, there was further pressure for the road network to be extended and improved. The rubber tyres of motor cars, instead of crushing and compacting the small-stone top layer of a McAdam-type road, tended to lift and disperse them. Roads for motor traffic consequently had to be made of concrete or of stones bound together with tar (the Tarmacadam process).

The modern road system gradually took shape in the course of the 20c. New York adopted a traffic code in 1903. **Mussolini** built the first fast roads especially designed for motor traffic, and the first *autostrada* opened in 1924. By 1930 there were approximately 300 mi/480 km of motorways in Italy. **Hitler's** Germany enthusiastically adopted the idea and began building the first *Autobahn* in 1934. After **World War II** roads finally replaced **railways** as the preferred medium for overland transportation of both passengers and goods, and all developed countries of the world followed the German and Italian example in providing special high-speed roads for motor vehicles.

Having previously affected human settlements mainly by linking them with other places, roads have gradually become an important determinant of the shape and organization of towns in themselves. Ring roads built to take through-traffic away from town centres have attracted businesses out of towns and cities, as commercial developments have sprung up on the outskirts. The centres of some cities have been radically reshaped to accommodate the automobile, whereas in others, roads have been returned to their original exclusively pedestrian function.

Previously a symbol of civilization, the road has, for many, become a symbol of the unnaturalness and destructiveness of modern society and its encroachment on the natural environment. In Britain, for example, the government has had to scale down and rethink its road-building programme as each new project, though welcomed by some, attracts vigorous protests from environmentally concerned citizens. ► **Canals**

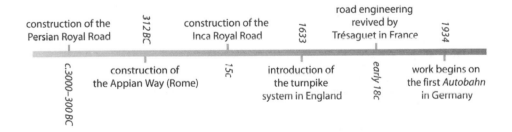

construction of the Persian Royal Road — *312 BC* — construction of the Inca Royal Road — *1633* — road engineering revived by Trésaguet in France — *1934*

*c.3000–300 BC* — construction of the Appian Way (Rome) — *15c* — introduction of the turnpike system in England — *early 18c* — work begins on the first *Autobahn* in Germany

---

**Robert of Anjou, the Wise** (1278–1343)
King of Naples. The grandson of **CHARLES OF ANJOU**, he succeeded his father, Charles II, to the throne in 1309. A leader of the Guelf papal party, he nonetheless broke with Pope **JOHN XXII** in 1330. A notable patron of learning and the arts, he was a friend of Boccaccio and Petrarch. ► **GUELFS**

**Roberts, Frederick Sleigh Roberts, 1st Earl** (1832–1914)
British field marshal. He took an active part in the **INDIAN UPRISING** of 1857–8, for which he was decorated with the Victoria Cross in 1858. He became Commander-in-Chief in India (1885–93), and served as Supreme Commander in South Africa during the second Boer War, relieving the Siege of **KIMBERLEY** (1900). He was created earl in 1901, and died while visiting troops in the field in France. ► **AFGHAN WARS**; **BOER WARS**

**Robespierre, Maximilien François Marie Isidore de** (1758–94)
French revolutionary leader. He became a lawyer, was elected to the **ESTATES GENERAL** (1789), became a prominent member of the Jacobin Club, and emerged in the National Assembly as a popular radical, known

as 'the Incorruptible'. In 1791 he was public accuser, and in 1792 presented a petition to the **LEGISLATIVE ASSEMBLY** for a Revolutionary Tribunal. Elected for Paris to the National Convention, he emerged as leader of the **MOUNTAIN**, strenuously opposed to the **GIRONDINS**, whom he helped to destroy. In 1793 he became a member of the Committee of **PUBLIC SAFETY** and for three months dominated the country, introducing the Reign of **TERROR** and the cult of the Supreme Being. However, as his ruthless exercise of power increased, his popularity waned. He was attacked in the National **CONVENTION**, arrested, and guillotined on the orders of the Revolutionary Tribunal. ► **FRENCH REVOLUTION; JACOBINS**

**Robin Hood** (c.1250–c.1350)
Semi-legendary English outlaw. The hero of a group of old English ballads, the gallant and generous outlaw of Sherwood Forest, he is said to have given generously to the poor and needy at the expense of proud abbots and rich knights, helping himself to their riches. The 'rymes of Robyn Hood' are named in *Piers Plowman* (c.1377) and the plays of Robin Hood in the *Paston Letters* (1473). The tradition may have had its origins in the popular discontent that led to the **PEAS-ANTS' REVOLT** (1381).

**Robinson, Arthur Napoleon Raymond** (1926– )
Trinidad and Tobago politician. Educated in Trinidad and at Oxford, he qualified as a barrister. On his return to the West Indies, he became politically active and in 1967, on independence, was Deputy Leader of the moderate-centrist People's National Movement (PNM). In 1984, with other colleagues, he broke away to form a left-of-centre coalition which became the National Alliance for Reconstruction (NAR), and which in the 1986 general election swept the PNM from power, making Robinson Prime Minister. Wounded in the 1990 attempted coup, he fought another election in Dec 1991, but he and the NAR were ousted by a rejuvenated PNM under Patrick Manning. When they returned to power under Basdeo Panday in 1995, Robinson served as adviser to the Prime Minister for two years; he was President from 1997 until 2003.

**Robinson, Sir John Beverley** (1791–1863)
Canadian politician. A prominent member of the **FAMILY COMPACT**, he became Attorney-General in 1818 and later Chief Justice (1829). In his determination to protect the imperial connection and the élite status of the Compact, he insisted on classifying American settlers as aliens and depriving them of both their property and their political rights. In 1830 he became President of the Executive Council and during the rebellion of 1837 he was responsible for the execution of two rebels and the banishment of 25.

**Robinson, Mary** (1944– )
Irish politician. She trained as a lawyer and was Professor of Law at Trinity College, Dublin, from 1969. She was a member of the Irish Senate (1969–89) and participated in numerous legal associations in the **EC** (European Community). She became an activist on many social issues, including women's and single parents' rights and the decriminalization of homosexuality. Nominated by the Labour Party, from which she had resigned in 1985 over the **ANGLO-**

**IRISH AGREEMENT**, she unexpectedly defeated the **FIANNA FÁIL** candidate Brian Lenihan in the presidential elections of Nov 1990. She held the post of President until 1997, and then became **UN** High Commissioner for Human Rights (1997–2002).

**Rob Roy**, properly **Robert MacGregor** (1671–1734)
Scottish outlaw. After his lands were seized by the Duke of Montrose, he gathered his clansmen and became a brigand. His career gave rise to many stories, often unsubstantiated, about his brave exploits, and of his generosity to the poor. Captured and imprisoned in London, he was sentenced to transportation, but pardoned in 1727. He is later thought to have become a Catholic.

**Rocard, Michel** (1930– )
French politician. He trained at the École National d'Administration, where he was a classmate of Jacques **CHIRAC**, and in 1967 became leader of the Unified Socialist Party (PSU). He joined the **SOCIALIST PARTY** (PS) in 1973, emerging as leader of its moderate social democratic wing, and unsuccessfully challenged François **MITTERRAND** for the party's presidential nomination in 1981. After serving as Minister of Planning and Regional Development (1981–3) and Agriculture (1983–5) in the ensuing Mitterrand administration, he resigned in Apr 1985 in opposition to the government's expedient introduction of proportional representation. In May 1988, however, as part of a strategy termed the 'opening to the centre', he was appointed Prime Minister by President Mitterrand. He was replaced as Prime Minister by Mme Edith Cresson in 1991. He became an MEP (Member of the European Parliament) representing the Party of European Socialists in 1994.

**Roca–Runciman Pact** (May 1933)
A commercial treaty between Britain and Argentina, referred to by the names of the chief negotiators, Vice-President Julio Argentino Roca (Argentina) and Walter Runciman (Britain). The pact guaranteed Argentina a share of the British meat market in return for various economic concessions. Nevertheless, the debates over the pact weakened the *Concordancia* or 'coalition' government of General Augustín Justo, which was faced with a vigorous nationalist campaign.

**Rochefort, Victor Henri, Marquis of Rochefort-Luçay** (1832–1913)
French journalist and politician. In 1868 he founded the satirical paper *La Lanterne*, which was quickly suppressed, but in 1869 on his election to the *Corps Législatif* he started the *Marseillaise*, in which he continued his attacks on the imperial regime. He was elected to the National Assembly (1871), but having sided with the **PARIS COMMUNE**, he was excluded, and sentenced to transportation to New Caledonia in the south Pacific. He escaped in 1874, returning to France after the amnesty of 1880. He continued his journalistic career with the popular and profitable newspaper *L'Intransigeant*, and became involved in the Boulangist movement. This produced a further period of exile in London (1889–95), after which he returned to French political journalism, moving to the extreme right, as a virulent anti-Semite and anti-Dreyfusard. He wrote his autobiography, *Adventures*

*of My Life* (trans 1896). ► BOULANGER, GEORGES; DREYFUS, ALFRED

### Rockefeller, John D(avison) (1839–1937)
US oil magnate and philanthropist. He became a clerk in a commission house in 1857 and then worked in a small oil refinery at Cleveland, Ohio. In 1870 he founded the Standard Oil Co. with his brother William, and this eventually gave him control of the US oil trade. He gave over US$500 million in support of medical research, universities and Baptist churches, and in 1913 he established the Rockefeller Foundation, avowedly 'to promote the well-being of mankind'.

### Rockingham, Charles Watson Wentworth, 2nd Marquess of (1730–82)
British politician. He was created Earl of Malton in 1750 and served as gentleman of the bedchamber to GEORGE II and GEORGE III. As leader of a prominent Whig opposition group, he was called upon to form a ministry in 1765. He repealed the STAMP ACT, affecting the American colonies, then court intrigues caused his resignation (1766). He opposed Britain's war against the colonists. His was the most consistent opposition Whig group to George III's government in the 1760s and 1770s, and leading spokesmen, such as FOX and BURKE, were adherents. He became Prime Minister again in 1782, the year he died. ► AMERICAN REVOLUTION

### Rodney, George Brydges Rodney, 1st Baron (1719–92)
British admiral. He joined the navy in 1732, became Governor of Newfoundland (1748–52), and won several victories during the SEVEN YEARS' WAR and after the AMERICAN REVOLUTION, when he defeated French fleets in the West Indies, notably off Dominica in 1782. He was made a baron after his return to England.

### Rodney, Walter (1942–80)
Guyanese historian and politician. Formerly Professor of African History at the University of Dar es Salaam, Rodney provoked a riot when he was deported from Jamaica in 1968 for his supposed connections with BLACK POWER. Although debarred from holding the history chair at the University of Guyana, he returned to his homeland and founded the Working People's Alliance which was antipathetic to the policies of BURNHAM's ruling PEOPLE'S NATIONAL CONGRESS. The author of *How Europe Underdeveloped Africa* (1972), he was killed by a bomb in mysterious circumstances in Guyana.

### Rodzianko, Mikhail Vladimirovich (1859–1924)
Russian politician. An OCTOBRIST, he was President of the third and fourth dumas and, after the outbreak of WORLD WAR I, he became the chairman of a special DUMA committee working to assist the war effort. The committee was, however, frustrated at every turn. In the wake of events of Feb 1917, Rodzianko appealed to NICHOLAS II to appoint a government that would enjoy public confidence; Nicholas simply refused to respond, and it fell to Rodzianko to ask him to abdicate, which he did. Thereafter, Rodzianko played little role in events.

### Roe v Wade (1973)
US Supreme Court decision legalizing abortion. It struck down state laws which prohibited abortion within the first three months of pregnancy on the grounds that the right to privacy, which included the right to have an abortion, was protected by due process.

### Roger I (1031–1101)
Norman ruler in Sicily. He joined his brother, Robert GUISCARD, in southern Italy, and helped him to conquer Calabria. In 1060 he was invited to Sicily to fight against the SARACENS, and took Messina. Everywhere the Normans were welcomed as deliverers from the Muslim yoke; in 1071 the Saracen capital, Palermo, was captured, and Robert made Roger Count of Sicily. After Robert's death (1085), Roger succeeded to his Italian possessions, and held the reins of Norman power in southern Europe.

### Roger II (1095–1154)
First Norman King of Sicily. The second son of ROGER I, he succeeded his older brother as Count of Sicily in 1105 and became Duke of Apulia in 1127, thus welding Sicily to the lands of Robert GUISCARD, his father's brother, and creating a strong Norman kingdom. He added Capua (1136), Naples and the Abruzzi (1140). He forced recognition of his royal titles from the pope and after the Byzantine Emperor had insulted Roger's ambassador, his fleet ravaged the coasts of DALMATIA and Epirus, took Corfu and plundered both Corinth and Athens (1146). In 1147 he took Tripoli, Tunis and Algeria. His court at Palermo was one of the most magnificent in Europe, and formed a critical point of contact for Christian and Arab scholars.

### Rogers, John (c.1500–1555)
English Protestant reformer and martyr. He was a London rector who converted to Protestantism at Antwerp, and helped to prepare the new translation called 'Matthew's Bible' in 1537. He returned to England in 1548, preached an anti-Catholic sermon at St Paul's Cross in 1553, just after the accession of MARY I, and was burnt. ► REFORMATION (England)

### Rogers, Robert (1731–95)
American frontier soldier. He was the leader of a 600-strong band of New England frontiersmen known as Rogers' Rangers, who fought bravely using Indian techniques in the FRENCH AND INDIAN WAR and in PONTIAC'S CONSPIRACY. Shortly after the outbreak of the AMERICAN REVOLUTION he was arrested by WASHINGTON on suspicion of espionage (1776) as he had had dealings with the British; this made him convert to the loyalist cause. He escaped and led a royalist force called the Queen's Rangers, which was defeated near White Plains, New York. After 1780 he lived in obscurity in England.

### Rogier, Charles Latour (1800–85)
Belgian politician. He trained and practised as a lawyer in Liège, worked in journalism, and was active in politics during the Belgian Revolution, joining both the Provisional Government and the National Congress. During the 1830s he was Governor of Antwerp, and became a cabinet minister (for Internal Affairs) for the first time in 1832–4. From the late 1840s onward he was the leading liberal politician of his day, forming and participating in governments (1847–52, 1857–61 and 1861–8). The LIBERAL PARTY dominated the middle of the 19c, and so Rogier presided over

their achievements: the industrial revolution, the 1848 constitution, free trade, and the battle with the Catholics over the SCHOOLS QUESTION. As a 'doctrinaire' liberal, he came into conflict with the radicals at the end of his career.

**Rohan-Gié, Henri, Duke of** (1579–1638)
French Duke of Léon, and Huguenot leader. On the surrender of La Rochelle (1628) a price was set on his head, and he made his way to Venice, but soon after was summoned by RICHELIEU to serve his king in the Valtellina, out of which he drove Imperialists and Spaniards. ▶ HUGUENOTS

**Rohan-Guéménée, Louis René Édouard, Prince of** (1734–1803)
French prelate. In 1778 he became a cardinal, and in 1779 became Bishop of Strasbourg. He fell prey to Cagliostro and the Comtesse de La Motte, who tricked him into believing that Queen MARIE ANTOINETTE, who knew nothing of the affair, wished him to stand security for her purchase by instalments of a priceless diamond necklace. The adventurers collected the necklace from the jewellers supposedly to give it to the Queen, but left Paris in order to sell the diamonds for their own gain. When the plot was discovered, Rohan-Guéménée was arrested, but was acquitted by the PARLEMENT of Paris (1786). He was elected to the ESTATES GENERAL in 1789, but refused to take the oath to the constitution in 1791, retiring to the German part of his diocese.

**Röhm, Ernst** (1887–1934)
German soldier, Nazi politician and paramilitary leader. He became an early supporter of HITLER and played a vital role in fostering good relations between the NAZI PARTY and the Bavarian authorities until Nov 1923. The organizer and commander of the SA or stormtroopers ('Brownshirts') during the mid-1920s and from 1931 to 1934, his plans to pursue policies independently of the NSDAP and his wish to supplant the traditional army led to his execution on Hitler's orders, in Munich. ▶ NIGHT OF THE LONG KNIVES

**Roh Tae Woo** (1932– )
South Korean politician. He was educated at the Korean Military Academy (1951–5), where he was a classmate of CHUN DOO-HWAN. He fought briefly in the KOREAN WAR and was a battalion commander during the VIETNAM WAR. He became commanding general of the Capital Security Command (1979), from which position he helped General Chun seize power in the coup of 1979–80. He retired from the army in 1981 and successively served, under President Chun, as Minister for National Security and Foreign Affairs (1981–2) and for Home Affairs (from 1982). He was elected chairman of the ruling Democratic Justice Party in 1985 and in 1987, following serious popular disturbances, drew up a political reform package which restored democracy to the country. He was elected President in 1987, and was succeeded by KIM YONG-SAM in 1992. In 1995 he was arrested on charges of accepting bribes in return for contracts, and apologized to the nation for his wrongdoing. He was imprisoned but released in 1998.

**Rojo, Vicente** (1894–1966)
Spanish soldier. The most brilliant strategist on the Republican side during the SPANISH CIVIL WAR. He organized the remarkable defence of Madrid in Nov 1936 as well as the Jarama and Guadalajara campaigns of 1937. Having been made Chief of the General Staff in May 1937, he not only reorganized the Popular Army, but planned the offensives of Brunete, Teruel and the Ebro. He returned to Spain from exile in 1957 and lived under virtual house arrest until his death in 1966.

**Rokossovsky, Konstantin Konstantinovich** (1896–1968)
Russian soldier. Born in Warsaw of a Polish father and a Russian mother, he served in WORLD WAR I in the Tsarist army and joined the Red Guards in 1917. He served in the RED ARMY cavalry during the RUSSIAN CIVIL WAR and after, but was lucky to survive imprisonment during the STALIN purges. In WORLD WAR II he was one of the defenders of Moscow, played a leading part in the Battle of STALINGRAD (1942–3), recaptured Orel and Warsaw, and led the Russian race for Berlin. In 1944 he was promoted Marshal of the USSR and then served as Commander-in-Chief of Soviet forces in Poland (1945–9). In 1949 he was appointed Polish Minister of Defence as Stalin's man in Warsaw, a post he was made to resign in 1956 during the anti-Soviet unrest in Poland, as part of the bargain under which GOMUŁKA became Premier, with greater control over Polish domestic affairs in return for supporting Soviet foreign policy. Rokossovsky then became a Deputy Minister of Defence of the USSR from 1956 to 1962, apart from a brief period in a military command in Transcaucasia.

**Roland, Manon** ▶ ROLAND DE LA PLATIÈRE, JEAN MARI

**Roland de la Platière, Jean Mari** (1734–93)
French politician. He married Marie Jeanne Phlipon (1754–93) in 1780. In 1791 Roland was sent to Paris by Lyons to watch the interests of the municipality; and Madame Roland established a salon patronized by the leading GIRONDINS. In Mar 1792 Roland became Minister of the Interior, but made himself hateful to the JACOBINS by his protests against the September Massacres (1792), in which demagogues had incited the Paris mob to invade the prisons, murdering innocent victims. He took part in the last struggle of the Girondins. On 31 May 1793, he was arrested, but escaped and fled to Rouen, hoping to organize insurrection, but in vain; the next day, Madame Roland was arrested. During her five months in prison she wrote her unfinished Memoirs, in which we have a serene and delightful revelation of her youth. On 8 Nov 1793 she was guillotined. Two days later her husband committed suicide.

**ROMANIA** official name **Socialist Republic of Romania**, also spelled **Roumania** or **Rumania**
A republic in south-eastern Europe, bounded to the south by Bulgaria; to the west by Serbia and Hungary; to the east by Moldova and the Black Sea; and to the north and east by the Ukraine. The Romanian people are descended from the Dacians, Romans, Vlachs, SLAVS and the other settlers in MOLDAVIA AND WALLACHIA (modern Romania) who speak Romanian. While the culture of the Slav settlers came to dominate elsewhere in the north Balkans, the Romanians'

ancestors assimilated to the Latin culture of the earlier Romanized inhabitants. Under the Ottomans (15–19c), the Romanians began their movement for national independence in the 1820s, aspiring to the unification of Moldavia, Wallachia and **TRANSYLVANIA**. In 1862 Moldavia and Wallachia merged to form the unitary Principality of Romania, and a monarchy was created in 1866. Romania joined the Allies in **WORLD WAR I**, and united with Transylvania, Bessarabia and Bukovina in 1918. In 1920 Transylvania, with its mixed Romanian and Magyar population, was finally joined to the Kingdom of Romania by the Treaty of **TRIANON**. Romania supported Germany in **WORLD WAR II** and Soviet forces occupied the country in 1944. After the war it lost territories to Russia, Hungary and Bulgaria. The monarchy was abolished and a People's Republic declared in 1947 under the autocratic President Nicolae **CEAUŞESCU**, leader of the Romanian Communist Party. Romania became a Socialist Republic in 1965. Becoming increasingly independent of the USSR from the 1960s, it formed relationships with China, and several Western countries. In 1989, violent repression of protest, resulting in the deaths of thousands of demonstrators, sparked a popular uprising and the overthrow of the Ceauşescu regime and execution of the President and his wife. Ion **ILIESCU** formed a National Salvation Front and was elected President, although unrest and demonstrations continued. In 1991 Romania became a multiparty democracy, although the government was dominated by former communists until 1996, when Iliescu was defeated in the elections by Emil Constantinescu. Iliescu was re-elected president in 2000 but was defeated in 2004 by Traian Basescu. Romania joined **NATO** in 2004. ▸ **BESSARABIA**; **BUKOVINA**; **DOBRUDJA**; **OLTENIA**; **REGAT**; **SUPPLEX LIBELLUS VALACHORUM**

**Romanov, Grigori Vasilevich** (1923– )
Soviet politician. The son of a Novgorod peasant, he educated himself as a shipbuilding engineer at night classes and by correspondence. It was 1955 before he agreed to be a party functionary, but by 1970 he was in charge of the Leningrad party as First Secretary and by 1976 in the **POLITBURO**. Yuri **ANDROPOV** made him a secretary of the Central Committee in 1983, a jumping-off platform for the general secretaryship, but he lacked Mikhail **GORBACHEV**'s skill and commitment to change and was simply brushed aside for the party succession in 1985.

**Romanov Dynasty**
The second (and last) Russian royal dynasty (1613–1917). The first Romanov Tsar, Mikhail, was elected in 1613 after the **TIME OF TROUBLES**. The Romanovs soon ruled as virtually absolute autocrats, allowing no constitutional or legal checks on their political power. Even when **NICHOLAS II** conceded the establishment of a national assembly or **DUMA** in 1905, he allowed it little power in practice. The dynasty ended with Nicholas II's abdication in Feb 1917, and his execution by Bolshevik guards in July 1918. ▸ **ALEXANDER I**; **CATHERINE II, THE GREAT**; **FEBRUARY REVOLUTION** (Russia); **NICHOLAS I** (of Russia); **PETER I, THE GREAT**; **REVOLUTION OF 1905**; **RUSSIAN REVOLUTION**

**Roman Question**
After the creation of a united Italian state in 1861, two substantial areas remained outside the kingdom: Venetia (which was acquired by war in 1866) and those areas of the **PAPAL STATES** not seized in 1860. The question of the acquisition of the latter came to be known as the 'Roman Question'. Two factors complicated the situation. The first was the loyalty felt by many Italians to the Roman Catholic Church and their consequent reluctance to use force to wrest the Eternal City from papal rule. The second was the presence since 1849 of a French garrison defending the pope, meaning any attack would result in a clash with France. Initial attempts to acquire Rome in 1860–1 hinged on negotiation and offers of purchase, but eventually it was taken by force (1870), when the French troops were withdrawn for use in the **FRANCO–PRUSSIAN WAR**. Even after Rome's annexation, the problem was not resolved since **PIUS IX**, already hostile to the Italian state which had first annexed much of his territory in 1860, became even more intransigent in his position that good Catholics should not recognize the Italian state or take any part in its politics. Tensions were to remain between Church and State until the **LATERAN PACTS** of 1929. ▸ **ASPROMONTE, BATTLE OF**; **MENTANA, BATTLE OF**

**Rome, Sack of** (1527)
The storming of the papal capital by the unpaid imperial mercenaries used by Emperor **CHARLES V** in the **ITALIAN WARS**. Pope **CLEMENT VII** had deserted the Habsburg cause and joined the League of Cognac after the Battle of **PAVIA** (1525), and the full wrath of his erstwhile allies was unleashed in the massacre of an estimated 8,000 civilians and widespread plunder. Clement escaped from the city and, after signing a treaty with Charles, fled to Orvieto. This was an event so shattering that in many ways it can be said to have brought the Italian **RENAISSANCE** to an end.

**Rommel, Erwin Johannes Eugen** (1891–1944)
German field marshal and Nazi sympathizer. Educated at Tübingen, he fought in **WORLD WAR I** and taught at Dresden Military Academy. He commanded **HITLER**'s headquarters guard during the early occupations, and led a Panzer division during the 1940 invasion of France. He then commanded the **AFRIKA CORPS**, where he achieved major successes. Eventually driven into retreat by a strongly reinforced 8th Army, the 'Desert Fox' was withdrawn, a sick man, from North Africa, and appointed to an Army Corps command in France. Returning home wounded in 1944, he condoned the plot against Hitler's life. After its failure and his implication in it, he committed suicide at Herrlingen. ▸ **EL ALAMEIN, BATTLE OF**; **WORLD WAR II**

**Roon, Albrecht Theodor Emil, Count of** (1803–79) Prussian army officer. He became War Minister (1859–73), and with **BISMARCK**'s support effectively reorganized the army, which helped make possible Prussian victories in the Danish, Austrian and Franco-Prussian Wars of the 1860s and 1870s. ► **AUSTRO-PRUSSIAN WAR**; **FRANCO-PRUSSIAN WAR**; **GERMAN–DANISH WAR**; **PRUSSIA**

**Roose, Pieter** (1586–1673) Southern Netherlands politician. He trained as a lawyer and was appointed to the Secret Council (*Geheime Raad*) of the Spanish Netherlands in 1622. From 1627 to 1631 he was a member of the High Council for Flanders and Burgundy in Madrid, and had the ear of King **PHILIP IV** of Spain. In 1632 he was President of the Secret Council, and after restoring Spanish power in the southern Netherlands, exercised it there in the later 1630s. He was relieved of his office in 1653.

**Roosevelt, (Anna) Eleanor** (1884–1962) US humanitarian and diplomat. The niece of Theodore **ROOSEVELT** and wife of Franklin D **ROOSEVELT**, she became active in politics during her husband's illness from polio and proved herself invaluable to him as an adviser on social issues when he became President. In 1941 she became Assistant Director of the Office of Civilian Defense and after her husband's death in 1945 extended the scope of her activities, becoming a US delegate to the **UN** Assembly (1945–53, 1961), Chairman of the UN Human Rights Commission (1946–51) and US representative to the General Assembly (1946–52).

**Roosevelt, Franklin D(elano)**, also called **FDR** (1882–1945) US politician and 32nd President, the fifth cousin of Theodore **ROOSEVELT**. He became a lawyer (1907), a New York State Senator (1910–13) and Assistant Secretary of the Navy (1913–20), and was Democratic candidate for the vice-presidency in 1920. Stricken with polio in 1921, he recovered partial use of his legs and went on to become Governor of New York (1929–33). During his first 'hundred days' as President (1933–45), he bombarded the economic crises with his **NEW DEAL** for national recovery (1933), and became the only President to be re-elected three times. At the outbreak of **WORLD WAR II** he strove to avoid US involvement and instead provided economic resources to the Allies in the form of a 'lend–lease' agreement, but Japan's attack on **PEARL HARBOR** (1941) left him no choice and the USA entered the war. He met **CHURCHILL** and **STALIN** at the **TEHRAN CONFERENCE** (1943) and **YALTA CONFERENCE** (1945) to formulate post-war plans, including the **UN**, but died three weeks before the German surrender. Throughout his presidency, his wife, Eleanor **ROOSEVELT**, was active in human rights and after his death became the US delegate to the UN. ► **LEND–LEASE AGREEMENT**

**Roosevelt, Theodore**, nicknamed **Teddy** (1858–1919) US politician and 26th President. Educated at Harvard, he became a member of the New York legislature (1881–84). In 1898 he raised a volunteer cavalry of cowboys and college athletes known as the **ROUGH RIDERS** in the **SPANISH–AMERICAN WAR**. Upon his return he was elected Governor of New York State (1898–1900). A Republican, he was elected Vice-President in 1900, became President on **MCKINLEY**'s assassination (15 Sep 1901), and was re-elected in 1904. During his presidency (1901–9), he strengthened the navy, initiated the construction of the **PANAMA CANAL**, and introduced a '**SQUARE DEAL**' policy for enforcing anti-trust laws. He received the **NOBEL PEACE PRIZE** in 1906 for his mediation during the **RUSSO-JAPANESE WAR** (1904–5). As organizer of the **PROGRESSIVE PARTY** as well as its candidate for the presidency in 1912, he was defeated by Woodrow **WILSON**. ► **NEW NATIONALISM**; **REPUBLICAN PARTY**

**Roosevelt Corollary** (1904) Amendment to the **MONROE DOCTRINE** enunciated by Theodore **ROOSEVELT** which stated that the USA had a duty to prevent political instability and financial mismanagement in the countries of its Caribbean 'backyard'. In its crudest form it was a justification for Roosevelt's 'big stick' and **TAFT**'s '**DOLLAR DIPLOMACY**' policies, and sanctioned US military intervention in Haiti (1915–34) and the Dominican Republic (1916–24). Such interference was theoretically reversed by F D **ROOSEVELT**'s '**GOOD NEIGHBOR POLICY**' of 1934, but this has not precluded further overt and covert interventions in Guatemala (1954), Cuba (1961), Dominican Republic (1965), Nicaragua (1979–87), Grenada (1983), Panama (1989) and Haiti (1994), not to mention a virtual blockade of Cuba for over 30 years, cemented into place by the **HELMS–BURTON ACT** (1996).

**Root, Elihu** (1845–1937) US politician and international lawyer. Educated in New York, he became a lawyer, US Secretary of War (1899–1904) and Secretary of State (1905–9). He helped to establish civilian government in Puerto Rico, as well as governing policies for Cuba and the Philippines. A supporter of the **LEAGUE OF NATIONS** and the development of the World Court, he was awarded the **NOBEL PEACE PRIZE** in 1912 for his promotion of international arbitration.

**Rosas, Juan Manuel de** (1793–1877) Argentine dictator. The son of an *estanciero*, he became an enterprising rancher and exporter of salted beef, with a loyal following among the *gauchos* on his lands. Rising to prominence as a federalist leader, he acted as Governor of Buenos Aires and *de facto* ruler of Argentina from 1829 until 1852, except for a brief interval in 1832–3. His regime was a form of personal terrorism, and witnessed a dramatic concentration of estanciero landholdings among major merchant families in Buenos Aires. Anti-foreign sentiment was encouraged, and Rosas' actions against local nationals and their interests resulted in an Anglo-French naval blockade in 1845–50. By 1850, opposition to his rule had coalesced around **URQUIZA**, Governor of Entre Ríos, while a generation of exiles, including **MITRE**, **SARMIENTO** and **ALBERDI** demanded modernization. Defeated by a force drawn from Brazil and the interior provinces at Monte Caseros in Feb 1852, he died in exile in England. ► **ESTANCIA**; **GAUCHO**

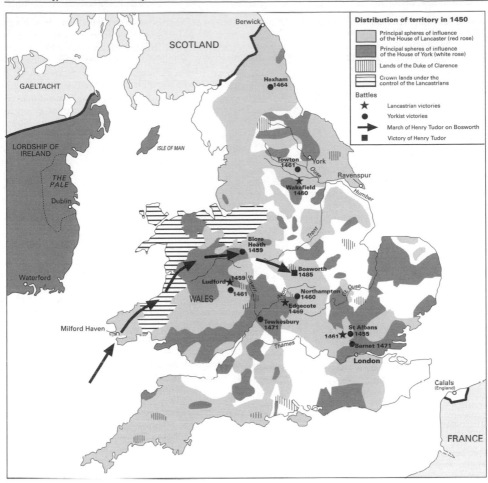

**Distribution of territory in 1450**

▧ Principal spheres of influence of the House of Lancaster (red rose)

▨ Principal spheres of influence of the House of York (white rose)

▥ Lands of the Duke of Clarence

▤ Crown lands under the control of the Lancastrians

**Battles**

★ Lancastrian victories

● Yorkist victories

→ March of Henry Tudor on Bosworth

■ Victory of Henry Tudor

**Wars of the Roses**

---

### Rosebery, Archibald Philip Primrose, 5th Earl of
(1847–1929)

British politician. He succeeded to the earldom in 1868, and after holding various educational and political posts, became Foreign Secretary (1886 and 1892–4) under **GLADSTONE**, whom he briefly (1894–5) succeeded as Premier before the Liberals lost the election of 1895. He was noted for his racehorse stables, and in his later years as a biographer of British statesmen. ► **LIBERAL PARTY** (UK)

### Rose-Innes, Sir James (1855–1942)

South African judge. Educated at the University of the Cape of Good Hope, he became Attorney-General (1890–3 and 1900–2), and then Judge President (later Chief Justice) of the Supreme Court of the Transvaal (1902–10), Judge of Appeal (1910–14) and Chief Justice of the Union of South Africa (1914–27). He advocated a liberal policy towards the Africans and, as head of a strong bench, was probably the greatest of all South African judges. His opinions are notable for their clarity and their willingness to rely on both the English and Roman-Dutch traditions in South African law.

### Rosenberg, Alfred (1893–1946)

German Nazi ideologue. A fervent advocate of national socialism, he joined the **NAZI PARTY** in 1920,

edited Nazi journals, for a time (1933) directed the party's foreign policy, and in 1934 was given control of its cultural and political education policy. In his *The Myth of the 20th Century* (1930) he expounded the extreme Nazi doctrines which he later put into practice in Eastern Europe, for which crime he was hanged at Nuremberg in 1946. ► **NUREMBERG TRIALS**

### Rosenberg Affair (1953)

US treason trial. Julius and Ethel Rosenberg were found guilty, like Klaus **FUCHS** in Britain, of passing atomic bomb secrets to the USSR. The worth of the information they had passed to the Russians was dubious and the sentence of death passed by Judge Irving Kaufman was more a measure of US fears of **COMMUNISM** and the anger felt at betrayal than a judicial decision. The Rosenbergs' prison letters aroused great sympathy in Europe, and their execution compounded the fears aroused by McCarthyism. ► **MCCARTHY, JOSEPH**

### Roses, Wars of the (1455–85)

A series of civil wars in England, which started during the weak monarchy of King **HENRY VI**; named from the emblems of the two rival branches of the House of Plantagenet, York (white rose) and Lancaster (red rose) – a symbolism that was propagated by the Tudor Dynasty (1485–1603), which united the two roses. The wars began when Richard, Duke of York, claimed the protectorship of the Crown after the King's mental breakdown (1453–4), and effectively ended with Henry Tudor's defeat of **RICHARD III** at Bosworth (1485). The armies were small, and the warfare intermittent, although marked by brutal executions. The wars were not purely dynastic in origin, and were exacerbated by the gentry and by aristocratic feuds, notably between the Neville and the **PERCY** families, and by the unstable 'bastard feudal' system, in which relations among landed élites were increasingly based upon self-interest – a system that the Tudors sought to control. ► **HENRY VII; LANCASTER, HOUSE OF; PLANTAGENET DYNASTY; TUDOR, HOUSE OF; YORK, HOUSE OF; WARWICK, RICHARD NEVILLE, EARL OF**

## Rosetti, Constantin A (1816–85)
Romanian politician, nationalist leader and journalist. In 1848, he led the radical Liberals during the period of political agitation and was General-Secretary of the Provisional Government (June 1848). He fled to Paris where he was active in Romanian revolutionary organizations and founded two Romanian newspapers (1850–1). He returned home in 1857 and took part in the *divan ad hoc*. He attacked Alexander **CUZA** for being too autocratic and made an alliance with Ion **BRĂTIANU** for the purpose of ousting the former. During the **INTERREGNUM** he was Minister of Education and, under Brătianu, Minister of the Interior (1878 and 1881–2). ► **MOLDAVIA AND WALLACHIA; ROMANIA**

## 'Rosie the Riveter'
US epithet. The generic name given to US women employed in defence production during **WORLD WAR II**. By 1944, over 50 per cent of workers in aircraft manufacture and shipbuilding were women and the number of married women in work had increased from around 15 per cent to almost 25 per cent. Their level of performance, in jobs for which they had previously been considered unsuitable, was so high that attitudes towards women in work were permanently altered.

## Ross, Sir John (1777–1856)
Scottish explorer and naval officer. He joined the navy at the age of nine and served with distinction in the **NAPOLEONIC WARS**. From 1812 he conducted surveys in the White Sea and the Arctic, leading an expedition in 1818 in search of the Northwest Passage. He led another such expedition (1829–33), during which he discovered and named Boothia Peninsula, King William Land and the Gulf of Boothia. ► **EXPLORATION**

## Rossbach and Leuthen, Battles of (5 Nov and 6 Dec 1757)
The battles took place in the **SEVEN YEARS' WAR**. At Rossbach, Prussia defeated Austrian and French forces. A month later, at Leuthen (Lutynia), Prussian forces routed a much larger Austrian army.

## Rossi, Pellegrino, Count (1787–1848)
Economist and politician. Forced to leave Italy in 1815 because of his sympathies for Joachim **MURAT**, he settled first in Geneva and then in France, where he was elected to the Upper House of the French Chamber (1839). In 1845 Guizot sent him as ambassador to Rome where he arrived just after the death of **GREGORY XVI**. He encouraged the new pope, **PIUS IX**, to undertake liberal reforms and (Sep 1848) became his Prime Minister at the head of a constitutional government but was assassinated by Roman radicals in Nov of the same year.

## Rostopchin, Feodor Vasilevich, Count (1763–1826)
Russian soldier, statesman and writer. He won great influence over the unbalanced Tsar **PAUL I** and was for two years his Foreign Minister. As a conservative, he was out of favour in **ALEXANDER I**'s early years, but as a patriot he regained favour in the war against Napoleon as Governor of Moscow. It was he who may have planned, or at least had a share in, the burning of Moscow against **NAPOLEON I** in 1812. He wrote historical memoirs and two comedies and other plays, in Russian and French.

## Rothschild, Meyer Amschel (1743–1812)
German financier. Named after the 'Red Shield' signboard of his father's house, he began as a moneylender, and became the financial adviser of the Landgrave of Hesse. The house transmitted money from the English government to Wellington in Spain, paid the British subsidies to Continental princes, and negotiated loans for Denmark (1804–12). His five sons continued the firm, establishing branches in other countries, and negotiated many of the great government loans of the 19c. ► **NAPOLEONIC WARS**

## Rouges
French-Canadian political party. The reform party of **CANADA EAST** which began to emerge from the late 1840s as the *Institut Canadien* acquired branches in the major towns of the province, and as the newspaper, *L'Avenir*, spread ideas derived from American republicanism and French radicalism. Under **PAPINEAU** and, after his retirement, A A Dorion, the party grew to be the major opposition to the conservative bloc, seeking repeal of the 1840 Act of Union, universal education for all and a democratic suffrage. Although the Rouges opposed confederation, they joined with the **CLEAR GRITS** and cooperated thereafter with the **LIBERAL PARTY** in federal politics. Within Quebec their liberalism earned the opposition of the Catholic Church and the ultramontane **CASTORS**.

## Rouget de Lisle, Claude Joseph (1760–1836)
French army officer. He composed the words and music of a battle hymn for the French Army of the Rhine at Strasbourg in 1792. This became the 'Marseillaise', the revolutionary and, eventually, the French national anthem.

## Rough Riders
The nickname created by the press for the First US Volunteer Cavalry Regiment, commanded during the **SPANISH–AMERICAN WAR** (1898) by Colonel Leonard Wood (1860–1927) and Lieutenant-Colonel Theodore **ROOSEVELT**. The fabled Rough Riders' 'charge' up San Juan Hill in Cuba (1 July 1898) was actually carried out on foot. Roosevelt emerged from the conflict a war hero.

## Rouher, Eugène (1814–84)
French politician. In 1848 he was returned to the Constituent Assembly, and until 1869 held various offices in the government. He negotiated the treaty

of commerce with England in 1860 and with Italy in 1863. In 1870 he was appointed President of the Senate. A staunch Napoleonist, after the fall of the French Second EMPIRE he fled abroad. Later he represented Corsica in the National Assembly.

**Roundheads ► CAVALIERS**

**Round Table Conferences** (1930–2)
A series of meetings in London between British government and Indian representatives to discuss the future constitution of India. It was prompted by the Simon Commission Report (1930) on the working of the 1919 Government of India Act. It helped in the formulation of the 1935 Government of India Act. ► **GOVERNMENT OF INDIA ACTS; MONTAGU–CHELMSFORD REFORMS**

**Rousseau, Jean Jacques** (1712–78)
French political philosopher, educationist and essayist. Largely self-taught, he carried on a variety of menial occupations until after he moved to Paris in 1741, where he came to know Diderot and the ENCYCLOPE-DISTS. In 1754 he wrote *Discourse on the Origin of Inequality* (1755), emphasizing the natural goodness of human beings and the corrupting influences of institutionalized life. He later moved to Luxembourg (1757), where he wrote his masterpiece, *The Social Contract* (1762), a great influence on French revolutionary thought, introducing the slogan '**LIBERTY, EQUALITY, FRATERNITY**'. The same year he published his major work on education, *Émile*, in novel form, but its views on monarchy and governmental institutions forced him to flee to Switzerland, and then England, at the invitation of David Hume. There he wrote most of his *Confessions* (published posthumously in 1782). He returned to Paris in 1767, where he continued to write, but gradually became insane. ► **PHILOSOPHES**

**Rowell–Sirois Commission** (1940)
Canadian Royal Commission on national economic problems. Appointed by Mackenzie KING in 1937, the commission was chaired by N W Rowell and, after his resignation in 1938, by J N Sirois. Its remit was to find a way by which the Dominion government, after R B BENNETT's NEW DEAL had been declared unconstitutional, could administer federal aid without infringing provincial rights. The commission's report analysed regional economic inequalities in depth and recommended a fundamental revision in the balance of federal and provincial powers. In particular it suggested that the Dominion should take over responsibility for social services (the major area of provincial expenditure), while in return the provinces should cease to levy income taxes and succession duties. A federal-provincial conference called to discuss the report in 1941 was torpedoed by the hostility of Ontario, Quebec and British Columbia (while Alberta had already boycotted the Commission itself), but in 1946 new revenue-sharing proposals were accepted by all the provinces except Ontario, which acceded in 1950, and Quebec, which made its own agreement in 1954.

**Rowlatt Act** (1919)
Passed by the British colonial government, the Anarchical and Revolutionary Crimes Act, popularly known by the name of its author, Sir Sidney Rowlatt, made the suspension of civil liberties during wartime by the Defence of India Act of 1915 a permanent feature of India's peacetime constitution. The Act aroused opposition amongst Indian nationalist politicians and caused M K GANDHI to organize the first all-India SATYAGRAHA, an initially peaceful protest involving strikes, demonstrations and the deliberate courting of arrest, in opposition to the measure. Popular support was widespread, partly because of economic distress but also due to anger amongst the Muslim community at the proposed post-war division of the empire of the Ottoman Sultan, Khalifa, the protector of Islam's holy places in the Middle East and the organization and involvement of India's Sikh community as part of a general movement of religious revivalism in India at this time. Unfortunately, the Satyagraha was accompanied by violent incidents, some of them committed by Ghadrites, which led to the imposition of martial law in the Punjab and the infamous AMRITSAR MASSACRE. Shocked at this outcome, Gandhi called the Satyagraha a 'Himalayan blunder', but the real blunder was committed by the British, as clumsy attempts to cover up the massacre and to absolve those involved from responsibility convinced many moderate and reformist Indian politicians (including Gandhi himself) of the impossibility of Indians ever securing justice under colonial rule.

**Rowntree, Joseph** (1836–1925)
English Quaker industrialist and reformer. Born in York, he was the son of Joseph Rowntree, a Quaker grocer. With his brother, Henry Isaac (d.1883), he became a partner in a cocoa manufactury in York in 1869, and built up welfare organizations for his employees. He was succeeded as chairman by his son, Seebohm ROWNTREE.

**Rowntree, (Benjamin) Seebohm** (1871–1954)
English manufacturer and philanthropist. Born in York, the son of Joseph ROWNTREE, he was educated at the Friends' School in York and Owens College, Manchester. He became chairman of the family chocolate firm (1925–41) and introduced enlightened schemes of worker participation. He devoted his life to the study of social problems and welfare, and wrote many books, including *Poverty: A Study of Town Life* (1901), *Poverty and Progress* (1941) and *Poverty and the Welfare State* (1951).

**Royal Niger Company**
A company founded to secure the Niger regions for the British against French competition. British traders on the River Niger had been amalgamated into the National African Company, which in 1886 obtained a royal charter to rule a large part of what later became Nigeria. They secured the navigable portions of the Niger, frustrated the French, and destroyed the power of African middlemen. The charter was wound up in 1898, and the various parts of Nigeria were later amalgamated as a British colony, which achieved independence in 1960.

**Roy Manabendra Nath**, also called **Narendranath Bhattacharya** (1887–1954)
Indian political leader. Involved with terrorist groups against British rule, he was sent in 1915 to request aid from the Germans in Batavia. His mission having

failed, he arrived in San Francisco in 1916, where he changed his name. He then went to Mexico, where he helped to found the Mexican Communist Party, and to Moscow, where he became a member of the Executive Committee of the **COMINTERN**, and founded the Communist Party of India in Tashkent (1920). He broke with the Comintern in 1929 but was arrested and imprisoned on his return to India. After independence, he abandoned **COMMUNISM**.

RPF; RPR ▶ GAULLISTS

**RSS** (*Rashtriya Swayamsevak Sangh*, 'National Self-Service Society')
A militant Hindu cultural organization, founded in Nagpur in the 1930s by K B Hedgewar with help from B S **MOONJE**, organized into cells, whose members practise martial arts, and which promotes an exclusively Hindu definition of the Indian nation. By 1940 its membership numbered 100,000 under the leadership of Golwalkar. The **JAN SANGH**, a political party which was originally an offshoot of the RSS, later became an independent political party and turned into the Bharatiya Janata Party (BJP). The RSS traditionally provided the Jan Sangh with the most vigorous canvassers at election time. ▶ **HINDU MAHASABHA**

**Rudolf I** (1218–91)
King of Germany (1273/91) and uncrowned Holy Roman Emperor. The founder of the **HABSBURG DYNASTY**, he was the most powerful prince in Swabia when he was elected King of Germany in 1273. He attempted to restore the power of the monarchy by the resumption of lands and rights usurped by the princes since 1245. His victory at **DÜRNKRUT** on the Marchfeld in 1278 over Ottokar II of Bohemia, who had occupied Austria and Styria, brought him control of these two duchies, which passed to his son, **ALBERT I**, and became the seat of Habsburg power.

**Rudolf II** (1552–1612)
Holy Roman Emperor (1576/1612). The eldest son of **MAXIMILIAN II**, he became King of Hungary in 1572, and King of Bohemia and King of the Romans (or German King) in 1575. A mentally unstable and incompetent ruler, he was soon faced with revolts, and Hungary, Bohemia, Austria and Moravia were taken from him by his brother **MATTHIAS**.

**Rudolf IV of Habsburg** (1339–65)
Duke of Austria. He assumed power at the age of 19 and, excluded from the Electoral College by the *Golden Bull* (1356), tried to establish Austria's independence by a series of forgeries, the most important of which was the **PRIVILEGIUM MAIUS**; these were, however, rejected by the emperor. He built up a number of dynastic links to strengthen Austria's position, founded Vienna University and rebuilt St Stephen's Cathedral in the city. ▶ **GOLDEN BULL**

**Rudolf of Rheinfelden** (1030–80)
Duke of Swabia and German anti-king. He was enfeoffed with Swabia in 1037 by the Empress Agnes, entrusted with the administration of Burgundy and given her daughter Matilda in marriage. After Matilda's death, he married **HENRY IV**'s sister-in-law, Adelaide (1066). From 1076 he went over to the papal side and had himself elected King when Henry IV

was deposed (1077). He enjoyed little support, though, and was not recognized by Pope **GREGORY VII** until 1080. Deposed as Duke of Swabia in favour of Frederick of Hohenstaufen, Rudolf was killed in battle in the same year.

**Ruffo, Fabrizio, Cardinal** (1744–1827)
Cardinal and leader of the army of **SANFEDISTI** that overthrew the **PARTHENOPEAN REPUBLIC** and restored the Bourbon monarchy in Naples. ▶ **FERDINAND I**

**Ruiz Zorrilla, Manuel** (1833–95)
Spanish politician. As Prime Minister (July–Oct 1871 and Aug 1872–Feb 1873), he reformed the Church, abolished slavery in Puerto Rico, and, on 11 Feb 1873, received the abdication of King Amadeus I. That same day, the First Republic was proclaimed. After the restoration of the monarchy in 1875, he went into exile in France. He continued to defend the Republican cause through military conspiracies, becoming a symbol of Republican idealism in the process. He returned to Spain in 1895, to die. ▶ **REPUBLIC, FIRST** (Spain)

**Rumelia**
Literally 'the land of the Romans', this was the name given by the Ottoman Turks to the province which included **THESSALY**, **EPIRUS**, Macedonia and **THRACE**. Divided into *timars* and later *vilayets*, it was lost to the Ottoman Turks in stages, beginning with the annexation of **EASTERN RUMELIA** by Bulgaria (1885). After the Treaty of Bucharest (1913), by which Greece gained Salonica and Serbia Monastir, the Ottoman Porte was left with only Edirne. ▶ **BUCHAREST, TREATIES OF**; **TIMAR**

**Rump Parliament**
The members of the English **LONG PARLIAMENT** who were left after **PRIDE**'s Purge of conservative and moderate 'Presbyterian' elements (Dec 1648). It numbered about 60, but by-elections brought it up to 125 by 1652. It abolished the monarchy and the House of **LORDS**. When it fell out with the army, **CROMWELL** dismissed it (Apr 1653). It was recalled in 1659 with the fall of the **PROTECTORATE**, and dissolved itself in 1660.

**Rum Rebellion** (1808)
An uprising in Sydney which deposed the Governor of New South Wales, Captain William **BLIGH**. Led by John Macarthur, a former army officer turned pastoralist, Major George Johnston and officers of the New South Wales Corps, the rebellion occurred because of personal antagonisms, and Bligh's attempt to end the use of rum as a currency. Bligh returned to England but was not reinstated as governor; Johnston was court-martialled and dismissed from the army; and Macarthur, on going to Britain, was forbidden to return to Australia until 1817.

**Rundstedt, (Karl Rudolf) Gerd von** (1875–1953)
German field marshal. He served in **WORLD WAR I**, and in the early 1930s became Military Commander of Berlin. In 1939 he directed the attacks on Poland and France. Checked in the Ukraine in 1941, he was relieved of his command, but in 1942 was given a new command in France. He was recalled after the success of the 1944 Allied invasion, but returned to direct the

Ardennes offensive. War crimes proceedings against him were dropped on the grounds of his ill health. ► **WORLD WAR II**

**Rupert** (1619–82)
Prince and royalist commander in the **ENGLISH CIVIL WARS**. He was the third son of the Elector Palatine **FREDERICK V** and Elizabeth, daughter of **JAMES VI AND I**. A notable cavalry leader, he won several victories in the major battles of the war, but was defeated at **MARSTON MOOR** (1644), contributed to the defeat at **NASEBY**, and after his surrender of Bristol was dismissed by **CHARLES I**. Banished by parliament, he led the small royalist fleet until it was routed by Robert **BLAKE** (1650). He escaped to the West Indies, returning to Europe in 1653, and living in Germany until the **RESTORATION**.

**Rupert I** (1352–1410)
King of Germany (1400/10). Elected King the day after the deposition of King **WENCESLAS IV** by the **ELECTORS** of Mainz, Trier and Cologne, he was crowned in Cologne in 1400. After an unsuccessful Italian campaign (1401–2), he was accepted by the pope in 1403. Rupert continued to support the pope in Rome during the **GREAT SCHISM**, unlike the majority of the German princes, who supported Alexander IV. His active efforts to strengthen the crown led to opposition from the princes and only his premature death prevented war with the Archbishop of Mainz.

**Rush, Benjamin** (1746–1813)
American physician and political figure. A member of the **CONTINENTAL CONGRESS**, he was a signatory of the **DECLARATION OF INDEPENDENCE**. In 1786 he set up the first free dispensary in the USA. His method of treatment of yellow fever was controversial, but he did pioneering work with the mentally ill and was the author of *Medical Inquiries and Observations upon the Diseases of the Mind* (1812).

**Rush–Bagot Convention** (1817)
An agreement between the USA and Britain to demilitarize the Great Lakes by limiting the number, tonnage and armament of ships on each side. The convention ended the threat of a Great Lakes arms race, but complete disarmament on the US–Canada border did not follow until decades later. The parties involved were the acting US Secretary of State, Richard Rush, and the British Minister to the USA, Charles **BAGOT**.

**Rushdie, (Ahmad) Salman** (1947– )
British writer. Born in Bombay, India, of Muslim parents, he was educated there and in England, at Rugby and Cambridge. He became widely known after the publication of his second novel, *Midnight's Children* (1981). *The Satanic Verses* (1988) caused worldwide controversy because of its treatment of Islam from a secular point of view, and in Feb 1989 he was forced to go into hiding because of a sentence of death passed on him by Ayatollah **KHOMEINI** of Iran. The *fatwa* has never been rescinded, despite the Iranian government having disowned the death penalty placed upon him.

**Russell, John Russell, 1st Earl** (1792–1878)
British politician. He became an MP in 1813. He was Home Secretary (1835–9) and Secretary for War (1839–41), and became Whig–Liberal Prime Minister (1846–52) after the **CONSERVATIVE PARTY** split over the repeal of the **CORN LAWS**. In **ABERDEEN**'s coalition of 1852 he was Foreign Secretary and leader in the Commons. He lost popularity over alleged incompetent management of the **CRIMEAN WAR**, and in 1855 he retired; but he became Foreign Secretary again in the second **PALMERSTON** administration (1859), and was made an earl in 1861. On Palmerston's death (1865), he again became Premier, but resigned the following year. ► **LIBERAL PARTY** (UK); **WHIGS**

**Russell, Lord William** (1639–83)
English politician. He travelled in Europe, and at the **RESTORATION** became an MP. A supporter of the 1st Earl of **SHAFTESBURY**, he was a leading member of the movement to exclude the Duke of York (later **JAMES VII AND II**) from the succession. He was arrested with others for participation in the **RYE HOUSE PLOT** (1683), found guilty by a packed jury, and beheaded in London. ► **WHIGS**

**RUSSIA**    official name **Russian Federation**
A republic occupying much of eastern Europe and northern Asia, bounded to the north by the Arctic Ocean; to the west by Norway, Finland, Estonia, Latvia, Belarus, the Ukraine and the Black Sea; to the south by Georgia, Azerbaijan, the Caspian Sea, Kazakhstan, China, Mongolia and North Korea; and to the east by the Sea of Okhotsk and the Bering Sea. Russia has been settled by many ethnic groups, initially the nomadic **SLAVS**, Turks and Bulgars (3–7c AD). The Byzantine Christian Church had been established by the end of the 10c. Moscow was established

as a centre of political power in the north during the 14c. The overlordship of the Mongol **GOLDEN HORDE** was challenged successfully from 1380. **IVAN III, THE GREAT** proclaimed himself 'Sovereign of all Russia' in 1480, and **IVAN IV, THE TERRIBLE** doubled the size of the empire between 1533 and his death in 1584. Internal disorder amongst a feudal nobility and constant warfare with border countries (eg Poland and Sweden) retarded Russian development until Tsar **PETER I, THE GREAT**. Under **CATHERINE II, THE GREAT** Russia became a great power, extending its territory into southern and eastern Asia. Defeat in the **RUSSO-JAPANESE WAR** (1904–5) precipitated a revolution which, although unsuccessful, brought Russia's first constitution and parliament. The **RUSSIAN REVOLUTION** in 1917 ended the monarchy, and within the communist Union of Soviet Socialist Republics (formed in 1920), Russia was the dominant political force, covering 75 per cent of the Soviet area with 50 per cent of its population. With the disbandment of the Union in 1991, Russia became an independent republic and assumed the Soviet Union's permanent seat on the **UN** Security Council. It also became a founding member of the **CIS** (Commonwealth of Independent States). Relations with some former Soviet republics deteriorated in the early 1990s, and the process of transition to a **MARKET ECONOMY** caused a severe economic crisis in 1993, followed by a national referendum to endorse President Boris **YELTSIN**'s economic reforms, and increased presidential powers. In 1994 ethnic unrest in **CHECHNYA**, where Muslim Chechens declared an independent republic, resulted in the **CHECHEN WARS**. Despite failing health during the 1990s, Yeltsin clung on to power until Dec 1999, when he resigned and Vladimir **PUTIN** became President after elections in Mar 2000. President Putin was re-elected in 2004 and has asserted an increasing degree of centralization. Through the **NATO**–Russia Council, established in 2002, Russia participates in global discussions about security threats. ► **USSR**

## RULERS OF RUSSIA

| Regnal Dates | Name |
|---|---|
| 1283/1303 | Daniel |
| 1303/c.1328 | Yuri |
| c.1328/1341 | Ivan I, Moneybag |
| 1341/53 | Simeon the Proud |
| 1353/9 | Ivan II, the Meek |
| 1359/89 | Dmitri Donskoi |
| 1389/1425 | Vasili I |
| 1425/62 | Vasili II |
| 1462/1505 | Ivan III, the Great |
| 1505/33 | Vasili III |
| 1533/84 | Ivan IV, the Terrible |
| 1584/98 | Fyodor I |
| 1598/1605 | Boris Godunov |
| 1605 | Fyodor II |
| 1605/6 | 'False Dimitri' |
| 1606/10 | Vasili IV |
| 1613/45 | Michael Romanov |
| 1645/76 | Alexei Mikhailovich |
| 1676/82 | Fyodor III |
| 1682/96 | Ivan V[1] |
| 1682/1725 | Peter I, the Great[1] |
| 1725/7 | Catherine I |
| 1727/30 | Peter II |
| 1730/40 | Anna Ivanovna |
| 1740/1 | Ivan VI |
| 1741/62 | Elizabeth Petrovna |
| 1762 | Peter III |
| 1762/96 | Catherine II, the Great |
| 1796/1801 | Paul |
| 1801/25 | Alexander I |
| 1825/55 | Nicholas I |
| 1855/81 | Alexander II |
| 1881/94 | Alexander III |
| 1894/1917 | Nicholas II |

► *Notes*
[1] Co-Tsar

## Russian Civil War

A war which took place in Russia following the 1917 **OCTOBER REVOLUTION**. Anti-Bolshevik forces (Whites) led mostly by Tsarist generals mounted a series of military and political campaigns against the new Soviet regime, supported by the intervention of Allied troops with the support of the governments of Britain, France, the USA and Japan. They were opposed by the Soviet **RED ARMY**, created by **TROTSKY**, which successfully fought back against them between 1918 and 1922. There were five main theatres of war: the Caucasus and southern Russia; the Ukraine; the Baltic provinces; the Far North; and Siberia. After the end of **WORLD WAR I**, the military justification for intervention disappeared and the Allied governments eventually lost heart. The Red Army, which increasingly enjoyed more popular support than the Whites, gradually defeated the counter-revolutionary forces on all fronts, and established Soviet military and political power throughout the whole of Russia and its borderlands, with the exception of Poland, Finland and the Baltic states, which received their independence. Among the legacies of the war was continuing Soviet–Western mutual suspicion, and the inclusion within the USSR of peoples such as the Ukrainians, Armenians and Georgians,

who had tried to regain their independence, which had been lost to Tsarist Russia. ► **BOLSHEVIKS**; **CZECHOSLOVAK LEGION**; **RUSSIAN REVOLUTION**; **WHITE RUSSIANS**

## Russian Constituent Assembly (1918)

Russia's first genuinely representative constitution-making body. One reason behind the **FEBRUARY REVOLUTION** (1917) was Tsar **NICHOLAS II**'s autocratic government. What emerged was the **RUSSIAN PROVISIONAL GOVERNMENT**, which was to hold power until a more democratic system could be decided upon by a representative constituent assembly. This was elected (Nov 1917) on the basis of proportional representation. The **SOCIALIST REVOLUTIONARY PARTY** gained over half of the seats (380 out of 703); the **BOLSHEVIKS** less than a quarter (168). **LENIN** still let the Assembly meet in Jan 1918 in the half-hearted hope that it would legitimize his new government. When it refused on the first day, he dissolved it on the second, thus ending all democratic experimentation for the next 70 years.

## Russian Imperial Academy of Science (1725)

The summit of the intellectual achievements of **PETER I, THE GREAT**, finally established just after his death. To bring Russia into mainstream Europe, Peter had already set up a School of Mathematics and Navigation, a Medical School and a Naval Academy. The new academy covered four main areas: mathematics, physics, history and art, and was the basis for the reputation that scientists built up during the 18c and 19c in sharp contrast to the backward state of politics. The same might be said of its direct successor, the Soviet Academy of Sciences, now the Russian Academy.

### Russian Orthodox Church

A Church originating in missionary activity on the part of the see of Constantinople and in political interest on the part of **KIEV RUS** in the 10c. In 988 Prince Vladimir declared Christianity the official faith; in the 14c Moscow became the see of the metropolitan; and in the 15c the Church effectively declared itself autonomous. In 1589 **BORIS GODUNOV** secured a patriarchate for Moscow, thus elevating the Russian Orthodox Church internationally. In 1667 Patriarch **NIKON** managed to reform the Church but was himself removed from office. And in 1721 **PETER I, THE GREAT** engineered a Spiritual Regulation that virtually brought the Patriarch and the Church under the tsar's control until 1917. Subsequently the Church was separated from the State and suffered considerable persecution. Gaining some recognition as a result of its support for **STALIN** during the Great Patriotic War (1941–5), it was still largely controlled by government agencies. In the mid-20c there was some revival of interest in the Church on the part of the intelligentsia, conscious of the role it formerly played in Russian art and culture. The contemporary Russian Church retains its former doctrine and liturgy, but since **GORBACHEV**'s time and the collapse of **COMMUNISM** it has become more popular, not least among young people.

### Russian Provisional Government (1917)

The government that was supposed to rule Russia until the **RUSSIAN CONSTITUENT ASSEMBLY** could produce a legitimate alternative, although its interim approach to revolutionary events flawed it from the start. It discussed minor issues, rather than making the big decisions that were required. It also lacked military power, was constantly opposed by the Soviets, and was too slow to move from modest liberal to reasonable centrist. In the end, it was swept away by **LENIN** and his **BOLSHEVIKS**.

### Russian Revolution (1917)

The revolution which overthrew the Russian imperial regime and brought to power the first communist government. Mass demonstrations of discontented and revolutionary workers and soldiers in Petrograd led to the abdication of **NICHOLAS II** in Feb 1917. There followed a period of power-sharing between a liberal-minded provisional government and the more socialist Petrograd Soviet, known as 'dual power'. **LENIN**'s **BOLSHEVIKS** soon refused to collaborate, and in Oct led an insurgency of armed workers, soldiers and sailors, removing the provisional government, seizing political power and establishing the first Soviet government. This very quickly shaped the revolution to its own Leninist–Stalinist prescription. ► **APRIL THESES**; **FEBRUARY REVOLUTION** (Russia); **JULY DAYS**; **MENSHEVIKS**; **OCTOBER REVOLUTION**

### Russian Serfs, Emancipation of the (1861)

The abolition by Tsar **ALEXANDER II** of the legal possibility of anyone owning serfs. A crucial, but belated, reform in Russia, this emancipated about 20 million serfs (half the population) from their landlords, thus signalling the beginning of Russia's transition from a feudal to a capitalist economy. Frequently ill-treated, the serfs formed an increasingly uneconomic labour force and they fought badly in the **CRIMEAN WAR**. The new tsar had little alternative but to free them, and in any case he was afraid of a massive peasant rising. However, although the emancipation manifesto freed the serfs from their human bondage, the liberated peasants were organized into communes (**MIR**) and obliged to find so-called redemption payments for the little land they received. This meant that economic bondage continued and, with it, economic backwardness and social discontent. It was not until the Russian **REVOLUTION OF 1905** that the payments were cancelled.

### Russo-Finnish War (Winter War) (1939–40)

The war between the USSR and Finland during the winter of 1939–40. Soviet forces invaded Finland in order to secure Finnish territory from which to defend Leningrad against a possible German attack. In spite of courageous and damaging Finnish resistance and early Russian bungling, and because of lack of support from Britain and France, Finland capitulated (Mar 1940) and was forced to cede valuable territory to the USSR. ► **CONTINUATION WAR**; **WORLD WAR II**

### Russo-Japanese War (1904–5)

The war between an expanding Russian Empire and a modernizing Japan over rival territorial claims and imperial ambitions in northern China. Tsar **NICHOLAS II** and most of his ministers were keen on a war that they expected to win and that they hoped would divert attention from internal unrest, but it turned out to be a series of military and naval disasters for Russia; it had little popular support, and was marked by ineffectual command and political confusion. The war ended in Japanese victory with the Treaty of **PORTSMOUTH** (1905). It also precipitated the Russian **REVOLUTION OF 1905**.

### Russo-Turkish Wars

A series of wars between an expanding Russian and a decaying Ottoman empire from the 17c to the 19c, principally for domination of the Black Sea and access to the Mediterranean. From the mid-18c they also involved national liberation struggles of the non-Turkish, Orthodox Christian peoples of the Balkans from Turkish, Islamic rule. As a result of the wars (the last in 1877–8), much of the northern Black Sea coast and the Caucasus was incorporated into the Russian Empire and the greater part of the Balkans gained its independence or was set firmly on the road to independence. ► **OTTOMAN EMPIRE**

### Ruthenia, Emergence and Disappearance of (1918–45)

An ethnically mixed area of about half a million people, moved through four countries' control in a quarter of a century. In 1918 Ruthenia was part of Austria-Hungary but was summarily transferred to the new Czechoslovakia. Between Sep 1938 and Mar 1939 it hovered uncertainly on the brink of independence, which it enjoyed for a few days, before it passed to Hungary. In 1945 it was transferred to the Ukraine, part of the USSR. Its population was 60 per cent Ruthenian, related to Ukrainians, but it had Slovak and Hungarian minorities (and Polish). It was neither Catholic nor Orthodox, but Greek Catholic (Uniate). Small and divided, its fate was decided by crude power politics. Post-1991, it provided some of the internal drive towards the separation of the Ukraine from Russia.

### Ruusbroec, Jan van (1293–1381)
Southern Netherlands mystic. He worked as a priest in Brussels from 1317, but in 1344 left to live in the woods south of the city in the Groenendaal Valley. In 1350 he became Prior of an order of Augustinians there, the Congregation of Groenendaal, which was a formative influence on the Modern Devotion. Van Ruusbroec's writings were well known even in his lifetime, and were characterized by his allegorical symbolism and his distinction between the holy and the profane life.

### Ruyter, Michiel Adriaanzoon de (1607–76)
Dutch admiral. He gave distinguished service in the **ANGLO-DUTCH WARS** of 1652–4, 1665–7 and 1672–8, winning notable victories in the Four Days' Battle off Dunkirk (1666) and a daring raid up the rivers Medway and Thames (Dutch Descent on **CHATHAM**, 1667), in which much of the English fleet was destroyed. In the third war, his victories prevented a seaborne invasion of the United Provinces, but he was mortally wounded in a battle against the French off Sicily.

**RWANDA** official name **Republic of Rwanda**

A landlocked republic in central Africa, bounded to the north by Uganda; to the east by Tanzania; to the south by Burundi; and to the west by the Democratic Republic of the Congo and Lake Kivu. In the 16c the Tutsi tribe moved into the country and took over from the Hutu, forming a monarchy. Rwanda became a German protectorate in 1899, and was mandated with Burundi to Belgium as the Territory of Ruanda–Urundi in 1919. It became a **UN** Trust Territory administered by Belgium after **WORLD WAR II**. Unrest in 1959 led to a Hutu revolt and the overthrow of Tutsi rule, and in 1962 the union with Burundi was broken as both nations gained independence. A military coup took place in 1973, and there was a gradual return to stability under a new Hutu President Juvenal **HABYARIMANA**, whose party, the National Revolutionary Movement for Development (MRND), was

the only legal party until 1991. The first multiparty elections took place in 1992 but were boycotted by the mainly Tutsi *Front Patriotique Rwandaise* (FPR). A coalition government was formed in 1992 but ethnic unrest, which had broken out a few years earlier, continued unabated, and was exacerbated by massacres of Tutsis by the Hutu-dominated army. There were moves towards a peace agreement in 1993, but President Habyarimana, who had been negotiating the accord, was killed in an air crash in 1994. The fighting between the Hutu and Tutsi peoples re-ignited, resulting in the loss of many thousands of lives and homes and the flight of hundreds of thousands of refugees to Burundi and Tanzania. Although attacks by extremist Hutu insurgents continued, many Hutu exiles were repatriated in the late 1990s and reconciliation efforts and political reforms began. The FPR, which now dominates politics, is regarded as authoritarian and some political parties are banned, but President Paul Kagame, elected in 2003, has been a stabilizing force.

### Ryan, Claude (1925–2004)
Canadian politician. Replacing Robert **BOURASSA** as the Quebec **LIBERAL PARTY** leader after the defeat of 1976, he was largely responsible, with Jean **CHRÉTIEN**, for the successful campaign against secession in **LÉVESQUE**'s referendum of 1980. However, his own suggestions for a decentralized federation with a Federal Council serving as a provincially based watchdog were not favourably received by Anglophones and he resigned the Liberal leadership after defeat by the **PARTI QUÉBECOIS** in the elections of 1981. He has remained a Minister of the National Assembly, and following the Liberal victory in 1985, he was Minister of Education in the Bourassa government.

### Rye House Plot (Apr 1683)
An alleged plot by **WHIGS** to murder **CHARLES II** of England and James, Duke of York, at Rye House near Hoddesdon, Hertfordshire. A counterpart to the alleged **POPISH PLOT** of 1678, it was foiled by the early departure of the royal pair from Newmarket. The conspirators were betrayed and captured; two of them, Algernon **SIDNEY** and Lord William **RUSSELL**, were executed. ▶ **JAMES VII AND II**

### Ryerson, Adolphus Egerton (1803–82)
Canadian educationist and politician. A Methodist minister and editor of the widely read *Christian Guardian*, Ryerson wielded tremendous influence. He constantly attacked the privileges of the Anglican Church, pressing for the secularization and sale of the **CLERGY RESERVES**, and for the proceeds to be used to support a compulsory school system. A reformer until a visit to England in 1833, he was absent during the rebellion of 1837, and condemned William Lyon **MACKENZIE**'s radicalism and readiness to use force. He opposed **RESPONSIBLE GOVERNMENT**, supporting Sir Charles **METCALFE** in the struggle with Robert **BALDWIN** and **LAFONTAINE**, who suspected that he had joined the **TORIES**. In 1844 he was appointed chief superintendent of education in **CANADA WEST**, a post he held until 1876 and in which he established the educational system of Ontario.

**Rykov, Alexei Ivanovich** (1881–1938)
Russian revolutionary and Communist Party and government official. Born in Saratov into a poor peasant family, he was educated at Kazan University and soon became involved in social democratic politics, being arrested, imprisoned and exiled several times. In mid-1917 he was elected to the Moscow Soviet and helped to organize the Bolshevik Revolution there, becoming People's Commissar for Internal Affairs in the first Soviet government. He held a number of senior government posts (1919–36), and was also a member of the **POLITBURO** (1919–29). But in 1928, together with **BUKHARIN** and Tomsky, he led the 'right opposition' to **STALIN**'s economic policies and had to give up his Party positions. In 1937 he was arrested for alleged anti-Party activities, and was shot the following year. He was among other prominent victims of Stalin's purges rehabilitated during the **GORBACHEV** era. ► **BOLSHEVIKS**; **FEBRUARY REVOLUTION** (Russia)

**Ryzhkov, Nikolai Ivanovich** (1929– )
Soviet politician. A Russian born in the Donetsk region in the Ukraine, he worked as a miner before studying engineering in Sverdlovsk. He then worked his way up from welding foreman in a heavy machine building plant to head of the giant Uralmash engineering conglomerate, the largest industrial enterprise in the USSR. A member of the Communist Party since 1956, he was brought to Moscow in 1975 to work as First Deputy Minister for Heavy Transport and Machine Building. Four years later, he became First Deputy Chairman of Gosplan, and in 1982 was inducted into the Party Secretariat by Yuri **ANDROPOV**, as Head of Economic Affairs. He was made a member of the **POLITBURO** by Mikhail **GORBACHEV** in Apr 1985 and became Prime Minister in Sep 1985, with the task of restructuring the Soviet planning process on the quasi-autonomous Uralmash model. He was not particularly successful in introducing economic change, and living standards declined. In the reform debate that followed in the autumn of 1990, Ryzhkov produced a very modest scheme compared with Stanislav **SHATALIN**'s radical plan. Gorbachev opted for a middle course and Ryzhkov was relieved of his post.

**SA** (*Sturmabteilung*, 'Storm Division')
German paramilitary league. Founded in 1921, the SA (sometimes dubbed the 'Brownshirts' because of its uniform) served as the paramilitary arm of the **NAZI PARTY**. In its early years it vied with the Nazi Party for supremacy within the movement and its leader, Ernst **RÖHM**, envisaged a military rising against the **WEIMAR REPUBLIC**. However, the failure of **HITLER'S MUNICH PUTSCH** in Nov 1923 persuaded the latter to seek power through electoral means. The SA was subordinated to the Nazi Party, in which role it gave excellent service as a proselytizer, propaganda vehicle, defence league and terrorist organization. Following Hitler's takeover, its 400,000, largely working-class, members were joined by over 2 million recruits, often blue-collar unemployed. Their impatience with Hitler's relative caution in political matters resulted in mounting lawlessness, which their leaders, still resenting their subordination to the party, did too little to control. Furthermore, Röhm openly aspired to replace the **REICHSWEHR** by the SA and carry the revolution further. All these factors combined to trigger the purging of the SA in mid-1934. After this it played a minor role in the Third **REICH**.

**Saarland**
Territory in south-west Germany, now a **LAND** of the Federal Republic. A heavily industrialized region on the north-eastern border of France, the Treaty of **VERSAILLES** placed the Saarland under a **LEAGUE OF NATIONS** administration and economically at France's disposal. The referendum scheduled for Jan 1935 to decide on the territory's ultimate future witnessed an overwhelming vote for, and a return to Germany. After **WORLD WAR II** the region was again detached from Germany, being constituted as an autonomous territory under French occupation, but the referendum of Jan 1957 saw the Saarland return to Germany.

**Sabah Family**
The ruling family of the oil-rich Gulf shaykhdom of Kuwait. Founded in the 18c, the current Amir (or Shaykh) of Kuwait is Jabir III bin Ahmad al-Sabah. A protectorate of Britain until 1971, Kuwait has been ruled by the Shaykh through his Prime Minister, Saad al-Abdullah al-Sabah, the Crown Prince. Most senior posts in Kuwait have been held by members of the ruling family, a matter which has given rise to much discontent not least in the aftermath of the **GULF WAR**, when members of the ruling family, who had amassed enormous wealth as a result of oil revenues, fled the country on the Iraqi invasion (1990), only to return after the coalition forces had duly expelled the

occupying Iraqis and, it would appear, to make few concessions to the political aspirations of the remainder of the population.

**Sabas, St ► SAVA, ST**

**Sabra**
Palestinian refugee camp on the outskirts of Beirut, Lebanon, created following the evacuation of Palestinians from the city after the June 1982 Israeli attack. It was the scene of a massacre of Palestinians by Christian Phalangists in Sep 1983.

**Sacajawea** (c.1786–1812)
Shoshone Native American, also known as Bird Woman. She was sold into slavery to a French-Canadian trader, who took her with him in 1804 when he joined the US transcontinental **LEWIS AND CLARK EXPEDITION**. Her participation was vital to the success of the expedition, which established an American presence in the Pacific north-west.

**Sacco and Vanzetti Affair** (1921–7)
US political *cause célèbre*. Nicola Sacco and Bartolomeo Vanzetti were arrested in 1920, during the **RED SCARE**, for a post office robbery and murder in South Braintree, Massachusetts. During the trial, the prosecutor was allowed to deliver inflammatory anti-communist speeches by the judge, who privately called the two defendants 'those anarchist bastards'. Their conviction and sentence to death therefore caused an uproar throughout the world. In response, Governor Fuller of Massachusetts appointed a committee to examine the case. It found that although the trial judge had been in grave breach of official decorum, justice had been done. The two men died in the electric chair in 1927. Debate on the case continues.

**Sacheverell, Henry** (c.1674–1724)
Church of England divine and Tory high-churchman. He was granted the Staffordshire parish of Cannock, and in 1709 delivered two sermons, one at Derby assizes, the other at St Paul's, attacking the Whig government with such rancour that he was impeached (1710) before the House of **LORDS**. He was found guilty and suspended from preaching for three years. Partly because of hostile Tory publicity generated by the trial, the Godolphin ministry fell that same summer, and in 1713 Sacheverell was selected by the House of **COMMONS** to preach the **RESTORATION** sermon. He was presented to the rich rectory of St Andrew's Holborn, where he squabbled with his parishioners, and was suspected of Jacobite sympathies.

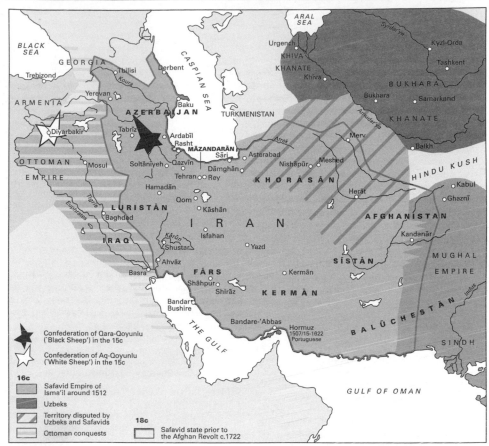

Confederation of Qara-Qoyunlu ('Black Sheep') in the 15c

Confederation of Aq-Qoyunlu ('White Sheep') in the 15c

**16c**

Safavid Empire of Isma'il around 1512

Uzbeks

Territory disputed by Uzbeks and Safavids

Ottoman conquests

**18c**

Safavid state prior to the Afghan Revolt c.1722

**Safavid State**

## Sachsenspiegel

Literally 'Saxon Mirror', the term refers to the most important of the medieval compilations of Saxon law, which was used by many towns as a basis for their constitutions. It was compiled by a knight, Eike von Repgow, between 1220 and 1225. Originally in Latin, it was later translated into the vernacular. It is divided into two sections, the first dealing with constitutional, criminal and civil law, and the second with feudal law.

## Sadat, Anwar el- (1918–81)

Egyptian politician. He trained for the army in Cairo, and in 1952 was a member of the coup which deposed King FAROUK. After becoming President in 1970, he temporarily assumed the post of Prime Minister (1973–4), after which he sought settlement of the conflict with Israel. He met Menachem BEGIN, the Israeli Premier, in Jerusalem (1977) and at CAMP DAVID, USA (1978), in which year he and Begin were jointly awarded the NOBEL PEACE PRIZE. Following criticism by other Arab statesmen and hard-line Muslims, he was assassinated by extremists while still in office. ► ARAB–ISRAELI WARS

## Sadowa, Battle of ► KÖNIGGRÄTZ-SADOWA, BATTLE OF

## Safavid Dynasty

The dynasty, possibly of Kurdish origin, which provided the Shahs of Persia from 1501 to 1722. Its eponymous founder, Safi al-Din, an Azerbaijani, mar-

ried the daughter of a leader of a Muslim Sufi order. After becoming the order's head in 1301, he gradually developed it into a revolutionary religious movement, the *Safaviyya*, under the hereditary leadership of his descendants, and was based at Ardabil near the Caspian Sea. Its military strength was provided by many of the Turkmen tribesmen of Azerbaijan and eastern Anatolia, who came to be known as Qizilbash ('redheads') from their distinctive headwear. By the end of the 15c the *Safaviyya* had grown strong enough to challenge for political power in Persia, and at Sharur in 1501 Isma'il I (1487–1524) defeated the leading Turkmen confederation, the Aq-Qoyunlu ('White Sheep'), and proclaimed himself shah. He proceeded to impose a variety of Islam called Twelver Shiism which has remained the predominant religion of Iran up to the present. Although Isma'il took over a Persian bureaucracy, military power remained with the Qizilbash leaders whose internecine struggles led to civil war in the reign of his son Tahmasp I (1514–76). Their supremacy was not ended until the reign of 'ABBAS I, THE GREAT, whose military and administrative reforms constituted a lasting achievement that enabled the Safavid state to survive a series of mediocre successors and pressure from Ottomans and Uzbeks until its overthrow by the Afghans in 1722.

## Sagasta, Práxedes Mateo (1827–1903)

Spanish politician. He was a member of from 1855 and took part in insurrection and 1866, having twice to flee to France. Se

Prime Minister (1871–2, 1874, 1881–3, 1885–90, 1892–5, 1897–9 and 1901–2), he introduced a number of reforms including universal male suffrage and trial by jury.

**Saguna, Andreiu** (1809–73)
Romanian political and religious leader. He studied philosophy, law and theology before being ordained priest (1833). During 1848, the year of revolutions, he took a leading role among the Transylvanian Romanian nationalists, becoming their chief spokesman at the Viennese court and presenting their case against the Hungarians. Loyalty to the Habsburg emperor remained his guiding principle and in 1849 he presented a petition for the political and religious autonomy of the Romanians within the Habsburg Empire. He worked for the recognition of the equality of the Romanian people and their two churches and was appointed the first Metropolitan of the ecclesiastical province of Transylvania (1864). His popularity among his own people later declined when he pledged loyalty to Emperor **FRANCIS JOSEPH** and supported the Austro-Hungarian settlement of 1867.

**Sa'id, Nuri al-** (1888–1958)
Iraqi politician. After military training at the Istanbul Staff College for the Turkish army, he fled to Egypt when his Pan-Arab activities became suspect, taking an active part in the **ARAB REVOLT** in which he served under T E **LAWRENCE** and the Amir, **FAYSAL I**. He followed Faysal to Iraq, where he was active in the establishment of the Iraqi army. In 1921 he became Iraq's first Chief of the General Staff and a year later Defence Minister. From 1930 onwards he held office as Prime Minister several times. Strongly pro-British and anticommunist in his sympathies, he fell foul of the Left and, in particular, those with pro-**NASSER** leanings. He was captured at the time of Abd al-Krim **QASSIM**'s coup d'état in 1958, and killed.

**Sa'id Pasha** (1822–63)
Ottoman Viceroy of Egypt (1854/63). He granted the concession for making the Suez Canal.

**Saigon, Battle of** (1975)
The final stage of the **VIETNAM WAR**, in which the city of Saigon, the headquarters of US (until 1973) and South Vietnamese military forces, fell to the communist forces of North Vietnam.

**Saigo Takamori** (1827–77)
Japanese **SAMURAI** leader. He commanded the proimperial forces that overthrew the **TOKUGAWA SHOGUNATE**. One of the most important leaders of the new Meiji government, Saigo resigned (1873) when his proposal for a punitive expedition to Korea to enforce the opening of diplomatic relations was turned down by his more cautious colleagues. He retired to **SATSUMA**, his native domain, and there he became increasingly critical of the government's reforms to create a centralized state and abolish the samurai class. His disaffected samurai followers resorted to open rebellion in 1877 which Saigo, initially reluctantly, agreed to lead. The rebellion, the last significant samurai uprising against the new Meiji government, was suppressed by the new (non-samurai) conscript army created in 1873, and Saigo committed suicide shortly afterwards. He has remained a popular hero Japan, the symbol of traditional virtues and resistance against arbitrary government.

**St Alban's Raid** (1865)
A Confederate attack made from Canada, on the town of St Albans, Vermont, during the **AMERICAN CIVIL WAR**. Such raids heightened tension between Great Britain and the USA during the civil war, and fears of retaliation were one of the factors leading Canadians to confederation.

**Saint Arnaud, Jacques Leroy de** (1796–1854)
French soldier. Louis Napoleon (**NAPOLEON III**) made him War Minister (1851–4) and he took an active part in the coup d'état of 2 Dec 1851 that gave Napoleon the crown. He was rewarded with a marshal's baton. In the **CRIMEAN WAR** he commanded the French forces, and cooperated with Lord **RAGLAN** at Alma, but nine days later died on his way home to France.

**St Bartholomew's Day Massacre** (24 Aug 1572)
The slaughter of French **HUGUENOTS** in Paris, ordered by King **CHARLES IX** and connived at by the Queen Mother, **CATHERINE DE' MEDICI**, to coincide with celebrations for the marriage of Margaret of Valois and Henry of Navarre (later **HENRY IV**) (18 Aug). An attempted assassination of the Huguenot leader Admiral **COLIGNY** failed (22 Aug), but mass butchery of Huguenots followed. ► **VALOIS DYNASTY**

**St Elijah's Day Revolt** ► **ILINDEN UPRISING**

**Saintes, Battle of the** (12 Apr 1782)
A major Caribbean Anglo-French naval action during the **AMERICAN REVOLUTION**. In that war, France and Spain sided with Britain's rebellious North American colonists and used the British preoccupation with the Americans to obtain naval supremacy and capture British colonies in the Caribbean. In 1782 the British admiral George **RODNEY** (who had taken St Lucia in 1778) returned from Europe to shadow the French commander, the Count de Grasse, who was planning to attack Jamaica with 35 warships. Battle was joined off the Saintes (the small rocky islets between Dominica and Guadeloupe) on 12 Apr and, after a day of heavy fighting, de Grasse, his flagship, the *Ville de Paris*, and six other ships were captured by the British. Rodney was hailed as the saviour of Jamaica.

**St Germain, Treaty of** (10 Sep 1919)
The treaty between the Allied victor powers and Austria, signed unwillingly by the latter, which defined the limits of the rump Austrian state, confirmed its separation from Hungary, and in effect blocked the desired union of German Austria with Germany. ► **WORLD WAR I**

**Saint-Just, Louis Antoine Léon Florelle de** (1767–94)
French revolutionary. He wrote poetry and essays, notably *L'Esprit de la révolution* (1791). He was elected to the National Convention (1792), attracted notice by his fierce tirades against **LOUIS XVI**, and as a devoted follower of **ROBESPIERRE** was sent on diplomatic and military missions. He joined the Committee of **PUBLIC SAFETY** (1793), contributing to the destruction of **DANTON** and **HÉBERT**. He became President of the National **CONVENTION** (1794), and sponsored the radical Ventôse Laws, redistributing

property to the poor. He was guillotined with Robespierre in the Thermidorian Reaction. ► **FRENCH REVOLUTION; THERMIDOR**

---

**ST KITTS AND NEVIS**    official name **Federation of St Christopher and Nevis**

An independent state in the North Leeward Islands in the eastern Caribbean Sea. It comprises the islands of St Christopher (St Kitts), Nevis and Sombrero. Originally inhabited by **CARIBS**, the islands were visited by Christopher **COLUMBUS** in 1493, who named the larger one Saint Christopher. The name was shortened to St Kitts by English settlers when the island became the first British colony in the West Indies, in 1623. Control was disputed between France and Britain in the 17–18c, and the island was ceded to Britain in 1783. St Kitts and Nevis were united in 1882, along with Anguilla (which became a separate British dependency in 1980). They became a state in association with the UK in 1967 and gained independence within the **COMMONWEALTH OF NATIONS** in 1983. In 1997 the government of Nevis voted to secede from St Kitts and the issue went to a referendum. Held on 10 Aug 1998, this failed to secure the two-thirds majority required, but Nevis, which already has its own administration and assembly, still hopes to achieve independence.

**Saint Laurent, Louis Stephen** (1882–1973)
Canadian lawyer and politician. In 1914 he became Law Professor at Laval University and was appointed counsel to the **ROWELL–SIROIS COMMISSION** between 1937 and 1940. In 1941 Mackenzie **KING** appointed him Minister of Justice and, unlike other Quebec Liberals, he supported King on conscription in 1944, for which he was made Secretary of State for External Affairs in 1946. King's own choice as his successor, Saint Laurent became Prime Minister in 1948, and enacted such social programmes as the extension of the old-age pension scheme and hospital insurance. Under his leadership, the Liberals were re-elected in 1949 and again, with a huge majority, in 1953; but he was defeated by the Conservatives under **DIEFENBAKER** in 1958 after a campaign that focused on the Liberals' arrogance in power.

---

**ST LUCIA**

An independent constitutional monarchy and the second-largest of the Windward Islands, situated in the eastern Caribbean Sea. Originally inhabited by Arawak Indians who were displaced by **CARIBS**, it was reputedly discovered by Christopher **COLUMBUS** in 1502. The British failed to settle it at first and it was

eventually settled by the French, but ownership was disputed between Britain and France from 1659. It became a British Crown Colony in 1814, and gained independence within the **COMMONWEALTH OF NATIONS** in 1979. Its economy has suffered since the **EU** phased out preferred access status for Windward Islands bananas, its main export.

**St Petersburg, Foundation of** (1703)
This city was the symbol of the advance of **PETER I, THE GREAT** into Europe and formed the basis of Russian naval power in the Baltic and beyond. He started building it near the mouth of the Neva River in a strategic position, but on swampy ground that cost thousands of lives. It was not until 1721, the year of the Treaty of **NYSTADT**, that the city was secure, and it took a century of construction, from Bartolomeo Rastrelli's **WINTER PALACE** through to Andrei Voronikhin's Kazan Cathedral, before it could claim to be one of the great cities of Europe. However, by that time, Tsar **ALEXANDER I**'s Russia was one of the great European powers.

**St Quentin, Battle of** (1557)
The battle fought near the town of that name in Picardy, resulting in a victory for the troops of **PHILIP II** of Spain, commanded by the Count of **EGMOND** and the Duke of Savoy, over the French troops commanded by the Dukes of Montmorency and Nevers. Philip II built his palace-monastery of El Escorial in part as a memorial of the battle, fought on the Feast of St Lawrence, to whom the building was dedicated.

**Saint-Simon, Claude Henri de Rouvroy, Count of** (1760–1825)
French social reformer and founder of French socialism. He served in the **AMERICAN REVOLUTION**, and during the **FRENCH REVOLUTION** was imprisoned as an aristocrat. His writing was a reaction against the great savagery of the revolutionary period, and proclaimed a brotherhood of man in which science and technology would become a new spiritual authority.

**St Stephen, Crown of** (1000)
The name given to the Hungarian royal title. Stephen (or Istvan in Magyar) was the baptismal name of Vajk, the son of Geza, who drew the Hungarian tribes together to form a feudal state. His baptism, like his marriage to a Bavarian princess, Giselle, was part of the process of raising the state's international standing. In 1000 he succeeded in obtaining the Emperor's permission to raise Hungary to the status of a kingdom, the crown allegedly being donated by the pope. This rare double achievement gave the new creation

some security at the time and, since Stephen was canonized in 1083 after his death, considerable pretensions thereafter.

### St Valentine's Day Massacre (14 Feb 1929)

Perhaps the most notorious gangland slaying in US history. It took place in Chicago, Illinois, where members of Al CAPONE's gang disguised themselves as policemen to gain admittance to a garage frequented by members of the rival 'Bugs' Moran gang. They lined the seven men they found there against a wall and then machine-gunned them to death. No one was ever convicted of the crime.

### ST VINCENT AND THE GRENADINES

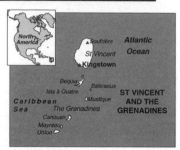

An island country in the Windward Islands, situated in the eastern Caribbean Sea. It was visited by Christopher COLUMBUS in 1498. The first European settlement was by British settlers in 1762, who entered into conflict with the native CARIBS and the French, defeating both in 1762. Most of the Caribs were deported in 1797, and black Africans were imported as slave labour. St Vincent and the Grenadines was part of the Windward Islands Colony (1880–1958) and then joined the West Indies Federation in 1958–62. It was a British colony from 1871 to 1956, when colonial rule ended, and gained its independence in 1979 under Prime Minister Milton Cato. He was succeeded in 1984 by James MITCHELL, who served until 2000, when his New Democratic Party was defeated by the United Labour Party. The economy has suffered since the EU phased out preferred access status for Windward Islands bananas, its main export.

### Saionji Kimmochi (1849–1940)

Japanese politician. The son of a court noble, Saionji studied law in France (1871–80) before becoming a member of the Privy Council and House of Peers. In 1903 he became leader of the largest party in the Diet, the SEIYUKAI, and served two terms as Prime Minister (1906–8 and 1911–12). After 1924, as the sole surviving GENRO (the only one not to have come from CHOSHU or SATSUMA), Saionji unsuccessfully attempted to restrain the military's increasing influence over politics.

### Sakharov, Andrei (1921–89)

Russian physicist and dissident. In 1948 he joined the nuclear weapons research group, and played a critical role in developing the Soviet hydrogen bomb. He received many honours and was elected a full member of the Academy of Sciences in 1953 at a very early age. While still supporting the USSR's possession of nuclear arms, he began opposing nuclear testing in the late 1950s because of the harmful effects of fall-out, thereafter supporting East–West cooperation and

human rights, and in 1975 he was awarded the NOBEL PEACE PRIZE. All of this brought him criticism and harassment at home and, exiled to Gorky in 1980 as a leading dissident, he lived under poor conditions until he was restored to favour, somewhat reluctantly, by Mikhail GORBACHEV in 1987. He was elected to the Congress of People's Deputies in 1989 as a representative of the Academy, and was active within it until he died of a heart attack. His contribution to the promotion of political tolerance in the USSR and the relaxation of East–West tension was almost unmatched. ►CIVIL RIGHTS

### Sakoku

The Japanese expression (literally, 'national seclusion') first coined in the early 19c to refer to the seclusion policy adopted by the TOKUGAWA SHOGUNATE and formalized in five directives issued between 1633 and 1639. The Tokugawa, fearing the subversive political impact of Christianity, excluded Spanish and Portuguese missionaries, persecuted Japanese Christians, and prohibited all Japanese from engaging in foreign trade or travelling abroad. The policy was also designed to strengthen Tokugawa control by preventing the DAIMYO from becoming too economically powerful through the profits of foreign trade. Not all foreign trade was banned, however. Carefully-regulated trade under Tokugawa control was permitted at Nagasaki (for the Dutch and Chinese) and at Tsushima (for the Koreans). It was through contact with the Dutch that Japan acquired a substantial body of Western knowledge during the 18c and early 19c. The seclusion policy was formally ended in 1854, when the KANAGAWA TREATY with the USA opened two ports to US ships. ►TREATY PORTS

### Saladin, properly Salah al-Din Yusuf ibn Ayyub (1137–93)

Sultan of Egypt and Syria and leader of the Muslims against the Crusaders in Palestine. Born in Mesopotamia, he entered the service of NUR AL-DIN, Amir of Syria, and on his death (1174) proclaimed himself Sultan, reduced Mesopotamia, and received the homage of the Seljuk princes of Asia Minor. His remaining years were occupied in wars with the Christians, whom he defeated at HITTIN in 1187, recapturing Jerusalem and almost all their fortified places in Syria. A third CRUSADE, headed by the kings of France and England, captured Acre in 1191, and he was defeated. He died soon after at Damascus. ►AYYUBID DYNASTY; CRUSADE, THIRD

### Salan, Raoul (1899–1984)

French general. From 1956 he was Commander-in-Chief of the French army in Algeria. In 1958 he played an important part in the crisis that brought Charles de GAULLE back to power, and was appointed by him as delegate of the government in Algeria, with full powers. An opponent of Algerian independence, he was brought back to France in 1959, and retired in 1960. In 1961 he joined in an attempted putsch led by General Challe. When this failed, he went underground in Algeria, and launched the OAS (*Organisation de l'Armée Secrète*), using terrorist methods in its struggle against de Gaulle's Algerian policy. He was arrested in 1962, condemned to life imprisonment, but later amnestied.

### Salandra, Antonio (1853–1931)

Italian politician and university professor. Elected a deputy in 1886, Salandra was a right-wing liberal who held various ministerial posts in the Pelloux and **SONNINO** governments. After 1910 he tried to become the focus for moderate and conservative forces, becoming Prime Minister in 1914. Together with Sonnino he was responsible for Italy's entry into **WORLD WAR I**, deciding to back France and Britain against Italy's former allies, Austria and Germany, feeling such a policy would bring greater territorial gains. He was replaced as Prime Minister in 1916, but formed part of the delegation to the **PARIS PEACE CONFERENCE**. He refused to form a government in Oct 1922 and made little effort to oppose **MUSSOLINI**, actually being on the fascist **LISTONE** in the Apr 1924 elections. After the murder of **MATTEOTTI**, Salandra withdrew his support from the fascists.

### Salasco Armistice (9 Aug 1848)

The armistice that brought fighting between the Piedmontese army of **CHARLES ALBERT** and the Austrian forces under **RADETZKY** to an end after the Battle of **CUSTOZZA**. The peace was not long-standing, Charles Albert declaring war again in 1849.

### Salazar, António de Oliveira (1889–1970)

Portuguese dictator. From the conservative, devout smallholding peasantry of the north, Salazar's seminary education allowed this reserved and studious individual to become a lecturer in economics at Coimbra, the university of the élite. He was active in a Catholic lay group and stood as a parliamentary candidate under the First Republic on three occasions. His economic expertise led to his ascendancy under the military dictatorship of General **CARMONA** (1926–32). During the early 1930s he laid the foundations of the **ESTADO NOVO** which he would dominate as dictator for over 35 years. The authoritarian and supposedly corporatist Salazarist state was underpinned by the army and the feared security police, the **PIDE**. Salazar's retrogressive economic policies made Portugal the poorest country in Europe (in 1960 per capita income was lower than that of Turkey), while greatly enhancing the wealth of its opulent oligarchy. Indeed, Salazar's economic failure made Portugal determined not to give up its African colonies. Yet it was the revolt of the army against the war in Africa against the independence movements (1961–74) that led to the downfall of the regime after his death. Although he fell from power in 1968 through ill health, he died in 1970 still thinking that he was dictator. ► **REPUBLIC, FIRST** (Portugal)

### Saldanha, João Carlos, Duke of (1790–1876)

Portuguese politician and soldier. He fought at Busaco (1810), helped Brazil against Montevideo (1817–22) and sided with Dom Pedro against Dom Miguel as a moderate constitutionalist. From 1846 to 1856, he was alternately head of the government and in armed opposition. Created a duke in 1846, he was twice ambassador in Rome, Prime Minister in 1870, and ambassador in London from 1871.

### Saleh, Ali Abdullah (1942–)

North Yemeni soldier and politician. A colonel in the army of the Yemen Arab Republic, he took part in the 1974 coup when Colonel Ibrahim al-Hamadi seized power, with rumours that the monarchy was to be restored. Hamadi was assassinated in 1977 and Colonel Hussein al-Ghashmi took over, only to be killed by a South Yemen terrorist bomb in 1978. Against this background of death and violence Saleh became President. Under his leadership, the war with South Yemen was ended and the two countries agreed to eventual reunion. He was re-elected in 1983 and 1988, later becoming President of the Council of the Republic of Yemen (1990–4) and President of the Republic of Yemen (1994– ).

### Salem Witch Trials (1692)

An outbreak of hysteria in colonial Massachusetts in which accusations were made that **WITCHCRAFT** was being practised. The situation quickly outran the control of the town authorities. Arrests were made on the unsupported testimony of young girls and 19 people were executed. Judge Samuel Sewall later publicly confessed that the trials had been in error and that he believed no witchcraft had been practised. The ramifications of the episode have been attributed to the breakdown of Puritan control, the tensions of economic and social change focused on conflict between Salem Village and Salem Town, and wider provincial fears (awakened by the recall of the charter) as to its future after the **GLORIOUS REVOLUTION**.

### Salians

(1) A Frankish tribe, first heard of in the 4c, which took over the leadership of the Frankish kingdom under the Merovingians. They are best known for the codification of Frankish law bearing their name, the *Lex Salica* (**SALIC LAW**). (2) The royal dynasty that came to power with **CONRAD II** and encompassed the reigns of **HENRY III**, **HENRY IV** and **HENRY V**, who was the last in the line. It is not clear whether the name of the dynasty refers to the Frankish tribe, to whom they were undoubtedly related, or whether it derives from the Old High German term *sal*, meaning 'lordship'. ► **FRANKS**

### Salic Law

In normal usage, a rule of succession to the throne barring women, and men whose royal descent is only through females. The principle was established in France from 1316, partly by ingeniously invoking the law-code of the Salian **FRANKS**, which was issued c.511 and given definitive form c.798 – Salic Law (Latin *Lex Salica*) in its original sense.

### Salisbury, Marquis of ► CECIL, ROBERT

### Salò, Republic of

The fascist 'Italian Social Republic' established in the north of Italy under German protection in autumn 1943, with **MUSSOLINI** as its puppet ruler. The republic had no single administrative centre, different ministries being located in different towns, eg Public Works in Venice, Finance in Brescia, Propaganda at Salò. It is from the last that it derived its usual name, a reflection of the fact that it was little more than a propaganda exercise, real power being located not in Italy but in Germany.

### SALT (Strategic Arms Limitation Talks)

The name given to two rounds of talks held between the USA and USSR to limit their nuclear weapons arsenals and slow down the arms race. The first began in Helsinki in 1969, designed to place a numerical limit on intercontinental nuclear weapons. An agreement (SALT I) was reached in 1972. SALT II talks began that same year, and agreement was reached in 1979. There developed, however, a hardening of attitudes in the West towards the USSR, brought on in large part by the Soviet refusal to allow on-site verification. Once the USSR invaded Afghanistan, US SEN-ATE ratification of SALT II was doomed. Both countries, nevertheless, initially kept to the limitations established in the agreement. The arms situation was ultimately transformed by the REAGAN–GORBACHEVarms reduction accord, the revolutions of 1989 and the break-up of the USSR in 1991. ► START

### Samarkand, Capture of (1497)
The capture of the old Timurid capital of Samarkand by BABUR, who was to be the first of the great Mughal rulers in India, represents the successful assertion of his authority over his kinsmen. Babur had earlier succeeded to his father's position as Mirza of Fergana, which position his uncles, Sultan Ahmad Mirza of Samarkand and Sultan Mahmud of Tashkent, were attempting to usurp. Although he only held Samarkand for a few months, Babur's success in wresting control of the city from his paternal uncle served notice of his promise for the future.

### samizdat
From the Russian *sam*, 'self' and *izdatelstvo*, 'publishing', the term refers to privately circulated editions of books and pamphlets not authorized for publication by the state censorship in the former USSR, and usually reproduced laboriously in typescript. The habit caught on in Poland and other communist countries, and helped to mould critical public opinion.

**SAMOA**  official name **Independent State of Samoa**, formerly (to 1997) **Western Samoa**

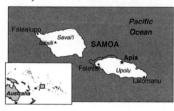

An island nation in the south-west Pacific Ocean, 1,600 mi/2,600 km north-east of Auckland, New Zealand. Inhabited since around 1000BC, Samoa was visited by the Dutch in 1772, and in 1889 was divided between Germany (which acquired Western Samoa) and the USA (which acquired Tutuila and adjacent small islands, now known as American Samoa). After 1914 Western Samoa was administered by New Zealand, from 1919 to 1946 under a LEAGUE OF NATIONS mandate and then as a UN Trust Territory, until it gained independence in 1962. Malietoa Tanumafili II became head of state for life in 1963. The legislative assembly voted to change the country's name to Samoa in 1997.

### Samori (c.1830–1900)
West African Islamic leader. Possessed of great military talent, he established in the 1870s an empire in the upper Niger region from Sierra Leone to Bamako and south into modern Côte d'Ivoire. After an initial confrontation in 1883, the French co-existed with Samori for a number of years, but between 1891 and 1894 conquered Samori's empire. Samori re-established himself further east between Côte d'Ivoire and northern Ghana, but he was captured by the French in 1898 and exiled to Gabon.

### Samsonov, Alexander (1859–1914)
Russian general. He was in charge of a force in the RUSSO-JAPANESE WAR (1904–5). In WORLD WAR I he commanded the army which, in order to take pressure off Russia's French ally, was given the task of invading East Prussia in Aug 1914, but was decisively defeated by HINDENBURG at the Battle of TANNEN-BERG (26–31 Aug). His shame and losses (100,000 prisoners) were so great, and his awareness that the last Battle of Tannenberg (Grunwald) in 1410 had been a huge Russian victory over the TEUTONIC KNIGHTS was so strong, that he committed suicide.

### Samuel (d.1014)
Emperor of Macedonia (c.976/1014). It appears that c.976 he became ruler of the small Slav state of Macedonia which had been under the nominal authority of Byzantium since 971. While the Byzantine Emperor Basil II was distracted by rebellions in Asia Minor, Samuel set out to increase his territory by conquest. He marched into Thessaly, central Greece and the Peloponnese and into the Bulgarian lands between the Danube and the Balkan Mountains. He took Larissa in Greece (985) but was unable to seize Salonica. By the end of the 10c, he had subdued Dioclea (modern Montenegro) and had marched as far as Zadar. He established his capital at Ohrid and proclaimed himself Emperor. Samuel's progress was halted when the armies of Basil II fell on Macedonia, crushing his forces at Strumica. According to legend, Samuel died from shock when he beheld the sorry spectacle of his returning men who, on the orders of the Emperor, had been blinded, except for one in every hundred who had been left with one eye so that he might lead the others home.

### Samuel, Herbert Louis Samuel, 1st Viscount (1870–1963)
British politician and philosopher. Educated at Oxford, he became an MP in 1902, and held various offices, including Postmaster-General (1910–14 and 1915–16), Home Secretary (1916 and 1931–2), and High Commissioner for Palestine (1920–5), where he pursued a policy of trying to establish a multinational commonwealth to include the Jews. He was Leader of the LIBERAL PARTY in the Commons (1931–5), and later Liberal Leader in the Lords (1944–55). He was created a viscount in 1937.

### samurai
Japanese warrior. Tokugawa Japan (1603–1868) had four hereditary classes: samurai, farmers, craftsmen and merchants (outcasts, or BURAKUMIN, were not part of this system). Only samurai were allowed to bear weapons, and they carried two swords. They had to serve their DAIMYO masters loyally and follow the warrior's code, BUSHIDO; in return they received lodging and income. ► MEIJI RESTORATION; TOKU-GAWA SHOGUNATE

## Sandinista National Liberation Front (*Frente Sandinista de Liberación Nacional*, FSLN)

A Nicaraguan guerrilla group which was formed in 1962 and quickly gained support among the landless peasantry. Its clashes with the National Guard resulted in civil war in 1976–9, until it seized power and became the ruling party of a socialist junta of national reconstruction under the leadership of Daniel ORTEGA. The peasants were rewarded with land expropriated from landowners, who from their positions of exile and dispossession organized an opposition group known as the CONTRAS and recruited a CIA-backed rebel army, which fought the Sandinista regime until ceasefires and disarmament were agreed in 1990 and 1994. The ceasefires were a result of the Sandinistas losing the 1990 elections to a coalition group led by Violeta Chamorro. Even so, it remained a powerful influence because of its control of the trade unions, police and military. ► IRAN–CONTRA AFFAIR; NICARAGUAN REVOLUTION

## Sandino, Augusto César (1895–1934)

Nicaraguan revolutionary. From the mountains of northern Nicaragua, he led guerrilla resistance to US occupation forces after 1926. His success in evading the US forces and the Nicaraguan National Guard generated sympathy for his cause, as well as a significant degree of anti-American feeling. After the withdrawal of the US Marines (Jan 1933), Anastasio SOMOZA, Chief of the National Guard, arranged a meeting with him, apparently to discuss peace. This was a ruse, however, and Sandino was murdered, on Somoza's orders, near Managua. The Nicaraguan revolutionary government of 1979–90 (later known as the *Sandinistas*) took him as their principal hero.

## Sand River Convention (1852)

An agreement whereby the British acknowledged the independence of the Boers beyond the Vaal River. After the GREAT TREK, the Boers had established a number of communities in the interior of southern Africa north of the Orange and the Vaal rivers. In 1848 Governor Sir Harry Smith of the Cape proclaimed the authority of Queen VICTORIA over these territories. Further frontier problems and Boer resistance under Andries PRETORIUS caused the British to reconsider their responsibilities beyond the borders of the Cape Colony. The Sand River Convention was followed within two years by the Bloemfontein Convention, under which the British relinquished authority over the Orange River Sovereignty. The British re-established imperial power over these territories between 1877 and 1881, and 1902 and 1906–7.

## Sandžak of Novi Pazar

Under the OTTOMAN EMPIRE, the administrative region (*sandžak* or *sanjak*) based around the town of Novi Pazar, now in modern Serbia. After gaining autonomy in 1830, the young state of Serbia soon aspired to the acquisition of the sandžak, but at the Congress of BERLIN (1878) it was awarded to Austria-Hungary (although it still remained under Ottoman suzerainty). By the Treaty of BUCHAREST (1913), it was divided between the Kingdoms of Serbia and Montenegro and in 1918 it became part of the Kingdom of Serbs, Croats and Slovenes (later Yugoslavia). With the redrawing of the internal boundaries of Yugoslavia at the end of WORLD WAR II, it became part of the Republic of Serbia within the Socialist Federal Republic of Yugoslavia.

## Sanfedisti

The name, applied in 1799, to the so-called 'Army of the Holy Faith' (*Santafede*) organized by the reactionary Cardinal Fabrizio RUFFO to overturn the PARTHENOPEAN REPUBLIC and to restore the Bourbon monarchy. Composed largely of peasants and Neapolitan poor, the irregular bands that made up the Santafede were often motivated by the chance to loot and settle vendettas rather than by genuine loyalty to the Bourbon throne.

## San Francisco, Treaty of (8 Sep 1951)

The treaty which brought to an end the war between Japan and 48 other nations. The other signatories were the nations that had declared war on Japan (with the exceptions of the USSR, the Republic of China (Taiwan) and the People's Republic of China) and those nations that had been created since the Japanese surrender in 1945 in territories which had been occupied by Japan. The San Francisco Treaty brought to an end the post-war occupation of Japan, and marked the restoration of Japan to the community of nations.

## Sanga of Mewar (1509/28)

Medieval Indian ruler. He was associated with the rise of Mewar during the 16c, which played an important part in the political history of north India. Rana ('King') Sanga, a grandson of Rana Kumbha, ascended to the throne of Mewar in 1508, and the following year began to defy the power of Delhi. The Lodi kings were, however, too involved with their own internal problems to bother much about Mewar, and Sanga contemplated an attack on Delhi. He allied himself with BABUR against Ibrahim Lodi, and agreed to attack Delhi from the south and west, whilst Babur attacked from the north. Trouble from Gujarat, however, prevented Sanga from keeping his part of the agreement and the Battle of PANIPAT ended in victory for Babur. Sanga did not expect Babur to stay in India and rule from Delhi. The alliance broke on this and in 1527 Sanga fought a war with Babur in which he was defeated. After his death, Mewar's power gradually declined to that of a minor state.

## Sanger, Margaret Louise (1883–1966)

US social reformer and founder of the birth control movement. Educated at Claverack College, she became a trained nurse, and married William Sanger in 1902. Appalled by the tragedies she encountered as a nurse, in 1914 she published a radical feminist magazine, *The Woman Rebel*, with advice on contraception, and two years later founded the first American birth-control clinic, in Brooklyn, New York, for which she was imprisoned. After later completing a world tour, she founded the American Birth Control League in 1921. Divorced in 1920, she married J Noah H Slee in 1922.

## Sanguinetti, Julio María (1936– )

Uruguayan politician. A member of the long-established, progressive Colorado Party (PC), which had its origins in the civil war of 1836, he was elected to the assembly in 1962, and headed the Ministry of Labour and Industry, and then Education and Culture (1969–73). The oppressive regime of Juan Maria

Bordaberry (1972–6) was forcibly removed, and military rule imposed before democratic government was restored in 1985. The 1966 constitution was, with some modifications, restored, and Sanguinetti was elected President. He took office in 1986, leading a government of national accord. Sanguinetti's major achievement was the restoration of democracy and human and **CIVIL RIGHTS**. However, the means by which he brought this about – a general amnesty to the military, rather than criminal trials – weakened his popular support. He lost the presidency in 1989, to Luis Alberto Lacalle of the Blanco Party, but regained it in 1994, serving until 2000.

**San Jacinto, Battle of** (21 Apr 1863)
The battle which completed the Texan struggle for independence from Mexico. An 800-strong Texan force led by Sam **HOUSTON** surprised and overwhelmed 1,400 Mexicans under **SANTA ANNA** at the San Jacinto River, capturing Santa Anna himself. The subsequent peace treaty established independence for Texas and made Houston President.

**Sanjak of Novi Pazar** ► SANDŽAK OF NOVI PAZAR

**Sanjurjo, José** (1872–1936)
Spanish soldier. As director of the **CIVIL GUARD** he played an important role in the establishment of the Second Republic in 1931 by refusing to place his forces at the service of the King, **ALFONSO XIII**. Nevertheless, he led an abortive monarchist rising against the new regime in 1932. Sentenced to life imprisonment, he was amnestied by the right-wing government of **LERROUX** in 1934. Popular in the army for his down-to-earth style, he accepted the leadership of the Nationalist rising of 17–18 July 1936 against the Republic, only to die on 20 July 1936 in an air crash. ► **REPUBLIC, SECOND** (Spain)

**Sankara, Thomas** (1950–87)
Burkina Faso soldier and politician. He joined the army in Ouagadougou in 1969 and attended the French Parachute Training Centre (1971–4) where he began to acquire radical political ideas. As a minister in Saye Zerbo's government, he increasingly came to believe in the need for a genuinely popular revolution to expunge the consequences of French colonialism. Leading a coup in 1983, he became Prime Minister and head of state, and introduced a wide range of progressive policies which made him enemies. Despite his great symbolic popularity among young radicals (outside Burkina Faso as much as inside the country), he was shot during a coup led by his close associate, Blaise **COMPAORÉ**, on 15 Oct 1987.

**SAN MARINO**    official name **Republic of San Marino**
A very small landlocked republic completely surrounded by central Italy, lying 12 mi/20 km from the Adriatic Sea. Its land boundaries measure 21 mi/34 km. Founded by a 4c Christian saint as a refuge against religious persecution, its independence was recognized by the pope in 1631, and in 1862 a treaty of friendship with the Kingdom of Italy preserved San Marino's independence. It is governed by two *capitani reggenti* elected every six months, who preside over a 60-member parliament called the Great and General Council

**San Martín, José de** (1778–1850)
Argentine soldier and politician. After military training, he served the Spanish crown against the Moors in Orán (1791), the British (1798), the Portuguese (1801) and the French during their occupation of Spain (1808–13). Rewarded for his distinguished service with high command, he travelled instead to Buenos Aires. In a dramatic change of allegiance, thereafter he played a major role in winning independence from Spain for Argentina, Chile and Peru. In 1817 he led an army across the Andes into Chile, defeating the Spanish at Chacubuco (1817) and **MAIPÚ** (1818). He then captured Lima, and became Protector of Peru (1821), but resigned the following year after failing to reach an agreement with **BOLÍVAR** over the future of Peru, and died in exile in France. ► **SPANISH-AMERICAN WARS OF INDEPENDENCE**

**San Remo, Conference of** (Apr 1920)
This conference, attended by representatives of Britain, France and Italy, reached agreement on the Middle East settlement after **WORLD WAR I**. The agreement covered the peace treaty with Turkey (eventually signed in Sèvres, Aug 1920), and the eventual independence of the Middle Eastern states. However, it also granted interim **MANDATES** to Britain over Iraq and Palestine, and to France over Syria and Lebanon (as had earlier been formulated in principle by the **SYKES–PICOT AGREEMENT**). Japan, Greece and Belgium were also party to the Conference, but not the USA or USSR.

**sans-culottes**
The French name (literally, 'without trousers') for the mass of the working populace in French towns at the time of the Revolution; it was, however, more specifically applied to small-time Parisian shopkeepers, craftsmen, wage-earners and unemployed who were politically active. Their demands for food controls and democratic government made them temporary allies of the **JACOBINS**. ► **FRENCH REVOLUTION**

**San Stefano, Treaty of** (1878)
A pre-emptive treaty concluding the Russo-Turkish War of 1877–8. Under its terms Russia gained considerable diplomatic advantages against the other European powers and weakened Ottoman power in the Balkans, particularly through the creation of a large Bulgarian state, ostensibly independent but arguably under Russian influence. Under pressure from Britain and Austro-Hungary, it was superseded by a multilateral treaty at the Congress of **BERLIN** (1878), the terms of which were less favourable to Russia, although they guaranteed the independence of a much smaller Bulgaria. Tsar **ALEXANDER II** particularly upset at **BISMARCK**'s false claim to have acted as 'honest broker' in mounting the Congress in Germany. ► **OTTOMAN EMPIRE**; **RUSSO-TURKISH WARS**

**Santa Anna, Antonio López de** (1794–1876)
Mexican soldier and dictator. The son of a colonial official, he served in the Spanish army and supported **ITURBIDE** in the struggle for Mexican independence, although he was one of those who deposed him in 1823. Dubbed the 'Hero of Tampico' because of his role in defending his country against Spanish attempts at reconquest, he was President from 1833 to 1836. Following a revolt in Texas by US settlers and the state's declaration of independence from Mexico (1836), Santa Anna defeated Texan forces at the **ALAMO**, but was routed at **SAN JACINTO**, and imprisoned. Dictator in 1839 and 1841–5, he returned to power on two occasions (1846 and 1853) at the head of Conservative groups, from Mexico and Puebla, anxious to preserve their *fueros* from Liberal attack and to preserve central control over the republic. An exile for many years, he was permitted to return to Mexico in 1872, and died in Mexico City. ► **FUERO**; **MEXICAN WAR**

**Santa Cruz, Andrés** (1792–1865)
Bolivian general and politician. He participated in the Peruvian revolution against Spain in 1820–3, and as President of Bolivia (1829–39) helped to quell an army rebellion against Peruvian President Luís José de Orbegoso (1835), then conquered Peru and set up and led a new union called the Peruvian–Bolivian Confederation. Fighting broke out between the Confederation and Chile in 1836, and after defeat at the Battle of Yungay in 1839 by a Chilean force under General Manuel Bulnes, the Confederation disintegrated and Santa Cruz went into exile in Europe.

**Santa Fé Trail**
A trading route from west Missouri through Kansas and Colorado to Santa Fé in New Mexico. The trail was pioneered by William Becknell in 1821, the year of Mexico's independence from Spanish rule. It remained a commercially important route for over 50 years, but declined after the Santa Fé railway was opened in 1880.

**Santander, Francisco de Paula** (1799–1840)
Colombian politician. He took part in the **SPANISH-AMERICAN WARS OF INDEPENDENCE**, acted as Vice President of **GRAN COLOMBIA** (1821–7) during **BOLÍVAR**'s campaigns, and was President of New Granada (modern Colombia) in 1832–7. An opponent of Bolívar, especially regarding the latter's decision to retain Venezuela in Colombia, Santander was the effective founder of Colombia, constructing a unitary regime in which the *fueros* of Church and army were set aside. ► **FUERO**

**Santarosa, Annibale de' Rossi di Pomarolo, Count Santorre di** (1783–1825)
Piedmontese general and politician. One of the key figures in the Piedmontese conspiracy of 1821 that forced the abdication of **VICTOR EMMANUEL I**, he became the *de facto* head of the Provisional Government established under the regency of **CHARLES ALBERT**. After the defeat of the revolution, he emigrated to France and then England. In 1824 he went to Greece to fight against Turkish rule and died in battle at Spakteria.

**Santer, Jacques** (1937– )
Luxembourg politician. He was educated at the universities of Paris and Strasbourg and at the Institute of Political Studies in Paris. After graduating he became an advocate at the Luxembourg Court of Appeal, but changed to a political career in 1963. As a *Parti Chrétien-Social* member he held several ministerial positions before becoming Prime Minister (1984–94). In 1995 he was elected President of the European Commission. Although he was considered a compromise candidate, he proved to be an able and judicious moderator of European politics at a time when the **EC** was moving towards greater cohesion and integration. He resigned from his post in Mar 1999 amidst allegations of fraud, and was succeeded by a former Prime Minister of Italy, Romano Prodi.

**Santerre, Antoine Joseph** (1752–1809)
French revolutionary and soldier. A wealthy brewer, he received a command in the **NATIONAL GUARD** in 1789, took part in the storming of the **BASTILLE** and was in charge at King **LOUIS XVI**'s execution. Appointed general of division (1793), he marched against the Vendéan royalists, but, miserably beaten, was recalled and imprisoned. ► **VENDÉE, WARS OF THE**

**Santiago, Order of**
One of the military orders founded in **CASTILE** during the **RECONQUEST**. It was founded in 1170, with a red cross in the shape of a sword as its symbol, and came to possess extensive estates (*encomiendas*), numbering 94 in 1616. Members were in theory subject to semi-monastic discipline. From 1523 the crown of Spain became, with papal permission, head of the order. The order was named after St James, one of the apostles of Jesus, who was said to have ended his days in Spain. From the 9c the alleged discovery of his tomb at Compostela made him the inspiration for the Reconquest, and he was known as Santiago Matamoros ('St James the Moor-Slayer'). ► **ENCOMIENDA**

**SÃO TOMÉ AND PRÍNCIPE**    official name **Democratic Republic of São Tomé and Príncipe**

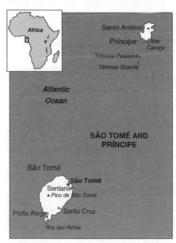

An equatorial island republic in the Gulf of Guinea, off the coast of west Africa. It comprises São Tomé, Príncipe, and several smaller islands. It was discovered by the Portuguese between 1469 and 1472, and became a Portuguese colony in 1522. From 1641 to 1740 it was held by the Dutch, then was recovered by Portugal. It later became a port of call en route to the

East Indies. Resistance to Portuguese rule led to riots in 1953, and the formation of an overseas liberation movement based in Gabon. It gained independence in 1975 and was a one-party state until a new constitution was introduced in the early 1990s. In Jul 2003 the government was overthrown by a military coup, but returned to power a week later after reaching an agreement with the coup leaders.

**Sapru, Tej Bahadur** (1875–1949)
Indian political leader and lawyer. He studied law and practised as a lawyer in Allahabad. Entering politics in 1907 as a moderate, he joined Annie **BESANT**'s Home Rule League Movement (1917) and became a member of Lord Reading's Executive Council in 1921. As a member of the government of India, Sapru took the initiative to remove restrictions on the press following the Press Act 1910, and to withdraw the Criminal Law Amendment Act, 1910. He represented India at the Imperial Conference London in 1923 and after M K **GANDHI**'s conviction and imprisonment, resigned from the Executive Council in 1923. At the Round Table Conference in London in 1930, he reiterated the demand for provincial autonomy with responsibility to the legislature at the centre. He was a member of the Privy Council in 1934 and was in favour of a new constitution under the Government of India Act in 1935. As a leader of the Non-Parties Conference at Allahabad in 1942, Sapru demanded that Winston **CHURCHILL** declare India's position equal to that of dominions. He was the first President of the Indian Council of World Affairs (1943), a position which he held until his death. He was a Persian and Urdu scholar, with a keen judicial mind free of religious and communal prejudices – one of the greatest statesmen of the Indian freedom movement. ► **COMMUNALISM**

**Saracens**
General term for Muslim forces, particularly during the Middle Ages. The name, which usually referred to Arab or Turkish groups, was used by Christians for all followers of Islam or Islamic subjects of the caliph.

**Saratoga, Battle of** (Oct 1777)
One of the most important engagements of the **AMERICAN REVOLUTION**. Actually fought near modern Schuylerville, New York, the battle brought the defeat of a large British army under John **BURGOYNE** by American Continental troops and militia under Horatio **GATES**. The outcome ended British plans to cut New England off from the rest of the states, and encouraged French intervention on the American side.

**Sardinia, Kingdom of**
The Italian kingdom created (1718–20) through the Duchy of Savoy's acquisition of Sardinia in exchange for Sicily. Despite its name, the kingdom's heart remained Savoy and Piedmont; to avoid confusion, it is generally called the Kingdom of Sardinia-Piedmont. During the course of the **RISORGIMENTO**, the kingdom became the driving force behind unification and in 1861 **VICTOR EMMANUEL II** of Sardinia became Italy's first king.

**Sarekat Islam**
The first mass political movement in the Netherlands East Indies (Indonesia), indeed the only mass movement in the colony prior to 1945. *Sarekat Islam* ('Islamic Union') was founded in 1912 by a prominent batik merchant from Surakarta, Hadji Samanhudi, to protect the economic interests of batik traders at a time of increasing organization within the Chinese commercial community. However, the movement soon moved beyond this narrow aim, attracting a wide range of frequently disparate elements. Indeed, at one time or another during its brief history, virtually every persuasion within the Indies population had come within it, and the membership had grown to more than 2 million in 1919. That figure may mean little; only a few tens of thousands were in any sense formal members while far more than 2 million were swept along by the movement. At the close of the 1910s, socialist elements achieved a growing influence within Sarekat Islam, provoking a major split with the Muslim wing. In 1921 the Indies Communist Party (PKI) was forced out of the central organization. However, by the late 1920s Sarekat Islam had largely faded into inactivity. ► **PARTAI KOMUNIS INDONESIA**

**Sarit Thanarat** (1908–63)
Thai military and political leader. Educated at the Royal Thai Military Academy, Sarit first saw combat during the suppression of the 1933 royalist Boworadet rebellion. Following distinguished service during the **PACIFIC WAR**, in the post-war years Sarit played an increasingly important role in military politics. He became Commander-in-Chief of the Army in 1954, and supreme commander of the armed forces in 1957. In Sep 1957, he staged a coup against **PHIBUNSONGKHRAM**. He became Prime Minister in 1958. Sarit ruled in a highly authoritarian manner, dealing harshly with all dissent. He was fiercely anti-communist. However, during his premiership, considerable attention was also given to improvement in the country's infrastructure and the development of the economy. He died in office, leaving a great fortune; most of it was confiscated by the government that succeeded him.

**Sarmiento, Domingo Faustino** (1811–88)
Argentine writer and politician. An outspoken critic of the dictator Juan Manuel de **ROSAS** and the **CAUDILLO** Juan Facundo Quiroga, he spent much of the early part of his life in exile in Chile (1831–6, 1840–5 and 1848–51), also travelling to Europe and the USA. He later served as Governor of San Juan (1862–4) before becoming, at a time of dramatic change, his country's first civilian President (1868–74). An especially vigorous promoter of education and immigration, he was also a prolific and forceful writer. With **ALBERDI** and **MITRE**, he was one of the most important architects of modern Argentina.

**Sarney (Costa), José** (1930–)
Brazilian politician. A follower of the UDN Bossa Nova (nationalist) group in the early 1950s, he became ARENA (National Renewal Alliance) Governor of Maranhão in 1965 under **CASTELO BRANCO**. A prominent Senator during the 1970s, he led the Social Democratic Party (PDS) under Figueiredo. Running-mate to Tancredo **NEVES** in 1985 on a breakaway ticket, he became President on Neves' sudden death.

Saddled with the latter's commitments, but without either the backing or skill to carry them through himself, he drifted from crisis to crisis. His attempt to retain the executive during the 1987–8 Constituent Congress succeeded, but at enormous political and economic cost. He was succeeded in 1990 by Fernando **COLLOR DE MELLO**.

### Sarrail, Maurice Paul Emmanuel (1856–1929)

French soldier. In **WORLD WAR I** he led the 3rd Army at the Battle of the **MARNE** (1914), commanded the Allied forces in the East (Salonica) from 1915 to 1917, where he deposed **CONSTANTINE I** of Greece. He was High Commissioner in Syria (1924–5), but was recalled after the bombardment of Damascus during a rising.

### Sassou-Nguesso, Denis (1943– )

Congolese soldier and politician. After completing his secondary education in the Congo Republic, he joined the army and trained in Algeria and France. An active member of the radical *Parti Congolais du Travail* (PCT), he was appointed Minister of Defence in 1975 and survived the military coup of 1977 in which President N'Gouabi was assassinated. In 1979, under popular pressure, power was transferred to the PCT and Sassou-Nguesso became President later in the year. He gradually moved politically towards the centre, rebuilding links with France and establishing more harmonious relations with the USA, and in 1990 introduced a multiparty political system. In the 1992 elections he lost his position to Pascal Lissouba, but in 1997 troops loyal to him ousted Lissouba and he returned to the presidency.

### Sastri, V S Srinivasa, in full Valangunian Sankarana-Rayana Srinivasa Sastri (1869–1946)

Indian politician. Greatly influenced by Annie **BESANT**, C P Ramaswami Aiyar and **GOKHALE**, he was the Secretary of the Madras session of Congress (1908). He took an active part in drawing up the Lucknow Pact between the Congress and the **MUSLIM LEAGUE**, which demanded 'responsive government for India', and was opposed to M K **GANDHI**'s policy of non-violence and non-cooperation. Elected to the Madras Council in 1913, he became a member of the Imperial Legislative Council in 1915 and of the Council of State in 1921. Sastri was a member of the delegation to South Africa that led to the Cape Town agreement, committing the South African government to shelve its Class Area Bill to segregate Indians. He also struggled for the cause of Indians living in Kenya and British East Africa and was President of the Servants of India Society for some years. In 1945, he strongly opposed Muhammad Ali **JINNAH**'s two-nation theory. ► **NON-COOPERATION MOVEMENT**

### Satavahana ► INDIA, PRE-ISLAMIC

### Sato Eisaku (1901–75)

Japanese politician. The younger brother of **KISHI NOBUSUKE**, he was an official in the Ministry of Railways before **WORLD WAR II**, and was first elected to the Diet in 1949. Indicted for corruption in 1954, he was released in 1956 before completion of his trial as part of a general amnesty celebrating Japan's entry into the **UN**. During Sato's premiership (1964–72), relations with South Korea were normalized (1965) and US-held **OKINAWA** was returned to Japan (1972). Although the 1960 security treaty with the USA was automatically extended in 1970, a dispute over Japanese textile exports and President Richard **NIXON**'s **NORMALIZATION** of relations with China without consulting Japan soured US–Japan relations during the last years of Sato's premiership. It is widely believed that Sato's three non-nuclear principles (non-manufacture, non-possession and non-introduction into Japan of nuclear weapons) earned him the **NOBEL PEACE PRIZE** in 1974.

### Satsuma

A feudal domain in south-west Japan created in the 7c. Designated an 'outside' (*tozama*) domain by the **TOKUGAWA SHOGUNATE** (ie one that had originally opposed the imposition of Tokugawa rule in 1603), its territory was much reduced in the 17c. **SAMURAI** activists from Satsuma played a leading role in the overthrow of the Tokugawa Shogunate in 1867 and then went on to dominate the new Meiji government along with former samurai from **CHOSHU**. The Satsuma–Choshu monopoly of power lasted virtually throughout the Meiji period (1868–1912).

### Satyagraha

Literally 'truth-force', the term refers to M K **GANDHI**'s philosophy of non-violent resistance to evil. It was conceived in South Africa in response to laws discriminating against Asians (1906), and used in campaigns against British rule in India. The approach involved fasting, economic boycotts, hand-spinning and hand-weaving.

**SAUDI ARABIA**   official name **Kingdom of Saudi Arabia**

An Arabic kingdom comprising about four-fifths of the Arabian Peninsula, bounded to the west by the Red Sea; to the north-west by Jordan; to the north by Iraq; to the north-east by Kuwait; to the east by the Arabian Gulf, Qatar and the United Arab Emirates; to the south-east and south by Oman; and to the south and south-west by Yemen. Famed as the birthplace of Islam with the holy cities of Mecca, Medina and Jedda, the modern state was founded by Saudi Arabia's first king, **IBN SAUD**, leader of the fundamentalist Wahhabi sect, who by 1932 had united the four tribal provinces of Hijaz in the north-west, Asir in the south-west, Najd in the centre and Al Hasa in the east. Saudi Arabia is governed as an absolute monarchy based on Islamic law and Arab **BEDOUIN** tradition, and has caused international concern over human rights abuses and public executions. King **FAHD** ibn Abd al-Aziz al-Saud became both head of state and Prime Minister in 1982; he suffered a debilitating stroke in 1996 and many of his official functions are now carried out by his brother, Crown Prince Abdullah. Since the discovery of oil in the 1930s, Saudi Arabia has become the world's leading oil exporter. The ruling family has preserved stability by suppressing dissent and resisted calls for greater democracy for many years, making limited concessions in 2005. The continued presence of foreign troops, particularly US troops, in the country after the GULF WAR was a cause of tension between rulers and people which was scarcely alleviated by a military redeployment to Qatar in 2003. The suppression of political dissent has fostered the rise of groups linked to AL-QAEDA that in recent years have carried out bombings and assassinations, often against the foreign business community.

### Sava, St (1174–1237)

Monk, founder of the Serbian Orthodox Church and member of the NEMANJA DYNASTY. Born Rastko Nemanja, the son of STEPHEN I NEMANJA, King of Serbia, he took the name Sava upon entering monastic life at Mount ATHOS. There, with the help of his father, he founded the Monastery of Hilandar which became a centre for Serbian culture and religious life. Returning to Serbia c.1208, he became head of the Studenica Monastery and founded a monastery at Žiča. Endeavouring to counter the influence of the BOGOMILS and of the Roman Church, he organized the Serbian Orthodox Church and, with the sanction of the Patriarch of CONSTANTINOPLE, he became its first Archbishop in 1219. He made a pilgrimage to the Holy Land and died at Trnovo in north Bulgaria. ► PEĆ, PATRIARCHATE OF

### Savage, Michael Joseph (1872–1940)

Australian-born New Zealand politician. In 1907 he emigrated to New Zealand, where he became a moderate trade unionist. He later moved into politics, and helped to found the Labour Party in 1916. He was elected to parliament in 1919 and in 1933 became leader of the New Zealand Labour Party. By cultivating the support of rural interests he secured a win for his party in the Nov 1935 general election, thus becoming the country's first Labour Prime Minister. His popularity grew and he was re-elected in 1938 but died in office two years later, to be succeeded by Peter FRASER.

### Savimbi, Jonas Malheiro (1934–2002)

Angolan soldier and nationalist. Educated in Angola and at Lausanne University, he returned to Zambia and became a leader of the Popular Union of Angola, being Foreign Minister of the Angolan government-in-exile (1962–4). After a period with the FNLA, he broke away to form UNITA and fought against the Portuguese until independence. Unable to agree with the leaders of the MPLA and the FNLA, he continued the struggle against the MPLA from bases in the south of Angola, supported by South Africa and the USA. A man of considerable charisma, he stood for a democratic and capitalist Angola, but his associations with South Africa and the USA made him a pariah in Third World circles. However, the strength of his position and diplomatic bargaining by the USA led to a series of meetings designed to end the civil war and remove the Cubans from Angola. Agreement for a ceasefire and democratic elections was finally achieved in 1991, but when Savimbi lost the subsequent elections the armed struggle broke out again. A further ceasefire began in 1995 with the confinement of UNITA troops and intervention of a UN peacekeeping force. However, in 1997 Savimbi boycotted the new government of national unity, even though he had been granted the special role of leader of the opposition, and fighting broke out again, continuing until after his death.

### Savonarola, Girolamo (1452–98)

Florentine religious and political reformer. He became a Dominican at Bologna in 1474, and came to be recognized as an inspiring preacher. He became Vicar-General of the Dominicans in Tuscany in 1493, and his preaching began to point towards a political revolution as the means of restoring religion and morality. When a republic was established in Florence (1494), he became its guiding spirit, fostering a Christian commonwealth, with stringent laws governing the repression of vice and frivolity. In 1495 he was called to Rome to answer a charge of heresy. He disregarded the order, was excommunicated in 1497, and burnt in Florence.

### Savornin Lohman, Alexander Frederik de (1837–1924)

Dutch Protestant politician. From 1879 to 1921 he sat in the Second Chamber, initially as a member of the Calvinist ANTI-REVOLUTIONARY PARTY (ARP). In 1884–95 he was also Professor of Law at the Calvinist Free University in Amsterdam. He was the leader of the more conservative tendency within the ARP, and as such objected to A KUYPER's schism from the Dutch Reformed Church in 1886, and his democratic politics; Savornin Lohman therefore led a splinter group away from the ARP in 1894, calling itself the Free Anti-Revolutionary Party, which in 1908 became the CHRISTIAN HISTORICAL UNION. In 1890–1 he was Minister for Internal Affairs in a confessional government.

### Savoy, House of

Rulers of the duchy of Savoy, a transalpine area in present-day Switzerland and France, from the 11c to the 19c. Its first heyday was from the mid-14c to the mid-15c; thereafter it was hemmed in by French and Spanish monarchies. In the 16c it suffered in the ITALIAN WARS and subsequently was often locked in conflict with Calvinist Geneva. The damage of the THIRTY YEARS' WAR added to a process of decline but this was reversed in the 18c when it extended its territories considerably, acquiring the kingdom of Sicily in 1713 and swapping it for Sardinia in 1720. Its mainland possessions were lost to the French in the NAPOLEONIC WARS but after its restoration in 1814 these became the base from which it overturned Austrian hegemony in northern Italy in the mid 19c. Its territorial ambitions coinciding with the RISORGIMENTO, Savoy became the ruling house of the kingdom of Italy until the country became a republic in 1946. ► VICTOR EMMANUEL II

### 'Saw-off'

Canadian political manoeuvre. It was used by the Conservative Party during the late 19c in order to deplete the already impoverished Liberal Party's funds. After a particularly close election result, they would file a petition alleging irregularities under the

## HOUSE OF SAVOY

| Regnal Dates | Name |
|---|---|
| 1553/80 | Emmanuel Philibert |
| 1580/1630 | Charles Emmanuel I |
| 1630/7 | Victor Amadeus I |
| 1637/8 | Francis Hyacinth |
| 1638/75 | Charles Emmanuel II |
| 1675/1730 | Victor Amadeus II |
| 1730/73 | Charles Emmanuel III |
| 1773/96 | Victor Amadeus III |
| 1796/1802 | Charles Emmanuel IV |
| 1802/21 | Victor Emmanuel I |
| 1821/31 | Charles Felix |
| 1831/49 | Charles Albert |
| 1849/78 | Victor Emmanuel II |
| 1878/1900 | Umberto I |
| 1900/46 | Victor Emmanuel III |
| 1946 | Umberto II |

Controverted Elections Act. Given the number of numerically small constituencies, there were many opportunities to use the device. Whether or not the petition was successful, the Liberal Party had to pay. If it was upheld then the election was void, and the expense of another election incurred. If the Liberals won, they still had to bear the legal costs.

**Saxe, (Hermann) Maurice, Count of**, also called **Marshal de Saxe** (1696–1750)
Marshal of France. He was an illegitimate son of **AUGUSTUS II, THE STRONG** King of Poland and Elector of Saxony. He served in the French army in the War of the **POLISH SUCCESSION** (1733–8), and in the War of the **AUSTRIAN SUCCESSION** (1740–8) invaded Bohemia, taking Prague by storm. In 1744 **LOUIS XV** appointed him commander in Flanders, where he won victories at **FONTENOY** (1745), Raucoux (1746) and Lauffeld (1747), and was promoted to Marshal of France.

**Saxe-Coburg-Gotha**
The name of the British royal family, 1901–17. King **EDWARD VII** inherited it from his father, Prince **ALBERT**, the second son of the Duke of Saxe-Coburg-Gotha. The obviously Germanic name was abandoned during **WORLD WAR I** as a means of asserting the 'Englishness' of royalty and playing down the extent of its German blood. ► **WINDSOR, HOUSE OF**

**Saxony**
A German ducal and electoral state which experienced many changes of fortune. Prominent from the 9c to the 11c, it was reduced by Emperor **FREDERICK I, BARBAROSSA** to two small areas on the River Elbe (1180–1422). Dynastic alliances enlarged the Saxon state on the Middle Elbe in the 15c. Frederick the Wise adopted Lutheranism (1524), establishing Saxony's Protestant leadership, and despite family divisions, it grew prosperous in the 16c. The reign of **JOHN GEORGE I** (1611/56) marked its steady eclipse by Brandenburg, and new duchies (eg Hanover) were formed out of Lower Saxony. Under the Catholic elector Frederick Augustus I (1694/1733), Saxony's prestige improved with his acquisition of the Polish crown as **AUGUSTUS II, THE STRONG**, but elector Frederick Augustus III (King **FREDERICK AUGUSTUS I** of Saxony) became a client of **NAPOLEON**, only to lose

two-fifths of his territory at the Congress of **VIENNA** (1814–15). Saxony was merged in the **NORTH GERMAN CONFEDERATION** (1866) and the German **REICH** (1871).

**Saya San Rebellion** (1930–1)
A major anti-colonial uprising in Burma (now Myanmar), named after its leader, Saya San. In inspiring rebellion, Saya San utilized both modern political organization at the local level and the millenarian expectations of folk belief, casting himself as the *Setkyamin*, the avenging king in Burman legend. However, the rebellion also took its strength from harsh economic conditions in the rural areas as the world depression struck Burma, and the burden of colonial taxation borne by the peasantry. In the course of the rebellion, some 3,000 were killed or wounded. A further 350 were executed for their part in the rebellion, including Saya San himself.

**Sayyid Dynasty**
An Indian dynasty that arose in Delhi after the Timurid invasion in the earlier half of the 15c. The first Sayyid sultan was a nominee of Timur. The Sayyids kept the **DELHI SULTANATE** going until the Lodis took over.

**Sazonov, Sergei Dmitriyevich** (1861–1927)
Russian diplomat and politician. He served in several diplomatic posts in Western Europe before becoming Foreign Minister in 1910. His role was somewhat ambivalent, helping to impose Russian control on Mongolia in 1911–13, encouraging the Balkan powers to turn against Turkey in 1912, and indicating his readiness to go to war with Germany in 1914, while at the same time attempting to restrain the Russian army and looking for peaceful settlements with both Austria and Germany. In this he simply reflected the Russian dilemma. Although he did everything possible after war broke out in 1914 to secure a Russian victory, he was dismissed by **NICHOLAS II** in 1916 on the issue of self-government for Poland.

**SBZ** (*Sowjetische Besatzungs Zone*, 'Soviet Zone of Occupation')
The territories in central Germany, between the western and Polish-occupied zones, which, in 1949, became the German Democratic Republic (East Germany, GDR). For many years thereafter the territory continued to be described by official and other sources in Federal (West) Germany as the SBZ so as to question the GDR's legitimacy.

**Scalawags**
US political epithet. A derogatory term for white Southerners who cooperated with occupying forces during the era of **RECONSTRUCTION** following the **AMERICAN CIVIL WAR**. Many Scalawags had never favoured secession, and some were principled opponents of **SLAVERY**.

**Schacht, (Horace Greely) Hjalmar** (1877–1970)
German financier. In 1923 he became President of the Reichsbank, and founded a new currency which ended the inflation of the mark. He was Minister of Economics (1934–7), but in 1939 was dismissed from his bank office for disagreeing with **HITLER** over rearmament expenditure. Involvement with the resistance led to his internment. He was acquitted of

war crimes at the **NUREMBERG TRIALS**. In 1953 he set up his own bank in Düsseldorf. ► **NAZI PARTY**

### Schaepman, Hermanus Johannes Aloysius Maria (1844–1903)

Dutch Roman Catholic priest and politician, journalist and poet. He took holy orders in 1867, and taught church history at the Roman Catholic seminary in Rijsenburg from 1870. As a journalist and editor his work was prodigious: he was editor-in-chief of *De Tijd* ('Time') and later of *Het Centrum* ('The Centre'), as well as being closely involved with several other publications. In 1880 he became the first Roman Catholic priest to enter the Dutch Second Chamber as an MP; he remained one until 1903, and effectively achieved the political emancipation of Dutch Roman Catholics. In 1883 he published a programme that called for Catholics to drop their alliance with the liberals, and to work with the Calvinist **ANTI-REVOLUTIONARY PARTY** to achieve their similar aims in the **SCHOOLS QUESTION** and in expanding the electorate. This position meant that very few of the Catholic élite, least of all the bishops, supported him. Nonetheless, in 1896 he managed to unite all the Dutch Catholic political groups around a single programme based on the 1891 papal encyclical *Rerum Novarum*.

### Scharnhorst, Gerhard Johann David von (1755–1813)

Prussian general and military reformer. He worked with **GNEISENAU** to reform the Prussian army after its defeat by **NAPOLEON I**, served as Chief of Staff to **BLÜCHER**, and was fatally wounded fighting the French at **LÜTZEN**. ► **PRUSSIA**

### Scheduled Castes and Tribes

Initially defined by the Government of India Act of 1919 and later by that of 1935, the schedule included all the castes and tribes in India considered by the British to be either of too inferior a social standing in the Indian **CASTE** system or too economically backward to be capable of exercising a vote and having a say in local government. Ostensibly, the scheduling of these groups was intended to protect them from exploitation and discrimination, but by insisting that the so-called 'untouchable' castes and those living in India's tribal areas should be represented by officials, the schedule also provided a convenient pretext for packing provincial councils with British nominees. On independence, the Indian government adopted a universal adult franchise and the scheduled castes and tribes were temporarily forgotten. Soon, however, the government realized that, to carry out its commitment to abolish all social discrimination, it would need to adopt measures of **POSITIVE DISCRIMINATION** and would have need of a convenient definition of those so disadvantaged. A proportion of all government posts and university and college places was therefore reserved for those from the tribal communities and 'backward' castes, and the 'schedule' of the 1930s was revived. The list of scheduled castes has expanded in accordance with political expediency. In 1991 the attempts to implement further increases in reservation, in line with the recommendations of the controversial 1980 Mandal Commission, led to widespread rioting in northern India and helped to bring down the minority **JANATA** **DAL** government under V P **SINGH**. ► **COMMUNALISM**; **GOVERNMENT OF INDIA ACTS**; **MANDAL COMMISSIONS**

### Scheel, Walter (1919–)

West German politician. After serving in the **LUFTWAFFE** in **WORLD WAR II** he went into business, joined the Free Democratic Party (**FDP**), and was elected to the **BUNDESTAG** in 1953. He was Minister for Economic Cooperation (1961–6) and Foreign Minister (1969–74), and in 1970, as part of the **OSTPOLITIK**, negotiated treaties with the USSR and Poland. Scheel was President of West Germany from 1974 to 1979.

### Scheer, Reinhard (1863–1928)

German naval commander. He went to sea as a naval cadet in torpedo craft. As Vice-Admiral he commanded the 2nd Battle Squadron of the German High Seas fleet at the outset of **WORLD WAR I**. He succeeded as Commander-in-Chief in 1916 and was in command at the Battle of **JUTLAND** (1916).

### Scheidemann, Philipp (1865–1939)

German political leader. A leading member of the Social Democratic Party (**SPD**), he proclaimed the German Republic in Nov 1918. He was Minister of Finance and Colonies in the Provisional Government of 1918, and first Chancellor of the Republic in 1919. He resigned rather than sign the Treaty of **VERSAILLES**.

### Scheldt Question

The dispute over the status of the Scheldt River, which connects the port of Antwerp with the sea, and which services a large and densely populated hinterland in Belgium and northern France. During the **EIGHTY YEARS' WAR**, the Sea-**BEGGARS** closed the river after the fall of Antwerp to the Spanish in 1585; the Treaty of **MÜNSTER** in 1648 confirmed their right to do this, until the French opened it again in the 1790s. A new chapter of the Scheldt Question began after the Belgian Revolution; in the settlement the Dutch were awarded Zeeland Flanders on the left bank of the river, which gave them control of its mouth; indeed, they imposed a toll on all shipping until 1863 (when the Belgians bought it off). Belgium tried without success to gain Zeeland Flanders after **WORLD WAR I**, there have been long negotiations concerning Belgium's access to the sea through Dutch territory. A 1963 treaty agreed the construction of a canal joining the Scheldt and the Rhine rivers, and this was completed in 1965.

### Schengen Agreement (1985)

An agreement permitting free movement of people between the signatory countries, without border, customs or immigration controls. The original signatories, at Schengen, Luxembourg, in 1985 were Belgium, France, Germany, Luxembourg and the Netherlands. These countries were subsequently joined by Austria, Denmark, Finland, Iceland, Italy, Greece, Norway, Portugal, Spain and Sweden. All except Norway and Iceland are **EU** members but the agreement is not part of the EU structure. The UK is not a signatory because of security concerns and retains the right to screen people entering the country.

### Schiller, Karl (1911–94)

German economist and politician. A distinguished academic career, latterly at the University of Hamburg, was complemented from 1949 by a growing involvement as an **SPD** member in municipal and national politics. In 1966 he became Economics Minister in the **CDU**/SPD coalition, retained the post in the SPD/**FDP** coalition (1969–72) and also served as Finance Minister (1971–2) before resigning from the government. He is credited with Germany's economic recovery from the 1966 recession and with introducing a Keynesian style of economic management to Germany.

**Schimmelpenninck, Rutger Jan** (1761–1825)
Dutch politician. He practised law in Amsterdam, and in the 1780s joined the **PATRIOT MOVEMENT** as a supporter of change from the *ancien régime*. In 1796 he became a member of the National Congress in the French-sponsored **BATAVIAN REPUBLIC**, and was appointed its representative in Paris in 1798, in London in 1802, and then in Paris again. In 1804 **NAPOLEON I** charged him with drawing up a constitution for the Netherlands, which came into effect in 1805 and which created Schimmelpenninck **GRAND PENSIONARY** at the head of the Republic. In 1806 Napoleon installed his own brother, **LOUIS NAPOLEON**, as King of Holland, and Schimmelpenninck retired to his estate near Deventer. He joined the First Chamber after the restoration in 1815. His achievement had been to introduce the Napoleonic administrative reforms to the Netherlands, for example in taxation and education.

**Schirach, Baldur von** (1907–74)
German Nazi politician. Born in Berlin, he became a member of the National Socialist Party in 1925 and a member of the **REICHSTAG** in 1932. In 1933 he founded and organized the **HITLER YOUTH**, of which he was leader until his appointment as *Gauleiter* of Vienna in 1940. He was captured in Austria in 1945 and found guilty at the **NUREMBERG TRIALS** of participating in the mass deportation of Jews; he was sentenced to 20 years' imprisonment. He was released from Spandau prison in 1966.

**Schleicher, Kurt von** (1882–1934)
German soldier and politician. He was on the general staff during **WORLD WAR I**. Politically active behind the scenes during **BRÜNING**'s chancellorship, he became Minister of War in von **PAPEN**'s government of 1932, then succeeding him as Chancellor. However, his failure to obtain either a parliamentary majority or emergency powers provided the preconditions for **HITLER**'s appointment as Chancellor in 1933. Schleicher and his wife were murdered by the Nazis in mid-1934 on a trumped-up charge of treason. ▶ **NIGHT OF THE LONG KNIVES**

**Schleswig-Holstein Problem**
The southern part of the Jutland Peninsula, linking Denmark and Prussia, whose ownership was hotly contested throughout the 19c and 20c. Since the Middle Ages, the two duchies had been ruled by the King of Denmark, despite their markedly different populations: Schleswig comprised a mixed population, while Holstein (which had joined the German Confederation in 1815) was almost completely German. Denmark sought, in 1848, to annex Schleswig, and war broke out between the Confederation and Denmark. A compromise was reached in 1852, although

the Danes' demands remained unresolved. War broke out again in 1863, prompted by a dispute over the right of **CHRISTIAN IX**, **FREDERICK VII** of Denmark's successor, to rule. At stake was the principle of the **SALIC LAW**, which did not recognize a female line of succession. The German population argued that the duchies should be ruled by the Duke of Augustenberg, and Prussia and Austria added their weight. A brief war followed, in which the Danes were defeated and, under the Treaty of Prague (1866), Schleswig-Holstein passed, as a province, under Prussian rule. Plebiscites following the Treaty of **VERSAILLES** (1919) led to the awarding of northern Schleswig to Denmark (July 1920); after a referendum, the remainder of Schleswig-Holstein was absorbed (1946) into West Germany as a state. **PALMERSTON** allegedly said of the problem: 'There are only three men who have ever understood it: one was Prince Albert, who is dead; the second was a German professor, who became mad. I am the third – and I have forgotten all about it.'

**Schlieffen, Alfred, Count von** (1833–1913)
Prussian field marshal. He advocated the plan which bears his name (1895), on which German tactics were unsuccessfully based in **WORLD WAR I**. He envisaged a German breakthrough in Belgium and the defeat of France within six weeks by a major right-wheel flanking movement, cutting off Paris from the sea, holding off the Russians meanwhile with secondary forces.

**Schlüter, Poul Holmskov** (1929– )
Danish politician. After studying at Aarhus and Copenhagen universities, he qualified as a barrister and Supreme Court attorney but was politically active at an early age, becoming leader of the youth movement of the Conservative People's Party (KF) in 1944. He became its national leader in 1951 and in 1952 a member of the Executive Committee of the KF. He was elected to parliament (**FOLKETINGET**) in 1964 and ten years later became Chairman of the KF, and in 1982 Prime Minister, heading a centre-right coalition which survived the 1987 election but was reconstituted, with support from one of the minor centre parties, *Det Radikale Venstre*, in 1988. After the 1990 election the coalition consisted of only two parties: Schlüter's Conservative Party and the Danish Liberal Party, *Venstre*, led by the Foreign Minister, Uffe Elleman-Jensen. Schlüter resigned with the rest of his government in 1993.

**Schmalkaldic League** (1531)
The league was created by the Protestant German princes who wished to defend their Protestantism against the attempts of Emperor **CHARLES V** to reintroduce Catholicism. It was led by **PHILIP THE MAGNANIMOUS**, Landgrave of Hesse and **JOHN FREDERICK I**, Elector of Saxony. Charles was forced to grant it a form of recognition in 1544 but was able to destroy it militarily a few years later (1547) at the Battle of **MÜHLBERG**.

**Schmerling, Anton von** (1805–93)
Austrian politician. After a training in law and an early career in the Civil Service, Schmerling served between July and Dec 1848 as a liberal minister in the Frankfurt Parliament. He then served in various

# Science

Science & Technology

The word 'science' derives from the Latin *scientia*, 'knowledge', from the verb *scire*, 'to know'. For many centuries 'science' meant knowledge and what we now call science was usually known as 'natural philosophy', as in the title of Newton's famous work of 1687, *Naturalis Philosophiae Principia Mathematica* ('The Mathematical Principles of Natural Philosophy'). It is doubtful, in fact, whether the word was widely used in its general modern meaning until the 19c, and that usage is symptomatic of the prestige that the scientific method and scientific observation, experimentation and development had by then acquired.

### Early civilizations
Astronomy was the first exact science to begin to emerge in ancient civilizations. The heavens were studied for astrological purposes – that the will of the gods might be foreknown – and in order to make a **calendar**, which had both practical and religious uses. The ancient Egyptians, for instance, who were not on the whole great mathematicians, wished to be able to predict the annual flooding of the Nile. They gave us the seven-day week. Chinese records and observations provide valuable references in modern times for eclipses, comets and the positions of stars. In India and even more so in Mesopotamia, mathematics was used to create a more descriptive astronomy. The ancient Mesopotamian number system was based on 60; from it the system of degrees, minutes and seconds was developed.

### The ancient Greeks
In all these civilizations, however, the emphasis was on observation and description. The tendency was to explain phenomena as being in the nature of things or the will of the gods. The Greeks sought more immediate explanations. (Perhaps partly as a result of the lack of sophistication of their own theology compared with that of their predecessors.) They examined phenomena – and the theories propounded by other or earlier thinkers – in a critical way. Thales of Miletus began the study of geometry in the 6c BC. At the same time Pythagoras was discovering the mathematical relationship of the chief musical intervals, crucially relating number relationships to physically observed phenomena. The early Greek natural philosophers passed on two major concepts to their successors. The universe was an ordered structure, and the ordering of it was organic not mechanical; all things had a purpose and were imbued with the propensity to develop in accordance with the purpose they were fated to serve.

The chief conduit for such ideas to later ages was Aristotle (384–322 BC). He provided a cosmology with the earth at its centre in which everything above the moon was subject to circular motion, and everything beneath it (on earth) was composed of one of four elements: earth, air, fire or water. The whole system was set in motion by a 'prime mover', usually identified with God. (This concept was developed and given a mathematical basis by Ptolemy (c.90–168 AD), an Egyptian astronomer and geographer working in Alexandria, whose main work, the *Almagest*, was revered until the 17c.) Aristotle also taught that living creatures were divided into species, organized hierarchically throughout creation and reproducing unchangingly after their own kind – an idea that remained unchallenged until the great debate on evolution in the 19c. For him scientific investigation was a matter of observation. Experimentation, by altering natural conditions, falsified the truth of things.

The greatest mathematician of ancient Greece was Archimedes (c.287–212 BC). As well as founding the science of hydrostatics, he discovered formulae for the areas and volumes of spheres, cylinders and other plane and solid figures, anticipated calculus, and defined the principle of the lever. His principal contribution to scientific advance lies perhaps in demonstrating how physical properties can be rendered in terms of mathematics, and how the formulae thus produced can then be subjected to mathematical manipulation and the results translated back into physical terms.

### Islam and the Middle Ages
The pursuit of mathematical theory and pure science was not of great interest to the Romans, who were of a more practical bent and tended to concentrate on technology. After the fall of the Roman Empire, ancient Greek texts were preserved in monasteries and in the Arab world. There the number system, derived from ancient Hindu sources, had given more flexibility to mathematics than was possible using Roman numerals. It was combined with an interest in astronomy and astrology, and in medicine.

---

Austrian offices between 1849 and 1851 before resigning in protest at the neo-absolutist policies of the Habsburg monarchy. However, in Feb 1861 he was the author of the February Patent, which failed to settle the monarchy's nationality problems but marked the beginning of constitutional government. Schmerling thereafter resumed his legal career as President of the Supreme Court and, from 1867, served as a member of the Upper House of the Austrian parliament. ► **HABSBURG DYNASTY**

### Schmidt, Helmut Heinrich Waldemar (1918– )
West German politician. After service in **WORLD WAR II**, he studied at Hamburg, joined the Social Democratic Party in 1946, and became a member of the **BUNDESTAG** in 1953. He was Minister of Defence (1969–72) and of Finance (1972–4), in which role he created a firm basis for Germany's continued eco-nomic growth. He succeeded Willy **BRANDT** as Chancellor in 1974, describing his aim as the 'political unification of Europe in partnership with the United States'. In 1982 his **SPD/FDP** coalition collapsed, to be replaced by a **CDU**/FDP administration. ► **KOHL, HELMUT**

### Schnaebele Affair (20–30 Apr 1887)
A war scare between France and Germany. Following the arrest of the French (Alsatian-born) commissioner for the Franco-German border, Schnaebele, on German soil on suspicion of espionage, French public opinion and even the Prime Minister, **BOULANGER**, called for war. However, the French President merely made a formal protest and since Schnaebele had been promised safe conduct while in Germany on official business, **BISMARCK** agreed to his release, thereby defusing the crisis.

Aristotelian thought re-emerged in the Christian West in large measure through the work of St Thomas Aquinas in the 13c. Christianity assimilated what it could from Aristotle, as Islam had done some centuries before. Scientific knowledge was still regarded as part of a total system embracing philosophy and theology: a manifestation of God's power, which could be observed and marvelled at, but not altered. Gradually Aristotle emerged as the ultimate authority and last word in natural philosophy. His enormous prestige combined with the conservatism of academics and of the Church laid something of a dead hand on the advance of science for several centuries, though in the later medieval era and the **Renaissance** period ancient Greek scientific thought was refined, and advances were made both in the Christian Mediterranean and in the Islamic **Ottoman Empire**. The European voyages of **exploration** and discovery stimulated much precise astronomical work, done with a view to assisting navigation. Jewish scholars who could move between the Christian and Muslim worlds were often prominent in this work.

### The Scientific Revolution

After the Renaissance, the conduct of scientific inquiry in the West underwent a significant change, resulting in the **Scientific Revolution** of the 16c and 17c. In astronomy, Nicolaus Copernicus (1473–1543) refuted many aspects of the Ptolemaic description of the universe, making the sun its centre. His work influenced Johannes Kepler (1571–1630), a German mathematician who concluded that the planets' orbits are elliptical rather than circular. **Galileo** Galilei, an Italian philosopher, mathematician and scientist, improved on the telescope that had been invented in Holland and used it to make observations that included the Milky Way and Jupiter's satellites. His later research convinced him of the truth of the Copernican system, but under threat from the **Inquisition** he recanted.

In England, William Gilbert (1544–1603) established the magnetic nature of the earth and was the first to describe electricity; William Harvey (1578–1657) described the circulation of the blood; and Robert Boyle (1627–91) analyzed the behaviour of gases under pressure – all in the early 17c. From England too came Sir Isaac Newton (1642–1727), who was to replace Aristotle as the supreme authority in natural philosophy for the next two centuries. Newton established the universal law of gravitation as the key to the secrets of the universe. In 1687 he published his *Principia*, which stated his three laws of motion. Simultaneously with Gottfried Leibniz (1646–1716) he invented calculus, and he also did enormously influential work on optics and the nature of light.

Cooperation and discourse between scientists had been fostered by the formation of societies where they could meet to discuss their work. For example, the Royal Society in London, incorporated by Royal Charter in 1662, and the Académie des Sciences in Paris, founded in 1666. Scientists used each others' discoveries to advance more quickly to new theories, and science obtained a new status and prestige.

### The 18–19c

The writers of the 18c **Enlightenment** played a major part in bringing the scientific advances of the previous century to a wider public and enhancing further the prestige of science. The scientific method – observation, research, even experimentation and the use of reason, unfettered by preconceptions or dogma to analyse the findings – was applied to almost all aspects of human life.

In the latter part of the century significant advances were made in chemistry – notably the discovery of oxygen, associated with the names of Lavoisier in France, Priestley in Britain and Scheele in Sweden. Scientific knowledge also contributed substantially to the **Industrial Revolution**. The discovery of aniline dye revolutionized the textile industry, an example of the usefulness of science which led to increased public support in the form of government funding. The École Polytechnique was founded in France in 1794 to give the benefits of scientific discovery to society. Technical schools followed elsewhere, and institutes were funded for scientific work. A new era of professional scientists had begun.

Botany also advanced during the 18c, when Linnaeus invented his system of binomial nomenclature (1735), and much interest was aroused by the many new species of plants and animals observed by explorers, particularly by Captain **Cook**. Work by the French naturalist Jean Baptiste Lamarck (1749–1829) foreshadowed Charles Darwin's theories of evolution and made the first break with Aristotle's notion of immutable species. The science of geology also emerged at this time; William Smith (1769–1839), 'the father of English geology', was drawn to investigate strata while working as an engineer on the Somerset coal canal. He was the first to identify strata by the different fossils found in them. Darwin (1809–82) published *The Origin of Species* in 1859. Its epoch-making conclusions – that once again

---

### Schoelcher, Victor (1804–93)

French politician. A republican, he was an advocate of the emancipation of the slaves of French colonies, which he accomplished as a member of the Provisional Government of 1848. He opposed the 1851 coup d'état, and remained in exile throughout the French Second Empire. He returned to France in 1870, was elected to the National Assembly in 1871, as Deputy for Martinique, and became a life Senator in 1875. ► EMPIRE, SECOND (France)

### Schönbrunn, Peace of ► VIENNA, TREATY OF

### Schools Question (Belgium)

The extended political conflict between the supporters of neutral state education and of Roman Catholic schools, dominating the third quarter of the 19c, and also the 1950s. The French revolutionary period had

removed the traditional monopoly held by the Catholic Church over education; during the union with the northern Netherlands (1815–30) King **WILLIAM I** insisted that education be regulated by the state, which became one of the contributory causes of the Belgian Revolution. The liberals held sway in Belgian politics around the middle of the 19c, and much of their anticlericalism was manifested in Education Acts that progressively reduced the influence of the Church in primary education. During the years 1878–84 more anti-Catholic provisions in education brought the Schools Question to a head; at the elections of 1884 the liberals were soundly beaten and the Catholics, embarking on 30 years of uninterrupted power, reversed the legislation. After **WORLD WAR II** the battleground switched to secondary education, and in 1954–8 education dominated Belgian

brought science into conflict with the Church – were eventually accepted by almost all biologists. The work of Gregor Mendel (1822–84) on the laws of heredity was not appreciated in his lifetime, but proved the foundation for later genetic research. The French chemist Louis Pasteur (1822–95) moved into biology and formulated the germ theory of disease.

The 19c also saw tremendous advances in physics. Alessandro Volta (1745–1827) developed the current theory of electricity, and invented the electric battery and electrolysis. Michael Faraday (1791–1867) experimented with magnetism and electricity, and enabled the building of generators and motors. James Clerk Maxwell (1831–79) proposed the field theory of electromagnetism which related the phenomena of electricity, magnetism and light mathematically. He also predicted the existence of radio waves, subsequently demonstrated by Heinrich Hertz (1857–94).

Though exact science had not been very important in the early stages of the Industrial Revolution in 18c Britain, technology by the end of the 19c – building on the work of these scientists – had developed many of the machines that were to transform life for the vast majority of humankind in the following century. Particulary in Imperial Germany between 1870 and 1914, scientific education and applied science became important parts of the educational system, right up to tertiary level. A research culture, capable of generating change, became institutionalized.

### Atomic physics and relativity

The ancient Greeks had proposed the theory that all matter is made up of minute particles which they termed atoms and held to be indivisible. Various early 19c scientists, notably Newton, John Dalton (1766–1844), Amedeo Avogadro (1776–1856) and William Prout (1785–1850), contributed to refining the concept of the atom and the molecule, and in 1869 the Russian chemist Dmitri Mendeleyev (1834–1907) began to draw up a periodic table relating the chemical properties of the elements to their atomic weight.

The theoretical work of Albert Einstein (1879–1955) at the beginning of the 20c heralded the development of quantum theory. His theory of relativity incorporated Maxwell's electromagnetic theory and Newton's mechanics, and predicted departures from the classical behaviour of materials at velocities approaching the speed of light. He also provided the century with its most famous formula – $E = mc^2$ – to define the mass equivalence of energy. During the same period experiments with ionizing radiations led to the postulation of the existence of subatomic particles, the building blocks of atoms and their nuclei. The splitting of the atomic nucleus by Ernest Rutherford (1871–1937) in 1919 demonstrated the large release of energy predicted by Einstein. Subatomic particles and their related force fields were studied in the second half of the 20c using vast particle accelerators up to 17 mi/27 km in length, with a view to forming a unified theory to describe all forces including gravity. Such a theory would produce a shift comparable to the change from Newton's to Einstein's paradigm.

In addition to the search for knowledge of the universe on the microscopic scale, astronomical observations from spacecraft (eg Voyager and Cassini-Huygens) and the Hubble telescope have provided data that has increased understanding of the universe on a cosmic scale.

Understanding the atom in terms of light electrons surrounding a heavy nucleus has led to a deeper understanding of the chemical and electronic properties of materials and ways of modelling them. At the end of the 20c this enabled the 'tailor-making' of materials, substances and devices exploited in chemical, pharmaceutical and electronic products.

### Genetics and beyond

Exploration of the atom in the 20c influenced, and had its counterpart in, the study of the basic building blocks of organic life. An understanding of the nature of the chemical bond and molecular structure, applied in the field of biology, led to work on DNA. Research by Francis Crick (1916–2004), James Watson (1928– ) and Maurice Wilkins (1916–2004) in the early 1950s revealed its helical structure. A particular feature of the structure – its composition from pairs of bases in varying orders – showed the existence of a genetic code. An explosion in genetic science followed in the second half of the century, and by 2003 the Human Genome Project had succeeded in identifying this genetic code, presenting opportunities for medical research to overcome previously incurable conditions as well as opening the possibility of the cloning and indeed 'tailor-making' of living beings.

Science, like religion, arose out of the desire to explain the world in which we live. The battles between the two have been hard fought, though by the 20c science could be said to have replaced religion as the dominant orthodoxy. However, with the incorporation of uncertainty factors and the development of chaos theory, science at its highest levels is probably less dogmatic now than at any time since the Renaissance.

---

politics once more. In 1958 the Schools Pact was signed, by which the three major parties (Catholics, socialists and liberals) agreed to a free choice of education at secondary level, with largely equivalent state funding.

### Schools Question (Netherlands)

The extended political conflict surrounding Calvinist and Roman Catholic attempts to gain equal status for confessional education, especially in terms of state funding. In Napoleonic times primary education had been made a state monopoly; from the 1820s both Catholics and Calvinists began to raise objections to this, for example by means of petitions. The issue dominated Dutch domestic politics from 1850 to 1917; the confessionals objected to the 'neutral' religious content of state education, and so set up their own schools, demanding state funds to run

them. The liberals refused; the Schools Question became a battleground in the emancipation of the Catholics and orthodox Calvinists. Further Education Acts in 1857 and 1878 only served to sharpen the conflict, and in 1889, during the first confessional government in the Netherlands, an Act was introduced giving partial subsidy to 'free' or non-state schools. During the government of 1901–5 led by Abraham **KUYPER** there were more laws increasing subsidies to religious schools; in 1917 a great compromise was struck, granting universal male suffrage, and financial equality to 'free' and state education: the constitution was amended accordingly. Since the pacification of 1917 the heat has left the debate, but education continued to be a highly divisive issue in the Netherlands in the interbellum and after **WORLD WAR II**.

# *The Scientific Revolution*

*Science & Technology*

The Scientific Revolution is a name given to the change in the nature of intellectual enquiry – of the way in which people thought about and investigated the natural universe – that began in Europe at the end of the 15c and gave birth to science as we know it today. Until this revolution was accomplished, or at least under way, it is doubtful whether any of the thinkers and scholars of Christian Europe can properly be called scientists.

### The medieval mindset

It is not true to say that there were no original thinkers in the **Middle Ages**. It is true in the main, however, that scholasticism – the name given to the theological and philosophical thought of the period – operated within a tightly closed system: the universe was created by God, and the primary truths relating to its nature and working were revealed in the Bible. As a source of knowledge, the Bible was supplemented by the writings of certain authors of immemorial and unimpeachable authority, notably Aristotle, Galen and the Church Fathers. To establish the truth of something, one first sought support from such an authority. If such support was found, the case was essentially closed. One did not, as the modern cliché has it, attempt to push back the frontiers of knowledge. One attempted, rather, to move closer to the true meaning of the already authoritatively established or formulated. When, as late as the 1650s, Bishop James **Ussher** attempted to establish the age of the world, he looked no further than Holy Scripture and, by diligently studying Biblical chronology, he arrived at a precise date for the Creation – 4004 BC.

Furthermore, it was axiomatic that in God's original perfect Creation there were no loose ends. Though the Fall of Man had introduced elements of uncertainty into the cosmos, evidence of the intended order was still discernible. Everywhere there was an underlying order, pattern and correspondence. Consequently, things could often best be understood or described by analogy with another. As God is ruler of the universe, so the sun is the chief and most powerful of the planets circling the earth, so the king is chief and ruler among men, so reason should rule over the inner life of humankind, and so the lion is the king of beasts. In modern terms, it is not saying very much about the lion to assert that its position in the animal kingdom is equivalent to that of a king among men or the sun among the planets, in medieval times there was very little else to be said.

### The Renaissance and the Reformation

The process of opening up the closed system began with the **Renaissance**, the **Reformation**, and the voyages of exploration and discovery. The people of the Renaissance possessed new knowledge or had new access to old sources. Many thought of themselves as belonging to an age that was making a significant break with the past. They began a process of secularizing knowledge, prising it away from its basis in theology, and making the study of subjects such as history and mathematics a thing of value in its own right. In northern Europe the Reformers rejected outright the traditional authority of the Church and instilled in believers the confidence to study the Word of God – and, by extension, His works – for themselves. Finally, voyages of discovery made known the existence on earth of new worlds entirely unsuspected by the ancients, consequently calling into question not only the value of geographical authorities but of other authorities as well.

### Copernicus, Kepler and Galileo

In 1530 the Polish astronomer Nicolaus Copernicus (1473–1543) completed his work *De Revolutionibus Orbium Coelestium* ('On the Revolutions of the Heavenly Spheres'). It represented the mature expression of an idea expressed earlier in a brief commentary, namely, that the sun was the centre of the universe and the earth and the other planets

---

**Schumacher, Kurt Ernst Karl** (1895–1952)
German politician. He studied law and political science at the universities of Leipzig and Berlin, and from 1930 to 1933 was a member of the **REICHSTAG** and of the executive of the Social Democratic parliamentary group. An outspoken opponent of National Socialism, he spent ten years from 1933 in Nazi concentration camps, where he showed outstanding courage. He became in 1946 Chairman of the Social Democratic Party (**SPD**) and of the parliamentary group of the **BUNDESTAG**. He strongly opposed **ADENAUER**'s policy of integration with Western Europe at the expense of reunification.

**Schuman, Robert** (1886–1963)
French politician. He was a popular Christian Democrat Deputy (1919–40) and then (1945–62) one of the leaders of the **MRP** ('Popular Republican Movement'). After holding office as Prime Minister (1947–8), he remained Foreign Minister (1948–53), during which time he carried through the Schuman Plan (1950) for pooling the coal and steel resources of Western Europe, one of the predecessors of the European Community. He was Minister of Justice

(1955–6) after which he concentrated on the European movement, becoming President of the **EEC** assembly (1958–60). ► **EC (EUROPEAN COMMUNITY)**

**Schuschnigg, Kurt von** (1897–1977)
Austrian politician. He served in **WORLD WAR I**, practised law, was elected a Christian Socialist Deputy (1927), and became Minister of Justice (1932) and of Education (1933). He was Chancellor of Austria from 1934 to 1938. His attempt to prevent **HITLER** occupying Austria led to his imprisonment until 1945. He then lived in the USA, where he became Professor of Political Science at St Louis (1948–67).

**Schwabenspiegel**
A south German reworking of the law code known as the **SACHSENSPIEGEL**, it originated in Augsburg in the second half of the 13c. Originally called the *Deutschspiegel*, the document was later revised (c.1287) and the name *Schwabenspiegel* became established for the revised version in the 17c. It is not as coherent as the *Sachsenspiegel*, but it served as a basis of law in southern Germany and as far north as Hessen until the 17–18c.

revolved around it. The book was published in Frankfurt in 1543 by a Lutheran printer, shortly before Copernicus's death.

Copernicus's theory, if accepted, not only demolished the old earth-centred Ptolemaic cosmology: it set at nought all the analogies based on that cosmology. It was accepted by very few, not even by Tycho Brahe (1546–1601), who himself contributed substantially to the advance of astronomy during the 16c by his observations of the stars and their movements. *De Revolutionibus* was banned by the Roman Catholic Church and remained so until 1835.

The Copernican theory was, however, accepted by Johannes Kepler (1571–1630), a German mathematician and astronomer who was Tycho Brahe's assistant and on his death succeeded him as imperial mathematician and court astronomer in Prague. Kepler's work on planetary orbits took the theory further and provided it with a mathematical foundation. His work on the laws of planetary motion, published in *Astronomia Nova* ('New Astronomy') in 1609 and *Harmonice Mundi* ('The Harmony of the World') in 1619, formed an essential foundation for the later discoveries of Isaac Newton (1642–1727). Kepler also made significant discoveries in optics, general physics and geometry. It is also noteworthy – and symptomatic of the still transitional status of science in the 17c – that he was appointed astrologer to Albrecht **Wallenstein**, the Catholic general who commanded in the **Thirty Years' War**. Newton himself was likewise a student of alchemy.

Copernicus's theory was also eventually and more famously accepted by Kepler's slightly older Italian contemporary, **Galileo**. Galileo first took issue with Aristotle as a student of medicine in Pisa. Appointed Professor of Mathematics there in 1589, he disproved Aristotle's theory that the speed of descent of an object is proportional to its weight – demonstrating this to his students, according to legend, by dropping objects of differing weight off the Leaning Tower of Pisa. In 1592 he was forced to give up his professorial chair by his Aristotelian colleagues and made his way to Florence. By this time he had also inferred that a pendulum could be used for the exact measurement of time, invented a hydrostatic balance, and written a treatise on specific gravity.

In Padua, where he was mathematics professor from 1592 to 1610, he perfected the refracting telescope on the basis of reports of its invention in Holland in 1608. Using the telescope – an aid denied to Copernicus and to Tycho Brahe – he made numerous discoveries, notably of four of the moons of Jupiter and of sunspots, that further confirmed his preference for the Copernican system first formed in 1595. From about 1613, while employed as court mathematician in Florence, his writings began to bring him into conflict not only with traditionalist academics, but also with the Church. In 1616 he was warned by Cardinal Bellarmine that he should no longer support Copernicus's view that the earth moved. After remaining silent on the subject for many years, in 1632 he published the *Dialogo sopra i due massimi sistemi del mondo* ('Dialogue on the Two Chief World Systems') in which, in the context of a discussion of the operation of tides, he again came down in favour of Copernicus. Summoned by the **Inquisition**, Galileo was compelled to abjure his position and sentenced to indefinite imprisonment – a sentence commuted almost immediately to house arrest. After abjuring he is said to have muttered 'eppur si muove' ('it does move nonetheless').

**Further advances**

Astronomy was not the only branch of science in which great strides were made during the 16c. The Belgian Andreas Vesalius (1514–64) was one of the first to dissect human cadavers. On the basis of his observations he published *De Humani Corporis Fabrica* (1543, 'On the Structure of the Human Body'), the same year that Copernicus's *De Revolutionibus* appeared. In it he effectively repudiated the anatomical principles of Galen and paved the way for William Harvey's discovery of the circulation of the blood, described in a book published in 1628. Galileo's work inspired Evangelista Torricelli (1608–47), the inventor of the barometer, another vital tool for use in experimentation, and the Dutch physicist Christiaan Huygens (1629–93), the inventor of the pendulum clock, the discoverer of the polarization of light and the first to propound its wave nature. Meanwhile, Robert Boyle (1627–91), an Irish experimental philosopher and chemist, and the formulator of 'Boyle's Law', was investigating the characteristics of air and of the

---

**Schwarzenberg, Felix Ludwig Johann Friedrich** (1800–52)
Austrian politician. During the **REVOLUTION OF 1848**, he was made Prime Minister, and created a centralized, absolutist, imperial state. He then sought Russian military aid to suppress the Hungarian rebellion (1849), and demonstrated Austrian superiority over **PRUSSIA** at the Olmütz Convention (1850). His bold initiatives temporarily restored Habsburg domination of European affairs. ► **HABSBURG DYNASTY**

**Schwarzenberg, Karl Philipp, Prince of** (1771–1820)
Austrian soldier and diplomat. He entered the army in 1787 and took part in the War of the Second Coalition (1792–1802). He was Ambassador to Russia in 1808, and when Austria declared war on France in 1809 he participated in the unsuccessful campaign. After the peace treaty, he pursued a diplomatic career until **NAPOLEON I** demanded him as general of the Austrian contingent in the invasion of Russia in 1812. When Austria turned on Napoleon, he became generalissimo of the allied armies that won the Battles of Dresden and **LEIPZIG** in 1813. In 1814 he helped to occupy Paris.

**Schwimmer, Rosika** (1877–1948)
Hungarian feminist and pacifist. As a journalist she was active in the Hungarian women's movement, and was a co-founder of a feminist-pacifist group. She became Vice-President of the Women's International League for Peace and Freedom, and in 1918–19 was Hungarian minister to Switzerland. In 1920, fleeing from the country's anti-Semitic leadership, she emigrated to the USA, but was refused citizenship since, as a pacifist, she could not promise to fight should war break out. For the rest of her life she continued to campaign for pacifism and before the outbreak of **WORLD WAR II** was outspoken in her criticism of growing European fascism.

**Science** ► *See panel*

**Scientific Revolution, The** ► *See panel*

**SCLC (Southern Christian Leadership Conference)**
US **CIVIL RIGHTS** organization. Formed in 1957 by Martin Luther **KING** and other ministers to pursue

vacuum by means of an air pump, constructed with the aid of his assistant Robert Hooke (1635–1703). Boyle took an active part in the meetings of the anti-scholastic 'invisible college' of Oxford intellectuals, a precursor of the Royal Society. His air pump became a powerful symbol of the 'experimental philosophy' promoted by the Royal Society from its founding in 1660. Hooke in 1662 became the Society's first curator of experiments.

The Royal Society (incorporated by Royal Charter in 1662) provided a focus and forum for scientific debate and a means of disseminating scientific knowledge – its *Philosophical Transactions* was the first professional scientific journal. Along with comparable institutions in other countries, notably the *Académie des Sciences* of Paris, founded in 1666, it promoted the systematization of scientific method and the way in which experiments and discoveries were reported. If experiments were to be reproducible and their results verifiable, they had to be described in plain language. The foundation of scientific academies also marked a great step forward in the social and political acceptance of science, though opposition from Aristotelians and other academic traditionalists, and from the Church, continued into the 18c.

### Newton

The culmination of the Scientific Revolution is generally taken to lie in the work of Sir Isaac Newton. His early mathematical studies led to the invention – simultaneously with Gottfried Leibniz (1646–1716) – of differential calculus. Turning his attention to the study of light and prisms, he constructed the first reflecting telescope, an invaluable aid to the astronomers that followed him. In 1684 he published his gravitation theory, and in 1687 his *Philosophiae Naturalis Principia Mathematica* ('Mathematical Principles of Natural Philosophy'). It stated his three laws of motion, which became the foundation of modern physics and were not challenged until the publication of Einstein's work in the early 20c.

Above all, Newton established a new synthesis. His was a universal law of gravitation; it not only explained the movements of the planets within the Copernican system, but it also explained such humble – and, for Newton himself, inspirational – events as the fall of an apple from the branch of a tree. Moreover, it did not exclude God from the universe. All Newton's work was undertaken within the framework of devout Christian belief, though his private theological beliefs were complex and heterodox.

By the time of Newton's death in 1727, the scientific method, as currently understood, was firmly established. The thinkers and writers of the **Enlightenment** took it for granted that an epoch had dawned in which observation, experiment and the free exercise of human reason were the foundations of knowledge. In popularizing science and spreading the knowledge of the discoveries made in the previous century, they helped to establish the prestige which it and its practitioners have enjoyed to the present day.

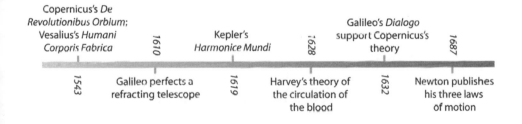

Copernicus's *De Revolutionibus Orbium*; Vesalius's *Humani Corporis Fabrica* — 1543 · 1610 — Galileo perfects a refracting telescope · Kepler's *Harmonice Mundi* — 1619 · 1628 — Harvey's theory of the circulation of the blood · Galileo's *Dialogo* support Copernicus's theory — 1632 · 1687 — Newton publishes his three laws of motion

racial integration, primarily in the South, through non-violent protest. As ministers they were natural leaders in their communities, able to explain their aims in terms of the Christian creed, and in a rhetoric which their people understood. An unsuccessful campaign in Albany, Georgia, in 1961 demonstrated the need for careful planning and preparation. In later campaigns the movement sought to develop a 'creative tension', inciting whites to overreact, attracting the media, and forcing the federal government to intervene. The success of this strategy was seen in Birmingham and Selma. However, it did not succeed in Chicago where blacks lacked unity, the issues were far more complicated and white opposition was far more skilful. After the death of Martin Luther King, the organization lost much of its moral authority, though it still remained an important platform for leaders such as Ralph Abernathy and, later, Jesse **JACKSON**.

### SCOTLAND

The northern constituent part of the United Kingdom, comprising all the mainland north of the border that runs from the Solway Firth to Berwick-upon-Tweed, and the island groups of the Outer and Inner Hebrides, Orkney and Shetland. Roman attempts to limit incursions of northern tribes were marked by the building of the Antonine Wall (AD142), which extended from the Forth estuary to the Clyde, and Hadrian's Wall (AD122–8), which extended from the Solway Firth to the River Tyne and was the principal northern frontier of the Roman province of Britain. There were the beginnings of unification in the 9c, but wars were fought between England and Scotland during the **MIDDLE AGES** until Scottish independence was restored by Robert **BRUCE**, and recognized by England in 1328. The Stuarts succeeded to the throne in the 14c and united the crowns of Scotland and England in 1603; the parliaments were united under the Act of **UNION** in 1707. There were unsuccessful Jacobite rebellions in 1715 and 1745. A proposal for devolution failed in a referendum in 1979, but another in 1997 gave it overwhelming approval and a Scottish parliament with tax-raising powers opened on 1 July 1999. Scotland's legal and educational system have always been different from and separate from those

of England and Wales, and many of its other institutions are distinct from those of England or Wales. A fundamental change was made to Scottish land ownership in 2004 when feudal tenure was abolished. ► ENGLAND; FIFTEEN REBELLION; FORTY-FIVE REBELLION; NORTHERN IRELAND; SCOTTISH WAR OF INDEPENDENCE; STUART, HOUSE OF; UNITED KINGDOM; WALES

### Scott, Robert Falcon (1868–1912)
English explorer. Born near Devonport, Devon, he joined the navy in 1881. In the *Discovery* he commanded the National Antarctic Expedition (1901–4) which explored the Ross Sea area, and discovered King Edward VII Land. In 1910 he embarked upon his second expedition in the *Terra Nova*, and with a sledge party reached the South Pole on 17 Jan 1912, only to discover that the Norwegian expedition under Roald Amundsen had beaten them by a month. All members of his party died, and their bodies and diaries were found by a search party eight months later. ► EXPLORATION

### Scott, Thomas (c.1842–1870)
Canadian Orangeman. He became an Protestant martyr when he was executed in 1870 during the RED RIVER REBELLION. This disastrous incident was the root of later troubles which split the country, such as the execution of Louis RIEL, the campaign of D'Alton MCCARTHY, and the MANITOBA SCHOOLS ACT.

### Scott, Winfield (1786–1866)
US general. He became a national hero for his part in the WAR OF 1812, distinguishing himself at the Battle of LUNDY'S LANE (1814). After framing the General Regulations and introducing French tactics into the US Army, he commanded the war against the Seminoles and the Creeks in Florida (1835–37), and helped to settle the disputed boundary line of Maine and New Brunswick (1839). In the MEXICAN WAR he took Veracruz (26 Mar 1847), put Antonio de SANTA ANNA to flight, and entered the Mexican capital (14 Sep). Known as 'Old Fuss and Feathers' because of his insistence on military punctilio, he was an unsuccessful Whig candidate for the presidency (1852). He retained nominal command of the army until Oct 1861, and was author of the 'Anaconda Plan' to envelop and strangle the Confederacy, which was eventually implemented.

### Scottish National Party (SNP)
A political party formed in 1928 as the National Party of Scotland, which merged with the Scottish Party in 1933. It first won a seat at a by-election in 1945 and made its first proper showing in the 1974 general election, when it took nearly a third of Scottish votes and won 11 seats. Its support appeared to decline for a time, with all but two of its candidates being defeated in 1979 and 1983. In 1988, however, it achieved a surprise victory in the Govan by-election. Having won three seats in 1987 and in 1992, in 1997 it

## RULERS OF SCOTLAND

| Regnal Dates | Name |
|---|---|
| 1005/34 | Malcolm II |
| 1034/40 | Duncan I |
| 1040/57 | Macbeth |
| 1057/8 | Lulach |
| 1058/93 | Malcolm III, Canmore |
| 1093/4 | Donald III (Donald Bane) |
| 1094 | Duncan II |
| 1094/7 | Donald III (Donald Bane) |
| 1097/1107 | Edgar |
| 1107/24 | Alexander I |
| 1124/53 | David I |
| 1153/65 | Malcolm IV, the Maiden |
| 1165/1214 | William I, the Lion |
| 1214/49 | Alexander II |
| 1249/86 | Alexander III |
| 1286/90 | Margaret, Maid of Norway |
| 1290/2 | Interregnum |
| 1292/6 | John Balliol |
| 1296/1306 | Interregnum |
| 1306/29 | Robert I, the Bruce |
| 1329/71 | David II* |
| 1371/90 | Robert II |
| 1390/1406 | Robert III |
| 1406/37 | James I |
| 1437/60 | James II |
| 1460/88 | James III |
| 1488/1513 | James IV |
| 1513/42 | James V |
| 1542/67 | Mary, Queen of Scots |
| 1567/1625 | James VI |

\* Edward Balliol, son of John Balliol, was crowned King of Scots in Sep 1332 but expelled in Dec; restored as king 1333–6

replaced the Conservative Party as the main opposition party to Labour in Scotland by winning six of the 72 Scottish seats; in the 2001 election it won five. Its principal policy aim is complete independence for Scotland from the UK, which was partially realized in 1999 with the introduction of the Scottish parliament, in which the SNP won 35 of the 129 seats. It was less successful in the 2003 elections to the Scottish Parliament but remained the second-largest party. ► **HOME RULE**

### Scottish War of Independence

The conflict between the Scots and English in the late 13c and early 14c. After heavy defeats by **EDWARD I** at the Battle of **DUNBAR** (1296) and Falkirk (1298), the Scots regrouped first under William **WALLACE** and then Robert **BRUCE**. The fall of Stirling Castle (1304) led to the capture and execution of Wallace but Bruce was crowned (1306) and, after Edward I's death (1307), increasingly asserted his authority. His victory at the Battle of **BANNOCKBURN** (1314) secured Scotland from English rule and the Scottish barons declared their allegiance to Bruce in the face of papal opposition to his kingship (Declaration of **ARBROATH**, 1320). A truce between England and Scotland (1323) was broken when the Scots crossed into Northumberland and ravaged it (1327–8). Queen **ISABELLA OF FRANCE** and her lover Roger Mortimer sued for peace. The English renounced all claims to feudal superiority over Scotland (1328) and recognized Bruce as its king. In 1329 Pope **JOHN XXII** issued a Bull authorizing Robert to be crowned and anointed. ► **EDWARD II**

### Scottsboro Case (1931)

A criminal case in Alabama involving nine African-American males who were falsely accused of raping two white women on a train. Having had the services of two volunteer lawyers only from the first day of the trial, they were all sentenced (by all-white juries) to long-term imprisonment or death. A series of retrials and the intervention of the US Supreme Court eventually overturned the guilty verdicts, but the last of the convicted defendants was not released from prison until 1950. The Scottsboro case opened many Americans' eyes to the injustices suffered by African-Americans in the segregated South.

### Scramble for Africa ► AFRICA, PARTITION OF

### Sculpture ► See panel

### SDI (Strategic Defense Initiative)

The proposal first made by President **REAGAN** in 1983 (dubbed by the press 'Star Wars') that the USA should develop the technologies for a defensive layered 'shield' of weapons based primarily in space, able to shoot down incoming ballistic missiles. SDI was highly controversial because it seemed to overthrow the principle of 'mutual assured destruction' on which the idea of deterrence rested, and also potentially undermined the Strategic Arms Reduction Talks (**START**). Also the technologies it would need to perfect, such as directed energy, as well as being extremely difficult to achieve, might ultimately be used for offensive as well as defensive purposes. SDI funding was reduced during George H **BUSH**'s administration when the project was scaled down and renamed GPALS (Global Protection Against Limited Strikes) in 1991, and, having cost around US$30 billion, was terminated in 1993 when the project was replaced by a new Ballistic Missile Defense Organization.

### Seaga, Edward Philip George (1930–)

US-born Jamaican politician. He went to school in Kingston, Jamaica and then studied at Harvard University. On the staff of the University of West Indies before moving into politics, he joined the **JAMAICA LABOUR PARTY** (JLP) and became its leader in 1974. Seaga entered the House of Representatives in 1962 and served in the administration of Hugh Shearer (1967–72) before becoming leader of the opposition. In 1980 he and the JLP had a resounding, and surprising, win over Michael **MANLEY**'s People's National Party (PNP), and Seaga became Prime Minister. He called a snap election in 1983 and won all the assembly seats, but in 1989 Manley and the PNP returned to power with a landslide victory.

### Sebastian (1554–78)

King of Portugal (1557/78). The grandson of Emperor **CHARLES V** and nephew of **PHILIP II** of Spain, he succeeded his grandfather, John III. Following the regencies of his grandmother, Catalina (1557/62) and great-uncle, Cardinal Henry (1562/8), he took control of the government at the age of 14. Lost in dreams of conquest and crusading zeal, he launched a futile

# *Sculpture*

*Art & Literature*

From the earliest times, the favourite subject for sculptors was the human form, often very stylized, but always representational. In the past, materials used depended on what was available, until trade and improved transport meant that materials could be moved as required. Throughout most of Oceania, sculptures were carved from wood. In the Marquesas and Hawaii, wooden statues of gods were erected in the sacred enclosures. In New Zealand, gods' heads decorated the war canoes, then the storehouses and the meeting-houses, with symbols of plenty and ancestral power. But where stone existed, monumental stone figures were created, most dramatically on Easter Island from around AD 900. The colossi were up to 40 ft/12 m in height, in a rigid style, each with a massive head merging into the torso.

In most parts of the world the earliest examples of sculpture are thought to have been associated with religion. Examples range from small fertility symbols and votive offerings (eg the *Venus of Willendorf* c.25,000 BC) to the relief carvings on temples in Egypt c.3100 BC, representing both traditions in sculpture: that done in the round, and that done in relief.

Both types are found throughout Asia. In China, stone-working was considered a lowly task, and clay modelling was initially more common. The cult of ancestor worship meant that burial sites were filled with art. Pottery grave figurines were made during the Zhou Dynasty, but the most impressive grave figures yet discovered are those around the tomb of Qin Shi Huangdi (259–210 BC): 7,000 life-size terracotta figures, with 400 horses and 100 chariots, all fully painted with realistic features. After the establishment of Buddhism, a new tradition of sculpture began, culminating in massive stone representations of the Buddha (c.563–c.483 BC). Such enormous statues are also found in Nepal, Tibet, Japan, Burma (now Myanmar), Thailand and Java, as well as the birthplace of Buddhism, India. Differences of style depended on how much the artists were permitted, or wished, to depart from the original ideal.

In India, sculpture was the supreme art form, applied to temple walls and cut into rocks. The subject was religious stories, and the intention narrative. The reliefs on the stupa at Bharhut (2c BC) use stylized planes and angles, and there are no expressions on the faces of the many people depicted. In contrast, the four gateways of the Great Stupa at Sanchi are covered in a sculpture more naturalistic and flowing, with landscapes filled with animals.

Originality and artistic self-expression were not the most common features of ancient sculpture. The representation of human figures tended to be formulaic; Egyptian statuary changed little during the 3,000 years of ancient **Egyptian civilization**, although there were periods when the faces on the statues of kings (and some important commoners) had truer portraits. The statues became larger as the pharaohs made themselves bigger and better pyramids; the four seated statues of Ramesses II (c.1304–c.1237 BC) at the Abu Simbel temple are each 66 ft/20 m high. But the style remained dignified and stylized. So too throughout the Middle East: faces looked very much the same in the reliefs of kings and priests. More freedom came with the representation of animals.

The oriental convention for the frontal pose, with the hair stiff, was also followed in ancient Greece. The influence of Egyptian statuary can be seen in the *kouroi* (life-size statues of young men) made for dedications in sanctuaries. Proportions were based on theory rather than observation; the aim was to present an ideal rather than represent a real person, even though a model was invariably used. A tendency to more realistic representation came in the classical period. Relief sculptures on pediments and friezes gave scope for narrative work, as at the Temple of Zeus at Olympus and the Parthenon in Athens, where the sculpture is conceived as part of the architectural whole. Athens was the centre for Greek art and culture, and the sculptors who worked there were greatly admired in their time and immediately after, although many of their works are lost, and others known only in the form of Roman copies. At that time, the ideal remained more important than the individual, but more realism was apparent in the treatment of female figures and clothing (eg on the frieze from the balustrade of the temple of Athene Nike), and before long the next generation of sculptors – Praxiteles, Scopas and Lysippus (all 4c BC) – began to put emotion and realism into their work. Praxiteles showed a new and sensual treatment of the female nude with his Aphrodite, and Lysippus made several studies of Alexander the Great. In the period after Alexander's death, the realistic style – full of movement – continued to develop.

---

and costly war against the **MOORS** of North Africa, and fell in the Battle of **ALCAZARQUIVIR** in Algeria. His death without an heir opened the way for the union of Portugal with Spain under his uncle, but continuing rumours that he was still alive fuelled Portuguese nationalism and gave rise to a series of impostors. The popular belief that he would return revived as late as 1807–8 when Portugal was occupied by the French.

## Secession, Right of

A US constitutional doctrine that enabled individual states to leave (or secede from) the Federal Union. Espoused by 11 Southern slave-holding states when Abraham **LINCOLN** was elected President (1861), the doctrine hastened the **AMERICAN CIVIL WAR**, during which it was discredited.

**Secularization** ► *See panel*

## Securities and Exchange Commission (SEC)

A body set up in 1934 in the USA during the **GREAT DEPRESSION** to regulate and control the issue of shares by corporations. It ensures that statements about the stocks being sold are accurate, and generally regulates the way US stock markets operate.

**SED** (*Sozialistische Einheitspartei Deutschlands*, 'Socialist Unity Party of Germany')

East German political party. Formed in East Germany in 1946 out of the **KPD** and a somewhat unwilling **SPD**, the SED became the Marxist–Leninist party of government in East Germany. Led initially by Wilhelm **PIECK** and Otto Grotewohl, it then saw Walter **UL-BRICHT** become General-Secretary in 1950 (1963 renamed First Secretary) and Erich **HONECKER** replace him in 1971 (1976 renamed General-Secretary). The SED claimed its moral authority as the German proponent of Soviet-style socialism, but despite a

It can be seen on the *Altar of Zeus* (now in Berlin, Germany) made for the temple at Pergamum, in the *Nike of Samothrace* (in the Louvre, Paris), and in the *Laocoön* statue (in the Vatican Museum, Rome), with its vigorous, writhing action.

Following the Roman conquest, Greek artists found rich patrons requiring accurate portraits. Funeral masks had been carved from the 1c BC, and from this custom evolved funerary busts that depicted ugliness as well as beauty. However, statues of the emperors tended to be idealized; there are no representations of Augustus as an old man, for example. All the Roman rulers erected monuments to celebrate their power and that of the empire. The Roman narrative style of sculpture is shown to its fullest extent in *Trajan's Column* (AD 103), where a spiral band of marble 4 ft/1.2 m wide winds up the 125 ft/38 m shaft, showing in great detail Trajan's Dacian campaigns. The figures were designed to be seen from a distance, and brightly painted.

After the fall of the Roman Empire, the Byzantine style of the Eastern Church held sway, with its stylized iconographic forms in figure representation and abstract stylized forms in architectural relief sculpture (eg in the Hagia Sophia, Istanbul). Abstract decoration was also a feature of Celtic carving and relief in Ireland and Scotland, and of Anglo-Saxon work in England, featured on stone crosses.

Ecclesiastic building was in the Romanesque style, characterized by heavy columns and rounded arches. Relief compositions in the tympanums over church doorways show each feature stylized and presented according to the symbolic meaning intended. The Gothic style that followed was adorned with more realistic figures, and particularly foliage, carved in stone, as at Reims Cathedral, France.

In Italy, the beginnings of a return to classical influences are apparent in the works of Nicola Pisano and his son Giovanni in the 13c. But with the period known as the **Renaissance**, the classical ideals became revered in all art, and the style of the preceding centuries was rejected in favour of a new realism based on the ideals of Greek art (as described by the Romans). In this new manifestation, however, the natural, rather than painted, surface of the material was preferred.

Donatello's marble *St George* (c.1415) and his bronze *David* (the first nude heroic statue since Roman times) are based on accurate observation of the human body. The new realism is apparent in all the great works of the time, for example Lorenzo Ghiberti's gilded bronze *Gates of Paradise* (1425–52) for the Florence Baptistery and Jacopo della Quercia's low relief over the doorway of San Petronio, Bologna (1425–38). Movement and realism had become the dominant features once again, incorporated into all works by Michelangelo (1474–1563). Michelangelo – sculptor, painter, architect and poet – produced works that epitomize the Renaissance. His earliest work shows the influence of the classical masters, but the *Pietà* (now in St Peter's, Rome) shows a realism and emotion more in keeping with Gothic art, so that the two are synthesized. His strong compositions are designed to be viewed from several angles, as is his 13 ft/4 m tall *David* (1501–4), carved from a block of spoiled marble. Balance, dignity and strength are evident in his works, which influenced sculptors throughout the 16c.

Some tried to emulate Michelangelo's massive figures, but Benvenuto Cellini (1500–71) moved towards a lighter, airier style. His bronze *Perseus* was also designed to be seen from several angles, and its spirit of movement was carried further by Giambologna (1529–1608) with his bronze *Flying Mercury*, balanced on tiptoe. The Mannerist style of Giambologna and his Florentine studio had influence throughout Italy and into northern Europe; the elaborate twisted poses were reflected in the movement of the art form known as Baroque, dating from around 1600. The supreme sculptor in this genre was Gian Lorenzo Bernini (1598–1680), who created pictorial effects (eg *Apollo and Daphne*), and appealed to the emotions (eg *Ecstasy of St Teresa*). The style was somewhat more restrained in France, and evolved into Rococo around 1700.

Around the middle of the 18c, a reaction to the extreme ornateness of some Rococo work encouraged a conscious attempt to revive both the style and spirit of classical art. The search for the ideal was on again, and calm rationalism was the keynote. Neoclassicism favoured a severe unemotional style, rejecting the pictorial and sensual approach of Bernini. A convention began that the subjects of monumental statues should be depicted naked or in classical dress, although uniform was acceptable depending on the purpose of the monument and the country where it was being erected. Throughout the 19c monumental sculptures were produced to honour heroes and their nations. Sculptors displayed their works in Academy exhibitions, eager for publicity. The chief patron was no longer the Church, but government.

---

membership of over 2 million in 1987, its style of government was never popular. Following the **REVO-LUTION OF 1989**, the SED reconstituted itself as the PDS (Party of Democratic Socialism), but enjoys only limited support. ► **MARXISM**

## Sedan, Battle of (1870)

The crucial French defeat of the **FRANCO-PRUSSIAN WAR**, bringing the end of the Second Empire in France. **MACMAHON's** plan to relieve the French Rhine Army, besieged in Metz, was foiled when German forces under **MOLTKE** encircled Sedan. **NAPOLEON III** surrendered the town with 83,000 men; the Germans then advanced on Paris. ► **EMPIRE, SECOND** (France)

## Seddon, Richard John (1845–1906)

British-born New Zealand politician. He emigrated to Australia in 1863, arriving in New Zealand in 1866.

He entered national politics in 1879 and in 1890 became a minister in Ballance's reforming Liberal government, succeeding Ballance as Prime Minister in 1893. Under Ballance and Seddon, New Zealand gained its reputation as a pioneer of state experiments in social reform. Their governments facilitated the extension of small farming by graduated land and income taxes, the repurchase of alienated Crown lands, the purchase of further Maori lands, reform of land law and cheap credit. They introduced the enfranchisement of women (1893); compulsory conciliation and arbitration (1894), old-age pensions (1898) and free secondary education (1903). These last two were Seddon's personal concerns, but his main contribution was political, disciplining the party and overcoming opposition in the Legislative Council. An imperialist, he sent troops to South Africa during the **BOER WARS** (1899–1902), but his aim of

New technology enabled the reproduction of large works at a reduced size and made them suitable for the drawing room.

At the end of the 19c, Impressionism flourished in painting in France. Auguste Rodin (1840–1917) was influenced by this, by Romanticism, and by the works of the Renaissance masters, to produce sculpture that was a complete break with all that had been done that century. His portrait busts and statues created controversy, and his extreme realism was criticized. He was to have influence on the work of many 20c sculptors, including Pablo Picasso (1881–1973) and Sir Jacob Epstein (1880–1959).

Picasso's work, like that of others in the 20c, was influenced by 'primitive' art, particularly that of Africa, where since ancient times there had been a rich tradition of sculpture in wood, unfired clay, copper alloys and wrought iron. Wood was the material most commonly used for masks, of which Picasso formed a varied collection. In their places of origin the masks were not made as 'art for art's sake', but to be used in ritual. The **Igbo** and Ibibio of Nigeria carved fearsome masks to represent evil characters in their dances, and beautifully featured ones to depict the virtuous. Dogon masks illustrated the Dogon view of the world and its creatures, and also had symbolic intent, as with the 'Great Mother' mask, representing death, and the Kanaga mask, representing creation. On the western Atlantic coast, in Sierra Leone, the women of the Mende made elegant polished black wooden masks to be worn by the leaders of their initiation ceremonies. The Bambara of Mali wore their Chi Wara antelope masks for the ceremonies of planting and harvesting. Both representational and non-representational forms were used in other forms of sculpture. The Yoruba in Nigeria strove in particular for certain effects in their work (both in wood-carving and bronze casting), and valued straightness, symmetry and smoothness over realism.

'Primitive' art was an important influence on many artists in the move away from the representational to the abstract during the 20c; Brancusi's symbolic, non-representational pieces, for example, show the influence of African art. The work of Henry Moore (1898–1986) draws upon the archaic Greek and Egyptian styles, but was also highly influenced by the Toltec–Maya statuary, particularly the reclining 'Chac Mools'.

Other ways were developed to break with the 19c 'academic' art, rooted as it was in classicism and literature. Constructivism reflected the beauty of the machine with constructions related to engineering and mathematics. A different means of reacting was the assemblage style, associated with Dadaism, where the assemblies of material were supposedly accidental and spontaneous, rather than rational. Reason was also rejected by the Surrealists, and their compositions juxtaposed familiar objects in an unfamiliar way.

The principles of Surrealism were shared by some sculptors, such as Moore and Alexander Calder (1898–1976), but expressed in a different way. The influence of the machine world was seen in Calder's 'mobiles': hanging wire sculptures with a continually changing composition – a style known as 'kinetic sculpture' – and adaptable for use in major public spaces.

After **World War II** a new medium became popular: metalwork. Using an oxyacetylene torch, sculptors worked in steel, providing their works with strength and flexibility. The development of this medium in the 1950s saw sculptors looking for a way to express ideas in abstract terms. From the 1960s onwards, innovation came in the use made of the 'environment', as natural features (trees, rocks, ice, etc) were used as the medium of expression, rather than as the subject they had been for hundreds of years. ► **Architecture**; **Painting**

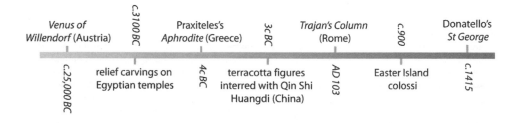

| *Venus of* *Willendorf* (Austria) | *c.3100 BC* | Praxiteles's Aphrodite (Greece) | *3c BC* | *Trajan's Column* *(Rome)* | *c.900* | Donatello's *St George* |
|---|---|---|---|---|---|---|
| *c.25,000 BC* | relief carvings on Egyptian temples | *4c BC* | terracotta figures interred with Qin Shi Huangdi (China) | *AD 103* | Easter Island colossi | *c.1415* |

annexing Fiji and Samoa to New Zealand was frustrated by the British government. As 'King Dick' he dominated New Zealand politics from 1893 until his death in office. ► **REEVES, WILLIAM PEMBER**

**Sedgemoor, Battle of** (5 July 1685)
A battle near Bridgwater, Somerset, which ended the Duke of **MONMOUTH**'s rebellion against James VII of Scotland and II of England. The rebel army received popular support and outnumbered the royal army by 4,000 to 2,500, but desertions provoked an abortive night attack. Monmouth was executed, and his supporters suffered under Judge **JEFFREYS**' 'BLOODY ASSIZES'. ► **JAMES VII AND II**

**Seeckt, Hans von** (1866–1936)
German army officer. After serving with merit as a staff officer in **WORLD WAR I**, Seeckt acted as military expert to the German delegation at the Treaty of **VER-** SAILLES before becoming Army Chief of Staff in 1920. His equivocal attitude to the republic saw him uphold order with emergency powers during the troubles of late 1923 and early 1924, but also saw him fail to act decisively against far-right conspirators (**KAPP PUTSCH**, 1920). Eventually this equivocation forced his resignation in 1926. As Chief of Staff he had been a strong advocate of military cooperation with the USSR, not least to undermine Poland. He sat in the **REICHSTAG** (1930–2), and functioned briefly thereafter as a military adviser in China.

**segregation**
The cultural, political, and typically geographical separation imposed by one racial or ethnic group on another. The term is most often applied to the subjugation of blacks by a politically dominant white élite, particularly through **APARTHEID** (literally, 'separateness') in South Africa in c.1948–91, and in the

# Secularization

Culture & Society

### Secularization and religion

Secularization denotes the process of change whereby authority passes
from a religious source to a secular source; it becomes an issue or a need
only where religion and the religious have acquired a powerful or dominant position in a society and penetrate all
aspects of life, including the processes of government. In ancient Greece and Rome, for instance, religion seems never to
have dominated the state. The chief religious offices were held by men who also held political office. While piety was
considered a virtue and due observance to the gods was to be paid, religion was seldom an all-consuming concern.
Moreover, polytheism was a flexible system. New gods and goddesses were admitted to the pantheon to accommodate
local cults, and an individual might freely choose a particular deity as his or her special patron, although prudence
demanded that other divinities should not be unduly neglected. None of this caused political problems.

With the rise of the great monotheistic proselytizing religions of Christianity and Islam the situation became very
different. The State, to put it crudely, had to guarantee salvation; it became the pillar of right religion. In practice, this
massively enhanced the power of Christian kings. There emerged a body of clerical men who claimed to exercise a
spiritual ministry on earth on behalf of God. Individuals, organizations and rulers in Christian countries gave large
amounts of land, money and other property to the Church in the hope of acquiring spiritual rewards, thereby increasing
its temporal influence. Normally, the clerical estate owed so much to the Crown that they were its servants and
propagandists.

In the Eastern Roman (Byzantine) Empire, the Church accepted the principle of 'Caesaropapism': subordination to an
Emperor thought of as a representative of divine authority on earth. In the West, the popes were generally not content
with a subordinate status. Quarrels between sovereigns and the papacy over the limits and jurisdiction of royal and
papal power (both, of course, claiming to be rooted in a divine mandate) were frequent, as exemplified in the clash
between **Henry II** of England and his Archbishop of Canterbury, Thomas à **Becket**. The Church's power was perhaps at
its peak during the pontificate of **Innocent III**, who claimed that the Holy Roman Emperor was subordinate to him. He
deposed the Emperor **Otto IV**, forced **Philip II** of France to reinstate his divorced second wife, Ingeborg of Denmark,
and placed England under an interdict and excommunicated King **John** (John Lackland) in order to secure the office of
Archbishop of Canterbury for his candidate, Stephen **Langton**. Such clashes over jurisdictional limits diminished in
frequency when the papacy needed royal help to defeat the Conciliar Movement.

Other cultures tended to avoid such conflicts between rulers and the professional religious classes. Islam has no
priesthood, although the *ulama*, or body of exponents of the five Islamic schools of law, could be influential. Religion
and the state were united in pursuit of Islamic righteousness. The Ottoman Sultan in Istanbul claimed to be the Caliph, or
supreme head of all Sunni Muslims (**Sunnis**). In Iran, the Safavid Sultans were intimately identified with the Shia form of
Islam (**Shiites**). In Buddhist Tibet, gifts to monasteries and numbers of monks reached the point where monastic leaders
who were regarded as incarnations of Buddha, such as the **Dalai Lama** and the Panchen Lama, became the rulers of the
country, although in China and Japan religious beliefs tended to reinforce loyalty to the righteous ruler. In China,
Buddhism, and more particularly Confucianism, taught civic virtues which were also inculcated by Buddhism and
Shinto in Japan.

### The Reformation

When **Henry VIII** of England denied the authority of the pope, abolished the payment of annates to Rome, proclaimed
himself supreme head of the Church of England (1534), and suppressed the monasteries, he was carrying to extremes
the traditions of his predecessors throughout Europe. Since Henry had no doctrinal differences with Rome and dealt as
severely with those who advocated Lutheranism as with those who supported the pope, his **Reformation** was

---

Southern states of the USA c.1900–60. Segregation of
blacks has been most apparent in housing, public
facilities and transportation, and education. **►** **CIVIL
RIGHTS**; **JIM CROW LAWS**

### Segu

A West African state, founded (c.1650) by the Bambara, a Mande-speaking agricultural people. They
also formed the state of Kaarta (now in Mali)
c.1753–4.

### Seguí, Salvador (1887–1923)

Spanish anarcho-syndicalist. He took part in the **TRA-
GIC WEEK** of 1909 and had to flee the repression afterwards. Having participated in the foundation of the
**CNT** in 1910, he became President of the Federation
of Construction Workers of Barcelona in 1914. Seguí
was the architect of the Pact of Saragossa (1916) with
the Socialist trade union movement, the **UGT**, which
led the two movements to pressure the government
jointly in the fight against inflation and unemployment. Indeed, he believed that common action
against capitalism not only required cooperation
with the Socialists, but even with groups beyond the

organized working class. Consequently, in 1917 he
participated in the general strike committee, even
though the CNT was not officially part of the
Republican-Socialist coalition. After **WORLD WAR I**,
the down-to-earth Seguí was the most prominent figure in the CNT, and in 1919 almost single-handedly
persuaded it to accept the agreement reached in the
La Canadiense strike, only to be undermined by the
revolutionary anarchists. On 10 Mar 1923 Seguí, despite his moderation, was assassinated in Barcelona
by the employers. His 'libertarian possibilism' maintained that the working class should not renounce
politics in order to achieve its ends, and his untimely
death robbed the Spanish anarcho-syndicalists not
just of an outstanding organizer, but of their most
gifted figure.

### Seipel, Ignaz (1876–1932)

Austrian politician. After an early career as a theologian, Seipel played a leading role in Austrian politics
from 1918 until his death. A member of the Christian
Social Party, he served in the Constituent Assembly
(1919–20) and as the Federal Chancellor (1922–4,

essentially an assertion of Divine Right kingship, with the king the only vice-regent of God on earth.

In general, the Reformation and **Counter-Reformation** revitalized the power of religion in the domestic and international politics of the Western world, making the concept of purely 'secular' power unthinkable. However, the intensity of competition between religious factions, an endemic problem since the earliest period of the Christian Church, reached unprecedented heights.

### Wars of religion

Wars of religion had been a recurrent phenomenon in Christendom, always based on the assumption that a given group or rival religion had no right to exist or control certain symbolically important sites. They were often manipulated for the advantage of specific powers. The 'crusade' against the **Albigenses** in the south of France was used to extend the power of the French crown. The Venetians successfully diverted the scandalous Fourth **Crusade** of 1204 to sack Orthodox Christian Constantinople and institute the Latin Occupation of **Constantinople**. Nevertheless, the other movements known to historians as 'The Crusades' were directed against the Islamic Middle East. They had a peripheral impact on Europe proper.

Wars of religion in the 16c and 17c saw the crusading mentality turned against fellow Western Christians. The wars seemed endless, often achieving unmistakeable genocidal ferocity. With the **Thirty Years' War** (1618–48), levels of destruction and hatred were reached which were bound to create a backlash. Small groups began to question the rightfulness or even the acceptability to God of the standard combination of dogmatic intolerance and potentially genocidal violence in the name of religion. Atheism as such was an almost unthinkable option even in the late 17c, but secret groups like 'The Family of Love' (many of whose members worked close to **Philip II** of Spain, champion of the Counter-Reformation) had begun to doubt the need to identify state power and dogmatic religious beliefs. The Dutch Republic simply did not try to enforce conformity on its religiously divided population.

### Enlightenment and revolution

Only in the 18c can we talk of secularization, and then only in Europe or European-derived state systems. Those who began to practise it belonged to different schools of thought. Many, like the Holy Roman Emperor **Joseph II**, were devout Christians who did not believe it was right for the state to coerce consciences. The moderate clergy of the Church of Scotland agreed, and looked on the butcheries of the 17c religious wars as a blasphemous parody of Christianity. Others, motivated by scientific and intellectual developments of the late 17c and the spirit of the **Enlightenment**, were sceptical about revealed religion, but even Voltaire was a sincere deist.

When the **Jacobins** under **Robespierre** came to power in France they went further, actively sponsoring the Cult of Reason as a replacement for Christianity and replacing the Gregorian **calendar** with a revolutionary and republican one in which 1793 became Year 1. The first 'secular' state in Western culture was the federal government of the USA after 1783, not because the bulk of its people were irreligious, but because they were deeply divided in religion.

### The 19c

The Roman Catholic Church recovered a lot of the ground it had lost at the end of the 18c in the more conservative climate that prevailed in Europe after the final defeat of **Napoleon I**. Identification of Church and State was seen as a bulwark against revolution. As a result, bourgeois liberalism tended, because of its anticlericalism, to demand the creation of a secular state with no sectarian affiliations, on the American model. The struggle between Church and State over matters such as control of education went on in France, as in other countries, throughout the 19c. In Britain the **Test Act** (1673) that required holders of public office (including military officers and Members of Parliament) to be communicating members of the Church of England was repealed in 1828. French education finally became 'compulsory, free and secular' under the Third **Republic**, as a result of a series of acts passed between 1878 and 1886, with Jules **Ferry** as their prime mover. In countries such as Mexico, with a hugely powerful colonial Church, post-independence

1926–9). Throughout the period he was a determined opponent of social democracy and gradually came to question the efficacy of democracy as such. His foreign policy achievements included the Geneva Protocol (1922) which obtained foreign credit and stabilized the Austrian economy, but at the cost of economic deflation and social suffering.

### Seiyukai

Literally, 'Association of Political Friends', the leading political party in Japan between 1900 and 1940. Created by **ITO HIROBUMI** in 1900 as a pro-government party in the Diet, the *Seiyukai* attracted the support of bureaucrats and landowners. Under the leadership of **HARA KEI** after 1914, the Seiyukai became the largest single party in the Diet. In 1918 Hara became Prime Minister of a Seiyukai-dominated cabinet, the first time a government had been formed from the majority party in the Diet. Despite high hopes, his government (1918–21) proved to be conservative on issues of political and social reform. The Seiyukai supported the military cabinets of the 1930s and advocated a hardline policy in China. The party was dissolved in 1940 as part of a government attempt to bring all political parties under the umbrella of the **IMPERIAL RULE ASSISTANCE ASSOCIATION**.

### Sekigahara, Battle of (Oct 1600)

A decisive battle in Japan in which the forces of **TOKUGAWA IEYASU** (mainly from the eastern part of the country) defeated their rivals in the west. One year later, Tokugawa Ieyasu was awarded the title of **SHOGUN** by the emperor, allowing him to impose a military hegemony over the country that was to last until 1867.

### Selden, John (1584–1654)

English jurist, historian and antiquary. He was an opponent of the '**DIVINE RIGHT OF KINGS**', and was twice imprisoned for his views. In 1623 he was elected MP for Lancaster, and in 1628 he helped to draw up the Petition of Right, for which he was committed to the Tower of London. He entered the **LONG PARLIAMENT** (1640) for Oxford University, sat as a lay member in the **WESTMINSTER ASSEMBLY** in 1643, and was appointed keeper of the records in the Tower and, in 1644, an Admiralty commissioner.

liberalism tended to demand secularization of the state.

As the 19c drew to a close, anticlericalism and secularism again became strong in many countries with the rise of socialist movements. Darwinism and **Marxism** provided an explanation of human rights and human history, and a blueprint for progress from which religion was excluded. The **Dreyfus** affair united all the progressive elements in French society against the reactionary and Catholic right, and the final separation of Church and State in France took place in 1905.

### The 20c
The culmination of socialist-inspired secularism can be seen in the establishment of the USSR after the **Russian Revolution** as an avowedly atheist state. In 1923, Mustafa Kemal **Atatürk**, the modernizing and westernizing founder of the modern republic of Turkey, abolished the Sultanate. In 1924 he abolished the office of the Caliph, the former **Ottoman Empire**'s spiritual head, closed all religious schools in Istanbul, and removed the Minister for Religion from the cabinet. In 1928 he repealed the provision in the Turkish constitution making Islam the state religion. Deputies elected to the parliament no longer took an oath in the name of Allah but made a secular affirmation.

The example of Turkey is of particular interest, because there was a strong movement against secularism in Muslim countries in the latter part of the century. Several countries that gained independence and developed into secular states on the Western or socialist pattern have since undergone processes of Islamicization, the most notable being Iran, where the overthrow of Shah Muhammad Reza **Pahlavi** in 1979 ushered in an Islamic republic – a virtual theocracy. The success of the **Iranian Revolution** gave an enormous boost to fundamentalist Islamic movements in countries such as Pakistan, Egypt and Algeria, where governments have either had to make concessions to religious militants or take up arms against them. Radical Islam has successfully presented itself as a populist alternative to corrupt, dictatorial regimes lacking both compassion and righteousness.

Ultimately, secularization at any level deeper than the state depends on a collapse of religious belief as a serious factor in individual lives. The USA has a secular government, set up by often deistic **Founding Fathers** who would be surprised at the strength, vitality and influence of orthodox, evangelical Christianity of various kinds in the modern republic. Nominally secular states often have religious roots. Only perhaps in most of Western Europe has the collapse of religious belief and practice been so relentless as to create fundamentally secular societies.

### Secularization of everyday life in post-Christian Europe
The importance of the religious dimension in everyday public and private life has diminished in the developed world, and people have looked for an alternative context for their living and alternative ways of marking rites of passage. In 1836, the passing of the Marriage Act for the first time allowed marriages to be solemnized in Britain otherwise than by a religious ceremony. Six hundred district register offices opened on 1 July 1837, as this and other acts concerned with civil administration came into force. Divorce, other than by Act of Parliament, became obtainable in the UK by 1857, although with difficulty and only when requested by husbands. Liberalizing social legislation on issues such as divorce and abortion has generally been opposed by the Church, especially in Catholic countries. But fewer and fewer people turn to institutionalized religion for guidance when education is universal, science provides the new orthodoxy, and the triumphs of technology have made life in the secular world so comparatively easy and comfortable.

One of the most difficult adjustments required for those raised in the ever more secular societies of Western Europe when they come to deal with other parts of the world is to realize that, so far, they are the exception, not the rule. In most of the world, including the USA, religious beliefs continue to exert a great influence, giving meaning to human life, with all the positive and negative implications that that fact carries. ► **Religion**; **Separation of Church and State** (France) (1905)

---

### selectors
Men or women who selected land made available on credit terms by the Australian states in Land Acts (1859–72) to encourage small farming. Selectors had to live on and work the farms. Many came from the goldfields, and too often inexperience, squatter opposition, limited acreage or unsuitable land resulted in a depressed rural proletariat rather than yeoman farmers. They provided the social environment of the **BUSHRANGERS** (1860–80). ► **CLOSER SETTLEMENT; SQUATTERS**

### self-determination
A doctrine dating back to the 18c that cultural communities and national groupings have the right to determine their own destiny, including political independence and the right to self-rule. The principle that each nation has the right to fashion its own state is incorporated in the **UN** Charter, and is a major plank in anti-colonialism.

### Self-Strengthening Movement
The ultimately abortive attempt by the **QING DYNASTY** between the 1860s and 1890s to strengthen China militarily and economically against foreign encroachment, through the selective importation of Western military technology and the establishment of modern economic enterprises. First rationalized by the Chinese scholar-official **FENG GUIFEN** as a means to 'learn the techniques of the barbarians in order to control them', self-strengthening was supported by Prince **GONG** at court and carried out by several high-ranking provincials, many of whom had participated in the suppression of the **TAIPING REBELLION**. Military projects included the construction of a shipyard at Fuzhou (1866) and arsenals at Shanghai (1865) and Nanjing (1867). Economic projects included the founding of the China Merchants Steam Navigation Company (1872) to compete with foreign shipping, and the opening of modern coal mines at Kaiping (1877) near Beijing. The period also witnessed the beginnings of institutional change. In 1861 a proto-Foreign Office (*Zongli Yamen*) was created, to which was attached a foreign language school for the training of interpreters. At no time, however, was a fundamental overhaul of China's institutions or education system envisaged. This, together with

the piecemeal and uncoordinated nature of the projects themselves, bureaucratic corruption, and persistent conservative opposition both at court and in most of the provinces to any modernizing change, contributed to the movement's failure, which was dramatically illustrated by China's military defeats at the hands of France (1885) and Japan (1895).

**Selim I, the Grim** (1467–1520)
Ottoman Sultan (1512/20). Having dethroned his father, **BAYEZID II**, and caused him, his own brothers, and nephews to be put to death, in 1514 Selim declared war against Persia, and took Diyarbakir and Kurdistan. In 1517 he conquered Egypt, Syria and the Hijaz, including the holy cities of Medina and Mecca, receiving the keys of the latter from the Sharif, and thus winning from the nominal 'Abbasid caliph at Cairo, al-Mutawakkil III, the headship of the Muslim world. Selim chastised the insolence of the **JANISSARIES**, sought to improve the condition of the peoples he had conquered, and cultivated the poetic art. He was succeeded by his son, **SÜLEYMAN I, THE MAGNIFICENT**. ► **MARJ DABIQ, BATTLE OF**

**Selim II** (1524–74)
Ottoman Sultan (1566/74). The son of **SÜLEYMAN I, THE MAGNIFICENT**, he proved to be an indolent drunkard, who delegated the handling of state affairs to his able Grand Vizier, Mehmed Sokollu. During Selim's reign Cyprus was sacked by Turkish troops and 30,000 inhabitants of Nicosia were massacred. A naval force mustered by the pope, Italian states and Spain, under Don **JOHN OF AUSTRIA**, succeeded in defeating the Turkish fleet at the Battle of **LEPANTO** in 1571. However, the victors did not follow up their success; Venice was forced to recognize Ottoman supremacy in the Mediterranean in 1573 and, the following year, Ottoman forces recaptured Tunisia from the Spanish (who had taken it in 1574).

**Selim III** (1761–1808)
Ottoman Sultan (1789/1807). Having succeeded his uncle, Abd ul-Hamid I, he prosecuted the war with Russia. However, the Austrians joined the Russians, and Belgrade surrendered to them, while the Russians took Bucharest, Bender, Akkerman and Ismail. Inspired by the reformist zeal of his father, Mustafa III (1757/74), and the changes brought about by the **FRENCH REVOLUTION**, Selim embarked on a plan of westernization for his country. Having established a committee for reform in 1792–3, he set about implementing a series of changes, known as the New Order (*Nizam-i Cedid*). These reforms affected the organization of the army, and the system of tax and land tenure. To promote contact with the West, he also opened Ottoman embassies in the major European capitals. However, these attempts at change engendered the hostility of conservative elements, such as the **JANISSARIES** and *ulama* (religious leaders), and Selim was forced in 1807, after a series of mutinies, to abandon his programme of reorganization. His dream of a New Order was ultimately to cost him both his throne and his life (by strangulation, on the orders of his successor, Mustafa IV).

**Seljuks**
A family of Turkish mercenary soldiers that rose to prominence and conquered much of Asia Minor in

the 11–12c. They were converted to the Muslim faith, and became established as sultans in the area of present-day Syria and eastern Turkey. Their decline in the 13c was brought on by Mongol pressure from the east and their defeat at Kösedagh (1243). ► **MONGOLS**

**Seminole**
A Muskogean-speaking Native North American group of south-east USA, descended from Creeks who settled in Florida in the late 18c, many intermarrying with runaway Negro slaves. One of the **FIVE CIVILIZED TRIBES**, they were drawn into war after aiding their fellow Creeks and fought against troops led by Andrew **JACKSON**. They eventually surrendered to US forces in the 1820s and 1830s, and were moved to reservations in Oklahoma. Population in 2000 was c.12,500. ► **CREEK; NATIVE AMERICANS**

**Semites**
A group of peoples found in south-west Asia. In antiquity they included the Ammonites, Amorites, Assyrians, Babylonians, Canaanites and Phoenicians; today the most prominent Semitic peoples are the Jews and the Arabs.

**Sempach, Battle of** (1386)
This battle was the culmination of a dispute between the city of Lucerne and the Duke of Austria, Leopold III. In it, Lucerne and the Swiss cantons inflicted a crushing defeat on the Austrians, losing only 200 of their 1,600 men, while Austrian losses amounted to around 1,800.

**Senanayake, Don Stephen** (1884–1952)
Sri Lankan politician. Born in Colombo, he was educated there and then worked on his father's rubber estate. Entering the Legislative Council in 1922, he founded the cooperative society movement in 1923, and was elected to the State Council in 1931 where he was Minister of Agriculture for 15 years. Following independence, he was Sri Lanka's first Prime Minister (1947–52), and also held the posts of Minister of Defence and External Affairs. He died after falling from his horse in Colombo.

**Senate**
One of the two chambers of the US **CONGRESS** in which legislative power is vested. It consists of two Senators from each state (100 in all) chosen by the people to serve for six years; the terms of a third of the members expire every two years. It has powers of 'advice and consent' on presidential treaties and appointments. It is presided over by the US Vice-President, who has no part in its deliberations but can cast the deciding vote if there is a tie. Legislation must pass both the **HOUSE OF REPRESENTATIVES** and the Senate before being signed by the President and becoming law.

**Sendero Luminoso ('Shining Path')**
A Maoist rural guerrilla movement of uncompromisingly revolutionary character, operating in the Peruvian central Andes (though capable, also, of mounting terrorist actions in cities) during the 1980s and 1990s. Its leader, Abimael Guzmán, was captured in Sep 1992 and sentenced to life imprisonment. By this time the Senderistas had caused around 30,000 deaths and seriously threatened the Peruvian economy. Over 6,000 Senderistas gave themselves up

during the subsequent government amnesty, others were caught and tried during the 1990s, including Guzmán's successor, Oscar Ramirez, in July 1999. A few remain active in remote areas causing sporadic terrorist attacks.

### Seneca
Iroquoian-speaking Native American group, who settled in present-day western New York State and eastern Ohio. A member of the IROQUOIS CONFEDER-ACY, they expanded through warfare in the 17c, and supported the British during the AMERICAN REVOLU-TION, which led to the destruction of their villages by US troops, and their settlement on reservations in 1797. The current population is c.9,500. ► NATIVE AMERICANS

### Seneca Falls Women's Rights Convention (1848)
US feminist conference. It was organized by Elizabeth Cady STANTON and Lucretia MOTT, who met after they had been denied seats at the World Anti-Slavery Conference in London. Stanton and Mott protested against the contradiction of fighting for the rights of blacks when they themselves did not have the right to vote. The Convention adopted a Declaration of Senti-ments modelled on the DECLARATION OF INDEPEN-DENCE, maintaining that 'all men and women are created equal'. It not only claimed the vote for women but demanded equality in property, marriage and education. ► SLAVERY

### SENEGAL official name Republic of Senegal

A country in West Africa, bounded to the north by Mauritania; to the east by Mali; to the south by Gui-nea and Guinea-Bissau; and to the west by the Atlan-tic Ocean. It surrounds the Gambia on three sides. Senegal was part of the Mali Empire in the 14–15c. The French established a fort at Saint-Louis in 1659, and it was incorporated as a territory within French West Africa in 1902. It became an autonomous state within the French community in 1958, and joined with French Sudan as the independent Federation of Mali in 1959, but withdrew in 1960 to become a sepa-rate independent republic. Its first President was Léopold SENGHOR, who was succeeded in 1981 by Abdou DIOUF. From 1982 to 1989 Senegal joined with the Gambia to form the Confederation of SENEGAM-BIA. Politics was dominated for 40 years by the Socia-list Party until Abdoulaye Wade was elected President in 2000 and a coalition led by his Senegalese Demo-cratic Party won the election in Apr 2001. In 1989 a violent dispute with neighbouring Mauritania began following the killing and expulsion of hundreds of Senegalese people living in Mauritania; virtual war

continued throughout 1990 and peace was restored in 1991–2. In the late 1980s a violent separatist insur-gency broke out in southern Senegal led by the Move-ment of Democratic Forces of Casamance; a peace agreement was signed in Dec 2004.

### Senegambia, Confederation of
An association between the Gambia and Senegal, begun in 1982, designed to integrate military, eco-nomic, communications and foreign policies and to establish joint institutions, while preserving inde-pendence and sovereignty. It proved to be of limited value and was ended by mutual agreement in 1989.

### Senghor, Léopold Sédar (1906–2001)
Senegalese poet and politician. Educated in Roman Catholic schools in Dakar, he went to the University of Paris and, after graduation, taught in France itself (1935–9). He joined the French army at the outbreak of war and was a prisoner (1940–2). A member of the Resistance (1942–4), he was a member of the French Constituent Assembly in 1945 and was Deputy for Senegal in the French Assembly (1948–58), during which period he was a university lecturer. He was one of the founders of *Présence Africaine* in 1947 and wrote widely in that and other intellectual magazines, establishing himself as a major poet and an exponent of the philosophy of NEGRITUDE. He formed the *Union Progressiste Senegalaise* in 1958 and, as its lea-der, became President of Senegal on the country's in-dependence in 1960. He retained cordial links with France and, although nominally a socialist, espoused a mixed economy. In 1981 he retired from politics.

### senhores de engenho
In colonial Brazil (1500–1822), these mill-owners were men of significant political power. Of varied ori-gins, their investment in capital stock, including slaves, made them risk-taking entrepreneurs. They rented their lands to *lavradores de cana*, who owned slaves and equipment to cultivate cane; this ensured a large supply of sugar to the *engenho* ('mill') throughout the long harvest period. Free labour was contracted for specialized and occasional tasks. Mill-owners also controlled cattle ranches (*fazendas*) in the interior, so that their activities dominated the economy and society of major regions of Brazil. By the mid-18c many had evolved into strong *parentelas*. ► FAZENDA; PARENTELA

### Senussi
A Sufi order found in North Africa, particularly the Sahara. Founded by Muhammad al-Sanusi (1791–1855), the Senussi is to be regarded as one of the reforming modern movements in Islam, preach-ing as it does a simple and purified form of the reli-gion. Its political importance lies in its opposition to the Italians in Libya and the fact that after WORLD WAR II the then leader of the Sanusiyya, Muhammad Idris al-Sanusi became King of Libya as Idris I. He ruled Libya until 1969, when he was deposed by a military coup and Muammar GADDAFI came to power.

### Separation of Church and State (France) (1905)
The conflict between the Church and the French Re-public had been renewed as a result of the DREYFUS affair (1898–9) and the Law on Associations (1901), which was used to dissolve the religious orders. COM-BES's government (1902–4) opened a conflict with

the papacy which led to the law of 1905 abrogating the **CONCORDAT** (1801), ending the position of the Roman Catholic Church as an established Church, financially supported and to some extent controlled by the State. The separation was at first fought bitterly by the Church, but the mollifying policies of **BRIAND**, Minister of Religious Worship in the **CLEMENCEAU** government (1906–9), reduced the confrontation, and in a short time the new regime proved acceptable to both sides. ► **REPUBLIC, THIRD** (France)

## separation of powers

A political doctrine, associated with the 18c philosopher Montesquieu, which argues that, to avoid tyranny, the three branches of government (legislature, executive, and judiciary) should be separated as far as possible, their relationships governed by checks and balances. The **US CONSTITUTION** is a practical example of an attempt at separation of powers. Parliamentary systems such as that of the UK do not have a complete separation, as the heads of the executive (ie government ministers) sit as members of the legislature. Nonetheless, most systems claim independence of the judiciary.

## Séparatisme

French-Canadian independence movement. It has played a significant role in Canadian politics since the 1960s. Some groups such as the **FRONT DE LIBÉRATION DE QUÉBEC** (FLQ) were prepared to resort to the sort of violence that resulted in the **OCTOBER CRISIS**. One of the largest groups was the *Rassemblement Démocratique pour l'Indépendance* which was important in the defeat of **LESAGE**, and became even stronger after the defeat of the **PARTI QUÉBECOIS** by the Liberals in 1985. Initially the federal government responded by attempting to remedy French-Canadian dissatisfactions through such initiatives as the Royal Commission on **BILINGUALISM AND BICULTURALISM**. As Prime Minister, Pierre **TRUDEAU** reasserted the tradition of tolerant Canadianism for which **LAURIER** had stood, in the hope that the province might be prevented from becoming racist and introverted. As a Québecois Liberal, his own success controverted the image of disadvantage that the separatist groups attempted to convey. During the 1990s *Séparatisme* rose in popularity and the *Parti Québecois* came to power after winning the 1994 provincial election. The following year a referendum on negotiating secession from Canada was rejected by only a very narrow margin.

## Sephardim

The name (from Hebrew *Sepharad*, 'Spain') given to the Jews of Spain and Portugal, and hence applied to all Jews who trace their descent from the Iberian Peninsula, more particularly to those descended from the Jews expelled in 1492. Their language and culture were Spanish (*Ladino*), distinguishing them sharply from the Jews of Eastern European origin (**ASHKENAZIM**). ► **JEWS, EXPULSION OF THE**

## sepoy

An Indian mercenary soldier employed by a European organization in India and trained and disciplined in the same way as regular European line infantry. They were first developed on any scale by the French *Compagnie des Indes Orientales* in the Car-

natic in the 1740s. Then, the British **EAST INDIA COMPANY** developed sepoy battalions as the cores of its three presidency armies. Their great advantage was that they were as good as European troops but cheaper. The term survived as the one of choice for an Indian private soldier in the new British Indian Army after the abolition of the Company state in 1858. ► **EAST INDIA COMPANY, FRENCH**

## September 11 attacks also known as 9/11

Suicide attacks by 19 members of **AL-QAEDA** on financial and military targets in the USA on 11 September 2001 (September (9) 11th in US date notation). Four passenger planes on domestic flights were hijacked; two were deliberately flown into the north and south towers of the World Trade Center, New York, and a third into the Pentagon, Washington DC; a fourth plane crashed without survivors in rural Pennsylvania and is presumed to have been brought down by its passengers. Following the crashes in New York the twin towers of the World Trade Center collapsed, destroying several adjacent buildings; the crash at the Pentagon also destroyed a section of the building. It is estimated that more than 3,000 people, including over 400 emergency service personnel, died either in the plane crashes or in the buildings' collapse. The shock of the attacks on the US psyche was compared with the attack on **PEARL HARBOR**, and saturation coverage by the world's media ensured that the shock was shared worldwide, prompting expressions of sympathy for the USA even from states such as North Korea. President George W **BUSH**, buoyed by global support, declared a war on **TERROR**, the first direct consequence of which was the **AFGHAN WAR** (2001). Internally, wide-ranging security measures and restrictions of civil liberties culminated in legislation such as the **PATRIOT ACT** and the establishment of the Department of Homeland Security.

## Septennial Act (1716)

Legislation repealing the Triennial Act (1694) which extended the maximum life of parliament from three years to seven. Remaining in force until the Parliament Act (1911) restricted parliaments to five years, it was important in easing the transition to political stability and to Whig supremacy in the early years of the Hanoverian monarchy. ► **HANOVER, HOUSE OF**; **TRIENNIAL ACTS**; **WHIGS**

## Septinsular Republic

The name given to the separate state formed from the Ionian Islands in 1800 on the basis of a treaty between the Russian Tsar and the Ottoman Sultan. First a protectorate of the Porte, then of Russia, the history of the short-lived republic was bloody and brutal. By the Treaty of Tilsit (1807) the islands were returned to France and became part of the **ILLYRIAN PROVINCES**. ► **TILSIT, TREATIES OF**

## Sequoia or Sequoyah, also called George Guess (c.1770–1843)

**CHEROKEE** leader. He was a major figure behind the decision of the Cherokee to adopt as much as possible of white culture, while retaining their own identity, and personally invented an alphabet for their language. ► **INDIAN WARS**

## SERBIA

A central European republic federated with the

republic of Montenegro, a mountainous area with deep river valleys. It is bounded to the north-west by Croatia; to the north by Hungary; to the north-east by Romania; to the east by Bulgaria; to the south by Macedonia; and to the west by Albania, Montenegro and Bosnia and Herzegovina. It includes the provinces of **KOSOVO** and **VOJVODINA**. The medieval Kingdom of Serbia was part of Byzantium until the 12c, when the **NEMANJA DYNASTY** established its authority over the emerging Serbian state. After the fall of **STEPHEN DUSHAN**, the state disintegrated and fell to the Turks (1389). In the 19c, after the Serbs' long struggle for independence from the Ottoman Turks, the Kingdom of Serbia was re-established at the Congress of **BERLIN**, with its capital at Belgrade. After **WORLD WAR I** it became part of the Kingdom of Serbs, Croats and Slovenes, and in 1945 the Federal People's Republic of **YUGOSLAVIA** (Croatia, Slovenia, Bosnia and Herzegovina, Macedonia, Montenegro and Serbia) was established under **TITO**, with the different national identities being severely stifled. After this federation disintegrated in 1991–2, only Serbia and Montenegro remained as the Federal Republic of Yugoslavia, declared on 27 Apr 1992, but this was restructured with effect from Feb 2003 into a loose federation of the republics of Serbia and Montenegro, with the federation responsible for defence, foreign and economic affairs, while each republic is responsible for internal matters. In the late 1980s Serbia withdrew the autonomous status of its province of Kosovo, which had a 90 per cent Albanian population, and the Kosovars' unequivocal vote for secession in 1992 resulted in brutal suppression by Serbian forces. In early 1998 the Kosovars were subjected to a renewed crackdown by Serbian forces which by the following year had developed into a brutal and systematic process of **ETHNIC CLEANSING** in which Kosovars were murdered or forced by Serbs to leave their homes and head for safety in neighbouring countries and further afield. In Mar–Jun 1999 **NATO** forces mounted air strikes on Serbia in an attempt to stop the atrocities. During the air strikes, Slobodan **MILOŠEVIĆ** and his successor as President of Serbia, Milan Milutinovic, were indicted for human rights atrocities by the **UN** war crimes tribunal. Hostilities ended with Serbia accepting an agreement, partially brokered by Russia, that allowed a UN peacekeeping force to enter Kosovo and guarantee human rights there. Prime Minister Zoran Djindjic authorized the extradition of Milošević to the war crimes tribunal in 2001; Djindjic was

assassinated in 2003 and replaced in 2004 by Vojislav Kostunica.

### Serbia and Montenegro
A loose federation of the republics of **SERBIA** and **MONTENEGRO** which came into effect from Feb 2003. The federation is responsible for defence, foreign and economic affairs, while each republic is responsible for internal matters; the ultimate aim is independence. The two republics had declared themselves the Federal Republic of Yugoslavia on 27 Apr 1992 after the secession in 1991–2 of the other four republics that had constituted **YUGOSLAVIA**, but this had not been recognized by the **UN**.

### Serbian Uprisings (1804 and 1815)
When the Serbs of the *pašaluk* of Belgrade rose in protest against the abuses of the local Ottoman administration, they were brutally suppressed by the **JANISSARIES**. This led to the first Serbian uprising of 1804 under the leadership of **KARAGEORGE**. What began as little more than a peasant revolt, attracted in time the support of Russia and of educated Romanians, Greeks and Serbs under Habsburg rule. By 1806, the insurgents had seized Belgrade and in 1807 the first Serbian constitution declared Karageorge the hereditary leader of Serbia. The Turks retook Belgrade in 1813 and the first uprising collapsed. The second uprising took place in 1815 under Miloš **OBRENOVIĆ** and ended with his recognition as the 'supreme prince of Serbia'. ➤ **KARADŽIĆ, VUK STEFANOVIĆ; OBRADOVIĆ, DOSITEJ; ŠUMADIJA**

### Sergei (1876–1944)
Russian Orthodox religious leader. Already a bishop in 1901, he managed to survive the **RUSSIAN REVOLUTION** (1917) and the subsequent campaigns against religion. In 1925 he became Patriarch by default when Patriarch **TIKHON** died, and in 1927 made a declaration of loyalty to the state that allowed something of Orthodoxy to continue. During **WORLD WAR II**, **STALIN** sought his support in defence of the country and allowed him to call a council in 1943 at which he was finally properly elected.

### Serrano, Francisco, Duke de la Torre (1810–85)
Spanish politician. He fought against the Carlists and, nominally a liberal, was favoured by **ISABELLA II** and played a conspicuous part in various ministries. Banished in 1866, in 1868 he drove out Isabella and was regent until the accession of Amadeus I of Savoy (1870). He waged successful war against the Carlists in 1872 and 1874; again regent in 1874, he resigned power into the hands of **ALFONSO XII**. ➤ **CARLISM**

### Settlement, Act of
An important statute of 1701 which determined the succession of the English throne after the death of Queen **ANNE** and her heirs, if any. It excluded the Catholic Stuarts from the succession, which was to pass to the Electress **SOPHIA** of Hanover, descendant through the female line of James VI of Scotland and I of England. Future monarchs were to be communicant members of the Church of England, and were not permitted to leave the country without the consent of parliament. ➤ **JAMES VI AND I; STUART, HOUSE OF**

### Sevastopol, Siege of (1854–5)
The centre-piece of the **CRIMEAN WAR**. Britain, France

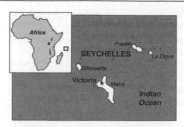

and Turkey chose to attack Russia's main naval base in the Black Sea in order to reduce its alleged threat to the status quo in the **OTTOMAN EMPIRE** and the Mediterranean. Time was lost through opting to surround it, and initial successes were not followed up. The result was that General Totleben was able to build formidable defences which Admiral Nakhimov used to good effect. In the event it took 12 months and many casualties to capture Sevastopol. Although Russia therefore lost the war, the battle honours were shared. The Russian surgeon, Nikolai **PIROGOV**, played a similar role inside the fortifications to Florence **NIGHTINGALE** outside.

### Seven Days' Battles (25 June–1 July 1862)
The final conflict in the **PENINSULAR CAMPAIGN** during the **AMERICAN CIVIL WAR**, in which the Union drive to capture Richmond was halted.

### Seven Years' War (1756–63)
A major European conflict rooted in the rivalry between Austria and Prussia and the imminent colonial struggle between Britain and France in the New World and the Far East. Hostilities in North America (1754) pre-dated the Diplomatic Revolution in Europe (1748–56), which created two opposing power blocs: Austria, France, Russia, Sweden and Saxony against Prussia, Britain and Portugal. British maritime superiority countered Franco-Spanish naval power and prevented a French invasion. The European war, precipitated by Prussia's seizure of Saxony, was marked by many notable pitched land battles. Saved from total defeat when Russia switched sides, **FREDERICK II, THE GREAT** of Prussia retained Silesia in 1763. ► **ELIZABETH PETROVNA**; **GEORGE II** (of Great Britain); **GRANBY**; **LOUIS XV** (of France); **MARIA THERESA**; **MONTCALM, MARQUIS OF**; **PARIS, TREATY OF**

### Seward, William Henry (1801–72)
US politician. He won the governorship of New York State in 1838 and during the 1850s became a major spokesman for the anti-**SLAVERY** movement and a leader of the **REPUBLICAN PARTY**. His 'irrepressible conflict' speech was thought by many Democrats to be responsible for John **BROWN**'s violence at the **HARPERS FERRY RAID**. He served as a very effective Secretary of State under Abraham **LINCOLN**, taking an uncompromising attitude towards French support for Archduke **MAXIMILIAN** as Emperor of Mexico, which he saw as a breach of the **MONROE DOCTRINE**. Severely injured during the assassination of Lincoln, he recovered to remain Secretary of State in President Andrew **JOHNSON**'s cabinet. In 1867 he secured the purchase of Alaska from Russia, known as 'Seward's folly', by persuading a reluctant **CONGRESS** of its vast mineral wealth.

### SEYCHELLES   official name Republic of Seychelles
An island group in the south-west Indian Ocean, north of Madagascar, comprising 115 islands. It was visited by Vasco da **GAMA** in 1502, and colonized by the French in 1768. The population is largely descended from 18c French colonists and their freed African slaves. Captured by Britain in 1794, it was incorporated as a dependency of Mauritius in 1814 and became a separate British Crown Colony in 1903. It

became an independent republic within the **COMMONWEALTH OF NATIONS** in 1976. Following a coup in 1977, when France-Albert **RENÉ** became President, it became a one-party state. Opposition parties have been permitted since 1991, however, and in 1993 the first multiparty elections were won by René's Seychelles People's Progressive Front. President René was re-elected in 1998 and 2001 but stepped down in 2004 and was replaced by James Michel. Some areas were damaged by the Indian Ocean tsunami in Dec 2004.

### Seymour, Edward, 1st Duke of Somerset, known as Protector Somerset (c.1506–1552)
English soldier and statesman. The brother of Jane **SEYMOUR**, he enjoyed high office under his brother-in-law, **HENRY VIII**. As warden of the Scottish marches, he led the invading English army that devastated southern Scotland and Edinburgh in the 'Rough Wooing' of 1543–4, after the Scots rejected a proposed marriage between Prince Edward (the future **EDWARD VI**) and the infant **MARY, QUEEN OF SCOTS**. At Henry's death in 1547 he was named Protector of England during the minority of Edward VI and was king in all but name. He defeated a Scottish army at **PINKIE** (1547), and furthered the **REFORMATION** with the first Book of Common Prayer (1549). Also in 1549 his younger brother Thomas was executed for attempting to marry Princess Elizabeth (the future Queen **ELIZABETH I**), and soon he himself was indicted for 'over-ambition' and deposed by John Dudley, Earl of Warwick (1549), and eventually executed.

### Seymour, Jane (c.1509–1537)
Queen of England. She was the third wife of **HENRY VIII**, the mother of **EDWARD VI**, and the sister of Protector Somerset. She was a lady-in-waiting to Henry's first two wives, and married him 11 days after the execution of Anne **BOLEYN**. She died soon after the birth of her son.

### Seyss-Inquart, Artur von (1892–1946)
Austrian politician. He practised as a lawyer in Vienna and saw much of **SCHUSCHNIGG**. When the latter became Chancellor in 1938, he took office under him, informing **HITLER** of every detail of Schuschnigg's life in the hope of becoming Nazi leader in Austria after the **ANSCHLUSS**. Instead, he was appointed Commissioner for the Netherlands in 1940. In 1945 he was captured by the Canadians, tried at the **NUREMBERG TRIALS** and executed for war crimes.

### Seyyid Said (1791–1856)
Sultan of Oman and Zanzibar (1806/56). The greatest of the sultans of the al-Busaid Dynasty, he was a merchant prince who ruled in both the Arabian Peninsula and East Africa between 1806 and his death. He visited the East African coast, over which Oman

had a vague suzerainty dating from the late 17c, in 1827–8. He recognized the potential of the islands of Zanzibar and Pemba and encouraged members of his Omani aristocracy to found clove plantations there. By 1840, he had moved his capital to Zanzibar. Under his rule, Indian merchants and capitalists moved into his dominions and Zanzibar became the major strategic and commercial port of the East African coast. The USA opened trading relations and the British established a powerful consulate. On Said's death, the British arbitrated the succession dispute. Under the Canning 'Award' of 1862, the combined sultanate of Oman and Zanzibar was divided between two of his sons.

**SFIO** ► SOCIALIST PARTY (France)

**Sforza, Carlo** (1872–1952)
Italian diplomat and politician. As Foreign Minister (1920–1), he negotiated the RAPALLO Treaty. In 1922 he was made Ambassador to Paris, but resigned on MUSSOLINI's seizure of power and chose to live in exile. After the fall of Mussolini, he returned to Italy and was a member of the first democratic governments. As Foreign Minister (1947–51), he backed European unity and Italian membership of NATO.

**Sforza, Francesco** (1401–66)
Duke of Milan (1450/66). The illegitimate son of Muzio Attendolo Sforza, he was the father of Galeazzo Maria and Ludovico SFORZA. He sold his sword to the highest bidder, fighting for or against the pope, Milan, Venice and Florence. From the Duke of Milan he obtained his daughter's hand and the succession to the duchy; and before his death had extended his power over Ancona, Pesaro, all Lombardy and Genoa.

**Sforza, Galeazzo Maria** (1444–76)
Italian nobleman, son of Francesco SFORZA and Duke of Milan (1466/76). A competent ruler, he was nonetheless notorious for debauchery and prodigality, and was assassinated.

**Sforza, Ludovico**, also known as **the Moor** (1451–1508)
Ruler of Milan (1481/99). The son of Francesco SFORZA, he acted as regent for his nephew Gian Galeazzo (1469–94) from 1476, but expelled him in 1481 and usurped the Dukedom for himself. He made alliance with Lorenzo de' MEDICI of Florence; under his rule, Milan became the most glittering court in Europe. He helped to defeat the attempts of CHARLES VIII of France to secure Naples, but in 1499 was expelled by LOUIS XII and imprisoned in France, where he died.

**Shaba** ► KATANGA

**Shackleton, Sir Ernest Henry** (1874–1922)
Irish explorer. He was a junior officer under Commander Robert SCOTT, on the *Discovery*, in the National Antarctic Expedition of 1901–4. In 1908–9, in command of another expedition, he reached a point 97 mi/156.2 km from the South Pole, which was at that time a record. During a further expedition (1914–16), his ship *Endurance* was crushed in ice, and he and five others made a perilous voyage of 800 mi/1,288 km to bring relief for those remaining on Elephant Island. He died in South Georgia while on a fourth Antarctic expedition.

**Shaftesbury, Anthony Ashley Cooper, 1st Earl of** (1621–83)
English statesman. He became a member of the SHORT PARLIAMENT (1640) and of the BAREBONE'S PARLIAMENT (1653), and was made one of CROMWELL's Council of State, but from 1655 was in opposition. At the RESTORATION he became a baron and Chancellor of the Exchequer (1661–72), a member of the CABAL (1667), an earl (1672), and Lord Chancellor (1672–3). He was dismissed in 1673, and led the opposition to the succession of James, Duke of York (later JAMES VII AND II). Charged with treason in 1681, he was acquitted, but fled to Holland in 1682, and died soon after in Amsterdam. ► ENGLISH CIVIL WARS

**Shaftesbury, Anthony Ashley Cooper, 7th Earl of** (1801–85)
British factory reformer and philanthropist. He entered parliament in 1826, and become the main spokesman of the factory reform movement. He piloted successive FACTORY ACTS (1847 and 1859) through parliament, regulated conditions in the coalmines (1842), and provided lodging houses for the poor (1851). A leader of the evangelical movement within the Church of England, he succeeded to his earldom in 1851.

**Shagari, Alhaji Shehu Usman Aliyu** (1925– )
Nigerian politician. Educated in northern Nigeria, he became a schoolmaster before being elected as a member of the Federal Parliament (1954–8). He was Minister of Economic Development (1959–60), of Establishments (1960–2), of Internal Affairs (1962–5) and of Works (1965–6). After the 1966 coup, he was both State Commissioner for Education in Sokoto province and Federal Commissioner for Economic Development and Reconstruction (1968–70) and then Commissioner for Finance (1971–5). He was a member of the Constituent Assembly that drew up the constitution for the Second Republic and was the successful presidential candidate for the National Party of Nigeria in 1979. He was President of Nigeria from 1979 until 1983, when he was overthrown in a military coup.

**Shah Jahan** (1592–1666)
Mughal Emperor of India (1627/58). His reign saw two wars in the Deccan (1636 and 1655), the subjugation of Bijapur and Golconda (1636), and attacks on the Uzbegs and Persians. A ruthless but able ruler, the magnificence of his court was unequalled. His buildings included the Taj Mahal, the tomb of his beloved third wife, Mumtaz Mahal. In 1658 he was held prisoner by his son AURANGZEB, until his death, at Agra. ► MUGHAL EMPIRE

**Shah Wali Ullah** (1703–62)
Muslim theologian. He took refuge in the concept of the community of the faithful looking only to God. He sought to meet the Hindu intellectual challenge by maintaining that the mystical experience of the divine union did not imply or involve absorption in the deity. Thus, Sufi practice, the Islamic religion of the heart, could be reconciled with the orthodox doctrine of God's sovereignty over his creation. He called for a return to the religion of the *Quran*, which he translated into Persian. Historians trace the seed of

Pakistan to the work of Shah Wali Ullah and his school of theologians.

### Shaka (1727–1828)

King of the Zulu (1817/28). The most famous of the Zulu kings, he built on the military achievements of his predecessor **DINGISWAYO**, extended the Zulu state, and contributed to the great dispersal of **NGUNI** peoples in southern Africa known as the *Mfecane*. Shaka was the illegitimate son of Senzangakona, the chief of the small clan known as the Zulu that was conquered by Dingiswayo's Mthethwa. When Dingiswayo was killed in battle with the rival Ndwandwe, Shaka's military genius enabled him to take over the Mthethwa army. In 1819 his troops, using the short stabbing assegai and the encircling attacking formation that he introduced, defeated the Ndwandwe and welded together a considerable state in northern Natal. His rule became a by-word for ruthlessness although he maintained reasonably good relations with the European traders settled at Port Natal. His victories sent waves of Nguni people into southern Natal, the Transvaal and areas of Central and East Africa as far north as Lake Victoria.

### Shalaev, Stepan Alexevich (1929–)

Soviet trade union leader. He spent his early years working in the timber industry, became a manager and then, in 1963, changed occupations to become a trade union official. Yet his function remained that of running the workforce. So in 1980 he became Minister of the Timber Industry and two years later was chairman of the whole trade union movement. This kind of dual role could not survive the reform period, and in 1990 he was pushed out.

### Shamil, also known as Imam Samuel (c.1797–1871)

Caucasian chief. He led Avar and Chechen tribesmen in the Caucasus in their 30-year struggle against Russia. Having become a Sufi mullah or priest, he strove to end the tribal feuds. A passionate believer and brilliant soldier, he was prominent in the defence of Gimry against the Russians in 1831. In 1834 he was chosen head of the Lesghians and, by abandoning open warfare for guerrilla tactics, secured numerous successes for the mountaineers. In 1839, and again in 1849, he escaped from the stronghold of Ahulgo after the Russians had made themselves masters of it, to continue preaching a **JIHAD** against the infidels. The Russians were completely baffled, their armies sometimes disastrously beaten, though Shamil began to lose ground. During the **CRIMEAN WAR** the Allies supplied him with money and arms, but after peace was signed the Russians compelled the submission of the Caucasus. In 1859, Shamil's chief stronghold, Vedeno, was taken. He was hunted for several months and, after a desperate resistance, was captured and exiled to Kaluga, south of Moscow. In 1870 he was finally allowed to go to Mecca, where he died. He and his like provide some of the inspiration for current Caucasian feelings against Russia.

### Shamir, Yitzhak (1915–)

Israeli politician. Born in Ruzhany, Russia (now Belarus), he studied law at Warsaw University and, after emigrating to Palestine, at the Hebrew University of Jerusalem. In his twenties he became a founder-member of the **STERN GANG**, the Zionist terrorist group that carried out anti-British attacks on strategic targets and personnel in **PALESTINE**. He was arrested by the British (1941) and exiled to Eritrea in 1946, but given asylum in France. He returned to the new state of Israel in 1948 but spent the next 20 years on the fringe of politics, immersing himself in business interests. He entered the Knesset in 1973, becoming its Speaker (1977–80). He was Foreign Minister (1980–3), before taking over the leadership of the right-wing **LIKUD** Party from Menachem **BEGIN**, and becoming Prime Minister (1983). From 1984, he shared power in an uneasy coalition with the Israel Labour Party and its leader, Shimon **PERES**. In 1990 the 'national unity' government collapsed, and in June 1992 Likud was defeated in the general election by the Labour Party, led by Yitzhak **RABIN**. Renowned for his forthright views, Shamir consistently refused to enter into discussions with the **PLO** (Palestine Liberation Organization). ►– **MAPAI PARTY**

### Shan

A Tai-speaking people, the second largest minority group in Myanmar (formerly Burma). Buddhists, with a strong cultural identity, they are mainly concentrated in the Shan state, constituting half of its population of 3.8 million. Most are rice farmers.

### Shang Dynasty ►– CHINESE DYNASTIES PRE-1000AD

### Shaposhnikov, Boris Mikhailovich (1882–1945)

Russian officer and Soviet marshal. Once he went over to the **BOLSHEVIKS** after 1917, he rose rapidly through the ranks until in 1928 he became Chief of Staff. He was commandant of the Frunze Military Academy (1932–7) and was promoted to be Chief of the General Staff (1937–40 and 1941–2). His role was particularly important in the wake of **STALIN**'s army purge. During **WORLD WAR II** his subservience to Stalin made him less valuable than several other commanders.

### sharecropping

A post-**SLAVERY** system of tenant farming in the USA in which short-term tenants (usually black) worked land for landlords (usually white) for a percentage of the crop raised. As much a means of labour and racial control as of economic production, sharecropping provided the economic basis of post-slavery white supremacy, although it also provided a limited economic autonomy for tenants.

### Sharett, Moshe (1894–1965)

Israeli politician. Born in the Ukraine, he settled in **PALESTINE** in 1906. Sharett served in the Turkish army during **WORLD WAR I**, after which he studied at the London School of Economics. Returning to Palestine, he was prominent in the **JEWISH AGENCY** in the 1930s and 1940s, and was arrested by the British authorities along with other Jewish leaders in 1946. Sharett was Israel's first Foreign Minister, and was then Prime Minister (1954–5). From 1960 he headed the executive of the **WORLD ZIONIST ORGANIZATION** and the Jewish Agency, spending his remaining years engaged in Zionist work. ►– **BEN-GURION, DAVID**; **ZIONISM**

### Sharm al-Shaykh

This area, which commands the western side of the Straits of Tiran, was occupied by the Egyptians in

May 1967 by order of President Gamal Abd al-NAS-SER. Because of the threat posed to the rights of passage through the Straits of Tiran and hence the effect on shipping passing from the Gulf of Aqaba to the Red Sea, particularly from the Israeli port of Eilat, the Israelis regarded this as a provocative act. The SIX-DAY WAR of 1967 can be seen as having in some measure the Egyptian occupation of Sharm al-Shaykh and the implied threat to Israeli shipping as its pretext.

**Sharon, Ariel** (1928–)
Israeli general and politician. Prominent in the War of Independence (1948) and SINAI CAMPAIGN (1956), he became a major-general shortly before the SIX-DAY WAR of 1967, during which he commanded an armoured division in the Sinai Peninsula. Leaving the army (July 1973), he was recalled to fight in the YOM KIPPUR WAR. That year he helped to form LIKUD and was voted into the Knesset. As Defence Minister (1981–3) under Menachem BEGIN, Sharon planned Israel's invasion of Lebanon in 1982. He became a leading member of the right-wing Likud Party and served in ministerial posts in successive governments in the 1990s. A remark of his in 2000 is held to have triggered the second INTIFADA, against which he took a hard line after becoming Prime Minister in 2001, including the controversial building of a high wall between Israeli and Palestinian territories. But in 2004 he attempted to overcome one of the obstacles to peace by initiating moves to evacuate Jewish settlements in Palestinian areas, in the face of fierce Israeli opposition.

**Sharpeville**
An African township outside Johannesburg in South Africa. It was here, on 21 Mar 1960, that the police opened fire on a crowd demonstrating against laws restricting non-white movements and requiring non-whites to carry identification cards (the so-called pass laws), killing 69 people and wounding 180 others. It led to the banning of both the ANC and the PAN-AFRICANIST CONGRESS (PAC) and became a symbolic day for all black nationalists in South Africa as a mark of their determination for self-rule and white intransigence.

**Sharpsburg, Battle of** ► ANTIETAM, BATTLE OF

**Shastri, Lal Bahadur** (1904–66)
Indian politician. He joined the independence movement at the age of 16, and was often imprisoned by the British. He excelled as a Congress Party official, and in NEHRU's Cabinet became Minister of Transport (1957), Commerce (1958), and Home Affairs (1960). He succeeded Nehru as Prime Minister (1964–6), but died of a heart attack in Tashkent, USSR, the day after signing a 'no war' agreement with Pakistan. ► INDIAN NATIONAL CONGRESS

**Shatalin, Stanislav Sergeevich** (1934–97)
Soviet economist. In 1989 he was appointed Secretary of the Economics Division of the Academy of Sciences and in 1990 he was made a member of Mikhail GORBACHEV's new presidential council. He acquired particular fame in the autumn of 1990 when he proposed a very radical economic reform, the '500-days plan', as an alternative to RYZHKOV's more conservative one. Gorbachev promised to amalgamate the two but retreated before his right-wingers, in this way undermining both the cause of PERESTROIKA and his own position.

**Shatt al-Arab**
Tidal river formed by the union of the Tigris, Euphrates and Karun rivers, in south-east Iraq; part of the Iraq–Iran border in its lower course. An international commission in 1935 gave control to Iraq, but disputes over navigational rights continued, and were one of the issues that led to the outbreak of the IRAN–IRAQ WAR (1980–8).

**Shays, Daniel** (c.1747–1825)
American revolutionary soldier. A farmer who became a captain in the American army, after the AMERICAN REVOLUTION he returned to farming in Pelham, Massachusetts. However, like many of his fellows, he found himself subject to impossible economic demands. In 1786–7 he led a short-lived rural insurrection, known as Shays' Rebellion, against his state's policies on taxes and debt repayment. The rebellion was crushed by state troops, but it provided a major impetus to the drafting of the federal constitution at the CONSTITUTIONAL CONVENTION of 1787.

**Shcharansky, Natan**, originally **Anatoli Borisovich Shcharansky** (1948–)
Soviet dissident. A brilliant mathematician who was disillusioned with Soviet society, in 1973 he applied for a visa to emigrate to Israel. This was repeatedly refused, prompting him to become increasingly active in the Soviet dissident movement. In 1976 he joined Yuri Orlov's Helsinki Watch Group, a body formed to monitor Soviet human rights violations, and in 1977 was sentenced to 13 years in a labour colony for allegedly spying on behalf of the CIA. He was freed from confinement in Feb 1986 as part of an East–West 'spy' exchange and joined his wife, Avital, in Israel, where he assumed the name Natan. Entering Israeli politics, he served in various ministerial posts, including as Deputy Prime Minister (2001–3).

**Shchelokov, Nikolai Anisimovich** (1910–84)
Soviet politician. A Ukrainian metallurgist, he had close associations with Leonid BREZHNEV in party work based in Dnepropetrovsk, as political officers in the army during WORLD WAR II, and subsequently in party work in Moldavia. In 1966 Brezhnev brought him to Moscow to become Minister of Internal Affairs (and a Central Committee member from 1968). He utilized his position to help himself and his friends to have an easy life; his corruption became notorious. In 1983 Yuri ANDROPOV dismissed him immediately on entering office; a year later he killed himself before charges could be brought against him.

**Shcherbitsky, Vladimir Vasilevich** (1918–90)
Ukrainian politician. A chemical engineer and wartime soldier, after 1945 he climbed up the Communist Party bureaucratic ladder until, by 1971, he was a member of the POLITBURO and, by 1972, First Secretary for the Ukraine. He silenced both dissidence and nationalism, and in dealing with the latter he was also of help to Mikhail GORBACHEV. He was typical of the obstacles facing PERESTROIKA, paying it lip-service, but resisting it by all possible means. He was the last of the old guard, and Gorbachev was only able to get rid of him a few months before his death.

**Sheffield Disturbances** (1866–7)
The name given to an outbreak of violence against non-unionized labour in the cutlery trade which prompted the British government to establish the first ever Royal Commission on trade unionism.

**Shehu, Mehmet** (1913–81)
Albanian politician. Born into a prosperous Muslim family, he studied at the American school in Tirana and later at an Italian military college, from which he was expelled for communist activities. He fought with the communists in the SPANISH CIVIL WAR and returned to Albania to fight in the resistance during WORLD WAR II. After the war, he studied at the military academy in Moscow (1945–6) and returned to Albania to become Chief of Staff in the Albanian army. With the ascendancy of the pro-Yugoslav faction within the Albanian Communist Party, he was expelled from party meetings but after the purges that followed Yugoslavia's expulsion from COMINFORM (Jun 1948), Shehu was readmitted and replaced XOXE as Minister of the Interior. He resumed his position as Chief of Staff and in 1954 became Prime Minister. He survived successive purges but it is a matter of speculation whether his suicide in 1981 was entirely voluntary. ► HOXHA, ENVER

**Shelburne, William Petty, 2nd Earl of** (1737–1805)
British politician and Prime Minister. He entered parliament, succeeded to his earldom in 1761, became President of the Board of Trade (1763) and Secretary of State (1766). Made Premier on the death of ROCKINGHAM (1782), he resigned in 1783 when outvoted by the coalition between FOX and NORTH. In 1784 he was made Marquis of Lansdowne.

**Shelest, Petr Yefimovich** (1908–96)
Ukrainian politician. A poor peasant, he became a Communist Party official and won Nikita KHRUSHCHEV's patronage. By 1957 he was First Secretary in Kiev, by 1963 First Secretary in the Ukraine, and by 1964 a Central Committee member. In 1968, under Leonid BREZHNEV, he took an interventionist approach in the Czechoslovak crisis. However, he tended to be soft on Ukrainian nationalism and lost Brezhnev's backing in 1972. In any case Brezhnev had his own more subservient candidate, SHCHERBITSKY.

**Shepilov, Dmitri Trofimovich** (1905–95)
Soviet politician. Educated at Moscow University, from 1926 to 1931 he was a public prosecutor in Siberia and later became a lecturer in political economy. During WORLD WAR II he was a political commissar in the Ukraine, where he came into contact with Nikita KHRUSHCHEV, and in 1945 he joined the Central Committee Secretariat. In 1952 he became Chief Editor of *Pravda*, in 1954 a member of the Supreme Soviet, and in 1956 Foreign Minister. But, disillusioned with Khrushchev, he participated in the ANTI-PARTY PLOT in 1957, was 'purged' by the Party leadership and banished to a distant teaching post.

**Sherbrooke, Sir John Coape** (1764–1830)
British general and Lieutenant-Governor of Nova Scotia (1811–16). His reputation was made during the PENINSULAR WAR and in the WAR OF 1812 he conducted a vigorous defence, which included the capture of Castine (Maine). He served as Governor-

in-Chief at Quebec from 1816 until he suffered a stroke in 1818.

**Shere Ali** (1825–79)
Amir of Afghanistan (1863/79). He was the younger son of DOST MUHAMMAD, whom he succeeded as Amir. Disagreements with his half-brothers soon arose, which kept Afghanistan in anarchy. Shere Ali fled to Kandahar, but in 1868 regained possession of Kabul with assistance from the viceroy of India, Sir John Lawrence. In 1879 his eldest son, Yakub Khan, rebelled but was captured and imprisoned. Shere Ali's refusal to receive a British mission (1878) led to war and, after severe fighting, he fled to Turkestan, where he died. He was succeeded by Yakub Khan.

**Sheridan, Philip Henry** (1831–88)
US general. Educated at the US Military Academy at West Point, he commanded a Federal division at the beginning of the AMERICAN CIVIL WAR, and took part in many of the campaigns. In 1864 he was given command of the Army of the Shenandoah, turning the valley into a barren waste, and defeating General Robert E LEE. He had a further victory at Five Forks in 1865, and was active in the final battles that led to Lee's surrender. He died at Nonquitt, Massachusetts, never having lost a battle.

**Sherman, Roger** (1721–93)
American Revolutionary patriot and public official. He was the only person to sign all four of the great US documents: the Articles of Association, the DECLARATION OF INDEPENDENCE, the ARTICLES OF CONFEDERATION and the US CONSTITUTION. Prominent in business and politics in Connecticut, he served in the state legislature and senate, was a judge, and became a member of the US HOUSE OF REPRESENTATIVES (1789–91) and US SENATE (1791–3). He was elected to the First CONTINENTAL CONGRESS (1774), where he helped to draft the Declaration of Independence and Articles of Confederation; he (and Oliver Ellsworth) introduced the Connecticut Compromise, which established the states' representation in CONGRESS.

**Sherman, William Tecumseh** (1820–91)
US general. Trained at the US Military Academy at West Point, he became a general in the Union Army during the AMERICAN CIVIL WAR. His most famous campaign was in 1864, when he captured and burned Atlanta. He then commenced his famous 'March to the Sea', in which his 60,000 men totally destroyed everything in their path en route to the coastal town of Savannah. His forces then moved north through the Carolinas causing even more devastation and gaining further victories which helped to bring forward the Confederate surrender. ► INDIAN WARS; MARCH THROUGH GEORGIA

**Sher Shah** (c.1486–1545)
Emperor of North India (1540/5). From the power base he had established in eastern North India, he contested the supremacy of the Mughals, defeating Emperor HUMAYUN at Chausa on the Ganges in 1539 and forcing him into exile. A formidable warrior and able administrator, he also built a new city at Delhi and a fine mausoleum at Sahasram in Bihar. Only his death in battle and the inefficiency of his successors allowed the Mughals to emerge triumphant.

**Shevardnadze, Eduard Amvrosievich** (1928– )
Soviet politician. Having studied history at the Kutaisi Institute of Education, he joined the Communist Party in 1948, and rose rapidly through the Komsomol youth league to the party apparatus during the 1950s and to the Georgian Ministry of the Interior in 1964 as minister. There from 1965 to 1972, he gained a reputation as a stern opponent of corruption, including that on the part of Mahavanadze, the Georgian Party Secretary. For his courage, he became Georgian Party Secretary himself in 1972 and introduced imaginative agricultural experiments. In 1978 he was brought into the **POLITBURO** as a candidate member and, having enjoyed long-standing connections with Mikhail **GORBACHEV**, was promoted to full Politburo status and appointed Foreign Minister in 1985, contrasting starkly with his dour predecessor, Andrei **GROMYKO**. He rapidly overhauled the Soviet foreign policy machine and, alongside Gorbachev, was responsible for the Soviet contribution to the ending of the **COLD WAR**. He was also a powerful influence for political reform inside the USSR and over the winter of 1990–1 constantly warned Gorbachev against the danger of a coup. In 1992 he returned to Georgia in the midst of a virtual civil war and, eventually becoming President of the newly independent state, took on himself the task of making it stable. He survived assassination attempts in 1995 and 1998, but, facing massive demonstrations over alleged electoral fraud, he was forced to resign in 2003.

**Shidehara Kijuro** (1872–1951)
Japanese politician. From a wealthy landlord family who had close links (through marriage) with the Mitsubishi financial combine, Shidehara was ambassador to the USA and a delegate to the **WASHINGTON CONFERENCE** (1921–2) before becoming Foreign Minister in the reforming **KENSEIKAI** government of 1924–6, and again in 1929–31. He adopted a policy of cooperation with the Western powers in China and aroused the ire of ultra nationalists when he supported the 1930 London Naval Treaty, which placed restrictions on Japan's naval build-up. He served as the second post-war Prime Minister in 1945–6 (because of his pro-Western reputation), seeing as his main task the preservation of the emperor system. This may have been behind Shidehara's suggestion that a disarmament clause (the eventual Article 9) be included in the 1947 **PEACE CONSTITUTION**. Shidehara was defeated in Japan's first post-war election in Apr 1946.

**Shigemitsu Mamoru** (1887–1957)
Japanese diplomat and politician. During the 1930s, as vice-Foreign Minister, Shigemitsu was associated with the Asia faction of diplomats, who favoured an aggressive and independent foreign policy in China rather than working with the West. As Ambassador to the USSR (1936) and Britain (1938), however, he also cautioned against war with the USA and opposed the alliance with **HITLER**'s Germany in 1940. He served as Foreign Minister in 1943–5, trying unsuccessfully during the last year of **WORLD WAR II** to involve the USSR as a mediator to bring about an early peace. Convicted as a war criminal in 1946, Shigemitsu served four years of a seven-year sentence before being released in 1950. He was Foreign Minister

again in the cabinet of **HATOYAMA ICHIRO** (1954–6), helping to normalize relations with the USSR in 1956.

**Shiites**
Members of an Islamic religious movement prominent in Iran and Iraq. After the murder of 'Ali, the son-in-law and nephew of the Prophet Muhammad, his followers continued to support his claim to the Muslim caliphate and became known as *Shi'at 'Ali* ('partisans of 'Ali'), usually anglicized as Shiites. They believe that 'Ali and his followers were both temporal rulers and imams. Today about 89 per cent of Iranians and 60 per cent of Iraqis are Shiites. The most important group is the 'Twelver' Shiites, who believe that there were twelve imams – 'Ali and his descendants – after the Prophet Muhammad, and that the twelfth did not die but disappeared, and one day will return to bring justice to the world. Since the 16c, Twelver Shiism has been Iran's state religion. ➤ **IMAM**; **RELIGION**; **SUNNIS**

**Shiloh, Battle of** (6–7 Apr 1862)
An engagement in the **AMERICAN CIVIL WAR** in Tennessee, near Corinth, Mississippi, between Union forces under General Ulysses S **GRANT** and Confederate forces under Albert Sidney Johnston (1803–62). Losses were heavy on both sides, with 13,000 Union and 11,000 Confederate casualties.

**Shimabara Rebellion** (1637–8)
A peasant uprising in Japan that broke out on the Shimabara Peninsula (in present day Nagasaki prefecture). Its leader, Amakusa Shiro, was an impoverished **SAMURAI** whose millenarian teachings drew huge support from amongst the inhabitants of a region suffering from famine, over-taxation and religious persecution. Forces of the **TOKUGAWA SHOGUNATE** finally took the rebel stronghold of Hara castle in Apr 1638, sparing no one; 37,000 rebels perished. Since the Shimabara region had been Christianized before official persecution began in 1614, the Tokugawa viewed the uprising as a Christian-inspired rebellion, reinforcing its decision to sever all contacts with the West.

**Shimonoseki, Treaty of** (17 Apr 1895)
The treaty that concluded the **SINO-JAPANESE WAR** (1894–5), fought over which country would exercise dominant influence in Korea. Japan's victory in the war brought it considerable gains. The treaty formally ended Korea's tributary relationship with China; henceforth Japan was to be the dominant power in Korea. China also had to pay an indemnity and to cede to Japan the island of Taiwan and the Liaodong Peninsula (southern Manchuria). More significantly, Japan gained the same treaty rights as the Western powers in China's **TREATY PORTS**. Although Japan was forced to return the Liaodong Peninsula to China in 1896 as a result of pressure from Russia, France and Germany (known as the Triple Intervention), this treaty was a significant turning-point in the emergence of Japan as an imperialist power in China.

**Shining Path** ➤ **SENDERO LUMINOSO**

**Shinto**
The indigenous religion of Japan, so named in the 6c to distinguish it from Buddhism, from which it subsequently incorporated many features. It emerged

# Ships

*Transport & Travel*

When the first human beings attempted to travel over water, it is reasonable to assume that they used rafts or dug-out canoes made from hollowed tree trunks. From these they graduated to simple craft made from a wooden frame covered with animal hide, such as the Celtic coracle or **Inuit** kayak, or with a sheath of planks covered in bark like Native American canoes. Perhaps the earliest vessels that can be called ships are the reed boats used by the ancient Egyptians, constructed of bundles of papyrus stems securely lashed together, and large enough to carry passengers or cargo under sail or with oars. As Thor Heyerdahl demonstrated in 1970, it would have been possible for ancient Egyptian sailors to cross the Atlantic in a vessel of this type. From 3000 BC the Egyptians also constructed ships with wooden-shell hulls, stiffened by bracers and rope tension. These were early galleys rowed by up to 20 oarsmen, with a sail hung from a double mast shaped like an inverted 'V' or attached to a single mast by a yard, and with a single steering oar or a connected pair of oars at the stern.

### The Phoenicians

The most accomplished seafaring nation on the Mediterranean in ancient times were the Phoenicians, who lived in modern-day Lebanon. Independent of Egypt in around 1100 BC, the Phoenicians rapidly developed as a seafaring and trading nation. They are known to have traded outside the Mediterranean, reaching at least as far as the south-western coast of Britain, and probably some way along the western coast of Africa. They built the best ships both for trade and for warfare in the Mediterranean of their time. Innovations credited to them are the development of the so-called 'round ship' – a ship considerably wider than most of its contemporaries, less dependent on oars and more on the wind, and with a larger cargo capacity – and of ships with oarsmen arranged in banks. As a rule, throughout European history ships designed for war have been long and narrow, ships for trade, broader and more rounded. This pattern was followed by the Greeks and Romans, and later by the Norsemen.

### The Greeks and Romans

The Greeks and Romans continued the development of galleys equipped with sails on the Egyptian pattern. The Greeks added a small superstructure at the rear of their vessels to afford some protection for the captain, and braced their ships with ropes that girdled the hull lengthwise and could be tightened to give extra strength in heavy seas or in battle. The Romans added a spritsail and a triangular topsail to the square mainsail on some of their ships. They increased the size of ships used in both trade and war. A large Roman merchant vessel could be up to 175 ft/53 m in length and 45 ft/14 m in breadth and depth. Some Roman warships carried **artillery** in the form of catapults, and a form of covering to protect against flaming missiles hurled from enemy vessels.

### The Chinese junk

In China a very different type of vessel was developed. The design of the junk is thought to have evolved from building up a box-shaped hull on top of two or more dug-out canoes lashed together. It was much squarer than European vessels and had no keel and no stempost or sternpost, that is, no main vertical structural timbers at front and rear. Strength and stability were obtained by fitting bulkheads lengthwise and crosswise inside the vessel, thus dividing the hull into watertight compartments and providing extra protection against sinking, a design feature not incorporated into Western ships until the 19c. By the 1c AD, junks carried a rudder which was let down in a well through the hull on the centreline of the vessel. This in-board rudder also compensated for the lack of a keel. The sails of a junk were made up of separate panels of linen or matting on bamboo yards, each with its own line, so that the sail could be furled rather in the manner of a Venetian blind. Marco **Polo** commented on the fact the Chinese ships had more than one mast. By his time Chinese traders had been sailing their junks as far as Indonesia and India for several centuries, and by the 15c they had reached the east coast of Africa.

---

from the nature-worship of Japanese folk religions, and this is reflected in ceremonies appealing to the mysterious powers of nature (*kami*) for benevolent treatment and protection. By the 8c divine origins were ascribed to the imperial family, the emperor believed to be descended from the Sun Goddess, and in time became the basis for State Shinto and its loyalty and obedience to the emperor. In the 19c it was divided into Shrine (*jinga*) Shinto and Sectarian (*kyoho*) Shinto, with the former regarded as a 'state cult' and the latter officially recognized as a religion but ineligible for state support. In 1945, State Shinto lost its official status and now worship is a private affair, although it remains a significant part of Japanese life.

**Shipov, Dimitri N** (1851–1920)
Russian political philanthropist. Chairman of the board of the **ZEMSTVO** in St Petersburg, he organized a meeting of his fellow chairmen in the summer of 1896 to exchange views and present them to the Tsar.

They encountered many official obstacles but held to their view that consultation was essential. Some became more radical and formed the Union of Liberation in 1903 to seek full representative government. In 1905 they went on to form the **KADETS**. But Shipov split to join **GUCHKOV** in establishing the **OCTOBRISTS** who were altogether less radical.

**Ships** ➤ *See panel*

**Shivaji** (1627–80)
Indian King and founder of the Maratha Kingdom (1674/80). He was the son of Shahaji Bhonsle, a Maratha nobleman who had defied the power of the Mughals in Bijapur. Shivaji was able to gather a considerable following among the Mawali hill-dwellers of the region, and, when the Bijapur authorities sent a large army against him in 1659, he succeeded in killing their general and ambushing the leaderless army. During the 1660s Maratha power continued to increase and he had himself crowned as Raja in 1674.

## Evolution of the sailing ship in Europe
Different climatic conditions affected the development of ships in European waters through the **Middle Ages**. The comparatively light winds in the Mediterranean meant the galley enjoyed a long life there; the Battle of **Lepanto** fought off the coast of Greece in 1571, between ships of the **Ottoman Empire** and the **Holy League**, almost exclusively involved galleys. The more variable winds in northern European waters and the Atlantic encouraged the development of sail; the Spanish **Armada** that sailed in 1588 was a fleet of sailing galleons and it was defeated by an English fleet of ships of a similar type.

The typical northern European ship of the early Middle Ages was the Hanseatic *cog*, a broad and sturdy trading ship with a raised structure or 'castle' at bow and stern, a single mast with a large square sail and, from around 1200, a rudder attached to the sternpost. The ship used in the first of the great voyages of discovery of the later Middle Ages were *caravels* – small sailing vessels with two or three masts and a lateen rig (a triangular sail mounted on a long diagonal spar) on all but the foremast – or *carracks* – somewhat larger, usually three-masted vessels, square-rigged on the foremast and mainmast, and with a lateen rig on the after mast. The galleon, developed from the carrack, carried the trade of Europe around the world during the 16–17c.

Ships began to carry guns from the middle of the 14c. Soon afterwards various European nations began to make a clearer distinction between sailing ships used for war and those used for commerce, a process accelerated by the need to defend sea routes and trading interests abroad. The men-of-war of the 17–18c carried cannon lined up along both sides of the ship on two or three decks, firing through openings in the side of the hull. By the end of the 18c the largest ships of the line carried over a hundred guns, were around 200 ft/60 m in length, 52 ft/16 m in width, and had a displacement of over 2,000 tonnes.

In the 19c, the emphasis in the construction of sailing ships tended to be on speed. Clippers built first in US yards and later in Europe were comparatively slim ships with tall masts designed to carry the maximum amount of sail. Wooden hulls gradually gave way to composite hulls, in which wooden planks were attached to an iron frame. Clippers achieved record sailing times on long-distance routes, and were used in the tea trade to Canton and the Australian wool trade, but ultimately were unable to compete with steamships for speed and reliability of service, and by the end of the 19c the age of sail was over.

## Steamships
The first steam-powered craft were being developed experimentally towards the end of the 18c. A Frenchman, the Marquis de Jouffroy d'Abbans, successfully sailed a paddle-boat on the River Saône in 1783. His achievement was soon emulated by the US inventors John Fitch and Robert Fulton. The first commercial steam-powered vessel in operation was the *Charlotte Dundas*, which ran on the Forth and Clyde canals in 1802. By 1816 steamships were making Channel crossings, and by 1819 the steamship *Savannah* was the first to cross the Atlantic, albeit mainly under sail. All the earliest steamships had paddle-wheels and wooden hulls. To carry the weight of steam engines, iron hulls were built, the first all-iron steamer entering service in 1820. The invention of a successful form of screw propeller in 1836 gave steam navigation a further boost. Brunel's *Great Western*, built specifically for transatlantic passenger service in 1838, was a paddle-steamer; the design of his next big ship, the *Great Britain*, was hastily altered and it was built in 1845 as the first ocean-going screw-driven steamer.

The advantages of steam propulsion and iron hulls soon also became apparent to military designers. The Royal Navy ordered its first class of paddle-steamers (used for towing sailing ships of the line) in 1820. The first battle between two **ironclad** steamers took place during the **American Civil War** when the Union's *Monitor* and the Confederate *Virginia* (known as *Merrimack*) fought an inconclusive duel off Hampton Roads, Virginia.

The design of steam engines continued to be refined. In the late-19c Atlantic trades, the advent of steel-hulled cargo ships with economical triple-expansion engines made US agricultural exports, especially wheat and cattle, much more competitive in European markets. Larger, faster steamships for cargo and passenger movement continued to be built until the early years of the 20c, when motor-powered vessels with internal-combustion engines began to take over.

---

He profited from the conflict between the Mughal emperor, AURANGZEB, and the Afghans to make extensive conquests in the south before his death. Although his empire remained essentially a 'robber-state', exacting 'protection-money' from areas under its control, he was also intensely devoted to the cause of Hinduism, and the Maratha Empire that he created maintained its independence until 1818.

**Shmelev, Nikolai Petrovich** (1936– )
Soviet academic reformer and politician. An economist graduate of Moscow University, he had a short period in the 1960s in the propaganda section of the Central Committee. But he spent most of his career from the time of Nikita KHRUSHCHEV to that of Mikhail GORBACHEV between three of the major institutes of the Soviet Academy, latterly having the opportunity to influence people in high places with his liberal ideas. From 1989 to 1991 he was a member of the Soviet Congress of Deputies.

**shogun**
A Japanese general; the head of a system of government which dates from 1192, when a military leader received the title *seii-tai-shogun* ('Barbarian-Quelling Generalissimo') from the Emperor. Most important were members of the TOKUGAWA SHOGUNATE (1603–1868), who ruled as military dictators, the Emperor remaining a figurehead, without power. The shoguns' rule strictly regulated and controlled life down to the smallest detail. The system ended in 1868. ► MEIJI RESTORATION

**Short Parliament** (Apr–May 1640)
The brief parliament summoned by CHARLES I of England to vote supplies for his campaigns against the Scots. It refused to do so, however, whereupon the King dissolved it after only three weeks, adding to parliament's sense of grievance.

**show trials**
Originally a series of political trials held in Moscow

Motor-powered vessels now account for the vast majority of the world's shipping fleet.

**Submarines**

The submarine, first described in 1578, first sailed in 1620 when a Dutch inventor, Cornelis Drebbel, took 12 oarsmen and a number of passengers on a trip beneath the River Thames in a leather-encased boat provided with air by a number of tubes attached to floats on the surface. The US inventor David Bushnell used a one-man, egg-shaped submarine driven by a primitive hand-cranked screw device to attack a British ship in New York harbour during the **American Revolution**. Another American, Robert Fulton, demonstrated a cigar-shaped submarine with a supply of compressed air and rudders for horizontal and vertical steering in 1800; it was not taken up by either the French or British governments.

The Confederate Navy possessed four submarines during the **American Civil War**, one of which blew up a Union ship but sank itself in the process. Development of the modern submarine, used with great effect especially by the German navy in both World Wars, awaited the development of the internal-combustion engine and the adaptation for use in submarines of the self-propelling torpedo, which was invented by the English engineer Robert Whitehead in 1866.

**Modern developments**

The great days of passenger transportation in ships lasted from the early 19c to the mid-20c. Air transport then effectively took over. Cargo transportation in the latter part of the 20c has continued to be entrusted to ships that have over time become progressively larger and simpler. Since **World War II**, more and more ships have been built with displacements of over 100,000 tonnes, the engines and accommodation located at the stern and the rest of the hull devoted to storage space especially for crude oil, bulk goods or containers.

Greater speed over water has become possible through designs such as the hydrofoil (the first of which was built in 1906) and the hovercraft (first patented by Sir Christopher Cockerell in 1955), which lift the hull of the vessel partly or wholly above the surface of the water. These designs are mainly employed in smaller craft. Nuclear units have also been used since the 1950s to provide power for submarines, and to a very limited extent to power surface vessels. ► **Monitor, USS v CSS Merrimack;Navy**

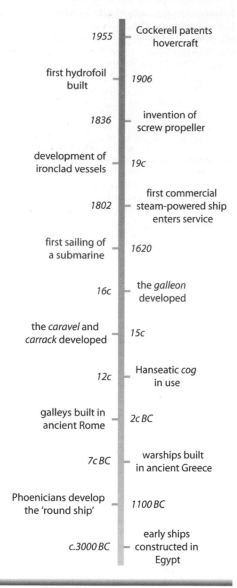

in the late 1930s under **STALIN**'s direct control. Because of what happened, the term came to refer to any political trial where the accused under pressure made public confessions of their alleged crimes, although their guilt would not have been established in any normal court. The process was an attempt to obscure personal vendettas and to justify political repression by demonstrating the use of apparently proper and just judicial procedures in dealing with so-called enemies of the state. ► **STALINISM**

**Shuvalov, Pyotr Andreevich, Count** (1827–89)

Russian officer, politician and diplomat. He served in the **CRIMEAN WAR**, became head of the Third Department or secret police in 1866 and proved himself a dangerous opponent of reform. In 1873, sent on a secret mission to London, he was able to do less damage and arranged the marriage between the Duke of Edinburgh and the only daughter of **ALEXANDER II**. In general he proved a sound diplomat; in 1878 he was one of the Russian representatives

at the Congress of **BERLIN**.

**Sicilian Vespers** (1282)

The wholesale massacre of the French in Sicily which began the Sicilian revolt against **CHARLES OF ANJOU**, King of Naples and Sicily, and a war ending in 1302. It was so called because the first killings occurred during a riot in a church outside Palermo at vespers (evensong) on Easter Monday 1282. ► **ANGEVINS**

**Sidi Muhammad** (1757–90)

Sultan of Maghrib (Morocco). He restored peace and prosperity after a period of political chaos. He developed Mogador as the principal port for trade with Europe, strengthened central authority and limited the intervention of Europeans in Moroccan affairs.

**Sidi Muhammad ben Yusuf** (1911–61)

Sultan of Morocco (1927/61). A member of the Alouite Dynasty, he exercised both spiritual and temporal power; privately supporting the nationalist Istaqlal Party, he constantly obstructed French hegemony. Hostility to him among Berber tribesmen gave the French the chance to depose him in 1953, but he was restored in 1955, and when Morocco attained independence in 1957 he became King Mohammed V. He died suddenly after a minor operation and was succeeded by his eldest son, Prince Moulay Hassan (HASSAN II), who had already emerged as the spokesman of chauvinistic Moroccan youth. His eldest daughter, Princess Lalla Ayesha, repudiated the yashmak and became a leader of the women's emancipation movement.

### Sidmouth, Henry Addington, 1st Viscount (1757–1844)

British politician. He left law for politics, and became an MP in 1783. He was Speaker of the House (1789–1801) when, upon the resignation of PITT, THE YOUNGER, he was invited to form a ministry. His Tory administration negotiated the Treaty of AMIENS (1802), which held for barely a year. His government ended in 1804, when he was created a viscount. He later became Home Secretary under LIVERPOOL (1812–21), unpopular for coercive measures such as the Six Acts (1819), which restricted newspaper publication and the holding of political meetings. It was during his period of office that the PETERLOO MASSACRE took place in Manchester. ► NAPOLEONIC WARS

### Sidney, Algernon (1622–83)

English politician. He became a cavalry officer in the ENGLISH CIVIL WARS on the parliamentary side, and was wounded at the Battle of MARSTON MOOR (1644). In 1645 he entered parliament, and served as governor in several cities. An extreme republican, he resented CROMWELL's usurpation of power, and retired from public life (1653–9). After the RESTORATION he lived on the Continent, but in 1677 was pardoned and returned to England. However, in 1683, he was implicated on very little evidence in the RYE HOUSE PLOT, and beheaded in London. ► WHIGS

### Siegfried Line

A fortified defensive line on Germany's western border with Belgium and France, known in German as the *Westwall* or 'Western Wall'. Built from 1936, to a large degree with conscripted labour, the Westwall turned out to be of limited military significance upon the Allied invasion of Germany (1944–5). ► WORLD WAR II

### SIERRA LEONE official name Republic of Sierra Leone

A coastal republic in West Africa, bounded to the north by Guinea; to the south-east by Liberia; and to the south and south-west by the Atlantic Ocean. The area was visited by Portuguese navigators in the 15c and British slave traders in the 16c and 17c. In the 1780s coastal land was bought from local chiefs by English philanthropists who established settlements for freed slaves; thus, Freetown was established. Sierra Leone became a British Crown Colony in 1808, and the hinterland was declared a British protectorate in 1896. The latter remained separate from the Freetown colony until 1951. The country gained independence in 1961 and became a republic in 1971 under the one-party regime of President Siaka STEVENS, who retired in 1985 and was succeeded by

Joseph Saidu MOMOH as President. Following the adoption of a new constitution in 1991 with provision for multiparty politics, there was a military coup in 1992 led by Captain Valentine Strasser; this resulted in the suspension of political activity and the dissolution of the new constitution until 1995. Despite the legalization of opposition parties, rebel forces grew in power and Strasser was ousted in 1996. Later that year Ahmad Tejan Kabbah was democratically elected as President, but he had to flee the country in 1997 after another coup; he was restored to power in 1998 with the help of forces sent by ECOWAS, and was re-elected in 2002. UN peacekeeping troops replaced ECOWAS forces in 2000 to police a peace accord agreed in 1999 but the rebels fought the peacekeeping forces until 2001, when another peace agreement was reached. The state of emergency in force since 1998 was lifted in 2002 and disarmament of rebel forces was completed in 2004.

### Sieyès, Emmanuel Joseph, Count of, called the Abbé Sieyès (1748–1836)

French cleric and political theorist. His pamphlet *Qu'est-ce que le tiers-état?* (1789, 'What is the Third Estate?') stimulated bourgeois awareness and won him great popularity. He was elected to the ESTATES GENERAL, and suggested the name National Assembly when it united into one body. He was a prominent figure in the early years of the FRENCH REVOLUTION, being one of the founders of the Jacobin club. However, as the Revolution became more extreme, he withdrew from centre stage, being famous for his reply to the question of what he had done during the Revolution, 'I survived'. He became one of the Directors, and in 1799 was a leading figure in the BRUMAIRE COUP that brought NAPOLEON I to power. He withdrew from public life under the First Empire, but was exiled at the Bourbon Restoration (1815) and lived in Brussels until 1830, when the JULY REVOLUTION allowed him to return to Paris. ► EMPIRE, FIRST (France); JACOBINS

### Sifton, Sir Clifford (1861–1929)

Canadian politician. As Manitoba's provincial Attorney-General (1891–6) he vigorously defended the province's educational policy during the MANITOBA SCHOOLS ACT. After the problem was resolved, LAURIER appointed him Minister of the Interior, and he established a very effective immigration policy that drew large numbers of Ukrainians and Doukhobors to the north-west. He broke with the Liberal government first in 1905, when he resigned over the restoration of separate schools in the north-west, and again when his defection over **RECIPROCITY** helped the Conservatives to win the election of 1911. ► **LIBERAL PARTY** (Canada)

**Sigismund** (1368–1437)
Holy Roman Emperor (1410/37). The son of **CHARLES IV**, he became King of Hungary in 1387, German King in 1410 and King of Bohemia in 1419. In 1396 he was defeated by the Ottoman Turks at Nicopolis, but later conquered Bosnia, Herzegovina and Serbia. As German King, he induced the pope to call the Council of Constance to end the Hussite schism (1414), but in the end made no effort to uphold the safe conduct he had granted to Jan **HUS**, and permitted him to be burnt at the stake in 1415. As a result, his succession in Bohemia was opposed by the **HUSSITES** in 1420 and he was only accepted in 1436, a year before his death.

**Sigismund I, the Old** (1467–1548)
King of Poland (1506/48). His court was filled with factions stirred up by his second wife, the daughter of the Duke of Milan, and the **REFORMATION** raised new troubles. In a war with Russia he lost Smolensk, but gained eastern Prussia (1525) and Moldavia (1531). A great patron of the **RENAISSANCE**, he died at Kraków.

**Sigismund II Augustus** (1520–72)
King of Poland (1548/72). During his reign Lithuania was joined to Poland, and Poland acquired Livonia, thus greatly expanding the kingdom. He died at Knyszyn.

**Sigismund III Vasa** (1566–1632)
King of Poland (1587/1632). Born in Sweden, from 1592 he was also King of Sweden, but was deposed by his uncle in 1599. This led to wars between the two countries until 1629, during which he lost Livonia (1621), and gave up his right to the Swedish crown. He died in Warsaw.

**Sigurd I, the Crusader** (c.1090–1130)
King of Norway (1103/30). The youngest of the three sons of **MAGNUS III, BARELEGS**, he ruled jointly with his brothers until their deaths (1115 and 1122). Between 1107 and 1111 he made an expedition with 60 ships to the Holy Land, the first Scandinavian king to take part in the Crusades (hence his nickname, *Jorsalafari*, 'Jerusalem-farer'). At home he did much to strengthen the Church, building cathedrals and imposing tithes for the first time.

**Sigurdsson, Jón** (1811–79)
Icelandic politician and scholar. Born in the west of Iceland, he was educated in Copenhagen, where he spent the rest of his life. As a politician, he led the struggle for autonomy under the Danish crown, earning himself the title 'the Father of Icelandic Independence'. He persuaded King **CHRISTIAN VIII** to restore the **ALTHING** as a consultative assembly in 1843, and King **CHRISTIAN IX** to give it legislative powers in internal affairs in 1874, on the thousandth anniversary of the traditional date of the founding of Iceland's first settlement. His birthday, 17 June, is Iceland's National Day.

**Sihanouk, Norodom** (1922–)
Cambodian politician. Educated in Vietnam and Paris, he became King of Cambodia in 1941. He negotiated the country's independence from France (1949–53), before abdicating in 1955 in favour of his father so as to become an elected leader under the new constitution. As Prime Minister and then, from 1960 after his father's death, also as head of state, he steered a neutralist course during the **VIETNAM WAR**. In 1970 he was deposed in a right-wing military coup led by the US-backed Lieutenant-General Lon Nol. Fleeing to Peking (Beijing), he formed a joint resistance front with **POL POT**, which overthrew Lon Nol in Apr 1975. Prince Sihanouk was reappointed head of state, but a year later was ousted by the **KHMER ROUGE** leadership. In 1982, while living in North Korea, he became head of a broad-based Democratic Kampuchea (Cambodia) government-in-exile, which aimed to overthrow the Vietnamese-installed regime in Cambodia. Following the Vietnamese troop withdrawal in 1989, he was involved in the attempts to negotiate a settlement of the country's civil war, and became its King in 1993. He abdicated in 2004 in favour of his son, Norodom Sihamoni.

**Šik, Ota** (1919–2004)
Czechoslovak economist and politician. Imprisoned in a concentration camp during **WORLD WAR II**, he joined the Communist Party in 1945. His main claim to fame was then as an economist, becoming Director of the Institute of Economics of the Academy of Sciences in 1962. This put him at the heart of the minor economic reform in the early 1960s and of the major political reform in 1968. He became a member of the Central Committee and a deputy premier. Not all of his ideas would necessarily have prospered, but he and they were swept away by the Soviet invasion in Aug; he then found it wiser to go abroad and never returned.

**Sikandar Hayat Khan** (1892–1942)
Indian politician. He came from a rich, landed family and after matriculating from school in Aligarh, entered University College, London to study medicine, but returned after two years. In **WORLD WAR I** he offered his services to the British government. He was appointed an honorary recruiting officer and was granted a commission. During the third of the **AFGHAN WARS** he acted as a company commander (1919). He was elected to the Punjab legislative council in 1921, and was appointed chairman of Punjab Reforms Committee to work with the Simon Commission. He was knighted in 1933 and was appointed Governor of Reserve Bank in 1935. He was elected Chief Minister of Punjab at the start of **WORLD WAR II** and held this office until 1942. During this time he launched rural reconstruction programmes, extended irrigation facilities, laid new roads, and established and strengthened *panchayats* (village councils). In his lifetime, the **MUSLIM LEAGUE** could not secure control of the Punjab province. After his death Punjab plunged into political turmoil.

**Sikhism**
A monotheistic religion combining elements from Hinduism and Islam, founded in the late 15c by Guru Nanak in the Punjab area of North India. It is called a religion of the gurus, and doctrinally, seeks union with God through worship and service. God is the true guru, and his divine word has come to humanity

through the ten historical gurus. The line ended with the death of **GOBIND SINGH** in 1708, after which the Sikh community and the Sikh scripture, the *Adi Granth*, were accorded the status of gurus. The Sikh way of life is closely related to Punjab identity and forms the basis of the movement for Punjab separatism. ► **RELIGION**

**Sikh Wars** (1845–6 and 1848–9)
Two struggles between the British and the Sikhs which led to the British conquest and annexation of the Punjab, north-west India (Mar 1849).

**Sikorski, Władysław Eugeniusz** (1881–1943)
Polish general and politician. Educated at Kraków and Lvov, he fought in the Russian-Polish War (1920–1), became Commander-in-Chief (1921), and Premier (1922–3). After **PIŁSUDSKI**'s coup (1926) he retired and wrote military history in Paris. He returned to Poland in 1938, but on being refused a command, fled to France, becoming Commander of the Free Polish forces and from 1940 Premier of the Polish government in exile in London. He was killed in an air crash at Gibraltar.

**Silesia**
Region of east-central Europe on both banks of the River Oder in south-west Poland and north-central Czechoslovakia, bounded on the south by the Sudetes Mountains. It was a disputed area between Austria and **PRUSSIA** in the 17–18c, passing largely to the latter. In 1921 Poland received part of industrial Upper Silesia and in 1945 the greater part was granted to Poland, with the removal or flight of the German population. ► **SILESIAN WARS**

**Silesian Wars** (1740 2, 1744–5 and 1756–63)
In these three wars, two campaigns in the War of the **AUSTRIAN SUCCESSION** and the **SEVEN YEARS' WAR**, Austria and **PRUSSIA** fought to control **SILESIA**, an area rich in minerals and ores. In the first war, Prussia conquered the area by 1742, and it extended its gains in the second war. In the Treaties of Berlin (1742) and **DRESDEN** (1745), Austria recognized Prussia's control of Silesia. In the third war, Austrian troops failed to retake Silesia and, once again, Austria was forced to acknowledge, by the Treaty of Hubertusberg (1763), Prussian sovereignty in the province.

**Sillon**
A French Catholic review, founded in 1894. In 1899 it was taken up by Marc Sangnier (1873–1950) to express his ideas of democratic Catholicism, and developed into a movement of clubs with a membership of students and workers. Condemned by Pope Pius X in 1910, it is seen as one of the roots of later Christian democracy.

**Simcoe, Sir John Graves** (1752–1806)
British colonial administrator. As Lieutenant-Governor of Upper **CANADA** (1792–94), his intention was to re-create British social and political patterns in the colony, but his disagreements with both London and Canadian administrators caused his recall in 1796. His most positive accomplishment was the use of the army in a huge road-building programme.

**Simeon II**, also known as **Simeon Saxecoburggotski** (1937–)
King of Bulgaria (1943/6). The son of **BORIS III** and

Tsaritsa Giovanna, he was proclaimed King on 28 Aug 1943 but was never crowned. Since he was too young to rule, Prince Kiril, together with the former Prime Minister, Bogdan Filov, and the former War Minister, General Nikola Mikhov, formed a council of regents. In Dec 1944 the **FATHERLAND FRONT** regime put the regents on trial and secured their execution. After a plebiscite (Sep 1946), Bulgaria was declared a People's Republic and Simeon went with his mother to Spain, where he became a businessman. After the fall of the communist regime, he returned to Bulgaria in 2001 and became involved in national politics, founding the National Movement for Simeon II. After leading his party to victory in elections later that year, he became Prime Minister at the head of a coalition government.

**Simmonds, Kennedy Alphonse** (1936–)
St Kitts and Nevis politician and physician. He practised medicine in the USA and Caribbean before entering politics and founding (1965) the People's Action Movement (PAM) as a centre-right alternative to the Labour Party. After a series of unsuccessful elections, in 1980 Simmonds and PAM won enough seats in the Assembly to form a coalition government with the Nevis Reformation Party (NRP) and he became Prime Minister. Full independence was achieved in 1983 and Simmonds' coalition was re-elected in 1984. He retained his post as Prime Minister until 1995.

**Simnel, Lambert** (c.1477–c.1525)
English pretender. The son of a joiner, he bore a resemblance to **EDWARD IV**, and was carefully coached (1487) by an Oxford priest, Roger Symonds, before being set up in Ireland as, first, the younger son of Edward IV, and then as the Duke of Clarence's son, Edward, Earl of Warwick (1475–99). Backed by Margaret of Burgundy, his supposed aunt, Simnel achieved some success in Ireland and was crowned in Dublin as Edward VI (1487), but, landing in Lancashire with 2,000 German mercenaries, he was defeated at Stoke Field, Nottinghamshire (1487), and subsequently became a royal scullion and falconer.

**Simon, John Allsebrook Simon, 1st Viscount** (1873–1954)
British politician and lawyer. A Liberal, he entered parliament in 1906, and was knighted in 1910. He was Attorney-General (1913–15) and Home Secretary (1915–16), before resigning from the cabinet for his opposition to conscription. Deserting the Liberals to form the Liberal National Party, he supported Ramsay **MACDONALD**'s coalition governments and became Foreign Secretary (1931–5), Home Secretary in the Conservative government (1935–7), Chancellor of the Exchequer (1937–40), and Lord Chancellor in Winston **CHURCHILL**'s wartime coalition (1940–5). He was created a viscount in 1940. ► **LIBERAL PARTY** (UK)

**Simon, Jules François** (1814–96)
French politician and philosopher. A lecturer at the Sorbonne in 1839, he became a Republican Deputy in 1848, and later one of the opposition Deputies in the *Corps Législatif* of the Second Empire. He was a member of the Government of **NATIONAL DEFENCE**

(1870–1), and was elected to the National Assembly (1871). He was Minister of Public Instruction (1871–3), and Prime Minister (1876–7). Describing himself as 'profoundly republican and profoundly conservative', he was nevertheless dismissed by President **MACMAHON** on 16 May 1877, initiating a major constitutional crisis. ► **EMPIRE, SECOND** (France)

## Sinai Campaign (1956)

This campaign, which can be seen as forming a prelude to the **SUEZ CRISIS**, took Israeli armour to the Suez Canal. Terrorist raids from Gaza in 1955 were put forward as the reason for Israel's move into the **GAZA STRIP**, which caused the Egyptians to close the Gulf of Aqaba. Egypt consulted on a joint military response with Syria and Jordan, but secret talks between Britain, France and Israel (so effectively secret that it appears that not even the British Ambassador in Cairo knew of them) resulted in an Israeli attack on the Sinai Peninsula on 29 Oct 1956. By 5 Nov, when the **UN** imposed a ceasefire, the Israelis under the leadership of Moshe **DAYAN** had occupied Sinai and reached the Suez Canal.

## Sindia

The title of the Maratha princes of Gwalior. Their founder was Ranaji Sindia, who rose to high rank in the bodyguard of the Peshwa, and had a grant of half the province of Mala. ► **SINDIA, BAJI RAO**; **SINDIA, DAULAT RAO**; **SINDIA, MADHAVA RAO**; **SINDIA, MAHADAJI**

## Sindia, Baji Rao (d.1886)

Maratha Prince of Gwalior. During the **INDIAN UPRISING** of 1857–8 he took the field against the rebels, but most of his troops deserted him, and he fled to Agra. He was reinstated, and was succeeded by his adopted son.

## Sindia, Daulat Rao (1779–1827)

Maratha Prince of Gwalior. The grandnephew of Ranaji Sindia, he ravaged Indore and Pune, but was routed by Holkar (1802), and next year brought upon himself the vengeance of the British **EAST INDIA COMPANY**. The Marathas were routed at Assaye and Argaum by Sir Arthur Wellesley (**WELLINGTON**), and were scattered at Laswari by Lord Lake. Thereupon Sindia ceded all his possessions in the Doab and along the right bank of the River Jumna to the British. Gwalior was restored in 1805.

## Sindia, Madhava Rao (d.1794)

Maratha Prince of Gwalior. The illegitimate son of Ranaji Sindia, he joined the Maratha confederation, and was crippled for life at the Battle of **PANIPAT** (1761). In 1770, along with the Peshwa and Holkar (the chief general), he helped the Mughal to expel the Sikhs and became virtually supreme in Hindustan. He came into conflict with the British in 1779, and was defeated by Warren **HASTINGS**, but by the Treaty of Salbai (1783) was confirmed in all his possessions. In 1784 he captured Gwalior, in 1785 marched on Delhi, and subsequently seized Agra, Aligarh and nearly the whole of the Doab. He raised and drilled an army in European fashion and crushed Jodhpur, Udaipur and Jaipur (all Rajput states), while Holkar remained his ally. He died (possibly murdered) at Pune.

## Sindia, Mahadaji (1727–94)

Maratha Ruler of Gwalior (1761/94). He succeeded Madu Rao in 1772 as Peshwa ('commander') of the combined Maratha forces. In addition to Maratha lieutenants, he used mercenary troops, hired adventurers and obtained assistance from the battalions of the French officer de Boigne. He used his trained troops in the decisive encounters that made him dominant in the Delhi kingdom and secured his supremacy in Rajputana. His dominion soon stretched from the River Sutluj to the Narmada and he became the recognized Mughal agent as Deputy Regent of the empire. However, his ambition was to control Pune and in 1792 he marched there to assert his claims against Holkar and Fadnavis in the Pune court. His death left his lands in the far less capable hands of Daulat Rao **SINDIA**, and his disciplined troops passed to the correspondingly weak Perron.

---

**SINGAPORE** official name **Republic of Singapore**

A republic at the southern tip of the Malay Peninsula, South-East Asia. It consists of the island of Singapore (linked to Malaysia by a causeway and a bridge) and about 50 adjacent islets. Originally part of the Sumatran Srivijaya kingdom, in 1819 it was leased by the British **EAST INDIA COMPANY**, on the advice of Sir Stamford **RAFFLES**, from the Sultan of Johore. Singapore, Malacca and Penang were incorporated as the Straits Settlements in 1826; they became a British Crown Colony in 1867, and were occupied by the Japanese during **WORLD WAR II**. Self-government was established in Singapore in 1959, led by **LEE KUAN YEW** who became Prime Minister in 1965, and it was part of the Federation of Malaya from 1963 until it withdrew and became an independent state in 1965. The People's Action Party has dominated politics since independence. After 25 years' service, Lee Kuan Yew resigned as Prime Minister in 1990 and was succeeded by Goh Chok Tong. In 2004 Lee Kuan Yew's son, Lee Hsien Loong, became Prime Minister.

## Singh, Charan (1902–87)

Indian politician. Born into a poor peasant family in Meerut District, Uttar Pradesh, he obtained a law degree in 1925. He started practising law in Ghaziabad, and soon became involved in the freedom movement. He courted arrest in the Salt **SATYAGRAHA** in 1932. In 1929 he joined the Congress, and was elected to the Uttar Pradesh Legislative Assembly in 1937, going on to represent his constituency for 40 years until 1977, when he was elected for the Lok Sabha (federal parliament). He joined both the **NON-COOPERATION MOVEMENT** and **QUIT INDIA MOVEMENT** in 1940. He was Chief Minister of Uttar Pradesh twice, and in 1969 formed the ministry of *Bharatiya Kranti Dal* (BKD). Charan Singh's *Bharatiya Lok Dal* revolted against Morarji **DESAI**'s 28-month-old Janata government and he was sworn in as the fifth Prime Minister of India in July 1979. He served in this capacity until the Congress (I) Party won the general elections in 1980.

### Singh, V(ishwanath) P(ratap) (1931– )
Indian politician. The son of an influential Raja in Uttar Pradesh, he was educated at Pune and Allahabad universities and was elected (1971) to the Lok Sabha (federal parliament) as a representative of the Congress (I) Party. During the administrations of Indira GANDHI and Rajiv GANDHI, he served as Minister of Commerce (1976–7 and 1983), Chief Minister of Uttar Pradesh (1980–2), Minister of Finance (1984–6) and Minister of Defence (1986–7), instigating a zealous anti-corruption drive in the finance and defence posts. In 1987 he was ousted from the government and Congress (I) when he unearthed the 'Bofors Scandal', which involved the payment of alleged arms deal 'kickbacks' to senior officials closely connected to Rajiv Gandhi. Respected for his probity and sense of principle, as head of the broad-based JANATA DAL coalition he emerged as the most popular opposition politician in India. He was elected Prime Minister in 1990, but in Nov that year he was defeated on a vote of confidence and was succeeded by Chandra Shekhar.

### Sinhala
A language of North Indian origin. The speakers of the language, the Sinhala or Sinhalese, form the largest group in the population of Sri Lanka and have dominated the country's politics since independence in 1948. Most Sinhala people are Buddhists and modern Buddhist nationalists believe that the Buddha himself entrusted the care of the island to the Sinhala people as custodians of his teaching. The election of S W R D BANDARANAIKE in 1956, with a promise to make Sinhala the sole language used in government, led to opposition from the country's predominantly Hindu TAMIL minority, which has continued ever since.

### Sinn Féin
Irish political party (literally, 'We Ourselves') which developed during the period 1905–8 under the direction of Arthur GRIFFITH in support of Irish independence from Britain. By the end of WORLD WAR I it had become the main Irish nationalist party. In the 1918 election, 73 of its candidates were elected to the UK parliament but refused to take their seats, instead setting up the DÁIL EIREANN in Dublin and declaring an Irish republic. Following the Anglo-Irish Treaty (1921), it split to form the two main Irish parties, and in 1970 it split again into official and provisional wings. As the political wing of the Provisional IRA, it has remained active in Northern Ireland, supported by hardline Irish nationalists. Following the peace initiative, in 1994 its President Gerry ADAMS announced an IRA ceasefire. This was broken in Feb 1996 and it was excluded from talks in 1996, but following a new ceasefire in 1997 was allowed to participate in the multiparty talks that resulted in the 1998 GOOD FRIDAY AGREEMENT. In the 1998 elections to the Northern Ireland Assembly it won 24 seats, retaining this number in 2003, but the activities of some supporters (STORMONTGATE) and the Provisional IRA's refusal to decommission weapons cast

doubt on the sincerity of its commitment to a peaceful settlement and led to the suspension of power-sharing in 2002. Its negotiating position in subsequent cross-party talks was undermined by the Provisional IRA's responsibility for a bank robbery in Dec 2004, which increased distrust of Sinn Féin and caused the British and Irish governments to harden their attitudes towards it. ➤ FIANNA FÁIL; FINE GAEL

### Sino-Japanese War (1894–5)
A long-standing conflict between Chinese and Japanese interests in Korea, which resulted in war during the Qing period. China suffered a humiliating defeat, and by the Treaty of SHIMONOSEKI (1895) recognized Korean independence and ceded Taiwan, the Liaodong Peninsula and the Pescadores to Japan.

### Sino-Japanese War (1937–45)
The war proper broke out in 1937 with the Japanese invasion of Tianjin (Tientsin) and Beijing, but this was only the ultimate phase of Japan's territorial designs on China. Manchuria had already been occupied (1931) and the puppet-state of MANZHUGUO created in 1932. Nanjing was invaded in Dec 1937, and most of northern China was soon under Japanese control. From Dec 1941, US intervention became the major factor in the PACIFIC WAR, which ended with Japan's surrender in 1945. ➤ UNITED FRONTS; WORLD WAR II

### Sino-Soviet Dispute (1960–89)
The period of extreme tension between the USSR and China, even leading to border war in 1969. STALIN had been a half-hearted supporter of the Chinese Communist Party; Nikita KHRUSHCHEV had subsequently been more generous; but both had been patronizing. MAO ZEDONG objected to being treated as inferior, and he had developed his own somewhat different brand of COMMUNISM. Ideological sparring led to Khrushchev withdrawing all Soviet assistance and advisers in 1960. Behind the border dispute also lay serious territorial differences. The situation only improved after DENG XIAOPING launched China on an outward-looking reform programme in 1978 and Mikhail GORBACHEV started his revolutionary upheaval in 1985. Their meeting in Beijing in 1989 signalled the end of the dispute, though internal developments in both countries have since renewed the strain. Moves were made to relieve the situation, however, and in 1997 the Presidents of China, Russia, Kazakhstan, Kyrgyzstan and Tajikistan met and signed an agreement to reduce the number of troops stationed along the border.

### Sioux
A cluster of Siouan-speaking Native North American groups belonging to the Plains culture. Having moved from further north into present-day north and south Dakota, they acquired horses, fought wars against other native groups, and hunted buffalo. They were later involved in clashes with advancing white settlers and prospectors, and were finally defeated at WOUNDED KNEE (1890). Their population in 2000 was c.108,500. ➤ DAKOTA; NATIVE AMERICANS

### Sipahi
Ottoman cavalryman. In return for service in the army, Sipahis drew their income from a grant of land, a TIMAR, which they held on a non-hereditary basis.

**Siraj ud-Daula**, originally **Mirza Muhammad** (c.1732–1757)
Nawab (Ruler) of Bengal under the nominal suzerainty of the **MUGHAL EMPIRE** (1756/7). He came into conflict with the British over their fortification of Calcutta, and marched on the city in 1756. The British surrender led to the infamous **BLACK HOLE OF CALCUTTA**, for which he was held responsible. Following the recapture of Calcutta, the British under **CLIVE OF PLASSEY** joined forces with Siraj ud-Daula's general, Mir Jafar, and defeated him at the Battle of **PLASSEY** in 1757. He fled to Murshidabad, but was captured and executed.

**Široký, Viliám** (1902–71)
Czechoslovak politician. As a young Slovak railway worker, he helped create the Communist Party in Bratislava in 1921 and by 1935 he was both a secretary of the Central Committee and a communist member of parliament. His experiences in **WORLD WAR II** included imprisonment in Slovakia and service in Moscow. Široký's subsequent rise made him Deputy Prime Minister (1945–53), Foreign Minister (1950–3), following the executed **CLEMENTIS**, and Prime Minister (1953–63), in succession to **ZÁPOTOCKÝ**. He survived the purges, but his bureaucratic credentials were inadequate to cope with the transitional needs of the late 1950s/early 1960s and he was dropped in favour of another Slovak, **LENART**, whose supposed reform credentials achieved little more.

**Sistova, Peace of** (1791)
The peace established between the Habsburg and the Ottoman Empires at Sistova on the borders of modern Bulgaria and Romania. Emperor **LEOPOLD II**, eager to end the war begun by his brother, **JOSEPH II**, agreed to return Belgrade to the Turks in exchange for modest gains in Bosnia. ► **HABSBURG DYNASTY**; **OTTOMAN EMPIRE**

**Sisulu, Walter Max Ulyate** (1912–2003)
South African nationalist. After working as a labourer in Johannesburg and then running his own real estate agency, he joined the **ANC** in 1940, becoming Treasurer of the Youth League in 1944. A leader of the Programme of Action in 1949, he was elected Secretary-General of the ANC in the same year. He resigned his post in 1954 because of banning orders, but continued to work underground. Sisulu was captured in 1963 and, found guilty of treason, was sentenced in 1964 to life imprisonment. He was released in 1989 and took responsibility for the party's internal organization after its legalization in 1990. He was Deputy President of the ANC from 1991 to 1994.

**Sithole, Ndabaningi** (1920–2000)
Zimbabwean cleric and politician. He worked as a teacher (1941–53) before going to the USA to study theology (1953–6) and was ordained a Congregational minister in 1958. He wrote *African Nationalism* in 1959, when he was also President of the African Teachers' Union. Sithole was Treasurer of the National Democratic Party in 1960 and, after it was banned, formed with Joshua **NKOMO** the Zimbabwe African People's Union (**ZAPU**), from which he split in 1963 and formed the Zimbabwe African National Union (**ZANU**). Imprisoned by the Rhodesian Front government from 1964 to 1975, during which time the lea-

dership of ZANU was wrested from him by Robert **MUGABE**, he went into exile in Zambia in 1975, forming his own faction of the **AFRICAN NATIONAL COUNCIL**. He negotiated with Ian **SMITH** and was a member of the Executive Council of the transitional government in Rhodesia-Zimbabwe (1978–80). Although he was elected to the first post-independence parliament, he ceased thereafter to play a major role in politics.

**sitiante**
The Spanish term used to describe a South American small-scale livestock or mixed farm. In the interior of north-eastern Brazil, it denotes an estate usually devoted to stockraising as its primary economic activity. *Sitiantes* in the southern states commonly cultivated cash crops, but historically employed a few slaves and engaged in subsistence agriculture, such as planting beans, manioc or maize. Sitiantes normally made up the following of local *coroneis* or *fazendeiros*, who often controlled credit and communications. In the Planalto and south, small-scale proprietors were known as *lavradores* or *camponeses* ('peasants'). By the mid 1960s, such lands had been subdivided to such an extent that they could not support the families of their owners. ► **FAZENDEIRO**

**Sitting Bull**, Sioux name **Tatanka Iyotake** (c.1834–1890)
Native American warrior. The chief of the **DAKOTA** Sioux, he was a leader in the **SIOUX** War of 1876–7. He is remembered especially for his role in the Battle of the **LITTLE BIGHORN**, following which he escaped to Canada, but surrendered in 1881. After touring with Buffalo Bill's Wild West Show, he returned to his people, and was present in 1890 when the army suppressed the '**GHOST DANCE**' messianic religious movement inspired by the Paiute leader **WOVOKA**. Sitting Bull was killed during the army's action. ► **CODY, WILLIAM F**; **INDIAN WARS**; **NATIVE AMERICANS**

**Six-Day War** (5–10 June 1967)
Arab–Israeli war. In May 1967 President Gamal Abd al-**NASSER** of Egypt blocked the Tiran Straits to Israeli shipping and massed troops in the Sinai Peninsula, while King **HUSSEIN** allowed Iraqi forces into Jordan. Taking preemptive action, Israel paralyzed the Egyptian air force and then, responding to Jordanian and Syrian attacks, captured East Jerusalem, the **WEST BANK**, Golan Heights and Sinai. Israel's unexpected victory was achieved in six days. Afterwards, Arab states refused to negotiate peace with Israel, which has therefore held on to the so-called 'occupied territories', except Sinai which was returned to Egypt after the peace agreement of 1979. ► **ARAB–ISRAELI WARS**; **ISRAEL**; **SHARON, ARIEL**

**Sixtus IV**, originally **Francesco della Rovere** (1414–84)
Italian pope (1471/84). A Genoese, he became a renowned Franciscan preacher, and was made a cardinal in 1467. His was a worldly pontificate. He fostered learning and built the Sistine Chapel, but his nepotism led to many abuses. He lowered the moral authority of the papacy, especially through his involvement in the Pazzi conspiracy against the **MEDICI** in Florence in 1478, and his sale of indulgences. ► **FRANCISCANS**

**Sixtus V**, originally **Felice Peretti** (1521–90)
Italian pope (1585/90). Elected for his apparent feebleness, his rule proved vigorously reformist. He repressed licence and disorder, reformed the law and the disposal of patronage, and secured a surplus for the treasury. A fierce opponent of Protestantism, he extended a measure of liberty to the Jews. He also instigated the building of the Vatican Library at the Lateran Palace.

**Skanderbeg**, originally **George Kastrioti** (1405–68)
Albanian patriot, of Serb descent. Carried away by Ottoman Turks at the age of seven, he was brought up a Muslim, and became a favourite commander of Sultan **MURAD II**, who gave him his byname, a combination of *Iskander* ('Alexander') and the rank of bey. In 1443 he changed sides, renounced Islam, and drove the Turks from Albania. For 20 years he maintained Albanian independence, but after his death, opposition to the Turks collapsed.

**Skobeleff, Mikhail Dmitriyevich** (1843–82)
Russian soldier. He fought against the Polish insurgents (1863), and from 1871 to 1875 was at the conquest of Khiva and Khokland. In the Russo-Turkish War of 1877–78 he played a conspicuous part at Plevna, in the Shipka Pass, and at Adrianople; in 1881 he stormed the Turcoman stronghold of Göktepe. He was an ardent Pan-Slavist. ► **RUSSO-TURKISH WARS**

**Skobtsova, Maria** (1891–1945)
Russian Orthodox nun. She early identified herself with the Social Revolutionaries when a student in St Petersburg, where she was the first woman to enrol at the Ecclesiastical Academy. Bolshevik excesses having disillusioned her, she was among those who escaped to France. She began work with the Russian Orthodox Student Christian Movement, which administered also to refugees, and in 1932, despite having had two divorces, became a nun. Unconventional and radical, she worked among society's cast-offs whom she fed and housed. Nazi measures against the Jews in wartime Paris provided a new challenge. She was arrested and sent to Ravensbrück **CONCENTRATION CAMP** in 1943, where she brought Christian light and hope despite appalling conditions. She was gassed on the eve of Easter 1945, reportedly going voluntarily 'in order to help her companions to die'.

**Skúli Magnússon** ► **MAGNÚSSON, SKÚLI**

**Slankamen, Battle of** (20 Aug 1691)
This battle, fought between the Ottoman army under Mustafa **KÖPRÜLÜ** and Habsburg forces under Louis of Baden, resulted in the ambush and defeat of the Ottomans and the death of Mustafa. His expedition had been aimed at reversing the Ottoman failures of the previous decade in Hungary and the Balkans by carrying Ottoman arms into Hungary, and the defeat was significant in that, since the Habsburgs were preoccupied by affairs in the west and since the Ottoman advance had been halted by the battle, the Danube became established as the boundary between the Ottoman and Habsburg Empires. ► **HABSBURG DYNASTY; OTTOMAN EMPIRE**

**Slánský, Rudolf** (1901–52)
Czechoslovak politician. Born in Moravia, an intellectual, he joined the Communist Party when it was founded in 1921 and, in 1929, became one of Klement **GOTTWALD**'s chief aides in revolutionizing or 'bolshevizing' it. He spent much of **WORLD WAR II** in Moscow but in 1944 was flown in to assist the Slovak uprising. From 1945 to 1951 he held the most important party post as Secretary-General, masterminding much of what produced and followed the **FEBRUARY REVOLUTION** in 1948. However, he was arrested, then executed during the purges, a victim of **STALIN**'s dislike of independent-minded communists, especially Jewish intellectuals. It was little comfort to the majority of his countrymen that he suffered the self-same fate he had imposed on others.

**Slave Rebellions**
The normal slave response to bondage was indirect resistance through sham illness, non-cooperation, vandalism and maroonage but when driven to extremes by white brutality or unfulfilled expectations, such as the **AMELIORATION** proposals of 1823 in the British West Indies, outright rebellion erupted. There were major slave uprisings in Cuba virtually every ten years from 1792 to 1844, and in Jamaica from 1655 to 1831; indeed, these were commonplace in almost every Caribbean colony. The only successful revolt was the Haitian Revolution of 1791, but the rebellion of Cuffy in Berbice (1763) came near to triumph and the revolt of Sam Sharpe in Jamaica (1831) seriously frightened the Jamaican plantocracy.

**Slavery** ► *See panel*

**Slavonia** ► CROATIA

**Slavonic Congresses** (1848, 1868 and 1908)
The series of meetings of Slav delegates in Prague, aimed at showing the unity of the Slav peoples in their struggles against other ethnic ruling groups. The Czechs were probably the least self-centred of the Slav peoples, but they also had local anti-Austrian and anti-German reasons for calling the congresses. The first congress was organized by František **PALACKÝ**, the second was addressed by him, and the third was summoned by **KRAMAR**. All of them drummed up general sentiments of solidarity, but showed evidence of international divisions. In Czech terms, the first two were the more successful in strengthening national feeling; the third, however, was too much dedicated to Kramar's personal political views.

**Slavophils and Westerners**
Opposing schools of thought in Russia during the 1840s. The Westerners argued that backward Russia should emulate the political, legal, scientific and rational traditions of Western Europe. The Slavophils believed in the superior quality of traditional Russian religious and social values, including Orthodox worship, a benevolent autocracy, and social and spiritual community (*sobornost*).

**Slavs**
The largest group of European peoples sharing a common ethnic and linguistic origin, consisting of Russians, Ukrainians, Belorussians, Poles, Czechs, Slovaks, Bulgarians, Serbs, Croats, Montenegrins and Macedonians. The ancient Slavs, inhabiting central and Eastern Europe, were first mentioned in 2c AD sources. After **WORLD WAR II**, most of the Slav nations

# Slavery

Culture & Society

### Slavery in ancient times

Slavery probably dates from prehistoric times, and all ancient
civilizations used slaves. Slavery is recorded in China from the time of the
Shang Dynasty, and in ancient Egypt, Mesopotamia and India, as well as among the Aztecs and Incas in pre-Columbian
America. Slaves were obtained through the enslavement of peoples conquered in war (the word 'slave' derives from the
medieval Latin word 'sclavus', meaning a Slavonic captive, conquered **Slavs** from Eastern Europe forming a large
proportion of the slave population in the early **Middle Ages**), as a punishment for crime, through the voluntary self-
enslavement of individuals or families for debt, or by trade. Though slave populations eventually became self-
reproducing, there was usually a demand for fresh supplies from outside. All but the poorest of families in ancient
Greece owned at least one slave. In fact slaves were something of a luxury consumer item, the possession of one creating
the demand for more.

Slaves were generally employed in two distinct spheres: as household servants or in large-scale industrial or
construction projects, such as the building of pyramids and royal palaces of ancient Egypt. The treatment and conditions
of the former were very much better than those of the latter. Excavations at the Laurium silver mines near Athens have
shown the appalling conditions in which gangs of slaves were compelled to work underground. Slaves in ancient Greece
and Rome also worked as craftsmen, agricultural labourers, oarsmen in galleys, and in some instances as tutors to
children. The economy of ancient Rome was heavily dependent on slave labour and this dependence is thought to have
contributed substantially to the empire's eventual decline.

The coming of Christianity improved conditions for slaves to some extent, but by no means eliminated the
institution. In the **Domesday Book**, 10 per cent of the population of England are recorded as slaves. Islam recognized
the existence of slavery, and Muhammad commanded his followers to treat their slaves well.

### The slave trade

The trade in African slaves began in ancient times. Slaves were sent across the Sahara to be traded in the Mediterranean
by Phoenicians, while Graeco-Roman traders in the Red Sea and beyond traded slaves from East Africa to Egypt and the
Middle East. The advent of the European age of exploration in the 15c added a new dimension to the trade. The
Portuguese exploring the western coast of Africa discovered a plentiful source of slaves, while at the end of the century
Christopher **Columbus** discovered what was to become the main market for them. During roughly the same period,
Arab traders and explorers sailing along the eastern coast of Africa and penetrating into central Africa from the east and
north supplied markets in India, Arabia and Iran. The Islamic slave trade always had a large white as well as a black
element. White slaves were drawn from European prisoners of war (especially in North Africa), and from the Black Sea
and Caucasus mountain areas (especially in the Ottoman dominions).

Throughout the ensuing three centuries, European nations vied and fought for control of the lucrative trade of
supplying slaves to the labour-intensive plantations in the West African islands of São Tomé and Príncipe; the Spanish
and Portuguese colonies in South America; the Caribbean; and the southern colonies of North America, following the
development of the plantation system there too from the second half of the 17c. The Portuguese dominated the trade in
the 16c, the Dutch in the early 17c, while the late 17c saw a period of intense competition as the French, British, Danes
and Swedes joined in. The trade reached its peak in the second half of the 18c. A typical voyage for a British ship would
involve a triangular course; south to the slave coast of West Africa to pick up a cargo of slaves who were transported
across the Atlantic in the most appalling conditions to the West Indies or the North American colonies, from where
sugar, cotton, tobacco or similar commodities would be shipped home. Abolition in the early 1800s effectively stopped
the Atlantic trade, but the East African trade continued until the middle of the 19c and beyond, especially during the
period of Omani power up to the 1860s.

Estimates vary concerning the number of slaves removed from Africa, the most reliable figure being around 12.5
million between 1650 and 1850. Many other people must have lost their lives in the wars stimulated by the trade, and the
total drain meant that at the very least the African population remained static for over two centuries.

### Abolition

The movement for the abolition of the slave trade and of slavery itself began, for practical purposes, in the 18c. The ideals
of the **Enlightenment**, as set forth, for example, in the American Declaration of Independence, were essentially
incompatible with the existence of slavery as an institution, though this was by no means evident to all Americans. The
Quakers had always opposed slavery. Evangelical Christianity inspired the 'Clapham Sect' in Britain, whose members
included Thomas **Clarkson**, James Stephen, Sir Thomas Fowell Buxton and, most famously, William **Wilberforce**, to
found in 1787 the Society for Effecting the Abolition of the Slave Trade. Wilberforce, MP for Hull, led the campaign in

---

were ruled by socialist governments imposed by the
Soviet Union, but with its collapse they have developed pluralistic political systems.

### SLFP (Sri Lanka Freedom Party)

Left-of-centre Sri Lankan political party formed by S
W R D **BANDARANAIKE** after his departure from the
UNP in 1951. The SLFP formed the largest party in
government in 1956–9, 1960–5 and 1970–7. Each
time, the party achieved power as leader of a coalition
formed with smaller left-wing parties, and each time
the coalition was undermined by internal friction and

gradual defections to the opposition. The leadership
of the party has been dominated by Bandaranaike, his
widow, Sirimavo **BANDARANAIKE**, and their children
and close relatives. In 1994 their daughter Chandrika
Bandaranaike **KUMARATUNGA**, as leader of the nine-
party People's Alliance, a coalition that included the
SLFP, was elected first Prime Minister and then President of Sri Lanka, thus ending the 17-year rule of the
United National Party (UNP). In the 2004 parliamentary elections the SLFP formed part of the United
People's Freedom Alliance, which won a majority of
seats.

parliament. Lacking support from Pitt's Tory administration, Wilberforce had to wait for the change of government in 1806, which brought Charles James **Fox** and the **Whigs** into power, to get his bill through. It became law in 1807 and the last British slave trader, the *Kitty Amelia*, left Liverpool in 1808. To Denmark, however, belongs the honour of being the first country to abolish the trade, which it did in 1804. The USA closely followed Britain, abolishing the trade in 1808. France abolished it in 1818 and Spain in 1820. British naval squadrons patrolled the coasts of West and East Africa to enforce the ban.

The abolition of slavery itself took most of the rest of the century. Slavery was officially ended in Britain and its territories one month after Wilberforce's death in 1833, and in France in 1845. In Brazil it was not abolished until 1888. In the USA, the existence of slavery in the Southern states and its integration into their culture and economy was a cause of contention throughout the first half of the 19c and one of the main causes of the **American Civil War**. Measures such as the **Missouri Compromise** of 1820 helped to keep the Union together uneasily for a time, but the election of the anti-slavery Republican candidate Abraham **Lincoln** to the presidency led to the secession of the Southern states and to war. In the course of the war, Lincoln issued in 1863 an **Emancipation Proclamation** that spelled the doom of the South's 'peculiar institution', and victory for the North led to the ratification of the 13th Amendment abolishing slavery throughout the United States in 1865.

### Slave revolts

Slaves throughout history periodically attempted to free themselves by rising up against their masters. Slaves were sometimes feared, especially when, like the *helots* of Sparta, they outnumbered the ruling class. The most famous slave revolt of ancient times was led by the Roman gladiator Spartacus, who in 73 BC defeated several Roman armies and caused havoc throughout large parts of Italy before being defeated in his turn and crucified along with large numbers of his followers. The most successful slave revolt of modern times was at the same time a war of national independence. **Toussaint L'Ouverture** was the best-known figure in a revolt against the French colonial regime in the island of Santo Domingo which led to the establishment of the republic of Haiti.

### African settlements for freed slaves

Two colonies were set up in Africa for liberated slaves: Sierra Leone and Liberia. In 1787 the British established a colony in Freetown which, first administered by the Sierra Leone company, became a Crown Colony in 1808 and achieved independence in 1961. Under the auspices of the **American Colonization Society**, the first settlement was established in Liberia in 1821 and the country became an independent republic in 1847.

### Slavery in the 20c

The **League of Nations** promulgated the International Slavery Convention in 1926, finally prohibiting slavery and the slave trade worldwide. Slavery in its old form can be declared with some confidence to be no longer in existence. Forms of servitude akin to slavery are far less certain to have been eradicated entirely, though these are subject to a Supplementary Convention of 1956 and to action in the **International Court of Justice**. The people, especially black and white people, whose relationship in the past was largely defined by slavery, have still not, however, altogether succeeded in coming to terms with its legacy.

International Slavery Convention promulgated — 1926

1865 — the USA abolishes slavery

slavery is abolished in the British Empire — 1833

1823 — establishment of the Anti-Slavery Society

Britain abolishes the slave trade — 1807

1804 — Denmark abolishes the slave trade

slave revolution in Haiti achieves independence — 1791–1804

1787 — establishment of the Society for Effecting the Abolition of the Slave Trade

European colonists establish plantations in the Americas and import slave labour — 16c

---

**Slim, William Joseph Slim, 1st Viscount** (1891–1970)

British field marshal. He served during **WORLD WAR I** in the **GALLIPOLI CAMPAIGN** and in Mesopotamia. In **WORLD WAR II**, his greatest achievement was to lead his reorganized forces, the famous 14th 'forgotten' army, to victory over the Japanese in Burma (now Myanmar). He was Chief of the Imperial General Staff (1948–52) and a highly successful Governor-General of Australia (1953–60). Knighted in 1944, he became a viscount in 1960.

**Slingelandt, Simon van** (1664–1736)

Dutch politician and political thinker. From 1690 to 1725 he was Secretary to the Council of State, then became Thesaurier-General to the republic, and in 1757 **GRAND PENSIONARY** of the Province of Holland. He believed firmly that the Dutch Republic should have a much stronger central authority, which he suggested could be vested in the Council of State. His best chance of achieving this programme was at the Great Meeting held in 1716 on the structure of the republic; however, the particularism of the provinces carried the day. His works were admired in the 1780s by members of the **PATRIOT MOVE-MENT**.

**SLOVAKIA** official name **Slovak Republic**
A landlocked republic in eastern Europe, bounded to the north by Poland; to the east by the Ukraine; to the south by Hungary; to the south-west by Austria; and to the west by the Czech Republic. It formed part of Great Moravia in the 9c, belonged to the Magyar Empire from the 10c, and from 1918 to 1993 formed part of Czechoslovakia. A Slovak national movement gradually grew up during the 19c and 20c, and was dependent on support from US Slovaks, through the **PITTSBURGH AGREEMENT**, and from **MASARYK** and **STEFANIK**. Slovakia finally managed to break away from Hungarian rule when the Austro-Hungarian Empire collapsed after **WORLD WAR I**. It became a province of Czechoslovakia in 1918, but many Slovaks (not only the nationalists) had genuine complaints – the Czechs had established a centralized state in 1918, were less devoutly Catholic and were economically better off – and in 1939, on **HITLER**'s instructions, a supposedly independent republic under German protection was carved out of Czechoslovakia. However, those who led the new republic (such as **TISO** and **TUKA**) soon lost popularity as the Germans exploited the Slovak economy and expected Slovaks to fight on the hated Russian front. Resistance produced the **SLOVAK UPRISING** in 1944. Although it was put down by the Germans, their presence and brutality simply recruited more volunteers to fight against them and Tiso. Little was done after 1945 to meet legitimate Slovak aspirations, but with the collapse of the communist regime in Czechoslovakia in 1990, nationalist demands intensified again. In Jan 1993 Slovakia finally gained its independence under President Michal Kováč. The Movement for a Democratic Slovakia (HZDS) dominated the coalition governments that held office in the early 1990s, but the centre-right coalition that came to power in 1998 and was re-elected in 2002 introduced the constitutional and economic reforms required for **NATO** and **EU** membership, both of which Slovakia achieved in 2004.

**Slovak Uprising** (Sep–Oct 1944)
A rising against **TISO**, President of the Slovak Republic, and his German masters. The rebels comprised partisans, civilians, Allied helpers and insurgent regiments from the Slovak army. Their aim was to free eastern Slovakia as the **RED ARMY** advanced and to block German reinforcements. For two months they held a large area around Banska Bystrice. But the Germans moved quickly, the Russians slowly, and there were divided counsels. Despite great heroism, the rising was put down. Many fighters escaped to the

mountains; inevitably the civilians suffered. The Slovaks gained little except an important historical memory.

**SLOVENIA** official name **Republic of Slovenia**

A mountainous republic in central Europe, bounded to the north by Austria; to the west by Italy; to the south by Croatia; and to the east by Hungary. Settled by Slovenians in the 6c, it was later controlled by **SLAVS** and **FRANKS** and was part of the Austro-Hungarian Empire until 1918 when it joined with Croatia, Montenegro, Serbia and Bosnia and Herzegovina to form the Kingdom of Serbs, Croats and Slovenes. This was renamed Yugoslavia in 1929 and became a communist republic in 1946. In July 1991, President Milan **KUČAN** declared the Republic's independence from the Yugoslav Federation. The Yugoslav National Army invaded but, after the so-called 'Ten-Day War', Serbia's President **MILOŠEVIĆ** acknowledged Slovenia's independence in the vain hope that he could arrest the secession of the republics of Croatia and Bosnia and Herzegovina. The Liberal Democracy of Slovenia party has been the major party in every government, all coalitions, since 1991. Slovenia joined **NATO** and the **EC** in 2004.

**Slovo, Joe** (1926–95)
South African nationalist. Born in Lithuania, he emigrated to South Africa in 1935, where he worked as a clerk before volunteering for service in **WORLD WAR II**. After joining the South African Communist Party (SACP), he qualified as a lawyer and defended many figures in political trials. He married Ruth First, daughter of the SACP Treasurer, and was a founding member of the Congress of Democrats in 1953. Charged in the treason trial of 1961, he nevertheless escaped the country in 1963, working for the **ANC** and SACP abroad. In 1985 he became Chief of Staff of **UMKHONTO WE SIZWE** but resigned to become General Secretary (1986–91) and later Chairman (1991–5) of the SACP. He returned to South Africa after the legalization of the SACP and was a major figure in the negotiations between the nationalist parties and the government. The first white member of the ANC's National Executive (from 1986), he was appointed Minister of Housing in 1994. When he died his dedication to the cause of black liberation was posthumously rewarded with a state funeral.

**Sluys, Battle of** (1340)
A naval battle fought in the Zwyn estuary in Flanders, the first major English victory in the **HUNDRED YEARS' WAR**. **EDWARD III**, King of England, personally commanded the English fleet, which wiped out or captured all but 24 of 200 French ships. However, he

failed to follow up his victory, either on land or sea.

**Smalls, Robert** (1839–1915)
US sailor and politician. A slave in Charleston, South Carolina, who with his brother shanghaied a Confederate paddle steamer, the *Planter*, and sailed it through Confederate guns to the Union fleet blockading the port. Later he enlisted as a pilot in the Union Navy. Smalls was one of the 200,000 blacks who crossed to the Union lines and served as spies and guides in unfamiliar territory, as well as working as labourers. After the war his military service provided a springboard for a local political career in South Carolina, in the course of which he served in the **HOUSE OF REPRESENTATIVES**.

**Smeral, Bohumir** (1880–1941)
Czechoslovak politician. A lawyer, he joined the Social Democratic Party in 1897 and was editing its paper by 1906. During **WORLD WAR I** he was slow to join the struggle for Czechoslovak independence, and following the 1917 **RUSSIAN REVOLUTION** his loyalty swung increasingly towards the left. In 1921 he helped found the Communist Party and became very active in Czechoslovak politics in the 1920s. In the 1930s he was also very active in the **COMINTERN**, which involved much travelling. Although he fled to Moscow in 1938 and died there, he was never a Stalinist, preserving some traces of his social democratic moderation. ➤ **STALINISM**

**Smirnov, Georgi Lukich** (1922–)
Soviet communist ideologue. Of Cossack stock with a long career in the Communist Party bureaucracy, he became adviser to Mikhail **GORBACHEV** in 1985 and Director of the Institute of **MARXISM–LENINISM** in 1987. In both positions he attempted to modify Brezhnevite orthodoxy; he was still trying, with only moderate success, when the party was closed down in 1991.

**Smith, Adam** (1723–90)
Scottish economist and philosopher. He was born in Kirkcaldy, Fife, and became Professor of Logic at Glasgow in 1751, and Professor of Moral Philosophy the following year. In 1776 he published *An Inquiry into the Nature and Causes of the Wealth of Nations*, a textbook of political economy. This superseded previous works by political economists like his rival Sir James Steuart. Smith was influenced by French political economists known as the **PHYSIOCRATS**. His work accepts a structured society led by a leisured aristocracy, whom alone he thought fit to rule. He is suspicious of businessmen, advocating freer markets and freer trade as a way of disciplining them by competition. Neither the inventor of economics, nor a major influence in his lifetime, he became an icon for businessmen and free-market economists in the 19–20c. After 1778 he was a Commissioner of Customs in Edinburgh.

**Smith, Alfred Emanuel** (1873–1944)
US politician. He rose from newsboy to be Governor of New York State (1919–20 and 1923–8) with an impressive record of liberal reform. 'Al' Smith was beaten as Democratic candidate for the US presidency in 1928, and later became an opponent of President Franklin D **ROOSEVELT**'s **NEW DEAL**.

**Smith, Goldwin** (1823–1910)
Canadian publicist. Regius Professor of Modern History at Oxford (1858–66), he settled permanently in Canada in 1871, and founded a chair of history at Toronto. He became one of the major figures in **CANADA FIRST**, and in *Canada and the Canadian Question* (1891) he argued for the union of Canada with the USA.

**Smith, Ian Douglas** (1919–)
Rhodesian politician and farmer. Educated at Chaplin High School and Rhodes University, he served with the Royal Air Force in **WORLD WAR II** before returning to his farm. He was elected a member of the Southern Rhodesian Legislative Assembly in 1948 for the United Party and then, for the United Federal Party (UFP), to the Federal Parliament in 1953, becoming Chief Whip. He broke with the UFP, ostensibly on the question of Britain's failure to grant independence to the white minority-ruled states of central Africa, and helped found the **RHODESIAN FRONT** in 1962. He replaced Winston Field as leader after a putsch and was Prime Minister from 1964 to 1978, when he became a member of the Executive Council of the transitional government in Zimbabwe-Rhodesia. A cautious and secretive man, he declared **UDI** (Unilateral Declaration of Independence) in 1965, negotiated without success with successive British governments and was immensely popular with his white voters. He was elected to the post-independence parliament and remained a vigorous opponent of Robert **MUGABE** and his government.

**Smith, Jedediah Strong** (1799–1831)
US fur-trader and explorer. Born in Jericho, New York, he went to St Louis to trade furs, and undertook two major explorations in the far south-west of North America between 1823 and 1830, covering more than 16,000 mi/25,760 km, first in the Central Rockies and Columbia River areas, trapping and providing intelligence on the activities of the **HUDSON'S BAY COMPANY**. He later became the first white man to reach California overland across the Sierra Nevada Mountains and Great Basin to the Pacific Ocean. He was killed by Comanches while leading a wagon train to Santa Fé.

**Smith, John** (1580–1631)
English colonist and explorer. He fought in Transylvania and Hungary, where he was captured by the Turks, and sold as a slave. After escaping to Russia, he joined an expedition to colonize Virginia (1607), and helped found **JAMESTOWN**. He was saved from death by **POCAHONTAS**. His energy and tact in dealing with the Indians led to his being elected President of the colony (1608–9). He wrote valuable accounts of his travels, and died in London.

**Smith, Joseph** (1805–44)
US religious leader, regarded as the founder of the **MORMONS**. Born in Sharon, Vermont, he received his first 'call' as a prophet in 1820. In 1823 he claimed that an angel told him of a hidden gospel written on golden plates, and in 1827 the sacred records were apparently delivered into his hands on a hill near Palmyra, New York. This, the so-called *Book of Mormon* (1830), contains a postulated history of America to the 5c of

the Christian era, claimed to have been written by a prophet named Mormon. Smith was to be the instrument of the Church's re-establishment, and despite ridicule and hostility, and sometimes open violence, 'the new Church of Jesus Christ of Latter-day Saints' (founded in 1830) rapidly gained converts. In 1831 it established its headquarters at Kirtland, Ohio, and built Zion in Missouri. Hostility became intense, and in 1838 a general uprising took place in Missouri against the Mormons. In 1840 they moved to Illinois, and within three years the Mormons there numbered 20,000. He was shot dead by a mob who broke into Carthage jail, where he was under arrest on charges of conspiracy. ► YOUNG, BRIGHAM

**Smrkovsky, Josef** (1911–74)
Czechoslovak politician. A baker's assistant, he joined the Communist Party in 1933 and was active in the resistance during WORLD WAR II. He was one of the leaders of the Prague rising in 1945 and held a series of party and government posts until, in 1951, he was imprisoned during the Stalinist purges. It was 1963 before he was rehabilitated and 1966 before he was readmitted to the party. In 1967–8 he was a prime mover in the reforms and became a popular chairman of parliament. His very moderation made him a Soviet target, and like Alexander DUBČEK he was taken to Moscow in Aug 1968 and then removed from power at the first opportunity the following year.

**Smuts, Jan Christian** (1870–1950)
South African general and politician. Educated at the University of Cambridge, England, he became a lawyer, fought in the second Boer War (1899–1902), and entered the House of Assembly in 1907. He held several Cabinet posts, led campaigns against the Germans in South West Africa and Tanganyika, was a member of the Imperial War Cabinet in WORLD WAR I, and succeeded Louis BOTHA as Prime Minister (1919–24). He was a significant figure at Versailles, and was instrumental in the founding of the LEAGUE OF NATIONS. As Minister of Justice under HERTZOG, his coalition with the Nationalists in 1934 produced the United Party; he was Premier again from 1939 to 1948. ► BOER WARS

**Snamek, Jan** (1870–1956)
Czechoslovak politician. Born and educated in Moravia, he was variously a priest, professor of theology and papal negotiator, and helped found Christian democracy in the late 1890s. A deputy from 1907, he supported MASARYK during WORLD WAR I and, as leader of the Populist Party in the interwar period, held several ministerial appointments. During WORLD WAR II he was Prime Minister in BENEŠ's government-in-exile in London, and Deputy Prime Minister (1945–8) in the National Front government. Usually a moderate, he nevertheless joined those resigning in 1948 and precipitating the FEBRUARY REVOLUTION. The middle road had not been easy and it became impossible under COMMUNISM.

**Snorri Sturluson** ► STURLUSON, SNORRI

**Soares, Mário Alberto Nobre Lopes** (1924– )
Portuguese politician. Educated at Lisbon University and in the Faculty of Law at the Sorbonne, Paris, he was politically active in the democratic socialist movement from his early twenties and was imprisoned for his activities on twelve occasions. In 1968 he was deported by SALAZAR to São Tomé, returning to Europe in 1970 and living in exile in Paris until 1974 when he returned to co-found the Social Democratic Party (PSD). In the same year he was elected to the Assembly and was soon brought into the government. He was Prime Minister (1976–8 and 1983–5), and then in 1986 was elected Portugal's first civilian President for 60 years, a post he held until 1996.

**Sobchak, Anatoli Alexandrovich** (1937–2000)
Russian politician. A talented law graduate who became Dean of the Faculty of Law in Leningrad (now St Petersburg), long before turning to politics. In the GORBACHEV period he became critical of many past communist practices and was chosen in 1989 as a member of both the Congress of Deputies and the Supreme Soviet, where he demonstrated his investigative and debating skills. In May 1990 he was elected Mayor of St Petersburg, a post he held until 1996, and in July 1990 abandoned the Communist Party to become both locally and nationally one of the driving forces for serious reform.

**Sobhuza II** (1899–1982)
King of Swaziland. Educated at Lovedale College, he was installed as Paramount Chief or Ngwenyama of the Swazi people in 1921. He was head of state when Swaziland became independent in 1968, but in 1973 he assumed full executive and legislative powers and introduced a new Constitution in 1978 which re-established traditional authorities, rather than universal suffrage, as the basis of legitimate authority.

**Sobukwe, Robert** (1924–77)
South African nationalist leader. Educated at mission schools and Fort Hare College, he was President of the Students' Representative Council in 1949 and a member of the ANC Youth League. He was dismissed from his teacher's post in 1952 because of his participation in the Defiance Campaign, but taught for the next seven years at Fort Hare College. He helped found the PAN-AFRICANIST CONGRESS (PAC) in 1959 and was elected its President. He was banned in 1960 and then imprisoned until 1969 when he was released, but restricted to Kimberley where he died in 1977.

**Social and Liberal Democratic Party (SLDP)** ► LIBERAL PARTY (UK)

**Social Credit Party**
Canadian political party. The monetary theory known as social credit (regarded as nonsense by most economists) was developed by a British engineer, Major Clifford H Douglas, during the early 1930s. It held that government should issue payments (social credits) to everyone, in order to balance consumers' buying power with agricultural and manufacturing productivity. It attracted the attention of an Albertan radio-evangelist, William Aberhardt, who spread the doctrine to the depression-hit prairie farmers. In the provincial election of 1935, the Social Credit Party came to power. The federal government, however, disallowed its attempts to implement its policies, and in a short time the party became just another free enterprise neo-conservative political party. As such, it retained power and had cleared the province's

debts by the mid-1950s. In 1952 it also defeated the Liberal–Conservative coalition in British Columbia, and throughout the 1950s it grew in federal strength. By 1962 **DIEFENBAKER** required its support to maintain his fragile hold on power, but in 1979 it contributed to a Conservative defeat when Joe **CLARK** refused to bargain for its support in a vote of confidence. By the 1980s, however, the party had all but disappeared and it was formally dissolved in 1993. ► **CRÉDITISTES**

## Social Darwinism
A school of thought which developed within 19c sociology based on the belief that social evolution depended on society adapting most efficiently to its environment. The associated 'eugenics movement' argued that Western society had developed because of the superior abilities of whites compared with other 'racial' groups.

## Social Democratic Labour Party (*Socialdemokratiskar Arbetarparti*, SAP)
The party was founded in Stockholm in 1889. Under the leadership of Hjalmar **BRANTING**, who became its first parliamentary representative in 1896, it came to adopt a reformist programme and was the largest party in the directly elected chamber of the parliament by 1915. Social Democratic ministers sat in a coalition government with the Liberals in 1917, and Branting headed purely Social Democrat administrations in 1920–5. Under Per Albin **HANSSON**, Tage **ERLANDER** and Sven Olof **PALME** the Social Democrats enjoyed continuous power from 1932 to 1976 (except for a brief break in 1936) either alone or in coalition with the Agrarians, but only rarely have they enjoyed an overall majority. They returned to power in 1982–91 (led by Palme until 1986, then by Ingvar Carlsson), and from 1994 (led by Carlsson until 1996, then by Göran Persson).

## Social Democratic Party (Austria) ► SPÖ

## Social Democratic Party (Denmark)
Founded in 1871 as a section of the socialist First International, in 1878 it was divided into a trade union wing and a political party wing, which in 1884 for the first time became represented in the Danish parliament (**FOLKETINGET**). After the general election in 1924, the Social Democrats became the largest party in parliament and formed their first government, with Thorvald **STAUNING** as Premier. The party has remained Denmark's largest. During the interwar period the party, under Stauning's leadership, moved away from the socialist idea of a class struggle. Instead, it became the party's ambition to create a welfare state for all social groups through democratic, parliamentary reforms. This ambition was fulfilled during the post-war period under the party leaders Hedtoft, Hansen, Kampmann and **KRAG**, all of whom were also prime ministers. After 1973, when the Danish economy was hit by recession, the party, led by **JØRGENSEN** (1972–87) and Auken (1987–92), became the chief defender of the welfare system, from 1982 as the main opposition party. In 1992 Poul Nyrup Rasmussen was elected as party leader and the party was in power again from 1993 to 2001.

## Social Democratic Party (Finland)
Founded in 1899, the party adopted a revolutionary

Marxist programme. It collaborated with Russian socialists against the Tsarist regime but was also committed to achieving Finland's independence from the Russian Empire. By 1916 it had won an absolute majority in the Finnish parliament, but was taken by surprise by the 1917 **RUSSIAN REVOLUTION**. Despite its collaboration with the bourgeois parties, the SDP's radicalism alarmed its partners in government, who achieved a parliamentary majority in the elections of Oct 1917. At this point, the SDP was urged by the new Bolshevik regime in Russia and by its own working-class supporters to seize power in its own right. The workers took control of the country through a revolutionary general strike, but the party leadership hesitated. When the bourgeois parties gave in to their demands for reform, the SDP called off the strike and a bourgeois government was formed. In Jan 1918 the Social Democrats declared this government deposed and set up a provisional workers' government. Civil war followed, in which the Reds were supported by the **BOLSHEVIKS** and the Whites by the Germans. The Reds were defeated (Apr 1918) and much of the leadership went into exile in Russia; in Aug 1918 they formed the Finnish Communist Party. The SDP in Finland was suppressed after the civil war but was revived, largely through the efforts of Väinö **TANNER**, in late 1918. From this point dates the deep division between the two wings of the Finnish workers' movement and the hostility of the communists towards Tanner's revisionism. Although the SDP retained the loyalties of the majority of the working class, an important minority was attracted to the communist-influenced Finnish Socialist Workers' Party, formed in 1920. Tanner formed a minority government, with the support of the Swedish People's Party, in 1926–7, but lost the leadership of the SDP for four years. SDP support grew steadily in the 1930s despite the attempt by the **LAPUA MOVEMENT** to repeat against the SDP the success of its anti-communist agitation. Excluded from office in 1936 by the opposition of President Svinhufvud, the Social Democrats formed a stable, broad-based coalition with the Agrarians and the Progressives following Svinhufvud's defeat in the presidential election of 1937, and were in government throughout Finland's two disastrous wars with the USSR in 1939–40 and 1941–4. A minority of the party opposed the war and linked up with the Communist Party when the latter was legalized after Finland's defeat, forming part of the communists' parliamentary organization, the Finnish People's Democratic League (SKDL). Tanner regained control of the SDP in Nov 1944 but was imprisoned as a war criminal (1946–9). Throughout the 1950s the party was weakened by internal struggles and was under the shadow of Soviet suspicion, heightened by the re-election of Tanner as Party Chairman in 1957. A major realignment of Finnish politics occurred in 1966; from this point onwards, the majority of Finnish governments were coalitions of Social Democrats, SKDL and the Centre Party, usually with a Social Democrat as Prime Minister. The 1980s saw a strong revival of the Finnish Conservative Party (which had also been the object of Soviet mistrust), but the SDP remained the largest party. In 1982 a Social Democrat, Mauno **KOIVISTO**, was elected President. He stepped down in 1994 and was succeeded by another Social

Democrat, Martti Ahtisaari. In the 1995 election the Social Democratic Party displaced the Centre Party, which had been in power since 1991 under Esko Aho, to become the largest group in parliament; Paavo Lipponen became Prime Minister (1995–2003). In 2003 the party formed a coalition government with the Centre Party, whose leaders have served as prime minister. ▶ COMMUNIST PARTY (Finland)

### Social Democratic Party (SDP)
UK political party formed in 1981 by a 'gang of four', comprising David OWEN, Shirley WILLIAMS, Roy JEN-KINS and Bill Rogers. They broke away from the LA-BOUR PARTY primarily over disagreements on policy and the degree of influence exerted on party policy by the trade unions. The party was a moderate centrist one, with a conservative market-oriented economic policy, and a more left-wing policy on social issues. The SDP formed an electoral pact with the Liberals in 1981, but despite some early electoral successes failed to break the two-party 'mould' of British politics. It merged with the LIBERAL PARTY in 1988, becoming the Social and Liberal Democratic Party, although a rump, led by David Owen, continued in existence as the SDP until 1992.

### Social Democratic Party of Japan
▶ JAPAN SOCIALIST PARTY

### Social Gospel
An early 20c movement in the USA concerned with the application of Christian principles to the social and political order in the service of the Kingdom of God. Among its most prominent leaders were Washington Gladden (1836–1918), Walter Rauschenbusch (1861–1918) and Shailer Matthews (1863–1941).

### socialism
A wide-ranging political doctrine which first emerged in Europe during industrialization in the 18c. Most socialists would agree that social and economic relationships play a major part in determining human possibilities, and that the unequal ownership of property under CAPITALISM creates an unequal and conflictive society. The removal of private property or some means of counterbalancing its power, it is held, will produce a more equal society where individuals enjoy greater freedom and are able to realize their potential more fully. A socialist society will thus be more cooperative and fraternal. Possibly the major division within socialism is between those who believe that to bring it about revolution is necessary, and those who believe change can be achieved through reforms within the confines of democratic politics. There are also differences as to how far capitalist production needs to be eradicated to bring about a socialist society.

### Socialism in One Country (post-1918)
The slogan epitomizing Soviet policy after the RUS-SIAN REVOLUTION. LENIN forced the events of late 1917 on the basis that a few workers and a mass of poor peasants constituted a genuine 'working class'. However, he still expected communist revolutions in more advanced industrial countries. When these did not materialize, he and STALIN opted for a policy of building socialism within formerly Tsarist Russia, using their 'working class' to build the industry that

the country needed to have a genuine proletariat. What resulted was not socialism, but a personal dictatorship within a forcibly industrialized country. The USSR also developed a very defensive foreign policy.

### Socialism with a Human Face (1968)
The description applied to the reform COMMUNISM proposed by Alexander DUBČEK in Czechoslovakia in 1968. It included genuine elections, an end to censorship, and freedom of assembly and travel. The threat this seemed to pose to communist parties everywhere provoked the Soviet invasion in Aug of the same year and the end of reform. Ironically, Mikhail GORBACHEV adopted a somewhat similar but more radical approach which helped to destroy his party.

### Socialist Party (France) (*Parti socialiste*, PS)
Officially known (1905–71) as the SFIO (*Section française de l'Internationale ouvrière*, 'French Section of the Workers' International'). Organized socialist parties emerged from 1879, but were for 20 years only tiny sects, divided among themselves, usually known by the name of their leaders, as Guesdists, Broussists, Allemanistes, etc, with very little representation in parliament. By 1901, two main parties had emerged, the *Parti socialiste de France* ('Socialist Party of France') under GUESDE, more dogmatically Marxist, and the *Parti socialiste français* ('French Socialist Party') under JAURÈS, more prepared to work within the existing system, and supporting the entry of a socialist, MILLERAND, into the cabinet. Under pressure from the Second International (the umbrella organization, created in 1889, in which all recognized socialist parties of the world are represented) they united in 1905, accepting in theory the intransigent MARX-ISM of Guesde, but in reality more influenced by Jaurès. Nevertheless the policy of refusing to accept office in 'bourgeois' cabinets was accepted, and maintained until 1936, except for WORLD WAR I, leading to defection from the party of many of its Deputies who had ministerial ambitions. The majority of the party agreed to support the government in 1914 *Union Sacrée* ('Sacred Union'), but as the war continued, a growing minority turned to opposition. This split foreshadowed the division of 1920 between socialists and communists. The majority of party members voted to join the Third International, and founded a new party. The leading figures in the Socialist Party after 1920 were Léon BLUM, the leader of the parliamentary group, and Paul Faure, the General-Secretary of the party. In opposition for most of the interwar period, the socialists overtook the radicals as the largest party of the Left in 1936, allowing Blum to form a coalition government, the POPULAR FRONT (1936–7, 1938). The party was divided over support for PÉTAIN in 1940, but emerged in 1945 as one of the three large parties that ruled France (1946–7) in a coalition (Tripartism). In 1947 the communists were excluded from that coalition, and the division of the Left between socialists and communists reduced the political influence of both parties for over 30 years. By 1971 the SFIO, which had been led by Guy MOLLET since 1946, appeared almost moribund; it combined in that year with other small parties and was renamed the *Parti socialiste* ('Socialist Party') with François MITTERRAND as leader. From 1981 to 1993 it

achieved the feat of holding a majority of seats in parliament, something very rarely achieved in France by a single party, although the majority was lost during the period of 'cohabitation' in 1986–8. It was defeated in 1993 by the **GAULLIST** Rally for the Republic (RPR) led by Édouard Balladur, but returned to power in 1997 at the head of a coalition led by Lionel Jospin, and governed in 'cohabitation' with the right-wing President Jacques **CHIRAC**. This arrangement ended in 2002 when Chirac's supporters achieved a parliamentary majority. ➤ **SOCIALISM**

### Socialist Revolutionary Party (SR)

A neo-populist revolutionary party in Russia, founded in 1902 and led by Victor Chernov (1873–1952). The SR's radical agrarian programme envisaged the uncompensated redistribution and 'socialization' of the land among a communally organized peasantry. Their 'fighting detachments' carried out a number of spectacular political assassinations between 1902 and 1918. In 1917 Chernov was Minister of Agriculture in the Provisional Government. ➤ **RUSSIAN REVOLUTION**

### social market economy (*Soziale Marktwirtschaft*)

Otherwise known as neo-liberalism, the social market economy was adopted first in the western zones of Germany (1948) and then by the Federal Republic (1949). Its guiding principle is that economic stability should be achieved through market forces, although the state is accorded a role in ensuring the smooth operation of a competitive market and in providing social security and welfare benefits in as far as they did not flout market principles. In the 1950s the **CDU** government and its Economics Minister, **ERHARD**, were staunch proponents of the social market economy and credited it with Federal Germany's 'economic miracle' (**WIRTSCHAFTSWUNDER**) and by the end of the 1950s all major German parties accepted the principle of a market economy. In practice, however, there had always been and there continue to be deviations from this principle in areas such as competition policy, social policy and labour policy.

### Sokolov, Sergei Leonidovich (1911– )

Soviet military commander. He rose rapidly during **WORLD WAR II** and was subsequently given a series of staff posts. In 1965 he became Commander of the Leningrad district and in 1967 Deputy Defence Minister. He was long retired when he was chosen to succeed **USTINOV** as Defence Minister in 1984. This represented a downgrading of the army, a process that was completed when dismissal came in 1987 because of the forces' failure to intercept a German light plane that landed provocatively in Red Square.

### Sokolovski, Vasili Danilovich (1897–1968)

Soviet marshal. He was already a staff officer by 1921 and led several assaults against Germany in **WORLD WAR II**, aiding the capture of Berlin. From 1945 to 1949 he was head of the Soviet military administration in Germany and was held responsible for the failure of the **BERLIN BLOCKADE**. Despite this, he became a Deputy Defence Minister (1949–60) and Chief of the General Staff (1952–60). He wrote standard studies of Soviet military strategy.

### Solemn League and Covenant (Sep 1643)

An alliance between the English parliament and the Scottish rebels against King **CHARLES I**. Parliament promised £30,000 a month to the Scots and the introduction of full Presbyterianism in England; the Scots agreed to provide an army to the hard-pressed Parliamentarians to fight Charles. The pact facilitated Parliamentary victory in the first of the **ENGLISH CIVIL WARS**, but Presbyterianism was never fully implemented. ➤ **COVENANTERS**

### Solferino, Battle of (20 June 1859)

An indecisive engagement between Austrians and invading Franco-Piedmontese forces in Lombardy. Extremely heavy casualties on both sides so revolted **NAPOLEON III** that he was encouraged to offer the Austrians an armistice without even consulting his Piedmontese allies. ➤ **VILLAFRANCA ARMISTICE**

### Solidarity

An organization established in Poland (Sep 1980) as the National Committee of Solidarity (*Solidarność*) to coordinate the activities of the emerging independent trade union following protracted industrial unrest, notably in the Lenin shipyard in Gdańsk. Its first President was Lech **WAŁESA** (later to become President of Poland). It organized a number of strikes in early 1981 for improved wages and conditions, and became a force for major political reform. It attempted to seek reconciliation with the Polish government through proposing a council for national consensus, but suffered continuous harassment and was rendered largely ineffective by the declaration of martial law (Dec 1981) and by being made illegal. It remained underground, but came back into the political arena in mid-1988. Following its successes in the 1989 elections, Solidarity entered into a coalition government with the communists, with one of its members (Tadeusz Mazowiecki) in 1989–91 becoming the first non-communist premier of Poland since 1947. A split between the newly elected President Wałesa and Mazowiecki prevented the formation of a new Solidarity-backed coalition in 1991 and the importance of the organization, renamed the Civic Parliamentary Forum, declined as it divided into various factions in the early 1990s. Although a Solidarity-led coalition led by Jerzy Buzek was in power from 1997 to 2001, its influence has continued to dwindle.

### SOLOMON ISLANDS

An independent country consisting of an archipelago of several hundred islands in the south-west Pacific Ocean. Inhabited since at least 1500BC, they were discovered by the Spanish in 1568. The southern Solomon Islands were placed under British protection in 1893, and the outer islands were added to the protectorate in 1899. The Battle of **GUADALCANAL** and other fierce fighting in **WORLD WAR II** took place here. The islands gained their independence within the

COMMONWEALTH OF NATIONS in 1978. Ethnic tensions on Guadalcanal descended in 1998 into conflict between militias which the government was unable to stem, and in Jun 2000 one militia staged an attempted coup. A peace agreement signed in Oct 2000 was fragile and when economic and social problems worsened in early 2002, violence and disorder increased until, in mid 2003, the government requested peacekeeping assistance from neighbouring countries. Although order was restored within a few months, the situation was still unstable and peacekeeping forces remained in the country.

### Solzhenitsyn, Alexander Isayevich (1918– )
Russian writer. Educated at Rostov in mathematics and physics, he fought in WORLD WAR II, and was imprisoned (1945–53) for unfavourable comment on STALIN's conduct of the war. On his release, he became a teacher, and started to write. His first novel, *Odin den iz zhizni Ivana Denisovicha* (1962, 'One Day in the Life of Ivan Denisovich'), set in a prison camp, was acclaimed both in the USSR and the West; but his subsequent denunciation of Soviet censorship led to the banning of his later, semi-autobiographical novels, *Rakovy korpus* (1968, 'Cancer Ward') and *V kruge pervom* (1968, 'The First Circle'). He was expelled from the Soviet Writers' Union in 1969, and awarded the Nobel Prize for Literature in 1970 (received in 1974). His later books include *Arkhipelag Gulag* (1973–8, 'The Gulag Archipelago'), a factual account of the Stalinist terror, for which he was arrested and exiled to West Germany (1974). He later lived in the USA and returned to Russia in 1994.

---

**SOMALIA**    official name **Somali Democratic Republic**

A north-east African republic, bounded to the northwest by Djibouti; to the west by Ethiopia; to the south-west by Kenya; to the east by the Indian Ocean; and to the north by the Gulf of Aden. The country was settled by Muslims in the 7–10c, and was the object of Italian, French and British interests after the opening of the Suez Canal in 1869. After WORLD WAR II, the modern Somali Republic was formed by the amalgamation of the Italian and British protectorates. It gained its independence in 1960, since when there has been territorial conflict with Ethiopia (which has a large Somali population) and Kenya. A military

coup took place in 1969 led by Muhammad Siad BARRE, who established a dictatorship and renamed the country the Somali Democratic Republic. In 1988 a civil war began between government forces and rebel groups, particularly the Somali National Movement (SNM), forcing Barre to flee in 1991. Two regions subsequently declared themselves independent: the north-east region (the Somaliland Republic) in 1991 under the SNM, and the south-east region (Puntland) in 1998. With agriculture disrupted by the fighting as well as severe drought, the population of Somalia faced starvation and thousands ended up in refugee camps. During the early 1990s UN peacekeepers attempted unsuccessfully to secure a ceasefire; UN troops were withdrawn in early 1995. Fighting continued in the late 1990s between rival clan-based factions in a land in which the state had effectively disintegrated. A 1999 peace plan attracted considerable support and moves towards restoration under a transitional government began in 2000 but fighting between pro- and anti-government militias resumed in 2001. The peace talks that began in 2003 were hampered by disputes and boycotts, but reached an agreement in early 2004 to establish a federal government and form a transitional parliament that would appoint a federal president.

### Somers, John Somers, 1st Baron (1651–1716)
English politician. A Whig, he became a lawyer (1676) and an MP (1689). He helped to draft the DECLARATION OF RIGHTS (1689), and after the GLORIOUS REVOLUTION (1688) held several posts under WILLIAM III, culminating as Lord Chancellor (1697). William's most trusted minister, he was the object of frequent attacks, which led to his IMPEACHMENT (and acquittal) in 1701. He was President of the Privy Council under Queen ANNE (1708–14). ► WHIGS

### Somme, Battle of the (1 July–19 Nov 1916)
A major WORLD WAR I British offensive against German troops in north-western France which developed into the bloodiest battle in world history, with more than a million casualties. It was launched by the British Commander-in-Chief, Douglas HAIG. When the attack was abandoned, the Allies had advanced 10 miles from previous positions. The battle formed part of the war of attrition on the Western Front.

### Somoza (García), Anastasio (1896–1956)
Nicaraguan dictator. The son of a wealthy coffee planter, he was educated in Nicaragua and the USA. As Chief of the National Guard (Nicaragua's army), he established himself in supreme power in the early 1930s. With army backing, he deposed President Juan Bautista Sacasa, replacing him at the beginning of 1937. Exiling most of his political opponents and amassing a huge personal fortune, he retained power until his assassination. His sons, Luis Somoza Debayle (1923–67) and Anastasio Somoza Debayle (1925–80), continued dynastic control of Nicaragua until the 1979 revolution.

### Sonderbund
A political and military league of seven Swiss Catholic cantons (Uri, Schwyz, Unterwalden, Zug, Fribourg, Lucerne, Valais), formed in 1845 to resist

liberal plans for centralization. The 25-day Sonderbund War (1847) ended with the government's defeat of the Sonderbund, and the creation of a federal state (1848).

### Song (Sung) Dynasty (960–1279)
The Chinese dynasty founded by Zhao Kuangying, with its capital at Kaifeng. From the beginning, it was threatened by the **KHITAN**, who in 1125 conquered all northern China, which they then ruled from Beijing. The Song court was re-established at Hangzhou (then called Linan), but the 'Southern Song Dynasty' was destroyed by the **MONGOLS**, who had earlier overcome the Khitan.

### Songhai
A West African state which rose to power in the region formerly dominated by Mali in the second half of the 15c, commanding the trade routes of the Sahara, the great market at Timbuktu, and the area westwards to Senegal. It declined as a result of the Portuguese re-orientation of trade routes, and was attacked by Moroccan forces in the 1590s. Songhai peoples still control much of the Saharan caravan trade. ► **BERBERS**

### Song Jiaoren (Sung Chiao-jen) (1882–1913)
Chinese revolutionary and champion of parliamentary government. He was a leading member of **SUN YAT-SEN**'s revolutionary anti-Manchu organization, the *Tongmenghui* ('Alliance League'), before 1911, helping to set up a branch in central China. Following the establishment of the republic in 1912, the Tongmenghui was transformed into a political party, the **GUOMINDANG** (Nationalist Party). Song became its principal spokesman in the elections of Dec 1912, carrying out a vigorous Western-style electioneering campaign calling for a figurehead presidency, a responsible cabinet system and local autonomy. The Guomindang won the elections and Song was widely tipped to become Prime Minister. Song's programme, however, was a direct challenge to the hegemonic ambitions of the President, **YUAN SHIKAI**. On his way to Beijing in Mar 1913, Song was assassinated at Shanghai railway station by Yuan's henchmen.

### Song Qingling (Soong Ch'ing-ling) (1892–1981)
Chinese politician. The wife of the Chinese revolutionary leader, **SUN YAT-SEN**, she played an increasingly active political role after his death (1925) and became associated with the left wing of the **GUOMINDANG**. After a Christian education in the USA, she became Sun Yat-sen's English-language secretary (1913) and married him in 1914. She was elected to the Central Executive Committee of the Guomindang (1926) and was a member of the left-wing Guomindang government established at Wuhan in 1927 in opposition to **CHIANG KAI-SHEK**. (Ironically her younger sister, Meiling (1897–2003), married Chiang Kai-shek in 1927.) After the collapse of the Wuhan government, Song Qingling spent two years in the USSR (1927–9). During the 1930s she was a prominent member of the China League for Civil Rights, which was constantly harrassed by Chiang Kai-shek's government. She stayed on in China following the victory of the Chinese communists (1949), becoming one of three non-communist vice-chairpersons of the People's Republic. As the widow

of Sun Yat-sen, of whom the communists claimed to be the legitimate heirs, she was accorded much respect by the Chinese Communist Party, although her presence in the new government remained an honorary one.

### Song Ziwen (Sung Tzu-wen/Soong, T V) (1894–1971)
Chinese financier and politician. His sister, **SONG QINGLING**, married **SUN YAT-SEN**, and through this Song became closely associated with the **GUOMINDANG**. He provided the financial stability which made possible the 1926 **NORTHERN EXPEDITION** that reunited China under the Nationalists. A second sister, Meiling (1897–2003), married **CHIANG KAI-SHEK** in 1927. Song served as Finance Minister of the new government until 1931, and was Foreign Minister from 1942 to 1945. When the Nationalist government was overthrown in 1949, he moved to the USA, where he died.

### Sonnino, Giorgio Sidney (1847–1922)
Italian diplomat and politician. He entered parliament in 1880 and occupied various ministerial posts, including Treasury Minister (1894–6). He was twice Prime Minister (1906 and 1909–10), and as Foreign Minister was responsible with **SALANDRA** for bringing Italy into **WORLD WAR I** on the side of the Allies. He remained Foreign Minister throughout the war and was part of the Italian delegation to the post-war conference in Paris.

### Sons of Liberty
An organization in the **AMERICAN REVOLUTION** that provided popular leadership in the resistance movement against Britain. Composed mainly of merchants, lawyers, artisans and small traders, it operated as an organized inter-colonial group in 1765–6, opposing the **STAMP ACT**. Thereafter, the men who had taken part continued to provide popular leadership, helping to organize the First **CONTINENTAL CONGRESS** in 1774. The term was also used to describe all Americans involved in the revolutionary movement.

### Soong, T V ► SONG ZIWEN

### Soong Ch'ing-ling ► SONG QINGLING

### Sophia (1630–1714)
Electress of Hanover. The youngest daughter of **FREDERICK V**, Elector Palatine and King of Bohemia, and Elizabeth, daughter of James VI of Scotland and I of England, in 1658 she married Ernest Augustus, Duke of Brunswick-Lüneburg, afterwards Elector of Hanover (1692). She was the mother of **GEORGE I** of Great Britain.

### Sophia Alexeevna (1657–1704)
Regent of Russia (1682/9). She was the daughter of Tsar **ALEXEI MIKHAILOVICH** and his first wife, Maria Miloslavskaya. On the death of her brother, Tsar Fyodor Alexeyevich (1682), Sophia opposed the accession of her half-brother Peter (the future **PETER I, THE GREAT**), and took advantage of a popular uprising in Moscow to press the candidature of her mentally deficient brother Ivan. A compromise was reached whereby both Ivan (V) and Peter were proclaimed joint Tsars, with Sophia as Regent. Supported by leading **BOYARS**, she became the *de facto* ruler of

Russia. A faction of the nobility succeeded in removing her from power in 1689, and (apart from a failed attempt to regain power in 1698) she spent the rest of her life in a convent in Moscow.

### Sophie Frederica Mathilda (1818–77)
Queen of the Netherlands (1849/77). The daughter of King William of Württemberg and Catherine Pavlovna of Russia, she married the future Dutch King **WILLIAM III** on 18 June 1839. They succeeded to the Dutch throne in 1849. Sophie bore her husband three sons, none of whom outlived their father. Their marriage was not a success, and she lived estranged from her husband until her death in The Hague.

### Sorbs
A slavic minority concentrated near Dresden in Lusatia who were never forced out or assimilated by German immigration in the Middle Ages. They maintain their own linguistic and cultural identity to this day.

### Sorsa, (Taisto) Kalevi (1930–2004)
Finnish politician. After graduating from Tampere University, he worked in publishing and with the **UN** in the Ministry of Education. In 1969 he became Secretary-General of the Social Democratic Party and went on to become its President (1970–91). He was elected to the *Eduskunta* in 1970, and served four terms as Prime Minister between 1972 and 1987. When the SPP formed a government with the conservative National Coalition Party in 1987, he became Deputy Prime Minister. He retired in 1991.

### Soult, Nicolas Jean de Dieu (1769–1851)
French marshal. Created Marshal of France by **NAPOLEON I** (1804), he led the French armies in the **PENINSULAR WAR** (1808–14) until defeated at Toulouse (1814). A skilled opportunist, Soult turned royalist after Napoleon's abdication, but joined him in the **HUNDRED DAYS**, acting as his Chief of Staff at the Battle of **WATERLOO**. Exiled until 1819, he was gradually restored to all his honours, and presided over three ministries of **LOUIS-PHILIPPE** (1832–4, 1839–40 and 1840–7).

### Souphanouvong, Prince (1909–95)
Lao prince and politician. On graduating as a civil engineer in 1937, he worked under the French administration in Vietnam. Following the capitulation of the Japanese in Aug 1945, he was returned to Laos, with the assistance of **HO CHI MINH**, to assist in the liberation of his country from the French. He was badly wounded when his forces were routed by the French in Mar 1946. In the early 1950s he became head of a Vietnamese front organization (later known as the **PATHET LAO**), accompanying the Vietnamese invasion of Laos in 1953–4. Souphanouvong entered the government in 1957, but his strongly pro-Vietnamese communist ties inevitably caused great tensions and he was imprisoned in 1959–60. In the 1960s it proved impossible to secure an integrated government in Laos, which consequently was driven apart by civil war, and Souphanouvong and the Pathet Lao left for the hills. The communist victory in Vietnam in 1975 brought the Pathet Lao to power in Laos and Souphanouvong became President of the Lao People's Democratic Republic, in effect a Vietnamese colony, a position he held until 1986. ► **VIETNAM WAR**

### SOUTH AFRICA   official name **Republic of South Africa**
A republic in the south of the African continent, divided into the four provinces of Cape, Natal, Orange Free State and Transvaal. It is bounded to the north-west by Namibia; to the north by Botswana; to the north-east by Zimbabwe, Mozambique and Swaziland; to the east and south-east by the Indian Ocean; and to the south-west and west by the southern Atlantic Ocean; Lesotho is landlocked within its borders. It was originally inhabited by **KHOISAN** tribes, and many Bantu tribes arrived from the north after c.1000. The Portuguese reached the Cape of Good Hope in the late 15c, and it was settled by the Dutch in 1652. The British arrived in 1795 and annexed the Cape in 1814. In 1836 the Boers or **AFRIKANERS** undertook the **GREAT TREK** north-east across the Orange River to Natal, and the first Boer republic was founded in 1839. Natal was annexed by the British in 1846, but the Boer republics of Transvaal (founded 1852) and Orange Free State (1854) received recognition. The discovery of diamonds in 1866 and gold in 1886 led to rivalry between the British and the Boers which resulted in the **BOER WARS** of 1880–1 and 1899–1902. In 1910 Transvaal, Natal, Orange Free State and Cape Province were united to form the Union of South Africa, a dominion of the British Empire; it became a sovereign state within the **COMMONWEALTH OF NATIONS** in 1931 and formed an independent republic in 1961. South African politics became dominated by the treatment of the non-white majority. Between 1948 and 1991 the **APARTHEID** policy resulted in the development of separate political

institutions for different racial groups, for example Africans were considered permanent citizens of the 'homelands' to which each tribal group was assigned and were given no representation in the South African parliament; nominal independence was granted to Transkei (1976), Bophuthatswana (1977), Venda (1979) and Ciskei (1981), but was not recognized internationally. Continuing racial violence and strikes led to the declaration of a state of emergency in 1986. Several countries imposed economic and cultural sanctions (especially in the field of sport) in protest at the apartheid system. The progressive dismantling of apartheid by the government of F W **DE KLERK** took place from 1990, but negotiations towards a non-racial democracy were marked by continuing violent clashes. In 1993 a new constitution gave the vote to all South African adults, and in 1994 free democratic elections resulted in the formation of an **ANC**-led multiracial government, and Nelson **MANDELA** became President. In the same year, South Africa rejoined the Commonwealth. Mandela was succeeded in 1999 by Thabo **MBEKI**, who was re-elected in 2004. In 2003, after years of official denial, the government announced programmes to tackle the high levels of **HIV/AIDS** infection in the country.
➤ **AFRIKANER BOND ; APARTHEID LAWS**

### South Africa Act (1909)

The act of the British parliament which created the Union of South Africa, with dominion status, in 1910. After the Boer War, the Liberal government that came to power in 1905 moved rapidly to restore responsible self-government to the Transvaal (1906) and the Orange Free State (1907). A series of constitutional conventions then set about federating the two Boer territories with the British colonies of the Cape and Natal; a union constitution was agreed upon, with the parliamentary capital in Cape Town, the administrative capital in Pretoria and the major law courts in Bloemfontein. The Union constitution ensured that the **AFRIKANERS** would remain the dominant political force in South Africa. It was hailed as a colonial triumph for **ASQUITH**'s government in keeping South Africa within the British Empire and ultimately ensuring its participation in two World Wars. However, the British failed to establish black political rights or protect the franchise enjoyed by limited numbers of Africans at the Cape. It led not to a liberalizing of the South African system, as the British had hoped, but to white supremacist rule and **APARTHEID**. ➤ **BOER WARS**

### South-East Asia pre-1000AD ➤ *See panel*

### South-East Asia Treaty Organization (SEATO)

An organization founded in 1954 to secure South-East Asia against communist 'aggression'. The eight signatories to the treaty were Australia, France, New Zealand, Pakistan, the Philippines, Thailand, UK and USA. It was phased out in the mid-1970s.

### Southern African Development Community (SADC) previously known as Southern African Development Coordination Conference (SADCC)

An association of 14 states (Angola, Botswana, Democratic Republic of Congo, Lesotho, Malawi, Mauritius, Mozambique, Namibia, Seychelles, South Africa, Swaziland, Tanzania, Zambia and Zimbabwe)

with its headquarters in Gaborone. The first meeting of its nine founding member states was held in Arusha in 1979, and its Lusaka Declaration (Apr 1980) set forth a commitment to a peaceful transition to majority rule in Zimbabwe and opposition to **APARTHEID** in South Africa. Originally set up to help limit members' dependence on South Africa, it is based upon sectoral coordination and acts as a conduit for international aid to the region. The organization adopted the title Southern African Development Community on 17 Aug 1992.

### South Pacific Forum

An organization set up in 1971 to bring together the heads of government of the independent and self-governing states of the South Pacific. Its headquarters are in Suva, Fiji, and its members are Australia, the Cook Islands, Fiji, Kiribati, the Marshall Islands, the Federated States of Micronesia, Nauru, New Zealand, Niue, Palau, Papua New Guinea, the Solomon Islands, Tonga, Tuvalu, Vanuatu and Samoa (formerly Western Samoa). In 1973 the South Pacific Bureau for Economic Cooperation was established to deal with economic matters and to oversee cooperation in such areas as trade and tourism. Over the years its discussions have included the rise in sea-level due to global warming, nuclear issues (in 1985 it declared the South Pacific a nuclear-free zone and in 1995 condemned France for testing nuclear weapons there) and overfishing. It is now known as the Pacific Islands Forum.

### South Sea Bubble (1720)

A financial crisis in Britain arising out of speculation mania generated by parliament's approval of the South Sea Company proposal to take over three-fifths of the National Debt. Many investors were ruined in the aftermath, but Robert **WALPOLE**'s plan for stock transfer retrieved the situation and made his reputation.

### South Slavs

The **SLAVS** began to establish themselves as farmers in the Balkans in the first decades of the 6c and eventually covered the entire peninsula. In the 7c a second wave of invaders, including the Croats and Serbs, who were Slavs, and the Turkic Bulgars, who assimilated to the earlier Slav settlers, entered the Balkans and established the first South Slavic states, Bulgaria, Croatia and Serbia. During the 15–17c, Croat, Slovene and Serb scholars became conscious of their common Slav ancestry and referred to themselves as Illyrians or simply Slavs, in addition to their more specific national names. In the 19c, under the influence of romantic nationalism, this Slav consciousness grew and gave rise to various movements for South Slav unification which led to the establishment of the Kingdom of Serbs, Croats and Slovenes (later Yugoslavia) at the end of **WORLD WAR I**. ➤ **BOSNIA AND HERZEGOVINA ; CARINTHIA ; CARNIOLA ; DALMATIA ; ISTRIA ; MONTENEGRO ; SERBIAN UPRISINGS ; YUGOSLAVISM**

### South Tirol

That part of the Tirol south of the Brenner Pass and currently in Italy. Although overwhelmingly German-speaking, the region passed to Italy after **WORLD WAR I** (Treaty of **ST GERMAIN**). Under **MUSSOLINI**, a

# South-East Asia pre-1000AD

*Culture & Society*

The region known today as South-East Asia comprises the area previously known as **Indochina** (lying as it does between the Indian subcontinent to the west and China to the north), together with the Malay Peninsula and the Malay Archipelago. Since most of the historical record about the earliest times in South-East Asia is based on Chinese sources, including accounts by ambassadors, traders and conquerors, much of our knowledge of the period is confined to their areas of interest.

## CAMBODIA

### Funan

The earliest known state in South-East Asia. Located in the delta of the Mekong River, Funan was founded in the 1c AD. It evolved a pattern of statecraft from the Indian model, although it is not accepted by all scholars that Indian Brahmins were actually resident in large numbers. Some have argued that Funan's rulers constructed complex irrigation systems to sustain large-scale, wet-rice agriculture, but again not all scholars agree. It is accepted, however, that Funan was a major international trading centre, from which the state, at the height of its power in the late 5c, derived great prosperity. Funan went into decline in the 6c and came under the control of Chenla.

### Chenla

Based on the region that is now north-eastern Cambodia, Chenla expanded west and south under Isanavarman (fl. AD 554), whose capital, Isanapura, was a centre of scholarship as late as the 14c. It endured into the 7c as a rich and artistic society, with such technological accomplishments as the distribution by canals of dammed water. By the end of the century the death of Jayavarman I saw the state split into minor principalities, of which the northernmost were relatively stable and the southernmost unsettled and weak. Partly as a consequence of this, the trade routes changed and travellers went to China by way of Sumatra. Cultural contact with India declined but local art continued to flourish until its dramatic revival in the kingdom of Angkor.

### Angkor

Rising to a dominant position over much of mainland South-East Asia, Angkor shows a remarkable combination of human creativity and religious belief. Using hydraulic techniques learned two centuries before, the Khmers turned the unproductive Angkor region into one of the most successful rice-growing areas ever known. Three crops a year were grown, supporting a population of a million and providing the agricultural economic base that allowed the state to build the great 'temple mountains' that still stand in Cambodia.

Jayavarman II (c.770–850) was the first king of Angkor, and reunified the old kingdom of Chenla to form the **Khmer Empire**. He was consecrated in his capital, Mahendraparvata, according to the Hindu rite, in order to establish Khmer independence of the growing hegemony of Java. His heirs continued the development of the state's artistic and religious life to the 10c, with Yashovarman I (c.890–910) building Yasodharapura, the first Khmer city in Angkor. With the collapse of the Tang Dynasty in China at the start of the 10c, the historical record becomes incomplete, but it is known that six more Khmer kings ruled throughout the 11c. The Angkorean Empire endured until the 13c, when it fell through internal rebellion.

### LAOS

The Laotian people, linguistically related to the Thais, had established the kingdom of Nanchao in south-west China by the 8c. Driven south by Chinese colonization, they crossed the mountains into the high reaches of the Mekong and Menam rivers, and began to set up kingdoms from about 1360 in a succession of narrow river valleys. They were poorer and more divided than the main Thai stock, and the culture they developed was a provincial version of the one that developed in Siam.

---

ruthless policy of Italianization, later condoned by **HITLER**, was pursued but ultimately failed. Since 1945 considerable tension in the area has been largely defused by various agreements between Austria and Italy that accord the region far-reaching cultural autonomy.

## soviet

Originally, a workers' council established in Russia after the 1905 revolution. They reappeared as workers' and soldiers' councils, important instruments of the 1917 revolution. Members of soviets were elected by popular vote, and lower soviets could not control higher ones. The highest was the Supreme Soviet, the legislative body of the USSR, which comprised representatives from all the constituent republics.

## Soviet–Chinese Friendship Treaty (1950)

The treaty bringing together the longest-established communist power and the most important new one, and settling some of their differences. **STALIN** had been less helpful to **MAO ZEDONG** than most had ex-

pected, but he now promised him protection against Japan and gave him US$300 million in aid. However, he did not offer protection against the USA, and kept him waiting for ten weeks in the middle of a Moscow winter to give him less aid than Poland. On the other hand he did agree to abandon Soviet positions within China. Relations prospered for a few years but gradually deteriorated into the **SINO-SOVIET DISPUTE**.

## Soviet–Finnish War ► CONTINUATION WAR

## Soviet Union ► USSR

## Soweto Riots (Apr 1976)

The student disturbances which took place in the Transvaal African township of Soweto, when several hundred people were killed resisting the teaching of Afrikaans in schools. The township (whose name derives from *South West Township*) remained a source of tension and violence in South Africa as well as a focus of agitation for black equality until white minority rule came to an end in 1994. ► **APARTHEID**

**MALAY PENINSULA**

Malay contact with India probably started well before the 1c AD, with southern Indians arriving throughout South-East Asia in some numbers. Chinese reports of the 3c indicate that Hinduism had been introduced a century before and that Indians married into local families, bringing the culture at least into trading posts and important townships. The first Indianized kingdom was Langkasuka, which had walled towns. The king went about on an elephant in procession with musicians and nobles decked out in gold. Excavations in the province of Kedah (now in Thailand) show that Buddhism flourished alongside Hinduism.

**THAILAND**

During the first millennium AD this was a collection of small states widely dispersed but linked by a common language. They appear to have been well established though situated as far apart as Burma, Assam and Yunnan. The religion of the bulk of the people was primitive animism, but there is evidence that Theravada Buddhism was introduced by Mon-Khmers in the central peninsula. The family was the main social unit and women enjoyed high status.

**VIETNAM**

Written history begins with the Chinese annals of 207 BC, when the general Chao T'o conquered the area for the Qin (Ch'in) Dynasty. When that dynasty fell, the general sought to rule the region as an independent state, but the Han emperor Wu Ti re-established imperial control in 111 BC. Census reports show that it comprised modern North Vietnam around the Red River delta, another province based on the former North–South border, and a province further south with a capital near Hue. At that time the Vietnamese were moving into the Iron Age, a process accelerated by contact with China. Indian influences would have come from contact with the Champas, who occupied territory on Vietnam's coast and lived by commerce and plunder.

The Chinese were constantly resisted, but persisted in their conquest since the highly fertile Red River delta was rich in precious metals, pearls and forests, as well as providing a trading post en route to the spice islands. At first they let the conquered Vietnamese run the country, but from about AD 110 direct rule was enforced and Chinese dress, language, religion, and handwriting were imposed. In AD 39 the Vietnamese took advantage of Han difficulties elsewhere to regain their freedom, but the Chinese soon reasserted their supremacy. This pattern of events continued until the 10c, with Sino-Vietnamese governors leading revolts at dynastic crises, until in 939 the demise of the Tang Dynasty led to a Vietnamese military victory over a Chinese army and the end of Chinese rule.

**BORNEO**

Chinese tradition maintains that trade with Borneo (for gold, resins and camphor) existed as early as the 1c BC. Buddhist pilgrims visited the island in the 4c AD and cultural contacts with India date from around 400, as shown by Sanskrit inscriptions and Gupta-style statues of the Buddha. Hindu influences came in from Java, and on the north coast there was political contact with China. A principality in what is now known as Brunei was reported to be paying tribute to China in the 6c.

**JAVA AND SUMATRA**

These islands are referred to by Pliny and Ptolemy as sources of medicinal and culinary spices. China traded for the same materials as well as camphor, as recorded from the 5c. The Chinese established trading posts but did not attempt to conquer the islands. By the 7c control of much of the trade was in the hands of Malays, whose centre of power was in southern Sumatra. The state of Srivijaya dominated the maritime trade passing through the region between the close of the 7c and the early 11c. The task of locating the precise site of the capital of Srivijaya continues to tax students of early South-East Asian history, but it was somewhere in the region of Palembang, in south-east Sumatra. Srivijaya's power was built on well-developed political and trading relationships with China, its ability to dominate local trade (that involved a capacity to suppress sea piracy), and its wide reputation as a centre of culture, learning and civilization. It was also an important centre of Buddhist observance and study, sustained and sponsored by the great wealth created by trade. When I-ching visited Srivijaya in 671, he found a very substantial community of Buddhist monks.

---

**Spaak, Paul Henri** (1899–1972)

Belgian politician. He became Belgium's first socialist Premier (1938–9) and was Foreign Minister with the government-in-exile during WORLD WAR II. In 1945 he was chairman of the first General Assembly of the UN. After his later periods as Premier (1946 and 1947–9), he was again Foreign Minister (1954–7 and 1961–8), in which role he became one of the founding fathers of the EEC. Secretary-General of NATO in 1957–61, he was sometimes known as 'Mr Europe'.

**Space Exploration** ► *See panel*

**Spahi** ► SIPAHI

**SPAIN** official name **Kingdom of Spain**

A country in south-western Europe, bounded in the north by France across the Pyrenees, and in the west by Portugal. Spain's early inhabitants included Iberians, Celts, Phoenicians, Greeks and Romans. From the 8c there was Muslim domination, and then Christian reconquest, which was completed by 1492. Spain assumed its modern form with the dynastic union of the crowns of ARAGON and CASTILE, a union that was effective by 1479. In the 16c the Spanish exploration of the New World led to the growth of the Spanish Empire. There was a period of decline after the Revolt of the Netherlands in 1568 (leading to the EIGHTY YEARS' WAR). Significant set-backs included the defeat of the Spanish ARMADA in 1588, defeat by France, acknowledged in the Treaty of the PYRENEES (1659), the War of the SPANISH SUCCESSION in 1702–13, Spain's involvement in the Peninsular War against NAPOLEON I in 1808–14, and the SPANISH–AMERICAN WAR in 1898 that led to the loss of Cuba, Puerto Rico and the remaining Pacific possessions. The dictatorship of Miguel PRIMO DE RIVERA (1923–30) was followed by the exile of the King and the establishment of the Second Republic in 1931. A military revolt headed by General FRANCO in 1936 led to the SPANISH CIVIL WAR and a fascist dictatorship. Prince JUAN CARLOS of Bourbon, nominated in 1969 to succeed

# Space Exploration

Science & Technology

Exploring beyond the bounds of the earth became a practical reality after **World War II**, using rocket science techniques that had been developed for the delivery of bombs. Both the USA and USSR developed the missile technology used by the Germans, but the Americans had the German rocket team, led by Wernher von Braun (1912–77). The USSR had heavier rockets and was the first to launch a space satellite, Sputnik, in 1957. This spurred the USA to greater endeavours, especially after the USSR achieved the first animal in orbit (the dog Laika in Sputnik 2), the first impact on the moon (Luna 2, 1959), the first photographs of the far side of the moon (Luna 3, 1959), and the first man in space (Vostok 1, Apr 1961). In response, a month later, President John F **Kennedy** declared a race to land a man on the moon and bring him home within the decade.

The American space programme is run by NASA (National Aeronautical and Space Administration), set up in 1958. Its headquarters are in Washington, with research centres around the country, but mission control is in Houston at what is now called the Johnson Space Center. From the 1960s this was the scene for the direction of manned space flights: the Mercury series (orbital flights); the Gemini series (first orbital docking, 1966); and the Apollo series. The first Apollo mission ended in disaster, with all three crew members dying in a fire in the capsule during a countdown test. Although this caused an 18-month delay to the programme, Neil Armstrong and Edwin 'Buzz' Aldrin were the first men on the moon as Kennedy had promised, landing on the surface in a lunar module from Apollo 11 in 1969. There were 20 Apollo missions in all, the last in 1975, but after the moon landing the US space effort faltered.

It was the turn of Russia to re-establish its ascendancy with the construction of the first space stations. Their moon programme had been abandoned after the successful US moon landing. It was decided to use the Soyuz spacecraft, originally designed to go to the moon, to send the crew to and from orbiting space stations. A docking system incorporated a hatch so that the crew could enter the station without a space walk. The first space station, Salyut 1, was launched in 1971, but only received one crew. The crew of Soyuz 11 docked successfully and spent 24 days on board, but suffocated during re-entry to earth's atmosphere when a valve opened, allowing their air to escape from the capsule. Problems arose with subsequent attempts, and the next successful space station was Salyut 4, launched in 1974. The two-man crew of Soyuz 17 spent a month on board in 1975 performing scientific experiments.

The same year saw the first major cooperation between the USA and USSR, the **Apollo–Soyuz Project**. NASA had launched its own space station, Skylab 1, followed by 2, 3 and 4, in 1973. A joint mission had been planned since 1970, one of its aims being to make a space rescue a possibility. The successful docking and transfer were shown live on television, and hopes were high for further cooperation. But none was forthcoming until 1995 and the rendezvous of Discovery with the Russian space station.

The focus on putting people into space had been continued by the Russians, whose cosmonauts spent very long periods on the Mir space stations, the first of which was launched in 1986. Titov and Manarov remained on Mir 1 for a year, being visited by other cosmonauts. These long spells in space were invaluable for the gathering of information about the effect of prolonged space flight on the human body. The station was continuously occupied until 1989, then a second phase of missions began, performing experiments, even repairing space craft on space walks.

Meanwhile, the US effort had moved on to the development of space shuttles to act as space laboratories, and economic launch vehicles for commercial satellites, as well as to ferry crew members to space stations. First the Columbia series was tested, then the larger Challenger. On the 25th space shuttle mission in 1986, the Challenger lifted off with seven crew and exploded 73 seconds later. The inquiry following this disaster found the cause of the explosion –

Franco, acceded to the throne in 1975, and survived attempted military coups in 1978 and 1981. A democratic constitution was implemented in 1978 and Spain joined the **EC** in 1986. Since the 1960s, the Basque separatist movement, **ETA**, has carried out numerous terrorist attacks and kidnappings; in 2003 its political front, *Herri Batasuna*, or *Euskal Herritarrok*, was banned. There was strong opposition to Spain's involvement in the **IRAQ WAR** and the governing Popular Party was defeated by the Socialist Workers' Party in the 2004 election, which took place only days after the Madrid train bombings by **AL-QAEDA**; Spanish troops were withdrawn from Iraq within two months.

## Spanish–American War (1898)

In 1898 Spain lost the final remnants – Cuba, Puerto Rico and the Philippines – of its empire to the USA. If the war signalled the emergence of the USA as an imperial power, it marked the eclipse of Spain as one. Although the material loss to Spain was substantial, the psychological blow was devastating. The end of the once vast empire confronted Spaniards not just with their declining power and status, but also their

sheer backwardness. There emerged a generalized, if unfocused, demand for the 'regeneration' of a 'decadent' nation. The 'Disaster of 1898' thereby triggered off a protracted internal crisis which culminated in the fall of the monarchy in 1931.

## Spanish-American Wars of Independence (1810–26)

The wars fought in South America, following **NAPOLEON**'s invasion of Spain (1808). Reformers in the major South American colonies set up semi-independent governments (1810), which were rejected both by royalists in the colonies and by the Spanish King **FERDINAND VII** when restored in 1814. The ensuing wars were fought in two main theatres: Venezuela, New Granada and Quito, where Simón **BOLÍVAR** was the leading patriot general, and Argentina and Chile, from where General José de **SAN MARTÍN** mounted an invasion of the Viceroyalty of Peru, still held by Spain (1820–1). The final liberation of Peru was effected in 1824 by Bolívar. The last Spanish garrisons in South America, at Callao (Peru) and on the island of Chiloé (Chile), surrendered to the patriots in 1826.

failed O-ring seals between two sections of the rocket boosters – and exposed other potentially dangerous problems. The programme was delayed for two years and started again with the Discovery and Atlantis series.

The unmanned space programme had, however, been very successful, with flights past Venus, Mars, Mercury, Saturn and Jupiter returning data of extreme interest to astronomers and geologists. The Mars Global Surveyor carried out a two-year mapping programme of the surface, and the Mars Pathfinder landed in 1997, sending back measurements and images.

In the 1970s space technology began to offer new possibilities for international communications, weather forecasting and navigation. The USA and the USSR/Russia were responsible for almost 90 per cent of payloads put into space between 1957 and 1996. The balance was provided by Australia, Canada, China, France, Germany, India, Japan, the UK and the European Space Agency (ESA).

The ESA was formed in 1964 and developed the Ariane rocket so that Europe could put its own satellites into orbit. Its aim is to carry out scientific research, and deploy weather and communications satellites. International cooperation has in general become more common, with astronauts of one nation flying in the spacecraft of another.

NASA and Europe combined on the work for the Hubble Space Telescope, which was launched in 1990 to provide a large facility free from the distortions of the earth's atmosphere. Initial problems with the focus of the mirror and the gyroscopes that control its attitude were corrected during EVAs (Extra Vehicular Activity) by Akers from the Endeavour in 1993, and further servicing in five EVAs from Discovery in 1997 increased its capabilities.

French and Soviet technology combined to put gamma ray detectors into space, and the NASA Gamma Ray Observatory was launched in 1991 to map the entire sky.

The Infrared Astronomy Satellite (IRAS) was a collaboration between the USA, the Netherlands and the UK, and was followed by the European Infrared Space Observatory in 1994. NASA arranged to launch an Infrared Telescope Facility in 2000

By the last decade of the 20c, plans abounded for space experiments and for manned space flight, such as a US one for a crewed mission to Mars in the 21c.

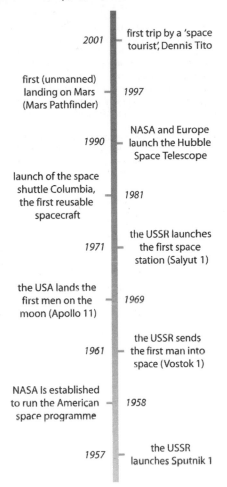

| | |
|---|---|
| 2001 | first trip by a 'space tourist', Dennis Tito |
| first (unmanned) landing on Mars (Mars Pathfinder) | 1997 |
| 1990 | NASA and Europe launch the Hubble Space Telescope |
| launch of the space shuttle Columbia, the first reusable spacecraft | 1981 |
| 1971 | the USSR launches the first space station (Salyut 1) |
| the USA lands the first men on the moon (Apollo 11) | 1969 |
| 1961 | the USSR sends the first man into space (Vostok 1) |
| NASA is established to run the American space programme | 1958 |
| 1957 | the USSR launches Sputnik 1 |

**Spanish Civil War** (1936–9)
The conflict between supporters and opponents of the Spanish Second Republic (1931–6). The 'Republicans' included moderates, socialists, communists, and Catalan and Basque regionalists and anarchists. The 'Nationalist' insurgents included monarchists, Carlists, conservative Catholics, and fascist Falangists. The armed forces were divided. Both sides attracted foreign assistance: the Republic from the USSR and the INTERNATIONAL BRIGADES; the Nationalists from fascist Italy and Nazi Germany. The Nationalist victory was due to the balance of foreign aid; to 'non-intervention' on the part of the Western democracies; and to greater internal unity, achieved under the leadership of General FRANCO. The war took the course of a slow Nationalist advance. The Nationalists initially (July 1936) seized much of north-west Spain and part of the south-west, then (autumn 1936) advanced upon but failed to capture Madrid. They captured Malaga (Mar 1937) and the north coast (Mar–Oct 1937); advanced to the Mediterranean, cutting Republican Spain in two (Apr 1938); overran Catalonia (Dec 1938– Feb 1939); and finally occupied Madrid and south-east Spain (Mar

1939). ► BASQUES; CARLISM; FALANGE ESPAÑOLA; FASCISM; REPUBLIC, SECOND (Spain)

**Spanish Succession, War of the** (1702–13)
The war fought nominally over the throne of Spain, but which involved worldwide interests in trade and the colonies. The succession, in dispute for a generation because of the lack of an heir to CHARLES II, the last Habsburg ruler of Spain, had initially been resolved by partition treaties between the major European powers. Charles II's will aimed to avoid any carve-up of the monarchy by settling the throne on LOUIS XIV of France's grandson, Philip, Duke of Anjou; in 1700, the latter became King PHILIP V of Spain, thereby provoking a declaration of war by the other disappointed powers. The Grand Alliance of the Hague (1701) united England, the HOLY ROMAN EMPIRE and the UNITED PROVINCES OF THE NETHERLANDS against France and Spain. The main centre of land operations was in the Netherlands, where the Duke of MARLBOROUGH inflicted major defeats on the French at Blenheim (1704) and Ramillies (1706), but there were also crucial spheres of conflict in Italy and the Iberian Peninsula. In Italy the successful Imperial

forces, commanded by **EUGÈNE OF SAVOY**, defeated the French at Turin (1706) and subsequently drove the Spanish out of the greater part of Italy. In the Iberian Peninsula, the Allies were supported by the Portuguese and the Catalans, enabling their armies to capture all the major cities of the peninsula by 1706. Gibraltar fell into Allied hands in 1704. Strong Franco-Spanish forces under the Marshal Duke of **BERWICK**, however, won a decisive victory at **ALMANSA** (1707), and the Bourbon forces laid siege to Barcelona, which fell in 1714. The general European war was settled by the Treaty of **UTRECHT** (1713), which confirmed the Bourbon succession in Spain, and by the Treaty of **RASTATT** (1714). ► **BOURBON, HOUSE OF**

## Spartacists

A left-wing revolutionary faction (the *Spartakusbund*), formed by Rosa **LUXEMBURG** and Karl **LIEBKNECHT** in 1917, which advocated ending **WORLD WAR I** and worked for a German socialist revolution. Initially part of the Independent **SPD**, it formed the core of the German Communist Party (**KPD**) when the latter was founded in 1919. Luxemburg and Liebknecht were murdered in disturbances during the German revolution in early 1919. ► **REVOLUTION OF 1918** (Germany)

## SPD (*Sozialdemokratische Partei Deutschlands*, 'Social Democratic Party of Germany')

German political party. In 1875 the two main workers' parties in Germany (Association of German Workers, Social Democratic Workers' Party) merged to form the SAP (Socialist Workers' Party). Despite severe persecution by the Bismarckian state, the party steadily gained support and because of this persecution its politics became increasingly Marxist and revolutionary in tone. In 1890 the SAP was renamed the SPD and in 1891 formally adopted a Marxist ideology (the **ERFURT PROGRAMME**). However, the more pragmatic stance of the trade unions and the increasing involvement of south German Social Democrats in public affairs encouraged the growth of 'revisionism' within the party, as advocated by Eduard **BERNSTEIN**. By 1914 the SPD had over 1 million members and the

support of 34.8 per cent of voters and although it split in 1917 on whether to tolerate the war effort, the majority SPD played the pre-eminent role in the founding of the **WEIMAR REPUBLIC** (1918–19). During the Weimar Republic the SPD pursued a reformist policy that found little favour either among political conservatives or the radicals of other parties. Banned by **HITLER** in 1933, the SPD was refounded in 1945 and in 1959, at Bad Godesberg, formally abandoned its Marxist ideology and committed itself to achieving reforms in the existing social order. In 1966 it entered government in coalition with the **CDU/CSU** and from 1969 to 1982 governed in coalition with the **FDP** when it achieved noteworthy successes in foreign policy (**OSTPOLITIK**) and domestic policy (**MITBESTIMMUNG**). In 1990 the former East Germany's new Social Democratic Party merged with it, and it returned to power in 1998 led by Chancellor Gerhard Schröder. Although it narrowly won the 2002 election, its membership is in decline. ► **BISMARCK, OTTO EDWARD LEOPOLD VON; MARXISM**

## Special Operations Executive (SOE)

An organization set up with British war cabinet approval in July 1940 in response to Winston **CHURCHILL**'s directive to 'set Europe ablaze'; it later also operated in the Far East. It promoted and coordinated resistance activity in enemy-occupied territory until the end of **WORLD WAR II**. ► **FFI; FREE FRENCH; MAQUIS; RESISTANCE MOVEMENT** (France)

## special relationship

A term used mainly by UK academic and media commentators to describe Anglo-American relations, reflecting historical ties of language and culture as well as shared values and interests, and (pejoratively) an alleged lack of realism on the part of British politicians (who rarely, if ever, use the term) about the harsh realities of international relations. Winston **CHURCHILL** during **WORLD WAR II** deluded himself into hoping for an enduring bilateral partnership, but the illusion did not survive peace, although closer political and military ties were created by the stresses of the **COLD WAR** and were exemplified by sharing nuclear weapons technology. Cultivating a special relationship with so dominant a power as the USA was a rational strategy for many countries, though it was always more important to them than to the USA, which by the late 20c had intimate political and economic ties with countries such as Canada, Israel, Mexico and the Republic of Ireland. UK membership of the EU was much favoured by the USA, because the UK was likely to moderate its protectionist and anti-US views in favour of an 'Atlantic' and open vision of Europe's future. The aftermath of the SEPTEMBER 11 ATTACKS, when the UK generally supported US actions, out of conviction on the part of its government, but France and Germany did not, demonstrated that the Anglo-American relationship could still be important, though only when perceived mutual interests coincided.

**Speenhamland System**

The most famous of many local expedients in Britain to improve the operation of the old POOR LAWS at a time of crisis. The name was taken from the Berkshire parish whose magistrates in 1795 introduced scales of relief for labourers dependent both on the prevailing price of bread and the size of labourers' families. The principles spread to many southern and eastern parishes in the early 19c. It was much criticized by political economists for encouraging the poor to breed!

**Speer, Albert** (1905–81)

German Nazi official. An architect by training, he joined the NAZI PARTY in 1931 and became HITLER's chief architect (1934) and Minister of Armaments (1942). Always more concerned with technology and administration than ideology, he openly opposed Hitler in the final months of WORLD WAR II, and was the only Nazi leader at the NUREMBERG TRIALS to admit responsibility for the regime's actions. He was imprisoned for 20 years in Spandau, Berlin, and after his release in 1966 became a writer.

**Speke, John Hanning** (1827–64)

English explorer. In 1854 he joined Richard Burton in a hazardous expedition to Somaliland, and in 1857 the Royal Geographical Society sent them out to search for the equatorial lakes of Africa. They discovered Lake Tanganyika (1858), then Speke travelled on alone. He found the lake which he named Victoria and identified as the source of the Nile. In 1860 he returned with James Grant, explored the lake, and tracked the Nile flowing out of it. He was about to defend the identification against Burton's doubts at a British Association meeting at Bath when he accidentally shot and killed himself. ➤ EXPLORATION

**Spence, William Guthrie** (1846–1926)

British-born Australian trade unionist and politician. His family emigrated to Australia in 1852. Without formal education and working by the age of 13, his beliefs stemmed from his experiences, eclectic reading and Nonconformist background. Secretary of the Amalgamated Miners Association (1882–91), and first President of the Amalgamated Shearers Union (1886–93), his activities contributed to the maritime strike of 1890 and the shearers' strike of 1891, both of which ended in defeat for the workers. In 1894 he founded the AUSTRALIAN WORKERS' UNION, becom-

ing Secretary (1894–8) and President (1898–1917). A member of the New South Wales assembly (1898–1901), he entered federal politics in 1901, but although he became Postmaster-General (1914–15), his major contribution to the Australian labour movement lay in his leadership and organization of rural unionism. Forced out of the union and the AUSTRALIAN LABOR PARTY for supporting conscription in 1916–17, he sat as a Nationalist until defeated in 1919.

**Speransky, Mikhail Mikhailovich** (1772–1839)

Russian politician. He entered government service in 1797, and was soon to achieve distinction, in 1807 becoming Secretary of State to ALEXANDER I, who commissioned him to draft a plan for governmental reform. However, the plan was shelved, and in 1812 a conservative conspiracy brought about his banishment. In 1819 he was appointed Governor-General of Siberia, where he initiated a programme of far-reaching administrative reforms. In 1821 he was recalled to St Petersburg where he was restored to Imperial favour. Now a firm supporter of absolute autocracy, he continued to serve both Alexander and NICHOLAS I in a number of senior posts. His greatest achievement at this time was the publication of a 30-volume collection of the laws of the Russian Empire (1830). ➤ DECEMBRISTS; NICHOLAS II; ROMANOV DYNASTY

**Spiegel Affair** (Oct–Nov 1962)

A political scandal in the Federal Republic of Germany. Following the publication of an article in the periodical *Der Spiegel* on 10 Oct 1962, which questioned the efficacy of West German defence policy, the authorities reacted by arresting its publisher (Rudolf Augstein) and several journalists. Augstein was charged with treason and *Der Spiegel* in effect subjected to censorship. However, a vigorous public re action and opposition from SPD and FDP members of parliament revealed government complicity in the affair, in particular by Franz-Josef STRAUSS, the Minister of Defence. The government backed down, delivering a setback to Strauss's wider political ambitions, undermining the authority of the Chancellor, ADENAUER, but consolidating individual and press freedoms and wider democratic values in post-war Germany.

**Spinola, Ambrogio, Marquis of Los Balbases** (1539–1630)

Genoese soldier in Spanish service. In 1602 he raised and maintained at his own cost 9,000 troops and fought against MAURICE, Count of Nassau and Stadholder of the United Provinces, in the Spanish Netherlands. He was one of the plenipotentiaries at the Hague Conference that made the TWELVE YEARS' TRUCE in 1609. In the early stages of the THIRTY YEARS' WAR he served the Habsburg cause by subduing the Lower Palatinate. He was recalled to the Netherlands to fight once more against Maurice of Nassau, who, however, died of a fever while attempting to relieve Breda, which fell to Spinola in 1625, an event commemorated in Velázquez's famous painting. ➤ HABSBURG DYNASTY

**Spinola, António Sebastião Ribeiro de** (1910–96)

Portuguese general and politician. From a well-to-do

landed family which was a pillar of the Establishment, he fought on the side of **FRANCO** during the **SPANISH CIVIL WAR** and was sent to Nazi Germany for training. A teetotaller and non-smoker, Spínola's trade-marks were his monocle, riding crop and African cane. As Governor-General of Guinea-Bissau (1968–73) he endeavoured to halt the independence movement through a combination of welfare and community projects (designed to win over the local population) and the latest counter-insurgency methods. Though he believed the war was militarily unwinnable, he returned to Portugal a war hero. After the bloodless coup of 25 Apr 1974 toppled the remnants of the **SALAZAR** regime, the conservative Spínola became President as a compromise candidate. He proved a limited and naive politician. Moreover, he clashed gravely with the Armed Forces Movement (MFA) over the granting of independence (July 1974) to Angola, Mozambique and Guinea. The ensuing power struggle led to his resignation (30 Sep 1974). After staging an unsuccessful coup attempt (Mar 1975), he fled into exile. He returned the following year, but played no further part in events.

### Spinoza, Benedict de (1632–77)

Dutch-Jewish philosopher and theologian. His deep interest in the new natural sciences (including astronomy and optics) and Cartesian rationalist philosophy made him unpopular in traditional religious circles, and he was expelled from the Jewish community in 1656 and persecuted by Calvinists. His major works include the *Tractatus Theologico-Politicus* (1670), which despite its anonymity made him famous, and his *Ethica* (published posthumously, 1677). In 1673 he refused the chair of philosophy at Heidelberg University in order to keep his independence.

### Spion Kop, Battle of (1900)

A battle of the second Boer War which was part of the British attempt to relieve the Siege of **LADYSMITH**, a town in Natal besieged by the Boers since Oct 1899. British forces attempted to take a hill a few miles from the town, and although they were close to success at one stage, the Boers succeeded in beating them off. There were 1,500 British casualties, and together with the reverse at Vaal Krantz in the same week, it continued the succession of defeats that the British suffered during the early months of the war. ► **BOER WARS**

### Spiritualia

The staff and ring, symbols of a bishop's spiritual authority. The practice of laymen investing bishops with these symbols was at the centre of the **INVESTITURE CONTROVERSY**.

### Spiritual Regulation (1721)

The reform by **PETER I, THE GREAT** of the **RUSSIAN ORTHODOX CHURCH**, which greatly reduced its former power. In the previous century Patriarch **NIKON** had tried and failed to make the Church superior to the State but he had nevertheless made it extremely powerful and rich. Peter extracted much of its wealth to pay for his wars; but in 1721 he also abolished the independent patriarchate and replaced it with a body of ten clerics, the Holy Synod, with a state official, the Procurator, to ensure that it obeyed the Tsar's will.

Thereafter, the Church was more or less automatically a loyal organ of State, though the patriarchate was reinstated in 1943 when a beleaguered **STALIN** was looking for patriotic support.

### SPÖ (*Sozialistische Partei Österreichs*, 'Socialist Party of Austria')

Austrian political party. Founded in 1889, the SPÖ functioned as a democratic Marxist party which attracted substantial support before 1914 and held power between 1919 and 1920 at the birth of the Austrian Republic. In opposition thereafter, it was opposed by the Right with increasing stridency and crushed in 1934 when it tried to resist by force the institution of crypto-fascist constitutional measures. Refounded in 1945, the SPÖ has held office in Austria for much of the post-war period, either alone or in coalition. In 1978 it eschewed **MARXISM**, supporting instead the democratization of society at all levels and the furtherance of workers' co-determination in the private sector. It changed its name to the Social Democratic Party of Austria in 1991 and remained in power in a two-party coalition with the Austrian People's Party (**ÖVP**) until 1999.

### spoils system

The practice in US politics of filling public offices on the basis of loyalty to the party in power. Such appointments were made beginning with the early presidencies but became widespread in Andrew **JACKSON'S** administration. The term itself derives from Senator William Marcy's defence of the system: 'to the victors belong the spoils'. The corruption and scandals in Ulysses S **GRANT**'s administration led to the passage of civil service reforms and examination requirements, resulting in the establishment of a career structure in government bureaucracies. ► **ALBANY REGENCY; MUGWUMP**

### Sporazum (1939)

The agreement reached on the eve of **WORLD WAR II** between the Yugoslav government led by Dragiša **CVETKOVIĆ** and the Croatian Peasant Party (HSS) led by Vladko **MAČEK**. The Croats agreed to cooperate with the Belgrade government in return for a large measure of self-government. The internal administration of Yugoslavia was reorganized to include **DALMATIA**, Slavonia and parts of Bosnia and Herzegovina within Croatia, and a Croatian assembly met at Zagreb to regulate Croatian domestic affairs. ► **SUBAŠIĆ, IVAN**

### Spurs, Battle of the (16 Aug 1513)

A battle between France and England, who had joined the **HOLY LEAGUE** of the pope, Spain and Venice against the French. **HENRY VIII** laid siege to Thérouanne, near St Omer (Pas-de-Calais), and beat off the French relieving force in this battle, which was so called because of the precipitate French retreat. Thérouanne and Tournai were taken, but these successes had no lasting significance.

### Spurs, Battle of the Golden ► **GOLDEN SPURS, BATTLE OF THE**

### squadristi

The term applied to members of the fascist paramilitary movement that developed in Italy in the period after 1919. *Squadrismo* was often no more than a manifestation of political thuggery and intimidation, often directed against members of left-wing groups, strikers and ethnic minorities. However, in some cases, particularly in rural areas, it represented an understandable reaction to intimidation by similar left-wing groups. Local 'squad' leaders came to be known as **RAS**. After **MUSSOLINI**'s seizure of power, he tried to reduce the threat to order posed by these militant supporters of **FASCISM**, channelling them with considerable success into the **MVSN**.

### Square Deal
The popular name for the domestic policies of US President Theodore **ROOSEVELT**, especially the enforcement of the **ANTI-TRUST ACTS**. The term was coined by Roosevelt during a speaking tour in the summer of 1902.

### Squatters
In Australian history, pastoralists who occupied unallocated land initially beyond the limits of Crown land grants; their position was formalized by the late 1840s. The term was subsequently used to denote large-scale landholders in general. Squatters formed a social and economic élite and used their power to impede government efforts to settle small farmers.
► **CLOSER SETTLEMENT; SELECTORS**

### Squillace, Leopoldo de Gregorio, Marquis of ►
ESQUILACHE, LEOPOLDO DE GREGORIO, MARQUIS OF

### SRI LANKA official name **Democratic Socialist Republic of Sri Lanka**, formerly (to 1972) **Ceylon**

A pear-shaped island state in the Indian Ocean situated off the south-east coast of India. The Sinhalese (from northern India) colonized part of the island in the 5c BC and dominated the northern plain until around AD 1200, when they gradually moved southwestwards due to the many **TAMIL** invasions from southern India. Buddhism spread amongst the Sinhalese from about 200BC. Some coastal areas of the country were conquered by the Portuguese in the 15c, then it was taken over by the Dutch in 1658. British occupation began in 1796, and the island became a British colony in 1802. The whole island was united for the first time in 1815, when it was named Ceylon. Tamil labourers were brought in from southern India during colonial rule, to work on coffee and tea plantations. Ceylon was given Dominion status within the **COMMONWEALTH OF NATIONS** in 1948, and became an independent republic as the Republic of Sri Lanka

in 1972. Acute political tension exists between the Buddhist Sinhalese majority and the Hindu Tamil minority, who wish to establish an independent state in the Tamil majority areas in the north and east. In the early 1980s Tamil separatists began fighting government forces for control of these areas. The fighting between the **LTTE** Tamil guerrillas and government forces remained mainly in the Jaffna Peninsula at first, though sporadic terrorist attacks took place nearer the capital. The civil war continued, despite an attempt by India in 1987 to enforce a compromise based on a united but somewhat decentralized Sri Lanka which would publicly acknowledge Indian regional hegemony, and various attempts at peace talks throughout the 1990s. A state of emergency was declared in 1996. In 1994 Chandrika Bandaranaike **KUMARATUNGA**, as leader of the nine-party People's Alliance, a coalition which includes the Sri Lanka Freedom Party (**SLFP**), was elected first Prime Minister and then President of Sri Lanka, thus ending the 17-year rule by the United National Party (**UNP**). Peace talks with the LTTE, the first formal negotiations in seven years, began in Sep 2002 but stalled in Nov 2003 and violence resumed. Parts of the country were devastated by the Indian Ocean tsunami in Dec 2004.
► **ANURADHAPURA; DRAVIDA MUNNETRA KAZHAGAM; INDO-SRI LANKAN PEACE ACCORD; KANDYAN KINGDOM; POLONNARUWA; SINHALA**

### Sri Lanka Freedom Party ► SLFP

### Srivijaya ► SOUTH-EAST ASIA PRE-1000AD

### Srobar, Vavro (1867–1950)
Slovak politician. As a medical student in Prague he was greatly influenced by **MASARYK**, and in 1898 he established a journal for Slovak youth that developed the idea of collaboration with the Czech national movement. During and just after **WORLD WAR I** he was able to give effect to the idea in the establishment of the Czechoslovak state. He did the same during and just after **WORLD WAR II** to get Czechoslovakia re-established. On both occasions, other Slovak attitudes were pushed aside.

### SS (*Schutzstaffel*, 'Protective squad')
A Nazi organization founded in 1925 as **HITLER**'s personal bodyguard. From 1929 it was transformed and expanded by **HIMMLER** into an élite force. Within the Third **REICH** it became an independent organization, controlling the police forces, and responsible for concentration camps and racial policy. It formed its own armed detachments, which after 1939 became the *Waffen* ('armed') SS. During **WORLD WAR II** it became an alternative army, an autonomous power within the Third Reich, and the principal agent of racial extermination policy. ► **NAZI PARTY**

### Stabilization Plan (1959)
The economic autarky sought after 1939 by the **FRANCO** regime by means of a heavily protected command economy had failed so signally by the late 1950s that the country was on the verge of bankruptcy. The Stabilization Plan of 1959 was the cornerstone of the regime's programme of capitalist modernization. This dramatic change in policy was engineered above all by Mariano Navarro Rubio (Minister of Finance, 1957–65) and Alberto Ullastres (Minister of Commerce, 1957–65), both prominent members of **OPUS**

**DEI**. Although the regime's switch to **LAISSEZ-FAIRE** capitalism proved economically successful, the short-term social cost was extremely high. However, the economic modernization of Spain did more than anything else to undermine the political foundations of the Franco dictatorship.

### Stack, Lee (d.1924)

British soldier. He was Sirdar (British Commander-in-Chief of the Egyptian Army) in 1924, at a time when a combination of the first Wafdist government in Egypt and the first Labour government in Britain was resulting in a certain amount of British sympathy being shown for Egyptian nationalist aspirations. Unfortunately for both sides, when Sa'd **ZAGHLUL** came to London for negotiations his demands were well beyond what the British government was prepared to concede. The upshot was increased hostility to the British in Egypt and particularly to the rank and status of the Sirdar. Stack was murdered in Cairo in late 1924 to some extent as a result of this. The subsequent ultimatum presented to Egypt by the British, although certainly not strong enough for the British expatriates in Egypt, was sufficient to jolt the Egyptian government. This, coupled with the complicity in a number of political murders with which certain Wafdists were charged, was enough to bring down the Wafdist government.

### Stadholder (*Stadhouder*)

The office of the chief executive of the Dutch Republic. Originally the Stadholder had been the King's representative and military commander in a given district; when the northern Netherlands broke formally with their Spanish monarch in 1581 the provincial assemblies (states) took it on themselves to appoint the Stadholder. This meant that his position was highly ambivalent; he was appointed by the states, but had the right to appoint officials, often including the members of the states themselves. Each province could appoint its own Stadholder, but in practice the offices always went to a prominent member of the House of Orange-Nassau (the northern provinces often chose a different member). The Stadholder was not a monarch, but successful ones like **FREDERICK HENRY, WILLIAM II** and **WILLIAM III, OF ORANGE** had many of the trappings of kings; conversely, powerful leaders of the states party like Johan de **WITT** tried to reduce the centralizing power of the Stadholders. There were two periods when no Stadholder ruled in most of the provinces: 1650–72 and 1702–47. Under William III the office became hereditary; in 1815 the son of the last Stadholder, **WILLIAM V**, became King **WILLIAM I**.

### Stahlberg, Kaarlo Juho (1865–1952)

Finnish politician. Having established his reputation as Professor of Law at Helsinki University, as well as a judge and a member of the Finnish Diet, in 1919 he drafted Finland's constitution and served as the republic's first President until 1925. Kidnapped by members of a pro-fascist movement in 1930, he was narrowly defeated in the elections of 1931 and 1937.

### Stahlhelm Bund der Frontsoldaten

German paramilitary league (literally, 'Steel Helmet League of Front-line Soldiers'). This monarchist para-

## HOUSE OF ORANGE-NASSAU

| Regnal Dates | Name |
|---|---|
| ▸*Stadholder* | |
| 1572/84 | William I, the Silent |
| 1585/1625 | Maurice |
| 1625/47 | Frederick Henry |
| 1647/50 | William II |
| 1672/1702 | William III |
| 1747/51 | William IV |
| 1751/95 | William V |
| ▸*King/Queen* | |
| 1815/40 | William I |
| 1840/9 | William II |
| 1849/90 | William III |
| 1890/1948 | Wilhelmina |
| 1948/80 | Juliana |
| 1980/ | Beatrix |

military veterans' association was founded in Nov 1918 to resist radical left-wing unrest. It then quickly became the main focus of anti-republican paramilitary activity in the **WEIMAR REPUBLIC**, propagating extreme nationalist and racist views, and did much thereby to undermine the democratic parliamentary order. Its political links to the **DNVP**, which formed a coalition with the **NAZI PARTY** in Jan 1933, allowed the *Stahlhelm* a minor role in **HITLER**'s consolidation of power after which its members were either absorbed into the **SA** (1933) or eventually saw their units disbanded (1935).

### Stakhanov, Alexei Grigorievich (1906–77)

Russian coalminer. He started an incentive scheme (1935) for exceptional output and efficiency by individual steelworkers, coalminers, etc. Such prize workers were called Stakhanovites.

### Stakhanovism

An economic system in the USSR designed to raise productivity through incentives. It was named after the first worker to receive an award, coalminer Alexei Grigorievich **STAKHANOV**, who in 1935 reorganized his team's workload to achieve major gains in production. The movement lasted only until 1939.

### Stalin, Joseph, originally Iosif Vissarionovich Dzhugashvili (1879–1953)

Georgian Marxist revolutionary and virtual dictator of the USSR. The son of a cobbler and ex-serf, he was educated at Tiflis Orthodox Theological Seminary, from which he was expelled in 1899. After joining a Georgian Social Democratic organization (1898), he became active in the revolutionary underground, and was twice exiled to Siberia (1902 and 1913). As a leading Bolshevik he played an active role in the **OCTOBER REVOLUTION**, and became People's Commissar for Nationalities in the first Soviet government and a member of the Communist Party **POLITBURO**. In 1922 he became General-Secretary of the Party Central Committee, a post he held until his death, and also occupied other key positions which enabled him to build up enormous personal power in the party and government apparatus. After **LENIN**'s death (1924) he pursued a policy of building '**SOCIALISM IN ONE COUNTRY**', and gradually isolated and disgraced his political rivals, notably Leon **TROTSKY**. In 1928 he launched the campaign for the collectivization of agriculture during which millions of peasants perished, and the first five-year plan for the forced industrialization of the economy. Between 1934 and 1938 he inaugurated a massive purge of the party, government, armed forces, and intelligentsia in which millions of so-called 'enemies of the people' were imprisoned, exiled or shot. In 1939 he signed the Non-Aggression Pact with **HITLER** which bought the USSR two years respite from involvement in **WORLD WAR II**. After the German invasion (1941), the USSR became a member of the Grand Alliance, and Stalin, as war leader, assumed the title of Generalissimus. He took part in the **TEHRAN CONFERENCE**, **YALTA CONFERENCE** and **POTSDAM CONFERENCE** which with other factors resulted in Soviet military and political control over the liberated countries of post-war Eastern and central Europe. From 1945 until his death he resumed his repressive measures at home, and conducted foreign policies which contributed to the **COLD WAR** between the USSR and the West. He was posthumously denounced by Nikita **KHRUSHCHEV** at the 20th Party Congress (1956) for crimes against the party and for building a 'cult of personality'. Under Mikhail **GORBACHEV** many of Stalin's victims were rehabilitated, and the whole phenomenon of '**STALINISM**' officially condemned by the Soviet authorities. ► **BOLSHEVIKS**; **RUSSIAN REVOLUTION**

### Stalingrad, Battle of (1942–3)
One of the great battles of **WORLD WAR II**, fought between Nazi German and Soviet troops in and around Stalingrad (now Volgograd) on the River Volga during the winter of 1942–3. After savage fighting, which cost 70,000 German lives, the German 6th Army surrendered (Feb 1943), yielding 91,000 prisoners of war to the Russians. The battle is regarded as a major turning-point in the Allied victory over Germany.

### Stalinism
A label used pejoratively outside (and ultimately inside) the USSR to refer to the nature of the Soviet regime during the period 1929–53. It referred to a monolithic system, tightly disciplined and bureaucratic, with the party hierarchy having a monopoly of political and economic power. It also encompassed the total subservience of society and culture to political ends, the suppression of political opponents and total disregard of human rights, and especially the promotion of an individual above the party. ► **COMMUNISM**; **STALIN, JOSEPH**

### Stalwarts
In the USA, members of a conservative faction within the **REPUBLICAN PARTY** which operated while President **HAYES** was in office (1877–81). The Stalwarts' leaders were Roscoe **CONKLING** and Chester **ARTHUR**, and their rivals were the more liberal Republicans nicknamed the 'Half-Breeds'. The Stalwarts' chief policies were support of the **SPOILS SYSTEM**, opposition to reconstruction in the South, and opposition to civil service reform of any kind. The term Stalwart was not used after 1881, when a faction-member and disappointed office-seeker assassinated President **GARFIELD** (the Half-Breeds' presidential candidate) – an action which facilitated the passage of the **PENDLETON CIVIL SERVICE REFORM ACT**.

### Stamboliski, Alexander (1879–1923)
Bulgarian politician. A staunch republican, in 1906 he took over the leading role in the Bulgarian Agrarian National Union (BANU). During **WORLD WAR I**, he was imprisoned by the pro-German King **FERDINAND I** for his outspoken support of the Allies. In 1918 he led a march on Sofia and forced the King to abdicate, briefly declaring a republic. After the 1919 elections, he became Prime Minister and represented defeated Bulgaria at the **PARIS PEACE CONFERENCE**. He established an authoritarian regime, organizing the anti-communist Orange Guard, undermining the position of the urban middle class and introducing a programme of radical reform designed to turn Bulgaria into a model agricultural state. Abroad, he tried to improve Bulgaria's international position, joining the **LEAGUE OF NATIONS** and attempting to mend relations with Yugoslavia. The military and the parties of the Centre and Right united against him while the Communist Party and **VMRO** agitated against his policies. In 1923 he was overthrown in a military coup and was tortured and decapitated by members of VMRO. ► **TSANKOV, ALEXANDER**

### Stambolov, Stephan Nikolov (1854–95)
Bulgarian politician. He took part in the rising of 1875–6 and became the leading member of the Russophobe regency (1886). As Premier (1887–94), he ruled with a strong hand. Forced to retire, he was assassinated.

### Stamp Act (1765)
A British Act passed by the administration of George **GRENVILLE**, which levied a direct tax on all papers required in discharging official business in the American colonies. It was the first direct tax levied without the consent of the colonial assemblies, and it caused much discontent in the colonies, six of which petitioned against it. (The measure provoked the colonists' famous slogan, 'No taxation without representation'.) The Act was withdrawn by the **ROCKINGHAM** government in 1766. ► **AMERICAN REVOLUTION**

### Standish, Myles or Miles (c.1584–1656)
English soldier and colonist. Born probably in Ormskirk, Lancashire, he served in the Netherlands, and in 1620 was hired by the Pilgrim Fathers to accompany them on the *Mayflower*. He was appointed military captain of the settlement at Plymouth, supervised the defences, and negotiated with the **NATIVE AMERICANS**. In 1625 he went to London to negotiate ownership of their land. He became Treasurer of Massachusetts (1644–9), and in 1631 was one of the founders of Duxbury, Massachusetts.

### Stanfield, Robert Lorne (1914–2003)
Canadian politician. In 1967 he took over the leadership of the Conservative Party from John **DIEFENBAKER** after a bitter fight. He sought French-Canadian support by proposing to accept bilingualism and special conditions for Quebec, but in doing so, he lost the support of many anglophone Conservatives. A successful Premier of Nova Scotia, he failed to project himself in national politics and in 1976 was replaced by Joe **CLARK**.

### Stanhope, Charles Stanhope, 3rd Earl (1753–1816)
British scientist and politician. He became an MP and

married the daughter of William **PITT, THE ELDER**. A strong enthusiast for the **FRENCH REVOLUTION**, he advocated peace with **NAPOLEON I** (1800). As a scientist, he invented a new microscope lens, two types of calculating machine, the first iron hand-printing press, and several other devices.

**Stanhope, James Stanhope, 1st Earl** (1675–1721)
British soldier and politician. He entered parliament as a Whig in 1701, and commanded in Spain during the War of the **SPANISH SUCCESSION** (1702–13). He was Secretary of State for Foreign Affairs under **GEORGE I**, and became his Chief Minister in 1717. ▸ **WHIGS**

**Stanisław II August Poniatowski** (1732–98)
Last King of Poland (1764/95). He was the son of Stanisław **PONIATOWSKI**. In St Petersburg in 1755, while in the suite of the British ambassador, he became much favoured by Empress **CATHERINE II, THE GREAT**. Largely through her influence and that of his father, he was elected king in 1764. A cultured and enlightened individual with reforming ideas and an independent streak, he was not necessarily the person most suited to countering the intrigues of his neighbours and the unruliness of the *sejm* or diet. **FREDERICK II, THE GREAT**, who had gained the consent of Austria to a partition of Poland, soon made a similar proposal to Russia, and despite Stanisław the first partition was effected in 1772. The sejm then agreed to try, too late, to introduce reforms. The intrigues of discontented nobles were used to facilitate Russian and Prussian intervention, and a second fruitless resistance was followed in 1793 by the second partition. The Poles now became desperate; under **KOŚCIUSZKO**'s leadership a much more widespread rising took place in 1794, the Prussians were driven out, and the Russians were several times routed. But Austria again intervened, Kościuszko was defeated, Warsaw was taken, and the independent Polish state and with it the Polish monarchy were at an end. Stanisław abdicated in 1795 and died in St Petersburg.

**Stanisław Leszczyński** (1677–1766)
King of Poland (1704/9 and 1733/5). After his election in 1704, under the influence of **CHARLES XII** of Sweden, he was driven out by **PETER I, THE GREAT**. Re-elected in 1733, he lost the War of the **POLISH SUCCESSION**, and formally abdicated in 1736, receiving the Duchies of Lorraine and Bar.

**Stanley, Sir Henry Morton**, originally **John Rowlands** (1841–1904)
Anglo-American explorer and journalist, born in Denbigh, Wales. In 1859 he went as cabin boy to New Orleans, where he was adopted by a merchant named Stanley. He served in the Confederate Army and US Navy, and in 1867 joined the *New York Herald*, accompanying Lord **NAPIER**'s Abyssinian expedition in 1868. In Oct 1869 he received the laconic instruction, 'Find **LIVINGSTONE**'; on his way he visited Egypt for the opening of the Suez Canal, and travelled through Palestine, Turkey, Persia and India. On 10 Nov 1871 he 'found' Livingstone at Ujiji in Tanganyika, and the two explored Lake Tanganyika. In 1874 he returned to Africa, determined the shape of Lake Tanganyika, and traced the Congo to the sea. In 1879, on a third expedition, working for King **LEOPOLD II** of the Belgians, he helped set up the Congo Free State. ▸ **EXPLORATION**

**Stanton, Elizabeth Cady** (1815–1902)
US feminist. Educated at Troy (New York) Female Seminary, she involved herself in the anti-**SLAVERY** and temperance movements, and in 1840 married the abolitionist Henry B Stanton. In 1848 she and Lucretia **MOTT** organized the first **WOMEN'S RIGHTS** convention in Seneca Falls, NY. She was personally responsible for the emergence of women's suffrage as a public issue, but she regarded women's rights as a much larger problem. ▸ **ABOLITIONISM**; **NATIONAL AMERICAN WOMAN SUFFRAGE ASSOCIATION**; **SENECA FALLS WOMEN'S RIGHTS CONVENTION**

**Starace, Achille** (1889–1945)
Italian politician. An interventionist in 1914 and a **BERSAGLIERI** officer in **WORLD WAR I**, Starace was one of the most energetic of the **FASCIST PARTY** (PNF) bosses in the immediate post-war era, dominating the PNF in both the Veneto and Venezia-Tridentina. Party Vice-Secretary (1921–2 and 1926–31), and Secretary (1931–9), he was most renowned for his profound stupidity and was a constant butt of popular jokes. In May 1941 he was made head of the **MVSN**, but was imprisoned under the Republic of **SALÒ** for insufficient attachment to the regime. He was captured and executed by partisans in Milan.

**Starčević, Ante** (1823–96)
Croatian nationalist. At first a follower of Ljudevit **GAJ** and the **ILLYRIAN MOVEMENT**, in 1861 with Eugen Kvaternik he founded the Croatian Party of Right (ie state-right). An extreme nationalist, he advocated the creation of an independent Croatia that would include not only all the Croats but also all the Slovenes and Serbs, whom he considered to be of Croatian nationality. During the anti-Croat regime of Ban **KHUEN-HÉDERVÁRY**, membership of his party grew to dominate Croatian political life in the 1880s.

**Star Chamber, Court of**
The royal prerogative court in Britain for hearing subjects' petitions and grievances, of uncertain date but increasingly prominent under the Tudors and early Stuarts. It consisted of privy councillors and two chief justices, who dealt swiftly and efficiently with cases, particularly those involving public order. **CHARLES I** used it against government opponents. It was abolished by the **LONG PARLIAMENT** in 1641. ▸ **STUART, HOUSE OF**; **TUDOR, HOUSE OF**

**Starhemberg Family**
A prominent Austrian family. Ernest Rüdiger (1638–1701) is the most notable member. He was the field marshal who defended Vienna when it was attacked by the Turks (during the Turkish Wars), for the last time, in 1683.

**START (Strategic Arms Reduction Talks)**
Discussions held between the USA and the USSR, beginning in 1982–3 after President Ronald **REAGAN** came to power, resuming after Mikhail **GORBACHEV** became General-Secretary in 1985 and continuing after 1991 between the USA and the four republics that had inherited nuclear weapons from the USSR:

Belarus, Ukraine, Russia and Kazakhstan. The talks were concerned with a reduction in the number of long-range missiles and their nuclear warheads and were complicated partly by issues of mutual distrust and partly by the need to deal also with other types of weapons. Agreements were reached on the abolition of intermediate-range nuclear missiles in 1987 (the **INF** Treaty) and on conventional forces in Europe in 1990 (the **CFE TREATY**). The way was then open for President George H W **BUSH** to agree the START I Treaty with President Gorbachev in Jul 1991 and the START II Treaty with President Boris **YELTSIN** in Jan 1993. Broadly speaking, the two powers agreed to cut their long-range nuclear capability by two-thirds within ten years. The other three former Soviet republics signed up to START I in Nov 1993 and agreed either to destroy their nuclear weapons or to hand them over to Russia. ► **SALT**

**Star Wars** ► **SDI**

**States General** ► **ESTATES GENERAL**

### States Reorganization Act (1956)
The process of linguistic reorganization of states in India was a prolonged and divisive one and raised fundamental questions of centre-state relations. The first step occurred in the aftermath of a major movement in the Andhra region of the former province of Madras. This led to the appointment of the States Reorganization Commission, which published its report in 1955. Following the States Reorganization Act, the boundaries of the southern states were reorganized in closer conformity with traditional linguistic regions. The bifurcation of Bombay province into the present states of Gujarat and Maharashtra followed in 1960. In 1966, Punjab was reorganized and its several parts distributed among three units: Punjab, the new state of Haryana, and Himachal Pradesh. Several new states have also been carved out in response to tribal demands in the north-eastern region of the country from time to time. Presently India has 25 states and seven union territories.

### states' rights
A US constitutional doctrine based on the Tenth Amendment that the separate states enjoy areas of self-control which cannot be breached by the federal government. Debate has surrounded the interpretation of this doctrine. At issue are the concepts of the implied power of the federal government and the extent or limitations of that power. The doctrine has been applied inconsistently and in support of opposing points of view. It was adopted by white Southerners between **RECONSTRUCTION** and the **CIVIL RIGHTS MOVEMENT**, and amounted to a code term for white supremacy.

### Statists
A late 18c southern Netherlands conservative political faction, also known as Nootists after their leader Hendrik van der Noot (1731–1837). In reaction to the rationalist reforms of Emperor **JOSEPH II**, two groups rose up in the **BRABANT REVOLUTION** of 1789; the **VONCKISTS** and the Statists. The latter wanted a return to the old situation where effective power had been in the hands of the provincial assemblies or states, hence their name.

### Statuto
In Italy, the name given to the constitution granted by **CHARLES ALBERT** in Mar 1848. It remained more or less unaltered as the constitution of united Italy after 1860. Extensive powers were vested in the king and the right to vote was limited by a very high property qualification.

### Statutum in favorem principum (1231–2)
A document enacted by **FREDERICK II**, at the instigation of lay and clerical princes on whom the Emperor depended for his Italian policy. The statute places limits on the role and influence of the towns and the extent to which they can intervene in what the princes regarded as their prerogatives.

### Stauffenberg, Claus, Count von (1907–44)
German soldier. Initially welcoming the advent to power of **HITLER**, he quickly became alienated by Nazi brutality. He was a colonel on the German general staff in 1944, and placed the bomb in the unsuccessful attempt to assassinate Hitler at Rastenburg (20 July 1944). He was shot the following day. ► **NAZI PARTY; WORLD WAR II**

### Stauning, Thorvald (1873–1942)
Danish politician. He became a member of the Danish parliament, the **FOLKETINGET** (1906), leader of the Danish Social Democratic Party (1910) and Scandinavia's first Social Democratic minister in 1916. After the general election of 1924, he became Premier of Denmark's first Social Democratic government. The longest-serving Danish Premier of the 20c (1924–6 and 1929–42), one of the achievements of the parliamentary reform policies of the Stauning administration was the social reform bill of May 1933 based upon the principle of the needy citizen's right to public support. In the general election of 1935, fought by the Social Democrats under the slogan 'Stauning or Chaos', the party's popularity reached its peak when 46 per cent of the electorate voted for it. Stauning's reform policy was interrupted (Apr 1940) with the German occupation of Denmark, but he continued as Premier of a national coalition government. He died on 3 May 1942 and his funeral became a manifestation of popular and national solidarity. ► **DENMARK, GERMAN INVASION OF**

### Steel, David Martin Scott, Baron Steel of Aikwood (1938– )
British politician. He became an MP in 1965, sponsored a controversial Bill to reform the laws on abortion (1966–7), and was active in the anti-**APARTHEID** movement. He became Liberal Chief Whip (1970–5), before succeeding Jeremy Thorpe as Liberal Party leader (1976–88). In 1981 he led the party into an alliance with the **SOCIAL DEMOCRATIC PARTY**. Following successful merger negotiations between the two parties (1987–8), he was the last leader of the Liberal Party. He remained active in national politics as an MP and party spokesman until he retired as an MP in 1997. He was a member of the Scottish Parliament and its Presiding Officer in its first term (1999–2003).

### Steel, Pact of (22 May 1939)
An offensive alliance concluded between fascist Italy and Nazi Germany and based on the earlier Rome–Berlin Axis. It committed either power to join the other should it become involved in hostilities.

**Stefanik, Milan Rastislav** (1880–1919)
Hero of the Slovak national movement. Born in Slovakia and educated in Prague, he migrated to Paris in 1904 and became a French citizen in 1910. An astronomer, then civil servant, he volunteered for the French air force in 1914 and was appointed general in 1918. He also worked with **MASARYK** and **BENEŠ** as a representative of the Slovaks. A spokesman at the **PARIS PEACE CONFERENCE** in 1919, his words carried great weight with the French and with his own Slovaks. In 1919 he was killed in an air crash while travelling back to Slovakia.

**Stein, (Heinrich Friedrich) Karl, Baron von** (1757–1831)
Prussian politician. He studied law at Göttingen, and entered the service of **PRUSSIA** in 1780, becoming Secretary for Trade (1804–7) and Chief Minister (1807–8), when he carried out important reforms in the army, economy, and both national and local government. In 1812 he went to St Petersburg, and built up the coalition against **NAPOLEON I**. He was later adviser to **ALEXANDER I** (1812–15), then retired to Kappenberg in Westphalia, where he died. ➤ **NAPOLEONIC WARS**

**Steinem, Gloria** (1934– )
US feminist and writer. A journalist and activist in the 1960s, she emerged as a leading figure in the women's movement. She co-founded *New York* magazine in 1968, was a co-founder of Women's Action Alliance in 1971, and was a founder of the feminist *Ms* magazine.

**Stephen** (c.1097–1154)
Last Norman King of England (1135/54). He was the son of Stephen, Count of Blois, and Adela, the daughter of **WILLIAM I, THE CONQUEROR**. He had sworn to accept **HENRY I**'s daughter, Empress Matilda, as Queen, but seized the English crown and was recognized as Duke of Normandy on Henry's death in 1135. Though defeated and captured at the Battle of Lincoln (Feb 1141), he was released nine months later, after Matilda's supporters had been routed at Winchester. However, Matilda strengthened her grip on the West Country; **DAVID I** of Scotland annexed the northern English counties by 1141; and Matilda's husband, Count Geoffrey of Anjou, conquered Normandy by 1144–5. Stephen was also repeatedly challenged by baronial rebellions, and after 18 years of virtually continuous warfare, he was forced in 1153 to accept Matilda's son, the future **HENRY II**, as his lawful successor. His reputation as the classic incompetent king of English medieval history is nevertheless undeserved. He was remarkably tenacious in seeking to uphold royal rights, and his war strategy was basically sound. His inability to defend the Norman Empire was due largely to the sheer weight of his military burdens, especially the major offensives of the Scots in the north and the **ANGEVINS** in the south.

**Stephen I** (977–1038)
First King of Hungary (997/1038). He formed Pannonia and Dacia into a regular kingdom, organized Christianity, and introduced many social and economic reforms. He received from the pope the title of 'Apostolic King' and, according to tradition, the crown of **ST STEPHEN**, now a Hungarian national treasure. He died at Esztergom, and was canonized in 1083.

**Stephen I Nemanja** (d.1200)
King of Serbia (1169/96). He was the founder of the Kingdom of Serbia and of the **NEMANJA DYNASTY**. After receiving a grant of land from the Byzantine Emperor **MANUEL I COMNENUS**, with his brothers he drew together the Serbian *župani* ('chieftains') in the **RAŠKA** region and established himself as their king in 1169. He abdicated in favour of his second son (1196) and, taking the name Simeon, became a monk on Mount **ATHOS**. ➤ **SAVA, ST**

**Stephen IV, the Great** (1435–1501)
Prince of Moldavia (1457/1504). He defended Moldavia against invasions by Hungary in 1467 and 1471 and by the Ottoman Turks, defeating the latter at Vaslui (1475) and Valca Alba (1476). He won a reputation as the 'Athlete of Christ' because of his determination to drive back the Turks from Christendom. ➤ **MOLDAVIA AND WALLACHIA; ROMANIA**

**Stephen Báthory** (1533–86)
Hungarian King of Poland (1575/86). Elected Prince of Transylvania in 1571, he succeeded to the Polish throne four years later. An able administrator and fine soldier, he easily suppressed a revolt of dissident burghers in Danzig and went on to defeat an attempted Russian invasion of Livonia under **IVAN IV, THE TERRIBLE** and retake Polotsk. He was responsible for many administrative reforms and was notably successful in achieving a tolerant resolution of the religious divisions brought about by the **REFORMATION** in Poland.

**Stephen Dushan** (c.1308–1355)
King (1331/46) and Emperor (1346/55) of Serbia. He was the greatest of the **NEMANJA DYNASTY**, who extended Serbian rule into Macedonia, Bulgaria and Albania and instituted a legal code.

**Stephensen, Magnús** (1762–1833)
Icelandic administrator. The first Icelandic governor of the island, he was the leading representative in Iceland of the European **ENLIGHTENMENT**. After studying in Copenhagen, he was sent by the Danish government to report on the effects of the great volcanic eruption of 1783. In 1789 he was appointed Justice for the southern and western areas of the island and in 1800 was made President of the new Supreme Court, which replaced the **ALTHING**. He encouraged reform in a number of fields and published Iceland's first monthly journal. He was, however, an arrogant man, who was somewhat insensitive to the traditions dear to his countrymen.

**Stepinac, Aloysius** (1898–1960)
Yugoslav prelate and cardinal, and Primate of Croatia. He was imprisoned by **TITO** (1946–51) for alleged wartime collaboration and, with failing health, was released but lived the remainder of his life under house arrest.

**Stepnyak ('Son of the Steppe'),** nom de guerre of **Sergei Mikhailovich Kravchinsky** (1852–95)
Russian revolutionary. An artillery officer, born Sergius Mikhailovich, he adopted this nom de guerre. Having become obnoxious to government as an

apostle of freedom, he was arrested, and subsequently kept under such surveillance that he left Russia and settled (1876) in Geneva, and then (1885) in London. He was, however, held to be the assassin of General Mesentzieff, head of the St Petersburg police (1878). He was run over by a train in a London suburb. Among his works were *La Russia Sotteranea* (1881, Eng trans *Underground Russia*, 1883), studies of the Nihilist movement; *Russia under the Tsars* (trans 1885); and the novel *The Career of a Nihilist* (1889).

### Stern Gang

Palestinian covert organization formed under Avraham Stern in 1940 after disagreement with the **IRGUN** over a ceasefire with the British during **WORLD WAR II**. Conflict between the Stern Gang and the British climaxed in 1942, when British forces sought and killed members of the group, including Stern himself. Thereafter, his followers adopted the name *Lohamei Herut Yisrael* ('Fighters for Israel's Freedom'), but others dubbed them the Stern Gang/Group. Their aim was to attack British installations and personnel in **PALESTINE** in the struggle for a Jewish state. Although collaborating with the **HAGANAH** and Irgun during 1945, many found the Stern Gang unnecessarily brutal. After 1948 the group was disbanded.

### Stevens, Henry Herbert (1878–1973)

Canadian politician. A member of **MEIGHEN**'s Conservative administrations in 1921 and 1926, he was Minister of Trade and Commerce in **BENNETT's** government from 1930. In 1934 he became Chairman of the **PRICE SPREADS COMMISSION**, and after the controversy surrounding its recommendations, he resigned to found the Reconstruction Party. He was its only successful candidate in the 1935 election, and returned to the Conservative Party in 1939.

### Stevens, Siaka Probyn (1905–88)

Sierra Leone politician. Educated in Freetown, he was a railwayman and miner, founding the Mineworkers Union in 1943. Appointed a representative in the Protectorate Assembly, he then went to study at Ruskin College, Oxford in 1945. On his return, he helped found the Sierra Leone People's Party (APC) in 1951. The APC won the 1967 general election but the result was disputed by the army and Stevens withdrew from the premiership. In 1968 an army revolt brought him back and in 1971 he became President. He established a one-party state and remained in power until his retirement at the age of 80.

### Stevens, Thaddeus (1792–1868)

US politician. After graduating from Dartmouth College, he began a law practice at Gettysburg, Pennsylvania. He was an outspoken opponent of **SLAVERY** throughout his years in **CONGRESS** (1849–53 and 1859–68). A radical Republican leader during **RECONSTRUCTION**, he actively pressed for the **IMPEACHMENT** of President Andrew **JACKSON** (1868).

### Stevenson, Adlai Ewing (1900–65)

US politician. Educated at Princeton, he became a lawyer, took part in several European missions for the State Department (1943–5), and was elected Governor of Illinois (1948) as a Democrat. He helped to found the **UN** (1946), ran twice against **EISENHOWER** as a notably liberal presidential candidate (1952 and 1956), and was the US ambassador to the UN in 1961–5.

### Stewart, Charles Edward, 'the Young Pretender' ► STUART, CHARLES EDWARD

### Stewart, House of ► STUART, HOUSE OF

### Stewart, James Francis Edward, 'the Old Pretender' ► STUART, JAMES FRANCIS EDWARD

### Steyn, Martinus Theunis (1857–1916)

South African politician. Born in Winburg, Orange Free State, he was state President (from 1896), joining with the Transvaal in the war (1889–1902). He promoted the Union of 1910, but later encouraged Boer extremists and their rebellion of 1914. His son, Colin Fraser (1887–1959), mediated between Generals **BOTHA** and **DE WET**, and was Minister of Justice in the **SMUTS** government (1939–45) and Minister of Labour (1945–8). ► **BOER WARS**

### Stilwell, Joseph Warren, nicknamed Vinegar Joe (1883–1946)

US soldier. Born in Palatka, Florida, he graduated from West Point in 1904. He was military attaché to the US Embassy in Peking (Beijing) from 1932 to 1939. In 1941 he became US military representative in China and in 1942 commander of the 5th and 6th Chinese Armies in Burma (now Myanmar). He was also Chief of Staff to **CHIANG KAI-SHEK**, for whom he planned the Ledo Road (later known as the Stilwell Road). In the Burma counter-offensive in 1943 he was commanding general of the US forces in China, Burma and India, but he was recalled in 1944.

### Stimson, Henry Lewis (1867–1950)

US politician. Appointed a US District Attorney in New York by President Theodore **ROOSEVELT**, he made his reputation in anti-trust actions. In 1911 he became Secretary of War in President **TAFT**'s administration and modernized the army in which, as an artillery colonel, he fought in France in 1917. President **COOLIDGE** sent him to Nicaragua to negotiate an end to the civil war, and then to the Philippines as Governor-General. He became Secretary of State in President **HOOVER**'s cabinet, and was the chief negotiator for the USA at the London Naval Conference (1930). At the 1932 Geneva Conference on arms limitation, he issued the 'Stimson Doctrine', condemning the Japanese occupation of Manchuria. Recalled as Secretary of War (1940) by President Franklin D **ROOSEVELT**, his experience made him a formidable influence on wartime policy, and (fearing that an invasion would be too costly in Allied lives) his advice was crucial in President **TRUMAN**'s decision to use the atom bomb against Japan.

### Stirling, William Alexander, 1st Earl of (1567–1640)

Scottish statesman, poet and scholar. Having gained the patronage of King **JAMES VI AND I** through his poetry and his kinship to the Earl of Argyll, he gained the King's support for his aim of acquiring a colony for Scotland, along the lines of **NEW FRANCE** and New England. He was granted (1621) the proprietorship of Nova Scotia ('New Scotland'), the three Atlantic provinces and the Gaspé Peninsula. The last was also claimed by the French, and the renewal of their claim eventually led to the failure of his ambitions. Alexander's major problem was to find Scots willing to settle in the colony, and James sought to help him by the promise of hereditary baronetcies and territory in the colony to Scots who would support a number of settlers. However, this measure failed under both James and his son, **CHARLES I**. In 1631 Alexander was commanded to yield Port-Royal to the French, after a challenge from **RICHELIEU**'s Company of One **HUNDRED ASSOCIATES**. He died with his dream unfulfilled, surrounded by creditors.

### Stockholm Bloodbath (1520)
After the fall of Stockholm to King **CHRISTIAN II** at the beginning of 1520 and his coronation in Nov, he allowed the trial and execution of 82 leading Swedes, including two bishops. The main charge against them was one of heresy and the main instigator was probably Archbishop Gustav Trolle, but the King also in this way disposed of many of his opponents. The event led on to the successful rebellion by **GUSTAV I VASA**, whose father had been a victim.

### Stojadinović, Milan (1888–1961)
Serbian politician and economist. After studying law at Belgrade University, he began his career in finance, becoming a minister in the Serbian Treasury (1914), Director of the English bank in Belgrade (1919) and Finance Minister in successive Yugoslav governments (1922–35). As head of the Yugoslav Radical Union, he was Prime Minister and Foreign Minister (1935–9). He led Yugoslavia away from the **LITTLE ENTENTE** and **BALKAN ENTENTE** towards the Axis camp, but his consent to Italian domination in Albania lost him the support of the regent, Prince **PAUL KARAGEORGEVIĆ**, and he was dismissed. Interned by the **CVETKOVIĆ–MAČEK** government (1939), he made his way to the British at Athens, who deported him to Mauritius and held him there until 1948. He then went to Argentina, where he worked as an economist and journalist. ► **LJOTIĆ, DIMITRIJE**

### Stolypin, Peter Arkadevich (1862–1911)
Russian politician. After service in the Ministry of the Interior (from 1884) he became Governor of Saratov province (1903–6), where he ruthlessly put down local peasant uprisings and helped to suppress the revolutionary upheavals of 1905. As Premier (1906–11), he introduced a series of agrarian reforms, which had only limited success. In 1907 he suspended the second **DUMA**, and arbitrarily limited the franchise. He was assassinated in Kiev. ► **NICHOLAS II; REVOLUTION OF 1905**

### Stormberg, Battle of (1899)
One of the battles of the 'black week' when the British suffered several reverses during the Boer War. They were defeated while attempting to take an important railway junction to the south of the Orange River, one of the keys to Bloemfontein. ► **BOER WARS**

### Stormont
A suburb of east Belfast and site of a castle which housed the seat of government in Northern Ireland from 1921 to 1972 and from 1999 and 2002. The Northern Ireland parliament, created by the Government of Ireland Act 1920, comprised a Senate and a House of Commons, both dominated by Protestants. It had jurisdiction over domestic affairs in the province until suspended by the Northern Ireland (Temporary Provisions) Act, 1972 which established direct rule from Westminster. Stormont Castle housed the Northern Ireland Assembly established in 1998 following the **GOOD FRIDAY AGREEMENT**, until its suspension in 2002. ► **BLOODY SUNDAY (1972); ULSTER 'TROUBLES'**

### Stormontgate
Northern Ireland political scandal. Following some months' surveillance of **IRA** sympathizers owing to suspicions that their spies had infiltrated the Northern Ireland administration at Stormont, police seized documents and computer disks in raids in Belfast on 4 Oct 2002. As a consequence, **SINN FÉIN**'s head of administration at the Northern Ireland Assembly and three others were charged with possessing documents that could be useful to terrorists. The incident implied that Sinn Féin was not sincerely committed to the **GOOD FRIDAY AGREEMENT** and that the IRA was targeting possible victims for a new round of violence. This led to the collapse of power-sharing. On 14 Oct 2002 Northern Ireland's self-government was suspended and direct rule from Westminster was restored.

### Strachan, John (1778–1867)
Canadian bishop. Prominent in the **FAMILY COMPACT**, he sought to maintain the ascendancy of the Anglican Church against the challenge of the Methodists (whom he accused of being American in origin and loyalty). As President of the Board of Education, his policy of keeping education under the clergy's control caused resentment throughout Upper **CANADA**. In 1839 he became first Bishop of Toronto and opposed the Reformers over such issues as the secularization of King's College in 1849 and the **CLERGY RESERVES** in 1854.

### Strafford, Thomas Wentworth, 1st Earl of (1593–1641)
English statesman. He was knighted in 1611, and in 1614 succeeded to his baronetcy, and entered parliament. He acted with the opposition (1625–8), but after being appointed President of the North and Baron Wentworth (1628), he supported **CHARLES I**. In 1632 he became Lord Deputy of Ireland, where he imposed firm rule. In 1639 he became the King's principal adviser, and Earl of Strafford. His suppression of the rebellion in Scotland failed, and he was impeached by the **LONG PARLIAMENT**. Despite a famous defence at Westminster, he was executed on Tower Hill. ► **BISHOPS' WARS; IMPEACHMENT**

### Straits Convention (1841)
By this treaty, the Straits, the passage from the Bosphorus to the **DARDANELLES** which links the Black Sea to the Mediterranean, was placed under international control. The treaty between the Great Powers closed the Straits to foreign warships during peacetime, a provision intended to reconcile Russian and British shipping interests since neither country would be able to menace the other's fleet on the Black Sea or the Mediterranean.

### Straits of Tiran, Closure of the (22 May 1967)
The Straits of Tiran, which control entry to the Red Sea from the Gulf of Aqaba, were closed in May 1967 by the Egyptian President Gamal Abd al-**NASSER** operating from the vantage point of Sharm al-Shaykh which commands the western side of the straits. The

closure of the straits, whereby the Israeli port of Eilat was effectively cut off from the sea, was seen by Israel as direct provocation and may be regarded as, in part at least, the *casus belli* of the SIX-DAY WAR of 1967 between Israel and the Arabs which resulted in the Israeli occupation of Golan, the WEST BANK, the Old City of Jerusalem, the GAZA STRIP, and Sinai as far as the Suez Canal.

## Straits Settlements
The name given to the former British Crown Colony which consisted of Singapore, Malacca, the Dindings, Penang and Province Wellesley. Singapore became a separate city state in 1965; the remaining components are now part of Malaysia.

## Strauss, Franz-Josef (1915–88)
West German politician. He served in the German army during WORLD WAR II and in 1945 joined the CDU's Bavarian-based sister party, the Christian Social Union (CSU), being elected to the BUNDESTAG (federal parliament) in 1949. He became leader of the CSU in 1961 and held a succession of ministerial posts. His career was seriously blighted when, for security purposes, he authorized a raid on the offices of the journal *Der Spiegel*, leading to his sacking as Minister of Defence in 1962. Throughout the 1970s he vigorously opposed the *Ostpolitik* initiative of the BRANDT and SCHMIDT administrations. In 1980 he sought election as Federal Chancellor for the CDU and CSU alliance, but was heavily defeated. Nevertheless, from 1978 he had success as State Premier of Bavaria, using this base to wield significant influence within the BUNDESRAT (federal upper house) and, from 1982, in the coalition government headed by Chancellor KOHL. ► SPIEGEL AFFAIR

## Streicher, Julius (1885–1946)
German Nazi journalist and politician. He was associated with HITLER in the early days of Nazism, taking part in the 1923 putsch. A ruthless persecutor of the Jews, he incited anti-Semitism through the newspaper *Der Stürmer*, which he founded and edited, and also served as Nazi *Gauleiter* (Party Regional Leader) for Nuremberg–Franconia. He was hanged at Nuremberg as a war criminal. ► GAU; MUNICH PUTSCH; NAZI PARTY; NUREMBERG TRIALS

## Streltsy (1550–1698)
The first regular regiment of Russian soldiers who gradually took upon themselves a political role. Musketeers, they were recruited by IVAN IV, THE TERRIBLE and initially helped the expansion and the consolidation of the Russian state. During the minority of PETER I, THE GREAT they became involved in attempting to keep SOPHIA ALEXEEVNA, his half-sister, on the Russian throne; and in 1698, when Peter was abroad, they tried in effect to prevent him coming back. Peter extracted a terrible revenge and disbanded what was left of them. However, he proceeded to build up the guards as his own élite military unit.

## Stresa, Conference of (11–14 Apr 1935)
Following HITLER's declaration of German rearmament (16 Mar 1935), the Italian, French and British governments condemned the move at a meeting in Stresa. They guaranteed Austria's independence and agreed on future cooperation (Stresa Front). The Front was quickly undermined by the Anglo-German

Naval Treaty (18 June 1935) and Italy's invasion of Abyssinia and intervention in the SPANISH CIVIL WAR.

## Stresemann, Gustav (1878–1929)
German politician. Entering the REICHSTAG in 1907 as a National Liberal, he became leader of the party, and later founded and led its successor, the German People's Party. He was Chancellor of the new German Republic in 1923, then Minister of Foreign Affairs (1923–9). He pursued a revisionist policy through the medium of diplomacy, helped to negotiate the LOCARNO PACT (1925), and secured the entry of Germany into the LEAGUE OF NATIONS (1926). He shared the NOBEL PEACE PRIZE in 1926. ► WEIMAR REPUBLIC

## Strijdom, Johannes Gerhardus (1893–1958)
South African politician. Educated at Stellenbosch and Pretoria universities, he was first a farmer and then a lawyer. Elected to parliament in 1929, he became the major spokesman for the least flexible members of the NATIONAL PARTY (NP) but was nonetheless made Minister of Lands and Irrigation when the NP came to power in 1948. He was chosen to succeed MALAN as leader and so became Prime Minister in 1954. He saw one of his cherished objectives achieved, namely APARTHEID, but died before South Africa became a republic.

## Stroessner, Alfredo (1912– )
Paraguayan dictator. The son of a German immigrant, he took up a military career, fighting in the CHACO WAR (1932–5). He became President in 1954 after leading an army coup which deposed Federico Chávez. He was re-elected at regular intervals (having had the constitution modified to allow this) but was forced to stand down after a military coup in 1989, led by Andrés Rodríguez.

## Stroganov, Pavel, Count (1779–1817)
Russian landowner and political adviser. With extensive property in the Urals and Siberia, he acted as adviser to ALEXANDER I both before and after his accession in 1801. A believer in autocratic government retraining the privileged and benefiting the downtrodden, he advocated the 'unofficial committee' of four that established the Tsar's liberal reputation in the years 1801–3. He soon became disillusioned because of the lack of fundamental change, and sought alternative outlets in military and diplomatic service.

## Strossmayer, Josip Juraj (1815–1905)
Croatian politician, prelate and man of letters. As leader of the Croatian National Party, he defended Croatian interests by pursuing a course of compromise and tactical opportunism towards Vienna. A passionate believer in South Slav unity, he developed the Illyrism of Ljudevit GAJ and is considered the intellectual founder of Croatian YUGOSLAVISM; the strength of his commitment is manifest in his efforts to reconcile the Catholic and Orthodox SOUTH SLAVS. ► ILLYRIAN MOVEMENT

## Štrougal, Lubomír (1924– )
Czechoslovak politician. A lawyer, he entered the Communist Party bureaucracy in 1955 and government office in 1959. In 1961 he took over the Ministry of the Interior at a sensitive time, managing to correct

some of its worst excesses before reverting to a Central Committee function in 1965. His reputation was sufficient to make him a Deputy Prime Minister in 1968, but he was a half-hearted supporter of the **PRAGUE SPRING**. In Aug he took the **HUSÁK** line of ostensibly trying to save something through working with the Soviet authorities. He was Prime Minister (1970–87) and was regarded as the man who might yet reinvigorate the reform movement; he never did.

**Strozzi, Filippo, the Younger**, properly **Giovanni Battista** (1489–1538)
Florentine nobleman. He was prominent in the revolt that overthrew the **MEDICI** in 1527, but the republic then established lasted only three years. The restored Medici, Alessandro, having been assassinated in 1537, Strozzi judged the time opportune to launch an attack on his successor, Cosimo I de' **MEDICI**, but was captured and executed.

**Strozzi, Piero** (1510–58)
Italian soldier. The son of Filippo **STROZZI** the Younger, he fought the **MEDICI** and escaped to France. There he was made a marshal of France by **HENRY II** in 1556 after campaigns in Italy. Strozzi found out the weaknesses of the defences of Calais before its capture by Francis, 2nd Duke of **GUISE** in 1558, and was killed at the siege of Thionville.

**Struensee, Johann Friedrich, Count** (1737–72)
German-born Danish politician. The son of a Halle pastor, in 1768 he became physician to **CHRISTIAN VII** of Denmark. He soon gained the confidence of the young king and queen and, with their backing, sought to free Denmark from Russian influence and win Sweden as an ally. Court intrigue, however, thwarted his ambitions and he was found guilty of treason and beheaded.

**Struve, Peter Bergardovich** (1870–1944)
Russian political economist. The grandson of Friedrich Struve, he was a leading Marxist and wrote *Critical Observations on the Problem of Russia's Economic Development* (1894), which **LENIN** attacked for its 'revisionism'. He edited several political magazines with liberal tendencies, was professor at the St Petersburg Polytechnic (1907–17) and was closely connected with the 'White' movement in south Russia after the **RUSSIAN REVOLUTION**. After 1925 he lived in exile in Belgrade and Paris, where he died during the Nazi occupation. His principal work is *Economy and Price* (1913–16).

**Stuart, Charles Edward Louis Philip Casimir**, known as **the Young Pretender** (1720–88)
Claimant to the British crown. The son of James Francis Edward **STUART**, he became the focus of Jacobite hopes. In 1744 he went to France to head the planned invasion of England, but after the defeat of the French fleet he was unable to leave for over a year. He landed with seven followers at Eriskay in the Hebrides (Jul 1745) and in Aug raised his father's standard at Glenfinnan. The clansmen flocked to him, Edinburgh surrendered, and he kept court at Holyrood. Victorious at Prestonpans, he invaded England, but turned back at Derby for lack of evident English support, and was routed by the Duke of **CUMBERLAND** at the Battle of **CULLODEN** (1746). The rising was ruthlessly suppressed, and he was hunted for five months. With the help of Flora **MACDONALD** he crossed from Benbecula to Portree, disguised as her maid. He landed in Brittany, then lived in France and Italy, where (after his father's death in 1766) he assumed the title of Charles III of Great Britain. ➤ **FORTY-FIVE REBELLION**; **JACOBITES**; **STUART, HOUSE OF**

**Stuart, House of**
The Scottish royal family, commencing with **ROBERT II** (1371/90), which succeeded to the English throne in 1603 with the accession of **JAMES VI AND I**, the cousin of **ELIZABETH I**, and the great-grandson of **HENRY VIII**'s sister Margaret. As English monarchs the family's fortunes were mixed. James VI and I and **CHARLES II** were both successful politicians (although the second spent his first 11 years as king in exile). But **CHARLES I** and **JAMES VII AND II** were not, and both lost their thrones. The Stuart monarchy ended in 1714 with the death of Queen **ANNE**, although pretenders laid claim to the throne and invaded Britain in support of their claims as late as 1745. ➤ **STUART, CHARLES EDWARD**; **STUART, JAMES FRANCIS EDWARD**

### HOUSE OF STUART

| Regnal Dates | Name |
| --- | --- |
| 1371/90 | Robert II |
| 1390/1406 | Robert III |
| 1406/37 | James I |
| 1437/60 | James II |
| 1460/88 | James III |
| 1488/1513 | James IV |
| 1513/42 | James V |
| 1542/67 | Mary, Queen of Scots |
| 1567/1625 | James VI of Scotland (as James I of England, 1603/25) |
| 1625/49 | Charles I |
| 1649/59 | Commonwealth and Protectorate |
| 1660/85 | Charles II |
| 1685/8 | James VII and II |
| 1689/94 | Mary II (co-sovereign) |
| 1689/1702 | William III (co-sovereign 1689/94) |
| 1702/14 | Anne |

**Stuart, James Ewell Brown**, known as **Jeb Stuart** (1833–64)
US Confederate soldier. Born in Patrick County, Virginia, he graduated from West Point in 1854 and served in the US cavalry in Texas and Kansas, resigning his commission at the outbreak of the Civil War in 1861. He became a valued intelligence officer in the Confederate Army, and the Confederacy's best-known cavalry commander, scouting Union forces of General George **MCCLELLAN** and performing brilliantly in Pennsylvania, at **FREDERICKSBURG** and Chancellorsville, and in the Wilderness Campaign. He was criticized at the Battle of **GETTYSBURG**, however, for arriving too late from a raid. He was mortally wounded at Yellow Tavern.

**Stuart, James Francis Edward**, known as **the Old Pretender** (1688–1766)
Claimant to the British throne. He was the only son of James VII of Scotland and II of England and his second wife, Mary of Modena. As a baby he was conveyed to St Germain, and proclaimed successor on

his father's death (1701). After failing to land in Scotland in 1708, he served with the French in the Low Countries. In 1715 he landed at Peterhead during the Jacobite rising, but left Scotland some weeks later. Thereafter he lived mainly in Rome, where he died.
► **FIFTEEN REBELLION**; **JACOBITES**; **JAMES VII AND II**; **STUART, CHARLES EDWARD**; **STUART, HOUSE OF**

**Stur, Ludovit** (1815–56)
Slovak writer and politician. One of a small group of educated Slovaks who resisted the growing policy of Magyarization in Hungary in the 1840s. He started publishing the Slovak *National News* in 1845 and chose the central Slovak dialect as the basis on which to found a proper literary language. In 1848 he helped to formulate demands for Slovak autonomy and appealed to Vienna for help. He also made contact with his Czech opposite members and helped found the Czechoslovak idea. Despite Slovak help for the Habsburg Emperor there was no concession after the defeat of the Magyars in 1849.

**Sturdza, Mihail** (1795–1884)
Ruler of Moldavia (1834/49). He was chosen as **HOSPODAR** ('governor') of Wallachia by Russia and the Ottoman Porte at the Convention of St Petersburg (1834). During his rule, the Danubian Principalities were a Russian protectorate and Sturdza showed himself adept at working with the Russians to his own benefit and to that of his subjects. Following the guidelines of the **ORGANIC STATUTES**, he attempted internal reforms and achieved genuine improvements in the standard of education, roads and postal service. In 1848 he quelled by force the petitioners led by Alexander **CUZA** who had called for moderate social and political reform. ► **MOLDAVIA AND WALLACHIA**

**Sture, Sten, the Elder** (c.1440–1503)
Regent of Sweden (1471/97 and 1501/3). On the death of his uncle, King **KARL KNUTSSON**, in 1470, Sten claimed the regency and defeated his opponents (who wished to restore the **KALMAR UNION** under the Danish king, **CHRISTIAN I**) at the Battle of Brunkeberg north of Stockholm (1471). In 1497 King Hans of Denmark and Norway successfully reasserted his claim to Sweden and forced Sten to step down. In 1503 the Swedish nobility again revolted and Sten was again chosen to be regent. Traditionally pictured as a selfless patriot fighting for Sweden's independence, recent research has revealed a ruthless opportunist with a driving personal ambition.

**Sture, Sten Svantesson, the Younger** (c.1492–1520)
Regent of Sweden (1512/20). He was the son of Svante Nilsson, Swedish regent (1504–12). An able but ambitious and ruthless man, he forced the nobles of the Council to accept him as regent on his father's death. He attempted to turn the regency into a hereditary monarchy and, while he enjoyed support among the commons and the lower nobility, he encountered growing opposition from the great nobles and Archbishop Gustav Trolle, whom he imprisoned in 1518. King **CHRISTIAN II**, who sought to restore the **KALMAR UNION**, took up the Archbishop's cause. After several unsuccessful attacks, he invaded Sweden in 1520 and defeated the Regent at the Battle of Åsunden

(1520). Sten was mortally wounded in the encounter and died on the journey back to Stockholm. His wife, Christina Gyllenstierna, bravely defended the city against Christian for eight months.

**Sturluson, Snorri** (1179–1241)
Icelandic chieftain and historian. He was born in western Iceland and fostered at Oddi in the south by the powerful Jón Loptsson. He acquired the estates of Borg and Reykholt, where he lived much of his life. He was Lawspeaker of the **ALTHING** for 15 years and became deeply involved in the turbulent politics of Iceland in the period which led to its loss of independence, first as an ally of the King of Norway and then as his opponent. He was finally slain at Reykholt by one of the King's followers. He is the author of two of the most important works of Icelandic literature, the *Prose Edda*, from which much of our knowledge of the Old Norse religion derives, and *Heimskringla*, a history of the early kings of Norway.

**Stuyvesant, Peter** (c.1592–1672)
Dutch administrator. He became Governor of Curaçao, Aruba and Bonaire (1643), and from 1646 directed the New Netherland colony. He proved a vigorous but arbitrary ruler, a rigid sabbatarian, and an opponent of political and religious freedom, but did much for the commercial prosperity of New Amsterdam until his reluctant surrender to the English in 1664.

**Suárez, Adolfo** (1932– )
Spanish politician. He was a high-ranking Francoist bureaucrat who owed much to his good looks, great charm and single-minded ambition. Appointed Prime Minister in Mar 1976, Suárez carried out a swift transition from the **FRANCO** dictatorship to democracy, the elections of June 1977 proving a personal triumph. Backed by the newly established **UCD** centrist party, he undertook the creation of the new democratic state. Having embodied consensual change in the constitution of 1978, Suárez triumphed again in the general election of 1979. However, economic and regional problems, divisions within both the government and UCD, as well as his own secretiveness and authoritarian style, led to his resignation in Jan 1981. The following year he founded the CDS ('Democratic and Social Centre Party'), which has won little support. The most important politician of the transition, Suárez helped establish democracy in Spain through pragmatism and conciliation.

**Subašić, Ivan** (1882–1955)
Croatian politician. A leading member of the Croatian Peasant Party (HSS) between the two World Wars, he became *ban* ('governor') of Croatia after the 1939 **SPORAZUM** between **CVETKOVIĆ** and **MAČEK**. During **WORLD WAR II**, he served in the Yugoslav government-in-exile in London and, as its Prime Minister, met **TITO** on the British-occupied island of Vis where he agreed to recognize **AVNOJ** as the only political authority within Yugoslavia (June 1944). In accordance with the provisions of the Vis Agreement, in Mar 1945 he and two colleagues from the London-based regime joined Tito's Provisional Government, but he resigned as Foreign Minister six months later and was under house arrest until after the communist victory in the Nov 1945 elections. Obliged to retire from public life, he settled in Croatia.

## Sucre, Antonio José de (1793–1830)

South American soldier-patriot, born in Venezuela. He was **BOLÍVAR**'s lieutenant, defeated the Spaniards at Ayacucho (1824), and became the first President (1826) of Bolivia. He tried to establish stability in the country, but was beset by warring political factions, as well as an incursion by Peruvian troops, and resigned in 1828. He took service with Colombia, and won the Battle of Tarqui (1829) against Peru. He was assassinated at Berruecos, near Pasló, possibly on the orders of José María Obando, a Colombian soldier. ►
**SPANISH-AMERICAN WARS OF INDEPENDENCE**

## **SUDAN** official name **Republic of The Sudan**

A north-east African republic, bounded to the north by Egypt; to the north-west by Libya; to the west by Chad; to the south-west by the Central African Republic; to the south by the Democratic Republic of the Congo and Uganda; to the south-east by Kenya; to the east by Ethiopia, Eritrea and the Red Sea. Sudan was Christianized in the 6c, and came under Muslim influences from the 13c. Egyptian control of northern Sudan began in the 19c when **MOHAMMED AHMED**, a religious leader who announced himself the **MAHDI** (the 'expected one'), began to unify western and central areas of the country. In 1881 he initiated a revolution which led to the fall of Khartoum in 1885. A combined British–Egyptian offensive was mounted against the Mahdists, defeated them at the Battle of **OMDURMAN** in 1898, and led to a jointly administered condominium under a British governor. Sudan gained its independence in 1956, and since then parts of the country have been almost constantly ravaged by civil war. After seizing power in 1969, General **NIMERI** managed to bring the civil war in the south to an end in 1972. However, fighting restarted in the 1980s and Nimeri was overthrown in 1985. Another coup, led by General Omar Hassan Ahmad al-Bashir in 1989, resulted in a strongly Islamic regime and the banning of all political parties until 1996, when Bashir and his supporters won the elections. The north–south rivalry (the Muslim Brotherhood's National Islamic Front (NIF) is based in the Arab, Muslim north, while the Sudan People's Liberation Army (SPLA) has its stronghold in the non-Arab, Christian and Animist south) has caused years of instability, several coups, and severe food shortages, the last mentioned exacerbated by drought and by the influx of refugees from Ethiopia and Chad in the early 1990s. A framework agreement signed in 2002 provides for an independence referendum in south Sudan after six years' of power-sharing; peace talks

continue. A separate conflict that broke out in the western **DARFUR** region in 2003 provoked severe reprisals by the government, operating through Arab militias, which attracted international condemnation and accusations of **ETHNIC CLEANSING** and even **GENOCIDE**. ► **CONDOMINIUM**; **MAHDI'S REVOLT**

## Sudan People's Liberation Movement

The proclamation of an Islamic state in Sudan in 1977, led to unrest in the south which found its expression in the emergence of the Sudan People's Liberation Movement. This movement initially represented a political refusal to accept the dictates of the government in Khartoum but subsequently moved to armed rebellion under Colonel John **GARANG**.

## Sudetenland

Mountainous territory on the Polish–Czech border. After **WORLD WAR I**, the name also applied to the parts of Bohemia and Moravia occupied by German-speaking people. It was occupied by Germany after the **MUNICH AGREEMENT** in 1938, and restored to Czechoslovakia in 1945, when the German-speaking population was expelled. ► **WORLD WAR II**

## Suez Crisis (1956)

A political crisis focused on the Suez Canal. Intensive rearmament by Egypt, the Egyptian nationalization of the Suez Canal, and the establishment of a unified command with Jordan and Syria aimed at surrounding and eliminating Israel, led in Oct to a pre-emptive strike by Israel in Sinai. Following this attack, the UK and France asked both sides to withdraw from the Canal Zone and agree to temporary occupation. When this was rejected by Egypt, the British and French invaded, but had to withdraw following diplomatic action by the USA and USSR. Israel was also forced to relinquish the Sinai Peninsula. There have been many allegations of collusion between Israel, France and the UK. ► **ARAB–ISRAELI WARS**; **CANALS**; **EDEN, ANTHONY**; **NASSER, GAMAL ABD AL-**

## suffragettes

Those women who identified with and were members of the late 19c movement to secure voting rights for women. In the UK the vote was 'won' after the end of **WORLD WAR I** (1918), though it was limited to those women of 30 years of age or over. There were many men and women opponents of female suffrage, and in the UK it was not until 1928 that women over 21 achieved the right to vote. ► **PANKHURST, EMMELINE**; **WOMEN'S RIGHTS**

## Suffren de Saint Tropez, Pierre André de (1729–88)

French naval commander. He served six years in Malta amongst the Knights **HOSPITALLERS**; he was captured in Admiral **BOSCAWEN**'s destruction of the Toulon fleet (1759), took part in the bombardment of Sallee (1765), was another four years in Malta, and returned to France as captain in 1772. In 1781 he was placed in command of a French squadron for service in the Indian Ocean, and captured Trincomalee. Returning to Paris in 1784, he was received with great honour as one of France's greatest admirals.

## Sugar Act (1764)

British statute that attempted for the first time to raise colonial revenue without reference to the colonial assemblies. Its main aim was to impose and collect customs duties and to prevent illegal trade. The colonials responded with protest, but not outright resistance, and the Act was sporadically enforced until the complete breakdown of British–American relations. ► **AMERICAN REVOLUTION; BOSTON TEA PARTY; STAMP ACT; TOWNSHEND ACTS**

## Sugar Revolution

The term used to denote the change from diversified, smallholding, family agriculture to large-scale, plantation/estate sugar monoculture which took place throughout the Caribbean c.1650. Prior to this date, European colonists had grown maize and ground food as subsistence crops, and tobacco and cotton as cash crops on small farms of a few acres using their own and indentured labour. However, the demand for sugar in Europe, its profitability and the suitability of the Caribbean coastal plains for its cultivation led to a widespread switch to the crop once its technology had been mastered. The change replaced the smallholder with the capitalist planter, the smallholding with the estate or plantation of several hundred acres and the indentured white labourer with the black African slave. The cultivation of 'King Sugar' was responsible for the slave trade, slavery, a dependent monoculture export economy and a hierarchical, racist and class-ridden society.

## Suger (c.1081–1151)

French prelate and politician. As Abbot of St Denis from 1122, he reformed the abbey and rebuilt its church in the first example of the Gothic style. **LOUIS VI** and **LOUIS VII** both employed him on diplomatic missions, and during Louis VII's absence on the Second **CRUSADE**, Suger served as Regent, displaying particular skills in financial administration.

## Suharto, Thojib N J (1921–)

Indonesian soldier and statesman. Educated for service in the Dutch colonial army, in 1943 he was given a command in the Japanese-sponsored Indonesian army and played an important role in the revolutionary struggle against the Dutch. He became a major political figure during the crises of 1965 and 1966, and assumed full executive power in 1967, ordering the mass arrest and internment of alleged communists. He became President in 1968, thereafter being re-elected every five years. Suharto's virtual dictatorship under the 'New Order' saw an improvement in Indonesia's relations with her neighbours in South-East Asia, the republic's return to membership of the **UN**, and considerable economic advance, sustained in large part by buoyant oil revenues. However, his period in office was threatened by Islamic fundamentalist extremists and by the long-running civil war in **EAST TIMOR**, and in 1998 he was ousted from power amidst calls for political reform and allegations of political and financial impropriety.

## Suhrawardy, Husein Shaheed (1893–1963)

Pakistani politician. Born in East Bengal, he was educated at Oxford University in England. In 1921 he became a member of the Bengal Assembly. He was Pakistan's Minister of Law (1954–5) and Prime Minister (1956–7).

## Sui Dynasty ► CHINESE DYNASTIES PRE-1000AD

## Sukarno, Ahmed (1902–70)

Indonesian statesman and first President of Indonesia (1945–66). He formed the Indonesia National Party (PNI) in 1927, was imprisoned by the Dutch in Bandung (1929–31), and lived in forced exile until 1942, when he emerged as a major nationalist leader during the Japanese occupation. He became President when Indonesia was declared independent in 1945 and was a crucial unifying figure during the subsequent struggle against the Dutch. His popularity waned as the country suffered increasing internal chaos and poverty in the late 1950s and 1960s, while his governments laid themselves open to charges of corruption and extremism. An abortive coup (1965) led to widespread violence and a takeover by the army, Sukarno's powers gradually devolving to General **SUHARTO**. Sukarno finally retired in 1968.

## Sukhothai

An ancient state and ruined city of Thailand, 273 mi/ 440 km north of Bangkok. Founded in the mid-13c, Sukhothai's power waned with the emergence of the southern state of **AYUDHYA** in the mid-15c.

## Sulaiman (1838–92)

Turkish soldier. He joined the army in 1854, fought in Montenegro, Crete and Yemen, and in peace taught at the military academy in Constantinople, of which he became director. He distinguished himself against the Serbians in 1876. When the Russians declared war (1877), Sulaiman checked them at Eski Zagra, but destroyed his army in heroic attempts to force them from the Shipka Pass. In Oct 1877 he became Commander-in-Chief of the Army of the Danube, but suffered defeat near Philippopolis (Jan 1878). Court-martialled, he was condemned to 15 years' imprisonment, but the Sultan pardoned him.

## Süleyman I, the Magnificent (1494–1566)

Ottoman Sultan (1520/66). He added to his dominions, by conquest, Belgrade, Budapest, Rhodes, Tabriz, Baghdad, Aden and Algiers. His fleets dominated the Mediterranean, although he failed to capture Malta. His system of laws regulating land tenure earned him the name *Kanuni* ('lawgiver'), and he was a great patron of arts and architecture. He died during the siege of Szigeth in his war with Austria. ► **OTTOMAN EMPIRE**

## Süleyman II (1641–91)

Ottoman Emperor (1687/91). The son of Ibrahim I, he succeeded his brother **MEHMED** when he was deposed in 1687. He was defeated by the Austrians in 1688, but from 1689 his Grand Vizier, Mustafa **KÖPRÜLÜ**, drove the Austrians out of Bulgaria, Serbia and Transylvania and retook Belgrade; Köprülü also introduced numerous liberal reforms, but was killed in battle in 1691.

## Sulh, Taqi al-Din al- (1909–88)

Lebanese Sunni politician. He was a fervent campaigner on behalf of the Arab peoples against any form of foreign interference in their affairs. Initially focusing on the way in which the Ottoman Turks had kept the Arab peoples in subjection, when the problems of Ottoman dominion had receded, he turned his attentions to the French and British. A moderate who aimed at reconciliation between Christians and Muslims in Lebanon, Taqi al-Din, together with his brother Kazim, maintained that, although the Lebanese people were part of the great Arab nation, the regional peculiarities of Lebanon made the country's independence an essential concomitant of its peaceful development. Politically active throughout his life, he played a prominent role in the late 1960s and early 1970s, and was Prime Minister in 1973–4.

**Sully, Maximilien de Béthune, Duke of** (1560–1641) French Huguenot soldier, financier and politician. He fought in the later stages of the Wars of RELIGION (1574–98) and was wounded at Ivry (1590). Instrumental in arranging HENRY IV's marriage to Marie de' Medici (1600), he became the King's Chief Minister and trusted counsellor. His major achievement was the restoration of the economy after the civil wars. In 1606 he was created duke, but after Henry's assassination (1610) was forced to retire to his estates. ► HUGUENOTS

**Sultan-Galiev, Mivza Said** (1892–1939) Tatar intellectual and politician. He attempted to synthesize Islam and COMMUNISM. He joined the BOLSHEVIKS in 1917 in his native Kazan and soon had an official post. STALIN welcomed him on to the commissariat of nationalities in 1920 as one of the few non-Russians and then had him arrested in 1923 for his dissident Islamic views. Freed, he continued to preach communism as a means of liberating his fellow non-Russian Muslims. However, he was rearrested in 1929 and disappeared. His name has been much revered among Muslims ever since.

**Šumadija** Literally 'the forested land', this term describes the region of central Serbia which lies to the south of Belgrade. After the fall of Serbia to the Ottoman Turks (1389), it was ruled from the 15c to 1697 by the Crnojević Dynasty of Montenegro. In 1804 the first of the SERBIAN UPRISINGS began in Šumadija and its chief town, Kragujevac, was the capital of Prince Miloš OBRENOVIĆ.

**Sumner, Charles** (1811–74) US politician. Born in Boston, he graduated from Harvard and was admitted to the Bar in 1834. He took little interest in politics until the threatened extensions of SLAVERY over newly acquired territory. In 1848 he joined with others to form the FREE-SOIL PARTY. Nominated for CONGRESS, he was defeated by the Whig candidate, but in 1851 was elected to the SENATE by the combined Free-Soil and Democratic votes of the Massachusetts legislature, a post he held for life. Alone in the Senate as the uncompromising opponent of slavery, in 1856 he was struck on the head in the Senate chamber by Preston S Brooks, a South Carolina member of Congress, and was incapacitated for nearly four years. The secession of the Southern states left the REPUBLICAN PARTY in full control of both houses of Congress and in 1861 Sumner was elected chairman of the Senate committee on foreign affairs. He supported the RECONSTRUCTION policies of the Radical Republicans, favoured the IMPEACHMENT of President Andrew JOHNSON, and opposed President Ulysses S GRANT's project for the acquisition of San Domingo. His criticisms of Grant's administration created a rift with leading Republican

politicians, which was deepened by his support of Horace GREELEY as candidate for the presidency in 1872.

**Sunday School** A class for the religious instruction of children, held on Sundays, usually in church buildings. The first Sunday School was probably that organized in Gloucester, England, in 1780, by Robert Raikes, whose aim was to provide elementary education as well as religious instruction to the children who worked in factories every other day of the week. Other 'schools' soon sprang up throughout Britain, assisted by the foundation of the London Sunday School Union (1803). Increasingly they became associated with the Protestant Churches. In the USA, the Sunday School movement began to spread in the 1790s, and was assisted from 1817 by the American Sunday School Union.

**Sunderland, Robert Spencer, 2nd Earl of** (1641–1702) English statesman. He became an influential adviser, successively, of CHARLES II, JAMES VII AND II and WILLIAM III. He was dismissed as Secretary of State in 1681 for voting to exclude James from the succession, but reinstated in 1683, becoming Chief Minister under James in 1685, and a Catholic (1688). On William's accession, he fled to Europe, but after renouncing his Catholicism was allowed to return in 1691. He was Lord Chamberlain for several months in 1697.

**Sung Chiao-jen ►** SONG JIAOREN

**Sung Dynasty ►** SONG DYNASTY

**Sung Tzu-wen ►** SONG ZIWEN

**Sunnis** Members of an Islamic religious movement representing 'orthodoxy' in Islam, comprising about 80 per cent of all Muslims. They recognize the first four caliphs as 'rightly guided' (*rashidun*), and base their *sunnah* (the 'path' of the Prophet Muhammad) upon the *Quran* and the *hadith* or 'traditions' of the Prophet. They are organized into four legal schools which all enjoy equal standing. The other major Islamic group is made up of SHIITES. ► RELIGION

**Sun Yat-sen (Sun Yixian)** or **Sun Zhongshan (Sun Chung-shan)** (1866–1925) Chinese politician. The founder and early leader of China's Nationalist Party, the GUOMINDANG, he first trained as a doctor in Hawaii and Hong Kong. Alarmed by the weakness and decay of China, he founded the Society for the Revival of China, and sprang to fame when, on a visit to London, he was kidnapped by the Chinese legation, and released through the intervention of the Foreign Office. He then helped to organize risings in southern China. He returned to China after the 1911 Wuhan rising, realized that he would not be widely acceptable as President, and voluntarily handed over the office to YUAN SHIKAI. After the assassination of his follower SONG JIAOREN, civil war ensued (1913), and he set up a separate government at Guangzhou (Canton). He died in Beijing, widely accepted as the true leader of the nation.

## superpowers

The description applied during the **COLD WAR** period to the USA and the USSR, the two nations with economic and military resources far exceeding those of other powers. With the collapse of the USSR in 1991, it is sometimes argued that there is only one superpower left. But arguments concerning gross national product and real or potential military strength suggest that China, Japan and the **EC** (European Community) might merit the description if still in use.

## Supilo, Frano (1870–1917)

Croatian politician. A Croat from **DALMATIA**, he worked closely with Ante **TRUMBIĆ**, co-founding with him the Social Democrat Party in 1895 and, during **WORLD WAR I**, the **YUGOSLAV COMMITTEE** which, from its base in London, tried to win Allied support for South Slav unification. ► **SOUTH SLAVS**

## Supplex Libellus Valachorum (1791)

The petition addressed from the Romanians in Transylvania to Emperor **LEOPOLD II**, in which they demanded the same rights as those enjoyed by the privileged nations of the province, the Magyars, Saxons and **SZEKLERS**. This was an attempt by the Romanians to seek representation in Transylvania's political institutions, which were then dominated by Magyar nobles.

## Supreme Court

In the USA, the highest federal court established under the constitution, members of which are appointed by the President with the advice and consent of the **SENATE**. In addition to its jurisdiction relating to appeals, the court exercises oversight of the **US CONSTITUTION** through the power of judicial review of the acts of state and federal legislatures, and the executive. It was created in 1789 and has comprised nine members since 1869.

## Surat

A coastal town in present-day Gujarat, which was subordinated by the British in 1709. Surat was a big trading and export centre under the Mughals and its value as a fort and as a strategic point between the Deccan and Gujarat was very high. In its heyday, ships from Surat traded with East Africa, the Middle East and throughout the Indian Ocean, and fortunes were made from the sale of textiles, precious metals and spices. In 1664 Surat was sacked by the Maratha leader **SHIVAJI**. Although it subsequently recovered from this, in the declining years of the **MUGHAL EMPIRE** the port became increasingly vulnerable. After the death of Muhammad Ali, the last great merchant of Surat, at the hands of the Mughal governor in 1733, a British blockade in 1734 and an attack on the merchant fleet in 1735, the majority of merchants fled to the relative safety of the British-controlled port of Bombay. After the establishment of British paramountcy in western India in 1803, the fortunes of the port then slowly recovered. Surat became important to the Indian national movement when a famous session of the **INDIAN NATIONAL CONGRESS** was held there in 1907. This session witnessed a clash between so-called 'moderates' and 'extremists'. The meeting broke up in disorder because of extremist attempts at coercion, but the episode ended with the assertion of the supremacy of the 'moderate' faction under

**GOKHALE, BANERJEA**, Sinha and **MEHTA**

**SURINAME**    official name **Republic of Suriname**

A republic in north-eastern South America, bounded to the west by Guyana; to the south by Brazil; to the east by French Guiana; and to the north by the Atlantic Ocean. Sighted by **COLUMBUS** in 1498, Suriname was first settled by the British in 1651. It was taken by the states of Zeeland in 1667, captured by the British in 1799, and restored to the Netherlands in 1818. It became an independent republic in 1975, after which around 40 per cent of the population emigrated to the Netherlands. A military coup took place in 1980, civilian government was restored in 1988, but another coup was staged in 1990. The following year elections brought a coalition called the New Front for Democracy and Development to power, led by Ronald Venetiaan, who became President. He implemented an unpopular austerity programme that brought economic stability, but lost power in 1996. By the time of his re-election in 2000, the economy was again in difficulties.

## Suslov, Mikhail Andreevich (1902–82)

Soviet politician. He joined the Communist Party in 1921, and was a member of the Central Committee from 1941 until his death. An ideologist of the Stalinist school, he became a ruthless and strongly doctrinaire administrator. Very different from Nikita **KHRUSHCHEV** in temperament and political outlook, he opposed Khrushchev's 'de-Stalinization' measures, economic reforms and foreign policy, and was instrumental in unseating him in 1964. ► **STALINISM**

## Suspects, Law of (17 Sep 1793)

This French law, drafted in sweeping terms, allowing the arrest of all who supported tyranny or federalism, former nobles or émigrés or their relatives, was the basis of the Reign of **TERROR**; it was repealed in 1795.

## Sustainable Development, UN Commission on

The Commission is part of the UN Economic and Social Council and was formed in Dec 1992 to monitor progress in implementing the measures agreed at the **EARTH SUMMIT**. Full sessions of the Commission are held annually. The Commission has 53 members: 13 from African states, eleven from Asian states, ten from Latin American and Caribbean states, six from Eastern European states, and 13 from Western European and other states.

## Suvorov, Alexander Vasilevich, Count (1729–1800)

Russian general. He fought in the **SEVEN YEARS' WAR**,

and in Poland and Turkey, then aided the Austrians against the French in Italy (1799), where he won several victories. Directed to join other Russian forces in Switzerland, he found them already defeated, and was forced into a winter retreat across the mountains to Austria, which he completed with great success. ► FRENCH REVOLUTIONARY WARS

**Suzman, Helen** (1917– )
South African politician. Educated at Parktown Convent and Witwatersrand University, she lectured part-time at the University (1944–52) but became deeply concerned by the rightward shift of the NATIONAL PARTY (NP); she joined the opposition United Party and was elected to parliament in 1953. Closely involved with the South African Institute of Race Relations in the 1970s, she was often a solitary voice against the NP's policy of APARTHEID in parliament. A formidable debater, Suzman earned the respect of opponents of apartheid and received the UN Human Rights Award in 1978. She retired from parliament in 1989 after 36 uninterrupted years of service.

**Suzuki Zenko** (1911–2004)
Japanese politician. He was elected in 1947 to the lower house of the Diet as a Socialist party deputy, but moved to the Liberal Party in 1949 and then, on its formation in 1955, to the conservative LIBERAL DEMOCRATIC PARTY (LDP). During the 1960s and 1970s he held a succession of ministerial and party posts, including Post and Telecommunications (1960–4), Chief Cabinet Secretary (1964–5), Health and Welfare (1965–8) and Agriculture, Forestry and Fisheries (1976–80). Following the death of his patron, OHIRA MASAYOSHI, he succeeded to the dual positions of LDP President and Prime Minister in 1980. His premiership was marred by factional strife within the LDP, deteriorating relations with the USA and opposition to his defence policy. He stepped down in 1982, but remained an influential LDP faction leader.

**Švehla, Antonín** (1873–1933)
Czechoslovak politician. Born near Prague, he was active in the Agrarian Party from its foundation in 1899, establishing its newspaper in 1906 and chairing its executive committee from 1909 until his death in 1933. Half-way through WORLD WAR I he threw his weight behind MASARYK's drive for complete independence. As Minister of the Interior (1918–20), he protected the new state against threats from the revolutionary Left. As Prime Minister for most of the period 1922–9, he gave it economic prosperity and social stability, based on a combination of middle-of-the-road agrarian and socialist interests.

**Svein I Haraldsson, Forkbeard** (d.1014)
King of Denmark (985/1014) and, for five winter weeks, of England (1014). He was the son of Harald Bluetooth, but rebelled against his father and deposed him in 985. His reign was notable for a series of military campaigns against England from 994 onwards. On each occasion, King ETHELRED THE UNREADY paid escalating amounts of *Danegeld* to buy off the Danish invaders but each time they returned for more. In 1013 Svein Forkbeard launched another expedition with imperial intent, taking with him his son CANUTE. By the end of the year, King Ethelred had fled to safety in Normandy, leaving Svein to take up the crown; but five weeks later, on 3 Feb 1014, Svein died, and Canute returned for a time to Denmark.

**Svein II Ulfsson**, also known as **Estridsson** (d.1074)
King of Denmark (1047/74). The son of a regent of Denmark, Earl Ulf, and nephew of CANUTE (his mother was Canute's sister, Estrid), he was appointed Regent of Denmark in 1045 by King MAGNUS I, THE GOOD of Norway (and Denmark), and was himself acclaimed King when Magnus died in 1047. HARALD HARDRADA, who became sole King of Norway, laid claim to Denmark as well, and now began a long and unrelenting war of attrition against Svein. Svein lost every battle, but never lost the war, and in 1064 peace was made and Harald accepted Svein's right to the throne of Denmark. In 1069, after the conquest of England by WILLIAM I, THE CONQUEROR, Svein's army descended on the north of England and captured York, but Svein made peace with William the following year and withdrew. He was succeeded by five of his sons in turn.

**Sveinn Björnsson** ► BJÖRNSSON, SVEINN

**Sverdlov, Yakov Mikhailovich** (1885–1919)
Bolshevik politician. Born and brought up in Nizhni Novgorod, he embraced socialism early and was arrested for the first time when he was 17 years old. Between 1902 and 1907 he was often in prison or in exile. In 1917 he rose rapidly to become Chairman of the Central Executive Committee, running both the party and the country while others fought their military and political battles. However, in 1919 he died suddenly, leaving a serious gap at the top which was never really filled.

**Sverdrup, Johan** (1816–92)
Norwegian politician. A combative and charismatic figure, Sverdrup was elected to parliament (the *Storting*) in 1850. His prolonged fight to establish parliamentary sovereignty in Norway was rewarded with success in 1884. Since Norway was ruled by the King of Sweden, this entailed challenging both the prerogatives of the crown and the union with Sweden. In 1869 Sverdrup became leader of Norway's first organized political party, the Left (*Venstre*). Following repeated challenges by Sverdrup and his supporters, King OSCAR II was finally obliged, in 1884, to turn to Sverdrup as the only leader who commanded the support of a majority in the Storting. Sverdrup was Prime Minister of Norway from 1884 to 1889.

**Sverrir Sigurdsson**, known as **the Usurper** (c.1150–1202)
King of Norway (1184/1202). Brought up in the Faroes, he claimed to be the illegitimate son of Sigurd Haraldsson, the Mouth (d.1155), King of Norway. He emerged from obscurity in 1179 to lay claim to the throne from MAGNUS V ERLINGSSON, whom he finally defeated and killed in 1184. He turned out to be one of Norway's greatest kings, strengthening the Crown against both Church and nobles with the support of the freeholding farmers. He commissioned one of the first Icelandic sagas – a biography of himself, *Sverris saga*, written during his lifetime by his contemporary and friend, Karl Jónsson, Abbot of the Monastery of Thingeyrar in Iceland.

## Švestka, Oldřich (1922–83)

Czechoslovak editor and politician. A journalist, he joined the Communist Party in 1945 and became one of the editors of its daily *Rudé Právo*. In 1958 he became editor-in-chief, and in 1962 he became a member of the Central Committee, and so held an influential political position. In 1968 he was admitted to the presidium of the party, but his allegiance to the **PRAGUE SPRING** was only formal. With **BIL'AK** and others he welcomed the Soviet invasion, and by 1975 he was once more editor-in-chief of *Rudé Právo*.

## Svoboda, Ludwik (1895–1979)

Czechoslovak soldier and politician. He fought with the **CZECHOSLOVAK LEGION** in Russia in 1917 before becoming a professional soldier. After escaping from Czechoslovakia in 1939 he became commanding general of the Czechoslovak army corps attached to the **RED ARMY** in 1943, and helped to liberate Košiče, Brno and Prague from 1944 to 1945. In 1948 he joined the Communist Party and was Minister of Defence until 1950. From 1952 to 1963 he lived in obscurity, mistrusted by the Stalinists; but, with Nikita **KHRUSHCHEV**'s backing, he was subsequently brought forward as a 'safe' patriotic father-figure and in 1968 he succeeded the discredited Antonín **NOVOTNÝ** as President. He gave loyal support to the abortive reforms of Alexander **DUBČEK** and, after the hostile Soviet intervention in 1968, he travelled to Moscow to seek relaxation of the repressive measures imposed on the Czechoslovaks. He remained in office until 1975, when failing health forced his retirement.

## Swabia

A south-western medieval German duchy, extending from the River Rhine in the west to the Alps in the south, Bavaria in the east, and Franconia in the north, containing the cities of Strasbourg, Constance and Augsburg. The **PEASANTS' WAR** of 1524–5 began there, because landlords and peasants were at odds, imperial authority was increasing, and Lutheran doctrines were spreading.

## Swabian League (1488)

Various leagues existed throughout the Middle Ages but in 1488, at Esslingen, 22 Imperial towns joined with the Imperial Knights' League of St George and some ecclesiastical princes (eg Mainz, Bavaria, Baden) to create a new league. This body, governed by three colleges of knights, princes and towns, possessed its own army. It was actively involved in the suppression of the **PEASANTS' WAR** (1524–5). The league was disbanded in 1534 as a result of tensions produced internally by the **REFORMATION** and the introduction of Lutheranism into some of the member states.

## Swadeshi

A Hindi term meaning 'of one's own country', this was a slogan used as part of an Indian campaign of boycotting foreign-made goods, initiated in protest against the partition of Bengal into two separate administrative divisions by the British in 1905 in defiance of Indian public opinion. The policy was viewed as an attempt to perpetuate British rule by dividing the Indian population, particularly the Muslims of East Bengal from the Hindus of West Bengal. Advocates of *Swadeshi* urged the Indian people to wear *khadi* or home-made country-cloth, amongst other things. The first example of mass opposition to British rule, the campaign led eventually to the abandonment of the partition of Bengal in 1911. ► **BENGAL, PARTITION OF**

## Swahili

A language spoken in East Africa, especially in Tanzania. A hybrid of Arabic and local languages, it has provided a bridge across tribal divides and has been seen by many East Africans as a national, or even regional, language that is indigenous rather than imported from the colonial power.

## SWAPO (South West Africa People's Organization)

Founded in 1958 as the Ovambo People's Organization, SWAPO became the main nationalist movement for South West Africa (Namibia) and organized the guerrilla war against the South African administration of the country. Based initially in Tanzania and then Zambia, the guerrilla movement established bases in Angola in the 1970s and became embroiled in the general conflict involving South Africa, **UNITA**, and the **MPLA** government in Luanda with its Cuban and Soviet support. Recognized by the **ORGANIZATION OF AFRICAN UNITY** (OAU), and later by the world community, as the authentic voice of Namibian aspirations, an international agreement was reached in 1988 that linked Namibia's independence with Cuban withdrawal from Angola and the cessation of South African support for UNITA. In the ensuing 1989 election, SWAPO won over half the votes and a majority of seats, forming the first independent government, and has been in government ever since.

## Swaraj

A Hindi term meaning 'self-government' or 'home rule'. It was used by Indian nationalists to describe independence from British rule.

## Swatantra Party

The only authentic Indian political party of the traditional Right, as the term would be understood in Europe. It was a coalition of big urban business and rural aristocratic and landlord elements in which the latter were dominant. The Swatantra Party was formed on an all-India basis in 1959 and was of consequence nationally only in three general elections: 1962, 1967 and 1972. In 1967 it succeeded in winning 44 seats in the Lok Sabha (the lower house of Parliament), emerging as the second largest party in the House after Congress. During its heyday, the Swatantra Party was the leading party of the Right, offering a full scale critique of the Congress policies of centralized planning, nationalization of industries, agrarian reform and non-alignment.

## SWAZILAND  official name **Kingdom of Swaziland**

A monarchy in south-east Africa, bounded to the north, west, south and south-east by South Africa, and to the north-east by Mozambique. The Swazi people probably arrived in the area in the 16c. Boundaries with the Transvaal were decided in the 19c, and independence was guaranteed in 1881 and again in 1884, when the country became a South African protectorate. The British agreed to the Transvaal administration of Swaziland in 1894 but, after the

second Boer War, Swaziland, though retaining its monarchy, came under British rule as a British High Commission territory in 1903. It gained independence in 1968 under King **SOBHUZA II**. Mswati III acceded to the throne in 1986 and faced increasingly strong demands for the democratization of the constitution, but political parties remain illegal. The country faces serious problems because of the very high levels of **HIV/AIDS** infection. ➤ **BOER WARS**

## SWEDEN official name **Kingdom of Sweden**

A constitutional monarchy in northern Europe, occupying the eastern side of the Scandinavian Peninsula, bounded to the east by Finland, the Gulf of Bothnia, and the Baltic Sea; to the south-west by the Skagerrak and Kattegat; and to the west and north-west by Norway. Formed from the union of the kingdoms of the Goths and Svears in the 7c, it did not include the southern parts of the peninsula (Skåne, Halland and Blekinge) which were part of Denmark until conquered in 1658. Sweden was united with Denmark and Norway under Danish leadership in the **KALMAR UNION** (1397). This union ended in 1527, following a revolt led by **GUSTAV I VASA**, founder of modern Sweden. The Swedish state also included Finland until all Finnish areas were finally lost to Russia in 1814. Norway was separated from Denmark in 1814 and united in personal union with Sweden as compensation for the loss of Finland, but that union was dissolved in 1905. Sweden has been a neutral country since 1814, including during both World Wars. It became a member of the **EC** in 1995, but in a 2003 referendum rejected membership of the **EURO ZONE**.

## Swing Riots (1830–1)
A movement of agricultural workers, especially in the south and east of England, consisting of a series of

arson attacks and the destruction of threshing machines. The uprising was put down by the Whig government, resulting in 19 executions and nearly 500 transportations, but the labourers won some wage concessions and delayed the introduction of mechanization. ➤ **LUDDITES**

## Swiss Guards
The papal police corps, originally instituted by Pope **JULIUS II** and recruited from the mercenaries of the cantons of the Swiss confederacy, whose reputation as infantrymen was established after their victories over the Burgundian calvary in 1476. Their dark blue, yellow, and red uniforms were designed by Michelangelo.

## SWITZERLAND official name **Swiss Confederation**, ancient name **Helvetia**

A landlocked European republic, bounded to the east by Liechtenstein and Austria; to the south by Italy; to the west by France; and to the north by Germany. Part of the **HOLY ROMAN EMPIRE** in the 10c, the Swiss Confederation was created in 1291 when the cantons of Uri, Schwyz and Unterwalden formed a defensive league. The Confederation expanded during the 14c and was the centre of the **REFORMATION** in the 16c. Swiss independence and neutrality was recognized under the Treaty of **WESTPHALIA** in 1648. The country was conquered by **NAPOLEON I**, who in 1798 instituted the Helvetian Republic. In 1815 it was organized as a confederation of 22 cantons, and in 1848 a federal constitution was adopted. Switzerland was neutral in both World Wars. A new President of Switzerland is elected every year. Many policy decisions are made by national referenda. A 2001 referendum rejected **EU** membership, while a 2002 referendum led to Switzerland joining the **UN**.

## Sykes–Picot Agreement (1916)
A secret agreement concluded by diplomat Sir Mark Sykes (for Britain) and Georges Picot (for France) on the partitioning of the **OTTOMAN EMPIRE** after **WORLD WAR I**. France was to be the dominant power in Syria and Lebanon, and Britain in Transjordan, Iraq and northern Palestine. The rest of Palestine was to be under international control, and an Arab state was to be established.

## Syllabus of Errors
Appended to the papal encyclical *Quanta cura* of 1864 was a 'Catalogue of the Principal Errors of Our Time' in which Pope **PIUS IX** not only condemned **SOCIALISM** and nationalism, but also rejected any notion that the Roman Catholic Church could tolerate 'progress, liberalism and modern civilization'. Rather than halting the forces that Pius feared, the Syllabus served to foster greater anticlericalism both within Italy and the rest of Europe.

**Sylvester II**, originally **Gerbert Aurillac** (c.940–1003)
French pope (999/1003). Renowned for his achievements in chemistry, mathematics and philosophy, he is said to have introduced Arabic numerals and to have invented a species of clock. As pope, he upheld the primacy of Rome against the separatist tendencies of the French Church.

**syndicalism**
A revolutionary socialist doctrine that emphasized workers taking power by seizing the factories in which they worked; developed in the 1890s, and common in France, Italy and Spain in the early 20c. The state was to be replaced by worker-controlled units of production. Often a general strike was advocated as part of the strategy. By 1914 it had lost its political force. The name, deriving from *syndicat* (French, 'trade union'), has also been applied to various non-revolutionary doctrines supporting worker control.

---

**SYRIA** official name **Syrian Arab Republic**

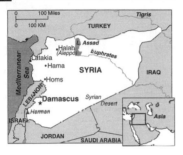

A republic in the Middle East, bounded to the west by the Mediterranean Sea and Lebanon; to the southwest by Israel and Jordan; to the east by Iraq; and to the north by Turkey. The country has been part of the Phoenician, Persian, Roman and Byzantine empires. It was conquered by Muslim Arabs in the 7c, when Damascus became the capital of the Umayyad Dynasty, and was subsequently ruled by foreign dynasties including the Egyptian Fatimids and **MAMLUKS**, before being conquered by Turks in the 11c. The scene of many battles during the Crusades in the **MIDDLE AGES**, it was part of the **OTTOMAN EMPIRE** in 1517 and enjoyed a brief period of independence in 1920, before being made a French mandate. Syria gained its independence in 1946. It merged with Egypt and Yemen to form the United Arab Republic in 1958, but re-established itself as an independent state under its present name in 1961. Syria suffered setbacks in the **SIX-DAY WAR** of 1967, when the Golan Heights region was seized by Israel, and in the **YOM KIPPUR WAR** of 1973. After the outbreak of civil war in Lebanon in 1975, Syrian troops were sent to restore order; Syrian soldiers were also part of the international coalition force that opposed Iraq in the **GULF WAR**. Syria cautiously took part in the Middle East peace talks in 1992, which gave rise to hopes of a peace agreement being reached with Israel. President Hafez al-**ASAD** seized power in a coup in 1970, formally taking office in 1971 and remaining President until his death in 2000, when he was succeeded by his son. Bashar al-Asad has introduced some openness into political life and eased restrictions on

debate. However, the USA remains hostile, and imposed economic sanctions in 2004 in protest at Syria's alleged support for terrorism and failure to prevent terrorists entering **IRAQ**. ► **AXIS OF EVIL**; **BA'ATH PARTY**; **FATIMID DYNASTY**

**Syrian National Bloc**
Formed in 1931, the National Bloc (*al-kutla al-wataniyya*) was a heterogeneous assortment of regional factions bound together by the common cause of the independence to which Syrian nationalists opposed to the French mandate aspired. After the national strike of 1936, which was not of the Bloc's making, the French invited delegates from the Bloc to negotiations in Paris. Despite the preparation of a draft treaty granting Syria a form of independence (while providing guarantees for the special position of France), by the outbreak of **WORLD WAR II** the Syrian nationalist aim of freedom from France had been frustrated. After the invasion of the Free French and British in 1940, the Bloc continued to press for independence, despite opposition from the Free French. The British, however, began to lend their support to the Bloc, which was led from 1940 by Shukri al-**QUWWATLI**, who was later to become President of the Syrian Republic. Independence was achieved in 1946, but the failure of the old élite, who came to power in 1946, to recognize the need for reform in the face of pressing social and economic difficulties led to military coups in 1949. As a result of the third of these, Colonel Adib Shishakli was to hold power until 1954. Despite the re-emergence of al-Quwwatli in 1955 and the reforming efforts of Khalid al Azm, the **BA'ATH PARTY** in Syria, by dint of proposing a **UNITED ARAB REPUBLIC** of Egypt and Syria in 1958, managed in due course to supplant the existing party structure.

**Szabo, Ervin** (1877–1918)
Hungarian intellectual. A lawyer by training and a librarian by occupation, he was very active in shaping socialist ideas from 1899 onwards. After a few years he switched from support for the Social Democratic Party to **SYNDICALISM**. He translated **MARX** and **ENGELS** and wrote extensively about **MARXISM**. He left behind a circle of young critics of bureaucracy, opportunism and militarism.

**Szalasi, Ferenc** (1897–1946)
Hungarian soldier and politician. A major on the general staff, he joined a secret racist group in 1930, and in 1933 published his *Plan for the Building of the Hungarian State*, which became the ideological handbook for Hungarian fascism. Retired from military service in 1935, he formed the first of a series of fascist parties culminating in the **ARROW CROSS** in 1938. Under Nazi pressure he became Prime Minister in 1944 and instituted a racist reign of terror. In 1946 he was executed as a war criminal.

**Szechenyi, Istvan, Count** (1791–1860)
Hungarian landowner, soldier, innovator and reformer. He was responsible for establishing the Hungarian Academy of Sciences, which from 1825 onwards contributed a cultural core and a broadening social base to aristocratic protests against Habsburg rule. He was also behind the building of Adam Clark's famous Chain Bridge across the Danube, joining the political weight of Buda to the

commercial weight of Pest to form a new capital. He eventually despaired both of the aristocracy and of the new nationalists and committed suicide. ► **HABSBURG DYNASTY**

## Szeklers

A tribe in **TRANSYLVANIA** which served as frontiersmen in medieval Hungary, then assimilated to the Magyars and came to speak the Hungarian language. The medieval kings of Hungary granted them the right of self-government in their districts; they elected their own count, who was responsible to the king, and their land was administered by the Transylvanian diet. During the **REFORMATION**, many became members of the Lutheran and Unitarian Churches. Today many Szeklers remain in Transylvania and form a Hungarian-speaking majority in the counties between Tîrgu Mureş and Braşov. ► **SUPPLEX LIBELLUS VALACHORUM**

**Taaffe, Eduard Franz Josef, Count von** (1833–95)
Austrian politician. Born 11th Viscount Taaffe and Baron of Ballymote in the Irish peerage, he became Austria's Minister of the Interior (1867) and Chief Minister (1869–70 and 1879–93). He showed great tact in an attempt to unite the various nationalities of the empire into a consolidated whole.

**Table of Ranks** (1722)
The grading by **PETER I, THE GREAT** of the Russian nobility into 14 different ranks for military and civil service. Peter was intent on exploiting all the resources of his state. In accordance with the Table, the nobility had to carry out service from a very young age; new men who did not happen to be nobles could also get on to the ladder; and promotion was dependent on performance. The fifth rank brought ennoblement, the ninth rank made it hereditary. Two-thirds served in the army or navy, the rest in the bureaucracy. Peter's successors were less able to dominate and exploit the nobility in this way; and **CATHERINE II, THE GREAT** produced a **CHARTER OF THE NOBILITY** mainly to keep them out of power.

**Tacna–Arica Question**
A prolonged diplomatic dispute between Peru and Chile concerning sovereignty over Tacna and Arica provinces, occupied by Chile in the War of the **PACIFIC**. It was finally resolved in 1929 by the award of Tacna to Peru and Arica to Chile.

**Taewon-gun**, also called **Yi Ha-ung** (1820–98)
Korean courtier. The father of the Korean king Kojong (1864/1907), he became the dominant figure at court in his capacity as Grand Prince (*Taewon-gun*). He favoured an exclusionist foreign policy, rejecting requests from Japan and the Western powers for the opening of diplomatic and commercial relations and preferring to maintain Korea's tributary relationship with China. His formal retirement in 1873 paved the way for the Treaty of **KANGHWA** (1876) with Japan, which signalled the end of Korean seclusion.

**Taft, Robert Alphonso** (1889–1953)
US politician. The son of President William **TAFT**, he studied law at Yale and Harvard and in 1917 became assistant counsel of the US Food Administration in Europe under **HOOVER**. A conservative Republican, he was elected to the **SENATE** from Ohio in 1938, and co-sponsored the **TAFT–HARTLEY ACT** (1947) directed against the power of the trade unions and the 'closed shop'. A prominent isolationist, he was Republican leader from 1939 to 1953, failing three times (1940, 1948 and 1952) to secure the Republican

nomination for the presidency.

**Taft, William Howard** (1857–1930)
US politician and 27th President. Educated at Yale, he became a lawyer, Solicitor-General (1890), the first civil Governor of the Philippines (1901), and then Secretary of War (1904–8) under President Theodore **ROOSEVELT**. As President (1909–13), he continued Roosevelt's aggressive foreign policy and his policies favouring conservation and regulation of big business, and achieved an excellent record of legislation. But he was handicapped by having followed the flamboyant and popular Roosevelt. While he was in fact a fairly progressive President, the public, in favour of reform as a result of Roosevelt's politics, perceived him as conservative, and he was not re-elected. From 1913 he was Professor of Law at Yale, and from 1921 Chief Justice of the US Supreme Court, where he made administrative improvements. He was the father of Robert Alphonso **TAFT**, the US Senator and Republican leader. ► **REPUBLICAN PARTY**

**Taft–Hartley Act** (1947)
US labour legislation. It outlawed 'unfair' labour practices such as the closed shop, and demanded that unions supply financial reports and curtail their political activities. It also gave the US government the power to postpone major strikes endangering national health or safety for a cooling-off period of 80 days. The National Management Relations Act, its official name, was passed over President **TRUMAN**'s veto by the first Republican-controlled **CONGRESS** in almost 20 years to limit the power of the **NATIONAL LABOR RELATIONS ACT** (the 'Wagner Act') of 1935, which the Republicans believed had shifted the balance between employers and workers far too much in favour of the unions.

**Tagliacozzo, Battle of** (1268)
The victory of **CHARLES OF ANJOU** over the armies of **CONRADIN OF SWABIA** secured for him the crown of Sicily and Naples, and marked the ruin of the empire in Italy. Conradin, the last legitimate Staufen heir, was taken. He appealed to the pope to intervene with his captors, but Clement IV did not respond and the 16-year-old and his entourage were publicly hanged in Naples. The papal triumph over the Staufen was complete but short-lived, for Charles of Anjou cared even less for ecclesiastical rights and privileges than the heirs of **FREDERICK II**.

**Ta'if Accord** (1989)
When Amin **GEMAYEL** left office as President of Lebanon in Sep 1988, the country found itself without a

government. Michel Aoun, then Commander-in-Chief of the Lebanese Army and a Maronite Christian, took over the presidential palace and went on to attack Syrian forces in Beirut. In response to the crisis, the **ARAB LEAGUE**, represented by King **FAHD** of Saudi Arabia and King **HASSAN II** of Morocco, together with President **CHADLI BENJEDID** of Algeria, proposed a peace plan (Oct 1989) and the Lebanese members of parliament gathered in Ta'if in Saudi Arabia. The Ta'if Accord was the result of their talks on the reduction of Maronite Christian domination in government. The essence of the agreement was that the cabinet and the National Assembly, to whom the President would be subject, would be equally divided between Christian and Muslim members. Not surprisingly, this proposal was criticized by both **DRUZE** and Shi'a, and rejected by Aoun.

## Taifa Kings
The name (literally, 'party' or 'faction' kings) given to the rulers of the petty kingdoms that were formed in Muslim Spain after the fall of the Caliphate of Córdoba in 1031. There was a total of 23 Taifa realms, many of which were conquered by the invading **ALMORA-VIDS** under Yusuf ibn Tashfin in the late 11c.

## Taiping Rebellion (1850–64)
A rebellion that spread all over southern China, led by **HONG XIUQUAN**. Its programme, which aimed at ushering in a 'Heavenly Kingdom of Great Peace' (*Taiping tianguo*) was a mixture of religion and political reform. The rebels took Nanjing (Nanking) in 1853 and made it their capital, but internal strife, foreign intervention, and the Qing forces under **ZENG GUOFAN** eventually brought the downfall of the movement. ➤ **QING DYNASTY**

## Taisho Emperor (Yoshihito) (1879–1926)
Emperor of Japan (1912/26). The only son of the **MEIJI EMPEROR** (Mutsuhito), he was proclaimed Crown Prince in 1889 and succeeded his father on the imperial throne in 1912. His 14-year reign saw the emergence of Japan as a great world power. Unlike his father, however, he took little part in active politics, for his mental health gave way in 1921. In the last five years of his life, Crown Prince **HIROHITO** was regent.

## TAIWAN official name **Republic of China**, formerly **Formosa**

An island republic consisting of Taiwan Island and several smaller islands, lying c.80 mi/130 km off the south-east coast of China. It was discovered by the

Portuguese in 1590 and conquered by Manchus of the **QING DYNASTY** in the 17c. Ceded to Japan in 1895, it was returned to China in 1945. The Nationalist government (the **GUOMINDANG**) was moved there after being defeated by the communists in China in 1949, and martial law was in force until replaced by National Security law in 1987. Demands for democratization in the late 1980s led to the first multiparty elections in 1992, which were won by the Guomindang. In 1991 Taiwan officially recognized the communist People's Republic of China for the first time in over 40 years. **LEE TENG-HUI** became President on the death of **JIANG JING'GUO** in 1988, and won the first democratic presidential elections in 1996. From the early 1990s power has shifted from the mainlanders to the native Taiwanese and 50 years of Guomindang rule ended in 2000 when Chen Shui-ban of the Democratic Progressive Party, a pro-independence party, was elected President.

## TAJIKISTAN official name **Republic of Tajikistan**

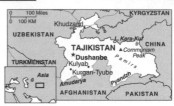

A republic in south-eastern Middle Asia, bounded to the west and north by Uzbekistan; to the north by Kyrgyzstan; to the east by China; and to the south by Afghanistan. Inhabited by Tajiks, who originated in Iran, it was conquered by Arabs in the 7c and 8c, then by the khanate of Bukhara from the 15c to the 18c. The area was then conquered by the Afghans, but by 1868 had come completely under Russian control. It became a Soviet Socialist Republic in 1929, joined the USSR in 1936, and achieved full independence in 1991, the year it became a member of the **CIS** (Commonwealth of Independent States). Civil war between government forces and forces loyal to the former communist regime began in 1992. A ceasefire in 1994 allowed elections to take placed, but fighting resumed in 1995 until a peace agreement was signed in Dec 1996. This agreement has held since, although there have been sporadic outbreaks of violence. The former communists have dominated the presidency and the government since 1991, with some elections either being boycotted by opposition parties or failing to meet international standards.

## Talat Pasha, Mahmud (1872–1921)
Initially a civil servant, he was a supporter of the liberal **YOUNG TURKS** movement along with **ENVER PASHA** who had been a military attaché in Berlin. An associate of Enver, who as Minister of War was regarded as having been largely responsible for bringing Turkey into **WORLD WAR I** on the German side, Talat was excluded from the peace negotiations after the conclusion of the **MUDROS ARMISTICE** in Oct 1918 and fled to Germany. He was assassinated by an Armenian in Berlin.

## Taliban
An Islamic fundamentalist group that first appeared in Afghanistan in late 1994. Its adherents came

originally from religious schools in Pakistan (*taliban* is Persian for 'students' or 'seekers'). Their objective was to replace the destructive factionalism which had characterized Afghan political life since the fall of the communist regime in 1992 with Islamic law. Within two years, and the loss of many thousands of lives, they had taken Kabul and controlled the Pashtun south and east of Afghanistan, about two-thirds of the country. Meanwhile the Tajik, Uzbek, Turkmen and Hazara (ie non-Pashtun) areas in the north remained under Afghani government control and were united in an alliance of forces opposed to Taliban rule called the United Islamic Front for the Salvation of Afghanistan (UIFSA). In 1997 the Taliban government was headed by *de facto* head of state Mullah Muhammad Rabbani, and was recognized by Pakistan, Saudi Arabia and the United Arab Emirates. In 1999 the Taliban appeared to agree to a power-sharing formula, but fighting soon resumed. Under strict Islamic law, crimes were punished with public floggings and executions, and women were denied many of the rights (eg to education and employment) that they might enjoy elsewhere. The Taliban regime was ousted by a US-led coalition and the Afghan Northern Alliance in the **AFGHAN WAR** (2001) but it continued a guerrilla war against the country's new government and international peacekeeping forces.

## Talleyrand (-Périgord), Charles Maurice de (1754–1838)

French politician. Educated for the Church, he was ordained (1779), appointed Bishop of Autun (1788), elected to the **ESTATES GENERAL**, and made President of the National Assembly (1790). He lived in exile in England and the USA until after the fall of **ROBESPIERRE**. As Foreign Minister under the **DIRECTORY** (1797–1807), he helped to consolidate **NAPOLEON I**'s position as Consul (1802) and Emperor (1804); but alarmed by Napoleon's ambitions, he resigned in 1807, becoming leader of the anti-Napoleonic faction. He became Foreign Minister under **LOUIS XVIII**, representing France with great skill at the Congress of **VIENNA** (1814–15). He then lived largely in retirement, but was **LOUIS-PHILIPPE**'s chief adviser at the **JULY REVOLUTION** (1830), and was appointed French Ambassador to England (1830–4). ▶ **FRENCH REVOLUTION**

## Tallien, Jean Lambert (1767–1820)

French revolutionary politician. As President of the National **CONVENTION** (1794), he was denounced by **ROBESPIERRE**, but conspired with **BARRAS** and **FOUCHÉ** to bring about the former's downfall. He became a member of the Council of Five Hundred under the **DIRECTORY** (1795–9), and accompanied **NAPOLEON I** to Egypt (1798). ▶ **FRENCH REVOLUTION**

## Talukdars

A class of landholders in eastern India which grew in the first half of the 18c. *Zamindars* (literally, 'lords of the land') were at the apex of a pyramid of revenue collecting agents. Below them were hundreds of small tenure holders, usually called *Talukdars*. Sometimes Talukdars paid directly to the government, although they more often did so through the Zamindars. Some 18c Taluks originated from older revenue rights that had been incorporated into a new Zamindari, but most appear to have been recent creations, granted to those who had settled new lands, or sold by existing Zamindars who wished to raise money. Even in the great Zamindaris in the last years of the Nawabs, men who wished to invest in revenue rights seem to have been able to purchase Taluks. ▶ **ZAMINDAR**

## Tambo, Oliver (1917–93)

South African politician. The son of a peasant farmer, he went to Johannesburg to attend a school set up by the Community of the Resurrection, where he came under the influence of Trevor Huddleston. Having graduated from Fort Hare College, he embarked upon a teaching diploma but was expelled for political activity. He joined the **ANC** Youth League in 1944, rising to be a member of the ANC executive (1949), Secretary-General (1955) and Deputy President (1959). He then went into exile and was President of the ANC in exile from 1977. He returned to South Africa in 1989 as titular leader of the party, but gave up this position at the meeting of the party in exile in 1990.

## Tamburlaine, Tamerlane ▶ TIMUR

## Tamil

A Dravidian language originally found in south India and Sri Lanka. The term 'Tamil' also refers to the speakers of the language, most of whom live in the south Indian state of Tamil Nadu, although there are substantial Tamil populations in Sri Lanka, where some have been agitating for secession from the state dominated by the Sinhala majority, and Malaysia. Nationalist political aspirations have been promoted by Tamil parties like the **DRAVIDA MUNNETRA KAZHAGAM** (DMK) in India as well as the militant **LTTE** ('Tamil Tigers') in Sri Lanka.

## Tammany Hall

US **POLITICAL MACHINE** of the **DEMOCRATIC PARTY** in New York City and State. It was originally a club (the Society of Tammany) founded in 1789, and in the late 19c and early 20c became notorious for its political corruption. Its power declined in the 1932 election, and although revived for a short time, it has ceased to exist as a political power in New York politics.

## Tanaka Giichi (1864–1929)

Japanese militarist and politician. A member of the **CHOSHU** clique, Tanaka served in both the **SINO-JAPANESE WAR** (1894–5) and the **RUSSO-JAPANESE WAR** (1904–5) and became a vigorous supporter of army expansion. He became leader of the **SEIYUKAI** in 1925 (signalling that party's close association with the military) and Prime Minister in 1927. During his premiership (1927–9) thousands of suspected communists were arrested under the **PEACE PRESERVATION LAWS**. Tanaka also initiated the policy of direct Japanese military intervention in China when he sanctioned three expeditions (1927–8) to east China (Shandong province), ostensibly to protect Japanese residents in the wake of **CHIANG KAI-SHEK**'s **NORTHERN EXPEDITION**.

## Tanaka Kakuei (1918–93)

Japanese politician. After training as a civil engineer and establishing a successful building contracting business, he was elected to Japan's House of Representatives in 1947. He rose swiftly within the dominant **LIBERAL DEMOCRATIC PARTY** (LDP), becoming

Minister of Finance (1962–5), Party Secretary-General (1965–7, 1968–71) and Minister of International Trade and Industry (1971–2), before serving as LDP President and Prime Minister (1972–4). He was arrested in 1976 on charges of accepting bribes as part of the **LOCKHEED SCANDAL**, and eventually in 1983 was found guilty and sentenced to four years' imprisonment. He had resigned from the LDP in 1976, becoming an independent deputy, but remained an influential, behind-the-scenes, faction leader. His appeal against the 1983 verdict was rejected by the High Court in 1987, but a further appeal was lodged and was still on-going at the time of his death.

**Tancred** (c.1076–1112)
Norman Crusader. The grandson of Robert **GUIS-CARD**, he went on the First **CRUSADE**. He distinguished himself in the sieges of Nicaea, Tarsus, Antioch, Jerusalem and Ascalon, and was given the principality of Tiberias (1099). He also ruled at Edessa and Antioch, where he died. ► **NORMANS**

**Taney, Roger Brooke** (1777–1864)
US jurist. He was admitted to the Bar in 1799 and Andrew **JACKSON** made him Attorney-General in 1831, and Secretary of the Treasury in 1833. The **SENATE**, after rejecting his appointment as Chief Justice in 1835, confirmed it in 1836. His most famous decision was in the Dred Scott case, when he ruled that the **MISSOURI COMPROMISE** was unconstitutional and that slaves and their descendants had no rights as citizens. This precipitated the Civil War, and injured the reputation of the Court for years thereafter. ► **DRED SCOTT V SANDFORD**

**Tanganyika African National Union (TANU)**
This party, founded in 1954, grew out of the Tanganyika African Association and was the dominant party in Tanganyika during the period leading to independence. Under the leadership of Julius **NYERERE**, it became first *de facto* and then, in 1966, *de jure* the only party in the country. Noted for the internal competition it provided at election time and for its unique brand of socialist ideology, laid out in the **ARUSHA DECLARATION**, the party merged in 1977 with the Afro-Shirazi Party of Zanzibar to form **CHAMA CHA MAPINDUZI** (CCM).

**Tannenberg, Battle of** (26–30 Aug 1914)
A **WORLD WAR I** battle between Russian and German forces. The Russian army under General Alexander **SAMSONOV** was completely routed; 100,000 prisoners of war were taken, and Samsonov himself committed suicide. German nationalists claimed the victory as revenge for the defeat of the **TEUTONIC KNIGHTS** by Russian, Polish and Lithuanian forces at the first Battle of Tannenberg (Grunwald) in 1410.

**Tanner, Väinö** (1881–1966)
Finnish politician. A controversial figure in Finnish politics, he emerged as leader of the **SOCIAL DEMOCRATIC PARTY** after the end of the civil war in 1918. Tanner distanced the party from the radical Left in order to cooperate with the Centre, a policy which enabled the Social Democrats to participate in a majority government in 1937. He was identified by the USSR as one of those who had blocked a peaceful

outcome to the negotiations which resulted in the **RUSSO-FINNISH WAR** (1939–40). Tanner earned further Soviet hostility through his role in government, first as Foreign Minister and later, during the **CONTINUATION WAR** of 1941–4, as Minister of Finance. In 1946 he was one of eight Finnish war leaders who were tried and convicted as war criminals. Following his release from prison in 1949 Tanner returned to parliament, and in 1957 was re-elected leader of the Social Democratic Party.

**Tantia Topee**, real name **Ramchandra Pandurangez** (d.1859)
Indian Brahmin soldier and rebel. Hailing from Gwalior, he was **NANA SAHIB**'s lieutenant in the **INDIAN UPRISING** (1857–8). He took part in the massacre of the British at Cawnpore (July 1857). With the Rani of Jhansi he occupied Gwalior and then held the field after his chief had fled. After a skilful campaign and march through central India and Khandesh, in an attempt to raise up the Marathas in revolt, he was betrayed, captured and executed in Apr 1859. ► **KANPUR, MASSACRE OF**

**Tanucci, Bernardo** (1698–1783)
Neapolitan politician and administrator. From 1754, he was the principal minister of Charles IV (1716–88; King of Spain as **CHARLES III**, 1759/88), under whom he pursued a lively anticlerical policy. After Charles's departure for Spain, he remained the main adviser of **FERDINAND I** (IV of Naples), and continued to pursue anticlerical and enlightened policies, including the expulsion of the Jesuits and the introduction of civil marriage. In 1776 he fell from favour and was forced to resign; henceforth affairs were increasingly dominated by the Queen, **MARIA CAROLINA**, and her lover, Acton.

**TANZANIA**     official name **United Republic of Tanzania**

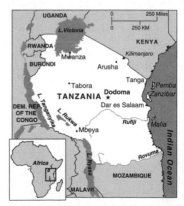

An East African republic, consisting of the mainland region of Tanganyika, and Zanzibar, just off the coast in the Indian Ocean, which includes Zanzibar Island, Pemba Island and some small islets. The country is bounded to the south by Mozambique and Malawi; to the south-west by Zambia; to the west by the Democratic Republic of the Congo; to the north-west by Burundi, Rwanda and Uganda; to the north by Kenya; and to the east by the Indian Ocean. Inhabited by Caucasoid peoples and then in the 5c by Bantus from western Africa, it had early links with Arab,

Indian and Persian traders. The Swahili culture developed in the 10–15c, and Portuguese explorers arrived in the 15c. The island of Zanzibar was the capital of the Omani empire in the 1840s. Exploration of the interior by German missionaries and British explorers took place in the mid-19c, and Zanzibar became a British protectorate in 1890. German East Africa was established in 1891 and by 1907 Germany controlled the whole country. After **WORLD WAR I** Tanganyika (mainland Tanzania) became a British mandate (1919) and in 1961 it became the first East African country to gain independence and become a member of the **COMMONWEALTH OF NATIONS**; it became a republic in 1962. Zanzibar was given independence as a constitutional monarchy, with the Sultan as head of state; the Sultan was overthrown in 1964, and an Act of Union between Zanzibar and Tanganyika led to the United Republic of Tanzania. A multiparty system was approved in 1992 and an agreement was reached in 1993 to set up a separate government for Tanganyika. In the mid-1990s hundreds of thousands of refugees from war and ethnic violence in Rwanda and Burundi arrived in Tanzania, exacerbating mounting internal tensions. Since the mid 1990s the economy has been liberalized by removing government controls instituted by Julius **NYERERE**'s policy of African socialism. ▶ **CHAMA CHA MAPINDUZI**; **TANGANYIKA AFRICAN NATIONAL UNION (TANU)**

**Tanzimat**

The term (literally, 'reorganization') used to describe the reforms in the **OTTOMAN EMPIRE** during the period 1839–78. Sultan **ABD UL-MAJID I** (1839/61) showed that he was determined to carry on the reforms of his father, **MAHMUD II**, when he issued the Noble Rescript (*Hatt-i Sherif*) in 1839. This marked a radical break with Islamic tradition, which had always regarded non-Muslims as separate and inferior. The Rescript recognized the equality of all religious groups before the law. Equal treatment for Muslims and non-Muslims was again promised in the Imperial Rescript (**HATT-I HUMAYUN**) of 1856, and in 1867 Christians began to be appointed to state councils. The aim was to integrate them (40 per cent of the Sultan's subjects were Christians early in the century) in the Ottoman Empire and this meant replacing the traditional educational and legal systems, dominated by the *ulama* (religious leaders), by secular organizations. From 1840, Western-type courts and codes were introduced and administration was centralized on the French model, with prefects and departments. A new educational system, with elementary and secondary schools to prepare students for higher technical education, grew slowly and painfully to create a new élite committed to reform. The economy was also improved, as land was reclaimed, new factories set up, postal (1834) and telegraph (1855) systems established and railways begun (1866). All these reforms were revolutionary, as they seemed to secure the triumph of the Christian enemy over Islam by imposing, often with the help of European advisers, European practices and institutions. Most Turks were unaffected by the Tanzimat – their lives, beliefs and loyalties were still dominated by Islam – but power had nevertheless passed to secular bureaucrats.

**Tardieu, André** (1876–1945)

French politician. A well-known journalist before 1914, he was a Deputy (1914–24 and 1926–36), High Commissioner in the USA (1917–18), and one of **CLEMENCEAU**'s chief advisers during the negotiation of the peace treaties. His political position was right-of-centre; he was Minister of Public Works (1926–8), Prime Minister (1929–30), Minister of the Interior (1928–30), of Agriculture (1931–2), and of Foreign Affairs during his own second term as Prime Minister (1932), thus clearly being the dominant figure throughout the 1928–32 parliament. During that time, he practised what he called a 'prosperity policy', providing government assistance for the modernization of agriculture and industry, the electrification of rural areas, etc, and put through measures to abolish fees in state secondary schools and to improve social insurance. The victory of the Left in the 1932 elections put him in opposition, but after the crisis of Feb 1934 he was brought back to office in the **DOUMERGUE** cabinet with the task of producing proposals for constitutional reform. When it became evident that they were not going to be adopted, he left active politics to defend his plans for a stronger executive power in books and articles.

**Tariff Policy** (Canada)

After 1846, Britain's policy of free trade allowed the colonial governments to cease imposing duties on foreign imports. Canada, however, needing revenue for development, raised tariffs from a general level of 10 per cent in 1846 to 20 per cent or 25 per cent by 1859. British manufacturers protested through the Duke of Newcastle to the Finance Minister, A T **GALT**, but he asserted Canada's economic independence. In the early years of confederation tariffs produced three-quarters of all federal government revenue, and by 1879 they had been raised to an average of 25 per cent through the **MACDONALD** government's National Policy, despite the complaints of fishermen and farmers. In 1897 **FIELDING** sought to solve their problems by introducing a two tier system, which he also tried to embody in an agreement with the USA in 1911. Later tariff agreements within the **COMMONWEALTH OF NATIONS** were negotiated through **IMPERIAL CONFERENCES**, and since **WORLD WAR II** within the framework of the General Agreement on Tariffs and Trade (**GATT**). The Tokyo round, completed in 1979, envisaged an average of nine per cent on dutiable goods (comprising 35 per cent of Canadian imports) by 1987. These tariff reductions, however, have been coupled with Canadian import restrictions on textiles, clothing and agricultural products.

**tarimbeiro**

Brazilian army slang for an officer who had risen through active service, rather than through formal qualifications gained at the military schools in Rio de Janeiro, Fortaleza or Rio Grande do Sul. *Tarimbeiros*, men who had seen service in the War of the **TRIPLE ALLIANCE** (or Paraguayan War) (1864–70), became sceptical of the ability of the Brazilian Empire to sustain a modern army and formed an alliance with the *doutores* (those who had studied under the guidance of well-known but bookish teachers) to overthrow the regime in 1889. Both groups became

# Technology

Science & Technology

The development of a particular technology requires resources to implement it and a social environment which will embrace it. Inventions before their time are not developed, but those that can be applied spread from one part of the world to another, taken by traders or conquerors, sometimes deliberately sought out.

A hand-axe dating from 250,000 BC establishes that the earliest human beings made and used tools. Weapons in the form of bows and arrows, spears, traps and slings have been found, as well as the more obvious tombs, burial mounds and religious buildings requiring technical skill. Stone as a material was replaced by iron, then copper, then bronze. Lands that were the source of metals (such as Crete, for copper) gained wealth and influence.

To transport this material, **ships** were developed from the rafts and reed boats used on the rivers. Phoenicians, Egyptians, Greeks and Romans made ships with square-rigged sails to run before the wind, with other power being supplied by oarsmen. Arabs made ships with triangular sails, the angles of which could be changed. Eventually, in the 13c, these designs were combined in the construction of the European ships that made the voyages of discovery.

On land, the use of the wheel (represented on a clay tablet from Ur dating from 3500 BC) provided flexibility of transport where the terrain was suitable. Where it was not, domesticated beasts such as the horse and camel carried the loads.

Building techniques developed according to the materials available: brick in Sumeria, stone in Egypt. The making of buildings and war machines was aided by the inventions of Archimedes in Syracuse: his pulley, screw and lever. The Romans developed building technology further with fired brick and tile, cement that would set under water, the use of the dome, arch and vault, and created aqueducts, tunnels, bridges, **roads**, sewers and public works to benefit their citizens. Some of these constructions have remained largely intact right up to the 21c.

All early civilizations used slaves for labour, so there was no incentive to create labour-saving devices. In Europe, after the fall of the Roman Empire, there were still slaves, but not much technological advance until the later medieval period, when commercial and industrial development stimulated change in fields ranging from shipbuilding to cannon-founding. The invention of movable type enabled the dissemination of knowledge outside Church control. The first Bible was printed in 1455 and by 1500 there were more than 6,000 published **books**, and large numbers of printers in many European cities. The development of this **printing** technology was a key factor in the **Reformation**.

Maps were printed too which, together with advances in ship design that allowed ships to sail closer to the wind and dispense with rowers, and the improvement in navigation techniques, provided the incentive for rulers and merchants to finance the voyages of discovery.

Wind power was harnessed on land by windmills. In use in the Middle East and China for some centuries previously, they began to be used in Europe in the 12c and were a great advance in areas that had little surface water, or were very flat. Watermills had been developed and improved by the Romans, and both types of mill were used for many types of manufacture until the advent of steam, then electricity, provided alternative power sources.

Coal was used as a power source in homes in Europe from the 16c, later fuelling potteries, glass-making and brick-making, and used in furnaces instead of charcoal. Deeper mines were dug, using technology from metal mines, to gain access to coal seams. Raw materials and manufactured goods had to be transported and the easiest way was by water. **Canals** were built by the Phoenicians, Assyrians, Sumerians, and extensively by the Chinese. In Europe, the Romans had

---

convinced that the army, rather than political élites, had become the defender of national interests. Their influence was broken in 1897–8, with the **CANUDOS CAMPAIGN** and the advent of **CAMPOS SALLES**.

**Tartar ▶ TATAR**

**Tasman, Abel Janszoon** (1603–c.1659)
Dutch navigator. In 1642 he discovered Tasmania, named Van Diemen's Land until 1855, and New Zealand, and in 1643 Tonga and Fiji, having been dispatched in quest of the 'Great South Land' by Antony Van Diemen (1593–1645), Governor-General of Batavia. Tasman made a second voyage (1644) to the Gulf of Carpentaria and the north-west coast of Australia. ▶ **EXPLORATION**

**Tatar**
A Turkic-speaking people living in the USSR. Sunni Muslims since the 14c, they were a highly stratified medieval society. Traditionally farmers and pastoralists, in the 18–19c they became important as political agents, traders, teachers and administrators in the Russian Empire.

**Taylor, Zachary** (1784–1850)
US general, politician and 12th President. He joined the army in 1808 and fought in several campaigns

against the **NATIVE AMERICANS**. In the **MEXICAN WAR** (1846–8) he captured Matamoros, and won a major victory at Buena Vista, though heavily outnumbered. He emerged from the war as a hero, and was given the Whig presidential nomination. The main issues of his presidency (1849–50) were the status of the new territories and the extension of **SLAVERY** there, but he died only 16 months after taking office. He was succeeded by Millard **FILLMORE**. ▶ **WHIG PARTY**

**Teamsters' Union (International Brotherhood of Teamsters, Chauffeurs, Warehousemen and Helpers of America)**
The largest US labour union, with over 1.4 million members. Founded in 1903, it was expelled from the **AFL-CIO** in 1957 for corruption, but was reaffiliated in 1987.

**Teapot Dome Scandal** (1923)
US political scandal. One of several in the administration of President Warren G **HARDING**, it involved the lease of naval oil reserves at Teapot Dome (Wyoming) and Elk Hills (California) by the Secretary of the Interior, Albert B Fall. He allowed no competition to the bids of Harry F Sinclair (Mammoth Oil) and Edward Doheny (Pan-American Petroleum), who had both lent him considerable sums of money.

built canals to link rivers, and the invention of the mitre lock was followed by extensive work across Europe, beginning with the Canal du Midi in France (1666–92). In Britain, the opening of the Bridgewater Canal (1761) was the beginning of canal construction that would continue for a century. The system of canals, linking manufacturing areas to the sea, served the businesses created by the events of the **Industrial Revolution**. The Industrial Revolution ushered in a new type of technology dominated by iron, steel and coal.

The movement towards centralized manufactories, away from cottage industries, was spurred on by the development of steam power, following James Watt's improvements (1769) to the steam engine. This in turn created a demand for the raw cotton for the textile industry, and after the invention of the cotton-gin, encouraged the development of cotton plantations in the south of the USA, fixing the demand for slave ownership there. Steam powered the spinning-jennies and the looms in the factories of northern Britain, and also powered locomotives for the **railways**. The first steam-locomotive service for passengers and freight was provided by the Liverpool and Manchester Railway (1830). During the next 100 years, railways were built all over the world, their tracks eventually made stronger by the use of steel.

Cheap iron had been available in Great Britain for industry, but with the invention of the Bessemer converter (1856), steel became available in bulk. Soon after, the open-hearth process made it possible to use the ores available in Europe, particularly Lorraine, and prompted the development of German heavy industry in the Ruhr.

Steel was the material of the precision tool. The creation of these tools was an industry in itself, but they were also vital to the production of many different goods and to the setting up of mass-production lines. Iron and steel helped travel and transport. They were used in the creation of better-engineered bridges and in ocean-going steamships. After the invention of refrigeration, such ships were able to transport meat long distances, from Australia and Argentina to Europe, and butter from New Zealand to Britain, encouraging growth of farming in those countries.

Steam-powered traction engines were made for the road and farm too, but they did not become very popular. Coal was used to produce gas that provided lighting in factories, streets and homes, remaining the method of lighting many streets in Europe until the mid-20c. It also made longer working hours more practicable.

Throughout the 19c, technological developments, increasingly generated by scientific research, led the way to an even greater acceleration of change in the 20c, when new inventions enabled faster travel, communication and spread of ideas.

In 1884 Sir Charles Parsons invented the steam turbine; this was developed in the early part of the following century to provide marine engines for massive ocean-going liners. It was also used (and is still used) in electricity-generating plants. Electricity had been popularized by the invention of the filament bulb, making it a practical fuel for lighting as well as an affordable means of powering factories and industrial processes.

New construction materials were produced: stainless steel, then aluminium. The latter was to be of great importance in the development of the **aircraft** industry. The early flying exploits of Wilbur and Orville Wright were translated into practical use by **World War I**. After that a small civil aviation industry began, then **World War II** caused an intensification of effort in aircraft design. After Sir Frank Whittle designed the gas turbine, faster planes made air travel more practicable, and soon the technology of military jets was translated to passenger movement. Planes became bigger and bigger, and were used as buses had been at the beginning of the century.

The fuel for this was kerosene. It had been used in oil lamps since the middle of the 19c, particularly in country regions far from town gas. After the **American Civil War**, a side product of kerosene, petroleum, became important, and a new industry was created, beginning in the USA.

Petroleum was the fuel most suitable for the internal-combustion engines that began to be manufactured to power

---

A **SENATE** investigation uncovered the scandal and Fall was eventually sentenced to prison for one year and fined US$100,000. Sinclair and Doheny were cleared of bribery charges, although Sinclair did serve nine months in jail for contempt of the Senate. In 1927 the Supreme Court found that neither of the leases was valid and the oilfields were returned to the government.

**Technology** ➤ *See panel*

**Tecumseh** (1768–1813)
Native American chief of the Shawnee and a gifted orator. He joined his brother, 'The Prophet', in a rising against the whites, which was suppressed at the Battle of **TIPPECANOE** in 1811. He then passed into British service, commanding the Native American allies in the **WAR OF 1812** and fell fighting at the Thames in Canada. ➤ **INDIAN WARS**; **NATIVE AMERICANS**

**Tehran Conference** (28 Nov–1 Dec 1943)
The first inter-allied conference of **WORLD WAR II**, attended by **STALIN**, **ROOSEVELT** and Winston **CHURCHILL**. The subjects discussed were the coordination of Allied landings in France with the Soviet offensive against Germany, Russian entry into the war against Japan, and the establishment of a post-war interna-

tional organization. Failure to agree on the future government of Poland foreshadowed the start of the **COLD WAR**.

**Teleki, Paul, Count** (1879–1941)
Hungarian politician. He became Professor of Geography at the Budapest University in 1919 and, combining politics with an academic career, was in the same year appointed Foreign Minister and, from 1920 to 1921, Premier. The founder of the Christian National League and chief of Hungary's boy scouts, he was Minister of Education in 1938 and again Premier in 1939. He was fully aware of the German threat to his country, but all measures to avert it, including a pact with Yugoslavia, were unavailing through lack of support. When Germany marched against Yugoslavia through Hungary, he took his own life.

**Tel el-Kebir, Battle of** (1882)
An engagement between British and Egyptian forces which resulted in the British becoming the effective rulers of Egypt. It followed a period of increasing Egyptian ambition to extend her power, which had led to a financial crisis. In 1875 the Egyptian Khedive **ISMA'IL PASHA** sold his Suez Canal shares to the British government, and in 1880 an international debt commission was established. These inroads on

cars at the end of the 19c. City streets saw the mingling of horseless carriages along with the horse-drawn ones, and mass-production techniques were developed for articles such as sewing-machines and typewriters. These techniques were applied to car manufacture by Henry Ford, and his less expensive vehicles became available to a greater range of people. Throughout the 20c more roads were built and more cars were made. The railways had been replaced in many Western countries by road transport, both for passengers and freight.

In the Western world, trains, then cars, enabled people to live at a distance from their place of work. In the 20c it became possible to stay at home and work as the cottage workers had done before the Industrial Revolution. Electronic communication linked them to their employer, a continuation of the developments that had brought the world into the home, first with radio, then **television**, then **computers**.

Radio signals were first transmitted in 1898, and by the 1940s most people in the West had a radio in their homes. Television continued the work begun by radio of making the same information quickly available to a large number of people at the same time. Foreign conflicts and foreign culture were familiar to everyone who owned a television set. By 1996, 98 per cent of US households owned at least one, and television-watching had become a source of entertainment and education for both adults and children.

All electronics development was made possible by one product of the petrochemical industry, plastic. The development of polymers in the 20c produced many new materials used in diverse fields from clothing and construction, including the construction of electrical and electronic goods; these also benefited from the discovery of semiconductors, which are used in transistors and silicon chips. An oil-fuelled, electronically controlled, science- and consumer-driven, multi-material-using technology had grown out of the older steel and coal technological complex, and electricity had been the bridge between them.

In a comparatively short time, the massive valve-filled computers developed in the 1940s became small enough to fit on a desk, and cheap enough to be owned by many individuals. A system of linking them was created in 1983, used at that time mainly by academics; it became known as the Internet. By the end of the 1990s it linked millions of computers across the globe and provided a means of exchanging a vast amount and huge variety of information; this inevitably includes materials that have no regulation or that circumvent legal controls previously enjoyed by governments, authors and publishers. Computer systems were incorporated into many areas of daily life: the telephone system, banking, shopping, domestic appliances. Then the spectre of the 'millennium bug' arose, predicting chaos caused by many computers' inability to cope with the date 2000. It was another example, according to critics, of technology out of control, although in the event the alarm proved unfounded.

Distrust of technology and science had been voiced by writers and filmmakers since the 1930s (eg Aldous Huxley's *Brave New World* and Charlie Chaplin's *Modern Times*) but spread to a much larger public after the creation of the first atomic bomb and its detonation over **Hiroshima** in 1945. The implications and dangers of nuclear weapons hung over the world during the years of the **Cold War** and persisted after its end, with fears concerning the safety of nuclear power generation – fears intensified by the disaster at **Chernobyl** – and the disposal of nuclear waste.

Disposal of waste in general was a problem, particularly the waste created by technical processes and the global effects of national industries. The conflict between the comforts of modern life, largely due to the leaps in technical advances, and the ecological dangers the processes cause, remains a major concern at the beginning of the 21c. ► **Environmental Awareness and Politics, The Emergence of**; **Science**; **Scientific Revolution, The**

---

Egyptian independence stirred the nationalism of young army officers. In 1881 an army faction under Colonel 'URABI PASHA forced Khedive Tewfik Pasha to appoint a new ministry with 'Urabi as Minister for War. The British regarded this as a dangerous destabilization of the country; the Royal Navy bombarded Alexandria and landed a British army under Sir Garnet **WOLSELEY**, who defeated 'Urabi at Tel el-Kebir. ► **'URABI REVOLT**

### Telengana Disturbances
Telengana, in northern Hyderabad, India, was the scene of the most widespread, violent and long-lived peasant insurrection in South Asia in the 20c. (It was also possibly one of the largest communist-led insurrections seen in all Asia (outside China and Vietnam) in modern times.) Beginning in 1946, at its height, the movement against the Nizam, the pro-British ruler of the independent princely state of Hyderabad, covered 3,000 villages spread over 16,000 sq mi/ 41,440 sq km. A peasant army was established, and communes set up in the villages under communist control which, among other things, raised agricultural wages and redistributed waste lands to the poor. Unwilling to come to terms even after the granting of independence from Britain and the formal incor-

poration of Hyderabad into the Union of India, central government troops were sent to the area in Sep 1948, although the movement was not finally suppressed until 1951. Nonetheless, a guerrilla movement is still active in the hills and communist MPs are regularly elected to the Lok Sabha (or Parliament) in Delhi. Since the STATES REORGANIZATION ACT of 1956, Hyderabad has been part of the modern Telugu-speaking state of Andhra Pradesh, and Telengana has seen continuing protest movements against immigration to the region and the alleged control of the Andhra state by what are said to be politicians and business interests originating in the north.

**Television** ► *See panel*

### Temesvár, Banat of
Within the Habsburg Empire, this was the province between Transylvania, Wallachia and the Danube, Tisza and Mures rivers. Settled by the Goths, SLAVS and Huns, from the 9c it was tied to Hungary, becoming in 1233 the Banat of Severin. From the mid-16c it was subject to the Ottomans, but by the Treaty of PASSAROWITZ (1718) it passed to Austria and was administered as the Banat of Temesvár. After 1779, it was attached to Hungary. By the Treaty of TRIANON (1920), Hungary retained the region around Szeged

# *Television*

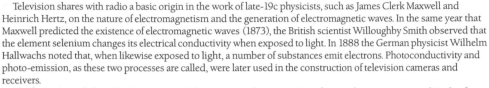

Science & Technology

### Pioneers

No single individual can be credited with the invention and development of television. Rather, by a gradual process of development, refinement and cross-fertilization, a workable system of transmitting and receiving visual images came into being between the 1880s and the 1930s.

Television shares with radio a basic origin in the work of late-19c physicists, such as James Clerk Maxwell and Heinrich Hertz, on the nature of electromagnetism and the generation of electromagnetic waves. In the same year that Maxwell predicted the existence of electromagnetic waves (1873), the British scientist Willoughby Smith observed that the element selenium changes its electrical conductivity when exposed to light. In 1888 the German physicist Wilhelm Hallwachs noted that, when likewise exposed to light, a number of substances emit electrons. Photoconductivity and photo-emission, as these two processes are called, were later used in the construction of television cameras and receivers.

The first proposals for television envisaged the capture and transmission of a complete image on a multitude of circuits simultaneously. In 1880 the scientists W E Sawyer and Maurice Leblanc suggested that if an image were rapidly scanned, the resulting data could be passed down a single wire and reassembled at the other end. By 1888 a crude but workable television apparatus was already in existence. In 1884 the German engineer Paul Nipkow invented a mechanical scanning device known as the Nipkow disc. The disc was perforated with small holes in a spiral pattern. Revolving 15 times per second, the disc was able to collect an image of a brightly lit object and transmit it to a receiver in which a similar disc rotated in front of a light source controlled by a light-sensitive device, producing a recognizable picture. Nipkow discs were used by early developers of experimental television systems such as John Logie Baird in the UK and Charles F Jenkins in the USA.

In the meantime, a system of electronic scanning was being developed by a number of engineers. The cathode ray tube was invented in 1897. Based on suggestions made in 1908 by the British engineer A A C Swinton, in the USA Philo T Farnsworth and Vladimir Zworykin independently developed types of television camera in which an electric charge on a screen was neutralized by an electron gun and converted into electrical impulses. A television receiver incorporating a cathode-ray tube was developed by another American, Allen B Dumont, in the 1930s.

### The beginnings of television broadcasting

The Scottish engineer John Logie Baird (1888–1946) is usually credited with demonstrating the first true television system in 1926. It was an electrical system based on the Nipkow disc with 30 lines scanning 10 times a second. The first television broadcasts to home receivers took place in the town of Schenectady, New York State, in 1928. The station WGY began broadcasting to homes in the area owning a domestic television set of a type developed by the Swedish-born US engineer Ernst F W Alexanderson for the General Electric Company. In 1935 regular television broadcasting began in Berlin, Germany. Transmissions went out three days a week on a 180-line system.

The BBC began broadcasting television programmes to the London area in 1936, experimenting at first with broadcasts produced in a 240-line format by Baird Television and 405-line broadcasts from Marconi–EMI. The superiority of the latter led to its adoption as the standard format for Britain until the 625-line format was adopted in 1962.

When the BBC began broadcasting in 1936, it reached an audience of a few thousand. It was not considered an

---

while Romania acquired the eastern portion, with the remainder going to Yugoslavia. The population is a mixture of nationalities; as well as Hungarians, Romanians, Vlachs, Tsintsars and Serbs, there remain the descendants of those Germans sent by the Habsburg emperors to repopulate the devastated Banat during the 18c.

### temperance movement

An organized response to the social disruption caused by the alcoholism so widespread in the 18c and 19c. Temperance societies were started first in the USA, then in Britain and Scandinavia. The original aim was to moderate drinking, but **PROHIBITION** became the goal. Federal prohibition became a reality in the USA in 1919, but was impossible to enforce and was repealed in 1933.

### Templars

The Poor Knights of Christ and of the Temple of Solomon; an international religious-military order, whose members were subject to monastic vows. The order was founded c.1120 chiefly to protect pilgrims to the Holy Land; its name derives from the location of its headquarters near the site of the Jewish Temple in Jerusalem. It developed into a widespread institution, acquiring wealth and property all over Europe,

and was suppressed by Pope **CLEMENT V** in 1312.

### Temple, Sir William (1628–99)

English diplomat and essay writer. A diplomat from 1655, he became ambassador at The Hague and negotiated the Triple Alliance (1668) against France. In 1677 he helped arrange the marriage of the Prince of Orange (**WILLIAM III**) to the Princess **MARY**, daughter of James, Duke of York (later **JAMES VII AND II**). After the **GLORIOUS REVOLUTION** he declined a political post in order to devote himself to literature.

### Temple, William (1881–1944)

English prelate and Archbishop of Canterbury. Ordained in 1908, he was Bishop of Manchester (1921–9), Archbishop of York (1929–42) and Archbishop of Canterbury (1942–4). An outspoken advocate of social reform, he crusaded against usury, slums and dishonesty, and in favour of the reform of Church structures and the ecumenical movement.

### Ten Days' Campaign (2–12 Aug 1831)

The militarily successful Dutch expedition against the Belgians during the Belgian Revolution, but one which failed to suppress the revolt. The Great Powers had recognized Belgium, but King **WILLIAM I** of the Netherlands refused to accept their terms and

important medium – some suggested it would never match the popularity of radio – and transmissions were halted abruptly (in the very middle of a broadcast) soon after the outbreak of **World War II**. The same thing happened in the USA, where RCA began large-scale public broadcasting from the New York World's Fair in 1939, only for the service to be suspended in 1941. The German service, however, continued broadcasting until the transmitter was destroyed by Allied bombing in 1943.

### The growth of the television audience

Television broadcasting resumed in both Britain and the USA shortly after the end of World War II. The viewing audience was at first small, but it began to expand as the post-war economic recovery got under way, first in the USA and later in Europe. There were approximately one million television sets in the USA in 1949, 10 million in 1951 and 50 million in 1959. The televising of the coronation of Queen **Elizabeth II** in 1953 gave a considerable boost to television sales in the UK. (The ceremony was also seen live on television in France, Holland and West Germany.)

Early programming included many transfers of popular radio shows: *Amos 'n' Andy*, *I Love Lucy*, *The Jack Benny Program* and *The Burns and Allen Show* all began life as US radio shows, were transferred to television in the 1950s and appeared on British screens shortly afterwards. The BBC initially had a monopoly of television broadcasting in the UK. Commercial television, financed by advertising, began in Britain in 1955. In the USA the three networks NBC, CBS and ABC enjoyed a virtual monopoly of national broadcasting until the mid-1980s, despite the rapid growth of local TV stations from the 1960s.

### Colour television

The possibility of colour television was mooted as early as 1904, and in 1928 John Logie Baird demonstrated a colour television transmission using a Nipkow disc with three sets of openings to capture the primary colours red, blue and green. Colour broadcasting first began in the USA in 1951 using a system developed by the Hungarian-born inventor Peter Carl Goldmark. Broadcasts made with Goldmark's system could not, however, be received by black-and-white sets. It was not until a compatible system had been perfected that regular colour broadcasting took off in the USA in 1954. Colour broadcasting began in Japan in 1960, and in the UK, France, Germany and the USSR in 1967.

### Video and other developments

The use of videotape for recording television pictures began in the 1950s. At first the complexity of the equipment, the high cost of the tape and the speed at which it had to revolve restricted its use to television broadcasting companies. Video cassette recorders for domestic use became available in the 1970s and began to become common only in the 1980s.

The first television broadcast by satellite was made in 1962 using the US satellite Telstar, briefly transmitting live pictures from the USA to Britain and France. The development of the principle of a geostationary satellite (one that remains in a fixed position above the earth's surface) in 1964 enabled a virtually worldwide television satellite network to be in place by the 1970s. The 1980s saw the development both of cable television and of satellite broadcasting, vastly increasing the number of channels from which viewers could choose.

### Other uses of television

Television is said to be unique among telecommunications media in having been developed primarily as a medium for entertainment and information in a domestic context. It has acquired many other uses, especially with the increased sophistication and miniaturization of television cameras and transmitting equipment. The discovery that television pictures could be transmitted from space enabled NASA to prepare the way for a landing on the moon by sending

ordered the campaign, led by his son, the future King **WILLIAM II**. Two Belgian armies were defeated at Hasselt and Leuven (Louvain); a French army arrived to help the Belgians, but the Dutch pressed their attack anyway. After 13 Aug the Dutch largely withdrew; the campaign gained them some concessions in the eventual settlement.

### tenentismo

Deriving from the Portuguese *tenente* ('lieutenant'), this term originally referred to the generation of young Brazilian army officers who graduated from the military school in Realengo after 1919. Trained by the 'indigenous mission' of officers who had been seconded to the Imperial German Army before **WORLD WAR I**, they emerged to general service highly critical of both superior officers and the regime they served. As a result, they took leading roles in the 1922 Copacabana Revolt, the Revolt of São Paulo, the Prestes Column and Revolution of 1930. Many continued in politics until the 1960s. Such men included Luís Carlos Prestes (leader of the Communists), Eduardo Gomes (*éminence grise* of the UDN), Cordeiro de Farias (the major support for **CASTELO BRANCO**), Jauréz Távora and Juraci de Maghalães, and were the progenitors of the military regime of 1964–85.

### Teng Hsiao-p'ing ► DENG XIAOPING

### Tennessee Valley Authority

An independent US government agency created by Act of Congress in 1933. It is responsible for development in the Tennessee River basin and has provided hydroelectric power cheaply, changing the basis of the state economy from agriculture to industry.

### Tennis Court Oath (1789)

An oath taken in a tennis court at the Palace of Versailles by representatives of the Third Estate locked out of their assembly place. Declaring themselves to be the National Assembly, the Deputies swore never to separate until a constitution was established for France. ► **ESTATES GENERAL**; **FRENCH REVOLUTION**

### Tenochtitlán

The capital of the Aztec empire. It was originally founded c.1325 on two small islands in Lake Texcoco, which were connected to the mainland by causeways; by 1519 it had spread over at least five square miles and was home to around 400,000 people. The ceremonial city centre consisting of pyramid temples and palaces was surrounded by a grid of streets and canals, and by *chinampas*, artificial island gardens

unmanned spacecraft to transmit pictures back from the moon's surface. The actual landing was also seen live as it took place in 1969.

Television cameras have also been in use in reconnaissance and weather satellites from the 1960s, and closed-circuit television has developed rapidly as a means of surveillance and a weapon in the war against crime. It is also now possible to insert miniature television cameras into the human body in order to assist in medical examinations and surgical operations. In short, there are very few environments which cannot now be visually explored in real time by means of television.

### The impact of television

Though radio was the first medium to bring the outside world directly into people's sitting rooms, the impact of bringing both sound and vision into the home has been much greater. Television is a fact of contemporary life, indeed a defining characteristic of life as lived in the late 20c and 21c. In 1998, 98 million homes in the USA were estimated to have television sets, and by the age of 18 the average child in the USA is estimated to have watched 17,000 hours of television.

Not surprisingly, television is seen as a potent force by many and a baneful influence by a few. The political influence that television can exert is frequently exemplified by citing the debates that took place between John F **Kennedy** and Richard M **Nixon** before the US presidential election of 1960. The debates were broadcast simultaneously on radio and television; radio listeners opined that Nixon had won the debate, television viewers decided in favour of Kennedy. Television is also credited with hardening opposition to the **Vietnam War** in the USA; television pictures of that war and of subsequent conflicts, disasters, or happier occasions have had a greater and more immediate impact on the public perception of events than words alone could have had. Above all, television has contributed to the globalization of events and people's experience. The funeral of Princess Diana in 1997, for instance, was watched by an estimated television audience of 6 billion in 44 different countries. Perhaps more significant is the perceived dominance of television time in the mounting of successful political campaigns in many Western countries, with consequences that are disturbing. One is the primacy of physical image, which has to be attractive and sympathetic in any successful political leader. The other is the sheer cost of political campaigning, which due to the expense of buying television time has led in political systems like that of the USA to politicians devoting a high proportion of their time to continuous fund-raising, and to massively enhanced influence for well-funded pressure groups.

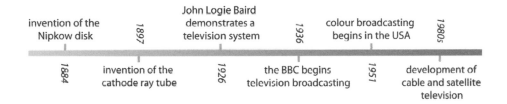

built on the lake. In 1521 the city was taken by rebellious subject peoples and the Spanish conquistador Hernán **CORTÉS**. Its fall marked the end of the empire. Virtually erased during the siege, it was replaced by a new Spanish city built over its site — Mexico City. ➤
**PRE-COLUMBIAN CIVILIZATIONS**

### Tenth Penny
The most famous of a series of taxes which were an important cause of the **EIGHTY YEARS' WAR**. In 1559 the Duke of **ALBA** introduced a new tax system in the Netherlands designed to centralize and standardize all the anomalous local ones which existed in the various provinces. The largest was the Tenth Penny, a 10 per cent tax put on all commercial transactions except in real estate. In the first two years it brought in 2 million gilders; in 1571 there were widespread revolts against it. The Spanish gave up trying to collect it in 1574.

### Ten Years' War (1868–78)
Nationalist Cuban uprising against Spanish illiberal rule provoked by the Special Laws of 1867. Led by Carlos Manuel de **CÉSPEDES**, 'The Father of the Country', Maximo Gomes, Antonio Maceo and Tomás **ESTRADA PALMA**, the 10,000-strong rebel force conducted an intermittent, desultory campaign against the Spanish army for ten years but, holding

no port, having no seat of government and unable to enlist international support, it could not prevail. Hostilities were brought to an end when a new Spanish commander, Martínez Campos, promised reform and representation. The Peace of Zanjón (Feb 1878) reiterated these promises but they proved a dead letter and the only positive outcome of the conflict was the abolition of **SLAVERY**.

### tercios
The name given to the élite regiments formed in the Spanish army in the 1560s, consisting of 12–15 companies, each of 250–300 men. Recruited exclusively from Castilians, they were used mainly in the battlefields of northern Europe, where they were feared and respected. In the early 18c, they were superseded by regiments based on the French model.

### Territorial Princes
Rulers of various secular principalities in the **HOLY ROMAN EMPIRE**. Some, such as those of Bohemia and Saxony, were **ELECTORS** who chose the Holy Roman Emperor; others did not belong to the electoral college. With the Ecclesiastical Princes, the Imperial Knights, the free cities and the Imperial towns, they constituted the level of overlordship beneath the Emperor.

## territory

In US history, the political status of an area prior to the attainment of statehood. It was held in two stages: in the first, an 'unorganized territory' was ruled by a judge; in the second, an 'organized' territory could elect its own legislature and non-voting delegate to CONGRESS. ► NORTHWEST ORDINANCE OF 1787

## Terror, Reign of (1793–4)

The extreme phase of the FRENCH REVOLUTION, characterized by the systematic execution of political opponents of the JACOBINS and supposed sympathizers of the Counter-Revolution, who were brought before the Revolutionary Tribunal and guillotined. Around 40,000 people are thought to have been killed in Paris and the provinces.

## terror, war on

A term describing efforts to counter terrorism. Used in the 1940s of British efforts to eliminate the IRGUN in Palestine and by President REAGAN in the 1980s, the term was adopted in 2001 by President George W BUSH in his response to the SEPTEMBER 11 ATTACKS to describe the measures that the USA would take against terrorism worldwide. These included the use of military force against those involved in the attacks, denying terrorists 'safe havens', restricting or stopping their funding, breaking up terrorist networks, coordinating information-gathering and improving domestic and international policing. The AFGHAN WAR (2001), legislation such as the PATRIOT ACT (2001), the creation of the Department of Homeland Security (2002), the use of agencies such as the FINANCIAL ACTION TASK FORCE and the Terrorist Finance Operations section (TFOS) of the FBI, and the authorization of the trial by military tribunals of foreigners suspected of having terrorist connections (2001) illustrate the methods adopted. Criticism centres on the failure to define sufficiently the concept of a war on terror, fear of the loss of civil liberties during a 'wartime' of unknown duration, and scepticism about the true aims of US policy in the Middle East and towards other countries it considers 'rogue' states. ► AXIS OF EVIL; IRAQ WAR

## Terror, White

In French history, a term first used in 1795, when the JACOBINS were pursued by those they had persecuted in the revolutionary Reign of TERROR of 1793–4. It revived on a larger scale (1815–16), against those who had supported NAPOLEON I during the HUNDRED DAYS, especially in the south of France.

## terrorism

The systematic, organized, unlawful and often indiscriminate use or threatened use of violence and intimidation against persons, groups or property, in an attempt to force a government or community to act in a certain way or accept certain demands, driven by political or ideological motives. Differing from the use of terror as an instrument of power by states, terrorism may be 'state sponsored', or 'unofficial', as employed by various opposition and underground movements. It may be confined to a specific territory ('domestic terrorism') or it may have an international dimension ('international terrorism'), manifest in air piracy and hostage-taking. The persecution of LOYALISTS by Patriot groups in the AMERICAN REVOLUTION was probably the first modern example of politically motivated terrorism designed to eliminate a rival tradition. Populism underpinned the terrorist tactics used against negroes by the KU KLUX KLAN following the AMERICAN CIVIL WAR. Anarchists in Europe in the 19c, particularly Russia, began to use terror as a means of mobilizing popular opinion against regimes perceived as tyrannical and reactionary. In the 20c terrorism changed, aided by automatic weapons, electronically detonated explosives, and the media, through which terrorist acts were given immediate, usually international, publicity. Prominent terrorist groups campaigning against the established social and political structure of their countries include the BAADER–MEINHOF GROUP of West Germany and the SENDERO LUMINOSO ('Shining Path') in Peru. Prominent nationalist groups fighting for liberation or independence include the Basque separatist group ETA in Spain, the TUPAMAROS in Uruguay, the LTTE ('Tamil Tigers') in Sri Lanka, and the FRONT DE LIBÉRATION DU QUÉBEC. There are many others, including those with quasi-sectarian objectives such as the IRA in Northern Ireland, and al-FATAH (which operates under the PLO), IRGUN and the STERN GANG in Israel. Although most countries attempt to combat terrorism, international collaboration between them is often hampered by legal and administrative difficulties, and with some states by a wish to keep open the option of attacking enemies without the risks of formal war by sponsoring terrorism against them; an example is Colonel GADDAFI's refusal for years to extradite for trial the Libyans suspected of planting the 1988 Lockerbie bomb. But the SEPTEMBER 11 ATTACKS in 2001 that brought AL-QAEDA to prominence caused a sea change in global attitudes and strategic thinking, vigorously promoted by the USA. The resulting war on TERROR largely swept away ideological or sectarian justifications for unlawful, indiscriminate, organized violence in an effort to provide global political and economic security, though the concept of terrorism continues to defy definition as some countries insist that terrorism is often legitimate national resistance.

## Tessin, Carl-Gustaf (1695–1770)

Swedish politician. He was the son of the architect Nicodemus Tessin, the Younger. As a young man he travelled extensively in France, Germany and Italy, and on his return to Sweden assumed a leading position in the pro-French and anti-Russian Hat Party, which hoped to regain territory lost to Russia at the end of the GREAT NORTHERN WAR. He was elected chairman of the Estate of Nobles when the Hats gained a majority in 1738. As envoy in Paris, he secured French support for the war launched against Russia in 1741. He gained the favour of King ADOLF FREDERICK and Queen LOVISA ULRIKA, and in 1746 was appointed governor to the future King GUSTAV III, a post he held until 1755. By then, his relations with the court had cooled, and he spent much of the rest of his life on his estate at Åkerö. He had immense influence on the Swedish culture of the period; his interior decoration of the Royal Palace in Stockholm introduced the Rococo style into the country and the collections he sold to the royal family formed the basis of the National Museum and Royal Library in Stockholm.

**Test Act** (1673)
A British Act passed by a parliament anxious to curb Catholic influence at **CHARLES II**'s court. Every office holder had to take Oaths of Supremacy and Allegiance, and to take communion according to the rites of the Church of England. A declaration against transubstantiation also had to be made. The passage of the Act necessitated the resignation of the King's brother, James, Duke of York, as Lord High Admiral. The Act remained in force until 1829. ► **CATHOLIC EMANCIPATION**

**Tet Offensive** (Jan–Feb 1968)
A campaign in the **VIETNAM WAR**. On 30 Jan 1968, the Buddhist 'Tet' holiday, the Viet Cong launched an attack against US bases and more than 100 South Vietnamese towns (which had been considered safe from guerrilla attack), the targets including the US Embassy in Saigon and the city of Hue. There were heavy casualties, including large numbers of civilians. US public opinion was shocked by the scale of death and destruction, and support for the war declined rapidly. The offensive proved to be a turning-point in the war; on 31 Mar 1968, President Lyndon B **JOHNSON** announced an end to escalation and a new readiness to negotiate.

**Teutonic Knights**
The Order of St Mary of the Germans, a religious-military order founded in Acre in 1190. The Order grew quickly in Germany and the Mediterranean and, as a result of Conrad of Mazovia's appeal for help in 1226, also gained a foothold in northern Europe. The *Golden Bull* of Rimini (1226) confirmed its position there and granted the Order all lands conquered from the heathen Prussians outside the borders of the Empire. With the loss of the Holy Land in 1291 all the Order's efforts were concentrated there and by the end of the 14c they controlled the Baltic lands of the **LIVONIAN KNIGHTS**, Prussia and East Pomerania. The Order's power declined after the Battle of **GRUNWALD** (1410), and the secularization of the Order in Prussia in 1525 led to Prussia becoming part of the **HOLY ROMAN EMPIRE**. The Order was dissolved in Germany in 1809 but re-established in Austria in 1834. ► **GOLDEN BULL**; **WINRICH OF KNIPRODE**

**Tewfik Pasha, Mohammed** (1852–92)
Khedive of Egypt (1879/92). The eldest son of **ISMA'IL PASHA**, he succeeded his father on the latter's abdication in 1879. The chief events of his reign were 'Urabi's insurrection (1882), the British intervention, the war with the Mahdi **MOHAMMED AHMED** (1884–5), the pacification of the Sudan frontiers, and the improvement of Egypt under British administration. He was succeeded by his son, **'ABBAS II**. ► **'URABI REVOLT**

**Tewkesbury, Battle of** (4 May 1471)
A decisive battle in the Wars of the **ROSES** at which **EDWARD IV** defeated Lancastrian forces hastily assembled by Queen Margaret, wife of **HENRY VI**. Their son, Prince Edward, was killed, as were many other leading Lancastrian supporters. Soon afterwards, Edward IV was able to re-enter London, order the death of Henry VI in the Tower of London and resume his reign, which was not thereafter seriously challenged.

**Texas Rangers**
A mounted paramilitary police force formed in the

1820s by Texas settlers to provide protection from Native American raids. The Rangers gradually evolved into a frontier militia, reaching their peak in the 1870s; then they were merged into the state's official police force (after 1874), and were finally merged with the state highway patrol (1935). Since then the Rangers have figured prominently in Texas history and folklore.

---

**THAILAND** official name **Kingdom of Thailand**, formerly **Siam**

A kingdom in South-East Asia, bounded to the west by the Andaman Sea; to the west and north-west by Myanmar; to the north-east and east by Laos; to the east by Cambodia; and to the south by Malaysia. There is evidence that Thailand had Bronze Age communities in c.4000BC. By the 7c Buddhism had spread to the country from India. Today 95 per cent of the population are Theravada Buddhists. Thailand's successful nationalist and reform movements have often had Buddhist leaders, and the work of the monastic order or *sangha* remains highly regarded in social terms. The Thai nation was founded in the 13c, and is the only country in south and south-east Asia to have escaped **COLONIZATION** by a European power. It was occupied by the Japanese during **WORLD WAR II**, and had a military-controlled government for most of the time from 1945 until mass demonstrations in 1992 resulted in the fall of the regime and led to a reduction in the power of the military. King **BHUMIBOL ADULYADEJ** became head of state in 1946. The economy was badly hit by the 1997 Asian economic crisis, but has recovered following remedial action by the government and **IMF**. Western areas were damaged by the Indian Ocean tsunami in Dec 2004. ► **SOUTH-EAST ASIA PRE-1000AD**

**Thakurdas, Purshottamdas** (1879–1961)
Indian industrialist and social reformer. He joined the family cotton business and started rooting out evil practices in the cotton industry. At the age of 28, the 'Cotton King of Bombay' was elected Vice-President of the Indian Merchants Chamber, Bombay. A founding member of the Federation of Indian Chambers of Commerce and Industry (FICCI), he went on to become its President. He was a member of the Retrenchment Committee (1922) and served on the Royal Commission on Indian Finance,

# Theatre

*Art & Literature*

The ancient origins of theatre are thought to lie in religious ritual, which to this day retains dramatic elements of its own. Early **drama** was always associated with **music** and **dance**, an association fully maintained in the traditional theatre of the East.

In India and Bali religious ritual remains a part of some theatrical performances, imbuing them with a deep significance alongside their entertainment value. Legends and religious stories were the subject matter of the classical Sanskrit drama that flourished between the 1c and 9c AD. The appeal was very visual, and depended on the formalized movements of the actors and their magnificent costumes. Folk theatre has maintained some of the same elements, combining music, dance, the use of costumes and masks into a total theatre experience of the kind Western theatre has more recently sought to regain. Roles were always played by men, except in the erotic *tamasha* plays, in which the leading female role was played by a woman. Originally developed as army entertainment, they were considered too bawdy for respectable women to attend.

The theatre of China, Japan and Korea also maintained the totality of display, and for much of the time relied on male actors. The roots of drama in religion meant that in China the plays were moral, setting the observer an example of how to behave; virtue always triumphed over evil. Nonetheless, theatre provided very popular entertainment in all its manifestations. When traditional theatre was banned during the **Cultural Revolution** (1966–76), and revolutionary operas performed instead, these were not met with the same enthusiasm.

Japan borrowed its first theatrical forms from China and Korea, but developed its own distinctive styles. Buddhist chants were incorporated into drama cycles of five plays that showed the fleeting nature of life and the inevitability of sorrow in the *Noh* drama, popular from the 14c. Noh plays were performed on a bare stage under a roof held up by four pillars, symbolism being used to tell the story: a paddle might indicate a boat, whereas a man walking round the stage with a riding whip might depict a long journey. Actors, always men, who learnt their craft over many years' apprenticeship, wore masks and rich costumes. This type of theatre was the province of the **samurai** class, and after their disbandment in 1867 there were no performances until the form was revived after **World War II**. At the beginning of *kabuki* theatre, which originated in the entertainment arranged by prostitutes for their clients, women briefly appeared on stage. When women were banned from the stage in 1629, their place was at first taken by young boys, but from 1653 all actors were adult males. The plays were always based on stories familiar to the spectators, and the interest was in the presentation. So too in South-East Asia, the formalized, long dance dramas were based on myths and legends, where all the skill of the actors was in the arrangement of the material. Gods, kings, princes, clowns and devils were represented, with costumes, make-up and body language as the means of communication. Throughout Asia, Western influence meant that new forms of theatre were seen in the 19c and 20c, but traditional forms remained popular.

The origins of theatre in ancient Greece, according to Aristotle (384–322 BC), the first theoretician of theatre, are to be found in the festivals that honoured Dionysus. The dancers and singers who acted out the stories were augmented by one actor who could play the characters, and a chorus to give the narrative. The first drama festival, at the Athenian Great Dionysia, was in 543 BC. At the drama festivals poets competed to have their (verse) plays performed, and the actors competed to win the crown for best performance. The performances were given in semi-circular auditoria cut into hillsides, capable of seating 10,000–20,000 people. The stage consisted of a dancing floor (*orchestra*), dressing room and scene-building area (*skene*). Since the words were the most important part, good acoustics and clear delivery were

Currency and Practice (1925), where he fought for a better exchange rate for the Indian rupee. He was appointed Sheriff of Bombay in 1920. Secretary of the Gujarat Famine Relief Fund in 1911, he also made generous contributions to schemes involving education and self-help. It was thanks to his initiative that the Indenture Act was abolished.

**Thalmann, Ernst** (1886–1944)
German politician. After joining the **SPD** in 1903, he switched to the **KPD** in 1920, joining its Central Committee in 1921. Convener of the KPD from 1925, he was heavily reliant on the **COMINTERN** in Moscow for his authority and steered the party increasingly along lines acceptable to the USSR. Arrested by the National Socialists in 1933, he was shot in **BUCHENWALD** concentration camp in 1944. ► **NAZI PARTY**

**Thames, Battle of the** (5 Oct 1813)
A battle of the **WAR OF 1812** fought near Chatham on the Thames River in present-day Ontario, Canada. US forces led by General William **HARRISON** won a significant victory over retreating British and Indian forces under General Proctor and **TECUMSEH** (who was killed), and thus defeated the British–Indian alliance and established control over the north-west.

**Thani, Khalifa bin Hamad al-** (1932–)
Sheikh and Prime Minister of Qatar (1972/95). The oil-rich Persian Gulf state of Qatar entered into treaty relations with Britain in 1916, having earlier been under Ottoman control. As with the Trucial States (now the United Arab Emirates), it was arranged that the foreign affairs of Qatar would be conducted by the British in return for naval protection, while internal affairs should be regulated by the state itself (and thus by extension the al-Thani family). The discovery of oil made Qatar extremely wealthy and the state became fully independent in 1971. Thani was deposed in 1995 by his son, Sheikh Hamad bin Khalifa al-Thani.

**Thanjavur** or **Tanjore**
Capital of the Chola Dynasty, situated by the River Kaveri. The Cholas built a number of Shiva and Vishnu temples, the most famous of which is the Brihadiswara temple at Thanjavur which was completed in 1010. Probably the largest temple built in India up to that time, it contains elaborate pillared halls and beautiful decorations. This was possibly the richest temple during this period, had an income of 500 lb/227 kg troy of gold, 250 lb/114 kg troy of precious stones, and 600 lb/272 kg troy of silver, which was

paramount. The actors (always men) wore masks appropriate to the characters they represented, and each might play several parts. The themes, as in Chinese theatre, were the weaknesses of man, retribution for wrongdoing, and the inevitability of sorrow. In his *Poetics*, Aristotle describes rules for tragedy which were to have a profound influence on theatre after the **Renaissance**.

The Greek tragedies that have survived are by Aeschylus (c.525–c.456 BC), Euripides (480/484–406 BC) and Sophocles (c.496–405 BC). Comedy developed in the mid-5c BC as light relief, with buffoonery, satire, parody and bawdy jokes; the only complete Greek comedies to have survived are by Aristophanes (c.488–c.388 BC). By the next century comedy was generally preferred to tragedy.

This style was also preferred in Rome, where plays were imitations of Greek tragedy that had lost all touch with their religious roots. The public taste for spectacle was indulged, actors raised themselves up on blocked shoes, and masks became bigger to make more impact. The style of the theatre had changed; the stage was raised and backed by an architectural façade. Plays that have survived are by Plautus (c.250–184 BC) and Terence (c.195–159 BC), who based many of his plots on the plays of Menander (c.343–291 BC). In turn his plots and conventions were used by Molière (1622–73) and Richard Brinsley Sheridan (1751–1816). The plays of Seneca the Younger (c.4 BC–c.65 AD), much plundered for plot in Elizabethan times, were a reaction against the vulgarization of the drama. He presented the Greek stories in five-act plays in which rhetoric was an important feature, and reason was shown to be at war with passion. The plays were probably intended to be read aloud by discerning admirers, rather than performed in public.

On stage, mime and pantomime developed. Often these involved satire directed at the Christian Church. The Church developed a distrust of the stage and excommunicated all mime performers in the 5c, and then closed all theatres in the 6c. However, actors did not disappear; travelling entertainers continued a folk tradition, combined with music, acrobatics and juggling. Folk dances from ancient rituals also survived, acting out events that had sometimes lost their original meaning.

Ironically, the revival of theatre in the West began in churches. The development of antiphonal music brought an element of dialogue to the mass. A three-line Easter trope, the *Quem Quaeritis?*, is thought to be the origin of liturgical drama, which became so successful and such a popular a way of teaching Biblical stories to the illiterate congregations in the 11c and 12c that it was thought best to move it outside the Church as well (the first recorded instance was *Adam* in France in 1170). Actors were laymen, exposition was in the vernacular, and cycles of stories were performed on holy days (particularly Corpus Christi) in France, Germany, Spain and England. These mystery plays, in cycles of about 50 performed over several days, told the story of the Bible from the Creation to the Resurrection. Increasingly elaborate performances were undertaken in England by the craft guilds on pageant wagons that moved from one part of town to another. The comic characters were especially popular. In the 15c the morality plays were less popular, being little more than dramatized sermons emphasizing the religious themes of good fighting evil, with death always in wait.

The time was ripe in England for another type of theatre. The flight of Greek scholars from Constantinople after 1453 had seen the re-emergence of the texts of Terence, Plautus and Seneca the Younger, distributed in printed form all over Europe in the 15c. In Italy and France the attempts to create plays based on the Aristotelian unities of time, place and action were stilted and dull. Creativity was in the court masques, ballets and opera, and in the improvisations of the Italian *commedia dell'arte*, with its acrobats, songs and stock characters.

In England the mystery plays declined after the suppression of the religious feast of Corpus Christi in 1548, morality plays were suppressed, and religious topics were banished from the stage. But the taste for theatre was still keen, and was catered to in London by professional companies of actors performing in inn yards. These actors were close to their

acquired through donations and contributions in addition to the revenue from hundreds of villages. Thanjavur became an important centre of art and culture in south India during the Chola reign. ➤ **PRE-ISLAMIC INDIA**

### Thant, U (1909–74)

Burmese diplomat. He was a teacher who became a civil servant when Burma (now Myanmar) became independent in 1948; he became Burma's **UN** representative in 1957. As Secretary-General of the UN (1962–71), he played a major diplomatic role during the **CUBAN MISSILE CRISIS**. He also formulated a plan to end the Congolese civil war (1962) and mobilized a UN peacekeeping force in Cyprus (1964). He died in New York City. The return of his body to Burma provoked major anti-government demonstrations.

### Thatcher, Margaret Hilda Thatcher, Baroness (1925–)

British politician. Elected to parliament in 1959, and after holding junior office, she became Minister of Education (1970–4). In 1975 she replaced Edward **HEATH** as leader of the **CONSERVATIVE PARTY** to become the first woman party leader in British politics. Under her leadership, the Conservative Party moved

towards a more 'right-wing' position, and British politics and society became more polarized than at any other time since **WORLD WAR II**. Her government (1979–90) privatized several nationalized industries and utilities, made professional services, such as healthcare and education, more responsive to market forces, and reduced the role of local government as a provider of services. Her election for a third term of office in 1987 was aided, as in 1983, by divisions in the **LABOUR PARTY** and a more equal division of votes between the opposition parties than had hitherto been usual. She became the longest-serving 20c Prime Minister in 1988, but her popularity waned and her anti-European statements caused damaging division within the Conservative Party. She resigned soon after failing to win a sufficiently large majority in the Conservative leadership contest of Nov 1990, and retired from her parliamentary seat of Finchley in 1992. That same year she was made a life peer.

### Theatre ➤ *See panel*

### Thebaw (1858–1916)

Last King of Burma (now Myanmar). He reigned from 1878 to 1885, when he was deposed by the British and sent into exile.

audience, and used facial expressions to communicate emotions; no masks were worn in this type of drama. During **Elizabeth I**'s reign, theatres were modelled on the inn yard, with raised platform stages and the minimum of scenery, and usually played to a somewhat rowdy audience. It was to these audiences that the plays of William Shakespeare (1564–1616) were presented, plays with plots taken from the Roman models or based on history, and dealing with contemporary issues. Organized in five acts like those of Seneca, they ignored Aristotle's unities and incorporated aspects of popular drama, such as the use of clowns and the wise fool. Women's roles were taken by boys whose voices had not broken. The language and characters of Shakespeare's plays enjoyed enormous success in his own time, forming part of the identity of the English nation.

Theatre in England was banned under Oliver **Cromwell**, but the **Restoration** in 1660 of **Charles II**, who had spent his exile on the Continent, saw new theatres built and a new type of play in which actresses appeared alongside actors. The French theatre with which Charles was familiar had flourished in a France made prosperous under the **Richelieu** regime. Pierre Corneille (1606–84) ignored the unities to produce very popular plays full of adventure, and with his masterpieces Molière raised comedy to the same heights as tragedy. After Molière's death, **Louis XIV** created the first European national theatre, the Comédie Française (1680), from his theatre company and other troupes. At around the same time, Jean Racine (1639–99) worked strictly within Aristotle's unities to produce severe tragedies.

The influence of Molière's work can be seen in the English Restoration comedies, such as William Congreve's *Way of the World* (1700). Tragedy was less successful, and many attempts were made to adapt Shakespeare to the neoclassic 'ideal'. A reaction against the aridity of this standard was evidenced in plays with more sentiment, part of the Romantic movement that culminated in Germany in the works of Johann Wolfgang von Goethe (1749–1832) and Friedrich von Schiller (1759–1805). The passions exhibited in those plays were transformed by other writers to the excesses of melodrama, the most popular drama form ever seen in the West (and having much in common with modern soap operas on **television**) with its stock characters and sensational events.

During the 19c many new theatres were built. Until the 18c plays had been performed in daylight, but evening performances started to be given by candlelight and lantern, and later by gaslight. Theatres were made more comfortable, with padded seats, boxes for those who wanted privacy, and a dress circle for the richer patrons. The era of actor managers like William Charles Macready (1793–1873) saw an improvement in the general standard of productions, and Henry Irving (1838–1905) was the first actor to receive a knighthood. The increased demand for spectacle and technical effects meant that it became difficult for one man to do it all. The stage manager came into being, followed by the director.

At the end of the century the advent of electricity (installed in the Savoy Theatre, London, in 1881) provided not only a safer, cleaner method of lighting the interior but presented new possibilities for lighting stage productions. A reaction against elaborate sets and the rantings of melodrama was seen in the realist drama of Henrik Ibsen (1828–1906), Anton Chekhov (1860–1904) and August Strindberg (1849–1912). The three had in common the ability to present psychological realism and create a rather gloomy mood. Chekhov's work was mounted at the Moscow Art Theatre, whose director, Konstantin Stanislavsky (1863–1938), held theories on acting that would reach far into the 20c, from theatre to **cinema**. The director became increasingly important; it was an era of experimentation and innovation. In Germany Richard Wagner (1813–83) used symbolism in his operas, combined with ambitious sets, art and costume in an attempt to create the 'complete theatre' that had always existed in China and Japan.

Symbolist theatre flourished in France, producing Alfred Jarry's *Ubu Roi* (1896), a piece highly shocking in its time; it also influenced the 1950s Theatre of the Absurd plays by Eugène Ionesco, Samuel Becket and Harold Pinter that examined the meaninglessness of life.

---

**Theodore, Kassai** (1816–68)
King of Abyssinia, as Theodore II (1855/68). In 1853 he crushed the vice-regent, Ras Ali, and, overthrowing the Prince of Tigray in 1855, had himself crowned Negus of Abyssinia as Theodore II. At first he was guided by two Englishmen, Plowden and Bell; but after they were killed in a rebellion (1860) he became more hostile to Europeans. He had made several vain attempts to procure the alliance of England and France against his Muslim neighbours, but without success. A letter sent to Queen **VICTORIA** in 1862 went somehow unnoticed, and a fancied slight was also received from **NAPOLEON III**. Theodore imprisoned the consuls along with other Europeans. Negotiations failed, and a British military expedition under General **NAPIER** landed in Abyssinia in the spring of 1867, and reached Magdala in Apr. An Abyssinian attack was repulsed. Theodore sued for peace and released the prisoners, but, as he declined to surrender, the fort was stormed and Theodore shot himself.

**Thermidor** (16–17 July 1794/8–9 Thermidor Year II)
The coup d'état when **ROBESPIERRE** and his Jacobin supporters were overthrown, ending the most radical phase of the **FRENCH REVOLUTION**. Among the insti-

gators of Thermidor were such former **JACOBINS** as Joseph **FOUCHÉ** and Paul **BARRAS** who, with members of the National **CONVENTION**, set about dismantling the machinery of the Reign of **TERROR**. ► **FRENCH REPUBLICAN CALENDAR**

**Thessaly**
In antiquity, an area of northern Greece noted for its cavalry, its chief cities being Larissa and Pherae. The aristocratic Aleuadae family actively supported the Persian invasion of Greece in 480BC. A tyranny established at Pherae in the late 5c challenged the power of the Aleuadae: Jason of Pherae (tyrant c.380/370BC) briefly united Thessaly into a powerful state, but was assassinated before this power could be consolidated. From c.353BC, Thessaly came under the influence of neighbouring Macedonia; the Thessalian cavalry accompanied Alexander III, the Great on his conquest of Persia. In 196BC the Romans liberated Thessaly from Macedonian control; in 146BC it became part of the Roman province of Macedonia. In the 7–13c it was invaded by the **SLAVS**, **SARACENS** and Bulgars, and then the Vlachs who took control of the region and made it part of Great Wallachia. In the 14c it was invaded by the Catalans and Serbs and fell to the Ottoman Turks after the collapse of the

An avant-garde mood prevailed in Europe at this time. In Italy Luigi Pirandello (1867–1936) explored the contradictions between outward appearance and inward reality in his most successful play, *Six Characters in Search of an Author* (1922). In Germany Bertolt Brecht (1898–1956) wanted the audience to see the stage as simply a stage, and not to be swept away by illusion. He experimented with the 'alienation effect' that would remind audiences that they were watching a play. His appeal was to reason, not the emotions, and had a major influence on other writers. In France the works of Jean Anouilh (1910–87), Jean Giraudoux (1882–1944) and Jean Genet (1910–86) presented ideas and ignored realism.

In the UK and USA, the commercial theatre tended to concentrate on realism for the first half of the century, with George Bernard Shaw (1856–1950) examining the realities of society rather than the individual. By the 1930s and 1940s this had given way to the 'comedy of manners' of Noël Coward (1899–1973). In the US theatre, psychological insights into characters were paramount. Both Eugene O'Neill (1888–1953), with his depiction of steamy passion, and Arthur Miller (1915–2005), with his ordinary man as tragic hero, used symbolism to underline their intended meaning.

In the UK a repertory system had developed at the beginning of the 20c, with theatres built in many cities; the middle of the century saw a bloom of great actors. There was a revival of Shakespearean drama, begun by Harley Granville-Barker (1877–1946), first at the Old Vic and then with the Royal Shakespeare Company, founded in the 1960s. The National Theatre, advocated since the time of the 17c actor David Garrick, was finally inaugurated under the direction of Laurence Olivier (1907–89) in 1962.

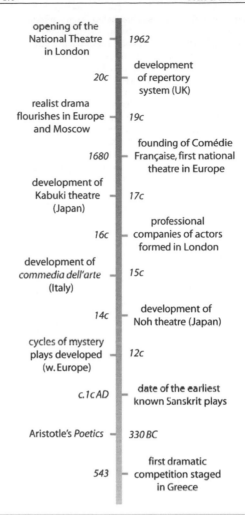

| | |
|---|---|
| opening of the National Theatre in London | 1962 |
| | 20c — development of repertory system (UK) |
| realist drama flourishes in Europe and Moscow | 19c |
| | 1680 — founding of Comédie Française, first national theatre in Europe |
| development of Kabuki theatre (Japan) | 17c |
| | 16c — professional companies of actors formed in London |
| development of *commedia dell'arte* (Italy) | 15c |
| | 14c — development of Noh theatre (Japan) |
| cycles of mystery plays developed (w. Europe) | 12c |
| | c.1c AD — date of the earliest known Sanskrit plays |
| Aristotle's *Poetics* | 330 BC |
| | 543 — first dramatic competition staged in Greece |

Kingdom of Serbia (1389). After the Congress of **BERLIN** (1878), the Ottoman Porte ceded Thessaly to Greece in stages: the greater part in 1881 and the remainder north of the Vale of Tempe in accordance with the Treaty of **LONDON** (1913).

**Theux de Meylandt, Barthélemy Théodore, Count** (1798–1874)
Belgian politician. In 1828 he and other liberal Catholics in the southern Netherlands formed a union with the liberals and so assisted the Belgian Revolution. From 1830 to 1850 he led the Belgian right in politics, and was a cabinet minister (usually of Internal Affairs) in 1831–2, 1834–40 and 1846–7. He formed his final government in 1871.

**Thiers, (Louis) Adolphe** (1797–1877)
French politician and historian. He held several posts in the government of **LOUIS-PHILIPPE**, and was twice Prime Minister (1836 and 1839). He supported **NAPOLEON III**'s candidacy as President of the republic in 1848, but was arrested and banished at the coup d'état of 1851, only to re-enter the Chamber in 1863 as a critic of Napoleon's policies. After the collapse of the Second Empire and the demise of the Government of **NATIONAL DEFENCE**, he was elected Chief of the Executive Power by the National Assembly, sup-

pressed the **PARIS COMMUNE**, and was elected first President of the Third Republic (1871–3). ► **CHARLES X**; **EMPIRE, SECOND** (France); **REPUBLIC, SECOND** (France); **REPUBLIC, THIRD** (France)

**Third Department** (1826–81)
The department of Russian government, established by **NICHOLAS I**, with responsibility for state security. It was part of his reaction against **ALEXANDER I**'s attempts at reform and, although it professed to be concerned with welfare and collected information for this purpose, it became in effect the secret police. Even under **ALEXANDER II** it had a very nasty reputation. He abolished it before his own assassination in 1881, but it was quickly replaced by the **OKHRANKA**.

**Third Rome** (1510)
The concept of Moscow as the successor to Rome and Constantinople. In 1510 Philotheus, an abbot from Pskov, wrote passionately to Basil III, Grand Prince of Moscow, about Rome falling to heresy and Constantinople to Islam, which left his dominion as the sole survivor and the heart of Christendom. Basil's father, **IVAN III**, had married a Byzantine princess and adopted the title Tsar from Caesar. So Basil was prepared to harness the Third Rome myth and give it political significance. It was a view of Russia's role in

the world that survived down to the 20c.

## Third World debt

A term for the debt burden of low-income countries since the 1970s. Large loans were made to Latin American, African and Asian countries in the 1960s, ostensibly for development but also to cement alliances during the **COLD WAR** and to absorb surplus income from commodity sales, particularly of petroleum. These loans were often in excess of need, and lack of accountability encouraged corruption and inflated military spending in the recipient states. By the 1980s higher energy costs, lower export commodity income and US domestic anti-inflation measures caused many banks to curtail these loans, which resulted in a tripling of interest rates and a fall in income in recipient countries that brought some, most notably Mexico in 1982, close to bankruptcy. The failure of traditional mechanisms to solve the problem led the **INTERNATIONAL MONETARY FUND** and the **WORLD BANK** to institute in 1996 the highly indebted poor country (HIPC) initiative by which some debt could be written off in return for the implementation of stringent economic measures. **JUBILEE 2000** and non-governmental organizations have called for total debt cancellation for 52 of the most hard-pressed countries, many located in subSaharan Africa. ➤ **BRANDT COMMISSION**; **NORTH–SOUTH DIVIDE**; **UNCTAD**

## Thirteen Colonies

The American provinces that revolted against British rule and declared independence in 1776. From North to South they were New Hampshire, Massachusetts, Rhode Island, Connecticut, New York, New Jersey, Pennsylvania, Delaware, Maryland, Virginia, North Carolina, South Carolina and Georgia. There was actually a fourteenth, as Vermont separated from New York. ➤ **AMERICAN REVOLUTION**

## thirty-eighth parallel

The boundary line proposed for the partition of Korea at the **POTSDAM CONFERENCE** in 1945, after the defeat of Japan (who had annexed Korea in 1910). In 1948 the Democratic People's Republic of North Korea was proclaimed (but not recognized by the Western powers). Since the **KOREAN WAR**, the 38th parallel again forms the line of division between North and South Korea.

## Thirty Years' War (1618–48)

A complex phase, specifically German in origin, of a long and intermittent power struggle between the kings of France and the Habsburg rulers of the **HOLY ROMAN EMPIRE** and Spain (1491–1715). It was triggered by the **BOHEMIAN REVOLT** (1618) against the Habsburgs, but the background was complicated by the developing confrontation between militant Calvinism and reinvigorated, post-Tridentine Catholicism. It was also complicated by the underlying constitutional conflict between the Holy Roman Emperor and the German princes. With the defeat of the newly elected King Frederick I of Bohemia (Elector **FREDERICK V** of the Palatinate) in 1620 by pro-Habsburg forces, and subsequent intervention by other powers (eg Sweden, Transylvania, Denmark and France), the conflict intensified, spreading to other theatres. Isolated as Spain collapsed, the Em-

peror opened negotiations (1643–8) which ended the German war, at the Peace of **WESTPHALIA**. ➤ **HABSBURG DYNASTY**; **TRENT, COUNCIL OF**

## Thokoly, Imre, Count (1657–1705)

Hungarian landowner. He was typical of those who used Turkish support to try to diminish Habsburg dominance. Basing himself in Transylvania, he managed to establish control over northern Hungary for much of the period 1677–83. Although he even became Prince of Transylvania for a short time in 1690, he was soon forced into powerless exile in Turkey. ➤ **HABSBURG DYNASTY**

## Thorbecke, Johan Rudolf (1798–1872)

Dutch politician. He studied at Amsterdam, Leiden and several German universities, and in 1825 was appointed Professor of History at Ghent University (then part of the United Kingdom of the Netherlands). In 1831 he moved to Leiden University. In the 1830s he became a liberal, and from 1840 sat in parliament. In 1844 he (with eight others) produced a proposal for a new constitution; in 1848 King **WILLIAM II** panicked at riots in other European capitals and made Thorbecke chairman of a constitutional committee; the resulting constitution was a classic liberal document and the foundation of modern democratic politics in the Netherlands. Thorbecke, who is often referred to as the founder of the modern Dutch state, led three governments (1849–53, 1862–6 and 1871–2). During his periods of office most of the crucial bills were passed concerning free trade, the abolition of **SLAVERY**, centralized government, the separation of Church and State, and the construction of the transport infrastructure. Towards the end of his career, despite great respect from all parts of the House, he came into conflict with the more radical wing of the liberals.

## Thorez, Maurice (1900–64)

French politician. Having worked briefly as a coalminer, he joined the **COMMUNIST PARTY** in 1920; he was made General-Secretary in 1930, when the earlier generation of leaders fell foul of **STALIN**, and remained in undisputed command of a highly disciplined party until his death. He was one of the creators of the **POPULAR FRONT**, thus bringing the party out of the political wilderness, although communists tended not to join in the Popular Front governments. He survived the difficult period of the **GERMAN–SOVIET PACT** (1939–41) by deserting from the French army into which he had been conscripted and fleeing to the USSR. He was amnestied, and returned to France in 1944, becoming Deputy Prime Minister in the cabinet of the socialist Ramadier (Nov 1946–May 1947). After the exclusion of the party from office he led it through its most Stalinist period, adopting a position of unwavering support for the USSR on all questions until 1956, when he refused to accept Nikita **KHRUSHCHEV**'s denunciation of Stalin.

## Thousand, Expedition of the (1860)

In Italian history, the expedition of volunteer **RED SHIRTS** led by **GARIBALDI** to assist Sicilian rebels against Bourbon rule.

## Thrace

The region which lies between the Maritsa and

Nestos rivers, the Aegean and the Stara Planina range, now divided between Greece, Bulgaria and Turkey. Annexed by the Roman Emperor Claudius (AD46), Thrace was settled by the Visigoths and **SLAVS** and in the 7c became part of Bulgaria. It fell to the Turks (1453) and parts of it remained under Ottoman rule until the 20c. An integral part of Greece according to the **MEGALE IDEA**, it was also the object of Russian and Bulgarian territorial ambitions throughout the 19c. By the Treaty of **BUCHAREST** (1913), Thrace was awarded to Bulgaria but was then ceded to Greece at the end of **WORLD WAR I** by the Treaty of **NEUILLY** (1919); at the end of the **GRAECO-TURKISH WAR**, however, the eastern part went to Turkey (1922).

### Thrane, Marcus (1817–90)
Norwegian labour reformer. An outstanding figure in the history of pre-Marxist socialism, he was a pioneer of the labour movement in Norway. Between 1848 and 1850 he organized 'workers' unions' to campaign for adult male suffrage and improved working and living conditions for labourers and poor farmers. Despite Thrane's advocacy of non-violent methods, he alarmed the authorities and was imprisoned without trial (1850–4). He was then sentenced to a further four years in prison. Thrane emigrated to the USA in 1862 and became politically active in the Norwegian-American community. He returned only once to Norway (1882–3), to find himself a largely forgotten figure.

### Three Emperors' League (Dreikaiserbund)
An entente (1873, renewed 1881 and 1884) between Emperors **WILLIAM I** of Germany, **FRANCIS JOSEPH** of Austria-Hungary, and **ALEXANDER II** of Russia. It was designed by **BISMARCK** to protect Germany by isolating France and stabilizing south-east Europe. Largely superseded by the **DUAL ALLIANCE** (1879) of Germany and Austria-Hungary, it lapsed in 1887.

### Three Feudatories, Rebellion of the (1673 81)
A rebellion in China that threatened the newly established Manchu **QING DYNASTY**. As a reward for helping them to consolidate their rule in south China, the Manchus awarded three Chinese generals (Wu Sangui, Shang Zhixin and Geng Jingzhong) control of the entire region. Known as 'the Three Feudatories', these generals resorted to open rebellion in 1673 when Emperor **KANGXI** made it known that their bailiwicks were to be brought under central control. Wu Sangui (Wu San-Kuei), the northern frontier general who had originally allowed the Manchus to pass through the Great Wall in 1644 on their way to capture Beijing, declared himself emperor of a new dynasty in 1678. For a while it seemed the Manchus might be driven from China but poor coordination amongst the rebel armies and Kangxi's vigorous counter-attack led to the rebellion's collapse in 1683. The Qing Dynasty was henceforth firmly entrenched in China and was not to be seriously threatened again until the mid-19c with the outbreak of the **TAIPING REBELLION**.

### Three Mile Island
The site of a nuclear power plant near Harrisburg, Pennsylvania, the name of which has entered the lexicon as a synonym for nuclear disaster. In Mar 1979 a series of mechanical problems, human errors and poor decisions led to a partial meltdown of the plant's

reactor core and the release of dangerous radioactive gases. Although no one was killed, the incident turned public opinion against the continued use of nuclear power. ► **CHERNOBYL**

### Throckmorton, Sir Nicholas (1515–71)
English diplomat. He fought at the Battle of **PINKIE** (1547), was knighted in 1547, and became Ambassador to France and Scotland. In 1569 he was imprisoned for promoting the scheme to marry **MARY, QUEEN OF SCOTS** to the Duke of Norfolk, but was soon released. His daughter, Elizabeth, married Sir Walter **RALEIGH**; his nephew, Francis (1554–84) was executed for planning a conspiracy to overthrow **ELIZABETH I**.

### Thuggee
A form of banditry in rural central India, said to be a cult which combined robbery and ritual murder (usually by strangling) in the name of Kali (the Hindu goddess of destruction). Under British Governor-General Lord William **BENTINCK** (1833–5), and his agent Captain William Sleeman, vigorous steps were taken to eradicate the problem.

### Thuringia
A historic area of Germany, including the Harz Mountains and Thuringian Forest, a march or frontier region against the **SLAVS**. Controlled by various dynasties, from the 10c Dukes of Saxony to the House of Wettin (1265), it was divided between Saxony, Hesse-Kassel, and others from 1485–1920, and was subsequently a part of East Germany.

### Tiananmen Square
The largest public square in the world, covering 99 acres/40 hectares and lying before the gate to the Imperial Palace in central Beijing. It was here that the People's Republic was proclaimed in Oct 1949. In June 1989, it was the scene of mass protests by students and others against the Chinese government. The demonstrations were crushed by troops of the Chinese army, leaving an undisclosed number of people dead.

### Tianjin, Treaty of (1858)
The second unequal treaty imposed on China by the Western powers following the invasion of an Anglo-French expeditionary force in 1856 to enforce revision of the Treaty of **NANJING** (1842) to allow for an expansion of foreign trade. Under the terms of the treaty, China was compelled to open ten new **TREATY PORTS** and to allow permanent foreign legations in the capital. Furthermore, foreigners could travel in the interior (where they would continue to enjoy the privilege of extraterritoriality), while the Yangzi River was opened to foreign navigation. When the Qing court refused to ratify the treaty, a second Anglo-French offensive was launched, which led to the occupation of the Chinese capital in 1860. The Beijing Convention (1860) confirmed the terms of this treaty, although additional concessions were wrung from the Qing; Britain acquired the Kowloon Peninsula (which became part of the colony of Hong Kong), while missionaries gained the right to travel and own property in the interior. ► **QING DYNASTY**

### Tianjin Massacre (1870)
A major anti-foreign and anti-Christian incident in

China, one of a number of 'missionary cases' during the second half of the 19c in which the arrogance of Western missionaries aroused the hostility of the local population already whipped up by grotesque rumours spread by conservative gentry élites. In 1869 a French Catholic cathedral with an attached orphanage had been built in Tianjin on the site of a razed Buddhist temple. When it became known that missionaries were offering payment to receive orphans, rumours abounded that Christians were maiming and torturing Chinese children. As Tianjin had already been occupied twice by Anglo-French forces in 1858 and 1860 during the **ARROW WAR** (1856–60), anti-foreign feeling was already rife. In an altercation with the local magistrate, the French consul (Henri Fontanier) accidentally shot and killed a bystander. An angry mob then killed the consul and several French traders, before destroying the cathedral and orphanage, in the process also killing ten nuns. The Chinese government was compelled to pay an indemnity and send a mission of apology to France.

**Tibet**, also known as **Xizang**

An autonomous region of China situated on a remote high plateau in central Asia between India and China, with its capital at Lhasa. Buddhism was introduced into Tibet by Indian missionaries in the 7c. In the 13c the Mongols conquered Tibet and appointed lamas (Buddhist priests and monks) to rule the country. Tibet reverted to secular rule following the end of the Mongol empire but when the Mongol Altan Khan invaded in the 16c, he converted to Buddhism and appointed the **DALAI LAMA** as ruler. The Panchen Lama, second only in importance to the Dalai Lama, was first appointed in the mid 17c. In the early 18c China established a resident commissioner (**AMBAN**) in Lhasa and controlled Tibet as a subject state. Chinese sovereignty over Tibet was challenged in the 19c by Britain and Russia but was finally acknowledged by them in a 1907 treaty. In 1910 China established direct rule over Tibet, but with the collapse of the Chinese imperial regime in 1911 Tibet proclaimed its independence and the Dalai Lama reigned undisturbed until communist rule was established in China. The **PEOPLE'S LIBERATION ARMY** invaded Tibet in 1950 and in 1951 representatives of the Dalai Lama and the Panchen Lama signed a treaty establishing joint Chinese-Tibetan rule. An armed Tibetan rebellion broke out in 1956, but this was crushed and the Dalai Lama fled to India in 1959; the Panchen Lama remained as a figurehead in Lhasa and Tibet became an autonomous region formally annexed to China in 1969. Since the 1980s large numbers of Chinese have been encouraged to move to Tibet, a development the Tibetan government-in-exile regards as an attempt to eradicate the culture of the Tibetan people. It underlines the continuing strength of Chinese imperial ambition in central Asia.

**ticket of leave**

A pass issued to convicts in Australia as a reward for good behaviour; it was a form of parole which could be issued after four, six or eight years depending on whether the sentence was for seven years, 14 years or life, respectively. About 30 per cent of convicts received tickets of leave by 1840. ► **TRANSPORTATION**

**Tientsin, Treaty of** ► TIANJIN, TREATY OF

**Tientsin Massacre** ► TIANJIN MASSACRE

**Tigray**

Tigray is the northernmost of Ethiopia's nine states and some of the territory is the subject of a border dispute between **ETHIOPIA** and **ERITREA**. Eritrea has not accepted changes to the border made in the 1980s when Eritrean and Tigrayan separatists were fighting the **MENGISTU** regime and wishes to return to the colonial boundary in force before Eritrea's incorporation into Ethiopia in the early 20c. Conflict from 1996 to 1998 left thousands dead or displaced and fighting continued despite both countries accepting an **OAU** peace settlement in 1999. A peace agreement in Dec 2000 set up a neutral boundary commission, but fighting has broken out since on several occasions.

**Tikhon** (1865–1925)

Patriarch of the **RUSSIAN ORTHODOX CHURCH**. He was the first to have to deal with the new communist regime. A bishop by 1898, he had few crises to face until he became patriarch in 1918. His first approach was to condemn the new Soviet state; but before his death he called on the faithful to show it political loyalty. Neither policy was to prove successful, and his *de facto* successor, **SERGEI**, faced the same problem.

**Tikhonov, Nikolai Alexandrovich** (1905–97)

Soviet politician. He began his career as an assistant locomotive driver, before training in the late 1920s at the Dnepropetrovsk Metallurgical Institute, where he met Leonid **BREZHNEV**, then a Communist Party (CPSU) organizer. Tikhonov worked for two decades in the ferrous metallurgy industry, before being appointed Deputy Minister for the Iron and Steel Industry (1955–7), Deputy Chairman of Gosplan (1963–5) and Deputy Chairman of the Council of Ministers (1965–80). He was inducted into the CPSU **POLITBURO** as a full member by party leader Brezhnev in 1979 and appointed Prime Minister in 1980, a post which he held until 1985. A cautious, centralist Brezhnevite, his period as state Premier was characterized by worsening economic stagnation.

**Tilak, Bal Gangadhar** (1856–1920)

Militant Indian nationalist, scholar and philosopher. After teaching mathematics, he became owner and editor of two weekly newspapers. A member of the so-called 'extremist' wing within the **INDIAN NATIONAL CONGRESS**, he was twice imprisoned by the British for his nationalist activities. He helped found the Home Rule League in 1914, and died in Bombay.

**Tillett, Benjamin** (1860–1943)

English trade union leader. He worked as brickmaker, bootmaker, sailor and Labour MP (1917–24, 1929–31). He was notable as organizer of the Dockers' Union in London and leader of the great dockers' strike in 1889, and of the London transport workers' strike (1911). He was expelled from Hamburg and from Antwerp (1896) for supporting dock strikes.

**Tilley, Sir Samuel Leonard** (1818–96)

Canadian politician. He was one of the few who supported confederation in New Brunswick and this lost him the 1865 election. John A **MACDONALD** ensured that he was given massive aid, including direct grants to help him win the 1866 election and he joined the federal government in 1867. When Macdonald fell in 1873, he became Lieutenant-Governor of New Brunswick, but on Macdonald's return to power he again entered government as Minister of Finance, bringing in the National Policy tariff. Ill health forced his retirement in 1885, although he remained as Lieutenant-Governor until 1893. ► **TARIFF POLICY (CANADA)**

**Tilly, Johann Tserclaes, Count von** (1559–1632)
Bavarian general. He was the chief commander of the **CATHOLIC LEAGUE**'s army in the **THIRTY YEARS' WAR**. He campaigned in 1594 with Emperor **RUDOLF II** against the Turks. He reorganized the Bavarian army in 1610 into a disciplined, efficient fighting force. He became Imperial commander in 1630 after **WALLENSTEIN**'s fall. His string of victories ended when he was decisively beaten by the Swedes at Breitenfeld (1631). He was subsequently fatally wounded in battle at the Lech River.

**Tilsit, Treaties of** (1807)
Agreements of France with Russia and Prussia, following the break-up of the Third Coalition. After spectacular victories at **JENA AND AUERSTÄDT** and the Battle of **FRIEDLAND, NAPOLEON I** imposed a blockade on continental trade with Britain, and established the Grand Duchy of Warsaw and the Kingdom of Westphalia. The treaties contained secret clauses intended to mollify Russia. ► **GRAND ALLIANCE, WAR OF THE; NAPOLEONIC WARS**

**timar**
In the **OTTOMAN EMPIRE**, the right to a share in the income drawn from taxation upon an area of land acquired by conquest. The holder of a *timar* (a *timariot*) was usually obliged to serve in the Ottoman cavalry. A *zaim* was a timariot granted a *zeamet*, a timar yielding an annual income of more than 20,000 *akchas*. After the introduction of gunpowder, the military importance of the timariots was eclipsed by the **JANISSARIES**. ► **AYANS; SIPAHI**

**Time of Troubles** (1598–1613)
A period of intense social and political turmoil in Russia, involving a series of successive crises, civil war, famines, Cossack and peasant revolts, foreign invasions, and widespread material destruction. The period ended with a national uprising against the invading Poles, and the election of the first Romanov tsar. ► **COSSACKS; ROMANOV DYNASTY**

**Timişoara, Banat of** ► **TEMESVÁR, BANAT OF**

**Timoshenko, Semyon Konstantinovich** (1895–1970)
Russian general. He joined the Tsarist army in 1915, and in the **RUSSIAN REVOLUTION** took part in the defence of Tsaritsyn. In 1940 he smashed Finnish resistance during the **RUSSO-FINNISH WAR**, then commanded in the Ukraine, but failed to stop the German advance (1942). He also served as People's Commissar of Defence, improving the system of army training. He retired in 1960. ► **WORLD WAR II**

**Timur**, also called **Timur Lenk**, Turkish for **Timur the Lame**, English **Tamerlane** or **Tamburlaine** (1336–1405)
Tatar conqueror. Born near **SAMARKAND**, in 1369 he ascended the throne of Samarkand, and in a series of devastating wars (in which he sustained the wounds that gave him his nickname) subdued nearly all Persia (1392–6), Georgia, and the **TATAR** Empire, and conquered all the states between the Indus and the lower Ganges (1398). He won Damascus and Syria from the Mamluk sovereigns of Egypt, then defeated the Turks at **ANKARA** (1402), taking Sultan **BAYEZID I** prisoner. He died while marching to conquer China. ► **MAMLUKS; TIMURIDS**

**Timurids**
The dynastic group descended from **TIMUR**, which ruled in Persia and in Central Asia following his death. The major achievement of the Timurids, of whom Shah-Rukh (1404/47) was arguably the greatest, lay in the realms of learning, architecture and the arts; despite the steady erosion of the empire as a result of rivalries between individual Timurids, these were cultivated at a high level until the end of the sultanate of Husayn Bayqara. The latter's son, Badi al-Zaman (who died in 1517 in Constantinople, a prisoner of **SELIM I, THE GRIM**), was the last of the Timurids to rule in Persia, although a descendant of Timur, **BABUR** was to found the Mughal Dynasty in India. ► **MUGHAL EMPIRE**

**Tindale, William** ► **TYNDALE, WILLIAM**

**Tindemans, Leo** (1922– )
Belgian politician. He studied economics and social sciences at Antwerp, Ghent and Leuven universities; in 1958 he became Secretary to the **CHRISTIAN PEOPLE'S PARTY** (CVP). In 1961 he entered parliament for Antwerp. From 1968 he regularly held cabinet posts, and led the government from 1974 to 1978. In 1979 he became Chairman of the CVP, and is particularly known for his role in the **EC** (European Community). He was President of the Group of European People's Party in the European Parliament from 1992 until 1994.

**Ting Ling** ► **DING LING**

**Tippecanoe, Battle of** (7 Nov 1811)
A conflict at which US forces led by General William **HARRISON** succeeded in suppressing an uprising by the Shawnee, who were supported by the British and led by **TECUMSEH** and his brother the 'Prophet' Tenskawatawa. The US victory was intended to halt Native American resistance to US westward expansion, but the threat to the north-west frontier remained for two more years, until the decisive Battle of the **THAMES**.

**Tippoo Sahib** (1749–99)
Sultan of Mysore (1782/99). The son of **HAIDAR ALI**, he continued his father's policy of opposing British rule, and in 1789 invaded the British-protected state of Travancore. In the ensuing war (1790–2) he was defeated by **CORNWALLIS** and had to cede half his kingdom. After recommencing hostilities in 1799, he was killed during the siege of Scringapatam.

**Tippu Tib** (1837–1905)
One of the most powerful of the traders and plantation owners of Zanzibar in the 19c. He created a personal empire in the eastern Congo region in the years before the Partition of **AFRICA**. Tippu began to lead large and powerful trading caravans, financed by Indian capitalists, into the interior of East Africa from the 1850s. Together with other Zanzibari traders, he

helped to establish networks of trade in ivory and slaves throughout eastern central Africa. In 1869 he settled in the rich ivory grounds of eastern Congo, became powerful in the markets there, and virtually ruled a large area for some 12 years. By the 1890s, he was back in Zanzibar and owned seven plantations and some 10,000 slaves.

### Tipú Sultán ▶ TIPPOO SAHIB

### Tirpitz, Alfred Friedrich von (1849–1930)
German admiral. He joined the Prussian navy in 1865, was ennobled in 1900, and rose to be Lord High Admiral (1911). As Secretary of State for the Imperial Navy (1897–1916), he raised a fleet to challenge British supremacy of the seas, and acted as its commander (1914–16). He advocated unrestricted submarine warfare, and resigned when this policy was, initially, opposed in government circles (to be implemented later, from 1 Feb 1917); he later sat in the REICHSTAG.
▶ WORLD WAR I

### Tiso, Józef (1887–1947)
Slovak priest and politician. Like many other Slovak priests he was attracted to politics by Catholic and ethnic feelings against the Czechs in the united state established in 1918. In 1938 he succeeded HLINKA as leader of the Populist Party and began talks with HENLEIN, the Sudeten leader, whose objective was to enable HITLER to destroy Czechoslovakia. Following the MUNICH AGREEMENT, ably assisted by DURCANSKY, he conspired with Hitler and in Mar 1939 obeyed the order to declare Slovakia independent, leaving Czechs to Hitler's mercy in the BOHEMIAN PROTECTORATE. As President of the new Slovakia he eventually, in 1944, invited the Germans in to suppress the patriotic SLOVAK UPRISING. In 1947 he was tried and executed in Bratislava. The Slovak–Czech relationship had been little improved by his efforts.

### Tisza, Kalman (1830–1902)
Hungarian politician. The father of Stephen TISZA, he was Premier and virtual dictator of Hungary from 1875 to 1890.

### Tisza, Stephen (1861–1918)
Hungarian politician. He was the son of Kalman TISZA. A patriotic Magyar, he was Premier of Hungary in the periods 1903–5 and 1913–17. He supported Germany and was assassinated on 31 Oct 1918, the first day of the Hungarian Revolution.

### Tito, originally Josip Broz (1892–1980)
Yugoslav politician. In WORLD WAR I he served with the Austro-Hungarian army, was taken prisoner by the Russians, and became a communist. He was imprisoned for conspiring against the regime in Yugoslavia (1928–9), and became Secretary of the Communist Party in 1937. In 1941 he organized partisan forces against the Axis conquerors, and after the war became the country's first communist Prime Minister (1945), consolidating his position with the presidency (1953–80). He broke with STALIN and the COMINFORM in 1948, developing Yugoslavia's independent style of COMMUNISM ('Titoism'), and played a leading role in the association of non-aligned countries. ▶ AXIS POWERS; CHETNIKS

### Titulescu, Nicolae (1883–1941)
Romanian politician. At the end of WORLD WAR I, he was one of the Romanian representatives at the peace negotiations in Paris and later signed the Treaty of TRIANON (1920). He worked at the Romanian Embassy in London (1922–6 and 1928–32), returning to Romania to serve as Foreign Minister (1927 and 1932–6). He negotiated Romania's membership of the LITTLE ENTENTE and the BALKAN ENTENTE and courted the support of France and the USSR. He was dismissed by CHARLES II of Romania in 1936.

### Tlatelolco, Treaty of (1967)
A treaty establishing a nuclear weapons-free zone in Latin America and the Caribbean. It was signed by 22 Latin American nations at first, by Argentina, Brazil and Chile in early 1994, and by Cuba in 1995.

### Tobruk, Battles of (1941–2)
A key city in Libya, Tobruk was taken from the Italians in Jan 1941 by WAVELL, then in command of the 8th Army. The arrival, however, in Libya of ROMMEL with his AFRIKA CORPS in Mar of the same year saw the British withdrawing eastward. The subsequent siege of Tobruk, which was garrisoned largely by Australian troops, lasted for some eight months until the garrison was able to break out. AUCHINLECK, who was now in command of the 8th Army and whom they managed to join, mounted a major offensive which was to extend British control over Cyrenaica as far as Benghazi, bringing back Tobruk with it. However, Rommel's counter-offensive towards Egypt meant that Tobruk was again placed under siege, this time falling in June 1942. In the event, Auchinleck was able to check Rommel's advance at the first Battle of EL ALAMEIN and it was the successful western drive of MONTGOMERY which finally recaptured Tobruk in Nov 1942.

### Tocqueville, Alexis Charles Henri Maurice Clérel de, (1805–59)
French historian and political scientist. In 1831 he went to the USA to report on the prison system. On his return he published a penetrating political study, *Democracy in America* (1835), which gave him a European reputation. He became a member of the Chamber of Deputies in 1839, and in 1849 was Vice-President of the Assembly and briefly Minister of Foreign Affairs. After Napoleon III's coup, he retired to his estate, where he wrote the first volume of *L'Ancien Régime et la Révolution* (1856, 'The Old Regime and the Revolution').

### Todarmal (d.1589)
Indian administrator. A brilliant revenue officer, he first served under SHER SHAH and then joined the court of AKBAR THE GREAT. He was instrumental in devising the 'Zabti System' or 'Todarmal's Bandobast', a system of revenue assessment and collection introduced during Akbar's reign. According to this system, the peasant was required to pay taxes on the basis of local produce as well as local prices. There were a number of advantages of this system. As soon as the area sown by the peasant had been measured, both the peasant and the state knew what the dues were. The peasant was, furthermore, given remission in the land revenue if crops failed on account of drought, floods, etc. Akbar successfully introduced this system in the area from Lahore to Allahabad, and in Malwa and Gujarat. A very efficient system of

revenue administration thus evolved under his guidance.

**Todd, Sir (Reginald Stephen) Garfield** (1908–2002)
Rhodesian politician. Born in New Zealand, he was educated there and in South Africa. Having gone to Southern Rhodesia in 1934 as a missionary, he was elected to the Legislative Assembly (1946) and then to the leadership of the United Rhodesia Party (1953) which made him Prime Minister of Southern Rhodesia. He was removed from the leadership by an internal putsch because of his liberalism and he helped form the overtly liberal Central African Party in 1959. After the party's failure in 1962, he returned to farming but remained the spokesman for white liberalism in the country, as a result of which he was restricted by the **RHODESIAN FRONT** government under Ian **SMITH** (1965–6 and 1972–6). A close friend and ally of Joshua **NKOMO**, he supported the latter in the 1980 elections.

**Todleben, Eduard Ivanovich** (1818–84)
Russian soldier and military engineer. Born of German descent in Mitau in Courland, he served in the Caucasus, and in the Danubian Principalities in 1853. He conducted with skill and energy the defence of **SEVASTOPOL** until he was severely wounded (June 1855); thereafter, he completed the fortification of Nikolaieff and Cronstadt. During the Russo-Turkish War of 1877–8 he was called to besiege Plevna, which he took after a brilliant defence. ► **MOLDAVIA AND WALLACHIA; RUSSO-TURKISH WARS**

**Togliatti, Palmiro** (1893–1964)
Italian politician. A member of the Italian Socialist Party in 1914, he was one of the founders of the Italian Communist Party (**PCI**) in 1921. Forced to flee Italy by the fascists in 1926, he organized the activities of the party from abroad and was part of the **COMINTERN** secretariat in charge of communists fighting in the **SPANISH CIVIL WAR**. In Mar 1944 he returned to Italy, played a key part in the coalition governments that controlled Italy until 1947 and was instrumental in stressing the need to avoid insurrectionary attempts. Until his death (while visiting Nikita **KHRUSHCHEV** in Yalta), he was Party Secretary, presiding over the PCI's development from a relatively small group of militants into the largest communist organization in the West. ► **BERLINGUER, ENRICO**

**TOGO**   official name **Republic of Togo**
A republic in West Africa, bounded to the west by Ghana; to the north by Burkina Faso; and to the east by Benin. Formerly part of the Kingdom of Togoland, it was a German protectorate from 1884 to 1914. After **WORLD WAR I** it was divided between France (French Togo) and Britain (part of British Gold Coast) by mandate of the **LEAGUE OF NATIONS** (1922). In 1946 the British and French governments placed their territories under **UN** trusteeships. French Togo became an autonomous republic within the French Union in 1956, while British Togoland voted to join the Gold Coast (Ghana) when Ghana gained independence in 1957. French Togo gained independence in 1960. Relations between Ghana and Togo gradually worsened, particulary in the 1990s when Ghana was accused of harbouring Togolese rebels. There were military coups in Togo in 1963 and 1967, the latter

bringing General Gnassingbé **EYADÉMA** to power. In 1979 a new constitution was adopted and Eyadéma proclaimed the third Togolese Republic, with himself as President. He was re-elected in 1986 and, having been forced by violent demonstrations to legalize other political parties, won the first multiparty presidential elections in 1993. Re-elected in 1998 and 2003, Eyadéma was President until his death in Feb 2005, when the army appointed his son, Faure Gnassingbé, to complete his final term of office.

**Togo Heihachiro** (1848–1934)
Japanese admiral. After training at the Royal Naval College at Greenwich, London, he served against China (1894). As commander during the **RUSSO-JAPANESE WAR** (1904–5), he bombarded Port Arthur. Togo defeated the Russian fleet at the Battle of **TSUSHIMA** (1905), the first victory of an Asian power over a European nation in modern times.

**Tojo Hideki** (1885–1948)
Japanese general and politician. He attended military college, became military attaché in Germany (1919), served in **MANCHURIA** as Chief of Staff (1937–40), and during **WORLD WAR II** was Minister of War (1940–1) and Prime Minister (1941–4). Arrested in 1945, he attempted to commit suicide, but was hanged as a war criminal in Tokyo.

**Tokugawa Ieyasu** (1542–1616)
Japanese warrior leader. The third of the three great historical unifiers of Japan, after **ODA NOBUNAGA** and **TOYOTOMI HIDEYOSHI**, he was a noble from eastern Japan. He took power after the Battle of **SEKIGAHARA** (1600), and founded the **TOKUGAWA SHOGUNATE**. He completed Edo Castle (the present Tokyo Imperial Palace) as his headquarters, and instituted an all-pervading centralized control of Japanese life whose effects are still felt.

**Tokugawa Shogunate** (1603–1867)
Japan's third warrior government, established by **TO-KUGAWA IEYASU** when he was awarded the hereditary title of **SHOGUN** in 1603 by the Emperor, following his military victory over rival warrior families at the Battle of **SEKIGAHARA** (1600). The Tokugawa Shogunate (or *bakufu*, 'tent government') was located in **EDO**

(present-day Tokyo) and proved to be the most durable of the three shogunates (the other two being the **KAMAKURA SHOGUNATE** and the **ASHIKAGA SHOGUNATE**), providing peace and stability until the mid-19c, when domestic social and economic change together with external pressure from Western powers combined to bring about its collapse. Tokugawa Japan has been described by historians as a centralized **FEUDALISM**; although the **DAIMYO** (feudal lords) were allowed considerable autonomy, they were subject to restrictions on the size of their castle towns and the number of retainers they could have. The Tokugawa also retained the right to reduce or confiscate their domains. Furthermore, daimyo were forbidden to engage in foreign trade and were obliged to reside in Edo for six months of every year (**ALTERNATE ATTENDANCE SYSTEM**). From the mid-18c, however, Tokugawa control gradually loosened as its financial situation worsened and attempts to impose a rigidly hierarchical social order foundered on the rocks of social and economic change, while the **SAMURAI** élite became indebted to an emerging merchant class. Dissatisfaction with the status quo led to an imperial loyalist movement in the early 19c which was to culminate in the overthrow of the Tokugawa and the **MEIJI RESTORATION** (1868).

## TOKUGAWA SHOGUNATE

| Regnal Dates | Name |
|---|---|
| 1603/5 | Tokugawa Ieyasu |
| 1605/23 | Tokugawa Hidetada |
| 1623/51 | Tokugawa Iemitsu |
| 1651/80 | Tokugawa Ietsuna |
| 1680/1709 | Tokugawa Tsunayoshi |
| 1709/12 | Tokugawa Ienobu |
| 1713/16 | Tokugawa Ietsugu |
| 1716/45 | Tokugawa Yoshimune |
| 1745/60 | Tokugawa Ieshige |
| 1760/86 | Tokugawa Ieharu |
| 1787/1837 | Tokugawa Ienari |
| 1837/53 | Tokugawa Ieyoshi |
| 1853/8 | Tokugawa Iesada |
| 1858/66 | Tokugawa Iemochi |
| 1866/7 | Tokugawa Yoshinobu |

**Tolbert, William Richard** (1913–80)
Liberian politician. Educated at Liberia College in Monrovia, he was a civil servant (1935–43) before becoming a member of the House of Representatives for the True Whig Party (1943–51). Vice-President from 1951 to 1971, he became President in 1971 and remained in this post until he was assassinated in a military coup on 12 Apr 1980.

**Toledo (Manrique), Alejandro** (1946– )
Peruvian economist and politician. From a poor, Quechuan (native Peruvian Indian) background, scholarships enabled him to receive a university education in the USA, following which he worked for the **UN, WORLD BANK, INTERNATIONAL LABOUR ORGANIZATION** and **OECD**. In 1998 he returned to Lima to an academic post before taking advantage of the political chaos in Peru to lead the centrist *Perú Posible* (PP) party and run for the presidency. After withdrawing from the 2000 presidential campaign over the smear tactics of other parties, he was elected president, the

first of Quechuan descent, in 2001 after a bribery scandal forced President **FUJIMORI** to resign. His populist appeal rested on promises to end corruption in the military, police and government, improve economic performance and create jobs. But economic slowdown in Latin America, along with increased activity by the **SENDERO LUMINOSO** and incursions by **FARC** (Revolutionary Armed Forces of Colombia) in support of illegal drug-trafficking, have made his presidency increasingly precarious.

**Tolpuddle Martyrs**
Agricultural labourers at Tolpuddle, Dorset, in England, who were organized in 1833 into a trade union by a Methodist local preacher, George Loveless (1796–1874), convicted of taking illegal oaths, and transported. The action provoked substantial protests, and the labourers were eventually pardoned.

**Tolstoy** or **Tolstoi**
A family of Russian nobles. Count Peter (1645–1729) was a trusted agent of **PETER I, THE GREAT**. Count Peter Alexandrovich (1761–1844) was one of **SUVOROV**'s generals and, under **NICHOLAS I**, head of a government department. Count Dmitri Andreevich (1823–89) was a reactionary Minister of Education, champion of Russian Orthodoxy and a 'Russifier' of the Poles.

**Toltecs** ► **PRE-COLUMBIAN CIVILIZATIONS**

**Tombalbaye, N'Garta François** (1918–75)
Chadian politician. Educated locally, he was a teacher before becoming a trades union organizer. He then helped organize the **RASSEMBLEMENT DÉMOCRATIQUE AFRICAIN** (RDA) in Chad in 1947 and was elected to the territorial assembly (1953). He rose to be Prime Minister in 1959 and then President on Chad's independence in 1962. He remained in this position until the military coup of 13 Apr 1975, during which he was killed.

**Tomsky, Mikhail Pavlovich** (1880–1937)
Soviet trade unionist. Born into a poor working-class family in St Petersburg, he organized factory strikes from his mid-teens. From 1909 to 1917 he was either in prison or in exile. He returned to trade union activity in Moscow in 1917, and by 1919 was Chairman of the Central Council of Trade Unions and by 1922 a full member of the **POLITBURO**. In these capacities he destroyed the unions in the Western sense and made them vehicles for party and government control. In the period 1928–30 he changed his stance and defended workers' rights. He was thereupon dismissed and committed suicide in protest against **STALIN**'s purges.

**Tone, (Theobald) Wolfe** (1763–98)
Irish nationalist. He acted as Secretary of the Catholic Committee, helped to organize the Society of **UNITED IRISHMEN** (1791), and had to flee to the USA and to France (1795). He induced France to invade Ireland on two occasions, and was captured during the second expedition (1798). He was condemned to be hanged, but committed suicide in Dublin.

**TONGA**   official name **Kingdom of Tonga**, also called **Friendly Islands**
An independent island group in the south-west Pacific Ocean. Inhabited from as early as 1000BC, the

islands were visited by Captain James **COOK** in 1773 and named the Friendly Islands. They received missionaries and were established as a nation under King George Tupou I. Tonga became a British protectorate in 1899, under its own monarchy, and gained independence in 1970. Taufa'ahau Tupou IV acceded to the throne in 1965. Tonga's first political party was formed in 1994 and its pro-democracy movement gained momentum by 1996, although only nine members of the parliament are popularly elected.

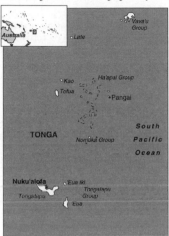

### Tooke, John Horne (1736–1812)
British politician. Born John Horne, he became a lawyer, and in 1760 a vicar. A radical, in 1771 he formed the Constitutional Society, supporting the American colonists and parliamentary reform. His spirited opposition to an enclosure bill procured him the favour of the rich Mr Tooke of Purley in Surrey, which led to his new surname and *The Diversions of Purley* (1786), written while in prison for supporting the American cause. He was tried for high treason in 1794, acquitted, and became an MP in 1801. ▶ **AMERICAN REVOLUTION; WILKES, JOHN**

### Topa Inca Yupanqui (d.1493)
Inca ruler. He acceded to the throne c.1471 on the abdication of his father, Pachacuti Inca, who had ruled since 1438. Topa Inca was a great conquerer and vastly expanded the Inca empire to include most of the central Andes region, bringing in all of highland Bolivia, most of north-western Argentina, and northern Chile down to the Maule River, which marked the Inca boundary. On his death he was succeeded by Huayna Capac. ▶ **PRE-COLUMBIAN CIVILIZATIONS**

### Tories (UK)
The British political party which emerged in 1679–80 as the group opposed to the exclusion of James, Duke of York from succession to the throne. The name was taken from 17c Irish outlaws who plundered and killed English settlers. The party developed after the **GLORIOUS REVOLUTION** (1688) as the supporters of the divine right of monarchy, and had particular support from the country squirearchy and most sections of the Anglican Church. It opposed religious toleration for Catholics and Dissenters. The Tories enjoyed periods of power in the reign of Queen **ANNE**, but the party went into decline after the Hanoverian succes-

sion, when some of its supporters became **JACOBITES**. It is generally agreed to have revived under **PITT, THE YOUNGER** as the leading opposition to French revolutionary ideology in the 1790s, and Lord **LIVERPOOL** became the first Prime Minister to acknowledge the title 'Tory' in the early 19c. Toryism developed into conservatism under **PEEL**, but survived as a nickname for the Conservatives. ▶ **CONSERVATIVE PARTY** (UK); **DIVINE RIGHT OF KINGS; JAMES VII AND II; WHIGS**

### Tories (USA)
Also known as Loyalists, those who remained loyal to the Crown during the **AMERICAN REVOLUTION**. After the **DECLARATION OF INDEPENDENCE**, loyalty to the Crown became treason, punishable by imprisonment and confiscation of property. It was estimated that one third of the colonial population were loyalists. Many chose to leave the country during or after the revolution and sufficient numbers enlisted in the British Army to make up several regiments.

### Torquemada, Tomás de (1420–98)
The first Inquisitor-General of Spain. He entered the Dominican Order in Valladolid, was later appointed Prior of the Convent of Santa Cruz in Segovia, and at about the same time was chosen to be a confessor of **ISABELLA I, THE CATHOLIC** and **FERDINAND II, THE CATHOLIC**. In 1482 he was appointed as one of the seven new inquisitors to continue the work of the recently founded (1480) **INQUISITION**. In 1483 he was chosen to head it as Inquisitor-General, and played a key role in forcing through the introduction of the new Inquisition in the realms of the crown of **ARAGON**. No evidence exists for attributing to Torquemada the evidently anti-Semitic philosophy of the early Inquisition, or responsibility for its excesses, but it is unquestionable that he was a major force behind the Expulsion of the **JEWS** in 1492.

### Tosks
Part of the Albanian nation from southern Albania, during the years of Ottoman rule they mainly lived as peasants working on large estates. Both Sunni and Bektashi Muslims, they were loyal to the Sultan and less open to political reform. Their dialect was the basis for the Albanian literary language. ▶ **GHEGS**

### Tostig (d.1066)
Earl of Northumbria. He was the son of Godwin and brother of **HAROLD II**. After return from banishment in 1052, **EDWARD THE CONFESSOR** created him Earl of Northumbria (1055) over which he ruled both violently and as a frequent absentee. He was supplanted by Morcar, whose title was confirmed by Edward and Harold. Tostig was banished and, upon Harold's succession (1066), plotted to overthrow him. He aided **HARALD HARDRADA**'s invasion from Norway in Sep and was killed at the Battle of Stamford Bridge (25 Sep 1066).

### totalitarianism
In its modern form, a political concept first used to describe the USSR's communist regime and Italy and Germany's fascist regimes during the period between the two World Wars. It is difficult to distinguish empirically from related concepts such as authoritarianism and dictatorship, but certain common features can be identified. These relate to the use of power

# Trade and Globalization

*Culture & Society*

Trade – the bartering, buying and selling of goods and services – has been a vital human activity since earliest times. An ancient series of trade routes, designated the 'Silk Road' by a 19c historian, ran from the Mediterranean through Bukhara and Samarkand to Dunhuang and on to Xian (Chang'an) in central China and was used by Alexander the Great to conquer Persia. Silks, spices and perfumes, precious stones such as amber and coral, gold, ivory and other commodities, such as glass, were traded along these routes. As well as commodities, knowledge, art, science, disease and religious cultures also travelled along the Silk Road; Buddhism was brought to China from India in this way, and later bubonic plague travelled west. The rise of **Kiev Rus** in the 10c was founded on its position straddling the trade routes between Sweden and Constantinople. By 1350 a intricate web of global trade routes had developed which started with the **Hanseatic League** in north-west Europe and stretched to the Far East. In Pre-Columbian America, in the area of present-day Ecuador, the Valdivias culture established routes which linked the Andes and Amazonian tribes, trading ornaments made from the red shell of the Spondylus oyster. By 600 BC these routes ran from Mexico to Chile, and supported sophisticated urban cultures. Around the same time, Mayans were carrying jade and brightly coloured feathers along extensive trade routes.

Early trade was not confined to overland routes, which were often beset by bandits despite the efforts of early warlords and rulers to protect such lucrative traffic. The Greeks and, particularly, the Phoenicians were renowned maritime traders, and the sea connected coastal city-states along well-known routes. Trading routes ran through the Red Sea and across the Indian Ocean, where the Romans would catch the monsoon winds to carry cargo to Deccan in India. Indian traders ventured through the Malacca Straits to the China coast. The rise of Islam in Asia Minor and Africa initially facilitated trade, but the success of the new religion's spread and conflict with Christianity in Asia meant that by the 14c land routes that ventured across religious borders had became unsafe. Europeans had not traded direct with Asia in any case; the great medieval mercantile states of Genoa and Venice acted as intermediaries, providing European access to the trading network, monopolized in the Mediterranean by Alexandria. Trade here was conducted by payment in specie (coin), and it has been postulated that the European voyages of **exploration**, seeking alternative routes to the Far East, were driven not only by a need to find markets for their goods, but also to find the gold needed to pay for the spices and luxury imports of the east through Alexandria.

The 16c brought two dramatic changes in global trade. The first was the **colonization** of North and South America by the major European states following the discovery of the Americas by Christopher **Columbus**. The import of precious metals, especially gold and silver, to Europe through Spain supported an expansion of commercial production and commodities trading, underpinned by new governmental financial systems and the existing private banks. In the 17c, France, Britain and the Dutch used chartered joint-stock companies to provide backing for overseas trade and colonization, and each founded a national **East India Company**; other chartered companies included the

---

and the means of government employed by the leadership, which claims exclusive rights to govern, usually on behalf of the party and its ideology. Furthermore, all aspects of social, political, industrial, military and economic life are controlled or permeated by the state apparatus. Political opposition is suppressed, and decision-making is highly centralized. ► **AUTHORITARIANISM**; **COMMUNISM**; **FASCISM**

**Touré, Ahmed Sékou** (1922–84)
Guinean politician. Educated in Quran schools and at Conakry (1936–40), he turned to trade union activity and attended the *Confédération Générale des Travailleurs* (CGT) Congress in Paris in 1947, after which he was imprisoned for a brief period. He was a founder-member of the **RASSEMBLEMENT DÉMOCRATIQUE AFRICAIN** (RDA) in 1946 and became its Secretary-General in 1952, as well as Secretary-General of the local CGT branch. He was a member of the Territorial Assembly from 1953, Mayor of Conakry in 1955 and then Deputy in the French National Assembly in 1956. In 1958 he organized an overwhelming 'non' vote to de **GAULLE**'s referendum on self-government within a French Community. Guinea was granted its independence at once, the French removing as many of their possessions as possible. Touré was President from 1958 to 1984, and retained his uncompromisingly radical views of domestic and foreign politics. He survived several attempts, supported by outside powers, to overthrow him. Soon after his death, the military did take control.

**Tours, Congress of** (25–30 Dec 1920)
The Congress of the French **SOCIALIST PARTY** (SFIO) at which the majority of members decided to join the Third International, and thus to create a new party, the **COMMUNIST PARTY** (SFIC). His impassioned oratory against this decision made Léon **BLUM** the most influential figure among those who decided to stay with the 'old firm', the Socialist Party. The subsequent general election (1924) revealed that the majority of socialist voters agreed, and the Communist Party had little support until the **POPULAR FRONT** period (1934–6).

**Toussaint L'Ouverture**, originally **François Dominique Toussaint** (1746–1803)
Haitian black revolutionary leader. He was born of African slave parents but was freed in 1777. In 1791 he joined the free black insurgents, becoming their leader. He rallied insurgent slaves to his cause after the French Republic abolished **SLAVERY** in 1794 and by 1797 was effective ruler of the former colony. He drove out British and Spanish expeditions, restored order, and aimed at independence. **NAPOLEON I** sent a new expedition to St Domingue, and proclaimed the re-establishment of slavery. Toussaint was eventually captured, and died in prison in France. His surname comes from his bravery in once making a breach (*ouverture*) in the ranks of the enemy.

**Townsend, Francis Everett** (1867–1960)
US physician and reformer. In 1933 he proposed a federally administered old-age pension plan, which he believed would stimulate the economy and end

Massachusetts Bay Company, founded in 1629 to extend trade and colonize along the Charles River, and the **Hudson's Bay Company**, established in 1670 in an attempt by the English to control the North American **fur trade**. Britain's influence took in most of the Atlantic seaboard, from Newfoundland to the Carolinas. France controlled the St Lawrence seaway and fortified trading posts along the Great Lakes system and the Mississippi basin. By the early 18c these European powers controlled the Atlantic economy, which was based on trade in slaves, sugar, cotton and tobacco, ships tracing a triangular route from Africa to the New World and thence to Europe. The European trading posts originally established along Africa's west coast to trade for gold gradually became the ports through which slaves were exported to the plantations in British, Portuguese and Spanish colonies.

The second major 16c change in global trade was the development of direct European trade with Asia. The Portuguese and Dutch opened up trade routes to the east which were exploited by all the major European countries so that by the early 18c trade links once again stretched around the globe, but now they were dominated by the European nations, which protected their commercial interests with national navies at sea and armies on land. European capital invested in these companies secured goods produced on commission for sale not only at home but also in the Asian markets, and merchantmen returned with goods purchased well below their European market value and therefore capable of yielding substantial profit to repay investors. By the beginning of the 19c, both the Atlantic and the Asian markets had been linked by the operations of the East India companies. The companies' customs dues could be a useful source of cash for Asian rulers, but the volume of their trade was tiny compared with Asian domestic markets.

For governments or rulers wishing to retain control over domestic trade, a common means was to put in place some form of protectionism. Early Muslim traders would not allow Genoese ships to take goods beyond Alexandria, requiring the goods to be moved to native carriers to continue their journey. Protectionism was not unusual in Europe; the **Navigation Acts**, for example, stated that only English shipping or shipping of the country where the cargo originated could bring goods into English ports, an attempt to exclude Dutch carriers from English colonial trade. The governments of Japan and China were equally reluctant to open up their domestic markets to acquisitive, mainly European, trading companies or allow the establishment of 'factories' for new goods in their ports. The **Tokugawa Shogunate** in Japan, fearing the subversive impact of Christianity, not only expelled all European missionaries but also prohibited Japanese involvement in foreign trade or travel, permitting only carefully regulated trading through two ports with the Dutch, Chinese and Koreans. This isolationist policy (**sakoku**) lasted until 1854, when Commodore Matthew **Perry**'s 'gunboat diplomacy' led to the Treaty of **Kanagawa**, which brought Japan back into the global trading network. The same tactics were used by the European powers to open up Chinese markets and by the Japanese to open up Korean markets.

It was the **Industrial Revolution** that during the 19c began to integrate these separate regions into a truly global economy. Along with the steamship, railways and telegraph, there were land surveys, census data collection and national legal systems that supported a new kind of organizational matrix, and the beginning of a system of global regulations and operating systems, underpinned by a new kind of international link: foreign investment. North America, especially the USA, was the main early destination for European capital, but by 1900 Latin America, British India and China were also

---

the Depression. The Townsend Plan was repeatedly defeated in **CONGRESS**, but its popularity helped bring about the passage of the Social Security Act (1935).

### Townshend, Charles Townshend, 2nd Viscount (1674–1738)

English politician. He succeeded his father as viscount (1687), was made Secretary of State by **GEORGE I** (1714–16 and 1721–30), and became a leading figure in the Whig ministry with his brother-in-law, Robert **WALPOLE**. After a resignation engineered by Walpole, he became known as 'turnip Townshend' for his interest in agricultural improvement, and his proposal to use turnips in crop rotation. ► **WHIGS**

### Townshend Acts (1767)

British statutes imposing taxes on five categories of goods imported into the American colonies, after successful colonial resistance to the **STAMP ACT** (1765). The Townshend Taxes likewise met resistance from the colonists, and four categories were repealed in 1770. The fifth, on tea, remained in effect until the **BOSTON TEA PARTY**. The Acts are named after British Chancellor of the Exchequer, Charles Townshend (1725–67), who sponsored them. ► **AMERICAN REVOLUTION**

### Toynbee, Arnold (1852–83)

English economic historian and social reformer. Born in London, he lectured in economic history at Balliol College, Oxford, and to numerous workers' adult education classes, and undertook social work

in the East End of London with Samuel Barnett. He is best known for the phrase '**INDUSTRIAL REVOLUTION**', coined in his work *The Industrial Revolution in England* (1884).

### Toyotomi Hideyoshi (1536–98)

Japanese warrior leader. The second of the three great historical unifiers of Japan, between **ODA NOBUNAGA** and **TOKUGAWA IEYASU**, sometimes called 'the Napoleon of Japan'. Unusually, he was an ordinary soldier who rose to become Oda's foremost general. His law forbade all except **SAMURAI** to carry swords (1588), and he banned Christianity for political reasons (1597). His armies invaded Korea (1592–8), but withdrew after his death at Fushimi Castle, Kyoto. ► **NAPOLEON I**

### Trade and Globalization ► *See panel*

### Trade Unions (Belgium)

As one of the first industrialized nations, with strong mining and heavy industrial sectors in Wallonia and Ghent, Belgian socialism developed early, having a radical syndicalist trade union movement as one of the moving forces. In 1898 the various socialist organizations joined a Syndical Committee, which in 1938 became the Belgian Labour League, and after **WORLD WAR II** the General Belgian Labour League (*Algemeen Belgisch Vakverbond; Fédération Générale du Travail de Belgique*). The Roman Catholics were much slower to adopt organizations exclusively for workers, but after the papal encyclical *Rerum Novarum* in 1891 work started, and in 1904 the General

attracting investment. Mounting nationalist tensions in Europe stimulated competitive bids for privilege, footholds and, eventually, territory even in Africa, where the volumes of trade were limited outside the South African diamond fields. Financial investment could speed development when it flowed from advanced economies to poorer ones, but increasingly during the 19c investment flowed from developed economies to ones without the power to resist or direct the flow of investment for their own benefit, and these areas were often colonized to maintain control over capital flow. When European governments began to guarantee loans and investments to overseas enterprises, the need arose for political control to safeguard those investments. Wars were fought to retain and expand access to markets, for example in China by Britain during the **Opium Wars**, or by the USA in north and central America. European rivalries rather than the inherent value of capital flows to areas with weak or vulnerable governments explains the surge in European colonialism around 1900, but after **World War I** direct empire was increasingly seen as a burden and the European powers granted independence to most of their former colonies in the second half of the 20c. In most cases, it was possible to secure an adequate degree of protection of assets by indirect influence over other governments. The problem of unbalanced relationships, often managed through the **International Monetary Fund**, remained as serious as ever.

Globalization is not a modern development but technological advances in transport and communications, particularly in information technology, have deepened it greatly, making it quicker and easier to complete international transactions, whether in goods or capital. Neither the swings between 19c **laissez-faire** economics, nor the protectionism exemplified by the **Hawley-Smoot Tariff Act** during the inter-war years, nor the swing back to free-market capitalism after 1945 were able to smooth out economic cycles. Nor could these models guarantee that the benefits of global trade were shared by everyone. In earliest times, the rise of globalization of consumption left the asset, whether a gold field or a cinnamon tree, in the hands of the producer. Modern globalization of production and ownership can mean that the asset is owned and controlled by a foreign concern, an objection levelled against many modern multinational companies. It is in the interests of global corporations to influence national governments to set up tariff-free zones, such as **NAFTA** or the **EU**, and to homogenize consumer preference. To its critics, globalization has no philosophical basis and is merely a new form of cultural and economic colonialism using intellectual property laws to impinge on basic areas such as food, in the patenting of genetically modified grains, and health, eg the refusal of pharmaceutical companies to supply cheaper retroviral drugs to AIDs suffers in subSaharan Africa. Since 1945, supranational organizations have been founded in part to address inequality between the developed and less developed countries. The **UN** has sponsored many organizations such as the **World Bank** and the **World Trade Organization** as well as research into the **north–south divide** by the **Brandt Commission** to heighten awareness of the issues surrounding globalization and to advocate solutions. While **interdependency theory** speculates that globalization can have a positive effect on closing the gap between the First and Third Worlds, other solutions to halt rising inequality and **Third World debt**, such as the **fair trade** movement and **Jubilee 2000**, have increased in grass-roots popularity. ► **Industrialization; Slavery**

---

Secretariat for Christian Professional Organizations was set up, which, after several changes, in 1923 became the General Christian Labour League (*Algemeen Christelijk Vakverbond*; *Confédération des Syndicats Chrétiens*). The importance of heavy industry to the Belgian economy meant that the more radical socialist Belgian trade unions always had a strong political influence, albeit sometimes rather negative, eg in the strikes of the 1880s; in the 20c both branches became integrated into Belgian political culture and the power-sharing mechanism of Belgian society.

**Trade Unions** (Netherlands)
Due to late industrialization, the trade union movement was slow to achieve strength in the Netherlands; it has always been characterized by ideological fragmentation (**VERZUILING**) into socialist, Calvinist, Catholic and liberal/neutral organizations. The first unions were found in the skilled trades in Amsterdam in the 1860s; in 1871 the General Netherlands Workers' League (*Algemeen Nederlandsch Werkliedenverbond*, ANWV) was set up as the first nationwide organization. Mainly out of fear of socialism, in 1877 the Calvinists set up *Patrimonium* as their national umbrella for workers, which in 1909 gave way to the Christian National Labour League (*Christelijk Nationaal Vakverbond*, CNV); the Roman Catholics were much slower and did not achieve a proper workers' national organization until the 1920s, which in 1963 became the Netherlands Catholic Labour League (*Nederlands Katholieke Vakverbond*, NKV). The socialists set up a National La-

bour Secretariat in 1893, which in 1905 led into the Netherlands League of Trade Unions (*Nederlandse Verbond van Vakverenigingen*, NVV). There was also a neutral league, the 'General' (*Algemeen Nederlands Vakverbond*, NVC, 1919), but it had limited influence. In 1975 the socialists and Catholics merged into the Federative Netherlands Labour Movement (*Federatie Nederlands Vakbeweging*, FNV). Dutch trade unionists in the 20c and early 21c have had close relations with their political parties and have often sent their leaders into parliament; by means of the consultative system within *Verzuiling* they are very well represented in policy-making, for example in the Social and Economic Council (SER).

**Trafalgar, Battle of** (21 Oct 1805)
The most famous naval engagement of the **NAPOLEONIC WARS**, which destroyed **NAPOLEON I**'s hopes of invading England and established British naval supremacy for a century. Fought off Cape Trafalgar, Spain, between the British and Franco-Spanish fleets, the British triumph was marred by the death of **NELSON** at the moment of victory.

**Tragic Week, The** (July 1909)
Spanish popular protest. The Tragic Week (*La Semana Trágica*) took place when a public demonstration in Barcelona against the conscription of soldiers for the war in Morocco developed into a violent popular protest with the widespread burning of churches and convents. This was largely a spontaneous backlash against the oppressive and anti-regionalist policies of the monarchy (with the Church being seized

on as the most visible manifestation of the ancien régime), though the inflammatory anticlerical propaganda of the **RADICAL REPUBLICAN PARTY** had done much to create the volatile climate of opinion. The Tragic Week was a turning-point in the history of modern Spain because it brought the Republican and Socialist movements together, which eventually culminated in the establishment of the Second Republic in 1931. ► **REPUBLIC, SECOND** (Spain)

**Trail of Tears** (1838–9)
An obligatory 800-mi/1,290-km mid-winter migration undertaken by the **CHEROKEE** and other tribes of the eastern USA who were displaced by white settlers, particularly after gold was discovered on their land. They were removed by US troops and forced to move west to unsettled **INDIAN TERRITORY** in Oklahoma. Around 4,000 are thought to have died from exhaustion, starvation and exposure during the march.

**transportation**
Sentence of banishment from England for those convicted of certain offences, introduced in 1597. Increasingly large numbers of English convicts were shipped to North America in the 17c and 18c, but the practice was ended by the **AMERICAN REVOLUTION**. As a result, the British government turned their attention to Australia; 162,000 convicts (137,000 males and 25,000 females) were transported to Australia from 1788 to 1868, mainly to New South Wales (1788–1840), Van Diemen's Land (1803–52) and Western Australia (1850–68). Most of the convicts were young, poorly educated urban-dwellers convicted of some form of theft. In the early years of settlement, convict labour was used on public works; subsequently the typical fate of most convicts was assignment to private service. ► **PENAL SETTLEMENTS**; **TICKET OF LEAVE**

**Transylvania**
A former province of northern and central Romania, separated from **MOLDAVIA AND WALLACHIA** by the Carpathian Mountains Transylvania was a principality that became part of the Austro-Hungarian Empire and was incorporated into Romania in 1918. It was part of the region ceded to Hungary by **HITLER** in **WORLD WAR II**.

**trasformismo**
The term applied to the Italian political practice of forming parliamentary alliances, almost regardless of political ideology, in order to guarantee a government majority. The origins of *trasformismo* can be traced back to the **CONNUBIO** and to some extent it exists even today; however, it reached its pinnacle in the late 19c governments of Agostino **DEPRETIS**. Because coalitions were not based on ideological considerations, trasformismo usually demanded extensive use of patronage and even blatant corruption to function effectively; it discredited the parliamentary system and led to a blurring of ideological distinction.

**treaty ports**
The ports opened by China during the 19c as a result of unequal treaties with the West. The first five (Canton, Amoy (Xiamen), Fuzhou, Ningbo and Shanghai) were opened by the Treaty of **NANJING** (1842) and by the end of the 19c there were over 50 treaty ports. Situated along China's coast and inland on major rivers, the treaty ports were places in which foreigners could reside, trade, and (after 1895) establish manufacturing enterprises whose goods were not subject to Chinese taxation. Foreigners enjoyed the privilege of extraterritoriality. In a number of treaty ports (eg Shanghai) foreign powers also leased land (known as concession areas) where they exercised legal jurisdiction and collected taxes. Condemned as bastions of foreign privilege by a growing Chinese anti-imperialist movement from the 1920s on, the treaty ports came to an end when the unequal treaties were formally abolished in 1943.

**Trenchard, Hugh Montague Trenchard, 1st Viscount** (1873–1956)
British marshal of the RAF. He joined the army in 1893, served in India, South Africa and West Africa, and developed an interest in aviation. He commanded the Royal Flying Corps in **WORLD WAR I**, helped to establish the RAF (1918), and became the first Chief of Air Staff (1918–29). As Commissioner of the London Metropolitan Police (1931–5), he founded the police college at Hendon. He became a baron in 1930 and a viscount in 1936.

**Trent, Council of** (1545–63)
A series of councils of the Roman Catholic Church, held at Trent, Italy. The Emperor **CHARLES V** had long advocated the convocation of such a council as a means of restoring the unity of the Church which the **REFORMATION** had broken. The popes tended to prevaricate because of the potential threat that a council posed to papal supremacy. After some efforts at compromise with Protestant doctrine, Jesuit influence helped to secure a powerful restatement of traditional dogma which included an emphatic reassertion of papal authority. The clarification on doctrinal matters was to form the ideological spearhead of the **COUNTER-REFORMATION**.

**Trent Affair** (1861)
An incident between the USA and Britain during the **AMERICAN CIVIL WAR**, in which the USS *San Jacinto* forcibly removed two officials of the Confederate states from the British ship *Trent* while in international waters. The issue provoked considerable British anger until the Confederate officials were released by the US Secretary of State.

**Treuga Dei**
During the early Middle Ages private wars and feuds were almost unrestricted. The reforming church in France at the end of the 10c introduced the *pax dei*, which compelled warriors to respect the rights and persons of non-combatants. The *Treuga Dei* (or 'truce of God') was a development of this, forbidding private warfare from Wednesday evening until the following Monday and during Lent. This was later extended to cover other seasons. The Salian Emperors were instrumental in trying to implement it in Germany. ► **LANDFRIEDE**; **SALIANS**

**Treurnicht, Andries Petrus** (1921–93)
South African politician. He studied at the universities of Cape Town and Stellenbosch and was a minister in the Dutch Reformed Church from 1946 until his election as a **NATIONAL PARTY** representative in 1971. Elected Transvaal provincial leader in 1978, he

held several cabinet posts under P W **BOTHA**, gaining a reputation as an unreconstructed supporter of **APARTHEID**. He opposed even Botha's partial liberalization of the regime and was forced to leave the party with 15 colleagues in 1982. He formed a new party, the **CONSERVATIVE PARTY OF SOUTH AFRICA**, which pressed for a return to traditional apartheid values and effective partitioning of the country. The party gained seats and votes, especially from among less well-off Afrikaners, over the next decade and took over from the moderate Progressive Federal Party as the official opposition within parliament.

**Triads ▶ HEAVEN AND EARTH SOCIETY**

### trialism
First formulated in 1894 by Josip Frank's Pure Party of Right, a breakaway group from **STARČEVIĆ**'s Party of Right, the proponents of trialism sought the creation within the Habsburg Empire of a Croatian state which would embrace all the Habsburg South Slavic possessions and would possess all the prerogatives that the Hungarians enjoyed under dualism. Frank and his followers hoped that Vienna would accept a trialist solution in order to secure the Croats as allies against the Hungarians. ▶ **KHUEN-HÉDERVÁRY, KÁROLY; NAGODBA**

### Trianon, Treaty of (1920)
The treaty agreed between the new state of Hungary and the Allies of **WORLD WAR I**, which reduced the territory of Hungary to about a third of its pre-war size. Romania received almost all that it had hoped to gain by entering the war, acquiring Transylvania with its mixed Romanian and Magyar population, Bessarabia, Crişana and **BUKOVINA** with part of the Banat, the rest of which was ceded to the Kingdom of Serbs, Croats and Slovenes (later Yugoslavia). Czechoslovakia also benefited from the treaty, gaining areas of mixed Czech and Magyar population.

### Tribur, Princes' Meeting at (1076)
In the face of the intensifying power struggle between **HENRY IV** and the German princes and the papacy, the king entered into negotiations with the princes, who had assembled with the papal legates at Tribur, in an attempt to stem his own increasing loss of support and in the hope of splitting the alliance between princes and papacy, thus preventing the election of an anti-king. After Henry had made concessions, including a promise to obey the pope, the princes agreed to recognize him as king, but only if his ban of excommunication was lifted within a year. The king responded with a submission to the pope at **CANOSSA** (1077), where he was absolved and his authority over the princes theoretically restored.

### Triennial Acts (1641, 1664 and 1694)
The collective name given to legislation passed requiring Parliament to assemble at least once every three years, as a reaction to the personal rule of **CHARLES I**. The 1694 Act also limited the life of each parliament to three years. ▶ **SEPTENNIAL ACT**

### Trieste, Free Territory of
This Adriatic port, at the north-west junction of the Istrian Peninsula, was promised to Italy in the Treaty of **LONDON** (1915). In the interwar years it was the subject of dispute between Italy and Yugoslavia and,

following **WORLD WAR II**, it was established as the 'Free Territory of Trieste', with the northern zone administered by the USA and Britain and the southern zone under Yugoslav control (1946). In 1954 the status of Trieste was revised and the northern zone was returned to Italy.

### Trikoupis, Spyridon (1788–1873)
Greek politician and writer. He was private secretary to Lord Guilford in the Ionian Islands, studied in Rome, Paris and London, and joined the patriots on the outbreak of the **GREEK WAR OF INDEPENDENCE** (1821). He was thrice Envoy-Extraordinary to London, was Minister of Foreign Affairs and of Public Instruction (1843), Vice-President of the Senate (1844–9), and Envoy-Extraordinary to Paris (1850). His son, Kharilaos (1832–96), was Foreign Minister (1866) and Premier repeatedly from 1875 to 1895.

### Trimble, David (1944– )
Northern Ireland moderate Unionist politician. He was qualified as a barrister, and in 1968 became a law lecturer. In 1975 he was elected as Vanguard Progressive Unionist Party member for South Belfast in the Northern Ireland Convention. He joined the more mainstream Ulster Unionist Party in 1978 and was elected MP for Upper Bann in 1990, becoming UUP party leader in 1995. He took part in the multiparty talks that resulted in the **GOOD FRIDAY AGREEMENT**, becoming the first Ulster Unionist leader to negotiate with **SINN FÉIN**, and shared the 1998 **NOBEL PEACE PRIZE** with the SDLP's John Hume. He was elected to the Northern Ireland Assembly in 1998, becoming First Minister of the devolved government. Although he had persuaded the UUP to accept it, widespread Unionist opposition to the Good Friday Agreement and scepticism about the sincerity of the nationalist parties continued and was strengthened by the lack of progress on IRA weapons decommissioning. He struggled to retain the support of a majority of the UUP Assembly members and faced a number of votes of confidence. He resigned as First Minister in Jul 2001 and was re-elected four months later only with the support of Alliance Party members. Power-sharing was suspended in Oct 2002 following **STORMONTGATE**, ending Trimble's tenure as First Minister. He remained UUP leader, but his party paid for its support of the Agreement when Ian **PAISLEY**'s **DEMOCRATIC UNIONIST PARTY** replaced it as the largest Unionist party in the Assembly in the Nov 2003 elections.

---

**TRINIDAD AND TOBAGO** official name **Republic of Trinidad and Tobago**

A republic comprising the southernmost islands of the Lesser Antilles chain in the south-east Caribbean

Sea, just off the South American mainland. Originally inhabited by Arawak and Carib Indians, the islands were visited by **COLUMBUS** in 1498. Trinidad was settled by Spain in the 16c, raided by the Dutch and French in the 17c, when tobacco and sugar plantations worked by imported African slaves were established, and ceded to Britain in 1802 under the Treaty of **AMIENS**. Tobago became a British colony in 1814. Trinidad and Tobago became a joint British Crown Colony in 1899, an independent member of the **COMMONWEALTH OF NATIONS** in 1962, and a republic in 1976 under the leadership of Eric **WILLIAMS**. ► **ARAWAKS; CARIBS; PEOPLE'S NATIONAL MOVEMENT**

### Tripartite Declaration (May 1950)

This represented an attempt by Britain, France and the USA to limit arms supplies to Israel and the Arab states in the wake of the emergence of the state of Israel, in the hope that this would ensure some stability for the area. Arms supplies were to be conditional on non-aggression, and the signatories to the Declaration undertook to take action both within and outside the framework of the **UN** in cases of frontier violation. Closer French relations with Israel subjected the Declaration to some strain, and with the Soviet arms deal with Gamal Abd al-**NASSER**'s Egypt in 1955 it became a dead letter.

### Triple Alliance (1882)

Following France's annexation of Tunisia, Italy joined the German–Austro-Hungarian **DUAL ALLIANCE** in order to protect her Mediterranean interests against France. The complex provisions of the resulting Triple Alliance protected Germany and Italy from French attack and all partners from unprovoked attack from a fourth party. Austro-Italian rivalries repeatedly threatened to destroy the Alliance and, with the coming of war in 1914, Italy's initial neutrality was followed by a declaration of war on Germany and Austria in 1915. ► **WORLD WAR I**

### Triple Alliance, War of the (1864–70)

A devastating war, fought by Paraguay against the combined forces of Brazil, Argentina and Uruguay (the Triple Alliance), which was provoked by the ambitions of the Paraguayan dictator, Francisco Solano **LÓPEZ**. The eventual victory of the Allies (most of the troops were provided by Brazil) was achieved at the cost of reducing the male population of Paraguay by nine-tenths.

### Triple Entente

A series of agreements between Britain and France (1904) and Britain and Russia (1907) initially to resolve outstanding colonial differences. It aligned Britain to France and Russia, who had concluded a military alliance in 1893–4. In 1914, the Triple Entente became a military alliance.

### Tripolitania

A region of North Africa, lying between Tunis and Cyrenaica; former province of western Libya. It was under Turkish control from the 16c until 1911, under Italian control until 1943, and under British control until 1952.

### Tripolitanian War (1911–12)

The war between Italy and Turkey, in which Italian forces invaded and occupied the Turkish province of **TRIPOLITANIA** (present-day Libya) to gain useful

ports and to prevent an extension of French influence in North Africa. After the declaration of war (Sep 1911), the initial invasion went smoothly but the Italians were surprised to discover that the local Arab population did not welcome them as liberators from Turkish rule. The Italians therefore found themselves fighting not only the Turkish army but also Arab tribesmen. **GIOLITTI**'s response was to try to put pressure on the Turks elsewhere, and in May 1912, 13 Turkish Aegean islands were seized. The outbreak of the Balkan war (Oct 1912) obliged Turkey to concentrate on resisting the threat from Bulgaria, Serbia, Montenegro and Greece, and so peace negotiations were begun with Italy, leading to the surrender of both Tripolitania and neighbouring Cyrenaica. Although the Italians were able to claim a considerable victory, the war brought them little real advantage; the colony was of little economic value and until the early 1930s required a constant and expensive military presence to combat a hostile native population.

### Triune Kingdom

During the 19c, the name given by Croatian nationalists to the kingdom which they hoped to create within the Habsburg Empire and which would consist of the three parts of the medieval Croat kingdom (Croatia, Slavonia and **DALMATIA**) with, according to some, Bosnia and Herzegovina. ► **TRIALISM**

### Trochu, Louis Jules (1815–96)

French soldier. After a distinguished military career in the Crimea and elsewhere, he entered the Ministry of War. However, the unpalatable truths contained in his *l'Armée française en 1867* set the court against him. On 17 Aug 1870 he was made Governor of Paris, and became President of the Government of **NATIONAL DEFENCE** (Sep 1870). Regarded as overcautious and timid, he resigned as Military Governor of Paris in Jan 1871; his functions as President of the Government of National Defence were ended by the election of the National Assembly (Feb 1871). ► **CRIMEAN WAR**

### Troelstra, Pieter Jelles (1860–1930)

Dutch politician. Trained as a lawyer, he disagreed with the anarchist tendencies of **DOMELA NIEUWENHUIS**, and helped set up the Social Democratic Workers' Party (SDAP) in 1894. From 1897 onwards he sat in parliament, and led the socialist group there. Often caught between the extreme left and the moderates, he never held a government post, but managed to keep the Dutch socialists together in their most turbulent period. In 1918 he tried to stage a coup, announcing the revolution in parliament, but support was insufficient and the effort collapsed; he remained an MP until 1925. ► **LABOUR PARTY** (Netherlands)

### Tromp, Cornelis Maartenszoon (1629–91)

Dutch naval commander. The son of Maarten **TROMP**, he shared the glory of Michiel de **RUYTER**'s Four Days' Battle off Dunkirk (1666), and won fame in the battles against the combined English and French fleets on 7 and 14 June 1673. On a visit to England in 1675 he was created baron by **CHARLES II** and was appointed Lieutenant-Governor of the United Provinces (1676).

**Tromp, Maarten Harpertszoon** (1598–1653)
Dutch admiral. In 1639 he defeated a superior Spanish fleet off Gravelines, and won the Battle of the Downs later that year. Knighted by **LOUIS XIII** of France (1640) and by **CHARLES I** of England (1642), he then fought the French pirates based on Dunkirk, while his encounter with Robert **BLAKE** in 1652 started the first of the **ANGLO-DUTCH WARS**. Victorious off Dover, he was defeated by a superior English fleet off Portland, and finally off Terheijde, near Scheveningen, where he was killed. His son, Cornelis (Maartenszoon) **TROMP**, was a Lieutenant-Admiral in the later **ANGLO-DUTCH WARS**.

**Tron, Andrea** (1712–85)
Venetian nobleman, diplomat and politician. He was perhaps the outstanding political figure of the 18c Venetian Republic. Known as 'el paron' for the way he dominated the Republic's councils, he was at various times ambassador to Vienna, Paris and Rome and was one of that minority of far-sighted patricians who recognized the need for wide-ranging reform of the Venetian state.

**Trotsky, Leon**, alias of **Lev Davidovich Bronstein** (1879–1940)
Russian revolutionary. Educated in Odessa, in 1898 he was arrested as a Marxist and exiled to Siberia. He escaped in 1902, joined **LENIN** in London, and in the abortive **REVOLUTION OF 1905** was President of the St Petersburg Soviet. He then worked as a revolutionary journalist in the West, returning to Russia in 1917, when he joined the **BOLSHEVIKS** and played a major role in the **OCTOBER REVOLUTION**. In the **RUSSIAN CIVIL WAR** he was Commissar for War, and created the **RED ARMY**. After Lenin's death (1924) his influence began to decline; he was ousted from the Party by **STALIN**, who opposed his theory of 'permanent revolution', exiled to Central Asia (1927), and expelled from the USSR (1929). He continued to agitate as an exile, and was sentenced to death in absentia by a Soviet court in 1937. He finally found asylum in Mexico, where he was assassinated by one of Stalin's agents. ► **RUSSIAN REVOLUTION**; **TROTSKYISM**

**Trotskyism**
A development of Marxist thought by Leon **TROTSKY**. Essentially a theory of permanent revolution, Trotskyism stressed the internationalism of **SOCIALISM**, avoided coexistence, and encouraged revolutionary movements abroad; this conflicted with **STALIN**'s ideas of '**SOCIALISM IN ONE COUNTRY**'. Trotskyism has since inspired other extreme left-wing revolutionary movements but they are factionally divided, and have little support outside some Western capitalist states. ► **COMMUNISM**; **MARXISM–LENINISM**; **STALINISM**

**Trucial States** ► **UNITED ARAB EMIRATES**

**Trudeau, Pierre Elliott** (1919–2000)
Canadian politician. Educated at Montreal, Harvard and London, he became a lawyer, helped to found the political magazine Cité Libre (1950), and was Professor of Law at the University of Montreal (1961–5). Elected a Liberal MP in 1965, he became Minister of Justice (1967) and an outspoken critic of Québécois **SÉPARATISME**. His terms of office as Prime Minister (1968–79 and 1980–4) saw the **OCTOBER CRISIS** (1970) in Quebec, the introduction of the Official Languages Act, federalist victory during the Quebec Referendum (1980), and the introduction of the **CONSTITUTION ACT OF 1982**. He resigned as leader of the **LIBERAL PARTY** and from public life in 1984.

**Trujillo (Molina), Rafael Leonidas** (1891–1961)
Dominican Republic dictator. He was dictator of the Dominican Republic from 1930 until his assassination in Santo Domingo, a city he had renamed Ciudad Trujillo. Born in San Cristóbal, Dominican Republic, he rose to prominence as commander of the police. His regime was both highly repressive and highly corrupt.

**Truman, Harry S** (1884–1972)
US politician and 33rd President. He fought in **WORLD WAR I**, was a presiding judge in the Jackson County Court in Missouri (1926–34), was elected to the **SENATE** as a Democrat in 1934 and became chairman of a Senate committee investigating defence spending. He became Vice-President (1944) and, on Franklin D **ROOSEVELT**'s death (Apr 1945), President. He was re-elected in 1948 in a surprise victory over Thomas E **DEWEY**. As President (1945–53) he ordered the dropping of the first atomic bomb on Japan in Aug 1945, which led to Japan's surrender. Following **WORLD WAR II**, he established a '**CONTAINMENT**' policy against the USSR, developed the **MARSHALL PLAN** to rebuild Europe and created **NATO** (1949). He authorized the sending of US troops to South Korea in 1950, and promoted the Four-Point Programme that gave military and economic aid to countries threatened by communist interference. He established the **CIA** (1947) and ordered the **BERLIN AIRLIFT** (1948–9). At home, he introduced his '**FAIR DEAL**' programme of economic reform. ► **DEMOCRATIC PARTY**

**Truman Doctrine** (1947)
A post-war foreign policy under which the USA promised military and economic aid to countries threatened by communism, and for which purpose US$400 million was appropriated by **CONGRESS**. It was announced by President Harry S **TRUMAN** during the early stages of the **COLD WAR** in response to the perceived threat of communist revolt faced by Greece, and to that of Soviet expansion in the Mediterranean region which was troubling Turkey.

**Trumbić, Ante** (1864–1938)
Croatian politician. A proponent of **TRIALISM**, with Frano **SUPILO** he founded the Croatian Social Democrat Party in 1895. During **WORLD WAR I** he was a founder and President of the **YUGOSLAV COMMITTEE**, helping to formulate the Declaration of Corfu in which the Committee and the Serbian government agreed to cooperate in establishing a South Slav state (July 1917). He was Minister for Foreign Affairs in the post-1918 Provisional Government but became disillusioned with the Serb nationalist programme of Nikola **PAŠIĆ** and **ALEXANDER I** and retired from political life in 1921.

**Trusteeship**
A system developed by the **UN** after 1945 for the international supervision of colonial territories that had been removed from the German and Ottoman empires at the end of **WORLD WAR I**. These territories

had been supervised originally under the **MANDATES** commission of the **LEAGUE OF NATIONS**, and mandates in the Middle East, Africa and the South Pacific were held by Britain, France, South Africa, Australia and New Zealand. Only South Africa refused to hand over South West Africa (now **NAMIBIA**) to the UN, leading to the long-running dispute over the independence of that territory. The British **PALESTINE** mandate became the setting for Arab/Jewish conflict and the British were forced to hand it over to the UN in 1948. The trusteeship system, in internationalizing key areas of colonial rule, has been seen as pressing forward decolonization.

**Truth, Sojourner**, originally **Isabella Van Wagener** (c.1797–1883)
US abolitionist. Born into **SLAVERY** in New York State, she escaped from her master in 1827 and settled in New York City, where she involved herself in the religious enthusiasms of the day until 1843, when she became a travelling preacher. She joined the abolitionist movement and became an effective anti-slavery speaker. She eventually settled in Battle Creek, Michigan, but remained active after the Civil War in the causes of freed slaves and also of **WOMEN'S RIGHTS**. ► **ABOLITIONISM**

**Ts'ai Ch'ang** ► CAI CHANG

**Tsai T'ien** ► ZAI TIAN

**Ts'ai Yuan-p'ei** ► CAI YUANPEI

**Tsankov, Alexander** (1879–1959)
Bulgarian politician. He became Prime Minister in 1923 after the military coup which overthrew **STAMBOLISKI**. Drawing his support from a coalition of parties called the Democratic Concord, his government tried to eliminate **VMRO** and the Bulgarian Communist Party. In Jan 1926 he was replaced by Andrei Liapchev.

**Tseng Kuo-fan** ► ZENG GUOFAN

**Tshombe, Moïse Kapenda** (1919–69)
Congolese politician. Educated in mission schools, he was a businessman who helped to found the *Confederation des Associations du Katanga* in 1957. When Belgium granted the Congo independence in 1960, he declared the copper-rich province of Katanga independent and became its President. On the request of **LUMUMBA**, **UN** troops were called in to reintegrate the province and Tshombe was forced into exile in 1963; he returned again in 1964, supported by some of the mining interests and white settlers of Katanga. Forced into exile again after **MOBUTU**'s 1966 coup, Tshombe was kidnapped in 1967 and taken to Algeria, where he died. A talented conservative, he became the representation of neo-colonialism's ugly face in the mythology of African nationalism throughout the continent.

**Tsiranana, Philibert** (1912–78)
Madagascar politician. Educated on the island and in France, he organized the Social Democratic Party, on whose ticket he was elected a member of the Representative Assembly in 1956, as well as the French National Assembly in 1957. He was Deputy President of Madagascar in 1958 and President in the following year. He remained in the post until he was overthrown in a military coup in 1972.

**Tsouderos, Emmanuel** (1882–1956)
Greek politician. A banker from Crete, he was a republican and follower of Eleuthérios **VENIZÉLOS**. In Apr 1940, after the suicide of Alexander Koryzis, he became Prime Minister and fled with King **GEORGE II** after Greece's surrender to Germany. He continued as Prime Minister in the Greek government-in-exile but, following the mutinies in the Greek army and navy in Egypt (Apr 1944), he was succeeded briefly by Sofoklis **VENIZÉLOS** and then by George **PAPANDREOU**.

**Tsushima, Battle of** (27 May 1905)
Admiral Togo's crushing victory over the Russian Baltic fleet, in the Tsushima Straits, during the **RUSSO-JAPANESE WAR**. It is remarkable for being the only instance in world history of a decisive engagement between all-gun **IRONCLAD** ships. The battle gave the Japanese naval supremacy and dashed Russian hopes of achieving a land victory.

**Tuan Ch'i-jui** ► DUAN QIRUI

**Tubman, Harriet** (c.1820–1913)
US abolitionist. She escaped from **SLAVERY** in Maryland (1849), and from then until the **AMERICAN CIVIL WAR** she was active on the slave escape route (the **UNDERGROUND RAILROAD**), making a number of dangerous trips into the South. She acquired fame among abolitionists, and counselled John **BROWN** before his attempt to launch a slave insurrection in 1859. During the Civil War she was a Northern spy and scout, but was denied a federal pension until 1897. ► **ABOLITIONISM**

**Tubman, William Vacanarat Shadrach** (1895–1971)
Liberian politician. Educated in a Methodist seminary, he was a teacher, lawyer and Methodist preacher. Tubman was elected for the True Whig Party, which protected the interests of the Americo-Liberian élite, and became a member of the Liberian Senate in 1922. In 1937 he was appointed Deputy President of the Supreme Court and, in 1944, was chosen as President of Liberia, a post he retained until his death.

**Tudeh**
The Communist Party of Iran, founded in 1920. It had the varying fortunes to be expected of a communist party in a primarily Islamic state and despite its temporary demise in 1930, it had its heyday with the Soviet intervention in northern Iran during **WORLD WAR II**. It helped, with the USSR, in the founding of the Kurdish Republic of Mahabad which lasted about a year, but was again outlawed in 1946. Surfacing yet again to support the left-wing leader **MOSADDEQ** in the early 1950s, the Tudeh Party was once more banned, this time by Shah Mohammad Reza **PAHLAVI**.

**Tudjman, Franjo** (1922–99)
Croatian politician and historian. He served in the partisan army led by **TITO** and in 1945 became the youngest general in the Yugoslav Federal Army. In 1972 he was imprisoned during the purge of the Croatian nationalist movement and in 1981 was again sentenced to three years' imprisonment in the first major political trial since Tito's death. A Professor of Modern History at the Faculty of Political Science at Zagreb, he became Chairman of the History of the Workers' Movement of Croatia. Following

the elections in Apr 1990, as leader of the right-wing Croatian Democratic Union, he became President of Croatia. He declared the Republic of Croatia's independence from the Yugoslav Federation (25 June 1991), but the republic soon found itself engaged in a brutal war against the Yugoslav Federal Army and Serb forces, which by Jan 1992 occupied virtually all of the ethnic Serb areas in Croatia (these had been recaptured by 1996). He was re-elected President in Sep 1992 and Aug 1997, and died in office after a short illness.

## Tudor, House of

A North Wales gentry family, one of whose scions married a Plantagenet in the early 15c. Elevated to the peerage in the mid-15c, they ruled England from 1485 to 1603. The dynasty began when Henry (later **HENRY VII**), 2nd Earl of Richmond and son of Margaret Beaufort (a Lancastrian claimant to the crown), overthrew **RICHARD III** in 1485. It ended with the death of **ELIZABETH I** in 1603. ► **EDWARD VI**; **HENRY VIII**; **MARY I**; **PLANTAGENET DYNASTY**

### HOUSE OF TUDOR

| Regnal Dates | Name |
|---|---|
| 1485/1509 | Henry VII |
| 1509/47 | Henry VIII |
| 1547/53 | Edward VI |
| 1553/8 | Mary I |
| 1558/1603 | Elizabeth I |

## Tu Duc (1829–83)

Emperor of Vietnam (1847/83). His reign saw the establishment of French rule over the whole of Vietnam. These years were marked by frequent outbreaks of internal rebellion and by a series of severe natural disasters. Allied with his own profoundly pessimistic and diffident nature, these circumstances fatally handicapped the Vietnamese court as it sought to come to terms with French commercial, religious and territorial ambitions from the late 1850s. By treaties concluded in 1862 and 1874 against a background of severe internal unrest, Tu Duc was forced into major concessions to France. His death provoked a major succession crisis, during which the French finally achieved complete domination over Vietnam.

## Tughlaq Dynasty

Indian dynasty, which came to power in Delhi in 1320 when Ghiyas ud-Din Tughlaq raised the banner of revolt against the much-weakened **KHALJIS** and defeated Khusrau. Ghiyas ud-Din Tughlaq established a new dynasty which ruled until 1412. The Tughlaqs provided three competent rulers: Ghiyas ud-Din, his son, **MUHAMMAD BIN TUGHLAQ** (1324/51), and his nephew, **FIRUZ SHAH TUGHLAQ** (1351/88). The first two of these rulers ruled over an empire that comprised almost the entire subcontinent; the empire of Firuz was smaller but still almost as large as that of **ALA AL-DIN KHALJI**. After Firuz's death, the **DELHI SULTANATE** disintegrated and north India was divided into a series of small states. Although the Tughlaqs continued to rule until 1412, the invasion of Delhi by **TIMUR** in 1398 may be said to mark the end of their empire.

## Tughrul Beg, Muhammad (c.990–1063)

He was the grandson of Seljuk, a leader of Ghuzz tribesmen in central Asia from whom the Great **SELJUKS** derive their name. Tughrul (or Toghril) moved westwards through Khurasan and Persia, and in 1055 was welcomed by the 'Abbasid caliph al-Qa'im, particularly because his arrival put an end to Buyid control of Baghdad and the central Islamic lands (a matter of some embarrassment to the (Sunni) caliph since the **BUYIDS** were Shiite). There was a hiccup in that during a temporary absence of Tughrul, the general al-Basasiri, previously in the Buyid camp but now a Fatimid supporter, re-emerged in Baghdad and forced the caliph to recognize the suzerainty of the Fatimid al-Mustansir in Cairo. This was however short-lived for with the return of Tughrul, Sunni control of Baghdad was restored. Tughrul was succeeded on his death by his nephew, **ALP ARSLAN**.

## Tuka, Vojtech (1880–1946)

Slovak politician. Of Magyar parentage and pro-Hungarian orientation, he was a member of **HLINKA'S** Slovak Populist Party during the 1920s and encouraged it to be more assertive in demanding Slovak autonomy. But in 1929 he was proved to be a Hungarian agent and was imprisoned, to the serious embarrassment of Hlinka and the whole party. In 1939 he reappeared as Deputy Prime Minister and then as Prime Minister and Foreign Minister in the puppet government of **TISO**. In 1946 he was condemned to death.

## Tukhachevsky, Mikhail Nikolaevich (1893–1937)

Soviet military leader. From 1926 he was Chief of Staff of the **RED ARMY**, which he was influential in transforming from a peasant army into a modern, mechanized force. His vigour and independence made him suspect to **STALIN**, and in 1937 he was executed, a victim of the great purge that decimated the Red Army's officer corps.

## Tulip Mania (1634–7)

A speculation bubble on the markets of the Dutch Republic; highly advanced financial institutions and an excess of capital led to spiralling prices for tulip bulbs, for which sometimes gigantic sums of money changed hands, based on the estimated resale price rather than on any intrinsic value. The bubble burst in 1637, ruining many throughout Dutch society.

## Tulsidas (1532–1623)

Indian poet. His most famous work is the *Ramcharitmanas*, which is the *Ramayana* retold in a simple and popular form. Pleading for a modified **CASTE** system based not on birth but on individual qualities, Tulsidas was essentially a humanistic poet, who upheld family ideals and complete devotion to the Hindu god Rama as a way of salvation open to all, irrespective of caste. He is considered a very prominent poet from the Bhakti Movement, whose religious ideas have had a profound and egalitarian effect on Indian social development.

## Tunglin Movement ► DONGLIN MOVEMENT

## TUNISIA official name Republic of Tunisia

A north African republic, bounded to the west by Algeria; to the south-east by Libya; and to the northeast and north by the Mediterranean Sea. Ruled at various times by Phoenicians, Carthaginians,

Romans, Byzantines, Arabs, Spanish and Turks due to its situation at the hub of the Mediterranean, it became a French protectorate in 1883 and gained independence in 1956. That year the monarchy was abolished and in 1957 a republic was declared, led by President Habib **BOURGUIBA**. The government's refusal to meet demands for the legalization of other political parties in the 1970s led to serious unrest, and in 1987 Bourguiba was deposed by his Prime Minister, General **BEN ALI**, who won unopposed elections in 1989 and 1994. Following the introduction of multiparty politics in 1994, President Ben Ali was re-elected in 1999 and 2004.

**Tupac Amarú**, assumed name from 1771 of **José Gabriel Condorcanqui** (c.1742–1781)
Peruvian Indian revolutionary. A *cacique* ('hereditary chief') in the Tinta region of southern Peru, he adopted the name of the last Inca ruler, of whom he was a maternal descendent, and was recognized by the Spanish as the Incas' legal heir. In 1780 he led the Peruvian peasants in a rebellion against Spanish rule and soon controlled large parts of Peru, Bolivia and Argentina, but the following year he was captured, tortured and executed. The **TUPAMAROS** of Uruguay are named after him.

**Tupamaros**
Uruguayan urban guerrillas belonging to the *Movimiento de Liberación Nacional* ('National Liberation Movement'). The movement was founded by Raúl Sendic, a labour organizer, in 1963 and was named after the 18c Peruvian Indian rebel **TUPAC AMARÚ**. The organization was suppressed by the military-controlled government of 1972–85, and since then has been re-created as a legitimate political party.

**Tupolev, Andrei Nikolaevich** (1888–1972)
Soviet military and civilian aircraft designer. The son of a lawyer and product of Moscow Higher Technical School, he was already working in a Moscow aircraft factory in the pre-revolutionary period. In the 1920s and 1930s he designed several bombers of world class, and even when imprisoned on false accusations of treason in 1937 and sent to the Gulag in 1939, he continued designing aircraft and was therefore released in 1943. Subsequently he worked on everything down to the supersonic passenger plane,

becoming the best-known international name in the business and keeping the Soviet air force at least on a par with that of the USA.

**Tupper, Charles** (1821–1915)
Canadian politician and diplomat. As Nova Scotia's Premier (1864–7), his was the primary responsibility for persuading it to join the confederation; but Joseph **HOWE**'s opposition had been so effective that he delayed until John A **MACDONALD** persuaded the imperial government to apply direct pressure, and terms more favourable to Nova Scotia had been included. He entered Macdonald's administration in 1870 and again in 1878. In 1884 he became High Commissioner in London and in 1896 Secretary of State in Mackenzie Bowell's short-lived government. In the same year he himself became Premier for ten weeks and committed the havering Conservative Party to remedial legislation in the controversy over the **MANITOBA SCHOOLS ACT**. The bill was talked out, however, and after the Liberals won the election of 1896, he led the Conservative opposition until 1900.

**Turati, Filippo** (1857–1932)
Italian politician. In 1892 he helped to found the party that three years later was to become the Italian Socialist Party (PSI). He was elected deputy in 1896 and remained one until he fled the country in 1926. In 1898 he was condemned to 12 years' imprisonment for his part in protests in Milan, but was released the following year. He refused to participate in **GIOLITTI**'s governments, but was always on the moderate wing of the socialist movement. He opposed the **TRIPOLITANIAN WAR** and Italian intervention in 1915. In the aftermath of **WORLD WAR I** and the Bolshevik Revolution, Turati found it hard to check the increasing radicalism of the PSI; he left the party when it joined the Third International (1919) and founded the Socialist Unity Party. With the assertion of fascist power, he fled Italy for France, where he died.

**Turenne, Henri de la Tour d'Auvergne, Viscount of** (1611–75)
French marshal. The grandson of **WILLIAM I, THE SILENT**, in the **THIRTY YEARS' WAR** he fought with distinction for the armies of the Protestant alliance. He captured Breisach (1638) and Turin (1640), and for the capture of Roussillon from the Spaniards (1642) was made Marshal of France (1643). In the civil wars of the **FRONDE**, he joined the *frondeurs* at first, but then switched sides; his campaigning (1652–3) saved the young King **LOUIS XIV** and **MAZARIN**'s government. In the Franco-Spanish war he conquered much of the Spanish Netherlands after defeating Louis II of Bourbon, Prince of **CONDÉ** at the Battle of the Dunes (1658). He won lasting fame for his campaigns in the United Provinces during the Dutch War (1672–5), but advancing along the Rhine he was killed at Sasbach.

**Turgot, Anne Robert Jacques** (1727–81)
French economist and politician. He became a magistrate in the **PARLEMENT** of Paris and was then promoted to Intendant at Limoges (1761–74), where he carried out reforms. Here he published his best-known work, *Réflexions sur la formation et la distribution des richesses* (1766, Eng trans *Reflections on the*

*Formation and Distribution of Wealth*). Appointed Controller-General of Finance by **LOUIS XVI** (1774), he embarked on a comprehensive scheme of national economic reform, but the opposition of the privileged classes to his Six Edicts led to his overthrow (1776), and he died forgotten, his reforms abandoned.

---

**TURKEY** official name **Republic of Turkey**

A republic lying partly in Europe and partly in Asia. The western area (Thrace) is bounded to the west by the Aegean Sea and Greece, and to the north by Bulgaria and the Black Sea; the eastern area (Anatolia) is bounded to the east by Georgia, Armenia, Azerbaijan and Iran, and to the south by Iraq, Syria and the Mediterranean Sea. Modern Turkey developed out of the **OTTOMAN EMPIRE** and includes the area known as Asia Minor. It was formerly part of the empire of Alexander III, the Great, and of the **BYZANTINE EMPIRE**. In the 13c, the Seljuk Sultanate was replaced by the Ottoman Sultanate in north-west Asia Minor. The Turkish invasion of Europe began with the Balkans in 1375, and in 1453 Constantinople fell to the Turks. The empire was at its peak in the 16c under **SÜLEYMAN I, THE MAGNIFICENT**, but in the 17c the Turks were pressed back by Russian and Austrian armies. In the 19c Turkey was regarded by Britain as a bulwark against Russian expansion but, following alleged Armenian massacres, Britain abandoned its support of Turkey. The **YOUNG TURKS** seized power in 1908 and became embroiled in the **BALKAN WARS** (1912–13). During **WORLD WAR I** Turkey allied with Germany. The Republic of Turkey was founded in 1923, led by Kemal **ATATÜRK**, who introduced a policy of westernization and economic development. Turkey was neutral throughout most of **WORLD WAR II**, before siding with the Allies, and its neutralist policy was abandoned when it joined **NATO** in 1952. There were military coups in 1960 and 1980. Relations with Greece were strained, leading to an invasion of Cyprus in 1974; this in turn strained relations with the Allies and resulted in a four-year US trade embargo. From the 1980s the south-east of Turkey suffered fierce fighting between government forces and the separatist PKK (Kurdish Workers' Party), who want to establish an independent Kurdistan for Turkey's 13 million **KURDS**; the PKK renounced violence in 2004 but the peace is fragile. Süleyman **DEMIREL** was made President of Turkey in 1993, the year Turkey's first woman Prime Minister, Tansu **ÇILLER**, took office; there have been several heads of government since Çiller departed in 1996. Since becoming a candidate for entry into the **EU** in 1999, Turkey has introduced human and civil rights reforms to strengthen its case for membership.

**Turkish Wars** (1662–4 and 1683–9)
The campaigns undertaken by Emperor **LEOPOLD I**

(1658/1705) to drive the Turks from Hungary. The first ended with an Austrian victory at St Gothard and the Peace of Vasvár (1664). In the second, persecution of Hungarian Protestants by the Emperor led them to ally with the Turks who marched, for the last time, on Vienna itself (1683). The Turkish Siege of **VIENNA** was lifted by **JOHN III SOBIESKI** on 12 Sep 1683. A string of Turkish defeats followed: Párkány (1683), Esztergom (1685), the fall of Budapest (1686), Mohács and the fall of Belgrade (1688), **SLANKAMEN** (1691) and Zenta (1697). The Treaty of **KARLOWITZ** (1699) ended the wars with substantial Turkish concessions.

**Turkmanchai, Treaty of** (Feb 1828)
The treaty under which Russia acquired eastern Armenia from the Persian Empire. Russian expansion southwards continued from **ALEXANDER I**'s reign into **NICHOLAS I**'s, and following almost three years of fighting the foundations were laid for control of the Caucasus. This kind of warfare also became almost standard training for the Russian army.

---

**TURKMENISTAN** official name **Republic of Turkmenistan**

A republic in south-west Middle Asia, bounded to the north by Kazakhstan and Uzbekistan; to the south by Iran and Afghanistan; and to the west by the Caspian Sea. About 80 per cent of the country is occupied by the Kara Kum Desert; the people live mainly around oases. Originally occupied by various tribes who were unified under the Russians in 1869, Turkmenistan was proclaimed a Soviet Socialist Republic in 1924. In 1991 it gained its independence under President Saparmurad Niyazov and became a member of the **CIS** (Commonwealth of Independent States). President Niyazov's regime has become increasingly autocratic, using authoritarianism and harrassment to suppress political opposition and freedom of the media, and in 1999 he became in effect president for life. The former Communist Party, renamed the Democratic Party, is the only legal party.

**Turner, Nat** (1800–31)
US slave insurrectionary. He learned to read, and in 1831 made plans for a slave uprising. He succeeded in killing his master's family and some 50 other whites. But as many as 100 slaves were killed and the revolt quickly collapsed. Captured after six weeks in hiding, he was brought to trial and hanged at Jerusalem, Virginia.

**Turner's Rebellion** (1831)
A slave uprising, the most famous in US history, in Southampton County, Virginia. Convinced by visions of a divine call to lead his people to freedom, the slave preacher Nat **TURNER** and a handful of followers led

75 slaves in a revolt that resulted in the deaths of 60 whites. The rebellion, which was put down by the militia at the cost of about 100 slaves' lives, did much to fuel anti-**ABOLITIONISM** in the South.

**Turner thesis** ►— FRONTIER THESIS

**Tutu, Desmond Mpilo** (1931– )
South African cleric. Educated in mission schools and at Pretoria Bantu Normal College, he studied at St Peter's Theological College and King's College, London. He was ordained a deacon in the Anglican Church in 1960 and held a variety of church positions in England, South Africa and Lesotho, including lecturing at the Federal Theological Seminary in Cape Province (1967–9), the University of Botswana, Lesotho and Swaziland (1970–2). He returned from England to South Africa in 1975 as Dean of Johannesburg, from where he went to be Bishop of Lesotho. As Secretary-General of the South African Council of Churches from 1978 to 1985, he spoke out strongly from the relative safety of his church position against the extremes of **APARTHEID** and was awarded the **NOBEL PEACE PRIZE** in 1984. Elected Bishop of Johannesburg (1984–6) and Archbishop of Cape Town (1986–95), he also chaired the Truth and Reconciliation Commission from 1995. A critic of the apartheid system, he nonetheless also criticized violence in the townships.

### TUVALU

A nation comprising a chain of nine low-lying atolls in the south-west Pacific Ocean, about 650 mi/1,050 km south of Fiji. The islands were settled by Polynesians by the 16c. They became a British protectorate as the Ellice Islands in 1877, were part of the British Protectorate of the Gilbert and Ellice Islands (see **KIRIBATI**) proclaimed in 1892 and were annexed as the Gilbert and Ellice Islands Colony in 1916. Following a vote by the Ellice islanders, the colonies were separated by 1975 and the Ellice Islands became independent as Tuvalu in 1978. Tuvalu is threatened by rising sea levels, which have already damaged its agriculture by increasing the soil's salinity. In 2002 Tuvalu, with **KIRIBATI** and the **MALDIVES**, began legal action against the USA for its refusal to sign the Kyoto Protocol.

**Tvardovsky, Alexander Trifonovich** (1910–71)
Soviet poet, editor and **SAMIZDAT** publisher. Writing during and after **WORLD WAR II**, he was editor of *Novy Mir* in the years 1958–70 when he exposed the excesses of **STALINISM**; for example, he secured the publication of Alexander **SOLZHENITSYN**'s *One Day in the Life of Ivan Denisovich*. His task became increasingly difficult following Leonid **BREZHNEV**'s rise to power in 1964, hence his resort to underground publication. However, he had laid the foundations for the

**GORBACHEV** years of open debate.

**Tver Manifesto** (1894)
An appeal made by the Tver **ZEMSTVO** to the new tsar, **NICHOLAS II**, that institutions such as theirs should have the opportunity and the right to express their opinions to him. It was composed by a talented lawyer, Fedor Rodichev, but it evoked the reply in 1895 that the zemstvo had been 'carried away by senseless dreams', and that Nicholas would 'uphold the principle of autocracy', which he did until he was forced to abdicate in 1917.

**Tvrtko I** (c.1338–1391)
King of Bosnia (1353/91). The greatest of all the Bosnian rulers, he assumed the royal title and laid claim to the thrones of Serbia, **DALMATIA** and Croatia. During his reign, Bosnia included all the Dalmatian towns except Zadar and Dubrovnik and became a stronghold of the heretical **BOGOMILS**.

**Tweed, William Marcy,** nicknamed **Boss Tweed** (1823–78)
US criminal and politician. Born in New York City, he trained as a chairmaker, became an alderman (1852–3), sat in **CONGRESS** (1853–5), and was repeatedly in the state Senate. One of the most notorious political bosses of the Tammany Society, he was made commissioner of public works for the city in 1870, and, as head of the 'Tweed Ring', controlled its finances. He made many fraudulent deals, and was exposed in 1871 and convicted. After escaping to Cuba and Spain (1875–6), he died in a New York jail while suits were pending against him for the recovery of US$6 million. ►— **TAMMANY HALL**

**Twelve Years' Truce** (1609–21)
Extended ceasefire in the **EIGHTY YEARS' WAR** between Spain and the Netherlands, thus giving a welcome rest to the war-exhausted parties and especially to the southern Netherlands after 41 years of being a theatre of war. The truce was against the wishes of the Dutch Stadholder **MAURICE** of Nassau, but forced by the states party which needed peace to restore its trade. During the truce, conflict flared up in the Dutch Republic between Maurice and the states party (led by **OLDENBARNEVELDT**), much of it manifested in the struggle between the **REMONSTRANTS** and the **COUNTER-REMONSTRANTS**. The Orange Party won the struggle, removed the states leaders from power, and renewed the war with Spain in 1621. ►— **STADHOLDER**

**Twenty-Four Parganas**
Revenue districts ceded to the British **EAST INDIA COMPANY** by Mir Jafar, Nawab of Bengal, in 1757.

**Twenty-One Demands**
A series of demands presented by Japan to China in 1915, which included: the recognition of Japanese control of **MANCHURIA**, Shandong, Inner Mongolia, south-eastern China and the Yangzi Valley; the imposition of Japanese advisers in the Chinese administration; and the compulsory purchase of 50 per cent of its munitions from Japan. President **YUAN SHIKAI** accepted them as the basis of a treaty, but the resulting popular patriotic protest movement gave impetus to the rise of Chinese nationalism.

**Two Sicilies, Kingdom of the**
The Bourbon kingdom in the south of Italy, restored

in 1815 after the collapse of Joachim MURAT's Kingdom of Naples, and comprising the island of Sicily and that part of the peninsula lying to the south of the PAPAL STATES. It ceased to exist in 1860 after it was successfully overrun by GARIBALDI and annexed by VICTOR EMMANUEL II.

### Tyler, John (1790–1862)

US politician and 10th President. He became a lawyer, member of the Virginia state legislature (1811–16), a US Congressman (1817–21), Governor of Virginia (1825–7), and then a US Senator (1827–36). Elected Vice-President in 1840, he became President in 1841 on the death of William Henry HARRISON, only a month after his inauguration. He remained in office from 1841–5. His most important accomplishments were the annexation of Texas and the WEBSTER–ASHBURTON TREATY. He later remained active in politics, adhering to the Confederate cause until his death.

### Tyler, Wat (d.1381)

English leader of the PEASANTS' REVOLT (1381). The rebels of Kent, after taking Rochester Castle, chose him as captain, and marched to Canterbury and London. At the Smithfield conference with RICHARD II blows were exchanged, and Tyler was wounded by the Mayor of London, William Walworth. He was taken to St Bartholomew's Hospital, where Walworth had him dragged out and beheaded.

### Tyndale, William (c.1494–1536)

English translator of the Bible. In 1523 he went to London to seek support for his project to translate the Scriptures into the vernacular. Bishop Cuthbert Tunstall refused his support, and Tyndale then went to Hamburg (1524), to Wittenberg, where he visited Martin Luther, and to Cologne (1525), where he began printing his English New Testament in the same year. Later he began work on an Old Testament translation in Antwerp (1531), but before it was finished he was accused of heresy, imprisoned and put to death in Vilvorde, Belgium.

### Tz'u Hsi ► CIXI

## U-2 Incident (1960)

On 1 May 1960 a US U-2 spy plane was brought down over Sverdlovsk in the USSR. After US denials, Premier Nikita **KHRUSHCHEV** produced the pilot, Francis Gary Powers, and his photographs of military installations. President **EISENHOWER** justified the flights as essential for US national security. Khrushchev took advantage of the situation at a scheduled Paris summit meeting a few days later, when he withdrew Eisenhower's invitation to visit the USSR and demanded that he condemn the flights. The President's refusal allowed Khrushchev to walk out of the summit and to blame the USA for its failure.

## U-boat

An abbreviation of the German *Unterseeboot* ('submarine'). The German navy launched large-scale submarine offensives in both World Wars, and each time the U-boats came close to victory.

**UCD** (*Unión Central Democrática*, 'Central Democratic Union') (1977–82)

A coalition of liberal, regional, Christian and social democratic groups under the leadership of Adolfo **SUÁREZ** which formed a political party after its success in the 1977 Spanish general election. Having formed the minority governments of 1977–82, numerous schisms and defections, caused by struggles over the party apparatus and ideological differences, led to the Union's rout in the 1982 election and its disbandment shortly thereafter. However, although it had failed as a party, the UCD had succeeded in transforming Spain from a dictatorship into a democracy.

## UDI (Unilateral Declaration of Independence) (11 Nov 1965)

The declaration by Ian **SMITH**'s Rhodesia Front government which attempted to maintain white supremacy in Southern Rhodesia (Zimbabwe). After the dissolution of the **CENTRAL AFRICAN FEDERATION** at the end of 1963, Nyasaland and Northern Rhodesia achieved independence as Malawi and Zambia. The British government then expected that Southern Rhodesia would also pursue unimpeded progress to black majority rule, but the white settlers attempted to maintain their dominance of the economy and politics of the territory. Harold **WILSON**'s British Labour government declined to use force against them, but imposed sanctions. Because of South Africa's initial support of Rhodesia, these took some time to take effect, but the Smith regime was ultimately defeated by guerrilla incursions from Zambia and Mozambique and by economic collapse. Zimbabwe achieved its independence in 1980.

**UDR ►** GAULLISTS

**UGANDA** official name **Republic of Uganda**

A landlocked East African republic, bounded to the south by Rwanda, Tanzania and Lake Victoria; to the east by Kenya; to the north by Sudan; and to the west by the Democratic Republic of the Congo. Bantu speaking peoples migrated into south-west Uganda c.500BC and by the 14c AD were organized into several kingdoms. Uganda was discovered by Arab traders in the 1830s, explored by John Hanning **SPEKE** in the 1860s and granted to the **IMPERIAL BRITISH EAST AFRICA COMPANY** in 1888. The Kingdom of **BUGANDA** became a British protectorate in 1893, and other territory was included by 1903. Uganda gained its independence in 1962 as a federation of the kingdoms of Ankole, Buganda, **BUNYORO**, Busoga and Toro, announced by Prime Minister Dr Milton **OBOTE**, who in 1966 deposed the President, King **MUTESA II**, and assumed all powers himself. In 1971 a coup was led by General Idi **AMIN** Dada, who expelled all Asian residents who were not Ugandan citizens. Reacting to Amin's repressive regime, Tanzanian troops and Ugandan exiles marched on Kampala, overthrowing the government in 1979. Obote returned to power but failed to restore stability and another coup took place in 1985. A military government ruled until 1986 when it was overthrown by Yoweri **MUSEVENI**, who became President and began the process of rebuilding the country but kept a ban on other political parties. Museveni was re-elected in the first free presidential elections in 1996, and re-elected again in 2001. A 2000 referendum favoured the continuation of the 'Movement' system under which political parties are allowed to exist but not to contest elections, although moves towards allowing parties to become active again were made in 2003. Rebel insurgency in the north and west by the Lord's

Resistance Army has displaced over one million people since 1986.

## Uganda Martyrs

A group of 22 African youths, converted to Roman Catholicism, who were killed for their faith in Uganda between 1885 and 1887. Canonized in 1964, they were among a number of Christians put to death in the reign of King Mwanga of Buganda.

## Ugolino della Gherardesca, Count (d.1289)

Ghibelline Count of Donoratico. By intriguing with Pisa's enemies and treachery in the city itself, Ugolino came to power in 1284. The tyrant was overthrown in 1289, and he and his relations starved to death in the tower to which they were confined. The grisly episode is recalled in Dante's *Inferno*. ► **GHIBELLINES**

## UGT (*Unión General de Trabajadores*, 'General Union of Workers')

Spanish socialist trade union movement. The UGT grew extremely slowly after its foundation in 1888, not achieving a national presence until the Second Republic of 1931–6. Throughout this period it was distinguished by its rigid centralism, ideological confusion, and practical moderation. The pragmatism of the UGT was shown above all by its collaboration with the dictatorship of Miguel **PRIMO DE RIVERA** (1923–30) in an effort to reshape the trade unions along corporatist lines. Under the Second Republic the UGT grew spectacularly, especially among landless day labourers. The failure of reform led to demands for action from an increasingly militant rank and file, culminating in the agricultural strike of June 1934 and the general strike and rising of Oct 1934. The defeat of these protests and their savage repression led the UGT to adopt a revolutionary line in 1935, though it still backed the Popular Front in the general election of Feb 1936. Once the Popular Front came to power, the UGT's rural section, frustrated by the lack of reform, encouraged landless labourers to take the law into their own hands, thereby polarizing the political climate further. During the **SPANISH CIVIL WAR** the UGT lost more and more influence to the **PCE**, and by the end of the war it had been torn apart by internal divisions. Like the **PSOE**, it played an extremely limited role in the opposition to the **FRANCO** regime. With the restoration of democracy in Spain in 1977, the UGT was re-established. By 1982 it had become the largest trade union body in Spain, but it fell out with the socialist government in 1988 over its modernization programme, and since then relations with the PSOE have not been as close. ► **REPUBLIC, SECOND** (Spain)

## Uighurs

One of China's national minorities, now numbering over 7.7 million and for the most part settled in Xinjiang. They are a people of Turkic origin who emerged as an independent force as early as the 7c. They developed their own script, and practised a religion which was a form of Manicheism, though the Uighurs in Xinjiang are now Sunni Muslims. There are also around 300,000 Uighurs living in Uzbekistan, Kazakhstan and Kyrgyzstan.

## Uitlanders

The name given to Europeans of a variety of national origins who flocked to the Transvaal after the discovery of gold there in 1886. They soon came to outnumber the Boers, who feared that they would be politically and culturally swamped. Their grievances, particularly relating to the franchise and citizenship rights, were used by Sir Alfred **MILNER** and the British as a pretext for the escalation of tension which led to the **BOER WARS**.

## Ujamaa

A **SWAHILI** word, usually translated as 'familyhood', which is applied to the special brand of African Socialism espoused by Julius **NYERERE** in Tanzania. It emphasizes cooperation and equality and is based upon his conception of traditional African society.

**UK** ► **UNITED KINGDOM**

## UKRAINE

A republic in eastern Europe, bounded to the southwest by Moldova and Romania; to the west by Hungary, Slovakia and Poland; to the north by Belarus; to the east by Russia; and to the south by the Black Sea. Inhabited by Scythians in ancient times, the country was then invaded by Goths, Huns and Khazars. Kiev became the centre of power, but it was overrun by the **GOLDEN HORDE** in the 14c. Ruled by Lithuania in the 14–15c, Ukraine came under Polish rule in the 16c, when many people fled and formed resistance movements (**COSSACKS**). It gradually became part of Russia in the 17–18c. Ukraine declared its independence in 1918, but Kiev was occupied by Soviet troops and the country became a Soviet Socialist Republic in 1922. In 1986 the **CHERNOBYL** nuclear disaster occurred, leaving a huge area of the country permanently contaminated. On the disintegration of the USSR, Ukraine successfully declared its independence in 1991 under President Leonid Kravchuk and became a founding member of the **CIS** (Commonwealth of Independent States). This was soon followed by a dispute with Russia over control of the Black Sea fleet and the status of the largely Russian-populated Crimean peninsula, whose declaration of autonomy in 1992 was rejected by Ukraine. There is a marked division in the country between the Russian-influenced east and the European-influenced west. This came to a head after the presidential election in Nov 2004 when, amid allegations of polling irregularities, the Russian-backed Viktor Yanukovych was declared the winner. The announcement sparked mass demonstrations and civil disobedience (the 'Orange Revolution'), which continued until the result was annulled and a re-run poll in Dec was won by the pro-Western Viktor Yushchenko.

## Ulbricht, Walter (1893–1973)

East German politician. At first a cabinetmaker, he

entered politics in 1912, and in 1928 became communist Deputy for Potsdam. He left Germany on **HITLER**'s rise in 1933, spending most of his exile in the USSR. In 1945 he returned as head of the German Communist Party (**KPD**), and became Deputy Premier of the German Democratic Republic and General-Secretary of the Socialist Unity Party (**SED**) in 1950. He was largely responsible for the 'sovietization' of East Germany, and had the **BERLIN WALL** built in 1961. ▶ **COMMUNISM**

### Ulrich of Württemberg (1487–1550)
Duke of Württemberg, his excessive taxes sparked a peasant rebellion in 1514. He was expelled from his possessions in 1519 by the **SWABIAN LEAGUE** and did not recover them until 1534. He was a Lutheran and a member of the **SCHMALKALDIC LEAGUE**.

### Ulrika Eleonora (1688–1741)
Queen of Sweden (1719/20). The younger sister of, and successor to, **CHARLES XII**, she married Prince Frederick of Hesse in 1714, and declared herself Queen after her brother's death. She was, however, compelled by the Estates to renounce her hereditary right to the throne. She was subsequently elected to the throne on condition that she accepted a new constitution which severely limited royal power. She found these limitations difficult to accept and in 1720 agreed to abdicate in favour of her husband, who ascended the throne as Frederick I.

### Ulster 'Troubles'
The name conventionally given to violence in Northern Ireland from 1968. The violence originated in conflict between Catholics and Protestants over **CIVIL RIGHTS** and perceived discrimination against the Catholic minority in the Province. Ulster Premier Terence **O'NEILL** initiated reforms but alienated loyalists in his Unionist Party and he resigned in 1969. Rioting and sectarian violence began to overwhelm police capabilities and the British Army was sent to maintain peace in 1969, but continuing violence resulted in the imposition of internment without trial, employed almost entirely against Catholics, under Brian Faulkner's administration. Anti-British Army feeling among the Catholics and mainland **IRA** attacks increased markedly after the **BLOODY SUNDAY** demonstrations (30 Jan 1972) and direct rule was imposed in Mar. In Dec 1973 the British, Ulster and Irish governments signed the power-sharing Sunningdale Agreement, providing for representation in the Province's government of both the Catholic and Protestant populations, but continued Protestant Unionist resistance to the agreement led to the collapse of the **STORMONT** executive in May 1974. Ulster reverted to direct rule from Westminster and sectarian killings continued. The IRA from time to time concentrated its attention on England with bombings and assassinations of prominent Conservative politicians, such as Airey Neave in 1979 and Ian Gow in 1990. Political initiatives to find a solution to an apparently intractable problem were frustrated over the years, until the **DOWNING STREET DECLARATION** of 1993 opened the way for more peace talks and an IRA ceasefire in 1994–6 provided hope that a solution could be found. Following renewed bomb attacks and rioting in 1996–7, the ceasefire recommenced in 1997 and cross-party talks resulted in the 1998 **GOOD FRIDAY**

**AGREEMENT** and the end of direct rule. Although the devolved government was suspended in 2002, the ceasefire has generally been observed and the British military presence reduced, allowing a return to normality for the society and economy of the region.

### Ultramontanism
Literally, 'beyond the mountains'; a movement, deriving from France, asserting the centralization of the authority and power of the Roman Catholic Church in Rome and the pope. It gained impetus after the **FRENCH REVOLUTION** (1789), and reached its high point with the First Vatican Council (1870) and the declaration of Papal Infallibility.

### Ultras
The name given to the extreme Right in French politics (1815–30), because they were more royalist than the King, while **LOUIS XVIII** reigned; **CHARLES X** adopted Ultra policies and lost his throne in 1830; the leading Ultras were Villèle and **POLIGNAC**.

### Umar ibn Tal, al-Hajj (c.1795–1864)
A Tukulor from Futa Toro who made the pilgrimage to Mecca, he was a member of the highly disciplined Tijaniyya order, and led one of the important jihads in the western Sudan. He conquered Bambara, Segu and the territories formerly welded together by **AHMADU IBN HAMMADU**. His conquests brought him into conflict with the French, but he recognized that he was not strong enough to dislodge them. ▶ **JIHAD**

### Umberto I (1844–1900)
King of Italy (1878/1900). The son and successor of **VICTOR EMMANUEL II**, he distinguished himself at the Battle of **CUSTOZZA**. He is often portrayed as a model constitutional monarch who, despite his conservative sympathies and considerable pressure from reactionary politicians, rarely interfered in parliamentary affairs. In reality, he was perfectly content to block ministerial appointments and to use the royal prerogative, especially in matters concerning the army or foreign affairs. Despite a genuine concern for his subjects (manifest particularly at times of natural disaster: earthquakes, floods and epidemics), there were attempts on his life in 1878 and 1897, before he was finally assassinated by an anarchist.

### Umberto II (1904–83)
King of Italy (May/Jun 1946). Made de facto Regent ('Lieutenant-General of the Realm') by his father, **VICTOR EMMANUEL III**, in June 1944, he ascended the throne on the latter's abdication in 1946, at a time when the monarchy had become widely unpopular. In a referendum later the same year 12,718,641 Italians voted in favour of a republic and 10,718,502 for the retention of the monarchy, most support for the latter stance being located in the **MEZZOGIORNO**. Umberto was forced to leave Italy, setting up residence in Portugal as the self-styled Count Di Sarre.

### Umkhonto we Sizwe
The military wing (literally, 'Spear of the Nation') of the **ANC** (African National Congress), which was established when the party was banned. Its main bases were in Angola and its Chief of Staff in the 1980s was Joe **SLOVO**. It has provided a number of the new generation of leaders in the ANC.

## UNITED NATIONS MEMBERSHIP

Grouped according to year of entry.

| Date | Member | Date | Member |
|---|---|---|---|
| 1945 | Argentina, Australia, Belgium, Byelorussian SSR (Belarus, 1991), Bolivia, Brazil, Canada, Chile, China (Taiwan to 1971), Colombia, Costa Rica, Cuba, Czechoslovakia (to 1993), Denmark, Dominican Republic, Ecuador, Egypt, El Salvador, Ethiopia, France, Greece, Guatemala, Haiti, Honduras, India, Iran, Iraq, Lebanon, Liberia, Luxembourg, Mexico, Netherlands, New Zealand, Nicaragua, Norway, Panama, Paraguay, Peru, Philippines, Poland, Saudi Arabia, South Africa, Syria, Turkey, Ukrainian SSR (Ukraine, 1991), USSR (Russia, 1991), UK, USA, Uruguay, Venezuela, Yugoslavia (to 1992) | 1964 | Malawi, Malta, Zambia, Tanzania |
| | | 1965 | The Gambia, Maldives, Singapore |
| | | 1966 | Barbados, Botswana, Guyana, Lesotho, Yemen (South, to 1990) |
| | | 1968 | Equatorial Guinea, Mauritius, Swaziland |
| | | 1970 | Fiji |
| | | 1971 | Bahrain, Bhutan, China (People's Republic of), Oman, Qatar, United Arab Emirates |
| | | 1973 | The Bahamas, German Democratic Republic (within GFR, 1990), German Federal Republic |
| | | 1974 | Bangladesh, Grenada, Guinea-Bissau |
| | | 1975 | Cape Verde, Comoros, Mozambique, Papua New Guinea, São Tomé and Príncipe, Suriname |
| | | 1976 | Angola, Seychelles, Western Samoa (Samoa, 1997) |
| 1946 | Afghanistan, Iceland, Sweden, Thailand | 1977 | Djibouti, Vietnam |
| 1947 | Pakistan, Yemen (North, to 1990) | 1978 | Dominica, Solomon Islands |
| 1948 | Burma (Myanmar, 1989) | 1979 | St Lucia |
| 1949 | Israel | 1980 | St Vincent and the Grenadines, Zimbabwe |
| 1950 | Indonesia | 1981 | Antigua and Barbuda, Belize, Vanuatu |
| 1955 | Albania, Austria, Bulgaria, Kampuchea (Cambodia, 1989), Ceylon (Sri Lanka, 1970), Finland, Hungary, Ireland, Italy, Jordan, Laos, Libya, Nepal, Portugal, Romania, Spain | 1983 | St Kitts and Nevis |
| | | 1984 | Brunei |
| | | 1990 | Liechtenstein, Namibia, Yemen (formerly North Yemen and South Yemen) |
| 1956 | Japan, Morocco, Sudan, Tunisia | 1991 | Estonia, Federated States of Micronesia, Latvia, Lithuania, Marshall Islands, North Korea, Russia, South Korea |
| 1957 | Ghana, Malaya (Malaysia, 1963) | | |
| 1958 | Guinea | | |
| 1960 | Cameroon, Central African Republic, Chad, Congo, Côte d'Ivoire (Ivory Coast), Cyprus, Dahomey (Benin, 1975), Gabon, Madagascar, Mali, Niger, Nigeria, Senegal, Somalia, Togo, Upper Volta (Burkina Faso, 1984), Zaire (Democratic Republic of Congo, 1997) | 1992 | Armenia, Azerbaijan, Bosnia-Herzegovina, Croatia, Georgia, Kazakhstan, Kyrgyzstan, Moldova, San Marino, Slovenia, Tajikistan, Turkmenistan, Uzbekistan |
| | | 1993 | Andorra, Czech Republic, Eritrea, Former Yugoslav Republic of Macedonia, Monaco, Slovakia |
| 1961 | Mauritania, Mongolia, Sierra Leone, Tanganyika (within Tanzania, 1964) | 1994 | Palau |
| 1962 | Algeria, Burundi, Jamaica, Rwanda, Trinidad and Tobago, Uganda | 1999 | Kiribati, Nauru, Tonga |
| | | 2000 | Tuvalu, Serbia and Montenegro |
| 1963 | Kenya, Kuwait, Zanzibar (within Tanzania, 1964) | 2002 | East Timor, Switzerland |

**UMW ► UNITED MINE WORKERS OF AMERICA**

## UN (United Nations Organization)

An organization formed to maintain world peace and foster international cooperation, formally established on 24 Oct 1945 with 51 founder countries. The UN Charter, which was drafted during WORLD WAR II by the USA, UK and USSR, remains virtually unaltered despite the growth in membership and activities. There are six 'principal organs'. The General Assembly is the plenary body which controls much of the UN's work, supervises the subsidiary organs, sets priorities, and debates major issues of international affairs. The 15-member Security Council is dominated by the five permanent members (China, France, UK, USSR and USA) who each have the power of veto over any resolutions; the remaining ten members are elected for two-year periods. The primary role of the Council is to maintain international peace and security; its decisions, unlike those of the General Assembly, are binding on all other members. It is empowered to order mandatory sanctions, call for ceasefires, and establish peacekeeping forces (these forces were awarded the NOBEL PEACE PRIZE in 1988). The use of the veto has prevented it from intervening in a number of disputes, such as the VIETNAM WAR. The Secretariat, under the Secretary-General, is based at the UN's headquarters in New York City. The staff are answerable only to the UN, not national governments, and are engaged in considerable diplomatic work. The Secretary-General is often a significant person in international diplomacy and is able to take independent initiatives. The INTERNATIONAL COURT OF JUSTICE consists of 15 judges appointed by the Council and the Assembly. As only states can bring issues before it, its jurisdiction depends on the consent of the states who are a party to a dispute. It also offers advisory opinions to various organs of the UN. The Economic and Social

Council is elected by the General Assembly; it supervises the work of various committees, commissions, and expert bodies in the economic and social area, and coordinates the work of UN specialized agencies. The Trusteeship Council oversees the transition of Trust territories to self-government. In addition to the organs established under the Charter, there is a range of subsidiary agencies, many with their own constitutions and membership, and some pre-dating the UN. The main agencies are the **FOOD AND AGRICULTURE ORGANIZATION**, the UN Industrial Development Organization, the International Maritime Organization, the **INTERNATIONAL ATOMIC ENERGY AGENCY**, the World Bank (the **INTERNATIONAL BANK FOR RECONSTRUCTION AND DEVELOPMENT**, the **INTERNATIONAL DEVELOPMENT ASSOCIATION**, the International Finance Corporation, the Multilateral Investment Guarantee Agency, and the International Centre for Settlement of Investment Disputes), the International Civil Aviation Organization, the International Fund for Agricultural Development, the **INTERNATIONAL LABOUR ORGANIZATION**, the **INTERNATIONAL MONETARY FUND**, **UNESCO**, the Universal Postal Union, the International Telecommunication Union, the World Intellectual Property Organization, the World Meteorological Organization, the **WORLD HEALTH ORGANIZATION** and the **WORLD TRADE ORGANIZATION**. The UN currently has 191 members. It is generally seen as a forum in which states pursue their national interest, rather than as an institution of world government, but it is not without considerable impact.

### UNITED NATIONS: SECRETARIES-GENERAL

| Dates | Name |
| --- | --- |
| 1946–53 | Trygve Lie |
| 1953–61 | Dag Hammarskjöld |
| 1962–71 | U Thant |
| 1972–81 | Kurt Waldheim |
| 1982–91 | Javier Pérez de Cuéllar |
| 1992–6 | Boutros Boutros-Ghali |
| 1997– | Kofi Annan |

### UNCTAD (United Nations Conference on Trade and Development)

A permanent organ of the **UN** General Assembly, established in 1964 to promote trade, investment and development in developing countries. Its work covers globalization and development strategies for the least developed nations and for those with transitional economies, international trade investment, technology and enterprise development, and provision of services such as research, policy analysis and data collection. It has consistently challenged the view presented by the **INTERNATIONAL MONETARY FUND** and the **WORLD TRADE ORGANIZATION** that free-market globalization and economic liberalization will result solely in benefits for developing countries and it is increasingly seen as a more democratic and inclusive organization, dealing even-handedly with issues of **FAIR TRADE**, law and corporate influence. Its headquarters are in Geneva, Switzerland, and it has 192 members. ➤ **BRANDT COMMISSION; JUBILEE 2000; NORTH–SOUTH DIVIDE; THIRD WORLD DEBT**

### Underground Railroad

In US history, a loose network of safe houses, hiding places, and routes to aid fugitive American slaves to reach freedom in the North or Canada. Never formally organized, it was active as early as 1786, but was most widespread and active between 1830 and 1860. Estimates suggest that it may have assisted some 50,000 runaways.

### Unequal Treaties ➤ NANJING, TREATY OF; TIANJIN, TREATY OF

### UNESCO (United Nations Educational, Scientific and Cultural Organization)

A **UN** specialized agency founded in 1946 to promote collaboration among nations through education, science and culture. In the 1980s, concern among the non-communist industrialized countries over the organization's administrative inefficiency and its allegedly inappropriate political aims led to the departure of the USA (1985), which had a major impact financially, and also of the UK (1985) and Singapore. The UK rejoined in 1997 and the USA in 2003. In 2005 there were 191 member states.

### Unidad Popular

Literally 'Popular Unity', this was a coalition of six left-wing political parties in Chile (Communists, Socialists, Radicals, and three minor groups) formed to support the presidential candidacy and government (1970–3) of Salvador **ALLENDE**.

### Uniformity, Acts of (1549, 1552, 1559 and 1662)

A series of acts passed by English parliaments which sought to impose religious uniformity by requiring the use of the Church of England liturgy as contained in the Book of Common Prayer (various editions, 1549–1662). The act of 1552 penalized Catholic recusants; that of 1662 excluded dissenting Protestant clergy.

### Unilateral Declaration of Independence (Rhodesia) ➤ UDI

### Union, Acts of (1707 and 1800)

The Acts which joined England in legislative union with Scotland (1707) and Great Britain with Ireland (1800). The 1707 Act brought 45 Scottish MPs to join the new House of **COMMONS** of Great Britain, and 16 peers became members of the House of **LORDS**; the Scottish legal system, however, remained separate. The 1800 Act created the United Kingdom of Great Britain and Ireland, which came into effect in 1801, and lasted until 1922. Union was brought about after the collapse of the Irish rebellion (1798) in order to increase British security during the **FRENCH REVOLUTIONARY WARS**. The Irish parliament was abolished; 100 Irish MPs were added to the UK House of Commons, and 32 peers to the Lords. The Churches of England and Ireland were united.

### Union for French Democracy ➤ INDEPENDENT REPUBLICAN PARTY

### Union Movement

A party formed by Sir Oswald **MOSLEY** in 1948 as a successor to his New Party (1931) and the British Union of Fascists (1932). It put up a handful of candidates during the period 1959–66, but failed to secure a significant number of votes. The party's main platform was opposition to immigration, but it also included a call to unite Europe into a vast market to buy from and sell to Africa. Mosley gave up the leadership in 1966, and the movement went into decline, dying out by the end of the 1960s. ► **BLACKSHIRTS**

## Union Nationale

French-Canadian political party. It was formed by a coalition of the Conservatives and *Action Libérale Nationale* to fight the 1935 provincial elections in Quebec. Its failure to win led to an amalgamation under Maurice **DUPLESSIS**. With the support of the rural and small-business sector, it won an easy victory in 1936 on a platform of political, social and economic reform. In practice, this turned out to be antiradicalism and pro-corporatism. In 1939 it was defeated after the intervention of Quebec Liberals in the federal government, but it returned to power in 1944 after accusing them of betraying nationalist rights, and it was to emphasize nationalist leanings thereafter. Duplessis maintained a very personal control of the party until his death in 1959, following which the party lost the 1960 election. In 1966 it regained power under Daniel Johnson, but he died in 1968 and very soon the **PARTI QUÉBECOIS** had seized the nationalist mantle. The *Union Nationale* lost the 1970 election and its support declined precipitously. Despite an attempt to revive it in 1999, it no longer exists.

## Union of Arms (July 1624)

The proposal drawn up by the Count-Duke of **OLIVARES** for a force of 140,000 men to be raised and maintained by each component state of the Spanish monarchy, in proportion to its resources. The plan was intended to solve the serious financial difficulties of the crown of **CASTILE**, which shouldered most of the defence burden. The plan was partially put into effect in Spanish America, Flanders and Italy. The strongest opposition came from the crown of **ARAGON**, notably from Catalonia. The proposal was one of the major grievances leading to the Revolt of **CATALONIA** in 1640.

## Union of Liberation (1903)

A loose alliance of Russian liberals coming together to advocate some form of representative government. They included the former Marxist Peter **STRUVE**; but predominantly they were well-to-do **ZEMSTVO** activists annoyed at **NICHOLAS II**'s incompetence and continued refusal to meet them. As the Russian **REVOLUTION OF 1905** developed, they split: **SHIPOV** and **GUCHKOV** to form the moderate **OCTOBRISTS**, and **MILIUKOV** and Muromtsev the more far-seeking **KADETS**. The Union represented an important transitory stage in Russian politics.

## Union of Soviet Socialist Republics ► USSR

## UNIP (United National Independence Party)

Formed in 1959 with Kenneth **KAUNDA** as its leader, UNIP was the strongest party in the last years of Northern Rhodesian colonial rule and provided the first post-independence government of Zambia. It became the only legal party in 1972, but in 1991, after pressure from the international community and widespread signs of dissatisfaction within the country, multiparty elections were held and UNIP was convincingly defeated.

**UNITA** (*União Nacional para a Independência Total de Angola*, 'National Union for the Total Independence of Angola')
An Angolan nationalist party, founded in 1966 by Jonas **SAVIMBI**. Its support was based in south-eastern Angola and, even after Angola gained independence from Portugal in 1975, it waged a guerrilla war against the **MPLA** government, receiving backing from the USA and South Africa. When the civil war seemed to have reached an inconclusive stalemate, after long and difficult negotiations, UNITA and the MPLA agreed upon a ceasefire in early 1991. In 1992 the multiparty elections were won by the MPLA, but UNITA refused to accept the results, and fighting resumed. During 1993 there were both sporadic outbreaks of violence between UNITA and the government, and peace talks, which resulted in a peace accord signed in Lusaka in 1994. In 1995 a **UN** peacekeeping force entered Angola, and in 1997 a new government of national unity was formed, which was boycotted by Savimbi. However, after Savimbi was killed in 2002, UNITA agreed to adhere to the 1994 ceasefire and started to demobilize its forces.

**Unitas Fratrum** ► **MORAVIAN BRETHREN**

## UNITED ARAB EMIRATES (UAE)

A federation in the eastern central Arabian Peninsula comprising seven internally self-governing emirates. It is bounded to the north by the Arabian Gulf; to the east by Oman; and to the south and west by Saudi Arabia. As early as the third millennium BC it was crossed by many Sumerian trade routes. It came under Muslim influence from the 6c and was visited by the Portuguese in the 16c. The British **EAST INDIA COMPANY** arrived in the 17c. Various peace treaties with Britain were signed from 1820 by the ruling sheikhs of what became known thereafter as the Trucial States – Abu Dhabi, Ajman, Dubai, Fujairah, Ras al Khaimah, Sharjah and Umm al Qaiwain on the Persian Gulf and Gulf of Oman – which accepted British protection in 1892. Abu Dhabi's huge oilfields were discovered in 1958. The new state formed by six emirates was established in 1971, when the special peace treaties ended and a Treaty of Friendship with Britain was signed; the emirate of Ras al Khaimah joined the following year. The UAE is governed by a Supreme Council comprising the hereditary rulers of the seven emirates and it elects a president from among its members every five years. Sheikh Zayed bin Sultan al-**NAHYAN** of Abu Dhabi was President from 1971 until his death in 2004, when his son, Sheikh Khalifa, was elected in his place.

## United Arab Republic (UAR)
The short-lived union between Egypt and Syria proclaimed in 1958. Gamal Abd al-NASSER was elected as head of state and the union generated considerable euphoria in both countries. Syria seceded, however, in late 1961, although Egypt retained the name until 1971 when it adopted the name Arab Republic of Egypt (ARE).

## United Australia Party
Australian political party formed in 1931 from the Nationalist Party and dissident Australian Labor Party members under the former Labor minister, Joseph LYONS. Although the party governed through the 1930s (in coalition with the Country Party after 1934), it was never stable, and merged into the LIBERAL PARTY OF AUSTRALIA (1944–5).

## United Automobile Workers (UAW)
US labour union. Originally formed by the AFL under the aegis of the NATIONAL LABOR RELATIONS ACT (the 'Wagner Act'), an attempt to impose a president on the UAW led to a revolt in the spring of 1936, when the members elected their own leader, Homer Martin, and enrolled in the CIO. The UAW had to operate in an industry dominated by three aggressively anti-union companies, General Motors, Chrysler and Ford. However, by Dec 1936 the union had become strong enough to demand official recognition from General Motors. This was refused, despite the Wagner Act, so an official strike began in Jan 1937, the workers sitting in rather than walking out. The employers brought in the police, who used tear gas, but ineffectually. Michigan Governor Frank Murphy refused to use the state militia to remove the strikers and demanded negotiations between the employers and John L LEWIS, President of the CIO. Backed also by President Franklin D ROOSEVELT, these discussions led to the UAW being recognized by General Motors, who also promised not to discriminate against union workers. Later that year, the same tactic was used to gain recognition from Chrysler. ► AFL–CIO

## United Empire Loyalist
A title adopted by some 50,000 Americans, mainly from New England and New York, who moved to Canada during the AMERICAN REVOLUTION and who declared their loyalty to the British King, GEORGE III. They settled mainly in what are now the Maritime Provinces, southern Quebec and Ontario. Those who had arrived by 1783 were entitled to put the initials 'UE' after their names, which became a mark of honour.

## United Fronts
Two political movements in China, which promoted cooperation between the Chinese COMMUNIST PARTY (CCP) and GUOMINDANG. In the first, begun in 1924, to promote the defeat of regional militarists and reunify the country, SUN YAT-SEN agreed to members of the Communist Party joining the Guomindang as individuals, while still retaining CCP membership, in exchange for Soviet military and organizational aid. The alliance relied heavily on Sun's personal prestige, however, and after his death (1925) friction developed between the right wing of the Guomindang and the communists, culminating in Mar 1926 when CHIANG KAI-SHEK, commander of the Guomindang army, expelled communists from senior positions within the organization. After the success of Chiang's NORTHERN EXPEDITION, he initiated (Apr 1927) a purge of all communists in areas under his control; the alliance was subsequently officially dissolved (July 1927). In Dec 1936 the XI'AN INCIDENT ended with an anti-Japanese alliance between the two parties and, after the outbreak of the SINO-JAPANESE WAR in 1937, the Communist Party initiated the second United Front. Clashes between Guomindang and communist forces made it an uneasy alliance from the start, and by 1941 it had virtually disintegrated, although efforts were made to revive it in 1943.

## United Fruit Company
The company organized in 1899, by the legendary Minor Cooper Keith, to cultivate and ship bananas from eastern Costa Rica. Keith extended his ventures into Honduras and Salvador, against competition from the USA, using refrigerated ships to transport the crop to the US market. The combination of buccaneering tactics and chicanery practised by the company during its early years earned it the sobriquet *el pulpo* ('the octopus'). At the height of its activities, United Fruit held extensive terrain and feeder railroads in many parts of Central American countries; Minor Keith was known as 'the uncrowned King of Central America', and the company remained a powerful force in the region and the Caribbean through the 1950s. It played a significant role in the US intervention of 1954 against Guatemala's President Jácobo ARBENZ.

## United Gold Coast Convention (UGCC)
A political party founded in 1947, which was led originally by Dr J B Danquah. It was the first organization to seek self-government within a short time frame (for what is now Ghana). For a while its General-Secretary was Kwame NKRUMAH, but he broke away to form the more radical CONVENTION PEOPLE'S PARTY (CPP) and defeated the UGCC in the 1951 elections, after which the latter was dissolved.

## United Irishmen, Society of
A society formed in Belfast in 1791 by Protestant lawyer Wolfe TONE, which supported the FRENCH REVOLUTION and espoused both religious equality and parliamentary reform. Its early support was primarily located in Ulster. As agitation increased, so United Irishmen became increasingly associated with support for Catholicism. The society was instrumental in organizing French support for the unsuccessful Irish rebellion of 1798, and afterwards went into decline.

## UNITED KINGDOM (UK) official name United Kingdom of Great Britain and Northern Ireland
A kingdom in Western Europe, comprising England, Scotland, Wales and Northern Ireland. Wales was effectively joined to England in 1301, then Scotland was joined under one crown in 1603 (and by legislative union in 1707) and Ireland in 1801 (the United Kingdom of Great Britain and Ireland). The present name dates from 1922, following the establishment

of the **IRISH FREE STATE**. The UK has a population of 59.6 million (2003 estimate). It is a kingdom with a monarch as head of state, governed by a bicameral parliament comprising an elected 659-member House of **COMMONS** and a House of **LORDS** whose members are life peers, plus 92 hereditary peers, Anglican bishops and law lords. A Cabinet is appointed by the Prime Minister. The UK joined the **EC** in 1973, but has chosen not to join the **EURO ZONE**. ► **ENGLAND**; **NORTHERN IRELAND**; **SCOTLAND**; **UNION, ACTS OF**; **WALES**

### United Mine Workers of America (UMW)

A US labour union, formed in 1890 by an amalgamation of mining unions within the AFL and the **KNIGHTS OF LABOR**. After unexpectedly successful strikes in 1897 and 1900, and the election in 1898 of a vigorous young president, John Mitchell, the union consolidated its position in 1902 with a strike in the anthracite fields. When it demanded recognition, an increase in wages and shorter hours, the coalfield operators responded aggressively and lost public sympathy when violence broke out. President Theodore **ROOSEVELT** saw the conflict as of national economic importance, and the intransigence of the operators led him to force arbitration. This established an important precedent for government intervention in the future. Under the leadership of John L **LEWIS** (1920–60) the union became part of the CIO, which merged with the AFL in 1957. Its membership, which

was as high as 500,000 in the 1930s, declined steeply in the latter half of the 20c, along with the decline of the labour movement itself. ► **AFL–CIO**

### United National Party (Sri Lanka) ► UNP

### United Nations Educational, Scientific and Cultural Organization ► UNESCO

### United Provinces of the Netherlands

Seven sovereign states of the Dutch Republic (Holland, Zeeland, Gelderland, Utrecht, Friesland, Groningen and Overijssel), roughly comprising the present kingdom of the Netherlands, but originally part of the Burgundian lands until they achieved independence from the Spanish crown in the **EIGHTY YEARS' WAR**. Also known as the Dutch Republic, it declined in the 18c, collapsing during the **FRENCH REVOLUTIONARY WARS** (1795).

### United Service Organizations (USO)

In the USA, an association of agencies, founded in 1941. It includes the YMCA, YWCA and the Salvation Army, and aims to provide for the social and recreational needs of the US armed forces.

### United States of America ► USA

### Universal Declaration of Human Rights

A declaration detailing individual and social rights and freedoms, principally written by René **CASSIN** and adopted by the **UN** General Assembly in Dec 1948, with Saudi Arabia, South Africa and the six

## UNITED KINGDOM: PRIME MINISTERS

| Dates | Name | Party | Dates | Name | Party |
|---|---|---|---|---|---|
| 1721–42 | Robert Walpole | Whig | 1855–8 | Viscount Palmerston (Henry John Temple) | Lib |
| 1742–3 | Earl of Wilmington (Spencer Compton) | Whig | 1858–9 | Earl of Derby | Con |
| 1743–54 | Henry Pelham | Whig | 1859–65 | Viscount Palmerston | Lib |
| 1754–6 | Duke of Newcastle (Thomas Pelham-Holles) | Whig | 1865–6 | Lord John Russell | Lib |
| 1756–7 | Duke of Devonshire (William Cavendish) | Whig | 1866–8 | Earl of Derby | Con |
| 1757–62 | Duke of Newcastle | Whig | 1868 | Benjamin Disraeli | Con |
| 1762–3 | Earl of Bute (John Stuart) | Tory | 1868–74 | William Ewart Gladstone | Lib |
| 1763–5 | George Grenville | Whig | 1874–80 | Benjamin Disraeli | Con |
| 1765–6 | Marquess of Rockingham (Charles Watson Wentworth) | Whig | 1880–5 | William Ewart Gladstone | Lib |
| 1766–70 | Duke of Grafton (Augustus Henry Fitzroy) | Whig | 1885–6 | Marquess of Salisbury (Robert Gascoyne-Cecil) | Con |
| 1770–82 | Lord North (Frederick North) | Tory | 1886 | William Ewart Gladstone | Lib |
| 1782 | Marquess of Rockingham | Whig | 1886–92 | Marquess of Salisbury | Con |
| 1782–3 | Earl of Shelburne (William Petty-Fitzmaurice) | Whig | 1892–4 | William Ewart Gladstone | Lib |
| 1783 | Duke of Portland (William Henry Cavendish) | Coal | 1894–5 | Earl of Rosebery (Archibald Philip Primrose) | Lib |
| 1783–1801 | William Pitt | Tory | 1895–1902 | Marquess of Salisbury | Con |
| 1801–4 | Henry Addington | Tory | 1902–5 | Arthur James Balfour | Con |
| 1804–6 | William Pitt | Tory | 1905–8 | Henry Campbell-Bannerman | Lib |
| 1806–7 | Lord Grenville (William Wyndham) | Whig | 1908–15 | Herbert Henry Asquith | Lib |
| 1807–9 | Duke of Portland | Tory | 1915–16 | Herbert Henry Asquith | Coal |
| 1809–12 | Spencer Perceval | Tory | 1916–22 | David Lloyd George | Coal |
| 1812–27 | Earl of Liverpool (Robert Banks Jenkinson) | Tory | 1922–3 | Andrew Bonar Law | Con |
| 1827 | George Canning | Tory | 1923–4 | Stanley Baldwin | Con |
| 1827–8 | Viscount Goderich (Frederick John Robinson) | Tory | 1924 | James Ramsay MacDonald | Lab |
| 1828–30 | Duke of Wellington (Arthur Wellesley) | Tory | 1924–9 | Stanley Baldwin | Con |
| 1830–4 | Earl Grey (Charles Grey) | Whig | 1929–31 | James Ramsay MacDonald | Lab |
| 1834 | Viscount Melbourne (William Lamb) | Whig | 1931–5 | James Ramsay MacDonald | Nat |
| 1834–5 | Robert Peel | Con | 1935–7 | Stanley Baldwin | Nat |
| 1835–41 | Viscount Melbourne | Whig | 1937–40 | Arthur Neville Chamberlain | Nat |
| 1841–6 | Robert Peel | Con | 1940–5 | Winston Churchill | Coal |
| 1846–52 | Lord John Russell | Lib | 1945–51 | Clement Attlee | Lab |
| 1852 | Earl of Derby (Edward George Stanley) | Con | 1951–5 | Winston Churchill | Con |
| 1852–5 | Lord Aberdeen (George Hamilton-Gordon) | Peelite | 1955–7 | Anthony Eden | Con |
| | | | 1957–63 | Harold Macmillan | Con |
| | | | 1963–4 | Alec Douglas-Home | Con |
| | | | 1964–70 | Harold Wilson | Lab |
| | | | 1970–4 | Edward Heath | Con |
| | | | 1974–6 | Harold Wilson | Lab |
| | | | 1976–9 | James Callaghan | Lab |
| | | | 1979–90 | Margaret Thatcher | Con |
| | | | 1990–7 | John Major | Con |
| | | | 1997– | Tony Blair | Lab |

Notes
| | |
|---|---|
| Coal | Coalition |
| Con | Conservative |
| Lab | Labour |
| Lib | Liberal |
| Nat | Nationalist |

Soviet members abstaining. It includes and defines the civil and political rights found in most democracies (eg the right to life, liberty and security of person; freedom from arbitrary arrest, detention or exile; the right to a fair and public hearing by an independent and impartial tribunal; freedom of thought, conscience and religion; and freedom of peaceful assembly and association), and in addition certain economic, social and cultural rights such as the right to social security, the right to work, the right to education, the right to rest and leisure, and the right to share in scientific advancement and its benefits. Although the Declaration is not legally binding, the International Covenant on Civil and Political Rights, and the International Covenant on Economic, Social and Cultural Rights, which embody the essence of the Declaration, were adopted in 1966 by the UN General Assembly and do have legal power.

# *Urbanization*

*Culture & Society*

The tendency to equate 'civilized' life with town living, in the Western tradition, goes back to ancient Greece and Rome, where ruling élites preferred to dominate their agrarian communities from their bases in towns. (Indeed, the Latin word 'civis', meaning city, gives us the English word 'civilization' and its cognates in other Germanic and Latin tongues.) Undoubtedly, this led to unmerited contempt for non-urban culture patterns. Nevertheless, the evolution of writing and the construction of buildings in stone and similar long-lasting materials presupposes that people come together in one place and remain there over a long period of time, needing not only to communicate with each other but to leave records of what has been said or done, and lasting structures in which to conduct public as well as domestic life. In other words, they presuppose the foundation of urban communities. The relationship between cities and civilized living throughout history has by no means always been a straightforward one, but by and large the link has been retained. Even in non-European cultures, such as the Maya of Central America around AD 1000, advanced architectural and intellectual achievements were the product of urban élites, parasitic upon a peasantry which eventually seems to have refused to support the urban superstructure, which had withered before Europeans made contact with the area.

### The first urban settlements

The growth of the first towns took place at a time when human beings had advanced far enough agriculturally to have gone beyond subsistence living and were able to produce a surplus that could feed the population of a town. Since the surplus had to be transported from the countryside to the town, the beginnings of urbanization are generally dated to about the same time as the invention of the wheel, around 3500 BC.

Urban communities began in southern Asia, in the fertile plains near large rivers: in the basin of the Tigris and Euphrates rivers in modern-day Iraq; in Egypt along the Nile; in the Indus Valley in modern-day Pakistan; and along the Yellow River in China. They were centres of trade and, besides providing a market place, they also encouraged specialization in particular crafts. They were centres of religious and intellectual life, and were, or soon became, centres of administration. They were walled and more easily defensible than scattered communities. Lastly, they frequently offered more civilized living. Excavations at Harappa and Mohenjo-Daro in the Indus basin have revealed brick-paved streets built on a grid plan with a drainage system, public granaries, and baths dating from between 2550 BC and 1550 BC.

Many cities doubtless began as independent city states. City-states tended to be the norm in early Mesopotamia. With the evolution of kingdoms and empires, the notion of a capital city took shape. In around 3100 BC Menes, the king of Upper Egypt, subdued Lower Egypt. Rather than rule his new unified state from either of the previous capitals he built a new one at Memphis, south of modern Cairo.

The population figures for early cities are difficult to determine. It has been suggested that cities c.2000 BC were extremely crowded places with population densities of up to 128,000 per sq mi/49,400 per sq km, given the limited amount of space available within the encircling walls. The population of ancient Athens at its height in the 5c BC is estimated to have been about 200,000 (of whom 50,000 were adult male citizens). The population of ancient Alexandria,

---

**Unkiar-Skelessi, Treaty of** (1833)
The treaty of alliance concluded between Tsar **NICHO-LAS I** and Sultan **MAHMUD II** at a time when the **OTTO-MAN EMPIRE** was under serious threat from **MUHAMMAD 'ALI**'s Egyptian revolt. To the chagrin of the other European powers, Russia gained not only the closure of the straits of the **DARDANELLES** against them but also a virtual protectorate over what was left of the Ottoman Empire. This helped to produce the Russophobia, particularly in Britain, that led to the **CRIMEAN WAR**.

**UNP (United National Party)**
Sri Lankan political party. A right-of-centre alliance, it was originally formed out of the disbanded Ceylon National Congress at independence in 1948. The UNP held power from then until 1956, when it was defeated by a coalition headed by S W R D **BANDARA-NAIKE**'s **SLFP**. It only enjoyed one sustained period of government in the next 20 years, under the leadership of Dudley Senanayake from 1965 to 1970, but after J R **JAYAWARDENE**'s landslide victory of 1977 it won all subsequent elections until 1994, when it was defeated by the People's Alliance, a nine-party coalition which included the SLFP, led by Chandrika Bandaranaike **KUMARATUNGA**. It won the majority of seats in the 2001 election and formed a government under Ranil Wickremasinghe, but lost the 2004 election.

**UNR ➤ GAULLISTS**

**Unrepresented Nations' and Peoples' Organization (UNPO)**
An organization founded in 1991 to which ethnic or minority groups that are unrepresented at an international level may belong. Members include **TIBET**, the Australian **ABORIGINALS**, the Ogoni people of Nigeria, and various former Soviet groups aspiring to independent nationhood from Russia. In 2004 there were over 60 members, representing over 100 million people. Former members include Armenia, Estonia and Latvia.

**untouchables ➤ CASTE**

**'Urabi Pasha**, in full **Ahmad 'Urabi Pasha al-Misri** (1839–1911)
Egyptian soldier and nationalist leader. An officer in the Egyptian army, he fought in the Egyptian–Ethiopian War of 1875–9 and took part in the officers' revolt that deposed the Khedive, **ISMA'IL PASHA**, in 1879. He was the leader of a rebellion against the new Khedive, **TEWFIK PASHA**, in 1881 (the **'URABI REVOLT**); this led to the setting up of a nationalist government, in which he was War Minister. The British intervened to protect their interests in the Suez Canal, and he was defeated at **TEL EL-KEBIR** in 1882. Sentenced to death, he was exiled to Ceylon instead and was pardoned in 1901.

founded by Alexander the Great in 332 BC, is said to have grown to be in the region of 500,000, and that of Rome to have been 800,000 or more.

## Roman towns

The Romans not only made their capital city the largest in the ancient world, they founded towns throughout their empire, in particular bringing urban civilization to Europe beyond the Mediterranean rim. As the evidence from the Indus Valley and elsewhere shows, towns, especially new towns, were laid out to a plan from the earliest times. Roman towns often began life as military encampments, rectangular areas surrounded by ramparts with a gate in each side, a central forum with public buildings, main streets leading from the forum to each of the gates, and lesser streets laid out on a grid plan.

Roman civilization was town-based, but the Romans were also aware of the reverse side of town living. The satirist Juvenal paints a vivid picture of the discomforts of life in Rome: the crowded unhealthy tenements, the dangers of walking about at night, and the danger of fire. Large areas of Rome were destroyed in a disastrous fire in AD 64. Yet it is typical of Rome that when the city was rebuilt regulations were enforced limiting the size of residential buildings, insisting that they should have their own walls and be built at least in part of non-flammable materials and requiring all householders to keep fire-fighting equipment available.

## The Middle Ages and the Renaissance

In Western Europe urban civilization declined rapidly after the fall of the Roman Empire. When Charlemagne became Emperor in AD 800, the greatest city in the world was perhaps Baghdad, founded in AD 762 on a circular plan over an area about 1.6 mi/2.5 km in diameter and continually outgrowing itself, or Chang'an, the capital of the Tang Dynasty in China, built as an enormous rectangle 6 mi/9.4 km by 5 mi/8.4 km, with a main thoroughfare 500 ft/153 m wide. In Europe only Constantinople and Córdoba, the latter with a mainly Muslim population, were of comparable size. The city of Rome itself was in severe decline and Charlemagne's capital, Aix-la-Chapelle (Aachen), was home to probably only two or three thousand people.

As Europe revived in the 11–12c, towns began to grow again, often in the shadow of a castle or a monastery, sometimes on the sites of previous Roman settlements. As forest was cleared and new land was made available for cultivation, new towns were also founded (over 100 new towns were thought to have been founded in England and Wales between 1066 and 1190). The motive for their foundation was generally commercial, and merchants benefited most from the process, acquiring considerable political power in addition to their wealth, especially where central royal government was weak. The rise of the towns of the **Hanseatic League** and that of the city-state of Venice are cases in point.

Medieval towns were seldom laid out to a plan, though a type of zoning existed insofar as practitioners of different trades tended to cluster together in one street or area. The science of town-planning was rediscovered from classical sources in the **Renaissance**. Thereafter, new settlements tended to be laid out in accordance with a geometrical plan, the commonest being the grid pattern. William Penn is often credited with popularizing this pattern in North America, having chosen it for the layout of Philadelphia. Its simplicity and capacity for almost infinite extension made it almost universal in towns across the length and breadth of the USA. The grid pattern was also the normal layout for the cities of colonial Latin America.

---

### 'Urabi Revolt (1881–2)

A demonstration in Egypt, led by Colonel Ahmad **'URABI PASHA**, an officer of Egyptian peasant origin, which forced the Khedive to accept a nationalist government. 'Urabi was initially an Under-Secretary and subsequently became Minister for War. The revolt was in essence a reaction of junior officers of native Egyptian origin against the Turko-Circassians who tended to monopolize the senior ranks of the army. Unfortunately for 'Urabi, these developments occasioned disquiet among the British and French, who demanded that the Khedive dismiss the nationalist government. This dismissal provoked xenophobic disorder and 'Urabi prepared to face the possibility of direct British and French intervention. The British eventually moved against 'Urabi, destroying the defences of Alexandria he had prepared and defeating the Egyptian army at **TEL EL-KEBIR**.

### Urban II, originally **Odo of Lagery** (c.1035–99)

French pope (1088/99). He became a monk at Cluny, and was made Cardinal Bishop of Ostia in 1078. As pope, he introduced ecclesiastical reforms, drove foreign armies from Italy, and launched the First **CRU-SADE**.

### Urban IV, originally **Jacques Pantaléon** (c.1200–64)

French pope. Born in Troyes, he was Bishop of Verdun (1253) and Patriarch of Jerusalem (1255). He insti-

tuted the feast of Corpus Christi (1264).

### Urban V, originally **Guillaume de Grimoard** (c.1310–70)

French pope. Born in Grisac, he was abbot of St Victor at Marseilles, and was elected pope at Avignon (1362). He made a determined attempt to move the papacy to Rome (1367/–70), but had to return to Avignon a few months before his death.

### Urban VIII, originally **Maffeo Barberini** (1568–1644)

Italian pope (1623/44). As pope, he supported **RI-CHELIEU**'s policy against the Habsburgs in the **THIRTY YEARS' WAR**, and took no action against the French alliance with Protestant Sweden in 1631. He carried out much ecclesiastical reform, revising the breviary and rewriting some of the hymns himself, and offered firm support to missionary activity. His condemnations of heresy included the works of **GA-LILEO** (despite a long-standing personal friendship) and those of Jansen. ➤ **HABSBURG DYNASTY; JANSEN-ISM**

### Urbanization ➤ See panel

### Uribe (Velez), Alvaro (1952– )

Columbian politician. Educated in Columbia and at Harvard and Oxford, he served as mayor of Medellín and as a senator (1986–94) before being elected governor of Antioquia district in 1995. In a country

**Urbanization after the Industrial Revolution**

It is estimated that in 1800 only some 3 per cent of the world's population lived in towns of 20,000 inhabitants or more. During the 19–20c the urbanization of the world's population accelerated exponentially, so that by 1960, 25 per cent were town-dwellers, increasing to 40 per cent in 1980, and approximately 50 per cent in the year 2000.

The later stages of the **Industrial Revolution** accelerated a process that had been going on for centuries, creating a demand for labour in the factories of industrial towns that sucked in workers from the countryside. The mechanization of **agriculture** reduced the need for workers on the land, sending more immigrants into the cities.

The squalid, polluted conditions and overcrowding in early industrial towns are well-known. It has been suggested that after the arrival of the first wave of immigration from the countryside, the increase in the overall number of inhabitants was relatively slow because the mortality rate in cities was so high – new recruits from the healthier countryside were always needed to sustain the labouring population at the required level. It was only in about 1900, after advances in **medicine** and improvements in public health, that the populations of cities first became self-sustaining.

**The city in modern times**

In earlier ages the suburbs of a city tended to be where the poorer people lived, often outside the city wall. With the advent of modern modes of transportation, suburban living became a more attractive proposition for the urban middle classes. Cities like London underwent enormous expansion in the late 19c and early 20c, swallowing up small towns and villages on their outskirts and filling the intervening space with streets and streets of houses of varying size and quality. It was only in 1909 that a Town Planning Act was passed in Britain, allowing municipalities to control the type and extent of building allowed within their jurisdiction and to ensure that adequate provision was made for open spaces and other communal facilities, and enshrining the concept of the 'green belt'. Similar action was undertaken at the same time in the USA.

New towns continued to be founded throughout the 20c, in some instances, such as in Britain after **World War II**, to cope with the over-spill of population from existing cities; in others, such as in the USSR, to establish a working population near to a valuable source of raw materials. In general, new towns have been planned with the quality of life of their inhabitants in mind, inspired, for instance, by the Garden City movement of Sir Ebenezer Howard (1850–1928) in Britain, whose first model town at Letchworth, Hertfordshire, was laid out in 1903.

The quality of life to be had in a large city became a matter of major concern during the latter part of the 20c. In the decades following World War II, the flight to the suburbs of more and more of the middle classes seemed to be leaving inner-city areas prey to gradual dereliction and the growth of crime and violence. In the developed world, urban renewal schemes, the decline of older smokestack industries and changing employment patterns have brought about some changes and rehabilitated a number of previously run-down inner-city districts. In the developing world, an earlier stage of city expansion is still being played out, with the city acting as a magnet for those no longer able to make a living off the land, or simply wishing to take advantages of the opportunities afforded by an urban area. This trend was particularly marked in China in the late 20c and early 21c, which saw the mass migration to the cities of rural dwellers seeking work. In parts of South America, Asia and Africa already huge and crowded cities are often surrounded by a ring of shantytowns filled with people clinging onto the city as a lifesaver and desperately hoping ultimately to be provided with the amenities that most modern city-dwellers now take for granted. ➤ **Industrialization**

---

plagued by civil conflict, poverty and drug cartels, he ran for president on a platform of economic development and ridding the country of the left-wing FARC guerrillas and paramilitaries such as the right-wing Self-Defence Forces of Colombia (AUC), and was elected in 2002. Despite cooperation with the USA's war on **DRUGS** and increased military spending, his government has been unable to suppress or to reach peace settlements with FARC or the AUC, which is suspected of having ties with the security forces. Since the **SEPTEMBER 11 ATTACKS** he has called for more international aid to fight terrorism in Columbia and declared a state of emergency in 2002. His critics argue that the country is too dependent on the USA and allege that he has links to the paramilitaries and drug-trafficking.

**Urquiza, Justo José de** (1801–70)

Argentine general and politician. A prominent businessman, he gained political experience early and after arriving in Buenos Aires became a confidant of the dictator **ROSAS**. From 1841 to 1854 he was Governor of Entre Ríos, where he suppressed all other military forces and encouraged educational and administrative reform. He formed alliances with other provincial governors and in 1852 rebelled against Rosas, defeating him at the Battle of Monte Caseros. Once installed as provisional dictator, Urquiza called a constitutional congress at Santa Fé

(1853) where a constitution modelled on that of the USA was adopted, creating the Argentine Confederation. From 1854 to 1860 he served as Argentina's first constitutional President and negotiated treaties that opened Argentina's ports to world trade, then became Commander-in-Chief of national forces and returned as Governor of Entre Ríos. In 1861 war between the provinces and Buenos Aires broke out, and Urquiza was defeated by **MITRE** in the Battle of Pavón. He commanded the Argentine army in a war with Paraguay in 1865–8, and in 1870 he and his sons were assassinated at home in Entre Ríos by political rivals.

**URUGUAY** official name **Oriental Republic of Uruguay**

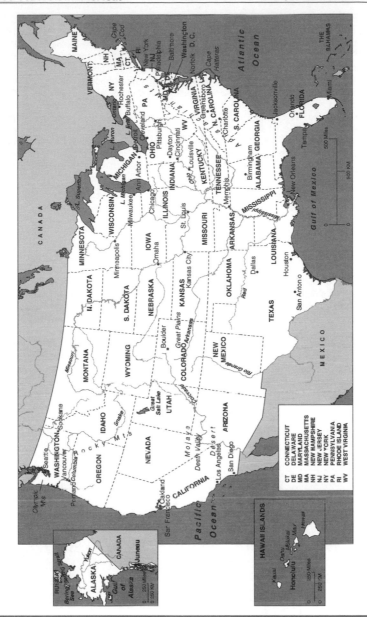

A republic in eastern South America, bounded to the south and east by the Atlantic Ocean; to the north by Brazil; and to the west by the River Uruguay and Argentina. Originally occupied by various Indian tribes known collectively as the Charrúas people, it was discovered by the Spanish in 1515 and became part of the Spanish Viceroyalty of Río de la Plata in 1726. Between 1814 and 1825 it was a province of Brazil, gaining its independence in 1828. During the 19c there was a struggle for political control between the liberals (the 'redshirts', or *Colorados*), and the conservatives (the whites, or *Blancos*), which was resolved when the former took office for 86 years (1872–1958). There was unrest caused by the Marxist terrorist **TUPAMAROS** in the late 1960s and early 1970s, and military rule prevailed from 1971 until civilian rule was restored in 1985, with Julio María **SAN-GUINETTI** as President until 1990. The 2004 presidential election was won by Tabaré Vazquez, the first left-wing candidate to hold the office.

**USA (UNITED STATES OF AMERICA)** also called **United States**, and often **America**
A federal republic in North America and the fourth-largest country in the world. It includes the detached states of Alaska and Hawaii. The mainland is bounded to the north by Canada; to the east by the Atlantic Ocean; to the south by Mexico and the Gulf of Mexico; and to the west by the Pacific Ocean. The country was first settled by migrant groups from Asia over 25,000 years ago. These **NATIVE AMERICANS** remained undisturbed until the country was explored by the Norse (9c) and the Spanish (16c), who settled in Florida and Mexico. In the 17c, there were settlements by the British, French, Dutch, Germans and Swedish. Many black Africans were introduced as slaves to work on the plantations. In the following

## UNITED STATES OF AMERICA: PRESIDENTS

Vice-Presidents in parentheses

| Dates | Name | Party | Dates | Name | Party |
|---|---|---|---|---|---|
| 1789–97 | George Washington (1st) (John Adams) | | 1889–93 | Benjamin Harrison (23rd) (Levi P Morton) | Rep |
| 1797–1801 | John Adams (2nd) (Thomas Jefferson) | Fed | 1893–7 | Grover Cleveland (24th) (Adlai E Stevenson) | Dem |
| 1801–9 | Thomas Jefferson (3rd) (Aaron Burr, 1801–5) (George Clinton, 1805–9) | Dem-Rep | 1897–1901 | William McKinley (25th) (Garret A Hobart, 1897–9) no Vice-President 1899–1901 | Rep |
| 1809–17 | James Madison (4th) (George Clinton, 1809–12) no Vice-President 1812–13 (Elbridge Gerry, 1813–14) no Vice-President 1814–17 | Dem-Rep | | (Theodore Roosevelt, 1901) | |
| | | | 1901–9 | Theodore Roosevelt (26th) no Vice-President 1901–5 (Charles W Fairbanks, 1905–9) | Rep |
| | | | 1909–13 | William Howard Taft (27th) (James S Sherman, 1909–12) no Vice-President 1912–13 | Rep |
| 1817–25 | James Monroe (5th) (Daniel D Tompkins) | Dem-Rep | | | |
| 1825–9 | John Quincy Adams (6th) (John C Calhoun) | Dem-Rep | 1913–21 | Woodrow Wilson (28th) (Thomas R Marshall) | Dem |
| 1829–37 | Andrew Jackson (7th) (John C Calhoun, 1829–32) no Vice-President 1832–3 (Martin Van Buren, 1833–7) | Dem | 1921–3 | Warren G Harding (29th) (Calvin Coolidge) | Rep |
| | | | 1923–9 | Calvin Coolidge (30th) no Vice-President 1923–5 (Charles G Dawes, 1925–9) | Rep |
| 1837–41 | Martin Van Buren (8th) (Richard M Johnson) | Dem | 1929–33 | Herbert Hoover (31st) (Charles Curtis) | Rep |
| 1841 | William Henry Harrison (9th) (John Tyler) | Whig | 1933–45 | Franklin D Roosevelt (32nd) (John Nance Garner, 1933–41) (Henry A Wallace, 1941–5) (Harry S Truman, 1945) | Dem |
| 1841–5 | John Tyler (10th) no Vice-President | Whig | | | |
| 1845–9 | James K Polk (11th) (George M Dallas) | Dem | 1945–53 | Harry S Truman (33rd) no Vice-President 1945–9 (Alben W Barkley, 1949–53) | Dem |
| 1849–50 | Zachary Taylor (12th) (Millard Fillmore) | Whig | | | |
| 1850–3 | Millard Fillmore (13th), no Vice-President | Whig | 1953–61 | Dwight D Eisenhower (34th) (Richard M Nixon) | Rep |
| 1853–7 | Franklin Pierce (14th) (William R King, 1853) no Vice-President 1853–7 | Dem | 1961–3 | John F Kennedy (35th) (Lyndon B Johnson) | Dem |
| | | | 1963–9 | Lyndon B Johnson (36th) no Vice-President 1963–5 (Hubert H Humphrey, 1965–9) | Dem |
| 1857–61 | James Buchanan (15th) (John C Breckinridge) | Dem | | | |
| 1861–5 | Abraham Lincoln (16th) (Hannibal Hamlin, 1861–5) (Andrew Johnson, 1865) | Rep | 1969–74 | Richard M Nixon (37th) (Spiro T Agnew, 1969–73) no Vice-President Oct–Dec 1973 (Gerald Ford, 1973–4) | Rep |
| 1865–9 | Andrew Johnson (17th) no Vice-President | Dem-Nat | 1974–7 | Gerald Ford (38th) no Vice-President Aug–Dec 1974 (Nelson A Rockefeller, 1974–7) | Rep |
| 1869–77 | Ulysses S Grant (18th) (Schuyler Colfax, 1869–73) (Henry Wilson, 1873–5) no Vice-President 1875–7 | Rep | | | |
| | | | 1977–81 | Jimmy Carter (39th) (Walter F Mondale) | Dem |
| 1877–81 | Rutherford B Hayes (19th) (William A Wheeler) | Rep | 1981–9 | Ronald Reagan (40th) (George H W Bush) | Rep |
| 1881 | James A Garfield (20th) (Chester A Arthur) | Rep | 1989–93 | George H W Bush (41st) (J Danforth Quayle) | Rep |
| 1881–5 | Chester A Arthur (21st) no Vice-President | Rep | 1993–2001 | Bill Clinton (42nd) (Al Gore) | Dem |
| 1885–9 | Grover Cleveland (22nd) (Thomas A Hendricks, 1885) no Vice-President 1885–9 | Dem | 2001– | George W Bush (43rd) (Dick Cheney) | Rep |

Notes

| | |
|---|---|
| Dem | Democrat |
| Fed | Federalist |
| Nat | National Union |
| Rep | Republican |

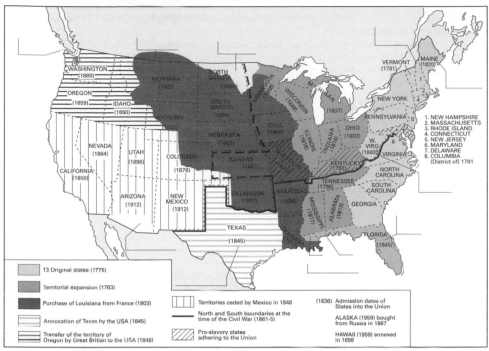

**USA: Entry of States into the Union**

Map legend:

13 Original states (1775)

Territorial expansion (1783)

Purchase of Louisiana from France (1803)

Annexation of Texas by the USA (1845)

Transfer of the territory of Oregon by Great Britian to the USA (1846)

Territories ceded by Mexico in 1848

North and South boundaries at the time of the Civil War (1861-5)

Pro-slavery states adhering to the Union

(1836) Admission dates of States into the Union

ALASKA (1959) bought from Russia in 1867

HAWAII (1959) annexed in 1898

States shown on map: WASHINGTON (1889), MONTANA (1889), NORTH DAKOTA (1889), MINNESOTA (1858), WISCONSIN (1848), MICHIGAN (1837), VERMONT (1791), MAINE (1820), NEW YORK, OREGON (1859), IDAHO (1890), SOUTH DAKOTA (1889), IOWA (1846), PENNSYLVANIA, WYOMING (1890), NEBRASKA (1867), ILLINOIS (1818), INDIANA (1816), OHIO (1803), W. VIRG. (1863), VIRGINIA, NEVADA (1864), UTAH (1896), COLORADO (1876), KANSAS (1861), MISSOURI (1821), KENTUCKY (1792), NORTH CAROLINA, CALIFORNIA (1850), TENNESSEE (1796), SOUTH CAROLINA, ARIZONA (1912), NEW MEXICO (1912), OKLAHOMA (1907), ARKANSAS (1836), MISSISSIPPI (1817), ALABAMA (1819), GEORGIA, TEXAS (1845), LOUISIANA, FLORIDA (1845)

1. NEW HAMPSHIRE
2. MASSACHUSETTS
3. RHODE ISLAND
4. CONNECTICUT
5. NEW JERSEY
6. MARYLAND
7. DELAWARE
8. COLUMBIA (District of) 1791

century, British control grew throughout the area. A revolt of the English-speaking colonies in the **AMERICAN REVOLUTION** (1775–83) led to the creation of the United States of America, which then lay between the Great Lakes, the Mississippi and Florida; the **DECLARATION OF INDEPENDENCE** was made on 4 July 1776. Louisiana was sold to the USA by France in 1803 (the **LOUISIANA PURCHASE**) and the westward movement of settlers began. Florida was ceded by Spain in 1819, and further Spanish states joined the Union between 1821 and 1853. In 1860–1, 11 Southern states seceded from the Union over the **SLAVERY** issue, and formed the Confederacy; the Civil War (1861–5) ended in victory for the North, and the Southern states later rejoined the Union. As a result of the North's victory, slavery was abolished in 1865. In 1867 Alaska was purchased from Russia, and the Hawaiian Islands were annexed in 1898 (both admitted as states in 1959). The USA entered **WORLD WAR I** on the side of the Allies in 1917. Native Americans were given the right to become US citizens in 1924. In 1929 the stockmarket on Wall Street crashed, resulting in the **GREAT DEPRESSION**. After the Japanese attack on **PEARL HARBOR** in 1941, the USA entered **WORLD WAR II**. The campaign for black **CIVIL RIGHTS** developed in the 1960s, accompanied by much civil disturbance. From 1964 to 1975 the USA intervened in the **VIETNAM WAR**, supporting non-communist South Vietnam. The USA led the **SPACE EXPLORATION** programme of the 1960s and 1970s (in 1969 US astronaut Neil Armstrong was the first person on the moon). The **WATERGATE** scandal (1972–4) forced President **NIXON** to resign; there was further scandal in 1986 over arms sales to Iran to fund Contra rebels in Nicaragua. The **COLD WAR** between the USA and the USSR came to an end in 1990; since then US military force has been deployed in **UN** peacekeeping missions in countries such as

Bosnia. In the 1991 **GULF WAR**, US troops led the assault against Saddam **HUSSEIN** following Iraq's invasion of Kuwait. After Democratic President Bill **CLINTON** came to power in 1993, the White House was dogged by various financial and sexual scandals, one of which resulted in the President's **IMPEACHMENT** and acquittal in 1999. Following the **SEPTEMBER 11 ATTACKS**, Republican President George W **BUSH** declared a war on **TERROR**, as part of which the USA led multi-national forces in the **AFGHAN WAR** and the **IRAQ WAR**. ► **CIVIL RIGHTS MOVEMENT; INDIAN WARS; IRAN–CONTRA AFFAIR**

## US Constitution

The US Constitution embodies the concepts on which the US system of government is based. The law of the land since 1789, it establishes a federal republic, balancing the power of the states and that of the federal government. In the federal government, power is divided among three independent branches: legislative, executive and judicial. The constitutional document comprises a short preamble followed by seven articles which include: the organization, powers and procedures of the legislative branch (**CONGRESS**); the powers of the President and executive; the powers of the judiciary, including the Supreme Court; the rights of the states; and procedures for amending the Constitution. The articles are followed by 26 amendments, the first ten of which are known as the **BILL OF RIGHTS** (although later amendments also deal with **CIVIL RIGHTS** issues). The others cover such matters as the election, death or removal of the President, and eligibility to stand for election to Congress. Drafted at the **CONSTITUTIONAL CONVENTION** of 1787 held in Philadelphia, the Constitution was adopted after it had been ratified by nine of the states. ► **ARTICLES OF CONFEDERATION**

## Usher, James ► USSHER, JAMES

### US–Japan Security Treaty (1960)
An agreement signed between Japan and the USA which allows the USA to operate military bases in many parts of Japan, thus helping to maintain Japan's national defence. It is a revised version of a 1951 treaty formulated following Japan's **WORLD WAR II** defeat and return to independence. Since the treaty was reaffirmed in 1970, either country may give one year's notice to terminate the agreement.

### Usman dan Fodio (1754–1817)
Ruler of Hausaland. He was the leader of a **JIHAD** or holy war in northern Nigeria, which resulted in the creation of a large Islamic empire extending over some 180,000 sq mi/466,200 sq km and 10 million people. A member of an Islamic brotherhood in the small state of Gobir, Usman began to preach about 1775. His repeated calls for reform in line with strict Islamic doctrine were resisted by successive Hausa rulers. In 1804 he launched a jihad against the ruling Hausa aristocracy and founded his capital at Sokoto. Many similar jihads followed and Usman, as *Shehu* (or Chief) of Sokoto, was able to establish client Muslim rulers over a vast area. This was an important part of the late 18c and early 19c movements to create African Islamic states, which were to prove resistant to the advance of European rule.

### USO ► UNITED SERVICE ORGANIZATIONS

### Ussher or Usher, James (1581–1656)
Irish prelate. In 1605, he drew up the Articles of Doctrine for the established Protestant Church of Ireland. In 1620 he was made Bishop of Meath, in 1623 Privy Councillor for Ireland, and in 1625 Archbishop of Armagh, in succession to his uncle Henry Ussher (c.1550–1631). He went to England (1640), and for about eight years was preacher at Lincoln's Inn. He was constant in his loyalty to the throne, yet was treated with favour by **CROMWELL**. Of his numerous writings, the best known is the *Annales Veteris et Novi Testamenti* (1650–4), which fixed the Creation precisely at 4004BC.

### USSR (Union of Soviet Socialist Republics), Russian Soyuz Sovyetskikh Sotsialisticheskikh Republik, also called Soviet Union
A federation of 15 republics which formed the world's largest sovereign state from the 1920s until its dissolution in 1991; the federation comprised Russia, Armenia, Azerbaijan, Belorussia (now Belarus), Estonia, Georgia, Kazakhstan, Kirghizia (now Kyrgyzstan), Latvia, Lithuania, Moldavia (now Moldova), Tajikistan, Turkmenistan, Ukraine and Uzbekistan. Russia had become a great power by the 18c, its territory extending from eastern Europe into southern Asia and throughout northern Asia to the Pacific. In 1917 the **RUSSIAN REVOLUTION** overthrew imperial rule of this empire, which was replaced after Bolshevik victory in the **RUSSIAN CIVIL WAR** by a Soviet government headed by **LENIN**, then after his death by **STALIN**. Stalin began vigorous socialist reforms, including **COLLECTIVIZATION** of agriculture and rapid industrialization. Soviet influence was extended after **WORLD WAR II** with the creation of a corridor of communist-dominated countries between the USSR

## USSR: POLITICAL LEADERS

► *President*

| | |
|---|---|
| 1917 | Lev Borisovich Kamenev |
| 1917–19 | Yakov Mikhailovich Sverdlov |
| 1919–46 | Mikhail Ivanovich Kalinin |
| 1946–53 | Nikolai Shvernik |
| 1953–60 | Kliment Yefremovich Voroshilov |
| 1960–4 | Leonid Ilich Brezhnev |
| 1964–5 | Anastas Ivanovich Mikoyan |
| 1965–77 | Nikolai Viktorovich Podgorny |
| 1977–82 | Leonid Ilich Brezhnev |
| 1982–3 | Vasili Vasilevich Kuznetsov *Acting President* |
| 1983–4 | Yuri Andropov |
| 1984 | Vasili Vasilevich Kuznetsov *Acting President* |
| 1984–5 | Konstantin Ustinovich Chernenko |
| 1985 | Vasili Vasilevich Kuznetsov *Acting President* |
| 1985–8 | Andrei Andreevich Gromyko |
| 1988–90 | Mikhail Sergeevich Gorbachev |

► *Executive President*

| | |
|---|---|
| 1990–1 | Mikhail Sergeevich Gorbachev |
| 1991 | Gennadi Ivanovich Yanaev *Acting President* |
| 1991 | Mikhail Sergeevich Gorbachev |

► *Chairman (Prime Minister) – Council of Ministers*

| | |
|---|---|
| 1917 | Giorgiy Yevgenievich Lvov |
| 1917 | Alexandr Fyodorovich Kerensky |

► *Chairman (Prime Minister) – Council of People's Commissars*

| | |
|---|---|
| 1917–24 | Vladimir Ilich Lenin |
| 1924–30 | Alexei Ivanovich Rykov |
| 1930–41 | Vyacheslav Mikhailovich Molotov |
| 1941–53 | Joseph Stalin |

► *Chairman (Prime Minister) – Council of Ministers*

| | |
|---|---|
| 1953–5 | Giorgiy Maximilianovich Malenkov |
| 1955–8 | Nikolai Alexandrovich Bulganin |
| 1958–64 | Nikita Khrushchev |
| 1964–80 | Alexei Nikolaevich Kosygin |
| 1980–5 | Nikolai Alexandrovich Tikhonov |
| 1985–91 | Nikolai Ivanovich Ryzhkov |
| 1991 | Valentin Pavlov |
| 1991 | Ivan Silaev *Acting Chairman* |

► *General-Secretary*

| | |
|---|---|
| 1922–53 | Joseph Stalin |
| 1953 | Giorgiy Maximilianovich Malenkov |
| 1953–64 | Nikita Khrushchev |
| 1964–82 | Leonid Ilich Brezhnev |
| 1982–4 | Yuri Andropov |
| 1984–5 | Konstantin Ustinovich Chernenko |
| 1985–91 | Mikhail Sergeevich Gorbachev |

and Western Europe, which heralded the **COLD WAR**. A process of détente from the 1970s produced a series of disarmament agreements (**SALT**; **START**), and international tensions between the USSR and the West eased, particularly after the policies of **GLASNOST** and **PERESTROIKA** were introduced by **GORBACHEV** in the 1980s. These policies introduced some political and economic reforms but also weakened Communist Party control, both in the USSR and in its satellite states, and encouraged local independence movements. The communist regimes in the Eastern European satellite states were all overthrown in 1989 and some of the Soviet republics began to agitate for independence. Conservatives attempted to reverse the process of reform in the 1991 **AUGUST COUP** in Moscow, but achieved the opposite effect so undermining the USSR that its constituent republics began to declare themselves independent, and the Union was formally dissolved in Dec 1991. ► **BOL-SHEVIKS; CIS; COMMUNIST PARTY OF THE SOVIET UNION; RUSSIA; YELTSIN, BORIS**

### Ustaša

The name (meaning 'uprising') of the Croatian fascist movement which was organized in the 1930s by Ante **PAVELIĆ** and supported by **MUSSOLINI**'s Italy, and Hungary. Its right-wing nationalist ideology was an extension of the politics of Ante **STARČEVIĆ**'s Croatian Party of (State) Right. A terrorist organization, it carried out the assassination of the Yugoslav King **ALEXANDER I**. During **WORLD WAR II** it upheld the regime of Pavelić in Croatia and brutally massacred many thousands of Serbs, Jews, gypsies, communists and non-Ustaša Croats.

### Ustinov, Dmitri Fedorovich (1908–84)

Russian politician and Soviet marshal. Born into a working-class family, he acquired a technical education in his twenties, and by 1938 he was manager of an arms factory in Leningrad. In 1941 he was appointed as People's Commissar for Armaments; from then until 1976, when he became Minister of Defence, his primary function was to develop the arms industry. He gave it a civilian element and secured it an unfair share of the Soviet budget. He also helped find it an outlet by supporting the invasion of Afghanistan in 1979. His death removed from the ministry and the **POLITBURO** a fierce opponent of Mikhail **GORBA-CHEV**'s campaign to reduce expenditure on the military.

### US War of Independence ► AMERICAN REVOLUTION

### Utrecht, Peace of (11 Apr 1713)

The treaty which ended the War of the **SPANISH SUCCESSION**, signed between England, the Dutch Republic, Spain and France, with the other powers agreeing in due course. By its terms Philip of Anjou became King **PHILIP V** of Spain, but the southern Netherlands went to the Austrian Habsburgs, along with Spanish parts of Italy. England obtained Gibraltar, and parts of Canada (from France). The Dutch contained France, obtained some possessions in Gelderland, and gained English support for the **BARRIER TREATIES**. ► **HABSBURG DYNASTY**

### Utrecht, Union of (1579)

The defensive alliance of the northern Dutch provinces against Spain in the **EIGHTY YEARS' WAR**, provoked by the Union of **ARRAS** which threatened to take the southern Netherlands back into the Spanish fold. The union was signed by the provinces of Holland, Zeeland, Utrecht, Groningen and Gelderland, and later by Ghent, some Frisian towns, Antwerp, Breda, Bruges, Lier, Drenthe, and eventually Prince **WILLIAM I, THE SILENT**, Prince of Orange. The union arranged taxes for defence purposes, and stipulated freedom of religion. Later the union gained the status of a sort of constitution for the northern Dutch Republic.

---

**UZBEKISTAN**   official name **Republic of Uzbekistan**

A republic in central and northern Asia, bounded to the south by Afghanistan; to the south-west by Turkmenistan; to the west and north by Kazakhstan; and to the east by Kyrgyzstan and Tajikistan; the Aral Sea lies in the north-west of the republic. In the 12–13c it was the centre of **GENGHIS KHAN**'s empire, and its cities of Samarkand and Tashkent grew rich from the silk caravan trade. It was divided into the khanates of Bukhara, Khiva and Kokand, which were subjected to attacks by Russia from the early 18c until they were annexed in 1876. The Uzbeks rebelled against Russian rule in 1918 but were suppressed and the country was proclaimed a Soviet Socialist Republic in 1924. It declared its independence from the USSR in 1991 under President Islam Karimov, and became a member of the **CIS** (Commonwealth of Independent States). A multi-party constitution was introduced in 1992, but despite this the two main opposition parties remain banned, little political opposition is tolerated, and human rights abuses by the authorities are reported regularly.

**Vaal Kraantz Reverse** (5–8 Feb 1900)
An incident in the Boer War in which the British general Sir Redvers Buller attacked Boers on a ridge of kopjes a few miles east of Spion Kop in an attempt to relieve Ladysmith. He was forced to withdraw and the British Commander-in-Chief, **ROBERTS**, was given authority to dismiss Sir 'Reverses' Buller. ➤ **BOER WARS**

**Vafiadis, Markos** (1906–92)
Greek politician. Like many other Greeks driven from Anatolia in 1923, he found work in the Greek tobacco industry. He joined the **KKE** (Communist Party of Greece) in 1928 and was frequently imprisoned during the 1930s for his communist activities. In 1941 he escaped from the island where he was being held and went to Macedonia where he became Captain of the **ELAS** 10th Division operating there. During the **GREEK CIVIL WAR** (1944–9), he led the Democratic Army of Greece which was founded by the KKE (Oct 1946). He organized communist bases in the villages and was one of those responsible for the abduction and forced enrolment in the army of many Greek youths and girls. Often at variance with the KKE leadership, he fled to Albania in 1949 after the KKE made a clumsy attempt on his life. He was expelled from the KKE the following year and was condemned for never having been 'a real communist'. ➤ **LAUSANNE, TREATY OF**; **ZACHARIADIS, NIKOS**

**Vakataka** ➤ **INDIA, PRE-ISLAMIC**

**Valckenier, Johan** (1759–1821)
Dutch politician. He made his career in academic law, holding chairs at the universities of Franeker (1782–7), Utrecht (1787) and Leiden (1795–6). Politically he was a fervent supporter of the **PATRIOT MOVEMENT**, following the ideals of the **FRENCH REVOLUTION** in the Netherlands, and working for a new unitary Dutch state. During the period of French domination of the Netherlands (1795–1813) he held political office; he was a member of the National Assembly in 1796, ambassador to Spain in 1796 and 1799–1801, and was a close adviser to King **LOUIS NAPOLEON** in 1806–10.

**Valdemar I, the Great** (1131–82)
King of Denmark (1157/82). The son of King Knut Lavard, he emerged victorious from 30 years of civil strife to give Denmark an unparalleled period of prosperity and expansion. In 1169 he destroyed the power of the Wends by capturing the island of Rügen. He strengthened the defences of the Danevirke and increased the size and effectiveness of the Danish army. He was succeeded by his eldest son, Knud VI.

**Valdemar II, the Victorious** (1170–1241)
King of Denmark (1202/41). The son of **VALDEMAR I, THE GREAT** and the brother of King Knud VI, he continued the expansionist policies of his predecessors, culminating in the conquest of Estonia (1219). He created a Danish Baltic empire which at its climax (c.1220) stretched from Holstein in the west to Estonia in the east. This empire, however, crumbled rapidly after the kidnapping of King Valdemar by a German vassal in 1223. In 1225 a huge ransom and the relinquishing of the bulk of the conquered territories secured the King's release. Only Estonia remained under Danish rule (until 1346). At the domestic level, however, Valdemar was not weakened, keeping a firm hold on power. He was succeeded by his brother, Erik (1216–50).

**Valdivia, Pedro de** (c.1510–1559)
Spanish soldier. He went to Venezuela (c.1534) and then to Peru, where he became **PIZARRO**'s lieutenant. He won renown at Las Salinas (1538), and was in real command of the expedition to Chile. He founded Santiago (1541) and other cities, including Concepción (1550) and Valdivia (1552). In 1559, attempting, with a small force, to relieve Tucapel, which was besieged by the **ARAUCANIANS**, he was captured and killed by the Indians. ➤ **EXPLORATION**

**Valencia, Conquest of** (1233–53)
The campaigns to conquer the Muslim Kingdom of Valencia were begun by **JAIME I, THE CONQUEROR**, and continued until the siege of Valencia city (Apr 1238). The city capitulated on 28 Sep and Jaime I entered in triumph on 9 Oct. Campaigns continued in later years until the whole of the kingdom was reduced by 1253.

**Valle, José Cecilio del** (d.c.1834)
Honduran attorney, intellectual and politician. A Conservative, he contested the first presidential election of the United Provinces of Central America (**CENTRAL AMERICAN FEDERATION**) in 1825, but lost to Manuel José Arce, a Liberal Salvadoran army officer. In 1834 he gained electoral victory over President Francisco **MORAZÁN**, but he died before taking office.

**Valley Forge**
An area in Chester County, Pennsylvania, USA, which was the winter headquarters of George **WASHINGTON** in 1777–8. His troops are renowned for the endurance and loyalty they showed while stationed there during the severe winter. ➤ **AMERICAN REVOLUTION**

## Valois Dynasty

The ruling dynasty of France from the accession of **PHILIP VI**, Count of Valois (1328), to the death of **HENRY III** (1589). The succession was maintained in the direct male line from the 14c until **LOUIS XII** of the Orléans branch assumed the crown (1498). The last three Valois kings – **FRANCIS II** (1559/60), **CHARLES IX** (1560/74) and **HENRY III** (1574/89) – were all childless. ► **ORLÉANS, HOUSE OF**

### VALOIS DYNASTY

| Regnal Dates | Name |
|---|---|
| 1328/50 | Philip VI |
| 1350/64 | John II, the Good |
| 1364/80 | Charles V, the Wise |
| 1380/1422 | Charles VI, the Foolish |
| 1422/61 | Charles VII, the Victorious |
| 1461/83 | Louis XI |
| 1483/98 | Charles VIII |
| 1498/1515 | Louis XII |
| 1515/47 | Francis I |
| 1547/59 | Henry II |
| 1559/60 | Francis II |
| 1560/74 | Charles IX |
| 1574/89 | Henry III |

### Van Buren, Martin (1782–1862)

US politician and 8th President. He became a lawyer, state Attorney-General (1816–19), Senator (1821), Governor of New York (1828), Secretary of State (1829–31) and Vice-President (1833–7). He was a supporter of Andrew **JACKSON** and a member of the group which evolved into the **DEMOCRATIC PARTY**. His presidency (1837–41) began during the financial panic of 1837 and in response to this, he introduced the Independent Treasury system. This crisis overshadowed his term in office and he was overwhelmingly defeated for re-election by the **WHIG PARTY** in 1840. In 1848 he ran unsuccessfully for President as the candidate of the **FREE-SOIL PARTY**, which opposed the spread of **SLAVERY**.

### Vandenberg, Arthur Hendrick (1884–1951)

US Republican politician. Born in Grand Rapids, Michigan, he studied at the university there and was elected to the **SENATE** (1928). An isolationist before **WORLD WAR II**, he strongly supported the formation of the **UN**, and was a delegate at the San Francisco Conference and at the UN Assembly from 1946.

### Vanderbilt, Cornelius (1794–1877)

US financier. Born on Staten Island, New York, he bought a boat at the age of 16 and ferried passengers and goods between Staten Island and New York City. By the age of 40 he had become the owner of steamers running to Boston and up the Hudson. In 1849, during the **GOLD RUSH**, he established a route from Lake Nicaragua to California, and during the **CRIMEAN WAR**, a line of steamships to Havre. In 1862 he sold his ships and entered on a great career of railroad financing, gradually obtaining a controlling interest in a large number of **RAILWAYS**. He gave a large sum of money to found Vanderbilt University at Nashville, Tennessee.

### Vandervelde, Émile (1866–1938)

Belgian politician. Having studied law, he joined parliament as a socialist in 1894 and became the leader of the **BELGIAN SOCIALIST PARTY**. He repeatedly held cabinet posts from 1916 to 1937, and was also a noted theorist in revisionist **MARXISM**. He published widely and was Chairman of the Second International from 1900.

### Vane, Sir Henry (1613–62)

English statesman. He travelled in Europe, became a Puritan, and sailed for New England in 1635, where he was Governor of Massachusetts; but his advocacy of religious toleration lost him popularity, and he returned in 1637. He entered parliament, became joint Treasurer of the Navy, and was knighted (1640). He helped to impeach **STRAFFORD**, promoted the **SOLEMN LEAGUE AND COVENANT** (1643), and was a strong supporter of the parliamentary cause in the **ENGLISH CIVIL WARS**. During the **COMMONWEALTH** he was appointed one of the Council of State (1649–53), but he opposed **CROMWELL**'s becoming Lord Protector in 1653, and retired from politics. On Cromwell's death he returned to public life (1659), opposed the **RESTORATION**, and was imprisoned and executed. ► **PROTECTORATE**

**VANUATU**  official name **Republic of Vanuatu**

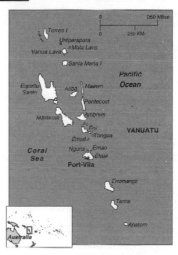

A chain of over 80 islands in the south-west Pacific Ocean, east of Australia. Many islands are actively volcanic. Visited by the Portuguese in the early 17c, the islands were named the New Hebrides in 1774 by Captain Cook. The islands were settled in the 19c by the British and French, who established plantations, and came under Anglo-French administration as the Condominium of the New Hebrides in 1906. Limited self government was introduced in 1978 and the New Hebrides became independent as Vanuatu in 1980.

### Vanunu, Mordechai (1948– )

Israeli nuclear technician. A relatively junior member of the technical staff developing Israel's nuclear arsenal, Vanunu's disillusionment with the duplicity of his country's government, which had always claimed that it would not be the first Middle East country to acquire atomic weapons, led him to resign his post in 1986, and later that year the *Sunday Times* published an interview with Vanunu in which he revealed that Israel had already stockpiled up to 200 atomic bombs at an underground factory in the Negev Desert. In Sep 1986 he was abducted at Rome airport by agents of Mossad, the Israeli secret service, and returned to Jerusalem. After a secret trial, Vanunu was found guilty of treason and sentenced to 18 years in solitary confinement. He was released in Apr 2004 but re-arrested in Nov, accused of breaching restrictions on his speech and movements.

### Vargas, Getúlio Dornelles (1883–1954)
Brazilian politician. After serving in the army and training as a lawyer, he was elected a Federal deputy in 1923. He was Minister of Finance under Washington Luís Pereira de Souza and headed the Liberal Alliance ticket for the presidency in 1930. Defeated in the polls, he won the support of significant military force to govern with the army from 1930–45. A man who stood aloof from party politics, he sought a **CONCI-LIAÇÃO** based upon support from the army, major industrial groups in São Paulo and Minas Gerais to achieve a more centralized state. Ousted in 1945 by the army, he returned as constitutional President in 1951. Four years later, in the face of mounting opposition from the right wing, he committed suicide. He created two political parties, the **PSD** and PTB, but his political heirs were Leonel **BRIZOLA** and João **GOULART**.

### Varna, Battle of (1828)
A three-month siege and battle between Russian and Turkish troops during the Russo-Turkish War, which took place at Varna, a fortress on the Black Sea coast of Bulgaria. The Turkish garrison fell in Oct 1828, and was occupied by Russian forces. ► **RUSSO-TURKISH WARS**

### Varotnikov, Vitali Ivanovich (1926– )
Soviet politician. He began work as a fitter in 1942, joined the Communist Party in 1947, and started to climb the bureaucratic and political ladder in his native Voronezh and Kubyshev. In 1975 he was brought to Moscow to become Deputy Chairman of the Russian Ministerial Council, but quickly clashed with Leonid **BREZHNEV** and was sent to Cuba as ambassador in 1979. Yuri **ANDROPOV** brought him back as full Chairman in 1983, and Mikhail **GORBACHEV** then made him Chairman of the Presidium of the Supreme Soviet in 1988. Not quite able, however, to accept full-blooded reform, he was dropped in 1990.

### Vasa Dynasty
A royal dynasty which provided Sweden's monarchs, with two exceptions, from 1523 to 1818. Originally a minor noble family, it gained the throne for the first time in the person of **GUSTAV I VASA**, who finally broke the Danish-dominated **KALMAR UNION** and carried through the **REFORMATION**. He was succeeded by three of his sons: **ERIK XIV, JOHN III** and (after the deposition of John's son, **SIGISMUND III VASA**) **CHARLES IX**. The latter's son, **GUSTAV II ADOLF**, was a great statesman and soldier, whose daughter, **CHRISTINA**, abdicated in 1654 in favour of her cousin, **CHARLES X GUSTAV**. His son, **CHARLES XI**, introduced absolute monarchy, but this was again abolished after the death of his childless son, **CHARLES XII**. The abdication of the latter's sister, **ULRIKA ELEONORA**, in 1720 brought a breach in the line with the accession of

her husband, Frederick I. His successor, **ADOLF FREDERICK**, was descended from Charles XI's sister, and his son, **GUSTAV III**, had even less of the blood in his veins. The line ended with his brother, **CHARLES XIII**, who died without heirs.

### VASA DYNASTY

| Regnal Dates | Name |
|---|---|
| 1523/60 | Gustav I Vasa |
| 1560/9 | Eric XIV |
| 1569/92 | John III |
| 1592/1604 | Sigismund |
| 1604/11 | Charles IX |
| 1611/32 | Gustav II Adolf |
| 1632/54 | Christina |
| 1654/60 | Charles X |
| 1660/97 | Charles XI |
| 1697/1718 | Charles XII |
| 1718/20 | Ulrika Eleonora |
| 1720/51 | Frederick |
| 1751/71 | Adolf Frederick |
| 1771/92 | Gustav III |
| 1792/1809 | Gustav IV Adolf |
| 1809/18 | Charles XIII |

### Vasilevski, Alexander Mikhailovich (1895–1977)
Soviet marshal. An ensign in the Tsarist army in 1915, he joined the **RED ARMY** in 1919 and served in the war with Poland. He subsequently demonstrated great skill in staff work. By 1940 he was Deputy Chief of the General Staff, and in 1942 he was confirmed as Chief. Along with **ZHUKOV** he planned the **STALINGRAD** counter-offensive; he went on to liberate White Russia and take Königsberg. In 1945 he directed the rapid defeat of the Japanese in the Far East. After **WORLD WAR II** he supervised the reorganization of the Soviet forces, eventually serving as Deputy Defence Minister in 1953–6. In 1959 he retired from active service, disenchanted with Nikita **KHRUSHCHEV**'s military doctrine.

### VATICAN CITY STATE

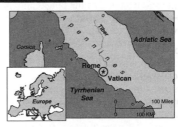

An independent papal sovereign state, and the smallest state in the world. Surrounded on all sides by Rome, Italy, it is a World Heritage Site and includes St Peter's, the Vatican Palace and Museum, several buildings in Rome, and the Pope's summer villa at Castel Gandolfo. The city state was created in 1929 by the **LATERAN PACTS** signed by Pope Pius XI and **MUSSOLINI**. These pacts or treaties ended the dispute arising from Italian occupation of the **PAPAL STATES** and the seizure of Rome in 1870, for the papacy had always refused to recognize the loss of the Papal States and their unification into Italy; however, in 1871 the Vatican papal state had been granted extraterritoriality. The Vatican is now protected by the 1954 La Haye

Convention. The head of state is the Supreme Pontiff of the Roman Catholic Church, the Pope, who is elected for life by the Sacred College of Cardinals and has full legislative, judicial and executive powers.

## Vatican Councils

Two councils of the Roman Catholic Church. The first, called by **PIUS IX** in 1869 to deal with a wide range of ecclesiastical and doctrinal issues, produced the decree of Papal Infallibility. The second (1962–5), called by **JOHN XXIII**, was aimed at renewing religious life and bringing the belief, structure and discipline of the Church up to date.

## Vauban, Sébastien le Prestre de (1633–1707)

French soldier and military engineer. After serving in the **FRONDE** (1651), he joined the government forces in 1653, and by 1658 was chief engineer under Turenne, serving with him at the siege of Lille (1667). He brought about a revolution in siege warfare and **FORTIFICATION**; he directed siege operations throughout **LOUIS XIV**'s campaigns, and surrounded the kingdom with a cordon of fortresses (1667–88). He was created Marshal of France in 1703.

## Vaudreuil, Philippe de Rigaud, Marquis of (c.1643–1725)

French soldier and colonist. He resented the French government's aim of controlling the colony of Canada while failing to support it adequately. The failure to resolve the differences between the French forces under the Marquis of **MONTCALM** and the *Canadiennes* under Vaudreuil did much to weaken their defences against British invasion. After the defeat, he attained the best possible terms for the **HABITANTS**, securing both their religious and their property rights.

## Vedic Age ► INDIA, PRE-ISLAMIC

## Velchev, Damian (1883–1954)

Bulgarian politician. A member of the Military League, in 1934 he led the military coup supported by **ZVENO**. In the 1944 government of the **FATHERLAND FRONT**, he became Minister of War but lost his position in 1946 during the communist purge and was sent to Switzerland as the Bulgarian representative. ► **DIMITROV, GEORGI; KOSTOV, TRAICHO; PETKOV, NIKOLA**

## Veldkornet

A Boer functionary during the period of Dutch **EAST INDIA COMPANY** rule at the Cape. It was a powerful, though part-time position, generally filled by a farmer, important in matters relating to legal affairs and black labour.

## Vellore Uprising (1806)

The rebellion at Vellore, a small town in the state of Tamil Nadu in India, was fostered by changes in regulations which were thought to reflect upon religion and encouraged by the proximity of the exiled Mysore princes. It was not comparable to the later **INDIAN UPRISING** of 1857–8 because the discontent was wholly military, but it cost Lord William **BENTINCK** his governorship of Madras.

## Veloukhiotis, Aris ► KLARAS, ATHANASIOS

## Velvet Revolution (1989)

The sudden, almost bloodless, process by which the communist regime in Czechoslovakia collapsed.

Ever since the **PRAGUE SPRING** was blighted in 1968 by the Soviet invasion, **COMMUNISM** had been tolerated but lacked popularity. Its mainstay remained the USSR with local military and police assistance. As Mikhail **GORBACHEV** tolerated change elsewhere in Eastern Europe, the public in Czechoslovakia saw their opportunity. On 17 Nov a crowd of 50,000 in Wenceslas Square was attacked by the police, but for the last time. The crowds grew, Miloš **JAKEŠ** and the rest of the Communist Party leadership resigned on 24 Nov, and Václav **HAVEL** became the new President on 30 Dec.

## Vendée, Wars of the

French counter-revolutionary insurrections in the western provinces against the central government in Paris. The brutal rising in La Vendée (1793), when priests and nobles encouraged the conservative peasantry to rebel against the National **CONVENTION**'s conscription and anticlerical policies, was a precedent for other provincial revolts in 1795, 1799, 1815 and 1832. ► **FRENCH REVOLUTION**

## Vendémiaire, 12th and 13th (4–5 Oct 1795)

In France, a royalist rising in protest against a decree of the National **CONVENTION**, stating that in the elections for a new assembly at least two-thirds of the seats should be reserved for the out-going members of the Convention. It was crushed by **BARRAS**, who brought in Napoleon Bonaparte to quell the uprising; he used cannon to disperse the insurgents gathered in front of the church of St Roch, Paris. ► **NAPOLEON I**

## Vendôme, Louis Joseph, Duke of (1654–1712)

French general. The great-grandson of **HENRY IV** (of France), he commanded in Italy and Flanders during the War of the **SPANISH SUCCESSION** (1701–14) and was defeated at Oudenarde by **MARLBOROUGH** (1708). Sent to Spain in 1710 to aid **PHILIP V**, he recaptured Madrid, defeated the English at Brihuega and the Austrians at Villaviciosa, but died soon after.

## vendus

A derogatory term for those French-Canadians who, like Sir George Étienne **CARTIER**, were alleged to have 'sold out' to anglophone Canada.

## Venezia Giulia

The name given by Italy to **ISTRIA** and Gorizia, two regions which the Italians gained from Austria at the end of **WORLD WAR I**. With Venezia Tridentina and Venezia Euganea, it was part of the so-called *Le Tre Venezie* (the Three Venices). At the end of **WORLD WAR II**, Italy ceded Istria to Yugoslavia and reorganized the remaining parts of Venezia Giulia as Friuli-Venezia Giulia.

## VENEZUELA official name Republic of Venezuela

The most northerly country in South America, bounded to the north by the Caribbean Sea; to the east by Guyana; to the south by Brazil; and to the south-west and west by Colombia. Originally inhabited by **CARIBS** and **ARAWAKS**, it was seen by **COLUMBUS** in 1498, and settled by the Spanish in 1520. There were frequent revolts against Spanish colonial rule, and in the early 19c an independence movement arose under Simón **BOLÍVAR**; this led to the establishment of the state of **GRAN COLOMBIA** (Colombia,

Ecuador and Venezuela) in 1819. Following the collapse of Gran Colombia in 1829, Venezuela became an independent republic in 1830 under President José **PÁEZ**. Since the 1960s there has been relative political stability, with the two major parties, the Democratic Action and the Christian Democrats, each holding power in turn. President Carlos Andrés Pérez, who came to power in 1989 soon faced rioting in response to his austerity measures. He survived two attempted coups in 1992, but was removed from office charged with corruption in 1993 (and imprisoned in 1996). He was succeeded in 1994 by Rafael Caldera. In 1998 Hugo **CHÁVEZ**, imprisoned for his part in one of the 1992 coup attempts, was elected President. He instituted unpopular economic reforms that provoked strikes and demonstrations but survived an attempted military coup in 2002 and a national referendum in 2004 on his tenure of office.

**Venezuelan Boundary Dispute**
A dispute between Britain and Venezuela over the boundary of British Guiana (now Guyana). In 1895 this provoked a brief but acute crisis in Anglo-American relations, the USA forcing Britain to accept arbitration. The dispute was settled in 1899.

**Venizélos, Eleuthérios Kyriakos** (1864–1936)
Greek politician. He became a lawyer and journalist, joined the Cretan Chamber of Deputies and took a prominent part in the rising against the Turks in 1896. As Prime Minister (1910–15) after the 1909 military coup, he restored law and order, promoted the Balkan League against Turkey and Bulgaria (1912–13), extended Greek territory and enacted land reform. His sympathies with France and Britain in **WORLD WAR I** clashed with those of King **CONSTANTINE I** and led him to establish a rival government (1917–20), forcing the King's abdication. During the 1920s and early 1930s, he was leader of the antiroyalist political faction. In 1935 he came out of retirement to support a military revolt staged by his sympathizers, but after its failure he fled to Paris, where he died.

**Venizélos, Sofoklis** (1894–1964)
Greek politician. The son of Eleuthérios **VENIZÉLOS**, in 1944 he was briefly Prime Minister of the Greek government-in-exile, resigning in favour of George **PAPANDREOU**. In the elections of Mar 1946 he led the National Political Union with Papandreou and Panayiotis Kanellopoulos. After the **GREEK CIVIL WAR** (1944–9), in the elections of Mar 1950, as leader of the Liberal Party he joined the coalition government with the National Progressive Centre Union and Papandreou's Democratic Socialist Party, becoming Prime Minister later that year.

**Vercors**
A mountain plateau near Grenoble in the Alps which became a stronghold of the French **WORLD WAR II** resistance movement. It was captured by the German army after a heroic struggle with great loss of life (13 Jun–5 Aug 1944).

**Verdinaso**
Belgian fascist political party, founded in 1931 by Joris Van Severen (1894–1940). The name is a shortened form of the League of Low Countries National Solidarists (*Verbond van Dietsch-Nationaal Solidaristen*). The party was influenced by French and Italian right-wing politics, and opposed parliamentary processes and all forms of liberalism and socialism; it never achieved a large membership. Originally heavily supportive of the **FLEMISH MOVEMENT**, Van Severen later championed a neo-Burgundian nationalist ideal; at the outbreak of **WORLD WAR II** he was executed by French forces (20 May 1940), and *Verdinaso* rapidly disappeared.

**Verdun, Battle of** (1916)
A battle in **WORLD WAR I**. The German army chose to attack a salient in the French line at this point because it was thought that its symbolic value would force the French to defend it to the bitter end. This did happen but, in spite of huge losses on both sides, Verdun did not fall. General **PÉTAIN**, the French commander for most of the battle, earned his reputation at Verdun.

**Vereeniging, Peace of** (1902)
The peace treaty which ended the second Boer War, signed at Pretoria. The Boers won three important concessions: an amnesty for those who had risen in revolt within the Cape Colony; a promise that the British would deny the franchise to Africans until after the Boer republics were returned to representative government; and additional financial support for reconstruction. The Peace ensured that there would be no significant change in the political relationship of whites and blacks in South Africa. ► **BOER WARS**

**Vergennes, Charles Gravier** (1717–87)
French politician. As **LOUIS XVI**'s Foreign Minister, he sought to humble Britain by promoting the independence of the USA. He negotiated the Peace of Paris (1783) and also **PITT**'s commercial treaty (1786). ► **AMERICAN REVOLUTION**

**Vergniaud, Pierre Victurnien** (1753–93)
French politician. He settled as an advocate at Bordeaux in 1781, and was sent to the National Assembly in 1791. His eloquence made him the leader of the **GIRONDINS**. In the National **CONVENTION** he voted for King **LOUIS XVI**'s death, and as President announced the result. When the Girondins clashed with the rival revolutionary faction known as the **MOUNTAIN**, who wanted to retain power by dictatorial means, Vergniaud and his party were arrested and guillotined (31 Oct 1793). ► **FRENCH REVOLUTION**; **JACOBINS**

**Vernon, Edward** (1684–1757)
British admiral. He joined the navy in 1700, and also became an MP (1727–41). In 1739, during the War of **JENKINS' EAR**, he was sent to harry the Spaniards in the Antilles, and his capture of Portobello made him

a national hero. During the Jacobite **FORTY-FIVE REBELLION**, Vernon's effective dispositions in the Channel successfully kept the standby Gallic reinforcements in their ports. He was nicknamed 'Old Grog', from his grogram coat, and in 1740 ordered the dilution of navy rum with water, the mixture being thereafter known as 'grog'.

**Verrazano, Giovanni da** (c.1480–1527)
Italian navigator and explorer. Born in Greve, Italy, he entered the service of **FRANCIS I** of France, and led an expedition to North America in 1524, exploring the coast from Cape Fear northward, probably as far as Cape Breton, becoming the first European to enter New York Bay. He later made voyages to Brazil and the West Indies, and is thought to have been captured and eaten by cannibals in the Lesser Antilles. ➤ **EXPLORATION**

**Versailles, Treaty of** (1919)
A peace treaty drawn up between Germany and the Allied powers at Paris. Of the 434 articles, the most controversial was article 231 assigning to Germany and her allies' responsibility for causing **WORLD WAR I**, and establishing liability for reparation payments. Germany lost all overseas colonies, and considerable territory to Poland in the East. The **RHINELAND** was demilitarized and to be occupied by Allied troops for up to 15 years, and German armed forces were strictly limited. ➤ **PARIS PEACE CONFERENCE**

**Verwoerd, Hendrik Frensch** (1901–66)
South African politician, born in Amsterdam, the Netherlands. He was educated at Stellenbosch, where he became Professor of Applied Psychology (1927) and Sociology (1933), and edited the nationalist *Die Transvaler* (1938–48). Elected Senator in 1948, he became Minister of Native Affairs (1950) and Prime Minister (1958–66). His administration was marked by the highly controversial policy of **APARTHEID**, an attempt on his life (1960), the establishment of South Africa as a republic (1962) and his assassination in Cape Town.

**Verzet, Het** ➤ **RESISTANCE MOVEMENT** (Netherlands)

**Verzuiling**
Literally 'pillarization', this is a Dutch term which describes the division of society into vertical ideological groups, rather than into horizontal socio-economic ones, particularly used of the Netherlands. The term is also known as vertical pluralism and consociationalism. Dutch *verzuiling* consists of two things: the division of society into four camps characterized by an ideology such as Roman Catholicism, Calvinism, socialism or humanism; and a complex of rules, regulations, committees and consultative processes which allow the efficient running of the country despite the vertical differences, and with proportional input from each group. Historically, the system arose out of demands made in the course of the 19c by the Roman Catholics, the Calvinists and the socialists for a share in the power held by the ruling liberals; in the 20c the institutions in the 'pillars' continued to expand until c.1960, since when there has been a process of de-pillarization (*ontzuiling*). The term *verzuiling* is also used of Belgian politics, but refers more to the development of the pillars than to the

mechanism of consultation for running the country.

**Vesey, Denmark** (c.1767–1822)
US insurrectionist. Born probably in St Thomas, West Indies, he was taken to Charleston, South Carolina, as a slave in 1783, and he bought his freedom in 1800 after winning a street lottery. A prosperous carpenter and preacher, he denounced **SLAVERY** as a violation of Christianity, and in 1822 he and ten slaves were arrested and charged with plotting an uprising against whites. Thousands of blacks were rumoured to have been involved, and though Vesey protested his innocence, he was hanged. The affair led to the passage of more stringent slave codes in many Southern states.

**Vespucci, Amerigo** (1451–1512)
Spanish explorer after whom the continent of America was named. Born in Florence, Italy, he was a contractor in Seville from 1495 to 1498 and provisioned one (or possibly two) of the expeditions of Christopher **COLUMBUS**. Although not a navigator or pilot himself, in 1499 he promoted an expedition to the New World commanded by Alonso de Hojeda and sailed there in his own ship, in which he explored the coast of Venezuela. His name (Latinized as 'Americus') was given to the American continents by the young German cartographer Martin Waldseemüller, after the publication at St Diè in Lorraine of a distorted account of his travels, based on forged versions of his letters. ➤ **EXPLORATION**

**Vichy**
The informal name of the French political regime between 1940 and 1945; officially the **FRENCH STATE** (*État français*). Established at the spa town of Vichy following Germany's defeat of France (1940), its head of state was Marshal Philippe **PÉTAIN** and its other dominant political figure Pierre **LAVAL**, Prime Minister from 1942. Although a client regime of Germany, Vichy at first succeeded in maintaining a degree of autonomy. ➤ **COLLABORATION** (France); **RIOM TRIAL**; **WORLD WAR II**

**Vicksburg, Battle of** (1863)
A major success for Union forces during the **AMERICAN CIVIL WAR**, in which General Ulysses S **GRANT** captured Vicksburg and thus the Mississippi River, splitting the Confederate forces in two. Pressured by an impatient President **LINCOLN**, Grant circumvented the impregnable cliffs protecting the city, captured the nearby city of Jackson and only then laid siege to Vicksburg. With bombardment from Unionist gunboats on the Mississippi River that lasted for six weeks, he forced the Confederate general, Pemberton, to surrender. The victory proved Grant's abilities as a general and Lincoln placed him in command of all the Union's western forces. The cause of emancipation was also helped by the use of black units in the campaign.

**Victor Amadeus II** (1666–1732)
Duke of Savoy (1675/1730), King of Sicily (1713/20) and King of Sardinia (1720/30). He reigned under the influence of his mother, Jeanne de Nemours, until 1684. After taking power in his own right, he pursued a domestic policy of administrative rationalization, fiscal reform and economic development. For most of his reign, his foreign policy was based on switching allegiance between **LOUIS XIV** of France and the

Habsburgs, according to the demands of the moment. Despite defeats at the hands of both imperial and French armies, he managed to extend his territories considerably, becoming King of Sicily by the Treaty of **UTRECHT** in 1713. Feeling Sicily too distant from Savoy, he swapped it for Sardinia in 1720, but retained his royal title. From 1720 he avoided involvement in international conflict and concentrated on domestic reform, establishing a new legal code (1723–9) and a land register (1730). In 1730 he abdicated in favour of his son, **CHARLES EMMANUEL III**, on condition that the latter kept him well informed of his actions. When Charles Emmanuel failed to do so, Victor Amadeus tried to restore his own rule, but was captured by his son and imprisoned at the fortress of Rivoli, where he died. ► **HABSBURG DYNASTY**

### Victor Amadeus III (1726–96)
King of Sardinia (1773/96). The son and successor of **CHARLES EMMANUEL III**, from the outset of the **FRENCH REVOLUTION** he offered sanctuary to aristocratic émigrés, including **LOUIS XVI**'s brother, the Count of Artois, who wished to use Savoy as a base from which to launch a counter-revolutionary invasion. Attacked by the revolutionary regime in 1792, Victor Amadeus was driven into the arms of the Habsburgs, but defeat by Napoleon Bonaparte forced him to leave the anti-French coalition in 1796. By the Treaty of Paris of May that year he was forced to cede Nice and Savoy and to accept the presence of a French garrison. ► **HABSBURG DYNASTY; NAPOLEON I**

### Victor Emmanuel I (1759–1824)
King of Sardinia (1802/21). The son of **VICTOR AMADEUS III**, he took part in wars against the French from 1793 to 1796. He became King on the abdication of his brother, **CHARLES EMMANUEL IV**, and until 1814 lived at Cagliari in Sardinia, as his mainland possessions were in the hands of the French. After the Vienna Settlement (which awarded Genoa and the Ligurian littoral to the Kingdom of Sardinia), he returned to Turin, where he pursued a policy of extreme reaction, rejecting any legacy of French rule and appointing to high office almost only conservative aristocrats who had followed him to Sardinia. In this climate of reaction, discontent grew, especially among those of his subjects who had served the Napoleonic regime; it found expression in the liberal insurrection led by **SANTAROSA** in 1821. Faced with an army mutiny and demands for a liberal constitution, Victor Emmanuel abdicated in favour of his brother, **CHARLES FELIX**, appointing the young **CHARLES ALBERT** as Regent until his brother's return from Modena.

### Victor Emmanuel II (1820–78)
King of Sardinia (1849/61) and King of Italy (1861/78). He came to the throne on his father's abdication, after the defeat of the Battle of **NOVARA**. He did not, as was once commonly held, have to defend the retention of the **STATUTO** against Austrian pressure to abolish it, but rather saw eye-to-eye with **RADETZKY** on the need to repress democracy and revolution. The early years of his rule did, however, witness a series of more or less liberal ministries under **D'AZEGLIO** and **CAVOUR**, although he was often unhappy about the anticlerical nature of much of their legislation. It was largely on his own initiative that Piedmont sent

troops to fight alongside the British and French in the **CRIMEAN WAR** in 1855. In 1859 he went to war in alliance with France to drive out the Austrians from the north of Italy, securing Lombardy but failing to take Venetia. In return for French assistance, he ceded Nice and Savoy to **NAPOLEON III**. During the spring of 1860 he also acquired Parma, Modena and Tuscany, their transfer to his rule being engineered largely by the **ITALIAN NATIONAL SOCIETY**. Later that year, Umbria, the Papal Marches and the Kingdom of the **TWO SICILIES** were annexed and in Mar 1861, he was crowned King of Italy. He did not, however, change his title to Victor Emmanuel I. Nor did he control the entire peninsula, having to wait until 1866 before acquiring Venetia, and 1870 until he gained Rome. ► **ROMAN QUESTION**

### Victor Emmanuel III (1869–1947)
King of Italy (1900/46). He came to the throne after the assassination of his father, **UMBERTO I**. After Italy's entrance into **WORLD WAR I**, he took an active part in the campaign, appointing his uncle, the Duke of Aosta, as Regent. With the arrival of peace, he took little active part in politics. In 1922, however, faced with **MUSSOLINI**'s bid to seize power he refused to declare a state of emergency, which would have enabled the army to crush the fascist movement. Instead, when **SALANDRA** declined to form a government, he asked Mussolini to do so, opening the way for the creation of the fascist regime. Among suggested motives for Victor Emmanuel's ready capitulation to the fascists are his fear that the alternative to Mussolini might have been a socialist revolution, anxieties about the loyalty of the army and rumours that the Duke of Aosta was planning to depose him. Mussolini's regime effectively deprived the monarchy of its powers, but it did make Victor Emmanuel Emperor of Ethiopia (1936) and King of Albania (1939). Eventually, however, the King was to play a part in toppling the **DUCE**: on 24 July 1943, the **FASCIST GRAND COUNCIL**, disillusioned by the progress of the war and dissatisfied with Mussolini's gutless readiness to accept orders from **HITLER**, begged Victor Emmanuel to assume power. On 25 July Mussolini was summoned by the King and dismissed; shortly afterwards, with Mussolini under arrest, Victor Emmanuel invited General **BADOGLIO** to form a government. However, he was irredeemably tarnished by his association with **FASCISM** and did little in the final stages of the war to improve his or his dynasty's popularity. In May 1946, in a last effort to save the monarchy, he abdicated in favour of his son, **UMBERTO II**. He died in exile in Egypt.

### Victoria, in full Alexandrina Victoria (1819–1901)
Queen of Great Britain (1837/1901) and Empress of India (1876/1901). She was the only child of **GEORGE III**'s fourth son, Edward, and Victoria Maria Louisa of Saxe-Coburg, sister of **LEOPOLD I**, King of Belgium. Taught by Lord **MELBOURNE**, her first Prime Minister, she had a clear grasp of constitutional principles and the scope of her own prerogative, which she resolutely exercised in 1839 by setting aside the precedent which decreed dismissal of the current ladies of the bedchamber, thus causing **PEEL** not to take up office as Prime Minister. In 1840 she married Prince **ALBERT of SAXE-COBURG-GOTHA**, and had four sons and

five daughters. Strongly influenced by her husband, with whom she worked in closest harmony, after his death (1861) she went into lengthy seclusion, neglecting many duties, which brought her unpopularity and motivated a republican movement. However, with her recognition as Empress of India, and the celebratory golden (1887) and diamond (1897) jubilees, she rose high in her subjects' favour, and increased the prestige of the monarchy. She had strong preferences for certain prime ministers (notably **MELBOURNE** and **DISRAELI**) over others (notably Peel and **GLADSTONE**), but did not press these beyond the bounds of constitutional propriety. At various points in her long reign she exercised some influence over foreign affairs, and the marriages of her children had important diplomatic, as well as dynastic, implications in Europe. She was succeeded by her son, **EDWARD VII**.

## Vieira, Antonio de (1608–97)
Portuguese Jesuit missionary. Born in Lisbon, he grew up in Bahia in Brazil, where he attended the Jesuit College and became a missionary. He returned to Portugal after the restoration of independence (1640), was appointed court preacher (1641–52) to King **JOHN (JOÃO) IV** and became influential. In 1653 he returned to Brazil as Superior of Jesuit missions, but in defending the local Indians fell foul of the colonists. Eventually, after years of conflict, Vieira and his fellow Jesuits were expelled from the Amazon and sent back to Lisbon in 1661. There he was put under house arrest and imprisoned by the **INQUISITION** (1663–8). He subsequently went to Rome where he was well received, and in 1681 was able to return with the Jesuits to Brazil, where he remained until his death.

## Vieira, João Bernardo (1939–)
Guinea-Bissau politician. He joined the Party for the Independence of Portuguese Guinea and Cape Verde (PAIGC) in 1960, and in 1964 became a member of the political bureau during the war for independence from Portugal. After independence in 1974, he served in the government of Luis de Almeida **CABRAL**, but in 1980 led the coup that deposed him. In 1984 constitutional changes combined the roles of head of state and head of government, making Vieira Executive President. He held on to power until May 1999, when he was ousted in coup.

## Vienna Award (1st) (2 Nov 1938)
The alteration of the Czechoslovak–Hungarian frontier following the **MUNICH AGREEMENT**. HITLER's success against Czechoslovakia encouraged other predators, and Hungary laid claim to **RUTHENIA** and part of Slovakia. **RIBBENTROP** and **CIANO** acted as arbitrators, although Hitler was still not sure what he wanted to happen to Ruthenia. But the Vienna Award gave Hungary a fertile slice of Slovakia with almost a million inhabitants, just over half of whom were, admittedly, Hungarian. Most of the area was restored to Czechoslovakia in 1945.

## Vienna Award (2nd) (29 Aug 1940)
The alteration of the Hungarian-Romanian frontier following the **GERMAN–SOVIET PACT**. When **STALIN** moved his forces into **BESSARABIA** (July 1940) in accordance with the terms of his pact with **HITLER**, Hungary saw its opportunity to reclaim Transylvania,

which had been lost to Romania at the end of **WORLD WAR I**. Hitler was anxious to weaken Romania to his own advantage but not to encourage Hungary (or **MUSSOLINI**) excessively. Eventually **RIBBENTROP** and **CIANO** again acted as arbitrators. This 2nd Vienna Award gave Hungary two-thirds of Transylvania. Most of this area, too, was restored to Romania in 1945.

## Vienna, Congress of (1814–15)
A European assembly convened at the instigation of the four victorious powers to redefine the territorial map of Europe after the defeat of **NAPOLEON I**. The negotiators were concerned to create a balance of power and to avoid alienating any major state. **METTERNICH** in particular was concerned to contain the forces of nationalism and liberalism and to preserve the prerogatives of the monarchies of Europe. ➤ **NAPOLEONIC WARS**

## Vienna Convention for the Protection of the Ozone Layer (1985)
A convention promoting the protection of the Earth's ozone layer. The impetus for the Convention was international concern at the depletion of the ozone layer, which became apparent in the 1970s and was ascribed to the action of chemicals such as chlorofluorocarbons (CFCs). The Convention, signed in 1985, provides for international cooperation in research and observation to safeguard the ozone layer. The **MONTREAL PROTOCOL ON SUBSTANCES THAT DEPLETE THE OZONE LAYER** was adopted in 1987 to control the phasing-out of ozone-depleting chemicals. The secretariat, based at the **UN** Environment Programme offices in Nairobi, serves both the Convention and the Montreal Protocol.

## Vienna, Siege of (1529)
The first Ottoman siege of Vienna, undertaken by **SÜLEYMAN I, THE MAGNIFICENT**, was indirectly the result of an agreement made by John **ZAPOLYA**, King of Hungary, with the Ottomans, whereby Zapolya was prepared to recognize Süleyman's suzerainty in return for the latter's help against the Habsburgs. Süleyman was, for his part, content that Hungary should be autonomous under Zapolya and act as a buffer state against the Habsburgs. An expedition against Hungary ensued, with the object of expelling **FERDINAND I**; Buda was occupied (Sep 1529) and Süleyman went on to lay siege to Vienna. The main reason behind the failure of the siege was climatic in that the season was too well advanced. Despite early success in the suburbs of Vienna, Süleyman, who was having difficulties with his own troops, particularly the **JANISSARIES**, decided to return to Istanbul for the winter. ➤ **HABSBURG DYNASTY**; **OTTOMAN EMPIRE**

## Vienna, Siege of (1683)
The second Ottoman siege of Vienna, undertaken by the Grand Vizier **KARA MUSTAFA** in the reign of **MEHMED IV**, was the culmination of a campaign provoked by the emergence of a Hungarian nationalist movement against the Habsburgs. As with the first siege of Vienna in 1529, Ottoman help was sought on the condition that Ottoman suzerainty would be recognized. After a campaign in Hungary in late 1682, a great army was mustered in Edirne (Adrianople) and the Ottomans eventually advanced on Vienna in

June 1683. Faced by a European coalition (Pope **IN-NOCENT XI** had managed to get men and money from Poland, Portugal and Spain to aid the beleaguered Habsburgs) and a vigorous defence of the city, the Ottomans were forced to retire. Polish assistance, led by **JOHN III SOBIESKI**, had been instrumental in saving Vienna and also played a major part in the subsequent defeat of the Ottomans at Gran. Kara Mustafa was made the scapegoat for the whole debacle, being dismissed and then executed in Belgrade in 1683. ➤ **HABSBURG DYNASTY; OTTOMAN EMPIRE**

### Vienna, Treaties of (1735 and 1738)

These two treaties began and ended the negotiations which concluded the War of the **POLISH SUCCESSION**. They recognized the claim of Frederick Augustus I of Saxony (**AUGUSTUS III** of Poland) to the Polish throne.

### Vienna, Treaty of (14 Oct 1809)

A peace treaty between **AUSTRIA** and France following the French victory at the Battle of **WAGRAM**. Austria lost most of her remaining Alpine and Adriatic lands as well as some northern border territories. She accepted French hegemony in Europe and adjusted her foreign policy to French requirements, as well as paying **REPARATIONS**. On 12 Aug 1813 Austria renounced the treaty.

### Viet Cong or Vietcong ('Vietnamese Communists')

The name commonly given in the 1960s to the communist forces that fought the South Vietnamese government during the **VIETNAM WAR**.

### Viet Minh or Vietminh

The abbreviation of Vietnam Doc Lap Dong Minh ('League for the Independence of Vietnam'), a politico-military organization formed by **HO CHI MINH** in 1941. It included nationalists and communists, and aimed at liberating Vietnam from the Japanese and then gaining independence from France. In 1945, on the Japanese surrender, it formed a government in Hanoi. Its army defeated the French at **DIEN BIEN PHU** in 1954. ➤ **VIETNAM WAR**

**VIETNAM** official name **Socialist Republic of Vietnam**

An independent socialist state in Indochina, bounded to the east by the South China Sea (including the Gulf of Tonkin in the north); to the west by

Laos and Cambodia; and to the north by China. Under the influence of China for many centuries, it was visited by the Portuguese in 1535. Dutch, French and English traders arrived in the 17c, with missionaries. In 1802 the regions of Tonkin in the north, **ANNAM** in the centre, and **COCHIN-CHINA** in the south united as the Vietnamese Empire, which was conquered by the French in the 19c. French protectorates were established in Cochin-China in 1867, and in Annam and Tonkin in 1884, and the French Indo-Chinese Union with Cambodia and Laos was formed in 1887. Vietnam was occupied by the Japanese in **WORLD WAR II**, and after the war the **VIET MINH** under **HO CHI MINH** fought for independence from France in the Indo-China War (1946–54), which resulted in the withdrawal of the French. In 1954 an armistice divided the country between the communist 'Democratic Republic' in the north and the 'State' of Vietnam in the south. Civil war in 1964–75 (the **VIETNAM WAR**) led to US intervention on the side of South Vietnam from 1965 until US troops were withdrawn in 1973. Saigon in South Vietnam fell in 1975, and with the defeat of South Vietnam nearly 200,000 Vietnamese fled the country. The country was reunified as the Socialist Republic of Vietnam in 1976. Large numbers of refugees tried to find homes in the West in the late 1970s, and the Chinese invasion of Vietnam in 1979 greatly increased the number of **BOAT PEOPLE** attempting to leave the country by sea. After the collapse of the USSR in 1991, Vietnam improved its relations with China and the USA. A new constitution was adopted in 1992 that approved many economic and political reforms but effective power remains with the ruling Communist Party. ➤ **INDOCHINA; SOUTH-EAST ASIA PRE-1000AD**

### Vietnam War (1964–75)

A war between communist North Vietnam and non-communist South Vietnam which broadened to include the USA. It was preceded by the Indo-China War (1946–54) between France and the **VIET MINH**, which ended with the defeat of the French at **DIEN BIEN PHU**. The Geneva Conference left North Vietnam under the rule of **HO CHI MINH**, while the South was ruled first by **BAO DAI** and then by **NGO DINH DIEM**. Elections were planned to choose a single government for all of Vietnam, but when they failed to take place, fighting was renewed. From 1961, in an attempt to stop the spread of **COMMUNISM**, the USA increased its aid to South Vietnam and the number of its 'military advisers'. In 1964 following a North Vietnamese attack on US ships, President Lyndon **JOHNSON** ordered retaliatory bombing of North Vietnam. Although the US **CONGRESS** never declared war officially, it passed the **GULF OF TONKIN RESOLUTION** which authorized US forces in South-East Asia to repel any armed attack and to prevent further aggression. US bombing of North Vietnam was continued, and in 1965 the USA stepped up its troop commitment substantially. By 1968 over 500,000 US soldiers were involved in the war. As the conflict dragged on, victory against the elusive communist guerrilla forces seemed unattainable. Opposition to the war within the USA badly divided the country, and pressure mounted to bring the conflict to an end. In 1968 peace negotiations were begun in Paris, and in 1973 a ceasefire agreement was signed. Hostilities did not

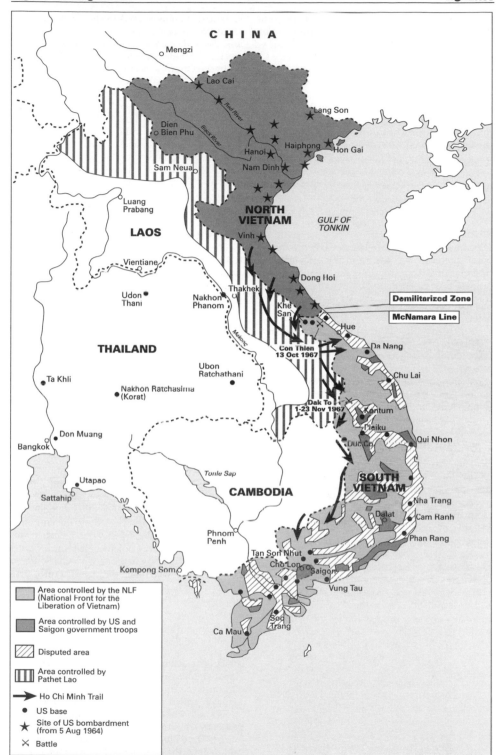

**Vietnam War (approximate situation, Dec 1967)**

end until two years later when North Vietnam's victory was completed with the capture of Saigon (renamed Ho Chi Minh City).

**Vigdís Finnbogadóttir ➤ FINNBOGADÓTTIR, VIG-DÍS**

**vigilante**

A self-appointed enforcer of law and order. In the mid-19c US West, official policing was slow to develop and so local citizens formed vigilante committees who meted out their own form of justice in an attempt to keep criminals, such as outlaw gangs, under control. They were gradually replaced in the late 19c by official law-keeping bodies.

**Vijayanagar** ► INDIA, PRE-ISLAMIC

**Vike-Freiberga, Vaira** (1937–  )
Latvian politician. She was born in Riga, Latvia, but fled with her family to German refugee camps in 1944. The family moved to Morocco before settling in Canada in 1954. She was professor of psychology at the University of Montreal from 1965 to 1998 and was active in the émigré community. Following retirement in 1998 she accepted an invitation to head the Institute of Latvia, an organization promoting Latvia overseas. Following deadlock in the 1999 presidential election, she stood successfully for election and became the first woman president in Eastern Europe. She was active in foreign policy, criticizing Russia and pursuing Latvian membership of NATO and the EU, both of which Latvia joined in 2004. She was re-elected in 2003.

**Vikings**
Raiders, traders and settlers from Norway, Sweden and Denmark, who between the late 8c and the mid-11c conquered and colonized large parts of Britain, Normandy and Russia; attacked Spain, Morocco and Italy; traded with Byzantium, Persia and India; discovered and occupied Iceland and Greenland; and reached the coast of North America. As sea-borne raiders they gained a deserved reputation for brutality and destructiveness, but as merchants and settlers they played an influential and positive role in the development of medieval Europe. Their earliest overseas settlements were in the Orkney and Shetland islands, which remained united to the Norwegian crown until 1472. ► CANUTE; DANELAW; NORMANS

**Villa, Pancho**, also known as **Francisco Villa**, originally **Doroteo Arango** (1877–1923)
Mexican revolutionary. The son of a field labourer, he followed a variety of modest occupations until he joined MADERO's uprising against DÍAZ (1911) and the MEXICAN REVOLUTION made him famous as a military commander. In a fierce struggle for control of the revolution, he and ZAPATA were defeated (1915) by Venustiano CARRANZA, with whom Villa had earlier allied himself against the dictatorship of General Victoriano HUERTA. Both Villa and Zapata withdrew to strongholds in north and central Mexico, from where they continued to direct guerrilla warfare. In 1916 Villa was responsible for the shooting of a number of US citizens in the town of Santa Isabel, as well as an attack on the city of Columbus, New Mexico, which precipitated the sending of a US punitive force by President Woodrow WILSON. The troops failed to capture Villa and he continued to oppose Carranza's regime until the latter's death (1920), when he laid down his arms and was pardoned. He was murdered at his hacienda in Chihuahua.

**Villafranca Armistice** (11 July 1859)
The armistice between NAPOLEON III and FRANCIS JOSEPH of Austria after the Battle of SOLFERINO that brought to an end the 1859 campaign to seize Lombardy and Venetia. By seeking peace with the Austrians, Napoleon III broke the promises he made in the PLOMBIÈRES Agreement to secure the whole of the Kingdom of LOMBARDY-VENETIA for the Kingdom of SARDINIA; indeed, his actions led to the resignation of a furious CAVOUR. However, the armistice did provide the basis for Piedmontese acquisition of most of Lombardy by the Treaty of Zurich (Nov 1859).

**Villalar, Battle of** (23 Apr 1521)
A relatively small engagement fought between the forces representing Emperor CHARLES V (Charles I of Spain) and the rebel *Comuneros*, commanded by Juan PADILLA. In bad weather conditions, the dispirited *Comunero* force was routed by the royal cavalry, suffering about 500 losses to about 20 on the royalist side. Padilla and his principal colleagues, Juan Bravo and Francisco Maldonado, were summarily executed the next day in Villalar. ► COMUNEROS, REVOLT OF THE

**Villars, Claude Louis Hector, Duke of** (1653–1734)
French soldier. He fought with distinction in the third Dutch War (1672–8) and in the War of the SPANISH SUCCESSION (1701–14). In 1711 he headed the last army France could raise, and with it fell upon the British and Dutch at Denain (July 1712). He became principal adviser on military affairs and foreign policy, and fought again in his eighties at the outbreak of the War of the POLISH SUCCESSION (1733–8). He died at Turin. ► MARLBOROUGH, DUKE OF

**Villehardouin, Geoffroi de** (c.1160–1213)
French nobleman and historian. Born in the castle of Villehardouin in Aube, he participated in the Fourth CRUSADE as one of its leaders. His *Conquête de Constantinople* ('Conquest of Constantinople') – he was present at the capture – describes the events from 1198 to 1207, and is one of the first examples of French prose.

**Villeneuve, Pierre Charles Jean Baptiste Sylvestre de** (1763–1806)
French admiral. He commanded the rear division of the French navy at the Battle of the Nile, and in 1805 was in charge of the French fleet at the Battle of TRAFALGAR, where he was taken prisoner. Released in 1806, during his return journey to Paris to face NAPOLEON I, he committed suicide at Rennes. ► NAPOLEONIC WARS

**Vimy Ridge**
An escarpment 5 mi/8 km north-east of Arras (Pas-de-Calais), and a strongly held part of the German defence line on the Western Front in WORLD WAR I. It was successfully stormed during the Battle of Arras by the Canadian Corps of the British 1st Army (1917). This feat of arms had great symbolic significance in establishing Canada's identity as an independent nation.

**Vínland**
A generalized Norse name meaning 'Berry' or 'Vine Land', applied to the eastern coast of North America from the time of its first sighting by the Viking Leif ERIKSSON in c.1000. Though the 'Vinland Map', purportedly of the 1440s, is a 20c forgery, accounts in two Icelandic sagas of the Norse discovery and attempted COLONIZATION of America, 500 years before COLUMBUS discovered the New World, are confirmed by archaeological evidence. Other Icelandic settlers tried to establish a colony in 'Vínland', but

withdrew in the face of hostility from the **NATIVE AMERICANS**.

## Violencia, La

The name given in Colombia to the undeclared civil war between Conservatives and Liberals, at its most intense between 1948 and 1955. The period was marked by numerous atrocities, especially in the countryside. Deaths attributable to the conflict probably exceeded 200,000.

## Virginius Incident (1873)

The seizure during the **CUBAN REVOLUTION** of the Cuban ship *Virginius* by Spanish authorities, and the execution of 53 people on board, among them US and British citizens. The ship had been fraudulently flying the US flag. The diplomacy of US Secretary of State Hamilton Fish succeeded in averting a war with Spain; the ship was returned and over US$80,000 compensation was paid to the families of the US and British crew and passengers who had been killed, but the Spanish officers were never punished.

## Visconti

Lords of Milan and Lombardy from 1277, and the most powerful family in northern Italy. The foundations were laid by Ottone, Archbishop of Milan (d.1295). Giovanni (1290–1354), who was archbishop, brought Genoa and Bologna under his jurisdiction. From 1395, the Visconti were hereditary Dukes of Milan (then probably the largest city in Italy) and Gian Galeazzo Visconti threatened for a time to conquer the whole of the peninsula. The male line died out in 1447, and after a brief republican interlude the succession passed to the Sforza. ► **VISCONTI, GIAN GALEAZZO**

## Visconti, Gian Galeazzo (1351–1402)

Milanese statesman. He succeeded his father, Galeazzo II, as joint ruler (1378/85) with his uncle Bernabò, whom he put to death (1385), thereafter ruling alone. As Duke, he made himself master of the northern half of Italy, bringing many independent cities into one state, arranging marriage alliances with England, France, Austria and Bavaria, and acting as a great patron of the arts.

## Vittorio Veneto, Battle of (Oct 1918)

The major victory for the Italians and their allies under General Armando **DÍAZ** over Austrian forces at the end of **WORLD WAR I**.

## Viviani, René (1862–1925)

French politician. As Prime Minister at the outbreak of **WORLD WAR I**, in order to demonstrate France's peaceful intentions he withdrew French forces from the German frontier. He was Minister of Justice in 1915 and French representative at the **LEAGUE OF NATIONS** in 1920.

## Vladimir I, the Great, in full Vladimir Svyatoslavich (d.1015)

Grand Prince of Kiev (c.978/1015). One of ancient Russia's most illustrious rulers, he consolidated the state, and led victorious campaigns against the Viatichi, Lithuanians and Bulgars. Under his rule the economy and culture of Kievan Russia generally flourished. In 988 he was converted to Christianity, and adopted the Greek Orthodox rite from Byzantium as the official religion of Russia. After his death,

Kievan Russia was torn apart by dynastic rivalries among his 12 sons. He was later canonized.

## Vladimir II, Monomachus (1053–1125)

Grand Prince of Kiev (1113/25). The great-grandson of **VLADIMIR I, THE GREAT**, he became by popular demand Grand Prince of Kiev in 1113 instead of the prior claimants of the Syiatoslav and Izyaslav families, thus founding the Monomakhovichi Dynasty. A popular, powerful, enlightened and peaceful ruler, he colonized, built new towns, dethroned unruly princes and introduced laws against usury. He left careful instructions to his son and cousin in the manuals *Puchenie* and *Poslanie*.

## Vladimirescu, Todor (1780–1821)

Romanian national leader. Born into a family of free peasants in Wallachia, he led the ill-fated 1821 revolt in **MOLDAVIA AND WALLACHIA**. Drawing on the support of the peasants and small landowners and cooperating with Greek leaders of the **FILIKI ETAIRIA**, he raised an insurrection against Ottoman rule which was the prelude to the **GREEK WAR OF INDEPENDENCE**. When Russia did not lend its support, he realized that the revolt would fail and so he opened negotiations with the Ottoman Porte. When the Greek leader Alexander **YPSILANTI** (1783–1828) learnt of this, he had Vladimirescu kidnapped and murdered. ► **PORTE, THE SUBLIME**

## Vlasov, Andrei Andreevich (1900–46)

Soviet general. During **WORLD WAR II** he distinguished himself defending his country until he was captured during 1942 when he emerged as the leader of a Russian group intending to overthrow **STALIN**. It was only subsequently in 1944 that he was allowed to raise two divisions to serve on the Russian front. In 1945 he surrendered to the Americans who handed him over to the Soviet authorities, who tried and hanged him in 1946. He was seen as a traitor to his country, but later revelations concerning Stalin and the more recent collapse of **COMMUNISM** have caused some observers to question that judgement.

## VMRO (Vnutrašnja Makedonska Revolucionarska Organizacija, 'Internal Macedonian Revolutionary Organization')

Founded in Salonica in 1893, the organization's goal was 'Macedonia for the Macedonians'. The failure of the **ILINDEN UPRISING** of 1903, however, divided its membership; the federalists wanted autonomy within a Balkan federation; the centralists wanted annexation to Bulgaria. After the **BALKAN WARS** and **WORLD WAR I**, when Macedonia was divided, VMRO, with Italian and Hungarian backing, waged a terrorist campaign from Bulgaria against the Yugoslav government. It kidnapped, tortured and murdered **STAMBOLISKI** after he signed the Treaty of Niš (1923) and was involved in the assassination of King **ALEXANDER I** of Yugoslavia (1934). ► **TSANKOV, ALEXANDER**

## Vogel, Hans-Jochen (1926–)

West German politician, successor to Helmut **SCHMIDT** as leader of the Social Democratic Party (**SPD**), from 1983 to 1991. A former Minister of Housing and Town Planning (1972–4) and Minister of Justice (1974–81), he also served briefly as governing Mayor of West Berlin (1981).

**Vogel, Sir Julius** (1835–99)
British-born New Zealand politician. He emigrated to Australia in 1852 and on to New Zealand in 1861. He edited and founded newspapers in both countries, entered the New Zealand parliament in 1863 and became Colonial Treasurer in 1869. He embarked on an extensive but inadequately regulated programme of public works funded by overseas borrowing, successfully stimulating rapid economic development on uncertain foundations. Conflicts with the provinces led to the abolition of provincial governments in 1875. He became Prime Minister in 1873, but retired in 1876 to become Agent-General in London. He returned to New Zealand politics and office in 1884 but renewed borrowing failed to stem the recession. The ministry fell in 1887 and Vogel retired from politics in 1889.

**Vogt**
In German history, an official appointed by the king or the emperor to administer imperial lands or a royal abbey. The most extensive of the lands administered in this way was the so-called *Vogtland*, which during the Hohenstaufen period was centred on the River Elster and had its administrative centre in Plauen. ►
**HOHENSTAUFEN DYNASTY**

**Vojvodina**
Literally 'duchy', the name refers to the region bounded by Hungary, Croatian Slavonia, and the River Danube, with its chief town at Novi Sad. Settled by the **SLAVS** (6–7c) and by the Magyars (9–10c), it fell to the Turks in 1526. By the Treaties of **KARLOWITZ** (1699) and **PASSAROWITZ** (1718), it came under the rule of Vienna. Under the Habsburgs, its fertile plains were settled by Germans, Slovaks, Hungarians, Ruthenians and Romanians. In Nov 1918, at the end of **WORLD WAR I**, the National Assembly of the Vojvodina voted to join the Kingdom of Serbs, Croats and Slovenes (later Yugoslavia). Occupied by the Germans during **WORLD WAR II** (Apr 1941), it was divided between the Nazi-collaborating governments of Hungary and the Independent State of Croatia. In 1945 it became an autonomous unit within the Republic of Serbia in the Socialist Federal Republic of Yugoslavia, and in 1963, with the regionalization of Yugoslavia, it virtually became an independent republic. In 1989 Serbia reasserted full control over Vojvodina, and during the 1990s many of the Croats and Hungarians in the province fled or were expelled, and their homes allocated to Serb refugees from Croatia. ► **HABSBURG DYNASTY**

**Volkspartij voor Vrijheid en Democratie** ► **LIBERAL PARTY** (Netherlands)

**Volksraad**
The ruling council of the Boer republics in South Africa. *Volksraads* were established by the various Boer communities in the interior of southern Africa after the **GREAT TREK** which commenced in 1835. They became the legislative bodies of the Transvaal and the Orange Free State up to the Boer War of 1899–1902. Volksraads were also created by the **GRIQUA** or half-caste republics established on the frontier of the Cape in the 19c. ► **BOER WARS**

**Volstead, Andrew John** (1860–1947)
US politician. A lawyer, he entered **CONGRESS** for the

Republicans in 1903 and is best remembered as the author of the 1919 Volstead Act, which prohibited the manufacture, transportation and sale of alcoholic beverages. The purpose of the legislation, which remained in force until 1933, was to placate the influential **TEMPERANCE MOVEMENT**, and to divert grain to food production in the wake of **WORLD WAR I**. In fact, **PROHIBITION** proved impossible to enforce effectively, and did little other than to create enormous profits for bootleggers and speakeasies, and provide Hollywood with the inspiration for countless gangster movies.

**Vonckists**
A late 18c southern Netherlands progressive political faction, named after its leader J F Vonck (1743–92). In reaction to the rationalist reforms of Emperor **JOSEPH II**, two groups rose up in the **BRABANT REVOLUTION**: the **STATISTS** and the Vonckists. The latter were mainly from the middle classes, and represented the forces of the **FRENCH REVOLUTION** in the southern Netherlands. In 1790 many had to flee to France, but they returned with the revolutionary armies in 1792 and 1794.

**Vo Nguyen Giap** (1912– )
Vietnamese military leader. He studied law at Hanoi University, joined the Vietnamese Communist Party, and trained in China. He led the **VIET MINH** against the French after 1945, and planned and executed the decisive defeat of their garrison at **DIEN BIEN PHU** in 1954. As Vice-Premier and Defence Minister of North Vietnam, he masterminded the military strategy that forced US forces to leave South Vietnam (1973) and led to the reunification of Vietnam in 1975. He was a member of the politburo from 1976 to 1982. He wrote *People's War, People's Army* (1961), which became a textbook for revolutionaries. ► **VIETNAM WAR**

**Voortrekkers**
The Boer migrants who left the Cape Colony from 1835 onwards to escape British rule and create independent republics in the interior of southern Africa. The British took the Cape during the **NAPOLEONIC WARS** and held it after the Congress of **VIENNA**. New land-owning systems, legal and administrative concepts, the English language, British settlers and more missionary activity were all introduced under their rule. The Boers took particular exception to the new legal status of their black workers, the emancipation of slaves in 1833 and the inability of the British to introduce acceptable frontier policies. A number of columns of Voortrekkers left under a series of leaders, including Louis Tregardt, Piet **RETIEF**, Gerrit Maritz and Hendrik Potgieter. About 6,000 left the Colony and established a number of small republics in the region across the Orange and Vaal rivers and Natal. Many withdrew from Natal when it was declared a British colony in 1843, and the republics coalesced into the Orange Free State and the South African Republic or Transvaal. For the rest of the 19c, the British made repeated and largely unavailing attempts to bring them back within their jurisdiction. The Voortrekkers are commemorated by a powerful and romantic monument in Pretoria.

**Voroshilov, Kliment Yefremovich** (1881–1969)
Soviet Marshal and politician. He joined the Russian

Social Democratic Labour Party in 1903, but political agitation soon brought about his exile to Siberia, where he remained a fugitive until 1914. He played a military rather than a political role in the 1917 **RUS-SIAN REVOLUTION**, and as Commissar for Defence (1925–40) was responsible for the modernization of the **RED ARMY**. He was removed from office after the failure to prevent the German Siege of **LENINGRAD**, but stayed active in the party, and after **STALIN**'s death became head of state (1953–60). ► **WORLD WAR II**

### Vorrink, Jacobus Jan (1891–1955)

Dutch politician. Beginning as a schoolteacher, he joined the Socialist Party (SDAP) in 1918, and was highly active in the socialist youth movements, eventually becoming Party Chairman in 1934. He sat in the First Chamber of parliament from 1935 to 1946, and was a member of the Second Chamber (1946–54). Despite having spent the period 1943–5 in a **CONCENTRATION CAMP**, after **WORLD WAR II** a press campaign accused him of having harboured fascist sympathies; perhaps this was the reason that he never held a cabinet post. ► **LABOUR PARTY** (Netherlands)

### Vorster, John, originally Balthazar Johannes Vorster (1915–83)

South African politician. Educated at Stellenbosch University, he became a lawyer and was a leader of the extreme Afrikaner group *Ossewa Brandwag* in **WORLD WAR II**, as a result of which he was interned for the duration of the war. He was elected to parliament for the **NATIONAL PARTY** in 1953 and was Minister of Justice (1961–5) before becoming Prime Minister (1966–78) and, for a brief moment, President. He was largely responsible for the imposition of the repressive **APARTHEID** laws and did not hesitate to employ state power to protect white interests. However, he was implicated in the 'Muldergate' scandal in which government funds had been misappropriated and was forced to resign.

### Voting Rights Act (1965)

US suffrage legislation. The law prohibited all means by which the segregationist Southern states had been able to prevent blacks from registering to vote. The Attorney-General was empowered to dispatch federal registrars anywhere that local officials were obstructing registration of blacks; the act was so effective that 250,000 new black voters had been able to register before the end of the year.

### Voznesenksy, Nikolai Alexeevich (1903–50)

Soviet economist. Educated after the **RUSSIAN REVOLUTION** (1917) in the Institute of Red Professors, he lectured there until in 1935 **ZHDANOV** recruited him as a planning assistant. He then became Chairman of the State Planning Bureau (1938–49), with one short interval in 1941–2 when Giorgiy **MALENKOV** was in the ascendant. He managed both the war-time economy and the post-war recovery, but **STALIN** had him arrested in 1949 and executed in 1950, seemingly because of the Zhdanov connection.

### Vranitzky, Franz (1937–)

Austrian politician. Educated at what is now the University of Commerce, Vienna, he embarked on a career in banking and in 1970 became adviser on economic and financial policy to the Minister of Finance. After holding senior appointments in the banking world he became Minister of Finance himself in 1984 and two years later succeeded Fred Sinowatz as Federal Chancellor. He resigned in 1997.

### Vyshinsky, Andrei Yanuaryevich (1883–1954)

Russian jurist and politician. He studied law at Moscow, joined the Communist Party in 1920, and became Professor of Criminal Law and then Attorney-General (1923–5). He was the public prosecutor at the state trials (1936–8) which removed **STALIN**'s rivals, and later became the Soviet delegate to the **UN** (1945–9 and 1953–4), and Foreign Minister (1949–53).

**Wacha Dinshaw Edulji** (1844–1936)
Indian politician. A member of the Bombay Legislative Council and the Imperial Legislative Council, he worked in close association with Dadabhai **NAOROJI** and Pherozeshah **MEHTA** for the peaceful development of his country through social reform, education and participation in politics. A founder-member of the **INDIAN NATIONAL CONGRESS**, he was its President in 1901. He criticized the British government's economic and financial policies and freely expressed his nation's viewpoint before the Welby Commission in London.

**Wade, Benjamin Franklin** (1800–78)
US politician. As a senator from Ohio (1851–69) and a leader of the Radical Republicans, he advocated harsh punishment for the Confederacy after the **AMERICAN CIVIL WAR**. In 1864 he was joint author of the Wade–Davis Manifesto demanding congressional rather than executive control of **RECONSTRUCTION**.

**Wafd Party**
The name of the Egyptian nationalist party which sent a delegation under the nationalist leader Sa'd **ZAGHLUL** to the British High Commissioner in 1919; the word means 'delegation'. The 'New Wafd' became Egypt's official opposition party in 1984, but was replaced as such in 1987 by an alliance headed by the **MUSLIM BROTHERHOOD**.

**Wagner, Robert Ferdinand** (1877–1953)
US politician. Born in Hesse, Nassau, Germany, he emigrated to the USA with his family in 1885 and settled in New York City. He was a Democratic senator from New York (1927–49) and one of President Franklin Roosevelt's most trusted allies in **CONGRESS**. He helped to win passage of many important pieces of **NEW DEAL** legislation, including the **NATIONAL LABOR RELATIONS ACT** (Wagner Act) of 1935, which guaranteed the right of labour to bargain collectively.

**Wagner Act** ► **NATIONAL LABOR RELATIONS ACT**

**Wagram, Battle of** (1809)
A victory achieved by **NAPOLEON I** over the Austrians under Archduke Charles (1771–1847), fought northeast of Vienna, notable for the unparalleled concentration of artillery fire. Napoleon forced Austria to seek an armistice and negotiate the Treaty of **VIENNA** (1809). ► **NAPOLEONIC WARS**

**Wahhab, Muhammad ibn Abd al-** (1703–92)
Eponymous founder of the strict Wahhabi sect in Islam. Born at Uyayna, he received his early education in Medina whereafter he travelled widely in Iraq and Persia, teaching and studying. He also became an advocate of the Hanbali school of jurisprudence and returned to Uyayna whence he was expelled for disruptive activities. Moving to Dar'iyya where the local chieftain, Muhammad ibn Saud, accepted his doctrine and undertook its defence and propagation, he aimed to get rid of *bid'a* ('innovation') later than the 3c AD and was vigorous in his opposition to the cult of saints. Abd al-Wahhab's religious views (which were of extreme simplicity) underpinned the aggressive and expansionist policies of Ibn Saud, and by the time of Abd al-Wahhab's death, Ibn Saud's son, Abd al-Aziz, was master of the whole of Najd. ► **WAHHABIS**

**Wahhabis**
An Islamic movement which derives from Muhammad ibn Abd al-**WAHHAB**, a religious reformer from Uyayna near Riyadh, and Muhammad ibn Saud, the ancestor of the present rulers of Saudi Arabia. The alliance was to lead to the unification in the 18c of most of the peninsula under the Saudi banner. The modern reunification of the kingdom was carried out (1902–32) by King Abd al-Aziz, otherwise known as '**IBN SAUD**'. Arabs call the followers of Abd al-Wahhab *muwahhidun* or 'unitarians' rather than *Wahhabis*, which is an anglicism. The movement maintains that legal decisions must be based exclusively on the Quran and the *Sunna*. The original Wahhabis banned music, dancing, poetry, silk, gold and jewellery, and in the 20c, the *ikhwan* ('brotherhood') have attacked the telephone, radio and television as innovations not sanctioned by God.

**Waitangi, Treaty of** (1840)
The treaty that marked the formal assumption of sovereignty over New Zealand by a reluctant British government. Based on the fiction that Maori society resembled European in concepts of sovereignty and organization of government, it recognized Maori property rights in which they were promised undisturbed possession, gave the Crown the sole right of purchase should they wish to sell, and bestowed upon them the rights and privileges of British subjects. The land question nevertheless remained a source of contention and warfare between settlers and **MAORIS** for much of the 19c. ► **MAORI WARS**

**Wajed, Hasina**, known as **Sheikh Hasina Wajed** (1947– )
Bangladeshi politician. The daughter of **MUJIBUR RAHMAN**, she was educated at Dhaka University. She

married the scientist M A Wajed Miah in 1968 and has two children. She was briefly imprisoned during the struggle for independence from **PAKISTAN** before her father became President of newly independent **BANGLADESH** in 1971. She escaped assassination in the 1975 military coup in which her father was killed, and during the following six years in exile was elected president of the **AWAMI LEAGUE**. She returned to Bangladesh in 1981 and worked to restore democracy. She became Leader of the Opposition after the 1986 elections but in 1991, in the first free general election for 16 years, her party failed to win a majority. The Awami League won the 1996 elections and she became Prime Minister, resigning in 2001.

### Wakefield, Edward Gibbon (1796–1862)
English colonial politician. Sentenced for abduction in 1827, he wrote in prison *A Letter from Sydney* (1829), which outlined his theory (expanded in several other books) of systematic **COLONIZATION** by the sale of Crown lands at a price sufficient to oblige intending purchasers to work for wages while amassing capital. The intention was to re-create English society as a basis for future self-government, attracting landowners by ensuring a supply of respectable labour, both male and female, and assisting labourers to emigrate from the proceeds of the land sales. He influenced the South Australian Association (which founded South Australia in 1836) and, as secretary (1838) to Lord Durham, the **DURHAM REPORT** on Canada. He formed (1837) the New Zealand Association and sent a shipload of colonists there (1839) to force the British government to recognize it as a colony. With George William, 4th Baron Lyttleton, he founded (1850) the Anglican colony of Canterbury, where he emigrated in 1853.

### Waldeck-Rousseau, Pierre Marie René (1846–1904)
French politician. A successful lawyer, he was a Deputy (1879–89) and Senator (1894–1904), first holding office in **GAMBETTA**'s cabinet (1881–2) and then under **FERRY** (1883–5) as Minister of the Interior. In 1884 he was responsible for a law legalizing trade unions. He retired from politics in 1889 to concentrate on his legal practice, but was brought back as Prime Minister (1899–1904) at the high point of the crisis caused by the **DREYFUS** affair. His ministry, known as the Ministry of Republican Defence, pardoned Dreyfus and survived the noisy attacks of the nationalist and anti-Semitic **LEAGUES**. It was a coalition that included a wide spectrum of opinion from the conservative republicans of which he was himself one, through the radicals to the socialist **MILLERAND**, and was supported by the Bloc des gauches ('Left-wing Bloc'). It passed the law on associations, which Waldeck-Rousseau saw as a way of legalizing the position of Roman Catholic religious orders in France. The law was used instead to begin a process that led to the dissolution of the great majority of the orders. Profoundly out of sympathy with the fervent anticlericalism that had developed in his majority, he resigned after winning the 1902 elections.

### Waldheim, Kurt (1918–)
Austrian politician. He entered the Austrian foreign service (1945) and became Minister and subsequently Ambassador to Canada (1955–60), Director of Political Affairs at the Ministry (1960–4), Austrian representative at the **UN** (1964–8 and 1970–1) and Foreign Minister (1968–70), and then UN Secretary-General (1972–81). His presidential candidature was controversial, because of claims that he had lied about his wartime activities, and had been involved in anti-Jewish and other atrocities in the Balkans. He denied the allegations and, despite international pressure, continued with his campaign, winning the presidency in 1986. He was defeated in elections in 1992, and in 1994 a US Justice Department report confirmed that Waldheim had served as an officer in the German army and had been involved in atrocities against Jews, civilians and Allied soldiers during **WORLD WAR II**.

### Waldo, Peter (fl.1175)
French religious leader. He became a preacher in Lyons (1170) and practised voluntary poverty. He was eventually excommunicated and banished from Lyons in 1184 with his followers, who because of their vow of poverty were known as 'The Holy Paupers'. They became known as the Waldenses.

### WALES
A principality and western constituent part of the United Kingdom; it also includes the island of Anglesey off the north-west coast. Celtic in origin, the original people of Wales, who had managed to resist the Romans, increased in number around the 4c when Anglo-Saxon invaders of Britain drove the Brythonic Celts into Wales, calling them *Waelisc*, 'foreign'. In the 8c Welsh territory was lost to Offa, King of Mercia, who built a frontier dyke from the Dee to the Wye, and in the 9c Rhodri Mawr united Wales against the Saxons, Norse and Danes. **EDWARD I** of England established authority over Wales, building several castles in the 12–13c, and his son was created the first Prince of Wales (1301). In the early 15c there was a Welsh revolt against **HENRY IV** led by Owen **GLENDOWER**. Wales was politically united with England by the Act of Union in 1535. It became the centre of Nonconformist religion in the 18c. A political nationalist movement developed, embodied in **PLAID CYMRU**, which returned its first MP in 1966. A referendum in 1979 opposed devolution, but another in 1997 narrowly approved it, and the opening session of the Welsh Assembly was held in June 1999. ► **ENGLAND**; **NORTHERN IRELAND**; **SCOTLAND**; **UNITED KINGDOM**

### Wałesa, Lech (1943–)
Polish trade unionist and politician. A former Gdansk shipyard worker, he became the leader of the independent trade union **SOLIDARITY**, which in 1980 openly challenged the Polish government's economic and social policies. He held negotiations with the leading figures in the Communist Party and had tacit but strong support from the Roman Catholic Church, but was detained by the authorities when martial law was declared in 1981. He was released in 1982, and was awarded the **NOBEL PEACE PRIZE** in 1983. Despite restrictions imposed on him, he continued to be a prominent figure in Polish politics, and was mainly responsible for the success of the negotiations which led to Solidarity effectively forming the first Polish non-Communist government in Sep 1989. This not only transformed the course of events

in Poland but was an important contributory factor in the whole East European revolution in the winter of 1989–90. Wałesa became President in Dec 1990, a position he retained until 1995 when he lost to Aleksander Kwaśniewski.

**Wallace, George Corley** (1919–98)
US politician. Born in Clio, Alabama, he served as a flight engineer in **WORLD WAR II** and practised law in Alabama before becoming involved in state Democratic politics. He served four terms as Governor of Alabama (1963–7, 1971–9, 1983–7), earning notoriety in the early 1960s by seeking to block **DESEGREGATION** in the Alabama public schools. He ran for President as a member of the American Independent Party in 1968, capitalizing on white backlash to garner more votes than expected for a third-party candidate, and in 1972 he was shot and paralysed in an assassination attempt while campaigning for the Democratic presidential nomination. His final term as governor was marked by a renunciation of his earlier racism, and an effort to win support from African-American voters.

**Wallace, Henry Agard** (1888–1965)
US agriculturist and politician. Born in Adair County, Iowa, he edited *Wallace's Farmer* from 1933 until 1940, serving as Secretary of Agriculture (1933–41) under Franklin D **ROOSEVELT**, whose **NEW DEAL** policies he supported. As Vice-President under Roosevelt from 1941 to 1945, he served as Chairman of the

Board of Economic Warfare. He failed to obtain renomination as Vice-President in 1944 but he became Secretary of Commerce (1945–6). He unsuccessfully stood for President in 1948.

**Wallace, Sir William** (c.1274–1305)
Scottish knight and champion of the independence of Scotland. He routed the English army at Stirling (1297), and took control of the government of Scotland as 'Guardian', but was defeated by **EDWARD I** at Falkirk (1298). He was eventually captured near Glasgow (1305), and was hanged, drawn, and quartered at Smithfield, London. Many legends collected around him due to his immense popular appeal as a national figure resisting foreign oppression.

**Wallenberg, Raoul** (1912–?47)
Swedish diplomat. He was a member of a prominent Swedish business family. In 1944 he was sent to Hungary under the auspices of the American War Refugee Board to attempt to rescue the 700,000 Jews put at risk by the German occupation of the country. With the help of special passports and warnings to the occupying power of post-war retribution, he managed to save over 100,000 Hungarian Jews. He was arrested by the Russians when they marched into Budapest in 1945, and disappeared. In spite of Russian claims that he died in 1947 as their prisoner, rumours continued to circulate that he was alive even in the 1970s.

**Wallenstein** or **Waldstein, Albrecht Wenzel Eusebius von, Duke of Friedland and of Mecklenburg, Prince of Sagan** (1583–1634)
Bohemian general. During the **THIRTY YEARS' WAR** he became Commander of the Imperial armies and won a series of victories (1625–9), gaining the titles of the Duke of Mecklenburg and 'General of the Baltic and Oceanic Seas'. His ambition led to his dismissal in 1630, but he was reinstated to defend the Empire against Swedish attack. He recovered Bohemia, but was defeated by **GUSTAV II ADOLF** at **LÜTZEN** (1632), and was again dismissed. His intrigues led to an Imperial proclamation of treason, resulting in his assassination at Eger by Irish and Scots mercenaries.

**Walloon Movement**
Belgian political movement, formed largely in reaction to the progress made by the **FLEMISH MOVEMENT**. Ever since Flemish rights were claimed in the early 19c, Walloon (southern Belgian, French-speaking) counter-claims have been lodged; since the early 20c there have been Walloon congresses each year in Liège. The movement has often been rather negative, perhaps because of the decline of Wallonia in economic and demographic terms in relation to Flanders in the 20c. After **WORLD WAR II** a National Walloon Congress spoke out for such alternatives as federalism, Walloon independence, or even annexation of Wallonia by France. In 1961 the Popular Walloon Movement was founded, agitating for the federal solution. In 1968 all the various Walloon organizations came together in the **RASSEMBLEMENT WALLON**; its power to win seats had declined by the late 1970s. The movement helped to accelerate the political federalization of Belgium; this eventually took place in 1993, when a separate regional government for Wallonia was established.

**Wall Street Crash**
The collapse of the US stock market in Oct 1929. The crash followed an artificial boom in the US economy (1927–9) fuelled by speculation. Panic-selling resulted in 13 million shares changing hands on 24 Oct, and 16 million on 29 Oct, causing widespread bankruptcy and a massive rise in unemployment. ► **GREAT DEPRESSION**

**Walpole, Sir Robert, 1st Earl of Orford** (1676–1745)
English politician. He became a Whig MP in 1701, and was made Secretary for War (1708) and Treasurer of the Navy (1710). Sent to the Tower for alleged corruption during the Tory government (1712), he was recalled by **GEORGE I**, and made a Privy Councillor and (1715) Chancellor of the Exchequer. After the collapse of the South Sea Scheme, he again became Chancellor (1721), and was widely recognized as 'Prime Minister', a title (unknown to the constitution) which he hotly repudiated. A shrewd manipulator of men, he took trouble to consult backbench MPs, and followed policies of low taxation designed to win their favour. He was regarded as indispensable by both George I and **GEORGE II**. His popularity began to wane in the 1730s over the Excise Scheme and also over his determination to avoid foreign wars. He did not fully recover from the outbreak of a war he had opposed in 1739, and resigned in 1742. His period in office is widely held to have increased the influence of the House of **COMMONS** in the constitu

tion. He was created Earl of Orford. ► **SOUTH SEA BUBBLE**

**Walsingham, Sir Francis** (c.1530–1590)
English statesman. He studied at Cambridge, became a diplomat, and was made a Secretary of State to **ELIZABETH I** (1573–90), a member of the Privy Council, and knighted. A Puritan sympathizer, and a strong opponent of the Catholics, he developed a complex system of espionage at home and abroad, enabling him to reveal the plots of **THROCKMORTON** and **BABINGTON** against the Queen, and was one of the commissioners to try **MARY, QUEEN OF SCOTS** at Fotheringay. ► **PURITANISM**

**Walter, Hubert** (c.1140–1205)
English churchman and statesman. He became Bishop of Salisbury (1189), and accompanied **RICHARD I, THE LIONHEART** on the Third **CRUSADE**. Appointed Archbishop of Canterbury in 1193, he played key roles in raising the ransom to secure Richard's release from captivity, and in containing the rebellion of the King's brother **JOHN**. At the end of 1193, he became justiciar of England, and was responsible for all the business of government until his resignation in 1198. On John's accession (1199), he became Chancellor, and was consulted on important matters of state.

**Wandervogel**
German and Austrian youth movement. Founded in Germany in 1901 and Austria in 1909, this movement asserted youthful values in society and an affinity with nature. Organized hikes, rural trysts and a search for adventure attracted a significant membership to the various *Wandervogel* associations. These continued to function during the **WEIMAR REPUBLIC**, but were closed by the **NAZI PARTY** in 1933, with members being transferred to the **HITLER YOUTH**.

**Wang Ching-wei** ► **WANG JINGWEI**

**Wang Jingwei (Wang Ching-wei)** (1883–1944)
Chinese politician. An associate of the revolutionary and Nationalist leader **SUN YAT-SEN**, he studied in Japan, where he joined Sun's revolutionary party, and from 1917 became his personal assistant. In 1927 he was appointed head of the new **GUOMINDANG** government at Wuhan, and in 1932 became the party's President, with his main rival for control of the Guomindang, **CHIANG KAI-SHEK**, in charge of the military. In 1938, after the outbreak of war with Japan, Wang offered to cooperate with the Japanese, and in 1940 he became head of a puppet regime ruling the occupied areas.

**Warbeck, Perkin** (c.1474–1499)
Flemish impostor. Pretender to the English throne, he was born in Tournai. He appeared in 1490 claiming to be Richard, Duke of York, the younger of the two sons of **EDWARD IV** murdered in the Tower. The Irish and the French, under **CHARLES VIII**, supported him, and in July 1495 he landed in Kent. In Scotland, **JAMES IV** married him to a daughter of the Earl of Huntly. In 1498 he attempted to besiege Exeter, but ran away to the sanctuary at Beaulieu in Hampshire, surrendered, and was imprisoned. Charged with attempting to escape, he was thrown into the Tower of London and executed.

# *Warfare*

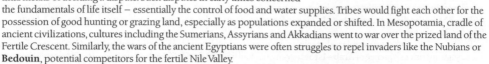

War & Warfare

### The nature of warfare

The origin of warfare has continued to be the reason for its existence: the final means of deciding a dispute. Such disputes in early times concerned the fundamentals of life itself – essentially the control of food and water supplies. Tribes would fight each other for the possession of good hunting or grazing land, especially as populations expanded or shifted. In Mesopotamia, cradle of ancient civilizations, cultures including the Sumerians, Assyrians and Akkadians went to war over the prized land of the Fertile Crescent. Similarly, the wars of the ancient Egyptians were often struggles to repel invaders like the Nubians or **Bedouin**, potential competitors for the fertile Nile Valley.

With the development of more sophisticated cultures, the spoils of war came to include control of trade and trade routes, as well as simple possession of land. The growth of great empires, like the Persian, the Roman and the Incan, was fuelled by conquest, with the mightier military powers taking control of, and absorbing, the resources of the weaker.

In time, religion came to be the catalyst for war, a prime example being the spread of Islam, inspired by the concept of the **jihad**, through North Africa, the Middle East and into Spain in the 7–8c. The **Thirty Years' War** (1616–48) began as a struggle between Catholic and Protestant before developing into a dispute over the balance of power in Europe.

On the boundless steppes of the Eurasian landmass, cavalry warfare was highly developed, especially in the shape of the horse-archer. Mounted nomad archers repeatedly overran agricultural and urban communities, culminating in the huge Mongol Empire established by **Genghis Khan** and his successors in the 13c. Earlier the Magyar cavalry had overrun the Hungarian plain, and in the 16c the **Mughal Dynasty** used Central Asian cavalry to take control of the plains of Hindustan. The Manchu nomads overran China in the 17c, and when they established the **Qing Dynasty** asserted their imperial sway over Tibetan and Islamic peoples.

With the evolution of states as political bodies, as opposed to aggregations of peoples or territories under one ruler, war between states for political, religious and economic hegemony became more important, as in the long duel for hegemony between Bourbon and Habsburg. In the **French Revolutionary Wars** (1792–9), the newborn First **Republic** of France struggled to repel invasion and consolidate its frontiers before going on to conquer large areas of Europe in the name of 'liberation'.

Competition for empire and trade was a major cause of war between European states from the 17c. Permanent navies of specialized warships, some mounting over 100 guns, evolved in states able to fund them. The **Seven Years' War** (1756–63) saw fighting between the British and the French in such distant theatres as Canada and India, as well as on the continent of Europe. The **Industrial Revolution** helped ensure war became mechanized, with huge armoured battle fleets and formidable conscript armies deployed by train networks.

The 20c saw the emergence of total war in both World Wars. Not only did nations send armies of hitherto unimagined size into combat in many different areas of the world, but their civilian populations were increasingly involved in the struggle. The idea of the 'home front' emerged in **World War I** with governments exerting tight control over vital industries, fixing hours of work and wage levels, and outlawing strikes. In Britain, licensing laws were introduced in 1916 to prevent drunkenness in the workplace, women were brought in to do the jobs of absent men, and the Military Service Act (1916) brought in **conscription**.

---

### Ward, Sir Joseph George (1856–1930)

New Zealand statesman. Born in Melbourne, he entered parliament in 1887 and held many prominent posts, including Minister of Public Health (the first in the world). He was Liberal Prime Minister from 1906 to 1912, and 1928 to 1930. With William Ferguson **MASSEY**, he represented New Zealand at the **PARIS PEACE CONFERENCE**.

### Warfare ► *See panel*

### warlords

Chinese provincial military rulers who engaged in a bitter power struggle and civil war after the death of President **YUAN SHIKAI** in 1916. They were eventually subdued by the 1926–8 **NORTHERN EXPEDITION** of **CHIANG KAI-SHEK**.

### War Measures Act (1914)

Canadian statute. Enacted in the first weeks of **WORLD WAR I**, it gave the federal government extraordinary powers. It could bypass the normal legislative process, suspend *habeas corpus* and deport without trial. It also included emergency economic regulations. Under the Act, immigrants from Germany and Austria-Hungary were forced to carry special identity cards and to register at regular intervals, while 8,300 aliens were interned in special camps. During **WORLD WAR II**, 6,414 orders were made under the War Measures Act; and it was still in force in 1945 when a de-

fector from the USSR, Igor Gouzenko, informed on a Soviet spy ring in Canada. The findings of a Royal Commission led to the arrest, under the Act, of the single communist MP, a prominent scientist and members of the civil and military service. In 1970 the Act was again invoked to deal with the **OCTOBER CRISIS** in Quebec.

### War of 1812

The name given to the hostilities between the UK and the USA between 1812 and 1814. Its deepest causes went back to some unfulfilled provisions of the Treaty of Paris of 1783, which secured American independence. However, war was eventually provoked by the persistent refusal of Britain to recognize American neutral and maritime rights. After 1793, in the course of the Anglo-French war, American trade was incessantly disrupted and American ships continually subjected to boarding and their crews to impressment. The most notorious of these incidents, the surrender of the USS *Chesapeake* to HMS *Leopard* in 1807, provoked commercial retaliation with President Thomas **JEFFERSON**'s embargo policy. The failure of both this and the subsequent Non-Intercourse Act to alter British policies eventually left the USA no other option but to declare war, if independence was to mean anything at all. Ironically, war began as British policy was changed with the

World War II saw even more of the globe caught up in the struggle, and the same pattern emerged of a government mobilizing the whole state for the war effort. Civilian involvement was even greater, with the mass bombing of cities and industrial centres, and the participation of many in acts of resistance against occupying armies.

After 1945, the threat of nuclear annihilation changed the face of war from open conflict to '**Cold War**' tension between the West and the communist bloc. The struggle became economic and political, with limited wars arising as smaller countries were incited to attack or rebel and were supplied with arms by one side or the other. The **Korean War** (1950–3) saw the direct intervention of Chinese forces but their **UN** opponents were forbidden by their own leaders to invade Chinese territory.

In the late 20c, global war was largely replaced by wars limited by time and space, as exemplified in such conflicts as the savage but brief sequence of **Arab–Israeli Wars**; the **Falklands War** (1982), which was over in a little more than two months and was confined to the South Atlantic; the **Gulf War** (1991), fought in parts of Kuwait and Iraq; the **Afghan War** (2001) and the **Iraq War** (2003), both lasting only a few months.

### The technology of warfare

The weapons of war began as the implements of hunting turned against other men instead of animals, such as stone axes and knives, and blades and spearheads made of horn, bone and flint. As metal smelting was developed, better weapons were made, first of bronze, then of iron, and metal **armour** was created to withstand them.

The ordinary foot-soldier was limited to what he could carry, and to attack fortifications siege weapons such as the catapult were developed. The invention of the composite bow allowed arrows to be fired with greater power, range and accuracy, ensuring that enemies could be attacked from a distance. The horse was brought into battle, first to pull the war chariots of the Mesopotamians, later as the steed of the cavalry warrior.

The heavily armoured *hoplite* phalanx of the ancient Greeks dominated the battlefield until a combination of heavier cavalry and lighter, more mobile infantry neutralized its power. The development of the stirrup allowed a heavily armoured horseman to keep his seat in battle, and the victory of the Goths over the Romans at Adrianople (AD 378) marked a period of armoured cavalry dominance that was ended only in the 14c by such infantry weapons as the English longbow and the Swiss pike.

The 14c also saw the introduction of the firearm to European war, and over the next 600 years **artillery** and small arms proliferated. Improvements in the accuracy, power and speed of firing of hand-held weapons led from the arquebus to the rifle and the submachine gun. Artillery became lighter and more mobile; at one end of the scale was the field gun, at the other end the 'Big Berthas' of World War I.

Artillery and machine guns dominated the battlefields of the 20c, killing soldiers on a hitherto unseen scale, particularly in World War I. The tank, the military **aircraft**, the guided missile, the submarine, and the aircraft-carrier all came to prominence in World War II, which closed with the most destructive weapon of all, the atomic bomb. The post-war period saw the development of intercontinental ballistic missiles with nuclear warheads, chemical and biological weapons, and depleted-uranium artillery rounds. By the end of the 20c conventional conflicts between states were dominated by air strikes with 'smart' weapons targeted with unprecedented precision by satellites and GPS (Global Positioning System). ► **Army**; **Air Force**; **Fortification**; **Navy**

---

suspension of the Orders in Council, while the most decisive military engagement, the American victory at the Battle of **NEW ORLEANS**, occurred after peace had been made at the Treaty of **GHENT** (Dec 1814). Apart from this defeat, the British were militarily more effective, victorious with their Native American allies against American attempts to gain Canadian land, and even burning down the Capitol and the White House in Washington. The peace treaty marked a change in the attitude of Britain towards the USA, allowing a mutually beneficial commercial relationship to develop and for the USA marking the achievement of substantive, as well as formal, independence.

### War of Independence, US ► AMERICAN REVOLUTION

### War Powers Act (1973)

US legislation requiring that **CONGRESS** be consulted before the President dispatch US forces into battle, and that Congress approve any continuance of war beyond 60 days. Public confidence in the executive branch had been greatly diminished after the **VIETNAM WAR** and **WATERGATE** and, like the Freedom of Information Act, this Act aimed to limit its power.

### Warren, Earl (1891–1974)

US jurist. He attended the University of California law school and was admitted to the Bar. An active Republican, he became Governor of California (1943–53)

and made an unsuccessful run for the vice-presidency in 1948. He became Chief Justice of the US Supreme Court in 1953. The Warren Court (1953–69) was active and influential, notably in the areas of **CIVIL RIGHTS** and individual liberties. It was responsible for the landmark decision in **BROWN V BOARD OF EDUCATION OF TOPEKA, KANSAS** (1954), which outlawed school segregation, and for Miranda v Arizona (1966), which ruled that criminal suspects be informed of their rights before being questioned by the police. Warren was chairman of the federal commission (the Warren Commission) that investigated the assassination of President John F **KENNEDY**.

### Warsaw Pact

The shorthand name for the East European Mutual Assistance Treaty signed in Warsaw in 1955 by Albania, Bulgaria, Czechoslovakia, East Germany, Hungary, Poland, Romania and the USSR; Albania withdrew in 1968. The pact established a unified military command for the armed forces of all the signatories who were committed to giving immediate assistance to one another in the event of an attack in Europe. It was a Soviet bloc response, in part, to the formation of **NATO** by the West. But it also had a political purpose, as was demonstrated when it was used in Czechoslovakia to restore communism, allegedly endangered by the **PRAGUE SPRING** in 1968. In the wake of the East European revolution in the winter of 1989–90, the pact effectively disintegrated before it was officially terminated in 1991.

**Wars of the Coalition**
A series of wars against Revolutionary France. The First Coalition (1793) began to collapse as a result of **NAPOLEON I**'s victories in 1797. In 1799, a Second Coalition arose after **NELSON**'s victory over the French in Egypt (**ABOUKIR BAY**) but dissolved with the overthrow of the French First Republic by Napoleon. A Third Coalition was created in 1805 to defeat Napoleon. ► **REPUBLIC, FIRST** (France)

**Wartburg**
A castle near Eisenach on a hill first fortified in 1080. After 1485 the castle belonged to the Dukes of Saxony. Martin **LUTHER**, after the Diet of Worms, hid at the Wartburg (May 1521–Mar 1522) to avoid Imperial persecution.

**Warwick, Richard Neville, Earl of**, known as **the Kingmaker** (1428–71)
English soldier and politician. He exercised great power during the first phase of the Wars of the **ROSES**. Created Earl of Warwick in 1450, he championed the Yorkist cause. In 1460 he defeated and captured **HENRY VI** at Northampton, had his cousin, Edward of York, proclaimed King as **EDWARD IV** (1461), and then destroyed the Lancastrian army at Towton. When Edward tried to assert his independence, Warwick joined the Lancastrians, forced the King to flee to Holland, and restored Henry VI to the throne (1470). He was defeated and killed by Edward IV at the Battle of Barnet. ► **LANCASTER, HOUSE OF**; **YORK, HOUSE OF**

**Washakie** (c.1804–1900)
Native American chief (from the 1840s) of the eastern Shoshone. A renowned warrior in conflicts with enemy tribes, he was friendly and generous towards white settlers and travellers, and helped the US Army in wars against other **NATIVE AMERICANS** on the Great Plains and in the **SIOUX** War of 1876. In 1868 he signed the Fort Bridger Treaty, which gave up Shoshone land in the Green River Valley in eastern Utah and southern Wyoming, to allow the building of the Union Pacific Railroad. He spent his later years as a dictator on the Shoshone Reservation.

**Washington, Booker T(aliaferro)** (1856–1915)
US black leader and educationist. He was born a slave in Franklin County, Virginia. After emancipation (1865), he was educated at Hampton Institute, Virginia, and Washington, DC, then became a teacher, writer and speaker on black problems and the importance of education and vocational training. In 1881 he was appointed principal of the newly opened Tuskegee Institute, Alabama, and built it into a major centre of black education. The foremost black leader in the late 19c, he encouraged blacks to focus on economic equality rather than fight for social or political equality. He was strongly criticized by W E B **DU BOIS**, and his policies were repudiated by the 20c **CIVIL RIGHTS MOVEMENT**. He was the author of *Up from Slavery* (1901).

**Washington, George** (1732–99)
US general and 1st President of the USA. He had an informal education, worked as a surveyor, and first fought in the campaigns of the French and Indian War (1754–8). He then managed the family estate at Mount Vernon, Virginia, becoming active in politics as a member of the Virginia House of Burgesses (1758–74). He represented Virginia in the first (1774) and second (1775) Continental Congresses. In 1775 he was given command of the American forces, where he displayed great powers as a strategist and leader of men. Following reverses in the New York area, he retreated through New Jersey, inflicting notable defeats on the enemy at Trenton (1776) and Princeton (1777). He suffered defeats at **BRANDY-WINE** and **GERMANTOWN**, but held his army together through the severe winter of 1777–8 at **VALLEY FORGE**. After the alliance with France (1778), he forced the surrender of **CORNWALLIS** at Yorktown in 1781, marking the end of the war. He then retired to Mount Vernon, and sought to secure a strong government by constitutional means. In 1787 he presided over the Constitutional Convention, and became the first President, an office he held from 1789 to 1797. He tried to remain neutral as political differences increased between the Federalists and Jeffersonians, and refused to continue for a third term in office. He retired to Mount Vernon and died two years later. ► **AMERICAN REVOLUTION**; **CONTINENTAL CONGRESS**; **YORKTOWN CAMPAIGN**

**Washington, Treaty of** (1871)
Treaty between the USA and Great Britain (whose delegation included the Canadian Prime Minister John A **MACDONALD**). The USA demanded compensation for the damage inflicted during the **AMERICAN CIVIL WAR** by Confederate raiders using arms manufactured in Britain, together with arbitration of the boundary south of Vancouver Island and the possession of the strategic island of San Juan. Canada hoped to negotiate a trade agreement in return for the admission of US fishermen to her inshore waters. Macdonald was well aware that Britain, above all, wished to establish good relations with the USA and he was determined that Canadian interests should not suffer. While the USA secured compensation and a favourable settlement of the boundary question, Macdonald ensured that Canada gained free navigation of the rivers of Alaska (crucial for the **HUDSON'S BAY COMPANY**) in exchange for free US use of the St Lawrence. Fishing and trade agreements were also negotiated between Canada and the USA which formed the basis for a consultative arrangement to resolve problems before they became international crises involving the British.

**Washington Conference** (Nov 1921–Feb 1922)
A naval conference held in Washington, DC, to consider the reduction of naval armaments in the Pacific, and to discuss political stability in the Far East. The UK, USA, Japan, France and Italy agreed to reduce the number of their capital ships (battleships and aircraft-carriers) and not to construct any more for ten years. A Nine-Power treaty was drawn up to ensure the independence of, and fair trading in, China, and the **ANGLO-JAPANESE ALLIANCE** of 1902 was replaced by a Four-Power Pact between the UK, Japan, the USA and France.

**Watauga Association** (1772)
An agreement among settlers of present-day north-

east Tennessee, USA, to establish civil government in the absence of regular institutions, and to obtain land directly from the **NATIVE AMERICANS** rather than from the British crown.

## Watergate (1972–4)
US political scandal. It led to the first resignation of a President in US history (Richard **NIXON**, in office 1969–74). The actual 'Watergate' is a hotel and office complex in Washington, DC, where the **DEMOCRATIC PARTY** had its headquarters. During the presidential campaign of 1972, a team of burglars was caught inside Democratic headquarters, and their connections were traced to the White House and to the Committee to Re-elect the President. Investigations by the *Washington Post*, a grand jury and two special prosecutors revealed that high officials who were very close to Nixon were implicated, and that Nixon himself was aware of illegal measures to cover up that implication. A number of officials were eventually imprisoned. Nixon himself left office when it became clear that he was likely to be impeached and removed.

## Waterloo, Battle of (18 June 1815)
The final defeat of **NAPOLEON I**, ending the **NAPOLEONIC WARS** and the Emperor's last bid for power in the **HUNDRED DAYS**. A hard-fought battle, in which **BLÜCHER**'s Prussian force arrived at the climax to support **WELLINGTON**'s mixed Allied force. A number of crucial blunders by the French contributed to their defeat.

## Wavell, Archibald Percival Wavell, 1st Earl (1883–1950)
British field marshal. He served in South Africa and India, became **ALLENBY**'s Chief of Staff in Palestine, and in 1939 he was given the Middle East Command. He defeated the Italians in North Africa, but failed against **ROMMEL**, and in 1941 was transferred to India, where he became Viceroy (1943). He was made field marshal and viscount (1943), earl (1947), Constable of the Tower (1948) and Lord-Lieutenant of London (1949). ► **WORLD WAR II**

## Wayne, Anthony, known as Mad Anthony (1745–96)
American Revolutionary general. During the **AMERICAN REVOLUTION**, he served at **BRANDYWINE**, **GERMANTOWN** and **MONMOUTH**, and in 1779 led a brilliant attack which captured Stony Point, New York, a British defence post on the Hudson River. In 1794 he fought **NATIVE AMERICANS** in the Ohio Valley and won a pivotal victory at the Battle of Fallen Timbers. The next year he negotiated a treaty with them which opened up the north-west to white settlers.

## Webb, Sidney James, Baron Passfield (1859–1947) and (Martha) Beatrice (1858–1943)
British social reformers, historians and economists, married in 1892. Sidney became a lawyer, and joined the **FABIAN SOCIETY**, where he wrote many powerful tracts. Beatrice interested herself in the social problems of the time. After their marriage they were committed to advancing the causes of **SOCIALISM** and trade unionism, publishing their classic *History of Trade Unionism* (1894), *English Local Government* (1906–29, 9 vols), and other works. They also started the *New Statesman* (1913). Sidney became an MP (1922), President of the Board of Trade (1924),

Dominions and Colonial Secretary (1929–30) and Colonial Secretary (1930–1), and was created a baron in 1929.

## Weber, Max (1864–1920)
German sociologist. Educated at Heidelberg and Berlin, he held university posts at Berlin (1893), Freiburg (1894), Heidelberg (1897) and Munich (1919). His best-known works include *Die protestantische Ethik und der Geist des Kapitalismus* (1904, Eng trans *The Protestant Ethic and the Spirit of Capitalism*, 1930) and *Wirtschaft und Gesellschaft* (1922, Eng trans *Economy and Society*, 1968) which were major influences on sociological theory. He helped to draft the constitution for the **WEIMAR REPUBLIC** (1919).

## Webster, Daniel (1782–1852)
US lawyer and statesman. He was called to the Bar in 1805, and served in the **HOUSE OF REPRESENTATIVES** (1813–17). Settling in Boston as an advocate in 1816, he distinguished himself before the US Supreme Court in the Dartmouth College case (1818) and **MCCULLOCH V MARYLAND** (1819), and as an orator became famous by his oration on the bicentenary of the landing of the **PILGRIM FATHERS**. He returned to **CONGRESS** (Dec 1823) as a Massachusetts Representative, and in 1827 he became a Senator. Having previously favoured free trade, in 1828 he defended the new protective tariff. His career was marked by a deep reverence for established institutions and for the principle of nationality. When the **WHIG PARTY** triumphed in 1840, Webster was called into William Henry **HARRISON**'s cabinet as Secretary of State (1841–3), a position he retained when Harrison died a few months later. Under President **TYLER**, he negotiated the **WEBSTER–ASHBURTON TREATY** (1842) with Britain, but resigned in May 1843. In 1844 he refused his party's nomination for President and supported Henry **CLAY**. He opposed the **MEXICAN WAR**. In 1850 he voiced his abhorrence of **SLAVERY**, and unwilling to break up the Union to abolish it, supported compromise measures. Under President **FILLMORE**, he was recalled as Secretary of State (1850–2) to settle differences with Britain. He was one of the greatest of US orators.

## Webster–Ashburton Treaty (1842)
An agreement between Britain and the USA which established the boundary between north-east USA and Canada. Among specific issues were disputed territory between Maine and New Brunswick and at the north end of Lake Champlain, navigation rights on the St John's River, and control of the Mesabi iron deposits. The treaty also established provisions for later joint action between the USA and Britain.

## Weerstand, Het ► RESISTANCE MOVEMENT (Belgium)

## Wehrmacht
Literally 'defence force', this is the term used to describe the German armed forces during the period 1935–45. Recruited by conscription, the *Wehrmacht* constituted the military strength of the National Socialist state and conducted the victorious **BLITZKRIEG** campaigns of the period 1939–41. However, from 1938 the *Waffen-SS* ('Armed' **SS**) was developed as a parallel Nazi army which, in the closing months of the war, came to overshadow the Wehrmacht. The

members of the Wehrmacht were bound to **HITLER** by a personal oath of loyalty and its commanders generally carried out Hitler's orders willingly, although individuals, such as those involved in the July 1944 plot against him, did offer resistance. ► **NAZI PARTY**

**Wei Ching-sheng** ► WEI JINGSHENG

**Wei Jingsheng (Wei Ching-sheng)** (1949– )
Chinese dissident. A Red Guard during the **CULTURAL REVOLUTION**, Wei served in the **PEOPLE'S LIBERATION ARMY** during the early 1970s before becoming an electrician at Beijing Zoo. During the **DEMOCRACY WALL MOVEMENT** (1978–9) he called for greater democracy (what he called the 'fifth modernization') and became the editor of an outspoken unofficial journal. He was arrested in Mar 1979 and brought to trial six months later on charges of divulging state secrets to foreigners and spreading counter-revolutionary propaganda. He was sentenced to 15 years in prison and was released in 1993. The following year he was arrested without charge, and in 1995 was sentenced to 14 years' imprisonment for alleged subversion. In 1997 he was released and allowed to emigrate to the USA.

**Weil, Simone** (1909–43)
French philosophical writer and mystic. She taught philosophy in several schools, interspersing this with periods of manual labour to experience the working-class life. In 1936 she served in the republican forces in the **SPANISH CIVIL WAR**. In 1941 she settled in Marseilles, where she developed a deep mystical feeling for the Roman Catholic faith, yet a profound reluctance to join an organized religion. She escaped to the USA in 1942 and worked for the **FREE FRENCH** in London, before her death at Ashford, Kent. Her posthumously published works include *La Pesanteur et la grâce* (1946, Eng trans *Gravity and Grace*, 1963) and *L'Attente de dieu* (1950, Eng trans *Waiting for God*, 1959).

**Weimar Republic**
The name by which the German Federal Republic of 1918–33 is known. In 1919 a National Constituent Assembly met at Weimar, on the River Elbe, and drew up a constitution for the new republic. The government moved from Weimar to Berlin in 1920. In 1933, two months after becoming Chancellor, **HITLER** passed an Enabling Act suspending the Weimar constitution.

**Weinberger, Caspar Willard** (1917– )
US politician. Born in San Francisco, he entered politics as a member of the California state legislature in 1952. He served as Finance Director (1968–9) in the California administration of Ronald **REAGAN** and then moved to Washington, to work first as Director of the Office of Management and Budget (1972–3) and then as Secretary of Health, Education and Welfare (1973–5) in the **NIXON** and **FORD** administrations. Following a period in private industry, he was appointed Defense Secretary by President Ronald Reagan with the brief to oversee a major military build-up. This he successfully did, developing such high-profile projects as the Strategic Defense Initiative (**SDI**), though there was Congressional criticism of the budgetary consequences and of **PENTAGON** inefficiency. A 'hawk' with respect to East–West issues,

Weinberger opposed a rapprochement with the USSR during the final years of the Reagan administration and resigned in 1987. In 1988 he was awarded an honorary knighthood (KBE) by the British monarch for 'service to British interests', most notably during the **FALKLANDS WAR** (Apr–June 1982).

**Weisse Rose**
The German anti-Nazi resistance group (literally, 'White Rose'), centred on Professor Kurt Huber and the students Hans and Sophie Scholl of Munich University. From autumn 1942 until their arrest on 18 Feb 1943 the group pursued a leafleting campaign in which they called for resistance against a morally bankrupt National Socialism. Arrested by the **GESTAPO**, the Scholls were executed on 22 Feb 1943 and Huber on 13 July 1943.

**Weizmann, Chaim Azriel** (1874–1952)
Israeli politician. Born near Pinsk, Russia (now Belarus), he studied in Germany and Switzerland, then lectured on chemistry at Geneva and Manchester. He helped to secure the **BALFOUR DECLARATION** of 1917, and became President of the **WORLD ZIONIST ORGANIZATION** (1920–30 and 1935–46), and of the **JEWISH AGENCY** (from 1929). He played a major role in the establishment of the State of Israel (1948), and was its first President (1949–52). ► **ZIONISM**

**Weizsäcker, Richard Freiherr, Baron von** (1920– )
West German politician, the son of a baron-diplomat who was tried at Nuremberg. He was educated at Berlin, Oxford, Grenoble and Göttingen universities, studying history and law. During **WORLD WAR II** he served in the **WEHRMACHT**. After the war he worked as a professional lawyer and was active in the German Protestant Church, becoming President of its congress (1964–70). A member of the conservative Christian Democratic Union (**CDU**) from 1954, he served as a Deputy in the **BUNDESTAG** from 1969, as CDU Deputy Chairman (1972–9) and, from 1981, as a successful Mayor of West Berlin, before being elected federal President in May 1984. He was re-elected in May 1989 and stepped down in 1994.

**Welensky, Sir Roy (Roland)** (1907–92)
Rhodesian politician. Born in Bulawayo, he was educated in local schools and then started work on the railways at the age of 14. He became leader of the Railway Workers' Union in Northern Rhodesia in 1933, by which time he had also been heavyweight boxing champion (1926–8). Elected to the Northern Rhodesia Legco in 1938, he founded the Northern Rhodesia Labour Party in 1941 and was appointed Director of Manpower by the Governor. He became Chairman of the unofficial opposition in 1946. A strong supporter of the proposed Federation of Rhodesia and Nyasaland, he was elected to its first parliament. Welensky was appointed Minister of Transport and Development in 1953, to which he soon added the portfolios of Communications and Posts. Promoted to Deputy Prime Minister in 1955, he succeeded Sir Godfrey **HUGGINS** (Lord Malvern) as Prime Minister in 1956, which post he held until the Federation's demise at the end of 1963. Although considered a doughty champion of white rule, he was strongly opposed to Southern Rhodesia's **UDI** and tried, unsuccessfully, to return to politics as an opponent of Ian **SMITH**. He

retired to a smallholding near Salisbury (now Harare).

## Welfs

A Frankish aristocratic family. They were the chief rivals of the **HOHENSTAUFEN DYNASTY** in Germany and Italy, with extensive lands in Saxony and Bavaria. They were at their most powerful under **HENRY THE LION**, whose son, **OTTO IV**, became king and emperor. The Welfs and Hohenstaufen were reconciled when **FREDERICK II** enfeoffed Otto's grandson with the Duchy of Brunswick-Lüneburg, the shrunken remains of his ancestors' lands. The term Guelf came to be used in Italy for supporters of the papacy against the emperor. ➤ **GUELFS**

## Wellesley, Richard Colley Wellesley, 1st Marquis
(1760–1842)
British administrator. He became an MP (1784), a Lord of the Treasury (1786), a marquis (1799) and Governor-General of India (1797–1805). Under his administration British rule in India became supreme; the influence of France was extinguished, and the power of the princes reduced by the crushing of **TIPPOO SAHIB** (1799) and the Marathas (1803). After his return to England, he became Ambassador to Madrid (1805), Foreign Minister (1809) and Lord-Lieutenant of Ireland (1821 and 1833).

## Wellington, Arthur Wellesley, 1st Duke of
(1769–1852)
British general and politician. He joined the army in 1787, was sent to India with his regiment, and there defeated **TIPPOO SAHIB**, became Governor of Mysore, and broke the power of the Marathas. Knighted in 1804, he became an MP (1806), and Irish Secretary (1807). He defeated the Danes during the Copenhagen expedition (1807), and in the **PENINSULAR WAR** drove the French out of Portugal and Spain, gaining victories at Talavera (1809), Salamanca (1812) and Toulouse (1814). For his role in this campaign he was given many honours, and created Duke of Wellington. After **NAPOLEON I**'s escape from Elba, he defeated the French at the Battle of **WATERLOO**. He supported **LIVERPOOL**'s government, and joined it as Master-General of the Ordnance (1818). He also became Constable of the Tower (1826) and army Commander-in-Chief (1827). His period as Prime Minister (1828–30) significantly weakened the Tory Party, which split over the question of **CATHOLIC EMANCIPATION** (1829), and was further weakened by disagreements over trade and parliamentary reform. Wellington's opposition to parliamentary reform brought down his government, which was succeeded by the **WHIGS**. He was Foreign Secretary under **PEEL** (1834–5), and retired from public life in 1846. ➤ **NAPOLEONIC WARS**

## Wells, Fargo & Co
A US stagecoach company founded by Henry Wells (1805–78) and William G **FARGO** in 1852. It was the most successful company of its kind in the West, thriving by carrying passengers, mail and money initially between California and the eastern states, and later serving other areas in the West and Latin America. In 1918 it merged with other companies to become the American Railway Express Company.

## Welser Family
A powerful banking family established in Augsburg in 1498 by Anton Welser. They were noted for their involvement in projects in the New World.

## Weltpolitik
A concept (literally, 'world policy') widely promoted in post-Bismarckian Imperial Germany and taken to mean the acquisition of new colonies, a greater German share in international trade, and parity with the other major powers, especially Britain. The creation of a large, high-seas battle fleet by **TIRPITZ** was seen as essential to the realization of these aims, but this attempt led in turn to a costly and ultimately futile arms race with Britain. *Weltpolitik* was further seen as a means of diverting public attention from the steadily growing constitutional tensions within Germany, but its limited success led to failure in this regard. The resulting crises in domestic and foreign policy led to calls for war from sections of the Establishment from 1912 onwards. ➤ **BISMARCK, OTTO VON**

## Wenceslas IV (1361–1419)
Holy Roman Emperor (1378/1400). The son of Emperor **CHARLES IV** and elder brother of Emperor **SIGISMUND**, he was crowned King of Bohemia in 1378 and Emperor in the same year. In the papal schism he followed his father's policy of supporting the pope in Rome, Urban VI, although he negotiated secretly with the antipope Clement VII in Avignon. He intervened ineffectually in the conflict between the princes and the towns by attempting to impose peace. Although capable, he was inactive and increasingly given to bouts of drunkenness. He allowed Germany to slide into anarchy and was deposed in 1400.

## Wends ➤ SORBS

## Wentworth, William Charles (1793–1872)
Australian politician, born at sea, his mother being a transported convict. He took part in 1813 in the first crossing of the Blue Mountains, and in 1816 returned to England where he had been educated, to study law. When called to the Bar in 1822, he had already published his classic *Statistical Historical and Political Description of the Colony of New South Wales* (1819). A staunch protagonist of self-government, which he made the policy of his newspaper *The Australian* (established 1824), he demanded an elected legislature, taxation by consent and trial by jury. He entered the Legislative Council in 1843, was chairman of the committee that drafted the New South Wales constitution, and as a wealthy landowner and defender of squatter interests, proposed a lower house elected on a property-owning franchise and an upper house of colonial peers, derisively called the 'bunyip aristocracy' by his opponents who deleted this provision. Wentworth accompanied the constitution to London where it was passed in the House of **COMMONS** in 1855, and retired to Dorset. A firm believer in education, he played a leading role in the foundation of Sydney University, and in establishing a state primary education system.

## Wesley, John (1703–91)
British evangelist and founder of Methodism. He was ordained deacon (1725) and priest (1728), and in 1726 became a fellow at Oxford and lecturer in Greek. Influenced by the spiritual writings of William Law, he became leader of a small group which had

gathered round his brother Charles, nicknamed the Methodists, a name later adopted by John for the adherents of the great evangelical movement which was its outgrowth. On their father's death, the brothers went as missionaries to Georgia (1735–8), but the mission proved a failure. In 1738, at a meeting in London, during the reading of **LUTHER**'s preface to the epistle to the Romans, he experienced an assurance of salvation which convinced him that he must bring the same assurance to others; but his zeal alarmed most of the parish clergy, who closed their pulpits to him. This drove him into the open air at Bristol (1739), where he founded the first Methodist chapel, and then the Foundry at Moorfields, London, which became his headquarters. His life was frequently in danger, but he outlived all persecution, and the itineraries of his old age were triumphal processions throughout the country. He was a prolific writer, producing grammars, histories, biographies, collections of hymns, his own sermons and journals, and a magazine.

## West Bank

The region of the Middle East west of the River Jordan and the Dead Sea. Administered by Jordan (1949–67), the area was seized by Israel in the **SIX-DAY WAR**. Because of Arab refusal to negotiate peace terms, Israel retained it, administered it as the district of Judea-Samaria and has allowed Jewish settlement. The West Bank includes Old (East) Jerusalem, as well as Bethlehem, Jericho, Hebron and Nablus, and is a focus of territorial aspirations by the Palestinians. Since 1987 there has been an intermittent **INTIFADA** against the Israelis, resulting in numerous deaths and the intermittent closure of schools and shops. In 1993 the **OSLO ACCORDS** between Israel and the **PLO** led to Palestinian self-government from May 1994 in the Jericho area of the West Bank, and this was subsequently extended to some other West Bank towns. Talks on the final status of Palestinian areas stalled in the late 1990s and became deadlocked when Israel and the USA refused to negotiate any longer with Yasser **ARAFAT**. His death in Nov 2004 and the election in Jan 2005 of a moderate successor, Mahmoud Abbas, has led to renewed talks with Israel. ➤ **ARAB–ISRAELI WARS**; **PALESTINIAN AUTONOMOUS AREAS**; **ZIONISM**

## Western European Union (WEU)

An organization of Western European states originally formed to promote Western European defence coordination and to give mutual assistance in the face of Soviet moves to dominate central Europe. The signatories of the original treaty in 1948 were Belgium, France, Luxembourg, the Netherlands and the UK. Talks between these states and the USA and Canada led to the formation of **NATO** in 1949. West Germany and Italy joined the original signatories in 1954 to form the WEU. After the creation of the **EEC** in 1958, the WEU became a forum for discussions between the six EEC states and the UK. After the UK's entry into the EEC in 1973, the WEU lost much of its purpose and was moribund until 1984 when it was reactivated as the forum for bi-annual discussions of the **EC** foreign and defence ministers on Western European security and the integration of defence policies. As an arm of the **EU**, the WEU has had an operational role in several trouble spots, clearing

mines, providing support and training for police, and enforcing **UN** sanctions against former Yugoslavia.

---

**WESTERN SAHARA**  formerly (until 1976) **Spanish Sahara**

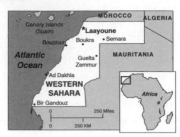

A disputed desert territory on the coast of north-west Africa, administered by Morocco. It is bounded by Morocco in the north, Algeria in the north-east, Mauritania in the east and south, and the Atlantic Ocean in the west. It was visited by Portuguese navigators in 1434 and claimed as a protectorate by Spain in 1884. After its Spanish status ended in 1975, Mauritania and Morocco divided between them a large area in the south under the name of Tiris el Gharbia. In 1979 conflict with the Algerian-backed **POLISARIO** independence movement caused Mauritania to withdraw and renounce all rights to the region, leaving Morocco to annex it. In 1976 Polisario, whose guerrillas operate from within Algeria, had renamed the region the Saharan Arab Democratic Republic and set up what they called a 'government in exile'. In 1988 the **UN** proposed a peace deal and a referendum for the indigenous Sahrawi people to decide whether they wanted an independent Western Sahara under Polisario leadership, or whether the region should officially become part of Morocco. This peace proposal was accepted by both Morocco and Polisario, and the referendum was planned for 2000 but following disagreements on both sides, the referendum has yet to be held. A UN-brokered ceasefire has been in force since 1991.

## Western Samoa ➤ SAMOA

## West India Regiment

Founded in 1795 in response to the need for local defence in the war with France, the force had 12 regiments by 1799. However, after mutinies in Dominica (1802) and Jamaica (1808), parts of the force were disbanded (1815). Of the remaining units, the 1st Regiment mutinied in 1837 in Trinidad, led by Daaga (Donald Stewart), and the 3rd Regiment was disbanded in 1870. In the Ashanti Wars (1873–4), the 1st and 2nd Regiments again saw action and in 1888 the two regiments were reconstituted to form the rank and file of two battalions led by white officers. That regiment served in both East and West Africa in **WORLD WAR I** and was finally disbanded in 1927.

## West Indies, Federation of the (1958–62)

Ill-fated union of the British West Indies devised at the Montego Bay Conference (Sep 1947). Damaged from the outset by the failure of Guyana, Belize, the Bahamas and the British Virgin Islands to join, the Federation was further weakened by disputes. These ranged from the powers of the federal government, taxation and the constitutional backwardness of the union relative to constitutional progress in Jamaica, Trinidad and Barbados, to the under-representation in the federal parliament of these states, given their contribution in population and finance. As it was, the West Indian Federal Labour Party led by Grantley **ADAMS** relied on small island support to maintain its majority over the Democratic Labour Party of Alexander **BUSTAMANTE**; when the latter withdrew Jamaica from the Federation (1961) and Eric **WILLIAMS** took out Trinidad (1962), the union collapsed and was dissolved.

**Westminster, Statute of** (1931)
Legislation which clarified that Dominions in the **BRITISH EMPIRE** were autonomous communities and effectively independent, though owing common allegiance to the Crown. The statute closely followed the formulation made by Arthur **BALFOUR** in the 1920s about the relationship of the Dominions to Britain and it also established a free association of members in the **COMMONWEALTH OF NATIONS**.

**Westminster, Statutes of** (1275, 1285 and 1290)
Part of a comprehensive programme undertaken by **EDWARD I** to reform English law and administration. The first statute (1275) was concerned mainly with criminal matters, notably compulsory trial by jury; the second (1285) covered many fields of law, and facilitated the creation of entailed estates; the third (1290) protected lords' feudal incidents.

**Westminster Assembly**
A body of clerics (120) and laymen (30) convened by the English **LONG PARLIAMENT** in 1643 to arrange a religious settlement to replace the Church of England. Dominated by Presbyterians, it produced a directory of public worship to replace the Book of Common Prayer, and the Westminster Confession of Faith. Its influence declined when the power of the army, which favoured toleration, increased after 1648.

**Westphalia**
A north-west German principality, first settled by Saxons c.700, given to the Archbishop of Cologne (1180), and later forming part of the Lower Rhine-Westphalian Circle of the **HOLY ROMAN EMPIRE** (1512). In 1803–6 it was divided between Brandenburg-Prussia and neighbouring states. Although the name was coined for Napoleon's satellite kingdom (1807), the princes regained possession (1814–15). ► **NAPOLEON I**

**Westphalia, Peace of** (1648)
A series of treaties ending the **THIRTY YEARS' WAR** between France and the Empire, and the **EIGHTY YEARS' WAR** between Spain and the Dutch, negotiated at the Westphalian towns of Münster and Osnabrück. The Peace marked the triumph of the French Bourbons over the Habsburgs, and enshrined the concept of *raison d'état* – the primacy of the interests of the sovereign state over other considerations, such as dynastic or religious factors. ► **BOURBON, HOUSE OF**; **HABSBURG DYNASTY**; **MÜNSTER, TREATY OF**

**Wettin Dynasty**
The Wettin family gained the electorate of Saxony in 1423. Later, in 1485, the family divided into two branches, the Ernestines and the Albertines. The Ernestines lost the electorship in 1547 to the Albertines. The Albertines were to produce two Polish kings (1697–1763) and numerous Saxon kings (1806–1918). The Ernestines provided kings for Belgium, Portugal, Bulgaria and Britain in the 19c and 20c.

**Weygand, Maxime** (1867–1965)
French soldier. As Chief of Staff to **FOCH** (1914–23), he rendered great services in **WORLD WAR I**. Then he was High Commissioner in Syria (1923–4), and appointed Chief of Staff (1930), and then designated Commander-in-Chief in a future war (1931). Retired in 1935, he was recalled and sent to command in Syria in 1939. In May 1940, in the middle of the battle for France, he was recalled to replace **GAMELIN** as Commander-in-Chief, but arrived too late to do much more than recommend an armistice. The **VICHY** government sent him as its delegate to North Africa, but he was recalled in response to German pressure and imprisoned in Germany until the end of **WORLD WAR II**. In 1948 he was brought before the High Court for his role in 1940, but the case was dropped.

**Whig Party** (USA)
One of two major US political parties during the decades prior to the **AMERICAN CIVIL WAR**. The name was adopted in 1834 to signify opposition to President Andrew **JACKSON** (1829–37). The Whigs stood for greater governmental intervention in the economy than did the Democrats, who followed Jackson, but both parties agreed on the necessity of keeping the **SLAVERY** issue out of politics. The Whigs collapsed in 1854, precisely because the slavery issue could no longer be contained. Daniel **WEBSTER** and Henry **CLAY** were prominent members of the party.

**Whigs** (UK)
A British political party which emerged in 1679–80 as the group agitating for the exclusion of James, Duke of York (later **JAMES VII AND II**), on the grounds of his Roman Catholicism. The name was probably a contraction of 'Whiggamores' – militant Scottish Presbyterians. The party benefited from the political changes of the **GLORIOUS REVOLUTION** of 1688 and, during its long period of dominance in British politics after 1714, drew much strength from defending 'the principles of 1688', which included limited monarchy and the importance of parliament. Whiggery is better seen as a general set of beliefs along these lines, rather than as a unified party. Most of its leaders were great landowners who used political patronage to create family-based groupings in parliament. The party was supported by many in the moneyed and commercial classes, and by Nonconformists who looked to the Whigs (usually mistakenly) to provide religious toleration. Whig fortunes waned in the late 18c, and Whigs became leading members of the new **LIBERAL PARTY** from the mid-19c. ► **TORIES**

**Whiskey Rebellion** (1794)
An insurrection of farmers in western Pennsylvania and Virginia, USA, against the excise tax imposed by the federal government on whiskey, which they made in large quantities from their crops of grain. The rebellion was suppressed by government forces led by Henry Lee and Alexander **HAMILTON**.

**Whiskey Ring** (1875)
A conspiracy of distillers and tax officials during the administration of President Ulysses S **GRANT** to defraud the government of taxes due on liquor; 238 people were indicted, including Grant's private secretary.

**White Australia Policy**
The unofficial national policy of Australia from 1901 until the late 1960s, designed to exclude non-European migrants; it was particularly aimed at Asians and Pacific Islanders. It also assumed the decline and ultimate extinction of the native **ABORIGINALS**. The policy enjoyed general support, including that of the trade union movement to protect union wage rates. In the late 1960s the policy was progressively dismantled, and race was replaced as a basis for admission by other, largely economic, criteria. ► **DICTATION TEST**

**Whitefield, George** (1714–70)
English evangelist, one of the founders of Methodism. He was associated with Charles and John **WESLEY** at Oxford and became an enthusiastic evangelist. Many of his adherents followed the Countess of Huntingdon in Wales and formed the Calvinistic Methodists, so she appointed him her chaplain, and built and endowed many chapels for him. He also played an important role in the **GREAT AWAKENING** in America.

**Whitehead, Edgar** (1905–71)
Southern Rhodesian politician. Born in England, he emigrated to Southern Rhodesia in 1928 and, after two years in the civil service, went into farming. He was elected to the legislative assembly in 1939 and, after war service, became the country's High Commissioner in London (1945–6) before being called back as Minister of Finance (1946–53). After a further period of farming, he was asked to be the **CENTRAL AFRICAN FEDERATION**'s representative in the USA, from where he was recalled again, this time to be Prime Minister. His term of office introduced several liberalizing measures but, lacking charisma and facing a more avowedly racist opposition in the Rhodesian Front, he lost office in the 1962 elections and retired, yet again, to his farm.

**White Mountain, Battle of the** (1620)
The battle in which Duke **MAXIMILIAN I** of Bavaria, acting on behalf of the Emperor, **FERDINAND II**, defeated the motley forces of **FREDERICK V**, Elector Palatine and recently elected King of Bohemia and Moravia, and put paid to what remained of Czech independence for three centuries. Frederick fled ignominiously and Ferdinand succeeded him as King, proceeding to execute or expel all those who had led the last-ditch fight for the right to pursue their own Czech Protestant faith. This was also an important first Habsburg victory in what was subsequently termed the **THIRTY YEARS' WAR**. ► **HABSBURG DYNASTY**

**White Russians**
The name collectively given to counter-revolutionary forces led by ex-Tsarist officers, which fought unsuccessfully against the Bolshevik **RED ARMY** during the **RUSSIAN CIVIL WAR** (1918–22). The Whites were supported by the military intervention of British, US,

French and Japanese troops; when these withdrew, White resistance to the Red Army collapsed. ► **BOLSHEVIKS**

**White Terror** ► **TERROR, WHITE**

**Whitlam, (Edward) Gough** (1916– )
Australian politician. A lawyer, he entered politics in 1952 and led the **AUSTRALIAN LABOR PARTY** (1967–77), forming the first Labor government since 1949. His administration (1972–5) was notable for its radicalism, ending conscription and withdrawing Australian troops from the **VIETNAM WAR**, recognizing communist China, relaxing the restrictions on non-white immigrants, abolishing university fees and creating Medibank (the state-funded healthcare system). He was controversially dismissed by the Governor-General in 1975 after the Senate had blocked his money bills, and lost the subsequent election. He retired from politics in 1977 and became Australian Ambassador to **UNESCO** in Paris (1983–6) and a member of its executive board (1985–9).

**WHO** ► **WORLD HEALTH ORGANIZATION**

**Wichale, Treaty of** (1889)
The friendship treaty between Italy and Abyssinia, which, according to the Italians, established Abyssinia as an Italian protectorate. The treaty was used by subsequent Italian governments to legitimize further extension of influence in East Africa, although the Abyssinians claimed that the Amharic text had been falsely rendered in the Italian version.

**Wilberforce, William** (1759–1833)
British politician, evangelist and philanthropist. He became an MP (1780), and in 1788 began the movement which resulted in the abolition of the slave trade in the British West Indies in 1807. He next sought to secure the abolition of all slavery, but declining health compelled him in 1825 to retire from parliament. He died one month before the Slavery Abolition Act was passed in parliament. A lifelong friend of **PITT, THE YOUNGER**, he was, like him, a strong opponent of reformers in the 1790s. His evangelical beliefs led him to urge the aristocracy to practise 'real Christianity', and to give a moral lead to the poor. ► **SLAVERY**

**Wilderness, Battle of** (1864)
An indecisive conflict in the **AMERICAN CIVIL WAR** between the Union Army under General Ulysses S **GRANT** and the Confederate Army under General Robert E **LEE**, fought in the Wilderness area of Virginia. Both sides sustained heavy losses in a month of relentless fighting.

**Wild West**
The part of the USA west of the Mississippi settled during the 19c and legendary for the adventures of its cattlemen and the struggle to gain and defend territory. The kind of society at America's last frontier was mythologized first of all by Ned Buntline's dime novels – Buntline was a pseudonym of Edward Z C Judson – about the exploits of William **CODY**, or 'Buffalo Bill'. Eleven years after starring in Buntline's play *The Scouts of the Prairie* (1872), Cody organized his own Wild West show featuring fancy shooting (the show was joined by Annie Oakley in 1885), a buffalo hunt, cowboys, a Pony Express ride, and **NATIVE AMERICANS** such as **SITTING BULL**, who toured with

the show for a while from 1885. Although the show went on, by 1890 the real Wild West had disappeared due to the increase in population, the decline of long-distance cattle drives, the building of RAILWAYS, and the end of hostilities with the Native Americans.

## Wilhelm, Crown Prince of Germany and Prussia
(1882–1951)
After serving as an army field commander during WORLD WAR I, he sought exile in the Netherlands on 13 Nov 1918 and renounced his claims to the German and Prussian thrones in Dec. He returned to Germany in 1923 and despite identifying with monarchist groups and, for a time, with the NAZI PARTY, he played a limited role in political life. ➤ PRUSSIA

## Wilhelmina, in full Wilhelmina Helena Pauline Maria (1880–1962)
Queen of the Netherlands (1890/1948). She succeeded her father WILLIAM III at the age of ten, her mother EMMA acting as Regent until 1898. In 1901 she married Duke Henry of Mecklenburg-Schwerin. An upholder of constitutional monarchy, she especially won the admiration of her people during WORLD WAR II. Though compelled to seek refuge in Britain, she steadfastly encouraged Dutch resistance to the German occupation. In 1948 she abdicated in favour of her daughter JULIANA, and assumed the title of Princess of the Netherlands. ➤ RESISTANCE MOVEMENT (NETHERLANDS)

## 'Wilhelmus'
The Dutch national anthem. It was originally a song of the BEGGARS (irregulars in the early part of the EIGHTY YEARS' WAR of the Dutch against Spain), composed c.1570 by an admiring follower of WILLIAM I, THE SILENT, Prince of Orange. The melody is derived from a French army marching song. In 1932 it became the official Dutch anthem, emphasizing the bond between Dutch nationalistic feeling and the House of Orange-Nassau.

## Wilkes, John (1727–97)
British politician and journalist. He studied at Leiden, became an MP (1757), and attacked the ministry in his weekly journal, North Briton (1762–3). He was imprisoned, released, then expelled from the House of COMMONS for libel. Re-elected on several occasions, and repeatedly expelled, he came to be seen as a champion of liberty, and an upholder of press freedom. In 1774 he became Lord Mayor of London, and in the same year finally gained readmission to parliament, where he remained until his retirement in 1790.

## Wilkins, Roy (1901–81)
US CIVIL RIGHTS leader. He began working for the NAACP in 1931, and became its executive director (1965–77). Throughout his career he fought to end segregation, rejecting the concept of separate development for blacks and opposing the black nationalism of both Marcus GARVEY and the BLACK POWER movement. Because of his insistence on using constitutional means to effect change, he fell out of favour in the 1960s with the more militant civil rights leaders.

## Wilkinson, James (1757–1825)
American soldier, adventurer and double agent. He served with distinction in the AMERICAN REVOLUTION and after the war became involved in politics in Kentucky. He conspired with the Spanish Governor of Louisiana to bring Kentucky under Spanish, instead of American, jurisdiction, but whilst secretly in the pay of Spain he also re-entered the American army. After the LOUISIANA PURCHASE he governed the Louisiana Territory (1805–6). There he became involved in a conspiracy with Aaron BURR to conquer the Mexican provinces of Spain and set up an independent government, but betrayed Burr to President JEFFERSON and became the chief witness at Burr's trial. After his own acquittal, he commanded US forces on the Canadian frontier in the WAR OF 1812, but his failure in the Montreal campaign (1813–14) resulted in his being discharged from service.

## Willard, Emma Hart (1787–1870)
US pioneer of higher education for women. Born in Berlin, Connecticut, and educated at Berlin Academy (1802–3), she married Dr John Willard in 1809. From her husband's nephew, who was studying at Middlebury College, she learned about the subjects studied there, including geometry and philosophy, which at that time were not taught to women. In 1814 she opened Middlebury Female Seminary, offering an unprecedented range of subjects, in order to prepare women for college. Unsuccessful in gaining funding for her school, she moved to Troy, New York, where she received financial help. The school developed quickly, and she wrote several highly regarded history textbooks. Her campaign for equal educational opportunities for women paved the way for co-education. ➤ WOMEN'S RIGHTS

## William I, in full Willem Frederik (1772–1843)
King of the Netherlands (1806/40), Grand Duke of Luxembourg and Prince of Orange-Nassau. He was the son of the last STADHOLDER, WILLIAM V, and Princess Wilhelmina of Prussia; the FRENCH REVOLUTION and Napoleonic period obliged him to spend his youth in exile from the Netherlands. In 1793–4 he led the Dutch forces against the French, but had to flee to England in 1795. He then entered the Prussian army as a general and moved to Berlin; in 1802 he became sovereign of the small German states of Fulda and Corvey, and chose the Prussian side against NAPOLEON I. He entered Austrian service in 1809, but then left for England again. In 1813 he was invited back to the Netherlands to lead the post-Napoleonic government as sovereign prince. When the Congress of VIENNA (1814–15) decided to unite the southern and northern Netherlands (present-day Belgium and the Netherlands) as a buffer against France, William took the title of King of the United Kingdom of the Netherlands. In 1791 he had married his cousin Princess Wilhelmina of Prussia, who died in 1837; in 1841 he was married again, controversially, to the Roman Catholic Duchess Henriëtte d'Oultremont. He was an exceptionally able monarch, but wanted no interference from parliament, and ruled by decree as a self-styled enlightened despot. His economic politics were interventionist; he founded the Netherlands Bank, the Netherlands Trading Company, the CULTURE SYSTEM in the Dutch East Indies, and was known as the King-Merchant. His policies were also of benefit to modern Belgium;

he founded the *Société Générale* in 1822, and gave great support to the industrial revolution there. His relentless centralization (in finance, religion and administration) created discontent, especially in the southern provinces, which led to the Belgian Revolution in 1830. William became increasingly unpopular in the 1830s as he refused to relinquish Belgium and maintained an armed peace; finally he abdicated in 1840 in favour of his son WILLIAM II, and moved to Berlin, where he died.

### William I (1797–1888)
King of Prussia (1861/88) and first German Emperor (1871/88). The second son of FREDERICK WILLIAM III, his use of force during the REVOLUTION OF 1848 made him unpopular, and he was forced to leave PRUSSIA temporarily for London. As King, he consolidated the power of the monarchy following the relative failure of the 1848 Revolution, and strengthened the army; renewed constitutional tensions led to his appointing (1861) BISMARCK as Prussian Minister-President, who initiated victorious wars against Denmark in 1864, Austria (1866), and France (1871), after which William was proclaimed Emperor. A semi-absolute monarch, he entrusted his Chancellor, Bismarck, with the reins of government. He survived two attempts at assassination in 1878. ► AUSTRO-PRUSSIAN WAR; FRANCO-PRUSSIAN WAR; SCHLESWIG-HOLSTEIN PROBLEM

### William I, the Conqueror (c.1027/8–1087)
Duke of Normandy and the first Norman King of England (1066/87). He was the illegitimate son of Duke Robert of Normandy. EDWARD THE CONFESSOR, who had been brought up in Normandy, most probably designated him as future King of England in 1051. When Harold Godwin, despite an apparent oath to uphold William's claims, took the throne as HAROLD II, William invaded with the support of the papacy, defeated and killed Harold at the Battle of HASTINGS, and was crowned King (25 Dec 1066). The key to effective control was military conquest backed up by aristocratic colonization, so that by the time of DOMESDAY BOOK (1086), the leaders of Anglo-Saxon society south of the Tees had been almost entirely replaced by a new ruling class of NORMANS, Bretons, and Flemings, who were closely tied to William by feudal bonds. He died while defending Normandy's southern border. ► NORMAN CONQUEST

### William I, the Lion (c.1142–1214)
King of Scots (1165/1214). He was the brother and successor of MALCOLM IV, THE MAIDEN. In 1173–4 he invaded Northumberland during the rebellion against HENRY II of England, but was captured at Alnwick, and by the Treaty of Falaise (1174) recognized Henry as the feudal superior of Scotland. Despite his difficulties with England, he made Scotland a much stronger kingdom, and in 1192 Celestine III declared the Scottish Church free of all external authority save the pope's. ► DAVID I

### William I, the Silent (1533–84)
Prince of Orange. First of the hereditary Stadholders of the United Provinces of the Netherlands (1572/84). He joined the aristocratic protest at the oppressive policies of PHILIP II of Spain, and in 1568 took up arms against the Spanish crown. After initial reverses, he began the recovery of the coastal towns with the help of the Sea-BEGGARS, and became the leader of the northern provinces, united in the Union of UTRECHT (1579) in revolt against Spain in the EIGHTY YEARS' WAR. He was assassinated at Delft by a Spanish agent. His byname comes from his ability to keep secret HENRY II of France's scheme to massacre all the Protestants of France and the Netherlands, confided to him when he was a French hostage in 1559. ► STADHOLDER; UNITED PROVINCES OF THE NETHERLANDS

### William II (1626–50)
STADHOLDER and Captain-General of the Netherlands (1647/50). He was the son of the Stadholder Frederick Henry, who had succeeded his brother, MAURICE of Nassau, in 1625. Anglo-Dutch diplomacy established what would prove a fateful marital linkage of the houses of Orange and Stuart by William's marriage in 1641 to Mary, daughter of CHARLES I, and William was elected to follow his father in office, which he duly did in 1647. Dutch independence was recognized at the end of the THIRTY YEARS' WAR in the Peace of WESTPHALIA (1648), but William wished to support the French in their continued war with Spain, in the hope of conquering the remaining Spanish Netherlands. He arrested his leading opponents in Holland, laid siege to Amsterdam and won an advantageous compromise, but died of smallpox before he could make much use of its results. His posthumous son, the future WILLIAM III of Britain and Ireland, would spend his life in opposition to France, for whose alliance William II had laboured in vain.

### William II, in full Willem Frederik George Lodewijk (1792–1849)
King of the Netherlands (1840/9), Grand Duke of Luxembourg and Prince of Orange-Nassau. The son of King WILLIAM I and Princess Wilhelmina of Prussia, he married the Russian Princess ANNA PAVLOVNA in 1816. He had a distinguished early career as a soldier, fighting under WELLINGTON in Spain (1811–13), present at Quatre-Bras and the Battle of WATERLOO, and as leader of the TEN DAYS' CAMPAIGN against the Belgians (1831). On 7 Oct 1840 he succeeded his father as King; his interests were not overtly political, and he generally maintained his father's autocratic line, although he was more tolerant in matters of religion. The European REVOLUTIONS OF 1848–9 seem to have panicked him into entrusting charge of the new Dutch constitution to the liberal Johan THORBECKE, and thus William was responsible for allowing the liberal floodgates to open in the Netherlands. He was succeeded by his son, WILLIAM III, in 1849.

### William II (1859–1941)
German Emperor and King of PRUSSIA (1888/1918). He was the eldest son of FREDERICK III and Victoria (the daughter of Britain's Queen VICTORIA), and grandson of WILLIAM I. He dismissed BISMARCK (1890), and began a long period of personal rule, later displaying a bellicose attitude in international affairs. He and his government pledged full support to Austria-Hungary after the assassination of the Archduke FRANCIS FERDINAND at Sarajevo (1914), thereby setting Europe on the road to war. During WORLD WAR I he became a mere figurehead, and when the

German armies collapsed, and US President Woodrow **WILSON** refused to negotiate while he remained in power, he abdicated and fled to the Netherlands, living as a country gentleman until his death. ► **JAMESON RAID**

**William II, Rufus** (c.1056–1100)
King of England (1087/1100). He was the second surviving son of **WILLIAM I, THE CONQUEROR**. His main goal was the recovery of Normandy from his elder brother, Robert Curthose, and from 1096, when Robert relinquished the struggle and departed on the First **CRUSADE**, William ruled the duchy as *de facto* duke. He also led expeditions to Wales (1095 and 1097); conquered Carlisle and the surrounding district (1092); and after the death of **MALCOLM III, CANMORE** exercised a controlling influence over Scottish affairs. Contemporaries condemned his government of England as arbitrary and ruthless. He exploited his rights over the Church and the nobility beyond the limits of custom, and quarrelled with Anselm, Archbishop of Canterbury. His personal conduct outraged many, for he was most likely a homosexual. He was killed by an arrow while hunting in the New Forest. It has been supposed that he was murdered on the orders of his younger brother, who succeeded him as **HENRY I**, but his death was almost certainly accidental.

**William III** (1817–90)
King of the Netherlands and Grand Duke of Luxembourg (1849/90). The son of King **WILLIAM II** and **ANNA PAVLOVNA**, he married his cousin, **SOPHIE FREDERICA MATHILDA** of Württemberg, with whom his relations were not good; after her death (1877), he married Princess **EMMA** of Waldeck-Pyrmont. Three sons from his first marriage failed to outlive him; from the second a daughter, the future Queen **WILHELMINA**, was born in 1880. William was a difficult sovereign; he wanted to rule directly, but found it hard to adapt to the conditions of constitutional monarchy. He had furious rows with his ministers, and took a personal dislike to the leading liberal of the day, Johan **THORBECKE**. His inability to operate with parliament led to the end of royal ministries, which were replaced by parliamentary ones; after the Luxembourg question of 1866–8 (in which William's government was heavily criticized from all sides) Dutch governments had to be able to count on a parliamentary majority. William's health deteriorated; in the months before he died, Queen Emma was made regent during Wilhelmina's minority.

**William III, of Orange** (1650–1702)
**STADHOLDER** of the United Provinces (1672/1702) and King of Great Britain (1689/1702). Born in The Hague, he was the son of **WILLIAM II** of Orange by Mary, the eldest daughter of **CHARLES I** of England. In 1677 he married his cousin Mary (1662–94), the daughter of **JAMES VII AND II** by Anne Hyde. Invited to redress the grievances of the country, he landed at Torbay in 1688 with an English and Dutch army, and forced James VII and II to flee; William and Mary were proclaimed joint rulers early the following year. He was defeated by James's supporters at Killiecrankie (17 July 1689) but overcame James at the Battle of the **BOYNE** (1 July 1690), then concentrated on the War of the Grand Alliance against France (1689–97),

in which he was finally successful. In later years, he had to withstand much parliamentary opposition to his proposals. He died, childless, the crown passing to Mary's sister, **ANNE**. ► **GLORIOUS REVOLUTION**

**William IV** (1711–51)
**STADHOLDER** and Captain-General of the Netherlands. He was born Charles Henry Friso, of a cadet branch of the House of Orange (Nassau-Dietz). In 1711 he was named Friesland's Stadholder in succession to his father, John William Friso. He was chosen as Stadholder in the other provinces at various intervals, all these posts having been untenanted since the death of **WILLIAM III, OF ORANGE** in 1702. His appointments were not completed until 1747 when Holland, Zeeland and Utrecht bowed to popular Orangist pressure in the riots after a French invasion. His offices were then declared hereditary in male and female lines, a tribute to the historical reputation of the House of Orange. Thus, in possession of near-absolute power, he failed to arrest the general decline of the Dutch Republic.

**William IV**, known as **the Sailor King** (1765–1837)
King of Great Britain and Ireland, and King of Hanover (1830/7). The third son of **GEORGE III**, he entered the navy in 1779, saw service in the USA and the West Indies, became Admiral in 1811, and Lord High Admiral in 1827–8. His elder brother having died, he succeeded **GEORGE IV** in 1830. Widely believed to have Whig leanings to his accession, he developed Tory sympathies, and did much to obstruct the passing of the first Reform Act (1832). He was the last monarch to use prerogative powers to dismiss a ministry with a parliamentary majority when he sacked **MELBOURNE** in 1834 and invited the **TORIES** to form a government. He was succeeded by his niece **VICTORIA**. ► **REFORM ACTS**; **WHIGS**

**William V** (1748–1806)
Last hereditary **STADHOLDER** and Captain-General of the Netherlands. He succeeded his father, **WILLIAM IV**, in 1751 but did not rule until 1766. He abandoned the old alliance of Orange and Britain, leaning instead towards alliance with Prussia, itself hostile to Britain after its loss of British support towards the end of the **SEVEN YEARS' WAR**. During the **AMERICAN REVOLUTION**, Britain declared war on the Netherlands because of its financial and moral support for the American rebels, but it was the pro-French 'Patriots', pressing for domestic reforms, who led William to leave The Hague in order to live outside what was now the hostile Province of Holland. Prussian armed intervention restored him in 1787. French revolutionary armies invaded the Netherlands in 1794, and in 1795 William fled to England, whose occupation of the Dutch provinces he took part in, including the abortive Anglo-Russian invasion of 1799. After that he lost heart, and allowed his followers to accept office in the **BATAVIAN REPUBLIC**, the French client state which had been formed in his absence.

**William, Count of Holland** (1228–56)
German King. The son of Count Florence IV of Holland, he was elected King (1247) after the death of the anti-king **HENRY RASPE**, and crowned in Aachen in 1248. He was unable to assert his claim until the death of **FREDERICK II** (1250) and was recognized

by Pope **INNOCENT IV** in 1251. He won the support of north Germany by his marriage to the daughter of the Duke of Brunswick, and that of the Hohenstaufen towns after the death of **CONRAD IV** (1254). He died in 1256 on a campaign against the Frisians, sinking unnoticed with his horse into a frozen swamp.

**William of Wickham ► WILLIAM OF WYKEHAM**

**William of Wied** (1876–1945)
Prince of Albania (7 Mar/3 Sep 1914). He arrived in newly independent Albania in Mar 1914, as a 35-year-old captain in the German army, with 75 million francs for financing the government. Seeing him as an Austrian protégé, the Italian government intrigued against him. He never gained control of the country, which was split into factions, and after losing the support of the Emperor **FRANCIS JOSEPH**, he left Albania in 1914. Fan **NOLI**'s verdict upon him was that 'he can be criticized only for being unable to perform miracles'.

**William of Wykeham** (1324–1404)
English churchman and statesman. Possibly the son of a serf, he rose to become the chief adviser of **EDWARD III** of England. He was appointed Keeper of the Privy Seal (1363), Bishop of Winchester (1367), and was twice Chancellor of England (1367–71 and 1389–91). He founded New College, Oxford, and Winchester College, both of which were fully established by the 1390s.

**Williams, Eric Eustace** (1911–81)
Trinidadian politician and historian. Educated in Trinidad and at Oxford, he studied history and political science before joining the faculty of Howard University in Washington, DC. His scholarly work included *Capitalism and Slavery*. After his return to Trinidad he founded the PNM (People's National Movement) in 1956. The new party won the general election and he was appointed chief minister, taking Trinidad into the Federation of the **WEST INDIES** (1958), insisting on a powerful centralized government. When that failed to materialize, Williams took Trinidad out of the federation and obtained independence (1962) with the slogan 'Discipline, Production and Tolerance'. He became Prime Minister, a post he held until his death in 1981. By practicing what he called 'pragmatic socialism' he helped to create one of the more successful economies in the Caribbean. ► **WILLIAMS THESIS**

**Williams, Roger** (c.1604–1683)
English colonist, founder of Rhode Island. A member of the Anglican Church, his espousal of Puritan beliefs led him to emigrate in 1630 to the Massachusetts Bay colony. He refused to participate in the Church in Boston, believing it had not separated from the English Church, and moved to Salem where, after challenging the authority of the Puritan magistrates over matters of personal conscience, he was persecuted and eventually banished. He took refuge with **NATIVE AMERICANS**, then purchased land from them on which he founded the city of Providence in 1636. His colony was a model of democracy and religious freedom; he went to England in 1643 and 1651 to procure a charter for it and served as its President (1654–7).

**Williams, Shirley Vivien Teresa Brittain Williams, Baroness** (1930–)
British politician. A former journalist, and Secretary of the Fabian Society (1960–4), she became a Labour MP in 1964. After many junior positions, she was Secretary of State for Prices and Consumer Protection (1974–6), and for Education and Science (1976–9). She lost her seat in 1979, became a co-founder of the Social Democratic Party in 1981, and the Party's first elected MP later that year. She lost her seat in the 1983 general election, but remained as the SDP's President (1982–7). She supported the merger between the SDP and the Liberal Party. She was awarded a life peerage in 1993. ► **LABOUR PARTY** (UK); **LIBERAL PARTY** (UK); **SOCIAL DEMOCRATIC PARTY** (UK)

**Williams Thesis**
Revolutionary argument postulated by Eric **WILLIAMS** in *Capitalism and Slavery* (1944) that British emancipation was more the consequence of 'laissez-faire' self-interest than imperial altruism. The idea that the abolition of the slave trade and **SLAVERY** was simply the result of the high-minded idealism of the abolitionists had been set in historical perspective by books such as Reginald Coupland's *The British Anti-Slavery Movement* (1933); Williams argued that while slavery and the slave trade had provided the necessary capital to finance the **INDUSTRIAL REVOLUTION** in England, by the beginning of the 19c the British West Indies sugar plantocracy with its expensive production, captive, monopolistic market and inefficient labour force had become an obstacle to a booming industrial society and its metropolitan, free-trading entrepreneurs.

**Wilmot Proviso** (1846)
A motion introduced in the US **CONGRESS** by David Wilmot (Democrat, Pennsylvania) to forbid the expansion of **SLAVERY** into territory acquired during the **MEXICAN WAR**. It passed the **HOUSE OF REPRESENTATIVES** but not the **SENATE**, where the South and the North had equal strength. The debate was a major step in the politicization of the slavery issue.

**Wilson, Arnold** (1884–1940)
British administrator. Having carried out surveying work in southern Persia as a young Indian army officer, he was appointed, by the British, to the commission charged with looking into the Ottoman–Persian Shatt al-Arab frontier dispute in 1913. He was a member of **COX**'s civil administration in 1915–16 and became (mid-1918) Acting Civil Commissioner on Cox's departure to Tehran. Wilson's administration, although generally fair and efficient, was distinctly unsympathetic towards local, and particularly nationalist, aims. After **WORLD WAR I**, he urged opposition both to the Anglo-French Declaration and to the notion of an Iraq run by a prince from the Sharifian family. His government appeared increasingly intolerant, giving rise to Iraqi fears that they had merely exchanged a Turkish master for a British, and that their political aspirations would be thwarted; this helped to bring about the insurrection of 1920. Later that year, Cox returned to Iraq, relieving Wilson of the task of carrying out the proposed constitutional programme for the country. Wilson went on to become an MP, was arrested early in **WORLD WAR II** because of alleged fascist sympathies and was killed in action,

having volunteered as a rear-gunner in the RAF.

**Wilson, Sir Henry Hughes** (1864–1922)
British field marshal. He joined the Rifle Brigade in 1884, and served in Burma (1884–7) and South Africa (1899–1901). As Director of Military Operations at the War Office (1910–14), he elaborated plans for the rapid support of France in the event of war with Germany. By the end of **WORLD WAR I**, he was Chief of the Imperial General Staff. Promoted field marshal and created a baronet (1919), he resigned from the army in 1922, and became an MP. His implacable opposition to the leaders of **SINN FÉIN** led to his assassination on the doorstep of his London home.

**Wilson, Henry Maitland Wilson, 1st Baron** (1881–1964)
British field marshal. He fought in South Africa and in **WORLD WAR I**, and at the outbreak of **WORLD WAR II** was appointed Commander of British troops in Egypt. Having led the initial British advance in Libya (1940–1) and the unsuccessful Greek campaign (1941), he became Commander-in-Chief Middle East (1943) and Supreme Allied Commander in the Mediterranean theatre (1944). Wilson headed the British Joint Staff Mission in Washington (1945–7), and was raised to the peerage in 1946.

**Wilson, (James) Harold, Baron Wilson of Rievaulx** (1916–95)
British politician. He became a lecturer in economics at Oxford in 1937. An MP in 1945, he was President of the Board of Trade (1947–51), and the principal opposition spokesman on economic affairs. An able and hard-hitting debater, in 1963 he succeeded **GAITSKELL** as leader of the **LABOUR PARTY**, then he became Prime Minister (1964–70). His economic plans were badly affected by balance of payments crises, leading to severe restrictive measures and devaluation (1967). He was also faced with the problem of Rhodesian independence, opposition to Britain's proposed entry into the Common Market, and an increasing conflict between the two wings of the Labour Party. Following his third general election victory, he resigned suddenly as Prime Minister and Labour leader in 1976. Knighted in 1976, he became a life peer in 1983. ► **EC (EUROPEAN COMMUNITY); EEC (EUROPEAN ECONOMIC COMMUNITY); RHODESIA CRISIS**

**Wilson, (Thomas) Woodrow** (1856–1924)
US politician and 28th President. He practised law in Atlanta, later became a university professor and, in 1902, President of Princeton University. He served as Democratic Governor of New Jersey (1911–13), and was elected President in 1912, running against Theodore **ROOSEVELT** and William **TAFT**, and served two terms (1913–21). His 'New Freedom' programme, establishing equality and opportunity for all men, created the Federal Reserve Board and the Clayton Anti-Trust Act (1914), which accorded many rights to labour unions. Wilson tried to keep the USA out of **WORLD WAR I** but was compelled to enter the war in Apr 1917 to make the world 'safe for democracy'. He laid out his peace plan proposal in the **FOURTEEN POINTS**, and actively championed the idea of forming a **LEAGUE OF NATIONS**, which was part of the Treaty of **VERSAILLES**. When the **SENATE** rejected the treaty, his idealistic vision of world peace was shattered. In 1919 he was awarded the **NOBEL PEACE PRIZE**, but thereafter his health declined severely, and he never recovered. ► **ANTI-TRUST ACTS**

**Windischgrätz, Prince Alfred** (1787–1862)
Austrian soldier. As commander in Bohemia from 1840, he suppressed the **REVOLUTION OF 1848–9** in Prague, and another in Vienna. In 1848 he helped to bring **FRANCIS JOSEPH** to the throne. He defeated the Hungarians repeatedly, but was superseded after his defeat by them at Gödöllö.

**Windsor, House of**
The name of the British royal family since 1917. This unequivocally English name resulted from a declaration by **GEORGE V**, a member of the House of **SAXE-COBURG-GOTHA**, during **WORLD WAR I**. It was felt that a Germanic surname for the British monarchy was inappropriate during a war against Germany.

### HOUSE OF WINDSOR*

| Regnal Dates | Name |
|---|---|
| 1910/36 | George V |
| 1936 | Edward VIII |
| 1936/52 | George VI |
| 1952/ | Elizabeth II |

* Name changed from House of Saxe-Coburg-Gotha to House of Windsor in 1917

**Windthorst, Ludwig** (1812–91)
German Catholic politician. He became distinguished as an advocate and politician in Hanover. After the absorption of Hanover by **PRUSSIA**, he became leader of the Ultramontanes in the German parliament and, as leader of the Catholic **CENTRE PARTY**, chief opponent of **BISMARCK** during the **KULTURKAMPF**.

**Wingate, Orde Charles** (1903–44)
British general. He was commissioned in 1922, and served in the Sudan (1928–33) and Palestine (1936–9), where he helped create a Jewish defence force. In the Burma theatre (1942) he organized the *Chindits* – specially trained jungle-fighters who were supplied by air, and thrust far behind the enemy lines. He was killed in a plane crash in Burma. ► **WORLD WAR II**

**Winnipeg General Strike** (1919)
One of the most significant Canadian strikes, it began when the employers in the building and metal trades refused to negotiate a collective bargaining procedure or to raise wages. After two weeks, the Winnipeg Trades and Labour Council voted to strike in sympathy. Fearing, like business leaders, that unionization would damage industrial profitability, the federal government immediately intervened. Despite the strikers' non-violence, specials were brought in to replace the city police force. A peaceful march was broken up, one spectator killed and 30 injured. The strike came to an end with its leaders jailed for sedition and the premier's promise of a Royal Commission. It did, however, politicize the issues, and in Manitoba's provincial elections of 1920 four of the jailed strike leaders were elected as socialists. The following year James S **WOODSWORTH** became the first socialist

# *Witchcraft*

*Culture & Society*

### Witchcraft in early times and folklore

Almost all early societies believed that certain individuals possessed more than natural powers and the ability to work magic for good or evil ends. The existence and practice of magic and witchcraft were taken to be part of the natural and social order. This was true of ancient Mesopotamia and Egypt, and also of ancient Greece and Rome, where the working of magic was only punishable if intended to do harm. It remained true among non-literate peoples into the 20c. Some societies, such as that of the Azande of southern Sudan studied by Sir Edward Evans-Pritchard in the 1920s and 1930s, distinguished between witchcraft, an innate and often hereditary power to work magic possessed by certain individuals, and sorcery, a black art which could be learned and practised by almost anyone. A European language as sophisticated as French uses the same word, *sorcellerie*, for both, but *maleficia*, or evidence of evil intent, was the touchstone of European witch persecution.

Among peasant people in Europe, an image of the witch evolved that is familiar from fairy stories, and similar to the image in other parts of the world. Witches were thought of as primarily (but not exclusively) female, and generally older women. They were reputed to fly by night, to have animals (familiars) who assisted them, to require parts of the human body to carry out their magic, and to attack or kill people, especially children, or dig up corpses. In Europe, witches were deemed to fly on broomsticks and their familiars were usually cats, dogs or toads; in Africa, baskets were used for flying in and the attendants were often baboons and hyenas. Their intentions and works were for the most part malign. They were held responsible for causing illness or death to other members of the community, crop failure, the failure of cows to provide milk, impotence in men and infertility or miscarriages in women, and for raising storms. On the other hand, almost all rural communities believed in the availability of benign magic for purposes such as easing childbirth, curing people and animals, and finding lost objects.

In a community where everyone believes in it, witchcraft can, to some degree 'work', as the victim may unconsciously collaborate in his or her own affliction. Likewise, some people undoubtedly were, or claimed to be, witches, often genuinely believing they could do the fantastic things they were claimed to do, believing, for example, that they were flying while they were actually in a state of sometimes drug-induced trance. A great many accusations of witchcraft, however, arose from personal jealousy, greed, or spite or from the stresses of living in a small enclosed community. In the 20c anthropologists discovered that in many non-literate societies, those who have become wealthier or better educated than the majority are often those most afraid of witchcraft, precisely because the progress they have made has alienated them to some degree from the rest of the community.

### The demonization of witches in Europe

The persecution of those accused of witchcraft, which began in the 15c, stood in a direct line of descent from the persecution of heretics in the earlier **Middle Ages**, when sects such as the **Albigenses** and Waldenses (whose style of life was generally characterized by strictness and asceticism) were hunted down and put to trial usually by the ecclesiastical and civil authorities working together. From 1231 the pursuit of heretics was entrusted to the **Inquisition**, and from 1252 it was authorized to use torture to extract confessions. The use of an inquisitorial procedure backed up by

---

member of the federal House of Commons, as a representative from Winnipeg. ► **MEIGHEN, ARTHUR**

**Winrich of Kniprode** (c.1310–1382)
Grand Master of the Teutonic Order. After a career in the Order as Commander in Danzig (Gdansk), Balga and Königsberg, he became Supreme Commander in Marienburg in 1346 and Grand Master in 1351. He presided over the period of the Order's great successes, when it became the centre for crusading chivalry from all over northern Europe. He was active as a diplomat and did much to enhance the prosperity of the German towns and the Order's trading links, especially with England and Flanders. He maintained peace with Poland and had many successes against the pagan Lithuanians. ► **HERMANN OF SALZA**; **TEUTONIC KNIGHTS**

**Winter, Jan Willem de** (1750–1812)
Dutch naval commander. He was defeated by Adam Duncan at the Battle of **CAMPERDOWN** (1797) and was ambassador to France from 1798 to 1802.

**Winter Palace, Storming of** (1917)
A symbolic victory for the Bolshevik revolutionaries. The Tsar's residence had become the headquarters of the **RUSSIAN PROVISIONAL GOVERNMENT**. With the Neva River on one side, and an open square on the other, it could have been defended. However, before the attack began on the night of 7 Nov (25 Oct old

style), **KERENSKY**, the Prime Minister, had already fled, and those left to face the attacking soldiers, sailors and workers' red guards were mainly young cadets and a women's battalion. An easy triumph subsequently made good political theatre. The Winter Palace is now the Hermitage Museum, one of the richest storehouses of art and artefacts in the world. ► **BOLSHEVIKS**

**Winter War** ► **RUSSO-FINNISH WAR** (1939–40)

**Winthrop, John** (1588–1649)
English colonist. Educated at Cambridge, England, he became a lawyer, and in 1629 the first Governor of the Bay Company. He crossed the Atlantic to settle what would become Massachusetts and Massachusetts colony, and was re-elected Governor 12 times. His political and religious conservatism greatly influenced the political institutions that were formed in the northern states of America.

**Wirth, Josef** (1879–1956)
German politician. After an early teaching career, he entered politics in Baden as a member of the **CENTRE PARTY** (1913) and national politics as a member of the **REICHSTAG** (1914). National Finance Minister after **WORLD WAR I**, he became Chancellor in May 1921. As such he headed a minority coalition of the republican parties (Centre, **SPD**, **DDP**) which tried to fulfil Allied **REPARATIONS** demands so as to demonstrate

torture had a radical effect on the judicial process and its outcome.

Under torture many heretics confessed to having been initiated into their sects at ceremonies at which a devil figure presided, noxious preparations often containing human remains were eaten or drunk, and a promiscuous orgy took place. The reliability of such confessions obtained under torture is, of course, highly doubtful. Many confessions were later withdrawn; to withdraw one's confession, however, was to recant, and led almost inevitably to death at the stake. Not surprisingly, many confessions were allowed to stand.

When the heretics had been all but eradicated, the notion of a diabolical anti-religion or conspiracy against the true Church was transferred, in the minds of religious fanatics, to witchcraft, and combined with existing folkloric beliefs. The notion of the *sabbat*, a kind of coven or gathering of witches at which the Devil was supposedly present in person, to accept the worship of his devotees, encourage them in evil-doing and finally copulate with them all, attained special prominence. It bears an obvious resemblance to the rites of which heretical sects were accused. The difficulty of establishing how such assemblies of large numbers of people were convened at night, in secret, and often in remote locations was overcome by assuming that the witches flew to them on their broomsticks or by using animal transport provided by their devilish masters.

### Witch hunts

Witch trials had already begun in France by 1486 when the book *Malleus Maleficarum* ('The Hammer of Witches') was published by two Dominican friars, Heinrich Kraemer and Johann Sprenger. This book, a sort of witch-hunter's manual, became widely known and read throughout Europe. It provided ammunition for witch-hunters, and its appearance, prefaced by a papal bull published at the two Dominicans' instigation two years previously, indicates how seriously witchcraft was taken at the time by the ecclesiastical establishment.

Witches were generally found out by denunciation. When a person was denounced as a witch, tests could be made to determine guilt or innocence. These included searching for 'the Devil's mark' (a spot on the body where the witch could feel no pain) or an additional teat (to suckle a familiar), or the water test in which the accused would be thrown into water with hands and feet bound. Those who sank were assumed to be innocent; those who floated were presumed guilty and executed. Under heavy interrogation or torture the accused were encouraged to name others they had seen at the sabbat. Most named names, and the process perpetuated itself. The great Scottish witch hunts only occurred after King **James VI and I** introduced continental inquisitorial procedure in the late 16c. Before that, witch hunts had been as rare as they were, and remained, in England.

Witch hunts took place in most countries of western Europe. The **Reformation** crisis, with its accompanying ideological conflicts and competition between Protestant and Roman Catholic regimes for legitimacy, saw witch hunts reach unprecedented proportions. Thousands of innocent people died as a result of the persecution, some estimates put the number as high as 200,000. In England, where white or harmless magic was recognized by common law as not identical with the *maleficia* of witchcraft proper, witch-hunting was quite rare, and the witch hunt carried out between 1644 and 1647 in East Anglia by the 'witch-finder general's mark' – Matthew Hopkins – was exceptional. After discovering and causing the death of hundreds of alleged witches, Hopkins was himself suspected of witchcraft on account of his success in smelling people out, failed the water test and was duly hanged. The famous **Salem Witch Trials**

their excessiveness. He resigned in Nov 1922, held further ministerial posts between 1929 and 1931 and then sought exile in Switzerland (1933) when **HITLER** took power. He returned to Germany in 1948, where he advocated a policy of German neutrality.

### Wirtschaftswunder

Literally 'economic miracle', this is the term given to Federal Germany's rapid economic recovery from the devastation of **WORLD WAR II**. Rapid growth from 1948 onward appeared to confirm the efficacy of the **SOCIAL MARKET ECONOMY** and helped to legitimize the democratic-parliamentary order.

### Wishart, George (c.1513–1546)

Scottish reformer. As a schoolmaster in Montrose (1538), he incurred a charge of heresy for teaching the Greek New Testament, and he then went to Cambridge, where he met the reformer Hugh **LATIMER**. The next few years he spent on the Continent, and in 1543 accompanied a commission sent to Scotland by **HENRY VIII** to negotiate a marriage contract between his infant son Prince Edward (the future **EDWARD VI**) and **MARY, QUEEN OF SCOTS**. He preached the Lutheran doctrine of justification by faith in several places, but, at the insistence of Cardinal David **BEATON**, he was arrested in 1546, and burned at St Andrews on 1 Mar. John **KNOX** was first inspired by Wishart.

### Witchcraft ▶ *See panel*

### Witt, Johan or Jan de (1625–72)

Dutch statesman and mathematician. The son of Jacob de Witt, he was made Pensionary of Dordrecht in 1650, and in 1653 **GRAND PENSIONARY** of the Province of Holland. As such, he was the leader of the States (republican or oligarchic) Party from 1653 to 1672, a party which strove to reduce the influence of the House of Orange in the Dutch Republic, and to leave power in the hands of the merchant élite of the towns and provinces. De Witt was effectively the Foreign Minister of the Dutch Republic during its most powerful period, and his authority was largely unchallenged. In foreign policy he supported the economic interests of the republic, playing England and France off against each other. At the close of the first of the **ANGLO-DUTCH WARS**, at Oliver **CROMWELL**'s insistence, he put through an Act of Seclusion, which prevented members of the House of Orange from holding office in the republic; the Act was repealed after the end of Cromwell's reign in 1660. As the young **WILLIAM III, OF ORANGE** came of age and was supported strongly by his uncle, **CHARLES II** of England, the Orange Party gained influence in the Netherlands, and in 1672, as scapegoats for a situation in which a French army was threatening the southern borders, de Witt and his brother Cornelius were lynched by an Orangist mob in The Hague (20 Aug 1672). William III then became the uncontested leader of the republic.

in Massachusetts, in 1692, as a result of which 19 people were executed, were the last major outbreak. The emerging rationalist and humanitarian spirit of the **Enlightenment** largely put paid both to a belief in witchcraft and to attempts to suppress it. The great early modern continental European witch hunts had always depended on an inquisitorial procedure and a refusal to distinguish between white and black witchcraft.

### Witchcraft in the 20c

Witchcraft in modern times has attracted a good deal of interest from anthropologists. Much interesting work has been done by scholars studying the beliefs of non-literate peoples in Africa and elsewhere, and the sociological significance and impact of occult practices. However, the most striking and perhaps surprising result of anthropological research during the 20c was a revival of the practice of witchcraft and its acceptance by many as a religion.

Led in the 1920s by the British Egyptologist Margaret Murray, various scholars offered a reinterpretation of its nature and history. According to their theory, witchcraft was a relic of an ancient, almost universal, pre-Christian religion whose main purpose was to ensure the fertility of the earth, mankind and beast. Witchcraft was an organized movement, and the sabbats were the celebrations of its immemorial rites, misrepresented by a Church that feared the influence of devil-worship.

Though there is some evidence of the survival of pagan practices into the Middle Ages, most historians now believe this thesis to be historically unfounded. Nevertheless, it provided a basis on which witchcraft – or Wicca, as it is often known – has been practised in the West from the 1950s and 1960s as a form of neo-paganism: a nature religion based on worship of a 'Mother Goddess', often with a strong feminist and environmentalist slant.

Demonization of unpopular individuals or groups has flourished most in technologically advanced societies, where it is an almost automatic reflex for politicians, newspapers or television networks to confront forces they dislike and do not understand. In that sense, witch hunts are still very much with us.

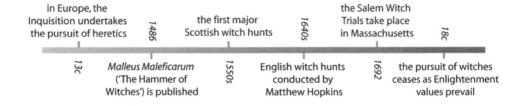

Timeline:
- **13c** — in Europe, the Inquisition undertakes the pursuit of heretics
- **1486** — *Malleus Maleficarum* ('The Hammer of Witches') is published
- **1550s** — the first major Scottish witch hunts
- **1640s** — English witch hunts conducted by Matthew Hopkins
- **1692** — the Salem Witch Trials take place in Massachusetts
- **18c** — the pursuit of witches ceases as Enlightenment values prevail

---

### Witte, Sergei Yulevich (1849–1915)

Russian politician. He became a recognized authority on transport economics, and was appointed Minister of Transport and then of Finance (1892). He actively encouraged the development of capitalism in Russia, and presided over the industrialization boom of the late 1890s, attracting foreign investment, and launching the construction of the Trans-Siberian Railway. Under the 'Witte system', Russia became a leading industrial power. As Prime Minister (1905–6) during the **REVOLUTION OF 1905**, he combined repression of popular disturbances with a policy of urging political concessions to the middle classes. He also headed the Russian delegation that signed the Treaty of **PORTSMOUTH** (1905) ending the **RUSSO-JAPANESE WAR**. He resigned in 1906, unable to satisfy either conservative or liberal opinion with his policies, but remained active in government circles until his death in Petrograd. ► **DUMA**; **NICHOLAS II**

### Wittelsbach

The premier Bavarian family, the Wittelsbachs provided successive dukes and kings for Bavaria from medieval times until the early 20c. They still have a disputed claim to the Spanish throne.

### Wittenberg

A city south-west of Berlin, chartered in 1293. It was the residence of the Dukes and **ELECTORS** of Saxony (1212–1547). The university, founded in 1502, is famous for its associations with **LUTHER** and **MELANCHTHON**. Luther nailed his 95 theses to the doors of Wittenberg's Church of All Saints on 31 Oct 1517.

### Witwatersrand, also called the Rand

The region (literally, 'white water's reef') centred on a ridge of gold-bearing rock in southern Transvaal province, South Africa. Johannesburg is located near its centre and it is the power house of the South African economy, with many black townships nearby providing a reserve of labour. Gold was discovered in 1886 (currently producing over half the world's supply).

### Władysław IV Vasa (1595–1648)

King of Poland (1632/48). The son of **SIGISMUND III VASA** of Sweden, he was elected to the Polish throne in 1632. His reign was a peaceful one, since Poland, despite attempts to draw the country into the conflict, remained neutral during the **THIRTY YEARS' WAR**. At home, he suffered from the religious controversies between Catholics and Protestants, but crushed the Cossack rebellions in 1637–8, initiating ten years of 'golden peace' in the Ukraine. Although he harboured grandiose plans to gain the Swedish throne and to drive the Turks from the Balkans, he lacked sufficient support amongst the Polish gentry to achieve this aim.

### WMD (weapons of mass destruction)

A blanket term for nuclear, biological, chemical and

radiological weapons. It describes weapons whose primary purpose is indiscriminate killing of both military personnel and civilians but which may also destroy infrastructure or make large areas of land unusable. The concept is an ancient one but the first modern use of the term was in a 1937 newspaper article describing the aerial bombardment of cities and the use of chemical weapons during the **SPANISH CIVIL WAR**. By the 1960s use of the term was mostly confined to diplomats and negotiators concerned with arms control, such as the **SALT** talks, and it came into general use again only in 2002 in the months before the **IRAQ WAR**. Attempts to place constraints on the use of WMDs include bilateral agreements between states with nuclear weapons stockpiles and multilateral treaties such as the **BIOLOGICAL AND TOXIN WEAPONS CONVENTION** (1975) and the Chemical Weapons Convention (1997).

### Wojtyła, Karól Jozef ► JOHN PAUL II

### Wolfe, James (1727–59)
British general. Commissioned in 1741, he fought against the **JACOBITES** in Scotland (1745–6) and was sent to Canada during the **SEVEN YEARS' WAR** (1756–63). In 1758 he was prominent in the capture of **LOUISBOURG** in Nova Scotia; the following year he commanded at the famous capture of **QUEBEC**, where he was killed.

### Wollstonecraft, Mary (1759–97)
Pioneer advocate of **WOMEN'S RIGHTS**. After working as a teacher and governess, she became a translator and literary adviser. In 1792 she published *Vindication of the Rights of Woman*, which advocated equality between the sexes, radical social change and economic independence for women. She also supported the **FRENCH REVOLUTION** and her ideas were vilified by the authorities. After a failed first marriage, she married William Godwin in 1797 and died giving birth to a daughter, Mary (later Mary Shelley, author of *Frankenstein*).

### Wolof
A West Atlantic language-speaking agricultural people of Senegal and the Gambia, traditionally grouped into a state with elaborate hierarchical distinctions. They developed a powerful empire (14–16c), were involved in the European slave trade, and later worked in factories and on European trading vessels.

### Wolseley, Garnet Joseph Wolseley, 1st Viscount (1833–1913)
British field marshal. He joined the army in 1852, and served in the second Anglo-Burmese War (1852–3), the **CRIMEAN WAR** (where he lost an eye), and the **INDIAN UPRISING** (1857–8), and the Chinese War (1860). He put down the **RED RIVER REBELLION** (1870) in Canada, and commanded in the Ashanti War (1873). After other posts in India, Cyprus, South Africa and Egypt, he led the attempted rescue of General **GORDON** at Khartoum. He became a baron (1882) and, after the Sudan campaign (1884–5), a viscount. As Army Commander-in-Chief (1895–1901), he carried out several reforms, and mobilized forces for the second Boer War (1899–1902). ► **ANGLO-BURMESE WARS**; **BOER WARS**

### Wolsey, Thomas (c.1475–1530)
English cardinal and statesman. He was ordained in 1498, appointed chaplain to **HENRY VII** in 1507, and became Dean of Lincoln. Under **HENRY VIII**, he became Bishop of Lincoln, Archbishop of York (1514), and a cardinal (1515). Made Lord Chancellor (1515–29), he pursued legal and administrative reforms. He was Henry VIII's leading adviser, in charge of the day-to-day running of government. He aimed to make England a major power in Europe, and also had ambitions to become pope, but his policy of supporting first Emperor **CHARLES V** (1523) then **FRANCIS I** of France (1528) in the Habsburg–Valois conflict was unsuccessful, and high taxation caused much resentment. When he failed to persuade the pope to grant Henry's divorce, he was impeached and his property forfeited. Arrested on a charge of high treason, he died while travelling to London. ► **HABSBURG DYNASTY**; **VALOIS DYNASTY**

### Women's Rights ► *See panel*

### Woodsworth, James Shaver (1874–1942)
Canadian social worker, Methodist minister and politician, who emerged as the country's conscience following the **WINNIPEG GENERAL STRIKE** and the federal elections of 1921. His social work in the cities showed him that his Church's complicity with capitalist society compromised any capacity for reform. He then turned to politics, but in 1917 lost his job in provincial government for criticizing conscription. He also resigned his ministry as a protest against the Church's support for the war. Arrested for sedition (as an editor of the Winnipeg strikers' bulletin), although not convicted, the resulting publicity helped to spread his reputation as a spokesman for the disadvantaged. Well informed also on the problems of the prairie farmers, he was a founder and President of the **CCF**. In 1926 he and A A Heaps were able to take advantage of the government's tiny majority to extract a promise from Mackenzie **KING** to introduce an Old Age Pensions Act and rescind the 1919 amendments to the Immigration Act and the Criminal Code; Woodsworth argued that both parties were corrupt and that it was his duty to use his parliamentary position to promote the cause of socialism. Although it took ten years to repeal the 1919 amendments, the Old Age Pensions Act was passed in 1927. Winning his last election in 1940, Woodsworth was the one MP who voted against Canada's involvement in **WORLD WAR II**, and his speech of conscience was heard in respectful silence.

### Worcester, Battle of (3 Sep 1651)
The last battle of the **ENGLISH CIVIL WARS**, fought between the English army, supported by local militia, under Oliver **CROMWELL** and an invading Scottish army led by **CHARLES II**, who had been crowned King of Scotland at Scone (1 Jan 1651). The English forces decisively overpowered their opponents and Charles was a fugitive for several weeks before escaping to Normandy to begin an exile in France, Germany and the Spanish Netherlands that lasted for almost nine years.

### Works Projects Administration (WPA) (1935–43)
A US federal agency established under President Franklin D **ROOSEVELT** to combat unemployment

# Women's Rights

*Culture & Society*

Most societies in historic times were male-dominated hierarchies. This form of social organization was prevalent for many millennia and was reinforced by world religions; Christianity, Judaism and Islam are all monotheistic faiths that depict a male god, and once they were firmly established they reinforced the existing social order which taught submission of the female. Palaeolithic statues of female goddesses, and the persistence of female deities in some religions, indicate that this was perhaps not always the case. In the ruling classes of some civilizations, for example Egypt and Polynesia, the women had equal authority and rights of inheritance, but even there the majority of women enjoyed fewer privileges and suffered more restrictions than their fathers and husbands.

In Western society the model for many institutions has been classical Greece and Rome. In neither place did women have the vote, nor were they educated in the same way as men. In Roman law a woman was the possession of her husband. This was to have an effect hundreds of years later, after the **French Revolution**, when women's revolutionary groups had proposed that 'Liberty, **Equality, Fraternity**' should be the goal for all, but the **Code Napoléon** that had been adapted was based on Roman law. Around the same time in England, Mary **Wollstonecraft** published *Vindication of the Rights of Woman* (1792). It advocated equality of the sexes and equality in education, but its revolutionary tone made it unacceptable to most.

This was a time of social as well as political change. Women started to work in factories for a wage (less than a man's, on the grounds that a man had a family to support). Such women had always taken their share of daily labour, whether in the fields or manufacturing goods in the home, as well as being responsible for domestic management and child care. Middle and upper class women were still expected to stay at home and support their husbands; however, this provided many with the leisure to involve themselves in fighting for social justice in many arenas.

Resistance to change in society was greatest in agricultural communities and in Roman Catholic countries. In Protestant industrialized countries like the USA and the UK there was more support. The first women's rights convention was held in 1848 in Seneca Falls, New York, led by Lucretia **Mott** and Elizabeth Cady **Stanton**. Both had been active in the anti-**slavery** movement in the USA, but both had been refused their seats at the 1840 Anti-Slavery Convention in London because they were women. The convention called for equality for women, including the vote. Stanton also collaborated with Susan B **Anthony** to publish the magazine *The Revolution*. Anthony was a tireless campaigner, believing, 'there will never be complete equality until women themselves help to make the laws and elect the law makers'. Her efforts were recognized by later generations; in 1978 she became the first woman to be commemorated on US coinage.

The first meeting of British campaigners in 1855 had a more limited goal of fairer property laws, but soon suffrage became an important argument there too, with support from some reforming politicians. John Stuart Mill wrote *The Subjection of Women* (1869) against this background, advocating the emancipation and equality of women.

Reforms were made in both countries, in the divorce laws, in provision for divorced women and their children, and in control over property. Colleges for women were founded and some voting rights were gained in some American states and in the UK. However, the first country to grant women suffrage for national elections was New Zealand (1893), followed by Australia (1902). Among the reasons holding up progress in the UK was the female franchise opposition of Queen **Victoria**, which her prime ministers did not challenge as they were not interested in the idea anyway. (As late as 1914, the Liberal Prime Minister H H **Asquith** was hostile to women's claims.) Faced with refusal, the suffragette movement sought to draw attention to its demands. Emmeline **Pankhurst**, with her daughter Christabel, formed the Women's Social and Political Union in 1903. Its militant campaigning led to imprisonment for many of the suffragettes, and their hunger strikes were countered by force-feeding. With the outbreak of **World War I** they turned their energies to support for the war effort. Their attitude then, and the work done by thousands of women during the war, paved the way for limited voting rights in 1918 (for women over 30), with full rights in 1928. Similarly, the war work of women in the USA was recognized by the approval of the 19th Amendment to the **US Constitution** which gave votes to women in 1919. Women had gained voting rights in Russia at the **Russian Revolution** (1917). Gradually other countries followed suit,

---

during the **GREAT DEPRESSION**. Originally called the Works Progress Administration, it built transportation facilities, parks and buildings. Some 8,500,000 people were employed during its history, including artists and writers as well as manual workers. ► **NEW DEAL** (USA)

**World Bank** ► **INTERNATIONAL BANK FOR RECONSTRUCTION AND DEVELOPMENT** (IBRD); **INTERNATIONAL DEVELOPMENT ASSOCIATION** (IDA)

**World Health Organization (WHO)**
A **UN** specialized agency formed in 1948 to advance international cooperation for the improvement in health of peoples in all countries. Primarily concerned with the control of epidemic diseases, vaccination and other programmes, worldwide sanitation, and water supplies, it also acts as a clearing house for information on such topics as drugs,

nuclear hazards and cancer research.

**World Trade Organization (WTO)**
The successor to **GATT**, the organization is affiliated to the **UN** and was formally established on 1 Jan 1995. It administers international trade agreements and provides a forum for trade negotiations and the settling of disputes between member states. Since the late 1990s, its conferences have been the target of demonstrations by opponents of globalization. As at 2004, membership totalled 148 countries.

**World War I** (1914–18)
A war whose origins lay in the increasingly aggressive foreign policies pursued by Austria-Hungary, Russia and, most significantly, Germany. The assassination of the heir to the Habsburg throne, **FRANCIS FERDINAND**, at Sarajevo in Bosnia (28 Jun 1914), triggered the war, which soon involved most European

although women did not obtain suffrage in catholic France, Italy and Ireland until after **World War II**, nor in Switzerland until 1973.

With this great political right achieved, the attention of women's rights campaigners moved to wider social issues: to the position of women in society and their right to control their own lives. The publication by French writer Simone de Beauvoir of *Le deuxième sexe* (1949, Eng trans *The Second Sex*, 1953) had a tremendous impact on feminists everywhere, inspiring others to write. In the USA Betty Friedan wrote *The Feminine Mystique* (1963), analysing the role of women in American society and attacking their conditioning to a submissive domestic role. In 1966 she helped to found the National Organization for Women (NOW), which fought to end discrimination in employment, pay, contraception and abortion. In the UK, Australian-born Germaine Greer published *The Female Eunuch* (1970), a study attacking the denial and misrepresentation of female sexuality by a male-dominated society, and attacking the institution of marriage as legalized slavery. Feminists objected to the view of women as 'sex objects', particularly to the focus in the media on the sexual attractiveness (or otherwise) of any woman, whatever the context. More radical groups attacked men as oppressors in a society pervaded by sexism. Feminists did not always agree with each other, and priorities varied in the fight for change. In the USA an **Equal Rights Amendment** to the Constitution (first introduced in 1923) was passed by both **Congress** and **Senate** in 1972, but failed to be ratified by the necessary 38 states. There was strong conservative opposition, particularly from women who felt they might lose privileges, be forced into responsibilities they did not want, or who resented what they saw as the denigration of the role of wife and mother by the activists. Not surprisingly, there was a backlash from men who felt themselves under constant attack.

Nonetheless, the complaints of the campaigners did have an effect on what was judged acceptable in society, evidenced in the 1990s by sexual harassment and sexual discrimination law suits, both high- and low- profile. Women had achieved equal opportunities in education in the West and used them to gain careers of their choice. However, the situation remained that women continued to occupy lower-paying jobs. In the USA in the 1980s the average pay of a woman was only 62 per cent of that of a man (although a better situation existed in Sweden, where it was 87 per cent). The 'glass ceiling', noted by Elizabeth Dole in the USA in 1990, continued to exist there and in many other countries, and in many professions. Even where women formed the majority of the work force, eg in teaching, libraries and publishing, they held a very small proportion of the top posts.

In the developing world, many rights already obtained in the West are still lacking. The impact of fundamentalist political movements in Islamic countries, often heavily supported by traditional women, has been quite contrary to trends in the Western world. In extreme cases such as the **Taliban** regime in Afghanistan, with its draconian restrictions on women's social and educational opportunities, it is reasonable to talk of the deliberate oppression of women. On the other hand, the very different Islam of Indonesia has shared in the generally emancipated role of women in the rest of South-East Asia. The vote has been achieved for women in all but the most reactionary of regimes, although the rights of women to control their own lives often remains an aspiration rather than a fact. ▶ **Seneca Falls Women's Rights Convention**

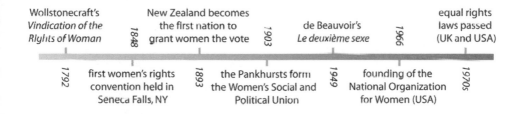

states following Austria's declaration of war on Serbia (28 July). Russia mobilized in support of Serbia (29–30 July); and Germany declared war on Russia (1 Aug), and on France (3 Aug). The German invasion of neutral Belgium (4 Aug) brought the British into the war on the French side. Japan joined Britain, France and Russia under the terms of an agreement with Britain (1902, 1911), and Italy joined the Allies in May 1915. Turkey allied with Germany (Nov 1914), and they were joined by Bulgaria (Oct 1915). Military campaigning centred on France, Belgium and, later, Italy in Western Europe, and on Poland, western Russia and the Balkans in Eastern Europe. The French army prevented the Germans from executing the **SCHLIEFFEN** Plan and then, with the **BRITISH EXPEDITIONARY FORCE**, at the first Battle of **YPRES**, from reaching the Channel ports. By the end of 1914, a static defence line had been established from the Bel-

gian coast to Switzerland. The Allies attempted to break the stalemate by the **GALLIPOLI CAMPAIGN** aimed at resupplying Russia and knocking out Turkey (Apr 1915– Jan 1916), but failed. On the eastern and south-eastern fronts, the **CENTRAL POWERS** occupied Russian Poland and most of Lithuania, and Serbia was invaded. After staunch resistance, Serbia, Albania and, latterly, Romania were overrun. For three years, an Allied army was involved in a Macedonian campaign, and there was also fighting in Mesopotamia against Turkey. Naval competition had played a crucial role in heightening tension before 1914, but in the event, the great battle fleets of Germany and Britain did not play an important part in the war. The only significant naval encounter, at **JUTLAND** in 1916, proved indecisive. The Allies organized a large offensive for the Western Front in 1916, but were forestalled by the Germans, who attacked

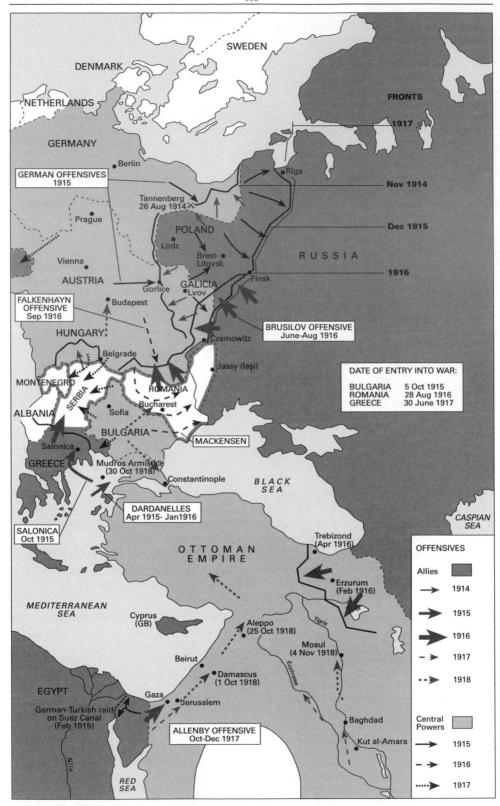

**World War I: Eastern Europe and the Middle East, 1914–18**

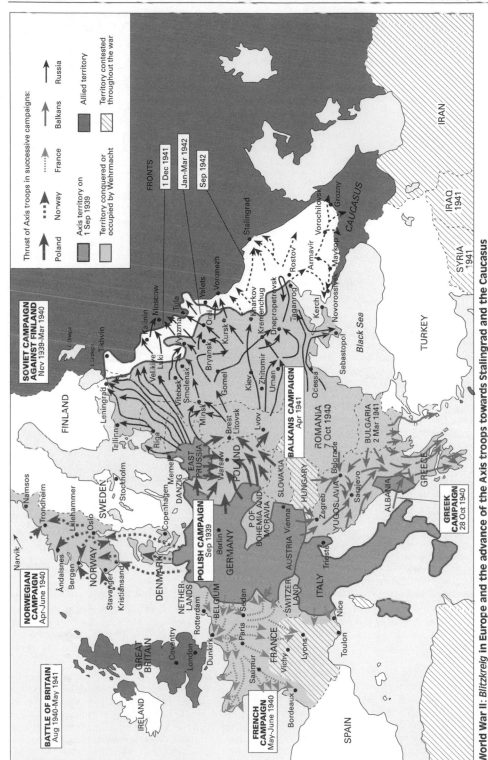

World War II: *Blitzkrieg* in Europe and the advance of the Axis troops towards Stalingrad and the Caucasus

France at Verdun (Feb–July). To relieve the situation, the Battle of the **SOMME** was launched, but proved indecisive. The Germans then unleashed unrestricted submarine warfare (Jan 1917) to cripple Britain economically before the USA could come to her aid. The USA declared war on Germany (2 Apr 1917) when British food stocks were perilously low, and the German submarine menace was finally overcome by the use of convoys. Tanks were used effectively by the Allies at the Battle of Cambrai (1916). By 1917, the Russian armies were broken and revolution broke out in St Petersburg and Moscow. In late 1917 **LENIN**'s Bolshevik government sued for peace and in Mar 1918 Germany and her allies imposed the punitive Treaty

# Writing Systems

Art & Literature

Examples of graphic expression found at archaeological sites throughout the world mingle art and the desire to convey information. It is thought that the development of drawn expression to form a coherent system that would represent the spoken word occurred independently at several sites, notably in Mesopotamia, China and Mesoamerica.

Earliest examples found of written symbols used for a conventional purpose are on clay tablets discovered in the Middle East and Europe, dating from around 3500 BC. Tablets made by the Sumerians seem to have been used for recording commercial transactions, and bear a strong resemblance to the clay tokens that were used in the same area for several thousand years before the tablets were made. The inscriptions on these tablets are mainly abstract, consisting of lines or circles.

Most early systems used pictographs or pictograms, symbols to represent an object that exists in the real world. The earliest known form of pictograph writing is from Egypt, dating from around 3000 BC. Prominent in temples and tombs, this system is known as hieroglyphic. Hieroglyphs are usually written from left to right, but vertical columns are also found. This system was not deciphered until the 19c, when members of **Napoleon I**'s army discovered a stone at Rashid (Rosetta) carved in three different scripts: one of them hieroglyphic, one demotic script and one Greek.

The same hieroglyphic signs, with few deviations, were used as the basis for both writing and fine art, and so the two practices developed simultaneously. The style of the former reflected the style of the latter, mainly because the same craftsmen were used for the inscription of both writing symbols and pictures.

Pictographic symbols have been found on bones and turtle shells in China dating from around 1500 BC, although by this time the writing system had been standardized for many centuries. There are also many later examples from Middle and North America, as well as from Minoan Crete and Easter Island. It is not always possible to decipher ancient pictographs in modern times because of a lack of knowledge of the cultural context in which they were written.

Pictographs do not relate to the sounds of language, as do most modern writing systems, but the later development of pictography, known as ideography, represented an abstract idea related to a concrete object, and then the name for that object. Thus Sumerian, Egyptian and Hittite scripts were a mixture of elements. Cuneiform (a term derived from the Latin 'wedge-shaped'), used throughout the Near East by the Sumerians, Babylonians, Assyrians and Hittites, began as a development of pictographic symbols, but came to be used to write words and syllables. Early examples were written on soft clay with a stylus, at first from top to bottom, but then left to right. Like hieroglyphics, the script could not be read by historians until the 19c.

Pictograms in China developed into a complex system where the written symbol represents a complete word, or part of a word. This means that in modern Chinese, a knowledge of 2000 characters is required, and in Japanese, where the writing system developed from the Chinese one, 1850 characters are considered essential for everyday use. Japanese has four writing systems, and two of them, *hiragana* and *katakana*, represent syllables. Such a syllabic system existed in Mycenaean Greek, and one was invented for Cherokee in 1821 and has 85 symbols.

By the 3c BC the technique of brush calligraphy had developed in China, and from that time occupied a place of particular importance as a visual art, particularly among the literati; it also became widely practised in Japan and Korea. Originally, ink was made from boiled soot and applied using a very fine brush attached to the end of a piece of bamboo.

In the Middle East, Arabic script became the most important medium for artistic expression, derived from the emphasis placed on 'the Word' as the medium of Allah's revelations to Muhammad, and from Islamic restrictions on the use of images. The flowing script of Arabic calligraphy is principally found in books and manuscripts, particularly the *Quran*, but is also to be found on minarets and mosques.

The most economical and versatile writing system to be devised is the alphabet, as it breaks down words into their phonic components, each being assigned a letter or group of letters to represent the sounds of speech. This means that most alphabets can manage with 30 or fewer symbols.

---

of **BREST-LITOVSK** on the USSR (annulled after Germany's defeat). Following this, in the spring of 1918, the Germans launched a major attack in the west, but after several months of success were driven back, with the USA providing an increasing number of much-needed troops. By Sep, the German army was in full retreat, and signified its intention to sue for peace on the basis of President **WILSON**'s **FOURTEEN POINTS**. By Nov, when the armistice was signed, the Allies had recaptured western Belgium and nearly all French territory. Military victories in Palestine and Mesopotamia resulted in a Turkish armistice (31 Oct 1918); Italian victories and a northward advance by Franco-British forces finished Austria-Hungary (and Bulgaria). Estimated combatant war losses were: British Empire, just under 1 million; France, nearly 1.4 million; Italy, nearly $\frac{1}{2}$ million; Russia, 1.7 million; USA, 115,000; Germany 1.8 million; Austria-Hungary 1.2 million, and Turkey 325,000. About double these numbers were wounded. ►

ANZAC; MARNE, BATTLE OF THE; PARIS PEACE CONFERENCE (1919–20); PASSCHENDAELE, BATTLE OF; REPARATIONS; TRIPLE ENTENTE; VERDUN, BATTLE OF; VERSAILLES, TREATY OF; VIMY RIDGE, BATTLE OF

### World War II (1939–45)

A war whose origins lay in three different conflicts which merged after 1941: **HITLER**'s desire for European expansion and perhaps even world domination; Japan's struggle against China; and a resulting (**SINO-JAPANESE WAR**) conflict between Japanese ambitions and US interests in the Pacific. The origins of the war in Europe lay in German unwillingness to accept the frontiers laid down in 1919 by the Treaty of **VERSAILLES** and the **NAZI PARTY**'s hegemonial foreign policy. After the German invasion of rump Bohemia-Moravia (Mar 1939), Britain and France pledged support to Poland. Germany concluded an alliance with the USSR (Aug 1939), and then invaded Poland (1 Sep), with Soviet troops joining in the attack on 17

The first alphabet developed was the North Semitic, around 1700 BC, in Palestine and Syria, with 22 consonant letters. From this base developed the Hebrew, Arabic and Phoenician alphabets. These were all consonantal, as Hebrew and Arabic still are, with the diacritical marking of vowels optional. The Greeks based their alphabet (c.1000 BC) on the Phoenician one, but added letters for vowels. Around 800 BC this became the model for the Etruscan alphabet, from which the Roman one was derived, and subsequently all modern Western European alphabets.

In parts of Eastern Europe, the Cyrillic alphabet is used, so-called because it is traditionally attributed to St Cyril, apostle to the **South Slavs** (c.860 AD). Based on the Greek alphabet, it includes extra symbols to represent Slavic sounds not found in Greek. It is used for Russian, Ukrainian, Serbian and Bulgarian.

In Western Europe, the Roman alphabet was adapted to accommodate differences in the local languages. A runic alphabet was used in north-western Europe from around AD 300 and continued in use on charms and monuments until the 17c. The version used in Britain contained extra letters to embrace the range of Anglo-Saxon sounds. The earliest English alphabet was devised by Christian missionaries who used the Irish form of the Latin alphabet and included extra letters.

Most Western alphabets have been based on preceding ones, and have often failed to keep pace with the spoken tongue, so that changes in speech have led to discrepancies in spellings and pronunciations. This is especially so with English, but not with Spanish and Finnish, for example, where the letter groupings are more consistent in their phonological values.

Artificial alphabets, ones that have been developed to use in a language with no previous history of writing, have attempted to be consistent with the phonetic values given to letters or groups of letters. Examples of these are the Armenian alphabet invented by St Mesrob in AD 405, the Mongolian hP'ags-Pa, devised in China in 1269, and the Fijian alphabet, devised by Wesleyan missionaries David Cargill and William Cross in the 1830s. Special alphabets have been created for a specific form of communication, for example 'Braille' for the blind, invented by Louis Braille c.1830.

A variant system of writing is shorthand. Such a system was used by Xenophon in the 4c BC to write the memoirs of Socrates, and another system was used by Julius Caesar in the 1c BC. Its development in more modern times was prompted by the needs of commercial correspondence and the recording of law proceedings, but modern technology has replaced it in many cases. The alphabet itself remains in constant use in electronic communication as well as on the page. ► **Books**; **Printing**

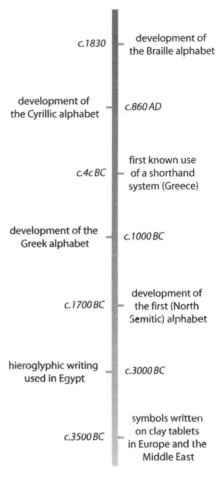

| | |
|---|---|
| c.1830 | development of the Braille alphabet |
| development of the Cyrillic alphabet | c.860 AD |
| c.4c BC | first known use of a shorthand system (Greece) |
| development of the Greek alphabet | c.1000 BC |
| c.1700 BC | development of the first (North Semitic) alphabet |
| hieroglyphic writing used in Egypt | c.3000 BC |
| c.3500 BC | symbols written on clay tablets in Europe and the Middle East |

---

Sep. Britain and France declared war on Germany (3 Sep), but could not prevent Poland from being overrun in four weeks. For six months there was a period of 'phoney war', when little fighting took place, but the Germans then occupied Norway and Denmark (Apr 1940), and Belgium and the Netherlands were invaded (10 May), followed immediately by the invasion of France. A combination of German tank warfare and air power brought about the surrender of the Netherlands in four days, Belgium in three weeks, and France in seven weeks. Italy declared war on France and Britain in the final stages of this campaign. There followed the Battle of **BRITAIN**, in which Germany tried to win air supremacy over Britain, but failed. As a result, German attempts to force Britain to come to terms came to nothing, not least because of Winston **CHURCHILL**'s uncompromising stance. Germany launched submarine (**U-BOAT**) attacks against British supply routes, but then moved east and invaded Yugoslavia (Apr 1941) and, following an Italian

military fiasco there, Greece. British military efforts were concentrated against Italy in the Mediterranean and North Africa. After early reverses for Italy, **ROMMEL** was sent to North Africa with the German **AFRIKA CORPS** to reinforce Italian military strength, and fiercely contested campaigning continued here for three years until Allied troops finally ejected German and Italian forces in mid-1943, invaded Sicily and then Italy itself, and forced Italy to make a separate peace (3 Sep 1943). In June 1941, in line with Hitler's long-held hostility to the USSR, and in his quest for **LEBENSRAUM**, Germany invaded her ally Russia along a 2,000 mi/3,220 km front, and German armies advanced in three formations: to the outskirts of Leningrad in the north, towards Moscow in the centre, and to the Volga River in the south. After spectacular early successes, the Germans were held up by bitter Soviet resistance, and by heavy winter snows and Arctic temperatures, for which they were completely unprepared. From Nov 1942 they were gradually driven back, suffering decisive reverses at STALINGRAD (winter 1942–3) and Kursk (May 1943). Leningrad was under siege for nearly two years (until Jan 1944), and about a third of its population died from starvation and disease. The Germans were finally driven out of the USSR (Aug 1944). A second front was launched against Germany by the Allies (Jun 1944), through the invasion of Normandy, and Paris was liberated (25 Aug). Despite German use of flying bombs and rockets against Allied bases, the Allies advanced into Germany (Feb 1945) and linked with the Russians on the River Elbe (28 Apr). The Germans surrendered unconditionally at Rheims (7 May 1945). In the Far East, Japan's desire for expansion, combined with a US threat of economic sanctions against her, led to her attack on PEARL HARBOR and other British and US bases (7 Dec 1941), and the USA declared war against Japan the next day. In reply Japan's allies, Germany and Italy, declared war on the USA (11 Dec). Within four months, Japan controlled South-East Asia and Burma (now Myanmar). Not until June 1942 did naval victories in the PACIFIC WAR stem the advance, and Japanese troops defended their positions grimly. Bitter fighting continued until 1945, when, with Japan on the retreat, the USA dropped two atomic bombs on HIROSHIMA and NAGASAKI (6 and 9 Aug). Japan then surrendered (14 Aug). Casualty figures are not easy to obtain accurately, but approximately 3 million Russians were killed in action, 3 million died as prisoners of war, 8 million people died in occupied Russia, and about 3 million in unoccupied Russia. Germany suffered $3\frac{1}{4}$ million military casualties, around 6 million total casualties, and lost a million prisoners of war. Japan suffered just over 2 million military casualties and just over $\frac{1}{4}$ million civilian deaths. France lost a total of $\frac{1}{2}$ million dead, and Britain and her Commonwealth just over 600,000. The USA suffered just over 300,000 casualties. It is also estimated that in the course of the German occupation of a large part of Europe, about 6 million Jews were murdered in extermination and labour camps, along with a million or more other victims. ► ANSCHLUSS; APPEASEMENT; ATLANTIC, BATTLE OF THE; ATLANTIC CHARTER; BLITZKRIEG; BULGE, BATTLE OF THE; BURMA CAMPAIGNS; CASABLANCA CONFERENCE; D-DAY; DESERT RATS; EL ALAMEIN, BATTLE OF; FREE FRENCH; GESTAPO; HOLOCAUST; KAMIKAZE; LEND–LEASE AGREEMENT; MAGINOT LINE; MUNICH AGREEMENT; NORMANDY CAMPAIGN; NORTH AFRICAN CAMPAIGN; NUREMBERG TRIALS; PARIS PEACE CONFERENCE (1946–7); POTSDAM CONFERENCE; SPECIAL OPERATIONS EXECUTIVE; SS; TEHRAN CONFERENCE; YALTA CONFERENCE

**World Zionist Organization**
The political institution established under the leadership of Theodor HERZL, its first President, at the First Zionist Congress, held in Basle (29–31 Aug 1897). The goal of the organization was the establishment of a national home for world Jewry in PALESTINE. For this purpose, the first Zionist bank and the JEWISH NATIONAL FUND were also formed. With time, the World Zionist Organization opened offices all around the world and, in the years before his death (1904), Herzl shaped it into an efficient and effective political institution. ► ZIONISM

**Worms, Concordat of** (1122)
This agreement, negotiated under Emperor HENRY V, brought a temporary end to the INVESTITURE CONTROVERSY. It was decided that bishops were to be invested with their fiefs, symbols of their secular office, by the emperor, but were to receive the ring and staff, the symbols of their spiritual authority, from the pope. The emperor retained a limited control over ecclesiastical appointments, but his power in this sphere was considerably weakened.

**Wörner, Manfred** (1934–94)
West German politician. He studied law at the universities of Heidelberg, Paris and Munich, then joined the conservative Christian Democratic Union (CDU) and was elected to the BUNDESTAG (federal parliament) in 1965. Establishing himself as a specialist in strategic issues, he was appointed Defence Minister in 1982 by Chancellor KOHL and then oversaw the controversial deployment of US Cruise and Pershing-II nuclear missiles in West Germany, an extension of military service from 15 to 18 months to compensate for a declining birth-rate, and, in 1984, the dismissal of General Gunter Kiessling, for alleged, though subsequently disproven, homosexual contacts. Wörner succeeded Lord CARRINGTON as Secretary-General of NATO in 1988.

**Wounded Knee** (29 Dec 1890)
The site in South Dakota (USA) of the final defeat of the SIOUX. The 'battle' was in fact a massacre of men, women and children by US troops, finally suppressing the GHOST DANCE cult inspired by the visions of the Paiute religious leader WOVOKA. In 1973 members of the American Indian Movement occupied the site to protest at the conditions of NATIVE AMERICANS. Two people were killed in the ensuing siege by FBI agents and federal marshals. ► INDIAN WARS

**Wovoka**, also known as **Jack Wilson** (c.1858–1932)
Native American religious leader. Born into the Paiute tribe near Walter Lake, Nevada, he was the son of a religious mystic, and at the age of 14, after the death of his father, he went to live and work on the ranch of a local white family. He had a religious vision in late 1888 that prompted him to found the messianic GHOST DANCE religion. He promised that if NATIVE AMERICANS lived peacefully and performed the Ghost Dance ritual, whites would disappear, the buffalo would return, and the dead would rise. He won followers among many tribes, especially the SIOUX, but after the massacre at WOUNDED KNEE, when many were killed wearing 'ghost shirts' from which they expected supernatural protection, the movement came to an end.

**Wrangel, Pyotr Nikolaievich, Baron** (1878–1928)
Russian army officer. He entered military service in 1904 and commanded a cavalry corps during WORLD WAR I. In the RUSSIAN CIVIL WAR, he commanded cavalry divisions and the Volunteer Army in the Ukraine, and in 1920 became Commander-in-Chief of the White armies in the south. After the RED ARMY victory, he fled to Turkey with the remnants of his troops. He died in Brussels, and was buried in Belgrade.

**Writing Systems** ► *See panel*

**WTO** ► WORLD TRADE ORGANIZATION

**Wu P'ei-fu** ► WU PEIFU

**Wu Peifu (Wu P'ei-fu)** (1874–1939)
Chinese warlord. A major figure in the warlord struggles of China (1916–27). He joined the BEIYANG ARMY, newly created by YUAN SHIKAI, and rose rapidly in its ranks. After Yuan's death (1916), when DUAN QIRUI sought by force and with Japanese assistance to recreate a united China that would accept a measure of political subordination to Japan, Wu and other northern generals refused Duan's orders. In the civil war that followed, he was unable to sustain his government of national unity (1923). He died in Japanese-occupied Beijing. ► WARLORDS

**Württemberg**
Originally part of Swabia, Württemberg became a Duchy in 1495. Duke Ulrich seized Church lands and introduced Lutheranism. Duke Christopher (1550/68) made substantial reforms while Duke Frederick (1593/1608) freed the Duchy from the titular overlordship of the Habsburgs. The dukedom was devastated in the THIRTY YEARS' WAR and by the French during the Wars of the Coalition (the War of the GRAND ALLIANCE). ► HABSBURG DYNASTY

**Wycliffe, John** (c.1330–1384)
English religious reformer. He taught philosophy at Oxford, then entered the Church, becoming Rector of Lutterworth, Leicestershire, in 1374. He was sent to Bruges to treat with ambassadors from the pope about ecclesiastical abuses, but his views were found unacceptable, and he was prosecuted. He then attacked the Church hierarchy, priestly powers, and the doctrine of transubstantiation, wrote many popular tracts in English (as opposed to Latin), and issued the first English translation of the Bible. His opinions were condemned, and he was forced to retire to Lutterworth, where he wrote prolifically until his death. The characteristic of his teaching was its insistence on inward religion in opposition to the formalism of the time. His followers were known as 'LOLLARDS', and the influence of his teaching was widespread in England, in many respects anticipating the REFORMATION.

**Wyszynski, Stefan** (1901–81)
Polish cardinal. Educated at Włocławek and Lublin, he was ordained in 1924, and became Bishop of Lublin (1946), Archbishop of Warsaw and Gniezno (1948), and a cardinal (1952). Following his indictment of the communist campaign against the Church, he was imprisoned (1953). Freed in 1956, he agreed to a reconciliation between Church and State under the GOMULKA regime, but relations remained uneasy.

## Xi'an Incident (12–25 Dec 1936)

The incident during which the **GUOMINDANG** leader **CHIANG KAI-SHEK** was kidnapped and held hostage in Xi'an by some of his own troops, under the 'Young Marshal', Zhang Xueliang (Chang Hsueh-liang). The hostage-taking was designed to force Chiang Kai-shek into acceding to demands for an alliance between the Guomindang and the communists against the Japanese, who had occupied Manchuria in 1931. He was released after 13 days thanks to intervention by the Communist leader, **ZHOU ENLAI** (further to urging by **STALIN**). Chiang Kai-shek made a verbal agreement to review Guomindang policy, and the second of the **UNITED FRONTS** followed.

## Xoxe, Koci (d.1949)

Albanian politician. A member of the Communist Party, and a wartime protégé of the Yugoslav partisan leader **TITO** he was Minister of the Interior in the post-war government, presiding over the trials of 'war criminals' which consolidated the position of Enver **HOXHA**. As a supporter of Albania's ties with Yugoslavia, his position weakened after Yugoslavia was expelled from **COMINFORM** and Hoxha moved closer to **STALIN**. From being second only to Hoxha in importance, he was demoted, then tried for treason and executed in 1949, a victim of Stalin's purge of 'Titoists'.

## XYZ Affair (1797)

A diplomatic incident between the USA and France. It arose when French agents, identified as 'X', 'Y' and 'Z', solicited a bribe from US agents sent to negotiate an end to maritime hostilities.

# Yaba Higher College

A college founded in Lagos, Nigeria in 1934 by the British Governor General, Sir Donald Cameron, with the intention of training Africans for administrative work. By **WORLD WAR II** it offered some degree courses.

# Yadava ► INDIA, PRE-ISLAMIC

# Yagoda, Genrikh Grigorevich (1891–1938)

Soviet police chief. A shadowy figure of Jewish origin, he became number two in the OGPU (or secret police) in 1924 and head of its successor, the NKVD, in 1934. He was **STALIN**'s agent in the great purges that started in that year. Yagoda was dismissed as inefficient in 1936 and brought before a firing squad in 1937. His successor, **YEZHOV**, was a much nastier figure.

# Yahya Khan, Agha Muhammad (1917–80)

Pakistani soldier. The son of a Pathan police superintendent, he was educated at Punjab University and the Indian Military Academy, Dehra Dun. He was commissioned in 1938, fought with the British 8th Army during **WORLD WAR II** and afterwards rose to become Chief of the Army General Staff (1957–62). He supported General **AYUB KHAN**'s successful coup in 1958, became army Commander-in-Chief in 1966 and, in 1969, with popular unrest mounting, replaced Ayub Khan as military ruler. In 1970 he sanctioned the nation's first national elections based on universal suffrage, but his mishandling of the Bangladesh separatist issue led to civil war and the dismemberment of the republic in 1971. After defeat by India in the third of the **INDO-PAKISTAN WARS** (1971), Yahya Khan resigned and was sentenced to five years' house arrest.

# Yakovlev, Alexander Nikolaevich (1923–)

Soviet party official and intellectual. Born into a simple peasant family in the Yaroslavl area, he first became an apparatchik after being invalided out of the army and by 1953 had been called to Moscow where, with the exception of four years of academic leave, he spent the period to 1973 servicing the Central Committee of the Communist Party. He was then exiled as Ambassador to Canada for a decade for offending communist hardliners. It was on Mikhail **GORBACHEV**'s advice that he was brought back to the Central Committee to assist with ideological work and by 1987 he was a full member of the **POLITBURO**. Although previously anti-American, he did much to give body to Gorbachev's new thinking on home and foreign affairs. He was eventually more reformist than

Gorbachev but still did everything possible to rescue him politically after the attempted **AUGUST COUP** in 1991. In 1995 he formed and became Chairman of the Russian Party of Social Democracy. ► **APPARAT**

# yakuza

Literally 'good-for-nothing', the Japanese word used to describe a gangster. Like the **MAFIA**, its Western equivalent, Japanese organized crime has a long history. Gangsters belong to recognized groups of racketeers (*boryokudan*). Often tattooed, gangsters cultivate a **SAMURAI**-like loyalty and are proud of their traditions. Like the Mafia, they are widely involved in such activities as gambling, extortion, racketeering, and the 'protection' of pachinko halls.

# Yalta Conference (4–11 Feb 1945)

A meeting at Yalta, in the Crimea, during **WORLD WAR II**, between Winston **CHURCHILL**, **STALIN** and **ROOSEVELT**. Among matters agreed were the disarmament and partition of Germany, the Russo-Polish frontier, the establishment of the **UN**, and the composition of the Polish government. In a secret protocol it was also agreed that Russia would declare war on Japan after the war with Germany ended. ► **CURZON LINE**

# Yamagata Aritomo (1838–1922)

Japanese soldier and politician. Made commanding officer of the **KIHEITAI** in 1863, he went on to become Vice-Minister of War (1871) and then Army Minister, issuing in 1878 the 'Admonition to the Military', which emphasized the traditional virtues of bravery and loyalty to the **MEIJI EMPEROR**, in an attempt to counteract the trend of liberalization. As Chief of Staff, he was the driving force behind the promulgation of the 1882 **IMPERIAL RESCRIPT TO SOLDIERS AND SAILORS** and the 1890 **IMPERIAL RESCRIPT ON EDUCATION**. He was Home Minister (1883–9) and was Japan's first Prime Minister (1889–91 and 1898–1900). His modernization of the military system led to Japanese victories in the **SINO-JAPANESE WAR** (1894–5) and **RUSSO-JAPANESE WAR** (1904–5), for which he was made Prince (*Koshaku*), and the emergence of Japan as a significant force in world politics. From 1903 he alternated with **ITO HIROBUMI** as President of the Privy Council; after the latter's death (1909), he was the dominant senior statesman, with the backing of the military and bureaucracy. His downfall came about in 1921, when he interfered in the marriage of the Crown Prince; he was publicly censured and died in disgrace the following year.

# Yamamoto Isoroku (1884–1943)

Japanese naval officer. Educated at the Japanese Naval

Academy, Etajima, he was wounded in the Battle of TSUSHIMA in the RUSSO-JAPANESE WAR (1904–5). He studied at Harvard (1917–19), serving thereafter as a language officer (1919–21) and as naval attaché at the Japanese Embassy in the USA (1926–2). He became Chief of the Aviation Department of the Japanese navy in 1935, and was vice-Navy Minister from 1936 to 1939. Opposed to the Japanese entry into WORLD WAR II, Yamamoto was nevertheless made Admiral (1940) and Commander-in-Chief Combined Fleet (1939–43). A great strategist, it was he who planned and directed the attack on PEARL HARBOR in Dec 1941. His forces were defeated at the Battle of MIDWAY (June 1942), and he was killed when his plane was shot down over the Solomon Islands.

### Yamani, Sheikh Ahmed Zaki (1930– )
Saudi Arabian politician. Educated in Cairo, New York and at Harvard, he worked as a lawyer before entering politics. Yamani was Minister of Petroleum and Mineral Resources from 1962 until 1986, and an important and 'moderate' member of OPEC (the Organization of Petroleum Exporting Countries).

### Yamashita Tomoyuki (1885–1946)
Japanese soldier. After serving in the RUSSO-JAPANESE WAR, WORLD WAR I and SINO-JAPANESE WAR, he commanded the Japanese 25th Army which overran Malaya and captured Singapore (15 Feb 1942). He then took over the Philippines campaign, capturing Bataan and Corregidor. Still in charge when General MACARTHUR turned the tables in 1944–5, he was captured and hanged in Manila for atrocities perpetrated by his troops.

### Yaméogo, Maurice (1921–93)
Burkina Faso politician. Educated in Upper Volta (now Burkina Faso), he was a civil servant and trade unionist before turning to politics and being elected to the Territorial Assembly in 1946. He was Vice-President of the Upper Volta section of the *Confédération Français du Travailleurs Chrétiens* and was active within the RASSEMBLEMENT DÉMOCRATIQUE AFRICAIN (RDA). Founder of the *Mouvement Démocratique Voltaique*, he was Minister of Agriculture (1957–8), Minister of the Interior (1958) and President (1958–66), before being toppled by a military coup on 4 Jan 1966 led by Lt-Col Sangoule Lamizana. He was imprisoned until 1970, when he went into exile in Côte d'Ivoire.

### Yanaconazco
A Peruvian term, originally signifying the Indian servants of Spaniards. By the mid-17c, the term had come to mean city labourers and servants dependent upon Spanish artisans or traders; and by the late 19c, the term *yanacona* signified a dependent sharecropper, producing a cash crop. Yanaconas were lent money by the estate to buy seed and fertilizers and to hire day-labourers from the sierra. In return, they serviced the loan and paid their shares in cotton.

### Yanaev, Gennadi Ivanovich (1937– )
Soviet lawyer and politician. He made his career in the COMMUNIST PARTY OF THE SOVIET UNION as a KOMSOMOL official and union apparatchik. That he had some genuine popularity was proved in 1989, when he was elected by the unions to the Congress of Deputies. In 1990 his promotion was unbelievably fast: Chairman of the Trade Unions, a POLITBURO member, and Soviet Vice-President. In all these positions he attempted to steer a middle course between reform and reaction; but in 1991 he opted for reaction, whether of his own free will or under pressure. His leadership of the attempted AUGUST COUP was so disastrous as to suggest that neither his heart nor his mind was in it. He was arrested with the others from the 'JUNTA', and was released in 1994. ➤ APPARAT

### Yang Shangkun (Yang Shang-k'un) (1907–98)
Chinese politician. The son of a wealthy Sichuan province landlord, he joined the Chinese COMMUNIST PARTY (CCP) in 1926 and studied in Moscow (1927–30). He took part in the LONG MARCH and the liberation war (1937–49), and became an alternate member of the CCP's secretariat in 1956, but during the CULTURAL REVOLUTION was purged for alleged 'revisionism'. He was rehabilitated in 1978, and in 1982 inducted into the CCP's Politburo and Military Affairs Commission. A year later he became a vice-chairman of the state Central Military Commission and in 1988 was elected state President, a position he held until 1993. Viewed as a trusted supporter of DENG XIAOPING, he had strong personal ties with senior military leaders and in June 1989 it was 27th Army troops, loyal to him, who carried out the brutal massacre of pro-democracy students in TIANANMEN SQUARE, Beijing.

### Yankee
The nickname for an inhabitant of New England, or Northerner in general (especially during and since the AMERICAN CIVIL WAR). It is also a general term for people of the USA, especially among non-Americans. The source is obscure, but it may derive from the Dutch *Janke* (a derivation of *Jan*), used as a nickname by early settlers.

### Yazov, Dmitri Timofeevich (1923– )
Soviet marshal. Of peasant stock from Omsk, he fought in WORLD WAR II as a young officer. He subsequently rose through various junior and senior commands, went through the General Staff Academy in 1967, and in 1984 became commander of the important Far East military district. In 1987 Mikhail GORBACHEV appointed him Deputy Minister, then Minister of Defence to bring the army into line with his reforms. However, Yazov supported only limited changes and was particularly unpopular with radical deputies. In Aug 1991 he felt that reform had proceeded to the point of endangering the army, but in the event his men would not obey him and fire on the pro-reform crowd. When the attempted AUGUST COUP failed, he was arrested. He was released in 1994.

### Yegorov, Alexander Ilich (1883–1939)
Soviet marshal. Of relatively humble origins in Samova, he was a colonel in the Tsarist army by 1917. He then threw in his lot with the BOLSHEVIKS and rose rapidly in the course of the RUSSIAN CIVIL WAR, during which he came into close contact with STALIN. By 1935 he was Chief of the General Staff and in 1937 he succeeded the executed TUKHACHEVSKY as Deputy Defence Minister, only to be shot himself two years later. The loss of his fighting experience and his organizational talent was sorely felt.

### Yehenala ➤ CIXI

**Yeltsin, Boris Nikolaevich** (1931– )
Soviet politician. He joined the **COMMUNIST PARTY OF THE SOVIET UNION** in 1961 and was appointed First Secretary of the Sverdlovsk region in 1976. He became a full member of the Central Committee in 1981 and was made its Secretary by Mikhail **GORBACHEV** in 1985 for a few months, before being appointed Moscow Party Chief, replacing the disgraced Viktor **GRISHIN**. Yeltsin, a blunt-talking, hands-on reformer, rapidly set about renovating the corrupt 'Moscow machine' and was elected a candidate member of the **POLITBURO** in 1986, but in 1987–8, after he had bluntly criticized party conservatives at two meetings of the Central Committee for sabotaging political and economic reform, he was downgraded to a lowly administrative post. No longer in the Politburo, he returned to public attention in 1989 by being elected to the new Congress of People's Deputies and becoming an outspoken critic of Gorbachev's failings. In May 1990 he was elected President of the Russian Federation and achieved even greater fame. But his moment of triumph came in Aug 1991, when he took the open stand that foiled the anti-Gorbachev coup and in Dec effectively put an end to both Gorbachev and the USSR. He was re-elected in the first post-Soviet presidential elections in 1996, but resigned in 1999 due to ill health. ► **AUGUST COUP**

**YEMEN**  official name **Republic of Yemen**

A republic in the south of the Arabian Peninsula, bounded to the north by Saudi Arabia; to the west by the Red Sea; to the south by the Gulf of Aden; and to the east by Oman. From c.750BC there were advanced civilizations in southern Arabia. It came under the control of the Muslim caliphate in the 7c AD, and was ruled by Egyptian caliphs from c.1000. Part of the **OTTOMAN EMPIRE** from the 16c until 1918, it was then ruled by the Hamid al-Din Dynasty until the revolution in 1962, when the Yemen Arab Republic (North Yemen) was proclaimed by the army. Fighting between royalists and republicans continued until 1967, when the republican regime was recognized. Aden was under British occupation from 1839 (therefore avoiding Ottoman rule), and had formed part of the Federation of South Arabia in 1963. British troops withdrew in 1967, but the area was overrun by the National Liberation Front, and the People's Republic of Yemen (South Yemen) was formed from Aden and its neighbouring emirates. It was renamed the People's Democratic Republic of Yemen in 1970. During the 1970s South Yemen had border disputes with Oman and North Yemen, but in 1990 the Yemen Arabic Republic (North Yemen) and the People's Democratic Republic of Yemen (South Yemen) formally united as the Republic of Yemen. Ali Abdullah **SALEH** became the first President of the united country, and

the first free, multiparty elections took place in 1993. There was another brief but violent civil war between the north and south of the country in 1994.

**Yevtushenko, Yevgeny Alexandrovich** (1933– )
Russian poet. His early poetry, such as *The Third Snow* (1955), made him a spokesman for the young post-**STALIN** generation. His long narrative poem *Stantsiya Zima* (1956, 'Zima Junction'), considering issues raised by the death of Stalin, prompted criticism, as did his *Babi Yar* (1962) which attacked anti-Semitism. In 1960 he began to travel abroad to give readings of his poetry. ► **BABI YAR**

**Yezhov, Nikolai Ivanovich** (1894–1939)
Soviet police chief. He first emerged in 1933 as a member of a small group charged by **STALIN** with the task of purging the Communist Party of undesirable elements, essentially those opposed to him. In 1936 he succeeded **YAGODA** as head of the NKVD (secret police) and turned the confined purges into mass terror. The bloodletting took on the title of the *Yezhovshchina*. Succeeded by **BERIA** in 1938, he too disappeared for ever in 1939.

**Yi Dynasty** (1392–1910)
The dynasty that ruled Korea under the official dynastic name of *Choson* ('morning serenity'). Founded by Yi Song-gye (1335–92), a prominent general under the preceding Koryo Dynasty (918–1392), the Yi Dynasty provided Korea with a long period of political and social stability until the incursions of Japan and the Western powers in the late 19c and its annexation as a Japanese colony in 1910. The Yi rulers were assisted by a centralized bureaucracy recruited through competitive civil service examinations on the Chinese pattern. Until the late 19c, the Yi maintained Korea's traditional tributary relationship with China.

**Yippies**, nickname for **Youth International Party**
A pressure group founded in 1968 by Abbie **HOFFMAN**, Jerry Rubin and others which campaigned against the **VIETNAM WAR** and against the US political and economic system in general. They joined the demonstration against the Vietnam War at the Democratic Convention in Chicago in 1968, but the demonstration turned into a riot and was suppressed by the police. Hoffman summarized the Yippies' ideology in *Steal this Book* (1971), in which he condemned the exploitation of the American people by their capitalist rulers, and proposed the transformation of the USA into a place where everything was free.

**Yishuv**
The Hebrew term (literally, 'settlement') used to describe the Jewish community living in **PALESTINE** before 1948. It was also used for the declaration of the State of Israel in that year. ► **BALFOUR DECLARATION**; **ISRAEL**; **JEWISH AGENCY**

**Yogyakarta**
A court city and sultanate in Java, founded in the mid-18c following the partition of central Java at the Treaty of Giyanti (1755). In 1810 and again in 1812, Yogyakarta was invaded by European forces. On the second occasion, British troops took and looted the *kraton* (court) itself and Yogyakarta subsequently lost considerable territory. During the Java War (1825–30),

many officials in Yogyakarta made common cause with Prince **DIPANAGARA**. Following the defeat of the rebel forces, Yogyakarta therefore lost all its remaining outlying territories as well as a great deal of its income. In the early 20c Yogyakarta became an important centre for the emerging nationalist and religious reformist movements. During the war against the Dutch for independence, following the Japanese surrender in 1945, the Indonesian Republic government resided in Yogyakarta.

**Yohannes IV** ► JOHN IV (of Ethiopia)

**Yom Kippur War** (1973)
This war, which followed the launching of a surprise attack by Egypt and Syria on Israel on the Jewish Day of Atonement (*Yom Kippur*), gave the Arabs an important lift in morale as a result of some initial success. The Israeli counter-attack could not, however, be contained by the Egyptian and Syrian forces, and the USA was persuaded by the Saudis to influence Israel to cease her military activities pending mediation by the **UN**. The importance of the war from the Egyptian point of view was that it went some way to salving the national pride which had taken a severe pounding in the **SIX-DAY WAR** (June 1967). ► **ARAB–ISRAELI WARS**

**Yonai Mitsumasa** (1880–1948)
Japanese naval officer and politician. Of **SAMURAI** descent, he was educated at the Japanese Naval Academy, Etajima and served in Russia (1915–17). He was Commander of the Imperial Fleet (1936–7), Navy Minister (1937–9 and 1944–5), and was briefly Prime Minister in 1940.

**York, Alvin Cullum**, known as **Sergeant York** (1887–1964)
US soldier. Born in Fentress County, Tennessee, he applied for conscientious objector status in **WORLD WAR I**. His petition was denied, and he was inducted into the army and sent to France, where he killed 25 Germans and captured 132 prisoners almost single-handedly at the Battle of the Argonne (1918). He was awarded the Congressional Medal of Honor and the Croix de Guerre, and became the most popular US hero of World War I.

**York, House of**
The younger branch of the **PLANTAGENET DYNASTY**, founded by Edmund of Langley, the fourth son of **EDWARD III** and first Duke of York, whence came three kings of England: **EDWARD IV**, who usurped the Lancastrian king **HENRY VI**; **EDWARD V**; and **RICHARD III** killed at the Battle of **BOSWORTH FIELD**, and succeeded by **HENRY VII**, first of the Tudors. ► **LANCASTER, HOUSE OF**; **ROSES, WARS OF THE**; **TUDOR, HOUSE OF**

## HOUSE OF YORK

| Regnal Dates | Name |
| --- | --- |
| 1461/70 | Edward IV |
| 1470/1 | Lancastrian rule |
| 1471/83 | Edward IV (restored) |
| 1483 | Edward V |
| 1483/5 | Richard III |

**Yorktown Campaign** (30 Aug–19 Oct 1781)
The final campaign of the **AMERICAN REVOLUTION**, in which the British Army under General **CORNWALLIS** was trapped at Yorktown in Virginia, by troops under George **WASHINGTON** and a French fleet under Admiral de Grasse (1722–88). The defeat destroyed the political will on the English side to continue the war. It brought the fall of Lord **NORTH**, Prime Minister since 1770, and opened the way for peace negotiations.

**Yoruba City States**
A cluster of politically autonomous units in Nigeria and Benin, inhabited by Kwa-speaking peoples, and each ruled by a king who is both political and religious head. The dominant state in the 17–18c was the kingdom of **OYO**, which broke up in the early 19c. Ibadan was the largest pre-colonial city in Black Africa, and the states are famed for their art. Missionaries were highly active in Yorubaland in the 19c, but Islam and traditional religions are also represented.

**Yoshida Shigeru** (1878–1967)
Japanese politician. Educated at Tokyo Imperial University, he served as a diplomat in several capitals. Vice-Foreign Minister (1928–30), in 1930–2 he was Ambassador to Italy and in 1936–8, after the army had blocked his appointment as Foreign Minister, he was Ambassador in London. As a fervent advocate of Japanese surrender, he was imprisoned (Jun 1945) for this view in the closing stages of **WORLD WAR II**. He was released (Sep 1945) under the US occupation and was appointed Foreign Minister. After **HATOYAMA**'s removal from public office by the US authorities, he stepped into his shoes as leader of the Liberal Party. As Prime Minister (1946–7 and 1949–54), he was instrumental in the socio-economic development of post-war Japan and in fostering relations with the West. In 1954 Hatoyama (who had been rehabilitated in 1951) forced him out of office and, when the **LIBERAL DEMOCRATIC PARTY** was formed in 1955, with Hatoyama as its leader, Yoshida withdrew from politics.

**Youlou, Abbé Fulbert** (1917–72)
Congo politician. Educated in Catholic seminaries and ordained a priest in 1946, he became Mayor of Brazzaville in 1957 and formed a moderate party to oppose the local socialists. He was elected to the territorial assembly in 1957 and was, in turn, Minister of Agriculture (1957–8), Prime Minister (1958–9) and President of the Congo Republic (1959–63), before being forced into exile in Spain as the result of popular opposition within the country.

**Young, Brigham** (1801–77)
US Mormon leader. Born in Whitingham, Vermont, he became a carpenter, painter and glazier in Mendon, New York. He first saw the *Book of Mormon* in 1830, and in 1832, converted by a brother of Joseph **SMITH**, was baptized and began to preach near Mendon. He was made an elder in Kirtland, Ohio, and preached in Canada (1832–3). In 1835 he was appointed to the Quorum of the Twelve Apostles of the Mormon Church, directed the settlement at Nauvoo, Illinois, and in 1844 succeeded Joseph Smith as President. When the **MORMONS** were driven from Nauvoo, he led them to Utah (1847) where they founded Salt Lake City. In 1850 President **FILLMORE** appointed Brigham Young Governor of Utah Territory, but the

Mormon practice of polygamy caused growing concern, and in 1857 a new governor was sent with a force of US troops to suppress it. Young bequeathed around US$2,500,000 to 17 wives and 56 children.

**Young, Whitney Moore, Jr** (1921–71)
US **CIVIL RIGHTS** leader. Born in Kentucky, he was a graduate in social work from the University of Minnesota. Executive director of the **NATIONAL URBAN LEAGUE** from 1961 until his death, some of his social welfare proposals were incorporated into President **JOHNSON**'s anti-poverty programmes.

**Young Ireland**
An Irish protest movement, founded in 1840, which produced *The Nation* magazine, arguing for repeal of the Act of Union. It set up an Irish Confederation in 1847, which returned several nationalists to parliament, and an unsuccessful Young Ireland rising took place in Tipperary (1848). ▶ **O'CONNELL, DANIEL**; **UNION, ACTS OF**

**Young Italy** (*Giovine Italia*)
The organization founded by the Italian patriot Giuseppe **MAZZINI** in 1831 after he had grown dissatisfied with the poor organization and muddled programme of the **CARBONARI**. Limited in all but exceptional circumstances to individuals under 40 years of age, the organization sought to develop Italian national feeling, aiming to generate a national, republican uprising. In reality, it merely inspired a handful of invariably abortive conspiracies, but it did play an important part in fostering patriotic sentiment among many future leaders of the **RISORGIMENTO**, including **GARIBALDI**. During the early 1830s, various sister organizations (Young Switzerland, Young Germany, Young Poland, Young Europe) were formed but they never achieved the same degree of support. Young Italy itself fell victim to the repressive measures of the Piedmontese government in the period 1833–5 and never again attained the widespread support of its earliest years.

**Young Plan** (1929)
A revision of the **DAWES PLAN** drawn up by an international commission chaired by US financier Owen D Young (1874–1962). It reduced the post-**WORLD WAR I** reparations payment due from Germany by 75 per cent, to 121 billion Reichsmark, to be paid in 59 annual instalments. The first payment was made in 1930, but then Germany lapsed into recession. The **LAUSANNE CONFERENCE** of 1932 promised to reduce the payments yet further, but when **HITLER** came to power in 1933 he repudiated all political and economic obligations made under the Treaty of **VERSAILLES** and no more payments were made.

**Young Pretender** ▶ **STUART, CHARLES EDWARD LOUIS PHILIP CASIMIR**

**Young Turks**
The modernizing and westernizing reformers in the early 20c **OTTOMAN EMPIRE**. With the support of disaffected army elements under **ENVER PASHA**, they rebelled against Sultan **ABD UL-HAMID II** in 1908, and deposed him (1909). The Young Turk revolution helped precipitate Austria-Hungary's occupation of Bosnia and Herzegovina (1908), the somewhat similar Greek officers' revolt of 1909, the Italian attack on

Libya (1911), and the **BALKAN WARS** (1912–13).

**Ypres, Battle of** (Oct–Nov 1914)
In **WORLD WAR I** the halting of a German offensive to outflank the **BRITISH EXPEDITIONARY FORCE**. It left Ypres (Belgium) and its salient dominated on three sides by German-occupied heights.

**Ypres, Battle of** (Apr–May 1915)
A series of German attacks, using poison gas (chlorine) for the first time in warfare. It forced the British to shorten their defence line in the Ypres salient.

**Ypres, Battle of** ▶ **PASSCHENDAELE, BATTLE OF**

**Ypsilanti, Alexander** (1725–1805)
Greek administrator. He became Ottoman **HOSPODAR** (governor) of Wallachia, but was put to death on suspicion of fostering Greek ambitions.

**Ypsilanti, Alexander** (1783–1828)
Greek soldier. The eldest son of Constantine **YPSILANTI**, he served with distinction in the Russian army (1812–13), and was chosen by the Greek 'Hetairists' as their chief in 1820. In 1821 he led a Romanian uprising in the Danubian Principalities, but was defeated by the Turks. He took refuge in Austria, where he died. ▶ **MOLDAVIA AND WALLACHIA**

**Ypsilanti, Constantine** (d.1816)
Greek administrator. The son of Alexander **YPSILANTI** (1725–1805), he became Ottoman **HOSPODAR** (governor) of **MOLDAVIA AND WALLACHIA**. Deposed in 1805, he came back with some thousands of Russian soldiers and stirred the Serbs to rebellion; he made another plan for restoring Greece, but had to flee to Russia.

**Ypsilanti, Demetrius** (1793–1832)
Greek soldier. The younger son of Constantine **YPSILANTI**, he served in the Russian army, and aided the schemes of his brother, Alexander **YPSILANTI** (1783–1828), for emancipating the Christian population of Turkey. In Greece, he took part in the capture of Tripolita (Oct 1820). His gallant defence of Argos stopped the victorious march of the Turks, and from 1828 to 1830 he was Commander-in-Chief of the Greek Army.

**Yrigoyen, Hipólito** (1852–1933)
Argentine politician. A lawyer and teacher, he was the principal leader of the **RADICAL PARTY** (*Unión Cívica Radical*) from 1896. He mounted a successful attack on the dominant conservative governments of the time, ushering in a period of Radical dominance. Yrigoyen was President in 1916–22, during which term he maintained Argentine neutrality in **WORLD WAR I**, and again in 1928–30. His second presidential term was ended by a military coup, precipitated by the country's prevailing economic depression and Yrigoyen's growing senility and weakening grasp on national affairs.

**Yuan Dynasty** (1279–1368)
The Chinese dynasty founded by **KUBLAI KHAN**, who completed the conquest of the Southern Song, and built a new capital (Marco **POLO**'s 'Cambaluc') at Beijing. The Chinese never accepted their foreign rulers, however, and after Kublai's death (1294) Mongol power rapidly declined. Civil war between Mongol princes broke out in 1328, and the dynasty was

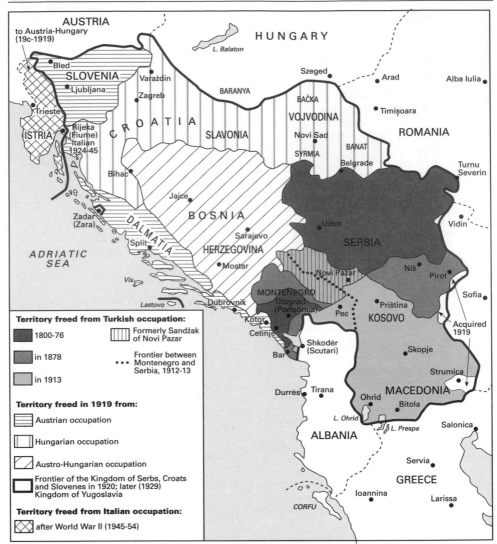

**Territory freed from Turkish occupation:**

- 1800-76
- in 1878
- in 1913
- Formerly Sandžak of Novi Pazar
- ••• Frontier between Montenegro and Serbia, 1912-13

**Territory freed in 1919 from:**

- Austrian occupation
- Hungarian occupation
- Austro-Hungarian occupation
- Frontier of the Kingdom of Serbs, Croats and Slovenes in 1920; later (1929) Kingdom of Yugoslavia

**Territory freed from Italian occupation:**

- after World War II (1945-54)

**Formation of Yugoslavia**

eventually overthrown by a Chinese uprising led by Zhu Yuanzhang. ► **MONGOLS**

**Yuan Shih-k'ai** ► **YUAN SHIKAI**

**Yuan Shikai (Yuan Shih-k'ai)** (1859–1916)
Chinese politician and soldier. He was careful to remain neutral during the **BOXER RISING**, from which he thus emerged with his army intact and with the gratitude of the foreign powers. On the death of his patron, the Empress-Dowager **CIXI** (1908), he was removed from influence, but recalled after the successful **CHINESE REVOLUTION** of 1911. As the first President of the Republic (1912–16), he lost support by procuring the murder of the parliamentary leader of the **GUOMINDANG** (**SONG JIADREN**) and making war on them, accepting Japan's **TWENTY-ONE DEMANDS**, and proclaiming himself Emperor (1915). Forced to abdicate, the humiliation may have hastened his death. ► **HUNDRED DAYS OF REFORM**; **QING DYNASTY**

**Yugoslav Committee**
Established during **WORLD WAR I** (Apr 1915) in Paris by, among others, Ivan Meštrović, Ante **TRUMBIĆ** and Frano **SUPILO**, the Yugoslav Committee held that the **SOUTH SLAVS** were entitled to their own state on the principles of national right and self-determination. Claiming to represent the interests of the South Slavs in the Habsburg monarchy, it moved to London where it campaigned to win the support of the Allies for the political unification of the South Slavs. By the Declaration of Corfu, it agreed to cooperate with the Serbian government in establishing a South Slav state (Jul 1917). At the end of **WORLD WAR I**, the National Council of Slovenes, Croats and Serbs in Zagreb authorized the Yugoslav Committee to act as its representative in international negotiations. After the Serbian regent, **ALEXANDER I KARAGEORGEVIĆ**, accepted the Council's proposals (1 Dec 1918), the South Slavs were united for the first time within the Kingdom of Serbs, Croats and Slovenes (later Yugoslavia).

**Yugoslavia**
Formerly a federal republic in the Balkan Peninsula of south-eastern Europe, bounded to the north by

**Break-up of Yugoslavia**

Austria and Hungary; to the east by Romania and Bulgaria; to the south by Greece and Albania; and to the west by the Adriatic Sea. After **WORLD WAR I** the Serbs of Montenegro and the Kingdom of Serbia were joined with the **SOUTH SLAVS** of the former Habsburg monarchy, the Croats, Slovenes and some Serbs, to become the Kingdom of Serbs, Croats and Slovenes, who were united under one monarch, **PETER I**, the King of Serbia and head of the Karageorgević Dynasty. Formal unification was proclaimed by the regent **ALEXANDER I KARAGEORGEVIĆ** (1 Dec 1918), who later, as King, renamed the kingdom the Kingdom of Yugoslavia (1929). The term 'Yugoslavs', literally the 'South Slavs', was the collective name for the inhabitants of Yugoslavia, who were members of several different nations; while the Serbs, Croats, Slovenes, Bosnian Muslims and Macedonians are all South Slavs, Yugoslavia had many non-Slav inhabitants including the Hungarians in the **VOJVODINA** and the Albanians in **KOSOVO**. Yugoslavia was occupied by Germany during **WORLD WAR II**, but resistance to the occupation was complicated by fighting between Serbian royalists (**CHETNIKS**), Croatian na-

tionalists and communists, as the resentment that had built up during the interwar years among different nations within Yugoslavia combined with long-standing national rivalries to erupt in a 'civil war' of brutal reprisals; the only semblance of 'Yugoslav' unity remained in the communist-led partisan army under **TITO**, which waged a brave and effective tactical campaign against the occupying Axis forces. After the war, Tito's version of **COMMUNISM** promised to neutralize old national rivalries and to unite the nations of Yugoslavia in pursuit of a common future; in 1945 a Federal People's Republic (Croatia, Slovenia, Bosnia and Herzegovina, Macedonia, Montenegro and Serbia) was established under Tito. In this federation of six republics and two autonomous provinces, each based around a core nation, the different national identities were strictly repressed. After Tito's death in 1980, however, nationalisms resurfaced and Yugoslavia fell into political and economic decline. At the end of the 1980s, political disagreement between the federal republics increased; in 1989 Slovenia declared its sovereignty and its strong opposition to the Communist Party. Despite the government's attempt to preserve Yugoslav unity by planning a multiparty system with direct elections, ethnic unrest in Serbia and Croatia placed further strains on the federal system. Of the six republics that made up Yugoslavia as established in 1945, four seceded in 1991–2, only Serbia and Montenegro remaining as the Federal Republic of Yugoslavia, which was declared on 27 Apr 1992 but was not recognized by the UN. This rump state was restructured with effect from Feb 2003 into a loose federation of the republics of SER-BIA and MONTENEGRO, with independence the ultimate aim. ➤ ALBANIA; SANDŽAK OF NOVI PAZAR

## Yugoslavism

During the 19c, the ideology of a primarily Croatian movement which sought to promote closer cultural and political ties among the SOUTH SLAVS. An extension of the Illyrianism of Ljudevit GAJ, its chief proponents were Bishop Juraj STROSSMAYER and Canon Franjo Rački. Originally aimed at unifying the South Slavs through their common culture and literary language, Yugoslavism developed into a political movement for the unification of the South Slavs of the Habsburg monarchy within a South Slav state that would remain part of a federalized monarchy. In time, its ultimate goal became a federal South Slav state including Serbia and Montenegro. ➤ ILLYRIAN MOVE-MENT

## Yusuf bin Hassan, also called Jerónimo Chingulia (1526/31)

Last sheik of the Malindi Dynasty of Mombasa (Kenya). As a youth he studied under Portuguese tutelage in Goa and was baptized a Christian as Dom Jerónimo Chingulia. Following his succession in 1526 he took up arms in 1531 against Portuguese domination. He was driven out of Mombasa and direct Portuguese rule was established.

## Zachariadis, Nikos (1903–73)
Greek political leader. The son of a tobacco worker, he was one of the many Greeks who were forced to leave Anatolia in 1923 after the **GRAECO-TURKISH WAR** and who became communists. He was Secretary-General of the **KKE** (Communist Party of Greece) from 1931 to 1941. Imprisoned during **WORLD WAR II** in **DACHAU** concentration camp, he lived to return home in 1945 to direct communist opposition to the British-backed Greek government and resumed his post as Secretary-General of the KKE. Believing that the communists would achieve their victory in the towns, he quickly came into conflict with Markos **VAFIADIS**, who was based in the country, and succeeded Vafiadis as commander of the Democratic Army in 1949. ▶ **LAUSANNE, TREATY OF**

## Zaghlul, Sa'd (c.1857–1927)
Egyptian politician and lawyer. Effectively the founder of the Egyptian **WAFD PARTY**, he headed a campaign to change the political position of Egypt, leading the delegation (*wafd*) of Egyptians who petitioned Britain for an end to the protectorate. This petition failed and, as a result, he was banished to Malta (1919). Anti-British riots followed and he was released, later achieving the desired recognition of independence for Egypt. After varying fortunes, during the course of which he was once more arrested and banished, Zaghlul eventually led his Wafd Party to success in Egypt's first election. By 1924 Zaghlul had become Egypt's first Prime Minister; a modern campaign conducted during the first Wafd government meant, however, that despite the success once more of the Wafdists in the 1926 election, the British refused to accept Zaghlul as Prime Minister. He was allowed, though, to become President of the Chamber, a cabinet containing six members of the Wafd, three Liberals and an independent, with the cabinet as a whole headed by the Liberal leader. Zaghlul, however, relinquished office shortly afterwards.

## Zaharoff, Sir Basil, originally Basileios Zacharias (1850–1936)
French armaments magnate and financier. Born in Anatolia, Turkey, of Greek parents, he was educated in Istanbul and England. He entered the munitions industry in the 1880s and became a shadowy but influential figure in international politics and finance, amassing a huge fortune in arms deals, oil, shipping and banking. He became a French citizen in 1913, and was knighted by the British in 1918 for his services to the allies in **WORLD WAR I**. He donated large sums of money to universities and other institutions.

## Zahir Shah, Mohammed (1914–)
King of Afghanistan (1933/73). Educated in Kabul and Paris, he was Assistant Minister for National Defence and Education Minister before succeeding to the throne in 1933 after the assassination of his father, **MOHAMMED NADIR SHAH**. His reign was characterized by a concern to preserve neutrality and promote gradual modernization. He became a constitutional monarch in 1964, but, in 1973, while in Italy receiving medical treatment, was overthrown in a republican coup led by his cousin, General Daud Khan, following a three-year famine. He lived in exile in Rome and remained a popular symbol of national unity for moderate Afghan opposition groups. He returned to Afghanistan in 2002 as a private citizen.

## Zahle, Carl Theodore (1866–1946)
Danish politician. After studying law, he became a member of the Danish parliament, **FOLKETINGET**. In Jan 1905, he and seven other members were expelled from the then leading Danish political party, *Venstrereformpartiet* ('Left Reform Party'), because they advocated a reduction in Denmark's defence expenditure. In response to the expulsion, in May 1905 Zahle became one of the founding members of a new centre party, *Det Radikale Venstre* ('The Radical Left'), which was to develop into a major middleground force of Danish pre-war and interwar politics. It was a socially committed, non-socialist party that wanted Denmark declared 'lastingly neutral' and the working-class party, *Socialdemokratiet*, drawn into the democratic process. The party's core electorate was made up of an unusual alliance of smallholders, schoolteachers and Copenhagen academics. As early as Oct 1909, Det Radikale Venstre formed its first, short-lived government, with Zahle as Premier. After the general election in 1913, he headed a much stronger government which, supported by the Social Democrats, secured the Danish policy of neutrality during **WORLD WAR I**. After the war, there was in financial and nationalistic circles a growing dissatisfaction with Zahle's government which resulted in his being dismissed by the King, **CHRISTIAN X**, on 29 Mar 1920, causing the so-called Easter Crisis.

## zaibatsu
A Japanese term for the large family-owned centrally controlled corporations that arose after the **MEIJI RESTORATION** to spearhead industrialization in Japan. Developing originally from **SAMURAI** noble houses, the *zaibatsu* controlled finance, manufacturing, mining and shipping, and exploited interlocking directorships and lifetime guarantees of employment to

become economically formidable. It was usual for a *zaibatsu* to own its own bank. Close ties with the state allowed them to secure monopolies, subsidies and, in the 1870s, cheap state assets. By 1930 four *zaibatsu*, Mitsubishi, Mitsui, Sumitomo and Yasuda, dominated the Japanese economy. After 1945 the US occupation authorities intended to dissolve the *zaibatsu* but faced with the rise of communism in China, allowed them to continue but as more loosely-organized institutions eventually known as **KEIRETSU**.

**Zaire** ▶ CONGO, DEMOCRATIC REPUBLIC OF THE

**Zai Tian (Tsai T'ien)** ▶ GUANGXU (KUANG-HSU)

**Zalygin, Sergei Pavlovich** (1913–2000)
Soviet fiction writer. Born in the Bashkin autonomous region, he spent much of his life in Siberia. He came into his own under Mikhail **GORBACHEV**, being one of the main campaigners against the project to reverse the Siberian rivers. He was Chief Editor of *Novy Mir* (1986–8) and was responsible for securing the publication of Solzhenitsyn's previously banned works.

**Zambezi Expedition**
An official British expedition (1858–64), led by David **LIVINGSTONE**, to investigate the potentiality of the Zambezi River for steamship communication with the interior of Africa, in order to promote the destruction of the slave trade, its replacement by 'legitimate' commerce, and the extension of missionary activity in the region. The expedition was a failure; the Zambezi was found to be non-navigable, Livingstone's relations with his associates were difficult and helped to thwart the scientific objectives, and the earliest missionary endeavours met with disaster.

**ZAMBIA** official name **Republic of Zambia**, formerly (to 1964) **Northern Rhodesia**

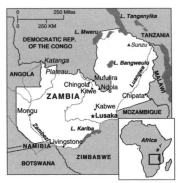

A landlocked republic in southern Africa, bounded to the west by Angola; to the south by Namibia; to the south-east by Zimbabwe and Mozambique; to the east by Malawi; to the north-east by Tanzania; and to the north-west by the Democratic Republic of the Congo. Most ethnic groups at present in Zambia arrived there between the 16c and the 18c. Arab slave-traders arrived in the 19c, as did European settlers, following David **LIVINGSTONE**'s discovery of the Victoria Falls in 1855. The country was administered by the **BRITISH SOUTH AFRICA COMPANY** under Cecil **RHODES**. Known as Barotseland, it was declared a British sphere of influence in 1888 and named Northern Rhodesia in 1911. It became a British pro-

tectorate in 1924. Massive copper deposits were discovered in late 1920s. Between 1953 and 1963 Northern Rhodesia joined with Southern Rhodesia (now Zimbabwe) and Nyasaland (now Malawi) as the Federation of Rhodesia and Nyasaland. Northern Rhodesia gained its independence in 1964 as the Republic of Zambia under President Kenneth **KAUNDA**. The first multiparty elections since independence were held in 1991, bringing Frederick Chiluba to power as President. He survived coup attempts in 1993 and 1997. Kaunda was implicated in the latter and placed under house arrest until 1998, when charges were dropped. Chiluba was succeeded by Levy Mwanawasa, who narrowly won presidential election in 2001 amid accusations of election irregularities, and who has tried to eliminate corruption. The country faces serious problems because of the high levels of **HIV/AIDS** infection.

**Zamindar**
A Persian term meaning 'holder/occupier of the land'. Its use in India ranged from hereditary tax collectors (Bengal) to large landowners with full proprietory rights (parts of northern India) to all local hereditary revenue officers (western and central India). The term was adopted by the British to mean 'landowner', notably in the permanent settlement of the land revenue in Bengal in 1793, designed to provide an aristocracy of improving landlords.

**Zamyatin, Evgeny Ivanovich** (1884–1937)
Russian novelist and short-story writer. He was exiled in 1905 after joining the Bolshevik Party, and again in 1911, but on each occasion soon returned to Russia. In 1921 he was a founder-member of the Modernist group, the Serapion Brothers, and was briefly imprisoned by the Soviets in 1922. In 1932 he travelled to Paris, where he remained until his death. He is best known for the novel *My* (1920, Eng trans *We*, 1924). ▶ **BOLSHEVIKS**

**Zanardelli, Giuseppe** (1826–1903)
Italian politician. He took part in the anti-Austrian uprisings in his native Brescia during the **REVOLUTIONS OF 1848–9** and supported the Piedmontese invasion of Lombardy in 1859. In 1860 he was elected to the new Italian parliament. Following the electoral victories of the Left in 1876, he held a number of ministerial posts until finally becoming Prime Minister in 1901. A left-wing liberal, he was violently anticlerical and a supporter of divorce. He was also responsible for the reform of the penal code. As Prime Minister, he was particularly concerned with improving the economic conditions of the **MEZZOGIORNO**.

**Zangid Dynasty**
Also known as the Atabeg Dynasty, it was established by 'Imad al-Din Zangi, who became Governor of Mosul in 1127 and took control of Aleppo in 1128. His power in the Fertile Crescent, resulting from his control of these two major cities, brought him into not always happy contact in the east with the great Seljuk sultanate, and in the west with the Crusaders and the Burid Dynasty which controlled Damascus. Chiefly remembered in the West for his capture of Edessa (1144), which feat precipitated the preaching of the unsuccessful Second **CRUSADE**, Zangi was murdered in 1146 and the dynasty's influence was then split

between Syria and the Jazira. He had expended much effort in endeavouring to gain control of Damascus but this was only finally achieved by his son, **NUR AL-DIN**. Zangid influence waned after the latter's death, chiefly as a result of the rise in power of one of his lieutenants, **SALADIN**, who subsequently gained control not only of Damascus, but also Aleppo. This finally confined Zangid influence once more to Mosul and and the northern Jazira. The Zangids can, however, be credited with the first effective prosecution of holy war (**JIHAD**) against the crusading **FRANKS**.

**Zanj** ► AZANIA

**ZANU (Zimbabwe African National Union)**
The party that was formed in 1963, under the leadership of Ndabaningi **SITHOLE**, as a breakaway from **ZAPU** in opposition to ZAPU's strategy. The party split again, as a result of which Robert **MUGABE** became leader. Banned from Southern Rhodesia, the party relocated to Mozambique and became, through its military wing, the Zimbabwe African National Liberation Army (ZANLA), the most effective guerrilla movement. Associated with ZAPU in 1976 to form the **PATRIOTIC FRONT**, it nevertheless fought the 1980 elections separately as ZANU and won 57 of the 80 seats available to black voters. It has been the dominant party since then. In 1988, after long discussions, it absorbed **NKOMO**'s wing of the Patriotic Front, and was thereafter known as ZANU (PF), with Mugabe as President. Its electoral successes in recent years have attracted allegations of electoral fraud.

**Zapata, Emiliano** (1879–1919)
Mexican revolutionary. The son of a mestizo peasant, he became a sharecropper and local peasant leader. After the onset of the **MEXICAN REVOLUTION**, he occupied estates by force and mounted a programme for the return of land in the areas he controlled to the native Indians. He initially supported Francisco **MADERO** and, with a small force of men was largely responsible for toppling the dictatorship of Porfirio **DÍAZ**. Along with Pancho **VILLA**, he subsequently fought the **CARRANZA** government. Meanwhile, he continued to implement agrarian reforms in the southern area under his control, creating impartial commissions responsible for land distribution and setting up the Rural Loan Bank. He was eventually lured to his death at the Chinameca hacienda in Morelos.

**Zapatista National Liberation Army** ► EZLN

**Zapolya, John** (1487–1540)
King of Hungary (1526/40). A prince of Transylvania, he was proclaimed king despite the superior Habsburg claim of Emperor **FERDINAND I**, who drove him out in 1527. John was, however, supported by **SÜLEYMAN I, THE MAGNIFICENT**, who reinstated him as a puppet ruler.

**Zapolya, John Sigismund** (1540–71)
King of Hungary. The son of John **ZAPOLYA**, he succeeded his father. However, as **SÜLEYMAN I, THE MAGNIFICENT** had made Hungary a Turkish province, he had to content himself with the voivodship of Transylvania.

**Zapolya, Stephen** (d.1499)
Hungarian soldier. He gained renown as a military leader under **MATTHIAS I, CORVINUS** by his defeat of the Turks and his conquest of Austria, of which he was made Governor (1485). He was the father of John **ZAPOLYA**, King of Hungary.

**Zapotecs** ► PRE-COLUMBIAN CIVILIZATIONS

**Zápotocký, Antonín** (1884–1957)
Czechoslovak trade unionist and politician. A stonemason from Kladno, he was active in the socialist youth movement from 1900 and in the Socialist Party from 1907. In 1920 he was a major organizer of an unsuccessful general strike, and in 1921 helped found the Communist Party. Imprisoned during **WORLD WAR II**, he emerged in 1945 to become the President of the revolutionary trade union organization that played a key role in seizing power in 1948. He was appointed Prime Minister and succeeded to the presidency when Klement **GOTTWALD** died unexpectedly in 1953. His responsibility for the purges was probably less than Gottwald's, but despite the moderation of old age, he lost much of the opportunity to make amends.

**ZAPU (Zimbabwe African People's Union)**
Founded in 1961 with Joshua **NKOMO** as its leader, in the 1960s it was the most popular party in Southern Rhodesia, espousing the end of white minority rule. It was banned in 1964 and moved to Zambia where it organized, through its military wing, the Zimbabwe Independent People's Revolutionary Army (ZIPRA), guerrilla attacks within Southern Rhodesia. It reassociated itself with **ZANU** to form the **PATRIOTIC FRONT** (PF) in 1976, but fought the independence elections in 1980 independently from its partner, although under the Patriotic Front label. It became effectively an **NDEBELE** party and finally fused with **ZANU** (PF) in 1988.

**Zaslavskaya, Tatyana Ivanovna** (1927–)
Soviet economist, sociologist and political reformer. Born into an academic family in Kiev, she was educated and researched in economics in Moscow until in 1963 she joined **AGANBEGYAN** in Novosibirsk and turned her attention to sociology. In the early 1980s she came into contact with Mikhail **GORBACHEV** through her writings on the countryside and at the same time earned herself a reputation for criticism of Soviet life. In 1988 she returned to Moscow to head a centre devoted to the study of public opinion and became in effect a most influential member of Gorbachev's reform team, including the Congress of Deputies.

**Zaydis**
A moderate Shiite grouping who take their name from Zayd, son of the fourth Imam, 'Ali Zayn al-Abidin. 'Ali's son, Muhammad al-Baqir, is the traditionally accepted fifth Imam of both the Seveners (Isma'ilis) and the Twelvers (Ithna 'Ashariyah). Of a more militant disposition than his elder brother Muhammad, Zayd attracted his own following. In modern times most Zaydis are to be found in the Yemen. Under Turkish rule from 1517 to 1918, the Zaydi Imam Yahya was established as ruler of the Yemen as a kingdom, principally with support from the British in Aden. Assassinated in 1948, Yahya was succeeded by

his son Ahmad, who ruled until 1962. Despite the subsequent proclamation of Yemen as a republic, discontent having been principally fomented by Gamal Abd al-**NASSER**'s Egypt, the religious basis of the Yemen continues to be principally Zaydi, with pockets of Isma'ilism, principally in the Jabal Haraz.

**Zeeland, Paul van** (1893–1973)
Belgian politician. He studied law and political science at Leuven (Louvain) University, where he held a chair from 1928 to 1963. He first became a cabinet minister (without portfolio) in 1934, and in 1935–7 was Prime Minister and Minister of Foreign Affairs. Having spent **WORLD WAR II** in England, he became Minister of Foreign Affairs (1949–54), and was intensively involved in the moves towards European union during those years.

**Zelanti**
The Italian term (literally, 'zealots') used to describe the ultra-reactionary cardinals who resisted the more reforming tendency typified by Cardinal **CONSALVI** after the Congress of **VIENNA** (1814–15).

**Zemski Sobor** (1550–1694)
A Russian form of estates that helped to strengthen central government until it was itself discarded by a forceful **PETER I, THE GREAT**. It can be traced back to 1471, but assumed importance only in 1550 when **IVAN IV, THE TERRIBLE** summoned it to help him in his law-making. It frequently played this role, but in 1613 it elected the first of the **ROMANOV DYNASTY** to be Tsar. In 1649 it assisted in codifying the laws, but it often met mainly to deal with disturbances. Although it was appointed, not elected, it nonetheless represented a cross-section of opinion, sometimes including peasants, and gave a flavour of popular participation in government, which was lost in Peter's time.

**zemstvo**
An organ of rural local self-government established in Russia following the emancipation of the serfs (1861). The zemstvos consisted of elected councillors, paid officials, and professional employees responsible for such matters as local education, health care, sanitation and public welfare. Their activities were, however, severely curtailed by the bureaucratic and financial constraints imposed by central government. ► **DUMA**; **RUSSIAN SERFS, EMANCIPATION OF THE**

**Zeng Guofan (Tseng Kuo-fan)** (1811–72)
Chinese politician, soldier and philosopher. When ordered in 1852 to raise a militia with which to quell the **TAIPING REBELLION**, he built a force as committed to Confucianism as the rebels were to their form of Christianity. His successes led to his appointment as Governor-General of the Nanjing (Nanking) area (1860); Nanjing was besieged and recovered from the rebels in 1864.

**Zenkl, Peter** (1884–1975)
Czechoslovak politician. Born in Tabor and educated in Prague, he was a relatively late entrant to politics. He was elected to the city council in 1923 as a National Socialist (Czechoslovak-style, totally different from **NAZI PARTY**) and became mayor in 1937. He became a government minister just before the **MUNICH**

**AGREEMENT** and remained one for a few more months. He was then imprisoned in **BUCHENWALD** concentration camp. In 1945 he resumed as Mayor but became a Deputy Prime Minister in the National Front government in 1946. In 1948 he was one of those who resigned to provoke a fresh election and instead gave the communists an excuse for their **FEBRUARY REVOLUTION**. He died in exile.

**Zentrum** ► **CENTRE PARTY** (Germany)

**Zervas, Napoleon** (1891–1957)
Greek resistance leader. In 1926 with General Kondylis he led a coup against the military dictatorship of General Pangalos (1925–6). During **WORLD WAR II** he was the leader in Greece of the non-communist resistance movement **EDES**, the National Republican Greek League. At the end of the war he bitterly opposed the communists in their attempts to seize power. ► **EAM**; **EKKA**; **ELAS**; **PLASTIRAS, NIKOLAOS**

**Zeta**
The name of the medieval state ruled by the Crnojević family until the Ottoman incursions in the late 15c and which from the 1690s formed part of Montenegro. The last ruler of Zeta, Ivan Crnojević, retreating from the Turks, transferred his court to Cetinje which later became the capital of Montenegro and seat of the **PETROVIĆ-NJEGOŠ DYNASTY**.

**Zhang Guotao (Chang Kuo-t'ao)** (1897–1979)
Chinese politician. As a student he played a part in the **MAY FOURTH MOVEMENT** of 1919, and in 1921, as a founding member, joined the new Chinese Communist Party. He rose to prominence as a labour leader and played a leading role in the Nanchang Mutiny (1927). He opposed the elevation of **MAO ZEDONG** as leader of the Party, but his army was destroyed by Muslim forces in the north-west. He defected to the **GUOMINDANG** in 1938. When the Chinese Communist Party won national power in 1949, he moved to Hong Kong.

**Zhang Zhidong (Chang Chih-tung)** (1837–1909)
Chinese scholar and provincial official. A pioneer of industrialization in late 19c China, he was successively Governor of Shanxi (1882–4), Guangdong and Guangxi (1884–9), and Hunan and Hubei (1889–1907). An impassioned patriot, he led the 'Purist' party, opposed to French encroachments in Indo-China, with disastrous results. After China's defeat in 1885, he turned his attention to education and industrialization, building a steelworks, mills and factories, but his efforts met with only limited success. ► **KANG YOUWEI**; **LI HONGZHANG**

**Zhao Ziyang (Chao Tzu-yang)** (1918–2005)
Chinese politician. He joined the Communist Youth League (1932) and worked underground as a Chinese Communist Party (CCP) official during the liberation war (1937–49). Zhao rose to prominence implementing land reform in Guangdong, becoming the province's CCP First Secretary in 1964. As a supporter of the reforms of **LIU SHAOQI**, he was dismissed during the **CULTURAL REVOLUTION**, paraded through Canton in a dunce's cap and sent to Nei Monggol. However, enjoying the support of **ZHOU ENLAI**, he was rehabilitated (1973) and appointed Party First Secretary of China's largest province, Sichuan (1975).

Here he introduced radical and successful market-orientated rural reforms, which attracted the eye of **DENG XIAOPING**, leading to his induction into the CCP Politburo as a full member in 1979 and his appointment as Prime Minister a year later. As Premier, he oversaw the implementation of a radical new 'market socialist' and 'open door' economic programme, and in 1987 replaced the disgraced **HU YAOBANG** as CCP General-Secretary, relinquishing his position as Premier. However, in June 1989, like his predecessor, he was controversially dismissed for his allegedly over-liberal handling of the **TIANANMEN SQUARE** pro-democracy demonstrations, and he remained under house arrest until his death.

**Zhdanov, Andrei Alexandrovich** (1896–1948)
Soviet politician. A school inspector's son, he joined the **BOLSHEVIKS** in 1915 and took part in the 1917 **RUSSIAN REVOLUTION** and the **RUSSIAN CIVIL WAR**. He then rose through the Communist Party bureaucracy until in 1934 he became Secretary of the Central Committee and in 1939 was appointed to the **POLITBURO**. He played a prominent role in the defence of **LENINGRAD** from 1941 to 1944, and subsequently assumed responsibility for ideological purity, bitterly attacking the West and its alleged imitators in the USSR.

**Zheng Chenggong (Cheng Ch'eng-kung)** ► **KOXINGA**

**Zheng He (Cheng Ho)** (1371–1433)
Chinese eunuch. He led a series of maritime expeditions to South-East Asia, India, and the east coast of Africa between 1405 and 1433 during the **MING DYNASTY**. He came from a Muslim family and became a close aide of Emperor **MING YONGLE** (1402/24). Ming Yongle promoted the maritime expeditions as a means both to assert the universality of the Chinese empire and expand trade. The expeditions were thought to be too extravagant by critics at court and were ended in the 1430s. China would never again have ambitions of being a seafaring power. ► **EXPLORATION**

**Zhivkov, Todor** (1911–98)
Bulgarian politician. A Communist Party member since 1932, in **WORLD WAR II** he fought in the resistance movement that in 1944 overthrew the pro-German Sofia regime. He was made Party Secretary in 1954 and Prime Minister in 1962 and, as Chairman of the Council of State from 1981, he was effectively the republic's President. In 1989 Zhivkov was replaced by Petar Mladenov as leader of the Bulgarian Communist Party, and in 1990 he was indicted on charges of 'especially gross embezzlement'. In 1992 his seven-year prison sentence was commuted to detention under house arrest.

**Zhou Dynasty** ► **CHINESE DYNASTIES PRE-1000AD**

**Zhou Enlai (Chou En-lai)** (1898–1976)
Chinese politician. One of the leaders of the Chinese Communist Party (CCP), he was Prime Minister of the Chinese People's Republic from its inception (1949) until his death. After pursuing his studies in Japan, he returned to China after the 1919 **MAY FOURTH MOVEMENT**. Imprisoned in 1920 as an agitator, on his release he spent four years in Europe, where he dedicated himself to the communist cause. In 1927, under the first of the **UNITED FRONTS**, he organized the revolt in Shanghai for the **GUOMINDANG**; he became a member of the CCP Politburo later the same year. In 1932 he was appointed to succeed **MAO ZEDONG** as Political Commissar of the Red Army, but after 1935, following Mao's elevation, he served him faithfully, becoming the Party's chief negotiator and diplomat. As Prime Minister (1949–76) and Minister of Foreign Affairs (1949–58) he vastly increased China's international influence. Perhaps his greatest triumph of mediation was in the **CULTURAL REVOLUTION** in China, when he worked to preserve national unity and the survival of government against the forces of anarchy. ► **CHIANG KAI-SHEK**; **COMINTERN**; **COMMUNISM**; **XI'AN INCIDENT**

**Zhu De (Chu Teh)** (1886–1976)
Chinese soldier. He was one of the founders of the Chinese Red Army and was closely associated throughout his later career with **MAO ZEDONG**. Zhu took part in the Nanchang Mutiny (1927) and his defeated troops joined with those of Mao to found the **JIANGXI SOVIET**. There, he and Mao evolved the idea of 'people's war', beating off attacks by **CHIANG KAI-SHEK**'s vastly superior **GUOMINDANG** forces until finally driven out in 1934. The Red Army then undertook the **LONG MARCH**, in which Zhu De was the leading commander. During the **SINO-JAPANESE WAR** (1937–45), he was in charge of the **EIGHTH ROUTE ARMY**. After the Japanese surrender and the renewal of civil war in China (1946), Zhu was Supreme Commander of the renamed **PEOPLE'S LIBERATION ARMY**, which expelled the Nationalists from mainland China. He was Chairman of the Standing Committee of the National People's Congress from 1959. 'Purged' at the beginning of the **CULTURAL REVOLUTION**, he was rehabilitated in 1967.

**Zhukov, Giorgiy Konstantinovich** (1896–1974)
Soviet marshal. He joined the **RED ARMY** in 1918, commanded Soviet tanks in Outer Mongolia (1939), and became army Chief of Staff (1941). He lifted the siege of Moscow, and in 1943 his counter-offensive was successful at the Battle of **STALINGRAD**. In 1944–5 he captured Warsaw, conquered Berlin, and accepted the German surrender. After the war he was Commander of the Russian zone of Germany, and became Minister of Defence (1955), but was dismissed by Nikita **KHRUSHCHEV** in 1957. ► **WORLD WAR II**

**Zia, (Begum) Khaleda** (1945–)
Bangladeshi politician. The widow of General **ZIAUR RAHMAN** who was President of Bangladesh from 1977 until his assassination in 1981, she became leader of the Bangladesh Nationalist Party (BNP) in 1982. In 1990, when President Hussain Muhammad **ERSHAD** was forced to resign, elections were called. The BNP's main contestant was the **AWAMI LEAGUE** led by Sheikh Hasina **WAJED**; in the event, the latter only gained 30 per cent of the seats and in 1991 Begum Zia became the first woman Prime Minister of Bangladesh. She held the post until 1996, and was re-elected in 2001.

**Zia ul-Haq, Muhammad** (1924–88)
Pakistani general and President. He served in Burma (now Myanmar), Malaya and Indonesia in **WOR**

**WAR II**, and in two of the **INDO-PAKISTAN WARS** (1965, 1971), rising rapidly to become general and Army Chief of Staff (1976). He led a bloodless coup in 1977, became President (1978–88), imposed martial law, banned political activity, and introduced an Islamic code of law. Despite international protest, he sanctioned the hanging of former President **BHUTTO** in 1979. He was killed in an air crash near Bahawalpur.

**Ziaur Rahman** (1935–81)
Bangladeshi soldier and President. He played an important part in the emergence of the state of Bangladesh. Appointed Chief of Army Staff after the assassination of **MUJIBUR RAHMAN** (1975), he became the dominant figure within the military. President from 1977 to 1981, his government was of a military character, even after the presidential election of 1978 which confirmed his position. He survived many attempted coups, but was finally assassinated in Dhaka.

**ZIMBABWE** official name **Republic of Zimbabwe**, formerly (to 1980) **Southern Rhodesia**

A landlocked republic in southern Africa, bounded to the south by South Africa; to the south-west by Botswana; to the north-west by Zambia; and to the east by Mozambique. From the 12c to 16c the country was a medieval Bantu kingdom, with its capital at Great Zimbabwe. In the 19c it was taken over by the **NBEBELE** people under King **MZILIKAZI** and named the Kingdom of **MATABELELAND**, which was often in dispute with the Shona people of Mashonaland to the north. It was visited by David **LIVINGSTONE** in the 1850s, and came under British influence in the 1880s when the **BRITISH SOUTH AFRICA COMPANY** under Cecil **RHODES** began its exploitation of the rich mineral resources of the area. The British South Africa Company invaded Mashonaland in 1890 and by 1900 controlled much of Central Africa. Its area was divided into Northern and Southern Rhodesia in 1911. Southern Rhodesia became a self-governing British colony in 1923, and in 1953 Northern and Southern Rhodesia formed a multiracial federation with Nyasaland. Nyasaland and Northern Rhodesia gained their independence in 1963. Opposition to the independence of Southern Rhodesia under African rule resulted in a Unilateral Declaration of Independence (**UDI**) by the white-dominated government of Prime Minister Ian **SMITH** in 1965. Economic sanctions and internal guerrilla activity forced the government to negotiate with the main African groups of the **PATRIOTIC FRONT**. Power eventually transferred to the African majority, and the country gained its independence as Zimbabwe in

1980. Robert **MUGABE** became Prime Minister on independence, and President in 1987. Criticized for an increasingly autocratic style of leadership, Mugabe was re-elected in 1990, 1996 and again in 2002 in elections whose integrity was questioned. Plans to redistribute land from white farmers to blacks were announced in the early 1990s but no action was taken until 2000, when the appropriation of white-owned farms was accompanied by intimidation and violence, and defied Supreme Court rulings that the appropriations were illegal. The appropriations caused an agricultural collapse that led to widespread food shortages. The country also faces the serious problems associated with high levels of **HIV/AIDS** infection.

**Zimbabwe African National Union** ► ZANU

**Zimbabwe African People's Union** ► ZAPU

**Zimmermann, Arthur** (1864–1940)
German politician. After diplomatic service in China, he directed from 1904 the eastern division of the German Foreign Office and was Foreign Secretary (Nov 1916– Aug 1917). In Jan 1917 he sent the famous 'Zimmermann telegram' to the German minister in Mexico with the terms of an alliance between Mexico and Germany, by which Mexico was to attack the USA with German and Japanese assistance in return for the US states of New Mexico, Texas and Arizona. This telegram finally brought the hesitant US government into the war against Germany. ► **WORLD WAR I**

**Zinoviev, Grigoriy Yevseyevich** (1883–1936)
Russian revolutionary and politician. Educated at Berne University, in 1924 he was made a member of the ruling **POLITBURO**, but because of opposition to **STALIN**'s policies was expelled from the **COMMUNIST PARTY OF THE SOVIET UNION** (1926). Reinstated in 1928, he was again expelled in 1932, and in 1935 was arrested after the assassination of **KIROV**. Charged with organizing terrorist activities, he was executed following the first of Stalin's great purge trials in Moscow. The so-called 'Zinoviev letter' urging British communists to incite revolution in Britain contributed to the downfall of the Labour government in the 1924 general elections. ► **BOLSHEVIKS**; **LENIN**; **OCTOBER REVOLUTION**

**Zinzendorf, Nicolaus Ludwig, Count von** (1700–60)
German religious leader. Educated at Wittenberg, he later held a government post at Dresden. He invited the persecuted Moravians to his estates, and there founded for them the colony of Herrnhut ('the Lord's keeping'). His zeal led to conflict with the government, and he was exiled from Saxony in 1736. Ordained at Tübingen (1734), he became Bishop of the **MORAVIAN BRETHREN**, wrote over 100 books, and died at Herrnhut.

**Zionism**
The movement which sought to recover for the Jewish people its historic Palestinian homeland (the *Eretz Israel*) after centuries of dispersion. The modern movement arose in the late 19c with plans for Jewish colonization of **PALESTINE**, and under Theodor **HERZL** also developed a political programme to obtain sovereign state rights over the territory. Gaining support after **WORLD WAR I**, its objectives were supported by the British **BALFOUR DECLARATION** in

1917, as long as rights for non-Jews in Palestine were not impaired. After **WORLD WAR II**, the establishment of the Jewish state in 1948 received **UN** support. Zionism is still active, as a movement encouraging diaspora Jews to immigrate to and take an interest in the Jewish state. ► **ALIYAH**; **ISRAEL**

**Ziska** or **Žižka, John, Count** (c.1370–1424)
Bohemian Hussite leader. He fought against the Poles, Turks and French, and soon after the murder of Jan **HUS**, became Chamberlain to King **WENCESLAS IV**. During the civil war he was chosen leader of the popular party, captured Prague (1421), and erected the fortress of Tabor, his party coming to be called Taborites. Having lost both his eyes in battles, he continued to lead his troops in a series of victories, compelling Emperor **SIGISMUND** to offer the **HUSSITES** religious liberty, but he died at Przibislav before the war was over.

**Zoë** (980–1050)
Byzantine Empress (1028/50). The daughter of the Byzantine Emperor Constantine VIII, in 1028 she married Romanus III. She had him murdered in 1034 and made her paramour Emperor as Michael IV. When his successor, Michael V, was deposed in 1042 she became Empress jointly with her sister Theodora, and married her third husband, Constantine IX.

**Zog I** (1895–1961)
King of Albania (1928/39). Educated in Istanbul, he became leader of the Nationalist Party, and formed a republican government in 1922. Forced into exile in 1924, he returned with the assistance of Yugoslavia, and became President (1925–8), proclaiming himself King in 1928. After Albania was overrun by the Italians (1939), he fled to Britain, and later lived in Egypt and France. He formally abdicated in 1946, and died in France.

**Zollverein**
A German customs union, based on the enlarged **PRUSSIA** of 1814, and officially constituted in 1834. It comprised all of Germany except the Austrian Empire, Hanover, Brunswick, Oldenburg, and three northern maritime states: a total of 17 states embracing 26 million people. It represented an important stage in the German unification process.

**Zouaves**
A body of troops in the French army, first raised from Algerian tribes in 1830, who dressed in flamboyant Moorish costume. During the **AMERICAN CIVIL WAR**, several 'Zouave' style volunteer regiments were raised on the US side.

**Zubatov, Sergei Vasilevich** (1863–1917)
Russian colonel. He was in the **OKHRANKA**, which organized trade unions to try to direct revolution. As unrest increased at the turn of the century, he was authorized to set up a 'Society for Mutual Help of Workers in Mechanical Production' to organize loyalist demonstrations. But another 'union' became entangled in a strike in Odessa, and Zubatov was dismissed and his idea dropped in 1904. Ironically the net effect was to increase union activity during the Russian **REVOLUTION OF 1905**.

**Zulu Kingdom**
The Zulu kingdom was formed in the early 19c, when

**SHAKA**, building on the military achievements of his predecessor, **DINGISWAYO**, welded the northern **NGUNI** into an expansive and highly militarized state. His troops became a formidable fighting force, dispersing many of the other peoples of southern Africa far afield; however, they were defeated by the Boers and British, and much of their territory annexed. They have retained a strong self-identity, and are organized politically into the modern **INKATHA FREEDOM PARTY** under their leader Chief Gatsha **BUTHELEZI**. Their territory, greatly contracted, became one of the 'homelands' of modern South Africa, **KWAZULU**. ► **AFRIKANERS**

**Zulu War** (1879)
A war between British forces and the Zulu kingdom characterized by initial reverses for the British but final defeat for the Zulu. From the time of the arrival of Boer settlers in northern Natal in 1836, there had been uneasy border relations between white and black. The boundary was set at different times on the Tugela, Black Umfolosi and Buffalo rivers, but Boer farmers continued to penetrate Zululand in search of land. A boundary commission was appointed (1878), but the colonial authorities refused to accept its recommendations because the High Commissioner, Sir Bartle Frere, considered that they were too favourable to the Zulu. When a party of Zulu crossed the Natal border to kidnap two wives of a Zulu chief, war was declared. After initial reverses at **ISANDHLWANA** and Rorke's Drift, the British forces under Lord Chelmsford defeated the Zulu at Ulundi. **CETEWAYO**, King of the Zulu, was exiled and Zululand was divided into 13 chieftaincies. The removal of the Zulu military threat encouraged the Boers to throw off British power in the Transvaal, leading to the first Boer War and the British defeat at **MAJUBA HILL** (1881). ► **BOER WARS**

**Zumalacárregui, Tomás de** (1788–1835)
Spanish soldier. He fought against **NAPOLEON**, and on the re-establishment of absolutism was made Governor of Ferrol, but in 1832, with other Carlists, was dismissed from the army. Head of the Carlist insurrection (1833), he kept his opponents at bay, and gained a series of victories over the Madrid generals. This turned the head of Don **CARLOS** and led him to interfere with the plans of his general, who was anxious to strike for Madrid; ordered to lay siege to Bilbao instead, Zumalacárregui died of a wound sustained as he observed enemy lines nearby. ► **CARLISM**

**Zurich, Peace of** (10 Nov 1859)
A treaty between Austria, Piedmont and France at the end of the north Italian war. Lombardy passed from Austrian, through French, into Piedmontese hands in return for compensation paid to Austria on Piedmont's behalf by France. This peace marked the first significant permanent reduction in Austrian power in northern Italy in the post-Napoleonic age and paved the way for Italian unification during the 1860s.

**Zveno**
Literally 'the Link', this is the name given to the Bulgarian civilian organization, formed in 1927 under the leadership of Colonel Kimon Georgiev, which aimed at the modernization of Bulgaria through the

development of technology and industry. The government of Colonel Damian **VELCHEV**, who had come to power in the 1934 military coup, implemented the Zveno programme and depended on the support of its members. During **WORLD WAR II**, members of Zveno joined the communist-backed **FATHERLAND FRONT** and Georgiev became Prime Minister in the new Bulgarian government organized by the Front (Sep 1944). In 1946, when Zveno became the target of the communists, Georgiev was demoted in stages as the Soviet-backed Georgi **DIMITROV** established himself in power.

**Zwangendaba** (d.c.1845)
General in the Ndwandwe army of northern Natal. After defeat at the hands of **SHAKA** in 1819, he took his followers northwards and settled near Delagoa Bay in Portuguese Mozambique. In 1831 Zwangendaba moved on, attacked the Shona in Zimbabwe, crossed the Zambezi River in 1835 and established military states in what are now Malawi and Tanzania. These states resisted the establishment of European rule in the Partition of **AFRICA**.

**Zwide** (d.1819)
Chief of the Ndwandwe, one of the northern Nguni tribes of northern Natal. The Ndwandwe and the Mthethwa under **DINGISWAYO** battled for power in the emerging **NGUNI** state. Dingiswayo was killed when attacked by Zwide in 1817, thus enabling **SHAKA** to take over the Mthethwa army and forge the Zulu state, which was one of the most celebrated of all African states in the 19c.

**Zwingli, Huldreich** or **Ulrich**, Latin **Ulricus Zuinglius** (1484–1531)
Swiss reformer. Ordained in 1506, he became a chaplain to Swiss mercenaries and was elected preacher in Zurich (1518). He opposed the selling of indulgences, espoused Reformed doctrines, and obtained the support of the civil authorities, but in 1524 he disagreed with Martin **LUTHER** over the question of the Eucharist, for he rejected the idea of any kind of real 'presence'. War between the cantons followed and he was killed in an attack on Zurich. ➤ **REFORMATION**

*International Organizations*

*and World Population Maps*

# International Organizations

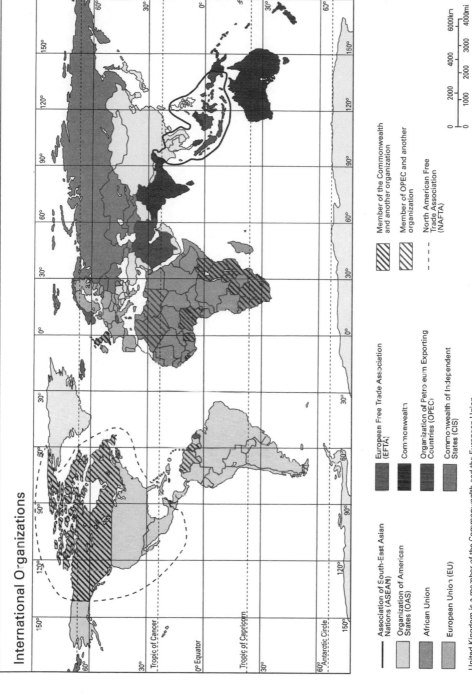

Association of South-East Asian
Nations (ASEAN)

Organization of American
States (OAS)

African Union

European Union (EU)

European Free Trade Association
(EFTA)

Commonwealth

Organization of Petroleum Exporting
Countries (OPEC)

Commonwealth of Independent
States (CIS)

Member of the Commonwealth
and another organization

Member of OPEC and another
organization

North American Free
Trade Association
(NAFTA)

United Kingdom is a member of the Commonwealth and the European Union.

## Population

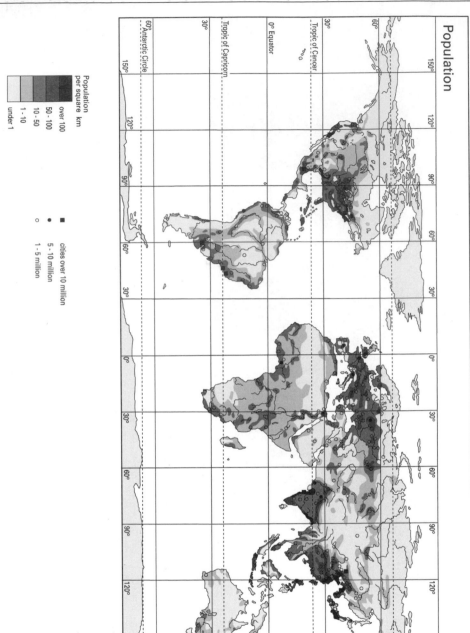

60° Antarctic Circle

30°

Tropic of Capricorn

0° Equator

Tropic of Cancer

30°

60°

Population
per square km

over 100
50 - 100
10 - 50
1 - 10
under 1

cities over 10 million
5 - 10 million
1 - 5 million

# Concise Chronology of World Events
## (AD1000 to 2000)

| | AMERICAS | EUROPE | AFRICA |
|---|---|---|---|
| **1000 – 1600** | c.1000 Leif Eriksson reaches North America | 1028 Canute, King of Denmark and England, conquers Norway<br>1066 Norman conquest of England | c.1055–1200 North Africa dominated by Almoravids then Almohads |
| | | | 1240 Mali Empire founded in W Africa<br>13c Kingdom of Benin founded in S Nigeria |
| | 1325 Aztec capital Tenochtitlán is founded in Mexico | 1337–1453 Hundred Years' War<br>1347–50 Black Death affects most of Europe<br>1378–1417 Great Schism | |
| | 1438 Inca Empire begins to expand<br>1492 Columbus reaches the New World | 1455–85 Wars of the Roses in England | 1448 First European fort built by Portuguese at Arguin in Mauritania |
| | 1521 Aztec Empire conquered by Cortés<br>1533 Inca Empire conquered by Pizarro | 1517 Protestant Reformation begins<br>1562–98 French Wars of Religion<br>1571 Battle of Lepanto<br>1588 Defeat of Spanish Armada | 1578 Moroccans overcome Portuguese in NW Africa |
| **1600 – 1900** | 1607 Virginia becomes first English colony in North America<br>1624 New Amsterdam (New York City) founded: second Dutch colony | 1618–48 Thirty Years' War<br>1642–8 English Civil Wars<br>1652–74 Anglo-Dutch Wars | 1600 Oyo Empire in W Africa begins to flourish<br>1652 Cape Town founded by Dutch East India Company<br>1689 Ashanti confederacy founded by Osei Tutu |
| | | 1702–13 War of the Spanish Succession<br>1707 Union of England and Scotland | |
| | 1775–83 American Revolution<br>1776 US Declaration of Independence | 1740–8 War of the Austrian Succession<br>1756–63 Seven Years' War<br>c.1775 Industrial Revolution begins<br>1789 French Revolution | 1776–86 Fulani Emirates founded |
| | 1803 Louisiana Purchase<br>1808–28 Independence movements in South America<br>1861–5 American Civil War<br>1867 Dominion of Canada formed | 1815 Battle of Waterloo<br>1848 Revolutions in Europe<br><br>1882 Triple Alliance formed | 1830 Algeria invaded by France<br>1838 Zulus and Boers start fighting<br>1880–1, 1899–1902 Anglo-Boer Wars<br>1884–5 Congress of Berlin divides up Africa |
| **1900 – 2005** | 1910–20 Mexican Revolution<br>1914 Panama Canal is opened<br>1917 USA declares war on Germany | 1912–13 Balkan Wars<br>1914–18 World War I<br>1917 Russian Revolution | 1910 South Africa becomes an independent dominion<br><br>1922 Egypt becomes independent<br>1935 Ethiopia invaded by Italy<br>1942 Battle of El Alamein in Egypt |
| | 1941 USA enters World War II<br>1945 UN formed<br>1949 NATO formed | 1939–45 World War II<br><br>1949 NATO formed; Germany divided into East and West until 1990<br>1957 EEC established | 1949–91 Policy of apartheid in South Africa<br>1957–75 Independence movements |
| | 1959 Cuban Revolution | | 1960 Sharpeville Massacre |
| | 1982 Falklands War | 1969 Violence begins in Northern Ireland in protest at British rule<br><br>1991 USSR breaks up; civil war in Yugoslavia | 1980 Black majority rule in Zimbabwe |
| | 1994 World Trade Organization formed | 1992 Yugoslavia breaks up; Czechoslovakia splits in two | 1994 Ethnic massacres in Rwanda and Burundi; ANC wins first multi-racial elections in South Africa |
| | 2001 Terrorist attacks on USA | 1999 NATO attacks Serbia over treatment of Albanians in Kosovo | 2004 Ethnic massacres in Darfur, Sudan |